BECK'SCHE RECHTS-
UND WIRTSCHAFTSWÖRTERBÜCHER

ALFRED ROMAIN

TEIL I

ENGLISH – GERMAN

ENGLISCH – DEUTSCH

DICTIONARY

OF LEGAL COMMERCIAL TERMS

PART I

ENGLISH – GERMAN

BY

ALFRED ROMAIN

Dr. jur., B. A., Attorney at Law

Fourth revised edition

in collaboration with

Hans Anton Bader

M. A. (Rockford)
County Court Judge in Munich

LONDON

BUTTERWORTHS

1989

WÖRTERBUCH

DER RECHTS- UND WIRTSCHAFTSSPRACHE

TEIL I

ENGLISCH – DEUTSCH

VON

ALFRED ROMAIN

Dr. jur., B. A., Rechtsanwalt

Vierte, neubearbeitete Auflage

unter Mitwirkung von

Hans Anton Bader

M. A. (Rockford)
Richter am Amtsgericht in München

C. H. BECK'SCHE VERLAGSBUCHHANDLUNG

MÜNCHEN 1989

CIP-Titelaufnahme der Deutschen Bibliothek

Romain, Alfred:
Wörterbuch der Rechts- und Wirtschaftssprache / von Alfred Romain. – München : Beck.
(Beck'sche Rechts- und Wirtschaftswörterbücher)
Parallelsacht.: Dictionary of legal and commercial terms
NE: HST

Teil 1. Englisch-Deutsch / unter Mitw. von Hans Anton Bader. – 4., neubearb. Aufl. – 1989
ISBN 3 406 33478 4

ISBN 3 406 33478 4

Druck der C. H. Beck'schen Buchdruckerei, Nördlingen

Vorwort zur 4. Auflage

Die neubearbeitete vierte Auflage des 1. Bandes des Wörterbuchs wurde um ca. 4500 Eintragungen erweitert. Der Inhalt ist aktualisiert und der neuesten Entwicklung auf den Gebieten von Recht, Wirtschaft und Verwaltung angepaßt. Um die Handlichkeit des Buches zu erhalten, hat der Verfasser den bisherigen Text gestrafft – vor allem durch Weglassung obsolet gewordener Begriffe – und zur Reduzierung von Verweisungen zusammengesetzte Ausdrücke in der Regel beim Substantiv eingeordnet.

Bei der Vorbereitung haben mitgewirkt:

Anton Bader M. A. (vgl. Titelseite), der bereits die Vorauflage rechtsvergleichend und redaktionell mitgestaltet hatte, durch Überarbeitung von Teilen des neuen Manuskripts, Herbert Breese als Fachübersetzer durch Einbringung seiner aus langjähriger Berufserfahrung und neuen Auswertungen stammenden Stichwortsammlung, insbesondere aus amerikanischen Quellen, Birgit Burger, M. A., als Fachübersetzerin mit Beiträgen aus dem internationalen Urheber- und Medienrecht, Prof. Dr. Murad Ferid (mein verehrter Doktorvater), mit Hinweisen aus der britischen Rechtsprechung, Assessor Stefan Löchner durch Überprüfung amerikanischer Terminologiequellen und Vorschläge für deutsche Entsprechungen, Rudolf Sachs, Fachübersetzer und Fachakademielehrer für Wirtschaft, Autor einschlägiger Werke, durch Beiträge aus dem Gebiet der Buchführung und der Handelsgesellschaften, Dipl.-Kfm. Dr. Wolfgang Schmidt, früherer langjähriger Leiter der Übersetzerabteilung der Esso-AG Hamburg, mit Beiträgen aus dem Gebiet der Betriebswirtschaft, die Münchener Rückversicherungsgesellschaft mit Hinweisen aus ihrem Rechtsgebiet, Dietlinde Bökenkamp durch abschließendes Korrekturlesen.

Für alle diese wertvollen Beiträge bedanke ich mich herzlich.

Wie bei den Vorauflagen ergaben sich in den Unterrichtsgesprächen mit meinen Studierenden an der Fachakademie des Sprachen- und Dolmetscher-Instituts München ebenfalls verwertbare Anregungen.

Möge sich auch diese Auflage als nützlich erweisen und wie die Vorauflagen freundliche Aufnahme finden.

Sommer 1989 *Alfred Romain*

Preface to the Fourth Edition

The revised fourth edition of the first volume of the dictionary has been expanded by about 4500 entries. The contents have been updated and brought into line with current developments in the fields of law, economics and administration. To preserve the handiness of the book in use, the text has been condensed – obsolete concepts have been omitted and the number of cross-references has been reduced by including most compound expressions under the corresponding nouns.

The following have helped in the preparation of this edition:

Anton Bader M. A. (see title page), who helped to shape the previous edition both editorially and from the point of view of comparative law, and has revised parts of the new manuscript; Herbert Breese, a legal translator, who brought to the work his collection of entry-words, especially from American sources, derived from his long experience and recent analyses; Birgit Burger, M. A., a legal translator who contributed material from the field of international copyright and media law; Prof. Dr. Murad Ferid (my doctoral supervisor), who provided material from British court decisions; Assessor Stephan Löchner, who checked sources of American terminology and made suggestions for German translations; Rudolf Sachs, a teacher and translator in the field of economics and the author of standard works of reference, who contributed material from the field of accountancy and trading companies; Dipl.-Kfm. Dr. Wolfgang Schmidt, formerly for many years the head of the translation department of the German Esso AG Hamburg, who provided material from the field of business administration; the Münchener Rückversicherungsgesellschaft, who provided material from their special field; Dietlinde Bökenkamp, who did the final proofreading.

For all these valuable contributions I am most grateful.

As with the previous editions, many useful ideas arose out of conversations with my students at the Fachakademie of the Sprachen- und Dolmetscher-Institut in Munich.

I hope this new edition will prove useful and receive as positive a reception as its predecessors.

Summer 1989 *Alfred Romain*

Abbreviations – Abkürzungen

ant	antonym	Antonym
adj	adjective	Adjektiv
adv	adverb	Adverb
allg	general(ly)	allgemein
bes.	especially	besonders
betr	concerning	betreffend
bil	accounting	Bilanzwesen
brit	British usage	britischer Sprachgebrauch
bzgl	referring to	bezüglich
bzw	respectively	beziehungsweise
ca	approximately	circa
canad	Canadian usage	kanadischer Sprachgebrauch
c. f. (cf)	compare	vergleiche
civ	civil law	Zivilrecht
crim	criminal law	Strafrecht
D	German Federal Republic	Bundesrepublik Deutschland
dgl.	(and) similar things	dergleichen
dh	that means (i. e.)	das heißt
e–r, e–e	a (indefinite article)	einer, eine
eccl	ecclesiastical	kirchlich bzw. kirchenrechtlich
econ	economic	wirtschaftlich
etw	something	etwas
evt.	possibly	eventuell
exch	exchange usage	Börsensprache
f, fem	feminine (gender)	weiblich (Genus)
feud	feudal	lehensrechtlich
fig	figuratively	im übertragenen Sinn
GB	Great Britain	Großbritannien
hist	historical	rechtsgeschichtslich
infra	infra	siehe unten
ins	insurance	Versicherungswesen
int	international law	Völkerrecht
inv.	investment funds	Investmentgesellschaften
jmd	someone	jemand
jmdm	to someone	jemandem
jmdn	someone (accusative)	jemanden
jur	legal term	juristisches Fachwort
l	-lich (German suffix in all declensions)	-lich, -licher, -liche, -liches, -lichen
lat	Latin	lateinisch
m	masculine (gender)	männlich (Genus)
med jur	forensic medicine	Gerichtsmedizin

mar	maritime	Seefahrt
mil	military	militärisch
min	mining	Bergbau
n	neuter	sachlich (Genus)
naut	nautical	nautisch
obs	obsolete	veraltet
parl	parliamentary	parlamentarisch
part	participle	Partizip
pat	patents	Patentwesen
pl	plural	Plural
pol	political	politisch
qv	quod vide	siehe dort
s	noun	Substantiv
sl	slang	Jargon
scot	Scots law	schottisches Recht
s. o.	someone	jemand
s. th. (sth)	something	etwas
tax	taxation	Steuerrecht
u	and	und
ua	and others	und andere(s)
US	American usage	amerikanischer Sprachgebrauch
usw	and so on (etc)	und so weiter
v	verb	Verb
vulg	vulgar	vulgär

Special abbreviations will be found at the beginning of some lengthy entries.
Besondere Abkürzungen sind am Anfang einiger längerer Titel angegeben.
(=) means that the same word may be used in German;
(=) bedeutet, daß im Deutschen das gleiche Wort stehen kann.
Italics indicates an explanation or circumscription;
Kursivsatz bedeutet eine Erläuterung oder Umschreibung.

A

ab initio von Anfang an, ex tunc.

abandon preisgeben, aufgeben, derelinquieren, verzichten, verfassen; ~ **a case** ein Verfahren nicht weiter betreiben; ~ **a claim** e–n Anspruch fallen lassen; ~ **a patent** auf ein Patent verzichten; ~ **a right** ein Recht aufgeben; ~ **an attempt** vom Versuch zurücktreten; ~ **an option** e–e Option verfallen lassen; ~ **the defense** die Verteidigung niederlegen; ~**ed property** → *property*; ~**ed shipwreck** aufgegebenes Schiff.

abandonee *jmd, demgegenüber ein Recht (oder e–e Sache) aufgegeben wird; Assekurant (dem Schiffswrack überlassen wird).*

abandoning a child Kindesaussetzung *f*.

abandonment Preisgabe *f*, Aufgabe *f*, Dereliktion *f*; Überlassung *f*, Verzicht *m*; Verlassen *n*, Aussetzen *n*; Nichtweiterbetreiben *n e–s Prozesses*; Ausbuchung *f*; ~ **of a legal title** Rechtsverzicht, Eigentumsverzicht; ~ **of action** Klagerücknahme; Ruhenlassen des Verfahrens; ~ **of an option** Verfallenlassen einer Option; ~ **of appeal** Rücknahme des Rechtsmittels, Berufungsrücknahme, Revisionszurücknahme; ~ **of attempt** Rücktritt vom Versuch ~ **of cargo** Abandon, Preisgabe der Ladung; ~ **of claim** Anspruchsverzicht; ~ **of domicile** Aufgabe des Wohnsitzes; ~ **of excess** Verzicht auf den Mehrbetrag; ~ **of mines** Auflassung von Bergwerken; ~ **of possession** Besitzaufgabe; ~ **of railways** Stillegung von Eisenbahnen; ~ **of the gold standard** Abgang vom Goldstandard; ~ **of the option money** → *option;* **constructive** ~ *schwere Eheverfehlung, die zum Getrenntleben führt*, indirektes bösliches Verlassen; **malicious** ~ böswilliges Verlassen; **voluntary** ~ grundloses Verlassen.

abatable umstoßbar, aufhebbar, einstellbar, abziehbar.

abate (ver)kürzen, erlassen, abziehen, herabsetzen, mindern; ~ **a grievance** e–n Übelstand abstellen.

abatement Herabsetzung *f*, Abschaffung *f*, Beseitigung *f*, Abschlag *m*, Nachlaß *m*, Ermäßigung, Kaufpreisminderung *f*; Zollrückerstattung *f*; unberechtigte Inbesitznahme e–s Nachlaßgrundstücks; ~ **and revival** Aussetzung des Verfahrens; ~ **notice** Beseitigungsanordnung *wegen e–r Belästigung;* ~ **of action,** einseitige Prozeßbeendigung *bzw* Ruhenlassen des Verfahrens; ~ **of cause of action** Untergang des Streitgegenstands; ~ **of debts** teilweiser (*proportionaler*) Schuldenerlaß; ~ **of legacies** anteilige Kürzung von Geldvermächtnissen; ~ **of nuisances** Beseitigung von Belästigungen, Selbsthilfe gegen Besitzstörungen; ~ **of the purchase price** (Kaufpreis)Minderung; ~ **pro rata** anteilige Herabsetzung (*von Forderungen*); **plea in** ~ → *plea*; **without** ~ ohne Preisnachlaß.

abator *jmd, der e–n Mißstand abstellt* (*nuisance*); widerrechtlicher Besitzer e–s Nachlaßgrundstücks.

abbacy Amt *n* (*Privilegien und Gerichtsbarkeit*) e–s Abts; Amtsdauer *f* e–s Abts.

abbreviature Kurzentwurf *m*.

abdication Abdankung *f*, Amtsniederlegung *f*, Verzicht *m*; ~ **of the throne** → *throne*.

abduct (*gewaltsam oder heimtückisch*) entführen.

abduction Entführung *f*; ~ **of child** Kindesentziehung.

abductor Entführer.

abesse abwesend sein.
abet Beihilfe leisten, anstiften; Vorschub leisten.
abetment Beihilfe *f*; Anstiftung *f*.
abettor Tatgehilfe *m*; *am Tatort anwesender* Anstifter.
abeyance Anwartschaft *f*, Schwebezustand *m*, Ungewißheit *f*; **in ~** schwebend unwirksam, aufschiebend bedingt; **to be left in ~** in der Schwebe bleiben; **to fall into ~** zeitweilig ausgesetzt werden.
abeyant unentschieden, in der Schwebe.
abidance Aufenthalt *m*; Befolgung *f*; **~ by the rules** Einhaltung von Vorschriften.
abide einhalten; bleiben, verbleiben, wohnen; **~ abroad** sich ständig im Ausland aufhalten; **~ and satisfy** vollstrecken, vollziehen; **~ by an award** e–n Schiedsspruch einhalten; **~ by one's promise** an seiner Zusage festhalten; **to be and ~** sich aufhalten; wohnhaft sein (in).
ability Fähigkeit *f*, Befähigung *f*; finanzielle Leistungsfähigkeit *f*; **mental ~** Geistesfähigkeit.
abjudge aberkennen.
abjudicate aberkennen.
abjudication *gerichtliche* Aberkennung *f*, Absprechung *f*; Entziehung durch Urteil.
abjuration Verzichtleistung *f* unter Eid, Abschwören *n*; **~ of allegiance** eidliche Erklärung e–s Einzubürgernden, daß er keinem anderen Staat oder Herrscher Treue schuldig ist; **~ of the realm** freiwillige Verbannung.
abjuratory abschwörend, entsagend.
abjure abschwören, verzichten, preisgeben, widerrufen; **~ continuation of patent advertising** die Unterlassung der Patentberühmung unter Eid versprechen; **~ the state** für immer ins Exil gehen.
able fähig, tauglich, befähigt; **~-bodied** tauglich, wehrfähig; **~-bodiedness** Tauglichkeit, körperliche Leistungsfähigkeit; **~-minded** geistig leistungsfähig; **~ to earn** erwerbsfähig; **~ to pay** zahlungsfähig; **~ to purchase** zahlungskräftig (*Käufer*); **~ to sue** parteifähig.
abnegate aufgeben, verzichten, ableugnen.
abnegation Ableugnung *f*, Verzicht *m*.
abnegative leugnend, entsagend, negativ.
abode Unterkunft *f*, Aufenthalt(-sort) *m*, Wohnsitz *m*; **fixed ~** dauernder Aufenthalt, Wohnsitz; **habitual ~** gewöhnlicher Aufenthalt; **permanent ~** ständiger Aufenthaltsort, Wohnsitz; **of unknown ~** unbekannten Aufenthalts; **settled ~** (fester) Wohnsitz; **the last known place of ~** der letzte bekannte Aufenthaltsort; **without fixed ~** ohne festen Wohnsitz.
abolish abschaffen, aufheben.
abolishment Abschaffung *f*, Aufhebung *f*; *US hist* Abschaffung der Sklaverei.
abolition Abschaffung *f*, Aufhebung.
abolitionism *US hist* Abolitionismus *m*, Politik *f* der Sklavenbefreiung.
aborticide Herbeiführung *f* e–r Fehlgeburt, Abtreibung *f*; Abteibungsmittel *n*.
abortient abtreibend.
abortifacient Abtreibungsmittel *n*.
abortion Abtreibung *f*; Schwangerschaftsabbruch *m*, Fehlgeburt *f*; **~ for social reasons** soziale Indikation; **legal ~** zulässiger Schwangerschaftsabbruch; **self-induced ~** Abtötung der eigenen Leibesfrucht, Eigenabtreibung.
abortive mißlungen, fruchtlos, verfehlt; **~ trial** ergebnislose Hauptverhandlung.
above über, höher; **~ all incumbrances** mehr als alle Belastungen, **~ average** überdurchschnittlich; **~ captioned** oben aufgeführt, obengenannt; **~ cited**

obenzitiert; ~ **mentioned** obenerwähnt; **par** → *par*; ~ **the line** zum ordentlichen Haushalt gehörig (*cf budget*).

abrade abnutzen, abschaben, schädigen.

abrasion Abnutzung *f*; Hautabschürfung *f*, Schürfwunde *f*.

abreast dicht bei, nebeneinander.

abridge abkürzen, kondensieren, einschränken; ~**d version** Kurzfassung.

abridgment Beeinträchtigung *f*, Beschränkung *f*; gekürzte Fassung *f*, Auszug *m*; ~ **of damages** Recht auf Schadenherabsetzung; ~**s of patent** Patentschriftenauszug: **fair** ~ eigenschöpferische Kürzung bzw. Zusammenfassung.

abro(a)chment spekulatives Aufkaufen *n*.

abrogable abschaffbar, aufhebbar.

abrogate aufheben (*Gesetz*), abschaffen, außer Kraft setzen.

abrogation Aufhebung *f e–s Gesetzes*, Außerkraftsetzung *f*.

abrogative auf Abschaffung hinzielend.

abscond sich entziehen, flüchtig sein, entweichen; ~**ing debtor** sich seinen Gläubigern entziehender (Gemein)Schuldner.

absconding Entweichen *m*, Sichverbergen *m*, Flucht *f*

absence Abwesenheit *f*, Ausbleiben *n*, Nichterscheinen *n*, Fernbleiben *n*; Vermißtsein *n*; Fehlen *n*, Nichtvorhandensein *n*, Ermangelung *f*; ~ **money** Auslöse, Trennungsgeld; ~ **of mind** Geistesabwesenheit, Bewußtlosigkeit; ~ **without leave** unerlaubte Entfernung von der Truppe, eigenmächtige Abwesenheit; **in the** ~ **of consideration** mangels Gegenleistung, mangels Deckung; **in the** ~ **of evidence** mangels Beweises; **in the** ~ **of proof to the contrary** mangels Beweises des Gegenteils.

absente reo in Abwesenheit des Angeklagten.

absentee Abwesende(r); nicht Erschienene(r); ~ **ballot** Briefwahl, Wahlschein *bei Briefwahl*; ~ **landowner** abwesender Grundherr; ~ **list** Abwesenheitsliste; ~ **taxpayer** im Ausland wohnhafter Steuerpflichtiger; ~ **voter** Briefwähler.

absenteeism Absentismus *m*, Wohnen *n* im Aulsand; unentschuldigtes Fernbleiben *n* (*von der Arbeit*).

absolute absolut, endgültig, bedingungslos, streng, unumschränkt.

absolution Absolution *f*, Lossprechung *f*.

absolutism Absolutismus *m*.

absolve Absolution erteilen, lossprechen, entbinden.

absorb absorbieren, in sich aufnehmen; ~ **border areas** Randgebiete eingemeinden; ~ **buying power** Kaufkraft abschöpfen; ~**-ing capacity** Aufnahmefähigkeit (*des Marktes*); ~**ing company** übernehmende Gesellschaft.

absorption Absorption *f*, Fusion *f* durch Aufnahme, Auffangen *n* (*Preise*); ~ **account** Wertberichtigungskonto; ~ **costing** Vollkostenrechnung; Produktionskostenaufteilung auf unfertige Erzeugnisse; ~ **value** berichtigter Wert; **cost** ~ Auffangen von Kosten.

abstain sich enthalten; ~ **from voting** (= *to abstain*) sich der Stimme enthalten.

abstention Stimmenthaltung *f*.

abstract Zusammenfassung *f*, Auszug *m*, Übersicht *f*; ~ **in chief** unmittelbarer Auszug aus den (*vollständigen*) Originalurkunden; ~ **of accounts** → *account(s)*; ~ **of balance** Bilanzauszug, Vermögensübersicht; ~ **of balance sheet** Bilanzauszug; ~ **of record** Zusammenfassung des Akteninhalts, Tatbestand (*e–s Urteils für die Rechtsmittelinstanz*); ~ **of title** Zusammenfassung der Grundeigentumsurkunden; **equated** ~ **of account** Staffelauszug.

abstract *v* entziehen; ~ **electricity** elektrische Energie entziehen.

abstracting electricity Energieentziehung *f*, Stromentwendung *f*.

abstraction Untreue *f*, Unterschlagung *f*, widerrechtliche Entnahme *f*; ~ **of documents** Urkundenunterschlagung; ~ **of water** Wasserentnahme (*aus öffentl. Gewässern*).

abundance Ergiebigkeit *f*, Überfluß *m*; ~ **of labour supply** Überangebot an Arbeitskräften.

abuse *s* Fehlgebrauch *m*, Mißbrauch *m*, Beschimpfung *f*; ~ **in respect of honours** Bestechung bei der Verschaffung von Orden, Ehrenzeichen und Amtswürden; ~ **of authority** Amtsmißbrauch; ~ **of confidence** Vertrauensbruch; ~ **of corporate franchise** Mißbrauch d. Rechtsfähigkeit e–r Körperschaft; ~ **of credit** Kreditmißbrauch; ~ **of discretion** Ermessensmißbrauch; ~ **of distress** widerrechtliche Benutzung e–r gepfändeten Sache; ~ **of elective franchise** Wahldelikte; ~ **of patent** mißbräuchliche Patentbenutzung; ~ **of power** Machtmißbrauch; ~ **of process** Verfahrensmißbrauch, mißbräuchliche Anrufung des Gerichts; ~ **of rights** unzulässige Rechtsausübung; ~ **of rules** mißbräuchliche Anwendung der Geschäftsordnung; ~ **of title** Rechtsmißbrauch.

abuse *v* mißbrauchen, beschimpfen.

abusee mißbrauchte Person *f*, beschimpfte P., Verführte(r).

abusing children unzüchtige Handlungen an Kindern.

abusive täuschend, mißbräuchlich, grob, beschimpfend; ~ **language** → *language*.

abut angrenzen, berühren.

abuttal Grundstücksgrenze *f*, Angrenzung *f*.

abutter Angrenzer *m*, Nachbar *m*, Anlieger *m*.

academic *s* (Rechts)Wissenschaftler *m*, Akademiker *m*.

accede einwilligen, beipflichten, beitreten; ~ **to a treaty** e–m Übereinkommen beitreten; ~ **to an opinion** sich e–r Meinung anschließen; ~ **to terms** Bedingungen zustimmen.

accedence Beitritt *m*, Einwilligung *f*, Zustimmung *f*; Antreten *n* e–s Amtes.

accelerate beschleunigen; ~**d cost recovery system** beschleunigte Abschreibung von Anschaffungskosten; ~**d depreciation** → *depreciation*; ~**d succession** vorzeitig, herbeigeführter Übergang des Nachlasses (*auf den Schluß- od. Nacherben*).

acceleration vorzeitige Fälligkeit *f*; ~ **clause** Fälligkeitsklausel, Verfallsklausel; ~ **of maturity** vorzeitiger Eintritt der Fälligkeit; ~ **premium** Lohnzuschlag für höhere Produktivität.

accept annehmen, abnehmen, akzeptieren; ~ **a risk** ein Risiko auf sich nehmen; ~ **as pledge** als Pfand annehmen; ~ **bills for collection** Wechsel zum Einzug hereinnehmen; ~ **delivery** (*Ware*) abnehmen; ~ **the tender** den Zuschlag erteilen (*Ausschreibung*).

acceptability Abnehmbarkeit *f*, Akzeptanz *f*, Vorteilhaftigkeit *f*.

acceptable annehmbar, beleihbar, lombardfähig; ~ **to monetary authorities** zentralbankfähig.

acceptance Annahme *f*, Abnahme *f* (*Ware, Werk*); Akzept *n*; Übernahme *f*; ~ **account** Akzeptkonto, Schuldwechselkonto; ~ **and receipt** Abnahme (*der Ware*); ~ **bill** → *bill* (3); ~ **commission** Akzeptprovision; ~ **commitments** Wechselverbindlichkeiten; ~ **credit** Akzeptkredit; ~ **due** fälliger Wechsel; ~ **for hono(u)r** Ehrenannahme; ~ **in case of need** Annahme im Falle der Not; ~ **institution (house)** Akzeptbank, Wechselbank; ~ **ledger** Akzeptbuch; ~ **line** Akzepthöchstkredit, Annahmegrenze; ~ **market** Bankakzeptmarkt; ~ **maturity tickler** Wechselverfallbuch; ~ **note** Annahmeschein, quittierter Lieferschein; ~ **of bid** Zuschlag (*Versteigerung*); ~ **of bills** Wechselannahme, Akzept; ~ **of charge** Festnahmebericht (*Polizei*); ~ **of deposits** Depositengeschäft; ~ **of goods** Annahme von

Waren; ~ **of offer** Annahme e–s Angebots; ~ **of plea of guilty** Zulassung e–r Schuldigerklärung; ~ **of reports and accounts** Entlastungserteilung; ~ **of service** Zustellungsbestätigung e–s Rechtsanwalts *mit der Verpflichtung zum Erscheinen im Termin*; ~ **of tender** Zuschlag (*an den Submittenten*), Auftragserteilung; ~ **of the claims** Anerkennung von Ansprüchen; ~ **receivable** offener Wechsel; ~ **subject to contract** Annahme vorbehaltl. e–s formgültigen Vertragsschlusses; ~ **supra protest** Ehrenannahme; ~ **tolerance** Annahmetoleranz; **accommodation** ~ → *accommodation;* **anticipated** ~ vor Fälligkeit bezahltes Akzept; **banker's (bank)** ~ Rembours, Bankakzept; **blank** ~ Blankoakzept; **clean** ~ unbeschränktes Akzept; **collateral** ~ Wechselbürgschaft, Avalakzept; **commission on** ~ Akzeptprovision; **conditional** ~ bedingte Annahme, Annahme unter Vorbehalt; **denial of** ~ Annahmeverweigerung; **discounting of ~s** Wechseldiskontierung; **documents against** ~ Dokumente gegen Akzept; **express** ~ ausdrückliche Annahmeerklärung; **general** ~ uneingeschränkte, unbedingte Annahme, unbeschränktes Akzept; **implied** ~ Annahme durch schlüssiges Verhalten; **local** ~ Platzakzept; **outright** ~ vorbehaltlose Annahme; **partial** ~ Teilannahme; **plant** ~ Abnahme (*nach Montage und Probelauf*) im Betrieb des Auftraggebers; **presentation for** ~ → *presentation*; **qualified** ~ eingeschränkte *bzw. bedingte* Annahme; **rebated** ~ vor Fälligkeit bezahltes Akzept; **returned for want of** ~ „mangels Annahme zurück"; **special** ~ Annahme e–s Domizilwechsels; **to find general** ~ **in trade** allgemeine Verkehrsgeltung erhalten; **tacit** ~ stillschweigende Annahme; **to provide with** ~ mit Annahme versehen; **trade** ~ → *trade*; **unconditional** ~ vorbehaltlose Annahme.

acceptation gebräuchlicher Sinn *m* (*e–s Wortes*); **literal** ~ **of the law** Buchstabe des Gesetzes.

accepted angenommen, akzeptiert, mit Akzept versehen.

acceptilation Schulderlaß *m*.

accepting house Akzeptbank *f*.

acceptor Akzeptant; ~ **for honour** Honorant; ~ **supra protest** Honorant; **collateral** ~ Wechselbürge.

access Zugang *m*, Zutritt *m*; Zufahrt; Umgang, Besuchsrecht, Verkehrsrecht; Gelegenheit zur Beiwohnung; ~ **and use of light** ungehinderter Lichteinfall; ~ **dispute** Verkehrsrechtsstreit; ~ **order** Besuchsrechtsbeschluß; ~ **routes** Anfahrtswege; ~ **to a highway** Zufahrtsrecht zu e–r Hauptstraße; ~ **to counsel** Recht auf Zuziehung e–s Anwalts; ~ **to courts** Zugang zu den Gerichten, staatlicher Rechtsschutz; Rechtsweg; ~ **to the books** Einsichtsrecht in die Bücher, Recht auf faires Verfahren; **except for** ~ nur Anlieger(verkehr); **interim** ~ einstweilige Besuchsrechtsregelung; **reasonable** ~ ausreichendes Besuchsrecht.

Access account Kreditkartenkonto *brit Großbanken*.

accessible zugänglich, erreichbar, verfügbar; ~ **to bribery** bestechlich.

accession *int* Beitritt *m*; Antritt *m*; originärer Eigentumserwerb *m durch Verbindung, Verarbeitung oder Vermischung*, Zuwachs *m*; ~**s** Neuerwerbungen, Neuanschaffungen, Zugänge; ~ **by confusion** Eigentumserwerb durch Vermischung; ~ **by merger** = ~ *by confusion qv*; **A** ~ **Council** Thronbesteigungsrat; ~ **of property** Vermögenszuwachs; ~ **of the sovereign** Thronbesteigung; ~ **to an international treaty** Beitritt zu e–m Staatsvertrag; ~ **to office** Amtsantritt; **A** ~ **Treaty** Beitrittsvertrag (*EG*); **Act of A** ~ Beitrittsakte (*EG*).

accessoriness Nebensächlichkeit *f*; Mitschuld *f*; Vorschubleistung *f*.

accessory *adj* zusätzlich, akzessorisch;

Begleit..., Zusatz.., Hilfs..., Neben...

accessory *s* Zubehör *n*; Tatgehilfe, Gehilfe *m*, Teilnehmer *an e–r Straftat*; ~ **after the fact** Begünstiger; ~ **before the fact** Tatgehilfe vor der Tat; ~ **during the fact** Gehilfe während der Tat (*am Tatort anwesend*).

accident Unfall *m*, unvorhergesehenes Ereignis *n*; ~ **action** Verkehrsunfallprozeß; ~ **annunity** Unfallrente; ~ **avoidance** Unfallvermeidung; ~ **benefit** Unfallentschädigung, Unfallrente; ~ **death** Unfalltod; ~ **hazard** Unfallrisiko; ~ **indemnity** Unfallentschädigung; ~ **insurance** → *insurance;* ~ **in the course of employment** Arbeitsunfall; ~**s on the roads** Unfälle außerhalb von Ortschaften; ~ **policy** → *policy* (1); ~ **prevention** Unfallverhütung; ~**-prone** unfallgefährdet, gefahrgeneigt; ~ **record** Unfallbericht; ~ **scene** Unfallfort, Unfallstelle; ~ **statistics** Unfallstatistik; **automobile** ~ Autounfall; **by** ~ **or mistake** zufällig oder irrtümlich; **fatal** ~ tödlicher Unfall; **fatigue** ~ auf Ermüdung zurückzuführender Unfall; **industrial** ~ Arbeitsunfall, Betriebsunfall; **inevitable** ~ unabwendbares Ereignis; **killing by** ~ zufällige Todesverursachung, unverschuldete Tötung; **motoring** ~ Autounfall; **noncompensible** ~ nicht zum Schadenersatz verpflichtender Unfall; **occupational** ~ Berufsunfall, Arbeitsunfall; **off-the-job** ~ Unfall außerhalb der Arbeitszeit; **on-the-job** ~ Betriebsunfall; **traffic** ~ Verkehrsunfall; **unavoidable** ~ unabwendbares Ereignis.

accidental zufällig, beiläufig, unwesentlich.

acclamation Zuruf *m* **vote by** ~ → *vote.*

accomenda Verkaufskommission an e–n Schiffskapitän (*über die Ladung, mit Gewinnbeteiligung*).

accommodate unterbringen, beherbergen, anpassen; Streit schlichten; ~ **with** versehen mit; ~**d party** durch Gefälligkeitsabrede Begünstigter.

accommodating gefällig, entgegenkommend; ~ **movements** Gold- und Devisenversendung zum Zahlungsbilanzausgleich; **on** ~ **terms** zu annehmbaren Bedingungen.

accommodation (*1*) Entgegenkommen *n*, finanzielle Hilfe *f*, Verständigung *f*, Schlichtung *f*; Ausstattung *f*, Versorgung *f*; ~ **acceptance** Gefälligkeitsakzept; ~ **address** Gefälligkeitsadresse; ~ **bill** → *bill (3);* ~ **indorsement** Gefälligkeitsindossament; ~ **indorsement loan** Kredit gegen Wechselbürgschaft; ~ **indorser** Gefälligkeitsgirant; ~ **line** kulanzweise Übernahme e–s Versicherungsrisikos; ~ **loan** Überbrückungskredit; ~ **maker** Gefälligkeitszeichner; ~ **note** Gefälligkeits(sola)wechsel; ~ **on each side** gegenseitiges Nachgeben; ~ **paper** Gefälligkeitswechsel; ~ **party** Gefälligkeitszeichner; ~ **road** gestattete Zufahrt; ~ **works** Bahnanlagen zum Schutz der Gleisanlieger.

accommodation (*2*) Wohnung *f*, Wohnraum *m*; Unterbringung *f*, Unterkunft *f*; ~ **lands** Bauland (*bes. für Bodenspekulation aufgekaufte Grundstücke*); ~ **registry** Wohnungsnachweis; ~ **unit** Wohnungseinheit; **alternative** ~ Ersatzwohnraum; **comparable** ~ Vergleichswohnung; **living** ~ Wohnung; **private rented** ~ privater Mietwohnraum; **rent-free** ~ mietfreies Wohnen; **sleeping** ~ Schlafmöglichkeit, Unterkunft; **tied** ~ Werkmietwohnung, Werkdienstwohnung.

accomplice Komplice *m*, Mittäter *m*, Tatbeteiligter *m*; ~ **witness** → *witness;* **corroboration of** ~ Erhärtung der Aussage e–s Tatbeteiligten; **evidence of** ~ Aussage e–s Tatbeteiligten; **feigned** ~ Agent provocateur (*als scheinbarer Mittäter*).

accomplish ausführen, vollenden,

erfüllen; ~ **a bill of lading** ein Konnossement durchführen; ~ **a promise** e–e Zusage einlösen; ~ **a purpose** ein Ziel erreichen, e–n Zweck erfüllen.

accomplishment Erfüllung *f*, Durchführung *f*, Ausführung *f*, Vollendung *f*; ~ **of one's duty** Pflichterfüllung; **industrial** ~ wirtschaftlicher Erfolg; **to avert** ~ die Vollendung der Tat abwenden; **withdrawal from** ~ Rücktritt vom Versuch.

accord *s* Einigkeit *f*, Übereinstimmung *f*, Einverständnis *n*; Einvernehmen *n*; Vergleich *m*; ~ **and satisfaction** vergleichsweise Erledigung (*e–r Verbindlichkeit*), Abfindungsvergleich; **executory** ~ noch nicht erfüllter Vergleich; **registration of ~s** *int* Registrierung von Übereinkünften; **to be in ~ with** übereinstimmen mit.

accord *v* einräumen, beipflichten, zustimmen, gewähren, zubilligen; ~ **a respite** e–e Zahlungsfrist einräumen.

accordance Übereinstimmung *f*, Einverständnis *n*; **in ~ with** gemäß, laut, in Übereinstimmung mit; **in ~ with regulations** nach Vorschrift; **in ~ with the accounts** rechnungsmäßig.

accordant einverstanden, beipflichtend (*in Kollegialentscheidungen*).

according übereinstimmend, gemäß, laut; ~ **to circumstances** je nach den Umständen; ~ **to contract** vertragsgemäß; ~ **to custom** herkömmlicherweise; ~ **to directions** weisungsgemäß; ~ **to law** gemäß dem Gesetz, nach gesetzlicher Vorschrift, von Rechts wegen; ~ **to my knowledge and belief** nach bestem Wissen und Gewissen; ~ **to the custom of the country** nach der Verkehrssitte; ~ **to the terms thereof** gemäß den Bestimmungen dieses Vertrages.

accost *v/t* jmdn ansprechen.

accouchement Niederkunft *f*.

account *v* Rechenschaft ablegen, sich verantworten, Rechnung legen, abrechnen, belegen, buchen.

account *s* (*1*) Rechenschaft *f*, Rechenschaftsbericht *m*, Rechnungslegung *f*; ~ **adjournment** Verweisung an den Einzelrichter im Rechnungslegungsprozeß; ~ **and discharge** *scot* jährliche Rechnungslegung; **~s and inquiries** Rechnungslegungs- und Aufklärungsbeschluß; ~ **stated** Schuldanerkenntnis; **action of** ~ Klage auf Rechnungslegung; **application of** ~ Antrag auf Rechnungslegung; **claim for an** ~ Anspruch auf Rechnungslegung; **detailed** ~ detaillierte Rechnungslegung; **final** ~ Schlußbericht; **leaving ~s in Chambers** die Rechnungslegung wird dem Einzelrichter *zur Prüfung* überlassen; **nil** ~ Erklärung des Rechnungslegungspflichtigen, daß nichts eingenommen wurde; **order for ~s** → *order* (*1*)); **preliminary ~s** Rechnungslegung im Vorverfahren; **prospective** ~ zukünftige Rechnungslegung; **residuary** ~ Rechnungslegung über den Nachlaß; **summons to proceed with ~s and inquiries** Ladung und prozeßleitende Anordnung im Rechnungslegungsverfahren; **to call to** ~ zur Rechenschaft ziehen; **to pass an** ~ Rechnung legen; **to render** ~ Rechnung legen, Rechenschaft ablegen; **variation in ~s** Änderung der Rechnungslegungsmethode; **verification of ~s** Versicherung der Richtigkeit der Rechnungslegung; **vouching ~s** Beibringung von Belegen für die Rechnungslegung.

account *s* (*2*) Konto *n* (= *K bzw. k*); Rechnung *f*, Abrechnung *f*, Saldo *m*, Außenstand *m*; **~s** *Bücher n/pl*, Gesamtheit der Buchhaltungsaufzeichnungen, Buchungsabschluß *m*, Rechnungsabschluß *m*; Abrechnungszeitraum (*brit Börse*); laufendes Kundenkredit*k*; **~s** Rechnungswesen *n*; **~s agreed upon** Rechnungsabschluß; ~ **and**

risk Rechnung und Gefahr; ~ **balance** Saldo; ~ **book(s)** Bücher e–s Kaufmanns oder Gewerbetreibenden; ~ **closed** abgeschlossenes *K*; ~**s code structure** *K–n*bezeichnungsschema; ~**s coding** Nummernschema für Haushaltstitel; ~ **current** *K*korrent, laufende Rechnung; ~ **day** Zahlungstag; Abrechnungstag (*brit. Börse: jeweils der 2. Dienstag nach dem Ende des „account" = Abrechnungszeitraums*); Abrechnungstag; ~ **duties** *brit* Schenkungsteuer; ~ **executive** Kundensachbearbeiter, Kontaktmann, Börsenauftragsnehmer, Kundenberater (*Börsengeschäfte*); Kontakter (*bei Werbeagenturen*); ~ **group** Kontengruppe; ~ **in arrears** Rechnungsrückstand; ~ **in bank** Bank*k*; ~ **in participation** gemeinsames *K*; ~ **manager** Kundenbetreuer; ~ **number** *K*nummer; ~ **of charges** Kosten*k*, Gebührenaufstellung, Spesenrechnung; ~ **of disbursement** Auslagennota; ~ **of redraft** Rückrechnung e–s Wechsels; ~**s payable** Verbindlichkeiten; ~**s payable department** Kreditorenbuchhaltung; ~ **payee (only)** (*Scheck*) nur zur Gutschrift auf *K* des genannten Zahlungsempfängers; ~ **period** Abrechnungsperiode; ~**s receivable** → *accounts receivable infra*; ~ **rendered** Rechnung; vorgelegte Rechnung; Abrechnungsvorschlag des Gläubigers; Rechnungsaufstellung; ~ **sales** Abrechnung des Kommissionärs; ~ **settled** beglichener Saldo; ~ **stated** (*vorgelegter und*) anerkannter Rechnungssaldo; **(~) statement** *K*auszug; ~ **turnover** *K*umsatz; ~ **year** Rechnungsjahr, Wirtschaftsjahr; **abridged** ~**s** Kurzform der Bilanz, **abstract of** ~**s** Buchauszug, Rechnungsauszug; **access to** ~**s** Zugang zu den Geschäftsbüchern; **active** ~ *K* mit laufenden Umsätzen; **adjustment** ~ Berichtigungs*k*; **adjustment of property** ~ Wertberichtigungs*k*; **advance** ~ Vorschuß*k*; **aging** ~**s** Einteilung der Außenstände nach Fälligkeiten; **annual** ~**s** Jahresabschluß; **appropriation** ~ Bereitstellungs*k*; **as per** ~ laut Rechnung; **assigned** ~**s** abgetretene Außenstände; **audit of** ~**s** → *audit;* **balance** ~ Ausgleichs*k*; **balance sheet** ~**s** Bestandskonten, der Bilanz zugrunde liegende Konten; **bills payable** ~ Akzept*k*; **bills receivable** ~ Rimessen*k*; **blocked** ~ Sperr*k*; **book** ~ → *book;* **book of** ~**s** Handelsbuch; **budget** ~ *Sonderk mit Auftrag, die laufenden Zahlungen d. Kunden zu leisten gegen monatl. regelmäßige Abbuchungen vom lfden K*; **capital** ~ Kapital*k*; **cash** ~ Kassen*k*, Kassa*k*, Kassenbuch; **charge** ~ → *charge;* **checking** ~ *US* Giro*k*, Scheck*k*; **cheque** ~ Giro*k*, Scheck*k*; **class of** ~ Kontenklasse; **clearing** ~ Verrechnungs*k*; **clearing up of** ~**s** Kostenbereinigung; **client** ~ Ander*k*, Fremdgeld*k* (*des Anwalts*); **closed** ~**s** ausgeglichenes *K*; **closing of** ~**s** Abschluß, Buchungsabschluß; **collection of** ~**s** Einziehung von Außenständen; **collective** ~ Sammel*k*; **commission** ~ Provisions*k*, Provisionsrechnung; **consignment** ~ Konsignations*k*; **consolidated** ~**s** konsolidierter Konzernabschluß; **contingencies** ~ Rückstellungs*k* für unvorhergesehene Verpflichtungen; **contingency** ~ Delkredere*k*; **contingent** ~ *K* für Unvorhergesehenes; **continued** ~**s** Übertrag; **contra** ~ Gegenrechnung, Gegen*k*; **control** ~ Kontroll*k*; **controlling** ~ Gegenrechnung; **cost** ~**s** Bücher der Betriebsbuchhaltung; **currency** ~ Devisen*k*, Fremdwährungs*k*; **current** ~ *K*korrent; *K*korrent*k*; laufende Rechnung; **custody** ~ Verwahrungs*k*; **dead** ~ umsatzloses *K*; **debit** ~ Debitoren*k*; **deferred** ~**s** → *deferred;* **deficiency** ~ Aufstellung über die Verlustentwicklung beim Gemeinschuldner; **delinquent** ~**s** überfällige Forderungen; notleidendes Darlehens*k*, überfälliges *K*; **delivery of** ~**s** Vorlage des

Rechnungsabschlusses; **deposit** ~ Depositen*k*, Festgeld*k*; **depositor's** ~ Kunden*k*, Scheck*k*; **depreciation** ~ → *depreciation;* **discount** ~ Disagio*k*; **discretionary** ~ *K* zur freien Verfügung; **dormant** ~ umsatzloses *K*; **drawing** ~ *K* für Privatentnahmen, *K* Entnahmen; Kundenkredit*k* (*in e–m Geschäft oder Warenhaus*); **equalization** ~ Ausgleichs*k*, Abschreibungs*k*; **escrow** ~ → *escrow*; **expense** ~ → *expense;* **external** ~ Ausländer*k*; **fabricated** ~ → *fabricate;* **falsification of ~s** Kontenfälschung; *Urkundenfälschung oder Vernichtung von Geschäftsbüchern bzw. Unterlagen;* **final** ~ Schlußrechnung, Endabrechnung; **final ~s** Jahresabschluß; **fitted ~s** → *fit;* **General A** ~ Generalk*k*; **for the** ~ zum nächsten Abrechnungstag; **frozen** ~ eingefrorenes *K*; gesperrtes *K*; **general ~s** allgemeine *K–n*, Hauptrechnung, Bücher der Geschäftsbuchhaltung; **general ledger ~s** Hauptbuch*k–n*; **goods** ~ Waren*k*; **group ~s** Konzernabschluß; Konzernbilanz, konsolidierte Bilanz; **guaranty** ~ Sicherstellungskonto: **impersonal** ~ Sach*k*; **in full discharge of our ~s** zum Ausgleich unserer Rechnung; **inactive** ~ *K* mit geringem Umsatz; **income statement** ~ Erfolgs*k*; **individual** ~ Einzel*k*; **individual retirement** ~ (*IRA*)) Altersvorsorge*k* (*steuerbegünstigt*); **insured** ~ versichertes *K* (*Fed. Deposit Insurance, USA*); **instalment ~s** Außenstände aus Abzahlungsgeschäften; **intercompany ~s** *K–n* im Konzernbereich, interne *K–n*; **interim ~s** Zwischenabschluß; **intermediate** ~ Zwischenabrechnung; **investment** ~ Depot*k*; **itemized** ~ spezifizierte Rechnung; **joint** ~ Gemeinschafts*k*, Meta*k*, Konsortial*k*; **liability** ~ → *liabilitiy;* **liquidated** ~ → *liquidated;* **liquidation** ~ Liquidations*k*; **loan** ~ Darlehens*k*, Kredit*k*; **long** ~ Kontokorrentverhältnis; **looseleaf** ~ Loseblatt*k*; **loro** ~ Loro*k*; **manufacturing** ~ Herstell*k*, Fertigungs*k*; **margin** ~ → *margin*; **multiple-party** ~ *K* mit mehreren Berechtigten; **mutual ~s** Kontokorrentverhältnis, gegenseitige Verrechnungskonten; **next** ~ nächste Rechnung, kommende Monatsrechnung; **nominal** ~ benannte Debitoren, Kreditoren*k*, Sach*k*, totes *K*; **nostro** ~ Nostro*k*; **numbered** ~ Nummern*k*; **omnibus** ~ Sammel*k*; **on** ~ auf Abschlag, a conto; **open** ~ offene Rechnung, *K* in laufender Rechnung; unbeglichene Rechnung; Exportlieferung auf Rechnung (*ohne Dokumentar-Sicherung*); **open-end** ~ offener Bestand; **operating ~s** Betriebsbuchführung; **our** ~ Nostroguthaben; **outstanding** ~ offene Rechnung; **overhead charges** ~ Gemeinkosten*k*; **partial** ~ Teilabrechnung; **participating** ~ Beteiligungs*k*, Konsortial*k*; **per** ~ **rendered** laut Rechnung; **personal** ~ Kunden*k*, Kredit*k*, Privat*k*; **petty** ~ Kassa*k*; **pledged ~s receivable** verpfändete Kundenforderungen; **post office giro** ~ *brit* Postgiro*k*; **private** ~ Privat*k*; **profit and loss** ~ Gewinn- und Verlustrechnung; **property** ~ Liegenschafts*k*, Vermögens*k*, Anlage*k*; **public ~s** Staatshaushalt, öffentl. Rechnungswesen; **real** ~ Bestands*k*; **realization** ~ Liquidations*k*; **received on** ~ in Gegenrechnung empfangen, a conto; **reserve** ~ Rückslagen*k*; **revenue** ~ Gewinn- und Verlust*k*; **running** ~ laufende Rechnung, Kontokorrent; **salary** ~ Gehalts*k*; **sale for the** ~ *exch* später zu begleichendes Geschäft; **sales** ~ Warenausgangs*k*; **savings** ~ Spar*k*; **securities** ~ Depot*k*; **secondary** ~ Nebenbuch*k*; **separate** ~ besonderes *K*, eigenes *K*.; **sequestered** ~ gerichtl gesperrtes *K*; **settled** ~ abgerechnetes *K*, schriftl. Saldenbestätigung; **share** ~ → *share;* **short** ~ → *short;* **sleeping** ~ totes *K*; **special** ~ Sonder*k*; **special checking** ~ *US* Scheck*k* mit Buchungsbelastung; **Special Drawing A~** (*Sonderziehungsk*) SZR-Konto beim IWF (*Internationaler Währungsfonds*); **statement of ~** *K*auszug, Rechnungsauszug; **sterling ~** → *sterling;* **stock ~** Kapital*k*, Lager*k*; Effektenrechnung; **subsidiary ~** Hilfs*k*; **subsidiary ledger ~** Nebenbuch*k*; **summary ~** zusammenfassendes *K*; **sundries ~** *K* „Verschiedenes", *K* pro Diverse; **survivorship ~** gemeinsames *K* mit Verfügungsrecht des Überlebenden; **suspended ~** transitorisches *K*; **suspense ~** Zwischen*k*, Interims*k*, Durchgangs*k*, Hinterlegungs*k* zur Abwendung der Vollstreckung; **tandem ~** Kontokorrentkredit*k*; **tax-sheltered ~** steuerfreies *bzw steuerbegünstiges K*; **thrift ~** Spar*k*; **to adjust an ~** ein *K* ausgleichen; **to "age" ~s** Konten nach ihrer Fälligkeit aufgliedern; **to audit ~s** Rechnungsprüfung vornehmen; **to balance an ~** ein *K* ausgleichen; **to block an ~** ein Guthaben sperren; **to bring into ~** (*against*) anrechnen (*auf*); **to clear ~s** abrechnen; **to cook the ~s** Unregelmäßigkeiten bei Kontenführung begehen; **to credit an ~** e–m *K* gutschreiben; **to debit an ~** ein *K* belasten; **to discharge an ~** → *to discharge;* **to dot ~s** Rechnungsposten nachprüfen; **to freeze an ~** ein Guthaben sperren; **to make out an ~** e–e Rechnung ausstellen; **to make up the cash ~** Kasse machen; **to open an ~ with s.o.** bei jmdm ein *K* eröffnen; **to overdraw an ~** ein *K* überziehen; **to pay into ~** auf ein *K* einzahlen; **to pay on ~** anzahlen; **to render an ~** Rechnung legen, abrechnen; **to set up an ~** → *to set up;* **to verify an ~** e–e Rechnung prüfen; **trading ~** Erfolgs*k*, Liefer*k*; Kundenabrechnung des Börsenmaklers; **two-name ~** gemeinsames *K*; **uncollectible ~s** uneinbringliche Forderungen; **unsettled ~** offenstehende Rechnung; **valuation ~** Wertberichtigungs*k*; **vostro ~** Vostro*k*; Sonder*k* „Löhne und Gehälter"; **wages and salaries ~** *Sonderk bei konkursgefährdeten Unternehmen im Auftrag von Gläubigerbanken.*

accountability Rechenschaftspflicht *f*, Rechnungslegungspflicht *f*, Haftungsumfang *m*; Verantwortlichkeit *f*; **~ commission** Disziplinarausschuß.

accountable verantwortlich, haftbar, haftpflichtig, zurechenbar.

accountancy Buchhaltung *f*, Buchführungswesen *n*, Rechnungswesen *n*; **~ adjustment** Buchkorrektur.

accountant Buchhalter *m*, Buchführungshelfer *m*, Wirtschaftsprüfer *m*, Abschlußprüfer *m*; **~'s certificate** Prüfvermerk; **A ~'s Certificate Rules** Vorschriften über Bestätigung der Rechnungsprüfung (*in Anwaltssachen*); **A ~ in Bankruptcy** Verwalter der Erträge aus Konkursveräußerungen; **~'s lien** Wirtschaftsprüferpfandrecht (*an Unterlagen*); **A ~ of Court** *scot* gerichtl Überwachungsbeamter für treuhänderische Verwaltungen; **~'s report** Prüf(ungs)bericht; **~ to the Crown** der Krone zur Rechnungslegung verpflichtete Person; **cash ~** Kassenbuchhalter; **certified (public) ~** Wirtschaftsprüfer; **chartered ~** Wirtschaftsprüfer; **cost ~** Betriebskalkulator; **court expert ~** gerichtl bestellter Buchführungs- und Bilanzsachverständiger; **private ~** betriebseigener Prüfer; **public ~** Wirtschaftsprüfer; *independent ~ ~: unabhängiger Abschlußprüfer.*

accounting Rechnungswesen *n*, Rechnungslegung *f*, Buchführung *f*; **~ date** Bilanzstichtag; **A ~ Directives Law** Bilanzrichtliniengesetz; **~ entity** buchführendes Unternehmen *bzw* buchführende Stelle; **~ equation** Ausgleichung der Buchhaltung, Kontenabstimmung; **~ evidence** Rechnungsnachweis; **~ for inventories** Inventurerstellung; **~ for units** Einheitsrechnung; **~ information** Buchführungsangaben, B.-daten; ~ **machine** Buchungsmaschine; ~ **methods** Buchungsmethoden; ~ **operation** Rechnungsvorgang; ~ **period** Abrechnungszeitraum, Veranlagungszeitraum; ~ **plan** Kontenrahmen; ~ **principles** Buchführungsgrundsätze; ~ **procedure** Buchhaltungsverfahren; ~ **process** Buchhaltungsvorgang; ~ **records** Geschäftsbücher, Buchungsunterlagen; ~ **reference period** Abrechnungszeitraum; ~ **report** Bilanzbericht; ~ **sheet** Abrechnungsbogen; ~ **supervisor** Leiter des Rechnungswesens; ~ **system** Buchführungssystem; ~ **unit** Rechnungsposten, Verrechnungseinheit; ~ **value** Buchwert; **accrual** ~ periodenechte Rechnungslegung, periodenechte Aufwands- und Ertragsrechnung; **activity** ~ Nachkalkulation; **actual-cost** ~ Nachkalkulation; **basic** ~ **requirements** grundlegende Erfordernisse der Buchführung; **branch** ~ Filialbuchführung; **budgetary** ~ Haushaltsrechnungsführung, Finanzplanung; **cash basis** ~ (schlichte) Einnahmen-Ausgaben-Rechnung; **cost** ~ Kostenrechnung, Selbstkostenberechnung, Rentabilitätsberechnung, Kalkulation, Betriebskostenermittlung; **current cost** ~ Wiederbeschaffungsprinzip; **deliveries** ~ wertmäßige Abrechnung; **depreciation** ~ *das systematische Verteilen von Anlagen auf die wirtschaftliche Nutzungsdauer;* **false** ~ Buchhaltungsfälschung; Abrechnungsbetrug; Fälschung bzw Vernichtung von Abrechnungen oder Buchungsunterlagen, Falschbuchung; **financial** ~ Finanzbuchhaltung; **general** ~ **department** Finanzbuchhaltung; **generally accepted** ~ **principles** Grundsätze ordnungsmäßiger Buchführung; **good** ~ ordnungsgemäße Buchführung; **governmental** ~ Staatsrechnungswesen, kameralistische Buchführung; **governmental** ~ **records** Buchhaltungsunterlagen und Bücher der öffentl Hand; **historical cost** ~ Anschaffungskostenprinzip; **inflation** ~ → *inflation;* **industrial** ~ betriebliche Buchführung, Betriebsbuchhaltung; **management** ~ betriebliches Rechnungswesen (*für Unternehmensleitung*); **merger** ~ Bilanzierung bei Fusionen; **municipal** ~ kommunales Rechnungswesen; **national income** ~ volkswirtschaftliche Erfolgsrechnung; **personnel** ~ Personalbuchhaltung; **property (plant)** ~ Anlagenbuchhaltung; **responsibility (activity)** ~ Wirtschaftlichkeitskontrollrechnung; **shop** ~ Betriebsabrechnung; **social** ~ Sozialbilanz, gesellschaftsbezogene Aufwendungen; **sound** ~ **practice** Grundsätze ordnungsmäßiger Buchführung; **tax** ~ Steuerbuchhaltung, Buchführung unter Beachtung vorwiegend steuerlicher Gesichtspunkte.

accounts receivable Debitoren *m|pl*; Forderungen *f|pl*, Außenstände *m|pl*, *kurz für: trade accounts receivable qv;* ~ **accounting** Debitorenbuchhaltung; ~ **clerk** Debitorenbuchhalter; ~ **discounted** zedierter Debitorenbestand; ~ **financing** Faktorierung; ~ **loan** Beleihung der Außenstände; ~ **management** Debitorenmanagement, Kreditmanagement; ~ **risk** Debitorenwagnis; ~ **turnover** Debitorenumschlag; **trade** ~ offene Buchforderungen.

accredit akkreditieren, offiziell bevollmächtigen; ~ **one's allegations** seine Angaben glaubhaft machen.

accredited akkreditiert, beglaubigt, autorisiert; ~ **representative** bevollmächtigter Vertreter.

accretion Anwachsung *f*, Zunahme *f*, Verlandung *f*, Anlandung *f*, Anschwemmung *f*, Anwachsung e–es Vermächtnisses bzw Erbteils (*durch Wegfall des Bedachten*) *m*.

accroach anmaßen, usurpieren, sich neigen.

accrual Anwachsung *f*, Zuwachs *m*,

Zugang *m*, Anfall *m*; ~ **accounting** → *accounting;* ~ **basis** Gewinnermittlung (*bzw Erfolgsermittlung*) durch Betriebsvermögensvergleich; periodengerechte Aufwands- und Ertragsrechnung; ~ **date** Fälligkeitstag; ~ **method** Gewinnermittlung durch Betriebsvermögensvergleich; ~ **of (a cause of) action** Zeitpunkt der Entstehung des Klageanspruchs; ~ **of a dividend** Entstehung e–s Dividendenanspruchs (*bei Vorzugsaktien*); ~ **of a right** Anfall e–s Rechts, Entstehung e–s Rechts; ~ **of inheritance** Erbfall, Anfall der Erbschaft; ~ **of interest** Auflaufen von Zinsen; ~**s payable** entstandene (*noch nicht fällige*) Verbindlichkeiten; ~**s receivable** entstandene (*noch nicht fällige*) Forderungen; **accounting for** ~**s** buchhalterische Darstellung von transitorischen Posten; **bank** ~**s** automatische Kontenerhöhungen; **clause of** ~ Anwachsungsklausel *in Testamenten.*

accrue zuwachsen, anfallen, hinzufügen, verbinden, zufließen, entstehen, auflaufen; ~ **by way of succession** im Erbgang anfallen.

accrued *adj* angefallen, aufgelaufen; ~ **holiday remuneration** anteilige Urlaubsvergütung (*bei Ausscheiden*); ~ **pension rights** Pensionsanwartschaft.

accruer Landzuwachs *m*, Erbzuwachs *m*.

accruing entstehend, anwachsend, e–e Anwartschaft bildend.

accumulate akkumulieren, anhäufen, (sich) ansammeln; aufzinsen.

accumulation Anhäufung *f*, Kumulation *f*, Thesaurierung *f*, Kapitalansammlung *f*, neugebildetes Vermögen aus investierten treuhänderischen Mitteln; ~ **for payment of debts** Rückstellung für Schuldentilgung; ~ **for raising portions** Bildung e–s Sonderfonds für (*nacherbberechtigte*) Abkömmlinge; ~ **of an annuity** Endwert e–r Annuität; ~ **of arrears** Anhäufung von Rückständen, Ansammlung von unerledigten Sachen; ~ **of funds** Kapitalansammlung; ~ **of reserves** Reservenbildung; **excessive** ~**s** unzulässige (*überlange*) Thesaurierung (*von Treuhandgeldern*).

accumulative kumulativ; ~ **judgment** zusätzliches Strafurteil, *dessen Vollstreckung bis zur Verbüßung e–r früheren Strafe ausgesetzt bleibt*; ~ **sentence** = ~ *judgment q.v.*

accusable anklagbar, strafbar.

accusation Anklage *f*, öffentliche Klage *f*, Beschuldigung *f*; **false** ~ falsche Anschuldigung; **formal** ~ Anklageerhebung; **malicious** ~ falsche Anschuldigung; **to reject** ~**s** Anschuldigungen zurückweisen.

accusatory part Anklagetenor *m* (*Bezeichnung der Straftat in e–r Anklageschrift*).

accuse *v* Anklage erheben, beschuldigen, bezichtigen.

accused *s* Angeklagte(r), Beschuldigte(r), Angeschuldigte(r); **evidence of** ~ Aussage des Angeklagten; **solicitor-access-denied** ~ *Beschuldigter, dem bei der polizeilichen Vernehmung die Zuziehung e–s Anwalts verweigert wurde*; **statement of** ~ Einlassung des Beschuldigten.

accuser Ankläger *m*, Anzeigeerstatter *m*, Privatkläger *m*.

accustomed üblich, gewohnheitsmäßig.

acid rain saurer Regen.

acid test Säuretest *m*, strenge Prüfung der Liquidität (*Bilanz*).

acknowledge anerkennen, zugestehen, bestätigen; ~ **the receipt** den Empfang bestätigen.

acknowledgment Bestätigung *f*, Beglaubigung *f*, Anerkenntnis *f*, Zugeständnis *n*; ~ **for production** anerkannte Verpflichtung zur Urkundenvorlegung; ~ **of debt** *schriftliches* Schuldanerkenntnis; ~ **of indebtedness** → *indebtedness;* ~ **of order** Auftragsbestätigung; ~ **of receipt** Empfangsbestätigung, Empfangsbescheinigung, Quittung; ~ **of receipt of mail** Postempfangsbescheinigung, Quittung für Postsendungen; ~ **of satisfaction** Abfindungsbestätigung; ~ **of service** Zustellungsbestätigung, Zustellungsnachweis; ~ **of signature** Unterschriftsbeglaubigung, (*nachträgliche*) Bestätigung der eigenen Unterschrift; ~ **of title** Anerkennung e–s dinglichen Rechts; **separate** ~ getrennte Beglaubigung (*der Ehefrau*).

acquaintance Bekanntschaft *f*, Kenntnis *f*.

acquainted persönlich bekannt, vertraut.

acquiesce dulden, stillschweigend billigen, einwilligen, sich fügen, etwas hinnehmen, etwas auf sich beruhen lassen.

acquiescence Duldung *f*, stillschweigende Billigung *f*, Verwirkung *f* durch Duldung.

acquire erwerben, an sich bringen, gewinnen, bekommen; ~ **(the) title** Eigentum erwerben.

acquirer Erwerber *m*; **hostile** ~ feindlicher Erwerber (*von Aktien bei Übernahmeangebot*); **potential** ~ Erwerbsinteressent.

acquisition (Eigentums)Erwerb *m*, Erwerbung *f*, Anschaffung *f*, Beschaffung *f*, Ankauf *m*; ~ **and operational phase** Beschaffungs- und Fertigungsphase; ~ **by absorption** Erwerb durch Verschmelzung; ~ **commission** Abschlußprovision; ~ **cost** Anschaffungskosten; ~ **of land** Grunderwerb *bes im Zwangsverfahren*; ~ **of ownership** Eigentumserwerb; ~ **of territory** Gebietserwerb; **derivative** ~ abgeleiteter (= *derivativer*) Eigentumserwerb, derivativer Gebietserwerb; **new** ~ Neuanschaffung, Neuerwerb; **for the** ~ **of gain** zu Erwerbszwecken; **original** ~ originärer (= *ursprünglicher*) Eigentumserwerb.

acquisitive gewinnsüchtig, auf Erwerb gerichtet.

acquisitor Erwerber *m*, spekulativer Aufkäufer, Unternehmenserwerber.

acquit freisprechen, freigeben, erfüllen, abtragen, quittieren; ~ **s. o. of a charge** jmdn von e–r Anklage freisprechen.

acquittal Freigabe *f*, Befreiung *f* von e–r Verbindlichkeit; Freispruch *m*; ~ **contract** Erlaßvertrag, Freigabevertrag; ~ **in fact (= in deed)** Freispruch aus tatsächlichen Gründen; ~ **in law** Freispruch aus Rechtsgründen; ~ **of an official duty** Erfüllung e–r Amtspflicht; **directed** ~ Freispruch (*aus Rechtsgründen*) auf Weisung des Richters *an die Geschworenen*; **hono(u)rable** ~ Freispruch wg. erwiesener Unschuld; **judgment of** ~ freisprechendes Urteil, Freispruch; **plea of (previous)** ~ Einrede bereits ergangenen Freispruchs (*in gleicher Sache*).

acquittance Quittung *f*, schriftl Freistellung *f* von e–r Verbindlichkeit; Schulderlaß *m*; Entlastung *f*; **sum of** ~ Abfindungssumme.

acreage restrictions Anbaubeschränkungen *f/pl*.

acronym Akronym *n*.

across the board „durch die Bank", global, in nicht differenzierter Weise; **~-the-board increase** generelle (Lohn)Erhöhung.

across-the-border commuter Grenzgänger *m*.

act *s* Handlung *f* (*e–s Menschen*), Handeln *n*, Tat *f*, Urkunde *f*, Verwaltungsakt *m*; Rechtsgeschäft *n*; Gesetz *n*; **~s and omissions** Handlungen und Unterlassungen; ~ **and warrant** *scot gerichtliche Bestätigung der Einsetzung e–s Sequesters*; ~ **book** *scot* Protokollbuch des Gerichts; **~, default or sufferance** Handeln, Unterlassen oder Dulden; ~ **done within the jurisdiction** e–r innerhalb der Gerichtsbarkeit begangene Tat; **~s falling short of homicide** Vorbereitung *bzw* Versuch der Tötung; ~ **in the law** Willenserklärung; **~, neglect or default** Handeln, Vernachlässigen oder Unterlassen; **A ~ of Adjournal** *scot Verfahrensordnung*; ~ **of ad-**

ministration Verwaltungsakt; **A ~ of Attainder** Ächtung, Bestrafung durch Einzelgesetz; **~ of bankruptcy** → *bankruptcy*; **A ~ of Congress** *US* Bundesgesetz; **~ of court** Maßnahme des Gerichts (*von Amts wegen*); **~s of court** gerichtliche Niederschriften (*im brit Seegericht*); **~ of curatory** *scot* Bestellung e–s Vormunds oder Pflegers; **~ of God** höhere Gewalt (*Ereignis der Naturgewalten ohne menschliches Dazutun*); **~ of God or other causes beyond s.o.'s control** höhere Gewalt; **~ of Government** *hist* Gnadenerlaß; **A ~ of Grace** Gnadenerlaß, Amnestie (*bei Thronbesteigung*); **~ of honour** Ehrenannahme *e–s Wechsels*; die notarielle Urkunde über e–e Ehrenannahme; **A ~ of Indemnity** (= *Indemnity Act*) Indemnitätsgesetz, Legalisierungsgesetz; **~ of insolvency** Zahlungsunfähigkeitsindiz (*e–r Bank*); **~ of law** gesetzliche Wirkung; **A ~ of Legislature** Gesetz *e–s US-Einzelstaates;* **~ of nature** Naturereignis; **~ of negligence** fahrlässige Handlung; **A ~ of Parliament** Gesetz (*formelles, parlamentarisch erlassenes* G); **~ of party** Willenserklärung; **~s of possession** Handlungen des Eigenbesitzers; **~ of protest** Protest, Protesturkunde; **~ of providence** unabwendbarer Zufall; **~s of rulers** höhere Gewalt, Verfügung von hoher Hand, Handlung e–s Herrschers; **~ of sale** (*Lousiana*) notariell beurkundete Auflassung; **A ~ of Settlement** (=) *brit Thronfolgegesetz von 1701*; **~ of state** Hoheitsakt, Staatsakt, hoheitsrechtliches Handeln des Staates; **A ~ of Supremacy** (=) *Gesetz über die Oberhoheit des englischen Königs gegenüber der Kirche von 1558*; **~s of terrorism** terroristische Anschläge; **~s of the King's enemy** *brit* Feindesgewalt; **~ of the law** Gesetzeswirkung (*unmittelbar durch das Gesetz bewirkte Übertragung oder sonstige Rechtsänderung*); **~ of transfer** Übertragungsakt, Abtretungserklärung; **A ~s of Union** (=) *brit Unionsgesetze zur Vereinigung Großbritanniens* (*mit Wales 1336, Schottland 1706, Irland 1800*); **~ of volition** Willensäußerung, konkludentes Handeln; **~ of war** kriegerische Handlung, feindlicher Akt; **~ or default** Handlung oder (*bzw*) Unterlassung; **~ or omission** Handlung *bzw* Unterlassung; **administrative ~** Verwaltungsakt, Verwaltungshandeln; **adoptive A ~** Übernahmegesetz; **a single ~** ein und dieselbe Tat; **any ~ or thing done** irgendeine Handlung; **bilateral ~** zweiseitiges Rechtsgeschäft, Vertrag; **blanket ~** Blankettgesetz; **by ~ of law** kraft Gesetzes, gesetzlich; **colourless ~** unauffällige Handlung, unspezifische H.; **concurrent ~** rechtlich zusammentreffende, ideal konkurrierende Tathandlungen; **congressional A ~** *US* Bundesgesetz; **consensual ~s** Handlungen im beiderseitigen Einverständnis, beiderseitige Willenserklärungen; **contractual ~** zweiseitiges Rechtsgeschäft; **criminal ~** strafbare Handlung, Straftat; **culpable ~** schuldhafte Handlung; **declaratory A~** (*die Rechtslage*) feststellendes Gesetz; **deliberate ~** vorsätzliche Handlung; **executive A~** Durchführungsgesetz; **felonious ~** Verbrechen; **general A ~** (allgem.) Gesetz; **general revival ~s** → *general;* **general survival ~s** → *general;* **hostile ~** Feindhandlung; **illegal ~** widerrechtliche Handlung; **immoral ~** sittenwidrige Handlung; **injurious ~** Verletzungshandlung; **in the very ~** auf frischer Tat, in flagranti; **innocent ~** schuldloses Handeln, gutgläubiges Handeln; **interpretation A~** Auslegungsgesetz; **judicial ~** richterliche Handlung, gerichtliche Entscheidung, Ermessensentscheidung nach Gewährung rechtlichen Gehörs, Maßnahme; **juristic ~** Rechtsgeschäft; **lawful ~** rechtl zulässige Handlung, **legal ~** R-shandlung, R-sgeschäft, Willenserklärung; **legislative** ~ Gesetz; **malicious** ~ vorsätzliche rechtswidrige Handlung, böswillige Handlung; **ministerial** ~ weisungsgebundene Handlung; **negligent** ~ fahrlässige Handlung; **official** ~ Amtshandlung; **overt** ~ offen begangene Tat, wahrnehmbare Handlung; **parallel ~s** gleichlaufende Erklärungen; **penal** ~ strafbare Handlung; **personal A~** Gesetz zur Verleihung der Rechtsfähigkeit; **preliminary** ~ vorläufiges Handeln; Tatbestandsurkunde *über Schiffskollision*; **private** ~ Willenserklärung, Rechtsgeschäft, rechtsgeschäftliche Erklärung von Einzelnen; **private A~** Spezialgesetz (*für eine Einzelperson oder Körperschaft*); **public** ~ Erklärung, die öffentlichen Glauben genießt; öffentliche Urkunde; **public A** ~ *allgemein geltendes* Gesetz, gesetzliche Vorschrift; **revenue A~s** → *revenue;* **special A~** = *private A~ qv;* **successive ~s** fortgesetzte Handlung; **unilateral** ~ einseitige Willenserklärung, Verfügung; **unlawful** ~ widerrechtl Handlung; **voluntary and formal** ~ freie Willenserklärung in gehöriger Form, formgebundene Willenserkl.; **wilful** ~ vorsätzl. Handlung, vorsätzl Tat; **wrongful** ~ schuldhafte Handlung

act *v* handeln (= *e–e Handlung vornehmen*), tätig sein, auftreten; ~ **as agent or on behalf of a third person** im fremden Namen handeln *vgl agent*; ~ **as chairman** den Vorsitz haben; ~ **as curtain** abschirmen, ausschließen; ~ **as principal and agent** mit sich selbst kontrahieren; ~ **in good faith** im guten Glauben handeln; gutgläubig handeln; ~ **innocently** gutgläubig und redlich handeln; ~ **in one's official capacity** kraft seines Amtes handeln, in amtl Eigenschaft handeln; ~ **on one's own behalf** im eigenen Namen handeln; ~ **under duress** unter Nötigung handeln.

"acte clair" klare, nicht auslegungsbedürftige Rechtsnorm; ~ **doctrine** direkte Anwendbarkeit e–r EG-Norm durch die nationalen Gerichte ohne Vorlage b Eur Gerichtshof.

acting handelnd, stellvertretend, amtierend; ~ **appointment** Einstellung auf Widerruf; ~ **generally in the action or matter** *allgemein für einen Mandanten* in einer Sache tätig sein; ~ **in the execution of an act** in Vollziehung e–s Gesetzes handelnd; ~ **partner** → *partner;* ~ **president** amtierender Präsident; ~ **through** vertreten durch; ~ **through agent** in mittelbarer Täterschaft handelnd; ~ **trustee** amtierender Treuhänder.

action Klage *f* (= *Kl bzw . . . kl*), Prozeß *m*, Streitsache *f*; amtliches Handeln *n*; Verfahren *n*, Maßnahme *f*; Handeln *n*, Tun *n*; ~ **begun by writ** *Kl* im ordentlichen Verfahren; ~ **brought without authority** *Kl*-erhebung ohne Prozeßvollmacht; ~ **by beneficiary** *Kl* e–s Treuhandbegünstigten; **A~ Department** Prozeßabteilung, Zentralgeschäftsstelle des High Court; ~ **ex contractu** *Kl* aus Vertrag; ~ **ex delicto** *Kl* aus unerlaubter Handlung; ~ **for a declaratory judgment** Feststellungs*kl*; ~ **for affiliation** Abstammungsfeststellungs- und Alimenten*kl* für ein uneheliches Kind; ~ **for an account** Rechnungslegungs*kl*; ~ **for annulment** Anfechtungs*kl*, Nichtigkeits*kl*; ~ **for arrears of interest** *Kl* auf Zahlung von Zinsrückständen; ~ **for arrears of rent** *Kl* auf Zahlung von Miet-(Pacht)rückständen; ~ **for breach of contract** *Kl* wegen Vertragsverletzung, *Schadenersatzkl wegen Nichterfüllung, Verzug oder positiver Vertragsverletzung*; ~ **for calls** *Kl* auf Leistung der Einzahlung (Aktien); ~ **for conversion** → ~ *of conversion*; ~ **for damages** Schadenersatz*kl*; ~ **for divorce** *US* Scheidungs*kl*; ~ **for infringement** Verletzungs*kl* (*gewerbliche Schutzrechte*); ~ **for li-**

bel → *libel*; ~ **for money had and received** *Kl* auf Rückzahlung wegen ungerechtfertigter Bereicherung; ~ **for nullity of marriage** Ehenichtigkeits*kl*; ~ **for partition** Teilungs*kl*, Aufhebungs*kl*, Auseinandersetzungs*kl*; ~ **for personal injuries** Schadensersatzklage wg. Körperverletzung; ~ **for poinding** Zwangsvollstreckung; Antrag auf Zwangsverwaltung; ~ **for recovery** Herausgabe*kl*; ~ **for recovery of land** *Kl* auf Herausgabe e–s Grundstücks, Räumungs*kl*; ~ **for redemption** *Kl* auf Wiedereinräumung des Besitzes an e–m verpfändeten Grundstück; *Kl* auf Rückgabe der verpfändeten Sache; ~ **for restitution** *Kl* auf Herausgabe; ~ **for restitution of conjugal community (or rights)** *Kl* auf Wiederherstellung der ehelichen Lebensgemeinschaft; ~ **for specific performance** *Kl* auf (*genaue*) Vertragserfüllung; *Kl* auf Vornahme e-r geschuldeten Handlung; ~ **for trover** → ~ *of trover*; ~ **for use and occupation** *Kl* auf Nutzungsentschädigung; ~ **in personam** schuldrechtliche *Kl*; ~ **in rem** dingliche *Kl*; ~ **in tort** → *tort*; ~ **of a writ** Einwendung wegen formaler Unzulässigkeit e–r *Kl*; ~ **of adherence** *scot Kl* auf Wiederherstellung der ehelichen Lebensgemeinschaft; ~ **of assumpsit** Schadenersatz*kl* wegen Nichterfüllung (*e–s schriftlichen oder formlosen Vertrages);* ~ **of book debt** Einklagung von Außenständen; ~ **of contract** *Kl* aus (einem) Vertrag; ~ **of conversion** *Kl* auf Wiedereinräumung des Besitzes; Herausgabe*kl bzw* Schadenersatz*kl* wegen widerrechtlicher Aneignung oder Verfügung (*vgl trover*); ~ **of debt** *Kl* auf Zahlung e–r Geldschuld, Zahlungs*kl;* ~**of division** → *division*; ~ **of ejectment** Räumungs*kl*; ~ **of recovery** Herausgabe*kl*, Erbschafts*kl*; ~ **of replevin** → *replevin*; ~ **of trespass** *Kl* wegen Besitzstörung; ~ **of trover** Bereicherungs*kl*, Schadenersatz*kl* wegen rechtswidriger Aneignung (*cf trover; nach 1852* = ~ *of conversion qv*), ~ **on contract** Vertrags*kl*, *Kl* aus Vertrag; ~ **on covenant** *Kl* aus gesiegelter Urkunde; ~ **on the case** deliktische *Kl*; ~ **or suit** *Kl* im ordentlichen Verfahren; ~ **possessory** = *possessory* ~ *qv*; ~ **prejudicial** Verfahren über e–e Vorfrage (*Kaufrecht*); ~ **rescissory** *scot* Feststellungs*kl* auf Grund e–r Anfechtung; ~ **thereon** diesbezügliche Amtshandlung (*zB des Patentamts*); ~ **to quiet title** Eigentumsfeststellungs*kl*; **abandonment of** ~ → *abandonment*; **abortive** ~ vergebliche *Kl*, Wegfall der Anspruchsgrundlage nach Rechtshängigkeit; **accessory** ~ Nebenverfahren; **administration** ~ *Kl* auf Anordnung der Nachlaßverwaltung; **administration** ~**s** Nachlaßverwaltungssachen, Pflegschaftssachen; **admiralty** ~ seerechtlicher Prozeß, *Kl* aus Ansprüchen des Seerechts; **an** ~ **lies** e–e *Kl* ist zulässig; **assignment of** ~**s** Geschäftsverteilung, Zuweisung e–r Sache; **bailable** ~ *Kl* gegen Sicherheitsleistung; **barring of** ~**s** Unzulässigkeit der *Kl*; **bringing of an** ~ Erhebung e–r *Kl*; **by way of** ~ im *Kl*–wege; **cause of** ~ *Kl*–grund; **chose in** ~ → *chose*; **civil** ~ Zivilkl; Zivilprozeß, bürgerliche Rechtsstreitigkeit; **class** ~ → *class*; **coercive** ~ Zwangshandlung; **collision** ~ Schadenersatz*kl* wegen Verkehrsunfall; **collusive** ~ auf Kollusion gestützter Prozeß; **commencement of** ~ *Kl*–erhebung; **commercial** ~**s** Handelssachen; **concerted** ~ gemeinschaftliches Vorgehen; **concurrent** ~**s** Parallelverfahren; **concomitant** ~**s** verbundene *Kl-n*; **conduct of** ~**s** Prozeßführung, **consolidation of** ~**s** *Kl*-verbindung; **contested** ~ streitige *Kl*; **continuing** ~ Fortsetzung des Prozesses (*zB bei Parteiänderung*); **criminal** ~ Strafverfahren; **cross** ~ Wider*kl*; **debenture** ~ *Kl* aus Schuldurkunde; **default** ~

Zahlungs*kl*, *Kl* wegen Zahlungsverzug; **declaratory** ~ Feststellungs*kl*; **derivative** ~ Prozeßstandschafts*kl*; **direct** ~ Direkt*kl* (*gegen den Versicherer*); **disciplinary** ~ → *disciplinary*; **discontinuance of** ~ Aussetzung des Verfahrens; **discretionary** ~**s** Ermessenshandlungen; **dismissal of** ~ *Kl*–abweisung; **droitural** ~ auf Eigentum gestützte Grundstücksherausgabe*kl*; **ejectment** ~ Räumungs*kl*; **equitable** ~ *Kl* im Equity-Verfahren; auf billigkeitsrechtlichen Anspruch gestützte *Kl*; *Kl* des Drittbegünstigten; **faint** ~ Scheinprozeß; **false** ~ Schein*kl*; **feigned** ~ Scheinprozeß; **feudal** ~ → *feudal*; **fictitious** ~ Scheinprozeß, fiktive *Kl*; **fixed-date** ~ *etwa Kl* mit festem Termin; Leistungs*Kl* (*ohne Zahlungskl*); **frivolous** ~ leichtfertige *Kl*; **foreclosure** ~ Pfandverfallsverfahren, Vollstreckung aus e–m Grundpfandrecht; **hypothecary** ~ Hypotheken*kl*; **in** ~ im Streit befangen; **independent** ~ unabhängige *Kl*; **industrial** ~ Arbeitskampfmaßnahmen; **joint** ~ Prozeß mit Streitgenossen; **legal** ~ *Kl* im ordentl Zivilprozeß; **local** ~ *Kl* am Gerichtsstand der belegenen Sache *bzw* der unerlaubten Handlung; **mixed** ~ (*gemischte*) schuldrechtliche und zugleich dingliche *Kl*; **multi-plaintiff** ~ Kollektiv*kl*; **nullity** ~ Nichtigkeits*kl*; **official** ~ Amtshandlung; **partition** ~ Teilungs*kl*; **penal** ~ Strafverfahren; **personal** ~ persönliche (= *schuldrechtliche*) *Kl*, Leistungs*kl*; nur vom Geschädigten selbst zu erhebende Kl; **petitory** ~ *Kl* auf Eigentumsfeststellung; *scot* Schadensersatz*kl*; **plenary** ~ *Kl* im ordentlichen Verfahren; **popular** ~ öffentliche *Kl* e–r Privatperson; *US*: Popular*kl*; **possessory** ~ Besitz*kl*, possessorische *Kl*, Räumungs*kl*; **previous** ~ Voraus*kl*, Vorverfahren; **private** ~ privatrechtliche *Kl*; **probate** ~ Nachlaß*kl*; streitiges Testamentsverfahren, *Kl* auf gerichtl Testamentsfeststellung; **prohibitory** ~ Unterlassungs*kl*; **quia timet** ~ vorbeugende Unterlassungs*kl*; **real** ~ dingliche *Kl*, *Kl* auf Herausgabe e–s Grundstücks; **redhibitory** ~ Wandlungs*kl*; **regulatory** ~ Regelung durch Vorschriften; **relator** ~ Popular*kl*, Verbands*kl* (*wegen Verletzung e–s öffentl Rechts zur Beseitigung e–s Übelstands; GB formell im Namen des Attorney General*); **rent** ~ *Kl* auf Mietzahlung; **representative** ~ *Kl* in Prozeßstandschaft; **rescissory** ~ Anfechtungs*kl*; **revived** ~ wiederaufgenommenes Verfahren; **revocatory** ~ Vertragsaufhebungs*kl*; **salvage** ~**s** *Kl–n* auf Bergelohn; **secondary** ~ mittelbare Arbeitskampfmaßnahme, Aufforderung zur Arbeitsniederlegung bei nichtbestreikten Betrieben; **state** ~ → *state (2)*; **statutory** ~ durch Parlamentsgesetze gegebene *Kl*; **stay of** ~ Aussetzung des Verfahrens; **subsequent** ~ später anhängig gewordener Prozeß; **summary** ~ *Kl* im abgekürzten Verfahren; **survival** ~ Schadensersatzkl über den Tod des Verletzten hinaus; **to institute** (= *bring*) **an** ~ *Kl* erheben, klagen; **to take** ~ klagen, gerichtlich vorgehen; **transitory** ~ *Kl* ohne örtlichen Anknüpfungspunkt (*für die überall die örtliche Zuständigkeit gegeben ist*); **vexatious** ~ schikanöse *Kl*; **voluntary** ~ *crim* freiwilliges (*nicht erzwungenes*) Handeln; **waiver of an** ~ *Kl*–verzicht; **withdrawal of an** ~ *Kl*-rücknahme (*vor der mündlichen Verhandlung*).

actionable klagbar, e–n Klagegrund bildend, gerichtlich verfolgbar; ~ **loss** einklagbarer Schaden; ~ **misrepresentation** gravierende falsche Angaben *bei Vertragsschluß*; ~ **negligence** → *negligence*; ~ **nuisance** rechtserhebliche Störung oder Belästigung; ~ **per se** selbständig e–n Klagegrund bildend;

~ **tort** unerlaubte Handlung, Delikt des Zivilrechts; ~ **words** ehrverletzende Worte, *die ohne weiteres e–n Schadenersatzanspruch begründen.*

actionary Aktionär *m* (*als Fremdwort für nicht-englische Aktionäre*).

activation Aktivierung *f.*

active tätig, aktiv; wirksam; rechtshängig (*Strafsachen*).

activity Tätigkeit *f,* Beschäftigung *f,* Aufgabengebiet *n;* ~ **rate** Prozentsatz der Berufstätigen; **field of** ~ Arbeitsgebiet, Tätigkeitsfeld; **independent** ~ selbständige Tätigkeit; **industrial** ~ gewerbliche Tätigkeit; **investigating** ~ Ermittlungstätigkeit; **sphere of** ~ Wirkungskreis; **professional** ~ Berufstätigkeit.

actor Kläger *m,* Stellvertreter *m,* Beauftragter *m.*

actrix Klägerin *f,* Stellvertreterin *f,* Beauftragte *f.*

actual tatsächlich, wirklich, effektiv; unmittelbar, gegenwärtig; ~ **change of possession** unmittelbarer Besitzübergang, tatsächlicher Besitzwechsel; ~ **costs and expenses** Istkosten, effektive Kosten; ~ **deviser of the invention** der tatsächliche Urheber der Erfindung, der wirkl Erfinder; ~ **man hours** Iststunden; ~ **market value** Verkehrswert; ~ **military service** Militärdienst; ~ **net cost** reine Selbstkosten; ~ **state of affairs** tatsächliche Lage der Dinge; ~ **takings** Effektiveinnahmen; ~ **total loss** Totalschaden, physischer Totalverlust; ~ **use or occupation** Benutzung und Gewahrsam.

actuarial versicherungsmathematisch; ~ **calculation** Versicherungskalkulation; ~ **method** Tafelmethode; ~ **practice** Versicherungstechnik; ~ **rate** Tafelziffer; ~ **society** Berufsverband von Versicherungsmathematikern; ~ **tables** versicherungsstatistische Tabellen; ~ **theory** Versicherungsmathematik; ~ **value** Versicherungswert.

actuary Versicherungsmathematiker *m;* ~**'s index** *exch* (=) *Verzeichnis von Papieren, die von Versicherungen aufgekauft werden.*

actus reus objektiver Tatbestand *m* (*cf mens|rea*), äußere Tatbestandsmerkmale.

ad (= *advertisement*) Anzeige *f,* Inserat *n;* ~ **man** Werbefachmann; ~ **writer** Anzeigentexter.

ad hoc (=) für den Einzelfall, von Fall zu Fall; ~ **assurances** Auflassungserklärung über e–n für den Einzelfall bestellten Treuhänder; ~ **settlement** treuhänderische Festlegung für den Einzelfall; ~ **trust** Treuhandsbildung für den Einzelfall.

adhocracy *System der innovativen Einzelfall-Lösungen.*

ad interim Zwischen-, bis dahin, vorläufig, einstweilig; ~ **copyright** vorläufiger Urheberrechtsschutz; ~ **protection for an invention** vorläufiger Schutz für e–e Erfindung.

ad litem für den (*diesen*) Rechtsstreit; **guardian** ~ → *guardian.*

ad valorem nach dem Wert; ~ **duty** → *duty;* ~ **tax** → *tax.*

adapt anpassen; ~ **for sale** für den Verkauf herrichten.

adaptation Anpassung *f,* Bearbeitung *f* e–s literarischen oder musikalischen Werks.

adapted angepaßt; ~ **figures** bereinigte Werte; ~ **from the original** nach dem Original bearbeitet; ~ **to be inhabited** für Wohnzwecke hergerichtet; ~ **to distinguish** Unterscheidungsfähigkeit erhalten habend, unterscheidungsfähig gestaltet.

adaptor Bearbeiter *m;* ~**'s copyright** Bearbeiterurheberrecht *n.*

addendum Zusatz *m,* Nachtrag *m; pl* **addenda** Zusätze, Zusatzbestimmungen; ~ **to a policy** Nachtragspolice.

addict Süchtiger *m;* **drug** ~ → *drug.*

addiction Sucht *f,* ~ **to alcohol** Alkoholismus.

addition Beifügung *f,* Zusammenrechnung *f,* Zugang *m;* ~**s at cost**

zusätzliche Leistungen zum Selbstkostenpreis; **future ~s** zukünftige Zugänge, Neuerwerbungen; **subsequent ~s** *bil* Zugänge.

additionales nachträgliche Vereinbarungen *f/pl*.

add ons miteinander verbundene Abzahlungsverträge *m/pl*.

address *s* (*1*) Adresse *f*, Anschrift *f*, **~ for payment** Zahlstelle, Zahlungsadresse; **~ for service** zustellungsfähige Anschrift, Zustellungsadresse; **abbreviated ~** Telegrammadresse; **business ~** Firmenanschrift; **cable ~** Drahtanschrift, Telegrammadresse; **code ~** Deckadresse; **delivery ~** Lieferanschrift; **home ~** Privatanschrift, Heimatanschrift, Wohnsitzadresse; **in case of change of ~** falls verzogen; **mailing ~** Postanschrift; **street ~** Anschrift.

address *s* (*2*) Ansprache *f*; Bittschrift *f*, Eingabe *f*, Bezeichnung *f* des angerufenen Gerichts; **~ in mitigation** Plädoyer über strafmildernde Umstände; **~ of counsel** Plädoyer; **~ to the crown** Dankesresolution *des engl Parlaments* an den Monarchen; **closing ~** Schlußplädoyer; **final ~** Schlußvortrag.

address *v* anreden, ansprechen; **~ the court** plädieren, bei Gericht (*mündlich*) vortragen.

addressee Adressat(in); **~ in case of need** Notadresse, Notadressat.

addressograph Adressiermaschine *f*.

adduce vorlegen, anbieten, vorbringen, beibringen; **~ evidence** → *evidence*.

adeem wegnehmen, widerrufen, entziehen, e–e Ersatzerfüllung e–s Vermächtnisses vornehmen (*durch den Erblasser bei Lebzeiten*), ein Vermächtnis unter Lebenden vorwegnehmen.

ademption Widerruf *m*, Ungültigkeitserklärung *f*; Entziehung *f* (*e–r Zuwendung*) wegen anderweitiger Verfügung des Erblassers über den vermachten Gegenstand; **~ of legacy** Entziehung e–s Vermächtnisses, Erledigung e–s Vermächtnisses durch Vorwegnahme unter Lebenden.

adequacy Angemessenheit *f*, Zweckdienlichkeit *f*.

adequate hinreichend, ausreichend, angemessen.

adhere sich anschließen, zu e–r Gruppe (Partei) gehören; **~ to a rule** sich an e–e Regel halten.

adherence Beitritt *m*, Anschluß *m*; **~ to a treaty** Beitritt zu e–m (*völkerrechtlichen*) Vertrag.

adherent verbunden, begleitend, fest verbunden mit.

adherent Anhänger(in); **~ to the King's (Queen's) enemies** Landesverräter.

adhesion Beitritt *m* (*zu e–m völkerrechtlichen Vertrag*); Assoziierung *f*; **~ contract** Standardvertrag mit einseitig auferlegten Bedingungen.

adjacency Angrenzung *f*, angrenzendes Grundstück *n*; gezielte Plazierung (*e–s Werbespots*).

adjacent benachbart, angrenzend.

adjective adjektivisch, unselbständig; verfahrensmäßig; **~ law** → *law*.

adjoin unmittelbar angrenzen; **~ing or contiguous** angrenzend oder unmittelbar benachbart; **~ing owners** Grenznachbar, Grundstücksnachbar, Anrainer.

adjourn vertagen, e–n Termin verlegen; **~ a case** die mündliche Verhandlung vertagen; **~ sine die** auf unbestimmte Zeit vertagen; **~ed meeting** Fortsetzung der Sitzung, Sitzung nach e–r Vertagung; **~ed summons** Terminsanberaumung; **~ed term** verlängerte Sitzungsperiode des Gerichts.

adjournment Vertagung *f*, Unterbrechung *f* (*der Hauptverhandlung*), Aussetzung *f* (*des Verfahrens*), Verlegung *f* e–s Termins, Beendigung *f* der Sitzungsperiode; **~ day** neuer *außerordentlicher* Termin (*e–s Gerichts*); **~ day in error** Sondertermin für Revisionssachen; **~ debate** formlose Debatte vor Schluß der Parlamentssitzung; **~ into chambers** Verweisung an den Einzelrichter *bzw* Rechtspfleger; ~ **into court** Kammervorlage; ~ **motion** Antrag auf allgemeine Debatte zum Sitzungsschluß; ~ **of appeal** Vertagung der Berufungsverhandlung; ~ **of the House** Vertagung der Parlamentssitzung; ~ **of trial** Verlegung des Verhandlungstermins; ~ **sine die** Vertagung auf unbestimmte Zeit, endgültiger Sitzungsschluß, Abschluß der Sitzungsperiode.

adjudge gerichtlich entscheiden, zuerkennen, verurteilen, zusprechen; ~ **s.o. bankrupt** über jmds Vermögen den Konkurs eröffnen; ~ **damages** Schadenersatz zusprechen.

adjudgment Zuerkennung *f*, Aburteilung *f*; Urteil *n*.

adjudicate gerichtlich entscheiden; ein Urteil fällen; zuerkennen; zuschlagen (*Versteigerung*); **~d bankrupt** Gemeinschuldner.

adjudication gerichtliche Entscheidung *f*, Zuerkennung *f*, Zuschlag *m*, Konkurseröffnung *f*; ~ **in bankruptcy** → *bankruptcy*; ~ **of guilt** Schuldausspruch (*im Urteil*); ~ **order** Konkurseröffnungsbeschluß; **administrative** ~ Verwaltungsentscheidung(sVerfahren); **free** ~ freihändige Vergabe e–s Auftrags; **qualified** ~ beschränkte Auftragsvergabe (*bei Ausschreibungen*).

adjudicative erkennend, richterlich, die gerichtliche Entscheidung betreffend; ~ **claims arbitration** Schiedsverfahren für Kleinforderungen.

adjudicator Schiedsrichter *m*, Verwaltungsrichter *m*, über e–e Beschwerde entscheidender Beamter.

adjudicatory gerichtlich zu entscheiden, gerichtsähnlich.

adjunct Zusatz *m*, Kollege *m*, Mitarbeiter *m*, Amtsgehilfe *m*.

adjunction Verbindung *f* von Sachen (*durch Aufnahme, Einbau und dgl, auch: Bearbeitung*).

adjuration eidliche Versicherung *f*, eidliche Beteuerung *f*.

adjure beschwören, vereidigen.

adjust anpassen, regulieren, ausgleichen, festsetzen, eichen; ~ **an account** → *account* (*2*); ~ **an entry** e–e Buchung berichtigen; ~ **the average** Dispache aufmachen; **seasonally ~ed** saisonbereinigt.

adjusted bereinigt, berichtigt.

adjuster Regulierungsbeauftragter *m* (*e–r Versicherung*); **average** ~ → *average* (*2*); **claim** ~ Regulierungsbeauftragter.

adjustment Anpassung *f*, Vergleich *m*, Ausgleich *m*, Schadensregulierung *f*, Kontenabstimmung *f*, Glattstellung *f*, ~ **account** → *account*; ~ **board** Schlichtungskommission; ~ **bonds** bei e–r Sanierung ausgegebene Obligationen; ~ **bureau** Schadensbüro; ~ **for currency losses (or gains)** Devisenwertberichtigung; ~ **of average** (= *average* ~) → *average* (*2*); ~ **of depreciations** Abschreibungskorrekturen; ~ **of interest** Zinsausgleich; ~ **of loss** Schadensregulierung; ~ **of prices** Preisanpassung; ~ **process** Anpassungsprozeß; **amicable** ~ gütliche Beilegung; **average** ~ → *average* (*2*); **cash** ~ Barausgleich; **compensatory** ~ ausgleichende Regelung; **currency** ~ Währungsangleichung; **financial** ~ Finanzausgleich; **foreign-exchange-rate** ~ Wechselkurskorrektur; **period of vocational** ~ Einarbeitungszeit; **property** ~ Vermögensausgleich; **wage** ~ Lohnangleichung.

admanuensis Eid *m* durch Handauflegen auf die Bibel; der (*auf diese Weise*) Schwörende.

admeasure abmessen, eichen; zuteilen.

admeasurement Messen *n*, Zumessen *n*, Bemessen *n*, Maß *n*, Eichung *f*, **~s** Maßangaben *f/pl*; **bill of** ~ Meßbrief (*e–s Schiffes*).

administer verwalten, e–e Amtshandlung vornehmen; verabreichen; ~ **an estate** e–n Nachlaß abwickeln; ~ **justice** Recht sprechen, die Rechtspflege ausüben; ~ **poi-**

son Gift beibringen; ~ **the oath** → *oath.*

administration Verwaltung *f* (= *Verw bzw . . . verw*), Behörde *f*, Regierung *f*; Nachlaßpflegschaft *f*; Nachlaßabwicklung bei gesetzlicher Erbfolge, Nachlaß*verw* (*gerichtlich angeordnete treuhänderische Verw und Abwicklung des Nachlasses, in diesem Sinne auch im folgenden gebraucht*); ~ **action** → *action*; ~ **ad colligenda bona defuncti** Nachlaßpflegschaft (*zur Sicherstellung des Nachlasses*); **ancillary** ~ gegenständlich beschränkte Nachlaß*verw*; ~ **and coordination department** Organisationsabteilung; ~ **bond** → *bond* (*2*); ~ **cum testamento annexo** gerichtlich angeordnete *Verw* des Nachlasses nach Maßgabe des Testaments; ~ **de bonis non** nachträgliche *Verw* von bisher nicht erfaßten Nachlaßgegenständen; ~ **durante absentia** Nachlaß*verw* während der Abwesenheit des Test.-Vollstreckers; ~ **expense** → *expense*; ~ **of an insolvent estate in court** Nachlaßkonkursverfahren; ~ **of assets** Vermögens*verw*, Nachlaß*verw*, Intestatsnachlaß*verw*; ~ **of estate** Nachlaßpflegschaft, Intestatsnachlaß*verw*; ~ **of justice** Rechtspflege, Rechtsprechung; ~ **of the law** Rechtsprechung, Rechtspflege; ~ **of the oath** → *oath*; ~ **order** Anordnung der Nachlaß*verw*, Anordnung der Geschäftsführung durch gerichtl bestellten Verwalter (*drohende Insolvenz*); ~ **suit** Klage auf Anordnung e–r Nachlaß*verw*; ~ **with the will annexed** = ~ *cum testamento annexo qv*; **ancillary** ~ gegenständl beschränkte Nachlaß*verw*; **board of** ~ → *board* (*1*); **business** ~ → *business*; **ancillary** ~ Nebennachlaß*verw*; **domiciliary** ~ Nachlaß*verw* am Wohnort des Erblassers; **executive** ~ die Minister und hohen politischen Beamten; **fiscal** ~ Finanz*verw*; **foreign** ~ Nachlaß*verw im Auftrag e–s ausländischen Gerichts*; **general** ~ unbeschränkte Nachlaß*verw*; **grant of** ~ Anordnung der Nachlaß*verw bzw* Nachlaßpflegschaft; Einsetzung des Intestat-Nachlaßabwicklers; **letters of** ~ Nachlaßverwalterzeugnis, Bestallungsurkunde des Intestat-Nachlaßabwicklers; *to take out* ~ ~ ~: *das Amt des Nachlaßverwalters* (*-abwicklers*) *antreten*; **limited** ~ zeitlich beschränkte Nachlaß*verw*; **local** ~ Gemeinde*verw*; **oath of** ~ → *oath*; **penal** ~ Strafvollzug, Strafvollzugsbehörde(n); **public** ~ von Amts wegen angeordnete Nachlaß*verw* (*bei Intestatnachlaß*); **requesting** ~ ersuchende *Verw*; **self** ~ Selbst*verw*; **special** ~ Nachlaß*verw* über einzelne Vermögensgegenstände, gegenständlich beschränkte Nachlaß*verw*; **summary** ~ abgekürztes Insolvenzverfahren.

administrative Verwaltungs . . ., (= *Verw–s*), verwaltend, die Verwaltung (= *Verw*) betreffend; ~ **destruction of property** Vernichtung von Gegenständen auf behördliche Veranlassung; ~ **international institutions** internationale Behörden; ~ **revocation of licenses** Entziehung der Zulassung durch die *Verw–s*behörde.

administratively auf dem Verwaltungswege.

administrator Verwalter *m*, Beamter *m*, gerichtlich eingesetzter Nachlaßtreuhänder (= *N*), Intestatnachlaßabwickler *m* (*in diesem Sinne Nachlaßverwalter* = *N*), Nachlaßverwalter *m*, Nachlaßpfleger *m* (*bes bei Intestatserbfolge*), Kurator *m*; ~ **ad colligenda bona** Nachlaßpfleger wegen Fehlens e–s Testamentsvollstreckers; ~ **ad litem** Prozeßpfleger; ~**'s bond** → *bond*; ~ **cum testamento annexo** = → *with the will annexed qv*; ~ **de bonis non** Teilnachlaßpfleger (*über noch nicht erfaßte Gegenstände*); ~ **durante absentia** Nachlaßpfleger wegen Abwesenheit eines Testamentvollstreckers; ~**in law** *scot* gesetzl Vertreter (*von Minderjährigen*); ~ **of a bankrupt's estate** Konkursverwalter; ~ **of an estate** *N*; ~ **pendente lite** Prozeßpfleger im Erbschaftsprozeß, Nachlaßprozeßpfleger; ~ **with the will annexed** *N* mit Testamentsbindung (*nach Ausfall e–s Testamentsvollstreckers bzw teilweisem Intestat*); **domestic** ~ *N* am letzten Wohnsitz des Erblassers; **principal** ~ Haupt*N*; **Public A**~, ~ *N*, amtlicher Nachlaßabwickler, öffentlicher Nachlaßtreuhänder.

administratorship Verwalteramt *m*, Stellung, Funktion des *administrator qv*.

administratrix Nachlaßverwalterin *f*, *cf administrator*.

admiralty Admiralität *f*; Seegerichtsbarkeit *f*; ~ **action** → *action*; ~ **bond** Garantieschein für Seetransport; ~ **cause** Seerechtssache; **A**~ **Chart** Seekarte der Royal Navy; ~ **court** Seegericht; **A**~ **Court** Seegericht (*als Abt. der Queen's Bench Division, seit 1970*); **A**~ **Division** Seerechtsabteilung des High Court London; ~ **jurisdiction** Seegerichtsbarkeit; ~ **law** → *law*; ~ **offence** seerechtliches Delikt; ~ **regulations** seerechtliche Vorschriften; ~ **rules** *US*-Verfahrensordnung für Seegerichtssachen; **droits of** ~ Einziehungsrecht (*der brit Krone*) von Prisen und Schiffswracks; **First Lord of the A**~ Erster Lord der Admiralität (*Marineminister*).

admissibility Zulässigkeit *f*; ~ **of evidence** Zulässigkeit von Beweismitteln *bzw* Beweisanträgen.

admissible zulässig, erlaubt, annehmbar; ~ **evidence** zulässiges Beweismittel.

admission Einlaß *m*, Aufnahme *f*, Zulassung *f*, Zulässigkeit *f*, Zugeständnis *n*, Eingeständnis *n*, Geständnis *n*; ~ **by conduct** Zugestehen durch schlüssiges Verhalten; ~ **of case of other party** Anerkenntnis (*im Zivilprozeß*); ~ **of documents** Nichtbestreiten der Echtheit von Urkunden; ~ **of fact** Zugestehen von Tatsachen, Erklärung des Nichtbestreitens; ~ **of guilt** Schuldgeständnis, Schuldbekenntnis; ~ **of liability** Haftungszugeständnis; ~ **of securities to the stock exchange** Börsenzulassung von Wertpapieren; ~ **to bail** Verschonung von der Untersuchungshaft gegen Kautionsleistung; ~ **to membership** Aufnahme als Mitglied (*bzw Gesellschafter oder Aktionär*); ~ **to the bar** Zulassung zur Anwaltschaft; **compulsory** ~ Einweisung (*Heilanstalt*); **direct** ~ ausdrückliches Geständnis; **incidental** ~ beiläufiges Zugeständnis, ungewolltes Zugestehen; **judicial** ~ → *judicial*; **partial** ~ Teilgeständnis; **plenary** ~ umfassendes Geständnis; **tacit** ~ stillschweigendes Zugeständnis; Zugestehen durch Nichtbestreiten; **to make no** ~ (*as to*) etw nicht einräumen; **true** ~ Geständnis *im Zivilprozeß*; **withdrawal of** ~ Widerruf e–s *gerichtlichen Geständnisses*.

admissive zulässig, statthaft.

admit gestatten, zugestehen, zulassen; aufnehmen, einweisen; ~ **a claim** e–n Klageanspruch anerkennen; ~ **evidence** Beweismittel zulassen; ~ **ted set-off** unbestrittene Aufrechnung; ~**ted to the stock exchange** zum Börsenhandel zugelassen, börsenfähig.

admittable zulässig, zuzulassen.

admittance Zutritt *m*; ~ **by authorized credentials only** Zutritt nur mit Sonderausweis.

admittedly zugegebenermaßen.

admittee der (die) Zugelassene.

admixture Mischung *f* (*nicht chemische Verbindung*), Beimischung *f*, Vermischen *n*.

admonish verwarnen, mahnen, belehren, über Rechtsfolgen belehren; ~ **s.o. of infringement of patent** jmdn wegen Patentverletzung verwarnen; ~ **to tell the truth** zur Wahrheit ermahnen.

admonition Ermahnung *f*, Belehrung *f* (*über die Folgen*), Verwarnung *f*; **letter of** ~ Abmahnungsschreiben.

adolescence Adoleszenz *f*, Alter *n* von Jugendlichen und Heranwachsenden.

adolescent Jugendliche(r), Heranwachsende(r).

adopt annehmen, aneignen, einbeziehen, übernehmen, aufnehmen, genehmigen, beschließen; adoptieren, an Kindesstatt annehmen; **resolution** e–n Beschluß fassen; ~ **the reports and accounts** (*dem Vorstand*) Entlastung erteilen.

adoptable annehmbar.

adopted children's register Adoptionsregister; ~ **country** Wahlheimat *f*.

adoptee Adoptierte(r), Adoptivkind *n*.

adopter Adoptierende(r).

adopting parents Adoptiveltern.

adoption Annahme *f*, Übernahme *f*, Billigung *f*, Adoption *f*; **A–~Act** Adoptionsgesetz; ~ **agency** Adoptionsvermittlungsstelle; ~ **of children** Annahme an Kindesstatt; ~ **of contract** Übernahme e–s Vertrages; ~ **of Table A** → *table*; ~ **of transaction** Billigung e–s Rechtsgeschäfts (*insbes beim Kauf auf Probe*); ~ **order** Adoptionsbeschluß; Adoptionsdekret; ~ **probationary period** Probezeit vor der Annahme; Adoptionsprobezeit; ~ **service** (*komunale*) Adoptionshilfe; Adoptionsfürsorge; ~ **relationship** durch A. begründete Beziehung, Adoptionsverhältnis; **society** Adoptionsverein; **equitable** ~ formlose Adoption; **granting letters of** ~ gerichtliche Genehmigung der Adoption.

adoptive übernehmend; Adoptions . . ., Adoptiv . . .

adstipulate als Gläubiger beteiligt werden.

adstipulation Mitberechtigung *f* e–s Gläubigers, Hereinnahme *f* e–s Gläubigers.

adult *adj* erwachsen.

adult *s* Erwachsene(r), Volljährige(r); ~ **education** → *education;* ~ **maintenance** → *maintenance;* **juvenile** ~ Heranwachsender (17–21).

adulterate *v* verfälschen; panschen.

adulteration Beimischung *f*, Verpanschung *f*, Verfälschung *f*; ~ **of food and drugs** unzulässige Beimischung bei Lebensmitteln *bzw* Arzneien.

adulterator Fälscher *m*; Falschmünzer *m*.

adulterer Ehebrecher *m*.

adulteress Ehebrecherin *f*.

adulterine im Ehebruch gezeugt; ~ **children** Kinder aus ehebrecherischer Verbindung.

adulterous ehebrecherisch; ~ **bastards** in Ehebruch gezeugte (nichteheliche) Kinder.

adultery Ehebruch *m*; **double** ~ beiderseitiger Ehebruch; **to commit** ~ Ehebruch begehen; **to live in** ~ in ehebrecherischen Beziehungen leben.

advance *s* Fortschritt *m*; Rangvortritt *m*; Vorausempfang, Vorschuß *m*; (*kurzfristiger*) Kredit *m*, *exch* Kursbesserung *f*; ~ **against costs** Kostenvorschuß; ~ **agent** auf Vorschußbasis arbeitender Vertreter; ~ **bill** vor Lieferung ausgestellte Tratte; **~s brought into hotchpot** Anrechnung des Vorausempfanges *bei der Erbauseinandersetzung*; ~ **guaranty** antizipierte Garantie (*Warentermingeschäft*); ~ **in the art** technischer Fortschritt; ~ **note** Verpflichtungsschein auf Vorschuß von Heuer; Steuergutschein; **~s on account of freight** Bevorschussung der Frachtvergütung; ~ **on costs** Kostenvorschuß; ~ **on current account** Kontokorrentkredit; ~ **on freight** Vorschuß auf Seefracht; ~ **on securities** Effektenbeleihung; **~s to employees** Arbeitnehmervorschüsse, Arbeitnehmerdarlehen; ~ **payment** Vorauszahlung; ~ **premium** → *premium*; ~ **tax collection** Steuervorauszahlung; **by way of** ~ vorschußweise, als Vorschuß; **cash** ~ Kassenvorschuß; **collateral** ~ Lombardkredit, Effektenlombard; **industrial ~s** Kreditgewährung der öffentlichen Hand an Betriebe der gewerblichen Wirtschaft; **secured ~s** Lombardkredit; **technical ~** technische Weiterentwicklung; **uncovered ~** ungedeckter Kontokorrentvorschuß.

advancement Vorrücken, **~n**, Beförderung *f*, Förderung *f*; Schenkung unter Anrechnung auf das Erbteil, vorweggenommene Erbfolge; Ausstattung *f*, Vorausempfang *m*; **~ by portion** Ausstattung, Aussteuer; **~ clause** → *clause*; **~ in life** Ausstattung; **~ of education** Förderung der Bildung; **~ of knowledge** Verbreitung von Kenntnissen; **~ of the legal system** Fortbildung der Rechtsordnung; **~ of trial** Beschleunigung des Verfahrens, frühzeitige Terminanberaumung; **equitable doctrine of ~** *Vermutung treuhänderischer Begünstigung bei Rechtsgeschäften von Eltern für Kinder u.ä.*; **power of ~** *Befugnis des Treuhänders, das Treugut teilweise für Ausstattung von Kindern zu verwenden.*

advantage Vorteil *m*, Vorzug *m*; **to gain pecuniary ~** e-n Vermögensvorteil erlangen; **to take ~ of s.o.** jmds Gutgläubigkeit ausnützen; **unfair ~** Übervorteilung.

advantageous vorteilhaft, günstig, gewinnbringend.

adventitious zufällig, durch Glücksfall erworben.

adventure *s*, Abenteuer *n*, Gefahr *f*, Risiko *n*, Spekulationsgeschäft *n*; **~ or concern** Unternehmung; **bill of ~** Risikoausschluß des Absenders, *Erklärung des Absenders, daß die Versendung auf Gefahr e-s Dritten erfolgt, dem die Ware gehört;* **gross ~** → *gross*; **joint ~** → *venture.*

adventurer Abenteurer *m*, Spekulant *m*, Unternehmer *m*.

adversarial kontradiktorisch; **~ system** kontradiktorisches Verfahren.

adversary *s* Gegner *m*, Prozeßgegner *m*; *adj* kontradiktorisch.

adverse entgegenstehend, entgegengesetzt, gegnerisch, ungünstig, unglücklich; **~ occupation of residential premises** Hausbesetzung.

adversely affected benachteiligt, beschwert.

adversus bonos mores sittenwidrig.

advertise öffentlich bekannt machen, inserieren; werben, Reklame machen; **~ for claims** zur Anmeldung von Ansprüchen auffordern.

advertisement Anzeige *f*, Inserat *n*; Werbung *f*; öffentliche Mitteilung *f*, Bekanntmachung *f*; **~s** Anzeigenteil *m*; **~ before suit** vorprozessuale Bekanntgabe durch Zeitungsannonce; **~ of change of name** Bekanntmachung der Firmenänderung; **comparative ~** vergleichende Werbung; **indecent ~s** anstößige Sexualwerbung; **institutional ~** Vertrauenswerbung; investorische Werbung; **keyed ~** Chiffre-Anzeige; **notice by ~** → *notice*; **official ~** amtliches Inserat; **public ~ of a reward** Auslobung; **~ sales executive** Anzeigenleiter, Leiter der Anzeigenabteilung.

advertiser Inserent *m*.

advertising|agency Werbefirma; **~ agent** Anzeigenvertreter; **~ agreement** Inseratsvertrag, Einschaltvertrag; **~ allowance** Werberabatt; **~ appropriation** Werbeetat; **~ by enticement** Lockvogelwerbung; **~ campaign** Werbefeldzug; **~ circular** Werbebrief; **~ expert** Werbefachmann; **~ gift** Werbegeschenk; **A~ Investigation Department** (*AID*) Britischer Werberat (*Überwachung nach ethischen Grundsätzen*); **~ media** Werbemittel, Werbeträger, Media; **~ on perimeter boards** Bandenwerbung; **above-the-line ~** (Agentur-Kommission für) Werbung in den klassischen Medien; **ambush ~** „hinterhältige" Werbung; **commercial ~** Wirtschaftswerbung; **cooperative ~** Gemeinschaftswerbung; **illuminated ~** Leuchtwerbung; **outdoor ~** Außenwerbung; **pictorial ~** Bildwerbung; **patent ~** → *patent.*

advice Rat *m*, Beratung *f*; gutachtliche Stellungnahme *f*, *kaufmännische* Benachrichtigung *f*; Avis *m|n*; ~ **note** → *note*; ~ **of collection** Einziehungsanzeige; ~ **of court** gerichtliche Feststellung; ~ **of delivery** Rückschein (*Zustellung*), Lieferanzeige; ~ **of dispatch** Versandanzeige; ~ **of draft** Trattenavis; ~ **of non-delivery** Unzustellbarkeitsmitteilung; ~ **of non-payment** Mitteilung über nicht erfolgte Zahlung; ~ **on evidence** Bericht über den Prozeßstand nach Beweisaufnahme; **credit** ~ → *credit*; **debit** ~ Lastschrift; **expert** ~ fachkundiger Rat; **for non-**~ mangels Avis; **independent** ~ unparteiische (*juristische*) Beratung; **legal** ~ Rechtsberatung, juristischer Rat; **letter of** ~ → *letter*, **ministerial** ~ Rat der Minister; **on the** ~ **of** auf Vorschlag von; **preliminary** ~ Voravis, Voranzeige; **shipping** ~ → *shipping*; **with the** ~ **and consent** mit Zustimmung von.

advise raten, beraten, mitteilen, benachrichtigen; avisieren; **"~ fate"** sofortige Auskunft über Deckung (*für e–n Scheck*) erbeten; Mitteilung erbeten, ob die Dokumente aufgenommen wurden (*Dokumenteninkasso*); ~ **in due course** rechtzeitig avisieren.

advisedly mit Überlegung, absichtlich, vorsätzlich.

advisement Überlegung *f*, Beratung *f*, Urteilsberatung *f*.

adviser Berater *m*; ~ **on consumer's problem** Kundenberater; **financial** ~ Finanzberater; **economic** ~ Wirtschaftsberater; **industrial** ~ Betriebsberater; **legal** ~ Rechtsberater; **vocational** ~ Berufsberater.

advising bank avisierende Bank.

advisive ratend, mahnend.

advisor = *adviser qv*.

advisory beratend; **A~, Conciliation and Arbitration Service** Beratungs-, Schlichtungs- und Schiedsgerichtsdienst (*für Arbeitsstreitigkeiten, GB, seit 1975*).

advocacy Anwaltstätigkeit *f*, forensische A.; Befürwortung *f*.

advocate *s* Befürworter(in), Advokat *n*, Rechtsanwalt *m*, Prozeßanwalt *m*; *scot: beim Supreme Court zugelassener Rechtsanwalt*; **A~ General** Rechtsberater der Krone, erster Kronanwalt im Admiralitätsgericht (*vgl Queen's Advocate*); jur. Berater e–s Richters am Europ. Gerichtshof; **College of A~s** → *college*; **Crown A~** Zweiter Kronanwalt im Admiralitätsgericht; **Faculty of A~s** *scot* Anwaltskammer; **Lord A~** *scot Generalstaatsanwalt;* **public** ~ (*selbsternannter*) Vertreter des öffentlichen Interesses.

advocate *v* befürworten, verteidigen, sich einsetzen für, geltend machen.

advocation *scot* Verweisung *f* an ein höheres Gericht.

advocator *scot* Berufungsführer *m*.

advocatus diaboli (=) Teufelsadvokat *m*.

advowee Kirchenpatron *m*, Person *f* mit Vorschlagsrecht für Kirchenpfründe; ~ **paramount** der höchste Kirchenpatron (*der Souverän*).

advowson Pfründenbesetzungsrecht *n*, Vorschlagsrecht *n* für eine Kirchenpfründe; ~ **appendant** mit dem Herrensitz verbundenes Vorschlagsrecht für eine Kirchenpfründe; ~ **collative** Einsetzung in eine Pfründe durch den Bischof; ~ **donative** Pfründenschenkung; ~ **in gross** vom Herrensitz gelöstes Pfründenrecht; ~ **presentative** Pfründenvorschlagsrecht.

aequitas (= *equity qv*) Billigkeit *f*, Billigkeitsrecht *n*; ~ **sequitur legem** (= *equity follows the law*) das strenge Recht (= *common law*) geht dem Billigkeitsrecht vor.

aerospace Weltraum *m*; ~ **industries** Raumfahrtindustrie.

affair Angelegenheit *f*, Sache *f*; Liebesverhältnis *n*; **domestic ~s** innere Angelegenheiten; **external ~s** auswärtige Angelegenheiten; **pecuniary** ~ Geldangelegenheiten; **private ~s** Privatangelegenheiten.

affect berühren, beeinflussen, beeinträchtigen, in Mitleidenschaft ziehen, unmittelbare Auswirkungen auf etwas haben; ~ **unfavorably** beeinträchtigen.

affection Zuneigung *f*; Verpfändung *f*; körperliche Beeinträchtigung *f*; **injurious** ~ wertmindernder Eingriff; **natural** ~ natürliche Zuneigung (*als Familienmitglied*).

affectus Affekt *m*, nervliche und seelische Disposition *f*.

affeer bemessen, schätzen, beitragsmäßig festsetzen, bestätigen, eidlich bestätigen; ~ **an account** eine Rechnungslegung unter Eid bestätigen.

affiance *s* beiderseitiges Eheversprechen *n*.

affiance *v* verpfänden; sich verloben.

affiant der (die) eidlich Erklärende (*jmd, der e–e schriftl Erklärung unter Eid abgibt*).

affidavit schriftliche unter Eid abgegebene Erklärung *f*, beeidete Erklärung *f*, *entspricht praktisch der eidesstattlichen Versicherung*; ~ **evidence** → *evidence*; ~ **in support** Glaubhaftmachung des Vorbringens; ~ **-man** *hist* Berufszeuge; ~ **of defence** beeidete Versicherung (*der Begründetheit der Einwendungen*) des Beklagten; ~ **of documents** Verlangen der eidlichen Beglaubigung von vorgelegten Urkunden; ~ **of increase** Glaubhaftmachung zusätzlicher Anwaltskosten; ~ **of merits** beeidete Versicherung *der Begründetheit des Vorbringens*; ~ **of notice** *beeidete Erklärung, der Gegenpartei Termin gegeben zu haben*; ~ **of plight and condition** *eidliche Erklärung über unveränderten Zustand des Testaments*; ~ **of service** beeidete Zustellungserklärung; ~ **of service and indorsement** eidliche Versicherung der erfolgten Zustellung; ~ **to hold to bail** eidlich versicherter Antrag auf Haftanordnung (*zur Arrestvollziehung*); ~ **to support application** Glaubhaftmachung des Antrags; ~ **verifying statement of affairs** Glaubhaftmachung des Gesellschaftsstatus *bei der Liquidation*; **argumentative** ~ eidlich versicherte Erklärung mit Ausführungen zur Sache; **defective** ~ fehlerhafte eidliche Versicherung; **defendant's** ~ eidlich versicherte Gegenerklärung des Beklagten *im summarischen Verfahren*.

plaintiff's ~ eidliche Versicherung der Richtigkeit der klagebegründenden Behauptungen (*im summarischen Verfahren*), Glaubhaftmachung der Klagebegründung.

affiliate *s* Mitglied *n*, Zweigorganisation *f*, Beteiligungsgesellschaft *f*, Tochtergesellschaft *f*, Filiale *f*, Mitglied *n*; ~**s** Konzernfirmen *f*|*pl*, verbundene Unternehmen *n*|*pl*, lokaler vertragsgebundener Anbieter (*von Sendungen*).

affiliate *v* sich zusammenschließen, sich für e–e politische Partei erklären; die Vaterschaft feststellen *bzw* behaupten.

affiliated|company Beteiligungsgesellschaft, Konzerngesellschaft; ~ **group** Beteiligungskonzern, Konzern; ~ **interest** Konzernbeteiligung; ~ **person** Besitzer e–r erheblichen Kapitalbeteiligung (*von mindestens 5%*); ~ **society** Zweiggesellschaft, Tochtergesellschaft, Konzerngesellschaft; ~ **union** → *union*.

affiliation Vaterschaftsfeststellung *f e–s nichtehelichen Kindes*; Unterhaltspflicht *f* für ein nichteheliches Kind; Angliederung *f*, Verschmelzung *f*; ~ **case** Unterhaltssache e-s nichtehelichen Kindes, Vaterschaftsprozeß; ~ **order** gerichtl Vaterschaftsfeststellung *i. d. R. verbunden mit Unterhaltsbeschluß*; **A~ Proceedings Act** Vaterschaftsverfahrensgesetz; **religious** ~ Religionszugehörigkeit *f*.

affinitas affinitatis Verwandtschaft *f* im weiteren Sinne, Schwippschwägerschaft *f*.

affinity Schwägerschaft *f*; **collateral** ~ Schwägerschaft in der Seitenlinie; **direct** ~ (*eigentliche*) Schwägerschaft; **quasi** ~ Beziehung zu den Verwandten des Verlobten; **re-**

lationship by ~ Verschwägerung, Schwägerschaft; **secondary** ~ *Beziehung zwischen dem Ehegatten und Verschwägerten des anderen Ehegatten, Schwippschwägerschaft.*

affirm bestätigen, bekräftigen, genehmigen; ~ **upon oath** eidlich bekräftigen, eidlich versichern.

affirmable vertretbar, bestätigungsfähig.

affirmance Bestätigung *f*, Bekräftigung *f*, Genehmigung *f*.

affirmant der Erklärende, Aussteller e–r eidesstattlichen Versicherung.

affirmation Beteuerung *f*, eidesgleiche Bekräftigung; ~ **of fact** Zusicherung in tatsächlicher Hinsicht; **solemn** ~ feierliche Versicherung, *etwa* eidesgleiche Beteuerung; ~ **sworn** ~ beschworene Behauptung, Versicherung unter Eid.

affirmative bestätigend, bejahend, positiv, beweispflichtig; ~ **action** Antidiskriminierung, ausgleichende Bevorzugung von bisher Benachteiligten; ~ ~ *program Antidiskriminierungsprogramm (USA)*; ~ **authorization** ausdrückliche Ermächtigung; ~ **charge** positive Rechtsbelehrung der Geschworenen, daß eine Verurteilung ausscheidet; ~ **defence** → *defence*; ~ **duty** rechtliche Verpflichtung; ~ **pregnant** eine Behauptung, aus der sich ein indirektes Zugeständnis zugunsten der Gegenseite ergibt; ~ **relief** die beantragte Rechtshilfe, Gegenstand der Leistungsklage; ~ **statute** Gebotsgesetz; **to answer in the** ~ bejahen, mit Ja antworten; **to hold the** ~ Beweisführer sein.

affix beifügen, anheften, beidrücken, versehen mit, verbinden; ~ **a seal to a document** e–e Urkunde siegeln.

afflicted mit e–m Gebrechen behaftet, leidend, schwer geschädigt; **person** ~ das Opfer (e–r Verletzung).

afforest aufforsten; zum Jagdbezirk machen.

afforestation Aufforstung *f*; Unterstellung *f* unter die Jagd- und Forstrechte.

affranchise befreien.

affray Raufhandel *m*, Rauferei *f*, Schlägerei *f*; **mutual** ~ Zweikampf *m*.

affreight zum Frachttransport chartern, befrachten.

affreightment Befrachtungsvertrag *m*, Seefrachtgeschäft *n*.

afore|execution had vor (*erfolgreicher*) Zwangsvollstreckung; **~-mentioned** obenerwähnt.

aforesaid vorstehend, vorgenannt, bereits erwähnt, vorerwähnt.

aforethought *crim* (mit) Vorbedacht, (mit) Überlegung, geplant, vorsätzlich; ~ **infringement** mit Vorbedacht ausgeführte, vorsätzliche Verletzung; **malice** ~ → *malice*.

after später, nachträglich; **~-acquired** nachträglich erworben; **~-acquired clause** Pfanderstreckungsklausel (*auf nachträglich erworbenes Gut*); **~-acquired property** → *property*; ~ **all deductions** nach sämtlichen Abzügen (*jedoch vor Steuern*), netto; ~ **any marriage** nach Verheiratung; **~-born child** nach dem Tode des Erblassers geborenes Kind; ~ **brother's and sister's children** entfernter verwandt als Geschwisterkinder; ~ **care condition** Nachsorgeauflage (*planning*); ~ **date** nach dem heutigen Datum; ~ **deduction of income tax** nach Abzug der Einkommensteuer (*verbleibender Betrag*); ~ **due consideration** nach gebührender Berücksichtigung; ~ **his decease** nach seinem Ableben; ~ **making provision** vorbehaltlich der Verfügungen (*zugunsten von*); ~ **raising as aforesaid** vorbehaltlich der Aufbringung der vorstehend erwähnten (*Beträge*); ~ **sight** nach Sicht (*Wechsel*).

after-care Gefangenenfürsorge *f*, Resozialisierungsbemühungen.

after-market *s* Sekundärmarkt (*nach Ausgabe durch Emissions-Konsortium*), Anschlußmarkt *m*.

aftermarket *adj* nachbörslich.

aftermath Grummet *n*, Recht *n* auf die letzte Grasmaht; Nachwirkungen *f*|*pl*.

afternoon Nachmittag *m*, Zeit von Mittag bis Mitternacht.

against gegen; ~ **documents** gegen Dokumente; ~ **morals** sittenwidrig; ~ **the form of the statute** gegen den gesetzlich formulierten Tatbestand (*Anklageschrift*); ~ **the peace** Verletzung der öffentlichen Ruhe und Ordnung; ~ **the provisions of this Act** unter Verletzung der Bestimmungen dieses Gesetzes.

age Alter *n*, Lebensstufe *f*; Volljährigkeit *f*; ~ **admitted** zugestandenes, einverständl festgestelltes Alter (*Lebensversichg*); ~ **allowance** → *allowance*; ~ **error arrears** Prämienrückstände wegen irrtümlicher Altersangabe; ~ **grouping** Altersaufbau; ~ **limit** → *limit*; ~ **of consent** *Mindestalter für die Einwilligung zum Geschlechtsverkehr (GB: 16)*; ~ **of criminal responsibility** Beginn der Strafmündigkeit; ~ **of discretion** Strafmündigkeit; ~ **of marriage** heiratsfähiges Alter; ~ **prayer** Einwendung der Minderjährigkeit; ~ **pyramid** Alterspyramide; ~ **relief** Altersfreibetrag; **coming of** ~ Erreichen der Volljährigkeit; **mental** ~ altersbezogner Intelligenzgrad; **of full** ~ volljährig; **to attain full** ~ volljährig werden; **not of (full)** ~ minderjährig; **under** ~ minderjährig.

agency (*1*) Stellvertretung *f*, Bevollmächtigung *f*; Auftragsverhältnis *n*; ~ **business** Kommissionsgeschäft, Geschäftsbesorgung; ~ **by estoppel** Vertretungsmacht kraft Rechtsscheins; ~ **by holding out** Anscheinsvollmacht; ~ **by operation of law** gesetzliche Vertretungsmacht; ~ **of necessity** Geschäftsführung ohne Auftrag; Schlüsselgewalt der Ehefrau; ~ **of wife** Vertretungsmacht der Ehefrau (*für den Ehemann*), Schlüsselgewalt; ~ **terms** Gebührenvereinbarung des Korespondenzanwalts mit dem örtlichen (*bes. Londoner*) Rechtsanwalt; **actual** ~ echte Stellvertretung; **disclosed** ~ offene Vertretung; **exclusive** Alleinvertretung, Alleinauftrag (*Makler*); **executive** ~ Verwaltungsbehörde; **general** ~ Prokura, Handlungsvollmacht; **implied** ~ stillschweigend erteilte Vollmacht, stillschweigende Vertretung; Vollmacht kraft Stillschweigens oder konkludenten Verhaltens; **joint** ~ Gesamtvertretung, **mercantile** ~ Handelsvertretung; Handlungsvollmacht; Kreditauskunftei; **ostensible** ~ Anscheinsvollmacht, Duldungsvollmacht, Stellvertretung auf Grund e–r Anscheinsvollmacht; **sole** ~ Einzelvertretungsmacht, Alleinvertretung; **statutory** ~ gesetzliche Vertretung; **unauthorized** ~ Vertretung ohne Vertretungsmacht; **undisclosed** ~ verdeckte Stellvertretung, unechte St.; **universal** ~ Universalvollmacht.

agency (2) Dienststelle *f* Amt *n*, Behörde *f*; **administrative ~s** Verwbehörden Körperschaften bzw. Anst. d. öffent. Rechts; **A~ to-Agency arrangements** Vereinbarungen zwischen Behörden; **commercial** ~ Handelsvertretung, Kreditauskunftei; **fiscal** ~ Finanzbehörde; **governmental** ~ Behörde; staatl Dienststelle; **independent** ~ mittelbare (Bundes)Behörde; **national** ~ staatl Organ; **public** ~ Behörde; **regulatory** ~ Aufsichtsbehörde, halbstaatl Verwaltungsbehörde.

agenda Tagesordnung *f*, Verhandlungspunkte *m*|*pl;* ~ **paper** schriftl Tagesordnung.

agent Stellvertreter(in), Vertreter(in), Bevollmächtigte(r), Beauftragte(r); Handelsvertreter(in), Handlungsreisende(r), Agent(in); ~ **and patient** selbstkontrahierender Beauftragter; Insichgeschäft; **~s and servants** Verrichtungsgehilfen; **~'s commission** Vertreterprovision; ~ **contract** Handelsvertretervertrag; ~ **for collection** Inkassobevollmächtigter; ~ **general** Generalbevollmächtigter, Generalagent, Geschäftsführer; ~ **intrusted** der mit Ware (*oder Traditionspapieren*) versehene Beauftragte; ~ **of an independent status** selbstständiger Vertreter, Handelsvertreter; ~ **of foreign principal** Beauftragter ausländischer Auftraggeber; ~ **of necessity** Geschäftsführer ohne Auftrag; ~ **of State** staatliches Organ, Behörde; ~ **solicitor** Behördenjurist; ~ **without authority** vollmachtloser Vertreter, falsus procurator; **apparent** ~ Anscheinsvertreter; **"as ~ only"** nur als Vermittler, im fremden Namen, auf fremde Rechnung; **authorized** ~ Bevollmächtigter; **buying** ~ Einkäufer, Einkaufsvertreter; **chartered patent** ~ → *patent*; **chief** ~ Generalagent; **closing** ~ Abschlußagent; **co-~** Gesamtvertreter; **collecting** ~ Inkassobevollmächtigter; **commercial** ~ Handelsvertreter; **commission** ~ → *commission*; **common** ~ → *common;* **confidential** ~ Vertrauensmann; **consular** ~ Konsul, Konsulagent; **dependent** ~ abhängiger Vertreter; **diplomatic** ~ diplomatischer Vertreter; **estate** ~ Grundstücksmakler; **exclusive sales** ~ Alleinvertreter, Inhaber e-s Alleinvertretungsrechts; **financial** ~ Kreditmakler; **fiscal** ~ Vertreter des Fiskus, Zahlstelle; **foreign** ~ Lobbyist für ausländ. Interessen; **legal** ~ gesetzl Vertreter; **forwarding** ~ Spediteur; **general** ~ Generalbevollmächtigter, Handlungsbevollmächtigter; Generalvertreter; **head** ~ Hauptvertreter, Generalvertr.; **high managerial** ~ Geschäftsführer, leitender Angestellter; **independent** ~ nicht weisungsgebundener Beauftragter; **innocent** ~ *crim* schuldloses Werkzeug (*bei mittelbarer Täterschaft*); **local** ~ Bezirksvertreter, örtlicher Vertreter, Platzvertreter; **managing** ~ Handlungsbevollmächtigter, Prokurist, Geschäftsführer, Generalbevollmächtigter, Vertreter; **manufacturer's** ~ Werksvertreter, Firmenvertreter; **mercantile** ~ Handelsvertreter (*meist mit Konsignationslager*); Kommissionär; **no ~s** Vertreterbesuche zwecklos; ohne Makler; **ostensible** ~ Anscheinsvertreter; **parliamentary** ~ Beauftragter für Privatvorlagen; **patent** ~ → *patent*; **paying** ~ Zahlstelle; **power of an** ~ Handlungsvollmacht; **private** ~ privatrechtlicher Stellvertreter, Bevollmächtigter; **process** ~ Zustellungsbevollmächtigter; **public** ~ Beamter, Beauftragter der öffentl Hand; **purchasing** ~ Einkäufer, Einkaufsvertreter; **real estate** ~ Grundstücksmakler, Immobilienmakler, Immobilienhändler; **regular** ~ ständiger Vertreter; **resident** ~ Ortsvertreter; Inlandsvertreter; **responsibility for the** ~ Haftung für den Erfüllungsgehilfen; **sales** ~ → *sale*; **secret** ~ Geheimagent; **shipping** ~ → *shipping*; **sole** ~ Alleinvertreter; **soliciting** ~ Vermittlungsagent; **special** ~ Inhaber e-r Spezialvollmacht, Bevollmächtigter für den Einzelfall; **statutory** ~ gesetzlicher Vertreter; **sub-~** Unterbevollmächtigter, Untervertreter; **to act as** ~ im fremden Namen handeln; **to be ~ to (a firm)** (e-e Firma) vertreten; **undercover** ~ verdeckter Ermittler, V-Mann, **universal** ~ Generalbevollmächtigter; **vicarious** ~ Erfüllungsgehilfe bzw Verrichtungsgehilfe; **would-be** ~ Vertreter ohne Vertretungsmacht.

agent provocateur Agent provocateur *m*, Lockspitzel *m*.

aggravate erschweren, verschärfen.

aging Altersgliederung *f* (*von Außenständen*).

aggravation Erschwerung **~, strafverschärfende** *bzw* schulderhöhende Umstände *m|pl;* ~ **of damages** schadenersatzerhöhende Umstände; **matter of** ~ erschwerender Umstand.

aggregate *adj* gesamt; ~ **amount** →

amount; ~ **corporation** Körperschaft; ~ **demand** Gesamtnachfrage; ~ **funding** Fundierung der Altersversorgungslasten; ~ **mortality table** *ins* Aggregattafel; ~ **wages tax** Lohnsummensteuer.

aggregate *s* das Gesamte, Gesamtsumme *f*; ~ **of votes cast** Gesamtstimmenzahl.

aggregate *v*|*t* zusammenfassen, verbinden.

aggregation Zusammenfassung *f* bekannter Erfindungen *bzw* Erfindungselemente (*kein Kombinationspatent*); ~ **of interests** Interessengemeinschaft.

aggression Aggression *f*, Angriff *m*.

aggressor Aggressor *m*, Angreifer *m*.

aggrieve *v* kränken, benachteiligen; **the ~d party** die beschwerte Partei; **to consider oneself ~d** sich beschwert fühlen.

aggrieved *s* Geschädigte(r).

aging Alterung *f*, Altersstruktur *f*, Altersgliederung *f*; ~ **schedule** Fälligkeitstabelle *f*; **extreme** ~ Überalterung.

agio Agio *n*, Aufgeld *n*; ~ **account** Aufgeldkonto.

agiotage Spekulation *f* in Staatspapieren; Wechselgeschäft *m*; Börsenspekulation *f*.

agitate agitieren, bewegen, erregen.

agitation Agitation *f*, Aufregung *f*, Bewegung *f*.

agnate *s* Agnat *m*, **~s** männliche Nachkommen m|*pl* desselben Stammvaters.

agnate *adj* agnatisch, väterlicherseits verwandt, von dem gleichen Vorfahren abstammend.

agnation Agnation *f*, Verwandtschaft *f* in gerader Linie väterlicherseits.

agnomination Zusatzname *m*, Vorname *m*.

agrarium Grundsteuer *f*, Grundlast *f*.

agree zustimmen, beipflichten, billigen, sich einigen; sich verpflichten; vereinbaren; **~d and declared** erklärt wie vereinbart; **~d case** Scheinprozeß, Kollusionsprozeß; **~d damages** vereinbarter (pauschalierter) Schadenersatz; **~d liquidated damages** vereinbarter pauschalierter Schadenersatz; ähnl: Konventionalstrafe; **~d minutes** → *minutes;* **~d order** → *order;* **~d statement of facts** vereinbarter Sachverhalt; **as may be ~d** je nach Vereinbarung; **unanimously ~d** einstimmig angenommen.

agreeably einverständlich, genehm.

agreement Einigung *f*, Willensübereinstimmung *f*, Vereinbarung *f*; Vertrag *m* (= *V bzw . . . v*), Abkommen *n*, Übereinkunft *f*, Verpflichtung *f*; **~currency** Verrechnungswährung; ~ **for (a) lease** Pacht*v*; ~ **for a lien** Vereinbarung über die Gewährung e–s Pfandrechts *bzw* Zurückbehaltungsrechts, rechtsgeschäftliches Pfandrecht; ~ **for insurance** Versicherungsvor*v*; ~ **for purchase** Kaufvorvertrag; ~ **for remuneration** Honorarvertrag; ~ **for separation** Trennungsvereinbarung, Vereinbarung über das Getrenntleben; ~ **for the sale of goods** Warenkauf*v*; **~, made and dated . . .** Vertrag vom . . .; ~ **not to assign** vertragl Abtretungsverbot; ~ **not to compete** Konkurrenzverbotsklausel; ~ **of consolidation** Fusions*v*; ~ **of sale** Kauf*v*; ~ **of service** Dienst*v*; ~ **on non-violence** Gewaltverzicht*v*; ~ **to commit crime** Verabredung zur Begehung e–r Straftat; ~ **to compound or stifle prosecution** vereinbarte Begünstigung oder Unterdrückung der Strafverfolgung; ~ **to create a legal mortgage** Vor*v* zur Bestellung e–s Grundpfandrechts; ~ **to sell** Kauf*v*, (*noch nicht erfüllter*) obligatorischer Kauf*v*; ~ **under hand** schriftlicher *V*; **additional** ~ Nebenabrede, Zusatzvereinbarung; **administrative** ~ Verwaltungsabkommen; **amicable** ~ gütliche Einigung, gütliche Regelung; **antenuptial** ~ vorehelicher *V*; **basic** ~ Grundvertrag, Rahmenvertrag; **closing** ~ Schlußvereinbarung; **collateral** ~ Nebenvereinbarung,

Nebenabrede; **collective** ~ Kollektivv, Tarifv; *int* kollektives Übereinkommen; **conciliated** ~ Schlichtungsvereinbarung, **continuing** ~ Dauerv; **executed** ~ bei *V*–sschluß erfüllter *V*, unterzeichneter *V*; **executive** ~ Regierungsabkommen; **executory** ~ noch zu erfüllender *V*, Verpflichtungsgeschäft; **express** ~ ausdrückliche Vereinbarung; **implicit** ~ = *implied* ~ *qv*; **implied** ~ stillschweigend getroffene Vereinbarung; **in** ~ einig sein; **interdepartmental** ~ *int* zwischenstaatliches Verwaltungsabkommen; **invalid** ~ ungültiger *V*; **joint** ~ Mantel(tarif)*v*; **marketing** ~ Vertriebsvereinbarung, Marktabsprache; **master** ~ Hauptvertrag; **multilateral** ~ multilaterales Abkommen, mehrseitiger *V*; **mutual** ~ **procedure** Verständigungsverfahren; **off-set** ~ (Devisen)Ausgleichsabkommen; **operating** ~ Betriebsübereinkommen; **open-end** ~ unbefristete *V*, Dauervertrag; **oral** ~ mündliche Vereinbarung; **partial** ~ Teilvereinbarung; **pocket** ~ Revers, Nebenabrede; **preliminary** ~ Vor*v*; **reciprocal** ~ gegenseitiger *V*, wechselbezüglicher *V*, synallagmatischer *V*, Vereinbarung auf Gegenseitigkeit; **seamen's** ~ Heuer*v*; **service** ~ Dienst*v*, Anstellungs*v*; Wartungs*v*; **small** ~ Kleinkredit für Konsumenten, **solemn** ~ förmlicher *V*; **special** ~ Sonder*v*, Einzelschieds*v*; **standard** ~ Einheits*v*; **strike-free** ~ Streikverzichtsvereinbarung; **substitution for prior** ~ Novation; **tacit** ~ stillschweigende Vereinbarung; **tentative** ~ vorläufige Abmachung, Probevertrag; **trade** ~ Handelsabkommen; Kollektiv*v*; **tying** ~ Ausschließlichkeits*v*; **verbal** ~ mündliche Vereinbarung, mündlicher *V*; **wage** ~ Arbeitstarifvertrag.

agrément Agrément *n, Zustimmung des Empfangsstaates vor Ernennung des Chefs e–r diplomatischen Vertretung.*

agribusiness Agroindustrie *f*.

agricultural landwirtschaftlich (= *landw*), Landwirtschafts . . ., Land . . ., Agrar . . .; ~ **bank** Landwirtschaftsbank; ~ **bond** ~ *bond* (*1*); ~ **children** in der Landwirtschaft beschäftigte Kinder; ~ **credit society** *landw–e* Genossenschaftsbank; ~ **credits** Agrarkredit; ~ **duty** Agrarzoll; ~ **economy** Agrarwirtschaft; ~ **fixtures** → *fixture*; ~ **gang** Landarbeitergruppe; ~ **holding** → *holding*; ~ **insurance law** *landw–e* Risikoversicherung; ~ **labo(u)rer** → *labo(u)rer;* ~ **land** *landw* genutzte Grundstücke, *landw–er* Grundbesitz; **A**~ **Land Commission** Behörde zur Verwaltung *landw–er Güter;* ~ **levy** → *levy*; ~ **lien** → *lien*; ~ **marketing** Agrarmarktregelung; ~ **marketing association** *landw–e* Absatzorganisation; ~ **mortgage corporation** *landw–e* Bodenkreditanstalt; ~ **produce** Agrarprodukte; ~ **rates** Kommunalabgaben für *landw–e* Grundstücke; ~ **society** Landwirtschaftsverband; ~ **wages board** Agrarlohnbehörde.

agriculture Landwirtschaft *f*.

agriculturist Landwirt *m, in der Landwirtschaft beschäftigte Person.*

agronomy Ackerbaukunde *f*, Agronomie *f*.

aground auf Grund gelaufen, auf Grund gesetzt.

ahead voraus, vor (*in der Fahrtrichtung*).

aid *s* Hilfe *f*, Unterstützung *f*, Beihilfe *f*; ~ **fund** Unterstützungsfonds; ~ **prayer** Pächterschutzantrag; ~ **societies** gemeinnützige Unterstützungsvereine; ~ **by verdict** Heilungs e–s Verfahrensmangels durch Urteil; ~ **to dependent children** Kinderfürsorge; ~ **to overseas countries** Auslandshilfe, Entwicklungshilfe; ~ **to the blind** Blindenhilfe; **grant-in-**~ Staatszuschuß; **legal** ~ → *legal aid*; **mutual** ~ → *mutual*; **public** ~ öffentliche Unterstützung; **to give** ~ **and comfort to the enemy** Landesverrat

begehen, e–r feindlichen Macht Vorschub leisten.
aid *v* helfen, unterstützten; ~ **and abet** Beihilfe leisten; ~ **and assist** unterstützen.
aide-mémoire Denkschrift *f*, Aide-mémoire *n*.
aider and abettor Tatgehilfe.
aids *hist* Hilfeleistungen f|*pl* des Lehensträgers für seinen Lehensherrn oder dessen Erben.
aim *s* Aufgabe *f*, Ziel *n*, Zweck *m*.
aim *v* zielen, abzielen.
air | **cargo** Luftfracht; ~ **cargo rates** Lufttransporttarif; ~ **carrier** Lufttransportunternehmen; ~ **commerce** Lufttransport; ~ **consignment note** Luftfrachtbrief; ~ **corps** Luftwaffe; ~ **courses** Luftwege; Luftschächte in Bergwerken; ~ **force** Luftwaffe; **A~ Force Board** Luftwaffenamt; ~ **lift** Luftbrücke; ~ **mail** Luftpost; ~ **navigation** Luftnavigation, Luftfahrt, Flugzeugwesen; ~ **piracy** Luftpiraterie; ~ **pollution** Luftverschmutzung, Luftverpestung; ~ **rights** Rechte am Luftraum über dem Grundstück; ~ **safety board** Flugsicherungsbehörde; ~ **service** Flugdienst; ~ **sovereignty** Lufthoheit; ~ **space** Luftraum; ~ **traffic** Luftverkehr; ~ **traffic control engineers** Fluglotsen; **A~ Traffic Services Agency** Agentur für Luftverkehrs-Sicherungsdienste; ~ **transportation** Luft(fracht)verkehr, Lufttransport; ~ **travel** Luftreiseverkehr; **A~ Travel Reserve Fund** Hilfsfond für geschädigte Flugreisende; ~**waybill** Luftfrachtbrief; ~ **worthiness** Lufttüchtigkeit; ~ ~ *certificate: Lufttauglichkeitszeugnis*
airbill Luftfrachtbrief *m*.
Air Call Funkaufruf (*an Rechtsanwälte zur sofortigen Vertretung*).
aircraft Luftfahrzeug *n*, Flugzeug *n*; ~ **cargo manifest** Frachtmanifest des Luftfahrzeugs; ~ **general declaration** allgemeine Ein- und Ausflugserklärung; **overflying** ~ (*ein Grundstück*) überfliegendes Flugzeug.
airline Luftverkehrsgesellschaft *f*; ~ **company** Luftverkehrsgesellschaft.
airport Flughafen *m*, Flugplatz *m*; ~ **of destination** Bestimmungsflughafen; ~ **of dispatch** Verladeflughafen; ~**s of entry** Einreiseflughäfen; **shipping** ~ Versandflughafen.
airway Flugzeugroute *f*; Luftzuführung *f* (Bergwerk); ~**s** Fluglinie, Luftverkehrslinie.
akin (bluts-)verwandt, entsprechend.
Alabama Case der Fall der Alabama (*völkerrechtliche Regeln über Neutralität im Seekrieg*).
alarming the Sovereign Majestätsbedrohung *f*.
alcohol counselling agency Alkoholberatungsstelle *f*.
alcoholic *adj* alkoholisch; ~ **beverage tax** Steuer auf alkoholische Getränke; ~ **delirium** Trinkerdelirium; ~ **strength** Alkoholgehalt.
alcoholic *s* Alkoholiker(in).
alcoholism Alkoholismus *m*, Trunksucht *f*.
alderman Stadtratsmitglied *n*, Beigeordneter *m*, Stadtrichter *m*, höherer Kommunalbeamter *m*.
ale silver Schankgebühr *f* (*Bierausschank in London*).
aleatory aleatorisch, zufallsbedingt; ~ **contract** → *contract*.
alert Alarmbereitschaft *f*.
alias alias (*Hinweis auf Decknamen*); ~ **execution** zweiter Vollstreckungsversuch; ~ **passport** Reisepaß auf e–n Decknamen; ~ **warrant** Haftbefehl zur Ergreifung unter einem Decknamen; ~ **tax warrant** zweiter Steuervollstreckungsauftrag; ~ **writ** → *writ*.
alibi Alibi *n*; **failure to establish** ~ Mißlingen des Alibibeweises; **plea of** ~ Berufung auf ein Alibi.
alien *adj* ausländisch, fremd, wesensverschieden; **A~ Agency Act** Gesetz zur Registrierung ausländischer Agenten und Beauftragter; ~ **ami** freundlicher Ausländer, *Angehöriger e–s befreundeten oder neutralen Staates*; ~ **corporation** ausländi-

sche Gesellschaft; im Ausland gegründete Körperschaft; ~ **enemy** *im Inland ansässiger* Angehöriger e–s Feindstaates; ~ **friend** = *alien amy qv*; ~ **née** Person ausländischer Geburt; ~ **property** Ausländervermögen, Feindvermögen; ~ **property administration** Verwaltungsbehörde für Ausländervermögen; **A~ Property Custodian** Treuhänder für Feindvermögen.

alien *s* Ausländer(in) Fremde(r), nicht eingebürgerter Bewohner des Landes; **A~ Immigration Act** Einwanderungsgesetz; **expulsion of ~s** Abschiebung von Ausländern; **migration of ~s** Ein- und Ausreise von Ausländern; **resident** ~ im Inland ansässiger Ausländer; **taxation of ~s** Ausländerbesteuerung.

alien *v* = *alienate qv*.

alienability Veräußerlichkeit *f*, Abtretbarkeit *f*.

alienable veräußerlich, übertragbar, abtretbar.

alienage Ausländereigenschaft *f*, Ausländerstatus *m*; **declaration of** ~ → *declaration*.

alienate veräußern, übertragen, übereignen; entfremden, abspenstig machen.

alienation Veräußerung *f*, Übertragung *f* (*bes von Grundstücken*); Entfremdung *f*, Abwerbung *f*; ~ **by devise** Übertragung durch letztwillige Verfügung; ~ **in mortmain** Grundstücks-(Lehens-)übertragung an e–e *kirchl oder weltl* Körperschaft; ~ **of affections** Entfremdung, Verlust der ehelichen Zuneigung und Lebensgemeinschaft; **A~ Office** *hist* Amt für die Einziehung von Abgaben bei Grundstücksveräußerungen; ~ **of title** Übereignung; **fraudulent** ~ Vermögenshinterziehung, Vollstreckungsvereitelung; Untreue; **liable to** ~ veräußerlich; **mental** ~ Geistesgestörtheit, Geisteskrankheit; **restraint of** (= *on*) ~ → *restraint*.

alienee (rechtsgeschäftlicher) Erwerber *m*; **fraudulent** ~ bösgläubiger Erwerber (*veruntreuten Nachlaßgutes*); **voluntary** ~ unentgeltlicher Erwerber.

alieni juris *lat* unter fremdem Recht (*des Vaters, Ehegatten oder Lehensherren*) stehend.

alienism Ausländereigenschaft *f*, Ausländerbesonderheiten *f/pl*.

alienist forensischer Psychiater *m*.

alienor Veräußerer *m*, rechtsgeschäftlich Verfügender *m*.

alight aussteigen, landen.

alignment Linienführung *f*, Anpassung *f* (*an eine Linie oder Richtung*); ~ **of customs duties** Angleichung von Zollsätzen; ~ **of positions** Harmonierung der Standpunkte.

alike ähnlich; ebenso, in gleicher Weise.

aliment *scot s* Unterhalt *m* (*bes für die Ehefrau*), *v* Unterhalt leisten.

alimentation Beköstigung *f*, Verpflegung *f*.

alimentary zum Unterhalt dienend; Nahrungs . . .; ~ **trust** → *trust*.

alimony Unterhaltszahlung *f* für die *getrennt lebende bzw geschiedene* Ehefrau; ~ **pendente lite** Unterhalt auf Grund einstweiliger Anordnung im Eheprozeß; ~ **pending suit** = *maintenance pending suit qv*; **temporary** ~ einstweilen zu zahlender U.; **permanent** ~ Unterhaltsrente bei Getrenntleben (*von Ehegatten*).

aliquot *adj* ohne Rest aufgehend; **an ~ part** Bruchteil, bestimmter Anteil

aliter wie anderweitig entschieden.

alliunde woandersher (*aus e–r anderen Rechtsquelle*); **evidence** ~ → *evidence*.

all alle, alles, gesamt, vollständig, ganz, sämtlich; ~ **actions** sämtliche *rechtshängigen und sonstigen Ansprüche*; ~ **actions and demands** alle Ansprüche; ~ **actions, suits and quarrels** alle Prozesse und Streitigkeiten; ~ **and every risk** sämtliche Gefahren; ~ **and singular** sämtliche, ausnahmslos; ~ **blue slate** reinamerikanische (*puritanische*) Kandidatenliste; ~ **causes of**

action sämtliche anhängigen Ansprüche; ~ **claims thereunder** alle daraus resultierenden Ansprüche; ~ **commodity rate** = *commodity rate qv*; ~ **damages** voller Schadenersatz; ~ **debts, personal estate and effects** das gesamte bewegliche Vermögen; ~ **effects** die gesamte bewegliche Habe; **A~ England Reports** (=) *umfassende private Entscheidungssammlung in GB*; ~ **estate clause** Globalklausel, *Klausel in Auflassungsurkunden, daß sämtliche Eigentums- und Besitzrechte am Grundstück auf den Erwerber übergehen;* ~ **estate, effects and property** das gesamte bewegliche und unbewegliche Vermögen; ~ **fours** (*to be on ~ fours = to run on ~ fours*) völlig gleichgelagert sein (*Präzedenzfall*); ~ **I am worth** alle meine Habe (*einschließlich Grundbesitz*); ~ **I possess** alles was ich besitze, meine gesamte Habe, mein gesamtes Vermögen; ~ **-in** (= *all inclusive*) alles eingeschlossen, pauschal; ~ **-in insurance** Globalversicherung; ~ **leases** sämtliche (*gegenwärtigen und zukünftigen*) Pachturkunden; ~ **loss** der gesamte Schaden; ~ **matters in difference** sämtliche Meinungsverschiedenheiten; ~ **my estate and interest** mein gesamtes (*Grundvermögen und bewegliches*) Vermögen; ~ **my personal property** mein gesamtes bewegliches Vermögen; ~ **my relations** alle meine Verwandten (*diejenigen, welche Intestaterben geworden wären*); ~ **other effects** die gesamte übrige Habe (*Reinnachlaß);* ~ **our requirements** unser gesamter Bedarf; ~ **participation clause** Allbeteiligungsklausel (*Vertrag nur gültig, wenn alle Beteiligten beitreten*); ~ **-party talks** Allparteiengespräche; ~ **rates, taxes and outgoings** alle (Grundstücks)lasten; ~ **reasonable care** jede zumutbare Sorgfalt; ~ **risk whatever of the passage** sämtliche Gefahren der Schiffsreise; ~ **risks** alle (durch *zufällige Ereignisse bedingten) Gefahren;* ~ **risks by land and water** alle Gefahren zu Wasser und zu Lande; ~ **sales final** kein Umtausch; ~ **savers certificates** Sparbriefe (*US, teilw. steuerfrei*); ~ **the estate** sämtliche Rechte *an Grundstücken*; ~ **the estate and interest of the vendor** sämtliche Rechte des Verkäufers (*am Grundstück*); ~ **the interest** sämtliche Rechte (*am Grundstück*); ~ **the property** das Gesamtvermögen; ~ **the rest** der verbleibende Teil des gesamten (*bewegl. und unbewegl*) Vermögens; ~ **the year round** das gesamte Jahr hindurch; ~ **transporting to be at owner's risk** jede Beförderung erfolgt ausschließlich auf die Gefahr des Eigentümers; ~ **which may remain of my money** was von meinem Geld übrigbleibt (*nach Abzug der Nachlaßverbindlichkeiten*).

allegation Behauptung *f*, tatsächliches Vorbringen *n*; ~ **of faculties** behauptete Leistungsfähigkeit *des Ehemannes zur Unterhaltszahlung*; **alternative** ~**s** Hilfsvorbringen; **false** ~ fälschliche Beschuldigung; **inconsistent** ~**s** widersprüchlicher Sachvortrag; **irrelevant** ~ nicht entscheidungserhebliches Vorbringen; **material** ~ wesentl Prozeßbehauptung; **primary** ~ Hauptbegründung (*der Klage*).

allege behaupten, darlegen, vortragen, erklären, anführen.

alleged behauptet, angeblich, mutmaßlich.

allegiance Untertanentreue *f*, Staatstreue *f*, Treuepflicht *f* des Lehensträgers; **acquired** ~ erworbene Treuepflicht; **actual** ~ = *local* ~ *qv*; **double** ~ doppelte Treuepflicht (*dem Bund und den Einzelstaaten gegenüber*); **local** ~ Respektierung der Gesetze des Gastlandes, Ausländertreuepflicht; **natural** ~ originäre (*angeborene*) Untertanenpflicht; **oath of** ~ → *oath*; **perpetual** ~ = *natural q. v.*; **temporary** ~ =*local q. v.*; **to owe** ~ treupflichtig sein; Staatstreue schuldig sein.

allegiant treu, loyal.

alleviate mildern, lindern.
alleviation Milderung *f*, Linderung *f*.
alley Gasse *f*, öffentlicher Weg *m*.
alliance Bündnis *n*, Allianz *f*; **defensive ~** Verteidigungsbündnis; **offensive and defensive ~** Schutz- und Trutzbündnis; **treaty of ~** → *treaty*.
allied verbündet, verwandt; **~ companies** Konzerngesellschaft; Mutter- und Tochtergesellschaft; **A~ Forces** Alliierte Streitkräfte; **A~ High Commission** Alliierte Hohe Kommission (*in Deutschland nach 1945*); **~ industries** verwandte Industrien.
allision seitliche Schiffskollision *f*, *Auffahren e–s Schiffes auf ein nicht in Fahrt befindliches Schiff*.
allocate zuteilen, zuweisen, zuordnen, zurechnen.
allocation Zuteilung *f*, Zuweisung *f*, Aufteilung *f* von Ausgaben auf Unterkonten, Zurechnung *f*; **~ by tenders** → *tender*; **~ of blame** Schuldzuweisung; **~ of business** Geschäftsverteilung; **~ of contracts** Auftragslenkung; **~ of currency** Devisenzuteilung; **~ of funds** Geldbewilligung; **~ of manpower** Arbeitskräfteverteilung; **~ of responsibility** Verteilung der Zuständigkeit (*bei Behörden*), **~ of shares** Aktienzuteilung; **~ of time order** Verhandlungszeitbeschränkung (*Parlamentsausschuß*); **~ office** Ausgleichsstelle.
allocution Erteilung *f* des letzten Worts an den Angeklagten.
allodial allodial, lehensfrei, erbeigen.
allograph Allographum, *von dritter Seite geschriebene Urkunde*.
allonge Allonge *f*, *e–m Wechsel angehängtes Blatt*.
allot zuteilen, auslosen, einteilen; **~ to the highest bidder** dem Meistbietenden zuschlagen.
allotment Zuteilung *f* (*bei Wertpapieremissionen*), Zuweisungen *f* von Mitteln (*in der öffentl. Verwaltung*); zugeteilte Landparzelle; **~ certificate** Bezugsbescheinigung (*Aktien*); **~ garden** Kleingarten, Schrebergarten; **~ letter** Zuteilungsschein; **~ money** Zuteilungsbetrag; **~ note** Urkunde über Abtretung der Heuer, Lohnanteilsanweisung; **~ notice** Zuteilungsanzeige, Bestätigung der Aktienübertragung (*bei Emission*); **~ of appropriation** Budgetaufschlüsselung; **~ schedule** Etatzuweisungsplan; **~ sheet** Aktienzeichnungsliste; **application for ~** → *application (1)*; **irregular ~** verfahrenswidrige Zuteilung; **return of ~s** Meldung an das Registergericht über die Begebung von Aktien (*oder sonstigen Kapitalanteilen*); **subscribed ~** Repartierung *f*, *Zuteilung bei überzeichneter Emission*.
allottee (Zuteilungs)empfänger *m*, Erwerber *m*, Abtretungsbegünstigter *m* (*Lohnabtretung e–s Seemanns*).
allotted days (*für Budgetberatungen*) vorbehaltene Sitzungstage.
allotter Zuteiler *m*, Ausloser *m*, Verteiler *m*.
allow gewähren, zulassen, gestatten; vermachen, zugestehen; **~ a claim** e–n Anspruch anerkennen; **~ a discount** Nachlaß gewähren; **~ an appeal** e–r Berufung (*bzw Beschwerde, Revision*) stattgeben; **~ costs** Auslagen bei der Kostenfestsetzung berücksichtigen; als Kosten festsetzen; **~ extenuating circumstances** mildernde Umstände zubilligen; **~ 3% on deposits** Einlagen mit 3% verzinsen; **time ~ed** → *time*.
allowable zulässig, absetzbar, anrechenbar; **~ in full against taxable profits** steuerlich voll absetzbar; **~ tolerance** zulässige Abweichung.
allowance Gewährung *f*, Zuschuß *m*, Entschädigung *f*, Steuerfreibetrag *m*, Absetzung *f*, Gewichtsabzug *m* für Verpackung; Toleranz *f*, zulässige Abweichung *f*; **~ for depreciation** Wertberichtigung; **~ for exchange fluctuations** Rückstellung für Devisenschwankungen; **~ for good will** Vergütung für den Firmenwert (*bzw Markenwert*); ~

for inflation Inflationsausgleich; ~ **for social duties** Repräsentationsgeld; ~ **for tare** Taravergütung; ~ **of claim(s)** Forderungsanerkennung; ~ **pendente lite** Freigabe von Einkünften während des Rechtsstreits; ~ **to cashier for errors** Nachlaß für Rechenfehler des Kassierers, Fehlgeld, Mankogeld; **after ~ for ...** nach Abzug von; **age** ~ Altersfreibetrag; **bad debt** ~ Wertberichtigung; **balancing** ~ → *balancing*; **children's** ~ Kinderfreibetrag; **combat** ~ Frontzulage, Kriegszulage; **daily** ~ Tagegeld; **dependant relative** ~ Freibetrag für Unterhaltspflichtige; **depreciation** ~ Absetzung, Abschreibung für Abnutzung; Abschreibungen für Wertminderung; **duty-free ~s** Freigrenzen im Reiseverkehr; **earned income** ~ Freibetrag bei Einkünften aus Arbeitsleistung (*landwirtschaftliche oder gewerbliche, selbständige oder nicht selbständige Arbeit*); **exchange** ~ Wert der Inzahlungnahme; **expense** ~ → *expense*; **extra** ~ Sondervergütung, Zusatzvergütung; **fixed** ~ Fixum; **initial** ~ erste Abschreibung bei Neubauten; **just** ~ berechtigte Aufwendungen *des Rechnungslegungspflichtigen*; **living** ~ Unterhaltszuschuß; **marginal** ~ verringerter Steuersatz bei Einkünften an der unteren Besteuerungsgrenze; **married man's** ~ Freibetrag für Ehemann; **mileage** ~ Kilometergeld; **personal** ~ persönlicher Freibetrag (*gemäß Personenstand*); **pass-through** ~ weiterzuleitender Aufschlag, überwälzbarer Zuschlag; **purchase** ~ (Kauf)Preisnachlaß; **rent** ~ Wohnungsbeihilfe, Wohngeld; **residential** ~ Ortszulage; **separation** ~ → *separation*; **single person's** ~ Freibetrag für Alleinlebende; **special** ~ besondere Kostenerstattung; **supplementary** ~ Nachbewilligung; Zusatzrente; **to make ~ for the period of custody** die Untersuchungshaft anrechnen; **voluntary** ~ ohne Anerkennung e–r Rechtspflicht geleistete Zahlung; **wear and tear** ~ Absetzung für Abnutzung (*AfA*), Abschreibung; **wife's earned income** ~ Freibetrag für Einkünfte der Ehefrau *aus Arbeitsleistungen*; **writing-down ~s** Abschreibungsmöglichkeiten.

allowedly anerkanntermaßen.

allude unbestimmt andeuten, auf etwas anspielen.

allurement Verlockung *f Kinder* anziehende Gegenstände oder Anlagen (*Haftpflicht*).

alluvion Verlandung, Anlandung, Anschwemmung.

ally Verbündeter *m*, Bundesgenosse *m*; Angehöriger *m* e–s verbündeten Staates.

almoin Lehensland *n* mit kirchlichen Dienstpflichten.

almoner Almosenverteiler *m*, Sozialbetreuer *m*.

almonry soziale Fürsorge *f*.

alms Almosen *m*, Armenhilfe *f*; ~ **fee** Kirchensteuer, Peterpfennig; ~**house** Fürsorgeheim, Armenhaus; ~ **land** Kirchenland.

alod Allod *n*, lehensfreies Land *n*, Freigut *n*, Erbgut.

alodiary Freigutsbesitzer *m*.

alodification Allodifikation *f*, Bodenreform *f*, *Beseitigung lehensrechtl Lasten*.

alongside längsseits; ~ **delivery** Abladung längsseits des Schiffes am Kai.

alter *s* Gegenpartei *f*.

alter *v* ändern, abändern.

alterable abänderbar, veränderlich.

alteration Änderung *f*; ~**s and improvements in the building** Änderung und Wertverbesserung am Gebäude; ~ **of cheques** Scheckfälschung; ~ **of instruments** unbefugte Änderung von Urkunden; ~ **of objects** → *object*; ~ **of share capital** Änderung (*Erhöhung oder Herabsetzung*) des Grundkapitals; ~ **of status** Statusänderung (*von Gesellschaften nach Konkurseröffnung*); **colourable** ~ geringfügige Änderung (*zur Umgehung des Patentschutzes*); **external** ~ Änderung an der

Außenseite; **material** ~ wesentl Änderung, rechtserhebl Änderung.
altercation heftiger Streit *m.*
alternat *int* Alternat *n*, Unterschriftenfolge *f.*
alternate *adj* abwechselnd; wechselweise.
alternate *v* abwechseln.
alternative *adj* alternativ, wahlweise, hilfsweise.
alternative *s* Alternative *f.*
altitude rules Flughöhenvorschriften *f/pl.*
alto et basso vorbehaltlose Unterwerfung *f* unter Schiedsgericht.
altum mare die hohe See, das offene Meer.
always | afloat ohne auf Grund zu setzen; ~ **hereafter** stets (*während der Laufzeit des Vertrages*); ~ **occupied** ständig bewohnt; ~ **thereafter** stets danach.
amalgamate verschmelzen, vereinigen, fusionieren; ~ **shares** Aktien zusammenlegen.
amalgamation Zusammenschluß *m*, Verschmelzung *f*, Fusion *f.*
ambassador Botschafter *m*; ~ **extraordinary** Sonderbotschafter; ~ **plenipotentiary** außerordentlicher und bevollmächtigter Botschafter; **libel upon** ~ Botschafterbeleidigung.
ambassadorial Botschafts ..., Gesandtschafts ...
ambidexter *s* mit beiden Händen geschickte Person *f*; Anwalt *m* (*bzw Geschworener*), der von beiden Seiten Geld nimmt.
ambiguity Unklarheit *f*, Mehrdeutigkeit *f*, Zweifelhaftigkeit *f*, Mißverständlichkeit *f*; ~ **upon the factum** grundlegende Mehrdeutigkeit; **latent** ~ versteckte Mehrdeutigkeit; Mißverständlichkeit; **patent** ~ offensichtliche Mehrdeutigkeit.
ambiguous unklar, mehrdeutig, mißverständlich, auslegungsbedürftig.
ambit Grenze *f*, Zuständigkeitsgrenze *f*; Zuständigkeitsbereich *m*; ~ **of the law** Bereich des Rechts.
ambulance Ambulanz *f*, Krankenwagen *m*; ~ **chaser** ein auf Unfallmandate erpichter Anwalt (*bzw dessen Gehilfe*); ~ **chasing** standeswidrige Bemühung um Unfallsmandate; ~ **services** Krankentransportdienste.
ambulatory beweglich, umherziehend, Wander ...; abänderbar; widerruflich (*Testament*).
ambush Hinterhalt *m*, Überraschungs ...
amelioration Verbesserung *f*, Bodenverbesserung *f*; ~ **works** Meliorationen.
amenability Zugänglichkeit *f*, Verantwortlichkeit *f* (*gegenüber Vorgesetzten*).
amenable verantwortlich, rechenschaftspflichtig; leicht zu beeinflussen, gefügig; ~ **to the jurisdiction** der Gerichtsbarkeit unterliegend.
amend verbessern, abändern.
amendable verbesserungsfähig.
amende honorable Buße *f*, Entschuldigung *f*, Ehrenerklärung *f.*
amendment Abänderung *f*, Zusatz *m*, Verbesserung *f*; ~ **by the court of its own motion** gerichtliche Abänderung (*bzw. Berichtigung*) von Amts wegen; **A~ Act** Änderungsgesetz, Novelle; ~ **of a bill** Abänderung e–r Vorlage; ~ **of action** Klageänderung; ~ **of appearance** Änderung des formalen Einlassungsschriftsatzes; ~ **of judgment** Urteilsberichtigung; ~ **of pleadings** Änderung des schriftsätzlichen Vorbringens; ~ **of statement of claim** Änderung der Klagebegründung; ~ **of statute** Gesetzesänderung; ~ **of writ** Änderung der Klage(schrift); ~ **of writ as to cause of action** Änderung des Streitgegenstandes der Klage; ~ **of writ as to parties** Parteiänderung *in e–r Klage*; Berichtigung der Parteibezeichnung, ~ **of writ without leave** Abänderung des Klageerhebungsschriftsatzes ohne gerichtliche Genehmigung; ~ **to a proposed** ~ Änderung des Abänderungsantrages; **Constitutional**

A~ Zusatzartikel der US-Verfassung; **drafting ~s** redaktionelle Änderungen; **technical ~** formaljuristische Änderung (*des Vorbringens*); **to move an ~** → *to move*; **with latest ~s** neueste Fassung.

amends Satisfaktion *f*, Schadloshaltung *f*, Genugtuung *f*, Wiedergutmachung *f*, Schadenersatz *m*; **tender of ~** Angebot (*nebst Hinterlegung*) e–r Bußgeldzahlung (*an den Beleidigten oder Geschädigten*); **to make ~** *for something* Schadenersatz leisten, *etw* wiedergutmachen.

amenit|y Annehmlichkeit *f*, Gebrauchsvorteil *m*, **~ies** natürliche Vorzüge *m|pl*, Voraussetzungen *f|pl* für den Besitzgenuß; **~ value** Gebrauchswert (*e–s Grundstücks*); **loss of ~** → *loss*; **preservation of ~** → *preservation*; **environmental ~ies** umweltfreundliche Bedingungen.

amercement *obs* Geldbuße *f*, Disziplinarstrafe *f* (*Zahlung*), gerichtliche Dienststrafe *f*; **~ royal** Strafe für ein Beamtenvergehen.

American *adj* amerikanisch (*meist auf USA bezogen*); **A~ Bar Association** Amerikanische Anwaltsvereinigung; **~ clause (=)** *Klausel bei Seeversicherung, die Ausgleichspflicht von Mitversicherten ausschließt;* **A~ type share certificate** Namensaktie mit Blankoübertragungs-Allonge (*ähnl Inhaberaktie*).

American *s* Amerikaner(in) amerikanische(r) Staatsangehörige(r).

ami Freund *m* nächster Angehöriger *m*; **prochain ~** → *next friend qv*.

amiable compositeur = *amicable compounder qv*.

amicable freundlich, gütlich; **~ action** einverständliche Durchführung e–s Rechtsstreits (*zur Klärung der Rechtslage*); **~ agreement** → *agreement*; **~ compounder** Schlichter.

amicably freundschaftlich, gütlich, außergerichtlich.

amicus curiae (=) sachverständiger Berater *m* des Gerichts (*über Spezialfragen oder fremdes Recht*).

amittere curiam *hist* Verlust *m* des Rechtsweges.

amnesia Amnesie *f*.

amnesty Amnestie *f*, allgemeiner Straferlaß *m*; **A~ Act** Amnestiegesetz.

amortization Amortisation *f*, planmäßige Tilgung *f*, *hist* Überführung *f* in den Besitz der toten Hand; **~ fund** Tilgungsfonds; **~ of debt** Schuldtilgung; **~ of premium** Tilgung des Agios; **~ plan** Tilgungsplan; **~ reserve** Tilgungsrücklage; **~ table of payments** Amortisationstabelle.

amortize amortisieren, tilgen.

amotion Besitzentziehung *f*, verbotene Eigenmacht, Entsetzung, Wegnahme *f*, Amtsenthebung *f*, Abberufung *f*.

amount *s* Betrag *m*, Gesamtsumme *f*, Ergebnis *n*; **~s advised** avisierte Zahlungen; **~ at issue** strittiger Betrag; **~ brought in** Vortrag (*aus vorjährigem Rechnungsjahr*); **~ carried forward** Vortrag auf neue Rechnung, Saldovortrag; **~ column** Betragsspalte; **~ covered** Deckungssumme, Versicherungssumme; **~ due** fälliger Betrag; **~ in cash** Barbetrag; **~ in controversy** Klagebetrag, Streitwert; **~ in dispute** Streitwert; **~ involved** Gegenstandswert; **~ of annuity** Ablösungssumme; **~ of claim** Klagebetrag, Streitwert; **~ of damages** Schadenersatzsumme; **~ of indebtedness** → *indebtedness*; **~ of loss** Schadenssumme, Schadensbetrag, Schadenshöhe; **~ of punishment** Strafmaß; **~ owing** Forderung, zahlbarer Betrag; **~ realized** erzielter Betrag, Veräußerungsertrag; **~ received** Betrag (dankend) erhalten, Quittung; **actual ~** Istbestand, Effektivbestand; **annual ~** Jahresbetrag; **aggregate ~** Gesamtbetrag; **basic ~** Grundbetrag; **clear ~** Nettobetrag; **compensatory ~s** Ausgleichsbeträge; **corrective ~** Berichtigungsbetrag; **disregardable ~** unschädlicher Betrag (*bei e–r Freigren-*

ze); **estimated** ~ veranschlagte Summe; **foreign** ~ Betrag in ausl-er Währung, Devisenbetrag; **gross** ~ Bruttobetrag; **guaranteed** ~ Haftsumme; **jurisdictional** ~ Streitwert *zur Bestimmung der Zuständigkeit*; **net** ~ → *net*; **nominal** Nennwert, Nennbetrag, Nominalwert; **partial** ~ Teilbetrag; **principal** ~ Hauptbetrag, Hauptsache(betrag), Hauptsumme; **pro-rata** ~ anteiliger Betrag; **real** ~ wirkl Betrag, Sollbestand; **residual** ~ Restbetrag; **short** ~ Fehlbetrag; **specific** ~ bestimmter Betrag; **subscribed** ~ gezeichneter Betrag; **substantial** ~ erheblicher Betrag; **total** ~ Gesamtbetrag.

amount *v* anwachsen, sich belaufen auf; ~ **to** betragen, den Gesamtbetrag bilden; ~ **to invention** Erfindungshöhe erreichen; ~**ing to** in Höhe von.

amovability Absetzbarkeit *f*, Abberufbarkeit *f*.

amovable absetzbar, abberufbar.

amove absetzen, abberufen.

ample ausgedehnt, weit, weitläufig, reichlich; ~ **safe and convenient means of ingress and egress** ausreichender, sicherer und bequemer Zugang; **to have ~means at one's disposal** über beträchtliche Mittel verfügen.

ampliation weitere Sachaufklärung *f*, Verschiebung *f* der Entscheidung wegen weiterer Sachaufklärung.

amplify nähere Ausführungen machen.

Amtrack = *US* halbstaatl Eisenbahngesellschaft.

anacrisis Inquisition *f*, scharfes Verhör *n*.

anagraph Register *n*, Inventur *f*, Kommentar *m*.

analogism Analogismus *m* (*Argument von Ursache und Wirkung*).

analogous analog, entsprechend; **to apply ~ly** entsprechend anwendend.

analogy Analogie *f*, Entsprechung *f*; **argument by** ~ Analogieschluß.

analysis Analyse *f*, Unterschuchung *f*; ~ **of expenses** Kostenanalyse; ~ **sheet** Bilanzzergliederung; **certificate of** ~ Analysen-Zertifikat; **comparative** ~ Gegenüberstellung.

anarchy Anarchie *f*, Gesetzlosigkeit *f*; **criminal** ~ kriminelle Anarchie, Herbeiführung der Anarchie durch Gewaltverbrechen.

anathema Bannfluch *m*; Kirchenbann *m*.

anathematize den Bann (über jmdn) aussprechen, exkommunizieren.

anatocism Zinseszins *m*, Wucher .

ancestor Vorfahre *m*, Aszendent *m*, Verwandter in aufsteigender Linie, Erblasser *m*, Vorbesitzer *m*; **collateral** ~ aufsteigende Verwandte in der Seitenlinie.

ancestral angestammt, ererbt, die Vorfahren betreffend, von den Vorfahren abstammend; ~ **estate** ererbter Grundbesitz, Erbhof; ~ **property** ererbter Landbesitz.

anchorage Ankerplatz *m*; Ankergebühr *f*, Liegegeld *n*; ~ **toll** Ankergebühr, Liegegeld.

ancient alt, historisch, uralt, seit unvordenklicher Zeit *bestehend*.

ancients Seniormitglieder *n|pl* (*engl Anwaltsinnungen*).

ancillary zusätzlich, ergänzend, untergeordnet; Hilfs . . ., Neben . . .; ~ **credit business** Kreditnebengewerbe (*Inkasso, Kreditberatung, Kreditvermittlung, Kreditauskunft u. a.*).

and und, sowie, einschließlich; ~**/or** und/oder, beziehungsweise (bzw), gegebenenfalls, (*das eine oder das andere oder beides*); ~ **"reduced"** → *reduce;* ~ **so forth** und weitere gleiche (*oder ähnliche*) Gegenstände; ~ **upwards** wenigstens.

anew neuerlich; **to try a case** ~ einen Fall neu verhandeln (*nach Zurückverweisung*).

angaria Angarienrecht *n* (*das Recht einer kriegsführenden Macht, das Eigentum Neutraler zu beschlagnahmen, zu benützen oder zu zerstören*); Zwangsgestellung *f* von Schiffen.

anger Zorn *m*, Affekt *m*.

aniens nichtig.

animadversion Verweis *m*, Tadel *m*, Rüge *f*, Kritik *f*.
animal Tier *n*; **~s ferae naturae** wilde Tiere; **~s mansuetae naturae,** gezähmte Tiere, Haustiere; **~s of base nature** Tiere niedriger Art; **base ~** niedriges Tier, unedles T.; **dangerous wild ~** gefährliche, wildlebende T–e.; **dead ~** Tierkörper, erlegtes Wild; **wild ~s** freilebende Tiere (außer Vögel); **cruelty to ~s** Tierquälerei; **domestic ~s** Haustiere; **liablility for ~s** Tierhalterhaftung; **reclaimed ~s** gezähmte Tiere, Haustiere.
animo vorsätzlich.
animus Vorsatz *m*, Wille *m*; **~ furandi** Diebstahlvorsatz; **~ lucrandi** gewinnsüchtige Absicht; **~ manendi** Absicht der Wohnsitzbildung; **~ possidendi** Besitzwille.
annals Annalen *pl*, Jahrbücher *n*|*pl*.
annex *s* Anhang *m* Anlage *f*, Nebengebäude *n*.
annex *v* beifügen, verbinden, hinzufügen; annektieren.
annexation (*dingliche*) Verbindung *f*, Hinzufügung *f*; Annexion *f*; **~ during the war** Kriegsannexion; **forced ~** gewaltsame Annexion; **premature ~** verfrühte Annexion (*vor Besiegung des Gegners*).
anniented nichtig gemacht.
anniversary Jahrestag *m*, Jubiläum *n*; **~ date** Jahrestag, jährl wiederkehrender (Abschluß)Tag; **~ days** (*geschützte*) Gedenktage; **~ publication** Jubiläumsschrift.
annotate mit Anmerkungen versehen, kommentieren, erläutern; **~d edition** Auflage mit Anmerkungen.
annotation Kommentar *m*, Erläuterung *f*, Anmerkung *f*; *hist*: Bestimmung *f* e–s Deportationsortes; Aufruf *m* e–s Abwesenden; Rechtsäußerung *f* des Monarchen.
announce verkünden, ankündigen; **~ shares** Aktien auflegen.
announcement Ankündigung *f*, Verkündung *f*, Bekanntmachung *f*; **~ of sale** Verkaufsanzeige; **newspaper ~** Bekanntmachung durch Zeitungsinserat; **official ~** Verlautbarung.
annoy ärgern, belästigen, stören.
annoyance Belästigung *f*, Störung *f*.
annual jährlich (= *j*); **~ average earnings** Jahresdurchschnittsverdienst; **~ close season** Schonzeit; **A~ Digest of Approbations** *j–e* Budgetzusammenstellung; **~ licence fee** Jahreslizenzgebühr; *j–e* Gebühr für Weiderechte; **~ net value** = *net ~ value → net;* **~ percentage rate** effektiver Jahreszins; **~ popular report** *j–er* Rechenschaftsbericht e–r Gemeinde; **The A~ Practice** Das Verfahrensrecht am Supreme Court London (*j–e Ausgabe mit Kommentar*); **~ profits or gains** *j–e* Erträge; **~ rack rent** *j–e* Bodenrente; **~ wage guarantee** Jahreslohngarantie.
annualise *v*|*t* aufs Jahr umrechnen.
annuitant Empfänger(in) e–r Jahresrente, Rentner(in).
annuity Jahresrente *f*, Rentenzahlungen *f*|*pl*; **~ies** Rentenpapiere *n*|*pl*; **~ bond** → *bond* (*1*); **~ certain** Zeitrente; **~ for life** = *life ~ qv*; Leibrentenvertrag; **~ies of tiends** *scot* Jahresabgabe an die Krone; **~ trust** → *trust*; **action of ~** *hist* Klage auf Zahlung e–r Bodenrente; **amortizable ~** Tilgungsrente; **attachment of ~** Rentenpfändung; **cash refund ~** Rückerstattungsrentenversicherung; **clear ~** *jährliche Zuwendung unter Freistellung von Steuern*; **contingent ~** aufschiebend bedingte Annuität; **Consolidated A ~ies** (*Consols*) konsolidierte brit Staatsanleihe; **contract of ~** Rentenvertrag, Leibrente; **deferred ~** aufgeschobene Rente, Anwartschaftsrente; **government ~** Staatsrente; **immediate ~** sofort fällige Rente; **irredeemable ~** unablösbare Rente; **life ~** Leibrente, lebenslängliche Rente; **noncontributory ~** Rente ohne Beitragspflicht; **ordinary ~** Annuität, Rente (*nachträglich fällige Rente*); **perpetual ~** Ewigrente, unkündbare Rente; **redeemable ~** ablösbare

Rente; **refund ~ contract** → *refund*; **register of ~ies** Register der Rentenschulden; **retirement ~** Rentenversicherung; **reversionary ~** Rente auf den Überlebensfall, einseitige Überlebensrente; **single payment ~** Rente auf Grund einmaliger Kapitalzahlung; **survivorship ~** Rente an den hinterbliebenen Lebensversicherungsbegünstigten; **temporary ~** zeitlich begrenzte Rente, Zeitrente; **terminable ~** Zeitrente; mit dem Tode des Begünstigten endende R., Leibrente.

annul annullieren, ungültig machen, nichtig machen, aufheben.

annulation Annullierung *f*; Aufgebot bei Verlust von Wertpapieren.

annulability Annullierbarkeit *f*, Anfechtbarkeit *f*, Aufhebbarkeit *f*.

annulment Ungültigkeitserklärung *f*, Aufhebung *f*, Annulierung *f*, Anfechtung *f*; **~ of adjudication (in bankruptcy)** Aufhebung des Konkursverfahrens; **~ of a judgment** Aufhebung e–s Urteils; **~ of marriage** Aufhebung e–r Ehe, Nichtigerklärung der Ehe; **~ of wrong** *int* Aufhebung e–s Gesetzes *bzw* e–r Gerichtsentscheidung (*aus Reparationsgründen*).

annulus et baculum (*Ring und Krummstab*) Investitur *f* e–s Bischofs.

annus|deliberandi *scot* Erbannahmefrist von e–m Jahr; **~ luctus** *hist* Trauerjahr der Witwe.

annomalous ungewöhnlich, regelwidrig, außerordentlich; **~ indorser** außergewöhnlicher Indossant (*nach Begebung, vor Fälligkeit und vor Remittentenindossament*); **~ plea** → *plea*.

another action pending (Einrede der) Rechtshängigkeit.

answer *s* Antwort *f*; Klageerwiderung *f*, Einwendung *f*, Beantwortung *f* e–s Rechtshilfeersuchens; **~ in the affirmative** zustimmende Antwort; **~ in the negative** ablehnende Antwort; **~ tending to incriminate** selbstbelastende Antwort (*durch die sich der Zeuge der Gefahr strafrechtlicher Verfolgung aussetzen würde*); **~ to a charge** Einlassung; **frivolous ~** offensichtlich unschlüssiges Gegenvorbringen; **insufficient ~** ungenügende Beantwortung (*zB von Fragen der Zeugen im Rechtshilfeverkehr*); **irrelevant ~** irrelevantes, neben der Sache liegendes Gegenvorbringen; **sham ~** Scheineinrede, *nur scheinbar schlüssiges Gegenvorbringen*; **voluntary ~** spontanes Gegenvorbringen.

answer *v* antworten, erwidern; verantwortlich sein, haften, sich verantworten; honorieren; **~ a summons** e–r gerichtlichen Ladung Folge leisten; **~ for** einstehen für.

answerable verantwortlich, haftbar; **to be ~** sich verantworten müssen.

ante vorher, oben (*bei Literaturzitaten*); **~ litem motam** vor Rechtshängigkeit.

antecede vorhergehen, den Vorrang haben.

antecedent vorherig, früher, bereits vorher bestehend.

antecessor Vorfahre *m*, Vorgänger *m*.

antedate zurückdatieren (*auf einen früheren Zeitpunkt datieren als den der Ausstellung*), früheres Datum einsetzen.

antenati vor e–m Zeitpunkt Geborene *m|pl*, *bes* voreheliche Kinder *n|pl* der Ehegatten.

antenuptial vorehelich; **~ contract** vorehelicher Vertrag, ehebezogener (Familien)Vertrag, Ehevertrag; **~ debts** voreheliche Schulden; **~ settlement** Ehevertrag *Bildung von Treuhandvermögen vor der Ehe zugunsten der zukünftigen Ehefrau und der Kinder,* Güterrechtsvertrag unter Verlobten.

anthropometry Anthropometrie *f* (*Körpermessungssystem zur Identifizierung*).

anti|A~ Blackout Law Verbot von Sendesperren bei ausverkauften Sportveranstaltungen *US*; **~ burglary device** Alarmanlage; ~

-**dumping law** Dumpingverbotsgesetz; Gesetz gegen wildes Müllabladen; ~ **-lobbying act** Gesetz gegen den Lobbyismus; ~ **-manifesto** Gegenmanifest, *Gegenerklärung e–r kriegführenden Macht über defensiven Charakter ihrer Kampfhandlungen;* ~ **-room** Abstimmungsraum für die Gegner der Vorlage; ~ **-social** antisozial, gesellschaftsfeindlich.

antichresis Antichrese *f*, Nutzpfand *m*, (Immobiliar-)Nutzungspfandrecht *n*.

anticipate vorwegnehmen, antizipieren; ~ **a bill** Wechsel vor Verfall einlösen; ~ **the payment** vor Fälligkeit zahlen; ~**d earnings** Anwartschaft auf Erträge; ~**d freight** die zu erwartenden Frachterträge; ~**d profits** → *profit*; ~**d slippage** zu erwartende Verzögerung.

anticipation Vorwegnahme *f*; Abschlagszahlung *f*; ~ **note** Rabatt für Vorauszahlung; ~ **of assets** Vorgriff auf Aktiva, Guthaben, Reserve; ~ **of life** mutmaßliche Lebensdauer; ~ **of property** Vorausverfügung über Vermögenserträge; ~ **(rate)** Nachlaß für Vorauszahlung (*evtl zusätzl zum Skonto*); **by (in)** ~ im voraus, im vorhinein; **restraint upon** ~ Beschränkung oder Veräußerungsfreiheit (*bei Vorbehaltsgut, GB, vor 1949*); **rule against** ~ Unzulässigkeit der Vorwegnahme von Tagesordnungspunkten.

anticipatory breach (of contract) Erfüllungsverweigerung *f*, vorsätzliche Erfüllungsvereitelung *f*, vorweggenommener Vertragsbruch *m*.

anticompact laws Antikartellgesetze; *Gesetze gegen Tarifabsprachen von Versicherungsgesellschaften.*

antigraphy zweite Ausfertigung *f*. (*e–r gesiegelten Urkunde*).

antimergerite Fusionsgegner *m*.

antinomy Antinomie *f*, Gegensätzlichkeit *f*, Widerspruch *m*, Widerspruch zweier Gesetze (*bzw Vorschriften eines Gesetzes*).

antisocial gesellschaftsfeindlich; ~ **driving behaviour** rowdyhaftes Fahrverhalten.

antitheses Gegensatz *m*, Antithese *f*.

antithetical gegensätzlich.

antitrust|Acts Antitrustgesetze (*Gesetze gegen Monopole und Wettbewerbsbeschränkungen in USA*); ~**action** Kartellklage; ~ **affidavit** eidlich versicherte Erklärung, daß den Antitrustgesetzen entsprochen wurde.

Anton Piller order (=) einstw. Verfügung zur Urkundenbeweissicherung (*auf dem Grundstück des Beklagten*).

any|agreement to the contrary etwaige entgegenstehende Vereinbarungen; ~ **debt owing or accruing** alle gegenwärtigen und zukünftigen Forderungen; ~ **difference** alle etwaigen Meinungsverschiedenheiten; ~ **estate or interest whatsoever** Vermögensrechte jeder Art; ~ **husband** der (*zu dem betreffenden Zeitpunkt etwa vorhandene*) Ehemann; ~ **interest** alle Rechte an Grundstücken, alle (*in Betracht kommenden*) Vermögenswerte; ~ **lawful purpose** jeder gesetzlich zulässige Zweck; ~ **moneys due** alle zur Zahlung fälligen Beträge; ~ **other** derartig(er, e, es); ~ **other article** ein anderer Gegenstand, ein weiterer Gegenstand der gleichen Art; ~ **other article or thing** alle sonstigen Gegenstände; ~ **other business** Verschiedenes (*Tagesordnung*); ~ **other cause** sonstige Ursache (*dieser Art*); ~ **other creditor** ein sonstiger Gläubiger; ~ **other person whatsoever** wer auch sonst; ~ **person who** wer . . . (*in gesetzlichen Strafnormen*); ~ **provincial authorities** Provinzbehörden und Provinzparlamente; ~ **provision however worded** jede Bestimmung gleich welchen Wortlauts; ~ **relation of mine** alle meine (*ehelich geborenen*) Verwandten; ~ **trade or business** ein (*derartiges*) Handelsgeschäft oder Gewerbe; **of** ~ **other year** eines anderen (*früheren oder späteren*) Jahres; **upon** ~

security of the company wofür sämtliche Vermögenswerte der Gesellschaft als Sicherheit dienen (*einschließlich Ansprüchen auf Kapitaleinzahlungen*).

anything irgend etwas; ~ **done** etwas, was geschieht; Amtshandlung; ~ **in anywise relating** alles, was damit zusammenhängt.

apart getrennt, einzeln, abgesondert; ~ **from** abgesehen von; **to live** ~ getrennt leben; **to set** ~ absondern.

apartment Apartment *n*, Etagenwohnung *f*; ~ **building** Mietshaus, Mietblock; ~ **hotel** *US* Apartmenthotel; **cooperative** ~ Genossenschaftswohnung.

apex das Oberste, Gipfel *m*; ~ **juris** der Gipfel der juristischen Spitzfindigkeit; ~ **rule** Normen über Schürfrechtsgrenzen (*von der Spitze e–r Erzader aus*).

aphasia Verlust *m* der Sprechfähigkeit (*gehirnbedingt*); **motor** ~ nervlich bedingte Schreibunfähigkeit; **sensory** ~ Ausfall der Sinneswahrnehmung.

aphonia Verlust *m* der Sprechfähigkeit (*durch Ausfall der Stimmorgane*) Stimmlosigkeit *f*.

apograph Abschrift *f*, Umschrift *f*, Inventur *f*.

apology Entschuldigung *f*, Ehrenerklärung *f*.

apostille Amtsbekräftigung *f* (*durch den Ursprungsstaat, cf legalization*).

apparatus Apparat *m*, Aggregat *n*, Maschine *f*; ~ **claim** Vorrichtungsanspruch; **life-support** ~ lebenserhaltende Apparate.

apparent offensichtlich, augenscheinlich, ersichtlich, anscheinend.

appeal Rechtsmittel *n*, Berufung *f*, Revision *f*; Beschwerde *f*, Einspruch *m*; ~ **against sentence** Strafmaßberufung; ~ **and error** Berufung und Revision; ~ **authority** Rechtsmittelinstanz; ~ **board** Berufungsstelle; ~ **bond** Sicherheitsleistung des Berufungsklägers; ~ **committee** Berufungsgericht gegen Urteile der Friedensrichter; ~ **in part** Teilberufung; ~ **on points of law** Revision, (*evt*) Rechtsbeschwerde; ~ **out of time** Berufung nach Fristablauf (*besondere Zulassung notw*); ~ **shall lie to ...** Berufung (Revision) zum ... ist zulässig; **consolidated** ~ streitgenössisches Rechtsmittel; **interlocutory** ~ Rechtsmittel gegen e–e Zwischenentscheidung; **cross-** ~ Anschlußberufung, Anschlußrevision; **tax** ~ Steuereinspruch, Berufung im Finanzgerichtsverfahren; **with possible** ~ rechtsmittelfähig; **without** ~ nicht rechtsmittelfähig, rechtskräftig.

appeal *v* ein Rechtsmittel (Berufung, Revision, Beschwerde) einlegen, appellieren.

appealable rechtsmittelfähig, berufungsfähig, revisibel, beschwerdefähig.

appear erscheinen, vor Gericht auftreten, schlüssig vortragen; ~ **against s. o.** gegen jmdn auftreten; ~ **by their clerk** Erscheinen *e–s Ausschusses vertreten* durch den Geschäftsführer; ~ **for** für jmdn vor Gericht auftreten, jmdn gerichtlich vertreten; ~ **in person** persönlich erscheinen; ~ **of record** aktenkundig werden; ~ **on remand** → *remand*; ~ **specially** sich unter Vorbehalt (*des Bestreitens der Zuständigkeit*) am Verfahren beteiligen.

appearance Erscheinen *n* vor Gericht, Beteiligung *f* am Rechtsstreit als Partei, Anzeige *f* der Prozeßbeteiligung des Beklagten, Einlassungserklärung *f*; ~ **by bench warrant** Erscheinen des Angeklagten auf Grund richterlichen Haftbefehls, Zwangsvorführung; ~ **by counsel** anwaltschaftliche Vertretung; ~ **by handing in** Einlassung durch Einreichung e–r Erklärung; ~ **by post** Einlassung auf dem Postwege; ~ **by third party** Streitbeitritt des Streitverkündeten; ~ **day** Verhandlungstermin; Gerichtstag; ~ **docket** Sitzungsliste; ~ **gratis** vorbehaltlose Einlassung *unter Verzicht auf Ladungs- und Einlassungsfristen;* ~ **in person** persönl Erscheinen; Einlassung des nicht anwaltschaftlich vertretenen Beklagten; ~ **to warning** Beitritt im Testamentsprüfungsverfahren (*gegen das Testament gerichtet*); ~ **under protest** Prozeßbeteiligung unter Vorbehalt *der Rüge der Unzuständigkeit des Gerichts*; **common** ~ unterstellte Prozeßeinlassung des säumigen Beklagten; **compulsory** ~ gerichtl angeordnetes persönliches Erscheinen; **conditional** ~ bedingte Einlassung (*unter Vorbehalt der Rüge der Unzuständigkeit*); **corporal** ~ (*physisches*) persönliches Erscheinen unter Vorbehalt; **court** ~ Auftreten vor Gericht; **general** ~ vorbehaltlose Einlassung; **late** ~ verspätete Einlassung; **limited** ~ gegenständlich beschränkte Einlassung; **memorandum of** ~ (*formularmäßige*) Einlassungserklärung; **notice of** ~ Einlassungsanzeige des Beklagten; **optional** ~ fakultatives Prozeßbeteiligungsrecht *e–s Nebenintervenienten*; **personal** ~ persönliches Erscheinen; **special** ~ beschränkte Einlassung (zur Rüge formeller Mängel); **to enter an** ~ *obs* sich einlassen; sich der gerichtl. Zuständigkeit unterwerfen; **to put in an** ~ e–r gerichtl. Ladung Folge leisten; **unconditional** ~ vorbehaltlose Einlassung; **voluntary** ~ freigestelltes persönliches Erscheinen.

appease schlichten, beilegen, beschwichtigen.

appeasement Beschwichtigung *f*, Versöhnung *f*.

appellant Berufungskläger(in), Revisionskläger(in); Beschwerdeführer *m*; Angeklagte(r) in der Berufungs-(Revisions)instanz, Berufungsführer(in); ~ **debtor** Schuldner als Beschwerdeführer.

appellate ein Rechtsmittel betreffend, zur Berufung (*oder sonstigen Rechtsmitteln)* gehörig, Berufungs . . ., Revisions . . ., Beschwerde . . .

appellation Anrufung *f*, Bezeichnung *f*.

appellee Berufungsbeklagter, Revisionsbeklagter, Beschwerdegegner.

append beifügen, anhängen.

appendage Anhang *m*, Nebengebäude *n*, Zubehör *n*, zugehöriges Recht *n*.

appendant *adj* zugehörend, zugehörig; ~ **and appurtenant** zugehörig, Zubehör bildend.

appendant *s* Beifügung *f*, Nebenrecht *n*, Zubehör *n*.

appendix Anhang *m*, Anlagen *f/pl* (*gedruckter*) Anlagenband zur Revisionsschrift, *GB*.

appertain (zu etw) gehören.

appertaining zugehörig.

appliance Gerät *n*, Vorrichtung *f*, Apparat *m*, Instrument *n*.

applicability Anwendbarkeit *f*, Eignung *f*.

applicable anwendbar, geeignet; ~ **mutatis mutandis** entsprechend anwendbar.

applicant Antragsteller(in), Bittsteller(in); ~ **countries** antragstellende Staaten; ~ **for a patent** Patentanmelder; ~ **for shares** Aktienzeichner; ~ **for silk** Anwärter auf den Rang e–s Queen's Counsel *qv*.; ~ **husband** antragstellender Ehemann; **civil service** ~ Bewerber für den öffentlichen Dienst, Laufbahnbewerber; **co-**~ Mitanmelder; **joint** ~**s** gemeinsame Anmelder; **selected** ~ erfolgreicher Bewerber; **subsequent** ~ späterer Anmelder (*Pat*).

application (*1*) Antrag *m*, Ersuchen *n*, Anwendung *f*, Verwendung *f*; ~ **by motion** → *motion*; ~ **by petition** Antrag auf gerichtliche Entscheidung (ordentl. Prozeß); ~ **by summons** Antrag auf Erlaß einer gerichtl Verfügung im Bürowege; ~**s consultation** Einsatzberatung; ~ **for admission** Zulassungsantrag; ~ **for allotment** Zuteilungsantrag; ~ **for annulment** Aufhebungsklage (*Ehe*); ~ **for certiorari** Antrag auf Zulassung e–r Revision; ~ **for citizenship** Einbürgerungsantrag; ~ **for directions** Einholen von Weisungen, Bitte um Auflagen des Gerichts; ~ **for discharge** Rehabilitierungsantrag (*des Gemeinschuldners*); ~ **for judgment by motion** Antrag auf Erlaß e–s (*Versäumnis*)Urteils; ~ **for leave** Antrag auf gerichtl Zulassung (*e–r Prozeßhandlung*); ~ **for listing** Antrag auf offizielle Einführung an der Börse; ~ **for maintenance** Antrag auf Anordnung der Unterhaltszahlung; ~ **for membership** Aufnahmeantrag; ~ **for particulars** → *particulars;* ~ **for receiver** Antrag auf Bestellung e–s (Konkurs)Verwalters; ~ **for registration** Anmeldung zum (Handels)Register; ~ **for registration of trademark** Warenzeichenanmeldung; ~ **for relief** Einspruch, Beschwerde, Abhilfeantrag; ~ **for renewal** Erneuerungsantrag, Verlängerungsantrag; ~ **for respite** Stundungsgesuch; ~ **for security** Antrag auf Anordnung e–r Sicherheitsleistung *durch den Prozeßgegner*; ~ **for shares** Antrag auf Zuteilung von Aktien; ~ **for substantive relief** Klageantrag, Bewilligungsantrag; ~ **for variation** Abänderungsantrag; ~ **of payments** Bestimmung der Tilgungsreihenfolge; ~ **to discharge order** Antrag auf Aufhebung e–s Beschlusses; ~ **to presume death** Antrag auf Todeserklärung; ~ **to set aside service** Antrag auf Feststellung der Unwirksamkeit der Zustellung; ~ **to stay proceedings** Antrag auf Einstellung des Verfahrens; **dishonest** ~ mißbräuchlicher Antrag; **economic** ~ wirtschaftliche Verwendung, Nutzanwendung; **ex parte** ~ Antrag im Verfahren der freiwilligen Gerichtsbarkeit; **field of** ~ Anwendungsgebiet; **grounds for** ~ Begründung des Antrags; **industrial** ~ **of invention** Nutzbarmachung e–r Erfindung; **initial** ~ Erstanmeldung; **originating** ~ verfahrenseinleitender Antrag; **practical** ~ Nutzanwendung; **range of** ~ Anwendungsbereich; **simple** ~ formloser Antrag; **table** ~ schriftlicher Antrag.

application (*2*) Patentanmeldung *f*; ~ **fee** Anmeldegebühr; ~ **for a patent** Patentanmeldung; ~ **for registration** Eintragungsantrag; ~ **for review** Antrag auf Überprüfung; ~ **for revocation** Löschungsantrag; ~ **in home country** Inlandsanmeldung; **additional** ~ Zusatzanmeldung; **basic** ~ Hauptanmeldung; Stammanmeldung; **divisional patent** ~ Teilanmeldung; Patentanmeldung für den ausgeschiedenen Teil; **foreign** ~ Auslandsanmeldung; **in-part** ~ Anschlußanmeldung; **interfering** ~ entgegenstehende, kollidierende Anmeldung; **original** ~ Erstanmeldung; **provisional** ~ vorläufige Anmeldung; **publication of** ~ Bekanntmachung der Anmeldung.

applied angewandt, verwendet; ~ **as productive capital** zur Kapitalinvestierung verwendet; ~ **art** angewandte Kunst, Kunstgewerbe; ~ **to charitable purposes only** nur für mildtätige Zwecke verwendet.

applot aufteilen, zuteilen, zuweisen.

apply beantragen, anwenden, verwenden; *v*/*i* anwendbar sein, Anwendung finden, gelten; ~ **money to a particular debt** die Zahlung zur Tilgung e–r bestimmten Schuld bestimmen.

appoint ernennen, bestellen, einsetzen; ~ **a hearing** e–n Termin zur mündlichen Verhandlung anberaumen; ~ **s.o. as one's agent** jmdn bevollmächtigen.

appointee der(die) Ernannte, der(die) Bestellte, der(die) Eingesetzte, Kandidat(in), Amtsinhaber(in).

appointment Ernennung *f*, Anstellung *f*, Bestellung *f*, Berufung *f*, Einsetzung *f*, Amt *n*, Stelle *f*; Bestimmung des Berechtigten; Terminsanberaumung *f*, Verabredung *f* (*e–s Treffens*), Termin *m*; ~ **book** Terminkalender; ~ **for life** Ernennung auf Lebenszeit; ~ **of a guardian** Bestellung e–s Vormunds; ~

of an heir Erbeinsetzung, **by special ~ to Her Majesty** königlicher Hoflieferant; **honorary ~** Ehrenamt; **mistaken ~** Fehlbesetzung; **permanent ~** Dauerstellung.

appointor der(die) Ernennende; Bestallungsbehörde *f*.

apportion aufteilen, umlegen, anteilig festlegen; **~ losses evenly** Verluste gleichmäßig verteilen.

apportionable aufteilbar.

apportionment Aufteilung *f*, anteilige Verteilung *f*; Zuweisung *f*; **~ of contracts** anteilige Festlegung der Vergütung (*bei teilbarem Vertrag*); **~ of costs** Kostenverteilung (*im Urteil*); **~ of funds** Zuweisung von Mitteln; **~ of salvage** gerichtliche Zuteilung des Bergelohns; **~ of tax** Festlegung der Besteuerung einzelner Vermögensgegenstände.

apposite einschlägig, geeignet.

appraisable schätzbar, bewertbar.

appraisal Wertschätzung *f*, Bewertung *f*; **~ of damage** Schadensschätzung; **condemnation ~** Enteignungstaxe.

appraise schätzen, bewerten.

appraisement Bewertung *f*, Schätzung *f*; Taxwert *m*; **official ~** amtliche Schätzung.

appraiser amtlicher Schätzer *m*, Bewertungsbeamter *m*; **~'s store** Zollager; **general ~** Zollbewertungsbeamter; **merchant ~** kaufmännischer Sachverständiger für Bewertungen und Zollangelegenheiten.

appreciable wahrnehmbar, merklich, bestimmbar.

appreciate würdigen, erkennen, im Wert steigen; **~ fully** würdigen; **~d surplus** Mehrbetrag, Mehrwert.

appreciation Einschätzung *f*, Würdigung *f*; Kursgewinn *m*, Werterhöhung *f*; Aufwertung *f*; Zuschreibung *f* (*Gegenteil von Abschreibung*); **~ in value** Wertsteigerung, Wertzuwachs; **~ of peril** wissentliches Aufsichnehmen e–r Gefahr; **~ of the inventive level** Beurteilung der Erfindungshöhe; **recorded ~** nachgewiesener Wertzuwachs; **taxes on capital ~** Steuern auf den Wertzuwachs.

appreciative anerkennend.

apprehend begreifen, wahrnehmen, befürchten, ergreifen, festnehmen, verhaften.

apprehensible begreiflich, verständlich.

apprehension Befürchtung *f*, Erkennen *n* e–s bevorstehenden Ereignisses; Auffassungsvermögen *n*; Festnahme *f*, Verhaftung *f*, **~ of death** das Wissen um den bevorstehenden Tod; **~ of offenders** Festnahme (*von Strafverdächtigen*); **provisional ~** vorläufige Festnahme.

apprehensive besorgt, furchtsam.

apprentice Lehrling *m*, Auszubildender *m*; **~ en la ley** *hist* Jurastudent, Anwalt.

apprenticeship Lehre *f*, Lehrverhältnis *n*, Lehrzeit *f*; **~ training** Lehrlingsausbildung; **contract of ~** Lehrvertrag; **period of ~** Lehrzeit, Ausbildungsdauer.

apprise in Kenntnis setzen, benachrichtigen.

approach sich nähern, annähern.

approach Annäherung *f*, Zutritt *m*; **right of ~** *int* Visitationsrecht; **subjectivist ~** subjektive Betrachtungsweise.

approbation Billigung *f*, Genehmigung *f*, Bestätigung (*e–r aufhebbaren Ehe*); Sanktionierung *f*; **on ~** auf Probe, zur Ansicht; **to buy on ~** auf Probe kaufen (*Rückgaberecht*).

appropriate *adj* angemessen, geeignet, passend.

appropriate *v* aneignen; (*Geldmittel für e–n bestimmten Zweck*) festlegen, bereitstellen; konkretisieren (*Gattungsschuld*); zuteilen, bewilligen; **~ money** sich Geld aneignen, Geld unterschlagen; **~ to one's use** sich zueignen; **~d surplus** → *surplus*.

appropriateness Angemessenheit *f*; **~ of the billing** Angemessenheit der Anwaltskostenrechnung.

appropriation Aneignung *f*, Eigentumserwerb *m*; Zweckbestimmung *f*, Anrechnungsbestimmung *f* (*bei*

Zahlungen); Zuteilung *f*, Verwendung *f*, Bewilligung *f*, Konkretisierung *f*; ~ **account** → *account* (*2*); ~ **act** Haushaltsgesetz; ~ **bill** Haushaltsvorlage, Bewilligungsvorlage; ~**s committee** Haushaltsausschuß; ~ **expenditure ledger** Kostenblatt über Ausgaben öffentlicher Mittel; ~ **-in-aid** Eigenverwaltung budgetfreier Mittel; ~ **of funds** Mittelzuweisung, Bereitstellung von Mitteln, Bewilligung von Geldern; ~ **of land** Landerwerb der öffentlichen Hand, Enteignung; ~ **of payments** Bestimmung der Tilgungsreihenfolge; ~ **of profits** Bereitstellung von Gewinnen zur Verteilung, Verwendung des Gewinns, Gewinnverteilung; ~ **of water** Ableitung von Wasser aus öffentlichen Wasserläufen *zu privaten Zwecken*; ~ **ordinance** Zuweisung von Haushaltsmitteln durch Gemeindebeschluß; **budgetary** ~ bewilligte Haushaltsmittel; **continuing** ~**s** nicht verbrauchte Haushaltsmittel; **deficiency** ~ → *deficiency*; **fraudulent** ~ widerrechtliche Zueignung (*Unterschlagung*); **specific** ~ ausdrückliche Zweckbestimmung.

appropriator der (die) *sich etwas widerrechtlich* Aneignende.

approval Genehmigung *f*, Billigung *f*; **agreement subject to** ~ Vereinbarung vorbehaltlich Bestätigung; **prior** ~ Einwilligung; **regulatory** ~ behördl Genehmigung; **sale on** ~ → *sale*.

approve zustimmen, billigen, genehmigen, gutheißen; Entlastung erteilen; **the board was** ~**d** dem Vorstand wurde Entlastung erteilt.

approved indorsed note (*zur Sicherheit) von Drittem indossierter Solawechsel*.

appurtenance (*Grundstücks*)Bestandteil *m* und Zubehör *n*, zugehöriges Recht, Pertinenz *f*; ~**s** Realrechte (*an Liegenschaften*).

appurtenant zugehörig, dazugehörend, dem Eigentum am Grundstück folgend; ~ **and appendant** zugehörig, Zubehör bildend.

apt geeignet, tauglich.

aptitude Eignung *f*, Hang *m*, Neigung *f*; ~ **test** Eignungsprüfung; **vocational** ~ berufl Eignung.

apud acta bei den Akten, zu Protokoll erklärt.

aquae|ductus Dienstbarkeit der Wasserführung über fremdem Grund; ~ **haustus** Wasserentnahmedienstbarkeit; ~ **immittendae** Wasserabflußdienstbarkeit.

aquatic rights Wasserrechte *n|pl, Privatrechte an Gewässern und deren Untergrund*.

arable ackerbaulich nutzbar, anbaufähig (*Land*).

arbiter Schiedrichter *m*, Schiedsgutachter *m*.

arbitrable schiedsrichterlich zu entscheiden.

arbitrage Arbitrage *f* (*Ausnutzung von Kursunterschieden an verschiedenen Börsenplätzen*); ~ **dealings** Arbitragegeschäfte; ~ **in securities** Effektenarbitrage; **direct** ~ einfache Devisenarbitrage (*an e–m Ort*); **compound** ~ Mehrfacharbitrage; **exchange** ~ Devisenarbitrage.

arbitrageur (*US also:* **arbitrager**) Arbitrageur *m*; Aktienaufkäufer für Übernahme-Spekulation.

arbitral schiedsrichterlich, Schieds . . .

arbitrament Schiedsspruch *m*; ~ **and award** Einrede des Schiedsgerichts.

arbitrariness Willkürlichkeit *f*.

arbitrary willkürlich, eigenmächtig.

arbitrate schiedsrichterlich entscheiden; **obligation to** ~ Schiedsklausel, Verpflichtung, durch Schiedsgericht entscheiden lassen.

arbitration Schiedsgerichtsverfahren *n*, Schiedsgericht *n*, schiedsrichterliche Entscheidung *f*; ~ **and award** Einrede der Schiedsklausel, Berufung auf den Schiedsvertrag; ~ **agreement** Schiedsvertrag, Schiedsvereinbarung, Schiedsabrede; ~ **award** Schiedsspruch; ~

board Schlichtungsstelle, Schiedsstelle; ~ **by head of state** Schlichtung *e–r internationalen Streitigkeit* durch das Oberhaupt e–s unbeteiligten Staates; ~ **(-only) clause** Schiedsklausel, Schiedsgerichtsklausel; ~ **committee** Schlichtungsausschuß; ~ **treaty** *int* Schiedsgerichtsvertrag; ~ **tribunal** Schiedsgericht; **commercial** ~ kaufmännisches Schiedsgerichtswesen; **compulsory** ~ Schiedsgerichtszwang, Zwangsschlichtung; **submission to** ~ Vorlage des Streitfalles an ein Schiedsgericht; **voluntary** ~ freiwillige Schiedsgerichtsbarkeit.

arbitrator Schiedsrichter *m*; **~'s award** Schiedsspruch, Schiedsurteil; ~ **of averages** Dispacheur; **third** ~ Schiedsobmann.

arbitrium Schiedsspruch *m*; ~ **est judicium** der Schiedsspruch hat Urteilskraft.

archives Archiv *n*, Archivbestände *m|pl*, Registratur *f*.

archivist Archivar *m*.

area Fläche *f*, Gebiet *n*; Bauplatz *m*; ~ **bargaining** regionale Tarifverhandlungen; ~ **code** Vorwahl; ~ **manager** Gebietsleiter; ~ **of application** Anwendungsgebiet, Geltungsbereich; ~ **of assessment** Veranlagungs-Steuerbezirk; ~ **of dispute** Streitstoff; ~ **of responsibility** Verantwortungsbereich, Zuständigkeit(sbereich), Z.sgebiet; ~ **of supply** Auslieferungsgebiet; ~ **rehabilitation** Flächensanierung; ~ **variance** gebietsweise Abweichungen (*vom Bauleitplan*); **built-up** ~ bebautes Gelände, geschlossene Ortschaft; **deprived ~s** unterversorgte Gebiete; **grey** ~ Grauzone (*juristische Zweifelsfälle*); **special ~s** Notstandsgebiete *GB*.

arguability Plausibilität *f*.

arguable vertretbar, plausibel.

argue begründen, geltend machen, argumentieren, vortragen; über etw mündl verhandeln.

arguendo als erläuternde (*nicht entscheidungserhebliche*) Ausführungen des Gerichts.

argument Argument *n*, Begründung *f*, Ausführungen *f|pl*, Vorbringen *n*, Vortrag *m*, Plädoyer *n*; ~ **in summation** Schlußplädoyer; ~ **of counsel** Plädoyer; **~s of the parties** Parteivorbringen; **closing** ~ Schlußplädoyer; **cogent** ~ schlüssige Begründung; **factual** ~ Ausführungen zum Sachverhalt; **legal** ~ → *legal*; **oral** ~ mündliche Ausführungen, Plädoyer; **sound** ~ stichhaltiges Argument; **tenable** ~ vertretbare Begründung, stichhaltiger Rechtsgrund.

argumentation Argumentierung *f*, Folgerung *f*, Debatte *f*.

argumentative argumentativ, plädierend, nicht tatsächlich begründet; polemisch, streitig.

argumentum e contrario Umkehrschluß *m*.

arise entstehen, sich ergeben; stammen; ~ **from the circumstances** sich aus den Umständen ergeben.

arising entstehend, entstanden und noch entstehend; ~ **in an appeal** Gegenstand des Berufungsverfahrens sein; ~ **out of the contract** sich aus dem Vertrag ergebend; ~ **out of this Act** auf Grund dieses Gesetzes; ~ **upon distinct occasions** aus verschiedenen Anlässen.

aristocracy Aristokratie *f*, Adel *m*; **landed** ~ Großgrundbesitzer(tum).

armchair principle Testamentsauslegung nach den Lebensverhältnissen des Testators.

armistice Waffenstillstand *m*; **A~ Day** Gedenktag des Waffenstillstandes von 1918; **general** ~ allgemeiner Waffenstillstand; **partial** ~ Teilwaffenstillstand.

arms Waffen *f|pl*; **armour and** ~ persönliche Waffen, Recht des Waffentragens; ~ **control** Rüstungskontrolle; ~ **race** Rüstungswettlauf; **by force of** ~ mit Waffengewalt; **poaching with** ~ bewaffneter Widerstand beim Wildern; **robbery with** ~ schwerer

Raub mit Waffen; **under** ~ bewaffnet, *mil* einsatzfähig.

arm's length deal Geschäft wie mit Außenstehenden.

army Heer *n*, Landstreitkräfte *f|pl*; ~ **council** Heeresrat; **regular** ~ stehendes Heer, Berufsheer; kriegsrechtlich organisierte Truppe.

arraign die Anklage eröffnen, *dem Beschuldigten die Anklage eröffnen und seine formale Einlassung entgegennehmen*.

arraignment Verlesung *f* der Anklageschrift und formale Erklärung des Beschuldigten zur Anklage; ~ **of peers** Adelsprivileg, vor dem Oberhaus vor Gericht gestellt zu werden (*Hochverrat u. a.*); ~ **of persons unfit to plead** Befragung e–s Unzurechnungsfähigen zur Anklage.

arrange ordnen, vereinbaren, sich verständigen, sich vergleichen; ~ **amicably** gütlich beilegen.

arrangement Arrangement *n*, Anordnung *f*, Vergleich *m* zur Abwendung des Konkurses, Liquidationsvergleich *m*, Vereinbarung *f*, Abmachung *f*; **internal** ~**s** interne Regelungen, Innenverhältnis; ~ **plan** Vergleichsvorschlag; ~ **to avert bankruptcy** Vergleich zur Abwendung des Konkurses *US*; ~ **of claims** Rangfolge von Konkursforderungen; ~ **with creditors** Gläubigervergleich (*zunächst außergerichtlich, bei Zustandekommen: Eintragung*); **amicable** ~ gütliche Erledigung; **appeal against** ~ Beschwerde gegen e–n Vergleich; **as per** ~ vereinbarungsgemäß; **banking** ~ bankmäßige Abwicklung; **binding** ~ bindende Abmachung; **living** ~**s** Wohnverhältnisse, Zusammenleben; **private** ~ außergerichtliche Regelung; **scheme of** ~ → *scheme*; **voluntary** ~ Vergleichsverfahren.

array *s* geordnete Aufstellung *f*, Gesamtheit der Geschworenen, Geschworenenliste *f*.

array *v* aufstellen, die Geschworenenliste aufstellen.

arrears Zahlungsrückstände *m|pl*; ~ **certificate** Verpflichtungsschein über rückständige Obligationszinsen; ~ **of interest** rückständige Zinsen, Zinsrückstände; ~ **of rent** Miet- *bzw* Pachtrückstände; ~**s to tax** Steuerrückstände; **in** ~ im Rückstand, in Verzug; **tax** ~ = ~ *to tax q. v.*; **to fall into** ~ in Rückstand geraten.

arrest *s* Arrest *m*, Verhaftung *f*, Festnahme *f*, Arrestbeschlagnahme *f*, Schiffsarrest *m*, Arrestpfändung *f*; ~ **by private person** vorläufige Festnahme durch Privatperson; ~ **for debt** persönl Arrest; ~ **of goods** Warenbeschlagnahme; ~ **of judgment** Aufschub der Urteilsverkündung; ~**s of kings, princes and peoples** Beschlagnahme durch staatlichen Hoheitsakt; ~ **of ship** Arrestpfändung eines Schiffes (*an die Kette legen*); ~ **record** Festnahmeprotokoll; ~ **under civil process** zivilrechtl Verhaftung, Verhaftung zur Vollziehung einer Beugestrafe; ~ **under criminal process** Verhaftung im Strafverfahren; ~ **under unexecuted judgment** Festnahme zur Strafverbüßung; ~ **under (by) warrant** Festnahme auf Grund (richterlichen) Haftbefehls; ~ **without warrant** vorläufige Festnahme; **commitment after** ~ Haftbefehl nach Festnahme; **exemption from** ~ Immunität (von Verhaftung); **freedom from** ~ Schutz vor willkürlicher Verhaftung; **malicious** ~ rechtsmißbräuchliche Festnahme, Freiheitsberaubung im Amt; **open** ~ Hausarrest; **order for** ~ Haftbefehl; **parol** ~ mündlicher Haftbefehl (*des Richters während der Sitzung*); **power of** ~ Verhaftungsbefugnis; **preventive** ~ vorbeugende Inhaftierung, Schutzhaft; **privilege from** ~ → *privilege*; **probable cause for** ~ dringender Tatverdacht; **resisting** ~ → *resisting*; **submission to** ~ Sich-Verhaften-Lassen; **summary** ~ vorläufige Festnahme; **to flee** ~ sich der Verhaftung durch die Flucht entziehen; **to lay ~ on** in Beschlag nehmen; **under ~** in Haft, verhaftet.

arrest *v/t* verhaften, festnehmen; hemmen; **~ the running of time** den Fristablauf hemmen.

arrestable offence → *offence*.

arrestation Verhaftung *f*.

arrestee *scot* Drittschuldner *m*, Dritter *m* als Besitzer gepfändeter Sachen bei Arrestvollziehung; Pfandschuldner.

arrestor der Festnehmende.

arrival Ankunft *f*, Eintreffen *n*; **~ draft** nach Ankunft der Waren zu akzeptierende *bzw* einzulösende Tratte; Tratte mit beigefügten Verschiffungsdokumenten; **actual ~** tatsächliche Ankunft.

arrive eintreffen, ankommen.

arrogate sich anmaßen; sich unrechtmäßig aneignen.

arrogation Anmaßung *f*; Adoptierung *f* e–s Volljährigen; **~ of power** Machtanmaßung.

arson Brandstiftung *f* (*am Hause e–s Dritten*); **~ with intent** (vorsätzl) Brandstiftung.

arsonist Brandstifter *m*.

art Kunst *f*, Kunstfertigkeit *f*; **~ and part** Beihilfe leistend; **~ unions** Künstlergenossenschaften; **applied ~** angewandte Kunst, Kunstgewerbe; **commercial ~** Werbegraphik; **prior ~** *pat* Stand der Technik; **promotion of ~s** Kunstförderung.

article *s* Artikel *m*, Abschnitt *m*, Warenart *f*; **~s, goods or things** Gegenstände; **~ demanded** der bestellte Artikel; **~ of average quality** Durchschnittsware; **~s of consumption** Verbrauchsartikel; **~s of domestic use and ornament** Hausrat; **~s of food** Lebensmittel; **~s of functional utility** Gebrauchsartikel; **~s of furniture** Möbel, Einrichtungsgegenstände; **~s of high quality** hochwertige Artikel; **~s of manufacture** fabrikmäßig hergestellte Gegenstände, hergestellte Waren; **~s of merchandise** Handelsware; **~s of perishable nature** verderbliche Waren; **~s of personal property** bewegliche Habe (*ohne Geld und Wertpapiere*); **~s of quick sale** Zugartikel, Verkaufsschlager; **~s of sale** Verkaufsgegenstände; **~s of vertu** kunstgewerbliche Gegenstände; **~s on commission** Kommissionsgut; **branded ~** Markenartikel; **knockdown ~s** Massenware; **proprietary ~s** *geschützte* Markenartikel, patentierte Monopolerzeugnisse; **scarce ~s** Mangelwaren; **semi-finished ~s** Halbfertigfabrikate.

article *v* Vereinbarung bezüglich der Lehrzeit treffen; **~d** vertraglich verpflichtet, in der Lehre; **~d clerk** → *clerk*.

articles *s/pl* Satzung *f*, Vertrag *m*, Schriftsatz *m* bei Gericht; *eccl* Klageschrift *f*; **~ and bylaws** Satzung; **~ of agreement** Vertragsniederschrift, Vorvertrag, Vereinssatzung; **~ of apprenticeship** Lehrvertrag; **~ of association** Satzung; interne Satzungsbestimmungen e–r company *qv*; **A~ of Confederation** =) *hist US, Föderationsvertrag der 13 Kolonien*; **~ of impeachment** Parlamentsanklage; **~ of incorporation** Satzung, Gründungsurkunde (*e–r Körperschaft*); **~ of consolidation** Fusionsvertrag; **~ of dissolution** Liquidationserklärung e–r Kapitalgesellschaft; **~ of marriage** (= *marriage ~*) Ehevertrag; **~ of partnership** Gesellschaftsvertrag; **~ of separation** Vereinbarung über das Getrenntleben; **~ of the navy** Marineordnung; **~ of the peace** Anrufung des Gerichts zum Schutz gegen Bedrohung; **A~ of Union** (=) *hist Vereinigung des schottischen Parlaments mit dem englischen, 1707*; **to go into ~s** sich zum Anwalt (*solicitor*) ausbilden lassen; **to sign the ~** sich anheuern lassen.

articulate *adj* klar, deutlich, verständlich.

articulately abschnittsweise, im einzelnen.

artifact Ausstellungsstück *m*.

artifice Raffinesse *f*, Kunstgriff *m*, Trick *m*, Täuschungsmanöver *n*; **to obtain by** ~ → *to obtain.*

artificer Handwerksmeister *m*, gewerbl Fachmann *m*, Mechaniker *m*; Kunstgewerbler *m*; Erfinder *m*, Urheber *m*, Künstler *m*.

artisan Handwerker *m*; **~'s routine work** gewöhnliche handwerksmäßige Arbeit.

artist Künstler *m auch*: Handwerker *m*.

as wie, weil, da, als; ~ **aforesaid** wie vorstehend erwähnt; ~ **against (a stranger)** gegenüber (Dritten), in Richtung gegen (*e–e Partei*); ~ **agents** im Auftrag von, in Vertretung von; ~ **alleged** wie behauptet, wie bereits vorgetragen; ~ **and when** bei, sobald wie; ~ **at present used and enjoyed** wie zur Zeit genutzt; ~ **before** wie bisher; ~ **between** im Verhältnis zu, gegenüber; ~ **between solicitor and client** üblicherweise vom Mandanten geschuldete Gebühren (*evt nicht erstattungsfähig*); ~ **counsel shall advise** anwaltschaftlich empfohlen; ~ **customary** üblich; ~ **devised** gemäß letztwilliger Verfügung; ~ **earned** gemäß erworbenem Anspruch; ~ **far as possible** nach Möglichkeit; ~ **far as practicable** soweit durchführbar; ~ **from now** von jetzt ab; ~ **he shall think fit** nach seinem Ermessen; ~ **held** nach dem jeweiligen Besitzstand; ~ **if and when** falls und zum Zeitpunkt daß, per Erscheinen, *unter dem Vorbehalt des Zustandekommens und auf den betreffenden Zeitpunkt;* ~ **it stands** wie die Ware steht und liegt, tel-quel; ~ **may seem just** berechtigt erscheinend; ~ **occasion may require** → *occasion*; ~ **of** (= *per) als zu e–m Zeitpunkt abgegeben,* zum; ~ **of course** von selbst, selbstverständlich; ~ **of right** rechtmäßig, von Rechts wegen, rechtlich; ~ **per** gemäß, bezogen auf; ~ **per advice** gemäß Benachrichtigung; *Bezogener wurde von der Ausstellung benachrichtigt;* ~ **per agreement** gemäß Vereinbarung; ~ **per catalogue** nach Katalog; ~ **per indorsement** (*zum Umrechnungskurs des Wechsels*) bei Indossierung; ~ **per memorandum of agreement** vereinbarungsgemäß, satzungsgemäß; ~ **received** jeweils bei Erhalt; ~ **required** → *required*; ~ **shall be begotten** (*Nachkommen*) die bis dahin gezeugt sind; ~ **shall be just** so wie recht und billig; ~ **soon as practicable** sobald wie praktisch möglich; ~ **such** als solcher, in seiner (der) Eigenschaft als; ~ **such trustee but not otherwise** nur in ihrer Eigenschaft als Treuhänder; ~ **the case arises** von Fall zu Fall; ~ **the case may be** entsprechend, je nach Sachlage, beziehungsweise; ~ **the case requires** wie jeweils erforderlich; ~ **the crow flies** in Luftlinie; ~ **the law directs** nach gesetzlicher Vorschrift.

ascend aufsteigen.

ascendant Aszendent *m*, Vorfahre *m*, Verwandter *m* der aufsteigenden Linie.

ascending line aufsteigende Linie *f*; **related in the** ~ in aufsteigender Linie verwandt.

ascent Aufstieg *m*, Erbanfall *m* an Aszendenten.

ascertain feststellen, festsetzen, ermitteln, bestimmen; ~ **a balance** e–n Saldo feststellen; ~ **the price** den Preis festsetzen; **~ed goods** → *goods.*

ascertainable feststellbar, bestimmbar.

ascertainment Ermittlung, Festlegung, Konkretisierung; ~ **of damage** Schadensfeststellung; ~ **of applicable law** Ermittlung des anwendbaren Rechts.

ascribe zuschreiben, zutrauen, zurückführen auf.

asexualization Sterilisierung *f* (*e–s Mannes*).

ashore|and afloat auf See oder an Land; ~ **or overside** an Land oder Schiffsentladeseite (*Überbordlieferung*).

aside seitlich, getrennt.

ask bitten, beantragen, ersuchen; ~ **the banns of s.o.** für jmdn das Aufgebot bestellen; ~**ed and bid** *exch* Brief und Geld; ~**ed price** *exch* Briefkurs; ~**ed quotation** Briefkurs.

asking a bribe passive Bestechung *f*.

aspect Aspekt *m*, Gesichtspunkt *m*.

asperse verleumden, verdächtigen.

aspersion Verleumdung *f*, Schmähung *f*, kritische Äußerung *f*.

aspiration (*pol*) inneres Streben *n*, Bestrebung *f*.

asport (*widerrechtlich*) fortschaffen.

asportation Wegnahme *f* und Fortschaffen *n* der gestohlenen Sache.

assail angreifen, überfallen.

assailable angreifbar, anfechtbar.

assailant (= assailer) Angreifer *m*, Gegner *n*.

assassin Meuchelmörder *m*, Attentäter *m*; **hired** ~ gedungener Mörder.

assassinate ermorden, heimtückisch umbringen, durch Attentat töten.

assassination Mord *m*, gedungener Mord *m*, politischer Mord *m*, Meuchelmord *m*, Mordattentat *n*.

assassinator = *assassin qv*.

assault (rechtswidriger) Angriff, Tätlichkeit *f*, gewaltsame Drohung *f*; Gewaltanwendung *f*; ~ **and battery** gewaltsame Körperverletzung; ~ **by misadventure** ungewollte Gewaltanwendung; ~ **in defence of property** Notwehr beim Angriff gegen Sachen; ~ **in resisting arrest** gewaltsamer Widerstand gegen die Festnahme; ~ **in self-defence** gewaltsame Notwehrhandlung; ~ **with intent to commit felony** Gewaltandrohung, Gewaltanwendung in verbrecherischer Absicht; ~ **with intent to commit murder** Mordversuch; ~ **with intent to ravish** versuchte Vergewaltigung; ~ **with intent to rob** räuberische Erpressung, versuchter Raub; **aggravated** ~ erschwerter Fall der Gewalttätigkeit bei Körperverletzung; **common** ~ (*einfache*) Gewaltanwendung oder Bedrohung; **criminal** ~ versuchte Körperverletzung; **felonious** ~ → *felonious*; **indecent** ~ sexuelle Nötigung; **secret** ~ geheimer Mordanschlag; **sexual** ~ sexuelle Nötigung (*durch Gewalt*); **simple** ~ = *common assault qv*.

assay *chem* Prüfung *f* der Reinheit von Metallen (*bes Edelmetallen*), Metallprobe *f*; ~ **commissioner** Münzprüfkommission (*US*); ~ **office** Münzmetallprüfanstalt; ~ **mark** Feingehaltszeichen; ~ **office bar** *amtlich auf Feingehalt* geprüfter Goldbarren; ~ **office value** Feingehaltswert; ~ **value** Münzwert.

assayer Edelmetallprüfer *m*; **A~ of the King** königlicher Münzprüfer.

assecurate verpfänden, beteuern.

assecuration Transportversicherung *f*.

assecurator Transportversicherer *m* (*bes Seetransport*).

assemblage Versammlung *f*; öffentliche Ansprache; ~ **value** Sammelwert.

assemble zusammentreten, sich versammeln; montieren.

assembly (*1*) Versammlung *f*; **Church A~** = *National Assembly of the Church of England (engl. Kirchenparlament)*; **constituent** ~ verfassungsgebende Versammlung, Gründungsversammlung; **deliberative** ~ beratende Versammlung; **general** ~ Vollversammlung; **General A~** *scot oberstes Kirchengericht*; **legislative** ~ gesetzgebende Versammlung; **plenary** ~ Plenarversammlung, Vollversammlung; **political** ~ Versammlung, Sitzung e–s Verfassungsorgans; **popular** ~ Volksversammlung; **riotous** ~ gewalttätige Zusammenrottung, Aufruhr; **unlawful** ~ unerlaubte Ansammlung.

assembly (*2*) Montage *f*; ~ **line** Fließband.

assemblyman Abgeordneter *m*.

assent *s* Zustimmung *f*, Genehmigung *f*, Billigung *f*; *bes.* Vollziehung d. letztwilligen Verfügung durch d. Test.vollstrecker; **con-**

structive ~ konkludente Zustimmung; **mutual** ~ Einigung (bei Vertragsschluß); **royal** ~ Königliche Zustimmung cf Royal; **vesting** ~ Grundstücksübertragungsurkunde des Nachlaßabwicklers.

assent *v* beipflichten, zustimmen, genehmigen.

assented genehmigt; (*bes Änderung auf e–r Wechselurkunde genehmigt*); ~ **bonds** *treuhänderisch hinterlegte Obligationen, deren Emissionsbedingungen mit Zustimmung der Obligationäre geändert wurden.*

assentient zustimmend.

assert erklären, behaupten, geltend machen; ~ **a claim** e–n Anspruch geltend machen; ~ **a right** sich auf ein Recht berufen, ein Recht geltend machen.

assertible verfechtbar, vertretbar.

assertion Behauptung *f*, Bekräftigung *f*, Erklärung *f*, Geltendmachung *n*; ~ **not proved** unbewiesene Behauptung; ~ **of fact** Tatsachenbehauptung; **negative** ~ negative Behauptung *tatsächlicher Art*; **positive** ~ bestimmte Behauptung; **solemn** ~ Beteuerung; **to make an** ~ e–e Behauptung aufstellen.

assertory|covenant Versprechen in gesiegelter Form; ~ **oath** → *oath*.

assess feststellen, bewerten, schätzen, veranlagen, festsetzen, umlegen; ~ **a building** e Gebäude schätzen, den Verkehrswert feststellen; ~ **taxes** zur Steuerveranlagen besteuern.

assessable steuerpflichtig, umlagepflichtig, nachschußpflichtig; ~ **site value** steuerlicher Grundstückswert.

assessed bewertet, veranlagt, besteuert, steuerlich; ~ **valuation of property** (steuerliche) Grundstücksbewertung.

assessee Zahlungspflichtige(r), Umlageschuldner(in).

assessment Bemessung *f*, Schätzung *f*, Veranlagung *f*, Umlage *f*, Festsetzung *f*; anteilige Kostenbelastung *f*; Anliegerbeitrag; ~ **bonds** Schuldverschreibungen für Umlagen, *bes für Erschließungskosten*; ~**s charged on the premises** Erschließungskostenbeiträge; ~ **company** Sterbegeldversicherung mit Umlageverfahren, Umlagekasse; ~ **contract** Vertrag mit Beitragspflicht *im Umlageverfahren*; ~ **district** Steuerbezirk, Umlagebereich; ~ **for tax** Steuerschätzung, Steuervorauszahlungsbescheid; ~ **fund** Umlagevermögen; ~**s, impositions and outgoings** die Grundstückslasten und -kosten; ~ **insurance** Versicherung im Umlageverfahren; ~ **insurance company** Versicherung auf Gegenseitigkeit *mit Nachschußpflicht*; Umlagekasse; ~ **list** Steuerliste, Veranlagungsliste; ~ **of costs** Kostenfestsetzung; ~ **of damages** Schadenersatzbemessung; ~ **of duty** Zollfestsetzung; ~ **of income tax** Einkommensteuerveranlagung; ~ **of profit** Gewinnberechnung; ~ **of property** Bewertung von Grundvermögen; ~ **of the penalty** Strafzumessung; ~ **of value** Bewertung, Wertschätzung; ~ **on landed property** Veranlagung zur Grundsteuer; ~ **period** Veranlagungszeitraum; ~ **procedure** Erschließungskostenbeitragsverfahren; ~ **system** Umlageverfahren; ~ **work** Arbeit zur Erhaltung des Abbaurechts (*US min*); **deficiency** ~ → *deficiency*; **local** ~ Gemeindeumlage, Kommunalabgabe; **parochial** ~ Gemeindeumlage, Pfarrgemeindeabgabe, Kirchgeld; **rate of** ~ Steuersatz, Umlagesatz; **special** ~ Sonderumlage; **subsequent** ~ Nachveranlagung; **tax** ~ Steuerveranlagung.

assessor Schätzbeamter *m*, Sachverständiger *m* für Bewertungen; Beisitzer *m*; **lay** ~ Laienrichter als Beisitzer; Schöffe; **mercantile** ~**s** kaufmännische Beisitzer, Handelsrichter; **nautical** ~**s** schiffssachverständige Beisitzer.

asset Vermögenswert *m*, Wirtschaftsgut *n*, Nachlaßgegenstand *m*, Aktivposten *m*; ~ **retirement** Ausscheiden von Vermögensgegenständen (*wegen Neuanschaffungen*); ~ **account** Anlagekonto, Bestandskonto; ~ **accountability** Bestandsführung, buchmäßige Erfassung von Anlagen; ~ **depreciation range** Abschreibungszeitraum; ~ **share** *ins* Prämienreserve; ~ **stripping** *Herauskauf von Betriebsanlagen u. sonstigen Vermögenswerten*; ~ **value** Wert *des Vermögensgegenstandes*.

assets Vermögen *n*, Aktiva *n|pl*, Vermögenswerte *m|pl*, Betriebsvermögen *n*, Wirtschaftsgüter *n|pl*; Ressourcen; ~ **abroad** ausländisches Vermögen; ~ **and liabilities** Aktiva und Passiva; ~ **employed** eingesetztes Aktivvermögen; ~ **entre mains** Nachlaßaktiva; ~ **in kind** Sachwerte; ~ **of the business** Firmenvermögen; ~ **per (= by) descent** vererbliches Vermögen; *für Nachlaßverbindlichkeiten haftendes Vermögen;* **absence of** ~ Vermögenslosigkeit, „mangels Masse"; **accrued** ~ antizipative Aktiva; **actual** ~ Reinvermögen; **afteracquired** ~ später erworbene Vermögensgegenstände; **attachable** ~ beschlagnahmefähige Werte; **available** ~ verfügbare Aktiva; **bankrupt's** ~ Vermögen des Gemeinschuldners, Konkursmasse; **business** ~ → *business*; **capital** ~ → *capital*; **cash** ~ → *cash*; **chargeable** ~ abgabenpflichtige Vermögenswerte, nicht von der *capital gains tax qv* befreite V.; **current** ~ Umlaufvermögen; **dead** ~ nicht realisierbare Vermögenswerte; **commercial** ~ Betriebsvermögen; **deferred** ~ transitorische Passiva; **earning** ~ gewinnbringende Kapitalanlagen, e–n Ertrag abwerfende Aktiva; **economic** ~ Wirtschaftsgüter, wirtschaftl Werte; **equitable** ~ nichtdingliche Vermögenswerte, nur billigkeitsrechtlich erfaßbare V.; **estate** ~ Nachlaß(Erbschafts-)-gegenstände; **external** ~ Auslandsvermögen; **fixed** ~ Anlagevermögen; **fixed tangible** ~ Anlagevermögen an Sachwerten; **floating** ~ Umlaufsvermögen; **foreign** ~ Auslandsvermögen; **frozen** ~ illiquides Vermögen; **hidden** ~ stille Reserven; **intangible** ~ immaterielle Vermögenswerte; **legal** ~ → *legal*; **liquid** ~ liquide Mittel, sofort realisierbare Aktiva; **long-lived** ~ langlebige Wirtschaftsgüter; **low-value** ~ geringwertige Wirtschaftsgüter; **net** ~ → *net*; **no** ~ kein Guthaben; **nominal** ~ Buchwerte; **non-current** ~ Anlagevermögen; **non-ledger** ~ nicht buchungsfähige Wirtschaftsgüter; **physical** ~**s** Sachvermögen; **operating** ~ Betriebsvermögen; **original** ~ Anfangskapital; **partnership** ~ → *partnership*; **permanent** ~ Anlagevermögen; **personal** ~ bewegliches Vermögen; **probate** ~ haftende Nachlaßmasse; **quick** ~ liquide Mittel; Forderungen aus Warenlieferungen und Leistungen; **real** ~ → *real*; **short-lived** ~ kurzlebige Wirtschaftsgüter; **slow** ~ Anlagevermögen; **sundry** ~ *bil* sonstige Vermögenswerte; **surplus** ~ **for distribution** zur Verteilung gelangende Überschüsse; **tangible** ~ Sachwerte, Sachanlagen; **to shed** ~ Vermögenswerte abstoßen; **wasting** ~ zeitl begrenzt vorhandene Ressourcen, abbaufähige Wirtschaftsgüter; **working** ~ Betriebsvermögen, Güter des Umlaufvermögens.

asseverate beteuern, versichern.

asseveration feierliche Versicherung *f*.

assign übertragen, abtreten, zuweisen, beiordnen; benennen, geltend machen, rügen; ~ **a case** (*e–m Richter*) e–e Sache zuweisen; ~ **a claim** e–e Forderung abtreten; ~ **a counsel to the accused** dem Angeklagten e–en Pflichtverteidiger beiordnen; ~ **a day for trial** e–n Verhandlungstermin festsetzen, terminieren; ~ **a lease** ein Pachtrecht übertragen, alle Rechte und Pflichten aus e–m Pachtvertrag übertragen; ~ **a patent (to)** ein Patent abtreten (an), ein Patent übertragen (auf); ~ **error** Revisionsgründe geltend machen; ~ **in blank** blanko übertragen; ~ **property** Vermögen übertragen; **agreement not to** ~ → *agreement*.

assignability Übertragbarkeit *f*, Abtretbarkeit *f*.

assignable übertragbar, abtretbar.

assignee Erwerber(in), Abtretungsempfänger(in), Zessionar, Rechtsnachfolger; ~ **by deed** gewillkürter Rechtsnachfolger, Zessionar; ~ **in fact** Zessionar; ~ **in law** Erwerber beim gesetzlichen Forderungsübergang; ~ **of invention** Erwerber der Rechte an e–r Erfindung.

assignment Rechtsübertragung *f*, Forderungsübertragung *f*, Abtretung *f*, Zession *f*, Vermögensübertragung *f*, Globalübertragung *f*; nähere Bezeichnung *f*; ~ **by operation of law** gesetzlicher Forderungsübergang, cessio legis; ~ **for the benefit of creditors** Liquidationsvergleich vgl *general assignment*; ~ **in blank** Blankoindossament; ~ **of accounts receivable (as collateral)** Sicherungsabtretung v. Außenständen; ~ **of action** → *action*; ~ **of application** Übertragung der Rechte an e–r Patentanmeldung; ~ **of bond** Übertragung e–s Schuldscheins; ~ **of breach** Spezifizierung der Vertragsverletzung; ~ **of business** Geschäftsverteilung (*e–s Gerichts*); ~ **of choses in action** Zession, Forderungsabtretung; ~ **of claims** Forderungsabtretung; ~ **of contract** Übertragung der vollen Vertragsstellung; ~ **of copyright** Übertragung des Urheberrechts; ~ **of debts** Forderungsabtretung; ~ **of dower** Bestimmung des Witwenteils; ~ **of errors** Revisionsrüge, Revisionsbegründung; ~ **of funds** Übertragung des Guthabens (*des Angewiesenen an den Remittenten*); ~ **of income** Einkommensübertragung (*aus Steuergründen*); ~ **of land** Landzuweisung; ~ **of lease** Weiterübertragung der Rechte aus e–m Miet- bzw Pachtvertrag; Miet-, Pachtabtretung; ~ **of matter** Zuweisung (*bzw Verweisung*) e–r Sache *an die zuständige Gerichtsabteilung;* ~ **of patent** Patentübertragung; ~ **of policy** Abtretung e–r Versicherungspolice; ~ **of title** Übereignung; ~ **of treaties** Vertragsüberleitung; ~ **of wages** Abtretung von Lohn- und Gehaltsansprüchen; ~ **of waste** Festlegung und Beschränkung von Entnahmerechten bei Brachland; ~ **with preferences** Vermögensübertragung *zur Gläubigerbefriedigung mit Auflagen* zur bevorzugten Befriedigung; ~ **without recourse** Abtretung unter Ausschluß des Rückgriffsrechts; **absolute** ~ unwiderrufliche (Forderungs)abtretung; **blanket** ~ Globalzession; **deed of** ~ → *deed*; **equitable** ~ formlose Abtretung; **fiduciary** ~ Sicherungszession; **foreign** ~ im Ausland vorgenommene Abtretung; **fraudulent** ~ Veräußerung in Gläubigerbenachteiligungsabsicht; **general** ~ Bereitstellung des Gesamtvermögens zur allgemeinen Gläubigerbefriedigung; **improper** ~ Zuweisung an e–e unzuständige Gerichtsabteilung; **legal** ~ schriftliche Abtretung *mit Schuldnerbenachrichtigung;* **involuntary** ~ gesetzlicher Vermögensübergang (*auf den trustee in bankruptcy qv*); **permanent** ~ Dauerstellung; **preferential** ~ gläubigerbegünstigende Abtretung *bzw* Verfügung; **prohibition of** ~ Abtretungsverbot; **special** ~ Anweisung zur Befriedigung einzelner Gläubiger; **undisclosed** ~ stille Zession; **voluntary** ~ freiwilliges Zurverfügungstellen des Vermögens zur Gläubigerbefriedigung; **wage** ~ Lohnabtretung; **wrong** ~ **of action** fehlerhafte geschäftsordnungsmäßige Zuweisung e–r Sache.

assignor Zedent *m*, Abtretender *m*.

assigns Zessionare, Rechtsnachfolger *m*|*pl*.

assimilate anpassen, angleichen.

assise (= *assize) hist* Assisengericht *n*, *Gerichtstage in der Provinz; seit 1971 abgelöst für Strafsachen durch die Crown Courts qv*.; Schwurgericht *n*, Thing *n*; ~ **rents** Grundrente; **certificate of** ~ *hist* Wiederaufnahme des Verfahrens; **civil** ~**s** *Gerichtsverhandlung in Zivilsachen vor entsandten Richtern des High Court;* **commissioner of** ~**s** beauftragter Richter; **criminal** ~**s** Assisen-Gerichtsverhandlung in Strafsachen.

assist helfen, unterstützen, beitragen zu; ~ **in carrying on business** Beihilfe leisten beim Betreiben e–s (*verbotenen*) Gewerbes.

assistance Hilfe *f*, Unterstützung *f*; ~ **authority** Fürsorgeamt; ~ **to developing countries** Entwicklungshilfe; **governmental** ~ staatliche Unterstützung; **intercourt** ~ Rechtshilfe; **judicial** ~ Rechtshilfe; **national** ~ staatliche Fürsorge, Sozialhilfe; **official** ~ Amtshilfe; **public** ~ Fürsorge, Sozialhilfe.

assistant Gehilfe (Gehilfin), Assistent(in), Mitarbeiter(in); ~ **judge** → *judge;* ~ **solicitor** → *solicitor*.

assisted person Partei *f* im Armenrecht, Prozeßkostenhilfe-Empfänger *m*.

assize = *assise qv*.

associate *s* Gesellschafter, Partner, Sozius, Anwaltassessor, Ausbildungsanwalt; Teilhaber, Genosse, Beteiligter, Beisitzer; ~ **company** Konzernunternehmen; ~ **in office** Mitinhaber e–s Amtes; ~ **judge** → *judge;* **A**~ **Justice** Richter am Obersten Bundesgericht, *US*.

associate *v* (sich) vereinigen, verbinden; ~ **in business (with)** sich geschäftlich verbinden (mit); ~**d company** nahestehende Gesellschaft; ~**d country** assoziiertes Land; ~**d trade-marks** verbundene Warenzeichen.

associateship Teilhaberschaft *f*, auswärtige Mitgliedschaft *f*.

association Zusammenschluß *m*, Vereinigung *f*, Verband *m*, *nicht rechtsfähiger* Verein *n*, Gesellschaft *f*, Gemeinschaft *f*, Sozietät *f*; ~ **agreement** Assoziierungsabkommen; ~ **clause** Gründerzeichnungsklausel, Gründungsvereinbarungsformel, Beitrittsklausel; **articles of** ~ → *articles;* **bar** ~ → *bar;* **building and loan** ~ Bausparkasse; **collective bargaining** ~ Tarifvereinigung; **incorporated** ~ rechtsfähiger, eingetragener Verein; **industrial** ~ Industrieverband, Wirtschaftsverband; **memorandum of** ~ → *memorandum;* **miner's** ~ → *miner;* **mining** ~ Bergwerksverein; **mutual** ~ Versicherungsverein auf Gegenseitigkeit; **non-profit** ~ **(=** ~ **not for profit)** Idealverein, gemeinnützige Vereinigung; **special** ~ Zweckverband, Gelegenheitsgesellschaft; **temporary** ~ Gelegenheitsgesellschaft; **trading** ~ Handelsgesellschaft; **unlawful** ~**s** Geheimbündelei; **vocational** ~ Berufsverband; **unincorporated** ~ nicht rechtsfähiger Verein.

assort sortieren, zuordnen, klassifizieren.

assortment Sortiment *n*, Klassifizierung *f*; ~ **of patterns** Musterkollektion.

assuetude Gewohnheit *f*, Verkehrssitte *f*.

assume annehmen, vermuten, übernehmen, voraussetzen; ~ **a debt** e–e Schuld übernehmen; ~ **a succession** e–e Erbschaft antreten; ~ **an obligation** eine Verbindlichkeit eingehen; ~**d address** Deckadresse; ~**d name** → *name;* ~**d risk** Risikoübernahme, Handeln auf eigene Gefahr; ~**d value** fiktiver Wert.

assumedly vermutlich, mutmaßlich.

assumpsit formloses Versprechen (*e–r vertraglichen Leistung*); Schadensersatzklage *f* wegen Nichterfüllung; **common** ~ Zahlungsklage aus formlosen Verträgen; **express** ~ → *express;* **general** ~ = *common qv;* **special** ~ Klage wegen Nichterfüllung e–r ausdrücklicher Zusage.

assumption Annahme *f*, Vermutung *f*; Übernahme *f*; ~ **clause** Übernahmeklausel; ~ **fee** Übernahmegebühr (Hypothek); ~ **of authority** Amtsanmaßung; ~ **of debt** Schuldübernahme; ~ **of indebtedness** Schuldübernahme; ~ **of mortgage** Hypothekenübernahme; ~ **of power** → *power*; ~ **of risk** → *risk*; ~ **of skill** Vermutung besseren Fachwissens des Dienstherrn (*bzgl Arbeitsunfallgefahren*); **gratuitous** ~ willkürliche Annahme.

assurable versicherbar; ~ **interest** versicherbares Interesse.

assurance (*1*) Zusicherung *f*, Versicherung *f* (= *V bzw . . .v); vgl insurance;* ~ **company** *V*-sgesellschaft; ~ **for third party** *V* auf fremde Rechnung; ~ **payable at death** Todesfall*v*; **combined endowment and whole life** ~ gemischte Erlebens- und Todesfall*v*; **contingent** ~ bedingte *V*; **convertible term** ~ *brit* Risikoumtausch*v*; **deferred** ~ aufgeschobene *V*; **fixed-term** ~ befristete Lebens*v*; **industrial** ~ Kleinlebens*v*; **last survivor** ~ *V* d. zuletzt Lebenden *von zwei oder mehreren Personen*; **ordinary life** ~ → *life insurance;* **pure endowment** ~ Erlebensfall*v*; **whole life** ~ Lebens*v* auf den Todesfall.

assurance (*2*) Auflassungsurkunde *f*, Eigentumsübertragungsklausel *f*; **collateral** ~ zusätzliche Auflassungserklärung; Garantievertrag; **common** ~**s** Übertragung von Grundeigentum, Auflassung in üblicher Form (*ohne Ausschluß der Rechtsmängelhaftung*), übliche Nachweise bei Auflassung; **common law** ~ Auflassung, *Liegenschaftsübertragung mit Formalakten nach dem Common Law*; **disentailing** ~ Liegenschaftsübertragung zur Lösung von Fideikommißbindungen; **further** ~**s** zusätzliche zur Wirksamkeit der Grundeigentumsübertragung erforderliche Erklärungen.

assure versichern, beteuern; zusichern.

assured – der(die) Versicherte (*Lebensversicherung*).

assurer Versicherer *m*.

astipulation Vereinbarung *m*.

astitution formale Vernehmung *f* zur Anklage (= *arraignment qv*).

asylum Asyl *n*, Zufluchtsort *m*; Asylrecht *n (Schutz vor Auslieferung*); ~**s board** Armenasylbehörde; **insane** ~ Heil- und Pflegeanstalt; **law of** ~ das (*objektive*) Asylrecht; **political** ~ politisches Asyl.

at bei; zu; an; ~ **a discount** mit Rabatt, mit Disagio; ~ **a premium** → *premium*; ~ **all times** zu jeder (*zumutbaren*) Zeit; ~ **all times convenient** zu genehmen Zeiten; ~ **an interval of** nach e–r Zwischenfrist von; ~ **anchor** vor Anker; ~ **any time** zu jeder Zeit; ~ **any time previously** zu früherer Zeit; ~ **arm's length** rein geschäftlich, unabhängig, (wie) zwischen unabhängigen Geschäftsleuten (*keine Sonderkonditionen!*); ~ **bar** rechtshängig, anhängig; ~ **best** bestens; **(money)** ~ **call** jederzeit abrufbare, jederzeit fällige Gelder, Tagesgelder; ~ **charterer's risk** auf Gefahr des Charterers (*kein Ausschluß der Verschuldenshaftung des Schiffseigners*); ~ **discretion** nach freiem Ermessen; ~ **expiration** bei Ablauf; ~ **his decease** bei seinem Tode; ~ **his own disposal** zu seiner freien Verfügung; ~ **home** zu Hause, nicht in Händen Dritter; ~ **issue** streitig, entscheidungserheblich; ~ **large** in Freiheit, auf freiem Fuße, freizügig, uneingeschränkt, im ganzen, *US:* den ganzen Staat vertretend; ~ **law** nach strengem Recht (*im Gegensatz zum Billigkeitsrecht = equity*); ~ **long date** auf weites Ziel; ~ **maturity** bei Fälligkeit; ~ **mercantile convenience** (*sobald*) wie unter Kaufleuten üblich und möglich; ~ **merchant's risk** auf Gefahr des Befrachters; ~ **once** sofort, umgehend, unverzüglich; ~ **or before** spätestens; ~ **owner's risk** auf Gefahr des Eigentümers; ~ **par** pari; ~ **present** zur Zeit; ~ **sea** auf hoher See; ~ **ship's expense but shipper's risk** auf Kosten des Reeders aber auf Gefahr des Befrachters; ~ **ship's risk** bei gleicher Gefahrenhaftung wie an Bord; ~ **sight** auf Sicht; ~ **the commencement** zu Beginn; ~ **the convenience of the purchaser** sobald es für den Käufer zumutbar ist; ~ **the costs** auf Kosten; ~ **the earliest possible moment** zum frühest möglichen Zeitpunkt; ~ **the King's (Queen's) pleasure** im Belieben des Königs, auf unbestimmte Zeit; ~ **the market** *Order an Makler*, zum Tageskurs *zu kaufen bzw zu verkaufen*; ~ **the rate of** zum Betrage von jeweils; ~ **the suit of** auf Antrag des . . ., auf Klage des . . .; ~ **the utmost** höchstens; ~ **variance** abweichend von; ~ **will** frei widerruflich, jederzeit kündbar.

atone Sühne tun (für), etwas sühnen; Ersatz leisten.

antonement Sühne *f*, Genugtuung *f*, Buße *f*.

atrocious scheußlich, gräßlich, grausam; ~ **assault and battery** schwere Körperverletzung.

atrocity Greueltat *f*, Scheußlichkeit *f*, gemeine Grausamkeit *f*.

attach, beschlagnahmen, pfänden, mit etw verbinden, anhängen; ~ **a debt** e–e Forderung pfänden; ~ **an account** ein Konto pfänden; **~ed hereto** anliegend; **~ing creditor** → *creditor*; **liabilities ~ing to a right** mit e–m Recht verbundene Verpflichtungen.

attachability Pfändbarkeit *f*.

attachable beschlagnahmefähig, pfändbar.

attaché Attaché *m*; **commercial** ~ Handelsattaché.

attachment Beschlagnahme *f*; Arrest *m*, Arrestvollziehung *f* (*persönl und dingl*); ~ **bond** Arrestsicherheit; Sicherheitsleistung zwecks Aufhebung d Arrests; ~ **execution** Forderungspfändung; ~ **for contempt** Beugehaft wegen Mißachtung des Gerichts; ~ **of debt** Forderungspfändung; ~ **of earnings order** Lohnpfändungsbeschluß; ~ **of privilege** Gerichtsstand auf Grund e–s Privilegs; ~ **of risk** Beginn des (Versicherungs)Risikos, Deckungsbeginn, Gefahrübergang; ~ **of witness** Anordnung der Beugehaft gg Zeugen (*zur Erzwingung des Erscheinens*); **ancillary** ~ vorläufige Pfandverstrikkung; **foreign** ~ Beschlagnahme auß des Hoheitsgebiets.

attack *s* Angriff *m*; Anfechtung *f* (*e–r Entscheidung, e–s Verwaltungsaktes*).

attack *v* angreifen, anfechten.

attain erreichen, erlangen; ~ **the age of 30** das 30. Lebensjahr vollenden.

attainder *hist* Verlust *m* der bürgerlichen Ehrenrechte und Vermögenseinziehung (*bei Todesurteil*), Ehrloserklärung; **bill of** ~Parlamentsverurteilung (*zum Tode*).

attaint zum Tode und zur Ehrlosigkeit verurteilen.

attainture Ehrloserklärung *f*.

attempt *s* Versuch *m*; ~ **impossible of fulfilment** untauglicher Versuch; ~ **to commit crime** Versuch (der Begehung) e–r Straftat; ~ **to deceive or defraud** Täuschungsversuch; **criminal** ~ strafbarer Versuch.

attempt *v* versuchen.

attend besuchen, teilnehmen, anwesend sein; ~ **a hearing** an e–r mündlichen Verhandlung teilnehmen; ~ **on the registrar** sich beim Registerrichter einfinden; ~ **the House** e–r Parlamentssitzung beiwohnen; ~ **to a person's interest** jmds Interessen wahrnehmen.

attendance Anwesenheit *f*, Bereitschaft *f*, Aufsicht *f*, Dienst *m*; ~ **allowance** Pflegegeld; Anwesenheitsgeld, Sitzungsgeld, Anwesenheitsprämie; ~ **bonus** Anwesenheitsprämie; ~ **centre** Freizeitarrestheim; ~ **fee** Tagegeld, Präsenzgeld; ~ **list** Anwesenheitsliste; ~ **money** Arbeitsbereitschaftsgeld; ~ **record** regelmäßiger Hochschulbesuch; ~ **time** Anwesenheitszeit; ~ **notes** Aktennotizen über Anwaltsbesuche; **compulsory** ~ Zwangsvorführung; **enforcing** ~ **of witnesses** Zeugen vorführen lassen; **obstructing** ~ **of witnesses** Zeugenbehinderung; **need for** ~ Anwesenheitserfordernis, A–spflicht; **officer of** ~ diensthabender Beamter.

attendant *adj* dazugehörig; ~**circumstances** Begleitumstände.

attendant *s* Bedienstete(r); **court** ~ Gerichtsdiener.

attention Aufmerksamkeit *f*, Beachtung *f*; **to give immediate** ~ zur sofortigen Veranlassung; **to give one's best** ~ **to orders** Aufträge bestens ausführen; **to give urgent** ~ **to sth.** etw vordringlich erledigen; **(to the)** ~ **of** zu Händen von.

attenuat|**e** mildern: ~**ing circumstances** mildernde Umstände.

attenuation Verminderung *f*, Abschwächung *f*, Milderung *f*.

attest bezeugen amtl beglaubigen, bestätigen; ~ **a will** e–e Testamentserrichtung unterschriftlich bezeugen; ein Testament als Zeuge bestätigen; ~**ed by notary public** notariell beglaubigt: ~**ed copy** beglaubigte Abschrift; ~**ing notary** der beglaubigende Notar; ~**ing witness** → *witness*; ~ **the truth of a statement** die Wahrheit e–r Aussage bestätigen.

attestation Zeugenvermerk *m*, Unterschriftsbeglaubigung *f* durch (*zwei*) Zeugen; ~ **clause** Beglaubigungsvermerk, Zeugenunterschriftsformel; ~ **of a deed** Urkundenbeglaubigung; ~ **of weight** Wiegeschein; ~ **of will** Beglaubigung der Testamentsunterschrift *durch* Zeugen; ~ **on hono(u)r** ehrenwörtliche Versicherung; **due** ~ ordnungsgemäße Beglaubigung durch e–n Unterschriftszeugen; **notarial** ~ notarielle Beglaubigung; **public** ~ öffentliche Beglaubigung.

attestor Unterschriftszeuge *m*.

attire Kleidung *f*, Tracht *f*, **official** ~ Amtstracht.

attitude Stellung *f*, Haltung *f*, Einstellung *f*; **mental** ~ innere Einstellung.

attorn ein Pacht- oder Mietverhältnis mit dem neuen Eigentümer fortsetzen (*ursprüngl: die Vasallentreue auf e–n neuen Lehensherrn übertragen*); beauftragen, betrauen.

attorney Bevollmächtigte(r); Anwalt; ~ **ad hoc** Spezialbevollmächtigter (*nur für den Einzelfall bestellt*); ~ **at large** an allen Gerichten zugelassener Anwalt; ~**at law** *US* Rechtsanwalt; ~**'s certificate** Bescheinigung für e–n Anwalt (*über Entrichtung der jährl Zulassungsgebühr*); ~**-client privilege** Anwaltsgeheimnis; ~ **fee** Anwaltsgebühr(en); **A**~ **General** *US*: Justizminister; *GB*: Kronanwalt, Generalstaatsanwalt; ~~*'s reference Revisionsvorlage des Att. Gen.* (*bei Freispruch*); ~ **in fact** Bevollmächtigter; ~**'s lien** anwaltschaftliches Zurückbehaltungsrecht; ~ **of record** Prozeßbevollmächtigter; **assigned** ~ beigeordneter Rechtsanwalt; *duty of* ~ *to serve: Pflicht e–s beigeordneten Anwalts zur Vertretung des Mandanten;* **lead** ~ Chefanwalt, Hauptprozeßbevollmächtigter; **letter of** ~ (*schriftl*) Vollmacht, Prozeßvollmacht; **patent** ~ Patentanwalt; **permanent** ~ Justiziar; **personal** ~ privater anwaltlicher Betreuer; **power of** ~ → *power*; **private** ~ Sachwalter, Beauftragter; **public** ~ Rechtsanwalt; **public interest** ~ Anwalt für öffentl Anliegen; **represented by** ~ anwaltschaftlich vertreten sein.

attorneyship anwaltschaftliche Tätigkeit *f*, Stellvertretung *f*, Anwaltschaft *f*.

attornment Fortsetzung *f* des Pacht-(Miet)verhältnisses (*mit neuem Eigentümer vgl to attorn*); ~ **clause**

Besitzmittlungsklausel bei der Sicherungsübereignung, Anerkenntnis der Eigentümerstellung des Gläubigers.

attract anziehen, anlocken.

attractive nuisance doctrine besondere Verkehrssicherungspflicht gegenüber Kindern; *Haftung des Grundstückeigentümers für Anziehungspunkte (für Kinder).*

attributable anrechenbar, zurechenbar, zuschreibbar.

attribute zuschreiben, anrechnen, zurechnen; ~ **false motives** falsche Beweggründe unterschieben.

attribution Zuweisung *f*, Zuerkennung *f*, Befugnis *f*.

auction *s* Versteigerung *f*; ~ **bill** Auktionsliste; ~ **broker** Auktionator; ~ **buyer** Ersteigerer; ~ **fees** Auktionsgebühren; ~ **mart** Auktionslokal; ~ **price** Auktionspreis; ~ **sale** Auktion; **compulsory** ~ Zwangsversteigerung; **Dutch** ~ Auktion mit absteigendem Ausbietungspreis; **major disposal** ~ Räumungsausverkauf; **mock** ~ Scheinauktion, Auktion mit Scheinbietern; **public** ~ öffentliche Versteigerung; **to go on the** ~ **block** versteigert werden; **unreserved** ~ Versteigerung ohne Mindestgebot.

auction *v* (*meist:* ~ *off*) versteigern; ~ **to the highest bidder** meistbietend versteigern.

auctioneer Auktionator *m*, Versteigerer *m*.

auctioneering Versteigern *m*.

audi alteram partem rule Grundsatz des (beiderseitigen) rechtlichen Gehörs.

audience Audienz *f*, Anhörung *f*; rechtliches Gehör *n*; **A~ Court** *hist engl kirchliches Gericht;* ~ **of leave** Abschiedsaudienz; **farewell** ~ Abschiedsaudienz; **public** ~ öffentl Audienz; allgemeine Zuhörerschaft; **right of** ~ → *right*; **valedictory** ~ Abschiedsaudienz.

audio-cassette (*Hör*)kassette *f*.

audit *s* Rechnungsprüfung *f*, Revision *f*; ~ **adjustment** durch die Revision veranlaßte Berichtigungsbuchung; ~ **day** (Ab)Rechnungstag; ~ **of accounts** Rechnungsprüfung; Kontenprüfung; ~ **opinion** *bil* Bestätigungsvermerk (*des Abschlußprüfers*); ~ **report** → *report;* ~ **system** Rechnungsprüfungswesen; ~ **working papers** Arbeitsunterlagen des Bücherrevisors; **annual** ~ Jahresabschlußprüfung; **cash** ~ → *cash;* **completed** ~ Abschlußprüfung, *zum Jahresschluß durchgeführte Prüfung*; **external** ~ außerbetriebliche Revision, Außenrevision; **field** ~ Außenprüfung, Betriebsprüfung; **general** ~ Jahresabschlußprüfung; **internal** ~ betriebsinterne Revision, Innenrevision; **inventory** ~ Inventarprüfung; **office** ~ Steuerprüfung; **preliminary** ~ Vorprüfung; **storage** ~ Inventurüberprüfung; **system** ~**s** auf das Buchhaltungssystem bezogene Prüfung; **tax** ~ → *tax*.

audit *v* prüfen, revidieren; e–e Rechnungsprüfung vornehmen; ~**ed and found correct** geprüft und für richtig befunden; ~**ed balance sheet** geprüfte Bilanz.

auditing Rechnungsprüfung *f*, Revision *f*; ~ **company** Revisionsgesellschaft, Prüfungsgesellschaft; ~ **department** Revisionsabteilung, Finanzprüfungsabteilung; ~ **invoices** Prüfung von Rechnungen; ~ **of accounts** Rechnungsprüfung; ~ **payrolls** Prüfung der Lohnkonten; ~ **procedure** Prüfungsverfahren, Revisionsverfahren; **post-**~ Jahresabschlußprüfung; **pre-**~ vorherige Prüfung und Genehmigung von (Staats)Ausgaben; **store** ~ Lagerbestandsumfrage.

auditor Rechnungsprüfer *m*, Revisor *m*, Abschlußprüfer *m*; ~**'s certificate** Prüfungsvermerk (e–s Wirtschaftsprüfers), Prüfungsbescheinigung; **A~ General** Präsident des Rechnungshofs; ~**'s report** → *report;* **appointment of** ~ Bestellung e–s Rechnungsprüfers; **field** ~ Außenprüfer; **independent** ~ neutraler (*externer*) Wirtschaftsprüfer; **professional** ~ öffentlicher

Bücherrevisor, Wirtschaftsprüfer; **public** ~ Betriebsprüfer; **relief of** ~ gerichtl Entlastung e–s Prüfers; **state** ~ staatl Rechnungsprüfer, Beamter des Rechnungshofes.

austerity strenge Einschränkung *f*, Selbstbeschränkung *f*; ~ **program(me)** Einschränkungsprogramm, Sparprogramm.

autarkical autark, selbstgenügsam.

autarky Autarkie *f*, Eigenversorgung.

authentic authentisch, maßgebend, echt, gültig.

authenticate die Echtheit bestätigen, beglaubigen; nachweisen, belegen.

authentication Beglaubigung *f*, Legalisation *f*; Echtheitzeugnis *n*; Nachweis *m*; ~ **of claims** Glaubhaftmachung von Ansprüchen.

authenticity Echtheit *f*, Gültigkeit *f*.

authenticum Urschrift *f*.

author Urheber(in), Verfasser(in), Autor(in); ~ **of repute** angesehener Autor (*gilt als "authority"*); ~**-publisher** Selbstverleger; ~**'s right** das Recht des Urhebers; **joint** ~**s** Miturheber, Mitverfasser.

authorisable zulassungspflichtig.

authoritative maßgebend, kompetent, verbindlich.

authorities (*the* ~) Rechtsprechung *f* und Rechtslehre *f*, herrschende Meinung *f vgl authority*.

authority Vollmacht *f* (= *V hzw . . . v*), Vertretungsmacht *f*; Präzedenzfall *m*, Lehrmeinung *f*, Vorentscheidung *f*, Rechtsquelle *f*; Behörde *f*; ~*ies: Behörden;* ~ **by estoppel** Vertretungsmacht kraft Rechtsscheins; ~ **coupled with an interest** *V* mit eigenen Interessen des Bevollmächtigten, entgeltliche Ermächtigung; ~ **to accept service** Zustellungsvollmacht, Zustellungsempfangsermächtigung; ~ **to collect debts** Inkasso*v*; ~ **to negotiate** Verhandlungs*v*, Negoziierungsermächtigung, Ankaufsermächtigung; ~ **to pay** Zahlungsermächtigung; ~ **to purchase** Ankaufsermächtigung (*zB von Wechseln bei der Exportfinanzierung*), Trattenankaufsermächtigung; ~ **to represent** *V*, Vertretungsbefugnis; **abuse of** ~ → *abuse*; **acquiring** ~ Enteignungsbehörde, Zwangserwerbsbehörde; **actual** ~ Vertretungsmacht im Einzelfall, faktische *V*; **administrative** ~ Verwaltungsbehörde; **apparent** ~ Anscheins*v*, Vertretungsmacht kraft Rechtsscheins; **central** ~ Zentralbehörde; **citation of** ~ Zitat, Quellenangabe; **commercial** ~ kaufmännische Handlungs*v*; **competent** ~ zuständige Behörde; **constructive** ~ Anscheins*v*; **controlling** ~ Aufsichtsbehörde; **defiance of** ~ Autoritätsverletzung; **excess of** ~ *V*-süberschreitung; **executive** ~ vollziehende Gewalt; **express** ~ ausdrückliche *V*, ausdrücklich eingeräumte Befugnis; **fiscal** ~ Steuerbehörde; **full** ~ uneingeschränkte Ermächtigung; **general** ~ General*v*; **governmental** ~ Staatsbehörde, Regierungsbehörde, Staatsgewalt; **High A**~ → *high*; **implied** ~ stillschweigende Vertretungsmacht; **incidental** ~ vorausgesetzte *V*, Annex*v*; **inherent** ~ immanente *V*; **joint** ~ Gesamt*v*; **judicial** ~→*judicial;* **key** ~ Hauptfundstelle; **legal** ~ Rechtsmeinung, Fundstelle; *legal* ~*ies: Rechtsprechung und Rechtslehre; Präzedenzentscheidungen;* **legislative** ~ Legislative; **limited** ~ beschränkte *V*, weisungsgebundene *V*; **local** ~ →*local*; **lower** ~**ties** untere Behörden; **naked** ~ schlichte *V* (*ohne eigene wirtschaftliche Beteiligung des Bevollmächtigten*); **official** ~ Amtsgewalt, Behörde; **on good** ~ glaubwürdig, aus guter Quelle; **on one's own** ~ aus eigener Machtbefugnis; **ostensible** ~ Anscheinsvollmacht; **parental** ~ elterliche Gewalt; **persuasive** ~ beachtliche aber nicht bindende richterliche Äußerung; **postal** ~**ies** Postbehörde(n); **public** ~ öffentliche Gewalt, Obrigkeit, Behörde; **representative** ~ Vertretungsmacht, Vertretungsbefugnis; **signed on** ~ amtlich bescheinigt; **signing with** ~ auf Grund e–r Ermächtigung unterzeichnend; **sole** ~ Alleinvollmacht; **special** ~ Spezial*v*; **statutory** ~ gesetzl Befugnis; **subordinate** ~ unterstellte Behörde; **superior** ~ vorgesetzte Behörde; **supervisory** ~ Aufsichtsbehörde; **under the** ~ **of** im Auftrag von; **under the** ~ **of this Act** auf Grund der in diesem Gesetz enthaltenen Ermächtigung; **unlimited** ~ unbeschränkte Vertretungsmacht, Generalvollmacht; **want of** ~ Mangel der Vertretungsmacht; **without** ~ unbefugt, unberechtigt, ohne Vertretungsmacht; **written** ~ schriftliche Vollmacht.

authorization Ermächtigung *f*, Bevollmächtigung *f*, Einwilligung *f*; **drawing** ~ Negoziierungskredit, Ziehungsermächtigung (*Ermächtigung, Dokumententratten auf die Korrespondenzbank bzw den Käufer zu ziehen*); **official** ~ amtl Genehmigung; **special** ~ ausdrückliche Ermächtigung.

authorize ermächtigen, autorisieren, genehmigen; ~**d** autorisiert, bevollmächtigt, beauftragt, befugt; ~**d to sign** zeichnungsberechtigt; **duly** ~**d** ordnungsgemäß ermächtigt, bevollmächtigt.

authorship Urheberschaft *f*, Verfassereigenschaft *f*.

auto stage im Linienverkehr eingesetztes Kraftfahrzeug.

autocracy Autokratie *f*, Alleinherrschaft *f*.

autograph eigenhändige Schrift *f*, Originalhandschrift *f*.

automated teller machine elektronische Bankschalter.

automatic automatisch; ~ **boy** Verkaufsautomat; ~ **error** absoluter Revisionsgrund; ~ **currency** elastische Währung; ~ **machine** Automat, Spielautomat; ~ **premium loans** automatische Beleihung des Deckungsstocks *zur Aufrechterhaltung der Prämienzahlungen*; ~ **separation** automatisches Ausscheiden aus dem Dienst; ~ **teller machine** elektronischer Bankschalter; ~ **ticket dispenser** Fahrkartenautomat; ~ **vending machine** Verkaufsautomat.

automatically automatisch, ohne weiteres; ~ **triggered shotguns** Selbstschußanlage; **to extend** ~ stillschweigend verlängern.

automation Automatisierung *f*.

automatism Automatie *f*, Automatismus *m*, unbewußte Bewegungen *f/pl*.

automobile Auto(mobil) *n*, Kraftfahrzeug *n*, Personenkraftwagen (PKW) *m*; ~ **accident** → *accident*; ~ **insurance** → *insurance*; **A**~ **Safety Act** Straßenverkehrszulassungsordnung.

autonomous autonom, unter Selbstverwaltung stehend; ~ **investment** *von wirtschaftlichen Zusammenhängen* unabhängige Investition.

autonomy Autonomie *f*, Selbstregierung *f*, Selbstverwaltung *f*.

autopsy Obduktion *f*, Leichenöffnung *f*, Autopsie *f*; ~ **and disenterment for evidential purposes** Obduktion und Exhumierung zu Beweiszwecken.

autre | action pendant Einrede der Rechtshängigkeit; ~ **droit** aus fremdem Recht; **pur** ~ **vie** auf Lebenszeit e–s Dritten.

autrefois zu anderer Zeit, früher, bereits einmal; ~ **acquit** Einwendung des früheren Freispruchs (*wegen der gleichen Tat*); ~ **convict** *ne bis in idem!* Einwendung, wegen der Tat bereits verurteilt worden zu sein.

auxiliary hilfsweise, subsidiär; Hilfs ...

avail *s* Nutzen *m*, Vorteil *n*, Gewinn *m*, Wert *m*; **to no** ~ zwecklos.

avail *v* etwas wert sein, sich eignen, nützen; ~ **oneself of a right** von e–m Recht Gebrauch machen.

availability Verfügbarkeit *f*, Verwendbarkeit *f*; (*für Werbung*) zur Verfügung stehende Sendezeiten; ~ **date** Wertstellung, Valuta; **deferred** ~ **schedules** Verfügbarkeitsaufstellungen.

available verfügbar, verwertbar; lieferbar, vorrätig; zulässig, statthaft; ~ **balance in hand** verfügbare Mittel; ~ **for distribution** verteilbar, zur Gewinnausschüttung verfügbar; ~ **for dividends** für Dividenden verfügbar; ~ **on request** auf Wunsch erhältlich (*gilt als ausreichende Bezugnahme auf allg Geschäftsbedingungen*).

availment Inanspruchnahme *f.*

aval Aval *m*, Wechselbürgschaft *f*; ~ **account** Avalkonto.

aver *v* vortragen, behaupten.

average *adj* durchschnittlich; ~ **daily balance** Durchschnittstagessaldo (*für Zinsberechnung*); ~ **due date** mittlerer Zahlungstermin; ~ **weekly earnings** durchschnittlicher Wochenverdienst.

average *s* (*1*) Durchschnitt *m*; ~ **of mean prices** mittlerer Preisdurchschnitt; **calculation of** ~ Durchschnittsrechnung; **common** ~ einfacher Durchschnitt; **rough** ~ angenäherter Durchschnitt; **weighted** ~ das gewogene Mittel, das gewichtete Mittel, gewogener Durchschnittswert.

average *s* (*2*) Havarie *f*, Haverei *f* (= *H bzw* . . .*h*), Beschädigung *f* (*von Schiff und Ladung*); ~ **adjuster** Dispacheur, *H*sachverständiger; ~ **adjustment** Schadensabwicklung als große *H*, *H*berechnung, Dispache; ~ **stater** = *average adjuster qv*; **adjustment of** ~ *H*verteilung, Dispache der großen *H*; **free from (general)** ~ frei von großer *H*; **free from** ~ **and free of all** ~ nicht gegen große und besondere *H* versichert; **free from** ~ **unless general** unter Ausschluß von *H* außer bei großer *H*; **free from (of) particular** ~ frei von Teilschaden; frei von Schäden in besonderer Havarie; **free of all** ~ **general** ~ → *general average* (*nach "general"*); **gross** ~ = *general average qv*; **particular** ~ besondere *H*; **petty** ~ kleine *H*; **simple** ~ = *particular average qv*, einfache *H*.

average *v* den Durchschnitt bilden, durchschnittlich betragen.

averment Sachvortrag *m*, Behauptung *f*; **alternative** ~ Hilfsvorbringen, Wahltatbestand; **immaterial** ~ unerhebliches Vorbringen; **impertinent** ~ = *immaterial averment qv*; **negative** ~ negative Behauptung; formelles Bestreiten; **particular** ~ substantiierter Sachvortrag.

aversion Abneigung *f*, **insurmountable** ~ unüberwindliche A.

avert abwenden; ~ **a damage** *ins* e–n Schaden abwenden; **an accident** e–n Unfall abwenden.

aviation Flugverkehr *m*, Luftfahrt *f*, Flugwesen *n*; ~ **convention** Luftfahrtabkommen; ~ **legislation** Luftfahrtgesetzgebung; ~ **treaty** Luftverkehrsabkommen; ~ **risks** → *risk*; **civil** ~ Zivilluftfahrt.

avionics Luftfahrt-Elektronik *f*.

avocation Nebenbeschäftigung *f* Hobby *n*.

avocatory abberufend, Abberufungs. . .

avoid vermeiden; nichtig machen, anfechten; ~ **a contract** e–n Vertrag anfechten; ~ **a patent** Antrag auf Nichtigerklärung e–s Patents stellen.

avoidable vermeidbar; anfechtbar.

avoidance Vermeidung *f*; Anfechtung *f*, Ungültigerklärung; ~ **of an agreement** Annullierung e–r Vereinbarung; ~ **of disposition of property** Anfechtung e–r Vermögensverfügung; ~ **of double taxation** Vermeidung der Doppelbesteuerung; ~ **of tax** (*zulässiges*) Vermeiden von Steuern; **power of** ~ Anfechtungsrecht.

avoirdupois Gewicht *n*; Gewichtssystem *n*; ~ **pound** → *pound*; ~ **weight** gesetzliches Handelsgewicht (*1 Pfund = 16 Unzen, 1 Unze = 16 Drams*); **dram** ~ → *dram*.

avow sich zu etw bekennen, rechtfertigen.

avowal Geständnis *n*, Bekenntnis *n*; ~ **of principles** Grundsatzbekenntnis.

avowed *adj* erklärt, anerkannt.

avowedly *adv* eingestandenermaßen.

avowry Rechtfertigung *f* der Vollziehung des Vermieterpfandrechts.

avulsion plötzliche Strombettverlagerung.

await erwarten, warten auf, entgegensehen; ~ **arrival** nicht nachsenden!; ~ **instructions** Anweisungen abwarten!.

award *s* Schiedsspruch *m*; Zumessung *f*; Verleihung *f*; Belohnung *f*, Prämie *f*; ~ **by umpire** Schiedsspruch; ~ **of balance due on account** Verurteilung zur Zahlung des Rechnungssaldos; ~ **of costs** Kostenentscheidung zugunsten e–r Partei; ~ **of damages** Zubilligung von Schadensersatz; ~ **of entry of judgment** Erlaß e–s Urteils; ~ **of hono(u)rs** Ordensverleihung, Verleihungsurkunde; ~ **of mutual releases** Abgeltungsklausel; ~ **of punishment** Strafzumessung; ~ **of referees** Schiedsspruch, Schiedsgutachten; ~ **of sum in full of all demands** dem Antrag in voller Höhe stattgebende Entscheidung; ~ **of the contract** Zuschlag, Auftragsvergabe *bei Ausschreibungen*; ~ **to inventors** Erfindervergütung; **arbitral** ~ Schiedsspruch; **arbitration** ~ → *arbitration* (*1*); **enforcement of** ~ Vollstreckung e–s Schiedsspruchs; **final** ~ (*abschließender*) Schiedsspruch; **industrial** ~ tarifrechtlicher Schiedsspruch; **protective** ~ Verurteilung zu Lohn- Gehaltsfortzahlung (*bei Nichtkonsultierung der Gewerkschaft vor Entlassung*); **reasoned** ~ mit Gründen versehener Schiedsspruch.

award *v* zusprechen, zuerkennen.

awardable entschädigungspflichtig (*Enteignung etc*).

aware (of) in Anbetracht, angesichts, in Kenntnis, in dem Bewußtsein, in der Erkenntnis.

awareness Erkenntnis *f*, Gewahrwerden *n* Bewußtsein (*als subjektives Tatbestandsmerkmal*); ~ **level** Bekanntheitsgrad (*e–r Marke etc*).

away-going crop *beim Ende des Pachtverhältnisses noch nicht eingebrachte Ernte*; Ernte *f* auf dem Halm.

axe Etatkürzung *f*.

axle weight Achsgewicht *n* Achslast *f*.

aye *parl* Ja-Stimme *f*; **the ~s have it** die Ja-Stimmen sind in der Mehrheit; der Antrag ist angenommen.

B

baby|bonds Kleinobligationen *f|pl;* ~ **boomers** geburtenstarke Jahrgänge; ~ **stock** neu ausgegebene Aktien.

bachelor Junggeselle *m*; Lediger *m*; Bakkalaureus; ~**'s degree** Bakkalaureat; ~ **of laws** (*LL.B.*) *unterster juristischer Grad.*

back *v* indossieren; dafür eintreten, unterstützen; sich zurückziehen; ~ **out of a contract** sich vertraglich übernommenen Verbindlichkeiten entziehen; ~ **the currency** die Währung stützen; ~ **ed bill** → *bill (3).*

backbiting Verleumdung *f.*

back|-bond treuhänderische Gegenverpflichtung (*bei Eigentumsverfügung*) förmliche Treuhandbestätigung; ~ **calculation** Rückrechnung (Blutalkohol); ~ **charge** Rückspesen; ~ **duty** Steuerrückstand; ~ **freight** Rückfracht; ~ **interest** rückständige Zinsen; ~ **lands** Hinterland, rückwärtige Grundstücke; ~**-letter** Rückbürgschaft; ~ **log of demand** Nachholbedarf; ~ **office** Hinterzimmer e–s Büros; Buchhaltung e–r Maklerfirma; ~ **pay** rückständiger Lohn, Lohnnachzahlung; ~ **roads** Nebenwege; ~ **taxes** Steuerrückstände, Nachversteuerung; ~ **to** ~ **credit** Gegenakkreditiv; ~ **to** ~ **houses** Häuser mit rückwärtiger Kommunmauer; ~ **to** ~ **loan** wechselseitiges Darlehen (*mittelbare Exportfinanzierung*); ~ **to-** ~ **reinsurance** → *reinsurance*; ~ **to work movement** Antistreikbewegung.

backdate *v/t* rückdatieren.

backer Helfer *m*, Hintermann *m*; Indossant *m*, Wechselbürge *m.*

background Hintergrund *m*; Werdegang *m*; Erfahrung *f*; **educational** ~ Vorbildung, Bildungsgang; **practical** ~ praktische Erfahrung.

backing Unterstützung *f*, Förderung *f*; Indossierung *f*; Stützungskäufe *m|pl*; ~ **a warrant** richterliche Bestätigung e–s Haftbefehls (aus *e–m anderen Bezirk*); ~ **and filling** *exch* geringfügige spekulativ bedingte Kursschwankungen; ~ **support** Währungsdeckung.

backlock Rückstand *m*; ~ **of orders** Auftragsrückstand; ~ **or unmet demand** Nachfragestau.

backspread unternormaler Kursunterschied *bei Arbitrage.*

backwardation *exch* Depot *m*, Kursabschlag *m*; Prolongationsgebühr *f* des Baissiers; ~ **business** Deport, Kostgeschäft; ~ **rate** Prolongationsgebühr.

bad schlecht, mangelhaft, mangelbehaftet, bösartig; unzulässig, rechtsfehlerhaft; ~ **debt expense** Forderungsausfallkosten; ~ **debt losses** Debitorenverluste, Forderungsausfälle; ~ **debt ratio** Forderungsausfälle in % vom Umsatz.

badge Abzeichen *n*; ~ **of fraud** Verdachtsmomente für betrügerisches Verhalten des Gemeinschuldners; **party** ~ Parteiabzeichen.

bag Sack *m*, Behälter *m*, Tasche *f*; ~ **cargo** in Säcke gefüllte Ladung; **mail** ~ Postsack.

bagatelle Bagatelle *f*, Geringfügigkeit *f.*

baggage Reisegepäck *n*; ~**s are matched to the passengers** das Handgepäck wird für jeden Fluggast festgestellt; ~ **car** Gepäckwagen; ~ **carousel** Gepäckkreisel; ~ **control** Handgepäckkontrolle; ~ **delivery area** Gepäckausgabebereich; ~ **insurance** → *insurance* **accompanied** ~ mitgeführtes Gepäck (*Handgepäck und aufgegebenes Gepäck*); **unaccompanied** ~ nicht mitgeführtes Gepäck.

bail *s* Bürgschaft *f*, Sicherheitsleistung *f*, Kaution *f*; Haftkaution *f*, Verschonung *f* von der Untersuchungshaft durch Sicherheitsleistung; Bürge *m*; ~ **above** (= ~ *to the action* = *special* ~) Sicherheitsleistung für den Beklagten (*zur Erfüllung evtl Urteilsverpflichtungen*); ~ **absolute** Kautionsstellung für e–n treuhänderischen Verwalter; ~ **below** (= ~ *to the sheriff*) Kaution zur Sicherung des Erscheinens des Beklagten; ~ **bond** → *bond* (*2*); ~ **common** fingierte Prozeßbürgenstellung als Einlassung auf e–e Klage; ~ **court** (*frühere*) Unterabteilung des Queen's Bench; ~ **dock** Anklagebank, Beschuldigtenzelle; ~ **hostel** Unterkunft für Beschuldigte, denen Haftverschonung gewährt wurde; ~ **in criminal proceedings** Kaution zur Haftverschonung; ~ **in error** Sicherheitsleistung des Revisionsklägers; ~ **of sureties** Verpflichtungserklärung der Kautionsbürgen; ~ **on appeal** Kaution zur Haftverschonung in der Berufungsinstanz; ~ **piece** Urkunde über die Sicherheitsleistung im Zivilprozeß; ~ **with or without sureties** Haftverschonung gegen Sicherheitsleistung mit bzw ohne persönliche Verbürgung des Erscheinens in der Hauptverhandlung; **backed for** ~ (*Haftbefehl mit*) Haftverschonungsvermerk gegen Sicherheitsleistung; **civil** ~ Sicherheitsleistung im Zivilprozeß; **common** ~ *hist* Erscheinen des Beklagten; **conspiracy to indemnify** ~ strafbare Verabredung e–n Kautionsbürgen zu entschädigen (*falls er in Anspruch genommen wird*); **continuous** ~ Kautionsstellung für die Dauer des Verfahrens; **insufficient** ~ ungenügende Kaution; **personation of** ~ Vorspiegelung, für jmdn Kaution zu leisten; **perfecting** ~ Feststellung der Kautionsstellungsfähigkeit; **release on** ~ Haftentlassung gegen Sicherheitsleistung; **second** ~ Afterbürge, Nachbürge; **shopping for** ~ wiederholte Bemühungen um die Erlaubnis zur Kautionsstellung; **special** ~ → *bail above*; **straw** ~ wertlose Kaution *beruflicher, vermögensloser Prozeßbürgen*; **to admit to** ~ gegen Sicherheitsleistung von der Untersuchungshaft verschonen; **to be out on** ~ sich nach Kautionsstellung auf freiem Fuß befinden; **to be remanded on** ~ gegen Kaution von der Haft verschont werden; **to jump** ~ die Kaution verfallen lassen (*durch Ausbleiben bei der Hauptverhandlung*); **to stand** ~ e–n Bürgen stellen, als Prozeßbürge eintreten, Sicherheit leisten, die persönliche Verantwortung für das Erscheinen übernehmen.

bail *v* von der Untersuchungshaft gegen Sicherheitsleistung verschonen; die Freilassung der Beschuldigten aus der Untersuchungshaft bewirken; e–e Sache in Verwahrung geben; ~ **out** durch Sicherheitsleistung aus der Haft freibekommen.

bailable für Kautionsstellung zugelassen; ~ **offence** Straftat, bei der Verschonung von der Untersuchungshaft gegen Sicherheit angeordnet werden darf; ~ **process** Verfahren mit Rechtsanspruch auf Kautionsstellung.

bailee Verwahrer *m*, Fremdbesitzer *m*, treuhänderischer Besitzer *m cf bailment*; ~ **clause** Gewahrsamsklausel; **embezzlement by** ~ (*strafbare*) Verpfändung von verwahrtem Gut; **unconscious** ~ unwissentlicher Verwahrer.

bailiff Gerichtsvollzieher *m*; Zustellungsbeamter *m*; ~**-errant** Stellvertreter e–s Bailiff; **bound** ~ gegen Kaution bestellter Gerichsvollzieher; **certificated** ~ diplomierter Gerichtsvollz.; **high** ~ Leiter der Gerichtsgeschäftsstelle, Obergerichtsvollzieher *GB: bis 1958, jetzt* → *registrar*; **jury** ~ Gerichtswachtmeister für die Geschworenen; **special** ~ (*zur Vornahme einzelner Handlungen*) beauftragter Gerichtsvollzieher; *von der Partei* beauftragter Zustellungsbeamter.

bailiwick Amtsbereich *m* e–s Bailiff *bzw* Sheriff; Geschäftsbezirk *n*; Spezialgebiet *n*, Fach *n*.

bailment Hinterlegung *f*; Verwahrung, Verwahrungsverhältnis; Kaution *f*; Besitzmittlungsverhältnis *n*, Besitzüberlassung *f an bewegl Sachen* auf Zeit, treuhänderischer Besitz *an bewegl Sachen*; ~ **by sovereigns** mittelbarer Besitz des Staatsouveräns; ~ **for hire** entgeltliche Verwahrung; ~ **for sale** Verkaufskommission; ~ **on trust** treuhänderische Besitzüberlassung; **actual** ~ Übertragung von Fremdbesitz; **constructive** ~ gesetzliches Eigentümer-Besitzer-Verhältnis an bewegl Sachen; **gratuitous** ~ Leihe; (unentgeltliche) Verwahrung; **involuntary** ~ = *constructive* ~ *qv*; ~ **lucrative** ~ entgeltliche Verwahrung; **naked** ~ = *gratuitous* ~ *qv*; **unconscious** ~ unwissentliche Verwahrung.

bailor Hinterleger *m*; mittelbarer Besitzer *m*.

bailout Rettungsaktion *f*, Notverkauf *n*, Notliquidation *f*, Nothilfesicherheit *f*; *Abstoßen von Aktien ohne Rücksicht auf Verluste*; steuergünstige Kapitalveräußerung anstelle von Dividenden; ~ **fund** Rettungsfonds; ~ **stock** Vorzugsaktien als steuerfreie Gratisaktien.

bailsman Bürge *m*.

bait and switch Lockvogelverkaufstrick *m*.

balance *s* Ausgleich *m*, Rechnungsabschluß *m*, Saldo *m*, Kontostand *m*, Rest *m*; ~ **account** → *account*; ~**s and obligations** Außenstände und Verbindlichkeiten; ~ **brought forward** Saldovortrag; ~ **carried forward to new account** Vortrag auf neue Rechnung; ~ **certificate** Aktienübertragungsurkunde mit Bestätigungsvermerk des Restbestandes *nach Teilveräußerung*; ~ **deficit** Verlustabschluß; ~ **due** geschuldeter Restbetrag, Debetsaldo; ~ **in cash** Kassenbestand, Kassensaldo; ~ **in hand** Überschuß, Kassenbestand; ~ **in your favour** Ihr Saldoguthaben; ~ **of accounts** Rechnungsabschluß, ~ **of goods and services** Leistungsbilanz; ~ **of convenience** Verhältnismäßigkeit e–r Entscheidung; ~ **of interests** Interessenausgleich; ~ **of international payments** = ~ *of payments qv*; ~ **of invoice** Rechnungssaldo; ~ **of my real and personal property** mein gesamtes übriges Vermögen; ~ **of payments** → *balance of payments*; ~ **of power** Mächtegleichgewicht, politisches Gleichgewicht; ~ **of probabilities** (*überwiegende*) Wahrscheinlichkeit, Wahrscheinlichkeitsbeweis; ~ **of the profits and gains** Überschuß der Einnahmen über die Betriebskosten, Rohgewinn; ~ **of trade** Handelsbilanz; ~ **on current account** Kontokorrentsaldo; ~ **order** vollstreckbarer Beschluß auf Zahlung von Nachschüssen (*Gesellschaftsliquidation*); ~ **owing** Restbetrag, Restschuld; ~ **payable** Debetsaldo; ~ **scrip** Restzertifikat bei e–r Teilveräußerung von Aktienbesitz; ~ **ticket** provisorisches Teilaktienzertifikat; **abstract of** ~ → *abstract*; **active** ~ Aktivsaldo; **actual** ~ Istbestand, Effektivbestand; **adverse** ~ schlechter Jahresabschluß, Unterbilanz, Defizit; **bank** ~ → *bank*; **cash** ~ Kassenbestand, Barbestand; **compensating deposit** ~ nicht abgehobene Teilbeträge e–s Kredits; **cooking of** ~**s** Bilanzverschleierung; **counter** ~ Gegensaldo, Aktivsaldo; **credit** ~ Kreditsaldo, Habensaldo, Guthaben; Gewinnabschluß; **current** ~ Kontokorrentguthaben, derzeitiger Saldo; **debit** ~ Debetsaldo; **dormant** ~ umsatzloses Guthaben; **favourable** ~ Aktivbilanz; **forward** ~ Saldovortrag; **general** ~ das gesamte übrige (*nicht von der Haftung erfaßte*) Vermögen; **gross** ~ Bruttoüberschuß; **interbank** ~**s** gegenseitige Bankforderungen; **loss** ~ Verlustsaldo; **minimum** ~ Mindestguthaben (*auf e–m Bankkonto*); **negative** ~ Minussaldo, Defizit; **net** ~

Reinertrag, Überschuß; **nominal** ~ Sollbestand; **rough** ~ Rohbilanz; **surplus** ~ überschüssiges Guthaben; **trial** ~ Rohbilanz; **ultimate** ~ Abschluß, Restsaldo; **unpaid** ~ offener Restbetrag.

balance *v* ausgleichen; ~ **the books** die Bücher abschließen; ~ **the cash** die Kasse übernehmen; ~ **the ledger** das Hauptbuch saldieren; ~**d budget** → *budget*; ~**d in account** saldiert.

balance of payments Zahlungsbilanz *f* (Z; *prädikativ* ~-~-~) ~ **deficit** Zdefizit; ~ **disequilibrium** Zungleichgewicht; ~ **equilibrium** Zgleichgewicht; ~ **policy** Zpolitik; ~ **surplus** Züberschuß; ~ **theory** Ztheorie; **overall** ~ Gesamtzahlungsbilanz.

balance sheet Bilanz *f*; ~ **audit** Bilanzprüfung; ~ **date** Bilanzstichtag; ~ **item** Bilanzposten; ~ **ratio** Bilanzkennzahl, Bilanzverhältniszahl; ~ **total** Bilanzsumme; **annual** ~ Jahresbilanz, Jahresabschluß; **bankrupt's** ~ Status des Gemeinschuldners; **commercial** ~ Handelsbilanz; **comparative** ~ Vergleichsbilanz; **condensed** ~ Kurzbilanz; **consolidated** ~ konsolidierte Bilanz, Konzernbilanz; **interim** ~ Zwischenbilanz; **proforma** ~ Vorausbilanz (*bei Emissionsprospekten*); **tax** ~ Steuerbilanz; **veiled** ~ verschleierte Bilanz.

balancing *adj* Ausgleichs... Saldo...; ~ **amount** Ausgleichsbetrag; ~ **charge** Aktivierung von Abschreibungen bei der Veräußerung; ~ **entry** Gegenbuchung, Ausgleichsposten.

balancing *s* **of accounts** Kassenabschluß, Saldierung; ~ **the books** Rechnungsabschluß, Buchungsabschluß; ~ **the equities** Billigkeitsabwägung, Nachteilsabwägung.

bale *s* Ballen *m*, *v* in Ballen verpacken.

balk Grenzstreifen zwischen Feldern, Rain *m*.

ballast Ballastladung *f*; **going in** ~ Ballast geladen haben.

balloon erhöhte Leasing-Schlußrate (*bei Übergang des Eigentums*); ~ **mortgage** Hypothek mit hoher Endtilgung; ~ **note** *Schuldschein mit niedrigen Amortisationsraten aber hoher Resttilgung*.

ballot *s* geheime Wahl *f*; Wahlzettel *m*, Wahlschein *m*; Wahl *f*, Wahlrecht *n*; Wahlgang *m*; Bestimmung *f* durch das Los; ~ **Act** Wahlgesetz; ~ **and sale society** (*unzulässige*) Bausparkasse mit Auslosung der Kreditzuteilung; ~ **-box** Wahlurne, Verlosungskasten; ~ **paper** Wahlschein, Stimmzettel; **election by** ~ geheime Wahl; **individual** ~ persönl Stimmabgabe, Einzelabstimmung; **in the first** ~ im ersten Wahlgang; **joint** ~ gemeinsame Abstimmung (*mehrerer Gesetzgebungskammern*); **mailed-in** ~**s** Briefwahlscheine; **mutilated** ~ ungültiger Stimmzettel (*von dem ein Stück entfernt wurde*); **office block** ~ Ämterwahlformular; **offical** ~ amtlicher Wahlschein; **open** ~ offene Wahl; **party column** ~ Listenwahlschein; **postal** ~ **papers** Wahlscheine zur Briefwahl; **second** ~ zweiter Wahlgang, Stichwahl; **secret** ~ geheime Wahl; **strike** ~ Urabstimmung.

ballot *v* abstimmen; ~**ted bills** durch das Los in die Tagesordnung aufgenommene Initiativanträge.

ban *s* Verbot *n*, Sperre *f*, Bann *m*, Bannmeile *f*, befriedetes Gebiet *n*; ~ **from driving** Fahrverbot; ~ **on overtime** Überstundenverbot; **outright** ~ absolutes Verbot; **import** ~ Einfuhrverbot.

ban *v* verbannen, verbieten.

banc Richterbank *f*, Gerichtssitzung *f*; **sitting in** ~ Plenarsitzung (*aller Richter*), Sitzung als Kollegialgericht.

bancomat Bargeldautomat *m*.

band Bande *f*; **raising armed** ~**s** Bildung bewaffneter Haufen.

banding Abstufung *n* nach (Steuer)-Tarifen.

bandit Bandit *m*, Gesetzloser *m*.

banging a market offene Baisseverkäufe.

banish verbannen, ausweisen.

banishment Landesverweisung *f*, Verbannung *f*; **sentence of** ~Urteil mit Aufenthaltsverbot.

bank Bank (= *B bzw b*), Bankhaus *n*, Kreditanstalt *f*; ~ **acceptance** *B*akzept; **account** *B*konto; ~ **assets** Vermögenswerte der *B*; ~ **audit(s)** *B*revision; ~ **balance** *B*guthaben, Kontostand bei e–r Bank, Banksaldo; ~ **bill** *B*wechsel, von e–r *B* indossierter Wechsel; ~ **book** Kontobüchlein, Sparbuch; ~ **branches** Zweigbanken; ~ **burglary insurance** Bankeinbruchsversicherung; ~ **call** behördliche Bilanzprüfungsaufforderung an e–e *B*; ~ **certificate** *B*bestätigung; ~ **charges** *B*spesen; ~ **charter** *B*konzession; ~ **cheque** *B*scheck, *auf e–e B gezogener Scheck*; ~ **circulation** ausgegebene *B*effekten; **commercial** ~ Geschäfts*b*, Universal*b*; **confirming** ~ bestätigende *B*; ~ **consolidation;** *B-en*fusion; ~ **crash** *B*krach; ~ **credit** *B*kredit; ~ **credit files** Akten über den Kreditkunden; ~ **deposit** *B*einlage: ~ **deposit note** *B*einlagenzertifikat, *B*einlagenschein; ~ **director** *B*direktor; ~ **draft** → *draft*; ~ **failure** *B*zusammenbruch, *B*krach; ~ **for co-operatives** Genossenschafts*b*; **B** ~ **for International Settlements** *B* für internationalen Zahlungsausgleich; ~ **funds** von der *B* verwaltete Gelder; ~ **giro** *B*giro, bargeldloser Zahlungsverkehr über e–e *B*, *B*verrechnungsverkehr; ~~ *credit slip Büberweisungsformular*; ~ **group** *B-en*konsortium; ~ **guaranty fund** *B*garantiefonds (*zum Schutz gegen Bzusammenbrüche*); ~ **holiday** → *holiday*; ~ **holiday break** *Kurzferien vom letzten Wochentag vor dem Bfeiertag bis zum 1. Wochentag danach;* ~ **in failing condition** insolvente *B*; ~ **indorsement** Giro e–r *B*; ~ **interest** *Bzinsen*; ~ **interest certificate** *B*bestätigung über Schuldzinsen d Kunden; ~ **investments** Anlage von *Bgeldern*; ~ **loans and discounts** Ausleihe- und Diskontgeschäft; ~ **merger-agreement** *B-en*fusionsvertrag; ~-**note** *B*note; **B** ~ **of England bill** bei der Zentralbank (*B. of E.*) diskontfähiger Wechsel; ~ **of issue** Noten*b*, Emissions*b*; ~ **officer** *B*beamter (*bes in leitender Stellung*); ~ **paper** *B*wechsel, bankfähiges Papier; ~ **payment order** Banküberweisungsauftrag, Zahlungsauftrag; ~ **post bill** Solawechsel der *B* (*von England*) zur Geldübermittlung auf dem Postwege; ~ **rate** (Mindest) Rediskontsatz der Zentral*b*, Diskontsatz *führender Banken* (*US*), Bankrate; *seit 1972: minimum lending rate qv*; ~ **receipt** *B*quittung; ~ **reconciliation** Kontoabstimmung; ~ **reference** *B*auskunft; **B** ~ **Return** Wochenbericht der Bank von England; ~**'s sorting code(number)** Bankleitzahl; ~ **statement** *B*auszug; *B*bilanz; ~ **stock** *B*aktien, Kapitalanteile an der *B*, Anteile am Vermögen der *B*; Aktien der *B* von England; ~ **teller** *B*kassier; ~ **transfer** *B*überweisung; ~ **trustee department** Treuhandabteilung e–r *B*; ~**vault** *B*tresor; **acceptance** ~ Akzept*b*; **advising** ~ avisierende *B*, Gutschrifsanzeige machende *B*, anzeigende *B*; **agricultural** ~ Landwirtschafts*b*; **associated** ~ (*e–r Clearinghausvereinigung*) angeschlossene *B*; **bonding of** ~ **officers** Kautionsstellung für leitende *B*beamte; **cash in** ~ *B*guthaben; **central** ~**s** Zentral*b-en*; **chartered** ~ konzessionierte *B*; **clearing** ~ *Br* Clearing*b*, Geschäfts*b*, Giro*b*, Mitglieds*b* e–r Scheckverrechnungsorganisation; **commercial** ~ Geschäfts*b*, allgemeine *B*; Handels*b*, Kredit*b*; **confirming** ~ bestätigende *B*; **conversion of** ~ **deposits** Überführung von *B*guthaben (*in Bargeld oder Gold*); **co-operative** ~ Genossenschafts*b*; **correspondent** ~ Korrespondenz*b*; **day-to-day** ~ **advances** kurzfristige *B*vorschüsse; **deposit** ~ Depositen*b*, Giro*b*; **fiduciary services of** ~**s** → *fiduciary*;

floating ~ Emissions*b*; **foreign** ~ Ausland*b* (*GB: mit Niederlassung in London*) → *joint* (*1*); **group** ~**s** Konzern*b-en*; **industrial** ~ Kundenkredit*b*; **intermediary** ~ zwischengeschaltete *B*; **joint-stock** ~Aktien*b*, *B*gesellschaft; **labo(u)r** ~ Gewerkschafts*b*; **lead** ~ Konsortialführer, federführende *B*; **member** ~ Mitglieds*b* (*US: Federal Reserve System*); **mutual savings** ~ Sparkasse, Genossenschaft*b*; **National B**~ National*b*, Staats*b*; **national** ~**s** im gesamten Staatsgebiet zugelassene und tätige *B-en*, Groß*b-en*; **negotiating** ~ negoziierende *B*; **non-member** ~ Nichtmitglied*b* (*US: Federal Reserve System*); **payor** ~ bezogene *B*, zahlende *B*; **presenting** ~ vorlegende *B*; **private** ~ Privat*b*; **public-sector** ~ *B* im Bereich der öffentl Hand; **recognized** ~ *von der Bank v Engl anerkannte B*; **redemption of** ~ **deposits** Auszahlung von Einlagen; **redemption of** ~ **notes** Einlösung von *B*noten; **run on** ~**s** → *run*; **shoe-string** ~ dubiose Klein*b*; **spite** ~ Konkurrenz*b* e–r Oppositionsgruppe; **state** ~ → *state*; **state-owned** ~ staatseigene *B*; **The B**~ die Bank von England.

bankable | assets für Banksicherheiten geeignete Vermögenswerte; ~ **bill** → *bill* (*3*); ~ **paper** bankfähige Wechsel *bzw sonstige bankfähige Wertpapiere;* ~ **securities** bankfähige Wertpapiere.

banker Bankier *m*, Bank *f*, Bankunternehmer *m*, Inhaber *m* e–r Bank; ~**'s acceptance** → *acceptance*; ~**'s bank** Bank der Banken (= *Zentralbank*); ~**'s bill of exchange** auf e–e Bank gezogener Wechsel; ~**'s blanket bonds** pauschale Kautionsversicherung für Bankangestellte; ~**s' books** Geschäftsbücher und Konten e–r *B*; **B**~**s' Books Evidence Act (=)** *Gesetz über die Verwendung von Bankauskünften im Beweisverfahren;* ~**'s cash notes** Bankkassenscheine (*Vorläufer des Schecks*); ~**'s (commercial) credit** Akkreditiv; ~**'s discretion** Bankgeheimnis; ~**'s draft** → *draft*; ~**'s lien** Bankenpfandrecht; ~**'s loan** Bankkredit; ~**'s note** verkehrsfähiger Schuldschein e–r Bank;~**'s order** *B*-Dauerauftrag; ~**'s payment** Zahlungsauftrag e–r Bank (*im Verrechnungsverkehr*); ~**'s reference** *B*referenz; ~**'s ticket** Rückrechnung (*beim Wechselregreß*); **collecting** ~ die *e–n Scheck zur Zahlung vorlegende Bank*; **commercial** ~ = *commercial bank* → *bank*; **individual** ~ Privatbank(ier), (*konzessioniertes*) Bankunternehmen (*als Einzelkaufmann*); **my** ~**s** meine Hausbank.

banking | business *B*geschäfte; Bankwesen *n*, Bankgeschäft *n*; ~ **center** Bankplatz; ~ **commission** Bankprovision; ~ **company** Bank(aktien)gesellschaft; ~ **concentration** Bankzusammenschlüsse; ~ **custom (~usage)** Bankusancen; ~ **hours** Geschäftsstunden; ~ **instrument** → *instrument*; ~ **partnership** Bankgesellschaft (*Personalgesellschaft*); ~ **operation** → *operation*; ~**secrecy** → *secrecy*; ~ **services** bankbetriebliche Leistungen, Dienstleistungen von Banken; ~ **supervision** Bankenaufsicht; ~ **syndicate** Bankenkonsortium; ~ **transactions** Bankgeschäfte; **branch** ~ → *branch*; **chain** ~ Filialbanksystem; lose Bankzusammenschlüsse; **commercial** ~ das Bankgewerbe; Bankgeschäfte (*vorwiegend für die kurzfristige Kreditversorgung*); **merchant** ~ → *merchant*; **sound** ~ seriöse Bankgeschäfte; **wholesale** ~ → *wholesale*.

banking a deal Finanzierung e–s Geschäftsabschlusses.

bankroll *v/t* finanzieren, mit Geld ausstatten.

bankrupt *adj*, bankrott, im Konkurs befindlich; **to be adjudicated** ~ das Konkursverfahren über *jmds* Vermögen eröffnen; **to declare oneself** ~ den Konkurs anmelden.

bankrupt Gemeinschuldner *m* (*der konkursreife oder im Konkurs befindliche Schuldner*), Bankrotteur *m*, zahlungsunfähiger Schuldner *m*; ~ **absconding with property** Flüchtigwerden e–s bankrotten Schuldners (*unter Mitnahme von Vermögensstücken*); ~**'s assets** → *assets*; ~**'s estate** Konkursmasse; **adjudged** ~ Gemeinschuldner; **adjudicated** ~ Gemeinschuldner; **creditor to a ~'s estate** Konkursgläubiger; **discharged** ~ Gemeinschuldner nach Aufhebung des Konkursverfahrens (*und Erlaß der Restschuld*); **fraudulent** ~ betrügerischer Bankrotteur; **list of creditors of a** ~ Gläubigerliste, Konkurstabelle; **to be in the ~'s order and disposition** nicht aussonderungsfähig sein; **undischarged** ~ nicht befreiter Gemeinschuldner (*dem Restschuld nicht erlassen wurde*); **voluntary** ~ Gemeinschuldner auf eigenen Antrag.

bankruptcy Konkurs *m* (= *K*); Zahlungsunfähigkeit *f*; **B ~ Act** Konkursordnung; ~ **court** Konkursgericht; ~ **discharge** Restschulderlaß durch das *K*gericht; ~ **distribution** Schlußverteilung im *K*verfahren; ~ **filing** *K*- bzw Vergleichsantrag; ~ **law** Konkursrecht; ~ **notice** Zahlungsaufforderung mit *K*androhung; ~ **of contributory** *K* e–s Gesellschafters, der noch Zahlungen auf seinen Kapitalanteil zu leisten hat; ~ **offences** *K*straftaten, *K*vergehen; ~**petition** *K*antrag; ~ **proceedings** → *proceedings*; ~ **rules** *K*vorschriften; ~ **schedule** Status des Gemeinschuldners; **act of** ~ *K*grund, Tatbestand, der zum *K*antrag berechtigt; **adjudication of** (= *in*) ~*K*eröffnung; **commissioner of** ~ → *commissioner*; **criminal** ~ **order** Feststellung e–r *K*forderung im Strafverfahren gegen Schädiger; **date of** ~ Tag der Einreichung des *K*antrags, **debtor in** ~ → *debtor*; **declaration of** ~ (*eigene*) *K*anmeldung; **discharge in** ~ → *discharge*; **dividend in** ~ → *dividend*; **fraudulent** ~ betrügerischer Bankrott; **involuntary** ~ *K* auf Antrag e–s Gläubigers; **preferential payments in** ~ bevorrechtigte Forderungen im *K*verfahren; **presentment on** ~ Wechselvorlage bei *K* des Bezogenen; **referee in** ~ → *referee*; **set-off in** ~ *K*-aufrechnung; **small** ~ Klein*k* *(im summarischen Verfahren)*; **straight** ~ (*voller*) *K*; **to file a petition in** ~ *K*antrag stellen (*vgl petition*); **to lodge a proof in** ~ e–e *K*forderung anmelden; **trustee in** ~ → *trustee*; **verging on** ~ konkursreif; **voluntary** ~ *K* auf Antrag des Schuldners.

banner Banner *n*, Transparent *n*; Werbespruchband *n*.

banning|action Gewerbeverbotsverfahren; ~**order** Verbotsverfügung.

banns|of marriage kirchliches Aufgebot *n*; ~ **of matrimony** = ~ **marriage** *qv*; Aufgebot; **to forbid the** ~ Einspruch gegen die Eheschließung erheben; **to publish the** ~ **of marriage** das Aufgebot (*von der Kanzel*) bekanntmachen.

baptism Taufe *f*; **proof of** ~ Nachweis der Taufe; **register of** ~ Taufregister.

baptismal Tauf . . .; ~ **name** Taufname; ~ **records** Taufurkunden.

bar (*1*) Anwaltschaft *f*; ~ **admission** Zulassung zur Anwaltschaft; ~ **association** Anwaltsverein, Rechtsanwaltskammer; ~ **committee** Ausschuß für anwaltschaftl Standesrecht; **B~ Council** Anwaltskammer, *Organ der Standesvertretung der barristers*; ~ **exam(ination)** Zulassungsprüfung; ~ **review courses** juristisches Repetitorium; **member of the** ~ (*zugelassener*) Rechtsanwalt; **parliamentary** ~ praktizierende Anwälte in Parlamentsausschüssen; **The B** ~ die Anwaltschaft, der Anwaltsstand; **the criminal** ~ die Strafverteidiger, Anwaltschaft in Strafsachen; **to be called to the** ~ als Anwalt zugelassen werden; **to qualify for the B**~ →*qualify*.

bar (*2*) Schranke *f*, Hindernis *n*; Ausschluß *m*; peremtorische Einrede *f*; ~ **at large** Einwendung der mangelnden Substantiierung; ~ **of ex-**

ecution Unzulässigkeit der Zwangsvollstreckung; Vollstreckungshindernis; ~ **of judgment** Einwendung der Rechtskraft (*res judicata*); ~ **of the House** Grenzstrich im englischen Unterhaus *für Nichtmitglieder*; ~ **of trial** Unzulässigkeit der Strafverfolgung, Prozeßhindernis; ~ **period** Ausschlußfrist; **~s to divorce** Scheidungshindernisse; ~ **to marriage** Ehehindernis; **common** ~ Einwendung der mangelnden Substantiierung; **ples in** ~ → *plea*.

bar (3) Bar *f*, Schankausschank *n*; **public** ~ Trinkstube, Bar, Trinkausschank.

bar *v* sperren, versperren, hindern, verbieten, ausschließen; **~red by lapse of time** durch Fristablauf ausgeschlossen; **~red by limitation** verjährt; **~red by the Statute of Limitations** verjährt.

barbarous barbarisch, bösartig, gnadenlos, grausam.

Barclay card Barclays Bank-Kreditkarte *f*.

bar code Strichkode *m* (*auf Warenpakkungen*), Balkenkode *m*.

bareboat charter (=) Mietvertrag *m* über ein leeres Schiff, Schiffsmiete *f*.

bargain *s* gegenseitige Verpflichtung *f*, Vereinbarung *f*, Vertrag *m*; billiger Einkauf *m*, Gelegenheitskauf *m*; *pl exch* Börsentransaktionen; ~ **and sale** *hist* Grundstücksübertragungsmethode *GB bis 1925*; ~ **basement prices** gewinnbringende Anfangskurse; ~ **book** Schlußnotenregister; ~ **counter** Verkaufstisch für verbilligte Sonderangebote; **~s done** gehandelte Kurse; ~ **for account** Termingeschäft; ~ **money** → *money*; ~ **or contract** vertragliche Vereinbarung; ~ **relationship** beidseitig verpflichtendes Verhältnis; ~ **sale** → *sale*; ~ **work** Kontraktarbeit (*Bergbau*); **bad** ~ schlechtes Geschäft; **cash** ~ → *cash*; **catching** ~ Übervorteilung; gewissenloses Geschäft; **dead** ~ spottbilliger Preis; **firm** ~ *exch* fester Abschluß; **unconscionable** ~ sittenwidriges Ausbeutungsgeschäft.

bargain *v* ein (*Kauf*)Geschäft abschließen; handeln, feilschen; ~ **away** billig abgeben; **as ~ed for** wie abgemacht, wie ausgehandelt.

bargainee (Grundstücks)Käufer *m*, Erwerber *m*.

bargaining *s* Handeln *n*, Verhandeln *n*, Verhandlungen *f*|*pl*, Feilschen *n*; **collective** ~ Tarifverhandlungen; **industry-wide** ~ Manteltarifvertragsverhandlungen; **single-plant** ~ Einzeltarifvertragsverhandlung.

bargaining agent ausschließlicher gewerkschaftlicher Tarifverhandlungsführer, Tarifpartner.

bargainor Verkäufer *m*, Veräußerer *m*.

bark die Rinde *f*; das Drumherum eines Schriftsatzes.

barkery Gerberei *f*.

barleycorn (=) *Längenmaß: ⅓ Zoll*; symbolische Pachtzahlung bzw Gegenleistung.

Barnard's Inn (=) *eine der Anwaltsinnungen in London*.

barometer stocks US Standardwerte.

baron Baron *m*, Freiherr *m*; *hist* Richtertitel; ~ **et feme** *hist* Mann und Frau, Ehegatten; **B~s of the Cinque Ports** *privilegierte Abgeordnete und Einwohner der südengl Hafenstädte;* **B~ of the Exchequer** Richter am Exchequer Gericht; **chief** ~ oberste Lehensträger.

barony Freiherrenwürde *m*, Grundbesitz *m* eines Freiherrn; ~ **of land** *Flächenmaß: 15 acres;* Unterbezirk einer Grafschaft.

barracuda Scharfmacher *m*, aggressive Person *f*, aggressiv verhandelnder Anwalt *m*.

barrator Querulant *m*, Prozeßstifter *m*; **common** ~notorischer Querulant, „Prozeßhansel".

barratrous betrügerisch, Prozeßanstiftung betreibend.

barratry *obs* Schacher *m* mit Kirchenämtern; Anstiftung *f* zu grundloser Prozeßführung; Baratterie *f*, betrügerische Handlungen *f/pl* eines Schiffskapitäns oder der Mannschaft.

barrier Schranke *f*, Hindernis *n*, Schlagbaum *m*, Grenzflötz *n* (*zwischen zwei Gruben*); **customs** ~ → *customs;* **restraining** ~ Absperrgitter; **trade** ~**s** Handelsschranken.

barring *prep* abgesehen von, ausgenommen; ~ **accidents** von zufälligen Ereignissen abgesehen; ~ **errors** Irrtum ausgenommen; Irrtum vorbehalten.

barring of claims Anspruchsverjährung, Ausschluß von Ansprüchen *vgl bar v;* ~ **of entailed interests** Aufhebung der Fideikommißbindung.

barrister Rechtsanwalt *m*, Prozeßanwalt *m* vor höheren Gerichten; ~ **–at-law** *Rang und Titel e–s barrister qv verliehen von e–m Inn of Court qv;* ~**'s professional obligations** Standes-(Berufs-)pflichten des Rechtsanwalts; ~**'s fee** Honorar des Prozeßanwalts (*Ehrensache, nicht gerichtlich durchsetzbar*); **consulting** ~ beratender Anwalt; **inner** ~ = *King's* (*Queen's*) *Counsel, privilegierter Prozeßanwalt, etwa Justizrat,* ranghöherer Anwalt; **junior** ~ rangjüngerer Anwalt, Nebenanwalt; **outer** (= **utter)** ~ nicht als King's (Queen's) Counsel zugelassener Anwalt, **vacation** ~ (Ferienanwalt), neu zugelassener Anwalt.

barter *s* Tausch *m*, Tauschgeschäft *n*; Koppelgeschäft (*Anbieten e–s fertigen Programms mit Werbespots*); ~ **transaction** Tauschgeschäft, Kompensationsgeschäft.

barter *v* tauschen, Tauschhandel treiben.

barterer Tauschhändler *m*.

bartering Tauschgeschäft *n*, Tauschhandel *m*; **international** ~ zwischenstaatlicher Warenaustausch.

base *adj* niedrig, niederträchtig; unehelich; falsch.

base *s* Basis, Grundmauern *f*, *mil* Stützpunkt *m*; ~ **line** Basislinie (*Vermessung*); ~ **period** Ausgangsfrist, Zeitraum als Berechnungsgrundlage; ~ **rate** → *rate;* ~ **year** Vergleichsjahr; **monetary** ~ monetäre Basis (*des Banksystems*) Geldbasis *f*.

baseless grundlos, unbegründet.

basement Souterrain *n*; Erdgeschoß *n*.

basic grundlegend; Grund ... Basis ...

basing point system Preisberechnungsverfahren *n* auf einheitlicher Frachtbasis.

basis Basis *f*, Grundlage *f*, ~ **of agreement** Vertragsgrundlage; ~ **of assessment** Bemessungsgrundlage; ~ **of charge** Berechnungsgrundlage; ~ **of bargain** Vertragsgrundlage, Grundlage für zugesicherte Eigenschaften; ~ **of contract** Vertragsgrundlage; ~ **of negotiations** Verhandlungsgrundlage; ~ **of valuation** Bewertungsgrundlage; ~ **period** *tax* Bemessungszeitraum; **contractual** ~ vertragliche Grundlage; *on a* ~~ *auch:* freiberuflich; **cost** ~ Bewertungsgrundlage, Selbstkostenpreis; **gold** ~ → *gold;* **legal** ~ Rechtsgrundlage.

basket Korb *m*, Warenkorb *m*; ~ **clause** → *clause;* ~ **formula** Korbformel.

basset verbotenes Glücksspiel *n*.

bastard *adj* unehelich; *s* uneheliches Kind *n*, Bastard *m*.

bastardization Unehelichkeitserklärung *f*.

bastardize für unehelich erklären.

bastardy Unehelichkeit *f*, uneheliche Geburt *f*, Vergehen *n* der unehelichen Zeugung; ~ **bond** Schuldurkunde zur Unterhaltssicherung für ein nichteheliches Kind; ~ **case** Vaterschaftsprozeß; ~ **order** Gerichtsbeschluß auf Unterhaltszahlung für ein nichteheliches Kind; ~ **proceedings** Unterhaltsprozeß gegen den Kindsvater.

batch proof gruppenweise Verprobung *f* von Bankeingängen.

baton Schlagstock; ~ **rounds** Schlagstock-Einsatz; ~**–round launcher** Plastikgeschoßwerfer.

battel *hist* Zweikampf *m* (*als Ordal = Gottesurteil*).
battery gewaltsame Körperverletzung *f*, tätliche Beleidigung *f*; **aggravated** ~ schwere Körperverletzung; **criminal** ~ gefährliche Körperverletzung; **simple** ~ einfache Körperverletzung; **technical** ~ Körperverletzung durch Heilungseingriff.
battle of forms *„Krieg der Formulare"*, Kollision widersprechender AGB.
bear *s* Baissespekulant *m*, Baissier *m*; ~ **market** fallende Börse; Baisse; ~ **operation** Baissespekulation; ~ **point** Baissemoment; ~ **raiding** Angriff des Baissiers; ~ **sale** Leerverkauf; ~ **seller** Baissespekulant; **uncovered** ~ Blankoverkäufer.
bear *adj* flau, fallend.
bear *v* tragen, führen, bringen; ~ **arms** Waffen führen; ~ **interest** Zinsen tragen; ~ **the costs** die Kosten tragen; ~ **the damage** den Schaden tragen, für den Schaden aufkommen; ~ **the name** den Namen führen; ~ **upon** Bezug haben auf; ~ **witness** bezeugen, Zeugnis ablegen.
bearer Inhaber *m*, Überbringer *m*; ~-**bill** Inhaberwechsel; ~ **bond** → *bond* (*1*); ~ **certificate** Inhaberpapier, Inhaberzertifikat; ~ **debenture** Inhaberschuldverschreibung; ~ **paper** Inhaberpapier; ~ **policy** Inhaberpolice; ~ **scrip** Interimschein; ~ **shares** → *share;* ~ **security** → *security* (*2*); ~ **warrant** Inhaberberechtigungsschein, Inhaberaktienzertifikat *vgl share warrant;* **bill payable to** ~ Inhaberwechsel; zahlbar an Überbringer; **cheque to** → *cheque;* **to** ~ an Überbringer; **to make out to** ~ auf den Inhaber ausstellen.
bearing|date of mit Datum vom; ~ **even date** gleichen Datums; ~ **interest** verzinslich.
bearish Baisse . . .; ~ **market** Baissebörse.
bearishness Baissestimmung *f*.
beast Tier *n*, Haustier *n*, Arbeitstier *n*, jagdbare (Säuge)tiere *n*|*pl;* ~**s of the chase** jagdbares Wild; ~**s of the forest** jagdbare Waldestiere; ~**s of the plow** Pflugtiere; ~**s of the warren** (*bestimmte*) jagdbare Tiere; *Hasen, Kaninchen, Rehe.*
beat *s* Runde *f* (*eines Wächters*); Unterbezirk *m*, Wahlbezirk *m*.
beating of the bounds Abschreiten der Gemeindegrenze.
beating the index *d. Erzielen besserer Anlageportefeuille-Ergebnisse als dem Börsenindex entspricht.*
become werden; ~ **entitled** ein Recht erwerben; ~ **final** rechtskräftig werden; ~ **incapable** geschäftsunfähig werden; ~ **liable to pay** haftbar werden, haften; ~ **payable** *zur Zahlung* fällig werden; ~ **vested** übergehen auf, erworben werden.
„bed and breakfast" deals *kurzfristiger Verkauf und Rückkauf von Aktien zur Ausnutzung der Jahresfreigrenze der capital gains tax qv.*
bedel Gerichtsdiener *m*.
bed-sit Wohnschlafzimmer *n*.
beer Bier *n*, bierartiges Getränk *n*; ~ **house** Bierwirtschaft; ~ **in bulk** Bier en gros, Brauereibier; ~ **-shop** Bierladen, Gassenschänke; ~ **tax** Biersteuer.
befall zustoßen.
before ehe, vor; ~ **hours** Vorbörse, vorbörslich; ~ **marriage** vorehelich, vor der betreffenden Ehe; ~ **the court** vor Gericht.
beg betteln, bitten, beantragen; ~ **leave** um Erlaubnis bitten, beantragen; ~ **the question** so tun, als ob etwas schon bewiesen sei (*und Schlußfolgerungen daraus ziehen*); etwas Unbewiesenes als ausgemachte Tatsache hinstellen; **we** ~ **to advise** wir erlauben uns mitzuteilen . . .
behalf *s* Behuf *m*, Nutzen *m*, Vorteil *m*; **on** ~ **of** im Namen von, für, in Vertretung von, zugunsten von; **to act on one's own** ~ im eigenen Namen handeln.
behavio(u)r Verhalten *n*, Benehmen *n*; ~ **decree** Scheidungsurteil wegen ehewidrigen Verhaltens; **bad** ~

schlechte Führung; **during good** ~ (*Amt*) auf Lebenszeit (*vorbehaltl Abruf bei Fehlverhalten*); **good** ~ Wohlverhalten, gute Führung; **unreasonable** ~ unzumutbares Benehmen (*als Scheidungsgrund*).

behoof Behuf *m*, Vorteil *m*, Nutzen *m*; **on** ~ **of the applicant** im Interesse des Anmelders.

belief Glaube *m*, Überzeugung *f*, Annahme *f*, **bona fide** ~ **of right** redliche Überzeugung, ein Recht zu haben; **mistaken** ~ **as to criminal character of act** Rechtsirrtum über die Strafbarkeit der Handlung; **reasonable ground of** ~ ausreichende Gründe für die Annahme.

believability Glaubwürdigkeit *f*.

belittle herabsetzen, verächtlich machen, bagatellisieren.

belligerency Kriegszustand *m*, Status *m* als Kriegsführender; **recognition of** ~ Anerkennung als kriegsführende Macht.

belligerent *adj* kriegsführend; ~ **occupation** → *occupation;* ~ **rights** Rechte e–s kriegsführenden Staates.

belligerent *s* kriegführender Staat *m*; ~**s** Bewaffnete *m*|*pl*, denen Kombattantenstatus zugebilligt wird; **unlawful** ~**s** völkerrechtswidrige Teilnehmer an Kampfhandlungen.

bellum justum gerechter Krieg *m*, völkerrechtlich zulässiger Krieg.

bellwether discount rate Leit-Diskontsatz (*US*).

belong *v* zugehören; ~**ing** gehörend, gehörig, zustehend, im Besitz von, im Eigentum von.

belongings Habe *f*, Habseligkeiten *f*|*pl;* ~ **remaining** (meine) übrige Habe; **personal** ~ persönliche Habe.

bench Bank *f*, Richterstuhl *m*, Richterschaft *f*; ~ **conference** Besprechung am Richtertisch mit den Anwälten; ~ **trial** Hauptverhandlung ohne Jury; ~ **warrant** → *warrant;* **elected to the** ~ zum Richter ernannt (*bzw gewählt*); **front** ~ Regierungsbank; die ersten Sitzreihen im Unterhaus (*für Minister bzw führende Oppositionsabgeordnete); ministerial* ~ Regierungsbank; **the** ~ **and the bar** Richter und Anwaltschaft; **to be raised to the** ~ zum Richter bestimmt werden; **to take the** ~ das Richteramt übernehmen.

Benchers Vorstandsmitglieder *n*|*pl* der Inns of Court qv. Kammervorstand *der barristers;* **federal** ~**s** Richter an den US Bundesgerichten.

benchmark Vermessungspflock *m*, Nivellierungszeichen an der Meßplatte; Bezugszins *m*, Bezugswert *m*; ~ **prime rate** Leitzins (Primarate); ~ **rate** Ecklohn.

bend Kurve *f*; **deceptive** ~**s** unübersichtliche Kurven;

benefactor Wohltäter *m*, Mäzen *m*;

benefice *eccl* Pfründe *f*, Wohltat *f*, Vorteil *m*.

beneficial wohltätig, vorteilhaft, zuträglich, nutznießend; ~ **association** Wohltätigkeitsverein; ~ **enjoyment** eigene Nutznießung; ~ **estate** Anrecht; ~ **freehold owner** (*unbeschränkter*) Grundstückseigentümer; ~ **interest** Treuhandbegünstigung; Eigennutzung, Nutzungsrecht, Nießbrauch; ~ **interest arising or accruing on the death** die beim Tode entstehende oder anfallende Begünstigung; ~ **interest in land** das Nutzungsrecht an Liegenschaften; ~ **owner** → *owner;* ~ **ownership** → *ownership;* ~**ly entitled** aus eigenem Recht zustehend; ~**ly held shares** Aktien im Eigenbesitz; **to be** ~**ly interested** ein eigenes Recht *an etwas haben*.

beneficiary *s* Begünstigter, Treuhandbegünstiger, Berechtigter, Bedachter *m*, Leistungsempfänger *m*; ~ **entitled in possession** nutzungsberechtigter Besitzer; ~ **heir** der Erbe; ~ **of trust** treuhandbegünstigter, Treuhandberechtigter; ~ **under the will** der testamentarisch Bedachte; **authorized** ~ der Berechtigte, der Empfangsberechtigte; **contingent** ~ bedingt Begünstigter; **first** ~ Erstbegünstigter; **net** ~ Begünstigter nach Abzug von Abgaben; **primary** ~ Erstbegünstigter; **residuary** ~ Erbe (*des Reinnachlasses*); **sole** ~ Alleinerbe, Alleinbegünstigter; **ultimate** ~ Letztbegünstigter.

beneficium *hist* Benefizium *n*, Lehen *n*, Begünstigung *f*, kirchliche Immunität *f*; ~ **excussionis** Einrede der Vorausklage.

benefit *s* Unterstützung *f*, Beihilfe *f*, Zuwendung *f*, Vorrecht *n*, Nutzen *m*, Gewinn *m*; Versicherungsleistung *f*; ~ **association** Wohltätigkeitsverein; ~ **building society** Baugenossenschaft; ~ **certificate** schriftliches Zahlungsversprechen; ~ **clause** Begünstigungsklausel; ~ **district** Erschließungsbeitragsbereich; ~ **fund** Unterstützungsfonds, Versicherungsfonds auf Gegenseitigkeit; ~**s in cash** Barleistungen; ~**s in kind** Sachleistungen; ~ **in money's worth** geldwerte Vorteile; ~ **of an invention** Nutzen e–r Erfindung; ~ **of clergy** *hist* Kirchenasyl; ~ **of counsel** Recht auf Stellung e–s Pflichtverteidigers; ~ **of discussion** → *discussion;* ~ **of division** Einrede von Mitbürgen, nur anteilig zu haften; ~ **officer** Sozialhilfebeamter; ~ **of inventory** die Rechtswohltat der Inventarerrichtung; ~ **of law** Rechtswohltat; ~ **of the choir** Spende (*Stiftung, Vermächtnis*) zugunsten des Kirchenchores; ~ **of doubt** (*die Rechtswohltat des*) „in dubio pro reo", im Zweifel zugunsten des Angeklagten; ~ **of the execution** Ansprüche aus der Zwangsvollstreckung; ~ **rates** Leistungssätze (*Social Security*); ~ **society** → *society;* ~ **year** Bezugsjahr (*Sozialversich.-Leistungen);* **accident** ~ → *accident;* **accrued** ~**s** erworbene Leistungsberechtigung; **contributory** ~ beitragspflichtige Leistung; **death** ~ Sterbegeld; **disability** ~ Invalidenrente; zusätzliche Leistungen bei Invalidität durch Unfall; **dismemberment** ~ Rentenzahlung bei Gliederverlust; **double accident** ~ → *double;* **extended** ~ Mehrleistung; **financial** ~Vermögensvorteil; **immediate** ~ sofortiger Versicherungsschutz; **indemnity** ~ Entschädigungsleistung; **insurance** ~ Versicherungsleistung; **legal** ~ Rechtsvorteil; **long** ~ langfristige Leistung; **maternity** ~ → *maternity;* **minimum** ~ Mindestunterstützungssatz; **mutual** ~ **society** → *mutual;* **non-contributory** ~ beitragsfreie Leistung; **nursing** ~ Stillgeld; **old age** ~ Altersrente, Altersfürsorge; **pecuniary** ~ Vermögensvorteil; **preferential** ~ Voraus, Vorwegentnahme; **primary** ~ *ins* Grundrente; **provident** ~**s** Sonderunterstützung bei Arbeitsunfähigkeit u. a.; **public** ~ Gemeinnutz, gemeinnütziger Zweck; **short-time** ~ Kurzarbeitergeld; **supplementary** ~ Sozialhilfe(leistung); **survivor** ~**s** Hinterbliebenenrente, Leistungen an Hinterbliebene; Witwen- und Waisengeld; **to take the** ~ **of the Act** gesetzliche Bestimmungen für sich in Anspruch nehmen; **unjustified** ~ ungerechtfertigte Bereicherung, ungerechtfertigter Vorteil.

benefit *v* begünstigen, Nutzen bringen, nutzen, sich etwas zunutze machen.

benevolence Wohltätigkeit *f*, Menschenliebe *f*, *hist* Zwangsabgabe an die Krone.

benevolent wohlwollend, Wohltätigkeits . . ., Unterstützungs . . .; ~ **instrumentality** Wohltätigkeitsorganisation.

bequeath vermachen (*von bewegl Vermögensgegenständen*); ~ **a legacy** ein Vermächtnis aussetzen.

bequest Vermächtnis *n*, → *legacy* (*Zusammensetzungen gelten entsprechend*).

Berne Convention Berner (Verbands)Übereinkunft *f* (*Copyright*); ~ **Union** Berner Verband (*Kreditversicherungsunternehmen*) *seit 1937*.

berth Ankerplatz *m*, Liegeplatz *m*; **customs** ~ → *customs;* **discharging** ~ Löschplatz.

berthage Kaigebühren *f/pl*.

Bertillon system *Identifizierungssystem n nach Körpermessungen.*
beset belagern, freien Zutritt behindern.
beseech dringend bitten, ersuchen.
besetting Umzingelung *f*, konzentrierter Angriff *m.*
besides zusätzlich, davon abgesehen, daneben, auch, gleichermaßen.
best best(er, –e, –es), am besten; ~ **bid** das beste Angebot; ~ **endeavours** größte Bemühungen; ~**evidence** → *evidence;* ~ **practible means** die praktisch möglichen Mittel; ~ **price** → *price;* ~ **title** → *title;* **at** ~ bestenfalls.
bestiality Unzucht mit Tieren, Sodomie *f.*
bestials Großtiere *n|pl, Rinder n|pl.*
bestow verleihen, übertragen, erteilen, verteilen.
bestowal Schenkung *f*, Verleihung *f.*
bet *s* Wette *f*; *v* wetten.
betray verraten, offenbaren.
betrayal Verrat *m*; ~ **of confidence** Vertrauensbruch; ~ **of state secrets** Verrat von Staatsgeheimnissen.
betrothal Verlöbnis *n.*
betrothed *s sg* die Verlobte, die Braut, *pl* die Verlobten, das Brautpaar.
betterment Verbesserung *f*, Melioration *f*, Wertsteigerung *f*, Werterhohung *f* e–s Grundstücks *(durch Erschließung)*; ~ **acts** Gesetze zur Sicherung von Ansprüchen für wertverbessernde Aufwendungen von Pächtern; ~ **levy** Investitionsumlage; ~ **tax** Wertzuwachssteuer.
betting Wetten *n*, verbotenes Wetten *n*; ~ **book** Wettbuch; ~ **by way of wagering** Wetten; ~ **debt** Wettschuld; ~ **house** Wettsalon; ~ **office** Wettannahme; ~ **slip** Wettschein; ~ **tax** Wettsteuer.
beyond jenseits, außer; ~ **a reasonable doubt** ohne vernünftigen Zweifel; ~ **dispute** → *dispute;* ~ **doubt** unzweifelhaft; ~ **expectation** wider Erwarten; ~ **the seas** Übersee, überseeisch, im Ausland *(außerhalb des U. K., der Kanalinseln und der Insel Man).*
bi-annual zweimal jährlich, halbjährlich.
bias Befangenheit *f*, Parteilichkeit *f*, Voreingenommenheit *f*; **free from** ~ unparteiisch, unvoreingenommen; **to impeach a witness for** ~ e–n Zeugen wegen Voreingenommenheit als unglaubwürdig hinstellen; **personal** ~ persönliches Vorurteil.
bias(s)ed befangen, parteiisch, voreingenommen.
bicameral system Zweikammersystem *n.*
bid *s* Preisangebot *n (des Kaufinteressenten)*, Submissionsangebot, Gebot *n (bei Versteigerungen)*, Lieferungsangebot *n*, festes Kursangebot bei Übernahmeversuch; Geldkurs; ~ **acceptance period** Angebotsbindungsfrist; ~**s and offers** *exch* Kauf- und Verkaufsangebote; ~ **bond** → *bond (2);* ~ **price** *(vom Käufer gebotener)* Geldkurs; ~ **rigging** Submissionsabsprachen; **alternative** ~ Alternativangebot; **call for** ~**s** (öffentliche) Ausschreibung; **closing** ~ Höchstgebot; **feigned** ~ Scheingebot; **first** ~ Erstgebot; **fixed** ~ festes Gebot; **friendly** ~ Übernahmeangebot von befreundeter Seite; **highest** ~ Meistgebot; **hostile** ~ unfreundliches Übernahmeangebot; **last** ~ Höchstgebot, das letzte Gebot; **lowest** ~ Mindestgebot; **open** ~ Submissionsangebot mit Preisreduzierungsvorbehalt; **opening** ~ erstes Gebot; **performance** ~ Leistungsangebot; **provisional** ~ vorläufiges Höchstgebot *(unter d. Mindestgebot)*; **referential** ~ Mehrgebot; **rigged** ~ Scheingebot, betrügerisches Gebot; **sham** ~ Scheingebot; **to offer a** ~ ein Gebot abgeben; **to retract a** ~ ein Gebot zurückziehen; **upset** ~ nachträgliches Mehrgebot *(vor Rechtskraft des Zuschlags).*
bid *v* bieten, steigern; ~ **and asked** *exch* Geld und Brief; ~ **in** erstei-

gern; ~ **off** den Zuschlag erhalten; ~ **up** steigern, e–n höheres Gebot legen.

bidder Bietender *m*, Bieter *m*; Bewerber *m*, Submittent *m*; **best** ~ Meistbietender; **bona fide** ~ echtes Submissionsangebot; **last and highest** ~ Letztbietender; **mock** ~ Scheinbieter; **no ~s** keine Kaufinteressenten.

bidding Bieten *n*, Steigern *n*, Mitbieten *n*; Gebot *n* (*bei Auktionen*); ~ **in property for unpaid taxes** Grundstücke in der Zwangsversteigerung wegen Steuerschulden erwerben; ~ **period** Ausschreibungsfrist; ~ **requirements** Ausschreibungsbedingungen; ~ **war** Übernahmekampf; **by-~** Hochtreiben (*der Versteigerung*) durch Scheingebote; **competitive** ~ freie Ausschreibung, Submissionen, Mitbieten; **dumb** ~ Versteigerung mit verdecktem Mindestgebot; **opening the** ~ Wiederaufnahme der Versteigerung; **reserved ~s** beschränkte Versteigerung (*freiwillige Versteigerung vorbehaltlich e–s Mindestgebots bei Mitbietungsrecht des Veräußerers); **upset** ~ höheres Gebot zwecks Wiederaufnahme der Versteigerung.

bid-proof gegen Übernahmeversuche abgesichert.

biennially alle zwei Jahre, im zweijährigen Turnus.

big groß; **B~ Bang** (=) *Börsenliberalisierung London 27. 10. 1986;* **The B~ Board** die New Yorker Börse; **The B~ Four** die 4 (*brit*) Großbanken (*Barclay, Lloyds, Midland, National, Westminister*).

bilateral zweiseitig, gegenseitig.

bill (*1*) Gesetzesvorlage *f*; Gesetzesentwurf *m*; ~ **heading** Titel e–r Vorlage; ~ **in Parliament** Parlamentsvorlage; ~ **of attainder** Parlamentsverurteilung (*zum Tode und zur Einziehung des Vermögens; verboten in US-Verfassung*); ~ **of indemnity** *hist* Gesetz zur Heilung von Formmängeln bei Amtseinsetzung; Entlastungsbeschluß (*für e–n Minister); ~ **of oblivion** Amnestievorlage; ~ **of pains and penalty** *hist* Verurteilung durch Parlamentsbeschluß (*zu geringeren Strafen als zum Tode*); **B~ of Supply** Nachtragshaushaltsvorlage; **appropriations** ~ Finanzvorlage; **companion** ~ Parallelvorlage; **emergency** ~ Notstandsvorlage; **finance** ~ Finanzvorlage; Steuervorlage; **government** ~ Regierungsvorlage; **hybrid** ~ → *hybrid;* **ministerial** ~ Regierungsvorlage, ausgabewirksame Vorlage; **money** ~ Finanzvorlage; **obstruction of ~s** Obstruktionstaktik im Parlament; **parliamentary** ~ Parlamentsvorlage; **personal B~** Privatvorlage (*Status bzw. Vermögen e–r Person*); **private** ~ Privatvorlage, Spezialvorlage, *Gesetzesantrag in privatem Interesse,* Initiativvorlage e–s Abgeordneten; **private ~ office** Parlamentsbüro für Privatvorlagen; **private member's** ~ Initiativantrag *e–s Abgeordneten;* **provisional ~ order** Antrag auf gesetzliche Bestätigung von Ministerbeschlüssen; **public** ~ Gesetzesvorlage (*für ein allgemeines Gesetz*); **public ~ office** Geschäftsstelle für allgemeine Vorlagen; **Scottish** ~ → *Scottish;* **to bring in a** ~ ein Gesetz einbringen; **to pass a** ~ ein Gesetz verabschieden; **trade** ~ Vorlage für ein Außenhandelsgesetz; **unopposed** ~ unstreitige Vorlage, Vorlage ohne Gegenstimmen.

bill (*2*) gerichtlicher Antrag *m*, Klageschrift *f* (*Equity Prozeß*); ~ **chamber** *scot* Gerichtsabteilung für Zwischenverfahren; ~ **for a new trial** Antrag auf Wiederaufnahme des Verfahrens; ~ **in aid of execution** Antrag im Gläubigeranfechtungsverfahren; ~ **in chancery** Antrag vor dem Chancery-Gericht; ~ **in equity** Antrag nach Billigkeitsrecht; **~s in eyre** *hist* Anträge im Verfahren vor dem königl Reiserichter; ~ **in nature of a ~ of review** Wiederaufnahmeantrag e–s Dritten; ~ **in nature of a supple-**

mental ~ Einbeziehung Dritter in ein Gerichtsverfahren; ~ **of certiorari** → *certiorari;* ~ **of complaint** → *complaint;* ~ **of conformity** Antrag auf Nachlaßverwaltung (*zur einheitlichen Gläubigerbefriedigung*); ~ **of cravings** *hist* Aufwendungsersatz für Unterbringung beauftragter Richter; ~ **of discovery** Antrag auf Offenlegung und Urkundenvorlage; ~ **of exceptions** (*zu Protokoll erklärte*) Verfahrenseinreden (*gerichtlich bestätigte Liste vorgebrachter Verfahrensrügen*); ~ **of foreclosure** Vollstreckung aus e–m Pfandrecht, *Antrag auf Pfandverfallserklärung bzw auf Pfandverkaufserlaubnis;* ~ **of grand jury** Entwurf der Anklageschrift *in der gerichtlichen Voruntersuchung durch Grand Jury;* ~ **of indictment** (*der Grand Jury zur Entscheidung vorliegende*) Anklageschrift; ~ **of information** Strafverfolgungsantrag *seitens des Staates;* ~ **of interpleader** Antrag des Gewahrsamsinhabers, Anspruchsteller auf den Prozeßweg zu verweisen; ~ **of particulars** substantiiertes Klagevorbringen, nähere Beschreibung der Straftat in der Anklageschrift; ~ **of peace** Feststellungsklage (*bei bestrittenen Rechtstiteln*); ~ **of privileges** *hist* Verfahren gegen Richter und Anwälte unter Immunität; ~ **of proof** *hist* Interventionsklage; ~ **of review** Antrag auf gerichtliche Überprüfung; Revisionsantrag (*obs;* → *appeal*); ~ **of revivor** Antrag auf Wiederaufnahme e–s (*ruhenden*) Verfahrens; ~ **quia timet** vorbeugende Unterlassungsklage; ~ **to establish a will** Antrag auf Feststellung der Gültigkeit e–s Testaments; ~ **to perpetuate testimony** Beweissicherungsantrag; ~ **to quiet possession and title** Feststellungsklage zur Beseitigung von Zweifeln an Besitz- oder Eigentumsrechten; ~ **to suspend a decree** Aussetzungsantrag; ~ **to take testimony de bene esse** Beweissicherungsantrag; **ancillary** ~ Antrag in e–m Nebenverfahren; **creditor's** ~ → *creditor;* **cross-**~ Widerklage; **supplemental** ~ Klageerweiterungsschriftsatz; **true** ~ Eröffnung des Hauptverfahrens (*Billigung der bill of indictment durch die Grand Jury*).

bill (*3*) (= *bill of exchange*) Wechsel *m* (= *W bzw. . . . w*), Tratte *f*; ~ **after date** Datowechsel; ~**s and notes** *W (jeder Art)*; ~ **at sight** Sichtw.; ~ **book** *W*buch, *W*obligobuch; ~ **broker** *W*makler; ~ **brokerage** *W*courtage; ~ **credit** *W*kredit; ~ **dealer** *W*makler, *W*kreditvermittler; Geldhändler; ~ **debt** *W*schuld; ~ **discounted** diskontierter *W*; ~ **drawn after date** Dato*w*; ~ **drawn on a nonexisting person** Keller*w;* ~ **for collection** *W* zum Einzug; Inkasso*w*; ~ **guarantee** → *guarantee;* ~**s in a set** *W* in mehrfacher Ausfertigung; ~**s in circulation** in Umlauf befindliche *W*; ~ **in distress** notleidender *W*; ~ **in suspense** notleidender *W*; ~ **jobber** *W*reiter, *W*spekulant; ~ **obligatory** gesiegeltes Schuldversprechen; ~ **of acceptance** Akzept, angenommener *W*; ~ **on goods** Waren*w*; ~ **or notes** gezogene *bzw* eigene *W*; Tratten bzw Sola*w*; ~**s payable** geschuldete *W*, *fällige oder künftig zahlbare W*, Akzeptobligo; ~ **payable at sight** Sicht*w*; ~ **payable on demand** Sicht*w*; ~ **rate** Wechseldiskontsatz; ~**s receivable** *W*forderungen, Besitz*w*, ausstehende *W*, Rimessen; ~ **surety** → *surety*; **acceptance** ~ zum Akzept vorzulegender *W*, Tratte; **accommodation** ~ Gefälligkeits*w*; **addressed** ~ Domizil*w*; **after sight** ~ Nachsicht*w*; **advance** ~ → *advance*; **approved** ~ bankfähiger *W*; **backed** ~ avalierter *W*; **bankable** ~ bankfähiger *W*, diskontfähiger *W*; **banker's** ~ Bankakzept; **blank** ~ Blanko*w*; **bogus** ~ Keller*w*; **branch** ~ Zahlstellen*w*; **clean** ~ *W* ohne Dokumentensicherung, reiner *W*; **commercial** ~ Handels*w*; **continental** ~ Festlandsw, W auf Plätze des europ. Kontinents; **date(d)** ~ Datow; **demand** ~ Sichtw; **discount** ~ Diskontw; **dishono(u)red** ~ → *dishono(u)r;* **documentary** ~ Dokumententratte; **domestic** ~ Inlandw (*im gleichen Staat ausgestellter und zahlbarer W*); **domiciled** ~ Domizilw; **domiciliary** ~ Domizilw; **eligible** ~ rediskontfähiger W; **fair** ~ → *fair s;* **fictitious** ~ Kellerw; **finance** ~ Finanzw, Finanzierungsw, Schatzw; **fine** ~ prima W, erstklassiges Akzept; erste Adresse; **fine bank** ~ → *fine;* **fine trade** ~ → *fine;* **first** ~ Primaw; **first class commercial** ~ erstklassiger Warenw; **foreign** ~ Auslandsw (*W dessen Bezogener in e–m anderen Staat ansässig ist als der Aussteller*); **guaranteed** ~ Avalw; **inchoate** ~ unvollständig ausgefüllter W; **indirect** ~ Domizilw; **industrial** ~ Industrieakzept; **inland** ~ Inlandsw (*Aussteller und Bezogener im Inland ansässig*); **investment** ~ Finanzw; **jobbing in** ~**s** W-arbitrage; W-reiterei; **local** ~ Platzw; **long (dated)** ~ langfristiger W; **made** ~ im Ausland zahlbarer Inlandsw; **matured** ~ fälliger W; **mercantile** ~ Warenw; **non-value** ~ Gefälligkeitsw; **order** ~ Orderw; **ordinary** ~ Handelsw; **original** ~ Primaw; **overdue** ~ fällig gewesener W; **past due** ~ verfallener W; *W, der nach Verfallstag noch nicht eingelöst ist;* **payment** ~ **(of exchange)** direkt zur Zahlung vorzulegender W, Solaw; **prime** ~ erstklassiger W; **private** ~ Kundenw; **protest of a** ~ W-protest; **provisional** ~ Sekundaw; **sales** ~ → *sales;* **second** ~ Sekundaw; **secured** ~ durch Dokumente gesicherter W; **short** ~ W mit kurzer Laufzeit; W kurz vor Fälligkeit; **sight** ~ Sichtw; **sola** ~ W in nur einer Ausfertigung; **sold** ~ vor Fälligkeit zur Kreditbeschaffung verkaufter W, diskontierter W; **three month's** ~ Dreimonatsw; **to cash a** ~ e–n W einlösen; **to collect a** ~ e–e W-forderung einziehen; **trade** ~ Warenw, Handelsw, Kundenw (*ohne Bankindossament*); **triplicate** ~ Tertiaw; **undue** ~ noch nicht fälliger W; **unexpired** ~ noch nicht fälliger W.

bill (*4*) Schuldversprechen *n*, Schuldverschreibung *f*, Schuldschein *m*, Kreditbrief *m*, Anweisung *f*; ~ **obligatory** gesiegeltes Schuldversprechen; ~ **of adventure** → *adventure;* ~ **of amortization** Amortisationsschein; ~ **of credit** Kreditbrief, Schatzanweisung; ~ **of debt** Schuldbrief; ~ **of gross adventure** Bodmereibrief; ~ **penal** Schuldurkunde mit Konventionalstrafklausel; ~ **single** gesiegeltes Schuldversprechen; **Exchequer** ~**s** (*verzinsliche*) Schatzanweisungen; **hand** ~ Schuldschein; **treasury** ~**s** Schatzwechsel (*kurzfristige Inhaberschuldverschreibungen des brit Staates*).

bill (*5*) Faktura *f*, Rechnung *f*, Aufstellung *f*, Deklaration *f*; ~ **for services** Kostenrechnung, Honorarrechnung; ~ **head** Rechnungsvordruck; ~ **of costs** Kostenrechnung (*e–s Anwalts*); ~ **of entry** Zolldeklaration, Einfuhrliste; ~ **of materials** Materialaufstellung; ~ **of parcels** Lieferschein mit Rechnung, Faktura, spezifizierte Warenrechnung; Paketliste; ~ **of quantity** Massenberechnung; ~ **of sight** schriftliche Warenaufstellung *des Importeurs gegenüber dem Zollamt; (nach bestem Wissen und Gewissen, ohne Detailkenntnis)*; ~ **of stores** Ausfuhrbestätigung des Zollamts; ~ **of sufferance** *zollamtl Erlaubnis zum zollfreien Warenverkehr zwischen engl Häfen,* Zollpassierschein; Erlaubnis zur zollfreien Rückeinfuhr; ~ **rendered** Rechnung(sstellung); **back** ~**s** unbezahlte Rechnungen; **creditor's** ~ gerichtlich festgestellter Gläubigeranteil; **grand** ~ **of sale** Schiffsverkaufsurkunde; **legal** ~ Anwaltsrechnung; **non-negotiable** ~ Rekta-Eigentumspapier; Frachtbrief; **receipted** ~ quittierte Rechnung; **to make out a** ~ e–e Rechnung ausstellen.

bill *v/t* berechnen, liquidieren, e–e Kostenrechnung an jmdn ausstellen; **~ed** in Rechnung gestellt; **~ed weight** Rechnungsgewicht; **~ one's client for work done** Kosten für anwaltschaftl Dienste berechnen, Leistungen in Rechnung stellen.

bill of admeasurement Meßbrief.

bill of exchange → *bill* (*3*).

bill of health Hafengesundheitsbescheinigung *f*, Quarantäneattest *n*; **clean ~** (*positive*) Hafengesundheitsbescheinigung (*mit Vermerk „ohne Krankheit"*), vorbehaltloses Gesundheitszeugnis; **foul ~** negative Hafengesundheitsbescheinigung (*mit Vermerk „Verdacht auf ansteckende Krankheit"*).

bill of indictment Anklageschrift *f*.

bill of lading Konnossement *n* (= *Kon bzw kon*); Seefrachtbrief *m*; *US auch* Frachtbrief; **claused ~** unreines *Kon*; **clean ~** reines *Kon;* **collective ~** Sammel*kon*; **combined transport ~** kombiniertes Transport*kon* (*Container-See- und Landtransport*); **destination ~** Bestimmungsort-*Kon* (*dort ausgestellt*); **dirty ~** unreines *Kon*; **forwarder's ~** Spediteur*kon*; **foul ~** unreines *Kon*, eingeschränktes *Kon*; **general ~** Sammel*kon*, Sammelfrachturkunde (*als Traditionspapier*); **groupage ~** = *grouped qv*; **grouped ~** Sammel*kon*; **inland waterways ~** Ladeschein; **inward ~** Import*kon*; **liner ~** Linienschiffahrts*kon*; **ocean ~** See*kon*, Seefrachtbrief; **omnibus ~** Sammel*kon*; **on-board ~** Bord*kon*; **order ~** Order*kon*; **outward ~** Export*kon*; **railroad ~** Eisenbahnfrachtbrief; **receipt for shipment ~** Übernahme*kon* (*des Reeders*); **received for shipment ~** Übernahme *Kon;* **river ~** Ladeschein; **shipped ~** Verschiffungs*kon*, Bord*kon*; **spent ~** erloschener Frachtbrief; **straight ~** nicht negoziierbares Namens*kon*, Rekta*kon*, **through ~** durchgehendes *Kon*; Durch*kon*, Transit*kon*, Durchfuhr*kon*; **transshipment ~** Umlade*kon*; **trucking companies ~** Ladeschein von Güterverkehrsunternehmen; **uniform ~** Einheits*kon*.

bill of rights Erklärung über Grundrechte, Grundrechtskatalog; **B~ of Rights** (GB, 1688) = brit. Grundrechtsakte; **bill of sale** besitzlose Übertragungsurkunde (e–r bewegl. Sache); **absolute ~** unbedingte Überweisungsurkunde; **conditional ~** Sicherungsübereignung(surkunde).

billet (*1*) Barren *m* (*auch Edelmetall*).

billet (*2*) Quartierzettel *m*, Quartier *n*; **billeting** Einquartierung *f*.

billing Rechnungsstellung *f*; **~ division** Rechnungsabteilung; **~ machine** Fakturiermaschine.

bimetallism Bimetallismus *m*, Zweimetallsystem *n*.

bind binden, verpflichten; **~ out** in fremde Dienste verpflichten; **~ over** gerichtl zum Erscheinen im Termin bzw zur Einhaltung von Auflagen verpflichten; **~ over on probation** auf Bewährung entlassen, Bewährungsfrist erteilen, Bewährungsauflagen anordnen; **~ such debts in the garnishee's hands** die Beschlagnahme der Forderungen an den Drittschuldner herbeiführen.

binder *ins* Deckungszusage *f*, vorläufige Versicherungspolice *f*, Vorverkaufsvertrag *m*.

binding zwingend, verbindlich; **~ receipt (= ~ slip)** vorläufige Deckungszusage; **~ Tuesday** der zweite Dienstag nach Ostern, halbjährlicher Pachtzahlungstermin.

binding over Einstellung des Verfahrens unter der Auflage ordnungsgemäßen Verhaltens.

biodegradable biologisch abbaufähig.

biosheer Lebenslauf *m*.

Biological Standards Act *GB, 1975:* Gesetz über Normen bei biologischen Substanzen (*zB Impfstoffen*).

bipartite zweiseitig, in zwei Ausfertigungen.

birching Verabreichen von Rutenschlägen.

birth Geburt *f*; ~ **certificate** Geburtsurkunde; ~ **control** Geburtenregelung; ~ **date** Geburtsdatum; ~ **place** Geburtsort; ~ **rate** → *rate;* ~ **record** Geburtenregister; **concealment of** ~ Verheimlichung einer Geburt; **live** ~ Lebendgeburt; **notification of** ~Anzeige e–r Geburt; **proof of** ~ Geburtsnachweis.

bissextile|day Schalttag; ~ **year** Schaltjahr.

black|acre (= *Blackacre aut Whiteacre*) Grundstück B; ~ **cap** schwarze Richterkappe (*bei Todesurteilen*); ~ **list** *s* schwarze Liste, Insolventenliste; *v* jmdn auf die schwarze Liste setzen; jmdn boykottieren; **B~ Maria** „Grüne Minna", Gefangenentransportauto; Münze; **B~ Rod** = *Gentleman Usher of the B~-Rod qv*.

black *v/t* boykottieren.

blackballed durch schwarze Wahlkugeln verworfen; ausgeschlossen.

blacking Boykottieren *n* (*durch Gewerkschaft*); ~ **of goods** Bearbeitungsboykott (*an Waren bestreikter Betriebe*).

blackleg Spieler *m*, Gauner *m*; Streikbrecher *m*.

blackmail *s* Erpressung *f*, finanzielle Erpressung; *hist* Naturalpacht *f*; *v* erpressen; **raw** ~ grobe Erpressung.

blackmailer Erpresser *m*.

blackout (*gezielte*) Sendesperre *f* (*TV, US*).

blame *s* Tadel *m*, Vorwurf *m*, Rüge *f*, Schuld *f*.

blame *v* tadeln, rügen; verantwortlich machen (für).

blank *adj* leer, blanko, unausgefüllt, offen, Blanko . . .; **to accept in** ~ blanko akzeptieren; **to draw in** ~ blanko trassieren; **to sign in** ~ blanko unterschreiben.

blank *s* Vordruck *m*, Formular *n*.

blanket generell, umfassend, pauschal.

blasphemous libel Gotteslästerung *f*.

blasphemy Gotteslästerung *f*.

blazon Wappenschild *n*, Amtsplakette *f*.

blemish verleumden.

blend Mischung *f*; Zusammenstellung *f*, Verschnitt *m*.

blended fund einheitliches Geldvermögen *n* (*nach Versilberung des Nachlasses*).

blight notice Ankündigung e–s (Grundstücks-)Zwangserwerbs.

blind *adj* blind; uneinsichtig; ~ **bargain** Katze im Sack (gekauft); ~ **car** Waggon ohne Plattform; ~ **corner** unübersichtliches Straßenstück, nicht einsehbare Straßenecke; ~ **entry** Blindbuchung; ~ **person** Blinder; ~ **pool** gemeinsames Sondervermögen für Spekulationen, die den Mitgliedern unbekannt bleiben; ~ **selling** Verkauf tel quel (*ohne Untersuchungsmöglichkeit*); ~ **tiger** verbotener Ausschank.

blindcraft Blindenarbeit *f*.

blinker *v* **the jury** die Geschworenen täuschen.

block *s* Block *m*, Paket *n*; Straßenquadrat *n*; ~ **capitals** (große) Blockbuchstaben; ~ **grant** pauschale Ausgleichszuweisung an Gemeinden; ~ **of shares** → *share;* ~ **of surveys** Sammelvermessung; ~ **proof** Massenprüfung nach Rubriken von Zahlungsmitteln; ~ **tariff** → *tariff;* ~ **to** ~ **rule** Festsetzung von Erschließungskosten nach Abrechnungsverbänden; **currency** ~ Währungsblock.

block *v* blockieren, sperren; ~ **an account** ein Konto sperren; ~**ing note** Sperrvermerk; ~**ing of bills** Einspruch gegen die Behandlung als nichtstreitige Vorlage; ~**ing of property** Vermögenssperre.

blockade Blockade *f* (= *Bl bzw . . . bl*); **commercial** ~ Handelsblokkade; **economic** ~ Wirtschafts*bl;* **pacific** ~ *Bl* im Frieden; **paper** ~ nicht erzwingbare *Bl*; **public** ~ offizielle *Bl*; **simple** ~ lokalisierte (de facto) *Bl*.

blockage *Wertminderung für schwer veräußerliche große Aktienpakete.*

blood Blut *s n*; *adj* blutsverwandt; ~ **feud** → *feud;* ~ **group evidence** Blutgruppengutachten (*Vaterschaft*); ~ **grouping test** Blutgruppenuntersuchung; ~ **guilt** Blutschuld; ~ **money** Wergeld, Blutgeld, Kopfgeld für die Tötung oder Ergreifung e–s Verfolgten; Mordlohn; ~ **relationship** Blutsverwandtschaft; ~ **stain** Blutfleck, Blutspur; ~ **test** Blutprobe, Blutgruppenuntersuchung; ~ **typing** Blutgruppeneinteilung; **full~** Vollblut, von gleichen Eltern abstammend; **half** ~ → *half;* **(of) mixed** ~ gemischter Abstammung; **(of) whole** ~ von den gleichen Eltern abstammend, vollbürtig.

bloodhound Bluthund *m*, Spürhund *m*, Schweißhund *m*; ~ **evidence** Aussagen über die Spurenaufnahme durch Spürhunde.

blot Fleck *m*, Makel *m*, Streichung *f*, Rasur *f* (*bei Geschriebenem*); ~ **of title** Rechtsmangel (*Grundstückskauf*); **legal** ~ Rechtsmangel.

blotter Löschblatt *n*, Schmierbuch *n*; Kladde *f* (*für Börsengeschäfte*); **cash** ~ Börsenhändlerjournal, Kassenjournal; **police** ~ Protokollbuch.

blow *v/t* **in the bag** „ins Röhrchen blasen".

bludgeon *s* Knüppel *m*; *v* niederknüppeln, nötigen.

blue blau; puritanisch; ~ **book** Blaubuch, amtliche Denkschrift, Dokumentensammlung; ~ **button** Bediensteter an der Londoner Börse; ~ **chips** Spitzenpapiere, Standardwerte; ~ **collar worker** Handarbeiter; ~ **laws** Gesetze gegen die Entheiligung des Sonntags; ~ **notes** Schuldurkunden gesichert durch Beleihung von Deckungsstock (*zur Aufrechterhaltung von Versicherungen*); ~ **pencil test** Teilnichtigkeitstest; *(Ausstreichen von Teilen möglich, ohne Sinn und Zweck zu beeinträchtigen);* ~**print** Lichtpause, Plan, Entwurf; ~ **ribbon jury** Sondergeschworenenbank (*für schwierige Fälle mit bes qualifizierten Personen*); ~ **sky laws** *US*: *Gesetze gegen Mißbrauch im Wertpapierhandel.*

board (*1*) Behörde *f*, **B~** Zentralbehörde *f*, Verwaltungsbehörde *f*, Gremium *n*, Rat *m*, Vorstand *m*, Direktorium *n*; Ausschuß *m*; ~ **meeting** Vorstandssitzung; Verwaltungsratssitzung; ~ **of adjustment** Bauleitplan-Spruchstelle; ~ **of administration** Kuratorium, Verwaltungsrat; ~ **of aldermen** Stadtrat; ~ **of appeals** Widerspruchsstelle; ~ **of audit** Rechnungshof; ~ **of awards** Spruchstelle (*bei Ansprüchen gegen Fiskus*); ~ **of civil authority** Ortsbehörde; ~ **of complaint** Beschwerdeausschuß; ~ **of control** Aufsichtsbehörde, Aufsichtsamt, Aufsichtsrat; **B~ of Customs and Excise** = *GB*: oberste Zoll- und Verbrauchsteuerverwaltung; ~ **of directors** → *director*; **B~ of Education** → *education;* ~ **of equalization** Behörde zur Vereinheitlichung örtlicher Steuersätze; ~ **of examiners** Prüfungsausschuß, Prüfungskommission; **B~ of Immigration Appeals** Einwanderungsbeschwerdestelle; ~ **of fire underwriters** Feuerversicherungsamt; Vorstand der Feuerversicherungsanstalten; ~ **of governors** Direktorium, Gouverneursrat, Verwaltungsrat; **B~ of Green Cloth** königlicher Haushaltsrat; *hist* Palastpolizeiamt; ~ **of guardians** Vormundschaftsrat, Fürsorgeausschuß; **B~ of Health** → *health;* **B~ of Inland Revenue** *GB* Oberste Finanzbehörde; ~ **of inquiry** → *inquiry;* ~ **of managers** Direktorium; ~ **of pardon(s)** → *pardon;* **B~ of Patents Appeal** Beschwerdesenat in Patentsachen; ~ **of referees** Schiedsstelle; ~ **of review** Beschwerdeausschuß in Bewertungssachen; ~ **of special inquiry** Sonderuntersuchungsausschuß (*zB für Einwanderer*); ~ **of supervisors** Aufsichtsamt, Rechnungsprüfungsamt; **B~ of Tax Appeals** Rechtsmittelinstanz in Steuersachen; **B~ of Trade** *US*:

Handelskammer; *GB früher*: Handelsministerium; → *Department of Trade;* ~ **of trustees** Kuratorium; Treuhänderausschuß; **B~ of Visitors** Gefängnisaufsichtsbehörde; ~ **of works** Gemeindebüro; Kommunalbehörde für öffentl Anlagen und Arbeiten; ~ **room** Vorstandszimmer, *pl* Chefetage; **administrative** ~ Verwaltungsrat; **advisory** ~ Beratungsstelle, Beirat; **arbitration** ~ → *arbitration;* **executive** ~ Vorstand; **member of the** ~ → *member;* **parole** ~ Gnadeninstanz, Gnadenausschuß.

board (*2*) Kost *f*, Logis *n*, Pension *f*; ~ **and lodging** Unterkunft und Verpflegung, Vollpension.

boarder Pensionsgast *m*, Zimmerherr *m*.

boarding|-clerk *brit* Hafenzollbeamter; ~ **officer** Prisenoffizier; ~ **and search** Überholung und Nachschau (*Luftfahrzeuge, Schiffe*).

boarding school Internat *n*.

bodily körperlich, physisch; ~ **fear** Furcht vor körperlicher Gewaltanwendung; ~ **feelings** körperliche Empfindungen; ~ **harm** Körperverletzung; ~ **heirs** → *heir;* ~ **injury** Körperverletzung, Körperbeschädigung; **actual** ~ **harm** (*vollendete*) Körperverletzung; **great** ~ **harm** schwere Körperverletzung; **great** ~ **injury** schwere Körperverletzung; **grievous** ~ **harm** → *grievous*.

body Körper *m*, Leib *m*, Person *f*; Leiche *f*; Gremium *n*, Körperschaft *f*; Inbegriff *m*, Gegenstand *m*; ~ **corporate** Körperschaft, juristische Person; ~ **execution** Zwangsvollstreckung gegen die Person des Schuldners; Taschenpfändung; **(the)** ~ **of a county** der Bezirk als Ganzes; **(the)** ~ **of an instrument** der Hauptteil der Urkunde (*ohne Eingangs- und Schlußformulierung*); ~ **of laws** Gesetzessammlung, Gesetzgebungswerk, Kodifizierung; ~ **of persons** Personengemeinschaft; ~ **of the offence** begangene Straftat, Tatbestand; ~ **politic** öffentl-rechtl Körperschaft, Gebietskörperschaft, Staat; ~ **responsible** (die) verantwortliche Stelle; ~ **search** → *search*; **administrative** ~ Behörde, Verwaltungsbehörde; **advisory** ~ beratendes Gremium; **constituent** ~ Gründungsgremium; **dead** ~ Leiche; **electoral** ~ Wahlgremium; **employer-led** ~ Gremium unter Leitung von Unternehmern; **executive** ~ ausführendes Organ; **legislative** ~ gesetzgebende Körperschaft; **public** ~ Behörde, amtliches Gremium, Anstalt *bzw* Körperschaft des öffentlichen Rechts; öffentl Rechtsträger, gemeinnützige Körperschaft; **self-elected** ~ sich selbst (*durch Kooption*) regenerierende Körperschaft; autonome Körperschaft; **representative** ~ Vertretungsorgan; **unincorporated** ~ nicht rechtsfähiger Verein.

bogus falsch, unecht, Schwindel ...; ~ **firm** Schwindelfirma; ~ **refugees** Scheinflüchtlinge, Scheinasylanten; ~ **signature** Gefälligkeitsunterschrift; ~ **transactions** Scheingeschäfte, Schwindelgeschäfte.

boilerplate *sl* Anwaltschinesisch *n*, umständliche Juristensprache *f*.

boiler-room transaction *dubioser Aktienverkauf per Telefon.*

bolter abtrünniger Wähler.

bolting private Rechtsgeschäfte in den Inns of Court; sich seinen Gläubigern durch Flucht entziehen.

bomb Bombe *f*; **gasoline~** Benzinbombe, Molotowcocktail; **petrol~** = *gasoline qv;* ~ **hoax** Bombenschabernack, falscher Bombenalarm.

bona Vermögensgegenstände *m|pl;* ~ **confiscata** eingezogenes Vermögen; ~ **mobilia** bewegliche Sachen; ~ **vacantia** herrenloses Gut, erbenloser Nachlaß.

bona fide bona fide, wirklich, echt, im guten Glauben, redlich, ohne Mißbrauchsabsicht; ~ **creditor** gutgläubiger Forderungsinhaber; ~ **error** unbeabsichtigter Fehler; ~

holder for value Inhaber eines (*gutgläubig erworbenen*) Wertpapiers; der wechselmäßig berechtigte Inhaber; ~ **let** wirklich vermietet; ~ **offer** solides Angebot; ~ **owner** → *owner;* ~ **possessor** gutgläubiger Besitzer; ~ **purchaser** → *purchaser;* ~ **residence** Wohnsitz; ~ **transaction** wirklich gewolltes (echtes) Rechtsgeschäft; ~ **traveller** redlicher Handelsreisender; ~ **use** gutgläubige Benutzung; **business** ~ **conducted by himself** wirklich von ihm selbst geführtes Geschäft.

bonanza besonders großer Goldfund *m*; unerwartet großer Gewinn *m*.

bond (*1*) gesiegeltes Schuldversprechen *n*; Schuldverschreibung *f* (= *Sch bzw ...sch, pl: Sch-n*) Teilschuldverschreibung *f*, Obligation *f* (= *Obl bzw obl; pl: Obl-n*), festverzinsliches Papier; ~ **and disposition in security** Schuldverpflichtung mit Hypothek; ~ **and mortgage** Pfandbrief; ~ **anticipation note** Zwischenschein (*bei öffentl Anleihen*); ~ **authorization** Ermächtigung zur Emission von *Sch-n;* ~ **creditor** Schuldscheingläubiger, Pfandbriefgläubiger; ~ **discount** → *discount;* ~ **for deed** (*obligatorischer*) Kaufvertrag auf Raten (*Grundstück*); ~ **for title** (Grundstücks)Kaufvertrag; ~ **funds** → *fund;* ~**-holder** Obligationär; ~**s outstanding** begebene (*noch nicht zurückgezahlte*) *Obl-n;* ~**s payable** fällige *Sch-n;* ~ **premium** Agio bei (*der Emission von*) *Sch-n;* ~ **rating** Qualitätsgruppierung von festverzinslichen Papieren; ~ **redemption** Rückzahlung e-r verbrieften Schuld, Tilgung v. *Sch;* ~ **retirement** Kündigung von *Obl-n durch den Schuldner;* ~**s to bearer** *Sch-n* auf den Inhaber; ~ **warrant** → *warrant;* ~ **washing** (=) *Steuerumgehung durch Verkauf von Obl-n mit Anspruch auf nächste Zinsfälligkeit und sofortigen Rückkauf ohne diesen Zinsanspruch;* **adjustment** ~**s** → *adjustment;* **agricultural** ~ Agrar-Immobilienzertifikat; **annuity** ~ Rentenanleihe (*Anleihe ohne festen Rückzahlungstermin*); Rentenversicherungssparbrief; **assented** ~**s** → *assented;* **assumed** ~**s** (*von der fusionierenden Gesellschaft*) übernommene *Obl-n*; *auch: durch Bürgschaft e-r anderen Gesellschaft gesicherte Obligation;* **baby** ~**s** Klein*obl-n;* **balanced** ~ Zertifikat e-s gemischten Versicherungsfonds; **bearer** ~ Inhaber*sch* mit Zinskupon; **bonus** ~**s** Kommunalanleihepapiere zur Finanzierung von Zuschüssen (*Bahnbau, Verkehrsanlagen*); **bottomry** ~ → *bottomry;* **bridge** ~**s** Brückenbauanleihepapiere; **bullet** ~**s** *Obl mit Endfälligkeit ohne laufende Tilgung; zwischentilgungsfreie Anleihepapiere;* **callable** ~ (*vom Schuldner*) kündbare *Obl-n*; **car trust** ~**s** durch das rollende Material gesicherte Bahnanleihepapiere; **charter** ~**s** *Obl-n* für Staatsanleihen (*als Kaution für Konzessionierung von Banken*); **clean** ~ ungirierte *Obl* mit Kuponschein, *US:* Inhaber*obl;* **collateral mortgage** ~**s** Pfandbriefe; **collateral (trust)** ~**s** gesicherte *Obl-n* (*durch treuhänderische Effektenhinterlegung*); **consolidated first mortgage** ~**s** durch erststellige Generalhypothek gesicherte *Obl-n*; **consolidated mortgage** ~**s** durch Generalverpfändung (*mehrerer Unternehmen*) gesicherte *Obl-n;* **continued** ~ Dauer*sch* (*mit gleichbleibender Verzinsung und verlängerter Laufzeit*); **convertible** ~**s** Wandel*sch*, Wandelanleihen; **corporate** ~**s** Industrie*obl-n*, *Sch-n* von Kapitalgesellschaften; **coupon** ~**s** *Sch-n* mit Zinscoupon; **currency** ~**s** Fremdwährungs*obl-n;* **debenture** ~ → *debenture;* **defaulted** ~**s** nicht mehr bediente *Obl-n;* **defence** ~**s** → *defence;* **deferred** ~**s** *Obl-n* mit aufgeschobenem Verzinsungbeginn; **definitive** ~ (*die endgültige*) Anleiheurkunde; **dividend** ~**s** Gewinn*sch-n mit verbriefter Dividendenbeteiligung an Sammelvermögen;* **double** ~ *scot* Schuldurkunde mit Strafklausel; **drawn** ~ ausgeloste, fällige *Obl;* **eligible** ~ mündelsichere *Sch;* **endorsed** → *festverzinsliches Papier mit Sonderbedingungen; garantierte Obligation;* **equal instalment** ~s Tilgungsanleihen; **equipment** **~s** Ausrüstungsobligationen (*durch Schiffe bzw rollendes Material gesichert*); **exchequer** **~s** *brit* langfristige Schatzanweisungen, **extended** **~s** *Obl–n* mit verlängerter Laufzeit; **external** **~s** Auslands*sch–n;* **farm mortgage** **~s** Agrarpfandbriefe; **federal** **~s** Bundesanleihen (*US*); **fiduciary** ~ Kaution; **first mortgage** **~s** erststellig gesicherte Pfandbriefe; **first lien collateral trust** **~s** erstrangig gesicherte Obligationen; **flat** ~ *Obl, in deren Preis aufgelaufene Zinsen berücksichtigt sind;* **founders'** **~s** Gründerobligationen, Schuldverschreibungen als Gegenleistung für Sacheinlagen; **friendly society** ~ Sparbrief e–s Kleinversicherungsvereins; **general mortgage** ~ Pfandbrief (*durch Generalhypothek gesicherte Schuldverschreibung*); **gold** **~s** → *gold;* **government** **~s** → *government;* **guaranteed** ~ garantierte Obligation; **guaranteed property** ~ Immobilienversicherungsfonds-Zertifikat (*mit garantiertem Mindestrückkaufkurs*); **heritable** ~ *scot* durch Grundpfandrechte gesicherte Schuldurkunde; **improved mortgage** ~ hypothekarisch gesicherte Schuldverschreibung für werterhöhende Investitionen; **improved property** **~s** an bebautem Grundstück dinglich gesicherte *Sch–n*; **income** ~ Gewinn*sch–n*; **indeterminate** **~s** *Obl–n* mit unbestimmter Laufzeit; **indexed-income** **~s** indexierte Gewinn*sch–n;* **industrial** **~s** Industri*obl–n;* **industrial development** **~s** Kommunalanleihen für Industrieansiedlungen; **interchangeable** **~s** → *interchangeable;* **interest** ~ *Sch* zur Abgeltung e–r Zinsschuld; **interest-bearing** **~s** festverzinsliche *Obl–n;* **interim** ~ kurzfristige Überbrükkungsanleihe; **investment** **~s** Anlagepapiere; **irredeemable** **~s** unkündbare (*nicht zurückzahlbare*) *Obl–n;* **irrigation** **~s** Anleihen für Bewässerungsprojekte; **joint** **~s** von mehreren Gesellschaften ausgegebene *Obl–n;* **junior** **~s** *Obl–n,* die durch e–e nachrangige Hypothek abgesichert sind; **junior lien** **~s** nachrangig gesicherte *Sch–n;* **land development** **~s** Landentwicklungsanleihepapiere; **land grant** **~s** Landschenkungs*obl–n* (*Eisenbahnbau*); **large** **~s** *Obl–n* in großer Stückelung; **legal** **~s** mündelsichere *Sch–n;* **liberty** **~s** Kriegsanleihen; **Lloyd's** ~ (=) *verzinsl Sch für erbrachte Leistungen;* **local** **~s** Kommunal*sch–n;* **long** ~ langfristige *Obl,* Langläufer; **long-term** **~s** *Obl–n mit langer Laufzeit;* **mortgage bank** ~ Pfandbrief; hypothekarisch gesicherte Schuldverschreibung; **mortgage** ~ Pfandbrief; **municipal** **~s** Kommunalanleihepapiere; **naked** ~ einseitige, ungesicherte Verpflichtung; **negotiable** ~ Order*sch*; **non-assented** **~s** *Obl–n* ohne Zustimmung zu e–m Sanierungsplan; **non-callable** **~s** nicht vorzeitig kündbare *Sch–n;* **optional** **~s** kündbare Anleihepapiere; **order** **~s** Orderschuldverschreibungen; **outstanding** **~s** noch nicht eingelöste *Obl–n;* **overlying** ~ vorrangig gesicherte *Sch;* **partial** ~ Teil*sch;* **participating** **~s** Investment*obl–n, Sch–n* mit Gewinnbeteiligung; **passive** ~ zinslose *Sch;* **plain** ~ ungesicherter Schuldschein; **preference income** ~ ertragsbedingte Vorzugs*obl;* **premium** **~s** Prämienanleihe, Losanleihe; **prior lien** ~ vorrangig gesicherte *Sch;* **prize** **~s** Auslosungsanleihe; **profit-sharing** **~s** Gewinnbeteiligungs*obl–n* (*Gewinn aus Sondervermögen*); **property** ~ Immobilienfonds-Zertifikat; **public** **~s** öffentliche Anleihepapiere; *Obl–n* der öffentl Hand; **public utility** **~s** *Obl–n* der öffentlichen Versorgungsbetriebe; **purchase**

money ~ Restkaufgeld-Schuldschein; **purchased line ~s** *Obl–n* zur Finanzierung des Erwerbs von Bahnlinien; **rail ~s** Eisenbahn*obl–n* (= *railroad ~s, railway ~s*); **real estate ~s** Pfandbriefe, *Obl–n* von Immobilientrusts; **redeemable ~s** *vorzeitig* kündbare *Obl–n*, Tilgungsanleihe(papiere), rückzahlbare *Obl–n;* **redemption ~s** → *redemption;* **refunding ~s** → *refunding;* **registered** ~ Namens-*Obl;* **registered coupon** ~ *US* Namens*sch* mit Inhaberzinscoupons; **respondentia** ~ Bodmereibrief mit Globalverpfändung (*von Schiff und Ladung*); **revenue ~s** Anleihen auf zukünftige Steuereinnahmen; Industrie*obl–n* auf Ertragsgrundlage; **savings ~s** → *savings;* **second mortgage** ~ durch zweite Hypothek gesicherte *Sch;* **secured ~s** dinglich gesicherte Anleihepapiere; **senior ~s** Vorzugs*obl–n;* **senior lien ~s** erstrangig gesicherte *Sch–n;* **serial ~s** Tilgungsanleihen, Serienanleihen; **series ~s** Serienanleihen; **sewer ~s** Kommunalanleihen zur Finanzierung der Kanalisation; **short-term ~s** *Obl–n* mit kurzer Laufzeit; **simple** ~ ungesicherte *Sch*, Schuldurkunde, Schuldschein; **single** ~ (*unqualifizierte*) gesiegelte Schuldurkunde, ungesicherte *Sch;* **sinking fund** ~ → *sinking fund;* **special** ~ Sonder*sch;* **special assessment** ~ Erschließungskostensch, Umlageverpflichtung; **stamped** ~ *US* Anleihepapiere mit (*auf die Urkunde gestempelten*) Sonderbedingungen; **tax-free ~s** steuerfreie *Obl–n;* **term ~s** gleichzeitig fällige *Obl–n;* **to float a** ~ e–e *Sch* auf den Markt bringen, e–e *Sch* begeben; **underlying ~s** vorrangige Pfandbriefe, bevorrechtigte *Obl–n;* **unified ~s** → *unified;* **unifying** ~ gesamtschuldnerische *Obl; Obl mit Gesamtverpfändung und gesamtschuldnerischer Haftung mehrerer Unternehmer;* **unredeemable ~s** unkündbare *Obl–n;* **war** ~ Kriegsanleihe(papier); **water ~s** *Obl–n* kommunaler Wasserwerke.

bond (*2*) Kaution *f*, Sicherheitsleistung *f*; ~ **for surrender of premises in good condition** Mieterkaution; ~ **for title** Kautionsstellung zur Sicherung des Eigentumsübergangs, Kaufvorvertrag (*Grundstück*), Eigentumsverschaffungsvertrag; ~ **hearing** Anhörung wegen Kautionsstellung; ~ **paper** Zollbegleitpapier; ~ **tenants** Hintersassen; ~ **to perform lease** Pächterkaution; **administration** ~ Sicherheitsleistung durch Testamentsvollstrecker (*bzw. Nachlaßverwalter*); **administrative** ~ = **administrator** ~ = *administration ~ qv*; **appeal** ~ → *appeal*; **average** ~ Havarieschein; **back** ~ Rückbürgschaft; **bail** ~ Haftkaution, Kautionsurkunde; **bid** ~ Bietungsgarantie, Submissionsgarantie; **blank** ~ → *blank;* **blanket ~s** pauschale Kautionsversicherung; **blanket position** ~ *US* Globalversicherungsschein gegen Veruntreuungsschäden; **claim** ~ Prozeßsicherheit; **completion** ~ Fertigstellungsgarantie; **construction** ~ Bauunternehmer-Kaution; **contract** ~ Werkunternehmerkaution; **contractor's** ~ Submissionsgarantie, Sicherheitsleistung des Bau(Werk)-unternehmers; **court** ~ Sicherheitsleistung bei Gericht; **dissolving** ~Sicherheitsleistung zur Lösung e–s Arrests *bzw* zur Pfandfreigabe; **fidelity** ~ Kaution für Veruntreuungsfälle; **financial** ~ Kaution; **forth-coming** ~ Sicherheitsleistung des Vollstreckungsschuldners (*damit Schuldner die Pfandsache vorläufig behalten kann*); **general average** ~ Havariebond; **guaranty** ~ Werkunternehmerkaution, Bietergarantie; Garantieschein; **indemnity** ~ Schadloshaltungsverpflichtung; Werkvertragserfüllungsgarantie; Ausfallbürgschaft; **insurance** ~ Garantieversicherung, Kautionsversicherung; **judgment** ~ → *judgment;* **judicial** ~ → *judicial;* **liability** ~ Sicherheitsleistung gegen Haftpflicht; **license** ~ Konzessionssicherheitsleistung; **master** ~ Unternehmergarantieschein; **name** ~ Veruntreuungskaution für namentlich benannte Personen; **official** ~ Kaution für Inhaber e–s öffentlichen Amtes; **payment** ~ Bietungsgarantie; **peace** ~ Kautionsstellung gegen Störung der öffentlichen Ordnung; **penal** ~ Verfalls-Sicherheit (*als Sanktion bei Vertragsverletzung*); **performance** ~ Erfüllungsgarantie, Sicherheitsleistung des Submittenten, Submissionsgarantie; **position** ~ → *position*; **redelivery** ~ Sicherheitsleistung für den Fall der Wiederherausgabepflicht; **removal** ~ Sicherheitsleistung bei Herausnahme unverzollter Güter aus dem Zoll-Lager; **salvage** ~ Kaution für Bergelohn, Bergungsvertrag; **security** ~ Kautionsurkunde (*Arbeitsverhältnis*); **straw** ~ fiktive Kautionsverpflichtung; **submission** ~ Sicherheitsleistung für Schiedsgerichtsverfahren und -urteil; **supersedeas** ~ Sicherheit des Rechtsbehelfsführers; **surety** ~ Vertrauensschadenkaution *für Haftung aus dem Arbeitsverhältnis*; Erfüllungsgarantie; **suretyship** ~ Bürgschaftsurkunde, Garantie, Verpflichtungsurkunde; **to furnish a** ~ e–e Kaution stellen; **to post a** ~ Sicherheit leisten (*zur Abwendung der Vollstreckung*).

bond *v* Sicherheit leisten, Kaution stellen; ~**ed goods** → *goods*; ~**ed warehouse** → *warehouse*.

bondholder Obligationär *m*.

bondsman Bürge *m*, gewerblicher Kautionssteller *m*.

bond-tenant Pächter *m* von Lehensland.

bonification Prämiengewährung *f*, Steuererlaß *m* zur Exportfinanzierung.

bonus Bonus *m*, Prämie *f*, Gratifikation *f*; ~ **certificate** Gewinnbeteiligungsbescheinigung (*Versicherung*); ~ **for completion before the time specified** Prämie für vorzeitige Fertigstellung; ~ **in cash** *ins* ausgezahlter Gewinnanteil; ~**-issue** Ausgabe von Gratisaktien; ~ **loading** Prämienzuschlag bei Policen mit Gewinnbeteiligung; ~**-penalty-contract** Werkvertrag mit Prämie (*für vorzeitige Fertigstellung*) und Vertragsstrafe (*für verspätete Fertigstellung*); ~ **share** Gratisaktie; ~ **stock** US: Aktien als Gratifikation; **capital** ~ Gratisaktien; **Christmas** ~ Weihnachtsgratifikation; **cost-of-living** ~ Teuerungszulage; **ex** ~ ohne Prämie; Kurs ohne Gratisaktienbezugsrecht; **hazard** ~ Risikoprämie, Gefahrenzulage; **local** ~ Ortszulage; **loyalty** ~ Treueprämie; **no claim** ~ Schadensfreiheitsrabatt; **non-production** ~ Prämie für Produktionsstillegung; **reversionary** ~ Summenzuwachs, Gewinngutschrift durch Erhöhung der Versicherungssumme; **sales related** ~ umsatzabhängige Prämie; **special** ~ Sonderzulage; **starting** ~ Einstellungsprämie; **uni-**~ Uni-Kurs mit Gratisaktienbezugsrecht.

boodle Bestechungsgeld *n*.

boodling Parlamentskorruption *f*.

book *s* Buch *n*; ~ **account** Kontokorrent; ~**s actually made up** tatsächlich erfolgter Buchabschluß; ~ **cost** Buchwert; ~ **debt** *in der Buchhaltung ausgewiesene* Forderung ~ **debts** Außenstände aus Warenlieferungen; ~ **loss** buchmäßiger Verlust; ~**s of account** Geschäftsbücher; ~ **of acts** Gerichtsakten (*Surrogate Court*); ~ **of adjournal** *scot* Strafakten; **B**~ **of Assize** *hist* (*liber assisarum*) *Entscheidungssammlung 1517*; **B**~ **of Common Prayer** (=) *Gottesdienstordnung der engl Hochkirche;* **B**~ **of Council and Session** *scot* Urkundenregister; **B**~**s of Feuds** *das Lehensbuch* (1152) *unter Kaiser Heinrich III;* ~ **of original entries** Tagebuch, Journal; ~ **of rates** Zolltarif; ~ **of remittances** Überweisungsbuch; **B**~ **of the Council** *hist Sammlung von Kronratsprotokollen 1421–1435*; ~**s open** Öffnung der Effektentransferbücher e–r Gesellschaft; ~

or other debts Außenstände und sonstige Forderungen; ~ **profit** Buchgewinn; ~ **rights** Buchveröffentlichungsrecht; ~ **sizes** die üblichen Buchformate; ~ **value** → *bookvalue*; **charge on ~ debts** Verpfändung der Außenstände; **minute** ~ → *minute;* **office** ~ → *office;* **petty** ~ kleines Kassabuch; **public** ~ öffentl Buch, öffentl Register; **poll** ~ Wahlliste; **statute** ~ →*statute;* **statutory ~s** gesetzl vorgeschriebene Bücher und Verzeichnisse e–r Kapitalgesellschaft (*Aktienbuch, Vorstands- bzw Verwaltungsratsmitglieder, Beteiligungen an stimmberechtigtem Kapital, Dienstverträge d. Verwalt.ratsmitgl*); **The B~s** *die Gesamtheit der englischen Entscheidungssammlungen.*

book *v* buchen, aufschreiben (*Polizei*), notieren, vormerken, vorbestellen, anmelden, *Grundbesitz* urkundlich übertragen; ~ **the prisoner for theft** den wegen Diebstahls Festgenommenen ins Polizeitagebuch aufnehmen; **~ed** gebucht, zum Abschluß verpflichtet; **to throw the ~ at s.o.** geg jmdn Anklage erheben.

booking Buchung *f*, Eintragung *f*, *scot* Pachtbesitz *m* kraft Registereintragung; ~ **contract** Agenturvertrag (*Künstler*).

bookkeeper's trial balance Kontenverprobung *f* der Buchhaltung, Probebilanz *f* der Buchhaltung.

bookkeeping (= *book-keeping*) Buchhaltung *f*, Buchführung *f*; ~ **by single entry** einfache Buchführung; ~ **department** Buchhaltung; ~ **entry** Buchungsposten, Buchung; ~ **voucher** Buchhaltungsbeleg; **double entry** ~ doppelte Buchführung; **duplicating ~ system** Durchschreibebuchführung; **electronic** ~ elektronische Maschinenbuchhaltung; **mechanical** ~ Maschinenbuchführung; **punched-card** ~ Lochkartenbuchführung.

bookmaker Buchmacher *m*, Wettvermittler *m*.

bookmaking Buchmacherei *f*, Wettannahme(stelle) *f*.

book value Buchwert *m*, Restbuchwert *m*, Nettobuchwert *m*; fortgeführter Anschaffungswert *m*; **net** ~ Restbuchwert; **remaining** ~ Restbuchwert; **year-end** ~ Restbuchwert.

boom Boom *m*, Hochkonjunktur *f*, Hausse *f*, wirtschaftlicher Aufschwung *m*, Reklamerummel *m*; ~ **in stocks** Aktienhausse; ~ **market** Haussemarkt; ~ **profit** Konjunkturgewinn; **cyclical** ~ Hochkonjunktur; **specious** ~ Scheinkonjunktur.

boost *s* Steigerung *f*, Werterhöhung *f*, Förderung *f*, Unterstützung *f*.

boosting Preistreiberei *f*, künstliches Hochtreiben *n* von Kursen.

bootleg wages außertarifliche Löhne *m|pl*.

bootlegger Alkoholschmuggler *m*.

bootlegging illegaler Handel *m* mit alkoholischen Getränken.

bootstrap *adj* aus eigenen Mitteln, intern finanziert.

border *s* Grenze *f*; ~ **control** Grenzkontrolle; ~ **crossing point** Grenzübergang; **~-line** Grenzlinie; **~line case** Grenzfall; ~ **post** Grenzstelle; ~ **search** Durchsuchung im Grenzgebiet; ~ **warrant** Durchsuchungsermächtigung in Grenzbezirken.

border *v* (an)grenzen; **~ing** angrenzend; **~ing state** Anliegerstaat, Randstaat.

bordereau Bordereau *m oder n*, Verzeichnis *n*, Resümee *n* der Geschäftsbeschreibung.

born geboren, *im Mutterleib lebensfähig entstanden*; ~ **alive** lebend geboren; ~ **out of wedlock** nichtehelich geboren; **to be** ~ künftig geboren.

borough Stadt *f*, (Stadt)Gemeinde *f*, Stadtbezirk *m*; ~ **council** Stadtrat; ~ **court** Stadtgericht (*bis 1973*); **B~ English** *hist* Vererbung auf den jüngsten Sohn; ~ **fund** Gemeindevermögen, Gemeindekasse; **B~ Funds Acts** Gesetze über die

Verwendung von Gemeindegeldern *u.a. für politische Zwecke;* ~ **head** *hist* Vorstand der Zehntschaft, Gemeindepolizist, Schulze; ~ **holder** *hist* Lehensbesitzer von städtischem Land; ~ **rate** Gemeindesteuer; ~**-reeve** *hist* Bürgermeister (*von Kleinstädten*), Schulze; ~ **session** Stadtgericht; **county** ~ → *county*; **municipal** ~ Stadtgemeinde; **parliamentary** ~ Parlamentswahlkreis; **pocket** ~ *hist* von e–m Grundherrn beherrschter Wahlkreis; **rotten** ~**s** *hist (=) überrepräsentierte, gering besiedelte Wahlkreise;* **royal** ~ durch königlichen Freibrief privilegierte Stadt; **rural** ~ ländlicher Bezirk.

borrow *v* ausleihen, entleihen, ein Darlehen aufnehmen; ~ **money flat** zinslosen Kredit erhalten; ~ **on a policy** e–e Police beleihen; ~ **on securities** Effekten lombardieren.

borrower Entleiher *m*, Darlehensnehmer *m*, Kreditnehmer *m*, Schuldner *m*; ~**'s note** → *note;* **joint** ~**s** Konsortialkreditnehmer; **sovereign** ~**s** Staaten als Kreditnehmer, Schuldnerländer; **would-be** ~ Kreditsuchender.

borrowing Leihe *f*; Entleihen *n*, Kreditaufnahme *f*; ~**s** *aufgenommene* Schulden, Darlehensschulden; ~ **arrangements** Kreditvereinbarungen; ~ **by false pretences** Kreditbetrug; ~ **control** staatliche Kontrolle von Emissionen; ~ **demand** Kreditbedarf; ~ **powers** → *power*; ~ **reserve** Kreditreserve; **inter-fund** ~ → *interfund*; **legal debt margin of** ~ gesetzliche Verschuldungsgrenze; **long-term** ~ langfristige Kreditaufnahme; **short-term** kurzfristige Geldaufnahme.

Borstal institution Jugendstrafanstalt *f*; ~ **training** Jugendstrafvollzug.

booth Verkaufsbude *f*, Fernsprechzelle *f*, Wahlzelle *f*.

boothage Marktstandgebühr *f*.

bottleneck Engpaß *m*; ~ **in production** Produktionsengpaß; ~ **in supplies** Versorgungsengpaß.

bottom Boden *m*; Tiefpunkt *m*, Tiefstand *m*, niedrigster Stand *m*; Tal *n*; **false** ~ Doppelboden (*Zollkontrolle e–s Fahrzeugs*); ~ **hole contract** *Bohrerlaubnisvertrag mit Abgabe bei best. Bohrtiefe;* ~**land** Talgrund, Auenland; ~ **price** → *price* (*1*).

bottoming out das Erreichen der Talsohle.

bottomry *obs* Bodmerei *f*; Bodmereivertrag *m*; Schiffsverpfändung *f*; ~ **bill** Bodmereibrief; ~ **bond** Bodmereibrief; ~ **insurance** Bodmereiversicherung; ~ **interest** Bodmereizinsen.

bough of a tree Baumzweig *m* (*Auflassungssymbol*).

bought and sold note *exch* Schlußschein, Schlußnote (des Maklers); ~ **by auction** ersteigert; ~ **deal** direkte Plazierung an Außenstehende; ~ **note** Schlußschein (*Ausfertigung für Käufer*); ~ **or received** käuflich erworben oder auf andere Weise erhalten.

Boulevard rule Stoppgebot an Hauptstraßen.

bounce *v/i platzen* (*Schecks*).

bouncer **"Rausschmeißer"** *m*.

bound gebunden, verpflichtet; ~ **bailiff** → *bailiff*; ~ **for** bestimmt nach; ~ **from** aus . . . erwartet; **homeward** ~ auf der Heimreise befindlich; **jointly and severally** ~ gesamtschuldnerisch (= samtverbindl) verpflichtet; ~ **over** durch gerichtl Auflagen verpflichtet (*bes zum Erscheinen in der Hauptverhandlung*).

bound *s* Grenze *f*, Schranke *f*; ~**s** Grenzlinie(n); **out of** ~**s** kein Eintritt, verbotenes Gebiet, Sperrgebiet; **working out of** ~**s** *min* Schürfung in fremdem Bereich.

boundary Grenze *f*, Grenzlinie *f*, Bannmeile *f*; **B**~ **Commission** Wahlbezirksabgrenzungskommission; ~ **customs** Grenzzoll; ~ **dispute** Grenzstreitigkeit; ~ **stone** Grenzstein; ~ **law** das Recht der Staatsgrenzen; **artificial** ~ künstliche Grenze; **case of** ~ Gerichtsentscheidung über Grenzen; **coastal** ~

Küstengrenze; **maritime** ~ Seegrenze; **natural** ~ natürliche Grenze; **private** ~ Privatgrenze; **public** ~ öffentl Grenze, Staatsgrenze; **river** ~ Flußgrenze.

bounded tree Grenzbaum (*an der Ecke e–s Grundstücks*).

bounders Grenzpunkte *m/pl.*

bounding angrenzend, Grenz ...; **charter** Konzessionsurkunde mit Grenzangabe; ~ **or abutting** unmittelbar angrenzend.

bounty Güte *f*, Zuwendungsabsicht *f*; Bonus *m*, Prämie *f*, Belohnung *f*, Subvention *f*, Exportprämie *f*; ~**-fed** subventioniert; ~ **lands** → *land*; **B~ of Queen Anne** *Zuwendung von Kroneinkünften für Unterhalt von Geistlichen, Unterstützungsfonds für arme Geistliche;* ~ **on exports** Ausfuhrprämie.

bourse Börse *f* (*ausländische Wertpapier- oder Produktenbörse*).

bowie knife langes Jagdmesser *n*, Schlachtmesser *n*.

box *s* Kasten *m*, Postfach *n*, Portefeuille *n*; ~**-day** *scot* Kalendertag für Urkundeneinreichung; ~ **number** Chiffrenummer; ~ **office** Vorverkaufsstelle; ~ **strapping** Stahlband um Verpackungskisten; **"against the ~"** *exch* Effektenverkauf unter Zurückhaltung der Wertpapiere (*die der Börsenhändler zwischenzeitlich leihweise beschafft*); **private** ~ Postschließfach.

box *v scot* bei Gericht einreichen.

boxing of pine trees widerrechtl Harzanzapfung *f*.

boycott *s* Boykott *m*; **consumer** ~ Konsumentenboykott, Käuferstreik; **negative** ~ Boykott durch schwarze Liste; **primary** ~ unmittelbarer Boykott; **secondary** ~ mittelbarer Boykott.

bracery Geschworenenbeeinflussung *f*, Geschworenenbestechung *f*.

bracket Gruppe *f*, Emissionskonsortium v. Banken.

brain Gehirn *n*, Verstand *m*, Intellekt*m*; ~ **drain** Abwandern von Kapazitäten; ~ **trust** Beraterstab, Gehirntrust; ~ **washing** Gehirnwäsche; ~ **worker** Geistesarbeiter.

branch Zweig *m*, Zweigstelle *f*, Abteilung *f*, Niederlassung *f*, Filiale *f*; ~ **banking** Filialbanksystem; ~ **of a river** Flußverzweigung; ~ **of the sea** Meeresarm (*einschließlich Flußbett bis zur Gezeitenzone*); ~ **office** Zweigstelle, Zweigniederlassung; **foreign** ~ Auslandsfiliale.

branch and screwdriver economy *e–e vom Auslandskapital abhängige Wirtschaft der Zweigniederlassungen und Wartungsarbeiten.*

brand *s* Marke *f*, Klasse *f*, Sorte *f*, Schutzmarke *f*, Warenzeichen *n*; Brandmal *n*; ~ **of merchandise** Markensorte; ~ **name** Marke, Handelsmarke, Sortenbeschreibung; ~ **recognition** Bekanntheitsgrad e–r Marke; **fighting** ~ *vorläufig eingeführte Warensorte zur Markteroberung durch Unterbieten;* **flagship** ~ führende Marke e–s Hauses, Hauptmarke; **manufacturer's** ~ Fabrikmarke; **national** ~ Marke (Sorte) mit weiter Verkehrsgeltung (*im ganzen Land*); **own** ~ Hausmarke; **packer's** ~ Handelsmarke des (*ursprünglichen*) Verpackers; **private** ~ Händlermarke, Hausmarke; **wildcat** ~ unsolide Markensorte (*die auf den Markt geworfen wird*).

brand *v* brandmarken, markieren.

branding Warenhersteller-Kennzeichnung *f*.

brandish *v* schwenken, schwingen; ~**ing of deadly weapon** Drohung *f* mit einer tödlichen Waffe.

brass knuckles Schlagring *m*.

brassage Münz(Präge)steuer *f*.

brawl Tumult *m*, Streit *m*, Auflauf *m*, Raufhandel *m*, Schlägerei *f*.

brawling Ruhestörung, lärmender Streit *m*.

breach *s* Bruch *m*, Verletzung *f*, Rechtsverletzung *f*; ~ **of an oath** Eidbruch; ~ **of an undertaking** Bruch eines gerichtl Versprechens; ~ **of close** widerrechtl Betreten fremden Besitztums; ~ **of confidence** Vertrauensbruch, Verletzung der Geheimhaltungspflicht; ~ **of contract** vorsätzl Vertragsbruch, (positive) Vertragsverletzung, Vertragsbruch durch Erfüllungsverweigerung; ~ **of covenant** Nichteinhaltung einer (*ausdrücklich erklärten*) Vertragspflicht; ~ **of duty** Pflichtverletzung, Verletzung der Treuepflicht, Untreue; ~ **of injunction** Zuwiderhandlung gegen eine gerichtliche Verfügung; ~ **of law** Gesetzesverletzung, Rechtsverletzung, Rechtsbruch; ~ **of planning control** Verletzung der Bauplanungsvorschriften (*unbefugte Erschließung*); ~ **of pound** Verstrickungsbruch, Einbruch in einen Pfandstall; ~ **of prison** Ausbruch aus dem Gefängnis; ~ **of privilege** Verletzung von Parlamentsprivilegien; ~ **of professional etiquette** standeswidriges Verhalten; ~ **of professional secrecy** Bruch des Berufsgeheimnisses; ~ **of promise** (of marriage) *obs* Bruch des Eheversprechens, Verlöbnisbruch; **~es of regulations** Ordnungswidrigkeiten; ~ **of statutory duty** unerlaubte Handlung durch Schutzgesetzverletzung; ~ **of the peace** Störung der öffentlichen Ruhe und Ordnung; ~ **of trust** Verletzung von Treuhänderpflichten; Nichterfüllung des Treuhand-Auftrags; Untreue; ~ **of warranty** Verletzung e–r Gewährleistungspflicht, Nichteinhaltung e–r Zusicherung, Garantieverletzung; ~ **of warranty of authority** Vollmachtüberschreitung, *Handeln ohne Ermächtigung gestützt auf Vollmacht;* ~ **proceedings** Verfahren wegen Widerrufs der Strafaussetzung zur Bewährung (*Nichteinhaltung von Bewährungsauflagen*); **anticipatory** ~ Erfüllungsverweigerung; **continuing** ~ andauernde Vertragsverletzung; **constructive** ~ Quasivertragsverletzung; **fraudulent** ~ betrügerische Vertragsverletzung; **once-and-for-all** ~ einmalige grundlegende Vertragsverletzung; **repudiatory** ~ positive Vertragsverletzung durch Erfüllungsverweigerung; **wilful** ~ vorsätzliche Regelverletzung.

breach *v/t* brechen, verletzen; ~ **a duty of care** e–e Sorgfaltspflicht verletzen.

breadwinner Ernährer der Familie.

break *s* Bruch *m*, Unterbrechung *f*, Pause *f*; ~ **in prices** Kurseinbruch, Preissturz; ~ **of service** Unterbrechung des Dienstverhältnisses; **clean** ~ endgültiger Abschluß (*ehelicher u. nachehelicher Verpflichtungen*).

break *v* brechen, einbrechen; ~ **an account** e–n Konkokorrent abbrechen; ~ **a case** über ein Urteil beraten; ~ **and take** Kauf mit Verlosungsrecht; ~ **even** ohne Gewinn und Verlust abschließen; ~ **ground** mit den Ausschachtungsarbeiten beginnen; ~ **out** ausbrechen.

breakage Bruch *m*, Refaktie *f Gewichtsabzug* (*bzw Preisabzug oder Vergütung*) *wegen Bruchschadens;* ~ **clause** Bruchklausel; ~ **during removal** Bruch anläßlich des Abtransports; **free from** ~ bruchfrei, frei von Bruch.

breakdown Zusammenbruch *m*, Maschinenschaden *m*; Aufgliederung *f*, Aufschlüsselung *f*; ~ **clause** Maschinenschadensklausel (*Schiffschartervertrag*); ~ **of costs** Kostenaufgliederung; ~ **of machinery** *totaler* Maschinenschaden; ~ **of marriage** Scheitern der Ehe; ~ **service** Notdienst (*Elektrizitätswerk*); ~ **value** Substanzwert.

break-even point Rentabilitätsgrenze *f*, Gewinnschwelle *f*.

breaking Einbrechen *n*; ~ **a quorum** Herbeiführung der Beschlußunfähigkeit; ~ **and entering** Einbruch; ~ **bulk** → *bulk;* ~ **doors** gewaltsames Öffnen von Türen; ~ **jail** = *jail-breaking* → *jail;* ~ **of arrestment** *scot* Verletzung der Arrestverstrickung; ~ **out of building** gewaltsames Verlassen eines Hauses; ~ **up highways** das Aufreißen von Landstraßen; ~ **the close** widerrechtl Betreten fremden Grundes, Besitzstörung; **constructive** ~ *als Einbruch geltende Handlungen*, Einschleichen, durch Trick Einlaß verschaffen; **seal** ~ Siegelbruch.

break-up value Schrottwert *m*, Liquidationswert *m*.

breast of the court das Gewissen des Gerichts, das gerichtl Ermessen.

breathalyser Gerät zur Atemprüfung.

breath|machine Atemmeßgerät wg. Alkohol, ~ **specimen** Atemprobe.

breath test Alkohol-Atemtest *m*, **roadside** ~ Alkoholtest an Ort und Stelle.

brethren Brüder *m|pl*, Geschwister *pl* (*bei letztwilliger Verfügung*); **B~ of Trinity House** (=) *engl Piloten- und Leuchtturmbehörde* (= *Elder Brethren of the Holy and Undivided Trinity* = *Corporation of the Trinity House of Depford Strand, vgl Trinity House*).

brevet Brevet *n*, Patent *n*; ~ **(rank)** Titularrang; ~ **d'invention** Erfindungspatent.

brevi manu kurzer Hand.

brewer Brauer *m*, Brauerei *f*.

brewster sessions Gerichtstage zur Entscheidung über Schankkonzessionen.

bribe *s* Bestechungsgeld *n*, Schmiergeld *n*; ~ **taker** bestechliche Person, Bestochener.

bribe *v* bestechen.

bribee Bestochener.

briber Bestechender *m*, Bestechung praktizierende Person *f*.

bribery Bestechung *f* (= . . .*b*), Vorteilsgewährung *f*; Vorteilsannahme *f*; ~ **at elections** Wahl*b*; ~ **of constable** Polizisten*b*; ~ **of juror** Geschworenen*b*; ~ **of ministerial officers** Beamten*b*; ~ **of public officials** Beamten*b*; ~ **of witnesses** Zeugen*b*; **commercial** ~ Bestechung von Geschäftspartnern zu Wettbewerbszwecken; **judicial** ~ Richter*b*.

bridewell Arbeitshaus *n*, Besserungsanstalt *f*.

bridge Brücke *f*; ~ **financing** Zwischenfinanzierung; **~-master** Brückenmeister, Brückenwärter.

bridging|advance Überbrückungsvorschuß, kurzfristige Ü.; ~ **loan** Überbrückungsdarlehen, Zwischenfinanzierung; ~ **transaction** Überbrückungsmaßnahme, Überbrückungskredit *m*.

bridle|path Reitweg *m*, Wegerecht *n* für Reiter; ~ **way** Reitweg.

brief *s* Schriftsatz *m*, Informationen *f|pl* für den Prozeßanwalt, Mandat(serteilung); Auszug *m*, Memorandum *n*; ~ **of title** Zusammenfassung der Grundeigentumsurkunden; ~ **on appeal** Berufungsbegründung; ~ **papal** päpstliches Sendschreiben; **appellate** ~ Schriftsatz in der Berufungsinstanz, *(Berufungsbegründung bzw. Berufungserwiderung)*; **counsel's** ~ Mandat; **legal** ~ Schriftsatz bei Gericht; *bes* Berufungsschriftsatz; **to file a** ~ Schriftsatz einreichen; **to hold a** ~ **(for)** vor Gericht vertreten, als Anwalt auftreten (für); **to take a** ~ die Vertretung vor Gericht übernehmen; **trial** ~ Prozeßmandat; Schriftsatz in erster Instanz; **written** ~ Schriftsatz.

brief *v* (*a barrister*) (*e–n Prozeßanwalt*) mandieren und mit Informationen versehen; informieren, instruieren.

briefing Beauftragung *f*, Einweisung *f*, Unterweisung *f*, Einsatzbesprechung *f*, Lagebesprechung *f*; ~ **a lawyer** Bestellung e–s Anwalts *mit Informationserteilung;* ~ **pack** Informationsmappe.

briefless unbeschäftigt (*Anwalt*).

brigand Brigant *m*, Straßenräuber *m*, Bandit *m*.

brigandage Brigantentum *m*, Straßenräuberei *f*, Banditentum *n*.

bring (*vgl brought*) bringen, überbringen, verbringen, (*Klage*) erheben, (*Prozeß*) anstrengen; ~ **a procedure** ein Verfahren anstrengen; ~ **about a reconciliation** e–e Versöhnung herbeiführen; ~ **an ac-**

tion Klage erheben; ~ **forward** vortragen; ~ **in the verdict** den Spruch verkünden (*Geschworene*); ~ **pressure to bear** Druck ausüben; ~ **suit** → *suit* (*1*); ~ **to account** in Rechnung stellen, zur Rechenschaft ziehen; ~**ing an action** Klageerhebung; ~**ing money into court** gerichtliche Hinterlegung; ~**ing up** das Aufziehen von Kindern.

brinkmanship Politik *f* am Rande des Abgrunds.

Bristol bargain *Darlehensvertrag mit pauschalierter Verzinsung.*

Britain Großbritannien und Nordirland = *United Kingdom of Great Britain and Northern Ireland qv.*

British *adj* britisch; ~ **citizen** brit Staatsbürger; ~ **citizenship** brit Staatsbürgerschaft (*seit 1. 1. 83*); ~ **Commonwealth** das brit–e Commonwealth; ~ **custom** nach britischen Usancen; ~ **dependent territories citizen** brit Staatsbürger e–s abhängigen Territoriums (*seit 1. 1. 83*); ~ **Funds** brit. Staatsanleihen; ~ **national** brit. Staatsangehöriger; ~ **national by birth** gebürtiger Brite, brit Volkszugehöriger, Brite; ~ **nationality** brit Staatsangehörigkeit; ~ **overseas citizen** brit Staatsbürger überseeischer Gebiete (*seit 1. 1. 83*); ~ **possessions** brit Besitzungen; ~ **protected person** Staatsangehöriger e–s brit Schutzgebiets bzw ehem Protektorats oder Freihandelsgebiets; ~ **protectorate** brit Protectorat, ~ **subject** britischer Staatsbürger (*bisher* = *Commonwealth citizen*).

broad arrow Kurzpfeil *m*, *Kennzeichen für Staatseigentum.*

Broadmoor *Sondernervenheilanstalt für gefährliche kriminelle Geisteskranke.*

broadsheet großes bedrucktes Blatt *n*, Plakat *n*.

broken gebrochen, angebrochen, fragmentarisch, zerrüttet; ~ **account** umsatzloses Konto; ~ **home** ein zerrüttetes Familienleben; ~ **lot** kleinerer Effektenposten; ~ **stowage** Leerraum im Schiff.

broker Makler *m*, Handelsmakler *m*; Wertpapierhändler *m* (*für fremde Rechnung*); Gerichtsvollzieher bei Mietvollstreckung; ~**'s** ~ = *floor trader qv;* ~**'s collateral loans** US Lombardkredite der Wertpapierhändler, *US* Effektenverpfändung; ~**'s commission** Maklerlohn, Maklerprovision, Courtage; ~**'s fee** = ~**'s** *commission qv*; ~**'s loan** Maklerdarlehen; ~**'s loan market** Effektenlombardmarkt; ~**'s contract note** Schlußschein, Schlußnote; **bill** ~ Wechselmakler; **commercial** ~ Handelsmakler; **credit** ~ Finanz(ierungs)makler; **curb-(stone)** ~ Freiverkehrsmakler; **discount** ~ Wechselmakler; **exchange** ~ Devisenhändler für Rechnung Dritter, Devisenmakler; **floor** ~ *US (NYSE)* Börsen(auftrags)makler; **industrial** ~ Makler für gewerbliche Grundstücke; **inside** ~ amtlich zugelassener Makler; **insurance** ~ Versicherungsmakler; **investment** ~ Investmentvermittler, Finanzmakler, **loan** ~ Finanzmakler; **mercantile** ~ Handelsmakler = *Handelsmäkler*; **merchandise** ~ Warenmakler, Handelsmakler; **money** ~ Finanzmakler, Geldvermittler, Geldverleiher, Kreditvermittler; **note** ~ Wechselmakler; **odd-lot** ~ Börsenmakler für kleinere Aufträge unter dem Mindestnennbetrag (*„Schluß"*); **outside** ~ nicht zur Börse zugelassener Makler; Winkelmakler; **pawn** ~ Pfandleiher; **placing** ~ Versicherungsmakler, der Teilrisiken unterbringt; **produce** ~ Produktenmakler, landwirtschaftlicher Großhändler; **real estate** ~ Immobilienmakler, Grundstücksmakler; **securities** ~ → *security* (*2*); **ship** ~ → *ship*; **stock** ~ → *stock* (*1*); **two-dollar** ~ = *floor broker qv;* **unlicensed** ~ nicht an der Börse zugelassener Makler.

brokerage Maklergeschäft *n*, Maklergebühr *f*, Courtage *f*, Maklerlohn *m*; ~ **account** Courtagerechnung, Courtagekonto; ~ **contract** Maklervertrag; ~ **fee** Vermittlungsgebühr; ~ **statement** Courtagerechnung; **buying** ~ Einkaufsprovision; **exchange** ~ Wechselcourtage.

brokering Vermittlung *f*, Weitervermittlung von Mandanten.

brothel Bordell *n*; ~ **keeping** Bordellhaltung.

brother Bruder *m*; ~**s german** Brüder gleicher Eltern; ~ **in law** Schwager; ~ **of the half blood** halbbürtiger Bruder; ~ **of the whole blood** vollbürtiger Bruder.

brought gebracht, eingeleitet; ~ **before a magistrate** dem Amtsrichter vorgeführt; ~ **forward** Vortrag, Übertrag; ~**-in capital** eingebrachtes Kapital; ~ **into charge of tax** der Besteuerung unterworfen; ~ **into question** fraglich geworden; ~ **to the attention of** zur Kenntnis gebracht.

bruise Prellung *f*.

bubble Seifenblase *f*, Luftschloß-Spekulation *f*; (Finanz)Schwindel *m*; ~ **company** Schwindelgesellschaft.

buckete(e)r nicht zugelassener Börsenmakler *m*; unreeller Börsenmakler *m*.

budget Haushalt *m* (= *H bzw h*), Staatshaushalt *m*, Haushaltsplan *m*, Budget *n*, Etat *m*, Voranschlag *m*; ~ **calendar** Zeitplan für die *H-s*-vorbereitung; ~ **commission** *H-s*-ausschuß; ~ **cut** Etatkürzung; ~ **debate** → *debate*; ~ **document** die *H-s*vorlage nebst Anlagen; ~ **estimates** *H-s*voranschläge; ~ **message** Begründung der *H-s*vorlage, *H-s*botschaft; ~ **proposal** *H-s*vorschlag; ~ **resolution** *H*verabschiedung; ~ **statement** *H-s*rede (*des Finanzministers zu Beginn der Haushaltsdebatte*); ~**surplus** *H-s*überschuß; ~ **year** *H-s*jahr; **adoption of** ~ Annahme des *H-s*plans; **adverse** ~ unausgeglichener *H*, Defizit*h*; **advertising** ~ Werbeetat; **balanced** ~ ausgeglichener *H*; **cash** ~ Kassenbudget, Liquiditätsbudget; **executive** ~ Regierungs*h*; **extraordinary** ~ außerordentlicher *H*; **federal** ~ Bundes*h*; **general** ~ der allgemeine *H-s*plan; **interim** ~ Nachtrags*h*; **legislative** ~ *H-s*gesetz; **national** ~ Gesamt*h* e–s Staates, Bundes*h*; **on** ~ im Rahmen der Haushaltsmittel, in der Finanzplanung; **ordinary** ~ ordentlicher *H*; **sales** ~ →*sale*; **special** ~ außerordentlicher *H*; **special** ~**s** besondere Budgets (*halbautonomer Dienststellen*); **state** ~ Staatshaushaltsplan; **supplementary** ~ Nachtragshaushalt; **to open the** ~ das Budget vorlegen.

budgetary etatmäßig, haushaltsmäßig, Haushalts . . .

budgeting Budgetierung *f*, Finanzplanung *f*; ~ **for bond funds** Budgetplanung für Anleihemittel; ~ **for expenditure** Ausgabenbudget; ~ **for personal services** Haushaltsmittel für Personalkosten; **cyclical** ~ antizyklische Haushaltsgestaltung.

buffer Puffer *m*; ~ **state** Pufferstaat.

bug Gewerkschaftsetikett *n* (*an Waren*).

buggery Sodomie *f*, widernatürliche Unzucht, Analverkehr *m*.

bugging elektronisches Abhören *n*; ~ **devices** Abhörmethoden, Abhöranlage.

build bauen, erbauen, schaffen.

builder Bauunternehmer *m*, Baufirma *f*; ~**'s estimate** Baukostenvoranschlag; ~**'s risk insurance** → *insurance*; **private** ~**s** gewerbliche Bauunternehmer, Wohnungsbaufirmen.

building | **agreement** Bauvertrag; ~ **and loan association** *genossenschaftl organisierte Bausparkasse*; ~ **block process** Baukostenverfahren; ~ **bye-laws** örtl Bauvorschriften; ~ **code** Bauordnung; ~ **contract** → *contract*; ~ **estimate** Baukostenvoranschlag; ~ **funds** Baugelder; ~ **land** Bauland, Baugrund; ~ **lease** → *lease*; ~ **licence** Bauerlaubnis, Baugenehmigung; ~ **lien** Bauunternehmerpfandrecht; ~ **line** Fluchtlinie, Baulinie; ~ **loan** Baudarlehen; ~ **loan agreement** Baudarlehensvertrag, Bauzwischenfinanzierung; ~ **materials** Baumaterial; ~ **operations** Bauarbeiten; ~ **or erection** Bauwerk; ~ **or structure** Bauwerk; ~ **owner** Bauherr, Besitzer e–s Kommunmauergrundstücks; ~ **permit** Baugenehmigung; ~ **purposes** Bauzwecke; ~ **quota** Baukontingent; ~ **regulation approval** Baugenehmigung; ~ **regulations** Bauvorschriften; (*B~ R ~s:*) Bauordnung; ~ **restrictions** Baubeschränkungen; ~ **scheme** Bauvorhaben, Bebauungsplan; ~ **site** Baustelle, Bauplatz, ~ **society** Baugenossenschaft, Bausparkasse; ~ **under construction** im Bau befindliches Haus; ~ **volume** umbauter Raum; **adjacent** ~ angrenzendes Gebäude; **commercial** ~ handelsgewerblich genutztes Gebäude, Gewerbegebäude; **domestic** ~ Wohnhaus, Privatgebäude; **historic** ~ Baudenkmal, Gebäude unter Denkmalschutz; **listed** ~ als denkmalschutzwürdig verzeichnetes Gebäude; **multiple-unit** ~ Appartmenthaus, *Wohn- bzw Geschäftsgebäude mit mehreren Einheiten*; **non-government** ~ privates Bauwesen; **obstructive** ~ gefährdendes Anliegergebäude; **public ~s** öffentliche Gebäude.

bulge Ausweitung *f*; Kursbuckel *m*; plötzliches Steigen *n* der Kurse; geburtenstarke Jahrgänge *m|pl*.

bulk Masse *f*, Menge *f*, Hauptteil *m* der Lieferung; ~ **article** Massenartikel; ~ **buying** Massenankauf, Mengeneinkauf; ~ **cargo** Massengutladung, Waggonladung; ~ **consignment** Massenlieferung; ~ **consumer** Großverbraucher; ~ **mail** Postwurfsendung; ~ **material** Rohmaterial; ~ **mortgage** Fahrnispfand; ~ **sale** Gesamtverkauf des Lagerbestandes; ~ **sales acts** gesetzl Formvorschriften bei Gesamtvermögensveräußerung; ~ **sampling** Stichprobenentnahme; **breaking** ~ Löschen der Ladung; widerrechtliche Transportmittelöffnung; **by the** ~ im ganzen, in Bausch und Bogen; **in** ~ gesamt, lose, unverpackt; **open** ~ (noch) unverpackte Massenware.

bull Haussier *m*, Haussespekulant *m*; ~ **and boar** Bullen und Eber *hist Verpflichtung zur Haltung dieser Zuchttiere;* ~ **campaign** Kurstreiberei; ~ **market** Hausse(markt); ~ **operation** Haussespekulation; ~ **pen** Haftraum im Gefängnis, Beruhigungszelle; ~ **ring** Hassepartei; **on** ~ **support** infolge von Stützungskäufen der Haussepartei.

bulldoze *v/t* mit Gewalt durchbringen (~ *an amendment through*).

bullet Anleiheemission ohne Tilgungsfonds.

bulletin Bulletin *n*, amtl Tagesbericht *m*; **official** ~ amtliches Mitteilungsblatt.

bullion Gold *n* und Silber *n* für Münzzwecke; Gold- *m* bzw Silberbarren *m*; ~ **dealer** Edelmetallhändler; ~ **fund** Fonds zum Ankauf von Edelmetall für Münzzwecke; ~ **market ratio** das Verhältnis des Goldpreises zum Silberpreis; ~ **reserve** Gold- bzw Silberbestand; ~ **trade** Handel mit ungemünztem Gold und Silber; **base** ~ unreines Metall (*in Barrenform*); **gold** ~ **standard** → *gold*.

bullishness Haussestimmung *f*.

Bullock order *Kostenentscheidung bei teilweisem Obsiegen gegen mehrere Beklagte*.

bum-bailiff Schuldbeitreiber *m*, Gerichtsvollzieher *m* zur Verhaftung des Schuldners.

bumping *Personalabbau m* durch Verdrängung der zuletzt Eingestellten.

bunco game Schwindel *m*.

bundle Konvolut *n*, Aktenbündel *n*; ~ **of papers** Aktenbündel.

bunker *s* (Kohlen)Bunker *m*; *v* bunkern, Kohle für Fahrtzwecke aufnehmen; **for ~ing or other purposes** zum Bunkern und (dazugehörigen) anderen Zwecken.

buoyancy steigende Tendenz *f*, inflationsbedingte Aufwärtsbewegung.

buoyant steigend (*Kurse, Preise*); ~ **market** feste Börse.

burden Last *f*, Belastung *f*, Ladung *f*,

Gewicht *n*; Auflage *f*, Bürde *f*; ~ **of adducing evidence** Beweisantrittslast; ~ **of going forward** weitere Darlegungslast als Replik; ~ **of persuasion** Überzeugungslast; ~ **of producing evidence** Beweisführungslast; ~ **of proof** Beweislast; ~ **of taxation** Steuerlast; ~**s of war** Kriegslasten; ~**-sharing** Lastenausgleich; Lastenbeteiligung; **public** ~**s** öffentl Lasten, ö. Grundstückslasten; **specific** ~ Beweisführungslast im Einzelfall; **any** ~ **or liability** sämtliche Lasten und sonstige (*mit der Sache verbundenen*) Verbindlichkeiten; **evidential** ~ Beweis(beibringungs)last.

burden *v* belasten, (Rechte) einschränken, beeinträchtigen.

bureau Schreibtisch *m*; Amt *n*; ~ **-de change** (*ple bureaux*) Wechselstube; **B~ of the Census** *US*: Statistisches Bundesamt; **B~ of Customs** *US* Bundeszollbehörde; **B~ of Workmen's Compensation** *US, etwa*: Berufsgenossenschaft; **B~ of Standards** *US* staatl Eichamt; **legislative** ~ Interessenvertretung beim Parlament.

bureaucracy Bürokratie *f*, Verwaltungssystem *n*.

burgess *obs GB*: Stadtbürger *m*, wahlberechtigter Stadtbürger *m*, Parlamentsabgeordneter *m* e–r Stadt; *US*: Ratsherr *m*, Bürgermeister *m*; ~ **roll** Bürgerliste.

burgher Stadtbürger *m*, Gemeindebürger.

burglar (*nächtlicher*) Einbrecher *m*; ~ **alarm service** Alarmanlagedienst; ~**-proof** einbruchsicher.

burglariously mit Einbruchsvorsatz.

burglary Einbruchdiebstahl, (*bei Nacht: GB, bis 1968*); Hausfriedensbruch *m* bei Nacht zum Zwecke der Begehung eines Verbrechens; ~ **in daytime** Einbruch bei Tage; ~ **insurance contract** Einbruchsversicherung; ~ **tools** Einbruchswerkzeuge; **aggravated** ~ schwerer (*verbrecherischer*) Hausfriedensbruch (*mit Schußwaffe bzw Sprengstoff*).

burial Begräbnis *n*, Beerdigung *f*; ~ **authority** Friedhofsverwaltung; ~ **fund** Sterbekasse; ~ **insurance** → *insurance*.

burking Mord zum Leichenverkauf.

burlaw court Nachbarschaftsgericht *n*.

burlaws Gesetze *n|pl* von Nachbarschaftsversammlungen.

burn *s* Brandwunde *f*, Brandstelle *f*.

burn *v* brennen, verbrennen.

burning/to defraud insurer Brandstiftung als Versicherungsbetrug; **wilful** ~ vorsätzliche Brandstiftung.

bursar Universitätskassenverwalter *m*.

bushel Bushel *m*, Scheffel *m*.

business Geschäft *n*, Handel *m*, Gewerbe *n*, Beruf *m*; Handelsbetrieb *m*, Tagesordnung *f*; ~ **acumen** geschäftl Gewandtheit, kaufmännische Geschicklichkeit; ~ **administration** Betriebswirtschaftslehre; ~ **agent** Handelsvertreter; ~ **allowance** Werbungskosten; ~ **assets** Geschäftsvermögen, Betriebsvermögen; ~ **association** Wirtschaftsverband; ~ **capital** → *capital*; ~ **committee** Parlamentsausschuß für die Einteilung der Sitzungszeit; ~ **concern** Geschäftsbetrieb, Handelsunternehmen; ~ **connected with the lease** die mit dem Pachtvertrag zusammenhängende *anwaltschaftl* Tätigkeit; ~ **consultant** Betriebsberater, Unternehmensberater; ~ **credit** Kredit im Geschäftsleben; ~ **cycle** Konjunkturzyklus, K.verlauf; ~ **day** Arbeitstag; ~ **dealings** geschäftliche Transaktionen; ~ **development loan** Mittelstandskredit; ~ **done** Umsatzbetrag, tatsächlich getätigte Börsenabschlüsse; ~ **economist** Betriebswirt; ~ **efficacy** beabsichtigte Wirkung; Wirksamkeit für die praktische Anwendung; ~ **entertainment** geschäftliche Einladungen; ~ ~ *expenses: Bewirtungsspesen;* ~ **expense** Betriebsausgabe; ~ **failure** Zahlungseinstellung, Konkurs; ~ **gains** Betriebseinnahmen, ~ **gift** Geschenk an Geschäftsfreunde; ~ **hazard** allgemeines

Unternehmerwagnis; ~ **hours** → *hour*; ~ **in futures** Termingeschäft; ~ **interruption insurance** → *insurance;* ~ **investment policy** betriebliche Investitionspolitik; ~ **letters** geschäftliche Korrespondenz, Geschäftsbriefe; **liability** → *liability*; ~ **licence** → *licence;* ~ **losses** Geschäftsverluste; ~ **management** → *management;* ~ **manager** kaufmännischer Direktor; ~ **meals and entertainment cost** Aufwendungen für Bewirtung von Geschäftsfreunden, Bewirtungsspesen; ~ **name** Firmenname, Firma; ~ **of a session** die Tätigkeit e–r Sitzungsperiode; ~ **of the borough** e–e Angelegenheit der Gemeinde; ~ **of the House** Angelegenheit des Unterhauses; ~ **on joint account** Konsortialgeschäft; ~ **or calling** gewerbliche oder berufliche Tätigkeit; ~ **policy** → *policy* (*2*); ~ **practices** Geschäftspraktiken; ~ **premises** Geschäftsräume; ~ **property** Betriebsvermögen; ~ **purposes** geschäftl Zwecke; ~ **records** Geschäftsbücher, Geschäftsunterlagen; ~ **reply card** Werbeantwortkarte; ~ **resulting through our efforts** durch unsere Bemühungen zustandekommende Geschäftsabschlüsse; ~ **risk** → *risk*; → **scheme** Geschäftsvorhaben; ~ **secret** → *secret;* ~ **situs** Sitz des Unternehmens; ~ **standing** Rang e–s Unternehmens, geschäftl Prestige; ~ **start-up scheme** Unternehmensgründungs-Hilfsprogramm; ~ **sub-committee** Geschäftsverteilungsunterausschuß; ~ **tenancy** gewerbliches Mietverhältnis; ~ **transaction** Geschäft; ~ **travel** Geschäftsreise; ~ **trust** → *trust*; ~ **usage** Handelsbrauch; ~ **user** gewerblicher Benutzer; ~ **venture** → *venture;* ~ **year** → *year;* **actual** ~ Effektivgeschäft; **administrative** ~ Nachlaßangelegenheiten; Verwaltungsangelegenheiten; **commercial** ~ Handelssachen; **common form** ~ ordentliches Verfahren, unstreitige Nachlaßsachen; **contango** ~ → *contango;* **core** ~ Hauptgeschäftsbereich; **current** ~ laufende Geschäfte; **current** ~ **year** laufendes Geschäftsjahr; **exempted** ~ Punkte außerhalb der Tagesordnung; **financial** ~ Finanzangelegenheiten; **for** ~ **and pleasure** für geschäftl und private Zwecke; **foreign** ~ Auslandsgeschäft(e); **general** ~ allg Versicherungsgeschäft (*Unfall etc, ohne Lebensv*); **going** ~ arbeitender Betrieb; **government** ~ Regierungsvorlagen; **increase in** ~ Konjunkturbesserung; **industrial** ~ (I. B.) Kleinlebensversicherung; **interruption of** ~ → *interruption*; **joint** ~ Betriebsgemeinschaft; **local** ~ Platzgeschäft; **long** ~ Personenversicherungen; **long term** ~ langfristige Versicherungsverträge (*Lebensversicherung*); **non-contentions** ~ → *non-contentions*; **new** ~ neue Abschlüsse, Neugeschäft(e); **no** ~ **done** ohne Umsatz; **offensive** ~ belästigender Gewerbebetrieb; **official** ~ Dienstsache; **one-line** ~ Spezialgeschäft, Fachgeschäft; **order of** ~ Reihenfolge der Tagesordnungspunkte, Einteilung des Sitzungstages; **over-the-counter** ~ ungeregelter Freiverkehr, „Tafelgeschäft"; **paying** ~ rentables Geschäft; **private** ~ Privatunternehmen, Privatbetrieb; geschäftsordnungsmäßige Behandlung von Spezialvorlagen; **public** ~ Unternehmen der öffentlichen Hand; öffentlichen Zwecken dienendes Unternehmen, gewerbliches Unternehmen; **retail** ~ Einzelhandelsgeschäft; **rival** ~ Konkurrenzunternehmen; **routine** ~ Routineangelegenheiten, laufende Geschäftsangelegenheiten; **service** ~ Dienstleistungsbetrieb, Dienstleistungsgewerbe; **sham** ~ Scheingeschäft; **small** ~ Kleingewerbe, Klein- und Mittelbetriebe; **special** ~ besonderer Tagesordnungspunkt; **to conduct a** ~ ein Geschäft betreiben, ... führen; **to run a** ~ ein Geschäft betreiben;

unincorporated ~es Einzelunternehmen und Personal-Gesellschaften; **unofficial** ~ Freiverkehr; **unopposed** ~ unstreitige Punkte (*der Tagesordnung*); **whole-sale** ~ → *wholesale.*

business entry rule Zulässigkeit von Buchungen als Beweismittel.

business judgment rule Haftungsausschluß für redliche Geschäftsführungsentscheidungen.

buttals Grenze *f* (*an der Schmalseite e–s Grundstücks*).

butts unbebaute Randstücke *n*|*pl* an der Schmalseite von Äckern; ~ **and bounds** Grundstücksgrenzen.

buy *v* kaufen; ~ **a borough** Wahlstimmen kaufen; ~ **at a premium** über Pari kaufen; ~ **by sample** nach Muster kaufen; ~ **firm** fest kaufen; ~ **for ready money** gegen bar kaufen; ~ **for the account** auf Termin kaufen; ~ **for the rise** auf Hausse spekulieren; ~ **in** sich eindecken; (*bei Auktion*) zurückkaufen, selbst ersteigern; ~ **off** (*Teilhaber*) abfinden; ~ **on a fall** auf Baisse kaufen; ~ **out** auskaufen (*Teilhaber*); ablösen; ~ **outright** gegen sofortige Lieferung kaufen, fest kaufen; ~ **out the execution** Pfändung durch Zahlung abwehren; ~ **over** bestechen; ~ **sell, or deal in** kaufen, Geschäfte tätigen; ~ **subject to inspection** auf Besicht kaufen; ~ **up** aufkaufen; **inclined to** ~ kaufbereit.

buy and sell agreement *käufliche Übernahme des Kapitalanteils des ausscheidenden Gesellschafters durch die Mitgesellschafter bzw die Firma und dessen Veräußerung.*

buy back *s* Rückkauf *m* Gegengeschäft *n* Pensionsgeschäft.

buyer Käufer *m*, Abnehmer *m*; Einkäufer *m*; ~ **credit** Bestellerkredit; Exportfinanzierungskredit; ~ **furnished property** vom Käufer gestellte Gegenstände; **~'s market** Käufermarkt; **~'s option** → *option;* **~s over** bezahlt und Geld (*Börsennotiz: „bez G"*); **~'s strike** Käuferstreik; **~-up** Aufkäufer; **active ~s** lebhafte Käufe; **at ~'s option** nach Wahl des Käufers; **cash** ~ Barkäufer; **first-time ~s** Erstkäufer; **forward** ~ Terminkäufer; **intending** ~ Kaufinteressent; **intermediate** ~ Zwischenkäufer; **let the** ~ **beware** auf Risiko des Käufers; **option** ~ → *option;* **potential** ~ möglicher Käufer; **prospective** ~ Kaufinteressent; **resident** ~ ortsansässiger Einkäufer; **sole** ~ alleiniger Abnehmer; **special** ~ Schatzwechselmakler *GB*; **undisclosed** ~ ungenannter Kunde; **wholesale** ~ Großeinkäufer; **would-be** ~ Kaufinteressent.

buying *s* Kaufen *n*, Einkauf *m*, Ankauf *m*, Erwerb *m*; *adj* Kauf ..., käuflich; ~ **agent** → *agent*; ~ **an option** Erwerb e–r Option; ~ **back** Rückkauf, Eindeckung; ~ **commission** → *commission*; ~ **in** (*zwangsweiser*) Deckungskauf (*für in Lieferverzug befindlichen Wertpapierhändler*); ~ **incentive** Kaufanreiz; ~ **locations** Bezugsstandorte; ~ **of pleas** käuflicher Erwerb von Klageansprüchen, unzulässige Prozeßeinmischung; ~ **of votes** Stimmenkauf; ~ **on margin** Effektenkauf teils bar, teils auf Kredit (*des Maklers*); ~ **order** Kaufauftrag; ~ **outright** Kassakauf; ~ **power** → *power*; ~ **quota** Einkaufskontingent; ~ **rate** → *rate*; ~ **spree** plötzliche Kauflust; ~ **titles** Ankauf von Besitzansprüchen an Grundstükken.

buy-in notice Nachfristsetzung (*zur Lieferung gekaufter Effekten*) unter Androhung anderweitiger Beschaffung.

buy-out (= *buyout, US*) Aufkauf *m*, Aktienübernahme *f*, Spekulationserwerb *m*, aufgekauftes Unternehmen; **leveraged** ~ fremd finanzierter Unternehmensaufkauf, ... Aktienaufkauf.

by *prep (1)* durch, spätestens bis, per, mit, bei, während; ~ **accident** durch zufälliges Ereignis; ~ **act and operation of law** = *by operation of law* → *law*; **(agreed)** ~ **and**

between (vereinbart) zwischen; ~ **authority** im Auftrag; ~ **color of office** ohne Kompetenz; ~ **consent** einverständlich; ~ **contract** vertraglich; ~ **day** bei Tage, tagsüber; ~ **desire of** auf Wunsch von; ~ **estimation** geschätzt, circa; ~ **force of the statutes** kraft Gesetzes; ~ **indirection** auf Umwegen; ~ **July 31st** bis 31. Juli (*einschließlich*); ~ **law so devised** in gesetzlich zulässiger Weise vermacht; ~ **leave of a judge** mit richterlicher Erlaubnis; ~ **means of a vehicle** mittels e–s Fahrzeugs; ~ **or in consequence of whose order** durch wessen Veranlassung; ~ **or through an agent** durch einen Vertreter (*bzw Vermittler*); ~ **or through whom** durch welchen, über welchen; ~ **purchase** durch Kauf, käuflich erworben; ~ **reason of** wegen; ~ **reason of wear and tear** wegen Abnutzung; ~ **return of post** postwendend; ~ **stealth** heimlich, unbemerkt; ~ **these presents** mit dieser Urkunde; hiermit, hierdurch; ~**, through, or under** mittelbar; ~ **virtue of** wegen, durch, gemäß; ~ **virtue of office** in (*mißbräuchlicher*) Ausübung (*seines*) Amtes; ~ **virtue of law** kraft Gesetzes; ~ **way of damages** als Schadenersatz; ~ **way of gift** schenkungsweise; ~ **way of succession** durch Erbschaft, durch Rechtsnachfolge.

by (*2*) nahebei, neben; ~ **-bidder** Scheinbieter (*jmd, der zu hohem Bieten reizen soll*); ~**-bidding** Steigern durch Scheingebote; ~ **-election** Nachwahl, Ersatzwahl; ~ **-product** Nebenprodukt.

bye-laws Statuten, Ortsvorschriften, Satzungsbestimmungen (*US, corporation*).

bypass Umgehungsstraße *f*.

byroad Anliegerweg *m*, Nebenweg *m*.

bystander in der Nähe Stehender *m*, Zuschauer *m*, Unbeteiligter *m*; ~**'s statement** Aussage eines unbeteiligten Unfallzeugen.

C

cab-rank Taxistand *m*; ~ **principle** Reihenfolge der Mandierung nach Abruf

cable Kabel *n*, Telegramm *f*; ~**address** Drahtadresse; **C~ Authority** (*CA*) Kabelfernsehbehörde *US*; ~ **franchise** Kabelfernseh-Konzession *GB*; ~**-gram** Telegramm; ~ **transfer** telegrafische Überweisung; ~ **TV** Kabelfernsehen; **interference with** ~**s** vorsätzliche Störung von Seekabeln; ~ **vetting** (Übersee)-Kabelverkehr-Überwachung; **basic** ~ Minimalangebot von Kabelprogrammen.

cabotage Kabotage *f*; Küstenschifffahrt *f*; Küstenfahrtlizenz *f*; Binnenluftverkehr *m*; Luftkabotage *f*.

cache (Waffen)Versteck *n*.

cachepolus Hilfsgerichtsvollzieher *m*.

cadastral ein Kataster betreffend, Kataster . . .; ~ **plan** Katasterplan; Vermessung; ~ **survey** Katasterplan.

cadastration Landvermessung *f*.

cadaver Leiche *f*, Kadaver *m*.

cadet Kadett *m*, Kriegsschüler *m*.

cadi Kadi *m*, Richter *m*.

caduca vererbliches Gut *n*; Verfall *m* e–r Erbschaft.

caduciary *adj* verfallend, Verfalls . . .

cafeteria plan Gehaltsnebenleistungen zur Auswahl.

calaboose Kittchen *n*, Knast *m*.

calamity Kalamität *f*, schwerer Unglücksfall *m*; **common** ~ gemeinsamer Unglücksfall, Todesvermutung für gleichzeitiges Versterben bei Massenunglück; **unforeseen** ~ Katastrophe(nfall).

calculate rechnen, berechnen, errechnen, kalkulieren, bestimmen; ~**d on a freehold basis** zu Grundeigentumspreisen berechnet; ~**d to cause fear** als Einschüchterung; ~**d to deceive** in Täuschungsabsicht, zwecks Irreführung, zwecks Marktverwirrung.

calculating the time Frist(en)berechnung *f*.

calculation Berechnung *f*; ~ **basis** Berechnungsgrundlage; ~ **of charges** Kostenberechnung; ~ **of probabilities** Wahrscheinlichkeitsrechnung; ~ **of proceeds** Ertragsrechnung; ~ **of profits** Rentabilitätsrechnung, Gewinnkalkulation; ~ **of the net return** Rentabilitätsrechnung; **back-**~ Rückrechnung (*Blutalkohol*); **rough** ~ Voranschlag.

calendar Kalender *m*, Terminkalender *m*; Liste der Angeklagten; ~ **days** Kalendertage; ~ **month** Kalendermonat; ~ **of causes** Sitzungsliste; ~ **of motions to discharge** Liste der Anträge auf Vorlage an das Plenum; ~ **of prisoners** Gefangenenliste; ~ **quarter** (Kalender-)Vierteljahr; ~ **year** Kalenderjahr; **approximate** ~ Überschlagsrechnung; **call of the** ~ Aufruf der Gesetzesvorlagen (*Parlament*); **consent** ~ Liste von voraussichtlich unstreitigen Vorlagen; **court** ~ Sitzungsliste; **private** ~ Liste der selbständigen Anträge von Abgeordneten; **special** ~ Liste zur sofortigen Behandlung; **to go on the** ~ in e–e Tagesordnung aufnehmen.

call *s* Ruf *m*, Aufruf *m*, Abruf *m*, Aufforderung *f*, Forderung *f*, Nachfrage *f*, Zahlungsaufforderung *f*, Einzahlungsaufforderung *f*, Bezugsoption *f*, Vorprämie *f*; Verleihung des Grades e–s barrister-of-law *qv*; ~ **deposits** jederzeit abrufbare Einlagen; ~ **for bids** → *bid*; ~ **for funds** Einforderung von Geldern; ~ **for proof in bankruptcy** Aufforderung zur Anmeldung von Konkursforderungen; ~ **for redemp-**

tion Aufforderung zum Rückkauf; ~ **letter** schriftliche Aufforderung zur Einzahlung auf Aktien; ~ **loan** jederzeit kündbares Darlehen, Abrufkredit *an Börsenmakler*; ~ **market** Markt für Tagesgeld; **money** Tagesgeld, tägl. kündbarer Kredit (*Börse*); ~ **of bonds** Aufruf von Obligationen; ~ **of more** Nachgeschäft; ~ **of the House** namentlicher Aufruf der Abgeordneten; ~ **on contributories** Nachschußaufforderung; ~ **on shares** Einzahlungsaufforderung an Aktionäre; ~ **option** Kaufoption, Vorprämiengeschäft; ~ **-over** Namensaufruf; ~ **price** Rücknahmekurs; ~ **rate** Tagesgeldsatz; ~ **receipt** Einzahlungsquittung; ~ **to arms** Einberufung; ~ **to order** Ordnungsruf; ~ **to the bar** Anwaltszulassung (*barrister*); **at** ~ auf Abruf, sofort fällig; **charge on unpaid ~s** Verpfändung der Ansprüche auf Kapitaleinbezahlung; **cold** ~ unangemeldeter Werbebesuch; *telephone* ~ ~: *unangemeldeter Telephonanruf zu Werbezwecken*; **directory ~s** → *directory*; **due at** ~ → *due*; **forfeiture for nonpayment** of **~s** Kaduzierung wegen Nichteinzahlung von Einlagen; **official** ~ Dienstgespräch; **payment in advance of ~s** vorzeitige Einzahlung auf Kapitalanteile; **personal** ~ Gespräch mit Voranmeldung; **power of court to make ~s** Befugnis des Gerichts zur Einzahlung von Kapitalanteilen aufzufordern (*Gesellschaftskonkurs*); **public** ~ Kursfestsetzung durch Zuruf; **put and** ~ Rück- und Vorprämie, Stellage; **roll** ~ Namensaufruf, namentliche Abstimmung.

call *v* rufen, aufrufen, einberufen, abrufen, zur Einzahlung auffordern; ~ **a case** e–e Sache *bei Gericht* aufrufen; ~ **a witness** e–n Zeugen aufrufen; ~ **an election** e–e Wahl ausschreiben; ~ **an expert** e–n Sachverständigen beiziehen; ~**ed upon to pay** zur Zahlung gezwungen *bzw* verpflichtet; ~ **for payment** zur Zahlung auffordern; ~ **in** einfordern; ~ **in a mortgage** e–e Hypothek kündigen; ~ **off a strike** e–n Streik abbrechen; ~ **the docket** die Sitzungsliste (*zu Beginn der Sitzung*) verlesen; ~ **the jury** die Geschworenen auslosen; ~ **the plaintiff** die Sache aufrufen (*bei Nichterscheinen des Klägers*); ~ **to account** zur Rechenschaft ziehen; ~ **to order** zur Ordnung rufen; ~ **to testify** e–n Zeugen benennen, jmdn zur Aussage auffordern; ~ **to the bar** als Anwalt zulassen; ~ **upon a prisoner** den Angeklagten auffordern, sich zu erklären, *ob er Einwendungen gegen seine Verurteilung habe* (*nach dem Schuldspruch*); **~ed on to act** obliegend, zu e–r Handlung veranlaßt; **hereinafter ~ed** nachstehend; nachstehend genannt.

callable jederzeit abrufbar; **~bonds** kündbare Obligationen; ~ **by lot** auslosbar.

calling *s* Beruf *m*, Berufsausgabe *f*; **common** ~ Berufsangabe; **ordinary** ~ ständige Arbeitsverrichtung, gewöhnlich ausgeübter Beruf.

calling the jury Einberufung der Geschworenen.

calumniate verleumden.

calumniator Verleumder *m*, jmd, der falsche Anschuldigung erhebt.

calumnious verleumderisch.

calumny Verleumdung *f*, falsche Anschuldigung *f*.

Calvo Clause Calvo-Klausel; Verzicht auf diplomatische Schutzrechte eines Ausländers; ~ **Doctrine** Calvo-Doktrin (*Verneinung der Staatshaftung und eines Interventionsrechts bei Unruhen*).

cambist Wechsler *m*, Wechselmakler *m*; Devisenhändler *m*.

cambium Wechsel *m*, Tausch *m*.

camera Richterzimmer *n*; ~ **regis** (*e–e Kammer des Königs*) ein privilegierter Ort oder Markt; ~ **stellata** = *Star Chamber qv*; **in** ~ im Richterzimmer; unter Ausschluß der

Öffentlichkeit; bei e–m Bürotermin.

cameralistics Kameralistik *f*, Abgabewesen *n*; Lehre von der kameralistischen Buchführung.

camouflage *s* Tarnung *f*; ~ **measures** Verschleierungsmaßnahmen; **danger of** ~ Verdunkelungsgefahr.

campaign *s* Aktion *f*, Kampagne *f*; Wahlkampf *m*; ~ **expenditure** Wahlkampfausgaben; ~ **for funds** Sammelaktion; ~ **for members** Mitgliederwerbung; ~ **mantras** Wahlkampftiraden; ~ **overkill** Wahlkampfdestruktion; **election** ~ → *election*; **sales** ~ Verkaufsaktion.

campers Anteil *m* am Ertrag eines Prozesses.

cancel für ungültig erklären, streichen, annullieren; ~ **a hearing** e–e mündliche Verhandlung absetzen; ~ **an order** e–n Auftrag stornieren; e–e Anordnung aufheben; **to be** ~**led out** sich gegenseitig aufheben; **until** ~**led** bis auf Widerruf.

cancellable annullierbar.

cancellation Annulierung *f*, Stornierung *f*; Ungültigkeitserklärung *f*; Rücktrittserklärung *f*; Durchstreichen *n*, Löschung *f*; Einziehung *f*; ~ **clause** Verfallsklausel, Rücktrittsklausel; ~ **of an entry** Löschung e–r Eintragung; ~ **of debts** Stornierung von Schulden; ~ **of loan** fristlose Darlehenskündigung; ~ **of orders** Annullierung (Stornierung) von Aufträgen; ~ **of securities** Kraftloserklärung von (*abhanden gekommenen*) Wertpapieren; ~ **of shares** Kaduzierung; ~ **of the sale** Wandelung des Kaufvertrages.

cancelling price Abstandssumme *f*.

candidate Kandidat *m*, Anwärter *m*; ~ **body** sich bewerbendes Gremium; ~ **for a teaching appointment** Lehramtsanwärter; **strong** ~ aussichtsreicher Kandidat; **unopposed** ~ alleiniger Kandidat.

candidature Kandidatur *f*, Bewerbung *f*.

candour Offenheit *f*, Aufrichtigkeit *f*; **positive duty of** ~ Offenbarungspflicht.

caning Züchtigung *f* mit dem Rohrstock.

cannabis Haschisch *n*.

cannot kann nicht, darf nicht; ~ **be found** nicht auffindbar, nicht erreichbar; **"~ handle"** Hereinnahme (*des Schecks*) abgelehnt.

canon *s* Regel *f*, Richtschnur *f*, kirchenrechtl Gesetz *n*; ~**s of construction** Auslegungsregeln; ~**s of descent** Regeln der gesetzlichen Erbfolge; ~**s of inheritance** Erbfolgenormen; ~**s of professional ethics** standesrechtliche Grundsätze; ~**s of taxation** Besteuerungsprinzipien.

canon *adj* kanonisch; **C~ Law** kanonisches Recht.

cannonshot rule *Grundsatz zur Bestimmung von Hoheitsgewässern: innerhalb der Reichweite der Küstenartillerie.*

"Can't Pays" Zahlungsunfähige *m/pl*.

cant *s* Schräge *f*, Biegung *f*, geneigte Fläche *f*; Jargon *m*, Zunftsprache *f*, Pöbelsprache *f*; Aufteilung *f* von Gemeinschaftseigentum.

canvass *v* Kundenwerbung durch Hausbesuche vornehmen; Wahlpropaganda von Tür zu Tür durchführen; ~ **orders** Aufträge hereinholen.

canvasser Kundenwerber *m*, Akquisiteur *m*, Wahlstimmenwerber *m*.

canvassing Stimmenwerbung an der Haustür; ~ **campaign** Werbefeldzug *m*, Werbeaktion *f*, Werbung an der Wohnungstür.

cap Obergrenze *f*.

capable fähig, tauglich, leistungsfähig; ~ **of being rendered fit** sanierungsfähig; ~ **of contracting** geschäftsfähig; ~ **of crime** schuldfähig, zurechnungsfähig; ~ **of distinguishing** unterscheidungsfähig (*Warenzeichen*); ~ **of making a will** testierfähig; ~ **of proof** beweisfähig; ~ **of taking effect** potentiell wirksam; **legally** ~ geschäftsfähig.

capacity Eigenschaft *f*, Funktion *f*; rechtl Fähigkeit *f*, Handlungsfähigkeit *f*, Fassungsraum *m*; ~ **of child in criminal law** Strafmündigkeit; ~ **of succession** dauernde Rechtsfähigkeit (*Körperschaft*); ~ **of trustee** (rechtl) Eignung als Treuhänder; ~ **to act as party** Parteifähigkeit; ~ **to be sued** → *to sue*; ~ **to commit crime** Schuldfähigkeit; ~ **to consent** Einwilligungsfähigkeit zum Geschlechtsverkehr; ~ **to contract** Geschäftsfähigkeit; ~ **to marry** Ehefähigkeit; ~ **to pay** Zahlungsfähigkeit; ~ **to sue** → *to sue*; **contractual** ~ Geschäftsfähigkeit; **criminal** ~ Schuldfähigkeit; **disposing** ~ Testierfähigkeit, Geschäftsfähigkeit; Rechtsstellung; geschäftliche Befugnisse; **earning** ~ Erwerbsfähigkeit; **executive** ~ Eigenschaften e-s leitenden Angestellten, Führungsqualität; **fiduciary** ~ Eigenschaft als Treuhänder; **idle** ~ ungenützte Kapazität; seiner Eigenschaft als; **fiduciary** ~ Treuhändereigenschaft; **legal** ~ Geschäftsfähigkeit; **limited** ~ beschränkte Geschäftsfähigkeit; **mental** ~ Zurechnungsfähigkeit, Schuldfähigkeit; **proprietary** ~ Verfügungsrecht über das eigene Vermögen; **public** ~ Gemeinnützigkeit; **purchasing** ~ Kaufkraft; **substantial** ~ Zurechnungsfähigkeit; **taxable** ~ Steuerkraft; **testamentary** ~ Testierfähigkeit.

capias Festnahmeverfügung *f*, persönl Arrestverfügung, Haftbefehl; ~ **ad audiendum judicium** Haftbefehl zur Vorführung bei der Urteilsverkündung; ~ **ad respondendum** Vorführung und Vernehmung zur Sache, Vorführung zur Einlassung auf Deliktsklagen; ~ **ad satisfaciendum** Befehl zur Verhaftung des Schuldners; ~ **extendi facias** Vollstreckungsauftrag der Krone; ~ **pro fine** Haftbefehl zur Vollziehung der Ersatzfreiheitsstrafe; ~ **utlagatum** Haftbefehl gegen einen für vogelfrei Erklärten; **writ of** ~ Haftbefehl.

capital Kapital *n* (= *K bzw* . . . *k*), Eigen*k n*, Anlage*k n*, Gesellschafts*k n*; ~ **accounts** Konten für das Anlagevermögen; ~ **allowance** Abschreibung auf Anlagegüter; ~ **appreciation** Werterhöhung des Anlagevermögens, Vermögenszuwachs; ~ **assets** Anlagevermögen; ~ **balance** Bilanzsaldo; ~ **base** *K*basis; ~ **brought in** *K*einlage; eingebrachtes *K*; ~ **budget** Investitionsplan; ~ **budgeting** Investitionsrechnung; ~ **clause** Satzungsbestimmung über die *K*struktur der Gesellschaft; ~ **contribution** Einlage e-s Gesellschafters; ~ **costs** werterhöhende Investitionskosten; ~ **element** Tilgungsanteil; ~ **employed** investiertes *K*; ~ **equipment** *K*ausstattung; ~ **expenditure** Investitionsaufwand; *K*aufwendungen; ~ **expenditure undertaking** Unternehmen mit Einsatz von Gesellschafts*k*; ~ **flotations** Emissionen; ~ **flight** *K*flucht; ~ **flow** = *flow of capital qv*; ~ **gain** Vermögenszuwachs, *K*zuwendung; Veräußerungsgewinn *von Anlagegütern*, ~ **gains** *realisierte* Kursgewinne; ~ **gains and losses** Zuwachs und Verminderung des Anlagevermögens *bzw des Eigenkapitals*; ~ **gains distribution** Ausschüttung realisierter Kursgewinne; ~ **gains distribution accepted in shares** ausgeschüttete, in Anteile umgewandelte Kursgewinne; ~ **gains dividend** Dividende des erhöhten Eigen*k-s*; ~ **gains tax** → *tax*; ~ **gearing** → *gearing*; ~ **goods** *K*güter; Investitionsgüter. Anlagegüter; ~ **grant** Investitionszuschuß; ~ **impairment** Unterbilanz, Auszehrung des Grund*k*; ~ **intensive** *k*intensiv; ~ **invested** *K*einsatz; ~ **investment** *K*anlage, langfristig angelegtes *K*; **C~ Issues Committee** Emissionskontrollausschuß; ~ **levy** → *levy*; ~ **loans** Investitionskredit, Darlehen für Anlagevermögen; ~ **money** *K*betrag, Hauptsumme (*außer Zinsen*), Hauptsache, Darlehensschuld; zum

Treuhandk gehörende Gelder; ~ movement Kbewegung; ~ **not called up** nicht zur Einzahlung aufgerufene Kanteile; ~ **outlay** Aufwendung auf das Anlagevermögen; ~ **outstanding** begebenes K; ~ **paid** einbezahltes K; ~ **project** Investitionsvorhaben; ~ **realisation account** Veräußerungsgewinnkonto; ~ **recovery** Krückfluß; Krückgewinnung; Realisierung von Dubiosen; ~ **redemption reserve fund** Rücklage für Rückkauf von Kanteilen; ~ **reduction** Kherabsetzung; ~ **reserve** Kreserve, nicht ausschüttbare Rücklage; ~ **reserve liability** nicht begebene Kreserve; ~ **resources** (Kapital)-Vermögen; eigene Mittel, Reinvermögen, EigenK; ~ **stock** Grundk, Aktienk, Stammk, genehmigtes K; ~ **structure** Kstruktur; ~ **surplus** Überschuß des Eigenk-s (*über das Nenn-Kapital*); ~ **tie-up** Kbindung; ~ **tied up in accounts** Kbindung in Debitoren; ~ **transactions** Kverkehr; ~ **transfer** Kübertragung; ~ **transfer tax** → *tax*; ~ **turnover** Kumschlag; ~ **yield** Kertrag; ~ **yield tax** → *tax*; **accumulation of** ~ Kbildung; **active** ~ Betriebsk, Umlaufk; **application of** ~ **money** (*treuhänderisch gebundene*) Verwendung von Geldern aus Treuhandk; **authorized** ~ Grundk, Stammk; **borrowed** ~ Fremdk; **business** ~ Geschäftsk, Betriebsk; **circulating** ~ Umlaufvermögen; **contribution of** ~ → *contribution*; **corporate** ~ Gesellschaftsk; **domestic** ~ Inlandsk; **dormant** ~ totes (*nicht investiertes*) K; **exodus of** ~ Kabwanderung; **fixed** ~ Realvermögen; **floating** ~ Umlaufvermögen, Betriebsk; **free** ~ frei verfügbares Geldkapital; **frozen** ~festliegendes K; eingefrorenes K; **fully paid up** ~ voll eingezahltes Aktienk; **idle** ~ totes K; **initial** ~ Anfangsk; **invested** ~ Anlagevermögen, angelegtes K; **issued** ~ ausgegebenes K; **joint** ~ Gesellschaftsk e–r Personalgesellschaft, Gesamthandsvermögen; **legal** ~ ausreichendes Eigenvermögen; **liquid** ~ K in Form von Geld, Geldk; **nominal** ~ Grundk, Nennk, Stammk, **ordinary** ~ Stammk; **original** ~ Gründungsk; **paid-in** ~ für Kanteile bezahlter Betrag; **paid-up** ~ einbezahltes K, **permanent** ~ unkündbares K, Anlagek; **private** ~ PrivatK, Privatvermögen; **proprietary** ~ Eigenk; **raising** ~ Kaufbringung; **reflux of** ~ Krückwanderung; **registered** ~ Nominalk, Grundk; **reserve** ~ *nur bei Liquidation verwendbare* Krücklage, Stammk; **share** ~ Grundk, Stammk; Aktienk; **shareholder's** ~ Aktienk; **seed** ~ Startkapital; **special** ~ Sondervermögen, Kommanditeinlage; **stock** ~ Aktienk; **subscribed** ~ gezeichnetes K; Grundk; **trading** ~ Betriebsk; **uncalled** ~ die noch nicht eingeforderten Keinlagen; **unemployed** ~ ungenutztes K, totes K; **unissued** ~ noch nicht ausgegebene Kanteile; **unpaid** ~ noch nicht einbezahltes K; **unproductive** ~ totes; **unrepresented** ~ ungedecktes Gesellschaftsk, verlorenes K; **watered** ~ verwässertes Grundk; **working** ~ → *working*.

capitalisation Kapitalisierung *f*; Kapitalausstattung *f*; ~ **issue** Ausgabe von Gratisaktien bei Kapitalerhöhung; ~ **of interest** Kapitalisierung von Zinsen; ~ **of profits** Kapitalisierung von Gewinnen (*mit Ausgabe von Gratisaktien*); Thesaurierung; **market** ~ Börsenkapitalisierung (*des Unternehmenswerts*).

capitalist Kapitalist *m*, Kapitalrentner *m*.

capitalize kapitalisieren, aktivieren (*von Anlagevermögen*); ~ **an annuity** e–e Rente kapitalisieren.

capitation Kopfsteuer *f*; ~ **grant** Zuschuß pro Kopf; ~ **levy** kopfsteuerartige Abgabe; ~ **tax** Kopfsteuer.

capititium zeremonielle Kleider- und Rangordnung *f*.

capitula Gesetzessammlung *f.*
capitulary Kodex *m.*
capitulation Kapitulation *f*, Kapitulationsurkunde *f.*
capitulations *hist* Kapitulationen *pl*, *Verträge über europäische Immunitätsrechte in der Türkei und in China.*
capper Betrugsköder *m.*
capriciously willkürlich, mutwillig.
captain Kapitän *m*, Schiffskapitän *m*, Hauptmann *m*, Anführer *m*; **~'s effects** persönliche Habe des Kapitäns; **~'s patent** Schifferpatent für große Fahrt; **~'s report** Seeprotest, Verklarung.
captator Erbschleicher *m.*
captio Ergreifung *f.*
caption (*1*) Ergreifung *f*; **~ and asportation** Wegnahme und Wegschaffung; **letters of ~** *scot* Haftbefehl gegen einen Schuldner; **warrant of ~** Steckbrief.
caption (*2*) Rubrum *n*, Rubrik *f*; Bildunterschrift *f*; Kopf *m* (*e–r Urkunde*).
captive *s* Gefangener *m*, Kriegsgef.
captive *adj* intern, firmeneigen, konzerneigen, abhängig.
captivity Gefangenschaft *f*, Kriegsgefangenschaft *f.*
captor Kaperer *m*, Prisennehmer *m*; Beschlagnahmestaat *m*, Gewahrsamsmacht *f.*
capture *s* Beschlagnahme *f*, Beute *f*, Prise *f*; **~ in port** militärische Beschlagnahme im Hafen; **~, seizure and detention** Beschlagnahme; **right of ~** Prisenrecht, Beuterecht.
car Wagen *m*, Waggon *m*, Auto *n*, Kraftfahrzeug *n*; **~ load** Wagenladung; **~ pollution** Autoabgas – Luftverschmutzung; **~ pound** Verwahrungsplatz für abgeschleppte Fahrzeuge; **~ tax** → *tax*; **~ theft** Autodiebstahl; **~ trust** Finanzierungsgesellschaft für Eisenbahnbedarf; **~ trust certificate** (= *car trust securities*) Eisenbahninvestmentpapier *dinglich gesichert an rollenden Material;* **compact ~** Kleinwagen; **executive ~** Vorstandswagen, Prestigefahrzeug; **one-owned ~** Wagen, der nur e–n Besitzer gehabt hat, Erstbesitz; **trade-in ~** Eintauschwagen.
caravan Wohnwagen *m*; **~ site** Wohnwagenabstellplatz.
carcer Karzer *m*, Untersuchungsgefängnis *n.*
card Karte *f*; **~s** Spielkarten *f/pl*; **~-carrying member** eingetragenes Mitglied; **~ holder** Mitglied; **~ index** Kartei, Kartothek; **~ outlet** Kreditkartenteilnehmer; **green ~** grüne Versicherungskarte.
cardinal hauptsächlich, vornehmlich.
care *s* (*1*) Sorgfalt *f* **common duty of ~** allgemeine Sorgfaltspflicht; **ordinary ~** verkehrsübliche Sorgfalt: *to exercise ~ ~ die verkehrsübliche Sorgfalt beachten;* **proper ~** hinreichende Sorgfalt, verkehrsübliche S.; **reasonable ~** → *reasonable;* **slight ~** Sorgfalt wie in eigenen Angelegenheiten; **special ~** besondere Sorgfalt(spflicht); **utmost (degree of) ~** äußerste Sorgfalt(spflicht), größtmögliche Sorgfalt.
care *s* (*2*) Aufsicht *f*, Pflege *f*, Sorge *f*, Obhut *f*; Personensorge *f*; **~ allowance** Pflegeentschädigung; **~ and control order** Sorgerechtsbeschluß; **~ and protection** Obhut; **~ assistant** Altenpfleger; **~, custody or control** Obhut, Gewahrsam, Herrschaftsbereich, Verantwortungsbereich; **~ order** Jugendfürsorgeanordnung; **~ proceedings** Fürsorgeerziehungsverfahren; **ante-natal ~** Schwangerenfürsorge; **compulsory ~** Amtspflegschaft; **nursing ~** Pflege; **to be under ~ and treatment** Patient einer (*geschlossenen*) Heil- und Pflegeanstalt sein; **under ~** entmündigt; **voluntary ~** freiwillige Fürsorgeerziehung.
careenage Kielgeld *n.*
career Laufbahn *f*, Karriere *f*; **~ and promotion rules** Laufbahnvorschriften; **~ consul** → *consul*; **~ officer** Berufsoffizier; **to enter upon a ~** eine Laufbahn einschlagen.

careful achtsam, sorgsam; sorgfältig; **upon ~ consideration** nach reiflicher Überlegung.
carefulness Sorgfalt *f*, Achtsamkeit *f*, Sorgsamkeit *f*.
careless fahrlässig, nachlässig, unachtsam; **~ and inconsiderate driving** rücksichtslose Fahrweise.
carelessness Fahrlässigkeit *f*, Nachlässigkeit *f*, Unachtsamkeit *f*.
caretaker Verwalter *m*, Wärter *m*, Kustos *m*.
cargo Ladung *f*, Frachtgut *n*; **~ book** Ladebuch; **~ hatch** Ladeluke; **~ insurance** → *insurance*; **~ lien** Ladungspfandrecht; **~ list** Ladeverzeichnis; **~ lost or not lost** ohne Rücksicht auf Verlust der Ladung; **~ policy** Ladungspolice; **~ space** Frachtraum; **~ stage** Ladegerüst; **~ underwriter** Frachtversicherer; **bulky ~** sperrige Ladung; **~** → *bulk;* **chilled ~** Kühlgut; **deck ~** → *deck*; **floating ~** unterwegs befindliche Ladung; Unterwegsware; schwimmende Ladung; **general ~** Stückgutladung; **inflammable ~** feuergefährliche Ladung; **mixed ~** gemischte Ladung, Stückgutladung; **outward ~** Hinfracht; **return ~** → *return*; **shifting ~** lose Ladung.
carnal körperlich, fleischlich, geschlechtlich; **~ abuse** Verletzung weibl Geschlechtsorgane bei Unzuchthandlungen; **~ knowledge** Geschlechtsverkehr, versuchter Geschlechtsverkehr ~ly sexual, den Geschlechtsverkehr betreffend; **to know;** ~ly *adv* den Geschlechtsverkehr ausüben, den Beischlaf vollziehen.
carnet Zollpassierschein *m*.
carousel Gepäckkreisel *n*.
carpetbagger Geschäftemacher *m* (*bes in e–m besiegten Land*), Abenteurer *m*, Schwindelbankier *m*.
carriage (*1*) Beförderung *f*, Fracht *f*, Frachtkosten *pl*, Beförderungskosten *pl*; Transport *m*, *GB* Fracht(gebühr) *bei Güterbeförderung zu Lande*; **~ and duty prepaid** franko Fracht und Zoll; **~ by air** Lufttransport; **~ by sea** Beförderung auf dem Seeweg, Seetransport; **~ charges** Frachtkosten; **~ forward** unfrei, Fracht zahlt der Empfänger; **~ of goods** Gütertransport, Beförderung von Waren, Frachtgeschäft; **~ of goods by air** Luftfrachtgeschäft; **~ of goods by road** Güterkraftverkehr; **~ paid** frachtfrei, Fracht bezahlt; **express ~** Eilgutbeförderung.
carriage (*2*) Annahme *f*; **~ of a bill** Annahme e–s Gesetzantrages, Verabschiedung e–r Vorlage; **~ of a motion** Annahme e–s Antrags.
carriageway Fahrbahn *f*; **dual ~**: geteilte Fahrbahn.
carrier Beförderer *m*, Frachtführer *m*, Luftfrachtführer *m*, Transportunternehmer *m*; **~'s charge** → *charge*; **~'s lien** → *lien*; **common ~** gewerbsmäßiger Frachtführer, Transportunternehmer, Verkehrsunternehmen; **common ~ of passengers** Personenverkehrsunternehmen; **contract ~** Sondervertragsfrachtführer; **initial ~** der erste (*in der Reihe der*) Frachtführer; **marine ~** Seefrachtführer; **no-frills ~** Luftlinie mit schlichtem Service; **private ~** nicht gewerblicher Beförderer, Gelegenheitsspediteur; **special ~** Gelegenheitsspediteur; **specific commodity ~** Spezialtransportunternehmen.
carry tragen, transportieren; **~ a gold-value guarantee** goldwertversichert sein; **~all** Reisetasche; **~ a member** für ein Mitglied aufkommen; **~ a motion** e–n Antrag annehmen; **~ an election** e–e Wahl gewinnen, e–n Kandidaten durchbringen; **~ arms** Waffen führen; **~ costs** → *cost*; **~ forward** vortragen auf; **~ forward to new account** auf neue Rechnung vortragen; **~ insurance** versichert sein; **~ interest** → *interest*; **~ into effect** wirksam werden lassen, ausführen; **~ into port** in den Hafen bringen; **~ on a business** gewerblich tätig sein, ein Geschäft betreiben; **~ on an action** e–n Rechtsstreit führen;

~ **out** durchführen, durchsetzen; ~**-over** → *carry-over*; ~ **weapons** Waffen führen.

carry-back (of losses) Verlustrücktrag; *m*; ~ **adjustment** rückwirkender Verlustausgleich (*tax, US*), Verlustrücktrag.

carrying | away das Wegschaffen (*der Diebesbeute*); ~ **capacity** Tragfähigkeit, Ladefähigkeit, Nutzlast; ~ **charges** Transportkosten, Speditionskosten, Lagerkosten, Preisaufschlag beim Abzahlungskauf; Grundbesitzlasten; Wohnungseigentumsgebühren; Verwahrungsnebenkosten; ~ **costs** mit Kostenentscheidung; ~ **of a bill** Annahme einer Vorlage; ~ **value** → *value*.

carry-over (= *carryover*) Vortrag *m*, Übertrag *m*; Überbestand *m*; Prolongation *f*, Report *m*; ~ **business** Reportgeschäft; ~ **day** Reporttag; ~ **rate** Reportsatz, Prolongationsgebühr.

cart *v* anrollen; *s* Wagen *m*, Güterwagen *m*; ~**ed goods** Rollgut.

carta Urkunde *f*, gesiegelte Urkunde *f*.

cartage Rollgeld *n*; Transportkosten *pl*; ~ **contractor** Rollfuhrmann; ~ **limit** Zustellbezirk.

carte blanche Blankovollmacht *f*, unlimitierte Ermächtigung.

cartel (*1*) Kartell *n*; ~ **agreement** Kartellvertrag; ~ **participant** Kartellmitglied; ~ **price** Kartellpreis, gebundener Preis; **price** ~ Preiskartell.

cartel (*2*) Abkommen *n* zwischen kriegführenden Mächten; ~**-ship** Parlamentärschiff *n*, Schiff *n* zum Austausch von Kriegsgefangenen.

cartman Fuhrunternehmer *m*.

cartulary Urkundentruhe *f*.

case (Gerichts)Sache *f*, Fall *m*, Rechtsstreit *m*; Ereignis *n*, Sachverhalt *m*, Tatbestand *m*, Vorbringen *n*, Sachvortrag *m*; Schadenersatzklage (= *trespass on the case qv*); ~ **advance** Kostenvorschuß; ~ **agreed on** unstreitiger Sachverhalt; ~**s and controversies** Rechtsstreitigkeiten; ~ **at bar** der vorliegende Fall; ~ **at issue** der zur Entscheidung stehende Rechtsstreit, der vorliegende Fall; ~**-book** Entscheidungssammlung; ~**-by-case approach** fallweises Vorgehen; ~ **for motion** schriftsätzliche Begründung e–s Antrages; ~ **history** Vorgeschichte, Krankheitsgeschichte; ~ **in chief** Beweisvorbringen des primär Beweisbelasteten; ~ **in dispute** der vorliegende Fall; ~ **law** Fallrecht, Präzedenzrecht, Richterrecht; ~ **monitoring** statistische Erfassung der Prozeßerledigung; ~ **note** → *note*; ~ **number** → *number*, ~ **of need** Notfall, Notadresse; ~ **on appeal** Berufungssache; ~**s pending** anhängige Verfahren; ~ **record** → *record;* ~ **reserved** *gemeinsame Sachverhaltsdarstellung* (*von den Parteien dem Gericht zur Entscheidung über Rechtsfragen vorgelegt*); ~ **retainer** Anwaltsgebührenvorschuß (*bereits verdient*); ~ **stated** Revisionsvorlage (*Tatbestand, der dem höheren Gericht zur Entscheidung über e–e Rechtsfrage vorgelegt wird*) Vorlage zum Rechtsentscheid; ~ **system** Rechtsunterricht nach Präzedenzfällen; ~ **to move for new trial** Begründung e–s Wiederaufnahmeantrages; ~ **under consideration** der vorliegende Fall; ~ **work** Fürsorgearbeit (*am einzelnen Fall*); a ~ **to answer** schlüssiges Vorbringen; **a good** ~ aussichtsreiches Vorbringen; **action on the** ~ → *action*; **arguable** ~ vertretbares Argument; **a strong** ~ e–e schlüssige, überzeugende Begründung; **as the** ~ **may be** je nach Sachlage, je nachdem; **civil** ~ bürgerlicher Rechtsstreit, Zivilsache, Zivilprozeß; **conduct of a** ~ → *conduct*; **criminal** ~ Strafsache, Strafprozeß; **ex parte** ~ einseitiges Verfahren, Fall der freiwilligen Gerichtsbarkeit, **high-security** ~**s** wichtige, abgeschirmte Staatsschutzfälle, Hochsicherheitsfälle; **in** ~ wenn, falls; **in** ~ **of death** im Todesfalle, bei Ableben; **in** ~ **of doubt** im Zweifel; **in** ~ **of emer-**

gency in e–m Notstand, im Notfall; **in ~ of need** im Notfalle, notfalls, falls *der Wechsel* notleidend wird; **juvenile** ~ Jugendsache; **law** ~ Rechtsfall, Rechtssache; **lead** ~ Präzedenzfall, Leitfall; **leading** ~ Präzedenzfall, Leitfall; **legal** ~ Rechtsangelegenheit; **multi-reason** ~ mehrfach begründete Klage; **negligible** ~ Bagatellfall; **"no ~ to answer"** *Strafrecht*: hoffnungsloser Fall, bei dem nichts zu machen ist; *Zivilrecht*: unschlüssiges oder unbewiesenes Vorbringen (*das keiner Replik bedarf*); **"one-off"** ~ einmaliger Fall; **particular** ~ Einzelfall; **petty** ~ geringfügige Streitsache, Bagatellsache; **ruling** ~ maßgeblicher Präzedenzfall; **running-down** ~ Verkehrsunfallsache (*Verletzung e–s Fußgängers*); **seminal** ~ bahnbrechender Fall; **special** ~ Sachverhalt für ein Zwischenurteil über den Grund, Vorlage e–s Sachverhalts zur richterl Entscheidung; **the instant** ~ der vorliegende Fall; **to bring on the** ~ mit der Bearbeitung des Falles vorankommen; **to call a** ~ → *call v*; **to conduct the** ~ den Prozeß führen; **to have a good** ~ das Recht auf seiner Seite haben; **to hear a** ~ in e–r Sache verhandeln; **to lose one's** ~ seinen Prozeß verlieren; **to make out a** ~ e–e Sache schlüssig vortragen; **to remit a** ~ e–e Sache verweisen *bzw* zurückverweisen; **to reopen a** ~ → *reopen*; **to state the** ~ den Fall vortragen; **written** ~ schriftsätzl Begründung.

cases and casks Rollgut *n*, (*Kisten und Fässer*).

caseload Zahl der bearbeiteten Fälle, Arbeitslast an Prozessen, Überlastung der Gerichte.

caseworker Sozialarbeiter *m*.

cash *s* Bargeld *n*; Zahlungsmittel *n|pl*; ~ **account** → *account*; ~ **against bill of lading** Kasse gegen Konossement; ~ **against documents** Kasse gegen Dokumente; ~ **and carry** (=) Barzahlung und Selbstabholung; ~ **assets** Barwerte, Barguthaben, liquide Mittel erster Ordnung; ~ **at maturity** zahlbar bei Fälligkeit; ~ **at my bankers** jederzeit fälliges Guthaben bei meiner Bank; ~ **audit** Kassenprüfung; Kassenrevision; ~ **balance** → *balance*; ~ **bargain** Barabschluß; ~ **basis** Barzahlungsbasis; ~ **before delivery** Vorauskasse; ~ **blotter** → *blotter*; ~ **bonus** Barprämie; ~ **book** Kassenbuch, Kassabuch; ~ **card** Geldautomatenkarte; ~ **consignment** Sendung gegen Barzahlung; ~ **contract** Barzahlungsvertrag; ~ **credit** Barkredit; ~ **demand** Bedarf an Zahlungsmitteln, Liquiditätsbedarf; ~ **deposit** Bareinlage, Bareinzahlung, Barhinterlegung; Bardepot; ~ **disbursements** → *disbursement*; ~ **discount** → *discount*; ~ **dispenser** Geldautomat; ~ **down** Baranzahlung; ~ **drawings** Barentnahmen, Barabhebungen; ~ **earnings** Bareinnahmen; ~ **flow** (=) Gewinneinbehalt (*nicht ausgeschütteter, versteuerter Reingewinn*); Kapitalfluß aus Umsatz, Barmittelfluß; ~ ~ *problems*: *Liquiditätsprobleme;* ~ **forecast** Liquiditätsprognose; ~ **in bank** Bankguthaben; ~ **inflows** Einnahmen, Zuflüsse von Zahlungsmitteln; ~ **in hand** Kassenbestand, Barbestand; ~ **in house** alle im Hause befindlichen Barmittel; ~ **in tills** Kassenbestand; ~ **indemnity** Mankogeld, Fehlgeldentschädigung; ~ **inflow** Geldzugang; ~ **injection** Liquiditätsspritze; ~ **loan** → *loan*; ~ **management** (=) Kassenhaltung, Liquiditätssteuerung, kurzfristige Finanzdisposition; ~ **margin** Bareinschuß; ~ **market** → *market*; ~ **note** Kassenobligation; ~ **on delivery** (*COD*) Nachnahme, zahlbar bei Übergabe; Lieferung gegen Barzahlung; ~ **or moneys so called** Bargeld oder bargeldgleiche Mittel; ~ **order** Zahlungsanweisung, Kassaorder, Warenbezugsanweisung bei Abzahlungsvereinbarungen; ~ **out-**

flows Ausgaben, Abflüsse von Zahlungsmitteln; ~ **over** Kassenüberschuß; ~ **paid** erfolgte Barzahlung, Quittung; ~ **paid and received** Einzahlungen und Abhebungen; ~ **payment** Barzahlung; ~ **price** Barpreis, Preis bei Barzahlung; ~ **procurement** Geldbeschaffung, Liquiditätsbeschaffung; ~ **ratio** Primärliquidität (*von Banken*); ~ **receipts** Zahlungseingänge, Kasseneingänge; ~ **records** Kassenbelege, Kassenaufzeichnungen; ~ **refund** Barerstattung; ~ **register** → *register*, ~ **remittance** Barüberweisung, Geldsendung; ~ **report** → *report*; ~ **requirements** Mindestvorschriften für liquide Mittel; ~ **sale** → *sale*; ~**-settled** bar reguliert; ~ **settlement** Barabfindung, Kapitalabfindung, prompte Erfüllung (*von Börsengeschäften*); ~ **short** Kassenmanko, Kassenfehlbetrag; ~ **shortfall** Liquiditätsmangel; ~ **squeeze** Liquiditätsengpaß; ~ **statement** Kassenbericht, Kassenzettel, Kassenausweis, Liquiditätsstatus; ~ **surrender value** Rückkaufswert (*einer Police*), Barablösungswert; ~ **system** Barzahlungssystem; ~ **transaction** Bargeschäft; ~ **tube system** Rohrpostbeförderung von Bargeld (*zB in Warenhäusern*); ~ **under the control of the court** gerichtlich hinterlegtes Geld; ~ **value** Barwert, Barverkaufspreis; Verkehrswert bei *Barzahlung*; *ins* Rückkaufswert; ~ **with options of bill** bar oder nach Wahl des Käufers in Wechseln; ~ **with order** Barzahlung bei Bestellung; **actual** ~ **value** → *value*; **adverse** ~ Kassendefizit; **fair** ~ **value** Verkehrswert, *angemessener Barveräußerungswert*; **foreign** ~ Bardevisen, Geldsorten, Sorten; **net** ~ netto Kasse; **operating** ~ vorhandene Betriebsmittel; **petty** ~ geringe Beträge, Portokasse, Handkasse; **prompt** ~ sofortige Barzahlung (*auch*: 7 *Tage Ziel*); **segregation of** ~ Aufteilung *und Zweckbindung* von Barmitteln; **spot** ~ netto Kasse, bar ohne Abzug, sofortige Bezahlung; **treasury** ~ Gold und jederzeit fällige Guthaben der Staatsbank.

cash *v* kassieren, einlösen.

cash-in Einlösung *f*, Rückgabe *f*.

cashier *s* Kassierer *m*, Kassenbeamter *m*, Schalterbeamter *m*; ~**'s cheque** → *cheque* (2).

cashier *v* entlassen, ausstoßen (*Offizier*).

casing Verpackung *f*; ~ **point** (=) Verrohrungspunkt (*Erdöl*).

casino Spielbank *f*; Spielkasino *n*.

casket Behälter *m*, Sarg *m*.

cassation Kassation *f*, Ungültigerklärung *f*.

casual zufällig, gelegentlich.

casualty Zufall *m*, unabwendbares Ereignis; Unfall *m*; ~ **company** Unfallversicherungsgesellschaft (*alle Sparten außer Feuer-, Lebens- und Transportversicherung*); ~ **insurance** → *insurance*; ~ **list** Verlustliste, Liste der Toten und Verwundeten; **unavoidable** ~ unabwendbares (zufälliges) Ereignis.

casus|belli Kriegsfall *m*, Kriegsgrund *m*; ~ **foederis** Bündnisfall.

casuistry Kasuistik *f*, Spitzfindigkeit *f*.

cat Katze *f*, Peitsche *f*; ~**s and dogs** billige Spekulationspapiere; **C~ and Mouse Act** *Gesetz über Strafvollzugaussetzung wegen Krankheit, GB 1913*; ~ **burglar** Fassadenkletterer; ~ **–o'-nine-tails** neunschwänzige Katze; ~**'s paw** willenloses Werkzeug (*bei mittelbarer Täterschaft*).

catalogue Katalog *m*, Verzeichnis *n*, Liste *f*; ~ **ordering concern** Versandhaus; ~ **shop** Versandhaus-Niederlassung.

catapult Präzisionsschleuder *f*.

catastrophe Katastrophe *f*; ~ **limit** Risikobegrenzung bei Katastrophen; ~ **reinsurance** Rückversicherung bei Katastrophen und Großschäden; ~ **reserve** außerordentliche Reserve.

catch *v* fangen, einfangen, ertappen,

ergreifen; ~ **red-handed** auf frischer Tat ertappen; ~ **the chairman's** (**the Speaker's**) **eye** das Wort erhalten.

catchings Fang *m* (*Hochseefischerei*).

catchment area Einzugsgebiet, Erfassungsgebiet; ~ **board** Entwässerungsbehörde *f*.

catchpoll (= *catchpole*) Polizist *m* (*zu Verhaftungen abgestellt*).

categorical kategorisch, unbedingt; ~ **denial** entschiedenes Bestreiten.

categor|y Kategorie *f*, Art *f*, Gruppe *f*; ~ **of risks** *ins* Gefahrenklasse; **by ~ies of trade** nach Branchengruppen.

cater cousin Vetter *m* vierten Grades, weitläufiger Verwandter *m*.

cater *v* Lebensmittel liefern, *Parties, Empfänge und dgl mit Speisen und Getränken versorgen*.

caterer Lebensmittellieferant *m*; Lieferant *m* von Fertigmahlzeiten, Party-Service-Unternehmen *n*, Proviantmeister *m*.

catering trade Hotel- und Gaststättengewerbe.

cattle Großvieh *n*; Rinder *n|pl*; ~ **gate** Rinderweidegerechtigkeit, Weideallmende; ~ **levant and couchant** Grunddienstbarkeit des Weiderechts; **~-lifting** Viehdiebstahl; ~ **range** Weideland für Rinder; ~ **trespass** Eindringenlassen von Vieh auf fremdes Weideland.

Caucasian *s* Weißer *m*; **non-** ~ Farbiger; *adj* kaukasisch; zur weißen Rasse gehörend, weiß (*Hautfarbe*).

caucus Parteiversammlung *f*, Wählerversammlung *f*, Zusammenkunft *f* des führenden Gremiums, Parteiausschuß *m*.

caucusdom Parteicliquenwesen *n*.

causa Grund *m*, Ursache *f*, Anlaß *m*, Sache *f*; ~ **causans** unmittelbare Ursache, Hauptursache; ~ **mortis** von Todes wegen; angesichts des Todes; ~ **proxima** unmittelbare Ursache; ~ **sine qua non** (=) absolute Ursache.

causal|connection Kausalzusammenhang; ~ **relation** Kausalzusammenhang.

causality Ursächlichkeit *f*, Kausalzusammenhang *m*.

causation Kausalität *f*, Verursachung *f*; **chain of** ~ Kausalzusammenhang; **line of** ~ Kausalität.

cause *s* Grund *m*, Ursache *f*; Rechtsstreit *m*, Prozeß *m*; ~ **and effect** Ursache und Wirkung ~ **-book** Ladungsbuch, Prozeßverzeichnis; ~ **célèbre** (=) berühmter Fall; **~-list** Terminverzeichnis, Verhandlungsliste; ~ **of action** Klagegrund, Sachverhalt e–r Klage, Klageberechtigung, Klagerecht; ~ **of appeal** Anlaß der Berufung, angefochtene Entscheidung; ~ **of complaint** Anlaß für die Beschwerde, Beschwer; ~ **or matter** Sache, Fall; ~ **pending** anhängige Sache; ~ **shown** schlüssige Begründung; **accidental** ~ Vorgang mit unvorhergesehener Folge; **commercial ~s** (*gerichtl*) Handelssachen; **common** ~ gemeinsame Sache; **common ~s** Zivilprozesse (*ohne Prozesse mit der Krone*); **concurrent** ~ Mitursache; **continuing** ~ **of action** Dauerzustand als Klagegrund; **direct** ~ unmittelbare Ursache; **final** ~ eigentliche Ursache; **for** ~ aus triftigem Grund, aus rechtlich erheblichem Grund; **immediate** ~ unmittelbare Ursache; **in one's own** ~ in eigener Sache; **intervening** ~ dazwischentretende *den Kausalzusammenhang unterbrechende* Ursache; **legal** ~ rechtserhebliche Ursache; **matrimonial ~s** → *matrimonial*; **no reasonable** ~ **of action or defence** Unschlüssigkeit des Klagevorbringens wie der Einwendungen; **on** ~ **shown** nach erfolgter Prüfung; **pecuniary ~s** → *pecuniary*; **pending** ~ anhängiges Verfahren; **petty** ~ Bagatellsache; **principle** ~ Hauptklage, Klage (*im Gegensatz zu Widerklage*); **probable** ~ → *probable*; **procuring** ~ Hauptursache; **producing** ~ echte (*e–e Wirkung herbeiführende*) Ursache; **proximate** ~ → *proximate*; **remote** ~ entfernte mittelbare Ursache; **short** ~ kurzer Fall; *im abge-*

kürzten Verfahren zu behandelnde Sache; **small** ~ Bagatellsache; **sole** ~ Alleinursache; **testamentary** ~ Nachlaßsache wegen letztwilliger Verfügung; **to show** ~ → *show*; **to plead a** ~ → *plead*; **ultimate** ~ die eigentliche Ursache; **undefended** ~ einwendungslose Klage, Klage bei Säumnis des Beklagten.

cause *v* veranlassen, verursachen, begründen; ~ **and procure** veranlassen; ~ **any proceedings to be taken** ein Gerichtsverfahren herbeiführen; ~ **or encourage** veranlassen oder dazu anstiften; ~ **or permit** veranlassen oder gestatten; ~ **or procure s. th. to be done** etw bewirken oder durch Dritte geschehen lassen; ~ **or suffer** verursachen oder dulden; ~ **to be imported** die Einfuhr veranlassen.

causeway Straßendamm *m*.

cautio Sicherheitsleistung *f*; ~ **judicatum solvi** Prozeßkostensicherheit; ~ **pro expensis** Prozeßkostensicherheit.

caution *s* Verwarnung *f*, (*Rechts*)Belehrung *f*, Vormerkung *f* im Grundbuch; *scot* Kaution *f*, Bürgschaft *f*.

caution *v* warnen, belehren, auf Rechte hinweisen.

cautionary *adj* vorsorglich; ~ **judgment** Urteil auf vorbeugende Unterlassung, Arresturteil.

cautioning Abmahnung *f*, Verwarnung *f*.

caveat Widerspruch in e–m Register; vorläufige Anmeldung *f* einer *noch unvollständigen* Erfindung; Schutzschrift *f*; ~ **actor** den Handelnden auf Bedenken aufmerksam machen; ~ **emptor** Mängelprüfungspflicht des Käufers; *Mängelrisiko liegt grundsätzl beim Käufer;* ~ **to will** Vorbehalt gegen Testamentsbestätigung; ~ **venditor** Gewährleistungshaftung des Verkäufers; ~ **viator** Sorgfaltspflicht und Schadensabwendungspflicht des Reisenden; **to enter a** ~ **against** Verwahrung einlegen, sich verwahren gegen; **to lodge a** ~ einen Widerspruch einlegen.

caveator *jmd, der Vormerkung bzw Widerspruch einlegt, canad* Patentanmelder *m*.

cavil *s* überkritische, frivole Einwendungen *f/pl*, kritische Spitzfindigkeiten *f/pl*; *v* sophistische Kritik üben, bekritteln.

cease aufhören; ~ **and desist order** → *order* (*1*); ~ **to be in force** außer Kraft treten; ~ **to exist** erlöschen, wegfallen, nicht mehr bestehen; ~ **to do business** die Geschäftstätigkeit einstellen; ~ **to hold office** aus dem Amt ausscheiden.

cede abtreten, zedieren, überlassen; ~**d territory** abgetretenes Gebiet.

ceiling Plafond *n*, Höchstgrenze *f*; ~ **price** → *price* (*1*); ~ **on loans** Kreditplafond; ~ **wages** festgesetzte Höchstlöhne.

celation Verbergen *n* von Schwangerschaft bzw Geburt.

celebration of marriage → *marriage*.

cell Zelle *f*, **drunk** ~ Ausnüchterungszelle; **prison** ~ Gefängniszelle; **single** ~ Einzelzelle; **sobering-up** ~ Ausnüchterungszelle.

censor *s* Zensor *m*; *v* Zensur ausüben.

censorship Zensur *f*; ~ **of the press** Pressezensur; **postal** ~ Briefzensur.

censurable der Zensur unterworfen.

censure Tadel *m*; Rüge *f*, Verweis *m*; **motion of** ~ Tadelsantrag.

census Erhebung *f*, Zählung *f*, Volkszählung *f*; ~ **of distribution** Betriebszählung im Warenhandel; ~ **of population** Volkszählung; ~ **of production** statistische Erfassung der Produktion; ~ **regalis** Jahreseinkünfte der brit Krone; **Bureau of C**~ → *bureau*.

center of gravity doctrine (Lehre vom) Schwerpunkt des Vertragsverhältnisses (*IPR*).

central zentral; **C**~ **Accounting Office** Bundesrechnungshof der

USA; ~ **authorities** Zentralbehörden; ~ **bank** Zentralbank; **C~ Criminal Court** → *court*; **C~ Government** die (*brit*) Regierung; **C~ Land Registry** Zentralgrundbuchamt *in London*; **c~ office** Zentralamt, Zentrale; Hauptgeschäftsstelle (*des Gerichts*); **C~ Office of Information** *GB* Informationsministerium; ~ **rates** → *rate*; **C~ Valuation Board** Hauptbewertungsstelle.

centralization Zentralisierung *f*, Zentralisation *f*.

centrist gemäßigter Politiker *m*.

ceremonial occasion förmlicher Anlaß; offizielle Festlichkeit.

ceremony Förmlichkeit *f*, Feier *f*; **official** ~ feierlicher Staatsakt, feierl Handlung.

certain bestimmt; ~ **rent** bestimmte Pacht; ~ **services** der Höhe nach begrenzte Dienste (*des Pächters*).

certainty Gewißheit *f*, Sicherheit *f*; ~ **in a bill** Bestimmtheit beim Wechsel; ~ **in trust** Bestimmtheit bei der Treuhandbestellung; ~ **to a certain intent in general** allgemeine Bestimmtheit einer Willenserklärung; ~ **to a certain intent in particular** Bestimmtheit einer Willenserklärung im Einzelnen; ~ **to a common intent** Bestimmtheit aus allgemeinem Bedeutungsinhalt; **legal** ~ Rechtssicherheit.

certificate *s* Bestätigung *f*, Bescheinigung *f*, Zeugnis *n*; ~ **for costs** *gerichtliche Bescheinigung zwecks Kostenfestsetzung*; ~ **from last employer** Arbeitsbescheinigung; ~ **into chancery** Vorlagebeschluß an das Kanzleigericht; ~ **of acknowledgment** Beglaubigungsvermerk; ~ **of apprenticeship** Lehrbrief; ~ **of approval** Genehmigungsbescheinigung; ~ **of authority** Vollmacht, Bescheinigung der Ermächtigung zur Geschäftsaufnahme; ~ **of average** Havariezertifikat; ~ **of birth** (= *birth* ~) Geburtsurkunde; ~ **of bonds** Zertifikat über Namensobligation(en); ~ **of charge** Bescheinigung über eingetragene Pfandrechte (*am Gesellschaftsvermögen*); ~ **of clearance inwards** Bestätigung über die Einklarierung (*e–s Schiffes*); ~ **of conformity** *obs* Entlastungsbescheinigung für e–n Gemeinschuldner; Konformitätsbescheinigung (Zoll); ~ **of consent to bail** Beschluß der Zulassung e–r Haftversicherungskaution; ~ **of conviction** schriftliches Strafurteil, Bescheinigung e–r Verurteilung; ~ **of (taxed) costs** Kostenfestsetzungsbeschluß; ~ **of damage** Schadensprotokoll; ~ **of death** (= *death* ~) Sterbeurkunde; ~ **of deposit** Depositenzertifikat, Einlagenzertifikat (*CD*), *floating rate CD*: *variabel verzinsliche CD*; Depotschein = (*verkehrsfähiges, e–e Festgeldanlage belegendes Papier*); ~ **of discharge** Bescheinigung der Urteilsbefriedigung; *mil* Entlassungsschein; ~ **of election** Wahlbestätigungsurkunde; ~ **of employment** Arbeitsbescheinigung; Beschäftigungsnachweis; ~ **of exemption** Befreiungsbescheinigung; Ausnahmebescheinigung; Bescheinigung über Befreiung von Prospektpflicht; ~ **of existence** Lebensbescheinigung; ~ **of funds** Hinterlegungsbescheinigung; ~ **of good conduct** Führungszeugnis; ~ **of hardship** Bescheinigung über das Vorliegen e–s Härtefalles; ~ **of health** Gesundheitsattest; ~ **of identification** Personalausweis, Nämlichkeitszeugnis; ~ **of identity** Identitätsnachweis; ~ **of incorporation** Gründungsurkunde, Gründungsbescheinigung; ~ **of indebtedness** Schuldurkunde, Schuldschein; Schuldanerkenntnis; ~ **of inspection** Beschaffenheitszeugnis, Prüfungszeugnis; ~ **of insurance** vorläufige Bescheinigung über den Abschluß e–r Seeversicherung, vorläufige Deckungsbescheinigung; ~ **of interest** Schürfanteilsurkunde, Bohrungsanteilsurk.; ~ **of inventory** Bescheinigung über die Inventuraufnahme; ~ **of marriage** Heiratsurkunde, Trauschein; ~ **of master** *Feststellungen des Rechtspflegers bzw. beauftragten Richters* (*über seine Untersuchung*); ~ **of naturalization** Einbürgerungsurkunde; ~ **of need** Bedarfsbestätigung; ~ **of nulla bona** Pfandabstandserklärung; ~ **of origin** Ursprungszeugnis; ~ **of occupancy** Bezugsfähigkeitsbescheinigung; ~ **of posting** Posteinlieferungsschein, postamtliche Absendebescheinigung; ~ **of poverty** Armutszeugnis; ~ **of priority** Dringlichkeitsbescheinigung; ~ **of protest** notarieller Wechselprotest; ~ **of purchase** Zuschlagsbescheinigung (*Zwangsversteigerung*); ~ **of quality** Qualitätszertifikat; ~ **of receipt** Empfangsbescheinigung, Annahmebescheinigung; ~ **of redemption** Tilgungsbescheinigung; ~ **of registration** Eintragungsbescheinigung; ~ **of registry** Schiffsregisterbrief; ~ **of sale** Zuschlagsbescheinigung (*Zwangsversteigerung*); ~ **of search** grundbuchamtl Nachforschungsbescheinigung; ~ **of service** Zustellungsurkunde; ~ **of shares** Aktienzertifikat, Kapitalanteilsbescheinigung; ~ **of shipment** Ladeschein; Verschiffungsbescheinigung; ~ **of stock** → *stock certificate*; ~ **of stowage** Stauattest; ~ **of survey** hafenamtliches Zustandsattest bei Löschung; ~ **of taxation** Kostenfestsetzungsbeschluß; ~ **of a tax deposit** (verzinsl) Steuergutschein; ~ **of title** = *title* ~ → *title*; ~ **of tonnage** Meßbrief; ~ **of warranty** Garantieschein; ~ **of weight** Gewichtsbescheinigung; ~ **to commence business** Erlaubnisschein für den Geschäftsbeginn (Geschäftsgründung); ~ **year** Jahresabschnitt seit Begebungsdatum; Jahresabschnitt der Rateneinzahlung; **auditor's** ~ → *auditor*; **bankrupt's** ~ Konkursaufhebungsbescheinigung; **bearer** ~ → *bearer;* **clearance** ~ → *clearance*; **common stock** ~ Stammaktien-(zertifikat); **face amount** ~ *investm* Nennwertzertifikat; **interim** ~ vorläufige Bescheinigung, Zwischenschein, Interimsschein; **land** ~ → *land*; **life** ~ Lebensbescheinigung; **marriage** ~ Heiratsurkunde; **medical** ~ ärztliches Attest; **MOT** ~ *etwa* TÜV Bescheinigung, Zulassungsbescheinigung für Kfz; **notarial** ~ notarielle Bescheinigung; **participation** ~ Beteiligungs-Genußschein; **official** ~ amtliche Bescheinigung; **participating** ~ Genußschein; **practising** ~ Zulassungsurkunde (*solicitor*), (*jährl*) Berufsausübungserlaubnis; **provisional** ~ Interimsschein; **registered** ~ Namenspapier, Namenszertifikat; **title** ~ → *title*; **trading** ~ Erlaubnis (*des Handelsregisteramts*) zum Geschäftsbeginn (*e–r neugegründeten Kapitalgesellschaft*); **treasury** ~ (**of indebtedness**) → *treasury; voting* **trustee's** ~ Stimmberechtigungsschein (*zur treuhänderischen Übertragung des Stimmrechts an Aktienkapital*).

certificate *v* bereinigen, Bescheinigung *bzw* Zeugnis ausstellen; **~d** staatlich zugelassen, Diplom . . .; **~d bankrupt** rehabilitierter früherer Gemeinschuldner.

certification Bescheinigung *f*, Beglaubigung *f*, Zulassung *f*; ~ **mark** → *mark*; ~ **of cheques** (*checks*), Scheckbestätigung (*durch die Bank*); ~ **of copy** Beglaubigung e–r Abschrift; ~ **tests** Zulassungsprüfungen.

certif|y (*certified, certifying*) bestätigen, bescheinigen, beglaubigen; **~ied bankrupt** = *certificated b. qv*; **~ied broker** amtlich zugelassener Makler; **~ied cheque** → *cheque* (*check*); **~ied copy** → *copy*; **~ied public accountant** Wirtschaftsprüfer; **~ied question** Vorlagebeschluß in e–r Rechtsfrage; **~ying committee** Armenrechtsprüfungsausschuß; **~ying officer** Urkundsbeamter; **~ying surgeon** Vertrauensarzt.

certiorari außerordentliches Revisionsverfahren *n*, Revisionsantrag *m*, Aktenanforderung *f*; **bill of ~** Revisionsantrag, Antrag auf rechtliche Überprüfung; **order of ~** Revisionszulassungsbeschluß; **writ of ~** *Verfügung an eine niedrigere Instanz, die Akten der höheren Instanz vorzulegen GB: seit 1938 order of ~*; Zulassung der Revision.

cert worthiness Revisionsfähigkeit *f*.

cessation Beendigung *f*, Einstellung *f*, Aufhören *n*; **~ of cohabitation** Beginn des Getrenntlebens; **~ of delivery** Einstellung der Lieferung; **~ of domestic life** Aufhebung der häuslichen Gemeinschaft; **~ of hostilities** Einstellung der Kampfhandlungen; **~ of payments** Zahlungseinstellung.

cesser Aufhören *n*, Beendigung *f*, Ablauf *m*; **~ clause** Cesser-Klausel (*Haftungsbeendigung bei Abladung*); **~ on redemption** *etwa* Löschung des Grundpfandrechts bei Tilgung; **previous ~ of a patent** vorzeitiger Ablauf eines Patents; **proviso for ~** Heimfallklausel bei Pfandeinlösung *bzw Hypothekentilgung*.

cessio bonorum Überlassung *f* des Schuldnervermögens an Treuhänder zur Gläubigerbefriedigung, Liquidationsvergleich.

cession Überlassung *f*, Aufgabe *f*, Preisgabe *f*; **~ of administration** Übertragung der Verwaltungshoheit; **~ of goods** Preisgabe des Schuldnervermögens zur Gläubigerbefriedigung; **~ of territory** Gebietsabtretung; **recognition of ~** Anerkennung einer Gebietsabtretung.

cestui|que trust Treugeber *m*, Treuhandbegünstigter *m*; **~ que use** *Begünstigter bei einer treuhänderischen Nutzungsüberlassung;* **~ que vie** Treuhandbegünstigter auf Lebensdauer des Treugebers.

ceteris paribus unter sonst gleichen Umständen.

chaffer *s* Handeln *n*, Feilschen *n*, Handelsware *f*; *v* handeln, feilschen.

chafferer Händler *m*, Schacherer *m*.

chaffery Verkehr *m*, Kaufgeschäfte *n|pl*.

chain Kette *f*, lückenlose Folge *f*; Kette von Filialgeschäften *n|pl*; **~ banking** → *banking*; **~ of causation** → *causation*; **~ of events** Folge von Ereignissen; **~ of representation** unterbrochene Folge von Testamentsvollstreckern; **~ of title** Folge von Eigentumsnachweisen, lückenloser Nachweis von Berechtigungen; **~ store** Kettenladen, Filialladen; **low-price ~** Billig-Ladenkette; **voluntary ~** Zusammenschluß von Einkaufsvereinigungen.

chair Vorsitz *m*, Präsidium *n*; Lehrstuhl *m*; **the question is put from the ~** der Vorsitzende stellt den Antrag zur Abstimmung; **to address the ~** sich an den Vorsitzenden wenden; **to be in the ~** den Vorsitz haben, vorsitzen.

chairman Vorsitzender *m*, Präsident *m*; **~ of a committee** Ausschußvorsitzender; **~ of committees** Gesamtausschußvorsitzender; **~ of the board of directors** Verwaltungsratsvorsitzender; **~ of the meeting** Leiter der Versammlung; **~'s panel** Vorstandschaft; **deputy ~** → *deputy*; **honorary ~** Ehrenvorsitzender.

chairmanship Vorsitz *m*.

challenge *s* Herausforderung *f*, Aufforderung *f*, Ablehnung von Geschworenen (*vor Vereidigung*); Einwendungen *f|pl*, Bestreitung *f*, Anfechtung *f*; **~ as to the facts** Angriff in tatsächl Hinsicht; **~ for cause** Ablehnung (*von Geschworenen*) unter Angabe eines bestimmten Grundes; **~ for favour** Ablehnung wegen Besorgnis der Befangenheit; **~ for the array** Gesamtablehnung der Geschworenen; **~ of identification** Aufforderung zur Legitimation; **~ of voters** Beschuldigung wegen Wahlbetrugs; **~ propter affectum** Ablehnung wegen Besorgnis der Befangenheit; **~ propter defectum** Ablehnung wegen mangelnder *vermö-*

gensmäßiger Voraussetzungen *für das Geschworenenamt*; ~ **propter delictum** Ablehnung e–s Geschworenen als vorbestraft; ~ **to fight** Herausforderung zum Zweikampf; Forderung zum Duell; ~ **to the array** Gesamtablehnung der Geschworenen; ~ **to the favour** Ablehnung wegen Besorgnis der Begünstigung; ~ **to the panel** = ~ *to the array qv*; ~ **to the separate polls** Ablehnung e–s einzelnen Geschworenen; **general** ~ grundsätzl Ablehnung eines Geschworenen; **peremptory** ~ Ablehnung von Geschworenen ohne Angabe von Gründen; **principal** ~ Ablehnung von Geschworenen wegen Besorgnis der Befangenheit.

challenge *v* herausfordern; bestreiten, ablehnen, anfechten; ~ **an election** die Gültigkeit einer Wahl anfechten; ~ **the competence** die Zuständigkeit bestreiten.

chamber Kanzlei *f*, Büro *n*, Amtszimmer *n*, Kammer *f*, Schatzkammer *f*, ~**s** Dienstzimmer des Richters, Anwaltskanzlei (*e–s Barristers*); ~**s business** Amtshandlungen des Richters im Bürowege; ~**-clerks** Sekretäre des Richters; ~**s counsel** beratender Anwalt; **heard in** ~**s** im Richterzimmer verhandelt, Zimmertermin; ~ **practice** beratende Anwaltspraxis; ~ **of commerce** Handelskammer; ~ **of shipping** Reedereiverband; ~**s of the King** = *King's Chambers qv*; **lower** ~ Unterhaus; **the elected** ~ das Unterhaus; **upper** ~ Oberhaus; **widow's** ~ Witwenvoraus, Anteile der Witwe an persönlichen Haushaltsgegenständen des Verstorbenen.

chamberlain Kämmerer *m*; **C~ of the City of London** Stadtkämmerer von London; **C~ of the Exchequer** *hist* Kämmerer des Schatzamtes; **Lord C~ of the Household** → *lord*.

champertor *jmd, der e–n fremden Prozeß aus eigennützigen Motiven führt*.

champertous *eine Ergebnisbeteiligung am fremden Prozeß betreffend*; ~ **contract between counsel and client** *(meist unzulässige)* Mandatsvereinbarung gegen Erfolgsbeteiligung.

champerty *Übernahme f einer Streitsache auf eigene Kosten gegen Ergebnisbeteiligung*, Prozeßkauf *m*, *GB bis 1967*.

chance *s*. *Zufall m*, zufälliges Ereignis *n*; Aussicht *f* Chance *f*, Möglichkeit *f*, Risiko *n*; ~ **bargain** Gelegenheitskauf; ~ **customer** Laufkunde; ~ **-medley** Raufhandel; *Körperverletzung bzw. Tötung aus Notwehr oder im Affekt bei zufälligem Streit*; ~ **verdict** durch Los bestimmter Spruch der Geschworenen; **game of** ~ → *game*; **last clear** ~ letzte Ausweichmöglichkeit, letzte Möglichkeit der Schadensverhinderung; **to take close** ~**s** ein großes Risiko eingehen.

chance *v* sich ereignen, sich zutragen.

chancellery Kanzleramt *n*; Dienstgebäude *n* e–s Kanzlers; Botschaftskanzlei *f*, Konsulatskanzlei *f*.

chancellor Kanzler *m*, Präsident *m* des Kanzleigerichts; Richter *m* (*beim Chancery Gericht*); *scot* Obmann *m* e–r Jury; Rektor *m*, Sekretär *m*, Kanzleivorstand *m*; = *Lord High Ch*. → *Lord oder* = *Ch. of the Exchequer*; ~**'s courts in the two universities** Amtsgerichte in den Universitäten Oxford und Cambridge; ~ **of a diocese** Rechtsberater e–s Bischofs; ~ **of a university** Rektor, Präsident *e–r Universität*; **Ch~ of the Duchy of Lancaster** Präsident des Gerichtes der Grafschaft L. (*zuständig für Kronland u.a.*); **Ch~ of the Exchequer** Finanzminister *GB*.

chancery Kanzlei *f*, Kanzleigericht *n*, Praxis *f* der Kanzleigerichte, Billigkeitsrecht *n*; **Ch~ Division** = *Chancery – Abteilung des High Court of Justice für Nachlaß-, Treuhand- und andere billigkeitsrechtl. Sachen;*

Chancery Lane Amtssitz und Behörde des Lord Chancellor, *etwa:* Justizministerium.

change *s* Änderung *f*, Veränderung *f*,

Abänderung *f*; Wechsel *m*, Geldwechsel *m*, Kleingeld *n*; ~ **funds** Kleingeld, Wechselgeld; ~ **in** (= *of*) **ownership** Eigentumswechsel, Besitzwechsel; ~ **in solicitor** Anwaltswechsel; ~ **-making machines** Münzwechselgerät; ~ **of address** Anschriftsänderung; ~ **of government** Regierungswechsel; ~ **of name** Namensänderung; ~ **of parties** Parteiwechsel; ~ **of plea** Änderung der Einlassung, Änderung der Erklärung zur Anklage; ~ **of position** Stellungswechsel, berufliche Veränderung (= *changing*); ~ **of solicitor** Anwaltswechsel; ~ **of title** Eigentumswechsel; ~ **of use** Gebrauchsänderung; Zweckentfremdung; ~ **of user** Nutzungsänderung; ~ **of venue** Verweisung (*wegen örtlicher oder sachlicher Unzuständigkeit*); ~ **of voyage** Änderung des Reiseziels; ~ **-over** Wechsel, Änderung, Umstellung; **short** ~ zu wenig Wechselgeld; **small** ~ Kleingeld, Wechselgeld.

change *v* ändern, wechseln; ~ **hands** in andere Hände übergehen.

channel Kanal *m*, Weg *m*, Fahrrinne *f*; ~**s of commerce** Handelswege, Handelsverbindungen; ~**s of trade** Handelswege, Absatzwege; **administrative** ~**s** Verwaltungsweg; **Green C**~ Durchgang für Reisende ohne zollpflichtige Ware (*Dover*); **main** ~ Hauptschiffahrtsrinne, Hauptbett; **natural** ~ Hauptbett (*e–s Stroms*); **normal** ~**s** Instanzenweg, Dienstweg; **opening of new** ~**s of trade** Erschließung neuer Absatzgebiete; **Red C**~ Durchgang für Reisende mit zollpflichtiger Ware (*Dover*); **through diplomatic** ~**s** auf diplomatischem Wege; **through official** ~**s** auf dem Dienstwege; im Instanzenzug; **usual** ~**s** der übliche Weg (*Interfraktionsabsprachen im engl Parlament*).

chapel Kapelle *f*, Kirche *f*, Gotteshaus *n*; **free** ~ Kapelle außerhalb der Gerichtsbarkeit; **proprietary** ~ in Privatbesitz stehende Kapelle.

chapitre zusammenfassender Vortrag *m*; *Zusammenfassung des Vorbringens vor beauftragten Richtern.*

chaplain Kaplan *m*, Hofkaplan *m*; **speaker's** ~ der Parlamentsgeistliche.

chapman Höker *m*, ambulanter Händler *n*.

chapter Kapitel *n*; Domkapitel *n*; Abschnitt *m* e–s Gesetzes **"C~ 11"** Vergleichsverfahren zur Konkursabwendung (*US Bankruptcy Code*).

character Merkmal *n*, Charakter *m*, Kennzeichen *n*, Art *f*, bezeichnende Eigenschaft *f*; ~ **assassination** Rufmord; ~ **of neighbourhood** die Art der benachbarten Besiedlung; **certificate of** (= *as to*) ~ Leumundszeugnis; **evidence of** ~ Leumundsbeweis(e); **false** ~ Arbeitszeugnisfälschung, Benutzung e–s gefälschten Arbeitszeugnisses; **out of** ~ unvereinbar (*mit der Art der vorhandenen Bebauung*); **personal** ~ persönliche Eigenschaften **public** ~ zeitgeschichtliche Persönlichkeit, P. des öffentl. Lebens;

characteristic Merkmal; **essential** ~ wesentliches Merkmal.

charge *s* Last *f*, dingliche Belastung *f*; Beschuldigung *f*, Anklage *f*, Anklageschrift *f*, Gebühr *f*, Rechnungsbetragen *m* Kontobelastung *f*; Rechtsbelehrung des Richters (*an die Geschworenen*); ~**s** Kosten und Auslagen; ~ **account** Kundenkonto (*zum Anschreibenlassen*); ~ **and discharge** Klärung von Forderung und Gegenforderung *im Vorverfahren*; ~ **and discharge statement** Rechnungslegung e–s Treuhänders; ~**s and expenses** Kosten; ~**s and mortgages** Grundpfandrechte und sonstige Grundstückslasten; ~ **by way of legal mortgage** Grundpfandrecht, Hypothek; ~ **card** Kreditkarte; **certificate** Grundbuchauszug über Belastungen; ~**s collected** Gebühren zahlt der Empfänger; ~**s deducted** abzüglich der Spesen; ~ **for credit** Kreditkosten; effektiver Kreditzins; ~ **for delivery** Zustellgebühr, ~ **for**

diverting mail to a new address Nachsendegebühr; **~s forward** Frachtkosten zahlt der Empfänger; **~ not proven** *scot* Freispruch mangels Beweisen; **~ of an indictment** Anklagepunkt; **~s of any kind** Belastungen jeder Art; **~ of debts on real estate** dingl Sicherung von Forderungen; **~ on goodwill** Verpfändung des Goodwill; **~ on land** Grundschuld, Grundstückslast; **~ on patents** Verpfändung von Partenten; **~ on uncalled share capital** Verpfändung von Ansprüchen auf Kapitaleinzahlung; **C ~s Register** Register der Grundstücksbelastungen (*vgl Grundbuch Abt II und III*); **~ -sheet** Haftliste (*Polizei*); Anklageschrift; **~ to enter heir** *scot* Auflage das Erbe anzutreten; **account of ~s** → *account* (*2*); **additional ~s** Nebenkosten, Mehrkosten; **agricultural ~** Generalverpfändung des landwirtschaftlichen Vermögens; **alternative ~** Alternativanklage; **bill of ~s** Kostenrechnung; **capital ~** Kapitalaufwand; **carrier's ~** Zustellgebühr; **collecting ~s** Inkassospesen, Einzugskosten; **collective ~** Gesamthypothek bzw. -grundschuld; **counter ~** Widerklage, Gegenklage, Gegenbeschuldigung; **criminal ~** (s) Anklage, Beschuldigung; **deferred ~s** → *deferred;* **depreciation ~s** → *depreciation;* **differential ~** Differenzabgabe (*EG*); **equitable ~** formlose Verpfändung, Pfandbestellung ohne Sicherungsübereignung; **excessive ~** überhöhte Gebühren, Überforderung; **fiscal ~s** Steuerlasten; **fixed ~** (*konkretisierte*) dingliche Belastung, feste regelmäßige Lasten; **floating ~** Generalverpfändung *der Vermögenswerte e–s tätigen Unternehmens, aufschiebend bedingte Globalverpfändung;* **free from any ~ or liability** netto, frei von allen Verbindlichkeiten; **flat ~** Pauschale; **flat-rate ~** Pauschalsatz; **free of ~** unentgeltlich, gratis, kostenfrei, gebührenfrei; **holding ~** Nebenbeschuldigung zwecks Aufrechterhaltung der Hauptermittlungen; **incidental ~s** Nebenkosten; **legal ~** Grundschuld (*langfristige Verpfändung e–s Grundstücks*); **legal ~s** → *costs*; **liable to ~s** gebührenpflichtig; **limited owner's ~** gesetzl Sicherungshypothek des Nießbrauchers am Nießbrauchsgrundstück (*für bezahlte Erbschaftssteuer*), **local ~s** Platzspesen; **note of ~s** → *note*; **prior ~** vorrangige Belastung; **public ~** Fürsorgeempfänger; **public ~s** öffentl Lasten, öffentl Ausgaben; **register of ~s** → *register,* **registered ~** eingetragene Reallast; **release from ~s** Freistellung von Pfandrechten, Entlassung aus dem Pfandverband; **salvage ~s** Bergungskosten; **special ~** besondere Kosten; Belehrung der Geschworenen zu e–r Einzelfrage; **to defray the ~s** die Kosten bezahlen; **to have ~ or conduct of** (*the ship*) die Kommandogewalt über (*ein Schiff*) haben; **to have ~ or control of** verantwortlich sein für, etw in seinem Herrschaftsbereich haben, (*ein Fahrzeug*) führen; **to hold an accused on unstated ~** *e–n* Beschuldigten wegen e–r nicht eröffneten Beschuldigung in Haft halten; **voluntary statutory ~** rechtsgeschäftl bestelltes Pfandrecht in gesetzl. Form.

charge *v* belasten, berechnen, in Rechnung stellen; beschuldigen, anklagen; **~ an account** ein Konto belasten; **~ off** eine Abschreibung vornehmen; absetzen; **~ or encumber** (*dinglich*) belasten; **~ the jury** die Geschworenen (*durch den Richter*) belehren; **~d upon land** an Grundstücken gesichert; **~d with income tax** einkommensteuerpflichtig.

chargeable anrechenbar, abgabenpflichtig, nicht befreit, zu berechnen, zu verantworten; **~ accounting period** Veranlagungszeitraum; **~ to income tax** einkommenssteuerpflichtig.

chargee (dinglich) Berechtigter *m*, dingl gesicherter Gläubiger *m*, Beschwerter *m*.

charging *s* Belastung *f*, Berechnung *f*, Anrechnung *f*, ~ **clause** Bestimmung über Treuhändervergütung; ~ **lien** → *lien;* ~ **order** → *order* (*1*).

charging part of the bill Klagerubrum.

charitable karitativ, mildtätig; gemeinnützig; ~ **and deserving** karitativ und förderungswürdig; ~ **company** → *company;* ~ **contribution** Beiträge zu karitativen Zwecken; ~ **gift** karitative Schenkung; ~ **institution** → *institution;* ~ **organization** Wohltätigkeitsverein, Hilfswerk; ~ **persons** Personen, die sich karitativen Zwekken widmen; ~ **purpose** karitativer Zweck; ~ **trust** → *trust;* ~ **uses** mildtätige (*gemeinnützige*) Zwecke.

charity Wohltätigkeit *f*; Wohlfahrtspflege *f*; karitative Stiftung *f*, wohltätige Stiftung; gemeinnützige Treuhand; ~ **appeal** Spendenaufruf; **C**~ **Commissioners** *GB* Stiftungsaufsichtsbehörde; ~ **performance** Wohltätigkeitsaufführung; ~ **shop** Wohltätigkeitsladen, ~ **state** Sondervermögen für mildtätige *bzw* gemeinnützige Zwecke; ~ **school** schulgeldfreie Schule bzw Hochschule (*für Bedürftige*); **assurance of land to** ~ Verfügung über ein Grundstück zugunsten einer Stiftung; **foreign** ~ Stiftungsvermögen mit Sitz im Ausland; **mixed** ~ Stiftungsvermögen aus Kapitaleinkünften gemischt mit Einkünften aus freiwilligen Beiträgen; **public** ~ öffentliche Wohlfahrt; *Wohlfahrtspflege für einen unbestimmten Personenkreis;* **pure** ~ völlig gebührenfreie gemeinnützige Einrichtung; **recreational** ~ treuhänderische Zuwendung zu Erholungszwecken; **religious** ~ mildtätige Stiftung für religiöse Zwecke.

chart *s* Tabelle *f*, graphische Darstellung *f*, Schaubild *n*, Seekarte *f*.

charta (*hist: carta*) konstitutive Urkunde *f*, gesiegelte Urkunde *f*, Charta *f*.

charter *s* Verleihungsurkunde *f*, Konzession *f*; Gesellschaftssatzung *US*, Gründungsurkunde *f* (*e–r jur Person*); Charter *f*, Chartervertrag *m*; = ~ *party qv;* ~ **by progress scot** Konzessionsverlängerungsurkunde; ~ **-land** Liegenschaften im freien Lehensbesitz; ~ **money** Schiffsmiete; ~ **of incorporation** Gründungsurkunde, Satzung; ~ **of pardon** Begnadigungsurkunde; ~ **rolls** *Urkundenverzeichnis 1199 bis 1516;* ~ **services** Charterfluggesellschaft; **bank** ~ → *bank* (*1*); **blank** ~ Freibrief; **catch time** ~ Zeitscharter; **demise** ~ Vermietung des gesamten Schiffes ohne Besatzung; **dry** ~ Vermietung e–s Schiffs bzw Flugzeugs ohne Besatzung; **head** ~ Hauptfrachtvertrag; **original** ~ Erstbelehnung, Erstkonzession **outside** ~ Schiffsvermietung an Dritte, **time** ~ → *time;* **voyage-** ~ → *voyage;* **wet** ~ Vermietung e–s Schiffs bzw Flugzeugs mit Besatzung.

charter *v* bevorrechtigen, privilegieren, chartern, mieten, befrachten; Privileg (*bzw*) Konzession erteilen; ~**ed civil engineer** Ingenieur (*Mitglied der Institution of Civil Engineers, London*).

charterer Charterer *m*, Schiffsmieter *m*, Flugzeugmieter *m*.

chartering | **broker** Befrachtungsmakler *m*; ~ **business** Schiffsfrachtgeschäft.

charter-party Charterpartie *f*, Chartervertragsurkunde *f*; ~ **by way of demise** Schiffscharter mit Besatzung.

chase Jagd *f*, Jagdrecht *n*, **common** ~ freie Jagdausübung für jedermann.

chaste keusch, unbescholten; ~ **character** Tugendhaftigkeit, Unbescholtenheit.

chastity Tugend *f*, sittsamer Lebenswandel *m*.

chastisement Züchtigung *f*.

chattel Mobile *f*, bewegliche Sache *f*, Gegenstand *m* des beweglichen Vermögens; *pl* bewegl Vermögen; ~ **interest** ein Recht an beweglichen Sachen; ~ **lien** Unternehmerpfandrecht; ~**mortgage** → *mortgage;* ~ **mortgagee** Sicherungsnehmer; ~ **mortgagor** Sicherungsgeber; ~**s personal** bewegliche Sachen; ~**s real** beschränkte Rechte an Grundstücken, Pachtgrundstücke; **incorporeal** ~**s** Immaterialgüterrechte; **land and** ~**s** Liegenschaften und bewegliche Sachen; **liability for** ~**s** → *liability;* **personal** ~**s** persönliche Habe; **property in** ~**s** Eigentum an bewegl Sachen; **real** ~**s** Rechte an e–m Grundstück.

chaud-medley Tötung *f* im Affekt *während e–s Raufhandels*.

cheap billig, preisgünstig.

cheapen billiger werden, im Preis sinken; ~**ing of money** Verbilligung der Geldsätze.

cheat *s* Betrug *m*, Betrüger *m*; **common** ~ notorischer Schwindler.

cheat *v* betrügen, übervorteilen.

check (*1*) *s* Kontrolle *f*, ~ **book** *brit* Kontrollbuch; ~ **of cash** Kassenrevision; ~**-off (system)** Einbehaltung der Gewerkschaftsbeiträge; ~ **on delivery** Abnahmekontrolle; ~ **over** Nachprüfung; ~ **register** Ausgabenkontrollbogen; ~ **roll** Liste der Bediensteten; ~**s and balances** → *system;* ~ **weigher** Gewichtskontrolleur (*bes im Kohlebergbau*).

check (*2*) *s US Schreibweise für cheque qv*.

check *v* prüfen, kontrollieren, abhaken, kollationieren, hemmen; **"~ed by"** (*Vermerk:*) „geprüft von"; ~**ing device** Prüfvorrichtung; ~**-weigh** nachwiegen (*von Wagenladungen*).

checkpoint Kontrollpunkt *m*; **roadside** ~ Straßenkontrollpunkt.

cheque *brit Scheck m* (= *Sch bzw sch*); ~ **book** *Sch*heft; ~ **book money,** Giralgeld; **account-only** ~ Verrechnungs*sch*; **bad** ~ ungedeckter *Sch* ~ **collection** *Sch* inkasso ~ **-kiting** *Sch*reiterei; ~ **made out to cash** Bar*sch*; ~ **on a banker** Bank*sch;* ~ **on no-par points** *hist Sch* mit Disagio ~ **rate** Auslands*sch*kosten; ~ **to bearer** Inhaber*sch*; ~ **to order** Order*sch*; ~ **writing machine** *Sch*austellungsmaschine; **blank** ~ Blanko*sch*; **bouncing** ~ ungedeckter *Sch*, Rück*sch*; **cash** ~Bar*sch*; **cashier's** ~ *US*: Bank*sch*, von e–r Bank auf sich selbst ausgestellter *Sch*.; **certified** ~ von der Bank bestätigter und garantierter *Sch*, *US*; **clearance of** ~**s** *Sch*-Clearing, *Sch*abrechnungsverkehr; **collection-only** ~ Verrechnungs*sch*; **counter** ~ (*check*) *US*: im Bankschalter verwahrter Bank*sch*, Kassen*sch*; **crossed** ~ gekreuzter *Sch*, Verrechnungs*sch*; **drawee of a** ~ *Sch*bezogener; **drawer of a** ~ Aussteller e–s *Sch–s*; **drawing of** ~**s where no funds** Ausstellung von ungedeckten *Sch–s*; **forged** ~ gefälschter *Sch*; **generally crossed** ~ allgemein gekreuzter *Sch;* **holder of a** ~ *Sch*inhaber; **marked** ~ bestätigter *Sch*; **memorandum** ~ als Sicherheit ausgestellter *Sch*, Sicherungs*sch*; **negotiable** ~ girierfähiger *Sch*; **non-negotiable** ~ Rekta*sch*; **obtaining money by worthless** ~ *Sch*betrug; **open** ~ Bar*sch*; **order** ~ Order*sch*; **overdue** ~ verspätet vorgelegter *Sch*; **paid** ~ eingelöster *Sch*; **pay** ~ Gehalts*sch*, Lohn*sch*; **personal** ~ gewöhnlicher *Sch*, *Sch* e–s Bankkunden; **presentation of** ~Vorlage e–s *Sch–s*; **post-dated** ~ vordatierter *Sch*; **raised** ~ gefälschter erhöhter Scheck; **registered** ~ (*check*) Bank*sch*; **regular** ~ ordnungsgemäßer *Sch;* **returned** ~ Rück*sch*, retournierter *Sch*, unbezahlter *Sch*; **specially crossed** ~ besonders gekreuzter *Sch*; **stale** ~ verspätet vorgelegter *Sch*, nicht innerhalb der Vorlegungsfrist (*bzw angemessener Zeit*) vorgelegter *Sch*; **stopped** ~ gesperrter *Sch*; **town** ~ *brit*

Platz*sch*; **traveler's** ~ Reise*sch*; **uncovered** ~ ungedeckter *Sch*; **uncrossed** ~ Barscheck.

cherry picking Einkauf ausgewählter TV-Programme auf dem freien Markt.

chest Geldkasse *f*, Kassette *f*, Fonds *m*; Truhe *f*, Kommode *f*.

cheze pfändungsfreies Wohnrecht *n* an einem Anwesen.

chicanery Rechtsverdrehung *f*, unredliches Manöver *n*, juristische Tricks *m|pl*.

chief *adj* hauptsächlich, Haupt ... ~ **administration office** Hauptverwaltung(ssitz); **C~ Baron (of the Exchequer)** Präsident des Exchequergerichts; **C~ Justice of England** = *Lord C~ Justice of England* → *Lord;* **C~ Land Registrar** Leiter der brit. Grundbuchbehörde; ~.

chief *s* Leiter *m*, Chef *m*, Vorgesetzter *m*, Vollmachtgeber *m*; ~ **of bureau** Amtsleiter; ~ **of a department** Abteilungsleiter; ~ **of mission** Missionschef; **C~ of Staff** Stabschef.

child Kind *n*, (*GB bis 14*) eheliches Kind *n*, Minderjähriger *m*; ~**abduction** Kindesentführung; ~ **abuse** Kindesmißhandlung; ~ **allowance** Kinderfreibetrag; ~ **benefit** Kindergeld *für schulpflichtige K–r*; ~ **Benefit Act** Kindergeldgesetz *GB, 1975*; ~ **-bearing** Gebärfähigkeit; **C~ Care Act** JugendfürsorgeG, *GB 1980*; ~ **care inspectorate** Jugendwohlfahrtsamt; ~ **destruction** Abtreibung, Tötung der Leibesfrucht; ~ **en ventre sa mère** Nasciturus; ~ **in care** unter Fürsorge stehender Jugendlicher; ~ **minder** Kinderbetreuer; ~ **labor legislation** Jugendarbeitsschutzgesetze; ~**'s long-term welfare** das Kindeswohl auf lange Sicht; ~ **of tender age** Kind bzw Jugendlicher (*bis 14 Jahre*); ~ **of the marriage** aus der Ehe hervorgegangenes Kind; ~**'s part** Witwenpflichtteilsrecht *in Höhe des Reinnachlaßwerts e–s Kindeserbteils*; ~ **placing** Unterbringung von Kindern bei Pflegeeltern; ~ **relief** Kinderfreibetrag; ~**snatching** geheimes Wegholen von Kindern; ~**'s special allowance** Kindergeldzulage; ~ **stealing** Kindesraub; K-sentführung; ~ **support** Kindesunterhalt; ~ **welfare** Jugendfürsorge; **baseborn** ~ uneheliches Kind; **delinquent** ~ verwahrloster, straffälliger Jugendlicher; **illegitimate** ~ nichteheliches Kind; ~ **legitimate** ~ eheliches Kind; **mongol** ~ mongolides Kind; **natural** ~ leibliches Kind, nicht eheliches Kind; **noncontributory** ~ **benefit** (staatliches, beitragsfreies) Kindergeld; **orphaned** ~ Waisenkind; **posthumous** ~ nach dem Tode des Vaters geborenes Kind; **protected** ~ (*zur Adoption vorgesehenes*) Kind, das beim Adoptionsbewerber wohnt, geschütztes K.

children Kinder *n|pl*; **Ch~ Act** Gesetz über die Rechtsstellung des Kindes *GB*; **Ch~ and Young Persons Act** Jugendschutz- und Jugendgerichtsgesetz *GB*; ~**'s endowment assurance** Aussteuerversicherung; ~ **in care** Jugendliche unter Fürsorgeerziehung; ~**'s maintenance payments** Kinderunterhaltszahlungen; ~ **of the family** zur Familie gehörende Kinder; ~ **of the marriage** aus der Ehe hervorgegangene Kinder; ~ **now living** zur Zeit lebende Kinder (*einschließl der Nachgeborenen*); **allowances for** ~ Kindergeld; **custody, charge or care of** ~ Personensorge, elterl Gewalt; **evidence of** ~ Aussagen von Kindern; **guardianship of** ~ Vormundschaft über Minderjährige; **handicapped** ~ behinderte Kinder **latchkey** ~ Schlüsselkinder; **nonmarital** ~ nichteheliche Kinder.

chilling a sale Verabredung *f* geringen Bietens.

Chiltern Hundreds *nominelles Kronamt, Pfründe;* **acceptance of stewardship of** ~ *Mandatsniederlegung im House of Commons.*

chimney money Schornsteinsteuer *f*.
Chinese copy täsuchend ähnliche Nachahmung *f*.
chippingavel *hist* Warenzoll *m*, Handelssteuer *f*.
chirograph eigenhändige Urkunde *f*, gesiegelte Urkunde *f*, Urkundenschluß *m* = *indenture*.
chivalry ritterlicher Dienst *m*, Ritterlichkeit *f*, ritterliches Lehen *n*; **orders of** ~ Ritterorden; **tenure of** ~ ritterliches Leben.
choice Wahl *f*, Auswahl *f*, Sortiment *n*, Auslese *f*, ~ **brand** vorzügliche Sorte; ~ **of courts** Wahl des Gerichtsstandes; ~ **of law** Rechtswahl (*welches Recht anwendbar sein soll*); **occupational** ~ Berufswahl.
choke *v* würgen, erwürgen, drosseln, erdrosseln.
choos|e aussuchen, Auswahl treffen; ~**ing curators** *scot* Antrag auf Bestellung eines Vormunds; **chosen freeholders** *etwa*: Kreisrat.
choreographic works Werke *n|pl* der Tanzkunst, choreographische Werke.
chose *s* Gegenstand *n* des beweglichen Vermögens, Fahrnis *f*, ~ **in action** obligatorischer Anspruch, Forderungs(recht), Immaterialgüterrecht; ~ **in possession** bewegliche Sache, Fahrnis; ~ **in suspense** = *chose in action qv;* ~ **local** ortsfeste Sache; ~ **transitory** transportable Sache.
chrematistics Krematistik *f*, Wissenschaft *f* vom Wohlstand.
Christmas|appeals Weihnachtsspendenaufrufe; ~ **bonus** → *bonus*.
church Kirche *f*; Gotteshaus *n*; ~ **affiliation** Zugehörigkeit zu einer Kirche; **C~ Assembly** → *assembly*; ~ **authorities** Kirchenbehörde(n); ~ **briefs** kirchliche Abkündigungen für wohltätige Zwecke; ~ **discipline act** Kirchendisziplinargesetz; ~ **door notices** Kundmachung durch Anschlag an die Kirchentür; ~ **lands** Kirchenländereien; ~ **marriage** Eheschließung in der Ch. of E. mit standesamtlicher Erlaubnis; ~ **meeting** Gemeindeversammlung; **Ch~ of England** (=) anglikanische Kirche (*engl Staatskirche*); ~ **property** Kirchenvermögen; ~ **rates** *hist*. Kirchensteuern; Kirchgeld, Umlagen zur Erhaltung des Kirchengebäudes; ~ **reeve** Kirchenaufseher; ~ **register** Kirchenbuch; ~ **robbery** Kirchendiebstahl; ~ **-scot** *hist* Kirchenabgabe; ~ **wardens** Kirchenvorsteher, Gemeindevorsteher; ~ **yard** Friedhof; **breaking into** ~ Kirchen(einbruchs)diebstahl; **community** ~ Kirchenverband; **disturbing service in** ~ Störung des Gottesdienstes; **national** ~ Staatskirche; **The Established Ch~** = *Church of England av*.
churn ständige Fluktuation von Kunden.
churning Vertrauensmißbrauch des Börsenmaklers *durch hohe Einsätze*.
Cinematograph|Act Gesetz über Lichtvorführungen; **c~ exhibition** Filmvorführung; **c~ film** Film, Lichtbildfilm.
cipher *s* Ziffer *f*, Chiffre *f*, Geheimschrift *f*; **in** ~ chiffriert.
cipher *v* chiffrieren; rechnen.
circuit Rundreise *f* eines beauftragten Richters, Bezirk *m*, Gerichtsbezirk *m*; *GB: etwa Oberlandesgerichtsbezirk*; ~ **breaker** Unterbrechermechanismus (*gegen unerwünschte Kursausschläge bei komputerisiertem Börsenhandel*); **court** → *court;* **C~ Court of Appeals** → *court*; ~ **flow of money** Geldkreislauf; ~ **judge** Richter kraft Auftrags; *GB*: *am Crown Court bzw. Country Court qv; US*: *am Circuit Court of Appeals qv*; Richter *bei e–m circuit court qv*; ~ **justice** beauftragter Richter des obersten US-Bundesgerichts; ~ **paper** Sitzungsplan für Assisen-Gerichte; ~ **system** Einteilung in Obergerichtsbezirke.
circuitous umständlich, weitläufig.
circuity of action Umständlichkeit *f* des Verfahrens, mangelnde Prozeßökonomie.

circular Zirkular *n*, Runderlaß *m*, Rundschreiben *m*.
circulat|e *v* zirkulieren, zirkulieren lassen, in Umlauf bringen; ~ **bills** Wechsel girieren; ~ **reports** Meldungen verbreiten; ~**ing assets** Umlaufvermögen; ~**ing capital** Umlaufvermögen; ~**ing medium** Zahlungsmittel; ~**ing notes** Banknoten; Notenumlauf.
circulation Umlauf *m*, Verbreitung *f*; ~ **of bank notes** Banknotenumlauf; ~ **of capital** Kapitalverkehr; ~ **privilege** Umlaufberechtigung; Banknotenprivileg; ~ **rates** Auflagenziffer; ~ **tax** → *tax*; **active** ~ Notenumlauf; **bills in** ~in Umlauf befindliche Wechsel; **fiduciary** ~ ungedeckter Notenumlauf; **free** ~ (*zollrechtlich*) freier Verkehr, **general** ~ Auflage einer allgemeinen Zeitung **paid** ~ abgesetzte Auflage; **restricted** ~ beschränkter Umlauf (*vertraulich*); **withdrawal from** ~ Außerkurssetzung.
circumlocution indirekte Redeweise *f*, Umschreibung *f*.
circumstance Umstand *m*, Tatumstand *m*, Sachlage *f*, Sachverhalt *m*; ~**s beyond control** unabwendbares Ereignis; nicht beherrschbare Umstände, Force majeure; ~**s creating a legal liability** haftungsbegründender Sachverhalt; ~**s of the case** Sachverhalt; ~**s permitting** soweit es die Umstände zulassen; **aggravating** ~**s** strafverschärfende Umstände; **attendant** ~**s** Begleitumstände, Nebenumstände; **collateral** ~**s** Begleitumstände; **exenuating** ~**s** mildernde Umstände; **financial** ~**s** Vermögensverhältnisse; **indigent** ~**s** ärmliche Verhältnisse; **mitigating** ~**s** mildernde Umstände; **particular** ~**s** besondere Umstände; **pecuniary** ~**s** Vermögensverhältnisse; **surrounding** ~**s** Begleitumstände.
circumstantiate umständlich beschreiben; durch Indizien beweisen.
circumvent *v* umgehen, vereiteln.
circumvention Umgehung *f*, *scot* Erschleichung *f* eines Urteils; ~ **of a patent** Patentumgehung; ~ **of the law** Umgehung des Gesetzes, Rechtsbeugung.
cital Vorladung *f*.
citation Ladung *f* der Beteiligten; Aufforderung *f*; Zitat *n*, Belegstelle *f*; Vorbemerkung *f*, Präambel *f*; *pat* entgegengehaltene Druckschrift, ~ **of Act** Zitierweise von Gesetzen (*GB: früher nach Regierungszeit des Monarchen, seit 1. 1. 1963: Jahr des Erlasses*). ~ **of authorities** Anführen von Fundstellen *höchstricherlicher Rechtsprechung*; **public** ~ Aufgebotsverfahren, Ladung durch öffentl. Zustellung.
citator Fundstellensammlung *f*.
cite laden, zitieren.
citizen Bürger *m*, Bürgerin *f*, Stadtbürger *m*, (*-in f*), Staatsbürger *m* (*in f*); Staatsangehöriger *m* (*–e f*); **c~'s action (group)** Bürgerinitiative; **C~'s Advice Bureaux** *brit* Rechtshilfeberatungsstellen; **~'s arrest** Festnahme durch jedermann; ~ **complaint** Strafanzeige e–s Unbeteiligten; **C~s for Tax Justice** *etwa*: Bund der Steuerzahler; ~ **of the United Kingdom and Colonies** britischer Staatsangehöriger (*grundsätzl jedoch ohne Bürgerrecht in den Dominions*), **private** ~ Privatmann, Bürger.
citizenry Bürgerschaft *f*, Volk *n*.
citizenship Staatsbürgerschaft *f*, Staatsangehörigkeit *f*, Status *m* eines Bürgers; ~ **by birth** Staatsangehörigkeit durch Geburt; ~ **by descent** Staatsangehörigkeit kraft Abstammung; **law** Staatsbürgerschaftsrecht; **federal** ~ (Bundes)-Staatsangehörigkeit der USA; **plural Commonwealth** ~ Zugehörigkeit zu mehreren Commonwealth Ländern; **state** ~ → *state* (*2*).
city Stadt *f*, Großstadt *f*, Innenstadt *f*; Börsen- und Finanzzentrum *n* von London; "City", City von London, autonome Körperschaft von London; **C~ Code** Übernahme und Fusionsregeln der Fusionskontrollstelle (*Panel on Take-overs*

and Mergers pv); ~ **courts** Stadtgerichte; ~ **company** Gilde; ~ **manager** Oberstadtdirektor; ~ **news** Börsenmeldungen; **C~ of London Court** Londoner Stadtgericht (*bis 1921*).

civic bürgerlich, staatsbürgerlich; ~ **enterprise** gemeinnütziges Unternehmen *der Bürger einer Stadt;* ~ **rights** →*right;* ~**s** Staatsbürgerkunde; **C~ Trust** → *trust.*

civil bürgerlich; zivilrechtlich; zivil; ~ **damage acts** *Gesetze betr Haftung für Alkoholverkauf,* **C~ Evidence Act** BeweisaufnahmeG (*GB 1976*); ~ **procedure convention** Übereinkommen über den Zivilprozeß.

Civil List Zivilliste *f*; ~ **pension** Ehrensold der Krone.

civil servant Angehörige des öffentlichen Dienstes, Staatsbediensteter; Beamter; **career** ~ Berufsbeamter; **unestablished** ~ außerplanmäßiger Staatsbeamter, Angestellter im öffentlichen Dienst.

civil service öffentlicher Dienst *m.*

civilian Zivilist *m*; Kenner des römischen Rechts.

civiliter in einer Zivilsache.

civilization Zivilisation *f*; Überführung eines Strafverfahrens in ein Zivilverfahren.

claim Anspruch *m*, Forderung *f*; Klagebegehren *n*, Schadensforderung *f*, Reklamation *f*; Vorrecht *n*; Patentanspruch *m*, Mutung *f*; ~ **against the estate** Forderung gegen den Nachlaß; ~**s agent** Schadensreferent; ~ **and delivery** Klage auf Herausgabe e–r bewegl Sache; ~ **check** Aufbewahrungsschein, ~**s department** Schadensbüro; ~ **expense** → *expense;* ~ **-expense reserve** Rückstellung für die Schadensabwicklung; ~ **for compensation** Schadensersatzanspruch, Entschädigungsanspruch; ~ **for damages** Schadensersatzansspruch; ~ **for interest** Zinsforderung; ~ **for possession** Räumungsklage (*bes gegen Grundpfandschuldner*); ~ **for uncalled capital** Kapitaleinzahlungsanspruch; ~**s form** Antragsformular, Anspruchsbegründungsformular; ~ **in detinue** Klage auf Herausgabe bewegl Sachen; ~ **in equity** billigkeitsrechtlicher Anspruch; ~ **in tort** Schadensersatzforderung aus unerlaubter Handlung; ~ **jumping** Vorwegnahme von Schürfrechten; ~ **of conusance** Hauptintervention, Rüge der Unzuständigkeit durch den Hauptintervenienten; ~ **of equity** billigkeitsrechtlicher Anspruch; ~ **of liberty** Antrag an die Krone auf Bestätigung von Privilegien; ~ **of negligence** Schadensersatzanspruch wegen fahrlässigen Verschuldens; ~ **of ownership, right and title** Eigentumsklage, Kl auf Herausgabe des Eigentums; ~ **of privilege** Berufung auf Aussageverweigerungsrecht, Recht zur Verweigerung der Urkundenvorlage; ~ **of right** Rechtsanspruch; **(any)** ~ **or demand** Ansprüche jeder Art; ~**s panel** Anspruchsprüfungsausschuß; **property bond** Sicherheitsleistung des Beklagten (*bei Herausgabeklage und Zwangsvollstreckung*); ~ **provable in bankruptcy** Konkursforderung; ~**s service** Schadensabteilung; ~ **to inheritance** Erbschaftsanspruch; ~ **to priority** Prioritätsanspruch; **adverse** ~ Interventionsanspruch (*auf gepfändete Sache*); **alternative** ~ wahlweiser Anspruch; **aucillary** ~ Hilfsanspruch, Nebenanspruch; **anterior** ~ ältere Forderung; **assignment of** ~**s** → *assignment;* **bad** ~ unbegründeter Anspruch; **contingent** ~ bedingter Anspruch, Eventualforderung; **colourable** ~ → *colourable;* **continual** ~ → *continual*; **contractual** ~ vertraglicher Anspruch; **damage** ~ Schadensersatzanspruch; **deferred** ~ gestundete Forderung; **delictual** ~ deliktischer Anspruch; **dependent** ~ *pat* Unteranspruch, abhängiger Anspruch; **diplomatic** ~ auf diplomatischem Wege geltend zu machender Anspruch; **disputed** ~

strittige Forderung; **dormant** ~ → *dormant;* **equitable** ~ billigkeitsrechtlicher Anspruch; **first** ~ Vorhand; **forfeited** ~ verfallener Anspruch; **fraudulent** ~**s** betrügerische Ansprüche, Versicherungsbetrug; **government** ~ von der Regierung geltend gemachter Anspruch; **independent** ~ *pat* Nebenanspruch, unabhängiger Anspruch; **insurer's** ~ (Regreß) Ansprüche des Versicherers; **legal** ~ Rechtsanspruch; **main** ~ Hauptanspruch; **matured** ~ fällige Forderung; **minimum** ~ Mindestanforderung; **mixed** ~**s** Anspruchshäufung; **monetary** ~ Geldforderung; **patent** ~ → *patent* **pecuniary** ~ Geldforderung; **possessory** ~ Besitzschutzanspruch, Besitzentziehungsanspruch, possessorischer Anspruch; **preferred** ~ bevorrechtigte Konkursforderung, **prior** ~ vorgehender Anspruch; **privileged** ~ bevorrechtigte Forderung; **provable** ~ beweisbare Forderung; Konkursforderung; **secured** ~ gesicherte Forderung; **small** ~**s** kleinere Forderungen (*bis £ 500*); amtsgerichtl Schiedsverfahren; **sound** ~ begründeter Anspruch; **statement of** → *statement;* **subordinate** ~ Unteranspruch **subsequent** ~ Nachforderung; **substantiated** ~ begründeter Anspruch; **supplementory** ~ Nachforderung; **sustainable** ~ vertretbarer Anspruch; **tortious** ~ deliktischer Anspruch, Forderung aus unerlaubter Handlung; **unliquidated** ~ bestrittener Anspruch; **unmeritorious** ~ Anspruch, der keine Anerkennung verdient; **unsecured** ~ ungesicherte Forderung, gewöhnliche Konkursforderung.

claim *v* beanspruchen, verlangen, fordern, behaupten.

claimable zu beanspruchen, beanspruchbar.

claimant Kläger *m*, Antragsteller *m*; (Parent)Anmelder *m*; Leistungsberechtigter, Anspruchsberechtigter; **fault in** ~ Mitverschulden des Anspruchsstellers.

clamp *s* Parkkralle *f*; *v/t* durch Parkkrallen blockieren; **C~ Rescue Company** Parkkrallen–Nothilfegesellschaft.

clamping Parkkrallensperre *f*.

clandestine heimlich; ~ **mortgages** verheimlichte vorrangige Grundstücksverpfändung; **C~ Outlawries** Gesetzesvorlage gegen Geheimbündelei (*symbolische Lesung im Unterhaus*).

clarification Klarstellung *f*, Klärung *f*.

clarify klären, klarstellen.

clarity Deutlichkeit *f*, Klarheit *f*.

clash *v* zusammenstoßen, kollidieren, im Widerspruch stehen; ~**ing interests** widerstreitende Interessen.

class *s* Kategorie *f*, Klasse *f*, Stand *m*, Gruppe *f*, Grad *m*; ~ **action** Gruppenklage (*Klage im Interesse einer Gruppe von Beteiligten*), Modellprozeß für eine Personenmehrheit, Klage der Aktionäre einer Gattung; ~ **affiliation** Klassenzugehörigkeit; ~ **fee** Klassengebühr; ~ **gift** = *gift to a class* → *gift*; ~ **index of patents** Verzeichnis der Patentklassen; ~ **legislation** Klassengesetzgebung; ~ **meeting** Versammlung der Aktionäre der gleichen Aktiengattung; ~**es of creditors** Kategorien von Gläubigern; ~ **of goods** Warenklasse Warengattung; ~ **of persons** Personenmehrheit der gleichen Kategorie; ~ **resolution** Beschluß der Aktionäre der gleichen Aktiengattung; ~ **rights** Rechte der Aktionäre der gleichen Aktiengattung; ~ **suit** Klage in Prozeßstandschaft für eine Personengruppe *vgl class action;* ~ **suspended** Zuordnung zu einer Schiffsklasse vorläufig aufgehoben; **administrative** ~ höherer Dienst (*brit öffentl Dienst*); **clerical** ~ Beamte und Angestellte des Kanzleidienstes; **executive** ~ gehobener Dienst; **the labouring** ~**es** die Arbeiterklasse, die Werktätigen (*Ar-*

beiter, Handwerker und Kleingewerbetreibende).

class *v* klassifizieren, rubrizieren, einstufen.

classification Klassifizierung *f*, Klassifikation *f*, Gliederung *f*, Einteilung *f*, Rubrizierung *f*, Eingruppierung *f* von Verfahrensbeteiligten; ~ **certificate** Klassifikationsattest (*für Schiffe*); ~ **of expenses** Kostenaufgliederung; ~ **of goods** Warenklasseneinteilung; ~ **of patents** Patentklassifikation; ~ **of risks** Risikoeinstufung (*der versicherten Personen und Gegenstände*); **International Patent C~** (*IPC*) Internationale Patentklassifikation; **security** ~ Geheimhaltungseinstufung; **vocational** ~ Berufsgruppeneinteilung.

classify klassifizieren, einteilen, einstufen; **~ied advertisement** Kleinanzeige; **~ied information** Verschlußsache; **~ied report** → *report;* **~ied roads** Straßen des Fernverkehrs, Hauptverkehrsstraßen.

clause Klausel *f* (*Kl bzw . . . kl*) Satz *m*, Nebensatz *m*, Absatz *m*, Paragraph *m*; **C~s Acts** konsolidierte Gesetze; ~ **as to venue of action** Gerichtsstandskl; **claims control** ~ *Kl betr die Mitwirkung der Rückversicherer bei der Schadensregulierung des Erstversicherers;* ~ **compromissoire** Schieds*kl*; ~ **of devolution** *scot* Amtsübergangs*kl*, Nachfolgebestimmungen; ~ **of return** *scot* Heimfalls*kl*; ~ **potestative** Potestativbedingung, Rücktritts*kl*; ~ **reserving errors** Irrtumsvorbehalts*kl*; ~ **resolutive** auflösende Bedingung; ~ **rolls** *hist Aufzeichnung geheimer königl Verbriefungen;* **accelerating** ~ Fälligkeits*kl*, Verfalls*kl*; **advancement** ~ *Ermächtigungskl zur vorzeitigen Auszahlung e–s Erbteils zwecks Ausstattung des Bedachten;* **agreed amount** ~ Selbstbeteiligungs*kl*; **arbitration** ~ →*arbitration;* **arson** ~ Brandstiftungs*kl*; **attestation** ~ → *attestation;* **average** ~ → *average*; **basket** ~ General*kl*; **blanket** ~ General*kl*; **break** ~ Kündigungs*kl*; **choice of law** ~ Rechtswahl*kl* (*Bestimmung des anzuwendenden Rechts*); **codicillary** ~ Nachtragsbestimmung (*zum Testament*); **coinsurance** ~ → *coinsurance*; **collision** ~ → *collision*; **commodities** ~ → *commodities*; **conscience** ~ → *conscience*; **contestable** ~ Widerrufs*kl* des Versicherers; **contractual** ~ Vertrags*kl*; **contribution** ~ Schadensteilungsabkommen; Schadensverteilungs*kl* bei Mehrfachversicherung; **convertibility** ~ Konversions*kl*; **cost of living** ~ Lebenshaltungskosten*Kl* (*mit automatischer Anpassung*); **cover-all** ~ General*kl*; Umwandlungs*kl*; **craft** ~ Leichter*kl*; **defeasance** ~ → *defeasance;* **demand** ~ Fälligkeits*kl*, Verfall*kl*; **deviation** ~ → *deviation*; **dispositive** ~ → *dispositive;* **due-on-sale** ~ Rückzahlung bei Verkauf (*Hypothekenkl*); **dum casta** ~ → *dum casta;* **entire contract** ~ Vollständigkeits*kl*, (*keine Nebenabreden*); **fluctuating** ~ Kostenerhöhungs*kl*, Schwankungs*kl*; **escalator** ~ → *escalator clause*; **escape** ~ Ausweich*kl*; **excepting** ~ Vorbehaltskl; **excess** ~ (= *Excess* ~) Selbstbehaltungs*kl*, Eigenanteils*kl*; **exclusion** ~ Freizeichnungs*kl*; **exclusive** ~ Ausschließlichkeits*kl*: **exemption** ~ Freizeichnungs*kl*; **exculpatory** ~ Entlastungs*kl* (*e–s Treuhänders*), Haftungsausschluß*kl* (*bei Gutgläubigkeit*); **exemption** ~ Freizeichnungs*kl*, Haftungsausschluß(*kl*); **F. I. A.** ~ (*full interest admitted*) Versicherungsinteresse anerkannt; **final** ~ Schlußbestimmung; **forum** ~ Gerichtsstands*kl*; **F. P. A.** ~ (*free of particular average claim*) frei von Beschädigung außer im Strandungsfall; **gold** ~ → *gold;* **grand father** ~ Besitzstand*kl*, **granting** ~ dingliche Verfügungs(*kl*); **habendum** ~ Eigentumsüberganskl; **hold harmless** ~ Schadloshaltungs*kl*; **incontestable** ~ (= *incontestability clause*) *ins* Unanfechtbarkeits*kl*; **interpretation** ~ → *interpreation*; **joint account** ~ → *joint*;

jurisdictional Gerichtsstands*kl*; **leakage** ~ Leckage-*Kl*; **limitation** ~ (vertragl) Haftungsbeschränkung; **loss payable** ~ Auszahlungsempfangs(berechtigungs)*kl*; **memorandum** ~ *ins* Freizeichnungs*kl*, Haftungsausschluß*kl*; **merger** ~ Schriftform*kl*, Gesamtvertrags*kl*; (*ins*); *Kl*, daß keine Nebenabreden bestehen; **mobility** ~ *Kl über Arbeitseinsatz außerhalb des Wohnorts*; **most-favoured-nation** ~ → *most;* **name and arms** ~ Namen- und Wappen*kl im Testament, zur Führung e–s bestimmten Namens und Familienwappens*; **national treatment** ~ Inländerbehandlungs*kl*; **negative** → *negative*; **no-action** ~ Vorausklage*kl* in Haftpflichtversicherungen; **non-contestable** ~ Unanfechtbarkeits*kl*, Widerrufausschluß*kl*; **non-liability** ~ Haftungsausschlußbestimmung; **not to order** ~ Rekta*kl*; **objects** ~ Bestimmung des Gesellschaftszwecks; **omnibus** ~ Sammel*kl*; **onerous** ~ lästige Bedingung; **operative** ~ dingl wirksame Übertragungs*kl*; **optional** ~ Fakultativ*kl*; **overreaching** ~ → *overreaching*; **overside-delivery** ~ → *overside*; **parcels** ~ → *parcels*; **penal** ~ Strafbestimmung, Vereinbarung e–r Vertragsstrafe; Vereinbarung von pauschaliertem Schadenersatz; **penalty** ~ Konventionalstraf*kl*; **policy proof of interest** ~ (*P.P.I.*) Versicherungsinteresse anerkannt; **protective** ~ Schutz*kl*; **reciprocity** ~ Gegenseitigkeits*kl*; **red** ~ (*rote Kl*); Vorschuß*kl* auf Akkreditiv; **reduced rate average** ~ Selbstbeteiligung gegen verringerte Prämie; **rent review** ~ Mietüberprüfungs*kl*; **restraint** ~ Wettbewerbsverbot **saving** ~ Vorbehalts*kl*, Salvatorische *Kl*, Freizeichnungs*kl*; Trenn*kl*; Besitzstand*kl*, Ausnahmebestimmung; **separability** ~ → *separability*; **sharp** ~ → *sharp*; **shifting** ~ → *shifting;* **simultaneous death** ~ Kommorientenvermutungs*kl* (*Testament*), **standard average** ~ Unterversicherungs*kl*; *Versicherungssumme prozentual zum Barwert* (*Feuerversicherung, US*), **submission** ~ → *submission;* **subrogation** ~ Rechtsnachfolge*kl*, Rechtsübergangs*kl*; **sue and labour** ~ = *suing and labo(u)ring* ~ *qv*; **supremacy** → *supremacy*; **testamentary** ~ Testamentsbestimmung; **testimonium** ~ → *testimonium;* **threefourths value** ~ → *three*; **tie-in** ~ Koppelungs*kl*; **topping-up** ~ Deckungsaufstockungs*kl* (*mit Fälligkeitssanktion*); **violating law** ~ Freizeichnungs*kl* bei Rechtsverletzung des Versicherten; *Haftungsausschluß bei Tod e–s widerrechtlich handelnden Versicherten* (*Lebensversicherung*); **waiver of premium** ~ Prämienverzichts*kl* bei Invalidität.

clausula *Klausel f*, Urteilstenor *m*.

clean rein, fehlerfrei, einwandfrei, vorbehaltlos; **C~ Air Act** *US*: Bundesgesetz gegen Luftverschmutzung; ~ **bill of health** → *bill of health;* ~ **bill of lading** → *bill of lading;* **to be** ~ keine Vorbehalte aufweisen.

clear *v* für einwandfrei befinden, rehabilitieren, bereinigen; räumen; einklarieren; ~ **a cheque** einen Scheck verrechnen; ~ **accounts** → *account* (*2*); ~ **goods** Waren verzollen; ~ **in** einklarieren; ~ **off** abstoßen, bezahlen, wegschaffen, wegräumen; ~ **oneself** sich rechtfertigen; ~ **the courtroom** den Sitzungssaal räumen lassen; ~ **the estate** alle Nachlaßverbindlichkeiten berichtigen; ~ **the title** →*title*.

clear *adj* rein, klar, zweifelsfrei, unbelastet, ohne Abzug, netto; ~ **after debts paid** netto nach Abzug der Schulden; ~ **amount** Nettobetrag; ~ **annual sum free from income tax** Nettobetrag pro Jahr unter Freistellung von Einkommensteuer; ~ **annual value** Nettojahresertragswert; ~ **of all costs and expenses of raising the same** abzüglich aller zur Mittelbeschaffung erforderlichen Kosten; ~ **of all de-**

ductions whatsoever rein netto, ohne Abzüge jeder Art; ~ **of all taxes and outgoings** ohne Steuern und Kosten; ~ **space clause** Mindestabstandsklausel (*Flugversicherung*); ~ **yearly income** Jahresertrag des Reinvermögens; ~ **yearly sum** jährlicher Nettobetrag; ~ **yearly value** nach dem Reinertrag berechneter Jahresertragswert.

clearance Tilgung *f*, Abrechnung *f*; Räumung *f*, Freigabe *f*, Verrechnung *f*; Ausreiseerlaubnis *f* für ein Schiff; Ausklarierung *f*, Verzollung *f*, Zollschein *m*, Abfertigung *f*; lichte Höhe *f*; ~ **area** zum Abbruch freigegebener Bereich ~ **bank** → *bank;* ~ **card** Arbeitsbescheinigung; ~ **certificate** Unbedenklichkeitsbescheinigung, Freigabeerklärung; ~ **inwards** das Einklarieren; ~ **of goods** Abfertigung der Waren; ~ **of stocks** Lagerräumung; ~ **on exportation** Ausfuhrabfertigung; ~ **order** Räumungsurteil; ~ **outwards** Ausklarieren *s, n*; ~ **sale** → *sale;* **customs** ~ → *customs;* **special** ~ vorgezogene Scheckabrechnung.

clearing Clearing *n*, Abrechnungsverfahren *n*, Abrechnungsverkehr *m*; ~ **account** → *account*; ~ **agreement** Verrechnungsabkommen; ~ **assets** Clearingguthaben; ~ **balance** Verrechnungssaldo; ~ **house** Abrechnungsstelle *von Kreditinstituten;* ~ **office** Verrechnungsstelle; ~ **sheet** *exch* Abrechnungsbogen; ~ **system** Verrechnungsverfahren; **after** ~ Nachverrechnung; **in** ~ Scheckeingang von der Verrechnungsstelle; **international** ~**s** internationaler Verrechnungsverkehr; **out** ~ Schecksammelabsendung an die Verrechnungsstelle; **clear-up rate** Aufklärungsquote *f*.

clemency Milde *f*, Nachsicht *f*, Gnade *f*.

cleptomania Kleptomanie *f*.

clergy Klerus *m*, Geistlichkeit *f*.

clergyable kirchenasylfähig.

clercial klerikal, geistlich; kanzleimäßig, Büro ....

clerk Büroangestellter *m*, Sekretär *m*, Schreiber *m*, Kanzleibeamter *m*, Leiter *m* der Geschäftsstelle (*eines Gerichts oder einer Behörde*); ~ **in holy orders** Geistlicher, Ordensgeistlicher; ~ **of court** Urkundsbeamter der Geschäftsstelle; Leiter der Geschäftsstelle des Gerichts; ~ **of records and writs** (*bis 1925*) Urkundsbeamter der Geschäftsstelle; **C~ of the Crown in Chancery** Sekretär des Lordkanzlers, Leiter des Wahlamts für Unterhauswahlen; **C~ of the House of Commons** Leiter der Verwaltung des Unterhauses; ~ **of the market** Marktaufseher, *Hofbeamter für Märkte und Eichwesen;* ~ **of the Parliaments** Leiter der Verwaltung des Oberhauses; ~ **of the privy seal** Sekretär des Lordsiegelbewahrers; ~ **of the table** *Gehilfe des Unterhaus-Präsidenten für Geschäftsordnungsangelegenheiten;* ~ **to the justices** (= *justices' clerk*) *Leiter der Geschäftsstelle und juristischer Berater der Friedensrichter;* **articled** ~ Anwaltsreferendar (*Solitor in Ausbildung*); **authorized** ~ zugelassener Gehilfe e–s Börsenmakler; **cause** ~ Terminkalenderführer des Gerichts; **checkout** ~ Kassierer (*Selbstbedienungsladen*); **chief** ~ Geschäftsleiter e–s Gerichts; Amtmann, Rechtspfleger (*jetzt: master*); **copying** ~ Expedient; **junior** ~ Bürogehilfe; **judge's** ~ jur Gehilfe höherer Richter; **managing** ~ Geschäftsführer, Bürovorsteher; **polling** ~ → *polling;* **principal** ~ *etwa* Urkundsbeamter der Geschäftsstelle; **senior** ~ Bürovorsteher, Hauptbuchhalter; **settlement** ~ → *settlement;* **signing** ~ zeichnungsberechtigter Handlungsgehilfe; Handlungsbevollmächtigter; **town** ~ → *town;* **unsalaried** ~ Volontär.

clerkship Ausbildungsverhältnis *f bei e–m Solicitor;* **articles of** ~ Anwaltsausbildungsvertrag.

client Klient *m*, Kunde *m*, Besteller *m*, Auftraggeber *m*, Mandant *m*; *auch*: *Solicitor im Verhältnis zu Barris-*

ter; ~ **account** (= *client's account*); Anderkonto *des Rechtsanwalts* (*bzw. Wirtschaftsberaters, Immobilienmaklers*) bei e–r Bank, Treuhandkonto; **~'s privilege** Recht des Mandanten auf anwaltschaftlicher Geheimhaltung; ~ **security fond** *Entschädigungsfonds d. Anwaltskammer für Mandanten unredlicher Anwälte;* **dead beat** ~ zahlungsunwilliger Mandant; ~ **entertainment** Mandantenbewirtung.

clientele Kundschaft *f*, Mandantschaft *f*.

cliff-hanger *pol* Zitterpartie *f*.

clinch *v* entscheiden, entgültig regeln; ~ **an argument** zwingend argumentieren.

cloak *v* verschleiern, bemänteln.

clock stamp Eingangsstempel *m* (*mit Zeitangabe*).

clocking (vehicles) Zurückstellen des Kilometerstandes.

clogs on the equity of redemption (unzulässige) Behinderung des Pfandauslösungsrechts.

close *adj* abgegrenzt, eng, verborgen; ~ **jail execution** Strafvollzug im Zuchthaus.

close *s* Abschluß *m*, Anzeigenschluß *m*; abgeschlossener Grundbesitz *m*, eingefriedetes Grundstück *n*; ~ **of pleadings** Beendigung der schriftsätzlichen Vorbereitung; ~ **of the escrow** → *escrow;* ~ **of school** Schulschluß; ~ **of the Exchange** Börsenschluß.

close *v* schließen, abschließen *vi* die Auflassung vollziehen (*US*); ~ **an account** eine Rechnung (ein Konto) abschließen, ein Konto auflösen; ~ **bankruptcy proceedings** Konkursverfahren einstellen; ~ **the case** die Beweisaufnahme schließen.

closed-end adj geschlossen, begrenzt; nicht zur Rücknahme von Anteilen verpflichtet.

closet (*~tted*) *v/reflex oneself, themselves with* in Klausursitzung tagen.

close out Glattstellung *f*, Kontenabschluß *m*.

closing an account Kontenabschluß, Schließung e–s Kontos; ~ **of books** Abschluß der Bücher; ~ **the file** Abschluß der Sache; Abtragen; ~ **trial balance** bereinigte Probebilanz.

closure Schließung *f*, Betriebsstillegung; ~ **of debate** Schluß der Debatte; ~ **for cargo** Verladeschluß; ~ **motion** Antrag auf Schluß der Debatte, ~ **order** Verschlußsachen-Anordnung; **to move the** ~ Schluß der Debatte beantragen.

cloth cap banking bankmäßige Lohnkontenführung *für gewerbliche Arbeiter*.

clothing allowance Kleidergeld *n*.

cloture Verfahren *n* zwecks Schluß der Debatte.

cloud on title Rechtsmangel *m*, Belastung *f* mit Rechten Dritter.

clout Einfluß *m*, Macht *f*; **political** ~ Machtpolitik, Korruption.

club Klub *m*, (*nicht rechtsfähiger*) Verein *m*; ~ **insurance** → *insurance*; **members** ~ Verein; nicht wirtschaftl V., Idealverein; **proprietary** ~ wirtschaftl. Verein zugunsten e–s Einzelnen; geschlossene Gesellschaft *f*; **social** ~ Verein, Klub; **unincorporated members'** ~ nicht rechtsfähiger Verein; **unincorporated proprietary** ~ nicht rechtsfähiger Verein (*wobei das dem Vereinszweck dienende Vermögen einem einzelnen gehört*).

club Knüppel *m*; Polizeistock *m*; ~ **in the closet** Knüppel im Sack.

co-administrator gemeinsamer Nachlaßverwalter *m*, *cf administrator*.

co-adventurer Gelegenheitsgesellschafter *m*.

coal Kohle *f*; ~ **and steel industry** Montanindustrie; ~ **mine** Kohlenbergwerk; ~ **pit** Kohlengrube; **~-whippers** Kohlenabladearbeiter.

coalesce sich vereinigen, zusammenwachsen.

coalescence Vereinigung *f*, Verbindung *f*.

coalition Koalition *f*, Verbindung *f*;

~ **cabinet** Koalitionsregierung; **government** ~ Regierungskoalition.
co-applicant Mitanmelder *m*.
co-assignee Miterwerber *m*, Mitzessionar *m*; Mitverschwörer *m*.
coast Küste *f*; ~ **blockade** Küstenblockade; ~ **guard** Küstenwache, Küstenpolizei; ~ **line** Küstenlinie (*bei Flut*); ~ **protection** Küstenschutz (*gegen Erosion*); ~ **waters** Küstengewässer, für Hochseeschiffahrt benutzbare Meereszugänge.
coastal | shipping Küstenschiffahrt; ~ **trade** Küstenhandel; ~ **waters** Küstengewässer.
coaster Küstenfahrer *m*, Küstendampfer *m*.
coat of arms Wappen *n*; **national** ~ Staatswappen.
co-belligerency *Status e–r mitkriegführenden (doch nicht verbündeten) Macht.*
co-beneficiary Mitberechtigter *m*, Mitbegünstigter *m*.
co-chairman Kopräsident *m*.
cocket *hist* Zollspiegel *n*, Zollbescheinigung *f*.
cockpit *Bezeichnung für Judicial Committe of the Privy Council qv.*
co-creditor Mitgläubiger *m*.
C.O.D. = *cash on delivery → cash.*
code *s* Kodex *m*, Kodifzierung *f*, Kodifikation *f*; Geheimschrift *f*; ~ **name** Deckname; Geheimname; ~ **of civil procedure** Zivilprozeßordnung; ~ **of conduct** Verhaltenskodex, Standesrichtlinien; ~ **of criminal procedure** Strafprozeßordnung; ~ **of ethics** Ehrenkodex, standesrechtliche Grundsätze; ~ **of good lending practice** Leitsätze für die Kreditvergabe; ~ **of law** Gesetzbuch, Kodex; ~ **of obligations** (Kodex von) Verhaltensregeln, Pflichtenkodex; ~ **of practice** Regeln der Baukunst, Verhaltensregeln; **C~ of Professional Responsibility** Standesrichtlinien; ~ **word** (*Telegramm*) Schlüsselwort; **civil** ~ Zivilgesetzbuch, bürgerliches Gesetzbuch; **commercial** ~ Handelsgesetzbuch; **criminal** ~ Strafgesetzbuch; **industrial** ~ Gewerbeordnung; **penal** ~ Strafgesetzbuch; **United States C~** *amtliche Sammlung der US Bundesgesetzgebung.*
code *v* kodifizieren; chiffrieren, verschlüsseln; kontieren; ~ **documents** Belege kontieren.
co-debtor Mitschuldner *m*.
codefendant Mitbeklagter *m*, Mitangeklagter *m*.
codex Kodex *m*; Codex Justianus *m*.
codicil Kodizil *n*, Testamentsnachtrag *m*, Zusatz *m*, Anhang *zu e–r Urkunde.*
codification Kodifikation *f*, Kodifizierung *f*.
codif|y kodifizieren; ~ **ied law** kodifiziertes Recht.
co-emption Aufkauf *m*, Erwerb *m* der Gesamtmenge.
coercion Nötigung *f*, Zwang *m*; ~ **of officials** Beamtennötigung; ~ **of witnesses** Zeugennötigung; **measure of** ~ Zwangsmaßnahme.
coercive Zwangs ..., mit Zwang verbunden.
co-executor Mittestamentsvollstrecker *m cf executor.*
coexistence Koexistenz *f*; **peaceful** ~ friedliche Koexistenz.
cogency Zwang *m*, überzeugende Kraft *f*, Stichhaltigkeit *f*.
cogent zwingend, überzeugend, triftig; ~ **argument** zwingendes Argument; ~ **reason** wichtiger Grund.
cogitate upon nachdenken über.
cogitation Nachdenken *n*, Überlegung *f*.
cognate *adj* verwandt, blutsverwandt; ~ **inventions** verwandte Erfindungen.
cognate *s* Verwandter mütterlicherseits, Kognat *m*.
cognation Verwandtschaft *f*; **civil** ~ rechtliche Verwandtschaft; **mixed** ~ gleichzeitige blutsmäßige und familienrechtliche Verwandtschaft; **neutral** ~ Blutsverwandtschaft.
cognition Erfassen *n*, Erkennen *n*.
cognizable gerichtlich verfolgbar,

der Gerichtsbarkeit unterliegend, zuständig sein für, justiziabel.

cognizance Erkenntnis *f*, richterliche Zuständigkeit *f*, Verhandlung *f*, Anerkenntnis *f*; **claim of ~** Rüge der Unzuständigkeit durch den Hauptintervenienten; **judicial ~** Gerichtskundigkeit; **to take ~ of the matter** etwas zur Kenntnis nehmen.

cognizant unterrichtet, wissend; zuständig; **to be ~ of** Kenntnis haben von.

cognomen Zuname *m*, Beiname *m*, Familienname *m*.

cognose untersuchen, erkennen.

cognovit Anerkenntnis *n* mit Stundungsvereinbarung, Schuldanerkenntnis *f*.

co-guarantor Mitbürge *m*.

co-guardian Gegenvormund *m*, Mitvormund *m*.

cohabitate *v*|*i* (*wie Mann und Frau*) zusammenleben.

cohabitation Zusammenleben *n* (*als Mann und Frau*); **~ contracts** Verträge für eheänliches Zusammenleben von Unverheirateten; **extramarital ~** nichteheliche Lebensgemeinschaft; **illicit ~** Konkubinat, gesetzwidriges Zusammenleben als Mann und Frau; **lascivious ~** (*strafbares*) Konkubinat, wilde Ehe; **unsafe and intolerable ~** öffentliches Ärgernis erregendes Konkubinat, **unlawful ~** *verbotenes* Konkubinat.

cohabitee Partner e–r außerehelichen Lebensgemeinschaft.

cohabiting couple zusammenlebendes Paar; **~ in state of adultery** ehebrecherisches Konkubinat.

co-heir Miterbe *m*.

co-heiress Miterbin *f*.

cohere logisch verbunden sein, zusammenhängen.

coherence logische Verbundenheit *f*, Zusammenhang *m*.

coherent logisch zusammenhängend.

cohesion Zusammenhang *m*.

coif *s hist* Kappe *f*; Juristenstand *m*; **brother of the ~** Jurist, Rechtsgelehrter.

coin *s* Münze *f*, Geldstück *n*, Metallgeld *n*, **~ laundry** Münzwaschsalon; **~ -operated amusement and gaming device(s)** Spielautomat(en); **~ -operated machine** Münzautomat (*für Musikwiedergabe*); **~ -operated telephone kiosk** Münzfernsprechstelle; **base ~** schlechte Münze, Scheidemünze; **copper ~** Kupfermünze; **counterfeit ~** falsche Münze, Falschgeld; **current ~** gangbare Münze, gültiges Hartgeld; **defacing ~s** Unkenntlichmachen von Münzen; divisional **~s** Scheidemünzen; **false ~**Falschgeld; **foreign ~s** ausländisches Münzgeld, Kurs ausländ. Münzen; **foreign ~s or notes** Sorten; **gold ~** Goldmünze, Goldstück; **impairing ~s** Münzverringerung; **minor ~**Kleingeld (*in Münzen*); **possessing counterfeit ~** unbefugter Besitz oder Gewahrsam von Falschgeld; **silver ~** → *silver;* **small ~** Kleingeld, Scheidemünzen; **subsidiary ~** Kleingeld, Scheidemünzen; **token ~** → *token;* **to pass the ~** Münzen weitergeben, in Verkehr bringen; **uttering counterfeit ~** → *uttering*.

coin v prägen, münzen, Münzen schlagen.

coinage Prägung *f*, Münzgeld *n*; **~ offence** → *offence*.

coincide zusammenfallen, zufällig zusammentreffen.

coincidence Zusammentreffen *n*, Zufall *m*.

coincident übereinstimmend.

coinheritance Miterbschaft *f*, gemeinsame Erbschaft *f*.

coinsurance gemeinsame Versicherung; proportionale Risikobeteiligung des Versicherten; Selbstbehalt; **~ clause** Selbstbeteiligungsklausel.

co-inventor Miterfinder *m*.

co-legatee Mitvermächtnisnehmer *m*.

collaborate zusammenarbeiten, mitarbeiten.

collaborateur Mitarbeiter *m*, Arbeitskollege *m pol* Kollaborateur *m*.

collaboration Mitarbeit *f*, Zusammenarbeit *f*; ~ **agreement** Kooperationsvereinbarung *f*.

collapse *s* Zusammenbruch *m*, Einsturz *m*; ~ **of a bank** Bankkrach; ~ **of prices** Preissturz, Kurssturz.

collapse *v* zusammenbrechen, einstürzen.

collar Kragen *m*, Halsband *n*, Ordenskette *f*; ~ **of S. S.** Amtskette des Lord Chief Justice.

collate kollationieren, vergleichen; *eccl* e–e Pfründe übertragen.

collateral *adj* nebenbei, Neben ..., Begleit ..., zusätzlich, akzessorisch, Sicherungs ..., kreditsichernd, Aval ...; Lombard ...; ~ **attack on judgment** Anfechtung eines Urteils außerhalb des Rechtsmittelverfahrens; ~ **loan market** Markt für kurzfristige Kredite, Lombardgeschäft; ~ **security note** Lombardwechsel; ~ **source rule** *keine Vorteilsausgleichung für Zuwendungen Dritter an den Geschädigten,* ~ **trust bond** durch Effekten gesicherte Schuldverschreibung; ~ **trust certificate** Treuhandzertifikat; ~ **trust loan** treuhänderisch gesicherte Anleihe.

collateral (security) *s* Sicherheit *f*, zusätzl Sicherheit; Sicherungsabstand *m*, Nebenbürgschaft *f*; **acceptable as** ~ beleihbar, lombardfähig, lombardierbar; **bankable** ~ Bankdeckung, Banksicherheit; **banking** ~ Banksicherheit; **industrial** ~ Sicherheit durch Hinterlegung von Industrieaktien; **pledged** ~ Faustpfand; **regular** ~ Sicherheit durch Effektenhinterlegung; **mixed** ~ Sicherheit durch Hinterlegung verschiedenartiger Effekten; **to call in** ~ die Sicherheiten heranziehen; **to give** ~ Sicherheit leisten; **to lend on** ~ → *lend;* **to serve as** ~ als Deckung dienen.

collateral security margin Sicherheitsmarge *f* (*bei Beleihungen*).

collation Kollation *f*, Vergleich *m* (*e–r Abschrift mit der Urschrift*), Kollationieren *n*; ~ **of seals** Siegelvergleich.

collect kassieren, sammeln, einziehen, das Inkasso vornehmen; ~ **debts** Forderungen einziehen; ~ **evidence** Beweismaterial sammeln; ~ **on delivery (C.O.D.)** per Nachnahme.

collectible einziehbar, beitreibbar.

collection Abholung *f*, Sammlung *f*; Inkasso *n*, Einziehung *f*, Beitreibung *f*; ~ **s** Forderungseingänge; ~ **agency** Inkassostelle, Inkassobüro; ~ **at source** Steuererhebung an der Quelle, Quellenbesteuerung; ~ **district** Zollbezirk; ~ **draft** Inkassowechsel; ~ **expenses** Inkassospesen, Einziehungskosten; ~ **letter** Anweisungsschreiben bei Einzelinkasso eines Schecks; ~ **of patterns** Musterkollektion; ~ **of premiums** Prämieneinziehung, Beitragseinziehung; ~ **of statistics** statistische Erhebung; ~ **period** durchschnittliche Inkassozeit; ~ **policy** Inkassopolitik; ~ **procedure** Beitreibungsverfahren; **clean** ~ **draft** nicht dokumentärer (Inkasso-)-Wechsel; **documentary** ~ **draft** Dokumententratte; **for** ~ zum Inkasso, zur Einziehung; **forcible** ~ Zwangsbeitreibung; **ready for** ~ zum Abholen bereit.

collective gesammelt, vereint, gemeinsam, zusammengefaßt, kollektiv.

collective wage agreement Entgelt-Tarifvertrag *m*.

collector Zolleinnehmer *m*, Steuereinnehmer *m*, Einziehungsbeamter *m*, Sammler; ~ **of decedent's estate** Nachlaßpfleger; ~ **of the customs** Zolleinnehmer; ~ **'s value** Liebhaberwert.

co-legatary Mitvermächtnisnehmer *m*.

college College *n*, rechtsfähiger Universitätsteil *m*; Universität *f*, Hochschule *f*, Fachschule *f*, wissenschaftliche Gesellschaft *f*, Akademie *f*; **C~ of Advocates** Anwaltsvereinigung (*an kirchlichen Gerichten und in der Seegerichtsbarkeit*); **C~ of Arms** = *Herald's C~ qv*; **C~ of Justice** *scot formelle Bezeichnung für Court of*

Session, Richterschaft am Court of Session; **technical** ~ techn. Fachhochschule.

collid|e kollidieren, aufprallen, zusammenstoßen, im Widerspruch stehen; **~ing interests** widerstreitende Interessen; Interessenkollision; **~ing statements** widerstreitende Darstellungen.

colliery Kohlenbergwerk *n*, Kohlenzeche *f*; ~ **guarantee** Garantie für die Mindestzeit der Beladung eines Schiffes mit Kohle; ~ **working days** gewöhnliche Werktage (im Kohlenbergwerk).

collision Kollision *f*, Zusammenstoß *m*, Widerstreit *m*; ~ **at sea** Schiffszusammenstoß *m*; ~ **clause** Kollisionsklausel (*Deckung bei Schiffszusammenstoß*); ~ **insurance** → *insurance*; ~ **liability** Kollisionshaftpflicht; **head-on** ~ Frontalzusammenstoß; **rear-end** ~ Auffahrunfall.

collocation Anordnung *f*, Reihenfolge *f*, *bes* Reihenfolge *f* der Konkursgläubiger.

colloquium Kolloquium *n*, Sachvortrag *m* bei Verleumdungsklage.

collude in heimlichem Einverständnis handeln.

collusion Kollusion *f*, geheimes (unerlaubtes) Einverständnis *n*, *sittenwidriges Zusammenwirken zur Vortäuschung eines Sachverhalts bzw. Beweismittels*; **risk of** ~ Kollusionsgefahr.

collusive verabredet, abgesprochen, sittenwidrig herbeigeführt; ~ **action** abgekartetes Vorgehen; ~ **bidding** manipulierte Angebotsangabe; ~ **conviction** Erschleichung einer Verurteilung (*um Strafverfolgung wegen schwerer Tat zu vermeiden*); ~ **legal proceedings** Kollusion im gerichtl Verfahren.

colonial kolonial, Kolonial . . ., *US*: ursprüngl die 13 Kolonien betreffend; **C~ Loans Acts** (=) *brit Gesetze über Staatsbürgschaften für Kolonialanleihen* (*1949–1952*); **C~ Preference** Vorzugszölle zwischen dem Mutterland und den Kolonien; ~ **register (companies)** Register der in den Kolonien ansässigen Gesellschaften; **C~ Stock Acts** (=) *brit Gesetze über die Zulässigkeit von Kolonialpapieren als mündelsichere Anlagen* (*1877–1948*).

colonize besiedeln, kolonisieren.

colore officii in amtlicher Eigenschaft.

colo(u)r *v* beschönigen, schönfärben.

colo(u)r *s* Farbe *f*, dunkle Hautfarbe *f*; Vorwand *m*, Anschein *m*; ~ **bar** Rassenschranke; ~ **blindness** Farbenblindheit; ~ **of authority** Anschein der Amtlichkeit; ~ **of law** das Mäntelchen des Rechts, Schein des Rechts; ~ **of title** Rechtsschein, Substantiierung des Eigentumsanspruches; *no* ~ ~ ~: *nicht das geringste dingl Recht*; ~ **prejudice** Rassenvorurteil; **by** ~ **of office** Amtsanmaßung, unter dem Vorwand einer Amtshandlung, Schein des Rechts; **to give** ~ Farbe bekennen, substantiiert erwidern; **without** ~ **of right** ohne das geringste Recht.

col(u)rable anscheinend echt, plausibel, schlüssig; nur zum Schein, vorgetäuscht; ~ **invocation of jurisdiction** Glaubhaftmachung von zuständigkeitsbegründenden Tatsachen; ~ **variation** geringfügige (*zu Täuschungszwecken vorgenommene*) Veränderung (*Warenzeichen*).

co-manager Mitgeschäftsführer *m*, 2. Konsortialführer *m*.

combatants Kombattanten *m*|*pl*, aktive Kriegsteilnehmer *m*.

combination Kombination *f*, Verbindung *f*, Unternehmenszusammenschluß *m*, Vereinigung *f*, Interessengemeinschaft *f*, Zusammenschluß *m*, Verschmelzung *f*, ~ **in restraint of trade** wettbewerbsbeschränkender Zusammenschluß; ~ **sales** Kopplungsverkäufe; **industrial** ~ Industriezusammenschluß; **lateral** ~ horizontaler Unternehmenszusammenschluß; **loose** ~ lockerer Zusammenschluß; **unlawful** ~ widerrechtliche Vereinigung.

combine Firmenzusammenschluß *m*, wettbewerbsbeschränkender Unternehmenszusammenschluß, Kartell *n*.
combine *v* vereinigen, verbinden.
combustibles feuergefährliche Güter *n*|*pl*.
come kommen (*vor Gericht*) erscheinen; ~ **by** erlangen, erwerben; ~ **in** *als Partner* eintreten, eintreffen (*Ware*), eingehen, einlaufen; ~ **in question** fraglich werden, bestritten sein; ~ **in for inheritance** → *inheritance;* ~ **into force** in Kraft treten; ~ **into operation** wirksam werden, in Kraft treten; ~ **of age** volljährig werden; ~ **to** zufallen; ~ **to know** erfahren, in Erfahrung bringen; ~ **to terms** sich einigen, sich vergleichen, verständigen; ~ **under...** fallen unter ...; ~ **up for discussion** Besprechungsthema sein; ~ **up to the expectations** den Erwartungen entsprechen; ~ **within the scope of a law** unter ein Gesetz fallen; ~**s and defends** es erscheint (*der Beklagte*) und läßt sich wie folgt auf die Klage ein.
comfort Unterstützung *f*, Genuß *m*, Hilfe *f*, Komfort *m*, Begünstigung *f*; ~ **letter** Patronatserklärung; *Schreiben, wonach keine Bedenken (gegen e–e Kreditgewährung) bestehen,* Kreditempfehlungsschreiben; *Schr. wonach e–e vorläufige Prüfung keine Unregelmäßigkeiten gezeigt hat.*
comity Courtoisie *f*, Respekt *m*; Entgegenkommen *n*; ~ **of nations** comitas gentium, Völkersitte; völkerrechtliche Courtoisie; *Konventionalregeln der entgegenkommenden Anerkennung von Rechten bzw Gerichtsentscheidungen fremder Staaten im eigenen Hoheitsgebiet*; Völkerrechtsgemeinschaft; **judicial** ~ internationale richterliche Courtoisie.
command *s* Befehl *m*, Befehlsgewalt *f*, Anordnung *f*; **by** ~ **of Her Majesty** auf Anordnung Ihrer Majestät; **C**~ **Papers** auf königl Befehl dem Parlament vorgelegte Schriftstücke (*Weißbücher u. a.*).
command *v* befehlen, gebieten, anordnen, verfügen; einbringen; ~ **the market** den Markt beherrschen.
commandeer requirieren.
commandment Gebot *n*, gerichtliche Anordnung *f*, Anstiftung *f* durch befehlsartige Beeinflussung.
commarchio Grundstücksgrenze *f*.
commence beginnen; ~ **legal proceedings** e–n Prozeß anstrengen.
commencement Beginn *m*; ~ **clause** Eingang, Kopf e–r Urkunde, Präambel; Klagerubrum; ~ **of a policy** Versicherungsbeginn; ~ **of business** Inbetriebnahme des Geschäfts, Geschäftsbeginn; ~ **of proceedings** Verfahrensbeginn, Rechtshängigkeit; ~ **of proof in writing** schriftliche Glaubhaftmachung; ~ **of prosecution** Beginn der Strafverfolgung; Anklageerhebung; ~ **of sentence** Strafantritt; ~ **of service of sentence** Strafantritt; ~ **of winding up** Liquidationsbeginn; **C**~ **oder** Anordnung des Inkrafttretens; **at the** ~ **of...** bei Inkrafttreten.
commendable empfehlenswert, löblich.
commendation Empfehlung *f*, Lob *n*; *hist* Huldigung *f* (*des Vasallen*).
commendatory empfehlend.
comment Bemerkung *f*, Stellungnahme *f*, Meinungsäußerung *f*, Werturteil *n*; **fair** ~ sachliche Kritik, zulässige Meinungsäußerung (*in Wahrnehmung berechtigter Interessen*), gutgläubiges Werturteil; **garbled** ~ entstellter Kommentar; **permissible** ~ zulässige erläuternde Berichterstattung, zulässiger Kommentar.
comment *v* kommentieren, Stellung nehmen.
commentary Kommentar *m*, Erläuterung *f*, Erläuterungswerk *n*, Aktennotiz *f*.
commentator Erläuterer *m*, Kommentator *m*.
commerce Handel *m*, Wirtschaft *f*, Handelsbeziehungen *f*|*pl*; ~ **among the States** = *interstate* ~ *qv;* **auxiliary branch of** ~ Hilfs-

gewerbe; **chamber of ~** Handelskammer, **Department of C~** *US* Handelsministerium; **domestic ~** Binnenhandel; **foreign ~** Außenhandel; *auch: Handel mit anderen Bundesstaaten der USA*; **internal ~** Binnenhandel; **international ~** zwischenstaatlicher Handel; Welthandel; **interstate ~** Handel zwischen den Gliedstaaten der USA; **intrastate ~** Handel innerhalb der Gliedstaaten der USA, Binnenhandel; **treaty of ~** → *treaty*.

commercia belli Kriegsverträge *m|pl*; *Verträge zwischen kriegführenden Staaten bzw deren Staatsangehörigen*.

commercial kommerziell, Handels..., Wirtschafts..., Geschäfts..., kaufmännisch, geschäftlich, wirtschaftlich.

commercial paper verkehrsfähige Wertpapiere *n|pl*, verbriefte Kredite des Handelsverkehrs; kurzfristige negozierbare Schuldscheine bzw Solawechsel *als Geldmarktpapiere von Großunternehmen*.

commercialese Geschäftssprache *f*, Kaufmannsstil *m*.

commercialism Handelsgeist *m*, Geschäftsgeist *m*.

commercialize in den Handel bringen, kaufmännisch nutzen.

commercials Werbespots *m|pl*.

commingle vermischen; **~d goods** vermischt gelagerte Waren (*insb landwirtschaftliche Erzeugnisse*).

commingling of securities Sammelverwahrung; **~ of funds** Vermischung von Fremdgeld *bzw* Treuhandmitteln mit eigenem Geld.

commissary Kommissar *m*, Beauftragter *m*, Offizier *m* der Indentatur; Verpflegungsamt *n*, Verpflegungsstelle *f*; *scot* Richter *m* e-s Grafschaftsgerichts; *brit* Universitätsrichter *m*, Kirchenkommissar *m*; **~ court** *scot* Kirchengericht; **~ store** *mil* Kantine.

commission *s* Kommission *f*, Beauftragung *f*; (entgeltliche) Geschäftsbesorgung *f*; Bestallung *f*; Provision, Courtage *f*; *mil* Offizierspatent *n*, *scot* Vollmacht *f*; *crim* Begehung *f*, Verübung *f*; Rechtshilfeersuchen *n*; **~ account** → *account;* **~ agency** Kommission; **~ agent** Handelsvertreter, Provisionsvertreter, (Verkaufs)Kommissionär; **~ buyer** Einkaufskommissionär; **~ day** Tag des Sitzungsbeginns im Assisengericht; **~ for appraisement and sale** Bestellung eines Schätzers und Verkaufsbeauftragten *für die Versteigerung oder freihändige Verwertung*; **~ for closing business** Abschlußprovision; **~ for examination of witnesses** Rechtshilfeersuchen zur Zeugenvernehmung; **C~ for Racial Equality** K. für Rassische Gleichbehandlung, Anti-Rassismus K.; **~ for subscribing debentures** Provision für die Vermittlung von Emissionsübernehmern bei Schuldverschreibungen; **~ for taking proof** Rechtshilfeersuchen für Beweisaufnahme; **~ government** Gemeindeverwaltung nach Delegationen von Stadtrechtsbefugnissen; **~ house** Börsenhändler, (*Devisen*)-Maklerfirma; **~ in lunacy** → *lunacy;* **~ merchant** Kommissionär (*US*); **~ of anticipation** Berechtigung zur vorzeitigen Abgabenerhebung; **~ of appraisement and sale** gerichtlicher Auftrag durch Schätzung und Verwertung (*Seerecht*); **~ of array** *hist* Musterungskommission; **~ of assize** Bestellung zum Reiserichter; **~ of bankruptcy** Einsetzung eines Untersuchungsbeauftragten in Konkurssachen; **~ of charitable uses** *Verfügung des Court of Chancery zur Feststellung von Mißbrauch bei Kirchenstiftungsland*; **~ of delegates** *hist* Berufungsinstanz gegen Urteile kirchlicher Instanzen; **C~ of EEC** Kommission der Europäischen Gemeinschaft; **~ of eyre** *hist* königl Beauftragung von Reiserichtern; **~ of gaol delivery** *hist* vom High Court entsandter Richter in Strafsachen; **~ of inquiry** Untersuchungskommission; ~ **of lieutenancy** Musterungskommission; ~ **of lunacy** → *lunacy;* ~ **of oyer and terminer** Entsendung e–s Strafrichters; ~ **of partition** Grundstücksteilungsverfahren; ~ **of rebellion** *hist* Beschlagnahmeverfahren zur Erzwingung von Gerichtsbeschlüssen; ~ **of review** *hist* kirchenrechtliche Revisionsinstanz, Überprüfungskommission; ~ **of rogatoire** = ~*s rogatory qv*; ~ **of the peace** Einsetzung eines Friedensrichters (*in e–m bestimmten Bezirk*); ~ **of unlivery** gerichtlich angeordnete Schiffsentladung in Seegerichtsverfahren; **C~ on Human Rights** Kommission für Menschenrechte; C~ **on Narcotic Drugs** Suchtstoffkommission; ~ **on overdraft** Überziehungsprovision; ~ **on sale** Verkaufsprovision, Umsatzprovision; ~ **quamdiu de bene gesserit** *Ernennung vorbehaltlich guter Führung*; ~**s rogatory** zwischenstaatliche Rechtshilfe bei Beweisaufnahme; ~ **sale** Kommissionsverkauf; ~ **-sharing arrangement** Provisionsbeteiligungsvereinbarung; ~ **to examine witnesses** Ersuchen zur Vernehmung von Zeugen auf dem Rechtshilfeweg; ~ **to take depositions** Rechtshilfeersuchen zur Aufnahme schriftlicher Zeugenaussagen; **acquisitive** ~ Abschlußprovision; **agent's** ~ → *agent*; **assent to bills by** ~ delegierte königliche Zustimmung zu Parlamentsgesetzen; **buying** ~ Einkaufskommission, Einkaufsprovision; **by way of** ~ auftragsweise, im Auftrag; **claim for** ~ Provisionsanspruch; **contingent** ~ bedingte (*von Schadensentwicklung abhängige*) Provision; **double** ~**s** Doppelprovision (Verkäufer u. Käufer); **Countryside C** ~ Behörde für Landschaftsschutz und Erholungsflächen, *GB*; **functional** ~ Fachkommission; **goods on** ~ Kommissionswaren; **in** ~ im Auftrag; **Industrial C~** Sozialversicherungsbehörde (*betr Arbeitsunfälle*); **mediation** ~ Vermittlungskommission; **military** ~ Militärgericht, Kriegsgericht; **on** ~ in Kommission, gegen Provision; **monetary** ~ Währungskommission; **on a** ~ **basis** in Kommission, auf Provisionsgrundlage; **overriding** ~ → *overriding*; **permanent** ~ ständige Kommission; **Royal C~ (of enquiry)** königliche Untersuchungskommission; **secret** ~ Schmiergeld; **special** ~ Sonderkommission, Sondergericht; **to obtain a** ~ *mil* zum Offizier befördert werden; **underwriting** ~ Provision aus Konsortialbeteiligungen, Provision für Übernahme e–r Effektenemission; königliche Vollmacht für summarisches Strafgericht.

commission *v* beauftragen, *jmdm* ein Mandat erteilen; ~**ed judge** → *judge;* ~**ed officers** → *officer.*

commissioner Beauftrager *m*, Behördenleiter *m*; beauftragter Richter *m*; ~ **for matrimonial causes** Einzelrichter in Ehesachen; **C~ for Oaths** *zur Beeidigung u. Abnahme von Affidavits ermächtigter Solicitor*; *etwa:* Notar; ~ **in** (= *of*) **bankruptcy** beauftragter Konkursrichter; ~**s in lunacy** Mitglieder von Entmündigungskommissionen; **C~ of Accounts and Deposits** *Abteilung für Rechnungswesen des US-Finanzministeriums*; ~ **of bail** Hinterlegungsbeamter (*Kautionen in Zivilsachen*); ~ **of bankrupts** = ~ *in bankruptcy qv*; ~ **of conciliation** Schiedsbeauftrager; ~ **of deeds** Urkundsperson, Beauftrager für Beurkundung im Rechtshilfeverkehr; ~ **of highways** Leiter der Straßenbaubehörde **C~s of Inland Revenue** *brit* Finanzamt; Ministerialabteilung für Steuern; Richter in Steuersachen; ~ **of internal revenue** Leiter der Steuerbehörde, Bundesfinanzamt *US*; **C~ of Patents** → *patent*; ~ **of public safety** Leiter der Schutzpolizei, Amt für öffentliche Ordnung; **C~ of Sewers** → *sewer*; **county** ~ → *county;* **General C~s** Finanzgericht, obere Finanzbehörde; Hochkommissar, **Lord High C~** Beauftragter der britischen Krone *beim schottischen Kirchentag*; **royal ~** *brit* Staatsbeauftragter; Angehöriger e–r königl Untersuchungskommission (*vgl Royal Commission*); **special ~** beauftragter Richter; **Special C~s** Finanzamt, Steuerbehörde für Veranlagungen.

commissive durch ein Tun verursacht; **~ waste** → *waste*.

commit begehen, verüben; einweisen, verhaften lassen, übergeben, anvertrauen, verpflichten; **~ adultery** Ehebruch begehen; **~ an act collectively** etw gemeinschaftlich begehen; **~ an act of bankruptcy** den Tatbestand eines Konkursgrundes verwirklichen; **~ for trial** in Untersuchungshaft nehmen, dem Strafgericht zur Hauptverhandlung überstellen; **~ to custody** in Haft nehmen, zur Verwahrung nehmen; **~ in trust** zu treuen Händen übergeben; **~ to prison** in Haft nehmen; **~ting magistrate** Ermittlungsrichter, Haftrichter.

commitment (*1*) Überweisung *f*, Überstellung *f*, Einlieferung *f*, Einweisung *f* (*in eine Anstalt*); Inhaftnahme *f*, Haftbefehl *m*; **~ after preliminary hearing** Anordnung der Untersuchungshaft; **~ paper** Bescheinigung der Vollstreckbarkeit e–r Freiheitsstrafe; **~ to prison** Inhaftierung, Einlieferung in ein Gefängnis; **civil ~** Einweisung, Verwahrung(sbeschluß) *in Heilanstalt etc*; **order of ~** Haftbefehl, **own ~** Eigenobligo (*Kreditvertrag*); **warrant of ~** → *warrant*.

commitment (*2*) Festlegung *f*, (vorläufige) Bindung *f*, Engagement *n*, Verpflichtung *f*; **~ appropriation** Verpflichtungsermächtigung; **~ charge** Bereitstellungsgebühren; **~ ceiling** Bereitstellungsplafond; **~ commission** Bereitstellungsprovision; **~ credit** Bereitstellungskredit; **~ fee** Bereitstellungsprovision; **~s for future delivery** Terminengagements; **foreign exchange ~** Devisenengagement; **without any ~** unverbindlich.

committal Begehung *f* (e–r Tat), Überstellung, Einweisung, Haftanordnung; **~ for sentence** Überstellung an den Crown Court (*qv*) zum Urteilsspruch, Überstellung zur Hauptverhandlung nach Voruntersuchung; **instant ~** Eröffnung der Hauptverhandlung ohne Voruntersuchung; **short ~** Anordnung der Hauptverhandlung ohne gerichtl. Voruntersuchung.

committee Ausschuß *m* (= *A bzw a*) Komitee *n*; **~ of contributions** Beitragss*a*; **~ of control** Kontroll*a*; **~ of experts** Fach*a*, Sachverständigen*a*, Sachverständigenbeirat; **~ of four** Vierer*a*; **C ~ of Governors of Central Banks** *A* der Notenbankpräsidenten; **~ of inland transport** Transport*a*, Binnenverkehrs*a*; **~ of inquiry** Untersuchungs*a*; **~ of inspection** Gläubiger*a*; **~ of lunatic** Vormund(srat) e-s Entmündigten; **C~ of Permanent Representatives** *A* der Ständigen Vertreter; **C~ of Privileges** Privilegien*a* *cf parliamentary privileges;* **C~ of Selections** Auswahl*a* für die Besetzung von Parlaments*a*-*n*; **C~ of Supply** Haushalts*a*; **C~ of the Whole (House)** Plenar*a*, das als *A* tagende Plenum; Gesamt*a*; **~ of three** Dreier*a*; **C~ of Ways and Means** Haushalts*a*, Bewilligungs*a*; **~ office** Abteilung für Ausschüsse im Parlamentssekretariat; **C~ on Appropriations** Haushalts*a*; **~ on origin** *A* für Ursprungsfragen (*EG*); **~ stage** Beratungsstadium e–r Vorlage; **ad hoc ~** Ad-hoc-*A*; **adjustment ~** Schlichtungs*a*; **administrative ~** Verwaltungs*a*; **advisory ~** beratender *A*, Beirat; **arbitral ~** Schieds*a*; **armaments ~** Rüstungs*a*; **auditing ~** Rechnungsprüfungs*a*; **auxiliary ~** Hilfs*a*; **budget(ary) ~** Haushalts*a*; **conciliation ~** Vergleichs*a*; **conference ~** Vermittlungs*a*; **consultative ~** Beratungs*a*; **coordinating ~**

Koordinierungs*a*; **council** ~ Rats*a*; **credentials** ~ Vollmachtenprüfungs*a*; **directing** ~ Direktions*a*; **drafting** ~ Redaktions*a*; **economic** ~ Wirtschafts*a*; **estimates** ~ *parl* Haushalts*a*; **executive** ~ Exekutiv*a*, Vollzugs*a*, Verwaltungs*a*, Gemeinde*a*, geschäftsführender *A*; **executory** ~ geschäftsführender *A*; **fact-finding** ~ Untersuchungs*a*; **financial** ~ Finanz*a*; **four-power** ~ Viermächte*a*; **general** ~ Präsidial*a*; **good offices** ~ *A* für gute Dienste; **hybrid** ~ gemischt zusammengesetzter *A*; **interdepartmental** ~ interministerieller *A*; **intersessional** ~ *parl* Ferien*a*; **joint** ~ gemeinsamer *A* (*mehrerer gesetzgebender Körperschaften*); **judicial** ~ Rechts*a*; **Judicial C** ~ = *Judicial Committee of the Privy Council → judicial;* **kitchen** ~ Verpflegungs*a*; **legal** ~ Rechts*a*; **liaison** ~ Verbindungs*a*; **main** ~ Haupt*a*; **manpower** ~ Arbeitskräfte*a*; **mediation** ~ Vermittlungs*a*; **mixed** ~ gemischter *A*; **monetary** ~ Währungs*a*; **negotiating** ~ Verhandlungs*a*; **parliamentary** ~ Parlaments*a*; **permanent** ~ ständiger *A*; **planning** ~ Planungs*a*; **policy** ~ Grundsatz*a*; **preparatory** ~ Vorbereitungs*a*; **presidential** ~ Präsidiums*a*; **Presidential C~** *A* der Präsidenten (*EWG*); **procedural** ~ Verfahrens*a*; **protective** → *protective;* **provisional** ~ ad hoc *A*; **quadripartite** ~ Vierer*a*; Vierparteien*a*; **registered** ~ engerer *A*; **secret** ~ geheimer Untersuchungs*a*; **select** ~ (*normaler*) Parlaments*a* (*GB*), engerer *A*, Sonder*a*; Untersuchungs*a*, **senior** ~ Ober*a*; **sessional** ~ → *sessional;* **shop** ~ Betriebsrat; **sifting** ~ Vorprüfungs*a*, Tagesordnungs*a*; **small** ~ engerer *A*; **social** ~ Sozial*a*; **specialized** ~ Fach*a*; **standing** ~ ständiger *A*; **standing orders** ~ Geschäftsordnungs*a*; **steering** ~ Lenkungs*a*; **sub-** ~ Unter*a*; **subordinate** ~ nachgeordneter *A*; **subsidiary** ~ Neben*a*; **supervisory** ~ Überwachungs*a*; **technical** ~ Fach*a*; **Technical Assistance C~** *A* für Technische Hilfe; **the House goes into** ~ **on a bill** das Unterhaus tritt als Gesamt*a* in die Beratung e–s Gesetzentwurfs zusammen; **Welsh C~** Parlaments*a* für Angelegenheiten von Wales; **working** ~ Arbeitsausschuß.

committitur Haftanordnung *f*, *Aktenvermerk:* „Haft"; ~ **piece** Haftstrafe urkunde gegen e–n säumigen Schuldner; **interim** ~ Anordnung der Untersuchungshaft.

commixtio(n) Vermengung *f*, Vermischung *f* (*von festen Stoffen verschiedener Eigentümer*).

commixture Gemisch *n*, Vermischung *f*.

commodious brauchbar, geräumig, breit.

commodities *pl von commodity qv,* Waren *f|pl*, Güter *n|pl*, Rohstoffe *m|pl*; bewegl Sachen *f|pl*; Grundstoffe *m|pl*; ~ **in bulk** Massengüter; **basic** ~ Rohstoffe.

commodity Ware *f*, Gut *n*, Handelsartikel *m*; Annehmlichkeit *f*, Vorteil *m*; ~ **agreement** Rohstoffabkommen; ~ **exchange** Warenbörse; ~ **exchange administration** Aufsichtsbehörde für die Produktenbörsen; ~ **futures** Warentermingeschäfte; ~ **futures option** Warenterminoption; ~ **loans** Warenkredit, durch Waren gesicherte Darlehen; ~ **market** Warenmarkt; Warenbörse, Produktenbörse; ~ **marketing** Warenabsatz; ~ **money** Warengeld, Indexwährung; ~ **papers** durch marktgängige Produkte gesicherter Wechsel, Verschiffungsdokumente; ~ **prices** Rohstoffnotierungen; ~ **rate** Sondergütertarif, Waggonfrachtsatz; ~ **standard** Naturalgeld; ~ **value** Warenwert; Sachwert; **scarce** ~ Mangelware.

common *adj* gemeinsam, allgemein, üblich, gemein.

common *s* Allmende *f*, gemeinschaftliches Nutzungsrecht, Gemeindeservitut, Gemeindeland *n*,

Ortspark *m*, gemeinschaftliche Gerechtsame *f*, ~ **appendant** Benutzungsrecht (*Weiderecht*) am fremden Grundstück, beschränkte persönliche Dienstbarkeit *f*; ~ **appurtenant** = ~ *appendant qv*; ~ **at large** (= ~ *in gross qv*); ~ **in gross** höchstpersönliches Allmendrecht subjektiv-dingliches Nutzungsrecht; ~ **of digging** Entnahmerecht am fremden Grundstück, Schürfrecht, Abbaurecht, allgemeines Recht auf Entnahme von Mineralien; ~ **of estovers** allgemeines Holzschlagerecht, Waldgerechtigkeit, Holzlesegerechtigkeit; ~ **of fishery** = ~ *of piscary qv*; ~ **of fowling** Jagdrecht auf Federwild und Wildkaninchen; ~ **of pasture** allgemeines Weiderecht, Weidegerechtigkeit; ~ **of piscary** allgemeines Fischereirecht, Fischereigerechtigkeit, Fischwasser; ~ **of shack** nachbarliches Nachweiderecht; ~ **of turbary** gemeindliches Torfentnahmerecht; ~ **sans nombre** unbeschränktes Weiderecht; ~ **without stint** unbeschränktes Weiderecht.

common communications carriers Fernmeldebetriebsgesellschaften.

common ground gemeinsame Basis, etwas Unstreitiges, unbestritten.

commonhold association (Wohnungs)Eigentümergemeinschaft *f*.

commonhold-freehold flat Eigentumswohnung *f* auf Erbpachtgrundstück.

common law *auch*: *Common Law*, das gemeine Recht (*Englands*), das englische allgemeine Recht, das (*vom Billigkeitsrecht unterschiedene*) strenge Recht; ~ **action** bürgerlicher Rechtsstreit; zivile Streitsache, Zivilklage; ~ **assignment** gewohnheitsrechtlich anerkannte Liquidationsabtretung an die Gläubiger; ~ **contempt** Strafverfahren als Folge einer Widersetzlichkeit gegen gerichtliche Verfügungen; ~ **copyright** → *copyright;* ~ **corporations** originäre juristische Personen (*zB Krone, Bischof*); ~ **courts** Common Law Gerichte, allg ordentliche Zivilgerichte; ~ **marriage** → *marriage*; ~ **mortgage** vertragliches Grundpfandrecht (*außerhalb eines Grundbuchs*); ~ **power of arrest** Festnahmerecht ohne Haftbefehl; ~ **remedy** Rechtsbehelf (*jeder Art*); ~ **right** originäres (*unabhängig von Gesetzen bestehendes*) Recht; ~ **trust** = Massachusetts Trust → *trust*; ~ **wife** (als Ehefrau anerkannte) Lebensgefährtin.

common learning Allgemeinbildung *f*.

Common Market (*EEC*) der Gemeinsame Markt (*EWG*).

common ownership enterprise belegschaftseigenes Unternehmen (*genossenschaftlich*).

common parts of blocks of flats Gemeinschaftsanlagen e–r Wohnanlage.

Common Serjeant Londoner Stadtrichter in Strafsachen; *circuit judge qv von Amts wegen*.

commonable im Mitbesitz stehend; zur Gemeindeweide zugelassen.

commonalty die Gemeinen *m|pl*, Bürgerschaft *f*; die einfachen Mitglieder *n|pl* (*eines Vereins usw*).

commoner Bürger *m*, Bürgerlicher *m*; **C**~ Mitglied *n* des Londoner Stadtrats; Mitglied *n* des Unterhauses; Teilhaber *m* an Gemeindeweideland.

commonwealth Volk *n*, Nation *f*, Staat *m*, Republik *f*; Commonwealth *n*, Staatenbund *m*; **the C**~ das brit. Commonwealth; ~ **citizen** Staatsangehöriger des Commonwealth; britischer Staatsbürger; ~ **countries** Mitgliedstaaten des brit Commonwealth; **C**~ **Development Corporation,** *GB 1982* Commonwealth Entwicklungsanstalt.

commorientes Kommorienten, *m|pl*, gleichzeitig miteinander Versterbende *m|pl*.

commote Landbesitz *m*, große Grundherrschaft *f* (*Wales*).

commotion Unruhen *f/pl*, Aufruhr *m*; **civil** ~ innere Unruhen.

communalism Selbstverwaltung(sprinzip) *n* der Gemeinden.

communalization Vergemeindung *f*, Eingemeindung *f*, Übernahme *f* durch eine Gemeinde.

communia dem Gemeingebrauch *m* dienende Güter *n/pl*.

communicate mitteilen, erklären, in Verbindung stehen, verkehren mit.

communicatee Mittelsmann *m*, Verbindungsmann *m*, Empfänger *m* von Mitteilungen.

communication Benachrichtigung *f*, Übermittlung *f*, Mitteilung *f*, Verkehr *m*, Verbindung *f*; ~ **by counsel to judge** Mitteilungen des Verteidigers an den Richter (*außerhalb des Verfahrens*); ~ **of information** Nachrichtenübermittlung; **confidential** ~ vertrauliche Mitteilung; **foreign** ~**s** Nachrichtenverkehr mit dem Ausland; **means of** ~ → *means*; **postal** ~ Postverbindung, Postverkehr, Mitteilung per Post; **privileged** ~**s** dem Zeugnisverweigerungsrecht unterliegende Mitteilungen; Berufsgeheimnis; **upward and downward** ~ behördeninterne Durchlässigkeit (des Informationsweges).

communicator Mitteilender *m*, Übermittler *m*.

community Gemeinsamkeit *f*, gemeinsamer Besitz *m*, Gemeinde *f*, Gemeinwesen *n*, Nachbarschaft *f*; Gemeinschaft *f*; Gütergemeinschaft *f*; ~ **centre** Gemeindehaus, Freizeitheim; ~ **charge** Gemeindeabgabe (*Gemeindekopfsteuer*); ~ **chest** *US* Armenunterstützungsfonds; ~ **credit policy** kommunale Kreditgewährungsrichtlinien; ~ **debt** gemeinschaftliche Schuld (*von Ehegatten*); ~ **home** Gemeinde-Jugendfürsorgeanstalt; ~ **lease** Gemeinschaftsverpachtung; ~ **of goods** Gütergemeinschaft; ~ **of heirs** Erbengemeinschaft; ~ **of income and profits** Errungenschaftsgemeinschaft; ~ **of interest** Interessengemeinschaft; ~ **of profits** Gewinngemeinschaft; gesamthänderische Bindung von Gewinnen; ~ **of property** (*eheliche*) Gütergemeinschaft; ~ **policing on foot** Polizeistreife zu Fuß; ~ **property** Gemeinschaftsgut, Gesamtgut; ~ **service (order)** Gemeinschaftsdienst, soziale Dienstleistung als Bewährungsauflage; ~ **trust** → *trust*; **conjugal** ~ eheliche Lebensgemeinschaft; **conventional** ~ vertraglich vereinbarte Gütergemeinschaft; **financial** ~ Finanz(welt); **general** ~ **of goods** allgemeine Gütergemeinschaft; **international** ~ Völkergemeinschaft; **legal** ~ die Juristen (*Anwälte und Richter*).

Community (die Europäische) Gemeinschaft *f* (= *G*); ~ **authorisation** *G*-*s*genehmigung; ~ **ceiling** *G*-*s*plafond (Zollpräferenzen); ~ **goods** *G*-*s*waren; ~ **instrument** Urkunde der EG; ~ **law** *G*-*s*recht; ~ **legislation** Gesetze der (Europ) Gemeinschaft, Gesetzgebung der EG; ~ **origin** *G*-*s*ursprung; ~ **procedure** *G*-*s*verfahren; ~ **product** *G*-*s*erzeugnis; ~**'s cohesion** *G*-*s*zusammenhalt; ~ **rules** *G*-*s*regelungen; ~ **tariff quota** *G*-*s*zollkontingent; ~ **treatment** *G*-*s*behandlung.

communize in Gemeineigentum überführen, vergesellschaften.

commutabe umwandelbar, ablösbar.

commutation Strafumwandlung *f*, Strafherabsetzung *f*, Strafaussetzung *f*; Austausch *m*, Ablösung *f*, Kapitalisierung *f*; Pendeln *n* (*Vorortwohnung – Arbeitsplatz*); ~ **debt** Ablösungsschuld; ~ **loan** Ablösungsanleihe; ~ **of annuity** Ablösung einer Rente; ~ **of death penalty** (*to life imprisonment*) Umwandlung der Todesstrafe (*in lebenslängliche Freiheitsstrafe*); ~ **of penalty** = ~ *of sentence qv*; ~ **of punishment** = ~ *of sentence qv*; ~ **of sentence** Strafumwandlung, Strafermäßigung, Herabsetzung des Strafmaßes, teilweiser Straferlaß; ~ **of ta-**

xes pauschalierte Vorwegzahlung von Steuern (*als Ablösung*); ~ **of tithes** Zehntablösung (*durch Geldrente*); ~ **ticket** Zeitkarte, Bezirkskarte.

commutative auswechselbar, Ersatz..., Tausch..., gegenseitig, wechselseitig.

commute austauschen, (*Strafe*) umwandeln, abfinden.

compact *adj* kurz, bündig, kompakt, konzentriert.

compact *s* Vertrag *m*, Pakt *m*, Übereinkunft *f*.

Companies House *GB* Amt für Kapitalgesellschaften.

companion Gesellschafter *m*, Begleiter *m*, Inhaber *m* e-r Ordensklasse; **C~ of the Garter** Ritter des Hosenbandordens.

compan|y Gesellschaft *f* (= *G bzw g*), Handelsgesellschaft *f*, Kapitalgesellschaft *f*; *brit* Aktiengesellschaft *f bzw* Gesellschaft *f* mit beschränkter Haftung; **C~ies Act** (= *CosA*) Gesetz über Kapital*g-en*; **C~ies Court** → *court;* ~ **duly constituted by law** ordnungsgemäß gegründete Kapital*g*; ~ **foundation** *G-s*gründung; ~ **incorporated by Act of Parliament** durch Parlamentsakte geschaffene Kapital*g*; ~ **law** → *law*; ~ **limited by guarantee** *gemeinnützige G* mit beschränkter Nachschußpflicht; ~ **limited by shares** Aktien*g*, GmbH; ~ **meeting** Hauptversammlung, Gesellschaftervers; ~ **name** (= ~*'s*) Firma der (*Kapital*)*G*; ~ **not having share capital** *G* ohne *G-s*kapital; ~ **not trading for profit** nicht gewerbliche *G*; **C~ of Porters** *Körperschaft zur Ausübung von Eichgerechtigkeiten in London*; **C-ies Register** Verpfändungsregister von *G-n*; ~ **register of members** Gesellschafterverzeichnis, Aktienbuch; ~ **searches** Recherchen zur Gesellschaftsgründung; ~ **secretary** *G-s*sekretär; ~ **union** Betriebsgewerkschaft; ~ **within the stanneries** *hist* Bergbau*g*, Gewerkschaft; **accepting** ~ Rückversicherer, **affiliated** ~ → *to affiliate;* **alien** ~ auswärtige *G*; **associated** ~ verbundene *G*, Konzern*g*; ~ **auditing** ~ → *auditing*; **banking** ~ → *banking*; **British** ~ Kapital*g* nach brit Recht *u von Commonwealth-Bürgern beherrscht*; **casual** ~ Gelegenheits*g*; **ceding** ~ Erstversicherer; **charitable** ~ gemeinnützige Körperschaft, mildtätige Stiftung; **chartered** ~ Handelskompagnie; *durch Hoheitsakt gegründete G*; **city** ~ → *city*; **close** ~ *GB; (US close corporation); Kapitalgesellschaft, die von wenigen Personen (höchstens 5) beherrscht wird; etwa:* Familien-GmbH; **closed-end** ~ → *investment company*; **constituent** ~ Konzern*g*; **controlled** ~ abhängige *G*, fremdbeherrschte *G*; Unter*g*; **controlling** ~ beherrschende G, Dach*g*; **defunct** ~ stillgelegte *G*; **diversified** ~ Investment*g*, mit gesetzlicher Risikostreuung; **dormant** ~ stillgelegte *G*; **dummy** ~ Schein*g*, Schwindel*g*; **exempt private** ~ Familien-GmbH; *von der Bilanzoffenlegung befreite, vinkulierte GmbH*; *GB bis 1980*; **face-amount certificate** ~ Investment*g*, die Nennbetragszertifikate bei Rateneinzahlung ausgibt; **family** ~ → *family*; **group** ~ Konzern*g*; **holding** ~ → *holding company*; **incorporated** ~ Kapital*g*, Aktien*g*; *brit* rechtsfähige *G*; **insurance** ~ → *insurance;* **joint stock** ~ *brit* Aktien*g*; *US* körperschaftlich organisierte Personen*g*, *etwa*: Kommandit*g* auf Aktien; **limited (liability)** ~ Aktien*g bzw G* mit beschränkter Haftung (*vgl public* ~ *bzw private* ~); **lead** ~ Haupt*g*, Konsortialführer; **listed** ~ börsennotierte *G*; **medium-sized** ~ Aktiengesellschaft mittlerer Größe (*bis 250 Mitarbeiter*); **money-lending** ~ Kreditinstitut, Kundenfinanzierungs*G*; **loss-making** ~ verlustbringende *G*; **mutual** ~ genossenschaftliche Versicherung auf Gegenseitigkeit; **mutual life insurance** ~ Lebensversicherungs*g* auf Gegenseitigkeit; **non-commercial**

~ nicht gewerbliche G; **non-profit-making** ~ nicht gewerbliche G; **non-resident** ~ ausländische G, G mit Sitz im Ausland; **off-the shelf** ~ Leerfirma, Firmenmantel; **one-man** ~ Einmanng; **overseas** ~ Auslandsg (*außerhalb GB gegründete Kapitalgesellschaft mit Niederlassung in GB*); **parent** ~ Mutterg, Stammhaus; **private** ~ G mit beschränkter Haftung; **proprietary** ~ → *proprietary*; **prospectus** ~ G mit Prospekt; *brit* Gründungsg; **public limited** ~ = *public* ~ (*plc*) *brit* Aktieng; **public utility** ~ öffentlicher Versorgungsbetrieb; **quoted** ~ zum Börsenhandel zugelassene G; **registered** ~ eingetragene G; *nach dem Companies Act gebildete und beim Registrar of Companies registrierte* G; **related** ~ Schwesterfirma; befreundete G; **resident** ~ inländische (Handels)G; **shell** ~ → *shell company*; **shipping** ~ → *shipping*; **small** ~ mittelständische Kapitalg (*bis 50 Mitarbeiter*); **statutory** ~ privat betriebene G der öffentlichen Versorgung (*konzessioniert durch das brit Parlament*); **struck-off** ~ gelöschte G; **subsidiary** ~ Tochterg; **underlying** ~ Tochterg; **trading** ~ Handelsg; **trust** ~ Treuhandg, Vermögensverwaltungsg; **to take ~ies private** *Aktien in GmbH-ähnliche G-n umwandeln*; **unicorporated** ~ nicht rechtsfähige G, Personalg; **unlimited** ~ G mit unbeschränkter Haftung; **unquoted** ~ G, deren Aktien nicht an der Börse notiert werden; **unregistered** ~ nicht *im Handelsregister* eingetragene G.

comparable *s* Vergleichsobjekt *n*.

comparable *adj* vergleichbar; ~ **period** Vergleichszeitraum; ~ **property** Vergleichsgrundstück, Vergleichsmietobjekt.

comparative vergleichend; ~ **knowledge** Abwägen des Mitverschuldens *nach dem Grad der beiderseitigen Kenntnis des gefahrbegründenden Umstandes*; ~ **rectitude** Schuldabwägung.

comparator Vergleichsmaßstab *m*, Vergleichsperson *f*.

compartmentalization übertriebenes Ressortdenken *n*.

compare vergleichen, kollationieren.

comparison Vergleich *m*, Gegenüberstellung *f*; ~ **of handwriting** Schriftvergleichung.

compass planen, im Schilde führen.

compassionate mitfühlend, humanitär; ~ **allowance** Zuwendung aus humanitären Gründen; Unterhaltszahlung an (*schuldig*) geschiedene Ehefrau, Notunterhalt; ~ **leave** Strafunterbrechung wegen Tod oder Krankheit naher Angehöriger.

compaternity geistige Verwandtschaft *f*, Patenschaft *f*.

compatibility Verträglichkeit *f*, Kompatibilität *f* (*auch pol*), Vereinbarkeit *f*.

compatible vereinbar, im Einklang stehend.

compel zwingen, etw erzwingen; ~ **payment** Zahlung erzwingen; ~ **the attendance** die Anwesenheit erzwingen (*Zeugen*).

compellability of witness Erzwingbarkeit *f* des Erscheinens von Zeugen.

compellable erzwingbar (*zB durch Ordnungsstrafe*).

compelling *adj* zwingend.

compendium Kompendium *n*, Abkürzung *f*, Abriß *m*; ~ **of law** Gesetzessammlung.

compensable zur Entschädigung berechtigend.

compensat|e entschädigen, vergüten, ersetzen, ausgleichen, aufrechnen; ~ **for damages** Schadenersatz leisten; **~ing balance** ständiges Kontokorrent-Mindestguthaben; **~ing errors** sich per Saldo ausgleichende Fehler; **~ing tax** Ausgleichssteuer.

compensatio criminis Aufrechnung *f* von Straftaten; Vorwurf *m*, selbst die gleiche Ehewidrigkeit begangen zu haben.

compensation Vergütung *f*, Schadensersatz *m*, Ausgleich *m*, Abfindung *f*, Entschädigung *f*; Leistungsentgelt *n*; Belohnung *f* für die Ergreifung von Straftätern; ~ **authority** Schankkonzessionsbehörden; ~ **claim** Entschädigungsanspruch; Schadenersatzanspruch; ~ **deal** Kompensationsgeschäft; ~ **for damage** Schadenersatz; ~ **for damage in kind** Naturalrestitution; Schadenersatz in natura; ~ **for disturbance** Entschädigung an weichenden Landpächter; ~ **for expense of attending trial** Zeugenentschädigung; ~ **for expropriation** Enteignungsentschädigung; ~ **for improvements** Ersatz für werterhöhende Aufwendungen; ~ **for loss of office** Entschädigung für Verlust des Amtes (*der Vorstandsmitgliedschaft*); ~ **for loss or damage** Schadensersatz; ~ **for pain and suffering** Schmerzensgeld; ~ **for use** Nutzungsentschädigung; ~ **insurance** (*Arbeiter*)Unfallversicherung; ~ **order** Entschädigungsbeschluß (*im Adhäsionsverfahren*); ~ **payable** geschuldete Entschädigung; ~ **period** Entschädigungszeitraum; ~ **trading** Kompensationsgeschäfte; **basic** ~ Grundvergütung; **deferred** ~ aufgeschobene (*noch nicht zu versteuernde*) Vergütung; **due** ~ volle Entschädigung; **fair** ~ angemessene Vergütung (für Dienstleistungen); **Just C~ Clause** *US* Verfassungsbestimmung über gerechte Enteignungsentschädigung; **monetary** ~ finanzielle Entschädigung, Schadensersatz in Geld; **"no fault"** ~ **system** Entschädigungssystem ohne Verschuldensprüfung; **pecuniary** ~ Entschädigung in Geld; **reasonable** ~ angemessene Entschädigung; **to award ~s** Schadenersatz zuerkennen; **to provide** ~ Entschädigung gewähren; **workmen's** ~ → *workmen*.

compensatory ausgleichend, Ersatz . . ., Entschädigungs . . .; ~ **fiscal policy** antizyklische Konjunkturpolitik.

compet|e im Wettbewerb stehen, konkurrieren; **~ing business** Konkurrenzbetrieb.

competence Zuständigkeit *f*, Kompetenz *f*, Befugnis *f*, Befähigung *f*, Qualifikation *f*; **occupational** ~ berufliche Eignung.

competency Zurechnungsfähigkeit *f*, Qualifikation *f*, Zuständigkeit *f*; ~ **proceedings** Verfahren (*Verhandlung*) zur Feststellung der Zurechnungsfähigkeit; ~ **to stand trial** Verhandlungsfähigkeit *des Angeklagten*; ~ **of witness** Zeugnisfähigkeit; Brauchbarkeit e–s Zeugen.

competent kompetent, zuständig, qualifiziert, fähig, zurechnungsfähig, befugt, sachkundig; ~ **to contract** geschäftsfähig; zum Vertragsschluß befugt; ~ **to dispose** verfügungsberechtigt; ~ **to dispose by will** testierfähig; berechtigt, *über etw* letztwillig zu verfügen.

competition Wettbewerb *m*, Konkurrenz *f*, Preisausschreiben *n*; ~ **clause** Konkurrenzklausel; ~ **for prizes** Sportprämienwette; ~ **in armaments** Wettrüsten; ~ **law** Wettbewerbsrecht; **conditions of** ~ Wettbewerbsbedingungen; **cutthroat** ~ mörderischer Wettbewerb, ruinöse Konkurrenz, **fair** ~ lauterer Wettbewerb; **fraudulent** ~ unlauterer Wettbewerb *mit Täuschungsabsicht*; **free** ~ freier Wettbewerb; **imperfect** ~ Chancenungleichheit im Wettbewerb; unvollkommene Wettbewerbsfreiheit; **open** ~ freier Wettbewerb; **perfect** ~ vollkommene Wettbewerbslage; **restraint of** ~ Wettbewerbsbeschränkung; **unfair** ~ unlauterer Wettbewerb.

competitive konkurrierend, auf Wettbewerb eingestellt, Konkurrenz . . ., wettbewerbsfähig, konkurrenzfähig.

competitiveness Konkurrenzfähigkeit *f*, Wettbewerbseigenschaft *f*.

competitor Konkurrent *m*, Mitbewerber *m*, Konkurrenzfirma; **to undercut a ~ in trade** einen Konkurrenten unterbieten.

compilation Kompilation *f*, Sammlung *f*, Zusammenstellung *f*, Aufstellung *f*.

compile zusammentragen, sammeln; **~d statutes** Gesetz- und Verordnungssammlung.

complain klagen, sich beschweren, Beschwerde führen.

complainant Beschwerdeführer *m*, Kläger *m*, Anzeigeerstatter *m*.

complaint Klage *f*, Klageschrift *f* (*GB: magistrates' courts, US: einzelstaatl*), Strafanzeige *f*, Strafanklage *f*, Beschwerde *f*; **~ by or on behalf of the party aggrieved** Klage, Beschwerde (*einer beschwerten bzw verletzten Partei*); **~s, if any** eventuelle Beschwerden; **~ of unfair dismissal** Kündigungsschutzklage; **~ procedure** Beschwerdeverfahren.

complement Ergänzung *f*, Vollständigkeit *f*.

complementary ergänzend, Ergänzungs-; **~ goods** zusammenhängende Waren; **~ insurance** → *insurance*; **~ rules** Ergänzungsvorschriften; **~ statements** ergänzende Ausführungen.

complete *adj* vollendet, vollkommen, vollständig; **~ and regular** vollständig und ordnungsgemäß; **~ copies of published work** vollständige Exemplare eines veröffentlichten Werkes; **~ determination of cause** abschließende Entscheidung, rechtskräftige Erledigung eines Prozesses; **~ in itself** vollständig, umfassend, abschließend.

complete *v* vollenden, abschließen, ergänzen, vervollkommnen, vervollständigen, ausfüllen; **~ a form** ein Formular ausfüllen; **~ a task** e-e Aufgabe erfüllen; **~d application form** ausgefüllter Antrag; **~d audit** → *audit;* **~d contract method** *Gewinn- bzw. Verlustermittlung erst bei Abschluß langfristiger Verträge;* **~d execution** beendigte Vollstreckung; **~d mortgage** *vollständig* bestelltes Grundpfandrecht; **~d offence** → *offence;* **~ in writing** (*bitte*) handschriftlich ausfüllen!

completeness Vollkommenheit *f*, Vollständigkeit *f*.

completion Beendigung *f*, Vollendung *f*, Abschluß *m*; Vollziehung *f*, e-s Grundstückskaufvertrages (*durch Besitzüberlassung, Eigentumsübertragung und Zahlung*); Ablauf *m*, Vervollständigung *f*, Fertigstellung *f*, Erfüllung *f*, Ergänzung *f*; **~ bond** → *bond* (*2*); **~ notice** Erschließungsfristbescheid; **~ of an attempt** Vollendung eines Versuches; **~ of an offence** Vollendung (*des Tatbestandes*) einer Straftat, Ausführung e-r Tat; Tatbeendigung; **~ of contract** Vertragserfüllung; **~ of sale** Kaufabschluß; **~ of sentence** Beendigung der Strafverbüßung; **~ of service** Ablauf der Dienstzeit.

compliance Erfüllung *f*, Einwilligung *f*; **~ cost** abgeführte Mehrwertsteuer; **~ officer** Kontrollbeamter *m*; **in-house ~** firmeninterner Kontrolleur; **~ visit** Kontrollbesuch; **~ with a condition** Erfüllung einer Bedingung; **~ with formalities** Einhaltung von Förmlichkeiten; **~ with the requirements** Erfüllung der Voraussetzungen; **declaration of ~** Erklärung, daß die Gründungsvorschriften eingehalten wurden; **in ~ with** gemäß, in Übereinstimmung mit; **on due ~ with the regulations** bei ordnungsmäßiger Einhaltung der Vorschriften; **~ with the requirements of the acts** Einhaltung der gesetzlichen Vorschriften; **substantial ~** → *substantial*.

compliant nachgiebig, willfährig, zuvorkommend.

complice Komplize *m*, Mittäter *m*.

complicity, Mittäterschaft *f*, Teilnahme *f*; **~ theory** Teilnahmelehre.

comply (*with*) erfüllen, entsprechen, nachkommen, einhalten, befolgen; **~ with a law** ein Gesetz befolgen; **~ with a summons** einer Ladung nachkommen; **~ with regulations** Vorschriften befolgen, Vorschriften einhalten; **~ with conditions** Bedingungen erfüllen.

component *s* Bestandteil *m*; **add-on ~s** Zusatzteile, Anbauteile.

compose zusammensetzen, beilegen, schlichten; ~ **differences** Differenzen beheben; ~ **the documents** Unterlagen abfassen, aufsetzen; ~**d of** bestehend aus.

composite | **demand** zusammengesetzte Nachfrage; ~ **rates of depreciation** allgemeine Abschreibungssätze; ~ **work** Sammelwerk.

composition Zusammensetzung *f*, Gesamtvergleich *m*; Vergleichssumme *f*, Pauschalsumme *f*, Sühnegeld *n*; Ausgleich *m*; ~ **by deed of arrangement** außergerichtlicher Gläubigervergleich; ~ **deed** Vergleichsurkunde (*mit Gläubigern*); ~ **for stamp duty** Stempelsteuerpauschalierung; ~ **in bankruptcy** Liquidationsvergleich, Zwangsvergleich; ~ **of matter** *pat* chemische Zusammensetzung, Stoffverbindung, Mischung; ~ **of tithes** Ablösung des Zehnten; ~ **proceedings** Vergleichsverfahren; ~ **with assignment and release** Liquidationsvergleich mit Abgeltungsklausel; ~ **with creditors** Gesamtvergleich mit Gläubigern; **amicable** ~ gütliche Regelung, einverständlicher Gläubigervergleich; **joint** ~ Gesamtvergleich.

compound *s* künstliche Mischung *f*, synthetische Mischung *f*, Verbindung *f*, Zusammensetzung *f*; **chemical** ~ chemische Verbindung.

compound *v* beilegen, zusammensetzen, sich einigen, vergleichen; ~ **a dispute** e–n Streit beilegen; ~ **a felony** *von Strafverfolgung (durch den Geschädigten) gegen Vergütung Abstand nehmen,* begünstigen; ~ **claims** Ansprüche abfinden; ~ **creditors** e–n Gesamtvergleich schließen; ~ **for a debt** e–e Abfindung vereinbaren; ~**ed settlement** pauschale Abgeltung.

compounder (*außergerichtl*) Vergleichsschuldner *m*.

compounding Aufzinsung *f*.

compounding | **a felony** (= ~ *of felony*) eigennützige Begünstigung (*durch eigennütziges Unterlassen der Strafanzeige*); ~ **of claims** vergleichsweise Forderungsbefriedigung.

comprehend erfassen, begreifen; enthalten, umfassen.

comprehensible begreiflich, faßlich, verständlich.

comprehension Auffassung *f*, Verständnis *n*, Begriffsvermögen *n*.

comprehensive umfassend; ~ **coverage** → *coverage*; ~ **international institutions** internationale Einrichtungen mit legislativer und administrativer Zuständigkeit.

comprint Piratendruck *m*, Raubdruck *m*.

comprise enthalten, insichschließen; ~**d and|or arranged total loss** *Totalschaden auf Grund eines Vergleichs bzw. einer Vereinbarung oder beidem*; vereinbarter Totalschaden.

compromise *s* Kompromiß *m*; *außergerichtlicher* Vergleich *m*; ~ **and settlement** Vergleich; ~ **in court** Prozeßvergleich; **offer of** ~ Vergleichsangebot.

compromise *v* (sich) vergleichen, e–n Kompromiß schließen; e–n Streit beilegen; ~ **on terms** e–n Vergleich zu Bedingungen und Auflagen abschließen.

comptroller Revisor *m*, Rechnungsprüfer *m*; **C~ and Auditor General** Präsident des Rechnungshofes; **C~ General** Präsident des Rechnungshofes; C~ **General of Patents** → *patent*; ~ **in bankruptcy** *Leiter der Aufsichtsbehörde für Konkursverwalter;* **C~ of (the) Currency** Bankaufsichtsamt (*US*); **C~ of Patents, Designs and Trade Marks** Präsident des brit Patentamts; Patentamt (*GB*); **State C~** Präsident des Rechnungshofes, Überwachungsbeauftragter für einzelstaatliche Finanzen (*bes zur Regelung von Ansprüchen gegen den Staat*).

compulsion Zwang *m*; **crime committed under** ~ im Nötigungszustand begangene Straftat; **forcible** ~ Nötigung mit Gewalt; **moral** ~ zwingende moralische Verpflichtung; **under** ~ unter Zwang, gezwungen.

compulsory obligatorisch, pflichtgemäß, zwingend, Zwangs...; ~ **measures short of war** Zwangsmittel bis an die Grenze e–s Krieges; ~ **school age** schulpflichtiges Alter; ~ **wearing of seat belts** Anschnallpflicht, Zwang zum Anlegen von Sicherheitsgurten; ~ **winding up** → *winding-up*; ~ **working of a patent** Ausübungszwang für ein Patent.

computable berechenbar, zu berechnen.

computation Errechnung *f*, Berechnung *f*, Überschlag *m*, Schätzung *f*, ~ **of cost** Kostenberechnung, Kostenanschlag; ~ **of interest** Zinsberechnung; ~ **of time** Berechnung von Fristen und Terminen; **basis of** ~ → *basis;* **period of** ~ → *period.*

compute errechnen, berechnen, kalkulieren, überschlagen; ~ **interest** Zinsen berechnen; **rule to** ~ Feststellung der Höhe des Urteilsbetrages nebst Zinsen (*im Beschlußverfahren*).

computer | **documents** beweiskräftige EDV-Angaben, Computer-Aufzeichnungen; ~ **integrated manufacturing** (*CIM*) computerintegrierte Fertigung; ~ **print-out** Computer-Ausdruck; ~ **produced records** EDV-Ausdrucke als Urkunden; **designing** ~ Konstruktionsentwurf-Computer.

computerisation Umstellung *f* auf EDV; (~ *of PAYE,* ~ *of the land register).*

conceal verheimlichen, verschweigen, verbergen, verschleiern; ~ **a person** Unterschlupf gewähren; ~ **evidence** Beweismittel unterdrükken; ~**ed assets** unsichtbare Aktiva, stille Reserven; verschleierte Vermögenswerte, schwarze Bestände.

concealment Versteck *n*, Verschweigen *n*, Verheimlichen *f*; ~ **of a criminal** Verbergen e–s Täters; ~ **of assets** Verheimlichung von Vermögenswerten; ~ **of creditors** Verschweigen von Gläubigern; ~ **of documents** Urkundenunterdrückung; ~ **of evidence** Unterdrücken von Beweismaterial; ~ **of material circumstances** Verheimlichung wesentlicher Tatumstände; ~ **of property by judgment debtor** Verheimlichen von Vermögenswerten durch Vollstreckungsschuldner; ~ **of wills** Verheimlichen *oder* Beiseiteschaffen von letztwilligen Verfügungen; **fraudulent** ~ arglistiges Verschweigen; **material** ~ *ins* Verschweigen eines wesentlichen Umstandes (*beim Versicherungsantrag*).

concede einräumen, gewähren, zugestehen; ~ **as true** als wahr zugeben, ~**d facts** zugestandene Tatsachen.

concededly zugestandenermaßen.

conceive empfangen, schwanger werden; begreifen, vorstellen.

concentration Anhäufung *f*, Ansammlung *f*; ~ **camp** Konzentrationslager.

concept Auffassung *f*, Inbegriff *m*; ~ **of justice** Gerechtigkeitsbegriff.

conception Vorstellung *f*, Auffassung *f*, Anschauung *f*, Empfängnis *f*; **date of** ~ Empfängniszeit; **general** ~ Allgemeinbegriff; **legal** ~ Rechtsauffassung, Rechtsbegriff; **power of** ~ Auffassungsvermögen; **statutory period of** ~ gesetzliche Empfängniszeit, einrechnungsfähige Zeit.

concern *s* Angelegenheit *f*, Belang *m*, Betreff *m*; Unternehmen *n*; **business** ~ → *business*; **industrial** ~ Industrieunternehmen, Wirtschaftsunternehmen; **commercial** ~ Handelsunternehmen; **matter of** ~ Sache von Belang; **operating** ~ laufendes Unternehmen, in Betrieb befindliches U, lebendes U; **paying** ~ rentables Unternehmen; **private** ~ Privatangelegenheit; **public** ~ öffentl Angelegenheit.

concern *v* betreffen, angehen, interessieren; ~**ed in business** mit einem Geschäft etwas zu tun haben; ~**ed or interested** direkt oder indirekt beteiligt.

concert *s* Einverständnis *n*, Verabredung *f*; heimliches Einverständnis *n*; ~**party** Konzertzeichner; verdeckte Kombination von Aktienaufkäufern; **C~ of Europe** das europäische Mächtekonzert (ab 1815); **in ~ with** im Einvernehmen mit.

concert *v* gemeinsam planen, verabreden, aufeinander abstimmen; ~**ed action** gemeinsames Vorgehen; konzentrierte Aktion.

concession Zugeständnis *n*, Nachgeben *n*, Konzession *f*; Bewilligung *f*, Zulassung *f*; Verleihung *f*; Zollzugeständnis *n*; ~ **agreements** Konzessionsverträge; ~ **of a licence** Einräumung einer Lizenz; **extra-statutory** ~ außergesetzliche Steuererleichterung; **mining** ~ → *mining*; **oil** ~Erdölkonzession.

concessionaire Konzessionär *m*, Inhaber *m* einer Konzession, Konzessionierter *m*.

concessionary travel facilities Reisevergünstigung, kostenlose (*bzw verbilligte*) Bahnfahrten.

concessive einräumend.

conciliation Versöhnung *f*, Schlichtung *f*, Vermittlung *f*; Güteverfahren *n*; Sühneverfahren *n*; ~ **board** Schlichtungsstelle; ~ **officer** Schlichtungsbeamter (*in Arbeitsstreitigkeiten*); ~ **proceedings** Vermittlungsverfahren, Schlichtung, Sühneverf., Güteverfahren.

conciliatory gütlich, versöhnlich, vermittelnd.

concise kurz, knapp.

conciseness Knappheit *f*, Kürze *f*, Prägnanz *f*.

conclave geheime Versammlung *f*, *eccl* Konklave *n*.

conclude binden, beenden, beschließen, folgern; ~ **a contract** e-n Vertrag schließen; ~ **a marriage** e–e Ehe eingehen; ~ **a treaty** ein Abkommen abschließen; ~**d contract** zustandegekommener Vertrag.

conclusion Abschluß *m*, Schluß *m*, Schlußfolgerung *f*; Schlußantrag *m*; abschließende Erklärung *f*; Schlußplädoyer *n*; ~ **of a deal** Geschäftsabschluß; ~ **of an agreement** Vertragsabschluß; ~ **of fact** Folgerung aus Tatsachen; ~**s of law** rechtliche Schlußfolgerung; rein theoretische juristische Argumente; ~ **of peace** Friedensschluß; ~ **to the country** die Vorlage des Falles an die Geschworenen; **false** ~ Trugschluß, Fehlschluß; **legal** ~ rechtliche Schlußfolgerung, Rechtsansicht; **in** ~ zum Schluß; **inescapable** ~ absolut zwingende Schlußfolgerung.

conclusive endgültig, abschließend, schlüssig, zwingend; ~ **argument** zwingendes Argument.

conclusiveness Endgültigkeit *f*, Schlüssigkeit *f*; ~ **of decision** Endgültigkeit einer Entscheidung; ~ **of judgment** Rechtskraft des Urteils; ~ **of the grounds of decision** Schlüssigkeit der Begründung der Entscheidung.

concoct zusammenbrauen, erfinden; ~ **a letter** e–n Brief fingieren.

concoction Erfindung *f* (*bei e-r Aussage*), Zusammengereimtes *n*.

concomitant *adj* begleitend; ~ **circumstances** Begleitumstände; ~ **with** im Zusammenhang mit.

concomitant *s* Begleitumstand *m*.

concord *s* Übereinstimmung *f*, Vergleich *m*; *hist* Auflassung *f*.

concordant übereinstimmend.

concrete konkret, gegenständlich, greifbar.

concubinage Konkubinat *n*, eheähnliches Zusammenleben *n*.

concur übereinstimmen, beipflichten, zustimmen, gleicher Meinung sein, beitragen, mitwirken; **to the success** zum Gelingen beitragen; ~**ring opinion** → *opinion*.

concurator Gegenvormund *m*, Gegenpfleger *m*.

concurrence Zusammentreffen *n*, Übereinstimmung *f*, Zustimmung *f*, (zeitliches) Zusammenwirken *n*, Mitwirkung *f*; Konflikt *m* (*von Normen*), Kollision *f*; ~ **of jurisdiction** Kompetenzstreit; **to act in ~ with** gemeinschaftlich vorgehen mit; **with the ~ of** unter zustimmender Mitwirkung von.

concurrent konkurrierend, parallel

laufend, übereinstimmend, zusammenwirken, gleichzeitig.

concurrently gleichzeitig, Zug um Zug; **to hold** ~ Miteigentümer sein, gemeinschaftlich berechtigt sein.

concussion Nötigung *f*, räuberische Erpressung *f*; Erschütterung *f*, Schock *m*; ~ **of brain** Gehirnerschütterung; ~ **of the spine** Rückgratsverletzung durch Prellung oder Stauchung; **cerebral** ~ Gehirnerschütterung.

condemn verurteilen, zum Abbruch bestimmen; einziehen; für Entscheidungszwecke in Anspruch nehmen; schuldig sprechen, mißbilligen; ~ **the defendant to pay** den Beklagten zur Zahlung verurteilen.

condemnable strafbar, verwerflich.

condemnation Verurteilung *f*, Enteignung *f*; Mißbilligung *f*; Beschlagnahme *f*; *int* Kondemnation *f*; prisengerichtliche Einziehung *f* (*e–s Schiffes*); ~ **money** Schadensersatzbetrag (*Urteil*); ~ **order** Abbruchanordnung, Beseitigungsverfügung; ~ **proceeding** Verfahren zur Feststellung der Enteignungsentschädigung; **inverse** ~ enteignungsgleicher Eingriff.

condemnatory verurteilend.

condensation Kondenswasserbildung *f*, Schwitzwasserbildung *f* (*Baumangel*).

condictio (=) Herausgabeanspruch *m*.

condiction = *condictio qv*.

conditio Bedingung *f*; ~ **sine qua non** absolute Bedingung.

condition *s* (*1*) Bedingung *f*, (= *B bzw... b*); Voraussetzung *f*; wesentliche Vertragsbedingung *f*, Vorbehalt *m*; ~ **attached to acceptance** Annahme mit *B–en*; ~ **attached to offer** Angebot mit *B–en*; ~ **in deed** tatsächliche *B*; ~ **in law** Rechts*b*; ~ **inherent** inbegriffene *B*; ~**s of a contract** Vertrags*b–en*; ~ **of avoidance** auflösende *B*, Rücktritts*b*; ~**s of carriage** Transport*b–en*; ~**s of delivery** Lieferungs*b–n*; ~ **of employment** Einstellungsvoraussetzung; ~**s of sale** Liefer*b–en*; Versteigerungsbedingungen (*bei Liegenschaften*); ~ **precedent** aufschiebende *B*, Vor*b*, Voraussetzung; ~ **subsequent** auflösende *B*; **affirmative** ~ *Vertragsbedingung, die ein Tun beinhaltet*; **basic** ~ Grund*b*; **casual** ~ Zufall*sb*; **collateral** ~ Neben*b*; **compulsory** ~ zwingende *B*, zwingend vorgeschriebene Verpflichtung; **concurrent** ~ gegenseitige (*reziproke*) *B*, gleichzeitig zu erfüllende *B*, *B* der Zug um Zug Leistung; **consistent** ~ konforme *B*; **copulative** ~ gekoppelte *B*; **dependent** ~ subsidiäre *B*; Abhängigkeitsverhältnis; **dependent** ~**s** sich gegenseitig bedingende Verpflichtungen; **disjunctive** ~ wahlweise zu erfüllende *B*; **dissolving** ~ auflösende *B*; **express** ~ ausdrückliche *B*; **illegal** ~ rechtl unzulässige *B*; **implied** ~ stillschweigende *B*; **impossible** ~ auf Unmögliches gerichtete *B*; **independent** ~ selbständige *B* (*von e–r anderen Bedingung unabhängig*); **judgment on** ~ bedingtes Urteil; **lawful** ~ rechtlich zulässige *B*; **main** ~ Haupt*b*, Grund*b*; **mixed** ~ gemischte *B* (*teilweise zufälliges Ereignis, teilweise vom Willen abhängig*); **mutual** ~ Zug um Zug *B*, gegenseitige *B*; **negative** ~ *Vertragsbedingung, die ein Unterlassen beinhaltet*, negative *B* (*für den Fall, daß ein Ereignis nicht eintritt*); **on** ~ **that** unter der *B*; daß...; **positive** ~ positive *B* (*an den Eintritt eines Ereignisses oder die Vornahme einer Handlung geknüpft*); **possible** ~ mögliche *B*; **potestative** ~ Potestativ*b*, Willkür*b*; **precedent** ~ aufschiebende *B*, Vor*b*, Voraussetzung; **repugnant** ~ unvereinbare *B*; **resolutory** ~ auflösende *B*; **restrictive** ~ Unterlassungsverpflichtung, einschränkende *B*; **single** ~ Einzel*b*; **statutory** ~ gesetzliche Voraussetzung; **stringent** ~ harte *B*, strenge *B*; **subsequent** ~ auflösende *B*; **sus-**

pensive ~ aufschiebende *B*; **suspensory** ~ aufschiebende *B*; **to make it a ~ that** ... es zur *B* machen, daß ...; **to satisfy a** ~ e-e *B* erfüllen; **unlawful** ~ rechtlich unzulässige *B*.

condition *s* (*2*) Beschaffenheit *f*, Zustand *m*|*p auch* Gegebenheiten; ~ **as supplied** Lieferungszustand; ~ **of the mind** Geisteszustand, Willensbildung; ~ **of vehicle** Zustand des Fahrzeuges; ~ **of visibility** Sicht; **apparent good order and** ~ in offenbar gutem Zustand; **changing ~s** Änderung der Geschäftsgrundlage, Veränderung der Risiken; **financial** ~ Finanzlage, Vermögenslage; **legal and real ~s** rechtliche und tatsächliche Verhältnisse; **local ~s** örtl Verhältnisse; **market ~s** Konjunktur, Marktlage, Zustand des Marktes; **operating** ~ betriebsbereiter Zustand; **perfect** ~ einwandfreier Zustand, mängelfreie Beschaffenheit; **physical** ~ Gesundheitszustand; **sound** ~ einwandfreier Zustand, unbeschädigter Z, Unversehrtheit; **statement of** ~ → *statement*.

condition *v* (*1*) bedingen, Bedingungen stellen, etw zur Bedingung machen, gewissen Bedingungen unterwerfen; **~ed upon the fulfilment of a requirement** von der Erfüllung e-r Voraussetzung abhängig.

condition *v* (*2*) etw auf seinen Zustand prüfen, den gewünschten Zustand herstellen; **well ~ed** in gutem Zustand.

conditional bedingt, abhängig; ~ **acceptance** bedingte Annahme; ~ **sale agreement** Vorbehaltskauf, Kaufvertrag mit Eigentumsvorbehalt(sklausel); ~ **sale note** Schuldschein über den Vorbehaltskauf.

conditionality Bedingtheit *f*.

condo Eigentumswohnung *f*.

condominium *int* Kondominium *n*, gemeinsame (Mandats)Verwaltung *f*, Wohnungseigentum *n*, Eigentumswohnung, Wohnungseigentumsanlage; ~ **apartment** Eigentumswohnung; ~ **association** Wohnungseigentümergemeinschaft; ~ **bye-laws** Gemeinschaftsordnung.

condonation Verzeihung *f*; ~ **and settlement** Verzeihung verbunden mit einer außergerichtlichen Regelung.

condone vergeben, verzeihen; ~ **a misuse** einen Mißbrauch dulden.

conduce (*to*) beitragen (*zu*), mitwirken (*bei*), dienen.

conducive förderlich, dienlich.

conduct *s* Verhalten *n*, Betragen *n*, Geleit *n*, Führung *f*, Leitung *f*, ~ **and affairs** persönliches Verhalten und Geschäftsgebaren; ~ **conducing** *Absehen vom Scheidungsurteil wegen eigenen Verschuldens der Klagepartei;* ~ **involving dishonesty** unredliches Verhalten; ~ **money** → *money*; ~ **of a case** Prozeßführung; ~ **of the meeting** Abhaltung e-r Versammlung; ~ **of the parties** Verhalten der Parteien; ~ **rules** standesrechtliche Richtlinien; ~ **unbecoming an officer and a gentleman** standeswidriges, ehrenrühriges Betragen; ~ **unbefitting a solicitor** standeswidriges Verhalten eines Anwalts; **certificate of (good)** ~ Leumundszeugnis, Führungszeugnis; **criminal** ~ strafwürdiges Verhalten, Lebensführungsschuld; **disorderly** ~ ordnungswidriges Betragen, Erregung e-s öffentlichen Ärgernisses; **expulsive** ~ *Verhalten das dem Arbeitnehmer das Verbleiben unzumutbar macht;* **good** ~ Wohlverhalten, gute Führung; **guilty** ~ schuldbewußtes Verhalten; **infamous** ~ → *infamous;* **illegal** ~ rechtswidriges Verhalten; **immoral** ~ sittenwidriges Verhalten; **improper** ~ ungehöriges Verhalten; **indecent** ~ unzüchtige Handlungen (*mit bzw an Kindern*); **involuntary** ~ nicht willensmäßig beherrschbares Verhalten; **professional** ~ standesgemäßes Verhalten; **repudiatory** ~ = *expulsive* ~ *qv*; **safe** ~ → *safe*; **unbecoming** ~ ungebührliches Betragen; **unfair** ~ unlauteres Verhalten; **unnatural** ~ ungewöhnliches Verhalten (*e–s Tatverdächtigen*); **unobjectionable** ~ einwandfreies Verhalten; **unprofessional** ~ standeswidriges Verhalten; **unreasonable** ~ ehewidriges Verhalten als Scheidungsgrund (*außer böslichem Verlassen*).

conduct *v* führen, leiten, verwalten; sich betragen, sich führen; ~ **a business** ein Geschäft führen.

conductor Leiter *m*; Schaffner *m*; Kapellmeister *m*, Dirigent *m*.

conduit concept *tax*: Prinzip der durchlaufenden Zurechnung.

confect *v/i* errichten (*Urkunde*), fertigen, unterfertigen; **a document is ~ed** e–e Urkunde wird errichtet.

confederacy Föderation *f*, Bündnis *n*, Staatenbund *m*; Komplott *n*, Verschwörung *f*, Verabredung *f* zu widerrechtlichem Tun; **permanent ~ of supreme governments** Staatenbund; **the C ~** *US* Südstaatenbund, die Südstaaten (*im Bürgerkrieg*).

confederate Verbündeter *n*, Bundesgenosse *m*, Tatbeteiligter *m*, *hist US* Konföderierter *m*, Südstaatler *m*; **the ~ states** die Gliedstaaten (*der USA*).

confederation Föderation *f*, Bund *m*, Staatenbund *m*; **Articles of C ~** *hist US: Bundesurkunde der 13 Kolonien (1777)*.

confer *vt* übertragen, verleihen; *vi* verhandeln; ~ **jurisdiction on a court** die Zuständigkeit eines Gerichtes begründen; ~ **a peerage** in den Adelsstand erheben; ~ **a power** bevollmächtigen; ~ **a right** ein Recht übertragen; ~ **authority** ermächtigen, bevollmächtigen; ~ **the right to vote** Stimmrecht gewähren; ~ **with one's counsel** sich mit seinem Anwalt besprechen.

conferee Erwerber *m*, Empfänger *m* *(eines Rechts)* Teilnehmer am Vermittlungsausschuß.

conference Konferenz *f*, Tagung *f*, Beratung *f*, Besprechung *f*, *auch; Übermittlung wichtiger Angelegenheiten an die andere Gesetzgebungskammer;* ~ **committee** → *committee*; **to convene a** ~ eine Konferenz einberufen.

confess gestehen, ein Geständnis ablegen, anerkennen, einräumen; ~ **error** der Gegenseite Zustimmung zur Revisionseinlegung erteilen (*seitens der obsiegenden Partei*).

confessant Beichtender *m*, Geständiger *m*.

confessedly zugestandenermaßen.

confession Geständnis *n (= G)*, Anerkenntnis; Beichte; ~ **and avoidance** Rechtseinwendungen ohne Bestreiten der Klagetatsachen; ~ **induced by promises of reward** durch Versprechungen herbeigeführtes *G*; ~ **induced by threats** durch Nötigung herbeigeführtes Geständnis; **~s made in custody** *G* während der Haft; ~ **obtained by deception** durch Täuschung herbeigeführtes *G*; ~ **obtained by violence** gewaltsam erzwungenes Geständnis; ~ **of defence** *obs* Klagerücknahme wegen Einwendungen nach Rechtshängigkeit; ~ **of judgment** Anerkenntnis (*eines Klageanspruchs*); ~ **to priests** Beichte; ~ **under oath** unter Eid abgegebenes *G*; **credibility of** ~ Glaubwürdigkeit eines *G–es*; **extra-judicial** ~ außergerichtliches *G*; **implied** ~ unterstelltes *G (durch Bitte um mildes Urteil)*; **inadmissible** ~ nicht verwertbares *G*; **indirect** ~ mittelbares *G (aus dem Verhalten des Angeklagten)*; **judgment by** ~ → *judgment*; **judicial** ~ → *judicial*; **naked** ~ blosses *G*; **oral** mündliches *G*; **plenary** ~ umfassendes *G*; **pretrial** ~ *G* vor dem Prozeß; **relative** ~ *hist G* eines Mitangeklagten (*um seine Haut zu retten*); **simple** ~ formelles Schuldbekenntnis; **to retract a** ~ → *to retract*; **to volunteer a** ~ von sich aus ein *G* ablegen; **voluntary** ~ freiwilliges *G*, unbeeinflußtes *G*; **weight of** ~ Bedeutung eines Geständnisses.

confessor Geständiger *m*; Beichtvater *m*.
confidant Vertrauensmann *m*, Empfänger von geheimhaltungsbedürftigen Informationen.
confide vertrauen, anvertrauen.
confidence Vertrauen *n*; vertrauliche Mitteilung *f*; ~ **game** Schwindelmethode; ~ **man** Schwindler; **abuse of** ~ Vertrauensmißbrauch; **breach of** ~ → *breach;* **public** ~ Vertrauen der Öffentlichkeit; **to keep** (= *to retain*) **in** ~ vertraulich behandeln.
confidential vertraulich.
confidentiality Vertraulichkeit *f*.
confider *jmd, der geheimhaltungsbedürftige Informationen e–m anderen anvertraut.*
configuration Form *f*, Gestalt *f*, Gestaltung *f*, Konfiguration *f*, ~ **control** Sicherung gleichmäßiger Gestaltung (*Flugzeugmontage*).
confinable begrenzbar.
confine begrenzen, beschränken; einsperren, inhaftieren; ~**d as a patient** in stationärer Behandlung in einer geschlossenen Anstalt.
confinement Haft *f*, Anhaltung *f*; Begrenzung *f*, Freiheitsbeschränkung *f*; Anstaltsunterbringung *f*; ~ **for life** lebenslange Freiheitsstrafe; ~ **in a fortress** Festungshaft; ~ **in asylum** Unterbringung in einer Heilanstalt; ~ **in jail** Freiheitsentzug, Gefängnishaft; ~ **in prison** Gefängnishaft; ~ **pending further investigation** Untersuchungshaft; ~ **to barracks** Stubenarrest; **close** ~ strenge Haft; **place of** ~ Haftort, Unterbringungsort; **pre-trial** ~ Untersuchungshaft; **sentence of** ~ Freiheitsstrafe; **solitary** ~ Einzelhaft.
confirm bekräftigen, aufrechterhalten, bestätigen, genehmigen; ~ **by documents** urkundlich bestätigen; ~ **by oath** eidlich erhärten; ~ **in writing** schriftlich bestätigen.
confirmation Bekräftigung *f*, Genehmigung *f*, Bestätigung *f*, *eccl* Konfirmation *f*, Firmung *f*, *scot* gerichtl Testamentsbestätigung; ~ **by oath** eidliche Bekräftigung; ~ **dative** Nachlaßverwalterzeugnis (*scot*), ~ **hearing** *parl* Anhörung bei Amtseinsetzungen; ~ **nominative** Testamentsbestätigung (*scot*); ~ **of a judgment** Bestätigung (= *Aufrechterhaltung*) eines Urteils; ~ **of acts** Bestätigung des Handelns eines Bevollmächtigten; ~ **of bishop** bischöfliche Bestätigung *e–r Amtseinsetzung*; ~ **of order** Auftragsbestätigung; ~ **of sale** gerichtliche Bestätigung von Versteigerungs- oder Zwangsverkaufsbedingungen; ~ **of signature** Unterschriftsbeglaubigung; **in** ~ **of** zur Bestätigung von; **letter of** ~ Bestätigungsschreiben; **negative** ~ Negativattest; **positive** ~ vorbehaltlose Bestätigung.
confirmatory bestätigend; ~ **meeting** Versammlung zur Bestätigung eines früher gefaßten qualifizierten Beschlusses.
confirmee Bestätigungsempfänger *m*, *Adressat einer Urkunde, durch die Auflassungsmängel geheilt werden.*
confirming|authority Bestätigungsbehörde (*für Schankkonzession*); ~ **house** *brit* Exportkontor, Vertretung von überseeischen Importfirmen (*„bestätigt" Aufträge überseeischer Importeure und übernimmt dadurch die Zahlungsgarantie*).
confirmor Bestätigender *m*, *derjenige, der eine Urkunde zur Heilung eines Auflassungsmangels errichtet.*
confiscable beschlagnahmefähig, der Einziehung unterliegend.
confiscate konfiszieren, einziehen; enteignen, beschlagnahmen.
confiscatee der von e–r Enteignung Betroffene.
confiscation Konfiszierung *f*, Einziehung *f*, Beschlagnahme *f*.
confiscatory konfiskatorisch; ~ **authority** Beschlagnahmebehörde, Enteignungsbehörde.
conflagration Feuersbrunst *f*, Brand *m*; ~ **line limits** Risikobegrenzung bei Häufung von Bränden; **cause of** ~ Brandursache.
conflicts *s* Widerspruch *m*, Konflikt

m, Widerstreit *m*; ~ **of interest** Interessenkonflikt; ~ **of jurisdiction** Zuständigkeitsstreit, Kompetenzstreit; ~ **of personal laws** interpersonales Recht; ~ **of laws** Kollisionsrecht, internationales Privatrecht; ~ **of presumptions** Kollision von Vermutungen, *Regeln über die Rangfolge von gesetzlichen Vermutungen*; ~**s questions** kollisionsrechtliche Fragen; **armed** ~ bewaffneter Zusammenstoß; **industrial** ~ Arbeitskonflikt; **labo(u)r** ~ Arbeitskampf.

conflict *v* kollidieren, miteinander in Widerspruch stehen; ~**ing claim** entgegenstehender (kollidierender) Anspruch; ~**ing decisions** einander widersprechende Entscheidungen; ~**ing evidence** → *evidence*; ~**ing opinions** entgegengesetzte Meinungen.

conform sich anpassen, übereinstimmen.

conformable übereinstimmend, entsprechend.

conformation Anpassung *f*, Gestaltung *f*.

conforming *adj* vertragsmäßig, vertragsgerecht.

conformity Übereinstimmung *f*.

confront gegenüberstellen, entgegentreten; ~ **the witnesses** Zeugen konfrontieren, Zeugen einander gegenüberstellen.

confrontation Gegenüberstellung *f*, Konfrontation *f*; Hinweis *m* zur Identifizierung; ~ **of accused by witness** Gegenüberstellung von Zeugen und Angeklagten; **rule of** ~ Grundsatz der Zeugenvernehmung in Anwesenheit der Parteien.

confuse verwechseln, vermischen.

confusio Vermischung *f*.

confusion Verwirrung *f*, Verwechslung *f*; Verschmelzung *f*, Vermischung *f*; ~ **of boundaries** Grenzverwirrung, gerichtliche Zuständigkeit für Grenzstreitigkeiten; ~ **of debts** Konfusion, Vereinigung von Forderung und Schuld; ~ **of goods** Vermischung (*bewegl Sachen*), Vermengung, Verbindung; ~ **of rights** Konfusion; ~ **of titles** Konsolidation absoluter Rechte; **accession by** ~ → *accession;* **danger of** ~ **of trade marks** Verwechslungsgefahr bei Warenzeichen.

confutable widerlegbar; ~ **assertion** widerlegbare Behauptung.

confutation Widerlegung *f*.

confute widerlegen.

congested value centres Ballungszentren hoher Versicherungsrisiken.

congestion Stauung *f*, Überfüllung *f*; ~ **of population** Überbevölkerung.

conglomerate Großkonzern *m*, Firmengruppe *f*, Mischkonzern *m*.

congregate sich versammeln.

congregation Versammlung *f*, Kirchengemeinde *f*.

congress Kongreß *m*, Tagung *f*, Zusammenkunft *f*; Botschafterkonferenz *f*; **C** ~ das Bundesparlament *US*, der Kongreß (*beide Häuser des US Parlaments*); **C** ~ **of Industrial Organizations** *US* Gewerkschaftsbund (AFL-CIO).

congressional district ~ *district*; ~ **power** Gesetzgebungskompetenz des Kongresses, *US*.

congressman Kongreßabgeordneter *m US*.

congruence (= *congruity*) Folgerichtigkeit *f*, Übereinstimmung *f*, Kongruenz *f*.

congruent passend, übereinstimmend, kongruent.

conjectural mußmaßlich.

conjecture *s* Vermutung *f*, Mutmaßung *f*, Annahme *f*.

conjecture *v* mutmaßen, vermuten, erraten.

conjointly gemeinsam, gemeinschaftlich.

conjoints Ehegatten *pl*.

conjugal ehelich, Ehe ....

conjunctive verbindend; ~ **denial** globales Bestreiten; ~ **obligation** → *obligation*.

conjuncture Zusammenfallen von Umständen.

conjuration Verschwörung *f*; Geisterbeschwörung *f*; Zauberformel *f*.
connate *adj* angeboren, artverwandt.
connect verbinden, sich verbinden, in Zusammenhang stehen; **~ed by marriage** → *marriage*; **~ing carriers** Verbindungstransportunternehmen; **~ing line** Anschlußstrecke.
connected lender liability Mithaftung des Kundenkreditfinanzierers bei Sachmängeln.
connection Zusammenhang *m*, Beziehung *f*, Verbindung *f*, Anschluß *m*; **illicit ~** unzüchtige Verbindung, Konkubinat; **proximate ~** unmittelbarer Kausalzusammenhang; **~s** Schwägerschaft, Verwandtschaft.
connivance (*strafbares*) geheimes Einverständnis *n* (*bes mit Ehebruch der Ehefrau, GB bis 1973; rechtsvernichtende Einwendung gegen Scheidungsklage des Mannes*); (*stillschweigende*) Zustimmung *f*, Begünstigung *f*.
connive (*etw Unerlaubtes*) stillschweigend dulden, zustimmen.
connotation Bedeutung *f*, Nebenbedeutung *f*.
connote bedeuten.
connubial intercourse eheliches Zusammenleben *n*, ehelicher (*Geschlechts*)Verkehr *m*.
connubium Ehefähigkeit *f*.
conpossessio Mitbesitz *m*.
conquest Eroberung *f*, gewaltsamer Erwerb *m*.
consanguinity Blutsverwandtschaft *f*; **collateral ~** Verwandtschaft in der Seitenlinie; **lineal ~** Verwandtschaft in gerader Linie; **relationship by ~** Blutsverwandtschaft.
conscience Gewissen *n*, Rechtsempfinden *n*; **~ clause** Entscheidung des Minderjährigen über Teilnahme am Religionsunterricht; **~ money** (*anonyme*) Steuernachzahlung; **right of ~** → *right*.
conscientious gewissenhaft, Gewissen ...; **~ objector** Kriegsdienstverweigerer; **~ obligation** Gewissenspflicht, Treueverpflichtung; **~ scruple** Gewissensbedenken.
conscious bewußt, absichtlich, vorsätzlich, wissentlich; **~ of** in dem Bewußtsein, eingedenk.
consciousness of guilt Schuldbewußtsein *n*.
conscript Rekrut *m*, Wehrpflichtiger *m*.
conscription Wehrpflicht *f*, Einberufung *f*.
consecutive nacheinanderfolgend, aufeinanderfolgend, zusammenhängend; **~ journeys** aufeinanderfolgende Fahrten; **~ sentence** ~ → *sentence*; **to number ~ly** fortlaufend numerieren.
consensual einverständlich, einvernehmlich, freiwillig; **~ contract** → *contract*.
consensus Konsens *m*, Übereinstimmung *f*, (Willens)Einigung; **~ ad idem** Einigung; Willensübereinstimmung; **~ builder** Konsens schaffende Persönlichkeit; **~ candidate** im allgemeinen Einvernehmen aufgestellter Kandidat; **~ of opinion** übereinstimmende Meinung.
consent *s* Zustimmung *f*, Einwilligung *f*, Einvernehmen *n*, Einverständnis *n*; **~ decree** Prozeßvergleich, einverständliche Entscheidung; Anerkenntnisurteil, Unterwerfungsentscheidung; **~ dividend** → *dividend*; **~ form** formularmäßige Zustimmungserklärung; **~ judgment** → *judgment*; **~ or agreement** Einwilligung; **~ order** = *order by consent qv*; **~ rule** gerichtlich protokolliertes Räumungsanerkenntnis; **~ stock** → *stock* (*1*); **~ to marriage** Heiratserlaubnis; **~ without reserve** vorbehaltlose Zustimmung; **age of ~** Ehemündigkeit; **by (common) ~** einverständlich; **by mutual ~** im beiderseitigen Einvernehmen, einverständlich; **express ~** ausdrückliche Zustimmung; **full ~** restloses Einverständnis, volle Zustimmung; **implied ~** stillschweigende Zustimmung, Zustimmung kraft konkludenten Verhaltens; **informed ~** Einwilligung (*für e–n Ein-*

griff); nach fachgerechter Aufklärung; **mutual** ~ gegenseitiges Einvernehmen, Willenseinigung; **prior** ~ vorherige Zustimmung, Einwilligung; **tacit** ~ stillschweigende Zustimmung, **unanimous** ~ (*einstimmiger*) Konsens, einhellige Zustimmung.

consent *v* zustimmen, einwilligen.

consequence Folge *f*, Folgerung *f*, Konsequenz *f*, Bedeutung *f*, Kausalzusammenhang *m*; **immediate** ~ direkte Folge; **legal** ~ Rechtsfolge; **probable** ~ adäquate Folge; **in** ~ **of** als Folge von; **that is of no** ~ das ist unwichtig; **to take the** ~**s** die Folgen auf sich nehmen; **unintended** ~**s** ungewollte Folgen.

consequent folgerichtig, folgend, konsequent; ~ **on loss of time** als Folge von Zeitverlust; ~ **upon** infolge.

consequential Folge ..., folgend ..., folgerichtig, kausal bedingt; ~ **damage or injury** Folgeschaden; Nebenfolgen e–s schädigenden Ereignisses.

conservancy authority Strom-schiffahrts- und Uferbehörde *f*.

conservation Umweltschutz *m*; Denkmalschutz *m*; Naturschutz *m*; ~ **area** denkmalgeschützter Ortsteil; **C**~ **of Wild Creatures and Wild Plants Act** *CB, 1975* Gesetz zum Schutz nicht jagdbarer wilder Tiere und wildwachsender Pflanzen; ~ **zone** *v* Naturschutzgebiet; Fischereizone.

conservator *US* Konservator *m*, Aufsichtsbeamter *m*; *US* Vormund *m*, Pfleger *m* (*eines Geistesschwachen bzw. Gebrechlichen*); ~**s of rivers** Flußbauamt; ~**s of the peace** *hist* Friedensrichter; Bewahrer des Friedens (*Titel des Monarchen*).

conservatorship Pflegschaft *f* (*Volljährige*).

consider betrachten, berücksichtigen, erwägen, in Betracht ziehen, erkennen, aburteilen; ~ **ex officio** von Amts wegen prüfen; ~ **in mitigation** strafmildernd berücksichtigen; ~**ing that** in Anbetracht dessen, in der Erwägung, daß ...

considerable erheblich, beträchtlich, bedeutend.

consideration Erwägung *f*, Berücksichtigung *f*, Rücksicht *f*; Gegenleistung *f* (= G), Entgelt *n*; ~ **of "blood"** = *meritorious qv*; ~ **for return of premium** *ins* Ristornogebühr; ~ **in contract** G bei Verträgen; ~ **money** G in Geld; ~ **of evidence** Beweiswürdigung; **adequate** ~ adäquate G; wertangemessenes Entgelt; **concurrent** ~ Zug-um-Zug-G; **continuing** ~ G *als Dauerschuld*; **equitable** ~ nur aus Billigkeitsgründen anerkannte G; **executed** ~ erbrachte G; vorgeleistete G; **executory** ~ zukünftige G, noch zu erbingende G; **express** ~ im Vertrag erwähnte G; **fair** ~ angemessene G, ohne Gläubigerbenachteiligung gewährte G; **fair and valuable** ~ angemessene G; **for valuable** ~ entgeltlich; **for want of** ~ mangels G; **good** ~ G auf Grund von Liebe und Zuneigung (*rechtl nicht genügend*); **gratuitous** ~ unentgeltliches Leistungsversprechen; **illegal** ~ rechtlich unzulässige G; **in** ~ **of** als G für; in Anbetracht, angesichts, im Hinblick, in der Erwägung, mit Rücksicht auf; **legal** ~ rechtl zulässige G; **meritorious** ~ G *auf Grund e–r Anstandspflicht*; **money** ~ G in Geld; **moral** ~ auf sittlicher oder Anstandspflicht beruhende G; **nominal** ~ geringfügige G, symbolische G; **over-valued** ~ überbewertete G; **partial** ~ unvollständige G; **past** ~ e–e bereits in der Vergangenheit erbrachte G; **pecuniary** ~ G in Geld, Zahlungsverpflichtung als G; **reasonable** ~ angemessene Rücksichtnahme; **statement of** ~ → *statement*; **sufficient** ~ rechtlich ausreichende G; **the first and paramount** ~ der oberste Gesichtspunkt (*z.B. Kindeswohl*); **time for** ~ → *time*; **to come into** ~ in Betracht kommen; **to submit for** ~ **and ap-**

proval zur Prüfung und Genehmigung vorlegen; **valid** ~ = *good* ~ *qv*; **valuable** ~ rechtserhebliche G (*ein Tun, Dulden oder Unterlassen*), (vermögenswertes) Entgelt.

consign übergeben, anvertrauen; versenden, verfrachten; konsignieren, in Kommission geben; *scot (Geld)* hinterlegen.

consignatary Verwahrer *m*; *econ*: Repositar *m*; Konsignat *m*.

consignee Empfänger *m*, Adressat *m*; Konsignatar *m*, Kommissionär *m*; ~ **pays carriage** Fracht bezahlt der Empfänger.

consignment Versand *m*, Versendung *f*, Sendung *f*; Verfrachtung *f*; Konsignation *f*, Verkaufskommission *f*; ~ **account** → *account*; ~ **contract** Kommissionsvertrag; ~ **for approval** Ansichtssendung; ~ **goods** Konsignationswaren; ~ **note** Frachtbrief; ~ **of replacement** Ersatzlieferung; ~ **store** Konsignationslager; **collective** ~ Sammelladung; **merchandise received on** ~ Kommissionsware; **small** ~**s** kleine Sendungen, Stückgut; **successive** ~**s** Teilsendungen.

consignor Absender *m*, Versender *m*; Kommittent *m*, Konsignator *m*, Konsignant *m*; *scot* Hinterleger *m*.

consistency Folgerichtigkeit *f*, Kontinuität, Vereinbarkeit *f*, Übereinstimmung *f*; ~ **of valuation** Bewertungsstetigkeit.

consistent folgerichtig, feststehend, im Einklang stehend, vereinbar; ~ **practice (of a court)** ständige Rechtsprechung; **on a** ~ **basis** unter Wahrung der (Bilanz)Kontinuität.

consolation Befriedigung *f*, Trost *m*.

consolidate vereinigen, (*Schulden*) konsolidieren, fundieren; (*Aktien*) zusammenlegen; (*Gesetzesvorlagen, Klagen*) verbinden; ~**d annuities** → *annuity*; ~**d balance sheet and accounts** konsolidierter Konzernabschluß; konsolidierte Konzernbilanz mit Gewinn- und Verlustrechnung; ~**d debt** konsolidierte Schuld, fundierte Sch. ~**d financial statements** Konzernabschluß; **C**~**d Fund** (=), Gesamtheit der brit. Staatseinnahmen; zentraler Haushaltsfonds; britische Staatskasse; ~**d group** Konzern; ~**d laws** kodifizierte Gesetze; ~**d loan** fundierte Anleihe; ~**d mortgage** Gesamthypothek; ~**d orders** Verfahrensordnung *des Chancery Court*; ~**d return** → *return*; ~**d shipments** Sammelladungen; ~**d statements** Konzernabschluß; ~**d statutes** → *statute*.

consolidation Vereinigung *f*, Zusammenlegung *f*; Konsolidierung *f*, Konsolidation *f*; Fusion *f*, Verschmelzung *f* (durch Neubildung); Klageverbindung *f*; ~ **Act** Kodifizierungsgesetz, zusammenfassendes Gesetz, Bereinigungsgesetz; ~ **bill** Vorlage zur Zusammenfassung von Gesetzen; ~ **of actions** Klageverbindung; ~ **of banks** Bankenfusion; ~ **of benefices** Vereinigung von Kirchenpfründen; ~ **of corporations** Fusion durch Neugründung; **C**~ **of Enactments (Procedure) Act** *GB, 1949* Gesetz über Gesetzesbereinigungsverfahren; ~ **of indictments** Anklageverbindung; ~ **of mortgages** Vereinigung von Grundpfandrechten, Bildung von Gesamthypotheken; ~ **of shares** Zusammenlegung von Aktien; ~ **of the market** Festigung des Marktes; ~ **of two firms** Verschmelzung zweier Firmen.

consols *brit* Konsols *f*, konsolidierte Staatsanleihe *f*.

consort *v* mit jmdm verkehren, sich zusammenschließen mit.

consortium (*pl consortia*) Konsortium *n*; eheliche Gemeinschaft *f*, Arbeitsgemeinschaft *f*, ad hoc Gesellschaft *f*; **loss of** ~ Verlust der ehelichen Lebensgemeinschaft; **right of** ~ Recht auf eheliche Gemeinschaft.

consortship Bergegemeinschaft *f*.

conspiracy Verschwörung *f*, Komplott *n*; Absprache *f*; Verabredung *f* zu Straftaten; ~ **in restraint of trade** wettbewerbsbeschränkte

Abrede (*bzw* Absprachen); ~ **to defraud** Verabredung zum Betrug; ~ **to murder** Mordkomplott; **civil** ~ Verabredung zu unerlaubter Handlung; Zusammenwirken zum Schaden Dritter, (verbotene) Absprache; **criminal** ~ Verabredung zu einer strafbaren Handlung.

conspirational konspirativ.

conspirator Verschwörer *m*, Beteiligter *m* an einem verbotenen gemeinschaftlichen Vorhaben.

conspire sich zu strafbarem Tun verabreden; sich verschwören.

constable Polizeibeamter *m*, Polizist *m*, *hist* Polizeiminister *m*; ~ **of a castle** Burgkastellan; **C~ of England** *hist* königlicher Polizeiminister in England; ~ **on patrol-duty** Polizeibeamter im Streifendienst; ~ **on point-duty** Polizist im ortsgebundenen Einsatz; **bribery of** ~ → *bribery*; **chief** ~ Polizeipräsident e–r Grafschaft oder Stadt; **duty to aid** ~ Rechtspflicht zur Hilfeleistung gegenüber einem Polizeibeamten; **high** ~ *hist* Kreispolizeichef; **petty** ~ örtlicher Polizeichef, Gerichtsdiener, Gerichtsvollzieher; **probationer** ~ Polizeibeamter auf Probe; **special** ~ Hilfspolizist.

constablewick örtlicher Polizeibezirk *m*.

constabulary Polizei *f*, Polizeimannschaft *f*; **country** ~ Gendarmerie; **Inspector of C~** Oberster Inspekteur der Polizei.

constat Aktenfeststellung *f*, Ausfertigung *f*.

constate *v* konstituieren, begründen.

constating instruments rechtsbegründende Urkunden, Gründungsurkunden.

constituency Wählerschaft *f*, Wahlkreis *m*, Wahlbezirk *m*; **parliamentary** ~ (Parlaments) Wahlkreis.

constituent *adj* einen Teil bildend; konstituierend.

constituent *s* Vollmachtsgeber *m*, Auftraggeber *m*, Aussteller *m*; Wähler *m*; Wahlberechtigter *m* für Parlamentswahlen.

constitute konstituieren, rechtsgeschäftl begründen, bestellen, ernennen, darstellen, beinhalten, bevollmächtigen. ~ **a person judge** jmdn als Richter einsetzen; ~ (*the elements of*) **a crime** den Straftatbestand erfüllen; ~**d authorities** Behörden.

constitution Errichtung *f*, Bildung *f*, Gründung *f*; Satzung *f*, Zusammensetzung *f*; *pol* Verfassung *f*, Grundgesetz *n*; **draft** ~ Verfassungsentwurf; **Federal C~** Bundesverfassung; **political** ~ Staatsverfassung.

constitutional verfassungsmäßig, konstitutionell, verfassungsrechtlich; ~ **amendment** Zusatz zur Verfassung, Verfassungsänderung; ~ **bar** die Schranke der Verfassungswidrigkeit; ~ **charter** Verfassungsurkunde; ~ **convention** verfassungsgebende Versammlung; ~ **liberties** Grundrechte, verfassungsmäßig garantierte Freiheitsrechte; ~ **monarchy** konstitutionelle Monarchie; ~ **officer** Inhaber eines durch die Verfassung geschaffenen Amtes; ~ **right** verfassungsmäßig garantiertes Recht, Grundrecht; ~ **state** Rechtsstaat.

constitutionality Verfassungsmäßigkeit *f*.

constitutive konstituierend; konstitutiv, (rechts)begründend.

constrain zwingen, nötigen.

constraint Zwang *m*, Nötigung *f*; **acting under** ~ im Nötigungsstand handelnd.

construct bauen, errichten; ~**ed or adapted** gebaut oder (*zu dem betreffenden Zwecke*) umgebaut.

construction (*1*) Bau *m*, Gebäude *n*; Bauausführung *f*, Baugewerbe *n*; Auslegung *f*, Deutung *f*; ~ **account** Baukonto; ~ **company** Baufirma, Bauunternehmen; ~ **contract** Werkvertrag über Bauleistungen, Bauvertrag; ~ **costs** Baukosten; ~ **equipment** Baugeräte, Bauausrüstung; ~ **industry** Baugewerbe; **residential** ~ Wohnungsbau.

construction (*2*) Auslegung *f*; ~ **of**

sentence Auslegung des Urteils; ~ **of statute** Gesetzesauslegung; **artificial** ~ gekünstelte Auslegung; **benevolent** ~ wohlwollende Auslegung; **equitable** ~ sinngemäße Auslegung; **favourable** ~ wohlwollende Auslegung; **liberal** ~ weite Auslegung; **literal** ~ wörtliche Auslegung, Wortauslegung; **strict** ~ enge Auslegung, strenge *A*, wörtliche *A*.

constructionist Auslegungsspezialist *m*.

constructive aufbauend, hypothetisch, gefolgert, präsumptiv, fingiert, indirekt, gesetzlich unterstellt.

constructively lost als Totalverlust geltend.

construe *v/t* auslegend.

constuprate notzüchtigen.

consul Konsul *m*; ~ **-general** Generalkonsul; **career** ~ Berufskonsul; **honorary** ~ Wahlkonsul; **salaried** ~ Berufskonsul.

consular konsularisch; ~ **agencies** konsularische Behörden; ~ **certificate** konsularische Bescheinigung; ~ **convention** Konsulatsvertrag, Konsularabkommen; ~ **court** Konsulargericht; ~ **invoice** Konsulatsfaktura; ~ **legalisation** Legalisation, konsularische Beglaubigung; ~ **officer** Konsularbeamter; ~ **post** konsularische Vertretung; ~ **protection** konsularischer Schutz; ~ **representative** konsularischer Vertreter; ~ **status** Konsularstatus; ~ **visa** Konsulatssichtvermerk.

consulate Konsulat *n*.

consult sich beraten, Rücksprache nehmen, um Rat fragen, konsultieren; ~ **an expert** e–n Sachverständigen zu Rate ziehen.

consultant Berater *m*, beratender Arzt *m*; **technical** ~ technischer Berater.

consultary response gerichtliche Äußerung zur Rechtslage.

consultation Beratung *f*, Rücksprache *f*; Fühlungnahme *f*, Konsultation *f*; ~ **machinery** *int* Konsultationsmechanismen; **procedure of mutual** ~ Konsultativverfahren.

consultative beratend; ~ **assembly** beratende Versammlung; ~ **machinery** Konsultationseinrichtungen.

consumable verbrauchbar.

consume verbrauchen.

consumer Verbraucher *m*, Konsument *m*; ~ **advocate** Anwalt der Verbraucher; **C~'s Association** Verbraucherschutzverband; ~ **campaign** Verbraucherschutzaktion; ~**s cooperative** Konsumgenossenschaft; ~**s' councils** Marktberatungsstellen; ~ **credit** Verbraucherkredit, Konsumentenkredit, Kundenkredit; **C~ Credit Act** Abzahlungs- und Warenkreditgesetz *GB* (~ ~ *Code, US*); ~ **credit agreement** Kundenfinanzierungsvertrag; ~ **credit register** Kundenkreditregister; ~ **credit licence** Konzession für Kundenkreditgeschäfte; ~ **debt** Schuld für Privatzwecke; ~ **demand** Verbrauchernachfrage; ~ **dispute** Streit mit Kunden; ~ **finance company** (*US*) Teilzahlungsfinanzierungsgesellschaft, Kundenkreditbank; ~ **hire agreement** Mietkaufvertrag mit Endverbraucher *bis £ 500*; Abzahlungsvertrag; ~ **inquiry** Verbraucherbefragung; ~ **investigation** Marktforschung; ~ **lease** Konsumentenleasing; ~ **loan company** Warenkreditgesellschaft; ~ **price** Einzelhandelspreis; ~ **price index** Lebenshaltungskostenindex, Verbraucherpreisindex; **C~ Product Safety** Commission US-Verbraucherschutz-Behörde; ~ **protection** Verbraucherschutz; ~ **sale** → *sale*; ~**'s terminal** Endpunkt der Stromzuleitung; ~ **trade practice** Geschäftsgepflogenheiten gegenüber Verbrauchern; ~ **safety** Verbraucherschutz; **bulk** ~ → *bulk*; **final** ~ Endverbraucher; **ultimate** ~ Endverbraucher, Letztverbraucher.

consumerism Verbraucherschutztendenz *f*, Konsumerismus *m*.
consummate vollziehen, durchführen, vollenden.
consummation Vollzug *m*, Durchführung *f*; Vollendung *f*; ~ **of felony** Vollendung e–s Verbrechens; ~ **of marriage** Vollziehung der Ehe *durch Beischlaf*; ~ **of plan** Erfüllung e–s Plans (*Gläubigervergleichs*).
consumption Verbrauch *m*, Konsum *m*; ~ **credit** Kundenkredit; ~ **finance** Kundenfinanzierung; ~ **in use** Substanzverzehr; **intravenous** ~ intravenöse Zuführung (*e–r Droge*); ~ **loans** → *loan*; **domestic** ~ Inlandsverbrauch; **home** ~ Inlandsverbrauch; **personal** ~ Eigenverbrauch; **private** ~ Selbstverbrauch, Eigenverbrauch.
container (=) Behälter *n*; ~ **bill of lading** Container-Frachtbrief; **light-weight** ~ Leichtbehälter; **tamper-proof** ~ diebessicherer Behälter.
containerization Verladung und Transport in Containern.
containment policy Eindämmungspolitik.
contamination Ansteckung *f*; **radioactive** ~ atomare Verseuchung.
contango *brit exch* Report *m*, *Kurszuschlag beim Prolongationsgeschäft*; ~ **business** Reportgeschäft, Prolongationsgeschäft; ~ **day** jeweils der erste Tag eines neuen *"account" qv* (*Abrechnungsperiode*); ~ **money** → *money*; ~ **rate** Reportsatz, Prolongationsgebühr.
contemnor ungehorsame Person *f*, *die sich der Mißachtung des Gerichts schuldig gemacht hat.*
contemplate betrachten, auffassen, beabsichtigen, billigend in Kauf nehmen.
contemplation Auffassung *f*, Sinn *m*, rechtsgeschäftlicher Wille *m*, Vorhaben *n*; ~ **of bankruptcy** in Kenntnis der konkursreifen Lage, im Hinblick auf den Konkurs (*bzw die Insolvenz*). ~ **of disfigurement** Schmerzensgeld für das Wissen um eine entstellende Verletzung; ~ **of insolvency** im Hinblick auf die Zahlungsunfähigkeit; ~ **of the parties** das, was sich die Parteien vorgestellt haben; **in** ~ **of death** → *death*; **in** ~ **of marriage** im Hinblick auf die bevorstehende Eheschließung.
contempt Mißachtung *f*, Geringschätzung *f*, Verachtung *f*; ~ **in face of the court** Ungebühr vor Gericht; ~ **of Congress** Mißachtung der Parlamentshoheit; ~ **of court** Mißachtung des Gerichts, Ungebühr vor Gericht, Ungehorsam gegenüber dem G.; ~ **of legislature** vorsätzl Ungehorsam gegenüber den gesetzgebenden Körperschaften; ~ **of parliament** Mißachtung der Parlamentshoheit; ~ **of the High Court of Parliament** = ~ *of parliament qv*; ~ **of the House** = ~ *of the Parliament;* ~ **power** Ordnungsstrafgewalt, Strafgewalt wegen Ungehorsam gegenüber dem Gericht; ~ **proceedings** Sonderverfahren wegen contempt of court *qv*; **civil** ~ Ungehorsam gegenüber gerichtlichem Gebot; **constructive** ~ Ungehorsam gegen gerichtliche Anordnungen; **criminal** ~ strafbare Mißachtung des Gerichts; Störung der Rechtspflege, Ungebühr vor Gericht; **direct** ~ Ungebühr vor Gericht.
contend behaupten, vorbringen, geltend machen; ~**ing parties** → *party*.
content *s* Inhalt *m*, Gehalt *m*; Fassungsvermögen *n*; ~**s** Inhalt; ~ **of my house** alles in meinem Haus Befindliche; ~ **thereof** dessen Inhalt; "~ **unknown"** „Inhalt unbekannt"; ~ **validation** Bewerbertestauswertung.
content adj zufrieden, bereit, einverstanden, „dafür" (*Ja-Stimme im House of Lords*); **not** ~ „dagegen" (*Nein-Stimme im House of Lords*).
contention Behauptung *f*, Vorbringen *n*; **ground of** ~ Streitgrund, Streitgegenstand; **in support of a**

~ als Unterstützung einer Behauptung; **point of** ~ Streitpunkt; **relief from further** ~ Befreiung von weiteren Streitigkeiten.

contentious streitig, strittig; ~ **business** streitige Zivilsache, streitige Sache der freiwilligen Gerichtsbarkeit; ~ **jurisdiction** → *jurisdiction*; ~ **possession** strittiges Besitzrecht; ~ **probate business** streitiges Testamentsverfahren; ~ **suit** streitiges Verfahren.

contentment Zufriedenheit *f*, Annehmlichkeit *f*, Zufriedenstellung *f*.

conterminous angrenzend.

contest *s* Streit *m*, Anfechtung *f*; ~ **of probate** Testamentsanfechtung; ~ **prizes** Preise eines Preisausschreibens; **adversarial** ~ kontradiktorischer Rechtsstreit.

contest *v* kämpfen, streiten, bestreiten, anfechten; ~ **a claim** einen Anspruch bestreiten; ~ **a will** ein Testament anfechten; ~**ed case** streitiges Verfahren.

contestable anfechtbar, bestreitbar.

contestant die anfechtende Partei *f*, streitende Partei *f*; *parl* Kandidat *m*.

contestation Streitfrage *f*, Streit *m*.

context Zusammenhang *m*.

contiguity Kontiguität *f*, Angrenzen *n*, Nähe *f*, Nachbarschaft *f*.

contiguous benachbart, angrenzend; ~ **and compact** angrenzend und zusammenhängend (unmittelbar).

contingency ungewisses, zukünftiges Ereignis *n*, Möglichkeit *f*, Aussicht *f*, Bedingung *f*; Zufallsbedingung **a** ~ **comes to pass** e–e Bedingung tritt ein; ~ **contract** aufschiebend bedingter Vertrag, Erfolgshonorarvertrag; ~ **fee** Erfolgshonorar; ~ **fund** Fonds für unvorhergesehene Ausgaben; **a** ~ **happens** e–e Bedingung tritt ein; ~ **insurance** Versicherung gegen besondere Risiken; ~ **insured against** das versicherte Risiko; ~ **planning** Vorausplanung für den Bedarfsfall; ~ **plan** Eventualplan, Krisenplan, ~ **reserve** Sicherheitsrücklage; ~ **sum** Vorsorgepauschale (*für Unvorhergesehenes, Werkvertrag*); ~ **with double aspect** subsidiäres Heimfallsrecht, Zuwendung mit bedingter Ersatzzuwendung, Nacherbeneinsetzung mit Ersatznacherbenbestimmung; **civil** ~**ies** Sonderfond des brit Finanzministeriums zur Zwischenfinanzierung unvorhergesehener, noch nicht bewilligter Ausgaben.

contingent *adj* bedingt; zufallsbedingt, eventuell; ~ **lists of balances** *exch* Wertpapierclearinglisten; ~ **on the result of the matter** vom Ausgang des Prozesses abhängig.

contingent *s* Kontingent *n*, Quote *f*, Anteil *m*, Beitrag *m*.

continual fortwährend, andauernd, kontinuierlich; ~ **claim** (*jährliche*) Wiederholung des Anspruchs zur Verhinderung der Ersitzung.

continuance Vertagung *f*, Aufschub *m;* Anberaumung *f* e–s neuen Termins; Fortsetzung *f*; Fortdauer *f*, Anhalten *n;* Stetigkeit *f*; ~**s** Termineintragungen in der Prozeßakte (*nach dem ersten Termin*); ~ **of case for sentence** Terminanberaumung zur Urteilsverkündung; ~ **of injury or damage** Fortdauer der verletzenden oder schädigenden Handlung oder Unterlassung; ~ **of the proceedings** Vertagung der Sitzung, Unterbrechung des Verfahrens; ~ **upon own motion of court** Vertagung der Sitzung von Amts wegen.

continuando behaupteter Fortsetzungszusammenhang *m*.

continuation Fortdauer *f*, Weiterführung *f*, Fortsetzung *f*, Prolongation *f*; ~ **application** Weiterbehandlungsantrag; ~ **clause** Verlängerungsklausel; ~ **day** Prolongationstag, Reporttag; ~**-in-part application** *pat* Antrag auf Teilweiterbehandlung; *approx* Ausscheidungsanmeldung; ~ **of tenancy** (*gerichtl angeordnete*) Fortsetzung des Mietverhältnisses; ~ **sheet** Zusatzblatt; ~ **school** → *school;* ~ **tenancy** (*gerichtl*) verlängertes Mietverhältnis.

continue fortsetzen, andauern; fortdauern, weiterbestehen, prolongieren; ~ **the case** die mündl Verhandlung wiederaufnehmen; die Sitzung fortsetzen; ~ **to hold** weiter in Besitz behalten; ~**d use** → *use;* **to be** ~**d** Fortsetzung folgt.

continuing andauernd, fortgesetzt, ständig; ~ **cause of action** Klagegrund bei e–r fortgesetzten Handlung; ~ **effects of injury** Dauerfolgen e–r Verletzung; ~ **legal education** juristische (Berufs)Fortbildung.

continuity Kontinuität *f*, Stetigkeit *f*; ~ **of employment** Beschäftigungskontinuität; ~ **of states** Staatenkontinuität; **price** ~ Preisstabilität.

continuous ununterbrochen, fortgesetzt, fortdauernd, laufend, stetig; ~ **adverse use** fortgesetzte bestrittene Nutzung; ~ **audits** laufende Rechnungsprüfung; ~ **consent** Dauererlaubnis; ~ **employment** ständige Beschäftigung; ~ **force of law** (ständige) Rechtskraft; ~ **injury** Dauerverletzung; ~ **period of unemployment** ununterbrochene Arbeitslosigkeit; ~ **record** fortlaufend geführte Akte; ~ **residence** dauernder Aufenthalt; ~ **temporary service** ununterbrochene Dienstleistung *von Gelegenheitsarbeitnehmern;* ~ **voyage** einheitliche Reise.

contra gegen, anderer Meinung *f* (a. M.); Gegenbuchung *f*; ~ **account** → *account;* ~ **bonos mores** gegen die guten Sitten, sittenwidrig; ~ **pacem** *hist* gegen den Königsfrieden; ~ **proferentem (rule)** Auslegung gegen den Verfasser der Urkunde *zB allg. Geschäftsbedingungen;* ~ **submissions** Gegenvorbringen.

contraband *adj* Schmuggel ..., illegal; ~ **trade** → *trade.*

contraband *s* Konterbande *f*, unter Einfuhrverbot *n (bzw Ausfuhrverbot)* stehende Ware *f*; ~ **of war** Kriegskonterbande; **to run** ~ Schleichhandel betreiben.

contrabandist Schmuggler *m*, Schleichhändler *m*.

contracausator Straftäter *m*, Angeklagter *m*.

contra-flow Gegenverkehr *m*.

contract *s* Vertrag *m (= V bzw ... v, V–e = Verträge)*, Vereinbarung *f*, förmlicher Vertrag *m*, schuldrechtlicher Vertrag *m;* ~ **bond** → *bond* (*1*); ~ **by Crown** *V* mit dem (*königl*) Staatsfiskus; ~ **by deed** förmlicher *V*, gesiegelter *V;* ~ **by post** auf dem Postwege geschlossener *V;* ~ **clause** *V*–sklausel; *US Verfassungsbestimmung über Unantastbarkeit von V–n durch einzelstaatl. Gesetzgebung;* ~, **dealing or transaction** Rechtsgeschäft; ~ **debt** *V*–sschuld, vertragl geschuldete Leistung; ~ **for deed** Grundstücksabzahlungskauf *Eigentumsurkunden (deeds) erst bei Restzahlung;* ~ **for future delivery** *V* auf künftige Lieferung, Sukzessivlieferungs*v;* ~ **for hire** (Geräte) Miete, (reine) Miete (*von bewegl Sachen*); ~ **for labour and material** Werklieferungs*v;* ~ **for work and material** = ~ *for labour and material qv;* ~ **for sale** Kauf*v (gegenwärtige bzw. künftige Leistung);* ~ **for sale of goods** Kauf*v* über bewegliche Sachen, Warenkauf*v;* ~ **for sale of land** Grundstückskauf*v;* ~ **for services** Werk*v*; *V* über Nebenleistungen; ~ **for supply of a service** Dienstverschaffungs*v;* ~ **for the benefit of third party** *V* zugunsten Dritter; ~ **for the rendering of services** Geschäftsbesorgungs*v*, Dienstverschaffungs*v;* ~ **for the supply of goods** Liefer*v;* ~ **for the supply of work and materials** Werklieferungs*v;* ~ **for work done and materials supplied** Werklieferungs*v;* ~ **fraud** betrügerische Auftragsvergabe; ~ **in restraint of trade** wettbewerbsbehindernde Vereinbarung, Kartellabsprache; ~ **in writing** schriftl *V;* ~ **involving literary property** Urheberrechts*v;* ~ **note** *exch* Schlußnote, Schlußschein, Auftragsbestätigung;

~ **not to compete** vertragl Wettbewerbsverbot; ~ **of affreightment** Charterv, Seefrachtv; Frachtv; ~ **of agency** Auftragsverhältnis, Bevollmächtigungsvereinbarung, Vertreterv *auch: Geschäftsbesorgungsv zur Herbeiführung einer Stellvertretung;* ~ **of apprenticeship** Lehrv; ~ **of bailment** Verwahrungsv; ~ **of benevolence** einseitig begünstigender V; ~ **of brokerage** Maklerv; ~**of carriage** Frachtv, Beförderungsv, Seefrachtv; ~ **of consignment** Kommissionsv; ~ **of donation** Schenkungsv; ~ **of employment** Dienstv, Arbeitsv; ~ **of guarantee** Garantiev, Bürgschaftsv; ~ **of indemnity** Garantiev, Haftungsfreistellungsv; ~ **of indemnity only** ein auf die Übernahme des Schadensrisikos beschränkter V; ~ **of lease** Pachtv, langfristiger Mietv; ~ **of loan** Darlehensv; ~ **of loan for use** Leihv; ~ **of marine insurance** Seeversicherungsvertrag, Seetransportversicherungsvertrag; ~ **of marriage** Eheschließung; ~ **of partnership** Gesellschaftsv; ~ **of purchase** Kaufv; ~ **of record** gerichtlich protokollierte Vereinbarung; gerichtliche Unterwerfungserklärung; ~ **of sale** Kaufv über Waren, bewegl Sachen; ~ **of service** ~ *of services* Arbeitsv; ~ **of tenancy** Pachtv Mietv; ~ **of warranty** vertragliche Garantie; ~ **period** Vertragszeit; ~ **placing authority** öffentlicher Auftraggeber; ~ **processing work** → *work;* ~, **promise or agreement** V oder V–sversprechen; ~ **required to be in writing** V mit (vorgeschriebener) Schriftform; ~ **sheet** Börsenumsatzliste; ~ **surgeon** V–sarzt; ~ **system** Akkordsystem; ~ **terms** V–sbedingungen; ~ **to sell** Lieferv; noch zu erfüllender Kaufv; ~ **to supply** Lieferv, Beschaffungsv; ~ **uberrimae fidei** Vertrauensvereinbarung, V mit voller Offenbarungspflicht (*bes des Versicherungsnehmers), V, der in besonders hohem Maße dem Grundsatz von Treu und Glauben unterworfen ist;* ~ **under hand** schriftlicher V; ~ **under seal** gesiegelter V; **accessory** ~ Nebenv, akzessorische Verpflichtung; Sicherungsverhältnis; **action of** ~ Klage aus V; **adhesion** ~ → *adhesion;* **administrative** ~ Verwaltungsabkommen; **aleatory** ~ aleatorischer V, Risikov, **alternative** ~ V mit Wahlschuld; **annulment of** ~ Annullierung des V–s; **bare** ~ schlichter V; **bilateral** ~ zweiseitig verpflichtender V; gegenseitiger V; **building** ~ Bauv; **by** ~ vertraglich, durch Ausschreibung; **certain** ~ unbedingter V, V mit bestimmtem (*nicht von ungewissen Ereignissen abhängigem*) Inhalt; **civil** ~ bürgerlich-rechtlicher V; **collateral** ~ Nebenv; **commutative** ~ gegenseitiger V, zweiseitig verpflichtender V *(mit Gleichwertigkeit von Leistung und Gegenleistung*); **conclusion of a** ~ V–sabschluß; **conditional** ~ bedingter V; **conditional sales** ~ Kaufv unter Eigentumsvorbehalt; **consensual** ~ Konsensualv, obligatorischer V; **constructive** ~ gesetzlich fingiertes V–sverhältnis, gesetzliches Schuldverhältnis; **continuing** ~ Sukzessivlieferungsv, Dauerv mit sukzessiven Leistungen; **contracting** ~ Industrieanlagenbauv; **cost plus** ~ → *cost;* **cost reimbursable** ~ → *cost;* **defective** ~ mit Mängeln behafteter V; **dependent** ~ *von der Erfüllung e–s anderen* abhängiger V; **destination** ~ Lieferv mit Gefahrübergang am Bestimmungsort; **divisible** ~ teilbarer V; **draft** ~ V-sentwurf; **entire** ~ einheitlicher V, unteilbarer V; V ohne Nebenabreden; Zug um Zug zu erfüllender V; **estate** ~ V zur Einräumung bzw Übertragung des Eigentumsrechts am Grundstück, Grundstückskaufv; **evergreen** ~ sich jährl stillschweigend verlängernder V; **executed** ~ bereits bei Abschluß erfüllter V, sofort vollzogener V; **execution of a** ~ Unterfertigung e–s *V–s, selten: V–*sausführung; **executory** ~ obligatorischer *V*, noch zu erfüllender *V;* **express** ~ ausdrücklicher *V;* **fictitious** ~ Schein*v*, fingierter *V;* **fiduciary** ~ Treuhand*v;* **final** ~ endgültiger *V;* **fixed-term** ~ Zeit*v;* **formal** ~ förmlicher *V;* formbedürftiger *V;* **freedom of** ~ *V–s*freiheit, Kontrahierungsfreiheit; **frustration of** ~ Wegfall der Geschäftsgrundlage; **gaming** ~ Wett*v*, Wette; **governmental** ~ Staatsauftrag, *V* des Staatsfiskus; **gratuitous** ~ *V* über e–e unentgeltliche Leistung; **hazardous** ~ Risiko*v*, *V* dessen Zweck von e–m ungewissen Ereignis abhängt; **illegal** ~ widerrechtl *V*, *V* mit gesetzlich verbotenem Inhalt; **immoral** ~ sittenwidriger *V;* **implied** ~ stillschweigender *V*, konkludent geschlossener *V;* **indemnity** ~ → *indemnity;* **independent** ~ *V* mit beiderseits unabhängigen Vertragspflichten; **indivisible** ~ unteilbarer Gesamt*v;* **infant's** ~ *V* e–s Minderjährigen; **informal** ~ formfreier *V*, nicht förmlicher *V*, ohne Formalitäten getroffene Vereinbarung; **insurance** ~ Versicherungs*v;* **integrated** ~ Gesamt*v*; abschließender *V;* **joint** ~ Gemeinschafts*v*; zusammengefaßter *V*, Gesamt*v;* **labor** ~ Tarif*v*, Kollektiv*v* (US); **life insurance** ~ Lebensversicherungs*v;* **literal** ~ *V* in Schriftform; **management** ~ Geschäftsführungs*v;* Betriebsleitungs*v;* **marketing** ~ Vermarktungs*v;* **marriage** ~ → *marriage;* **master** ~ einheitl Haupt*v;* **mixed** ~ *V* mit ungleicher beiderseitiger Leistung; Zuwendung mit Auflage; **multiple delivery** ~ Bezugs*v*, Sukzessivlieferungs*v;* **mutual** ~ gegenseitiger *V*, synallagmatischer *V;* **naked** ~ = *nude* ~ *qv;* **negative** ~ *V* mit Unterlassungsverpflichtung; **nominate** ~ typischer *V;* **nude** ~ Konsensual*v* ohne Gegenleistungsversprechen, einseitiger *V;* **onerous** ~ entgeltlicher *V;* beiderseits verpflichtender *V (mit ungleichen Verpflichtungen)*; **open** ~ Grundsatzvereinbarung, Vor*v* (*ohne Einzelregelungen*); **open end** ~ ergänzungsbedürftiger *V;* Dauerliefervertrag zu festen Preisen; **oral** ~ mündl *V;* mündl vervollständigter oder geänderter *V;* **(entire) output** ~ Gesamtproduktionskauf*v;* **parol** ~ ungesiegelter *V* (*mündlich oder schriftlich*); **participating** ~ Gewinnbeteiligungs*v;* **party to a** ~ → *party;* **passenger** ~ → *passenger;* **personal** ~ *V* über bewegliches Vermögen; höchstpersönlicher *V;* **pignorative** ~ Pfand*v;* **placing of** ~**s** Auftragsvergabe; **pre-incorporation** ~ Vorgründungs*v;* **preliminary** ~ Vor*v;* **prime** ~ Haupt*v*, General*v;* **principal** ~Haupt*v;* **proposed** ~ beabsichtigter *V;* **public** ~ *V* der öffentl Hand; **real** ~ Real*v;* *V* über Liegenschaften; **reciprocal** ~ gegenseitiger *V;* **restricted** ~ beschränkter *V;* an Möbelmiete oder Dienstleistung gekoppelter Wohnungsmiet*v;* **service** ~ → *service* (*1*); **severable** ~ teilbarer *V;* **several** ~ Einzel*v;* **sham** ~ Schein*v;* **simple** ~ nicht gesiegelter *V (mündl oder schriftl)*; **social** ~ → *social;* **special** ~ gesiegelter *V;* **speciality** ~ *V* in gesiegelter Form; **standard** ~ Standard*v*, Muster*v;* **standing** ~ laufender *V*; **supplementary** ~ Zusatz*v;* **synallagmatic** ~ synallagmatischer *V;* **testamentary** ~ Erb*v;* **to award a** ~ (*bei Ausschreibungen*) den Zuschlag erteilen; **to draw up a** ~ → *to draw;* **to enter into a** ~ e–n *V* abschließen; **tying** ~ Exklusiv*v;* **unconscionable** ~ mit Treu und Glauben nicht zu vereinbarender *V;* **underwriting** ~ Emissions*v*, Konsortial*v*, Versicherungs*v;* **unenforceable** ~ nicht erzwingbarer *V*, Natural*v;* **unfair** ~ unbilliger *V*, ungerechter *V;* **unilateral** ~ einseitig verpflichtender *V;* konkludent angenommenes *V–s*angebot; **union** ~ → *union;* **unreasonable** ~ unzumutbarer *V;* **usage** ~

Gebrauchsüberlassungs*v*, Benutzungs*v;* **verbal** ~ mündlicher *V;* **vicious** ~ anfechtbarer *V*, schwebend unwirksamer *V;* **void** ~ nichtiger *V;* **voidable** ~ anfechtbarer *V*, vernichtbarer *V;* **wagering** ~ Spiel*v*, Wett*v;* **written** ~ schriftlicher *V*.

contract *v* kontrahieren, e–n Vertrag (ab)schließen; durch Vertrag begründen, erlangen; sich vertraglich verpflichten; ~ **a loan** e–e Anleihe aufnehmen; ~ **a marriage** → *marriage;* ~ **away** abbedingen; ~ **debts** Schulden machen; ~ **for** e–n Vertrag schließen auf, sich verpflichten (zu); ~ **liabilities** Verpflichtungen eingehen; ~**ring agency** Auftragnehmer, die den Auftrag vergebende Dienststelle; **the ~ing states** die Vertragsstaaten.

contracting Vergabe(wesen), Vergabe von Bauverträgen; Baugewerbe; ~ **out** Untervorgabe, Abbedingung (von AGBs).

contraction Kontraktion *f*, das Zusammenziehen *n*, Verringerung *f*, Schrumpfung *f;* ~ **of credit** Kreditverringerung.

contractor Kontrahent *m*, vertragschließende Partei *f;* (Werk)-Unternehmer *m*, Generalunternehmer *m;* ~**'s basis** geschätzte, angemessene Unternehmervergütung; ~**'s estimate** (Bau)kostenvoranschlag; ~**'s plant** Baumaschinen und Baustelleneinrichtung; **builder and** ~ Bauunternehmer; **general** ~ Generalunternehmer; Hauptunternehmer; **independent** ~ (*Werkvertrags*)unternehmer, unabhängig Handelnder; **joint** ~ Mitunternehmer; **main** ~ Hauptlieferant, Generalunternehmer; **original** ~ Hauptunternehmer, Hauptlieferant; **prime** ~ Hauptunternehmer *ant Subunternehmer*.

contractual vertraglich, vertragsmäßig, Vertrags . . .; ~ **due date** vereinbarte Fälligkeit; ~ **duty of care** vertragl Sorgfaltspflicht.

contradict widersprechen, widerlegen.

contradiction Widerspruch *m*, Widerlegung *f;* ~ **in terms** innerer Widerspruch *m*, logische Unmöglichkeit *f;* **flagrant** ~ krasser Widerspruch

contradictory widersprüchlich.

contradistinction Gegensätzlichkeit *f*, Unterschied *m;* **in** ~ **to** im Gegensatz zu.

contra-indication Gegenanzeige *f*, ~**s** dagegen sprechende Gesichtspunkte.

contrariety Gegensätzlichkeit *f*, Unverträglichkeit *f*, Widerspruch *m*, Widersprüchlichkeit *f*, ~ **of interests** Interessengegensatz.

contrariwise im Gegenteil, umgekehrt.

contrary gegen; im Gegenteil; entgegengesetzt; zuwiderlaufend; ~ **to law** gesetzeswidrig, rechtswidrig; ~ **to one's duty** pflichtwidrig; ~ **to one's knowledge** wider besseres Wissen; ~ **to public policy** dem öffentl Interesse zuwiderlaufend, sittenwidrig; ~ **to regulations** vorschriftswidrig; ~ **to rule** regelwidrig; ~ **to the evidence** im Widerspruch zum Ergebnis der Beweisaufnahme; ~ **to the public interest** dem öffentl Interesse zuwiderlaufend; ~ **to the principle of good faith and confidence** gegen Treu und Glauben.

contrary *s* Gegenteil *n;* **unless the** ~ **appears** außer im gegenteiligen Fall.

contravene verletzen, zuwiderhandeln, übertreten; ~ **a law** gegen ein Gesetz verstoßen; ~ **selection 32** gegen § 32 verstoßen.

contravener Zuwiderhandelnder *m*.

contravening equity *für den gegnerischen Standpunkt sprechende Billigkeitserwägung f*.

contravention Übertretung *f*, Zuwiderhandlung *f*, Verstoß *m;* ~ **(of rules and regulations)** Ordnungswidrigkeit.

contribute mitwirken, beisteuern, beitragen, einbringen; ~ **cash** e-e Bareinlage leisten; ~**d property** → *property*.

contribution Gesellschafseinlage *f*, Beitrag *f*, Einlage *f*, Gesamtschuldneranteil *m*, Ausgleich *m*, Ausgleichszahlung *f*, Nachschuß *m;* ~ **from joint tortfeasor** *Ausgleich durch einen deliktisch haftenden Gesamtschuldner an den leistenden Gesamtschuldner;* ~ **in kind** Sacheinlage; ~ **of capital** Einlage, Kapitaleinbringung; ~ **order** Beschluß über e–n Kostenbeitrag des Angeklagten (*zu den Verfahrenskosten*); ~ **to general average** Havarie-Grosse-Beitrag; ~**s to periodicals** (*literarische*) Beiträge in Zeitschriften; ~ **week** Beitragswoche (*Sozialversicherung*); **charitable** ~ Beiträge zu karitativen Zwecken; **compulsory** ~ Pflichtbeitrag; **employee's** ~ Arbeitnehmeranteil; **employer's** ~ Arbeitgeberanteil; **financial** ~ Beitrag; **flat-rate** ~**s** Einheitsbeiträge (*Sozialversicherung*); **initial** ~ Stammeinlage; **pro rata** ~ anteilmäßiger Beitrag; **voluntary** ~ freiwilliger Beitrag, Spende;

contributive value *Steuerwert auf Grund des wirtschaftlichen Zusammenhanges einer Vielzahl von Vermögenswerten,* Sammelsteuerwert.

contributor Beitragender *m*, Spender *m;* **voluntary** ~ freiwillig Versicherter.

contributory *adj* mitwirkend, beitragend, beitragspflichtig, nachschußpflichtig.

contributory *s* Beitragspflichtiger *m;* beitragspflichtiges Mitglied *n;* nachschußpflichtiger Gesellschafter *m (bei Liquidation) für den nicht erbrachten Teil seiner Einlage haftender Gesellschafter;* ausgleichspflichtiger Gesamtschuldner *m*.

contrition Reue *f*, Schuldgefühl *n*.

contrivance Erfindung *f*, Kunstgriff *m*, Vorrichtung *f*; **crafty** ~s raffinierte Machenschaften.

control *s* Beherrschung *f*, Kontrolle *f*, Verfügung *f*, Aufsicht *f*; *pl* ~*s* Kontrollmechanismen, Kontrollsystem, Bewirtschaftungsvorschriften; ~ **agent** Agentenführer; ~ **of borrowing order** Kreditkontrollverordnung; ~ **of car** Herrschaft über ein Fahrzeug; ~ **of exports** staatliche Exportregelung; ~ **of foreign exchange** Devisenbewirtschaftung; **budgetary** ~ Budgetkontrolle; **credit** ~ Kreditkontrolle, Steuerung des Kreditvolumens; **currency** ~ Devisenbewirtschaftung; **economic** ~ Wirtschaftslenkung; **foreign exchange** ~ → *foreign exchange;* **housing** ~ → *housing;* **immediate** ~ vollständige, unmittelbare Beherrschung (*des Fahrzeugs*); **industrial** ~ Gewerbeaufsicht; **internal** ~ innerbetriebliche Aufsicht; **joint** ~ gemeinsame Verfügungsgewalt; **legal** ~ rechtliche Beherrschung; Rechtsaufsicht; **legislative** ~ Beherrschung durch das Parlament, Kontrolle durch die Legislative; **occupational** ~ betriebliches Weisungsrecht, Weisungsgebundenheit; **parental** ~ elterliche Gewalt; **parliamentary** ~ Parlamentskontrolle (*der Regierung*); **physical** ~ tatsächliche Gewalt, Gewahrsam; **price** ~ → *price;* **rent** ~ Mietpreisbindung, Mieterschutz; **to have corrective** ~ **over** zuständig sein für Maßnahmen der Sicherung und Besserung; **wartime** ~ Kriegsbewirtschaftung.

control *v* beherrschen, beeinflussen, regeln, beschränken, über etw verfügen, kontrollieren, nachprüfen.

controller Kontrolleur *m*, Aufsichtsbeamter *m*, Leiter *m des Rechnungswesens, Rechnungsprüfer m;* Person mit beherrschendem Einfluß auf e–e Körperschaft; ~ **of accounts** Rechnungsrevisor.

controversial bestritten, streitig, strittig, umstritten.

controversy Streitfall *m*, Streitfrage *f*; **without** ~ unbestritten, unstreitig.

controvert bestreiten, streiten.

controvertible bestreitbar, strittig.

contumacious widersetzlich, aufsässig, ungehorsam, (*trotz Ladung*) nicht erschienen.

contumacy Widersetzlichkeit *f*, Ungehorsam *m*, Kontumaz *f*, Unge-

bühr *f*; vorsätzliches Nichterscheinen.
contumalious unverschämt, schikanös.
contumax Beschuldigter *m*, der sich der Hauptverhandlung entzieht.
contusion Quetschung *f*, Prellung *f*.
conurbation städtisches Siedlungsgebiet *n*, städtischer Großraum *m* (*zB London*), Ballungsraum *m*.
conusance Zuständigkeit *f*.
conusant wissentlich, in Kenntnis von.
convalescence Genesungszeit *f*.
convalescent home Sanatorium *n*, Genesungsheim *n*.
convenable genehm, geeignet.
convene versammeln, einberufen.
convenience Zweckmäßigkeit *f* Annehmlichkeit *f*; ~ **store** Nachbarschaftsladen; **as a matter of** ~ aus Zweckmäßigkeitsgründen; **public** ~ Bedürfnis der Allgemeinheit; (öffent) Bedürfnisanstalt; **to pay at** ~ nach Belieben zahlen, gelegentlich bezahlen.
conventicle geheime Zusammenkunft *f*.
convention Übereinkunft *f*, Vereinbarung *f*, Konvention *f*; Parteitag *m*, Kongreß *m*, Versammlung *f*; **C**~ Übereinkunft, Verband *meist bezogen auf Berner Übereinkunft (Copyright) oder Pariser Verbandsübereinkunft (gewerbl Rechtsschutz)*; **C~ application** Verbandsanmeldung, **C~ country** Verbandsland, Abkommensland; **C~ date** Datum der Verbandspriorität; ~ **of estates** *scot* Ständeversammlung; **commercial** ~ Handelsabkommen; **judicial** ~ → *judicial;* **monetary** ~ Münzkonvention; **National C**~ US Bundesparteitag (*zur Nominierung des Präsidentschaftskandidaten);*
conventional vertraglich, vereinbart, konventionell, herkömmlich, üblich; ~ **way of acting** verabredetes, vertragsmäßiges Vorgehen.
convergence Konvergenz *f*; Annäherungsprozeß *m*.
conversant vertraut, wohnhaft.
conversation Verkehr *m;* Gespräch *n*, Unterhaltung *f*, Unterredung *f*, Besprechung *f*; Lebensweise *f*, Umgang *m;* **criminal** ~ Verführung der Ehefrau eines anderen; **private** ~ vertrauliche Unterredung.
conversion Umwandlung *f*, Konversion *f*, Umrechnung *f*, Konvertierung *f*; unbefugte Geltendmachung *f* von Eigentumsrechten; Eigentumsentziehung *f*; Veruntreuung *f*; Unterschlagung *f*, Exzeß des Fremdbesitzers; Änderung *f* der Zugehörigkeit; ~ **account** Umstellungsrechnung; ~ **balance** Konversionsguthaben; ~ **chart** Umrechnungstabelle; ~ **damages for infringements of copyright** Schadensersatz wegen Urheberrechtsverletzung; ~ **loan** (Konversions-) Konvertierungsanleihe; ~ **in bankruptcy** *Umwandlung von Geschäftsvermögen zu Privatvermögen und umgekehrt;* ~ **of debts** Schuldumwandlung; ~ **of goods** vorsätzl Verletzung fremden Eigentums an bewegl Sachen; ~ **of merchant ships** Umwandlung von Handelsschiffen in Kriegsschiffe; ~ **of penalty** Strafumwandlung; ~ **of pledge (to own use)** Pfandunterschlagung; ~ **of premises** Umwandlung, Umbau, Zweckentfremdung von Baulichkeiten; ~ **of shares into stock** Umwandlung von voll einbezahlten Kapitalanteilsrechten in Aktien (*verkehrsfähige, gleichmäßig gestückelte Anteile*); ~ **of stock** Änderung der Stückelung der Aktien; ~ **privilege** Umwandlungsrecht (*Wandelschuldverschreibungen*); ~ **rate** Umrechnungskurs; ~ **right** Umwandlungsrecht, Tauschrecht; ~ **stocks** Umtauschtilgungsanleihe; **constructive** ~ mittelbare widerrechtliche Aneignung; **doctrine of** ~ Fiktion der Umwandlung von Grundvermögen in Geld (*trust*); **equitable** ~ Vermögensumwandlung, Versilberung, Verwertung; **forced** ~ Zwangskonvertierung; **fraudulent** ~ betrügerische Entziehung, Veruntreuung; **possibility of** ~ Konversionsmöglichkeit.

convert konvertieren, umwandeln, umrechnen, umtauschen, widerrechtl vorenthalten, unterschlagen, unrechtmäßig verwenden; ~ **into capital** in Kapital umwandeln; ~ **into cash** realisieren, flüssig machen, versilbern, liquidieren; ~**ed insurance** → *insurance*.

converter der Unterschlagung Begehende, widerrechtl Verfügender, Besitzentzieher *m*.

convertibility Konvertibilität *f*, Konvertierbarkeit *f*; ~ **into cash** Liquidierbarkeit; **external** ~ freie Konvertibilität für Ausländer; **free external** ~ freie Konvertierbarkeit *der Währung*.

convertible konvertierbar, umtauschbar.

convey begleiten, transportieren, mitteilen, übertragen; ~ **the files to the court** dem Gericht die Akten übermitteln; ~**ed** befördert; ~ **by sea only** ausschließliche Seebeförderung.

conveyance Übertragung *f*, Übereignung *f*; Auflassung *f*, Liegenschaftsübertragung Veräußerung; dingl Verfügung; dingl Belastungsurkunde; Transport *m*, Transportmittel *n*|*pl*; ~ **by devise** Übertragung durch Verfügung von Todes wegen: ~ **by operation of law** gesetzlicher (Eigentums)übergang; ~ **by record** gerichtl beurkundete Grundstücksübertragung; *Übertragung durch Spezialgesetz bzw königl Verfügung;* ~ **in pais** Auflassung an Ort und Stelle; ~ **of property** Übertragung von Vermögen, Eigentumsübertragung; ~ **on sale** kaufweise (*kaufähnliche*) Übereignung; ~ **or transfer of property** Veräußerung; ~ **to oneself** Eigentumsübertragung an sich selbst (*zB beim Treuhänder,* **absolute** ~ Übertragung des Grundeigentums, Auflassung; **conditional** ~ bedingte Übereignung; **deed of** ~ Auflassungsurkunde, Eigentumsübertragungsurkunde; **derivative** ~ = *secondary* ~ *qv;* **fraudulent** ~ Vollstreckungsvereitelung; Grundstücksveräußerung zur Gläubigerbenachteiligung; **mesne** ~ Übereignung durch Mittelspersonen; **ordinary** ~ (*privatrechtliche*) Veräußerung, außergerichtliche Auflassung; **overreaching** ~ → *overreaching;* **primary** ~ Auflassung, rechtsbegründende Grundstücksverfügung; **public** ~ öffentl Transportmittel, öffentl Beförderung; **secondary** ~ sekundäre (abändernde) Grundstücksverfügung; abgeleiteter Grundstückserwerb; **voluntary** ~ unentgeltliche Grundstücksübertragung.

conveyancer *Spezialanwalt m für Grundstücksübertragungen, Bodenverkehrsfachmann, Immobilienanwalt.*

conveyancing (*Spezialgebiet der*) Grundstücksübertragung, Grundstücksverkehr, Bodenverkehr; ~ **Acts** Grundstücksübertragungsgesetze; ~ **costs** Anwaltsgebühren bei Grundstücksübertragungen, Verbriefungskosten (*bei Auflassung*); **matters** Grundstücks(übertragungs)angelegenheiten; **private** ~ Bodenverkehr ohne Grundbuch (*by deed*); **registered** ~ Bodenverkehr mit Grundbuch

conveyer Beförderer *m,* Überbringer *m,* Veräußerer *m;* ~ **belt** Fließband, Montageband.

convict *s* Verurteilter *m, Sträfling m;* ~ **made goods** von (Straf)gefangenen angefertige Waren; ~ **prison** Strafanstalt; ~ **under licence** bedingt mit Meldeauflage Entlassener.

convict *v* überführen, verurteilen, schuldig sprechen; ~ **of an offence** überführen, wegen einer Straftat schuldig sprechen, verurteilen; ~**ed** verurteilt; vorbestraft; ~**ed of a crime** (vor)bestraft; ~**ed of felony** wegen eines Verbrechens (vor)bestraft; ~**ed on indictment** anklagegemäß verurteilt; im Geschworenenverfahren verurteilt; ~**ed person** Vorbestrafter; **previously** ~**ed** vorbestraft.

conviction Verurteilung *f*, Schuldspruch *m;* Überzeugung *f*; **former**

~ Vorstrafe; **political** ~ politische Überzeugung; **previous** ~**s** Vorstrafen; **spent** ~ gelöschte Vorstrafe; **summary** ~ Verurteilung im summarischen Verfahren (*vor dem Einzelrichter ohne Geschworene*); **wrongful** ~ widerrechtliche Verurteilung.

convince *v/t* überzeugen.

convocation Einberufung *f* (*e–r Versammlung*), *eccl* Provinzialsynode *f*; akademischer Senat *m*.

convoke einberufen, zusammenrufen.

cook *v sl* (*Bilanz, Rechnung*) verschleiern, fälschen; ~**ed accounts** gefälschte Bücher, ~**ing of balance sheets** Bilanzfälschung.

co-obligor Mitschuldner.

cool blood Kaltblütigkeit *f*.

cooling-off|agreement Stillhalteabkommen (*Arbeitskampf*); Schlichtungsvertrag *m*; ~ **period** Wartezeit, in der keine Kampfmaßnahmen durchgeführt werden dürfen, Abkühlungsfrist, Überdenkungsfrist, Widerrufsfrist des Schuldners bei Kreditgeschäften.

co-op Genossenschaft *f*, Genossenschaftswohnung *f*.

co-operate zusammenarbeiten, mitarbeiten; mitwirken, beitragen zu.

co-operation Zusammenarbeit *f*, Mitarbeit *f*, Mitwirkung *f*, Zusammenschluß *m*; **ongoing** ~ bestehende Zusammenarbeit.

co-operative *adj* genossenschaftlich, kooperativ, mitarbeitend; ~ **association** Genossenschaft; ~ **bank** → *bank* (*1*); ~**buying association** Einkaufsgenossenschaft; ~ **company** Gemeinschaft; ~**enterprise** Genossenschaft(sunternehmen). ~ **insurance** genossenschaftliche Versicherung; ~ **market organisation** Vertriebsgenossenschaft, ~ **society** → *society*.

co-operative (= *cooperative*) *s* Genossenschaft *f*; Coop *f*; **industrial** ~ gewerbliche Genossenschaft.

co-opt *v* hinzuwählen, kooptieren.

co-optation Zuwahl *f*, Ergänzungswahl *f*, Kooptation *f*.

co-ordinate *adj* gleichgestellt, gleichrangig.

co-ordinat|e *v* koordinieren, aufeinander abstimmen.

co-ordination Koordination *f*, Koordinierung *f*, Abstimmung *f*, Gleichschaltung *f*; ~ **allowance** Ausgleichszahlung.

co-owners Miteigentümer *m/pl*.

co-ownership Miteigentum *n*; **matrimonial** ~ (ehe)güterrechtliches Miteigentum.

cop *s sl* Polizist *m*.

cop *v/t US sl* wegnehmen, stehlen, gewinnen; ~ **a plea** → *plea*.

coparcenary *obs* (*1*) gemeinschaftlich ererbtes Grundeigentum *n*; Miterbenstellung, Mitberechtigung (*am Nachlaßgrundstück*); (*2*) = *coparcener qv*.

coparcener *obs* Miteigentümer *m*, Miterbe *m*, Mitbeteiligter *m*.

coparties Streitgenossen *m/pl*

copartner Teilhaber *m*, Gesellschafter *m*, Sozius *m*.

copartnership Teilhaberschaft *f*, Sozietät *f*; Personalgesellschaft *f*.

coprincipal Mittäter *m*; Mitgeschäftsführer *m*.

coprolalia Coprolalie *f*, schwachsinnige Neigung zur Obszönität *f*.

copulation Paarung *f*; Koitus *m*, Beischlaf *m*.

copy *s* Kopie *f*, Imitation *f*, Abschrift *f*, Ausfertigung *f*, Durchschlag *m*; ~ **of indictment** Anklageschrift; ~ **of the file** Aktenabschrift, bes. Ausdruck des Gerichtskomputers; **archival** ~ Archivkopie; **attested** ~ beglaubigte Abschrift; **authenticated** ~ beglaubigte Abschrift, *evt* Ausfertigung; **autograph** ~ eigenhändige Abschrift; **bulky** ~ Exemplare im Großformat; **carbon** ~ Durchschlag; **certified** ~ beglaubigte Abschrift; **close** ~ anwaltschaftlich beglaubigte Abschrift; **conformed** ~ übereinstimmende Abschrift; **court-sealed** ~ Ausfertigung, gerichtlich beglaubigte Abschrift; **engrossed** ~ Ausfertigung; **examined** ~ beglaubigte Abschrift; **exemplified** ~ Ausfertigung, beglaubigte Abschrift; **fair** ~ Reinschrift, druckfertiges Manuskript; **file** ~ Aktendurchschlag, Abschrift für die Akten; **free** ~ Freiexemplar; **full** ~ vollständige Abschrift; **identical** ~ genaue Abschrift; **notarized** ~ notariell beglaubigte Abschrift; **office** ~ *amtl* Ausfertigung; **official** ~ amtl Abschrift; **pirate** ~ unerlaubter Nachdruck; **proof** ~ Belegexemplar, *ein aus Umbruchsabzügen zusammengeheftetes Buchexemplar zur Copyright Hinterlegung;* **rough** ~ Rohentwurf; **sample** ~ Probeexemplar; **true** ~ gleichlautende Abschrift; beglaubigte Abschrift.

copy *v* nachahmen, abschreiben; ~ **from memory** aus der Erinnerung reproduzieren; ~**ing clerk** → *clerk;* ~**ing fees** Schreibgebühren.

copyhold *GB bis 1926* Zinslehen *n,* Bauernland *n,* einer Grundherrschaft, Erbpachtbesitz *m,* Nutzungseigentum *n;* ~ **enfranchisement** Ablösung lehensrechtlicher Beschränkungen.

copyholder (*landwirtschaftlicher*) Erbpächter *m,* Lehensgutpächter *m.*

copying kopieren *n* vervielfältigen *n;* **unauthorised** ~ unerlaubtes Kopieren.

copyist Abschreiber *m,* Nachahmer *m,* Nachdrucker *m,* Plagiator *m.*

copyright *s* Urheberrecht *n, (= U bzw u),* literarisches Eigentum *n,* Urheber- und Verlagsrecht *n,* Musterschutz *m;* ~ **act** *U–s*gesetz; ~ **case** Klage wegen Verletzung des *U–s;* ~ **collecting society** Urheberrechtsverwertungsgesellschaft; ~ **convention** *U–s*abkommen; ~ **edition** urheberrechtlich geschützte Ausgabe; ~ **in designs** Geschmacksmusterschutz, eingetragenes Geschmacksmuster; ~ **law** (das) *U;* ~ **notice** *US* Copyright-Vermerk; Schutzvermerk; **C~ Office** Urheberschutzbehörde; ~ **owner** *U–s*inhaber; ~ **period** Schutzfrist; ~ **privilege** *U;* ~ **proprietor** Inhaber eines *U–s,* Berechtigter; ~ **protection** *U–s*schutz; ~ **records** Copyright-Akten; ~ **royalties** Lizenzgebühren für *U–e;* ~ **subsistence** Erhaltung des *U;* ~ **suit** *U–s*prozeß; ~ **term** Schutzfrist; ~ **tribunal** *U–s*-Schiedsstelle; **abandonment of** ~ Verzicht auf das *U;* **action for** ~ *U–s*klage; **ad interim** ~**s** Schutz ad interim, vorläufiger *U–s*schutz; **claim of** ~ urheberrechtlicher Schutzanspruch; **common law** ~ gwohnheitsrechtl *U, (US: anerkannt soweit vor 1. 1. 78 entstanden, unbegrenzt gültig);* **Crown** ~ *brit* Staats*u;* **inchoate right to renew** ~ Anwartschaft auf Verlängerung des *U–s;* **infringement of** ~ *U–s*-verletzung; **lapsed** ~ erloschenes *U;* **literary** ~ *U* an literarischen Werken; **manufacturing provisions of** ~ **law** Vorschriften über inneramerikanischen Druck englischsprachiger Werke; **musical** ~ *U* an Werken der Tonkunst; **notice of** ~ Copyright-Vermerk, Schutzzeichen; **original** ~ originäres *U;* **out of** ~ nicht mehr urheberrechtlich geschützt; **presumption of** ~ *U–s*vermutung; **renewal of** ~ Verlängerung eines Urheberrechts; **statutory** ~ gesetzliches *U;* **subsisting** ~ (*bereits bzw noch*) bestehendes *U;* **Universal C~ convention** → *universal.*

copyright *v* urheberrechtlich schützen, das Urheberrecht (*Copyright*) erwerben; ~**ed works** urheberrechtlich geschützte Werke.

copyrightable urheberrechtsfähig.

copywriting (Werbe)Textierung *f.*

coram | judice vor e–m *ordnungsgemäß besetzten* zuständigen Gericht; ~ **nobis** uns (*dem Gericht*) vorliegend; ~ **non judice** vor einem unzuständigen Gericht; ~ **vobis** *Berichtigungsverfügung an ein unteres Gericht.*

cordon *s* Abriegelung *f,* Absperrung *f;* **to** ~ **off** *v* abriegeln.

co-respondent Mitbeklagte(r), Mitschuldiger *m (GB vor 1971; am Ehebruch der Frau Beteiligter),* Ehebruchszeuge *m.*

corn Getreide *n,* Korn *n; US* Mais *m;* ~ **broker** Getreidemakler; ~ **exchange** → *exchange (3)*; ~**laws** *hist* Kornzölle; ~ **rent** Naturalgetreidezins; ~ **sales** Getreidehandelsvorschriften über Gewichte; ~ **tax** Getreidezoll; ~ **trade clause** Klauseln des Getreidehandels.

corner *s exch* (spekulative) Aufkäufergruppe *f;* Schwänze *f, planmäßig herbeigeführte Marktenge im Termingeschäft;* Vermessungseckpunkt *m.*

corner *v (bestimmte Warengattung zu spekulativen Zwecken)* aufkaufen; ~ **the adversary** den Gegner in die Enge treiben; ~ **the market** den Markt aufkaufen, spekulative Hausse herbeiführen, schwänzen.

corner shops kleine Ladengeschäfte, „Tante Emma" Läden.

cornerer Aufkäufer *m.*

corollary logische Folge *f,* natürliche F, sekundäre F, selbstverständliche F, Abteilung *f,* Ergebnis *n.*

corona Krone *f (als Partei der Strafverfolgungsbehörde).*

coroner *amtlicher Leichenbeschauer und Untersuchungsrichter bei ungeklärten Todesfällen,* Untersuchungsrichter *m* für Todesursachen; Kronverwalter; ~**'s court** Untersuchungsgericht *für Todesursachen;* ~ **'s depositions** *Niederschrift der beeidigten Aussagen bei der Untersuchungsverhandlung wegen ungeklärter Todesfälle;* ~**'s inquest** gerichtliche Untersuchung ungeklärter Todesfälle.

corpnership *etwa* GmbH & Co KG mit zahlreichen Kommanditisten.

corporacy interne Gruppe *f,* verschworene Gemeinschaft *f;* verbürokratisiertes Großunternehmen *n.*

corporal körperlich, physisch.

corporate körperschaftlich, zu einer juristischen Person gehörend; ~ **agent** *für e–e Körperschaft vertretungsberechte natürliche oder jurist Person;* ~ **articles** Satzung; ~ **assets** Firmenvermögen *(einer Kapitalgesellschaft)*; ~ **authority** Stadtrat, Gemeindebehörde; ~ **charter** *staatl Gründungsurkunde und Betriebserlaubnis e–r jurist Person (US);* ~ **citizenship** Staatszugehörigkeit e–r jurist Person; ~ **deed of trust** Treuhandsvertrag für die Emissionen einer Kapitalgesellschaft; ~ **domicile** Sitz e–r Körperschaft; ~ **entity** Rechtspersönlichkeit e–r Körperschaft; ~ **fiduciaries** Treuhandgesellschaften, juristische Personen mit Treuhandsfunktionen; ~ **franchise** *durch staatliche Konzession verliehene* Rechtsfähigkeit einer Körperschaft; ~ **image** das Erscheinungsbild e–r Gesellschaft; ~ **improvement notes** gewerblicher Pachtvertrag mit Instandhaltungspflicht des Verpächters; ~ **income tax** Körperschaftssteuer ~ **meeting** Hauptversammlung; ~**name** → *name;* ~ **office** Bürgermeisteramt, Amt eines kommunalen Wahlbeamten; ~**officer** leitender Funktionär einer juristischen Person, Vorstandsmitglied; ~ **powers** satzungsgemäße Befugnisse einer juristischen Person; ~ **purpose** Gesellschaftszweck, Gemeindeaufgaben; ~ **shell** Firmenmantel; ~ **sign** Firmensymbol; ~ **trustee** Kreditinstitut *(oder sonstige Körperschaft)* als Treuhandverwalter bzw Nachlaßverwalter; ~ **veil** Schleier der Geheimhaltung vor den Aktivitäten einer Körperschaft.

corporation Körperschaft *f (= Kö bzw kö), (rechtsfähige)* Stadtgemeinde *f,* Gilde *f,* Zunft *f,* Innung *f,* juristische Person *f,* Körperschaft des öffentl Rechts; **C~ Act** *hist* Gesetz über Wählbarkeit von Kommunalbeamten *(nach Konfessionszugehörigkeit)*; ~ **aggregate** *(von mehreren Personen gebildete) Kö;* ~ **bills** Kommunalschatzwechsel; ~ **bonds** Schuldverschreibungen einer Kapitalgesellschaft, **benevolent** ~ gemeinnützige *Kö;* ~ **bylaws** Ausführungsbestimmungen zur Satzung; ~ **by prescription** *Kö* seit unvordenklicher Zeit, gewohnheitsrechtlich betehende *Kö;* ~ **counsel** → *counsel;* ~ **court** Stadtgericht; ~ **duty** Erbschaftssteuerersatzabgabe von *Kö–en (u.*

nicht rechtsfähigen Vereinigungen); ~ **income tax** → *corporate income tax;* ~ **lawyer** auf Gesellschaftsrecht spezialisierter Anwalt; ~ **patent department** Firmenpatentabteilung; ~ **profits tax** → *tax;* ~ **sinking fund mortgage bond** Kommunalpfandbrief; ~ **sole** ein mit Rechtsfähigkeit ausgestattetes Amt (*Krone, Bischof*); ~ **tax** → *tax;* ~**s with high payout ratios** dividendenfreudige Gesellschaften; **banking** ~ Aktienbank; **business** ~ gewerbliche *Kö,* Kapitalgesellschaft; **chartered** ~ *durch Hoheitsakt geschaffene Körperschaft,* konzessionierte Gesellschaft, eingetragene Gesellschaft; **civil** ~ gewerbliche *Kö,* Kapitalgesellschaft, gewerblicher Verein; **close** ~ GmbH-ähnliche Kapitalges. *mit geschlossenem Gesellschafterkreis; von einem (sich selbst regenerierenden) Vorstand beherrschte private Kö;* Familiengesellschaft; **collapsible** ~ *Kö* für einmaligen Zweck; **commercial** ~ Kapitalgesellschaft; **common law** ~ → *common law;* **de facto** ~ faktische Gesellschaft, als *Kö* behandelte Ges.; **de jure** ~ *Kö,* juristische Person; **development** ~ (*Stadt*) Entwicklungsgesellschaft; **domestic** ~ inländische *Kö;* **ecclesiastical** ~ kirchliche *Kö,* geistliche Korporation; **eleemosynary** ~ karitative *Kö,* gemeinnützige *Kö;* **foreign** ~ außerhalb des jeweiligen Staates gegründete Kapitalges., *US in e-m anderen Bundesstaat bzw im Ausland gegründete Kapitalges;* ausländische *Kö;* **joint-stock** ~ Kapitalgesellschaft, Aktiengesellschaft; **lay** ~ (weltliche) *Kö;* **local** ~ Gemeinde; **membership** ~ (*eingetragener*) Verein; **moneyed** ~ Bank- und Versicherungsgesellschaft, Kreditinstitut; Kapitalgesellschaft; **municipal** ~ → *municipal;* **mutual** ~ Gegenseitigkeitsgesellschaft; **non-profit** ~ gemeinnützige *Kö;* **non-stock** ~ *US Kö* ohne Kapitalbegebung (*öffentlich-rechtlich oder privatrechtlich*), eingetragener Verein, Stiftung; **non-trading** ~ gemeinnützige *Kö,* eingetragener Verein; **not-for-profit** ~ gemeinnützige *Kö;* **open** ~ Kapitalges. mit offenem Kreis von Anteilseignern, Publikumsgesellschaft; **parent** ~ Muttergesellschaft; **political** ~ Gebiets*kö; Kö* des öffentlichen Rechts; **private** ~ privatrechtliche *Kö;* **professional** ~ freiberufliche GmbH; **public** ~ öffentlich-rechtliche *Kö;* **publicly held** ~ Publikumsgesellschaft (*US*); **public-service** ~ öffentliches Versorgungsunternehmen; **public utility** ~ öffentliches Versorgungsunternehmen; **quasi** ~ nichtrechtsfähiger Verein (*körperschaftl organisiert*), Selbstverwaltungsorganisation; **quasi public** ~ gemischt-wirtschaftlicher öffentlicher Versorgungsbetrieb, gewerblicher Betrieb einer *Kö* des öffentlichen Rechts, Regiebetrieb; **religious** ~ kirchliche *Kö;* **spiritual** ~ kirchliche *Kö;* **statutory** ~ öffentlich-rechtliche *Kö;* **thin** ~ unterkapitalisierte Aktiengesellschaft; **trading** ~ Handelsgesellschaft, *Handel betreibende Kapitalgesellschaft;* **tramp** ~ Briefkastengesellschaft *mit veränderlichem Standort;* **trust** ~ → *trust;* **wholly-owned** ~ → *wholly;* **wholly-owned government** ~ → *wholly.*

corporative körperschaftlich, korporativ; genossenschaftlich; gesellschaftlich; ständisch.

corporator Gründer *m;* Gründungsmitglied *n.*

corporeal physisch, greifbar, körperlich, materiell.

corps diplomatique diplomatisches Korps *n.*

corpus Kapital *n (eines Vermögens),* Gesetzessammlung *f;* ~ **delicti** objektiver Tatbestand einer Straftat; **C**~ **Juris** *e-e Rechtsenzyklopädie;* ~ **possessionis** Gegenstand des Besitzes.

correct *adj* richtig, fehlerfrei, korrekt, vorschriftsmäßig, einwandfrei; wahr; ~ **annual percentage**

rate effektiver Jahreszins; ~ **as to form and to the point** formgerecht und sachlich richtig; ~ **attest** „Richtigkeit beglaubigt", „für die Richtigkeit".

correct *v* berichtigen, richtigstellen; zurechtweisen, tadeln; strafen, züchtigen; ~**ing and adjusting entries** Buchungsberichtigungen; ~**ing entry** Berichtigungsbuchung.

correction Berichtigung *f*, Richtigstellung *f*, Abstellung *f von Mißbräuchen*, Fehlerverbesserung *f*, Korrektur *f*; Zurechtweisung *f*, Tadel *m*, Züchtigung *f*, Strafvollzug *m*, Besserung *f*; ~ **of proof sheets** Korrekturlesen *s|n*; ~ **or explanation** Berichtigung oder Erläuterung (*Patentbeschreibung*); ~ **proof** Korrekturabzug; **assault by** ~ (*Nichtstrafbarkeit der*) Züchtigung als Körperverletzung; **house of** ~ Besserungsanstalt, Gefängnis; **killing by** ~ körperliche Züchtigung mit Todesfolge; **lawful** ~ gesetzlich zulässige Züchtigung.

correctional institutions Strafvollzugsanstalten *f|pl*

corrective action Abhilfemaßnahmen; ~ **training** Jugendstrafe (*Borstal*).

correspond im brieflichen Verkehr stehen, übereinstimmen, entsprechen; ~**ing attorney** Korrespondenzanwalt; ~**ing member** korrespondierendes (*auswärtiges*) Mitglied; **C~ing Societies Act** Gesetz gegen Geheimbündelei.

correspondence Schriftverkehr *n*, Korrespondenz *f*; **retained** ~ banklagernd.

correspondent *s* Berichterstatter *m*, Korrespondent *m*; Absender *bzw* Empfänger e–s Briefes; ~ *adj* entsprechend, übereinstimmend; ~ **bank** Korrespondenzbank; ~ **banking** Bankverkehr duch Korrespondenzbanken.

corrigendium Berichtigung *f*.

corrigible berichtigungsfähig.

corroborat|e bestärken, bestätigen, unterstützen; ~ **an assertion** e–e Behauptung erhärten.

corroboration Beweisbestätigung *f*, Bekräftigung *f*; ~ **of prosecutrix** Erhärtung der Aussage der Privatklägerin; **absence of** ~ das Fehlen zusätzlichen Beweismaterials.

corrugations Rillen *f|pl (bei Fingerabdrücken)*, Handlinien *f|pl*, Falten *f|pl*, Runzeln *f|pl*.

corrupt *adj* korrupt, bestechlich.

corrupt *v* verderben, verleiten, verführen, korrumpieren, bestechen.

corruptibility Bestechlichkeit *f*.

corruptible korrumpierbar, bestechlich.

corruption Korruption *f*, Bestechung *f*; ~ **of agents** (*aktive oder passive*) Bestechung von Beauftragten; ~ **of blood** Makel der Ehrlosigkeit (*Folge des attainder qv*); ~ **of magistrate** Richterbestechung; ~ **of ministerial officers** Beamtenbestechung; ~ **of public morals** Sittenverderbnis; ~ **of witnesses** Zeugenbestechung.

corset control of credit allg mengenmäßige Kreditrestriktionen *f*.

cosh Totschläger *m*, Knüppel *m*.

cost *s* Kosten,; *pl* (= *K bzw* . . . *k*): Selbstkosten *pl*, Preis *m*, Einkaufspreis *m*; Kosten des Rechtsstreits, Prozeßkosten; Kostenentscheidung *f*, Kostenerstattungsanspruch *m*; Unkosten *pl*, Auslagen *f|pl*, Spesen *pl*; ~ **account** → *account*; ~ **accounting** → *accounting*; ~ **allocation** *K*umlage; *K*verteilung; ~**s and expenses** *K* und Auslagen; ~**s as between party and party** erstattungsfähige *K*; ~ **basis** → *basis*; ~ **bond** *K*sicherheitsleistung; ~**-book** Kalkulationsbuch; ~**-book mining company** *brit* bergrechtliche Gewerkschaft; ~ **breakdown** *K*aufgliederung; ~**s, charges, and expenses** *K* jeder Art; ~**s chart** *K*tabelle; ~ **control account** *K*gegenkonto; ~ **and freight** (*C & F. c & f*) Kosten und Fracht (*d.h. Lieferpreis enthält Versandkosten ohne Transportversicherung*); ~ **cutting** *K*senkung; ~**s de incremento** *K*erhöhung; ~**s distribution** *K*verteilung; ~**s draughtsman** Kostensachbearbeiter, Kostenfestsetzungsspezialist; ~**s due to a solicitor** Anwalts*k*; ~ **effective** *k*wirksam, *k*günstig; ~ **effectiveness analysis** Betriebskostenkalkulation; ~ **estimate** *K*(vor)anschlag; ~**-finding** *K*erfassung; ~**-finding division** Kalkulationsabteilung; ~**-floor rule** *Mindestkostenregel (Kostenmiete)*, Selbstkostenregel; ~ **free** kostenfrei, kostenlos; ~**s follow the event** → *~s shall follow the event;* ~**s in and about the action** die *K* des Rechtsstreits; ~**s in any event** die *K-n* hat die Partei selbst zu tragen unabhängig vom Ausgang des Rechtstreits; ~**s in the event** *K-n*entscheidung wie im Hauptprozeß; **cause** *~s K* des Rechtsstreits; ~**s in the discretion of the judge** im richterlichen Ermessen liegende *K*entscheidung; ~**s incurred in** ... bei ... angefallene, aufgelaufene *K*; ~, **insurance, freight (C.I.F.)** *K* (*der Verladung*), Versicherung u. Fracht *vom Verkäufer zu tragen (cif-Klausel)*; ~ **keeping** *K*buchhaltung; ~ **method** Bewertung zum Rechnungswert; ~ **of carriage** Bahnfracht*k*; ~**s of collection** Inkasso*k*; ~ **of debt** Fremdkapital*k–n*; ~ **of delivery** Liefer*k*, Versand*k*; ~ **of distribution** Vertriebs*k*; ~**s of execution** Zwangsvollstreckungs*k*; ~**s of issue** *K* des Rechtsstreits; ~ **of labo(u)r** Lohn*k*; ~**s of litigation** Prozeß*k*, *K* des Rechtsstreits; ~ **of living** → *cost of living infra*; ~**s of maintenance** Unterhalts*k*, Instandhaltungs*k*; ~**s of management** Verwaltungs*k*; ~ **of money** Geldbeschaffungs*k*; ~**s of poor prisoner's defence** *K* der Pflichtverteidigung; ~**s of professional witnesses** Entschädigung für sachverständige Zeugen; ~ **of production** Herstellungskosten; ~**(s) of promotion** Gründungs*k*; ~**s of realisation** Verwertungs*k*; ~**s of reference** Fürsorge*k*; ~**(s) of repairs** Instandhaltungs*k*; Instandsetzungs*k*; ~**(s) of replacement** Wiederbeschaffungs*k*; ~ **of sales** Absatz*k*; Vertriebs*k*; ~**s of suit** Prozeß*k*; ~**s of the action** Prozeß*k*; ~**s of the appeal** *K* der Berufungs-(Revisions-)Instanz; ~**s of the day** *K* für e–n Termin (*als Verzögerungsgebühr*); ~**s of the proceedings** *K* des Verfahrens; ~**s of umpirage** *K* des Schiedsverfahrens; ~**s of working** Betriebs*k*; ~ **of works payment** Kriegsschadensreparaturvergütung; ~**s on appeal** *K* in der Berufungsinstanz; ~**s on judgment for part only of claim** *K*entscheidung bei Teilurteil; ~**s on judgment for whole claim** *K*entscheidung bei Endurteil (*bzw Schlußurteil*); ~**s payable out of the estate** Masse*k*; ~**-plus (contract)** Auftrag auf Regie (*Material- und Arbeitskosten plus Marge)*; ~**-plus a percentage of cost** Selbst*k*, plus prozentualer Aufschlag; ~ **plus-fixed-fee contract** Selbstkostenvertrag mit festem Zuschlag; ~ **price** Selbstkostenpreis; ~ **push** *K*druck; ~ **reimbursable contract** Vertrag auf Selbstkostenerstattungsbasis; ~ **reimbursement management construction work** Generalunternehmer-Bauaufträge auf Kostenerstattungsbasis; ~**s reserved** *K*entscheidung dem Richter vorbehalten; ~ **saving** *K*einsparung; ~**s shall follow the event** *K*entscheidung nach Maßgabe des Prozeßausgangs; ~ **sharing** *K*beteiligung; ~ **statements** *K*aufstellungen; ~**s to abide the event** *K*entscheidung der Rechtsmittelinstanz für alle Instanzen; ~**s to abide the result** *K* bleiben der Endentscheidung vorbehalten; ~**s to be paid out of central funds** die *K* einschließlich der notwendigen Auslagen des Angeklagten trägt die Staatskasse; ~**s to be taxed** festzusetzende *K*; ~ **unit** *K–n*einheit, *K–n*träger; ~ **value** Selbstkostenwert; **actual** ~ Selbst*k*, Gestehungs*k*;

all-in ~ Gesamt*k–n; **alternative** ~ Alternativk; K* Herstellungs*k* alternativer Erzeugnisse; **amortized** ~ *K* zum (*abgeschriebenen*) Buchwert; **apportionment of ~s** → *apportionment;* **assessment of ~s** → *assessment;* **at** ~ zum Selbstkostenpreis, zu Anschaffungs*k;* **average ~s** Durchschnitts*k;* **bill of ~s** *K*rechnung des Anwalts; **certificate of ~s** → *certificate;* **closing ~s** Neben*k* beim Grundstückskauf; **common fund ~s** Gerichts*k;* **consequential ~s** Schadensfolge*k;* ~ ~ *basis of costs: Kostenfestsetzung nach Angemessenheit und Notwendigkeit;* **constant ~s** feste *K;* **differential** ~ Grenz*k;* **direct** ~ direkte *K*, Einzel*k;* Produktions*k* in Geld; **dismissed with costs** kostenpflichtig abgewiesen; **dives ~s** erstattungsfähige Anwalts*k* der obsiegenden Partei im Armenrecht; **double ~s** *K* zum doppelten Satz (= *Kosten zum anderthalbfachen Satz*); **entitlement to ~s** *K*erstattungsanspruch; **final ~s** endgültige *K*entscheidung; **first ~s** Gestehungs*k*, Selbst*k*, Anschaffungs*k;* **fixed ~s** Gemein*k;* **free of ~s** kostenfrei, kostenlos; **full** ~ sämtliche *K;* **general ~s** Gemein*k;* **historic(al)** ~ historische *K*, Istkosten der Vergangenheit; Anschaffungs*k;* **imprisonment for ~s** Freiheitsstrafe wegen nichtbezahlter Gerichts*k;* **imputed** ~ kalkulatorische *K;* **indirect** ~ indirekte *K*, Gemein*k;* **interlocutory ~s** *K* im Zwischenverfahren **invoice** ~ → *invoice;* **landed ~s** Preis bei Anlieferung; **legal ~s** Prozeß*k;* Verfahrens*k;* **legitimate ~s** rechtlich zulässige *K;* **net** ~ Netto*k;* **normal** ~ → *normal;* **operating ~s** Betriebs*k;* **order for ~s** *K*festsetzung durch das Gericht, **original** ~ Anschaffungs- oder Herstellungs*k;* **overhead ~s** Gemein*k;* **own** ~ Selbst*k;* **party to party** ~ → *party;* **predetermined** ~ vorkalkulierte *K;* **prime** ~ Einstandspreis, Beschaffungs*k*, Gestehungspreis; **primary** ~ effektive *K;* **recurring ~s** laufende Geschäftsun*k;* **reimbursement of ~s** *K*erstattung; **replacement** ~ Wiederbeschaffungs*k;* **residual** ~ Restbuchwert; **running ~s** laufende Un*k;* **scale of ~s** Gebührentabelle; **security for ~s** → *security* (*1*); **solicitor's ~s** Anwalts*k;* **solicitor and client ~s** eigene Anwalts*k;* **start-up ~s** Anlauf*k;* **sunk** ~ einmalige Produktions*k;* **taxation of ~s** Festsetzung der erstattungsfähigen *K;* **to carry ~s** die *K* hat die unterliegende Partei zu erstatten; **to fix the ~s** die *K* festsetzen; **to shave ~s** *K* einsparen; **to your** ~ auf Ihre *K;* **treble ~s** „dreifache *K*" (= *Kosten plus 2 × den halben Satz*); **undistributed ~s** Generalunkosten; **volume** ~ → *volume;* **with ~s** kostenpflichtig; mit Kostenerstattungsanspruch gegen die unterliegende Partei.

cost *v* kosten, kalkulieren, berechnen.

costermonger Straßenhändler *m* mit Obst und Gemüse.

costing Kostenberechnung *f*, Preisfestsetzung *f*, Berechnung *f* des Selbstkostenpreises, Herstellungskostenkalkulation; Kostenerfassung; **differential** ~ Grenzkostenkalkulation; **direct** ~ Grenzkostenkalkulation.

cost of living Lebenshaltungskosten; ~ **adjustment** Teuerungsausgleich; ~ **allowance** Teuerungszulage; ~ **bonus** Teuerungszulage; ~ **index** → *index*.

co-stipulator Mitkontrahend *m*.

costly kostspielig, teuer.

co-surety Mitbürge *m*.

co-tenancy Mitberechtigung *f*, gemeinsames Miet(Pacht)recht *n*.

co-tenant Mitberechtigter *n*, Mitmieter *m*, Mitpächter *m*.

cotland Häuslerland *m*, Kleinpächterland*m*, Zinslehensland *m*.

cottage Hütte *f*, Kate *f*, kleines Wohnhaus *n* ohne Grundbesitz; Landhaus *n;* ~ **industry** Heimarbeit; **tied** ~ Landarbeiter-Werkwohnung.

cottager Gutsarbeiter *m*, Landarbeiter *m*.
cottier Häusler *m*, Kleinbauer *m*, Pachthäusler *m*; ~ **tenancy** Kleinpachtvertrag (*Irland*); ~ **tenure** *irische* landwirtschaftliche Kleinpacht.
cotton Baumwolle *f*; Baumwollgarn *n*; **C~ Cloth Factories Act** *Arbeitsschutzgesetz für Baumwollfabriken 1889*; ~ **exchange** → *exchange* (*3*); ~ **factory** Textilwerk für Baumwolle; ~ **grades** Baumwollhandelsklassen; ~ **industry** Baumwolltextilindustrie; ~ **linters** Linters, Baumwollfaserreste; ~ **marks** Webereizeichenregister für (Baumwoll-Textilien; ~ **mill** Baumwollspinnerei und -weberei; ~ **notes** Lagerscheine für Baumwollballen; ~ **season** Saison für den Baumwollhandel (*1. Sept. bis 1. Mai*); **upland** ~ Hochlandbaumwolle.
co-trustee Mittreuhänder *m*.
couchette car Liegewagen *m*.
coulisse die Kulisse *f* (*Börse*).
council Versammlung *f*, Rat *m*, Stadtrat *m*, Gemeinderat *m*; ~ **care** kommunale Fürsorgeverwahrung; ~ **estate** kommunaler Wohnblock; ~ **flat** *GB* (gemeindeeigene) Sozialwohnung; ~ **housing** gemeindlicher sozialer Wohnungsbau; ~ **of conciliation** Schlichtungsausschuß; **C~ for Mutual Economic Assistance** Rat für gegenseitige Wirtschaftshilfe; **C ~ of Europe** Europarat; **C~ of Industrial Design (=)** *staatlich gefördertes Gremium für gewerbliche Formgebung (Industriedesign) GB*; ~ **of judges** Richterversammlung (*des Supreme Court zur Beratung über das Verfahrensrecht, der Rules qv*); **C~ of Legal Education** *Kommission der Anwaltskammern für juristische Ausbildung*; **C~ of Ministers** Ministerrat (*EG*); ~ **of the bar** Vorstand der Anwaltskammer; **C~ of the Community** Rat der Gemeinschaft; **C~ of the European Communities** Rat der Europäischen Gemeinschaften; ~ **of war** Kriegsrat; **C ~ on Tribunals** *Überwachungsgremium für tribunals qv*; ~ **school** → *school*; ~ **tenant** → *tenant*; **advisory** ~ Beirat; **advisory ~ of experts** Sachverständigenbeirat; **Aulic C~** Reichshofrat (*des alten deutschen Reichs*); **city** ~ Gemeinderat, Stadtrat; **common** ~ Stadtverordnetenversammlung; Stadtrat (*von London*); **County C~** → *county*; **local** ~ Stadtrat, Gemeinderat; **Privy C~** → *privy*; **select** ~ Stadtratsausschuß, obere Kammer eines Gemeindeparlaments (*US*).
councillor Stadtrat *m*, Ratsherr *m*.
counsel *s* Prozeßanwalt *m* (= *barrister qv*); Rat *m*, Berater *m*, Rechtsberater *m*, Rechtsbeistand *m*; **~'s brief** *brit* Mandierung, Beauftragung (*e-s barrister*) zur Vertretung vor Gericht; ~ **for accused** Verteidiger; **C~ for the Crown** öffentlicher Ankläger; ~ **for the plaintiff** Prozeßbevollmächtigter des Klägers; ~ **for the prosecution** Anklagevertreter; ~ **for witness** anwaltschaftlicher Beistand für Zeugen; ~ **of record** Prozeßbevollmächtigter; Rechtsanwalt der bei Gericht auftritt; **~'s opinion** Anwaltsgutachten, *Rechtsgutachten eines (noch) nicht mit der Prozeßführung betrauten Anwalts*; **~'s signature** anwaltschaftliche Unterschrift; **assigned** ~ beigeordneter Verteidiger, Offizialverteidiger; **congressional** ~ Parlamentssynikus, Spezialanwalt für Parlamentsangelegenheiten; **conveyancing** ~ Fachanwalt für Grundstücksübertragungen, **corporation** ~ Syndikus, Gesellschaftsjustitiar, (ständiger) Rechtsberater e-r Aktiengesellschaft; Syndikus e-r Stadtgemeinde; **house** ~ Syndikusanwalt; **general** ~ Leiter der Rechtsabteilung; **"I am ~ for"** ich vertrete anwaltlich . . .; **independent** ~ (*US*) (unabhängiger) Sonderstaatsanwalt; **junior** ~ Gehilfe des prozeßführenden Anwalts; **lead** ~ Chefanwalt, erster Verteidiger; **legal** ~ R-anwalt, Verteidiger; **legislative** ~ jurist Mitarbei-

ter e–s Abgeordneten; **"of ~"** Prozeßbevollmächtigter aus e–r Anwaltssozietät; **opposing** ~ Gegenanwalt, gegnerischer Prozeßbevollmächtigter; **outside** ~ (unabhängiger) Rechtsanwalt; **Parliamentary C~** *Parlamentsjustiziar zuständig für Formulierung von Gesetzesvorlagen*; **plaintiff's** ~ der Prozeßbevollmächtigte der Klagepartei.

counsel *v* beraten, anraten; ~ **and procure** durch Rat und Tat Beihilfe leisten.

counselling Beratung, Patientenberatung u -aufklärung über Risiken.

counsel(l)or Rechtsanwalt *m*, Rechtsberater *m*, juristischer Berater *m*.

count *s* Zählung *f*, Rechnung *f*, Zahl *f*; (Tatsachen)Vortrag *m*, Anklagepunkt *m*, Klagebegründung *f*, selbständiger Teil einer Klagebegründung; ~ **and reckoning** *scot* Rechnungslegungsklage gegen einen Beauftragten; ~ (*in an indictment*) Anklagepunkt, einzelner Tatvorwurf; **alternative** ~ alternativer Anklagepunkt (*aus anderen rechtl Gesichtspunkten*); **common ~s** stereotype Begründungsformeln, Klagebegründung bei schuldrechtl Klagen; **general** ~ allgemeine zusammengefaßte Klagebegründung; **money ~s** stereotype Begründungsformeln bei Zahlungsklage; **omnibus** ~ Klagebegründung aus allen denkbaren Anspruchsgrundlagen; **principal** ~ Hauptanklagepunkt; **several ~s** Bestandteile e–r Klage bei Anspruchshäufung; **to call a** ~ die Auszählung der Stimmen verlangen; **special** ~ substantiierte Begründung des einzelnen Klageanspruchs.

count *v* berechnen, zählen; vortragen, plädieren; ~ **against** anrechnen auf.

count-out Zählung *f* der anwesenden Parlamentsmitglieder (*zur Feststellung der Beschlußfähigkeit*); Vertagung *f* wegen Beschlußunfähigkeit.

countenance würdigen, wertschätzen; dulden, zulassen, begünstigen, Vorschub leisten.

counter Ladentisch *m*, Schalter *m*; Zählwerk *n*, Schranke *f* (*Börse*); ~ **congestion** Gedränge am Abfertigungsschalter; **over the** ~ an der Kasse, am Schalter, *US exch* im Freiverkehr, außerhalb der Börse, über den Ladentisch, bar; **to sell over the** ~ *US* im Laden verkaufen; freihändig verkaufen.

counter entgegengesetzt, zuwider.

counteract entgegenhandeln, entgegenwirken; ~ **a rule** e–r Vorschrift zuwiderhandeln.

counter-accusation Gegenbeschuldigung *f*.

counter-action Gegenwirkung *f*; Widerklage *f*.

counter-affidavit beeidigte Gegenerklärung *f*.

counterbalance ausgleichen, kompensieren.

counterbidding Gegenbieten *n*, Überbieten *n*.

counterbond gesiegelte Schadloshaltungsverpflichtung *f*; Rückbürgschaft *f*.

countercharge Gegenbeschuldigung *f*.

countercheck Gegenprobe *f*.

counterclaim (= *counter-claim*) *s* Gegenanspruch *m*; Gegenforderung *f*; Widerklage *f*; ~, **set-off or cross-demand** Gegenansprüche jeder Art, einschließlich Aufrechnungsansprüche(n); **compulsory** ~ konnexe Widerklage; **permissive** ~ zulässige, nicht konnexe Widerklage.

conunterclaim *v* e–n Gegenanspruch geltend machen; Widerklage erheben.

counterclaimant Widerkläger *m*.

counter-confirmation Gegenbestätigung *f*.

counter-deed geheime beurkundete Gegenerklärung *f*, geheimer Widerruf *m*.

counter demand Gegenforderung *f*.

counter-entry Gegenbuchung *f*.

counter-evidence Gegenbeweismittel *m*.

counter-executed gegengezeichnet.
counterfeit *adj* falsch, gefälscht; ~ **money** Falschgeld; ~ **notes** Falschgeld (*in Scheinen*); ~ **reprint** unberechtigter Nachduck, Raubdruck; ~ **ring** Falschmünzerbande.
counterfeit *s* gefälschter Gegenstand *m*, Fälschung *f*, gefälschte Münze *f*.
counterfeit *v* nachmachen, fälschen, falschmünzen; ~**ing coins** Falschmünzerei; ~**ing documents** Urkundenfälschung; ~**ing seals** Siegelfälschung; ~**ing trade marks** Warenzeichen-Nachahmung.
counterfeiter Falschmünzer *m*; Urkundenfälscher *m*.
counterfeiting Falschmünzerei *f*, Geldfälschung *f*, Ursprungsfälschung *f*, Nachahmung *f*.
counterfoil Kontrollabschnitt *m*, Kupon *m*, Zinsschein *m*, Empfangsquittung *f*, Gepäckschein *m*; ~ **book** Talonbuch; ~ **of cheque** (= *US: check*) Scheckabschnitt; ~ **waybill** Frachtbriefduplikat.
counter-indemnity Garantie für Schadloshaltungshaftung.
counter-inquiry Gegenuntersuchung *f*.
counter-insurance Rückversicherung *f*.
counter-intelligence Spionageabwehr *f*.
counter-letter Rückübertragungsverpflichtung *f*.
countermand *s* Aufhebung *f*, Widerruf , Annulierung *f*, Abbestellung *f*; ~ **of cheque** Schecksperrung.
countermand *v* widerrufen, aufheben, e–e Weisung rückgängig machen; **payment** ~**ed** Zahlung gesperrt; **until** ~**ed** bis auf Widerruf.
countermark Kontrollzeichen *n*, Zunftzeichen *n*.
counter-memorial Gegendenkschrift *f*.
counter-motion Gegenantrag *m*.
counter-notice Widerspruch (*gegen Kündigung*), Gegenerklärung *f*.
counter-offer Gegenangebot *n*.
counterorder Abbestellung *f*, Stornierung *f*.
counterpart Gegenstück *n*, Ausfertigung *f e–r Originalurkunde*; ~ **account** Gegenkonto; ~ **writ** (*weitere*) Ausfertigung e–r Klageverfügung (*vgl writ*); **in multiple** ~**s** in mehrfacher Ausfertigung.
counter-plea Gegeneinwand *m*, Replik *f*.
counter-proposal Gegenvorschlag*m*.
counter-purchase Gegenkauf *m*, Tausch *m*.
counter-question Gegenfrage *f*.
counter-remittance Gegendekkung.
counter-rolls Aktienduplikat *n*.
counter-security Gegensicherheit *f*; Rückbürgschaft *f*.
counter-sign *s* Vermerk *m* für die Richtigkeit; Beglaubigungsvermerk *f*; Gegenzeichnung *f*.
countersign *v* gegenzeichnen, mitunterzeichnen.
countersignature Gegenzeichnung *f*, Mitunterschrift *f*.
counterstatement Gegenerklärung *f*.
countersteering Gegensteuern *n*.
countersuit Widerklage.
counter surety Rückbürge *m*.
countertally Talon *m*.
counterterrorism Terrorismusbekämpfung.
countertrade Gegengeschäfte *n*|*pl*, Kompensationsgeschäfte *n*|*pl*.
contervail ausgleichen, kompensieren; *v*|*i* gleichwertig sein.
country Gegend *f*, Gebiet *n*, Landstrich *m*; Land *n*, Staat *m*, Volk *n*, Nation *f*; die Geschworenen *m*, *f*|*pl*; ~ **bank** Provinzbank; ~ **clearing house** Abrechnungsstelle der Provinzbanken; ~ **collection department** Abteilung für Einzelinkasso (*von Schecks*); ~ **of adoption** Wahlheimat; ~ **of consignment** Bestimmungsland; ~ **of origin** Ursprungsland; ~ **of sale** Käuferland; ~ **of shipment** Absenderland; ~ **whence arrived** Herkunftsland; **associated** ~ assoziiertes Land; **custom of the** ~ → *custom*; **foreign** ~ fremdes Land, Ausland, (*jedes Land außer dem UK, e–m abhängigen Gebiet, der Republic of Ireland und Ländern die in § 50 (1)*

Anlage 3 des British Nationality Act aufgeführt sind); **member** ~ → *member,* **native** ~ Heimatland, Heimat, Geburtsland; Vaterland; **"proclaimed"** ~ in *US* Urheberrechtsschutz einbezogenes Land; **recipient** ~ Empfängerstaat; **supplier** ~ Lieferland.

county Grafschaft *f*, Kreis *m*, Bezirk *m*; ~ **affairs** Selbstverwaltungsaufgaben einer Grafschaft; ~ **association** Wehrbezirk der brit Territorialarmee; ~ **at large** Landkreis; ~ **attorney** *US* Staatsanwalt; ~ **board** Kreisverwaltungsamt; ~ **board of equalization** Steuerbewertungsausgleichsamt (*e–r Grafschaft*); ~ **bonds** Schuldverschreibungen einer Grafschaft; Kommunalobligationen; ~ **borough** kreisfreie Stadt (*über 50000 Einw, GB: 1933–1972*) ~ **bridge** größere Brücke (*für die eine Grafschaft zuständig ist*); ~ **business** Selbstverwaltungsangelegenheiten e–r Grafschaft als Gebietskörperschaft; ~ **college** Fortbildungsschule; ~ **commissioner** Leiter der Grafschaftsverwaltung; *US* Friedensrichter; ~ **corporate** kreisfreie Stadt (*als Gebietskörperschaft*); ~ **council** *brit* Kreisrat, Grafschaftsverwaltungsbehörde; ~ **councillor** Mitglied eines Grafschaftsrates, Kreisrat; ~ **debentures** Kommunalschuldverschreibungen; ~ **district** Unterbezirk eines Landkreises *bzw* einer kreisfreien Stadt; ~ **farm bureau** landwirtschaftliche Beratungsstelle; ~ **franchise** aktives Wahlrecht für Kreistags- und Stadtratswahlen; ~ **general fund** Haushaltsmittel einer Grafsch.; ~ **jail** Stadt- *bzw* Kreisgefängnis, Distriktsgefängnis; ~**line** Grenzstreifen zwischen zwei Grafschaften (*mit beiderseitiger Zuständigkeit für Strafsachen*); ~ **of a city** Stadtkreis; **C~ of London** Groß-London (*als Gebietskörperschaft ohne die eigentliche Londoner City*); **C~ of London Sessions** Strafgericht der Grafschaft London; ~ **officers** Kreisbeamte, Kommunalbeamte; ~ **police** Grafschaftspolizei; ~ **powers** gesetzliche Befugnisse e–r Grafschaft; ~ **property** Grafschaftsvermögen; ~ **purpose** Kreisaufgaben; ~ **rate** Grundsteuer (*der Grafschaften*); ~ **road** Ortsverbindungsstraße; ~ **seat** Kreishauptstadt; ~ **site** Verwaltungssitz e–r Grafschaft, Gerichtsort (*e–r Grafschaft*); ~**-town** freie Kreisstadt *durch Privilegien der Krone*, Kreis(haupt)stadt; ~ **warrant** → *warrant*; **administrative** ~ Grafschaft, Landkreis, kreisfreie Stadt (*als Verwaltungseinheit*); **foreign** ~ fremde Grafschaft; **metropolitan** ~ Großstadtbezirk, städt. Regionalverwaltungsbehörde: *z. B. Greater Manchester, nicht: Gross-London*; **non-metropolitan** ~ Grafschaft, Kreis, Bezirk; **parliamentary** ~ Wahlbezirk (*für Parlamentswahlen*); **The Home C~ies** *die London am nächsten gelegenen Grafschaften;*

county court Amtsgericht für Zivilsachen; ~ **actions** Klagen am Amtsgericht; ~ **district** Amtsgerichtsbezirk; **C~ Rules** Prozeßordnung für Amtsgerichte.

coup de grace Gnadenstoß *m*, Gnadenschuß *m*.

couple Paar *n*, Liebespaar *n*; **live-in** ~ zusammenwohnendes Paar.

coupled with an interest *Vertretungsverhältnis* mit eigener Beteiligung des Beauftragten.

coupon Coupon *m*, Kupon *m*, Zinsschein *m*, Gewinnanteilschein *m*; ~ **bond** → *bond* (*1*); ~ **goods** markenpflichtige Waren (*im Krieg*); ~ **interest rate** Zinssatz für Obligationen; ~ **notes** Schuldscheine mit Zinsbogen; ~ **sheet** Couponbogen, Zinsbogen; ~ **teller** Couponkassierer; **dividend** ~ → *dividend*; **interest** ~ → *interest* (*2*); **international reply** ~ → *international*.

course Lauf *m*, Verlauf *m*; Gang *m*, Weg *m*, Kurs *m*; ~ **authorized or required** *naut* der zulässige oder erforderliche Kurs; ~ **of business** der (*übliche*) Geschäftsgang, im normalen geschäftlichen Verkehr; ~ **of**

commerce Handelsverkehr; ~ of employment Arbeitsbereich; Ausübung der Tätigkeit; ~ of justice Lauf der Gerechtigkeit; ~ of law Rechtsgang, Rechtsweg; ~ of procedure Verfahrensgang; ~ of the voyage (übliche) Route; ~ of trade Handelsverkehr.

court Hof *m*, Gericht *n* (*kurz: G bzw ...g; Gerichts = G–s*), Gerichtshof *m*, Gerichtssaal *m*; das erkennende Gericht *n*, Spruchkörper *m* e–s Gerichts, der (die) Richter; ~ **above** höhere Instanz; ~ **adjudication** Aburteilung, gerichtliche Entscheidung; ~ **administrator** Geschäftsstellenleiter d *G–s*; ~**'s agenda** Sitzungsliste; ~ **ambience** *G–s*atmosphäre; ~**-baron** Vasalleng, Patricyrimonial*g*, Hofmarks*g*; ~ **below** untere Instanz, Vorinstanz; ~ **decision** *G–s*entscheidung; ~ **declaration** gerichtliche Feststellung; ~ **escort duty** Vorführdienst; ~ **expert** → *expert*; ~ **fee** → *fee*; ~ **file** → *file*; ~ **for the correction of errors** Revisions*g*; **C~ Funds Office** Oberjustizkasse; ~**-hand** (*gotische*) Kanzleischrift; ~**-house** *G–s*-gebäude; ~ **in bank** Plenar*g*, großer Senat; ~**-lands** Domänenland (*für Eigennutzung des Gutsherrn*); ~**-leet** *hist* jährlicher *G–s*tag, örtliches *G*; ~**-martial** Militär*g*, Kriegs*g*, Stand*g*; **Courts Martial Appeal C~** Berufungskriegs*g*, Berufungswehrstraf*g*; ~ **not of record** Sonder*g*, *G–e unter dem Rang von ordentlichen G–en*; ~ **of admiralty** See*g*; ~ **of Aldermen** Ältestenrat (*City of London*); ~ **of ancient demesne** *hist* G für Inhaber von Königslehen; **C~ of Appeal** Berufungs*g*, Appellations*g*; ~ ~ ~ (*civil division*) *GB Berufungsg in Zivilsachen, Oberlandesg*); ~ ~ ~ (*criminal division*) *GB Berufungsg für Strafsachen; (seit 1968*); ~ **of arbitration** Schieds*g*; ~ **of arbitration of the chamber of commerce** Handelskammer-Schieds*g*; **C~ of Archdeacon** Dekanats*g* (*unterstes Kirchengericht*); **C~ of Arches** *G* des Erzbischofs von Canterbury (*für kirchenrechtliche Berufungen*); **C~ of Assistants** *Staatsrat und Gerichtshof der Kolonie von Massachusetts*; ~ **of assize and nisi prius** turnusmäßig von abgesandten Richtern geleitetes örtliches Geschworenen*g*; ~ **of attachments** unteres Forst*g*; ~ **of audience** oberes Kirchen*g*; ~ **of augmentation** *G* für Stiftungsvermögen; ~ **of bankruptcy** Konkurs*g*, Konkursabteilung des Zentral*g–s GB*; ~ **of brotherhood** „Bruderschaftsgericht", *gemeinsame Hafenbehörde der Cinque Ports qv*; **C~ of Chancery** Chancery-*G*, königliches Kanzlei*g* (*Equity-Recht*); **C~ of chivalry** ritterliches Ehren*g*; (~ **of Civil Appeals** Berufungs*g* in Zivilsachen, *US*; ~**s of civil jurisdiction** Zivil*g–e*; **C~ of Claims** *GB*: Kommission zur Feststellung von Lehensrechten *anläßlich der Krönung; US*: oberstes Bundesverwaltungs*g* (*für Ansprüche gegen die USA*), Verwaltungs*g* (*einzelstaatlich zuständig für Ansprüche gegen die öffentliche Hand*); ~ **of common council** (=) Londoner Stadtrat; **C~ of Common Hall** Zünfte und Stadtratsversammlung in London; **C~ of Common Pleas** *GB*: *hist* oberes Common Law *G*, *Common Bench Gericht bis 1875*; Land*g* (*US einzelstaatlich*); ~ **of competent jurisdiction** zuständiges *G*; ~ **of conscience** billigkeitsrechtliches *G*, *hist* Zivil*g* für Bagatellforderungen; ~ **of conciliation** G als Gütestelle; ~ **of construction** → *construction*; ~ **of convocation** Kirchenratsversammlung; ~**s of criminal jurisdiction** Straf*g–e*; **C~ of Criminal Appeal** Berufungs*g* für Strafsachen, Strafsenat; (*GB, vor 1966*); **C~ of Customs and Patent Appeals** *US* Beschwerde*g* in Zoll- und Patentsachen; **C~ of Customs Appeals** *G* für Berufung in Zollsachen; ~ **of Delegates** oberstes kirchliches Revisions*g GB*; ~ **of equal authority** gleichgeordnetes *G*; ~ **of equity** Equity-*G*,

Billigkeitsg, (*Billigkeitsrechtsprechung*); **C~ of Error** Appellationsg, Revisionsg; **C~ of Exchequer** (=) *höheres Zivilgericht; Finanzgericht (bis 1873)*; **C~ of Faculties** erzbischöfliches G (*für kirchliche Privilegien*); **~ of first instance** G erster Instanz, erstinstanzliches G; **~ of general jurisdiction** ordentliches G; **~ of general quarter sessions of the peace** allg G für Strafsachen; **~ of general sessions** erstinstanzliches G für Strafsachen (*in einigen US-Staaten*); **C~ of Great Sessions** Assiseng *in Wales*; **~ of guestling** Sonderg der Cinque Ports *qv*; **C~ of High Commission** oberstes Kirchendisziplinarg (*bes für Ketzereiverfolgung 1583–1640*); **~ of hono(u)r** Ehreng, Disziplinarg; **C~ of Hustings** Londoner Stadtg; **~ of inquiry** *mil* Untersuchungsg, kriegsrechtliche Voruntersuchung; **~ of justice** *ordentliches G, G–shof*; **C ~ of Justice of the European Communities** Europäischer Gerichtshof; **C~ of Justice Seat** *oberstes* Forstg; **C~ of Justiciary** *scot* Oberstes G für Strafsachen; **C~ of King's (Queen's) Bench** (=) königl Zentralg, London; **~ of last resort** letztinstanzliches G; **~ of law** ordentliches G, G–shof; **~ of limited jurisdiction** G mit beschränkter (*spezieller*) Zuständigkeit; **~ of lodemanage** Seeg (*Cinque Ports*); **C~ of Magistrates and Freeholders** Strafg (*für Sklaven und Freigelassene, South Carolina*); **C~ of (the) Marshalsea** königliches Hofg *für Angehörige des Hofes;* **C~ of Military Appeals** Berufungsg in Wehrsachen; **~ of nisi prius** Zivilg *erstinstanzlich,* Erstg, Tatsacheninstanz; **C~ of Ordinary** Nachlaßg (*US einzelstaatl*); **~ of original jurisdiction** erstinstanzliches G; **C~ of Passage** *Stadtgericht von Liverpool*; **C~ of Peculiars** (=) *engl Kirchengericht*; **C~ of Piepoudre** (= *Piedpoudre* = *Piepowder*) hist Markt- und Messeg *in allen engl Messen und Märkten*; **C~ of Probate** *GB* Nachlaßg (*bis 1857*) *vgl* = *probate court*, **~ of protection** Vormundschaftsg; *C ~ P~: Abteilung des High Court zur Verwaltung des Vermögens von Geisteskranken*; **~ of record** ordentliches G, staatliches G; **~ of referees** G für Streitfälle der Arbeitslosenunterstützung (*GB*), Vorprüfungsausschuß für Privatvorlagen im Parlament; **C~ of Regard** *ein historisches Forstgericht*; **~s of request** *untere Zivilgerichte (GB, jetzt county courts qv)*; **C~ od Review** Rechtsmittelg für Konkursfälle *GB*; **C~ of Session** Oberstes G für Zivilsachen *scot*; **C~ of Sessions** Kriminalg, Strafg (*US einzelstaatlich*); **~ of sewers** Abwässerüberwachungsbehörde; **C~ of Shepway** *oberstes Zivilgericht in den Cinque Ports*; **~s of special jurisdiction** Sonderg–*e*; **~ of special sessions** Sonderg, Einzelfallg; **C~ of Star Chamber** Staatsg–*shof*, Inquisitionsg *in Westminster, bis 1640*; **~ of summary jurisdiction** Amtsg = *magistrates courts qv*; **C~ of Survey** =) *Beschwerdegericht in Seeuntüchtigkeitssachen*; **C~ of the Chief Justice in Eyre** *oberstes Forstg in England* (*bis 1817*); **~ of the clerk of the market** Markt- und Messeg; **C~ of the Constable and Marshal** = *court of chivalry qv*; **~ of the coroner** → *coroner*; **C~ of the Counties Palatine** Pfalzgrafschaftsg; **~ of the Earl Marshal** *Militärg*; **C~ of the Lord High Admiral** Admiralitätsg; **C~ of (the) Lord High Steward** (=) *Gericht für Hochverratsfälle des Adels* (*Oberhaus*); **C~ of the Lord High Steward of the King's Household** Hofg *für Strafsachen*; **C~ of the Lord High Steward of the Universities** Sonderg *für Strafsachen in Universitäten* (*Oxford, Cambridge*); **C~ of the Lord Justices** *Appellationsinstanz in Equity-Sachen*; **C~ of the Official Principal** = *Court of Arches qv*; **C~ of the Steward and Marshal** Bezirksgericht (*des königlichen Hofes*) *für Zivilsachen*; ~ **of the steward of the king's household** *Hofgericht für Strafsachen*; **C~s of the United States** Bundes*g–e* der USA; **C~s of the Universities** → *university*; ~ **of trade** Gewerbe*g*; ~ **of ultimate resort** *G* letzter Instanz; **~s of Westminster Hall** die obersten *königl G–e* von England; ~ **practice** Praxis der *G–e*, *G–s*verfahren, *G–s*ordnung; ~ **procedure** *G–s*verfahren; **~records** *G-s-*akten; ~ **rolls** grundherrschaftliche Urkunden, Lehenskataster; ~ **room** *G–s*saal, Sitzungssaal; ~ ~ *lawyer*: *Prozeßanwalt*; ~ **rules** gerichtliche Verfahrensvorschriften, Prozeßordnung; ~ **ruling** gerichtliche Verfügung, *G–s*entscheidung; ~ **system** *G–s*verfassung, *G–s*system; **~usher** *G–s*diener; **Admiralty C~** → *admiralty*; **administrative** ~ Verwaltungs*g*; **appellate** ~ Berufungs*g*, Rechtsmittelinstanz; **base** ~ niederes *G* (*nicht zu den ordentl Gerichten gehörend*); **borough** ~ Stadt*g bis 1974*; **Central Criminal C~** (= *Old Bailey*) Zentralstraf*g* von Groß-London; **circuit** ~ *US* erstinstanzliches *G für mehrere Bezirke*; **circuit ~ of appeals** *US*, Bundesberufungs*g*; **City of London C~** → *city*; **civil** ~ Zivil*g*, ordentliches *G*; **closed** ~ unter Ausschluß der Öffentlichkeit tagendes *G*; **Commercial C~** Kammer für Handelssachen; **common law ~s** → *Common Law*; **Companies C~** Kammer für Handelssachen, Abt. Kapitalgesellschaften (*beim High Court*); **competent** ~ zuständiges *G*; **consistory** ~ Konsistorial*g*, unteres Kirchen*g*, Nachlaß*g*; **constitutional** ~ Verfassungs*g*, ordentliches (*durch die Verfassung vorgesehenes*) *G*; **co-ordinate** ~ gleichrangiges *G*; **county** ~ → *county court*; **criminal** ~ Straf*g*, Strafkammer; **Crown C~** →*crown*; **customary ~-baron** Patrimonial*g* für Zinslehen; **customs** ~ → *customs*; **de facto** ~ faktisch existierendes *G*; **diocesan** ~ Diözesan*g*; **District C~** Bezirks*g*; *US* Bundesgericht *erster Instanz*; **divided** ~ Mehrheitsentscheidung e–s *G–s*; **divisional** ~ Berufung *bzw* Beschwerdekammer; **divorce county** ~ Amts*g mit Zuständigkeit* für unstreitige Scheidungen; **domestic** ~ innerstaatliches *G*; Familien*g*; **equity** ~ Equity-*G*, *G–s*abteilung für billigkeitsrechtliche Sachen; **European C~ of Human Rights** Europäischer *G–s*hof für Menschenrechte; **examining** ~ Voruntersuchungs*g*; **family** ~ Familien*g*, Familien*g-s*abteilung; **federal** ~ Bundes*g–e*; **Federal District C~** Bundesbezirks*g* (*unteres Bundesgericht, US*); **foreign** ~ ausländ. *G bzw G e–s anderen US-Bundesstaats*; **freeholder's ~-baron** *hist* Patrimonial*g* für Freisassen; **full** ~ Plenar*g*, Vollsitzung aller Richter, Kammersitzung, Senatssitzung; **High ~ of Admiralty** Prisen*g*, Seegerichtshof; **High C~ of Judiciary** *scot* Oberstes *G* für Strafsachen; **High C~ (of Justice)** (=) *Zentralzivilgericht in London seit 1873*; **High C~ of Parliament** → *high*; **honour ~s** Herrschaftsgerichte; **industrial** ~ Schieds*g* für Streitigkeiten der Tarifpartner; **inferior** ~ unteres *G* = *Amtsgericht*, Instanz*g*; **instance** ~ unteres Prozeß*g*; **intermediate ~s** *etwa*: Land*g–e*; *G–e* mittlerer Instanz; **International C~ of Justice** Internationaler Gerichtshof *seit 1946*; **juvenile** ~ Amtsgericht für Jugendangelegenheiten; **labo(u)r** ~ Arbeits*g*; **Last C~** *Gericht in den Marschen von Kent*; **law** ~ *G–s*hof; **leave of** ~ → *leave;* **legislative ~s** gesetzlich geschaffene *G-e*; **limited** ~ *G* mit beschränkter Zuständigkeit; **local** ~ Amts*g*, örtliches *G*, einzelstaatliches *G*; **magistrates'** (*US*: *magistrate's ~ s*) ~ Amts*g für kleinere Strafsachen, teilw Zivilsachen wg Unterhalts, Bagatellansprüchen u. Ordnungswidrigkeiten*; **Mayor's and City of London C~** → *mayor*; **martial** ~ Kriegs*g*; **maritime** ~

→ *maritime;* **metropolitan ~s** → *metropolitan*; **middle-tier** ~ G mittlerer Zuständigkeit; **national** ~ innerstaatl G; **naval** ~ → *navigation*; **newly assembled** ~ G (*bzw Senat, Kammer*) in neuer Besetzung; **open** ~ öffentliche G–s-verhandlung; **ordinary** ~ ordentliches G; **original** ~ Erstg; **orphan's** ~ Vormundschaftsg und Nachlaßg (*in einigen Staaten der USA*); **parish** ~ Amtsg, Grafschaftsg (*Louisiana*); **Permanent C~ of Arbitration** Haager Schiedsgerichtshof; **Permanent C~ of International Justice** der Ständige Internationale Gerichtshof; *Vorläufer des International Court of Justice*; **plenary** ~ Plenarsitzung des G–s; Vereinigte Senate; **police** ~ Polizeig; Schnellg; **prefect's** NachlaßG (*New Mexico*); **pretorial** ~ Strafg (*Maryland, US*); **probate** ~ Nachlaßgg; **provincial** ~ Diözösang (*York, Canterbury*); **provisional** ~ vorläufiges G, Sonderg; **recess of the ~s** → *recess*; **regularly constitued** ~ ordnungsgemäß besetztes G; **requesting** ~ das ersuchende G; **reviewing** ~ Rechtsmittelgericht, Rechtsmittelinstanz; **secret** ~ Femeg; **sheriff's** ~ Londoner Stadtg *vor 1920, scot* Amtsg; **small debts ~s** → *small*; **sole ~ of competence** ausschließl zuständige G; **spiritual** ~ geistliches G, Kircheng; **standing civilian ~s** Militärg–*e* für Zivilsachen im Ausland *GB 1976*; **superior** ~ *GB*: oberes G; Obere G–*e*: *House of Lords, Court of Appeal, High Court, Crown Courts, Courts-Martial Appeal Court, Restrictive Practices Court*; *US*: (*1*) oberstes einzelstaatliches G, (*2*) Landg; **Supreme C~** Oberster Gerichtshof; Oberstes Bundesg *von USA*; oberstes *einzelstaatliches* G; höheres G; GB brit Zentralgerichtshof (*Court of Appeal, High Court of Justice, Crown Court*); **Supreme C~ of Errors** Revisionsg, *Kassationsgericht in Connecticut*; **Supreme ~ (of Judicature)** *Zentralgericht für England und Wales bestehend aus High Court of Justice, Crown Court und Court of Appeals*; **supreme ~ practice** höchstrichterliche Rechtssprechung; **supreme judicial** ~ oberstes (*einzelstaatliches*) G; **surrogate's** ~ Vormundschafts- und Nachlaßg; **tax** ~ Finanzg; **territorial ~s** → *territorial*; **the ~ is in session** die Sitzung ist eröffnet; **to appear in** ~ vor G erscheinen; **to go to** ~ vor G gehen, klagen; **to the satisfaction of the** ~ zur Überzeugung des Gerichts; **University ~s** → *university*.

courtesy Höflichkeit *f*, Entgegenkommen *n*, Courtoisie; **estate by the** ~ (= *right of* ~) Nießbrauchsrecht des Witwers am Grundvermögen der verstorbenen Ehefrau; **voluntary** ~ Gefälligkeit.

courtyard Hof *m*, Hofraum *m*.

cousin Cousin *m*, Cousine *f* (= *Kusine*), Vetter *m*, Base *f*, Geschwisterkind *n*; Adelsgenosse *m*, Euer Lieb-den (*Anrede königlicher Häupter oder des Hochadels*); **~-german** (= *first* ~ *qv*); Stammesverwandter; **country ~s** weitläufige Verwandte aus der Provinz; **first** ~ Vetter, Base, Cousin, Cousine (= *Kusine*) ersten Grades (*Kind e–s Onkels bzw e–r Tante*); **first ~ once removed** *Kind e–s first cousin qv*, Enkel eines Onkels bzw e–r Tante; **half ~s** entfernte Vettern und Basen (*umfaßt: first ~s once removed und second ~s qv*); **quarter ~s** entfernte Vettern 2. Grades (*Enkel e–s Großonkels*).

covenable angenehm, geeignet.

covenant *s* förmliches rechtsverbindl Versprechen *n*; Nebenvereinbarung *f*, Gewährleistungsversprechen *n*, Klausel *f* e–s gesiegelten Vertrages; ~ **against assignment** vertragliches Abtretungsverbot; ~ **against competition** vertragliches Wettbewerbsverbot; ~ **against encumbrances** Gewährleistung für Lastenfreiheit; ~ **against subletting** vertragliches Verbot der Untervermietung *bzw* -verpachtung; ~ **appurtenant** an Grundstück gebundene Verpflichtung; ~ **for further assurance** *Verpflichtung zur Abgabe aller (weiteren) Erklärungen, die zum vollständigen Eigentumsübergang und zur Lastenfreistellung notwendig sind*; ~ **for quiet enjoyment** Gewährleistung ungestörter Besitzausübung, vertragl Rechtsmängelhaftung: *vertragliche Pflicht des Veräußerers, Ansprüche Dritter auf den übertragenen Grundbesitz abzuwehren*; ~ **for securing payment or repayment of money** gesiegelte Urkunde zur Sicherung einer Geldforderung; ~ **for title** Rechtsmängelgewährleistung (*des Grundstücksverkäufers*); ~ **in gross** schuldrechtliche Nebenverpflichtung; ~ **in law** *auslegungsmäßig* festgestellte Verpflichtung; ~ **in restraint of trade** wettbewerbsbeschränkende Vereinbarung; ~ **negative in substance** Unterlassungsverpflichtung; ~ **not to compete** vertragl Wettbewerbsverbot; **not to sue** vertraglicher Klageverzicht; ~ **not to use premises for trade** Verpflichtung, gewerbliche Nutzung zu unterlassen; ~ **of marriage** Ehevertrag; Ehebund, Eheschließung; ~ **of nonclaim** Anspruchsverzicht (*Erklärung des Veräußerers, für sich und seine Erben und sonstige Rechtsnachfolger auf jegliche Ansprüche aus dem veräußerten Grundstück für immer zu verzichten*); ~ **of right to convey** verbindliche Erklärung der Veräußerungsbefugnis; ~ **of seisin** *verbindliche Erklärung, daß dem Veräußerer das zu übertragende Recht zusteht*, Garantie der Veräußerungsbefugnis; ~ **of warranty** Rechtsmängelgarantie des Verpächters (*daß die Ausübung des Pachtrechts nicht durch den Eigentümer beeinträchtigt wird*); **"~s performed"** „Verpflichtungen erfüllt", *bestreitende Einlassung auf eine Klage aus gesiegeltem Vertrag*; **~s running with the land** (*dinglich wirkende*) Rechte und Pflichten des jeweiligen Grundstücksbesitzers; ~ **to convey** Auflassungsvereinbarung, Verpflichtung zur Übertragung eines langfristigen Nutzungsrechtes; ~ **to honor guaranty** (*US*) Garantieübernahmeverpflichtung des Vertragshändlers ggüber dem Lieferanten; ~ **to indemnity** Schadloshaltungsverpflichtung; ~ **to insure** Vertragspflicht zur Aufrechterhaltung einer (Grundstücks)versicherung; ~ **to renew** Vertragsverlängerungsoption; ~ **to repair** = *repairing ~ qv*; **~s to run with the land** = *~s running with the land qv*; ~ **to stand seised** *hist* treuhänderische Übertragung von Grundstücken (*auf Ehefrau, Verwandte etc*); **action of** ~ Klage aus einem gesiegelten Vertrag; **affirmative** ~ (*1*) Anerkennung der Vertragsangaben; (*2*) Verpflichtung zu zukünftiger Leistung; **auxiliary** ~ Nebenpflicht; **collateral** ~ Nebenpflicht; **concurrent** ~ wechselseitig zu erfüllende Verpflichtung; **continuing** ~ Dauerverpflichtung; **declaratory** ~ Anerkennung der Einschränkung (*oder Weisungsgebundenheit*) von Nutzungen; **dependent** ~ (*von e–r Vorleistung oder Bedingung*) abhängige Verpflichtung; **disjunctive ~s** Wahlschuldverpflichtungen, Ersetzungsbefugnis des Gläubigers; **express** ~ ausdrückliche Verpflichtung *aus e–m gesiegelten Vertrag*; **full ~s** volle Rechtsmängelgewährleistung des Grundstücksveräußerers; **full ~ deed** Grundstücksübertragungsurkunde (*mit voller Gewährleistung des Veräußerers*); **full-repairing** ~ Verpflichtung des Mieters (Pächters), alle Instandhaltungsarbeiten zu übernehmen; **general** ~ allgemein schuldrechtliche Verpflichtung; **implied** ~ *in e–m gesiegelten Vertrag* stillschweigend enthaltene Verpflichtung; Rechtsmängelgewährleistung (*des Grundstücksverkäufers*); **independent** ~ abstrakte Verpflichtung; **inherent** ~ wesentliche Vertragspflicht; **intransitive** ~ nicht übertragbare Verpflichtung (*nur dem Berechtigten selbst gegenüber* *zu erfüllen*); **joint** ~ gemeinsame Verpflichtung; **landlord's** ~ Vermieter (Verpächter)verpflichtung; **mutual** ~**s** wechselseitige Verpflichtungen; **negative** ~ Unterlassungsverpflichtung; **obligatory** ~ eigenverbindliche Verpflichtung; **onerous** ~**s** Lastenübernahme durch den Pächter/Mieter; **particular** ~ besondere Vereinbarung; **personal** ~ schuldrechtliche Verpflichtung; persönlich zu erfüllende Verpflichtung; **principal** ~ Hauptpflicht; **real** ~ mit dem Grundstück verbundene Verpflichtung mit Wirkung (*für und gegen die betr Rechtsnachfolger*); **repairing** ~ Nebenpflicht des Mieters/Pächters zu Instandsetzungen u. Vornahme von Schönheitsreparaturen; **restrictive** ~ einschränkende Vereinbarung; nachbarliche Nutzungsbeschränkungen (*des jeweiligen Besitzers*); Wettbewerbsklausel nach Ende des Arbeitsverhältnisses; **separate** ~ = *several* ~ *qv*; **several** ~**s** Einzelverpflichtungen Mehrerer (*nicht samtverbindlich*); **specific** ~ Verpflichtung mit dinglicher Wirkung bzgl e–s Einzelgrundstücks; **transitive** ~ auf den Rechtsnachfolger übergehende Verpflichtung; **usual** ~**s** die üblichen Mieter/Pächterverpflichtungen; **vendor's** ~**s for title** → *vendor*, **writ of** ~ → *writ*.

covenant *v* vereinbaren, sich (förmlich) verpflichten, zusichern; ~ **jointly and severally** sich samtverbindlich verpflichten; ~**ed benefit** *ins* vertragsmäßiger Versicherungsgewinn.

covenantee der (die) *vertraglich* Berechtigte.

covenanter = *covenantor qv*.

covenantor der (die) *vertraglich Verpflichtete*.

cover *s* Umschlag *m*; Deckung *f*; Sicherheit *f*, Abschirmung *f*, Versicherungsschutz *m*; Vorwand *m*, Deckmantel *m*; ~ **address** Deckadresse; ~ **note** vorläufige Deckungszusage; ~ **of assurance** Deckungskapital; ~ **ratio** Deckungsverhältnis (*Währung*); **additional** ~ weitere Deckung, Nachschuß; **cash** ~ Bardeckung, Barsicherheit; **for want of** ~ mangels Deckung; **gold** ~ → *gold*; **provisional** ~ vorläufige Deckungszusage.

cover *v* decken, erfassen, umfassen, sich erstrecken auf; (*for absent colleagues*) vertreten; ~ **a bill** Deckung für e–n Wechsel anschaffen; ~**ed job** pflichtversicherte Tätigkeit.

coverage Deckung *f*, Deckungssumme *f*, Versicherungsschutz *m*; Gesetzesbereich *m*; Verbreitung *f*, Erfassung *f*; ~ **for bad risks** Deckung für schlechte Risiken; **comprehensive** ~ allg. Fahrzeugschadensdeckung außer Unfall; **full** ~ volle Risikoübernahme, volle Deckung; **restricted** ~ eingeschränkte Versicherung.

covering Verschluß *m*, Verpackung *f*, Hülle *f*, Futteral *n*, Gefäß *n*, Einwickelpapier *n*, Mantel *m*, Umschlag *m*, Deckung *f*, Glasur *f*.

covering | agreement Mantelvertrag; ~ **claim** Deckungsforderung; ~ **deed** Sicherungsvertrag (*bei Wertpapieremissionen*); ~ **-in process** Einzahlungsanweisungsverfahren; ~ **letter** → *letter*, ~ **purchase** Deckungskauf; ~ **warrant** Einzahlungsanordnung.

coverture Ehestand der Frau.

cover-up *pol* Deckungsmanöver *n*.

covin geheimes Einverständnis *n*, Kollusion *f*, betrügerische Verabredung *f*.

covinous betrügerisch, auf Grund betrügerischer Absprache.

crack *v/t* aufbrechen, entschlüsseln.

crackdown scharfes Durchgreifen *n*.

craft Handwerk *n*, Beruf *m*, Gewerbe *n*; ~ **fraternity** Handwerksinnung; **guild** Innung, Gilde; ~ **union** Berufsgewerkschaft, Gewerkschaft einer Fachrichtung; **small** ~ Kleinhandwerk, Kleingewerbe.

craftsman Gewerbetreibender *m*, Handwerker *m*.

crash Zusammenstoß *m*; Absturz *m*; (*Börsen*)Krach *m*; Zusammenbruch

m; ~ **barriers** Leitplanken; Absperrgitter; ~ **program** Sofortprogramm, Notprogramm.
crate Lattenkiste *f*, Lattenverschlag *m*.
crating Verpackung *f* in Kisten.
crave ersehnen, erflehen, dringend erbitten; ~ **leave to refer** bitten, Bezug nehmen zu dürfen.
create schaffen, schöpferisch tätig sein, hervorbringen; erzeugen, verursachen; gründen, begründen.
creation Gründung *f*, Begründung *f*, Schaffung *f*, Erschaffung *f*, Erhebung *f*, Errichtung *f*; ~ **of currency** Geldschöpfung; ~ **of new jobs** Arbeitsplatzbeschaffung.
creativeness schöpferische Kraft *f*, Produktivität *f*.
credence Glaube *m*; Beglaubigung *f*, **letters of** ~ Beglaubigungsschreiben *n*; **to give** ~ **to the witness** dem Zeugen Glauben schenken.
credentials Beglaubigungsschreiben *n*, Empfehlungsschreiben *n*; Zeugnisse *n*|*pl*; Ausweispapiere *n*|*pl*; **authorized** ~ Sonderausweis, berichtigte Beglaubigungspapiere.
credible glaubwürdig, glaubhaft.
credibility Glaubwürdigkeit *f*; ~ **gap** Glaubwürdigkeitslücke.
credit Kredit *m* (= *K bzw* ... *k*), Gutschrift *f*, Habenseite *f*, Akkreditiv *n*; guter Ruf *m*, Ansehen *n*, Verdienst *m*, Steuergutschrift *f*; ~ **acceptance** *K*zusage; ~ **accommodation** Zurverfügungstellung von *K*; ~ **advice** Gutschriftanzeige; ~ **against tax** Steuerfreibetrag; ~ **agency** Auskunftei; ~ **agreement** *K*vereinbarung, *K*abkommen; ~ **analysis** *K*prüfung; ~ **and debit** Soll und Haben; ~ **applicant** *K*antragsteller; ~ **arrangement** *K*abkommen; ~ **balance** → *balance*; ~ **bank** *K*bank; *K*anstalt; ~ **blotter** *exch* Gutschriftskladde; ~ **bureau** *K*auskunftei; ~ **brokerage** *K*vermittlung; ~ **buying** *K*kauf; ~ **by way of guarantee** Aval*k*; ~ **capacity** *K*fähigkeit; ~ **card** *K*karte; ~ **cardholder** *K*kartenbesitzer; ~ **commitment** *K*engagement; ~ **control** → *control*; ~ **crunch** *K*klemme; ~ **default register** Schuldnerliste; ~ **department** *K*abteilung; ~ **entry** Habenbuchung; ~ **examiner** *K*prüfer; ~ **expansion** *K*ausweitung; ~ **files** Unterlagen über die *K*würdigkeit; ~ **foncier** Boden*k*; ~ **for dependents** Steuerfreibetrag für Familienangehörige; ~ **guarantee** *K*garantie, *K*bürgschaft; ~ **in cash** Bar*k*; ~ **on current account** Kontokorrent*k*; ~ **information** *K*auskunft; ~ **instrument** *K*urkunde; ~ **insurance** *K*versicherung; ~ **interest** → *interest* (*2*); ~ **investigation** Untersuchung der *K*fähigkeit; ~ **investigator** *K*prüfungsermittler; ~ **item** Habenposten, Gutschriftposten; ~ **limit** *K*grenze, *K*limit; ~ **line** *K*grenze, *K*plafonds; ~ **loss** *K*verlust; ~ **margin** *K*grenze; ~ **memos** (= *memorandum*) Gutschriftzettel, Gutschein; ~ **money** *K*geld, Buchgeld; ~ **note** Gutschriftanzeige; ~ **on goods** Waren*k*; ~ **on joint account** Meta*k*; ~ **on landed property** Real*k*, Boden*k*, Immobilien*k*;~ **overdrawing** *K*überschreitung, *K*überziehung; ~ **period** Laufzeit e–s *K–s*, Zahlungsziel, Ziel; ~ **policy** *K*politik; ~ **rate** *K*zins; ~ **rating** Beurteilung der *K*fähigkeit; Bonitätseinstufung; ~ **reference agency** *K*auskunftsbüro; ~ **report** → *report*; **resources** → *resource*; ~ **restriction** *K*beschränkung; *K*restriktion; ~ **risk** *K*risiko; ~ **sale** Kauf auf *K*, Abzahlungskauf; ~-**sale agreement** Abzahlungsvertrag; ~ **scoring** *K*würdigkeitsbeurteilung; ~ **side** Habenseite; ~ **slip** Einzahlungsbeleg; ~ **squeeze** *K*verknappung; *K*beschränkung; ~ **standards** Bonitätsanforderungen; ~ **standing** *K*würdigkeit (*bei sofortigem Eigentumsübergang*); ~ **statement** ~ *K*auskunft; ~ **status** *K*würdigkeit; ~ **stringency** *K*knappheit; ~ **supply** *K*beschaffung; ~ **system** *K*wesen; ~ **terms** *K*bedingungen nach: *K*bedingun-

gen, Zahlungsbedingungen (*beim Lieferantenkredit*); ~ **token** *K*Karte bzw *K*wertzeichen; ~ **transfer** Banküberweisung; ~ **under caption** rubrizierter *K*; ~**union** Sparverein, *K*genossenschaft; **acceptance** ~ → *acceptance*; ~ **agricultural** ~ Agrar*k*; **anticipatory** ~ Vorfinanzierungs*k*; **availability of** ~ Verfügbarkeit von *K*; **availment of** ~ Inanspruchnahme von *K*; **back-to-back** ~ Gegenakkreditiv; konzerninterner Gegen*k*; **bank** ~ Bank*k*; **blank** ~ Blanko*k*; **book** ~ Buch*k*; **clean** ~ Wechselkreditkonto für reine Wechsel (*ohne Dokumente*); reines Akkreditiv; **collateral** ~ Lombard*k*; **commercial** ~ kurzfristiger Handels*k*, Waren*k*; **commercial acceptance** ~ Warenrembours*k*; **confirmed** ~ bestätigter Bank*k*; **consumer** ~ Kunden*k*; **countervailing** ~ der durch Gegen*k* gedeckte (*erste*) *K*; **deferred** ~**s to income** → *deferred*; **depreciated** ~ **money** wertverringertes *K*geld; **documentary** ~ Dokumenten*k*, Real*k*, Rembours*k*; **draft** ~ Rembours*k*; **extended** ~ prolongierter *K*; **extension of** ~ *K*gewährung, *K*verlängerung; **extortionate** ~ ausbeuterischer *K*; **fixed-sum** ~ Darlehen; **freezing of** ~**s** → *freezing*; **fresh** ~ neuer *K*; **general** ~ allgemeiner Leumund; **global** ~ Rahmen*k*, **guarantee** Aval*k*; **guaranteed** ~ Bürgschafts*k*; **imperilling of a person's** ~ **standing** *K*gefährdung; **industrial** ~ Industrie*k*; **instalment** ~ Teilzahlungs*k*, Abzahlungs*k*; **interim** ~ Zwischen*k*, Überbrückungs*k*; **intermediate** ~ mittelfristiger *K*, Zwischen*k*; **irrevocable** ~**s** unwiderrufliche Akkreditivstellung; **joint** ~ Konsortial*k*; **land** ~ Boden*k*; **letter of** ~ → *letter of credit*; **limit of** ~ *K*grenze; **line of** ~ *K*linie; **long** ~ langfristiger *K*; **long-term** ~ langfristiger *K*; **mutual** ~**s** gegenseitige Guthaben, gegenseitige Gutschriften; **notice of** ~ *K*kündigung; **open** ~ offener *K*, Kontokorrent*k*; **open account** ~ Buch*k*; **personal** ~ Personal*k*; **pre-finance** ~ Vorfinanzierungs*k*; **pre shipment** ~ (Import)Vorfinanzierungs*k*; **public** ~ öffentliches Ansehen; **redemption of** ~ Rückführung e–s *K–s*; **redemption of** ~ **money** Abzahlung e–s *K–s*; **restricted-use** ~ zweckbestimmter *K*; **retail** ~ Einzelhandels*k*; **revolving** ~ Revolving*k*; **running account** ~ Kontokorrent*k*; **secondary** ~ Gegenakkreditiv; **service** ~ kreditierte Dienstleistung; **short-term** ~ kurzfristiger *K*, Lieferanten*k*; **stand-by** ~ Abruf*k*, Überbrückungs*k*; Bereitschafts*k*; **starting** ~ Anlauf*k*; **storage** ~ *K* auf eingelagerte Ware; **store** ~ Anschreibenlassen, *K* beim Kaufmann; **supplemental** ~ Nachtrags*k*; **supplier** ~ Lieferanten*k* (*d. Exporteurs*); **temporary** ~ Zwischen*k*; **to extend** ~**s** Kredit(e) einräumen; **trade** ~ Lieferanten*k*; Finanzierung von Handelsgeschäften, Handels*k*; **transferable** ~ übertragbares Akkreditiv; **unrestricted-use** ~ Dispositions*k*; **unused** ~ nicht beanspruchter *K*; **volume of** ~ *K*volumen; **wholesale** ~ Großhandels*k*; **worthy of** ~ *k*würdig.

credit *v/t* gutbringen, gutschreiben; **to be** ~ **ed against** angerechnet werden auf.

creditable kreditwürdig, glaubhaft, respektabel.

creditor Gläubiger *m* (= *Gl bzw gl*); ~ **at large** gewöhnlicher (*nicht titulierter, ungesicherter*) *Gl*; ~ **beneficiary** der anspruchsberechtigte Drittbegünstigte; ~ **'s bill** Klage der Nachlaß*gl* auf Rechnungslegung und Verteilung des Nachlasses *GB*; Zwangsvollstreckungsantrag; Klage auf abgesonderte Befriedigung; ~ **by endorsement** Giro*gl*, *Gl* durch Indossament; ~**s'committee** *Gl*ausschuß; ~ **in (the) bankruptcy** Konkurs*gl*; ~**s' ledger** Kreditorenbuch; ~ **limit** *IMF* Begrenzung der Verpflichtungen für die *Gl*länder, „Gläubigerlimit"; **~'s meeting** *Gl*versammlung; **~ of the estate** Nachlaß*gl*; **~s' petition** Konkurseröffnungsantrag der *Gl*; **~s ranking equally** gleichrangige *Gl*; **~'s resolutions** Beschlüsse der *Gl*versammlung; *special ~ ~: Glbeschluß mit einfacher Mehrheit nach Köpfen und ¾ nach Forderung*; **~s' voluntary winding up** außergerichtliche Gesellschaftsliquidation durch die *Gl*; **~s' voting rights** *Gl*stimmberechtigung; **antecedent ~** bereits (*vor e–r verschleierten Vermögensverfügung des Schuldners*) vorhandener Gl; **appeal by ~s** *Gl*beschwerde; **arrangement with ~s** *Gl*vergleich; **attaching ~** Arrest*gl*, Pfändungs*gl*, Vollstreckungs*gl*; **availability of property for ~s** Zugriffsmöglichkeit für *Gl*; **catholic** *scot* dinglich gesicherter *Gl*; **certificate ~** Inhaber e–s kommunalen Schuldzertifikats; **claims by ~** *Gl*ansprüche; **conditional ~** *Gl* e–r Anwartschaft; **confidential ~** geheimer Kreditgeber, *jmd, der e–m Zahlungsunfähigen Kredit verschafft*; **double ~** doppelt gesicherter *Gl*; **execution ~** Vollstreckungs*gl*; **fraudulent ~** unredlicher *Gl*, *der im Konkursverfahren betrügerische Angaben macht*; **general ~** ungesicherter *Gl*, allgemeiner Konkurs*gl*; **joint ~s** Gesamt*gl*; **joint and several ~** → *joint and several*; **judgment ~** Vollstreckungs*gl*; **junior ~** nachrangiger *Gl*; **lien ~** dinglich gesicherter *Gl*, Pfand*gl*; **meeting of ~s** → *meeting*; **mortgage ~** → *mortgage*; **non-privileged ~ of a bankrupt** nicht bevorrechtigter Konkurs*gl*; **ordinary ~** gewöhnl (Konkurs)*Gl*; **petitioning ~s** betreibende *Gl*, antragstellende *Gl*; **preferential ~** bevorrechtigter *Gl*; **preferred ~** bevorrechtigter *Gl*; **principal ~** Haupt*gl*; **priority of ~s** Rang der *Gl*, *Gl*vorrang; **privileged ~** bevorrechtigter *Gl*; **secondary ~** zweitrangiger *Gl*; **secured ~** dinglich gesicherter *Gl*; absonderungsberechtigter *Gl*; **simple contract ~** *Gl* aus einem ungesiegelten Vertrag, gewöhnlicher (*nicht bevorrechtigter*) *Gl*; **single ~** (*nur*) einfach gesicherter *Gl*; **speciality ~** *Gl* aus e–m gesiegelten Vertrag, *Gl* e–r verbrieften Schuld; **subsequent ~** nachträglich gesicherter *Gl*; **sundry ~s** diverse *Gl*; **trade ~** Lieferantenkreditgeber; **~s** Lieferanten, Warengläubiger, Liefer- und Leistungsverbindlichkeiten; **unsecured ~** nicht gesicherter *Gl*.

creditrix Gläubigerin *f*.

creditworthiness Kreditwürdigkeit *f*.

crew Gruppe *f*, Kolonne *f*, Belegschaft *f*, Besatzung *f*, Mannschaft *f*, Dienstpersonal *n*; **~ list** Mannschaftsliste, Musterrolle.

crier Gerichtswachtmeister *m*, *der die Sachen aufruft*; Ausrufer *m*, Marktschreier *m*; **common ~** öffentl Versteigerer.

crime strafbare Handlung *f*, Straftat *f*, Verbrechen *n*, Vergehen *n*; **~s admitting of accessories** Straftaten, bei denen Beihilfe oder Begünstigung möglich ist; **~ against humanity** Verbrechen gegen die Menschlichkeit; **~ against nature** abartige Sexualpraktiken, bes. Sodomie; **~ against property** Vermögensdelikt; **~ against the other** Ehegattenstraftat; **~ busting** Verbrechensbekämpfung; **~ of basic intent** *Straftatbestand, bei dem nur allgemeiner Vorsatz bewiesen werden muß*; **~ of omission** Straftat durch Unterlassen; **~ of specific intent** *Straftatbestand, bei dem der Vorsatz alle Tatmerkmale umfassen muß*; **~ of strict liability** objektive Straftat (*ohne Schuldnachweis*); **~ of violence** Gewaltverbrechen; **~ prevention** Generalprävention, Verbrechensverhütung; **~ stoppers program** *etwa*: „Aktenzeichen unbekannt"; **~ victims compensation statute** Opferentschädigungsgesetz; **abatement of ~** Begünstigung; **abominable ~** widernatürliche Unzucht; **accomplished** ~ vollendete Tat; **attempted** ~ Versuch e–r Straftat; **blood** ~**s** Gewaltverbrechen, *Verbrechen mit Blutvergießen*, Mord und Totschlag; Terroristenmorde; **capital** ~ Kapitalverbrechen, mit Todesstrafe bedrohtes Verbrechen; **commission of a** ~ Begehung e–r Straftat; **common law** ~ (*crimen per se*) absolut strafbare Handlung (*auch ohne ausdrückliche Strafvorschrift strafbar*); **constructive** ~ *Straftatbestand auf Grund von Analogie;* **continuous** (= *continuing*) ~ Dauerstraftat; **extraterritorial** ~ Auslandsstraftat; **failure to consummate** ~ Nichtvollendung der Tat; **forcible** ~ Gewaltverbrechen; **high** ~**s** schwere Vergehen (*ohne als felonies zu gelten*); **inchoate** ~ Straftat im Versuchsstadium bzw als Anstiftung; **infamous** ~ ehrenrührige Straftat, Verbrechen mit Verlust der bürgerlichen Ehrenrechte; **major** ~ Verbrechen, schwere Straftat; **minor** ~ Vergehen; **notable** ~ schwere Straftat; **quasi** ~ Ordnungswidrigkeit; **serious** ~ Schwerkriminalität; **statutory** ~ gesetzlich normierte Straftat; **street** ~ Straßenkriminalität, auf offener Straße begangene Verbrechen; **terminated** ~ beendete Tat; **to detect a** ~ e–e Straftat aufdecken; **violent** ~ Gewaltverbrechen.

criminal *s* Täter *m*, Straftäter *m*, Verbrecher *m*; **big-time** ~ berüchtigter Verbrecher; **career** ~ Berufsverbrecher; **dangerous** ~ gemeingefährlicher Verbrecher; **habitual** ~ Gewohnheitsverbrecher; **professional** ~ Berufsverbrecher.

criminal *adj* strafbar, Straf . . ., strafrechtlich, verbrecherisch; ~ **information** Strafanzeige ~ ~ *against unidentified persons: Strafanzeige gegen Unbekannt;* ~ **identification division** Erkennungsdienst; ~ **justice system** Strafrechtspflege.

Criminal Attempts Act 1981 *GB* Gesetz über Strafbarkeit des Versuchs.

Criminal Injuries Board Entschädigungsstelle für Verbrechergeschädigte.

Criminal Investigation Department (*C. I. D.*) Kriminalpolizei.

Criminal Law Revision Committee Strafrechtreformausschuß.

criminality Kriminalität *f*; **white collar** ~ Wirtschaftskriminalität.

criminate beschuldigen, belasten, anklagen; ~**oneself** sich selbst belasten.

criminatory anklagend, beschuldigend.

criminology Kriminologie *f*.

crimping betrügerisches Anheuern *n* von Matrosen.

crisis Krise *f*; ~ **package of measures** Krisenpaket; **commercial** ~ Wirtschaftskrise; **economic** ~ Wirtschaftskrise; **monetary** ~ Währungskrise.

criterion Kriterium *n*, Kennzeichen *n*, Tatbestandsmerkmal *n*; **overriding** ~ übergeordneter Gesichtspunkt.

critic Kritiker *m*, Rezensent *m*.

critical kritisch, tadelsüchtig; entscheidend, ausschlaggebend; ~ **date** Feststellungsdatum, maßgeblicher Zeitpunkt, Stichtag.

cronyism Kumpanei *f*, Filz *m*.

crook Gauner *m*, Schwindler *m*, Hochstapler *m*.

crooked unehrlich, betrügerisch, korrupt.

crop Ernte *f*, Ernteertrag *f*, Feldfrüchte *f/pl*, Bodenertrag *m*, Bebauung *f*, Kultivierung *f*; ~ **insurance** → *insurance*; ~ **lien** Verpfändung der Ernte auf dem Halm; **industrial** ~ gewerbliche Naturerzeugnisse, nachwachsende Rohstoffe; **loan** Erntefinanzierung; **growing** ~ Ernte auf dem Halm; **main** ~ Haupternte, erste Ernte; **outstanding** ~ die Ernte auf dem Halm; **standing** ~ = *outstanding* ~ *qv*.

cropper Landarbeiter *m* für Naturallohn (*Beteiligung am Ernteertrag* = *share-cropper*).

cross *s* Kreuz *n*, Kreuz *n* als Handzeichen (*Analphabeten*), Schwindel *m*.

cross|acceptance Wechselreiterei; ~**action** → *action*; ~ **appeal** → *appeal*; ~ **applications** (*for custody*) entgegengesetzte Anträge (*auf Sorgerechtsübertragung*); ~ **bench** *brit* Querbank, Bank der Parteilosen; ~ **benchers** *brit* Neutrale; ~ **bill** Rückwechsel; Widerklage; ~-**border** grenzüberschreitend; ~ **bow** Armbrust; ~ **cause** Widerklage; ~ **claim** Gegenanspruch; Gegenforderung; ~ **collateral** wechselseitige Sicherheitsleistung; ~ **complainant** Widerkläger; ~ **defendant** Widerbeklagter; ~ **demand** → *demand*; ~ **dressing** Transvestismus; ~ **easement** gemeinschaftliches Benutzungsrecht, wechselseitige Grunddienstbarkeit; ~ **entry** Gegeneintragung, Gegenbuchung; ~ **errors** → *error*; ~ **examination** → *examination*; ~ **exchange** Kreuzparität, indirekte Parität; ~-**firing** Scheckreiterei; ~ **frontier** grenzüberschreitend; ~ **guarantees** samtverbindl Bürgschaften (*mehrerer Konzerngesellschaften*); ~ **holding** gegenseitiger Kapitalanteilsbesitz *n*; ~ **liability** beiderseitige Haftpflicht; ~ **licences** → *licence*; ~ **motion** → *motion*; ~ **order** Kompensationsorder; ~ **ownership** wechselseitige Kapitalverflechtung; ~ **petition** Gegenantrag, Widerklage; ~ **rate** Kreuzparität, indirekte Parität; ~ **reference** Querverweis, Verweisung; ~ **remainders** → *remainders*; ~ **sale** (*unzulässiger*) Selbsteintritt des Börsenmaklers; ~ **subsidize** quersubventionieren; ~ **trade** = *wash sale qv*; ~ **walk** Fußgängerüberweg.

crossing (*1*) (Straßen)Kreuzung; **controlled** ~ Kreuzung mit Ampelanlage, Kreuzung mit Verkehrsregelung; **level** ~ niveaugleicher Bahnübergang.

crossing (*2*) Kreuzung *f*, Scheckkreuzung *f*; **general** ~ allgemeine Kreuzung (*Scheck*); **special** ~ besondere Scheckkreuzung (*unter Angabe der alleinempfangsberechtigten Bank*).

crowd Menschenmenge *f*; ~ **reaction** spontane Reaktion e–r Menschenmenge; **the C**~ *eine der 4 Abteilungen der New Yorker Börse für Obligationen*.

crown Krone *f*, Monarch *m*, König *m*, Königin *f*, Souverän *m*; ~ **agent** Beauftragter der Krone; **C**~ **Agents** Kron-Agenten, *zentrales Beschaffungsamt, GB*; **C**~ **Appointments Commission** Personalvorschlagskommission der Krone; ~ **cases** Strafsachen; ~ **cases reserved** *Rechtsfragen in Strafsachen aus der Provinz, die der Entscheidung des Appellationsgerichts vorbehalten werden*; **C**~**hold** Kronlehen; ~ **debts** Forderungen der Krone; ~ **grant** Überlassung e–s Kronlehens, Zuweisung von Staatsgrund; **C**~ **immunity enforcement procedure** königl Immunitätsvorschriften; **C**~ **interest** Krongut, Vermögensrecht der Krone, Staatseigentum; ~ **jewel option** Kaufoption für wertvollste Vermögensgegenstände e–s Unternehmens zu günstigem Preis (*als Abwehr bei unerwünschtem Annahmeangebot*); ~ **lands** Grundbesitz der Krone, Krongüter, Staatsdomänen; ~ **law** Strafrecht *GB*; **C**~ **Office** *Kronamt*; ~ *oberste Justizbehörde für Schottland*; ~ **official** königlicher Beamter, Staatsbeamter; ~ **paper** Terminliste der Strafsachen; ~ **paper day** Terminstag für Strafsachen; ~ **private estates** Privatgrundbesitz der Krone; ~ **privilege** Widerspruchsrecht der Staatsanwaltschaft gegen Vorlage e–r Urkunde (*weil gegen öffentliches Interesse*), Beweismittelausschluß wegen Nachteils für die Krone; **C**~ **proceedings** *Zivilverfahren, an denen die Krone beteiligt ist*; **C**~ **Proceedings Act** Gesetz über Zivilverfahren der Krone (1947); **C**~ **servant** Bediensteter der Krone; **C**~ **service** Dienste für die Krone; **C**~ **Solicitor** = *solicitor to the Treasury*, → *treasury*; ~ **suits** Klagen der Krone; **appeal by way of** ~ **cases**

reserved Revision in Strafsachen; **demise of the** ~ → *demise*; **estate passes to the** ~ Nachlaß fällt an den Staatsfiskus; **plea of the C~** *scot* Strafklage beim High Court of Justiciary (*qv*); **the C~ in right of the United Kingdom** die Krone in ihren Rechten im Vereinigten Königreich; **the C~ side** *strafgerichtliche Abteilung des King's (Queen's) Bench Gerichts*.

Crown Court *(=)* Staatsgericht *für schwere Straftaten, Jugendgerichtssachen ua, allgemein in GB seit 1970 anstelle der Assises qv*; ~ **centre** Gerichtsgebäude e–s Crown Court (*auch für zivilgerichtl Verhandlungen*); ~ **rules** Gerichts- und Verfahrensordnung der Crown Court.

crucial entscheidend; ~ **date** Stichtag, das entscheidende Datum; ~ **issue** entscheidende Frage.

cruelty Mißhandlungen *f/pl*, Grausamkeit *f*, Quälerei *f*; ~ **to animals** Tierquälerei; ~ **to children** Kindesmißhandlung; **legal** ~ Mißhandlungen (*als schwere Eheverfehlung*); **mental** ~ schwere Kränkungen, seelische Grausamkeit, bösartige Herzlosigkeit; **persistent** ~ Dauermißhandlung.

cruise Kreuzfahrt; ~ **ship** Kreuzfahrten-Schiff; ~ **ship passenger** Kreuzfahrer.

cry *s* Schrei *m*, Ruf *m*, Zetergeschrei *n* (*bei der Verfolgung e–s Verbrechens*).

cubicle kleiner abgeteilter (*oben offener*) Raum *m*, Einzelzelle *f*, Abteil *n*, Teilkäfig *m*.

cudgel Keule *f*, *fig* Prügel.

cui bono? zu wessen Vorteil?

cul de sac Sackgasse *f*.

culpa Verschulden *n*, Fahrlässigkeit *f*.

culpability Schuld *f*, Schuldvorwurf *m*.

culpable schuldhaft.

culprit Angeklagter *m*, Angeschuldigter *m*, Täter *m*, Übeltäter *m*.

cultivate landwirtschaftlich bebauen, bestellen, bearbeiten.

cum|coupon mit Coupon; ~ **dividend** → *dividend*; ~ **new** mit Bezugsrecht; ~ **privilegio** Bibeldruckmonopol; ~ **rights** mit Bezugsrecht; ~ **testamento annexo** → *administration*.

cumulative sich anhäufend, zusätzlich, kumulativ.

cura Sorge *f*, Pflegschaft *f*, Vormundschaft *f*.

curable heilbar (*auch jur*).

curatio Pflegschaft *f*.

curative heilend, heilbar (*auch betr Formmängel*).

curator Verwalter *m*, Museumswärter *m*; Pfleger *m*, *scot* Vormund *m*; ~ **absentis** Abwesenheitspfleger; ~ **ad litem** = *guardian ad litem qv*; ~ **bonis** in Vermögensangelegenheiten, Abwesenheitspfleger, Pfleger.

curatorship Pflegschaft *f*.

curatrix (*weiblicher*) Pfleger *m bzw* Vormund *m*.

curb *s* Bordstein *m*, Gehweg *m*; ~ **(stone) broker** → *broker*; ~ **exchange** Nebenbörse *für nicht an der Börse von New York notierte Werte, ursprüngl:* Straßenbörse, *ungenau*: Freiverkehrsbörse; ~ **market** = ~ *exchange qv*; **New York C~ Exchange** *(=) inoffizieller Teil der Wertpapierbörse von New York*.

cure *s* Kur *f*, Heilverfahren *n*, Heilung *f*, Mängelbeseitigung *f*, Abhilfe *f*; ~ **by verdict** Heilung e–s Verfahrensmangels durch das Urteil; ~ **notice** → *notice*; ~ **of addiction** Entziehungskur; ~ **provision** Heilungsbestimmung (*bei Vertragsfehlern*).

cure *v* gutmachen, sanieren, heilen; ~ **a defect** einen Fehler verbessern, e–n Mangel heilen; e–m Mangel abhelfen; ~ **defective title** Mängel der Eigentumsnachweise heilen.

curfew Sperrstunde *f*, Ausgehverbot *n*; **dusk-to-dawn** ~ nächtliche Ausgangssperre.

curia Hof *m*, Palast *m*, Herrensitz *m*; ~ **regis** das Königsgericht.

currency Umlauf *m*; Laufzeit *f*; Währung *f*, gesetzliches Zahlungsmittel *n*; Devisen *f/pl*, Fremdwährung *f*; ~ **account** → *account* (2); ~ **agreement** Währungsabkommen; ~ **ar-**

bitrage Devisenarbitrage; ~ **bill** (Fremd)Währungswechsel; ~ **bonds** → *bond (1)*; ~ **check at border** Devisenkontrolle (*an der Grenze*); ~ **clause** Valutaklausel, Währungsklausel; ~ **control** → *control*; ~ **dealings** Devisenverkehr; ~ **draft** (Fremd)Währungswechsel; ~ **element** Devisenkomponente; ~ **hedging arrangements** Währungskurssicherungsgeschäfte; ~ **holdings** Devisenbestände; ~ **inflation** Inflation; ~ **notes** Geldscheine, Banknoten; ~ **of a bill** Laufzeit e–s Wechsels; ~ **of a contract** Laufzeit e–s Vertrages; ~ **offence** Devisenvergehen; ~ **policy** Währungspolitik; ~ **profiteer** Devisenschieber; ~ **racket** Devisenschiebung; ~ **rates** Devisenkurse; ~ **reform** Währungsreform; ~ **regulations** → *regulation*; ~ **risk in foreign trade** Kursrisiko im Außenhandel; ~ **transactions** Devisengeschäft; ~ **with multiple exchange rates** Währung mit mehrfachen Wechselkursen; **adjustable** ~ elastische Währung; **blocked** ~ *nicht frei konvertierbare Währung*; Währung mit Devisensperre, Währung mit gesperrten Auslandskonten; **controlled** ~ Währung mit Devisenkontrolle, staatlich gelenkte Währung; **convertibility of** ~ Umtauschbarkeit, Konvertierbarkeit; **debasement of** ~ → *debasement*; **depreciated** ~ entwertete Währung, abgewertete W; **domestic** ~ Binnenwährung, inländisches Geld; **double** ~ Doppelwährung; **floating** ~**ies** floatende Währungen; **fractional paper** ~ Kleingeldscheine; **fluctuations of** ~ Währungsschwankungen; **foreign** ~ → *foreign*; **hard** ~ harte Währung; **irredeemable** ~ nicht (in Gold) einlösbare Währung; **key** ~ Leitwährung; **lawful** ~ gesetzliche Währung, gesetzl Zahlungsmittel; **local** ~ Landeswährung; **managed** ~ manipulierte Währung; **metropolitan** ~ Währung des Mutterlandes; **multiple** ~ Währung mit gespaltenem Wechselkurs; **national** ~ Landeswährung; **normally drawable** ~ normalerweise für Ziehungen geeignete Währung (*Internationaler Währungsfonds*); **scarcity of** ~ Devisenmangel; Geldknappheit; **soft** ~ weiche Währung, schwache W.; **sound** ~ gesunde Währung; **unsupported paper** ~ ungedeckte Papierwährung.

current laufend, umlaufend, kursierend, gängig, aktuell, gegenwärtig, derzeit gültig.

current account payments deficit Leistungsbilanzdefizit *n*.

curse Fluch *m*, Bannfluch *m*, Kirchenbann *m*.

curtail abkürzen, beeinträchtigen, schmälern; ~ **one's expense** seine Ausgaben herabsetzen.

curtailment Schmälerung *f*, Beeinträchtigung *f*, Verminderung *f*, Herabsetzung *f*; ~ **of expenses** Ausgabenkürzung.

curtesy Nießbrauchsrecht *n* des Witwers am Grundbesitz der verstorbenen Ehefrau, Witwerrecht *n*.

curtilage umschlossener Hofraum *m*, eingezäunter Teil *m* e–s Anwesens.

custodes Kustode *m*, Verwalter *m*, Pfleger *m*.

custodial *adj* in Haft befindlich, mit Freiheitsentzug verbunden.

custodian Treuhänder *m*, amtlicher Verwahrer *m*; ~ **account** Treuhandverwahrungskonto; ~ **bank** Depotbank; ~ **for alimony** Unterhaltspfleger; **C~ of Enemy Property** Feindvermögensverwalter; ~ **of property** Vermögensverwalter; ~ **office** Treuhandstelle; ~ **trustee** amtlich zugelassener Treuhandverwahrer; **gratuitous** ~ unentgeltlicher Verwahrer; **legal** ~ amtliche Hinterlegungsstelle; **to be the legal** ~ **of** (gesetzlichen) Gewahrsam (inne)haben.

custodianship Amtszeit eines Verwahrers; Personensorge *f*; Pflegeelternschaft *f*; ~ **order** Pflegschaftsbestellung über Minderjährige; ~ **proceedings** Personensorgeverfahren.

custodier Gewahrsamsinhaber *m*, Verwahrer *m*.

custody Gewahrsam *m*, tatsächl Gewalt *f*; Haft *f*; Verwahrung *f*; Aufbewahrung *f*; Erziehungsgewalt *f*; Personensorge *f*, Aufenthaltsbestimmungsrecht *n*; ~ **account** → *account*; ~ **dispute** Sorgerechtsstreit, Sorgerechtsprozeß; ~ **fee** Aufbewahrungsgebühr; ~ **officer** Polizeigewahrsamsbeamter; ~ **of goods** Aufbewahrung von Gütern; ~ **of property** Vermögensverwaltung; ~ **of securities** Aufbewahrung von Wertpapieren; ~ **of the child** Sorge für die Person des Kindes, Aufenthaltsbestimmungsrecht; ~ **of the law** gerichtlicher Gewahrsam, amtliche *bzw* gerichtliche Verwahrung; ~ **or control** Personensorge, elterliche Gewalt; ~ **order** Personensorgerechtsbeschluß; ~ **proceedings** Sorgerechtsverfahren; ~ **receipt** Depotschein; **joint** ~ Gemeinschaftsdepot; **juvenile** ~ Freiheitsentzug für Jugendstraftäter; **divided** ~ geteiltes Sorgerecht; **entitled to** ~ sorgeberechtigt; **legal** ~ Personensorge(recht); **official** ~ amtliche Verwahrung; **place of** ~ Gewahrsamsort, Aufbewahrungsort; **preliminary** ~ vorläufiger Gewahrsam, Polizeigewahrsam; **preventive** ~ Unterbindungsgewahrsam; Sicherungsverwahrung; **protective** ~ Schutzhaft; **safe** → *safe*; **safe** ~ **receipt** → *safe*; **service of** ~ Depotverwaltung; **to commit to** ~ in Haft nehmen, die Haft anordnen; in Gewahrsam nehmen; **to surrender to** ~ sich (zur Inhaftnahme) stellen.

custom Sitte *f*, Gepflogenheit *f*, Gewohnheit(srecht) *n*, Usance(n) *f* (*pol*); Kundschaft *f*; ~**s and usages** Gewohnheitsrecht; ~**s and usages of war** Kriegsrecht; ~**s and services** Lehenspflichten; ~ **made** Sonderanfertigung, Bestellung nach Maß; **C~s of London** örtliches Gewohnheitsrecht von London; ~ **of merchants** Handelsbrauch, kaufmännisches Gewohnheitsrecht; ~ **of the country** gutsherrschaftliche Gepflogenheit; gewohnheitsrechtliche Landpachtbedingungen; ~**(s) of the port** Hafenusancen; ~ **of the Realm** Landesbrauch, *britisches* Gewohnheitsrecht; ~ **of the sea** Seemansbrauch; ~ **of the trade** Handelsbrauch, Usancen; **banking** ~ → *banking*; **British** ~ → *British*; **established** ~ **of trade** anerkannter Handelsbrauch; **general** ~ (*allgemeine*) Verkehrssitte, allgemeines Gewohnheitsrecht; das Common Law; **immemorial** ~ uralter Brauch; **international** ~ internationale Gepflogenheiten, völkerrechtliches Gewohnheitsrecht; **legal** ~ Gewohnheitsrecht; **local** ~ Ortsbrauch, Platzgebrauch, örtliche Gepflogenheit, ortsüblich; **loss of** ~ → *loss*; **maritime** ~ Seebrauch; **mercantile** ~ Handelsbrauch; **particular** ~ besondere Gepflogenheit (*im Einzelfall*), örtliches Gewohnheitsrecht; **recognized** ~ Gewohnheitsrecht; **special** ~ örtlich beschränkte Gepflogenheit, Platzgebrauch; **valid** ~ Gewohnheitsrecht.

customary gebräuchlich, herkömmlich, üblich, gewohnheitsmäßig.

customer Kunde *m*; ~ **agent** Kundenvertreter (*Export*); ~ **automated teller** elektronischer Bankschalter; ~ **base** Kundenbasis, Kulisse; ~**'s cheque** Kundenscheck; ~ **country** Abnehmerland; ~ **dissatisfaction** Unzufriedenheit von Kunden, Kundenverdruß; ~**'s ledger** Kundenkonto, Debitorenbuch; ~**s' loans** Kundenkredite, Darlehen an Kunden; ~**s' man** Kundensachbearbeiter, Anlageberater; ~ **ownership** Aktienbeteiligung der Geschäftskundschaft; ~ **protection** Schutz der (Börsen)Kunden; ~**'s sole risk** auf alleinige Gefahr des Kunden; ~**'s statement** Rechnung; **chance** ~ → *chance*; **delinquent** ~ säumiger Kunde; **launching** ~ Erstbesteller *(Flugzeugtyp)*; **occasional** ~ Laufkunde; **private**

~ Privatkunde, Stammkunde; **regular** ~ Stammkunde, Stammgast; **residential** ~**s** Kundenhaushaltungen; **"rustbelt"** ~**s** Kunden aus der eisenschaffenden Industrie; **stray** ~ gelegentlicher Kunde, Laufkunde.

customs Zoll *m*, Zölle *m|pl*; ~ **agent** Zollagent; ~ **airport** Zollflughafen; ~ **and excise duties** Zölle und Gebrauchssteuern; ~ **authorities** Zollbehörde; ~ **barrier** Zollschranke; ~ **berth** Zollandungsplatz; ~ **broker** Zollmakler, Zollagent; ~ **certificate** Bescheinigung der Zollstelle; ~ **charges** Zollgebühren; ~ **classification** Zolltarifierung; ~ **clearance** Zollabfertigung; ~ **control** Zollkontrolle, Zollüberwachung; ~ **convention** Zollabkommen; ~ **court** *US* Zollgericht; ~ **custody** Zollgewahrsam; ~ **debenture** Zollrückschein; ~ **declaration** → *declaration*; ~ **duty** Zoll; ~ **enclave** Zollanschlußgebiet; ~ **entry** Vorlage zur Verzollung; Zolldeklaration; ~ **examination** Zollrevision; ~ **facilities** Zollerleichterungen; ~ **fine** Zollstrafe; ~ **formalities and detentions** Zollformalitäten und Zurückbehaltung durch die Zollbehörden; ~ **fraud** Zollhinterziehung; ~ **frontier** Zollgrenze; **C** ~ **House** Hauptzollamt; (*auch: Custom-house*); ~ **import certificate** zollamtliche Einfuhrbestätigung; ~ **inspection** Zollbeschau; ~ **invoice** Zollfaktura; ~ **inwards** Eingangsausfertigung (*Zoll*); ~ **juridiction** Zollhoheit; ~ **laboratory** zolltechnische Prüfanstalt; ~ **laws and regulations** Zollvorschriften; ~**-locked** unter Zollverschluß; ~ **offence** Zollvergehen; ~ **office** Zollamt; ~ **officer** Zollbeamter; ~ **on merchandise** Zoll, Warenzoll; ~ **operations** Amtshandlungen der Zollbehörden; ~ **outwards** Ausgangsabfertigung (*Zoll*); ~ **penalty** Zollstrafe; ~ **permit** Zollabfertigungsschein; ~ **policy** Zollpolitik; ~ **procedure** Zollverfahren; ~ **rate** Zollsatz; ~ **receipt** Zollquittung; ~ **receipts** Zolleinnahmen; ~ **reduction** Zollsenkung; ~ **regime** Zollsystem; ~ **regulations** Zollvorschriften; ~ **revenue** Zolleinnahmen; ~ **seal** Zollverschluß; **C** ~ **Service** Zollbehörde; ~ **shed** Zollschuppen; ~ **tariff** Zolltarif; ~ **territory** Zollgebiet; ~ **treaty** Zollvertrag; ~ **union** Zollunion; ~ **value** Zollwert; ~ **violation** Zollvergehen; ~ **warehouse** Zollspeicher; ~ **warrant** Zollauslieferungsschein; **to attend to** ~ **formalities** die Zollformalitäten erledigen; **to clear through the** ~ verzollen.

customs duties Zölle *m|pl*, Zollgebühren *f|pl*, Zollabgaben *f|pl*; ~ **of a fiscal nature** Finanzzölle; **evasion of** ~ Zollhinterziehung; **liability to pay** ~ Zollpflicht; **reduction of** ~ Zollsenkung; **to levy** ~ Zölle erheben.

customs office Zollamt *n*; ~ **en route** Durchgangszollstelle; ~ **of departure** Abgangszollstelle; ~ **of destination** Bestimmungszollstelle.

cut *s* Schnitt *m*, Streichung *f*, Herabsetzung *f*, Abzug *m*; Anteil *m*; Kupon *m*; ~ **in prices** Preisherabsetzung; ~ **in salary** Gehaltskürzung.

cut *v* schneiden, herabsetzen, kürzen, reduzieren; ~ **a person off** jmdn enterben; ~ **one's expenses** seine Ausgaben reduzieren; ~ **off** abschneiden; enterben; ~ **off an entail** Fideikommißbindung aufheben.

cut-off point Endzeitpunkt *m*, Tag des Außerkrafttretens.

cutpurse Taschendieb *m*; Beutelschneider *m*.

cutting Unterbieten *n*.

cycle Zyklus *m*; ~ **policy** zyklische (Konjunktur)politik; ~ **upswing** Konjunkturaufschwung; **business** ~ → *business*; **economic** ~ Konjunkturzyklus.

cyclical zyklisch.

cy-près „so nahe wie möglich", wohlwollende (*dem Willen des Erblassers nahekommende*) Auslegung.

D

dactylogram Fingerabdruck *m.*

Dail (Eireann) *Parlament des irischen Freistaates.*

daily täglich (*in der Regel: einschließlich Sonn- und Feiertagen*).

daily balance interest calculation Staffel(zins)methode *f*, Zinsberechnung mit Saldoverzinsung *f.*

dairy Molkerei *f*, milchwirtschaftlicher Betrieb, Milchgeschäft; Milchwirtschaft *f*, Milchvieh *n*; ~ **farming** Milchwirtschaft.

Dale and Sale (=) *fiktive Grundstücksbezeichnungen für Rechtsausführungen.*

damage Schaden *m*, Schädigung *f*, Beschädigung *f*; Einbuße *f*; ~ **by reason of fire** Feuerschaden; ~ **by sea** Havarie; ~ **by water** Wasserschaden; ~ **-clear** *hist* quota litis; ~ **feasant** → *feasant*; ~ **control operation** Schadensbegrenzung(saktion); ~ **in fact** Schaden im Einzelfall; ~ **survey** Schadensprüfung; ~ **to cargo** Schäden der (Schiffs)Ladung; ~ **to cargo by jettison and sacrifice** Ladungsschäden durch Seewurf und Aufopferung; ~ **to cargo in discharging** Ladungsschäden beim Löschen (*große Havarie*); ~ **to goods** Schäden an beweglichen Sachen; ~ **to person** Personenschaden, Körperverletzung; ~ **to property** Sachschaden; ~ **to reputation** Rufschaden; ~ **to ship** Schaden am Schiff; **actual** ~ tatsächlicher, unmittelbarer Schaden; **criminal** ~ böswillige, strafbare Sachbeschädigung; **consequent** ~ daraus entstehender Schaden; **consequential** ~ Folgeschaden; **denial** ~ Aufopferspruch; **direct** ~ unmittelbarer Schaden; **irreparable** ~ nicht wiedergutzumachender Schaden; **malicious** ~ vorsätzliche, böswillige Schadenszufügung, Vandalismus; **negligible** ~ geringfügiger Schaden; **proximate** ~ adäquater Schaden; **permanent** ~ Dauerschaden; **pecuniary** ~ Vermögensschaden; **physical** ~ tatsächlicher Schaden, Sachschaden; **remote** ~ nicht adäquater Folgeschaden; **residual** ~ verbleibender Dauerschaden; **special** ~ Schaden im Einzelfall, ungewöhnlicher Schaden; **structural** ~ Bauschäden; **to be liable for the** ~ schaden(s)ersatzpflichtig sein; **to bear the** ~ → *to bear*; **to inflict** ~ Schaden zufügen; **to suffer** ~ Schaden erleiden, Schaden zugefügt erhalten.

damages Schadensersatz *m* (*in Geld*); gerichtl zuerkannter Schadensersatz *m*, Entschädigung *f*; (*Schadensersatz kurz: Sch*); Schadensfolgen *f/pl*; ~ **are awarded** *Sch* wird gewährt; ~ **at large** Pauschalentschädigung; ~ **for bereavement** *Sch* weg Unfalltod des Ehegatten; ~ **for breach of contract** *Sch* wegen (positiver) Vertragsverletzung, *Sch* wegen Nichterfüllung; ~ **for delay in finishing** *Sch* wegen verspäteter Fertigstellung; ~ **for illegal arrest** *Sch* wegen Freiheitsberaubung im Amt; ~ **for inconvenience and distress** *Sch* wegen Unannehmlichkeiten und nervlicher Belastung; ~ **for non-performance** *Sch* wegen Nichterfüllung; ~ **for pain and suffering** Schmerzensgeld; ~ **go to the plaintiff** dem Kläger wird *Sch* zugesprochen; ~ **in tort** *Sch* aus unerlaubter Handlung; ~ **on an unsparing scale** rigoros bemessener *Sch*; ~ **ultra** weitere *Sch*forderung (*über den gerichtlich hinterlegten Betrag hinaus*); **action for** ~ → *action*; **actual** ~ echter *Sch*, adäquater *Sch*; **adjudicated** ~ gerichtl zuerkannter *Sch*, zugesprochener *Sch*; **adjustment of** ~ Schadensregulierung; **affirmative** ~ geltend gemachter *Sch*; **aggravated** ~ *Sch* in e–m besonders schweren Fall; **assessment of** ~ → *assessment*; **civil** ~ Ersatz des Drittschadens; **claim for** ~ *Sch*anspruch; **compensatory** ~ (*adäquater*) *Sch*; **conjectural** ~ mutmaßlicher *Sch* , *Anspruch auf Schadensersatz, dessen Höhe nur vermutet, nicht bewiesen werden kann*; **consequential** ~ Ersatz für mittelbaren Schaden; **contemptuous** ~ mißbilligende Zuerkennung von *Sch* (*aus rein formalen Gründen*); **contingent** ~ *Sch*zubilligung vorbehaltlich der Entscheidung über den Schadensgrund; **continuing** ~ Ersatz für Dauerschaden, fortlaufende *Sch*zahlungen; **direct** ~ Ersatz des unmittelbaren Schadens; **double** ~ doppelter *Sch* (*pönalisierende Verurteilung in doppelter Höhe des tatsächlich entstandenen Schadens*); **excessive** ~ überhöhte *Sch*-Zuerkennung; **exemplary** ~ übernormal hohes *Sch*urteil (*zugleich als Strafe und Abschreckung*); **expectancy** ~ *Sch* für entgangenen Gewinn; **fair** ~ großzügig bemessener *Sch*; **final** ~ endgültiger *Sch*; **fee** ~ Ersatz für Substanzschaden am Grundstück; **future** ~ *Sch* für zukünftige Beeinträchtigungen; **general** ~ genereller *Sch*, *Sch* für typische Fälle dieser Art; **imaginary** ~ imaginäre *Sch*forderung; **incidental** ~ *Sch* für Neben- und Folgekosten; **indeterminate** ~ unbezifferter *Sch*; **intervening** ~ zwischenzeitlicher *Sch* (*Ersatz für die Erhöhung des Schadens während der Rechtsmittelinstanz*); **irreparable** ~ *Sch* (*in Geld*) für nicht wiedergutzumachenden Schaden, nur schätzbarer *Sch*; **judgment for** ~ → *judgment*; **land** ~ Grundstücks(enteignungs)entschädigung; **lawful** ~ gesetzlich begründeter *Sch*anspruch; **liable to pay** ~ *sch*pflichtig; **liquidated** ~ bezifferter *Sch*; (*im voraus vereinbarter*) pauschalierter *Sch*; *ungenau*: Vertragsstrafe, Konventionalstrafe; **measure of** ~ Höhe des *Sch*, *Sch*bemessung; **necessary** ~ Ersatz für alle notwendigen Schadensfolgen; **nominal** ~ ganz geringer (*nur aus Rechtsgründen*) zugesprochener *Sch*; **order to pay** ~ Verurteilung zu *Sch*; **pactional** ~ pauschalierter *Sch*; **payment of** ~ Entschädigungsleistung; **pecuniary** ~ *Sch* in Geld; **permanent** ~ Haftung e–s Grundstücks für Dauerschäden; **presumptive** ~ pönalisierende *Sch*zuerkennung; **prospective** ~ Ersatz für voraussichtlichen Folgeschaden; **provisional** ~ vorläufiger *Sch* (*Klage*); **proximate** ~ Ersatz des nächstursächlichen Schadens, Ersatz des unmittelbaren Schadens; **punitive** ~ tatsächlicher *Sch* zuzüglich e–r Zivilstrafe, pönalisierende Verurteilung zu *Sch*; **rescissory** ~ Naturalrestitution bzw Geldersatz; **recurring** ~ *Sch*rente; **remote** ~ Ersatz für indirekten Schaden, *Sch* für Spätfolgen; **retributive** ~ Buße; **sentimental** ~ *Sch* für Liebhaberwert; **special** ~ *Sch* für besondere Schadensfolgen; Ersatz für atypischen Schaden; **speculative** ~ Ersatz für vermeintlichen Folgeschaden, spekulativer *Sch*; **stipulated** ~ pauschalierter vereinfachter *Sch*; **substantial** ~ adäquater *Sch*; **temporary** ~ Ersatz für zeitweise erlittenen Schaden; **to award** ~ zu *Sch* verurteilen, *Sch* zusprechen; **to bring an action for** ~ *Sch*klage einreichen; **to hold s. o. for** ~ *jmdn* auf *Sch* in Anspruch nehmen; **to recover** ~ *Sch* zugesprochen bekommen; **treble** ~ *Sch* in dreifacher Höhe; **unaccrued** ~ noch nicht fälliger *Sch*; **unliquidated** ~ unbezifferte *Sch*forderung, *Sch* dem Grunde nach; **vindictive** ~ pönalisierender *Sch*.

damaging event Schadensereignis *n*.

dame Freifrau *f*; *Titel für weibliche Mitglieder des Order of the British Empire*; Bezeichnung für e–e Richterin.

damna Schadensersatzzuerkennung *f*.

damnification Schädigung *f*.
damnify schädigen, Schaden zufügen; **~ied** zur Bürgschaftsleistung verurteilt.
damp Baufeuchtigkeit *f*.
danger Gefahr *f*, Gefährdung *f*, Risiko *n*; ~ **money** Gefahrenzulage; ~ **of absconding** Fluchtgefahr; **~s of navigation** Gefahren der Seefahrt; **~s of the river** *die üblichen* Gefahren der Flußschiffahrt; ~ **of the defendant fleeing** Fluchtgefahr (beim Angeklagten); **~s of the roads** Gefahren durch den Straßenzustand; ~ **of the sea** Gefahren des Meeres (*Schiffahrt*); ~ **to life** Lebensgefahr; **alternative** ~ Gefährdung durch Selbsthilfe; **apparent** ~ → *apparent*; **apprehended** ~ Gefahr im Verzug; **causing public** ~ gemeingefährlich; **common** ~ gemeinsame Gefahr (*Havarie*); **immediate** ~ unmittelbar bevorstehende Gefahr; **imminent** ~ drohende Gefahr; **mortal** ~ Lebensgefahr; **unavoidable** ~ unabwendbare Gefahr; **unusual** ~ besondere Gefahrenquelle; **to pose** ~ e–e Gefahr darstellen.
dangerous gefährlich, gefährdend, riskant, unsicher; ~ **per se** von Natur aus gefährlich, gefahrgeneigt; **inherently** ~ immanent gefährlich.
data Angaben *f|pl*, Sachverhalt *m*, Daten *n|pl*; ~ **processing** Datenverarbeitung; ~ ~ *equipment: Datenträger;* ~ ~ *manager* → *manager*; **factual** ~ Tatsachenmaterial; **personal** ~ Personalien, Angaben zur Person; **to furnish** ~ Informationen beschaffen.
data protection Datenschutz *m*, **D~ P~ Act** Datenschutzgesetz; ~ **registrar** Datenschutzbeauftragter.
date *s* Datum *n*, Tag *m*, Termin *m*, Ausstellungstag *m*, Zeitpunkt *m*, Frist *f*, Sicht *f*; ~ **as per postmark** Datum des Poststempels; ~ **for completion** Fertigstellungstermin; ~ **for payment** Fälligkeitstermin; ~ **of adjudication** Tag der Urteilsverkündung; ~ **of birth** Geburtsdatum; ~ **of cleavage** Trennungsdatum (*Einreichung des eigenen Konkursantrages*); ~ **of commencement** Anfangstag; ~ **of delivery** Liefertermin; ~ **of execution of document** Datum der Ausstellung e–r Urkunde; ~ **of expiry** (*expiry* ~) Ende des Zeitablaufs, Tag des Erlöschens, Verfallstag, Verfallstermin; ~ **of invoice** Rechnungsdatum; ~ **of issue** (= *of issuance*) Ausgabetag *m*; ~ **of mailing** Datum der Aufgabe zur Post, Absendetag; ~ **of maturity** (*maturity* ~) Fälligkeitstermin, Fälligkeitstag, Fälligkeitsdatum; ~ **of publication** Veröffentlichungsdatum, Bekanntmachungstag; ~ **of receipt** Eingangsdatum, Empfangstag; ~ **of reference** Termin beim Einzelrichter; ~ **of shipment** Absendetag; ~ **of the review** Stichtag *zur Feststellung der hypothetischen Schadensentwicklung*; ~ **of trial** (Gerichts)Termin; ~ **term** Zeitbestimmung, vertragliche Festlegung der Frist; **appointed** ~ festgesetzter Termin; **at a set** ~ einem bestimmten Termin; **at the earliest practicable** ~ so bald wie möglich; **closing** ~ letzter Termin, Schlußtag (*zB bei e–r Ausschreibung*), Auflassungszeitpunkt (*US*); **cut-off** ~ Schlußtermin, Stichtag; **due** ~ Fälligkeit(stermin), Verfallstag; **effective** ~ Tag des Inkrafttretens; **extended** ~ Nachfrist; **final** ~ Schlußtermin, Endtermin; **fixed** ~ Termin, festgesetzte Frist, Stichtag; **insertion of** ~ Einsetzen des Datums; **key** ~ → *key*; **of even** ~ gleichen Datums; **of the same** ~ gleichen Datums; **of this** ~ vom Heutigen (*Tage*); **onset** ~ Datum des Eintritts der Erwerbsunfähigkeit; **out of** ~ veraltet, Einlösungsfrist abgelaufen (*Vermerk auf Scheck*); **presumption as to** ~ Vermutung für die Richtigkeit des Datums; **priority** ~ Prioritätsdatum; **proof of** ~ Datumsbeweis; **reckonable** ~ Stichtag; **relevant** ~ Stichtag; **record** ~ Stichtag (*für den*

Aktienerwerb); **to fix a ~** e–n Termin anberaumen; **to keep a ~ ~** e–e Frist einhalten; **trial ~** Hauptttermin, T. zur mündl. Verhandlung; Hauptverhandlungst.; **up to ~** → *up*; **without ~** undatiert.

date *v* datieren, das Datum tragen, mit Datums- und Ortsangabe versehen; **~ back** rückdatieren, zurückreichen; **~ forward** vordatieren; **~d** mit Datum versehen, datiert, vom . . .; unter dem (*Datum*); **~d bills** Wechsel mit Fälligkeitsdatum.

datum Gegebene *n*, Voraussetzung *f*, Angabe *f*, Einzelheit *f*, Unterlage *f*; **~ quantity** Bezugsmengen.

dawn raid Aktienaufkaufaktion gleich nach Börseneröffnung.

day Tag *m*, Kalendertag *m*, Datum *n*, Tageslicht *n*; **~ book** Journal; **~ care center** Tagesstätte; Kindergarten; **~ certain** Termin, festes Datum; **~s in bank** *hist* Gerichtstage, Einlassungsfrist; **~ in court** Gerichtstag, Gelegenheit zur Verteidigung, rechtliches Gehör; **~ labourer** Arbeiter, Tagelöhner; **~ letter** Brieftelegramm; **~ money** täglich fälliges Geld; **~ next appointed** der nächte Termin; **~ nursery** Kinderkrippe, Kinderzimmer; **~ of appearance** Verhandlungstermin; **~ of birth** Geburtsdatum; **of date** Tage der Datumangabe; **~s of demurrage** Extraliegezeit, Überliegezeit; **~ of election** Datum der Wahl; **~ of entry** Einklarierungstag; **~s of grace** Gnadenfrist, Respekttage; geduldete Verzugstage, Zahlungsfrist, Nachfrist; **~ of hearing** Gerichtstermin; **~ of issue** Ausgabetag, Erscheinungsdatum; **~ of nomination** Ernennungstag, Beförderungstag, Tag der Bekanntmachung der Kandidatur; **~ of settlement** Verrechnungstag, Liquidationstag; **~ off** freier Tag; **~ option** *brit* bis zum nächsten Tag 19.45 h laufendes Prämiengeschäft; **~ order** *exch* Tagesauftrag (*nur am Tag der Auftragserteilung gültig*); **~ -release** tageweise Freistellung; **~ -rule** Tagesurlaub (*aus dem Gefängnis für notwendige Angelegenheiten*); **~-shift** Tagesschicht; **~s' sight** → *sight*; **~ to ~ loan** täglich fälliges Maklerdarlehen; **~ to show cause** Einlassungstermin; **~ training centre** Tagesausbildungsheim (*Bewährungshilfe*); **~ -writ = ~ -rule** *qv*; **~, year and waste** *hist* = *year, day and waste qv*; **appointed ~** Stichtag, festgesetzter Tag, festes Datum; Tag des Inkrafttretens; **artificial ~** Tageszeit (*von Sonnenaufgang bis Sonnenuntergang*); **banking ~** Bankgeschäftsstunden; **calendar ~s** Kalendertage; **civil ~** Kalendertag (*von Mitternacht bis Mitternacht*); **clear ~s** volle Tage (*ohne den ersten und letzten Tag, auf den das Ereignis fällt, mitzuzählen*); **closing ~** letzter Tag; **common ~** *hist* gewöhnlicher Sitzungstag; **current ~s** aufeinanderfolgende Tage; **entire ~** ein 24-Stundentag, ein Kalendertag; **excluded ~** gesetzlicher Feiertag; **fixed ~** Frist, Termin; **intermediate ~** Zwischentag; *der dritte Tag der Börsenabrechnungsfrist*; **judicial ~s** Gerichtstage, Gerichtstermine, Sitzungstage; **juridical ~s** Sitzungstage; **law ~** → *law*; **lawful ~** Werktag; **lay ~s** Liegezeit, Löschtage; **legal ~** Gerichtstag, Sitzungsperiode; **natural ~** Kalendertag, Tageslichtzeit; **nonbusiness ~s** Sonn- und Feiertage; **non-enumerated ~** Sitzungstag außer der Reihe (*für besondere Anträge*); **non-judicial ~** gerichtsfreier Tag; **non-working ~s** gesetzliche Feiertage; **on the appointed ~** zum festgesetzten Datum; **pay ~** Zahltag, Lohn- und Gehaltsempfangstag, Abrechnungstag, Zahlungstermin; **peremptory ~** unverschiebbarer Terminstag; **record ~** Stichtag (*für den Aktienerwerb*); **running ~** laufende Kalendertage, Liegetage; **settling ~** Abrechnungstag; **solar ~** → *solar*; **this ~ week** heute in einer Woche; **to appoint a ~** e–n Termin festlegen; **to fix a ~ for a hearing** e–n Termin anberaumen; **working ~**

Werktag ohne Samstag und ohne gesetzl Feiertage.
daylight Tageslicht *m* (*einschl Morgengrauen und Abenddämmerung*); ~ **saving time** Sommerzeit.
daytime bei Tage, bei Tageslicht.
de bene esse vorläufig, für alle Fälle; **taking evidence** ~ Beweissicherungsverfahren.
de facto (=) faktisch; ~ **contract** faktisches Vertragsverhältnis, vertragsähnliche Beziehung; ~ **corporation** faktische Gesellschaft, als Körperschaft behandelte Gesellschaft; ~ **-government** de facto Regierung; ~ **-judge** faktisch als Richter amtierende Person; ~ **-marriage** eheähnliches Verhältnis; ~ **-officer** der tatsächliche (*nicht unbedingt rechtmäßige*) Amtsinhaber; ~ **recognition** ~ Anerkennung, Anerkennung als de facto Regierung; **blockade** ~ faktische Blockade, unerklärte Blockade; **wife** ~ „Ehefrau" bei nichtiger Ehe.
de jure von Rechts wegen, rechtlich; ~ **corporation** juristische Person, Körperschaft im Rechtssinne; ~ **government** rechtmäßige Regierung; ~ **recognition** de jure Anerkennung, endgültige völkerrechtliche Anerkennung.
de injuria Einwendung des eigenen Verschuldens des Verletzten.
de minimis rule Geringfügiges wird vom Gericht nicht beachtet.
dead tot, gestorben; unfruchtbar, unproduktiv; ungültig, leer, nichtssagend.
deadhead Freipassagier *m*; Inhaber e–r Freikarte, Fahrzeug ohne Ladung, Leerfahrt *f*.
deadline Frist *f*; ~ **for application** letzte Anmeldefrist, Anmeldeschluß.
deadlock Stillstand *m*, Blockierung *f*, Stockung *f*.
dead man's part = **dead's part** *scot* der freien Verfügung des Testators unterliegender Teil des Erblasservermögens.
deadweight cargo Bruttoladefähigkeit, Schwergutladefähigkeit; ~ **carrying capacity** Tragfähigkeit (*e–s Schiffes in Gewichtstonnen*); ~ **debt** der nicht rentierlich gedeckte Teil der Staatsschuld *GB*; ~ **loading capacity** Ladevermögen (*in Gewichtstonnen*); ~ **ton** → *ton*; ~ **tonnage** Leertonnage, Ladefähigkeit (*Schiff*), Gesamtzuladungsgewicht (*Ladung, Proviant, Treibstoff*).
deal *s* Handel *m*, abgeschlossenes Geschäft *n*; **arm's length** ~ → *arm's length*; **cash** ~ Barverkauf; **fair** ~ gerechte Ausgangslage; **interaffiliate** ~ konzerninternes Geschäft; **to make a** ~ ein Geschäft abschließen, ein besonders günstiges Geschäft machen.
deal *v* teilen, austeilen, handeln, geschäftlich tätig sein; ~ **at arm's length** auf rein geschäftlicher Basis verhandeln; ~ **in** handeln mit (*ein Sortiment führen*); ~ **with** behandeln, betreffen, bearbeiten.
dealer Händler *m*, Kaufmann *m*, Eigenhändler *m*, Börsenmakler *m*; ~**'s buyer** Wiederverkäufer; ~ **in securities** Wertpapierhändler, Effektenhändler; ~ **-order bank** Händlerauftragsreserve; ~**'s rebate** → *rebate*; ~**'s talk** Anpreisungen im Handel; **authorized** ~ autorisierter Händler, Vertragshändler; **franchised** ~ autorisierter Händler; **money** ~ Geldwechsler, Devisenhandler; **real estate** ~ Immobilienhändler; **retail** ~ Einzelhändler; **wholesale** ~ Großhändler.
dealing Geschäft *n*, Handel *m*, Geschäftsgebaren *n*, Börsengeschäft *n*; ~**s** Behandlung, Verfahrensweise; Geschäftsverkehr; ~**s for cash** Bargeschäft; ~**s for the account** Termingeschäft; ~ **in stocks** Effektengeschäft; ~ **or transaction** Rechtsgeschäft; **commercial** ~**s** Handelsgeschäfte; **exclusive** ~ Ausschließlichkeitsbindung; **fair** ~ redliches Geschäftsgebaren, zulässiger, redlicher Gebrauch (*geschützter Werke*); **illegal** ~ verbotener Handel (*mit etw*); **insider** → *insider;* **mutual** ~**s** gegenseitige Geschäfts-

beziehung; **unfair** ~ unlautere Geschäftsmethoden.

deal maker Händler *m*, Börsenhändler *m*.

dean Dekan *m*, Vorstand *m*, Präsident *m*, Doyen *m*; ~ **and chapter** Bischöfliche Ratsversammlung; **D~ of Faculty** *scot* Präsident der Anwaltskammer; **D~ of Guild** *scot* Ortsrichter, Leiter der Baupolizei; **D~ of the Arches** *Laienrichter des Court of Arches qv*; ~ **of the diplomatic corps** Doyen des diplomatischen Korps.

death Tod *m*; ~ **benefit** Sterbegeld *n*; ~ **by hanging** Tod durch den Strang; ~ **certificate** Sterbeurkunde; ~ **duty** Erbschaftssteuer *GB: bis 1975*; ~ **grant** Sterbegeld; ~ **litigation** Sterbefallprozesse, Erbschaftsprozesse; ~**'s part** = *dead's part qv*; ~ **penalty** Todesstrafe; ~ **penalty abolition** Abschaffung der Todesstrafe; ~ **rate** Sterblichkeitsziffer, Getötetenrate; ~ **records** Sterberegister; ~ **row** Zellentrakt der Todeskandidaten; ~ ~ *inmates: Todeskandidaten*; ~ **sentence** Todesurteil; ~ **warrant** → *warrant*; ~ **watch** Bewachung e–s Todeskandidaten; ~ **without issue** Tod ohne Nachkommenschaft; **accidental** ~ Unfalltod; T. durch zufälliges Ereignis; **brain** ~ Gehirntod; **cause of** ~ Todesursache; **certification of** ~ Totenschein; **civil** ~ bürgerlicher Tod, Entzug der Rechtsfähigkeit, Verlust der bürgerlichen Ehrenrechte, Friedlosigkeit; **compensable** ~ Arbeitsunfalltod; **day of** ~ Todestag; **determination of** ~ Todesbestimmung; **in contemplation of** ~ angesichts des Todes, in Todeserwartung; **in the event of** ~ im Todesfalle; **instantaneous** ~ sofortiger Tod; **natural** ~ natürlicher Tod; **presumption of** ~ → *presumption*; **presumptive** ~ Todesvermutung; **proof of** ~ → *proof*; **register of** ~**s** Sterberegister; **registration of** ~ standesamtliche Eintragung von Todesfällen; **to come by one's** ~ den Tod finden; **to put a person to** ~ jmdn umbringen, jmdn töten; **violent** ~ gewaltsamer Tod, unnatürlicher Tod.

death-bed Totenbett *n*, zum Tode führende Krankheit *f*; ~ **confession** Geständnis e–s Sterbenden; ~ **declaration** Äußerung e–s Sterbenden (*als Beweismittel*); ~ **deed** Urkunde auf dem Sterbebett; **law of** ~ *hist scot* Testamentsungültigkeitsvorschriften.

debar from ausschließen von.

debase entwürdigen, verfälschen.

debasement Erniedrigung *f*, Entwürdigung *f*, Verschlechterung *f*; ~ **of currency** Münzverschlechterung, Münzverfälschung; ~ **of the coinage** Münzverschlechterung.

debatable vertretbar, streitig; ~ **assertion** bestreitbare Behauptung, vertretbare Behauptung; **a** ~ **point** ein vertretbarer Gesichtspunkt; ~ **theory** umstrittene Theorie.

debate *s* Debatte *f*, Aussprache *f*; **budget** ~ Debatte über den Staatshaushalt, Budgetdebatte.

debat|e *v* debattieren, erörtern, erwägen; ~ **a bill** e–e Vorlage beraten; ~**ing society** Debattierklub.

debauch sittlich verderben, korrumpieren, verführen.

debauchery Ausschweifung *f*, Schwelgerei *f*, Zuchtlosigkeit *f*, Unzucht *f*.

debauchment Ausschweifung *f*, Orgie *f*, Unzucht *f*, Verderbtheit *f*.

debellatio Debellatio *f*, *Erlöschen des Völkerrechtssubjekts durch Eroberung bzw vernichtende Niederlage*.

debenture Obligation *f*, Schuldschein *m*; Schuldverschreibung *f*, Schuldurkunde *f* mit Verpfändungsklausel; Rückzollschein *m*; ~**s already issued** bereits begebene Obligationen (*Serien oder einzelne*); ~ **bond** Inhaberschuldverschreibung; ~ **containing any charge** dinglich gesicherte Schuldverschreibung; ~ **creditor** Obligationär; ~ **goods** → *goods*; ~ **holder** Inhaber e–r Schuldverschreibung, Obligationär, Schuldscheinberechtigter; Gläubiger e–r verbrieften Forderung; ~ **holder's action** Antrag auf abgesonderte Befriedigung von Schuldverschreibungsgläubigern; ~ **indenture** Schuldverschreibungsurkunde (*mit zusätzl Bedingungen ohne dingl Sicherheit*); ~ **issue** Emission von Schuldverschreibungen; ~ **stock** Obligationen mit Treuhandsicherung; ~ **trust deed** Schuldurkunde mit Treuhandsicherheit; **all-moneys** ~ Globalverpfändungsurkunde zur Deckung aller Verbindlichkeiten; **bearer** ~ → *bearer*; **convertible** ~ Wandelschuldverschreibung; **convertible subordinated** ~**s** nachrangige Wandelanleihe; **fixed** ~ immobiliengesicherte Schuldurkunde; **floating** ~ durch Verpfändung der am Umlaufvermögen gesicherten Schuldurkunde; **fractional** ~ (*klein*) gestückelte Schuldverschreibung; **guaranteed** ~**s** verbürgte Schuldverschreibungen; **income** ~ Gewinnschuldverschreibung, ertragsabhängige Schuldverschreibungen; **irredeemable** ~ Schuldverschreibung ohne Tilgungszwang, unkündbare Obligation; **mortgage** ~ → *mortgage*; **naked** ~ ungesichertes Schuldanerkenntnis; **partial** ~ Teilschuldverschreibung; **participating** ~ Gewinnschuldverschreibung; **perpetual** ~ (*auf unbeschränkte Zeit*) unkündbare Schuldverschreibung; **railway** ~ Eisenbahnobligation; **redeemable** ~ einzulösende Schuldverschreibung; **registered** ~ Namensobligation, Namensschuldverschreibung; **secured** ~ (konkret) dingl gesicherte Schuldurkunde; **simple** ~ ungesicherte Schuldurkunde, Schuldschein; **sinking fund** ~ Tilgungsfonds-Schuldverschreibung.

debit *s* Debet *n*, Soll *n*, Schuldposten *m*, Schuldsaldo *m*, Belastung *f*, Einzuggebiet *n* e–s Inkassovertreters; ~ **advice** Lastschrift; ~ **and credit** Soll und Haben; ~ **balance** → *balance*; ~ **blotter** Kladde für Sollbuchungen; ~ **card** Geldkarte; ~ **charge procedure** Lastschriftverfahren; ~ **entry** Lastschrift, Sollbuchung, Abbuchung; Abgang (*Lager*); ~ **item** Sollposten, Debetposten, Lastschriftposten, Passivposten; ~ **memo** Belastungsanzeige; ~ **note** Lastschriftanzeige, Belastungsaufgabe; ~ **rate** Sollzinssatz; ~ **side** Sollseite; ~ **voucher** Lastschriftbeleg; **bank** ~ Sollbuchung einer Bank; **direct** ~ Abbuchung im Bankeinzugsverfahren; **interest on** ~ **balances** Sollzinsen; **your** ~ **balance** Saldo zu Ihren Lasten.

debit *v* belasten; ~ **an account** → *account*.

debitor Schuldner *m*.

debitrix Schuldnerin *f*.

debitum geschuldet, Schuld *f*.

debrief *v*|*t* Informationen erfragen, vernehmen, „ausquetschen".

debt Schuld *f*, Geldschuld *f*, Verbindlichkeit *f*, Forderung *f* (*bes*) Geldforderung *f*; ~**s** Schulden *f*|*pl*, Forderungen *f*|*pl*; ~**s abroad** Auslandsschulden; ~ **adjusting** Schuldenregelung; ~**s admissable for proof** zur Konkursanmeldung geeignete Forderungen; ~ **breakdown** Schuldenaufschlüsselung; ~ **by simple contract** nicht verbriefte Schuld, Schuld ohne Brief und Siegel, formlos vereinbarte Schuld; ~ **by specialty** = *specialty debt qv infra*; ~, **claim or demand** Geldforderungen und sonstige Ansprüche; ~ **collecting** Inkassowesen, Inkassomandate; ~ **collection agency** Inkassobüro; ~ **collector** Inkassomandator, Inkassobeauftragter; ~ **conversion** Umschuldung; ~ **counselling** Schuldnerberatung; ~ **default** Einstellung des Schuldendienstes; ~, **default or miscarriage** Schuld, Pflichtversäumnis oder Haftung aus unerlaubter Handlung; ~ **due** Forderung, fällige Forderung, geschuldeter Betrag; ~**s due and owing** Forderungen, Außenstände; ~ **enforcement** Zwangsvollstreckung wegen Geldforderungen; ~ **(to) equity ratio** (= ~ *equity ratio*) Verhältnis von Fremdkapital zu Eigenkapital; Verschuldungsgrad, Verschuldungskoeffizient; ~ **equity swap** Tausch von Schulden gegen Aktienkapital; ~ **growing due** zukünftige Zahlungsforderung; ~ **instrument** Schuldurkunde; ~ **limit** Verschuldungsgrenze; ~ **limitation** Begrenzung der Staatsschuld; ~ **management** Schuldenstrukturpolitik; ~ **financing** → *financing*; ~ **margin** Verschuldungsspielraum; ~ **of hono(u)r** Ehrenschuld; ~ **of record** gerichtlich festgestellte Schuld, titulierte Forderung; ~**s of the estate** Nachlaßschulden; ~ **or liquidated demand** Geldforderung; ~**s owing or accruing** gegenwärtige und zukünftige Forderungen, fällige und fällig werdende Forderungen; ~ **provable in bankruptcy** (einwandfreie) Konkursforderung; ~ **ratio** Verhältnis von Fremdkapital zu Gesamtvermögen;~**s receivable** Außenstände, Forderungen (*aus laufender Geschäftstätigkeit*); ~ **recovery** Inkassowesen; ~ **relief** Erleichterungen für Schuldner; ~ **rescheduling** Umschuldung, Fälligkeitsstreckung; ~ **restructuring** Umschuldung; ~ **service** Schuldendienst; ~ **service charges** Schuldenbedienungskosten; ~ **situate within jurisdiction** im Zuständigkeitsbereich gelegene Forderung; ~ **standoff** Nichtbedienung von Anleihen; ~ **standstill** Schuldenstillhalteabkommen; ~ **swap** Schuldentausch, Eintausch von Anleihen gegen Beteiligungen (*in Schuldnerländern*); ~ **upon record** sich aus amtlichen Unterlagen ergebende Schuld; **acknowledgment of** ~ → *acknowledgment*; **action of** ~ → *action*; **active** ~ Geldforderung; geschuldeter Geldbetrag; Außenstände; **affidavit of** ~ **and danger** Antrag auf sofortige Beitreibung (*Forderung der Krone*); **ancestral** ~ Erblasserschuld; **antecedent** ~ frühere Schuld (*bereits bei Darlehensgewährung oder Wechselausstellung bestehende Verbindlichkeit*); **assigned** ~ abgetretene Forderung; **assumption of** ~ → *assumption*; **bad** ~**s** Dubiosen, uneinbringliche Forderungen; **bad** ~**s collected** eingegangene, schon abgeschriebene Forderungen; **barred** ~ verjährte Forderung; **bonded** ~ Obligationsschuld; **book** ~**s** → *book*; **civil** ~ bürgerlich-rechtl Geldforderung, privatrechtliche Schuld; **contingent** ~ bedingte Forderung, bedingte Schuld, Eventualschuld; **convertible** ~ Wandelschuldverschreibung; **deadweight** ~ → *deadweight*; **deferred** ~ nachrangige Konkursforderung; **desperate** ~ uneinbringliche Forderung; **disputed** ~ bestrittene Forderung; **doubtful** ~ dubiose Forderung; **doubtful** ~**s** Dubiosen; **existing** ~ fällige Schuld; **external** ~ Auslandsschuld, Außenschulden; **fiduciary** ~ Schuld aufgrund e–s Vertrauens- bzw Treuhandverhältnisses; **financial** ~ Geldforderungen des Kapitalverkehrs; **floating** ~ Kredit mit Globalverpfändung, kurzfristige Verbindlichkeiten, kurzfristige (nicht konsolidierte) Staatsschuld; **floating** ~**s** allgemeine Geschäftsschulden, kurzfristige Staatsschuld; **foreign** ~**s** Auslandsschulden; **fraudulent** ~ betrügerisch erlangter Kredit; **free from** ~ schuldenfrei; **frozen** ~**s** Stillhalteschulden; **funded** ~ fundierte Schuld, unkündbare Schuld, Anleiheschuld, Staatsanleihe ohne feste Laufzeit, konsolidierter Kredit; **future** ~ zukünftig fällig werdende Forderung *bzw* Schuld; **good** ~**s** sichere Forderungen; **hypothecary** ~ durch Grundpfand gesicherte Forderung; **imprisonment for** ~ → *imprisonment*; **in** ~ verschuldet; **in payment of** ~ Leistung an Erfüllungsstatt; **installment** ~ Abzahlungsschuld, Ratenschuld; **internal** ~**s** Inlandsschulden; **judgment** ~ gerichtlich festgestellte Schuld; Vollstreckungsschuld; **legal ~s** bei e–m (*common law*) Gericht einklagbare Schuld; **liability for ~s** → *liability*; **limitation on incurrence of ~** Verschuldungsgrenze; **liquid ~** fällige Forderung; **liquidated ~** der Höhe nach feststehende Schuld; **liquidation of ~** → *liquidation*; **local ~s** Schulden von Gebietskörperschaften; **localized ~** ortsbezogene Staatsschulden; **longterm ~s** langfristige Verbindlichkeiten; **mutual ~s** gegenseitige Schulden, beiderseitige Kontokorrentschuldposten; **national ~** Staatsschuld; **nonbusiness ~** nichtgeschäftliche Forderung; nichtgewerbliche Schuld; **odious ~s** *aus politischen Gründen abgelehnte Schulden*; **ordinary ~** nicht gesicherte Forderung, nicht bevorrechtigte Forderung, gewöhnliche (Konkurs)Forderung; **outstanding ~s** Außenstände, Forderungen; **passive ~** Schuld, unverzinsliche Schuld; **past ~** bereits bestehende Schuld; **pecuniary ~** Geldschuld; **permanent ~** Dauerschuld, fundierte Schuld; **preferential ~** bevorrechtigte Forderung; **preferred ~** vorrangige Forderung; **private ~** persönliche Schuld; **privileged ~** bevorrechtigte Forderung, vorweg zu befriedigende Nachlaßverbindlichkeit; **proof of ~s** → *proof*; **provable ~** Konkursforderung, nachweisbare Forderung; **public ~** Staatsschuld; **pure ~** *scot* fällige, unbedingte Forderung; **recoverable ~** beitreibbare Forderung, *pl* beitreibungsfähige Außenstände; **regimental ~s** → *regimental*; **reproductive ~** durch echte Vermögenswerte gedeckte Staatsschuld; **residual ~** Restschuld; **retainer of ~s** → *retainer*; **secured ~s** dingl gesicherte Forderungen; **secured public ~** dinglich gesicherte Staatsschuld; **settlement of ~s** → *settlement*; **short-term ~s** kurzfristige Verbindlichkeiten; **small ~s** Kleinforderungen; **solvent ~s** fällige, kurzfristige realisierbare Forderungen; **specialty ~** durch gesiegelte Urkunde ausgewiesene Schuld; verbriefte Forderung; **sperate ~** einbringliche Forderung; **stale ~** verwirkte Forderung; **statute-barred ~** verjährte Forderung; **suit for a ~** Klage auf Zahlung (*e–r Geldschuld*); **to attach a ~** → *to attach*; **to get into ~** sich verschulden; **to liquidate a ~** → *to liquidate*; **to prove a ~** eine Forderung (*im Konkurs*) anmelden und nachweisen; **trade ~s** Geschäftsschulden; **undischarged ~** unbeglichene Schuld; **undisputed ~** unbestrittene (Geld)-Forderung, unbestrittene (Geld)-Schuld; **undue ~** noch nicht fällige Schuld; **unfunded ~** nicht fundierte Staatsschuld; **unified ~** → *unified*; **unliquidated ~** Schuld unbestimmter Höhe; **war ~s** Kriegsschulden.

debtee Gläubiger *m*; **~ executor** zum Testamentsvollstrecker bestellter Gläubiger.

debtor Schuldner *m*, Kreditnehmer *m*, Verpflichteter *m*; **D~s Act 1869** *Gesetz zur Beseitigung des Schuldturms in England*; **~ by endorsement** Giroschuldner; Indossamentsschuldner; **~ country** Schuldnerland; **~'s court** Vollstreckungsgericht; **~ -creditor agreement** Kundenkreditvertrag, Verbraucherkreditvertrag: **~ -creditor-supplier agreement** gekoppelter Lieferfinanzierungsvertrag; **~ executor** *der zum Testamentsvollstrecker bestellte Schuldner des Erblassers;* **~ in bankruptcy** Gemeinschuldner; Schuldner, gegen den ein Konkurstatbestand vorliegt (*act of bankruptcy*); **~ of assignment** Zessionsschuldner; **~ primarily liable** selbstschuldnerisch Haftender; **~'s property** Schuldnervermögen; **~'s summons** (*bankruptcy notice*) Konkursankündigung; **~ who would not pay** zahlungsunwilliger Schuldner; **common ~** *scot* Gemeinschuldner;

co-principal ~ Solidarschuldner; **examination of** ~ *eidliche* Vernehmung des Gemeinschuldners; **execution** ~ Vollstreckungsschuldner; **fiduciary ~s** Beamter bzw Treuhänder als Schuldner; **fraudulent** ~ betrügerischer Schuldner; **joint ~s** gemeinsame Schuldner, Gesamtschuldner; **judgment** ~ Vollstreckungsschuldner; **primary** ~ primär haftender Schuldner; **principal** ~ Hauptschuldner; **secondary** ~ sekundär haftender Schuldner; **sole** ~ Alleinschuldner, Einzelschuldner; **sundry ~s** diverse Außenstände; **trade ~s** *bil* Liefer- und Leistungsforderungen.

decamp *v/i* sich aus dem Staube machen, „abhhauen".

decapitation Enthauptung *f*.

decartelization Konzernentflechtung *f*.

decasualisation Überführung *f* von Gelegenheitsarbeitern in feste Arbeitsverhältnisse.

decease *v* sterben, ableben, verscheiden.

decease *s* Ableben *n*, Tod *m*, Sterbefall *m*.

deceased *adj* verstorben.

deceased *s* der (die) Verstorbene, Erblasser *m*, Erblasserin *f*; **~'s estate** Nachlaß.

decedent der (die) Verstorbene; Erblasser *m*, Erblasserin *f*; **~'s estate** Nachlaß.

deceit Täuschung *f*, arglistige Täuschung *f*, Irreführung *f*, Betrug *m*; **wilful** ~ arglistige Täuschung.

deceitful plea Scheinvorbringen *n*, Prozeßbetrug *m*.

deceive täuschen, betrügen.

decency Anstand *m*, Anständigkeit *f*, Schicklichkeit *f*, Sittsamkeit *f*; **common** ~ Anstand und Sitte, öffentliche Sittlichkeit; **public** ~ allgemeine Anstandsgefühle, Sittlichkeit.

deception Täuschung *f*, Irrtumserregung *f*; **reckless** ~ bedingt vorsätzl Täuschung; **wilful** ~ arglistige Täuschung.

deceptive täuschend, betrügerisch.

decertify *v/t* die Zulassung entziehen (*Gewerkschaft*).

decide entscheiden, sich entschließen; ~ **a case** e–n Fall entscheiden.

decimal currency Dezimalwährung *f*.

decimalization Einführung *f* des Dezimalsystems.

decision Entscheidung *f* (= *E bzw e*); Beschluß *m*, Urteil *n*; Erkenntnis *f*; Bescheid *m*; ~ **affirmed** Entscheidung bestätigt; ~ **comes up for approval** (die) *E* liegt der Rechtsmittelinstanz vor; ~ **complained of** die angefochtende *E*; ~ **ex aequo et bono** Billigkeitse, Ermessens*e*; ~ **is pending** die *E* steht noch aus; ~ **maker** Entscheidungsträger; **~-making process** Verfahren zur Herbeiführung e–r Entscheidung; *E*-sfindung(sverfahren); ~ **of the majority** Mehrheits*e*, Mehrheitsbeschluß; ~ **on a question of law** Revisions*e*; ~ **on the merits** Sachentscheidung; **administrative** ~ Verwaltungs-*E*, Verwaltungsakt; **amending** ~ Änderungsbescheid; **appeal lies from this ~ to the ...** gegen diese *E* kann ein Rechtsmittel beim ... eingelegt werden; **confirmatory** ~ bestätigende *E*; **court** ~ → *court*; **discretionary** ~ Ermessens*e*; **final** ~ endgültige *E*, rechtskräftige *E*; *aber auch:* Endurteil, *gegen das noch Rechtsmittel möglich;* **grounds of the** ~ (*E–s*)Gründe; **interlocutory** ~ Zwischen*e*; **judicial** ~ → *judicial*; **leading** ~ Präzedenzfall; **legal** ~ gerichtliche *E*; **power of** ~ → *power*; **preliminary** ~ vorläufige *E*, Zwischen*e*; **provisional** ~ Vorbescheid; **reasoned** ~ abgewogene *E*, mit Gründen versehene *E*; **reasons for the** ~ (*E–s*)Gründe; **to arrive at a** ~ zu e–r *E* gelangen; **to pass a** ~ gerichtlich entscheiden, ein Urteil erlassen; **to refer for** ~ (*zur E*) e–m Schiedsrichter vorlegen; **to rescind a** ~ e–e *E* aufheben; **to reserve one's** ~ sich die *E* vorbehalten, die *E* in e–m besonderen Termin verkünden; **technical**

~formale *E*, formalistische *E*; **two – track** ~ Doppelbeschluß, *E* mit Alternative; **unreported** ~ nicht veröffentlichte E.

decisive entscheidend, maßgeblich.

deck|cargo Deckladung *f*; ~ **load** Deckladung.

declarant der (die) Erklärende, Anmelder *m*.

declaration Erklärung *f* (= *E bzw . . . e*), Willenserklärung *f*, unbeeidigte Aussage; Feststellung *f*; Anmeldung *f*; Klageschrift *f*; Anspruchsbegründung *f*; ~ **against interest** selbstbelastende, den eigenen Interessen zuwiderlaufende *E*; ~ **as to election expenses** *E* über die Wahlausgaben *e–s Abgeordneten*; ~ **as to rights** Feststellungsurteil; ~ **date** Tag der Dividenden-Beschlußfassung; ~ **in chief** Hauptbegründung e–r Klage; ~ **in lieu of oath** eidesstattliche Versicherung; ~ **inwards** (Zoll)Einfuhr*e*; ~ **of accession** Beitritts*e*; ~ **of alienage** Options*e* zugunsten e–s fremden Staates, Verzicht auf die Staatsangehörigkeit; ~ **of bankruptcy** Bankrott*e*; ~ **of charge** Feststellung des Rechts auf abgesonderte Befriedigung *aus dem Geschäftsvermögen*; ~ **of contents** Zolldeklaration; Inhaltsangabe; ~ **of death** Todes*e*; ~ **of deceased person** *E* e–s Verstorbenen; ~ **of dividend** Festsetzung e–r Dividende; ~ **of goods** Zolldeklaration; ~ **of inability to pay debts** Zahlungsunfähigkeits*e*; Insolvenz*e*; ~ **of indemnity** Schadloserklärung; ~ **of independence** Unabhängigkeits*e*; **D~ of Independence** Amerikanische Unabhängigkeitserklärung *vom 4. Juli 1776*; ~ **of insolvency** Insolvenz*e*; ~ **of intent** Absichts*e*; ~ **of intention** Absichts*e*, *US* Naturalisations*e*; ~ **of legitimacy** Ehelichkeitsfeststellung (*durch Urteil*); ~ **of majority** Volljährigkeits*e*, Mündig*e*; ~ **of non-infringement** Feststellungsurteil, daß keine Rechtsverletzung vorliegt; ~ **of nullity** Nichtigkeitsurteil; ~ **of options** Prämien*e*; ~ **of origin** Ursprungs*e* *(Ware)*; **D~ of Paris** Pariser Seerechtsdeklaration (1856); ~ **of paternity** Vaterschaftsanerkenntnis; ~ **of peace** Friedens*e*; ~ **of policy** Grundsatz*e*; ~ **of principal** Offenlegung des Auftraggebers; ~ **of principle** Grundsatz*e*; ~ **of priority** Prioritäts*e*; ~ **of property** Anmeldung von Vermögen; ~ **of purchase** Kauf*e*; ~ **of right** Feststellungsurteil (*gegen die Krone*); **D~ of Rights** Grundrechtskatalog; ~ **of secrecy** Geheimhaltungsgelöbnis (*Wahlbeauftragte*); ~ **of solvency** Solvenz*e* (*als Voraussetzung für freiwillige Gesellschaftsliquidation*); ~ **of taking** Entziehungsbeschluß, Inanspruchnahme; ~ **of title** Feststellungsurteil (*über das Bestehen e–s Rechtstitels*); ~ **of trust** Treuhands*e*, treuhänderische Übertragung; ~ **of understanding** Einvernehmens*e*; ~ **of uses** *E* der Nutzungsberechtigung, Nießbrauchbestellung; ~ **of validity** Gültigkeits*e*; ~ **of value** Wertangabe; ~ **of war** Kriegs*e*; ~ **outwards** (Zoll) Ausfuhr*e*; **bilateral** ~ beiderseitige *E*; **binding** ~ bindende *E*; **customs** ~ Zoll*e*, Zolldeklaration, *E* über die Mitführung zollpflichtiger Waren; **dying** ~ *E* e–r Person kurz vor ihrem Tode, *E* auf dem Sterbebette; **false** ~ falsche (*eidesstattliche*) Versicherung; mittelbare Falschbeurkundung; (*irrtümliche*) unrichtige Beschreibung; **interpretative** ~ Auslegungs*e*; **self-serving** ~ vorprozessuale *E* zum eigenen Vorteil, Schutzbehauptung; **statutory** ~ *uneidliche Versicherung der Richtigkeit nach bestem Wissen und Gewissen* (*ähnl eidesstattl Versicherung*); **to make a** ~ → *to make*; **unilateral** ~ einseitige Willens*e*; **vesting** ~ → *vesting*.

declarator|of property *scot* Eigentumsfeststellungsklage; ~ **of trust** Klage auf Feststellung e–r treuhänderischen Vermögensbindung.

declaratory erklärend, erläuternd, Feststellungs . . .; ~ **part of a**

judgment Urteilsbegründung; ~ **part of a law** die materiellen Vorschriften e–s Gesetzes.

declare erklären, aussagen, klären, feststellen, äußern, deklarieren; ~ **a dividend** e–e Dividende festsetzen; ~ **a trust** ein Treuhandsverhältnis begründen; ~ **one's interest** seine persönlichen Interessen (*als Vorstandsmitglied*) offenlegen; ~ **oneself biassed** sich für befangen erklären.

decline *s* Abnahme *f*, Rückgang *m*, Sturz *m*, Niedergang *m*, Verfall *m*, ~ **guaranty** Garantie gegen Preisrückgang (*Warenterminhandel*); ~ **in demand** Nachfragerückgang; ~ **in value** Wertminderung; ~ **list** Liste abzulehnender Risiken; **general** ~ allgemeiner Geschäftsrückgang.

decline *v* ablehnen, sich weigern; ~ **an answer** e–e Beantwortung verweigern; ~ **an offer** ein Angebot ablehnen; ~ **(all) responsibility** die Verantwortung ablehnen.

decoding Entschlüsselung *f*, Dechiffrierung *f*.

decollation Enthauptung *f*.

deconcentration Auflockerung *f*, Dezentralisierung *f*, Entflechtung *f*.

decontaminate entseuchen, entstrahlen, entgiften.

decontamination Entseuchung *f*, Entstrahlung *f*, Entgiftung *f*.

decontrol freigeben, die Zwangswirtschaft aufheben; ~**led** nicht mehr zwangsbewirtschaftet, freigegeben.

decorate dekorieren, schmücken, verschönern, Schönheitsreparaturen vornehmen; Orden verleihen.

decoy *s* Lockvogel *m*, Köder *m*; *v* ködern, verlocken, verleiten; ~ **letter** Fangbrief, Köderbrief; ~**ing child** das Weglocken zur Entführung Minderjähriger; ~ **team** Polizeifalle.

decrease *s* Abnahme *f*, Verminderung *f*; ~ **in demand** Nachfragerückgang; ~ **in value** Wertminderung; ~ **of value** Minderwert.

decrease *v* abnehmen, sich vermindern, zurückgehen.

decree Verordnung *f*, Dekret *n*; Urteil *n* (*im Equity-Verfahren*), Beschluß *m*; ~ **absolute** Endurteil (*nach Wegfall des Vorbehalts*), Scheidungsurteil (*evt Rechtsmittel möglich*); ~ **arbitral** *scot* Schiedsgerichtsentscheidung; ~ **conform** *scot* Urteilsbestätigung; ~ **dative** *scot* Einsetzung e–s Nachlaßverwalters; ~ **for judicial separation** Urteil über die Gestattung des Getrenntlebens; ~ **for the restitution of conjugal rights** → *restitution*; ~ **law** Verordnungsrecht; Rechtsverordnung; ~ **nisi** vorläufiges (Scheidungs)Urteil, (Scheidungs)Vorbehaltsurteil; ~ **of adjudication** Konkurseröffnungsbeschluß; ~ **of constitution** *scot* Urteil auf Feststellung e–r Schuld; ~ **of distribution** Nachlaßverteilungsbeschluß; ~ **of exoneration** *scot* Entlastung(sbeschluß); ~ **of forthcoming** *scot* Überweisungsbeschluß; ~ **of insolvency** Feststellung der Nachlaßüberschuldung, Nachlaßkonkurseröffnung; ~ **of locality** *scot* örtlicher Verteilungsbeschluß (*Verteilung der Nutzungen von Pachtland auf die Erben durch Gerichtsbeschluß*); ~ **of modification** *scot* Änderungsbeschluß (*Zuwendung*); ~ **of nullity** Ehenichtigkeitsurteil, Eheaufhebungsurteil (*ex tunc*); ~ **of registration** *scot* Verfahren zur Vollstreckbarkeitserklärung; ~ **pro confesso** Versäumnisurteil (*gegen den Beklagten*); **absolute** ~ = *decree absolute qv*; **by** ~ auf dem Verordnungswege; **consent** ~ → *consent*; **declaratory** ~ Feststellungsurteil; **deficiency** ~ gerichtliche Feststellung der (*durch die Pfandverwertung nicht befriedigten*) Restforderung; **emergency** ~ → *emergency*; **executive** ~ Durchführungsverordnung; **final** ~ Endurteil; **interlocutory** ~ Zwischenurteil, Beschluß (*während des Verfahrens*); **to issue a** ~ → *to issue*.

decrement Abnahme *f*, Ausfall *m*, Abgang *m*; ~ **table** Ausscheidetafel, Mortalitätstafel; **double** ~ *ins*

Ausscheidetafel mit zwei Ausscheidecursachen.

decriminalisation Entkriminalisierung *f.*

decrowning Entthronung *f,* Entziehung *f* der Königswürde.

decrypt entschlüsseln.

decryptment Entschlüsselung *f.*

decurrent ablaufend, nachschüssig; ~ **rent** nachschüssige Miete.

dedicate widmen, der Öffentlichkeit zur Verfügung stellen.

dedication Widmung *f (für öffentliche Zwecke)*; ~ **day** Kirchweih; ~ **of way** Widmung (als öffentliche Straße); **common-law** ~ gewohnheitsrechtliche Widmung; **statutory** ~ Widmung kraft Gesetzes; **tacit** ~ stillschweigende Widmung.

dedition Preisgabe *f.*

deduc|e abziehen, folgern; ~**ing title** Nachweis der Rechtsnachfolge.

deduct absetzen, abziehen, kürzen; ~**ed and paid** nach Abzug und Zahlung (*von Steuern*); **tax** ~**ed** nach (Abzug der) Steuern.

deductible absetzbar, abzuziehen; ~ **average** Selbstbehalt; ~ **clause** Selbstbehaltsklausel; **$ 10** ~ **comprehensive** Fahrzeugversicherung mit 10 Dollar Selbstbeteiligung.

deductibility Absetzbarkeit *f.*

deduction Abzug *m,* Absetzung *f;* Folgerung *f,* Deduktion *f,* Schluß *m;* ~ **at source** Quellensteuerabzug; ~ **for expenses** abzugsfähige Betriebsausgaben; ~ **for new** Abzug neu für alt; ~ **of unaccrued interest** Abzinsung; **admitted as** ~ abzugsfähig; **allowable** ~**s** zulässige Absetzungen; **itemized** ~**s** spezifizierte Ansetzung; **marital** ~ → *marital.* **payroll** ~ → *payroll*; **standard** ~ Pauschalfreibetrag; **statutory** ~**s** gesetzliche (Steuer)-abzüge.

deed *s* gesiegelte Urkunde *f,* Urkunde *f,* beurkundeter Vertrag *m;* Tat *f,* Handlung *f;* ~ **absolute** = *absolute deed qv* ~**s and simple contracts** gesiegelte, schriftliche sowie formlose Verträge; ~ **box** Urkundentresor, Schatulle; ~ **indented** = *indenture qv;* ~ **in fee** Grundstücksauflassungsurkunde; ~ **indented** mehrseitige gesiegelte Urkunde; ~ **of agency** Liquidationstreuhand (*e–s Schuldners*); ~ **of arrangement** beurkundeter außengerichtlicher Vergleich (*mit Gläubigern*); ~ **of assignment** Übertragungsurkunde, Abtretungsurkunde, Generalabtretung; ~ **of conveyance** → *conveyance;* ~ **of covenant** Nebenverpflichtungen (*in Form e–r gesiegelten Urkunde*); Subskriptionsverpflichtung; ~ **of discharge** (*förmliche*) Treuhandbeendigungserklärung; ~ **of donation** Schenkungsurkunde; ~ **of foundation** Stiftungsurkunde; ~ **of gift** Schenkungsurkunde; ≈ *notariell beurkundete Grundstücksschenkung;* ~ **of grant** Übertragungsurkunde; Auflassungsurkunde; ~ **of inspectorship** Bestellung(surkunde) eines vertraglichen Liquidators zugunsten der Gläubiger; ~ **of partnership** Gesellschaftsvertrag (*Personalgesellschaft*); ~ **of postponement** förmliche Rangrücktrittserklärung; ~ **of priorities** Rangvorhabensurkunde; ~ **of reconveyance** Rückauflassungsurkunde; ~ **of release** förmliche Freigabeerklärung, Rückauflassung an den Schuldner; löschungsfähige Quittung; ~ **of separation** (*förmliche*) Vereinbarung über das Getrenntleben; ~ **of settlement** Treuhanderrichtungsurkunde zugunsten der Ehefrau; ~ **of transfer** Auflassungsurkunde, Abtretungsurkunde, Übertragungsurkunde; ~ **of trust** = *trust deed qv;* ~ **poll** einseitig errichtete gesiegelte Urkunde; ~ **to correct error in prior** ~ Berichtigungsurkunde, Nachtragsurkunde zum Zwecke der Berichtigung; **absolute** ~ unbedingte und unbeschränkte Grundstücksübertragungsurkunde; Vollrechtsübertragungsurkunde, **abstraction of** ~ Eigentums-Urkundenauszug; **ancient** ~ ältere (*sicher verwahrte*) Urkunde (*etwa 20–30 Jahre alt*); **collective** ~ Sammelurkunde; **composition** ~ Gläubigervergleich; **contract by** ~ → *contract* **defeasible** ~ auflösende bedingte Übertragungsurkunde; **derivative** ~ ergänzende Urkunde; **enrolled** ~ gerichtlich *bzw amtlich* hinterlegte Urkunde; **execution of a** ~ → *execution;* **gratuitous** ~ Urkunde ohne Gegenleistung, unentgeltliche urkundliche Willenserklärung; **master** ~ Hauptauflassungsurkunde (*Wohnungseigentum*); **notarial** ~ notarielle Urkunde; not. beurkundete gesiegelte Urkunde; **privileged** ~ vom Formzwang freigestellte Urkunde; **quitclaim** → *quitclaim;* **title** ~**s** → *title;* **to execute a** ~ → *execute;* **to make a** ~ e–e Urkunde errichten; **supplemental** ~ Nachtragsurkunde; **vesting** ~→ *vesting,* **warranty** ~ → *warranty.*

deed *v* urkundlich übertragen.

deem beurteilen, (als etwas) ansehen, gelten (als), auslegen, glauben, halten (für); ~ **fit and proper** als einwandfrei gelten; ~**ed to be fraudulent** gilt als betrügerisch; ~**ed to belong** gilt als jmds Eigentum; ~**ed to have been caused** gilt als verursacht durch; ~**ed to pass** gilt als übergegangen (*zB ein Recht*).

deemsters Richter *m|pl* (*auf der Insel Man*).

deescalation Entspannung *f*, Abbau *m* der Krisensituation.

deescaltory eskalationsbremsend.

deface durchstreichen, ausstreichen; verunstalten, entstellen, unkenntlich machen.

defacement Entstellung *f*, Ausstreichen *n*, Unkenntlichmachen *n*, Entwerten *n*.

defalcate Untreue begehen, veruntreuen; aufrechnen.

defalcation Unterschlagung *f*, Untreue *f*, Aufrechnung *f*.

defalk aufrechnen.

defamacast Verleumdung im Rundfunk.

defamation Ehrverletzung *f*, Ehrenkränkung *f*, Beleidigung *f*, Verleumdung *f*, üble Nachrede *f*; ~ **of a competitor's reputation** Rufschädigung eines Konkurrenten; ~ **of character** Ehrabschneidung; **unintentional** ~ unbeabsichtigte Ehrverletzung.

defamatory beleidigend, ehrenrührig, verleumderisch; ~**libel** → *libel;* ~ **matter** beleidigendes Material; ~ **per quod** beleidigungsfähig auf Grund besonderen Sachverhalts; ~ **per se** an sich beleidigende Äußerung, Formalbeleidigung; ~ **upon its face** ohne weiteres verleumderisch.

default *s* Nichterbringung *f* e–r Leistung, Pflichtversäumnis *f*, Leistungsstörung *f*, Verzug *m*, pflichtwidrige Unterlassung *f*; Säumnis *f*; ~ **action** Mahnverfahren; ~ **by defendant** Säumnis des Beklagten; ~ **fine** Verzugsstrafe; Säumnisbuße; ~ **in delivery** Lieferverzug; ~ **in payment** Zahlungsverzug; ~ **in service of statement of claim** Unterlassen der Klagezustellung; ~ **notice** Vertragsverletzungsmitteilung, Abhilfeaufforderung; Androhung der Verfallsklausel; (*befristete*) Androhung des Auftragsentzugs wegen Schlechterfüllung und/oder Verzuges; ~ **risk** Ausfallsrisiko; ~ **surcharge** Säumniszuschlag; ~ **of appearance** Säumnis im Termin; ~ **of defence** Unterlassen rechtzeitiger Einwendungen; ~ **of issue** das Fehlen von Nachkommenschaft; ~ **risk** Ausfallrisiko (*Inkasso*), Debitorenrisiko; ~ **summons** Mahnbescheid; **persistent** ~ **in filing returns** ständige pflichtwidrige Nichtabgabe von Erklärungen (*Handelsregister*); **principal's** ~ Ausfall des Hauptschuldners; **to be in** ~ **of one's obligations** seinen Verpflichtungen nicht nachgekommen sein; **to make** ~säumig sein, in Verzug geraten, **wilful** ~ vorsätzliche Unterlassung e–r geschuldeten Leistung; bewußte Nachlässigkeit.

default *v* nicht erfüllen (*Vertrag*); verletzen, (*Verpflichtungen*) nicht einhalten, in Verzug geraten; nicht erscheinen; ~ **on one's loans** seine Anleihen nicht bedienen, die Zahlung für Anleihezinsen und Tilgung einstellen.

defaulter Säumiger *m*, Veruntreuender *m*; säumige Partei *f*; **declared** ~ zahlungsunfähiges Börsenmitglied.

defeasance Annulierung *f*, Aufhebung *f*; ~ **clause** Aufhebungsklausel, Rückauflassungsklausel, Heimfallsklausel, Gegenstandsloserklärung e–r Sicherungsübereignung.

defeasible annullierbar, unter einer auflösenden Bedingung stehend, mit Heimfallsrecht ausgestattet, bedingt rückübertragbar; ~ **fee** auflösend bedingtes Grundeigentum; ~ **title** auflösend bedingtes Eigentum.

defeat *s* Niederlage *f*; ~ **at the polls** Wahlniederlage; **voting** ~ Abstimmungsniederlage.

defeat *v* besiegen, zu Fall bringen; nichtig machen, vereiteln, rückgängig machen; ~ **a bill** e–n Antrag zum Scheitern bringen; ~ **a claim** e–n Anspruch zu Fall bringen; ~ **a creditor** e–en Gläubigeranspruch vereiteln; ~ **a right** ein Recht ungültig machen, ein Recht entziehen; ~ **and delay creditors** die Befriedigung der Gläubiger vereiteln oder verzögern; ~**ed party** die unterliegende Partei; ~**ing of a creditor** Gläubigerbenachteiligung, Vereitelung e–s Gläubigeranspruchs.

defect Fehler *m*, Mangel *m*, schadhafte Stelle *f*; Abfall *m*, Lossagung *f*; ~ **in indictment** technischer Fehler in der Anklageschrift; ~ **due to workmanship** Fertigungsfehler, Ausführungsmangel; ~ **in jurat** Mangel der eidlichen Beglaubigungsformel; ~ **in law** Rechtsmangel, Gesetzeslücke; ~ **in title** Rechtsmangel; Fehler im Rubrum; ~ **not apparent** nicht äußerlich erkennbarer Mangel; ~ **of design** Konstruktionsfehler, Gestaltungsmangel; ~ **of form** Formfehler, Formmangel; ~ **of parties** Mangel des Prozeßführungsrechts; ~ **of proceedings** Verfahrensmangel; ~ **of quality** Sachmangel, Qualitätsmangel; ~ **of (= in) substance** inhaltlicher Fehler; materiellrechtlicher Mangel, wesentlicher Mangel (*e–s Schriftstücks vor Gericht*); ~ **of title** Rechtsmangel; ~ **apparent** ~ äußerlich erkennbarer Mangel; **design** ~ Planungsfehler (*Architekt*) **fatal** ~ Nichtigkeitsgrund; **formal** ~ Formfehler; **hidden** ~ verborgener Mangel, versteckter Mangel; **intrinsic** ~ innerer Mangel; **latent** ~ verborgener Mangel, versteckter Mangel; **mental** ~ Geistesstörung, geistiger Defekt; **patent** ~ äußerlich erkennbarer Fehler; **physical** ~ körperliches Gebrechen; Körperbehinderung; **redhibitory** ~ zur Wandlung berechtigender Mangel.

defect *v/i* zum Feind überlaufen, abtrünnig werden.

defection Lossagung *f*, Abfall *m*, Parteiwechsel *m*, Abwandern *n* (*von Führungskräften*).

defective *adj* fehlerhaft, mangelhaft; geistesgestört; **D~ Premises Law;** Gebäudehaftpflichtgesetz *m*.

defectiveness Mangelhaftigkeit *f*, Unvollständigkeit *f*, Unzulänglichkeit *f*, Schadhaftigkeit *f*.

defector Abtrünniger *m*, Fraktionswechsler *m* Überläufer *m*; **double** ~ Doppelüberläufer.

defence (= *defense*) (1) *mil* Verteidigung *f*; **D~ Acts** Enteignungsgesetze für Verteidigungszwecke; ~ **area** für Neutrale gesperrte Seezone; ~ **bonds** Kriegsanleihen; **D~ Council** Staatsverteidigungsrat, (*GB* Verteidigungsministerium); ~ **expenditure** Verteidigungsausgaben; ~ **information** Verteidigungsnachrichten; ~ **procurement** das mil. Beschaffungswesen; ~ **regulations** Kriegsverordnungen; ~ **sales** Verkauf von Rüstungsgütern; **civil** ~ Zivilschutz; **national** ~ Landesverteidigung; Bundesverteidigung.

defence (= *defense*) (*2*) Verteidigung (*bei Gericht*), Verteidigungsvorbringen *n*; Rechtfertigungs(sgrund), Einwendung(en) *f*, Einrede *f*, Gegenvorbringen *n*; ~ **arising out of the contract** vertraglich begründete Einwendung(en); ~ **attorney** Verteidiger; ~ **by accused in person** persönliche Verteidigung des Angeklagten; ~ **by counsel** Wahlverteidigung, Verteidigung durch einen Rechtsanwalt; ~ **certificate** Armenrechtszeugnis für eine Pflichtverteidigung; ~ **counsel** Verteidiger; ~ **evidence** von der Verteidigung beantragte Beweiserhebungen, Beweismaterial der Verteidigung; ~ **in bar** prozeßhindernde Einrede; ~ **of accident** Verteidigungsvorbringen, es habe sich um e–n Unglücksfall gehandelt; ~ **of fraud** Einrede der Arglist; ~ **of insanity** Berufung auf Unzurechnungsfähigkeit; ~ **of privilege** Berufung auf Immunität; ~ **of obedience to orders** Berufung auf höheren Befehl; ~ **of set-off** Einrede der Aufrechnung; ~ **of tender** Einwendung, die Leistung angeboten zu haben; ~ **of truth** Berufung auf den Wahrheitsbeweis; ~ **of counterclaim** Einwendung von Gegenansprüchen; ~ **to crime** Verteidigung; ~ **"unfit to plead"** Einrede der Unzurechnungsfähigkeit, E. der mangelnden Prozeßfähigkeit; **affidavit of** ~ Bescheinigung, daß das Beklagtenvorbringen aussichtsreich ist; **affirmative** ~ Einwendungen mit Gegenansprüchen, Gegenvorbringen; **arguable** ~ vertretbares Gegenvorbringen; **complete** ~ *ein Gegenvorbringen, das den Anspruch zu Fall bringt,* absolute Einrede, peremptorische Einrede; **costs of** ~ Kosten der Verteidigung; **dilatory** ~ prozeßhindernde Einrede; hinhaltendes Taktieren des Beklagten; **equitable** ~ Einwendung nach Billigkeitsrecht, persönliche Einwendung, im Equity-Verfahren zulässige Einwendung; **full** ~ alle Einwendungen (*Generalklausel*); **frivolous** ~ frivoles Vorbringen des Beklagten; **good** ~ berechtigte Einwendung; **inadmissible** ~ unzulässige Einwendung, unzulässiges Verteidigungsvorbringen; **legal** ~ rechtlich ausreichendes Verteidigungsvorbringen; *Einwendungen, die nur in Common Law Gerichten zulässig waren;* **meritorious** ~ materiell-rechtliche Einwendung; **no** ~ ohne begründetes Gegenvorbringen; **partial** ~ Einwendung gegen einen Teil der Klage; **peremptory** ~ restloses Bestreiten des Klagevorbringens; *Behauptung, die Klage sei nicht schlüssig oder von vorneherein völlig unbegründet;* **personal** ~ persönliche Einwendung (*Wechsel*); **points of** ~ Klageerwiderung, Einzelpunkte des Verteidigungsvorbringens; **preliminary** ~ dilatorische Einreden; **pretermitted** ~ verspätetes *nicht mehr zulässiges* Gegenvorbringen; **private** ~ Berufung auf außerstrafrechtl Notwehrrechte; **public interest** ~ Berufung auf Wahrnehmung öffentl Interesses; **self-** → *self;* **sham** ~ offensichtlich unbegründetes Verteidigungsvorbringen; **special** ~ besondere (*ankündigungspflichtige*) Einwendung; **statement of** ~ → *statement;* **time for** ~ Frist zur Klagebeantwortung; **to plead a** ~ e–e Einrede erheben, einwenden; **to put forward a** ~ eine Einrede erheben, **to rebut the** ~ ein Verteidigungsvorbringen widerlegen; **to set up a** ~ → *to set up;* **witness for the** ~ → *witness.*

defend (sich) verteidigen, sich auf e–e Klage einlassen; ~ **a suit** e–n Prozeß als Beklagter führen.

defendant Beklagter *m* (= *Bekl bzw bekl*); Antragsgegner *m*; Beschuldigter *m*, Angeschuldigter *m*; Angeklagter *m*; ~ **added** nachträglich mitverklagte Partei; ~ **company** die verklagte Gesellschaft; ~ **in error** Revisions*bekl;* ~ **in person** persönlich erschienener *Bekl;* ~ **not served** *Beklagter, dem die Klage bzw Ladung nicht zugestellt wurde;* ~ **showing cause** der sich auf die Klage einlassende Beklagte; ~ **un-**

der disability nicht prozeßfähiger *Bekl;* **absconding** ~ *Bekl*, der sich durch Fernbleiben dem Prozeß entziehen will; **co-** ~ Mit*bekl*, Mitangeklagter; **indigent** ~ mittelloser *Bekl;* **joint** ~ Mitangeklagte; **nominal** ~ Beklagter als notwendiger Streitgenosse (*ohne sonstigen Klageanlaß*); **principal** ~ Haupt*bekl*; **remanded** ~ Beschuldigter in Untersuchungshaft; **representative** ~**s** Beklagte, die zugleich stellvertretend als Mitglieder einer Personenmehrheit verklagt sind.

defended verteidigt, streitig.

defender *scot* Beklagter *m*, Angeklagter *m*; Verfechter *m*, Verteidiger *m*; **D~ of the Faith** Verteidiger des Glaubens (*Titel der englischen Könige seit 1521*) **public** ~ Offizialverteidiger.

defeneration Zinswucher *m*.

defensible zu verteidigen, vertretbar, entschuldbar.

defensive defensiv, abwehrend.

defensor Verteidiger *m*; unbefugter Verteidiger *m*; Kirchenpatron *m*, Schutzherr *m; hist* Vormund *m*, Beklagter *m*.

defer unterbreiten, sich unterordnen; aufschieben, hinausschieben; ~ **sine die** auf unbestimmte Zeit verschieben; ~ **until further notice** bis auf weiteres zurückstellen.

deference Unterordnung *f*, Nachgeben *n*; Hochachtung *f*, Ehrerbietung *f*.

deferment Aufschub *m*, Verzögerung *f*, Zurückstellung *f* (*Wehrdienst*), Zurückgestellter *m*, UK-Gestellter *m*; ~ **in call-up** Aufschub der Aufbietung; ~ **of sentence** (= *deferring sentence*) Aufschiebung der Urteilsverkündung (*bis 6 Monate, zur Prüfung der Bewährungsvoraussetzungen*); **occupational** ~ berufliche Unabkömmlichkeit; **to apply for** ~ **of the hearing** Vertagung (*bzw* spätere Anberaumung) des Termins beantragen.

deferral Aufschub *m*; ~ **of payment** Zahlungsaufschub, Tilgungsstreckung.

deferred zurückgestellt, zurückverwiesen, verspätet, vertagt, der Zukunft vorbehalten, ausgesetzt, aufgeschoben; ~ **accounts** Zwischenkonten, Konten zwecks späterer Gutschrift; ~ **accounts receivable** künftig fällige Forderungen; ~ **assets** → *assets;* ~ **availability items** später verfügbare Inkassoposten; ~ **charges (to operations)** vorausbezahlte Betriebsausgaben, vorausbezahlte Aufwendungen, aktive Rechnungsabgrenzung; ~ **creditors in bankruptcy** Gläubiger mit Rang nach den gewöhnlichen Konkursgläubigern; ~ **credits to income** passive Rechnungsabgrenzungen, im voraus eingegangene Erträge; ~ **delivery** *exch* Lieferungsaufschub; ~ **income** transitorische Passiva; ~ **item** transitorischer Posten; ~ **life annuities** Anwartschaft auf Leibrente; ~ **ordinary share** → *share;* ~ **pay** Soldeinbehaltung; ~ **premiums** *ins* nachträglich zahlbare Prämien; ~ **rebate** nachträglicher Umsatzbonus; ~ **revenue** transitorische Passiva; ~ **shares** → *share;* ~ **taxes** → *tax*.

deficiency Fehler *m*, Fehlbetrag *m*; Mangel *m*, Unvollkommenheit *f*; ~ **account** → *account* (*2*); ~ **advances** Kassenvorschlüsse (*der Staatsbank*); ~ **appropriations** Nachtragsbewilligung; ~ **assessment** Mankoberechnung (*Steuerveranlagung*); ~ **bill** Antrag auf nachträgliche Deckung eines Defizits, Antrag auf Nachtragsbewilligung; ~ **claim** Mängelrüge; ~ **dividend** → *dividend;* ~ **guarantee** Ausfallbürgschaft; ~ **judgment** Ausfallurteil, *gerichtliche Feststellung der Höhe einer aus der Pfandverwertung oder Vollstreckung nicht gedeckten Restforderung;* ~ **in receipts** Mindereinnahmen; ~ **in the proceeds** Minderertrag; ~ **in title** Rechtsmangel; ~ **in weight** Fehlgewicht, Gewichtsmanko; ~ **let-**

ter Steuermahnschreiben; ~ **notice** Steuermahnung; ~ **of men** Fehlbestand (Schiffsbesatzung); ~ **reserve** Rückstellung für Ausfall von Einkünften; **mental** ~Geistesschwäche, Störung der Geistestätigkeit.

deficient mangelhaft, unzureichend.

deficit Defizit *n*, Unterbilanz, *f*, Ausfall *m*, Fehlbetrag *m*; ~ **financing** Defizitfinanzierung; ~ **spending** Defizitfinanzierung; konjunkturbelebende defizitäre Ausgaben der öffentlichen Hand; **budgetary** ~ Haushaltsdefizit; **cash** ~ Kassenfehlbetrag; **disposing of** ~ Ausgleich eines Minusbetrages; **external** ~ Zahlungsbilanzdefizit; **fiscal** ~ Haushaltsdefizit; **to meet a** ~ e–n Fehlbetrag ausgleichen; **to settle a** ~ e–n Fehlbetrag begleichen.

defile schänden, entehren (*Frau*), deflorieren, besudeln, verderben, beschmutzen.

defilement Unsauberkeit *f*, Unreinheit *f*, Verderbnis *f*, Verdorbenheit *f*, Befleckung *f*, Schändung *f*, Vornahme *f* unzüchtiger Handlungen; ~ **of girls** Verführung zur Unzucht und Unzucht mit Mädchen (*unter 16*).

define definieren, bestimmen, formulieren, vorschreiben, Bedeutung festlegen, begrenzen; ~ **a common policy** Grundsätze e–s gemeinsamen Vorgehens festlegen; ~ **an inventive idea** e–n Erfindungsgedanken definieren; ~**d mental element** subjektives Tatbestandsmerkmal; ~ **the scope of the invention** den Umfang der Erfindung abgrenzen; **as** ~**d in the Act** gemäß der Legaldefinition, gemäß der Begriffsbestimmung des Gesetzes.

definite bestimmt, deutlich; ~ **and certain amount** Betrag von bestimmter Höhe; **to become** ~ Bestandskraft erlangen.

definition Definition *f*, Erklärung*f*, Abgrenzung *f*, Begriffsbestimmung *f*, Erläuterung *f*; **absolute** ~ zwingende Begriffsbestimmung; **legal** ~ Legaldefinition; **non-statutory** ~ nicht im Gesetz enthaltene Begriffsbestimmung; **statutory** ~ Legaldefinition.

definitive endgültig, bestandskräftig entschieden, End ...; ~ **bond** Schuldverschreibungsurkunde (*eingetauscht gegen Zwischenschein*); ~ **publication of any order** Verkündung e–s Beschlusses.

deflation Deflation *f*.

deflationary *adj* deflationär.

deflection of trade Ablenkung *f* des Handels.

defloration Defloration *f*, Entjungferung *f*, Verführung *f*.

deflower deflorieren, entjungfern, schänden.

deforce widerrechtlich vorenthalten, widerrechtlich Landbesitz entziehen; *scot* Widerstand gegen Vollstreckungsbeamte leisten.

deforcement Entsetzung *n*, verbotene Eigenmacht durch Besitzentziehung *f*; *scot* Widerstand *m* gegen Vollstreckungsbeamte.

deforc(e)or *derjenige, der e–n anderen gewaltsam und widerrechtlich von e–m Grundstück vertreibt,* der Widerstand gegen Vollstreckungsbeamte Leistende.

deforestation Rodung *f*, Abholzung *f*.

deform verunstalten, deformieren, umgestalten, entstellen.

deformity Mißbildung *f*, Mißgestalt *f*.

defraud betrügen, übervorteilen, beschwindeln, hintergehen; ~ **the revenue** Abgaben hinterziehen; **attempt to** ~ Täuschungsversuch; **intent to** ~ → *intent;* **to act with intent to** ~ in Betrugsabsicht handeln; ~**ing the Revenue** Steuerhinterziehung.

defraudation Hinterziehung *f*, Unterschlagung *f*; betrügerisches Erlangen *n;* ~ **of the customs** Zollhinterziehung.

defrauder Betrüger *m*, Steuerhinterzieher *m*.

defray bestreiten, decken, bezahlen, für Bezahlung sorgen; ~ **expenses**

die Unkosten bestreiten, die Spesen übernehmen.

defunct verstorben, vergangen; erloschen, ausgelaufen; ~ **company** gelöschte Gesellschaft.

defy|competition der Konkurrenz die Stirn bieten; ~ **a ruling** sich über eine Anordnung hinwegsetzen.

degradation Degradierung *f*, Absetzung *f*, Entlassung *f* (*aus e–m Amt*); Degradation *f*, Erniedrigung *f*, Entziehung *f* der Priesterwürde.

degrade erniedrigen, entwürdigen, herabsetzen, degradieren; ~ **a witness** e–n Zeugen schlecht machen.

degrading entwürdigend, erniedrigend.

degree Maß *n*, Rang *m*, Stufe *f*, Grad *m*, Ausmaß *n*; akademischer Grad *m*, Personenstand *m*, Verwandtschaftsgrad *m*, Qualifikation *f*; ~ **of consanguinity** Verwandtschaftsgrad; ~ **of disability** Invaliditätsgrad; ~ **of kin** Verwandschaftsgrad; ~ **of risk** Gefahrenhöhe; **by ~s** allmählich, Schritt für Schritt; **doctor's** ~ Doktorgrad; **forbidden ~s** = *prohibited ~s qv;* **prohibited ~s** → *prohibited;* **to take a** ~ e–n akademischen Grad erlangen.

degression Degression *f*.

degressive degressiv; absteigend.

del credere Delkredere *n*; ~ **agent** Handelsvertreter mit Delkredere; ~ **commission** Delkredereprovision; **to stand** ~ Delkredere übernehmen.

delapidation Verschlechterung *f*, Abnutzung *f*, Verschleiß *m*.

delator Ankläger *m*, Beschuldigter *m*, Denunziant *m*, Schmeichler *m*.

delay *s* Aufschub *m*, Verspätung *f*, Verzögerung *f*, Verzug *m*; schuldhaftes Zögern *n*; ~ **due to own conduct** selbstverschuldete Verzögerung; ~ **in claiming** Anspruchsverzögerung, Verwirkung; ~ **in delivery** Lieferverzug; ~ **in (=** *of*) **payment** verspätete Zahlung, Zahlungsverzug; ~ **in performance** Leistungsverzögerung, Leistungsverzug; ~ **in transit** Transitverzögerung; ~ **of creditors** Gläubigerbenachteiligung; ~ **of proceedings** Prozeßverschleppung; **creditor's** ~ Gläubigerverzug; **damage caused by** ~ Verzugsschaden; **debtor's** ~ Schuldnerverzug; **compulsory** ~ *US* gesetzl Überlegungspflicht (*Arbeitskampf*); **excessive** ~ übermäßige (*an sich entschuldbare*) Verzögerung **excusable** ~ entschuldbare Verzögerung; **extension of** ~ Fristverlängerung, Nachfristgewährung; **grant of** ~ Stundung; **inordinate** ~ unerhörte Verzögerung, grober Fall des Verzugs; **oppressive** ~ Verzögerungen als Druckmittel (*im Stafprozeß*); **request for** ~ Stundungsgesuch; **to grant a** ~ e–e Frist bewilligen; **undue** ~ Verzug, schuldhaftes Zögern; **unreasonable** ~ schuldhaftes Zögern; **vexatious** ~ schikanöse Verzögerung, Obstruktionsverzögerung; **without undue (or unreasonable)** ~ unverzüglich, ohne schuldhaftes Zögern.

delay *v* aufschieben, hinhalten, zögern, hemmen, verzögern; ~ **hinder or defraud creditors** Gläubigerbehinderung betreiben; **~ed action** verspätetes Handeln; **~ed delivery** verspätete Lieferung; **~ed delivery bond** Lieferungskaution; **~ing effect of the appeal** aufschiebende Wirkung des Rechtsmittels.

delegate *s* Delegierter *m*, Abgeordneter *m*, Stellvertreter *m*; ~ **to a meeting** Abgeordneter, Konferenzteilnehmer.

delegate *v* abordnen, delegieren, bevollmächtigen, den Schuldner auswechseln, e–e Schuldübernahme durchführen; ~ **authority** Vollmacht weiterübertragen; ~ **powers** ermächtigen, Befugnisse übertragen, Untervollmacht erteilen.

delegation Delegierung *f*, Abordnung *f*, Bevollmächtigung *f*, Ermächtigung *f*, Weitergabe *f*, Übertragung *f*, Schuldübernahme *f*, Auswechseln *n* von Schuldnern; ~

of authority Vollmachtsübertragung; ~ **of legislative powers** Gesetzgebungsdelegation; ~ **of powers** Vollmachtsübertragung, Unterbevollmächtigung; **agent by** ~ Unterbevollmächtigter; **imperfect** ~ Erfüllungsübernahme, nicht befreiende Schuldübernahme; **perfect** ~ befreiende Schuldübernahme; **trade** ~ Handelsdelegation; **trustee by** ~ Nachfolgetreuhänder.

delete streichen, (aus)radieren, löschen; ~ **an entry** Eintragung löschen; ~ **from the agenda** von der Tagesordnung absetzen.

deleterious gesundheitsgefährdend.

deletion Streichung *f*, Weglassung *f*.

deliberate *adj* wohlüberlegt, mit Überlegung, absichtlich, vorsätzlich; bedächtig, besonnen.

deliberate *v* überlegen, beraten, reiflich bedenken, abwägen.

deliberation Überlegung *f*, Beratung *f*, Erwägung *f*, Bedächtigkeit *f*, Bedachtsamkeit *f*; **after due** ~ nach gebührender Beratung.

deliberative beratend.

delict Delikt *n*, unerlaubte Handlung *f*; **quasi** ~ → *quasi;* **state** ~**s** Staatsdelikte.

delicta juris gentium völkerrechtliche Delikte.

delimit abgrenzen, begrenzen.

delimitation Abgrenzung *f*, Begrenzung *f*, Grenzziehung *f*; ~ **of a frontier** Grenzfestlegung.

delinquency Kriminalität *f*, Pflichtverletzung *f*, Vergehen *n*, Gesetzesverletzung *f*; Zahlungsrückstand *m*, Verzug *m*; ~ **amount** Steuerrückstand, erschlichener Steuerabzug; ~ **charges** Verzugskosten; V.-sgebühren; **international** ~ völkerrechtliches Unrecht; **juvenile** ~ Jugendkriminalität; Verwahrlosung und Missetaten Jugendlicher; **tax** ~ → *tax*.

delinquent *s* Delinquent *m*, Straftäter *m*, Verbrecher *m*, **defective** ~ geistesgestörter Täter; **minor** ~minderjähriger Missetäter.

delinquent *adj* straffällig, verbrecherisch, säumig, nicht fristgerecht geliefert.

delist *v/t* die Börsennotierung aussetzen bzw streichen.

deliver übergeben, befreien, liefern, zustellen; entbinden; begeben, erlassen; ~ **a copy** e–e Abschrift erteilen; ~ **a judgment** ein Urteil erlassen; ~ **a speech** e–e Rede halten; ~ **an opinion** ein Gutachten abgeben; **land is** ~ **ed in execution** es wird in ein Grundstück vollstreckt, das Grundstück wird von der Vollstreckung erfaßt.

deliverable lieferbar; übergabefähig.

deliverables zu liefernde Gegenstände.

deliverability Lieferbarkeit *f*.

delivery (*pl deliveries* = ~s) Übergabe *f*, Aushändigung *f*, Zustellung *f*, Begebung *f*, Zusendung *f*, Überbringung *f*, Lieferung *f*, Entbindung *f*; ~ **and acceptance** (*of an estate*) Auflassung ~**ies and services** Lieferungen und sonstige Leistungen; ~**s and services rendered** Liefer- und Leistungsgeschäfte; **as required** Lieferung nach Abruf; ~ **bond** Kaution zur Freigabe beschlagnahmter Waren; ~ **by instalments** Sukzessivlieferung; ~ **by mistake** versehentliche Lieferung; ~ **charge** Zustellgebühr, *pl* Lieferkosten, Anlieferungkosten; ~ **cost** Lieferkosten, Lieferspesen; ~ **expenses** Lieferungskosten, Versandkosten; ~ **free domicile** Lieferung frei Bestimmungsort; ~ **free of charge** freie Lieferung; ~ **in escrow** Übergabe zur treuhänderischen Verwahrung; ~ **instructions** Liefervorschriften; Lieferungsanweisungen; ~ **note** Lieferschein; ~ **of accounts** Vorlage von Büchern; ~ **of a deed** Begebung e–r (*gesiegelten*) Urkunde; ~ **of a judgment** Urteilsverkündung; ~ **of a will** Errichtung e–s Testaments; ~ **of goods** (Waren)Lieferung; ~ **of notice** (*schriftliche*) Mitteilung; ~ **of possession** Einräumung des Besitzes, Herausgabe, Übergabe, Besitzübergang; ~**of**

the summing up Abgabe der Rechtsbelehrung an die Geschworenen; ~ **of things to innkeepers** Einbringung von Sachen bei Gastwirten; ~ **of wrong goods** Falschlieferung, Aliud-Lieferung; ~ **on sale** Auslieferung; ~ **order** → *order* (*2*); ~ **period** Lieferzeitraum, Lieferfrist; ~ **standards** Liefernormen; ~ **to arrive** rechtzeitige Übergabe der Dokumente bis zur Ankunft der Ware; ~ **to opposite party** Zustellung an die Gegenpartei; ~ **up** Herausgabe; ~~ *of documents for cancellation* Aufgebot von Urkunden zur Ungültigerklärung; **absolute** ~ bedingungslose Begebung (*e–r Urkunde*); **actual** ~ tatsächliche (*physische*) Übergabe; **conditional** ~ bedingte Begebung, vorläufige Aushändigung e–r Urkunde zu Händen e–s Dritten; **constructive** ~ mittelbare Besitzverschaffung, symbolische Übergabe (*als Übergabe geltende Surrogate*); **express** ~ Eilzustellung; **forward** ~ spätere Lieferung; **free** ~ portofreie Zustellung; **good** ~ einwandfreies Stück (*Wertpapierverkauf*); **immediate** ~ sofortige Lieferung; **late** ~ verspätete Ablieferung; **manual** ~ Übergabe; **multiple** ~ **contract** → *contract;* **negotiation by** ~ Negoziierung durch Übergabe (*des Papiers*), wertpapierrechtliche Übertragung durch (*Einigung und*) Übergabe; **oral** ~ mündlicher Vortrag; **order for** ~ Auslieferungsbefehl; **overdue** ~ rückständige Lieferung; **partial** ~ Teillieferung; **pending** ~ bis zur Übergabe; **place of** ~ → *place;* **port of** ~ → *port;* **presumption of** ~ → *presumption;* **priority** ~ Vorzugslieferung; **prompt** ~ sofortige Lieferung; **ready for** ~ → *ready;* **second** ~ zweite Übergabe, *endgültige Übergabe von zunächst hinterlegten Urkunden vom Verwahrer an den Erwerber* (*escrow*); **short** ~ kurzfristige Lieferung; unvollständige Lieferung; **special** ~ Eilzustellung; **specific** ~ Herausgabe e–r beweglSache; **subsequent** ~ Nachlieferung; **symbolic** ~ fiktive Übergabe; symbolische Übergabe, Übergabesurrogat; **tender of** ~ Lieferangebot, Übergabeversuch; **terms of** ~ → *term;* **time of** ~ → *time;* **to take** ~ → *to take;* **transfer by** ~ Übertragung durch Übergabe; **vendor** ~**ies** Warenlieferungen; **writ of** ~ → *writ*.

delude täuschen, hintergehen, betrügen.

delusion Einbildung *f*, Täuschung *f*, Sinnestäuschung *f*, Selbsttäuschung *f*; ~ **of grandeur** Größenwahn; **insane** ~ Wahnvorstellung, Zwangsvorstellung, Wahn; **mental** ~Sinnestäuschung; **systemized** ~ *systematisch richtige, in sich logische Gedankenfolge aus e–r Wahnvorstellung*.

demand *s* Aufforderung *f*, Anspruch *m*; Nachfrage *f*, Bedarf *m*, Begehren *n*, Vorlage*f*; ~ **and supply** Angebot und Nachfrage; ~ **deposit** Sichteinlage; Kontokorrentkonto; ~ **clause** → *clause;* ~ **draft** → *draft;* ~ **for capital** Kapitalnachfrage; ~ **for extradition** Auslieferungsersuchen; ~ **for** (= *of*) **payment** Zahlungsaufforderung, Mahnung zur Zahlung; ~ **in reconvention** Widerklage; ~ **in writing** schriftliche Aufforderung; ~ **loan** → *loan;* ~ **note** Sichtpapier, (*jederzeit bei Vorlage zahlbarer und sofort einklagbarer*) Schuldschein; Solasichtwechsel; Mahnschreiben; ~ **paper** bei Sicht zahlbares Papier; ~ **price** Geldkurs; ~ **quotation** *exch* Geldnotiz, Geldkurs; ~ **rate** Geldkurs; ~ **under his hand** persönlich unterschriebene Zahlungsaufforderung; **accumulated** ~ Nachholbedarf; **brisk** ~ lebhafte Nachfrage; **compulsory** ~ Intervention des Eigentümers; **cross-** ~ Widerklage; Gegenanspruch, Gegenforderung; **current** ~ laufende Nachfrage; **domestic** ~ Inlandsnachfrage; **home** ~ Inlandsnachfrage; inländischer Bedarf; **legal** ~ förmliche Aufforderung Mahnung; **liquidated** ~ bestimmte Forderung, bezifferte Forderung, fällige Geldforderung, Zahlungsanspruch; **mutual ~s** gegenseitige (*konnexe*) Forderungen; **on ~** auf Verlangen, bei Vorlage (*ohne vorherige Aufforderung*) zahlbar; **on official ~** auf amtliche Aufforderung; **payable on ~** → *payable;* **pent-up ~** Nachholbedarf; **personal ~** Zahlungsaufforderung gegen den Aussteller oder Akzeptanten; **reasonable public ~** (*for a bank*) ausreichendes öffentliches Bedürfnis; **sluggish ~** lustlose Nachfrage; **stale ~** alte (*evtl verwirkte*) Forderung; **statutory ~** (gesetzliche) Mahnung unter Konkursandrohung (*2 Tage Frist*); **steady ~** gleichbleibende Nachfrage; **symbolic ~** symbolische Übergabe (*Grundstücksübertragung*); **to pay on first ~** auf erste Aufforderung zahlen; **unliquidated ~** der Höhe nach unbestimmter Anspruch.

demand *v* beanspruchen, klagen auf; fragen, fordern, vorladen; **~ payment** zur Zahlung auffordern.

demandant Forderer *m*, Anspruchssteller *m*, Kläger *m*, betreibende Partei *f* (*bei dinglicher Klage*).

demanding|money with menaces Erpressung, versuchte Erpressung; räuberische Erpressung; **~ property by threats** Erpressung, versuchte Erpressung, räuberische Erpressung.

demand-led *adj* nachfrageabhängig, nachfragebedingt.

demandress Anspruchsstellerin *f*, Klägerin *f*, *fem von demandant qv*.

demarcation Grenzmarkierung *f*; **~ dispute** Zuständigkeits(Abgrenzungs)streit.

démarche diplomatisches Einschreiten *n*, Demarche *f*.

demeanour Verhalten *n*, Benehmen *n*, Auftreten *n*.

demens Schwachsinniger *m*.

demented geistesgestört.

dementi Richtigstellung *f*, Dementi *n*.

dementia Demenz *f*, Schwachsinn *m*; **~ praecox** Dementia praecox, Schizophrenie; **precocius** = **~** *praecox qv;* **senile ~** Altersschwachsinn.

demerger Entflechtung *f*.

demergerisation Entflechtung (*von Großkonzernen*).

demerit Verwerflichkeit *f*; Minuspunkt *m*.

demesne freier Grundbesitz *m*, Eigenbesitz *m*; Domäne *f*, Gut *n*, Grundbesitz *m*, Staatsgut *n*, Rittergut *n*, Hofmark *f*, *vom Gutsherrn* selbst genutzte Ländereien *f*|pl; **~ as of fee** *hist* Eigenbesitz, Eigenlehen; **~ lands** eigengenutzte Ländereien *des Gutsherrn;* **~ lands of the crown** Eigenländereien der Krone; **ancient ~** ursprüngliches Kronland, freies Lehen.

demesnial eigengenutzt, *adj von demesne qv*.

demisable übertragbar, verpachtbar.

demise *s* (*Grundstücks*) Überlassung *f*; Verpachtung *f*, Vermietung *f*; Ableben *n*, Tod *m* des Monarchen, Thronfolge *f*; **~ and redemise** Pacht und Rückverpachtung; **~ of the crown** Ableben des Monarchen; Thronfolge; **on the ~ of Smith** (= *dem. Smith*) beim Tode von Smith.

demise (*von Immobilien*) verpachten, in Erbpacht überlassen, vermieten, übertragen (*von Immobilien*) **~ed premises** → *premises*.

demission Demission *f*, Rücktritt *m*, Amtsverzicht *m*.

democracy Demokratie *f*, Volksherrschaft *f*; **industrial ~** betriebliche Mitbestimmung; **local ~** Demokratie auf örtl Ebene, demokratische Gemeinde und Kreisverfassung; **representative ~** repräsentative D., mittelbare D.

democratic demokratisch; **~ majority rule** demokratisches Mehrheitssystem.

demolition|order Abbruchsverfügung; **~ works** Abbrucharbeiten.

demonetization Demonetisierung *f* (*zB von Gold*) Entmonetisierung *f*.

demonetize demonetisieren, entmonetisieren.

demonstrable demonstrierbar, beweisbar, offensichtlich.

demonstrate demonstrieren, an den Tag legen, anschaulich machen, beweisen, darstellen, nachweisen; ~ **an embodiment of the invention** ein Ausführungsbeispiel der Erfindung vorführen.

demonstration Demonstration *f*, Vorführung *f*, Beweisführung *f*, Darstellung *f*.

demonstrative anschaulich, beweisend, überzeugend.

demonstrator Demonstrant *m*, Demonstrierender *m*, Beweisführender *m*.

demote degradieren, zurückversetzen, zurückstufen.

demur Einwendungen erheben, beanstanden, auf Unschlüssigkeit hinweisen, rechtliche Einwendungen erheben.

demurrable nicht schlüssig, rechtlich nicht ausreichend.

demurrage Überliegezeit *f*, Überliegegeld *n*, Standgeld *n*, Lagergeld *n* (*wegen nicht rechtzeitiger Abholung*); ~ **days** Überliegezeit; ~**lien** Überliegegeldpfandrecht, ~ **rate** Liegegeldsatz; **to be on** ~ Überliegezeit beanspruchen.

demurrant die einwendende Partei; *die sich auf mangelnde Schlüssigkeit berufende Partei.*

demurrer Einwand *m* der mangelnden Schlüssigkeit, rechtliche Einwendungen *f/pl;* ~ **to evidence** Geltendmachen des Mangels an Schlüssigkeit (*so daß es auf die Beweiserhebung nicht ankommt*); ~ **to interrogatories** Beanstandung der Fragestellung (*bei Rechtshilfevernehmung*); **general** ~ allgemeine Rüge der Unschlüssigkeit; **parol** ~ Aussetzung des Verfahrens (*insbesondere wegen Minderjährigkeit des Beklagten*); **speaking** ~ (*fehlerhafte*) Rüge der mangelnden Schlüssigkeit (*vermischt mit Gegenvorbringen*); **special** ~ *besonders begründete Rüge der Unschlüssigkeit oder Unzulässigkeit des gegnerischen Vorbringens;* auf Formfehler gegründeter Einwand.

denationalization (= *de-nationalisation*) Reprivatisierung *f*.

denationalize reprivatisieren.

denaturalization Ausbürgerung *f*.

denature *v* denaturieren, ungenießbar machen, vergällen.

deniability Bestreitbarkeit *f*, Bestreiten können *n*.

deniable *adj* bestreitbar.

denial Verweigerung *f*, Dementi *n*, Leugnen *n*, Ablehnung *f*, Bestreiten *n*, Abstreiten *n*; Absage *f*, abschlägige Antwort *f*, Verneinung *f*, ~ **of due process** Vorenthaltung e–s rechtsstaatlichen Verfahrens; ~ **of justice** Justizverweigerung, Rechtsverweigerung; ~ **of patentability** Aberkennung der Patentfähigkeit; ~ **of responsibility** Ablehnung der Verantwortung; ~ **of sexual intercourse** Verweigerung des ehelichen (Geschlechts)Verkehrs; ~ **upon oath** Bestreiten unter Eid; **general** ~ allgemeines Bestreiten, Bestreiten des gesamten Klagevorbringens; **official** ~ (amtliches) Dementi; **procedural** ~ verfahrensmäßige Diskriminierung; **special** ~ Bestreiten einzelner Klagebehauptungen; **specific** ~ = *special* ~ *qv*.

denigrate *vt* verleumden, schlecht machen.

denization Akt *m* der Gleichstellung e–s Ausländers mit den Untertanen; Teileinbürgerung *f*; **letter of** ~ Schutzbrief für e–n Ausländer.

denizen *n* Einwohner *m*, eingebürgerter Ausländer *m*.

denizen *v* den Untertanen gleichgestellt werden, einbürgern.

denominate bezeichnen, benennen.

denomination Name *m*, Benennung *f*, Klasse *f*, Kategorie *f*, Religionsgemeinschaft *f*, Konfession *f*; Stükkelung *f*, Sektion *f*; ~ **of goods** Warenbezeichnung; ~ **of shares** Aktiennennbetrag.

denominational konfessionell, e–r Religionsgemeinschaft zugehörig.

denotation Bedeutung *f*, Bezeichnung *f*.

denote bedeuten, bezeichnen.

denoting stamp aufgeprägte Stempelmarke *f*.

denounce kündigen, denunzieren, verurteilen; zum Verbrechen erklären; bei Gericht anzeigen; ~ **a treaty** e–n (*völkerrechtlichen*) Vertrag kündigen.

denouncement öffentliche Rüge *f*, Denunziation *f*; Kündigung *f*, Landenteignungsverfahren *n gegen Ausländer*; ~ **of a new work** Unterlassungsverfügung gegen Errichtung e–s Neubaus.

de novo von neuem, wiederaufgenommen; ~ **trial** (*vollständig*) neues Verfahren.

denuclearisation Abbau der Atomwaffen, Abschaffung von A.

denunciation Denunziation *f*, Strafanzeige *f*, Androhung *f*; Kündigung *f*, Ankündigung *f*, Verurteilung; *scot* Erklärung *f* zum Rebellen, öffentliche Verurteilung *f*; ~ **of treaties** Kündigung von Staatsverträgen; **to deliver a ~ against s.o.** gegen jmd e–e gerichtliche Anzeige erstatten; **to warn s.o. of a ~** jmd abmahnen; mit gerichtlicher Anzeige bedrohen.

deny bestreiten, in Abrede stellen, dementieren, abschlagen, verleugnen, sich weigern, verneinen, aberkennen; ~ **a motion** Antrag ablehnen; ~ **probate** → *probate;* ~ **the inventive level** die Erfindungshöhe verneinen.

depart weggehen, abweichen, abfahren, abgehen von; Klagebegründung ändern.

department (*1*) Abteilung *f*, Dienststelle *f*, Amt *n*, Fachbereich (*Universität*); **store** → *store;* ~ **trial** Disziplinarverfahren; **accounting** ~ Buchhaltung; **action** ~ Prozeßabteilung der Geschäftsstelle des Gerichts; **executive** ~ Ministerium; **filing** ~ Registratur, gerichtl Hinterlegungsstelle; **government** ~ → *government;* **issue** ~ Abteilung für Notenausgabe; **legal** ~ Rechtsabteilung **legislative** ~ Legislative *f*; **personnel** ~ → *personnel*; **scrivenery** ~ Gerichtskanzlei.

Department (*2*) Ministerium (= *Min bzw min, GB; bzw US soweit vermerkt ist*) ~ **of Agriculture,** Landwirtschafts*min (US)* ~ **of Commerce** Handels*min (US)* ~ **of Defense** Verteidigungs*min (US)* ~ **of Education and Science** *Min* für Erziehung und Wissenschaft, Kultus*min;* ~ **of Employment** Arbeits*min;* ~ **of Energy** Energie*min;* ~ **of Environment** Umweltschutz*min;* ~ **of Health and of Social Security** Gesundheits- und Sozial*min;* ~ **of Health, Education and Welfare** Bundes*min* für Gesundheit, Erziehung und Wohlfahrt (*US*); ~ **of Housing and Urban Development** Bundes*min* für Wohnungswesen und Stadtentwicklung (*US*); ~ **of Industry** Industrie*min;* ~ **of Justice** Justiz*min (US)*; ~ **of Labor** Bundesarbeits*min (US)*; **D~ of State** Außenministerium (*USA-Regierung*); Staatsministerium, Staatskanzlei (*USA-Einzelstaaten*); ~ **of the Interior** Innenministerium; ~ **of the Procurator General and Treasury Solicitor** Rechtsabteilung der brit. Regierung (*mit Ministerialrang*); ~ **of Trade** Handels*min;* ~ **of Transport** Verkehrs*min;* ~ **of Transportation** Bundesverkehrs*min (US);* **The Law Officers** ~ Generalstaatsanwaltsamt (*Ministerialrang*); **Treasury** ~ Bundesschatzamt, Bundesfinanz*min (US)*.

departmental Abteilungs. . ., Ministerial. . ., ministeriell, Regierungs. . .

departmentalization (*Arbeitsteilung durch*) Aufgliederung *f* in Abteilungen.

departure Abfahrt *f*, Abgehen *n*, Abweichung *f*; Klageänderung *f*; ~ **from the law** Rechtsbeugung; **minute** ~ geringfügige Abweichung; **notice of** ~ → *notice;* **place of** ~ Abfahrtsort; **port of** ~ → *port;* **time of** ~ → *time*.

depeculation *hist* Fürstenberaubung *f*, Amtsunterschlagung *f*.

dependant = *dependent qv*.

dependence Abhängigkeit **umbilical** ~ engste Abhängigkeit.
dependency Schutzgebiet *n*, Protektorat *n*; Abhängigkeit *f*; ~ **benefit** Leistung an Unterhaltsberechtigte (*des Versicherten*).
dependent *adj* abhängig.
dependent *s* (*brit dependant*) Abhängiger *m*, Unterhaltsberechtigter *m*; **lawful** ~**s** gesetzlich Unterhaltsberechtigte.
depletable *adj* abbaufähig; abschreibbar.
deplete leeren, erschöpfen, ausbeuten; ~**d cost** Anschaffungskosten nach Abzug der Substanzverringerung.
depletion Substanzverzehr *m*, Ausbeutung *f*, Kraftentzug *m; tax* Abschreibung *f* für Substanzverringerung; ~ **allowance** Absetzung für Substanzverringerung; ~ **loss** Abbauverlust; ~ **of capital** Kapitalentblößung.
depone schriftlich eidlich erklären.
deponent (*cf affidavit*), Aussageperson *f*, der (*schriftlich eidlich*) Erklärende.
depopulation Entvölkerung *f*, Verursachung *f* von Bevölkerungsschwund, Vertreibung *f*.
deport abschieben, deportieren, *hist* verbannen, ins Exil schicken, des Landes verweisen.
deportation Abschiebung *f*, Deportation *f*, Ausweisung *f*; ~ **order** Ausweisungsbeschluß; **informal** ~ Abschiebung.
deportee Ausgewiesener *m*, Deportierter *m*.
depose absetzen; schriftlich aussagen, unter Eid zu Protokoll geben.
deposit *s* Depot *n*, Hinterlegung *f*, Verwahrung *f*; der hinterlegte Gegenstand *m* Verwahrungsgut; Einzahlung *f*, Einlage *f*, Anzahlung *f*, Reugeld *n*; ~**s** Depositengeschäft; ~ **account** → *account;* ~ **against fees** Vorschuß (*Rechtsanwalt*); ~ **agreement** Hinterlegungsvereinbarung (*Mietkaution*); ~**s and drawings** Einzahlungen und Auszahlungen; ~ **at call** Sichteinlage; ~ **at notice** Einlage mit Kündigungsfrist; Kündigungsgeld; ~ **bank** Depositenbank; ~ **banking** Depositengeschäft; ~ **box** Stahlfach; ~ **company** Stahlfachverwahrungsgesellschaft; ~ **compensating balance** Bankguthaben zum Ausgleich für Kontokorrentkredit; ~ **creditor** Sonderberechtigter am Wertpapierfonds *e–r Investmentgesellschaft;* ~ **currency** Bankgeld, Giralgeld; ~ **for hire** entgeltliche Verwahrung; ~ **guaranty fund** Einlagensicherungsfond; ~ **in court** gerichtliche Hinterlegung; ~ **insurance** Einlagenversicherung; ~ **insurance corporation** Bankeinlagenversicherungsgesellschaft; ~ **liabilities** Einlagenverbindlichkeiten (*e–r Bank*); ~ **line** durchschnittlicher Kreditsaldo e–s Depositenkontos; ~ **money** Buchgeld, Giralgeld; Depositengelder; ~ **note** = *bank deposit note qv;* ~ **of a security** Sicherheitsleistung, Hinterlegung; ~ **of copy** Hinterlegung e–s Exemplars (*e–r Veröffentlichung zwecks Copyrights*); ~ **of securities** Wertpapierdeponierung; ~ **of title-deeds** Hinterlegung von Eigentumsurkunden (*als formlose Grundpfandbestellung*); ~ **of wills** Testamentshinterlegung; ~ **premium** vorläufige Prämie bei Abschluß; ~ **rate** Habenzins, Einlagenzins; ~ **receipt** Einzahlungsquittung, Depotschein; Hinterlegungsquittung; ~ **security arrangements** Einlagensicherung; ~ **security reserve** Sicherungsreserve; ~ **slip** Einzahlungsbeleg; ~ **society** Sparverein; ~ **ticket** Einzahlungsschein; ~ **-taking business** Depositengeschäft; ~ **warrant** Depotschein, Hinterlegungsschein, ~ **with bank** Guthaben bei e–r Bank; **bank** ~ Bankeinlage; **call** ~**s** → *call;* **collective** ~ Sammeldepot; **contract of** ~ Verwahrungsvertrag; **conventional** ~ vertragliche Hinterlegung; **current** ~**s** Kontokorrenteinlagen; **demand** ~**s** Sichteinlagen; täglich fällige Einlagen; **deri-**

vative ~s Gutschriften für Darlehen, Depositen durch Bankkredit, gutgläubig erworbene Kapitalerträge, indirekte Einlagen; **fixed ~** Festgeld; **general ~** Sammelverwahrung, uneigentliche Verwahrung; **government ~s** Bankguthaben *pl* staatlicher Organe; **gratuitous ~** unentgeltliche Verwahrung; **guaranty of ~s** → *guaranty;* **insurance of ~** Versicherung von Bankeinlagen; **involuntary ~** gesetzliches Verwahrungsverhältnis, unbeabsichtigtes Liegenlassen (*von Sachen*); Eigentümer-Besitzer-Verhältnis (*an bewegl Sachen*); **irregular ~** unregelmäßige Verwahrung, Summenverwahrung; **joint ~** gemeinschaftliche Einlage; **judicial ~** gerichtlich angeordnete Verwahrung; **misapplication of ~** unzulässige Verwendung e–r hinterlegten Sache; **naked ~** unentgeltliche Verwahrung; **natural ~** Privateinlage, nicht geldmarkmäßiger Finanzierungsbeitrag; **necessary ~** Aufbewahrung aus Geschäftsführung ohne Auftrag; **notice ~** → *notice;* **omnibus ~** Sammeldepot; **on ~** in Verwahrung; **parliamentary ~** Stellung von Sicherheiten für Privatvorlagen; **primary ~** direkte Einlage, effektive Einlage (*nicht auf Kredit gewährte Einlage*); **public ~** staatliche Einlage bei Banken, Guthaben der öffentlichen Hand; **quasi ~** verwahrungsähnliches Verhältnis; **regular ~** Verwahrung, Einzelverwahrung, eigentliche Verwahrung; **safe ~** → *safe;* **safe ~ box** → *safe;* **safe ~ vault** → *safe;* **savings ~** → *savings;* **savings bank ~** → *savings;* **secondary ~** sekundäre Einlage, Gutschrift für Kapitalerträge; **sight ~** → *sight;* **simple ~** Sammelverwahrung; **special ~** Einzelverwahrung; **special ~** *bei der Zentralbank hinterlegte und gesperrte* Mindestreserven; **straight ~** schlichte Einlage (*ohne Zertifikatserteilung*); **time ~** → *time;* **thrift ~** Spareinlage; **to hold a ~ in bank** über ein Bankguthaben verfügen; **to pay a ~** e–e Anzahlung leisten; **voluntary ~** vereinbarte Hinterlegung.

deposit *v* in Verwahrung geben, hinterlegen, ins Depot geben, e–e Einlage machen, einzahlen.

depositary Verwahrer *m*; **~ for public moneys** *Bezeichnung für Banken, die als Verwahrer öffentlicher Mittel zugelassen sind;* **~ state** Verwahrerstaat.

depositary agency beschränkte ausländische Bankniederlassung *US*.

depositing business Depotgeschäft *n*.

deposition Niederschrift *f* e–r außergerichtlichen eidlichen Aussage, schriftliche Zeugenerklärung, *etwa* eidesstattliche Versicherung *f*; **~ before justices** beeidigte schriftliche Aussage in der Voruntersuchung; **~ de bene esse** schriftl eidliche Aussage zur Verlesung in der Gerichtsverhandlung; **~ on oath** eidliche Erklärung, beeidete schriftliche Zeugenaussage; **dying ~** protokollierte Aussage e–s Sterbenden; **to take down on ~** e–e eidliche Aussage (*außerhalb der Verhandlung*) zu Protokoll nehmen.

depositor Deponent *m*, Depositeninhaber *m*, Einzahler *m*, Hinterleger *m*; jmd, der e–e Sache (*zB Rauschgift*) e–m anderen zum Aufbewahren gibt.

depository Aufbewahrungsort *m*, Hinterlegungsstelle *f*; Bankier *m*; Stapelplatz *m*, Lagerhaus *n*, Magazin *n*; Registratur *f*; **~ for wills of living persons** Testamentshinterlegungsstelle; **~ of records** Urkundenverwahrungsort; **"authorised ~"** (*zur Wertpapierverwahrung*) zugelassenes Kreditinstitut; **public ~** zur Verwahrung öffentl Gelder zugelassenes Kreditinstitut; **United States Depositories** *US* ausgewählte Banken zur Verwahrung von Bundesmitteln.

depot Depot *n*, Warenhaus *n*, Magazin *n*, Gerätepark *m*; Güterbahnhof *m*, Bahnhof *m*; **~ grounds** Bahnhofsgelände, Lagerplatz; **~ ship** Vorratsschiff, Versorgungsschiff.

deprave verderben, demoralisieren, pervertieren, Verachtung bezeugen; **~d conduct** entmenschtes Verhalten; **~ the Lord's Supper** Gotteslästerung, Verunglimpfung des heiligen Abendmahls; **of ~d mind** entmenscht.

depravity Scheußlichkeit *f*, Niedertracht *f*, Lasterhaftigkeit *f*, lasterhafte Handlung *f*; **exceptional ~** extrem niederträchtige (ehezerstörerische) Gesinnung.

depreciate geringschätzen, verachten, entwerten, im Wert sinken, abschreiben.

depreciation Abwertung *f*, Entwertung *f*, Abschreibung *f*, Wertverringerung *f*, Absetzung für Abnutzung *f*, Verschleiß *m*, Verschlechterung *f*; **~ account** Abschreibungskonto; **~ allowance** → *allowance*; **~ base** Bemessungsgrundlage für die Abschreibung; **~ charge** Abschreibungsbetrag; *A–s*aufwand; *A–ssumme;* **~ clause** Entwertungsklausel; **~ expense** Abschreibungsaufwand; **~ for cost accounting purposes** kalkulatorische Abschreibung; **~ for wear and tear** Abschreibung, Absetzung für Abnutzung (AfA); **~ for tax purposes** steuerl Abschreibung; **~ fund** Wertminderungsrückstellung; **~ in value** Wertverringerung; **~ of assets** Wertminderung von Vermögenswerten, Abschreibungen; **~ of coin** Geldentwertung; **~ of currency** Kursrückgang (= Kursverfall) e–r Währung, Kaufkraftminderung; **~ of money** Geldwertminderung; **~ rate** Abschreibungssatz; **~ reserve** Abschreibung, Wertberichtigung auf Posten des Anlagevermögens; **accelerated ~** beschleunigte Abschreibung, Sonderabschreibung; **accrued ~** Wertberichtigung; **accumulated ~** Wertberichtigung; **allowance for ~** Abschreibungssatz; **book ~** bilanzielle Abschreibung; **declining-balance ~** degressive Abschreibung, Buchwert-a.; **deducted ~** Wertminderungsabschlag; **extraordinary ~** außerordentliche Abschreibung, außerplanmäßige A.; **free ~** Steuerfreiheit bis zur Abschreibung der Investitionen; **functional ~** Absetzung für außergewöhnliche technische Abnutzung; **increasing-charge ~** progressive Abschreibung; **ordinary ~** ordentliche Abschreibung, planmäßige A.; **physical ~** natürliche Abnutzung; **provision for ~ = ~** reserve qv; **reducing-balance ~** degressive Abschreibung; **scheduled ~** planmäßige Abschreibung; **sum-of-the-years'-digits ~** digitale Abschreibung, arithmetisch degressive A.; **straight-line ~** lineare Abschreibung; **tax ~** steuerliche Abschreibung.

depredation Plünderung *f*, Raub *m*, Verheerung *f*, Raubzug *m*, Überfall *m*.

depression Depression *f*, Wirtschaftskrise *f*; **the D~** *die Weltwirtschaftskrise 1929–32.*

deprivation Entziehung *f*, Entzug *m*, Beraubung *f*, Verlust *m*, Mangel *m;* **~ of a right** Entziehung e–s Rechts; **~ of citizenship** Aberkennung der Staatsbürgerschaft, Ausbürgerung; **~ of civic rights** Aberkennung der bürgerl Ehrenrechte; **~ of liberty** Freiheitsentzug; **~ of pension** Aberkennung des Ruhegehalts; **~ of possession** Besitzentziehung, **~ of property** Enteignung; Einziehung von Sachen (*als Nebenstrafe*); **temporary ~ of capacity** zeitweilige Unzurechnungsfähigkeit; **unlawful ~** widerrechtliche Entnahme.

deprive berauben, wegnehmen, entziehen; **~ s.o. of a right** jmdm ein Recht aberkennen, jmdm ein Recht entziehen.

deputation Deputation *f*, Abordnung *f*.

deputize vertreten; jmdm zum Stellvertreter einsetzen; deputieren, abordnen.

deputy Stellvertreter *m*, Vertreter *m*, Delegierter *m*; Abgeordneter *m*; **~ chairman** stellvertretender Vorsitz(end)er; ~ **consul** Vizekonsul; ~ **judge** beauftragter Richter, kommissarischer R; ~ **mayor** 2. Bürgermeister; ~ **registrar** stellvertretender Urkundsbeamter; Standesbeamter; ~ **sheriff** Vize-Sheriff; Vizepolizeichef, Gerichtswachtmeister; Gerichtsvollzieher; ~ **steward** Vizerichter e–r Gutherrschaft; **general** ~ **sheriff** ständiger Vizepolizeichef; **special** ~ Sonderbeauftragter; **special** ~ **sheriff** Hilfspolizist, Sonderbeauftragter der Ortspolizei.

derangement Geistesverwirrung *f*, Geistesgestörtheit *f*; ~ **of the senses** Bewußtseinsstörung; **mental** ~ Geistesstörung, krankhafte Störung der Geistestätigkeit.

derate herabsetzen, senken (*Gemeindesteuern*).

derating Erlaß *m* örtlicher Steuern, Grundsteuerbefreiung *f*; ~ **reliefs** Steuererleichterungen (*bei Kommunalabgaben*).

deregister *v/t* im (Handels)Register löschen.

deregistration Löschung *f* im (Handels)Register.

deregulate *v/t*, deregulieren, liberalisieren, von Vorschriften befreien, aus der Bewirtschaftung entlassen.

de-regulation Deregulierung *f*, Deregulation *f*, Aufhebung von Kontrollen, Freigabe, Entbürokratisierung *f*, Liberalisierung *f*.

derelict *s* herrenlose (*derelinquierte*) Sache *f*; Vagabund *m*.

derelict *adj* aufgegeben, verlassen, herrenlos; nachlässig, untreu; ~ **land** herrenloser Grund; verlandetes Flußbett; ~ **property** derelinquierte Sache; ~ **vessel** verlassenes Schiff, treibendes Wrack; **quasi** ~ quasi-derelinquiert (*noch nicht endgültig aufgegebenes Schiff*).

dereliction Dereliktion *f*, (*einseitige*) Aufgabe dinglicher Rechte; Preisgabe *f*, Verlanden *n* (*Strand*); ~ **of duty** Pflichtvernachlässigung; ~ **of professional responsibilities** Vernachlässigung von Berufspflichten, Anwaltsverschulden durch Unterlassung.

derequisition Freigabe *f* von e–r Beschlagnahme; Aufhebung *f* der Wohnungszwangswirtschaft.

derestrict Beschränkungen aufheben; ~**a road** Straße freigeben.

derivation Ableitung *f*, Herkunft *f*.

derivative derivativ, abgeleitet; ~ **rights of action** Klagerechte in Prozeßstandschaft.

derive ableiten, herleiten, erzielen; ~ **a profit** e–n Gewinn erzielen; ~**d demand** Bedarf an zur Verarbeitung bestimmten Gütern; ~**d income** abgeleitetes Einkommen.

derogate Abbruch tun, abträglich sein, zum Nachteil gereichen, beeinträchtigen, schmälern; *ein Gesetz* teilweise aufheben *bzw* abändern.

derogation Beeinträchtigung *f*, Schmälerung *f*, Nachteil *m*; Entwürdigung *f*, Derogation *f*, Teilaufhebung *f*, Abänderung *f*, Wertminderung *f*; ~ **from a grant** nachträgliche Schmälerung eines übertragenen Rechts; ~ **from a material fact** Bagatellisierung e–r wesentlichen Tatsache; ~ **from a privilege** Beeinträchtigung e–s Vorrechts; **in** ~ **of** in (unter) Abänderung von.

derogatory nachteilig, abträglich, herabwürdigend, geringschätzig; ~ **clause** Ungültigkeitsklausel für spätere letztwillige Verfügungen.

descend anfallen, (kraft Erbfolge) übergehen, zufallen, herkommen, abstammen; **lineally** ~ **ed from** in direkter Linie abstammend von.

descendant Nachkomme *m*, Abkömmling *m*; ~ **of the first degree** Abkömmling ersten Grades, Kind; **lineal** ~ Abkömmling gerader Linie, direkter Abkömmling; **participating** ~ erbberechtigter Abkömmling; *pl:* Abkömmlinge als Miterben.

descendible vererbbar, vererblich.

descent Abstammung *f*, Abkunft *f*, Erbgang *m*, Beerbung *f*, Vererbung *f*, gesetzliche Erbfolge *f*;

Erbfall *m*; ~ **cast** Intestatvererbung von Grundbesitz; ~ **or devise** gesetzliche oder testamentarische Erbfolge; **collateral** ~ Abstammung in der Seitenlinie; **illegitimate** ~ nichteheliche Abstammung; **immediate** ~ unmittelbare Abstammung, unmittelbare Erbfolge; **legitimate** ~ eheliche Abstammung; **lineal** ~ Abstammung in gerader Linie; **mediate** ~ mittelbare Abstammung, mittelbare Erbfolge; **rules of** ~ Erbfolgenormen; **stock of** ~ Stamm; **to trace one's** ~ seinen Stammbaum zurückverfolgen.

describe beschreiben, schildern, bezeichnen; **hereinafter ~d as ...** nachfolgend als ... bezeichnet.

description Beschreibung *f*, Spezifikation *f*; Beschaffenheit *f*, Bezeichnung *f*, Gattung *f*, Art *f*, Sorte *f*; ~ **of commodities** Warenbezeichnung; ~ **of contents** Inhaltsangabe; ~ **of goods** Warenbeschreibung, ~ **of invention** Patentbeschreibung; **by** ~ nach Beschreibung, nach Angabe; **commercial** ~ handelsübliche Bezeichnung; **goods by** ~ Waren gemäß Beschreibung (*bzw Katalogangaben*); **of every** ~ von jeder Art, in jeder Qualität **official** ~ Amtsbezeichnung: **prior public printed** ~ Vorveröffentlichung in e-r Druckschrift (*Patent*).

desegregate die Rassentrennung aufheben.

desegregation Aufhebung *f* von Rassentrennung.

desert *v* verlassen, desertieren, im Stich lassen, abtrünnig werden; ~ **the colours** fahnenflüchtig werden; ~ **the diet** *scot* e-n Anklagepunkt aufgeben; **inciting soldiers to** ~ Anstiftung zur Fahnenflucht.

deserter Deserteur *m*, Fahnenflüchtiger *m*, Ausreißer *m*, Überläufer *m*.

desertion Desertion *f*, Fahnenflucht *f*; unbefugtes Abheuern *n*; Verlassen *n*, Imstichlassen *n*; Abtrünnigwerden *n*; böswilliges Verlassen *n*; ~ **of children** Kinderaussetzung, Verlassen von Kindern (*in hilfloser Lage*); ~ **without cause** grundloses Verlassen; **assisting in** ~ Beihilfe zur Fahnenflucht; **constructive** ~ *ehewidriges Verhalten, das den schuldlosen Teil zum Verlassen der ehelichen Wohnung veranlaßt und dies bezweckt;* **obstinate** ~ nachhaltiges böswilliges Verlassen, nachhaltiges unberechtigtes Getrenntleben; **wilful** ~ böswilliges Verlassen.

deserve verdienen, würdig sein.

design *s* (*1*) Absicht *f*, (Tat)Plan *m*; **common** ~ bewußtes und gewolltes Zusammenwirken; **unity of** ~ einheitlicher Vorsatz.

design *s* (*2*) Muster *n*, Design *n*, Dessin *n*; Konstruktionsentwurf *m*, Entwurf *m*, Konstruktion *f*; Geschmacksmuster *n* (= *Ge bzw ge*); Formgebung *f*, Gestaltung *f*; Machart *f*; **~s** *Ge*angelegenheiten; ~ **defect** Konstruktionsfehler; Planungsfehler (*Bauwerk*); **D~s Act** *Ge*gesetz; ~ **certificate** Musterzulassung; **D~ Council** Institut für industrielle Gestaltung; **~s for articles of manufacture** (*gewerbliches*) *Ge;* ~ **for works of art** kunstschutzfähiges Muster; ~ **patent** *(geschütztes) Ge, Ge*recht; **D~ Register** *Ge*rolle; ~ **requirements** *Ge*voraussetzungen; ~ **review** Konstruktionsüberprüfung, Musterzulassungsüberprüfung; ~ **type** Konstruktionstyp; **author of a** ~ Urheber e-s *Ge-s;* **copyright in** ~ → *copyright;* **Council of Industrial D~** → *council;* **crown user of** ~ Vorbehaltsrecht der Krone zwecks Benutzung von *Ge-n;* Zwangslizenz für staatliche Zwecke; **faulty** ~ fehlerhafte Konstruktion (*e-r Maschine*); **industrial** ~ Industriedesign, gewerbliche Formgebung, Gestaltung, *Ge;* **ornamental** ~ *Ge,* Ausstattung, Ziermuster; **proprietor of a** ~ Inhaber e-s *Ge-s;* **protection of ~s** *Ge*schutz; **registered** ~ eingetragenes *Ge*.

design *v* entwerfen, beabsichtigen, planen, vorhaben; gestalten.

designate bezeichnen, kennzeichnen,

markieren, designieren, ausersehen sein; ~ **a counsel for the defence** e–n Pflichtverteidiger bestimmen; ~ **an heir** zum Erben bestimmen; ~**d examiner** zuständiger Prüfer; ~**d time** angegebene Zeit; Frist.

designation Bezeichnung *f*, Bestellung *f*, ~ **of invention** Bezeichnung der Erfindung, Titel der Erf. **proprietary** ~ → *proprietary*.

designee vorgesehener Amtsinhaber, der künftige Nachfolger.

desist aufhören, Abstand nehmen von, ablassen von, unterlassen.

desistement Aufhebung *f* des jus fori (*bei Auslegung ausländischer Testamente*).

desk officer Referent *m*.

despacheur Dispacheur *m* = *average adjuster qv*.

Despatch Box Urkundentruhe *f im Unterhaus* (*auch als Rednerpult verwendet*).

despatch money Prämie *f* für vorzeitige Leistung.

despatches Depeschen *f/pl*, dienstliche Regierungsmitteilungen *f/pl* (*vgl dispatch*).

desperate verwegen, tollkühn, hoffnungslos, ausweglos, wertlos; ~ **debt** uneinbringliche Forderung.

despite *prep* trotz, ungeachtet.

despite *s* Beleidigung *f*, Schimpf *m*, Hohn *m*, Verachtung *f*, Trotz *m*, Herausforderung *f*.

despoil berauben, plündern, heimlich entziehen.

desponsation Verlöbnis *n* (*durch die Eltern der Brautleute*).

destination Bestimmung *f*, Zweckbestimmung *f*; Nachfolgeverfügung *f*; *scot* Ersatzeinsetzung *f*, Ersatzbestimmung *f* (*Erbrecht*); ~ **bill** → *bill of lading;* ~ **contract** → *contract;* ~ **control regulations** Endverbleibskontrollvorschriften; **final** ~ Bestimmungsort; ~ *certificate: Endverbleibsnachweis;* **place of** ~ → *place;* **port of** ~ → *port;* **ultimate** ~ (endgültiger) Bestimmungsort.

destitute mittellos, verarmt, notleidend, ermangelnd, unterhaltsbedürftig; ~ **or necessitous circumstances** Unterhaltsbedürftigkeit.

destitution Mangel *m*, Not *f*, bittere Armut *f*, Elend *n*.

destroy zerstören, demolieren, verwüsten, vernichten, zerrütten; ~**ed bill** vernichteter Wechsel.

destruction Zerstörung *f*, Demolierung *f*, Vernichtung *f*, Untergang *m*; ~ **of subject matter of contract** Untergang des Vertragsgegenstandes; ~ **of will** Vernichtung des Testaments; **child** ~ → *child*.

destructive zerstörend, verheerend, vernichtend; destruktiv, zersetzend, zerrüttend, verderblich, schädlich.

desuetude Ungebräuchlichwerden *n*, Nutzungsaufgabe *f*; ~ **of treaties** Unwirksamkeit von Verträgen durch lange Nichtanwendung; **to fall into** ~ obsolet werden, außer Gebrauch kommen, ungebräuchlich werden.

detail *s* Einzelheit *f*, Detail *n*; **to give full** ~**s** substantiieren, Einzelheiten bringen.

detail *v* substantiieren, ausführlich darstellen, einzeln aufführen.

detain sicherstellen, zurückbehalten, anhalten, feilhalten, in Haft halten, internieren; ~ **goods** Waren zurückbehalten; ~ **in custody** in (Untersuchungs)Haft behalten; ~**ing officer** Schiffsarrestierungsbeamter; ~**ing power** → *power* (*1*).

detainee Internierter *m*; **civilian** ~ Zivilinternierter; **pretrial** ~ Untersuchungshäftling.

detainer (widerrechtliche) Vorenthaltung *f* des Besitzes; **forcible** ~ *widerrechtlicher* gewaltsamer Gewahrsam (*an Liegenschaften*), widerrechtliche Herausgabeverweigerung, Besitzstörung; **lawful** ~ rechtmäßiger Freiheitsentzug; **unlawful** ~ widerrechtl Räumungsverweigerung; **writ of** ~ → *writ*.

detaining for questioning vorläufige Festnahme *zwecks Einvernahme*.

detainment Beschlagnahme *f*, Verfügungsbeschränkung *f*, Zurückbehaltung *f*, unfreiwilliger Aufenthalt *m*.

detect entdecken, aufdecken, ausfindig machen.

detection Entdeckung *f*, Aufdekkung *f*; ~ **of falsehood** Aufdekkung der Unwahrheit; ~ **rate** Aufklärungsquote.

detective Detektiv *m*, Ermittler *m*, Fahnder *m*; ~ **agency** Detektei; ~ **bureau** Kriminalabteilung; „Kripo"; ~ **police** Kriminalpolizei; **private** ~ Privatdetektiv.

detector dog Spürhund *m*.

detente *pol* Entspannung *f*.

detention Festhalten *n*; Haft *f*, Internierung *f*, (widerrechtliche) Vorenthaltung *f* des Besitzes; Einbehaltung *f* Beschlagnahme *f*, Gewahrsam; ~ **centre** Kurzarrestanstalt *für Heranwachsende;* ~ **charges** Kosten bei Beschlagnahme; ~ **for debt** Schuldarrest, Schuldhaft; ~ **for deportation** Abschiebehaft; ~ **for short periods** Kurzzeitarrest; ~ **home** Besserungsanstalt; ~ **hospital** geschlossene Anstalt (*zur vorübergehenden Unterbringung Nervenkranker*); ~ **in reformatory** Unterbringung in e–r Erziehungsanstalt; ~ **of a bill** Vorenthaltung e–s Wechsels; ~ **of a ship** Anhalten e–s Schiffes; ~ **on remand** Untersuchungshaft; ~ **pending trial** Untersuchungshaft; **actual** ~ tatsächliche Gewalt, Gewahrsam; **coercive** ~ Zwangshaft, Beugehaft; **compulsory** ~Verwahrung; **pretrial** ~ Untersuchungshaft; **preventive** ~ Unterbindungsgewahrsam; Sicherungsverwahrung *GB: abgeschafft 1967 → extended sentence;* **right of** ~ → *right;* **to compensate the** ~ die Untersuchungshaft anrechnen; **unlawful** ~ widerrechtliches Zurückbehalten; Freiheitsberaubung.

deter abhalten, abschrecken; ~ **ring effect** Abschreckungswirkung *f*.

deterioration Verschlechterung *f*, Verderb *m*, Wertminderung *f*; Verschleiß *m*; **inherent** ~ innerer Verderb, leichte Verderblichkeit; **intrinsic** ~ innerer Verderb, leichte Verderblichkeit; **natural** ~ innerer Verderb; natürlicher Verderb.

determent Abschreckung *f*, Abschreckungsmittel *n*.

determinable beendbar, bei Eintritt e–s Ereignisses endend; feststellbar; ~ **future time** bestimmbarer zukünftiger Zeitpunkt.

determinate *adj* bestimmt, festgesetzt, endgültig, entschlossen, entschieden.

determination Abgrenzung *f*, Bestimmtheit *f*, Entscheidung *f*, Festsetzung *f*, Feststellung *f*, Entschluß *m*; Beendigung *f*; ~ **letter** verbindl Auskunftschreiben der Finanzbehörde; ~ **of costs** Kostenfestsetzung; ~ **of counsel's fees** Festsetzung von Rechtsanwaltsgebühren; ~ **of conditions** Festsetzung von Bedingungen; ~ **of need** Armutszeugnis, Feststellung der Bedürftigkeit; ~ **of proceedings** Erledigung des Verfahrens; ~ **of rent** Mietfestsetzung; ~ **of will** Widerruf e–r Nutzungserlaubnis (*vgl estate at will*); **administrative** ~ Verwaltungsakt, Verw-sentscheidung; **final** ~ Endurteil, Endentscheidung.

determine bestimmen, entscheiden, abgrenzen, beendigen, enden; bedingen; ~ **a price** e–n Preis festsetzen; **as the court may** ~ nach Ermessen des Gerichts; **to hear and** ~ verhandeln und entscheiden; ~**d by lapse of time** durch Zeitablauf beendet.

deterrence Abschreckung *f*; **graduated** ~ abgestufte Abschreckung.

deterrent Abschreckung *f*, Abschreckungsprinzip *n*; **nuclear** ~ atomare Abschreckung.

detinue widerrechtliche Vorenthaltung *f* des Besitzes an beweglichen Sachen; **action of** ~ Vindikationsklage, Herausgabeklage *GB bis 1977.*

detour *s* Umleitung *f*, Umweg *m*; ~ *v* **the traffic** den Verkehr umleiten.

detoxification centre Entziehungsanstalt *f* (*Alkohol*).
detract entziehen, abziehen, wegnehmen, beeinträchtigen.
detraction Beeinträchtigung *f*, Schmälerung *f*, Verunglimpfung *f*, Verbringen *n* ins Ausland.
detriment Nachteil *m*, Schaden *m*, Vermögensnachteil *m*; **legal** ~ Rechtsnachteil; **material** ~ erheblicher Nachteil.
detrimental nachteilig, abträglich; ~ **to the public interest** dem öffentlichen Interesse abträglich.
detritus Schutt *m*, Abfall *m*.
de-unisation Abbau der Gewerkschaftsbindung.
deuterogamy Wiederverheiratung *f* nach dem Tod des Ehegatten, Deuterogamie *f*, zweite Ehe *f*.
devaluation Abwertung *f*; ~ **clause** Abwertungsklausel; ~ **profit** Abwertungsgewinn; **currency** ~ (Währungs)Abwertung.
devastation Verwüstung *f*, Verheerung *f*; Vergeudung *f* von Nachlaßmitteln; **general** ~ Verschwendung des Erbes.
devastavit pflichtwidrige Schädigung des Nachlasses durch den Nachlaßverwalter bzw Testamentsvollstrecker.
develop entwickeln, weiterbilden, erschließen, nutzbar machen; ~**ed land** erschlossenes Gebiet; ~**ed tract of land** erschlossenes Gelände; ~**ing country** Entwicklungsland.
developer (Bauland-)Erschließungsunternehmen *n*; **property** ~ Bauland-Erschließungsfirma, Bauträger *m*.
development Entwicklung *f*, Weiterbildung *f*, Erschließung *f*, Nutzbarmachung *f*, bauliche *bzw* gewerbl Bodennutzung, Ausbau *m*; ~ **aid** Entwicklungshilfe; ~ **area** wirtschaftlich rückständiges Gebiet; *special* ~ ~: *Notstandsgebiet*; ~ **banks** Entwicklungsbanken; ~ **charge** Erschließungsabgabe; **D**~ **Commissioners** Entwicklungsbehörde; ~ **corporation** → *corporation*; ~ **district** Gebiet mit hoher Arbeitslosigkeit; **D**~ **Fund** Entwicklungsfonds; ~ **land** Bauerwartungsland; ~ **land tax** Erschließungsgewinnabgabe; ~ **of building ground** Erschließung von Bauland; ~ **operation** Erschließung (*Stadtansiedlungen*) ~ **plan** Flächennutzungsplan, Baulanderschließungsplan; ~ **project** Entwicklungsvorhaben; ~ **risk** Produzentenrisiko wegen Neuentwicklung; ~ **value** Wertdifferenz durch Flächennutzungsbeschränkung, Erschließungswert, Grundstückswert durch Ortserschließung; **commercial** ~ wirtschaftliche Entwicklung; **housing** ~ Wohnsiedlung; **industrial** ~ industrielle Erschließung; **industrial** ~ **company** Industrieförderungsgesellschaft.
deviate abgehen, abweichen, ablenken; ~ **from instructions** von Weisungen abweichen; ~ **from justice** das Recht beugen.
deviation Abweichung *f*, Deviation *f*, Kursabweichung *f*, Abgehen *n* vom Kurs; selbständiger Handel *m* außerhalb des Arbeitsauftrags; ~ **clause** Abweichungsklausel, zulässige Abweichung; ~ **from the party line** Abweichung von der Parteilinie; ~ **of quality** Qualitätsabweichung; **permissible** zulässige Abweichung.
deviator *pol* Abweichler *m*.
device Plan *m*, Vorhaben *n*, Vorrichtung *f*; Kennzeichen *n*, Erfindung *f*, Apparat *m*; etwas Erdachtes; ~ **patent** → *patent*; **claim to a** ~ Vorrichtungsanspruch (*Patentanmeldung*); **curative** ~ Heilungsmöglichkeit, Abhilfemöglichkeit; **distinctive** ~ Unterscheidungsmerkmal; unterscheidungsfähige Vorrichtung; **fiscal** ~ Finanzplan, steuerliches Mittel; **fraudulent** ~ Schwindelunternehmen; betrügerischer Trick; **procedural** ~ Verfahrenstrick.
devil *s* Anwaltsvertreter *m*; Lohnschreiber *m*; ~**'s advocate** advocatus diaboli.

devil *v* Terminvertretungen (*für vielbeschäftigten Anwalt*) übernehmen; anwaltschaftliche Hilfsdienste leisten.

devious abwegig, ungewöhnlich, gewunden, verschlagen.

devisable vermachbar, vertretbar, erdenkbar, erdenklich.

devise *s* letztwillige Zuwendung *f* von Grundbesitz, Immobilienlegat *n*; Erbeinsetzung auf den unbeweglichen Nachlaß; ~ **to charity** letztwillige Verfügung über Immobilien für wohltätige Zwecke; ~ **to A and B between them** Grundstückslegat an A und B gemeinsam; ~ **to wife for life with remainder to sons** Einsetzung der Ehefrau als Vorerbin und der Söhne als Nacherben; **alienation by** ~ → *alienation*; **by** ~ **or descent** Testats- oder Intestatserbfolge *bei Grundbesitz*, Rechtsnachfolge; **conditional** ~ bedingte letztwillige Verfügung (*über Immobilien*); **contingent** ~ aufschiebend bedingte letztwillige Verfügung (*über Immobilien*); Nacherbeneinsetzung; **executory** ~ Vermächtnis einer Anwartschatft (*an Immobilien*), letztwillige Verfügung mit Auflagen, Nacherbeneinsetzung, Nachvermächtnis; **general** ~ letztwillige Verfügung über den gesamten Grundbesitz des Erblassers; **lapsed** ~ nicht wirksam gewordene letztwillige Verfügung (*über Immobilien*), durch Vorversterben hinfällig gewordene Erbeinsetzung; **residuary** ~ letztwillige Verfügung über den gesamten restlichen Grundbesitz des Erblassers; **specific** ~ Grundstücksvermächtnis; **vested** ~ unbedingte letztwillige Verfügung (*über Immobilien*).

devise *v* Grundbesitz letztwillig zuwenden.

devisee letztwillig mit Grundbesitz Bedachter *m* testamentarischer Grundstückserbe; ~ **in trust** treuhänderisch gebundener *devisee qv;* **residuary** ~ Testatserbe des unbeweglichen Restnachlasses.

deviser Erfinder *m*; **presumptive** ~ mutmaßlicher Urheber (der Erfindung).

devisor letztwillig über Grundbesitz Verfügender *m*.

devoid bar, ohne, ermangelnd.

devolution Anfall *m*, Heimfall *m*, gesetzliche Rechtsnachfolge *f*; Erbgang *m*, Übergang *m*; Delegation *f*; Dezentralisation *f*; ~ **agreements** Übereinkünfte über Rechtsnachfolge (*Völkerrecht*); ~ **of authority** Übergang von Befugnissen; ~ **of ownership** Eigentumsübergang; ~ **of the crown** Thronfolge; ~ **of the estate** Übergang e–s Vermögens, Anfall der Erbschaft (*an den personal representative qv);* ~ **of title** Rechtsübergang; ~ **upon death** Rechtsnachfolge bei Tod.

devolutive appeal Rechtsmittel *n* ohne Suspensivwirkung.

devolve übertragen, anfallen, zufallen; (*kraft Erbfolge bzw sonst gesetzlich*) übergehen, heimfallen.

devolvement Heimfall *m*.

dewarding Entlassung aus der Vormundschaft, Aufhebung der V.

dialling code Vorwahlnummer *f*, Ortskennziffer *f*; **direct** ~ **in** Durchwählen *n*.

diary Tagebuch *n* Terminkalender *m*.

dicta *pl von dictum qv*.

dictated but not signed nach Diktat verreist.

dictionary Lexikon *n*, Wörterbuch *n*; **legal** ~ juristisches Wörterbuch.

dictum (*pl:dicta*) richterlicher Ausspruch *m*, richterliche Meinung *f*, Spruch *m*, Maxime *f*, beiläufige Äußerung *f*, *Kurzform für obiter dictum qv*; **gratis** ~ e–e Erklärung ohne Obligo; **obiter** ~ → *obiter*, **simplex** ~ unbewiesene Behauptung, schlichte Meinungsäußerung.

die *v* sterben; ~ **a violent death** e–s gewaltsamen Todes sterben; ~ **by his own hands** Selbstmord begehen; ~ **childless** kinderlos sterben; ~ **leaving issue** Nachkommen hinterlassen; ~ **without (leaving) issue** ohne Abkömmlinge sterben.

dies Tag *m*, Gerichtstag *m*; Tagesration *f*; ~ **a quo** Fristbeginn, erster Tag e–r Frist; ~ **jurisdicus** (gewöhnlicher) Gerichtstag; ~ **ad quem** Fristende, letzter Tag e–r Frist; ~ **non (juridicus)** gerichtsfreier Tag; Tag, der bei Fristen nicht mitgezählt wird.

diet Landtag *m*, Parlament *n* (*Kontinentaleuropa*); **Federal D~** Bundestag.

Dieu Et Mon Droit Gott und mein Recht (*Motto im britischen Wappen*).

differ sich unterscheiden, nicht übereinstimmen, sich nicht einig sein; **I beg to** ~ ich bin anderer Ansicht; **the witnesses** ~ Zeugenaussagen sind widersprüchlich.

difference Differenz *f*, Unterschied *m*, Unterscheidung *f*; Meinungsverschiedenheit *f*, Streit *m*; **~s in exchange** Kursdifferenz; ~ **in prices** Preisunterschied; ~ **in rates** Kursdifferenz; ~ **in treatment** unterschiedliche Behandlung; ~ **of opinion** Meinungsverschiedenheit; **settlement of ~s** Beilegung von Streitigkeiten.

different unterschiedlich, verschieden, besonders, andersartig.

differential *s* Unterschiedlichkeit *f*, Lohn- u. Gehaltsverschiedenheit *f*, Niveauunterschiede *m*|*pl*.

differential *ad*, unterscheidend, unterschiedlich; ~ **freight rate** Ausnahmefrachtsätze; ~ **piece rate system** Stücklohnverfahren; ~ **rates** Ausnahmefrachtsätze.

difficult schwer, schwierig, problematisch.

difficulty Schwierigkeit *f*, Unverständlichkeit *f*, Problem *n*; Widerstand *m*, Widrigkeit *f*; ~ **in selling** Absatzschwierigkeiten; ~ **of supply** Versorgungsschwierigkeiten; **initial ~ies** Anlaufschwierigkeiten; **insuperable ~ies** unüberwindliche Schwierigkeiten.

digamy Wiederverheiratung *f* des Witwers, neue Ehe *f* des Witwers.

digest *v* kompilieren.

digest *s* Auswahl *f*, Anthologie *f*; Fallsammlung *f*, Gesetzessammlung *f*; ~ **of statistics** statistisches Jahrbuch; statistische Zusammenfassung; **the D~s** (*Dig*) die Digesten.

dignities Würden *f*|*pl*, Nebenrechte *n*|*pl*.

dignity of man Menschenwürde *f*.

digress abschweifen, abweichen; ~ **from the subject** vom Thema abkommen, abschweifen.

digression Abschweifung *f*, nicht zur Sache gehörige Ausführung *f*.

digressive abschweifen, nicht zur Sache gehörig.

dijudication gerichtliche Entscheidung *f*, Aburteilung *f*.

dilapidation Verfallenlassen *n*, Baufälligkeit *f*, schlechter Bauzustand *m*; Vergeudung *f*; notwendige Instandsetzung; **schedule of ~s** Liste der notwendigen Reparaturen.

dilatoriness Säumnis *n*, Säumigkeit *f*, Zaudern *n*.

dilatory dilatorisch, hinausschiebend, verzögerlich.

diligence Sorgfalt *f* (= *S*), Sorgsamkeit *f*, aufmerksame Tätigkeit *f*, Emsigkeit *f*, Eifer *m*; ~ **usual in ordinary intercourse** die im gewöhnlichen Verkehr erforderliche *S*; **due** ~ die im Verkehr erforderliche *S*; **extraordinary** ~ außerordentlich hoher Grad der *S*–spflicht; **great** ~ große *S*, gesteigerte *S* **high** ~ = *great* ~ *qv;* **incident** ~ erforderlicher Eifer bei der Vorlage von Urkunden; **in exercising reasonable** ~ bei Beachtung der im Verkehr erforderlichen *S*; **low** ~ geringe *S;* **necessary** ~ erforderliche *S*; **ordinary** ~ gewöhnliche *S*, übliche *S*; **reasonable** ~ angemessene *S*, zumutbare *S*, zumutbares Bemühen; **slight** ~ = *low* ~ *qv*; **special** ~ die besondere *S* des Fachkundigen; **want of** ~ Mangel an *S*, Fahrlässigkeit.

diligent sorgfältig, fleißig, arbeitsam; aufmerksam, nachhaltig.

dilute verdünnen, verwässern, verflüssigen; ~ **labour** ungelernte Arbeiter einstellen.

dilution Verdünnung *f*, Verwässerung *f*; ~ **doctrine** (*Lehre von der*)

Warenzeichenverwässerung (*Abschwächung der Unterscheidungskraft*).
diminish (ver)mindern, verringern.
diminution Minderung *f*, Verminderung *f*, Unvollständigkeit *f* (*der Akten*); Schwund *m*; ~ **in value** Wertminderung; ~ **of profits** Gewinnschrumpfung.
dimisi „ich habe (*das Pachtrecht*) übertragen" (*Urkundenformel*).
dinarchy Doppelherrschaft *f*.
dip *s* Abdachung *f*, Bodensenke *f*, Neigung *f* e–r Erzader; Tiefgang *m*; Taschendieb *m*; Geschäftsrückgang *m*.
diploma Diplom *n*, akademisches Diplom *n*, Zulassungsurkunde *f*, Ernennungsurkunde *f*; Verleihungsurkunde *f*; amtliches Schriftstück *n*, Verfassungsurkunde *f*, Staatsurkunde *f*; **to award a** ~ ein Diplom verleihen.
diplomacy Diplomatie *f*; diplomatisches Vorgehen *f*; **cultural** ~ Kulturpolitik; **secret** ~ Geheimdiplomatie.
diplomatic diplomatisch (= *d*); ~ **agency** *d–e* Auslandsdienststelle; ~ **agent** → *agent*; ~ **asylum** *d–es* Asyl; ~ **body** *d–es* Korps; ~ **business** Amtsgeschäfte des auswärtigen Dienstes; ~ **character** *d–r* Eigenschaft; *clothed witch* ~ ~: *mit d–er Eigenschaft versehen;* ~ **code** *d–er* Code (*Verschlüsselung*); ~ **couriers** Kuriere (*im diplomatischen Dienst*); ~ **immunity** Diplomaten-Immunität; ~ **intercourse** → *intercourse;* ~ **list** *d–e* Liste; ~ **mission** *d–e* Mission; ~ **note** *d–e* Note; ~ **officer** Beamter des Auswärtigen Dienstes; ~ **pouch** Kuriergepäck; ~ **privileges** → *privilege*; ~ **relations** *d–e* Beziehungen; ~ **representative** → *representative*; ~ **service** *d–er* Dienst, auswärtiger Dienst; **through** ~ **channels** auf *d–em* Wege; **to entertain** ~ **relations** *d–e* Beziehungen unterhalten; **to sever** ~ **relations** *d–e* Beziehungen abbrechen.
diplomatics Diplomatik *f*, Urkundenlehre *f*, Diplomatie *f*.
diplomatism Diplomatie *f*.
dipsomania Trunksucht *f*.
dipsomaniac Trunksüchtiger *m*.
direct *adj* direkt, gerade, unmittelbar, nächstliegend; persönlich; ~ **and sole cause** die (*unmittelbare und*) alleinige Ursache; ~ **debit card** Abbuchungskreditkarte; ~ **labour organisation** Beschäftigung von Arbeitskräften in eigener Regie (*Gemeinden*); ~ **loss or damage** unmittelbarer Schaden; ~ **-mail literature** Reklamematerial für Postwurfsendungen; ~ **or proximate cause** unmittelbare Ursache; ~ **personal supervision** unmittelbare Beaufsichtigung; ~ **proof of malice** zweifelsfreier Beweis der bösen Absicht; ~ **reporting agency system** unmittelbare Direktionszuständigkeit (*von Versicherungsvertretern*); ~ **restraint on alienation** absolutes (*gesetzliches*) Veräußerungsverbot; ~ **writing company** Hauptversicherer, Erstversicherer (*Rückversicherung*).
direct *v* anordnen, verfügen, hinweisen, leiten, richten, belehren; ~ **the jury as to law** den Geschworenen Rechtsbelehrungen erteilen; ~**ed verdict** Spruch der Geschworenen gemäß juristischer Anweisung des Berufsrichters; **as** ~**ed** vorschriftsmäßig, laut Verfügung; ~**ing the flow of capital** Kapitalsteuerung.
direction Leitung *f*, Weisung *f*, Belehrung *f*; Richtung *f*; ~**s for evidence** Beweisbeschluß; ~ **for use** Gebrauchsanweisung; ~ **in writing** schriftliche Weisung; ~ **of verdict** *Weisung des Berufsrichters an die Geschworenen, aus Rechtsgründen in e–m bestimmten Sinn zu entscheiden*; ~**s to a jury** Rechtsbelehrung der Geschworenen; ~**s to the constables** Anweisung an die Polizei, Übertragen von Aufgaben an die Polizei; **by** ~ **of** nach Weisung von, auf Veranlassung von; **summons for** ~**s** → *summons*.
directive Richtlinie *f*, Vorschrift *f*, Anordnung *f*; **administrative** ~ behördliche Weisung, Verwal-

tungsanordnung, Verwaltungsrichtlinie.

director Verwaltungsratsmitglied *n* (= *V*) *ungenau: Vorstandsmitglied bzw GmbH-Geschäftsführer bzw Aufsichtsratsmitglied;* Direktor *m*, Leiter *m*; **~s** Verwaltungsrat (*mit Funktionen des Vorstands und Aufsichtsrats; gemeinsam bzw einzeln*); **~ general** Generaldirektor; **D~-General of Fair Trading** Leiter der brit. *Verbraucherschutz-, Wettbewerbs- und* Monopolbehörde; **D~ Legal Services** Leiter der Rechtsabteilung; **~s' meeting** Verwaltungsratssitzung; **D~ of Census** Leiter des Statistischen Bundesamtes *US*; **D~ of Public Prosecutions** die Staatsanwaltschaft; der Generalstaatsanwalt; **D~ of Savings** Leiter der Postspardienste *GB*, **~ of the budget** US Leiter der Haushaltsabteilung; **D~ of the Mint** Präsident des Bundesmünzamtes *US*; **~s' report** → *report*; **board of ~s** Verwaltungsrat (*mit Funktionen des Vorstands und Aufsichtsrats*), *ungenau:* Vorstand *bzw* Aufsichtsrat; **alternate ~** ständiger Vertreter e–s *V–s*, Ersatzmann; **commercial ~** kaufmännischer Direktor; **continuing ~** verbleibendes *V*; **controlling ~** *V* mit beherschendem Einfluß: **delinquent ~** *V*, gegen das Verdacht der Untreue besteht; **disqualified ~** *V*, bei dem die Voraussetzungen für sein Amt nicht mehr vorliegen; *V*, das mangels Pflichtaktie auszuscheiden hat; **engineering ~** technischer Direktor; **executive ~s** (*aktive*) *V–er;* **divisional managing ~** Abteilungsleiter; **finance ~** Leiter der Finanzabteilung; **full-time working ~** hauptberufl *V*; **independent ~** betriebsunabhängiges (*externes*) *V*; **inside ~** der Gesellschaft angehörendes *V*; **managing ~** (geschäftsführender) Direktor, geschäftsführendes *V*, Generaldirektor; **non-executive ~** nicht an der Geschäftsführung beteiligtes *V*, nichtgeschäftsführendes *V*; (*kurz: non-exec*) *etwa*: Aufsichtsratsmitglied; **ordinary ~** (*gewöhnliches*) *V*; **outside ~** externes *V*; **proceedings of ~s** Geschäftsordnung des Verwaltungsrats; **production ~** Produktionsleiter; **quorum of ~s** → *quorum*; **removal of ~s** Entlassung von *V–n*; **retiring ~** ausscheidendes *V*; **salaried ~** hauptberufliches *V*; **sole ~** Einzelvorstand, Einzel(GmbH)Geschäftsführer; **technical ~** technischer Direktor.

directorate Direktorium *n*, Vostand *m*.

directorship Vorstandssitz *m*; **interlocking ~** Überkreuzverflechtung (*durch Aufsichtsratssitze*).

directory *adj* leitend, anweisend, bestimmend.

directory Adreßbuch *n*, Einwohnerverzeichnis *n*, Telefonverzeichnis *n*; Branchenverzeichnis *n*; **commercial ~** Branchenadressbuch; **trade ~** Branchenadressbuch.

dirigism Dirigismus *m*.

diriment nichtig machend.

disability Geschäftsunfähigkeit *f*, beschränkte Geschäftsfähigkeit *f*; Behinderung *f*, Arbeitsunfähigkeit *f*, Erwerbsunfähigkeit *f*, Invalidität; Unvermögen *n*; Prozeßunfähigkeit *f*; **~ benefits** → *benefit;* **~ clause** Invaliditätsklausel (*Beitragsfreiheit, sonstige Vergünstigungen*); **~ fund** Invaliditätsfonds; **~ insurance** → *insurance*; **~ retirement** Invalidisierung; **~ to sue** mangelnde Prozeßfähigkeit (*beim Kläger*); **absolute ~** Geschäftsunfähigkeit; **canonical ~** Ehehindernis nach kanonischem Recht; **civil ~** Ehehindernis nach bürgerlichem Recht, zwingendes Rechtshindernis; **congenital ~** erbbiologisch bedingte Behinderung; Genschäden; **general ~** Geschäftsunfähigkeit, beschränkte Geschäftsfähigkeit; **legal ~** Geschäftsunfähigkeit, Verfügungsunfähigkeit (*auch: Konkurs; evtl*: Entzug der bürgerlichen Ehrenrechte); **mental ~** Geschäftsunfähigkeit; **partial ~** partielle Geschäftsfähigkeit; Teilinvalidität, Arbeitsunfähigkeit; **permanent (and total)** ~ Erwerbsunfähigkeit; Vollinvalidität; **person under** ~ → *person*; **personal** ~ auf die Person beschränktes Unvermögen; **physical** ~ Invalidität, Erwerbsunfähigkeit, Arbeitsunfähigkeit; **special** ~ Unfähigkeit im besonderen; beschränkte Geschäftsfähigkeit; **temporary** ~ zeitweilige Arbeitsunfähigkeit; **total** ~ völlige Erwerbsunfähigkeit.

disable *v* unfähig machen, außerstand setzen, untauglich machen, zum Invaliden werden; entmündigen; **~d ex-service man** Kriegsinvalide; **~d from acting** handlungsunfähig; **~d person** Invalide, Erwerbsunfähiger, Arbeitsunfähiger, Schwerbehinderter, Schwerbeschädigter; **D~d Persons Employment Act** Schwerbehindertengesetz; **~d soldier** Kriegsversehrter **~d worker** schwerbeschädigter Arbeiter; **legally ~d** geschäftsunfähig, beschränkt geschäftsfähig.

disablement Unfähigkeit *f*, Invalidität *f*, Arbeitsunfähigkeit *f*, Erwerbsunfähigkeit *f*, Dienstunfähigkeit *f*, Untauglichkeit *f*, Schwerbehinderteneigenschaft *f*, Schwerbeschädigteneigenschaft *f*; ~ **benefit** Berufsunfähigkeitsrente (*wegen Arbeitsunfall bzw bestimmter Krankheiten*), Kriegsopferrente; ~ **gratuity** Beschädigtenrente *bei weniger als 20%er Minderung der Erwerbsunfähigkeit;* ~ **pension** Schwerbeschädigtenrente (*Kriegsopferversorgung, GB*); ~ **officer** Betreuer für Schwerbeschädigte; **D~ Resettlement Service** Abteilung für Umschulung und Vermittlung von Schwerbeschädigten; **total** ~ Vollinvalidität.

disadvantage *s* Nachteil *m*, Schaden *m*, Verlust *m*; **legal** ~ Rechtsnachteil; **to sell at a** ~ mit Verlust verkaufen.

disadvantage *v/t* benachteiligen.

disadvantageous nachteilig.

disaffection politische Unzufriedenheit *f*, staatsfeindliche Gesinnung *f*; **incitement to** ~ → *incitement*.

disaffirm aufheben, umstoßen, die Genehmigung verweigern; erklären, an etwas nicht gebunden zu sein; ~ **a court decision** e–e Gerichtsentscheidung aufheben.

disaffirmance Anfechtung *f*, Rücktritt *m*, Nichtanerkennung *f*, Aufhebung *f*.

disafforest *v* Wald wieder zu landwirtschaftlichem Grund machen, abforsten, Waldland von den Forstgesetzen ausnehmen.

disagree nicht übereinstimmen, ablehnen, einander widersprechen.

disagreement Meinungsverschiedenheit *f*, Uneinigkeit *f*, Unstimmigkeit *f*, Nichtübereinstimmung *n*.

disallow nicht gestatten, nicht gelten lassen, verbieten, zurückweisen, aberkennen; ~ **a claim** e–n Anspruch abweisen; ~ **an appeal** ein Rechtsmittel (*Berufung, Beschwerde, Revision*) zurückweisen.

disallowance Mißbilligung *f*, Nichtanerkennung *f*, Verwerfung *f*; ~ **of amendments** Nichtgestattung von Änderungen; ~ **of disbursement** Streichung von Ausgaben, Feststellung der Rechtswidrigkeit von Ausgaben (*Fiskus*).

disappear verschwinden.

disapply *v/t* nicht mehr anwenden, unanwendbar machen.

disappreciation technischer Preisrückgang *m* (*als Korrektur überhöhter Preise*), markttechnisch bedingter Kursrückgang.

disapprobation Mißbilligung *f*.

disappropriation Enteignung *f*, Entziehung *f* e–r Kirchenpfründe.

disapproval Mißbilligung *f*, Abweisung *f*, Ablehnung *f*.

disapprove mißbilligen, verwerfen, ablehnen.

disarmament Abrüstung *f*, Entwaffnung *f*.

disaster Unglück *n*, Mißgeschick *n*, Katastrophe *f*; ~ **area** Katastrophengebiet; **common** ~ gemeinsames Unglück (*Versterben in e–m*); **natural** ~ Naturkatastrophe.

disavow abrücken (von), ablehnen, in Abrede stellen, verleugnen, ableugnen.

disavowal Leugnen *n*, Verleugnen *n*, Nichtanerkennung *f*, Dementi *n*.

disbar aus der Anwaltschaft ausschließen.

disbarment Ausschluß *m* aus der Anwaltschaft.

disbench aus dem Anwaltsvorstand ausschließen.

disbursement|s Barauslagen *f|pl*, (*notwendige*) Kosten und Auslagen *f|pl* der Partei, Ausgaben des Treuhänders; ~ **clause** Auslagenklausel; ~ **voucher** Zahlungsanweisung, Kassenanweisung, Auszahlungsbeleg; **cash** ~**s** Zahlungsausgänge, Ausgaben.

disbursing|agent Auszahlungsbeauftragter; ~ **officer** zu Auszahlungen ermächtigter Beamter; ~ **records** Ausgabenbelege, Soldunterlagen.

discardment Außerbetriebsetzung *f*; ~ **overside** Ausladung über Schiffsseite.

discern erkennen, unterscheiden, wahrnehmen, feststellen.

discernment Einsicht *f*, Scharfsinn *m*, Verständnis *n*; Urteilskraft *f*, Erkennen *n*; Unterscheidungsvermögen *n*.

discharge *s* Entlassung *f*, Erledigung *f*, Erlöschen (*durch Erfüllung*); Haftungsfreistellung; Entlastung; Aufhebung e–r Grundstücksbelastung; Aufhebung e–r Entscheidung; Einstellung *f* des Verfahrens; Rechnungslegung *f* (*im Prozeß*); ~ **by alteration** Erlöschen (*der Wechselverpflichtung*) durch Änderung; ~ **by renunciation** Erlöschen (*der Wechselverpflichtung*) durch Verzicht; ~ **from** (= *in*) **bankruptcy** Aufhebung des Konkursverfahrens (*mit Erlaß restlicher Schulden*); ~ **from commonage** Aufhebung, Ablösung, von Allmendrechten; ~ **from custody** Haftentlassung; ~ **from prosecution** Einstellung des Verfahrens; ~ **of a contract** Erfüllung e–s Vertrages, Erlöschen e–s vertraglichen Schuldverhältnisses; ~ **of a debt** Schuldtilgung, Erlöschen e–r Forderung; ~ **of an obligation** → *obligation*; ~ **of bill by alteration** Ungültigwerden des Wechsels infolge unbefugter Änderung der Wechselurkunde; ~ **of cargo** Löschung der Ladung; ~ **of duty** Pflichterfüllung, Wahrnehmung von Aufgaben, Dienstausübung; ~ **of encumbrances** Lastenfreistellung; ~ **of jury** Entlassung der Geschworenen; ~ **of mortgage** Löschung e–s Grundpfandrechts, Freigabe von e–r Hypothek; ~ **of prisoner** Haftentlassung; ~ **of right** Erfüllung e–s Anspruchs, Erlöschen e–s Rechts; ~ **of the accused** Einstellung des Verfahrens gegen den Angeklagten; ~ **of trustee** Entlastung des Treuhänders; ~ **on account of bias or prejudice** Entlassung (*von Schöffen oder Geschworenen)* wegen Besorgnis der Befangenheit; **absolute** ~ Absetzen von Strafen (nach *Verurteilung*); **conditional** ~ bedingter Straferlaß; **dishonorable** ~ unehrenhafte Entlassung; **final** ~ entgültige Entlassung aus der Haft; **full** ~ bedingungslose Entlassung, restlose Erfüllung, vollständige Begleichung; **lawful** ~ Entlastung des Gemeinschuldners (*restl. Schulderlaß*); **personal** ~ Rehabilitierung; **to give a** ~ Entlastung erteilen; **unconditional** ~ Entlassung ohne Auflagen; absoluter Haftungsverzicht; **unilateral** ~ Entlassung aus einseitig erfüllter Verpflichtung.

discharge *v* entbinden, freisprechen, entlasten, löschen, erfüllen, begleichen, tilgen, befriedigen; **"~ afloat"** „Schiff muß schwimmend löschen", ~ **an account** e–e Rechnung quittieren; ~ **an obligation** e–e Verbindlichkeit erfüllen; ~ **an order** Beschluß aufheben; ~ **from all calls due** von jeder Haftung für bisherige Einzahlungsverpflichtungen freistellen; ~ **process of ex-**

ecution e–e Zwangsvollstreckungsmaßnahme aufheben, Zwangsvollstreckung einstellen; ~ **with ignominy** ausstoßen, unehrenhafte Entlassung aussprechen; **~d and acquitted** bezahlt und quittiert; **~d bill** bezahlter Wechsel; **~d prisoners aid** Gefangenenhilfe, Gefangenenfürsorge; **debt ~d** getilgte Schuld, nicht mehr beitreibbare Schuld; **until ~d in full** bis zur restlosen Schuldtilgung.

disciplinary disziplinarisch, Disziplinar . . .; ~ **action** Disziplinarmaßnahme, Disziplinarverfahren; ~ **board** Disziplinargericht; ~ **code** Disziplinarvorschriften, standesrechtliche Vorschriften; ~ **committee** Ehrengericht; ~ **control** Disziplinargewalt; ~ **measures** Disziplinarmaßnahmen; ~ **proceedings** Dienststrafverfahren; ~ **rules** Dienststrafordnung; ~ **transfer** Strafversetzung; **D~ Tribunal** Ehrengerichtshof (*solicitors*).

discipline *s* Erziehung *f*, Disziplin *f*, (*elterliches*) Züchtigungsrecht *n*; **D~ Committee** (*of the Law Society*) Ehrengericht (*der Anwaltskammer*).

discipline *v* maßregeln, erziehen.

disclaim ausschlagen, zurückweisen, verzichten; ~ **a right** auf ein Recht verzichten, ein Recht ausschlagen; ~ **a trademark** auf Warenzeichenschutz verzichten; ~ **an action** die Verantwortung für e–e Handlung ablehnen; ~ **an offer for sale** ein Verkaufsangebot nicht anerkennen; ~ **liability** Haftung ablehnen; **~ed property** → *property*.

disclaimer Verzicht *m*, Aufgabe *f*, Dereliktion *f*; Ablehnung *f* der Annahme, Haftungsablehnungserklärung; Ausschlagung *f*; *hist* Bestreiten des Obereigentums durch den Belehnten, Bestreiten *n* des Verpächterrechts durch den Pächter, Teilverzicht *m* auf Patentfähigkeit; ~ **by crown** Rechtsverzicht der Krone; ~ **by liquidator** Verzichtserklärung des Liquidators; ~ **by trustee** Nichtannahme des Treuhandamtes; ~ **clause** Verzichtsklausel, Haftungsausschlußklausel; ~ **of a right** Rechtsverzicht; ~ **of an estate** Nichtannahme e–r Grundstückszuwendung; ~ **of powers** Verzicht auf Befugnisse, **official ~ of a statement** amtliches Dementi e–r Behauptung.

disclamation Nichtanerkennung *f* (*von Grundherrschaftsrechten*).

disclos|e offenbaren, enthüllen, aufdecken; ~ **oneself** sich offenbaren, *zu erkennen geben, daß man selbst der wirkliche Berechtigte ist;* **duty to** ~ → *duty* (*1*); **~ing a defence** schlüssige Einwendungen vorbringen.

disclosure Enthüllung *f*, Offenlegung *f*, Aufdeckung *f*, Offenbarung (*der Erfindungsmerkmale*); ~ **of earnings** Gewinnausweis; ~ **of information** Auskunftserteilung, Offenbarung (Preisgabe) von Informationen; ~ **of information relating to trade** Preisgabe von wirtschaftlichen Kenntnissen; ~ **of offence by accused** Mitteilung der Straftat durch den Beschuldigten; ~ **of official secrets** Preisgabe von Staatsgeheimnissen; ~ **of vote** Preisgabe des Wahlgeheimnisses der Stimmabgabe; ~ **requirements** *bil* Angabepflichten; ~ **rules** Publizitätsvorschriften; **full** ~ vollständige Offenlegung; **required ~s** *bil* Pflichtangaben.

discommon *v* (*Allmende*) der öffentlichen Benutzung entziehen, ein gemeinsames Recht entziehen.

disconcert aus der Fassung bringen, vereiteln.

disconformity Unstimmigkeit *f*, mangelnde Übereinstimmung *f*.

discontinuance Nichtfortsetzung *f*, Rücknahme *f*, Absetzung *f*, Einstellung *f*, Unterbrechung *f*; ~ **by consent without leave** Klagerücknahme mit Zustimmung des Prozeßgegners ohne gerichtliche Erlaubnis; ~ **by interveners** Ausscheiden des Klägers zugunsten e–s Streithelfers; ~ **of action** Klagerücknahme; ~ **of counterclaim** Rücknahme der Widerklage; ~ **of**

estate (rechtswidrige) Verfügung zum Schaden künftig Berechtigter, Aushöhlung des Nachlasses; ~ **of execution** Einstellung der Vollstreckung; ~ **of subscription** Beendigung des Abonnements; ~ **with leave** Klagerücknahme mit Erlaubnis des Gerichts; **revival after** ~ erneutes Geltendmachen der Klage (*nach Aussetzung bzw Ruhen des Verfahrens*); **voluntary** ~ Klagerücknahme.

discontinue *v* unterbrechen, einstellen; aussetzen, auflösen; ~ **the proceedings** die Sache absetzen, das Verfahren unterbrechen, das Verfahren nicht fortsetzen; ~**d business** eingestellter Geschäftsbetrieb.

discontinuing a licence Konzessionsentzug, Nichtverlängerung e–r Konzession.

discontinuous gelegentlich, unterbrochen, unzusammenhängend.

discount *s* Preisnachlaß *m*, Rabatt *m*, Abzug *m*, Diskont *m*; Disagio *n*; ~ **bank** Diskontbank; ~ **bill** → *bill (3)*; ~ **bracket** Rabattgruppe; ~ **broker** → *broker*; ~ **charge** Diskontsatz; ~ **company** Finanzgesellschaft für Forderungsaufkauf; Kundenfinanzierungsbank; ~ **credit** Diskontkredit; ~ **expenses** Wechselspesen; ~ **holdings** Wechselbestände, Portfolio; ~ **house** Diskontbank, Wechselbank; ~ **ledger** Wechselbuch; ~ **level** Rabattstufe; ~ **market** Diskontmarkt; ~ **of draft** Wechseldiskont; ~ **of draft** Wechseldiskont; ~ **period** Skontofrist; ~ **piracy** unberechtigte Inanspruchnahme von Skonto; ~ **rate** Diskontsatz; ~ **store** Rabattladen, Diskont-Laden; ~ **"up front"** Rabatt vorab; ~ **window** Rediskontfazilität; **abnormal** ~ außergewöhnliche Preisnachlässe; **at a** ~ unter Pari, zu herabgesetztem Preis; **bill** ~ Wechseldiskont; **bond** ~ Kursdifferenz unter dem Nennwert e–r Obligation; **cash** ~ (Kassa)Skonto, Barzahlungsskonto; **dealer's** ~ Händlerrabatt; **extra** ~ Sonderrabatt; **functional** ~ Funktionsrabatt; **less** ~ abzüglich Diskont; **mini-fleet** ~ Versicherungsrabatt für e–n kleinen Wagenpark; **prepaid** ~ Wechseldiskont; **primary** ~ echtes Skonto; **quantity** ~ Mengenrabatt; **reinvestment** ~ Wiederanlagerabatt; **retail** ~ Einzelhändlerrabatt; **share** ~ → *share*; **special** ~ Sonderrabatt; **trade** ~ Handelsrabatt, Wiederverkäuferrabatt; **true** ~ offenes Disagio (*Darlehen*); **wholesale** ~ → *wholesale*.

discount *v* abrechnen, diskontieren, den Wert mindern, nicht mitrechnen; ~**ed cash flow method** (=) *Methode der Investitionsstatistik nach dem diskontierten gegenwärtigen Barwert des zukünftigen Ertrages;* ~ **ed value** Diskontwert.

discountability Diskontfähigkeit *f*, Diskontierbarkeit *f*.

discountable diskontfähig, diskontierbar, rabattfähig.

discounted payback method dynamische Amortisationsrechnung *f*.

discounting Diskontierung *f*; Abzinsung *f*; Rabattgewährung *f*; ~ **of drafts** Wechseldiskontierung; ~ **transaction** Diskontgeschäft.

discoverable erkennbar, sichtbar.

discovered peril (= *doctrine of* ~) Lehre von der letzten Ausweichmöglichkeit vor der erkannten Gefahr.

discovert alleinstehend, nicht verheiratet, ledig, verwitwet; **feme** ~ → *feme*.

discovery Entdeckung *f*, Offenlegung *f*, Offenbarung *f*, Auskunft *f*; ~ **against the Crown** Antrag auf Urkundenvorlage durch den Fiskus; ~ **and inspection** Vorlagezwang zwecks Augenscheinseinnahme; ~ **and production of documents** Mitteilungspflicht über Urkunden mit Urkundenvorlage; ~ **by interrogatories** gerichtliche Auflage, e–e Liste mit Fragen der Gegenpartei zu beantworten; ~ **in aid of execution** Schuldnervernehmung (*zwecks Vermögensoffenba-*

rung); ~ **of debtor's property** Vermögensoffenbarung; Offenlegung des Schuldnervermögens; ~ **of documents** Urkundenvorlage; ~ **of stolen goods** Auffinden gestohlener Güter; ~ **vein** Haupterzader (*e–r fündig gewordenen Schürfstelle*); **automatic** ~ **of documents** Urkundenvorlage ohne Antrag; **bill of** ~ → *bill* (*2*); **claim for** ~ Anspruch auf Auskunftserteilung *bzw* Urkundenvorlage; **liable to** ~ auskunftspflichtig, vorlagepflichtig; **mutual** ~ **of documents** beiderseitige Urkundenvorlage; **order for** ~ → *order*; **right of** ~ → *right*.

discredit *s* Mißkredit *m*, schlechter Ruf *m*, Unglaubwürdigkeit *f*.

discredit *v* in Mißkredit bringen, für unwahr erklären, diskreditieren; ~ **a witness** e–n Zeugen als unglaubwürdig hinstellen.

discrepancy Unstimmigkeit *f*, Diskrepanz *f*, Widerspruch *m*.

discretion Ermessen (= *E*) *n*, billiges Ermessen *n*, freie Entscheidungsgewalt *f*, Umsicht *f*, Vorsicht *f*, Klugheit *f*; Fähigkeit zwischen Recht und Unrecht zu unterscheiden; ~ **of court** gerichtliches *E*; ~ **of judge** richterliches *E*; ~ **statement** dem gerichtlichen *E* anvertraute Erklärung, *vertrauliches Geständnis eigenen Ehebruchs des Ehescheidungsklägers*; ~ **to arrest or to prosecute** Opportunitätsprinzip; **absolute** ~ uneingeschränktes *E*; **abuse of** ~ → *abuse;* **administrative** ~ behördliche *E*, Verwaltungse; **age of** ~ Strafmündigkeit (*GB*: *14 Jahre*); **at one's** ~ nach freier Wahl, nach Belieben; **at the** ~ **of the court** nach Gutdünken des Gerichts, im *E* des Gerichts; **banker's** ~ → *banker*, **criminal** ~ Strafmündigkeit; **exercise of** ~ → *exercise;* **judicial** ~ richterliches *E*; **legal** ~ richterliches *E*, rechtliches *E*; **residual** ~ inhärente Ermessensbefugnis; **to leave to the** ~ **of a person** dem Belieben überlassen, dem *E* überlassen; **to use one's own** ~ nach eigenem *E* handeln; **unfettered** ~ uneingeschränktes Ermessen.

discretionary ermessensmäßig, Ermessens . . .

discriminate unterscheiden, verschieden behandeln, ungerecht behandeln; ~ **against** benachteiligen.

discrimination Diskriminierung *f*, unterschiedliche Behandlung *f*, Verletzung des Gleichheitssatzes; Unterscheidung *f*, Benachteiligung *f*; ~ **by way of victimisation** Benachteiligung durch Schikane; ~ **of a party in interest** ungleiche Behandlung e–r beteiligten Partei, Diskriminierung e–r Prozeßpartei; **job** ~ diskriminierende Beschäftigung von Arbeitskräften; **administrative** ~ willkürliche Verletzung des Gleichheitssatzes, Diskriminierung durch die Behörde; **benign** ~ = reverse ~ *qv*; **racial** ~ Diskriminierung aus rassischen *bzw* ethnischen Gründen, Rassendiskriminierung; **reverse** ~ Gegendiskriminierung zum Ausgleich (rassischer) Nachteile; Ausgleichsbevorzugung; **sex-based** ~ geschlechtsbezogene Diskriminierung.

discriminative diskriminierend, unterschiedlich, benachteiligend.

discussion Besprechung *f*, Erörterung *f*; Meinungsaustausch *m*, Beratung *f*; *scot* Vorausklage *f*, Feststellung *f* der Nachlaßgläubiger; **benefit of** ~ Einrede der Vorausklage; **liberty of** ~ freie Aussprache, Redefreiheit; **preliminary** ~ Vorbesprechung.

disdain Geringschätzung *f*.

disease Krankheit *f*, Leiden *n*; **epidemic** ~ Seuche, Epidemie; **hereditary** ~ Erbkrankheiten; **industrial** ~ Berufskrankheit; **mental** ~ Geisteskrankheit; **notifiable** ~ meldepflichtige Krankheit; **occupational** ~ Berufskrankheit; **prescribed** ~ amtlich anerkannte Berufskrankheiten; **to contract a** ~ sich anstecken; **venereal** ~ Geschlechtskrankheit.

disemboweling Eviszeration *f*, Ausweidung *f*; Harakiri *n*.

disencumber von Belastungen freistellen, entschulden.
disengage freimachen, lösen, entladen; entloben.
disengagement Freimachung *f*; Entlobung *f*; Lösung *f*; *pol* Auseinanderrücken der Machtblöcke; ~ **agreement** Entflechtungsabkommen.
disentail Fideikommißbindung aufheben, Erbbeschränkung beenden, von festgelegter Erbfolge befreien.
disentailment Aufhebung *f* e–r festgelegten Erbfolge *bzw* Nacherbschaftstreuhand, Fideikommißauflösung *f*.
disentitle e–e Berechtigung absprechen; e–s Rechtes verlustig gehen, Rechtsschutz verlieren.
disentitlement Anspruchsverlust *m*, Zuspruchentziehung *f*, Rechtsverlust *m*.
disestablishment Abschaffung *f*, Aufhebung *f*; Entstaatlichung *f* (*der engl Hochkirche*).
disfame schlechter Ruf *m*.
disfavour Mißfallen *n*, Ungnade *f*.
disfigurement Entstellung *f*.
disfranchise ein Recht entziehen; das Wahlrecht aberkennen, *jmdn* der Grundrechte verlustig erklären; e–e Konzession entziehen.
disfranchisement Entzug *m* des Wahlrechts; Entrechtung *f*, Ausschluß *m* aus e–r Körperschaft.
disgavel ein Grundstück von erbrechtlicher Bindung freimachen, *den anteilsgleichen Erbgang auf die Söhne aufheben*.
disgorgement Herausrücken *n* (*v. Gewinnen*), Wiedervonsichgeben *n*.
disgrace *s* Schande *f*, Ehrlosigkeit *f*, Ungnade *f*.
disgrace *v* entehren, schänden; ~ **oneself** (*as witness*) sich Schande bereiten, *etwas aussagen sollen, was e–m (als Zeuge) zur Unehre gereicht.*
disgrade e–r Würde verlustig erklären.
disguise verkleiden, verschleiern, bemänteln, verstellen.
disguise *s* Verstellung *f*, Täuschung *f*, Irreführung *f*, Verschleierung *f*, Maske *f*.
disheritor der Enterbende, *jmd, der e–n anderen enterbt oder um sein gesetzliches Erbe bringt.*
dishoard *v* Gehortetes (*Geld, Gold, Rohstoffe*) wieder dem Wirtschaftskreislauf zuführen.
dishonest unehrlich, unredlich ~ **abstraction of electricity** Stromentwendung.
dishonesty Unehrlichkeit *f*, Untreue *f*, Unredlichkeit *f*.
dishonour of a bill Nichthonorierung e–s Wechsels (*Akzeptverweigerung bzw Nichtbezahlen*).
dishono(u)r *v*|*t* entehren; nicht honorieren, nicht akzeptieren, nicht einlösen, zu Protest gehen lassen; ~**ed by non-acceptance** Akzeptverweigerung.
dishono(u)rable ehrenrührig, unehrenhaft, schimpflich.
disincarcerate aus der Haft entlassen.
disincentive Anreizblockierung *f*, Gleichgültigkeit *f* hervorrufender Faktor.
disinclined *adj* abgeneigt.
disincorporation Vereinsauflösung *f*, Verlust der Rechtsfähigkeit, Auflösung und Löschung e–r Körperschaft (ohne Liquidationsverfahren).
disinflation Rückgang *m* e–r inflationären Entwicklung.
disinherison Enterbung *f*.
disinherit *v* enterben, von der Erbfolge ausschließen.
disinheritance Enterbung *f*, Ausschluß von der Erbfolge, Entzug *m* der Erbanwartschaft auf Grundvermögen.
disinstitutionalized adj nicht mehr (in geschlossener Anstalt) verwahrt.
disintegrate zersetzen, auflösen, zerfallen.
disintegration Zersetzung *f*, Zerfall *m*, Zerrüttung *f*.
disinter exhumieren.
disinterested unvoreingenommen, neutral, objektiv, am Ausgang des Rechtsstreits uninteressiert, uneigennützig.

disintermediation Ausschaltung von Zwischenkreditgebern; zwischengesellschaftliche Kreditgewährung *f*; Einlagenabzug zur Reinvestierung.
disinterment Exhumierung *f*.
disinvestment Desinvestition *f*; Zurückziehung *f* von Anlagekapital, Investitionsentzug *m*.
disjunctive allegations Haupt- und Hilfsvorbringen; ~ **terms** sich gegenseitig ausschließende Bedingungen, Alternativbedingungen.
dislocate verlagern, verrücken.
dislocation Verrückung *f*, Verschiebung *f*, Verrenkung *f*; ~ **of traffic** Verkehrsstörung, Verkehrsverlagerung.
disloyal untreu, treulos, illoyal, verräterisch.
disloyality Untreue *f*, Treulosigkeit *f*, verräterische Haltung *f*.
dismantle abbauen, demontieren, abbrechen, abwracken, abtakeln.
dismantlement Abbau *m*, Ausbau *m*, Demontage *f*; Abtakelung *f*, Abwracken *n*.
dismantling Demontage *f*, Abbruch *m*, Zerstörung *f*; ~ **list** Demontageliste.
dismember zerstückeln, zergliedern, zerreißen.
dismemberment Zerstückelung *f*, Gliederverlust *m*; ~ **benefit** → *benefit*; ~ **schedule** Gliedertaxe.
dismiss entlassen, abweisen, ablehnen; ~ **a case for want of evidence** Verfahren mangels Beweises einstellen; e–e Klage wegen Beweisfälligkeit abweisen; ~ **an action** e–e Klage abweisen; ~ **an appeal** ein Rechtsmittel (*Berufung, Beschwerde evt Revision*) zurückweisen; ~ **a petition** e–e Klage abweisen; ~ **a person from office** jmdn seines Amtes entheben; ~ **an appeal** e–e Berufung (*bzw e–e Revision, e–e Beschwerde*) zurückweisen (*bzw „verwerfen" aus Verfahrensgründen*); ~ **summarily** die Eröffnung der Hauptverhandlung ablehnen; ~ **the charge** das Verfahren einstellen; ~ **with costs** kostenpflichtig abweisen.
dismissal Entlassung *f*, fristlose Entlassung *f*, Klageabweisung *f*, Verfahrenseinstellung *f*, Freispruch *m*; ~ **agreed** unstreitiges klageabweisendes Urteil; ~ **by notice** ordentliche Arbeitgeber-Kündigung; ~ **claims** Ansprüche wegen unberechtigter Kündigung; ~ **compensation** Abfindung für Verlust d. Arbeitsplatzes; ~ **for want of prosecution** Zurückweisung *bzw* Abweisung wegen ungenügenden Betreibens des Verfahrens; ~ **from employment** Kündigung des Arbeitsverhältnisses; ~ **from a post** Amtsenthebung; ~ **notice** Kündigungsschreiben; ~ **of appeal** Zurückweisung des Rechtsmittels; ~ **of a convict** Entlassung aus dem Gefängnis; ~ **of a criminal case** Einstellung e–s Strafverfahrens; ~ **of action** Klageabweisung als unzulässig; ~ **of bill in equity** Klageabweisung im Equity-Verfahren; ~ **of involuntary bankruptcy case** Ablehnung des Konkursantrags; ~ **on grounds of pregnancy** Entlassung wegen Schwangerschaft; ~ **of proceedings** Klagerücknahme; ~ **on the merits** Klageabweisung als unbegründet; ~ **pay** Abfindung bei e–r Entlassung; ~ **statement** Kündigungsbegründung; ~ **with prejudice** klageabweisendes Sachurteil; Amtsentlassung; ~ **without notice** fristlose Entlassung; ~ **without prejudice** klageabweisendes Prozeßurteil ohne Sachentscheidung; ~ **without reasonable excuse** Klageabweisung als unzulässig; **constructive** ~ durch unzumutbares Arbeitgeberverhalten verursachte Arbeitnehmerkündigung; **fair** ~ berechtigte Entlassung; **instant** ~ fristlose Entlassung; **judgment of** ~ → *judgment*; **self** ~ freiwilliges Ausscheiden; **summary** ~ fristlose Entlassung; **unfair** ~ unzulässige Entlassung, sozialwidrige Arbeitgeberkündigung; **Unfair D~s Act** Kündigungsschutzgesetz; **unlawful** ~ unzulässige Kündigung;

wrongful ~ widerrechtliche fristlose Entlassung.

dismissed „abgewiesen" (*meist klageabweisendes Sachurteil*); ~ **for want of equity** klageabweisendes Sachurteil (*im Equity-Verfahren*).

dismission Entlassung *f*, Amtsenthebung *f*.

dismortgage e–e Hypothek ablösen, e–e Hypothek zurückzahlen, ein Grundpfandrecht löschen.

disobedience Ungehorsam *m*, Gehorsamsverweigerung *f*; ~ **to a judgment** Ungehorsam gegen e–n Urteilsspruch; ~ **to statute** Gesetzesungehorsam; **civil** ~ passiver Widerstand; ziviler Ungehorsam; **wilful** ~ vorsätzlicher Ungehorsam (*gegenüber dem Gericht*), Widersetzlichkeit.

disobedient ungehorsam.

disobey nicht gehorchen, verstoßen, verletzen, zuwiderhandeln.

disorder Unordnung *f*, Unruhe *f*, Störung *f*, Aufruhr *m*, Durcheinander *n*, Ruhestörung *f*, Tumult *m*, Krawall *m*, ungebührliches Benehmen *n*; **civil** ~ Landfriedensbruch; **mental** ~ Geistesstörung, krankhafte Störung der Geistestätigkeit; **public** ~ öffentliche Unruhen, Auflauf, Aufruhr, Landfriedensbruch.

disorderly unordentlich, ungebührlich, aufrührerisch, öffentliches Ärgernis erregend, ordnungswidrig.

disown nicht anerkennen, verleugnen; dementieren; ~ **one's signature** seine Unterschrift nicht anerkennen.

disparag|e schmälern, verunglimpfen, verachten, herabsetzen; Ungleiches verbinden; ~**ing competition** herabsetzende Werbung; ~**ing statement** geringschätzige, herabsetzende Äußerung.

disparagement Verunglimpfung *f*, Verruf *m*, Verächtlichmachen *n*, Unehre *f*; Mesalliance *f*, Standeswidrigkeit *f*; ~ **of a competitor** Anschwärzung; Geschäftsehrverletzung, Verunglimpfung e–s Mitbewerbers; ~ **of goods** unwahre herabsetzende Äußerung über die Ware e–s Mitbewerbers.

disparit|y Ungleichheit *f*, Unvereinbarkeit *f*, Disparität *f*; **structural** ~**ies** strukturbedingte Ungleichheiten.

dispark die Aufhebung e–s Parks anordnen; e–n *öffentlichen* Park entwidmen.

dispart trennen, spalten.

dispatch *s* Absendung *f*, Versand *m*, Abfertigung *f*, Beförderung *f*, rasche Erledigung *f*; Depesche *f*, Regierungserklärung *f*; ~ **agency** Depeschenbüro; ~ **agent** Abfertigungsspedition; ~ **by post** Versendung mit der Post; ~ **clerk** Abfertigungsangestellter; ~ **department** Versandabteilung, Abfertigungsabt.; ~ **money** Eilgeld, Beschleunigungsgebühr, Vergütung für schnelles Entladen; ~ **note** Verladeschein, Versandanzeige; Paketkarte; ~ **of business** prompte Erledigung der geschäftlichen Angelegenheiten; ~ **of goods** Warenabsendung; ~ **service** Abfertigungsdienst; **advice of** ~ → *advice*; **bearer of** ~**es** Kurier; **country of** ~ Versandland; **customary** ~ prompte Absendung nach den üblichen Gepflogenheiten unter Wahrnehmung der (*in der Schiffahrt*) üblichen Sorgfaltspflicht; **day of** ~ Abgangstag; **mode of** ~ Versandart; **quick** ~ Eilabfertigung.

dispatch *v* abfertigen, absenden, erledigen.

dispatching clerk Expedient *m*, Abfertiger *m*.

dispauper das Armenrecht entziehen.

dispensation Nachsicht *f*, Dispens *f*, Befreiung *f*, Erlaß *m*; **marriage** ~ → *marriage*.

dispense befreien, entbinden, dispensieren, abschaffen, von etwas absehen, ohne etwas auskommen; ~ **justice** Recht sprechen; ~ **with an oath** auf Vereidigung verzichten; ~ **with the service** von der Zustellung absehen; auf Zustellung verzichten; **it may be** ~**d with** es

ist nicht obligatorisch, es kann darauf verzichtet werden.
dispensing notice Verzichtserklärung *f* (*auf gesonderte Bankauszüge*).
dispersal Verbreitung *f*, Streuung *f*, Dekonzentration *f*; ~ **of assets** Streuung von Vermögensanlagen; ~ **of industry** Auflockerung von Industriegebieten; ~ **of ownership** Eigentumsstreuung; ~ **of stock ownership** Aktienstreuung.
displace absetzen, verdrängen, verschieben, vertreiben, deportieren; ~**d person** Verschleppe(r), D. P.
displacement Verschiebung *f*, Versetzung *f*, Verdrängung *f*, Verschleppung *f*; ~ **of funds** anderweitige Kapitalverwendung; ~ **ton** → *ton*; **light** ~ Leertonnage; **load** ~ → *load*.
display Auslage *f*, Ausstellung *f*, Zurschaustellung *f*; **indecent** ~ Zurschaustellung von unzüchtigem Material.
disposable frei verfügbar, veräußerlich, disponibel.
disposal Erledigung *f*, Verfügung *f*, Übertragung *f*, Veräußerung *f*, Beseitigung *f*; ~ **of business assets** Veräußerung von Betriebsvermögen; ~ **of child** gerichtliche Aufenthaltsbestimmung für ein Kind; ~ **of nuclear waste** Atommüll-Entsorgung; ~ **of premises** Übertragung der Benutzungsrechte an e–m Grundstück; ~ **of refuse** Müllabfuhr; ~ **period** Zeitraum zwischen Erwerb und Veräußerung; **restraint on** ~ → *restraint*; **sole right of** ~ → *right*.
dispose verfügen, veräußern, entscheiden, regeln, erledigen, aufgeben, verkaufen; ~ **by will** testamentarisch verfügen, letztwillig verfügen, vermachen; ~ **of a case** e–n Prozeß verhandeln, e–n Fall erledigen; ~ **summarily** e–e Sache summarisch erledigen; **to be ~d of by agreement** gütlich geregelt werden.
disposing|capacity → *capacity*; ~ **power** → *power*; **capable of** ~ testierfähig.
disposition Verfügung *f* (= *V bzw v*), Veranlagung *f*, Bestimmung *f*, Neigung *f*, Veräußerung *f*; ~ **clause** *scot* Auflassungsklausel; ~ **by will** testamentarische *V*, letztwillige *V*; ~ **in contemplation of death** *V* auf dem Sterbebett; ~ **mortis causa** letztwillige *V*; ~ **of profits** Gewinnverwendung; ~ **of property** Vermögens*v*; ~ **without trial** Erledigung ohne mündl Verhandlung (*im Bürowege*); ~**s of the land** Grundstücksverfügungen; **correspective** ~ gegenseitige *V* (*gemeinschaftliches Testament*); **criminal** ~ kriminelle Veranlagung; **final** ~ endgültige Erledigung; **free** ~ freie Verfügung; ~ **inter vivos** *V* unter Lebenden; **power of** ~ → *power* (*1*); **testamentary** ~ testamentarische *V*, letztwillige *V*; **voluntary** ~ unentgeltliche Verfügung.
dispositive|clauses verfügende Bestimmungen (*e–s Vertrags*); ~ **facts** → *fact*; ~ **treaty** → *treaty*.
disposses räumen, vom Grundbesitz ausschließen, den Besitz an Grund und Boden entziehen.
dispossession Räumung *f*, Vertreibung *f*, Entsetzung *f*, Besitzentziehung *f*, verbotene Eigenmacht *f*; ~ **proceedings** Räumungsverfahren; ~ **warrant** Zwangsräumungsauftrag.
disprobative beweisentkräftend, gegenbeweislich.
disproof Gegenbeweis *m*, Widerlegung *f*.
disprovable widerlegbar, als unrichtig beweisbar.
disprove widerlegen, das Gegenteil beweisen.
disproportion Mißverhältnis *n*.
disproportionate unverhältnismäßig.
dispunishable nicht (be)strafbar.
disputability Strittigkeit *f*, Unerwiesenheit *f*, Fraglichkeit *f*.
disputable debattierbar, bestreitbar.
disputant Gegner *m*, Disputierer *m*, Streiter *m*, Rechthaber *m*.
dispute *s* Streit *m*, Streitfall *m*, Mei-

nungsverschiedenheit *f*, Auseinandersetzung *f*; ~ **about jurisdiction** Zuständigkeitsstreit, Kompetenzkonflikt; **beyond** ~ unstreitig, unzweifelhaft, fraglos, außer Streit; **future ~s clause** Schiedsklausel; **in** ~ streitig, streitbefangen; **industrial** ~ Arbeitskampf; **jurisdictional** ~ Zuständigkeitsstreit; **legal** ~ Rechtsstreit, juristische Auseinandersetzung; **niggardly** ~ schäbiger Streit, äußerst kleinlicher Streit.

dispute *v* streiten, bezweifeln, erörtern; ~ **a will** ein Testament anfechten; **~d claims office** *ins* Rechtsabteilung.

disqualification Disqualifizierung *f*, Verlust *m* der Voraussetzungen, Ausschluß; ~ **from being a witness** Verlust der Zeugnisfähigkeit; ~ **from driving** Entzug der Fahrerlaubnis; ~ **from holding public office** Unfähigkeit zur Bekleidung öffentlicher Ämter; ~ **from succeeding** (*to the estate*) Erbunwürdigkeit; ~ **from taking** Erbunwürdigkeit; ~ **order** Betätigungsverbot für leitende Funktionen in Kapitalgesellschaften; **mandatory** ~ zwingend vorgeschriebener Entzug der Fahrerlaubnis; **~s on conviction** Verlust von bürgerlichen Ehrenrechten bei Verurteilung.

disqualif|y unfähig machen, disqualifizieren, ausschließen, die Voraussetzung für ein Amt verlieren; ~ **oneself** sich für befangen erklären; ~ **s. o. from holding office** jmdm (*die Voraussetzungen für*) ein Amt entziehen; **~ied by sex** durch das Geschlecht von e–m Amt ausgeschlossen; **~ied premises** nicht zugelassene Räume; **to become ~ied** die Voraussetzung für ein Amt verlieren.

disrate zurückstufen, degradieren, ausrangieren.

disrationare rechtfertigen, den Entlastungsbeweis führen.

disregard *s* Nichtbeachtung *f*, Außerachtlassen *n*, Mißachtung *f*, Gleichgültigkeit *f*; Ignorierung *f*; ~ **of court** Nichtbeachtung des Gerichts.

disregard *v* außer Acht lassen, mißachten, geringschätzen; ignorieren, übersehen.

disregardable geringfügig, unschädlich.

disrepair Baufälligkeit *f*, schlechter Erhaltungszustand *m*; Reparaturbedürftigkeit; **to fall into** ~ baufällig werden, herunterkommen.

disreputable verrufen, ehrlos, übel beleumdet.

disrepute Verruf *m*, Mißkredit *m*, schlechter Ruf *m*.

disruption Störung *f*, Verwerfung *f*; **~s of the world economy** Verwerfungen der Weltwirtschaft.

dissaving Entsparen *n*, Auflösung von Ersparnissen.

dissection Sektion *f*, Zergliederung *f*, Sezierung *f*; ~ **of accounts** Kontenaufgliederung; **judicial** ~ → *judicial*.

disseise den Besitz entziehen, widerrechtlich aus dem Grundbesitz verdrängen; *hist* entweren.

disseisee *jmd der widerrechtlich aus seinem Grundbesitz verdrängt wurde.*

disseisin Dejektion *f*, *widerrechtliche* Verdrängung *f* aus dem Grundbesitz, Entzug *m* der Gewere.

disseisitrix *fem von disseisor qv.*

disseisor *jmd, der e–n anderen widerrechtlich aus dem Grundbesitz verdrängt hist.*

dissemble verhehlen, verbergen, sich verstellen.

disseminate verbreiten.

dissemination Verbreitung *f*, Bekanntwerden *n*; ~ **of information** Verbreitung von Nachrichten; **innocent** ~ schuldlose Verbreitung.

disseminator Verbreiter *m*; **innocent** ~ gutgläubiger Verbreiter.

dissent *s* Dissens *m*; Nichtübereinstimmung *f*, Unstimmigkeit *f*, Meinungsverschiedenheit *f*, abweichende Meinung *f*; Abweichung *f* von der anglikanischen Kirche.

dissent *v* anderer Meinung sein, nicht zustimmen; von der anglikanischen Kirche abweichen.

dissenter Nonkonformist *n*, Andersdenkender *m*, Andersgläubiger *m*, Dissident *m*.

dissentient abweichend, nicht (*mit der Mehrheit*) übereinstimmend, andersdenkend.

dissipation Verschwendung *f*, Verschwindenlassen von Vermögen.

dissimulate verheimlichen, heucheln, sich verstellen, dissimulieren.

dissimulation Verheimlichung *f*, Heuchelei *f*, Verstellung *f*, Verschleierung *f*, Dissimulation *f*.

dissociate aus e–r Gesellschaft austreten, sich lossagen, absondern.

dissociation Trennung *f*, Austritt *m*, Lossagung *f*.

dissolution Auflösung *f*, Aufhebung *f*; ~ **of company** Auflösung e–r Gesellschaft, *Abschluß der Liquidation*; ~ **of marriage** Auflösung der Ehe, Scheidung, Eheaufhebung, Ehenichtigkeitserklärung; ~ **of Parliament** Parlamentsauflösung; ~ **of partnership** Auflösung e–r Personalgesellschaft; ~ **of the conjugal community** Aufhebung der ehelichen Lebensgemeinschaft; ~ **order** Auflösungsverfügung; **de facto** ~ Auflösung e–r Gesellschaft, Liquidationsbeginn, Aufgabe der Geschäftstätigkeit, faktische Geschäftsauflösung.

dissolve auflösen, rückgängig machen, aufheben, ungültig erklären, beenden.

dissuade abraten, widerraten; ~ **a witness** e–n Zeugen beeinflussen, nichts auszusagen.

distance Distanz *f*, Abstand *m*, Entfernung *f*, Strecke *f*, große Entfernung *f*; ~ **freight** Distanzfracht; **braking** ~ Bremszeit, **overall stopping** ~ Bremsweg; **thinking** ~ Reaktionszeit.

distemper Unruhe *f*, Aufruhr *m*.

distinction Unterscheidung *f*, Verschiedenheit *f*, Klarheit *f*, Deutlichkeit *f*; **class** ~ Klassenunterschied; **legal** ~ glänzende juristische Karriere; **to receive a** ~ e–n Orden verliehen bekommen; **without** ~ **of race** ohne Berücksichtigung von Rassenunterschieden.

distinctive kennzeichnend, charakteristisch, spezifisch, unterscheidbar.

distinctiveness charakteristische Eigenschaft *f*, Besonderheit *f*, Unterscheidungskraft *f*.

distinguish unterscheiden, auseinanderhalten (*können*); ~ **a case** sich von der höchstrichterlichen Entscheidung unterscheiden.

distort verdrehen, entstellen, verzerren, verformen.

distortion Entstellung *f*, Verdrehung *f*, Verzerrung *f*, Verformung *f*; ~ **of competition** Wettbewerbsverzerrung, Wettbewerbsverfälschung.

distract ablenken, verwirren.

distrain pfänden, die Mobiliarvollstreckung durchführen; Besitz ergreifen, beschlagnahmen; das Vermieterpfandrecht ausüben; ~ **for rent** wegen Mietschulden vollstrecken.

distrainable einem Gläubigerpfandrecht unterliegend, pfändbar.

distrainee Vollstreckungsschuldner *m*, Gepfändeter *m*.

distrainer Vollstreckungsgläubiger *m*, der sich aus einem Pfandrecht *n* befriedigende Gläubiger *m*, der beschlagnehmende Pfandgläubiger *m*.

distraint Pfändung *f* (*cf distress*), Beschlagnahme *f*; **warrant of** ~ gerichtliche Ermächtigung zur Beschlagnahme, Pfändungsbeschluß.

distress *s* (*1*) Pfändung *f*, Beschlagnahme *f durch den Gläubiger*, Pfandverwertung *f*, Steuerpfändung *f*, Geltendmachung *f* e–s Vermieter-(Verpächter-)Pfandrechts; ~ **borrowing** Kreditaufnahme in e–r Notlage (*zu überhöhten Zinsen*); ~ **damage feasant** Zurückbehaltung von schadensstiftenden Tieren; ~ **for rent** Pfändung wegen Miet-(Pacht-)schulden, Ausübung e–s Vermieterpfandrechts; ~ **infinite** unbeschränkte Beschlagnahme (*zur Erzwingung von gerichtlichen Anordnungen*); ~ **sale** Pfandverkauf; ~ **warrant** → *warrant*; **double** ~ →

double; **illegal** ~ unzulässige Vollstreckung; **levy of** ~ Pfändung, Vollstreckung, Beschlagnahme; **privileged from** ~ → *privileged*; **rescue of** ~ Verstrickungsbruch, Wegnahme sichergestellter Sachen; **second** ~ Anschlußpfändung; **writ of grand** ~ *hist* Gesamtbeschlagnahme von Haus und Hof (*als Erzwingungsmaßnahme*).

distress *s* (*2*) Not *f*, Elend *n*, Gefahr *f*, Seenot *f*; ~ **and danger** Not und Gefahr; ~ **call** Notruf; ~ **signal** = *signal of* ~ → *signal*; **port of** ~ → *port*; **simulated** ~ vorgetäuschte Notlage.

distributable verteilbar, verteilungsfähig, ausschüttungsfähig.

distribute aufteilen, verteilen, auseinandersetzen, vertreiben, absetzen, austragen.

distributee Erbe *m* (*Mobiliarnachlaß*); **legal** ~ Anspruchsberechtigter aus dem Reinnachlaß.

distributing agent Handelsvertreter, Gebietsvertreter; ~ **syndicate** Plazierungskonsortium.

distribution Verteilung *f*, Austeilung *f*, Vertrieb *m*, Zustellung *f*, Auseinandersetzung *f*; Verteilung des Intestatsnachlasses an erbberechtigte Angehörige; Zuteilung *f*, Gabe *f*; Ausschüttung *f*; ~ **cartel** Absatzkartell; ~ **expense** Absatzkosten, Vertriebskosten; ~ **in kind** Verteilung (*von Gewinn*) in natura; ~ **manager** Leiter der Vertriebsabteilung; ~ **network** Leitungsnetz, Verteilernetz; ~ **of assets** Verteilung des Vermögens, Auseinandersetzung; ~ **of bankrupt's estate** Verteilung der Konkursmasse; ~ **of business** Geschäftsverteilung (*bei Gericht*); ~ **of credit** Kreditlenkung; ~ **of industry** Industrieverteilung; ~ **of profits** Dividendenverteilung; Gewinnausschüttung; ~ **of risk** Risikoverteilung; ~ **of the dividend** Ausschüttung der Dividende; ~ **of the estate** Aufteilung des Intestatsnachlasses, Erbauseinandersetzung; ~ **of trading profits** Ausschüttung von Börsengewinnen; ~ **per stirpes** Nachlaßaufteilung nach Stämmen; **channels of** ~ Vertriebswege; **controlled** ~ Absatzlenkung; **equitable** ~ *gerichtliche, billigkeitsmäßige Verteilung des Ehegattenguts bei Scheidung ohne Verschulden*; **final** ~ Schlußverteilung; **preliminary** ~ Abschlagszahlung; **pro rata** ~ → *pro rata*; **ratable** ~ = *pro rata* ~ *qv*; **scheme of** ~ Verteilungsplan; **secondary** ~ *exch* Pakethandel, mittelbare Plazierung; **Statute of D~s** *GB hist, US,* gesetzliche Erbfolgeregeln, Intestatserbgesetz: *Intestatserbfolge bei Mobiliarnachlaß*.

distributive austeilend, verteilend; ~ **cost accounting** Zuschlagskalkulation; ~ **finding of the issue** (*teilweise dem Kläger teilweise dem Beklagten etw zusprechender Spruch der Geschworenen*), Quotenurteil.

distributor Verteiler *m*, Vertragshändler *m*, Wiederverkäufer *m*, Bezirksvertreter *m*, Filmverleiher *m*; ~ **discount** Händlerrabatt; **sole** ~ Alleinvertragshändler; **industrial** ~ Großhändler, der Industriebetriebe beliefert; **wholesale** ~ Großhändler; **ultimate** ~ Letztverteiler.

district Bezirk *m*; Ortsbezirk *m*, Distrikt *m*, Kreis *m*, Gerichtsbezirk *m*; *US* Zweckverband *m*; ~ **agreement** Ortstarif; ~ **attorney** *US* Staatsanwalt; ~ **auditor** Bezirks-Rechnungsprüfer; ~ **board** Zweckverbandsamt; ~ **clerk** Geschäftsleiter des District Court; ~ **council** Ortsgemeinderat, örtliche Gebietskörperschaft in e-r Grafschaft; ~ **court** → *court*; ~ **heating** Fernheizung; ~ **judge** → *judge*; ~ **land registry** Bezirksgrundbuchamt; ~ **manager** Bezirksleiter; **D~ of Columbia** District von Columbia (*bundesunmittelbares Gebiet der Hauptstadt Washington*); ~ **parish** *eccl* Untergemeinde, Teilgemeinde; ~ **registrar** Rechtspfleger beim Amtsgericht (*county court*); ~ **registry** Außenstelle des Londoner Zentralgerichts; **administrative** ~

Verwaltungsbezirk, Regierungsbezirk; **congressional** ~ Wahlbezirk für US Bundeswahlen; **judicial** ~ → *judicial*; **legislative** ~ Wahlbezirk; **official** ~ Amtsbezirk; **polling** ~ Wahlbezirk; **postal** ~ Postzustellbezirk; **residential** ~ Wohngebiet; **rural** ~ Landbezirk; *bis 1972: ländlicher Teilbezirk e–r Grafschaft*; **sewage** ~ Abwasserzweckverband; **urban** ~ Stadtbezirk; *bis 1972: städt Teilbezirk e–r Grafschaft.*

districting Wahlkreisabgrenzung *f.*

distringas Pfändungsauftrag (*obs*); ~ **jurators** Verfahren zur Erzwingung der Amtsfunktion von Schöffen.

disturb stören, beunruhigen.

disturbance Störung *f* der öffentlichen Ordnung, Ruhestörung *f*, Besitzstörung *f*, Unruhe *f*, Verwirrung *f*; ~ **claim** *Entschädigungsanspruch wg Besitzbeeinträchtigung bei Enteignung oder enteignungsgleichem Eingriff*; Aufopferungsanspruch; ~ **compensation** Entschädigung wegen Betriebsstörung (bei Enteignung); ~ **of common** unbefugte Nutzung der Allmende; ~ **of franchise** Beeinträchtigung e–r Konzession; ~ **of patronage** Beeinträchtigung des Patronatsrechts; ~ **of peace** Ruhestörung; ~ **of possession** Besitzstörung; ~ **of public meetings** Versammlungsstörung; ~ **of public or religious worship** Gottesdienststörung; ~ **of repose** Störung der Nachtruhe; ~ **of tenure** Verdrängen e–s Pächters; ~ **of the peace** Störung der öffentlichen Sicherheit und Ordnung, Ruhestörung; ~ **of the public** Störung der öffentlichen Ordnung; ~ **of ways** Behinderung e–s Wegerechts; **morbid** ~ **of the balance of the mind** krankhafte Störung der Geistestätigkeit; **public** ~**s** Unruhen; **to foment** ~ Unruhe schüren.

disturbant Störfaktor *m.*

disturber Störer *m*, Unruhestifter *m.*

disunion Uneinigkeit *f*, Zwietracht *f*, Spaltung *f*, Trennung *f.*

disunite entzweien, trennen, spalten.

disunity Uneinigkeit *f.*

disuse Nichtgebrauch *m*, Nichtverwendung *f*; **to fall into** ~ außer Gebrauch kommen, obsolet werden.

disutility Nutzlosigkeit *f*, Mißnutzen *m*, negativer Nutzen *m*, Lästigkeit *f.*

ditching Meliorationsarbeiten *f/pl.*

diurnal täglich, bei Tage.

divan *orient* Diwan *m*, Staatsrat *m*, Ratszimmer *n*, Kanzlei *f*, Gerichtssaal *m.*

diverge voneinander abweichen, auseinander gehen.

divergence Abweichung *f*, Divergieren *n*, Divergenz *f.*

divergent sich widersprechend.

diversification Diversifikation *f*, Diversifizierung *f*; Risikostreuung *f*; Abänderung *f*, verschiedenartige Gestaltung *f*; ~ **of risk** Risikoverteilung, Risikostreuung; ~ **of supplies** Diversifizierung der Versorgung.

diversion Ablenkung *f*, Ableitung *f*; ~ **of highways** (Straßen)Umleitung; ~ **of letters from addressee** Briefunterschlagung; ~ **program** Maßregeln der Resozialisierung.

diversity Verschiedenheit *f*, Mannigfaltigkeit *f*, Ungleichheit *f*; ~ **factor** Divergenz-Koeffizient (*bei statistischer Qualitätskontrolle*); ~ **jurisdiction** Wahlgerichtsbarkeit (*bei Verschiedenstaatlichkeit der Parteien*), ~ **of citizenship** (*Bundeszuständigkeit bei*) Verschiedenheit der (Glied)staatenzugehörigkeit der Prozeßparteien; **soup-to-nuts** ~ wahllose Anlagestreuung.

divert ableiten, entziehen, ablenken, umleiten.

divest entkleiden, berauben, entziehen; (Beteiligungen etc) abstoßen; ~ **o.s. of a privilege** auf ein Vorrecht verzichten; ~ **shares to the public** Aktien an die Allgemeinheit veräußern (Privatisieren).

divestible einziehbar, aufhebbar.

divestiture Abstoßen e–r Tochtergesellschaft *bzw* Beteiligung, Abstoßen von Kapitalvermögen.

divestitive entziehend, e–n Rechtsverlust bedingend; ~ **fact** → *fact.*

divestment Besitzentziehung *f*; Abstoßen e–r Beteiligung (*Tochtergesellschaft*), Kapitalabzug *m*; **corporate** ~ Abstoßen von Gesellschaftsbeteiligungen.

divide teilen, Reinertrag teilen; *parl* abstimmen (*lassen*); ~ **the cause of action** den Klagegegenstand aufteilen.

dividend Dividende *f* (= *D bzw d*), Anteil *m*, Konkursquote *f*; ~ **addition** *ins* zusätzliche Gewinnbeteiligung; ~ **bond** → *bond* (*1*); ~ **counterfoil** Abschnitt der *D–n*-Zahlungsanweisung (*mit Steuerangaben*); ~ **coupon** *D–n*schein, Gewinnanteilschein; ~ **cover** *D–n*-deckung (*im Verhältnis zum Reingewinn*); ~ **in bankruptcy** Konkursquote; ~ **in specie** Natural*d*; ~ **mandate** *brit D–n*überweisungsauftrag; ~**s net** Rein*d* (*abzüglich Steuer*); ~**s not yet collected** noch nicht abgehobene *D*; ~ **off** ohne (*die nächste*) *D*; ~ **on** einschließlich (*der nächsten*) *D*; ~**s on shares** Aktien*d*; ~ **on stock** *D*, Aktien*d*; ~ **passed** ausgefallene *D*; ~ **payable in kind** Natural*d*; ~ **payout for window-dressing purposes** *D–n*-optik; ~ **payout ratio** Ausschüttungsrate; ~ **payout restriction** Ausschüttungssperre; ~ **qualification** *D–n*berechtigung; ~ **rate** Höhe der *D*; ~ **reinvestment plan** *D–n*wiederanlageplan; ~ **reserve** Rückstellung für *D*; ~**s to policyholders** Versichertendividenden; ~ **warrant** *D–n*schein, *D–n*-Zahlungsanweisung; Koupon; ~ **yield** *D–n*rendite; **accrued** ~**s** aufgelaufene *D*; **accumulative** ~ = *cumulative* ~ *qv*; **accumulated** ~ noch nicht ausbezahlte *D*; **bond** ~ *D* in Form e–r Obligation; **cash** ~ Gewinnausschüttung, Bar*d*; **collected** ~ abgehobene *D*; **commodity** ~ Waren*d*; **consent** ~ beim Aktionär (*auf Grund seiner Zustimmungserklärung gegenüber dem Finanzamt*) versteuerte *D–n US*; **constructive** ~ als ausbezahlt geltende (*einbehaltene*) *D*; **contingent** ~ unvorhergesehene *D*; **cum** ~ einschließlich (*der nächsten*) *D*; **cumulation of** ~ *D–n*nachzahlung *in späteren Gewinnjahren*; **cumulative** ~ kumulative *D* (*mit Nachholungsrecht*); **declaration of** ~**(s)** → *declaration*; **deferred** ~ später fällige *D*, *D* mit aufgeschobener Fälligkeit; **deficiency** ~**s** nachbezahlte *D*; **equalizing** ~ Ausgleichs*d*; **ex** ~ ex *D* = xd.; **extra** ~ Sonder*d*; **extraordinary** ~ außerordentl *D*; **final** ~ Schluß*d*; **gross** ~ Brutto*d*; **guaranteed** ~ garantierte *D*; **interim** ~ Zwischen*d*, Abschlags*d*; **limited** ~ limitierte *D*; **nimble** ~ *D aus Nettogewinn trotz Kapitalverlust*; **noncumulative** ~ (gewöhnliche) *D ohne Nachbezugsrecht*; **optional** ~ Gratisaktie mit Wahlrecht der Barabfindung; **ordinary** ~ Stamm*d*; **passing of the** ~ Nichtausschüttung von *D*; **preferential** ~ Vorzugs*d*; **preferred** ~ Vorzugs*d*, *D* auf Vorzugsaktien; **property** ~ Natural*d*, Sachwert*d*; **provisional** ~ Abschlags*d*; **regular** ~ regelmäßige *D* gleicher Höhe; **reversionary** ~ Anwartschafts*d*; **scrip** ~ Gewinnanteilscheine; *D* durch Interimsscheine *für Gratisaktien*; **security** ~ Gewinnausschüttung in Wertpapieren; **special** ~ außerordentliche *D*, Bonus; **stock** ~ *D* in Form von Aktien, Gratisaktien; **to distribute** ~**s** *D*(*–n*) ausschütten.

Divine Right of Kings das Gottesgnadentum; göttliches Recht der Könige.

divisible teilbar.

divisim getrennt, einzeln.

division Teilung *f*, Auseinandersetzung *f*, Spaltung *f*, Einteilung *f*, Grenzlinie *f*; Abstimmung *f*; Gerichtsabteilung *f*, Kategorie *f*, Abteilung *f*, Unternehmensbereich *m*; Landschaft *f*, Teil *m* e–r Grafschaft; ~ **of an estate** Erbauseinandersetzung; ~ **of disbursement** Auszahlungsabteilung (*Staatskasse*); ~ **of labo(u)r** Arbeitsteilung; ~ **of**

opinion Meinungsverschiedenheit, Entscheidungsunfähigkeit; ~ **of profit** Gewinnausschüttung; ~ **of property** Vermögensteilung; Auseinandersetzung; **action of** ~ *scot* Teilungsklage, Auseinandersetzungsklage; **final** ~ Auseinandersetzung; **snap** ~ überraschende Abstimmung; **tie** ~ unentschiedene Abstimmung; **to press a** ~ auf Abstimmung drängen.

divisional court Rechtsmittelkammer, Kollegialgericht, Kammer; *Beschwerdekammer bzw Berufungskammer des High Court*; ~ **patent application** → *application* (*2*); **D~ Registry** Hauptregistratur der Familienabt. d. High Court.

divisionalisation Dezentralisierung in autonome Abteilungen.

divorce *s* Scheidung *f*, Ehescheidung *f*; Ehetrennung *f*; ~ **a mensa et thoro** Trennung von Tisch und Bett; ~ **a vinculo matrimonii** (*vollständige*) Ehescheidung; ~ **based on behaviour** auf ehewidriges Verhalten gestützte Scheidung; ~ **by (mutual) consent** Konventionalscheidung, einverständliche Scheidung; ~ **commissioner** beauftragter Richter in Ehesachen; ~ **court** für Ehescheidungen zuständiges Gericht; ~ **proctor** Vertreter des Staats im Scheidungsverfahren; ~ **rate** Scheidungsrate; ~ **towns** *Städte, in denen die Scheidungskammern des High Court Sitzungen abhalten können*; **defended** ~ streitige Scheidung; **ex parte** ~ Scheidung im einseitigen Verfahren; ~ **without reference to fault** Scheidung ohne Rücksicht auf Verschulden, Scheidung nach dem Zerrüttungsprinzip; **foreign** ~ ausländische Scheidung, Scheidung außerhalb des Staates (*bzw Gliedstaates*) der Eheschließung; **ground for** ~ Scheidungsgrund; **limited** ~ gerichtliche Anordnung des Getrenntlebens; **mail order** ~ Scheidung per Post, (*Sch. ohne Ortsansässigkeit und ohne Anwesenheit im Gericht – nicht anerkannt*); **migratory** ~ Scheidung ohne festen Wohnsitz; **no-fault** ~ Scheidung ohne Verschulden (*nach dem Zerrüttungsprinzip*); **petition for** ~ → *petition*; **to file a** ~ Scheidungsklage erheben; **to get a** ~ sich scheiden lassen; **uncontested** ~ unstreitige Scheidung; **undefended** ~ nicht streitige Scheidung.

divorce *v* trennen, scheiden, sich scheiden lassen; ~**d parties** geschiedene Ehegatten; **he** ~**d his wife** er ließ sich von seiner Frau scheiden.

divorcee der (die) Geschiedene.

divulge preisgeben, enthüllen; ~ **trade secrets** Geschäftsgeheimnisse preisgeben.

do *v* tun, machen; ~ **away with** veräußern, beseitigen; ~ **federal time** in e–r Bundes-Strafvollzugsanstalt (*US Gefängnis*) einsitzen; ~ **justice** Gerechtigkeit walten lassen; ~ **law** dem Recht Wirksamkeit verleihen, das Recht durchsetzen, das Recht verwirklichen; ~ **or suffer** tun oder dulden; ~ **the needful** das Erforderliche veranlassen.

dock *s* (*1*) Dock *n*, Hafenbecken *n*, Anlegestelle *f*, Kai *m*, Pier *f/m*, Laderampe *f*, Abstellgleis *n*; ~ **charges** Dockgebühren, Kaigebühren; ~ **dues** Dock-, Kaigebühren; ~-**master** Dockmeister *m*; ~ **receipt** → *receipt*; ~ **warrant** Docklagerschein, Dockempfangsschein; ~ **worker** Hafenarbeiter.

dock *s* (*2*) Anklagebank *f*; ~ **brief** Übernahme der (*kostenlosen*) Verteidigung; ~ **defense** unmittelbare Mandierung e–s Verteidigers im Gerichtssaal.

dock *v* docken, ins Dock bringen, kürzen.

dockage Hafen- und Kaigebühren *f/pl*, Docken *n*, Dockmöglichkeit *f*.

docker Hafenarbeiter *m*.

docket *s* Prozeßliste *f*, Urteilsverzeichnis *n*, Terminkalender *m*, Gerichtstagebuch *n*, Gerichtsprotokoll *n*, Aktenresümee *n*; Registerbuch *n*, Katasterverzeichnis *n*, Zollquittung *f*, Lieferschein *m*; ~ **fee** Prozeßgebühr; **appearance** ~ → *appearance*; **bar** ~ *nichtamtliche Prozeßliste e–r Sitzungsperiode (für die Anwaltschaft)*; **civil** ~ Liste der anhängigen Klagen; **execution** ~ Pfändungsliste; **judgment** ~ → *judgment;* **preferred** ~ Liste vorrangig angesetzter Gerichtssachen; **striking a** ~ → *striking*; **to clear the** ~ die anhängigen Sachen erledigen; **trial** ~ → *trial.*

docket *v* auszugsweise eintragen; in die Prozeßliste eintragen, resümieren, etikettieren, beschriften; ~ **a case** e–n Termin ansetzen; ~ **a judgment** ein Urteil ins Urteilsregister eintragen; ~ **goods** Waren etikettieren.

doctor *s* Doktor *m*, Arzt *m*, Akademiker *m*; ~**'s certificate** ärztliche Bescheinigung; ~**'s degree** Doktorgrad; ~ **of Laws** (*LL.D.*) Doktor der Rechte; **panel** ~ Kassenarzt; ~**-patient privilege** Recht des Patienten auf Einhaltung der ärztl. Schweigepflicht.

doctor *v* ärztlich behandeln, verordnen, praktizieren, zusammenflikken, zurechtmachen, fälschlich frisieren, verpanschen.

doctorate Doktorwürde *f*.

doctrine Lehre *f*, Doktrin *f*, Lehrsatz *m*, Prinzip *n*, Theorie *f*; ~ **of avoidable consequences** Grundsatz der Schadensminderungspflicht; ~ **of consideration** Lehre von der Gegenleistung bei Vertragsschluß; ~ **of corporate alter ego** Möglichkeit des Haftungsdurchgriffs (*bei jur. Person*); ~ **of declared intention** Erklärungstheorie; ~ **of election** Wahl des Verpflichteten bei verdeckter Stellvertretung; ~ **of necessity** notwendige Zuständigkeit (*wenn kein anderes Gericht bzw keine anderen Richter vorhanden*); ~ **of notice** Lehre vom Schutz des gutgläubigen Erwerbs; ~ **of real intention** Willenstheorie; ~ **of severance** Lehre von der Teilnichtigkeit (*Aufrechterhaltung von abtrennbaren Vertragsbestandteilen bei Teilnichtigkeit*); ~ **of transformation** Prinzip der Rezeption von Völkerrecht durch Staatsgesetz; ~ **of trap** Gefährdungshaftung für Fußangeln *u dgl*; **matrimonial offence** ~ Schuldprinzip (*Scheidungsrecht*).

document *v* dokumentieren, belegen, beurkunden.

document *s* Dokument *n* (= *D bzw* ...*d*), Urkunde *f* (= *U bzw* ...*u*), Schriftstück *n*, Unterlage *f*; ~**s against acceptance** *D–e* gegen Akzept; ~**s against payment** Zahlung gegen *D–e*; ~**s in proof of statement** Beweisschriftstück für die Aussage; ~ **of appointment** Ernennungsurkunde; ~ **of title** Eigentumsurkunde; Dispositionspapier, Traditionspapier; ~**s of title to goods** Traditionspapiere, kaufmännische Orderpapiere; ~ **of title to land** Grundstückseigentums*u*; ~ **privileged from production** *U*, deren Vorlage nicht verlangt werden kann; ~**s tax** *U–nsteuer*; ~ **under hand** nicht gesiegelte *U*, *U* in Schriftform; **accompanying** ~**s** Begleitpapiere; **affidavit of** ~**s** eidesstattliche Versicherung über den Verbleib von *U–n*; **altering a** ~ **with intent to defraud** *U–n*fälschung; **ancient** ~ uralte *U* (*mehr als 20 Jahre alte Urkunde mit Echtheitsvermutung*); **application** ~**s** Anmeldungsunterlagen; **authentic** ~ echte *U*; **average** ~**s** *ins* Schadenspapiere; **cash against** ~**s** → *cash*; **commercial** ~**s** kaufmännische Unterlagen; **concealment of** ~**s** → *concealment*; **confidential** ~ vertrauliche Schriftstücke; **conformed** ~ beglaubigte Abschrift; **contractual** ~ Vertrags*u*; **discovery of** ~**s** *U–n*vorlage; **disposal of** ~**s** Verfügung über Urkunden, *Regeln darüber, was mit den (Wahl-)-Urkunden weiter zu geschehen hat*; **evidentiary** ~ beweiserhebliche *U*; **foreign** ~ ausländische, öffentliche *U*; **impounded** ~ gerichtlich beschlagnahmte *U–n*; **inspection of** ~**s** → *inspection*; **judicial** ~ → *judicial*; **legal** ~ rechtsförmliche *U*;

lodging ~s Vorlage der Prozeßakte; **negotiable ~** begebbares Wertpapier, verkehrsfähiges Wertpapier; **notice to inspect ~s** Mitteilung, daß *U–n* eingesehen werden können; **official ~s** amtliche *U–n*; **original ~** Original*u*; **power to call für ~s** → *power (1)*; **pre-existing ~** bereits vorhandene *U–n*, vorprozessuale *U–n*; **priority ~s** Prioritätsbelege; **private ~s** Privat*u–n*; **private proof of ~** Echtheitsbeweis durch die Partei; **production of ~s** → *production*; **public ~** öffentliche *U*, Staats*u*; **public proof of ~** *U–n*beweis durch öffentliche Register; **putting in ~s** Beweisantritt durch *U–n*vorlage; **shipping ~s** → *shipping*; **substantiating ~** beweiskräftige Unterlage; **to draw up a ~** → *to draw*; **to execute a ~** e–e *U* unterfertigen; e–e *U* unterzeichnen.

documentary acceptance credit Rembourskredit.

documentation Glaubhaftmachung *f* durch Unterlagen, Dokumentation *f*, Dokumentenmaterial *n*.

doer Täter *m*; *scot* Stellvertreter *m*, Beauftragter *m*.

dog-Latin Küchenlatein *n*.

dog patrol Hundestreife *f*.

dogma Lehrsatz *m*, Glaubenssatz *m*, *hist* Senatsverordnung *f*.

doing Tat *f*, Tun *n*; **~s** Begebenheiten *f*|*pl*; *hist* Lehensdienste *m*|*pl*; **~ business** Geschäftstätigkeit.

dole *s* Anteil *m*, Spende *f*; Arbeitslosengeld *n*; **~-fish** Anteil am Fischzug; **~-meadow** Weidenanteil; **~ office** Arbeitsamtsbüro; **to be on the ~** arbeitslos sein, stempeln gehen.

doli|capax (bedingt) strafmündig; strafrechtlich verantwortlich; **~ incapax** absolut strafunmündig *GB: unter 8 Jahren.*

doll interview technique *Methode der Befragung von Kindesopfern bei Sexualdelikten mittels Demonstrationspuppen.*

dollar (US-)Dollar *m*; **~ acceptance** Dollarakzept; **~ balance** Dollarguthaben; **~ denominated** auf Dollar lautend; **~ diplomacy** Dollardiplomatie; **~ drain** Dollarabfluß; **~ drive** Exportförderung *um Dollar(s) zu verdienen*; **~ gap** Dollarlücke; **~ overhang** große ungebundene Dollarbestände; **~ scrips** *US* Besatzungsgeld; **~ store** *US* Einheitspreisgeschäft; **~ stringency** Dollarknappheit; **~ -a-year-man** *US ehrenamtlich für die US-Regierung Tätiger (z. B. prominente Persönlichkeit der Wirtschaft).*

dolus Dolus *m*, Vorsatz *m*; betrügerischer Vorsatz *m*.

domain Bereich *m*, Herrschaftsrecht *n*, Eigentum *n*, Fachgebiet *n*; **eminent ~** → *eminent*; **national ~** Staatsvermögen, Staatseigentum; **public ~** Gemeingut, Staatsbesitz, Grundeigentum der öffentlichen Hand, dem US-Bund gehörendes Land; gemeinfreie Werke; **to be in the public ~** gemeinfrei sein (*gewerblicher Rechtsschutz*); der Öffentlichkeit frei zugänglich sein (*Informationen*), nicht vertraulich sein.

Domesday Book (=) *hist erstes Kataster von England, 1086.*

domestic häuslich, die Familie betreffend, familienintern; inländisch; **~ arbitration agreement** Schiedsgerichtsvertrag ohne Auslandsberührung; **~ court** → *court*; **~ court panel** Liste von Laienrichtern in Unterhalts- und Vormundschaftssachen über Minderjährige; **~ international sales corporation** (*DISC*) *US-amerikanische Außenhandelsgesellschaft mit Sitz in USA bzw US Territorien (steuerliche Vorteile)*; **~ ordering** Inlandsaufträge; **~ violence** Gewalttätigkeiten im Familienbereich; Tätlichkeiten gegen Familienangehörige; **D~ Violence and Matrimonial Proceedings Act** Familienschutzgesetz *GB 1976.*

domestication Domestikation *f*; Ansässigwerden *n*, Assimilation, Anerkennung *f* als inländisch.

domicile Domizil *n*, Wohnsitz *m* (= *W bzw ... w*), Wohnsitzland *n*; Sitz *m* (*e–r Firma*), Hauptniederlassung *f*; Zahlstelle *f*; ~ **by birth** ursprünglicher (*durch Geburt erworbener*) *W*; ~ **by operation of law** gesetzlicher *W*, durch Heirat erworbener *W*; ~ **of a bill** Zahlungsadresse; ~ **of choice** gewählter *W*; ~ **of corporation** Sitz e–r Körperschaft; ~ **of dependency** (*von Angehörigen*) abgeleiteter *W*; ~ **of origin** Ursprungs*w*, *W* am Geburtsort; ~ **of succession** Nachlaß*w*, *W* als Anknüpfungspunkt für die Erbschaft; **commercial** ~ Sitz der Niederlassung, gewerblicher *W*; **corporate** ~ → *corporate*; **de facto** ~ (*faktischer*) *W*; **dependent** ~ abgeleiteter *W* (*e–s Minderjährigen*); **domestic** ~ inländischer *W*; **elected** ~ gewählter *W*; **fiscal** ~ steuerlicher *W*; **foreign** ~ Auslands*w*; **law of** ~ → *law*; **legal** ~ *W* im Rechtssinn; **legal** ~ **of a company** Sitz e–r Körperschaft; **matrimonial** ~ gemeinsamer ehelicher *W*; **municipal** ~ örtlicher *W innerhalb e–r Gemeinde; W* in e–r Gemeinde; **national** ~ inländischer *W*; **natural** ~ ursprünglicher *W*; **necessary** ~ gesetzlicher *W*; **quasi national** ~ dauernder Aufenthalt (*in e–m Staat*); **right of** ~ → *right*; **state of** ~ → *state* (*2*).

domiciled mit Wohnsitz in, mit Sitz in, ansässig, beheimatet, wohnhaft; ~ **bill** → *bill* (*3*); **to be** ~ **abroad** seinen Wohnsitz im Ausland haben.

domiciliary Heimats ..., Wohnsitz ...

domiciliate (*e–n Wechsel*) domizilieren, ~**d bill** Domizilwechsel.

domiciliation Domizilierung ~ (*Wechsel*).

domination Herrschaft *f*, Beherrschung *f*; Vorherrschaft *f*; **foreign** ~ Fremdherrschaft.

domineer despotisch herrschen, tyrannisieren.

dominical den Sonntag betreffend; ~ **rest** Sonntagsruhe.

dominicide Tötung *f* des Lehensherren *oder* Lehrmeisters, *hist*.

dominion Oberherrschaft *f*, Regierungsgewalt *f*, Hoheitsrecht *n*; Eigentumsrecht *n*; Hoheitsgebiet *n*, Dominium *n*; ~**s** Dominions, *Staaten im britischen Commonwealth*; **D~ Register** *Handelsregister für britische Körperschaften in den Dominions*.

dominium Verfügungsrecht *n*, Herrschaftsgewalt *f*, Eigentum *n*; ~ **directum** *scot* Obereigentum an Grundstücken.

dominus Herr *m*, Lehensherr *m*, Eigentümer *m*; Vertretener *m*; ~ **litis** *Herr des Rechtsstreits, die* (*eigentliche*) Partei; ~ **navis** Schiffseigentümer.

donate schenken, e–e Schenkung machen.

donatio(n) inter vivos Schenkung unter Lebenden; ~ **mortis causa** Schenkung von Todes wegen.

donation Schenkung *f*, unentgeltliche Zuwendung *f*; ~ **lands** → *land*; **by way of** ~ schenkungsweise; **deed of** ~ → *deed*; **executed** ~ Handschenkung; **executory** ~ Schenkungsversprechen; **gratuitous** ~ reine Schenkung; **onerous** ~ Schenkung unter Auflage; **remunerative** ~ belohnende Schenkung.

donative schenkungsweise, Schenkungs ...

donator Schenker *m*.

donatorius Beschenkter *m*.

donatory Empfänger von verfallenem Gut (*seitens der Krone*).

donatrix Schenkerin *f*.

done geschehen, errichtet, ausgefertigt; abgemacht; ~ **at ... this ... day of ...** geschehen zu ... am ...; ~ **by a person** von jmdm (*bzw seinem Vertreter*) getan; ~ **in duplicate** in zweifacher Ausfertigung; geschehen in zwei Urschriften; ~ **in three original texts** geschehen in drei Urschriften; ~ **or intended to be** ~ geschehen oder beabsichtigt.

donee Beschenkter *m*, Schenkungsempfänger *m*, Bedachter *m*, Treunehmer *m*, Belehnter *m*, Ermächtigter *m*; ~ **beneficiary** Drittbegünstigte(r); ~ **of power** der Bevollmächtigte.

donor Schenker *m*, Lehensgeber *m*, Treugeber *m*; Stifter *m*, Wohltäter *m*; ~ **of a power** der Ermächtigende, Vollmachtgeber.

doom Schicksal *n*, Urteil *n*, jüngstes Gericht *n*; Tag *m* des jüngsten Gerichts, *fig* Gerichtstag *m*.

door Tür *f*, Haustür *f*, Pforte *f*, Zugang *m*; **~-to-~ selling** Hausieren; **~-to-~ transport** Beförderung von Haus zu Haus; **the bank closes its ~s** die Bank stellt ihre Zahlungen ein; **to lay a charge at someone's ~** jmdn beschuldigen.

dope *s* Rauschgift *n*, Rauschgiftsüchtige(r); ~ **fiend** Rauschgiftsüchtiger.

dope *v* Rauschgift nehmen *bzw* verabreichen, Aufputschmittel verabreichen.

dormant schlafend, unbenutzt, untätig, still, verborgen, brach liegend.

dormitory halfway houses Nächtigungsheime für Freigänger.

doss-house Obdachlosenasyl *n*.

dossier Dossier *n*, Akte *f*; **personal** ~ Personalakte.

dot Mitgift *f*.

DoT = *Department of Trade qv*.

dotage Senilität *f*, geistige Altersschwäche *f*.

dotal eingebracht, zum Heiratsgut *bzw* zum Witwenteil gehörend; zur Aussteuer gehörend; ~ **property** eingebrachtes Gut der Frau.

dotation Einräumung *f* des Witwenpflichtteils, Dotation *f*, Stiftung *f*.

dotted line punktierte Linie *f* (*zum Unterschreiben*); **to sign on the** ~ *einfach* unterschreiben; Unterschrift leisten, ohne zu prüfen.

double doppelt, zweifach, zweimal; ~ **accident benefit** doppelte Leistung bei Unfalltod; ~ **account system** doppelte Buchführung; ~ **criminality rule** Grundsatz der identischen Norm (*Auslieferungsrecht*); **~-dealing** Doppelzüngigkeit, Unaufrichtigkeit; ~ **dipping** Doppelversorgung (*Pension, Rente etc*); ~ **patenting** Doppelpatentierung; **~-radius rule** Doppelradiusregel *Bestimmung der Grenze der Hoheitsgewässer in Bruchteilen*; ~ **recovery** *Schadensersatzleistung, die den gesamten Schaden mehrerer Betroffener übersteigt.*

doubt *s* Zweifel *m*, Bedenken *n*|*pl*.

doubt *v* bezweifeln, zweifeln.

doubtful zweifelhaft, dubios.

dove Taube *f*; **~s** Friedenspartei *f*.

dow stiften, ausstatten (*vgl to endow*).

dowable e–m Witwenpflichtteil (*vgl dower*) unterliegend.

dowager (*erbberechtigte*) Witwe *f*, Witwe *f* im Adelsstand; **queen-~** Königinwitwe.

dower Mitgift *f*, Wittum *n*, Witwenleibgedinge *n*, Witwenpflichtteil *m* (*nur bezüglich Grundvermögen*), Nießbrauchsrecht *n* der Witwe am Immobiliennachlaß des verstorbenen Ehemannes; *GB bis 1925*; gesetzliches Erbrecht *n* der Ehefrau; ~ **by custom** Witwennießbrauchsrecht nach Ortsbrauch; ~ **by the Common Law** gemeinrechtliches Witwennießbrauchsrecht (*zu ⅓ des Immobiliennachlasses*); **writ of** ~ Klage auf Einräumung des Witwenanteils (*am Grundstück*).

dowerless ohne Mitgift.

down *v* **tools** die Arbeit niederlegen.

down-grading niedrigere Einstufung *f*, Zurückstufung *f*, Abgruppierung *f*.

down payment Anzahlung *f*.

downsizing Verkleinerung *f*, Gesundschrumpfung *f*.

downswing Konjunkturabschwung *m*.

downturn Geschäftsrückgang *m*, Flaute *f*.

dowress Witwe mit Anspruch auf dower *qv*.

dowry Mitgift *f*, eingebrachtes Gut *n* der Ehefrau.

doyen Doyen *m* (*des diplomatischen Korps*), Sprecher *m*, Wortführer *m*, Rangältester *m*.

draft (*1*) Entwurf *m*; ~ **agreement** Vertragsentwurf, Entwurfsfassung e–s Vertrages; ~ **bill** Vorlagenentwurf; ~ **claim** vorläufige Anspruchsfassung (*Patent*); ~ **contract** → *contract*; ~ **directive** Richtlinienentwurf; ~ **law** Gesetzesentwurf; Entwurfsfassung e–s

Gesetzes; ~ **letter** Briefentwurf, Entwurfsschreiben; ~ **proposal** Vorschlagsentwurf; ~ **resolution** Entschließungsentwurf, **rough** ~ Vorentwurf.

draft (*2*) Anweisung *f*, gezogener Wechsel *m*, Tratte *f*, ~ **at sight** Sichttratte; ~ **credit** Rembourskredit, Trassierungskredit, Wechselkredit; **advice of** ~ Trattenavis; **bank** ~ Bankscheck (*auf eine ausländische Korrespondenzbank gezogener Scheck*), Bankwechsel; **banker's** ~ (*bestätigter*) Bankscheck (*gleich Bargeld*); **clean** ~ schlichter Wechsel, Tratte ohne Dokumente, nichtdokumentäre Tratte; **clean collection** ~ → *collection*; **collection** ~ → *collection*; **demand** ~ Sichtwechsel, Sichttratte; **discount of** ~**s** → *discount*; **documentary** ~ Dokumententratte, dokumentäre Tratte; **documentary collection** ~ → *collection*; **interest bearing** ~ Tratte mit Zinsvermerk; **long** ~ Auslandswechsel; **presentation** ~ Sichtwechsel; **sight** ~ Sichtwechsel; **time** ~ Terminwechsel.

draft (*3*) Musterung *f*, Rekrutierung *f*, Einberufung *f*; ~ **dodger** Drükkeberger vor dem Wehrdienst.

draftee der Einberufene *m*.

drafting Entwurfsabfassung *f*; ~ **office** ausfertigende Stelle *f*, federführendes Amt *n*; **faulty** ~ fehlerhafte Abfassung, Formulierungsfehler.

draftsman Entwurfsverfasser *m*, Urkundenverfasser *m*; **parliamentary** ~ Spezialist für Formulierung von Parlamentsvorlagen.

draftsmanship formulierungsmäßige Gestaltung *f*; Formulierungskunst *f*.

drag Hemmung *f*, Verschleppung *f*.

drag-net|technique Schleppnetz-Fahndung; ~ **clause** Sammelklausel.

drama Drama *n*, Schauspiel *n*, dramatische Dichtkunst *f*.

dramatic|composition Werk *n* der Schauspielkunst; ~ **copyright** Urheberrecht an Werken der Schauspielkunst; ~ **piece** Werk der Schauspielkunst, Werk der Theaterkunst; ~ **work** Werk der Schauspielkunst.

draughtsman = *draftsman qv*.

draw *v* ziehen, aufsetzen (*Schriftstück*), ausstellen; ~ **a bill of exchange** e–n Wechsel ausstellen, Wechsel nehmen; ~ **an instrument** e–e Urkunde (*förmlich*) aufsetzen; ~ **conclusions** Schlüsse ziehen; ~ **down** ausschöpfen e–s Kreditlimits; ~ **interest** Zinsen tragen; ~**n against uncollected funds** Deckung erst bei Zahlungseingang; ~ **on** ziehen auf; ~ **on the reserves** Reserven angreifen; ~ **one's salary** Gehalt beziehen; ~ **profits from** Gewinne erzielen; ~ **the profits** Gewinne entnehmen; ~ **up a contract** e–n Vertrag aufsetzen; ~ **up a document** e–e Urkunde errichten; ~**artificially** ~**n** in juristischer Fachsprache formuliert; **bank** ~**n upon** bezogene Bank.

drawback Hindernis *n*, Nachteil *m*; Rückzoll *m*, Zollrückvergütung *f bei Wiederausfuhr*, (*Umsatz*)*Steuerrückvergütung f* bei Ausfuhr.

drawee Bezogener *m*, Trassat *m*, Angewiesener *m*; **alternative** ~**s** Alternativbezogene; **joint** ~**s** gemeinsame Wechselnehmer; **release of** ~ Haftungsentlassung des Bezogenen.

drawer Wechselaussteller *m*, Scheckaussteller *m*, Trassant *m*, Anweisender *m*.

drawing Entnahme *f*, Ausstellung *f*, Ziehung *f*, Abhebung *f*; Zeichnung *f*, Abbildung *f*; ~ **a bill** Aufstellung e–r Rechnung; ~ **account** → *account* (*2*); ~ **and redrawing** Wechselreiterei; ~ **any lottery** Teilnahme am Lotteriespiel; ~ **authorization** → *authorization*; ~ **by partners** Privatentnahmen der Gesellschafter; ~ **commission** Trassierungsprovision; ~ **day** Ziehungstag; ~**s in cash** Barentnahmen; ~ **right** Abhebungsbefugnis, Ziehungsrecht; **cum** ~ inklusive Ziehung; **current** ~ die nächste Auslosung (Obligationen); **dollar** ~**s** Dollarabhebungen; **personal** ~**s** Privatentnahmen, Privatabhebungen; **redeemable by** ~**s** auslosbar.

drayage Rollgeld *n*.

drink *s* Getränk *n*; alkoholische Getränke; ~ **dispenser** Getränkeautomat; **subsequent** ~ Nachtrunk.

drink-drive conviction Verurteilung wegen Trunkenheit am Steuer; ~ **offence** Alkoholdelikt des Fahrzeugfahrers, Straftat des Fahrens bei alkoholbedingter Fahruntüchtigkeit.

drip Dienstbarkeit *f* der Duldung des Herabtropfens von Regenwasser.

drive *s* Fahrt *f*, Spazierfahrt *f*, Fahrstraße *f*; Treiben *n*, Treibjagd *f*; Tendenz *f*, Kampagne *f*, Sammelaktion *f*, Verkaufsaktion *f*; **export** ~ Exportförderungskampagne; **sales** ~ Verkaufsförderungskampagne.

drive *v* fahren, (*ein Kfz:*) lenken, führen.

drive-in bank Bank mit Autoschalter.

driver Fahrer *m*, Kfz-Führer *m*; Lokomotivführer *m*; ~**-only train operation** schaffnerloser Zugbetrieb.

driveway Fahrbahn *f*; **private** ~ Privateinfahrt.

driving Fahren *n*, Führen e-s Kraftfahrzeugs; **D~ and Vehicle Licensing Centre** Führerschein- und Kfz-Zulassungsstelle; ~ **rectification course** polizeilicher Fahrunterricht; ~ **disqualification** Entzug der Fahrerlaubnis; ~ **licence** Fahrerlaubnis, Führerschein; *clean* ~~: *Fahrerlaubnis ohne Punkteintrag;* ~ **while asleep** Einschlafen am Steuer; ~ **while drunk** Trunkenheit am Steuer; ~ **while under the influence of drink** Fahren unter Alkoholeinwirkung; ~ **whilst** (= *while*) **disqualified** Fahren nach Entzug der Fahrerlaubnis; ~ **with alcohol concentration above prescribed limit** Fahren bei Blutalkoholgehalt über dem Grenzwert; ~ **while intoxicated** Trunkenheit am Steuer; ~ **while unfit** Fahren bei (alkoholbedingter) Fahruntüchtigkeit; **careless** ~ unvorsichtiges Fahren; **dangerous** ~ verkehrsgefährdendes Fahren (= *Führen e-s Kfz*); **faulty** ~ schlechtes Fahren, fehlerhaftes F.; **furious** ~ wildes Fahren, rowdyhaftes F.; **inconsiderate** ~ rücksichtsloses Fahren; **reckless** ~ grob verkehrsgefährdendes Fahren.

droit Recht *n*, *hist* Gesetz *n*, Rechtsanspruch *m*; **autre** ~ fremdes Recht.

droitural rechtlich zustehend, auf das (Eigentums)Recht gestützt.

drop *s* Sturz *m* (*von Preisen*), plötzliches Fallen *n*; ~**-letter** Ortsbrief (*vom Aufgabepostamt zuzustellender Brief*); ~ **shipment** Lieferung im Streckengeschäft, Direktlieferung (an Endabnehmer); ~ **shipment delivery** = ~ *shipment qv*; ~ **shipper** Großhändler, der das Streckengeschäft betreibt.

drop *v* fallen, fallen lassen, einstellen; ~ **the action** die Klage nicht weiter betreiben, die Klage zurücknehmen; ~ **the charge** die Klage zurücknehmen, das Ermittlungsverfahren einstellen; ~ **-ped order** weggefallener Tagesordnungspunkt (*parl*); ~**ping ground** Holzzwischenlagerplatz; ~ **out rate** Durchfallquote; **a rule** ~**s** über e-n Antrag wird nicht entschieden (*wegen Stimmengleichheit*).

droplock stock *Anleihe mit variabler aber fixierbarer Verzinsung.*

drug Droge *f*, Arzneimittel *n*, pharmazeutisches Präparat *n*, Narkotikum *n*, Betäubungsmittel *n*, Rauschgift *n*; ~ **abuse** Drogenmißbrauch; ~ **addict** Rauschgiftsüchtiger; ~ **trafficker** Rauschgifthändler; ~ **trafficking** Rauschgifthandel; **administering** ~**s** das

Verabreichen von Narkotika; **controlled** ~ erlaubnispflichtiges Betäubungsmittel; **dangerous** ~**s** Rauschgifte, gesundheitsgefährdende Narkotika; **stupefying** ~ Betäubungsmittel.

drummer Handelsreisender *m*

drunkard Trinker *m*, Trunksüchtiger *m*; **habitual** ~ Gewohnheitstrinker.

drunkenness Betrunkenheit *f*; ~ **in charge of motor vehicle** Trunkenheit am Steuer; ~ **on duty** Trunkenheit im Dienst; **habitual** ~ Trunksucht, Alkoholismus; **voluntary** ~ verschuldete Trunkenheit.

drunk-ometer Blutalkoholmeßgerät *n*.

dry trocken; rein formell; ohne Vorteil; unter Alkoholverbot.

dual citizenship (= *dual nationality*) doppelte Staatsangehörigkeit.

dualism Dualismus *m* (*z. B. zwischen Völkerrecht und innerstaatlichem Recht*).

dubitante „zweifelhaft" (*Richtervermerk auf Entscheidungsbegründungen*).

dubitatur zweifelhaft (*in Fallsammlungen*).

duces tecum Ladung *f* mit Vorlageanordnung (*Urkunden, Geschäftspapiere*).

duchy Herzogtum *n*; **D~ Court of Lancaster** *obs Sondergericht für Kronrechte in der Grafschaft Lancaster*.

dud Blindgänger *m*, Niete *f*; ~ **cheque** ungedeckter Scheck; ~ **note** falsche Banknote; ~ **stock** unverkäufliche Waren.

due fällig, sofort zahlbar, schuldig, geschuldet, gebührend, ordnungsgemäß, vorschriftsmäßig, notwendig, erforderlich; ~ **and payable** zur Zahlung fällig; ~ **and reasonable care** im Verkehr erforderliche Sorgfalt; ~ **at call** jederzeit abrufbar, jederzeit fällig, täglich fällig; ~ **bill** Schuldschein, schriftl Schuldanerkenntnis; ~ **care and attention** (*die im Verkehr*) erforderliche Sorgfalt; ~ **cause shown** bei Nachweis e-s wichtigen Grundes; ~ **consideration** gebührende Beachtung, ausreichende Berücksichtigung; ~ **course of law** der Rechtsweg, rechtsstaatliches Verfahren; ~ **from banks** Guthaben bei anderen Banken, Nostroguthaben; ~ **on sale clause** zur Rückzahlung fällig bei (Grundstücks)-verkauf (*Hypothek*); ~ **process of law** → *process* (*1*); ~ **proof of service** Zustellungsnachweis; ~ **publication of banns** ordnungsgemäßes Aufgebot; ~ **to banks** Bankschulden, Nostroverpflichtungen; **to fall** ~ fällig werden.

duel *s* Duell *n*, Zweikampf *m*; **challenge to fight** ~ Herausforderung zum Zweikampf; **homicide in** ~ Tötung beim Zweikampf.

duelling Duellieren *n*, Zweikampf *m* (*mit tödlichen Waffen*).

dues Mitgliederbeiträge *m*|*pl*, Abgaben *f*|*pl*, Gebühren *f*|*pl*; **harbo(u)r** ~ → *harbo(u)r;* **membership** ~ Mitgliedsbeiträge; **union** ~ Gewerkschaftsbeiträge.

dull flau, lustlos, langweilig.

dullness Flaute *f*, Lustlosigkeit *f*, Geschäftsstille *f*, Stagnation *f*.

dulocracy Sklavenherrschaft *f*.

duly formgerecht, ordnungsgemäß, vorschriftsmäßig, gehörig; ~ **appointed** ordnungsgemäß bestellt; ~ **authorized** ordnungsgemäß bevollmächtigt; ~ **completed** formgerecht abgeschlossen; ~ **constituted by law** ordnungsgemäß konstituiert; ~ **determined by notice to quit** ordnungsgemäß gekündigt; ~ **made** (rechtlich) einwandfrei geschehen, bewirkt; ~ **received** richtig erhalten.

dummy Strohmann *m*, Statist *m*; ~ **activity** Scheintätigkeit; ~ **director** Proformadirektor; ~ **stockholder** Strohmann-Aktionär; ~ **transaction** Scheingeschäft.

dump *v* unterbieten (*am Weltmarkt*); zu Schleuderpreisen verkaufen, Dumping betreiben; kippen,

(*Schutt*) abladen, verklappen (*auf See*).

dump *s* Halde *f*, Schuttabladeplatz *m*, Munitionslager *n*.

dumping Dumping *n*, Schleuderausfuhr *f*, Preisunterbietung *f*; Abkippen *n* (*Müll, Schutt*); Verklappung *f*; ~ **at sea** Verklappung; ~ **duties** → *duty* (*2*); ~ **refuse** Müllablagerung; **hidden** ~ verschleiertes Dumping; **margin of** ~ Dumpingspanne; **price** ~ Preisdumping.

dun bedrängen, mahnen; ~ **for payment** zur Zahlung mahnen.

dunning Mahnwesen *n*; ~ **activity** Mahnwesen; ~ **letter** (*wiederholtes*) Mahnschreiben.

duopoly Marktbeherrschung *f* durch zwei Produzenten.

duplicate *s* Duplikat *n*, 2. Ausfertigung *f*; ~ **copy** Ausfertigung; ~ **recording system** Durchschreibebuchführung; ~ **will** in zwei Urschriften errichtetes Testament; e–es der beiden Originaltestamente; **done in** ~ → *done*; **made in** ~ in zweifacher Ausfertigung; ~ **original** zweite Originalausfertigung; **true** ~ gleichlautende Abschrift.

duplicate *v* kopieren, verdoppeln, vervielfältigen, reproduzieren.

duplicitous alternativ, mehrfach begründet.

duplicity Zweideutigkeit *f*, Doppelzüngigkeit *f*; unzulässige Häufung *f* (*im schriftsätzlichen Vortrag oder in e–r Gesetzesvorlage*); ~ **in indictment** unzulässige Vermischung von Anklagepunkten.

durability Lebensdauer *f*, Widerstandsfähigkeit *f*.

durables langlebige Wirtschaftsgüter.

duration Dauer *f*, Laufzeit *f*; ~ **of a bill** Laufzeit e–s Wechsels; Wechselfrist; ~ **of a copyright** Schutzfrist *e–s Urheberrechts;* ~ **of a cover** Deckungszeit (*Versicherung*); ~ **of offer** Gültigkeitsdauer e–r Offerte; ~ **of punishment** Strafdauer; ~ **of validity** Gültigkeitsdauer.

duress Nötigung *f* (*durch Drohung oder Zwang*); ~ **of goods** sittenwidrige Druckausübung beim Warenkauf; ~ **of imprisonment** Freiheitsberaubung; ~ **per minas** Nötigung zu e–r Handlung (*durch Bedrohung*); **economic** ~ wirtschaftl Pression; **hearing under** ~ Zwangsverhör; **mental** ~ widerrechtlicher psychischer Zwang; **moral** ~ psychische Nötigung; sittenwidrige Pression unter Ausnutzung e–r Notlage; **physical** ~ Nötigung durch körperliche Gewalt, physischer Zwang; **political** ~ politische Pression, politische Erpressung; **to act under** ~ im Nötigungsstand handeln, unter widerrechtlichem Zwang handeln; **to plead** ~ ein Geständnis wegen Zwangsanwendung widerrufen; **under** ~ genötigt, gezwungen, auf Grund e–r Nötigung.

duressor Nötigender *m*.

during während, im Laufe von; ~ **coverture** im Ehestand, während der Dauer dieser Ehe; ~ **currency of policy** während der Laufzeit e–r Versicherung; ~ **good behavior** bei einwandfreier Führung; ~ **her life and until she shall marry again** auf Lebenszeit bzw bis zur Wiederverheiratung; ~ **her Majesty's pleasure** auf unbestimmte Zeit; (*nach Belieben ihrer M.*); ~ **her widowhood** bis zum Tode *bzw* der Wiederverheiratung der Witwe; ~ **his natural life** auf Lebenszeit; ~ **my life** solange ich lebe; ~ **one year** im Laufe e–s Jahres; ~ **pleasure** solange nicht abberufen, im Belieben (*des Monarchen*); ~ **the bankruptcy** bis zur Beendigung des Konkursverfahrens; ~ **the hours of service** während der Dienstzeit; ~ **the possession of the tenant** während der Besitzzeit des Pächters; ~ **the trial** während der Hauptverhandlung (*von der Eidesleistung der Geschworenen bis zum Urteilsspruch*).

Dutch|auction Auktion *f* mit Abschlag (*Herabsetzen der Preise bis zum Zuschlag*); **D~ treat** jeder zahlt seine eigene Zeche.

dutiable abgabepflichtig, steuerpflichtig, zollpflichtig.

duty (*1*) Schuld *f*, Pflicht *f*, Verpflichtung *f*, Obliegenheitspflicht *f*; ~ **in law** Rechtspflicht; ~ **of care** Sorgfaltspflicht; ~ **of care for safety** Verkehrssicherungspflicht; ~ **roster** Diensteinsatzplan; ~**solicitor** → *solicitor;* ~ **of discovery** Verpflichtung zur Vorlage e–r Urkunde; ~ **of presentation** Vorlagepflicht; ~ **of secrecy** Geheimhaltungspflicht; ~ **to act** Rechtspflicht zu handeln; ~ **to assist** Pflicht zur Hilfeleistung; ~ **to cooperate** Mitwirkungspflicht; ~ **to disclose** Offenbarungspflicht, Aufklärungspflicht, Anzeigepflicht; ~ **to refrain** Unterlassungspflicht; ~ **to render assistance after accident** Pflicht zur Hilfeleistung bei Unglücksfällen; ~ **to take care** Sorgfaltspflicht; **absolute** ~ absolute Pflicht, einseitige Rechtspflicht; **administrative** ~**ies** Verwaltungsaufgaben; **breach of** ~ → *breach;* **conjugal** ~ eheliche Pflicht; **contrary to** ~ pflichtwidrig; **discharge of** ~ → *discharge*; **hotchpot** ~ → *hotchpot*; **in the course of** ~ in Ausübung des Dienstes; **judicial** ~ → *judicial*; **legal** ~ Rechtspflicht; **lifelong** ~ lebenslängliche Pflicht; **mandatory** ~ zwingende Verpflichtung; **ministerial** ~ Amtspflicht; **moral** ~ sittliche Pflicht; **negative** ~ Unterlassungspflicht; **occupational** ~**ies** Berufspflichten; Arbeitnehmerpflichten; **off** ~ außer Dienst, außerdienstlich; **official** ~ Amtspflicht, Dienstpflicht; **on** ~ im Dienst; **permissive** ~ nicht zwingend vorgeschriebene Pflicht; **positive** ~ Pflicht zum Handeln; **professional** ~ Berufspflicht; **proprietary** ~**ies** → *proprietary;* **public** ~ Dienstpflicht, Beamtenpflicht; (*öffentl*) Dienst; **report for** ~ sich zum Dienst melden; **superior** ~ Pflichtenkollision, übergesetzlicher Notstand.

duty (*2*) Zoll *m*, Abgabe *f*, Gebühr; Stempelsteuer *f*; ~ **-free** zollfrei; ~ **-free entry** zollfreie Einfuhr; ~ **of detraction** *Erbschaftssteuer bei Wegschaffung von Nachlaßgegenständen aus dem Staatsgebiet;* ~ **-paid** verzollt; **ad valorem** ~ Wertzoll, Stempelsteuer; **agricultural** ~ Agrarzoll; **assessment of** ~ Verzollung; **countervailing** ~ Ausgleichszoll; **customs** ~ → *customs*; **death** ~ → *death*; **differential** ~ Differentialzoll, Vorzugszoll; **discriminating** ~ Differentialzoll; **dumping** ~ Anti-Dumping Ausgleichszoll; **excise** ~ Verbrauchssteuer; **exempt from** ~ gebührenfrei, zollfrei; **external** ~**ies** Zölle, Außenzölle; **licence** ~ → *licence*; **maximum import** ~ Höchstzoll bei der Einfuhr; **penal** ~ Strafzoll; **port** ~**ies** Hafenzoll, Hafengebühren; **preferential** ~ Vorzugszoll; **protective** ~ Schutzzoll; **retaliatory** ~ Kampfzoll, Vergeltungszoll, Retorsionszoll; **unascertained** ~**ies** pauschalierte Zölle; **to impose** ~**ies** Zölle festsetzen.

dwell wohnen, sich aufhalten.

dweller Bewohner *m*.

dwelling Wohnung *f*, Wohnhaus *n*, Eigenheim *n*, Familienwohnung *f*; ~ **house** → *house*; ~ **-place** Wohnung, dauernder Aufenthaltsort, Wohnort; **movable** ~**s** fahrbare Wohngelegenheiten (*Zelte und Wohnwagen*); **private** ~ Privathaus, Eigenheim; Privatwohnung; **separate** ~ abgeschlossene Wohnung.

dwindling of assets Kapitalschwund, Vermögensverfall.

dysnomy schlechte Gesetzgebung *f*, fehlerhaftes Gesetz *n*.

E

earl Graf *m*; **E ~ marshal of England** Oberzeremonienmeister; *hist Gerichtsherr über Adelsgerichte*.
earldom Grafenwürde *f*.
earles-penny Kaufschilling *m*, Anzahlung *f* als Kaufbestätigung.
early|bird issue *US* Frühausgabe e–r Tageszeitung; **~ closing** frühzeitiger Arbeitsschluß; **~ leaver** Frührentner; **~ retirement scheme** Vorruhestand(sregelung); **~ warning** Frühwarnung (*vor Atomangriff*); Vorankündigung (*von Arbeitskämpfen*).
earmark *s* Kennzeichen *n*, Merkmal *n*; **~ rule** Identitätsverlust des Geldes durch Vermischung.
earmark *v* markieren, für bestimmte Zwecke festlegen, zurückstellen.
earn verdienen, erwerben.
earner Erwerbstätiger *m*, Verdiener *m* (*durch Leistung oder aus Kapital*); **employed ~s** Arbeitnehmer.
earnest *s* Draufgabe *f*, Handgeld *n*; **~ money** Handgeld, Kaufschilling, Draufgeld, Anzahlung.
earning capacity Erwerbsfähigkeit *f*, finanzielle Leistungsfähigkeit, Ertragsfähigkeit *f*, Rentabilität *f*; **decreased ~** geminderte Erwerbsfähigkeit; **impairment of ~** Minderung der Erwerbsfähigkeit; **loss of ~** Verlust (*bzw Minderung*) der Erwerbsfähigkeit.
earning power Erwerbsfähigkeit *f*; *auch*: Ertragskraft *f* (*e–s Unternehmens*).
earnings *s*|*pl* Verdienst *m*, Arbeitseinkommen *n*, Einnahmen *f*|*pl*; **~ coverage** *langfristige* Ertragsdeckung (*Börsenhandel*); **~ performance** Ertragsentwicklung; **~ picture** Ertragssituation; **~ potential** Gewinnpotential; **~ report** Gewinn- und Verlustrechnung; **~ yield** Nettogewinn; Ergebnisbericht; **accumulated ~** Gewinnvortrag; **actual ~** tatsächlicher Verdienst; **company ~** Gesellschaftseinkünfte; **gross ~** Bruttoeinnahmen; **incidental ~** Nebenverdienst; **retained ~** einbehaltener Gewinn, thesaurierter G., Nettoerträge, Reinverdienst, Nettoverdienst; **personal ~** Einkünfte aus eigener Arbeitstätigkeit; **professional ~** freiberufliche Einkünfte.
easement Dienstbarkeit *f*, Grunddienstbarkeit *f* (= *G*), Servitut *n*; **~ in gross** beschränkt persönliche Dienstbarkeit; **~ by necessity** Notwegerecht; **~ of access** Notwegrecht; Dienstbarkeit, den Zugang zum herrschenden Grundstück zu dulden; **~ of convenience** Dienstbarkeit zur Nutzungsverbesserung; **~ of light** Dienstbarkeit gegen Verbauung von Fenstern; nachbarrechtliches Verbot des Lichtentzugs, Lichtrecht; **~ of necessity** Dienstbarkeit als Notrecht; **~ of support** *G* zur Anliegerabstützung; **~ or right** servitutsähnliches Recht; **affirmative ~** = *positive ~ qv*; **apparent ~** *G*; äußerlich erkennbare *G*; **appurtenant ~** *G*, *als Bestandteil des herrschenden Grundstücks*; **continuous ~** *G* wegen e–s Dauerzustandes; **discontinuous ~** im Einzelfall ausgeübte *G*; **equitable ~** dienstbarkeitsähnliche Verpflichtung, formlose Dienstbarkeit; **floating ~** variable Wegerechts-Dienstbarkeit; **implied ~** stillschweigende dienstbarkeitsähnliche Verpflichtung (*zB des Verkäufers e–r Nachbarparzelle, bisherige Nutzung zu dulden*); **intermittent ~** (*nur*) zeitweilig ausgeübte Dienstbarkeit; **legal ~** (*dingl wirkende*) Dienstbarkeit; **negative ~** auf ein Unterlassen gerichtete *G*; **nonapparent ~** nichtständige Dienstbarkeit; **non-continuous ~**

nichtständige Dienstbarkeit (*die bei Nichtausübung erlischt*); **positive** ~ G, die zu einem Handeln (*auf dem dienenden Grundstück*) *berechtigt*; **private** ~ privatrechtliche G; **public** ~ *G der öffentlichen Hand, öffentlich rechtliches Servitut;* **quasi** ~ dienstbarkeitsähnliches Recht; **reciprocal negative** ~ G mit gegenseitiger Unterlassungsverpflichtung (*bei Verkauf von benachbarten Parzellen*); **secondary** ~ Nebenrecht zur Ausübung e–r Dienstbarkeit.

Easter|-dues (~ offerings) Ostergabe *f*, Osterkollekte *f* (*Gemeindeabgabe*); ~ **sittings** = ~ *term qv*; ~ **term** Gerichtssitzung des 2. Quartals (*15. April – 8. bzw 13. Mai*); ~ **vacation** Gerichtsferien an den Osterfeiertagen.

easy leicht, mühelos, günstig; ~ **market** → *market*; ~ **money** → *money*; ~ **profit** → *profit*; ~ **terms** → *term*; **in** ~ **circumstances** wohlhabend.

eat *v* **one's terms** die Vorbereitungszeit in der Anwaltsvereinigung ableiten (*unter Teilnahme an gemeinsamen Dinners*).

eating-house Speiselokal *n* (*ohne Schankkonzession*).

eaves Dachtraufe *f*, Dachübergang *m*; ~ **-drip** Dienstbarkeit auf Ableitung des Regenwassers, Rinnrecht, Traufrecht.

eavesdropper Lauscher *m*.

eavesdropping verbotenes Lauschen *n*, heimliches Horchen *n*.

ebb and flow Ebbe und Flut (*Grenze der Seegerichtsbarkeit*).

ebriety Trunkenheit *f*.

eccentricity Absonderlichkeit *f*, Wunderlichkeit *f*, Exzentrizität *f*.

ecclesiastic Kleriker *m*, Geistlicher *m*.

ecclesiastical kirchlich, geistlich; ~ **authorities** Klerus, Kirchenbehörden; **E~ Commission** = *High Court of Commission* → *Court;* **E~ Commissioners** Kirchenreformkommission, gemeinsamer Kirchenausschuß (*des engl Parlaments*); ~ **corporation** → *corporation*; ~ **court** Kirchengericht; ~ **dilapidations** (*kirchenrechtliche Sanktionen gegen*) Verwahrlosung von kirchlichen Gebäuden; ~ **division of England** kirchliche Gebietsgliederung Englands; ~ **jurisdiction** kirchliche Gerichtsbarkeit; ~ **law** Kirchenrecht; ~ **property** Kirchenvermögen; ~ **things** kirchliche Vermögensgegenstände.

echelon Staffel *f*, Befehlsebene *f*, Rang *m*; **higher ~s** höhere Chargen.

ecology Ökologie *f*; **natural** ~ Landschaftsökologie

econometrics Ökonometrie *f*.

economic wirtschaftlich, Wirtschafts ... (= *W*), volkswirtschaftlich, geschäftlich; wirtschaftswissenschaftlich; **E~ and Monetary Union** Wirtschafts- und Währungsunion; ~ **friction** wirtschaftlicher Reibungskoeffizient; ~ **interpenetration** wirtschaftliches Zusammenwachsen (*EG*); ~ **law** ökonomisches Gesetz; ~ **policy restraints** *w*politische Zwänge; ~ **self-sufficiency** Autarkie.

economical wirtschaftlich; sparsam, rationell.

economics Volkswirtschaftslehre *f*; Ökonomik *f*; Nationalökonomie *f*; ~ **minister** Wirtschaftsminister; **applied** ~ angewandte Volkswirtschaft; **consumer** ~ Verbrauchswirtschaft; **monetary** ~ Geldwirtschaft; **oil and gas** ~ die wirtschaftl Seite der Öl- und Erdgasförderung.

economising on cost Kostenersparnis.

economist Volkswirt *m*, Nationalökonom *m*; **business** ~ → *business;* **rural** ~ Agrarwirtschaftler.

economize sparsam wirtschaften.

economy Volkswirtschaft *f*, Wirtschaft *f* (= *W bzw ...w*); Wirtschaftlichkeit *f*, Sparsamkeit *f*; **~ies of scale** Größenvorteile, Großbetriebsvorteile; **agricultural** ~ Agrar*w*; **barter** ~ Tausch*w*; **competitive** ~ Wettbewerbs*w*; freie Markt*w*; **controlled** ~ gelenkte

W, Plan*w*, Zwangs*w*; **external** ~ Außen*w*; **internal** ~ Binnen*w*, innerbetriebliche Rationalisierung; **mixed** ~ gemischte *W-s*form; **monetary** ~ Geld*w*; **national** ~ Volkswirtschaft, Nationalökonomie; **political** ~ Volks*w*, Nationalökonomie, Volkswirtschaftslehre, *W-s*wissenschaften; **public** ~ Volkswirtschaftslehre, Nationalökonomie; **social** ~ Nationalökonomie; **uncontrolled** ~ freie Markt*w*; **world** ~ Welt*w*.

ECU (=) *European Currency Unit* Europäische Währungseinheit *f*.

edict Edikt *n*, Erlaß *m*, Verordnung *f*.

edit redigieren, herausgeben.

edition Auflage *f*, Ausgabe *f*; **abridged** ~ gekürzte Ausgabe; **best** ~ die beste Auflage (*Copyright-Hinterlegung*); **corrected** ~ verbesserte Auflage; **new** ~ Neuausgabe; **revised** ~ neu bearbeitete Auflage, revidierte Auflage; **surreptitious** ~ heimlicher Nachdruck.

editor Herausgeber *m*, Chefredakteur *m*, Redakteur *m*; ~ **in chief** Chefredakteur; **city** ~ Lokalredakteur; **prison** ~ „Sitzredakteur" (*Redaktionsmitglied, das Haftstrafe für die Redaktion verbüßt*); **sub** ~ Hilfsredakteur.

editus verkündet; geboren.

education Erziehung *f*, Bildungswesen *n*, Pädagogik *f*; Bildung *f*, Vorbildung *f*; ~ **code** Mindestanforderungen für Volksschulzuschüsse; ~ **committee** örtlicher Ausschuß für Unterrichtsfragen; ~ **department** Erziehungsministerium; ~ **in a reformatory** Erziehung in einer geschlossenen Anstalt; ~ **in approved school** Fürsorgeerziehung; ~ **of road users** Verkehrserziehung; **adult** ~ Erwachsenenbildung; **agricultural** ~ landwirtschaftliches Fachschulwesen; **board of** ~ Schulbehörde; **Board of** ~ Erziehungsministerium; **commercial** ~ Handelschulausbildung; **compulsory** ~ allgemeine Schulpflicht; **elementary** ~ Volksschulbildung, Grundschulbildung; Schulwesen der Elementarstufe; **further** ~ Berufs- u. Fachschulausbildung; **legal** ~ juristische Ausbildung; **Minister of E**~ Erziehungsminister; **primary** ~ Grundschulerziehung; **prisoners'** ~ Gefangenenschulwesen; **public** ~ öffentliches Schulwesen, Schulbildung an öffentlichen Schulen; **religious** ~ Religionsunterricht; **secondary** ~ höhere Schulbildung; **tertiary** ~ Hochschulausbildung; **vocational** ~ berufliche Schulbildung Berufsschulwesen.

educational background → *background*; ~ **endowment** Stiftung für Schulzwecke; ~ **establishment** Bildungseinrichtung; ~ **expenses** Fortbildungskosten; ~ **grants** Beihilfen im Bildungsbereich; ~ **institution** → *institution*.

EEC = *European Economic Community* → *European*.

efface auslöschen, tilgen.

effect *s* Wirkung *f*, Wirksamkeit *f*, Folge *f*, Ergebnis *n*, Resultat *n*, Inhalt *m* e–r Urkunde; Rechtswirksamkeit *f*; ~**s of the injury** Verletzungsfolgen; **collateral** ~ Nebenwirkung; **coming into** ~ Inkrafttreten; **legal** ~ rechtliche Wirkung, Rechtswirksamkeit; **retrospective** ~ rückwirkende Kraft, Rückwirkung; **to bring into** ~ zur Ausführung bringen; **to prosecute an action with** ~ erfolgreich klagen; **to take** ~ wirksam werden; **to that** ~ dementsprechend, mit der (*betr.*) Wirkung.

effect *v* bewerkstelligen, zustandebringen, bewirken; ~ **a payment** Zahlung leisten; ~ **an application** e–e Anmeldung tätigen; ~ **service (on)** Zustellung (an ...) vornehmen; **acceptance shall be** ~**ed** die Annahme hat zu erfolgen.

effective wirkungsvoll, rechtswirksam, tatsächlich wirksam; ~ **date** → *date;* ~ **in law** rechtswirksam; ~ **money** → *money*; ~ **rate (of interest)** → *rate*; ~ **value** Effektivwert; **being** ~ **forthwith** mit sofortiger Wirkung; **to become** ~ in Kraft treten.

effects Habe *f*; bewegliches Vermögen *n*; Wertpapiere *n/pl*, Wechsel *m*, Kassenbestand *m*; **personal** ~ persönliche Habe, persönliche Gebrauchsgegenstände; **real and personal** ~ das gesamte Vermögen; **uncleared** ~ eingezahlte, noch nicht eingelöste Schecks.
effectual wirksam, gültig.
effectuate bewirken, bewerkstelligen.
efficacious wirksam, wirkungsvoll.
efficacy Wirksamkeit *f*, Kraft *f*.
efficiency Leistungsfähigkeit *f*, Effizienz *f*, rationelles Wirtschaften *n*; ~ **bonus** Leistungsprämie, Leistungszulage; ~ **bonus plan** Leistungsprämiensystem; ~ **principle** Leistungsprinzip; ~ **rating** Leistungsbewertung (*Arbeitnehmer*); ~ **record** Leistungsangaben in der Personalakte; ~ **report** dienstliche Beurteilung *e–s Beamten*; **commercial** ~ Wirtschaftlichkeit; **operating** ~ betriebliche Leistungsfähigkeit.
efficient leistungsfähig, tüchtig; ~ **cause** die eine Kausalreihe auslösende Ursache; ~ **farming** leistungsfähige landwirtschaftliche Nutzung; ~ **instruction** wirksamer Unterricht (*Kinder*); ~ **intervening cause** = *intervening cause* → *cause*; ~ **state to resume servive** wieder fahrbereiter Zustand (*Schiff*).
effigy Nachbildung *f*, plastisches Abbild *n*.
effluent Ablaß *m*, Abfluß *m*; ~ **fees** Abwässergebühren, Kanalgebühren; **trade** ~ Absatzgebiet.
efflux Zeitablauf *m*, Abfluß *m*; ~ **of gold** Goldabfluß.
effluxion of time Zeitablauf *m*.
effort Bemühung *f*, Anstrengung *f*, Betreben *n*; **combined** ~ gemeinsame Anstrengung.
effraction gewaltsames Durchbrechen *n*, Aufbrechen *n bzw* Einbrechen *n*.
egalitarian gleichmacherisch.
egg-shell skull principle *Grundsatz der Haftungskausalität auch bei naturbedingter Verletzlichkeit des Opfers*.
egress Zugang *m*, Zutritt *m*; ~ **and regress** das Recht ein Grundstück wiederholt zu betreten.
eire *hist* Route *f* der Reiserichter.
eject hinauswerfen, zwangsräumen; ~ **a tenant** die Zwangsräumung gegen einen Mieter (bzw Pächter) betreiben.
ejection Zwangsräumung *f*, Besitzentziehung *f*.
ejectment Zwangsräumung *f*; ~ **bill** Räumungs- und Rechnungslegungsklage gegen Landpächter; **action of** ~ → *action*; **equitable** ~ Klage auf Herausgabe des verkauften Grundstücks; **justice** ~ Zwangsräumungsverfahren.
ejector Räumungsgläubiger *m*; **casual** ~ fiktiver Räumungskläger (*aus zufällig erworbenem Besitz*).
ejuration Verzicht *m*.
ejusdem generis (rule) *Auslegungsregel der Beschränkung e–s Sammelbegriffs auf Gegenstände der aufgezählten Art*.
elaborate *adj* sorgfältig ausgearbeitet; ~ **account** spezifizierte Rechnung.
elaborate *v* ausarbeiten, substantiieren, spezifizieren.
elaboration Ausarbeitung *f*, Vollendung *f*, Verfeinerung *f*.
elapse ablaufen.
elder statesman → *statesman*; ~ **title** Rechtstitel mit besserer Priorität.
eldest child das älteste (*beim Erbfall lebende*) Kind; ~ **male issue** der älteste männliche Nachkomme; ~ **male lineal descendant** der älteste männliche Nachkomme gerader Linie.
elect *adj* ausgewählt, designiert.
elect *v* wählen, auswählen, optieren, sich entscheiden (*für bzw gegen etwas*); ~ **a domicile** e–n Wohnsitz begründen; ~**ed official** Wahlbeamter; **right to** ~ → *right*.
electable wahlfähig, wählbar.
election Wahl *f*, Ausübung *f* e–r Ersetzungsbefugnis *f*; Ausübung *f* e–s Wahlrechts; ~ **agent** Wahlagent, Wahlkampfbeauftragter; ~ **auditor** Wahlprüfer; ~ **board** Wahlausschuß; ~ **bribe** Wahlbestechung *pl* (*unseriöse*) Wahlversprechungen; ~

by direct universal suffrage allgemeine Wahlen; ~ by party tickets Listenwahl; ~ campaign Wahlkampagne; ~ commission Wahluntersuchungskommission; ~ committee Wahlausschuß; ~ contest Wahlanfechtung; ~ district Wahlkreis; ~ dower Witwenpflichtteil (*alternativ zur letztwilligen Zuwendung*); ~ expenses Wahlkosten des Kandidaten; ~ judge Wahlprüfungsrichter; ~ manifesto Wahlmanifest, Wahlprogramm; ~ of remedies Festlegung auf e–n Rechtsbehelf; ~ officer Wahlleiter; ~ petition → *petition*; ~ platform Wahlprogramm; ~ pledges Wahlversprechungen; ~ rally Wahlversammlung; ~ returns Wahlergebnis; ~ turnout Wahlbeteiligung; by- ~ Nachwahl; close ~ knappe Wahl; closely contested ~ umstrittene Wahl; eligible for ~ → *eligible;* equitable ~ Entscheidung für e–e alternative Zuwendung; general ~s allgemeine Wahlen; local ~ Gemeindewahl; mayoral ~s Bürgermeisterwahl(en) off-year ~s Zwischenwahlen; parliamentary ~s Parlamentswahlen; preliminary ~s Vorwahl; primary ~s interne Parteiwahlen *zur Nominierung von Kandidaten,* Vorwahlen; recall ~ Abwahl; regular ~ regelmäßige Wahl; right of ~ Wahlbefugnis; special ~ Nachwahl, außerordentliche Wahl; to stand for ~ kandidieren; uncontested ~ Wahl ohne Gegenkandidaten.

electioneer Agitator *m*, Wahltaktiker *m*.

elective wählbar, von der Ausübung e–r Wahlbefugnis abhängig.

elector Wähler *m*; **~s' list** Wählerliste; **registered qualified ~** Wahlberechtigter.

electoral Wahl ...; **~ area** Wahlbezirk; **~ capacity** Wahlberechtigung; **~ college** Wahlmännerkollegium; **E~ Commission** (*richterliche*) Wahluntersuchungskommission; **~ corrupt practices** Wahlbestechung; **~ count** Wahlzählung; **~ division** Wahlbezirk (*für Neuwahlen*); **~ process** Wahlverfahren; **~ rot** Wählerschwund.

electorate Wählerschaft *f*.

electrocute auf dem elektrischen Stuhl hinrichten.

electrocution Hinrichtung *f* auf dem elektrischen Stuhl.

electronic data processing (*EDP*) elektronische Datenverarbeitung *f* (*EDV*).

eleemosynary karitativ, mildtätig, Almosen ...; **~ corporation** → *corporation*.

elegit Vollstreckungsverfahren *n* (*alternativ zu fieri facias qv, GB, bis 1956*); Zwangsverwaltung *f*; **~ creditor** Vollstreckungsgläubiger (*bei e–m Elegit-Verfahren*); **tenant by ~** zwangsverwaltender Gläubiger; **writ of ~** → *writ*.

element Bauelement *n*, Bestandteil *m*; Tatbestandsmerkmal *n*; **~ of an offence** (Straf-) Tatbestandsmerkmal; **common ~s** *Bestandteile des Anwesens im Gemeinschaftseigentum;* **constituent ~s** Tatbestandsmerkmale; **mental ~** innere Tatseite, subjektives Tatbestandsmerkmal; **essential ~s** Grundbestandteile; **structural ~s** Bauteile; **the ~s** die (*Natur*)Elemente.

elemental elementar, wesentlich, grundlegend.

eligibility passives Wahlrecht *n*, Wahlfähigkeit *f*; Qualifikation *f*, Eignung *f*; Fähigkeit *f* zur Bekleidung e–s Amtes; **~ for benefits** *ins* Leistungsvoraussetzungen; **~ for naturalization** Einbürgerungsfähigkeit; **~ for office** Voraussetzungen für ein Amt, Einstellungsfähigkeit **~ for vacation** Urlaubsberechtigung; **~ requirements** Berechtigungserfordernisse; **~ rules** Berechtigungsvorschriften.

eligible wählbar, die Voraussetzungen erfüllend, berechtigt, anwartschaftsberechtigt, bezugsberechtigt; geeignet, akzeptabel; **~ for a discount** rabattfähig; **~ for a pension** pensionsanwartschaftsberechtigt; ~ **for appointment** in Betracht kommender Bewerber; ~ **for discount** diskontfähig; ~ **for election** passiv wahlberechtigt; ~ **for membership** mitgliedschaftsfähig; ~ **for re-election** wiederwählbar; ~ **to serve as collateral** beleihbar; ~ **to sit the examination** prüfungsteilnahmeberechtigt; ~ **to vote** wahlfähig, wahlberechtigt.

elimination Eliminierung *f*, Ausschaltung *f*, Beseitigung *f*, Streichung *f*, Verbannung *f*; ~ **of competition** Ausschaltung der Konkurrenz; ~ **of customs barriers** Abbau der Zollschranken.

ellipsis Ellipse *f*, Auslassung *f* von Worten oder Teilsätzen ohne Sinnveränderung.

eloign entfernen, unbekannt verziehen.

eloignment Entfernung *f* (*aus dem Amtsbezirk bzw dem Zugriffsbereich*).

elongatus Unzustellbarkeitsbescheinigung *f* (*Adressat verzogen*).

elope entlaufen, durchgehen.

elopement böswilliges Verlassen *n zum Zwecke des ehebrecherischen Konkubinats*; Verlassen *n* der elterlichen Wohnung *zum Zwecke e–r nicht gestatteten Heirat*; Sich-Entführen-Lassen *n*, Fortlaufen *n*.

eloquence Beredsamkeit *f*, Redegabe *f*, Eloquenz *f*.

eloquent beredt, redebegabt, redegewandt.

elsewhere sonstwo, anderwärts, an e–m anderen Ort (*bzw Hafen*).

elucidate erläutern, klarstellen, deutlich machen.

elucidation Erklärung *f*, Erläuterung *f*.

elude sich entziehen, umgehen, ausweichen.

emanate ausgehen von, herrühren von, ausströmen, ausstrahlen von.

emanation of the Crown Organ *n* der Krone, Beauftragter *m* der Krone.

emancipation Emanzipation *f*, bürgerliche Gleichstellung *f*, Volljährigwerden *n*, Volljährigkeitserklärung *f*, Verzicht *m auf elterliche Gewalt*; ~ **proclamation** Sklavenbefreiungs-Proklamation (*zB USA 1863*); **partial** ~ Einräumung der partiellen Geschäftsfähigkeit.

embargo Embargo *n*, Sperre *f*, Handelssperre *f*, Handelsverbot *n*, Liefersperre *f*, Beschlagnahme *f*, Hafensperre *f*; ~ **on gold** = *gold* ~ *qv*; ~ **on ships** Schiffahrtssperre; **civil** ~ Schiffsarrest; **hostile** ~ Embargo gegen Schiffe e–s feindlichen (*oder voraussichtlich feindlichen*) Staates; **mandatory** ~ verbindliche Sperre.

embark sich einschiffen, an Bord gehen, einsteigen.

embarkation Einschiffung *f*.

embarrass in Verlegenheit bringen, Obstruktion treiben.

embassage Einsetzung *f* e–s Botschafters.

embassy Botschaft *f*, Botschaftsgebäude *n*; ~ **counsellor** Botschaftsrat; ~ **documents** konsularisch legalisierte Urkunden (*bes Außenhandelsrechnungen*); ~ **premises** Botschafts- *bzw* Gesandtschaftsgrundstück; ~ **staff** Botschaftspersonal.

embedded fest eingefügt.

embezzle Untreue begehen, veruntreuen; unterschlagen.

embezzlement Untreue *f*, Veruntreuung *f*, Unterschlagung *f* (*GB bis 1968*).

embezzler Veruntreuer *m*.

emblem of sovereignty Staatssymbol *n*, Staatswappen *n*, Staatsflagge *f*.

emblements Feldfrüchte *f/pl*, Ernte *f* auf dem Halm; **right to** ~ das Recht des Aberntens, das Recht auf Ernte der eigenen Saat.

embodiment Inkarnation *f*, Personifikation *f*, Verkörperung *f*, Realisierung *f*, Aufnahme *f*, Einfügung *f*.

embod|y verkörpern, eingliedern; **to be ~ied in a law** in e–m Gesetz enthalten sein.

embrace annehmen, ergreifen, umfassen, sich umarmen; ~ **an opportunity** e–e günstige Gelegenheit wahrnehmen.

embracery *obs* Geschworenenbestechung *f*.

emendation Textverbesserung *f*.

emendatory textverbessernd.

emerge auftauchen, sich herausstellen, hervorgehen aus.

emergency Notlage *f*, Notstand *m*, Ernstfall *m*, Notfall *m*, Krise *f*, Krisenfall *m*; ~ **address** Notadressat; ~ **assignment** Sondereinsatz (*in Notfällen*); ~ **board** Notstandskommission (*Schlichtung von Arbeitskämpfen); ~* **call** Notruf; ~ **clause** Gefahrenklausel; ~ **decree** Notverordnung; ~ **legislation** Krisengesetzgebung, Notstandsgesetze; ~ **measures** Notmaßnahmen; ~ **period** Dauer des Krisenzustandes; ~ **powers** Notstandsermächtigung, außerordentliche Vollmachten; ~ **provisions** Notstandsbestimmungen; ~ **ration** eiserne Ration; ~ **repairs** dringend notwendige Reparaturen; ~ **sale** Notverkauf; ~ **stocks** Krisenbestände; **national** ~ Staatsnotstand.

emigrant Emigrant *m*, Auswanderer *m*; ~ **agent** Fremdarbeiterwerber; ~ **runner** Auswanderungsvermittler; ~ **ship** Auswandererschiff; **advisory board of** ~**s** Auswanderungsberatungsstelle.

emigrate auswandern.

emigration Auswanderung *f*; ~ **of capital** Kapitalabwanderung; ~ **of companies** Sitzverlegung von Gesellschaften ins Ausland; ~ **officers** Beamte der Auswanderungsbehörde.

eminence Erhebung *f*, hohe Stellung *f*, hoher Rang *m*, Ruhm *m*.

eminent ausgezeichnet, herrschend, berühmt, hervorragend; ~ **domain** Enteignungsrecht des Staates; hoheitliches Obereigentum (*an Grund und Boden*).

emissary Abgesandter *m*.

emission Ausscheidung *f*, Auswurf *m*, Ausgabe *f*|*pl* Abgase; ~**s of gaseous pollutions** umweltschädliche Abgase; ~ **standards** Abgasnormen; **car** ~**s** Autoabgase; **gaseous** ~**s** Abgase; **particle** ~**s** Feststoff-Emissionen.

emit ausgeben, emittieren, begeben, auswerfen; ~ **bills of credit** Papiergeld emittieren.

emitter Aussteller *m*, Emittent *m*.

emmenagogues menstruationsfördernde Mittel (*zur Abtreibung verwendbar*).

emolument Vergütung *f*, Entlohnung *f*; ~**s** Einkünfte *f*|*pl*, Bezüge *m*|*pl*, Tantiemen *f*|*pl*, Ausschüttungen *f*|*pl*; **casual** ~**s** Gelegenheitseinkünfte; **foreign** ~**s** Auslandsbezüge; **official** ~**s** Bezüge; **pensionable** ~**s** Bezüge mit Pensionsberechtigung.

emphyteusis Erbpacht *f*.

emphyteuta Erbpächter *m*.

emphyteutic erbpachtlich; ~ **lease** Erbpacht.

empire Reich *n*, Imperium *n*, Kaiserreich *n*; **the E**~ das britische Weltreich; **E**~ **City** Beiname von New York; ~ **goods** Waren aus den Empire-Ländern; ~ **settlement** (*Förderung der*) Besiedlung der britischen überseeischen Gebiete; **E**~ **State** *Beiname des Staates New York.*

emplead anklagen.

employ *s* Dienste *m*|*pl*, Beschäftigungsverhältnis *n*.

employ *v* anwenden, verwenden; einstellen, beschäftigen, einsetzen; ~ **ed earner** Arbeitnehmer; ~~*'s employment: Arbeitsverhältnis;* ~ **ed in a process** bei (*bzw mit*) e–m Verfahren beschäftigt; ~**ed inventor** Arbeitnehmererfinder; ~**ed person** Arbeitnehmer; **gainfully** ~**ed** gegen Entgelt beschäftigt; **permanently** ~**ed** vollbeschäftigt; **self-**~**ed person** Freiberufler, Selbständiger.

employee Arbeitnehmer *m*, Angestellter *m*; ~ **achievement award** Leistungsauszeichnung für Betriebsangehörige; ~**s' beneficiary associations** Arbeiterwohlfahrtsvereine; ~**s' benefits** Sozialleistungen; ~ **consultation** beratende

Mitwirkung von Arbeitnehmern; **~'s duties** Arbeitnehmerpflichten; **~'s invention** Arbeitnehmererfindung, Betriebserfindung; **~ on short time** auf Kurzarbeit gesetzter Arbeitnehmer; **~ participation in company operations** betriebl Mitbestimmung; **~ profit sharing** Gewinnbeteiligung der Arbeitnehmer; **~s' representative** Arbeitnehmervertreter; **~s' security company** Arbeitnehmerpensionsfond (*in Form e–r Investmentgesellschaft*); **~ stock** Belegschaftsaktion; **~ stock bonus** Gratisaktion; **~ trust** Pensionsstiftung; **black-coated ~** *brit* höherer Angestellter; **borrowed ~** Leiharbeitnehmer; **casual ~** gelegentlich Beschäftigter; **executive ~** leitender Angestellter; **higher-paid ~s** höhere Angestellte; **loaned ~** Leiharbeitnehmer; **permanent ~** Beamter, Mitarbeiter in Dauerstellung; **salaried ~** Angestellter, Gehaltsempfänger.

employer Arbeitgeber *m*, Dienstherr *m*, Unternehmer *m*, (Werkvertrags-) Besteller *m*; **~s' association** Arbeitgeberverband; **~'s contribution** → *contribution*; **~ for hire** Auftraggeber (*bei Dienstvertrag*); **associated ~s** Konzernarbeitgeber; **~'s duties** Arbeitgeberpflichten; **E~s' (Compulsory Insurance) Act** Haftpflichtversicherungsgesetz für Unternehmer; **~'s liability** Arbeitgeberhaftung (*bei Arbeitsunfällen*); **~s' liability insurance** → *insurance*; **~'s prerogative to dismiss** das grundsätzliche Entlassungsrecht des Arbeitgebers; **British E~s' Confederation** brit. Arbeitgeberverband, *Dachverband der brit Unternehmer*.

employment berufliche Tätigkeit *f*, Arbeitsverhältnis *n*, unselbständige Arbeit *f*, Anstellung *f*, Einstellung *f*; Mandierung *f*; **~ agency** Stellenvermittlung, Arbeitsvermittlungsfirma; gewerblicher Arbeitsvermittler; **~ applicant** Arbeitssuchender; **~ bureau** Stellennachweis; **~ contract** Dienstvertrag, Arbeitsvertrag; **E~ Appeal Tribunal** Berufungsschiedstelle in Arbeitssachen; *etwa*: Landesarbeitsgericht; **~ exchange** Arbeitsamt; **~ for hire** Dienstvertrag; entgeltliche Beschäftigung; **~ in domestic service** Beschäftigung als Hausangestellte(r); **~ market** Stellenmarkt; **~ of a casual nature** Gelegenheitsbeschäftigung; **~ of capital** Kapitalanlage; **E~ of Children Act** JugendarbeitsschutzG; **~ of counsel** Mandierung e–s Wahlverteidigers; **~ of force** Gewaltanwendung; **~ of labo(u)r** Arbeitseinsatz; **~ office** Arbeitsamt, Stellenvermittlung(sbüro); **~ on trial** Probearbeitsverhältnis, Anstellung zur Probe; **~ opportunity** Beschäftigungsmöglichkeit; **~ permit** Arbeitserlaubnis; **~ placement service** amtliche Arbeitsvermittlung; **E~ Protection Act** Kündigungsschutzgesetz (GB, 1975); **~ protection compensation** Abfindung wegen Verlust des Arbeitsplatzes; **~ protection rights** Arbeitnehmerschutzrechte; KündigungsschutzG; **~ rate** Beschäftigungsrate (*Anteil der Beschäftigten am Arbeitskräftepotential*); **~ security** gesicherter Arbeitsplatz; **~ service** Stellenvermittlung; **~ tax** → *tax;* **~ situation** Arbeitsmarktlage; **~ volume** Beschäftigungsvolumen; **casual ~** Gelegenheitsbeschäftigung; **common ~** gemeinsames Beschäftigungsverhältnis; Haftungsausschluß für Verrichtungsgehilfen (*bei Schäden durch Arbeitskollegen*); **continuous ~** Dauerarbeitsverhältnis; Dauerbeschäftigung; **contracted-out ~** von der (Renten)-Versicherungspflicht freiwillig befreites Arbeitsverhältnis; **contract of ~** → *contract*; **full ~** Vollbeschäftigung; **full-time ~** hauptamtliche Beschäftigung; **hazardous ~** gefahrgeneigte Beschäftigung; **loan ~** Leiharbeitsverhältnis; **National Re-~ Service** Bundesumschulungsdienst *US*; **out of ~** stellenlos; **part-time ~** Nebenbeschäftigung;

pensionable ~ pensionsberechtigte Stellung; **permanent** ~ Dauerstellung; **place of** ~ → *place*; **primary** ~ Arbeitsplätze durch Direktinvestitionen; **private** ~ privates Arbeitsverhältnis; **probationary** ~ Probeanstellung; **professional** ~ Beschäftigung eines Akademikers; **public** ~ öffentlicher Dienst, Staatsdienst; **regular** ~ feste Anstellung, ständiges Arbeitsverhältnis; **safety in** ~ Arbeitsschutz; **salaried** ~ Beschäftigung im Angestelltenverhältnis; **sideline** ~ Nebenbeschäftigung; **suitable alternative** ~ geeignete Ersatzbeschäftigung; **terms and conditions of** ~ allgemeine Anstellungsbedingungen; **to enter into** ~ Arbeit aufnehmen (*Ausländer*); **to terminate the** ~ das Arbeitsverhältnis kündigen, das Arbeitsverhältnis beenden.

emporium Großhandelsgeschäft *n* in e–r Hafenstadt, Stapelplatz *m*, Magazin *n*.

empower bevollmächtigen, ermächtigen.

empties Leergut *n*; ~ **returned** Leergut zurück.

emptor Käufer *m*.

en autre droit in fremdem Recht.

en route unterwegs, en route.

en ventre sa mère im Mutterleib, nasciturus, noch nicht geboren

enable befähigen, ermächtigen.

enabling legislation Ermächtigungsgesetze; Anpassungsgesetze; ~ **power** Ermächtigung, Vollmacht; *bes* Ermächtigung des Grundeigentümers an den Pächter zur Bestellung dingl Rechte am Grundstück; ~ **statute** Gesetz mit delegierten Befugnissen, Gesetz mit dispositiven Rechtsvorschriften; Gesetz mit heilender Kraft.

enact verordnen, Gesetzeskraft verleihen, (Gesetz) in Kraft setzen, verabschieden, erlassen; ~**ed law** → *law*; **be it** ~**ed as follows** es wird folgendes Gesetz beschlossen.

enacting clause Gesetzesformel *f*; ~ **words** Gesetzesformel.

enactment Gesetz, Rechtsverordnung, gesetzliche Bestimmung *f*, Teil *m* e–s Gesetzes; ~ **date** Tag des Inkrafttretens; **legislative** ~ Gesetz, Rechtsverordnung.

enactor Gesetzgeber *m*.

encapsulation Konkretisierung *f*, Ausprägung *f*; **contractual** ~ vertragliche Einbeziehung, vertragl Fixierung; **legislative** ~ gesetzliche Fassung (*e–s Rechtsgedankens*).

encashment Inkasso *n*; Einlösung (*von Fondsanteilen bzw Schecks*); **prior** ~ vorzeitige Einlösung.

encipher verschlüsseln, chiffrieren.

enclave Enklave *f*.

enclose beifügen, beilegen; **scot** die Geschworenen einschließen; ~**d area** umbauter Raum; ~**d please find** anliegend erhalten Sie.

enclosure Anlage *f*, Beilage *f*; Einfriedung *f*, Umzäunung *f*, eingezäunter Grund *m*; Entlastung von Allmenderechten.

encourage ermutigen, anspornen, bestärken, fördern, aufreizen, anstiften; ~**ing commission of crime** Anstiftung.

encouragement Ermutigung *f*, Antrieb *m*, Anspruch *m*, Forderung *f*.

encroach beeinträchtigen, eingreifen, schmälern; ~ **upon another's right** ein fremdes Recht beeinträchtigen; ~ **upon a person's functions** in fremde Zuständigkeit eingreifen; ~ **upon adjoining land** ein Nachbargrundstück beeinträchtigen.

encroachment Eingriff *m*, Übergriff *m*, Rechtsverletzung *f*, Beeinträchtigung *f*.

encumber *cf incumber*, dinglich belasten.

encumbrance *cf. incumbrance*; dingliche Belastung *f*.

encumbrancer = *incumbrancer*; dinglich Berechtigter *m* e–r Grundstücksbelastung, Gläubiger e–s Grundpfandrechts.

end *s* Ende *n*, Ziel *n*, Zweck *m*, Konsequenz *f*, Folge *f*; ~ **in itself** Selbstzweck; ~ **of month** Ultimo; ~ **of the term** Fristende; ~ **of the**

year Jahresultimo; ~ **of will** Ende des Testaments; **~– of – terrace house** Reiheneckhaus; ~ **to** ~ von e–m Ende zum anderen; ~ **use** Verwendung; ~ **user** Letztabnehmer; ~ **user's certificate** Endverbleibsbescheinigung; **private ~s** Privatzwecke; **to gain one's** ~ sein Ziel erreichen; **to this** ~ zu diesem Zweck.

end *v* aufhören, beendigen, enden; **~ed or determined** durch Zeitablauf oder Kündigung beendet.

endeavour *s* Bemühung *f*; **to use one's best ~s** sich nach besten Kräften bemühen.

endeavour *v* **to persuade** anstiften.

endorsable (= *endorseable*) = *indorsable qv* eintragungsfähig, strafpunktträchtig; ~ **offence** → *offence*.

endorse = *indorse qv*; ~ **a driving licence** Strafpunkte auf Führerschein eintragen.

endorsee = *indorsee qv*.

endorsement = *indorsement qv*; Indossament *n*, rückseitiger Bestätigungsvermerk *m*; ~ **of writ** Vervollständigung des Klageformulars (*durch kurze Begründung*); ~ **of service** Angaben auf Zustellungsurkunde (*über Zeit und Ort der Z.*), Zustellungsbescheinigung; ~ **of a driving licence** Eintrag von Strafpunkten auf dem Führerschein; ~ **of claim** Anspruchsbegründung auf Klageformular; ~ **on passport** Passeintrag; **obligatory** ~ zwingend vorgeschriebene Eintragung.

endorser = *indorser qv*.

endow stiften, ausstatten, dotieren, ein Witwenteil einräumen; **~ed charities** mildtätige (*mit Vermögen ausgestattete*) Stiftung; **~ed school** → *school*.

endowment Stiftung *f*, Dotation *f*, Zuwendung *f* e–s Witwenteils; ~ **assurance** gemischte Lebensversicherung, Versicherung auf den Todes- und Erlebensfall; Terme-fix-Versicherung; ~ **capital** Dotationskapital; ~ **fund(s)** Stiftungsvermögen; ~ **insurance** gemischte Lebensversicherung (*auf den Erlebens- bzw Todesfall*); ~ **mortgage** → *mortgage;* ~ **policy** → *policy* (*1*); **charitable** ~ mildtätige Stiftung; **permanent** ~ Stiftungskapital.

endurance test Haltbarkeitsprüfung *f*, Zuverlässigkeitsprobe *f*.

enduring nachhaltig, dauerhaft.

enduring power of attorney Dauervollmacht *f* (*formgebundene eintragungsbedürftige Vollmacht, die bei eintretender Geschäftsunfähigkeit gültig bleibt*).

enemy Feind *m*, Feindstaat *m*, Angehöriger *m* e–s Feindstaates; ~ **action** feindliche Kampfhandlung;“ ~ **goods,** ~ **ship”** Waren e–s Feindstaates auf neutralem Schiff unterliegen der Beschlagnahme; **~'s property** Feindvermögen (*und gleichgestelltes sonstiges Vermögen*); **alien** ~ → *alien;* **public** ~ Feindstaat, Angehörige e–s Feindstaates; gemeingefährlicher *flüchtiger* Verbrecher.

energy Energie *f*; ~ **balance sheet** Energielage; ~ **consumption** Energieverbrauch; ~ **crisis** Energiekrise; ~ **resources** Ressourcen im Energiebereich; ~ **saving** Energieeinsparungen; ~ **sector** Energiebereich; ~ **supply** Energieversorgung.

enfacement Vermerk *m* auf der Vorderseite e–r Urkunde.

enfeoff belehnen.

enfeoffment Belehnung *f*.

enforce erzwingen, vollziehen, vollstrecken; ~ **a judgment** aus e–m Urteil vollstrecken; ~ **a lien** ein Pfandrecht vollziehen, die Pfandverwertung vornehmen; ~ **one's rights** seine Rechte gerichtlich durchsetzen.

enforceability Durchsetzbarkeit *f*, Klagbarkeit *f*.

enforceable durchsetzbar, klagbar, erzwingbar, vollstreckbar, vollziehbar; ~ **in proceedings** einklagbar; **legally** ~ → *legally;* **provisionally** ~ vorläufig vollstreckbar.

enforcement Erzwingung *f*, Durchsetzung *f*, Vollstreckung *f*, Vollziehung *f*; ~ **notice** (Gesetzes)Vollzug

→ *notice;* ~ **of judgment debts** Zwangsvollstreckung aus Zahlungstiteln; ~ **officer** Beamter der Schutzpolizei; ~ **order** Vollstrekkungsklausel ~ **proceedings** Zwangsvollstreckung; ~ **summons** Pfändungsauftrag, Zwangsvollstreckungsbenachrichtigung; **high profile** ~ strenger u effizienter Gesetzesvollzug; **reciprocal** ~ **of judgments** *int* gegenseitige (Anerkennung und) Vollstreckung von Urteilen.

enfranchise befreien, das Stimmrecht verleihen; Pachtbesitz in Grundeigentum umwandeln; ~**d land** von lehensrechtlichen Diensten freigestelltes Land.

enfranchisement Befreiung *f*; *hist* Sklavenbefreiung *f*; Verleihung *f* e–s Parlamentssitzes; Befreiung *f* von lehensrechtlichen Diensten; ~ **of tenancy** Umwandlung von Pachtrechten in Eigentum.

engage verpflichten, binden, einstehen für, versprechen, engagieren, anstellen, ausüben; ~ **and employ** jmdn beschäftigen; ~ **in negotiations** in Verhandlungen eintreten; ~ **seamen** Seeleute anheuern; ~**d in his employment** in Ausübung seiner Tätigkeit als Arbeitnehmer; ~**d in so discharging or receiving** während des Entladens oder Beladens; ~ **the services of a lawyer** e–n Anwalt nehmen, ... mandieren; **to be** ~**d in business** geschäftlich tätig sein.

engagement Verlöbnis *n*; Verbindlichkeit *f*, Verpflichtung *f*; Stellung *f*, Beschäftigung *f*, Engagement *n*; ~ **blank** Auftragsformular (*Prüfertätigkeit*); ~ **to marry** Verlöbnis; **contractual** ~ vertragliche Verpflichtung; **current** ~ laufende Verpflichtung; **fresh** ~ Neueinstellung; **implied** ~ stillschweigende Verpflichtung; **social** ~**s** gesellschaftliche Verpflichtungen; **without** ~ ohne Obligo, unverbindlich, freibleibend.

engender herbeiführen, hervorbringen.

engine Maschine *f*, Arbeitsvorrichtung *f*, Motor *m*, Lokomotive *f*; Folterwerkzeug *n*; **nuisance caused by** ~ Belästigung durch Maschineneinsatz.

engineer Techniker *m*, Maschinist *m*, Ingenieur *m*, Bauführer *m*; Baubetreuer *m*; Pionier *m*; **civil** ~ Bauingenieur (*für öffentliche Tiefbauarbeiten*).

engineering contract Werkvertrag (über Tiefbauarbeiten); ~ **change order** technischer Änderungsauftrag; ~ **department** Konstruktionsbüro, technische Abteilung; ~ **development** technische Entwicklung; ~ **operations** Tiefbauarbeiten; ~ **work** Tiefbau (*und sonstige Arbeiten*) mit Maschineneinsatz; **civil** ~ Tiefbau, Planung, Technik und Bauausführung öffentlicher Verkehrs- und Versorgungsanlagen; **industrial** ~ Betriebstechnik; **human** ~ Anthropotechnik; **reverse** ~ Nachkonstruktion, Nachahmung, Nachbau.

engross in Reinschrift erstellen, ausfertigen; ~**ed bill** gedruckte (Parlaments)-Vorlage; ~**ed resolution** gedruckter Entschließungsentwurf; ~**ing hand** Kanzleischrift.

engrosser Ausfertiger *m* e–r Urkunde.

engrossing Erstellung e–r Ausfertigung (*e–s Urteils etc*), Anfertigung e–r Reinschrift.

engrossment Ausfertigung *f*, Reinschrift *f*.

enhance steigern.

enhancement in value Werterhöhung, Wertsteigerung; ~ **of damages** schadenersatzerhöhende Umstände.

enjoin anordnen, durch gerichtliche Verfügung untersagen, auferlegen, verbieten.

enjoy sich (*e–s Gegenstands*) erfreuen, genießen, im Besitzgenuß sein, etwas haben, nutznießen; ~ **a privilege** ein (Vor)recht haben; ~ **a right** ein Recht haben, e. R. ausüben.

enjoyment Genuß *m*, Ausübung *f* e–

s Rechts, Nutzung *f*, Besitz *m*, Befriedigung *f*; ~ **as of right** in Ausübung e–s Nutzungsrechts; ~ **of land** Bodennutzung; **actual** ~ unmittelbarer Besitzgenuß; **adverse** ~ Ausübung e–r Grunddienstbarkeit; **beneficial** ~ eigene Nutznießung; **quiet** ~ ungestörter Besitz(genuß); Freiheit von Einwirkungen Dritter, Rechtsmängelgewähr.

enlarge erweitern, vergrößern, verlängern, befreien; ~ **an accused** e–n Angeklagten auf freien Fuß setzen; ~ **an estate** ein Herrschaftsrecht an e–m Grundstück rangmäßig verbessern (*eg Pachtbesitz zu Eigentum*); ~ **the scope of the invention** den Umfang e–r Erfindung erweitern; **~d acceptance** bedingte Annahme; **~d edition** erweiterte Ausgabe.

enlargement Ausweitung *f*, Vergrößerung *f*; ~ **of long terms** Umwandlung von langfristigen Erbpachtrechten in Grundeigentum; ~ **on bail** Aufhebung des Haftbefehls gegen Sicherheitsleistung, Freilassung gegen Bürgschaft.

enlarger l'estate Erweiterung *f* des Lebenstatus, Umwandlung *f* des Pachtbesitzes in Eigentum.

enlarging statute Erweiterungsgesetz *n*.

enlist den Wehrdienst antreten, sich zum Wehrdienst melden; **~ed men** Unteroffiziere und Mannschaften.

enlistment Anwerbung *f*, Rekrutierung *f*, Eintritt *m* in den Mannschaftsstand (*als Freiwilliger oder Eingezogener*); **foreign** ~ Anwerbung zu ausländischem Militärdienst; **foreign ~ act** Gesetz gegen Wehrdienst britischer Untertanen in fremden Staaten.

enormous enorm, schwer, erschwerend.

enquire = *inquire qv*.

enquiry = *inquiry qv*.

enrich o.s. sich bereichern.

enriched *adj* bereichert; **unjustly** ~ ungerechtfertigt bereichert.

enrichment Bereicherung *f*; **undue** ~ ungerechtfertigte Bereicherung; **unjust** ~ ungerechtfertigte Bereicherung.

enroll eintragen, registrieren, sich anmelden, sich melden; ~ **for a course** e–n Kurs belegen; ~ **in a college** immatrikulieren; **~ed bill** (*formgerecht erlassenes*) Gesetz; **~ed deeds** → *deed*; **~ed law agent** *scot* zugelassener Rechtsbeistand; **~ed member of a party** eingetragenes Parteimitglied.

enrolling officer Musterungsoffizier.

enrol(l)ment Eintragung *f*, Beitritt *m*, Hinterlegung *f* von Urkunden; ~ **of deeds** gerichtliche Eintragung und Hinterlegung von gesiegelten Urkunden (*GB bis 1925*); ~ **of vessels** Schiffseintragung (*Küsten- und Binnenschiffahrt*); ~ **office** Registratur, Gerichtsstelle zur Eintragung und Aufbewahrung von Urkunden; ~ **records** Anmeldungsunterlagen; **military** ~ **register** → *military*.

ens legis = *legal entity* → *entity*.

enschedule einfügen.

enseal mit dem Siegel versehen.

enshrinement feierliche Niederlegung (*in der Verfassung etc*).

ensue (from) folgen, danach kommen, erfolgen, sich ergeben aus.

entail *s* beschränkt (*nur an Abkömmlinge*) vererbliches Grundstückseigentum; Fideikommiß *n*, festgelegte Erbfolge *f*; **contractual** ~ **of policy** förmliche Konkretisierung von Absichten im Vertrag; **quasi** ~ fideikommißähnliche Festlegung, lebenslänglicher Nießbrauch für Erblasser und dessen leibliche Erben; **to break an** ~ Fideikommißbindung lösen.

entail *v* zur Folge haben; die Erbfolge beschränken, festlegen; **~ed estate** ~ = *estate tail qv*; **~ed interest** → *interest*.

entailment Einbeziehung *f* in ein Fideikommiß; *bes* Festlegung *f* der Erbfolge.

entangle verwickeln, verstricken, verwirren.

entanglement Verwicklung *f*, Verstrickung *f*, Verwirrung *f*; **external ~s** außenpolitische Verwicklung; **no foreign ~s!** keine Auslandsverstrickungen! (*Schlagwort der Isolationisten, US*).

enter betreten, eindringen, einreichen, eintragen; **~ a plea** Einrede erheben; **~ a protest** Protest erheben; **~ an appearance** → *appearance* sich auf e–en Prozeß einlassen; **~ into a contract** → *contract*; **~ into a recognizance** sich gegenüber dem Gericht verpflichten; **~ into an agreement** e–n Vertrag abschließen; **~ into negotiations** in Verhandlungen eintreten; **~ judgment** → *judgment*; **~ objections to a statement** Einwände gegen eine Darstellung erheben; **~ on the record** eintragen, registrieren, protokollieren; **~ on the reference** das Schiedsrichteramt annehmen; **~ upon an inheritance** Erbschaft antreten; **~ upon an office** ein Amt antreten; **~ing short** Gutschrift „Eingang vorbehalten", vorläufige Verbuchung eines Wechseleingangs; **to ~ short** unter Wert deklarieren.

enterprise Spekulation *f*, Unternehmen *n*, Unternehmungsgeist *m*, Geschäft *n*, gefahrengeneigte Arbeit *f*; **~ accounting** Rechnungswesen des Gesamtunternehmens; **~ zone** Gewerbegebiet, Gewerbeentwicklungsgebiet (*in sanierungsbedürftigen Stadtbezirken, Steuervergünstigungen, GB*); **business ~** Geschäftsunternehmung; **commercial ~** Handelsunternehmen; **corporate ~** Kapitalgesellschaft; **domestic ~** Inlandsunternehmen; **free ~** freies Unternehmertum; **free ~ economy** freie Wirtschaft, private Wirtschaft, Privatunternehmen; **industrial ~** Industrieunternehmen; **joint ~** Gelegenheitsgesellschaft; Gemeinschaftsunternehmen (*ähnlich BGB Gesellschaft*); **manufacturing ~** Fertigungsbetrieb; **mixed ~** gemischtwirtschaftliches Unternehmen; **mutual ~** genossenschaftliches Unternehmen; **national ~** Staatsbetrieb; **nonprofit ~** gemeinnütziges (*nicht gewinnbringendes*) Unternehmen; **publicly owned ~** öffentliches Unternehmen, Staatsbetrieb; **state ~** → *state* (*2*); **trading ~** Handelsunternehmen.

entertain aufrechterhalten; unterhalten.

entertainer Bühnenkünstler *m*, Darsteller *m*; **public ~** Schausteller.

entertainment Unterhaltung *f*, Vergnügung *f*; **~ allowance** Aufwandsentschädigung; **~ business** Vergnügungsindustrie; **~s duty** Vergnügungssteuer, Kinoabgabe; **~ tax** → *tax*, **exempt ~s** erlaubte Vergnügungsspiele.

entice (away) verleiten, verführen, abwerben, abspenstig machen.

enticement Verlockung *f*, Abwerbung *f*; **~ of servant** Abwerbung e–s Bediensteten.

entire ganz, vollständig, unvermischt; **~ loss of sight** (*so gut wie*) vollständiger Verlust des Sehvermögens.

entirely without understanding geschäftsunfähig, deliktsunfähig.

entirety das Ganze, Gesamtheit *f*; Ungeteiltheit *f*, etwas als Einheit, etwas Unteilbares; **~ of interest** Gesamthandsberechtigung; **tenancy by ~ies** Gesamtberechtigung von Ehegatten (*an Grundbesitz*); eheliche Gütergemeinschaft (*an Grundstücken*), (= *tenancy by the entirety*), *GB bis 1925*).

entitle berechtigen, ein Recht haben.

entitled berechtigt, anspruchsberechtigt; **~ for the time being** jeweils anspruchsberechtigt; **~ in (his) own right** aus eigenem Recht; **~ in immediate expectancy** anwartschaftsberechtigt; **~ in possession** besitzend, Anspruch auf Besitz habend; **~ party** die berechtigte Partei; **~ to a pension** pensionsberechtigt; **~ to act** handlungsfähig, handlungsbefugt; **~ to contribution** ausgleichsberechtigt; **~ to maintenance** unterhaltsberechtigt; **~ to possession** anspruchsberechtigt auf Besitz (*bzw Zahlung*); ~ **to prove** anmeldeberechtigt zur Konkurstabelle; ~ **to receive any payment** zahlungsempfangsberechtigt; ~ **to redeem** einlösungsberechtigt; ~ **to sue** aktiv legitimiert, Prozeßbefugnis habend; ~ **to the dividend** dividendenberechtigt; ~ **to the income** anspruchsberechtigt auf die Einkünfte; ~ **to the receipt** forderungsberechtigt; ~ **to vote** stimmberechtigt, wahlberechtigt.

entitlement Anrecht *n*, Berechtigung *f*; Anspruch *m*; ~ **programs** ~ das soziale Netz; soziale Rechtsansprüche; ~ **to benefits** *ins* Leistungsberechtigung; ~ **to costs** Kostenerstattungsanspruch; ~ **to preference** Präferenzberechtigung.

entity Wesen *n*, Gebilde *n*, Rechtsträger *m*, **distinct** ~ eigenständiges Ganzes, unverwechselbares Ganzes; **legal** ~ juristische Person, Rechtspersönlichkeit, rechtliche Existenz.

entrance Antritt *m*, Eintritt *m*.

entrant Eintretender *m*, Einreisender, einreisende Person; Besucher *m*, neues Mitglied *n*; **illegal** ~ widerrechtlich Einreisender.

entrapment das Provozieren e–r strafbaren Handlung (*zur Überführung des Täters*).

entrapping person agent provocateur, Lockspitzel *n*.

entreat bitten, ersuchen.

entrepot Lager *n*, Transitlager *n*, Umschlagplatz, Speicher *m*, Lager *n* im Freihafen; ~ **trade** Reexporthandel, Freihafenhandel, Transithandel, *bei dem die Ware über das Land des Transithändlers geleitet wird.*

entrepreneur Unternehmer *m*.

entrepreneurial unternehmerisch.

entrepreneurship Unternehmertum *n*, Unternehmergeist *m*.

entrust anvertrauen, betrauen.

entry Eintreten *n*, Betreten *n*, Besitzergreifung *f* (*von Pachtland durch den Verpächter*); Inbesitznahme, Besitzübernahme (*nur Grundstücke*); Eintragung *f*, Einbringung *f*, *scot* Erbbestätigung *f* durch den Grundherrn; ~ **by court** gerichtliche Besitzeinweisung (*bei Enteignung*); ~ **by intimidation** Eindringen durch Einschüchterung; ~ **by legal process** Zutritt im gerichtl Auftrag; ~ **clearance** Einreiseerlaubnis; ~ **clearance officer** Einreisebeamter; ~ **for marriage in speech** Herausgabeklage wegen Nichteinhaltung des Heiratsversprechens; ~ **of appearance** *formelle* Einlassungserklärung (*zu Beginn des Prozesses*); ~ **for trail** Terminsanberaumung; ~ **into possession** Besitzübernahme e–s Grundstücks durch den Hypothekengläubiger; ~ **into the Community** Eingang in die Gemeinschaft (*EG Warenverkehr*); ~ **of cause for trial** *Vorlage der Prozeßakten mit* Antrag auf Anberaumung des Verhandlungstermins; ~ **on the roll** Erklärung der Partei zu Protokoll des Gerichts; ~ **outwards** Zollausgangserklärung; ~ **permit** Einreiseerlaubnis; ~ **with intent to commit felony** Betreten in verbrecherischer Absicht; ~ **without breaking** Einschleichen; ~ **without warrant** polizeiliches Betretungsrecht ohne Durchsuchungsbefehl; **actual** ~ → *actual*; **bookkeeping** ~ → *bookkeeping*; **Books of E** ~ *hist Formularsammlung für Klagen bei Common Law Gerichten*; **closing** ~ Abschlußbuchung; **compound** ~ Sammelbuchung; **correcting** ~ → *to correct*; **credit** ~ Gutschrift; **customs** ~ → *customs*; **debit** ~ → *debit*; **double** ~ **bookkeeping** → *bookkeeping;* **false** ~ Falschbuchung; **forcible** ~ Hausfriedensbruch, gewaltsames Eindringen; **free** ~ zollfreie Einfuhr; **illegal** ~ illegale Einreise; **inferior** ~ im Rang nachgehende Eintragung; **homestead** ~ → *homestead*; **lawful** ~ gesetzlich zulässige Wiederinbesitznahme (von Grundstücken); **making false** ~ Falschbeurkundung; **mineral land** ~ *Einreichung* *e–s Besitzanspruchs auf Staatsgrund wegen Bergwerksrechts*; **no ~!** Eintritt verboten!; kein Eintrag, Fehlanzeige; **open ~** offenkundige Inbesitznahme (*unter Zeugen*); **original ~** Grundbuchung, Erstausfertigung; **perfect ~** unbeanstandete Zolldeklaration; **period-end adjusting ~** Berichtigungsbuchung (*am Ende e–r Rechnungsperiode*); **port of ~** →*port*; **pre-emption ~** Inbesitznahme von Staatsgrund und Ausübung e–s Vorkaufsrechts (*wegen Besiedelung und Erschließung*); **prime ~** vorläufige Angaben (*Zoll*); **reversing ~** Stornobuchung; **subsequent ~** spätere Eintragung, Nachtragsbuchung; **suspense ~** transitorische Buchung, vorläufige Buchung; **timber culture ~** Inbesitznahme von Staatsland auf Grund von Aufforstungsgesetzen; **to adjust an ~** e–e Buchung berichtigen; **unlawful ~** widerrechtl Landbesitznahme; **writ of ~** → *writ*.

entryman Siedler *m*, Landnehmer *m*.

enumerated aufgezählt, aufgeführt; **~ powers** Zuständigkeitskatalog.

enumeration Aufzählung *f*; **~ district** Zählbezirk.

enumerators amtliche Zähler *m*|*pl*.

enunciate ausdrücken, aussprechen, verkünden, öffentlich erklären, grundsätzlich feststellen.

enure (= *inure*) in Kraft treten, in Kraft setzen, zufallen, zugute kommen, gelten.

envelope Briefumschlag *m*, Kuvert *n*; **reply-paid ~** frankierter Rück-Antwort-Briefumschlag; **self-addressed ~** Briefumschlag mit Rücksendeadresse, Antwortumschlag; (*wenn frankiert:*) Freiumschlag.

envenom vergiften.

environment Umgebung *f*, Milieu *n* ~ policy Umweltpolitik; **marine ~** Meeresumwelt.

environmental/affairs Umweltfragen; **~ impact statement** Erklärung zu den Umweltauswirkungen (*e–s Vorhabens*); **~ influences** Umwelteinflüsse; **~ law** → *law*; **~ protection** Umweltschutz; **E ~ Protection Agency** Umweltschutzamt.

environmentally benign umweltfreundlich.

envisage beabsichtigen, betrachten, ins Auge fassen.

envoy diplomatischer Vertreter *m*, Gesandter *m*; Bote *m*, Bevollmächtigter *m*; **~ extraordinary** außerordentlicher Gesandter, bevollmächtigter Gesandter; **special ~** in besonderer Mission entsandter Vertreter, Sonderbotschafter.

episcopacy Episkopat *n*, bischöfliche Amtstätigkeit *f*.

episcopalia Kirchenabgaben *f*|*pl* an den Bischof.

epitome (of title) ununterbrochene Reihe von Eigentumsnachweisen.

equable *adj* beiden Teilen gerecht werdend, gerecht, ausgewogen.

equal gleich, paritätisch, gleichförmig, gleichmäßig, gleichwertig; **~ and uniform taxation** gleichmäßige Besteuerung; **~ benefit** gleichmäßige Begünstigung; **E ~ Opportunities Commission** (Enquête-)Kommission über ausbildungsmäßige und berufl Gleichberechtigung von Frauen (*GB seit 1975*); **E ~ Pay Act** Gleichbehandlungsgesetz für Lohnfortzahlung; **in ~ degree** gleichen Grades (*verwandt*); **in ~ parts** zu gleichen Teilen; **on ~ level** paritätisch gleichrangig.

equality Gleichheit *f*, Gleichmäßigkeit *f*, Gleichberechtigung *f*; Gleichwertigkeit *f*; **~ before the law** Gleichheit vor dem Gesetz; **~ clause** Gleichbehandlungsklausel für Frauen; **~ is equity** gleichmäßiger Berücksichtigung, entspricht dem Billigkeitsrecht; **~ of pay** Lohngleichheitsprinzip; **~ of rights** Gleichberechtigung; **~ of states** völkerrechtliche Gleichheit von Staaten; **~ of votes** Stimmengleichheit.

equalization Angleichung *f*, Gleichmachung *f*, Vereinheitlichung *f*; ~

claim Ausgleichsanspruch; ~ **of taxes** Steuerausgleich.

equalize *v/t* ausgleichen.

equate gleichsetzen, gleichmachen; **~d calculation of interest** Staffelzinsrechnung; **~d interest** Staffelzinsen, gestaffelte Zinsen.

equation Ausgleich *m*, Gleichung *f*; ~ **of payments** mittlerer Zahlungstermin; ~ **of prices** Preisausgleich; ~ **of supply and demand** Gleichgewicht von Angebot und Nachfrage; **monetary** ~ Geldausgleich.

equilibrium theory Gleichgewichtstheorie *f*, statische Preistheorie *f*.

equip ausrüsten, ausstatten.

equipment Einrichtung *f*, Ausstattung *f*, Ausrüstung *f*, Material *n*, Anlage *f*; ~ **bonds** ~ → *bond (1)*; ~ **frame** Rahmen, Chassis; ~ **operation costs** Betriebskosten für Fahrzeuge u Maschinen; ~ **records** Verzeichnis der Einrichtungsgegenstände; ~ **(trust) bonds** durch rollendes Material gesicherte Schuldverschreibungen e–r Eisenbahngesellschaft; **add-on** ~ Zusatzausrüstung; **capital** ~ Anlagegüter; **clerical** ~ Büroeinrichtung; **idle** ~ nicht ausgenutzte Betriebsanlagen.

equitable billigkeitsrechtlich, recht und billig, formlos; Equity ...; ~ **estates and interests** Rechte an (*fremder*) Sache; sachenrechtsähnliche (*obligatorische*) Rechte; **leasehold estate** billigkeitsrechtl Pachtrecht; ~ **rate of interest** Zinsanspruch gegen Treuhänder *bzw* Verwalter (*wegen Einbehaltung von Geld*).

equities Rechtsbehelfe *m/pl* nach dem Equity-Recht; Stammaktien *f/pl*, Anfechtungsrechte *n/pl*; **free from** ~ unter Ausschluß aller persönlichen Einwendungen; **industrial** ~ Industrieaktien; **junior** ~ Stammaktien nach Vorzugsaktien; **marketable** ~ börsenfähige Aktien, börsengängige Dividendenwerte; **to keep** ~ **off title** das Herrschaftsrecht (Eigentum) von Rechten Dritter freihalten.

equity Billigkeitsrecht *n*, Billigkeit *f*, Rechtschaffenheit *f*, Gerechtigkeit *f*, Fairness *f*, Treu und Glauben; der von der Verpfändung nicht erfaßte Restwert, Eigenkapital *n*; ~ **capital** Eigenkapital; ~ **debt ratio** Verschuldungsgrad; ~ **dilution** Wertverschlechterung durch Grundstücksbelastung; ~ **draftsman** Spezialanwalt für Klagen am Equity Gericht; ~ **financing** → *financing*; ~ **follows the law** analoge Anwendung des strengen Rechts im Billigkeitsrecht; ~ **holder** Anteilseigner; ~ **investment** Beteiligung am Gesellschaftskapital; ~ **jurisdiction** Zuständigkeit im Equity Verfahren; ~ **jurisprudence** Rechtsprechung von Equity Gerichten; ~ **market** Aktienmarkt; ~ **(method of) accounting** Bewertung nach der Eigenkapitalanteilsmethode; ~ **of a statute** entsprechende Anwendung e–s Gesetzes; ~ **of exoneration** unbeschränktes Auslösungsrecht (*des Pfandschuldners u Sicherungsübereigners*); ~ **of partners** Anspruch *der Gesellschafter auf Heranziehung des Gesellschaftsvermögens zur Deckung von Gesellschaftsschulden*; ~ **of redemption** Pfandauslösungsrecht; Tilgungsrecht des Grundpfandschuldners *auch nach Pfandverfall vgl mortgage*; Resteigentum des Sicherungsgebers; ~ **participation** Beteiligung am Eigenkapital; ~ **practice** Verfahren in Equity Sachen; ~ **ratio** Eigenkapitalquote, Verschuldungsgrad; ~ **securities** Aktien, Dividendenpapiere; ~ **share** Stammaktie; ~ **share capital** Stammkapital; ~ **stake** Aktienbeteiligung; ~ **term** Sitzungsperiode für Equity-Sachen; ~ **to a settlement** = *wife's* ~) Anspruch der Ehefrau auf treuhänderische Begünstigung aus Mannesvermögen (*für sich und Kinder*); ~ **to redeem** = ~ *of redemption qv*; ~ **under the policy** Rückkaufwert; **better** ~

rangbesserer Anspruch (*auf ein Recht an e–m Grundstück, nach Billigkeitsrecht*); **countervailing** ~ → *to countervail*; **latent** ~ verdeckter Anspruch im Innenverhältnis; **natural** ~ gesundes Rechtsempfinden, materielle Gerechtigkeit; Treu und Glauben; **paramount** ~ übergeordneter billigkeitsrechtl Anspruch; **perfect** ~ voller billigkeitsrechtlicher Anspruch; Anwartschaft des Käufers, *der bereits voll bezahlt hat, vor Verbriefung in e–r gesiegelten Urkunde*; **secret** ~ geheimer Anspruch im Innenverhältnis, geheimgehaltenes Anrecht; **wife's** ~ = ~ *to a settlement qv*.

equivalence Gleichwertigkeit *f*, gleiche Bedeutung *f*, gleicher Gegenwert *m*; ~ **of exchange** Kursparität.

equivalent *adj* äquivalent, gleichbedeutend, gleichwertig, identisch, entsprechend; ~ **price** Paritätskurs.

equivalent *s* Äquivalent *n*, Gegenwert *m*, volle Entsprechung *f*, gleicher Betrag *m*.

equivocal unbestimmt, zweideutig, doppelsinnig, zweifelhaft.

equivocate doppelsinnig reden, Ausflüchte machen; **"don't ~ with me"** „machen Sie keine Ausflüchte!"

equivocation Mehrdeutigkeit *f*, Doppelsinn *m*, Wortverdrehung *f*, Ausflüchte *f*|*pl*.

erase ausradieren, ausstreichen, löschen; ~ **from the register** im Register löschen.

erasing a person's name jmds Namen löschen; jmdm die Zulassung entziehen.

erasure Radierstelle *f*, Streichung *f*; Rasur *f* e–r Urkunde, Tilgung *f* im Strafregister.

erect errichten, aufstellen.

erection Errichtung *f*, Bau *m*, Gebäude *n*, Baulichkeit *f*.

ergonomics Ergonomie *f*, Arbeitsplatzanalyse *f*.

ermine Hermelinmantel *m*; richterliche Würde *f*.

err *v*|*i* sich irren; ~ **in law** rechtsfehlerhaft entscheiden.

errand Botengang *m*, Besorgung *f*.

errant umherreisend (*Reiserichter*), umhersuchend; irrend, irrig.

errata Errata *n*|*pl*, Druckfehlerliste *f*.

erroneous irrig, unrichtig; ~ **in (point of) law** rechtsfehlerhaft; ~ **judgment** rechtsfehlerhaftes Urteil.

error Irrtum *m*, Versehen *n*; Rechtsfehler *m*; Revisionsgrund *m*, Revisionsverfahren *n* (*GB bis 1875 bzw Strafverf bis 1907*); ~**s and omissions excepted** (*E & O.E.*) Irrtümer und Auslassungen vorbehalten; ~ **apparent of record** offensichtlicher (*die Revision tragender*) Rechtsfehler; ~ **coram nobis** Gegenvorstellungen bei Instanzgericht wegen Rechtsfehlern; ~ **coram vobis** Rechtsfehler der Vorinstanz; ~ **de persona (=** ~ *personae*); Identitätsirrtum; ~**s excepted** Irrtum vorbehalten (*Abrechnung*); ~ **fortunae** Irrtum über das Vermögen der Braut; ~ **in fact** Tatsachenirrtum, Tatbestandsfehler, Fehler bei der Feststellung des Sachverhalts; ~ **in (of) judgment** falsche Beurteilung, (Selbst)Täuschung; Fehlurteil; ~ **in law** Rechtsverletzung, Rechtsfehler (*als Revisionsgrund*); ~ **in negotio** Irrtum über die Rechtsnatur des Geschäftes; ~ **nominis** Irrtum über den Namen; ~ **of fact** Tatsachenirrtum, fehlerhafte Tatbestandsfeststellung; ~ **of judgment** Beurteilungsfehler; ~ **of law** Rechtsirrtum; ~ **of procedure** Verfahrensmangel; ~ **of quality** (*Eheanfechtungsgrund wegen*) Irrtum(s) über die Unbescholtenheit der Braut; **administrative** ~ fehlerhafter Verwaltungsakt; **assignment of** ~**s** → *assignment*; **automatic** ~ absoluter Revisionsgrund; **beneficial** ~ Rechtsfehler zugunsten des Angeklagten; **clerical** ~ Schreibversehen; **common** ~ allgemein anerkannter Revisionsgrund; **cross** ~**s** Anschlußrevision; **decision without** ~ Entscheidung (ist) rechtlich einwandfrei; **defendant in** ~ → *defendant*; **fatal** ~ revisibler Fehler; Restitutionsgrund; **fundamental** ~ grundlegender Rechtsfehler (*von Amts wegen zu berücksichtigen*), absoluter Revisionsgrund; **harmful** ~ Rechtsfehler, durch den e–e Partei beschwert ist; **harmless** ~ unerheblicher Rechtsfehler; **invited** ~ geflissentlich herbeigeführter Verfahrensfehler; **judicial** ~ → *judicial*; **jurisdictional** ~ irrtümliche Zuständigkeitsannahme; **prejudicial** ~ Rechtsfehler, durch den der Angeklagte beschwert wird; **reversible** ~ revisibler (Rechts)Fehler, Revisionsgrund; **special** ~**s** Erwiderung des Revisionsbeklagten (*mit verfahrensrechtlichen Rügen*); **technical** ~ rein theoretischer (*unbedeutender*) Verfahrensfehler; **to assign** ~ → *to assign*; **to bring** ~ sich auf Irrtum berufen, Revisionsgründe vorbringen; **to rectify an** ~ e–n Fehler berichtigen, e–n Irrtum richtigstellen; **writ of** ~ → *writ*.

escalator clause automatischer Ausgleich *m*, Indexklausel *f*, Gleitklausel *f*.

escape *s* Flucht *f*, Entweichenlassen *n*, Ausweg *m*, Notausgang *m*; ~ **clause** Rücktrittsklausel, Änderungsklausel, Ausweichklausel; ~ **from prison** Entweichen aus dem Gefängnis; ~ **of dangerous things** Entweichen(lassen) gefährlicher Stoffe; ~ **warrant** Haftbefehl gegen Flüchtlinge; ~ **way** Notausgang (*Bergwerk*); **allowing** ~ Entweichenlassen; **negligent** ~ fahrlässiges Entweichenlassen; **voluntary** ~ bewußtes Entweichenlassen.

escape *v* fliehen, vermeiden.

escheat *s* (*GB bis 1925*) Heimfall *m*, des Lebens; heimgefallenes Gut *n*, Staatserbrecht *n* (*mangels sonstiger Erben*), Einziehung *f* von herrenlosem (*oder dem Staat verfallenem*) Gut; **single** ~ Einziehung des Vermögens e–s Hochverräters; **writ of** ~ Heimfallsklage (*des Lehensherrn*).

escheat *v* heimfallen; ~ **to the Crown** dem Staat zufallen (*herrenloser Nachlaß*).

escheator Einziehungsbeamter *m* für Heimfallsgut der Krone.

escort Geleit *n*, Wache *f*; ~ **vessel** Geleitschiff; **police** ~ → *police*.

escot Gemeindesteuer *f*.

escrow vorläufige Hinterlegung *f* e–r Urkunde; Übergabe in treuhänderische Verwahrung; die treuhänderisch hinterlegte Urkunde *f*; ~ **account** Treuhand-Hinterlegungskonto; ~ **agent** (*treuhänderischer*) Zwischenverwahrer; ~ **bond** beim Treuhänder hinterlegte Obligation; ~ **deposit** Treuhandhinterlegung; **close of** ~ *Beendigung der treuhänderischen Hinterlegung der Grundstücksübereignungsurkunde* (*Eigentumsübergang des Grundstücks*) ~ **depositary** Verwahrungsstelle für treuhänderisch hinterlegte Wertpapiere; **delivery in** ~ vorläufige Hinterlegung; **to deposit in** ~ treuhänderisch hinterlegen; **to give in** ~ in treuhänderische Verwahrung geben.

espera Beibringungsfrist *f*.

espionage Spionage *f*; **counter** ~ Spionageabwehr; **industrial** ~ Werksspionage, Industriespionage.

espousals beiderseitiges Eheversprechen *n*, Verlöbnis *n*.

espy erspähen, entdecken.

esquire Esq. *Adelsprädikat*; *dem Namen nachgestellte Höflichkeitsbezeichnung in der Adresse von Herren, in US für juristische Amtsinhaber und Anwälte gebräuchlich*.

essence Inbegriff *m*, Wesenheit *f*, das Wesentliche *n*, Kern *m*; ~ **of the case** Kernpunkt des Rechtsstreits; ~ **of the contract** wichtigste Bestimmung e–s Vertragsinhalts; **of the** ~ wesentlich, absolut verbindlich; *time is of the* ~ → *time*.

essential höchst wichtig, absolut erforderlich; ~ **component part** wesentlicher Bestandteil; ~**s of a contract** wesentliche Vertragserfordernisse; ~ **part** Hauptbestandteil.

essentialit|y Sachlichkeit *f*, wesentliche Eigenschaft *f*, Hauptsache *f*; **~ies** Wesensmerkmale.

essoin *s hist* Entschuldigung *f* für Nichterscheinen, Vertagungsantrag *m*; ~ **day** Gerichtstag zur Verhandlung über Vertagungsanträge und über das Ausbleiben von Geladenen; ~ **roll** Protokoll über Nichterscheinen und Vertagung.

essoin *v* sich für das Nichterscheinen bei Gericht entschuldigen, um Vertagung bitten.

essoiniator Geladener *m*, der sich für sein Nichterscheinen entschuldigen läßt.

establish einrichten, gründen, stiften, etablieren, errichten, einsetzen, sich niederlassen, nachweisen, dartun, bestätigen; ~ **a claim** e–n Anspruch glaubhaft machen; ~ **a domicile** Wohnsitz begründen; ~ **a prima facie case** etwas schlüssig begründen und glaubhaft machen, den Beweis des ersten Anscheins erbringen; ~ **a rule** e–e Regel aufstellen; ~ **credit with a company** Warenkredit aufnehmen; ~ **one's identity** sich ausweisen, seine Identität nachweisen; **~ed custom** stehender Brauch; **~ed fact;** → *fact;* **~ed law** → *law*; **~ed merchant** selbständiger Kaufmann; **~ed practice** → *practice*; **~ed principles of law** feststehende Rechtsgrundsätze; **~ed use** lang bestehende Grundstücksnutzung; **well-~ed business** gut eingeführtes Geschäft; **well~ed interpretation** anerkannte Auslegung.

establishment Festsetzung *f*, Gründung *f*, Errichtung *f*, Unternehmen *n*, Niederlassung *f*; ~ **charge** Verwaltungsgemeinkosten, Gemeinkostenzuschlag; ~ **of a credit** Akkreditiveröffnung; ~ **of aliens** Niederlassung von Ausländern; ~ **of companies** Gesellschaftsgründungen; ~ **of damage** Schadensnachweis; ~ **of dower** die Einräumung des Witwennießbrauchs; ~ **of standards** Normenfestsetzung; ~ **of wills** (*Klage auf*) Feststellung der Gültigkeit e–s Testaments; **branch** ~ Zweigniederlassung; **business** ~ Geschäftsbetrieb; **domestic** ~ Heim, Wohnheim; **industrial** ~ Industrieunternehmen; **main** ~ Hauptniederlassung; **mercantile** ~ Handelsniederlassung, Handelsfirma; **military** ~ militärische Anlage; **new** ~ Geschäftsneugründung; **permanent** ~ Betriebsstätte, Niederlassung; **principal** ~ Hauptniederlassung; **right of** → *right*; **small** ~ Kleinbetrieb.

estate Stand *m*, Klasse *f*; Sondervermögen *n*; Landgut *n*, Besitztum *n*, dingliche Rechte *n|pl* am Grundstück; Besitzrecht *n*, Nachlaß *m*, Vermögensmasse *f*; ~ **agency** Immobilienfirma; ~ **agency conveyancing department** Immobilienverkehrsabteilung mit Notariat; ~ **agency work** Immobilienmaklertätigkeit; ~ **agent** Immobilienmakler; *residential* ~ ~: *Immobilienmakler für Wohngrundstücke; rogue* ~ ~s *unehrliche Makler*; ~ **and effects** persönliche Habe; Gesamtvermögen, abgesonderte Vermögensmasse; ~ **and interest** das gesamte Immobiliarvermögen; ~ **at sufferance** Duldungsbesitz; ~ **at will** jederzeit kündbares auf unbestimmte Zeit eingeräumtes Besitzrecht; ~ **bill** Vorlage zur Befreiung von Fideikommißbindung; ~ **by elegit** Zwangsverwaltungsbesitz; ~ **by purchase** rechtsgeschäftlich erworbenes Besitzrecht; ~ **by statute merchant** Zwangsverwaltungsbesitz nach Londoner Stadtrecht; ~ **by statute staple** Zwangsverwaltungsbesitz nach Marktrecht; ~ **by the curtesy** Witwennießbrauch (*gesetzlicher Nießbrauch des Witwers am Immobiliennachlaß der Ehefrau*); ~ **by the entirety** Gesamtgut (*Ehegattenrecht*); ~ **charges** Grundstückslasten; ~ **clause** Sammelklausel (*zur Übertragung sämtlicher dem Veräußerer zustehenden Rechte*); ~ **contract** Vertrag zum Erwerb von Rechten an e–m Grundstück, Grundstückserwerbsoption, Vorkaufsvertrag, *meist*: Grundstückskaufvertrag; ~ **duty (tax)** Nachlaßsteuer, Erbschaftssteuer (*GB bis 1975*); ~ **for life** = *life* ~ *qv*; ~ **for years** zeitlich begrenztes Besitzrecht, Pachtverhältnis auf feste Zeit; ~ **from year to year** jährlich ablaufendes Pachtverhältnis; ~ **in common** mehreren zustehendes Besitzrecht, Bruchteilsberechtigung, Bruchteilsgemeinschaft; ~ **in coparcenary** Gesamthandsberechtigung in der Erbgemeinschaft; ~ **in dower** Witwennießbrauch (*am Grundvermögen des Ehemannes*); ~ **in entirety** Gesamthandseigentum; ~ **in expectancy** Anfallsrecht, dingliches Anwartschaftsrecht; ~ **in fee simple** *unbeschränktes* Grundstückseigentum; ~ **in fee tail** Fideikommiß, erbfolgemäßig festgelegtes (Grund)Vermögen; ~ **in joint tenancy** Gesamthandsbesitz (*mit Anwachsungsrecht im Todesfall*); ~ **in land** Grundbesitz, (Herrschafts)Recht am Grundstück, voll angefallenes dingliches Recht; ~ **in possession** unmittelbarer Grundbesitz, Recht zum unmittelbaren Besitz; ~ **in remainder** zeitlich nachgeordnetes Besitzrecht, Recht zum Nachbesitz, dingliche Rechtsstellung des Nacherben; ~ **in reversion** Heimfallsrecht; ~ **in severalty** Einzelpachtbesitz, alleinige dingliche Berechtigung; ~ **of inheritance** Erblehen, gesetzlich vererbbarer Grundbesitz; Nachlaß; **E~s of the Realm** die Reichsstände; ~ **owner** → *owner*; ~ **planning** Nachlaßplanung; ~ **pur autre vie** Besitzrecht auf Lebenszeit e–s Dritten; ~ **(in) tail** Fideikommiß; erbfolgemäßig festgelegtes Vermögen, Majorat; ~ **tail female** nur auf weibliche Abkömmlinge und deren weibliche Nachkommen festgelegtes (vererbbares) Besitzrecht; ~ **tail male** auf männliche Nachkommen und deren männliche Nachkommen festgelegtes Besitzrecht; ~ **trust** → *trust*; ~ **upon condition** bedingtes Besitzrecht; **absolute** ~ absolutes Besitzrecht; Eigentum; **administration of** ~ → *administration*; **administrator of an** ~ → *administrator*; **augmented** ~ Reinnachlaß zuzüglich Wert von Schenkungen und Ehegattenvermögen; **bankrupt's** ~ → *bankrupt*; **base** ~ nachgeordneter Pachtbesitz, nachgeordnetes Lehen; **beneficial** ~ Anrecht; **claim against the** ~ Konkursforderung; Forderung gegen den Nachlaß; **clear** ~ unbelastetes Grundstück; **concurrent legal** ~ Miteigentum; **contingent** ~ aufschiebend bedingtes Besitzrecht; **conventional** ~ rechtsgeschäftl begründetes dingliches Recht am Grundstück; **credit on real** ~ Realkredit; **creditor of the** ~ → *creditor*; **debts of the** ~ → *debt*; **determinable** ~ kündbares Besitzrecht; **diseased persons' ~s** Nachlässe; **distribution of the** ~ → *distribution*; **dominant** herrschendes Grundstück; **entailed** ~ = → *tail qv*; **equitable** (*nur*) billigkeitsrechtlich anerkanntes Recht an Sachen; sachenrechtsähnliches obligatorisches Recht; Rechtsstellung des Treuhandbegünstigten; **executed** ~ ausgeübtes Eigentumsrecht, sofort ausübbares Besitzrecht; **executory** ~ aufschiebend bedingtes Grundstücksrecht; **expectant** ~ Anwartschaftsrecht (*an Liegenschaft*); **fast** ~ Immobilien, Grundvermögen; **fiduciary** ~ Treuhänderrecht am Treugut, Treuhänderstellung; **future** ~ dingl Anwartschaft auf Grundbesitz; **general** ~ Gesamtvermögen; **indeterminable** ~ nicht einseitig beendbares Herrschaftsrecht am Grundstück; eigentumsähnliches dingl Recht; **heirless** ~ erbenloser Nachlaß; **landed** ~ Grundvermögen; **leasehold** ~ pachtartiges Besitzrecht, Pachtgrundstück; Erbpacht; **legal** ~ Grundeigentum, eigentumsähnliches Grundbesitzrecht; **liabilities of the** ~ Nachlaßverbindlichkeiten; **life** ~ lebenslängliches Besitzrecht, Liegenschaftsnießbrauch;

mixed ~ Erbpachtbesitz (*auf 99 Jahre und verlängerbar*); **movable** ~ *bewegl* Habe, bewegl Vermögen; **net** ~ Reinnachlaß (*nach Abzug e–s Steuerfreibetrages und der Nachlaßverbindlichkeiten*); **non-ancestral** ~ rechtsgeschäftlich erworbene Liegenschaft; **original** ~ originäres Besitzrecht; **owner of an** ~ → *owner;* **particular** ~ Teilrecht an Grundstück; Zuwendung e–s Besitzrechts; das e–m Vorerben oder Zwischenberechtigten zugewendete Besitzrecht; **personal** ~ bewegliches Vermögen; **privity of** ~ → *privity*; **qualified** ~ beschränkt dingliches Recht, auflösend bedingtes Nießbrauchsrecht; **real** ~ → *real estate*; **rents of an** ~ Grundrente; **residential** ~ Wohngrundstück; **residual** ~ Restnachlaß; **residuary** ~ (allgemeiner) Nachlaß; Restnachlaß, Reinnachlaß; **royal** ~ englische Staatsdomäne; **separate** ~ Sondervermögen; **servient** ~ dienendes Grundstück (*Dienstbarkeit*); **settled** ~ treuhänderisch gebundenes Sondervermögen; **superior** ~ herrschendes Grundstück (*Dienstbarkeit*); **total** ~ Gesamtmasse, Gesamtnachlaß; **testamentary** ~ letztwillig verfügter Nachlaß, Nachlaß bei testamentarischer Erbfolge; **trust** ~ Treuhandsvermögen, Treugut, Treuhänderrechtsstellung; **vacant** ~ herrenloser Nachlaß; **vested** ~ angefallenes dingliches Recht, wohlerworbenes Besitzrecht, Herrschaftsrecht.

estimable schätzenswert, schätzbar.

estimate *s* Schätzung *f*, Voranschlag *m*, Kostenvoranschlag *m*; **~s committee** Haushaltsausschuß; ~ **of damage** Schadensschätzung; **~-to-complete** geschätzter Restaufwand; **building** ~ → *building*, → *builder*; **official** ~ amtliche Schätzung; **preliminary** ~ Voranschlag; **rough** ~ grobe Schätzung, überschlägiger Voranschlag, Überschlagsrechnung; **safe** ~ vorsichtiger Kostenvoranschlag; vorsichtige Schätzung; **select committee on ~s** Ausschuß für Haushaltsvoranschläge; **the E~s** Haushaltsvoranschlag.

estimate *v* schätzen, taxieren, berechnen, veranschlagen, beurteilen, bewerten; **~d amount** Schätzbetrag; **~d earnings** geschätztes Einkommen; **~d receipts** Solleinnahmen; **~d total** geschätzte Gesamtziffer.

estimation price Taxkurs.

estimator Schätzer *m*, Taxator *m*.

estop hindern; **to be ~ped** (nach Treu und Glauben) gehindert sein.

estoppel Unzulässigkeit *f* der Rechtsausübung, Hinderung *f*, Hemmung *f*, Präklusion *f*, Ausschluß *m*, Verwirkung *f*; ~ **by acceptor** Ausschuß wechselrechtlicher Einwendungen des Akzeptanten; ~ **by conduct** Unzulässigkeit der Rechtsausübung wegen eigenen Verhaltens; **by deed** Unzulässigkeit *bzw* Verwirkung des nachträglichen Bestreitens von Erklärungen, *die in gesiegelten Urkunden enthalten sind*; ~ **by election** Unzulässigkeit des Rückgängigmachens e–s ausgeübten Wahlrechts; ~ **by garnishee order absolute** Unzulässigkeit von Drittschuldnereinwendungen (*gegen e–e rechtskräftige gepfändete Forderung*); ~ **by judgment** innere Rechtskraftwirkung; ~ **by laches** (Einrede der) Verwirkung; Verschweigung; **by matter of record** Unzulässigkeit des nachträglichen Bestreitens gerichtlich protokollierter Erklärungen; ~ **by misrepresentation** Unzulässigkeit der Rechtsausübung wegen eigener falscher Angaben; ~ **by negligence** Unzulässigkeit von Einwendungen wegen eigenen fahrlässigen Verhaltens; ~ **by record** Präklusion durch gerichtliche Urkunde, Einrede der Rechtskraft; *vgl ~ by matter of record*; ~ **by representation** Verwirkung auf Grund eigener Angaben; *Unzulässigkeit von Einwendungen gegen Erklärungen e–s Vertreters bei Anscheinsvollmacht*; ~ **by silence** Unzulässigkeit, sich auf Schweigen zu berufen, *wenn Pflicht zum Reden besteht*; ~ **by verdict** Einrede der inneren Rechtskraft; ~ **by warranty** Unzulässigkeit der nachträglichen Beeinträchtigung e–r ausdrücklich gewährten Rechtsposition; ~ **certificate** Valutabescheinigung, Bescheinigung e–r tatsächl Feststellung; **collateral** ~ inzidenter getroffene Entscheidung; innere Rechtskraftwirkung; **equitable** ~ (*Einrede der*) Unzulässigkeit der Rechtsausübung, Verwirkung; ~ **in pais** Unzulässigkeit der Rechtsausübung aufgrund eigenen Verhaltens; **issue** ~ Einrede der materiellen Rechtskraft; **judicial** ~ → *judicial*; **legal** ~ = ~ *by deed qv*; **promissory** ~ Verhalten, das als Zusage aufgefaßt wird (*auf das sich die Gegenseite berufen kann*); Rechtscheinbindung auf Grund e–r Zusage.

estovers Holzentnahmerecht von fremdem Grund, Holzgerechtigkeit *f*; *Reallast für Unterhaltsbedürfnisse*.

estrangement Entfremdung *f*.

estray herrenloses Vieh; Aneignungsrecht *n* an entlaufenen *bzw* streunenden Haustieren.

estreat Ausfertigung *f*; ~ **of a recognisance** gerichtl Vollziehung e–r nicht eingehaltenen Sicherheitsleistung oder Verpflichtungserklärung.

estrepe zu Ödland machen, verwüsten.

estrepement Verwüstung *f*; **writ of** ~ (*Schadenersatz*)Klage wegen Verwüstung oder Verödung von Pachtland.

ethics Ethik, Sittenlehre, Sittengesetze, Moral; ~ **code** Standesrichtlinien; **E~ in Goverment Act** (*US 1978*) *Gesetz gegen unlautere Machenschaften in der Regierung*; **legal** ~ → *legal*; **professional** ~ Standespflichten e–s Anwalts; Berufsethos, Standesrecht.

ethnic volklich, volkstumsmäßig; ~ **German** Volksdeutscher; ~ **group** Volksgruppe; ~ **ticket balancing** ausgewogene Kandidatenaufstellung nach Volksgruppen.

etiquette/of the profession Standesregeln *f|pl* (*Anwälte, Ärzte usw*)); **professional** ~ Standesgepflogenheiten.

eundo, morando, et redeundo freies Geleit *n*.

eunomy gleiche Gesetze *n|pl* e–r ausgewogenen Verfassung.

Euro|bond Euro-Anleihe, Eurobond; ~ **card** Euroscheck-Karte; ~ **cheque** Euroscheck; ~ **currency** Eurowährung; ~ **notes** (=) kurzfristige Euromarkt-Schuldverschreibungen.

European|Atomic Energy Community (*Euratom*) Europäische Atomgemeinschaft; (*Europäisch* = *E*); ~ **Centre for Medium-Range Weather Forecasts** E–s Zentrum für mittelfristige Wettervorhersage; ~ **Civil Aviation Conference** E–e Zivilluftfahrt-Kommission; ~ **Coal and Steel Community** (Coal and Steel Pool, ECSC) E–e Gemeinschaft für Kohle und Stahl; ~ **Commission of Human Rights** E–e Kommission für Menschenrechte; ~ **Communities** E–e Gemeinschaften; ~ **Communities Act** *Anpassungsgesetz an die EG* (*GB 1972*); ~ **Company for the Financing of Railway Rolling Stock** E–e Gesellschaft für die Finanzierung von Eisenbahnmaterial; ~ **Company for the Chemical Processing of Irradiated Nuclear Fuels** E–e Gesellschaft für die Chemische Aufbereitung Bestrahlter Kernbrennstoffe; ~ **Convention on Human Rights** E–e Menschenrechtskonvention; ~ **Council** (*of heads of state*) E–r Rat; ~ **Court** Europäischer Gerichtshof; **Court of Human Rights** E–r Gerichtshof für Menschenrechte; ~ **Court of Justice** E–r Gerichtshof; ~ **Currency Unit** (*ECU*) E–e Währungseinheit (*EWE*); ~ **Customs Union** E–e Zollunion; ~ **Economic Com-**

munity (*EEC*) E-e Wirtschaftsgemeinschaft (*EWG*); ~ **Economic Council** (*EEC*) E–r Wirtschaftsrat; ~ **edifice** europ. Aufbauwerk; ~ **entity** das europäische Ganze; ~ **Free Trade Association** E–e Freihandelszone; ~ **Investment Bank** E–e Investitionsbank; ~ **judicial area** europäischer Rechtsraum; ~ **Molecular Biology Conference** E–e Konferenz für Molekularbiologie; ~ **Molecular Biology Laboratory** E–s Laboratorium für Molekularbiologie; ~ **Molecular Biology Organization** E–e Molekularbiologie-Organisation; ~ **Monetary Co-operation Fund** E–r Fonds für währungspolitische Zusammenarbeit; ~ **Monetary System** (*EMS*) E–s Währungssystem; ~ **Nuclear Energy Agency** E–e Kernenergie-Agentur; ~ **Nuclear Research Centre** E–s Atomforschungszentrum; ~ **Organization for Experimental Photogrammetric Research** E–e Organisation für experimentelle photogrammetrische Untersuchungen; ~ **Organization for Nuclear Research** E–e Organisation für kernphysikalische Forschung; ~ **Parliament** E–s Parlament; ~ **Patent Convention** E–s Patentübereinkommen; ~ **Patent Office** E–s Patentamt; ~ **Patent Organization** E–e Patentorganisation; ~ **Payments Union** (*EPU*) E–e Zahlungsunion; ~ **Southern Observatory** E–e Organisation für Astronomische Forschung in der Südlichen Hemisphäre; ~ **Space Agency** E–e Weltraumorganisation; ~ **Space Technology Centre** E–s Zentrum für Weltraumtechnik; ~ **unification** europ. Einigung, europ. Einigungsprozeß; ~ **Unit of Account** (*E. U. A.*) E–e Rechnungseinheit (*ERE*); ~ **Youth Centre** E–s Jugendzentrum; **Youth Foundation** E–s Jugendwerk.

Europeanisation Europäisierung *f*.

euthanasia Euthanasie *f*, Sterbehilfe *f*.

evacuate evakuieren, verlagern, räumen.

evacuation Evakuierung *f*, Verlagerung *f*, Räumung *f*.

evade vermeiden; ausweichen ~ **a rule** e–e Vorschrift umgehen; ~ **one's creditors** sich seinen Gläubigern entziehen; ~ **punishment** sich der Strafverbüßung entziehen; ~ **the law** das Gesetz umgehen.

evaluate bewerten, berechnen, abschätzen.

evaluation Wertbestimmung *f*, Wertermittlung *f*; ~ **of the evidence** Beweiswürdigung.

evasion Umgehung *f*, Ausflucht *f*, Unterdrückung *f* von Tatsachen; Hinterziehung *f*, Entziehung *n*; ~ **of customs duties** → *customs duties*; ~ **of law** Gesetzesumgehung; ~ **of liability** Haftungsvereitelung; ~ **of tax(es)** *unerlaubte* Steuerverminderung, Steuerverkürzung (*evtl mit Täuschungshandlung*), Steuerhinterziehung; **draft** ~ Drückebergerei vor dem Wehrdienst; **fiscal** ~ = → *of tax qv*.

evasive ausweichend; ~ **action** Ausweichmanöver; ~ **answer** ausweichende Antwort, Ausflucht.

eve Abend *m*, Vorabend *m*, Zeit *f* unmittelbar vor e–m Ereignis.

even *adj* eben, gerade; ausgeglichen, glatt; ~ **- handed** unparteiisch; **to be** ~ quitt sein, nichts mehr schulden; **to get** ~ **with s. b.** mit jmdm abrechnen.

even v **up** glattstellen; ~**ing up** Glattstellung.

evening Abend *m* (*von Sonnenuntergang bis zur normalen Schlafenszeit*); ~ **classes** Abendkurs; ~ **school** → *school*; ~ **trade** Abendbörse, Nachtbörse.

evenings Gewährung *f* e–s (*am Feierabend einzubringenden*) Teils der Ernte an den Pächter.

event Ereignis *n*, Fall *m*; Ergebnis *n*; Endentwicklung *f*; ~ **in issue** entscheidungserhebliches Ereignis; ~ **insured** Versicherungsfall; ~ **of death** Todesfall; ~ **of default** Leistungsstörung; **contingent** ~ ungewisses Ereignis; **fortuitous** ~ zufälliges Ereignis; **inevitable** ~ unabwendbares Ereignis; **natural** ~ Naturereignis; **specified** ~ bestimmtes E; **supervening** ~ zusätzl kausales Ereignis, Ereignis von überholender Kausalität.

eventual letztlich, endgültig; eventuell, gegebenenfalls.

eventuate ausgehen, endigen, stattfinden.

every jeder (jede, jedes), alle; ~ **other person** alle Sonstigen; ~ **other son** alle (anderen) Söhne; ~**thing else** alles sonst (*noch dazu gehörende*); **all and** ~ **person** jeder, jede Person.

everything I am possessed of alle meine Habe, mein gesamtes Vermögen; ~ **I die possesses of** mein gesamter Nachlaß; ~ **passing under this my will** mein gesamter beweglicher Nachlaß.

eaves-dropper Lauscher *m* (*an der Wand*).

evict räumen, die Herausgabe erlangen (*Grundstück*).

eviction Zwangsräumung *f*, Entsetzung *f*, Abmeierung *f*; ~ **proceedings** Räumungsverfahren; **actual** ~ faktische Zwangsräumung; **constructive** ~ schwere Besitzstörung, die zur Besitzaufgabe führt; **total** ~ restlose Zwangsräumung.

evidence Beweis *m* (= *B bzw b*), *gerichtlich zugelassenes* Beweismittel *n*, Beweismaterial *n*, Beweisführung *f*, Beweisaufnahme *f*, Beweisergebnis *n*; Nachweis *m*; Aussage *f*; ~ **aliunde** Neben*b* (*zur Auslegung e-r Urkunde*); ~ **as to character** Leumunds*b*; ~ **by affidavit** schriftlich beeidete Zeugenaussage; ~ **by inspection** Augenscheins*b*; ~ **for the prosecution** Belastungsmaterial, Beweisführung gegen den Angeklagten; ~ **in rebuttal** Gegen*b*-(mittel), Widerlegungs*b*; ~ **of a contract** Nachweis des Vertragsschlusses, Vertragsurkunde; ~ **of character** Leumunds*b*; ~ **of debt** Schuldurkunde; ~ **of grant of probate** Erbschein, gerichtl Testamentsbestätigung; ~ **of identity** Ausweis, Identitätsnachweis; ~ **of indebtedness** Schuldurkunde; ~ **of opinion** Meinungsäußerung des Zeugen; ~ **of ownership** Eigentumsnachweis; ~ **of previous conviction** Vorstrafennachweis; ~ **of prisoner** Vernehmung des Angeklagten zur Sache; Aussagen von *inhaftierten* Angeklagten; ~ **of professional qualifications** *B* der beruflichen Zulassung; ~ **of service** Zustellungsnachweis; ~ **of system** *B* der typischen Begehungsweise; ~ **of title** Eigentumsnachweis; ~ **of user** Verwendungsnachweis (e-r Urkunde); ~ **on adjournment** *B*mittel in weiterer Verhandlung; ~ **on application** Glaubhaftmachung des Antrags; ~ **on commission** Zeugenvernehmung durch beauftragten Richter; ~ **on oath** eidliche Aussage; ~ **rules** *B*regeln; ~ **viva voce** *B* durch mündliche Aussage; **adminicular** ~ *eccl* Hilfs*b*(mittel); **admissibility of** ~ → *admissibility*; **admissible** ~ → *admissible*; **admission of** ~ Zulassung e-s *B*mittels; **affidavit** ~ Glaubhaftmachung, Beweisführung durch beeidete schriftliche Erklärungen; **auto-optic** ~ Augenschein(*sb*); **best** ~ primäres *B*mittel, Originalurkunde; **best** ~ **rule** Unzulässigkeit sekundärer *B*mittel (*bei Vorhandensein primärer Beweismittel d. h. Originalurkunden*); **casual** ~ Zufallsbeweismittel; **character** ~ Leumunds*b*; **circumstantial** ~ Indizien*b*; **civil** ~ *B*recht im Zivilprozeß; **clear** ~ klares, widerspruchsloses Beweismaterial; **cogent** ~ zwingender *B*; **commissioner for taking** ~ Rechtshilfebeauftragter *(Richter, Konsul, Beamter oder Anwalt) zur Zeugenvernehmung;* **competent** ~ zulässiges (und schlüssiges) *Bmaterial*; **conclusive** ~ zwingender *B*, unwiderlegbare *B*; **conflicting** ~ widerstreitendes *B*material, widersprüchliche Aussagen; **contradicting** ~ widersprüchliches *B*material; **consideration of** ~ → *consideration;* **corroborative** ~ zusätzliches *B*material (*zur Unterstützung*); **counteracting** ~ Gegen*b*(mittel); **criminal** ~ *B*recht im Strafverfahren; **cumulative** ~ zusätzliches *B*material, Häufung von *B*material; **demonstrative** ~ Augenscheins*b*; **derivative** ~ (*von unzulässigem abgeleitetes*) unvertretbares *B*material; **destruction of** ~ Vernichtung von *B*mitteln; **detrimental** ~ abträgliche, Aussage; **direct** ~ unmittelbarer *B*; **directions for** ~ → *direction*; **documentary** ~ Urkunden*b*; Nachweis; **exculpatory** ~ Entlastungs*b*(mittel); **ex parte** ~ einseitige Zeugenvernehmung (Voruntersuchung); **expert** ~ Sachverständigen*b*; **external** ~ *B*mittel außerhalb e–r Urkunde; **extrajudicial** ~ außergerichtlicher Nachweis; **extraneous** ~ *B*mittel außerhalb e–r Urkunde; **extrinsic** ~ = *extraneous* ~ *qv*; **fabricated** ~ erfundenes *B*material, fälschlich hergestelltes *B*material; **fabricating false** ~ = *fabrication of* ~ *qv*; **facts in** ~ bereits bewiesene Tatsachen; **false** ~ falsche Aussage; **first-hand hearsay** ~ mittelbarer *B* ersten Grades; **for want of** ~ mangels *B*; **fresh** ~ neues *B*mittel; **hearing of** ~ → *hearing*; **hearsay** ~ *B* vom Hörensagen, mittelbarer *B*; **identification** ~ = *identifying* ~ → *identify;* **in** ~ dem Gericht vorliegendes *B*mittel; **incompetent** ~ unzulässiges *B*angebot, nicht zugelassenes *B*mittel; **incriminating** ~ Belastungsmaterial, belastendes *B*material; **incontrovertible** ~ unwiderleglicher B; **inculpatory** ~ Schuld*b*; **indirect** ~ Indizien*b*; **indispensable** ~ notwendiges Glied e–r *B*kette; **inferential** ~ Indizien*b*; **internal** ~ *B*kraft e–r Urkunde; **intrinsic** ~ unmittelbarer Urkunden*b*; **irrefutable** ~ unwiderlegbares *B*material; **judicial** ~ gerichtl zulässiges *B*mittel; **law of** ~ → *law*; **legal** ~ *B*mittel, zulässiges *B*angebot; **material** ~ rechtserhebliche *B*angebote; **mathematical** ~ wissenschaftlicher *B*, mathematisch zwingende *B*führung; **moral** ~ erheblich von der *B*würdigung abhängiger *B*stoff, Augenscheins*b*, Frei*b*, Wahrscheinlichkeits*b*; **multiple** ~ *B*material für mehrere *B*themen; **natural** ~ direkter *B*; **negative** ~ Negativ*b*, *B* des Nichtgeschehenseins, *B* des Nichtvorhandenseins; **newly-discovered** ~ neu entdecktes *B*mittel (*Wiederaufnahme des Verfahrens*); **not a shred of** ~ nicht der geringste *B*; **ocular** ~ Augenschein(seinnahme); **offer of** ~ → *offer*; **opinion** ~ gutachtliche *B*führung; **oral** ~ Aussage(n) vor Gericht, *B* durch Zeugen- *bzw.* Parteivernehmung; **original** ~ *B*material in Form von Originalurkunden; **parol** ~ mündlicher *B*, Zeugen*b*, *auch* = *extrinsic* ~ *qv*; **partial** ~ Teil*b*; *B* zu e–m Teilkomplex; **perjured** ~ Meineidsaussage; **persuasive** ~ überzeugender *B*; **positive** ~ direkter *B*, eindeutiger *B*; **preappointed** ~ gesetzlich vorgeschriebenes Beweismittel; **preponderance of** ~ → *preponderance*; **presentation of** ~ *B*angebot; **presumptive** ~ Indizien*b*; Wahrscheinlichkeits*b*, Primafacie*b*; *B auf Grund als wahr zu vermutender Umstände*; **prima facie** ~ → *prima facie*; **primary** ~ primäre *B*mittel; **primary documentary** ~ *B* durch Originalurkunden; **print-out** ~ Computer-Ausdruck als *B*urkunde; **probable** ~ Wahrscheinlichkeits*b*, Anscheins*b*, Glaubhaftmachung; **probative** ~ beweiskräftiges Material; **production of** ~ → *production*; **proffered** ~ angebotener *B*; **proper** ~ zulässiges *B*mittel; **reading** ~ Verlesung des *B*aufnahmeprotokolls; **real** ~ Augenschein(*sb*); **rebutting** ~ = ~ *in rebuttal qv*; **refusal to receive** ~ Ablehnung e–s *B*antrags; **relevant** ~ zur Sache gehöriges *B*angebot; **rules(s) of** ~ → *rule*; **satisfactory** ~ hinreichender *B*, ausreichender *B*; **scintilla of** ~ Spur e–s

B-s; **secondhand** ~ *B* aus zweiter Hand; *B* vom Hören und Sagen; **secondary** ~ sekundäres *B*mittel, indirektes *B*mittel; **secondary documentary** ~ mittelbarer Urkunden*b*; Urkunden*b* durch andere *B*mittel als durch Originalurkunden; **self-** ~ Selbstverständlichkeit; **skilled** ~ Sachverständigen*b*; **State's** ~ *B*material der Staatsanwaltschaft, belastende Aussage e–s Tatbeteiligten; **substantial** ~ Glaubhaftmachung, vorläufiger *B*; hinreichender *B*; **substantive** ~ Haupt*b*, erhebliches *B*material; **substitutionary** ~ hilfsweise angebotener *B*; **sufficient** ~ hinreichender *B*; **summary of** ~ Zusammenfassung der *B*aufnahme; **sworn** ~ eidliche Aussage; **tangible** ~ körperliche *B*gegenstände; **testimonial** ~ Zeugen*b*; **to adduce** ~ *B* antreten; **to admit in** ~ in *B*mittel entgegennehmen; **to be in** ~ dem Gericht als *B*mittel vorliegen; **to bear** ~ den Nachweis erbringen; **to call a person in** ~ jmdn als Zeugen vernehmen lassen; **to furnish** ~ → *to furnish*; **to hear** ~ Zeugen vernehmen lassen; in die *B*aufnahme eintreten; **to introduce** ~ → *to introduce*; **to lead** ~ *B* antreten; **to put in** ~ *B*mittel dem Gericht vorlegen, *B* antreten; **to receive in** ~ als (*zulässiges*) *B*mittel entgegennehmen; **to take** ~ *B* erheben; **to tender in** ~ *B* antreten; **to weigh the** ~ die *B*würdigung vornehmen; **traditionary** ~ *B* der Überlieferung; **transcript of** ~ → *transcript*; **unchallenged** ~ nicht angegriffene *Be*; nicht angegriffene Aussagen bzw Beweisurkunden; **unsworn** ~ unbeeidigte Aussage; **unused** ~ nicht verwendete *B*mittel; **verbal** ~ mündl Aussagen; **visual** ~ Augenscheins*b*, Augenscheinsobjekt; **weighing of** ~ *B*würdigung; **weight of** ~ das Ergebnis der B*aufnahme, das größere Gewicht bei der B*würdigung; **words of** ~ Worte, die zu beweisen sind; **written** ~ Urkundenbeweis.

evidence *v/t* dartun, nachweisen, bestätigen **~d in writing** in Schriftform.

evident augenscheinlich, evident; **self-** ~ aus sich selbst bewiesen, selbstverständlich, offensichtlich.

evidential beweismäßig.

evidentiary als Beweismittel geltend, Beweis . . .

evil schlecht, böse; ~ **fame** schlechter Leumund; ~ **liver** e–n unmoralischen Lebenswandel führende Person.

evince dartun, bekunden.

evoke hervorrufen; Rechtssachen an sich ziehen; sich die Sache (*von e–r unteren Instanz*) vorlegen lassen.

ex ab, ehemalig, außer, vorbehaltlich, ~ **abundante cautela** höchst vorsorglich; ~ **aequo et bono** nach billigem Ermessen; ~ **all** ausschließlich aller Rechte; ~ **ante** vorausberechnet; ~ **bonus** → *bonus*; ~ **capitalisation** ~ Berichtigungsaktien (*ex BA*); ~ **cars from alongside steamer** ab Waggon am Verladekai beim Schiff; ~ **contractu** aus Vertrag, vertraglich; ~ **coupon** ohne Koupon; ~ **delicto** aus unerlaubter Handlung; ~ **dividend** → *dividend*; ~ **drawing** ohne Teilnahme an der nächsten Auslosung; ~ **facie** offensichtlich; ~ **factory** → *factory*; ~ **gratia** freiwillig, ohne Anerkennung einer Rechtspflicht; ~ **interest** ohne demnächst fällige Zinsen; ~ **new** ohne Bezugsrechte (*ex B*); ~ **officio** von Amts wegen; ~ **officio member** Mitglied kraft Amtes; ~ **officio oath** Ausforschungseid; ~ **parte** einseitig, auf einseitigen Antrag (*ohne Anhörung der Gegenseite*), Antragsteller (*im Rubrum*); ~ **parte application** Antrag *in e–m einseitigen Verfahren*; ~ **parte case** → *case*; ~ **parte proceedings** einseitiges Verfahren, Antragsverfahren ohne Anhörung des Gegners; ~ **post facto clause** Verfassungsverbot rückwirkender Gesetze; ~ **post facto law** rückwirkendes Gesetz; ~ **proprio motu** von Amts wegen; ~ **quay** ab Kai; ~ **quay (duty paid)** ab Kai (verzollt); ~ **quay (duty on buyer's account)** ab Kai (unverzollt); ~ **relatione** ~ auf Anzeige, auf Bericht; ~ **rights** (=*xr*) ex Bezugsrecht; ~ **ship** ab Schiff; ~ **stock dividend** ausschließlich Gratisaktien; ~ **warehouse** ab Lager; ~ **works** ab Werk.

exact *adj* genau, sorgfältig.

exact *v* einfordern; ~ **payment** Zahlung betreiben.

exaction Beitreibung *f*; Beitreibung *f* als Amtsanmaßung.

exactor Steuerbeitreiber *m*.

examination Untersuchung *f*, Vernehmung *f*, Verhör *n*, Prüfung *f*, Einsichtnahme *f*; Beschau *m* (*Zoll u.a.*); ~ **by judge** richterliche Vernehmung; ~ **de bene esse** vorprozessuale Vernehmung e–s Zeugen; ~ **in chief** Hauptvernehmung der Zeugen (*durch die benennende Partei*); ~ **of accounts** Buchprüfung, Rechnungsprüfung; ~ **of a prisoner** polizeil bzw gerichtl Vorprüfung des Tatverdachts; ~ **of bankrupt** gerichtliche Vernehmung des Gemeinschuldners; ~ **of defendant** verantwortliche Vernehmung des Beschuldigten (in eigener Sache); ~ **of goods** Prüfung der Ware; ~ **of invention** Prüfung des Erfindungsanspruchs; ~ **of title** Prüfung der Eigentumsverhältnisse; ~ **of wife** (*getrennte*) Vernehmung der Ehefrau; ~ **on oath** eidliche Vernehmung; **competitive** ~ Bewerbungsprüfung; **compulsory** ~ Zwangsvernehmung; **cross-**~ Kreuzverhör, Vernehmung durch die Gegenpartei; **cursory** ~ oberflächliche Prüfung, Durchsicht; **direct** ~ Hauptvernehmung (*durch die benennende Partei*); **entrance** ~ Aufnahmeprüfung; **final** ~ Abschlußprüfung; **medical** ~ ärztliche Untersuchung; **post mortem** ~ Leichenschau; **preliminary** ~ Voruntersuchung, Vernehmung des Beschuldigten in der gerichtlichen Voruntersuchung, *pat* Vorprüfung; **private** ~ Vernehmung unter Ausschluß der Öffentlichkeit; **public** ~ öffentliche Vernehmung, Gemeinschuldnervernehmung *zur Offenbarung seines Vermögens und Offenlegung seines Verhaltens*; **random** ~ Stichprobe; **re-direct** ~ zweite Vernehmung durch die benennende Partei (*nach der cross* ~); **separate** ~ abgetrennte Vernehmung (*in Abwesenheit anderer*), gesonderte Beurkundung; **viva voce** ~ mündliche Prüfung, mündliche Zeugenvernehmung; **written** ~ schriftliches Examen.

examine prüfen, revidieren, vernehmen, verhören; ~**d and found** nach Prüfung festgestellt; ~**d copy** → *copy*.

examinee Prüfung *m*, Kandidat *m*.

examiner Untersuchungsführer *m*, Prüfender *m*, Vernehmer *m*, gerichtlich mit Zeugenvernehmungen beauftragter Rechtsanwalt *m*; **hearing** ~ Vorsitzender bei e–r behördlichen Anhörung; ~ **in chief** *pat* Hauptprüfer, Leiter der Prüfungsstelle; ~ **of petitions for private bills** Parlamentsvorprüfer für Privatvorlagen; ~ **s of the court** Vernehmungsrichter bei auswärtigen Beweisaufnahmen; **board of** ~**s** → *board* (*1*); **medical** ~ Vertrauensarzt, ärztlicher Leichenbeschauer; **National E**~**s** *US-Bundesprüfer für Kreditinstitute*; **primary** ~ *pat* Vorprüfer; **special** ~ kommissarische Vernehmungsperson; im Einzelfall beauftragter Vernehmungsrichter.

examining authority Prüfungsbehörde; ~ **board** Prüfungsstelle; ~ **surgeon** Werkarzt, Vertrauensarzt.

example Beispiel *n*, Muster *n*, Probe *f*, Exemplar *n*; **constructional** ~ konstruktives Beispiel: **illustrative** ~ Erläuterungsbeispiel: **numerical** ~ Zahlenbeispiel.

exannual roll Liste *f* der nicht beitreibbaren Forderungen und Strafen.

exceed überschreiten, übersteigen,

übertreffen; ~ **one's authority** seine Vollmacht überschreiten.

except ausgenommen, außer; ~ **as otherwise (herein) provided** vorbehaltlich anderslautender Bestimmungen; ~ **when** außer wenn; ~ **with the sanction of the court** außer mit gerichtlicher Genehmigung; ~ **ed perils clause** *ins* Gefahren – Freizeichnungsklausel.

excepting vorbehaltlich.

exceptio Einrede *f*; neues tatsächliches Gegenvorbringen *n*.

exception Ausnahme *f*, Einwendung *f*, Gegenvorstellungen *f/pl*; ~ **accounting** Gutschriftsbuchungen unter Vorbehalt; ~ **to bail** Einrede der ungenügenden Sicherheitsleistung; ~ **to the rule** Ausnahme, Sonderfall; **bill of ~s** → *bill* (*2*); **by way of** ~ ausnahmsweise; **declinatory** ~ Rüge der Unzuständigkeit; **dilatory** ~ aufschiebende Einrede; **general** ~ Einwendung der Unschlüssigkeit des Klagevorbringens; **negativing ~s** → *negative*; **peremptory** ~ peremptorische Einrede, rechtsvernichtende Einrede; **special** ~ Rüge formaler Mängel der Klage; **to take ~s** Gegenvorstellungen erheben, Anstoß nehmen, Rechtsmittel vorbehalten.

exceptional ausnahmsweise, außergewöhnlich, besonders; ~ **and not systematic** ausnahmsweise und nicht planmäßig; ~ **case** Ausnahmefall; ~ **circumstances allowance** Erstattung notwendiger Aufwendungen (*Angeklagter*); ~ **depreciation** außergewöhnliche Wertminderung, ~ **difficulty** besondere Schwierigkeit; ~ **grant** Ausnahmebewilligung; ~ **hardship** ungewöhnlicher Härtefall; ~ **provisions** Sonderbestimmungen, Ausnahmevorschriften; ~ **rate** Sondertarif, Ausnahmepreis.

excerpt Auszug *m*, Exzerpt *n*.

excess Exzeß *m*, Überschuß *m*, Ausschreitung *f*; *ins* Selbstbehalt *m*, Franchise *f*; ~ **capacity** Überkapazität; ~ **charge** Gebührenzuschlag; ~ **clause** → *clause*; ~ **depreciation** Kaufkraftschwund; ~ **export** Ausfuhrüberschuß; ~ **fare** → *fare*; ~ **freight** Frachtzuschlag; ~ **hours** Überstunden; ~ **insurance** → *insurance*; ~ **loan** zusätzlicher Kredit (*über der Kreditlinie*); ~ **of authority** Vollmachtsüberschreitung; ~ **of demand** Nachfrageüberhang; ~ **of loss reinsurance** Schadensexzedentenversicherung; ~ **of privilege** Beleidigung unter Immunitätsmißbrauch; ~ **postage** Strafporto; ~ **profit** Übergewinn, Sondergewinn; ~ **profits duty (=** ~ *profits levy* = ~ *profits lax*) Sondergewinnsteuer; ~ **reserves** → *reserve*; ~ **vote** Ausgabenüberschreitungsausgleich, Nachtragsbewilligung; (*Haushaltsposten*); ~ **weight** Übergewicht, Mehrgewicht.

excessive übermäßig; ~ **bail** überhöhte Kaution; ~ **charge** → *charge*; ~ **damages** → *damages*; ~ **indebtedness** Überschuldung; ~ **interest** überhöhte Zinsen; ~ **profits** Übergewinn; ~ **supply** Überangebot; ~ **tax** zu viel erhobene Steuer; ~ **use of intoxicants** Trunksucht; ~ **weight** Überlastung.

exchange *s* (*1*) Umtausch *m*, Tauschgeschäft *fn*. Fernsprechzentrale *f*; ~ **deal** Tauschgeschäft; ~ **land** Tauschgrundstück; ~ **of commodities** Güteraustausch; ~ **of goods and services** Waren- und Dienstleistungsverkehr; ~ **of letters** Briefwechsel; ~ **of livings** *eccl* Pfründentausch; ~ **of notes** Notenwechsel; ~ **of pleadings** Schriftsatzwechsel; ~ **of property** Tausch (*von Vermögensgegenständen*); ~ **privilege** Umtauschrecht; ~ **transaction** Tauschgeschäft; ~ **value** Tauschwert, Marktwert; **deed of** ~ Tauschurkunde (*Grundstücke*); **dry** ~ fingiertes Tauschgeschäft, als Tauschgeschäft getarnter Wucher, **like-kind** ~ (*steuerfreier*) Tausch von Produktionsgütern bzw Anlagegütern gleicher Art; **owelty of** ~ Wertausgleichszahlung bei Grundstückstausch; **trunk** ~ Fernamt.

exchange *s* (*2*) Wechsel *m*; Geldwechsel *m*, Devisen *f/pl*, Währungs ...; ~ **adjustment** Wechselkursanpassung; ~ **allowance** Devisenzuteilung, Devisenfreibetrag; ~ **arbitrage** → *arbitrage*; ~ **as per indorsement** Währungskurs nach Angabe auf dem Indossament; ~ **broker** → *broker*; ~ **certificate** Devisengenehmigung; ~ **clause** Währungsklausel, Kursklausel auf Auslandswechsel; ~ **clearing** Devisenclearing; ~ **commission** Provision für Geldwechseln; ~ **contact** Devisenmanipulationsvertrag, Devisenumtauschvertrag; ~ **control** Devisenbewirtschaftung; ~ **control authority** Devisenbehörde; ~ **dealer** Devisenhändler; ~ **equalisation account** Währungsausgleichskonto; ~ **equalisation fund** Währungsausgleichsfonds; **E~ Equalisation Account** Währungskursstabilisierungsfond (*GB, Abt. der Treasury qv*); ~ **equilibrium** ausgeglichene Zahlungsbilanz, ~ **for forward delivery** Termindevisen; ~ **forward-operations** Devisentermingeschäfte; ~ **for spot delivery** Kassadevisen, Devisenkassa; ~ **futures** Devisentermingeschäfte; ~ **guaranty** Kurssicherung; ~ **hedging** Kurssicherung; ~ **holdings** Devisenbestände; ~ **intervention** Intervention am Devisenmarkt; ~ **loss** Wechselkursverlust; ~ **management** Währungspolitik, währungspolitisches Instrumentarium; ~ **market** Wechselplatz, Devisenmarkt; ~ **office** Wechselstube; ~ **parity** Kursparität; ~ **permit** Devisengenehmigung; ~ **premium** Agio; Aufgeld; ~ **proceeds** Deviseneinnahmen; ~ **profit** (Devisen) Kursgewinn; ~ **rate** → *exchange rate*; ~ **regulations** Devisenbestimmungen; ~ **restriction** Devisenbeschränkung; ~ **risk** Kursrisiko, Devisenrisiko; ~ **rules** Devisenvorschriften; **E~ Stability** Währungskursstabilität; **E~ Stabilization Fund** Währungsausgleichsfonds (*E. S. F.*) *Entsprechung des Exchange Equalization Account qv*; ~ **stringency** Devisenknappheit; ~ **the same** Wechselkurs unverändert; ~ **transfer risk** Konvertierungsrisiko; ~ **variations** Wechselkursschwankungen; **arbitration of** ~ → *arbitration* (*2*); **bill of** ~ Wechsel, Tratte; → *bill* (*3*); **domestic** ~ US Inlandwechsel; **first** ~ Primawechsel; **foreign** ~ → *foreign exchange*; **indirect** ~ indirekte Devisenarbitrage; **nominal** ~ nomineller Umrechnungskurs; **par of** ~ → *par*; **second of** ~ Sekundawechsel, weitere Wechselausfertigung; **sole of** ~ Primawechsel; **third of** ~ Tertiawechsel.

exchange *s* (*3*) Börse *f*; ~ **report** Börsenbericht; **Consolidated E~** New Yorker Börse; **corn** ~ Getreidebörse; **cotton** ~ Baumwollbörse; **stock** ~ → *stock exchange*; **to list on the** ~ zum Börsenhandel zulassen.

exchange *v* tauschen, wechseln, umtauschen.

exchange rate Wechselkurs; Devisenkurs; ~ **appreciation** Aufwertung; ~-~ **guarantee** Wechselkursgarantie; ~-~ **management** Wechselkurssteuerung; ~-~ **parity** Währungsparität; ~-~ **policies** Wechselkurspolitik; **floating** ~ → *floating*; **fluctuations of** ~~ Devisenschwankungen, **grid of bilateral** ~ ~**s** Gitter bilateraler Wechselkurse; **indirect** ~~ → *indirect*; **managed** ~**s** manipulierte Wechselkurse, gelenkte W.; **multiple** ~~ gespaltener Wechselkurs; *ple*; **pegged** ~~**s** feste Währungskurse; **two-tiered** ~ gespaltener Devisenkurs.

exchequer Finanzbehörde *f*, Schatzamt *n*, Fiskus *m*, Zentralkonto *n* des britischen Staates *bei der Bank von England*; ~ **bill** Schatzanweisung; ~ **bonds** → *bonds* (*1*); **E~ Chamber** *engl Berufungsgericht bis 1873, Vorgänger des Court of Appeal*; ~ **division** Steuergerichtsabteilung; ~ **grants** Staatszuschüsse an Gemeinden; ~ **return** Wohnbericht über das Zentralkonto der britischen Regierung; **Chancellor of the E~** → *chancellor*; **Court ~ of E~** → *court*.

excise Verbrauchssteuer *f*, Konzessionsabgabe *f*; öffentl Abgabe *f*; ~ **bond** Zolldurchlaßschein; ~ **commission** örtlicher Ausschuß für Schankkonzessionen; ~ **duties** Verbrauchssteuern; ~ **duty on coffee** Kaffeesteuer; ~ **licences** Konzessions- u. Gebrauchserlaubnisabgaben (*Kfz-Steuer, Hundesteuer ua*); ~ **office** Regieverwaltung; ~ **warehouse** → *warehouse*.

exciseable liquor steuerpflichtige alkoholische Getränke *n*|*pl*.

excitation Aufforderung *f* (*zu e–r strafbaren Handlung*).

excit|e auffordern (*zu e–r strafbaren Handlung*); aufreizen; ~**ing disaffection** Aufforderung zum Ungehorsam.

exclosure abgeschlossenes Grundstück *n*.

exclud|e ausscheiden, ausschließen; ~**ing** unter Ausschluß von.

exclusion Ausschluß *m*, Ausschließung *f*; ~ **and ouster** Besitzentziehung; ~ **clause** → *clause*; ~ **from licensed premises** Lokalverbot *bes für Angehörige von terror. Vereinigungen*; ~ **of aliens** Einreiseverbot für Ausländer; ~ **of causes** Eliminierung anderer Ursachen; ~ **order** Aufenthaltsverbot, Landesverweisung; Verweisung aus der Ehewohnung durch Gerichtsbeschluß; Lokalverbot für Verurteilte.

exclusionary ausschließend, Ausschluß; ~ **stock tender** Abwehrkaufangebot von Aktien *zum festen Kurs*.

exclusive ausschließlich, exklusiv, ohne; ~ **bargaining agent** alleiniger Tarifpartner; ~ **dealer arrangement** Eigenhändlervertrag mit Ausschließlichkeitsklausel; ~ **legislative authority** ausschließliche Gesetzgebungsbefugnis; ~ **of costs** ohne Kosten; ~ **right to sell** Alleinvertriebsrecht; ~ **sales agreement** Alleinvertriebsvertrag.

exculpate entschuldigen, rechtfertigen.

exculpatory entlastend, exkulpierend.

excusable entschuldbar, unverschuldet.

excusatio Rechtfertigungsgrund *m*, Schuldausschließungsgrund *m*, Schuldaufhebungsgrund *m*.

excuse *s* Entschuldigung *f*, Rechtfertigung *f*, Ausflucht *f*, **lawful** ~ Rechtfertigungsgrund, Schuldausschließungsgrund; **legal** ~ = *lawful* ~ *qv*; **without reasonable** → *without*.

excuse *v* entschuldigen.

excuss beschlagnahmen.

excussio Beitreibung *f* vom Hauptschuldner.

excussion Beschlagnahme *f*.

executable vollziehbar, vollstreckbar.

execute ausführen, durchführen, vollstrecken, hinrichten, errichten, vollziehen, unterfertigen; ~ **a contract** e–n Vertrag unterzeichnen *bzw* ausführen; ~ **a deed** e–e Urkunde unterfertigen (*und siegeln*) e–e Urkunde errichten; ~ **a judgment** ein Urteil vollstrecken; ~ **judgment on s. o's assets:** in jmds Vermögen vollstrecken; ~ **a last will** ein Testament errichten *bzw* vollziehen, ~ **a mortgage to a person** jmdm e–e Hypothek bestellen; ~ **a power of attorney** e–e Vollmacht errichten; ~ **an instrument** e–e Urkunde unterfertigen, e–e U. errichten.

executed vollzogen, bereits durchgeführt; errichtet, unterfertigt, ausgefertigt.

execution (*1*) Ausführung *f*, Vollziehung *f*, Vollstreckung *f*, Pfändung *f*, Unterzeichnung *f*, Unterfertigung *f* e–r Urkunde, formgültige Errichtung *f* e–r Urkunde; ~ **by delivery** Vollstreckung durch Wegnahme; ~ **by public sale** Zwangsversteigerung; ~ **creditor** → *creditor*; ~ **debtor** → *debtor*; ~ **of a contract** → *contract*; ~ **of a deed** Unterfertigung einer (*gesiegelten*)

Urkunde; ~ **of a judgment** Vollstreckung aus e–m Urteil; ~ **of a policy** Ausstellung e–s Versicherungsscheines; ~ **of a trust** Ausführung e–r Treuhandverpflichtung; ~ **of an office** Ausübung e–s Amtes; ~ **of an order** Auftragserledigung; ~ **of decree** Vollstreckbarkeitsverfahren e–s Urteils; ~ **of (a) judgment** Zwangsvollstreckung aus e–m Urteil; ~ **of sentence** Strafvollstreckung; ~ **of the law** Gesetzesvollziehung; ~ **of wills** → *will*; ~ **on an award** Vollstreckung aus e–m Schiedsurteil; ~ **on bond** Vollstreckung gegen Sicherheitsleistung; ~ **paree** Unterwerfung unter die Zwangsvollstreckung; ~ **sale** → *sale*; ~ **warrant** Vollstreckungsbefehl; **abortive** ~ fruchtlose Vollstreckung; **attachment** ~ → *attachment*; **bar of** ~ Vollstreckungshindernis, Unzulässigkeit der Zwangsvollstreckung; **costs of** ~ Vollstreckungskosten; **discontinuance of** ~ → *discontinuance*; **dormant** ~ Pfändungsauftrag bei Zurückstellung der Verwertung; **equitable** ~ Einsetzung e–s Zwangsverwalters mit Veräußerungsbefugnis; **exempt from** ~ → *exempt;* **fee for** ~ Vollstreckungsgebühr; **fresh** ~ neuerliche Pfändung; **general** ~ Zwangsvollstreckung in das bewegliche Vermögen; Auftrag, in das gesamte Schuldnervermögen zu vollstrekken; **junior** ~ nachrangige Vollstreckung; **postponement of** ~ Strafaufschub; **protection from** ~ Vollstreckungsschutz; **special** ~ Auftrag, bestimmte Gegenstände zu pfänden; **speedy** ~ sofortige Vollstreckbarkeit; **stay of** ~ Vollstreckungsaufschub; vorläufige Einstellung der Zwangsvollstreckung, Sistierung; **stay of ~ during good behaviour** Aussetzung des Strafvollzugs bei guter Führung; **staying** ~ vorläufige Einstellung der Zwangsvollstreckung; **subject to** ~ → *subject*; **suspension of** ~ → *suspension*; **to have ~ issued** die Zwangsvollstreckung betreiben; **to commence** ~ die Zwangsvollstreckung einleiten, Vollstrekkungsauftrag erteilen; **to levy** ~ → *levy v*; **to suspend** ~ die Vollstrekkung vorläufig einstellen; **unsatisfied** ~ fruchtlose Pfändung; (*ganz oder teilweise*) erfolglose Zw.vollstreckung; **writ of** ~ → *writ*.

execution (*2*) Hinrichtung *f*; ~ **by lethal injection** Hinrichtung durch die Todesspritze.

executioner Scharfrichter *m*, Henker *m*.

executive *adj* vollziehend; exekutiv, vollstreckend, Vollstreckungs ..., Vollziehungs ...; ~ **head** Staatschef, Firmenchef; **E~ Mansion** Amtssitz des (US) Präsidenten, das Weiße Haus; ~ **officer** Vorstandsmitglied (*e–r amerikanischen Aktiengesellschaft, d.h. President, Vicepresident, Treasurer, Secretary, u.ä., nicht jedoch Chairman of the Board of Directors*); Beamter (*der öffentlichen Verwaltung*); ~ **organ** Organ der Exekutive.

executive *s* Exekutive *f*, vollziehende Gewalt *f*; Vorstand *m*; Leiter, leitender Angestellter; ~ **share incentive scheme** Beteiligungsplan für Führungskräfte; **banking** ~ Bankdirektor; **chief** ~ Vorstandsvorsitzender, Direktor, leitender Angestellter; **commercial** ~ kaufmännischer Angestellter in leitender Stellung, wirtschaftliche Führungskraft; **legal** ~ Anwaltsmitarbeiter; **the Chief E~** der (US) Präsident; **the national** ~ Gesamtvorstand (*Verband, Partei*).

executor Testamentsvollstrecker *m* (= *T bzw ...t*), letztwillig bestimmter Nachlaßabwickler; ~ **according to the tenor (of the will)** konkludent bestellter *T*; ~ **and trustee corporation** Testamentsvollstreckungs- u. Treuhand-Gesellschaft; **~s, administrators and assigns** *T*, Nachlaßverwalter und Sonderrechtsnachfolger; ~ **as such** in seiner Eigenschaft als *T*; **~'s bond** Kaution des *T*; ~ **by**

substitution Ersatzt; ~ **creditor** Nachlaßgläubiger als subsidiärer Nachlaßverwalter; ~ **dative** *scot* gerichtlich bestellter *T*; ~ **de son tort** unrechtmäßige handelnder *T*; ~**'s year** Jahresfrist zur Abwicklung der Testamentsvollstreckung; ~ **lucratus** *T* e–s deliktisch haftenden Erblassers; ~**-nominate** *scot* testamentarisch bestellter *T*; ~ **of an** ~ *T* des *T–s* (*Rechtsübergang*); ~ **to the tenor** *T* auf Grund sinngemäßer Anwendung der letztwilligen Verfügung; **corporate** ~ institutioneller *T* (*Bank*); **general** ~ unbeschränkter *T*; *T* für den Gesamtnachlaß; **instituted** ~ letztwillig eingesetzter *T*; **joint** ~ gemeinschaftlicher *T*, Mitvollstrecker; **limited** ~ (gegenständlich *bzw* zeitlich) beschränkter *T*; **sole** ~ alleiniger *T*; **special** ~ gegenständlich beschränkter *T*.

executorship Testamentsvollstreckeramt *n*; ~ **expenses** Kosten der Testamentsvollstreckung.

executory noch zu vollziehen, zukünftig erfüllbar, noch nicht vollständig erfüllt.

executress Testamentsvollstreckerin *f*.

executrix Testamentsvollstreckerin *f*.

exemplary exemplarisch, pönalisierend.

exemplification Erläuterung *f*, beglaubigte Abschrift *f*, Ausfertigung *f*.

exemplif|y a deed e–e Ausfertigung (*bzw beglaubigte Abschrift*) herstellen; ~**ied copy** → *copy*.

exempt *adj* befreit, ausgenommen, immun; ~ **from duty** gebührenfrei, zollfrei; ~ **from execution** unpfändbar; ~ **from military service** vom Wehrdienst befreit; ~ **from taxation** steuerfrei; ~ **private company** → *company*; ~ **property** → *property*; ~ **securities** nicht registerpflichtige Wertpapiere.

exempt *s* ein vom Wehrdienst Freigestellter *m*; unter Immunität stehende Person *f*.

exempt *v* befreien, freistellen, ausnehmen.

exemption Befreiung *f*, Freibetrag, Immunität *f*, Unpfändbarkeit *f*; ~ **clause** → *clause*; ~**s dependent uponsize** größenabhängige Befreiungen; ~ **from duty** Zollfreiheit; ~ **from judicial execution** Unpfändbarkeit; ~ **from liability** Haftungsausschluß; ~ **from punishment** Strafausschließungsgrund; ~ **laws** gesetzliche Unpfändbarkeitsbestimmungen; ~ **limit** Steuerfreigrenze; **customs** ~ Zollfreiheit; **flat** ~ Freibetrag; **full** ~ uneingeschränkte Befreiung; **legal** ~ gesetzliche Befreiung(sgründe); **old age** ~ Altersfreibetrag; **personal** ~ persönlicher (Steuer)-Freibetrag; **words of** ~ Immunitätsklausel; **writ of** ~ gerichtliche Freistellung vom Geschworenendienst.

exequatur Exequatur *n*; **to grant the** ~ das Exequatur erteilen.

exercise *s* Übung *f*, Gebrauch *m*, Anwendung *f*, Ausübung *f*; ~ **of a privilege** Ausübung e–s Rechts; Geltendmachung e–s Vorrechts; ~ **of a right** Rechtsausübung; ~ **of discretion** Ermessensgebrauch; ~ **of functions** Ausübung von Amtsbefugnissen; ~ **of jurisdiction** → *jurisdiction*; ~ **of options** Ausübung des Prämienrechts, Optionsausübung.

exercise *v* ausüben, gebrauchen, anwenden; ~ **a remedy** von e–m Rechtsbehelf Gebrauch machen; ~ **effective administrative control** staatliche Hoheitsrechte ausüben; ~ **pressure** Druck ausüben; ~ **proper care** die im Verkehr erforderliche Sorgfalt beachten; ~ **reprisals** Repressalien ergreifen; ~ **supervisory jurisdiction** als Aufsichtsinstanz tätig werden.

exercitorial power treuhänderische Befugnisse (*der Schiffskapitäne für die Reederei*).

exhaust erschöpfen, verbrauchen, aufbrauchen; ~ **the soil** Raubbau treiben.

exhaust emissions Abgase *n|pl beim Kfz.*
exhaustion of local remedies Ausnutzung des innerstaatlichen Rechtswegs.
exhibit *s* Beweisurkunde *f*, Beweisstück *n*, Asservat *n*, Anlage *f*; **list of ~s** Beweisurkunden- und Asservatenliste; ~ **section** Asservatenabteilung.
exhibit *v* vorlegen, zeigen, ausstellen, offenlegen; ~ **a bill** Klage erheben; ~ **a charge** gegen jmdn Anklage erheben; **to be kept constantly ~ed** ständig gut sichtbar anzubringen.
exhibitant derjenige, der eine Beweisurkunde *bzw* Asservat vorlegt; Antragsteller.
exhibition Ausstellung *f*, Schaustellung *f*, Vorführung *f*, Vorzeigen *n*; Zurschaustellung *f*; ~ **of an affidavit** Beibringung e–r beeideten schriftlichen Erklärung; ~ **of documents** Einreichung von Urkunden; ~ **value** erwartete Mindesteinnahmen, Mindesteinspielerlös (*Film*); **indecent** ~ sittenwidriges Zurschaustellen; **industrial** ~ Gewerbeausstellung.
exhibitioner Stipendiat *m*.
exhibitionist Exhibitionist *m*.
exhibitor Aussteller *m*, Darsteller *m*; die vorlegende Partei *f*.
exhumation Exhumierung *f*.
exhume exhumieren.
exigence Dringlichkeit *f*, dringlicher Fall *m*, Notlage *f*, kritische Lage *f*, Zwangslage *f*, Notfall *m*; ~ **of a bond** das durch die Kaution gesicherte Verhalten; ~ **of a writ** Tenor e–r gerichtlichen Anordnung.
exigency = *exigence qv*.
exigendary Gerichtsbeamter *m* zuständig für Zwangsladungen.
exigent *adj* dringend benötigt.
exigible fällig, geschuldet, eintreibbar.
exile *s* Verbrannter *m*; Verbannung *f*, Exil *n* (*freiwillig bzw zwangsweise*); ~ **government** Exilregierung; **internal** ~ Verbannung im eigenen Staatsgebiet.
exile *v* verbannen.
exilement Verbannung *f*, Landesverweisung *f*.
exist existieren, vorhanden sein, bestehen; **to cease to** ~ → *to cease*.
existence Existenz *f*, Dasein *n*, Vorhandensein *n*, Tatsächlichkeit *f*, Dauer *f*, Fortbestehen *n*; **continued** ~ Fortbestand.
existing bestehend; ~ **and accruing rights** Rechte und Anwartschaften; ~ **circumstances and conditions** die jeweiligen Umstände; ~ **debt** → *debt*; ~ **equity** Anspruch auf künftige Zahlung; ~ **law** → *law*; **liabilities** bestehende Verbindlichkeiten (*einschließlich späterer Fälligkeiten*); ~ **person** natürliche Person (*einschließlich nasciturus*); ~ **practice** Gepflogenheit, Übung; ~ **servants** jeweilige Bedienstete; ~ **use** derzeitiger Verwendungszweck.
exitus Nachkommenschaft *f*; Bodenerträge *m|pl*; Abschluß *m* e–s Verfahrens.
exodus Auswanderung *f*, Abwanderung *f* (*auch Kapital*); ~ **of capital** Kapitalflucht; **rural** ~ Landflucht.
exonerate (*from*) entlasten, rehabilitieren.
exoneration Freistellung *f* von Verbindlichkeiten, Entlastung *f*, Rehabilitierung *f*; ~ **clause** Freizeichnungsklausel.
exoneretur Haftungsfreistellung *f* des Bürgen.
exorbitant übertrieben, übermäßig, ungesetzlich; ~ **interest** überhöhte Zinsen; ~ **price** → *price* (*1*).
exorbitance of the charge außergewöhnliche Höhe der geforderten Vergütung.
exordium Einleitung *f* (*e–s Plädoyers*).
expansion Expansion *f*, Erweiterung *f*, Ausweitung *f*; ~ **investment** Erweiterungsinvestition; ~ **of business** Geschäftserweiterung; ~ **of credit** Kreditausweitung; ~ **of trade** Handelsausweitung; **monetary** ~ Geldausweitung.
expatriate *s* freiwillig im Ausland Lebender *m* Auslands*amerikaner*;

Ausgebürgerter *m*; jmd, der seine Nationalität gewechselt hat; *v* seine Nationalität aufgeben, auf seine Staatsbürgerschaft verzichten.

expatriation Ausbürgerung *f*, Aufgabe *f* der Staatsbürgerschaft.

expectancy Anwartschaft *f*; ~ **of life** *ins* Lebenserwartung; **estate in** ~ → *estate*; **immediate** ~ nächste Anwartschaft; **in** ~ zukünftig; **release of** ~ → *release*.

expectant *adj* zu erwarten, zukünftig, Anwartschafts ...; ~ **estate** → *estate*; ~ **heir** → *heir*; ~ **interest** zukünftiges Recht, Nacherbenrecht; ~ **mother** werdende Mutter; ~, **presumptive or vested share** zu erwartender, vermutlich bestehender oder effektiv übertragener Anteil; ~ **right** Anwartschaftsrecht; ~ **share or interest** Anwartschaftsanteil oder Anwartschaftsrecht.

expectation of life Lebenserwartung *f*.

expected|time of arrival (*ETA*) voraussichtliche Ankunftszeit; ~ **time of departure** (*ETD*) voraussichtliche Auslaufzeit.

expedience Zweckmäßigkeit *f*.

expedient *adj* zweckdienlich, zweckmäßig; *s* Hilfsmittel, Notbehelf; ~ **in the public interest** im öffentlichen Interesse liegend; ~ **to the ends of justice** der Herbeiführung e–r gerichtlichen Entscheidung dienlich, der Rechtspflege entsprechend.

expediment Mobiliarvermögen *n*.

expedit|e beschleunigen, abfertigen, befördern, ausstellen; ~ **a matter** e–e Sache beschleunigt behandeln; ~**ed service** Eildienst; ~**ing proceedings** Beschleunigung des Verfahrens.

expedition Beschleunigung *f*, Eile *f*, Gewandtheit *f*; Expedition *f*, Feldzug *m*.

expeditious rasch, emsig, prompt, förderlich.

expel ausweisen, vertreiben, ausstoßen, gewaltsam entfernen, relegieren, ausschließen.

expellee Vertriebener *m*, Ausgewiesener *m*, Ausgestoßener *m*.

expend ausgeben, aufwenden, verbrauchen.

expendable trust funds Treuhandfonds mit freier Ertragsverwendung.

expenditure Ausgaben *f|pl*, Aufwand *m*; ~ **account** → *account*; ~ **ceiling** Ausgaben-Plafonds, Etat; **additional** ~ Mehraufwand; **administrative** ~ Verwaltungskosten; **aggregate** ~ Gesamtaufwand; **average** ~**s** Havariegelder; **basic** ~ bleibende Unkosten; Gemeinkosten; **budgetary** ~ Haushaltsausgaben; **capital** ~ → *capital*; **cash** ~ Baraufwand; **consumer** ~ Verbraucherausgaben; **incidental** ~**s** unvorhergesehene Ausgaben; **living** ~**s** Lebenshaltungskosten; **national** ~ Staatsausgaben; **non-recurring** ~ einmalige Ausgabe; **office** ~ Bürounkosten; **operating** ~ Betriebsausgaben; **pre-trading** ~ Aufwendungen vor Geschäftseröffnung; **public** ~ Staatsausgaben, öffentl Ausgaben; **routine** ~ tägliche Ausgaben; **running** ~ laufende Betriebskosten; **to allocate one's** ~ Ausgaben aufschlüsseln.

expense Ausgaben *f|pl*, Aufwand *m*, Auslagen *f|pl*, Kosten *f|pl*; ~ **account** Unkostenkonto; ~ **allowance** Aufwandsentschädigung; ~**s attached to the meeting** Kosten der (Haupt)Versammlung; ~**s charged forward** gegen Vorausbezahlung der Kosten; ~ **covered** Kosten gedeckt; ~**s deducted** nach Abzug der Kosten; ~ **incurred** Aufwendungen, angefallene Kosten, entstandene Ausgaben; ~ **not otherwise received** nicht anderweitig erstattete Kosten; ~ **of maintenance** Erhaltungskosten; ~ **of management** Verwaltungskosten; ~**s of noting** Kosten der notariellen Wechselvorlage, Protestkosten (*vgl noting*); ~**s of noting and protest** Protestkosten; ~ **of production** Herstellungskosten;

~s **of re-exchange** *Rückwechselkosten und Protestkosten für e–n Auslandsprotestwechsel;* ~**s of selling** Vertriebskosten, Verkaufsunkosten; **accrued** ~ antizipative Passiva; **actual** ~**s** Barauslagen; **administration** ~ Kosten der Erbschaftsverwaltung, K. der Nachlaßabwicklung *cf administration;* **administrative** ~**s** Verwaltungskosten; **advanced** ~ Kostenvorschuß; **at my** ~ auf meine Kosten; **at ship's** ~ auf Kosten der Reederei; **business** ~ Betriebsausgabe(n); **cancelling** ~**s** Ristornogebühr; **cash** ~**s** Barauslagen; **claim** ~ Regulierungskosten, Bearbeitungskosten; **collection** ~**s** → *collection;* **contingent** ~ unvorhergesehene Ausgaben; **current** ~**(s)** laufende Ausgaben; **direct** ~ unmittelbarer Kostenaufwand; **entertainment** ~ Bewirtungsausgaben; **executive** ~**s** Geschäftsführungskosten; **funeral** ~**s** Bestattungskosten; **general** ~ Gemeinkosten, allg Unkosten; **incidence of** ~ Unkostenanfall; **incidental** ~**s** Vollstreckungsauslagen, Nebenauslagen; **initial** ~**s** *ins* Abschlußkosten; **legal** ~**s** Anwalts- und Gerichtskosten; **legislative** ~**s** Parlamentskosten; **living** ~ Lebenshaltungskosten; **loading** ~**s** Verladekosten; **necessary** ~**s** notwendige Auslagen; **operating** ~**s** Betriebskosten, betriebliche Aufwendungen; **ordinary** ~**s** Parlamentskosten; **organization** ~ Gründungskosten; **out-of-pocket** ~**s** Barauslagen; **out-of-town travel** ~**s** Reisespesen; **preliminary** ~ Gründungskosten; **prepaid** ~**s** transitorische Posten, aktive Rechnungsabgrenzung; **reasonable** ~**s** angemessene Auslagen; **reimbursed** ~**s** erstattete Kosten; **running** ~**s** laufende Ausgaben; **selling** ~**s** Vertriebskosten; **testamentary** ~**s** Kosten der Testamenserrichtung; Testamentsvollstreckerkosten; **to break down** ~**s** Kosten aufschlüsseln; **to charge to** ~ als Aufwand verbuchen; **to refund the** ~**s** Kosten zurückerstatten; **trifling** ~ geringfügige Unkosten; **unabsorbed** ~ nicht überwälzte Gemeinkosten; **unexpired** ~ transitorische Aktiva.

experience Erfahrung *f*; ~ **rate** Erfahrungssatz; **business** ~ **Geschäftserfahrung; commercial** ~ kaufmännische Erfahrung; **post qualification** ~ Erfahrung seit Zulassung (als *Anwalt*).

experiment Versuch *m*, Experiment *n*.

expert *adj* sachverständig, fachmännisch.

expert *s* Fachmann *m*, Sachverständiger *m*, Gutachter *m*; ~**'s judgment** Sachverständigenurteil; ~**'s opinion** Gutachten e–s Sachverständigen; ~**('s) testimony** Aussage des Sachverständigen; Sachverständigenbeweis; **court** ~ gerichtlich bestellter Sachverständiger; **handwriting** ~ Schriftsachverständiger; **report of** ~ Sachverständigengutachten; **the issue for the** ~ die zu begutachtende Frage.

expertise Sachverständigenwissen *n*, besondere Fachkunde *f*, Sachverständigengutachten *n*, Expertise *f*; **in-house** ~ firmeninterne Spezialkenntnisse.

expiate abbüßen, sühnen.

expilation Nachlaßuntersuchung *f*.

expiration Zeitablauf *m*, Ablauf *m*, Ende *n*, Erlöschen *n*, Außerkrafttreten *n*; ~ **date of a patent** Ablaufzeitpunkt e–s Patents; ~ **of a patent** Ablauf e–s Patents; ~ **of a period** Fristablauf; ~ **of a truce** Ablauf des Waffenstillstandes; ~ **of an agreement** Vertragsablauf; ~ **of the term (fixed)** Fristablauf; **at the** ~ **of . . .** nach Ablauf von . . .; **date of** ~ Fälligkeitstermin, Verfallstag.

expir|e verfallen, erlöschen, ablaufen, außer Kraft treten; **E** ~**ing Laws Continuance Act** Gesetz über Verlängerung auslaufender Gesetze.

expiry Fristablauf *m*, Zeitablauf *m*, Verfall *m*; ~ **date** → *date.*

explain erklären, erläutern.
explanation Erklärung *f*, Erläuterung *f*.
explanatory statement Erklärung *f*, Erläuterung *f*.
explicit deutlich, bestimmt, klar, ausdrücklich.
exploit ausbeuten, benutzen, verwerten.
exploitation Ausbeutung *f*, Verwertung *f*, Benutzung *f*; ~ **of the sea bed** Ausbeutung des Meeresbodens; **exclusive right of** ~ ausschließliches Nutzungsrecht; **illegal** ~ widerrechtliche Ausbeutung; **illegitimate** ~ unberechtigte Ausbeutung; **industrial** ~ industrielle Verwertung; **intermediate** ~ Zwischenbenutzung; **wasteful** ~ Raubbau.
exploiter Benutzer *m*; **intermediate** ~ Zwischenbenutzer; **joint** ~ Mitbenutzer.
exploration Untersuchung *f*, Erforschung *f*, Exploration *f*, Probe *f*, Probebohrung *f*, Orientierung *f*.
explosives Sprengstoffe *m/pl*.
Explosive Substance Act Sprengstoffgesetz.
export Export *m*, (Waren) Ausfuhr *f*; ~ **agent** Exportvertreter; ~ **bonus** Ausfuhrprämie; ~ **bounty** Ausfuhrprämie; ~ **clearance** Ausfuhrerlaubnis; ~ **controls** Ausfuhrkontrolle; ~ **council** Ausfuhrförderungsgemeinschaft; **E~ Credits Guarantee Department** *brit* Behörde für Ausfuhrbürgschaften; ~ **demands** Exportanforderungen; ~ **declaration** Ausfuhrerklärung; ~ **documents** Ausfuhrdokumente; ~ **duty** Ausfuhrzoll; ~ **earning stabilization** Stabilisierung der Exporterlöse; ~ **entry** Ausfuhrformular; ~ **guarantee** Exportbürgschaft; **E~ Guarantees Advisory Council** Beratungsstelle für Exportbürgschaften; *GB*; ~ **houses** Exportfirmen; **E~ Import Bank** (*Eximbank*) Ausfuhr- Einfuhr B. (*US*); ~ **licence** → *licence*; ~ **manager** → *manager*; ~ **order** Exportauftrag; ~ **permit** Ausfuhrerlaubnis, Ausfuhrgenehmigung; ~ **premium** Ausfuhrprämie; ~ **prohibition** Ausfuhrverbot; ~ **promotion** Ausfuhrförderung; ~ **quota** Ausfuhrkontingent; ~ **regulations** Ausfuhrbestimmungen; ~ **specie point** Goldausfuhrpunkt; ~ **specification** Zollausfuhrerklärung; ~ **subsidy** Exportsubvention; ~ **surplus** Ausfuhrüberschuß; ~ **tariff** → *tariff*; ~ **tax** → *tax*; **invisible ~s** unsichtbare Ausfuhren; **national** ~ Gesamtausfuhr; **personal ~s** Ausfuhrgegenstände zum Privatgebrauch; **unrequited ~s** Exporte ohne (Ausgleich durch) Gegenimporte.
export *v* exportieren, ausführen; ~ **outright** endgültig ausführen.
exportation Export *m*, Ausfuhr *f*.
exporter Exporteur *m*; Ausführer *m* (*Zoll*); **approved** ~ ermächtigter Ausführer; **~'s sale price** Verkaufspreis des Exporteurs.
expos|e ausstellen, zur Schau stellen; durch Aushang bekannt machen; aussetzen, sich entblößen; ~ **for sale** feilhalten; **~ing children** Kindesaussetzung (*Kleinkinder*); **~ing unfit food for sale** Feilhalten nicht zum Verbrauch geeigneter Lebensmittel.
exposition Ausstellung *f*, Erläuterung *f*, Erklärung *f*; **vocal** ~ mündl Vortrag.
expository statute Erläuterungsgesetz *n*.
ex post facto law → *ex*.
expostulate postulieren, Vorhaltungen machen.
expostulation Vorhaltung *f*, Verweis *m*; Klage *f*, Protest *m*.
exposure Ausgesetztsein *n*; Kreditrisiko *m*, Engagement *n*; Zur-Schau-Stellen *n*; ~ **hazard** Nachbarschaftsrisiko, Strahlungsrisiko; ~ **of a plot** Aufdeckung e–r Verschwörung; ~ **of person** unsittliche Entblößung als offenes Ärgernis; ~ **of child** Kindesaussetzung; **indecent** ~ öffentliche Erregung geschlechtlichen Ärgernisses, unsittliche Entblößung, Exhibitionis-

mus; **sovereign** ~ Staatsschuldrisiko; **voluntary** ~ **to unnecessary danger** Selbstgefährdung.
exposure draft Projektentwurf *m*, Arbeitspapier *n*.
expound auslegen, deuten, interpretieren.
express *adj* (*1*) ausdrücklich; ~ **provision to the contrary** ausdrückliche gegenteilige Bestimmung; ~ **ly prohibited** ausdrücklich untersagt, verboten.
express *adj* (*2*) Express ..., Schnell ... Eil ...; ~ **money order** Zahlungsanweisung der American Express Co; ~ **postal mail** Eilpost, Sonderzustellung; **E~ post messenger service** Eilbotendienst.
expromissio(n) private (= befreiende) Schuldübernahme) *f*.
expromissor Schuldübernehmer *m*.
expropriate enteignen.
expropriation (*entschädigungslose*) Enteignung *f*; **compulsory** ~ Enteignung.
expropriatory enteignend, enteignungsähnlich.
expulsion Vertreibung *f*, Ausstoßung *f*, Ausweisung *f*; ~ **of aliens** Abschieben von Ausländern.
expunge löschen, streichen.
expurgate säubern, reinigen, Unstatthaftes weglassen, zensieren.
expurgation Reinigung *f*, Läuterung *f*; **E~ Index** Index (*kirchlich verbotener Schriften*).
expurgator Zensor *m*, Säuberer *m*, Berichtiger *m*.
extant bestehend, noch vorhanden.
extend erweitern, verlängern, sich erstrecken, prolongieren, abschätzen, durch Vollstreckung erfassen; ~ **a loan to s.o.** jmdm ein Darlehen gewähren; ~ **a patent** ein Patent verlängern; ~ **the validity** die Gültigkeit verlängern; ~ **to and include** darüber hinaus bedeuten; erweiternd umfassen; ~**ed (term) insurance** → *insurance*; ~**ed value** voller Schätzwert; ~**ing protest** notarielle Wechselprotesterhebung *f* (*nach Notifizierung*).
extender of credit Kreditgeber *m*.
extension Erweiterung *f*, Ausdehnung *f*, Verlängerung *f*, Prolongation *f*, Stundung *f*, Fristverlängerung *f*; Nebenanschluß *f*, Nebenstrecke *f*, Erweiterungsbau *m*; ~ **agents** *US* Beauftragte für (*landwirtschaftliche*) Forbildungskurse; ~ **agreement** Fristverlängerungsabrede; ~ **of a judgment** Vollstreckbarkeitserklärung (*e–s Urteils in e–m anderen Staat*); ~ **of certificate** Verlängerung e–r Bescheinigung; ~ **of credit** Kreditgewährung; ~ **of jurisdiction** Zuständigkeitserweiterung; ~ **of mortgage** Einbeziehung in den Pfandverband; ~ **of permitted licensing hours** Verlängerung der Polizeistunde; ~ **of (a) patent** Patentverlängerung; ~ **of protest** = *extending protest qv*; ~ **of the term of payment** befristete Stundung; ~ **of time** Fristverlängerung, Nachfrist; ~ **of time for appeal** Verlängerung der Rechtsmittelfrist; ~ **of working hours** Arbeitszeitverlängerung; ~ **work** berufliches Fortbildungswesen.
extensive ausgedehnt, umfangreich; ~ **interpretation** → *interpretation*.
extent Höhe *f*, Größe *f*, Weite *f*, Umfang *m*; Immobiliarvollstreckung *f*, Zwangsverwaltung *f*; Schätzung von Grundbesitz zwecks Zwangsverwaltung (*GB bis 1947*); ~ **in aid** Vollstreckungsanordnung gegen einen Drittschuldner *e–s Staatsschuldners*; ~ **in chief** Zwangsbeitreibung von Kronforderungen; ~ **of damage** Schadenshöhe; ~ **of liability** Haftungsumfang, Haftung; **manorial** ~ → *manorial*.
extenuat|e verringern, mildern; ~**ing circumstances** → *circumstance*.
extenuation Strafmilderung *f*.
exterminate ausrotten, vernichten.
extermination Ausrottung *f*.
external äußerlich, außen befindlich; ~**s** *s* äußere Form, Äußeres; ~ **and visible injury** sichtbare durch äußere Einwirkung entstandene Verletzung; ~ **part of the premises** die Außenmauern und sonstige

Bauteile; ~ **payments are in deficit** die Zahlungsbilanz ist passiv.

exterritorial exterritorial.

exterritoriality Exterritorialität *f.*

extinct erloschen, ausgestorben, aufgehoben; ~ **firm** gelöschte Handelsfirma.

extinction Löschung *f*; ~ **value** → *value*; **legal** ~ Löschung, Ungültigkeitserklärung.

extinguish tilgen, löschen, auslöschen, aufheben, zum Erlöschen bringen.

extinguishment Erlöschen *n*, Vernichtung *f*, Aufhebung *f*; ~ **of common** Verlust des Allmenderechts; ~ **of debts** Erlöschen von Schuldverpflichtungen; ~ **of easements** Erlöschen einer Dienstbarkeit, Verhinderung des gewohnheitsrechtlichen Entstehens einer Dienstbarkeit; ~ **of estates** Fusion von Grundstücksrechten; ~ **of highways** Auflassung von Landstraßen; ~ **of legacy** Vermächtnisfortfall, Unwirksamkeit e–s Vermächtnisses; ~ **of manorial incidents** Aufhebung des Grundherrschaftsdienstes; ~ **of rent** Erlöschen der Bodenzinsen; ~ **of ways** Erlöschen von Wegerechten.

extirpate ausrotten, vertilgen.

extirpation Raubbau *m* (*seitens des Pächters*).

extirpatione gerichtliche Verfügung *f* wegen mutwilliger Beschädigung der Pachtsache.

extorsive erpresserisch.

extort erpressen, erzwingen; ~ **a confession** ein Geständnis erzwingen; ~**ing money by menaces** räuberische Erpressung.

extortion Erpressung *f*, Nötigung *f*; ~ **by public officials** Erpressung im Amt (*GB bis 1968*).

extortionate erpresserisch, sittenwidrig hoch; wucherisch.

extortioner Erpresser *m*, beamteter Erpresser *m*.

extra besonders, zusätzlich, Neben. . ., Sonder. . .; ~ **allowance** → *allowance;* ~ **budgetary** außeretatmäßig; ~ **costs** Sonderaufwendungen, außergerichtliche Kosten; ~ **dividend** → *dividend;* ~ **– dotal property** Vorbehaltsgut *der Ehefrau;* ~ **duty** Zollaufschlag; ~ **fare** Zuschlag; ~ **fee** Sondergebühr; ~ **-hazardous employment** gefahrgeneigte Tätigkeit; ~ **income** → *income*; ~ **-judicial** außergerichtlich → *extrajudicial*; ~ **lay-days** Überliegetage; ~ **-legal** außergesetzlich; ~ **-marital** außerehelich; ~ **-matrimonial** außerehelich; ~**-parliamentary** außerparlamentarisch; ~ **profit** Übergewinn, Nebenverdienst; ~ **services** Nebendienste; ~ **-statutory concessions** außergesetzliche (Steuer)Zugeständnisse; ~ **vires** außerhalb der Zuständigkeit *bei Überschreitung des Satzungszwecks*, ultra vires; ~ **work** außervertragliche Leistungen; Zusatzleistung, Arbeiten auf Grund von Sonderwünschen des Bauherrn.

extract *s* Auszug *m*, wesentlicher Inhalt *m*.

extract *v* extrahieren, gewinnen (aus), zitieren.

extraction Auszug *m*, Abkunft *f*, Herkunft *f*, Extrahieren *n*, Ausscheiden *n*; ~ **of blood** Blutentnahme.

extraditable auslieferbar.

extradite ausliefern.

extradition Auslieferung *f*; ~ **committal** Auslieferungshaft(befehl); ~ **of nationals** Auslieferung eigener Staatsangehöriger; ~ **proceedings** Auslieferungsverfahren; ~ **request** Auslieferungsersuchen; **bars to** ~ Auslieferungshindernisse.

extrajudicial außergerichtlich.

extralateral right *Recht an Erzadern oder Flözen, die schräg unter der Grundstücksgrenze hinweg führen.*

extraneous ausländisch, auswärtig, fremd, außerhalb der Urkunde liegend; ~ **expenses** Fremdaufwendungen; ~ **perils** → *peril.*

extraordinary außerordentlich, außergewöhnlich.

extraparochial außergemeindlich; von Gemeindeabgaben befreit.

extra-territorial exterritorial.
extra-territoriality Exterriorialität *f*.
extremit|y äußerste Not *f*, äußerste Maßnahme *f*, der weiteste Punkt *m*; **to proceed to ~ies** zu äußersten Maßnahmen greifen.
extrinsic äußerlich, nicht dazu gehörig.
eye-witness *s* Augenzeuge *m*; *v* Augenzeuge sein.
eyes only höchst persönlich und vertraulich.
eyre *hist* richterliche Rundreise *f*, Termin *m* von Richterkommissaren *m|pl* des Zentralgerichts.

F

Fabian policy Zauderpolitik *f*, Politik *f* der Entschlußlosigkeit.
fabric Struktur *f*, Gewebe *n*, Fabrikat *n*, Stoff *m*, Stahldrahtgewebe *n als Betonverstärkung*; ~ **lands** → *land*; **F~s (Misdescription) Act** Gesetz gegen falsche Gewebebezeichnungen; **social** ~ gesellschaftliche Struktur.
fabricate fälschlich erfinden, fälschen, erdichten; ~**ed account** gefälschte Rechnung; ~**ed document** Falschurkunde, unechte Urkunde; ~**ed fact** vorgespiegelte falsche Tatsache.
fabrication of evidence Herstellung falschen Beweismaterials; betrügerisches Fingieren von Beweisen.
face Vorderseite *f*, Außenseite *f*, Stirnseite *f*, Wortlaut *m*, Nennwert *m*; ~ **amount** Hauptsachebetrag *auf einer Schuldurkunde*, Gesamtbetrag; ~ **amount certificate** → *certificate*; ~ – **amount certificate company** → *company*; ~ **of book** erste Seite, Titelseite; ~ **of instrument** Wortlaut der Urkunde; ~ **of judgment** Urteilsbetrag (*ohne Zinsen*); ~**of policy** Wortlaut des (*gesamten*) Versicherungsscheines; ~ **of record** die *gesamte* Gerichtsakte; ~ **value** Nennwert, Nennbetrag, Nominalwert; **regular on its** ~ allem Anschein nach ordnungsgemäß; **void on its** ~ nichtig, wie sich aus dem Wortlaut der Urkunde ergibt.
facere Tun *n*, Pflicht *f* zum Handeln.
facia Ladenschild *f*, Firmenkennzeichnung *f*.
facile leicht, gewandt, geschickt; *scot* leicht überredbar.
facilit|y Leichtigkeit *f*, Gewandtheit *f*, günstige Gelegenheit *f*, Möglichkeit *f*, ~**ies** Einrichtung *f*, Anlage *f*; ~ **fee** Bereitstellungsprovision; ~ **letter** Kreditbestätigung; ~**ies of payment** Zahlungserleichterungen; **bilateral** ~ zweiseitige Kreditbeziehung; **idle** ~ stilliegende Betriebsanlage.
facsimile Faksimile *n*, genaue Nachbildung *f*, genaue Abschrift *f*; ~ **probate** wortgetreue Testamentsbestätigung, *genaue Wiedergabe von Form und Inhalt des Testaments durch das Nachlaßgericht*; ~ **signature** Faksimileunterschrift; ~ **stamp** Faksimilestempel.
fact Tatsache *f* (= *T bzw t*), Umstand *m*, Wirklichkeit *f*; ~ **finding** Sachverhaltsforschung, Feststellung des Sachverhalts; ~**s in evidence** → *evidence*; ~**s in issue** klageerheblicher Sachverhalt, die entscheidungserheblichen *T–n*; ~ **material to risk** für das Versicherungsrisiko wesentliche *T*; ~**s not in record** nicht aktenkundige *T–n*; ~ **situation** Sachverhalt; ~**s of accident** Unfall-Sachverhalt; ~ **of common knowledge** allgemeinkundige *T*; ~**s of the case** Sachverhalt, Tatbestand; **ablative** ~**s** *T–n*, die zum Rechtsverlust führen; **accomplished** ~ vollendete *T*; **adjudicative** ~**s** tatsächliche Feststellungen für den *verwaltungsrechtlichen* Einzelfall; **admission of** ~**s** → *admission*; **after the** ~ nach der Tat; **ascertainment of** ~**s** tatsächliche Feststellung; **before the** ~ vor der Tat; **collateral** ~**s** unstreitige *T–n* am Rande des Prozesses; **commercial** ~ handelsmäßige Tatsache (*Zoll*); **constituent** ~ Tatbestandsmerkmal; **dispositive** ~**s** *rechtsbegründende, rechtsändernde oder e–n Rechtsverzicht bedeutende Tatsachen*; **divestive** ~**s** e–n Rechtsverlust bedingende *T–n*; **essential** ~**s** die wesentlichen Tatbestandsmerkmale, der wesentliche Teil des Sachverhalts; **established** ~ feststehende

T; **evidential ~s** beweiserhebliche *T–n*, relevante *T–n*; **evidentiary ~** beweiserhebliche *T*, Hilfs*t* für den Beweis, beweisbare *T*; **immaterial ~s** nicht entscheidungserhebliche *T–n*; **inferential ~s** abgeleitete *T–n*, durch Schlußfolgerungen festgestellte *T–n*; **investive ~s** rechtsbegründende *T–n*; **issue of ~** → *issue (2)*; **jurisdictional ~s** zuständigkeitsbegründender Sachverhalt; **legislative ~s** *Tatsachenwissen der Verwaltungsorgane als Grundlage ihrer Verordnungen*; **litigation ~s** tatsächliche Informationen für den Rechtsstreit; **material ~** wesentliche *T*; **minor ~s** untergeordnete Beweis*t–n*; **notorious ~s** notorische *T–n*, offenkundige *T–n*; **physical ~s** physische *T–n*, sinnlich wahrnehmbare *T–n*; **primary ~** durch Zeugen bzw Augenschein beweisbare *T–n*; **principal ~** die entscheidende *T*; **probative ~** beweiserhebliche *T*; **real ~s** der (*wirkliche*) Sachverhalt, echte Tatsachen; **relative ~** Indiz; **suspicious ~** Verdachtsmoment; **the ultimate ~** die letztlich entscheidende *T*.

faction Clique *f*, Interessengruppe *f*, Zwietracht *f*.

factionist Parteigänger *m*.

factious zwieträchtig, aufrührerisch, parteisüchtig.

factiousness Parteisucht *f*.

factitious künstlich, nachgeahmt.

factor Faktor *m*, Einfluß *m*, Umstand *m*; Agent *m*, Verkaufskommissionär *m*; Absatzfinanzierungszessionar *m*, Factoring-Firma *f*; **~ cost** Faktorkosten; **F~s' Act** *brit G (ursprünglich von 1889) über Veräußerungsbefugnis und Verpfändung durch Kommissionäre*; **~ earnings** Einkünfte aus Arbeit und Vermögensnutzung; **~s of production** Produktionsfaktoren; **~ payments** Löhne, Gehälter, Gewinne, Zinsen und Mietzahlungen; **determining ~** maßgeblicher Umstand; **judicial ~** → *judicial*; **non-specific ~s** unspezialisierte Produktionsfaktoren.

factorage Provision *f* des Kommissionärs.

factoring Factoring *n*, Debitorenverkauf *m*, *Vorfinanzierung von abgetretenen Außenständen*; **~ with recourse** unechtes Factoring; **~ without recourse** echtes Factoring; **nonrecourse ~** echtes Factoring; **recourse ~** unechtes Factoring.

factorizing process Pfändung *f* von Sachen des Schuldners im Besitz e–s Dritten.

factory Fabrik *f*, Werk *n*, Werkstätte *f*, Betrieb *m*, Betriebsgrundstück *n*; Faktorei *f*; **F~ies Act** *GB (1961) cf Factory Acts*; **F~ Acts** Gewerbeordnung mit Arbeitsschutzbestimmungen GB; **~ committee** Betriebsrat; **~ cost** Herstellungskosten (*ohne Verpackung*); **~ expenses** Fabrikationskosten; **~ hand** Fabrikarbeiter; **~ legislation** → *legislation*; **~ management** Betriebsleitung; **~ manager** Werksleiter; **~ overhead** Fertigungsgemeinkosten; **~ owner** Fabrikbesitzer, Unternehmer; **~ plant** Werk, Werksanlage; **~ prices** → *price*; **~ regulations** gewerbepolizeiliche Bestimmungen; Betriebsordnung; **~ worker** Fabrikarbeiter; **ex ~** ab Werk; **supplying ~** Lieferwerk.

factual tatsächlich.

factum *hist* Handlung *f*; gesiegelte Urkunde *f*, Testamentserrichtung *f*; **~ probandum** die zu beweisende Tatsache; **~ probans** Indiz, Hilfstatsache für den Beweis.

facultative berechtigend, fakultativ, freigestellt, wahlfrei; **~ powers** Ermessensbefugnis; **~ reinsurance** Rückversicherungsoption.

faculty Erlaubnis *f*, Ermächtigung *f*, Befugnis *f*, *kirchenrechtl Dispens m*; Fakultät *f*, Fähigkeit *f*, Gabe *f*; **~ of hearing** Hörvermögen; **~ of law** juristische Fakultät; **imaginative ~** Vorstellungskraft; **inventive ~** erfinderische Begabung; **perceptive ~** Auffassungsgabe.

fail fehlen, mangeln, nicht tun, unerledigt lassen, nicht erfüllen, unterlassen, von e–r Möglichkeit keinen Gebrauch machen, entfallen, nicht anfallen, ausfallen, die Zahlungen einstellen, versäumen, versagen, scheitern; ~ **in a suit** e–n Prozeß verlieren; ~ **in business** geschäftlich scheitern; ~ **in limine** von vorneherein scheitern; ~ **in one's duty** seine Pflicht nicht erfüllen; ~ **or determine** ausfallen oder beendet sein; ~ **to yield the right of way** die Vorfahrt nicht beachten; ~ **to obtain relief** mit e–m Rechtsbehelf keinen Erfolg haben; **a provision ~s** e–e Bestimmung entfällt.

failing mangels, in Ermangelung; im Falle des Ausbleibens; versagend, ausbleibend; ~ **heirs** bei Nichtvorhandensein von (*gesetzlichen*) Erben; ~ **of record** Unvermögen der Beibringung e–r Urkunde; ~ **payment** → *payment*; ~ **proof** mangels Beweises, beweisfällig; ~ **proof of the contrary** bis zum Beweis des Gegenteils; ~ **special agreement** in Ermangelung e–r besonderen Vereinbarung; ~ **to appear** bei Ausbleiben im Termin; ~ **to comply with** bei Nichtbefolgung; ~ **to inform** bei Nichtanzeige; ~ **to report** Unterlassung der (Unfalls-)Meldung; ~ **to stop** unerlaubtes Entfernen vom Unfallsort; ~ **which** widrigenfalls; **in ~ circumstances** zahlungsunfähig, konkursreif.

failure Ausbleiben *n*, Ermangelung *f*, Mißerfolg *m*, Scheitern, Versäumnis *n*, Unwirksamkeit *f*, Versagen *n*, Betriebseinstellung *f* wegen Zahlungsunfähigkeit; wirtschaftlicher Zusammenbruch *m*; ~ **by lapse** Unwirksamkeit wegen Wegfalls des Bedachten; ~ **of consideration** Wegfall der Gegenleistung; ~ **of evidence** fehlender Beweisantritt, Beweisfälligkeit; ~ **of issue** das Fehlen von Abkömmlingen *als Erbanwärter*; ~ **of justice** Versagen der Justiz, Fehlurteil; ~ **of performance** Nichterfüllung; ~ **of proof** Beweisfälligkeit, Nichterbringung e–s prima facie Beweises; ~ **of record** Nichtvorlage e–r Beweisurkunde; ~ **of title** Nichtverschaffung des Eigentums durch den Verkäufer, Rechtsmangel; ~ **of trust** Ungültigkeit e–r Treuhandbindung; ~ **to appear in court** Nichterscheinen vor Gericht; ~ **to comply** (*with*) Nichteinreichung, Nichtbefolgung; ~ **to consult** Unterlassung e–r Aussprache; Nichtgewährung e–r Gelegenheit zur Stellungnahme; ~ **to file a return** Nichteinreichung e–r (*Steuer-*)Erklärung; ~ **to maintain** Vernachlässigung der Unterhaltspflicht; ~ **to make a claim** das Nichtgeltendmachen e–s Anspruchs; ~ **to make delivery** das Nichterfolgen der Übergabe; ~ **to make discovery** unterlassene Urkundenvorlage; ~ **to meet obligations** Zahlungseinstellung; ~ **to notify** unterlassene Meldung, Unterlassung der (e–r) Mitteilung; ~ **to obey** Ungehorsam, Nichtbefolgung, Zuwiderhandlung; ~ **to procure licence** Nichtbeschaffung e–r Konzession; ~ **to take delivery** Nichtabnahme; ~ **to wear seat belt** Nichtanlegen des Sicherheitsgurts; ~ **under a court order** von Amts wegen eingeleitetes Insolvenzverfahren; **bank** ~ Bankzusammenbruch; **commercial** ~ geschäftlicher Zusammenbruch; **crop** ~ Mißernte; **financial** ~ finanzieller Zusammenbruch.

faint pleader vorgetäuschtes schriftsätzliches Vorbringen (*zur Täuschung Dritter*).

fair *s* Markt *m*, Marktrecht *n*, Jahrmarkt *m*, Messe *f*, Ausstellung *f*; ~ **bill** Markt- und Messewechsel; **agricultural** ~ Landwirtschaftsmesse.

fair *adj* angemessen, fair, gerecht, billig, annehmbar, ehrlich, unparteiisch, anständig; ~ **and equitable** der Billigkeit entsprechend; ~ **and full equivalent for loss** voller angemessener Schadensausgleich; ~ **and proper legal assessment** gleichmäßige, rechtlich einwandfreie Bewertung; ~ **and reason-**

able angemessen; ~ **and reasonable compensation** angemessene Entschädigung; ~ **and reasonable contract** fairer Vertrag (*ohne Nachteile für e–n Minderjährigen*); ausgewogener Vertrag; ~ **and reasonable test** Inhaltskontrolle von allgemeinen Geschäftsbedingungen; ~ **and reasonable value** der beste erzielbare Barverkaufswert, Verkehrswert; ~ **average quality** gute Durchschnittsqualität; Handelsware mittlerer Art und Güte; ~ **credit reporting** nichtdiskriminierende Kreditauskünfte; ~ **current market price** angemessener Marktpreis, Verkehrswert; ~ **employment practices** nicht diskriminierende Behandlung von Stellenbewerbern; ~ **knowledge or skill** angemessene Sachkunde; ~ **market value** Verkehrswert; ~ **on its face** (*Gerichts- oder Zustellungsurkunde*) ohne offenkundige Mängel; ~ **preponderance of the evidence** überwiegendes Beweisergebnis; ~ **wages clause** Standardbetrag für angemessene Löhne *bei öffentlichen Aufträgen*; ~ **wear and tear** angemessene Abnutzung.

fairly gerechterweise, richtigerweise; ~ **to be excused** zu exkulpieren; ~ **workable** in zumutbarem Umfang abbaufähig.

fairness Billigkeit *f*, Gerechtigkeit *f*, Redlichkeit *f*; ~ **doctrine** Ausgewogenheitsgrundsatz, Grundsatz, unterschiedliche Standpunkte zu berücksichtigen.

fair trade *US*: Preisbindung der zweiten Hand; Nichtdiskriminierung im Außenhandel; ~ **Act** Preiskartellverbot(sgesetz) (*US Code*); ~ **agreement** *US*: Vereinbarung über Preisbindung der zweiten Hand; ~ **law** *US: Gesetz, das Preisbindung der zweiten Hand für Markenartikel gestattet*; ~ **product** *Ware mit zulässiger Preisbindung der zweiten Hand.*

Fair Trading Act *GB* Verbraucherschutz- und Kartellgesetz.

fairway Schiffahrtsrinne *f*.

faith Glaube *m*, Vertrauen *n*, Treue *f*, Versprechen *n*; **bad** ~ Bösgläubigkeit; **breach of** ~ Vertrauensbruch, Illoyalität; **freedom of** ~ Glaubensfreiheit; **full** ~ **and credit** *gegenseitige Anerkennung von Gesetzen und Gerichtsentscheidungen zwischen den Gliedstaaten der USA*; **good** ~ Redlichkeit, Gutgläubigkeit; **in bad** ~ bösgläubig; **in breach of** ~ mißbräuchlich, unter Vertrauensbruch; **in good** ~ gutgläubig, redlich; **on the** ~ **thereof** in (gutem) Glauben darauf; im Vertrauen auf; **public** ~ öffentlicher Glaube.

faithfully wahrhaftig, genau, zuverlässig, prompt.

fake *s* Fälschung *f*.

fake *v* fälschen, etwas Unechtes herstellen.

fake-out Bluff *m*, Täuschung *f*.

falcidian portion Mindesterbteil *m*.

fall *v* abnehmen, fallen, ein Recht verlieren; ~ **foul of an agreement** mit e–r Vereinbarung Probleme haben; ~ **vacant** frei werden (*Sitz in e–m Gremium*).

fallacious abwegig.

fall-out station nukleare Meßstation *f*.

fallow-land Brachland *n*, Brache *f*.

false falsch, unecht, täuschend, bewußt unwahr, heimtückisch; unrichtig, irrtümlich, rechtswidrig; ~ **accusation of crime** falsche Anschuldigung; ~ **assumption of authority** Amtsanmaßung; ~ **assumption to act** Anmaßung zum Handeln; ~ **in any material particular** in e–r wesentlichen Einzelheit falsch; ~**lights and signals** irreführende Schiffssignale; ~ **measures** Hohlmaßfälschung; ~ **trade description** Falschbezeichnung von Waren.

falsehood vorsätzliche Unwahrheit; ~, **fraud and wilful imposition** *scot* Betrug; **injurious** ~ Rufschädigung, Kreditschädigung; **malicious** ~ böswillige Unwahrheit.

false pretences arglistige Täuschung, Vorspiegelung falscher

Tatsachen; **under** ~ betrügerisch, durch Täuschung.

falsi crimen Fälschungsdelikt *n*, Arglist *f*, Täuschung *f*, Falschschwören *n*.

falsification Fälschung *f*, Verfälschung *f*, Anfertigung e–r unechten Urkunde; Nachweis *m* der Buchungsfälschung; ~ **of accounts** Buchhaltungsfälschung.

falsify fälschen, verfälschen, fälschlich anfertigen, als falsch beweisen, anfechten; ~ **a document** Urkundenfälschung begehen; ~ **a pedigree** Personenstandsfälschung begehen; Täuschung über die Abstammung begehen; e–e Rechtsnachfolgeurkunde verfälschen; ~ **any account** Buchungsaufzeichnungen fälschen; ~**ing a judgment** Aufhebung e–s Urteils; ~**ing a record** Falschbeurkundung, Fälschung einer öffentlichen Urkunde.

famacide Rufmörder *m*.

fame Gerücht *n*, Ruf *m*, Ruhm *m*; **ill** ~ schlechter Leumund,

familiarities Vertraulichkeiten; **improper** ~ unzulässige (ehewidrige) Vertraulichkeiten; ehewidriges Verhalten.

family Familie *f*, Großfamilie *f*; ~ **allowance** Kindergeld (*GB bis 1975*) Familienbeihilfe; ~ **arrangement** treuhänderische Regelung über das Familienvermögen; vorweggenommene (*vertragliche*) Nachlaßregelung, Erbvertrag; ~ **assets** Familienhabe *f*, Vermögen; ~ **bible** Hausbibel mit Familienbuch; ~ **case work agencies** Familienfürsorgeeinrichtungen; ~ **company** Familien-GmbH; ~ **council** Familienrat; ~ **court** → *court;* **F** ~ **Division** Familiengerichtsabteilung des High Court, London; ~ **expenditure survey** Indexvergleich der Familienlebensunterhaltskosten; ~ **expenses** Haushaltskosten; ~ **expense statutes** gesetzliche Haftungsbestimmungen für Familienanschaffungen; ~ **group** *ins* Haushaltsangehörige; ~ **law** Familienrecht; ~ **mansion** Herrensitz e–r Familie; ~ **meeting** Familienrat, Familienratssitzung; ~ **name** → *name*; ~ **owned enterprise** Familienbetrieb; ~ **physician** Hausarzt; ~ **protection policy** → *policy*; ~ **provision** *gerichtlich festgesetzte Versorgung unterhaltsbedürftiger Angehöriger aus dem Nachlaß*, Pflichtteilsunterhalt; Pflichtteil; ~ **purpose doctrine** Kfz-Halterhaftung für Familienangehörige; ~ **relation** Familienbeziehung, familienähnliche Beziehung; ~ **relocation** Umsiedlung von Familien; ~ **settlement** = ~ *arrangement qv*; ~ **supplement** Familienbeihilfe; ~ **tree** Ahnentafel; ~ **use** (*steuerlicher*) Eigenverbrauch; ~ **violence** Gewalttätigkeiten im Familienbereich; **F**~ **Welfare Association** Familienfürsorgeverband (*London*).

famine Hungersnot *f*, Mangel *m*; ~ **relief** Hilfe bei Hungersnot, Hilfsaktion bei Hungerkatastrophe.

fancy Phantasie . . ., phantasierend, ausgefallen; ~ **articles** Modewaren; ~ **bread** Spezialbrot; ~ **word** Phantasiewort (*bei Warenzeichen*).

fare Fahrpreis *m*, Schiffspassage *f*, Flugpreis *m*, Wassergeld *n*; **slashing** radikale Flugpreis-Senkung; ~ **stage** Teilstrecke; **bill of** ~ Speisekarte; **discount** ~**s** Rabattflugpreise; **excess** ~ Zuschlag; **full** ~ voller Fahrpreis; **discount** ~ Billigflug; herabgesetzter Fahr-/Flugpreis; **single** ~ einfacher Fahrpreis.

farm *s* Landgut *n*, Pachtgut *n, adj* landwirtschaftlich (= *landw*); ~ **crossing** niveaugleicher Bahnübergang auf dem Land; ~ **development loan** *landw* Betriebsmittelkredit; ~ **labo(u)rer** Landarbeiter; ~ **land** *landw–er* Grund, Bauernland, *landw–e* Betriebsfläche; ~ **lease** *landw–er* Pachtvertrag; ~ **loan** Agrarkredit; ~ **loan bond** *US* Agrarpfandbrief *e–r landw–en Genossenschaftsbank*; ~ **mortgage loans** Agrarhypotheken; ~ **products** *landw–e* Erzeugnisse; ~ **rent** → *rent;* ~**stead** Bauernhof; ~

stock *landw–es* Inventar; → **tenancy** Landpacht, Verhältnis; ~ **utensils** *landw–e* Geräte; **home** ~ selbst bewirtschaftetes Land; **model** ~ Mustergut; **stock** ~ Viehzuchtbetrieb.

farm *v* bebauen, bewirtschaften, betreuen, pachten; **to** ~ **let** verpachten; ~ **out** verpachten, (*e–n Auftrag*) weitervergeben.

farmer Pächter *m*, Bauer *m*, Pächter *m* e–r Konzession; ~**s' cooperative association** Landwirtschaftsgenossenschaft; ~ **general** Oberverpächter; ~**s' union** Bauernverband.

farming *s* Landwirtschaft *f*, Pachtbetrieb *m*; ~ **and breeding** Ackerbau und Viehzucht.

farming *adj* landwirtschaftlich (= *landw*); ~ **buildings** *landw–e* Betriebsgebäude; ~ **effects** Zubehör e–s *landw–n* Betriebes; ~ **lease** *landw–e* Pacht; ~ **stock** das lebende und tote Inventar e–s *landw–n* Betriebes; ~ **stock and effects** das gesamte (bewegliche) *landw–e* Betriebsvermögen.

farming out Untervergabe.

fascio (= *facio*) Firmenschild, Firmenzeichen *n*.

fastenings Befestigungsmittel *n*|*pl* (*Transport*).

fatal tödlich, mit tödlichem Ausgang, schicksalhaft.

fatality Todesfall *m*, Todesopfer *m*; **occupational** ~**ties** tödliche Arbeitsunfälle.

father Vater *m*, Kindsvater *m*, Adoptivvater *m*, Stiefvater *m*; ~ **of the House** der rangälteste Abgeordnete (*der am längsten ununterbrochen dem Unterhaus angehörende Abgeordnete*); **adoptive** ~ Adoptivvater; **biological** ~ biologischer Vater, leiblicher V.; **natural** ~ biologischer Vater; leiblicher V.; **reputed** ~ der vermutliche Vater; **the putative** ~ der vermutliche Kindesvater, Zahlvater.

fatigue Ermüdung *f*, Arbeitsminderung *f*; ~ **accident** Unfall durch Übermüdung.

fatuity Einfältigkeit *f*, Geistesschwäche *f*.

fault Fehler *m*, Schuld *f*, Verschulden *n*, schuldhaftes Verhalten, schuldhafte Handlung *f bzw* schuldhafte Unterlassung *f*; Sachmangel *m*; ~ **-based law** → *law;* ~ **finding** kleinliches Herumkritisieren, Krittelei, Nörgelei; ~ **in construction** Konstruktionsfehler; ~ **or privity of owner** schuldhaftes Handeln oder Unterlassen des Eigentümers; ~ **principle** Schuldprinzip (*Scheidung*); Verschuldensprinzip; ~ *system* = ~ *principle qv*; ~ **repair obligation** Instandsetzungspflicht, Reparaturverpflichtung; **both spouses equally at** ~ beiderseitiges Verschulden der Parteien (*obs, Scheidung*); **gross** ~ grobe Fahrlässigkeit; **hidden** ~ heimlicher Mangel; **intermittent** ~ gelegentl auftretender Mangel, immer wieder auftretender Betriebsfehler; **party not at** ~ der nichtschuldige Teil; **slight** ~ leichte Fahrlässigkeit; **the** ~ **lies with him** ihn trifft das Verschulden; **to be at** ~ schuld sein, verschulden; **very slight** ~ ganz geringfügiges (*nicht zur Haftung ausreichendes*) Verschulden; **with all** ~**s** unter Ausschluß jeder Sachmängelhaftung „wie es steht und liegt", ohne Gewähr, „wie besichtigt"; **without one's** ~ unverschuldet.

faultiness Fehlerhaftigkeit *f*, Mangelhaftigkeit *f*.

faulty schadhaft, fehlerhaft, mangelhaft, unrichtig.

favo(u)r *s* Gunst *f*, Begünstigung *f*, Voreingenommenheit *f*; **balance in your** ~ → *balance;* **challenge for** ~ → *challenge.*

favo(u)r *v* unterstützen, begünstigen.

favo(u)rable günstig, dienlich, förderlich.

favo(u)ritism Begünstigung *f*; Günstlingswesen *n*, Vetternwirtschaft *f*.

fealty Lehenstreue *f*; **general** ~ Untertanenentreue; **oath of** ~ → *oath;* **special** ~ Lehenstreue.

fear *s* Furcht *f*, Befürchtung *f*, Angst *f*; ~ **of death** Todesangst; **in ~ of one's life** in Todesängsten.
feasance Tun *n*, Erfüllung *f*, Errichtung *f*, Gesetzgebung *f*.
feasant tuend; **damage ~** schadenstiftend (*z. B. von fremdem Weidevieh*).
feasibility Durchführbarkeit *f*; ~ **study** Projektstudie *f*; Vorprüfung e–s Projekts, Machbarkeitsstudie.
feasible durchführbar.
feasor der Handelnde, Errichter *m* e–r Urkunde, Gesetzgeber *m*.
feast Feiertag *m*, Kirchenfeiertag *m*; ~**s** Quartalszahltage *m*|*pl*.
featherbedding Überbesetzung *f* von Arbeitsplätzen.
feature Charakterzug *m*, Wesenszug *m*, Eigenart *f*; ~ **picture** Hauptfilm; **distinctive ~** Unterscheidungsmerkmal; **novel ~** Neuheitsmerkmal; **special ~** Besonderheit.
federal Bundes . . . zur Bundeszuständigkeit gehörig; ~ **instrumentality** Organ der Bundesregierung.
Federal funds Tagesgeld *(US) n*.
Federal Reserve System *(=) Zentralbanksystem d. USA*.
federalism Föderalismus *m*, bundesstaatliche Staatsform *f*; Bundeszuständigkeit *f*.
federalist Föderalist *m*.
federalize föderalisieren, verbünden, dezentralisieren.
federate föderieren, sich zu e–m Staatenbund bzw Bundesstaat vereinigen; ~**d state** Bundesstaat.
federation Föderation *f*, Zusammenschluß *m*, Verband *m*, Staatenbund *m*, Eingliederung *f* in e–n Staatenbund.
federative föderalistisch, bundes . . .
fee *s* (*1*) Lohn *m*, Bezahlung *f*; Honorar *n*, Gebühr(en) *f*, Schulgeld *n*; Nebenkosten *pl*; ~ **arrangement** Gebührenvereinbarung; ~**s and actual expenses** Gebühren und Auslagen; ~**-bill** *gerichtliche* Gebührentabelle; ~ **charging** *s* Inrechnungstellung von Anwaltsgebühren; ~**-charging** *adj* entgeltlich; ~ **contract** Honorarvertrag; ~ **cutting** Gebührenreduzierung, Gebührenunterbietung; ~ **earner** Honorarverdiener, freiberufl Anwalt; Partner e–r Sozietät; ~ **schedule** Gebührentabelle; ~ **sharing** Gebührenteilung; ~ **splitting** Tantiemenaufteilung, Gebührenaufteilung; ~ **with brief** Mandierungsgebühr; **advance of ~** Honorarvorschuß; **annual ~** Jahreshonorar; **appeal ~** Berufungsgebühr; **application ~** Anmeldegebühr; **arbitration ~** Schiedsgerichtskosten; **arrangement ~** Kreditprovision; Vermittlungsprovision; **attendance ~s** Präsenzgelder; **attorney's ~** Anwaltshonorar; **auctioneer's ~** Provision des Auktionators; **author's ~** Tantieme, Autorenanteil; **basic ~** Grundgebühr (*TV*); **brief ~** Mandatierungsgebühr (*barrister*); **broker's ~** Maklerlohn; **civil court ~s** Gerichtskosten in Zivilsachen; **closing ~** Abschlußgebühr, Abschlußprovision; **club ~** Vereinsbeitrag; **collection ~** Inkassogebühr; **commitment ~** → *commitment*; **completion ~** Abschlußgebühr; **consular ~s** Konsulatsgebühren; **contingent ~** Erfolgshonorar; **counsel's ~** Anwaltsgebühr(en), Anwaltshonorar; **court ~s** Gerichtsgebühren, Gerichtskosten; **court-awarded ~s** gerichtl festgesetzte Anwaltskosten; **deposit ~** Hinterlegungsgebühr; **director's ~** Vergütung e–s Verwaltungsratsmitglieds; **discharging ~** Entladekosten, Löschungskosten; **docket ~** Prozeßgebühr; **entrance ~** Eintrittsgeld; Policengebühr; **excess ~** Gebührenzuschlag; **expert's ~** Sachverständigengebühr; **facility ~** → *facility*; **filing ~** Anmeldegebühr; **final ~** Schlußgebühr; **fixed ~** fest vereinbarte Vergütung zuzüglich Kosten und Auslagen; **flat ~** Pauschalgebühr, Pauschalhonorar; **forwarding ~** Vermittlungsgebühr für Mandatsweitergabe; **front-end ~** Abschlußgebühr; **inspection ~** Bauabnahmegebühr;

law ~**s** → *law;* **lawyer's** ~**s** Anwaltshonorar; **legal** ~**s** Anwaltsgebühren; **licence** ~ → *licence*; **negotiation** ~ Verhandlungsgebühr (*außergerichtl*); **notarial** ~ Notarskosten; **patent** ~ Patentgebühr; **pilot's** ~ Lotsengebühr; **plaint** ~ gerichtl Prozeßgebühr; **plan** ~ Bauplanbearbeitungsgebühr; **probate** ~ *Verwaltungsgebühr für Umschreibung (von Aktien) auf Erben*; **professional** ~**s** Honorar; **protest** ~ Protestkosten, Rückscheckgebühr; **publication** ~ → *publication*; **refund of** ~**s** Gebührenerstattung; **registration** ~ Eintragungsgebühr; **remission of** ~**s** Gebührennachlaß; **renewal** ~ Jahresgebühr, Verlängerungsgebühr; **retaining** ~ Mandierungsgebühr, Gebührenvorschuß (*für Anwalt*); laufendes Festhonorar; **safe deposit** ~ Aufbewahrungsgebühr; **sealing** ~ Gebühr für die Ausstellung e–r Patenturkunde, Siegelgebühr; **sessional** ~ Standardgebühr für e–e Sitzungsperiode; **sheriff** ~**s** Gerichtsvollzieherkosten; **standard** ~ Regelgebühr(en); **term** ~ → *term;* **to levy** ~**s** Gebühren erheben; **to set the** ~**s** die Anwaltsgebühren berechnen.

fee *s (2)*, Lehen *n*, lehnsrechtlicher Grundbesitz *m*, Grundeigentum *n*; ~ **absolute** Grundeigentum, Allodialgut; ~ **and life-rent** Eigentum und Nießbrauch; ~ **damages** → *damages*; ~ **expectant** Erbpachtbesitz; ~ **simple** → *fee simple*; ~ **tail** → *fee tail*; **base** ~ *hist Ausschluß der Fideikommißerbfolge durch den Pachtbesitzer*, befristetes Immobiliarnutzungsrecht; **conditional** ~ bedingtes Lehen, fideikommissarischer Besitz; **determinable** ~ auflösend, bedingtes Herrschaftsrecht am Grundstück; zeitlich begrenzte Erbpacht; **great** ~ Kronlehen; **knight's** ~ ritterliches Lehen; **limited** ~ beschränktes Besitzrecht am Grundstück; **plowman's** ~ Bauernerbpacht (*mit gleichen Erbteilen der Söhne*); **qualified** ~ auflösend bedingtes Grundbesitzrecht; **quasi** ~ widerrechtlich erworbener Landbesitz, Lehensland; Land unmittelbar beim Herrenhaus; **to hold the** ~ Grundstückseigentümer sein.

fee-farm Erbpacht *f*; Zinslehen; ~ **rent** Ewigrente als Zahlung für Grunderwerb.

fee-farmer Erbpächter *m*.

fee simple *kurz für: fee simple absolute in possession qv*: Grundstückseigentum *n*, unbeschränktes Erblehen *n*, Allodialgut *n*; ~ **absolute in possession** Grundeigentum; ~ **conditional** Fideikommißlehen; **determinable** ~ beendbares *eigentumsähnliches* Grundbesitzrecht (*mit Heimfallsklausel bzw Rechtsübergangsklausel*); **owner in** ~ Grundstückseigentümer.

fee tail Fideikommißbesitz *m*; beschränkt vererblicher Grundbesitz *m*.

feeble-minded geistesschwach; ~ **person** Geistesschwacher.

feeble-mindedness Geistesschwäche *f*, Schwachsinn *m*.

feed stützen, stärken, füttern; ~**ing the estoppel** Heilung bei mangelnder Veräußerungsbefugnis.

feeder line Nebenbahn; ~ **road** Zubringerstraße.

feel fühlen, sich fühlen; ~ **aggrieved** sich für beschwert halten.

feign heucheln, sich verstellen; ~ **disease** simulieren.

feigned fingiert, falsch, ~ **accomplice** → *accomplice*; ~ **action** → *action*; ~ **contract** Scheinvertrag; ~ **diseases** simulierte Krankheiten; ~ **issue** → *issue (2)*.

feint Finte *f*, Täuschungsmanöver *n*, Verstellung *f*; ~ **in law** Schauprozeß.

fellow Genosse *m*, Mitglied *n*, Teilnehmer *m*, Kollege *m*; ~ **citizen** Mitbürger; ~ **countrymen** Mitbürger, Landsleute; ~ **employee** Arbeitskollege; ~ **heir** Miterbe; ~ **lodger** Mitbewohner; ~ **owner** Miteigentümer; ~ **partner** Mitgesellschafter; ~ **servants** gemeinsame Arbeitnehmer; *superior fellow servant: übergeordneter Verrichtungsgehilfe*; ~ **servants rule** *Grundsatz der Nichthaftung der Arbeitgeber bei Arbeitnehmerschäden, die durch fahrlässiges Verhalten anderer Arbeitnehmer verursacht werden*; ~ **traveller** Mitreisender, Mitläufer, getarnter Kommunist, Kommunistensympathisant; ~ **unionist** Mitglied derselben Gewerkschaft; ~ **worker** Arbeitskollege.

felo-de-se Selbstmörder *m*.

felon Verbrecher *m*, Täter *m*.

felonia Felonie *f*.

felonious verbrecherisch, böswillig, mit Verbrechensvorsatz, in verbrecherischer Absicht; ~ **assault** verbrecherischer Angriff, Morddrohung, Mordversuch; ~ **homicide** → *homicide*; ~ **intent** Verbrechensvorsatz; ~ **taking** Wegnahme mit Diebstahlsvorsatz; ~ **wounding** gefährliche Körperverletzung.

feloniously verbrecherischerweise, in verbrecherischer Absicht.

felon|y (*GB: seit 1967 = misdemeanor*) Verbrechen *n*, Kapitalverbrechen *n*, Felonie *f*, Bruch *m* der Lehenstreue; **F~ Act** *brit Gesetz über die Abschaffung der Einziehung des Landbesitzes von Schwerverbrechern*; ~**ies committed with explosives** Sprengstoffverbrechen; ~ **drunk driving** (*US*) Verbrechen der Trunkenheit am Steuer; ~ **murder** Verbrechen mit Todesfolge; **capital** ~ mit Todesstrafe bedrohtes Verbrechen; **compounding of** ~ → *compounding*; **misprision of** ~ → *misprision*; **reducible** ~ ein evtl als Vergehen bestrafbares Verbrechen; **treason** ~ → *treason*.

felting Filzherstellung *f*.

female *s* weibliche Person *f*; *adj* weiblich; ~ **child** Mädchen; ~ **labour** → *labour*; ~ **suffrage** Frauenstimmrecht; **graduated** ~ Akademikerin; **unmarried** ~ ledige, verwitwete oder geschiedene Frau, alleinstehende Frau.

feme Frau *f*, verheiratete Frau *f*; ~ **covert** verheiratete Frau; ~ **discovert** geschiedene Frau, Witwe; ~ **sole** alleinstehende Frau; ~ **sole trader** selbständige Geschäftsfrau.

femicide Tötung *f* einer Frau; Frauenmörder *m*.

feminist Frauenrechtlerin *f*.

fence *vt* einzäunen, einfrieden, sichern, abwehren, zum Schongebiet erklären; *vi* ausweichend antworten; Sachhehlerei betreiben.

fence *s* Zaun *m*, Hecke *f*, Einfriedung *f*, Hehler *m*; ~**-month** (*-time, -season*) Schonzeit.

feneration Wucher *m*, Wucherzinsen *pl*.

feodal = *feudal qv*; ~ **action** lehnsrechtliche Klage; ~ **system** Feudalsystem, Lehenswesen.

feodality = *fidelity bzw fealty qv*.

feodatory Lehensträger *m*.

feodum Lehen *n*.

feoffee Lehnsmann *m*, Belehnter *m*, Erwerber *m*; ~ **to uses** *hist* treuhänderischer Erwerber von Grundvermögen.

feoffer Lehnsherr *m*, Grundeigentümer *m*.

feoffment Belehnung *f*, Lehensbesitzübertragung *f*, Investitur *f*; **charter of** ~ Belehnungsurkunde.

feoffor Veräußerer *m* von Lehensbesitz, Belehnender; ~ **to uses** Treugeber, Stifter.

ferial days Feiertage *m|pl*.

ferret *v|t* (*out*) ermitteln.

ferriage Fährgeld *n*, Überfahrt *f* (*mit Fähre*).

ferry *s* Fähre *f*, Fährrecht *n*; ~ **boat** Eisenbahnfähre, Trajekt; ~ **franchise** Fährkonzession; ~ **man** Fährmann; ~ **operator** Fährenbetriebsgesellschaft; **private** ~ Privatfähre; **public** ~ öffentliche Fähre; **roll-on, roll-off** ~ Autofähre.

ferry *v* Fährdienste leisten, überführen (*vom Werk*).

fesance Handlung *f* (= *feasance qv*).

festing|men *hist* Bürgen, Geiseln; ~**-penny** Handgeld bei Einstellung von Dienstboten.

fetch abholen, holen, einbringen; ~ **a high price** e–n hohen Preis erzielen.

feticide Abtötung *f* der Leibesfrucht, Abtreibung.
fetters Fußfesseln *f/pl*, Fesseln *f/pl*; ~ **upon the discretion** unzulässige Einengung des (Verwaltungs)Ermessens.
feud (*1*) Fehde *f*, Streit *m*; **blood** ~ Blutsfehde, Blutrache.
feud (*2*) Lehen *n*; **improper** ~ außerordentliches Lehen; Lehen minderen Rechts; **proper** ~ ordentliches Lehen, das eigentliche (*ursprüngliche*) Lehen.
feudal lehnsrechtlich, Lehens . . ., feudal; ~ **action** lehnsrechtliche Klage; ~ **courts** Lehensgerichte; ~ **grant** = *feoffment qv*; ~ **law** → *law*; ~ **lord** Lehnsherr; ~ **possession** Lehensbesitz, Gewere; ~ **service** lehnsrechtliche Dienste; ~ **system** Feudalsystem, Lehnswesen.
feudalism Feudalsystem *n*, Lehnswesen *n*; **continental** ~ das Lehnswesen auf dem europäischen Kontinent.
feudality Lehnswesen *n*, Lehnspflicht *f*.
feudalize in Lehnsbesitz überführen, in das Lehnssystem einbeziehen.
feudary Lehnsträger *m*.
feudatory lehnspflichtig.
feudist Lehnsrechtler *m*.
few einige, wenige; **the** ~ Elite, die Auserwählten.
fi. fa. = *fieri facias qv*.
fiancé Verlobter *m*, Bräutigam *m*.
fiancée (= *fiancee*) Verlobte *f*, Braut *f*.
fiat Bestätigung *f*, Zulassung *f*, Ermächtigung *f*, gerichtlicher Befehl *m*, Verfügung *f*, prozeßleitende Verfügung *f*, (*Rechtsmittel*) Zulassung *f*; ~ **in bankruptcy** Zulassung des Konkursverfahrens gegen Kaufleute; ~ **justitia** (=); *Zulassung e–r Revision durch königliches Dekret im Oberhaus*; ~ **money** Papiergeld, staatl. Geld, Zeichengeld; **joint** ~ Konkurseröffnungsbeschluß gegen Gesamtschuldner.
fiber Faser *f*; **man-made** ~ Kunstfaser.
FIBOR (*Frankfurt Interbank Offered Rate*) deutscher Referenzzinssatz *m*.
fiction Fiktion *f*, Unterstellung *f*; **legal** ~ gesetzliche Fiktion, ~ **of law** = *legal* ~ *qv*.
fictitious fiktiv, fingiert, nachgeahmt; ~ **action** Scheinprozeß (*zur Klärung e–r Rechtsfrage*); ~ **bargain** Scheingeschäft; ~ **bill** → *bill* (*3*); ~ **character** eine erfundene Person; ~ **firm name** *Firma, die nicht mit dem Namen des Geschäftsinhabers übereinstimmt*; ~ **plaintiff** fingierte Klagepartei; ~ **sale** Scheinverkauf, Proformaverkauf; ~ **transaction** Scheingeschäft; ~ **value** fiktiver Wert.
fiddle *v/i* schwindeln, manipulieren; ~**ling expenses** Geschäftsausgabenschwindel betreiben.
fide-commissary *s* Treugeber *m*.
fide-jussor Ausfallbürge *m*.
fide-promissor = *fide-jussor qv*.
fidelity Treue *f*, Pflichttreue *f*, Aufrichtigkeit *f*, Ehrlichkeit *f*, genaue Übereinstimmung *f*; ~ **bond** → *bond* (*2*); ~ **guarantee insurance** → *insurance*; **conjugal** ~ eheliche Treue.
fiducial = *fiduciary adj qv*; ~ **office** Vertrauensamt.
fiduciary *s* Treuhänder *m*; adj treuhänderisch, fiduziarisch.
fief Lehensgut *n*; ~ **tenant** Lehensträger, Besitzer e–s freivererblichen Lehens.
field Feld *n*, Acker *m*; Amtsbereich *m*, Fachgebiet *n*, Sachgebiet *n*; ~ **allowance** Frontzulage; ~ **book** (städtisches) Kataster, Flurnummern-Verzeichnis; ~ **damage** Flurschaden; ~ **executive** leitender Angestellter e–r Niederlassung; ~ **engineering service** technischer Kundendienst; ~ **garden allotment** Gemüsekleingarten, Schrebergarten; ~ **investigation** Nachforschung an Ort und Stelle, Marktforschung; ~ **of activity** Arbeitsfeld, Tätigkeitsbereich; ~ **of application** Anwendungsbereich; ~ **of knowledge** Wissensgebiet; ~ **of law** Rechtsgebiet; ~ **of operations** Tätigkeitsbereich; ~ **reeve** Beauftragter für das Weide-

land; ~ **sales executive** Außendienstleiter; ~ **service** Außendienst; ~ **sobriety test** (*US*) Alkoholtest an der Unfallstelle; ~ **staff** Mitarbeiter im Außendienst; ~ **ware housing** besitzlose Verpfändung e–s Warenlagers; ~ **work** Außenarbeit; **common** ~ Gemeindeland, Almende.

fierding courts *hist Gerichte unterster Instanz.*

fieri|facias = *fi. fa.* Vollstreckungsermächtigung *f* des Gerichtsvollziehers, Pfändungsauftrag *m*; ~ **feci** Pfändungsbericht.

fifo (*first-in-first-out*) Bewertungsverfahren *n* für Lagerbestände (*wobei unterstellt wird, daß die zuerst gekaufte Ware auch zuerst veräußert wird*).

fight Kampf *m*, Zweikampf *m*, Raufhandel *m*, Schlägerei *f*; ~ **for office** Kampf um die (politische) Macht.

fighting Kampfhandlungen *f*|*pl*.

figure Figur *f*, Zahl *f*, Ziffer *f*; Persönlichkeit *f*, Bildzeichen *n*; ~**head** repräsentative (*vorgeschobene*) Persönlichkeit; **nominal** ~ Merkposten *bil*; **public** ~ Person der Zeitgeschichte, P. des öffentlichen Interesses.

filch entwenden, klauen, stibitzen.

file *s* Akte *f*, amtliche Verwahrung *f*, Ordner *m*, Rolle *f*; ~ **clerk** Registraturbeamter; ~ **copy** → *copy*; ~ **index** Aktenverzeichnis; ~ **mark** Eingangsvermerk; ~ **wrapper** Aktenumschlag, Aktendeckel; **dead** ~**s** weggelegte Akten; **personal** ~**s** Personalakten; **supplementary** ~**s** Beiakten; **to lie on the** ~ weggelegt sein; auf unbestimmte Zeit zu den Akten genommen sein.

file *v* einreichen, registrieren, zu den Akten reichen; zur Eintragung anmelden, vorlegen; ~ **for protection under Chapter 11 of the Bankruptcy Code** (*US*) Vergleich anmelden (zur Abwendung des Konkurses); ~ **away** (*als erledigt*) weglegen; ~ **with the court** bei Gericht einreichen; ~ **with the Registrar** beim Registergericht einreichen.

filiate die Vaterschaft e–s unehelichen Kindes feststellen.

filiation Vaterschaft *f*, Abstammung *f*; gerichtliche Vaterschaftsfeststellung *f*; ~ **order** = *affiliation order qv*; ~ **proceeding** Vaterschaftsfeststellungsverfahren.

filibuster Marathondebatte *f*, *Obstruktion durch restlose Ausnutzung der parlamentarischen Redezeit.*

Filing and Record Department Registratur *f*.

filing officer Registraturbeamter.

filing compartment Ablegefach *n*.

filip Kurzerholung *f* (Börse).

filius nullius nichteheliches Kind *n*.

fill füllen, ausfüllen, vervollständigen; erfüllen, besetzen; ~ **an office** ein Amt besetzen.

fillage Hafenabgabe *f* für Schiffsladung.

film Membran *f*, dünne Schicht *f*, Film *m*; ~ **distributor** Filmverleiher; ~ **producer** Filmhersteller; ~ **rights** → *right*.

filthy schmutzig, unflätig, ordinär, ekelhaft, sittenverderbend, moralisch verwerflich.

final endgültig, End..., Schluß...; ~ **and conclusive** endgültig, rechtskräftig; bestandskräftig; ~ **appealable order** Endentscheidung (*mit Rechtsmittelmöglichkeit*).

finality Endgültigkeit *f*, Bestandskraft *f*, Unanfechtbarkeit; ~ **clause** Bestandskraftklausel.

finance Finanzwesen *n*, Finanzierung *f*, Finanzierungsmittel *n*|*pl*; ~ **Act** Finanzgesetz; ~ **bank** Kundenkreditbank; ~ **bill** → *bill (1)*; ~ **bill of exchange** → *bill (3)*; ~ **committee** Finanzausschuß, Investitionsausschuß; ~ **company** Finanzierungsgesellschaft, Kundenkreditbank; ~ **corporation** Finanzierungsgesellschaft (*Aufbau-, bzw Entwicklungsfinanzierung*); ~ **lease** Finanzierungsleasing(vertrag); **business** ~ Geschäftsfinanzen; **industrial** ~ Industriefinanzierung; **long-term** ~ langfristige Finanzierung; **short-term** ~ kurzfristige Finanzierung; **off-balance sheet** ~

nicht in der Bilanz ausgewiesene Finanzierung.

finance *v* finanzieren, mit Kapital ausstatten; Geldgeschäfte machen; ~ **away** (Geld) verschieben.

finances Finanzen *f/pl*, Staatseinkünfte *f/pl*; Staatsvermögen *n*, Geldmittel *n/pl*; **national** ~ Staatsfinanzen; **public** ~ Staatsfinanzen, Finanzwissenschaft, Finanzwirtschaft, öffentliche Finanzen.

financial finanziell; steuerlich; ~ **capital maintenance** nominelle Kapitalerhaltung; ~ **drain** Geldentzug, Abfluß von Finanzmitteln, finanzielle Inanspruchnahme; ~ **interrelation** Kapitalverflechtung; ~ **provision for a spouse** Ehegattenunterhalt; ~ **provision order** nachehelicher Unterhaltsbeschluß; ~ **provision order during marriage** Ehegattenunterhaltsbeschluß; ~ **responsibility law** *Gesetz zur finanziellen Absicherung von Großschadenshaftpflicht*; ~ **year** → *year*.

financier Finanzier *m*, Finanzexperte *m*.

financing Finanzierung *f*; ~ **by accrued depreciation** Finanzierung aus Abschreibungen; ~ **company** Finanzierungsgesellschaft; ~ **expenses** Finanzierungskosten; ~ **of exports** Exportfinanzierung; ~ **rate** Finanzierungs(zins)satz; **business** ~ betriebliche Finanzwirtschaft; **consumer** ~ Kundenkredit; **debt** ~ Fremdfinanzierung; **equity** ~ Eigenfinanzierung, Finanzierung mit Eigenkapital, Beteiligungsfinanzierung (durch Aktienemission); **external equity** ~ Eigenfinanzierung (*durch Emissionen, neue Einlagen*); **interim** ~ Zwischenfinanzierung; **non-recourse** ~ Forfaitierung (*Forderungsankauf bei Regreßverzicht*); **preliminary** ~ Vorfinanzierung; **trade credit** ~ Finanzierung mit Lieferantenkredit.

find finden, befinden, bemerken, erkennen; ~ **a true bill** die Anklage zur Hauptverhandlung zulassen (*Voruntersuchung durch die Grand Jury qv*); ~ **against a party** gegen e–e Partei entscheiden; ~ **bail** Bürgen stellen; ~ **distributively** teilweise zuerkennen, zum Teil abweisen; ~ **for a party** zugunsten e–r Partei entscheiden; ~ **guilty** schuldig sprechen; ~ **money** Geld beschaffen.

finder Finder *m*; Finanzmakler *m*; hist Zollfahnder *m*; ~ **of goods** Finder; ~ **of lost property** Finder; ~**'s reward** Finderlohn.

finding Fund *m*, Befund *m*; Wahrspruch *m*, Erkenntnis *f*; gerichtliche Feststellung *f*, Zwischenentscheid *m*; ~ **of lost property** Fund; ~ **of a jury** Geschworenenspruch; ~ **of facts** Feststellung des Sachverhalts; Tatbestand *e–s Urteils*; ~ **of guilt** Schuldspruch; ~ **of means** Kapitalbeschaffung; ~ **of the court** gerichtliche Feststellung, Gerichtsurteil; **alternative** ~**s** Wahlfeststellungen; **concurrent** ~**s** übereinstimmende Urteilsfeststellungen (mehrerer Kollegialrichter); **general** ~**s** zusammengefaßte Urteilsfeststellungen, Tatbestand; **interlocutory** ~**s** Zwischenentscheidung; **judicial** ~**s** → *judicial*; **special** ~ Geschworenenurteil zu Einzelpunkten.

fine (1) *s* Geldstrafe *f*, Buße *f*; **administrative** ~ Bußgeld; **determinate** ~ bestimmte Geldstrafe; **disciplinary** ~ Bußgeld, Ordnungsgeld; **hefty** ~ deftige Geldstrafe; **illeviable** ~ uneinbringliche Geldstrafe; **joint** ~ kollektive Geldstrafe; **liable to a** ~ mit Geldstrafe bedroht; **nominal** ~ unbedeutende Geldstrafe; **to assess a** ~ e–e Geldstrafe festsetzen; **to impose a** ~ zu e–r Geldstrafe verurteilen; **to remit a** ~ e–e Geldstrafe erlassen; **unlimited** ~ Geldstrafe in unbegrenzter Höhe.

fine *(2) s hist* Auflassung *f als (fingierter) Prozeßvergleich*, Abgabe *f* an den Grundherrn; ~ **and ransom** *hist* Strafe und Lösegeld; **F~s and Recoveries Act** *engl Gesetz zur Abschaffung der mittelalterlichen Auf-*

lassungsformen (1833); ~ **for endowment** *hist Abgabe der Witwe zur Erlangung des Lehnsbesitzes*; ~ **on alienation** *hist Abgabe an den Lehnsherren bei Veräußerung des Lehens*; ~ **rolls** *hist Verzeichnis von Zahlungen aus Lehensveräußerungen 1199–1641.*

fine *v* e–e Geldstrafe auferlegen.

fine *adj* fein, rein, erstklassig; ~ **bank bill** erstklassiges Bankakzept; erste Adresse; ~ **trade bill** erstklassiger Handelswechsel; ~**-tuning** Feinsteuerung (*Wirtschaft*).

fineness|of gold Feinheitsgrad des Goldes; ~ **of metal** Feinheitsgrad von Edelmetallen.

fingerprint Fingerabdrücke *m|pl*; **DNA** ~ genetischer Fingerabdruck.

finish *s* Nachbearbeitung *f*, Schlußbearbeitung *f*, Glanz *m*, Appretur *f*.

finish *v* enden, beendigen, fertigstellen, vervollkommnen, bearbeiten, ausarbeiten, perfektionieren, töten.

finishing Fertigstellung *f*, Vollendung *f*, Überarbeitung *f*, Veredelung *f*, Nachbearbeitung *f*; Installation *f*; Schlußbehandlung *f* bei der Stoffherstellung *f*, Ausstattung *f*, Appretieren *n*, Zurichtung *f*.

fink Streikbrecher *m*, Spitzel *m*.

fire Feuer *n*, Brand *m*; ~**-alarm system** Feuermeldesystem; ~ **arm** → *firearm*; ~ **authorities** Feuerschutzbehörde; ~ **brigade** Feuerwehr; ~ **damage** Feuerschaden; ~ **department** Feuerschadensabteilung; ~ **district** Feuerwehrbezirk; ~ **door** feuerfeste Tür, feuerhemmende Tür; ~ **escape** Feuerleiter; ~ **exit** Notausgang; ~ **fighter** Feuerbekämpfer; ~ **fighting machine** Feuerlöschapparat; ~ **hazards** Brandgefahr, Feuerrisiko; ~ **house** Feuerwache; ~ **inquest** Brandfeststellung; ~ **insurance** → *fire insurance*; ~ **lane** Feuerwehr-Anfahrtszone; ~ **or loss assessor** Brandschadensprüfer; ~ **ordeal** → *ordeal*; ~**-plugs** Hydranten; ~ **policy** Brandversicherung, Feuerversicherungspolice; ~**-proof** feuerbeständig; ~ **protection** Feuerschutz, Brandverhütung; ~ **raising** Brandstiftung; ~**-resisting** feuerbeständig, feuerhemmend; ~ **risk** Brandgefahr; ~ **sale** Ausverkauf wg Brandschadens, Notverkauf; ~ **station** Feuerwache; ~ **underwriter** Feuerversicherungsgesellschaft; ~**wall** Brandmauer; ~**-wood** Feuerholz; ~**-works** Feuerwerk, Leuchtmunition; plötzliche Hausse; **extinction of** ~ Feuerbekämpfung; **false alarm of** ~ vorsätzliche falsche Feuermeldung; **friendly** ~ Nutzfeuer; **hostile** ~ Schadenfeuer; **intentional** ~ Brandstiftung; **unfriendly** ~ Schadensfeuer.

firearm Schußwaffe *f*; ~**s certificate** Waffenbesitzkarte, Waffenschein; **imitation** ~ Spielzeugwaffe, Imitationswaffe.

fire-bomb *v|t* Brandbomben legen.

fire insurance Brandversicherung *f*, Feuerversicherung *f*; ~ **company** Brandversicherungsgesellschaft; ~ **fund** Brandkasse; ~ **loss adjustment** Brandversicherungsregulierung; **preferred** ~ **risks** günstige Feuerrisikoklasse.

firm *s* Firma *f*, Personalgesellschaft *f*, offene Handelsgesellschaft *f*; Sozietät *f*, Unternehmen *n*; ~ **debts** Firmenschulden; Gesellschaftsverbindlichkeiten; ~ **name** Firmenname, Firma (*bei e–r Personalgesellschaft*); **assets of a** ~ Firmenvermögen, Gesellschaftsvermögen; **commercial** ~ Handelsfirma; **competitive** ~ Konkurrenzfirma; **defunct** ~ erloschene Firma; **independent** ~ selbständige Firma (*bzw Personalgesellschaft*); **law** ~ → *law*; **member of a** ~ Teilhaber; **private** ~ Privatfirma, Einzelfirma; (*evtl:*) Offene Handelsgesellschaft; **property of the** ~ Geschäftsvermögen; **to sign for the** ~ im Namen der Firma zeichnen.

firm *adj* fest; ~ **belief** ehrliche Annahme, feste Überzeugung; ~ **offer** bindendes Angebot, Angebot zum festen Preis, Festangebot; ~ **price** Festpreis; ~ **quotation** verbindliches Preisangebot.

firmness Entschiedenheit *f*, Unnachgiebigkeit *p*.

first erster, erst . . ., führend, erstrangig, erststellig; ~ **accrued** erstmals entstanden; ~ **aid** erste Hilfe; ~ **allotment** ursprüngliche Emission; ~ **and nearest of kindred** nächste Verwandte; ~ **and readiest of means** die zuerst zur Verfügung stehenden Mittel; ~ **and true inventor** der Erfinder; ~ **appointment** erste Besetzung des Amtes; ~ **blush** nach dem ersten Anschein; ~ **born** erstgeboren; ~ **call** erster Abruf zur Kapitaleinzahlung; ~ **charge** erstrangige Globalverpfändung, vorrangig; ~ **come** ~ **served basis** „wer zuerst kommt, mahlt zuerst"; solange Vorrat reicht; ~ **consigned in** ursprünglich abgeschickt in; ~ **cost** → *cost* (*1*); ~ **cousin** → *cousin*; ~ **degree burn** Verbrennung ersten Grades; ~ **demised** bei der ersten Auflassung; ~ **devisee** Vorerbe; ~ **duly paid** wobei keine Zahlungsrückstände bestehen dürfen; ~ **fruits** erste Frucht des Jahres (Naturalabgabe); ~ **heir** nächster Erbanwärter; ~ **impression** erstmaliger Rechtsfall (*für den es keinen Präzedenzfall gibt*); ~ **instance** erste Instanz; ~ **let** erstmals vermietet; ~ **lien** → *lien*; ~ **lien collateral trust bonds** → *bond* (*1*); ~ **mortgage** → *mortgage*; ~ **mortgage bonds** → *bond* (*1*); ~ **name** Rufname; ~ **of exchange** Primawechsel; ~ **offender** → *offender*; ~ **open water** (*f. o. w.*) Verschiffung erst bei eisfreiem Wasser; ~ **option** → *option*; ~ **papers** vorläufige Einbürgerungspapiere; **"~-past-the-post" system** Mehrheitswahlrechtssystem; ~ **policy year** erstes Versicherungsjahr; ~ **port of clearance** der erste Ausfuhrhafen; ~ **premium** Erstprämie; ~ **processing** erste Verarbeitung; ~ **publication** Erstveröffentlichung; ~ **purchaser** → *purchaser*; ~ **rate** erstklassig; ~ **reading** erste Lesung; ~ **refusal** → *right of ~s*; ~ **refusal clause** Optionsklausel, Vorkaufsklausel; ~ **son** der älteste Sohn; ~ **trial** mündliche Verhandlung erster Instanz; **~-year capital allowance** volle Abschreibung im Anschaffungsjahr.

first-class erstklassig; ~ **mail** Briefpost; ~ **misdemeanant** Verurteilter im erleichterten Strafvollzug; ~ **water** bevorrechtigte Wasserentnahme.

firsts *pl* Waren *f*|*pl* erster Qualität.

fisc Fiskus *m*, Schatzamt *n*, Staatseinkommen *n*.

fiscal steuerlich; Finanz . . ., fiskalisch.

fiscal drag fiskalpolitische Bremswirkung *f durch heimliche Steuerprogression*.

fiscus Fiskus *m*, Kronvermögen *n*.

fish Fisch *m*, Seetiere *n*|*pl*; ~ **and game law** Fischerei- und Jagdgesetz; ~ **commissioner** Beauftragter für (*Binnengewässer-*)Fischzucht; **Royal** ~ dem königlichen Aneignungsrecht unterliegende (*gestrandete oder in Küstengewässern gefangene*) Wale und Störe.

fishery Fischerei *f*, Fischereirecht *n*, Fischfangrechte *n*|*pl*, Fischgründe *m*|*pl*; ~ **laws** Fischereigesetze; **costal** ~ Küstenfischerei; **common** ~ allgemeine Fischgründe; allgemeines Fischereirecht; **common of** ~ → *common*; **deep sea** ~ Tiefseefischerei; **free** ~ Fischereigerechtigkeit (*Binnengewässer*); **freshwater** ~ Binnenfischerei; **public** ~ allgem. Fischrecht; **right of** ~ Fischereirecht; **sea** ~ → *sea*; **several** ~ ausschließliches Fischereirecht des Grundeigentümers, selbständiges Fischereirecht.

fishing | **banks** flache Fischereigewässer; ~ **bill** Ausforschungsantrag; ~ **expedition** Ausforschungsfragen, A.-Beweisantrag; ~ **fleet** Fischfangflotte; ~ **grounds** Fischgründe; ~ **licence** Angelschein, Fischerlaubnis; ~ **rights** Fischereirecht, Fischereigerechtigkeit; ~ **trip** = ~ *expedition qv*.

fishtail *v*|*i* (*hinten*) ausscheren.

fit *adj* geeignet, passend, arbeitsfähig, einsatzfähig, tauglich; ~ **and convenient for the purpose** zweckentsprechend, geeignet; ~ **and proper person** geeignete Person; ~ **for habitation** für Wohnzwecke geeignet; ~ **for printing** zum Druck geeignet, druckreif; ~ **for service** diensttauglich; ~ **for work** arbeitsfähig; ~ **to be tried** (*in erster Linie*) sachlich zuständig sein; ~ **to be tried in superior court** *die Voraussetzung für die Verhandlung der Streitsache im oberen Gericht erfüllend*; ~ **to serve as a pledge** verpfändbar, lombardfähig.

fit *v* passen, anpassen, versehen mit; ~**ted accounts** *scot* unwidersprochener Kontokorrentsaldo; ~**ted or provided with** versehen sein mit.

fitments Einbauten *in e–r Wohnung*.

fitness Eignung *f*, Tauglichkeit *f*; ~ **for human habitation** Eignung für Wohnzwecke; ~ **for purpose** Zweckdienlichkeit, Eignung; ~ **of goods for use** Gebrauchsfähigkeit der Waren; **certificate of** ~ Tauglichkeitsbescheinigung; **physical** ~ (körperliche) Tauglichkeit.

fittings Ausstattung *f*, Einrichtungsgegenstände *m|pl*, Zubehör *n* (*zu beweglichen Sachen*); ~ **shop** → *shop*.

fix *v* festsetzen, festlegen, bestimmen, anberaumen; ~ **a date for a meeting** e–e Sitzung anberaumen; ~ **a day** e–n Termin anberaumen; ~ **a dividend** Dividenden festsetzen; ~ **a hearing** e–n Termin anberaumen; ~ **a limit** → *limit*; ~ **a penalty** e–e Strafe festsetzen, das Strafmaß bestimmen; ~ **damages** die Schadensersatzleistung festlegen; ~ **up** sich arrangieren; ~ **the price** den Preis bestimmen, Kurs festsetzen; ~**ing of a limit** Festsetzung von Höchstbeträgen; ~**ing of prices** Kursbildung, Preisfestsetzung, Preisabsprachen; ~**ing of quotas** Kontingentierung.

fixed fest, festgesetzt, gebunden, geordnet, erledigt, reguliert; ~ **and fastened** *mit dem Grundstück* verbunden; ~ **belief** vorgefaßte Meinung; ~ **exchange** direkte Notierung, Mengennotierung; ~ **penalty notice** Strafzettel, *etwa:* Bußgeldbescheid; ~ **penalty system** *etwa:* Bußgeldregelung; ~ **rate preference shares**, ~ **sum credit** Darlehen auf e–e bestimmte Summe; ~ **term maintenance order** befristeter Unterhaltsbeschluß; ~ **term tenancy** Festmietvertrag, befristetes Mietverhältnis; ~ **yield securities** Wertpapiere mit unveränderlichen Erträgen.

fixture Grundstückszubehör *n*, wesentlicher Bestandteil von Grundstücken; die eingebauten beweglichen Gegenstände *m|pl* des Mieters *bzw Pächters*; fest befristete Anleihe; ~**s and fittings** Einbauten, Zubehör des Mieters *bzw Pächters*, Scheinbestandteile e–s Grundstücks; **agricultural** ~**s** Einbauten des Landpächters *und sonstige trennbare Bestandteile* bei e–m landwirtschaftl Anwesen; **domestic** ~**s** Wohnungseinbauten und Zubehör der Mietsache; **immovable** ~**s** wesentlicher Grundstücksbestandteil; **movable** ~ entfernbarer Grundstücksbestandteil; **non-removable** ~ wesentlicher Grundstücksbestandteil; **ornamental** ~**s** Mietereinbauten zur Verschönerung; **tenant's** ~**s** → *tenant*; **trade** ~**s** gewerbliche Einbauten und Zubehörteile des Mieters.

flag Fahne *f*, Flagge *f*, Flaggensignal *n*; ~ **of convenience** *Schiffsflagge e–s anderen Landes als das des Schiffseigners*, „Billigflagge"; ~ **of the United States** Bundesflagge der USA; ~ **of truce** Parlamentärsfahne; **abuse of** ~ Flaggenmißbrauch; **bearer of the** ~ **of truce** Parlamentär; **duty of the** ~ Flaggenzeremonie (*der Anerkennung von Hoheitsgewässern*); **law of** ~ Flaggenrecht; **law of the** ~ das Recht der Flagge, *das nationale Recht des der Schiffsflagge zugehörigen Staates*, das Recht des Heimathafens; **mari-**

time ~ Seeflagge; **merchant** ~ Handelsflagge; **national** ~ Hoheitsflagge, Staatsflagge; **to display a** ~ flaggen, e–e Flagge führen; **to strike the** ~ die Fahne einziehen; **transfer to another** ~ *int* Wechsel des Flaggenstaates; **verification of the** ~ *int* Prüfung e–r Flagge; **yellow** ~ Quarantäneflagge.

flag down *v/t* zum Halten bringen (*a passing car for help*).

flagrant necessity Notstand *m*, Nötigungsstand *m*.

flagrante delicto auf frischer Tat.

flannel wortreiche elegante Ausführungen, täuschendes Gerede.

flashing blue beacon Blaulicht *n*.

flat *s* Etagenwohnung *f*; ~ **owner** Wohnungseigentümer; ~ **owner shareholder** Anteilseigner und Wohnungseigentümer e–r Wohnungsgesellschaft; ~ **ownership** Wohnungseigentum; ~ **property** Wohnungseigentum; ~ **share** Teilbewohnen, Wohnbeteiligung; **freehold** ~ Eigentumswohnung; **residential** ~ Privatwohnung.

flat *adj*; flach, platt, stumpf, lustlos, flau; pauschale Zinsen bereits eingeschlossen, einheitlich, Einheits . . .

flaw Formfehler *m*, Fabrikationsfehler *m*, Mangel *m*; ~ **in a title** Rechtsmangel.

flawed mangelhaft, rechtsfehlerhaft.

flee *v* die Flucht ergreifen, fliehen; ~ **arrest** sich der Festnahme durch die Flucht entziehen; ~ **from justice** flüchtig werden; ~ **to the wall** sich in äußerster Notwehrlage befinden.

fleece *v* ausplündern, „rupfen", betrügen, prellen.

fleet Flotte *f*, Kriegsflotte *f*, Luftflotte *f*, Fahrzeugpark *m*; Bucht *f*; **the F~** = *Fleet Prison qv*; **F~ Books** *standesamtl Bücher aus dem Fleet Gefängnis und Umgebung, 18. Jhd.*; ~ **marriage** → *marriage*; ~ **of cabs** Taxipark eines Unternehmers; ~ **policy** Sammelpolice (*für Wagenpark*); **F~ Prison** *altes Londoner Schuldgefängnis für Beugestrafen*; ~ **seller** Verkaufserfolg e–r Modellreihe (PKW); **F~ Street** *Presseviertel in London, „die britische Presse"*; **merchant** ~ Handelsflotte.

flexible flexibel, elastisch, anpassungsfähig, veränderlich; ~ **working hours** flexible Arbeitszeit.

flexitime Gleitzeit *f*, gleitende Arbeitszeit, flexible Arbeitszeit.

flight (*1*) Flucht *f*; ~ **from taxation** Steuerflucht; ~ **money** Fluchtgelder; ~ **of capital** Kapitalflucht.

flight (*2*) Flug *m*; ~ **cancellation** Flugstornierung; ~ **surveillance** Flugüberwachung.

flipping Refinanzierung von Kundenkrediten.

float *s* Floß *n*, schwimmende Landebrücke; die gutgeschriebenen aber noch nicht bezahlten Schecks; Schecks im Einzug; Bestand an laufender Produktion; der noch nicht plazierte Teil e–r Anleihe.

float *v* schweben, flott machen, umlaufen, (*Wertpapiere*) plazieren; (*e–n Unternehmen*) gründen; floaten (*Währung*); ~ **a company** e–e Gesellschaft gründen; ~ **a loan** e–e Anleihe auflegen.

floatable schwimmfähig, trittfähig, flößbar.

floatation = *flotation qv*.

floater(s) erstklassige Inhaberpapiere *n/pl*, Generalpolice *f/pl*; Wechselwähler *m/pl*; **perpetual** ~ ewiglaufender Zinswechsler.

floating *s* (=) flexible Wechselkurse.

floating *adj* schwebend, fluktuierend, variabel, aufschiebend bedingt; ~ **exchange rate** frei veränderlicher Devisenkurs; ~ **interest rate** variabler am Geldmarkt orientierter Zinssatz; ~ **rate note** (*FRN*) Schuldverschreibung mit variabler Verzinsung, zinsvariable Anleihe.

flode-mark Flutmarke, Höchstwasserstand.

flogging Auspeitschen *n*.

flood Überschwemmung *f*; ~ **waters** Überschwemmung(sfluten).

"flood gates" argument Berücksichtigung unabsehbarer Nachfolgefälle.

floor Fußboden *m*, Diele *f*, Grund *m*, Stockwerk *n*; Meeresboden *m*, Fahrbahn *f*; Sitzungssaal *m*, Börsenparkett *n*, Plenum *n*; Mindestkurs, Kurstiefstand; ~ **broker** → *broker*; ~ **leader** → *leader*; ~ **of protection** Grundversorgung (*„soziales Netz"*); ~ **of the court** *Teil des Sitzungssaales unmittelbar vor der Richterbank;* ~ **of the House** Plenarsaal; ~ **partner** Teilhaber e–r Maklerfirma; ~ **plan financing** Zwischenfinanzierung des jeweiligen Händlerbestandes (*an PKW oder dgl*) *mit Sicherheit am ausgestellten Objekt*; ~ **trader** → *trader*; ~ **walker** Rayonchef im Warenhaus, Aufsicht; **to cross the** ~ **of the House** zur Gegenpartei übergehen; **to have the** ~ das Wort haben; **to take the** ~ das Wort ergreifen.

flotage (= *floatage*) Treibgut *n*.

flotation Gründung *f*, Emission *f*; Begebung *f*; ~ **of a company** Gründung (*und Kapitalbeschaffung*) e–r Gesellschaft; **of an issue** Wertpapieremission; **foreign** ~ Auslandsemission.

flotsam Treibgut *n*.

flourish florieren, blühen; zu e–m (*Schwert-, Stock-*) Streich ausholen, mit e–m Schlage drohen.

flow Fließen *n*, Strömen *n*, Fluß *m*; ~ **chart** Flußdiagramm, Verarbeitungsdiagramm; ~ **of capital** Kapitalbewegung; Kapitalwanderung; ~ **of currency** Geldumlauf; ~ **of traffic** Verkehrsstrom; ~ **of work** Arbeitsablauf.

flowers of the Crown der Krone verfallenes Hab und Gut *von Verbrechern und Flüchtigen*.

fluctuation Fluktuation *f*, Flukturieren *n*, ständige Schwankungen *f/pl*; ~**s in rates of remuneration** Schwankungen der Vergütungssätze; ~ **margins** Bandbreiten; ~ **of currency** Währungsschwankungen, häufige Devisenkursänderung; ~ **of exchange** Devisenkursschwankungen; ~**s of the market** Konjunkturschwankungen; **cyclical** ~ zyklische Konjunkturschwankung; **seasonal** ~**s** jahreszeitlich bedingte Schwankungen.

flurry plötzliche kurze Belebung *f* (*Börse*).

flutter kurze Spekulation *f*.

fly fliegen, fliehen; ~ **for it** *hist* wegen der Tat flüchtig sein (*Frage an den Angeklagten deren Bejahung zur Einziehung des Vermögens führte*).

flying squad Überfallkommando *n*.

fly power Blankoübertragungsallonge (*Aktienzertifikat*).

f. o. b. = *free on board* → *free*.

fodder Futter *n* (*für Pferde und Rinder*); Futterentnahmerecht *n* des Herrschers.

foeneration Geldverleih *m* zu Wucherzinsen.

foeticide Abtreibung *f*.

foist andrehen, aufschwätzen.

folder Umschlag *m*, Mappe *f*, Aktendeckel *m*; Broschüre *f*, Faltprospekt *m*.

foliation Blattzählung *f*, Seitennumerierung *f*.

folio *s* Folioblatt *n*, Folioformat *n*, Blatt *n*, Kontobuchseite *f*, Kontobuchdoppelseite *f*, Einheitswortzahl *f* e–r Urkunde (*72 Wörter beim Royal Supreme Court London, sonst auch 90 Wörter*); ~ **size** Folioformat.

folio *v* paginieren; Dokument gemäß Worteinheitszahl abteilen und numerieren.

follow-on support nachvertragliche Unterstützung *f*.

follow-settlements clause Regulierungs-Folgepflichtklausel, *Klausel betreffend die Folgepflicht des Rückversicherers bei Schadensregulierungen des Erstversicherers*.

food Nahrung *f*, Lebensmittel *n*; **F~ and Environment Protection Act** Nahrungsmittel- und Umweltschutz Gesetz (GB *1985*); ~ **manufacturing industry** Lebensmittelindustrie; ~ **position** Ernährungslage; **unwholesome** ~ nicht zum Verzehr geeignete Lebensmittel.

foodstuff Lebensmittel *n/pl*; **adulteration of** ~**s** Lebensmittelverfälschung.

foolscap Propatriapapier *n gefaltete Schreibbogen, Kanzleibogen, engl Druckpapierformat (13½ × 17 Zoll).*

foot *s* Fuß *m*; (*Längenmaß 0,3048 m*), Ende *n*; ~ **and mouth disease** Maul- und Klauenseuche; ~ **or end** am Schluß (*e–s Testaments*); ~ **pound** (=) *Energieeinheit (um ein Pfund e–n Fuß zu heben).*

foot *v/t* die Spalten e–s Kontos addieren; ~ **the bill** die Rechnung begleichen, die Zeche bezahlen.

footing *s* (*1*) Spaltenaddition *f*, Summe *f* der Soll- oder Habenseite e–s Kontos.

footing (*2*) Grundlage *f*, Basis *f*, Stand *m*; Einstandsgeld *n*; **on an equal** ~ paritätisch.

footnote Fußnote *f*, Anmerkung *f*.

footpath Fußweg *m*, Gehweg *m*.

foot-prints Fußabdrücke *m/pl.*

foot-race Wettrennen *n*.

foot-tracks Fußspuren *f/pl.*

footway Bürgersteig *m*; Gehsteig *m*.

for für, an Stelle von, in Vertretung von, im Interesse von, im Auftrag von; während, auf die Dauer von; als Gegenleistung für; zuständig für, wegen, hinsichtlich dessen, zu gunsten von, in Anbetracht dessen; nach, in Richtung; ~ **appropriate action** zur weiteren Veranlassung; ~ **a turn** *US* als ganz kurzfristige Anlage; ~ **account of** auf Rechnung von, *Indossamentsvermerk des Zahlungsberechtigten*; ~ **an unlimited period** unbefristet, auf unbeschränkte Zeit; ~ **and during such time** vorübergehend, zeitweise; ~ **and on behalf of** im Auftrag; ~ **at least** mindestens (*bei Tagen: einschließlich Anfangs- oder Schlußtag*); ~ **behoof of** zu Gunsten; ~ **cause** aus begründetem Anlaß; ~ **charterer's account** auf Rechnung des Schiffsmieters; ~ **collection** → *collection*; ~ **default of all such issue** falls keine Nachkommen vorhanden sind, (*bei denen die Voraussetzungen vorliegen*); ~ **deposit only** nur zur Verrechnung; ~ **ever** auf alle Zeit (*konstitutive Worte bei Auflassung*); ~ **further action** zur weiteren Veranlassung; ~ **her separate use** (*treuhänderisch*) zu ihrer gesonderten Nutzung; ~ **hire and reward** zur gewerbl Personenbeförderung; ~ **money** → *money*; ~ **or in connection with** als Gegenleistung *bzw* im Zusammenhang mit; ~ **private information** zur vertraulichen Kenntnisnahme; ~ **purpose of** zwecks; ~ **sale** zum (*allgemeinen*) Verkauf; ~ **that** wegen (*es folgen tatsächliche Behauptungen*); ~ **the benefit of** zu gunsten von; ~ **the direct benefit** unmittelbar zu Gunsten von; ~ **the purposes of the Act** für die im Gesetz vorgesehenen Zwecke; ~ **the time being** → *time*; ~ **third account** auf fremde Rechnung; ~ **two successive weeks** in zwei aufeinanderfolgenden Wochen; ~ **use** zu Gunsten e–s Dritten, zum Gebrauch (*nicht Verbrauch*); ~ **use for trade** zum Handelsgebrauch; ~ **valuable consideration** entgeltlich; ~ **value** wertpapierrechtlich erworben, entgeltlich erworben; ~ **value received** entgeltlich; Wert erhalten; *vgl. value*; ~ **want of** in Ermangelung von, mangels, bei Nichteintreten; ~ **want of funds** mangels Deckung; ~ **want of provision** mangels Deckung; ~ **whom it may concern** für alle in Betracht Kommenden; **loan use** → *loan*.

forage *s* Futter *n*, Beutezug *m*.

forage *v* Proviant beschlagnahmen, Lebensmittel plündern.

forbear *s* Vorfahre *m*, Ahne *m*.

forbear *v* unterlassen, sich enthalten.

forbearance Unterlassung *f*, Duldung *f*, Nachsicht *f*, Abstandnehmen *n* von der Vollstreckung; ~ **to sue** Abstandnehmen von der Klage.

forbearing nachsichtig, geduldig.

forbid verbieten, untersagen.

force *s* Kraft *f*, Wirkung *f*, Rechtsgültigkeit *f*, Gewalt *f*, Zwang *m*, widerrechtliche Gewaltanwendung *f*; ~ **and fear** Gewalt oder Bedrohung; ~**-fed** zwangsernährt; ~

majeure (=) höhere Gewalt; ~ **of an argument** Überzeugungskraft e–s Arguments; ~ **of arms** Waffengewalt; ~ **of law** Gesetzeskraft; ~ **permissible** zulässige Gewaltanwendung; **deadly** ~ tödliche Gewaltanwendung; **legal** ~ Rechtsverbindlichkeit, Gesetzeskraft; **lethal** ~ Gewalt mit Todesfolge; tödliche Gewaltanwendung; **physical** ~ physischer Zwang; unmittelbare Gewalt; **police** ~ Schutzpolizei; **probative** ~ → *probative*; **reasonable** ~ angemessene Gewalt(anwendung); **retroactive** ~ Rückwirkung; **superior** ~ unwiderstehliche Gewalt; **to be in** ~ gültig, rechtsgültig sein, gelten, in Kraft sein; **to come into** ~ in Kraft treten; **use of** ~ Gewaltanwendung.

forc|e *v* zwingen, erzwingen, nötigen, Gewalt antun; ~**ed call** Anlaufen e–s Nothafens.

forced sale of collaterals Exekution, Zwangsverwertung von Sicherheiten.

forcible gewaltsam, gewalttätig, Zwangs...; eindringlich; ~ **resistance to arrest** Widerstandsleistung bei Verhaftung.

forecast Prognose *f*, Voraussage *f*, Prophezeiung *f*, Vorausberechnung *f*; **long-term** ~**ing** langfristige Prognose.

foreclosable vollstreckbar (*mortgage*), vor der Pfandverwertung stehend.

foreclose ausschließen, für verfallen erklären, aufbieten, das Einlösungsrecht ausschließen; ~ **a mortgage** aus e–r Hypothek vollstrecken, den Pfandgegenstand für verfallen erklären; ~ **s. o.** jmdm e–e Ausschlußfrist setzen.

foreclosure Ausschluß *m*, Aufhebung *f*, Grundpfandverfallserklärung *f*, Vollstreckung *f* aus e–m Grundpfandrecht; Abweisung *f*; ~ **absolute** rechtskräftige Pfandverfallserklärung; ~ **action** Vollstreckungsklage, Klage auf Feststellung des Pfandverfalls (*auf Ausschluß des Pfandauslösungsrechts [equity of redemption qv] des Schuldners)*; ~ **decree** gerichtliche Pfandverfallserklärung, Zwangsvollstreckungsverkauf; ~ **nisi** vorläufige Verfallserklärung; ~ **order** Pfandverfallsbeschluß; ~ **proceedings** Pfandverfallsverfahren, Zwangsvollstreckung in das Grundstück; ~ **sale** Zwangsversteigerung, Pfandverkauf; **statutory** ~ gesetzlich zugelassener Pfandverkauf (*in Vollmacht des Schuldners*); **strict** ~ Anordnung des endgültigen Pfandverfalls nach Ausschlußfrist.

forecourt Vorderhof *m*, Hofraum *m* vor dem Hause.

foredate zurückdatieren (*auf ein früheres als das Ausstellungsdatum*).

foregift Abstandszahlung *f* für Erlangen e–r Pacht.

foregone conclusion vorweggenommene Schlußfolgerung *f*, ausgemachte Sache *f*, unvermeidliche Folgerung *f*, Selbstverständlichkeit *f*.

foreign fremd, ausländisch (= *ausl*), auswärtig; ~ **affairs** auswärtige Beziehungen; ~ **aid** Auslandshilfe; ~ **born** im Ausland geboren; **Foreign Claims Settlement Commission** (*US*) Kommission zur Regelung von Auslandsansprüchen; ~ ~ ~ ~ *award: Zuerkennung e–s Entschädigungsanspruchs an e–n ausländischen Anspruchsteller*; ~ **coins** *ausl–es* Münzgeld, Kurs *ausl–er* Münzen; ~ **coins or notes** Sorten; ~ **currency** → *foreign currency (infra)* Fremdwährungsschulden; ~ **dollar bonds** Dollaranleihen fremder Staaten (*außer USA*); ~ **domination** Fremdherrschaft; ~ **dominion** britisches Herrschaftsgebiet außerhalb der britischen Inseln; **F~ Enlistment Act** Gesetz gegen die Anwerbung zu ausländ. Militärdienst *GB 1870*; ~ **exchange** → *foreign exchange*; ~ **general average** (FGA) Havarie grosse Regelung am fremden Bestimmungshafen; ~**-going ship** im Überseeverkehr eingesetztes Schiff; ~**-held** in

Auslandsbesitz (*befindlich*); ~ **international sale corporation** (*FISC*) *ausländische internationale Handelsgesellschaft (von USA aus gesehen)*; ~ **personal holding company** *US ausländische Körperschaft, an der höchstens 5 Steuerausländer eine Mehrheitsbeteiligung haben*; ~ **service of process** Klagezustellung im Ausland.

foreign currency Fremdwährung *f*, Devisen *pl*, ausländische Zahlungsmittel; ~ **accounts** Fremdwährungskonten; ~ **liabilities reserves** Devisenreserven; ~ **trade** Devisenhandel; ~ **translations** Devisenumrechnungen.

foreign exchange ausländische Zahlungsmittel *n*|*pl*, Devisen *pl* (= *D*); ~ **allotments** *D*-zuteilungen; ~ **arbitrage** *D*-arbitrage; ~ **bill** Fremdwährungswechsel; ~ **broker** *D*-makler; ~ **control** *D*-Kontrolle, *D*-bewirtschaftung; ~ **cushion** *D*-polster; ~ **dealer** *D*-makler; ~ **dealings** *D*-handel; ~ **equalisation fund** *D*-ausgleichsfonds; ~ **guaranty** Kurssicherung; ~ **holdings** *D*-guthaben; ~ **licence** *D*-bewilligung, *D*-genehmigung; ~ **markets** *D*-märkte; ~ **quota** *D*-kontingent; ~ **rates** *D*-kurse; ~ **shortage** *D*knappheit; ~ **transaction** *D* geschäft.

foreigner Ausländer *m*, Fremder *m*; **employment of** ~**s** Beschäftigung von Ausländern; **naturalisation of** ~**s** Einbürgerung.

Foreign Office *GB* Außenministerium, Auswärtiges Amt.

Foreign Secretary Außenminister.

Foreign Service Auswärtiger Dienst.

foreign trade Außenhandel; ~ **agreement** Außenhandelsabkommen; ~ **bank** Außenhandelsbank; ~ **zone** Freihandelszone.

forejudge gerichtlich entziehen, ausstoßen, verbannen; **to be** ~**d the court** *hist* vom Gericht ausgeschlossen werden.

forejudger Ausschlußurteil *n*, gerichtliche Entziehung *f*.

foreman Obmann *m* (*der Geschworenen*), Vorarbeiter *m*, Werkmeister *m*, Aufseher *m*.

fore-matron die Vorsitzende e–r Geschworenenbank.

fore-mentioned oben erwähnt.

forensic forensisch, gerichtlich.

fore-oath *hist* Voreid *m* (*des Klägers bei Klageerhebung*).

foresaid vorstehend, obengenannt.

foresee vorhersehen.

foreseeability Voraussehbarkeit *f*.

foreseeable voraussehbar; ~ **future** überschaubare Zukunft.

foreshore Gestade *n*, Küstenvorland *n*, Watt *n*.

foresight Voraussicht *f*, Vorsorge *f*, Umsicht *f*.

forest Forst *m*, Wald *m*; Jagdrecht *n*.

forestall zuvorkommen, aufkaufen, abfangen.

forestaller *hist* Behinderung *f*, widerrechtliche Straßensperre *f*, Abfangen *n* von Wild; Aufkäufer *m*.

forestalling Vorwegnahme *f*, Straßenbehinderung *f*; ~ **the market** (*spekulatives*) Aufkaufen.

forester Förster *m*, *königlicher* Forstbeamter *m*.

forestry Forstwirtschaft *f*; ~ **lease** Verpachtung von Wald an den Staat.

forfaiting Forfaitierung (*rückgriffsfreier Verkauf von Auslandsforderungen*)

forfeit *s* verwirktes Pfand *n*, Buße *f*; ~ **money** Reuegeld, Abstandsgeld.

forfeit *v* verwirkt sein, verfallen, straffällig werden; ~ **a pledge** ein Pfand für verfallen erklären; ~ **a right** e–s Rechts verlustig gehen.

forfeiture Einziehung *f*, Verwirkung *f*, Verfall *m*, Verfallserklärung *f*, Verlust *m*, Buße *f*; ~ **of a bond** Pfandverfall; Auslösung der Vertragsstrafe; ~ **of a deposit** Depotverfall; ~ **of a pension** Entziehung des Pensionsanspruchs; ~ **of citizenship** Aberkennung der Staatsangehörigkeit; ~ **of civic rights** Aberkennung der bürgerlichen Ehrenrechte; ~ **of lease** Pachtrechtsverfallsklausel (*bei Zahlungsverzug*), fristlose Verwirkung, sofortiger Verlust des Mietrechts; ~ **of marriage** *hist* Verlust von Standesrechten bei nicht genehmigter Heirat; ~ **of property** Einziehung des Vermögens; ~ **of shares** Kaduzierung von Aktien; **criminal** ~ Einziehung (*wegen Verwendung bei Straftat*).

Forfeitures Abolition Act *Gesetz über die Abschaffung der Vermögenseinziehung bei Verbrechern, GB 1870.*

forge fälschen, verfälschen, e–e Falschurkunde herstellen; ~ **a signature** e–e Unterschrift fälschen; ~ **coins** Münzen verfälschen; ~**d instrument** verfälschte Urkunde, unechte Urkunde; **F~d Transfers Acts** *brit Gesetze zur Entschädigung bei betrügerischen Aktienmanipulationen.*

forger Urkundenfälscher *m*, Falschmünzer *m*.

forgery Urkundenfälschung *f*, Siegelfälschung *f*, Fälschung *f*, verfälschte Urkunde *f*, Verfälschung *f* echten oder Herstellung falschen Beweismaterials; ~ **of a document** Urkundenfälschung; ~ **of a passport** Paßfälschung; ~ **of acceptance** Akzeptfälschung; ~ **of an instrument** Urkundenfälschung; ~ **of bills** Wechselfälschung; ~ **of indorsement** Indossamentsfälschung; ~ **of signature** Unterschriftsfälschung; ~ **of will** Testamentsfälschung, Herstellung und Verwendung e–s fingierten Testaments.

forgive vergeben, e–e Schuld erlassen.

forgiveness of interest Zinsverzicht *m*.

forgo von etw Abstand nehmen, verzichten; ~ **a debt** e–e Forderung erlassen.

forgoing the cash discount Skontoverzicht *m*.

form *s* Gestalt *f*, Modell *n*, Schablone *f*; Form *f*, Formular *n*, Vordruck *m*; gesetzlich festgelegter Wortlaut; ~ **letter** Formularbrief; ~**s of action** Klagearten, Klageformulare; ~ **of enterprise** Unternehmensform, Rechtsform des Unternehmens; ~ **of government** Regierungssystem, Staatsform; ~ **of oath** → *oath*; ~ **of payment** Zahlungsweise; ~**s of the court** gerichtl Formulare; ~ **of the statute** gesetzliche Formvorschrift; ~ **required by law** gesetzliche Form; ~ **requirements** Formerfordernisse; ~**-sheet** Formularblatt; ~ **stipulated by contract** gewillkürte Formvorschrift; **a mere matter of** ~ eine bloße Formalität; **application** ~ Anmeldeformular, Antragsformular; **cheque** ~ Scheckformular; **common** ~ schlicht, formlos, üblich, anerkannte Formulierung; unstreitiges (Nachlaß-) Verfahren; **contrary to** ~ formwidrig; **correct as to** ~ formgerecht; **false** ~ Formulierungsfehler bei Schriftstücken für das Gericht; **in bad** ~ unschicklich; **in due** ~ → *due*; **in the** ~ **hereinafter set forth** in der nachstehenden Formulierung; **legal** ~ vorgeschriebene Form, gesetzliche Form, gesetzliche Musterformulierung; **matter of** ~ Formsache, Förmlichkeiten (*der Schriftsätze usw*); **open** ~ ausfüllungsbedürftiges Formular; **order** ~ → *order* (2); **prescribed** ~ vorgeschriebenes Formular; vorgeschriebene Formulierung; unter Einhaltung von Formvorschriften; **printed** ~ Vordruck; **registered** ~ in Form e–r Registereintragung; **solemn** ~ förmlich, zeremoniell; **statutory** ~ gesetzliche Form(vorschrift).

form *v* bilden, gestalten; ~**ed action** Klage mit vorgeschriebener Formulierung; ~**ed design** Überlegung, vorher geplanter Vorsatz.

forma pauperis *obs* (im) Armenrecht *n*.

formal formal, konentionell, förmlich, offiziell, peinlich genau; ~ **call** offizieller Besuch; ~ **ending** Schlußformel; ~ **irregularities in the proceedings** (formale) Verfah-

rensfehler; ~ **requirements** Formvorschriften, Formerfordernis, Formzwang.
formalism leere Förmlichkeiten *f/pl*, Formalismus *m*.
formality Formvorschrift *f*, Formalität *f*, Förmlichkeit *f*, rechtstechnische Gestaltung *f*; **without** ~ formlos, schlicht.
format Verhandlungsplan *m*, Programm *m*.
formation Bildung *f*, Gründung *f*; ~ **of a company** Gesellschaftsgründung; ~ **of a contract** Zustandekommen e-s Vertrages, Vertragsschluß.
former erstgenannter, erster, vorerwähnt, früher, ehemalig, vorhergehend, vormalig, vormals, weiland; ~ **acquittal** Berufung auf e-n rechtskräftigen Freispruch in gleicher Sache; ~ **adjudication** Einrede der Rechtskraft (*e-r früheren Entscheidung*); ~ **jeopardy** → *jeopardy*.
formerly ehemalig, vormals.
formula Formel *f*, Klageformular *n*; **empty** ~ Leerformel.
formularies *hist* Formularsammlung *f*.
formulate formulieren, festsetzen, auf e-e Formel bringen.
formulation Formulierung *f*, Fassung *f*.
formulism Formelwesen *n*, Formelkram *m*, Formelhaftigkeit *f*.
fornication außerehelicher Geschlechtsverkehr *m*, Unzucht *f*, Hurerei *f*.
forsake im Stich lassen, aufgeben.
forswear abschwören, unter Eid verneinen; falsch schwören, meineidig werden.
forthcoming *adj* herauskommend, demnächst erscheinend, nächst(-er, -e, -es).
forthwith unverzüglich, umgehend, ohne schuldhaftes Zögern.
fortnightly vierzehntägig, alle 14 Tage, halbmonatlich; ~ **settlement** Medioabrechnung; ~ **(settlement) loan** Mediogeld.
fortuitous zufällig, zufallsbedingt, unbeabsichtigt, unvermeidbar.
fortune Glück *n*, Zufall *m*, Geschick *n*, Schicksal *n*, Reichtum *m*; Mitgift *f*; ~ **de mer** Schiffsvermögen, Vermögensteil des Reeders auf dem Seetransport; ~ **hunter** Mitgiftjäger; ~**-telling** (verbotene) Wahrsagerei.
forum Forum *n*, Gerichtsstand *m*; ~ **clause** → *clause*; ~ **contractus** Gerichtsstand des Erfüllungsortes; ~ **conveniens** ins gerichtliche Ermessen gestellte Zuständigkeit *bei Auslandszustellung an den Beteiligten*; ~ **originis** Gerichtsstand des Geburtswohnsitzlandes, Wohnsitzgerichtsstand des Beteiligten; ~ **non conveniens** Zuständigkeitsablehnung *im Interesse der Parteien und aus prozeßökonomischen Gründen*; ~ **rei** Gerichtsstand der belegenen Sache; ~ **rei gestae** Gerichtsstand des Tatorts; ~ **rei sitae** Gerichtsstand der belegenen Sache, dinglicher Gerichtsstand; ~ **shopping** (manipulierte) Wahl des für den Kläger günstigsten Gerichtsstandes; **natural** ~ allgemeiner Gerichtsstand, der einzig vernünftige Gerichtsstand.
forward budget Vorausschätzung des Finanzbudgets; ~ **business dealings** Terminhandel; ~ **buying** Terminkauf; ~ **combination** Fusion des Herstellungs- mit dem Vertriebsunternehmen; ~ **contract** Terminabschluß; ~ **cover** Terminsicherung; ~**deals** Zeitgeschäfte, Termingeschäfte; ~ **delivery** Terminlieferung; ~ **exchange market** Devisen-Terminhandel; ~ **exchange rate** Devisenterminkurs; ~ **market** → *market*; ~ **operation** Terminhandel, Terminabschluß; ~ **purchase** → *purchase*; ~ **quotation** Terminnotierung; ~ **rate** → *rate*; ~ **sale** → *sale*; ~ **securities** Terminwerte, Terminpapiere; ~ **strategy** Vorwärtsverteidigungsstrategie; ~ **transaction** → *transaction*; **from this day** ~ von heute an; **to buy** ~ e-n Terminkauf tätigen.
forward senden, befördern, absenden, verladen, übersenden; **to be**

~ed bitte nachsenden!; **not to be ~ed** bitte nicht nachsenden!
forwarder Spediteur *m*; **~'s receipt** Spediteur-Übernahmebescheinigung.
forwarding Beförderung *f*, Absenden *n*, Versenden *n*, Abfertigung *f*, Spedieren *n*, Speditions . . .; **~ advice** Versendungsanzeige; **~ agency** Speditionsfirma; **~ agent** Spediteur; **F~ Agent's Certificate of Receipt** (*FCR*) internationale Spediteur-Übernahmebescheinigung (*der FIATA*); **~ charges** Verladekosten, Versandspesen, Speditionskosten, Versendungskosten; **~ clerk** Expedient; **~ department** Versandabteilung, Expeditionsabteilung; **~ instructions** Versandvorschriften; **~ merchant** Spediteur, Speditionskaufmann; **~ note** Frachtbrief, Versandmitteilung; **~ station** Versandbahnhof; **mode of ~** Versendungsart.
foster *v/t* (*Kind*) an Pflegeeltern übertragen, in Pflege geben.
foster|-child Pflegekind; **~-father** Pflegevater; **~ home** Heim für Pflegekinder, Fürsorgeheim; **~-mother** Pflegemutter; **~-parents** Pflegeeltern.
fosterer Förderer *m*, Adoptivbruder *m*; Amme *f*, Pflegevater *m*.
fostering Förderung *f*, Anregung *f*; Inpflegegeben *n* von Kindern.
fosterland Nutzland *n* zur Eigenverpflegung.
fosterlean Vergütung *f* für Pflegekind; Witwenanteil *m* am Grundbesitz.
found *v* stiften, gründen, errichten; **~ed on an act of adultery** auf Ehebruch gestützt; **~ed on an affidavit** durch eidesstattliche Versicherung glaubhaft gemacht; **~ed on contract** (*Klage*) aus Vertrag, vertraglich; **~ed on tort** (*Klage*) aus unerlaubter Handlung, deliktisch; **an action is ~ed** ein Klageanspruch ist begründet, Klageanspruch ist gegeben; **ill ~ed** schlecht begründet, abwegig; **well ~ed** begründet.
found *part von to find* aufgefunden, vorgefunden, angetroffen, festgestellt, erkannt; **~ committing** auf frischer Tat ertappt; **~ in possession** im Besitze angetroffen; **~ neglected** als verwahrlost festgestellt; **~ on premises** im Lokal angetroffen (*oder gesehen*); **~ within the jurisdiction** im Gerichtsbezirk festgenommen; **not ~** kein hinreichender Tatverdacht.
foundation Grundlage *f*, Fundament *n*, Fundierung *f*; Anstalt *f*, Schenkung *f*; Gründung *f*, Stiftung *f*, Errichtung *f*; **~ charter** Gründungsurkunde, Stiftungsurkunde; **~ stone** Grundstein; **charitable ~** mildtätige Stiftung; **denominational ~** kirchliche Stiftung.
founder *s* Gründer *m*, Stifter *m*; **~'s preference rights** Gründervorzugsrechte; **~'s shares** → *share*.
foundership Stiftereigenschaft *f*.
foundling Findling *m*, Findelkind *n*; **~ hospital** Findelhaus.
four|corners Text e–r Urkunde; *das, was sich unmittelbar aus dem Text e–r Urkunde ergibt*; **~ day costs** innerhalb 4 Tagen zu erstattende Kosten (*nach Kostentabelle*); **~ day order** → *order* (*1*).
Fourteenth Amendment *der 14. Zusatzartikel der US-Verfassung (Grundrechte)*.
fourth|(bill) of exchange Quartettwechsel; **~ class matter** Paketporto *US*; **~ degree manslaughter** fahrlässige Tötung; **(the) F~ Estate** der „Vierte Stand" (*die Presse*).
fractional gebrochen, minimal; **~ amount** Bruchteil; **~ certificate** Teilschein; **~ coins** Kleingeldmünzen, Scheidemünzen; **~ currency** Kleingeld, Kleingeldnoten, Scheidemünzen; **~ lot** *Aktien:* kleines Paket *von weniger als 100 Stück*; **~ number** Bruchzahl; **~ paper money** Papierkleingeld; **~ rights** (Bezugsrechts)Spitze; **~ tract of land** Teilfläche, Parzelle.
frame *v* formulieren, entwerfen, verfassen; lügnerisch bezichtigen, falsche Anschuldigungen erheben,

jmdn verleumden, in e–e Falle lokken.

framework of planning Planungsrahmen *m*.

franchise Franchise *f*, Selbstbehalt *m*; Stimmrecht *n*, Wahlrecht *n*; Konzession *f*, Privileg *n*, Alleinvertretung *f*, verliehene Rechtsfähigkeit *f*; Marktrecht *n*; Gerechtigkeit *f*; ~ **clause** Franchiseklausel, Selbstbehaltsklausel; ~ **de l'hôtel** *int* Unverletzlichkeit der Amtswohnung des diplomatischen Vertreters; ~ **prisons** *hist* Schuldgefängnisse; ~ **tax** → *tax*; **elective** ~ allgemeines Wahlrecht; **electoral** ~ allgemeines Wahlrecht; **general** ~ staatlich verliehene Rechtsfähigkeit; **local government** ~ Wahlrecht bei örtlichen Wahlen; **parliamentary** ~ Wahlrecht für Parlamentswahlen; **personal** ~ *Berechtigung, als juristische Person gegründet zu werden und zu existieren;* Verleihung der Rechtsfähigkeit; **secondary** ~ Konzession (*bes bei öffentlichen Versorgungsbetrieben*); **special** ~ = *secondary* ~ *qv* (*siehe oben!*); **sports** ~ Spiellizenz (*an Verein*).

franchising Franchising-System *n* (*Vertriebssystem*); Überlassung von Verkaufsrechten; entgeltliche, befristete Knowhow-Konzession; **piggy back** ~ Huckepack-Franchising.

franchisee Franchisenehmer *m*, Konzessionsinhaber *m*.

franchisor Franchisegeber *m*, Konzessionserteiler *m*.

franco (=) *Lieferkosten trägt der Verkäufer*; ~ **price** Preis frei Lieferung am Lagerhaus des Käufers.

frank frei, offen, unverhohlen, aufrichtig, freimütig; ~**-almoigns** Landschenkung an die Kirche, zinsfreies Kirchengut; ~ **bank** = *freebench qv*; ~**-chase** Jagdduldungsdienstbarkeit (*Verbot der Beseitigung von Gehölzen*); ~**-fee** dienstfreies Lehnsland, freies Grundeigentum; ~**-law** das Recht der Freien; ~**-marriage** *Fideikommiß zugunsten der verheirateten Tochter und deren Ehemann beschränkt auf deren gemeinsame Abkömmlinge*; ~**-pledge** gegenseitige Bürgschaft und Geiselstellung; (*Mitglied e–r*) Zehnerschaft; Gesamtverbindlichkeit; ~**-tenant** Freisasse = *freeholder*; ~**-tenement** freies Leben, freies Grundeigentum.

frank *v/t* portofrei versenden.

franked investment income Kapitalerträge nach Steuerabzug.

franking | letters Freiportoprivileg der *Parlamentsabgeordneten*; ~ **machine** Frankiermaschine, Freistempler; ~ **officer** *Postbeamter für Freimachung privilegierter portofreier Post*; ~ **privilege** Freiportoprivileg (*von Parlamentsabgeordneten*).

fraternal brüderlich, bruderschaftlich, geschwisterlich; ~ **benefit association** Unterstützungsverein, Bruderschaft, Genossenschaft, logenähnlicher Verein, Sterbeverein; ~ **insurance** genossenschaftliche Sterbegeldversicherung; ~ **order** Loge, Bruderschaft.

fraternity Brüderlichkeit *f*, Studentenverbindung *f*, Korporation *f*, Bruderschaftsloge *f*, Berufsstand *m*; **the legal** ~ die Anwaltschaft.

fraternization Verbrüderung *f*, Fraternisierung *f*.

fraternize fraternisieren, sich verbrüdern (*bes mit der Bevölkerung des besetzten Gebietes*).

fratricide Brudermord *m*, Schwesternmord *m*.

fraud Betrug *m*, arglistige Täuschung *f*, Irreführung *f*; ~ **at common law** Betrug (*im allgemeinen*); ~ **in fact** Betrug, arglistige Täuschung; ~ **in law** *dem Betrug gesetzlich gleichgestellte Tatbestände*; Untreue; ~ **on a power** Vollmachtsmißbrauch; Mißbrauch der Amtseinsetzungsbefugnis; ~ **on minority** unlautere Machenschaften gegen Minderheitsbeteiligte; ~ **order** Postsperre wegen Betrugsverdacht, Aushändigungsverbot, Auszahlungssperre der Post; ~ **squad** Betrugsdezernat; **actionable** ~ (*erhebliche*) arglistige Täuschung, Betrug;

actual ~ arglistige Täuschung, (*vollendeter*) Betrug; **concealed** ~ von vorneherein beabsichtigter Betrug; **constructive** ~ Untreue, sittenwidriges Rechtsgeschäft; **exterritorial** ~ Betrug außerhalb der Strafgerichtsbarkeit *e–s Staates*; **extrinsic** ~ Prozeßbetrug (*außerhalb des Verfahrens*); **fiscal** ~ Steuerhinterziehung; **intrinsic** ~ Prozeßbetrug (*im Verfahren selbst*); **legal** ~ = ~ *in law qv;* **mail** ~ → *mail*; **moral** ~ arglistige Täuschung; **notice of** ~ Kenntnis der Täuschungsabsicht, Kenntnis der betrügerischen Wechselbegebung; **pious** ~ frommer Betrug; **positive** ~ = *actual* ~ *qv*; **Statute of F~s** gesetzliche Formvorschriften, Schriftform bei Bürgschaft; *hist Gesetz gegen Betrug 1677*; **tax** ~ Steuerhinterziehung, vorsätzliche Steuerverkürzung (= *criminal* ~~); *civil* ~~: *Steuerordnungswidrigkeit*; **to obtain by** ~ → *to obtain*.

fraudulent arglistig, betrügerisch, böswillig, bösgläubig; ~ **and void as against the assignee** relativ unwirksam (*lediglich*) gegenüber dem Rechtsnachfolger; ~ **credit statement** betrügerische Selbstauskunft bei Darlehensaufnahme; ~ **intent** → *intent*; **F~ Mediums Act** (*GB, 1961*) Gesetz gegen betrügerische Geisterbeschwörungen.

free frei, gratis, kostenlos, gebührenfrei, ungehindert; ~ **allowance of luggage** Freigepäck; ~ **alongside ship** (*F.A.S.*) frei Längsseite Schiff; ~ **and clear** frei von Rechten Dritter; ~ **and clear of all rates** frei von allen Steuern und Gebühren; ~ **astray** keine Sonderkosten für fehlgeleitete Sendungen; ~ **at domicile after clearance through customs** frei Haus verzollt; ~ **at factory gate** frei Werk; ~ **at point of dispatch** ab Werk; ~ **docks** frei Dock; ~ **domicile** frei Haus, frei Bestimmungsort; ~ **entry, egress and regress** das Recht, ein Grundstück jederzeit zu betreten (*und zu verlassen*); ~ **for public performance** mit freiem Aufführungsrecht; ~ **from all deductions** ohne Abzüge jeder Art; ~ **from average** *etc* → *average*; ~ **from breakage** → *breakage*; ~ **from defect(s)** mangelfrei, fehlerfrei; ~ **from duty** zollfrei; ~ **from encumbrances** lastenfrei (*von privatrechtl Lasten*); ~ **from legacy duty respectively** (*Vermächtnisse*) ohne Abzug anteiliger Erbschaftssteuern; ~ **frontier** frei Grenze; ~ **gift coupon** Gutschein; ~ **insurance period** beitragsfreie Versicherungszeit; ~ **market economy** freie Marktwirtschaft; ~ **market price** Freiverkehrskurs; ~ **market rate** Freiverkehrskurs; ~ **marketeering** *adj* freihändlerisch; ~ **men** die Freien; ~ **miners** freie (*mit Bergwerksrecht ausgestattete*) Bergleute; ~ **of all average** → *average*; ~ **of capture and seizure** Beschlagnahmerisiko ausgeschlossen; ~ **of charge** → *charge*; ~ **of commission** provisionsfrei; ~ **of customs duties** zollfrei; ~ **of damages** Schaden nicht zu unseren Lasten; ~ **of expense** spesenfrei; ~ **of income tax** einkommensteuerfrei; ~ **of interest** zinsfrei; ~ **of payment** franko; ~ **of particular average** → *average*; ~ **of riots and civil commotions** frei von Aufruhr und Bürgerkrieg; ~ **of tax** steuerfrei; ~ **on aircraft** frei Flugzeug; ~ **on board** *FOB Incoterms* frei an Bord; *US-Definition*: frei verladen (*Schiff oder anderes Transportmittel*), frei geliefert (*zB FOB inland point in country of importation*); ~ **on board and trimmed** frei an Bord einschließlich Verstauung (*Kohlenhandel*); ~ **on board** (*FOB*) **Buyer's plant;** ~ **on quay** frei auf den Kai; ~ **on rail** frei Waggon; ~ **on steamer** frei Schiff; ~ **on truck** *GB*: frei Waggon; *US*: frei LKW; ~ **overside** frei einschließlich Löschung im Ankunfthafen; ~ **post** portofrei; Porto bezahlt der Empfänger; ~ **ride** Freifahrt, kurzfristige Haussespekulation (*mit Gewinn-*

realisierung vor Bezahlung); ~ **rider** Schnorrer; *nicht gewerkschaftl Organisierter, der gewerkschaftl Vorteile ausnutzt,* Trittbrettfahrer; kurzfristiger Spekulant (*cf free ride*); ~ **trade area** Freihandelszone.

freedom Freiheit *f*, Unabhängigkeit *f*, ~ **from bias** Unvoreingenommenheit; ~ **from encumbrances** Lastenfreiheit; ~ **from fear** Freiheit von Furcht; ~ **from want** Freiheit von Not; ~ **of a borough** Bürgerrecht; ~ **of a company** Meisterrecht; ~ **of action** Handlungsfreiheit; ~ **of association** Vereinsfreiheit; ~ **of choice of profession** freie Berufswahl; ~ **of commerce** Handelsfreiheit; ~ **of competition** Wettbewerbsfreiheit; ~ **of contract** → *contract*; ~ **of cultivation** Recht der ackerbaulichen Nutzung; ~ **of establishment** Niederlassungsfreiheit; ~ **of expression** Meinungsfreiheit; **F~ of Information Act** G. über Informationspflicht der Behörden; ~ **of movement** Freizügigkeit, Niederlassungsfreiheit, Domizilfreiheit; ~ ~ ~ *for workers: Arbeitsfreizügigkeit;* ~ **of opinion** Meinungsfreiheit; ~ **of religion** Bekenntnisfreiheit; ~ **of settlement** Niederlassungsfreiheit; ~ **of speech** Redefreiheit, Meinungsfreiheit, Recht der freien Meinungsäußerung; ~ **of speech and of the press** Rede- und Pressefreiheit; ~ **of the air** Freiheit des Luftraumes; ~ **of the chair** Freiheit der Lehre; ~ **of the city** Freiheit von Gemeindeabgaben, Ehrenbürgerrecht; ~ **of the press** Pressefreiheit; ~ **of the seas** Freiheit der Meere; ~ **of trade** Handelsfreiheit, Gewerbefreiheit; ~ **of use** unbeschränktes Benutzungsrecht; ~ **to provide services** berufliche Freizügigkeit (*zB für freie Berufe*); **academic** ~ akademische Freiheit; **constitutional** ~ Grundrecht; **economic** ~ Gewerbefreiheit; **testamentary** ~ Testierfreiheit; **to confer the** ~ **of a city** das Ehrenbürgerrecht verleihen.

freehold Grundeigentum *n, Eigentumsrecht bzw langfristige Herrschaftsrechte an Grundstücken, hist* freies Lehen, Erblehen; ~ **estate** Grundeigentum; ~ **farm** freier Bauernhof; ~ **flat** → *flat*; ~ **houses** im Eigentum stehende Häuser; ~ **in law** gesetzlich vererbtes Grundeigentum (*von dem noch nicht Besitz ergriffen wurde*); ~ **land societies** Siedlungsgemeinschaften, Parzellierungsgemeinschaften; ~ **properties** Eigentumsgrundstücke; **absolute** ~ **title** unbeschränktes Grundstückseigentum; **actual** ~ Eigen(tümer)besitz an Grundstükken; **descendible** ~ *gesetzlich* vererbbares Grundstück; **determinable** ~ (*zeitlich auf Lebenszeit oder frühere Ereignisse*) beschränkte eigentumsähnliche Nutzung; **movable** ~ → *movable*; **registered** ~ im Grundbuch eingetragenes Grundstückseigentum.

freehold *adj* im Grundeigentum stehend, Eigentums . . .

freeholder Grundeigentümer *m*.

freeing child for adoption Freigabe des Kindes zur Adoption.

free lance *s* Freiberufler.

free-lance *adj* freiberuflich.

free-lance *v/i* freiberuflich tätig sein.

freely|convertible accounts unbeschränkt konvertierbare Konten; ~ **to be enjoyed or possessed** mit unbeschränktem Nutzungsrecht.

freeman Freisasse *m*, Allodialbesitzer *m*, freier Mann *m*; Stadtbürger *m*; **honorary** ~ Ehrenbürger.

freepost portofrei, Gebühr bezahlt.

freetrader Anhänger des Freihandels.

freeway Autobahn *f*.

freez|e *v* einfrieren (Kapital), beschlagnahmen, sicherstellen; ~ **out** ausschließen, kaltstellen; ~ **prices** Preisstopp durchführen; ~ **wages** Lohnstopp durchführen; ~**ing of credit** Kreditsperre.

freight Fracht *f*, Frachtkosten *f/pl*, Schiffsmiete; Ladung, Frachtgut; ~ **absorption** Frachtkostenübernahme durch den Verkäufer; ~ **al-**

lowed *Frachtabzug vom Angebotspreis vom genannten Punkt an gestattet, an dem die Gefahr übergeht*; ~ **and carriage** See- und Landfrachten; ~ **and demurrage** Fracht- und Liegegeld; ~ **at destination** Fracht zahlbar am Bestimmungsort; ~ **bill** Frachtbrief; ~ **booking** Frachtbuchung; ~ **broker** Transportmakler; ~ **by air** Luftfracht; ~ **capacity** Frachtraum; ~ **car** Güterwaggon; ~ **carrier** Frachtflugzeug; ~ **charges** Frachtkosten, Frachtgebühren; ~ **collect** Fracht wird eingezogen; ~ **contract** Frachtvertrag; ~ **declaration** Anmeldung der Ladung (*Zoll*); ~ **depot** Güterbahnhof; ~ **equalisation** Frachtausgleich; ~ **forward** Fracht bezahlt der Empfänger; ~ **forwarder** Güterspediteur; ~ **home** Rückfracht; ~ **indemnity** Fracht(zahlungs)garantie (*gegenüb. d. Reeder*); ~ **index futures** Frachtterminkontrakte; ~ **insurance** → *insurance*; ~ **note** Frachtrechnung; ~ **out and home** Hin- und Herfracht; ~ **paid** frachtfrei, Fracht bezahlt; ~ **payable at destination** Fracht bezahlt der Empfänger; ~ **prepaid** Fracht vorausbezahlt; ~ **pro rata** anteilige Fracht; ~ **quotation** Frachtnotierung; ~ **rate** Frachtsatz; ~ **reduction** Frachtermäßigung; ~ **release** Güterfreigabe; Frachterlaß; ~ **steamer** Frachtschiff; ~ **tariff** Güter-, Frachttarif; ~ **ton** Gewichtstonne, Frachttonne; ~ **traffic** Güterverkehr, Frachtverkehr; ~ **train** Güterzug; ~ **yard** Güterbahnhof; **additional** ~ Mehrfracht; **advance** ~ Frachtbezahlung im voraus; **by slow** ~ *US* als Frachtgut; **by** ~ **train** als Frachtgut; **dead** ~ Fautfracht, Leerfracht, Fehlfracht, Ballastladung, Reufracht, Vergütung für nicht ausgenutzten Schiffsraum; **fast** ~ Eilgut, Schnellgut; **home** ~ Rückfracht; **gross** ~ Bruttofracht; **joint** ~ gemeinsamer Frachttarif; **less-than-carload** ~ Stückgut(sendung); **local** ~ Eisenbahnzubringerfrachtverkehr, Rollgutverkehr; **lump sum** ~ Pauschalfracht, Gesamtchartervergütung (*für Schiffsmiete*); **outgoing** ~ Ausgangsfracht; **outward** ~ Hinfracht, abgehende Fracht; **prepaid** ~ vorausbezahlte Fracht; **phantom** ~ fiktive Transportkosten (*die nach den Geschäftsbedingungen in Rechnung gestellt werden*); **railroad** ~ Bahnfracht; **released** ~ Fracht zu herabgesetztem Wert; **revenue** ~ zahlende Ladung; **terms of** ~ Frachtbedingungen; **time** ~ Zeitfracht; **voyage** ~ → *voyage*.

freightage Ladung *f*, Transport *m*, Frachtgebühren *f/pl*.

freighter Charterer *m*, Ablader *m*, Versender *m*, Fuhrmann *m*; Frachter *m* (*Schiff*).

freighting Befrachtung *f*, Chartern *n*; ~ **ad valorem** Befrachtung nach dem Wert; ~ **by contract** Pauschalfracht; ~ **on measurement** Maßfracht; ~ **on weight** Befrachtung nach Gewicht; **voyage** ~ direkte Seefrachtbeförderung (*von Hafen zu Hafen*).

frequency Häufigkeit *f*; ~ **of accidents** Unfallhäufigkeit.

frequent *adj* häufig; *v* häufig aufsuchen, gewohnheitsmäßig besuchen.

fresh neu, frisch, ungebraucht, kürzlich; ~ **disseisin** *hist* Selbsthilfe zur Entsetzung e-s Besitzstörers; ~ **entry in a register** Neueintragung; ~ **evidence** → *evidence*; ~ **force** kürzlich erfolgte Gewaltanwendung (*innerhalb 40 Tagen*); ~ **pursuit** sofortige Verfolgung.

freshwater fishing Süßwasserfischerei *f*.

friend Freund(in), Bekannte(r); ~**s and relations** die Bekannten und Verwandten; ~ **of the court** = *amicus curiae qv*; **my honourable** ~ mein Fraktionskollege; **my learned** ~ → *learned*; **next** ~ → *next*.

friendless man Geächteter *m*.

friendly freundlich, freundschaftlich, wohlwollend, zuträglich.

fringe|benefits Nebenleistungen des

Arbeitgebers, Sozialleistungen; ~ **order** *Erlaubnis zur Versorgung einzelner Grundstücke außerhalb des Konzessionsgebiets.*

frisk *s* Leibesvisitation *f*, rasche Durchsuchung *f*, Filzung *f*.

frisk *v* eine Leibesvisitation vornehmen, filzen, abtasten.

frivolous belanglos, frivol, leichtfertig; ~ **appeal** offensichtlich aussichtslose Berufung; ~ **or vexatious action** frivole oder schikanöse Klage; ~ **plea** → *plea*.

from (a date) vom (Datum) an (*diesen Tag im allg nicht mitgezählt*); ~ **a parent** *unmittelbar* von einem Elternteil; ~ **a port** von außerhalb e–s Hafens; ~ **alongside ship** ab Längsseite Schiff; ~ **and after the passage of this Act** vom Inkrafttreten des Gesetzes an; ~ **and after their decease** nach ihrem Tode = *nach dem Tode des Letztverstorbenen*; ~ **any cause whatever** aus jedwedem Grund; ~ **day to day** auf den jeweils nächsten Tag, auf e–n späteren Tag; ~ **henceforth** von jetzt ab; ~ **necessity** im Notstand; ~ **place to place** von e–r Stelle zur anderen (*innerhalb der gleichen Stadt*); ~ **testator's death** seit dem Tode des Erblassers (*den Todestag nicht mitgerechnet*); ~ **the date of** ab ... (Datum) einschließlich; ~ **the day of the date** vom Datum der Urkunde einschließlich gerechnet; ~ **the expiration of a policy** seit Erlöschen der Police; ~ **the loading** ab Verladen; ~ **the neighborhood** aus benachbartem Gebiet; ~ **the part of the father** väterlicherseits; ~ **the time of the contract** vom Tage des Vertragsschlusses an (*diesen mitgezählt*); ~ **time to time** zu gegebener Zeit, bei Veranlassung, so oft wie erforderlich, von Zeit zu Zeit.

front Fassade *f*, Vorderseite *f*, Außenseite *f*, Front *f*, Strohmann *m*, Aushängeschild *n*, Unverfrorenheit *f*; ~ **bench** → *bench*; ~ **company** als Tarnung dienende Gesellschaft; ~ **foot rule** Erschließungskostenaufteilung nach Straßenangrenzungslänge; ~ **wages** Diskriminierungsausgleichslohn.

frontage Vorderfront *f*, Frontlänge *f*, Ausblick *m*; ~ **road** neben der Durchgangsstraße verlaufende innerörtliche Straße.

frontager Eigentümer *m* e–s Straßenanliegergrundstücks, Anlieger *m*.

front-end|finance Zusatzexportfinanzierung; ~ **loading** Vorausbelastung *f* mit Zinsen u. Spesen (*Abschlußgebühren, Vermittlungsprovision*); ~ **load plan** *investm* Nennwert-Gebühren-Vorabzugsplan *m*.

front-floor rule Umlegung der Erschließungskosten nach Länge des angrenzenden Straßenstücks.

front-seat passenger Beifahrer.

frontier Grenze *f*, Siedlungsgrenze *f*, Zivilisationsgrenze *f*; ~ **control** Grenzüberwachung; ~ **crossing** Grenzüberschreitung; ~ **crossing point** Grenzübergang; ~ **dispute** Grenzstreitigkeit; ~ **district** (Zoll) Grenzbezirk; ~ **formalities** Grenzformalitäten; ~ **incident** Grenzzwischenfall; ~ **pass** Grenzausweis; ~ **passage** Grenzübertritt; ~ **surveillance** Grenzaufsicht; ~ **worker** Grenzgänger; ~ **zone** Grenzgebiet; **land** ~ Landgrenze.

fronting and abutting unmittelbar (*an die Erschließungsanlagen*) angrenzend.

fructus Früchte *f*|*pl*, Erträge *m*|*pl*.

fruit Früchte *f*|*pl*, Obst *n*; Garten-, Feld- und Waldfrüchte; Rechtsfrüchte *f*|*pl*; Erträge *m*|*pl*; ~ **and tree doctrine** *steuerliche Unbeachtlichkeit von Einkunftsabtretungen*; ~ **fallen** Erträge nach der Trennung; ~**growing** Obstbau; ~**s of crime** bei der Straftat erlangte Gegenstände; ~ **of poisonous tree doctrine** Unverwertbarkeit gesetzwidrig erlangter Beweise; ~**s of the land** Bodenfrüchte; **natural** ~**s** Bodenfrüchte; **raw** ~**s** frisches Obst.

frustrate vereiteln; ~**d by the passage of time** durch Zeitablauf gegenstandslos, verwirkt; **a contract becomes** ~**d** die Geschäftsgrundlage für e–n Vertrag ist weggefallen.

frustration Vereitlung *f*, Verhinderung *f*; (*nachträgliche unverschuldete*) Unmöglichkeit *f* der Leistung; ~ **of contract** Wegfall der Geschäftsgrundlage, Vereitelung des Vertragszwecks; **commercial** ~ Wegfall der Geschäftsgrundlage; **self-induced** ~ Selbstvereitelung des Vertragszwecks.

fuel Brennstoff *m*, Kraftstoff *m*, Treibstoff *m*, Brennmaterial *n*; ~ **allotments** Zuteilung von Gemeindewald für die Brennstoffversorgung; **Minister of F~ and Power** Minister für Energieversorgung; **primary** ~**s** energiehaltige Bodenschätze; **secondary** ~**s** durch menschliche Tätigkeit gewonnene Energie bzw Brennstoffe; **unleaded** ~ bleifreier Kraftstoff, unverbleites Benzin.

fugitation gerichtliche Entziehung *f* des Vermögens eines flüchtigen Angeklagten.

fugitive *adj* flüchtig; ~ **criminal** flüchtiger Rechtsbrecher, *Angeklagter oder Verurteilter einer Auslandsstraftat, der sich im Inland aufhält*; ~ **goods** bei der Flucht aufgegebene Beute; ~ **offender** flüchtiger Tatverdächtiger, flüchtiger Straftäter.

fugitive *s* der (die) Flüchtige; ~ **from justice** steckbrieflich Gesuchter, flüchtiger Beschuldigter oder Verurteilter (*aus e–m anderen Land*); ~**'s goods** Vermögen e–s flüchtigen Beschuldigten.

fulfil erfüllen; ~ **the qualifications** die Bedingungen (*Voraussetzungen*) erfüllen.

fulfilment Erfüllung *f*, Ausführung *f*; **last day of** ~ letzter Tag e–r Leistungsfrist; **place of** ~ → *place*.

full voll, völlig, vollständig, vollendet, fällig; ~ **and absolute control** unbeschränkte Verfügungsgewalt; ~ **and complete cargo** volle Ladung (*Schiff*); ~ **and free liberty** *scot* unbeschränktes Entnahmerecht (*Rohstoffe*); ~ **annual value** voller Jahresertragswert; ~ **civil pay** volles Gehalt; ~ **compensation for damage** voller Schadenersatz; ~ **enjoyment of rights** uneingeschränkte Ausübung von Rechten; ~ **faith and credit** → *faith*; ~ **interest admitted** volles Versicherungsinteresse zugestanden; "~ **line forcing"** Warenabgabe nur bei komplettem Sortimentskauf; ~ **or valuable consideration** *Verkauf oder Verpfändung für eine* geldwerte Gegenleistung; ~ **payout lease** Vollamortisations-Leasing.

fully|administered (estate) Einrede der Erschöpfung des Nachlasses; ~ **entitled** berechtigt; ~ **estated** volle Aufrechterhaltung der Nießbrauchsrechte; ~ **licensed** *Gaststätte* mit unbeschränkter Schankkonzession; ~ **paid (up)** voll eingezahlt; ~ **subscribed** voll gezeichnet, liberiert.

function Funktion *f*, Obliegenheit *f*, Beruf *m*, Amt *n*, Aufgabe *f*, Tätigkeit *f*; **administrative** ~ Verwaltungsfunktion; **advisory** ~ beratende Funktion; **judicial** ~ → *judicial*; **legislative** ~ Gesetzgebungsfunktion; **ministerial** ~ weisungsgebundene Aufgabe; **official** ~ Repräsentation; **outside one's** ~**s** außerdienstlich; **regulatory** ~ Verwaltungsfunktion, Aufsichtsfunktion; **scope of** ~ Amtsbereich, amtliche Zuständigkeit; **separation of** ~**s** Ämtertrennung.

functional amtlich, fachlich, funktional, funktionell; ~ **classification** Gliederung nach Sachgebieten; ~ **discount** → *discount*; ~ **interpretation** funktionelle Auslegung; ~ **statement** Wirkungsangabe.

functionary Beamter *m*, Amtsträger *m*, Funktionär *m*.

functus officio seines Amtes entbunden (sein).

fund *s* Fonds *m*, Sondervermögen *n*, zweckgebundene Mittel; Investmentfonds *m*; ~**s** flüssige Mittel *n*|*pl*, Geld *n*, Ertrag *m*, Effekten *pl*, staatliche Vermögenseinkünfte *f*|*pl*, Staatspapiere *n*|*pl*; ~ **accounting**

buchhalterische Bearbeitung von selbständigen Etatposten; **~-holder** Inhaber von Staatsanleihen; **~ in court** bei Gericht hinterlegtes Geld; **~ in medio** *scot* Streitgegenstand e–r Hauptintervention; **~ of ~s** Dachfonds; **~ or estate** Sondervermögen; **~s voluntarily contributed** freiwillige Beiträge; **advisory ~s** *von der Bank verwaltete, nach ihrem Ermessen u. nach Rückfrage beim Kunden zu investierende Mittel*; **amortization ~** → *amortization*; **appropriation of ~s** → *appropriation*; **available ~s** verfügbare Mittel, liquide M.; **blended ~** → *blended*; **bond ~** *US*: Rentenfonds; **bonus ~** Dividendenfonds; **closed-end ~** Investmentfonds mit begrenzter Emissionshöhe; Anlagefonds ohne Verpflichtung ausgegebene Anteilscheine zurückzunehmen; **collateral ~** Sicherheitsfond; **Consolidated F~** → *consolidate*; **common ~** gemeinsame Kasse; gemeinsames Sondervermögen, Gemeinschaftsmittel; **company's ~s** Gesellschaftsvermögen; **cumulative ~** thesaurierender Fonds; **current ~s** liquide Mittel; **discretionary ~s** in das Ermessen der Bank gestellte Investitionsgelder; **depreciation ~** → *depreciation*; **diverted ~s** zweckentfremdete Mittel; **dormant ~** *gerichtl hinterlegte Gelder, über die lange Zeit (über 15 Jahre) nicht verfügt werden kann*, unverzinsliche Gelder; **endowment ~** → *endowment*; **expendable trust ~** → *expendable*; **Fed ~s** (*federal ~s*) Tagesgeld; **fixed ~** Investmentfonds mit feststehendem Portefeuille; **flexible ~** Investmentfonds mit auswechselbarem Portefeuille; **for want of ~s** → *want*; **general ~** allgemeine Etatmittel; **guarantee-deposits ~s** gesperrte Gelder im Wertpapierfonds für Garantieleistungen (*bei freien Ertragsentnahmen*); **income generating ~** ertragsbildende Investmentfonds; **liquid ~s** flüssige Mittel; **load ~** *Investmentfonds mit Gebührenberechnung bei Verkauf der Anteile*; **loan ~** Sondervermögen für Darlehensgewährung; **loan ~s** Kreditmittel; **managed ~** *Investmentfond mit auswechselbarem Wertpapierbestand*; **mixed ~** gemischter Fond; auch = *blended ~* → *blended*; **mutual ~** Investmentfonds der "open end" Kategorie; **no ~s** kein Guthaben, keine Deckung; **no-load ~** Investmentfonds mit gebührenfreiem Anteilsverkauf; **nonexpendable trust ~** → *non-expendable*; **off-shore ~s** Exotenfonds, Anlagefonds in überseeischer Steueroase; **open-end ~** Investmentfonds mit unbeschränkter Anteilsemission; **operating ~s** Betriebsmittel; **partnership ~s** Gesellschaftsvermögen; **pension ~** Pensionskasse; **permanent ~s** eiserner Bestand; **petty cash ~** Portokasse; **political ~** politischer Kampffonds e–r Gewerkschaft; **provident ~** Unterstützungskasse; **public ~s** öffentliche Mittel, Staatsfinanzen, Staatsanleihepapiere; **redemption ~** → *redemption*; **relief ~** Unterstützungsfonds, Unterstützungskasse; **reserve ~** → *reserve*; **revolving ~** Umlauffonds, Sondervermögen, dem laufend Mittel entnommen und zugeführt werden; **secret ~** Geheimfonds, Reptilienfonds; **sector ~s** Branchenfonds; **sick ~** Krankenkasse; **sinking ~** → *sinking*; **strike ~** Streikkasse; **tied up ~s** festgelegte Gelder; **(to be) in ~s** bei Kasse sein; **to raise ~s** Gelder aufbringen, finanzieren; **utility ~** → *utility*; **working capital ~** Betriebsmittelfonds.

fund *v* fundieren, finanzieren, kapitalisieren, zu verzinslichem Kapital machen; **~ ed dividends** in Obligationen umgewandelte Dividendenschulden; **~ed investment** mündelsichere Anlage; **~ed property** → *property*; **~ed trusts** treuhänderische Übertragung von Wertpapieren zur Deckung von Versicherungsprämien; **~ing bonds** Fundierungsschuldverschreibungen, Umschuldungsanleihe; ~**ing certificate** Fundierungszertifikat, Zertifikat für Kapitalisierung rückständiger Zinsen und Dividenden; ~**ing loan** → *loan*.

fundamental fundamental, grundlegend; ~ **law** Grundgesetz, Verfassung.

fundamus „wir gründen" (*funktioneller Ausdruck in Gründungssatzungen*).

funding Kostentragung *f*, Finanzierung *f*; Konsolidierung *f*, Refinanzierung *f*, Rückstellungsbildung *f*; ~ **gap** Finanzierungslücke; **public** ~ Kostenübernahme aus öffentl Mitteln.

funeral expenses Bestattungskosten *f/pl*.

fungible ersetzbar, vertretbar (*Sachen*), fungibel.

fungibles vertretbare Sachen *f/pl*, Gattungssachen *f/pl*.

furandi animus Diebstahlsvorsatz *m*.

furlough Urlaub *m* (*Militär oder Staatsdienst*), *vt*: zwangsbeurlauben.

furnish liefern, beibringen, versorgen, ausstatten, verschaffen; ~ **a surety** e–n Bürgen stellen; ~ **capital** Kapital bereitstellen, K. zur Verfügung stellen; ~ **documents** Urkunden beibringen; ~ **evidence** Beweismaterial beibringen; ~ **proof** Beweis erbringen, Beweis antreten.

furniture *n/pl*, Möbel, Wohnungseinrichtung *f*; ~**s and fixtures** Wohnungseinrichtung und Zubehör; ~ **depository** Möbellager (*bei Zwangsräumung*); ~ **of a ship** Schiffsausrüstung; **fixed** ~ fest eingebaute Möbelstücke; **household** ~ → *household*.

further *adj* zusätzlich, sonstig(–er, –e, –es); ~**advance** neue Darlehensgewährung *gegen die gleiche Sicherheit*; ~ **assurance** → *assurance* (*2*); ~ **charge** weitere Beleihung; ~ **consideration** Antrag auf Wiederaufnahme der mündlichen Verhandlung; Wiedereintritt in die mündliche Verhandlung; ~ **cover** Nachschuß; ~ **education** Fortbildung; ~ **evidence** neue Beweisangebote, neue Beweismittel; ~ **hearing** neue mündliche Verhandlung, vertagte Sitzung; ~ **instructions** nachträgliche weitere Belehrung der Geschworenen; ~ **particulars** weitere Einzelheiten; ~ **proceedings** nächste Sitzung (*anberaumt auf* ...); **covenant for** ~ **assurance** → *covenant*; **plea to** ~ **maintenance of action** Einwendung aus Sachverhalten nach Rechtshängigkeit; **until** ~ **advice** solange nichts anderes mitgeteilt wird; **until** ~ **order** → *order* (*1*).

further *v* fördern, begünstigen.

furtherance Beihilfe *f*, Förderung *f*, Unterstützung *f*.

furtive heimlich.

fusion Fusion *f*, *Vereinigung der barristers u. solicitors zur Einheitsanwaltschaft*.

futile vergeblich, wirkungslos; ~ **attempt** fruchtloser Versuch, vereitelter Versuch.

futures Termingeschäft *n*, Terminkontrakt(e); ~ **commission merchant** Terminkommissionär; ~ **contract** Terminkontrakt; ~ **exchange** Terminbörse, Terminmarkt; ~ **market** Terminmarkt; ~ **price** Terminkurs; ~ **quotation** Terminnotierung; ~ **trading** Terminhandel; **commodity** ~ → *commodity*; **stock-indexed** ~ Aktienindex-Termingeschäfte (*bzw -Terminkontrakte*).

G

gag *s* Knebel *m.*
gag *v* knebeln, freie Meinungsäußerung unterdrücken.
gage *v* verpfänden.
gain *s* Gewinn *m*, Einkünfte *f/pl*, Wertzuwachs *m*; **~s on disposals** Veräußerungsgewinn; **capital** ~ → *capital*; **chargeable ~s** steuerpflichtiger Kapitalzuwachs; **holding** ~ inflationsbereinigter Wertzuwachs; **ill-gotten ~s** dubioser Erwerb; **net ~s** Reingewinne, Reinertrag.
gain *v* gewinnen, verdienen, erwerben; Vorteil haben; ~ **the land** der Bodennutzung dienen.
gainful einträglich, gewerblich; ~ **activity** gewerbliche Tätigkeit; ~ **employment** Erwerbstätigkeit; ~ **occupation** Erwerbstätigkeit; **to carry on ~ undertakings** sich gewerblich betätigen.
gainings Ertrag *m.*
gale Bodenzins *m*, Pachtzahlung *f*, Schürfrecht *n*; **~-day** Fälligkeitstag (*für Zinszahlungen*).
gallery Galerie *f*, Tribüne *f*, Empore *f*; **distinguished strangers'** ~ Prominententribüne (*Parlament*).
gallon Gallone *f.*
gallows Galgen *m.*
gambit Eröffnungszug *m*, Gesprächsbeginn *m*, taktisches Manöver *m.*
gamble *s* Glücksspiel *n*, Spekulation *f.*
gamble *v* wetten, Glücksspiel betreiben, ein Hasardspiel treiben, spekulieren.
gambler Spieler *m*, Börsenspekulant *m*; **common** ~ gewerblicher Spielunternehmer.
gambling Glücksspiel *n*; ~ **contracts** Spiel- und Wettverträge; ~ **debt** Spielschuld; ~ **device** Glücksspielgerät; ~ **in futures** Differenzgeschäft, Terminspekulation; ~ **policy** spekulative Lebensversicherung *auf das Leben e–s Fremden*; **commercialized** ~ gewerbliches Glücksspiel; **exchange** ~ Börsenspiel, Jobben.
game (*1*) Wild *n*, jagdbare Tiere *n/pl*; ~ **certificate** Jagdschein; **~-keeper** Wildhüter, Förster; ~ **law** → *law*; ~ **licence** → *licence*; **fair** ~ jagdbares Wild.
game (*2*) Glücksspiel *n*; ~ **of chance** Glücksspiel *n*, Wettvertrag, Spielwette; **unlawful** ~ verbotenes Glücksspiel.
gaming Glücksspiel *n*; ~ **and wagering** Spiel- und Wettverträge; ~ **casino** Spielkasino; ~ **contract** → *contract*; ~ **debt** Spielschuld; ~ **house** Spielsalon, Spielbank; ~ **machine** Spielgerät; **common ~ house** Spiellokal.
ganancial property ehel Gütergemeinschaft *f.*
gang *s* Gang *m*, Gruppe *f*, Rotte *f*, Kolonne *f*, Bande *f*; ~ **boss** Kolonnenführer; Bandenchef; ~ **days** *Tage, an denen das Gemeindegebiet abgeschritten wird*; ~ **master** *jmd, der Jugendliche für Landarbeit anheuert und beschäftigt*; ~ **theft** Bandendiebstahl; **~-week** Woche für das Grenzabschreiten.
gangway Durchgang, Passage, Quergang im Parlament; Fallreep; Sohlenstrecke (*Bergbau*).
gaol (= *jail qv*), Gefängnis *n*, Haftanstalt *f* (*bes für kurzfristigen Freiheitsentzug*); ~ **delivery** Ermächtigung zur Strafverhandlung über Inhaftierte (*für beauftragte Richter des High Court*) GB bis 1971; ~ **liberties** = ~ *limits qv*; ~ **limits** Außenbezirk e–r Gefangenenanstalt; ~ **sessions** Friedensrichterkollegium zur Überwachung der Gefängnisverwaltungen.
gap Lücke *f*, Gesetzeslücke *f*; **to remedy a** ~ e–e Gesetzeslücke ausfül-

len; **unplugged** ~ unverschlossene Gesetzeslücke.

garbage disposal Müllbeseitigung.

garden Garten *m*; **allotment** ~ → *allotment*; **town** ~**s** öffentliche Gärten, Parks.

garnish *v* verwarnen, vorladen, Drittschuldnerpfändung vornehmen; Sachen des Schuldners im Gewahrsam e–s Dritten beschlagnahmen lassen.

garnishee *von der Pfändung benachrichtigter* Drittschuldner *m*, Drittbesitzer *m* von beschlagnahmtem Schuldnervermögen; ~ **order** = *garnishment order* → *garnishment*; ~ **proceeding** Forderungspfändungsverfahren; ~ **summons** Pfändungs- u. Überweisungsbeschluß (*d. Country Court*); **temporary** ~ **order** vorläufiges Zahlungsverbot.

garnishment Forderungspfändung *f*, Drittbesitzbeschlagnahme *f*; Vorladung *f*; ~ **order** Pfändungs- und Überweisungsbeschluß, Beschlagnahmebeschluß *bzw Sachpfändung* beim Drittbesitzer; **equitable** ~ Vermögensoffenbarungsverfahren *zur Aufdeckung von pfändbaren Ansprüchen*.

garnishor Vollstreckungsgläubiger *m* bei Forderungspfändung.

garranty = *guarantee qv*.

garrison Garnison *f*.

garroting Garottierung (*Hinrichtung durch Erwürgen*).

garth Gatter *n*, Einfriedung *f*, umfriedeter Raum *m*.

gas Gas *n*, Benzin *n*, Kraftstoff *m*; **G~ Consultative Council** Kundenberatungsstelle für Gasverbraucher; **G~ Council** Gasversorgungsbehörde; ~ **station** *US* Tankstelle; **casing-head** ~ Gas aus e–r Ölquelle; **lethal** ~ lebensgefährliches Gas; **natural** ~ Erdgas.

gate Tor *n*, Pforte *f*, Schranke *f*, Gatter *n*, Sperre *f*, Eingang *m*, Weg *m*, Zugang *m*, Eintrittsgeld *n*.

gauger Eichmeister *m*; ~**'s certificate** Eichzeugnis.

gavel *hist* Steuer *f*, Naturalabgabe *f/pl*, Bodenzins *m*, Tribut *m*; ~ **work** Frondienst.

gazette (= *official* ~) Staatsanzeiger *m*, amtliches Organ *n*, Amtsblatt *n*; **Federal G~** Bundesanzeiger; **London G~** brit. Staatsanzeiger.

gazette *v* amtlich bekanntgeben, in das Amtsblatt setzen.

gazumping *Drohung mit Nichtbeurkundung außer bei nachträgl Angebotserhöhung (Hauskauf)*.

gearing Fremdkapitalaufnahme, Leverage-Effekt *m cf leverage;* Verhältnis und Wirkung der Kapitalarten zueinander, Kapitalstruktur, Verhältnis von Fremd- zu Eigenkapital; **capital** ~ = *gearing s.o.;* **high** ~ hoher Verschuldungsgrad durch Fremdkapital.

gender gap Abstand zwischen männlichen und weiblichen Teilnehmern.

genealogie Genealogie *f*, Abstammung *f*, Stammbaum *m*.

genealogical | **research** Ahnenforschung *f*; ~ **tree** Ahnentafel, Stammbaum.

genearch Familienoberhaupt *n*.

general allgemein, gemeinsam, gemeinschaftlich, üblich, umfassend, nicht spezialisiert, ungefähr, annähernd; ~ **allowance for doubtful accounts** Pauschalwertberichtigung zu Forderungen; **G~ Accounting Office** (Bundes)Rechnungshof *US*; **G~ Agreement on Tariffs and Trade** (*GATT*) Allgemeines Zoll- und Handelsabkommen (*von 1947*); ~ **annual licensing meeting** jährliche Sitzung zur Vergabe von Schankkonzessionen; **G~ Arrangements to Borrow (GAB)** Allgemeine Kreditvereinbarungen; ~ **book-keeping department** Hauptbuchhaltung; ~ **building scheme** Gesamtbebauungsprojekt; ~ **carrying** allgemeines Frachtgeschäft; ~ **contingency reserve** Rücklage für ungewisse Verluste oder Aufwendungen; **G~ Council of the Bar** Zentrale Anwaltskammer (*GB*) c|*f Bar Council*; **G~ Development Order** Flächennutzungsplan; ~ **equitable charge** formloses Grundpfand; ~ **improvement area** sanierungsbedürftiges Wohngebiet; **G~ Index of Retail Prices** *allgem. Lebenshaltungskostenindex GB*; ~ **issue** → *issue (2)*; *mil* Ausgabe der Kleiderkammer (*daher: G. I. = US-Soldat*); **G~ Land-Office** Staatsländereien-Verwaltung *USA, jetzt: Bureau of Land Management*; ~ **liability policy** → *policy (1)*; ~ **limits** Stadtgebiet von London, *Umkreis von 6 Meilen von Charing Cross*; **G~ Medical Council** Ärztekammer *GB*; ~ **medical practitioner** praktischer Arzt; ~ **obligation utility bonds** Obligationen öffentlicher Versorgungsbetriebe mit Staatsgarantie; ~ **operating expense** allgemeine Betriebskosten; ~ **participation clause** = *all participation clause qv*; **G~ Post Office** Hauptpost; ~ **property tax** → *tax*; ~ **public knowledge** Allgemeinkundigkeit; ~ **purposes rate** allgemeine (Fahr)Tarife; ~ **restraint of trade** überall gültiges Konkurrenzverbot; ~ **revival acts** *Gesetze, die das Wiederaufleben von Schadensersatzansprüchen nach dem Tode des Unfallgeschädigten vorsehen*; ~ **safety certificate** Seetüchtigkeitsbescheinigung; ~ **survival acts** *Gesetze zur Erhaltung von Schadensersatzansprüchen nach dem Tode des Unfallgeschädigten.*

general average große Havarie *f*; ~ **contribution** Beitrag zur großen Havarie; ~ **loss** Verlust durch große Havarie (*Überbordwerfen der Ladung zur Rettung des Schiffes*).

generality allgemeine Feststellung *f*, Allgemeingültigkeit *f*, allgemeines Prinzip *n*, allgemeines Gesetz *n*, allgemeine Regel *f*, Mehrzahl *f*, Unbestimmtheit *f*.

generalize verallgemeinern.

generic die Gattung bestimmend, betreffend, allgemein, typisch; ~ **claim** Gattungsanspruch; ~ **goods** → *goods*; ~ **name** Gattungsbezeichnung.

genesis Genese *f*, Vorgeschichte *f*, Ursprung *m*, Herkunft *f*.

Geneva Agreement *Genfer Zoll- und Handelsübereinkommen (30. 10. 47)*; ~ **Conventions** die Genfer Konvention (*betr. Rotes Kreuz*).

genitor Erzeuger *m*.

genocide Völkermord *m*.

gens Rasse *f*, Stamm *m*, Volk *n*, Großfamilie *f*.

gentleman's agreement (= Gentlemens' Agreement), Gentleman Agreement, Absprache *unter Ehrenmännern,* Frühstückskartell.

gentry niederer Adel *m*, Landadel *m*.

genuine echt, authentisch, wahr, unverfälscht, rein; ~ **signature** → *signature.*

genuineness of signature Echtheit *f* der Unterschrift.

genus Gattung *f*, Art *f*, Klasse *f*; Nachkommen *m/pl* gerader Linie.

geographical name geographische Benennung *f*, Ortsbezeichnung *f*.

german vollblütig, gleicher Abstammung.

germane zusammenhängend.

gerrymander *s* manipulierte Wahlbezirksabgrenzung *f*.

gerrymander *v* Wahlbezirksgrenzen manipulieren.

gestation Gestation *f*, Schwangerschaft *f*, Trächtigkeit *f*; **period of** ~ die einrechnungsfähige Zeit, Empfängniszeit, Schwangerschaftsdauer; **term of** ~ = *period of ~ qv.*

gestio Verhalten *n*, Geschäftsführung *f*.

gestor Geschäftsführer *m* (ohne Auftrag), jmd, der Angelegenheiten e-s anderen erledigt.

get *v* bekommen, erlangen, gewinnen; ~ **a good title** volles Eigentum erwerben; ~ **down to business** zur Sache kommen; ~ **in** gewählt werden, ankommen; ~ **in lane** Einordnen!; ~ **in property** Vermögenswerte hereinholen; ~ **paid** bezahlt werden.

getaway Start *m*, Startfähigkeit *f*; Flucht *f*.

get-up *s* Aufmachung *f* von Waren, Ausstattung *f*; Initiative *f*.

gibbet Galgen *m*; ~ **law** Lynchgesetz.

gift Geschenk *n*, Schenkung *f*, unentgeltliche Zuwendung *f*, letztwillige Zuwendung; fideikomissarische Übertragung *f* von Grundvermögen; ~ **by will** letztwillige Zuwendung, Vermächtnis; ~ **enterprise** Verlosung, *bes als Verkaufsanreiz*; ~ **inter vivos** Schenkung unter Lebenden; ~ **mortis causa** Schenkung von Todes wegen; ~ **over** unentgeltliche Zuwendung auf Lebenszeit und nach dem Tode des Beschenkten an eine andere Person; aufschiebend bedingte Schenkung; ~ **sub modo** bedingte Schenkung unter Auflagen; ~ **tax** → *tax*; ~ **to a class** Schenkung an e–n bestimmten Personenkreis; **absolute** ~ Handschenkung; **anatomical** ~ testamentarische Organspende; **charitable** ~ mildtätige Schenkung, Liebesgabe; **free** ~ Zugabe; **imperfect** ~ unvollkommene Schenkung, noch nicht vollzogene Sch.; **lifetime** ~ Schenkung (*bei Lebzeiten*); **net** ~**s** *Gesamtbetrag der Schenkungen während e–s Kalenderjahres minus steuergesetzl Abzüge*; **onerous** ~ Schenkung unter Auflagen; **outright** ~ Handschenkung; **personal** ~ persönliches Geschenk, echte Schenkung (*nicht remuneratorisch*), Handschenkung; **residuary** ~ Zuwendung des Reinnachlasses (= *Restnachlasses*); **specific** ~ Einzelzuwendung; Zuwendung e–s bestimmten Gegenstandes; **substitutional** ~ Ersatzzuwendung; **substitutionary** ~ letztwillige Zuwendung nach Stämmen; **vested** ~ vollzogene Schenkung; angefallene Zuwendung; **voluntary** ~ Schenkung, unentgeltl Zuwendung.

gildable steuerpflichtig, tributpflichtig.

gilts brit. Staatsanleihen.

gilt-edged erstklassig, mündelsicher.

gipsies Zigeuner; Nichtseßhafte (*gleich welcher Herkunft und Rasse*).

girl Mädchen *n* (*jur: unter 16 Jahren*); **under-age** ~ Mädchen unter dem zustimmungsfähigen Alter.

giro Giro *n*, Verrechnungsverkehr *m*; Postgirodienst *m*; ~ **account** Postgirokonto; ~ **cheque** Postscheck, **National G** ~ *GB* staatl Postgirodienst; **postal** ~ Postgirodienst.

girth Gürtellänge *f* (*alte Maßeinheit*); ~ **and sanctuary** *scot hist* Zufluchtsrecht bei Affekttötung.

gisement entgeltliche Übernahme *f* der Viehweide.

gist Hauptpunkt *m*, Kern *m*; ~ **of action** Hauptinhalt der Klage.

give geben, unentgeltlich zuwenden; ~ **a bill of exchange** Wechsel ausstellen; ~ **a discharge** quittieren, Entlastung erteilen; ~ **a limit** limitieren; ~ **account** Rechenschaft ablegen; ~ **aid and comfort** begünstigen; ~ **aid and comfort to the enemy** den Feind begünstigen, Landesverrat begehen; ~ **an opinion** begutachten, ein Gutachten erstatten; ~ **and bequeath** vermachen, von Todes wegen schenken; ~**-and-take policy** Zug-um-Zug-Grundsatz, Gegenleistungspolitik; ~ **away** kostenlos abgeben, verschenken; ~ **authority to** bevollmächtigen; ~ **bail for** Bürgschaft leisten für, e–n Bürgen stellen, Kaution stellen; ~ **bonds** Sicherheiten bestellen; ~ **colo(u)r** den gegnerischen Sachvortrag zugestehen; ~ **credit** Glauben schenken; Kredit gewähren, Garantie übernehmen; ~ **employment** beschäftigen; ~ **evidence** bekunden, vor Gericht aussagen, als Zeuge auftreten, Zeugnis ablegen; ~ **for the call** *exch* Vorprämie kaufen; ~ **for the put** *exch* Rückprämie kaufen; ~ **full particulars** spezifizieren, detaillieren; ~ **grace** e–e Nachfrist gewähren; ~ **in continuation** in Report geben; ~ **in payment** in Zahlung geben; an Zahlungs statt hingeben; ~ **judgment** ein Urteil erlassen; ~ **notice** kündigen, Nachricht erteilen, erklären; ~ **notice to quit** dem Mieter (Pächter) kündigen; ~ **offence** Anstoß erregen, Ärgernis erregen; ~ **oneself up to the police** sich der Polizei stellen; ~ **rise** Anlaß geben; ~ **someone the benefit of the doubt** im Zweifel zugunsten jmds entscheiden; ~ **time** stunden; ~ **up** übergeben, aufgeben; ~ **up one's claims** auf seine Ansprüche verzichten; ~ **value for** Gegenleistung gewähren; ~ **way** *nav* ausweichen (*unter dem Heck des anderen Schiffes den Kurs kreuzen*); *parl* jmdm das Wort überlassen, sich unterbrechen lassen.

given under my hand von mir unterzeichnet, von mir unterschriftlich erklärt.

giver Schenker *m*, Aussteller *m* (*Wechsel*); ~ **of a call** Erwerber e–r Kaufoption; ~ **of a put** Erwerber e–r Verkaufsoption; ~ **of a bill** Wechselaussteller; ~ **of an option** Optionsgeber, Prämienkäufer, Käufer e–r Option.

giving rings Ringzeremonie bei Amtsübernahme.

glanders Rotz *m*, Zoonose *f* (*Pferdekrankheit*).

Glass-Steagal Act (*US Banking Act 1933*) (= *gesetzl Trennungslinie zw Investment- und Geschäftsbanken*).

gleaning Ährenlesen *n*.

glebe kirchliches Stiftungsland *n*.

global global, umfassend, pauschal; ~ **insurance** Pauschalversicherung; ~ **interdependence** weltweites Aufeinanderangewiesensein, weltweite Interdependenz; ~ **output** Gesamtproduktion; ~ **quota** Globalkontingent; ~ **settlement** Gesamtregulierung; ~ **sum** Gesamtsumme, Pauschalbetrag; ~ **total** Gesamtbetrag.

gloss Glosse *f*.

glossary Glossar *n*.

glut Überangebot *n*, Schwemme *f*; ~ **of money** → *money*; ~ **on the market** Marktschwemme.

go *v* gehen, ausgehen von, erlassen werden; ~ **all out for** sich restlos einsetzen für; ~ **armed** Waffen tragen; ~ **astray** fehllaufen, verlorengehen, abschweifen, abhanden kommen; ~ **bail** Kaution übernehmen; ~ **between** vermitteln; ~ **further into a question** sich genauer mit der Frage befassen; ~ **hence** von der persönlichen Anwesenheit entbunden werden, entlassen werden; ~ **in for law** Jura studieren; ~ **into partnership** sich assoziieren; ~**-slow** *„Arbeit streng nach Vorschrift", Langsamstreik;* ~ **over an account** e–e Abrechnung prüfen; ~ **through the hoops** Konkurs anmelden; ~ **to court** → *court*; ~ **to expenses** aufwenden, sich Unkosten machen; ~ **to law** den Rechtsweg beschreiten; ~ **to protest** zu Protest gehen; ~ **to the country** Neuwahlen veranlassen, Wahlen ausschreiben, Geschworenenverhandlung beantragen; ~ **under the name of** im Namen des ... auftreten; ~ **unpunished** straflos bleiben; ~ **without day** den Prozeß verlieren (*ohne weitere Verhandlung*).

go-between *s* Vermittler *m*.

God|and my Country *hist Nichtschuldigerklärung des Angeklagten*; **~'s penny** Gottespfennig, Handgeld; ~ **the Almighty and Omniscient** Gott der Allmächtige und Allwissende (*Eidesformel*); **act of** ~ höhere Gewalt, unabwendbares Naturereignis.

god-bote Kirchenstrafgeld *n*.

godchild Patenkind *n*.

godparents Taufpaten *m/pl*.

godpenny Handgeld *n* zur Verpflichtung e–s Dienstboten.

go-go fund dynamischer, thesaurierender Investment-Fond *m*.

going | concern in Betrieb befindliches Unternehmen; lebender Betrieb; ~-~*value* → *value*; ~ **equipped for cheat** gewohnheitsmäßig Betrügereien versuchen; ~ **equipped for stealing** Beisichführen von Einbruchs- oder Diebeswerkzeug; **~, ~, gone** zum ersten, zum zweiten und zum letzten! (*Versteigerung*); ~ **naked** Leerkauf von Optionen; ~ **price** üblicher Preis,

Verkehrswert; ~ **public** zur Publikumsgesellschaft werden; ~ **private** Herausnahme der Aktien aus der Börse und Aktienrückkauf; ~ **rate of interest** derzeitiger Zinssatz; ~ **short** Baissespekulation; ~ **through the bar** Befragung aller anwesenden Anwälte, welche Anträge gestellt wurden; ~ **to allotment** Vornahme der Aktienausgabe.

gold Gold *n* (= *G bzw g*); ~ **backing** Gdeckung; ~ **bar** Gbarren; ~ **basis** Gbasis; ~ **bloc** Gblockländer; ~ **bonds** Ganleihe, Gewährungsobligationen; ~ **bullion standard** Gkernwährung; ~ **buying price** Gankaufspreis; ~ **certificates** Gzertifikate (*des US-Schatzamts*); ~ **clause** Gklausel *in Schuldverschreibungen u. a.*; ~ **coin and bullion** Münz- und Barreng*;* ~ **coin clause** Gmünzenklausel (*effektive Zahlung mit Gmünzen*); ~ **coinage** Gmünzenprägung; ~ **content** Ggehalt; ~ **cover** Gdeckung; ~ **currency** Gwährung; ~ **embargo** Sperre des Gverkehrs, Gembargo, Gausfuhrverbot; ~ **exchanges** Gvaluten; ~ **exchange standard** Gdevisenwährung, Gdeckungswährung; ~ **export point** Gausfuhrpunkt, oberer Gpunkt; ~ **fixing** Festsetzung des Gpreises; ~ **flow** Gbewegung; **hoarding** Ghortung; ~ **market** Edelmetallbörse; ~ **parity** Gparität; ~ **point** Gpunkt; ~ **premium** Gagio, Gaufgeld; ~ **rate** Gkurs; ~ **reserve** Greserve, Gbestand; ~ **settlement fund** Gausgleichsfonds *USA*; ~ **shares** Aktien von Gbergwerken; ~ **specie** Münzg; ~ **standard** Gstandard, Gwährung; ~ **stock** Gbestand; ~**tranche rights** Gtranchen-Ziehungsrechte; ~ **value guarantee** Gwertgarantie; **bar** ~ Barreng*;* **earmarked** ~ G, das e–e Zentralbank für e–e andere verwahrt; **fine** ~ Feing; **ingot** ~ Barreng, Stangeng; **monetary** ~ Münzg; ~ **standard** ~ Münzg.

golden | **handcuffs** hohe Zuwendung zwecks Festhaltens in der Firma; ~ **handshake** *hohe Abfindung für ausscheidende leitende Angestellte*; ~ **hello** großzügige Einstellungsbedingungen; ~ **parachute** großzügige Abfindung (*für Führungskräfte bei „unfreundlicher" Übernahme*).

good *adj* gut, einwandfrei, zahlungsfähig, gültig; ~ **and clear record title** → *title*; ~ **and lawful men** zu Geschworenendiensten geeignete Männer; ~ **and sufficient cause** triftiger Grund; ~ **and sufficient reason** triftiger Grund; ~ **and tenantable repair** einwandfreier (*zur Vermietung geeigneter*) Erhaltungszustand; ~ **and valid** rechtsgültig; ~ **and workmanlike manner** werkgerecht, fachlich einwandfrei; ~ **leasehold title** langfristiger Pachtbesitztitel; ~ **marketable title** einwandfreier (*zur Weiterveräußerung geeigneter*) Rechtstitel; ~ **merchantable quality and condition** handelsübliche Güte und Beschaffenheit; ~ **moral character** einwandfreier Leumund; ~ **neighbourliness** gutnachbarliche Beziehungen; ~ **neighbour policy** Politik der guten Nachbarschaft; ~ **offices** *int* die guten Dienste, Vermittlungsdienste; ~ **operating order** guter Betriebszustand; ~ **order and condition** ordentlicher Zustand; ~ **order and decorum** wohlanständiges Verhalten; ~ **reason to the contrary** Glaubhaftmachung des Gegenteils; ~ **record title** unbelastetes Grundeigentum; ~ **root of title** rechtsgültige Basisurkunde; ~ **time allowance** teilweiser Straferlaß wegen guter Führung; ~ **until recalled** (= ~ *until cancelled*) gültig bis auf Widerruf.

good *s* das Wohl, das Gute; **common** ~ Gemeinwohl; *scot* Gemeindevermögen; **public** ~ das öffentliche Wohl; *conducive to the* ~ ~: *im öffentl Interesse liegend.*

Goodright *Name e–s fiktiven Klägers ähnlich John Doe.*

goods *s pl* Güter *n|pl*, Waren *bzw* Waren, (*handelbare*) bewegliche Sachen; ~ **account** → *account* (*2*); ~ **and capital movement** Güter- und Kapitalverkehr; ~ **and chattels** bewegliches Vermögen, Mobilien; ~ **and movables** = ~*s and chattels qv*; ~ **and services** Güter und Dienstleistungen, Waren- und Dienstleistungsverkehr; ~ **bargained and sold** für verkaufte und übereignete Ware (*Kaufpreisklage*); ~ **bought** Kaufgut; ~ **chargeable by weight** gewichtszollbare Waren; ~ **declaration** → *declaration;* ~ **exempt from execution** unpfändbare Sachen; ~ **exempted from seizure** unpfändbare Sachen; **in communion** *scot* eheliches Gesamtgut (*von beweglichen Sachen*); ~ **in process** unfertige Erzeugnisse (*Bilanzposten*); ~ **in progress** unfertige Erzeugnisse (*Bilanzposten*); ~ **in transit** Transitgüter, Transitware; ~ **in trust** Ware in jmds Verwahrung, Treugut; ~ **not possessed** nicht im Besitz (*des Inventarisierenden*) befindliche Ware; ~ **on hand** Lagerbestand, Warenlager, lieferbare Ware; ~ **on sale or return** Kommissionsware; ~ **or documents of title to goods** Waren oder Traditionspapiere; ~ **pledged** verpfändete Waren, sicherungsübereignete Waren; ~ **quota** Warenkontingent; ~ **rates** Gütertarif; ~ **received** Wareneingänge; ~ **returned** Retourewaren, Rückwaren, Remittenden; ~ **shed** Güterschuppen; ~ **sold and delivered** gelieferte Waren (*Kaufpreisanspruch für Waren*); ~ **taken in execution** gepfändete Sachen; ~ **to declare** anmeldepflichtige Waren; ~ **vehicles** Lastfahrzeuge; ~ **wares and merchandise** Warenbestand; **ascertained** ~ konkretisierte Gattungssachen, individuell bestimmte Ware; **bill on** ~ → *bill*; **bonded** ~ Waren unter Zollverschluß; **branded** ~ Markenware(n); **capital** ~ → *capital*; **carriage of** ~ → *carriage*; **carted** ~ Rollgut; **chargeable** ~ abgabenpflichtige Waren; **contraband** ~ Bannware; **convenience** ~ Waren des tägl Bedarfs (*die der Verbraucher zur bequemen Bedarfsdeckung im nächstgelegenen Laden kauft*); **debenture** ~ (= *debentured* ~) Rückzollgüter; **disposable** ~ sofort lieferbare Ware(n); **distressed** ~ Ausverkaufsware bei Geschäftsaufgabe; **dry** ~ Textilien, Kurzwaren, Schnittwaren; **durable** ~ langlebige Wirtschaftsgüter; **dutiable** ~ zollpflichtige Waren; **duty-free** ~ zollfreie Waren; **fashion** ~ Modeartikel; **finished** ~ Fertigwaren; **free** ~ beschlagnahmefreie Güter, zoll- u kontingentfreie Einfuhrware; **fungible** ~ vertretbare Sachen; **future** ~ zukünftig herzustellende oder zu erwerbende Waren; **hot** ~ heiße Ware, Kontrabandware; in gesundheitsgefährdender Weise hergestellte Ware; **improved** ~ veredelte Ware; **incoming** ~ Wareneingänge; **industrial** ~ gewerbliche Produktionsgüter; Industrieartikel; **job** ~ Ausschußware, Ramschware; **lawful** ~ *int* erlaubte Ware (*für ein neutrales Schiff, keine Konterbande*); **lot of** ~ Warenpartie; **marketable** ~ gängige Waren; **miscellaneous** ~ Sammelgut; **onerous** ~ unwirtschaftliche Güter; **outgoing** ~ Warenausgang; **perishable** ~ verderbliche Waren; **perished** ~ untergegangene Sachen *bzw* Waren; **petty** ~ Kurzwaren; **proprietary** ~ Markenwaren; **protected** ~ geschützte Waren (*auf welche Abzahlungsgeschäfts-Schutzbestimmungen Anwendung finden*); **returned** ~ retournierte Ware, zurückgegebene W.; **rummage** ~ Restwaren; **scarce** ~ Mangelware; **semifinished** ~ Halbfertigwaren, Halbzeug; **shoddy** ~ minderwertige Ware, Schund; **shopping** ~ Waren des nicht alltäglichen Bedarfs; von Kaufinteressenten besonders ausgesuchte Ware; **soft** ~ Textilware; **specialty** ~ Spezialartikel; **specific** ~ Speziessachen, Waren als Stückschuld; **unascertained** ~ nicht konkretisierte Gattungssachen,

Gattungsware; **uncollected** ~ nicht abgeholte Waren, nicht abgerufene Ware; **unrivalled** ~ konkurrenzlose Erzeugnisse; **unsolicited** ~ unbestellte Ware; **white** ~ weiße Ware (*Küchenherde, Kühlschränke etc*).

goodwill (=) Firmenwert *m*, Façonwert *m*; **acquired** ~ derivativer Firmenwert; **created** ~ originärer Firmenwert; **developed** ~ originärer Firmenwert; **negative** ~ → *negative*.

G.O.P. (*Grand Old Party*) die Republikanische Partei (*USA*).

gore nicht einvermeßbare Teilfläche *f*, Teilbezirk *m* einer Grafschaft.

govern regieren, verwalten, regeln, beherrschen, bestimmen, leiten, lenken; **~ing body** Kuratorium, Universitätssenat, Lenkungsausschuß; **~ing director** allein verfügungsberechtigtes Vorstandsmitglied; **~ing instrument** Kuratoriumsakte; **~ing law** anwendbares Recht; **self-~ing territories** → *territory*; **to be ~ed by** (*e–m Recht, e–r Vorschrift*) unterliegen; beherrscht werden.

government *s* Regierung *f*, Regierungsgewalt *f*, Regierungsausübung *f*; Staat *m*, Staatssystem *n*, Staatshoheit *f*; Verwaltung *f*, Staatsanwaltschaft *f*; *adj* Regierungs . . ., staatlich, (= *st*) amtlich; ~ **accountant** amtlicher Rechnungsprüfer; ~ **actuary** amtlicher Versicherungsmathematiker; ~ **agency** Behörde, Dienststelle, Amt; ~ **aid** *st–e* Unterstützung; ~ **annuities** *st–e* Rentenpapiere; ~ **annuities societes** Rentensparvereine; ~ **bank** Staatsbank; ~ **banking institution** *st–es* (*bzw halbstaatliches*) Kreditinstitut; ~ **bill** → *bill* (*1*); ~ **bonds** Staatspapiere, Bundesobligationen, Staatsanleihen; ~ **borrowing** *st–e* Schuldenaufnahme; ~ **broker** *Börsenmakler im Auftrag der Bank of England*; ~ **chemist** Amtsprüfer für Lebensmittel, Futter und Drogeriewaren; ~ **contract** öffentlicher Auftrag; Staatsauftrag; ~ **control** Staatslenkung; *st–e* Bewirtschaftung; ~ **department** Ministerium, Zentralbehörde; ~ **depository** amtliche Kapitalsammelstelle; ~ **deposits** → *deposit*; ~ **employee** Staatsbediensteter; ~ **enterprise** Regiebetrieb, Wirtschaftsbetrieb der öffentlichen Hand; ~ **expenditure** Staatsausgaben; ~ **funds** fundierte Staatspapiere; ~ **grant** Staatszuschuß, *st–e* Beihilfe; ~ **guarantee** → *guarantee*; ~ **in exile** Exilregierung; ~ **loan** → *loan*; ~ **monopoly** Staatsmonopol; ~ **notes** *brit* Schatzbriefe; ~ **obligations** Staatsanleihen; **G~ of a different persuasion** e–e „andere" Regierung; ~ **of laws** gesetzeskonforme Rechtsprechung; ~ **of the country** die (*betreffende*) Regierung; ~ **of the day** die derzeitige Regierung; ~ **official** Staatsbeamter, Regierungsbeamter; ~ **operation** *st–er* Betrieb (*von Unternehmungen*); ~ **order** Staatsauftrag; ~ **owned** staatseigen; ~ **ownership** Staatseigentum; ~ **paper** Staatspapiere, Staatsanleihen; ~ **printer** Staatsdruckerei; ~ **printing office** Staatsdruckerei; ~ **property** Staatseigentum; ~ **publications** amtliche Veröffentlichungen *der US-Bundesregierung*; ~ **regulations and restrictions** Vorschriften und Beschränkungen; ~ **relations manager** Leiter der Behördenbeziehungsarbeit, Lobbyist; ~ **representative** Regierungsvertreter; ~ **revenue** Staatseinkünfte; ~ **securities** → *security* (*2*); ~ **spending** öffentliche Ausgaben, Staatsausgaben; ~ **stock(s)** Staatspapiere; **G~ stocks** britische Staatsobligationen; **all-party** ~ Allparteienregierung; **arbitrary** ~ Willkürherrschaft; **caretaker** ~ Übergangskabinett; **central** ~ Regierung, Zentralverwaltung; **change of** ~ Regierungswechsel; **coalition** ~ Koalitionsregierung; **consensus-style** ~ einvernehmliche Regierung, auf Konsens gegründete R.; **consolidated** ~ *Ausübung der*

Staatsgewalt durch nur ein Ministerium; **constitutional** ~ verfassungsmäßige Regierung; **de facto** ~ → *de facto*; **de jure** ~ → *de jure*; **democratic** ~ demokratische Regierungsform; **depository** ~ Verwahrerregierung; **federal** ~ Bundesregierung; **form of** ~ → *form*; **interim** ~ Interimsregierung; **left-wing** ~ Linksregierung; **local** ~ Kommunalverwaltung, örtliche Verwaltung; **member** ~ Regierung eines Mitgliedstaates; **minority** ~ Minderheitsregierung; **mixed** ~ gemischte Staatsform (*aus Monarchie, Aristokratie und Demokratie*); **municipal** ~ Gemeindeverwaltung; **national** ~ Regierung, Staatsregierung, Bundesregierung, Regierung des gesamten Landes; **parliamentary** ~ parlamentarische Regierungsform; **proprietary** ~**s** → *proprietary*; **provisional** ~ Interimsregierung, vorläufige Regierung; **puppet** ~ Marionettenregierung; **representative** ~ Repräsentativsystem; repräsentative Staatsform; **republican** ~ republikanische Staatsform; **requisitioning** ~ ersuchende Regierung; **science of** ~ Staatswissenschaft; **self-**~ Selbstverwaltung; **signatory** ~ → *signatory*; **the incoming** ~ die neue Regierung.

governmental Regierungs . . ., Staats . . ., staatlich.

governor Gouverneur *m*; *Ministerpräsident e–s Gliedstaats der USA*; Kommandant *m*; Leiter *m*, Vorstand *m*; Regent *m*; Gefängnisdirektor *m*; ~**-general** Generalgouverneur; **board of** ~**s** → *board;* **colonial** ~ Gouverneur einer Kolonie.

gown Robe *f*, Amtstracht *f*, Talar *m*.

grab *v* klauen, verhaften.

grab-gains Trickdiebstahl *von Handtaschen*.

grab-raid Raubüberfall *m*.

grace Gnade *f*, Gnadenfrist *f*, Nachfrist *f*; **act of** ~ Gnadenakt, Gnadenerweis; **days of** ~ → *day*; **matter of** ~ Gnadensache; **period of** ~ → *period*, **petition of** ~ Gnadengesuch.

gradatim stufenweise.

gradation Abstufung *f*, Abtönung *f*, Einteilung *f*, Klassifizierung *f*, stufenweise Anordnung *f*, Staffelung *f*.

grade *s* Grad *m*, Rang *m*, Stufe *f*, Qualität *f*, Handelsklasse *f*, Steigung *f*, Gefälle *n*, Neigung *f*, Note *f*, Zensur *f*; ~ **designation marks** Warenklassenbezeichnung; ~ **label** Güteklassenbezeichnung; **first** ~ erstklassig; **low** ~ geringwertig, von minderer Qualität.

grad|e *v* einstufen; ~ **goods** Waren- und Güteklassen einteilen; ~**ing and marking** nach Güteklassen einteilen und bezeichnen; ~**ing of premiums** *ins* Beitragsstaffelung.

grade crossing *US* schienengleicher Übergang.

grading Klassierung *f*.

graduate Graduierter, Absolvent *m*.

graduate *v* abstufen; e–n akademischen Grad erwerben, graduieren.

graduated *adj* abgestuft, gestaffelt, graduiert.

gradus parentelae Stammbaum *m*.

graft Schmiergeld *n*, Schiebung *f*; Heilung *f* e–s Mangels bei der Hypothekenbestellung.

grafter Schieber *m*, korrupter Beamter *m*.

grain Korn *n*, Getreide *n*, Teilchen *n*, Faser *f*; Gran *n* (*Gewichtseinheit*); ~ **futures** Getreidetermingeschäfte; ~ **rent** Vergütung für Aberntenrecht.

gram (= *gramme*) Gramm (*des metrischen Systems*).

grand groß, bedeutend, endgültig; ~ **gang** 1000 Dollar; ~ **days** *Festtage der Inns of Court qv*; ~ **jury** → *jury*; ~ **larceny** → *larceny*; ~ **total** Endsumme, Gesamtsumme.

grandchild Enkel *m*, (*evt*) Urenkel *m*; ~**ren of any degree** alle Enkel (*jur*: eheliche Abkömmlinge außer Kindern).

grandfather Großvater *m*; ~ **clause** *Ausnahme von Wahlrechtsbeschrän-*

kungen in den Südstaaten für Abkömmlinge von Veteranen der südstaatlichen Streitkräfte; ~ **rights** Besitzstand.

grandparent Großelternteil *m*.

grange Viehzuchtfarm *f*.

grant *s* Bewilligung *f*, Erteilung *f*, (rechtsgeschäftliche) Einräumung, Verfügung, Zuwendung *f*; Übertragung (*von Grundstücksrechten*); Zuschuß *m*; Konzessionserteilung *f*; *scot* Schenkung *f*; ~ **by will** letztwillige Zuwendung; ~**-in-aid** öffentlicher Zuschuß, Beihilfe, Subvention; ~ **of a patent** Patenterteilung; ~ **of administration** → *administration*; ~ **of licence** Lizenzerteilung, Lizenzvergabe; ~ **of personal property** entgeltliche Übertragung von beweglichem Vermögen; ~ **of probate** → *probate*; ~ **of representation** Einsetzung eines Testamentsvollstrekkers; ~ **recycling** Beihilferückflußverwendung; ~ **to uses** (*GB vor 1925*), Grundstücksübertragung mit Treuhandsbedingungen; **ancillary** ~ = *ancillary probate* → *probate*; **block** ~**s** generelle Mittelzuweisungen an die Gemeinden; **general** ~ allgemeine Mittelzuweisung an Gemeinden; **governmental** ~ Staatszuschuß, staatliche Beihilfe; **improvement** ~ Modernisierungsbeihilfe; **maintenance** ~ Unterhaltsbeihilfe; **private land** ~ Übertragung von Staatsgrund an Privatpersonen; **public** ~ Gewährung oder Übertragung aus Vermögen der öffentlichen Hand; **rate-support** ~ Mittelzuweisung der Zentralregierung an die Kommunen; Finanzausgleichsmittel für Gemeinden; **royal** ~ königl Verleihung, Konzessionserteilung durch die Krone; **to obtain a** ~ e–e Testamentsbestätigung (*cf probate*) erlangen.

grant *v* bewilligen, erteilen, gewähren; ~ **a charter** Rechtsfähigkeit verleihen; ~ **a divorce** auf Scheidung erkennen, ein Scheidungsurteil antragsgemäß erlassen; ~ **a licence** e–e Lizenz erteilen; ~ **a loan** ein Darlehen geben, beleihen; ~ **a petition** e–m Antrag stattgeben; ~ **a request** e–m Antrag stattgeben; ~ **a respite** stunden, Zahlungsaufschub gewähren; ~ **an injunction** e–e einstweilige Verfügung erlassen; ~ **and demise** Pachtbesitz einräumen (*mit Rechtsmängelhaftung*); ~ **and to freight let** Schiffscharter erteilen, ~, **bargain and sell** die Auflassung erklären; ~ **grace** Nachfrist gewähren; ~ **leave** zulassen, für zulässig erklären; ~ **leave to appeal** die Revision für zulässig erklären; ~ **probate** → *probate*; ~**time** eine Frist bewilligen, stunden.

grantee Erwerber *m*, Empfänger *m*, Bedachter *m*, Zessionar *m*; Konzessionär *m*; ~ **of an annuity** Rentenberechtigter; ~ **of a patent** Patentinhaber; ~ **of licence** Lizenznehmer; ~ **to uses** *hist* Treuhänder, Treuhandeigentümer.

grantor Veräußerer *m*, Verfügender, Übertragender *m*, Verleiher *m*, Bewilligender *m*; ~ **of a licence** Lizenzgeber; ~ **of a power** Vollmachtgeber; ~ **of a trust** Treugeber, Stifter, Errichter e–er Treuhand; ~ **of real estate** Grundstücksveräußerer; ~ **of the lease** Verpächter; ~ **trust** → *trust*.

graph grafische Darstellung *f*, Diagramm *n*, Schaubild *n*.

grass *v/i* denunzieren, als Informant betätigen.

grass roots *pol* Basis *f*, politische Anhängerschaft *f*.

gratification Gratifikation *f*, Belohnung *f*; Befriedigung *f*, Genugtuung *f*.

gratis gratis, umsonst, unentgeltlich; ~ **dictum** → *dictum*.

gratuitous unentgeltlich, gratis, umsonst.

gratuit|y Unentgeltlichkeit *f*; Belohnung *f*, Geschenk *n*, Abfindungssumme *f*, Zuwendung *f*, Zulage *f*, Zuschuß *f*, Trinkgeld *n*; ~**ies** Trinkgelder.

gravamen Klagegrund *m*, Beschwer *f*, Schwerpunkt *m* der Anklage.
grave and weighty reason wichtiger Grund; ~ **impropriety or infamous conduct** höchst ungebührliches oder ehrloses Verhalten.
graveyard Friedhof *m*; ~ **insurance** *unredliche* Versicherung bei hohem Todesrisiko; ~ **shift** → *shift*.
grave plot Begräbnisstätte *f*, Begräbnisplatz *m*.
gravity Bedeutung *f*, Schwere *f*, Wichtigkeit *f*; ~ **of testimony** Gewicht e–r Zeugenaussage; ~ **of the infringement** Schwere der Verletzung.
gray mail *s* Erpressungsversuch durch geheimhaltungsbedürftiges Beweismaterial; ~ **statute** Gesetz über Verfahren in Geheimsachen.
Gray's Inn (=) Anwaltsinnung in London.
Great Britain Großbritannien (*England, Wales u. Schottland*).
greed Habgier *f*.
Green Book (=) Prozeßordnung der County Courts; ~ **field project** Unternehmenvorhaben „auf der grünen Wiese"; ~ **form scheme** Beratungshilfe.
green mail *s* Aktienaufkauf als Übernahmepression, *hochspekuliertes erpressungsähnliches Übernahmeangebot, Sonderprofit aus Abfindung für erpresserisches Übernahmeangebot, bes. Rückkauf überhöhter Aktien vom Übernahmespekulanten*.
greenbacks *US* Dollarnoten *f/pl*.
Greenwich Hospital (=) Pflegeheim für Seeleute; ~ **(mean) time** Greenwicher mittlere Sonnenzeit.
greffier Gerichtsschreiber *m*, Registrator *m*, Notar *m*.
grey legal area Grauzone *f*.
grid lock absolute Blockierung des Verkehrs.
grievance Klage *f*; Beschwer *f*; Beschwerde *f*, Mißstand *m*; ~ **committee** Schlichtungsausschuß, Disziplinarausschuß; ~ **proceedings** Schlichtungsverfahren bei Arbeitnehmerbeschwerden.
grieved = *aggrieved qv*.
grievous bodily harm schwere (*bzw gefährliche*) Körperverletzung *f* (*ohne genaue Abgrenzung*).
grill *v/t* e–m strengen Verhör unterziehen, in die Mangel nehmen.
grocer Lebensmittelgeschäft *n*; *hist* Grossist *m*.
groceries Lebensmittel *n/pl*, Kolonialwaren *f/pl*.
grog-shop Schnapsladen *n*, Bar *f*.
grogging verbotene Schnapsbrennerei *f* (*aus dem Holz der Schnapsfässer*).
gross brutto, roh, grob, gesamt; ~ **adventure** Bodmereidarlehen; ~ **annual value** Bruttomiet(pacht-)wert (*wobei Vermieter die Instandhaltungskosten, Mieter die öffentlichen Lasten trägt*); ~ **book value** Buchwert vor Abschreibung; ~ **breach of duty** grobe Pflichtverletzung; ~ **domestic product** Bruttoinlandsprodukt; ~ **domestic investments** Gesamtinlandsinvestitionen; ~ **inadequacy** unzumutbar geringe Entschädigung; ~ **merchandising margin** Bruttospanne ohne Skontoabzug; ~ **national product (GNP)** Bruttosozialprodukt; ~ **register ton** → *ton*; ~ **relevant distribution** Bruttogewinnverteilung; ~ **reserve assets** Bruttoreserven; ~ **terms** *Laden und Löschen geht zu Lasten des Schiffes*; ~ **trading profit** Bruttogeschäftsgewinn; ~ **value of premises** (*jährl*) Mietertragswert.
ground *s* (*1*) Boden *m*, Erde *f*; ~ **annual** *scot* Erbbaurechtszins; ~ **crew** Bodenpersonal; ~ **floor** Vorzugspreis, günstiger Ausgabekurs; ~ **game** Niederwild; ~ **landlord** Grundeigentümer *bzw* Eigentümer des Erbbaugrundstücks; ~ **lease** Erbbaurechtsvertrag; ~ **rent** *Pachtzins bei building lease qv, etwa*: Erbbauzins; Erbpachtzins, Ewigrente; ~ **writ** Antrag auf Zulassung auswärtiger Vollstreckung (*beim Prozeßgericht*); **above** ~ über Tage, oberirdisch; **common** ~ Gemeindeland, Allmende; Gemeinsamkeit(en), Unstreitiges.

ground *s* (*2*) Grund *m*, Begründung *f*; **~s for a judgment** Urteilsgründe; **~s for annulment** Aufhebungsgründe; **~ for divorce** Scheidungsgrund; **~s for litigation** Prozeßmaterial; **~ of action** Klaggrund; **~s of appeal** Rechtsmittelbegründung, R.-gründe; **~ of claim** Klaggrund; **~ of defence** Verteidigungsgrund; **~ of impugnment** Anfechtungsgrund; **~ of nullity** Nichtigkeitsgrund; **~s of** (= *for*) **opposition** *pat* Einspruchsbegründung; **legal ~** Rechtsgrund; **substantial ~s** erhebliche Gründe; **untenable ~** unhaltbarer Grund; **valid ~s** stichhaltige Gründe, triftige Gründe.

ground *v* begründen, gründen; **~ed upon** gestützt auf.

groundage Hafengeld *n*.

group Gruppe *f*, Konzern *m*; **~ accounts** → *account* (*2*); **~ annuities** Gemeinschaftsrenten; **~ banking** Bankkonzernbildung, Bankkonzerngeschäfte; **~ buying** Sammeleinkauf; **~ company** → *company*; **~ demand** Konzernbedarf; **~ depreciation** Gruppenabschreibung; **~ insurance** → *insurance*; **~ management report** Konzernlagebericht; **~ piecework** Gruppenakkord; **~ rate** Sammeltarif; **~ relief** Steuervorteil für Konzerngesellschaft bei Körpersch.St., Schachtelprivileg; **age ~** Altersgruppe; **interagency ~** aus verschiedenen Behörden gebildetes Gremium; **multinational ~** Multi, internationaler Konzern; **occupational ~** Berufsgruppe; **parliamentary ~** Fraktion.

groupage Sammelladung; **~ documents** Containerpapiere mit mehr als e–r Ladung; **~ shipment** Sammelladung zum selben Bestimmungsort.

grouping order Anordnung zur Bildung e–s Gemeindeverbandes.

growth Wachstum *n*, Vergrößerung *f*, Zuwachs *m*, Herkunft *f*; **~ areas** Entwicklungsgebiete; **~ half-penny** Abgabe für Mastvieh; **~ perspectives** Wachstumsperspektiven; **~ targets** Wachstumsziele; **rate of ~** → *rate*.

grub stake Gelegenheitsgesellschaft *f* von Schürfern und Ausrüstern; **~ agreement** Schürfbeteiligungsvertrag.

guarantee *v* (= *to guaranty*), garantieren, bürgen, gewährleisten; **~ a bill of exchange** Wechselbürgschaft leisten; **~ a legal title** e–n Rechtstitel sichern; **~ reciprocity** Gegenseitigkeit verbürgen; **~d accounts** verbürgte Außenstände; **~d analysis** garantiert richtige Analyse; **~d annual wage** garantierter Jahreslohn; **~d bonds** Obligationen mit Dividendengarantie; **~d credit** → *credit*; **~d employment** garantierte Mindestbeschäftigung; **~d employment account** Sonderbeitragskonto bei garantierter Dauerbeschäftigung (*Steuervergünstigung US*); **~d for** volle Gewähr für; **~d for cargo** garantiert ladebereit; **~d minimum wage** → *wage*; **~d securities** (= *~d stocks*) Aktien mit Dividendengarantie.

guarantee *s* (*cf guaranty*) Garantie *f*, Bürgschaft *f*, Kaution *f*; Garant *m*, Bürge *m*, Sicherheitsnehmer *m*; Gläubiger *m*, dem Bürgschaft geleistet wird; Kautionsnehmer *n*; **~ association** Kautionsversicherungsgesellschaft; **~ card** Bürgschaftskarte; **~ ceiling** Garantiehöchstgrenze; **~ commission** Delkredereprovision; **~ credit** → *credit*; **~ deposit** Kautionsdepot; **~ deposits funds** → *fund*; **~ for a bill** Wechselbürgschaft, Wechselbürge; **~ indebtedness** Bürgschaftsschuld; **~ insurance** → *insurance*; **~ of consumer goods** gesetzl Verbraucherschutz; **~ of supply** Liefergarantie; **~ of tender** Bietungsgarantie; **~ payment** Garantiezahlung, Mindestweiterbezahlung bei Ausstellung (*e–s Arbeitnehmers*); **~ period** Garantiezeit; **~ society** Kautionsversicherungsgesellschaft; **~ stock** *nicht rückzahlbare* Kapitaleinlage (*Baugenossenschaft*); **advance**

payment ~ Anzahlungsgarantie; **bank** ~ Bankbürgschaft; **beneficiary under a** ~ Garantiebegünstigter; **bill** ~ Wechselbürgschaft; **certificate of** ~ Garantieschein; **collective** ~ Mitbürgschaft, Kollektivbürgschaft; **company limited by** → *company*; **conditional** ~ Ausfallbürgschaft; **contract of** ~ → *contract*; **credit** ~ → *credit*; **delivery** ~ Bietungsgarantie; **government** ~ Staatsbürgschaft; **implementation of a** ~ Inanspruchnahme e–r Garantie; **joint and several unlimited** ~ samtverbindliche unbeschränkte Bürgschaft; **line of** ~ Avallinie; **ordinary** ~ einfache (*nicht selbstschuldnerische*) Bürgschaft; **payment** ~ Zahlungsgarantie, Anweisungsgarantie; **performance** ~ Leistungsgarantie; **simple** ~ einfache (*nicht selbstschuldnerische*) Bürgschaft; **tender** ~ Bietungsgarantie; **to furnish** (= *submit*) **a** ~ Garantie leisten; e–e Bürgschaft beibringen.

guarantor Bürge *m*; Sicherungsgeber *m*, Garant *m*, Garantiegeber *m*; Garantieverpflichteter *m*.

guaranty Garantie *f*, Garantievertrag *m*, Gewährleistung *f*, Kaution *f*; (*juristisch ungenau:*) Bürgschaft *f*; ~ **account** → *account* (2); ~ **bond** → *bond* (2); ~ **commission** Delkredereprovision; ~ **company** Kautionsversicherungsgesellschaft; ~ **fund** gesetzliche Gemeinschaftsrückstellung zur Sicherung von Bankeinlagen; ~ **insurance** → *insurance*; ~ **of collection** Delkredere, Zahlungsgarantie; ~ **of deposits** (*staatl*) Bankeinlagenversicherung; ~ **of title insurance** → *insurance*; **absolute** ~ selbstschuldnerische Bürgschaft; **collateral** ~ Garantievertrag; **conditional** ~ Ausfallbürgschaft; **continuing** ~ Dauergarantie, Kontokorrentbürgschaft; **fidelity** ~ Verläßlichkeitskaution; **general** ~ allgemeine Garantie; **implied** ~ stillschweigende Gewähr; **letter of** ~ Drittgarantieschein (*als Mängelgewährleistung*); **limited** ~ (*auf ein Rechtsgeschäft*) beschränkte Garantie; **special** ~ persönliche Garantie; **specific** ~ Garantie *für e–n konkreten Fall.*

guard *s* Beschützer *m*, Wächter *m*, Posten *m*, Wache *f*, Schutzvorrichtung *f*; ~ **dog** Wachhund; **coast** ~ Küstenwacht.

guardage Vormundschaft *f*.

guardian Vormund *m*; Pfleger *m*; Verwahrer *m*; ~ **ad hoc** Pfleger mit besonderem Auftrag; ~ **ad litem** Prozeßpfleger; ~**'s allowance** (Sozialversicherungs)Zuwendungen für Mündel; ~ **by appointment of court** gerichtlich bestellter Vormund; ~ **by election** vom Minderjährigen ausgewählter Vormund; ~ **by nature** der (*natürliche*) Inhaber der elterlichen Gewalt; ~ **for nurture** personensorgeberechtigter Elternteil (*bis zum 14. Lebensjahr*); ~ **in chivalry** *feud* herrschaftliche Vormundschaft; ~ **in socage** *gewohnheitsrechtlicher* Vormund *bis zum 14. Lebensjahr*; ~ **of infant** Vormund e–s Minderjährigen; ~ **of property** Vermögensverwalter; ~ **of the Cinque Ports** Richter der Seehäfen „Cinque Ports" *qv*; ~ **of the estate** Nachlaßpfleger; ~ **of the peace** Polizeibeamter; ~ **of the poor** Wohlfahrtspfleger, Fürsorgebeamter, Armenpfleger; ~ **of the public interest** Wahrer der öffentlichen Interessen; ~ **of the spiritualities** geistlicher Verwalter e–s vakanten Bistums; ~ **of the temporalities** königlicher Verwalter e–s vakanten Bistums bzw e–r Abtei; **ancillary** ~ Gegenvormund; **assistant** ~ Beistand; **chief** ~ Obervormund; **controlling** ~ Gegenvormund; **domestic** ~ vom Wohnsitzgericht bestellter Vormund; **exempted** ~ befreiter Vormund; **foreign** ~ gegenständlich beschränkter Pfleger bei ausländischem Mündel; **general** ~ (*unbeschränkter*) Vormund; **interim** ~ vorläufiger Vormund; **legal** ~ Vormund; **natural** ~ sorgeberechtigter Elternteil; **official** ~

Amtsvormund; **special** ~ Pfleger (*mit beschränkten Kompetenzen*); **testamentary** ~ testamentarisch bestellter Vormund.

guardianship Vormundschaft *f*, Obhut *f*; ~ **of minors** V. über Minderjährige; **exempted** ~ befreite Vormundschaft; **letters of** ~ → *letters*; **to receive into** ~ unter Vormundschaft stellen.

gubernatorial Regierungs . . ., Gouverneurs . . .

guest Gast *m*, Hotelgast *m*; ~ **house** Fremdenheim, Pension; ~ **statute** Gesetz über Haftungsausschluß bei Gefälligkeitsmitnahme (*außer für Vorsatz und grobe Fahrlässigkeit*); ~-**taker** = *agister qv*; **gratuitous** ~ Gefälligkeitsmitfahrer.

guestimate grobe (über den Daumen gepeilte) Schätzung *f*.

guidage Geleit *n*, Vergütung *f* für sicheres Geleit.

guidance Führung *f*, Leitung *f*, Anleitung *f*, Orientierung *f*, Richtlinie *f*, Beratung *f*; Leumund *m*; ~ **counsel** Jugendpsychologe; **vocational** ~ Berufsberatung.

guide Führer *m*, Leiter *m*, Berater *m*; Leitfaden *m*, Reiseführerbuch *n*; general *s* allgemeine Leitlinien; ~ **dog** Blindenhund.

guideline Richtlinie *f*, Richtschnur *f*; ~ **power** Richtlinienkompetenz, Befugnis zur Rahmengesetzgebung.

guild Gilde *f*, Zunft *f*, Innung *f*, Bruderschaft *f*; ~ **merchant** Kaufmannsgilde; ~ **rents** Zunftabgaben an die Krone; **trade** ~ Handwerkerzunft.

guildhall Rathaus *n*; **G~ Sittings** Gerichtssitzung im Londoner Rathaus (*in städtischen Angelegenheiten*).

guillotine *s* Guillotine *f*; Redezeitbeschränkung *f*; *v* ~ **a debate** e–e Debatte abwürgen.

guilt Schuld *f*; **admission of** ~ → *admission*; **collective** ~ Kollektivschuld; **consciousness of** ~ → *consciousness*; **finding of** ~ → *finding*; **joint** ~ Mitschuld, Mitverschulden, konkurrierendes Verschulden; **proof of** ~ →*proof*; **question of** ~ → *question*; **to shoulder the** ~ die Schuld auf sich nehmen.

guilty schuldig; ~ **but insane** *Feststellung der Unzurechnungsfähigkeit des überführten Täters;* ~ **through ignorance** *Feststellung des Verschuldens bei unbewußter Fahrlässigkeit*; ~ **with no criminal intent** *Feststellung der Unzurechnungsfähigkeit e–s überführten Täters*; **predominantly** ~ überwiegend schuldig.

guise Vorwand *m*, Tarnung *f*, Deckmantel *m*.

gun Geschütz *n*, Kanone *f*, Handfeuerwaffe *f*, Gewehr *n*, Flinte *f*, Pistole *f*, Revolver *m*; ~ **barrel** Gewehrlauf *bzw* Pistolenlauf; ~ **licence** → *licence*; ~ **man** Gangster; ~ **running** Waffenschmuggel; ~ **squad** Mordkommando; **at** ~ **point** angesichts vorgehaltener Pistole; **spring** ~**s** Selbstschüsse.

gunning for s.o. gezielte Spekulation zum Nachteil e–s anderen; ~ **for stocks** *US* Börsenmanöver der Baissepartei.

gynarchy Frauenherrschaft *f*; Staat *m* mit weiblichem Staatsoberhaupt.

gyp *v* beschwindeln; **to be** ~**ped** übers Ohr gehauen werden.

gyrations wilde Kurssprünge *m*|*pl*.

gyves Fußfesseln *f*|*pl*, Fußeisen *n*|*pl*.

H

habeas corpus (=) *Grundrecht des richterlichen Gehörs e–s Inhaftierten*; richterliche Haftprüfung; **writ of** ~ → *writ*.

habendum *Auflassungsklausel, dingliche Übertragungsklausel*; ~ **et tenendum** = *to have and to hold qv*.

habit Gewohnheit *f*, Übung *f*, geistige Beschaffenheit *f*; Amtstracht *f*.

habitability Bewohnbarkeit *f*.

habitable bewohnbar; ~ **repair** bewohnbarer Zustand.

habitancy dauernder Aufenthalt *m*.

habitation Wohnhaus *n*, Wohnung *f*, Aufenthaltsort *m*; dingliches Wohnrecht *n*.

habitual gewöhnlich, gewohnheitsmäßig; ~**ly leaving one's wife without means of support** fortgesetzte Verletzung der Unterhaltspflicht gegenüber der Ehefrau.

Hague|Conference Haager Friedenskonferenz *f* (*1899–1907*); ~ **Conventions** Haager Konventionen, Haager Abkommen; ~ **Regulations** Haager Landkriegsordnung; **H**~ **Rules on bills of lading** Haager Regeln (*betreffend Konnossemente, 1924*); ~ **Tribunal** der ständige Schiedsgerichtshof im Haag, Haager Schiedshof.

hairline cracks Haarrisse *m|pl*.

half halb, hälftig; ~ **a year** ein halbes Jahr (= *182 Tage*); ~**-blood** halbblütig, halbbürtig (*ein gemeinsamer Elternteil*); ~**-bred** halbblut, halbbürtig; ~**-breed** Mischling; ~ **brother** Halbbruder; ~ **caste** Mischling, Eurasier; ~ **chest** halbe Kiste (*Tee: 75 bis 80 lbs*); ~ **commission man** Vermittlungsagent e–s Effektenmaklers, Remisier; ~ **cousins** → *cousin*; ~ **defense** *scot* kurze Einlassungsformel (= *defends the force and injury, and says . . .*); ~ **dime** Fünfcentstück; ~**-dollar** halber Silberdollar; ~ **eagle** Fündollar(gold)münze; ~ **endeal** die Hälfte; ~ **fare ticket** Fahrkarte zum halben Preis; ~ **holiday** halber Arbeitstag; ~ **interest** Beteiligung zur Hälfte; ~ **pay** die Hälfte der Bezüge, Wartegeld; ~ **pilotage** *naut* halbe Pilotenvergütung (*für Bereitschaft*); ~ **proof** → *proof*; ~ **quarter day** Quartalshälftetag (*8. Febr., 9. Mai, 11. Aug., 11. Nov.*); ~ **section** (*320 acres*) die Hälfte e–r Landvermessungseinheit; ~ **sister** → *sister*; ~**-timer** halbtags arbeitender Jugendlicher; ~**-tongue** je zur Hälfte muttersprachlich verschieden besetzte Jury, Geschworenengericht für Ausländer; ~**-weekly** zweimal wöchentlich erscheinend; ~**-year lands** der gemeinsamen Weidenutzung unterliegendes Land.

hallmark Edelmetallprägezeichen (*zur Herkunftsangabe*), Feingehaltsstempel *n*.

halt at major road ahead Halt, Vorfahrt beachten!

hammer *s* Hammer *m*; Zwangsversteigerung *f*; ~ **price** *nach Börsenvorschriften bestimmter* Preis bei Liquidation eines Maklers, Realisierungspreis bei Liquidation; **sold under the** ~ zwangsversteigert; **the fall of the** ~ Zuschlag; **to bring to the** ~ unter den Hammer bringen, zwangsversteigern.

hammer|a defaulter die Zahlungsunfähigkeit bekanntgeben; ~ **the market** e–n Baisseangriff machen; ~**ing** (*of a stockbroker*) Insolvenzfeststellung e–s Maklers an der Börse.

hand *s* Hand *f*, Hilfe *f*, Arbeiter *m*, Gehilfe *m*; Handschrift *f*, Unterschrift *f*; *pl* Besitz *m*, Kontrolle *f*,

Obhut *f*, Gewalt *f*; ~**-made** handgearbeitet; ~ **money** Handgeld, Kaufschilling; ~**s-off attitude** Desinteresse; ~ **to mouth buying** Einkauf nur für notwendigen Bedarf; **by** ~ mit der Hand; durch Boten; **by one's** ~ eigenhändig; **cash in** ~ → *cash*; **dead** ~ tote Hand (Körperschaft des öffentlichen Rechts); **under** ~ → *under*; **with clean** ~**s** redlich.

hand *v* aushändigen; ~ **down** verkünden (*Urteil*); ~ **in** einreichen; ~ **out** herausgeben, überlassen; ~ **over** übergeben, herausgeben.

handbag snatching Handtaschenraub.

handbill Reklamezettel *m*, Flugblatt *n*.

handcuffs Handschellen *f/pl*.

handicraft Handwerk *n*.

handicraftsman Handwerker *m*.

handle *s* Handhabe *f*, Vorwand *m*.

handle *v* hantieren, handeln; ~ **a case** e–n Fall bearbeiten.

handler Hehler *m*; Tierhalter *m*; am Produktionsvertrieb Beteiligter *m*.

handling (*1*) Handhabung *f*, Bearbeitung *f*, Abfertigung *f*; ~ **charges** Umschlagsspesen; ~ **fee** Bearbeitungsgebühr; ~ **time** Bearbeitungszeit, innerbetriebliche Materialtransportzeit; **ordinary** ~ normale Abfertigung.

handling (*2*) Hehlerei *f*; ~ **of stolen goods** Hehlerei; **dishonest** ~ Hehlerei.

hand-sale Handkauf *m*, Kaufabschluß *m* durch Handschlag; Handgeld *m*.

handsel Handgeld *n*.

handwriting Handschrift *f*, handschriftlich geschriebenes Schriftstück *n*; ~ **expert** Schriftsachverständiger.

handwritten handgeschrieben, holographisch.

handyman Mann *m* für alles; Gelegenheitsarbeiter *m*.

hang anhängig sein; hängen.

hanged, drawn and quartered hingerichtet durch Hängen, Zangenreißen und Vierteilen.

hanger-on Mitläufer *m*.

hanging Hängen *n*, Hinrichtung *f* durch den Strang; **execution by** ~ Hinrichtung durch den Strang.

hanging the process während der Rechtshängigkeit.

hangman Henker *m*.

Hansard (=) *brit offizielles Parlamentsprotokoll*.

hansardize *parl* jmdm e–e frühere protokollierte Erklärung entgegenhalten.

happening of the accident das Unfallereignis *n*; ~ **of the contingency** Eintritt der Bedingung; ~ **of the event insured** (= *of the risk*) der Versicherungsfall.

harasser Belästiger *m*, Nötiger *m*.

harassment bösartige Belästigung *f*, Schikane *f*, schikanöse Pression *f*; ~ **of debtors** Schuldnernötigung; ~ **of occupier** Schikane gegen Bewohner; ~ **of tenant** Vermieterschikane; ~ **suit** Schadensersatzprozeß wegen Nötigung; **sexual** ~ sexuelle Nötigung, schikanöse Diskriminierung als Frau.

harbo(u)r *s* Hafen *m*; ~ **authority** Hafenbehörde, Hafenamt; ~ **barrage** Hafensperre; ~ **board** Hafenbehörde; ~ **dues** Hafengelder; ~ **line** Grenze der Hafengewässer; ~ **master** Hafenmeister, Hafenkapitän; ~ **of refuge** Nothafen, Zufluchtsort; ~ **of transshipment** Umschlaghafen; **commercial** ~ Handelshafen; **tidal** ~ Gezeitenhafen, Fluthafen.

harbouring Begünstigung *f* durch Unterschlupfgewährung; ~ **an employee** Arbeitsgewährung für vertragsbrüchigen Arbeitnehmer.

hard hart, streng; ~ **and fast** unbedingt, absolut, bindend; ~ **and fast rule** → *rule;* ~ **cases** unbillige Entscheidungen; ~ **cash** Barbestand, Hartgeld; ~ **facts** nackte Tatsachen; ~ **goods** Haushaltsartikel; ~ **labour** Zwangsarbeit (*US; GB vor 1948*); ~ **liquor** scharfe Getränke; ~ **money** Hartgeld; ~ **selling** Verkaufen um jeden Preis; ~ **shoulder** Bankett *n* (*Landstraße*).

harden sich festigen, anziehen (*Kurse*); **~ing of the market** Versteifung auf dem (Geld)markt.
hardpan steinhartes Erdreich *n*, (*Schürfrecht*).
hardship Härte *f*, Mühsal *f*, Beschwerde *f*; ~ **allowance** Härtebeihilfe; ~ **case** Härtefall; ~ **clause** Härteklausel; **exceptional** ~ außergewöhnlicher Härtefall; ~ **premium** Härteausgleichszulage; **grave** ~ schwerer Härtefall; **inequitable** ~ unbillige Härte; **iniquitous** ~ unbillige Härte; **undue** ~ unbillige Härte; **to relieve** ~ → *to relieve*.
hardy *parl* immer wiederkehrender Gegenstand *bzw* Antrag.
harm Schaden *m*, Nachteil *m*; **substantial** ~ beträchtlicher Schaden.
harmful schädlich.
harmless unschädlich, schadlos; **to hold s. o.** ~ jmdn schadlos halten.
harmonization Harmonisierung *f*; Angleichung *f*; ~ **of economic policies** Harmonisierung der Wirtschaftspolitik.
harmonize harmonisieren, übereinstimmen; ~ **conflicting evidence** widersprüchlichen Beweisstoff zur Übereinstimmung bringen.
harmony Harmonie *f*, Übereinstimmung *f*; **domestic** ~ häuslicher Friede, **in** ~ **with** übereinstimmend mit.
harsh and unconscionable von sittenwidriger Härte.
harvesting Einbringen *n* der Ernte; ~ **expenses** Erntekosten.
haul *s* Transport *m*, Straßengütertransport *m*; **short** ~ Kurzstreckenfracht.
haul *v*|*t* holen, transportieren.
haulage Beförderung *f*, Förderung *f*, Transport *m*; Beförderungskosten *pl*; ~ **contractor** Rollfuhrunternehmer; **long** ~ Fernlastverkehr.
hav|**e** haben, behalten, besitzen; ~ **a vote** stimmberechtigt sein; ~ **authority over** Befehlsgewalt über jmdn haben; ~ **charge of a vehicle** ein betriebsbereites Fahrzeug in Gewahrsam haben (*in der Absicht, es in Betrieb zu nehmen*); ~ **and hold** = *to* ~ *and to hold qv* → *to*; ~ **jurisdiction** zuständig sein; ~ **notice of** Kenntnis haben von; ~ **obtained** erlangt haben; ~ **or convey** in Gewahrsam haben oder veräußern; ~ **power to dispose** Verfügungsrecht haben; ~ **the quorum** beschlußfähig sein; **~ing authority** maßgebend; **~ing or holding** im Eigenbesitz (habend).
haver Besitzer *m*, Inhaber *m* (*e–r Urkunde*), vorlagepflichtige Partei *f*.
hawker Straßenverkäufer *m*; **~'s licence** Reisegewerbeerlaubnis.
hawking Straßenverkauf *m*.
hawks Falken *m*|*pl*, Kriegspartei *f*.
hazard Zufall *m*, Gefahr *f*, Risiko *n*, die versicherte Gefahr; Glücksspiel *n*; ~ **bonus** → *bonus*; **~s not covered** ausgeschlossene Risiken; **~s of the sea** Seegefahr; ~ **to human health** Gesundheitsgefährdung; ~ **warning lights** Warnblinkanlage; **changes in** ~ Änderungen hinsichtlich des (*Grades des*) Versicherungsrisikos; **industrial** ~ Betriebsrisiko; **moral** ~ *vom Willen des Versicherten abhängiges Risiko; mangelnder Schutzwille des Versicherten, subjektives Risiko des Versicherten;* **occupational** ~ Berufsrisiko.
hazardous gewagt, gefährlich, leichtfertig, gefahrgeneigt; ~ **contract** → *contract*; ~ **goods** gefährliche Güter; ~ **insurance** → *insurance*; ~ **negligence** Leichtfertigkeit; ~ **occupation** gefährlicher Beruf, gefahrgeneigte Beschäftigung; ~ **speculation** gewagte Spekulation.
head Spitze *f*, Oberhaupt *n*, Direktor *m*; Abteilung *f*, Rubrik *f*, Überschrift *f*; Staatschef; ~ **lease** Hauptmiete, Hauptpachtvertrag; ~ **money** Kopfgeld; ~ **note** Urteilszusammenfassung, Leitsatz; **~s of agreement** Präambel, Vertragsvorbemerkungen; vorvertraglich fixierte Hauptpunkte e–s Vertrages; ~ **of a family** Familienoberhaupt; ~ **of consular post** Leiter der konsularischen Vertretung; ~ **of department** Abteilungsleiter; ~ **of**

household Haushaltsvorstand; ~ **of legal section** Leiter der Rechtsabteilung; ~ **of loss** Schadenskategorie; ~ **of state** Staatsoberhaupt; ~ **of the government** Regierungschef; ~ **office** Direktion; **departmental** ~ Abteilungsleiter; **per** ~ pro Kopf; **to bring the case to a** ~ den Fall zur Entscheidung bringen.

headhunter Talentsucher *m*.

headhunting consultancy Talentsuche-Agentur *f*.

headlight (Front)Scheinwerfer *m*, **full** ~ Fernlicht.

headquarters Hauptsitz *m*, Direktion *f*, Haupt(geschäfts)sitz *m*, Hauptniederlassung *f mil* Oberkommando *n*, Hauptquartier *n*.

headright certificate (*Texas*) Siedlungsland-Schenkungsurkunde *f*.

headship Rektorat *n*.

headsman Scharfrichter *m*; Anführer *m*, Vorsteher *m*, Vormann *m*.

healing Act Gesetz *n* zur Heilung formaler Mängel (*e–s anderen Gesetzes*).

health Gesundheit *f*, Wohlbefinden *n*; ~ **and beauty lines** Gesundheits- und Kosmetikbranche; ~ **authorities** Gesundheitsbehörden; ~ **care benefits** Krankenversorgungsleistungen; ~ **care provider** Krankenkassenversorgungsträger; ~ **certificate** Gesundheitszeugnis; ~ **controls** gesundheitsrechtliche Kontrollen, ~ **insurance** Krankenversicherung, Krankheitsausfallversicherung; ~ **laws** Gesetzgebung auf dem Gebiet des Gesundheitswesens; ~ **officer** Beamter des Gesundheitsamts; ~ **professional** Arzt; ~ **service** staatlicher Gesundheitsdienst; **bill of** ~ → *bill of health*; **Board of H**~ Gesundheitsamt; **mental** ~ geistige Gesundheit, psychische Verfassung; **Minister of H**~ Gesundheitsminister; **National H~Service** *GB* staatlicher Gesundheitsdienst; **physical** ~ körperl Gesundheit; **public** ~ → *public*; **sound** ~ einwandfreier Gesundheitszustand.

healthy gesund, nicht krankheitsanfällig.

hear|a case → *case*; ~ **evidence** → *evidence*; ~ **the parties** den Parteien Gelegenheit zur Stellungnahme geben.

heard and finally determined verhandelt und durch Endentscheidung erledigt.

hearing Anhörung *f*; Gerichtssitzung *f*, mündliche Verhandlung *f*, Sitzung *f* in der Hauptverhandlung, Vernehmung *f*, Untersuchung *f*; ~ **in camera** Sitzung unter Ausschluß der Öffentlichkeit; Sitzung im Richterzimmer; Zimmertermin; ~ **in public** öffentliche Anhörung; ~ **in presence** *scot* Plenarsitzung e–s oberen Gerichts; ~ **of evidence** Beweisaufnahme; ~ **of complaint** mündl Verhandlung vor dem Amtsrichter; ~ **of such application** Verhandlung über den Antrag; ~ **of witness** Zeugenvernehmung; **adjudicatory** ~ Anhörung im Widerspruchsverfahren, Anhörung vor e–r Behörde mit Entscheidungsbefugnis; **administrative** ~ verwaltungsgerichtliche Verhandlung; behördliche Anhörung; **adversary** ~ streitige Verhandlung; **congressional** ~ öffentliche Ausschußsitzung des US Abgeordnetenhauses (*mit Vernehmung der Auskunftspersonen*); **expedited** ~ vorgezogener Termin; **fair** ~ rechtliches Gehör, gerechte Verhandlungsführung; **final** ~ letzte Schlußverhandlung; **full** ~ (volles) rechtliches Gehör; **inter partes** ~ Verhandlung in Anwesenheit beider Parteien, kontradiktorische Verh.; **omnibus** ~ allgemeine Anhörung; **opening of the** ~ Eröffnung der Sitzung; **original** ~ mündl Verhandlung erster Instanz; **preliminary** ~ Voruntersuchung; **public** ~ öffentliche Verhandlung, öffentl Anhörung.

hearsay Hörensagen *n*, Aussage *f* über Äußerungen Dritter; ~ **evidence** → *evidence*; ~ **rule** Nichtzulassung von Aussagen über Äußerungen Dritter.

hebdomad Woche *f* (*Zeitraum von 7 Tagen*).
hebdomadal wöchentlich.
heckle durch Zwischenrufe provozieren.
heckler Zwischenrufer *m*, bösartiger Fragesteller *m*.
hedge *s* Hecke *f*; *exch* Sicherungsgeschäft *n*; Kauf *m* gekoppelt an Termingeschäft zur Absicherung (*Warenbörse*); **~-bote** Holzentnahmerecht des Pächters; **~ buying** Dekkungskauf; **~ clause** Vorbehaltsklausel, Schutzklausel *zB von Maklern (keine Gewähr für Richtigkeit)*; **~ lawyer** Winkeladvokat; **~ marriage** heimliche Ehe; **~-priest** nicht akademisch gebildeter Ordenspriester (*Irland*); **~ selling** Deckungsverkauf.
hedge *v* sich nicht festlegen wollen; **~d in by clauses** verklausuliert.
hedging Abschluß *m* von Deckungsgeschäften, Kurssicherungsgeschäft *n*; **~ principle** Grundsatz der Fristenkongruenz; **~ sale** → *sale*.
heedless unachtsam, fahrlässig.
heedlessness Unachtsamkeit *f*, Fahrlässigkeit *f*.
heeler Lakai *m*, Schmarotzer *m*, Nachläufer *m*.
hegemony Hegemonie *f*, Vorherrschaft *f*.
heinous verabscheuungswürdig; **~ crime** verabscheuungswürdiges Verbrechen, Gewaltverbrechen.
heir Erbe *m* (= *E bzw e*), *ursprüngl* gesetzlicher Erbe des Grundvermögens; **~s and assigns** Rechtsnachfolger, Erwerber, gesetzliche Erben, die Treuhandsberechtigten des Nachlasses; **~s and successors** Leibeserben; **~ apparent** der nächste Erbanwärter; **~ at law** gesetzlicher *E*; **~ beneficiary** beschränkt haftbarer *E* (*nach Inventarerrichtung*); **~ by adoption** Adoptiverbe; **~ by custom** *brit E* entsprechend dem Ortsgebrauch; **~ by devise** Testamentserbe; **~ collateral** *E* in der Seitenlinie; **~ conventional** Vertragserbe; **~ female** Erbin, Erbanwärterin; **~ general** gesetzlicher *E* (*des unbeweglichen Nachlasses*); **~ hunter** Ermittler von (*fehlenden*) Erben; **~ in expectancy** Erbschaftsanwärter; **~ in mobilibus** Mobiliarerbe; **~ in tail** Vorerbe; **~ to personal** estate Mobiliarerbe; **~ institute** *scot* Testamentserbe; durch letztwillige Verfügung eingesetzter *E*; **~s male of the body** männliche Abkömmlinge als Erbanwärter; **~ of conquest** Immobiliarerbe vom nichtberechtigten Erblasser; **~ of line** *E* in gerader Linie (*erster Ordnung*); **~ of provision** letztwillig eingesetzter *E*; **~ of tailzie** *E* außerhalb der erbberechtigten Abkömmlinge; **~ of the blood** *E* auf Grund der Verwandtschaft; **~s of the body** leibliche *E–n*; **~ presumptive** mutmaßlicher Erbe; **~ special** *Fideikommißerbe, der den Nachlaß als Schenkung beansprucht*; **~ testamentary** testamentarischer *E*; **~ to personal estate** Mobiliarerbe; **~ unconditional** vorbehaltloser *E*; **apparent ~** = **~** *apparent qv*; **bodily ~s** leibliche *E–n*; **community of ~s** → *community*; **contractual ~** durch Erbvertrag eingesetzter *E*, Vertragse*e*; **expectant ~** Erbanwärter; **fiduciary ~** treuhänderischer Zwischen*e*; **final ~** Nacherbe; **forced ~** Pflichtteilsberechtigter; **his male ~ forever** der erstgeborene männliche *E* und zukünftig jeweils dessen erstgeborener männlicher *E*; **instituted ~** eingesetzter *E*, Testamentserbe; **irregular ~** außerordentlicher *E* (*durch gesetzliche Bestimmung berufener Erbe, nicht vom Erblasser abstammender E*); **joint ~s** Mit*e–n*; **lapse of an ~** Wegfall e–s *E–n*; **lawful ~s** rechtmäßige *E–n* (*die Abkömmlinge sind*); **legal ~** gesetzlicher *E* (*im Sinne des kontinentalen Rechts*); **legitimate ~s** *legitime E–n (eheliche Kinder, bzw Erben ehelicher Kinder)*; **limited ~** nicht befreiter Vorerbe; **living ~s** lebende Erbberechtigte; **male ~** männlicher *E*, nächster männlicher Erbberechtigter; **natural ~s** *E–n*, die mit

dem Erblasser in gerader Linie verwandt sind; **presumptive** ~ = *E*anwärter, vermutlicher *E*; **pretermitted** ~ → *pretermit*; **provisional** ~**s** Vor*e–n*; **reversionary** ~ Nach*e*; **right** ~ rechtmäßiger *E*; **rightful** ~ rechtmäßiger *E*; **sole** ~ Alleinerbe, Universalerbe; **substitute** ~ Ersatzerbe; **substitution of an** ~ → *substitution*; **substitutional** ~ Ersatz*e*; **testamentary** ~ testamentarischer *E*; **true** ~ rechtmäßiger *E*; **universal** ~ Alleinerbe, Universalerbe.

heirdom Erbfolge *f*.

heiress Erbin *f*.

heirless ohne Erben, erbenlos.

heirloom Hausrat und Zubehör zum Immobiliarnachlaß.

heirship Erbeneigenschaft *f*, Erbrecht *n*; ~ **movables** Zubehör des Immobiliarnachlasses.

held entschieden, erkannt, das Gericht entschied wie folgt; ~ **covered** Deckungsbestätigung (*betr Transportgüter*); ~ **for damages** schadensersatzpflichtig; ~ **in trust** in Treuhandsbesitz.

helpline Notruf *m*.

Helsinki Final Act Helsinki Schlußakte *f*.

henceforth in Zukunft, von nun an, künftig.

henchman Gefolgsmann *m*, Anhänger *m*, Konsorte *m*.

heptarchy Heptarchie *f*, Siebenherrschaft *f*, Bund *m* von 7 Staaten; *die 7 angelsächsischen Königreiche in England*.

Heralds' College Heroldsamt *n* (*königl Behörde für Adelsgenealogie und Wappenführung*).

heraldry Heraldik *f*, Wappenkunde *f*, heraldische Symbole *n|pl*, *hist Kauf von Vorrang der Reihenfolge für Gerichtsverhandlungen*.

herbage Weiderecht *n*, Dienstbarkeit *f* e–s Weiderechts.

herbenger königlicher Quartiermacher *m*.

herding Viehhüten *n*, Rinderzucht *f*.

here-and-there contract *Geldwechselgeschäft bei Zug um Zug Zahlung an verschiedenen Orten*.

hereafter nachstehend, zukünftig; ~ **to be begotten** die zukünftigen Abkömmlinge.

hereby hiermit, hierdurch.

hereditability Erblichkeit *f*.

hereditable vererblich.

hereditaments *gesetzl vererbbare* Vermögensgegenstände *m|pl* (*GB, bis 1925*); Immobiliargüter; dingliche Rechte *n|pl* am Grundstück, Erbgut *n*; **corporeal** ~ unbewegliche Vermögensgegenstände, Immobiliargüter; Liegenschaften; **incorporeal** ~ Grundstücksnebenrechte, Rechte des jeweiligen Grundstückseigentümers.

hereditariness Vererblichkeit *f*.

hereditary vererbbar, vererblich, erblich, ererbt, Erb . . .

herein hierin, in dieser Urkunde; ~ **before** vorstehend; ~ **before contained** im Vorstehenden enthalten; ~ **before mentioned** oben erwähnt; ~ **contained** in dieser Urkunde enthalten, in diesem Paragraphen enthalten; ~ **specified** in dieser Urkunde näher bezeichnet.

hereinafter nachstehend.

heretobefore vordem, ehemals, früher, in der Vergangenheit.

hereunder auf Grund dieser Vorschrift, hierunter fallend.

herewith hiermit, hierdurch.

heriot Naturalabgabe *f* an den Lehnsherrn beim Tode des Erbpächters; Geldzahlung aus gleichem Anlaß.

heritable vererblich, erblich.

heritage Erbe *n*, unbewegliches Vermögen *n*; ererbtes Kulturgut *n*; **National H**~ Landeskulturerbe *n*.

hermeneutics Hermeneutik *f*, Auslegungskunst *f*, Auslegungswissenschaft *f*; **legal** ~**s** juristische Auslegungsgrundsätze.

herring silver Ablösungszahlung *f* für Heringslieferung (*als Naturalabgabe an Kirche oder Kloster*).

hesitate zögern, Bedenken haben, unschlüssig sein.

hesitation Zögern *n*, Zurückhaltung *f*; **without** ~ ohne Bedenken.
heurematic law juristische Auslegungskunst *f*.
hiatus Bruch *m*, Lücke *f*; ~ **in diplomatic communications** Unterbrechung der diplomatischen Kommunikationen.
hide of land *hist* Landmaß *von 60–100 acres*.
hierarchy Hierarchie *f*, Kirchenhierarchie *f*.
higgle feilschen, aushandeln.
high hoch; berauscht (*Suchtstoffe*); **H~ Authority** Hohe Behörde (*Montanunion*); **H~ Church** → *church*; ~ **class investment** erstklassige Anlage; ~ **command** Oberkommando; **H~ Commission** Hohe Kommission; **H~ Commission Court** = *Court of H~ Commission* → *court*; ~ **commissioner** Hochkommissar; **H~ Court** = *High Court of Justice* → *court*; **H~ Court of Chancery** = *Court of Chancery qv*; **H~ Court of Delegates** = *Court of Delegates qv*; **H~ Court of Justice** → *court*; **H~ Court of Justiciary** → *court*; **H~ Court of Parliament** *das gesamte britische Parlament als Gericht; der Justizausschuß des Oberhauses als Revisionsgericht*; ~ **degree of care and diligence** Sorgfaltspflicht; ~ **fliers** extrem gestiegene Aktien; ~ **pressure salesmanship** aggressive Verkaufsmethoden; ~ **priced** hochstehend (Kurs); ~ **speed line** Schnellstrecke; **H~ Steward** *hist Richter in Hochverratssachen von Adligen, GB vor 1948; Lord High Steward of the Royal Household qv; Richter der Universität Oxford*; ~ **tension electricity pylon** Hochspannungsmast.
highbinder Erpresser *m*, Rowdie *m*.
highflyer agressiver Spekulant *m*.
highschool *US:* höhere Schule, Mittelschule *f*; **technical** ~ höhere technische Fachschule.
highway Fernverkehrsstraße *f*, Landstraße *f*; ~**s** öffentliche Verkehrswege *m|pl* (*einschließlich Bahn- und Wasserweg*); ~ **acts** Straßenbau- und Straßenunterhaltsgesetze; ~ **authorities** Straßenbehörde; ~ **board** Straßenbauamt; **H~ Code** amtliche Straßenverkehrsregeln; ~ **crossing** Kreuzung von Bahn und Straße; ~ **laws** = ~ *acts qv*; ~ **median** Mittelstreifen; ~ **offences** Straßenverkehrsdelikte; ~ **rate** Straßenunterhaltsabgabe (*von Grundbesitzern*); ~ **robbery** → *robbery*; ~ **tax** Straßenbausteuer; ~ **toll** Verkehrsunfallziffer; **Commissioners of H~s** Straßenbauamt; Straßenbehörde; **common** ~ Landstraße; **express** ~ Schnellverkehrsstraße, Autobahn; **favo(u)red** ~ vorfahrtsberechtigte Straße; **maintenance of ~s** Straßenunterhalt; **public** ~ Landstraße, öffentlicher Verkehrsweg.
highwayman Straßenräuber *m*.
hijacker (= *high-jacker*) Straßenräuber, Flugzeugentführer *m*.
hijacking Luftpiraterei *f*; Flugzeugentführung *f*; Fahrzeugentführung *f*, Piraterie *f*; **H~ Act** Gesetz gegen Flugzeugentführung *GB 1971*.
Hilary|Rules *brit prozeßrechtliche Vorschriften von 1834*; ~ **sittings** *Gerichtstermine in der Zeit vom 11. Januar bis Mittwoch vor Ostern*; ~ **term** Gerichtszeit im Winter = ~ *sittings qv*; Sitzungsperiode vom 11. Jan. bis Mittw. vor Ostern.
hinder and delay (versuchte) Vollstreckungsvereitelung begehen.
hindermost ganz hinten.
hindrance Behinderung *f*.
hinterland = das Landesinnere (*e–s unzivilisierten Festlandes*).
hipflask defence Berufung auf den Nachtrunk.
hire *s* Mietzins *m für bewegliche Sachen*; Lohn *m*, Mietvertrag *m*; über bewegl Sachen, Schiffsmiete *f*, Chartervergütung *f*; Lohnarbeitsvertrag *m*; Geschäftsbesorgungsvertrag *m*; ~**-car** Mietwagen; ~ **depot** Geräteverleihstation; **for ~ or gain** gewerblich; **for ~ or reward** entgeltlich.
hire *v* mieten, anheuern, als Lohnarbeiter einstellen; ~ **a murderer** e–n

Mörder dingen; ~ **a sailor** e–n Matrosen anheuern; ~ **an attorney** sich e–n Anwalt nehmen; ~**d man** *landwirtschaftlicher* Lohnarbeiter, Knecht.

hireling Söldner *m*, Mietling *m*.

hireman Untertan *m*.

hire purchase Abzahlungsgeschäft *n*, Kaufmiete *f*, Mietkauf *m*, Vorbehaltskauf.

hire-purchase|agreement Kaufmietvertrag; Ratenkaufvertrag; ~ **finance house** Kundenkreditbank, Abzahlungsfinanzierungsgesellschaft; ~ **transaction** Abzahlungsgeschäft.

hirer Mieter *m*, Dienstherr *m*, Arbeitgeber *m* von Gelegenheitsarbeiten.

hiring Mieten *n* von bewegl Sachen, Einstellung *f* von Personal; ~ **at will** Einstellung von Arbeitskräften auf unbestimmte Zeit; ~ **charge** Mietgebühr; ~ **fair** *hist* Markt zur Verdingung von Arbeitskräften; ~ **freeze** Einstellungsstop; ~ **hall** Stellenvermittlung; ~ **of a thing for use** Mobiliarmiete; ~ **of care and attention** Geschäftsbesorgungsvertrag; ~ **out** Vermietung.

his testibus in Gegenwart dieser Zeugen.

historical bays *Buchten f/pl, die gewohnheitsrechtlich als Hoheitsgewässer gelten.*

history|of law Rechtsgeschichte *f*; **legal** ~ Rechtsgeschichte.

hit and run driver Unfallflucht begehender Kraftfahrer.

hitherto bisher, bisherig, rückliegend.

hive-down Abschütteln der Verbindlichkeiten durch Einbringen der Masseaktiva in Firma gegen deren Aktien.

hive-off Absonderung u Aufkauf von Tochterfirmen; Funktionsabspaltung.

hoarding *s* (*1*) Hortung *f*, Hamstern *n*, Thesaurierung *f*; ~ **of money** Geldhortung; ~ **purchases** Hamsterkäufe.

hoarding *s* (*2*) Bauzaun *m*, Schutzwand *f*; **advertisement** ~ Reklamewand, Werbefläche *f*; Plakatwand.

hock *s* Pfand *n*; **in** ~ verschuldet, verpfändet; im Kittchen.

hock *vt* verpfänden, ins Leihhaus bringen.

hocus *v* (*Getränke*) fälschen, betrügen.

hodge-podge act Gesetz *n, das ein Sammelsurium beinhaltet,* Sammelgesetz *n*.

hogshead Oxhoft *n altes Flüssigkeitenmaß n für Wein*; *Oxhoftfass.*

hold halten, festhalten, besitzen, innehaben; bekleiden (*Amt*); erachten, halten für, schätzen, für Recht erkennen; ~ **a brief** vor Gericht vertreten, als Anwalt auftreten; ~ **a conference** e–e Besprechung abhalten; ~ **a meeting** tagen, e–e Sitzung abhalten; ~ **an accused on unstated charge** → *charge*; ~ **an office** ein Amt bekleiden; ~ **court** Gerichtsverhandlung abhalten; ~ **good** in Kraft bleiben, (noch) gelten, zutreffen; ~ **harmless** schadlos halten; ~ **in one's own right** aus eigenem Recht besitzen; ~ **in safe custody** verwahren; ~ **on lease** als Pächter besitzen; ~ **on trust** treuhänderisch besitzen; ~ **out** den Anschein geben, den Rechtsschein dulden; ~*ing oneself out as a partner: sich als Partner gerieren;* ~ **over** Mietsache nicht zurückgeben; nach Mietvertragsende besitzen; noch nach Beendigung der Amtszeit amtieren; ~ **pleas** vor Gericht verhandeln; ~ **possession** besitzen; ~ **responsible** verantwortlich machen; ~ **shares** Aktien besitzen, Aktionär sein; ~ **s.o. for murder** jmdn wegen Mordverdachts in Haft halten; ~ **the market** Stützungsaktion unternehmen; ~ **the purse** Kassenführer sein.

holder Inhaber *m*, Wechselinhaber *m*; Besitzer *m*; Pächter *m*; ~ **for the time being** der jeweilige Inhaber; ~ **for value** Wechselinhaber aufgrund entgeltlicher Übertragung; ~ **for value without notice** gutgläubiger rechtmäßiger Wechselinhaber; ~ **in due course** rechtmäßiger (*wertpapierrechtlich legitimierter*) Wechselinhaber bzw Scheckinhaber, wertpapiermäßig berechtigter gutgläubiger Inhaber; ~ **in good faith** gutgläubiger Inhaber *bzw* Empfänger; ~ **of a bill of exchange** Präsentierer, Inhaber e–s Wechsels; ~ **of a conditional purchase** Landbesitzer unter Vorbehaltskauf; ~ **of a licence** Konzessionsinhaber, Lizenznehmer; ~ **of a pension** Rentenempfänger, Rentenberechtigter; ~ **of a power of attorney** Inhaber e–r Vollmacht; ~ **of a right** Rechtsinhaber, Berechtigter; ~ **of an account** Kontoinhaber; ~ **of an annuity** Rentenberechtigter, Rentenempfänger; ~ **of order for goods** Auftragnehmer, Warenlieferant; ~ **of pledged property** Pfandnehmer; **actual** ~ gegenwärtiger Inhaber; **bona fide** ~ = ~ *in good faith qv*; **debenture** ~ → *debenture*; **former** ~ ursprünglicher Inhaber; **joint** ~**s** gemeinsame Wertpapierberechtigte; Miteigentümer, Mitbesitzer; **lawful** ~ rechtmäßiger Besitzer, legitimierter Inhaber; **legal** ~ rechtmäßiger Inhaber; **onerous** ~ Inhaber auf Grund e–r entgeltlichen Übertragung; **patent** ~ → *patent*; **policy** ~ → *policy* (*1*); **previous** ~ Vorbesitzer, Vordermann; **registered** ~ eingetragener Inhaber; **small** ~ Kleinpächter, Kleinbauer; Kleinaktionär; **sole** ~ Alleininhaber; **third** ~ Drittbesitzer; **true** ~ rechtmäßiger Inhaber.

holding Halten *n*, Besitzen *n*; landwirtschaftl Pachtbesitz *m*, Mietsache *n*, Anwesen *n*; Lehensbesitz *m*, Beteiligung *f*, Anteilsbesitz *m*, Kapitalbesitz *m*, Gerichtsentscheidung *f*; ~ **of the court** Gerichtsentscheidung; ~ **period** Besitzdauer; **agricultural** ~ landwirtschaftlicher Pachtbesitz, landwirtschaftlicher Betrieb, Bauernhof; **base** ~ nachgeordneter (*mittelbarer*) Pachtbesitz; **bill** ~**s** Wechselbestand, Wechselportefeuille; **collateral** ~**s** Lombardbestand; **foreign** ~**s** Auslandsbesitz; **monetary** ~ Geldbestand; **net** ~**s** Nettobestände, Nettoguthaben; **permanent** ~**s** Daueranlagen; **small** ~ landwirtschaftlicher Kleinbetrieb, Kleinbauernpacht.

holding company Holdinggesellschaft *f*, Dachgesellschaft *f*; **registered** ~ registrierte Holdinggesellschaft (*US Securities and Exchange Comm. Offenlegungspflichten*).

holding out Anscheinserweckung *f*; Ursprungstäuschung *f*.

holding over Verschiebung *f*; Wohnenbleiben nach Vertragsablauf.

holiday (kirchlicher) Feiertag *m*; Urlaub *m*, Ferien *pl*; ~ **entitlement** Urlaubsanspruch; ~ **lettings** Vermietung von Ferienwohnungen; ~**-maker** Urlauber; ~ **remuneration** Urlaubsvergütung; ~**s with pay** bezahlter Urlaub; **bank** ~ Bankfeiertag *GB* (*Engl* + *Wales*): *Ostermontag; der letzte Montag im Mai; der letzte Montag im August; 26. 12., außer wenn ein Sonntag,* dann der *27. 12.; Neujahrstag*; ~~ *break: arbeitsfreier Werktag vor e–m Bankfeiertag ua*; **legal** ~ gesetzlicher Feiertag; **national** ~ Staatsfeiertag, gesetzl geschützter Feiertag; ein zum Feiertag erklärter Tag; **public** ~ gesetzlicher Feiertag; **spoilt** ~ vertaner Urlaub.

holograph *adj* holographisch, handgeschrieben; *s* eigenhändig geschriebene Urkunde *f*, eigenhändiges (holographisches) Testament *n*.

homage Huldigung *f*, Ehrerbietung *f*; ~ **ancestral** originäres Lehen; ~ **jury** *Geschworene, die Lehensleute des gleichen Herrn sind.*

homager Lehensmann *m*, Vasall *m*.

home Heim *n*, Haus *n*, Wohnung *f*, Heimat *f*; ständiger Wohnort *m*, Aufenthaltsort *m*, Asyl *n*; ~ **address** → *address*; ~ **affairs** innere Angelegenheiten; ~ **beat police officers** Streifendienstpolizisten in Wohngebieten; ~ **bound** auf der Rückreise, auf dem Rückflug; ~

building and loan association Bausparkasse; ~ **buyer** Eigenheimkäufer; ~ **club cooperative appartment houses** Mehrfamilienhäuser von Baugenossenschaften; ~**s connected** (*an das KabelTV*) angeschlossene Haushalte; **H~ Counties** → *county*; ~ **country** Heimatland; ~ **currency** Landeswährung, Binnenwährung; ~ **defence** Landesverteidigung; ~ **demand** → *demand*; ~ **description** → *description*; ~ **economics** Hauswirtschaftslehre; ~**-equity loan** Eigenheimdarlehen auf 2. Hypothek; zweitstelliges Hypothekendarlehen; ~ **financing** Wohnungsbaufinanzierung; ~ **forces** Inlandsstreitkräfte; ~ **for the aged** Altenwohnheim; ~ **freight** → *freight*; **H~ Guard** Miliz, Bürgerwehr; ~ **improvement grant** Zuschuß zu Eigenheim-Investitionen; ~ **industry** einheimische Industrie, Heimindustrie; ~ **lot** Hausgrundstück e–s Landwirtschaftsbetriebes; ~ **loss** Verlust des eigenen Wohnhauses durch Enteignung; ~**-made** inländisch; ~ **manufacture** → *manufacture*; ~ **market** Inlandsmarkt; ~ **mortgage** *nachrangige* Eigenheimshypothek; ~ **mortgage loan** Hypothekendarlehen auf Wohngrundstück(e) in Eigenbesitz; **H~ Office** *GB* Innenministerium; ~ **owner** Hausbesitzer; ~ **ownership** Eigenheimbesitz; ~ **producer** Inlandserzeuger; ~ **requirements** Inlandsbedarf, eigener Bedarf; ~ **remedy makers** Drogerieartikel-Hersteller; ~ **rule** Selbstverwaltung, Autonomie; **H~ Secretary** Innenminister (*England u Wales*); ~ **securities** inländische Wertpapiere; ~ **state** Heimatstaat, Staat des Sitzes e–r Körperschaft; ~ **trade** Binnenhandel; ~ **trade ship** Küsten- und Nahverkehrsschiff; ~ **value** Inlandswert; ~ **work** Heimarbeit; **mental nursing** ~ Pflegeheim für geistig Behinderte; **nursing** ~ Pflegeheim; **principal** ~ Hauptwohnsitz; **residential** ~ Alters- u Behindertenwohnheim; **to set up** ~ gemeinsam zu wohnen anfangen; e–e Wohngemeinschaft bilden; **voluntary** ~**s** durch Spenden unterhaltene Jugendheime.

homeland Heimatland *n*; autonomes Siedlungsgebiet (*Südafrika*).

homeless obdachlos.

homelessness Obdachlosigkeit *f*.

homestall Wohnhaus *n* e–s landwirtschaftlichen Anwesens.

homestead Heimstätte *f*, Siedlungshof *m*, *pfändungsfreies, eigenbewirtschaftetes* landwirtschaftliches Anwesen *n*; ~**-aid benefit association** Heimstätten-Genossenschaft; ~ **corporation** gemeinnützige Siedlungsgesellschaft; ~ **entry** Geltendmachung e–r Anwartschaft auf Siedlungsland; ~ **exemption** Vollstreckungsschutz für Heimstätten; ~ **(exemption) laws** Gesetze über Vollstreckungsschutz von Heimstätten; ~ **right** → *right*; **business** ~ eigengenütztes gewerbliches Anwesen (*pfändungsfrei*); **probate** ~ → *probate*; **rural** ~ landwirtschaftliche (*unter Vollstreckungsschutz stehende*) Heimstätte; **urban** ~ städtische (*unter Vollstreckungsschutz stehende*) Heimstätte.

homesteader Siedler *m*, Kleinbauer *m*.

homesteading Wohnsiedlungsbildung.

homeward freight Rückfracht *f*, Rückladung *f*.

homeworker Heimarbeiter *m*.

homicidal die Tötung eines Menschen betreffend; ~ **attempt** Totschlagsversuch; Mordversuch.

homicide Tötung *f* (*e–s Menschen*); ~ **by misadventure** Tötung als zufällige Folge e–s rechtmäßigen Tuns; schuldlose Tötung als zufälliges Ereignis, Unfall mit Todesfolge; ~ **by necessity** rechtlich zulässige, notwendige Tötung; ~ **per infortunium** = ~ *by misadventure qv*; ~ **se defendendo** Tötung aus Notwehr; ~ **squad** → *squad*; ~ **through carelessness** fahrlässige Tötung; **casual** ~ *scot* schuldlose zufällige Tötung; **criminal** ~ Tötungsverbrechen, strafbare Tötung; **culpable** ~ Tötungsdelikt, Totschlag; **excusable** ~ gerechtfertigte *bzw* entschuldbare Tötung; **excusable** ~ **by misadventure** entschuldbare zufällige Tötung; **felonious** ~ Tötungsverbrechen; Mord *bzw* Totschlag; **involuntary** ~ ungewollte Tötung, fahrlässige Tötung; **justifiable** ~ Tötung bei Vorliegen e–s Rechtfertigungsgrundes; **lawful** ~ rechtmäßige Tötung, entschuldbare Tötung; **negligent** ~ fahrlässige Tötung; **unintentional** ~ unbeabsichtigte Tötung; **wilful** ~ vorsätzliche Tötung.

homologate homologieren, bestätigen, ratifizieren, beglaubigen.

homologation Bestätigung *f*, Genehmigung *f*, gerichtliche Bestätigung *f*, Beglaubigung *f*.

homologize homologieren, zur Übereinstimmung bringen.

homology Homologie *f*, Übereinstimmung *f*.

honesty Ehrlichkeit *f*; ~ **box** Kasten für freiwillige Zolldeklaration.

hono(u)r *s* Ehre *f*, Auszeichnung *f*, von der Krone verliehenes Adelsprädikat *n*, Lehensherrschaftsbereich *m*; Ordensverleihung *f*, Ehrenbezeigung *f*; ~ **courts** → *court*; **acceptance for** ~ → *acceptance*; **affair of** ~ Ehrenhändel; **award of** ~**s** → *award*; **code of** ~ Ehrenkodex; **court of** ~ → *court*; **debt of** ~ → *debt*; **declaration of** ~ ehrenwörtliche Erklärung; **office of** ~ Ehrenamt; **payment for** ~ → *payment*; **professional** ~ Berufsehre; **word of** ~ → *word*; **your H**~ Euer Gnaden; hohes Gericht!

hono(u)r *v* honorieren, akzeptieren, einlösen, bei Fälligkeit bezahlen, e–e Ehrenannahme vornehmen.

hono(u)rable ehrenvoll, ehrenwert, ehrbar; *Anrede für Parlamentsabgeordnete und Nachkommen des Hochadels; Höflichkeitsbezeichnung für Richter (bes USA)*; ~ **acquittal** Freispruch mit Ehrenerklärung (*Kriegsgericht*); ~ **discharge** ehrenhafte Entlassung; ~ **mention** ehrenvolle Erwähnung; ~ **understanding** Absprache, *deren Einhaltung Ehrensache ist*; **my** ~ **friend** mein Fraktionskollege; **the** ~ **member** der (Herr) Abgeordnete (*meist der Gegenfraktion*).

honorarium Honorar, Ehrenzuwendung *f*; ~ **clause** ehrenwörtliche Bestimmung.

honorary ehrenamtlich, ehrenvoll, unentgeltlich; ~ **and vital interests** *Vorbehalt, Ehrenangelegenheiten und lebenswichtige Interessen nicht vor den Internationalen Schiedsgerichtshof zu bringen*; ~ **appointment** Ehrenamt; ~ **canons** kirchlicher Würdenträger ohne Pfründenberechtigung; ~ **consul** → *consul*; ~ **degree** ehrenhalber verliehener akademischer Grad; ~ **doctor** Doktor h. c.; ~ **feuds** *Adelstitel, die auf den erstgeborenen Sohn übergehen*; ~ **freedom** Ehrenbürgerrecht; ~ **freemen** Ehrenbürger *pl*; ~ **member** Ehrenmitglied; ~ **office** → *office*; ~ **president** Ehrenvorsitzender; ~ **services** feudale Ehrenpflichten; ~ **title** ehrenhalber verliehener Titel; ~ **trustees** ehrenamtliche Treuhänder; **in an** ~ **capacity** ehrenamtlich.

hookland jährlich bebautes Ackerland *n*.

hooliganism Rowdytum *n*.

hootch Fusel *m* illegal (schwarz) hergestellter Branntwein *m*.

hope hoffen, die Hoffnung aussprechen (*treuhänderische Wirkung in Testamenten*).

horizontal property acts Wohnungseigentums- und Wohnungsgenossenschaftsgesetze.

hornbook law elementares Recht *n*, rudimentäre Rechtskenntnisse *f/pl*.

horning = *letters of* ~ → *letter*.

hornswoggle triumphieren über, überwältigen, schikanieren.

hors| de la loi geächtet; ~ **de son fee** nicht unter sein Lehen fallend (*als Einwendung*).

hortatory ermahnend, mahnend.

horticulture Gartenbau *m*.
hospital Krankenhaus *n*, Lazarett *n*; ~ **cost containment** Krankenhauskostendämpfung; ~ **order** Einweisungsverfügung in geschlossene Anstalt; ~ **ship** Lazarettschiff; **mental** ~ Nervenklinik, psychiatrisches Krankenhaus, Heil- und Pflegeanstalt; **public** ~ Krankenanstalt; gemeinnütziges (Stiftungs-)Krankenhaus; **special** ~ geschlossene Krankenanstalt, Krankenanstalt e–r Haftanstalt; **teaching** ~ Lehrkrankenhaus.
hospitalization stationäre Krankenhausbehandlung *f*; ~ **insurance** Versicherung für stationäre Krankenhausbehandlung.
hospiticide Mord *m* am Gast *bzw* Gastgeber.
host Gastgeber *m*, Hausherr *m*, Wirt *m*; ~ **country** Gastland; ~ **state** Gastland.
hostage Geisel *f*; **~-for-prisoner deal** Geiseltausch gegen Inhaftierte; **taking of ~s** Geiselnahme.
hostel Heim *n*, Herberge *f*.
hostile feindlich, feindselig, Feind . . .
hostilit|y Feindseligkeit *f*; **~ies** Kampfhandlungen, Kriegsführung; **active ~ies** Kampfhandlungen; **cessation of ~ies** → *cessation*.
hotchpot Vermischung *f* von Vermögensrechten; Einbeziehung *f* von Vorausempfängen bei Erbauseinandersetzungen; ~ **duty** (= ~ *liability*) Recht auf Ausgleichung, Ausgleichspflicht; **to put in** ~ e–e Ausgleichung vornehmen.
hotel Hotel *n*, Gasthof *m*; ~ **industry** Beherbergungsgewerbe; **~-keeper** Hotelbesitzer, Hotelier, Gastwirt; ~ **proprietor** Hotelbesitzer (*Eigentümer, auch Pächter*).
hour Stunde *f*; **~s of attendance** Anwesenheitszeit, Bürostunden, Sprechstunden; ~ **of cause** *scot* Terminstunde; **~s of darkness** Dunkelheit (*½ Std. nach Sonnenuntergang bis ½ Std. vor Sonnenaufgang*); **~s of duty** Dienstzeit; **~s of labor** gesetzl Arbeitszeit (*US*); **authorized ~s** Amtsstunden; **business ~s** Dienstzeit; Geschäftsstunden; **chargeable ~s** gebührenpflichtige Arbeitsstunden (*Stundenhonorar*); **closing** ~ Ladenschlußzeit; **man** ~ → *man*; **office ~s** Dienstzeit, Amtsstunden, Bürozeit; **official ~s** = *office ~ qv*; **reasonable ~ for presentment** Vorlage, die nicht zur Unzeit erfolgt; **rush** ~ Stoßzeit; **stock exchange ~s** Börsenstunden.
hourly stündlich, stundenweise, fortwährend; ~ **expense rate** Stundensatz (*des Anwalts*); ~ **rate** Stundentarif; ~ **wage** Stundenlohn.
house Haus *n*, Anwesen *n*, Wohnhaus *n*; Handelsfirma *f*; Börse *f*, *parl* Kammer *f*; **The House** *GB*: das Unterhaus; die (Londoner) Börse; *US*: das Abgeordnetenhaus; ~ **agent** Makler für Wohnhäuser, Wohnungsmakler; ~ **and farm** Haus und Hof; ~ **bill** Filialwechsel, eigenes Akzept; **~-bote** Holzentnahmerecht für Hausreparaturen; ~ **bound** unter Hausarrest stehend; **~-burning** Brandstiftung (*am fremden Wohnhaus*); ~ **committee** Parlamentsausschuß; **~-duty** Steuer auf Wohnhäuser, Gebäudesteuer (*GB bis 1924*); ~ **in multiple occupation** von Einzelpersonen bewohntes Haus; ~ **jobber** Häusermakler; ~ **let in lodgings** Mietshaus; **H~ of Commons** Unterhaus; **H~ of Commons Offices Commission** *Personal- und Gehaltskommission für Bedienstete des H. of C.*; **H~ of Convocation** Synode; ~ **of correction** Arbeitshaus, Gefängnis; **H~ of Delegates** Deputiertenhaus, Unterhaus (*in US-Gliedstaaten*); ~ **of ill fame** Bordell, Stundenhotel; ~ **of issue** = *issuing ~* → *issue*; **H~ of Keys** *Unterhaus auf der Insel Man*; **H~ of Lords** Oberhaus; **H~ of Lords Offices Committee** *Personalausschuß des Oberhauses*; **H~s of Parliament** das Parlament; ~ **of refuge** Jugendgefängnis, Besse-

rungsanstalt; Obdachlosenheim; **H~ of Representatives** *US* Abgeordnetenhaus, *Unterhaus des US Congress und einzelstaatlicher Parlamente*; ~ **of worship** dem Gottesdienst gewidmetes Gebäude; ~ **owner** Hauseigentümer, Hausbesitzer; ~ **plate** Hausplakette, Hausschild; ~ **renovation grant** Hausrenovierungszuschuß; ~ **tax** Wohnhaussteuer; ~ **to** ~ **collection** Haussammlung; ~ **to** ~ **search** systematische Durchsuchung von Häusern; **ancient** ~ uraltes Wohnhaus; historischer Altbau; **bawdy** ~ Bordell; **beer** ~ → *beer*; **boarding** ~ → *boarding*; **chief** ~ Stammhaus; **clearing** ~ → *clearing*; **commission** ~ → *commission*; **controlled** ~ der Wohnraumbewirtschaftung unterliegendes Gebäude, preisgebundener Altbau; **disorderly** ~ verrufenes Haus, Bordell, Stundenhotel, Spielhölle; **dwelling** ~ Wohnhaus; **duplex** ~ Doppelhaus; **frame** ~ Holzhaus, Fachwerkhaus; **furnished** ~ möbliertes Wohnhaus; **Inner H~** → *inner*; **issuing** ~ = ~ *off issue qv*; **lewd** ~ Bordell, Haus, in dem Prostituierte verkehren; **mansion** ~ → *mansion*; **occupied** ~ bewohntes Haus; **old trading** ~ alte Firma; **originating** ~ Konsortialführerin; **Outer H~** → *outer*; **public** ~ Gastwirtschaft; **remand** ~ Jugendbewahranstalt; **sponging** ~ Schuldgefängnis; **tied** ~ brauereigebundene Gaststätte; **tippling** ~ Trinkstube, Bar.

houseage Zwischenlagergebühr *f*.

housebreaking Einbruch zur Begehung e–s Verbrechens (*GB bis 1968*); ~ **implements** Einbruchswerkzeug.

household Haushalt *m*, Familiengemeinschaft *f*; ~ **allowance** Haushaltsgeld, Wirtschaftsgeld; ~ **effects** Haushaltsgegenstände; Inhalt und Zubehör eines Wohnhauses; ~ **employees** Hausangestellte; ~ **expenses** Haushaltungskosten; ~ **furniture** Haushaltseinrichtung; ~ **furniture and effects** Hausrat und sonstige persönliche Habe; **goods** Haushaltsgegenstände, Hausrat; ~ **remedies** Gesundheitsmittel, Kosmetikartikel; ~ **servants** Hausangestellte; Schloßbedienstete; ~ **stuff** Hausrat; ~ **troops** Leibgarde; ~ **utensils and requisites** Haushaltsgeräte; **common** ~ gemeinsamer Haushalt, häusliche Gemeinschaft, Wohngemeinschaft; **head of the** ~ Haushaltsvorstand.

householder Eigenbesitzer *m* e–s Wohnhauses; Haushaltsvorstand *m*, Hausbewohner *m*; **~'s protest** *Bescheinigung der Nichteinlösung e–s Wechsels durch Mitbewohner;* **compound** ~ Haushaltsvorstand in Häusern mit mehreren Mietparteien; **single** ~ Alleinwohnender; **substantial** ~ Hausbewohner (*Mieter*).

housekeeper Haushälterin *f*, Hausmeister *m*, (*ständiger*) Hausbewohner *m*; **~'s relief** Steuerfreibetrag für eine Haushälterin.

housekeeping allowance Wirtschaftsgeld *n*, Haushaltsgeld *n*.

houseless obdachlos.

housing Wohnungswesen *n*, Wohnungsbeschaffung *f*, Wohnungsverhältnisse *n/pl*; Wohnungsbau *m*; ~ **action area** Wohnraumsanierungsgebiet; **H~ Acts** *GB* Mieterschutzgesetzgebung; ~ **allocation** Wohnungszuweisung; ~ **association** Wohnungsgenossenschaft; ~ **benefit** Wohngeld; ~ **control** Wohnungsbewirtschaftung, Wohnungszwangswirtschaft; **H~ Corporation** Aufsichtsbehörde für Bausparkassen u. Wohnungsbaugenossenschaften; ~ **credit** Wohnungsbeschaffungskredit; ~ **credit institutions** Bausparkassen; ~ **disrepair** Wohnhausverfall, Instandsetzungsbedürftigkeit von Wohnhäusern; ~ **duty** Wohnungsbeschaffungspflicht; ~ **estate** Wohnsiedlung; ~ **for rent** Mietwohnungen; ~ **list** Mietervormerkliste; ~ **problem** Wohnungsproblem; ~

shortage Wohnungsnot; ~ **starts** Wohnungsneubau; ~ **trust** gemeinnützige Wohnungsbaugesellschaft; **privately rented** ~ privat vermieteter Wohnraum; **suitable alternative** ~ geeigneter Ersatzwohnraum.

however worded gleich welchen Wortlauts.

huckster *ambulanter* Obst- und Gemüsehändler *m*, Straßenhändler *m*; Werbefachmann *m*.

hue and cry Zetergeschrei *n*; Zetermordio *n*; Fahndungsausschreibung *f*, Steckbrief *m*; **H~ and C~** Londoner Polizeibericht (*mit Steckbriefen*).

hulks Richtstätte *f*, Schiffsgefängnis *n*.

hull Rumpf *m*, Körper *m*, Hülle *f*, Schiffskörper *m*; ~ **and machinery** Kasko und Maschinen; ~ **insurance** → *insurance*; ~ **interest** → *interest* (*1*); ~ **policy** → *policy* (*1*); ~ **underwriter** Schiffskaskoversicherer.

human menschlich; ~ **engineering** Arbeitsplatzgestaltung; ~ **relations** innerbetriebliche Mitarbeiterbeziehungen; **h~ rights** Menschenrechte; ~ **rights activists** Bürgerrechtler; **H~ Rights Convention** Menschenrechtskonvention.

humanitarian doctrine *die Beweisregel der letzten Ausweichmöglichkeit bei Verkehrsunfällen*.

humanity Menschheit *f*; Menschlichkeit *f*; **crime against** ~ Verbrechen gegen die Menschlichkeit.

humbug Schwindel *m*, Täuschung *f*.

hundred Hundertschaft *f*; **H~ Court** *Grundherrschaftsgericht über das Gebiet einer Hundertschaft*; ~ **gemot** Gerichtstag der Hundertschaft; ~ **penny** Hundertschaftssteuer.

hung *adj* blockiert, nicht entscheidungsfähig.

hunting Jagd *f*; ~ **ground** Jagdrevier; ~ **licence** Jagdschein, Jagderlaubnis; ~ **season** Jagdzeit.

hurt *s* Verletzung *f*, Schaden *m*.

hurtful schädlich, nachteilig.

husband *s* Ehemann *m*, Gatte *m*; ~ **and wife** Eheleute, Eheverhältnis, Ehe; **live-in** ~ mit Ehefrau zusammenlebender Gatte.

husbandman Landwirt *m*, Bauer *m*, Landpächter *m*.

husbandry Haushaltung *f*, Ackerbau *m*, Landwirtschaft *f*, Wirtschaftlichkeit *f*, Wirtschaftsführung *f*; **alternate** ~ Wechselwirtschaft; **animal** ~ Viehzucht; **good** ~ einwandfreie Wirtschaftsführung (*e–s Agrarbetriebes*).

hush-money Schweigegeld *n*.

hush up vertuschen.

hustings Ortsgericht *n*; Rednertribüne *f*, Wahltribüne *f*.

hybrid hybrid, ungleichartig, gemischt; ~ **bill** Interessenvorlage, ungleichartige Gesetzesvorlage.

hydrostatic test hydrostatischer Versuch *m* (*zur Feststellung, ob eine Lebendgeburt vorgelegen hat*).

hygiene Hygiene *f*, Gesundheitspflege *f*, Gesundheitswesen *n*; **industrial** ~ Betriebshygiene, betrieblicher Gesundheitsschutz.

hyperinflation galoppierende Inflation *f*.

hypothec besitzloses Pfandrecht *n* am Schuldnervermögen; Schiffshypothek *f*; *engl Bezeichnung für kontinentalrechtliche Hypothek*.

hypothecary|action Hypothekenklage; ~ **value** Beleihungswert, Lombardwert.

hypothecate verpfänden, verbodmen, lombardieren.

hypothecation besitzlose Verpfändung *f*, Bodmerei *f*; ~ **bond** Bodmereischein; ~ **certificate** Verpfändungserklärung, Lombardschein; **advances against** ~ Warenlombard; **letter of** ~ → *letter*.

I

idea Idee *f*, Vorstellung *f*, Gedanke *m*, Meinung *f*; **inventive** ~ Erfindungsgedanke; **leading** ~ Grundgedanke.

idem| **per idem** lediglich zusätzlich, erläuternd; ~ **sonans** gleichlautend (*Buchstabierung nicht entscheidend*).

identifiable identifizierbar, feststellbar.

identification Identifizierung *f*, Identitätsfeststellung *f*, Erkennung *f*, Legitimation *f*; ~ **card** Personalausweis; ~ **mark** Erkennungszeichen, Nämlichkeitszeichen; ~ **measures** Maßnahmen zur Nämlichkeitssicherung; ~ **number** Kennzeichen; ~ **of goods** Konkretisierung von Waren; ~ **of witnesses** Feststellung der Personalangaben eines Zeugen; ~ **papers** Legitimationspapiere; ~ **parade** Vorführung von Verdächtigen *zum Zwekke der Identifizierung,* Wahlgegenüberstellung; ~ **words** Buchstabierungswörter (*Ida, Nordpol etc*); **assumed** ~ übernommene falsche Personalien; **to produce** ~ sich ausweisen.

identify identifizieren; ~ **oneself** sich ausweisen; ~ **oneself with** sich solidarisch erklären; ~**ing evidence** Identitätsbeweismittel.

identity Identität *f*, Gleichheit *f*, Personengleichheit *f*, Individualität *f*, Persönlichkeit *f*; Ausweis *m*, Nämlichkeit *f*; ~ **card** Personalausweis, Kennkarte; ~ **control** Ausweiskontrolle; ~ **disk** Erkennungsmarke; **mistaken** ~ Personenverwechslung, Identitätsirrtum; **of known** ~ von Person bekannt; ~ **of person** Personengleichheit.

idiot (*GB: Begriff gesetzl nicht mehr gebräuchl seit 1959*) Idiot *m*, Schwachsinniger *m*; **natural** ~ von Geburt Schwachsinniger.

idle müßig, untätig, unausgenutzt, stillstehend, unproduktiv, tot, faul, arbeitsscheu; ~ **administrative formality** überflüssige Verwaltungsformalität; ~ **and disorderly person** Müßiggänger ohne geordnete Lebensverhältnisse, arbeitsscheue, liederliche Person; ~ **plant expenses** Stillstandskosten.

if wenn, falls, vorausgesetzt daß; ~ **alive** falls (dann) noch am Leben; ~ **and as called upon** bei Anforderung, bei Abruf; ~ **and when** falls, wenn; ~ **and whenever** wenn (auch immer); ~ **any** (*nachgestellt*), falls vorhanden, eventuell, zutreffendenfalls, gegebenenfalls; ~ **from any cause whatsoever** gleich aus welchem Grund; ~ **he thinks fit** wenn er es (*nach pflichtgemäßem Ermessen*) für angebracht hält; ~ **living** falls am Leben; ~ **necessary** falls erforderlich; ~ **so** bejahendenfalls, in diesem Fall.

ignominy Schmach *f*, Schande *f*, Schimpf *m*, Niederträchtigkeit *f*.

ignorance Unkenntnis *f*, Unwissenheit *f*, Nichtwissen *n*; ~ **of fact** Nichtkenntnis tatsächlicher Umstände; ~ **of law is no defence** Unkenntnis des Gesetzes schützt vor Strafe nicht; **accidental** ~ Nichtwissen nebensächlicher Fakten; **culpable** ~ schuldhafte Unkenntnis; **essential** ~ Unkenntnis e-s wesentlichen Umstandes; **involuntary** ~ zwangsläufige Unkenntnis; **non-essential** ~ Unkenntnis unerheblicher Umstände; **voluntary** ~ schuldhafte Unkenntnis.

ignorant nichtwissend, in Unkenntnis von, unwissend, unkundig.

ignore nicht kennen, nicht beachten, ignorieren, sich weigern, etwas zur Kenntnis zu nehmen; ~ **a bill of indictment** e-e Anklage nicht zulassen.

ignoring directions Nichtbeachtung *f* von Verkehrsanweisungen; ~ **traffic signs** Nichtbeachtung von Verkehrszeichen.

ill krank; **terminally** ~ todkrank.

illegal ungesetzlich, rechtswidrig, widerrechtlich, gesetzeswidrig, verboten.

illegality Ungesetzlichkeit *f*, Rechtswidrigkeit *f*, Gesetzwidrigkeit *f*, Illegalität *f*; **tainted with** ~ mit dem Makel der Gesetzwidrigkeit behaftet.

illegitimacy Nichtehelichkeit *f*.

illegitimate unrechtmäßig, unerlaubt, nichtehelich; ~ **statement** unberechtigte Erklärung.

illeviable unpfändbar, nicht beitreibbar.

illicit unerlaubt, verboten; ~ **continuance of use** rechtswidrige Weiterbenutzung; ~ **distillery** Schwarzbrennerei; ~ **practice of a profession** unerlaubte Ausübung e–s Berufes.

illiquid unbeziffert, zahlenmäßig unbestimmt, nicht ohne weiteres zu Geld zu machen; illiquide.

illness (*schwere*) Krankheit *f*; ~ **allowance** Krankenbeihilfe; ~ **frequency rate** Krankenausfallsquote; **mental** ~ Geisteskrankheit; **occupational** ~ Berufskrankheit; **previous** ~ Altleiden.

illocable nicht plazierbar, unvermietbar.

ill-treatment Mißhandlung *f*.

illusion Illusion *f*, Fehlvorstellung *f*, Sinnestäuschung *f*.

illusory täuschend, illusorisch, lediglich pro forma; ~ **appointment** nominelle Zuordnung e–s Vermögensgegenstandes (*bei Vollmacht bzw Treuhand*).

imbalance Ungleichgewicht *n*; ~ **in payments** unausgeglichene Zahlungsbilanz; **economic** ~ wirtschaftl Ungleichgewichte; **regional ~s** regionale Unausgewogenheiten, reg. Ungleichgewichte.

imbasing of money Münzverschlechterung *f*.

imbroglio Verwirrung *f*, Streit *m*.

imitate nachahmen, nachbauen, nachbilden.

imitation Nachahmung *f*, Nachbildung *f*, täuschende Nachahmung *f*, Fälschung *f*; ~ **firearm** imitierte Schußwaffe, Scheinpistole; ~ **of trade-marks** täuschende Nachahmung von Warenzeichen; **colo(u)rable** ~ täuschend ähnliche Nachahmung, sklavische Nachahmung; **fraudulent** ~ täuschende Nachahmung; **obvious** ~ offensichtliche Nachbildung; **slavish** ~ sklavische Nachahmung.

imitator Nachahmer *m*.

immaterial immateriell, unwesentlich, unerheblich; ~ **averment** → *averment*; ~ **issue** → *issue* (*2*); ~ **variance** geringfügige Abweichung.

immediacy Unverzüglichkeit *f*.

immediate unmittelbar, augenblicklich, umgehend; ~ **or cancel order** limitierter, nur sofort ausführbarer Börsenauftrag.

immemorial unvordenklich, uralt; ~ **custom** uralter Brauch; ~ **possession** → *possession*; ~ **usage** unvordenkliche Gewohnheit; **from time** ~ seit unvordenklicher Zeit.

immigration Einwanderung *f*; ~ **authorities** Einwanderungsbehörden; ~ **laws** Einwanderungsgesetze; ~ **offender** Straffälliger nach Einwanderungsrecht; ~ **officer** Einwanderungsbeamter; ~ **quota** Einwanderungskontingent; ~ **restrictions** Einwanderungsbeschränkungen; ~ **visa** → *visa*.

imminence of danger das Vorhandensein *n* gegenwärtiger Gefahr, Gefahr *f* im Verzug.

imminency of death das unmittelbare Bevorstehen des Todes.

imminent unmittelbar, bevorstehend, drohend, gegenwärtig; ~ **danger** gegenwärtige Gefahr; ~ **dispute** unmittelbar bevorstehender Streit.

imminently dangerous article lebensgefährlicher Gegenstand *m*.

immobilization Festlegung *f*, Einfrieren *n*, Einziehung *f*; ~ **of ille-**

gally parked vehicles Blockierung widerrechtl geparkter Fahrzeuge; ~ **of liquid funds** Liquiditätsbindung.

immobilize festlegen, immobilisieren; ~**d money** festgelegte Gelder.

immoral sittenwidrig, unsittlich, unmoralisch.

immorality Sittenwidrigkeit *f*; Unsittlichkeit *f*.

immovable *adj* unbeweglich, Immobilien . . ., Immobiliar . . .; ~ **fixture** → *fixture*.

immovable *s* Gegenstand *m* des unbeweglichen Vermögens, Immobilie *f*, Grundstück *n*|*pl*: ~**s**; unbewegliche Sachen, Liegenschaften, Immobilien, Grundeigentum.

immune immun, unverletzlich, befreit; ~ **from discovery** der Geheimhaltung unterliegend, nicht offenbarungspflichtig; **to be** ~ **from legal process** nicht der Gerichtsbarkeit unterworfen sein, immun.

immunity Immunität *f*, Privileg *n*, Befreiung *f*, Sonderrecht *n*; ~ **from jurisdiction** gerichtl Immunität; ~ **from legal liability** Haftungsfreiheit; ~ **from prosecution** gerichtliche Immunität; ~ **from suit** zivilrechtliche Immunität; ~ **from taxation** Steuerfreiheit; **blanket** ~ generelle Immunitat, Amtsimmunität; **diplomatic** ~ diplomatische Immunität; **fiscal** ~ persönliche Steuerfreiheit; **foreign** ~ Immunität; **interspousal** ~ Verbot der Deliktsklage gegen Ehegatten; **judicial** ~ → *judicial*; **jurisdictional** ~ gerichtliche Immunität; Befreiung von der Gerichtsbarkeit (*des Gastlandes*); **legislative** ~ Indemnität und Immunität der Abgeordneten; **parliamentary** ~ parlamentarische Immunität; **public interest** ~ Befreiung von der Vorlagepflicht im öffentl Interesse; Geheimhaltung im öffentl Interesse; **restrictive** ~ beschränkte Staatsimmunität; **sovereign** ~ → *sovereign adj*; **state** ~ → *state*; **vicarious** ~ Haftungsausschluß für Verschulden Dritter (*Erfüllungs- bzw. Verrichtungsgehilfen*).

impact Stoßkraft *f*; Aufprall (*Unfall*); ~ **of a tax** Steuerbelastung.

impair beeinträchtigen, vermindern, schwächen, entgegenstehen; ~**ed mental power** verminderte geistige Fähigkeit; ~**ing coins** → *coin*; ~**ing the obligation of contracts** die Beeinträchtigung von vertraglichen Pflichten, Leistungsstörung.

impairment Beeinträchtigung *f*, Schädigung *f*; ~ **in value** Wertminderung; ~ **of conjugal life** Ehewidrigkeit; ~ **of contract** Verletzung der Vertragsautonomie; *US Verfassungsverbot von Eingriffen in Verträge durch Gliedstaaten*; Leistungsstörung; ~ **of earning capacity** → *earning capacity*; **permanent** ~ Dauerschaden.

impanel die Geschworenen(liste) aufstellen; ~ **a jury** die Geschworenenliste zusammenstellen.

imparl *v* besprechen; Gelegenheit zu außergerichtlichen Vergleichsverhandlungen gewähren; e–e Vertagung erreichen.

imparlance Vergleichsbesprechung, Erwiderungsfrist, Vertagung; **general** ~ Vertagung zur Vorbereitung der mündlichen Verhandlung (*nach Einlassung*); **general special** ~ *Vertagung zur Klageerwiderung unter Vorbehalt aller Einwendungen*; **special** ~ *Vertagung, bei der dem Beklagten Einwendungen gegen die Klagebegründung vorbehalten bleiben*.

impartial unparteiisch, unvoreingenommen, vorurteilslos, unbefangen; ~ **jury** unvoreingenommene Geschworene.

impartiality Unparteilichkeit *f*, Objektivität *f*.

impartible feud unteilbares, nur auf den erstgeborenen Sohn vererbliches Lehen.

impatronization Einweisung *f* in e–e Kirchenpfründe.

impeach anklagen, verklagen; bestreiten, herabsetzen, anfechten; ~ **a witness** die Glaubwürdigkeit e–s Zeugen erschüttern; ~ **an official**

Amtsanklage erheben; ~ **the trustworthiness of a witness** die Unglaubwürdigkeit e–s Zeugen dartun.

impeachable anfechtbar, anklagbar; ~ **for waste** haftbar für Substanzschäden *cf waste*.

impeachment Amtsanklage *f*, Parlamentsanklage *f*, Anfechtung *f*, Bestreiten *n*, Infragestellen *n*; ~ **action** Anfechtungsklage; ~ **of a document** Bestreiten der Echtheit e–r Urkunde; ~ **of a witness** Erschütterung der Glaubwürdigkeit e–s Zeugen (*Zweck des Beweisantritts*); ~ **of annuity** Beeinträchtigung der Ertragsfähigkeit e–s Grundstücks; ~ **of waste** Haftung des Pächters für Substanzschäden, *diesbezügliche* Schadenersatzklage; **articles of** ~ Anklageschrift (*bei Amtsanklageverfahren*); **collateral** ~ indirekter Rechtsbehelf (*gegen ein Urteil, außerhalb des Rechtsmittelzuges*); **without** ~ **of waste** ohne Haftung wegen Substanzminderung (*Grundstück*).

impeccability Unfehlbarkeit *f*, Makellosigkeit *f*.

impeccable makellos, einwandfrei.

impecunious *adj* mittellos.

impecuniosity Mittellosigkeit *f*.

impecunity Mittellosigkeit *f*.

impede hindern.

impedient Obstruktion treibende Partei *f*.

impediment (gesetzliches) Hindernis *n*, Behinderung *f*; ~ **to marriage** Ehehindernis; **absolute** ~ absolutes (Ehe)hindernis; **certificate of no** ~ Ehefähigkeitsattest; **diriment** ~ Ehenichtigkeitsgrund, unheilbares Ehehindernis; **lawful** ~ gesetzl Ehehindernis; **prohibitive** ~ Eheverbot *mit Strafandrohung (keine Ehenichtigkeit)*; **relative** ~ relatives Ehehindernis (*gegenüber bestimmten Personen*).

impeding the service of process Zustellungsvereitelung *f*.

impending bevorstehend; ~ **apprehension or prosecution** dringender Tatverdacht.

imperative zwingend, streng anweisend, befehlend; ~ **provision** zwingende Bestimmung, Mußvorschrift.

imperceptible unmerklich; ~ **accretion** allmähliche (kaum feststellbare) Anwachsung.

imperfect unvollkommen, mangelhaft, unvollständig, schwach, nicht durchsetzbar.

imperfection Unvollkommenheit *f*, Schwäche *f*, Mangelhaftigkeit *f*, Mangel *m*, Fehler *m*.

imperil gefährden.

imperious gebieterisch, zwingend.

impermissible unzulässig.

impersonal unpersönlich, unbenannt.

impersonate personifizieren, sich ausgeben als; darstellen.

impersonation Personifikation *f*, Darstellung *f*, Identitätstäuschung *f*.

impertinence Unerheblichkeit *f*, Irrelevanz *f*, Unschlüssigkeit *f*, Belanglosigkeit *f*, Unverschämtheit *f*.

impertinent unerheblich, nicht zur Sache gehörig, irrelevant; unverschämt.

impetration Erlangung *f* durch Bitten und Gesuche.

impignoration Verpfändung *f*.

impingement Übergriff *m*, Auftreffen *n*.

implead anklagen, verklagen, mitverklagen; ~**ed** verklagt, mitverklagt.

implement *s* Gerät *n*, Werkzeug *n*, Bedarfsgegenstand *m*; *scot* Ausführung *f* (*e–s Vertrages etc*); ~**s of housebreaking** Einbruchswerkzeuge; ~**s of trade** Arbeitsgeräte; **agricultural** ~**s** landwirtschaftliche Geräte.

implement *v* ausführen, erfüllen; ~ **a law** ein Gesetz durchführen; ~**ing agency** ausführende Dienststelle; ~**ing order** → *order* (*1*); ~**ing regulation** Durchführungsbestimmung.

implementation Durchführung *f*; **expeditious** ~ zügige Durchführung.

implicate implizieren, mit inbegriffen sein, zur Folge haben.
implication Vermutung *f*, Folgerung *f*, Unterstellung *f*, stillschweigendes Inbegriffensein *n*; **by** ~ stillschweigend, impliziert; **necessary** ~ zwingende Bedeutung, (*durch Auslegung zu ermittelnde*) allein in Betracht kommende Bedeutung.
implicit impliziert, stillschweigend, vorbehaltlos, mit inbegriffen, mitverstanden; ~ **obedience** unbedingter Gehorsam.
implied *adj* stillschweigend, nicht ausdrücklich, konkludent, (gesetzlich) vermutet, gefolgert, mit inbegriffen, mitgemeint, impliziert.
imply besagen, stillschweigend enthalten, in sich einschließen, bedeuten.
import *s* Import *m*, Einfuhr (= *E*) *f*; ~**s** Importartikel *m*; ~ **agent** Importagent; ~ **ban** → *ban*; ~ **certificate** *E*-genehmigung; ~ **cuts** *E*-kürzungen; ~ **deposit** Barhinterlegung zwecks *E*-erlaubnis; ~ **duties** *E*-zoll; ~ **entry** *E*-deklaration; ~ **excise tax** *E*-steuer; ~ **gold point** Goldeinfuhrpunkt; ~ **goods** *E*-waren; ~ **house** Importfirma; ~ **licence** → *licence*; ~ **mark-up** Aufschlag auf den *E*-preis; ~**s of goods on hire** Einfuhren von Waren zur Vermietung; ~ **permit** *E*-erlaubnis; ~ **prohibition** *E*-verbot; ~ **quota** *E*-kontingent; ~ **regulation** *E*-bestimmungen; ~ **requirements** *E*-bedarf; ~ **restrictions** *E*-beschränkungen; ~ **surcharge** *E*-sonderabgabe; ~ **tariff** *E*-zoll; **bounty on** ~**s** *E*-prämie; **embargo on** ~**s** *E*-sperre; **free** ~ zollfreie *E*; **free-of-levy** ~ abschöpfungsfreie *E*; **invisible** ~**s** unsichtbare *E*; **non-quota** ~**s** nicht kontingentierte *E*-waren; **quantitative restriction on** ~ mengenmäßige *E*-beschränkung; **token** ~**s** symbolische Importe.
importation Import *m*, Einfuhr *f*; ~ **in bond** Einfuhr unter Zollverschluß.
importer Importeur *m*.
importing house Importhandelsfirma *f*.
importuning (*for purposes of prostitution*) Belästigung *f*, Anhalten *n* (*Prostitution*); **charges of** ~ Anklage wegen sexueller (*bzw homosexueller*) Belästigung.
importunity Drängen *n*, beharrliches Bitten *n*, Zudringlichkeit *f*.
impose auferlegen, aufbürden; verhängen; ~ **a fine** → *fine*; ~ **a penalty** → *penalty*; ~ **a tax on s. th.** etwas besteuern; ~ **an embargo** ein Embargo verhängen; (*ein Schiff*) beschlagnahmen, an die Kette legen; ~ **an obligation** e–e Verpflichtung auferlegen; ~ **charges** Abgaben erheben; ~ **conditions** Bedingungen auferlegen; ~ **restrictions** Beschränkungen auferlegen.
imposition Auferlegung *f*, Auflagen *f/pl*, Verhängung *f*; Abgabe *f*, Steuer *f*, Besteuerung *f*; Täuschung *f*, Betrug *m*.
impossibility Unmöglichkeit *f* (= *U*); ~ **in fact** objektive *U*; ~ **of performance** *U* der Leistung; **absolute** ~ absolute *U*; **legal** rechtl *U*; **manifest** ~ offenbare *U*; **partial** ~ teilweise *U*; **physical** ~ objektive *U*; **practical** ~ Unvermögen, praktische *U*, subjektive *U*, wirtschaftl *U*; **relative** ~ subjektive *U*, Unvermögen; **strict** ~ eigentliche *U*, echte *U*; **subsequent** ~ nachträgliche *U*.
impossible unmöglich; **juridically** ~ juristisch unmöglich; **legally** ~ rechtlich unmöglich; **physically** ~ physisch unmöglich.
imposter Betrüger *m*, Hochstapler *m*.
imposts Abgaben *f/pl*, Steuern *f/pl*, Einfuhrabgaben *f/pl*, Zoll *m*.
imposture Betrügerei *f*, Steuerhinterziehung *f*, Schwindel *m*, Hochstapelei *f*.
impound sicherstellen, beschlagnahmen, in Verwahrung nehmen; ~ **distress** gepfändetes Vieh verwahren und versorgen.

impracticability Undurchführbarkeit *f*; **commercial** ~ Wegfall der Geschäftsgrundlage; nachträgliches Unvermögen.

impracticable undurchführbar, praktisch unmöglich.

imprescriptibility Unersitzbarkeit *f*.

imprescriptible unersitzbar; ~ **rights** Rechte, die nicht durch Ersitzung erworben werden können.

impress (*Siegel*) aufdrücken, beidrücken; ~**ed seal** → *seal*; ~**ed stamp** → *stamp*.

impression Abdruck *m*, Eindruck *m*, Wirkung *f*; **fraudulent** ~ unerlaubter Nachdruck.

impressment Zwangsrekrutierung *f*, Zwangsanheuerung *f*, Requisition *f*.

imprest Vorschuß *m* (*aus öffentlichen Mitteln*); ~ **accountant** Vorschußempfänger; ~ **cash** (= ~ *fund*) Bargeldkasse; ~ **money** Handgeld (*bei zwangsweise angeheuerten Matrosen*), Soldvorschuß aus Krongeldern; ~ **office** Vorschußkasse *der Admiralität*; ~ **system** Kleingeldvorschuß an Kassierer *zwecks späterer Abrechnung*.

imprimatur Druckerlaubnis *f*; höchstrichterl Bestätigung e–r Rechtsprechung.

imprint Druckvermerk *m*, Impressum *n*, Aufdruck *m*, Stempel *m*.

imprison einsperren, inhaftieren, jmdn der Freiheit berauben; ~ **people against their will** Freiheitsberaubung begehen; **person** ~**ed** in Haft befindliche Person.

imprisonable mit Freiheitsstrafe bedroht; ~ **road traffic offence** mit Freiheitsstrafe bedrohtes Verkehrsdelikt.

imprisonment Inhaftierung *f*, Haft *f*, Gefängnis *f*, Gefängnisstrafe *f*, Freiheitsstrafe *f*; ~ **for debt** *obs* Inhaftierung im Schuld(ner)gefängnis; ~ **for default** Ersatzfreiheitsstrafe; ~ **for failure to pay fine** ersatzweise verhängte Freiheitsstrafe; ~ **for life** lebenslängliche Freiheitsstrafe; ~ **in default of payment of fine** Ersatzfreiheitsstrafe; ~ **in lieu of fine** Ersatzfreiheitsstrafe; ~ **in third division** Strafverbüßung in der 3. Abteilung (*allgemeiner Strafvollzug*); ~ **not exceeding two months** Freiheitsstrafe bis zu zwei Monaten; ~ **on bread and water diet** Kerker bei Wasser und Brot; ~ **with hard labour** Freiheitsstrafe mit Zwangsarbeit, Zuchthausstrafe; **false** ~ Freiheitsberaubung; **period of** ~ → *period*; **to serve one's term of** ~ seine Freiheitsstrafe verbüßen.

improbation *scot* Klage *f* auf Feststellung der Unechtheit e–r Urkunde.

improbative nicht beweiskräftig.

improper unpassend, unzulässig, vorschriftswidrig, ungebührlich; ~ **cumulation of actions** unzulässige Klagehäufung.

impropriation *eccl* Aneignung *f* e–r Kirchenpfründe durch Laien.

impropriety Ungehörigkeit *f*, Unschicklichkeit *f*; **judicial** ~ richterliches Fehlverhalten.

improvable verbesserungsfähig.

improve verbessern, vervollkommnen, veredeln, meliorieren; ~ **in value** im Wert steigen.

improvement Verbesserung *f*, Erschließung *f*, Wertsteigerung *f*, Melioration *f*; ~**s** werterhöhende Aufwendungen *f/pl*; **I~ Act District** Erschließungsbezirk; ~ **bonds** Kommunalanleihe *zur Verbesserung öffentlicher Anlagen*; ~ **in prices** Kursbesserung; ~ **in value** Werterhöhung; ~ **industry** Veredelungswirtschaft; ~ **notice** Abmahnung, Abhilfeanordnung; ~ **of houses** Werterhöhung von Wohnhäusern; ~ **of land** = *land* ~ → *land*; ~ **of towns** Stadtsanierung; ~ **patent** → *patent*; ~ **scheme** Abänderungsplan; **expenditure for** ~**s** werterhöhende Aufwendungen; **local** ~**s** Ausbau der Gemeindeanlagen (*für Grünflächen, Spazierwege etc*); **patentable** ~**s** patentfähige Verbesserungen; **permanent** ~**s** ständige Verbesserungen; **public** ~**s** öffentl Arbeiten; **technological**

~s Verbesserungen nach dem Stand der Technik; **valuable ~s** werterhöhende Investitionen; **unexhausted ~s** noch nicht abgewohnte werterhöhende Mieterleistungen.

improver Erschließungsfirma *f.*

improvidence Ungeeignetheit *f*, Unzuverlässigkeit *f*, Unbedachtsamkeit *f*, Unvorsichtigkeit *f*, Leichtsinn *m*.

improvident achtlos, unvorsichtig, unbedacht, leichtsinnig.

impubes Kind *n*, Minderjähriger *m* vor der Pubertät (*Knabe unter 14, Mädchen unter 12 Jahren*).

impugn anfechten, bestreiten, bekämpfen; **the ~ed decision** die angefochtene Entscheidung.

impugnable bestreitbar, anfechtbar.

impugnation Bestreitung *f*, Widerlegung *f.*

impulse Impuls *m*, Drang *m*, Regung *f*; **~ goods** spontan (*nach dem Aussehen*) verkaufte Ware; **irresistible ~** unwiderstehlicher Drang; **uncontrollable ~** Affekt, unwiderstehlicher Drang.

impunity Straffreiheit *f*, Straflosigkeit *f*; **~ law** Straffreiheitsgesetz; **with ~** ungestraft.

imputability Zurechenbarkeit *f.*

imputable zurechenbar, zuschreibbar.

imputation Zurechnung *f*, Beschuldigung *f*, Bezichtigung *f*; **~ of unchastity** Bezichtigung unsittlichen Lebenswandels; **~ of payment** Zweckbestimmung e–r Zahlung; **~ of wrong** Bezichtigung (*e–s Unrechts*); **~s on the character of the witness** Angriff auf den Leumund des Zeugen.

impute *v/t* zuschreiben, zumessen, zurechnen.

imputed zugerechnet, zurechenbar, zugeschrieben.

in in, auf, bei, an; im Besitz; **~ a representative capacity** stellvertretend, in Vertretung (*i. V.*); **~ a workman like manner** fachgerecht; **~ accordance with the form** nach dem Wortlaut des (*gesetzlichen*) Formulars; **~ accordance with the terms of the judgment** nach dem Inhalt des Urteils; **~ action** → *action*; **~ adversum** streitig (*gegen e–e Partei*); **~ alieno solo** auf fremdem Grund; **~ alio loco** an anderer Stelle, anderenorts; **~ all cases** in allen (*diesbezüglichen*) Fällen; **~ all respects** in jeder Hinsicht, unter allen Umständen; **~ an advisory capacity** in beratender Eigenschaft; **~ an independent capacity** in freiberuflicher Eigenschaft; **~ an (one's) official ~** in amtlicher Eigenschaft; **~ and about** anläßlich, zusammenhängend mit; **~ and out of court** gerichtlich und außergerichtlich; **~ apparent good order and condition** äußerlich in einwandfreiem Zustand; **~ arbitrio judicis** nach richterlichem Ermessen; **~ arrear** im Rückstand; **~ articulo mortis** im Augenblick des Todes; **~ attendance** anwesend; **~ autre** fremden Rechts; **~ autre droit** aus fremdem Recht; **~ bad faith** → *faith*; **~ bank** Plenarsitzung des Gerichts; **~ being** existent; **~ blank** blanko; **~ bond** unter Zollverschluß, in amtlicher Verwahrung; **~ bonis** bei den Vermögensgegenständen des ...; **~ bonis defuncti** bei den Nachlaßgegenständen; **~ breach of faith** → *faith*; **~ bulk** als Ganzes, en gros; **~ camera** → *camera*; **~ case** → *case*; **~ chief** Haupt ..., hauptsächlich; (*examination*) **~** *chief* → *examination*; **~ circulation** im Umlauf; **"~" clearer** Annahmebeamter e–s Clearinghauses; **"~" clearing** Gesamtbetrag der bei e–r Verrechnungsstelle eingehenden Schecks; **~ commendam** zu treuen Händen; **~ common** gemeinschaftlich, gesamthänderisch; **~ conformity with the contract** vertragsgemäß; **~ conjunction with** gemeinsam mit, gemeinschaftlich; **~ consequence of** → *consequence*; **~ consideration of** → *consideration*; **~ contemplation of death** angesichts des Todes, im

Hinblick auf den eigenen Tod; ~ **contemplation of marriage** im Hinblick auf die Eheschließung; ~ **contravention of law** gesetzeswidrig; ~ **course of delivery** bei Lieferung; ~ **curia** bei öffentlicher Gerichtsverhandlung; ~ **current use** allgemeingebräuchlich; ~ **custodia legis** in gerichtlichem Gewahrsam, in amtlicher Verwahrung; ~ **default of agreement** bei Nichteinigung; ~ **default of payment** mangels Zahlung; bei Nichtzahlung, im Verzugsfall; ~ **default of such issue** falls solche Nachkommen nicht vorhanden sind; ~ **default whereof** widrigenfalls, mangels, falls das nicht erfolgt; ~ **demand** begehrt; ~ **dubio** im Zweifel; ~ **due course** im normalen Verlauf, bei normalem Geschäftsgang; ~ **due form** formgerecht, vorschriftsmäßig; ~ **due time** termingerecht, rechtzeitig; ~ **equal moieties** je zur Hälfte; ~ **equal proportions** zu gleichen Teilen; ~ **equity** nach Billigkeitsrecht, billigerweise, fairerweise; ~ **esse** existent, tatsächlich vorhanden, *bereits* bestehend; ~ **evidence** bereits im Beweismaterial enthalten, dem Gericht zum Beweise vorliegend; (*facts*) ~ *evidence* → *evidence*; ~ **execution** durch Pfändung, bei der Zwangsvollstreckung; ~ **execution and pursuance of** zur Vollziehung und nach dem Inhalt (*e–r anderen Urkunde*); ~ **expeditione** im (*überseeischen*) Kriegseinsatz; ~ **extenso** von Anfang bis Ende; ungekürzt; ~ **faciendo** bei der Ausführung; ~ **fact** tatsächlich; ~ **favour of** zugunsten von, zahlbar an dessen Order; ~ **fee** als Eigentum, als Lehen; ~ **fieri** bei der Vollendung; ~ **flagrante delicto** → *flagrante*; ~ **force** → *force*; ~ **forma pauperis** *obs* im Armenrecht; ~ **front of** vor, auf der Vorderseite; ~ **full** vollständig; ~ **full confidence** in vollem Vertrauen; ~ **full life** am Leben und rechtsfähig; ~ **full of account** zum Ausgleich der Rechnung; ~ **furtherance of** zur Förderung; ~ **good faith** → *faith*; ~ **good working order** betriebsfähig; ~ **gross** dem Grundherrn persönl gehörend; ~ **hand** jederzeit verfügbar; ~ **his own right** aus eigenem Recht, im eigenen Namen; ~ **his trade or business** in seinem Gewerbe; ~ **invitum** gegen e–e nicht bereite Partei; ~ **judgment** bei Gericht; ~ **jure** rechtlich, juristisch; ~ **jus vocare** gerichtlich gegen jmdn vorgehen; ~ **keeping with** in Übereinstimmung mit; ~ **kind** → *kind*; ~ **law** rechtlich, gesetzlich; ~ **lieu of** → *lieu*; ~ **like good order and condition** in gleichem einwandfreiem Zustand; ~ **limbo** unentschieden, aufgeschoben; ~ **limine** von vorneherein, vorläufig; ~ **litem** im Rechtsstreit; (*oath*) ~ *litem* → *oath*; ~ **loco parentis** an Elternstatt, an Stelle e–s Elternteils; ~ **manner aforesaid** in vorstehend bezeichneter Weise; ~ **manner and form** nach Art und Weise; ~ **mercy** nach gerichtlichem Ermessen (*Strafe*); ~ **more than one name** unter mehr als einem Namen, nicht als Einzelunternehmer; ~ **motion** in Bewegung (*Maschinen*); ~ **need** → *need*; ~ **one's official capacity** in amtlicher Eigenschaft; ~ **one's private capacity** in privater Eigenschaft, als Privatperson (*nicht in amtlicher Eigenschaft*); ~ **open account** in laufender Rechnung, noch nicht abgerechnet; ~ **opposition** als Gegner, als Gegenpartei; ~ **or about** in oder in der Nähe von; ~ **or at** in *bzw* bei; ~ **or incidental to** bei oder anläßlich; ~ **or out of** innerhalb oder außerhalb; ~ **pais** ohne gerichtl Verfahren; ~ **paper** in Kladde, noch nicht ausgefertigt; ~ **pari delicto** beiderseits mitschuldig; ~ **pari materia** im analogen Fall; ~ **part** teilweise, zum Teil; ~ **perpetuity** → *perpetuity*; ~ **person** persönlich; ~ **personam** persönlich, schuldrechtlich; ~ **plant** innerbetrieblich; ~

pleno im Plenum, Plenar . . .; ~ **port** im Hafenbereich; ~ **posse** möglicherweise existent; ~ **possession** im unmittelbaren Besitz; ~ **praesenti** gegenwärtig; ~ **preference to any other person** vorrangig gegenüber anderen; ~ **private** geheim, unter vier Augen, nicht öffentlich; ~ **process of adjustment** bei der Regulierung; ~ **propria persona** in eigener Person, persönlich; ~ **public** öffentlich; ~ **pursuance (of)** gemäß; ~ **re** in Sachen (*bei einseitigen Verfahren*); in der Angelegenheit . . ., betreffs; ~ **receipt** erhalten, empfangen; ~ **regard to** → *regard*; ~ **rem** dinglich; ~ **render** ablieferungspflichtig; ~ **respect of** → *respect*; ~ **retentis** zur Beweissicherung; ~ **seaworthy trim** *so beladen, daß die Seetüchtigkeit nicht beeinträchtigt ist*; ~ **service date** Zeitpunkt der Inbetriebnahme; ~ **service training** betriebliche Berufsausbildung; ~ **sight** in Sicht; ~ **situ** an Ort und Stelle; ~ **specie** → *specie*; ~ **statu quo** im vorigen Stand; ~ **stirpes** nach Stämmen (*Erbfolge*); ~ **store** auf Lager; ~ **substance** im wesentlichen; ~ **substantial agreement** im wesentlichen übereinstimmend; ~ **terrorem** zur Abschreckung; ~ **the absence of anything to the contrary** soweit nicht ausdrückl etwas anderes bestimmt ist; ~ **the alternative** alternativ, hilfsweise; ~ **the body** *of the note* im Text *des (Sola)wechsels*; ~ **the conduct of the suit** bei der Führung des Prozesses; ~ **the course of** im Laufe von, während, anläßlich; ~ **the execution of his duty** bei Erfüllung seiner Amtspflicht; ~ **the field** im Felde, im Einsatzgebiet; ~ **the first place** erstens; ~ **the face of** angesichts (*der Tatsache, daß . . .*); ~ **the law** anwaltschaftlich tätig; ~ **the loading** bei der Ladung; ~ **the name of** → *name*; ~ **the peace of the state** bei Landfrieden, im Frieden; ~ **the presence of** in Anwesenheit von; ~ **the public interest** im öffentlichen Interesse; ~ **the usual manner** wie üblich; ~ **the very act** auf frischer Tat, in flagranti; ~ **transitu** unterwegs; ~ **trust** → *trust*; ~ **ventre sa mere** → *en ventre*; ~ **virtue (of)** Kraft, auf Grund von; ~ **vitro fertilisation** künstliche Befruchtung der Frau; ~ **witness whereof** zu Urkund dessen; **the ~s** die an der Macht Befindlichen.

inability Unfähigkeit *f*, Unvermögen *n*; ~ **to act** Unfähigkeit der Amtsausübung; ~ **to pay (debts)** Zahlungsunfähigkeit; ~ **to perceive legal wrong** fehlendes Unrechtsbewußtsein.

inaccessible unzugänglich.

inaction Untätigkeit *f*.

inadequacy Unangemessenheit *f*, Mißverhältnis *n*, Unvollkommenheit *f*, Mangelhaftigkeit *f*, Unanständigkeit *f*.

inadequate unzureichend, unzulänglich, unangemessen.

inadmissible unzulässig, nicht als Beweismittel zugelassen.

inadvertence Unachtsamkeit *f*, Unaufmerksamkeit *f*, Versehen *n*, Irrtum *m*.

inadvertent unachtsam, unbeabsichtigt, unvorsichtig, versehentlich, irrtümlich; ~ **default** unbeabsichtigtes Versäumnis, versehentliches Terminversäumnis; versehentliche Nichtleistung.

inalienability Unveräußerlichkeit *f*, Unübertragbarkeit *f*.

inalienable unveräußerlich, nicht übertragbar; ~ **provision** unabtretbare Zuwendung.

inanimate matt, flau, unbelebt.

inanimateness Flaute *f*.

inapplicability Unanwendbarkeit *f*, Unbrauchbarkeit *f*.

inapplicable unanwendbar.

inappreciable (*quantity*) ganz geringfügig, kaum merklich.

inappropriate ungeeignet, unpassend, unzweckmäßig, ungehörig, unsachlich.

inattention Unachtsamkeit *f*.

inauguration Einweihung *f*, Einführung *f*, Amtseinsetzung *f*; ~ **address** Antrittsrede (*bei Amtsübernahme*); **I~ Day** Tag des Amtsantritts des US-Präsidenten (*20. Januar nach der Wahl*).

inboard innenbords, das Schiffsbord nicht überragend; ~ **cargo** Innenladung.

inborow Vorhof *m*, Tor *n*; ~ **and outborow** Grenzbürger, Grenzwächter; *Grenzland zwischen England und Schottland.*

inbound | **common** abgegrenzte nicht umfriedete Allmende *f*; ~ **transportation** Eingangsfracht.

Inc. (= *incorporated qv*) *als nachgestellter Firmenbestandteil*: AG *bzw* GmbH, *bei Vereinen*: *e. V.*

incalculability Unberechenbarkeit *f*, Unbestimmbarkeit *f*.

incalculable unberechenbar, unzuverlässig, unmeßbar, ungewiß.

incapability Unfähigkeit *f*, Untauglichkeit *f*; ~ **of being elected** Nichtwählbarkeit; ~ **of forming intent** Unzurechnungsfähigkeit; ~ **of holding public office** Unfähigkeit zur Bekleidung e–s öffentlichen Amtes; ~ **of making a will** Testierunfähigkeit.

incapable ungeeignet, unfähig; ~ **of being ascertained** nicht feststellbar; ~ **of giving evidence** zeugnisunfähig; ~ **of self-support** unfähig, sich selbst zu unterhalten; ~ **of working** arbeitsunfähig; ~ **to contract** geschäftsunfähig.

incapacitate unfähig machen, untauglich machen, disqualifizieren, entmündigen.

incapacitated nicht (mehr) geschäftsfähig, unzurechnungsfähig.

incapacitation Unfähigmachen *n*, Aberkennung *f* der Geschäftsfähigkeit, Entmündigung *f*.

incapacity Unfähigkeit *f*; Geschäftsunfähigkeit *f*; Mangel *m* an rechtl Befugnis; ~ **for employment** Erwerbsunfähigkeit; ~ **for work** Arbeitsunfähigkeit, Erwerbsunfähigkeit; ~ **to consummate** Beiwohnungsunfähigkeit (*als Eheaufhebungsgrund*); ~ **to contract** Geschäftsunfähigkeit, beschränkte Geschäftsfähigkeit; ~ **to sue** fehlende Prozeßfähigkeit; **legal** ~ Geschäftsunfähigkeit, beschränkte Geschäftsfähigkeit; **lesser** ~ geminderte Erwerbsfähigkeit, Berufsunfähigkeit; **mental** ~ Geschäftsunfähigkeit *bzw* Unzurechnungsfähigkeit *wegen Geistesschwäche oder Geistesgestörtheit*; **partial** ~ Teilinvalidität; **senile** ~ Geschäftsunfähigkeit wegen Senilität; **testamentary** ~ Testierunfähigkeit; **total** ~ Erwerbsunfähigkeit, Vollinvalidität.

incarcerate inhaftieren, einsperren.

incarceration Einschließung *f*, Inhaftnahme *f*, Freiheitsentzug *m*.

incendiarism Brandstiftung *f*, Pyromanie *f*.

incendiary *adj* Feuer . . . brandstifterisch, aufwieglerisch; ~ **bomb** Brandbombe; ~ **letter** *scot* Drohbrief; ~ **loss** auf Brandstiftung beruhender Schaden.

incendiary *s* Brandstifter *m*, Brandbombe *f*; Aufwiegler *m*.

incentive | **bonus** Leistungsprämie; ~ **pay** Leistungslohn, Lohnerhöhung bei Leistungssteigerung; ~ **post** Dienststellung mit Aussicht auf Sonderbeförderung; ~ **wage** Erfolgslohn; **buying** ~ Kaufanreiz.

inception Anfang *m*, Prozeßbeginn m.

incertainty Unbestimmtheit *f*.

incest Inzest *m*, Blutschande *f*.

incestuosi in Inzest gezeugte Personen.

incestuous blutschänderisch; ~ **adultery** mit Blutschande verbundener Ehebruch; ~ **bastards** Abkömmlinge aus e–r blutschänderischen Verbindung.

inch Zoll *m* (*2,54 cm*); ~ **of candle** Versteigerung, *bei der bis zum Erlöschen e–r (ein Zoll langen) Kerze geboten werden kann.*

inchmaree clause Inchmaree-Klausel *f*, *Deckungsklausel für Schaden durch Kesselexplosion und Maschinendefekte.*

inchoate unvollständig, nicht vollendet, im Versuchsstadium.

incidence Anfall *m*, Belastung *f*, Vorkommen *n*, Häufigkeit *f*; ~ **of a tax** Anfall e–r Steuer, Steuerbelastung; ~ **of loss** Schadensanfall, Schadenshäufigkeit.

incident *adj* zufällig, abhängig, verbunden mit, gehörend zu.

incident *s* Zufall *m*, Vorfall *m*, Zwischenfall *m*, Ereignis *n*, Nebenpflicht *f*; ~**s** unvorhergesehene Ausgaben *f/pl*.

incidental zufällig, beiläufig, gelegentlich, nebensächlich; ~ **or conducive to** dazugehörig und zweckdienlich; ~ **to employment** zur Arbeitsausübung gehörig; erwerbsbedingt; ~ **to one's main business (or profession)** nebenerwerblich; ~ **to the sale** mit dem Kauf zusammenhängend.

incineration Verbrennung *f*, Einäscherung *f*, Feuerbestattung *f*.

incinerator Verbrennungsanlage *f*.

incipitur der Anfang e–r Gerichtsurkunde, Rubrum *n*.

incit|e anstiften, aufwiegeln, aufreizen, antreiben, anspornen; ~**ing to riot** Aufwiegelung zum Landfriedensbruch.

incitement Aufwiegelung *f*, Aufhetzung *f*, Anstiftung *f*, Anreizung *f*; ~ **of crime** Anstiftung; ~ **to disaffection** Anstiftung zum Hochverrat, Wehrkraftzersetzung; ~ **to disobedience of laws** Aufforderung zum Ungehorsam gegen Gesetze; ~ **to race** (= *racial*) **hatred** Aufstachelung zum Rassenhaß.

inclination to buy Kauflust *f*, Kaufinteresse *n*, Kaufneigung *f*.

inclose umgeben, einengen; ~ **a jury** die Geschworenen einschließen; ~**d ground** eingehegtes Grundstück; umfriedetes Grundstück.

inclosure Herausnahme *f* von Land aus der Allmende, Aufhebung von Allmendrechten; Einfriedung *f*, eingehegtes Grundstück *n*; ~ **acts** Gesetze über die Privatisierung von Gemeindeland.

include einschließen, umfassen, dazu gehören, enthalten; ~ **a person in a will** jmdn im Testament bedenken.

includible einschließlich, unter eine Bestimmung fallend.

including einschließlich.

inclusion Einbeziehung *f*, Einschließung *f*, Einsetzung *f*, Inbegriff *m*, Einfügung *f*; ~ **of conditions** Aufnahme von Bedingungen.

inclusive einschließend, einschließlich.

incoherence Unvereinbarkeit *f*, Widerspruch *m*, Zusammenhangslosigkeit *f*.

incoherent unzusammenhängend, zusammenhanglos.

income Einkommen *n*, Einnahmen *f/pl*, Ertrag *m*, Einkünfte *f/pl*; ~ **account** Ertragsrechnung; ~ **after taxes** Einkommen nach (Abzug von) Steuern; ~ **and adjustment bond** Besserungsschein; **I~ and Corporation Taxes Act** Einkommen- und Körperschaftssteuergesetz (*GB, 1970*); ~ **and expenditure account** Ertrags- und Aufwandsollrechnung; ~ **basis** Rendite (*e–s Wertpapiers*); ~ **bill** Einkommensteuerbescheid; ~ **bonds** → *bond* (*1*); ~ **bracket** Einkommensgruppe; ~ **debenture** → *debenture*; ~ **deduction** Abzüge vom steuerpflichtigen Einkommen; ~ **deductions** betriebsfremder Aufwand; ~ **deficiency** Einkommensteuerausfall; ~ **determination** Einkommensermittlung, Erfolgsermittlung; ~ **due to a bankrupt** dem Gemeinschuldner zustehende Einkünfte; ~ **earned** realisierter Ertrag; ~ **exempt from taxes** steuerfreies Einkommen; ~ **from a business** Gewerbeertrag; ~ **from capital** Kapitalertrag, Einkommen aus Kapitalvermögen; ~ **from dividends** Dividendeneinkünfte; ~ **from interest** Zinserträge; ~ **from investment** = *investment* ~ *qv*; ~ **from occupation of lands** Einkünfte aus Landbesitz; ~ **from ownership of land** Einkünfte aus Grundeigentum; ~ **from securi-**

ties Einkünfte aus Wertpapiervermögen; ~ **gearing** *Verhältnis von Zinszahlungen zu Reingewinn und Steuern*; ~ **group** Einkommensklasse; ~ **in kind** Naturaleinkommen; ~ **of non-recurrent nature** außergewöhnliche Erträge; ~ **return** Rendite; ~ **statement** Gewinn- und Verlustrechnung; ~ **tax** → *income tax*; ~ **value** Ertragswert; ~ **yield** Zinserträge; **actual** ~ echte Einkünfte; **additional** ~ Nebeneinkommen, Nebeneinnahmen; **adjusted gross** ~ bereinigter Bruttoertrag; **aggregate** ~ Gesamteinkünfte, *bes*: Ehegatteneinkommen bei Gesamtveranlagung; **annual** ~ Jahreseinkommen, Jahresertrag; ~ **assessable** ~ steuerpflichtiges Einkommen; **average** ~ Durchschnittseinkommen; **average gross annual** ~ durchschnittliche Bruttojahreserträge; **cash** ~ Bareinnahmen; **corporate** ~ Gesellschaftseinkommen; **derived** ~ abgeleitetes Einkommen; **discretionary** ~ frei verfügbares Einkommen; **disposable personal** ~ verfügbares persönliches Einkommen, Nettoeinkommen (nach Steuern); **dividend** ~ Dividendeneinkünfte; **earned** ~ Arbeitseinkommen; Einkünfte aus (*freiberuflicher und abhängiger*) Arbeit und gewerblicher Tätigkeit; **earned** ~ **allowance** Freibetrag für Berufstätige; **earned** ~ **relief** = *earned* ~ *allowance qv*; **extra** ~ Nebeneinkommen, Nebeneinnahmen; **factoral** ~ Faktoreinkommen; **fixed** ~ festes Einkommen; **foreign** ~ Einkünfte aus Investitionen im Ausland; **government** ~ Staatseinkünfte; **gross** ~ Bruttoeinkünfte (*vor Steuern*), Bruttoertrag; **individual** ~ Privateinkünfte, Privateinkommen; **independent** ~ arbeitsfreies Einkommen; **industrial** ~ Einkünfte aus Gewerbebetrieb; **median** ~ mittleres Einkommen; **national** ~ → *national*; **net** ~ Nettoeinkünfte, Einkommen; **nominal** ~ pro forma Bezüge, Nominaleinkommen; **nonoperating** ~ gewerbliche Einkünfte aus Investitionen; **non-recurring** ~ einmaliges Erträgnis; **operating** ~ betriebliche Einkünfte; **permanent** ~ ständige Einkünfte; **personal** ~ Einkünfte natürlicher Personen; **prepaid** ~ transitorische Passiva; **pretax** ~ Einkommen vor Steuern, unversteuertes Einkommen; **private** ~ Privateinkommen; **real** ~ Realeinkommen, effektives Einkommen; **regular** ~ festes Einkommen; **realized** ~ realisierter Gewinn; **retirement** ~ Ruhegeldbezüge; Altersversorgung; **revenue from** ~ Einkommen aus Kapitalvermögen; **secondary** ~ Nebeneinkommen; **source of** ~ → *source*; **split** ~ Ehegattensplitting; **statutory** ~ (*3jähriges*) Durchschnittseinkommen; **tax exempt** ~ steuerfreie Einkünfte; **taxable** ~ steuerpflichtiges Einkommen, zu versteuernder Einkommensbetrag; **total net** ~ Jahreseinkommen; **trading** ~ Einkommen aus Gewerbebetrieb; **unearned** ~ Einkommen aus Kapitalvermögen.

income tax Einkommensteuer *f*; *bzw* Körperschaftsteuer *f*; ~ **appeal tribunal** Finanzgericht (*für Einkommensteuer u. Körperschaftst.*); ~ **return** Einkommensteuererklärung; ~ **threshold** untere Besteuerungsgrenze *bei der Einkommensteuer*.

incomer Ankömmling *m*, Rechtsnachfolger *m*.

incoming einlaufend; ~ **exchanges** *Schecks, die bei e–r Bank von e–r Clearingstelle eingehen*; ~ **mail** Posteingang; ~ **partner** → *partner*; ~ **stocks** Zugänge zum Lagerbestand.

incomings Zahlungseingänge *m|pl*, Einnahmen *f|pl*.

incommodious unbequem, lästig, beengt, beeinträchtigt.

incommunicado streng von der Außenwelt abgeschlossen; in Isolierungshaft.

incommunication Isolierungshaft *f*.

incommutable nicht umwandelbar, nicht herabsetzbar.

incompatibility Inkompatibilität *f*,

Unvereinbarkeit *f*; ~ **of temperament** Unverträglichkeit.

incompatible inkompatibel, unvereinbar.

incompetence = *incompetency qv*.

incompetency Inkompetenz *f*, Unfähigkeit *f*, Ungeeignetheit *f*; **mental** ~ Schuldunfähigkeit.

incompetent unzuständig, nicht befugt, unfähig; ~ **to contract** geschäftsunfähig; ~ **to testify** zeugnisunfähig; **to be adjudicated** ~ gerichtlich für geschäftsunfähig erklärt werden.

incomplete unvollständig, mangelhaft.

inconceivable unbegreiflich, unvorstellbar.

inconclusive unschlüssig, nicht überzeugend.

inconclusiveness Unschlüssigkeit *f*, Mangel *m* an Beweiskraft.

incongruity Inkongruenz *f*, Mißverhältnis *n*, Unangemessenheit *f*.

incongruous inkongruent, nicht übereinstimmend, unangemessen.

inconsequence Folgewidrigkeit *f*, Inkonsequenz *f*, Zusammenhanglosigkeit *f*, Irrelevanz *f*.

inconsequential belanglos.

inconsistency Unvereinbarkeit *f*, mangelnde Folgerichtigkeit *f*, Widerspruch *m*.

inconsistent widersprüchlich, unvereinbar, inkonsequent, **previous statements** widersprüchliche Angaben; ~ **with** nicht im Einklang mit.

incontestability Unanfechtbarkeit *f*.

incontestable unanfechtbar; ~ **clause** → *clause*.

incontinence Unenthaltsamkeit *f*, Unkeuschheit *f*, Zügellosigkeit *f*.

inconvenience Beschwerlichkeit *f*, Ungelegenheit *f*, Unannehmbarkeit *f*, Schwierigkeit *f*, Hindernis *n*.

inconvertibility Nichtkonvertierbarkeit *f*.

inconvertible nicht konvertierbar, unveränderlich, unverwertbar.

incorporate *adj* unkörperlich, immateriell.

incorporate *v* einverleiben, einbeziehen, eingemeinden; Körperschaftsrechte (Rechtsfähigkeit) verleihen; zur juristischen Person machen; gründen; Rechtsfähigkeit verleihen; ~ **by reference** zum Bestandteil (e–s Vertrages) erklären; durch Bezugnahme zum Inhalt e–r Urkunde machen; ~ **into land** mit dem Boden verbinden.

incorporated accountant öffentlich bestellter Buchprüfer; ~ **authority** rechtsfähige Anstalt, Wirtschaftsunternehmen der öffentlichen Hand; ~ **bank** Aktienbank; ~ **body** Körperschaft; ~ **by Act of Parliament** parlamentarisch verliehene Rechtsfähigkeit; ~ **city** kreisfreie Stadt; ~ **company** → *company*; **I~ Council of Law Reporting** (=) *Stiftung für Gerichtsaufzeichnungen und Entscheidungssammlungen;* **I~ Law Society** Anwaltskammer (*für Solicitors*); ~ **society** eingetragener Verein; ~ **trades** Zunftgewerbe.

incorporation Gründung *f* e–r Körperschaft, Vereinigung *f*, Einbeziehung *f*, Übernahme *f*, Einverleibung *f*, Eingemeindung, Verbindung *f*, Angliederung *f*; ~ **by reference** Einbeziehung durch Bezugnahme; ~ **of a territory** Einverleibung e–s Gebietes; **articles of** ~ Satzung e–r Körperschaft; **certificate of** ~ → *certificate*; **compulsory** ~ Zwangseintragung.

incorporator Gründer *m*, Gründungsmitglied *n*.

incorporeal immateriell, unkörperlich.

incorrect or otherwise unjust ungenau beziehungsweise falsch.

incorrectness Unrichtigkeit *f*, Fehler *m*, Irrtum *m*.

incorrigible unverbesserlich, unerziehbar; ~ **rogue** → *rogue*.

incorruptible unbestechlich.

increase *s* Vergrößerung *f*, Vermehrung *f*; Steigen *n*, Zunehmen *n*, Erhöhung *f*, Wachsen *n*, Ertrag *m*, Nutzen *m*; ~ **in** (= *of*) **capital** Kapitalerhöhung, Kapitalaufstokkung; ~ **in demand** wachsende

Nachfrage; ~ **in efficiency** Leistungssteigerung; ~ **in taxation** Steuererhöhung; ~ **of burdens** Lastenerhöhung; ~ **of hazard** Risikosteigerung; ~ **of receipts** Mehreinnahmen; ~ **of rent** Mieterhöhung; ~ **of risk** *ins* Gefahrenerhöhung; ~ **of the bank rate** Diskonterhöhung; ~ **in value** Wertzuwachs; **affidavit of** ~ beeidete Versicherung über Kostenerhöhungen (*Steuer*); **costs of** ~ festgesetzte erstattungsfähige Kosten (*über dem Nominalsatz*); **real terms** ~ echte Erhöhung, Nettoerhöhung.

increase *v* vergrößern, vermehren; ~ **the borrowings** Kredite in erhöhtem Maße in Anspruch nehmen; ~ **the credit** den Kredit verbessern.

increment Erhöhung *f* (*vgl increase*), Erhöhungsbetrag *m*; ~ **taxes** Wertzuwachssteuern; **annual** ~ jährliche (Gehalts-)Steigerung; **unearned** ~ Wertzuwachs.

incremental cost nahe der Rentabilitätsgrenze liegende Kosten.

incriminate beschuldigen, belasten, inkriminieren; ~ **oneself** sich selbst belasten.

incriminating | **admission** (belastendes) Einräumen von Tatumständen; ~ **circumstance** belastender Umstand; ~ **evidence** → *evidence*; ~ **questions** *Fragen, durch deren Beantwortung der Zeuge seine eigene strafbare oder unehrenhafte Handlung offenbaren müßte.*

incrimination Beschuldigung *f*, rechtl Belastung *f*.

incriminatory statement belastende Erklärung *f*, belastende Aussage *f* zu Protokoll des Vernehmungsbeamten.

incroachment Beeinträchtigung *f*.

inculpate beschuldigen, anklagen, verstricken.

inculpation of states Staatenhaftung *f* aus Verschulden.

inculpatory beschuldigend, belastend.

incumbency Amtsinhaberschaft *f*, Amtszeit *f*.

incumbent obliegend, zufallend; **to be** ~ **on a person** jmdm obliegen.

incumbent *s* Amtsinhaber *m*, Amtsträger *m*; Pfründeninhaber *m*.

incumber = *encumber qv*, belasten.

incumbrance = *encumbrance qv*.

incumbrancer = *encumbrancer qv*.

incur sich zuziehen, auf sich laden, eingehen, entstehen (*z. B. unmittelbar durch Gesetz*); ~ **a penalty** → *penalty*; ~ **a risk** ein Risiko eingehen; ~ **criminal responsibility** strafrechtlich haften; ~ **debts** Schulden machen, Verpflichtungen eingehen; ~ **indebtedness** sich verschulden; ~ **liabilities** Verpflichtungen eingehen; haften; ~**red expenses** = *expense incurred* → *expense*; ~**red in and about the action** anläßlich des Prozesses entstandene (*Kosten*).

incursion Einfall *m*, Eingriff *m*, Übergriff *m*.

indebitatus assumpsit *hist* schuldrechtliche Klage *f*, Zahlungsklage *f*.

indebted verpflichtet, verschuldet, geschuldet.

indebtedness Schuld *f*, Verschuldung *f*, Verpflichtung *f*; **acknowledgement of** ~ Schuldanerkenntnis; **amount of** ~ Höhe der Verschuldung; **certificate of** ~ → *certificate*; **instrument of** ~ Schuldurkunde; **involuntary** ~ gesetzliche (unaufschiebbare) Zahlungsverpflichtung; **net** ~ echte Verschuldung; **voluntary** ~ aufschiebbare (nicht zwingende) Zahlungsverpflichtung.

indecency Unsittlichkeit *f*, Unanständigkeit *f*, Unzucht *f*, Anstößigkeit *f*; ~ **with children** unzüchtige Handlungen an Kindern, sexueller Mißbrauch von Kindern; **gross** ~ schwere Unzucht, (verbotene) gleichgeschlechtliche Handlungen zwischen Männern *bzw* sexueller Mißbrauch von Kindern; **public** ~ Erregung e–s öffentlichen Ärgernisses.

indecent unzüchtig, unsittlich, anstößig, obszön.

indecimable *hist* vom Zehnten befreit.
indefeasibility Unanfechtbarkeit *f*.
indefeasible unanfechtbar, unangreifbar, unaufhebbar; ~ **right** unangreifbares Recht.
indefensible unhaltbar, nicht vertretbar.
indefinite unbestimmt; ~ **failure of issue** das Ausbleiben von Nachkommen auf unbestimmte Zeit.
indefiniteness Unbestimmtheit *f*; ~ **of statute** Unbestimmtheit *f* gesetzlicher Tatbestände (*Strafrecht*).
indelible unauslöschlich, untilgbar, nicht radierbar; ~ **ink** Kopiertinte; ~ **pencil** Tintenstift.
indemnification Entschädigung *f*, Schadenersatz *m*, Schadloshaltung *f*, Schadlosstellung *f*, Abfindung *f*.
indemnifier Garant *m*, Garantiegeber *m*, Schadloshalter *m*.
indemnify schadlos halten, entschädigen; **liable to** ~ schadenersatzpflichtig, zur Schadloshaltung verpflichtet.
indemnitee der zur Schadloshaltung Berechtigte; Entschädigungsberechtigter *m*.
indemnitor der zur Schadloshaltung Verpflichtete, Entschädigungsverpflichteter *m*, Haftungsschuldner *m*.
indemnity Entschädigung *f*, Schadenersatz *m*, Schadloshaltung *f*, Garantievertrag *m*, Haftungsfreistellung *f*, Abfindungsgeld *n*, Sicherstellung *f*, Straflosigkeit *f*; **I~ Act** = *Act of Indemnity qv*; ~ **against liability** Haftungsfreistellung; ~ **bond** → *bond* (*2*); ~ **clause** Schadloshaltungsklausel; ~ **company** Insolvenz-Versicherungsgesellschaft; ~ **contract** Schadloshaltungsvertrag, Freistellungsvertrag; ~ **for costs** Kostensicherheit, Freistellung von der Kostenhaftung; ~ **for expropriation** Enteignungsentschädigung; ~ **for illegal arrest** Entschädigung für unschuldig verbüßte Untersuchungshaft; ~ **insurance** → *insurance*; ~ **lands** Ersatzgrundstücke (*bei Enteignung*); ~ **letter** *brit* Garantieverpflichtung, Ausfallbürgschaft; ~ **period** Leistungsdauer, Dauer der Haftung; ~ **policy** Haftpflichtversicherung (*beschränkt auf Erstattung von bezahltem Schaden*); ~ **schedule** Liste für die Regulierung bei Teilinvalidität; ~ **to retiring partner** Haftungsfreistellung des ausscheidenden Gesellschafters (*durch Sicherheitsleistung*); **cash** ~ → *cash*; **claim for** ~ Schadenersatzanspruch; **contract of** ~ → *contract*; **double** ~ doppelte Versicherungssumme bei Unfalltod; **letter of** ~ → *letter*; **monetary** ~ Geldabfindung; **patent** ~ Freihaltung von Ansprüchen wegen Patentverletzung; **sum of** ~ Abfindungssumme; **third party** ~ → *third*; **trustee's** ~ Haftungsfreistellung des Treuhänders; **war** ~ → *war*.
indenization (*vorläufige*) Freilassung *f*, Verleihung *f* des Status e-s freien Staatsbürgers, Einbürgerung *f*.
indent *s* Einrückung (*d. Zeile*); Vertragsurkunde *f*, Requisition *f*, Auslandsbestellung *f*; *hist* Staatsanleihe *f*; **closed** ~ Auslandsbestellung über Vertreter mit Herstellerbenennung.
indent *v* eine mehrseitige, gesiegelte Urkunde errichten; förmlich vereinbaren; als Lehrling verpflichten.
indenture mehrseitig errichtete Urkunde *f*; förmlicher Vertrag *m*; gesiegelte Vertragsurkunde *f*; Lehrbrief *m*; ~ **of apprenticeship** Lehrvertrag; ~ **of assumption** Übernahmevertrag; ~ **of mortgage** Hypothekenbewilligungsurkunde; ~ **security** Pfandbrief, Treuhandzertifikat; ~ **security holder** Pfandbriefinhaber, Treuhandzertifikatsbesitzer; **tripartite** ~ (*gesiegelte*) Vertragsurkunde in dreifacher Ausfertigung; ~ **trust** *Treuhandsondervermögen zur Sicherung von Wertpapieren*; ~ **trustee** Wertpapiersicherungstreuhänder.
indentured labour unfreie Arbeitskräfte *f/pl*, zwangsvertragliche Arbeitskräfte.

independence Unabhängigkeit *f* (= *U*), Selbständigkeit *f*; ~ **of states** souveräne *U*; **attainment of** ~ Erlangung der *U*; **declaration of** ~ → *declaration*.

independent unabhängig, selbständig; ~ **body politic** öffentlichrechtliche Körperschaft; ~ **brakes** voneinander unabhängige Bremsvorrichtungen; **I~ Broadcasting Authority** *GB*: *öffentl rechtl brit* Rundfunk- und Fernsehanstalt, *seit 1973*; ~ **clause** Hauptsatz; ~ **contractor** → *contractor*; ~ **of any other person** ohne Rücksicht auf Dritte; ~ **personal services** selbständige Arbeit; ~ **post audit** Außenrevision; ~ **public accountant** unabhängiger Abschlußprüfer; ~ **sovereign state** souveräner Staat; ~ **treasury system** *hist US* vom Bankensystem unabhängiges Staatsfinanzsystem (*auf Metallgeldbasis*).

independently owned in Alleineigentum stehend.

indeterminable nicht feststellbar, nicht entscheidungsfähig, zeitlich unbeschränkbar, unkündbar, unbefristet, offen; ~ **estate** → *estate*.

indeterminate unbestimmt; unbefristet; ~ **conditional release** bedingter Straferlaß.

indetermination Unbestimmtheit *f*.

index Index *m*, Inhaltsverzeichnis *n*; Nachweis *m*, Indexziffer *f*, Bibliografie *f*; ~ **card** Karteikarte; ~**-limited wage** Indexlohn; ~**(-) linked** indiziert, an den (Lebenshaltungskosten-)Index gekoppelt, indexgebunden, gleitend; ~ **map** Katasterübersichtsplan; ~ **number** Indexziffer, Meßzahl; ~ **of members** Aktienbuch; ~ **of minor interests** Verzeichnis von nachgeordneten Rechten eines Grundstücks; ~ **of names** Namensverzeichnis; ~ **of retail prices** Einzelhandelspreisindex; ~ **of wholesale prices** Großhandelsindex; **cost-of-living** ~ Lebenshaltungsindex; **crossed weight** ~ gekreuzter Index; **trade-weighted** ~ Index des Außenwerts; **weighted** ~ gewogener Index.

indexation Indexbindung *f*, Berücksichtigung des Lebenshaltungsindex; ~ **allowance** Bewertungsabschlag wegen Erhöhung des Lebenshaltungsindex.

index animi sermo *auf den Wortlaut abstellender Auslegungsgrundsatz*.

indicate anzeigen, hinweisen auf, zeigen, andeuten, bezeichnen, zum Ausdruck bringen; **amount ~d** der angegebene Betrag.

indication Anzeige *f*, Anzeichen *n*, Angabe *f*, Merkmal *n*, Indiz *n*; ~ **of denomination** Stückelung; ~ **of origin** Ursprungsbezeichnung; ~ **of price** Preisangabe; **letter of** ~ → *letter*.

indicative evidence angetretener Beweis *m*, Beweisanzeichen *n*.

indicium *pl indicia* Indiz *n*, Indizienbeweis *m*.

indict anklagen, die öffentliche Anklage *durch Geschworene* erheben.

indictable als schwere Straftat *zum Geschworenengericht* anklagbar.

indictee der Angeklagte.

indictment Anklage *f*, Anklageschrift *f*, Anklagebeschluß *m*, Eröffnungsbeschluß *m*, *US*: Anklage durch Voruntersuchungsgeschworene (*Grand Jury*); ~ **and information** Anklage (*jeder Art*); **bill of** ~ → *bill* (*2*); **consolidation of** ~ Verbindung von Anklagepunkten; **copy of** ~ → *copy*; **counts in** ~ Anklagepunkte; **finding of an** ~ Bestätigung des dringenden Tatverdachts; **joint** ~ Geschworenenanklage gegen mehrere Beschuldigte; **multicount** ~ Anklage mit mehreren Straftatbeständen; **plea to** ~ → *plea*; **preferment of bill of** ~ Anklageerhebung durch Geschworene; **return of** ~ = *finding of an* ~ *qv*; **to bring in an** ~ den dringenden Tatverdacht bestätigen, Anklage erheben; **trial of** ~ Hauptverhandlung.

indictor Ankläger *m*.

indifferent unparteiisch, unbeteiligt, uninteressiert, gleichgültig.

indigence Bedürftigkeit *f*, Armut *f*.
indigenisation Einbeziehung ins Inland; ~ **laws** *Gesetze zur Überführung von Firmenbeteiligungen an inländische Anteilseigner.*
indigenous einheimisch, eingeboren, angeboren.
indigent bedürftig, arm; ~ **insane person** mittelloser Geisteskranker.
indignit|y Beleidigung *f*, Beschimpfung *f*, Unwürdigkeit *f*; ~**ies to the person** beleidigende Tätlichkeiten.
indirect indirekt, mittelbar; ~ **exporting** unsichtbare Ausfuhr.
indirect production cost Fertigungsgemeinkosten.
indiscretion Indiskretion *f*, Verletzung *f* der Schweigepflicht, Unbesonnenheit *f*, Unüberlegtheit *f*, Vertrauensbruch *m*.
indiscrimination Mangel *m* an Unterscheidungsvermögen.
indispensability Unentbehrlichkeit *f*, Unabkömmlichkeit *f*.
indispensable unentbehrlich, unabkömmlich, unerläßlich.
indisputable unbestreitbar.
indisputability clause Rücktrittsverzichtsklausel (*Police*).
indistanter unverzüglich.
individual *adj* einzeln, individuell; ~ **account** → *account*; ~ **assets** Privatvermögen (*e–s Gesellschafters*); ~ **bank return** *Ausweis des New Yorker Clearinghauses*; ~ **bargaining** Einzeltarifverhandlung; **(the)** ~ **case** der vorliegende Fall, Einzelfall; ~ **consumer** Einzelverbraucher; ~ **debts** Privatschulden (*e–s Gesellschafters*); ~ **deposits** *Einlagen von Privatpersonen, Gesellschaften etc, nicht von Banken, Sparkassen etc*; ~ **earnings** Pro-Kopf-Einkommen; ~ **ledger** Kundenbuch; ~ **piece work** Einzelakkord; ~ **resident of the United States** Privatperson mit dauerndem Aufenthalt in den USA; **I**~ **Retirement Accounts** steuerfreie Altersvorsorgekonten (*US*).
individual *s* Individuum *n*, Person *f*, Einzelwesen *n*, natürliche Person *f* bzw juristische Person; Privatperson *f*; **claims of** ~**s** Ansprüche von natürlichen Personen; **group of** ~**s** Personenvereinigung; **international personality of** ~**s** völkerrechtliche Rechtsfähigkeit von natürlichen Personen; **private** ~ Privatperson, Einzelperson; **responsibility of** ~**s** Haftung von Privatpersonen.
individualism Individualismus *m*, Theorie *f* der unbeschränkten Unternehmerfreiheit.
individually persönlich, namentlich, jeder für sich; **to be** ~ **answerable for s. th.** persönlich für etwas haften.
indivisible unteilbar.
indivisum ungeteilter Gemeinschaftsbesitz *m*.
indorsable girierbar, indossierbar.
indorse indossieren, girieren; ~ **a bill of exchange** e–n Wechsel indossieren, einen Wechsel girieren; ~**d in blank** mit Blankoindossament versehen; **amount** ~**d** eingeklagter Betrag.
indorsee Indossatar *m*; ~ **in due course** der gutgläubige Erwerber auf Grund e–s Indossaments.
indorsement (= *endorsement*) Indossament *n* (= *Ind bzw ind*), Bestätigung *f*, Vermerk *m*; ~ **after maturity** Nach*ind*; ~ **as to service** Zustellungsbestätigung; **"**~ **confirmed"** „Giro bestätigt"; ~ **for collection** Inkasso*ind*; ~ **in blank** Blanko*ind*; ~ **in full** Voll*ind*; ~ **of address** Anschriftenvermerk des Klägers auf Klageladung; ~ **of claim** kurze Begründung des Klageanspruchs; ~ **of service** Zustellungsvermerk auf Klage; ~ **of warrant** Bestätigung *und Vollziehung* e–s auswärtigen Haftbefehls; ~ **per pro** Prokura*ind*; **"**~ **required"** „Giro fehlt"; ~ **supra protest** *Ind* nach Protest; ~ **without recourse** Giro (= *Ind*) ohne Obligo, *Ind* ohne Gewähr, *Ind* ohne Haftung; **absolute** ~ unbeschränktes *Ind*; **accommodation** ~ Gefälligkeits*ind*; **blank** ~ Blanko*ind*; **conditional** ~ bedingtes *Ind*, be-

schränktes *Ind, Ind vor Wechselannahme mit Auflagen für den Annehmer, Ind mit Bedingung für die Wechselhaftung*; **creditor by** ~ → *creditor*; **direct** ~ *US* Vollgiro; **full** ~ Vollgiro, Voll*ind*; **general** ~ Blanko*ind*; **holder by** ~ Indossatar; **official** ~ amtl Bestätigung; **order of** ~ Reihenfolge der *Ind–e*; **partial** ~ Teil*ind*; **pledge** ~ Pfand*ind*; **post** ~ Nach*ind*; **procuration** ~ → *procuration*; **proper** ~ ordnungsgemäßes *Ind* bzw Giro; **qualified** ~ beschränktes *Ind*, „Giro ohne Verbindlichkeit"; (Voll)*Ind* unter Haftungsausschluß; (Voll)*Ind* mit Angstklausel, *Ind* in stellvertretender Eigenschaft; **regular** ~ gewöhnliches Giro; **restrictive** ~ Rekta*ind*, Rektaklausel, negative Orderklausel; **special** ~ Voll*ind*, Namens*ind*; **special** ~ **of writ** abgekürzte Klagebegründung; **subsequent** ~ nachfolgender Indossant, Nachmann; **without** ~ ungiriert.

indorser Indossant *m*, Girant *m*; **~'s liability** Indossamentshaftung, Wechselhaftung, Giroverbindlichkeit; **preceding** ~ Vormann; **previous** ~ Vorindossant, Vormann; **second** ~ zweiter Indossant, Nachmann; **subsequent** ~ Nachindossant, Nachmann.

induce herbeiführen, veranlassen, anstiften.

inducement Motivierung *f*, Anreiz *m*; Verleitung *f*, Abfindungszahlung *f*; Veranlassung *f*, Interesse *n* (*am Vertragsschluß*); Beweggrund *m*, Tatmotiv *n*, einleitende Zusammenfassung *f* der Klagebegründung; ~ **leading to confession** Versprechungen als Beweggrund für ein Geständnis; **fraudulent** ~ arglistige Täuschung als Beweggrund.

induct (*in den Besitz*) einweisen, einführen, einsetzen; einberufen.

inductee Rekrut *m*, eingezogener Soldat *m*.

induction Einsetzung *f* in ein Kirchenamt bzw e–e Kirchenpfründe; Aufnahme *f* e–s Soldaten in die Streitkräfte, Einberufung *f*; ~ **order** Gestellungsbefehl.

indulgence Nachsicht *f*, Milde *f*, Stundung *f*; *eccl* Ablaß *m*.

industrial industriell, gewerblich, Industrie . . ., Gewerbe . . .; ~ **accident prevention** betriebliche Unfallverhütung; ~ **and provident societies** → *society*; ~ **and trade fairs** (gewerbliche) Messen; **I~ Common Ownership Act** Gesetz über belegschaftseigene Unternehmen *GB 1976*; ~ **death benefit** Arbeitsunfalls-Witwen(Witwer-)-rente; ~ **development certificate** Bescheinigung des Umweltschutzministeriums zur Industriestandortwahl; ~ **estates** Industriegebiet; ~ **diseases benefits** Sozialversicherungsleistungen an Arbeitgeber wegen arbeitsbedingter Erkrankungen; **I~ Estates Management Corporation** Industrieentwicklungsgesellschaft; ~ **finance company** gewerbl Kreditgenossenschaft; ~ **injuries benefit** Sozialversicherungsleistung bei Arbeitsunfall; ~ **injuries insurance** → *insurance*; ~ **life insurance** → *insurance*; ~ **property** gewerbliche Schutzrechte; ~ **property protection** gewerblicher Rechtsschutz; ~ **relations** Beziehungen zwischen den Sozialpartnern, Arbeitgeber-Arbeitnehmerbeziehungen; **I~ Relations Act** Betriebsverfassungs- und Arbeitskampfgesetz *GB, 1971*; ~ **relations officer** Schlichtungsbeamter bei Arbeitskämpfen; ~ **relations policy** Arbeitnehmerpolitik; **I~ Training Board** Industrieausbildungskommission; ~ **training levy** Ausbildungsumlage; ~ **tribunal** → *tribunal*.

industry Industrie *f* (= *Ind bzw ind*), Gewerbe *n*, Wirtschaftszweig *m*; **~ies in distress** notleidende Industriezweige; **basic** ~ Grund(stoff)-*ind*; **branch of** ~ Gewerbezweig, Erwerbszweig; **building** ~ Baugewerbe; **coal, iron and steel** ~ Montan*ind*; **consumer goods** ~ Verbrauchsgüter*ind*; **financial ser-**

vices ~ Kreditgewerbe; **finishing** ~ Veredelungs*ind*; **food manufacturing** ~ → *food*; **heavy** ~ Schwer*ind*; **primary** ~ Grundstoffindustrie; **processing** ~ Veredelungs*ind*, Verarbeitungs*ind*; **school of** ~ Berufsschulinternat; **service** ~ → *service*; **smoke stack** ~**ies** traditionelle Schwerindustrie; **supplying** ~ Zuliefer*ind*; **transforming** ~ verarbeitende *Ind*.

inebriate *adj* berauscht, betrunken; *s* Betrunkener *m*, Trunksüchtiger *m*; ~ **reformatory** Entziehungsanstalt für Alkoholiker; **asylum for** ~**s** Trinkerheilanstalt.

ineffective unwirksam, ungültig; **to become** ~ außer Kraft treten, unwirksam werden.

ineffectual wirkungslos.

inefficacious unwirksam, kraftlos.

inefficiency mangelnde Leistungsfähigkeit *f*.

inefficient unrationell, unfähig.

ineligibility Untauglichkeit *f*, Unwählbarkeit *f*, Ausschluß *m* vom passiven Wahlrecht, Unfähigkeit *f* zur Bekleidung e–s Amtes.

ineligible nicht wählbar, untauglich, unfähig zur Bekleidung e–s Amtes; ~ **paper** nicht diskontierfähiger Wechsel.

inequality Ungleichheit *f*.

inequitable unbillig, ungerecht.

inequity Unbilligkeit *f*, Ungerechtigkeit *f*.

inertia selling Verkaufsaktion durch Zusenden unbestellter Waren.

inevitable unvermeidlich, unvermeidbar, unabwendbar.

inexact ungenau, unrichtig, fehlerhaft.

inexcusable unentschuldbar.

inexpedience Unzweckmäßigkeit *f*.

inexpedient unzweckmäßig, ungeeignet.

infallibility Unfehlbarkeit *f*, Zuverlässigkeit *f*.

infallible unfehlbar, zuverlässig, untrüglich.

infamous verrufen, berüchtigt; schändlich; ~ **conduct** unehrenhaftes Verhalten; ~ ~ *in a professional respect: grob standeswidriges Verhalten (bei Medizinern)*; ~ **crime** → *crime*; ~ **crime against nature** widernatürliche Unzucht (*Sodomie*).

infamy Ehrlosigkeit *f*, Schande *f*; *hist* Verlust *m* der bürgerlichen Ehrenrechte, Verlust *m* der Zeugnisfähigkeit.

infancy Minderjährigkeit *f*; **natural** ~ Minderjährigkeit, Kindesalter (*bis einschließlich 7 Jahre*).

infant *adj* minderjährig → *minor*; ~ **children** Minderjährige; ~ **mortality** → *mortality*; ~ **state** junger Staat.

infant *s* Kind *n*; Minderjährige(r) *m*|*f*, Unmündige(r) *m*|*f*; **I**~ **Life (Preservation) Act** Abtreibungsverbotsgesetz *GB 1929*; ~ **welfare** → *welfare*.

infanticide Kindestötung *f*, *Töten e–s Kindes (bis 12) durch dessen Mutter unter mildernden Umständen*.

infeasible unausführbar, undurchführbar.

infection Infektion *f*, Ansteckung *f*; ~ **of goods** Beschlagnahmefähigkeit von Gütern als Konterbande; **auto** ~ Selbstinfektion.

in-feeding betriebs- oder konzerneigene Versorgung *f* mit Gütern *bzw* Dienstleistungen.

infeoffment Belehnung *f*.

infer ableiten, folgern, schließen.

inferable ableitbar, sich ergebend (*aus*).

inference Folgerung *f*, Schluß *m*; **to negative an** ~ e–e Folgerung (*bzw*. Vermutung) widerlegen; **wrong** ~ Fehlschluß.

inferential durch Folgerung festgestellt, gefolgert.

inferior untergeordnet, niedriger, geringer, minderwertig.

inferiority Untergeordnetsein *n*, Minderwertigkeit *f*.

infeudation Belehnung *f*.

infidelity Untreue *f*, Treulosigkeit *f*.

infighting interne Kämpfe *m*|*pl*.

infirm schwach, gebrechlich.

infirmative schwächend, entlastend; ~ **consideration** entlastender Gesichtspunkt, entlastende Überlegungen; ~ **fact** entlastende Tatsache; ~ **hypothesis** Nichtschuldhypothese bei Würdigung belastender Umstände.

infirmity Schwäche *f*, Gebrechlichkeit *f*; **mental** ~ Geistesschwäche.

inflaming the minds of others aufreizen.

inflation Inflation *f*, Geldentwertung *f*; ~ **accounting** inflationsbereinigte Bilanzierung, inflationsneutrale (= inflationsbereinigte) Rechnungslegung; **allowance for** ~ → *allowance*; **cost-push** ~ Inflation durch Kostensteigerungen; **credit** ~ Kreditausweitung; **creeping** ~ schleichende Inflation; **demand-pull** ~ Übernachfrage-Inflation; nachfrageinduzierte Infl.; **galloping** ~ galoppierende Infl.; **gradual** ~ schleichende Inflation; **homegrown** ~ hausgemachte Inflation; **hyper**~ galoppierende Inflation; **monetary** ~ Geldinflation; **runaway** ~ galoppierende Inflation; **wage-push** ~ durch Lohnsteigerungen bedingte Inflation.

inflation-linked inflationsgekoppelt, inflationsbezogen.

inflation-proofing Inflationsausgleichssicherung *f*.

inflationary spiral Inflationsspirale *f*, Preis-Lohnspirale *f*.

inflict auferlegen, aufzwingen, zufügen; verhängen; ~ **a penalty** e–e Strafe verhängen; ~ **damage** → *damage*.

infliction Auferlegung *f*, Verhängung *f*, Zufügung *f*.

influence Einfluß *m*, Einwirkung *f*; **sphere of** ~ Interessengebiet, Einflußgebiet; **improper** ~ sittenwidrige Beeinflussung; **undue** ~ unzulässige Beeinflussung, psychischer Zwang.

influx Zufluß *m*, Einströmen *n*; ~ **of capital** Kapitalzufluß.

inform benachrichtigen, verständigen, informieren; **liability to** ~ → *liability*; ~ **(against)** e–e Strafanzeige erstatten (gegen jmdn).

informal formlos, formfrei; ~ **contract** → *contract*; ~ **investigation** inoffizielle Untersuchung.

informality Formlosigkeit *f*, Formmangel *m*, Mangel *m* der gesetzlichen Form.

informant Informant *m*, Gewährsmann *m*, der Meldende.

information Mitteilung *f*, Nachricht *f*, Information *f*, Kenntnis *f*, Auskunft *f*, Meldung *f*, Benachrichtigung *f*, Erkundigung *f*, Bescheid *m*, Unterrichtung *f*; Wissen *n*, wissenswerte Tatsachen *f*/*pl*; Strafanzeige *f*, Strafklage *f*, ~ **agreement** Informationsaustauschvereinbarung (*bei Submissionen*); ~ **bureau** Informationsstelle; ~ **in rem** Aufgebot zur Einziehung (*von Schatzfund uä*) durch die Krone; ~ **in the nature of a quo warranto** öffentliche Klage wegen Anmaßung e–r Konzession *bzw Amtsanmaßung*; ~ **in the public domain** allgemein zugängliche Informationen; frei benutzbare Informationen; ~ **of intrusion** Räumungsklage *gegen unberechtigte Benutzer von Staatsgrund*; ~ **office** Auskunftsstelle, Informationsamt, Informationsstelle; ~ **service** Informationsdienst; **Central Office of I**~ Informationsministerium; **compounding** ~ Absehen von e–r Strafanzeige gegen Entgelt; **confidential** ~ vertrauliche Kenntnisse; **criminal** ~ Strafanzeige *GB, US*, auch *pl*; Anklage (*ohne Geschworenenverfahren*); **ex officio** ~ Strafanzeige von Amts wegen (*des Generalstaatsanwalts namens der Krone)*; **filing** ~ Einreichung e–r Strafanzeige; **for** ~ zur Kenntnisnahme; **industrial** ~ gewerbliche Öffentlichkeitsarbeit; **liable to render** ~ auskunftspflichtig; **non-public** ~ interne Information, vertrauliche Kenntnisse; **price-sensitive** ~ interne kursrelevante Information; **private** ~ vertrauliche Mitteilung; **privileged** ~ durch ein Aussageverweigerungsrecht geschützte Mitteilung; **to dismiss an** ~ das Verfahren (*mangels Tatverdachts*) einstellen; **to furnish ~ of s.th.** über etwas Auskunft erteilen; **to gather ~ about s.th.** Erkundigungen über etwas einziehen; **to lay an ~** Strafanzeige erstatten; **to obtain ~** Auskunft erlangen; **to prefer an ~** Strafanzeige erstatten; **to secure ~** (sich) Information beschaffen; **upon ~ and belief** nach bestem Wissen und Gewissen.

informatus non sum *Erklärung f des Anwalts des Beklagten, keine Information erhalten zu haben.*

informer Anzeigenerstatter *m*, V-Mann *m*, Spitzel *m*, Denunziant *m*; **~ evidence** Aussagen von Denunzianten bzw Spitzeln; **common ~** berufsmäßiger Denunziant, Spitzel; **paid ~** Spitzel, Polizeispitzel; **police ~** Polizeispitzel, Vertrauensmann der Polizei.

infra siehe unten (*Zitierhinweis*).

infract verstoßen gegen, (*Gesetze*) brechen.

infraction Verletzung *f*, Übertretung *f*, Verstoß *m* (*Gesetz*); **~ of a treaty** Verletzung e–s (völkerrechtlichen) Vertrages; **~ of the law** Gesetzesverletzung.

infrastructure Infrastruktur *f*; **~ projects** Infrastrukturvorhaben.

infring|e verletzen, übertreten; (*gegen e–e Vorschrift*) verstoßen, (*ein Recht*) beeinträchtigen; **~ a rule** gegen e–e Regel verstoßen, **~ a trust** e–e Treuhandpflicht verletzen; **~ing act** Verletzungshandlung.

infringement Übertretung *f*, Verstoß *m*, Zuwiderhandlung *f*; Verletzung *f* e–s gewerblichen Schutzrechtes; **~ litigation** Verletzungsstreit (*gewerblicher Rechtsschutz*); **~ of copyright** → *copyright*; **~ of patent** Patentverletzung; **~ of trademark** Warenzeichenverletzung; **~ proceedings** = *suit qv*; **~ suit** Patentverletzungsklage, Prozeß wegen Verletzung e–s gewerblichen Schutzrechtes; **action for ~** → *action*; **contributory ~ of patent** mittelbare Patentverletzung; **criminal ~** vorsätzliche, strafbare Urheberrechtsverletzung; **innocent ~** schuldlose Verletzung; **public ~** offenkundige Verletzung.

infringer Verletzter *m* (*meist: e–s gewerblichen Schutzrechts*).

ingenuity Einfallsreichtum *m*, Erfindungsgabe *f*, Scharfsinn *m*, sinnreiche Erfindung *f*.

ingoing neu, ein Amt antretend; **~ tenant** der neue Mieter (*bzw Pächter*).

ingot Barren *m*; **~ gold** → *gold*.

ingredient Bestandteil *m*, Tatbestandsmerkmal *n*; **~ of an offence** Tatbestandsmerkmal; Tatbestandsinhalt; **chief ~** Hauptbestandteil.

ingress, egress, and regress das Recht auf freie Zufahrt (*zu und von e–m Grundstück*).

ingross = *engross qv*.

ingrossing spekulative Preistreiberei *f*.

inhabit bewohnen; **~ed house duty** Wohnsteuer *f*; **to be ~ed** bewohnt, Wohnzwecken dienend.

inhabitant Bewohner *m*, Einwohner *m*.

inhere anhaften, innewohnen, zugehören, eigen sein, enthalten sein.

inherent innewohnend, inhärent, immanent, zugehörig; **~ logic** Natur der Sache; **~ vice** innerer Mangel (*infolge natürlicher Beschaffenheit*); versteckter Mangel.

inherit erben, vererben, beerben; **~ jointly** gemeinsam erben, Miterbe sein.

inheritability Erblichkeit *f*, Vererblichkeit *f*.

inheritable vererblich, auf den Erben übergehend; **not ~** unvererblich.

inheritance Erbe *n*, Erbgang *m*, Erbfall *m*, Erbrecht *n*, Beerbung *f*, Erbschaft *f*, Nachlaß *m* *speziell*: Intestatserbschaft *f* von Immobilien; **~ Act** *brit* Erbschaftsgesetz; **~ in abeyance** ruhende Erbschaft; **~ tax** → *tax*; **accrual of ~** → *accrual*; **certificate of ~** Erbschein; **compulsory right of ~** gesetzliches Erbrecht; **contract of ~** Erbvertrag; **devolution of an ~** Erbfall, Rechtsnachfolge durch Erbgang; **disclaimer of ~** Erbausschlagung;

estate of ~ → *estate*; **joint share in an** ~ Miterbenanteil; **partition of an** ~ Erbteilung, Erbauseinandersetzung; **possession by** ~ Erbbesitz; **scheme of** ~ Teilungsplan; **to come in for an** ~ e–e Erbanwartschaft haben; **to come into an** ~ erben.

inheritor Erbe *m*.

inheritrix (*pl: inheritrices*) Erbin *f*.

inhibit hindern, verbieten, untersagen.

inhibition Untersagung *f*, Verbot *n*; Widerspruch *m* (*Grundbuch*); Sperrvermerk *m* (*in e–m Register*); ~ **against a wife** *scot* Entzug der Schlüsselgewalt; *gerichtliches Verbot, Rechtsgeschäfte mit einer Ehefrau vorzunehmen und ihr Kredit zu gewähren*.

inhibitory verbietend.

in-house firmeneigen, intern, innerbetrieblich.

inhuman unmenschlich, menschenrechtswidrig.

iniquitous ungerecht, widerrechtlich, bösartig, schlecht, sündig, lasterhaft.

iniquity Ungerechtigkeit *f*, Widerrechtlichkeit *f*, Schlechtigkeit *f*, Frevelhaftigkeit *f*, Sünde *f*, Laster *n*; **to commit** ~ *scot* eine widerrechtliche Entscheidung fällen.

initial *adj* anfänglich, Erst . . .; ~ **export quota** Exportausgangskontingent; ~ **guarantee deposit** Anfangskaution; ~ **phase** Anlaufphase, Anfangsphase; ~ **placing of securities** Erstplazierung von Wertpapieren; **I~ (Provision for Family and Dependents) Act** Pflichtversorgungsgesetz für unterhaltsberechtigte Hinterbliebene; ~ **share issue** das ursprünglich begebene Aktienkapital, Grundkapital.

initial *v* paraphieren, abzeichnen; **~led ne varietur** als unabänderlich paraphiert.

initials Initialen *f*|*pl*, Anfangsbuchstaben *m*|*pl* (*bes des Namens*).

initiate beginnen, einleiten, einführen, einweihen; ~ **a legal action** ein Gerichtsverfahren beginnen; ~ **legislation** Gesetze(svorlagen) einbringen; ~ **negotiations** Verhandlungen beginnen.

initiation Einführung *f*, Aufnahme *f*, Beginn *m*; ~ **fee** Aufnahmegebühr, Eintrittsbeitrag; ~ **into an office** Amtseinführung; ~ **of crime** Herbeiführung e–r Straftat (*durch agent provocateur*).

initiative *adj* einleitend, selbständig; einführend, anfänglich.

initiative *s* Initiative *f*, erster Schritt *m*, einleitende Handlung *f*, Anregung *f*, Unternehmungsgeist *m*, Entschlußkraft *f*; Gesetzesinitiative *f*; Volksbegehren *n;* **legislative** ~ Einbringung e–r Vorlage; Volksbegehren.

initiatory einleitend.

injudicious nicht dem Richteramt entsprechend; ~ **conduct** richterliches Fehlverhalten.

injunction gerichtliche Verfügung *f*, gerichtl Anordnung, gerichtl Befehl; Unterlassungsurteil *n*, einstweilige Verfügung *f*; (= *einstw Vfg*); ~ **against execution of sentence** gerichtliche Einstellung der Strafvollstreckung; ~ **quia timet** vorbeugende Unterlassungsverfügung; ~ **to produce proof** gerichtliche Auflage, Beweis anzutreten; **blanket** ~ globale *einstw Vfg*; **final** ~ Endurteil auf Vornahme bzw Unterlassung e–r Handlung; **interim** ~ *einstw Vfg* (= ~ *ad interim*); **interlocutory** ~ *einstw Vfg*; **labour** ~ *einstw Vfg* in arbeitsrechtlichen Streitigkeiten; **mandatory** ~ *einstw Vfg* bzw Anordnung zur Vornahme e–r Handlung *bes auf Wiederherstellung des ursprünglichen Zustandes*; **matrimonial ~s** einstweilige Anordnung in Ehesachen (*bes betr Ehewohnung, Belästigung*); **negative** ~ gerichtl Verbot; **permanent** ~ *bis zum rechtskräftigen Endurteil im Hauptsacheverfahren gültige einstw Vfg*; **perpetual** ~ *Anordnung mit endgültiger Regelung auf unbestimmte Zeit*, Unterlassungsurteil; **preliminary** ~ *einstw Vfg* (*auf Unterlassung*); **preventive** ~ vorbeugende *einstw Vfg bzw* vorbeugendes Unterlassungsurteil; **prohibitory ~** *einstw Vfg* auf Unterlassung, gerichtliches Verbot; **provisional ~** *einstw Vfg*; **restrictive ~** *einstw Vfg* mit Unterlassungsanordnung; **special ~** *einstw Vfg bzw* einstw Anordnung, *meist nach Vorankündigung*; **temporary ~** *einstw Vfg*, einstw Anordnung; **to award an ~** e–e *einstw Vfg bzw* einstw Anordnung erlassen; **to grant an ~ ex parte** eine *einstw Vfg* ohne vorherige Benachrichtigung des Gegners erlassen.

injunctive anordnend, befehlend; verbietend, Verbots . . ., Unterlassungs . . ., auf Unterlassen gerichtet.

injure (*ein Recht*) verletzen, jmdn verletzen, beschädigen, benachteiligen, jmdm eine Körperverletzung zufügen; **~d party** der (die) Verletzte, der (die) Geschädigte; **fatally ~d** tödlich verletzt.

injurious schädlich, verderblich; beleidigend, verletzend; **~ to health** gesundheitsschädlich.

injuriously affected nachteilig betroffen, geschädigt.

injury Schaden *m*, Beschädigung *f*, Nachteil *m*, schädigende Handlung *f*, Schadensereignis *n*; Beschwer *f*, Beleidigung *f*, Verletzung *f*; **~ benefit** Arbeitsunfallsrente *bzw* Rente wegen Berufskrankheit *GB*: *bis 26 Wochen, dann (gfls) disablement benefit qv*; **~ by accident** Unfallsverletzung, unfallsbedingte Körperbeschädigung; **~ to any other land** Schaden an fremden Grundstücken; **~ to property** Sachbeschädigung, Sachschaden; **absolute ~** Verletzung absoluter Rechte der Person; **accidental ~** unfallsbedingte Körperverletzung, Arbeitsunfallverletzung; **ante-natal ~** vorgeburtliche Schädigung; **bodily ~** → *bodily*; **civil ~** zivilrechtlich verfolgbare Verletzung *bzw* Beschädigung; **compensable ~** entschädigungspflichtige Verletzung; **disabling ~** zu Arbeitsunfähigkeit führende Verletzung; **fatal ~** tödliche Verletzung, **industrial ~** Arbeitsunfallverletzung; **irreparable ~** nicht wiedergutzumachende Schädigung; **legal ~** Rechtsverletzung; **malicious ~** vorsätzliche Körperverletzung, böswillige Verletzung, absichtliche Schädigung; **multiple ~ies** Mehrfachverletzungen; **occupational ~** Arbeitsunfallverletzung; **on-the-job ~** Arbeitsunfallverletzung; **non-accidental ~** → *non-accidental*; **permanent ~** lebenslängliche Körperbeschädigung; **personal ~** Personenschaden, Körperverletzung, Gesundheitsbeschädigung; Verletzung des Persönlichkeitsrechts; **physical ~** Körperverletzung; **pre-existing ~** bereits vorhandene Verletzung; Vorschädigung; **prenatal ~** Verletzung des ungeborenen Kindes; **private ~** *Verletzung der Rechte von Privatpersonen, Verletzung im Sinne des Zivilrechts*; **public ~** Verletzung e–s Rechtsguts der Allgemeinheit; **real ~** Ehrverletzung; **relative ~** mittelbare Rechtsverletzung; **reparable ~** durch Geldzahlung wiedergutzumachende Beschädigung; **serious (bodily) ~** schwerer Fall der Körperverletzung; **to inflict an ~** Schaden zufügen; **verbal ~** Beleidigung, Rufschädigung.

injustice Unrecht *n*, Ungerechtigkeit *f*; **gross ~** grobe Ungerechtigkeit

inland *adj* inländisch, einheimisch; **~ bill (of exchange)** → *bill* (*3*); **~ carrier** Inlandfrachtführer; **~ commodities** einheimische Waren; **~ customs office** Binnenzollstelle; **~ marine insurance** Binnentransportversicherung; **~ navigation** Binnenschiffahrt; Schiffahrt in den USA (*ohne die Großen Seen*); **~ port** Binnenhafen; **~ produce** Landesprodukt; **~ rate** Binnentarif; **~ revenue** Steueraufkommen; inländ. Abgabenaufkommen; **I~ Revenue (Office)** Steuerbehörde, Finanzamt; **~ revenue minders** Finanzbeamte, Steuerreferenten; **~ revenue stamp** Steuerstempelmarke; ~ **trade** Binnenhandel; ~ **transport** Binnenverkehr; ~ **transport insurance** Binnentransportversicherung; ~ **waters** Binnengewässer; ~ **waterways bill of lading** → *bill of lading*; ~ **waterways insurance** → *insurance*; ~ **waterways transport** Binnenschiffahrtsverkehr.

inland *s* Inland *n*, Binnenland *n*.

in-law *s* Verschwägerte(r), angeheiratete(r) Verwandte(r).

inmate Hausgenosse *m*, Mitbewohner *m*, Insasse *m* (*Gefängnis*); ~ **of house of prostitution** Prostituierte e–s Bordells; **camp** ~ Lagerinsasse; **prison** ~ → *prison*.

inn Gasthof *m*; **I~s of Chancery** *Anwaltsvereinigungen (von Solicitors) in London*; **I~s of Court** (=) *Vereinigungen der Barristers in London*; die Gebäude der Inns of Court; **common** ~ Gasthof.

innate angeboren, natürlich, eigen.

innavigable unschiffbar; nicht seetüchtig.

inner|barrister → *barrister*; ~ **city housing estate** Innenstadtwohnanlage; **I~ House** *Gerichtssaal im Court of Sessions*; **I~ Temple** (=) *einer der Inns of Court qv*; ~ **urban area** Innenstadtgebiet.

innkeeper Gastwirt *m*; **~'s liability** Gastwirtshaftung; **~'s lien** → *lien*.

innocence Unschuld *f*, Schuldlosigkeit *f*; **presumption of** ~ → *presumption*.

innocent unschuldig, schuldlos, unverschuldet, gutgläubig; ~ **holder for value** gutgläubiger Wechselinhaber; ~ **mistake of the law** unverschuldeter Rechtsirrtum.

innominate nicht benannt, nicht klassifiziert; ~ **contracts** atypische Verträge.

innovation Neuerung *f*; *scot* Novation *f*; ~ **capital** Innovationskapital.

innovativeness Innovationsfähigkeit *f*.

innuendo versteckte Andeutung *f*, beleidigende Unterstellung *f*.

inobservance Nichtbeachtung *f*.

inoperative unwirksam, ungültig; **to become** ~ ungültig werden, außer Kraft treten.

inops consilii ohne (Rechts)beratung (*bei Testamentserrichtung*).

inordinatus Intestaterblasser *m*.

in-patient Patient *m* in stationärer Behandlung.

inpayment Einzahlung *f*.

inpenny and outpenny Pachtpfennig *m* (*gezahlt bei Übernahme und bei Abgabe von Pachtland*).

input-output analysis Input-Output-Analyse *f* (*Strukturanalyse der liefer- und leistungsmäßigen Verflechtungen im Produktionsbereich*).

inquest Untersuchung *f durch Geschworene*; Beweisaufnahme *f*; Inquisitionsverfahren *n*, amtliche Untersuchung *f* e–r Todesursache; Leichenschauverfahren *n*; ~ **into deaths** Untersuchung von Todesursachen; ~ **of lunacy** gerichtliche Untersuchung wegen Geisteskrankheit; ~ **of office** amtliche Untersuchung zur Feststellung angefallenen Kronvermögens; ~ **on the body** gerichtl Leichenbeschau; **arrest of** ~ Antrag auf Einstellung des Untersuchungsverfahrens; **coroner's** ~ *vgl coroner*; gerichtliche Untersuchung ungeklärter Todesfälle; **official** ~ amtliche Erhebung, Untersuchung.

inquire erkundigen, untersuchen, forschen, nachfragen; ~ **in writing** schriftlich anfragen.

inquiry Untersuchung *f*, Nachforschung *f*, Anfrage *f*, gerichtliches Aufklärungsersuchen *n*, parlamentarisch angeordnete Untersuchung *f*; ~ **agent** Ermittler, Ermittlungsbeamter; ~ **inspector** Prüfer, Rechercheur; **~-office** Auskunftsbüro; **board of** ~ Ausschuß, Untersuchungskommission; **Court of I~** → *court*; **due** ~ ordnungsgemäße Untersuchung; **judicial** ~ → *judicial*; **preliminary** ~ gerichtl Voruntersuchung; **public** ~ amtl *bzw* öffentl Untersuchung; **to institute an** ~ e–e Untersuchung einleiten; **to make ~ies** Nachforschungen anstellen.

inquisition Untersuchung *f*, Geschworenenuntersuchung (*bzgl der Todesursache*); ~ **after death** *Untersuchung über den Lehenbesitz anläßlich des Todes e–s Lehensträgers*; ~ **of lunacy** gerichtliche Untersuchung wegen Geisteskrankheit; **coroner's** ~ = *coroner's inquest* → *coroner*.

inquisitor gerichtlicher Untersuchungsführer *m*.

inquisitorial inquisitorisch, Inquisitions . . ., Untersuchungs . . .

inquorate beschlußunfähig.

inroad Eingriff *m*, Übergriff *m*.

insane wahnsinnig, geisteskrank, geistesgestört, unzurechnungsfähig; ~ **person** Geisteskranker; **incurably** ~ unheilbar geisteskrank; **to be certified** ~ für unzurechnungsfähig wegen Geisteskrankheit erklärt werden.

insanitary unhygienisch.

insanity Geisteskrankheit *f*, Geistesgestörtheit *f*; ~ **induced by intoxication** Unzurechnungsfähigkeit wegen Volltrunkenheit; **absolute** ~ völlige Verblödung; **affective** ~ Affektpsychose; **circular** ~ manisch-depressives Irresein; **choreic** ~ Veitstanz; **compulsive** ~ Zwangspsychose; **congenital** ~ erbliche Geisteskrankheit; **emotional** ~ Affektpsychose; **habitual** ~ chronische Geisteskrankheit; **involutional** ~ senile Geistesschwäche; **legal** ~ Unzurechnungsfähigkeit *bzw* Geschäftsunfähigkeit wegen Geisteskrankheit; **maniacal-depressive** ~ manisch-depressives Irresein; **moral** ~ moralischer Defekt, krankhafte Gewissenlosigkeit; krankhafte Hemmungslosigkeit (*nicht als Unzurechnungsfähigkeit anerkannt*); **partial** ~ teilweise in Erscheinung tretende Geisteskrankheit; Monomanie *bzw Übergangsstadium von Geisteskrankheit*; **perceptional** ~ halluzinatorische Psychose; **plea of** ~ → *plea*; **polyneuritic** ~ Korsakowsche Psychose; **puerperal** ~ Puerperalpsychose (*geistige Störung der Mutter während oder kurz nach der Geburt*); **recurrent** ~ Psychose mit lichten Perioden; in Schüben auftretende Geisteskrankheiten; **recurrent fits of** ~ sich wiederholende manische Anfälle; **senile** ~ Altersdemenz; **settled** ~ Geisteskrankheit durch chronischen Alkoholismus und Entziehungskuren, Delirium tremens; **standing mute on account of** ~ wegen Unzurechnungsfähigkeit unfähig, sich zur Anklage zu erklären; **syphilitic** ~ Geisteskrankheit durch Syphilis; **temporary** ~ → *temporary*; **test of** ~ Prüfung der Zurechnungsfähigkeit wegen möglicher Geisteskrankheit; **traumatic** ~ traumatische Geisteskrankheit *als Folge e–r Gehirnverletzung*.

inscribe einschreiben, eintragen.

inscription Inschrift *f*, Aufschrift *f*, Eintragung *f*.

insensible sinnlos, unverständlich.

inseparable untrennbar, unzertrennlich.

insert einfügen, einsetzen, einschalten, inserieren.

insertion Einfügung *f*, Einwurf *m*, Zusatz *m*, Einführung *f*, Anzeige *f*, Inserat *n*.

inshore fishing Küstenfischerei *f*.

insider Insider, *jmd, der interne börsenrelevante Kenntnisse hat*; ~ **dealing** Börsengeschäfte von Firmenangehörigen (*bzw Führungskräften*) aufgrund interner Informationen; ~ **trading** = *dealing qv*; ~ **transgressions** „Insider"-Delikte.

insidious heimtückisch, trügerisch, hinterlistig.

insight (*into*) Einsicht *f*, Einblick *m*.

insignia Insignien *n*|*pl*, Amtszeichen *n*|*pl*, Wappen *n*|*pl*, Abzeichen *n*|*pl*, Embleme *n*|*pl*, Merkmale *n*|*pl*.

insignificant unerheblich, unbedeutend, bedeutungslos.

insincerity Unaufrichtigkeit *f*, arglistige Täuschung *f*.

insinuate andeuten, indirekt zu verstehen geben, anspielen (auf).

insinuation Anspielung *f*, versteckte Andeutung *f*, Insinuation, Schmeichelei *f*, Eintragung *f* in ein Register; ~ **of a will** Vorlage e–s Testaments.

insist (*on*) bestehen (*auf*), drängen, verlangen, Wert legen (*auf*), betonen, beharrlich fortfahren; ~ **on one's innocence** seine Unschuld beteuern.

insolvency Zahlungsunfähigkeit *f*, Insolvenz; ~ **fund** Insolvenzrückstellung (*der brit Staatsbank*); ~ **laws** Gesetze über Vergleichs- und Konkursverfahren, Insolvenzrecht; ~ **of an estate** Nachlaßüberschuldung; **I~ Services Account** Masseguthabenskonto (*brit Staatsbank*); **commercial** ~ Zahlungsunfähigkeit e–s Kaufmanns; **in case of** ~ bei Zahlungsunfähigkeit; **involuntary** ~ von Gläubigerseite beantragtes Vergleichs- *bzw* Konkursverfahren; **national** ~ Staatsbankrott; **notorious** ~ amtsbekannte Zahlungsunfähigkeit; **open** ~ offenbare Zahlungsunfähigkeit, amtsbekannte Unpfändbarkeit; **practical** ~ zeitweise Illiquidität; **voluntary** ~ beantragtes Vergleichs- *bzw* Konkursverfahren.

insolvent zahlungsunfähig, insolvent.

inspect inspizieren, prüfen, beaufsichtigen, Einsicht nehmen, einsehen, besichtigen; ~ **a witness** e–n Zeugen vernehmen; ~ **the goods** die Ware prüfen.

inspectator Staatsanwalt *m*; Gegner *m*.

inspection Prüfung *f*, Besichtigung *f*, Einsichtnahme *f*; ~ **as of right** Einsichtnahme als Rechtsanspruch; ~ **by the judge** richterliche Augenscheinseinnahme; ~ **fee** Prüfgebühr; ~ **laws** gesetzliche Vorschriften über Warenprüfung; ~ **of child** Augenscheinseinnahme durch Betrachten des Kindes (*Vaterschaftsfeststellung*); ~ **of deeds** Einsicht in Urkunden; ~ **of documents** Urkundeneinsicht, *Recht der Einsichtnahme und Abschriftentnahme von Urkunden des Gegners*; ~ **of files** Akteneinsicht; ~ **of property** Augenscheinseinnahme; ~ **order** Beschluß auf Urkundeneinsicht; **certificate of** ~ → *certificate*; **committee of** ~ Gläubigerausschuß (*Konkurs*); **consignment for** ~ Ansichtssendung; **customs** ~ Zollrevision; **judicial** ~ richterlicher Augenschein; **local** ~ Ortsbesichtigung, Augenscheinseinnahme; **ocular** ~ Augenscheinseinnahme; **ordinary** ~ übliche Prüfung; **public** ~ jedermann zugängige Einsichtnahme; **right of** ~ Recht der Einsichtnahme; **to be open to** ~ zur Einsicht ausliegen; **to buy after** ~ nach Besicht kaufen; **trade** ~ Gewerbeaufsicht; **trial by** ~ → *trial*.

inspector Inspektor *m*, Prüfer *m*; ~ **of constabulary** Polizeiaufsichtsbeamter; **I~ General of the Forces** Generalinspekteur der Streitkräfte; ~ **of taxes** Leiter des Finanzamtes; ~ **of weights and measures** Eichmeister; ~ **of works** Bau(aufsichts)behörde; **customs** ~ Zollbeamter; **police** ~ Polizeikommissar.

inspectorship deed Liquidationsvergleichsurkunde *f*.

inspectorate Inspektion *f* (*als Behörde bzw Bezirk*), Dienstaufsichtsbehörde *f*.

install installieren, einrichten; einbauen, aufstellen, einweisen.

installation Einrichtung *f*; Betrieb *m*, Anlage *f*, Amtseinsetzung *f*; ~ **bonds** serienweise rückzahlbare Obligationen; ~ **charges** Montagegebühren; ~ **cost** Aufstellungskosten, Einbaukosten; **military** **~s** militärische Anlagen.

instalment Rate *f*, Teilzahlung *f*; ~ **business** Abzahlungsgeschäft; ~ **buying** Abzahlungskauf; ~ **credit** → *credit* (*2*); ~ **deliveries** Teillieferungen in regelmäßigen Abständen; ~ **finance company** Teilzahlungskreditbank; ~ **financing** Teilzahlungsfinanzierung; ~ **mortgage** → *mortgage*; ~ **options** wahlweise Zahlung der Versicherungssumme in Teilbeträgen; ~ **paper** Teilzahlungsfinanzierungsurkunde; **arrears of ~s** Ratenrückstand; **final** ~ letzte Rate, Schlußrate; **first** ~ Anzahlung, erste Rate; **monthly** ~ Monatsrate; **on the ~ plan** auf Abzahlungsbasis; **yearly** ~ Jahresrate.

instance *s* Beispiel *n*, Ansuchen *n*, Augenblick *m*, Instanz *f*; **at the ~ of** auf Veranlassung von, auf Antrag von; **causes of** ~ Antragsverfahren; **court of first** ~ → *court*; **for** ~ zum Beispiel; **higher** ~ obere Instanz; **in a given** ~ in e–m Einzelfall; **lower** ~ untere Instanz.

instance *v/t* als Beispiel anführen.

instant sofort, gegenwärtig, laufend.

instantaneous augenblicklich, umgehend, sofort.

instanter sofort, unverzüglich; **to plead** ~ *etwas* unverzüglich (*innerhalb von 24 Std.*) vortragen; **trial** ~ sofortige Hauptverhandlung.

instigate anstiften, aufreizen.

instigation Anstiftung *f*; Veranlassung *f*; Aufhetzung *f*; **at the ~ of** auf Veranlassung von, auf Antrag von.

instigator Anstifter *m*, Aufrührer *m*.

institorial power Geschäftsführungsbefugnis *f* (*Handlungsgehilfe*).

institute *s* Einrichtung *f*, Institut *n*; Vorerbe *m*; ~ **for defectives** Heil- und Pflegeanstalt; **I~ of Bankers** (=) *Berufsverband der Bankiers und Bankbeamten GB*; **I~s of Lord Coke** *Rechtsbücher von Lord Coke, 1628 (grundlegendes Werk über das Common Law)*; **I~ of Patent Agents** *brit* Patentanwaltskammer; **endowed** ~ Stiftung, Anstalt mit Stiftungskapital.

institute *v* einsetzen, einrichten, gründen, stiften, jmdn in ein Amt einsetzen; ~ **an action** (*a suit*) Klage erheben; ~ **bankruptcy proceedings** das Konkursverfahren einleiten, Konkursantrag stellen; ~ **criminal proceedings** Strafverfahren einleiten, Strafklage erheben, Strafantrag stellen.

institution Einsetzung *f*, Eröffnung *f*, Anstalt *f*, Institut *n*, Organ *n*; **~s not for profit** gemeinnützige Anstalten; ~ **of a prosecution** das Anhängigmachen e–r Klage; Einleitung e–s Strafverfahrens; ~ **of an action** Klageerhebung; ~ **of proceedings** Einleitung e–s Verfahrens; **charitable** ~ karitative Einrichtung, wohltätige Stiftung; **educational** ~ Bildungseinrichtung, Bildungsanstalt, Schule; **financial** ~ Kreditinstitut; **mental** ~ psychiatrische Klinik, Heil- und Pflegeanstalt; **penal** ~ Strafanstalt; **public** ~ öffentliche Anstalt; **vocational** ~ Jugendstrafanstalt.

institutor Gründer *m*, Stifter *m*.

instruct Weisungen erteilen, belehren, informieren, unterrichten; ermächtigen, als Anwalt aufzutreten; ~ **counsel** e–n Prozeßbevollmächtigten informieren.

instruction Vorschrift *f*, Weisung *f*, Unterrichtung *f*, Belehrung *f*; **~s for brief** Prozeßvorbereitung, Informationsbeschaffung; **~s for despatch** Versandanweisungen; **~s for use** Gebrauchsanweisung; ~ **manual** Gebrauchsanweisung(shandbuch); ~ **sheet** Anweisungsblatt; **~s to applicants** Anmeldebestimmungen; **~s to the jury** Rechtsbelehrung der Geschworenen; **cautionary** ~ Belehrung *zum Schutz des Beschuldigten*; **letter of** ~ Schreiben mit Weisungen, gerichtliche Verfügung an den Sachverständigen über das Beweisthema; **official** ~ Dienstvorschriften; **operating ~s** Bedienungsanweisung; **peremptory** ~ bindende Rechtsbelehrung (*an die Geschworenen*).

instructor Instrukteur *m*, Lehrer *m*, Dozent *m*.

instrument Urkunde *f*, konstitutive Urkunde *f*, Übereinkunft *f*, Beweisstück *n*; ~ **in writing** Schriftstück, Urkunde; ~ **not to order** Rektapapier; ~ **of abdication** Abdankungsurkunde; ~ **of acceptance** Annahmeurkunde; ~ **of accession** Beitrittsurkunde; ~ **of appeal** Berufungsschriftsatz *an das Plenargericht*; ~ **of appointment**

Bestallungsurkunde; ~ **of approval** Genehmigungsurkunde; ~ **of assignment** Zessionsurkunde; ~**of charge** Hypothekenbewilligungsurkunde; ~ **of debt** Schuldurkunde; ~ **of dissolution** Liquidationsurkunde; ~ **of evidence** Beweisurkunde; ~ **of gaming** Glücksspielapparat; ~ **of housebreaking** Einbruchswerkzeug; ~ **of indebtedness** Schuldurkunde; ~ **of payment** Zahlungsmittel; ~ **of ratification** Ratifikationsurkunde; ~ **of saisine** *scot* Auflassungsurkunde; ~ **of security** Sicherungsurkunde, Verpfändungsurkunde; ~ **of signature** Unterzeichnungsurkunde; ~ **of transfer** Übertragungsurkunde; ~ **(payable) to bearer** Inhaberpapier; ~ **to order** Orderpapier; **authentic** ~ echte Urkunde, beglaubigte Urkunde; **banking** ~ bankfähiges Wertpapier, Bankurkunde; **commercial** ~ kaufmännisches Wertpapier; Handelspapier; **common** ~**s** *int* Solidaritätsmechanismen; **deed,** ~ **or will** gesiegelte oder sonstige Urkunde oder letztwillige Verfügung; **false** ~ gefälschte Urkunde; **inchoate** ~ unvollständige Urkunde; eintragungsbedürftige U., noch nicht eingetragene U.; **legal** ~ (wirkende) Urkunde; **measuring** ~**s** Meßinstrumente; **negotiable** ~ → *negotiable*; **non-negotiable** ~ Rektapapier; **notarial** ~ Notariatsurkunde; Notariatsprotokoll, notariell beurkundetes Dokument; **perfect** ~ rechtsgültige Urkunde; **registered** ~ Namenspapier; **testamentary** ~ Testamentsurkunde.

instrumental dienlich, förderlich; ~ **cause** mitwirkende Ursache; **to be** ~ **to** beitragen, mitwirken.

instrumentality Mittel *n*, Mitwirkung *f*, Organ *n*, Behörde *f*; ~ **rule** Durchgriffshaftung auf die beherrschende Gesellschaft von Organgesellschaften; **administrative** ~ Verwaltungsorgan, Behörde; **governmental** ~ staatliche Behörde; öffentliche Behörde; **through the** ~ **of** durch Vermittlung von.

insubordination Gehorsamsverweigerung *f*, Ungehorsam *m* gegen Vorgesetzte.

insufficiency Unzulänglichkeit *f*, Unfähigkeit *f*, Unvollständigkeit *f*, mangelnde Substantiierung *f* (*der Klageerwiderung*); Dürftigkeit des Nachlasses; ~ **of assets** mangelnde Deckung (*e–s Schecks*); mangels Masse (*Konkurs*).

insufficient unzulänglich, ungenügend, ungültig; ~ **funds** ungenügende Deckung; ~ **packing** Verpackungsmangel.

insulate isolieren.

insulation Isolierung *f*; **thermal** ~ Wärmedämmung.

insult *s* Beleidigung *f*, Beschimpfung *f*, Ehrverletzung *f*; **gross** ~ schwere Beleidigung.

insult *v* beschimpfen, beleidigen; verhöhnen; ~**ing behaviour** ehrkränkendes Verhalten.

insuperable unüberwindlich.

insurable versicherbar, versicherungsfähig.

insurance Versicherung *f* (= *V bzw v*), Risikoversicherung *f*; **I~ Act** *V–s*vertragsgesetz; *V–s*aufsichtsgesetz; ~ **adjuster** Schadensgutachter, Schätzer; ~ **against breakage** Bruch*v*; ~ **against loss by redemption** Kursverlust*v*; ~ **against third-party risks** Haftpflicht*v*; ~ **agent** *V–s*vertreter; *V–s*agent; ~ **agreement** *V–s*vertrag; ~ **benefit** → *benefit*; ~ **bond** *V–s*beleihungsschuldschein; ~ **broker** → *broker*; ~ **business** *V–s*gewerbe; ~ **canvasser** *V–s*werber, *V–s*vertreter; ~ **carriers** *V–s*träger; ~ **certificate** *V–s*bestätigung; ~ **charges** *V–s*kosten; ~ **claim** *V–s*anspruch; ~ **commissioner** *V–s*aufsichtsbehörde; ~ **committee** Sozial*v–s*ausschuß (Kranken*V*); ~ **company** *V–s*gesellschaft; ~ **contract** → *contract*; ~ **contribution** → *contribution*; ~ **coupon** *V–s*vertragsabschnitt; ~ **coverage**

V–*s*deckung; ~ **department** *V*–*s*-aufsichtsbehörde; ~ **dodger** pflichtwidrig nicht versicherter Fahrer; ~ **expenses** *V*–*s*kosten; ~ **fraud** *V*–*s*betrug; ~ **fund** *V*–*s*deckungsmittel; ~ **holder** Versicherter; ~ **law** → *law*; ~ **legislation** gesetzliche Vorschriften über das *V*–*s*wesen; ~ **map** *V*–*s*lageplan; ~ **money** *V*–*s*summe; ~ **note** vorläufiger *V*–*s*schein; ~ **on freight** Fracht*v*; ~ **on hull and appurtenances** Kasko*v*; ~ **of merchandise** Waren*v*; ~ **period** *V*–*s*dauer; ~ **policy** *V*–*s*police; ~ **portfolio** *V*–*s*bestand; Wertpapierbestand e–r *V*; ~ **premium** *V*–*s*prämie; ~ **rate** *V*–*s*prämiensatz; ~ **rating** Prämienberechnung; ~ **regulations** *V*–*s*ordnung; ~ **shares** *V*–*s*aktien; ~ **tariff** *V*–*s*tarif; Prämientarif; ~ **to cover long-term at-home or nursing-home care** Pflegefall*v*; ~ **trust** Treuhandverwaltung von Lebensversicherungsvermögen; ~ **with participation in profits** *V* mit Gewinnbeteiligung; **accident** ~ Unfall*v*; **accounts receivable** ~ Delcredere*v*; Forderungsausfall*v*; **additional** ~ Nach*v*, (*verbotene*) Doppel*v*; **air passenger** ~ Fluggast*v*; **aircraft** ~ Luftfahrt*v*; **air-travel** ~ Luftunfall*v*; **all-in** ~ Gesamt*v*; **all-risk** ~ Gesamt*v*, Global*v*; **all loss** ~ Gesamtversicherung; **annuity** ~ Renten*v*; **assessable** ~ *V* mit Nachschußpflicht; **assessment** ~ Lebens*v* auf Gegenseitigkeit; **assessment life** ~ **policy** Lebens*v* im Umlageverfahren (*mit variabler V–sleistung*); **automobile** ~ Kraftfahrzeug*v* (*Sammelbegriff*); **automobile personal liability and property damage** ~ Haftpflicht*v* mit Kasko*v*; **auto-travel** ~ Kraftfahrreise*v*; **bad debts** ~ Kredit*v*; **baggage** ~ Reisegepäck*v*; **blanket** ~ Kollektiv*v*; **boiler** ~ Dampfkessel*v*; **bonds** ~ Kautions*v*; **builder's risk** ~ Bauhaftpflicht*v*; **buildings** ~ Gebäude*v* (*Brandversicherung*); **burglary** ~ Einbruchsdiebstahl*v*; **burial** ~ Sterbe*v*; **business** ~ Betriebsverlust*v*; **business closure** ~ Betriebsschließungs*v*; **business interruption** ~ *V* gegen Betriebsunterbrechung; **business partnership** ~ Teilhaber*v*; **capital redemption** ~ Spar*v*; **cargo** ~ Fracht*v*; **casualty** ~ Unfall*v*; Schadens*v*; **cattle** ~ Vieh*v*; **check-alteration and forgery** ~ *V* gegen Scheckfälschungen; **child endowment** ~ Ausstattungs*v*; **club** ~ Gegenseitigkeits*v* (*von Schiffseignern wegen besonderer Risiken*); **contract penalty** ~ Vertragsstrafen*v*; **co-** ~ → *coinsurance*; **collateral** ~ Neben*v*; **collective** ~ Gruppen*v*, Kollektiv*v*; **collision** ~ Kollisions*v*, Kasko*v*; **commercial** ~ Handelsrisiko*v*, Delkredere- und Vertrauensschaden*v*; **commercial accident** ~ Betriebsunfall*v*; **common carrier's legal liability** ~ gesetzliche Frachtführerhaftpflicht*v*; **compensation** ~ Schadens*v*; **complementary** ~ Zusatz*v*; **comprehensive** ~ Universal*v*; *GB*: kombinierte Haftpflicht*v* mit Vollkasko*v*, Insassenunfall*v* und Gepäck*v*; *US*: Kasko*v*; **compulsory** ~ Pflicht*v*, Zwangs*v*; **computer misuse** ~ Komputermißbrauch*v*; **compulsory liability** ~ Haftpflicht-Pflicht*v*; **concurrent** ~ gemeinsame *V durch mehrere Versicherer;* **consequential loss** (= *damage*) ~ Folgeschaden*v*, Vermögensschaden*v*; **contract of** ~ *V*–*s*vertrag; **contractor's all-risks** ~ pauschale Risiko*v* für Unternehmerleistungen; **contractor's public liability and property damage liability** ~ Unternehmerhaftpflicht*v*; **contributory** ~ *V* mit Selbstbehalt; **converted** ~ *US staatl Lebensv für Angehörige der Streitkräfte*; **convertible collision** ~ Kasko*v* mit Prämienerhöhung nach erstem Unfall; **convertible term** ~ Risikoumtausch*v*; **conveyance** ~ Transport*v*; Haftpflicht*v* im Grundstücksverkehr; **cooperative** ~ → *co-operative*; **credit** ~ → *credit*

(*2*); **crime** ~ Verbrechensschadenv; **crop** ~ Erntev; **decreasing term** ~ Lebensv mit abnehmender Todesfallzahlung; *V* mit abnehmender Versicherungssumme; **deferred** ~ im voraus bezahlte *V–s*-beiträge; **deferred annuity** ~ abgekürzte Lebensv; **disability** ~ Unfallv, Invaliditätsv; **double** ~ Doppelv, Mehrfachv; **earthquake** ~ Erdbebenv; **elevator** ~ Fahrstuhlv; **employer's** ~ Unternehmerhaftpflichtv; **employer's liability** ~ Unternehmerhaftpflichtv, Betriebshaftpflichtv (*für Körperverletzung*); **endowment** ~ → *endowment*; **errors and omissions** ~ *V* gegen Schäden durch Irrtum und Auslassungen; Kassenmanko-*V*; **excess** ~ Exzendentenv, Überv; **exempt from** ~ *v–s*frei; **expiration of an** ~ Erlöschen e–r *V*; **extended** ~ prolongierte *V*; **extended term** ~ als Einmalprämienv fortgesetzte *V*; **factory** ~ Betriebsv; **fidelity** ~ Kautionsv; **fidelity and guarantee** ~ Kautionsv, Vertrauensschadenv und Kreditv; **fire** ~ → *fire insurance*; **first loss** ~ Erstrisikov; **first part** ~ Eigenv; **fleet** ~ Kraftfahrzeugsammelv; **floater** ~ laufende *V*; **flood** ~ Überschwemmungsv; **fly-wheel** ~ Schwungradv; **fraternal** ~ → *fraternal*; **freight** ~ Frachtv; **general** ~ allgemeine Seeschadensv; **general conditions of** ~ allgemeine *V–s*bedingungen; **general liability** ~ allgemeine Haftpflichtv; **government** ~ staatl Veteranenlebensv; **greenhouse** ~ Gewächshausv; **group** ~ Gruppenlebensv; **group creditor** ~ Kollektivlebensv für Kleinkreditnehmer; **group disability** ~ Sammelunfallv; **group-term life** ~ Gruppenrisikolebensv; **growing crops** ~ Erntev; **guarantee** ~ (= *guaranty* ~) Kautionsv, Kreditv; **guarantee of title** ~ Rechtsmängelgewährleistungsv (*bei Grundstücksverkauf*); **hail (storm)** ~ Hagelv; **hazardous** ~ Risikov, *V* mit ungewöhnlich großem Risiko; **health** ~ → *health*; **householders' comprehensive** ~ Hausratv; **hull** ~ Schiffsv, Schiffskaskov; **indemnity** ~ Haftpflichtv; **individual** ~ Einzelv; **industrial injuries** ~ Betriebsunfallv; **inland waterways** ~ Binnenschiffahrtsv; **insolvency** ~ Insolvenzsicherung; **International Motor I**~ (*Green Card*) Internationale Autoversicherung; (*grüne V–s-karte*); **joint life** ~ → *life insurance*; **jewelry** ~ Schmuckv; ~ **leasehold** ~ Pachtausfallv; **legal** ~ Rechtsschutzv; **legal expenses** ~ Rechtsschutzv; **liability** ~ Haftpflichtv; **life** ~ → *life insurance*; **lightning** ~ Blitzschlagv; **live stock** ~ Viehv; **loss of profits** ~ Geschäftsausfallv; **luggage** ~ Reisegepäckv; **machinery** ~ Maschinenhaftpflichtv; **marine** ~ Seev, Seetransportv; **marine hull** ~ Schiffskaskov; **marriage portion** ~ Brautaussteuerv; **material damage** ~ Sachschadensv; **mercantile open-stock** ~ Diebstahlsv offener Warenlager; **miner's** ~ Knappschaftsv; **mobile** ~ Kraftfahrzeugv; **mortgage** ~ Hypothekenv; **motor car** ~ Kraftfahrzeugv; **motorcar liability** ~ Kraftfahrzeughaftpflichtv; **motor own damage** ~ Kfz-Kaskov; **motor passenger accident** ~ Kfz-Insassenv; **mutual** ~ *V* auf Gegenseitigkeit; **national health** ~ → *national*; **no fault** ~ *V* gegen Gefährdungshaftung; **no fault auto** ~ Autounfallv für den eigenen Versicherungsnehmer ohne Prüfung der Verschuldensfrage; **non-assessable** ~ *V* ohne Nachschußpflicht; **non-mandatory** ~ freiwillige *V*; **non-recurring premium** ~ Einmalprämienv; **obligatory** ~ Pflichtv; **old age** ~ Altersv; **old line life** ~ (normale) Todesfallv; **over** ~ Überv; **own** ~ Selbstv; Selbstbehalt; **own vehicle** ~ Kaskov; **paid-up** ~ voll eingezahlte *V*; **parcel post** ~ Paketpostv; **participating** ~ *V* mit Gewinnbeteiligung; **paymaster rob-**

bery ~ Lohnkassenraub*v*; **partnership** ~ → *partnership*; **personal hold-up** ~ *V* gegen Raubüberfall; **personal liability** ~ Privathaftpflicht*v*, persönliche Haftpflicht*v* (*Hauseigentümer-Haftpflicht ohne Kfz*); **plateglass** ~ Spiegelglas*v*; **private** ~ Privat*v*; **producers' liability** ~ → *producer*; **professional (indemnity)** ~ → *professional;* **property** ~ (damage) Sachschadens*v*; **property owner's liability** ~ Hauseigentümerhaftpflicht*v*; **protection and indemnity risks** ~ Reederhaftpflicht*v*; **public liability** ~ allgemeine Haftpflicht*v*; **pure endowment** ~ Kapital*v* auf den Erlebensfall; **rain** ~ Regen*v*; **reciprocal** ~ Gegenseitigkeits*v*; **rent** ~ Mietausfall*v*; **rental value** ~ Mietausfall*v*; **residence burglary** ~ Wohnungseinbruchs*v*; **retirement income** ~ gemischte Lebens- und Rentenversicherung; **safe deposit box** ~ Tresor*v*; **securities** ~ Wertpapierverwahrungs*v*; **self** ~ Selbst*v* durch Rückstellungen; **sickness** ~ Kranken*v*; **single-premium** ~ Lebens*v* gegen Einmalprämie; **small craft** ~ *V* für Kleinfahrzeuge und Sportboote; **social** ~ Sozial*v*; **special** ~ besondere Schadens*v*, zusätzliche Transport*v*; **specific** ~ spezielle Schadens*v* *mit ziffernmäßiger Verteilung der Versicherungssumme auf Einzelgegenstände*; **sprinkler leakage** ~ *V* gegen Wasserschaden aus Feuerlöschanlagen; **steam boiler** ~ Dampfkessel*v*; **storm and tempest** ~ Sturmschäden*v*; **strike** ~ Streik*v*; **subsequent** ~ Nachversicherung; **surety** ~ Kautions*v*, Untreue*v*; **surgical fees** ~ Operationskosten*v*; **survivorship** ~ Hinterbliebenen*v*; **tenant's liability** ~ Mieterhaftpflicht*v*; **term** ~ *V* auf Zeit, zeitlich begrenzte *V*, *V* für bestimmte Zeitdauer; **term of** ~ *V*–*s*dauer; **third party** ~ Haftpflicht*v*; **third party indemnity** ~ Haftpflicht*v*; **third party liability** ~ Haftpflicht*v*; **time** ~ = *term* ~ *qv*; **title** ~ *V* gegen Rechtsmängel bei Grundstückserwerb; **trade credit** ~ Debitoren*v*, Warenkredit*v*; **transport** ~ Transport*v*; **travellers' accident** ~ Reiseunfall*v*; **unemployment** ~ → *unemployment*; **use and occupancy** ~ → *use s*; **voluntary** ~ freiwillige *V*; **war risk** ~ Kriegsrisiko*v*; **water damage** ~ Wasserschadens*v*; **weather** ~ Reisewetter*v*; **whole life** ~ → *life insurance*; **whole life and endowment** ~ Kapital*v* auf den Todes- und Erlebensfall; **windstorm** ~ Sturmschäden*v*; **workmen's compensation** ~ Berufsunfall*v*; Unternehmerhaftpflicht*v*.

insurant Versicherungsnehmer *m*.

insure versichern, absichern; **~d bank** versicherte Bank (*der staatl Depositenversicherung angeschlossen*); **~d elsewhere** anderweitig versichert.

insured *s* der Versicherte, die Versicherte, Versicherungsnehmer(in).

insurer Versicherer *m*; **co-** ~ Mitversicherer; **direct** ~ Erstversicherer; **individual** ~ Einzelversicherer; **subrogated** ~ Versicherer als Rechtsnachfolger des Geschädigten.

insurgency Aufstand *m*.

insurgent *adj* aufständisch; *s* Aufständischer.

insurrection Erhebung *f*, Empörung *f*, Aufruhr *m*.

insurrectionary movement Aufruhrbewegung *f*.

insurrectionist Empörer *m*, Aufrührer *m*.

intaker Hehler *m*.

intangible immateriell, nichtmateriell, unkörperlich.

intangibles Immaterialgüter *n*|*pl*, unkörperliche Gegenstände *m*|*pl*.

integer integer, unverletzt, unberührt.

integral part wesentlicher Bestandteil *m*.

integrate integrieren, einbeziehen, eingliedern; **~d bar** einheitliche Gesamtanwaltschaft; **~d economy** einheitliches Wirtschaftssystem; ~**d public utility system** integrierte Versorgungsbetriebe; ~**d school** Schule ohne Rassentrennung.

integration Integration *f*, Einbeziehung *f*; Eingliederung *f*, Einordnung *f*; Aufhebung *f* der Rassenschranke; Zulassungsregelung *f* für die Anwaltschaft; **progressive** ~ fortschreitende Eingliederung; **vertical** ~ → *vertical*.

integrity Integrität *f*, Lauterkeit *f*, Rechtschaffenheit *f*; ~ **of witness** einwandfreier Leumund des Zeugen.

intellectual geistig, verstandesmäßig; ~ **property protection** Schutz geistigen Eigentums.

intelligence Intelligenz *f*; Nachricht *f*, Auskunft *f*, Nachrichtendienst *m*; ~ **agent** Geheimagent; ~ **office** Informationsbüro; ~ **officer** Nachrichtenoffizier; ~ **service** geheimer Nachrichtendienst; **counter-**~ Spionageabwehr; **industrial** ~ geheime Kenntnisse aus der Industrie; Industriespionage.

intelligencer Zwischenträger *m*, Kundschafter *m*, Spion *m*.

intelligibility Allgemeinverständlichkeit *f*, Deutlichkeit.

intelligible begreiflich, verständlich.

intemperance Unmäßigkeit *f*, Unenthaltsamkeit *f*.

intend beabsichtigen, wollen, den Vorsatz haben, bezwecken; ~**ed to be recorded** zur Eintragung vorgesehen; ~**ed wife** die Verlobte; ~**ing buyer** Kaufinteressent.

intendant Intendant *m*, hoher Ministerialbeamter *m*, Leiter *m*.

intendment die (wahre) Bedeutung, der (wirkliche) Wille; ~ **of law** der Sinn des Gesetzes, der Wille des Gesetzgebers; ~ **of testator** der wirkliche Wille des Erblassers; **common** ~ die allgemeine Bedeutung (*e–s Wortes*).

intent Vorsatz *m*, Absicht *f*, Bedeutung *f*, Zweck *m*; ~ **to commit an offence** strafrechtl Vorsatz; ~ **to deceive** Täuschungsvorsatz; ~ **to defraud** betrügerische Absicht; ~ **to injure** Verletzungsvorsatz; **common** ~ allgemeine Bedeutung (*e–s Wortes*); **constructive** ~ vermuteter Vorsatz (*zB bei Fortsetzungszusammenhang*); **contingent** ~ bedingter Vorsatz, dolus eventualis; **criminal** ~ strafrechtlicher Vorsatz; **evil** ~ böswillige Absicht; **felonious** ~ verbrecherische Absicht, Verbrechensvorsatz; **full** ~ feste Absicht Betrugsvorsatz; Täuschungsabsicht; **fraudulent** ~ → *fraudulent*; **general** ~ allgemeine Willensrichtung; **implied** ~ aus den Tatumständen gefolgerter Vorsatz; **legislative** ~ gesetzgeberische Absicht, Wille des Gesetzgebers; **malicious** ~ böswillige Absicht; **presumed** ~ mutmaßliche Absicht; **specific** ~ konkreter Vorsatz; **transferred** ~ *Verletzungsvorsatz gilt auch bei aberratio ictus*.

intentio Anklagepunkt *m*.

intention Absicht *f*, Vorsatz *m*, Wille *m*, Bedeutung *f*, Zweck *m*; ~ **of Parliament** Wille des Gesetzgebers; ~ **of possessing** Besitzwille; ~ **of the parties** Parteiwille; ~ **to create legal relations** rechtsgeschäftliche Absicht; ~ **to deceive** Täuschungsabsicht; **contrary** ~ gegenteilige Absicht; **criminal** ~ strafrechtl Vorsatz; **defective** ~ Willensmangel; **deliberate** ~ Vorsatz; **guilty** ~ *scot* Vorsatz; **testamentary** ~ Erblasserwille, Absicht des Testierenden.

intentional absichtlich, vorsätzlich, bewußt; ~ **improper use of monopoly** vorsätzlicher Monopolmißbrauch; ~ **physical harm** vorsätzliche Körperverletzung.

inter|alia unter anderem; ~ **se** unter sich; untereinander, im Innenverhältnis; ~ **partes** im Innenverhältnis der Parteien; ~ **vivos** unter Lebenden.

inter-agency agreement Verwaltungsabkommen.

inter-allied interalliiert, die Beziehung zwischen den Alliierten betreffend.

interbank | **clearing** Orts-Clearing;

~ **payments** Zahlungen im Bankverkehr; ~ **rate** Interbankrate (*Euromarkt*); ~ **relations** Bankverkehr; **in** ~ **dealings** im Bankverkehr.

interbourse securities → *security* (*2*).

intercede sich verwenden, vermitteln, Fürsprache einlegen; intervenieren.

interceder Fürsprecher *m*, Vermittler *m*.

intercedure Schuldübernahme *f*.

intercensal period Zeitspanne zwischen zwei Volkszählungen.

intercept abfangen, abhören, abschneiden.

interception Abfangen *n*, Abhören *n*, Abstoppen *n*, Behindern *n*, Abschneiden *n*; ~ **of documents** Urkundenunterdrückung.

intercession Vermittlung *f*, Fürsprache *f*, Interzession *f*.

intercessor Fürsprecher *m*, Vermittler *m*.

interchange Austausch *m*, Tauschhandel *m*, Abwechslung *f*; ~ **of civilities** Austausch von Höflichkeiten; ~ **of staff** Austausch von Mitarbeitern *verschiedener Unternehmen*.

interchangeable austauschbar, auswechselbar; ~ **bonds** Inhaberobligationen, auswechselbare Namensschuldverschreibungen.

intercitizenship Mehrstaatenangehörigkeit *f*.

intercom (Haus)Sprechanlage.

intercommon *v* gemeinsam *bzw* gegenseitig Nutzungsrechte gewähren.

intercommune mit jmdn verkehren.

intercommunicate miteinander in Verbindung treten, einander mitteilen.

intercompany zwischenbetrieblich; Konzern ...; ~ **receivables** Konzernforderungen; ~ **sales** konzerninterner Umsatz.

intercommunal zwischen Bevölkerungsgruppen.

inter-connections Verflechtung *f*.

intercorporate konzernintern; ~ **privilege** Schachtelprivileg; ~ **stockholding** Kapitalverflechtung (*durch Aktienbeteiligung*).

intercourse Verkehr *m*, Umgang *m*; **commercial** ~ Handelsverkehr, geschäftlicher Verkehr; **conjugal** ~ ehelicher Verkehr; **diplomatic** ~ diplomatischer Verkehr; **economic** ~ Wirtschaftsverkehr; **extramarital** ~ außerehelicher (Geschlechts)Verkehr; **marital** ~ ehelicher Verkehr; **non-consensual** ~ Geschlechtsverkehr ohne Einwilligung; **premarital** ~ vorehelicher (Geschlechts)Verkehr; **sexual** ~ Beischlaf, Geschlechtsverkehr; **unlawful** ~ verbotener G. V., außerehelicher G. V.; **unnatural** ~ außerehelicher G. V. bzw verbotener G. V.; **verbal** ~ mündlicher Verkehr, mündliche Mitteilungen.

interdenominational interkonfessionell.

interdepartmental interministeriell; ~ **agreement** → *agreement*.

interdependence wechselseitige Abhängigkeit *f*.

interdependent gegenseitig abhängig.

interdict *s* Interdikt *n*, *scot* gerichtliches Verbot *n*.

interdict *v* untersagen, verbieten.

interdiction Verbot *n*, Entmündigung *f*; ~ **of commercial intercourse** totales Embargo; ~ **of fire and water** Bann (*mit dem Verbot, Feuer oder Wasser zu gewähren*).

interesse termini Anwartschaft *f* bei Tod eines Pachtbesitzers.

interest *s* (*1*) Interesse *n*, dingliches Recht *n*, Anrecht *n*, Anspruch *m*; ~ **action** Klage auf Einsatz e–s Nachlaßverwalters; ~ **groups** Interessengruppen, Interessenverbände; ~ **in a business** Beteiligung, Vermögensinteresse; ~ **in expectancy** Anwartschaft; ~ **in land** Recht am Grundstück; ~ **in possession** Besitzrecht, Besitzanspruch; Mitbesitz; ~ **in result of case** Interesse am Ausgang des Rechtsstreits; ~ **in succession** Erbanwartschaft; ~ **in the patent exploitation** Beteiligung an der Patentverwertung; ~ **insured** versichertes Interesse; ~ **of the publisher** berechtigtes Interesse des Mitteilenden; ~**or no** ~ ohne Rücksicht darauf, ob versicherbares Interesse besteht; ~ **policy** → *policy* (*1*); ~ **suit** *Prozeß über die Berechtigung zur Nachlaßverwaltung*; **absolute** ~ absolutes Recht (*an e–r Sache*); **adverse** ~ Interesse e–s Zeugen am Ausgang e–s Rechtsstreits gegen die benennende Partei, Interesse e–s feindlichen Zeugen; **beneficial** ~ → *beneficial*; **clash of** ~**s** Interessenkonflikt; **common** ~ Interesse der Allgemeinheit, Kommunrecht, Recht am Gemeinschaftseigentum (*Wohnungseigentumsrecht*); **community of** ~ → *community*; **concurrent** ~**s** nebeneinander bestehende (dingl) Rechte; **conditional** ~ bedingtes Anrecht; **contingent** ~ bedingtes Recht; **controlling** ~ beherrschender Einfluß, beherrschende Beteiligung; **determinable** ~ → *determinable*; **disqualification for** ~ Ausschluß wegen eigenen Interesses; **entailed** ~ erbfolgemäßig festgelegtes Besitzrecht; **equitable** ~ billigkeitsrechtlicher Anspruch, sachenrechtsähnlicher obligatorischer Anspruch, Anwartschaftsrecht; **executory** ~ aufschiebend bedingtes dingliches Recht, noch einzuräumendes dingliches Recht; **financial** ~ Beteiligung; **foreign** ~**s** ausländ. Beteiligungen; **future** ~ Anwartschaft; **hull** ~ Kaskointeresse; **inchoate** ~ Anwartschaft; **insurable** ~ versicherbares Interesse; **joint** ~ Mitbeteiligung, Gemeinschaftsbeteiligung; **junior** ~ nachrangiges Anrecht; **legal** ~ dingliche Berechtigung; **legitimate** ~ berechtigtes Interesse; **life** ~ → *life interest*; **limited** ~ beschränktes Recht an e–r Sache; **long** ~ Engagement der Haussepartei; **minor** ~**s** nachrangige Grundstücksrechte; **national** ~ Landesinteresse, Staatsinteresse; **overriding** ~**s** → *overriding;* **partnership** ~ → *partnership*; **pecuniary** ~ finanzielles Interesse, geldwertes Interesse; **positive** ~ Erfüllungsinteresse, positives Vertragsinteresse; **possessory** ~ Besitzrecht; **private** ~ eigenes Interesse; **proprietary** ~**s** Eigentums- und eigentumsähnliche Rechte (*Anrechte*); **public** ~ öffentliches Interesse; **reversionary** ~ Heimfallsanspruch, Anwartschaft, zukünftiges Recht aus einer treuhänderischen Zuwendung; Nacherbschaft(srecht); **senior** ~ ranghöhere Sicherheit, rangbesseres Recht; **to have an** ~ ein Vermögensinteresse haben; dinglich berechtigt sein; beteiligt sein; **to impair a person's** ~**s** jmds Interessen beeinträchtigen; **undivided** ~**s** Gesamthandsbesitz, Gesamthandsrechte; **valuable** ~ Vermögensrecht, vermögenswertes Recht; **vested** ~ wohlerworbenes Anrecht, *pl* berechtigte Interessen; Interessengruppen.

interest (*2*) Zins *m*, Zinsen *pl*; ~ **balance** Zinssaldo, *der täglichen Zinsberechnung zugrundeliegender Kontosaldo*; ~ **band** Zinsstufe; ~ **bearing** verzinslich; ~ **bearing security** verzinsliches Wertpapier; ~ **component** Zinsbestandteil; ~ **coupon** Zinsschein, Zinskupon (= *Zinscoupon*); ~ **differential** Zinsgefälle; ~ **expense** Zinsaufwand; ~**-free loan** unverzinsliches Darlehen; ~ **for default** Verzugszinsen; ~ **for late payment** Verzugszinsen; ~ **hike** Zinsanstieg; ~ **of money** Geldzins; ~ **on costs** Zinsen auf (festgesetzte) Kosten; ~ **on arrears** Verzugszinsen; ~**on current account** Kontokorrentzinsen; ~ **on delinquent accounts** Verzugszinsen; ~ **on deposits** Einlagezins; ~ **on overdraft** Überziehungs(kredit)zinsen; ~ **on overdue accounts** Verzugszinsen; ~ **on principal** Kapitalverzinsung, Zinsen von der Hauptsache; ~ **on the** ~ Zinseszinsen; ~ **paid** Passivzinsen, Habenzinsen; ~ **payable** Passivzinsen, fällige Zinsen; ~ **payment** Zinszahlung, Zinsvergütung; ~ **premium** Zinsbonus; ~ **rate** Zinssatz, Zinsfuß; ~ **receivable** Aktivzinsen; Zinsforderung(en); ~ **relief on loans** Abzugsfähigkeit von Schuldzinsen (*Hauskauf etc*); ~ **sheet** Zinsbogen; ~ **statement** Zinsaufstellung, Zinsrechnung; ~ **table** Zinstabelle; ~ **ticket** Zinsschein; ~ **upon** ~ Zinseszinsen; ~ **voucher** Zinsbeleg; ~ **warrant** Zinskupon; ~ **yield** Zinsertrag; **accrued** ~ aufgelaufene Zinsen, Stückzinsen; **accruing** ~ anfallende Zinsen, noch nicht fällige Zinsen; **accumulated** ~ aufgelaufene Zinsen; **annual** ~ Jahreszins; **arrears of** ~ → *arrears*; **at** ~ verzinslich, gegen Zinsen; **balance of** ~ Zinsrest; **banking** ~**s** Bankzins; **broken-period** ~ Bruchzins, Ratazins, Stückzins, zeitanteiliger Zins; **calculation of** ~ Zinsberechnung; **compound** ~ Zinseszinsen; **computation of** ~ → *computation*; **contract** ~ vereinbarte Zinsen; **conventional** ~ vereinbarter Zinsfuß; **credit** ~ Habenzinsen; **creditor** ~ **rate** Habenzinssatz; **cum** ~ mit Stückzinsen; **current** ~ laufende Zinsen; **debit** ~ Sollzinsen; **debtor** ~ **rate** Sollzinssatz; **deferred** ~ transitorische (*im nächsten Rechnungsabschluß zu erfassende*) Zinsen; **discretionary** ~ Zinsen nach gerichtl Ermessen; **equated** ~ → *equated*; **ex** ~ → *ex*; **exact** ~ (Jahres)Zinsen *berechnet auf Basis von 365 Tagen*; **extortionary** ~ **rates** Wucherzinsen; **fixed** ~**-bearing** festverzinslich; **fluctuation of** ~ **rates** Zinsschwankungen; **free of** ~ → *free*; **graduated** ~ gestaffelte Zinsen; **gross** ~ Effektivzins; **illegal** ~ Wucherzinsen; **imputed** ~ kalkulatorische Zinsen; **interim** ~ Zwischenzins; **legal** ~ (*höchster*) gesetzlich zulässiger Zins; gesetzliche Kontokorrentzinsen; **loan** ~ Zinsen für Fremdkapital; **maritime** ~ bei Schiffbeleihung zulässiger Zinssatz, Bodmereizinsen; **mesne** ~ Zwischenzins; **natural rate of** ~ der natürliche Zins, *der den Status quo der Volkswirtschaft erhält*; **negative** ~ Negativzins; **net** ~ Nettoverzinsung (*nach Abzug der Quellensteuer, ohne Provisionsabzug*); **neutral rate of** ~ konjunkturneutraler Zinssatz; **no** ~ **shall be chargeable** Zinsen dürfen nicht berechnet werden; **nominal** ~ Nominalverzinsung; **ordinary** ~ Jahreszins *berechnet auf der Basis von 360 Tagen*; **outstanding** ~ rückständige Zinsen; **overdue** ~ Verzugszinsen; **past due** ~ Verzugszinsen; **paying** ~ verzinslich; **penal** ~ Verzugszinsen; **principal and** ~ → *principal;* **red** ~ Sollzinsen; **simple** ~ gewöhnliche Zinsen (*ohne Zinseszins*); **statutory** ~ gesetzliche Zinsen; **to carry** ~ Zinsen tragen, verzinslich sein; **true** ~ reine Zinsen; **unearned** ~ transitorische Zinserträge; **usurious** ~ Wucherzinsen; **yielding** ~ verzinslich.

interested beteiligt, interessiert; ~ **in contract** private Interessen an e–m Vertragsabschluß habend; ~ **in the matter in dispute** privat am Streitgegenstand interessiert; ~ **witness** → *witness*; **parties** ~ → *parties*; **to be** ~ **in** beteiligt sein.

interfactory comparative studies Betriebsvergleiche.

interfer|e stören, intervenieren, sich einmischen; sich um Belange Dritter kümmern; kontrollieren, behindern; ~ **in a dispute** sich in e–n Streit einschalten; ~ **with an application** e–r Anmeldung entgegenstehen; ~ **with or affect** eingreifen oder berühren; ~**d with** beeinträchtigt; ~**ing claims** widerstreitende Ansprüche; ~**ing inventions** kollidierende (*sich ganz oder teilweise überdeckende*) Erfindungen.

interference Zusammenstoßen *n*, Aufeinandertreffen *n*, Widerstreit *m*, Konflikt *m*, Beeinträchtigung *f*, Einwirkung *f*, Störung *f* (unbefugter) Eingriff *m*, Verletzung *f*, Einmischung *f*, Zugriff *m*; patentamtliche Feststellung *f* der Kollision von Patentansprüchen; ~ **of interest** Interessengegensatz; ~ **with air-**

space Störung des Luftraums über e–m Grundstück, Verletzung des Luftraums; ~ **with business** Eingriff in den Gewerbebetrieb; ~ **with individual liberty** Eingriff in die persönliche Freiheit; ~ **with industrial property** Verletzung gewerblicher Schutzrechte; ~ **with possession** Besitzstörung, Verletzung des Besitzes; ~ **with property under arrest** rechtswidrige Handlungen an beschlagnahmten Vermögensgegenständen; ~ **with receiver** Störung der Amtstätigkeiten des Verwalters; ~ **with (subsisting) contract** Verleitung zum Vertragsbruch; ~ **with the civil liberties** Eingriff in die grundrechtlich geschützten Freiheiten; ~ **with wards of court** widerrechtliche Verfügung über Mündel, *die unter gerichtlichem Schutz stehen*; ~ **with witnesses** Zeugenbeeinflussung; Abhaltung von Zeugen, Aussagen zu machen; **action to restrain** ~ Klage auf Unterlassung der Störung; **executive** ~ Eingreifen des US-Präsidenten (*zB durch Gnadenerweis*); **foreign** ~ ausländische Einmischung; **judicial** ~ gerichtl Eingriff (*in die Verwaltung*); **legislative** ~ Eingriff der Legislative *in richterliche Kompetenzen*; **outside** ~ äußere Beeinflussung; **state** ~ staatliche Einmischung; **unlawful** ~ verbotene Eigenmacht, Besitzstörung, Immission.

interfund|borrowing Kreditgewährung *f* innerhalb des Gesamtbudgets; ~ **settlement** Abrechnung zwischen den einzelnen Haushaltsposten; ~ **transactions** Rechtsgeschäfte zwischen Verwaltungsabteilungen.

intergenerational transfer program Generationenvertrag *m*.

intergovernmental|agreement Regierungsübereinkommen; ~ **bodies** zwischenstaatliche Organisationen *auf Ministerialebene*; ~ **conference** zwischenstaatliche Regierungskonferenz; ~ **consultations** zwischenstaatliche Beratungen *auf Verwaltungsebene*.

interim *adj* einstweilig, vorläufig Zwischen . . .; ~ **acceptance certificate** provisorische Abnahmebescheinigung; ~ **bridging finance** Zwischenfinanzierung; ~ **financial statement** Zwischenbilanz; ~ **injunction** → *injunction*.

interinsurance Gegenseitigkeitsversicherung; ~ **exchange** Schadensteilungsverband *m*.

interior decorative repairs Schönheitsreparaturen *f|pl*.

interline zwischen die Zeilen setzen.

interlineation Einfügung *f* zwischen den Zeilen.

interlocking|combine Konzern; ~ **directorates** Verflechtung durch Aufsichtsratsposten und Vorstandspersonalunion.

interlocution Unterredung *f*; *scot* Zwischenentscheidung *f*.

interlocutory einstweilig, vorläufig, Zwischen . . .

interlope Handel oder Gewerbe ohne Konzession betreiben.

interloper Eindringling *m*, Schwarzhändler *m*; jmd der den Handel anderer abfängt.

intermarriage Mischehe *f*, Eheschließung *f* zwischen verschiedenen Völkern; (*gewöhnliche*) Eheschließung *f*.

intermarry heiraten, die Eheschließung vornehmen, sich mit e–r ausländischen (*bzw e–r andersrassigen*) Person verheiraten.

intermeddle sich einmischen, sich unbefugt mit etwas befassen.

intermediary *adj* vermittelnd; zwischengeschaltet.

intermediary *s* Makler *m*, Vermittler *m*, Zwischenhändler *m*; **through the** ~ **of** durch Vermittlung von; **to act as** ~ vermitteln, makeln.

intermediate zwischen, eingeschaltet, mittelbar; ~ **credit bank** staatliche Landwirtschaftsbank (*zur Vermittlung von kurzfristigen Krediten*).

interministerial interministeriell.

intermission Aussetzen *n*, Unterbrechung *f*, Unterlassen *n*.

intermit aussetzen, unterbrechen, einstellen.
intermittent | **easement** → *easement*; ~ **unemployment** zeitweise Arbeitslosigkeit.
intermittently mit Unterbrechungen.
intermixture of goods Vermischung *f* von Waren (*verschiedener Eigentümer*).
intern *v* internieren.
internal intern, Binnen...; ~ **rate of duty** Binnenzollsatz; ~ **revenue** Steueraufkommen; ~ **revenue code** Abgabenordnung; ~ **revenue office** *US* Finanzamt; **I~ Revenue Service** *US* Steuerbehörden, Fiskus.
international international (= *int*) zwischenstaatlich; ~ **arbitration** *int–e* Schiedsgerichtsbarkeit; **I~ Bank for Reconstruction and Development** Internationale Bank für Wiederaufbau und Entwicklung, Weltbank; ~ **classification of goods** *int–e* Warenklasseneinteilung (*Warenzeichen*); ~ **comity** völkerrechtliche Usancen, völkerrechtliche Courtoisie; ~ **commerce** → *commerce*; ~ **community** Völkergemeinschaft; ~ **convention** *int–es* Übereinkommen; ~ **copyright** *int–es* Urheberrecht; **I~ Court of Justice** → *court*; ~ **courtesies** *int–e* Höflichkeiten; **I~ Criminal Police Organization** Internationale Kriminalpolizeiliche Organisation (*Interpol*); ~ **economics** Wirtschaftslehre der außenwirtschaftlichen Beziehungen; ~ **exchange market** *int–er* Devisenmarkt; ~ **expert** von der UNO beauftragter Sachverständiger; ~ **justice** völkerrechtliche Rechtspflege; ~ **law** → *international law*; ~ **legislation** Normensetzung durch multilaterale Verträge; ~ **lending** → *lending*; ~ **market** → *market*; ~ **minimum standards** völkerrechtlich üblicher Mindeststandard *für Ausländerbehandlung*; ~ **monetary conference** → *conference*; ~ **money order** Auslandspostanweisung; ~ **morality** Verhaltensregeln der völkerrechtlichen guten Sitten; ~ **official** Bedienstete *int–er* Behörden; **I~ Payment** internationale Postanweisung *GB*; ~ **personality** Völkerrechtssubjekt; ~ **public policy** übergeordnete bindende Völkerrechtsgrundsätze; **I~ Rapid Payment** internationale Eil-Postanweisung *GB*; ~ **recognition** *int–e* Anerkennung; ~ **reply coupon** *int–er* (Rück-)Antwortschein; ~ **river community** *int–e* Flußanliegergemeinschaft; ~ **rivers** → *river*; ~ **road signs** *int–e* Verkehrszeichen; ~ **sanitary conventions** *int–e* Übereinkommen auf dem Gebiet des Gesundheitswesens; ~ **securities** *int* gehandelte Effekten; ~ **settlement** *int–e* Schuldenregelung(en); ~ **standard** → *standard*; ~ **supply contract** Liefervertrag mit Auslandsberührung; ~ **trade unionism** *int–es* Gewerkschaftswesen; ~ **union** → *union*; ~ **usage** *int–e* Gepflogenheiten; ~ **waters** *int–e* Gewässer.
international law internationales Recht *n*; Völkerrecht *n*; **customary** ~ Völkergewohnheitsrecht; **explicit** ~ ausdrückliches Völkerrecht; **implicit** ~ stillschweigendes Völkerrecht; **intertemporal** ~ intertemporales Völkerrecht; **private** ~ internationales Privatrecht; **public** ~ Völkerrecht; **public** ~ **of the sea** Seevölkerrecht; **quasi** ~ völkerrechtsähnliche Beziehungen.
internationalization Internationalisierung *f*.
internationalize internationalisieren.
internee Internierte(r) *m bzw f*.
internment Internierung *f*.
internuncio Internuntius *m*, päpstlicher Gesandter *m* 2. Ranges.
internuncius Bote *m*, Vermittler *m*.
interpellate e–e Anfrage stellen, interpellieren, eine Zwischenfrage stellen.
interpellation Anfrage *f*, Zwischenfrage *f*, Interpellation *f*; Ladung *f*; parlamentarische Anfrage *f*; Erklä-

rung *f*, e–e Vereinbarung nach Zeitablauf nicht fortsetzen zu wollen.

interplea Einwand *m* der mangelnden Passivlegitimation; Desinteresse(erklärung) am Streitgegenstand (*der Dritten überlassen wird*); Interventionsklage *f*.

interplead den Streit verkünden, *vgl interpleader*; den Kläger und Drittinteressenten auf den Streitgegenstand verweisen.

interpleader Streitverkündung zur Verweisung auf den Prätendentenstreit, Einwand *m* der mangelnden Passivlegitimation *mit dem Antrag, Interessenten am Streitgegenstand zu veranlassen, den Rechtsstreit untereinander auszutragen;* ~ **issue** Beanspruchersteit, Prätendentenstreit; **sheriff's** ~ Verweisung des *gegen Pfändung* Intervenierenden auf den Rechtsweg; **stakeholder('s)** ~ Verweisung auf den Prätendentenstreit (*durch den Inhaber des Streitgegenstandes*).

Interpol = *International Criminal Police Organisation → international.*

interpolate einfügen, einschieben, interpolieren.

interpolation Einfügung *f*, Einschub (*in den Text e–r Urkunde*), die eingefügten Worte *n*|*pl*.

interpose einschieben, einschalten, vorbringen, intervenieren; ~ **a counterclaim** e–e Gegenforderung erheben; ~ **a veto** Veto einlegen; ~ **an objection** e–n Einwand vorbringen.

interposition Intervention *f*, Vermittlung *f*, Fürsprache *f*.

interpret auslegen; dolmetschen; ~ **extensively** weit auslegen; ~ **liberally** großzügig auslegen; ~ **restrictively** eng auslegen; ~ **strictly** eng auslegen.

interpretation Auslegung *f* (= *A*); mündliche Übersetzung *f*; **I~ Act, 1889** *brit Gesetz von 1889 über A von gesetzlichen Bestimmungen*; ~ **clause** *A–s*bestimmung; ~ **section** Paragraph mit Legaldefinitionen; **administrative** ~ behördliche *A* von Gesetzen; **artful** ~ wissentlich verzerrte *A*; **authentic** ~ gesetzliche *A*; **broad** ~ teleologische *A*, weite *A*; **close** ~ enge *A*; **comparative** ~ vergleichende *A*; **conceptual** ~ begriffliche *A*; **customary** ~ üblicherweise anerkannte *A*; **doctrinal** ~ begriffliche *A*; **extensive** ~ weite *A*, extensive Interpretation; **extravagant** ~ unzulässig weite *A*; **free** ~ freie *A nach Treu und Glauben*; **grammatical** ~ grammatikalische *A*; **historical** ~ historische *A*, *A* aus der Entstehungsgeschichte; **judicial** ~ gerichtliche *A*, richterliche *A*; **legal** ~ gesetzlich festgelegte *A*; **liberal** ~ großzügige *A*; **limited** ~ eng begrenzte *A*; **literal** ~ wörtliche *A*; **logical** ~ sinngemäße *A*; **narrow** ~ enge *A*; **orthodox** ~ konventionelle *A*; **predestined** ~ *A* auf Grund vorgefaßter Meinung; **purposive** ~ teleologische *A*; **restricted** ~ enge *A*; **restrictive** ~ einschränkende *A*; **strict** ~ enge *A*; **stringent** ~ einschränkende *A*; **teleological** ~ teleologische *A*; **unrestricted** ~ unbeschränkte *A*.

interpreter Dolmetscher(in) *m bzw f*; **allowance to** ~ Gerichtsgebühren für Dolmetscher; **chief** ~ Chefdolmetscher; **state-certificated** ~ staatl geprüfter Dolmetscher; **sworn** ~ vereidigter Dolmetscher.

interpreting Dolmetschen *n*.

interregnum Interregnum *n*, herrscherlose Zeit *f*, Übergangsregierung *f*.

interrelation Wechselbeziehung *f*.

interrogate verhören, vernehmen.

interrogation Verhör *n*, Vernehmung *f*; **police** ~ → *police*; **pretrial** ~ Vernehmung im Ermittlungsverfahren.

interrogator Vernehmungsbeamter *m*, der Vernehmende.

interrogatories schriftliche, *unter Eid zu beantwortende* Beweisfragen *f*|*pl*, Fragebogen *m*; **leave to administer** ~ *gerichtliche Erlaubnis, dem Beklagten Fragen zur schriftlichen Beantwortung unter Eid vorzulegen*; **fish-**

ing ~s ausforschende schriftl Befragung, **oppressive ~** unzulässige (*zB der Ausforschung dienende*) schriftliche Beweisfragen; **prolix ~** ungebührlich wortreiche Fragelisten.

interrupt unterbrechen.

interruption Unterbrechung *f*, *bes* Unterbrechung *f der Verjährung*; **~ of business** Unterbrechung des Geschäftsablaufs, Geschäftsunterbrechung (*als Schaden*); Unterbrechung e–r Parlamentsdebatte; **~ of proceedings** Ruhen des Verfahrens; **~ of sentence** Strafaussetzung, Strafunterbrechung.

intersection Kreuzung *f*, Kreuzungsbereich *m*, Abbiegung *f*; **point of ~** Kreuzungsmittelpunkt; Aufprallpunkt.

interspousal innerehelich.

interstate mehrere US-Einzelstaaten betreffend; **~ commerce** Handel zwischen den US-Bundesstaaten; **I~ Commerce Clause** *US-Verfassungsbestimmung (Art I 3) zur Regelung des grenzüberschreitenden Handels innerhalb der USA*; **~ compact** Vereinbarung zwischen Bundesstaaten; **~ extradition** Auslieferungs(recht) im Verhältnis der US-Bundesstaaten zueinander; **~ law** → *law*; **~ rendition** *Überstellung von Straftätern in einen anderen US-Bundesstaat*.

intertiare Unterlagen sicherstellen (*bei e–m Dritten*).

interval Intervall *n*, Zwischenzeit *f*, Pause *f*, Zwischenraum *m*; **~ ownership** zeitanteiliges Eigentum (*zB an Ferienwohnung*); *cf time-sharing qv*; **lucid ~** lichter Augenblick.

intervene intervenieren, vermitteln, dazwischentreten; **~ in a case of need** als Notadressat intervenieren.

intervener Intervenient *m*, Nebenintervenient *m*.

intervenient *s* Intervenient *m*.

intervening | **act** eine den Kausalzusammenhang unterbrechende Handlung; Interventionshandlung; **~ agency** *Sachverhalt, der den Kausalzusammenhang unterbricht*.

intervention Intervention *f*, Vermittlung *f*, Haupt- *bzw* Nebenintervention *f*, Prozeßbeitritt *m*; **~ board** Interventionsstelle (*EG*); **~ point** Interventionspunkt (*der Zentralbank*); **~ rate** Interventionskurs; **~ supra protest** Ehreneintritt; **economic ~** wirtschaftspolitische Intervention; **police ~** polizeiliches Eingreifen.

interview Interview *n*, Unterredung *f*, Besprechung *f*; pol. Vernehmung *f*.

interzonal | **agreement** interzonale Vereinbarung; **~ boundary** Interzonengrenze; **~ traffic** Interzonenverkehr.

intestable nicht testierfähig.

intestacy Intestat *n*, Intestatserbfolge *f*, gesetzliche Erbfolge; Erbfall *m* ohne Testament; **distribution on ~** Nachlaßauseinandersetzung bei gesetzlicher Erbfolge; **partial ~** teilweise Intestatsbeerbung; *Nachlaß, über den nur teilweise letztwillig verfügt ist*; **share under an ~** → *share*; **succession on ~** gesetzliche Erbfolge, Intestaterbfolge.

intestate *s* Intestaterblasser *m*, Erblasser *m* bei gesetzlicher Erbfolge.

intestate *adj* testamentslos, Intestats . . .; **~ estate** Intestatsnachlaß; **~ laws** Gesetze über die Intestaterbfolge; **to die ~** ohne Hinterlassung e–s Testaments sterben; **~ succession** → *succession*.

intimacy Intimität *f*; ehewidrige Beziehung *f*.

intimate *adj* eng befreundet, vertraulich.

intimate *v* andeuten, zu verstehen geben, kundtun, mitteilen.

intimation Andeutung *f*, Wink *m*, Nahelegung *f*, Mitteilung *f*, Anzeichen *n*, schriftlicher Hinweis *m* auf ein Recht; Anzeige des Zedenten an Schuldner; **letters of ~** *scot* Vorführungsbefehl *an die Staatsanwaltschaft*.

intimidation Einschüchterung *f*, Drohung *f*, Nötigung *f*; **~ of vot-**

ers Nötigung von Wählern; ~ **of witnesses** Zeugennötigung; **larceny by** ~ räuberische Erpressung.

intolerable unerträglich, unzumutbar.

intoxicat|e berauschen, betrunken machen; ~**ed person** unter Alkoholeinfluß stehende Person; ~**ing liquor** alkoholische Getränke.

intoxication Vergiftung *f*, Alkoholeinfluß *m* (Be)trunkenheit *f*; **voluntary** ~ schuldhafte Betrunkenheit.

intoximeter Alkoholtestgerät *n*, Alkohol-Atemmeßgerät *n*.

intra innerhalb, Inner...; ~**-Community** innergemeinschaftlich; ~**-Community treatment** Gemeinschaftsbehandlung (*EG*); ~**-European trade** innereuropäischer Handel; ~ **fidem** glaubhaft; ~ **firm comparison** innerbetrieblicher Rationalisierungstest; ~ **-industrial studies** Betriebsvergleich; ~ **vires** ermächtigt, befugt; innerhalb der satzungsgemäßen Befugnisse.

intralim rights *Schürfrechte innerhalb senkrechter Ebenen gemäß der Oberflächengrenze.*

intraliminal innerhalb der Grenzen.

intramural innerhalb der Mauern, innerstädtisch, innerhalb des Universitätsbezirks.

intransigence Unnachgiebigkeit *f*, Unversöhnlichkeit *f*, Radikalismus *m*.

intransigent politischer Starrkopf *m*, Radikaler *m*.

intrastate innerstaatlich (*im Sinne der US-Bundesstaaten*); ~ **commerce** → *commerce*.

intricate schwierig, verwickelt.

intrigue *s* Intrige *f*, Machenschaft *f*, geheimes Liebesverhältnis *n*, Ränkespiel *n*.

intrigue *v* intrigieren, verlocken, verwirren.

intriguer Intrigant *m*, Ränkeschmied *m*.

intrinsic inner, eigen, eigentlich, wirklich, wahr.

introduce einführen, bekanntmachen, einleiten, einbringen, vorbringen; ~ **a bill** e–e Vorlage einbringen; ~ **evidence** Beweis antreten, Beweisurkunden vorlegen.

introduction Einführung *f*, Einleitung *f*, Vorstellung *f*, Anbahnung *f*; ~ **of a motion** Einbringen e–s Antrags; Antragstellung; ~ **price** Einführungskurs, Einführungspreis; **letter of** ~ → *letter*.

introductory einführend; ~ **act** Einführungsgesetz.

intromission Geschäftsführung *f* ohne Auftrag; Einmischung *f* in fremde Vermögensangelegenheiten; Börsengeschäfte *n|pl* durch Beauftragte; **necessary** ~ notwendige Geschäftsführung ohne Auftrag.

intromit einfügen, *scot* Vermögen verwalten, über etwas verfügen.

intrude eindringen, (*den Besitz*) stören.

intruder Eindringling *m*, Besitzstörer *m an Grundstücken*, Usurpator *m*, (rechtswidriger) Erbschaftsbesitzer *m*.

intrusion Besitzstörung *f*, widerrechtliche Inbesitznahme *f von Immobilien bei Todesfall bzw. Heimfall*; **information of** ~ → *information*.

intrust zu treuen Händen überlassen, anvertrauen.

inure wirksam werden, zur Folge haben, nützen, dienen; ~ **to the benefit of** zugute kommen, zugunsten jmds wirken.

inurement Gewöhnung *f*, Gebrauch *m*; Wirksamwerden *n*.

invade Rechte verletzen, eindringen, einfallen; ~ **another person's rights** in jmds Rechte eingreifen.

invalid unwirksam, ungültig, rechtsunwirksam.

invalid carriage fahrbarer Krankenstuhl *m*.

invalidate für ungültig erklären, außer Kraft setzen, entkräften; ~**d bonds** für ungültig erklärte Schuldverschreibungen.

invalidation Kraftloserklärung *f*, Ungültigkeitserklärung *f*.

invalidism Invalidität *f*.

invalidity (Rechts)Ungültigkeit *f*, Unwirksamkeit *f*, Nichtigkeit *f*, Invalidität *f*; ~ **allowance** Erwerbsunfähigkeitsrente; **declaration of** ~ Kraftloserklärung, Nichtigkeitserklärung; **partial** ~Teilunwirksamkeit.

invariable unabänderlich, ständig, unwandelbar; ~ **practice (of a court)** ständige Rechtsprechung.

invasion Invasion *f*, Verletzung *f* e–s Rechtes; ~ **of personal liberty** Beeinträchtigung der persönlichen Freiheit.

invective Schmähung *f*, Beschimpfung *f*, Verleumdung *f*.

inveigle verlocken, verleiten; ~ **to gambling** zum Glücksspiel verleiten.

invent erfinden; ~**ed word** Worterfindung, erdachtes Wort, Kunstwort.

inventio Fund *m*, das Finden.

invention Erfindung *f* (= *E bzw* ...*e*), erfundener Gegenstand *m*; **amount of** ~ *E*-shöhe; **claim to the** ~ Anrecht auf die *E*; **definite** ~ fertige *E*; **developing** ~ zur Weiterentwicklung dienende *E*, zusätzliche *E*; **efficiency-promoting** ~ den Wirkungsgrad steigernde *E*; **employee's** ~ Arbeitnehmere; **factor-saving** ~ ein Hilfsmittel sparende *E*; **factor-using** ~ ein Hilfsmittel nutzende *E*; **joint** ~ gemeinsame *E*; **labour-saving** ~ arbeitssparende *E*, **lack of** ~ → *lack*; **level of** ~ → *level*; **no** ~ **is involved** es liegt keine patentfähige *E* vor; **object of an** ~ Aufgabe e–r *E*; **patent for** ~ → *patent*; **patentable** ~ patentfähige *E*; **priority of** ~ → *priority*; **right to the** ~ Recht an der *E*; **standard of** ~ (Maßstab der) *E*–shöhe; **subject matter of an** ~ → *subject matter*; **the** ~ **lacks novelty** *E* mangelt der Neuheit; **title by** ~ Rechtserwerb e–r *E bzw e–s Urheberrechts*; **to achieve an** ~ e–e *E machen;* **to amount to** ~ *E*–shöhe haben; **to exploit an** ~ e–e *E* nutzen; **to put an** ~ **into practice** e–e *E* in die Praxis umsetzen; **use of** ~ Benutzung der *E*; **vicious** ~ gegen die guten Sitten verstoßende *E*; **working of an** ~ Arbeitsweise e–r *E*, Ausübung e–r *E*; **works** ~ Betriebserfindung.

inventive erfinderisch, Erfindungs . . .

inventiveness Erfindungsgabe *f*.

inventor Erfinder *m* (= *E*); ~**'s certificate** Erfinderzeugnis; ~**'s oath** → *oath;* **dependent** ~ abhängiger *E*, unfreier *E*; **fellow** ~ Miterfinder; **first** ~ (der) Erfinder; **independent** ~ freier *E*; **joint** ~**s** gemeinsame *E*; **original** ~ der eigentliche *E*, der ursprüngliche *E*, der *E* der Haupterfindung; **prior** ~ Vorerfinder; **sole** ~ Alleinerfinder; **true and first** ~ der (eigentliche) *E*; *E*nennung.

inventorship Erfindereigenschaft *f*.

inventory Bestandsliste *f*, Bestandsverzeichnis *n*, Warenbestand *m*, Inventur *f*, Bestandsaufnahme *f*; ~ **accumulation** spekulatives Anwachsenlassen der Lagerbestände; ~ **and iron safe clause** Inventurpflicht und Panzerschrankverwahrungsklausel (*Versicherung*); ~ **control** Bestandskontrolle; Regelung der Lagerhaltung; ~ **cutting** = ~ *decumulation qv*; ~ **decumulation** Vorratsabbau, Abbau der Lagerbestände; ~ **item** Posten des Bestandsverzeichnisses; ~ **loan** Lagerfinanzierungsdarlehen; ~ **of parts** Ersatzteillager; ~ **of process** Liste der vorzulegenden Urkunden; ~ **of property** Vermögensverzeichnis; ~ **period** Inventarfrist; ~ **protection** Preisgarantie für Lagerbestände; ~ **rate** Inventarkurs (*bankintern*) für Bestände; ~ **reserve** Wertberichtigung auf Vorratsvermögen; ~ **sheet** Inventarverzeichnis; ~ **shrinkage** Bestandsverlust, Schwund; ~ **taking** Bestandsaufnahme; ~ **turnover** Lagerumsatz, (*Jahresumsatz geteilt durch Lagerbestände*); ~ **valuation** Lagerbestandsbewertung, Inventurbewertung; ~ **value** Lagerbestandswert, Inventarwert; ~ **verification** Inventurprüfung; **beginning** ~ = *opening* ~ *qv*; **book** ~

Buchinventur; **certificate of** ~ → *certificate*; **closing** ~ Schlußinventar, Schlußbestand; **contents of** ~ Inventarverzeichnis; **continuous** ~ fortlaufende Lagerbestandsfeststellung; **cradle-to-grave** ~ Generalinventur, lückenlose Erfassung der Lagerbestände; **estate** ~ Nachlaßverzeichnis; **estimated** ~ geschätzter Lagerbestand; **filing of the** ~ Inventarerrichtung; **opening** ~ Eröffnungsinventar, Anfangsinventar, Anfangsbestand; **perpetual** ~ permanente Inventur, Buchinventur; **physical** ~ physische Bestandsaufnahme; körperliche Bestandsaufnahme; **record** ~ Buchinventur; **taking of an** ~ Bestandsaufnahme; **target** ~ Sollbestand, Planbestand.

inveritare Beweis antreten.

inverse umgekehrt, entgegengesetzt; **in the** ~ **order** in umgekehrter Reihenfolge.

inversion Umkehrung *f*.

invest anlegen, investieren; ~ **a person with authority** jmdn ermächtigen; ~**ing institution** Kapitalsammelstelle; ~**ing member** Bausparer *vor Zuteilungsreife*; ~**ing public** das investierende Publikum.

investee Investitionsempfänger *m*; ~ **currency** Währung des Empfängerlandes *e–r Investition*.

investigat|e erforschen, untersuchen, aufklären, erheben, überprüfen, ermitteln; ~**ing activity** → *activity*; ~**ing authority** Ermittlungsbehörde; ~**ing committee** Untersuchungsausschuß; ~**ing magistrate** Untersuchungsrichter.

investigative reporting Fahndungsjournalismus *m*, Ermittlungsjournalismus *m*.

investigation Ermittlung *f*, Untersuchung *f*, Nachforschung *f*, Erforschung *f*, Erhebung *f*, amtliche Feststellung *f*; ~ **of a company** behördliche Ermittlungen über die Finanzen e–r Gesellschaft; ~ **of title** Prüfung der Eigentums- und Belastungsverhältnisse (*beim Grundstückskauf*); **criminal** ~ *polizeiliche bzw staatsanwaltschaftliche* Ermittlung; **legislative** ~ Untersuchung durch einen Parlamentsausschuß; **to mount an** ~ e–e Ermittlungsaktion starten; **on-site** ~ örtliche Erhebungen; **preliminary** ~ Voruntersuchung; **pre-sentence** ~ Ermittlungen zum Strafmaß *bzw zur Bewährung;* **runaway** ~ sich ausweitende Ermittlungen.

investigator Ermittlungsbeamter *m*; Rechercheur *m*; **private** ~ Privatdetektiv.

investitive rechtsbegründend; Bestallungs . . ., Verleihungs . . .

investiture Investitur *f*, Belehnung *f*.

investment Investition *f*, Anlage *f*, Kapitalanlage *f*, Beteiligung *f*; ~**s abroad** Auslandskapitalanlagen; ~ **account** → *account*; ~ **advisor** Anlageberater; ~ **allowance** Steuervergünstigung für Kapitalanlagen; ~ **analysis** Aufgliederung und Bewertung des Portefeuilles; ~ **bank(er)** Investitionsbank, Emissionsbank (*für Effekten*); ~ **banking** Kapitalanlage-Bankgeschäfte; ~ **bill** → *bill* (*3*); ~ **bonds** → *bond* (*1*); ~ **broker** → *broker*; ~ **business** Anlagegeschäft; ~ **buying** Anlagekäufe; ~ **capital** Anlagekapital; ~ **club** Verein für Kapitalanlageinteressenten; ~ **company** → *investment company*; ~ **contract** Kapitalanlagevertrag; ~ **counsel** Effektenanlageberater; ~ **credit** (*langfristiger*) Anlagekredit; ~ **dealer** Effektenhändler; ~ **department** Effektenabteilung; ~ **dollars** für Auslandsinvestitionen verfügbare Dollarguthaben; ~ **earnings** Anlageerträge; ~ **exchange** Anlagevermittlungsbüro; ~ **expenditure** Investitionsaufwand; ~ **expense** Investitionskosten; ~ **failure** Fehlinvestition; ~ **financing** Investitionsfinanzierung; ~ **from own sources** Eigeninvestition; ~ **funds** Anlagefonds; ~ **goods** Investitionsgüter; ~ **houses** *Spezialunternehmen für Emissionen;* ~ **in accounts receivable** Kapitalbindung in Debitoren; ~ **in default** notleidendes Wertpapier;

~ **in physical assets** Sachinvestition; ~ **in securities** Effektenanlage; ~ **income** Einkünfte aus Kapitalvermögen *sowie aus Vermietung und Verpachtung*; ~ **intentions** Kapitalanlagevorhaben; ~ **management** Verwaltung von Kapitalanlagen; ~ **middleman** Anlagevermittler; ~ **policy** Anlagepolitik; ~ **portfolio** Portefeuille von Anlagepapieren; ~ **property** Investitionsgüter; ~ **protection** Kapitalanlegerschutz; ~ **rating** Anlagebewertung; ~ **ratio** Investitionsquote; ~ **revenue** Ertrag von Kapitalanlagen; ~ **scheme** Anlageplan, Anlagekonzept; ~ **securities** Anlagewerte; ~ **share** Kapitalanteil an e–r Investmentgesellschaft; ~ **supervisory service** Investmentgesellschafts-Überwachung; ~ **tax credit** Steuergutschrift für Anschaffung von Anlagegütern; ~ **trust** Kapitalanlagegesellschaft; ~ **underwriters** Emissionshäuser; ~ **value** Anlagewert; **authorized ~s** mündelsicher angelegtes Geld; **capital** ~ → *capital*; **defaulted ~s** notleidende Kapitalanlagen; **evaluation of ~s** Bewertung von Anlagepapieren; **expansion** ~ → *expansion*; **fixed income** ~ festverzinsliche Anlagewerte; **fixed ~ trust** *Kapitalanlagefonds mit direkter Beteiligung der Zertifikatsinhaber am Wertpapierbestand*; **fixed property** ~ Anlagevermögen; **foreign** ~ Auslandsbeteiligung; **gilt-edged** ~ mündelsichere Kapitalanlage; **legal ~s** mündelsichere Kapitalanlagen; **listed ~s** zum Börsenhandel zugelassene Aktien; **long(-term)** ~ langfristige Anlage; **negative** ~ Lagerabbau; **nonspeculative** ~ Kapitalanlage als Dauerertragsquelle; **original** ~ Gründungseinlage; **pecuniary** ~ Vermögensanlage; **permanent** ~ Daueranlage, langfristige Kapitalanlage; **public ~s** Investitionen der öffentlichen Hand; **qualified ~s** gesetzl zulässige Kapitalanlagen (US: Investmentgesellschaften); **real** ~ Sachanlagen; **real estate** ~ Kapitalanlage in Grundbesitz; **rediscounting of ~s** Lombardierung und Rediskontierung von Anlagepapieren; **replacement** ~ → *replacement*; **selected ~s** ausgesuchte Anlagewerte; **speculative** ~ Kapitalanlage zu Spekulationszwecken; **statement of ~s** Kapitalanlagestatus; **temporary** ~ kurzfristige Kapitalanlage, Wertpapiere des Umlaufvermögens; **trustee** ~ mündelsichere Anlage; **unitised** ~ Anlage in Investmentfonds-Zertifikaten; **unprofitable** ~ Fehlinvestition; **unquoted** ~ nicht börsenfähige Wertpapiere.

investment company Investmentgesellschaft (= *I*), Kapitalanlagegesellschaft; **close(d)-end** ~ *I* ohne eigene Wertpapieremission, Kapitalanlageverwaltungs-Gesellschaft; **diversified** ~ → *company*; **mutual** ~ *Kapitalanlagefonds bei jederzeitigem Kündigungsrecht der Zertifikatsinhaber*; **open-end** ~ *I* mit eigener Wertpapieremission; **regulated** ~ *US* gesetzlich geregelte *I* (*steuerbegünstigt*).

investor Kapitalanleger *m*, Anleger *m*; **novice** ~ Investitionsneuling.

inviolability Unverletzlichkeit *f*, Immunität *f*; ~ **of diplomats** Immunität von Diplomaten; ~ **of letters** Briefgeheimnis.

inviolable unverletzlich, unverbrüchlich.

invitation Einladung *f*, Freigabe *f* für den allgemeinen Verkehr; ~ **for tenders** = ~ *to bid qv*; ~ **or call** Ausschreibung; ~ **to bid** Ausschreibung, Aufforderung zur Abgabe von Submissionen; ~ **to tender** → *invitation to tender*; ~ **to treat** Aufforderung zur Abgabe e–s Angebots.

invitation to tender Ausschreibung *f*, Vergabe *f*, **limited** ~ beschränkte Ausschreibung; **open** ~ freihändige Vergabe.

invite einladen, auffordern, herausfordern, erbitten; ~ **subscriptions** → *subscription*; **~d error** → *error*.

invitee der Eingeladene; *jmd, der sich auf e–m Grundstück auf Wunsch des Eigentümers aufhält.*

invocation Anrufung *f*, Aufforderung *f*; **colourable ~ of jurisdiction** → *colo(u)rable.*

invoice Lieferantenrechnung *f*, Faktura *f*; ~ **amount** Rechnungsbetrag; ~ **book** Rechnungsbuch, Einkaufsfakturenbuch; ~ **clerk** Fakturist; ~ **cost** Einkaufspreis; ~ **discounting** Verkauf von Außenständen, Factoring; ~ **price** Gestehungspreis, Großhandelspreis; **commercial** ~ Handelsfaktura, Handelsrechnung; **consular** ~ Konsulatsfaktura; **customs** ~ → *customs;* **final** ~ Endrechnung; **proforma** ~ Proformarechnung; **provisional** ~ vorläufige Rechnung; **purchase** ~ Eingangsrechnung; **sales** ~ Ausgangsrechnung; **shipping** ~ Versandrechnung; **supplier's** ~ Lieferantenrechnung; **verifiable** ~ prüffähige Rechnung.

invoice *v* in Rechnung stellen, fakturieren; **~d price** Rechnungspreis; **amount ~d** Rechnungsbetrag; **as ~d** laut Faktura.

invoicing Fakturierung *f*, Inrechnungstellung *f*.

invoke anrufen, sich berufen auf, heranziehen, Bezug nehmen auf; ~ **a precedent** e–n Präzedenzfall anführen; ~ **the provisions of a statute** sich auf gesetzliche Bestimmungen berufen.

involuntary unfreiwillig, unter Zwang; nicht vorsätzlich; ~ **act** unfreiwillige Handlung, willenlose *H.*; ~ **bankruptcy** → *bankruptcy*; ~ **confession** unfreiwilliges Geständnis; ~ **deposit** → *deposit*; ~ **discontinuance** Prozeßbeendigung von Amts wegen, Aussetzung des Verfahrens von Amts wegen; ~ **drunkeness** unfreiwillige Betrunkenheit; ~ **exposure** Aussetzung; ~ **homicide** → *homicide*; ~ **intoxication** = ~ *drunkeness qv*; ~ **liquidation** Zwangsliquidation, Gesellschaftskonkurs; ~ **manslaughter** → *manslaughter*; ~ **payment** unfreiwillige (*widerrechtlich herbeigeführte*) Zahlung, Zahlung auf Grund arglistiger Täuschung oder Drohung; ~ **servitude** → *servitude*; ~ **transfer** Übertragung kraft Gesetz, gesetzlicher Forderungsübergang (*ohne Willenserklärung*).

involve einschließen, enthalten; verwickeln, zur Folge haben; ~ **expense** Kosten zur Folge haben; ~ **the forfeiture of property** die Einziehung des Vermögens zur Folge haben; **~d in debts** verschuldet.

involvement Verwicklung *f*.

inward ins Inland, die Einreise betreffend; ~ **bound** auf der Heimfahrt befindlich; ~ **manifest** → *manifest.*

IOU (= *I owe you*), Schuldanerkenntnis.

ipse dixit lediglich eigenes Vorbringen *n*, nur von ihm selbst behauptet.

ipso facto (=) automatisch; *eccl* automatische Exkommunikation *f*.

ipso jure (=) unmittelbar kraft Gesetzes.

iron *adj* eisern; ~ **clad clause** unumgehbare Klausel; ~ **law of wages** eisernes Lohngesetz, *wonach die Löhne sich dem Existenzminimum angleichen*; ~ **note** erstklassig abgesicherter Schuldschein; **~-safe clause** Geldschrankklausel.

iron *s* Eisen *n*; **~s** Handschellen *bzw* Fußeisen; **leg ~s** Fußeisen, Fußfesseln.

irradiation injury Strahlenschädigung *f*.

irrational irrational, unvernünftig, töricht, absurd.

irrebuttable unwiderlegbar; ~ **presumption** → *presumption.*

irreconcilable unvereinbar, unversöhnlich, unüberbrückbar.

irrecoverability Nichtbeitreibbarkeit *f*.

irrecoverable uneinbringlich, nicht beitreibbar; ~ **debts** uneinbringliche Forderungen; ~ **loss** unersetzbarer Schaden, unersetzlicher Verlust.

irrecusable unwillkürlich, ohne Willenserklärung.
irredeemable unkündbar, nicht tilgbar, unablösbar (*Hypothek*); nicht rückkaufbar.
irrefragability Unwiderlegbarkeit *f*.
irrefragable unwiderleglich, unumstößlich.
irrefutable nicht widerlegbar.
irregular unregelmäßig, vorschriftswidrig, regelwidrig, unrichtig, uneinheitlich.
irregularity Unregelmäßigkeit *f*, Unrichtigkeit *f*, Vorschriftswidrigkeit *f*; Ungehörigkeit *f*, Verfahrensverstoß *m*, unübliches Verfahren *n*; ~ **in form** Formfehler; ~ **in service** Zustellungsmangel; **legal** ~ formaler Verfahrensverstoß; **material** ~ wesentlicher Verfahrensfehler; **to commit** ~**ies** sich vorschriftswidrig verhalten; **to waive the** ~ auf die Folgen des Verfahrensverstoßes verzichten.
irrelevancy Unerheblichkeit *f*, Belanglosigkeit *f*, Irrelevanz *f*.
irrelevant nicht zur Sache gehörig, neben der Sache liegend; rechtlich unerheblich, belanglos, irrelevant; ~ **to the issue** für die Entscheidung nicht rechtserheblich, nicht schlüssig.
irremovability Nichtabschiebbarkeit *f* (*von Fürsorgeempfängern*); Unabsetzbarkeit *f*.
irremovable nicht abschiebbar, unabsetzbar.
irreparable damages → *damages*; ~ **injury** → *injury*; ~ **loss** unersetzlicher Verlust; ~ **mischief** nicht wiedergutzumachende Nachteile.
irrepealable unwiderruflich.
irrepleviable unauslösbar, uneinlösbar, der Interventionsklage nicht unterliegend, nicht herausgebbar; ~ **pledge** uneinlösbares Pfand.
irreproachable untadelig; ~ **conduct** untadeliges Verhalten.
irresistible unwiderstehlich; ~ **force** unwiderstehliche Gewalt; ~ **impulse** unwiderstehlicher Trieb, Affekt.
irrespective of ohne Rücksicht auf, unabhängig von.
irresponsibility Unverantwortlichkeit *f*, Unzurechnungsfähigkeit *f*, Nichthaftbarkeit *f*.
irresponsible unverantwortlich, nicht verantwortlich, unzurechnungsfähig, nicht haftbar.
irretrievable unwiderbringlich, unersetzlich, nicht wieder gutzumachen; ~ **breakdown of marriage** Scheitern der Ehe, Ehezerrüttung.
irreverence Respektlosigkeit *f*.
irreversible irreversibel, nicht umkehrbar, nicht rückgängig zu machen.
irrevocability Unwiderruflichkeit *f*.
irrevocable unwiderruflich.
irrigation Bewässerung *f*; ~ **district** Bewässerungs(zweck)verband (*Gebietskörperschaft*).
is ist (*zum jeweils in Betracht kommenden Zeitpunkt*), *bzw* sein wird, gewesen ist.
island company *auf den Kanalinseln bzw der Insel Man gegründete Kapitalgesellschaft* (*als oversea company qv*).
isolated abgesondert, isoliert; **in** ~ **cases** in Einzelfällen; ~ **transactions** vereinzelte Rechtsgeschäfte.
isolation Isolierung *f*, Absonderung *f*.
isometric standard Preisindexwährung *f*.
issuable zur entscheidenden Frage führend, schlüssig; ~ **defense** sachlich-rechtliche Einwendung; ~ **plea** sachlich-rechtlicher Einwand, schlüssige Einwendung; ~ **terms** Prozeßzeiten der Gerichte (*Hilary und Trinity qv*).
issuance Ausgabe *f*, Erlaß *m*; ~ **of an order** Erlaß e–s Beschlusses.
issue *s* (1) Emission *f*; Ausgabe *f*, Begebung *f*, Ausstellung *f*; Erlaß *m*; ~ **above par** Überpariemission; ~**s and profits** (Boden)Erträge; ~ **at par** Pariemission; ~ **for sale** Feilhalten, Anbieten; ~ **of a cheque** Ausstellung und e–s Schecks; ~ **of a loan** Emission e–r Anleihe; ~ **of debentures** Begebung von Schuldverschreibungen; ~ **of loan capi-**

tal Begebung von Obligationen; ~ **of proceedings** Verfahrensbeginn, Klageerhebung; ~ **of securities** Effektenemission; ~ **of shares** Aktienemission; ~ **price** Emissionskurs, Ausgabepreis, Begebungspreis, Zeichnungspreis; ~ **to (the) public** öffentliche Zeichnung; **authorized** ~ genehmigtes Kapital; **bank of** ~ → *bank* (*1*); **capable of** ~ emissionsfähig; **country of** ~ Emissionsland; **date of** ~ → *date*; **domestic** ~ Inlandsemission; **fiduciary** ~ ungedeckte Notenausgabe (*der Bank of England*); **first** ~ erste Serie; **house of** ~ Wertpapieremissionsfirma, Emissionsbank; **index-linked** ~ Emission mit Preisindexklausel, *E.* mit Gleitklausel; **industrial** ~**s** Industriewerte; **inferior** ~ Unterpariemission; **internal** ~ Inlandsemission; **note** ~ → *note*; **original** ~ Erstemission; **Pink Form I**~ → *pink*; **place of** ~ → *place*; **privileged** ~**s** bereinigte Emissionen; **public** ~ öffentliche Emission; **rate of** ~ → *rate*; **rights** ~ → *right*; **second** ~ zweite Serie (*Wertpapieremission*); **superior** ~ Überpariausgabe.

issue *s* (*2*) Streitfrage *f*, Streitpunkt *m*, wesentliche bestrittene Behauptung *f*; Punkt *m* der Tagesordnung; ~ **estoppel** → *estoppel*; ~ **in fact** = ~ **of fact** *qv*; ~ **in law** = ~ **of law** *qv*; ~ **of a dispute** rechtliche Streitfrage; ~ **of conscience** Gewissensfrage; ~ **of fact** Tatfrage, entscheidungserhebliche Frage des Sachverhalts; ~ **of law** streitige Rechtsfrage; ~ **oriented** sachbezogen; ~ **preclusion** Einwand der materiellen Rechtskraft; **at** ~ strittig, im Streit befangen; **board-level** ~ ein Problem für die Vorstandsetage; **closed** ~ erledigte Frage; **collateral** ~ *Verteidigungsvorbringen zu e–r Vorfrage*; **common** ~ *die zu entscheidende Frage beim Bestreiten der Echtheit e–r Urkundenunterschrift;* **determinative** ~ entscheidungserhebliche Frage; **feigned** ~ hypothetische Streitfrage (*simulierter Zwischenstreit zur Herbeiführung e–r Geschworenenentscheidung*); **formal** ~ verfahrenstechnisch genaue Einlassung; **general** ~ allgemeines Bestreiten, Nichtschuldigerklärung; **genuine** ~ relevante, entscheidungserhebliche Streitfrage; **immaterial** ~ nicht entscheidungserhebliche Frage; **informal** ~ verfahrenstechnisch ungenaue Einlassung; **irrelevant to the** ~ für die Entscheidung der Streitfrage (rechtlich) unerheblich; **joinder of** ~ → *joinder*; **justiciable** ~ justiziable Frage, gerichtlich zu entscheidender Punkt, e–r gerichtlichen Entscheidung zugängliche Frage; **material** ~ entscheidungserhebliche Frage; **matter in** ~ → *matter*; **minor** ~ Nebenfrage; **multifarious issue** willkürliche Klagehäufung, willkürlich verbundene Streitgegenstände; **point at** ~ → *point*; **preliminary** ~ Vorfrage; **question at** → *question*; **real** ~ (die) eigentliche Streitfrage; **relevant to the** ~ → *relevant*; **special** ~ Bestreiten von Einzelpunkten; **the case at** ~ → *case*; **to be in** ~ streitig sein, zur Debatte stehen, Gegenstand von Verhandlungen sein; **to join the** ~ sich einlassen; die entscheidungserhebliche Frage feststellen; **to settle an** ~ die entscheidungserhebliche Frage festlegen; **triable** ~ rechtserhebliche Frage; zur Entscheidung anstehende Frage.

issue *s* (*3*) Nachkommen *m*|*pl*, Kinder *n*|*pl*, Erben *m*|*pl*; Abkömmlinge *m*|*pl* in gerader Linie; ~ **in tail** erbberechtigte Nachkommen bei Fideikommiß; ~ **in tail male** gebundene männliche Erbfolge; ~ **living** lebende Nachkommen; ~ **of cousins** Kinder von Vettern und Kusinen; ~ **risk** *Risiko, daß unbekannte Abkömmlinge vorhanden sind, bzw sein werden*; **lawful** ~ eheliche Nachkommen(schaft); **legitimate** ~ eheliche Nachkommen.

issue *v* begeben, emittieren; ausstellen, erlassen, erteilen; *auch v*|*i* Klage erheben; ~ **a bill** e–n Wechsel ausstellen; ~ **a decree** Urteil *bzw Beschluß* erlassen; ~ **a patent** ein Patent erteilen; ~ **a summons** gerichtlich laden, vorladen; ~ **a warrant of arrest** e–n Haftbefehl erlassen; ~ **a writ** zum Zwecke der amtlichen Zustellung übergeben; Klage erheben; ~ **and allot** begeben (*Aktien*); ~ **the execution** Vollstreckungsauftrag erteilen, die Zwangsvollstreckung betreiben; ~ **writ of summons** Klage erheben; **~d capital** → *capital*; **~d stock** ausgegebenes Aktienkapital.

issueless ohne Nachkommen, kinderlos.

issuer Aussteller *m*, Emittent *m*.

issuing ausstellend, emittierend, Emissions . . .; ~ **bank** Emissionsbank, Akkreditivbank; ~ **company** emittierende Gesellschaft; ~ **date** Ausstellungsdatum; ~ **house** Emissionshaus; ~ **place** → *place*; ~ **transactions** Emissionsgeschäfte.

item Punkt *m* (*e–r Aufzählung*), Nummer *f*, Ziffer *f*, Teil *m*, Gegenstand *m*, Bestandteil *m*, Posten *m*, Position *f*; ~ **of a bill** Rechnungsposten; ~ **of account** Rechnungsposten; ~ **of property** Vermögensgegenstand; ~ **of the budget** Haushaltstitel; ~ **on the agenda** Tagesordnungspunkt; **common** ~ den gleichen Teil des Streitgegenstandes betreffend (*Kostenrecht*); **credit** ~ → *credit* (*2*); **debit** ~ → *debit*; **free ~s** spesenfreie Inkassi; **news** ~ Nachricht, Pressenotiz; **patented ~s** patentierte Einzelheiten, einzelne Patentgegenstände; **sub-** ~ Unterposition; **to credit an** ~ e–n Posten gutschreiben.

itemize näher angeben, verzeichnen, listenmäßig aufstellen, aufgliedern; ~ **an account** Rechnung spezifizieren; ~ **costs** Kosten aufgliedern; **~d pay statements** aufgegliederte Lohn- u. Gehaltsabrechnung.

iter Fußweg *m*, Wegerecht *n*, Route *f*.

itinera Reiserouten *f/pl der Richter*.

itinerant reisend, im Umherziehen, Wander . . .; ~ **judge** Reiserichter, kommissarischer Richter *bei turnusmäßigem Besuch der zugewiesenen Gerichte*; ~ **peddling** Hausieren; ~ **trade** → *trade*; ~ **vendor** Reisender, Vertreter, Wandergewerbetreibender, Hausierer.

itinerary Reiseroute *f*; **prescribed** ~ vorgeschriebene Fahrstrecke.

itinerate umherziehen, e–e (*richterliche*) Rundreise vornehmen.

J

jactitation Berühmung *f*; ~ **of marriage** Ehesimulation *unbegründetes Vorgeben, mit jmdm verheiratet zu sein*; ~ **suit** Prozeß wegen e–r Berühmung; negative Feststellungsklage; **action of** ~ Feststellungsklage wegen Eigentumsberühmung.

jail Gefängnis *n*, Haftanstalt *f* (*vgl gaol*); ~ **bird** Knastbruder; ~ **breaking** Ausbruch aus e–m Gefängnis; ~ **delivery** → *gaol*; ~ **liberties** Außenbezirk e–r Gefangenenanstalt; ~ **sentence** → *sentence*; **commitment to** ~ Einweisung in ein Gefängnis; **to put in** ~ einsperren lassen, inhaftieren.

jailer Gefängnisdirektor *m*, Leiter *m* e–r Haftanstalt, Gefängniswärter *m*.

jay|walker unachtsamer Fußgänger; ~ **walking** unachtsames Gehen; **diagonal** ~ **walking** unachtsames Überqueren e–r Kreuzung.

Jedburgh justice Lynchjustiz *f*.

jeofail(e) Berichtigungserlaubnis *f* wegen formaler Klagemängel.

jeopardize gefährden, aufs Spiel setzen.

jeopardy Gefahr *f*, Risiko *n*, Gefahr *f* e–r Verurteilung, Risiko *n* des Strafurteils; ~ **assessment** Beurteilung des Steuerausfalls; ~ **of life or limb** Gefahr der Verurteilung zu e–r schweren Strafe; **double** ~ (*ne bis in idem*) Gefahr doppelter Verurteilung; **former** ~ Berufung auf ne bis in idem; **to be in legal** ~ e–m Strafverfahren ausgesetzt sein.

jerquer zollamtlicher Prüfer *m*.

jerry-built provisorisch, als Behelf errichtet.

jetsam Seewurfgut *n*, *bei Seenot über Bord geworfene Ladung*.

jettison Überbordwerfen *n* (*zur Rettung e–s Schiffes und der Ladung aus Seenot*) Seewurf *m*; ~ **and washing overboard** Überbordwerfen und Überbordspülen.

jigger boss Vorarbeiter *m*, Antreiber *m* (*Bergbau*).

Jim Crow Neger *m*; Nigger *m*; ~ **-ism** Rassentrennung, Rassendiskriminierung.

jingo Chauvinist *m*.

jingoism Chauvinismus *m*.

job Arbeit *f*, Geschäft *n*, Posten *m*, Beruf *m*, Beschäftigung *f*; ~ **analysis** Arbeitsplatzuntersuchung; ~ **card** Arbeitslaufkarte; ~ **classification** Berufsklassifikation; ~ **conditions** *äußere* Arbeitsbedingungen; ~ **control** Beherrschung e–s Betriebes (*oder Betriebsteils*) durch Gewerkschaften; ~ **cost system** Kostenrechnung für Einzelfertigung; ~ **counseling** Arbeitnehmerberatung; ~ **creation** Schaffung von Arbeitsplätzen; ~ **cutting** Stellenabbau, Personalabbau; ~ **description** Tätigkeitsbeschreibung; ~ **evaluation** Arbeitsplatzbewertung; ~ **goods** → *goods*; ~ **grade** Berufsklassifizierung; ~ **instruction** Arbeitsunterweisung; ~ **loss** Verlust des Arbeitsplatzes; ~ **lot** Warenposten mit kleinen Fehlern; ~ **or career prospects** Berufsaussichten; ~ **order** Verarbeitungsanweisung, Fabrikationsauftrag; ~ **placement** Arbeits(platz)vermittlung; ~ **preservation** Erhaltung der Arbeitsplätze; ~ **production** Einzelfertigung; Herstellung nach Angaben des Kunden; ~ **profile** Tätigkeitsrahmen; Arbeitsplatzbeschreibung; ~ **prospects** Arbeitsmarktaussichten, Aussichtung für die Beschaffung von Arbeitsplätzen; ~ **rate** Akkordrichtsatz; ~ **rating** Arbeitsplatzbewertung; ~ **referral service** Stellennachweis(dienst); **J~ Release Act** Gesetz über vorzeitiges Ausscheiden von Arbeitnehmern; ~ **release scheme** Plan für vorzeitige Aufgabe des

Arbeitsplatzes; ~ **security** Sicherheit des Arbeitsplatzes; ~ **seniority** Dienstalter; ~ **shop** Einzelanfertigungsbetrieb; **~-switching** häufiger Arbeitsplatzwechsel; ~ **ticket** Arbeitslaufzettel; ~ **wage** Akkordlohn, Stücklohn; ~ **work** Akkordarbeit; **odd ~s** → *odd*; **put-up** ~ abgekartetes Spiel; **rush** ~ Eilauftrag; **to work by the** ~ zum Festpreis arbeiten; im Akkord arbeiten.

jobber Jobber *m*, Börsenhändler *m* *(der nur im eigenen Namen und für eigene Rechnung Geschäfte abschließen darf, Mitglied der Londoner Börse)*, Börsenspekulant *m*, *US = stockjobber qv*; Viehhändler *m*; Großhändler *m*, Ramschpostenhändler *m*; Gelegenheitsarbeiter *m*; ~ **system** Börsenhändlersystem (*Londoner Börse*); **desk** ~ Grossist ohne eigenes Lager; **exchange** ~ Sortenhändler; **general line** ~ Großhändler für alle Warengattungen; **local** ~ Platzmakler; **rack** ~ *Großhändler, der Einzelhändler versorgt und Absatz organisiert*; Platzmakler; **wagon** ~ *Großhändler von Haushaltsartikeln*; *Belieferer von Hotels und Anstalten.*

jobbery *pol* Geschäftemacherei *f*; Aktienhandel *m*.

jobbing Gelegenheitsarbeit *f*, Akkordarbeit *f*; Effektenhandel *m*, Spekulation *f*; Großhandel *m*, Zwischenhandel *m*; Schiebung *f*, Wucher *m*; ~ **in bill's** → *bill* (*3*); ~ **in contangoes** *exch* Reportgeschäft; **stock** ~ → *stock* (*1*).

jobholder Arbeitnehmer *m*; **public** ~ Staatsbediensteter, Angehöriger des öffentlichen Dienstes.

jobless arbeitslos; Arbeitsloser; **joblessness** Arbeitslosigkeit *f*; ~ **level** Arbeitslosigkeitsstand.

John Doe (=) *fiktiver Name m e–r Prozeßpartei oder e–s sonstigen Beteiligten.*

join verbinden, sich verbinden, sich vereinigen, beitreten, eintreten; ~ **a firm as partner** in e–e Gesellschaft als Teilhaber eintreten; ~ **a law suit** e–m Rechtsstreit beitreten; ~ **A. B. as party** A. B. mitverklagen; ~ **an action** e–m Prozeß beitreten; ~ **in an undertaking** sich an e–r Unternehmung beteiligen; ~ **the issue** den Prozeß auf die entscheidungserhebliche Frage konzentrieren.

joinder Klageverbindung *f*, Klag(en)häufung *f*, Klagebeitritt *m*, Intervention *f*; ~ **in demurrer** das Eingehen auf e–e prozeßhindernde Einrede; ~ **in issue** *Einigung darüber, welcher streitige Sachverhalt zur Entscheidung gestellt wird*; ~ **in pleading** Festlegung des entscheidungserheblichen Sachverhalts, *nach vorbereitenden Schriftsätzen*; ~ **of accessory with principal in indictment** gemeinsame Anklage von Haupttäter und Tatgehilfe; ~ **of actions** = ~ *of causes of action qv*; ~ **of causes of action** Anspruchshäufung, objektive Klag(en)häufung; ~ **of charges** Zusammenfassung von Anklagepunkten; ~ **of claims** objektive Klagehäufung; ~ **of defendants** das Mitverklagen (*weiterer Parteien*); ~ **of documents** Verbindung von Urkunden (*bei Protokollierung*); ~ **of error** Revisionserwiderung im Strafverfahren; ~ **of indictments** Anklageverbindung; ~ **of issue** Kondensierung des Streitstoffes auf entscheidungserhebliche Punkte; ~ **of joint plaintiffs** (*bzw defendants*) notwendiger Prozeßbeitritt *aus sachlichrechtlicher Gemeinschaft*; ~ **of offenses** Einbeziehung von Einzelstraftatbeständen *in die gleiche Anklageschrift;* ~ **of offenders** gemeinsame Anklageerhebung gegen Tatbeteiligte; ~ **of parties** Bildung e–r Streitgenossenschaft, Nebenintervention; ~ **of parties in the alternative** Alternativverklagung *von zwei Parteien;* ~ **of trustees** notwendige Prozeßbeteiligung von Treuhändern; **compulsory** ~ notwendige Streitgenossenschaft; **permissive** ~ Streitgenossenschaft, subjektive Klagehäufung.

joint *adj* verbunden, gemeinschaftlich, gemeinsam, ungeteilt, zur gesamten Hand, kollektiv, solidarisch, Mit...; ~ **account clause** *Hypothekentilgungsklausel, wonach Zahlung an den überlebenden Mitgläubiger schuldbefreiend wirkt;* ~ **and several** → *joint and several*; ~ **and survivor annuity** Überlebensrente; ~ **annuity survivor pension plan** Pensionssystem mit Zahlung von Überlebensrente; ~ **industrial council** paritätisch besetzte Tarifvertragskommission; ~ **industry of husband and wife** Erwerbstätigkeit beider Ehegatten; ~ **life assurance** wechselseitige Überlebensversicherung; ~ **lives** solange beide (*bzw mehrere*) Personen am Leben sind; *ins*: verbundene Leben; ~ **negotiating panel** gemeinsamer Verhandlungsausschuß; Mitaktionäre, Aktionäre in Rechtsgemeinschaft; ~ **scrutiny committee** gemeinsamer Vorprüfungsausschuß für Parlamentsvorlagen; ~ **stock** Aktienkapital; ~ **stock bank** Aktienbank, Bankaktiengesellschaft; ~ **stock company** → *company*; ~ **tax return** gemeinsame Steuererklärung der Ehegatten; ~ **through rate** gemeinsame Frachtgebühr (mehrerer Frachtführer).

joint and several solidarisch, gesamtschuldnerisch; ~ **creditor** Gläubiger e–r Forderung, für die samtverbindlich gehaftet wird; ~ **guarantee** Solidarbürgschaft; ~ **liability** gesamtschuldnerische Haftung; ~ **negligence** samtverbindliche Haftung für Fahrlässigkeit; ~ **note** samtverbindlicher Schuldschein; ~ **obligation** → *obligation*; **to be ~ly and ~ly liable** gesamtschuldnerisch haften.

joint venture *(=)* Arbeitsgemeinschaft *f*, Gemeinschaftsunternehmen *n*, BGB-Gesellschaft *f*; ~ **distribution company** Gemeinschafts-Vertriebsgesellschaft.

jointist Inhaber *m* e–s verbotenen Alkoholausschanks.

jointress nießbrauchsberechtigte Ehefrau *f* (*mit lebenslänglichem Nießbrauch am Grundvermögen des Mannes*).

jointure Leibgedinge *n*; Wittum *n*; Nießbrauchsrecht *n* der Witwe am Grundvermögen des Ehemannes.

joker *Klausel f, durch die ein Gesetz ad absurdum geführt wird*; Hintertürchen-Paragraph *m*.

jouissance|rights Genußrechte *n|pl*; ~ **shares** Genußaktien, Genußscheine.

journal Tagebuch *n*, Journal *n*, Schiffstagebuch *n*, Tagesprotokoll *n*, Parlamentsbericht *m*; **J~s of the Houses of Parliament** Parlamentsprotokoll; ~ **entry** Journalbuchung; (*Buchung mit Gegenbuchung*); ~ **office** Protokollführerabteilung; **cash** ~ Kassenbuch; **Committee for the J~s** Protokollprüfungsausschuß *brit Oberhaus*); **ledger** ~ amerikanisches Journal, in Tabellenform geführtes Hauptbuch; **purchase** ~ Wareneingangsbuch, Einkaufsjournal; **purchase returns** ~ Rückwarenbuch (*für Verkäufe*); **sales** ~ Ausgangsjournal, Ausgangsfakturenbuch; **sales returns** ~ Retourenjournal, Rückwarenbuch.

journey Tagesreise *f*, Reise *f*; Route *f*.

journeyman Tagelöhner *m*, Geselle *m*.

joy-riding unbefugte Benutzung *f* e–s PKW; Schwarzfahrt *f*; Fahrt mit gestohlenem PKW.

judge Richter *m* (= *R bzw r*) Vorsitzender *m*, Einzelrichter *m*, Gericht *n*; ~ **ad quem** *R* der Rechtsmittelinstanz; ~ **advocate** → *judge advocate*; Strafvollzugsbehörde der Militärjustiz; Staatsanwalt beim Militärgericht; **J~ Advocate General** Oberste Militärstaatsanwaltschaft; ~ *Department: oberste wehrrechte Abteilung im Verteidigungsministerium;* **J~ Advocate of the Fleet** Marine-Staatsanwaltschaft; **~'s certificate** Kostenbeschluß, gemeinsame richterliche Stellungnahme; **~'s clerk** → *clerk*; ~ **de facto** als *R* fungierende Person; ~ **in chambers** Einzelr, *R* außerhalb des

Termins, im Bürowege entscheidender *R*; ~ **-made law** → *law;* **~'s minutes** handschriftliche Protokollnotizen des *R–s*; **~'s notes** = *~'s minutes qv;* **~'s oath** → *oath*; **~'s order** richterlicher Beschluß im Bürowege; ~ **ordinary** *R* am (früheren) Court of Probate; **J~s' Rules** richterliche Richtlinie für polizeiliche Vernehmungen und Anzeigeerstattung; ~ **trial** Verhandlung vor dem Einzel*r*; **administrative law** ~ Verwaltungs*r*; **appellate** ~ Berufungs*r*, Revisions*r*; **assistant** ~ Gerichtsassessor, Hilfs*r*; ~ **associate** ~ Beisitzer; **chief** ~ oberster *R*, Gerichtspräsident; **circuit** ~ → *circuit*; **commercial** ~ (Berufs)*R* in e–r Kammer für Handelssachen *n* (*commercial court*), Handels*r*; **commissioned** ~ beauftragter *R*, Rechtshilfe*r*; **deputy** ~ beauftragter *R*, kommissarischer *R*; **district** ~ Amts*r*, Bezirks*r*, *R* e–s District Court *qv*; **even-handed** ~ gerechter *R*; **impartial** ~ unvoreingenommener *R*; **junior** ~ Assessor; **lay** ~ Laien*r*; **national** ~ einem beteiligten Staat angehörender *R* (*internationaler Gerichtshof*); **non-lawyer** ~ Laien*r*; **original** ~ Erst*r*, Vorder*r*, Tat*r*; **presiding** ~ Gerichtsvorsitzender; **professional** ~ Berufs*r*; **puisne** ~ (*gewöhnlicher*) *R*, Beisitzer; **regular** ~ gesetzlicher *R*, Berufs*r*; **reporting** ~ Berichterstatter; **senior** ~ rangältester *R*, vorsitzender *R*; **side** ~ (Laien) Beisitzer; **single** ~ Einzel*r*; **sole** ~ Einzel*r*; **summary** ~ *R* des Schnellgerichts, Ermittlungs*r*; **to challenge a** ~ e–n *R* ablehnen; **trial** ~ Tat*r*, Vorder*r*, *R* erster Instanz; **vacation** ~ Ferien*r*, in den Gerichtsferien amtierender *R*; **waivers** ~ *sl* milder *R*.

judge *v* richten, judizieren.

judge advocate Militärstaatsanwalt *m*, Militärrichter; *US: auch* juristischer Stabsoffizier.

judgment Urteil *n* (= *U bzw u*), Endurteil *n*, Urteilsbegründung *f*, gerichtliche Entscheidung *f*; Urteilsvermögen *n*; ~ **admitting of no appeal** *U*, gegen das kein Rechtsmittel gegeben ist; *formell* rechtskräftiges *U*; ~ **after trial** kontradiktorisches *U*; ~ **bond** Sicherheitsleistung (*des Bekl*) zur Abwendung der Vollstreckung (*vor Rechtskraft*); ~ **-book** *U*-*s*register; ~ **by confession** Anerkenntnis*u*; ~ **by consent** gerichtl protokollierter Vergleich; ~ **by** (= *in*) **default** Versäumnis*u*; ~ **by motion** *U auf gesondert zugestellten Antrag wegen nicht ausreichenden Gegenvorbringens*; ~ **by nil dixit** *U* wegen Nichtverteidigung d. Beklagten; ~ **creditor** → *creditor*; ~ **debt** → *debt*; ~ **debtor** → *debtor*; ~ **debtor summons** Zahlungsbefehl mit Konkursandrohung; ~ **docket** *U*–*s*register, *U*–*s*verzeichnis; ~ **execution** Vollstreckungsklausel (*auf Urteil*); **J~s Extension Act** *Gesetz von 1868 über die Gültigkeit englischer U–e in Schottland u Irland*; ~ **for abstention from same act** Unterlassungs*u*; ~ **for amount to be ascertained** *U* auf Zahlung e–s (*von e–m Dritten*) festzustellenden Betrages; ~ **for damages** *U* auf (Zahlung von) Schadenersatz; ~ **for plaintiff** obsiegendes *U* des Klägers; ~ **for possession** *U* auf Besitzeinräumung; ~ **fund** Entscheidungsfonds (*auf Grund e–s Gerichtsurteils; Indianerabfindung*); ~ **in default of appearance** Versäumnis*u*; ~ **in default of defence** Versäumnis*u* gegen die beklagte Partei *wegen Nichtanzeige der Verteidigungsbereitschaft*; ~ **in error** Revisions*u*; ~ **in foreign currency** Fremdwährungs*u*; ~ **in personam** schuldrechtliches *U*, Leistungs*u*; ~ **in rem** *U* mit dinglicher Wirkung, Gestaltungs*u*; ~ **lien** → *lien*; ~ **note** Schuldschein mit Unterwerfungsklausel (*mit Vollmacht zum gerichtl Anerkenntnis*); ~ **of acquittal** freisprechendes *U*; ~ **of conviction** Verurteilung, Straf*u*; ~ **of dismissal** klageabweisendes *U bei*

Säumnis des Klägers; ~ **of his peers** *U* durch ranggleiche Richter; ~ **of nonsuit** → *nonsuit*; ~ **of nulle prosequi** klageabweisendes Versäumnis*u* (*nach Erklärung des Klägers, die Klage nicht weiter zu verfolgen*); ~ **of nullity** Nichtigkeits*u*; ~ **of repleader** Zwischen*u* auf Gestattung neuen schriftsätzlichen Vortrags; ~ **of respondent ouster** Zwischen*u* über die Verwerfung e–r dilatorischen Einrede; ~ **of retraxit** *U* nach Klageverzicht; ~ **on a case stated** *U* auf Grund e–s einverständlich unterbreiteten Sachverhalts; ~ **on a special verdict** *U* bei unstreitigem Sachverhalt; ~ **on default** Versäumnis*u*; ~ **on demurrer** klagabweisendes *U* wegen Unschlüssigkeit der Klage; ~ **on (the) pleadings** *U* im schriftlichen Verfahren (*nach dem Stand des schriftsätzlichen Vortrags*); ~ **on the merits** Sach*u*; ~ **over** Regreß*u*; ~ **paper** *U*–sblatt mit Rubrum *zur amtlichen Einsetzung des Urteils*; ~ **roll** Urteilsurkunde mit Klage und Ladungsnachweis (*aufzubewahrende Teile der Gerichtsakte*); ~ **seat** Richterbank, Gericht; ~ **subject to appeal** noch nicht rechtskräftiges *U*; ~ **summons** *Ladung des (angebl zahlungsunwilligen) Vollstreckungsschuldners auf Verhaftungsantrag des Vollstreckungsgläubigers*, Antrag auf Beugehaft gegen den zahlungsunwilligen Vollstreckungsschuldner; ~ **with costs** kostenpflichtige Verurteilung; **accumulative** ~ → *accumulative*; **agreed** ~ gerichtlich protokollierter Vergleich; **alternative** ~ Leistungs*u* mit alternativem Tenor; **approbating the** ~ *nachträgliche Einwendungen nach e–m Versäumnisu*; **arrest of** ~ Einstellung des Verfahrens (*wegen Verfahrensfehler nach Schuldspruch vor Verkündung des Strafmaßes*); **cautionary** ~ → *cautionary*; **conditional** ~ bedingtes End*u*; **confirmatory** ~ bestätigendes *U* (*der Rechtsmittelinstanz*); **consent** ~ einverständlich beantragtes *U*, Prozeßvergleich; **contradictory** ~ kontradiktorisches *U*; **declaration** ~ Feststellungs*u*; **declaratory** ~ Feststellungs*u*; **defended** ~ Urteil im streitigen Verfahren; **deferment of a** ~ Aussetzung der Verkündung e–s *U–s*; **deficiency** → *deficiency*; **dissenting** ~**s** voneinander abweichende *U–e* bzw *U–s*begründungen; **domestic** ~ inländisches *U bzw in dem betr Einzelstaat der USA erlassenes U*; **dormant** ~ lange Zeit nicht vollstrecktes *U*; nicht mehr vollstreckbares *U*; **enforcement of** ~ → *enforcement;* **entry of** ~ Eintragung des *U–s*, Erlaß des *U–s*; **false** ~ Fehl*u*; **favorable** ~ obsiegendes *U*; **final** ~ Endurteil (*Abschluß e–r Instanz*); (*doch auch:*) rechtskräftiges *U*; **foreign** ~ ausländisches *U bzw in einem anderen Einzelstaat der USA erlassenes U*; **interlocutory** ~ Zwischen*u*; **irregular** ~ verfahrenswidrig erlassenes *U*; **junior** ~ jüngeres *U* gegen den gleichen Beklagten; **level** ~ ausgeglichenes *U*; **money** ~ *U* auf Zahlung; **moral** ~ moralisch motiviertes (Gerichts)Urteil; **motion to correct** ~ Antrag auf *U–s*berichtigung; **personal** ~ Leistungs*u*; **pocket** ~ vollstreckbare Urkunde auf Zahlung; **precedent** ~ Vorentscheidung, Präzedenzfall; **provisional** ~ Vorbehalts*u*; **register of** ~**s** *U–s*register; **regular** ~ ordnungsgemäß erlassenes *U*; **rendition of** ~ → *rendition*; **reprieve of** ~ *befristete* Aussetzung *der Vollstreckbarkeit* e–s *U–s*; **reserved** ~ Urteil (*dessen Begründung sich der Richter vorbehalten hatte*), nachträglich verkündetes Urteil; **respite of** ~ Vertagung der *U–s*verkündung; **reversal of a** ~ → *reversal*; **summary** ~ *U* im abgekürzten Verfahren (*ohne Geschworenenverhandlung, z. T. ohne mündliche Verhandlung*); **to deliver a** ~ → *to deliver*; **to enter** ~ ein *U* erlassen (*im Urteilsbuch eintragen*); **to execute a** ~ → *to execute*; **to pronounce** ~ ein *U* verkünden; **to quash a** ~ ein *U* aufheben; **to reopen** ~ → *to reopen*; **to reverse the** ~ das *U* aufheben; **to set aside a** ~ ein *U* aufheben; **unexecuted** ~ noch nicht vollstrecktes *U*; **vacation of** ~ *U*-saufhebung; **villenous** ~ *hist U bei Verlust aller Ehrenrechte unter Einziehung des Vermögens*; **void** ~ nichtiges *U*; **voidable** ~ anfechtbares *U*.

judgment-proof unpfändbar, nicht der Zwangsvollstreckung unterworfen.

judgeship Richterschaft *f*, Richteramt *n*.

judicature Gerichtsbarkeit *f*, Justiz *f*, die Justizangehörigen, Gerichtshof *m*, Rechtsprechung *f*; **J~ Acts** *brit Gerichtsverfassungsgesetze (1875)*; **system of** ~ Gerichtsverfassung, Gerichtsordnung.

judicial gerichtlich (= *g*), richterlich, Gerichts . . .; scharf urteilend, kritisch, unparteiisch; ~ **act** → *act*; ~ **action** *g–es* Verfahren; ~ **activism** Richter als Sozialingenieure; ~ **admission** Geständnis vor Gericht; ~ **and extrajudicial** gerichtlich und außergerichtlich; ~ **assistance** → *assistance*; Vertragshilfe; ~ **authority** Justizbehörde, Gerichtsbarkeit; ~ **bond** Kaution, Sicherheitsleistung bei Gericht; ~ **business** *g–e* Tätigkeit; ~ **circuit** Gerichtsbezirk; ~ **code** Gerichtsverfassungsgesetz (*J~Code US Bundesprozeßordnung*); ~ **cognizance** Kenntnis des Gerichts; ~ **combat** Zweikampfordal; **J~ Committee of the Privy Council** Justizausschuß des englischen Kronrates (*Revisionsinstanz für Gerichtsentscheidungen außerhalb der britischen Inseln*); ~ **compulsion** *g–er* Zwang; **J~ Conference** Vermittlungsausschuß für Richterbestellung *US*; ~ **confession** *g–es* Geständnis; ~ **construction** richterliche Auslegung; ~ **control** richterliche Überprüfung(smöglichkeit); ~ **convention** Vereinbarung auf Grund *g–er* Auflage; ~ **council** Richterrat (*e–s Gerichtsbezirks*); ~ **courtesy** Anerkennung *g–er* Entscheidungen aus völkerrechtlicher Kourtoisie; ~ **custom** Rechtsgewohnheit, Gerichtspraxis; ~ **cypres** *g–e* Auslegung zugunsten des Erblasserwillens; ~ **decision** Gerichtsurteil, *g–e* Entscheidung, *bes* Entscheidung e–r höheren Instanz; ~ **declaration of law** ständige Rechtsprechung; ~ **decree** Gerichtsurteil (*in Equity-Verfahren*); ~ **department** die Justiz, Justizverwaltung; ~ **dictum** Dictum, *beiläufige Äußerung e–s Richters zu e–r Rechtsfrage*; ~ **discretion** richterliches Ermessen; ~ **dissection** *g–e* Obduktion; ~ **district** Gerichtsbezirk; ~ **divorce** Ehescheidung durch Gerichtsurteil; ~ **documents** Gerichtsurkunden, Gerichtsakten; ~ **duty** Pflicht der sachgerechten Prüfung e–r Entscheidung; ~ **error** Justizirrtum, Rechtsirrtum, Fehler des Gerichts; ~ **estoppel** *Unzulässigkeit späteren Bestreitens des Inhalts früherer eidlicher Erklärungen*; ~ **factor** *g* bestellter Pfleger in Vermögensangelegenheiten; ~ **finding** Richterspruch, Gerichtsurteil, richterliche Feststellungen; ~ **function** richterliche Funktion; Richteramt; ~ **hearing** mündliche Verhandlung; ~ **immunity** Immunität des Richters; ~ **independence** richterliche Unabhängigkeit; ~ **inquiry** *g–e* Wahrheitsfindung; *g–e* Untersuchung; ~ **inspection** *g–e* Besichtigung, richterlicher Augenschein; ~ **inspection of a locality** Ortstermin; ~ **investigation** *g–e* Untersuchung; ~ **knowledge** Kenntnis des Gerichts, gerichtsbekannte Tatsachen; ~ **notice** → *notice*; ~ **oath** → *oath*; ~ **office** richterliches Amt, Amt in der Justiz; ~ **officer** Richter; Justizbeamter; ~ **opinion** *g–e* Stellungnahme, Urteilsbegründung; ~ **order** → *order (1)*; ~ **power** richterliche Gewalt, Justizgewalt; ~ **precedent** Präzedenzfall; ~ **procedure** *g–es* Verfahren; ~ **proceedings** Gerichtsverfahren, Gerichtsverhandlung; ~ **question** *g* zu entscheidende Frage, der richterlichen

Gewalt zugeordnete Frage; ~ **record** Gerichtsurkunde, Gerichtsakte; ~ **reference** *g* angeordnetes Schiedsverfahren; ~ **reform** Justizreform; ~ **relief** Rechtsschutz(begehren); ~ **remedy** Rechtsweg, *g–er* Rechtsbehelf, Klagemöglichkeit; ~ **restraint** gerichtl Kontrolle, gerichtl–e Beschränkungen; ~ **review** richterliche Nachprüfung, Normenkontrolle, Revision; ~ **sale** Zwangsversteigerung, Zwangsverkauf; ~ **self-restraint** richterliche Zurückhaltung; ~ **separation** Trennung von Tisch und Bett, *g* gestattetes Getrenntleben; ~ **statistics** Statistik über abgeurteilte Täter; ~ **supremacy** Justizhoheit; *Überwachung der Einhaltung der Verfassung durch die Gerichte*; ~ **system** Gerichtswesen, Rechtspfleger; ~ **trustee** *g* bestellter Treuhänder; ~ **uncertainty** Unsicherheit der Gerichtspraxis, ... der Urteilsfindung; ~ **writ** → *writ*; **quasi** ~ gerichtsähnlich.

judiciary *adj* richterlich; *s* rechtsprechende Gewalt *f*, Gerichtswesen *n*, Justiz *f*, Richterschaft *f*, Richterstand *m*; **J~ Act** *US-Bundesgerichtsverfassungsgesetz (1789)*; ~ **law** richterlich festgestelltes Gewohnheitsrecht, Richterrecht.

judicium Dei Gottesurteil *n*.

juggling of accounts Kontenmanipulation *f*.

junction Einmündung *f*, Abzweigung *f*, Verbindung *f*, Knotenpunkt *m*; **traffic** ~ → *traffic*.

juncture kritischer Zeitpunkt *m*, Lage *f*, Stand *m* der Dinge.

junior *adj* jünger, niederer, nachrangig.

junior *s* Jüngere(r), Untergeordnete(r), Juniorpartner.

junk Schrott *m*; ~ **bonds** minderwertige Obligationen, Ramschanleihe, *ungesicherte, nachrangige hochverzinsliche Risikoobligationen;* ~ **dealer** Schrotthändler; ~ **securities** geringwertige Wertpapiere; ~ **shop** Schrotthandlung, Altwarenladen; ~ **value** Schrottwert.

junking Verschrottung *f*, *das Ausscheiden veralteter Maschinen und Ersatz durch neue.*

jura|regalia Staatshoheitsrechte; ~ **regia** Prärogativrechte der Krone.

jural (positiv)rechtlich, juristisch.

jurat Beurkundungsformel *f* der Eidesleistung.

juration Eidesabnahme *f*, Eidesleistung *f*.

jurator Geschworener *m*.

jurats Gemeindeälteste *m|pl*.

juridical gerichtlich, Justiz . . .

jurimetrics Jurimetrie *f*, *Anwendung der Mathematik und der EDV auf die Rechtsfindung.*

juris|et de jure nach jedem Recht, rechtlich und gesetzlich unwiderlegbar (*Vermutung*); ~ **utrum** *hist* Pfründenherausgabeklage.

jurisconsult Jurist *m*, Rechtsgelehrter *m*.

jurisdiction Gerichtsbarkeit *f*, Gerichtshoheit *f*, Gerichtsstand *m*, Zuständigkeit *f*; Kompetenz *f*; ~ **clause** Gerichtsstandsklausel; Begründung der Zuständigkeit (*in e–r Klage*); ~ **over the subject matter** Gerichtsbarkeit über den Streitgegenstand; ~ **to re-hear** Gerichtsbefugnis der erneuten Sachprüfung, Zuständigkeit als Berufungsgericht; **appellate** ~ Zuständigkeit als Rechtsmittelinstanz; **arbitral** ~ Schiedsgerichtsbarkeit; **civil** ~ Zivilgerichtsbarkeit; **comprehensive** ~ Allzuständigkeit; **compulsory** ~ ausschließliche Zuständigkeit; **concurrent** ~ konkurrierende Zuständigkeit, nicht ausschließliche Gerichtsbarkeit, Wahlgerichtsstand; **conflict of** ~ → *conflict*; **consent** ~ vereinbarter Gerichtsstand; **contentious** ~ streitige Gerichtsbarkeit; **co-ordinate** ~ konkurrierende Zuständigkeit; **court of** ~ zuständiges Gericht; **court of general** ~ → *court*; **criminal** ~ Strafgerichtsbarkeit; **delegated** ~ übertragene Gerichtsbarkeit; **disciplinary** ~ Disziplinargerichtsbarkeit; **discretionary** ~ Ermessensbefugnis; **domestic** ~ inländische

Gerichtsbarkeit, Gerichtsstand der inländischen Gerichte, Hoheitsbereich; **exclusive** ~ ausschließliche Zuständigkeit; **exercise of** ~ Ausübung der Gerichtsbarkeit, Gebrauchmachen von der Zuständigkeit; **federal** ~ Bundeszuständigkeit, Zuständigkeit der Bundesgerichte; **fiscal** ~ Steuerhoheit; **foreign** ~ fremde Zuständigkeit, außerhalb des Staatshoheitsgebiets ausgeübte Gerichtsbarkeit; **foreign ~ acts** *Gesetze über brit Gerichtsbarkeit außerhalb des UK*; **full** ~ (*unbeschränkte*) sachliche Zuständigkeit; **general** ~ allgemeine Zuständigkeit; **industrial** ~ Arbeitsgerichtsbarkeit; **inherent** ~ von Amts wegen bestehende Befugnisse; **in rem** ~ dinglicher Gerichtsstand; **instant** ~ ursprüngl Zuständigkeit; **lack of** ~ → *lack*; **limited** ~ Sonderzuständigkeit, funktionelle Zuständigkeit; **local** ~ örtliche Zuständigkeit; **maritime** ~ maritime Staatshoheit, Seegerichtsbarkeit, seegerichtliche Zuständigkeit; **matrimonial** ~ Zuständigkeit in Ehesachen; **national** ~ inländische Gerichtsbarkeit; **non-contentious** ~ freiwillige Gerichtsbarkeit; **original** ~ erstinstanzliche Zuständigkeit; **ouster of** ~ → *ouster*; **penal** ~ Strafgerichtsbarkeit; **pendent** ~ vorbehaltene, konkurrierende (Bundes)zuständigkeit; **personal** ~ Staatshoheitsrechte über natürliche Personen; **place of** ~ Gerichtsstand; **plea to** ~ → *plea*; **plenary** ~ unbeschränkte Zuständigkeit; **primary** ~ vorgeschaltete (*behördliche*) Zuständigkeit; **probate** ~ Zuständigkeit in Vormundschafts- und Nachlaßsachen; Zuständigkeit des Nachlaßgerichts, Nachlaßgerichtsbarkeit; **residuary** ~ subsidiäre Zuständigkeit; allgemeiner Gerichtsstand; **special** ~ Sondergerichtsbarkeit, besondere Zuständigkeit; **summary** ~ Zuständigkeit der Amtsgerichte, des Einzelrichters; niedere Gerichtsbarkeit; **supervisory** ~ Aufsichtsbefugnis; **territorial** ~ territoriale Gerichtshoheit; örtliche Zuständigkeit; **transient** ~ vorläufige Zuständigkeit; **to decline** ~ sich für unzuständig erklären; **to lie within the** ~ zum Gerichtsbezirk gehörend; **voluntary** ~ freiwillige Gerichtsbarkeit.

jurisdictional Gerichtsbarkeits . . ., Zuständigkeits . . ., Kompetenz . . .

jurisprudence Jurisprudenz *f*, Rechtswissenschaft *f*; allgemeine Rechtslehre *f*; **analytical** ~ Begriffsjurisprudenz; **comparative** ~ vergleichende Rechtswissenschaft, Rechtsvergleichung; **equity** ~ → *equity*; **medical** ~ Gerichtsmedizin.

jurist Rechtsgelehrter *m*, Jurist *m*.

juristic juristisch, rechtswissenschaftlich.

juror Geschworener *m*, Schöffe *m*, Eidesleistender *m*; **~'s book** Geschworenen-Verzeichnis; **~'s oath** Geschworeneneid; **alternate** ~ Ersatzgeschworener.

jury Geschworene *pl* (= *G bzw g*); die Geschworenen *m/f/pl*, Geschworenengericht *n*, Jury *f*; ~ **action** Zivilprozeß (mit *G–n*); ~ **box** *G–n*-bank; ~ **commissioner** Beamter, der für die Auswahl der *G–n* zuständig ist; **~'s deliberation** Beratung der *G–n*; ~ **list** *G–n*liste, Schöffenliste; ~ **nobbling** Geschworenenbestechung; ~ **of good and lawful men** zwölf G; ~ **of matrons** *Frauengeschworene* (*zur Feststellung der behaupteten Schwangerschaft e–r zum Tode Verurteilten*); ~ **panel** *G–n*liste; ~ **process** Ladung von *G–n*; ~ **tampering** Beeinflussung der Geschworenen; ~ **trial** Verfahren mit *G–n*, *G–n*prozeß; ~ **vetting** Auswahlprüfung der Geschworenen; ~ **wheel** Losziehungsmaschine zur Wahl der *G–n*; **challenge of** ~ Einwendungen gegen die Aufstellung von *G–n*, Ablehnung von *G–n*; **civil** ~ *G* in Zivilsachen; **common** ~ die *G–n*, *G–n*bank; **coroner's** ~ Leichenbeschau-G; **discharge of** ~ →

discharge; **foreign** ~ *G* aus e–m anderen Gerichtsbezirk; **foreman of a** ~ *G–n*obmann; **grand** ~ Voruntersuchungs*g* (*US; GB bis 1948*); **hung** ~ blockiertes *G–n*gericht (*das sich zu keinem Spruch durchringen kann*); **mixed** ~ mehrsprachiges *bzw rassisch verschieden besetztes G–n*gericht; **petit** ~ *G–n*gericht in Strafsachen, *G-n*bank; **petty** ~ = *petit* ~ *qv*; **pix** ~ Münzprüfungs*g*; **special** ~ außerordentliches *G–n*gericht; beruflich qualifizierte *G*, standesmäßig beschränktes *G–n*gericht; *GB vor 1971*; **striking a** ~ Auswahl von *G–n* (*durch Eliminierung*); **struck** ~ besonders (*durch Eliminierung*) ausgewählte *G*; **to impanel a** ~ → *to impanel*; **to instruct the** ~ die *G–n* belehren; **trial** ~ die *G–n* (*in der Hauptverhandlung bzw mündlichen Verhandlung*); **view by** ~ → *view*.

juryman der Geschworene.

jurywoman die Geschworene.

jus Recht *n* (*im objektiven bzw subjektiven Sinn*); ~ **accrescendi** Anwachsungsrecht; ~ **albinatus** *hist* Anspruch des Monarchen auf den Nachlaß e–s Ausländers; ~ **commune** = *common law qv*; ~ **coronae** Kronrecht; ~ **deliberandi** Ausschlagsrecht (*Erbschaft*); ~ **disponendi** Veräußerungsrecht, Verfügungsrecht; ~ **dividendi** Recht, über (Grund)Vermögen letztwillig zu verfügen; ~ **duplicatum** Eigentum und zugleich Besitz; ~ **evocandi** Rückrufungsrecht (*gegenüber eigenen Staatsangehörigen*); ~ **fiduciarium** Treuhandrecht; ~ **gentium** Völkerrecht; ~ **mariti** *Verwaltungs- und Nutznießungs-Recht des Ehemannes am eingebrachten Mobiliarvermögen der Frau*; ~ **osculi** „Kußrecht" *Ehehindernis wegen Verwandtschaft einschließlich zweiten Grades*; ~ **relicti** Ehegattenerbrecht; ~ **sanguinis** Abstammungsprinzip; ~ **soli** Bodenprinzip, Erwerb der Staatsangehörigkeit des Geburtslandes; ~ **spatiandi** Anwesenheitsrecht, Wegerecht; ~ **tollendi** Wegnahmerecht; **to set up the** ~ **tertii** die Aktivlegitimation bestreiten.

just gerecht, rechtlich zulässig, gesetzlich, rechtschaffen; ~ **allowances** → *allowance;* ~ **and equitable** recht und billig; ~ **and proper** gerecht und angemessen; ~ **and reasonable** gerecht und zumutbar; ~ **cause** ein begründeter Anlaß, erhebliche Gründe; rechtlich einwandfreie Begründung; ~ **cause of provocation** Provoziertsein aus erheblichem Anlaß (*bei Tötungsdelikten*); ~ **compensation** angemessene Entschädigung; **J~ Compensation Clause** → *compensation*; ~ **debts** rechtsgültige Verbindlichkeiten; ~ **excuse** berechtigter Anlaß, Rechtfertigung; ~ **or convenient** nach pflichtgemäßem Ermessen; ~ **reward** gerechte Vergütung; ~ **terms** gerechte Bedingungen; ~ **title** absoluter Rechtstitel; ~ **value** der (*echte*) Verkehrswert; **without** ~ **cause** ohne rechtfertigenden Grund; ohne wichtigen Grund.

justice (*1*) Gerechtigkeit *f*, Richtigkeit *f*; Rechtspflege *f*, Rechtsprechung *f*, Justiz *f*, Gerichtsbarkeit *f*; **administration of** ~ → *administration*; **civil** ~ Zivilgerichtsbarkeit; **commutative** ~ ausgleichende Gerechtigkeit; **court of** ~ → *court*; **Department of J~** → *department*; **distributive** ~ austeilende Gerechtigkeit; **equal** ~ gleiche Behandlung vor Gericht; Justiz-Gleichberechtigung; **fountain of** ~ (*King or Queen*) Schöpfer des Rechts; **in** ~ von Rechts wegen; **low** ~ Gerichtsbarkeit für Bagatellsachen; **miscarriage of** ~ → *miscarriage*; **natural** ~ (natürliche) Gerechtigkeit, wirkliche Gerechtigkeit, materielle G; Rechtstaatlichkeit; **open** ~ öffentlich zugängliche Rechtspflege; **perversion of** ~ → *perversion*; **preventive** ~ Vorbeugung, vorbeugende Justiz; **remedial** ~ korrektive Rechtspflege; **retributive** ~ vergeltende Gerechtigkeit;

substantial ~ (*materielle*) Gerechtigkeit; **to administer** ~ → *to administer*; **to bring to** ~ aburteilen; **to evade** ~ sich der Strafverfolgung entziehen; **to pervert the course of** ~ → *pervert*; **to temper** ~ **with mercy** Gnade für Recht ergehen lassen, Milde walten lassen; **to mete out** ~ Recht sprechen, judizieren.

justice (*2*) Richter *m*; Amtsrichter *m*; ~**s' clerk** = *clerk to the* ~*s* → *clerk;* ~**s' court** Amtsgericht, Friedensgericht; ~**s in eyre** *hist* Reiserichter, reisende Richterkommissare; ~ **of a circuit** = ~ *of assize qv*; ~**s of appeal** Berufungsrichter, *Richter am Court of Appeal, London*; ~**s of assize** *reisender* Richterkommissar; ~**s of gaol delivery** Richterkommissare in Strafsachen; ~**s of nisi prius** = ~ *of assize qv;* ~**s of oyer and terminer** *reisende* Richterkommissare in Strafsachen; ~**s of the bench** *Richter der Common Law Abteilung des High Court*; ~**s of the forest** Richter in Forstsachen; ~ **of the peace** (*J. P.*) Friedensrichter, *cf magistrate*; ~**s of the quorum** amtierende Friedensrichter (*deren Anwesenheit bei Kollegialgerichten erforderlich ist*); ~**'s warrant** *amtsrichterlicher Haftbefehl*; **chief** ~ Gerichtspräsident, Oberrichter; **examining** ~ Ermittlungsrichter.

justiceship Richteramt *n*, Richterwürde *f*.

justiciability Justizfähigkeit *f*, die *Eigenschaft, justitiabel zu sein*.

justiciable justitiabel, e–r Gerichtsbarkeit unterworfen; gerichtl entscheidbar, e–r gerichtl Entscheidung zugänglich.

justiciary (= *justiciar*) *hist hoher königlicher Gerichtsbeamter m*.

justiciatus Verfahren *n* zur Prüfung der Kautionsfähigkeit.

justifiable rechtlich vertretbar, zu rechtfertigen; ~ **cause** hinreichender Tatverdacht; ~ **homicide** → *homicide*; ~ **omission** entschuldbare Unterlassung; ~ **reason** vertretbarer Grund; ~ **sale of cargo** Notverkauf e–r Schiffsladung; **legally** ~ rechtlich vertretbar.

justifiability Rechtfertigungsmöglichkeit *f*, Exkulpationsmöglichkeit *f*.

justification Rechtfertigung *f*, Verteidigung *f*; **plea in** ~ Berufung auf die Wahrnehmung berechtigter Interessen; **to plead** ~ Rechtfertigungsgründe geltend machen.

justify rechtfertigen; ~ **bail** den Nachweis der ausreichenden Kautionsstellung führen.

justness Gerechtigkeit *f*, Rechtmäßigkeit *f*, Korrektheit *f*.

juvenile *s* Jugendlicher; *adj*, jugendlich, Jugend ...

juxtaposition Juxtaposition *f*, das Nebeneinanderstellen *n*; das Verbinden von Erfindungselementen ohne neue Funktion; *vgl aggregation*.

K

kangaroo Befugnis *f*, die Reihenfolge von Zusatzanträgen zu bestimmen (*in parl Ausschüssen*); ~ **closure** *Abkürzung der Debatte durch Nichtbehandeln von Änderungsanträgen;* ~ **court** Scheingericht, illegales Gericht; ~ **trial** Scheinprozeß.

keelage Ankerrecht *n*, Ankergebühr *f*.

keel-haul Strafe *f* des unter dem Kiel Durchziehens.

keep *s* Burgfrieden *m*, Zitadelle *f*; Lebensunterhalt *m*, Kost *f* und Wohnung *f*; Recht *n*, den Gewinn zu behalten.

keep *v* behalten, führen, fortsetzen, betreiben, halten, innehalten, bewahren, aufbewahren; ~ **a boarding house** e–e Pension betreiben; ~ **a disorderly house** ein Bordell betreiben; ~ **a common household** die häusliche Gemeinschaft aufrechterhalten; ~ **a law** ein Gesetz einhalten; ~ **a term** e–e Frist einhalten; ~ **an inn** e–e Gastwirtschaft betreiben; ~ **books** Bücher führen; ~ **down interest** Zinsen bei Fälligkeit bezahlen; ~ **efficient** leistungsfähig führen; ~ **for sale** feilhalten; ~ **house** *cf keeping house; infra*; ~ **in custody** in Haft halten; ~ **in order** in Ordnung halten; ~ **in repair** *ständig* in ordnungsgemäßem Zustand halten; ~ **in safe custody** verwahren, aufbewahren; ~ **in store** auf Lager halten; ~ **open** offen halten (*Laden*); ~ **records** amtliche Urkunden verwahren; ~ **s. th. in suspense** etwas in der Schwebe halten, etwas ungewiß lassen; ~ **term** *an offiziellen Diners der Anwaltsvereinigung teilnehmen als Zulassungsvoraussetzung*; ~ **the date** die Frist einhalten; ~ **the minutes** Protokoll führen; ~ **the peace** die öffentliche Ruhe und Ordnung bewahren; ~ **up** aufrechterhalten (*Versicherung*); ~ **up one's payments** seinen Zahlungsverpflichtungen nachkommen, regelmäßig zahlen; ~ **within a limit** ein Limit einhalten.

keeper Wärter *m*, Wächter *m*, Verwahrer *m*, Verwalter *m*; Inhaber *m*; ~ **of a bawdyhouse** Bordellhalter; ~ **of an animal** Tierhalter; **K~ of Public Records** Leiter des Staatsarchivs; ~ **of the forest** Forstverwalter; **K~ of the Great Seal** Staatssiegelbewahrer; **K~ of the King's Conscience** *Bezeichung für den Lordkanzler;* **K~ of the Liberty of England** *hist* Bewahrer der Freiheit Englands (*Titel von Staats- u Justizurkunden nach der Hinrichtung Karls I. 1649*); ~ **of the peace** Friedensbewahrer (*Bezeichnung des Amtsrichters ua*); **K~ of the Privy Purse** Intendant der Zivilliste; **K~ of the Privy Seal** = *Lord Privy Seal qv*; ~ **of the rolls** Verwahrer der amtlichen Urkunden in e–r Grafschaft; ~ **of the touch** Münzmeister; **Lord K~ of the Great Seal** Lordsiegelbewahrer.

keeping house das Sichverbergen e–s Schuldners in der eigenen Wohnung (*Konkursgrund*).

kerb|crawling Aufforderung zur Unzucht vom Auto aus; ~ **walker** jmd der (vermeintliche) Straßenprostituierte anspricht.

kerb market(s) Nachbörse *f*, Vorbörse *f*.

key Schlüssel *m*, Lösung *f*, Chiffre *f*; Schlüsselstellung *f*, Schlüsselmacht *f*; Kai *m*; ~ **date** Stichtag, Berichtszeitpunkt; ~ **industry** Schlüsselindustrie; ~ **man** Schlüsselkraft; ~ **money** Schlüsselgeld, Mietablösung; ~ **note** Grundgedanke, Parteilinie; ~ **note address** programmatische Rede; ~**s of court** *scot* Gerichtsbeamte; ~ **rate** → *rate*; ~

region(s) Schlüsselregion(en); ~ **symbols** grafische Zeichen; ~ **to a cypher** Kodeschlüssel; ~ **witness** → *witness*; ~ **word** Stichwort; **false** ~ Nachschlüssel; **skeleton** ~ → *skeleton*.

Keys die (*zwölf*) Abgeordneten der Insel Man; **House of** ~ *die gesetzgebende Versammlung der Insel Man*.

kickback geheime Provison *f*, geheime Gebührenbeteiligung *f*; Schmiergeld *n*.

kid-gloves handling Samthandschuh-Behandlung *f*.

kidder Getreideaufkäufer *m*, Spekulant *m*.

kidnapper Menschenräuber *m*, erpresserischer Entführer *m*.

kidnapping Menschenraub *m*, Entführung *f in ein anderes Land*, erpresserische Entführung *f*; ~ **for ransom** Lösegeld-Menschenraub; **simple** ~ Freiheitsberaubung; Entführung.

kill töten.

killing Töten *n*, Tötung *f*; ungewöhnlich großer und unerwarteter Spekulationsgewinn *m*; ~ **by misadventure** unverschuldete Tötung; ~ **child in womb** Tötung der Leibesfrucht; ~**in resisting arrest** Tötung beim Widerstand gegen Verhaftung (*meist als Mord bestraft*); ~ **of unborn persons** Tötung e–s lebensfähigen Kindes im Mutterleib (*nach mehr als 28 Wochen Schwangerschaft*); **malicious** ~ vorsätzliche Tötung; **wilful** ~ vorsätzliche Tötung.

kin *adj* (bluts)verwandt.

kin *s* die Verwandten, Blutsverwandtschaft *f*; Familienangehörigkeit *f* (*Verwandtschaft nebst Schwägerschaft*); **next of** ~ → *next*.

kind Art *f*, Gattung *f*, Klasse *f*, Sorte *f*; **in** ~ in natura, in Waren, in Sachgütern gleicher Art und Güte; **obligation in** ~ Gattungsschuld; **payment in** ~ Sachleistung, Naturalleistung; **remuneration in** ~ Sachbezug, Naturallohn, Deputat.

kindred and affinity Verwandtschaft *f* und Schwägerschaft *f*.

king König *m*; ~**'s** königlich (= *kgl*); **K~s-At-Arms** *kgl–e* Herolde; ~ **of arms** Wappenkönig; **K ~'s Bench** = *Queen's Bench* (*Division*) *qv*; **K~'s Bench Prison** *hist Schuldnergefängnis in London*; ~**'s books** *hist kgl-s Pfründenverzeichnis;* ~**'s briefs** (*letters*) *kgl–e* Spendenersuchen an Geistlichkeit; **K~'s chambers** Meeresbuchten als brit Hoheitsgewässer; **K~'s Council** Kronrat; ~**'s counsel** → *Queen's Counsel*; ~**'s enemies** Staatsfeinde; **K~'s English** reines Englisch (*der Gebildeten*); **K~'s peace** Landfrieden; **K~'s Proctor** → *Queen's Proctor*; **the** ~ **can do no wrong** Grundsatz der *kgl–en* Immunität, Ausschluß des Rechtswegs gegen den König.

kingdom Königreich *n*, Reich *n*, Gebiet *n*.

kingship Königswürde *f*, Königstum *n*.

kinsfolk Verwandte *pl*, Familienangehörige *pl*.

kinship Verwandtschaft *f*, Verwandtschaftsverhältnis *n*.

kinsman Sippenangehöriger *m*, Familienangehöriger *m*, Angehöriger *m* der gleichen Rasse; **collateral** ~ **men** Verwandte in der Seitenlinie; **remote** ~ entfernter Verwandter.

kinswoman Verwandte *f*.

kiosk Kiosk *m*; Telefonhäuschen *n*.

kissing the book das Küssen der Bibel (*bei der Eidesleistung*).

kite *s* Gefälligkeitswechsel *m*, Kellerwechsel *m*; ~ **-flying** Ausstellung von ungedeckten Schecks oder Wechseln, Wechselreiterei.

kite *v* sich Kredit durch die Clearingzeit e–s Schecks beschaffen; Verpflichtungen durch neue Schulden abdecken; e–e Scheckfälschung begehen.

kleptomania Kleptomanie *f*.

knacker Abdecker *m*, Notschlächter *m*, Tierkörperverwerter *m*; Abbruchunternehmer *m*.

knife *v/t* mit dem Messer auf jmdn einstechen, erstechen; ~ **to death** erstechen.

knight (*nicht vererbl niedrigstes Adelsprädikat*); Ritter *m*; Angehöriger *m* e–s Ritterordens; **~'s fee** → *fee*; **K~ Marshal** Hofmarschall *m* (*für Vergehen und Verstöße zuständiger Hofbeamter*); **~ of the post** käuflicher Zeuge; Meineidszeuge; **~s of the shire** Grundbesitzer und beauftragte Grafschaftsabgeordnete; **~ service** Ritterdienste; ritterschaftliches Lehen.

knock|down zuschlagen (*Auktion*), *den Preis* drücken; zerlegen; **~ off** schnell erledigen; e–n Preisabstrich vornehmen; **completely-~ed -down** (*CKD*) vollständig zerlegt; **semi-~ed-down** (*SKD*) teilzerlegt; **~ing advertising** herabsetzende Werbung.

knock for knock agreement Schadensteilungsvereinbarung *von Versicherungen*.

knockings *sl* Schlußplädoyer *n*.

knock-out|agreement Bietervereinbarung (*sich nicht gegenseitig hoch zu steigern bzw vorläufig nicht mitzusteigern*); **~ price** niedrigster Preis.

know *v* wissen, kennen, erkennen, erfahren, verstehen, können; geschlechtlich verkehren; **~ all men (by these presents)** hiermit sei kundgetan (*althergebrachte Einleitungsformel bei Urkunden*); **~ by experience** aus Erfahrung wissen.

know-how *s* Knowhow *n*, praktisches Erfahrungswissen *n*; **industrial ~** praktische Betriebserfahrung; **manufacturing ~** Spezialkenntnisse von der Herstellung; **technical ~** technisches Erfahrungswissen.

knowingly wissentlich, vorsätzlich; **~ allow** wissentlich gestatten, geflissentlich gestatten; **~ and wil(l)fully** vorsätzlich.

knowledge Wissen *n*, Kenntnis *f*, Bekanntschaft *f*, Erfahrung *f*, Wissenschaft *f*, Kenntnisse *f/pl*; **~ and consent** (mit) Kenntnis und Billigung; **~ of another's peril** in Kenntnis der Gefährdung e–s anderen; **~ of law** Rechtskenntnisse; **actual ~** unmittelbare Kenntnis; **carnal ~** → *carnal*; **chargeable with ~** zurechenbare Kenntnis habend; **common ~** allgemein Bekanntes, Allgemeinwissen; **comparative ~** → *comparative*; **contrary to one's ~** wider besseres Wissen; **expert ~** Sachkenntnis, Sachkunde, Spezialwissen; **general ~** Allgemeinkundigkeit, allgemein bekannte Tatsachen; **guilty ~** Schuldbewußtsein, subjektiver Tatbestand; **common ~** Allgemeinkundigkeit; **imputed ~** unterstellte Kenntnis, Fiktion des Kennens bzw des Wissens; **official ~** amtliche Kenntnis; **personal ~** Kenntnis aus eigener Wahrnehmung; **positive ~** sichere Kenntnis; **practical ~** praktische Kenntnisse; **public ~** Allgemeinkundigkeit; **technical ~** Fachwissen; **to the best of one's ~ and belief** nach bestem Wissen und Gewissen; **without ~ and consent** ohne Wissen und Willen.

knowledgable kenntnisreich, fachlich qualifiziert.

knuckle-duster Schlagring *m*.

kyth *adj* verwandt, *s* Verwandtschaft *f*.

L

label *s* Anhängezettel *m*, Etikett *n*, Bezeichnung *f*, angehefteter Zusatz *m*; Packzettel *m*; Klageschrift *f im Exchequer Gericht;* ~ **printer** Etikettenausdrucker (*elektron. Ladenkasse*); **protection of ~s** Ausstattungsschutz für Etikette und Beschriftung.

label *v* beschriften, bezeichnen, etikettieren.

label(l)ling Etikettierung *f*, Bezeichnung *f*, Markierung *f*, (Preis-)Auszeichnung *f*; **false** ~ Etikettfälschung, Etikettenschwindel; **informative** ~ (Waren)Herkunftsbezeichnung.

labo(u)r Arbeit *f*, Tätigkeit *f*, körperliche Anstrengung *f*, geleistete Dienste *m|pl*; Arbeitskräfte *f|pl*, Arbeitnehmer *m*; Arbeiterschaft *f*, Arbeiter *m*; ~ **and management** die Sozialpartner; ~ **arbitration** Schlichtung in Arbeitsstreitigkeiten; ~ **association** Arbeitnehmervereinigung, Gewerkschaft; ~ **bank** → *bank* (*1*); ~ **conditions** Arbeitsbedingungen; ~ **conflict** → *conflict;* ~ **copartnership** Gewinnbeteiligung der Arbeitnehmer; ~ **-costs per unit of output** Arbeitskosten pro Produktionseinheit; ~ **court** → *court*; **L~ Day** Tag der Arbeit (*in USA 1. Montag im September*); ~ **demand** Nachfrage nach Arbeitskräften; ~ **dispute** arbeitsrechtliche Streitigkeit; ~ **exchange** Arbeitsamt, Arbeitsvermittlung; ~ **force** Arbeitspotential; Arbeitskräfte; ~ **home** Arbeiterwohnheim; ~ **inspection** Arbeitsaufsicht; ~ **intensive** lohnintensiv; ~ **law** → *law*; ~ **leader** Gewerkschaftsführer; ~ **legislation** arbeitsrechtliche Gesetzgebung; ~ **management committee** gemischter Ausschuß der Arbeitgeber und Arbeitnehmer; ~ **market** Arbeitsmarkt; **~-mix** das innerbetriebliche Zahlenverhältnis der Angestellten zu Arbeitern; ~ **-only sub-contracting** selbständige Partiearbeit als Subunternehmer; ~ **organization** → *organziation*; ~ **permit** Arbeitserlaubnis; ~ **piracy** Abwerbung von Arbeitskräften; ~ **policy** Arbeitsmarktpolitik; ~ **recruitment** Anwerbung von Arbeitskräften; **L~ Relations Act** *etwa*: Betriebsverfassungsgesetz; ~ **representation** Arbeitervertretung, Gewerkschaftsvertretung; ~ **resources** Arbeitsmarkt; ~ **standards** arbeitsrechtliche Normen; ~ **surplus** Überschuß an Arbeitskräften; ~ **turnover** Arbeitsplatzwechsel; ~ **union** Gewerkschaft; ~ **union affiliation** Gewerkschaftszugehörigkeit; ~ **unit** Lohnkosteneinheit; **allocation of** ~ Zuteilung von Arbeit; **casual** ~ Gelegenheitsarbeit; **collective** ~ **contract** Tarifvertrag, Kollektivvertrag; **common** ~ körperliche Arbeit und gewerbliche Tätigkeit; **compulsory** ~ Zwangsarbeit, Arbeitspflicht; **conscription of** ~ Dienstverpflichtung; **convict** ~ Gefangenenarbeit; **cost of** ~ → *cost*; **deployment of** ~ Arbeitskräfteeinsatz; **division of** ~ → *division*; **fair** ~ **standards** gerechte Arbeitsnormen, arbeitsrechtl Vorschriften; **farm** ~ Landarbeit; **female** ~ weibliche Arbeitskräfte; **forced** ~ Zwangsarbeit; **foreign** ~ ausländische Arbeitskräfte, Fremdarbeiter; **free** ~ nicht *gewerkschaftlich* organisierte Arbeiterschaft; **hard** ~ Zwangsarbeit (*Zuchthaus*); **hire of** ~ Einstellung von Arbeitskräften; **indirect** ~ Gemeinkostenlohn, Hilfslohn; **manual** ~ körperliche Arbeit; **mobility of** ~ Freizügigkeit von Arbeitskräften; **organized** ~ gewerkschaftlich organisierte Arbeitnehmerschaft; **personal** ~ eigene Arbeit; **semi-skilled** ~ angelernte Arbeiter; angelernte Arbeitskräfte; **skilled** ~ gelernte Arbeiter, Facharbeiter; **to shed** ~ Arbeitskräfte abbauen; **unfair** ~ **practices** unlautere Arbeitskampfmethoden; **unorganized** ~ nicht gewerkschaftlich organisierte Arbeitnehmer; **unskilled** ~ ungelernte Arbeiter.

labo(u)r *v* **a jury** Geschworene zu beeinflussen suchen.

labo(u)rer Arbeiter *m*, Handarbeiter *m*, Lohnarbeiter *m*; **agricultural** ~ Landarbeiter; **casual** ~ Gelegenheitsarbeiter; **skilled** ~ Facharbeiter; **unskilled** ~ Hilfsarbeiter.

laches Verwirkung *f*; ~ **in bringing suit** Klageverwirkung; **estoppel by** ~ → *estoppel*; **to be barred by** ~ verwirkt sein (*durch unterlassene Rechtsverfolgung*).

lack *s* Bedürfnis *n*, Mangel *m*, Fehlen *n*; ~ **of authority** mangelnde Vertretungsmacht; ~ **of care** Vernachlässigung; Mangel an Sorgfalt; ~ **of conformity** Vertragswidrigkeit; ~ **of form** formaler Fehler, Formlosigkeit, Formmangel; ~ **of invention** fehlende Erfindungseigenschaft; Mangel an Erfindungshöhe; ~ **of jurisdiction** Unzuständigkeit; ~ **of means** Bedürftigkeit, Mittellosigkeit; ~ **of title** Rechtsmangel; **for** ~ **of evidence** mangels Beweises.

lacuna Sinnlücke, Inhaltslücke; ~ **in the law** Gesetzeslücke *f*.

lade *v* (*Schiff*) beladen, verladen; ~**n in bulk** beladen mit unverpackten Massengütern.

lading Beladen *n* (*e–s Schiffes*), Verladen *n*, Fracht *f*; ~ **charges** Ladekosten; **bill of** ~ → *bill of lading*.

lady|clerk kaufmännische Angestellte; **L~ Day** Quartalstag, 25. März; ~**'s friend** Kläger in Prozeßstandschaft für verheiratete Frau.

laesae majestatis (= *laesa majestas, lese-majesty*) Majestätsbeleidigung *f*.

lag Galgenvogel *m*, Zuchthäusler *m*; Zuchthausstrafzeit *f*.

lag Verzögerung *f*, Zurückbleiben *n*; Phasenverschiebung *f*; ~ **of investment** Investitionsnachholbedarf; **earnings** ~ Einkommensnachholbedarf, Lohnzahlungsverzögerung.

lagniappe kleines Geschenk als Zugabe (*des Verkäufers*).

laissez|-faire Laissez-faire *n* (*wirtschaftlicher Liberalismus*); ~ **-passer** Passierschein.

laity Laienstand *m* (*Nichtgeistliche*), Laien *m|pl*; Nichtfachleute *m|pl*.

lamb *exch* unerfahrener Spekulant *m*, Betrogener *m*.

lame duck *exch* ruinierter Spekulant *m*, Zahlungsunfähiger *m*; nicht wiedergewählter Amtsinhaber (*bes US Präsident*) *während der restlichen Amtszeit*; ~ **government** handlungsunfähige Regierung *f*, *am Schluß der Parlamentszeit*; ~ **session** *Sitzung des noch nicht neu konstituierten Parlaments*.

Lammas|Day *scot* 1. August (*Abrechnungstag*); ~ **lands** *Land, an dem Weiderechte vom 1. August bis zur Neusaat bestehen*.

land Land *n*, Grund *m* und Boden *m*; Grundstück *n*; Grundbesitz *m*; ~**s** Liegenschaften *f|pl*, Ländereien *f|pl*; ~ **-acquisition program** Bodenbeschaffungsplan; ~ **agency** Immobilienbüro; ~ **agent** Grundstücksmakler; *brit* Gutsverwalter; ~ **and buildings, real estate** *bil* unbebaute und bebaute Grundstücke; ~**s and tenements** (eigene) Liegenschaften; ~ **bank** Bodenkreditanstalt; staatliche Landwirtschaftsbank; ~ **bonds** landwirtschaftliche Pfandbriefe; ~ **broker** Immobilienmakler; ~ **buildings, plant and machinery** *brit bil* Sachanlagen; ~ **carriage** Landtransport; ~ **certificate** amtliche Grundstückseigentumsbescheinigung; Grundbuchauszug; ~ **charge** Grundstücksbelastung; Grundpfandrecht; Grundschuld; Reallast; **L~ Charges Register** *grundbuchartiges Regi-*

ster für Belastungen des Grundst. (ähnl. Abt. II u. III d. dt. Grundbuchs); **~s clauses Acts** brit Gesetze über Bodeninanspruchnahme durch die öffentliche Hand; **~ college** landwirtschaftliche Hochschule; **~ commissioner** *Treuhand-Grundstücksbehörde*; **~ compensation** Grundstücksentschädigung (*bei Enteignung*); **~ consolidation** Flurbereinigung; **~ contract** Grundstückskaufvertrag; **~ court** Gericht für Grundstückssachen; **~ credit company** Bodenkreditanstalt; **~ damages** → *damages*; **~ department** (Bundes)Amt für Staatsland; **~ development** Erschließung von Bauland; **~district** Bezirk für Staatslandverwaltung; **~ drainage** Bodenentwässerung; **~ for building sites** Bauland; **~ gabel** Bodenzins; **~ grabbing** spekulatives Aufkaufen von Land; **~ grant** *US* (*staatliche*) Landzuweisung, Landschenkung; **~-grant procedure** Landzuweisungsverfahren; **~ holding** Grundbesitz, landwirtschaftlicher Pachtbesitz; **~ improvement** Bodenverbesserung, Melioration; **~ Improvements Company** *GB* (=) *Agrarkreditanstalt;* **~ jobber** Grundstücksspekulant; **~ law** Immobilienrecht, Bodenrecht; **L~ law** Landesrecht (*Deutschland*); **~ mortgage bank** Bodenkreditbank; **~ office** Staatsbodenverwaltung; **~ on lease** Pachtland; **~ owner** → *owner*; **~ patent** *US* Landzuweisungsurkunde; **~ planning control** Planfeststellung; **~ price** Grundstückspreis, Bodenpreis; **~ racketeering** gewinnsüchtige Bodenspekulation; **~ records** Grundstücksregister; **~-reeve** Pachtgrund-Überwachungsbeamter; **~ reform** Bodenreform; **~ register** Grundbuch; **L~ R~ registry** Grundbuchbeiakten, grundbuchamtl Verzeichnisse (*betr Prozesse, Leibrenten, gerichtl Anordnungen, Vergleiche, dingl Belastungen*); **~registrar** Grundbuchsbeamter; **~ registration** Grundbuchsystem; **~ registry** Grundbuchamt **~ revenues** Kronlandeinkünfte, Grundstückseinkünfte; **~ settlement association** *staatliche Siedlungsgesellschaft*; **~ societies** Siedlungsgenossenschaften; **~ steward** Gutsverwalter; **~ surveying** Landvermessung; **~ surveyor** Vermessungsbeamter; **~ tenant** Grundpächter; unmittelbarer Grundstücksbesitzer; **~s tenements and hereditaments** Liegenschaften aller Art; **~ title** Grundstücksurkunde; dingl Grundstücksrecht, Grundeigentum; **L~ Titles and Transfer Act** Grundbuch- und Bodenverkehrsgesetz; **L~s Tribunal** *GB Schiedsstelle für Enteignungsentschädigungen*; **~ use** Grundstücksnutzung; **~ value** Bodenwert, Grundstückswert; **~ waiter** Hafenzollbeamter *für die Erfassung ankommender Ware;* **~ warfare** Landkrieg; **~ warrant** *US*: Landzuweisungsurkunde; **abutting ~** angrenzendes Grundstück; **accommodation ~s** →*accommodation*; **action for recovery of ~** → *action*; **adjacent ~** angrenzendes Grundstück; **agricultural ~** landw genutzte Grundstücke, landw-er Grundbesitz; **barren ~** nicht anbaufähiges Land; **bounty ~s** Schenkungsland: *Staatsland, das als Anerkennung für geleistete Dienste verschenkt wird;* **by ~** auf dem Landwege; **by ~ and sea** zu Wasser und zu Lande; **carrier by ~** Frachtführer; **common ~** Allmende; **crown ~(s)** → *crown*; **clear area of ~** unbebautes Gelände; **cut-over ~** abgeholztes Land; **demesne ~s** → *demesne*; **development ~** → *development;* **donation ~s** Stiftungsgrund, Landschenkungen; **fabric ~s** Kirchenschenkungsland *zur Erhaltung und Reparatur des Kirchengebäudes;* **fiscal ~s** Krongüter; **improved ~** durch Melioration gewonnenes Weideland, melioriertes Land; **interest in ~** → *interest (1)*; **mineral ~s** bergbaufähiges Land, Bodenschätze enthaltendes Land, Schürfgebiet, Abbaugelände; **near-ripe** ~ Bauerwartungsland; **place ~s** Eisenbahntrassenland; **public ~s** Grundstücke der öffentlichen Hand; **raw** ~ unerschlossenes, ungenütztes Bauerwartungsland US; **recorded** ~ eingetragenes Grundstück; **registered** ~ grundbuchamtlich erfaßtes Grundstück; **school ~s** öffentlicher Grundbesitz zur Finanzierung von Schulen; **seated** ~ genutzter Boden; **settled** ~ treuhänderisch gebundener Landbesitz; e–r Fideikommißbindung unterliegendes Grundstück; Fideikommißland; **Settled L~ Act** *GB Gesetz zum Abbau von Treuhand- und Fideikommißbindungen im 19. Jhd*; **tenemental** ~ Pachtland; **to take ~ out of production** Flächen still legen; **underused** ~ zu gering genutzter Boden, brachliegendes Land; **undeveloped** ~ nicht erschlossenes Grundstück; **unregistered** ~ nicht grundbuchmäßig erfaßte Grundstücke; **unseated** ~ ungenutzter Boden; **vacant** ~ unbebautes Grundstück.

landed terms franco Löschung, Verkaufspreis einschließlich Fracht- und Entladungskosten.

landholder Grundbesitzer *m*, Grundpächter *m*.

landing Landen *n*, Landung *f*; Löschung *f*, Landesteg *m*; ~ **certificate** Löschbescheinigung, Löschschein; ~ **charges** Landungskosten, Löschungskosten; ~ **notice** Frachtankunftsbenachrichtigung; ~ **order** → *order* (2); ~ **place** Landeplatz; ~ **waiter** Hafenzollbeamter *für ankommende Waren;* ~ **weight** Gewicht am Eingangsort.

landlady Hauswirtin *f*, Vermieterin *f*.

landlocked eingeschlossen von umgebenden Grundstücken, ohne Zufahrt.

landlord Grundeigentümer *m*, Gutsherr *m*, Hauswirt *m*, Vermieter *m*, Verpächter *m*; ~ **and tenant** Miet- u Pachtrecht; Miet- *bzw* Pachtverhältnis; **L~ and Tenant Acts** Mietgesetzgebung; **~'s fixtures** wesentliche Bestandteile des Grundstücks, installierte Einrichtungsgegenstände; **~'s warrant** Vollstreckungsauftrag aus Vermieterpfandrecht.

landman Bodenpächter *m*.

landmark Feldmarkung *f*, Grenzstein *m*; ~ **case** grundlegender Fall, Prozeß von historischer Bedeutung; ~ **conservation** Denkmalschutz für Einzelobjekte in der Landschaft; **removal of a** ~ Grenzverrückung.

landowner Grundbesitzer *m*, Grundeigentümer *m*, **neighbouring** ~ Grundstücksanlieger, Grundstücksnachbar.

landscape|areas Landschaftsschutzgebiete; ~ **protection** Landschaftsschutz.

lane Fahrspur *f*, Nebenstraße *f*, Weg *m*, Gasse *f*, Route *f*; ~ **change** Fahrbahnwechsel; ~ **switching** plötzlicher Fahrbahnwechsel.

language Sprache *f*, Ausdrucksweise *f*, Worte *n|pl*, Wortlaut *m*; Diktion *f*; Phraseologie *f*, Fachsprache *f*; ~ **of treaties** Wortlaut von Verträgen; **abusive** ~ Beschimpfung; **legal** ~ Gesetzessprache, Juristensprache; **offensive** ~ Beschimpfung; Schimpfworte; **official** ~ Amtssprache; **opprobrious** ~ herabsetzende Worte; Schmähung; **unparliamentary** ~ unparlamentarische Ausdrucksweise.

lappage sich überschneidende Herrschaftsrechte *n|pl*, Konflikt *m*.

lapse *s* Verlauf *m*, Ablauf *m*; Heimfall *m*, Rechtsverlust *m*, Wegfall *m* (*e–s Rechtes, des Bedachten*), Erledigung *f*, Ausfall *m*; Versäumnis *n*; ~ **of a patent** Erlöschen e–s Patents; ~ **of a right** Verfall e–s Rechtes; ~ **of copyright** Erlöschen e–s Urheberrechts; ~ **of gift** Ausfall e–s Vermächtnisses (*wegen Vorversterbens des Bedachten*); ~ **of memory** Gedächtnisausfall; ~ **of offer** Gegenstandsloswerden des Angebots, Ablauf der Annahmefrist; ~ **of**

time Zeitablauf, Fristablauf; ~ **patent** Anschlußkonzession; ~ **risk** Risiko der vorzeitigen Beendigung e–s Lebensversicherungsvertrages; ~ **statutes** *Gesetze gegen Erlöschen von Vermächtnissen bei Vorversterben des Begünstigten (Übergang auf den Erben des Begünstigten).*

lapse *v* gleiten, verstreichen, ablaufen; erlöschen, verfallen, hinfällig werden; heimfallen; **~d policies book** *ins* Versicherungsablaufregister; **this agreement ~s** diese Vereinbarung tritt außer Kraft; dieser Vertrag läuft ab ...

larcenous diebisch; ~ **intent** Diebstahlsvorsatz.

larceny (*US, GB bis 1968*) Diebstahl *m* (= *D bzw d*), *auch Unterschlagung f bzw Untreue f*; ~ **by a trick** Trick*d*; ~ **by bailee** Unterschlagung; ~ **by finder** Fundunterschlagung; ~ **by public servant** Amts*d*, Amtsunterschlagung; ~ **from the person** Tasche*nd*; **common-law** ~ = *larceny qv*; **compound** ~ qualifizierter *D* (*Wegnahme von der Person des Bestohlenen oder aus seinem Haus*); schwerer Diebstahl; **constructive** ~ *D, bei dem der Vorsatz des Täters aus den Tatumständen gefolgert wird*; **grand** ~ Groß*d* (*von Gegenständen mit hohem Wert*); **mixed** ~ schwerer *D*; **petit** (= *petty*) ~ Klein*d*; **simple** ~ (*einfacher*) *D*.

lascivious lustvoll, obszön, unmoralisch, unzüchtig; ~ **carriage** Unzuchthandlungen; ~ **cohabitation** → *cohabitation*.

lash system (=) Lash-System *n* (*Frachtschiffe mit Leichtern an Bord*).

last *adj* äußerst, letzt, vorig, zuletzt; ~ **antecedent rule** *Auslegungsgrundsatz der Bezogenheit auf das unmittelbar Vorangehende;* ~ **attention** äußerste Aufmerksamkeit; ~ **clear chance** → *chance;* ~ **consumer** Endverbraucher; ~ **day business** *exch* Ultimogeschäft; ~ **day money** Ultimogeld; ~ **day of term** letzter Gerichtstag vor den Gerichtsferien; ~ **entitled** letztberechtigt; ~ **heir** der Heimfallsberechtigte bei Erbenlosigkeit; der Staat als Erbe; ~ **in first out** (*inventory*) zuletzt eingekauft, zuerst verbraucht (*Lifo-Methode, US, Bewertung des Vorratsvermögens zum ältesten Einstandswert, also keine Aktivierung von Preissteigerungen*); (*dismissal:*) die zuletzt Eingestellten werden als erste entlassen; ~ **past** der letzte (*der Urkundenbegebung*) vorangegangene Tag; ~ **place of abode** der letztbekannte (*inländische*) Aufenthaltsort; ~ **survivor assurance** → *assurance*; (*right of*) ~ **word** das letzte Wort.

late spät, verspätet, vormalig, früher; verstorben; ~ **fee** Spät(*einlieferungs*)gebühr; ~ **of** ehemals wohnhaft in; **no(t) ~r than** spätestens bis, nicht später als; **~st day** letzter Tag, äußerster Termin; **at the ~st on** spätestens am, bis ... spätestens.

lately kürzlich, vor einiger Zeit, vor geraumer Zeit.

latent geheim, versteckt, verborgen; ~ **ambiguity** → *ambiguity*; ~ **deed** eine lange Jahre (*über 20*) im Safe verwahrte gesiegelte Urkunde; ~ **defect** → *defect;* ~ **equity** → *equity;* ~ **injury** nicht äußerlich erkennbare Verletzung *oder Verletzungsfolgen*; ~ **reserves** stille Reserven.

latitude of judgement Entscheidungsrahmen *m*, E.-spielraum *m*.

Latin *s* Latein *n*; ~ **church** römisch katholische Kirche; ~ **information** (*deliktische*) Schadensersatzklage der Krone; ~ **side** *die* „lateinische Seite" des *Chancery Gerichts* (*gemäß Common Law, nicht Equity*); **law** ~ Juristenlatein; **lawyers'** ~ Juristenlatein; **thieves** ~ Gaunersprache.

launderette Waschsalon *m*.

laundering the proceeds Geldwäsche *f*, Geldwaschanlage *f*, Ertragswäsche *f*.

law Gesetz *n*, Recht *n* (= *R bzw r*) *Recht im objektiven Sinn*; gemeines Recht (*gegenüber Billigkeitsrecht*); ~

abiding gesetzestreu; ~ **agent** *scot* *R*–*s*anwalt; ~ **and order** Recht und Ordnung; ~ **as amended on...** Gesetz in der Fassung vom...; ~ **breaker** *R*-*s*brecher, Gesetzesübertreter; ~ **centre** Rechtsberatungsstelle für Minderbemittelte; ~ **charges** Prozeßkosten; ~ **Christian** Kirchen*r*; ~ **code** Gesetzbuch, Kodex; **L~ Commission** (*permanente*) Rechtsreform-Kommission *GB seit 1965;* ~ **Committee** *R*-*s*beirat, *R*-*s*ausschuß; ~ **costs** die Kosten des *R*-*s*streits; ~ **day** Terminstag, Verfallstag; ~ **department** *R*-*s*abteilung; ~ **draft** Gesetzesvorlage; ~ **enforcement** Gesetzesvollzug; Rechtsanwendung; ~ **enforcement authorities** Vollzugsbehörden; ~ **fee** Gerichtsgebühr, Gerichtskosten; ~ **firm** Anwalts(groß)kanzlei; ~ **French** Gerichtsfranzösisch (*in England*); ~ **giver** Schöpfer des *R*-*s*; ~ **in force** geltendes *R*; ~ **Latin** → *Latin*; ~ **library** *R*-*s*bibliothek; **L~ List** Anwaltsverzeichnis; **L~ Lord** richterliches Oberhausmitglied; Revisionsrichter des Oberhauses; ~ **making** *R*-*s*schöpfung; ~ **making power** gesetzgebende Gewalt, Gesetzgebungsbefugnis; ~ **martial** Standrecht, Kriegs*r*; ~ **memorandum** *R*-*s*gutachten; ~ **merchant** Handels*r*; ~ **of agency** *R* der Stellvertretung; ~ **of arms** Kriegs*r*; ~ **of arrest** Haft*r*;; ~ **of bills of exchange** Wechsel*r*; **L~s of Canute** *Sammlung angelsächsischer Rechte unter König Knut, 11. Jhd;* ~ **of capture** Ausbeutungs*r* *n* an Bodenschätzen (*durch den Grundeigentümer*); ~ **of cause and effect** Gesetz von Ursache und Wirkung, Kausalität; ~ **of confidence** *R* über den Schutz der Vertraulichkeit; ~ **of contract** Vertrags*r*; Schuld*r*; ~ **of diminishing returns** Gesetz vom abnehmenden Ertragszuwachs; ~ **of diminishing utility** Gesetz des abnehmenden Grenznutzens; ~ **of domestic relations** Familien*r*; ~ **of domicile** *R* des Wohnsitzes; ~ **of evidence** Beweis*r*; ~ **of flag** → *flag*; ~ **of industrial property** *R* des gewerblichen Rechtsschutzes; ~ **of inheritance** Erb*r*; ~ **of libel** Beleidigungs*r* *vgl libel*; ~ **of local government** Gemeindeverwaltungs*r*; ~ **of marque** Retorsions*r* der Schiffsbeschlagnahme; ~ **of master and servant** Dienstvertrags*r*, privates Arbeits*r*; ~ **of meeting** (*öffentliches*) Versammlungs*r*; ~ **of nationality** Personalstatut; ~ **of nations** Völker*r*; ~ **of nature** Natur*r*, Naturgesetz; ~ **of negligence** *R* der Fahrlässigkeitshaftung; ~ **of obligations** Schuld*r*; ~ **of peaceful assembly** öffentl. Versammlungs*r*; ~ **of procedure** Prozeß*r*, Verfahrens*r*; ~ **of property** Sachen*r*; Liegenschafts*r*; **L~ of Property Act** *brit Bodenrechtsreformgesetzgebung von 1925*; ~ **of real property** Liegenschafts*r*; ~ **of status** *R* der *R*-*s*fähigkeit und Geschäftsfähigkeit (*int Privatr*); ~ **of supply and demand** Gesetz von Angebot und Nachfrage; ~ **of succession** Erb*r*, *R* der gesetzlichen Erbfolge; ~ **of taxation** Steuerrecht; ~ **of the air** Luft*r*; **L~s of the Bretts and Scotts** *schottische Rechtssammlung bis 14. Jhd*; ~ **of the case** rechtskräftiger Entscheidungssatz, materielle Rechtskraft; *r*-*s*kräftiger Schiedsspruch, unstreitiges Vorbringen in der Vorinstanz, Endentscheidung, nicht angefochtener Beschluß, unangefochtene *R*-*s*belehrungen; ~ **of the Commonwealth** Commonwealth-*R* (*von der Legislative eines Commonwealthlandes erlassenes oder bestätigtes Recht*); ~ **of the flag** → *flag*; ~ **of the land** das (*englische bzw amerikanische*) *R*, die allgemein in e–m Lande geltenden Normen; das öffentliche *R*, *r*-*s*staatliche Prinzipien; ~ **of the place of fulfilment** *R* des Erfüllungsortes; ~ **of the road** Straßenverkehrs*r*, Linksfahrgebot *bzw* Rechtsfahrgebot; ~ **of the sea** See(völker)*r*; ~**s of the several states** Gesetze (und Rechtsprechung) der

Einzelstaaten (USA); ~ **of the staple** *hist* Marktr, das in e–r Hafenstadt gültige *R*; Handelsr; ~ **of torts** R der unerlaubten Handlungen; ~ **of trade-marks** Warenzeichenr; ~**s of war** Kriegsr; Völkerr im Kriege; **L~s of Wisby** (=) *hist* Gesetze von Wisby (*Seerechtssammlung 13. Jhd*); ~ **office** Anwaltskanzlei; ~ **officer** Polizeibeamter; **L~ Officers of the Crown** *brit* die hohen juristischen Kronbeamten, Kronanwaltschaft = *Attorney General und Solicitor General, qv;* ~ **practice** Anwaltstätigkeit; ~ **question** *R-s*frage, rechtliche Frage; ~ **reform** Rechtsreform; ~ **reports** → *report;* ~ **review** juristische Zeitschrift; ~ **school** juristische Fakultät; ~ **sittings** → *sittings*; **L~ Society** Anwaltskammer (*für solicitors qv*), Anwaltsverein; ~ **spiritual** Kirchenr; ~ **stationers' charges** Kanzleiausfertigungsgebühren, Schreibgebühren e–r Anwaltskanzlei; ~ **suit** (= *lawsuit*) bürgerlicher Rechtsstreit, Zivilprozeß; ~ **terms** Sitzungsperiode der Gerichte; ~ **worthy** *r-s*schutzfähig; **absolute** ~ Naturr, grundlegende *R–s*sätze (*abstrakter Gültigkeit*); **according to** ~ → *according;* **adjective** ~ Verfahrensr, formelles *R*, **administration of the** ~ → *administration;* **administrative** ~ Verwaltungsr; **admiralty** ~ Seer; **agrarian** ~**s** Agrargesetze, Bodenreformgesetze; **agricultural** ~ Agrarr; **anti-compact** ~**s** → *anticompact*; **anti-cruising** ~ *Gesetz gegen das ziellose Herumfahren mit d. Auto*; **anti-discrimination** ~ Gesetz gegen Rassendiskriminierung; Gesetz gegen unlautere diskriminierende Tarifierung *im Versicherungsgewerbe;* **anti-injunction** ~ Gesetz zur Einschränkung gerichtlicher Unterlassungsverfügungen *in Arbeitskampfsachen*; **anti-rebate** ~ Gesetz über das Verbot von Provisionsabsprachen mit Kunden; **antitrust** ~ Kartellr; **arbitrary** ~ gesetztes R; **banking** ~ Bankr; **benefit of a** ~ *R-s*vorteil, *R-s*wohltat; **binding** ~ zwingendes *R*; **binding in** ~*r-s*verbindlich; **body of** ~**s** → *body*; **bound by** ~ gesetzlich, rechtlich verpflichtet; **branch of** ~ *R-s*gebiet; **budgetary** ~ Haushaltsr; **by** ~ durch Gesetz, von *R-s* wegen; **by(e)-laws** → *by* (*2*); **by act of** ~ kraft Gesetzes; **by operation of** ~ gesetzlich, kraft Gesetzes; **canon** ~ Kirchenr, kanonisches *R*; **case** ~ Fallr, Präzendenzr, Richterr; **civil** ~ bürgerliches *R*, Zivilr, römisches *R*, das kontinentale Rechtssystem; **club** ~ die Regeln der Gewaltanwendung; **codified** ~ kodifiziertes *R*; **cogent** ~ zwingendes *R*; **colonial** ~ Kolonialr; *R* der ursprünglichen 13 Kolonien in Nordamerika; **commercial** ~ Handelsr; **common** ~ → *common law*; **Community** ~ → *Community*; **company** ~ Gesellschaftsr; **comparative** ~ *R-s*vergleichung; **competition** ~ Wettbewerbsr; **constitutional** ~ Verfassungsr; Staatsr; **construction** ~ Baur; **consuetudinary** ~ Gewohnheitsr; **copyright** ~ Urheberr; **criminal** ~ Strafr; **crown** ~ → *crown*; **customary** ~ Gewohnheitsr; **decree** ~ → *decree*; **directly applicable** ~ unmittelbar anwendbares *R* (*EG*); **disciplinary** ~ Dienststrafr; **domestic** ~ innerstaatliches *R*, nationales *R*, Landesr, Heimatr; **draft** ~ → *draft*; **economic** ~ → *economic*; **EEC** ~ Gemeinschaftsr (*EG*); **electoral** ~ Wahlgesetz, Wahlr; **emergency** ~ Notstandsr; **enacted** ~ Gesetzesr; **environmental** ~ Umweltschutzr; **established** ~ bestehendes *R*, geltendes *R*, anerkanntes *R*; **ex post facto** ~ → *ex post facto;* **exchange** ~ Wechselr; **existing** ~ geltendes *R*; **family** ~ Familienr; **fault-based** ~ auf dem Schuldprinzip (= *Verschuldensprinzip*) beruhendes *R*; **federal** ~ Bundesr, Bundesgesetz; **feudal** ~ Lehnsr; **field of** ~ → *field*; **fiscal** ~ Steuerr; **flexible** ~ nachgiebiges *R*; **force of** ~ → *force*; **foreign** ~ ausländisches *R*, außerenglisches *R* (*zB schottisches R*); *R e–s* anderen Bundesstaates; **forest** ~ Forst*r*, Forstgesetz; **free** ~ *R* der Freien; **game** ~ Jagd*r*, Jagdgesetz; **general** ~ allgemein geltendes *R*; **governing** ~ anwendbares *R*; Vertrags*r*; **heir at** ~ → *heir*; **immutable** ~ unabänderliches *R*; **industrial** ~ Arbeits*r*, Gewerbe*r*, Wirtschafts*r*; **insolvency** ~**s** → *insolvency*; **inspection** ~**s** → *inspection;* **insurance** ~ Versicherungs*r*; **international** ~ → *international law*; **interpretation of the** ~ Gesetzesauslegung; **interstate** ~ interlokales US-Privat*r*, *R zwischen den US-Bundesstaaten*; **intestate** ~**s** → *intestate*; **judgemade** ~ Richter*r*; **labo(u)r** ~ Arbeits*r*; **Lidford L**~ Lynchjustiz; **local** ~ Orts*r*, Kommunal*r*; **maritime** ~ Se*r*, Seehandels*r*; **maritime international** ~ internationales See*r*; **martial** ~ → *martial*; **mercantile** ~ Handels*r*; **mining** ~ Berg*r*, Bergwerks*r*; **mistake of** ~ → *mistake;* **mixed** ~ gemischte Gesetze (*zugleich schuldrechtliche und sachenrechtl. Normen*); **monetary** ~ Münzgesetz; Münz*r*; **moral** ~ Sittengesetz; **municipal** ~ innerstaatliches *R*, Stadt*r*; lokales *R* e–r Gemeinde; **national** ~ innerstaatliches *R*, nationales *R*, Landes*r*; **native** ~ Eingeborenen*r*; **natural** ~ Natur*r*; Naturgesetz; **naval** ~ Mariner*r*; **naval prize** ~ Seeprisen*r*; **navigation** ~ Schiffahrtsgesetz; **operation of** ~ *unmittelbare* Wirkung des Gesetzes; gesetzlicher Rechtsübergang; **operative** ~ gültiges Gesetz; **organic** ~ → *organic*; **paramount** ~ ranghöchstes *R*, Verfassungs*r*; **parish** ~ → *parish*; **Patent** ~ Patentgesetz, Patent*r*; **penal** ~ Straf*r*, Strafgesetz; **pending at** ~ rechtshängig; **peremptory** ~ zwingendes *R*, unabdingbares *R*; **personal** ~ persönliches Immunitäts*r*; Ausnahme*r* fremder Staatsangehöriger; **political** ~ Staats*r*; **positive** ~ positives *R*, geltendes *R*, Satzungs*r*, gesetztes *R*; **prescriptive** ~ Gewohnheits*r*; **private** ~ Privat*r*, Zivil*r*, **private international** ~ → *international law*; **probate** ~ Nachlaß*r*, Testaments*r*; **prospective** ~ positives, nicht rückwirkendes *R*; **protection of** ~ *R*-sschutz; **provision of** ~ Gesetzesvorschrift, Gesetzesbestimmung; **public** ~ öffentliches *R*, Staats*r*; *US* Gesetz (*P.L. No* ...); **public international** ~ Völker*r*; **purview of a** ~ Inhalt e–s Gesetzes; Sinn e–s Gesetzes; **quarantine** ~ Quarantänevorschrift; **relevant** ~ anzuwendendes Gesetz; **remedial** ~ formelles *R*; **retroactive** ~ rückwirkendes Gesetz; **retrospective** ~ rückwirkendes Gesetz; **revenue** ~ Steuer*r*, Abgaben*r*; **Roman** ~ römisches *R*; **space** ~ Raum*r*; **special** ~ Nebengesetz, Spezialgesetz, Sonder*r*; **state** ~ *US* einzelstaatliches *R*; **statute** ~ gesetztes *R*; geschriebenes *R*, Gesetzes*r*; **strict** ~ strenges *R*; **substantive** ~ materielles *R*, sachliches *R*; **sumptuary** ~**s** → *sumptuary;* **supplementing and co-ordinating** ~ Ergänzungs- und Rahmengesetz; **supremacy of** ~ Vorrang des *R-s*, *R*-sstaatlichkeit; **tacit** ~ stillschweigendes *R*, Gewohnheits*r*; **territorial** ~ innerstaatliches *R*; **the proper** ~ **of the contract** das auf den Vertrag anzuwendende Recht; **to abrogate a** ~ ein Gesetz aufheben; **to apply a** ~ ein Gesetz anwenden; **to be at** ~ **with s.o.** mit jmdm prozessieren; **to go in for** ~ Jura studieren; **to invalidate a** ~ ein Gesetz außer Kraft setzen; **to practice** ~ den Anwaltsberuf ausüben; **to promulgate a** ~ ein Gesetz verkünden; **to repeal a** ~ ein Gesetz aufheben; **to recast the** ~ das *R* neugestalten, Gesetze novellieren; **to revise a** ~ ein Gesetz abändern; **to skirt the** ~ das Gesetz umgehen; **trademark** ~ Warenzeichen*r*; **tribal** ~ Stammes*r*; **trite** ~ elementares *R*; **unenacted** ~ = *unwritten* ~ *qv*; **unification of** ~ *R*-svereinheitlichung;

uniform ~ → *uniform*; **unwritten** ~ ungeschriebenes *R*, Gewohnheits*r*; ungeschriebenes Gesetz; **valid in** ~ *r-s*gültig, *r-s*kräftig; **versed in** ~ *r-s*gelehrt, *r-s*kundig; **written** ~ geschriebenes *R*, gesetztes *R*, Gesetzes*r*, Satzungs*r*.

lawful rechtmäßig, gesetzmäßig, gesetzlich, gesetzl zulässig, gesetzl erlaubt; ~ **ground of objection** gesetzlicher Einspruchsgrund (*Patentrecht*).

lawfully gesetzmäßig *adv*, in gesetzlich zulässiger Weise; ~ **begotten** ehelich gezeugt; ~ **demanded** in gesetzlicher Weise (*zur Zahlung*) aufgefordert, (an)gemahnt; ~ **detained** in gesetzlich zulässiger Weise in Verwahrung; ~ **due** rechtlich geschuldet; ~ **sworn as a witness** gesetzmäßig als Zeuge beeidigt.

lawfulness Gesetzmäßigkeit *f*, Rechtmäßigkeit *f*, Rechtswirksamkeit *f*.

lawless gesetzlos, ungesetzlich; ~ **man** Geächteter.

lawmaker Gesetzgeber *m*, Parlamentsabgeordneter *m*; **incumbent** ~ derzeitiger Abgeordneter.

lawsuit Zivilprozeß *m*, bürgerlicher Rechtsstreit *m*; **party to a** ~ Prozeßpartei; **pending** ~ anhängiger Prozeß.

lawyer Jurist *m*, Rechtsanwalt *m*; ~ **chairmanship** Vorsitz durch Juristen (*bzw Anwälte in Verwaltungsschiedsstellen*); **academic** ~ Rechtswissenschaftler; **aerospace** ~ Anwalt für Luft- und Weltraumrecht; **case-hardened** ~ prozeßerfahrener Anwalt; **commercial property** ~ Spezialanwalt für gewerbliche Vermögensverwaltung; **common** ~ Zivilrechtler; **family** ~ Anwalt für Familienrecht; **independent** ~ (freier) Rechtsanwalt; **industrial** ~ Wirtschaftsjurist; **in-house** ~ angestellter Anwalt, Syndikusanwalt; **inside** ~ = *in-house* ~ *qv*; **libel** ~ auf Verleumdungsprozesse spezialisierter Anwalt; **long-winded** ~ langatmiger Anwalt; **media** ~ auf Medienrecht spezialisierter Anwalt; **palimony** ~ *auf Unterhaltsklagen von Lebensgefährtinnen spezialisierter Anwalt*; **patent** ~ → *patent*; **pettifogging** ~ Winkeladvokat; **public interest** ~ Sozialanwalt; Anwalt der Bürgerinteressen; **country** ~ Kleinstadtanwalt; **employed** ~ = *in-house* ~ *qv*; **takecover** ~ auf Übernahmen von Aktiengesellschaften spezialisierter Anwalt; **to retain a** ~ e–n Anwalt mandieren, e–n A. beauftragen; **trial** ~ Prozeßanwalt, Anwalt mit überwiegender Gerichtspraxis.

lawyering Ausübung des Anwaltsberufs.

lawyerless anwaltslos, ohne Zulassung von Anwälten; ohne Anwaltszwang.

lay *adj* Laien . . ., weltlich; ~ **assessor** Laienbeisitzer, Schöffe; ~ **impropriator** pfründeberechtigter Laie; ~ **corporation** → *corporation;* ~ **fee** nichtkirchliches Lehen; ~ **investiture** die Übergabe der weltlichen Besitzungen e–r Diözese an den Bischof; ~ **involvement** Beteiligung von Laien (am Richteramt); ~ **judge** → *judge*; ~ **land** Brachland; ~ **magistracy** Laienrichtertum (*justice of the peace qv*); ~ **magistrate** Nichtjurist als Amtsrichter, Laienrichter; ~ **people** Geschworene; ~ **rector** *hist* pfründeberechtigter Laie; ~ **witness** nicht sachverständiger Zeuge; **The L~ Observer** Überprüfungsbeauftragter gegenüber der Law Society *qv*.

lay *s* Gewinnanteil *m* der Schiffsbesatzung am (Wal)Fischfang; ~ **system** Fischfangversteigerung mit Verteilung des Reinerlöses an den Schiffskapitän und Mannschaft.

lay *v* legen, vorbringen; ~ **aside** zurücklegen; ~ **attachment** mit Beschlag belegen; ~ **before the House** dem Parlament vorlegen, *e–e Vorlage* einbringen; ~ **claim to s. th.** auf etw Anspruch erheben; ~ **damages** die Schadenersatzforderung *in der Klage* beziffern, den Schadenersatz der Höhe nach geltend machen; ~ **down** (*Amt*) niederlegen; ~ **down a time-limit** e–e Frist setzen; ~ **down an indictment** Anklage erheben; ~ **embargo** Schiffsbeschlagnahme vornehmen, an die Kette legen, Schiffsarrest anordnen; ~ **off** ausstellen, (*vorübergehend*) entlassen; ~ **on the table** *parl* vorlegen, einbringen; ~ **out** vorschießen, auslegen; ~ **papers** *parl* informieren; ~ **up** stillegen.

layaway vereinbartes Zurücklegen von Waren.

lay-by Ausweichstelle; ~ **system** Abzahlungskauf (*bei Lebensmitteln*).

lay days Liegetage, Löschzeit gemäß Chartervertrag.

laying an information Erstatten e–r Strafanzeige.

layman Laie *m*, Nichtfachmann *m*; Nichtjurist *m*.

layoff Ausstellung *f* (*von Arbeitskräften*), (*vorübergehende*) Entlassung wegen Arbeitsmangels; ~ **by seniority** Abbau von Arbeitnehmern nach Altersstufen.

lazaret Quarantänelazarett *n*; Quarantänedesinfektionsabteilung *f*.

lazaretto Quarantänestation *f*.

lead Hinweis *m* (auf Abschlußmöglichkeiten *bzw*. *Aufklärungsspuren*); **to pursuea** ~ e–m Hinweis nachgehen; e–e Spur verfolgen.

lead case → *case*.

lead manage *v*|*j* die Konsortialführung ausüben.

lead manager → *manager*.

lead time → *time*.

leader Führer *m*, Leiter *m*; erster Anwalt *m*, Kronanwalt *m*; Leitartikel *m*; ~ **of a gang** Bandenführer, Rädelsführer; ~ **of a parliamentary group** Fraktionsführer; ~ **of the delegation** Delegationsführer; ~ **of the House** Fraktionsführer der Regierungspartei; **L~ of HM Opposition** Oppositionsführer *im brit Unterhaus*; **floor** ~ Fraktionsführer.

leaders *exch* führende Werte *m*|*pl*, Favoriten *m*|*pl*.

leaf-raking (Laubrechen) unproduktive Notstandsarbeiten *f*|*pl*.

leaflet Merkblatt *n*, Werbedrucksache *f*, Prospekt *m*, Flugblatt *n*.

leaf vegetables Blattgemüse.

leakage Leck *n*, Indiskretion *f*; Leckage *f*, Verlust *m*; ~ **and breakage** Leckage und Bruch; ~ **clause** → *clause*; **deliberate** ~ gezielte Indiskretion; **free from** ~ frei von Leckage.

lean sich stützen auf, tendieren, neigen zu; ~ **against a doctrine** eine Lehre mißbilligen.

leaning Neigung *f*, Tendenz *f*; **criminal** ~**s** kriminelle Neigungen.

leapfrog *v*|*i* Sprungrevision einlegen, (~ *to the House of Lords*).

leapfrog procedure Sprungrevisionsverfahren (*in Zivilsachen*).

learn erfahren, lernen, ersehen, feststellen.

learned gelehrt, rechtsgelehrt; ~ **in the law** juristisch ausgebildet; ~ **societies** wissenschaftliche Gesellschaften; **my** ~ **friend** *brit* mein verehrter Kollege (*unter Juristen*).

learner Anfänger *m*, Anlernling *m*; Fahrschüler *m*.

lease *s* Landpacht *f*, *befristete entgeltliche Nutzungsüberlassung*; langfristiger Grundstücksmietvertrag *m*, Mietvertrag *m*; Pacht *f*, Mietverhältnis *n*; Pachtzeit *f*, Mietzeit *f*; Miet/Pachtvertragsurkunde; Leasing *n*; Leasingvertrag *m*; ~ **by tenants in common** gemeinsamer Untermiet(pacht)vertrag *mehrerer Berechtigter*; ~ **for life** Pacht auf Lebenszeit; ~ **for lives** Erbpacht auf die Dauer des Lebens e–s Dritten; ~ **for term of years** Pacht auf Zeit; ~ **from month to month** monatlich kündbares Nutzungsverhältnis; ~ **in perpetuity** Erbpacht; ~ **in possession** Pachtverhältnis mit unmittelbarer Besitzerhaftung; **agreement for a** ~ Miet-/Pachtvertrag, schuldrechtlicher Miet-/Pachtvertrag; **agreement for** ~ **on expiration of present** ~ Miet(Pacht-)verlängerungsvertrag; **agricultural** ~ Landpacht; **bailment** ~ Mietkauf, Leasing; **building** ~ *langfristige Verpachtung mit*

Verpflichtung des Pächters zur Errichtung e–s Bauwerks; **commercial** ~ Mietvertrag über gewerblich genutzte Räume; **concurrent** ~ mehrfache Verpachtung; **conditional** ~ in Grundstückseigentum umwandelbares Pachtverhältnis; **equitable** ~ schuldrechtliches Pachtrecht; **farming** ~ → *farming*; **graduated** ~ gestaffelte Pacht, Staffelmiete; **ground** ~ → *building* ~; **heritable** ~ Erbpacht; **homestead** ~ Heimstättenpacht *US auf 28 Jahre vergebene Pacht e–s eigenbewirtschafteten Hofes*; **improvement** ~ mit Meliorationsauflagen vergebene Pacht; **improving** ~ *improvement* ~ *qv*; **legal** ~ dingliches Pachtrecht, Erbpacht; **long** ~ langfristiger (Miet-)Pachtvertrag; **master** ~ Hauptpacht; **mining** ~ Bergwerksberechtigung, Bergwerkspacht; **net** ~ Nettopacht (*Nebenkosten beim Pächter*); **ninety-nine year** ~ Pacht auf 99 Jahre; **one-off** ~ Einmalpacht, unverlängerbare Zeitpacht; **ordinary** ~ Miete, Mietvertrag; **parol** ~ formloser Landpachtvertrag (*bis zu 3 Jahren*); **pastoral** ~ Weidepacht; **perpetual** ~ Erbpacht; **perpetually renewable** ~ ständig verlängerbarer Miet-/Pachtvertrag *mit wiederholbarer Neuabschlußverpflichtung bzw ständiger Verlängerungsklausel*; **proprietary** ~ *Pacht- bzw Mietverhältnis direkt mit dem Eigentümer*, Hauptpacht, Hauptmiete; **renewal of a** ~ → *renewal*; **reversionary** ~ Anschlußpacht, Nachpachtrecht, *Pachtverhältnis mit zukünftigem Anfangstermin*; **running** ~ → *running*; **short** ~ Verpachtung auf höchstens 21 Jahre; **tenure by** ~ → *tenure*; **term of** ~ → *term*; **to assign a** ~ → *to assign*; **to grant a** ~ vermieten, verpachten; **usufructuary** ~ Pacht, Pachtvertrag.

lease *v* pachten, verpachten, mieten, vermieten.

leaseback Rückmiete *f*, Rückpacht *f*; **sale-**~ Verkauf mit Zurückmieten.

leasehold Pacht *f*, dingl Nutzungsrecht auf Zeit; Pachtgrundstück *n*; ~ **area** Pachtgebiet; ~ **enfranchisement** *brit* Pachtlandbefreiung; *Ablösung von Grundzins zur Verschaffung vollen Bodeneigentums*; (gesetzliche) Übertragung des Grundeigentums auf den (Erb)Pächter; ~ **enfranchisement** Umwandlung langfristiger Pachtrechte in Eigentum; ~ **estate** → *estate*; ~ **improvements** Werterhöhung des gepachteten Grundstücks; ~ **insurance** → *insurance*; ~ **interest** Recht an e–m Pachtgrundstück, Miet-(Pacht)besitz(recht) am Grundstück; ~ **land and buildings** *brit bil* Pachtbesitz; ~ **mortgage** Grundpfandrecht auf Pachtgrundstück; ~ **mortgage bond** *am Gebäude auf Pachtgrundstück gesicherte Schuldurkunde*; ~ **ownership** eigentumsähnliches Rechtsverhältnis; ~ **property** Pachtgrundstück, Pachtland; ~ **reversion** Heimfall des Unterpachtbesitzes; Verfügungsrecht des Verpächters für die Zeit nach dem Heimfall; ~ **security** Pachtvermögen; ~ **tenure** Pachtbesitz, Pachtverhältnis.

leaseholder Pächter *m*.

leasing Verpachtung *f*, Vermietung *f*, Leasing *n*; ~ **agreement** Leasingvertrag; ~ **broker** Leasing-Makler; ~ **company** Leasinggesellschaft; ~ **powers** gesetzliche Verpachtungsrechte; **big ticket** ~ Groß-Leasing, Groß-Charter ((*Tanker etc*); **car** ~ **contract** PKW-Leasingvertrag; **equipment** ~ Anlagen-Leasing, **vehicle** ~ Fahrzeug-Leasing, **finance** ~ Finanzierungsleasing; **fleet** ~ Vermietung von Fahrzeugparks; **operational** ~ Operating-Leasing; **plant** ~ Vermietung von Betriebsanlagen.

leave Urlaub *m*; Erlaubnis *f*, Rechtsmittelzulassung *f*; ~ **of absence** Sonderurlaub (*mil*), Dienstbefreiung; ~ **entitlement** Urlaubsanspruch; ~ **hurdle** Zulassungshürde (*für Revisionen*); ~ **of court** gerichtliche Erlaubnis; ~ **requirement** Zulassungserfordernis (*für Revi-*

sion); ~ **to appeal** Zulassung der Revision; ~ **to appeal out of time** Zulassung e–s verspäteten Rechtsmittels; ~ **to defend** Auflage, Einwendungen vorbringen; ~ **to issue writ (of summons)** Erlaubnis zur Klageerhebung; ~ **to join causes of action** Genehmigung der Klagehäufung; ~ **with pay** bezahlter Urlaub; ~ **without pay** unbezahlter Urlaub; **absence without** ~ unerlaubtes Fernbleiben; **annual** ~ Jahresurlaub; **on** ~ beurlaubt; **parental** ~ Kindererziehungsurlaub; **to grant** ~ **for a new trial** die Wiederaufnahme des Verfahrens zulassen.

leave *v* verlassen, überlassen, hinterlassen, vermachen, vererben; ~ **in abeyance** offen lassen, in der Schwebe lassen; ~ **issue** Nachkommen hinterlassen; ~ **on record** protokollieren lassen; ~ **s. th. undone** etwas unterlassen.

ledger Hauptbuch *n*, Gesamtheit *f* von Konten; ~ **abstract** Hauptbuchauszug; ~ **account** Hauptbuchkonto; ~**-book** *kirchenrechtliches* Urkundenbuch; ~ **folio** Hauptbuchfolio; ~ **of consignment of goods** Warenausgangsbuch; ~ **records** Hauptbücher; **accounts payable** ~ Kontokorrentbuch (Kreditoren); **accounts receivable** ~ Kontokorrentbuch (Debitoren); **creditor's** ~ → *creditor;* **customer's** ~ → *customer;* **general** ~ Hauptbuch, (*Sachkonten der*) Geschäftsbuchhaltung; **general** ~ **inventory account** Vorrätekonto in der Hauptbuchhaltung; **great** ~ Staatsschuldenbuch; **personal** ~ Privatkontenbuch; **plant** ~ → *plant*; **securities** ~ Effektenbuch; **shareholder's** ~ Aktienbuch; **subsidiary** ~ Hilfsbuch; **to balance the** ~ → *to balance.*

left|behind zurückgelassen (*in fremdem Hafen*); ~ **at station till called for** bahnlagernd; ~ **till called for** postlagernd.

leftist Linkspolitiker *m*, Linksradikaler *m*.

legacy Vermächtnis *n* (= *V bzw v*); Legat *n*; *letztwillige Verfügung über bewegliche Vermögensgegenstände;* ~ **duty** Erbschaftssteuer (*auf den beweglichen Nachlaß, GB bis 1949*); ~ **hunter** Erbschleicher; **abatement of** ~ *V*kürzung; **absolute** ~ unbedingtes *V*; **accumulative** ~ Zusatz*v*; **ademption of** ~ → *ademption*; **alternate** ~ Wahlvermächtnis; **charitable** ~ Mildtätigkeitsstiftung, *V* für mildtätige Zwecke; **conditional** ~ bedingtes *V auch: Vorerbschaft*; **contingent** ~ aufschiebend bedingtes *V*; **cumulative** ~ Doppelanfall e–s Vermächtnisses; **demonstrative** ~ beschränktes Gattungs*v*, aus bestimmten Mitteln zu erfüllendes Geld*v*; **disclaimer of** ~ Ausschlagung e–s *V–ses*; **general** ~ Gattungs*v*; **general pecuniary** ~ Geldsummen*v*; **indefinite** ~ Pauschal*v*, letztwillige Zuwendung des beweglichen Nachlasses; **lapsed** ~ ausgefallenes *V* (*durch den Tod des Bedachten erledigtes Vermächtnis*); **modal** ~ *V* mit Auflagen (*über die Art der Erfüllung*); **pecuniary** ~ Geld*v*, *V* e–s Geldbetrages; **preferential** ~ Voraus*v*; **residuary** ~ letztwillige Zuwendung des beweglichen Restnachlasses; **reversionary** ~ Ersatz*v*; **special** ~ = *specific* ~ *qv*; **specific** ~ Einzel*v*, Sonder*v* (*e–s einzelnen Vermögensgegenstandes*); **statutory** ~ gesetzl Erbanspruch d. überlebenden Ehegatten im Intestatnachlaß (*Kapitalzahlungen u bewegl Habe*)); **substitutional** ~ Ersatz*v*; **trust** ~ von e–m Treuhänder zu verwaltendes *V*; **universal** ~ Erbeinsetzung, letztwillige Zuwendung des gesamten Vermögens; **vested** ~ bestimmtes *V*, unbedingtes *V*.

legal gesetzmäßig, legal, gesetzlich, gerichtlich, rechtmäßig, rechtlich, juristisch, Rechts . . .; ~ **acumen** juristischer Scharfsinn; ~ **audio secretary** Anwaltsstenotypistin; ~ **clinic** Großkanzlei; ~ **cap** Kanzleibogen (*oben gefaltet*); ~ **chose in**

action ein von Dritten zu erlangender Gegenstand; ~ **advice and assistance** Beratungshilfe; ~ **costs drawer** Kostensachbearbeiter *e–r Anwaltskanzlei*; ~ **custody of the child** Personensorge; ~ **debt margin** Marge bis zur gesetzlichen Verschuldungsgrenze; ~ **drafting** Entwurf von *R–s*dokumenten; ~ **duty to support** gesetzliche Unterhaltspflicht; ~ **insurance** → *insurance*; ~ **lending limits** gesetzl Ausleihungsgrenzen für Banken; ~ **literature** rechtswissenschaftliche Literatur; ~ **logic** juristische Logik; ~ **notice to quit** gesetzlich zugelassene Kündigung; ~ **professional privilege** anwaltschaftliches Aussage- und Offenbarungsverweigerungsrecht; ~ **rate of interest** gesetzlicher Zinsfuß; ~ **scholar** Rechtswissenschaftler, Rechtsgelehrter.

legal aid Prozeßkostenhilfe *f*; **L~ A~ and Advice Act** Prozeßkostenhilfegesetz; ~ **certificate** Prozeßkostenhilfebescheinigung, *früher*: Armenrechtszeugnis; ~ **order** Prozeßkostenhilfebeschluß; ~ **to poor prisoners** Pflichtverteidigung, Prozeßkostenhilfe in Strafsachen; **criminal** ~ = ~ *to poor prisoners qv*.

legalese Juristensprache *f*.

legalism strenge Gesetzestreue *f*, Rechtsformalismus *n*, Paragraphenreiterei *f*.

legalistic legalistisch, formaljuristisch, positivistisch.

legality Legalität *f*, Rechtmäßigkeit *f*, Gesetzmäßigkeit *f*, Gesetzlichkeit *f*, Gültigkeit *f*.

legalization Legalisierung *f*, rechtliche Sanktionierung *f*; Legalisation *f*, Amtsbekräftigung *f*, (konsularische) Bestätigung (*der Echtheit e–r Beglaubigung*); Beglaubigung *f*, gerichtliche Bestätigung *f*.

legalize legalisieren, beglaubigen, rechtlich genehmigen, rechtlich sanktionieren; **~d nuisance** erlaubte Immission, zugelassene Einwirkung.

legally *adv* gesetzlich, rechtlich; ~ **bound** rechtlich verpflichtet; ~ **dead** verschollen, bürgerlichrechtlich tot; ~ **due** geschuldet; ~ **effective** rechtswirksam; ~ **enforceable** rechtswirksam, rechtlich durchsetzbar, vollstreckungsfähig; ~ **established** rechtmäßig errichtet; eingeführt; ~ **exempt** (gesetzlich) befreit; ~ **incapacitated** geschäftsunfähig; ~ **liable** gesetzlich verpflichtet, haftbar; ~ **protected** gesetzlich geschützt; ~ **qualified** zugelassen, die gesetzlichen Voraussetzungen erfüllend; ~ **represented** anwaltschaftlich vertreten; ~ **tenuous** rechtlich schwach begründet.

legalness Rechtmäßigkeit *f*.

legatary Vermächtnisnehmer *m*.

legatee Vermächtnisnehmer *m*, letztwillig (mit bewegl Vermögen) Bedachter; **joint** ~ Mitvermächtnisnehmer; **pecuniary** ~ Empfänger e–s Geldvermächtnisses; **residuary** ~ mit dem Nachlaßrest Bedachter; Testatserbe des bewegl Restnachlasses; **reversionary** ~ Nachvermächtnisnehmer, Nacherbe; **sole** ~ Alleinerbe; **specific** ~ Vermächtnisnehmer (*Einzelvermächtnis*); **universal** ~ Universalerbe.

legation Botschaft *f*, Gesandtschaft *f*, Botschaftspersonal *n*, Gesandtschaftspersonal *n*, Gesandtschaftsgebäude *n*; **right of** ~ → *right*.

legator Erblasser *m*, Vermächtnisgeber *m*, Testator *m*.

legerdemain Freizügigkeit *f*, Liberalisierung *f*.

legible deutlich lesbar.

legislate Gesetze geben, Gesetze erlassen.

legislation Gesetzgebung *f* (= *G bzw g*), Legislative *f*, Gesetze n|*pl*; ~ **by reference** Änderungs*g*; ~ **of an expropriatory discriminatory nature** enteignungsähnliche diskriminierende Gesetze; **autonomic** ~ Satzungs*g*, *G–s*autonomie; **act of** ~ Gesetzgebungsakt; **administrative** ~ *G* durch die Verwaltung; Verwaltungsverordnungen; **anti-**

violence ~ Gewaltbekämpfungsgesetze; **channel of** ~ *G–s*weg; **comparative** ~ Rechtsvergleichung; **consequential** ~ Folgegesetze, Anpassungsgesetze; **delegated** ~ → *to delegate*; **domestic** ~ inländische G, Landesg; **emergency** ~ → *emergency;* **factory** ~ Arbeitsschutzg; **landmark** ~ wegweisende Gesetze, fundamental wichtige G; **municipal** ~ innerstaatliche G; **national** ~ innerstaatliche Gesetzgebung, innerstaatliche Rechtsvorschriften; **penal** ~ Strafgesetzgebung; **permissive** ~ *Gesetze, deren Anwendung Ermessenssache der Behörden ist,* Kannbestimmungen; **preventive** ~ vorbeugende Gesetze; **primary** ~ Gesetzgebung (*durch formelle Gesetze*); **process of** ~ → *process* (*1*); **promulgation of** ~ Gesetzesverkündung; **retroactive** ~ rückwirkende G; **retrospective** rückwirkende G; **social** ~ Sozialg; **subordinate** ~ delegierte G, Verordnungen; **secondary** ~ Rechtsverordnungen, Gesetzgebung auf dem Verordnungswege; abgeleitete Rechtsetzung; **to enact** ~ Gesetze erlassen; **to initiate** ~ → *to initiate.*

legislative gesetzgebend, legislativ, Gesetzgebungs... (= *G–s*) ~ **act** Gesetz; ~ **and administrative provisions** Rechts- und Verwaltungsvorschriften; ~ **assembly** → *assembly*; ~ **authority** → *authority*; ~ **body** → *body*; ~ **budget** Haushaltsgesetz; ~ **bureau** Interessenvertretungen (*beim Parlament*); **L~ Committee** *G–s*ausschuß *der Church of England*; ~ **control** Beherrschung durch das Parlament; ~ **courts** gesetzlich geschaffene Gerichte, Verwaltungsgerichte, Sondergerichte; ~ **department** Legislative; ~ **enactment** Gesetz, Verordnung; ~ **expenses** Parlamentskosten; ~ **function** *G–s*funktion; ~ **history of an enactment** Gesetzgebungsvorgeschichte (*Auslegungsgrundsatz*); ~ **initiative** Einbringung e–r Vorlage; Volksbegehren; ~ **intent** → *intent*; ~ **investigation** Untersuchung durch einen Parlamentsausschuß; ~ **or other action** Erlaß von Rechtsvorschriften oder sonstige Maßnahmen; ~ **power** → *power* (*1*); ~ **provisions** Rechtsvorschriften; ~ **purpose** Absicht des Gesetzgebers; der gesetzgeberische Zweck; ~ **supremacy of Parliament** (gesetzgeberische) Oberhoheit des Parlaments; ~ **time-table** Zeitplan für die Parlamentsarbeit; ~ **treaty** → *treaty*.

legislator Gesetzgeber *m*, Abgeordneter *m*.

legislature Legislative *f*, gesetzgebende Körperschaft *f*, Parlament *n*; **emergency** ~ Notparlament; **The L~** das Parlament; der Kongreß (*USA*).

legist Rechtskundiger *m*, Rechtsgelehrter *m*.

legitim *scot* Pflichtteilsrecht der Kinder am väterlichen beweglichen Nachlaß.

legitimacy Legitimität *f*, Ehelichkeit *f*; **L~ Act** Nichtehelichengesetz; **declaration of** ~ → *declaration*; **presumption of** ~ → *presumption*; **status of** ~ → *status*; **to contest the** ~ die Ehelichkeit anfechten.

legitimate *adj* legitim, gesetzlich, ehelich, rechtmäßig; ~ **claim** berechtigter Anspruch; ~ **consignee** Empfangsberechtigter; ~ **descent** eheliche Abstammung; ~ **doubt** berechtigter Zweifel; ~ **heirs** → *heir*; ~ **interest** ~ → *interest* (*1*); ~ **issue** eheliche Nachkommen.

legitimate *v* legitimieren, für rechtmäßig erklären, für ehelich erklären; **to be ~d by subsequent marriage** durch nachfolgende Eheschließung ehelich werden.

legitimation Gültigkeitserklärung *f*, Berechtigung *f*, Legitimierung *f*, Ausweis *m*; Legitimation *f*; Ehelichkeitserklärung *f*; ~ **by subsequent marriage** Legitimation durch nachfolgende Eheschließung.

legitime Pflichterbanteil *m der Kinder am Nachlaß der Eltern bzw e–s Elternteils.*

leisure group Konzern der Freizeitindustrie.

lend verleihen, ausleihen, als Darlehen geben; vermachen; ~ **day-to-day money** Tagesgelder ausleihen; **L~ Lease Act** Leih- und Pachtgesetz; ~ **money on goods** Waren beleihen; ~ **on collateral (security)** lombardieren, Darlehen gegen Sicherheit gewähren, gesicherten Kredit gewähren; ~ **on interest** gegen Zinsen ausleihen; ~ **on mortgage** ein Grundstück beleihen, eine Hypothek geben.

lender Darlehensgeber *m*, Verleiher *m*, Ausleiher *m*, Gläubiger *m*; ~ **credit** Kundenkreditfinanzierung; ~ **of capital** Geldgeber, Kapitalgeber; ~ **of last resort** Kreditgeber letzter Instanz (*die Bank von England*); **mainstream ~s** reguläre Kreditgeber.

lending Ausleihen *n*, Verleihen *n*, Leihe *f*, Darlehensgewährung *f*; ~ **fee** Leihgebühr; ~ **ceilings** Ausleihungshöchstgrenzen; ~ **operation** Darlehensgeschäft; ~ **or loaning money on credit** Kreditgewährung, Kreditgeschäfte; ~ **rate** Zins für Ausleihungen; *base ~ ~*: *Basiszinssatz, Eckzins*; **~s' ratio** Ausleihquote (*im Verhältnis zur Depositen*); **international ~** internationales Kreditwesen.

length Länge *f*, Laufzeit *f*; ~ **of life** Lebensdauer; ~ **of service** Dienstzeit, Dienstalter.

lenience (= *leniency*) Nachsicht *f*, Milde *f*.

lenient milde, nachsichtig.

leonina societas leonistische Gesellschaft *f*.

lese majesty Majestätsbeleidigung *f*.

lesion Schädigung *f*, Verletzung *f*, Funktionsstörung *f*, Ungleichheit *f* von Verträgen.

less weniger, abzüglich; **~-than-carload lot** (l.c.l.) Stückgut, Waggonteilladung; **~-than-carload freight** Stückgutfracht; ~ **charges** abzüglich Kosten; ~ **discount** → *discount;* **~-than-truckload** LKW-Teilladung, LKW-Stückgutladung; ~ **value** Minderwert.

lessee Pächter *m*, Mieter *m*; Leasingnehmer *m*.

lessor Verpächter *m*, Vermieter *m*, Hauswirt *m*; Leasinggeber *m*; **~'s lien** → *lien*; ~ **of the plaintiff** *hist (fiktiver)* Verpächter des Klägers *bei Räumungsklage*; **immediate ~** der unmittelbare Vermieter (Verpächter).

let lassen, vermieten; Zuschlag erteilen (*bei Submissionen*); auflassen; zulassen; e–n Auftrag erteilen, anordnen; ~ **a prisoner escape** e–n Gefangenen entweichen lassen; ~ **in** den Beitritt zulassen; ~ **on hire** vermieten (*bewegl Sachen*); ~ **on lease** verpachten; ~ **s.o. off the hook** jmdn von Schulden entlasten; ~ **the defendant in** dem Beklagten die nachträgliche Rechtsverteidigung gestatten; ~ **the writ issue as prayed** der Beschluß wird antragsgemäß erlassen; ~ **to bail** Haftverschonung gegen Kaution zulassen; ~ **to be used** vertraglich zur Nutzung überlassen.

lethal tödlich, todbringend, lebensgefährdend; ~ **catapult** Präzisionsschleuder; ~ **weapon** → *weapon.*

let-off *s* Billig-Davongekommensein *n*; milde Bestrafung *f*.

letter *s* Brief *m*; Schreiben *n*; **~s** amtliche Urkunde, behördliches Ersuchen, Bestallungsurkunde, Sendschreiben; **~s ad colligenda bona** Nachlaßverwalterbestellung; **~-carrier** Briefträger; **~s close** königliches Privatprivileg; ~ **drop** Briefkasten(firma); ~ **from prison** Gefangenenbrief; **~gram** Brieftelegramm; ~ **missive** Vorlageschreiben *an höheres Gericht*, königliches Sendschreiben *über die Wahl e–s Bischoffs*; Vorladung an Oberhausmitglieder; ~ **in hand** den Erhalt Ihres Schreibens bestätigend; ~ **of acceptance** Annahmeschreiben; ~ **of accredition** Akkreditionsbrief; ~ **of acknowledgment** Bestätigungsschreiben; **~s of administration** Nachlaßpflegerzeugnis; **~ of advice** Anzeige, Benachrichtigungsschreiben; Avis; **~ of advocation** Zuständigkeitsfeststellung e-s Rechtsmittelgerichts; **~ of allotment** = *allotment letter → allotment*; **~ of application** Antrag, Bewerbungsschreiben; Antrag auf Zuteilung von Wertpapieren; Zeichnungserklärung; **~ of appointment** Ernennungsurkunde, Bestallungsurkunde; **~ of attorney** Vollmachtsurkunde; **~ of attornment** *cf attornment*; **~ of authority** Akkreditivermächtigung, Negoziierungskredit; **~ of bottomry** Bodmereivertrag; **~s of business** königliches Handschreiben an Kirchenversammlung *über Behandlung bestimmter Tagesordnungspunkte*; **~ of charge** Hinterlegungsbestätigung; **~ of comfort** = *comfort letter qv*; **~ of comment** Beanstandungsschreiben; **~ of complaint** Beschwerdebrief; **~ of consent** Einverständniserklärung; **~ of consignment** Frachtbrief; **~s of correspondence** (Privat)Korrespondenz; **~ of credence** Beglaubigungsschreiben; **~ of credit** → *letter of credit*; **~ of delegation** Ermächtigungsschreiben, Inkassovollmacht; **~ of exchange** Wechsel; **~s of fire and sword** *scot hist* Befehl zur gewaltsamen Entsetzung e-s Pächters *bzw* Lehensträgers *„mit Feuer und Schwert"*; **~s of guardianship** Pflegeschaftseinsetzungsbeschluß *über Mündelvermögen;* **~s of horning** *scot* gerichtliche Zahlungsaufforderung *mit Strafandrohung*; **~ of hypothecation** Verpfändungsurkunde, Bodmereibrief; *Antrag an die Bank auf Überlassung der verpfändeten Ware zu treuen Händen zwecks Verkaufs und Kredittilgung*; **~ of identification** beigefügte Unterschriftsprobe; Einführungsbrief (*e-m Reisekreditbrief beigefügt*); **~ of indemnity** *schriftliche* Schadloshaltungsverpflichtung; Indemnitätsbrief, Konossementsgarantie; **~s of indication** Korrespondentenliste (*Zirkularkreditbrief*); **~ of inquiry** Auskunftsersuchen; **~ of instruction** schriftliche Anweisung; **~ of intent** (schriftliche) Absichtserklärung; *L~ of I~: garantieähnliche Zusicherung e-r Muttergesellschaft über Bonität der Tochter*; **~ of intercession** Interventionsschreiben, Vermittlungsschreiben; **~ of introduction** Einführungsschreiben, Empfehlungsschreiben; **~ of licence** Moratorium; **~ of lien** Pfandurkunde; **~s of marque and reprisal** Kaperbrief; **~ of naturalization** Einbürgerungsurkunde; **~s of open doors** gerichtliche Ermächtigung zur gewaltsamen Öffnung; **~ of recall** Abberufungsschreiben, *Notifizierungsschreiben über den Abruf e-s diplomatischen Vertreters*; **~ of recommendation** Empfehlungsschreiben; **~ of recredentials** Bestätigungsschreiben über den Abruf e-s diplomatischen Vertreters; **~s of regress** → *regress*; **~ of regret** Mitteilung über die Nichtzuteilung von Effekten; **~ of reminder** Mahnbrief; **~ of renunciation** Verzichtsschreiben; **~s of request** Vorlageschreiben an Revisionsmittelinstanz; Rechtshilfeersuchen (*an ausländischen Staat*), Übernahmevertrag; **~ of respite** Moratorium, Stundung; **~ of rights** Bezugsrechtsurkunde; **~s of safe conduct** Geleitbrief; **~ of set-off** Ermächtigung zum Saldoausgleich; **~s of trust** Treuhandurkunde; **~s patent** Staatsurkunde; Patent, königl Zustimmung zu Gesetzen; Landkonzessionsurkunde; **~ requesting payment** Mahnbrief; **~s rogatory** Amtshilfeersuchen, Rechtshilfeersuchen zur Zeugenvernehmung; **~ stock** → *stock*; **~s testamentary** Testamentsvollstreckerzeugnis; **~ to be called for** postlagernder Brief; **begging ~** (*oft: betrügerischer*) Bettelbrief; **business ~s** → *business*; **circular ~** Rundschreiben; **covering ~** Begleitschreiben; **cut-out** ~ Brief mit ausgeschnittenen Buchstaben; **dead** **~s** unzustellbare Postsendung, Anmeldeschluß; **dimissory** **~s** *eccl* Dimissiorale *n*; **double** ~ Doppelbrief; **draft** ~ → *draft*; **dunning** ~ Mahnschreiben; **express** ~ Eilbrief; **incoming** ~ einlaufender Brief; **insured** ~ Wertbrief; **libellous** ~ beleidigendes Schreiben; **minded** ~ beanstandetes Schreiben; **official** ~ amtliches Schreiben, Amtsbescheid; **outgoing** ~ auslaufender Brief; **prepaid** ~ frankierter Brief; **registered** ~ Einschreibebrief; **rogatory** **~s** = *~s rogatory qv*; **side** ~ → *side*; **split** ~ Bezugsrechtsurkunde mit Aufteilungsbefugnis; **the** ~ **in hand** der vorliegende Brief; **unclaimed** ~ nicht abgeholter Brief; **unpaid** ~ unfrankierter Brief.

letter of credit Kreditbrief *m*, Akkreditiv *n*; **ancillary commercial** ~ Nebenakkreditiv, subsidiäres Akkreditiv; **circular** ~ Zirkularkreditbrief, Reisekreditbrief; **clean** ~ nichtdokumentäres Akkreditiv; **commercial** ~ Warenkreditbrief, Handelskreditbrief, Dokumentenakkreditiv; Rembourskredit, Bankrembours; **confirmed** ~ *unwiderrufliches* bestätigtes Akkreditiv; **direct** ~ an e–e bestimmte Bank gerichtetes Akkreditiv; **documentary** ~ Dokumentenakkreditiv; **export** ~ Exportkreditbrief; **general** ~ allgemeiner Kreditbrief (*an jedermann*); **import** ~ Importkreditbrief; **irrevocable** ~ unwiderrufliches Akkreditiv; **mutual** ~ Gegenakkreditiv; **non-revolving commercial** ~ nicht revolvierendes Akkreditiv; **open** ~ unbegrenzter Kreditbrief; **oriental** ~ Ankauf und Negoziierungsermächtigung (*Fernosthandel*); **reverse of a** ~ Rückseite e–s Akkreditivs; **revocable** ~ widerrufliches Akkreditiv; **revolving** ~ Revolving-Akkreditiv; sich erneuerndes Akkreditiv; **special** ~ Kreditbrief an bestimmte Adresse; **straight** ~ *Kreditbrief, dessen Gültigkeit sofort nach Finanzierung der darin spezifizierten Waren erlischt*; **traveler's** ~ Reisekreditbrief; **unconfirmed** ~ unbestätigtes Akkreditiv; **to cash a** ~ e–n Kreditbrief einlösen; **to confirm a** ~ ein Akkreditiv bestätigen; **to open a** ~ → *to open*.

letting Vermietung *f*, Verpachtung *f*; ~ **out** Zuschlagserteilung bei Submission; ~ **(out) of contracts** Untervergabe; ~ **out to hire** Vermietung von bewegl Sachen; ~ **scheme** Projekt e–r Mietwohnungsanlage; ~ **value** Mietwert (*e–r Wohnung*); ~ **with board or attendance** möbl Zimmervermietung mit Pension bzw Bedienung; **shorthold** ~ → *shorthold*.

level *s* gleiche Höhe *f*, Maßstab *m*, Niveau *n*; Stufe der Strafbemessung; ~ **of efficiency** Leistungsgrad; ~ **of employment** Beschäftigungsstand; ~ **of incomes** Einkommensniveau; ~ **of invention** Erfindungshöhe; ~ **of organization** Organisationsstufe; ~ **of output** Produktionsstand; ~ **of performance** Leistungsstand; **at government** ~ auf Regierungsebene; **bargain** ~ niedrigster Kurs; **inventive** ~ Erfindungshöhe; **prewar** ~ Vorkriegsstand; **price** ~ → *price (1)*.

level *v* ausgleichen, nivellieren; ~ **down** nach unten nivellieren; ~ **up** nach oben ausgleichen.

leverage Leverage *n*, Hebelwirkung *f*, Verschuldungshebel *n*, Maß der Fremdfinanzierung; Einfluß *m*, verdeckte Beeinflussung; Verhältnis *n* von Obligationen und Vorzugsaktien zu Stammaktien; ~ **fund** Risiko-Investmentfonds; ~ **stock** Stammaktien bei großem Anteil an Vorzugsaktien (*daher Hebelwirkung auf Ertrag*); **optimal** ~ optimaler Verschuldungsgrad.

leveraged buyout durch Leihkapital finanzierter Aufkauf (*von Gesellschaften*), Unternehmenserwerb unter Ausnutzung des Leverage-Effekts.

levered verschuldet.

leviable veranlagungsfähig, einhebbar, pfändbar.

levitical degress als Ehehindernis geltende Verwandtschaftsgrade *m|pl.*

levy *s* Beschlagnahme *f*, Pfändung *f*, Pfandverwertung *f*; gesetzliche Feststellung *f* der Steuern und Abgaben, Steuersatz *m*, Steuerveranlagung *f*, Besteuerung *f*, Umlage *f*; Eintreibung *f*; ~ **court** Verwaltungsgericht, Verwaltungsbehörde; Steueraufsichtsbehörde; ~ **of distress** → *distress* (*1*); ~ **of execution** Pfändung; ~ **of taxes** Besteuerung; **agricultural** ~ Abschöpfung (*EG*); **betterment** ~ kommunale Zusatzabgabe für Erschließungen; **capital** ~ Kapitalabgabe; **capital gains** ~ Kapitalzuwachssteuer; **equitable** ~ vorläufige Beschlagnahme; **property** ~ → *property*; **subsequent** ~ **of duties** Nacherhebung von Zöllen; **wrongful** ~ widerrechtliche Pfändung (*von Sachen e–s Dritten*).

levy *v* auferlegen, erheben, veranlagen, kassieren; pfänden, umlegen; ~ **a fine** e–e Geldstrafe auferlegen; ~ **by deduction at source** Quellenbesteuerung vornehmen; ~ **by direct assessment** (*zur Einkommensteuer*) veranlagen; ~ **distress** die Zwangsvollstreckung betreiben; beschlagnahmen, pfänden; ~ **execution against s. o.** die Zwangsvollstreckung gegen jmdn betreiben; bei jmdm pfänden lassen.

lewd unzüchtig; ~ **and lascivious cohabition** (*unzüchtiges*) Konkubinat.

lewdness Unzucht *f*; **open** ~ öffentlich (anstößiges) unzüchtiges Verhalten.

liability (*pl liabilities* = ~**ies** *in alphabetischer Reihenfolge dem Singular gleichgestellt*) Haftung *f* (= *H bzw h*), Verbindlichkeit *f*, Obligation *f*, Verpflichtung *f*, Schuld *f*, Verantwortlichkeit *f*, Haftpflicht *f*; Passivposten *m*, Schuldposten *m*; ~ **account** Passivkonto; ~**ies adjustment** Schuldenregelung (*in Kriegszeiten*); ~ **bond** Verpflichtungsschein; ~ **certificate** Vollständigkeitserklärung; ~ **coverage** *H*–ssumme; ~ **created by statute** gesetzliche *H*; ~ **for animals** Tierhalter*h*; ~ **for breach of duty** *H* für Verletzung e–r Pflicht; ~ **for chattels** Waren-Verkehrssicherungspflicht, Produzentenhaftung; ~ **for compensation** (Schadens)-Ersatzpflicht; ~ **for costs** Kosten*h*; ~ **for damages** Schadens*h*, *H* auf Schadenersatz; ~ **for debts** Schulden*h*; ~ **for defective equipment** *H* für schadhafte Arbeitsgeräte und Einrichtungen; ~ **for defects** Mängel*h*; ~ **for fault** Verschuldens*h*; ~ **for faults** Mängel*h*; ~ **for loss** *H* für Schaden; ~ **for manufactured products** Produzenten*h*; ~ **in solido** gesamtschuldnerische *H*; ~ **in tort** *H* aus unerlaubter Handlung; ~**ies incurred** eingegangene Verpflichtungen; ~ **insurance** → *insurance;* ~ **of an official** Beamten*h*; ~ **of contributory** *H* des nachschußpflichtigen Gesellschafters; ~ **of drawer** (*Wechsel*) Aussteller*h*; ~ **of indorser** (*Wechsel*) Indossanten*h*; ~ **of shipowner(s)** Reederhaftung; ~ **of stockholders** = *stockholders'* ~ → *stockholder*; ~ **of the estate** Nachlaßverbindlichkeiten; ~ **on account of acceptances** Akzeptverbindlichkeiten; ~ **on claims outstanding** Schadensreserve, Rückstellungen für ausstehende Verpflichtungen; ~ **over** Regreßpflicht; ~**ies payable on demand** täglich fällige Verbindlichkeiten, Sichtverbindlichkeiten; ~ **regardless of fault** *H* unabhängig vom Verschulden, Gefährdungs*h*; ~ **regime** *H*–sregelungen, *H*–ssystem; ~ **side** Passivseite (*Bilanz*); ~ **to account** Rechenschaftspflicht, Rechnungslegungspflicht; ~ **to contribute** Beitragspflicht, Nachschußpflicht; ~ **to discover** Auskunftspflicht, Vorlagepflicht; ~ **to indemnify** Schadenersatzpflicht; ~ **to inform**

Anzeigepflicht, Meldepflicht (*Verbrechen*); ~ **to insure** Versicherungszwang; ~ **to maintain** Unterhaltspflicht; ~ **to make good a loss** Schadenersatzpflicht; ~ **to provide maintenance** Unterhaltspflicht; ~ **to tax** Steuerpflicht, steuerliche *H*; **absolute** ~ strenge *H*; *H* ohne Verschulden, Gefährdungs*h*; **acceptance** ~ (Wechsel-)-Akzeptverpflichtung; **accounting** ~ Rechnungslegungsverpflichtung; **accrued** ~ antizipative Passiva; Rückstellung(en); **actual** ~ unbedingte Verbindlichkeit; **apportionment of** ~ Festlegung von *H–s*quoten; **assets and ~ies** Aktiva und Passiva; **assumption of** ~ Schuldenübernahme; **bank** ~ Bankverbindlichkeit; **business** ~ geschäftliche *H*; **~ies** Geschäftsschulden; **capacity to incur** ~ Geschäftsfähigkeit; **civil** ~ zivilrechtliche *H*; **collective** ~ Kollektiv*h*; **contingent** ~ Ausfall*h*, Eventualverpflichtung; **contractual** ~ vertragliche Verpflichtung, Vertrags*h*; **corporate** ~ Verbindlichkeit(en) e–r Körperschaft, körperschaftliche *H*; **criminal** ~ strafrechtliche Verantwortlichkeit, Zurechnungsfähigkeit; **current ~ies** kurzfristige Verbindlichkeiten; **deposit ~ies** → *deposit*; **deferred ~ies** im voraus eingegangene (*zunächst passivierte*) Einnahmen, aufgeschobene (*gestundete*) Schulden; **direct** ~ unmittelbare *H*; unbedingte Verbindlichkeit, unbestrittene V.; **discharge of a** ~ Erfüllung e–r Verpflichtung; **employer's ~ insurance** → *insurance*; **endorser's** ~ → *indorser*; **escape** ~ der Verantwortung entrinnen; **exclusion of** ~ *H–s*ausschluß; **exemption from** ~ → *exemption;* **existing ~ies** → *existing;* **fixed** ~ langfristige fundierte Verbindlichkeit; **floating** ~ aufschiebend bedingte Verbindlichkeit; **foreign ~ies** Auslandsverbindlichkeiten; **hotchpot** ~ Ausgleichspflicht (*Erbrecht*); **indirect** ~ Eventualverbindlichkeit; **individual** ~ persönliche *H*; **intercompany** ~ Konzernverbindlichkeit(en); **internal ~ies** Inlandsverbindlichkeiten; **joint** ~ gemeinsame Verbindlichkeit, gemeinsame *H*; **joint and several** ~ → *joint and several*; **judgment ~ies** vollstreckbare Verbindlichkeiten (*aus Urteilen*); **legal** ~ *H*, Haftpflicht; rechtliche Verpflichtung, gesetzliche *H*; **limited** ~ beschränkte *H*; **limited ~ company** → *company;* **limited tax** ~ → *tax;* **long term ~ies** langfristige Verbindlichkeiten; **matured** ~ fällige Schuld; überfällige Schuld; **monetary ~ies** Geldschulden; **non-contractual** ~ außervertragliche *H*; **non-monetary ~ies** Verbindlichkeiten außer Geldschulden; **outstanding ~ies** *bil* Verbindlichkeiten; **parental** ~ elterliche *H*; **personal** ~ persönliche *H*; **primary** ~ unmittelbare Verpflichtung; **private** ~ persönliche *H*; **product** ~ → *product;* **professional** ~ → *professional;* **public** ~ allgemeine Haftpflicht; **release from** ~ Entlassung aus *H*; **representative's** ~ Repräsentanten*h*; **reserve** ~ → *reserve*; **secondary** ~ sekundäre Verbindlichkeit, subsidiäre *H*, Eventualverbindlichkeit, Ausfall*h*; **secured ~ies** gesicherte Verbindlichkeiten; **several** ~ individuelle Verpflichtung, individuelle *H*, *auch*: samtverbindliche *H eines Mitschuldners*; **shareholders'** ~ Einzahlungspflicht der Aktionäre, Forderungen an die Aktionäre; **statutory** ~ gesetzliche *H*; **strict** ~ strenge *H*, *H* ohne Verschulden, Gefährdungs*h*; strafrechtliche Haftung, ohne daß Vorsatz bewiesen werden muß; **suspense** ~ transitorische Passiva; **tax ~ies** Steuerschuld; **tortious** ~ *H* aus unerlaubter Handlung, deliktische *H*; **unlimited** ~ unbeschränkte *H*; **unsecured** ~ ungesicherte Verbindlichkeit, gewöhnliche Konkursforderung, nicht bevorrechtigte Forderung; **vicarious** ~ *H* für Dritte, *H* für Verschulden Dritter;

(*Erfüllungsgehilfen, Verrichtungsgehilfen*); stellvertretende *H.*

liable verantwortlich, haftbar, haftpflichtig, verpflichtet; ~ **by estoppel** haftbar aus Rechtsschein; ~ **for compensation** schadenersatzpflichtig; ~ **for damages** schadenersatzpflichtig; ~ **in solidum** samtverbindlich haftbar; **criminally** ~strafrechtlich haftbar, ~ **in the second degree** subsidiär verpflichtet, subsidiär haftbar; ~ **to account** rechenschaftspflichtig; ~ **to be seized** beschlagnahmefähig; ~ **to commission** provisionspflichtig; ~ **to contribution** beitragspflichtig, nachschußpflichtig; ~ **to duty** zollpflichtig; ~ **to execution** der Zwangsvollstreckung unterliegend; ~ **to maintain** unterhaltspflichtig; ~ **to pay** zahlungspflichtig; ~ **to recourse** → *recourse*; ~ **to stamp duty** → *stamp*; **civilly** ~ zivilrechtlich haftbar; **criminally** ~ strafrechtlich haftbar, strafbar; **individually** ~ persönlich haftbar; **jointly** ~ gemeinsam haftbar, *auch*: samtverbindlich, gesamtschuldnerisch; **jointly and severally** ~ samtverbindlich, gesamtschuldnerisch; **secondarily** ~ subsidiär haftbar, verpflichtet; **severally** ~ einzeln haftbar (*nicht notwendigerweise samtverbindlich*); **to be** ~ **to prosecution** sich strafbar machen; **to be** ~ **to taxation** steuerpflichtig sein; **to be vicariously** ~ für (Verschulden) Dritte(r) einstehen müssen; **to become** ~ **on a bill** aus e–m Wechsel verpflichtet werden, wechselrechtlich haften.

liaison Verbindung *f* Anlaufstelle *f*; ~ **office** Verbindungsstelle, V.-büro.

libel *s* Klage *f* (*im Seerechtsverfahren*; *scot*: *allgemein*); schriftliche Beleidigung *f*, *Ehrverletzung in schriftlicher oder anderer dauerhafter Form* (*Druck, Bild, Tonträger ua*); Verleumdung *f*, üble Nachrede *f*, kreditschädigende unwahre Angaben *f/pl*; ~ **on administration of justice** Justizverleumdung; **action for** ~ Verleumdungsklage; **blasphemous** ~ gotteslästerliche Veröffentlichung; **criminal** ~ strafbare Verleumdung; **defamatory** ~ Verleumdung in Schrift oder Druck; **innuendo in** ~ beleidigende Andeutungen; **obscene** ~ unzüchtige Veröffentlichung; **publication of** ~ → *publication*; **seditious** ~ staatsgefährdende Veröffentlichung, hochverräterische (*bzw majestätsbeleidigende*) Veröffentlichung; **trade** ~ → *trade*.

libel *v* (*schriftlich usw vgl libel s*) beleidigen, verleumden; vorläufig sicherstellen (*Seerecht*).

libelant Kläger *m* (*Kirchenrecht, Seerecht*).

libelee Beklagter *m* (*Kirchenrecht, Seerecht*).

libeller Verleumder *m*, Verfasser *m* e–r Schmähschrift.

libel(l)ous verleumderisch, beleidigend (*vgl libel*); ~ **per quod** zweideutig (*verleumderisch nur, wenn der Beleidigungscharakter bewiesen wird*); ~ **per se** offensichtlich beleidigend (*ohne Beweislast*).

liberal freisinnig, freigebig, großzügig, liberal; ~ **arts** Geisteswissenschaften; ~ **construction** → *construction* (2); ~ **interpretation** → *interpretation;* ~ **profession** → *profession*; ~ **system of public schools** allgemein zugängliche Schulen; ~ **trade policies** liberale Handelspolitik.

liberalisation of trade Liberalisierung *f* des Handels.

liberalism Liberalismus *m*.

liberality Freisinnigkeit *f*, Freigebigkeit *f*.

liberate befreien; aus der Haft entlassen.

liberation Befreiung *f*, Freilassung *f*, Erlöschen e–r Schuldverpflichtung.

liberator Befreier *m*.

libertas Freiheit *f*, Privileg *n*, Vorrecht *n*.

liberty Freiheit *f*, Privileg *n*, Vorrecht *n*; (*pl liberties* = ~**ies** *alphabetisch wie Singular eingeordnet*); pfändungsfreie Bezirke *m/pl*; Zudringlichkeit *f/pl*; unzuchtähnliche Handlungen *fpl*, Ehewidrigkeit *f*; ~ **loan bonds** *US* Kriegsanleihen (*1917–19*); ~ **of a port** Hafenanlauferlaubnis; ~ **of action** Handlungsfreiheit; ~ **of conscience** Gewissensfreiheit; ~ **of contract** Vertragsfreiheit; Kontrahierungsfreiheit; ~ **of craft** Gewerbefreiheit; ~ **of speech** Redefreiheit; ~ **of the globe** geographisch unbeschränkter Versicherungsschutz; Berechtigung, sämtliche Häfen anzulaufen; ~ **of the press** Pressefreiheit; ~ **of the rules** Wohnen im festgelegten Bezirk außerhalb der Haftanstalt; ~ **of the subject** Untertanenfreiheit; ~ **of trade** Handelsfreiheit, Gewerbefreiheit; ~ **to apply** Antragstellung bleibt der Partei vorbehalten; ~ **to average** das Recht der Durchschnittsberechtigung der Liegetage; ~ **to call** (Hafen) Anlaufpflicht; ~ **to hold pleas** grundherrschaftliche Gerichtsbarkeit; ~ **to shift** Berechtigung, den Ankerplatz (*im gleichen Ankergebiet*) zu ändern; **chartered ~ies** verbriefte Freiheitsrechte; **civil** ~ Freiheit der Person; **civil ~ies** Bürgerrechte, Grundrechte; **contractual** ~ Vertragsfreiheit; **deprivation of** ~ Freiheitsentziehung; **natural** ~ natürliche Freiheit, Freiheit der Person; **personal** ~ persönliche Freiheit; **political** ~ staatsbürgerliche Freiheit, Bürgerrecht; **religious** ~ Religionsfreiheit; **social** ~ gesellschaftlich gebundene Freiheit.

LIBOR → *London interbank offered rate.*

licence (*US: license*) *s* Erlaubnis *f*, Ermächtigung *f*, Konzession *f*, Lizenz *f*, Zulassung *f*, Befähigungsnachweis *m*, Handlungsfreiheit *f*; bedingter Straferlaß *m*; ~ **agreement** Lizenzvertrag; ~ **by estoppel** Gestattung aus vorangegangener Duldung; ~ **collections** Inkasso von Konzessionsabgaben; ~ **conditions** Auflagen bei bedingtem Straferlaß; ~ **confiscation** Beschlagnahme des Führerscheins, Einziehung d. F.; ~ **duty** Lizenzgebühr; ~ **fee** Lizenzgebühr, einmalige Lizenzabgabe, Konzessionsabgabe; ~ **for exports** Ausfuhrgenehmigung; ~ **holder** Lizenzinhaber; ~ **in amortization** Erlaubnis zur Übertragung e–s Grundstücks in Kirchenbesitz; ~ **in mortmain** *staatliche e–r Körperschaft gewährte Erlaubnis, Grundstückseigentum zu haben und zu übertragen;* ~ **of law** anwaltschaftliche Zulassung; ~ **of qualification** Arbeitserlaubnis, Befähigungsschein; ~ **of right** Zwangslizenz; ~ **plate** Nummernschild, amtliches Kennzeichen; ~ **tax** → *tax*; ~ **to assign** Erlaubnis zur Weiter- bzw Untervermietung; ~ **to carry fire-arms** Waffenschein; ~ **to carry on a trade** Gewerbeschein; **L~ to Convocation** staatlicher Genehmigungszwang für Beschlüsse der Kirchenversammlung; ~ **to lessee to make alterations** Berichtigung des Pächters zur Vornahme von Änderungen; ~ **to manufacture** Herstellungslizenz; ~ **to marry** = *marriage licence qv*; ~ **to operate** Zulassung zum Geschäftsbetrieb; ~ **to practice medicine** Approbation; ~ **to print** Druckerlaubnis, Abdrucksrecht; ~ **to record** Gestattung der Aufzeichnung (*auf mechanischem oder elektronischem Wege*); ~ **to subdemise by way of mortgage** Erlaubnis zur Verpfändung d. Pachtrechts (*zur Bestellung e–r nachrangigen Hypothek*); ~ **to underlet** Untervermietungserlaubnis; ~ **to use** Benutzungslizenz; ~ **under a patent** Patentlizenz; **bare patent** ~ Patentlizenz ohne technische Nebenleistungen; **blox** ~ *pat* En-bloc-Lizenz, Pauschal-Lizenz; **broadcast receiving** ~ Radioempfangserlaubnis; **broadcast transmitting** ~ (Radio)Sendeerlaubnis; **building** ~ → *building;* **business** ~ Gewerbekonzession; **cinemas and films** ~ Filmvorführungskonzession; **clean patent** ~ Patentlizenz ohne technische Nebenleistungen;

common ~ einfache kirchl Heiratserlaubnis; **compulsory** ~ Zwangslizenz; *pauschale Abgeltung von Urheberrechten an TV Programmen mit freiem Einspeisungsrecht*; **contractual** ~ Lizenz, vertragliche Erlaubnis; **cross** **~s** gegenseitige Lizenzen, Austausch von Lizenzen; **cross ~ agreement** Lizenzabkommen auf Gegenseitigkeit; **dog** ~ Hundehaltererlaubnis; **driving (driver's)** → *driving*; **excise** ~ *brit Lizenz zur Herstellung oder Verkauf von Waren gegen Bezahlung e–r besonderen Steuer*; Schankkonzession; **exclusive** ~ ausschließliche Lizenz; **executory** ~ noch nicht auszuübende Lizenz; **exploitation of a** ~ Lizenzverwertung; **export** ~ Ausfuhr(Sonder)genehmigung; **express** ~ ausdrücklich gewährte Lizenz; **free** ~ Freilizenz; **game** ~ Jagdschein; Jagderlaubnis; **gratuitous** ~ unentgeltliche Nutzungserlaubnis; **gun** ~ Waffenschein; **hack** ~ *US* Taxikonzession; **hawker's** ~ → *hawker*; **high** ~ Sonderkonzession; **holder of a** ~ → *holder*; **implied** ~ stillschweigend gewährte Lizenz; **import** ~ Einfuhrlizenz, Einfuhrerlaubnis; **individual** ~ Einzelgenehmigung; **interim** ~ vorläufige Konzession; **issue of** **~s** Konzessionserteilung; **justices'** ~ *brit* Konzession zum Verkauf von alkoholischen Getränken; **letter of** ~ → *letter*; **manufactured under** ~ Lizenzbau; **manufacturing** ~ Herstellungslizenz; **marriage** ~ staatliche Heiratserlaubnis; **mining** ~ Mutung, Bergwerkskonzession; **motor vehicles** ~ Fahrerlaubnis, Betriebserlaubnis für Kraftfahrzeuge; **non-exclusive** ~ einfache Lizenz; **off** ~ Konzession zum Verkauf alkoholischer Getränke über die Straße; **on** ~ Schankkonzession; **operating** ~ Betriebserlaubnis; **ordinary** ~ einfache Lizenz; **pedlar's** ~ Wandergewerbeschein; **per unit** ~ Stücklizenz; **plenary** ~ uneingeschränkte Erlaubnis; **registrar's** ~ standesamtliche Heiratserlaubnis; **restricted** ~ beschränkte Lizenzgebühr; **rod** ~ Angelschein (*für geschützte Fischarten*); **royalty-free** ~ gebührenfreie Lizenzen; **semi-exclusive** ~ = *sole* ~*qv*; **simple** ~ jederzeit widerrufliche Erlaubnis; **sole** ~ ausschließliche Lizenz mit Herstellungs- und Vertriebsvorbehalt des Lizenzgebers; **special** ~ (kirchl) Sonderheiratserlaubnis (*ohne Aufgebot*); **subject to** ~ → *subject*; **to take out a** ~ sich e–e Erlaubnis *bzw* Konzession beschaffen; **trade mark** ~ Warenzeichenlizenz; **trading** ~ Gewerbeschein, Handelserlaubnis; **transfer** ~ Transferbewilligung; **unrestricted** ~ unbeschränkte Lizenz.

license *v* e–e Erlaubnis erteilen, e–e Konzession geben, lizenzieren, gestatten, berechtigen, genehmigen, konzessionieren; zulassen, öffentlich bestellen; **~d company** konzessionierte Gesellschaft; **~d deposit-taker** amtlich zugelassener Hinterleger; **~d hawker** behördlich zugelassener Marktverkäufer; **~d person** Konzessionsinhaber; **~d premises** → *premises*; **~d victualler** *Inhaber e–r Konzession zum Vertrieb alkoholischer Getränke*.

license = *licence qv*.

licensee Lizenzinhaber *m* (-in *f*), Lizenznehmer *m* (*-in f*), Konzessionsinhaber *m* (*-in f*), (Benutzungs)Berechtigter; ~ **by invitation** zutrittsberechtigte Person; **bare** ~ *lediglich* geduldeter Benutzer; **exclusive** ~ Inhaber e–r Ausschließlichkeitslizenz; **joint** ~ Mitinhaber e–r Lizenz; **mere** ~ = *bare* ~ *qv*; **occupying** ~ berechtigter vertragsloser Wohnungsinhaber; **sole** ~ alleiniger Lizenzinhaber.

licensing Lizenzgewährung *f*, Zulassung *f*, Konzessionierung *f*; **L~ Act** Gesetz über den Vertrieb alkoholischer Getränke; Gewerbegenehmigungsgesetz; Druckerlaubnisvorschriften; ~ **agency** Konzessionierungsbehörde; ~ **authority**

Behörde für Konzessionierung von Alkoholvertrieb an Verbraucher; ~ **body** Lizenzerteilungsstelle, Konzessionsvergabestelle; ~ **hours** Ausschankzeiten; ~ **justices** Friedensrichter in ihrer Eigenschaft als Schankkonzessionsbehörde; ~ **magistrate** Beamter für Erteilung von Konzessionen; ~ **of a meeting** Versammlungserlaubnis(erteilung); ~ **of premises** jährliche gerichtliche Schankkonzessionsvergabe; ~ **ordinance** Lizenzgewährung; ~ **power** Konzessionsbefugnis; ~ **requirements** gewerbepolizeiliche Voraussetzungen; ~ **test** Zulassungsprüfung; **compulsory** ~ Zwangslizenzgewährung; **cross** ~ gegenseitige Lizenzgewährung; Austausch von Sonderrechten zw. Programmanbietern; **multiple** ~ Erteilung von Parallellizenzen *an mehrere Lizenznehmer*, Zusammenfassung von Lizenzen.

licensor Konzessionserteiler *m*, Lizenzgeber *m*.

licentiate Inhaber *m* e–r Zulassung (*zur Ausübung e–r freiberuflichen Tätigkeit*), Lizentiat *m*.

licentiousness gewissenlose Willkür *f*, Zügellosigkeit *f*, Unzüchtigkeit *f*.

licet gesetzlich zulässig, erlaubt.

licitation Versteigerungsausgebot *n*; Auseinandersetzungsversteigerung *f*, Teilungsversteigerung *f*.

licking of thumbs *hist* (*Daumenlekken*) *Förmlichkeiten bei Vertragseinigung*.

lie *s* Lüge *f*; ~ **detector** Lügendetektor; **white** ~ Notlüge.

lie *v* liegen, vorhanden sein, zulässig sein; ~ **in franchise** herrenlos sein; ~ **in grant** nur urkundlich (*nicht physisch*) übertragbar sein; ~ **in livery** (*nur*) durch Besitzübergabe übertragbar sein; ~ **in wait** im Hinterhalt liegen; ~ **on the file** das Verfahren ruhen lassen; ~ **open to public inspection** zur öffentlichen Einsichtnahme ausliegen; ~ **over** aufgeschoben werden, überfällig sein (Wechsel); ~ **to** angrenzen, beiliegen; ~ **under suspicion** unter Verdacht stehen; **an action will not** ~ e–e Klage ist unzulässig; **no appeal shall** ~ ein Rechtsmittel ist nicht gegeben.

liege *adj* lehnspflichtig.

liege Leh(e)nsmann *m*, Vasall *m*; ~ **homage** Fürstenhuldigung; ~ **lord** Leh(e)nsherr; ~ **people** Untertanen.

liegeman Leh(e)nsmann *m*.

lien Pfandrecht *n* (= *Pfr*); dingliche Belastung *f*, Zurückbehaltungsrecht *n* (an Sachen); dingliche Sicherheit *f*; ~ **account** Geltendmachung des Pfandbetrags; ~ **by agreement** Vertrags*pfr*; ~ **attachment** Pfändungs*pfr* (*durch Arrestvollziehung*); ~ **by levy (of execution)** Pfändungs*pfr*; ~ **by operation of law** gesetzliches *Pfr*; ~ **covenant** Zusicherung des Nichtbestehens e–r dinglichen Belastung; ~ **creditor** dinglich gesicherter Gläubiger, Pfandgläubiger; ~ **holder** Pfandgläubiger, Zurückbehaltungsberechtiger; ~ **of a covenant** Eingangsformel e–r Vertragsurkunde; ~ **of holder** *Pfr* des Wechselinhabers; ~ **on a bill** *Pfr* an e–m Wechsel; ~ **on property** Grundstückslast; ~ **on real estate** Grund*pfr*; ~ **perfected** *Pfr* bei Pfandreife; **agricultural** ~ Ernte*pfr*; **artisan's** ~ Unternehmer*pfr* (*des Handwerkers*); **attorney's charging** ~ *Pfr* des Anwalts am Streitgegenstand; **attorney's retaining** ~ Zurückbehaltungsrecht des Anwalts an den Urkunden des Mandanten; **bailee's** ~ Verwahrer*pfr*; **carrier's** ~ *Pfr* des Frachtführers; **charging** ~ *Pfr* an bestimmten Sachen, dingliche Sicherung; Aktenzurückbehaltungsrecht; **common-law** ~ gesetzl Zurückbehaltungsrecht an Sachen; **concurrent** ~**s** gleichrangige *Pfr-e*; **consummate** ~ Vollstreckungs*pfr* auf Grund e–s rechtskräftigen Titels; **conventional** ~ Vertrags*pfr*, vertragliches Besitz*pfr*; **crop** ~ → *crop;* **enforcement of a** ~ Verwertung e–s Pfandes; **equitable** ~ Sicherungszusage (*an den nicht besitzenden Gläubiger*), vorläufiges Sicherungsrecht, besitzloses *Pfr*; **execution** ~ Vollstreckungs*pfr*, Zwangshypothek; **factor's** ~ Kommissionärs*pfr*; **frist** ~ erstrangiges *Pfr*; **floating** ~ Globalverpfändung (*einschl. späterer Zugänge*); **general** ~ allgemeines Zurückbehaltungsrecht (*wegen aller Forderungen aus dem Mandatsverhältnis bzw der Geschäftsbeziehung*); **implied** ~ gesetzlich vermutetes *Pfr*, stillschweigend begründetes *Pfr*; **inchoate** ~ *Pfr* auf Grund e–s noch nicht rechtskräftigen Titels; **innkeeper's** ~ *Pfr* des Gastwirts (*am eingebrachten Gut des Gastes*); **involuntary** ~ Zwangs*pfr*, Vollstreckungs*pfr*; **judgment** ~ Zwangshypothek; **judicial** ~ Vollstreckungs*pfr*; **junior** ~ nachrangiges *Pfr*; **landlord's** ~ Vermieter*pfr*; **lessor's** ~ Vermieter-/Verpächter*pfr*; **maritime** ~ Schiffs*pfr* (*an Schiff und Ladung*); **materialman's** ~ *Pfr* des Baustofflieferanten; **mechanic's** ~ gesetzliches Bauhandwerker*pfr*; *canad auch*: Bauwerkssicherungshypothek; **mercantile** ~ kaufmännisches Zurückbehaltungsrecht, kaufmännisches *Pfr*; **multiple** ~ Gesamt*pfr*; **municipal** ~ → *municipal*; **official receiver's** ~ Sequester*pfr* (für Kosten); **particular** ~ *Pfr* an e–r bestimmten Sache; Unternehmer*pfr*, spezielles *Pfr*, konkretes *Pfr*; **possessory** ~ Besitzpfand; **prior** ~ rangbesseres (*meist erstrangiges*) *Pfr*; **senior** ~ rangbesseres *Pfr*, älteres *Pfr*; **retaining** ~ Zurückbehaltungsrecht; **second** ~ *Pfr* an zweiter Rangstelle; **secret** ~ besitzloses, nicht offengelegtes Verkäufer*pfr* am (*bewegl*) Kaufgegenstand bis zur Kaufpreiszahlung; **seller's** ~ Zurückbehaltungsrecht des Verkäufers; **special** ~ *Pfr* an e–r bestimmten Sache *bzw e–r bestimmten Forderung*; **specific** ~ = *special* ~ *qv*; **statutory** ~ gesetzliches *Pfr*; **statutory factor's** ~ gesetzl. *Pfr* am Konsignationslager; **unpaid seller's** ~ Zurückbehaltungsrecht des Verkäufers; **vendor's** ~ Zurückbehaltungsrecht des Verkäufers; gesetzl *Pfr* des Verkäufers am aufgelassenen Grundstück (*für restl Kaufpreis*); **warehouseman's** ~ Lagerhalter*pfr*.

lienee Eigentümer *m* der mit e–m Pfandrecht (*lien qv*) belasteten Sache.

lienor Pfandgläubiger *m*; Zurückbehaltungsberechtigter *m*.

lieu Ort*m*, Stelle *f*; ~ **lands** Ersatzgrundstücke (*Enteignungsrecht*); ~ **tax** Ersatzsteuer; **in** ~ **of** an Stelle von, anstatt; **in** ~ **of an oath** an Eides Statt; **in** ~ **of payment** an Zahlungs Statt.

life Leben *n*, Lebensdauer *f*, Gültigkeitsdauer, Laufzeit *f*; ~ **and limb** Leib und Leben; ~ **annuitant** Leibrentenempfänger; ~ **annuity** Leibrente(nvertrag); ~ **assurance** Lebensversicherung (*vgl. assurance*); ~ **-belt** Kreditsicherheit; ~ **certificate** Lebensbescheinigung; ~ **beneficiary** lebenslang Begünstigter; ~ **care contract** lebenslänglicher Pflegevertrag; ~ **contingence** *ins* Lebensrisiko; ~ **contract** Vertrag auf Lebenszeit; ~ **director** lebenslang bestelltes Verwaltungsratsmitglied; ~**-estate** lebenslängliches Herrschaftsrecht am Grundstück, Grundstücksnießbrauch; ~ **expectancy** Lebenserwartung; ~ **-hold** lebenslange Grundpacht; ~ **imprisonment** lebenslängl Freiheitsstrafe; ~ **in being** verbleibende Lebenszeit *e–s Bedachten*; ~ **insurance** → *life insurance*; ~ **interest** → *life interest*; ~ **land** Pachtung auf Lebenszeit; ~ **member** → *member*; ~**'s necessities** allgemeiner Lebensbedarf; ~ **of an agreement** Laufzeit e–s Vertrages; ~ **or lives in being** *Lebenszeit einer oder mehrerer beliebiger (bereits gezeugter) Personen (rule against perpetuities)*; ~ **peer** → *peer*; ~ **peerage** → *peerage*; ~ **policy** → *policy*; ~ **rent** Nießbrauch auf Lebenszeit; ~ **renter** (*le-*

benslänglicher) Nießbraucher; ~ **savings service** Rettungsdienst; ~ **sentence** lebenslängliche Freiheitsstrafe; ~ **table** Sterblichkeitstabelle; ~ **tenancy** = *tenancy for life qv*; ~ **tenant** = *tenant for life qv*; ~ **tenure** Grundpacht auf Lebenszeit, Amt auf Lebenszeit; ~ **time** Lebenszeit; Laufzeit; **conditions of** ~ Lebensbedingungen; **conjugal** ~ eheliche Lebensgemeinschaft; **during the** ~**time** zu Lebzeiten; **expectation of** ~ → *expectation;* **for** ~ lebenslang, auf Lebenszeit; **natural** ~ natürliche Lebenszeit e–s Menschen; **operating** ~ Nutzungsdauer; **physical** ~ Lebensdauer, Gesamtnutzungsdauer; **presumption of** ~ → *presumption*; **remaining useful** ~ Restnutzungsdauer; **station in** ~ → *station;* **service** ~ Nutzungsdauer; **useful** ~ (betriebsgewöhnliche) Nutzungsdauer, Brauchbarkeitsdauer.

lifeboat operation solidarische Stützungsaktion (*Banken*).

life insurance *vgl assurance*, Lebensversicherung *f* (= *Lv bzw lv*); ~ **premium** *Lv*–sprämie; ~ **premium tax relief** Steuervergünstigungen für *Lv*–sprämien; ~ **proceeds** *Lv*leistung; ~ **reserves** *Lv*fonds, *Lv*deckungsfonds; ~ **trust** *Lv* streuhandfonds; ~ **with profits** *Lv* mit Gewinnbeteiligung; ~ **without profits** *Lv* ohne Gewinnbeteiligung; **governmental** ~ *Lv* für Staatsangestellte; **group** ~ Gruppen*Lv*; **industrial** ~ → *insurance;* **key man** ~ *Lv* für Schlüsselkräfte; **joint** ~ wechselseitige Überlebensversicherung; **limited pay** ~ *Lv* mit abgekürzter Prämienzahlung; **mutual** ~ *Lv* auf Gegenseitigkeit; **ordinary** ~ (= *assurance*) Groß*lv*; *Lv auf den Todesfall;* **renewable term** ~ → *renewable*; **straight** ~ Versicherung auf den Todesfall; **whole** ~ Todesfallversicherung.

life interest dingl Recht auf Lebenszeit (*das eigene oder ein fremdes Leben*); lebenslanges Nießbrauchsrecht *n*, Nießbrauch *m*; ~ **to survivor** Nießbrauch für den überlebenden Ehegatten; **determinable** ~ auflösend bedingtes lebenslängliches Nutzungsrecht; **holder of a** ~ *etwa*: Vorerbe.

lifer Lebenslänglicher *m*, zu „lebenslänglich" Verurteilter; lebenslange Freiheitsstrafe.

lifo = *last-in-first-out* → *last*.

lift *v* aufheben, beseitigen, stehlen; ein Plagiat begehen, tilgen; ~ **a ban** ein Verbot aufheben; ~ **a promissory note** e–n Schuldschein (*bzw Solawechsel*) bezahlen (*oder durch andere Schuldurkunde ersetzen*), prolongieren; ~ **cattle** Vieh stehlen; ~ **the bar** die Verjährung unterbrechen.

lifter Langfinger *m*, Dieb *m*, Ladendieb *m*.

lifting Aufhebung *f*; Plagiat *n*, Stehlen *n*; ~ **the veil** gerichtl Prüfung innergesellschaftl Vorgänge; **shop** ~ → *shop*.

ligan über Bord geworfene *an Boje befestigte* Güter *n*|*pl*, Seewurf *m*.

light industrial concern Unternehmen der Leichtindustrie.

lighter Leichter *m*.

lighterage Leichtergeld *n*; Leichtertransportgewerbe *n*, das Leichtern.

lighterman Leichterschiffer *m*.

lighting Beleuchtung *f*; ~ **control** Beleuchtungskontrolle; ~ **control offender** Lichtsünder.

lights Lichtrecht *n*, Recht auf Sonnenlicht *n*, Recht gegen Verbauung *n*; **ancient** ~ gewohnheitsrechtl Lichtrecht (*nach 20 Jahren*).

like grade and quality etwa gleiche Beschaffenheit und Güte.

likely to cause danger gefährlich.

likewise ebenfalls, desgleichen.

limb Glied *n*, Körperteil *m*, *für die Wehrtauglichkeit* notwendiger Körperteil *m*.

limit *s* Grenze *f*, Limit *n*, Beschränkung *f*; ~ **of credit** Kreditlimit, Beleihungsgrenze; ~ **of indemnity** Versicherungssumme, Haftungsgrenze; ~ **order** → *order* (*2*); **age** ~ Altersgrenze, Mindestalter;

debt ~ → *debt;* **in** ~**s** Zutritt gestattet; **off** ~**s** *für Militärpersonen* gesperrt; **prescribed** ~ fester Grenzwert (Blutalkohol); **speed** ~ → *speed*; **time** ~ → *time*; **to fix a** ~ limitieren, ein Limit festsetzen; **upper** ~ Höchstgrenze, obere Grenze, Höchstsatz.

limit *v* begrenzen, limitieren, befristen, beschränken; ~ **a price** ein Preislimit setzen.

limitary einschränkend.

limitation Begrenzung *f*, gesetzl Begrenzung e-s Klagerechts; Beschränkung *f*, Einschränkung *f*, Verjährung *f*, Ersitzung *f*, beschränkte Haftpflicht *f*; ~ **in law** gesetzliche Begrenzung, auflösend bedingtes Nutzungsrecht; ~ **of actions** Verjährung, Klageausschlußfrist; ~ **of authority** Vollmachtsbeschränkung, Zuständigkeitsbeschränkung; ~ **of claims** Anspruchsverjährung; ~ **of damages** Höchstbeträge für Schadenersatz; ~ **of estate** zeitliche bzw inhaltliche Beschränkung e-s Herrschaftsrechts (Besitzrechts) am Grundstück; ~ **of imports** Einfuhrbeschränkung; ~ **of indebtedness** Verschuldungsgrenze; ~ **of jurisdiction** Beschränkung der Zuständigkeit; ~ **of liability** Haftungsbeschränkung, beschränkte Haftung; ~ **of prosecution** Verfolgungsverjährung; ~ **of sentence** Vollstreckungsverjährung; ~ **of time** Verjährung, Ausschlußfrist; ~ **period** Verjährungsfrist; Ausschlußfrist (*für Klage bzw Antragsstellung*); ~ **title** voller Rechtstitel (*unter Ausschluß aller Rechtsmängelansprüche*); ~ **over** Anwartschaft, Nacherbschaft; **collateral** ~ *aufschiebende Bedingung bei zeitlich beschränkten Nutzungsrechten*; **conditional** ~ *auflösende Bedingung bei Einräumung e-s zeitlich begrenzten Nutzungsrechts*; **contingent** ~ bedingte zeitliche Beschränkung; **executory** ~ rechtsgeschäftliche Beschränkung e-s zukünftigen dingl Rechts; **period of** ~ = *limitation period qv, supra*; **special** ~ ipso facto wirkende Beendigung e-s Nutzungsrechtes; **Statute of** ~ → *statute*; **statutory** ~ (gesetzliche) Verjährung(svorschriften); **structural** ~ strukturbedingte Beschränkung; **term of** ~ → *term;* **time of** ~ Klage(ausschluß)frist, Verjährung; **words of** → *words.*

limited beschränkt, begrenzt, limitiert; (*als Firmenzusatz seit 1980 = private company limited*); ~ **by guaranty** mit beschränkter Nachschußpflicht; ~ **by shares** mit beschränkter Haftung, auf die Einlage beschränkt; ~ **company** → *company*; ~ **criminal liability** verminderte Zurechnungsfähigkeit; ~ **liability** → *liability*; ~ **liability company** → *company*; ~ **life assets** Kapitalanlagegüter mit beschränkter Lebensdauer; ~ **owner's charge** → *charge*; ~ **power of appointment** beschränkte Befugnis zur Bevollmächtigung bzw Delegation; ~ **price store** Kleinpreisgeschäft, Billigwarenhaus; ~ **tax liability** → *tax*; ~ **warranty deed** *Auflassungsurkunde mit persönlich beschränkter Zusicherung der Nichtbeeinträchtigung des Erwerbers, vgl warranty deed* → *warranty.*

Lincoln's Inn (=) *eine der englischen Anwaltsinnungen.*

line Linie *f*, Strich *m*, Gerade *f*, Richtlinie *f*, Grenze *f*, Stamm *m*, Strecke *f*, Bahnlinie *f*, Omnibuslinienverkehr *m*, Städteverbindung *f*, Warensortiment *n*, Telefonleitung *f*; Verwandtschaftslinie *f*; (=) *Längenmaß* = $^1/_{12}$ *Zoll*; Höchstbetrag *m*, Zeichnungsgrenze *f*; ~**s and corners** Grenzlinien und ihre Winkel; ~ **and staff** hierarchische Verwaltungsgliederung; ~ **dropping** Aufgabe von Produktionszweigen (*im Händlerangebot*); ~ **of action** Handlungsweise, Vorgehen; ~ **of argument** Argumentation, Beweisführung; ~ **of argumentation** allgemeine Begründung; ~ **of business** Geschäftszweig; ~ **of conduct** Verhalten, Lebensführung; ~ **of credit** → *credit*; ~ **of danger** Gefahrensgrenze; ~ **of demarcation** Demarkationslinie; ~ **of deposit** durchschnittlicher Kreditsaldo e-s Depositenkontos; ~ **of duty** Dienst(art); ~ **of industry** Industriezweig; ~ **of shares** Aktienpaket, Aktienposten; ~ **of succession** Abstammungslinie; **above the** ~ *brit* ordentlicher Etatposten; **ascending** ~ aufsteigende Linie; **building** ~ → *building;* **collateral** ~ Seitenlinie; **continuous** ~ ununterbrochene Linie (*Straße*); **descending** ~ absteigende Linie; **direct** ~ gerade Linie; **dotted** ~ → *dotted*; **exchange** ~ Hauptanschluß; **extension** ~ Nebenanschluß; **feeder** ~ → *feeder*; **general** ~ Baulinie; **gross** ~ *ins* Höchstgrenze der Annahme; **guiding** ~ Leitlinie (*Straße*); **head** ~ Überschrift, Schlagzeile; **in** ~ **with** in Übereinstimmung mit; **in the** ~ **of duty** dienstlich, in Ausübung der dienstlichen Pflichten; **in the ascending** ~ in aufsteigender Linie; **in the collateral** ~ in der Seitenlinie; **in the descending** ~ in absteigender Linie; **in the direct** ~ in gerader Linie; **main** ~ Hauptstrecke; **maternal** ~ mütterliche Linie, Abstammung mütterlicherseits; **net** ~ *ins* Höchstgrenze des Selbstbehalts; **on a straight** ~ **basis** *linear* (*Abschreibung*); **one~-business** → *business*; **paternal** ~ väterliche Linie, Abstammung väterlicherseits; **private** ~ Privattelefon; **stage** ~ Städteverkehr (Bus); **subscriber's** ~ Teilnehmeranschluß; **to take a strong** ~ energisch vorgehen; **trunk** ~ → *trunk*.

lineage Geschlecht *n*, Abstammung *f*, Stammbaum *m*, Sippe *f*.

lineal linear, geradlinig, in gerader Linie.

lineup Gegenüberstellung *f* zur Identifizierung; Aufstellung *f* in e–r Reihe.

lining up financing Bereitstellung der Finanzierung.

link Band *n*, Verbindung *f*, Zwischenglied *n*, Verbindungsstück *n*; ~ **in the chain of title** Verbindungsstück (*Urkunde*) beim Eigentumsnachweis von Grundstücken; **causal** ~ Kausalzusammenhang.

linkage of risks Risikoverbindung *f*.

liquet es ist klar; es ergibt sich klar daraus; es ist schlüssig.

liquid flüssig, liquide, sofort greifbar.

liquidate liquidieren, abwickeln, auflösen, tilgen, e-e Schuldenregelung vornehmen; versilbern, glattstellen; ~ **a debt** e-e Schuld tilgen.

liquidated festgestellt, beziffert, (der Höhe nach) geklärt, bestimmt, geregelt, getilgt; ~ **account** feststehender Saldo; ~ **claim** ziffernmäßig bestimmte Forderung; ~ **damages** → *damages*.

liquidating | **agent** Liquidator, liquidierende Stelle; ~ **distribution** Masseverteilung; ~ **dividend** Liquidationsquote, Konkursquote.

liquidation Liquidation *f*; Verflüssigung *f*, Glattstellung *f*, Realisation *f*, Abwicklung *f*, Auflösung *f*, Tilgung *f*, Bezahlung *f*; ~ **account** → *account*; ~ **dividend** Liquidationsdividende, Schlußquote; ~ **of a fund** Auflösung e-s Fondsvermögens; ~ **of an annuity** Rentenablösung; ~ **of debts** Schuldentilgung; ~ **of holdings** Flüssigmachen von Kapitalanlagen; ~ **of speculations** Glattstellung, Spekulationsbeendigung; ~ **price** Liquidationspreis, Zwangsverkaufspreis; ~ **value** → *value*; **amicable** ~ stille Liquidation; **compulsory** ~ Zwangsliquidation, Gesellschaftskonkurs; **insolvent** ~ Gesellschaftskonkurs; **inventory** ~ Lagerabbau; **voluntary** ~ freiwillige Liquidation, stille Liquidation.

liquidator Liquidator *m*, Abwickler *m*; ~ **in voluntary winding-up** freiwillig bestellter Liquidator; ~ **in winding up by court** Konkursverwalter, Zwangsliquidator; **official** ~ gerichtlich bestellter Liquidator, Konkursverwalter; **pro-**

visional ~ Sequester, vorläufiger Liquidator.

liquidity Liquidität *f*, Flüssigkeit *f*; ~ **afflux** Liquiditätszustrom; ~ **margin** Liquiditätsspielraum; ~ **pooling** Liquiditätsausgleich; ~ **position** Liquiditätslage; ~ **provision** Liquiditätsvorsorge; ~ **ratio** Liquiditätsquote; ~ **reserves** Liquiditätsreserven; **efflux of** ~ Liquiditätsabfluß; **excess** ~ Überliquidität; **reduced** ~ Liquiditätseinengung, Liquiditätsschwierigkeiten; **world** ~ internationale Liquidität.

liquor alkoholisches Getränk *n*, Alkohol *m*; ~**s** Spirituosen; ~ **dealer** Getränkehandelskaufmann; ~ **licence** Schankkonzession; ~**-shop** Spirituosengeschäft; ~ **treaties** Verträge gegen Alkoholschmuggel.

lis pendens anhängiger Rechtsstreit *m*, Rechtshängigkeit *f*.

list *s* Liste *f*, Verzeichnis *n*, Aufstellung *f*; *exch* Kursblatt *n*, Liste *f* der börsenfähigen Wertpapiere; ~ **of assets** Masseverzeichnis (*Konkurs*); Nachlaßverzeichnis; ~ **of assets and liabilities** Finanzstatus; ~ **of creditors** Gläubigerverzeichnis; ~ **of documents** Anlagenliste von Urkunden; ~ **of electors** Wahlliste, Wählerliste; ~ **of foreign exchange** Devisenkurszettel; ~ **of members** Mitgliederverzeichnis, Liste der Gesellschafter *bzw* Aktionäre; ~ **of orders** Bestelliste; ~ **of precedency** (= *precedence*) Rangliste; ~ **of prices** Preisliste, Kursblatt; ~ **of quotations** Kursblatt, Kurszettel; ~ **of sailings** Liste der Abgangsdaten; ~ **of securities** Effektenliste; ~ **of the crew** Musterrolle; **L**~ **of World Heritage in Danger** „Liste des gefährdeten Erbes der Welt"; ~ **price** → *price* (*1*); **active** ~ Verzeichnis der aktiven Offiziere; **annual** ~ Jahresverzeichnis; **black** ~ → *black*; **cargo** ~ Ladeverzeichnis; **cause** ~ Terminkalender (*des Gerichts*); **check** ~ Kontrolliste; **commercial** ~ Sitzungsliste der Kammer für Handelssachen; **free** ~ Freiliste (Zoll); **industrial** ~ Kurszettel der Industrieaktien; **legal** ~ Liste mündelsicherer Anlagen; **nominal** ~ Namensverzeichnis; **official** ~ amtliches Kursblatt, Liste der börsenfähigen Effekten; **registration** ~ Wählerliste; **single** ~ Einheitsliste; **statutory** ~ gesetzl Verzeichnis (*mündelsicherer Anlagen*).

list *v* notieren, quotieren, in e-e Liste aufnehmen, verzeichnen, an der Börse einführen; ~ **officially** amtlich notieren; ~ **property with a broker** Makler beauftragen, Grundbesitz zu verkaufen.

lister Steuerbeamter *m* (*zur Erfassung des steuerpflichtigen Vermögens*).

listing Eintragung in e-r Liste; Festlegung der Sitzungsliste; Registrierung *f*, *exch* Zulassung *f* (*von Wertpapieren*), Börseneinführung *f*; Grundstücksmaklervertrag (*Verkauf bzw Vermietung*); ~ **of cases** Terminanberaumung, Terminierung; ~ **of property** *Verpflichtung, an jeden vom Immobilienmakler gebrachten Interessenten zum ausgesetzten Preis zu verkaufen*; ~ **of securities** Zulassung von Wertpapieren an der Börse; ~ **procedure** Börsenzulassungsverfahren; ~ **property** (*for taxation*) Aufstellung des Vermögens, Inventaraufstellung; ~ **section** Terminierungsabteilung (*Chancery Chambers*); **exclusive** ~ Ausschließlichkeitsauftrag e-s Immobilienmaklers (zum Verkauf); **multiple** ~ Anhandgeben e-s Grundstücks an mehrere Makler; **net** ~ *Grundstücksmaklervertrag mit Nettoangebot, Mehrerlös als Maklerprovision;* **official** ~ **notice** Zulassungsbescheid (*für Effekten an der Börse*); **open** ~ offener Maklervertrag (*Ggs: Alleinauftrag*); **real estate** ~ Beauftragung e-s Immobilienmaklers (*z. Verkauf bzw Vermietung*).

literal buchstäblich, wörtlich.

literalness Wörtlichkeit *f*, Buchstäblichkeit *f*; **legalistic** ~ formaljuristisches Kleben am Buchstaben des Gesetzes.

literary literarisch, schriftstellerisch, gebildet; ~ **activity** schriftstellerische Betätigung; ~ **composition** Schriftwerk (*Urheberrecht*); ~ **merit** eigenschöpferische Leistung in e-m Schriftwerk; ~ **piracy** → *piracy*; ~ **property** → *property*; ~ **work** Schriftwerk.

literate *adj* des Lesens und Schreibens kundig.

literatim wörtlich, buchstäblich.

lithograph Lithographie *f*, Steindruck *m*.

litigant (Prozeß)Partei *f*; Prozeßanwalt *m*, vorwiegend forensisch tätiger Anwalt; ~ **in person** der Prozeßführende (*bes der Kläger*) persönlich, die nicht vertretene Partei; **successful** ~ obsiegende Partei; **unassisted** ~ Partei ohne Prozeßkostenhilfe; **vexatious** ~ ungebührliche Partei e-s Rechtsstreits, Querulant.

litigate prozessieren, streiten.

litigation Prozeß *m*, Rechtsstreit *m*; ~ **department** Prozeßabteilung; ~ **proceedings** → *proceedings*; **conduct of** ~ Prozeßführung; **contentious** ~ streitige Gerichtsbarkeit, kontradiktorische Prozeßführung; **death** ~ Rechtsstreitigkeiten anläßlich von Todesfällen; Erbschaftsprozesse; **in** ~ streitbefangen; **infringement** ~ → *infringement*; **international** ~ Prozeß vor dem internationalen Gerichtshof; **commercial** ~ Wirtschaftsprozesse, Führung von Wirtschaftsprozessen; **non-contentious** ~ echte Streitsache der freiwilligen Gerichtsbarkeit; **party to** ~ Prozeßpartei; **patent** ~ → *patent*; **plea of negligent** ~ → *plea*; **surge of** ~ Prozeßflut; **to trigger** ~ e-n Prozeß auslösen.

litigator Partei *f* (*e-s Rechtsstreits*).

litigious streitig, zum Rechtsstreit gehörig, querulatorisch *Prozesse führend*, prozeßfreudig; ~ **claim** streitgegenständliche Forderung; ~ **patent** → *patent*; ~ **person** Querulant; ~ **procedure** → *procedure*; ~ **right** *(nur) gerichtlich durchsetzbares Recht*.

litis contestatio streitige Prozeßführung *f*, Herausarbeitung *f* der entscheidungserheblichen Fragen.

litispendence Rechtshängigkeit *f*.

litter Abfall; ~ **bugs** Abfallsünder.

littering Wegwerfen bzw unbefugtes Abladen von Abfall, wilde Deponie.

live and dead stock totes und lebendes Inventar.

live *v* leben, wohnen; ~ **apart** getrennt leben; ~ **in adultery** in ehebrecherischem Verhältnis leben; ~ **separate** getrennt leben.

livelihood Lebensunterhalt *m*, Auskommen *n*; **ability to earn one's** ~ Erwerbsfähigkeit; **comfortable** ~ Wohlstand, gutes Auskommen; **means of earning a** ~ Erwerbsmöglichkeiten.

livery Übergabe *f*, Übertragung *f* (*von Grundstücken*), Belehnung *f*, Besitzübergabe *f*, Besitzurkunde *f*; Herausgabeklage *f*; Livree *f*, Gildenvorrecht *n*; Miete *f* von Arbeitstieren, Pensionsaufnahme *f* von Pferden; ~ **company** Zunft *der City of London*; ~ **conveyance** Fahrzeug zur öffentlichen Personenbeförderung; ~ **in chivalry** Freigabe von Mündelvermögen (*bei ritterlichen Lehen*); ~ **in deed** physische Besitzübergabe auf dem Grundstück (*mit Symbolhandlung*); ~ **in law** Besitzübergabe in Sichtweite vom Grundstück; ~ **of seisin** Besitzeinweisung, Übertragung des Lehens; ~ **stable** Mietstallung, Pferde- und Fahrzeugvermietung.

liveryman Mitglied *n* e-r Gilde (*London*).

livestock Nutztiere *n|pl*, Viehbestand *m*; ~ **breeding** Viehzucht.

living apart Getrenntleben *n*; ~ **together** (eheliches) Zusammenleben.

Lloyd's | **bond** → *bond* (*1*); ~ **brokers** Lloyd's Makler *m|pl*; **L~ Law Reports** (=) *Urteilssammlung*; ~ **List** Lloyd's Liste, Schiffsnachrichtenblatt; ~ **Register (of Shipping)** Lloyd's Register; ~ **underwriters** Lloyd's Versicherer, London.

load *s* Last *f*, Ladung *f*, Ladegewicht *n*, Belastung *f*; ~ **capacity** Ladefähigkeit, Tragfähigkeit; ~ **compartment** Laderaum (*LKW*); ~ **displacement** Ladetonnage; ~ **draught** Tiefgang des beladenen Schiffes; ~ **factor** Auslastung, Auslastungsfaktor; Kapazitätsausnutzungsgrad; ~ **line** Ladelinie; ~ **rate tariff** → *tariff*; **additional** ~ Beiladung; **deck** ~ → *deck*; **peak** ~ Spitzenbelastung; **permissible** ~ Höchstbelastung; **unit** ~ → *unit*.

load *v* laden, beladen, belasten, beschweren; ~**ed arm** geladene Waffe; ~**ed in bulk** als Masse *ohne Behälter* verladen.

loader Verlader *m*, Stauer *m*.

loading Beladen *n*, Ladung *f*, Fracht *f*; *ins* Anteil *n* der Prämie an Verwaltungskosten; ~ **and unloading** Aufladen und Abladen, Beladen und Entladen, Laden und Löschen; ~ **berth** Ladestelle, Ladeplatz; ~ **capacity** Ladevermögen; ~ **charges** Ladekosten; ~ **days** Ladefrist; ~ **limit** Belastungsgrenze; ~ **list** Ladeliste; ~ **on the berth** Stückgutbefrachtung; ~ **port** = *port of* ~ → *port*; ~ **ramp** Laderampe; ~ **risk** Verladerisiko; **maximum permissible** ~ höchst zulässige Belastung; **place of** ~ Ladeort; **time for** ~ → *time*.

loadmanage Lotsenlohn *m*.

loan *s* Darlehen *n* (= *D bzw d*), Anleihe *f*, Leihe *f*, Kredit *m*; ~ **account** → *account* (*2*); ~ **against borrower's note** Solawechselkredit, Schuldschein*d*; ~ **against collateral** besichertes = *gesichertes D*, Lombardkredit; ~ **against pledged bill** Wechselpension; ~ **against security** Kredit gegen Sicherheit, gesichertes *D*; ~ **agreement** Kreditvertrag, *D*-svertrag; ~ **application** Kreditantrag; ~ **arranger** *D*-svermittler; ~ **association** Bausparkasse; ~ **at interest** verzinsliches *D*; ~ **at notice** kündbares *D*; ~ **bank** Lombardbank, Kreditanstalt; ~ **business** Lombardgeschäft; ~ **capital** Fremdkapital, Anleihekapital; *D*-ssumme; ~ **ceiling** Kreditplafond; ~ **certificate** Clearingbank-Hinterlegungszertifikat; ~ **commissioners** (=) Finanzierungstelle für öffentliche Arbeiten; ~ **crowd brokers** *Makler (an der New Yorker Börse), die untereinander oder an Dritte Aktien borgen oder ausleihen*; ~**s en bloc** Globaldarlehen; ~ **for account of others** *D*-sgewährung für fremde Rechnung; ~ **for consumption** *D*; ~ **for exchange** Gefälligkeits-Warendarlehen; ~ **for use** Leihe; ~ **funds** → *fund*; ~ **guarantee** Anleihegarantie; ~ **holder** Obligationär, Gläubiger; ~ **insurance** Kreditversicherung; ~ **interest** *D*-szinsen; ~ **ledger** *D*-skonto; ~ **loss reserve** Rückstellung für Ausfall von Krediten; **internal** ~ Inlandsanleihe; ~ **of general working capital** allgemeiner Betriebskredit; ~ **officer** Kreditsachbearbeiter; ~ **on a gold basis** Goldanleihe; ~ **on collateral** Lombard*d*; ~ **on debentures** Obligationsanleihe; ~ **on mortgage** hypothekarisch gesichertes *D*, Hypotheken*d*; ~ **on respondentia** = *respondentia* ~ → *respondentia*; ~ **on securities** Effektenlombard; ~ **ratio** Beleihungsprozentsatz; ~ **redemption** Tilgung (*e-s Darlehens bzw e-r Anleihe*); ~ **repayable on demand** täglich kündbares *D*; ~ **rollover** Anleiheumschuldung; ~ **shark** Kreditwucherer, Kredithai; ~ **stock** Fremdkapital; ~ **society** Arbeitnehmerkreditgenossenschaft; ~ **syndication** Konsortialkredit-(Geschäft); ~ **terms** Anleihebedingungen; ~ **tickets** Kreditauskunftsbogen; ~ **value** Beleihungswert (*e-r Versicherungspolice*); ~ **with fixed repayment** Kredit mit fester Fälligkeit, befristeter Kredit; **accommodation** ~ → *accommodation*; **agricultural** ~ Agrarkredit; **allotted** ~**s not yet collected**

noch nicht abgehobene ausgeloste Anleihestücke; **amortization** ~ Tilgungsanleihe; **as a** ~ leihweise, *d*-sweise; **bailout** ~ Stützanleihe, Sanierungsanleihe; **bank** ~ Bank*d*, Bankkredit; **blocked** ~ kapitalersetzendes Darlehen; Stockdarlehen; **bridging** ~ Überbrückungskredit; **broker's** ~ → *broker*; **building** ~ Baugeld, Baukredit; **business** ~ Betriebsmittelkredit; **call** ~ → *call*; **cash** ~ bar ausbezahltes *D*; **clearing** ~ Emissionsüberbrückungskredit; **collateral** ~ besichertes *D*; Lombardkredit; **commercial** ~**s** Warenkredit, kurzfristige *D* für Wirtschaftsunternehmen; **commodate** ~ Leihe; **commodity** ~ durch Waren-Lagerschein gesichertes *D*; **construction** ~ Baukredit; **consumer** ~ Kleinkredit, Konsumgüterkredit; **consumption** ~**s** *D* für konsumptive Zwecke, Konsumptivkredite; **contractor** ~ Unternehmerkredit; **conventional** ~ Immobilienkredit ohne Beteiligung der staatl Kreditversicherung *US*; **corporation** ~ Kommunalanleihe; **cost of** ~ *D*-sgebühren, Kreditkosten; **customer** ~ *D* an Privatpersonen; **daily** ~ täglich kündbarer Kredit; **day-to-day** ~ Tagesgeld; **dead** ~ dubioses *D*, *wegen Nichtrückzahlung verlängertes kurzfristiges D*; **debtor of a** ~ *D*-sschuldner; **delinquent** ~ notleidende Anleihe; dubiose Darlehensforderung; **demand** ~ tägliches Geld, sofort fälliger Kredit; **endowment** ~ Darlehen mit Versicherungsdeckung; **external** ~ Auslandsanleihe; **feed** ~ Futtermittelkredit; **fiduciary** ~ ungesicherter Personalkredit; **fixed** ~ befristetes Darlehen; **forced** ~ Zwangsanleihe; **foreign** ~ Auslandsanleihe; **free** ~ zinsfreies *D*, unverzinsliches *D*; **funding** ~ Fundierungsanleihe, Kapitalisierungsanleihe; **general-purpose** ~ nichtzweckgebundene Anleihe; **government** ~ Staatsanleihe; **gratuitous** ~ Leihe; **industrial** ~ Industrieanleihe; **installment** ~ Abzahlungs*d*, Amortisations*d*, Ratenkredit; **intercompany** ~ konzerninternes *D*; **interim** ~ Zwischenkredit; **internal** ~ Inlandsanleihe; **international** ~ internationale Anleihe; **issue of a** ~ → *issue* (*1*); **jumbo** ~ Riesenkredit; **local** ~ Kommunalanleihe; **lombard** ~ → *lombard*; **long-term** ~ langfristiges *D*; **marine** ~ Bodmerei(darlehen), Bodmereigeld; **mixed** ~ *durch verschiedenartige Sicherheiten gedeckter Kredit*; **morning** ~ Tages*d* (*für Börsenmakler*); **mortgage** ~ → *mortgage*; **municipal** ~ Kommunalanleihe; **ninety days** ~ Dreimonatsgeld; **non-accruing** ~ nicht bediente Anleihe; **non-performing** ~ nicht bediente Anleihe; **overnight** ~ am nächsten Tage rückzahlbares *D*; **participation** ~ Beteiligungs*d* (*mehrerer Banken*); **permanent** ~ Daueranleihe; Stockdarlehen; Investitionsdarlehen; **perpetual** ~ unkündbare Rentenanleihe; **personal** ~ Personalkredit; Privat*d*; *D* mit Ratentilgung; **precarious** ~ Leihe zur jederzeitigen Rückgabe; **preference** ~ Vorzugsanleihe, Prioritätsanleihe, Vorrechtsanleihe; **proceeds of** ~ Nettokredit (*ohne Gebühren und Kosten*); **prohibited** ~ verbotene Kreditgewährung; **public** ~ Staatsanleihe, öffentliche Anleihe; **purchase money** ~ → *purchase*; **real estate** ~ → *real estate*; **redeemable** ~ Tilgungsanleihe; **redemption** ~ → *redemption*; **revolving** ~ Revolving-Kredit, sich automatisch verlängerndes *D*; **secured** ~ gesichertes *D*, garantierte Anleihe; **short-term** ~ kurzfristiges *D*; **small** ~**s** Klein*d*, Kleinkredit; **soft** ~ Kredit zu günstigen Bedingungen (*in nicht konvertierbarer Währung, niedriger Zins u. a.*); **straight** ~ tilgungsfreies *D*; **street** ~ kurzfristiges *D* an Börsenmakler; **subordinated** ~ nachrangiges *D*; **subscription to a** ~ Anleihezeichnung; **syndicated** ~ Konsortialanleihe; **term** ~ → *term*; **terms of a** ~ *D*-sbedingungen; **tied** ~ zweckgebundene Anleihe; **time** ~ *D* mit bestimmter Laufzeit, Festgeld, befristeter Bankkredit; **to float a** ~ → *to float*; **to recall a** ~ → *to recall*; **to redeem a** ~ → *to redeem*; **troubled** ~ notleidende Anleihe; **undersubscribed** ~ nicht voll gezeichnete Anleihe; **unsecured** ~ ungesichertes *D*; **war** ~ Kriegsanleihe.

loanable ausleihbar.

loanback Policenbeleihung *f*.

loaner Darlehensgeber *m*.

lobby *s* Wandelgang *m*, Vorraum *m*, ~ **banking** Geld- und Bankautomatendienst im Vorraum; ~ **reporter** Parlamentsreporter.

lobby *v* (*Abgeordnete*) bearbeiten, Interessen im Parlament vertreten.

lobbying Lobbyismus *m*.

lobbyist Lobbyist *m*, Interessenvertreter *m*.

local örtlich, lokal, Kommunal . . ., ortsgebunden; ~ **board of health** Gemeindegesundheitsamt; ~ **by-laws** Ortsstatuten; ~ **call** Ortsgespräch; ~ **freight train** Nahgüterzug; ~ **channel station** Regionalsender; ~ **land charges** kommunale Grundstückslasten; ~ **planning authority** Ortsplanungsbehörde, Kreisplanungsbehörde; ~ **taxation licences** kommunalgebührenpflichtige Konzessionen.

local authority örtliche Behörde *f*, Kommunal- bzw Kreisbehörde *f*; ~ **bonds** Kommunalanleihen, Kommunalpapiere; ~ **escalator loan** zinsvariable Kommunalanleihe; ~ **mutual loan** kündbare Kommunalanleihe.

localism örtliche Eigentümlichkeit *f*, Lokalpatriotismus *m*.

locality Örtlichkeit *f*, Ort *m*, Lage *f*; ~ **of a law** örtliche Gesetzeszuständigkeit.

localization Lokalisierung *f*.

localize lokalisieren, örtlich beschränken.

locally | **competent** örtlich zuständig; ~ **situate** belegen.

locate örtlich festlegen, lokalisieren, örtl-e Grenzen abstecken, ausfindig machen, herausfinden; **to be ~d** liegen, belegen sein, e-n Sitz haben.

location Lage *f*; Vermietung *f*, Verpachtung *f*; Mutung *f*; Standort *m*, Errichtung *f*, Grenzfestlegung *f*; ~ **factors** Standortfaktoren; ~ **of loss** Schadensort, Schadensstelle; ~ **notice** *min* Anschlag an der Fundstelle; **edge-of-town** ~ Stadtrandlage; **ordering** ~ Bestell(ungs)ort; **prime** ~ erstklassige Lage.

locative calls Geländepunkte *m|pl*, Grenzpunkte *m|pl*.

locator Vermieter *m*, Verpächter *m*, Landvermesser *m*.

lock *s* Schloß *n*, Verschluß *m*; Schleuse *f*; ~ **dues** Schleusengeld.

lock *v* verschließen, absperren, versperren; ~ **out** aussperren.

lock box Bankschließfach *n*.

lockfast verschlossen und verriegelt.

locking up of capital Festlegung von Kapital.

lockage Schleusengeld *n*.

lock-out Aussperrung *f*; **defensive** ~ Abwehraussperrung; **general** ~ Massenaussperrung.

lock-up Haftanstalt *f*, Polizeigefängnis *n*; Gewahrsam *m*, festgelegtes zinsloses Kapital *n*, eingefrorenes Kapital *n*; ~ **agreement** Absicherungsvereinbarung e–r Fusionsübernahme; ~ **house** provisorisches Gefängnis.

loco am Ort, ab, an; ~ **citato** (*loc. cit.*) am angeführten Ort, a. a. O.; ~ **parentis** an Eltern Statt; ~ **price** → *price*.

lococession Platzmachen *n*, Weichen *n*, Freigabe *f*.

locum tenens Stellvertreter *m*; **locum** bes. Terminsvertreter, Urlaubsvertreter *d. Anwalts*.

locus | **regit actum** (=) *die Form richtet sich nach dem Recht des Errichtungsortes* (*der Urkunde*); ~ **sigilli** (*L. S.*) Stelle für das Siegel (*Hinweis auf das Siegel in der Originalurkunde*); ~ **standi** das Recht, bei Gericht gehört zu werden, Postulationsfähigkeit; Prozeßführungsrecht.

lode Flöz *m*; (Erz)Ader *f*.

lodeman Hafenpilot *m*, Hafenschlepperführer *m*.
lodemanage Lotsengeld *n*, das Engagieren e-s Lotsen.
lodge einlegen, einreichen, hinterlegen; ~ **a credit with** bei jmdm e-n Kredit eröffnen; ~ **an entry** e-e Eintragung erwirken; ~ **a proof in bankruptcy** → *bankruptcy*; ~ **a protest** Protest erheben, Widerspruch einlegen; ~ **administrative powers with a board** e-r Behörde Verwaltungsbefugnisse übertragen; ~ **an appeal** Berufung einlegen; ~ **claims** Ansprüche erheben; ~ **documents** Urkunden vorlegen.
lodger Zimmermieter *m*, Zimmermieterin *f*.
lodging Wohnung *f*, Unterkunft *f*, Beherbergung *f*; Anmeldung *f*, Einreichung *f*; ~ **allowance** Wohnungsgeldzuschuß; ~ **place** Schlafstelle, vorübergehende Unterkunft; ~ **house** Pension, Fremdenheim; **common** ~ **house** Obdachlosenheim, Nachtasyl.
lodgment Hinterlegung *f*, Deponierung *f*; Einreichung *f*, Abgabe *f*; ~ **office** Hinterlegungsstelle; ~ **of funds in court** gerichtl Hinterlegung; ~ **of money into court** Einzahlung an die Hinterlegungsstelle; **cash** ~ (gerichtliche) Hinterlegungsverfügung.
log *s* Holzklotz *m*, gefällter Baumstamm *m*; ~**s** Rundholz *n*; **merchantable** ~**s** handelsübliche Holzstämme (*Mindestgröße* 9×32 *Zoll*).
log *v* (ins Logbuch) eintragen, vormerken; e-e Geldstrafe auferlegen.
log-book Logbuch *n*, Schiffstagebuch *n*, Bordbuch *n*; Kfz-Brief *m*; **official** ~ (*vorgeschriebenes*) Schiffstagebuch.
logging Holzfällerei *f*.
logjam Blockierung durch Arbeitsüberhäufung.
logo Firmenzeichen *n*, Signum *n*, Wortsymbol *n*.
log-rolling *das Einbeziehen umstrittener Anträge in e-e aussichtsreiche Gesamtvorlage.*
loitering Herumlungern *n*.
lombard Geldwechsler *m*, Pfandleiher *m*; ~ **loan** Lombarddarlehen; **L~ rate** Lombardsatz; **L~ Street** *der Londoner Geldmarkt*; **the L~** der (deutsche) Lombardsatz.
London London, Großlondon, die Verwaltungsgrafschaft London; ~ **Chamber of Commerce and Industry Business Registry** *(=) gesamtbritisches Firmenregister*; ~ **Commodities Exchange** Londoner Warenbörse; ~ **equivalent** Londoner Parität; ~ **Gazette** (=) *brit Staatsanzeiger;* ~ **interbank offered rate** *(Libor) Leitzins für den Eurogeldmarkt*; ~ **rates** Londoner Wechselkurs; ~ **Sessions** *Sitzungsperioden des Central Criminal Court in London*; ~ **sittings** Sitzungen der Guildhall; ~ **Stock Exchange** Londoner (Effekten-)Börse; ~ **Transport Executive** Londoner Stadtverkehrsbehörde.
long *adj* lang, langfristig, auf lange Sicht, gut versorgt sein mit, eingedeckt, auf Preissteigerung wartend; reich (an); ~ **and short haul** Nah- und Fernverkehrstransport; ~**-dated investment** langfristige Kapitalanlage; ~ **distance removal** Möbelfernverkehr; ~ **distance transport** Güterfernverkehr; ~ **end of the market** Geldmarkt für langfristige Staatspapiere; ~ **leasehold building land** *etwa:* Erbbaugrundstück; ~**-service anniversary** Dienstjubiläum.
long *s* Haussier *m*; Hausseposition *f*; Long Position *f*, Überbestand *m*; langfristige Staatspapiere.
longevity pay zusätzlicher Sold *m* für langfristig Dienende.
longhand Kurrentschrift *f*, Langschrift *f*, Schreibschrift *f*; **in** ~ handschriftlich.
longshoreman Dockarbeiter *m*.
longstop äußerste Frist für die Klageerhebung, Ausschlußfrist *f*.
long-term langfristig.
lookout Wache *f*, Schiffswache *f*, Beobachtungsposten *m*, Obacht *f*; **proper** ~ gehöriges Achtgeben.

loophole in the law Gesetzeslücke *f*, Hintertürchen *n*.

loose leaf Loseblattsammlung; ~ **system of bookkeeping** Loseblattbuchführung.

looting Plünderung; ~ **of a corpse** Leichenfledderei.

lord Lehensherr *m*, Gebieter *m*, Grundherr *m*, (=) Adelsprädikat m; Magnat *m*, Baron *m*, (=) *Titel für brit Richter;* **the L~s** das Oberhaus; **L~ Advocate** jur Vertreter d brit Krone in Schottland; ~ **and vassal** Lehensverhältnis; **L~ Chamberlain of the Queen's Household** Oberhofmeister, Haushofmeister; **L~ Chancellor** = *L~ High Chancellor qv*; *L~ Ch~'s office*: *etwa Justizministerium*; **L~ Chief Baron** *hist Präsident des Court of Exchequer*; **L~ Chief Justice (of England)** *Präsident des Court of Appeal und der Queen's Bench Abteilung des High Court*; **~s commissioners** Staatskommissare, *mit der gemeinschaftlichen Ausübung hoher Staatsämter Beauftragte*; **L~ Commissioner of Judiciary** *scot* Gerichtspräsident; **L~'s day** (*der Tag des Herrn*) Sonntag; **L~'s Day Act** *GB* Gesetz über Einhaltung der Sonntagsruhe; **L~ Great Chamberlain of England** Lord-Großkämmerer; **L~ High Admiral** königliches Marineamt; **L~ High Chancellor** *brit* Lordkanzler; *etwa* Justizminister, Kabinettsmitglied, Präsident des Oberhauses und hoher Gerichte; **L~ High Commissioner** *Vertreter der britischen Königin bei der schottischen Kirchenversammlung*; **L~ High Constable** Großkonnetabel von England (*Ehrentitel*); **L~ High Steward of the Royal Household** Großhofmeister von England, *stellvertretender Präsident des Oberhauses bei Anklage gegen Oberhausmitglieder*; **L~ High Treasurer** erster Lord des Schatzamts, *hist* Schatzkanzler; Schatzamt; ~ **in gross** oberster Lehnsherr; **Lord Justice** → *L~ Justices of Appeal*; **L~ Justice-Clerk** *scot Vizepräsident des Court of Justiciary*; **L~ Justice General** *scot Präsident des High Court of Justiciary*; **L~ Justices** *hist beauftragte Abwesenheitsvertreter des Monarchen*; **L~s Justices of Appeal** Richter des Court of Appeal; **L~ Keeper** = *Keeper of the Great Seal qv*; **L~ Lieutenant** *hist brit Vizekönig in Irland*; oberster Kronbeamter für e-e Grafschaft; **L~ Lieutenant of the Courts** königl Grafschaftskommissar (*empfiehlt Friedensrichterbestellung*); **L~ Lyon King of Arms** (=) *Präsident des Heraldikamts in Schottland*; **L~ Mayor** Oberbürgermeister, *Bürgermeister der City of London*; **L~ Mayor's Court** Londoner Stadtgericht; ~ **of the manor** Gutsherr, Grundherr, Patronatsherr; **~s of appeal** = *L~s of Appeal in Ordinary qv*; **L~s of Appeal in Ordinary** (= „Law-Lords") richterliche Oberhausmitglieder; **L~s of Erection** *scot* Laienbelehnte *kirchlicher Pfründen*, Verwalter von säkularisiertem Klostervermögen; **~s of parliament** Oberhausmitglieder; **~s of regality** *scot* beauftragte Richter; **L~ of Session** *scot* Richter des Court of Session; ~ **ordinary** *scot Richter erster Instanz des Court of Session*; ~ **paramount** oberster Lehnsherr; **L~ President of the Council** Lordpräsident des Kronrats; **L~ Privy Seal** Lordsiegelbewahrer (*Ministerrang*); **L~ Provost** *scot* Oberbürgermeister; **~s spiritual** geistliche Mitglieder des Oberhauses; **L~ Speaker of the House of Peers** Präsident des Oberhauses; **L~ Steward of the Queen's Household** Lordoberhofmeister (*mit richterlichen Funktionen am Hof*); **~s temporal** weltliche Mitglieder des Oberhauses; **L~ Treasurer** Erster Lord der Schatzkammer; Schatzamt; **chief** ~ der (*eigentliche*) Lehensherr; **First L~ of the Treasury** → *treasury*; **First L~ of the Admiralty** → *admiralty*; **very** ~ direktor Lehnsherr.

lordship Herrschaft *f*, Lehensherrschaft *f*, Herrschaftsbesitz *m*, Lordschaft *f*; **Your L~** *brit* Eure Lordschaft (*Anrede für Richter*).

loss Verlust *m* (= *V bzw v*), Einbuße *f*, Schaden *m*, Nachteil *m*, Untergang *m*, Ausfall *m*; Wertminderung *f*, Kursverlust *m*; Versicherungsschaden *m*, Schadensfall *m*; ~ **advice** Schadensanzeige; ~ **assessment** Schadensabschätzung, Schadenstaxierung; ~ **by fire** Brandschaden; ~ **by leakage** (*Gewichts*) *V* durch Auslaufen; ~ **carried forward** *V*vortrag; ~ **carry back** *V*rücktrag, rückwirkender *V*ausgleich, (*steuerliche*) Anrechnung von *V-en* auf frühere Gewinne; ~ **claimable on insurance** Schaden als Anspruch gegen e-e Versicherung; ~ **compensation** *V*ausgleich; ~ **event** Schadensereignis (= *occurrence qv*); ~ **in price** Preis*v*; Preisverfall, Kurs*v*; ~ **in transit** *V* auf dem Transport; ~ **in value** Wertminderung; ~ **leader** Lockartikel, Lockvogel-Angebot; ~ **on exchange** Kurs*v*; ~ **of amenity** Verlust an Lebensqualität; ~ **of consortium (and services)** *V* der ehelichen Lebensgemeinschaft; ~ **of custom** *V* der Kundschaft; ~ **of earnings** Verdienstausfall, Gewinnentgang; ~ **of employment** *V* des Arbeitsplatzes; ~ **on enjoyment of life** Verlust der Möglichkeit, das Leben zu genießen, Verlust an Lebensqualität; ~ **of expectation of life** verminderte Lebenserwartung; ~ **of faculty** *V* e-s Sinnesorgans; ~ **of franchise** *US V* der Konzession; ~ **of insurance benefits** Entgang von Versicherungsleistungen; ~ **of interest** Zins*v*; ~ **of law** *hist V* der Rechtsstellung e-s Freien; ~ **of markets** *V* von Absatzgebieten; ~ **of pay** Lohnausfall; ~ **of priority** Rang*v*; ~ **of profits** Gewinnentgang; ~ **of profits insurance** → *insurance*; ~ **of property** Vermögensschaden; *V* von (*beweglichen*) Sachen; ~ **of publicity** Schaden am Prestige, Öffentlichkeitsschaden; ~ **of rent** Mietausfall; ~ **of services** entgangene Dienste; *V* von Diensten (*zB im Haushalt*); ~ **of (sense of) taste** Verlust des Geschmacksinns; ~ **of the adventure** Ausfall des Unternehmens; ~ **of time** Zeit*v*; ~ **of use** Gebrauchsentzug, Nutzungsschaden, Nutzungsausfall; ~ **of useful value** *V* des Gebrauchswertes; ~ **of wages** Lohnausfall; ~ **of wife's services** Verlust der Tätigkeit der Ehefrau als Hausfrau; ~ **on exchange** Kurs*v*; ~ **on securities** Kurs*v*; ~ **or damage** Schaden jeder Art; ~ **or forfeiture (of a license)** *V bzw* Entzug (e-r Konzession); ~ **payee** Empfangsberechtigter im Schadensfall; ~ **ratio** Schadensquote; ~ **reserve** Verlustrückstellung, Schadensreserve, Rückstellung für laufende Risiken; ~ **settlement** Schadensregulierung; **accidental** ~ zufälliger Schaden; **actual** ~ Sachschaden, physischer Schaden; **actual total** ~ Totalschaden; **all** ~ **insurance** → *insurance*; **allowable** ~ absetzbarer Verlust; **amount of** ~ → *amount;* **appraisal in** ~ gutachterliche Schadensfeststellung; **arranged total** ~ verglichener Totalschaden; **ascertainment of** ~ Feststellung des Schadens; **at a** ~ zu e-m *V*preis; mit *V*; **book** ~ buchmäßiger *V*; **capital** ~ Kapital*v*; **casualty** ~ Zufallschaden; **clear** ~ Netto*v*; **constant** ~ Dauer*v*; **constructive** ~ = *constructive total* ~ *qv*; **constructive total** ~ als Total*v* geltender Schaden; angenommener Totalschaden; **corporate** ~ Firmen*v* (*bei Kapitalgesellschaften*); **dead** ~ vollständiger und endgültiger Verlust; **direct** ~ unmittelbarer Schaden; **economic** ~ wirtschaftlicher Schaden; **exchange** ~ Währungs*v*; **expectation of** ~ Schadenserwartung; **first** ~ **insurance** → *insurance*; **gross** ~ Brutto*v*, Roh*v*; **in case of** ~ bei Eintritt des Versicherungsfalles; **large** ~ Großschaden; **marine** ~ *V* auf See; **minimizing** ~ Schadensminderung,

Schadensbekämpfung; **minor** ~ Kleinschaden, Bagatellschaden; **natural** ~ natürlicher Schwund; **net** ~ Reinverlust, Netto*v*; **non-allowable** ~ nicht absetzbarer Verlust; **normal** ~ natürlicher Schwund; **notice of** ~ → *notice*; **operating** ~ Betriebs*v*, Geschäfts*v*; **partial** ~ Teilschaden, Teil*v*, *weniger als totaler Schaden*; **pecuniary** ~ Vermögensschaden; **prevention of** ~ → *prevention*; **probability of** ~ Schadenswahrscheinlichkeit; **proof of** ~ → *proof*; **redistribution of** ~ Schadensumschichtung, Schadensabwälzung; **salvage** ~ Bergungsschaden, Bergungsverlust; **stop** ~ **orders** *nach unten limitierter Effektenverkaufsauftrag*; **total** ~ Total*v*, Totalschaden; **trading** ~ Betriebs*v*.

lost verloren, abhanden gekommen; ~ **cause** hoffnungsloses Unterfangen, aussichtsloses Anliegen; ~ **corner** nicht mehr feststellbarer Endpunkt (*Kataster*); ~ **document** abhandengekommene Urkunde; ~ **grant** Ersitzung (*bei Dienstbarkeiten*); ~ **or not lost** *mar ins* rückwirkender Versicherungsschutz (*auch für den Fall e-s inzwischen eingetretenen nicht bekannten Schiffsverlustes*); ~ **profits** entgangener Gewinn; ~ **property** verlorene Sache, Fundsache; ~ **property office** → *office*; **action on** ~ **instrument(s)** (Wechsel)Klage bei Verlust der Originalurkunde; **irretrievably** ~ unwiederbringlich verloren; **keeping** ~ **property** Fundunterschlagung.

lot Los *n*, Partie *f*, Lieferposten *m*; Gruppe *f*, Anteil *m*, Parzelle *f*, Flurstück *n*; ~ **and scot** *hist* Bleibergwerksabgabe *an die engl Krone;* ~ **book** Kataster(buch); ~ **money** Partieprovision des Auktionators; ~ **of land** Parzelle, Grundstück; ~ **of stocks** Aktienpaket; **auction** ~ Auktionsposten; **building** ~ Bauplatz; **by casting** ~**s** durch das Los; **by drawing** ~**s** durch das Los; **full** ~ US(Börsen)Abschlußeinheit = *round lot* → *round;* **in** ~**s** partienweise, in Partien; **odd** ~ →*oddlot;* **regular** ~ Börsenabschlußeinheit, voller Börsenschluß; **round** ~ → *round*.

lot *v* verlosen; in Parzellen teilen.

lottery Lotterie *f*; ~ **bond** Lospapier, auslosbares Wertpapier; ~ **loan** Prämienanleihe; ~ **prize** Lotteriegewinn; ~ **sampling** Zufallsauswahl; **Dutch** ~ Klassenlotterie; **Genoese** ~ Zahlenlotterie (*das Setzen auf Gewinnzahlen*); **societies'** ~**ies** Vereinslotterien.

love | affair Liebesverhältnis; ~ **-day** Schiedstag; Tag für Nachbarschaftshilfe; ~ **match** Liebesheirat; **free** ~ freie Liebe, nichteheliche Geschlechtsverkehr.

low tief, niedrig, billig; ~ **duty goods** niedrig verzollte Waren; ~ **rent housing** sozialer Wohnungsbau; ~ **value lands** billiger Grund und Boden (*US*).

lower-tier contract nachgeordneter Subunternehmervertrag *m*.

loyal loyal, legal, staatstreu.

loyalist *hist* Anhänger *m* der brit Krone; treuer Parteianhänger *m*.

loyality Loyalität *f*, Treue *f*, Gesetzestreue *f*, Untertanentreue *f*; ~ **bonus** Treueprämie.

luck money Glücksgeld *n* (*Preisnachlaß beim Viehhandel*).

lucrative entgeltlich, lukrativ, gewinnbringend, einträglich; ~ **bailment** → *bailment*; ~ **office** → *office*; ~ **succession** lediglich vorteilhafter Erwerb.

lucrativeness Einbringlichkeit *f*, Rendite *f*.

lucre Gewinn *m*, (*sittenwidrige*) Bereicherung *f*.

lucrum cessans entgangener Gewinn *m*.

luggage Gepäck *n*; ~ **insurance** → *insurance*; ~ **locker** (*Gepäck-*)-Schließfach; ~ **office** Gepäckschalter, Gepäckabfertigung; ~ **ticket** Gepäckschein; **left** ~ **office** Gepäckaufbewahrung; **ordinary** ~ persönliches Gepäck, Reisegepäck; **personal** ~ Handgepäck.

lull Geschäftsstille *f*
lumber Bauholz *n*, Nutzholz *n*; ~ **man** Holzarbeiter, Holzfäller; ~ **scaler** Holzvermesser; ~ **trade** Holzhandel.
lumberjack Holzarbeiter *m*, Lumberjack *m* (*Sportweste*).
lump Kolonnenarbeit *f*, Partiearbeit als Subunternehmervertrag.
lump sum Pauschalbetrag *m*.
lump-sum *adj* pauschal, Pausch...; ~ **award** pauschaler Schadensersatz; ~ **contract** Pauschalvertrag, Globalvertrag; ~ **deduction** pauschaler Abzug; ~ **investment** Anteilserwerb durch einmalige Zahlung; ~ **order** einstweilige Anordnung auf einmalige (Pauschal)Zahlung; ~ **payment** Pauschalabfindung, Vorwegzahlung von Raten; ~ **settlement** Pauschalabfindung.
lunacy Geistesschwäche *f*, Geistesgestörtheit *f*, Geschäftsunfähigkeit *f*; ~ **proceedings** Gerichtsverfahren zur Feststellung von Geistesgestörtheit, Entmündigungsverfahren; **commission in (of)** ~ *GB, vor 1959* gerichtlicher Auftrag zur Untersuchung e-s angeblich Geistesgestörten, Beschluß über Einleitung e-s Entmündigungsverfahrens.
lunatic *s* Geistesgestörte(r) *f* bzw *m*, Geistesschwache(r); *adj* geistesgestört, geisteskrank, wahnsinnig, irrsinnig; ~ **asylum** Irrenanstalt, Heil- und Pflegeanstalt, Nervenkrankenhaus; **a** ~ **not found so** jmd, bei dem keine Geistesstörung festgestellt wurde; **a** ~ **so found** für geisteskrank erklärte Person; **criminal** ~ geisteskranker Straftäter.
lurch Hang *m*, Neigung *f*; unhaltbare Lage *f*, Taumeln *n*, Torkeln *n*.
lure Lockmittel *n*, Lockvogel *m*.
lying by Nachlässigkeit *f* bei der Geltendmachung von Rechten; Verwirkung *f*.
lying in grant nicht physisch übertragbar (*sondern nur durch Urkunde*).
lynch law Lynchgesetz *n*, Lynchjustiz *f*.
Lyon's Inn (=) *e-e Anwaltsinnung f in London*; ~ **King of Arms** *scot* Kronherold, Wappenherold.

M

mace *parl* Amtsstab *m*; **~-bearer** Träger des Amtsstabes *(zB im Unterhaus)*.

machine Maschine *f*, Apparat *m*; **~ tools industry** Werkzeugmaschinenindustrie; **automatic ~** Automat; **perfect ~** vollendete Erfindung (= *Maschine, die alle Erfindungsmerkmale in brauchbarer Form verwirklicht*).

machinery technische Ausstattung *f*, Maschinenpark *m*, Räderwerk *n*; Mechanismus *m*, (Trieb)Werk *n*; Maschinerie *f*, Maschinen *f/pl*; **~ and equipment** Maschinen und Geräte, Betriebsausrüstung, Betriebs- und Geschäftsausstattung; **~s and other erections** technische und sonstige Anlagen; **~ and plant** Maschinen und Betriebsanlagen; **~ insurance** → *insurance*; **~ of government** Regierungsapparat; **administrative ~** Verwaltungsapparat; **dangerous ~** gefahrenträchtige Maschine bzw Maschinenanlage; **official ~** Behördenapparat; *höchstrichterliche Regeln bei Berufung auf;* **party ~** → *party*.

M'Naghten Rules *Regeln betr Unzurechnungsfähigkeit wegen Geisteskrankheit.*

macro-economics Makroökonomie *f*, Makroökonomik *f*.

mad point Gegenstand *m* einer monomanischen Vorstellung, fixe Idee *f*.

made gemacht, hergestellt, erlassen, abgeschlossen, eingereicht; **~ good** wiederhergestellt, *(Schaden)* ersetzt, repariert; **~ known** zur Kenntnis gebracht, zugestellt; **~ up for sale** (*zum Verkauf*) verpackt *bzw* hergerichtet; **~ to-measure** maßgeschneidert, auf individuelle Kundenwünsche abgestellt.

Madrid Trade Mark Convention Madrider Markenabkommen *n* (*von 1891, zuletzt revidiert 1967*).

magister Herrscher *m*, Graduierter *m*, Wissenschaftler *m*.

magisterial obrigkeitlich, amtlich, behördlich, richterlich, maßgeblich, gebieterisch; **~ bench** Laienrichterschaft; **~ cases** (*wichtige*) Gerichtsentscheidungen; **~ function** staatsanwaltschaftliche Funktion; **~ precinct** → *precinct*.

magistracy Obrigkeit *f*, Exekutive *f*, Verwaltung *f*, Amtsgericht *n*, Amtsrichter *m*, Strafrichter *m*; höheres Amt *n*.

magistrate *m*, Amtsrichter *m* in Strafsachen (*und ähnl Angelegenheiten, teilweise behördl Art*), Polizeirichter *m*, Friedensrichter *m*; Verwaltungsbeamter *m*; **~'s clerk** juristischer Gehilfe des (Laien)Amtsrichters; **~s' court** → *court;* **chief ~** Regierungschef, Leiter der Exekutive, Bürgermeister; **committing ~** Ermittlungsrichter; **examining ~** Ermittlungsrichter; **investigating ~** Ermittlungsrichter; **metropolitan ~** (berufsmäßiger) Amtsrichter in London; **police ~** → *police*; **stipendiary ~** Stadtrichter, (*besoldeter städtischer*) Amtsrichter.

Magna Charta (=) *engl Verfassungsurkunde von 1215.*

maiden junge unverheiratete Frau *f*, Jungfrau *f* (*juristisch nicht notwendigerweise virgo intacta*); **~ name** Mädchenname *e–r verheirateten Frau;* **~ surname** Mädchenname, *Familienname bei Geburt e–r Frau.*

mail *s* Briefpost *f*, Postgut *n*; Paketbeförderung *f*; *scot* Grundzins *m*; **~ ballot** Wahlschein (*bei Briefwahl*); **~ fraud** betrügerische Postbenutzung; **~ matter** Postgut; **~-order** Bestellung zum Postversand; ~

order business Versandhandel; ~ **order sales** Versandhandelumsatz; ~ **robbery** Postraub; ~ **service** Postdienst, Postverkehr; ~ **survey** Meinungsumfrage per Post; ~ **transfer** Geldüberweisung per Post; **by return of** ~ postwendend; **certified** ~ Briefpost mit Zustellungsnachweis; **direct** ~ Wurfsendung; **first-class** ~ Briefpost; **fourth-class** ~ Paketpost; **"hate ~"** Beschimpfungsbriefe; **registered** ~ Einschreibsendung; **second-class** ~ Zeitungspost, Pressepostgut; **third-class** ~ Drucksache(n); **unrecorded** ~ gewöhnliche Post.

mail *v* bei der Post aufgeben, mit der Post versenden; ~**ed** per Post abgeschickt, ordnungsgemäß bei der Post aufgegeben.

mailable zum Postversand zugelassen.

mailcert Befreiungsvermerk *m* für Postsendung *im Kriege*.

mailing address Postanschrift; ~ **charges** Postgebühren; ~ **list** Adressenliste, Versandliste; ~ **machine** Frankiermaschine.

maim *v* verstümmeln, e–e schwere (Körper)Verletzung zufügen; ~ **or wound** e–e schwere (Körper)Verletzung zufügen.

main purpose rule *Aufrechterhaltung der dem Hauptzweck dienenden Bestimmung bei widersprechenden Vertragsklauseln.*

maintain behaupten, darauf bestehen, unterhalten, versorgen, instandhalten, aufrechterhalten, beibehalten, fortsetzen; ~ **a patent** ein Patent aufrechterhalten; ~ **an action** e–n Prozeß führen; ~ **diplomatic relations** diplomatische Beziehungen unterhalten; ~ **and keep efficient** (*zB als Schulträger*) für ordnungsgemäße Erhaltung und Gebäudeverwaltung verantwortlich sein; ~ **order** die Ordnung aufrechterhalten; ~**ed minimum resale prices** gebundene Mindestpreise der zweiten Hand.

maintainability Wartungsfreundlichkeit *f*.

maintainable haltbar, zu rechtfertigen, vertretbar, erhaltungspflichtig.

maintenance (*1*) Erhaltung *f*, Instandhaltung *f*, Beibehaltung *f*, Behauptung *f*, Aufrechterhaltung *f*, Wartung *f*, Betreuung *f*; ~ **activity costs** Wartungskosten; ~ **and repair** Instandhaltung; ~ **assessment** Erhaltungsumlage; ~ **charges** Wartungskosten; ~ **engineer** Wartungstechniker; ~ **laxity** Wartungsschlamperei; ~ **of value guarantee** Werterhaltungsgarantie; **current** ~ Wartungskosten, laufende Instandhaltung; **pre-accident** ~ rechtzeitige Wartung (*vor e–m Unfall*); **preventive** ~ vorbeugende Instandhaltung; **resale price** ~ → *resale*.

maintenance (*2*) Unterhalt *m*, Fürsorge *f*, Lebensunterhalt *m*; ~ **after termination of marriage** nachehelicher Unterhalt; ~ **agreement** Unterhaltsvereinbarung; ~ **clause** Versorgungsbestimmung (*Testament, Treuhand*); ~ **obligations** Unterhaltsverpflichtungen; ~ **payments** Unterhaltszahlungen; ~ **pending suit** einstweilige Anordnung auf Unterhaltszahlung (*an Ehegatten*); **award of** ~ Zuerkennung von Unterhalt; **comfortable** ~ standesgemäßer Unterhalt, **life-long** ~ lebenslänglicher Ehegatten-Unterhalt; **long-term** ~ Dauerunterhalt; **reasonable** ~ angemessener Unterhalt; **separate** ~ Unterhalt bei Getrenntleben (*der Ehegatten*).

maintenance (*3*) Prozeßanstiftung *f*, Prozeßförderung *f Dritter gegen Gewinnbeteiligung*; widerrechtl–e Unterstützung einer fremden Prozeßpartei.

maintainor außenstehender Prozeßanstifter *m*, Prozeßförderer *m*.

majesty Majestät *f*; **during Her M~'s pleasure** auf unbestimmte Dauer, bis auf Widerruf; **on Her M~'s service** amtlich, dienstlich, portofreie Dienstsache (*O.H.M.S.*).

major *addj* größer; mündig, volljährig geworden; ~ **and minor fault rule** Anscheinsbeweis für das Alleinverschulden des hauptsächlich Schuldigen (*Schiffzusammenstoß*); ~ **proposition** *scot abstrakte Tatbestandsangaben in e–r Anklageschrift.*

major *s* Volljähriger *m*, für volljährig erklärte Person *f*.

majoritarianism Majorisierungsprinzip *m*.

majority (*1*) Mehrheit *f* (= *M bzw ...m*) Majorität *f*; Mehrzahl *f*; *majority bedeutet in der Regel absolute Mehrheit, es kann jedoch auch relative Mehrheit gemeint sein*; ~ **action** Maßnahmen e–r *M*; ~ **holding** *M–s*-beteiligung; ~ **interest** *M–s*-beteiligung; ~ **of members** *M* nach Köpfen; ~ **of qualified electors** *M* der *an der Abstimmung teilnehmenden wahlberechtigten* Wähler; ~ **of shares** Aktien*m*; ~ **of stockholders** *kapitalmäßige M* von Aktionären (*außer wenn nach Köpfen abgestimmt wird*); ~ **of votes** Stimmen*m*, Mehrzahl der abgegebenen Stimmen; ~ **opinion** *M*svotum; Mehrheitsbeschluß; ~ **owned subsidiary** Tochtergesellschaft mit *M–s*beteiligung der Mutter; ~ **rule** → *rule;* ~ **view** Ansicht der *M* (*zB e–s Kollegialgerichtes*); ~ **vote** Stimmen*m*, einfache *M*; **bare** ~ einfache *M*; **clear** ~ einfache *M*; **comfortable** ~ sichere *M*; **decision of the** ~ → *decision*; **narrow** ~ knappe *M*; **necessary** ~ → *necessary*; **numerical** ~ zahlenmäßige *M*; **qualified** ~ qualifizierte *M*; **relative** ~ relative *M*; **special** ~ qualifizierte *M*; **to command a** ~ über e–e *M* verfügen; **two-thirds** ~ Zweidrittel*m*; **whooping** ~ überwältigende *M*; **working** ~ arbeitsfähige *M*.

majority (*2*) Mündigkeit *f*, Volljährigkeit *f*; **declaration of** ~ → *declaration;* **legal** ~ **for marriage** Ehemündigkeit; **on attaining one's** ~ bei Erreichen der Volljährigkeit; **to attain one's** ~ volljährig werden.

make *s* Machart *f*, Fasson *f*, Erzeugnis *n*, Fabrikat *n*; ~ **and year** Hersteller und Baujahr (*Kfz*); **foreign** ~ ausländisches Fabrikat; **standard** ~ Normalausführung.

make *v* machen, anfertigen, bilden, begründen, verursachen, leisten, errichten, ausstellen, unterfertigen, abschließen, verschaffen; ~ **a contract** e–n Vertrag schließen; e–n Vertrag schriftlich schließen; ~ **a declaration** e–e Erklärung abgeben; ~ **a market** e–e Absatzmöglichkeit schaffen; ~ **a price** e–n Preis bestimmen; ~ **a will** ein Testament aufsetzen, ein T. errichten; ~ **absolute** den Vorbehalt wegfallen lassen; ~ **allowance for** berücksichtigen, in Betracht ziehen, anrechnen; ~ **amends** → *amends;* ~ **an ass of the law** die Justiz blamieren, das Recht ad absurdum führen; ~ **an award** etwas im Urteil zuerkennen, ein Urteil erlassen; ~ **oath** den Eid leisten, schwören; ~ **answer** e–e Klageerwiderung einreichen, auf etwas erwidern; ~ **away** beiseite schaffen, sich aus dem Staube machen; sich wegschleichen; ~ **binding** verbindlich machen; ~ **complaint** sich beschweren; ~ **default** → *default;* ~ **distress** pfänden; ~ **distributions in stock** Gratisaktien verteilen; ~ **evident** dartun, beweisen; ~ **good a loss** e–n Verlust abdecken, für e–n Schaden aufkommen; ~ **good defects** Mängel beheben; ~ **known** bekanntgeben; ~ **oath and say** unter Eid aussagen; ~ **one's faith** *scot = make one's law qv*; ~ **one's law** *hist* e–n Reinigungseid ablegen, sich darauf berufen; ~ **out an account** e–e Rechnung ausstellen; ~ **out in blank** in blanko ausstellen; ~ **out to bearer** auf den Inhaber ausstellen; ~ **over a debt** e–e Forderung abtreten; ~ **payment** Zahlung leisten, zahlen; ~ **purchase** einkaufen; ~ **the cash** Kasse machen; ~ **to order** auf Bestellung fertigen; ~ **trumped up charges** bewußt unberechtigte Anklage erheben; ~ **up an account** ein Konto abschließen; ~ **up books** e–n Buchabschluß vornehmen; ~ **up for the deficit** den Fehlbetrag decken;

~ **up the average** die Dispache aufmachen; ~ **void** annullieren, anfechten.

maker Fabrikant *m*, Hersteller *m*, Aussteller *m*; ~**'s number** Fabriknummer; ~ **of a statement** der Erklärende, der Aussteller e-r Erklärung; ~ **of note** Aussteller e-s Solawechsels; ~**'s shift** Fabrikantentrick, Notbehelf bei der Herstellung.

makeshift Notbehelf *m*, Provisorium *n*.

make-ready time Vorbereitungszeit *f* (*zB für Maschineneinsatz*).

make-up wages Ausgleichslohn *m* (*bei geringem Akkordlohn*).

make-up work Aufholarbeit *f*.

makeweight (Gewichts)Zugabe *f*, Ersatz *m*, Ausgleich *m*; Zusatzargument *n*.

making Fertigung *f*, Herstellung *f*, Werk *n*; ~ **of a will** Testamentserrichtung; ~ **off without payment** sich ohne zu zahlen davonmachen; ~ **over** Übertragung, Übereignung; ~**-up day** Reporttag, Erklärungstag; ~ **up price** → *price* (*2*); ~ **up the accounts** Kontoabschluß.

mala|fide bösgläubig, unredlich; ~ **fide holder** bösgläubiger Inhaber; ~ **in se** (=) *originäre Straftaten, gewohnheitsrechtlich strafbare Handlungen*; ~**prohibita** *auf Grund e-s Strafgesetzes strafbare Handlung*.

maladjustment schlechte Anpassung *f*, Mißverhältnis *n*.

maladministration Verwaltungsfehler *m*, fehlerhafter Verwaltungsakt *m*, Mißwirtschaft *f*.

malapportionment mißbräuchliche Wahlkreiseinteilung *f*.

malconduct Fehlverhalten *n*.

male männlich; ~ **descendants** männliche Abkömmlinge (*des Mannesstammes*); ~ **heir** → *heir*; ~ **issue** männliche Nachkommen *im Mannesstamm*; ~ **line** Agnaten, Mannesstamm; ~ **lineal** = *male line qv*; ~ **nephews** Neffen im Mannesstamm, Söhne von Brüdern; ~ **servant** Diener.

malediction Fluch *m*, Verwünschung *f*; Verleumdung *f*.

malefaction Verbrechen *n*, Straftat *f*.

malefactor Täter *m*, Übeltäter *m*, Missetäter *m*.

malevolence Böswilligkeit *f*, Arglist *f*.

malfeasance Übeltat *f* Fehlverhalten *n* im Amt; rechtswidriges Handeln *n*, Begehung *f* e-r unerlaubten Handlung.

malformation (*körperl*) Mißbildung *f*.

malfunction *v/i* schlecht funktionieren, ausfallen.

malice böse Absicht *f*, Böswilligkeit *f*, Vorsatz *m*, böser Glaube *m*, Arglist *f*; ~ **aforethought** Mordvorsatz, verbrecherischer Vorsatz, kriminelle Grundeinstellung; ~ **in fact** Schädigungsabsicht; ~ **in law** böse Absicht, (vermuteter) Vorsatz; ~ **prepense** = ~ *aforethought qv;* **actual** ~ böse Absicht, Schädigungsabsicht; **constructive** ~ vermuteter Vorsatz, gesetzlich unterstellter Verbrechensvorsatz, vermutete böse Absicht; **express** ~ böse Absicht, Schädigungsabsicht; **general** ~ bösartige Veranlagung, krimineller Hang; **implied** ~ vermuteter Vorsatz, aus dem Gesamtverhalten gefolgerte böse Absicht; **legal** ~ vermuteter Vorsatz; **particular** ~ auf eine bestimmte Person gerichtete böse Absicht, Groll, Rachedurst; **preconceived** ~ vorbedachte böse Absicht; **premeditated** ~ Tötungsvorsatz nach Überlegung; **special** ~ = *particular* ~ *qv*; **transferred** ~ aberratio ictus; **universal** ~ allgemeiner Hang zu strafbaren Handlungen *bes zum Töten*.

malicious bösartig, böswillig, in böser Absicht; ~ **abuse of legal prozess** Prozeßmißbrauch, Mißbrauch des Rechtswegs.

malinger simulieren.

malingerer Simulant *m*, simulierender Drückeberger.

malpractice standeswidriges Verhalten *n*; grober ärztlicher Kunstfehler *m*; schwere Verletzung *f anwaltschaftlicher oder ärztlicher* Berufspflichten; ~ **suit** Prozeß wegen ärztl Kunstfehlers; ~ **judgment** Urteil wegen standesrechtl Verfehlung; **legal** ~ Anwaltspflichtverletzung; **medical** ~ ärztliche Pflichtverletzung.

malt|beverages Bier *n* und bierähnliche Getränke *n|pl*; ~ **liquor** Bier und bierartige Getränke; ~ **-shot** Bierherstellungsabgabe.

maltreatment Mißhandlung *f*; ärztlicher Kunstfehler *m*.

malversation Veruntreuung *f*, Amtsmißbrauch *m*, Fehlverhalten *m* im Amt (*bzw im Beruf*).

malvolence Böswilligkeit *f*, Boshaftigkeit *f*.

man *s* Mensch *m*, Mann *m*; erwachsene männliche Person; *hist* Lehensmann *m*, Vasall *m*; ~**-day** Tagesleistung einer Arbeitskraft; ~**-hour** Arbeitsstunde; ~ **in possession** Gewahrsamsinhaber; ~**-mistress relationship** Konkubinat, außerehel Lebensgemeinschaft; ~ **of skill** Sachverständiger; ~ **of straw** Strohmann, Berufszeuge; ~**-week** wöchentliche Arbeitsleistung *e–r Arbeitskraft*; **lawful** ~ freier Mann, eidesfähiger Ehrenmann; **patent** ~ Patentfachmann.

manacles Handfesseln *f|pl*.

manage führen, handhaben, leiten, bewirtschaften, behandeln, die Geschäftsführung ausüben; ~**d currency** → *currency*; ~**d fund** → *fund*.

management Geschäftsführung *f*, Geschäftsleitung *f*, Leitung *f*, Betriebsführung *f*, Verwaltung *f*, Direktion *f*, Behandlung *f*, Handhabung *f*; Führungskräfte *f|pl*, leitende Angestellte *m|pl*; Arbeitgeber(seite); ~ **accountancy** Unternehmensberatung durch Wirtschaftsprüfer; ~ **accounting** → *accounting*; **M**~ **and Administration Department** *gerichtliche* Abteilung für Verwaltung von Mündelvermögen; ~ **and labour** Arbeitgeber und Arbeitnehmer; ~ **body** Geschäftsführungsorgan; ~ **buyout** Aufkauf eigener Aktien durch die leitenden Angestellten *zur Übernahme und Sanierung*; ~ **committee** geschäftsführender Ausschuß; ~ **company** Verwaltungsgesellschaft, Hausverwaltungsges.; ~ **consultant** Betriebsberater, Unternehmensberater; ~ **consulting** Unternehmensberatung; ~ **contract** → *contract*; ~ **education** betriebswirtschaftl Studium; ~ **game** Betriebsplanspiel; ~ **inventory** Stellenbesetzungsplan für Führungskräfte; ~ **of a corporation** Verwaltungsspitze; Geschäftsleitung; ~ **of a ship** technische Bedienung e–s Schiffes; ~ **of property** Vermögensverwaltung; ~ **problems** Organisationsprobleme; ~ **ratio** *Verhältnis leitender Angestellter zu Gesamtbeschäftigtenzahl*; betriebswirtschaftliche Proportion(en); ~ **reserve group** Führungsnachwuchsgruppe; ~ **science** Betriebsführungslehre; ~ **team** Führungsgruppe; ~ **trust** Kapitalanlagegesellschaft mit eigenverantwortl Anlageverwaltung; **administrative** ~ Verwaltungspraxis, Leitung von Behörden; **advanced** ~ mittlere Führungsschicht; **board of** ~ Vorstand, Verwaltungsrat; **business** ~ Geschäftsführung, Betriebsführung; **debt** ~ Schuldenverwaltung; **earnings of the** ~ Tantiemen (*des Vorstandes*); **executive** ~ Geschäftsleitung; **multiple** ~ mehrstufige Betriebsführung; **personnel** ~ → *personnell*; **senior** ~ Firmenleitung; **top** ~ oberste Betriebsleitung, Unternehmensspitze; **under new** ~ unter neuer Geschäftsführung.

manager Betriebsführer *m*, Geschäftsführer *m*, Leiter *m*, Direktor *m*, Manager *m*; ~**s** Direktion; ~**'s discretionary limits** Grenzen der Beleihungsbefugnis von Zweigstellenleitern; ~ **in trust** treuhänderischer Verwahrer (*bzw Verwalter*); ~**s of a conference** Abgeordnete des Vermittlungsausschusses; ~**'s report** Geschäftsbericht, **advertis-**

ing ~ Werbeleiter; **bank** ~ Bankdirektor; **branch** ~ Filialleiter; **chief** ~ Hauptgeschäftsführer; **data processing** ~ Leiter der Datenverarbeitung; **departmental** ~ Abteilungsleiter (*Betrieb*); **deputy** ~ stellvertretender Direktor; **development** ~ Leiter der Entwicklungsabteilung; **export** ~ Leiter der Exportabteilung; **general** ~ Geschäftsführer, (*auch evt:*) Generaldirektor; **lead** ~ Konsortialführer; **marketing** ~ Leiter der Abteilung Absatzförderung; Leiter der Vertriebsabteilung; **official** ~**s** amtliche Liquidatoren; **personnel** ~ Personalchef; **resident** ~ örtlicher Geschäftsführer; **sales** ~ Verkaufsleiter, Leiter der Verkaufsabteilung; **special** ~ gerichtlich bestellter Geschäftsführer, Einzelliquidator, Sequester; **sub-** ~ Abteilungsleiter; **technical** ~ technischer Direktor; **top** ~ oberster Betriebsleiter; **works** ~ Betriebsleiter, Werksleiter.

managerial authority Führungsbefugnis; ~ **economics** allgemeine Betriebswirtschaftslehre; ~ **employee** leitender Angestellter; ~ **revolution** die Revolution der Manager; ~ **staff** leitende Angestellte; **in** ~ **capacity** in leitender Stellung.

managership Geschäftsführung *f*, Leitung *f*, Direktion *f*.

managing leitend, geschäftsführend; ~ **agent** → *agent;* ~ **clerk** → *clerk;* ~ **committee** Verwaltungsausschuß, Verwaltungsrat, Vorstand; ~ **director** → *director*; ~ **owner of ship** geschäftsführender Miteigentümer e–s Schiffes; ~ **partner** → *partner*; ~ **president** geschäftsführender Präsident.

mancipate verklaren, binden.

mandamus außerordentliches Rechtsmittel *n*; gerichtliche Anweisung *f* an ein unteres Gericht *bzw* eine Behörde; Beschwerderecht *n* gegen Beamte; gerichtlicher Hoheitsbefehl *m* bei Rechtsverweigerung; ~ **injunction** gerichtliche Sicherstellung; **action of** ~ Erzwingungsverfahren *gegen Gericht oder Behörde*, Untätigkeitsklage; **alternative** ~ *gerichtl–er Befehl, der Gegenvorstellungen gestattet*; **interlocutory** ~ einstweilige Verfügung; **peremptory** ~ absolut zwingender (*zweiter*) gerichtlicher Befehl *ohne Einwendungsmöglichkeit*; **writ of** ~ gerichtlicher Befehl auf Vornahme e–r Handlung.

mandatary Beauftragter *m*, Bevollmächtigter *m*, Mandatar *m*.

mandate *s* Weisung *f*, gerichtlicher Befehl *m*, = *mandamus qv*, unentgeltlicher Auftrag *m*, Vollmacht *f*, Mandat *n*; ~ **system** Mandatssystem; **allotment of** ~**s** *parl* Sitzverteilung.

mandate *v* e–m Mandat unterstellen, ~**d territories** Mandatsgebiete.

mandator Auftraggeber *m* (*bei unentgeltlichem Auftrag*), Vollmachtgeber *m*.

mandatory *adj* obligatorisch, vorgeschrieben, zwingend; ~ **duty** → *duty*; ~ **injunction** → *injunction*; ~ **instructions** verbindliche Anweisungen; ~ **order** → *order* (*1*); ~ **provision** zwingende Bestimmung, Mußvorschrift; ~ **seatbelt law** Anschnallpflichtgesetz; ~ **testing** Zwangstests(anwendung).

mandatory *s* Beauftragter *m* (= *mandatary qv*)

manhood Volljährigkeit *f* des Mannes, Männlichkeit *f*.

mania Manie *f*, Sucht *f*; ~ **a potu** Trinkerpsychose, Säuferwahn.

manifest *adj* offenbar, offensichtlich, augenscheinlich, unbestreitbar; ~ **injustice** offenkundige Ungerechtigkeit.

manifest *s* Kundgebung *f*, Manifest *n*, Ladungsverzeichnis *n*, Frachtliste *f*; ~ **of cargo** Ladungsmanifest; **inward** ~ Zolleinfuhrerklärung; **outward** ~ Zollausfuhrerklärung.

manifest *v* darlegen, kundtun, offenbaren.

manifesto Proklamation *f*, Kundgebung *f*, Manifest *n*, Grundsatzerklärung *f*; **election** ~ → *election.*

manifestation Kundmachung *f*, Offenbarung *f*; ~ **of intention** Ausdruck des Willens.
manipulate handhaben, behandeln.
manipulation Manipulation *f*, Beeinflussung *f*, Behandlung *f*, Handhabung *f*; ~ **of elections** Wahlmanipulierung; **fraudulent** ~ betrügerisches Geschäftsgebaren.
manner Art *f* und Weise *f*; Diebesbeute (*in der Hand des Diebes*); ~**s and customs of a country** Sitten und Gebräuche e–s Landes; "~ **and form**" *traditionelle Schlußworte im Bestreitungsschriftsatz, wonach die Formrichtigkeit des gegnerischen Sachvortrages bestritten wird;* ~ **of calculation** Berechnungsart; **business** ~**s** Geschäftsgebaren.
manning Tagesarbeit *f*; Gerichtsladung *f*; ~ **table** Stellenbesetzungsplan.
manor Haus *n*, Wohnung *f*, Sitz *m*; Lehensgut *n*, Herrensitz *m*, Rittergut *n*; Erbpachtland *n*.
manorial|documents *Urkunden e–s Herrenhofes und grundherrschaftlichen Gerichts*; ~ **extent** *Bestandsaufnahme der Rechtsverhältnisse von Herrenhöfen durch Geschworene*; ~ **incidents** *mit Herrenhof verbundene Gerechtsame*; ~ **rights** Gutsherrenrechte, Grundeigentümersrechte; ~ **waste** nicht bewirtschaftetes Gutsland.
manpower Arbeitskräfte *f/pl*, Menschenbestand *m*, Kriegsstärke *f*; **M~ Services Commission** Ausbildungs- und Umschulungsbehörde (*GB*); ~ **shortage** Arbeitskräftemangel.
mansion Wohnhaus *n*, Herrschaftssitz, Villa; ~ **house** Herrensitz, Wohnhaus auf e–m Gutshof, Villa, Mietshaus, Apartmenthaus; **the M~ House** *Amtssitz des Lord Mayor von London.*
manslaughter rechtswidrige Tötung *f* (*e–s Menschen*); Totschlag *m* (*wenn vorsätzl*); ~ **by an unlawful and dangerous drug** Todesverursachung durch Rauschgift; ~ **through negligence** = *negligent* ~ *qv*; **constructive** ~ leichte Körperverletzung mit Todesfolge; **first degree** ~ Totschlag *ohne mildernde Umstände*; **involuntary** ~ unbeabsichtigte Tötung *bei Begehung e–r Straftat*; fahrlässige Tötung; versehentliche Tötung; **negligent** ~ fahrlässige Tötung; **unintentional** ~ = *involuntary* ~ *qv*; **voluntary** ~ Totschlag im Affekt.
manslayer Totschläger *m*, *eine Person, die manslaughter begangen hat.*
manslaying Totschlag *m*.
manstealing Menschenraub *m*, Entführung *f*.
manticulate Taschendiebstahl begehen.
mantle children *durch nachfolgende Eheschließung* legitimierte Kinder *n/pl*.
mantrap Fußangel *f*, Falle *f*.
manu|opera in der Hand des Diebes angetroffene Beute *f*; ~ **propria** eigenhändig.
manual *adj* eigenhändig, mit der Hand, manuell; ~ **aptitude** manuelle Begabung; ~ **delivery** (*tatsächliche*) Übergabe; ~ **exchange** Fernamt mit Handvermittlung; ~ **gift** Schenkung von beweglichen Sachen (*mit Übergabe*), Handschenkung; ~**labo(u)r** → *labo(u)r*; ~ **mechanical bookkeeping** Durchschreibbuchhaltung; ~ **possession** unmittelbarer Besitz; ~ **rate** Tarif bei sozialer Unfallversicherung (*nach Gefahrenklassen gestaffelt*); ~ **training** Werkunterricht; ~ **work** Handarbeit; ~ **worker** → *worker*; ~**ly signed** eigenhändig unterzeichnet.
manual *s* Handbuch *n*, Leitfaden *m*, Dienstvorschrift *f*; **operating** ~ Betriebshandbuch, Betriebsanleitung; **sales** ~ Verkaufsbroschüre.
manufacture *s* Herstellung *f*, Fabrikation *f*, Fertigung *f*, Erzeugnisse *n/pl*, Fabrikat *n*; ~ **to customer's specification** Einzelanfertigung; **article of** ~ Industrieerzeugnis; **branch of** ~ Industriezweig; **cost of** ~ Herstellungskosten; **domestic** ~**s** einheimische Gewerbeprodukte; **home** ~ einheimisches Er-

zeugnis, inländisches Fabrikat; **semi-** ~ Halbfabrikate; **serial** ~ Serienherstellung.

manufacture *v* verarbeiten, herstellen, fertigen; **~d article** Fertigfabrikat; **~d goods** Industriewaren, Industrieerzeugnisse.

manufacturer Fabrikant *m*, Produzent *m*, Hersteller *m*, Industrieller *m*; **~'s agent** → *agent*; **~'s cost** Herstellungskosten; **~'s excise** Herstellungsumsatzsteuer; **~'s export agent** Exportvertreter; **~'s liability** Produzentenhaftung.

manufacturing|agreement Herstellungsvertrag; ~ **business** Industrieunternehmen; ~ **clause** Inlandherstellungsklausel (*bei Büchern in USA: Copyrightvoraussetzung*); ~ **concern** Fabrikationsbetrieb; ~ **corporation** Aktiengesellschaft für Industrieproduktion; ~ **costs** Herstellungskosten; ~ **country** Herstellungsland; ~ **department** Produktionsabteilung; ~ **enterprise** Fertigungsbetrieb, Werk; ~ **establishment** Fabrik, Industrieunternehmen, Verarbeitungsbetrieb; ~ **expense** Fertigungsgemeinkosten; ~ **industries** verarbeitende Industrie, Fertigungsindustrie; ~ **margin** Fertigungsüberschuß, Verarbeitungsspanne; ~ **order** innerbetrieblicher Auftrag, Fabrikauftrag; ~ **overhead** Fertigungsgemeinkosten; ~ **price** Fabrikpreis; ~ **process** Herstellungsverfahren, Fertigungsverfahren; ~ **right** Herstellungsrecht, Fabrikationsrecht; ~ **secret** → *secret*; ~ **statement** Aufgliederung der Herstellungskosten.

manumission Sklavenfreilassung *f*; Befreiung *f* von fremder Herrschaft.

manuscript *adj* handschriftlich; handgeschrieben oder maschinengeschrieben.

manuscript *s* Manuskript *n*, Autorenmanuskript *n*, Urschrift *f*, Satzvorlage *f*; Handschrift *f*.

map references Planquadrate.

march Grenze *f*, Markierungslinie *f*.

marches *hist* Grenzen *fpl*, Grenzland *n*, Marken *fpl*.

Mareva injunction *einstweilige Vermögenssperre bei Gefährdung der vorläufigen Vollstreckbarkeit,* dingl Arrest.

margin Grenze *f*, Spielraum *m*, Marge *f*, Überschuß *m*, Rand *m*; Handelsspanne *f*, Verdienstspanne *f*, Limit *n* des Maklers, Deckung *f*, Rentabilitätsgrenze *f*, Sicherheitsminimum *n*; Einschuß (*zu hinterlegende Summe bei Akkreditiven*); ~ **account** Hinterlegungskonto (*beim Börsenhändler*); ~ **business** Differenzgeschäft; ~ **call** Nachschußaufforderung *des Börsenmaklers*; ~ **of preference** Präferenzspanne; ~ **of profit** Verdienstspanne, Gewinnspanne; ~ **of safety** Sicherheitsspanne; ~ **requirements** Überdeckungsspanne *bei Darlehen an Mitgliedsbanken*; **gross** ~ Bruttomarge, Bruttospanne, Bruttogewinn; **to leave a** ~ e–n Gewinn abwerfen; **to purchase securities on** ~ Wertpapiere auf Kredit kaufen.

marginal|analysis Grenzplanungsrechnung; ~ **borrower** Grenzkreditnehmer; ~ **case** Grenzfall; ~ **constituency** *brit* umstrittener Wahlbezirk; ~ **consumer** marginaler Verbraucher (*der bei Preisänderung dazukommt oder wegfällt*); ~ **costing** Grenzkostenkalkulation, Mengenkostenrechnung; ~ **cost** Grenzkosten; ~ **deposit** Einschuß; ~ **disutility** Grenze der Arbeitswilligkeit (*lohnabhängig*); ~ **earnings** Grenzertrag; ~ **exceptions** geringfügige Ausnahmen; ~ **firm** marginales Unternehmen (*das als letztes in ein Produktionsgebiet eintritt oder es verläßt*); ~ **income** Grenzertrag; ~ **land** marginaler Boden; ~ **lender** letztbereiter Kreditgeber; ~ **net product** Nettogrenzprodukt; ~ **note** Randbemerkung, Vertragszusatz, Resumé e–r Entscheidung, kurze Inhaltsangabe am Rande von Gesetzestexten; ~ **payment** Differenzzahlung; ~ **produ-**

cer Grenzproduzent; ~ **product** Grenzprodukt; ~ **production** Produktion an der Kostengrenze; ~ **productivity** Grenzproduktivität; ~ **profit** Grenzertrag, knapper Gewinn, Gewinnminimum, Rentabilitätsgrenze; ~ **purchaser** Grenznachfrager, Grenzkäufer, unschlüssiger Käufer; ~ **rate of substitution** Grenzrate der Substitution; ~ **relief** *ermäßigter Steuersatz für unterste steuerpflichtige Einkommensgruppen*; ~ **revenue** *Differenz zwischen Umsatz und variablen Kosten*; *Spanne, aus der die fixen Kosten gedeckt werden müssen*; ~ **sales** gerade noch rentabler Absatz, Verkauf zum Selbstkostenpreis; ~ **significance** Grenzwert; ~ **theory of value** Grenznutzentheorie; ~ **trading** Differenzgeschäft (*Börsentermingeschäft, Teilhinterlegung*); ~ **unit** letzte Produkteinheit; ~ **unit cost** Grenzkosten; ~ **utility** Grenznutzen; ~ **value** Grenzwert, *die marginal niedrigsten Preise als Kaufanreiz*; ~ **yield** Grenzertrag; **operating** ~ Handelsspanne, Gewinnspanne.

marine Marine *f*, Schiffs. . ., See. . .; ~ **adventure** Seegefahr, Seerisiko; ~ **belt** Küstenhoheitsgewässer; ~ **board** Seeamt; ~ **cable** Seekabel; ~ **contract** seerechtlicher Vertrag, Seebeförderungsvertrag; **M~ Corps** Marine-Infanterie, Marinekorps; ~ **engineering** Schiffsmaschinenbau; ~ **inspector** Schiffsinspektor (*e–r Versicherung*); ~ **insurer** Seeversicherer; ~ **interest** Bodmereizinsen; ~ **peril** Seegefahr, Seerisiko; ~ **registry** Schiffsregister; ~ **stores** Schiffsbedarf, Schiffsvorräte; Schiffsbedarfsmagazin; ~ **survey** Schiffsinspektion (*des Versicherungsbeauftragten*); ~ **transport** Seetransport; Beförderung auf dem Seewege; **mercantile** ~ Handelsmarine.

mariner Seemann *m*, Matrose *m*, Seefahrer *m*; **~'s will** Seemannstestament; **master** ~ Kapitän.

marital ehelich, die Ehe betreffend, den Ehemann betreffend; ~ **coercion** Nötigung der Ehefrau durch den Ehemann; ~ **control** Verwaltungs- und Nutznießungsrecht des Ehemannes an dem eingebrachten Gut der Ehefrau; Verfügungsrecht des Ehemannes; ~ **deduction** Ehegattenfreibetrag; ~ **deduction trust** Ehegatten-Freibetragstreuhand *Treuhandzuwendung in Höhe des Ehegattenfreibetrages; gemäß Schenkungs- bzw Erbschaftssteuer*; ~ **duty** eheliche Pflicht (*allgemein*); ~ **home** eheliche Wohnung; ~ **portion** Witwenpflichtanteil am Nachlaß; ~ **privilege** → *privilege*; ~ **relations** eheliche Beziehungen, Verhältnis der Ehegatten zueinander; ~ **rights** Pflichtanteil des Ehegatten am Nachlaß des anderen; eheliche Rechte, Rechte des Ehemannes; ~ **property** → *property*; ~ **rights and duties** eheliche Rechte und Pflichten.

maritime|affairs Seesachen, Schiffahrtsangelegenheiten; ~ **adventure** Seeunternehmen; ~ **assistance** Bergung und Hilfeleistung (*aus Seenot*); ~ **belt** Küstenhoheitsgewässer; ~ **blockade** Seeblockade, Seesperre; ~ **cause** seerechtlicher Fall; ~ **claim** seerechtlicher Anspruch; ~ **commerce** Seehandel, Überseehandel; **M~ Commission** *Oberste US-Bundesbehörde für die Schiffahrt*; ~ **contract** Schiffahrtsvertrag; ~ **contract of affreightment** Seefrachtvertrag; ~ **court** Gericht für seerechtliche Angelegenheiten, Seeamt; ~ **domain** See(hoheits)gebiet; ~ **employees** Arbeitnehmer in der Schiffahrt; ~ **freight** Seefracht; ~ **frontiers** Küstengrenzen; ~ **international law** internationales Seerecht; ~ **lien** → *lien*; ~ **loan** Bodmerei(darlehen); ~ **matters** Schiffahrtsangelegenheiten, Seesachen; ~ **peril(s)** Seetransportgefahr; ~ **port** Seehafen; ~ **power** Seemacht; ~ **profit** Bodmereiprämie, Bodmereigewinn; ~ **regulations** Handelsschiffahrtsvorschriften; ~ **safety** Schiffssicherheit, Sicherheit auf See; ~ **sal-**

vage Bergung und Hilfeleistung (*aus Seenot*); ~ **service** seemännische Dienstleistung; **M~ Service** *US Handelsmarineausbildungsorganisation*; ~ **shipping** Seeschiffahrt; **M~ State** *die Offiziere und Mannschaften der britischen Kriegsmarine*; ~ **territory** Hoheitsgewässer; ~ **tort** *in schiffbaren Gewässern begangene unerlaubte Handlung*; ~ **trade** → *trade*; ~ **transactions** Schiffahrts- und Seehandelsangelegenheiten; ~ **usage** Seebrauch, Seemannsbrauch; **National M~ Board** (=) *Verhandlungs- und Schiedsstelle von Arbeitgebern und Arbeitnehmern der Handelsmarine*.

mark *s* Marke *f*, Zeichen *n*, Warenzeichen *n*, Schutzmarke *f*; Notierung *f*; Markierung *f*, Bezeichnung *f*, Merkmal *n*, Spur *f*, Rang *m*, Unterschriftszeichen *n*, Kreuze *n|pl* als Unterschrift; Prägezeichen *n*; ~ **of origin** Herkunftszeichen, Ursprungszeichen; ~ **of proof** Beweisindiz; ~ **of quality** Gütezeichen; ~ **on** Preisaufschlag *zum Einkaufspreis*; **boundary** ~ Grenzzeichen, Grenzmarke; **certification** ~ Gütemarke, Gütezeichen; Verbandsmarke; **check** ~ Kontrollzeichen; **collective** ~ Verbandszeichen, Kollektivmarke; **commercial** ~ Warenbezeichung; **deceptive** ~ irreführendes (Waren)Zeichen; **distinctive** ~ unterscheidungsfähiges Zeichen; spezifisches Warenzeichen; **national** ~ Kennzeichen des Erzeugerlandes (*made in . . .*); **manufacturer's** ~ Fabrikzeichen, Warenzeichen; **non-distinctive** ~ nicht deutlich unterscheidbares Warenzeichen; **old** ~ Warenzeichen, mit seit alters bestehender Verkehrsgeltung; **registered** ~ eingetragene Handelsmarke; **service** ~ Dienstabzeichen; **signature by** ~ → *signature;* **trade** ~ → *trademark*.

mark *v* kennzeichnen, auszeichnen, brandmarken, aufzeichnen, bezeichnen, markieren, mit e–m Zeichen versehen; ~ **a price** e–n Kurs notieren; ~**ed and numbered** gekennzeichnet und numeriert; ~**ed cheque** → *cheque*; ~ **down** e–n Preisabschlag vornehmen, Ware niedriger auszeichnen; ~**ed out** abgegrenzt; ~ **up** e–n Preisaufschlag vornehmen, die Preise heraufsetzen; e–n Gemeinkostenzuschlag vornehmen.

markdown Preisherabsetzung *f*, niedrigere Bewertung *f*, Preisnachlass *m*, Preisabschlag *m*.

market Markt *m* (= *M bzw . . . m*), Börse *f*, Absatz *m*; Handelsplatz *m*, Absatzgebiet *n*, Marktrecht *n*; ~ **agency** *M*stelle, *M*büro; ~**s and fairs** Märkte und Messen; **M~ and Trading Information System** (*MANTIS*) *(=) elektronisches Börsenhandels- und Informationssystem (London)*; ~ **average** Durchschnittspreis am *M*, Durchschnittskurs; ~ **conditions** → *condition (2)*; ~ **control** *M*beherrschung; ~ **day** *M*tag, Börsentag; ~ **dues** *M*gebühren, Standgebühren; ~ **economy** freie *M*wirtschaft; ~ **forces** (die) Kräfte des (freien) *M–s*; ~ **gardens** Gärtnereibetriebe; ~ **geld** *M*zoll; ~ **inspection certificates** Feststellungsbescheinigung von US Agrarbeauftragten über den Agrarmarkt; ~ **leader** Marktführer; *pl*: führende Börsenwerte; ~ **letters** (*tägliche*) *M*berichte; ~ **maker** "Markt-Macher", marktbestimmender Effektenhändler, Primärhändler (*zur Kurspflege*), führende Plazierungsbank für Eurobonds; ~ **making** Aufbau e–s Markts (*zB durch Kaufen u Verkaufen*); ~ **meltdown** Absacken der Kurse; ~ **of issue** Emissions*m*; ~ **off** *M* abgeschwächt; ~ **order** → *order (2)*; ~ **overt** öffentlicher *M*, *M*- und Ladengeschäfte (*gutgläubiger Erwerb möglich*); ~ **potential** Absatzmöglichkeit; ~ **power** Macht (*e–s Unternehmers*) auf dem *M*; ~ **price** *M*preis, Handelspreis, Börsenkurs, Verkehrswert; ~ **profit** Kursgewinn; ~ **quotation** Kursnotierung; ~ **rate** Börsenkurs, Kurswert; ~ **rate** (**of**

discount) Diskontsatz der Geschäftsbanken; ~ **report** *M*bericht, Börsenbericht; ~ **research** *M*forschung; ~ **rigging** Kurstreiberei; ~ **selling value** gewöhnlicher Verkaufswert; ~ **share** *M*anteil; ~ **sharing** Aufteilung des *M–es*; ~ **syndicate** Börsensyndikat; ~ **terms** Börsenbrauch, Börsenusance; ~ **tier** Börsensegment, *M*segment; ~ **towns** Städte mit *M*-recht; ~ **transactions** Börsengeschäfte, Börsentransaktionen; ~ **turmoil** Börsenturbulenzen; ~ **value** *M*wert; Verkehrswert, Kurswert, Tageskurs; ~ **watchers** Börsenbeobachter; **absorptive capacity of the** ~ Aufnahmefähigkeit des *M–es*; **active** ~ lebhafter *M*; **agricultural** ~ Agrar*m*; **assured** ~ zugesicherter Absatz*m*; **at** ~ *exch* billigst, bestmöglich; **at the** ~ *exch* zum Börsenkurs, bestens; **available** ~ Absatzmöglichkeit; **bear** ~ → *bear*; **bearish** ~ Baissestimmung; **bond** ~ Renten*m*; **brisk** ~ lebhafter Börsen*m*; **bullish** ~ haussierende Börse, Haussestimmung; **call** ~ → *call*; **capital** ~ Kapital*m*; **cash** ~ Kassa*m*; **clerk of the** ~ → *clerk;* **colonial** ~ *M* für Kolonialwerte, **commercial paper** ~ *M* für Schuldscheine erstklassiger Unternehmen; **commodity** ~ → *commoditiy;* **common** ~ allgemein zugänglicher *M*; **competitive** ~ freier *M* (*mit freiem Wettbewerb*); **concentration of** ~**s** Zusammenballung von Absatzgebieten; **discount** ~ → *discount*; **domestic** ~ Binnen*m*, Inlands*m*; **dominant** ~ **power** marktbeherrschende Stellung; **dull** ~ lustlose Börse; **easy** ~ *M* mit Überangebot; **equity** ~ Aktien*m*; **exchange** ~ → *exchange (2)*; **external** ~ Außenmarkt; **floating-rate** ~ zinsvariabler Euroanleihe*m*; **forward** ~ Termin*m*; **free** ~ → *free*; **futures** ~ Termin*m*, Warenbörse mit Terminhandel; **gilt-edged** ~ *M* für brit Staatspapiere; **glutted** ~ übersättigter *M*; **grey** ~ grauer *M*; **imperfect** ~ unvollkommener (*heterogener*) *M*; **inactive** ~ lustloser *M*; **insurance** ~ Versicherungs*m*; **interbank** ~ Interbanken*m*; **international** ~ Welt*m*; **issue** ~ Emissions*m*; **kerb** ~ → *kerb*; **limited** ~ enger *M*; **liquid** ~ Börse mit ausreichenden Umsätzen, *wegen Glattstellungen* schwache Börse; **narrow** ~ enger *M*; **national** ~ Absatz im ganzen Land; **nominal** ~ fast umsatzlose Börse; **open** ~ *vgl oben: market overt*; **open** ~ **value** Verkehrswert; **oversea** ~**s** Überseemärkte; **over-the-counter** ~ (= *OTC market*) Freiverkehrs*m*, Telefonverkehr; **parallel** ~ Parallel*m*, Neben*m*; **perfect** ~ theoretisch vollkommener (*homogener*) *M*; **primary** ~ Primär*m*, *M* für Neuemissionen; Aufkauf*m*, Rohstoff*m*; **property** ~ Immobilien*m*, Grundstücks*m*; **public** ~ öffentlicher *M*; **railroad** ~ = *railway* ~ *qv*; **railway** ~ *M* für Eisenbahnwerte; **real estate** ~ → *real estate*; **receptive** ~ aufnahmebereiter *M*; **regional** ~ regionaler Absatz; **sagging** ~ schwache Börse; **secondary** ~ Sekundär*m* (*für bereits emittierte Werte*); **share** ~ Aktien*m*; **small** ~ enger *M*; **spot** ~ Kassa*m*; **steady** ~ fester *M*; **stock** ~ →*stock market*; **strong** ~ feste Börse; **temporary** ~ *M*, gelegentlicher *M*, Jahr*m*; **thin** ~ enger *M*, knappe Auftragslage (*nur wenige vom Tageskurs abweichende Börsenaufträge*); **to be in the** ~ auf dem *M* sein; zum Verkauf angeboten werden; **to find a** ~ Absatz finden; **to play the** ~ → *to play*; **trading** ~ stagnierende, vom Berufshandel wahrgenommene Börse; **unofficial** ~ Freiverkehr; **virgin** ~ unbearbeiteter *M*.

marketability Marktfähigkeit *f*, Verkehrsfähigkeit *f*.

marketable marktfähig, marktgängig, gut verkäuflich, verkehrsfähig, börsenfähig; ~ **equities** → *equities*; ~ **parcel** börsenübliche Stückzahl; ~ **securities** → *security (2)*; ~ **title** freies Verfügungsrecht an Grundstücken, rechtsmängelfreier Grundbesitz; ~ **value** → *value;* **easily** ~ sofort realisierbar.

marketeers Befürworter *m/pl* des Gemeinsamen Marktes *in GB.*

marketing Marketing *n*, Marktversorgung *f*, Absatzpolitik *f*; Verkaufsstrategie *f*; ~ **agent** Absatzmittler; ~ **agreement** → *agreement*; ~ **association** Marketing-Verband, absatzwirtschaftlicher Verband; ~ **company** Vertriebsgesellschaft; ~ **consultant** Vertriebsberater; ~ **cooperative** Absatzgenossenschaft; ~ **cost** Vertriebskosten; ~ **manager** → *manager*; ~ **of securities** Effekteneinführung, Effektenvertrieb; ~ **operations** absatzwirtschaftl-e Maßnahmen; ~ **organization** Absatzorganisation, Vertriebsorganisation; ~ **plan** Vertriebsplan; ~ **ploys** Vermarktungstricks; ~ **policy** Absatzpolitik; ~ **quotas** Absatzkontingente; ~ **regulatory** Marktordnung; ~ **research** Absatzforschung; **agricultural** ~ Agrarmarktregelung.

market place Markt *m* Marktstandort *m*; Marktplatz *m*.

marking Kennzeichnung *f*, Bezeichnung *f*, *exch* Notierung *f*, Markierung *f*; ~ **clerk** Kursmakler; ~ **country of origin** Ursprungsbezeichnung; ~ **out** Grenzziehung, Vermarkung; **false** ~ **of goods** falsche Bezeichnung von Waren; **longitudinal** ~**s** Längsmarkierungen (*Straße*).

marksman Schreibunkundiger *m* (*der Unterschriftszeichen macht*); Scharfschütze *m*.

markup Handelsaufschlag *m*, Kalkulationsaufschlag *m*, Handelsspanne *f*; Preiserhöhung *f*.

marriage Ehe *f*, Eheschließung *f*, Heirat *f*; **M~ Act** Ehegesetz; ~ **articles** Ehevertrag (*unter Verlobten*); ~ **allowance** Ehegattenfreibetrag; ~ **brokage** Heiratsvermittlung, Heiratsvermittlungsprovision; ~ **brokage contract** Heiratsvermittlungsvertrag; ~ **broker** Heiratsvermittler; ~ **by certificate** standesamtliche Heirat; ~ **by proxy** Ferntrauung; ~ **ceremony** Trauung, Eheschließungsakt; ~ **certificate** Heiratsurkunde; Trauschein; ~ **consideration** Eheversprechen *als Gegenleistung;* ~ **contract** Ehevertrag; ~ **dispensation** Ehedispens, Befreiung vom Ehehindernis; ~ **duty** eheliche Pflicht, Eheverpflichtung; ~ **established by habit and repute** *scot* gewohnheitsrechtl anerkannte formlose Ehe; ~ **for love** Liebesheirat; ~ **guidance** Eheberatung; ~ **at a registry office** standesamtliche Trauung; ~ **law** Eherecht, Ehegesetz; ~ **licence** → *licence*; ~ **notice book** Aufgebotsbuch; ~ **of convenience** nur im Eigeninteresse erfolgte Eheschließung, Zweckheirat, Vernunftehe, Scheinehe; ~ **officer** *zur Vornahme der standesamtlichen Eheschließung ermächtigter diplomatischer oder konsularischer Vertreter*; ~ **over distance** Ferntrauung; ~ **portion** Mitgift, Heiratsgut; ~ **portion insurance** → *insurance*; ~ **prohibition** Eheverbot; ~ **promise** Eheversprechen; ~ **property register** Güterrechtsregister; ~ **records** Eheschließungsurkunden in amtlicher Verwahrung; ~ **registrar** Standesbeamter für Eheschließung; ~ **service** Trauung, Traugottesdienst; ~ **settlement** Ehevertrag, Güterrechtsvertrag, Güterrechtstreuhandvertrag (*treuhänderische Zuwendung anläßlich der Eheschließung*); ~ **ties** eheliche Bande; **age of** ~ heiratsfähiges Alter; **announcement of** ~ Heiratsanzeige, Aufgebot; **annulment of a** ~ Aufhebung e-r Ehe; **avail of** ~ → *avail*; **bigamous** ~ Doppelehe, bigame Ehe; **breach of promise to** ~ → *breach*; **breakdown of** ~ → *breakdown*; **celebration of** ~ Eheschließung; kirchliche Trauung, **civil** ~ standesamtliche Trauung; **connected by** ~ verschwägert; **common-law** ~ eheähnliche, gesellschaftl akzeptierte Lebensgemeinschaft; **consensual** ~ formlose

Heirat; **consular** ~ Konsularehe, Eheschließung vor dem Konsul; **consummation of** ~ Vollziehung der Ehe; **dissolution of** ~ → *dissolution*; **English** ~ → *English*; **fictitious** ~ Scheinehe; **fleet** ~ *hist* Proforma-Eheschließung; (*in der Nähe des Fleet-Prison London*), heimliche Eheschließung; Scheinehe; **foreign** ~**s** Eheschließungen im Ausland; **impairment of prospect of** ~ Beeinträchtigung der Heiratschancen; **impediment to** ~ → *impediment*; **incestuous** ~ blutschänderische Heirat; **irregular** ~ reine Konsensualheirat (*ohne kirchlichen oder staatlichen Akt*); **jactitation of** ~ → *jactitation*; **legal** ~ rechtsgültige Ehe; **manus** ~ *hist* Ehe mit Unterwerfung der Frau; **mixed** ~ Mischehe; **mock** ~ Scheinehe; **morganatic** ~ morganatische Ehe (*standesungleiche Ehe*); **party contracting a** ~ Eheschließender; **plural** ~ Polygamie, Mehrehe, *bigame oder poligame eheähnliche Verbindung*; **proxy** ~ Handschuhehe; **Scotch** ~ formlose Eheschließung; **sham** ~ Scheinehe; **to annul a** ~ e–e Ehe (*durch Gerichtsurteil*) aufheben; **to contract a** ~ eine Eheschließung vornehmen; **to celebrate a** ~ e–e Eheschließung vornehmen, sich verheiraten; **void** ~ *automatisch* nichtige Ehe; **voidable** ~ vernichtbare Ehe, aufhebbare Ehe, der gerichtl Aufhebung unterliegende Ehe.

marriageable ehefähig, heiratsfähig; ~ **age** Ehemündigkeit.

married | at a registry office standesamtlich getraut; ~ **couple** Ehepaar, Eheleute; ~ **state** → *state (1)*; ~ **women's property** güterrechtliche Stellung der Ehefrau, Frauenvermögen.

marshall *s* Marschall *m*; Gerichtswachtmeister *m*, Gerichtsvollzieher *m*; Polizeichef *m*; **U.S. M**~ *(=) Justizbeauftragter der US-Bundesregierung in jedem der Einzelstaaten, Polizeichef und Bundesgerichtsvollzieher*.

marshal *v/t* ordnen, geleiten, bereitstellen, erfassen, aufstellen; ~ **assets** e–n Verteilungsplan aufstellen, Vermögen zur Befriedigung der Gläubiger erfassen; ~ **evidence** die Beweisaufnahme zusammenfassend erläutern; ~ **property** Vermögen erfassen (*mit Wirkung e–r Beschlagnahme*); ~ **the facts** Tatbestände ordnen.

marshalling | liens Feststellung der Rangordnung von Grundpfandrechten; ~ **of assets** Erfassung von Vermögenswerten; ~ **securities** Feststellung der Befriedigungsrechte vorrangiger Gläubiger.

mart Markt *m*, Handelszentrum *n*, Auktionsraum *m*.

martial | law Kriegsrecht, Standrecht, Kriegsgesetz; **court** ~ → *court*; **state of** ~ **law** Belagerungszustand; **to proclaim** ~ **law** das Kriegsrecht verhängen.

Martinmas *der 11. November (ein Quartalszahltag)*.

martyria *rhetorische Methode, sich auf eigene Erfahrung zum Beweis zu berufen.*

mass collision Massenkarambolage *f*.

mass transit Massen(nah)verkehrsmittel *n*.

Massachusetts | Rule *Regel, daß beim Scheckinkasso jede Bank, die den Scheck hat, Vertreter des Kontoinhabers ist*; ~ **Trust** → *trust*.

masthead Impressum *n*.

mast-selling *hist* Verkauf *m* der Habe eines toten Seemannes (*am Mast*).

master *s* Herrscher *m*, Herr *m*, Meister *m*, Arbeitgeber *m*, Dienstherr *m*, Handwerksmeister *m*, Lehrherr *m*, Ausbildender *m*; Schiffer *m*, Kapitän *m*; Rechtspfleger *m*; ~ **and servant relationship** Dienstverhältnis, Arbeitsverhältnis; ~ **antenna TV** (Groß)Gemeinschafts-Antennenanlage; ~ **at common law** Rechtspfleger in engl Obergerichten; ~ **budget** Gesamtetat; ~**'s certificate** Kapitänspatent; ~**'s effects** Kapitängut; ~ **file** Zentralarchiv; ~ **in chancery** Rechtspfleger (*in der Chancery Abteilung des High*

Court); ~ *obs* **in lunacy** Gerichtsbeauftragter in Entmündigungssachen, Vormundschaftsrichter; ~ **of a ship** = *ship* ~ *qv*; ~ **of ceremonies** Zeremonienmeister; **M~ of Law** (*LL. M.*) Magister der Rechte, *juristischer akademischer Grad unter dem Doktorgrad*; **M~ of the Bench** *Titel eines bencher qv*; **M~ of the Court of Protection** *Präsident des Court of Protection qv*; ~ **of the Crown Office** *Staatsanwalt bei Antragsdelikten*; **M~ of the Faculties** *Beamter der erzbischöflichen Verwaltung von Canterbury, zuständig für Dispenserteilung*; **M~ of the Horse** Oberstallmeister; **M~ of the Household** Hofmarschall; **M~ of the King's Musters** = Musterungsbeauftragter *der Krone*; **M~ of the Mint** Leiter der königlichen Münze; ~ **of the ordnance** Feldzeugmeister; **M~ of the Posts** *hist* Oberpostmeister; **M~ of the Rolls** (=) *hist Bezeichnung e-s Chancery-Richters, jetzt: Richter am Court of Appeals mit administrativer Sonderfunktion als Staatsurkundenbewahrer*; **M~ of the Seal Office** Gerichtssiegelbewahrer; ~ **of the Supreme Court** Rechtspfleger *mit teilw richterl Funktionen ohne mdl Verhandlg* am Zentralgericht in London; **M~ of the Wards** *Richter des Court of Wards and Liveries qv*; **~'s protest** Verklarung.

match-maker Ehemakler *m*, Heiratsvermittler *m*.

match *v* passend machen, passend verheiraten; **~ed and lost** Ausscheiden durch das Los; **~ed order** Vortäuschung von Börsenumsätzen durch Kauf- und Verkaufsaufträge für die gleichen Wertpapiere; ~ **the sample** dem Muster entsprechen.

matching gleich, entsprechend.

mate Ehegatte *m*, Maat *m*, Steuermann *m*, Arbeitskamerad *m*, Gehilfe *m*; **~'s certificate** Schifferpatent für kleine Fahrt; **~'s patent** = *~'s certificate qv*; **~'s receipt** Steuermannsquittung, Auslieferungsschein, vorläufige Ladungsempfangsbescheinigung.

material *adj* erheblich, wesentlich, wichtig, materiell-rechtlich; ~ **change of user** *brit* wesentliche Änderung in der Person des Warenzeichenbenutzers; ~ **factor defence** materiell-rechtl Einwendung; ~ **irregularity of procedure** wesentlicher Verfahrensfehler; ~ **to the merits of the case** entscheidungserheblich.

material *s* Material *n*, Stoff *m*, Baustoff *m pl auch:* Unterlagen; ~ **cost burden rate** Materialgemeinkostensatz; ~ **costing** Materialkostenermittlung; ~ **in process** Halbfabrikate-Materialanteil; **~s manager** Materialverwalter; Leiter der Materialabteilung; ~ **on hand** Materialbestand; ~ **on order** bestelltes (*noch zu lieferndes*) Material; **~s testing office** Materialprüfungsamt; **bought-out ~s** Fremdmaterial; **defect in ~** Materialfehler; **indirect ~** Gemeinkostenmaterial, Hilfsmaterial; **raw ~** → *raw*.

materiality Erheblichkeit *f*, Wichtigkeit *f*; ~ **of evidence** Beweiserheblichkeit.

materialman Materiallieferant *m*, Schiffsausrüster *m*.

materiél Material *n*.

maternal mütterlich, mütterlicherseits.

maternity Mutterschaft *f*; ~ **allowance** laufendes Mutterschaftsgeld (*18 Wochen ab 11. Woche vor erwarteter Niederkunft*); ~ **benefit** Mutterschaftshilfe; ~ **care** Entbindungsfürsorge, Wöchnerinnenhilfe; ~ **grant** Mutterschaftshilfe; ~ **pay** Mutterschutzlohn(fortzahlung); **M~ Pay Fund** Mutterschutzlohn-Ausgleichsfonds; ~ **home** Entbindungsheim; ~ **leave** *arbeitsfreie Schutzfrist nebst* Mutterschaftsurlaub (*GB: 11 Wochen vor bis 29 Wochen nach Niederkunft*); ~ **period** Mutterschutzfrist; ~ **rights** Mutterschaftsansprüche; ~ **services** Fürsorge für werdende Mütter und Wöchnerinnen.

matricide Muttermord *m*, Muttermörder *m*.

matriculate Mitglied werden; immatrikulieren, sich einschreiben.

matriculation Immatrikulierung *f*.

matrimonial ehelich, die Ehe betreffend, Ehe . . .; ~ **actions** (Klagen in) Ehesachen; ~ **agent** Heiratsvermittler; ~ **breakdown** Zerrüttung e–r Ehe; ~ **cause(s)** Ehesache(n); **M~ Causes Act** Ehe(rechtsreform)gesetz (*GB 1973*); ~ **cohabitation** eheliches Zusammenleben, Zusammenleben wie Eheleute; ~ **domicile** → *domicile;* ~ **home** Ehewohnung; ~ **injunction** → *injunction*; ~ **jurisdiction** → *jurisdiction*; ~ **law** Eherecht; ~ **maintenance** ehelicher Unterhalt; ~ **matter** Ehesache; ~ **offence** → *offence*; ~ **order** → *order (1)*; ~ **property law** eheliches Güterrecht; ~ **proceedings** Verfahren in Ehesachen; ~ **regime** → *regime*.

matrimony Ehe *f*, Ehestand *m*.

matrix Matrize *f*, Urschrift *f*; Organisationszentrum.

matron verheiratete Frau *f*, ältere Dame *f*; Oberin *f*, Aufseherin *f*, Wärterin *f*; **jury of ~s** → *jury*.

matter Angelegenheit *f*, Materie *f*, Sache *f*, anspruchsbegründender Sachverhalt *m*, Sachvortrag *m*, tatsächliche Behauptung *f*, Streitgegenstand *m*; ~ **in controversy** Streitgegenstand, Streitfall; ~ **in deed** urkundlich nachweisbare Tatsache; ~ **in difference** Streitpunkt, streitige Angelegenheit; ~ **in dispute** = ~ *in controversy qv*; ~ **in hand** vorliegende (Gerichts)Sache; ~ **in issue** Streitgegenstand, Streitsache; ~ **in pais** mündlich zu beweisender Sachverhalt; tatsächliches Vorbringen, Tatsachenstoff; ~ **involving honour** Ehrensache; ~ **of abatement** Rechtsmangel; ~ **of common concern** Angelegenheit von allgemeiner Bedeutung; ~ **of complaint** streitige Angelegenheit; ~ **of consequence** wichtige Angelegenheit; ~ **of course** Selbstverständlichkeit; ~ **of discretion** Ermessensfrage; ~ **of fact** Tatbestand, Tatsache, *adj, adv*: sachlich, unemotional; ~ **of form** → *form*; ~ **of honour** Ehrensache; ~ **of law** Rechtsfrage; ~ **of moment** Angelegenheit von Bedeutung; ~ **of official concern** Dienstsache, amtliche Sache; ~ **of opinion** Ansichtssache; ~ **of practice and procedure** Verfahrensangelegenheiten, Verfahrensfrage; ~ **of prestige** Prestigefrage; ~ **of record** aktenmäßig (*bzw urkundlich*) feststehende Tatsache; ~ **of state** Staatsangelegenheit; ~ **of subsistence for man** Nahrung, Nahrungsmittel; ~ **stated** Sachvortrag; **added** ~ Beifügung, Zusatz; **collateral** ~ (unwesentliche) Nebensache; **commercial ~s** Handelssachen; **criminal** ~ Strafsache; **fiscal ~s** Steuerwesen; **foreign** ~ vor ein anderes Gericht gehörige Sache; **in the ~ of** in Sachen; **legal** ~ Rechtsangelegenheit; **monetary ~s** Geldangelegenheiten; **new** ~ neuer Sachvortrag; **official** ~ Dienstsache; **outstanding** ~ unerledigte Sache; **personal** ~ Privatangelegenheit; **printed** ~ Drucksache; **the factual** ~ der Sachverhalt.

mature adj fällig, reif, unbedingt geschuldet; ~ **economy** hochentwickelte Volkswirtschaft; ~ **idea** ausgereifte Idee; ~ **plan** fertiger Plan.

matur|e *v* fällig werden, reifen, volljährig werden; **~ed** verfallen, fällig; **~ing on** fällig werdend am.

maturity Fälligkeit *f*, Reife *f*, Verfallszeit *f*, Volljährigkeit *f*, Verfallstag e–s Wechsels; ~ **age** *ins* Endalter; ~ **date** = *date of maturity* → *date;* ~ **factoring** Fälligkeitsfactoring; umfassender Factoring-Dienst; ~ **index** Terminkalender, Verfallbuch; ~ **mismatch** Fristenkongruenz; ~ **of claim** Fälligkeit e–s Anspruchs; ~ **of one year** einjährige Laufzeit; ~ **transformation** Fristentransformation; ~ **value** Fälligkeitswert; **by** ~ *ins* durch Ablauf; **current** ~ innerhalb e–s

Jahres fällige Verbindlichkeit, **endorsement after** ~ → *endorsement*.
maverick Einzelgänger *m*, Außenseiter *m*.
maxim Maxime *f*, Rechtsgrundsatz *m*, Sentenz; ~**s of equity** sprichwörtliche Grundregeln des Billigkeitsrechts; ~ **of law** Rechtsgrundsatz.
maximum | amount Höchstbetrag; ~ **capacity** Höchstkapazität; ~ **carrying capacity** Höchsttragfähigkeit; ~ **demand** Spitzennachfrage (*der Verbraucher*); ~ **demand tariff** → *tariff*; ~ **duration of credit** Höchstlaufzeit des Kredits; ~ **limit** Höchstgrenze; ~ **load** Höchstbelastung; ~ **loan value** Beleihungsgrenze; ~ **output** Höchstleistung; ~ **price** Höchstpreis, Höchstkurs; ~ **quota** Höchstkontingent; ~ **interest rates** Höchstzinssätze; ~ **speed** Höchstgeschwindigkeit; ~ **value** Höchstwert, oberste Wertgrenze; ~ **wages** Spitzenlohn, Höchstlohn.
may können, dürfen, (*als fakultative Bestimmung in Verträgen und Gesetzen*), in der Lage sein, zuständig sein für, befugt sein, im stande sein; ~ **be** eintreten können, möglicherweise entstehen.
mayhem schwere Körperverletzung *f*, Verstümmelung *f*, Selbstverstümmelung *f*.
mayor Bürgermeister *m*; ~, **aldermen and burgesses** Bürgermeister, Ratsherren und Bürger (*kreisfreie Stadt*); ~ **of the borough** Oberbürgermeister; ~**'s court** Stadtgericht; **M~'s and City of London Court** *Londoner Amtsgericht (für Zivilsachen) bis 1971.*
mayoralty Bürgermeisteramt *n*, Amtszeit des Bürgermeisters.
mayoress Gattin *f* des Bürgermeisters; Bürgermeisterin *f*, Inhaberin des Bürgermeisteramts.
meal-rent Bodenzins *m* in Form von Mehl.
meals on wheels Essen auf Rädern.
mean *adj* durchschnittlich, mittel, mittelmäßig; ~ **due date** mittlerer Verfallstag; ~ **low tide** mittlere Ebbe, mittleres Niedrigwasser; ~ **low water** mittleres Niedrigwasser; ~ **price** mittlerer Preis; ~ **value** → *value*.
mean *s* Mittelwert *m*, Mitte *f*, Mittelmäßigkeit *f*.
meaning Bedeutung *f*, Sinn *m*; ~ **and intentions** Sinn und Wille; **legal** ~ rechtliche Bedeutung; **literal** ~ wörtliche Bedeutung; **prima facie** ~ prima-facie Bedeutung; **secondary** ~ Nebenbedeutung, sekundäre Bedeutung.
means Mittel *n|pl* (= *M bzw ... m*), Geldmittel *n|pl*, Vermögen *n*, Einkommen *n*; ~ **form** Vermögenserklärungsformular; ~ **of communication** Nachrichten*m*, Nachrichtenübermittlungsmedien; Verkehrs*m*; ~ **of mass communication** Massenmedien; ~ **of conveyance** Transport*m*, Beförderungs*m*; ~ **of evidence** Beweis*m*; ~ **of living** Erwerbsquelle; ~ **of payment** Zahlungs*m*; ~ **of production** Produktions*m*; ~ **of subsistence** Erwerbsquelle, Unterhalt; ~ **of support** Unterhalt; ~ **of transportation** Beförderungs*m*; ~**-related financial penalties** Geldstrafen(system) nach wirtschaftlichen Verhältnissen des Täters; ~ **test** Bedürftigkeitsprüfung; *tested benefits: vom Nachweis der Bedürftigkeit abhängige Leistungen,* **available** ~ verfügbare *M*; **current** ~ Umlaufvermögen; **limited** ~ begrenzte *M*; **to have ample** ~ **at one's disposal** über genügend *M* verfügen; **private** ~ Eigenmittel, private Mittel; **to live beyond one's** ~ über seine Verhältnisse leben; **without** ~ unbemittelt, mittellos.
measure *s* Maß *n*, Maßeinheit *f*, Grad *m*, Ausmaß *n*, Umfang *m*; Maßnahme *f*; Synodalverordnung *f*; ~ **of care** der Grad der (erforderlichen) Sorgfaltspflicht; ~ **of damages** Schadenshöhe; ~ **of public security** Sicherheitsmaßnahme; ~**s of safety and rehabilitation** Maßre-

geln der Sicherung und Besserung; ~ **of value** Wertmaßstab; **counter** ~ Gegenmaßnahme; **interim** ~ einstweilige Anordnung; **emergency** ~**s** → *emergency;* **instant** ~**s** Sofortmaßnahmen; **legal** ~**s** juristische Schritte, Rechtsweg; **preventive** ~**s** vorbeugende Maßnahmen.

measure *v* messen, bemessen.

measurement Messung *f*, Maß *n*; Vermessung *f*, Abmessung *f*; Schiffstonnage *f*; ~ **cargo** sperrige Güter, Sperrgut; ~ **goods** *Ware, die nach Raumfrachtsätzen verschifft wird;* ~ **list** Aufmaßliste; ~ **of performances** Leistungsmessung; **certificate of** ~ Meßbrief.

measurer Feldmesser *m*, Landmesser *m*, Tuchabmesser *m*.

meat inspection Fleischbeschau *f*.

mechanic Handwerker *m*, Mechaniker *m*; ~**'s lien** → *lien.*

mechanical handwerksmäßig, mechanisch, maschinell, schablonenartig; ~ **device** maschinelle Einrichtung, mechanische Vorrichtung; ~ **effect** Nutzwert; ~ **engineer** Maschinenbauer, Ingenieur; ~ **engineering** Maschinenbau; ~ **equivalent** mechanisch gleichwertiger Gegenstand (*ohne Erfindungshöhe*); ~ **power** mechanische Kraft; ~**ly propelled vehicle** Kraftfahrzeug; ~ **skill** handwerkliche Geschicklichkeit; ~ **strength** mechanische Stärke; ~ **treatment** Weiterverarbeitung; ~ **work** mechanische Arbeit; schablonenmäßige Arbeit.

medal Medaille *f*, Auszeichnung *f*, Orden *m*; ~ **of hono(u)r roll** Ordensliste.

media („*the* ~“) Medien *n*|*pl*, Werbeträger *m*, Reklamemittel *n*; ~ **analysis** Werbeträgeranalyse ~ **oriented** auf Meinungsmedien ausgerichtet; **advertising** ~ Werbemittel.

median familiy income mittleres Familieneinkommen.

median strip Mittelstreifen *m* (*Straße, Autobahn*).

mediate *adj* mittelbar; ~ **descent** → *descent*; ~ **powers** Nebenbefugnisse; ~ **testimony** Zeugenaussage als sekundäres Beweismittel.

mediate *v* vermitteln, schlichten.

mediation Vermittlung *f*, Schlichtung *f*; Güteverfahren *n*; ~ **committee** → *committee;* ~ **mission** Vermittlungsauftrag, V.-saktion; **offer of** ~ → *offer*.

mediator Schlichter *m*.

Medicaid staatl. Krankenhilfe *f* (*US*).

medical ärztlich, medizinisch; ~ **benefits** ärztliche Leistungen (*e-r Kasse*); ~ **care** ärztliche Betreuung; ~ **certificate** → *certificate*; ~ **director** Leiter der medizinischen Abteilung (*e-r Versicherungsgesellschaft*); ~ **evidence** medizinischer Sachverständigenbeweis; ~ **examiner** → *examiner*; ~ **expense** Arztkosten, Behandlungskosten; ~ **inspection** (amts)ärztliche Untersuchung; ~ **jurisprudence** → *jurisprudence;* ~ **officer of health** *brit* Amtsarzt, Beamter des Gesundheitsdienstes; ~ **opinion** → *opinion;* ~ **practices committee** Zulassungsausschuß für Kassenärzte; ~ **practitioner** → *practitioner*; ~ **profession** die Ärzteschaft; ~ **referee** Amtsarzt, Vertrauensarzt; ~ **report** Arztbericht, Ärztegutachten; ~ **service** Gesundheitsdienst, Sanitätswesen; ~ **services** ärztliche Leistungen.

Medicare (=) Krankenhauskostenübernahme für Sozialrentner durch die US-Sozialversicherung.

medicine Medizin *f*, Heilkunde *f*; Arznei *f*; ~**-chest** Bordapotheke; **forensic** ~ Gerichtsmedizin; **legal** ~ Gerichtsmedizin; **schools of** ~ ärztliche Lehrmeinungen.

medico-legal gerichtsmedizinisch.

medium | **dated** mittelfristig; ~ **price** mittlerer Preis, Durchschnittspreis; ~ **quality** Mittelqualität; ~ **size** mittlere Größe; ~ **-term** mittelfristig; ~ **-term bonds** Schuldverschreibungen mit mittlerer Laufzeit; ~ **term credit** mittelfristige Darlehen (*3–10 Jahre*).

medley Gemisch *n*, Mischmasch *m*; Durcheinander *n*, Handgemenge *n*.

meet treffen, begegnen, entgegenkommen, erfüllen, zusammentreten; ~ **a bill** e-n Wechsel einlösen; ~ **competition** konkurrenzfähig sein; ~ **due protection** honoriert werden (*Wechsel*); ~ **objections** Einwände ausräumen, e-r Beschwerde abhelfen; ~ **one's obligations** seinen Verpflichtungen nachkommen; ~ **the expenses** für die Kosten aufkommen; ~ **with an accident** e-n Unfall haben; ~ **with approval** Billigung finden.

meeting Versammlung *f* (= *V bzw v*), Hauptversammlung *f*, Mitgliederversammlung *f*, Sitzung *f*, Tagung *f*, Zusammenkunft *f*; ~ **in camera** Sitzung unter Ausschluß der Öffentlichkeit; ~ **of creditors** Gläubiger*v*; ~ **of members** Mitglieder*v*, Haupt*v*; ~ **of minds** Willenseinigung, Übereinstimmung; ~ **of shareholders** Haupt*v*; ~ **of the board** Vorstandssitzung, Verwaltungsratssitzung; **adjourned** ~ fortgesetzte Sitzung nach Vertagung; **annual general** ~ Jahres*v*; **called** ~ außerordentliche Haupt*v*; **class** ~ → *class;* **company** ~ *brit* Haupt*v*; **constituent** ~ Gründungs*v*; **extraordinary general** ~ außerordentliche Haupt*v*, außerordentliche Mitglieder*v*; **family** ~ → *family*; **final** ~ Schluß*v*; **general** ~ ordentliche Haupt*v*, ordentliche Mitglieder*v*; **inquorate** ~ beschlußunfähige *V*; **notice of** ~ Ladung zur Haupt*v*; **ordinary** ~ ordentliche Haupt*v*; **plenary** ~ Plenarsitzung, Voll*v*; **preliminary** ~ Vor*v*; **private** ~ nicht öffentliche Sitzung; **public** ~ öffentl Versammlung, öffentl Sitzung; **regular** ~ ordentliche Haupt*v*, ordentliche Mitglieder*v*; **shareholder's** ~ Haupt*v*, General*v*; **special** ~ außerordentliche Haupt*v*; Sondersitzung; **stated** ~ ordentliche Sitzung; **statutory** ~ gesetzlich vorgeschriebene erste Haupt*v*; **to adjourn the** ~ die Sitzung vertagen; **to address the** ~ das Wort ergreifen; **to attend a** ~ an e-r Sitzung teilnehmen, bei e-r *V* anwesend sein; **to summon a** ~ e-e *V* einberufen.

mega-bid Groß-Übernahmeangebot *n*.

mega-corporation Riesenunternehmen *n*, Großkonzern *m*.

mega-merger Fusion von Großunternehmen, „Elefantenhochzeit".

meliorat|e verbessern, veredeln, (*Boden*) meliorieren; ~**ing waste** = *ameliorating waste* → *waste*.

melioration Verbesserung *f*, Veredelung *f*, Melioration *f*.

melon-cutting Ausschüttung *f* e-r Sonderdividende, Zuteilung *f* von Gratisaktien, Ausgabe *f* von Bezugsrechten zu e-m niedrigen Sonderkurs.

meltdown Durchschmelzen des Reaktorkerns.

Meltdown Monday der schwarze Montag (*19. 10. 1987, Börsenkrach*).

member Mitglied *n*; Anteilseigner, Bausparer; Aktionär *m*, Gesellschafter *m*; Abgeordneter *m*; Glied *n*, Körperteil *n*, Organ *n*; ~ **as of right** Mitglied kraft Amt(e)s; ~ **bank** → *bank (1)*; ~ **country** Mitgliedstaat; ~ **firm** zugelassene Börsenmaklerfirma; ~ **of Congress** Abgeordneter (*bzw selten: Senator*) des US-Kongresses; ~ **of Parliament** Unterhausabgeordneter; ~ **of the (executive) board** Vorstandsmitglied, Verwaltungsratsmitglied; ~ **of the consortium** Konsortialmitglied; ~ **of the (assured's) household** Haushaltsangehöriger (des Versicherten); ~ **of the stock exchange** Börsenmitglied; ~**s' dues** Mitgliedsbeiträge; **alternate** ~ Ersatzmitglied; **dissenting** ~ auf Ablehnung beharrender Aktionär; **enrolled** ~ eingetragenes Mitglied; **full** ~ ordentliches Mitglied; **life** ~ Mitglied auf Lebenszeit; **original** ~ Gründungsmitglied; **private** ~ Parlamentsabgeordneter (*ohne Regierungsamt*); **register of** ~**s** → *register*; **senior** ~ (*of a company*) leitender Mitarbeiter (*e-r Gesellsch.*); **regular**

~ ordentliches Mitglied; **subscribing** ~ förderndes Mitglied; **unadvanced** ~ noch nicht zuteilungsberechtigter Bausparer; **union** ~ Gewerkschaftsmitglied; **voting** ~ stimmberechtigtes Mitglied.

membership ~ Mitgliedschaft *f*, Zugehörigkeit *f*; Mitgliederzahl *f*, Gesamtheit *f* der Mitglieder; ~ **association** (*nicht eingetragener*) Verein; ~ **corporation** → *corporation;* ~ **dues** Mitgliedsbeiträge; ~ **renewal** Verlängerung der Mitgliedschaft; **application for** ~ → *application;* **compulsory** ~ Zwangsmitgliedschaft, Beitrittszwang; **dual** ~ Doppelmitgliedschaft; **ex-officio** ~ Mitgliedschaft von Amts wegen.

memo Notiz *f*, Aktennotiz *f*; **intercompany** ~ interne Aufzeichnung.

memorandum Memorandum *n*, Aufzeichnung *f*, Note *f*, Verbalnote *f*; Denkschrift *f*, Schriftsatz *m*, Vermerk *m*; ~ **and articles** Satzung; ~ **articles** *ins* vom Versicherungsschutz ausgeschlossene (*verderbliche*) Gegenstände; ~ **bill** Lieferschein; ~ **buying** Kauf mit Rückgaberecht; Kauf auf Probe; ~ **clause** → *clause;* ~ **decision** gerichtliche Abordnung, Auflagenbeschluß; formlose Entscheidung ohne Gründe; Ankündigung e-r Entscheidung; ~ **for file** Aktenvermerk; ~ **in error** schriftliche Erklärung wegen Tatsachenirrtum; ~ **in writing** Aufzeichnung, Niederschrift, schriftliche Festlegung; ~ **of agreement** Vorvertrag; ~ **of alteration** Änderungsanmeldung (*Patent*); ~ **of appearance** Einlassungserklärung; ~ **of association** Gesellschaftsvertrag; Gründungsvertrag, Gründungssatzung, Satzungsbestimmungen für das Außenverhältnis; ~ **of charge** Grundstücksbelastungsurkunde; ~ **of deposit** Hinterlegungsurkunde; Wertpapierverpfändungsurkunde; ~ **of insurance** vorläufige Dekkungszusage; ~ **of law** Rechtsgutachten; ~ **of satisfaction** (*löschungsfähige*) Quittung; ~ **of understanding** Grundsatzvereinbarung; ~ **sale** → *sale;* **common** ~ *Ausschlußklausel bei Transportversicherung.*

memorial Denkschrift *f*, Bittschrift *f*, Kurzfassung *f* e-r Urkunde; Kurzfassung *f* e-r Gerichtsverfügung, Urkundenauszug *m*; ~ **publication** Festschrift.

memorization das Auswendiglernen; Gedächtniswiedergabe *f* von urheberrechtlich geschützten Werken.

memory Gedächtnis *n*, Andenken *n*, Erinnerungswert *m*, Geistesverfassung *f*; **beyond** ~ vor Menschengedenken, unvordenklich; **legal** ~ Menschengedenken, rechtlich relevante Vergangenheit; **living** ~ Menschengedenken; die Rückerinnerung heute noch Lebender; *within ~~: seit Menschengedenken*; **loss of** ~ Verlust des Erinnerungsvermögens, Gedächtnisschwund; **refreshing the** ~ → *refreshing;* **subconscious** ~ unterbewußte Erinnerung; **to search one's** ~ sein Gedächtnis erforschen.

menace *s* Bedrohung *f*, Drohung *f*, drohende Gefahr *f*.

menace *v* bedrohen.

mendicancy Bettelei *f*.

menial *s* Knecht *m*, Magd *f*, Diener *m*, Lakei *m*; ~ *adj* ~ **offices** niedrige Dienste.

mens|legis der Sinn des Gesetzes; ~ **legislatoris** der Wille des Gesetzgebers; ~ **rea** Schuldbewußtsein; subjektiver Tatbestand, kriminelle Absicht.

mensa et thoro gerichtliche Ehetrennung *f*, Gestattung *f* des Getrenntlebens (*von Tisch und Bett*).

mental geistig, Geistes ..., psychisch, seelisch, intellektuell, innerlich; ~ **aberration** krankhafte Störung der Geistestätigkeit; ~ **anguish** Schmerz, seelischer Schmerz, psychisches Leid; ~ **case** Geisteskranker, Fall für e-e Irrenanstalt; ~ **review tribunal** Beschwerdestelle gegen Unterbringung in Nervenheilanstalt; ~ **patient** Geistesgestörter.

mental health geistige Gesundheit, psychische Verfassung; **M~ H~ Commission** Aufsichtsamt für Nervenheilanstalten.

mentally deficient geistig behindert; ~ **disturbed person** Geistesgestörter, Geistesschwacher; ~ **ill** geisteskrank.

mentation Geisteszustand *m*.

mention *s* Erwähnung *f*, Meldung *f*, Vermerk *m*.

mention *v* erwähnen; **not to** ~ geschweige denn; ~**ed before** vorerwähnt; ~**ed below** unten erwähnt, nachstehend; nachstehend aufgeführt; **above** ~**ed** vorstehend erwähnt, vorstehend aufgeführt; **hereinafter** ~**ed** unten erwähnt, nachstehend erwähnt.

mentionable erwähnbar, erwähnenswert, anführenswert.

mercable handelsfähig, zum Verkauf bestimmt.

mercantile kaufmännisch, Handels ...

mercantilism Merkantilismus *m*.

mercantive zum Handel gehörig.

mercenary Söldner *m*.

merchandise *s* Handelsware *f*, Güter *n/pl*, Ware *f*, Handelsgüter *n/pl*, nicht zum sofortigen Verbrauch bestimmte Ware *f*; ~ **account** Warenkonto; ~ **advances** Vorschüsse auf Warenbestände; ~ **bond** Ware unter Zollverschluß; ~ **broker** → *broker*; ~ **budget** Mittel für Warenbeschaffung; ~ **cost** Einkaufskosten *abzüglich Warenskonto*; ~ **credit** Warenkredit, Lieferantenkredit; ~ **exchange** Warenbörse; ~ **manual** Warenhandbuch; ~ **marks** Warenauszeichnung, Etikettierung; ~ **on consignment** Kommissionsware; ~ **planning** Absatzplanung; ~ **procurement cost** Warenbeschaffungskosten; ~ **trade deficit** Warenhandelsdefizit; ~ **traffic** Warenverkehr, Güterverkehr; ~ **turnover** Warenumsatz; ~ **warehouse** Warenspeicher; **branded** ~ Markenartikel; **class of** ~**s** Warenklasse; **lawful** ~ gesetzlich zulässige Waren (*bezogen auf Verschiffungshafen*); **legal** ~ keinem gesetzlichen Verbot unterliegende Ware; **shop worn** ~ Ladenhüter, *vom langen Liegen im Laden wertgeminderte Waren;* **slowmoving** ~ langsam verkäufliche Waren; **unclaimed** ~ nicht abgeholte Ware.

merchandise *v* Handel treiben, kaufen und verkaufen; Absatzplanung betreiben.

merchandiser Verkaufsberater *m*.

merchandising Verkaufspolitik *f*, Verkaufsförderung *f*; ~ **margin** Handelsspanne; ~ **policy** Verkaufsgrundsätze.

merchant Händler *m*, Kaufmann *m*, Ladenbesitzer *m*; ~**s' accounts** kaufmännische Buchführung; ~ **adventurer** kaufmännischer Übersee-Spekulant, ~ **appraiser** → *appraiser;* ~ **bank** Handelsbank, Geschäftsbank; ~ **banking** Großfinanzierungs-Bankgeschäfte; ~ **fleet** → *fleet;* ~ **navy** Handelsmarine; ~**s' prices** Engrospreise; ~**'s risk** (*Transportgut*) auf Gefahr des Händlers (*Konossementinhabers*); ~**'s rule** *Anrechnungsusance bei Teilzahlungen* (*Hauptsache bleibt verzinslich bis zur Schlußabrechnung*); ~ **seaman** Angehöriger der Handelsmarine, Matrose; ~ **ship** → *ship;* **commission** ~ → *commission;* **feme sole** ~ selbständige Geschäftsfrau; **law** ~ → *law;* **statute** ~ → *statute*; **wholesale** ~ Großhändler, Großhandelskaufmann.

merchantability marktgängige Qualität *f*, handelsübliche Qualität *f*, mittlere Art und Güte.

merchantable marktgängig, verkäuflich, von mittlerer Art und Güte; ~ **quality** marktgängige Qualität, zum Weiterverkauf geeignete Qualität, mittlere Art und Güte, Tauglichkeit zum gewöhnlichen Gebrauch; ~ **title** rechtsmangelfreies Eigentum (*an Waren*), handelsübliches Verfügungsrecht.

merchanting überseeische Warenbörsengeschäfte *n|pl;* ~ **trade** Transithandel.

merchantman Handelsschiff *n*, Kauffahrteischiff *n*.

merchantry kaufmännisches Gewerbe *n*, Kaufmannschaft *f*.

mercy *s* Gnade *f*, Gnadenrecht *n*, Ermessensstrafe *f*; ~ **killing** Gnadentod, aktive Sterbehilfe; Euthanasie; **petition for** ~ → *petition;* **prerogative of** ~ → *prerogative;* **recommendation to** ~ → *recommendation.*

mere *adj* bloß, lediglich, rein; ~ **licensee** *jmd, der lediglich mit Duldung des Eigentümers ein Anwesen betritt;* ~ **motion** unbeeinflußte Handlung (*aus eigenem Willen*), von Amts wegen; ~ **right** schlichtes Recht, besitzloses Eigentumsrecht (*an Liegenschaften*).

meretricious unzüchtig, buhlerisch, hurenhaft, verführerisch.

merge aufgehen, verschmelzen, fusionieren.

merger Verschmelzung *f*, Fusion *f*, Vereinigung *f* (durch Aufnahme), Unternehmenszusammenschluß *m*; Konfusion *f*; ~ **agreement** Fusionsvertrag; ~ **clearance** Billigung der Konzentration; ~ **clause** → *clause*; ~ **of charges on property** Konfusion von Grundstückslasten; ~ **of contract** Erlöschen e-s Vertrages durch Novation; ~ **of offences** Konsumtion (*von nachrangigen Straftatsbeständen durch die höhere Norm*); ~ **of rights** Vereinigung (von Forderung und Schuld), Erlöschen von Ansprüchen durch Konfusion; ~ **of rights of action** Aufgehen der Klageansprüche im Urteilstenor; ~ **of sentences** Gesamtstrafe; ~**s mania** Fusionsmanie; **conglomerate** ~ Verschmelzung *nicht konkurrierender und nicht in Lieferbeziehungen stehender Gesellschaften;* **corporate** ~ Verschmelzung, Fusion von Kapitalgesellschaften; **horizontal** ~ Verschmelzung von Konkurrenzgesellschaften; **pre-~ notification** Anzeige e-s geplanten Zusammenschlusses; **vertical** ~ vertikale Verschmelzung, *Verschmelzung mit Belieferer bzw Abnehmer.*

mergerite Fusionsbefürworter *m*, Fusionär *m*.

merit Verdienst *m*, Wert *m*; Begründetheit *f*, rechtserhebliche Bedeutung *f*; ~ **bonus** (*einmalige*) Leistungszulage; ~ **increase** Leistungszulage *f*; ~**s of the case** der entscheidungserhebliche Sachverhalt; die (*materiellrechtliche*) Begründetheit; *to try the merits of a case: e-n Fall materiell-rechtlich prüfen*; ~ **pricing system** vom Schadensverlauf abhängige KFZ-Prämie; ~ **rating** Leistungseinstufung, Leistungsbeurteilung, Personal- und Befähigungsnachweis; ~ **system** Leistungsprinzip (*bei Beförderung*); ~ **affidavit of** ~**s** → *affidavit;* **inventive** ~ Erfindungshöhe; **literary** ~ → *literary;* **the** ~**s of plaintiff's claim** die Begründetheit des Klageanspruchs; **to deal with a case on its** ~**s** e-n Fall materiellrechtlich entscheiden; **to examine the** ~**s of a claim** die Schlüssigkeit e-s Anspruchs prüfen; **to establish** ~ schlüssig begründen; **without** ~ unbegründet.

merit *v* verdienen, Wert haben.

meritocracy Leistungsgesellschaft *f*.

meritorious verdienstvoll, berechtigt, begründet, schlüssig; ~ **cause of action** die Anspruchsgrundlage des ursprünglich Berechtigten; ~ **consideration** → *consideration*; ~ **defence** → *defence.*

mesne dazwischentretend, Zwischen . . ., Mittel . . .; ~ **assignment** dazwischenliegende Abtretung (*in e-r Kette von Abtretungen*); ~ **incumbrance** Zwischenbelastung; ~ **interest** → *interest* (*2*); ~ **lord** Zwischenlehensherr, Unterlehensherr; ~ **process** → *process* (*1*); ~ **profits** → *profit*; ~ **tenant** mittelbarer Vasall, Untervasall.

message Botschaft *f*, Nachricht *f*, Mitteilung *f*; ~ **delivery time** Postlaufzeit; ~ **from the crown** Botschaft des Monarchen *an das*

Parlament; **investigation** ~ Fahndungsmeldung; **President's** ~ Botschaft des Präsidenten an den Kongreß (*US*); **repeated** ~ Kontrolltelegramm.

messenger Bote *m*, Kurier *m*, Gerichtsdiener *m*, Gerichtsvollzieher *m*, Siegelbewahrer *m* des Gerichts; **~s-at-arms** *scot* Gerichtsvollzieher, Justizwachtmeister; ~ **service** Kurierdienst; **foreign ~s' service** Kurierabteilung.

Messrs. (= *messieurs*) Firma (*in Briefadresse an Personalgesellschaften*).

messuage Wohnhaus *n* mit Nebengebäuden, Hofraum u Hausgarten; Anwesen *n*.

metachronism Zeitberechnungsfehler *m*.

metage Meß- und Waagegeld *n*.

metalwork Metallarbeit *f*, Metallware *f*.

metalworker Metallarbeiter *m*; **~s' union** Metallarbeitergewerkschaft.

metayer system Naturalpachtsystem *n* für Kleinpächter.

mete *v* **out punishment** Strafe zumessen.

meter fraud Zählermanipulation *f*.

metering elektronische (*heimliche*) Aufzeichnung von angerufenen Telephonnummern und Dauer der Gespräche.

metes and bounds natürliche Grenzlinien *f/pl* (*e-s Grundstücks*).

method Methode *f*, Verfahren *n*; ~ **of application** Anwendungsverfahren; ~ **of calculation** Berechnungsart, Berechnungsmethode; ~ **of compensation** Ausgleichsrechnung; ~ **of depreciation** Abschreibungsmethode; ~ **of taxation** Besteuerungsverfahren; ~ **of voting** Abstimmungsart; **~s study** Arbeitsmethoden(untersuchung); **comparative** ~ Kostenvergleichsmethode; **declining balance** ~ degressive Abschreibungsmethode; **literal** ~ wörtliche Auslegungsmethode; **service-output** ~ (*of depreciation*) Mengenabschreibung; **short-cut** ~ Abkürzungsverfahren; **straight line** ~ lineare Abschreibungsmethode; **unit-of-production** ~ (*of depreciation*) Mengenabschreibung; **working** ~ Fabrikationsverfahren.

metropolis Hauptstadt *f*, Metropole *f*, Hauptzentrum *n*; **commercial** ~ Handelsmetropole.

metropolitan *adj* hauptstädtisch, großstädtisch, e-m städtischen Ballungsraum zugehörig; *London betreffend;* ~ **borough councils** Londoner Stadtbezirksräte; ~ **county** → *county;* ~ **courts** *etwa:* Londoner Amtsgerichte; ~ **district** Stadtgebiet von Großlondon; **M~ Police District** äußerer Polizeibezirk von Groß-London (*ohne City*); **M~Police Force** Polizei von Groß-London; **M~Police Magistrate** (besoldeter) Amtsrichter für Strafsachen in London; ~ **stipendiary magistrate** (*entgeltlich tätiger*) Londoner Bezirksrichter.

mezzanine Zwischengeschoß *n*; Zwischenabschluß *n*.

Michaelmas/Day St. Michaelstag *m* (*29. September, dritter Quartalszahltag*); ~ **sittings** Herbstsitzungsperiode (*bis 21. 12.*); ~ **term** *obs* Herbstsitzungsperiode *der englischen Gerichte*.

micro counsel EDV-Spezialanwalt *m*.

mid|-channel Schiffahrtsrinne, schiffbarer Teil e-s Flusses; ~ **-month** Medio ..., Monatsmitte; ~ **-month account** Medioabrechnung; ~ **-year demands** Anforderungen zum Halbjahresultimo.

middle|line of main channel Mittellinie des Hauptschiffahrtsweges; ~ **of the river** Flußmitte, Mitte der Schiffahrtsrinne des Flusses; **M~ Temple** (=) *e-e der hist Anwaltsinnungen in London;* ~ **price** → *price* (*2*); ~ **thread** Mittellinie der Flußströmung.

middleman (= middle man) Mittelsmann *m*, Vermittler *m*, Makler *m*, Hauptvertreter *m*; Oberpächter *m*; **~'s profit** Zwischengewinn.

middling *adj* mittelmäßig, gewöhnlich.

middlings *s pl* Ware(n) *f* mittlerer Art und Güte, Mittelsorte *f*.

midnight deadlinie Schlußtermin zu Mitternacht.

Midsummer Day Johannistag *m* (*24. Juni*), *2. Quartalstag*.

midwife Hebamme *f*; **certified** ~ zugelassene Hebamme.

migrant Person *f* ohne festen Wohnsitz; ~ **labo(u)rers** Wanderarbeiter.

migrate wandern, ziehen, übersiedeln.

mile Meile *f* (*Landmeile: 1,609 km*); **nautical** ~ *internationale* Seemeile (*1,852 km*); **statute** ~ *englische* Landmeile (*1,609 km*); **three** ~ **limit** Dreimeilengrenze.

mileage Meilenlänge *f*, bereits gefahrene Meilen *f/pl*, Kilometerstand *m* (*Kraftfahrzeug*), Leistung pro Meile (*Benzin*); ~ **rate** Schiffskanalgebühr (*pro Meile*); **constructive** ~ Fahrtkostenpauschale.

militancy Kriegszustand *m*, Kriegsführung *f*, Angriffskrieg *m*, Kampfgeist *m*.

mileston reports Meilensteinberichte *m*.

militant streitend, kämpfend, streitbar, aggressiv.

military|age militärisches Alter; ~ **authority** Militärbehörde; ~ **base** Militärstützpunkt; ~ **bounty land** (*geschenktes*) Land für Kriegsveteranen; ~ **board** Militärgerichtsstelle; **budget** Verteidigungshaushalt; ~ **causes** militärgerichtliche Sachen; ~ **code** Militärgesetzbuch; ~ **commission** → *commission*; ~ **court** Miltärgericht, Kriegsgericht; ~ **enrolment register** Stammrolle; ~ **execution** standrechtliche Erschießung; ~ **feuds** Lehen für militärische Dienste; ~ **government** Militärregierung; ~ **intelligence** (*militärische*) Abwehr, Gegenspionage; ~ **jurisdiction** Militärgerichtsbarkeit; ~ **law** Wahlrecht; ~ **necessity** übergesetzlicher Notstand in militärischen Angelegenheiten; ~ **offences** (*US: offenses*) Militärstraftaten; ~ **office** → *office;* ~ **officer** → *officer;* ~ **pay** Wehrsold; ~ **pay book** Soldbuch; ~ **police** → *police;* ~ **prison** Militärgefängnis; ~ **service** Wehrdienst; ~ **service (hardship) committee** Beschwerdeausschuß für Härtefälle bei Einberufungen; ~ **tenures** mit militärischen Diensten verbundene Lehen; ~ **testament** → *testament;* ~ **tribunal** → *tribunal;* **absence in** ~ **service** unerlaubte Entfernung von der Truppe; **compulsory** ~ **service** Militärdienstpflicht, allgemeine Wehrpflicht.

militia Miliz *f*, Bürgerwehr *f*; ~ **men** Milizsoldaten, Zeitsoldaten.

milk Milch *f* (*einschließlich Sahne und Magermilch, ohne Trockenmilch*); ~ **marketing board** Milchhandelsbehörde; **new** ~ Rohmilch, frische (*nicht abgerahmte*) Vollmilch.

milker Reisescheckdieb *m*.

mill Mühle *f*, Spinnerei *f*, Fabrik *f*, Industriewerk *n*; ~ **hand** Fabrikarbeiter; ~ **privilege** Mühlengerechtigkeit; ~ **site** Mühlengrundstück, Werksgrundstück; **rolling** ~ Walzwerk.

mind Geist *m*, Sinn *m*, Verstand *m*, Wille *m*, Absicht *f*, Geistesrichtung *f*; **disposing** ~ Testierfähigkeit; **guilty** ~ Schuldbewußtsein, **normal** ~ normale, durchschnittliche Geistesverfassung; **of sound** ~ → *sound;* **state of** ~ → *state* (*1*).

minder (*of an animal*) Tierhalter *m*; Versorger e-s Tieres.

mine *s* Grube *f*, Zeche *f*, Bergwerk *n*, Mine *f*; **law of** ~**s and minerals** Bergwerksrecht.

mine *v* abbauen; verminen.

miner Bergarbeiter *m*, Grubenarbeiter *m*, Kumpel *m*; ~**'s association** Knappschaft; ~**'s benefit fund** Knappschaftskasse.

mineral|district Bergbaugebiet *n*, Gebiet *n* mit Bodenschätzen; ~ **deed** Schürfrechtsurkunde; ~ **land entry** → *entry;* ~ **lands** → *land;* **lease** Pacht e-s Bergwerksrechts; ~ **lode** Ersatzader, *Mineralien führende Gesteinsschicht;* ~ **rights** → *right*; ~ **rights duty** Bergwerkssteuer; ~

servitude Schürfrechtsdienstbarkeit; Schuldverschreibung auf Grund e-r Sch.; ~ **substances** mineralhaltige Stoffe, Mineralien.

minibond Einmalprämienversicherung.

mini-maxi *Emissionsvereinbarung zum festen Kurs für eine Mindestmenge, im übrigen bestens.*

minimization of damages Schadensminderung(spflicht) *f.*

minimize auf ein Minimum bringen, als geringfügig darstellen, verharmlosen, herabsetzen, verkleinern.

minimum aggregate volume Mindest-Gesamtmenge; ~ **amount** Mindestbetrag; ~ **charge** Mindestsatz, Mindestgebühr; ~ **commercial quantity** handelsübliche Mindestmenge; ~ **inventory** Mindestbestand; ~ **lending rate** (Mindest-) Zentralbankdiskontsatz der Bank von England (*früher: "bank rate"*); ~ **margin requirement** Mindestdeckung; ~ **order policy** Mindestbestellrichtlinien; ~ **paid-in-capital** eingezahltes Mindestkapital; ~ **periods of notice** *gesetzl* Mindestkündigungsfristen (*gegenüber Arbeitnehmern*); ~ **rate** Mindestkurs, Mindestsatz; ~ **wage legislation** Gesetze über Mindestlöhne.

mining academy Bergakademie; ~ **claim** Mutung, Anspruch auf Schürfrechte; ~ **company** Bergwerksgesellschaft; ~ **concession** Nutzungsrecht, Bergwerkskonzession; ~ **district** Bergbaugebiet; ~ **industry** Montanindustrie, Bergbau; ~ **law** → *law*; ~ **lease** → *lease*; ~ **location** Mutung, Landnahme für Schürfzwecke; ~ **operations** Bergwerksarbeiten; ~ **partnership** → *partnership*; ~ **rent** Pachtzins für Bergwerksrechte; ~ **rights** → *rights*; ~ **share** → *share*; ~ **strip** ~ Tagebau, Abbau über Tage.

minister Minister *m*; Priester *m*; Diener *m*; diplomatischer Vertreter *m*, Gesandter *m*; internationaler Schiedsrichter *m*, Beauftragter *m*; Gerichtsvollzieher *m*; ~ **(of the Crown)** Minister; ~ **of State** Staatssekretär, Staatsminister (*e-r Zentralregierung*); ~ **plenipotentiary** Sonderbotschafter, Gesandter; ~ **resident** Ministerresident (*nächste Rangklasse nach Gesandten*); ~ **without portfolio** Minister ohne Geschäftsbereich; **cabinet** ~ Minister mit Kabinettsrang; **career** ~ Berufsdiplomat; **departmental** ~ Minister (*mit Geschäftsbereich*); **foreign** ~ Botschafter *bzw* Gesandter; **Interior M**~ Innenminister; **junior** ~ parlamentarischer Staatssekretär; **non-departmental** ~ *Minister ohne Geschäftsbereich*; *Regierungsmitglied mit Ehrenministerwürde*; **prime** ~ Premierminister, Ministerpräsident; **public** ~ diplomatischer Vertreter; **resident** ~ Ministerresident, Gesandter.

ministerial amtlich, weisungsgebunden, ausführend, ministeriell, Verwaltungs ...; geistlich, priesterlich.

ministerialist Regierungsanhänger *m*.

ministry Ministerium *n*; geistliches Amt *n*, Priesteramt *n*; **M**~ Regierung *f*, Gesamtheit *f* der politischen Beamten e-r Regierung; Amt e-s Gesandten; **executive** ~ *brit* die Minister und hohen politischen Beamten.

minor *adj* minderjährig, unmündig; unbedeutend, geringfügig; ~ **defects** geringfügige Mängel; ~ **fact** untergeordnete Beweistatsache; ~ **interests** → *interest* (*1*); ~ **issue** Nebenfrage; ~ **loss** Kleinschaden, Bagatellschaden; ~ **offence** → *offence*.

minor *s* Minderjähriger *m früher: infant*; **emancipated** ~ für volljährig erklärter Minderjähriger; sich selbst versorgender M.

minority Minderheit *f*, Minderzahl *f*, Minderjährigkeit *f*, Minorität *f*; ~ **and lesion** *scot* Nachteil, Ungleichheit der Vertragsleistungen; ~ **holding** Minderheitsbeteiligung; ~ **obstruction** Obstruktion durch eine (*Parlaments*)Minderheit; ~

vote Stimmenminderheit; **linguistic** ~ sprachliche Minderheit.

mint *s* Münze *f*, Münzamt *n*; ~ **condition** unbenutzt, neu (*Münzen, Briefmarken etc*); ~**-mark** Münzzeichen; ~ **-master** Münzmeister, Leiter des Münzamtes; ~ **par of exchange** Münzparität, Metallwährungsdevisenkurs; ~ **parity** Münzparität, Goldparität, festes Wechselpari; ~ **ratio** Münzfuß, Verhältnis von Goldmünzen zu Silbermünzen; ~ **remedy** Toleranz.

mint *v* münzen, prägen; ~**ing charges** Prägegebühren.

mintage Prägegebühr *f*, geprägtes Geld *n*.

minuta (*pl-ae*) kleinste Einzelheit; ~**ae of a section** die Feinheiten e–s Paragraphen.

minute *s* Konzept *n*, Notiz *f*, Entwurf *m*, Memorandum *n*, Protokolleintrag *m*; ~ **book** Protokollbuch *n*; *entry in the* ~~: *Aufnahme in das Protokollbuch*.

minute *v* protokollieren; **to have sth** ~**d** etwas protokollieren lassen.

minutes Protokoll *n* Niederschrift *f*; vereinbarte Entscheidungsformulierung; ~ **of evidence** Aussageprotokoll, Beweisaufnahmeprotokoll; ~ **of the meeting** Sitzungsprotokoll; ~ **of the proceedings** Verhandlungsprotokoll; **agreed** ~ vereinbarte Niederschrift; **duty to keep** ~ Pflicht der Protokollführung; **loose-leaf** ~ (*unzulässige*) Protokolle in losen Blättern; **reading the** ~ Protokollverlesung; **to adopt the** ~ das Protokoll genehmigen.

Miranda rule (= *ruling*) (*US*) *notwendige Rechtsbelehrung e-s Tatverdächtigen vor der polizeilichen Vernehmung über sein Aussageverweigerungsrecht: darüber daß seine Angaben vor Gericht gegen ihn verwendet werden können und über sein Recht auf Zuziehung e-s Rechtsbeistands*; ~ **warnings** Belehrungen des Beschuldigten über seine Rechte.

misadventure Unglücksfall *m*, unglücklicher Zufall *m* (*bei gesetzlichem Tun*).

misallege e-e falsche tatsächliche Behauptung aufstellen, falsch zitieren.

misapplication unzulässige Verwendung *f*, Untreue *f*, Unterschlagung *f* von Geldern.

misapprehension Mißverständnis *n*, falsche Auffassung *f*, Irrtum *m*.

misappropriate widerrechtlich verwenden, unterschlagen, veruntreuen.

misappropriation widerrechtliche Verwendung *f*, Veruntreuung *f*, Unterschlagung *f*; ~ **in office** Unterschlagung im Amt.

misbehaviour ungebührliches Verhalten *n*, Fehlverhalten *n*, schlechte Führung *f*.

misbranding irreführende Markenbezeichnung *f*, Falschetikettierung *f*.

miscalculation Fehlkalkulation *f*, falsche Berechnung *f*, Rechenfehler *m*.

miscarriage Fehlschlagen *n*, Fehler der Rechtspflege; Mißlingen *n*; fahrlässige Geschäftsführung *f*, Fehlverhalten *n*; ~ **of a criminal act** Fehlgehen e-r Tat, aberratio ictus; ~ **of justice** Rechtsbeugung, Fehlurteil; Justizirrtum.

miscasting Prüfirrtum *m*, Zählfehler *m*.

miscegenation Rassemischung *f*, rassenverschiedenes Konkubinat *n*.

miscellaneous | **expense** Unkosten, verschiedene Gemeinkosten; ~ **goods** Sammelgüter; ~ **income** sonstige Erträge; ~ **market** verschiedenartiger Börsenumsatz.

miscellany Gemisch *n*, Sammlung *f*, Sammelband *n*.

mischance Mißgeschick *n*, Unfall *m*, unglücklicher Zufall *m*.

mischarge fehlerhafte Anklage *f*.

mischief *s* Übel *n*, Unfug *m*, Verletzung *f*, schädigendes Tierverhalten; negativer Gesetzeszweck; ~ **rule** *Auslegungsregel: Frage nach dem Mißstand, dem das Gesetz abhelfen*

soll; **criminal** ~ strafbare Störung der öffentlichen Ordnung; **malicious** ~ mutwillige Sachbeschädigung; **public** ~ grober Unfung, Störung der öffentlichen Ordnung.
misclassify falsch rubrizieren; in die falsche Geheimhaltungsstufe einordnen.
miscognisant unwissend.
misconceive falsch auffassen, nicht richtig begreifen; **~d in law** rechtsfehlerhaft, rechtlich abwegig.
misconception of the law Rechtsirrtum *m*, juristische Fehlvorstellung.
misconduct Ungebühr *f*, schlechtes Benehmen *n*, Fehltritt *m*, schlechte Führung *f*, schlechte Amtsführung *f*, ordnungswidriges Verhalten *n*; ~ **in office** Amtsvergehen, Amtspflichtverletzung; ~ **in professional employment** standeswidriges Verhalten, Berufsvergehen; ~ **of public officer** Fehlverhalten im Amt, Beamtenvergehen; **official** ~ Disziplinarvergehen; **professional** ~ standeswidriges Verhalten; **wilful** ~ vorsätzliche schwere Dienstverfehlung.
misconstruction falsche Auslegung *f*, Mißdeutung *f*.
misconstrue falsch auslegen.
miscontinuance verfahrensfehlerhafte Vertagung *f*.
misconveyance Fehlleitung *f* (*e-r Sendung*).
misdate falsch datieren.
misdeclaration falsche Angaben in e–r Steuererklärung.
misdelivery ordnungswidrige Lieferung *f*, Fehlleitung *f*, falsche Ablieferung *f durch den Frachtführer*.
misdemeanant Straftäter *m* (*bei Vergehen*), Täter *m*, Delinquent *m*.
misdemeano(u)r Vergehen *n*, mittelschwere Straftat *f*; **gross** ~ Vergehen; **petty** ~ leichtes Vergehen.
misdescription falsche Angaben *f|pl*, Fehlbeschreibung *f* des Vertragsgegenstandes; irreführende Beschreibung *f*.
misdirect fehlleiten, Geschworene falsch belehren; ~ **oneself** von falschen rechtlichen Voraussetzungen ausgehen.
misdirection Irreführung *f*, falsche Adressierung *f*, unrichtige Rechtsbelehrung *f* der Geschworenen.
mise Prozeßkosten *pl*, Abgaben *f|pl*, Petitum *n* e-r Klage; ~ **-money** Geldzahlung *f* für Erwerb e-r Konzession.
misentry Fehleintragung *f*, unrichtige Buchung *f*.
misfeasance Delikt *n*, *unerlaubte Ausführung e-r an sich rechtmäßigen Handlung*; ~ **proceedings** → *proceedings;* ~ **summons** *Anordnung der gerichtl Überprüfung bei Verdacht auf Untreue von Vorstandsmitgliedern u. ä.*
misfortune Unglücksfall *m*, Unglück *n*, Mißgeschick *n*; ~ **without misconduct** unverschuldetes Mißgeschick.
misgivings Bedenken *n|pl*.
misgovernment schlechte Verwaltung *f*, Mißwirtschaft *f*.
misguidance Irreführung *f*, Verleitung *f*.
mishandle falsch behandeln, schlecht handhaben, fehlerhaft bearbeiten.
mishear sich verhören, falsch hören.
misinformation unrichtige Berichterstattung *f*, Fehlinformation *f*, falsche Angabe *f*.
misinterpretation falsche Auslegung *f*, Mißdeutung *f*, Verkennung *f*.
misjoinder unzulässige Klageverbindung *f*; unzulässige Einbeziehung *f* e-s Streitgenossen; ~ **of causes of action** unzulässige Anspruchshäufung; ~ **of counts** unzulässige Zusammenfassung von Anklagepunkten; ~ **of defendants** unzulässige gemeinsame Anklage gegen mehrere Beschuldigte; ~ **of inventor** unzulässige Einbeziehung e-r Person als Miterfinder; ~ **of parties** unzulässige Beteiligung am Rechtsstreit.

misjudge falsch beurteilen, verkennen.
misjudgment Fehlurteil *n.*
mislaid property verlegte Sache *f.*
mislay verlegen (*nicht wiederfinden können*).
misleading irreführend, verleitend; ~ **instruction** irreführende Belehrung der Geschworenen.
mismanagement schleche Verwaltung *f*, Mißwirtschaft *f.*
mismatching Fehlpaarung; ~ **maturities** inkongruente Verbindung, Fristeninkongruenz.
misnomer Fehlbezeichnung *f.*
mispleading (rechts)fehlerhafter schriftsätzlicher Vortrag *m.*
misprint *s* Druckfehler *m*; *v* verdrukken.
misprision Nichtanzeige *f* von Straftaten; Mißachtung *f* der Staatshoheit, Majestätsbeleidigung *f*, Hochverrat *m*, Amtsuntreue *f*, Amtsunterschlagung *f*; Begünstigung *f*; Pflichtversäumnis *f*; ~ **of felony** *obs* Verheimlichung des Verbrechens eines anderen; ~ **of treason** Nichtoffenbarung landes- oder hochverräterischer Taten; **clerical** ~ Fehler (*bzw Betrug*) seitens e–s Justizbeamten; **negative** ~ pflichtwidrige Nichtoffenbarung, Verheimlichung; **positive** ~ Mißachtung der Staatsgewalt, Majestätsbeleidigung, Hochverrat, Amtsuntreue, Amtsunterschlagung.
misreading (*vorsätzliches*) falsches Vorlesen e-r Urkunde.
misreception of evidence rechtsfehlerhafte Zulassung *f* von Beweismitteln.
misrecital unrichtige Vertragspräambel *f*, unrichtige Vorbemerkungen *fpl.*
misrepresent falsch darstellen, unrichtige tatsächliche Angaben machen.
misrepresentation falsche Angabe(n) bei Vertragsschluß, Irrtumserregung, unrichtige Darstellung *f*; (*Verleitung zum Vertragsschluß durch*) irreführende Angaben; ~ **damages** Schadensersatz wegen Falschangaben bei Vertragsschluß (*culpa in contrahendo*); **fraudulent** ~ arglistige Täuschung; **innocent** ~ schuldlose Angabe von unrichtigen Tatsachen, nicht zu vertretende Unrichtigkeit von Angaben; **material** ~ falsche Angaben über e-n wesentlichen Punkt; **negligent** ~ fahrlässige Unrichtigkeit von Angaben; **willful** ~ Irreführung.
misrepresentee Adressat e-r unrichtigen (vertragsanbahnenden) Erklärung.
misrule Mißwirtschaft *f*, Mißregierung *f.*
missing fehlend, abwesend, vermißt, verschollen, abgängig; ~ **items** fehlende Sendungen; ~ **ship** überfälliges Schiff; **to be reported** ~ als vermißt gemeldet werden.
mission Mission *f*, Delegation *f*, (ständige) Vertretung *f*, Auftrag *m*, Dienstreise *f.*
misstatement falsche Darstellung *f.*
mistake Fehler *m*, Mißverständnis *n*, Irrtum *m*, Einigungsmangel *m*, Dissens *m*; Mißgriff *m*; ~ **in the inducement** Motivirrtum; ~ **of fact** Tatsachenirrtum; ~ **of law** Rechtsirrtum; **bona fide** ~ rechtserheblicher Irrtum; **by** ~ irrtümlicherweise, versehentlich; **clearly proven** ~ erwiesener Irrtum; **clerical** ~ Schreibversehen; **common** ~ allgemein verbreiteter Irrtum, beiderseitiger Irrtum; **honest** ~ gutgläubiger Irrtum; **innocent** ~ unverschuldeter Irrtum; **mutual** ~ beiderseitiger Irrtum; **operative** ~ relevanter zur Unrichtigkeit führender Irrtum; **unilateral** ~ einseitiger Irrtum.
mistaken falsch, irrtümlich, fehlerhaft.
mistress Mätresse *f*, (ausgehaltene) Geliebte *f*, „Lebensgefährtin" *f.*
mistrial mit schweren Rechtsfehlern behaftetes Verfahren *n*, Fehlprozeß *m.*
misuse Mißbrauch *m*; **M~ of Drugs Act** Drogenmißbrauchsgesetz *GB 1974*; ~ **of position** Amtsmißbrauch.

misuser Mißbrauch *m*, unzulässige Rechtsausübung *f*, Mißbrauch e-r Befugnis; Mißbrauch e-r Lizenz.

mitigat|e mildern, lindern; ~ **the loss** den Schaden mindern; **~ing circumstances** → *circumstance*.

mitigation Schadensminderung *f*; Strafmilderung *f*; ~ **of damages** Schadensminderung; ~ **of punishment** Strafmilderung; ~ **of sentence** Stafmilderung; **address in** ~ → *address;* **to consider in** ~ → *to consider*.

mittimus Haftbefehl *m*, Einweisungsanordnung *f*; Strafakten *f/pl*; Verweisungsbeschluß *m*.

mixed gemischt, vermischt; ~ **arbitral tribunal** → *tribunal*; ~ **investment trust** gemischter Anlagefonds; ~ **life assurance contract** Lebensversicherung auf Erlebens- und Todesfall; **~-ownership government corporation** gemischtwirtschaftliches Unternehmen; ~ **residential and non-residential use** gemischtwirtschaftliche Nutzung; (*für Wohnzwecke und gewerbliche Zwecke*); ~ **question of law and fact** *Frage rechtlicher und zugleich tatbestandsmäßiger Art*; ~ **subjects of property** *Gegenstände, die zugleich Eigenschaften des beweglichen und des unbeweglichen Vermögens haben*.

mixtion Vermischung *f* (*von beweglichen Sachen*).

mixture Mischung *f*, Gemisch *n*, Beimischung *f*, Gemenge *n*, Mixtur *f*, Kreuzung *f*.

M'Nathen Rules richterliche Regeln bei angebl Unzurechnungsfähigkeit.

mob Mob *m*, Zusammenrottung *f*; ~ **law** Lynchjustiz.

mobbing and rioting Landfriedensbruch *m*.

mobile bank Bankschalterbus, Bankfiliale auf Rädern.

mobile crime prevention centre transportable Einbruchschutzzentrale.

mobile home Wohnwagen *m*.

mobility|allowance Sozialversicherungsbeihilfe für Bewegungsbehinderte; ~ **clause** → *clause*.

mock|auction Scheinversteigerung *f* (*strafbar GB*); ~ **trial** Scheinprozeß *m*.

mockery of the law Verhöhnung *f* des Rechts.

mode Art *f* und Weise *f*, Methode *f*, Brauch *m*, Modus *m*; ~ **of conveyance** Beförderungsart, Versendungsart; ~ **of election** Wahlverfahren; ~ **of payment** Zahlungsweise; ~ **of proceeding** Verfahrensweise; ~ **of process** Zustellungsart.

model *s* Modell *n*, Muster *n*, Vorbild *n*, Urbild *n*, Vorlage *f*, Typ *m*; Bauweise *f*, Konstruktion *f*; Mannequin *n*; ~ **act** Mustergesetz; ~ **plant** Musterbetrieb; ~ **year** Baujahr *n* (*Kfz*); **demonstrator** ~ Vorführmodell; **full size** ~ unverkleinertes Modell; **scale** ~ maßstabgerechtes (*verkleinertes*) Modell.

moderator Schiedsrichter *m*, Vermittler *m*, unparteiischer Diskussionsleiter *m*, Vorsitzender *m* e-r Bürgerversammlung, *eccl* Vorsitzender *m* e-s Kirchengerichts.

modification Änderung *f*, Abänderung *f*, Einschränkung *f*, Abwandlung *f*, Milderung *f*, teilweise Umwandlung *f*, Abart *f*, **retrospective** ~ nachträgl (rückwirkende) Änderung; **subject to ~s** Änderungen vorbehalten.

modify abändern, einschränken, umändern, abwandeln, näher bestimmen, mildern.

modo et forma allgemein und formalrechtlich (*bestreiten*).

modus Modus *m*, Art und Weise *f*; ~ **of an indictment** Sachverhaltsdarstellung in e-r Anklage; ~ **tenendi** Lehensart; **rank** ~ zu weit hergeholtes Beweismittel.

moiet|y die Hälfte, Hälfteanteil; ~ **acts** *Strafgesetze, bei denen die Hälfte des Strafbetrages dem Anzeigeerstatter (bzw Denunzianten) überlassen wurde;* **to hold by ~ies** zur Hälfte berechtigt sein, hälftig beteiligt sein.

mole Maulwurf *m*; Geheimagent.

molest belästigen.
molestation Belästigung *f*, Besitzstörung *f*; *scot* Verfahren *n* zur Verhinderung von Besitzstörungen *bei streitigem Grundbesitz*.
molester Sittenstrolch *m*; **child** ~ Kindsverderber.
moment Augenblick *m*, Zeitpunkt *m*; Bedeutung *f*.
momentum Eigendynamik *f*, Bewegungsgröße *f*, bewegende Kraft *f*, Wucht *f*, Schwung *m*.
monarchy Monarchie *f*; **absolute** ~ absolute Monarchie; **despotic** ~ absolute Monarchie; **elective** ~ Wahlmonarchie; **hereditary** ~ Erbmonarchie; **limited** ~ konstitutionelle Monarchie.
monetarism Monetarismus *m*, monetaristische Inflationstheorie.
monetary geldlich, monetär, pekuniär, finanziell, Geld ..., Währungs ..., Münz ...
monetization Münzprägung *f*.
monetize prägen, in Umlauf setzen.
money Geld *n* (= *G bzw g*), Münze *f*, Vermögen *n*; ~ **account** Grechnung; ~ **advance** Vorschuß; ~ **at call** Tages*g*; ~ **at call and short notice** kurzfristiges *G*; ~ **at credit at the bank** Bankguthaben; ~**-bill** → *bill*; ~ **broker** → *broker*; ~ **circulation** *G*umlauf; ~ **claim** Zahlungsanspruch; *G*Forderung; ~ **compensation** Barabfindung, Geldentschädigung; ~ **counts** Zahlungsklage(n) aus Vertrag; ~ **damages** Schadenersatz in *G*; ~ **debt** *G*schuld; ~ **demand** *G*nachfrage; ~ **expended** verbrauchte Mittel; ~ **had and received** Rückzahlungsanspruch (u. -klage) wegen Wegfalls der Gegenleistung; Bereicherungsanspruch wegen fehlgeleiteter Zahlung; ~ **in account** Giral*g*, Buch*g*; ~ **in court** bei Gericht hinterlegtes *G*; ~ **in hand** jederzeit verfügbares *G*; ~ **in the bank** Bankguthaben; ~ **invested** angelegtes *G*; ~ **into land** *G, das wie Liegenschaften behandelt wird*; ~ **in trust** Treuhand*g*; treuhänderisch verwahrtes *G*; ~ **laundering** *G*wäsche, *G*waschanlage; ~ **lent** wegen Darlehens(*Klageformel*); ~ **letter** Wertbrief; ~ **loan** Bardarlehen; Kassendarlehen; ~ **lodged in court** gerichtl hinterlegtes *G*, an die Gerichtskasse einbezahltes *G*; ~ **lying idle** totes Kapital; ~ **made** durch Vollstrekkung eingezogenes *G*; ~ **manager** Geldmarktspezialist, Währungsspezialist; ~ **market** *G*markt; ~ **market indebtedness** *G*marktverschuldung; ~ **market rate** *G*marktsatz, *G*marktzins; ~ **matters** *G*angelegenheiten; ~ **monger** *G*händler, Wucherer; ~ **of adieu** Kaufschilling; ~ **of account** Rechnungwährung, Buchhaltungswährungseinheit; ~ **of redemption** Valuta; ~ **of which I am possessed** mein Barvermögen; ~ **on call** (= *at call*) = *call* ~ → *call*; ~ **on deposit** Bankguthaben; ~ **on mortgage** hypothekarisch ausgeliehenes *G*, Hypothekarvermögen; ~ **on security** *G* gegen Sicherheit; ~ **only** nur gegen Barzahlung; ~ **or money's worth** in *G* oder Geldeswert; ~ **order** → *money order*; ~ **interest** verzinsliches Darlehen; ~ **owing** Außenstände; ~ **paid** verauslagtes *G* (*Klageformel auf Erstattung von Auslagen*); ~ **paid into court** gerichtlich hinterlegtes *G*; ~ **paid to defendant's use** *Bezeichnung e-r Klage auf Ausgleich unter Gesamtschuldnern*; ~ **payable periodically** regelmäßig zahlbare Beträge, Rente; ~ **put up** angelegtes *G*; ~ **rate** *G*marktsatz, *G*marktzins; ~**s received** *G*eingänge; ~ **reserve** *G*reserve, Barrücklage; ~ **secured** gesicherte Forderung; ~ **settlement** Treuhandanlage, *treuhänderische Festlegung von Geldvermögen*; ~ **shop** Kundenbank, Schnellkreditfirma; ~ **squeeze** *G*klemme, *G*knappheit; ~ **stock** *G*bestand (*e-s Landes*); ~ **substitute** *G*surrogat; ~ **supply** *G*versorgung, *G*mengenversorgung; ~ ~ *growth*: *Geldmengenzuwachs*; ~ **transactions** *G*ver-

kchr; ~ **transfer** Güberweisung; ~ **trust** Finanztrust; ~ **value** *G-s-*wert, Wert in *G*, finanzieller Wert; **advance of** ~ Vorschuß; **bank** ~ Giral*g*, Buch*g*; **bargain** ~ Anzahlung (*als Bestätigung der Verbindlichkeit*), Drauf*g*; **barren** ~ totes Kapital; **bottomry** ~ Bodmereigelder; **call** ~ → *call*; **capital** ~ → *capital*; **cheap** ~ billiges *G*; **claim for** ~ Zahlungsanspruch, *G*forderung; **clear** ~ Nettobetrag; **coined** ~ Hart*g*; **commodity** ~ → *commodity*; **conduct** ~ Reisekostenvergütung (*bei Vorladung*); **contango** ~ Prolongationskosten; **credit** ~ → *credit*; **current** gangbare Münze, Kurant*g*; **day to day** ~ tägliches *G*, Tagesgeld; **dead** ~ nicht arbeitendes *G*; nur hochverzinsl erhältliches *G*; **dealing for** ~ Kassageschäft; **deposit** ~ → *deposit*; **earnest** ~ → *earnest*; **easy** ~ billiges *G*, leicht verdientes *G*; **effective** ~ umlaufendes *G*; **emergency** ~ Not*g*; **entailed** ~ → *entail*; **equality** ~ Ausgleichsbetrag (*Grundstückstausch*); **excess** ~ Güberhang; **fiduciary** ~ Giral*g*, ungedeckte Banknoten, Kredit*g*; **floating** ~ nicht investierte Gelder; **flow of** ~ *G*strom; **for** ~ gegen Barzahlung, netto Kasse; **foreign** ~ ausländische Zahlungsmittel; **foreign** ~ **order** Auslandspostanweisung; **forfeit** ~ Abstandsgeld, Reugeld; **glut of** ~ *G*schwemme, *G*überhang; **grease** ~ Schmiergeld; **hoarding of** ~ → *hoarding;* **hot** ~ heißes *G*; **hush** ~ Schweige*g*; **key** ~ → *key;* **light** ~ billiges *G*; **lawful** ~ gesetzliches Zahlungsmittel; **long term** ~ langfristiger Kredit; **marked** ~ gekennzeichnete Geldscheine; **metal** ~ Münz*g*; **milled** ~ Münz*g*; **near** ~ Quasigeld, geldähnliche Werte; **outstanding** ~ *G*forderung; **paper** ~ Papier*g*; **pocket** ~ Taschen*g*; **possession** ~ Verwahrungsgebühr (*des Gerichtsvollziehers*); Aufwandsentschädigung bei Besitzentziehung durch Vollstreckung; **postal** ~ durch Postanweisung übersandtes *G*; **principal** ~ Darlehenskapital, Hauptsachebetrag; **public** ~ öffentliche Mittel; **purchase** ~ → *purchase*; **ready** ~ flüssige Mittel, Bar*g*; **regular** ~ Tages*g*; **representative** ~ Repräsentativ*g*, Zeicheng*g*, *G*surrogat; **salvage** ~ Bergelohn; **scarcity of** ~ *G*knappheit; **seed** ~ Startkapital; **shortage of** ~ *G*mangel; **stake** ~ →*stake*; **supply of** ~ *G*versorgung, *G*angebot; **telegraphic** ~ telegraphische Überweisung; **time** ~ befristetes Darlehen, Fest*g*; **trustee** ~ Treuhandvermögen; **unpaid purchase** ~ → *purchase*; **velocity of** ~ *G*umlaufgeschwindigkeit; **warehouse** ~ Lager*geld*.

moneyed | **capital** liquide Vermögenswerte; ~ **corporation** → *corporation;* ~ **interests** Finanzwelt.

moneylender gewerbl Geldverleiher *m*; **M~s Act** Gesetz zur Regelung von gewerblichen Kreditgeschäften (*GB, bis 1974; Banken und Pfandleiher fielen nicht darunter*).

money lending Kleinkreditwesen *n*.

moneyness Geldartigkeit *f*, Geldeigenschaft *f*.

money order (indossierbare) Anweisung auf Zahlung e-r bestimmten Geldsumme, limitierter Scheck (mit festem aufgedruckten Betrag); **postal** ~ beim Postamt einlösbare Zahlungsanweisung, *ungenau:* Postanweisung; **telegraph(ic)** ~ telegraphische Postanweisung.

monger Händler *m*, Krämer *m*; **fish** ~ Fischhändler.

moniment Urkunde *f*, Auszeichnung *f*.

monition Ladung *f*, Vorladung *f*, Abmahnung *f*, **general** ~ Ladung aller Verfahrensbeteiligten.

monitor Abhöranlage *f*, Mithöreinrichtung *f*; technische Meßüberwachung *f*.

monitoring Überwachung *f*; ~ **individual's performance** Leistungskontrolle.

monitum (=) Ermahnung *f*; **judicial** ~ *int* völkerrechtliche Ermahnung.

monkey business Gaunerei *f*, Schwindel *m*, Affentheater *n*.
monocracy Monokratie *f*.
monocrat Alleinherrscher *m*.
monogamy Einehe *f*, Monogamie *f*.
monogram Monogramm *n*.
monograph Monographie *f*, Abhandlung *f*.
monomachy Duell *n*, einmaliger Zweikampf *m*.
monometallism Monometallismus *m*.
monopolistic monopolistisch, marktbeherrschend, Monopol...; ~ **competition** Wettbewerb zwischen marktbeherrschenden Unternehmen; ~ **fund** monopolartige Versicherung, Zwangsversicherung (*Sozialversicherung*); ~ **use of patents** Ausschließlichkeitsnutzung von Patenten.
monopolization Monopolisierung *f*.
monopolize monopolisieren, den Markt beherrschen, ein Monopolrecht für sich in Anspruch nehmen.
monopoly Monopol *n*, absolutes ausschließliches Recht *m*; Alleinherstellungsrecht *n*, Alleinvertriebsrecht *n*; Monopolgesellschaft *f*; ~ **agreement** Kartell; **M~ies Commission** Monopolkommission; Kartellbehörde; **M~ies and Mergers Commission** *GB:* Kartellamt (*früher: M~ies Commission*); ~ **enterprise** marktbeherrschendes Unternehmen; **M~ies and Restrictive Practices Act** Kartellgesetz *GB;* ~ **situation** Marktbeherrschung (*zu ¼*), monopolartige Lage; ~ **value** Wert der (*Schank*)–Konzession; **commercial** ~ Handelsmonopol; **discriminating** ~ diskriminatorische Ausnutzung e–r Monopolstellung; **fiscal** ~ Steuermonopol; **government** → ~ *government;* **infringement of** ~ **rights** Verletzung von Ausschließlichkeitsrechten, Verletzung von gewerblichen Schutzrechten; **production** ~ Fabrikationsmonopol.
monopsony Monopson *n*, Nachfragemonopol *n*.
monster Monstrum *n*, Mißgeburt *f*.
monstrans de droit Nachweis *m* des Lehensrechts; Herausgabeklage *f* gegen den Staat *bis 1947*.
month Monat *m*, Kalendermonat *m*, Monatsfrist *f*; **...~s after date** heute in ... Monaten; **...~s after sight** ... Monate nach Sicht; ~ **order** → *order* (2); **a~'s credit** Einmonatskredit; **calendar** ~ → *calendar;* **civil** ~ Kalendermonat (*des gregorianischen Kalenders*); **current** ~ laufender Monat; **lunar** ~ Mondmonat (*28 Tage*); **one ~'s notice** monatliche Kündigungsfrist; **partial** ~ Teilmonat; **solar** ~ Kalendermonat; **this day** ~ heute in e–m Monat; **three ~s' date** drei Monate von heute an, Dreimonatswechsel; **three ~s' paper** → *paper,* **twelve~s** → *twelve;* **within a** ~ binnen Monatsfrist.
monthly monatlich; ~ **account** Monatsrechnung; ~ **balance sheet** Monatsbilanz, Monatsabschluß; ~ **instal(l)ment** → *instal(l)ment*; ~ **pay** monatliche Gelder, Monatslohn; ~ **settlement** → *settlement*.
monument Denkmal *n*, Grabstein *m*; Grenzstein *m*, Vermessungspunkt *m*; überlieferte Urkunde *f*. **ancient** ~ (geschütztes) Baudenkmal; **natural** ~ Naturdenkmal.
monumental inscription Grabinschrift *f*, Grabdenkmal *n*.
mood swing Stimmungswechsel *m* (*Börse*).
Moody Index (=) *US Preisindex für Stapelwaren des Welthandels*.
moonlighting Schwarzarbeit *f*, unerlaubte Nebentätigkeit; private Anwaltstätigkeit von Syndikus-Juristen; Auszug aus e–r Wohnung „bei Nacht und Nebel".
moonshine Fusel *m*, geschmuggelter *bzw* schwarzgebrannter Schnaps *m*.
moor *Gerichtsbeamter der Insel Man*.
moorage Anlagegebühr *f*, Liegeplatz *m*.
mooring das Festmachen (*e–s Schiffes*), das Vertäuen.
moot *adj* diskutierbar, unentschieden, streitig, strittig, umstritten; ~ **case** ein hypothetischer Fall; ~

court Gericht für hypothetische Fälle; ~ **point** = ~ *question qv*; ~ **question** strittige Frage, unentschiedene Frage, juristisches Problem.

moot *s hist* Volksversammlung *f*, Thing *n*; *brit* juristische Debattierübung, *f*; ~ **hall** Ratsversammlungsraum, juristisches Debattierzimmer; ~ **hill** *hist* Thingstätte; ~ **man** Teilnehmer an e–r juristischen Übungsdebatte.

mooting juristische Disputierübung *f*.

mop Stellenmarkt *m* für Bedienstete *bes Landarbeiter*.

mora Verzug *m*; ~ **accipiendi** Annahmeverzug, Gläubigerverzug; ~ **solvendi** Schuldnerverzug.

moral *adj* moralisch, charakterlich; ~ **actions** willkürliche Handlungen, willensabhängiges Handeln; ~ **certainty** an Sicherheit grenzende Wahrscheinlichkeit; ~ **defectives** Menschen mit krankhaften Charaktermängeln; ~ **imbeciles** geistesgestörte Triebtäter; ~ **improvement** sittliche Höherentwicklung; ~ **suasion** gütliches Zureden, Gewissensappell.

morale Moral *f*, Geist *m*, Kampfgeist *m*; **employee** ~ Arbeitsmoral.

morality Sittlichkeit *f*, sittliches Verhalten *n*, Ethik *f*.

morals squad Sittenpolizei, „Sitte".

moratorium Moratorium *n*, Stillhalteabkommen *n*, vertraglicher Zahlungsaufschub *n*, Stundung *f*.

morbidity Krankhaftigkeit *f*, Krankenstand *m*, Erkrankungsziffer *f*; ~ **rate** durchschnittlicher krankheitsbedingter Arbeitsausfall *pro Arbeitnehmer*.

more or less mehr oder weniger, ungefähr, annähernd, circa.

moreage Anlegegebühr *f*.

moreover außerdem, überdies, noch dazu.

morgue Leichenhaus *n*, Aufbahrungshalle *f*; Zeitungsarchiv *n*.

moron Schwachsinniger *m*, Idiot *m* (*Verstandesgrenze e–s Achtjährigen*).

morphinomania Opiumsüchtigkeit *f*, Morphinismus *m*.

Morris Plan Company Kleinkreditbank *f*.

mortal tödlich, sterblich, Todes . . .; ~ **remains** Leiche.

mortality Sterblichkeit *f*, natürlicher Tod *m*; ~ **rate** Sterbeziffer; ~ **table** Sterblichkeitstabelle; **infant** ~ Kindersterblichkeit.

mortgage *s* Grundpfandrecht *n* (= *Gpfr*); Grundpfand *n* (= *Gpfd*), Hypothek *f* (= *H bzw h*), Grundschuld *f*, Hypotheken- bzw Grundschuldurkunde; Sicherungsübereignung *f*, Verpfändung *f*; ~ **action** *H-n*-Klage (*Zahlung bzw Herausgabe*); ~ **advance** Vorschuß auf das Hypothekendarlehen, Zwischenfinanzierung; ~ **annuity scheme** hypothekarisch gesichertes Annuitätendarlehen; ~ **bank** *H-n*bank; ~ **banking** *H-n*bankgeschäft; ~ **bond** *und Zusammensetzungen → bond (1)*; ~ **broker** Immobilienkreditvermittler; ~ **by deposit of title deeds** *formloses Gpfr durch Hinterlegung von Eigentumsurkunden*; ~ **caution** *H-n*vormerkungsurkunde; ~ **certificate** *Gpf*brief; ~ **charge** *Gpfr*; ~ **claim** *H-n*forderung; ~ **company** *H-n*bank; ~ **credit** Immobiliarkredit, Hypothekarkredit; ~ **creditor** *H-n*gläubiger, *Gpfd*gläubiger; ~ **debenture** Pfandbrief; hypothekarisch und durch Globalverpfändung gesicherte Schuldurkunde; ~ **debt** *H-n*schuld, die (*durch Gpfd*) gesicherte Forderung; ~ **deed** *H-n*brief, *Gpfd*urkunde, Verpfändungsurkunde; ~ **instrument** *Gpf*bestellungsurkunde; *H-n*-brief, Grundschuldbrief; ~ **interest** *H-n*zins; ~ **interest relief** Erleichterungen bei *H-n*zinsen; ~ **lending** *H-n*kreditgeschäft, *H-n*-ausleihungen; ~ **lessee** nießbrauchsberechtigter *H-n*gläubiger; ~ **lien** Grundpfandrecht; ~ **loan** durch *Gpfd* gesichertes Darlehen, *H-n*darlehen; ~**money** *H-n*betrag (*durch Gpfd gesicherte Hauptsachefor-*

derung), persönliche Forderung; ~ **note** hypothekarisch gesicherter Schuldschein; ~ **obligation** durch *Gpfd* gesicherte Verbindlichkeit; ~ **of debt under contract** Verpfändung (*Sicherungsabtretung*) e–r vertraglichen Forderung; ~ **of equitable interest** *Verpfändung e–r treuhänderisch gebundenen Zuwendung bzw e–r Anwartschaft*; ~ **of goods** Sicherungsübereignung (*von beweglichen Sachen*); ~ **of land** *H, Gpfr;* ~ **of legacy** Vermächtnisverpfändung; ~ **of judgment debt** Sicherungsabtretung e–r Vollstreckungsforderung; ~ **of registered land** grundbuchmäßige *H*; ~ **of shares** Aktienverpfändung; Sicherungsübertragung von Kapitalanteilen; ~ **of ship** Schiffshypothek; ~ **on land** *Gpfr*, *H bzw Grundschuld;* ~**s payable** fällige *H-n*-schulden; ~ **real estate coupon bond** Pfandbrief mit Zinskupons; ~**s receivable** hypothekarisch gesicherte Forderungen; ~ **redemption insurance** Rückzahlungslebensversicherung bei Grundstücksverpfändung; ~ **term** Laufzeit e–r *H*; **aggregate** ~ Gesamt*h*; **aircraft** ~ Pfandrecht an Luftfahrzeugen; **amortization** ~ Tilgungs*h*; **blanket** ~ Global*h*; General*h*; **building society** ~ Bausparkassen-*H*; **chattel** ~ Sicherungsübereignung, Mobiliar*h*; **chattel** ~ **with after-acquired property clause** Sicherungsübereignung einschließlich Neuerwerb; **closed** ~ (= *closed-end* ~) abschließendes, nicht erweiterungsfähiges *Gpfr* (*keine weitere Beleihungsmögl.*); **collateral** ~ **bond** → *bond (1)*; **collective** ~ Gesamt*h*; **common law** ~ → *common law;* **compound** ~ Gesamt*h*; **consolidated** ~ → *consolidate; consolidation* **of** ~**s** → *consolidation*; **contributory** von mehreren Schuldnern mit festen Beträgen bediente *H*; **conventional** ~ vertragliches *Gpfr*, Konsensual*h*; **conveyance by way of** ~ dingliche Übertragung zur Sicherheit; **crop** ~ Verpfändung der Ernte auf dem Halm; **defaulted** ~ *H*, auf die nicht gezahlt wird; **discharge of a** ~ Tilgung e–r *H-n*-forderung, Erlöschen e–s *Gpfr–s*; **dry** ~ *Gpfr* ohne persönliche Forderung, Grundschuld; **endowment** ~ mit Lebensversicherung gekoppelte *H*; **equitable** ~ obligatorischer Verpfändungsvertrag, hypothekenähnliches Sicherungsrecht (*nur billigkeitsrechtlich anerkannt*); **first** ~ erststellige *H*, erstrangiges *Gpfr*; **first** ~ **bonds** → *bond (1)*; **general** ~ Global*h*, Gesamt*h*; **graduated payment** ~ *Gpfr* mit Staffelzahlungsplan; **instalment** ~ Tilgungs*h*; **joint** ~ *H* für gemeinsam haftende Schuldner; **judicial** ~ Zwangs*h*; **instalment** ~ Amortisations*h*; **junior** ~ rangschlechtere *H* (*bzw Gpfr*); **legal** ~ *H* (*bzw Gpfr*) (*nach strengem Recht*), erste *H*; **maximum** ~ Höchstbetrags*h*; **open** ~ nicht voll valutiertes *Gpfr*; **open-end** ~ variabel valutierbare *H*; **package** ~ Zubehör erfassende *H*; **participating** ~ *mehreren Gläubigern zustehendes Gpfr*, **participation** ~ *H* mit zusätzlicher Gewinnbeteiligung; **pension-related** ~ ruhegehaltsbezogene *H;* **priority of** ~**s** Rangstellung von *Gpfr–n*; **puisne** ~ nachrangige *H*; **purchase money** ~ → *purchase*; **regulated** ~ *Gpfr* an mietgebundenem Wohngrundstück; **running-account** ~ Höchstbetrags*h*; **second** ~ zweite *H*, zweitrangiges Gpfr; **senior** ~ rangbesseres *Gpfr*; **shiftability of** ~ **loans** Mobilität von *H-n*darlehen; **ship** ~ Schiffs*h*; **standing** ~ *Gpfr* mit Gesamtrückzahlung ohne Amortisation; **statutory** ~ *Gpfr auf gesetzl Formular*; **straight** ~ Festbetrags*h* ohne Amortisierung; **subsequent** ~ rangnächstes *Gpfr*; **tacit** ~ (*automatische*) *gesetzliche* Sicherungs*h*; **to complete a** ~ *e–e H* bestellen, ein *Gpfr* bestellen; **to discharge a** ~ ein *Gpfr* löschen lassen, ein *Gpfr* aufheben; **to foreclose a** ~ e–e *H* (= *Gpfr*) realisieren; sich aus e–r *H* befriedigen, aus e–r *H* vollstrecken; *das Einlösungsrecht bei e–r H (e–m Gpfr) durch Gerichtsbeschluß für verfallen erklären*; **to purchase on** ~ mit Hypothekenfinanzierung kaufen; **to redeem a** ~ → *redeem;* **underlying** ~ vorrangiges *Gpfr*; **variable rate** ~ zinsvariable *H*; **Welsh** ~ Nutzpfand, Antichrese; **wraparound** ~ Refinanzierungs*h*; zweite *H*.

mortgage *v* hypothekarisch belasten, (Grundbesitz) verpfänden.

mortgageable (*hypothekarisch*) beleihungsfähig.

mortgagee Grundpfandgläubiger *m*; ~ **clause** *ins Eintritts- und Rechtsübergangsklausel des Grundpfandgläubigers (bei Prämienverzug des Gpfschuldners)*; ~ **endorsement** *ins* Unterzeichnung e–r *mortgagee clause qv*; ~ **in possession** Grundpfandgläubiger in unmittelbarem Besitz (*der Pfandsache*).

mortgagor Grundpfandschuldner *m*, Hypothekenschuldner *m*, Sicherungsgeber *m*, Verpfänder *m*; ~ **entitled to redeem** einlösungsberechtigter Grundpfandschuldner.

mortification Übergang *m* e–s Vermögens zur toten Hand.

mortify zum Vermögen der toten Hand machen.

mortis causa von Todes wegen.

mortmain Grundstücksubereignung *f* auf e–e (*kirchliche oder weltliche*) Körperschaft; tote Hand *f*, unveräußerlicher Vermögensgegenstand *m*; ~ **Acts** (*verschiedene brit*) *Gesetze gegen Grundstücksveräußerung an kirchliche Körperschaften;* **M~ and Charitable Uses Act** *brit Gesetz über letztwillige Landschenkungen an Körperschaften von 1888*; **in** ~ unveräußerlich, nicht verkehrsfähig, zum Vermögen e–r Kirche bzw charitativen Organisation gehörend; **licence in** ~ → *licence*.

mortuary Leichenhalle *f*, ~ **table** Sterblichkeitstabelle.

most-favo(u)red-nation | **clause** Meistbegünstigungsklausel *f*; ~ **preference** meistbegünstigende Zollpräferenz; ~ **tariff** → *tariff*; ~ **treatment** Meistbegunstigung.

most favourable terms and conditions provisions Meistbegünstigungsklausel (*in Lizenzverträgen*).

most wanted list Spezial-Fahndungsliste *f*.

MOT certificate *etwa* TÜV Bescheinigung *GB*.

mother Mutter *f*, werdende Mutter *f*; ~**s' pension laws** *Fürsorgegesetze für alleinstehende Mütter*; ~**'s share** Erbanteil der überlebenden Ehefrau und Mutter; **house-tied** ~ häuslich gebundene Mütter; **surrogate** ~ Leihmutter; **unmarried** ~ ledige Mutter; **working** ~ berufstätige Mutter.

motion Antrag *m* (= *A bzw a*), *mündlicher* Verfahrensantrag *m*; ~ **denied on the law** als (rechtlich) unbegründet abgewiesener *A*; ~ **for a mistrial** Antrag auf Feststellung der Ungültigkeit des Verfahrens wegen schwerer Verfahrensverstöße; Nichtigkeitsklage; ~ **for adjournment** Vertagungs*a*; ~ **for decree** *A* auf Terminsanberaumung; ~ **for directions** *A* auf Erlaß e–r prozeßleitenden Verfügung; ~ **for judgment** Klage*a*, Sach*a* (*auf gerichtliche Entscheidung*); ~ **for more definite statement** (Einwendung und) Antrag auf bessere Substantiierung; ~ **for new trial** *A* auf Wiederaufnahme des Verfahrens; ~ **in error** Verfahrensrüge; ~ **of censure** Mißbilligungs*a*; ~ **of course** *A* im Bürowege, *über den ohne mündliche Verhandlung entschieden wird*; ~ **of no confidence** Mißtrauens*a*; ~ **on appeal** Berufungs*a*, *A* (*bzw* Gegen*a*) in der Berufungsinstanz; ~ **to arrest judgment** *A* auf Einstellung des Verfahrens (*vor Urteilsverkündung*); ~ **to commit** *A* auf Erlaß e–s Haftbefehls; ~ **to dismiss** Klageabweisungsantrag wegen Unzulässigkeit; ~ **to quash judgment** *A* auf Aufhebung e–s Urteils; ~ **to set aside** Verwerfungs*a*, Aufhebungs*a*; ~ **to set aside judgment** *A* auf Aufhebung e–s Urteils; ~ **to strike out evidence** *A* auf Streichung (von Aussagen) im Protokoll; ~ **to suppress** Antrag auf Ausschluß von unzulässig erlangtem Beweismaterial; **abandoned** ~ zurückgenommener *A bzw* nicht weiter verfolgter *A*; **adoption of a** ~ Annahme e–s *A–s*; **application by** ~ formloser *A* im Bürowege; **cross** ~ Gegen*a*; **dilatory** ~ *parl* verzögerlicher *A*, Obstruktions*a*; **early day** ~ Dringlichkeits*a*; **ex parte** ~ einseitiger *A* e–r Partei, *über den ohne mündliche Verhandlung entschieden wird*; **mover of a** ~ *A*steller; **notice of** ~ → *notice*; **on one's own** ~ auf eigenen *A*, von Amts wegen; **originating** ~ verfahrenseinleitender *A*; **private member's** ~ Initiativ*a* e–s Abgeordneten; **privileged** ~ *parl* Dringlichkeits*a*; **probate** ~ *A* im Nachlaßverfahren (*auf Testamentsbestätigung*); **procedural** ~ Verfahrens*a*; *parl A* zur Geschäftsordnung; **saving** ~ Vorbehalts*a*; **speaking** ~ Antrag, der nicht vorgetragene Tatsachen einbezieht; **substantive** ~ *parl A* zur Sache; **to present a** ~ e–n *A* vorlegen.

motion analysis Bewegungsstudie *f*.

motivate Gründe vorbringen, motivieren, begründen.

motivation Begründung *f*, Antrieb *m*; ~ **research** Motivforschung, *Marktforschung über Käuferinteressen*.

motive Beweggrund *m*; **base ~s** niedrige Beweggründe; **from ~s of lucre** in gewinnsüchtiger Absicht; **improper** ~ unlauterer Beweggrund; **inferred** ~ Beweggrund (*aus objektivem Tatbestand abgeleitet*); **interest ~s** eigennützige Beweggründe.

Motor Insurance Bureau Entschädigungsstelle der Kfz-Versicherer.

motoring | manslaughter grob fahrlässiges Verkehrsdelikt mit Todesfolge; ~ **offence** Verkehrsdelikt *n*, Vergehen *n* gegen die Straßenverkehrsordnung; ~ **summons** Strafbefehl wegen e–s Verkehrsdelikts.

motor vehicle Kraftfahrzeug *n*; **public** ~ Kfz der öffentl Hand.

motorway Autobahn, mehrbahnige Autostraße; ~ **offences** Verkehrsdelikte auf Autobahnen; **dual two-lane** ~ Autobahn; vierspurige Autostraße.

movable beweglich, Mobiliar ...; ~ **and immovable property** bewegliches und unbewegliches Vermögen; Vermögen (*jeder Art*); ~ **dwellings** → *dwelling*; ~ **equipment** bewegliche Ausrüstung; ~ **estate** → *estate*; ~ **freehold** veränderlicher Grund (*Land, dessen Umfang sich durch natürliche Einflüsse verändert*); ~ **property** → *property*.

movables bewegliches Vermögen *n*, Mobilien *f/pl*, Fahrnis *f*.

movant Antragsteller *m* (*-in f*).

move *s* Antrag *m*, Vorgehen *n* bei Gericht, Schritt *m*, Aktion *f*, Maßnahme *f*.

move *v* bewegen, sich bewegen; umziehen; beantragen, e–n Antrag stellen, übergehen auf, dazu beitragen; ~ **a censure** e–n Tadelsantrag stellen; ~ **about freely** sich frei bewegen; Freizügigkeit genießen; ~ **an amendment** e–n Änderungsantrag stellen; ~ **away** fortziehen, verziehen; ~ **for papers** *cf moving (1)*; **~d by the desire** von dem Wunsch geleitet (*Präambel*).

movement Bewegung *f*, Bestrebung *f*, Tendenz *f*, Fortschreiten *n*, Umsatz *m*; ~ **of capital** Kapitalbewegung; ~ **of goods** Warenverkehr, Güterverkehr; ~ **of prices** Kursbewegung, Preisbewegung; **downward** ~ Fallen (Kurs), Abwärtsbewegung; **free** ~ Freizügigkeit; **free** ~ **of goods** freier Warenverkehr; **upward** ~ Steigen, Aufwärtsbewegung.

mover Antragsteller *m* (*-in f*); Spediteur *m*, Fuhrunternehmer *m*.

moving (*1*) Antragstellung *f*, Antrag *m*; ~ **for an argument** Antrag auf besondere mündliche Erörterung des Falles; ~ **for papers** Antrag auf Vorlage von Unterlagen; *parl An-*

trag auf Sacherörterung ohne Beschlußfassung.

moving (*2*) Umzug *m*; ~ **allowance** Umzugskostenbeihilfe; ~ **day** Umzugstag; ~ **expenses** Umzugskosten.

muckraker *s* Schnüffler *m*, Saubermann *m*, Skandalkolporteur *m* (*jmd, der Korruption aufspürt*).

mudslinging Schmutzkampagne *f*, „Schlammschlacht" *f*.

mug book Verbrecheralbum *n*.

muggee Opfer e–r räuberischen Anrempelei.

mugger Großstadt-Straßenräuber *m*.

mugging Anrempeln *n* und Berauben *n*; **knife point** ~ räuberisches Anrempeln mit vorgehaltenem Messer.

mug shot Portraitaufnahme *bei Identifizierung*, Aufnahme für die Verbrecherkartei.

mugwump Unabhängiger *m*, Einzelgänger *m*, unzuverlässiges Parteimitglied *n*.

mulier Frau *f*, Ehefrau *f*, Witwe *f*, Jungfrau *f*, eheliches Kind *n*; ~ **puisne** nachgeborener ehelicher Sohn (*dessen Eltern ein gemeinsames voreheliches Kind hatten*).

multicorporate enterprise Konzern *m*.

multi-employer bargaining Tarifverhandlungen *f/pl* auf Verbandsebene.

multifariousness unzulässige Anspruchshäufung *f*.

multilateral multilateral, mehrseitig.

multiline telephone number Sammelnummer *f*.

multinational *adj* vielstaatlich, multinational; ~ **arrangements** mehrseitige Übereinkünfte; ~ **companies** Multis, Weltkonzern; ~ **group** → *group*; ~ **state** → *state (2)*.

multinational *s* Multi *n*; internationaler Großkonzern *m*.

multipartite aus mehreren Teilen bestehend, mehrseitig.

multiple vielfach, mehrfach; ~ **delivery contract** Sukzessivlieferungsvertrag; ~ **disaster claims** Sammelklagen aus Katastrophen; ~ **insertion rate** Sonderpreis für Dauerinserate; ~ **lease** Mietvertrag über mehrere Wohneinheiten; ~ **lines of credit** Kredit(begrenzung) bei mehreren Banken gleichzeitig; ~ **party system** Mehrparteiensystem; ~ **poinding** *Weigerung mehrerer Anspruchsteller, den Streit um die Sache unter sich auszutragen*; ~ **rate system** multiple Wechselkurse; ~ **shift operation** Mehrschichtbetrieb; ~ **system operators** (*MSD*) Kabelfernseh-Gesellschaften.

multiplicity *unzulässige Aufspaltung des Streitstoffes auf mehrere Prozesse*; ~ **of actions** (*unzulässige*) mehrfache Klage über den gleichen Streitgegenstand; ~ **of suits** = ~ *of actions qv*.

multiply multiplizieren; ~ **accessories** *Grundstücksbestandteile auf neugebildete Einzelgrundstücke erstrecken.*

multi-state *adj* mehrstaatlich; *US*: in mehreren Bundesländern einheitlich (geltend).

municipal kommunal, städtisch, Stadt . . ., Gemeinde . . ., innerstaatlich; ~ **administration** Kommunalverwaltung; ~ **affairs** Kommunalangelegenheiten; ~ **aid** Gemeindezuschuß; ~ **authorities** Kommunalbehörden, Stadtrat; ~ **bank** Kommunalbank; ~ **board** Magistrat, Stadtrat, Gemeinderat; ~ **bonds** → *bond (1)*; ~ **borough** → *borough*; ~ **bye-laws** Gemeindesatzung; ~ **charter** Gemeindekonzession; ~ **code** Gemeindesatzung; ~ **compensation** Abgabe an Gemeinde *für Konzessionserteilung*; ~ **corporation** (kommunale) Gebietskörperschaft, Gemeinde *als juristische Person*; kreisfreie Stadt; ~ **council** Gemeinderat, Stadtrat; ~ **court** Amtsgericht, Stadtgericht; ~ **credit** Kommunalkredit; ~ **domicile** → *domicile*; ~ **elections** Gemeindewahlen, Kommunalwahlen; ~ **eviction** Wohnungszwangsräumung durch die Gemeinde; ~ **functions** Kommunalaufgaben, eigene Gemeindezuständigkeiten; ~

government örtliche Selbstverwaltung, Kommunalverwaltung, Gemeindeverwaltung; ~ **law** → *law*; ~ **legislation** → *legislation*; ~ **lien** *gesetzliche Grundstückslast zugunsten von Gemeinden*, städtische Reallast; ~ **loan** → *loan*; ~ **officer** Stadtdirektor, leitender städtischer Beamter, Kommunalreferent; ~ **ordinance** → *ordinance*; ~ **privilege** Stadtprivileg; ~ **property** → *property*; ~ **purposes** öffentliche Zwecke; ~**rates** Gemeindesteuern, Gemeindeabgaben; ~ **savings bank** Stadtsparkasse; ~ **securities** → *security (2)*; ~ **services** städtische Einrichtungen; ~ **taxation** Kommunalsteuern; ~ **trading** gemeindliche Gewerbetätigkeit; ~ **warrant** → *warrant*; **quasi ~ corporation** Stadtwerke, Kommunalgesellschaft, Regiebetrieb.

municipality örtliche Gebietskörperschaft *f*, Stadtgemeinde *f*, Stadtverwaltung *f*, Stadtbezirk *m*.

municipalization Überführung *f* in städtische Verwaltung, Eingemeindung *f*.

municipalize eingemeinden.

municipals Kommunalanleihen *f/pl*.

muniment Urkunde *f*, Dokument *n*, Beweistitel *m*; *pl*: Urkundensammlung *f*, Archiv *n*; ~**s of title** Grundeigentumsurkunden.

muniment-room Archivraum *m*.

murder *s* Mord *m*, *evt Totschlag m*; ~ **by explosion** Sprengstoffmord; ~ **by poison** Giftmord; ~ **for hire** gedungener Mord, Mord auf Bestellung; ~ **in the first degree** Mord; ~ **in the second degree** Totschlag; ~ **jury** Geschworene in e–m Mordfall; ~ **trial** Mordprozeß; ~ **with** (= ~ *and*) **robbery** Raubmord; **attempt to** ~ Mordversuch; **capital** ~ Mord; **depraved heart** ~ ungeheuerlich grausamer Mord; **multiple** ~ mehrfacher Mord; **noncapital** ~ (gewöhnl) Mord; *evt Totschlag*; **sex** ~ Lustmord; **wilful** ~ vorsätzl Tötung; Mord.

murder *v* ermorden.

murderer Mörder *m*.

murderess Mörderin *f*.

mushroom enterprises (*schnell entstandene*) Spekulationsbetriebe *m/pl*.

musical | composition Musikwerk, musikalische Komposition; ~ **tabloid** Musical in Kurzform, Kurzoperette, Unterhaltungspotpourri mit Darbietungen; **composer of ~ works** Urheber von Werken der Tonkunst.

muster-roll *mar* Musterrolle *f*.

mutation Eigentumsübergang *m*, Rechtsnachfolge *f*, ~ **of libel** Klageänderung.

mutatis mutandis (=) analog, sinngemäß, in entsprechender Anwendung; **to apply** ~ entsprechend anwenden.

mute stumm; ~ **by malice** Einlassung (*zur Anklage*) verweigert; ~ **by visitation of God** taubstumm; **to stand** ~ die Einlassung zur Anklage (*bzw die Aussage*) verweigern.

mutilate verstümmeln; ~**d body** verstümmelte Leiche.

mutilation Beschädigung *f*; Verstümmelung *f*, schwere Körperverletzung *f*.

mutineer *s* Meuterer *m*.

mutineer *v* meutern.

mutinous rebellisch, aufsässig, aufrührerisch.

mutiny *s* Meuterei *f*, **M~ Acts** *GB: Meutereigesetze* (*1689 bis 1879*); **inciting to** ~ Anstiftung zur Meuterei.

mutiny *v* meutern.

mutual gegenseitig, auf Gegenseitigkeit, austauschbar, reziprok, wechselseitig; ~ **advance premium** Gegenseitigkeitsversicherung mit Vorausprämie; ~ **benefit association** Wohltätigkeitsverein auf Gegenseitigkeit; ~ **benefit society** Gegenseitigkeitsverein; ~ **currency account** gegenseitiges Währungskonto; ~ **improvement society** Fortbildungsverein; ~ **indemnity association** Berufsgenossenschaft, ~ **insurance** → *insurance*; ~ **investment company** → *investment*; ~ **life insurance** → *life insurance*; ~ **loan association and building society** Bausparkasse auf Gegenseitigkeit; ~ **loan society** Kreditgenossenschaft; ~ **non-profit company** gemeinnützige Körperschaft auf Gegenseitigkeit; ~ **relief association** Unterstützungskasse auf Gegenseitigkeit; ~ **reserve company** Versicherungs- und Sparverein; ~ **savings bank** → *bank (1)*.

mutuality Gegenseitigkeit *f*, Reziprozität *f*.

mutuant Darlehensgeber *m* (*bes von Naturalien*).

mutuary = *mutuant qv*.

mutuation Darlehensaufnahme *f*.

mutuum Darlehen *n* (*von vertretbaren Sachen oder Geld*).

my mein, mir gehörig, in meinem Besitz befindlich; ~ **duties** die mich *bzw meinen Nachlaß* treffenden Abgaben; ~ **estate and effects** mein gesamtes Vermögen; ~ **freehold house** mein Eigenheim; ~ **people** meine Familie, meine Angehörigen.

mysterious disappearance unerklärliches Verschwinden *n*.

mystery *u a*: Handwerk *n*, Beruf *m*, Gilde *f*, Zunft *f*.

mysticism vage Mutmaßung *f*, unbegründete Vermutung *f*.

mystification Irreführung *f*, absichtliche Täuschung *f*.

N

name *s* Name *m* Benennung *f*, Firmenname *m*; ~ **and address supplied** Name u. Anschrift sind der Redaktion bekannt; ~ **and arms clause** → *clause*; ~ **and description** Angaben zur Person; ~ **day** Abrechnungstag, Skontrationstag für Termingeschäfte; ~ **of maker** Name des Ausstellers; ~ **of place** Ortsname; ~ **recognition** Bekanntheitsgrad; ~ **withheld** Name der Redaktion bekannt; **assumed** ~ angenommener Name, Deckname, Pseudonym; **brand** ~ Markenname; **business** ~ Firma, Firmenname; **by** ~ mit Namen, namentlich; **Christian** ~ Taufname, Vorname, Rufname; **collective** ~ Sammelname, Sammelbegriff; **commercial** ~ Firma, Firmenname, Handelsbezeichnung; **company** ~ Firma e–r Kapitalgesellschaft; *„too-like"* ~ ~: *„zu ähnlicher"* (*verwechslungsfähiger*) *Firmenname e–r Kapital-Gesellschaft*; **corporate** ~ Firma einer Kapitalgesellschaft; **distinctive** ~ Marke, Warenbezeichnung; **family** ~ Nachname, Familienname; **fictitious** ~ Deckname, Pseudonym; **firm** ~ Firma, Firmenname; **full** ~ vollständiger Name; **given** ~ Rufname; **in the** ~ **and on behalf of** namens und im Auftrag; **in the** ~ **of** im Namen von; *für e–n anderen*; **in the** ~ **of the law** im Namen des Gesetzes; **legal** ~ (*ein*) Vorname und Nachname; **maiden** ~ → *maiden*; **my** ~ **and blood** männliche Nachkommen, die meinen Namen tragen; **pen** ~ Schriftstellername, Pseudonym (*e–s Schriftstellers*); **proper** ~ Eigenname, der richtige Name; **proprietary** ~ gesetzl geschützter (Firmen)Name; **specific** ~ der eigentliche Name; **trade** ~ → *trade name*; **true** ~ der richtige Name.

name *v* benennen, bezeichnen, nennen; namentlich zur Ordnung rufen; ~**d, appointed and constituted** ordnungsgemäß bestellt; **above** ~**d** obengenannt, obenerwähnt; **last** ~**d** letztgenannt.

naming Benennung *f*, Bezeichnung *f*, Namhaftmachung *f*; Ordnungsruf *m*; ~ **a Member** Erteilung e–s Ordnungsrufs.

Nansen passport Nansenpaß *m* (*Ausweis für Staatenlose*).

narcotic | **drug addict** Rauschgiftsüchtiger; ~ **drug** Betäubungsmittel, Rauschgift.

narcotic *s* Rauschgiftsüchtige(r); Betäubungsmittel *n*, Narkotikum *n*, Rauschgift *n*; **unlawful** ~**s traffic** unbefugter Verkehr mit Betäubungsmitteln.

nark *US sl* Polizeispitzel *m*.

narratio Tatsachenvortrag *m*, Klagebegründung *f*, mündlicher Vortrag vor Gericht.

narrative Bericht *m*, Erzählung *f*, *scot* Beschreibung *f* der Parteien des Rechtsgeschäftes, Beurkundung *f*; ~ **of facts** Tatsachenschilderung.

nascent state status nascendi, Entstehungszustand *m*.

natal care Mutterschaftshilfe *f*.

natality Geburtenziffer *f*.

nation *s* Volk *n*, Nation *f*, Gesamtstaat *m*, Bundesstaat *m*; ~ **state** Nationalstaat; ~ **wide** *adj* das ganze Land betreffend; **community of** ~**s** Völkergemeinschaft; **emerging** ~**s** Entwicklungsländer; **law of** ~**s** → *law*; **member** ~ Mitgliedstaat.

national *adj* national, staatlich, gesamtstaatlich, bundesweit; ~ **anthem** Nationalhymne; ~ **bank notes** Banknoten (*e–r Landeswährung*); ~ **banking system** das Bankwesen e–s Landes; **N~ Board of Fire Underwriters** *US*: Verband der Feuerversicherungsanstalten;

N~ Coal Board *GB*: Staatliche Kohlebehörde; ~ **colours** Nationalflagge, Nationalfarben, Landesfarben; ~ **consciousness** Nationalbewußtsein; ~ **debt commissioners** Staatsschuldenverwaltung; ~ **defense** Landesverteidigung; Bundesverteidigung; ~ **defense contribution** Rüstungssondersteuer; ~ **defense premises** Verteidigungsanlagen; ~ **device** Hoheitszeichen; ~ **emblem** Hoheitszeichen; ~ **emergency** Staatsnotstand; ~ **emergency council** zentrale Notstandsbehörde; **N~ Enterprise Board** (öffentl rechtl) Gesellschaft für Industrieförderung (*Holding, Darlehen u.a.*); ~ **expenditure committee** Ausschuß zur Kontrolle von Wahlausgaben; **N~ Giro Bank** Postgirodienst; ~ **health insurance** allgemeine (staatliche) Krankenversicherung; **N~ Health Service** *brit* staatlicher Gesundheitsdienst; ~ **income** Volkseinkommen, Nationaleinkommen, Sozialprodukt; ~ **income by distributive shares** Volkseinkommen nach Einkommensarten; ~ **incomes policy** konjunkturdämpfende Einkommenspolitik; **N~ Industrial Relations Court** oberes Arbeitsgericht *GB bis 1974*; ~ **insurance** *GB* gesetzliche Sozialversicherung; **N~ Insurance Act** *GB* Sozialversicherungsgesetz; ~ **insurance benefits** Leistungen der Sozialversicherung; ~ **insurance contributions** Sozialversicherungsbeiträge; ~ **insurance local tribunal** *etwa*: Sozialgericht; ~ **safety council** Unfallverhütungsrat; **N~ Savings Bank** *etwa* Postsparkasse *GB*; ~ **savings certificates** Sparkassengutscheine, Sparbonds; ~ **securities exchange** überregionale Börse; **N~ Trust** *GB* Stiftung für Denkmalschutz, *Treuhandorganisation zur Erhaltung von Kulturdenkmälern*; ~ **wellbeing** Volkswohlfahrt, Gemeinnützigkeit.

national *s* Staatsangehöriger, Volkszugehöriger; **foreign ~ s** Ausländer, fremde Staatsangehörige

nationalism Nationalismus *m*, nationale Politik *f*.

nationality Staatsangehörigkeit *f* (*Personen*), Staatszugehörigkeit *f* (*Sachen*); Nationalität *f*, Volkszugehörigkeit *f*, ~ **of companies** Staatszugehörigkeit von Kapitalgesellschaften; **acquisition of ~** Erwerb der Staatsangehörigkeit; **continuous ~** Dauerstaatsangehörigkeit; **double ~** doppelte Staatsangehörigkeit; **dual ~** = *double ~ qv*; **effective ~** gültige Staatsangehörigkeit; **forfeiture of ~** Aberkennung der Staatsangehörigkeit; **proof of ~** → *proof*; **release from ~** Entlassung aus dem Staatsangehörigkeitsverhältnis; **renunciation of ~** Verzicht auf e–e Staatsangehörigkeit.

nationalization (*auch –sation*) Verstaatlichung *f*, Sozialisierung *f*.

nationalize (*(auch –lise*) nationalisieren, verstaatlichen; **~d industry** verstaatlichte Unternehmungsgruppe.

native *adj* heimisch, inländisch, angeboren; ~ **born citizen** gebürtiger (amerikanischer) Staatsbürger.

native *s* Eingeborene(r), im Lande Geborene(r).

nativism Inländerbegünstigung; *Begünstigung der Einheimischen vor den Einwanderern.*

natural natürlich, physisch; ~ **and probable consequences** adäquate Folgen; ~ **marketing area** natürliches Vertriebsgebiet; ~ **milk shed** natürliches Milchversorgungsgebiet; ~ **object of testator's bounty** die normalerweise Erbberechtigten, *die nächsten Angehörigen.*

naturalization Naturalisierung *f*, Einbürgerung *f*; ~ **court** Einbürgerungsgericht; **act of ~** Bürgerbrief, Akt der Einbürgerung; **application for ~** Einbürgerungsantrag; **collective ~** Kollektiveinbürgerung; **eligibility for ~** → *eligibility*; **petition for ~** Einbürgerungsantrag.

naturalize einbürgern, naturalisieren; ~**d citizen** Staatsangehöriger kraft Einbürgerung.

nature Natur *f*, Wesen *n*, Art *f*, Beschaffenheit *f*, **N~ Conservancy Council** Britische Naturschutzbehörde; ~ **conservation** Naturschutz; **by** ~ von Natur aus; **from the ~ of the case** nach der Art des Falles; **law of** ~ → *law*; **power of** ~ Naturkraft.

naval | agreement Flottenabkommen; ~ **court** Marineuntersuchungsgericht; ~ **courts-martial** Flottengericht; ~ **discipline** Disziplinarordnung der Marine; ~ **enlistment** Aufnahme in die Kriegsmarine; ~ **estimates** Marineetatvoranschlag; ~ **intelligence** Marinenachrichtendienst; ~ **law** → *law*; ~ **officer** Marineoffizier; *US* Hafenzollbeamter; ~ **prize law** → *law*; ~ **supremacy** Seeherrschaft.

navicert Navicert *n*, Geleitschein *m* (*für neutrale Handelsschiffe*).

navigation Seefahrt *f*, Schiffahrt *f*, Navigation *f*; ~ **Acts** Schiffahrtsgesetze; ~ **agreement** Schiffahrtsabkommen; ~ **company** Schiffahrtsgesellschaft; ~ **court** Seeamt, Schiffahrtsgericht; ~ **dues** Schiffsabgaben; ~ **head** Schiffbarkeitsgrenze, Endhafen; ~ **law** → *law*; ~ **route** Schiffahrtsstraße; ~ **servitude** allgemeines Binnenschiffahrtsrecht; Gemeingebrauch öffentlicher Gewässer für die Schiffahrt; **commercial** ~ Handelsschiffahrt, Kauffahrteischiffahrt; **occasional** ~ Gelegenheitsschiffahrt, Trampschiffahrt; **regular** ~ Linienschiffahrt.

navy Flotte *f*, Kriegsmarine *f*, ~ **agency** Schiffsagentur für kriegsverpflichtete Schiffe; ~ **bill** Marinesoldanweisungen; Flottenvorlage; ~ **certificate** Ausfuhrgenehmigung (*in Kriegszeiten*); **N~ Department** *US* Marineministerium; ~ **estimates** = *naval estimates qv*; **N~ List** Marine-Rangliste; ~ **pension** Marineruhegeld; ~ **register** *US* Schiffsverzeichnis.

ne|exeat Ausreiseverbot *n*; gerichtliche Aufenthaltsbeschränkung; ~ **varietur** Änderung unzulässig (*notarieller Beglaubigungsvermerk*).

nearest nächst; ~ **accessible** nächst zugänglich; ~ **and next of kin** die nächsten (Bluts)Verwandten; ~ **as possible** weitmöglichst entsprechend; ~ **bid given** Übergebot.

neat rein, netto (*Gewicht bzw Menge*).

neatness knappe schlüssige Darstellung *f*.

necation Tötungshandlung *f*.

necessaries Bedarfsartikel *m|pl*, Bedürfnisse *n|pl*, lebensnotwendige Dinge *n|pl*; ~ **and comforts** Notwendigkeiten und Annehmlichkeiten des Lebens; ~ **of life** Lebensbedürfnisse; **bare ~ of life** notdürftiger Lebensbedarf; **to meet the ~ of life** die Lebensbedürfnisse befriedigen.

necessary notwendig, erforderlich, gezwungen; ~ **and convenient** *in zumutbarem Umfang* erforderlich und zweckmäßig; ~ **and expedient** notwendig und zweckmäßig; ~ **and proper** notwendig und geeignet; ~ **legal assistance** erforderlicher Rechtsbeistand.

necessitate erfordern, notwendig machen.

necessitous circumstances Bedürftigkeit *f*, Unterhaltsbedürftigkeit *f*.

necessity Notwendigkeit *f*, Zwang *m*, Erfordernis *f*, Zwangslage *f*, Not *f*, Notstand *m*, Unumgänglichkeit *f*, ~ **of writing** gesetzliche Schriftform; Erfordernis der Schriftlichkeit; **business** ~ betriebsbedingte Notwendigkeit; **mercantile** ~ kaufmännische Notwendigkeit; **physical** ~ naturgesetzl Notwendigkeit; **public** ~ Notwendigkeit für öffentliche Zwecke; **reasonable commercial** ~ zumutbare wirtschaftl Notwendigkeit; **state of** ~ → *state*; **urgent** ~ Notstand.

necklace Halsband *n*; *terroristische Mordmethode durch Anbrennen e–s benzingefüllten Autoschlauchs um den Hals des Opfers.*

necrocopsy (= *necropsy*) Leichenbesichtigung *f*, Autopsie *f*; Nekroskopie *f*, Obduktion *f*.
necrophilosm (= *necrophilia*) Nekrophilie *f*; krankhafte Vorliebe *f* für Leichen, Leichenschändung *f*.
nee (*née*) geborene (*Ehefrau*).
need *s* Bedürfnis *n*, Bedarf *m*, Angewiesenheit *f*, Bedürftigkeit *f*, Unterhaltsbedürftigkeit *f*, Armut *f*, Elend *n*, Not *f*, Notstand *m*, Notwendigkeit *f*, Mangel *m*; ~ **for coordination** erforderliche Koordinierung; **address in case of** ~ Notadresse; **anticipated** ~ voraussichtlicher Bedarf; **borrowing** ~ Kreditbedarf; **essential** ~**s** Grundbedürfnisse; **if** ~ **arises** nötigenfalls, wenn nötig; **in case of** ~ notfalls, gegebenenfalls; **in** ~ falls notwendig; falls der Indossant in Anspruch genommen werden muß; **in** ~ **of assistance** hilfsbedürftig; **in** ~ **of repair** reparaturbedürftig; **monetary** ~ Geldbedarf; **proof of** ~ → *proof*; **urgent** ~ dringender Bedarf.
need *v* benötigen, brauchen, erfordern, nötig sein, müssen.
needful notwendig, erforderlich, unerläßlich.
needless unnötig, nutzlos, sinnlos.
needy arm, bedürftig.
negate verneinen, negieren, leugnen.
negation Verneinung *f*, Ablehnung *f*, Verwerfung *f*, Annullierung; ~ **of law** Rechtsfeindlichkeit.
negative *adj* negativ, abschlägig, ablehnend, verneinend; ~ **clause** Negativklausel; ~ **certificate of origin** Negativattest über *isrealischen* Ursprung (*von Waren bzw Bestandteilen*); ~ **conflict of jurisdiction** negativer Kompetenzstreit; ~ **evidence of character** abträglicher Leumundsbeweis; ~ **goodwill** negativer Firmenwert (*Überschuß des Buchwerts über den Kaufpreis für die Firma*); ~ **liquidity of debt** Illiquidität; ~ **pledging clause** Nichtverpfändungsklausel, Nichtbelastungsversprechen; ~ **pregant** *ein Bestreiten, in dem ein ungewolltes Geständnis liegt.*
negative *v* negieren, verneinen, ablehnen, verwerfen, widerlegen; ~ **an appeal** e–e Berufung verwerfen; ~ **an exception** e–n Ausnahmetatbestand verneinen.
neglect *s* Verabsäumung *f*, Nachlässigkeit *f*, Achtlosigkeit *f*; Verzug *m*, Pflichtversäumnis *f*; ~ **of children** Vernachlässigung der Kinder, *Gefährdung des Lebensbedarfs der Kinder*; ~ **of duty** Pflichtversäumung, pflichtwidriges Unterlassen, Dienstvergehen; ~ **of proper precautions** Unterlassung der erforderlichen Vorsichtsmaßregeln; ~, **omission or error** pflichtwidrige Unterlassung oder Fehler; ~ **or default** pflichtwidriges Unterlassen; ~ **to observe** Nichtbeachten (*e–r Vorschrift*); ~ **to pay** Zahlungsverzug; ~ **to prosecute** Vernachlässigung der Prozeßführung, Säumnis des Klägers; ~ **to provide maintenance** Vernachlässigung der Unterhaltspflicht; **culpable** ~ schuldhaftes Unterlassen, selbstverschuldetes Nichtgeltendmachen; **excusable** ~ unverschuldetes Versäumnis (*Wiedereinsetzung in den vorigen Stand möglich*); **wilful** ~ vorsätzl Unterlassung.
neglect *v* versäumen, unbeachtet lassen, vernachlässigen, unterlassen, nicht sorgen für.
negligence Fahrlässigkeit *f*, fahrlässiges Verhalten *n*; ~ **by estoppel** unzulässige Rechtsausübung auf Grund eigenen fahrlässigen Verhaltens; ~ **clause** Freizeichnungsklausel; ~ **in law** Verletzung der gesetzlich festgelegten Sorgfaltspflicht; ~ **per se** gesetzlich vermutete Fahrlässigkeit; **action for** ~ Schadensersatzklage wegen fahrlässiger Schädigung; **actionable** ~ *rechtlich relevante* Fahrlässigkeit, fahrlässige Schädigung; **active** ~ fahrlässiges Handeln; **advertent** ~ Leichtfertigkeit, Gefahrenblindheit; **by** ~ fahrlässig; **collateral** ~ Dritthaftung für fahrlässige Schädigung; **common law** ~ allgemeine Fahrlässigkeit; **comparative** ~ Mitverschul-

den; **contributory** ~ Mitverschulden des Geschädigten (*das Schadenersatzanspruch mindert*); **concurrent** ~ mitwirkendes Verschulden mehrerer; **concurrent contributory** ~ Mitverschulden *durch mangelnde Abwendung des schädigenden Ereignisses;* **criminal** ~ strafbares Fahrlässigkeitsdelikt; **culpable** ~ Fahrlässigkeit; **gross** ~ grobe Fahrlässigkeit, Leichtfertigkeit; **hazardous** ~ Leichtfertigkeit; **homicide caused by** ~ fahrlässige Tötung; **imputed** ~ zu vertretende Fahrlässigkeit Dritter; **inadvertent** ~ unbewußte Fahrlässigkeit; **law of** ~ → *law*; **legal** ~ Fahrlässigkeit (*im Rechtssinne*), das Außerachtlassen der erforderlichen Sorgfalt; **mutual contributory** ~ beiderseitiges Mitverschulden; **ordinary** ~ leichte Fahrlässigkeit; **passive** ~ fahrlässiges Unterlassen; **personal** ~ eigene Fahrlässigkeit; **professional** ~ fachliche Nachlässigkeit, berufl Verschulden (Anwaltshaftung), Kunstfehler; ~ ~ *of solicitors*: *Anwaltsverschulden*; **slight** ~ geringer Grad von Fahrlässigkeit; *auch*: Fahrlässigkeit bei besonders strengem Maßstab an die Sorgfaltspflicht; **statutory** ~ Verletzung besonderer gesetzlicher Sorgfaltspflicht; **subsequent** ~ Haftung aus Ingerenz; **supervening** ~ überholendes (*Fremd*)Verschulden; **wanton** ~ Leichtfertigkeit, bewußte, grobe Fahrlässigkeit; **wil(l)ful** ~ (*bewußte*) Leichtfertigkeit.

negligent fahrlässig, nachlässig, unachtsam, säumig, schuldhaft; ~ **of duty** pflichtvergessen.

negotiability Begebbarkeit *f*, Negoziierbarkeit *f*, Verkehrsfähigkeit *f*, Umlauffähigkeit *f*, ~ **by custom** gewohnheitsrechtliche Verkehrsfähigkeit; ~ **by statute** gesetzliche Verkehrsfähigkeit.

negotiable begebbar, verkehrsfähig, umlauffähig, negoziierbar; ~ **bill** Wechsel; ~ **character** Verkehrsfähigkeit, Umlauffähigkeit, Begebbarkeit; ~ **check** → *check*; ~ **document** → *document*; ~ **instrument** umlauffähiges Wertpapier, begebbares Wertpapier; ~ **instruments law** Wertpapier; ~ **note** Solawechsel; ~ **on the stock exchange** börsenfähig; ~ **order of withdrawal account** (*NOW account*) NOW-Konto, *verzinsliches Kontokorrent Konto, US*; ~ **securities** umlauffähige Wertpapier; ~ **warehouse receipt** Orderlagerschein; ~ **words** Begebbarkeitsklausel, Orderklausel.

negotiate übertragen, begeben; verhandeln; ~ **a bill** e–n Wechsel begeben, e–n Wechsel durch Indossament übertragen; ~ **a loan** Darlehensverhandlungen führen, ein Darlehen aufnehmen; ~ **a sale** Kaufverhandlungen führen und zum Abschluß bringen; ~ **a transaction** ein Geschäft zustande bringen; ~ **further** weiterbegeben.

negotiating table Verhandlungstisch *m*.

negotiation Verhandlung *f*, Unterhandlung *f*; Begebung *f*, wertpapiermäßige Übertragung *f*, Girierung *f*, Giro *n*; ~ **by delivery** (*wertpapiermäßige*) Übertragung durch Übergabe; ~ **credit** Negoziierungskredit; ~ **fee** → *fee (1)*; ~ **of a bill** Begebung e–s Wechsels; ~ **of title** Negoziierung, Begebung (*e–s Wertpapiers*); **advice of** ~ Negoziierungsanzeige, Begebungsavis; **antecedent** ~**s** vorvertragliche Verhandlungen (*Kreditgeschäft*); **one-to-one** ~**s** persönliche Verhandlungen, direkte V; **open to** ~ verhandlungsbereit; **preliminary** ~**s** Vorverhandlungen.

negotiator Unterhändler *m*, Verhandlungsführer *m*.

negotiorum gestio Geschäftsführung *f* ohne Auftrag.

negotiorum gestor Geschäftsführer *m* ohne Auftrag.

neighbo(u)r Nachbar *m*; ~ **principle** (grundsätzl) Sorgfaltspflicht gegenüber dem Nächsten; ~ **state** Nachbarstaat.

neighbo(u)rhood Nachbarschaft *f*, nähere Umgebung *f*.

neighbo(u)ring benachbart, angrenzend; ~ **or adjoining houses** benachbarte *bzw* angrenzende Gebäude; ~ **right** verwandtes Recht.

neither party keine der Parteien, *vereinbartes Nichtauftreten beider Parteien.*

nemine contradicente (*to elect* ~ ~) ohne Widerspruch, einstimmig.

nepotism Vetternwirtschaft *f*, Nepotismus *m*.

net netto, rein, nach allen Abzügen; ~ **amount at risk** das Deckungskapital übersteigendes Versicherungsrisiko; ~ **level annual premium** Nettoprämie, Deckungsprämie bei Lebensversicherung; ~ **annual proceeds** jährlicher Reinertrag; ~ **annual value** jährlicher Nettoertragswert; ~ **asset value** Wert des Reinvermögens, Nettoinventarwert; ~ **avails** Diskonterlös, Gegenwert e-s diskontierten Wechsels, Nettoerlös; ~ **bonded debt** reine Anleiheschuld; ~ **book value** Buchwert; ~ **cash flow** Netto-Cashflow (*Jahresgewinn zuzügl Abschreibungen minus ausbezahlter Dividenden*); ~ **change in business inventories** bereinigte Inventarveränderungen; ~ **creditor position** Netto-Überschußposition; ~ **earnings rule** Nettoertragswertberechnung; ~ **income after taxes** Reineinkommen nach Steuern; ~ **income for the year** Jahresüberschuß; ~ **interest return** Nettoverzinsung; ~ **national product** Nettosozialprodukt; ~ **of indirect taxes** frei von indirekten Steuern; ~ **operation assets** Nettoaktiva des gewöhnlichen Geschäftsbetriebs; ~ **operating income** Nettobetriebsgewinn (*Einkommen vor Zinsen und Einkommenssteuern aber nach Abschreibung*); ~ **operating loss** Nettobetriebsverlust (*vor Zinsen u Steuern, nach Abschreibung*); ~ **relevant distribution** Nettoausschüttung; ~ **sale contract** Nettoverkaufsvertrag (*mit Handelsvertreter, er behält den Mehrerlös*); ~ **short-term capital gain** Spekulationsgewinn; ~ **take-home pay** Nettolohn, Nettogehalt; ~ **tangible asset value** Anlagevermögen; ~ **value added** Nettosozialprodukt; ~ **working capital** Betriebskapital, *Umlaufvermögen abzüglich kurzfristiger Verbindlichkeiten;* ~ **worth** Eigenkapital, Reinvermögen; echter Wert.

neutral *adj* neutral, parteilos, unparteiisch.

neutral *s* Neutraler *m*, neutraler Staat *m*.

neutrality Neutralität *f*; ~ **agreement** Neutralitätsabkommen; ~ **laws** Neutralitätsgesetze; **armed** ~ bewaffnete Neutralität; **friendly** ~ wohlwollende Neutralität; **permanent** ~ dauernde Neutralität.

neutralization Neutralisation *f*.

neutralize neutralisieren; ~**d state** neutralisierter Staat; ~**d zone** neutralisierte Zone.

never indebted *allg. Bestreiten des Schuldgrundes.*

new neu; ~ **and useful** neu und von praktischem Nutzen, gewerblich verwertbar; ~ **assignment** *Replik, daß Einwendungen des Beklagten die Klageansprüche nicht betreffen*; ~ **business commission** Abschlußprovison; ~ **cause of action** Klageänderung durch neuen Sachvortrag; **N**~ **Deal** Neubeginn (*Reformgesetzgebung unter F. D. Roosevelt ab 1933*); ~ **departure** neuer Weg, Neuorientierung; ~ **for old** neu für alt; ~ **go** = ~ *time qv*; ~ **or original** neu *bzw* ursprünglich (*schöpferische Leistung*); **of** ~ von neuem, vollkommen neues Verfahren.

New York Curb Exchange *New Yorker Freiverkehrsbörse, seit 1953: American Stock Exchange.*

next | **before** unmittelbar vorangehend; ~ **devisee** Testamentserbe; ~ **eldest** der nächstjüngere (*von letztwillig bedachten Söhnen*); ~ **entitled** nächstberechtigt, Nächstberufener (*Erbfolge*); ~ **friend** Prozeßpfleger, *Kläger in Prozeßstandschaft für e-n Minderjährigen*; ~ **heir** der nächste *gesetzlich* Erbberechtigte; ~ **male heirs** unmittelbar erbberechtigte Abkömmlinge; ~ **male kin** der nächste männliche Verwandte (*auch pl*); ~ **of kin** die nächsten Angehörigen; ~ **of kin in blood** nächste (Bluts)Verwandte; ~ **post** postwendend; ~ **presentation** Vorschlagsrecht *bei Pfründenvergabe;* ~ **session** nächste (*praktisch mögliche*) Sitzung; ~ **vacancy** Besetzungsrecht *e-r frei werdenden Pfarrstelle;* **end ~ (account)** *brit exch* Ultimo nächsten Monats.

nexus Band, Bindung *f*; **familiar ~** Familienband(e).

niche Marktlücke *f*; ~ **marketing** Absatzförderung für e-e Marktlücke, Ausnützung e-r M.

nient | comprise Einwendung der Unvollständigkeit des Klagevortrags; ~ **dedire** nichts bestreiten, sich e-m Versäumnisurteil aussetzen; ~ **le fait** Bestreiten der Echtheit der Urkunde.

night Nacht *f*; ~ **charge** Nachttarif; ~ **duty** Nachtdienst; ~ **magistrate** Nachtdienst habender Polizeibeamter; ~ **mail** Nachtpost, Nachtpostzug; ~ **man** Nacharbeiter, Arbeiter der Nachtschicht; ~ **poaching** nächtliche Wilderei; ~ **safe** Nachttresor; ~ **shelter** Nachtasyl; ~ **shift** Nachtschicht; ~ **stick** Schlagstock (*der Polizei*); ~ **time** Nachtzeit, Nacht (*30 Min nach Sonnenuntergang bis 30 Min vor Sonnenaufgang*); ~ **walker** Straßenmädchen; **„call ~"** Aufnahmeabend (*für Mitglieder von Anwaltsinnungen*), Festessen anläßlich der Anwaltszulassung.

nihil „amtsbekannt ohne pfändbare Habe"; ~ **dicit** Verurteilung mangels Einwendungen; ~ **est** Mitteilung der Unzustellbarkeit; ~ **debet** der Beklagte bestreitet, etw zu schulden.

nil rate band steuerfreie Stufe *f*, Nullsatz *m*.

no *s* Nein *n*, Neinstimme (*pl noes, nos*).

no|account kein Konto; ~ **admittance** Eintritt verboten; ~ **advice** kein Avis, mangels Avis zurück; ~ **agents** → *agent*; ~**arrival, no sale** bei Nichteintreffen keine Kaufverpflichtung; ~ **award** Bestreiten des Vorliegens e-s Schuldspruchs; ~ **bill** kein ausreichender Tatverdacht für eine Anklage, Verfahren eingestellt; ~ **case to answer** Einwand der Nichtschlüssigkeit *bzw* Beweisfälligkeit; ~ **change given** Geld abgezählt bereit halten!; ~ **claims bonus** (= *discount*) Schadensfreiheitsrabatt; ~ **costs** Kostenaufhebung; ~ **cure, no pay** Leistung auf Erfolgsbasis; ~ **evidence** kein Beweisstoff für die Geschworenen vorhanden; ~ **fault** ohne Verschulden *cf divorce; cf insurance*; ~ **funds** keine Dekkung, kein Guthaben; ~**-go area** Gebiet ohne Polizeischutz; ~**-go riot zone** Tumultzone *aus der sich die Polizei zurückgezogen hat*; ~ **good** unbrauchbar; ~ **goods** keine pfändbare Habe; ~ **goods exchange** Umtausch nicht gestattet; ~ **guarantee** ohne Gewähr; ~ **instruction to pay** keine Zahlungsanweisung; ~ **liability whatever** unter Ausschluß jeder Haftung; **N~ lobby** *Vorraum für die mit „Nein" stimmenden Abgeordneten*; ~ **nonsense court arbiter** Richter mit straffer Verhandlungsführung (*bei dem nicht lange gefackelt wird*); ~ **orders** (N/O) keine Aufträge; ~ **order as to costs** Kostenentscheidung ergeht nicht; ~ **par (value)** ohne Nennwert, nennwertlos; ~ **play, no pay** bei Nichtspielen keine Gage; ~ **profit treatment** *gewinnlose Produktion durch Arbeitskampf;* ~ **reasonable prospect** (*of ...ing*) keine hinreichende Aussicht; ~ **recourse** Ausschluß jeder Haftung, kein Regreß, kein Rechtsbehelf; ~ **salvage charges** *Ausschluß der Haftung für Bergungskosten bzw Kosten* *aus Schadensminderungsprozessen (vgl sue and labour clause)*; ~ **substantial miscarriage of justice** *keine gravierende Fehlentscheidung*; ~ **sufficient distress** zur Befriedigung (aus Vermieterpfandrecht) nicht ausreichend.

nobile officium (=) *scot* Ermessen nach Billigkeit.

nocent schuldhaft, verbrecherisch.

noctanter nächtlich, Zulassung der Vollstreckung zur Nachtzeit.

no fault ohne Verschulden (*Gefährdungshaftung, Zerrüttungsprinzip*).

noise Lärm *m*; ~ **abatement** Lärmbekämpfung; *~~zone: Lärmschutzbereich*; ~ **barrier** Lärmschutzwall; ~ **bill** Gesetzesvorlage gegen Lärmbelästigung; ~ **insulation grant** Lärmschutzisolierungsbeihilfe; ~ **protection** Lärmschutz; *~~ embankment*: Lärmschutzwall; *~~wall: Lärmschutzwand*; **disturbing** ~ ruhestörender Lärm.

noisome belästigend, gesundheitsschädlich.

nolle prosequi *Erklärung des Klägers, den Prozeß nicht fortzusetzen*; Einstellung des Verfahrens (*strafrechtlich*).

nolo contendere Nichtbestreiten *n* e-r Anklage, stillschweigendes Schuldgeständnis *n*, Schuldigerklärung *f*.

nom de plume Schriftstellername *m*

nomen | collectivum Sammelbezeichnung, Sammelbegriff, Oberbegriff; ~ **generale** Gattungsbezeichnung; ~ **juris** Rechtsbegriff, juristisches Kunstwort.

nomenclature Nomenklatur *f*, Namensverzeichnis *n*, Benennungssystem *n*, Fachsprache *f*, Terminologie *f*; Zolltarifschema *n*.

nominal nominell, nur dem Namen nach, nur auf dem Papier stehend, namens, Nenn . . .

nominate *v* benennen, vorschlagen.

nominatim namentlich, benannt.

nominating and reducing *Auswahlverfahren für Geschworene*.

nomination Nominierung *f*, Aufstellung *f* e-s Kandidaten, Benennung *f*; ~ **of beneficiary** *ins* Einsetzung e-s Begünstigten; ~ **paper** Wahlvorschlagsliste; **fresh** ~ erstmalige Kandidatenaufstellung.

nominative durch Ernennung eingesetzt.

nominee Designierte(r), Nominierte(r), Vorgeschlagene(r), vorgeschlagener Amtsinhaber; vorgeschobene Person *f*, Strohmann *m*; ~ **company** Strohmanngesellschaft; ~**s of a bank** *Treuhandagentur für den Effektentransfer*; ~ **shareholder** → *shareholder*; **voting by** ~**s** an der Abstimmung indirekt teilnehmen.

nomographer juristischer Schriftsteller *m*.

nomography juristische Abhandlung *f*, Gesetzbeschreibung *f*.

nomotheta Gesetzgeber *m*.

nomothetical gesetzgeberisch.

non-ability Prozeßunfähigkeit *f*, mangelnde Postulationsfähigkeit *f*.

non-acceptance Annahmeverweigerung *f*, Akzeptverweigerung *f*; **returned for** ~ mangels Annahme zurück.

non acceptavit Bestreiten *n* des Wechselakzepts.

non-access Nichtbeiwohnung *f*, fehlende Gelegenheit *f* zum Geschlechtsverkehr.

non-accidental nicht zufällig; ~**injury** schuldhafte Verletzung; *auf Grund gefahrgeneigter Tätigkeit entstandene Verletzung*.

non-accruing nicht bedient (Anleihe), ertragslos, notleidend.

non-acknowledgment Nichtanerkennung *f*.

non-act Unterlassung *f*.

non-actionable nicht einklagbar.

non-admission Zulassungsverweigerung *f*; Nichtzugestehen *n*, Bestreiten *n* mit Nichtwissen.

non-admitted assets *ins* ungeeignete Deckungsmittel *n*|*pl*.

non-adversarial nicht kontradiktorisch, nicht streitig.

nonage Minderjährigkeit *f*, fehlendes Alterserfordernis *n*.

non-aged minderjährig.

non-aggression pact Nichtangriffspakt *m.*
non-alienation Nichtveräußerung *f.*
non-aligned blockfrei.
non-alignment Blockfreiheit *f.*
non-ancestral estate → *estate.*
non-apparent easement → *easement.*
non-appealable (formell) rechtskräftig, nicht rechtsmittelfähig.
non-appearance Nichteinlassung *f*, Nichterscheinen *n.*
non-applicability Nichtanwendbarkeit *f.*
non-approval Nichtgenehmigung *f*, Ablehnung *f.*
non-assented ungenehmigt; ~**bonds** → *bond (1)*; Obligationen ohne Zustimmung zu e-m Sanierungsplan; ~ **stock** → *stock (1).*
non-assessable nicht nachschußpflichtig, nicht umlagepflichtig; ~ **stock** → *stock (1).*
non-assignable nicht abtretbar, nicht übertragbar.
non-assignability Nichtabtretbarkeit *f*, Abtretungsverbot *n.*
non assumpsit *Bestreiten des Verpflichtungsgrundes.*
non-attendance Fernbleiben *n*, Nichterscheinen *n*, Säumnis *n.*
non-bailable nicht zur Kautionsstellung zugelassen; ohne Kautionsverpflichtung.
non-basic nicht grundlegend (wichtig), nicht fundamental.
non-belligerence Nichtkriegführung *f*, *früher: wohlwollende Neutralität; Diskriminierung zwischen Kriegsführenden durch e-n neutralen Staat*; Zustand zwischen Krieg und Frieden, (*nach Beendigung des Kriegszustandes, vor bzw ohne Friedensschluß*).
non bis in idem (= *ne bis in idem*) Strafklageverbrauch *m*, materielle Rechtskraft *f* in Strafsachen.
non-business|days → *day*; ~**debt** → *debt.*
non-cancellable nicht stornierbar, unkündbar.
non-callable unkündbar (*Effekten*).
non-cash bargeldlos.
non cepit Bestreiten *n* der Wegnahme.
non-claim Verwirkung *f* des Klagerechts.
non-cohabitation Getrenntwohnen *n.*
non-combatants Nichtkombattanten *m*|*pl.*
non-commercial nicht gewerblich, privat.
non-commissioned nicht bevollmächtigt; den Unteroffiziersrängen angehörend.
non-committal unverbindlich, ohne Bindung.
non-committed ungebunden, blockfrei.
non-commutable nicht ablösbar, nicht umwandelbar.
non-competence Unzuständigkeit *f.*
non-competitive nicht am Wettbewerb teilnehmend, nicht wettbewerbsmäßig.
non-compliance Nichtbefolgung *f*, Zuwiderhandlung *f.*
non compos (mentis) unzurechnungsfähig, geisteskrank.
nonconforming nicht vorschriftsmäßig, abweichend.
non-conformist *s* Nonkonformist *m*, Dissident *m*; *adj* sektierisch.
non-consensual ohne Einwilligung, nicht zustimmend.
non-consent Nichtzustimmung *f.*
non-content Antragsgegner *m.*
non-contentious nicht streitig; ~ **business** nichtforensische Anwaltstätigkeit; freiwillige Gerichtsbarkeit; ~ **civil case** Verfahren der freiwilligen Gerichtsbarkeit.
non-contestable nicht anfechtbar, unanfechtbar, unwiderruflich.
non-contingent bedingungsunabhängig, unbedingt, absolut gültig.
non-continuous nicht dauernd, nicht auf Dauer bestehend, unterbrochen.
noncontracting nicht vertragsschließend, Nichtvertrags . . .
non-contractual nicht vertraglich, außervertraglich.
non-contributable nicht umlagepflichtig, beitragsfrei.

non-contributory nicht beitragspflichtig, beitragsfrei, nicht umlagenpflichtig, nicht nachschußpflichtig.
non-cultivation Brachliegenlassen *n*, Flächenstillegung *f*.
non-cumulative nicht kumulierend, nicht nachholbar.
non-custodial ohne Freiheitsentzug (→ *sentence*; *treatment*).
non-delegable nicht delegierbar.
non-delivery Nichtlieferung *f*, Nichtübergabe *f*, Nichteinräumung *f* des Besitzes; Unzustellbarkeit; Nichtzustellung (*Post*); ~ **in due contract time** nicht termingerechte Lieferung.
non-departmental ohne Ministerrang.
non-dependant *s* unterhaltsunabhängige Person *f*.
nondescript schwer zu beschreiben, nicht klassifizierbar.
non-deductible nicht abzugsfähig.
non-depository agency rechtl unselbständige ausländ. Bankniederlassung ohne Despositenerlaubnis (*US*).
non-detachable nicht abtrennbar, nicht demontierbar.
non-deterrables von Strafandrohung unbeeindruckte Gewohnheitstäter *m|pl*.
non-direction fehlende Rechtsbelehrung *f* an die Geschworenen
non-disabling nicht zur Erwerbsunfähigkeit führend bzw ausreichend.
nondischargeable (*debts*) nicht erlaßbar, nicht stornierbar.
non-disclosure Nichtoffenbarung *f*, Verletzung der Offenbarungspflicht, Nichtmitteilung *f*, Nichtpreisgabe *f*; Nichtweitergabe *f*.
non-discretionary nicht ermessensfrei, weisungsgebunden.
non-discrimination Nichtdiskriminierung *f*, Gleichbehandlung *f*; ~ **notice** Diskriminierungsverbotsbescheid.
non-distinctive nicht unterscheidungskräftig, nicht ausgeprägt.
non-diversified nicht diversifiziert, ohne Anlagestreuung.
non-durable kurzlebig.
non-dwelling nicht für Wohnzwekke bestimmt.
non-effective unwirksam.
non-elective nicht auf Wahl beruhend; ~ **self-perpetuating body** autonomes, sich selbst ergänzendes Gremium.
non-eligible nicht wählbar, nicht zulassungsfähig, nicht zugelassen.
non-employed arbeitslos.
non-enforceability Nichtvollstreckbarkeit *f*, Nichteinklagbarkeit *f*.
non-English speakers Personen, die der englischen Sprache nicht mächtig sind.
non-enumerated nicht beziffert, unbeziffert, nicht aufgezählt.
nonessentials nicht lebensnotwendige Güter *n|pl*.
non est factum *Bestreiten der Errichtung e-r Urkunde*.
non-exclusive nicht ausschließlich; ~ **occupation agreement** Gruppenwohnungsüberlassungsvertrag; Gruppenmietvertrag.
non-execution Nichtausführung *f*.
non-exempt nicht ausgenommen, pfändbar, zollpflichtig.
non-exhaustion Nichtverbrauch *m*, Nichtausschöpfung *f*, Nichterschöpfung *f*; ~ **of domestic remedies** Nichterschöpfung des innerstaatlichen Rechtswegs.
non-expendable nicht auszahlbar, nicht ausschüttungsfähig, **trust fund** Thesaurierungsfonds; nicht auszahlbares Treuhandvermögen.
non facere Nichteingreifen *n*; Unterlassungspflicht *f*.
nonfeasance schuldhaftes Unterlassen *n*.
non-fee earner angestellter Anwalt; ohne Gebührenanspruch Tätiger.
non-forfeitable nicht verfallend, ohne Verfallsmöglichkeit *f*.
non-forfeiture Nichtverfall *m*, Unverfallbarkeit *f*; ~ **law** Gesetz *n* gegen Verfall der Deckungssumme; ~ **provisions** *ins* obligatorische Rückkaufbedingungen.
non-freehold pachtbesitzmäßig, Pacht.

non-free unfrei, gebunden.
non-fulfilment Nichterfüllung *f*.
non-householder e-e Person ohne (selbständigen) Haushalt.
non-insurable (= *noninsurable, US*) nicht versicherbar, unversicherbar.
non-insurance Nichtversicherung *f*.
non-intercourse Verweigerung *f* von zwischenstaatlichen Wirtschaftsbeziehungen; Nichterfolgen des Geschlechtsverkehrs.
non-interest-bearing unverzinslich.
non-intervention Nichteinmischung *f*.
non-issuable nicht ausstellungsfähig, nicht erfaßbar.
non-joinder *unterlassene Einführung eines notwendigen Streitgenossen in den Prozeß*.
non-judicial nicht gerichtlich.
non-juror Eidesverweigerer *m* (*bei Ableistung des Treueids*).
non-jury list Gerichtsliste für Sachen vor dem Einzelrichter *evt* mit Beisitzer.
non-justiciable nicht justitiabel, keiner gerichtlichen Entscheidung zugänglich.
non-lawyer Nichtanwalt *m*, Nichtjurist *m*.
non-leviable unpfändbar.
non-liability Nichthaftung *f*, Nichtbestehen *n* e-r Steuerpflicht, Haftungsausschluß *m*.
non-licenced ohne (Schank)Konzession *f*.
non-liquet unklar, unschlüssig; *Geschworenenspruch, daß Sache noch einmal untersucht werden muß*.
non-litigious nicht-prozessfreudig, nichtstreitig; ~ **matters** Angelegenheiten *f/pl* der freiwilligen Gerichtsbarkeit.
non-local-authority-reliant nicht auf kommunale Betreuung angewiesen.
non-mailable vom Postversand ausgeschlossen.
non-marital nichtehelich.
non-marketable nicht begehbar, nicht verkehrsfähig, nicht börsenfähig.
non-medical nicht ärztlich (*bestätigt, untersucht, etc*).
non-member Nichtmitglied *n*.
non-member|bank *US* Bank *f*, *die dem Federal Reserve System nicht angeschlossen ist*; ~ **states** Nichtmitgliedstaaten.
nonmerchandise items nicht zum Warenverkehr gehörige Gegenstände.
non-merchant Nichtkaufmann *m*.
non-merchantable nicht verkehrsfähig, nicht handelbar.
non-metropolitan regional, nicht großstädtisch, provinziell, → *county*.
non-national Ausländer *m*, *adj* ausländisch.
non-natural unnatürlich, nicht der natürlichen Beschaffenheit entsprechend.
non-navigable nicht (*für Seeschiffe*) schiffbar.
non-negotiability notice Sperrvermerk *m*, Rektaklausel *f*.
non-negotiable nicht begebbar, nicht negoziierbar, nicht verkehrsfähig.
non-observance Nichterfüllung *f*, Nichtbefolgung *f*, Nichtbeachtung *f*.
non-observant ungehorsam, vorschriftswidrig.
non-occupational berufsfremd, nichtberuflich, privat.
non-occupying nicht im Besitz (*der Mietsache bzw Pachtsache*) befindlich; nicht Gewahrsam habend.
non-official nicht amtlich, inoffiziell.
non-operating betriebsfremd, nicht in Betrieb befindlich, nicht mit dem Betrieb verbunden, nichtbetrieblich.
non-owner Nichteigentümer *m*.
non-participating nicht partizipierend; *ins* ohne Gewinnbeteiligung *f*.
non-party nicht parteigebunden, überparteilich.
nonpayment Nichtzahlung *f*, Nichteinlösung *f*, Zahlungsverzug *m*.

non-performance Nichterfüllung *f*.
nonperishable nicht verderblich.
non placet nicht gebilligt, abgelehnt (*Stimmabgabe*).
non possumus attitude starre ablehnende Haltung *f*.
non-privileged nicht bevorrechtigt.
non-profit (*US: nonprofit*) keinen Gewinn anstrebend, nicht gewerblich, gemeinnützig; ~ **making** nicht auf Gewinn gerichtet, gemeinnützig.
non-profileration Nichtverbreitung (*von Atomwaffen*).
non-proprietary nicht aus dem Eigentum hergeleitet; eigentumsfremd.
non pros = *non prosequitur qv*.
non prosequitur Klageabweisung *f* wegen nachlässiger *bzw* säumiger Prozeßführung.
non-prospectus ohne Prospektzwang.
non-provable nicht zur Konkurstabelle anmeldungsfähig.
non-provided nicht versorgt, nicht subventioniert.
non-quota nicht unter das Kontigent fallend, non-quota.
non-quotation Nichtzulassung *f* zur amtlichen Notierung.
non-ratable Kommunalabgabenfrei.
non-rebuttable unwiderlegbar; ~ **presumption** → *presumption*.
non-recognition Nichtanerkennung *f*.
non-recourse regreßlos, ohne Rückgriff.
non-recurrent nicht wiederkehrend, einmalig.
non-recurring = *non-recurrent qv*.
non-redeemable unkündbar, nicht zurückrufbar, nicht rücknehmbar.
non-reimbursable nicht erstattungsfähig, nicht rückzahlbar, à fonds perdue, verloren (*Zuschuß*).
nonrepair schlechter Erhaltungszustand *m*, unterlassene Instandsetzung *f*.
non-repressive nicht repressiv.
non-residence Nichtansässigkeit *f*, Wohnsitz *bzw* dauernder Aufenthalt außerhalb des Gerichtsbezirks.
non-resident *adj* auswärtig, nicht (hier) ansässig, nicht hier wohnhaft; ~ **citizen** *US* Staatsbürger mit Wohnsitz im Ausland *bzw außerhalb des Gerichtsbezirkes*; ~ **company** *brit* nichtansässige Gesellschaft *ohne (Haupt-)Geschäftssitz im Inland*; ~ **taxpayer** → *taxpayer*.
non-resident *s* Nichtansässige(r), Gebietsfremder *m*, Person mit Auslandswohnsitz; Devisenausländer *m bzw* -in *f*; ~ **convertibility** freie Konvertierbarkeit für (Devisen-)-Ausländer.
non-retroactivity Nichtrückwirkung *f*, ohne rückwirkende Kraft.
non-reversible nicht revisibel, formell rechtskräftig.
non-sane unzurechnungsfähig.
nonsense Unsinn, *unverständliche Worte in e-r Urkunde*.
non sequitur nicht schlüssig; falscher Schluß, Trugschluß *m*.
non-signatory Nichtunterzeichner . . .
non-signer Nichtunterzeichner *m*.
non-solicitor licensed conveyancer nichtanwaltlicher Grundstücksübertragungsspezialist.
non-stock ohne Aktienkapital, ohne Grundkapital.
non-stop durchgehend, ohne Zwischenlandung.
non-striker Nichtstreikender *m*.
non-suit *s* (= *nonsuit*) Prozeßbeendigung *f* ohne Sachentscheidung; Klageabweisung *f*; **compulsory** ~ Klageabweisung wegen unschlüssigen bzw nicht substantiierten Vortrags; **involuntary** ~ klageabweisendes Urteil (*wegen Säumnis, mangelnder Schlüssigkeit, Beweisfälligkeit ua*); ~ **judgment of** ~ klageabweisendes Urteil; **peremptory** ~ klageabweisendes Urteil *mangels Substantiierung bzw wegen Beweisfälligkeit*; **voluntary** ~ Klagerücknahme.
non-suit *v* (= *nonsuit*) die Klage (*ohne Verzicht auf den Klageanspruch*) zurücknehmen; die Klage (*wegen Versäumnis des Klägers bzw wegen Unschlüssigkeit*) abweisen; ~ **a plaintiff** die Klage abweisen.

non-summons Einwendung *f* der nicht erfolgten bzw verspäteten Zustellung.

non-support Verletzung *f* der Unterhaltspflicht; **criminal** ~ strafbare Unterhaltspflichtverletzung.

non-taxability Steuerfreiheit *f*.

non-taxable nicht steuerbar, nicht zu versteuern.

non-tenure Bestreiten *n* der Pächtereigenschaft.

non-term sitzungsfreie Zeit *f*, Gerichtsferien *f*.

non-testamentary nichttestamentarisch, nicht letztwillig.

non-trader Nichtkaufmann *m*.

non-trading nichtgewerblich.

non-traffic nicht verkehrsbedingt, nichtgewerblich.

non-transferable nicht übertragbar.

non-union nicht organisiert, ohne Gewerkschaftsbindung; ~ **shop** *US* gewerkschaftsfreier Betrieb; ~ **worker** Nichtgewerkschaftler.

non-unitary nicht einheitlich.

non-use Nichtgebrauch *m*.

non-user Nichtgebrauch *m (von Rechten)*, Nichtbenutzung *f*, Nichtausübung *f*, unterlassene Inanspruchnahme *f*.

non-utility mangelnde Verwertbarkeit *f*, Nutzlosigkeit *f*.

non-value unbewertet, unbeziffert, ohne Wertangabe.

non-violence Gewaltlosigkeit *f*.

non-voting nicht stimmberechtigt; stimmrechtlos; ich enthalte mich der Stimme.

non-waiver vorbehaltlich, ohne Verzicht.

non-warranty Haftungsausschluß *m*.

norm Norm *f*, Verhaltensnorm *f*; Regel *f*, Muster *n*, Richtschnur *f*, Durchschnittsleistung *f*, Produktionsstandard *m*; **basic** ~ Grundnorm; **legal** ~ Rechtsnorm.

normal normal, regelrecht, vorschriftsmäßig, mustergültig; ~ **cost** Normalkosten, die niedrigsten durchschnittlichen Produktionskosten; ~ **distribution** Normalverteilung (Statistik); ~ **output** Normalleistung, Normalerzeugung; ~ **performance** Normalleistung; ~ **stock method** Methode e-s kontinuierlichen normalen Lagerbestandes; ~ **take-home pay** normaler Nettolohn; ~ **wear and tear** normale Abschreibung; gewöhnliche Abnutzung; ~ **working of the contract** das normale Funktionieren des Vertrages.

normalcy Normalität *f*, normale Verfassung *f*.

normally in der Regel, regelmäßig, normalerweise.

Norman French anglo-französisch (*englische Juristensprache im Mittelalter*).

nostrum Geheimmittel *n*, Patentrezept *n*, Quacksalbereimittel *n*.

not nicht, un . . .; ~ **accepted, medically unfit** aus ärztlichen Gründen untauglich; ~ **accountable** nicht rechenschaftspflichtig, keine Haftung für; ~ **ascertained** nicht festgestellt; ~ **assignable** nicht übertragbar; ~ **binding offer** freibleibendes Angebot; ~ **due** nicht fällig; ~ **earlier than** frühestens; ~ **exactly** zirka (*ca*), Zirkabetrag; Irrtum vorbehalten; ~ **exceeding** höchstens, bis zu; ~ **found** → *found*; ~ **guilty** nicht schuldig, unschuldig; ~ **guilty by reason of insanity** Freispruch wegen Schuldunfähigkeit durch Geisteskrankheit; ~ **guilty by statute** Bestreiten der Anklage unter Berufung auf ein besonderes Gesetz; ~ **in derogation of** unbeschadet; ~ **included in** nicht enthalten in, nicht darunter fallend; ~ **later than** spätestens, innerhalb der Frist von . . .; ~ **less than** mindestens, wenigstens; ~ **liable** ohne Haftung für, frei von Verbindlichkeiten für; ~ **marrying or dying** falls (*die Betroffene*) unverheiratet stirbt; ~ **more than** höchstens; ~ **negotiable** nicht negoziierbar, nicht begehbar, nicht verkehrsfähig, Rekta . . .; ~ **of public concern** ohne öffentliches Interesse; ~ **on the merits** nicht in der Sache selbst; ~

otherwise nicht anderweitig, nicht anders; ~ **possessed** nicht im Besitz, *Bestreiten des Besitzes*; ~ **proven** → *proven*; ~ **registrable** nicht eintragungsfähig; ~ **satisfied** fruchtlos gepfändet; ~ **settled** nicht treuhänderisch übertragen; ~ **sooner than** frühestens, nach e-r Frist von; ~ **sufficient funds** keine Deckung; ~ **to my knowledge** meines Wissens nicht; ~ **to order** nicht indossabel, Rekta ... *cf clause*; ~ **transferable** → *transferable*; ~ **tried** Hauptverhandlung (noch) nicht durchgeführt; ~ **under command** steuerlos, navigationsunfähig, treibend (*Schiff*); ~ **yet in esse** noch nicht erzeugt (*child*).

notarial notariell; von einem notary public *qv* beglaubigt; ~ **act** Amtshandlung e-s Notars; Notariatsurkunde; ~ **act of honour** notarielle Ehrenhandlung; ~ **attestation** → *attestation*; ~ **certificate** → *certificate*; ~ **charges not to be incurred** (*Vermerk auf Wechsel*) „ohne Kosten"; ~ **deed** → *deed*; ~ **instrument** → *instrument;* ~ **protest certificate** Protesturkunde; ~ **will** → *will*.

notarise = *notarize*; notariell beglaubigen, *evt* notariell beurkunden.

notary Notar *m*; **~'s chambers** Amtssitz des Notars; ~ **public** Notar (*Inhaber e-r Notariatskommission*) *solicitor mit Notariat;* öffentlicher Beurkundungsbeamter (*nicht dem dt Notar entsprechend*); **~'s seal** → *seal*.

notation Vermerk *m*, Aufzeichnung *f*, Aktenvermerk *m*.

notchell (= *nochell*) Anzeige *f*, nicht für die Schulden der Ehefrau aufzukommen.

note *s* Bescheid *m*, Note *f*, Notiz *f*; Schuldschein *m*, Solawechsel *m*; Rechnung *f*, Nota *f*, Banknote *f*; ~ **broker** → *broker*; ~ **for a patent** Schuldschein für Erwerb e-s Patents; ~ **for protest** Vormerkung zum Protest; ~ **holder** Inhaber e-s Eigenwechsels, Wechselbesitzer, Schuldscheininhaber; **~s in circulation** Banknotenumlauf; ~ **in reply** Antwortnote; ~ **issuance facility** Schuldschein-Rahmenarrangement; ~ **issue** Banknotenumlauf; ~ **issuing right** Notenbankprivileg; ~ **of allowance** Mitteilung der Rechtsmittelzulassung; ~ **of blocking** Sperrvermerk; ~ **of charges** Gebührenrechnung, Spesenrechnung; ~ **of entry** Eintragungsvermerk (*in e-m Register*); ~ **of expenses** Auslagenrechnung, Spesenrechnung; ~ **of fine** Auflassungsurkundenauszug; ~ **of hand** Schuldschein, eigener Wechsel; ~ **of issue** Mitteilung erfolgter Terminsfestsetzung; ~ **of protest** Protestnote; ~ **or memorandum** kurze Vertragsniederschrift; **~s payable** *bil* Wechselschulden; **~s payable to banks** Wechselverbindlichkeiten gegenüber Banken; ~ **payable on demand** auf Anforderung zahlbarer eigner Wechsel; ~ **providing for compound interest** Schuldschein mit Zinseszinsklausel; **~s receivable** *bil* Wechselforderung (*Solawechsel*); ~ **teller** Inkassobeamter für Wechsel; **~s tickler** Verfallbuch für Wechsel; ~ **verbale** Verbalnote; ~ **with agreement to execute renewal** Solawechsel mit Prolongationsvereinbarung; ~ **with surety** Schuldschein mit Bürgschaft; **advance** ~ Heuernote; **advice** ~ Anzeige, Benachrichtigungsschreiben; Ankündigungsschreiben, Mitteilung der Ankunft e-r Sendung bei der Bahn; **bond** ~ Zollbegleitschein; **bond-secured ~s** Banknoten mit Deckung durch Staatsanleihen *bzw* Hypotheken; **borrower's ~s against ad rem security** dinglich gesicherte Schuldscheine; **broker's** ~ → *broker;* **case** ~ Leitsatz, kurze Wiedergabe des Falles; **cautionary** ~ Verwarnung; **circular** ~ Zirkularkreditbrief; **collateral** ~ dingl gesicherter Schuldschein; **confirmation** ~ Bestätigungsschreiben; **cover** ~ → *cover*; **credit** ~ → *credit (2)*; **debit** ~ → *debit*; **delivery** ~

→ *delivery*; **demand** ~ → *demand*; **discounted** ~ diskontierter Solawechsel; **dispatch** ~ → *dispatch;* **executed** ~ begebener Solawechsel, ausgestellter und übergebener Schuldschein; **floating-rate** ~ zinsvariabler Schuldschein; Obligation, (FRN); **guaranteed** ~ durch Bürgschaft gesicherte Schuldverschreibung; **head** ~ Leitsatz (*e-s Urteils*); **installment** ~ Ratenschuldschein; **joint** ~ gesamtschuldnerischer Schuldschein; **judgment** ~ → *judgment*; **marginal** ~ → *marginal*; **mortgage** ~ → *mortgage*; **negotiable** ~ → *negotiable*; **official** ~ Amtsbescheid; **past due** ~ überfälliger Schuldschein *bzw* Solawechsel; **promissory** ~ → *promissory note*; **practice** ~ → *practice*; **protested** ~**s** → *protest v*; **serial** ~ Ratenzahlungsschuldschein; **take** ~ (*vorläufige*) Dekkungszusage; **term** ~ Eigenwechsel, Solawechsel; **time** ~ befristeter Schuldschein, Sch. mit fester Laufzeit; **to take** ~ **of sth** etwas zur Kenntnis nehmen; **trade customers'** ~**s** Warenkreditschuldscheine; **unpaid** ~ Rückwechsel (*Solawechsel*); **unsecured** ~ ungesicherter Schuldschein.

note *v* notieren, vermerken, zur Kenntnis nehmen, beachten, besonders bemerken; ~ **a bill** e-n Wechselprotest beurkunden.

notice *s* Wahrnehmung *f*, Kenntnis *f*, Information *f*, Notiz *f*, Bekanntmachung *f*, Anschlag *m*, Hinweis *n*, Benachrichtigung *f*, Bescheid *m*, Mitteilung *f*, Nachricht *f*, Ankündigung *f* (*e-s Antrags*), Anzeige *f*, Verfügung *f*, Vorladung *f*, Warnung *f*, Kündigung *f*; Kennzeichen *n*, Merkmal *n*, schriftliche Bemerkung *f*; ~ **before action** Klageandrohung; ~ **board** Schwarzes Brett; ~ **by advertisement** öffentliche Zustellung; ~ **by publication** öffentliche Bekanntmachung; ~ **deposit** Einlagenkonto mit Kündigungsfrist; ~ **for priority** Prioritätsankündigung; ~ **in lieu of distringas** Vorpfändung (*von Kapitalanteilen und Wertpapierrechten*); ~ **in writing** schriftliche Mitteilung; ~ **loan** Darlehen mit Kündigungsfrist; ~ **of abandonment** Abandonerklärung; ~ **of accident** (Arbeits)Unfallmeldung; ~ **of action** Klageankündigung (*gegen privilegierte Personen*); ~ **of admission** schriftsätzliche Aufforderung an den Beklagten, Tatsachen (*beschränkt auf diesen Prozeß*) zuzugestehen; ~ **of any trust** Hinweis auf ein Treuhandverhältnis; ~ **of appearance** → *appearance*; ~ **of arrival** Eingangsbestätigung; ~ **of assent** Zustimmungserklärung; ~ **of assessment** Steuerbescheid; ~ **of assignment** Abtretungsanzeige; ~ **of birth** Geburtsanzeige; ~ **of call** Einzahlungsaufforderung (*des Liquidators*); ~ **of cancellation** Rücktrittsanzeige, Rücktrittserklärung; ~ **of change of domicile** Anmeldung wegen Wohnungswechsel; ~ **of claim** Streitverkündung; ~ **of consignment** Anzeige über die Absendung; ~ **of curtailment to remain** (*in Britain*) Verkürzung der Aufenthaltserlaubnis; ~ **of death** Todesanzeige; ~ **of defects** Mängelrüge, Mängelanzeige; ~ **of deficiency** *Bescheid der Steuerbehörde über formale Mängel der Steuererklärung*; ~ **of delivery** Zustellungsurkunde; ~ **of denial** Ablehnungsbescheid; ~ **of departure** Abmeldung (*an das Melderegister*); ~ **of deposit** *brit* Vermerk über die Hinterlegung *der Eigentumsurkunde*; ~ **of desire to sever** Aufhebungsverlangen, Teilungsbegehren; ~ **of determination** Bescheid, Steuerbescheid; ~ **of disclaimer** (amtliche) Verzichterklärung; ~ **of discontinuance** Klageverzicht; ~ **of dishonour** Notanzeige, Nichthonorierungsanzeige (*Nichtakzeptierung bzw Nichtzahlung e-s Wechsels*); ~ **of dismissal** Arbeitgeberkündigung; ~ **of error** Berichtigungsanzeige; ~ **of foreclosure** Pfandverfallsankündigung; ~ **of hearing**

Ladung zum Termin; ~ **of intended prosecution** Strafverfolgungsankündigung (*wegen Verkehrsdelikts*); ~ **of intention to defend** Anzeige der Verteidigungsbereitschaft; ~ **of intention to proceed** befristete Ankündigung der Wiederaufnahme *des ruhenden Prozesses*; ~ **of intention to redeem** Rückkaufsankündigung; ~ **of judgment** Mitteilung *an den Prozeßgegner* über Urteilsverkündungsdatum; *gerichtliche* Mitteilung des Urteils; ~ **of lis pendens** Bekanntmachung der Rechtshängigkeit, Bekanntmachung der Streitbefangenheit des Eigentums; ~ **of loss** Schadensanzeige; ~ **of marriage** Heiratsanzeige; ~ **of motion** Benachrichtigung über e-n Antrag; Initiativantrag; Ankündigung des Datums der Antragstellung an den Gegner; ~ **of objections** Spezifizierung von Patenteinsprüchen; ~ **of payment in** Hinterlegungsbenachrichtigung; ~ **of prohibition** Sperrvermerk; ~ **of protest** Protestnotifizierung, Mitteilung über Wechselprotest; ~ **of redemption** Kündigung von Wertpapieren; ~ **of reference** Benachrichtigung über die Erhebung e-r Schiedsklage; Klagemitteilung; ~ **of rejection** Ablehnungsbescheid; ~ **of rescission** Anzeige (*bzw Androhung*) des Rücktritts vom Vertrag; ~ **of suspension** Benachrichtigung über die Zahlungseinstellung; ~ **of termination** Kündigung; ~ **of title** Kenntnis e-s Rechtsmangels; ~ **of trial** Klageankündigung; Ladung zum Termin; ~ **of withdrawal** Kündigung *e-s Bankguthabens*; *int* Rücktrittsanzeige, Kündigungsanzeige; ~ **of withdrawal of funds** Kündigung von Einlagen; ~ **of writ of summons** Mitteilung der Klage an Beklagten im Ausland (*anstatt Zustellung*); ~ **on forfeiture of shares** Androhung der Kaduzierung von Kapitalanleihen; ~ **period** Kündigungsfrist; ~ **to admit** = ~ *of admission qv*; ~ **to admit facts** = ~ *of admission qv*; ~ **to appear** Ladung des Beklagten; ~ **to consul** Benachrichtigung des *örtlichen* Konsulats; ~ **to defend action** Aufforderung, sich auf die Klage einzulassen; ~ **to members** Benachrichtigung von Aktionären; ~ **to pay** Zahlungsaufforderung; ~ **to plead** Androhung des Versäumnisurteils mangels Einlassung; ~ **to produce** Aufforderung zur Urkundenvorlage; ~ **to quit** befristete Kündigung durch den Vermieter (*bzw* Verpächter); Anzeige der bevorstehenden freiwilligen Räumung; ~ **to stop payment of cheque** Schecksperrung; ~ **to terminate contract** Kündigung e-s Vertrages; ~ **to third party** Streitverkündung; ~ **to treat** Inanspruchnahme e-s Grundstücks für öffentl. Zwecke; Aufforderung, in Verkaufsverhandlungen mit Enteignungsbehörde einzutreten; ~ **to vacate** Kündigung, Räumungsaufforderung; **a forthnight's** ~ 14tägige Kündigung; **actual** ~ (tatsächliche) Kenntnis; **at short** ~ kurzfristig; **averment of** ~ Behauptung, daß Mitteilung erfolgt ist; **completion** ~ Baufertigstellungsanzeige; **constructive** ~ unterstellte Kenntnis, gesetzlich vermutete Kenntnis, zurechenbare Kenntnis; **cure** ~ Abhilfemitteilung; Androhung von Maßregeln bei nicht fristgerechter Beseitigung von Mängeln; **defective** ~ Zustellungs- bzw Ladungsmängel; **deposits at** ~ → *deposit*; **doctrine of** ~ → *doctrine*; **draft** ~ Einberufungsbefehl; **due** ~ erforderliche Mitteilung, ordnungsgemäße Kündigung; **duty to give** ~ *ins* Anzeigenpflicht; *exch* Notifikationspflicht; **enforcement** ~ Zwangsbescheid, Vollziehungsbescheid; **expiration of** ~ Ablauf der Kündigungsfrist; **express** ~ ausdrückliche Mitteilung, Kenntnis auf Grund der Mitteilung; **final** ~ (endgültige) Kündigung mit Räumungsaufforderung; **immediate**

~ sofortige Benachrichtigung, *ins* unverzügliche Schadensmeldung; **implied** ~ tatsächlich vermutete Kenntnis; **imputed** ~ zurechenbare Kenntnis e-s Dritten; Kenntnis des Stellvertreters (*die der Vertretene gegen sich gelten lassen muß*); **judicial** ~ eigene Kenntnis des Gerichts; *of* ~~: gerichtsnotorisch, gerichtsbekannt; **legal** ~**s** Gerichtsbekanntmachung; **obituary** ~ Todesanzeige; **obligation to give** ~ Mitteilungspflicht; **official** ~ Amtskenntnis, von Amts wegen bekannt sein; **party wall** ~ Hinweis auf Kommunmauer; **period of** ~ → *period*; **personal** ~ *effektive* Benachrichtigung des Empfängers persönlich; **presumptive** ~ tatsächlich vermutete Kenntnis; **previous** ~ Vorankündigung, Voranzeige; **priority** ~ Rangvormerkung; **public** ~ öffentliche Bekanntmachung, Aufgebot, Aufruf; Ruf; **reasonable** ~ angemessene Kündigungsfrist; **seven days'** ~ wöchentliche Kündigungsfrist; **special** ~ besondere Ankündung mit Vorfrist; **third party** ~ → *third*; **to give** ~ → *to give*; **to receive** ~ Nachricht erhalten; **until further** ~ bis auf weiteres; **without** ~ ohne vorherige Ankündigung; fristlos; gutgläubig; **without previous** ~ ohne Ankündigung, ohne vorherige Mitteilung; **written** ~ **of withdrawal** Kündigungsschreiben, Kündigungsbenachrichtigung (*Einlagen, Kredit*).

notice *v* wahrnehmen, beachten, bemerken, anzeigen, melden, benachrichtigen.

notifiable meldepflichtig, anzeigepflichtig.

notification Bekanntgabe *f*, Benachrichtigung *f*, Notifizierung *f*, Verständigung *f*, Anzeige *f*, Mitteilung *f*; ~ **of protest** Protestanzeige; ~ **of readiness to despatch** Meldung der Versandbereitschaft; ~ **of setting-down** Terminbenachrichtigung; ~ **regulations** Meldebestimmungen; **official** ~ (amtlicher) Bescheid, Amtsbescheid; **public** ~ öffentliche Bekanntmachung; öffentliche Zustellung.

notify bekanntgeben, anzeigen, mitteilen, benachrichtigen, erklären, notifizieren; ~**ing accused of his right to counsel** Belehrung des Angeklagten über sein Recht, e-n Verteidiger zu haben; ~**ing bank** avisierende Bank.

noting *s* notarieller Beurkundungsvermerk *m* über erfolglose Wechselvorlage; *formularmäßige* Angabe des Grundes der Nichteinlösung (*Sichtwechsel*); ~ **a bill** Vorprotest e-s Wechsels (*Beiheftung des Nichtbezahlungsvermerks*); **date of** ~ Notifizierungsdatum; **expenses of** ~ → *expenses*.

notion Begriff *m*, Vorstellung *f*.

notional begrifflich, gedanklich, nur gedacht, hypothetisch, imaginär; ~ **settlement** → *settlement*.

notoriety Amtsbekanntheit *f*, Offenkundigkeit *f*, Gerichtskundigkeit *f*; **proof of** ~ *scot* = *judicial notice* → *notice*.

notorious offenkundig, allgemeinkundig, notorisch, bekannt, berüchtigt.

notwithstanding ungeachtet, unbeschadet, trotz, ohne Rücksicht auf, in Abänderung von, abweichend von, nichtsdestoweniger, dennoch, trotzdem; ~ **anything in the foregoing provisions** ohne Rücksicht auf etwa anderslautende vorstehende Bestimmungen; ~ **anything in the said policy to the contrary** in Ergänzung und teilweisen Abänderung der genannten Police; ~ **section 2** abweichend von Abschnitt (*Paragraph*) 2.

novation Novation *f*, Schuldumschaffung *f*; befreiende Schuldübernahme *f*.

novel *adj* neu, neuartig, ergänzend; ~ **fact situation** neuartige tatsächliche Lage.

novel *s* Novelle *f*, Nachtragsgesetz *n*; **the N~s** die Novellen Justinians.

novelty Neuheit *f*, Neuerung *f*; ~ **of invention** Neuheit der Erfindung;

degree of ~ Grad der Neuheit; **examination for** ~ Neuheitsprüfung; **infringement of** ~ Neuheitsschädlichkeit; **net rest of** ~ reiner Neuheitsrest; **objection for want of** ~ Einspruch wegen mangelnder Neuheit; **to negate the** ~ die Neuheit verneinen.

novice Neuling *m*, Anfänger *m*.

novitiate Lehrzeit *f*, Lehre *f*; Probezeit *f*; Novizenhaus *n*.

novus actus interveniens (=) Unterbrechung *f* des Kausalzusammenhangs *durch dazwischentretendes Ereignis*.

now jetzt, zum gegenwärtigen Zeitpunkt, im Todeszeitpunkt (*Testament*); ~ **owing** fällig, gegenwärtig geschuldet; zum Zeitpunkt des Ablebens geschuldet.

noxious schädlich, übelriechend, gesundheitsschädlich, unmoralisch; ~ **fumes** gesundheitsschädliche Dämpfe; ~ **plants** schädliches Unkraut; ~ **thing** schädlicher Gegenstand, schädlicher Stoff; ~ **trade** Gewerbe belästigender Art.

nubile ehefähig, heiratsfähig.

nubility Ehefähigkeit *f*; **certificate of** ~ Ehefähigkeitszeugnis.

nuclear | **arms-free zone treaty** Vertrag über atomwaffenfreie Zone; ~ **crimes** atomare Straftaten; ~ **deterrent** atomare Abschreckung; ~ **facilities** Kernkraft-Einrichtungen; ~ **force** Atomstreitkraft; ~-**free zone** atomwaffenfreie Zone; ~ **plant operation** Betreiben e-r Atomanlage; ~ **reprocessing plant** atomare Wiederaufbearbeitungsanlage; **N**~ **Regulatory Commission** *(US)* Atombehörde; ~ **sharing** Kernwaffenmitbesitz; ~ **test ban** Atomwaffenversuchsverbot; ~ **umbrella** atomare Abschirmung; ~ **waste** Atommüll; ~ **waste dump** Endlagerung; ~ **waste plant** atomare Wiederaufarbeitungsanlage.

nude nackt, ohne Einhaltung der Formvorschrift; ohne Gegenleistung; ~ **matter** Behauptung ohne Beweisantritt.

nudum pactum = *nude pact* → *pact*.

nugatory vergeblich, unwirksam, wertlos, gegenstandslos, ohne Überzeugungskraft.

nuisance Störung *f*, Unzuträglichkeit *f*, Gefahrenquelle *f*, (negative) Einwirkung (*meist durch Immissionen*); Besitzstörung *f*, Ärgernis *n*, Belästigung *f*, Polizeiwidrigkeit *f*; ~ **at law** = ~ *per se qv*; ~ **by furnace** Rauchbelästigung; ~ **in fact** *an sich zulässige, aber auf Grund der örtlichen Verhältnisse besitzstörende Tätigkeit oder Baulichkeit*; ~ **per se** *Sachverhalt, der auch ohne gesetzliches Verbot e-e rechtswidrige Störung bedeutet*; ~ **settlement** Abfindungsvergleich *zur Vermeidung e-s geringfügigen oder unsicheren Prozesses*; **abatement of a** ~ Beseitigung der Störung, Selbsthilfe (*zur Beseitigung des störenden Zustandes*); **actionable** ~ → *actionable*; **assize of** ~ *hist* Beweissicherungsantrag auf Feststellung e-r Besitzstörung durch Geschworene; **attractive** ~ *für Kinder attraktive* Gefahrenquelle; **civil** ~ Besitzstörung; **common** ~ = *public* ~ *qv*; **continuing** ~ Dauerbelästigung; **mixed** ~ *Besitzstörung und zugleich öffentliches Ärgernis*; **permanent** ~ Dauerbelästigung, ständige Gefahrenquelle; **private** ~ Besitzstörung, nachbarrechtliche Belästigung; **public** ~ öffentliche Störung *bzw* öffentliche Gefahrenquelle, öffentliches Ärgernis.

nul nein, nichts; ~ **award** *Klageabweisungsantrag im Schiedsverfahren*; ~ **disseisin** *Bestreiten der widerrechtlichen Entziehung von Liegenschaftsbesitz*; ~ **tiel corporation** *Einwendung des Nichtbestehens der betreffenden Körperschaft*; ~ **tiel record** *Bestreiten des Vorhandenseins e-r Beweisurkunde*; ~ **tort** *Einwendung gegen eine Grundstücksherausgabeklage, daß keine unerlaubte Handlung vom Beklagten begangen wurde*; ~ **waste** → *waste*.

null nichtig, unwirksam, ungültig; ~ **and void** (*null und*) nichtig.

nulla | **bona** keine pfändbare Habe

(*Pfandabstand*); ~ **poena sine lege** (=) keine Strafe ohne Gesetz.

nullification Nichtigkeitserklärung *f*, Ungültigmachung *f*, Nullifizierung *f*, Aufhebung *f*, Vernichtung *f*; Blockierung *f* e-s Bundesgesetzes durch Einzelstaat.

nullify für nichtig erklären, ungültig machen, vernichten; ~ **a patent** ein Patent für nichtig erklären lassen.

nullity Nichtigkeit *f*, Unwirksamkeit *f*, Ungültigkeit *f*; ~ **action** → *action*; ~ **appeal** *pat* Nichtigkeitsbeschwerde; ~ **of marriage** Ehenichtigkeit; ~ **procedure** Verfahren in Nichtigkeitssachen; ~ **suit** (*Prozeß über eine*) Nichtigkeitsklage; **absolute** ~ (absolute) Nichtigkeit; **complete** ~ Gesamtnichtigkeit, Ungültigkeit; **decree of** ~ → *decree*; **partial** ~ Teilnichtigkeit; **plea of** ~ → *plea*; **proceedings for** ~ **of marriage** Ehenichtigkeitsklage; Eheaufhebungsklage; **relative** ~ Anfechtbarkeit.

nullius filius uneheliches Kind *n, erbunfähiges Kind, dessen Eltern unbekannt sind*.

nullum | crimen rule „keine Strafe ohne Gesetz"; ~ **tempus occurrit regi** *die kön̈glichen Hoheitsrechte unterliegen keinem Zeitablauf und keiner Verjährung*.

number *s* Nummer *f*, Zahl *f*, Ziffer *f*, Anzahl *f*, Artikel *m*, Ware *f*; ~**s game** illegales Zahlenlotto; ~ **of action** Geschäftsnummer, Aktenzeichen; ~ **of units** Stückzahl; ~**s stamp** Zahlenstempel; **calculated** ~ Sollbestand; **case** ~ Aktenzeichen; **code** ~ (Konto)Nummer, Postleitzahl; **identifying** ~ Aktenzeichen; **inactive** ~ nicht mehr benützte Nummer; **indefinite** ~ unbestimmte Zahl, e-e frei abwandelbare Zahl; **invoice** ~ Rechnungsnummer; **reference** ~ → *reference*; **running** ~ (fort)laufende Nummer, laufende Zahl; **serial** ~ Eingangsnummer, laufende Nummer.

number *v* numerieren, zählen, betragen; **consecutively** ~**ed** fortlaufend numeriert; **marked and** ~**ed** mit Zeichen und Nummern versehen.

numeral Grundzahl *f*, Zahlwort *n*.

numerical numerisch, zahlenmäßig.

numero Nummer *f*, Kennziffer *f*.

nunc pro tunc (*now for then*) rückwirkend gültig.

nunciature Nuntiatur *f*, Amtsperiode *f* e-s Nuntius.

nuncupate öffentlich und feierlich erklären.

nuncupative mündlich; ~ **will** → *will*.

nuptial ehelich, die Ehe betreffend; Hochzeit . . .

nurse Krankenschwester *f*, Krankenpflegerin *f*, Kinderschwester *f*; **district** ~ Gemeindeschwester; **state registered** ~ staatlich geprüfte Krankenschwester.

nursery grounds Baumschulengrundstück.

nurture *s* Ernährung *f*, Nahrung *f*, Erziehung *f*.

nurture *v* nähren, aufziehen, erziehen.

O

oath Eid *m*, Schwur *m*; ~ **after statement** Nacheid; ~ **in supplement** Parteieid in eigener Sache; ~ **of administration** Nachlaßverwaltereid; ~ **of allegiance** Treueid, Fahneneid; ~ **of credulity** *scot* Eid nach bestem Wissen und Gewissen; ~ **of disclosure** Offenbarungseid; ~ **of enlistment** Fahneneid; ~ **of fealty** Lehnseid; ~ **of manifestation** Offenbarungseid; ~ **of office** Amtseid, Diensteid; ~ **on the colours** Fahneneid; ~**-rite** Eidesförmlichkeiten; **administration of** ~ Beeidigung, Eidesleistung; **assertory** ~ assertorischer Eid, Eid über die Bekundung e-r Wahrnehmung; außergerichtlicher Eid *vor e-r Behörde*, Amtseid; **by** ~ eidlich, unter Eid; **clerk's** ~ Eid des Urkundsbeamten; **coronation** ~ Krönungseid; **decisive** ~ Parteieid des Prozeßgegners; **decisory** ~ Eideszuschiebung auf den Prozeßgegner, Eid bei Vernehmung des Prozeßgegners; **extrajudicial** ~ außergerichtlicher Eid; **false** ~ Falscheid, Meineid; **form of** ~ Eidesformel; **interpreter's** ~ Dolmetschereid; **inventor's** ~ Erfindereid; **judge's** ~ Richtereid; **judicial** ~ gerichtlicher Eid, vor dem Richter geleisteter Eid; **non-judicial** ~ außergerichtlicher Eid; **official** ~ Diensteid; **on** ~ eidlich, unter Eid; **parliamentary** ~ Abgeordneteneid; **poor debtor's** ~ Offenbarungseid; **promissory** ~ Voreid, promissorischer Eid; **purgatory** ~ *hist* Reinigungseid, Läuterungseid; **qualified** ~ beschränkter Eid; **refusal to take an** ~ Verweigerung der Eidesleistung; **solemn** ~ (*feierliche*) Eidesleistung (*vor Gericht*); **suppletory** Ergänzungseid, eidl Vernehmung des Beweisführers; **to administer an** ~ den Eid abnehmen; **to bind s.o. by** ~ jmdn eidlich verpflichten; **to examine on** ~ eidlich vernehmen; **to execute an** ~ e-n Eid leisten; **upon** ~ unter Eid, eidlich; **voluntary** ~ Parteieid (*der beweispflichtigen Partei, zusätzlich zu anderen Beweismitteln*); **witness's** ~ Zeugeneid.

obedience Gehorsam *m*, Gesetzestreue *f*; ~ **to orders** Befehlsbefolgung.

obey gehorchen, befolgen, Folge leisten, beachten.

obit Beerdigungsfeierlichkeit *f*, Sterbetagsfeierlichkeit *f*.

obiter dictum (=) Nebenbemerkung, nicht tragender Entscheidungsgrund; *gelegentliche Rechtsäußerung e-s Richters*; *beiläufige nicht entscheidungserhebliche Bemerkung zu einer Rechtsfrage.*

obituary Nachruf *m*, Todesanzeige *f*.

objects *s* Objekt *n*, Gegenstand *m*, Ziel *n*, Zweck *m*, Gegenstand *m* der Wahrnehmung; ~ **at issue** Streitgegenstand; ~**s clause** Gesellschaftszweckbestimmung der Satzung; ~ **d'art** (kleiner) Kunstgegenstand; ~ **found** Fundsache; ~**s of a company** Gesellschaftszweck, Gegenstand e-s Unternehmens; ~ **of a power** Gegenstand e-r Vollmacht *bzw* e-r Begünstigung; ~ **of a statute** Gesetzeszweck; ~ **of an action** das Rechtsschutzbegehren; ~**s of general concern** Belange der Allgemeinheit; **convincing** ~ Überführungsstück, Beweisstück; **immediate** ~ Nahziel; **secondary** ~ Nebenzweck; **with the** ~ **of gain** in gewinnsüchtiger Absicht.

object *v* beanstanden, einwenden, Einspruch erheben, Widerspruch erheben, widersprechen, ablehnen, protestieren; ~ **to probate** ein Testament anfechten; **not** ~**ed to** unbeanstandet.

object lesson Anschauungsunterricht *m*, praktisches Beispiel *n*, Denkzettel *m*.

objection Widerspruch *m*, Einspruch *m*, Einwand *m*, Ablehnung *f*; Reklamation *f*, Beanstandung *f*; ~ **in (point of) law** rechtliche Einwendung; ~ **is sound** der Einwand ist berechtigt; ~ **to a juror** Ablehnung e-s Geschworenen; ~ **to probate** Testamentsanfechtung; **broadside** ~ generelles Bestreiten, Ablehnung ohne Angabe von Gründen; **no ~s** keine Bedenken; **preliminary** ~ prozeßhindernde Einrede; **right to** ~ Einspruchsrecht; **to allow an** ~ e-m Einspruch stattgeben; **to lodge an** ~ Widerspruch einlegen; **to meet ~s** → *to meet*; **to sustain an** ~ e-m Einwand stattgeben.

objectionable zu beanstanden, nicht einwandfrei, anstößig, unannehmbar.

objective *s* Ziel *n*, Zweck *m*, Zielsetzung *f*, Angriffsziel *n*, Operationsziel *n*.

objective *adj* objektiv, sachbezogen.

objector Widerspruchsführer *m*, Beschwerdeführer *m*, Gegner *m*, Opponent *m*; **conscientious** ~ Kriegsdienstverweigerer.

oblation Kirchgeld *n*, Kirchengebühren *f|pl*.

obligant Schuldner *m*.

obligate verpflichten, sich verpflichten, verbindlich machen.

obligation Verpflichtung *f* (= *V bzw . . . v*) Verbindlichkeit *f*; Schuld *f*, Schuldversprechen *n*, Schuldverhältnis *n*, Schuldurkunde *f*, Obliegenheit *f*, Obligation *f*, Schuldverschreibung *f*; ~ **in kind** → *kind*; ~ **of a contract** gesetzliche Pflicht, Verträge einzuhalten; Vertragspflicht; ~ **of a performance** Leistungspflicht; ~ **of secrecy** Verschwiegenheitspflicht; ~ **solidaire** solidarische (= *gesamtschuldnerische*) *V*; ~ **to buy** Kauf*v*, Kaufzwang; ~ **to disclose** Auskunftspflicht; ~ **to maintain** Unterhaltspflicht; ~ **under a contract** vertragliche *V*; **absolute** ~ zwingende *V*; **accessory** ~ akzessorische Verpflichtung, Nebenpflicht; **alternative** ~ Wahlschuld(-verhältnis); **assumption of an** ~ Eingehen e-r *V*; Schuldübernahme; **business** ~ Geschäftsverbindlichkeit; **cautionary** ~ Eventual*v*; **civil** ~ rechtlich durchsetzbare *V*, Rechtspflicht; **conditional** ~ bedingte *V*; **conjunctive** ~ gekoppelte *V*, Sammel*v*; **contractual** ~ Vertragspflicht, vertragliche *V*; **dependent** ~ (*von anderen Umständen*) abhängige Verpflichtung; **determinate** ~ Speziesschuld, *V* zu einer bestimmten Leistung; **direct** ~ Hauptpflicht; **discharge of an** ~ Erfüllung e-r *V*, Erlöschen e-s Schuldverhältnisses; Befreiung von e-r *V*; **divisible** ~ *V* zu e-r teilbaren Leistung; **equitable** ~ *V* nach Billigkeit; **express** ~ ausdrückliche *V*; **heritable** ~ vererbliche Verbindlichkeit; vererbliches Schuldverhältnis, *auf die Erben von Gläubigern bzw Schuldnern übergehendes Schuldverhältnis*; **imperfect** ~ nicht einklagbare *V*, Naturalobligation; **implied** ~ stillschweigende *V*, gesetzlich vermutete *V*; **indeterminate** ~ *V* zu e-r nicht spezifischen Leistung, Gattungsschuld; **indivisible** ~ *V* zu e-r unteilbaren Leistung; **joint** ~ gemeinsame *V*; Gesamtschuld(verhältnis); Gesamt*v*; **joint and several** ~ samtverbindliche *V*; **legal** ~ gesetzliche Pflicht, Rechtspflicht; **long-term** ~ langfristige Verbindlichkeit; **moral** ~ Anstandspflicht, moralische *V*; **mutual** ~ gegenseitige *V*; **natural** ~ Naturalobligation, nicht einklagbare *V*, unvollkommene *V*; **obediential** ~ Obliegenheit; **onerous** ~ belastende *V*; **pecuniary** ~ pekuniäre Verpflichtung, Geldschuld; **penal** ~ bewehrte *V*, *V* mit Konventionalstrafklausel; **perfect** ~ rechtlich durchsetzbare *V*; **personal** ~ persönliche (*auf das Leben des Schuldners beschränkte*) *V*; **primary** ~ Haupt*v*, Hauptpflicht, primäre *V*; **primitive** ~ Haupt*v*, *bei deren*

Nichterfüllung Schadenersatz verlangt werden kann; **principal** ~ Hauptpflicht, Hauptverbindlichkeit, Hauptschuld, Hauptsacheschuld; **pure** ~ unbedingte *V*; **real** ~ dingliche *V* (*auf Immobilien bezogen*); **secondary** ~ sekundäre *V*, Nebenpflicht; **several** ~ Einzel*v* Mehrerer, unabhängige *V*; **short-term** ~ kurzfristige Verbindlichkeit; **simple** ~ einfache (*nicht bedingte*) *V*; **single** ~ Einzel*v*, Schuldversprechen; *V* ohne Konventionalstrafklausel; **solidary** ~ samtverbindliche *V*; **specific** ~ Speziesschuld; **strictly personal** ~ höchst persönliche *V*; **superadded** ~ zusätzl *V*; **to meet one's ~s** → *to meet*; **to satisfy an** ~ e-r *V* nachkommen, e-e *V* erfüllen; **unifactoral** ~ einseitige *V*; **without** ~ unverbindlich, freibleibend, ohne Obligo.

obligatory bindend, verpflichtend, zwingend, obligatorisch, schuldrechtlich.

oblige verpflichten, binden; eine Gefälligkeit erweisen.

obligee Gläubiger *m*, Berechtigter *m* aus e-r gesiegelten Schuldurkunde (*bond*), Forderungsberechtigter *m*.

obligor Schuldner *m*, Verpflichteter *m* aus e-r gesiegelten Schuldurkunde (*bond*), Leistungsschuldner *m*; **primary** ~ Hauptschuldner.

obliterate ausstreichen, wegradieren, löschen, ungültig machen, entwerten, zerstören, unkenntlich machen; ~ **a document** e-e Urkunde zerstören.

obliteration Unkenntlichmachung *f*, Auslöschung *f*, Streichung *f*; ~ **of crossing** Unsichtbarmachen e-r Scheckkreuzung; ~ **of record** *widerrechtliche* Unkenntlichmachung von amtlich verwahrten Urkunden.

oblivion Vergessen *n*, Vergeßlichkeit *f*; Vernichtung *f*, Unachtsamkeit *f*, amtliches Ignorieren *n* e-r Straftat, Straferlaß *m*, Amnestie *f*, Gnadenerweis *m*.

oblivious vergessend, vergeßlich, nicht beachtend.

obloquy Verleumdung *f*, Schmähung *f*, Vorwurf *m*.

obnoxious anstößig, anrüchig, geschmacklos, verhaßt, abscheulich, unangenehm, schädlich, straffällig, tadelnswert.

obreption Erlangung *f* durch Betrug oder Überraschung.

obrogation Gesetzesaufhebung *f*, Änderung *f* e-s Gesetzes durch Novellierung *f*.

obscene obszön, unanständig, unzüchtig, pornografisch.

obscenity Obszönität *f*; Unzüchtigkeit *f*; ~ **case** Pornografieprozeß.

obscure unklar, verschwommen, unverständlich; **of** ~ **origin** von unbekannter Herkunft.

observable zu beachten, einzuhalten.

observance Beachtung *f*, Einhaltung *f*, Befolgung *f*, Observanz *f*, Herkommen *n*, Brauch *m*, Sitte *f*; Regel *f*, Vorschrift *f*; ~ **of commercial usages** Einhaltung von Handelsbräuchen; ~ **of contracts** Vertragstreue; ~ **of the laws** Einhaltung der Gesetze; ~ **or performance** Einhaltung *bzw* Erfüllung; **strict** ~ genaue Befolgung; **with due** ~ **of** unter gebührender Beachtung.

observant achtsam, aufmerksam.

observation Beobachtung *f*, Bemerkung *f*, Wahrnehmung *f* (*auch = observance qv*); **for your** ~ zu Ihrer Stellungnahme; **to keep under** ~ beobachten.

observe einhalten, beobachten, beachten, befolgen, erfüllen, nachkommen, bemerken, sagen, äußern.

obsignatory ratifizierend, genehmigend.

obsolescence Veralten *n*, Überalterung *f*; ~ **allowance** *Bewertungsfreibetrag bei Ersatzbeschaffung für veraltete Wirtschaftsgüter;* **functional** ~ technische Überalterung; **method** ~ Überalterung des Produktionsverfahrens; **planned** ~ absichtlich herbeigeführtes Altmodischwerden; **product** ~ Überalterung der Erzeugnisse.

obsolescent veraltet (*aber noch verwendet*).
obsolete veraltet, außer Gebrauch, nicht mehr angewendet, nicht mehr beachtet; ~ **law** überholtes, nicht mehr angewandtes Recht, veraltetes *aber noch nicht aufgehobenes Gesetz*; ~ **securities** aufgerufene und ungültig gemachte Wertpapiere.
obstante behindernd, dagegenstehend, nicht damit vereinbar.
obstinate eigenwillig, hartnäckig.
obstriction Verbindlichkeit *f*, Schuldverpflichtung *f*.
obstruct behindern, hemmen, blokkieren, sperren; Obstruktion betreiben; ~ **s.o.'s view** die Aussicht versperren.
obstructing | an officer Widerstand gegen Vollstreckungsbeamte, Widerstand gegen die Staatsgewalt; ~ **justice** Behinderung der Rechtspflege; ~ **proceedings of legislature** Parlamentsnötigung; ~ **process** Vollstreckungsbehinderung, Zustellungsbehinderung; ~ **the recruting or enlistment service** Behinderung der Wehrdiensterfassung.
obstruction Obstruktion *f*, vorsätzliche Behinderung *f*, Hindernis *n*; ~ **of a highway** Behinderung des Straßenverkehrs; ~ **of an easement** Behinderung der Ausübung e-r Grunddienstbarkeit; ~ **of bankruptcy** Behinderung des Konkursverfahrens; ~ **of course of justice** Behinderung der Rechtspflege; ~ **of members** Parlamentsnötigung (gegenüber Abgeordneten); ~ **of police** Behinderung der Polizei, Widerstand gg Vollstreckungsbeamte; ~ **of polling** Wahlbehinderung; ~ **of recovery of premises** (*strafbare*) Behinderung der Räumungsvollstreckung; **wilful** ~ vorsätzl Verkehrsbehinderung.
obstructionism Obstruktionspolitik *f*.
obstructionist Obstruktionspolitiker *m*.
obtain erlangen, erhalten, beschaffen, erreichen, bekommen, erwirken; ~ **a judgment** ein Urteil erwirken; ~ **acceptance** Akzept einholen; ~ **by artifice** erschleichen; ~ **by false pretences** betrügerisch erlangen, Betrug begehen; ~ **by fraud** erschleichen, betrügerisch erwerben; ~ **credit by false pretences** Kreditbetrug; ~ **probate** → *probate*; ~ **redress from a person** gegen jmdn Regreß nehmen; ~ **the contract** den Zuschlag erhalten.
obtainable erhältlich, beschaffbar.
obtaining | board and lodging (*by false pretences*) Zechprellerei *f*, betrügerisches Verschaffen *n* von Unterkunft und Verpflegung; ~ **(of) credit** Kreditbeschaffung, Krediterlangung; ~ **pecuniary advantage** Erlangung e-s Vermögensvorteils.
obtainment Erlangung *f*; **surreptitious ~ of a patent** Patenterschleichung.
obverse Vorderseite *f* (*Münze, Blatt*).
obvious offensichtlich, augenscheinlich, einleuchtend, offenkundig.
occasion *s* Gelegenheit *f*, Grund *m*, Ursache *f*, Ereignis *n*, Vorfall *m*, Veranlassung *f*; **as ~ arises** gegebenenfalls, bei Gelegenheit; **as ~ may require** nach Bedarf, je nach Veranlassung; **on** ~ bei Gelegenheit, gelegentlich; **on a privileged** ~ in Wahrnehmung berechtiger Interessen.
occasion *v* Gelegenheit geben, veranlassen, verursachen; ~ **loss** Schaden verursachen; **~ed by** als Folge von, veranlaßt durch.
occasional gelegentlich.
occupancy Gewahrsam *m* (*Wohnung, Grundstück*), Belegung *f*, Okkupation *f*, Aneignung *f*, Besitzergreifung *f*, unmittelbarer Besitz *m*, Innehabung *f*; ~ **rate** Belegungsprozentzahl (*Hotel*); **multiple** ~ Mehrfachbelegung.
occupant Inhaber *m*, Bewohner *m*, Okkupant *m*, Aneignender *m*, Besitzergreifer *m*; Besitzer *m*, Besetzer *m*; ~ **at sufferance** geduldeter Ge-

wahrsamsinhaber, jederzeit kündbarer Pächter, prekarischer Besitzer; ~ **at will** = ~ *at sufferance qv.*

occupatio Okkupation *f*, Aneignung *f vgl occupation.*

occupation (*1*) Gewahrsam *m*, Innehaben *n*, Besitz *m*, Besitznahme *f*, Besitzergreifung *f*, Okkupation *f*; Besetzung *f*, Besatzung *f*; ~ **authorities** Besatzungsbehörden; ~ **lease** Pacht verbunden mit Berufspraxis; ~ **licence** Weidepacht; ~ **road** → *road*; ~ **rent** Nutzungsentschädigung; **actual** ~ tatsächliches Innehaben, Gewahrsam; **belligerent** ~ kriegerische Besetzung; **beneficial** ~ Grundstücksbesitz mit vollem Nutzungsrecht; **exclusive** ~ Alleinbesitz; **original** ~ Okkupation, Aneignung; **personal** ~ eigenes Bewohnen, Eigennutzung.

occupation (*2*) Beschäftigung *f*, Tätigkeit *f*, Beruf *m*, Gewerbe *n*; (*2*) ~ **group** Berufsgruppe; **dangerous** ~ gefahrgeneigte Tätigkeit; **ostensible** ~ regelmäßige (*erkennbare*) Beschäftigung; **regular** ~ ständiger Beruf, überwiegend ausgeübte Berufstätigkeit.

occupational berufsbedingt, beruflich, Berufs ...; ~ **pensions scheme** betriebl Altersversorgungswerk; **O~ Safety and Health Act** *US:* Bundesarbeitsschutzgesetz.

occupier Bewohner *m*, Hausbewohner *m*; (Gewahrsams-)Inhaber *m*, Besitzer *m*, Nutznießer *m*; **~s' liability** Haftung des jeweiligen Besitzers *für Verkehrssicherheit*; **O Liability Act** Hausbewohner-Haftpflichtgesetz (*für Verkehrssicherheit*); Verkehrssicherungspflicht; ~ **of land** unmittelbarer Besitzer e-s Grundstücks; Gewahrsamsinhaber e-s Grundstücks; **contiguous ~s** Anlieger; **private** ~ (Eigen)Bewohner, Eigennutzer; **protected** ~ unter Mieterschutz stehender Wohnungsinhaber; **residential** ~ Wohnungsinhaber, Bewohner.

occupy innehaben, bewohnen, in Besitz nehmen, besitzen, beschäftigen; besetzen; ~ **a dual capacity** in doppelter Eigenschaft tätig sein, mit sich selbst kontrahieren; ~ **an office** ein Amt bekleiden, innehaben.

occupying | **claimant** *Nichteigentümer m, der Ansprüche auf Verwendungsersatz stellt*; ~ **claimant acts** *Gesetze über Aufwendungsentschädigung besitzender Nichteigentümer.*

occur vorkommen, sich ereignen, vorfallen, vor Augen kommen; **a condition ~s** e-e Bedingung tritt ein; **a loss ~red** ein Schaden ist entstanden.

occurence Vorfall *m*, Vorkommnis *n*, Ereignis *n*, Eintritt *m* e-s Ereignisses; ~ **of event insured against** Versicherungsfall.

ocean | **bill of lading** Konnossement, Seefrachtbrief; **~-carrying trade** Hochseeschiffahrt; **~-going steamer** Ozeandampfer; ~ **lane** Schiffahrtsroute; ~ **liner** Ozeandampfer, Passagierschiff; ~ **marine insurance** Seeversicherung; ~ **traffic** Seeverkehr.

ochlocracy Ochlokratie *f*, Herrschaft *f* des Pöbels.

octroi duties Stadtzölle *m|pl.*

odd ungerade, einzeln; ~ **job man** Gelegenheitsarbeiter; ~ **jobs** Gelegenheitsarbeit; ~ **money** restliches Geld; ~ **month** Monat mit 31 Tagen; **50** ~ etwas über 50.

odd lot *exch* weniger (*d. h. 1–99 Aktien*) als die handelsübliche Schlußeinheit (*100 Aktien = round lot → lot*); nicht offiziell gehandelte Posten *m*; weniger als ein „Schluß"; ~ **broker** Makler in kleinen Effektenposten; ~ **business** *Börsengeschäft mit kleineren als den üblichen Einheiten*; ~ **dealer** → *dealer*; ~ **doctrine** *Zumutbarkeit anderweitiger Beschäftigung e-s Arbeitsgeschädigten.*

oddments restliche Einzelstücke *n|pl*, Restbestände *m|pl.*

odometer Kilometerstandsanzeiger; ~ **sticker** Plakette mit Angaben des Kilometerstands *(bzw der gefahrenen Meilen).*

of | **a like description** gleicher Beschreibung; ~ **age** volljährig; ~ **counsel** → *counsel*; ~ **course** von Rechts wegen, ohne weiteres *zu gewähren*; ~ **force** → *force*; ~ **grace** gnadenhalber, im freien gerichtlichen Ermessen stehend; ~ **new** → *new*; ~ **no legal force** nicht rechtsverbindlich; ~ **no settled address** ohne festen Wohnsitz, nicht seßhaft; ~ **record** → *record(s)*; ~ **right** von Rechts wegen; ~ **sound and disposing mind and memory** testierfähig; ~ **sound health** *ins* gesund; ~**sound mind** geistig normal, geschäftsfähig; ~ **the body** abstammend von.

off | **balance sheet** nicht in der Bilanz auszuweisende Verbindlichkeit; ~-**board market** *Markt für nicht notierte Wertpapiere*; ~-**board securities** *US* amtlich nicht notierte Wertpapiere; ~-**chance** entfernte Möglichkeit; ~ **charges** abzurechnende Kosten; ~ **duty** → *duty (1)*; ~ **going crop** = *away going crop qv*; ~ **licence** → *licence*; ~ **limits** Zutritt verboten; ~-**market** *adj* nicht an der Börse (gehandelt); ~-**price store** Billigladen, Diskountladen; ~ **shade** nicht ganz dem Farbmuster entsprechend; ~ **standard** Qualitätsunterschreitung, Qualitätsabweichung; ~ **the berth** vor den Anliegeplätzen; ~ **the line** nicht im Gewahrsam der *betreffenden* Bahngesellschaft; ~ **the record** → *record s*; ~ **year elections** → *elections*; **for** ~-**consumption** zum Mitnehmen (*von alkoholischen Getränken*).

offence (*offense vorwiegend US-Schreibweise*) strafbare Handlung *f*, Straftat *f*, Vergehen, Zuwiderhandlung, Ärgernis *n*; ~ **against forest laws** Forstfrevel; ~**s against morality and decency** Sittlichkeitsdelikte; ~**s against property** Vermögensdelikt; ~**s against public order** Straftaten gegen die öffentliche Ordnung; ~**s against the person** Straftaten gegen die Person (*Leben, Körper*); ~**s against the state** Staatsschutzdelikte; ~ **charged with** die zur Last gelegte (Straf)Tat; ~ **committed** Straftat, vollendete Straftat; ~ **in office** Amtsvergehen; ~ **involving moral turpitude** sittlich verwerfliches Delikt; ~ **of juveniles** Jugendsache; ~ **of violence** Gewaltverbrechen; ~**s related to road traffic** Straßenverkehrsgefährdung; ~**s triable either way** vor dem Einzelrichter oder dem Geschworenengericht aburteilbare Straftaten; **accomplished** ~ vollendete Tat; **arrestable** ~ Verbrechen; schwere mit Freiheitsstrafe bedrohte Tat (*sofortige Verhaftung zulässig*); **civil** ~ unerlaubte Handlung; **coinage** ~ Münzdelikt, Münzvergehen; **completed** ~ vollendete Tat; **computer-related** ~**s** Computerstraftaten; **continuing** ~ Dauerstraftat; **criminal** ~ strafbare Handlung, Straftat; **cumulative** ~ in Realkonkurrenz begangene, wiederholte Straftat; **currency** ~ Devisenvergehen; **customs** ~ Zollvergehen; **disciplinary** ~ Diziplinarvergehen, Dienstvergehen, Ordnungswidrigkeit, Verstoß gegen die Gefängnisordnung; **divisible** ~ → *divisible*; **duplicated** ~ Gesetzeskonkurrenz bei Straftaten; **economic** ~ Wirtschaftsverbrechen; **„either way"** ~**s** = ~*s triable either way s.o.*; **endorsable** ~ strafpunktepflichtiges Verkehrsdelikt; **extradictable** ~ Auslieferungsdelikt; **federal** ~ Straftat nach (*US*) Bundesrecht; **first** ~ erstmalige Straftat; **fiscal** ~ Zoll- *bzw* Steuervergehen; **fresh** ~ neue Straftat; **higher** ~ schwerere Straftat; **hybrid** ~ mittelschwere Straftat (*summarisches Verfahren oder förmliche Anklage*), Vergehen; **included** ~**s** konsumierter Strafbestand; **inchoate** ~ unvollendete Straftat, Straftat im Versuchsstadium; **indictable** ~ Verbrechen, schweres Vergehen; **joint** ~ in Mittäterschaft begangene Straftat; **juvenile** ~ Jugendstraftat; **lesser included** ~ konsumierte Nebentat *bzw* strafbare Nachtat; **matrimonial** ~ schwere Eheverfehlung; **minor** ~ geringfügige Straftat, Bagatelldelikt, Übertretung; **motoring** ~ → *motoring*; **moving traffic** ~ Verkehrsdelikt; **necessarily included** ~ konsumiertes Delikt; **outstanding** ~**s** unerledigte Straftaten; **pecuniary** ~ mit Geldstrafe bedrohte Übertretung; **petty** ~ Bagatelldelikt; **notifiable** ~ meldepflichtige Straftat; **political** ~ politische Straftat; **public** ~ Offizialdelikt; **punishable** ~ Straftat; **quasi** ~ e-m Dritten zurechenbare Strafe; **revenue** ~ Vergehen gegen die Abgabenordnung, Zollvergehen, Zolldelikt; Steuerstraftat; **road traffic** ~ Straßenverkehrsdelikt; **same** ~ dieselbe Straftat (*wegen der schon ein Strafverfahren durchgeführt wurde*); *ne bis in idem*; **second** ~ Rückfallstat, *Straftat im ersten Rückfall*; **separate** ~ Realkonkurrenz; **sexual** ~ Sexualdelikt, Sittlichkeitsdelikt, Sittlichkeitsvergehen; **similar** ~**s** einschlägige Vorstrafen, ähnliche Straftaten; **splitting** ~**s** *getrennte Verhandlung realkonkurrierender Straftaten*; **street** ~**s** → *street*; **subsequent** ~ Nachtat, spätere Straftat; **substantive** ~ abgeschlossene Tat, Straftat; **substantive independent** ~ eigene strafbare Handlung (*e-s Mittäters*); Straftatbestand, Straftat; **summary** ~ Ordnungswidrigkeit, Übertretung; **target** ~ die geplante verabredete Straftat; **technical** ~ Formaldelikt; **to give** ~ → *to give*; **to remit an** ~ → *to remit*; **to take** ~ Anstoß nehmen; **tripartition of** ~**s** Dreiteilung der Straftaten; **unnatural** ~ = *buggery qv*; **voting** ~ → *voting*.

offend sich vergehen, verstoßen, zuwiderhandeln, beleidigen.

offender (Straf)Täter *m*; ~ **of the first degree** Haupttäter; **first** ~ nicht vorbestrafter Täter; **fugitive** ~ flüchtiger Täter; **habitual** ~ Gewohnheitstäter; **infrequent** ~ Gelegenheitstäter; **joint** ~ Mittäter; **juvenile** ~ Jugendlicher, jugendlicher Täter (*unter 17*); **persistent** ~ Gewohnheitsverbrecher (*obs*), Hangtäter; **political** ~ politischer Straftäter; **principal** ~ Haupttäter; **repeat** ~ Wiederholungstäter, Rückfalltäter; **second and subsequent** ~ Rückfalltäter; **violent-felony** ~ Gewaltverbrecher; **young adult** ~**s** Heranwachsende, heranwachsende Straftäter (*GB: 17–20*); **young** ~ Jugendlicher, jugendlicher Täter; **youthful** ~ Jugendlicher, jugendl Täter.

offense →*offence*.

offensive offensiv, Angriffs..., belästigend, beleidigend.

offer *s* Angebot *n* (= *A bzw ... a*), Vertragsantrag *m*; Offerte *f*, Gebot *n*; Vorbringen *n*; ~ **for sale** Verkaufs*a*, Emissionsofferte, Zeichnungsangebot; ~~ *by tender: Verkaufsausschreibung*; ~ **in blank** Blankoofferte; ~ **of amends** *A* der Wiedergutmachung; ~ **of assistance** Unterstützungs*a*; ~ **of compromise** Vergleichsvorschlag; ~ **of employment** Stellen*a*; ~ **of evidence** Beweisantritt, Beweis*a*; ~ **of mediation** Vermittlungs*a*, Schlichtungsvorschlag; ~ **of services** Anerbieten von Dienstleistungen; ~ **subject to prior sale** Zwischenverkauf vorbehalten; ~ **to buy** Kauf*a*, Kaufgesuch; ~ **to sell** Verkaufs*a*; ~ **to the public** Angebot an die Allgemeinheit, Auslobung; ~ **without engagement** freibleibende Offerte, nicht verbindliches *A*; **acceptance of** ~ → *acceptance*; **best** ~ Meistgebot, Höchstgebot; **binding** ~ festes *A*; **contractor's** ~ Submission, *A* e-s Werkunternehmers; **cross** ~**s** sich kreuzende Angebotsschreiben; **counter-**~ Gegen*a*; **delivery of an** ~ Zugehenlassen e-s *A-s*, Abgabe e-s *A-s*; **firm** ~ festes *A*; **free** ~ freibleibendes *A*; **general** ~ öffentliches *A*; **hostile** ~ unfreundliches Übernahmeangebot; **implied** ~ stillschweigendes *A*; **invitatiton to** ~ Aufforderung zur Abgabe e-s

A-s; **not binding** ~ freibleibendes *A*; **on** ~ zu verkaufen, verkäuflich; **personal** ~ Antrag unter Anwesenden; **original** ~ ursprüngliches *A*; **positive** ~ festes *A*; **qualified** ~ abgeändertes Angebot; **special** ~ Sonder*a*; **verbal** ~ mündliches *A*; **unconditional** ~ → *unconditional*; **voluntary** ~ unverlangtes *A*.

offer *v* anbieten, darbieten, offerieren, sich bereit erklären, vorbringen, vorlegen, bieten, ein Vertragsangebot machen; ~ **a reward** e-e Belohnung aussetzen; ~ **for sale** zum Verkauf anbieten, feilhalten; ~ **for subscription** zur Zeichnung auflegen; ~**to sell** zum Verkauf anbieten, feilhalten; ~**ed subject to prior sale** Zwischenverkauf vorbehalten.

offeree Angebotsadressat *m*; Antragsempfänger *m*.

offering Beitrag *m*; Schenkung *f*, Verkaufsangebot *n*, Emission *f*; ~ **price** Emissionskurs, Zeichnungskurs; **public** ~ öffentl Emission, öffentl Aufforderung zur Zeichnung; **private** ~ begrenzte Emission; **secondary** ~ Sekundäremission.

offeror Anbieter *m*, Antragender *m*.

office Behörde *f*, Amt *n*, Dienststelle *f*, Geschäftsstelle *f*, Büro *n*, Geschäftsraum *m*, Kontor *n*, Kanzlei *f*, Dienst *m*, öffentliches Amt *n*, Amtstätigkeit *f*, Beruf *m*, amtliche Stellung *f*, Posten *m*, Funktion *f*, Aufgabe *f*; ~ **bearer** Amtsinhaber; ~**-book** Amtsbuch, Amtsregister, Tagebuch e-r Behörde; ~ **burglary policy** gewerbliche Einbruchsversicherung; ~ **circular** Dienstanweisung; ~ **conference** Kanzleibesprechung; ~ **copy** Ausfertigung; öffentl beglaubigte Abschrift e-r amtl verwahrten Urkunde; ~ **floater** Globalversicherung der Büroeinrichtung; ~ **found** Feststellungsbefund von Geschworenen; ~ **grant** Auflassung von Amts wegen; ~ **hands** Büropersonal; ~ **hours** → *hour*; ~ **hunter** Postenjäger; ~**-jobbing** Ämterhandel; ~ **manager** Bürovorsteher; ~ **of destination** Bestimmungspostamt; **O**~ **of Fair Trading** (*OFT*) Wettbewerbskontrollamt (*GB*); ~ **of honour** Ehrenamt; ~ **of issue** Ausgabestelle; ~ **of judge** Richteramt; ~ **of payment** Zahlstelle, Auszahlungsstelle; ~ **of profit** Amtstätigkeit gegen Vergütung, bezahltes Amt; ~ **premises** Büroräume, Bürogebäude; ~ **sharing** Bürogemeinschaft; ~**s of the court** Amtsräume des Gerichts; ~ **standby** Bereitschaftsdienst (*e-r Kanzlei*); ~ **user** Benutzung für Bürozwecke; **abuse of** ~ Mißbrauch der Amtsgewalt, Ermessensmißbrauch; **assumption of** ~ Amtsantritt; Amtsanmaßung; **auditing** ~ Rechnungsprüfungsamt; **billeting** ~ Quartieramt; **by virtue of his** ~ kraft seines Amtes; **central** ~ Zentralamt, Zentralbüro; **civil** ~ Zivilbehörde; **county** ~ Grafschaftsamt, wählbares Amt der Kreisverwaltung; **court** ~ Geschäftsstelle des Gerichts; **discharge from** ~ Amtsenthebung; **district** ~ *wählbares* Amt e-s Bezirks; **elective** ~ Wahlamt; **executive** ~ Amt, leitende Dienststelle, Exekutivbüro; **federal** ~ Bundesbehörde; Amtsstellung in der Bundesverwaltung; **field** ~ Außenstelle; **home** ~ *US* Zentralbüro, Hauptsitz; **honorary** ~ Ehrenamt; **in virtue of his** ~ kraft seines Amt(e)s; **judicial** ~ → *judicial*; **local** ~ örtliche Behörde, Amt e-r Ortsbehörde; **lost property** ~ Fundbüro; **lucrative** ~ besoldetes *bzw* mit Gebührenrecht ausgestattetes Amt; **main** ~ Direktion, Hauptverwaltung; **materials testing** ~ → *material*; **military** ~ militärische Dienststellung; **ministerial** ~ weisungsgebundenes Amt, Amt e-r Verwaltungsbehörde; **paid** ~ besoldetes Amt; **pensionable** ~ pensionsberechtigte Dienststellung; **political** ~ politische Amtsstellung; **predecessor in** ~ → *predecessor*; **principal** ~ Hauptverwaltung,

Gesellschaftssitz; **public** ~ öffentliches Amt, Behörde; **regional** ~ regionale Geschäftsstelle; **registered** ~ eingetragene (ladungsfähige) Gesellschaftsadresse (*bzw Vereinsanschrift*); (*eingetragener*) Sitz (*e-r Kapitalgesellschaft*); Gesellschaftssitz; **revenue** ~ Finanzamt; **state** ~ *wählbares* Amt in e-m Einzelstaat der *US*; **successor in** ~ → *successor;* **taxing** ~ Geschäftsstelle des Kostenbeamten; **term of** ~ → *term*; **to cease to hold** ~ → *to cease*; **to come into** ~ ein Amt antreten, an die Regierung kommen; **to hold** ~ amtieren; **to vacate one's** ~ aus dem Amt ausscheiden; **vacation of** ~ Freiwerden e-s Amts.

officer Amtsinhaber *m*, Amtsträger *m*, Funktionär *m*; Wahlbeamter *m*, leitender Beamter *m*, leitender Angestellter *m*, Staatsbediensteter *m*; Offizier *m*, Vollzugsbeamter *m*; **~'s commission** Offizierspatent; ~ **de facto** faktischer Amtsinhaber; ~ **de jure** Amtsinhaber von Rechts wegen; ~ **of a company** (*or*) **corporation** *satzungsgemäßer Funktionsträger e-r Körperschaft; etwa:* Vorstandsmitglied; ~ **of a society** Vorstandsmitglied e–s Vereins; ~ **of justice** Gerichtsbeamter; **~s of the court** *Anwälte als Rechtspflegeorgan*; **~s of the United States** hohe US Beamte (*Minister, Dienststellenleiter und Bundesrichter der USA*); **adjudicatory ~s** Beamte mit richterlichen Befugnissen, Rechtspfleger; **administrative** ~ Beamter, Angehöriger des öffentlichen Dienstes; **cabinet** ~ Minister; **civil** ~ Beamter, Staatsbediensteter; **clerical ~s** *brit Beamte und Angestellte des mittleren Dienstes*; **commercial** ~ Handelssachbearbeiter e-s Konsulats; **commissioned** ~ Offizier; **corporate** ~ = ~ *of a corporation qv*; **custody,** ~ → *custody;* **customs** ~ → *customs*; **election** ~ → *election*; **executive** ~ → *executive*; **fiscal** ~ Finanzbeamter; **judicial** ~ → *judicial*; **liaison** ~ Verbindungsoffizier; **local government** ~ Kommunalbeamter; **military** ~ Offizier, Berufsoffizier; **ministerial** ~ Beamter, Verwaltungsbeamter; **noncommissioned** ~ Unteroffizier; **peace** ~ → *peace*; **preventive** ~ Beamter des Zollfahndungsdienstes; **public** ~ Beamter *bzw* Angestellter im öffentl Dienst; Bediensteter der öffentl Hand; **regular** ~ Berufsoffizier; **reserve** ~ → *reserve*; **revenue** ~ Beamter der Finanzverwaltung, Steuerbeamter; **safety** ~ → *safety*; **staff** ~ → *staff*; **taxing** ~ Kostenfestsetzungsbeamter; *parl: Schätzer des Finanzbedarfs von Privatvorlagen*; **warrant** ~ Feldwebel (*und vergleichbare Dienstränge*).

official *adj* amtlich; Amts . . .; Offizial . . .; offiziell, beamtet, amtsüblich, förmlich, vorgeschrieben; ~ **certificate of search** grundbuchamtl Prüfungsbescheinigung; **O~ Custodian for Charities** Amtsverwahrer für karitatives Stiftungsgut.

official *s* Beamter *m*, Funktionär *m*; **government** ~ Regierungsbeamter, Staatsbeamter.

officialdom Beamtenschaft *f*, Bürokratismus *m*, Amtsschimmel *m*.

officialese Amtssprache *f*, Amtsjargon *m*.

officially *adv* amtlich, von Amts wegen.

officiate *v*/*i* amtieren, e-e Amtshandlung vornehmen.

officialty Amtsbereich *m*, Amtszulässigkeit *f*.

officious halbamtlich, offiziös; diensteifrig, aufdringlich; ~ **will** Testament, in dem nur die eigene Familie bedacht wird.

offset *s* Aufrechnung *f*, Gegenrechnung *f*, Verrechnung *f*, Gegenposten *m*, Ausgleich *m*, Abzug *m*; ~ **account** Verrechnungskonto, Wertberichtigungskonto; ~ **credit** Verrechnungskredit.

offset *v* aufrechnen; **~ting claims** Aufrechnen *n*, Aufrechnungsforderungen; **~ting entry** Gegenbuchung, Storno, Änderungsbuchung; ~**ting transactions** Kompensationsgeschäfte, Verrechnungsgeschäfte.

offshore vor der Küste gelegen, außerhalb der Küste, Küstennähe *f*; ~ **fund** Investmentfirma außerhalb des UK (*Sitz in Steueroase*); ~ **orders** Offshore-Aufträge, Rüstungshilfsaufträge; ~ **purchases** Offshore-Käufe (*von den USA bezahlte, nicht die USA berührende Lieferungen für militärische und zivile Versorgung außerhalb USA*).

offspring Abkömmlinge *m*, Nachkommenschaft *f*.

oil Erdöl *n* Rohöl *n*; ~ **futures market** Ölterminmarkt; ~ **industry** Erdölindustrie; **live** ~ Erdgas enthaltendes Rohöl.

old | established firm alteingesessene Firma; ~ **people's welfare council** Altersfürsorgeausschuß; ~ **style** alte Zeitrechnung (*Jahresbeginn 25. März; in England vor 1752*).

Old Bailey (=) Londoner Zentralgericht für Strafsachen.

oligarchy Oligarchie *f*.

oligopolist Oligopolist *m*.

oligopoly Oligopol *n*.

ombudsman (=) Beschwerdekommissar *m*.

omissa Antrag *m* auf Ergänzungstestamentsvollstreckung.

omission Unterlassung *f*, Wegfall *m*, Versäumnis *n*, Übergehung *f*, Auslassung *f*; **accidental** ~ versehentliche Auslassung; **administrative** ~ Untätigkeit e-r Behörde, pflichtwidrige Unterlassung e-r Verwaltungsbehörde.

omit weglassen, unterlassen, versäumen; ~ **a dividend** e-e Dividende ausfallen lassen.

omittance Unterlassung *f*, Auslassung *f*.

omnium *brit exch Gesamtwert, der zur Sicherung e-s Darlehens herangezogenen Effekten.*

on | a scale *bei aufsteigend oder absteigend gestaffelter Limitierung* (*Wertpapierhandel*); ~ **account** → *account*; ~ **account of** für Rechnung von, wegen; ~ **account of performance** erfüllungshalber; ~ **account of whom it may concern** für wen es angeht; ~ **all fours** → *all fours*; ~ **allotment** bei Zuteilung; ~ **and from** seit, ab (*Zeitpunkt*); ~ **any account whatsoever** aus jedem Rechtsgrund; ~ **approval** auf Probe; ~ **behalf of** → *behalf*; ~ **board** an Bord; ~ **call** auf tägliche Kündigung, jederzeit fällig; auf Abruf zum dann gültigen Preis; ~ **consignment** auf Kommissionsbasis; ~ **conviction** bei (*rechtskräftiger*) Verurteilung; ~ **default** bei Nichtleistung, bei Nichterfüllung, bei Verzug; ~ **demand** auf Verlangen, auf Wunsch; jederzeit fällig, zahlbar ohne Kündigung; ~ **either side** auf beiden Seiten; ~ **file** bei den Akten; ~ **good authority** aus wohlunterrichteten Kreisen; ~ **goods** (*Versicherung*) von Waren; ~ **his retirement** bei seinem Ausscheiden aus dem Dienst; ~ **or about** etwa an (*Tag, Ort*), in der Nähe von; ~ **or about the person** bei sich (*am Leibe*); ~ **or after the ... (date)** ab ... (Datum); ~ **or before the ... (date)** bis zum ... (Datum); bis einschließlich; bis spätestens; ~ **or in or about** auf, in *bzw* bei; ~ **order** auf Bestellung; ~ **payment of** gegen Zahlung von; ~ **proportions of party strength** nach Partei-Proporz; ~ **sale or** (= *and*) **return** auf Kommissionsbasis, auf Probe; zum Wiederverkauf, *bzw* zur Rückgabe (*bei Nichtverkauf in angemessener Zeit oder bei Nichtgefallen*); ~ **shore** an Land; ~ **stand** mit Lagerungsrecht; ~ **the account of** namens, im Auftrage von; für; ~ **the books** Außenstände; ~ **the footing** auf der gleichen Grundlage, nach gleichen Grundsätzen; ~ **the person** am Leibe (*am oder im Körper oder in der Kleidung*); ~ **the same terms** zu gleichen Bedingungen; ~ **the spot** an Ort und Stelle.

on-carrier Weiterbeförderer *m*, Reeder *m*.

once | a highway, always a high-

way *Grundsatz der Beibehaltung der Widmung als öffentliche (Land-)Straße*; ~ **a mortgage, always a mortgage** *Grundsatz der Aufrechterhaltung des Verpfändungscharakters e-r Urkunde*; ~ **in jeopardy** *„ne bis in idem"*; **at** ~ sofort, umgehend.

oncost Gemeinkosten *pl*; Unkosten *pl*.

on-cost method *Bewertungsmethode für noch nicht abgeschlossene Aufträge (Material + Arbeit + Gemeinkostenanteil)*.

one|day loan Tagesgeld; ~**-line business** → *business*; ~ **man company** → *company*; ~**-name paper** *nicht indossierter* nur mit *einer* Unterschrift versehener Wechsel; ~**-night stand** einmaliges Gastspiel; ~ **off** einmalig; einmalige Leistung, einmalige Produktion nach Kundenwunsch; **„one off" act** einmalige Tat; ~**-parent benefit** Beihilfe an alleinerziehenden Elternteil; ~ **person, one vote** allgemeines gleiches Wahlrecht; ~**-price policy** *gleiche Preise für alle Kunden und Abnahmemengen*; ~**-price store** Einheitspreisgeschäft; ~**-sided** einseitig, parteiisch; ~**-stop banking** alle Bankgeschäfte in e-r Niederlassung *(in e-r Hand)*; ~**-stop shopping** Einkauf im Supermarkt, ~**-third guideline** Drittelregel *(Ehegattenunterhalt)*; ~**-time financing charge** einmalige Finanzierungsgebühr; ~ **thousand hour clause** *Höchststundenzahl von 1000 pro 26 Arbeitswochen für unregelmäßig Beschäftigte*; ~**-time rate** Preis für einmalige Inserierung; ~**-trip container** Wegwerfbehälter, Einwegflasche; ~**-way** Einbahn, einseitig, einfach, nur für Hinfahrt.

onerosity Beschwerlichkeit *f*, *scot* Entgeltlichkeit *f*.

onerous belastend, ungleichmäßig stärker verpflichtend, einseitig verpflichtend; drückend, beschwerlich, lästig.

on-lend *v/t* weiterverleihen.

onomastic *adj Eigenschaft e-r Unterschrift, die von der Handschrift der Urkunde verschieden ist.*

onus Last *f*, Beschwer *f*, Bürde *f*, Ladung *f*; ~ **of proof** Beweislast; ~ **probandi** Beweislast; ~ **to show** Beweislast; **reverse** ~ umgekehrte Beweislast.

op.cit. (=) *a.a.O.* am angeführten Ort.

open *adj* offen, öffentlich, sichtbar, offensichtlich, allgemein bekannt, zugänglich, noch nicht abgeschlossen, noch nicht entschieden; ~ **account credit terms** Kontokorrentkredit; ~ **and unbuilt upon** unbebaut; ~**-book account** offenes Konto, laufende Rechnung; ~ **charge account** offener Buchkredit; ~ **for signature** unterschriftsreif; zur Unterschrift bereit liegend; ~ **lot** allseits an Straßen angrenzendes Grundstück; ~ **mortgage clause** *Ermächtigung des Grundpfandschuldners zum Einzug der Versicherungssumme;* ~ **price system** Preisinformationssystem; ~ **price term** *(Kauf) Vertrag* ohne Preisbestimmung; ~ **to the public** dem Publikum zugänglich; ~ **to bribery** bestechlich; ~ **trade** noch nicht abgeschlossenes Spekulationsgeschäft, Termingeschäft vor Abschluß des Deckungsgeschäftes.

open *v* öffnen, eröffnen; ~ **a case** einleitende Ausführungen machen; ~ **a commission** die Sitzung eines beauftragten Gerichts eröffnen; ~ **a credit** e-n Kredit eröffnen; ~ **a crossing** die Scheckkreuzung rückgängig machen *(durch den Aussteller)*; ~ **a default** Wiedereinsetzung nach Versäumnisurteil bewilligen; ~ **a deposition** e-e *(versiegelte)* schriftliche Zeugenbekundung im Gericht eröffnen; ~ **a judgment** die Wiederaufnahme des Verfahrens zulassen; ~ **a letter of credit** ein Akkreditiv eröffnen; ~ **a rule** das Verfahren nach e-m Beschluß wieder aufnehmen; ~ **a street** e-e Straße dem öffentlichen Verkehr widmen, e-e Straße dem Verkehr freigeben; ~ **a will** ein Testament eröffnen; ~ **bids** die Versteigerung (*trotz bisherigen letzten Gebots*) fortsetzen; ~ **court** die Sitzung eröffnen; ~ **up new markets** neue Absatzgebiete erschließen; ~ **the budget** den Haushaltsplan vorlegen; ~ **the pleadings** mit dem Plädoyer beginnen; ~ **to the public** (*ein Patent*) zwangsweise der Öffentlichkeit zur Verfügung stellen.

open-end ohne bestimmte Dauer, unbestimmt hoch, ohne feste Grenze.

open-ended offen, auf unbestimmte Dauer, unbeschränkt; ~ **prison stay** Freiheitsentzug auf unbestimmte Zeit.

opening | balance Eröffnungsbilanz; ~ **bank** *das Akkreditiv* eröffnende Bank; ~ **capital** Anfangskapital, Grundkapital; ~ **ceremony** Eröffnungsfeierlichkeiten; ~ **inventory** → *inventory*; ~ **pleading** Anfangsplädoyer; ~ **sitting** Eröffnungssitzung; ~ **speech** einleitender Vortrag (*d StA bzw d Verteidigers*), Eingangsplädoyer; ~ **talks** einleitende Besprechungen.

opening a crossing Barzahlungsanweisung auf e-m Verrechnungsscheck.

opening an account Kontoeröffnung *f*.

opening of credit Krediteröffnung *f*, Kreditbereitstellung *f*.

open market Markt; Märkte und Ladengeschäfte; offener Markt, freier Markt; Freiverkehr; ~-~ **credit** Schuldscheindarlehen; ~-~ **loans** Offenmarktkredite; ~-~ **operations** Offenmarktgeschäfte; ~-~ **policy** Offen-Markt-Politik; ~-~ **rates** Geldsätze am offenen Markt, freier Kapitalmarktzins.

operate arbeiten, betreiben, führen, verwalten, in Betrieb sein, funktionieren, handhaben, betätigen, fahren, lenken, einwirken, bewirken, wirksam sein; verursachen; spekulieren; ~ **a business** ein Geschäft betreiben; ~ **for a fall** auf Baisse spekulieren; ~ **for a rise** auf Hausse spekulieren; **a law** ~**s** ein Gesetz findet Anwendung, ist in Kraft; **licence to** ~ → *licence*.

operating | ability Betriebsfähigkeit; ~ **activities** Betriebstätigkeit; ~ **company** Betriebsgesellschaft, Transportunternehmen; effektiv tätige Gesellschaft (*im Gegensatz zur Holding-Gesellschaft*); ~ **cost ratio** Betriebskostensatz; ~ **lease** Operating Leasing, Operate-Leasingvertrag (*mietvertragsähnlich, kündbar*); ~ **rate** Kapazitätsausnutzungsgrad.

operation Wirken *n*, Wirkung *f*, Wirksamkeit *f*, Rechtswirksamkeit *f*, Geltung *f*; Unternehmen *n*, Geschäft *n*, Transaktion *f*; Handlung *f*, Vorgang *m*, Verfahren *n*, Betrieb *m*, Tätigkeit *f*, Gang *m*, Arbeitsweise *f*, Arbeit *f*, Arbeitsprozeß *m*, Operation *f*, Bedienung *f*; ~ **credit** Betriebskredit; ~ **for own account** Nostrotransaktion; ~ **in futures** Termingeschäft; ~**s manager** Betriebsleiter; ~ **of act** Inkrafttreten e-s Gesetzes; ~ **of contract** Wirkung e-s Vertrages; ~ **of law** → *law*; ~ **of motor vehicle** Betrieb e-s Kraftfahrzeugs; ~ **of treaty** Geltungsbereich e-s Vertrages; ~**s research** Unternehmensforschung; **area of** ~ Tätigkeitsbereich, Wirkungsbereich; **banking** ~ Banktransaktion; **bearish** ~ Baissespekulation; **by** ~ kraft, auf Grund von; **by** ~ **of law** gesetzlich, kraft Gesetzes; **criminal** ~ Abtreibungseingriff; **financial** ~ Finanztransaktion; **forward** ~ → *forward*; **inter-company** ~**s** Konzerngeschäfte; **limited** ~ beschränkte Wirkung; **marketing** ~ → *marketing*; **reckless** ~ leichtsinniges Fahren, rücksichtsloses Fahren (*bzw Betreiben e-r Maschine*); **sphere of** ~ Tätigkeitsbereich, Wirkungsbereich; **to be in** ~ in Kraft sein; **to bring into** ~ in Kraft setzen; **to come into** ~ → *to come*; **to put in** ~ in Kraft setzen.

operational wirksam, betrieblich, Betriebs . . ., Operations . . ., Einsatz . . ., innerorganisatorisch; ~ **accounting** Betriebsabrechnung; ~ **audit** Prüfung der Betriebstätigkeit; ~ **hazards** Betriebsgefahren; ~ **procedure** Betriebsablauf; ~ **research** Betriebsforschung.

operative *adj* rechtswirksam, wirksam, in Wirkung befindlich; ~ **effect** Wirksamkeit; ~ **facts** Tatbestandsmerkmale; ~ **machinery** in Betrieb befindliche Maschinen; ~ **mistake** beachtlicher Irrtum; ~ **part** rechtsgestaltender Teil (*e-r Urkunde*), konstitutiver Teil; Tenor *m*; ~ **provisions** → *provision*; ~ **words** → *word*; **to be** ~ Geltung haben.

operative *s* Arbeiter *m*, Maschinist *m*, Detektiv *m*, Agent *m*; **covert** ~ Geheimagent, verdeckter Ermittler; V-Mann.

operator Unternehmer *m*, Betriebsführer *m*, Produzent *m*, Operateur *m*; Maschinist *m*, Maschinenführer *m*; Bedienungsperson *f*; Fahrzeugführer *m*, Fahrer *m*; berufsmäßiger Spekulant *m*; ~ **for a fall** Baissespekulant, Baissier; ~ **for a rise** Haussespekulant, Haussier; ~**'s licence** Führerschein; ~ **of a motor vehicle** Kraftfahrzeugführer; **crane** ~ Kranführer; **engine** ~ Maschinist; **radio** ~ Funker; **telephone** ~ Telefonist(in); **unlicenced** ~ Fahrer ohne Fahrerlaubnis.

opinion Ansicht *f*, Meinung *f*, Stellungnahme *f*, Meinungsäußerung *f*, Ermessen *n*, Gutachten *n*, Urteilsbegründung *f*; ~ **evidence** → *evidence*; ~**-formers** meinungsbildende Persönlichkeiten; ~ **list** Auskunftsbuch (*über Kunden*); ~ **of the court** Urteilsbegründung; Ansicht des Gerichts; ~ **of witness** Meinungsäußerung e-s Zeugen *im Gegensatz zu tatsächlichen Bekundungen*; ~ **poll** Meinungsumfrage; **advisory(expert)** ~ (Sachverständigen)-Gutachten, Rechtsgutachten; **biased** ~ Vorurteil; **concurring** ~ im Ergebnis zustimmendes Sondervotum zur Urteilsbegründung (*e-s Richterkollegiums*); **counsel's** ~ → *counsel*; **current** ~ gegenwärtige Meinung; **dissenting** ~ gegenteiliges Sondervotum zur Urteilsbegründung *mit der Mehrheitsentscheidung* (*des Kollegialgerichts*) *nicht übereinstimmende Stellungnahme e-s Richters*, abweichende Meinung; **draft** ~ Entwurf e-s Gutachtens; **expert** ~ Sachverständigengutachten; **expression of** ~ Meinungsäußerung, Werturteil; **fixed** ~ vorgefaßte Meinung; **free** ~ freie Meinungsäußerung; **legal** ~ Rechtsgutachten, Rechtsauffassung; **majority** ~ Mehrheitsansicht, Mehrheitsvotum; **medical** ~ ärztliches Gutachten; **minority** ~ Minderheitsansicht; **per curiam** ~ Urteilsbegründung des Kollegialgerichts; **public** ~ öffentl Meinung; ~~ *polls: Meinungsumfragen;* ~~ *research: Demoskopie*; **separate** ~ gesonderte Urteilsbegründung.

opponent *s* Gegner *m*, Widersacher *m*, Gegenpartei *f*, *adj* gegnerisch.

opportune opportun, günstig, passend, rechtzeitig.

opportunity Gelegenheit *f*, Möglichkeit *f*; ~ **costs** alternative Kosten; ~ **of being heard** rechtliches Gehör; ~ **to make representations** Gelegenheit, Einwendungen vorzubringen; ~ **to rebut** Gelegenheit zur Replik; ~ **to respond** Gelegenheit zur Erwiderung, G. zur Gegendarstellung; ~ **to wipe the slate clean** Rehabilitierungschance; **should the** ~ **arise** gegebenenfalls.

oppose bekämpfen, sich widersetzen; einwenden, Widerspruch erheben; entgegenstehen; ~ **an application** Einspruch gegen e-e (Patent)Anmeldung einlegen; ~ **a will** ein Testament anfechten; ~ **the divorce** der Scheidung widersprechen.

opposed entgegengesetzt, feindlich; ~ **business** *parl* streitig gewordene Individualvorlagen.

opposer Gegner *m*, Opponent *m*, *pat* Einsprechender *m*.

opposite entgegengesetzt, umgekehrt, gegnerisch, gegenüberliegend; ~ **party** → *party*.

opposition Opposition *f*, Gegensatz *m*, Widerstand *m*, Widerspruch *m*, Einspruch *m*; ~ **fee** *pat* Einspruchsgebühr; ~ **proceedings** *pat* Einspruchsverfahren; ~ **to grant new tenancy** Widerspruch gegen Fortsetzung des Mietverhältnisses; **notice of** ~ *pat* Einspruchseinlegung; **parliamentary** ~ Parlamentsopposition; **party in** ~ *pat* Einspruchspartei, Opposition; **rejoinder to an** ~ *pat* Einspruchserwiderung; **to meet with** ~ auf Widerspruch stoßen.

oppress unterdrücken, tyrannisieren.

oppression Unterdrückung *f*, Nötigung *f* im Amt, Freiheitsberaubung *f* im Amt; ~ **of minority shareholders** unfaire Pression gegen Minderheitsaktionäre.

oppressive unterdrückend, niederdrückend, tyrannisch; ~ **child labour** Ausbeutungskinderarbeit.

oppressor Unterdrücker *m*, Tyrann *m*.

opprobium Schande *f*, Verachtung *f*.

opt optieren, sich entscheiden; ~ **for a nationality** für e-e Staatsangehörigkeit optieren; ~ **out** *cf opting out*.

optant Optant *m*.

optimacy Adel *m*, Menschen *m*|*pl* der höchsten Stände.

optimum *adj* optimal, bestmöglich, günstigst(er, e, es); ~ **allocation of resources** optimale Rohstoffverteilung *f*.

optimum *s* Optimum *n*, Bestwert *m*.

opting out wahlweises Ausscheiden *n*, Freizeichnung *f*, Befreiung von der Versicherungspflicht auf Antrag.

option Option *f*, Wahl *f*, Wahlrecht *n*, Optionsrecht *n*, Bezugsrecht *n*, Prämie *f*, Prämiengeschäft *n*; Sonderausstattung *f*, Extra(s); ~ **agreement** Bezugsrechtsvereinbarung; ~ **bond** Optionsanleihe, Bezugsrechtsobligation; ~ **business** Prämiengeschäft; ~ **buyer** Prämienkäufer; ~ **by tenant to purchase premises** Vorkaufsrecht des Mieters; ~ **clause** Optionsklausel; ~ **day** Prämienerklärungstag; ~ **deal for the call** Vorprämiengeschäft; ~ **deal for the put** Rückprämiengeschäft; ~ **dealer** Prämienhändler; ~ **forward** Optionsgeschäft in Terminsdevisen; ~**-loaded** mit vielen Sonderausstattungsangeboten; ~**s market** Terminmarkt; ~ **money** Prämie; ~ **mortgage scheme** Hypothek mit Zinswahlrecht (*wg Steuerbegünstigung*); ~ **of exchange** Umtauschrecht; ~ **of nationality** Staatsangehörigkeitsoption; ~ **of owner to complete works** Recht des Bestellers zur Ersatzvornahme; ~ **of purchase** Kaufoption (*zB bei Pachtvertrag*); ~ **on new stock** Bezugsrecht; ~ **order** Auftrag auf Abruf; ~ **period** Optionsdauer; ~ **price** Prämienkurs; ~ **rate** Prämiensatz; ~ **right** Option, Optionsrecht; ~ **stock** → *stock* (*1*); ~ **to purchase** Ankaufsoption; Ankaufsmöglichkeit, Ankaufsrecht, Anwartschaft, Ablöserecht; ~ **to renew at competitive rental** Mietverlängerungs(options)recht zur ortsüblichen Miete; **abandonment of the** ~ **money** Aufgabe der Prämie, Prämienaufgabe; **at buyer's** ~ nach Wahl des Käufers; **at seller's** ~ nach Wahl des Verkäufers; **at the** ~ nach Wahl; **buyer's** ~ Kaufoption, Vorprämie; **buyer's** ~ **to double** Nochgeschäft in Käufers Wahl; **call** ~ → *call*; **compound** ~ Doppelprämie; **double** ~ Stellagegeschäft; **field-installed** ~**s** am Standort eingebaute Zusatzgeräte; **firm** ~ feste Option, alleiniges Ankaufsrecht; **first** ~ Vorhand (*beim Kauf*), Option beim ersten Verkaufsfall; **giver of an** ~ → *giver*; **grantee of the** ~ Optionsberechtigter; **local** ~ *brit* Ortsentscheid über Schankgerechtigkeit; **naked** ~ ungesicherte Option; **put** ~ → *put s*; Rückprämie(ngeschäft); **seller's** ~ Verkaufsoption, *exch* Rückprämie; **sel-**

ler's ~ to double Nochgeschäft in Verkäufers Wahl; **single ~** einfaches Prämiengeschäft; **stock ~** → *stock (1)*; **taker of an ~** *brit* Prämienverkäufer, Optionsnehmer; **traded ~** handelbare Option, an der Börse gehandelte Option.

optional fakultativ, wahlweise, freigestellt, wahlfrei; **~ standard provision** *ins* weglaßbare (*aber unveränderliche*) Standardbestimmung; **to leave it ~ with a person** *jmdm* die Wahl lassen.

optionee Optionsberechtigter *m*, Optionsempfänger *m*, durch Wahlrecht Begünstigter *m*.

optioner Optionsgeber *m*, Optionsgewährer *m*; durch Wahlrecht Verpflichteter *m*.

or oder, nämlich (*auslegungsmäßig manchmal: und*); **~ elsewhere** oder sonstwo; **~ order** oder dessen (*deren*) Order; **~ otherwise** oder in sonstiger Weise; **~ thereabouts** etwa, mehr oder weniger, circa.

oral mündlich.

orality Mündlichkeit *f*.

orator Redner *m*, Sprecher *m*; Kläger *m* (*im Equity-Prozeß*); **Public O~** Universitätssprecher (*Oxford, Cambridge*).

oratrix Klägerin *f* (*im Equity-Prozeß*); Rednerin *f*.

ordain anordnen, verordnen, errichten, e-e Verfassung geben, ordinieren.

ordeal *hist* Ordal *n*, Gottesurteil *n*; **fire ~** Feuerordal; **water ~** Wasserordal.

order *s* (*1*) Befehl *m*, Anordnung *f*, Erlaß *m*, Weisung *f*, Beschluß *m*, gerichtliche Entscheidung *f*; **~ absolute for dissolution of marriage** (endgültiges) Scheidungsurteil; **~ adding defendant** *Beschluß auf Zulassung des Mitverklagens von weiteren Beklagten*; **~ as to costs** Kostenentscheidung, Kostenbeschluß; **~ barring future actions** *Ausschluß weiterer Rechtsbehelfe durch Gerichtsbeschluß;* **~ blanks** Beschlußformulare; **~ book** *Buch über ausstehende Parlamentsbeschlüsse, Fragen u. Anträge*; **~ by consent** *Beschluß auf Grund der Zustimmung der beschwerten Partei*; **~ declaring rights** Zwischenfeststellungsurteil; **~ dismissing summons generally** *Beschluß auf Zurückweisung des Antrags auf Verfahrenseröffnung*; **~ ex parte** Beschluß auf einseitigen Antrag *ohne mündliche Verhandlung*; **~ extending time** Fristverlängerungsbeschluß; **~ for accounts** Rechnungslegungsbeschluß; **~ for attachment of earnings** Lohnpfändungsbeschluß; **~ for costs** Kostenfestsetzungsbeschluß; **~ for custody, maintenance and education of children** Personensorgebeschluß; **~ for directions** prozeßleitende Verfügung *(zur Vorbereitung der mündlichen Verhandlung)*; gerichtliche Anordnung; Auflagenbeschluß; **~ for discharge** Rehabilitierungsbeschluß (*e-s Konkursgerichts*); **~ for discovery** Auflagenbeschluß zur Urkundenvorlage; **~ for enforcement** Vollstreckungsklausel; **~ for evidence** Beweisbeschluß; **~ for examination** Beweisbeschluß *zur Vernehmung e-s Zeugen oder Sachverständigen*; **~ for further and better particulars** Substantiierungsauflage; **~ for judicial separation** Beschluß über Gestattung des Getrenntlebens; **~ for maintenance** Unterhaltsbeschluß, Unterhaltsurteil; Herausgabeverfügung; **~ for particulars** Beschluß mit Auflage der Substantiierung; **~ for payment** Zahlungsanweisung, Zahlungsanordnung; **~ for possession** gerichtlicher Räumungsbefehl; Räumungsurteil im summarischen Verfahren; **~ for re-engagement** Anordnung auf Wiedereinstellung (*e-s Entlassenen*); **~ for reinstatment** (gerichtl) Anordnung der Wiedereinsetzung in die Arbeitsstelle; **~ for renewal** Verlängerungsbeschluß; **~ for separate representation** Anordnung getrennter Prozeßvertretung; **~ for substituted service** Beschluß auf Zulassung der öffentlichen Zustellung; ~ **for time** Verfügung über die Gewährung e–r Fristverlängerung; ~ **for transfer of action** Verweisungsbeschluß; ~ **giving leave to defend** *Einlassungsbeschluß*; ~ **in bankruptcy** Beschluß im Konkursverfahren, Konkurseröffnungsbeschluß; ~ **in chambers** Beschluß im Bürowege; **O~ in Council** königlicher Erlaß (*auf Empfehlung des Kronrats*); ~ **in writing** schriftliche Verfügung; ~ **nisi** Vorbehaltsbeschluß; vorläufige Entscheidung; ~ **of adjudication of bankruptcy** *endgültiger* Beschluß über die Eröffnung des Konkursverfahrens; ~ **of arrest** Arrestbefehl, Haftbefehl; ~ **of attachment** Arrestbeschluß, Beschlagnahme, Forderungspfändung; ~ **of civil authority** Verwaltungsakt; ~ **of committal** Anordnung der Beugehaft; ~ **of Council** Verordnung (*des Kronrats*), Kronratsverfügung, Verwaltungsanordnung des Kronrats; ~ **of course** notwendiger Beschluß, *der auf einseitigen Antrag erlassen werden muß*; ~ **of discharge** Freistellungsbeschluß für den Gemeinschuldner; ~ **of distribution** Verteilungsbeschluß; ~ **of filiation** Unterhaltsurteil mit Vaterschaftsfeststellung; ~ **of mandamus** → *mandamus*; ~ **of reference** Verweisungsbeschluß, *Beschluß auf gerichtliche Bezifferung des Schadens*; ~ **of revivor** Beschluß auf Fortsetzung e–s ruhenden Verfahrens; ~ **of seizure** Arrestbefehl; ~ **of session** Beschluß e–s Assisengerichts; ~ **of the court** gerichtliche Verfügung, Gerichtsbeschluß; ~ **of the House** Geschäftsordnungsbeschluß des Unterhauses; ~ **to carry on proceedings** Prozeßfortsetzungsbeschluß; ~ **to deliver interrogatories** Beschluß auf Vorlage von Fragebögen (*für Zeugenvernehmung*); ~ **to dismiss** *Beschluß auf Verwerfung e–s Rechtsmittels*; klageabweisendes Urteil *wegen Unzulässigkeit*; ~ **to dismiss for want of prosecution** Klageabweisung mangels Betreibens des Verfahrens; ~ **to pay** Zahlungsanweisung, Zahlungsanordnung; ~ **to pay costs** Kostenentscheidung; ~ **to show cause** gerichtliche Verfügung, Einwendungen vorzubringen; **absolute** ~ zwingender Beschluß; **administrative** ~ Verwaltungsanordnung, Verfügung; **affiliation** → *affiliation;* **agreed** ~ Beschluß auf übereinstimmenden Antrag; **care and control** ~ → *care*; **balance** ~ → *balance*; **bastardy** ~ → *bastardy*; **attachment** ~ = ~ *of attachment, supra*; **binding** ~ → *binding over*; **carriage of** ~ *Recht auf Besitz an Beschlußausfertigung*; **cease and desist** ~ Unterlassungsverfügung; **charging** ~ vorläufiges Verfügungsverbot, dinglicher Arrest; Zwangsvollstreckungsbeschlagnahme (*bes von Rechten*); Zwangsverwaltungsbeschluß; **circular** ~ Umlauf, Runderlaß; **closing** ~ Benutzungsverbot für Wohnzwecke; örtl. Ladenschlußvorschrift; **custody** ~ → *custody*; **compulsory** ~ Zwangsliquidationsbeschluß, Konkurseröffnungsbeschluß (*gegen Kapitalgesellschaft*); **consolidated attachment** ~ zusammengefaßter Pfändungs- und Überweisungsbeschluß (*mehrere Titel*); **declaratory** ~ auf Feststellung lautendes Zwischenurteil; **decretal** ~ → *decretal*; **direct-child** ~ unmittelbare Kindesunterhaltsanordnung; **emergency** ~ Notverordnung; **executive** ~ Verordnung; **exclusion** ~ → *exclusion*; **final** ~ Endentscheidung in Form e–s Beschlusses; **final go-ahead** ~ endgültiger Startbefehl; **four-day** ~ Vollzugsfrist von vier Tagen; **garnishee** ~ → *garnishee*; **general ~s** gerichtliche Verfahrensordnung; **implementing** ~ Durchführungsverordnung; **injunctive** ~ Verbotsverfügung; **instalment** ~ Ratenzahlungsbeschluß; **interim** ~ einstweilige Anordnung, Zwischenverfügung; **interlocutory** ~

Zwischenentscheidung, Zwischenurteil, einstweilige Anordnung, Zwischenverfügung; **interpleader** ~ → *interpleader*; **judicial** ~ Gerichtsbeschluß; **legal** ~ gesetzliche Anweisung; **maintenance** ~ einstweilige Anordnung auf Unterhaltszahlung, Unterhaltsurteil; **mandatory** ~ *strafbewehrte* einstweilige Verfügung *auf Wiederherstellung des ursprünglichen Zustands*; **matrimonial** Beschluß in Ehesachen (*Gestattung des Getrenntlebens, Unterhalt, Sorgerecht*); **ministerial** ~ Ministerialerlaß, Verordnung; **non-cohabitation** ~ gerichtl Verweisung aus der Ehewohnung; **non-molestation** ~ Belästigungsverbot (*gegenüber getrennt lebender Ehefrau*); **ouster** ~ Besitzentziehungsbeschluß; Verbot des Betretens der Ehewohnung durch den Ehegatten *in e–r einstweiligen Anordnung*; **peremptory** ~ zwingender Beschluß; **preclusion** ~ Ausschließungsverfügung (*Ausschluß von Angriffs- und Verteidigungsmitteln*); **prerogative** ~ Beschluß aufgrund außerordentlicher Rechtsmittel (*mandamus, prohibition, certiorari qv*); **procedural** ~ Verfahrensbeschluß; **provisional** ~ einstweilige Anordnung; provisorische Verordnung; **receiving** ~ vorläufiger Konkurseröffnungsbeschluß; offener Arrest (*Konkursverfahren*), gerichtliche Sequestration; **registration** ~ Eintragungsbeschluß; **regulatory** ~ Verwaltungsvorschrift; **release** ~ Freilassungsbeschluß, Beschluß über die Aufhebung des Haftbefehls; **requisition** ~ → *requisition*; **restraining** ~ *brit* vorläufiges Verfügungsverbot, auf Unterlassung gerichtete einstweilige Verfügung; **seizing** ~ Arrestbefehl, Beschlagnahmeverordnung; **speaking** ~ Erläuterungsbeschluß; **special** ~**s** Verordnungen mit Gesetzeskraft; **statutory** ~ Rechtsverordnung, Verwaltungsverordnung *auf Grund gesetzlicher Ermächtigung*; **stop** ~ vorläufiges Verfügungsverbot, Zahlungsverbot, Veräußerungsverbot, Vertriebsverbot; **superior** ~ höherer Befehl; **supervision** ~ überwachte Auflage (*zB Aufenthaltsbestimmung bei Bewährung*); *Beschluß auf gerichtliche Überwachung e–r freien Liquidation*; **temporary** ~ einstweilige Anordnung; **time** ~ gerichtl Fristverlängerung; **to cease and desist** ~ Unterlassungsverfügung, Unterlassungsbefehl (*im Urteil*); **until further** ~ *rechtsgültig vorbehaltlich späterer Gerichtsentscheidung*; **"unless"** ~ Auflagenbeschluß mit Ausschlußfrist; **variation** ~ (Unterhalts-)Abänderungsbeschluß (*etwa: Abänderungsurteil*).

order *s* (2) Order *f*, Anweisung *f*, Bestellung *f*; Auftrag *m*; ~ **and disposition** Fremdbesitz (*des Gemeinschuldners*); ~ **at best** *exch* Auftrag bestens, Bestensauftrag; ~ **bill (of exchange)** → *bill (3)*; ~ **bill of lading** → *bill of lading*; ~ **bonds** → *bond (1)*; ~ **book** Auftragsbuch, Auftragsbestand; ~ **for collection** Inkassoauftrag; ~ **for payment of money** Zahlungsanweisung; ~ **for remittance** Überweisungsauftrag; ~ **for the account** *exch* Terminauftrag; ~ **form** Auftragsformular, Bestellschein, Bestellzettel; ~**s in hand** Auftragsbestand; ~ **release** Auftragsfreigabe; ~ **slip** *exch* Auftragszettel; ~ **to sell** Verkaufsauftrag; ~ **valid today** Tagesauftrag; **acknowledgment of** ~ Auftragsbestätigung; **additional** ~ Nachbestellung; **binding** ~ verbindliche Bestellung; **buying** ~ Kaufauftrag; **collective** ~ Sammelauftrag; **conditional** ~ freibleibender Auftrag; bedingte Anweisung; **contingent** ~ gekoppelter Auftrag; verbundener A., „Zug um Zug"-Geschäft; **counter** ~ → *counter-order*; **covering** ~ Deckungsauftrag; **crossed** ~ Selbsteintrittsangebot zu höherem Kurs; **delivery** ~ Lieferanweisung; Auslieferungsschein; Anweisung zur Auslieferung von Lagergut; Lagerschein; **day** ~ nur für e–n Tag gültiger Börsenauftrag, **disbursing**

~ Auszahlungsverfügung; **discretionary** ~ *Maklerauftrag, bei dem der Preis in das Ermessen des Maklers gestellt ist*; **dispatch** ~ Versandauftrag; **filled** ~ ausgeführter Auftrag; **firm** ~ fester Auftrag; **good** ~ limitierter Auftrag in Tageskursnähe; **immediate or cancel** ~ → *immediate*; **incoming** ~**s** eingehende Aufträge; **initial** ~ Anfangsbestellung; **landing** ~ Löschungserlaubnis, Zollpassierschein; **limit(ed)** ~ limitierter Auftrag, Limitauftrag; **long** ~ Verkaufsorder über eigene (*dem Auftraggeber gehörende*) Aktien; **made out to** ~ an Order lautend; **market** ~ Bestens-Order, unlimitierter Börsenauftrag; **money** ~ → *money*; **month** ~ Terminauftrag auf Monatsfrist, für e–n Monat gültiger Börsenauftrag; **"near"** ~ Zirkaauftrag; **no-limit** ~ unlimitierter Auftrag; **offshore** ~**s** → *offshore*; **open** ~ bis auf Widerruf gültige Order; **outstanding** ~**s** unerledigte Aufträge; **own** ~ eigene Order; **permanent** ~ Dauerauftrag; **postal** ~ Postanweisung; **purchase** ~ Kaufauftrag, Lieferauftrag; **repeat** ~ Nachbestellung; **roundlot** ~ *Börsenauftrag in runden* Mindestmengen; **rush** ~ Eilauftrag; **scale** ~ Gesamtbörsenauftrag mit differenzierten Kursinstruktionen; **short** ~ *Börsenauftrag, bei dem Besteller die Effekten noch nicht besitzt*; **standing** ~ → *standing order*; **stop** ~ (=) Limitsetzung, Kauf- oder Verkaufauftrag mit Kurslimit; Schecksperre; **stop-limit** ~ *stop order qv nach Erreichen des Kurslimit;* **stop-loss** ~ (=) Verlustbegrenzungsauftrag; **time** ~ fest terminierter Börsenauftrag; **unconditional** unbedingte Anweisung; **unfilled** ~**s** unerledigte Aufträge; **unlimited** ~ unlimitierte Order; **week** ~ für eine Woche gültiger Börsenauftrag, Börsenterminauftrag auf Wochenfrist; **written** ~ schriftliche Bestellung.

order *s* (*3*) Ordnung *f*, öffentliche Ordnung *f*, System *n*, Geschäftsordnung *f*, Aufstellung *f*, Zustand *m*, Klasse *f*, Reihenfolge *f*, Folge *f*; ~ **of administration** Reihenfolge der Regelung von Nachlaßverbindlichkeiten; ~ **of payment** Zahlungsrangfolge (*Konkurs*); ~ **of precedence** Rangordnung, Rangfolge; ~ **of precedence of motions** Reihenfolge der (*zu behandelnden*) Anträge; ~ **of registration** Reihenfolge der Eintragung; ~ **of sequence** zeitliche Reihenfolge; ~ **of succession** Erbfolgeordnung, Thronfolgeordnung; ~ **paper** Tagesordnung im Unterhaus, Sitzungsprogramm; **good working** ~ betriebsfähiger Zustand; **public** ~ öffentliche Ordnung; **social** ~ Gesellschaftsordnung, soziale Ordnung.

order *v* anordnen, verordnen, befehlen, regeln, lenken, bestellen, dekretieren; durch Beschluß bestimmen, verfügen; ~ **and direct** e–e Weisung geben; durch Beschluß anordnen; ~ **costs** über die Kosten entscheiden; ~**ed, adjudged and decreed** beschlossen und verkündet.

ordinance Verordnung *f*, Verfügung *f*; ~ **of the forest** Forstgesetz; **emergency** ~ Notverordnung; **municipal** ~ kommunale Verordnung, Gemeindesatzung; **police** ~ → *police*.

ordinary *adj* ordentlich, normal, angemessen, gewöhnlich, üblich; ~ **civil causes** Rechtsstreitigkeiten vor den ordentlichen Gerichten, Streitsachen; ~ **course of business** üblicher Geschäftsbetrieb; gewöhnlicher Geschäftsverkehr; ~ **course of post** bei normaler Postbeförderung und Zustellung; ~ **general meeting** ordentliche Hauptversammmlung, Jahresversammlung; ~ **hazards of occupation** gewöhnliches Berufsrisiko; ~ **life insurance** (= *assurance*) → *life insurance*; ~ **market value** Verkehrswert; ~ **meeting** = ~ *general meeting qv*; ~ **necessaries of life** die allgemeinen Lebensbedürfnisse; ~ **negligence** → *negligence*; ~ **per-**

sons Durchschnittsmenschen; **preferred share** → *share*; ~ **proceeding** allgemeines Streitverfahren; ~ **receipts** ordentliche (Staats)Einnahmen; ~ **repairs** gewöhnliche Erhaltungsarbeiten und Schönheitsreparaturen; ~ **residence** → *residence*; ~ **resolution** → *resolution*; ~ **risks** gewöhnliches Berufsrisiko; ~ **seaman** einfacher Matrose; ~ **services** übliche Leistungen; ~ **session** ordentliche Sitzungsperiode; ~ **shares** → *share s*; ~ **skill in the art** übliche handwerkliche Geschicklichkeit; ~ **travel** allgemein übliche Straßenbenutzung; ~ **use** gewöhnlicher Gebrauch; ~ **useful life** betriebsgewöhnliche Nutzungsdauer; ~ **value** gewöhnlicher Wert; ~ **way of trade** normaler Geschäftsverlauf; ~ **written law** gesetztes Recht; **to exercise** ~ **care** → *care*.

ordinary *s* Ordinarius *m* (*mit kirchengerichtlicher Zuständigkeit ausgestatteter Geistlicher*), geistlicher Richter *m*, *US*: Nachlaßrichter *m*, Vormundschaftsrichter *m*.

ordnance Feldzeugwesen *n*; ~ **datum** Vermessungsmarke, mittlere Höhe über Normalnull; ~ **debentures** Schatzanweisungen des Waffenamtes; **O~ Department** Zeugamt, Waffenamt; ~ **map** Generalstabskarte, Meßtischblatt; ~ **officer** Artillerieoffizier (*Marine*), Offizier der Feldzeugtruppe, Waffenoffizier; **O~ Survey** allgemeine amtliche Landvermessung *GB*; **Board of O~** Zeugamt (*GB bis 1855*).

ore-leave Erzschürfrechte *n*.

organ Organ *n*, Sprachrohr *n*, Werkzeug *n*, Instrument *n*, Hilfsmittel *n*, Handlanger *m*; ~ **donation** Organspende; ~ **donor** Organspender; **administrative** ~ Verwaltungsorgan; **executive** ~ Organ der Exekutive, Vollzugsorgan.

organic organisch, verfassungsmäßig; ~ **Act** *US Bundesgesetz zur Übertragung der Regierungsgewalt über ein Territorium*; Gründungsstatut; ~ **law** Grundgesetz, Verfassung.

organization Organisation *f*, System *n*, Aufbau *m*, innere Verfassung *f*, Anordnung *f*; Zusammenschluß *m*, Verband *m*; Verwaltungsapparat *m*, Parteiorganisation *f*; ~ **certificate** Konzessionsurkunde, Gründungsurkunde; **O~ for Economic Cooperation and Development** Organisation für wirtschaftliche Zusammenarbeit und Entwicklung (*OECD, Paris, seit 1960*); **O~ for the Maintenance of Supplies** *brit* Technische Nothilfe; ~ **tax** → *tax*; **administrative** ~ Verwaltungsapparat; **affiliated** ~**s** angeschlossene Verbände; **charitable** ~ Wohltätigkeitsverein, Hilfswerk; **head** ~ Spitzenverband; **industrial** ~ Betriebsorganisation; **labo(u)r** ~ Arbeitnehmerorganisation, Gewerkschaftsorganisation; **professional** ~Berufsverband; **proscribed** ~ verbotene (*terroristische*) Organisation; **voluntary** ~**s** private Fürsorgeverbände.

organize organisieren, einrichten; ausbauen, aufbauen, mit Organen versehen; gewerkschaftlich organisieren; ~**d county** ordnungsgemäß konstituierte Grafschaft; ~**d labo(u)r** → *labo(u)r*.

origin Ursprung *m*, Herkunft *f*, Abstammung *f*, Quelle *f*; ~ **brand** Herkunftsbezeichnung ~ **mark** Ursprungskennzeichnung; ~ **marking** Kennzeichnung des Herkunftslandes; **certificate of** ~ → *certificate*; **country of** ~ Ursprungsland; **foreign** ~ ausländische Herkunft; **national** ~ Abstammung, Ursprungsland; **state of** ~ → *state* (*2*).

original *s* Original *n*, Urschrift *f*, **in the** ~ im Original, urschriftlich; **single** ~ (*nur einmal vorhandene*) Originalurkunde.

original *adj* ursprünglich, echt, Original ..., selbständig, eigentümlich; ~ **equipment manufacturer** ~ (*OEM*) Originalgerätehersteller *m*.

originality Ursprünglichkeit *f*, Eigentümlichkeit *f*, Eigenart *f*.

originate entstehen, entstehen lassen, hervorbringen.

originating | **bank** Akkreditivbank *f*; ~ **notice of motion** *gerichtliche Mitteilung der prozeßeinleitenden Antragstellung an den Antragsgegner*; ~ **petition** Klage, Klageschriftsatz, Verfahrensantrag; ~ **summons** → *summons*.

originator Urheber *m*, Begründer *m*; Stifter *m*.

orphan *s* Waisenkind *n*, Vollwaise *m*, vaterloses Kind *n*, Halbwaise *m*; ~ **asylum** Waisenhaus, Waisenanstalt; ~**'s court** → *court*.

orphanage part Pflichterbteil *m* für Kinder.

orthodox orthodox, konventionell, allgemein anerkannt, üblich; ~ **interpretation** althergebrachte Auslegung.

ostensible scheinbar, anscheinend, angeblich.

ostracize verbannen, ächten.

other ander(er, e, es), verschieden von, zusätzlich zu, sonstig(er, e, es), gleicher Art; ~ **assets** sonstige Aktiva; ~ **evidence** weiteres Beweismaterial; ~ **matters in difference** sonstige streitige Angelegenheiten, ~ **payments** *bil* sonstige Ausgaben; ~ **receipts** *bil* sonstige Einnahmen; ~ **than** mit Ausnahme von; ~ **the issue of my body** meine sonstigen Nachkommen; ~ **things being equal** bei sonst gleichen Bedingungen.

otherwise anders als, sonst, andernfalls, im übrigen, anderweitig; ~ **acted innocently** (der sich) im übrigen gutgläubig verhalten hat; **A ~ B** A alias B.

oust *v* die Zwangsräumung durchführen, Besitz und Nutzung entziehen, exmittieren; vertreiben, entlassen (*aus e–m Amt*), absetzen, zwangsweise entfernen; ausschließen, abbedingen; ~ **s.o. from office** jmdn seines Amtes entheben, jmdn absetzen; ~ **the jurisdiction of the courts** den Rechtsweg ausschließen.

ouster Zwangsräumung *f*, Vertreibung *f* aus e–m Grundstück, Besitzentziehung *f*, Entsetzung *f*; gewaltsame Absetzung *f*, Entfernung *f* vom Amt; ~ **application** Antrag auf Verweisung aus der Ehewohnung; ~ **clause** Klausel über den Ausschluß des Rechtsweges; ~ **order** → *order* (*1*); ~ **of jurisdiction** Ausschluß des allgemeinen Gerichtsstandes, Entziehung der Zuständigkeit; **actual** ~ Eigenbesitzanmaßung.

out | **and out** hundertprozentig, ganz und gar, absolut, unentwegt; ~ **at interest** verzinslich ausgeliehen; ~ **of benefit** Versicherungsschutz vorläufig aufgehoben; ~ **of bounds** → *bound*; ~ **of court** außergerichtlich; ohne Aktivlegitimation, aussichtslos (*Klage*); ~ **of date** → *date*; ~ **of employment** → *employment*; ~ **of hand** kurzer Hand; ~ **of my estate** aus meinem Nachlaß; ~**-of-pocket expenses** Barauslagen; ~**-of-pocket loss rule** = *~-of-pocket-rule qv*; ~**-of-pocket rule** Schadenersatz für die Mehraufwendungen; ~ **of print** → *print*; ~ **of repair** → *repair*; ~ **of term** in den Gerichtsferien, außerhalb der Sitzungsperiode; ~ **of the state** außerstaatlich, ausländisch, jenseits der Staatsgrenzen; ~ **of time** überfällig; nicht mehr fristgerecht; ~ **of town bill** Distanzwechsel; ~ **of work** → *work*; **land ~ at rent** verpachtetes Grundstück; **speak** ~ sprich (*sprechen Sie!*) laut und deutlich!; **the party is** ~ die Partei ist nicht mehr am Ruder; **to be ~ on bail** → *bail*; **to be $ 10** ~ 10 Dollar eingebüßt haben.

outage-costs Ausfallwert e–r Betriebsanlage.

outbalance überwiegen, übertreffen.

outbid überbieten, ein niedrigeres Submissionsangebot machen.

outbidder Mehrbietende(r) *f* (*m*), Meistbietende(r) *f* (*m*).

outbound auslaufend (*Schiff*); ~ **transportation** Ausgangsfracht.

out-boundaries äußere Grenzen *f|pl.*

outbuilding Außengebäude *n*, Nebengebäude *n*.

outcast Ausgestoßener *m*, Verbannter *m*, Vagabund *m*; Abfall *m*, Ausschuß *m*.

outclearance Ausklarieren *n* (*aus e–m Hafen*).

out-clearing *brit Gesamtbetrag m der an die Verrechnungsstelle gerichteten Schecks.*

outcrop an die Oberfläche reichendes Flöz *n* (*bzw Erzader*).

outcry Schrei *m*, Entsetzensschrei *m*, Hilferuf *m*, Geschrei *n*; **open** ~ offener Zuruf, (*Börse, Terminhandel*); ~ ~ *trading system: Börsenhandel durch offenen Zuruf;* **sale by** ~ Straßenverkauf mit Ausrufen der Ware.

outer|bar jüngere Anwälte *m|pl*; *außerhalb der Schranke für Senioranwälte (Queens Counsel)*; ~ **districts of urban areas** städtische Außenbezirke; ~ **door** Haustür, Wohnungstür; **O~ House** *scot Gericht 1. Instanz im Court of Sessions*; ~ **space law** Weltraumrecht.

outfit Ausstattung *f*, Aussteuer *f*; Schiffsausrüstung *f*, Einrichtung *f*; Vergütung *f* für Aufwendungen *bei Auslandsversetzung von diplomatischen Vertretern.*

outflow Abfluß *m*; ~ **of capital** Kapitalabfluß.

outgo Aufwendungen *f|pl.*

outgoing ausscheidend, weggehend.

outgoings Ausgaben *f|pl*, Aufwendungen *f|pl*; Grundstückslasten *f|pl*; **excess** ~ (*Abwälzung von*) Erhöhungen der öffentl Lasten (*auf den Mieter*).

outhouse Nebengebäude *n*, Hintergebäude *n*; Klosett *n* außerhalb des Hauses.

outland äußere Äcker *m|pl* und Wiesen *f|pl*, Ländereien *f|pl* (*die nicht zu dem vom Herrenhof selbst bewirtschafteten Grund gehören*); Grenzland.

outlaw *s* Geächteter *m*, Vogelfreier *m*, Bandit *m*, Gewohnheitsverbrecher *m*.

outlaw *v* ächten, für vogelfrei erklären, die Rechtsgültigkeit entziehen, verbieten, verfemen; ~**ed debt** verjährte Forderung.

outlawr|y Ächtung *f*, Verbot *n*, Unzulässigkeitserklärung *f*, Nichteinklagbarkeit *f*; ~**ies bill** (=) *formale historische Vorlage zur Bekämpfung geheimer Verbrechen* (*bei jeder brit Parlamentseröffnung verlesen*); ~ **of war** Kriegsächtung.

outlay Auslagen *f|pl*, Aufwendungen *f|pl*, Unkosten *pl*; ~ **curve** Ausgabenkurve; **cash** ~ Barauslagen; **initial** ~ Anfangsausgabe, Anschaffungskosten; **professional** ~**s** Werbungskosten.

outlet Markt *m*, Absatzgebiet *n*.

outline|drawings Übersichtszeichnungen *f|pl*; ~**floor plan** Bauplan, Geschoßflächenplan.

outlook Aussicht *f*, Anschauung *f*, Standpunkt *m*; **business** ~ Geschäftsaussichten.

outlot außerhalb der Gemeindegrenzen beginnendes Grundstück *n*.

outnumber an Zahl übertreffen; **to be** ~**ed** in der Minderheit sein.

outplacement Entlassungshilfe *f*; ~ **consultancy** Entlassungshilfe und Neuvermittlung für leitende Angestellte; ~ **firms** Entlassungshilfefirmen, *Umschulung und Ersatzarbeitsplatzvermittlung.*

outport Seehafen *m* Außenhafen *m*.

output Ertrag *m*, Produktionsleistung *f*; ~ **cut** Produktionskürzung; ~ **evaluation** Leistungsermittlung; ~ **figures** Produktionszahlen; ~ **per hour** Stundenleistung; ~ **quotas** Förderquoten (*Erdöl*); ~ **target** Produktionsziel, Soll; **annual** ~ Jahresproduktion, Jahresförderung; **daily** ~ Tagesproduktion; **gross** ~ Bruttoproduktionswert; **industrial** ~ Industrieproduktion; **required** ~ Leistungbedarf.

outputter *US* Produzent *m*, Erzeuger *m*; Hehler *m*, Falschgeldabschieber *m*.

outsourcing Fremdbelieferung *f*, Beschaffung durch Fremdbezug, Verlegung von Bezugsquellen ins Ausland.

outrage *s* Freveltat *f*, Ausschreitung *f*, Greueltat *f*, Gewalttätigkeit *f*, Beleidigung *f*, Schimpf *m*, Schande *f*, Vergewaltigung *f*; ~ **upon decency** grobe Verletzung des Anstandes, öffentliches Ärgernis; ~ **upon personal dignity** Freveltat gegen die Menschenwürde.

outrage *v* freveln, sich vergehen an, grob beleidigen, schänden, mißhandeln.

outriders berittene Gerichtsboten *m*|*pl* (*zur Einführung von Geschworenen*); Eskortefahrer (*Polizei*).

outright völlig, gänzlich, total, vorbehaltlos, direkt; ~ **forward** Devisentermingeschäft mit vereinbartem Erfüllungstag; ~ **gold-value guarantee** volle Goldwertgarantie; **to buy** ~ e–n festen Kaufabschluß tätigen; gegen sofortige Lieferung kaufen; **to sell** ~ ganz verkaufen, in Bausch und Bogen verkaufen.

outrun übersteigen; ~ **one's credit** seinen Kredit überziehen; ~ **one's income** über seine Verhältnisse leben.

outsell e–n höheren Preis erzielen; mehr absetzen.

outside äußer(er, e, es) Außen . . ., fremd . . ., außenstehend; ~ **capital** Fremdkapital; ~ **countries** Drittländer; ~ **market** Freiverkehrsmarkt; Markt für unnotierte Werte; ~ **(stock) broker** freier Makler, an der Börse nicht zugelassener Makler; Winkelmakler; ~ **transactions** Freiverkehrsumsätze.

outsider Außenseiter *m*, Außenstehender *m*, Nichtfachmann *m*, Laie *m*; Freiverkehrsmakler *m*.

outsize Übergröße *f*.

outstanding ausstehend, unerledigt, offen, nicht (zurück)bezahlt, im Umlauf befindlich; auffallend, hervorragend; ~ **account** → *account* (*2*); ~ **bonds** → *bond* (*1*); ~ **capital stock** ausgegebene Aktien; ~ **crop** → *crop*; ~ **debts** → *debts*; ~ **interest** → *interest* (*2*); ~ **liabilities** → *liability*; ~ **matter** unerledigte Sache; ~ **money** → *money*; ~ **order** → *order* (2); ~ **payment** → *payment*; ~ **premiums** Prämienaußenstände; ~ **stock** → *stock* (*1*); ~ **term** = *term in gross qv*; restliche Pachtzeit; ~ **title** besseres Recht.

outstroke Bergwerksabbau *m* durch Stollen vom Nachbargrundstück.

outtrade *im Außenhandel* übertreffen; umsatzmäßig überflügeln.

outturn Ertrag *m*, Ausstoß *m*, Leistung *f*, Produktion *f*; sich herausstellende Beschaffenheit *f*.

outvote überstimmen.

outvoter Briefwähler *m*, nicht im Wahlkreis wohnender Wähler *m*.

outwall Außenmauer *f*.

outward auswärts, nach außen; ~ **bound vessel** auslaufendes Schiff; ~ **journey** Ausreise, Hinreise; ~ **mail department** Versandabteilung, Expedition.

outwear abnutzen, überdauern.

outweigh schwerer sein als, überwiegen.

outwork Außenarbeit *f*, Heimarbeit *f*.

outworker Heimarbeiter *m*.

over über, mehr, weiter; ~ **and above** extra, darüberhinaus; ~ **and short account** Kassendifferenzkonto; ~ **or upon** (*the pavement*) auf oder über (*der Straßenoberfläche*).

overage Überschuß *m*, Mehrbetrag *m*.

overagio Extraprämie *f*, Extraaufgeld *n*.

overbalance Übergewicht *n*, Mehr *n*; ~ **of exports** Ausfuhrüberschuß.

overbid *s* Mehrgebot *n*.

overbid *v* überbieten.

overbilling überhöhte Rechnungsstellung *f*.

overbooking Überbuchung *f*.

overbridge überbrücken.

overbuilt zu dicht bebaut.

overcapacity Überkapazität *f*.

overcapitalization Überkapitalisierung *f*.

overcapitalized überkapitalisiert.

overcertification Bestätigung e–s Überziehungsschecks.

overcharge überladen, zuviel berechnen; zu schwer anklagen.

overcharging Preistreiberei *f*; Zuvielberechnung *f*; Gebührenüberhebung *f*; ~ **of rent** Mietwucher, Mietpreisüberhöhung.
over-commitment übermäßige Bindung *f*, Überengagement *n*, übermäßige Verbraucherkreditaufnahme.
over-compensation Überentschädigung *f*.
overcrowding Überfüllung *f*, Überbelegung von Wohnraum.
overdraft (o/d) Überziehung *f* e–s Bankkontos; Kontokorrentkredit *m*, Überziehungskredit *m*; ~ **commission** Überziehungsprovision; ~ **facility** Kontokorrentkredit; ~ **limit** Kontokorrent(kredit)limit; ~ **on current account** überzogenes Kontokorrentkonto.
overdraw (*Konto*) überziehen.
overdue rückständig, fällig, überfällig, verfallen.
over-estimate Überbewertung *f*, zu hohe Schätzung *f*.
overfreight Überfracht *f*.
overfull employment Überbeschäftigung *f*.
overfunding Überfinanzierung *f*; *Geldmengenkontrollinstrument der Zentralbank*.
overhaul *s* Generalüberholung *f*, gründliche Revision *f*.
overhaul *v* überholen, gründlich nachsehen, untersuchen, renovieren.
overhead Gemeinkosten *pl*, Generalunkosten *pl*, fixe Kosten *pl*; ~ **costs** Gemeinkosten; ~ **distribution** Gemeinkostenumlage; ~ **expenses** Gemeinkosten, allgemeine Geschäftsunkosten; ~ **rate** Gemeinkostensatz; **departmental** ~ Abteilungsgemeinkosten; **overabsorbed** ~ Gemeinkostenüberdeckung.
overhead rail link Schwebebahnverbindung.
overindebtedness Überschuldung *f*.
over-insurance Überversicherung *f*.
over-invest überinvestieren.
over-investment Überinvestition *f*.
over-issue (= *overissue US*) *s* Überemission *f*, zu hohe Ausgabe *f* (*von Wertpapieren*); *v* mehr (*Effekten*) ausgeben als zulässig.
overlap übergreifen, überschneiden.
overleaf umseitig.
overleveraged übermäßig fremdkapitalisiert.
overline Kreditgewährung *f* über der Verschuldungsgrenze.
overlive überleben.
overload *s* Überlastung *f*, Überbeanspruchung *f*, zu hohes Gewicht *n*.
overload *v* überladen, überlasten, zu hohen Belastungen aussetzen.
overlord Oberlehnsherr *m*.
over-luggage Mehrgewicht *n*, Gepäck *n* mit Übergewicht; ~ **-luggaged** überladen, überlastet.
overlying mortgage nachstelliges Grundpfandrecht *n*; ~ **right** Wasserentnahmerecht *n* des Oberliegers.
over-market *v/c* übermäßig vermarkten.
overpay zu hoch bezahlen, überbezahlen; zu reichlich entschädigen.
overplus Überschuß *m*, Überfluß *m*.
overpower überwältigen; ~**ing drug** ein die Widerstandskraft lähmendes Rauschmittel.
over-proceeds Mehrerlös *m*, Mehrertrag *m*.
overproduction Überproduktion *f*.
overrate überschätzen, überbewerten, zu hoch veranschlagen, zu hoch besteuern.
overreach überragen, fortbestehen, übervorteilen; lastenfrei übertragen; ~ **oneself** sich übernehmen.
overreachable nachrangig, ungeschützt (*gegenüber dem Erwerber*).
overreaching *Ausschluß nachrangiger bzw. nicht durch Eintragung geschützter Rechte beim Verkauf*; ~ **clause** Erstreckungsklausel *f* (*Verfügungsrechte des Treugebers bezogen auf nachrangige Treuhand*), Vertragsbestimmung zur Erhaltung der vorrangigen Veräußerungsbefugnis des Verpächters bzw Treugebers; ~ **conveyance** lastenfreie Auflassung (*durch Verkaufstreuhand*); ~ **provisions** *Bestimmungen über den*

lastenfreien Erwerb beim Verkauf durch veräußerungsberechtigten Treuhänder.

override (*im Rang*) vorgehen, maßgeblich sein; ~ **a veto** ein Veto nicht beachten, ein Veto überstimmen.

override principle Grundsatz der absoluten Vorrangigkeit (*berufl. Verschwiegenheit*).

overriding | commission Überprovision, Gebietsprovision; ~ **interests** vorrangige Rechte (*am Grundstück*); ~ **royalty** zusätzliche Konzessionsabgabe; ~ **trust** rangbessere Treuhand.

overrule außer Kraft setzen, umstoßen, verwerfen, ungültig machen, aufheben, zurückweisen, nicht stattgeben; ~ **a plea** e–e Einrede zurückweisen; ~ **an application** e–n Antrag ablehnen, zurückweisen, verwerfen; ~ **the lower court** die Entscheidung der unteren Instanz aufheben *bzw.* abändern; **objection ~d** dem Einspruch wird nicht stattgegeben; die Frage wird zugelassen.

overs Mehrgewicht *n*; Mehrgewicht *n* durch Salzbeimengung (*Fleischkonserven*); ~ **and shorts** Konto zur vorläufigen Verbuchung unklarer Posten.

overseas | companies ausländische Kapitalgesellschaften *f/pl* (*mit Niederlassung in GB*); ~ **countries** Ausland, Überseeländer; **O~Development Administration** *GB* Entwicklungsministerium; ~ **relations** Auslandsbeziehungen *GB*; ~ **resources development** Entwicklungshilfe; ~ **territories** überseeische Hoheitsgebiete; ~ **trade** Überseehandel, *brit* Außenhandel; ~ **trading corporation** *brit* Außenhandelsgesellschaft.

oversee beaufsichtigen.

overseer Aufseher *m*, Inspektor *m*; **~s of highways** Straßenbauamt; **~s of the poor** Armenpfleger, Fürsorgeamt.

oversell mehr verkaufen als lieferbar; zuviel verkaufen.

overset aufheben (*Beschluß*).

overside Überbord; ~ **delivery clause** Überbord-Auslieferungsklausel.

oversize Übergröße *f*.

overspend sein Einkommen überschreiten; über seine Verhältnisse leben.

overstate zu hoch angeben, übertreiben, überschätzen; ~ **one's case** sein Anliegen übertreiben.

overstatement of claims Geltendmachung von überhöhten Forderungen, Überberechnung.

overstay (Zeit) überschreiten; zu lange bleiben.

overstayer überfälliger Ausländer (*dessen Aufenthaltserlaubnis abgelaufen ist*).

overstock zu viel auf Lager haben.

oversubscribe überzeichnen.

oversubscription Überzeichnung *f*.

oversupervise *v/i* zu scharf überwachen.

oversupply Überangebot *n*.

overt offen, offenbar, offenkundig, nicht verborgen.

overtake überholen.

overtax zu hoch besteuern.

overtaxation übermäßige Besteuerung *f*.

over-the-counter direkt über den Ladentisch, bar, im Freiverkehr gehandelt, außerbörslich.

overtime Überstunden *f/pl*, Mehrarbeit *f*; ~ **pay** → *pay*; ~ **premium** Überstundenzuschlag.

overtrade sich absatzmäßig übernehmen; *Geschäfte mit zu geringem Betriebskapital betreiben.*

overture Eröffnung *f* (Verhandlungs)Angebot *n*; formeller Heiratsantrag *m*; Friedensangebot *n*.

overvaluation Überbewertung *f*.

overvalue überschätzen, überbewerten.

overweight Übergewicht *n*, zu hohes Gewicht *n*, Mehrgewicht *n*.

overwork Mehrarbeit *f*, übermäßig viel Arbeit *f*, Überbeschäftigung *f*.

owe schulden, schuldig sein, verdanken, zurückzuführen auf; ~ **allegiance** → *allegiance*.

owelty Gleichheit *f*, Ausgleichsschuld *f*; ~ **of exchange** Wertausgleich bei Grundstückstausch; ~ **of partition** Wertausgleichsrecht bei Naturalteilung.

owing unbezahlt, schuldig, geschuldet; ~ **and accruing** geschuldet (*einschließlich noch nicht fälliger Schulden*); **amount** ~ → *amount*; **balance** ~ → *balance*; **sum** ~ → *sum*.

own *adj* eigen; wirklich; ~ **account trading** Eigengeschäft(e); ~ **branders** Hausmarkenhändler; ~ **brother** leiblicher Bruder; ~ **consent in writing** eigenhändige schriftliche Zustimmung; ~ **consumption** Eigenverbrauch; ~ **costs** Selbstkosten; ~ **cousin** Vetter ersten Grades; ~ **financing** Eigenfinanzierung; ~ **insurance** → *insurance*; ~ **name** Name, Eigenname, persönlicher Name; ~ **property** → *property*; ~ **reserves** eigene Reserven; ~ **retention** Selbstbehalt; ~ **resources** Eigenmittel; ~ **risk** → *risk*; ~ **sole use** zu alleiniger Verwendung; ~ **use and benefit** *nur* zur eigenen Nutzung; **by one's ~ hand** eigenhändig; **in his ~ right** aus eigenem Recht.

own *v* das Eigentum haben, Eigentümer sein, zu eigen haben, (dinglich) berechtigt sein; besitzen (*unjuristisch*); bekennen, zugeben; ~ **a claim against a person** e–n Anspruch gegen jmdn haben; ~ **a life estate** ein lebenslängliches Nießbrauchsrecht haben; **family- ~ed enterprise** → *family*; **federally-~ed** bundeseigen; **foreign- ~ed** in ausländischem Eigentum stehend; **jointly ~ed** im gemeinsamen Eigentum.

owner Eigentümer *m*, *Träger e–s eigentumsähnlichen Herrschaftsrechts*, (dinglich) Berechtigter, Rechtsinhaber *m*, Besitzer *m*, **~'s (land) charge** Eigentümergrundschuld; ~ **for the time being** derzeitiger Eigentümer, jeweiliger Eigentümer; ~ **in fee simple** → *fee simple*; ~ **-occupation** Eigenbesitz (*Wohnungen, Eigenheime*); ~ **-occupied** eigengenutzt, vom Eigentümer bewohnt; ~ **-occupier** Grundeigentümer als Eigenbesitzer; ~ **of a patent** Patentinhaber; ~ **of an account** Kontoinhaber; ~ **of an estate** Grundeigentümer, Grundherr, Inhaber e–s Herrschaftsrechtes am Grundstück, am Grundstück Berechtigter, *vgl estate*; ~ **of a right** Berechtigter; ~ **possessor** Halter, der selbst Eigentümer ist (*Kfz*); ~ **pro tempore** zeitweiliger Eigentümer; **~'s public liability insurance** Eigentümerhaftpflichtversicherung; **~'s title** Eigentum, Grundstückseigentum; **absolute** ~ Volleigentümer, (unbeschränkter) Eigentümer; **abutting** ~ Anlieger; **actual** ~ faktischer Inhaber; **adjacent** ~ angrenzender Eigentümer, Anlieger; **beneficial** ~ wirtschaftlicher Eigentümer, eigentümerähnlicher Treuhandbegünstigter; billigkeitsrechtlicher Eigentümer, materieller E.; **bona fide** ~wirklicher Eigentümer; **co-**~ Miteigentümer; **common ~s** Miteigentümer; **entailed** ~ Vorerbe; **equitable** ~ wirtschaftlicher Eigentümer, Eigentümer im Innenverhältnis, Eigentümer nach Billigkeitsrecht; **estate** ~ Grundeigentümer *bzw* dingl berechtigter Grundpächter; eigentumsähnlich Berechtigter; **general** ~ Eigentümer; **joint** ~ Miteigentümer, Mitberechtigter; **land** ~ Grundeigentümer, Grundbesitzer; **legal** ~ Eigentümer; treuhänderischer Eigentümer; **limited** ~ beschränkter Eigentümer; Nießbrauchsberechtigter; **outright** ~ Volleigentümer; **part** ~ Teileigentümer, Parteninhaber (*bei Schiffen*), Mitberechtigter, Miteigentümer; **policy** ~ → *policy* (*1*); **previous** ~ Voreigentümer; **putative** ~ mutmaßlicher Eigentümer; **real** ~ *wirklicher* Eigentümer; **record** ~ urkundl nachgewiesener Eigentümer; dinglich Berechtigter; **registered** ~ eingetragener Eigentümer; **reputed** ~ vermutlicher Eigentümer (*Gemeinschuldner von Sachen in seinem Gewahrsam*); **rightful** ~ rechtmäßiger Eigentümer; **riparian** ~ Flußanlieger, Eigentümer des Ufergeländes; **sole and unconditional** ~Alleineigentümer; **special** ~ dinglich Berechtigter, Eigentümer auf Zeit; **subsequent** ~ Besitznachfolger; **true** ~ wirklicher Eigentümer.

ownership Eigentum(srecht) *n*; ~ **interest** Eigentumsanteil; ~ **of property** Sacheigentum; ~ **representation** Vertretung des Anteilseigners; **absolute** ~ (unbeschränktes) Eigentum; **bare** ~ bloßes Eigentumsrecht (*ohne Nutzungen*); **beneficial** ~ selbstgenutztes Vermögensrecht, wirtschaftliches Eigentum; **change in** ~ → *change*; **circular** ~ multilaterale kapitalmäßige Konzernverflechtung; **collective** ~ Gemeinschaftsbesitz, Kollektiveigentum; **common** ~ Miteigentum; **concurrent** ~ Miteigentum, Mitberechtigung, Teilhaberschaft; **corporate** ~ Gesellschaftseigentum; **cross** ~ Eigentumsverflechtung; Besitz verschiedener Kommunikationsmittel auf demselben Markt; **evidence of** ~ → *evidence*; **exclusive** ~ unbeschränktes Alleineigentum; **imperfect** ~ belastetes Eigentum; Eigentum auf Zeit; **incorporeal** ~ eigentumsähnliches Herrschaftsrecht an immateriellen Gegenständen; **joint** ~ Miteigentum (*zur gesamten Hand*); Mitberechtigung; **legal** ~ (juristisches) Eigentum; **multiple** ~ Konzentration von Eigentumsrechten, Konzernbildung; **naked** ~ bloßes Eigentumsrecht (*ohne Nutzungen*); **national** ~ Staatseigentum; **part** ~ Teileigentum, Bruchteilseigentum; **perfect** ~ dingliches Vollrecht; volles uneingeschränktes Eigentum, lastenfreies Eigentum; **public** ~ Staatseigentum; **reputed** ~ vermutetes Eigentum *des Gemeinschuldners an Sachen in seinem Besitz;* **reservation of** ~ Eigentumsvorbehalt; **right of** ~ Eigentumsrecht; **shared** ~ Bruchteilseigentum, Alleineigentum; **sole and unconditional** ~ unbeschränktes Alleineigentum; **special** ~ beschränktes Eigentum, dingliches Sicherungsrecht; **stock** ~ Aktienbesitz; **title to** ~ Eigentumstitel; **transfer of** ~ → *transfer*; **uncertain** ~ ungeklärtes Eigentumsverhältnis; **undivided** ~ Miteigentum zur gesamten Hand.

oyer gerichtliche Untersuchung *f*, mündliche Verhandlung *f*, Vorlage *f* und Verlesung *f* e–r streitgegenständlichen Urkunde, Ausfertigung *f* e–r Urkunde für den Prozeßgegner; ~ **and terminer** *königliche Ermächtigung für die Gerichtsbarkeit der Assisengerichte* (*bis 1971*); ~ **de record** Antrag auf richterliche Berücksichtigung e–r Urkunde; **court of** ~ **and terminer** → *court*.

oyez „Achtung“, „Ruhe im Gerichtssaal“ (*Ausruf des Gerichtswachtmeisters bei Sitzungsbeginn*).

P

PACE = *Police and Criminal Evidence Act 1984, GB.*

pack *s* Packung *f*, Ballen *m*, Bündel *n*.

pack *v* packen, verpacken, konservieren, eindosen; betrügerisch zusammensetzen, ein Gericht parteilich besetzen; **~ed as usual in trade** handelsüblich verpackt; **~ed for exportation by sea** seemäßig verpackt; **~ed for retail sale** in Aufmachung für den Einzelverkauf; **~ the court** das Gericht nach politischen Gesichtspunkten besetzen; **false ~ed** mit unzulässiger Beimischung verpackt (*Baumwollballen*); **mixed ~ed** verschiedene Qualitäten enthaltend; **water ~ed** feuchtes Gut enthaltend (*Baumwollballen, durch Wasserzusatz schwerer gemacht*).

package Paket *n*, Packstück *n*; Pakkung *f*, Verpackung *f*, Emballage *f*, Frachtgut *n*; **~ car** Waggon für Stückgutladung; **~ deal** Koppelungsgeschäft; **~ goods** abgepackte Ware; **~ holidays organization** Pauschal(ferien)reisen-Unternehmen; **~ of rights** Bündel von Rechten; **~ parcel** Sammelpaket (*kleine Sendungen an verschiedene Empfänger*); **~ policy** → *policy*; **~ tour** Pauschalreise; **~ ~** *operator: Pauschalreisen-Veranstalter*; **deceptive ~** Mogelpackung; **original ~** Originalverpackung, originalverpacktes Paket, Paket üblicher Art und Größe; **overall ~** *pol* (Gesamt-)Paket *von Verhandlungsangeboten*.

packaging Verpackung *f*, Packungsgestaltung *f*, Ausstattung *f*; **misleading ~** irreführende Pakkungsgestaltung; **shoddy ~** schäbige Verpackung.

packcloth Packtuch *n*, Packleinwand *f*.

packer Packer *m*, Verpacker *m*, Fleischwarenhersteller *m*.

packing Einpacken *n*, Verpacken *n*, Verpackung *f*; **~ charges** Verpakkungskosten; **~ credit** Versandbereitstellungskredit; **~ house** Fleischwarenfabrik, Obstpackerei, Warenlager; **~ list** Paketinhaltsliste, Versandliste; **~ material** Verpackung; **~ sheet** Packtuch, Packleinwand; **~ slip** Packzettel; **original ~** in Originalverpackung; **seaworthy ~** seemäßige Verpakkung, Seeverpackung.

pact Vertrag *m*, Pakt *m*, Übereinkunft *f*; **~ of mutual assistance** Beistandspakt; **~ of non-aggression** Nichtangriffspakt; **nude ~** Konsensualvertrag ohne Gegenleistungsversprechen, einseitiger Vertrag; **obligatory ~** formlose obligatorische Vereinbarung, obligatorischer Vertrag, reiner Konsensualvertrag.

pactional vereinbart, konventionell.

pactions völkerrechtliche Realverträge *m*|*pl*, sofort erfüllte Übereinkommen *n*|*pl*.

pactitious vertraglich geregelt.

pactum | de contrahendo Vorvertrag *m*; **~ de non alienando** vertragliches Veräußerungsverbot; **~ de non petendo** (=) vereinbarter Klageverzicht; **~ nudum** = *nude pact* → *pact*.

padding Polster *n*, überflüssiges Beiwerk *n* (*in e–m Schriftsatz*).

page *v* seitenweise numerieren.

paid (ein)bezahlt, gezahlt, Zahlung erhalten; **~-in** einbezahlt; **~ in full** voll bezahlt; **~ or declared** ausbezahlt bzw beschlossen (*Dividende*); **~ up** (*auch: ~-up*) voll einbezahlt, bezahlt.

pain Schmerz *m*, Pein *f*; **~ and suffering** Schmerzen, Schmerzensgeld; **~ award** Schmerzensgeld (*-bemessung*); **~s of law** *scot* Strafe; **mental ~ and suffering**

psychische Leiden; **on ~ of forfeiture** bei Meidung des Verfalls, mit Verfallsandrohung; **prospective ~** voraussichtliche Schmerzen; **under ~ of imprisonment** unter Androhung e–r Freiheitsstrafe.
paint *s* Farbe *f*, Malerarbeiten *f/pl*; *v* ausmalen, Schönheitsreparaturen durchführen.
paintwork Malerarbeit(en) *f/pl*.
pairing(-off) verabredete Abwesenheit *f* (*bzw Stimmenthaltung*) von zwei Parteigegnern im Parlament.
palimony suit *US* Klage auf Unterhalt für die Lebensgefährtin.
pallet Palette *f*, Pritsche *f*, Laderost *m*, Lagerbock *m*, Trockenbett *n*; **~ load** Palettenladung.
palliate beschönigen, bemänteln, (*Schmerz*) lindern.
palm *v* schmieren, bestechen.
palm off etwas aufschwindeln, abschieben (*Falschgeld*), betrügerisch in Verkehr bringen, Erzeugerbenennungsschwindel treiben.
palm oil Schmiergeld; „Schutzgebühr" *an Erpresser*.
palmarium zusätzliche Erfolgsgebühr *f*.
palmistry Wahrsagen *n* aus der Hand, Handlesen *n*.
palmprint evidence Identifizierung *f* durch Handballenabdruck.
palpable offensichtlich, offenkundig.
pamphlet Broschüre *f*, Flugschrift *f*, Pamphlet *n*, Abhandlung *f*; **~ laws** halbjährliche Gesetzessammlung.
pandects Pandekten *f/pl*.
pandemonium Tumult *m* (*zB parl*).
pander *s* Zuhälter *m*, Kuppler *m*.
pander *v* Kuppelei treiben.
panderer Zuhälter *m*, Kuppler *m*.
pandering Kuppelei *f*.
panel Gremium *n*, Kollegialgericht *n* (*Kammer, Senat*), Spruchkörper *m* e–s Gerichts, Geschworenenliste *f*; Liste *f* von Anwälten, Kassenärzten etc; Forum *n*, **~ discussion** Podiumsdiskussion; **~ doctor** → *doctor*; **~ house** Bordell; **~ of arbitrators** Schiedsrichterliste; **P~ on Take-overs and Mergers** *Aufsichtsgremium für Fusionen und Übernahmen GB*; **~ patient** Kassenpatient; **advisory ~** Beirat, beratender Ausschuß; **closed ~** begrenzte Anwaltsliste *e–r Rechtsschutzversicherung*; **electoral ~** Wählerliste; **local valuation ~** kommunale Steuerbewertungsstelle.
panhandle *s* schmaler Landstreifen.
panhandle *v* schnorren, betteln.
panhandler Straßenbettler, arbeitsscheuer Herumtreiber *m*.
panier Bursche *m*, Kellner *m* (*in Anwaltsinnungen*).
panellation Auswahl und Einsetzung *f* der Geschworenen.
pantomime Pantomime *f*, Gebärdenspiel *n*.
paper Papier *n*, Urkunde *f*, Schriftstück *n*, Akte *f*, Dokument *n*, Banknote *f*, Wechsel *m*, Brief *m*, Kurszettel *m*, Wertpapier *n*; Zeitung *f*; Prüfungsarbeit *f*, wissenschaftlicher Vortrag *m*, wissenschaftliche Arbeit *f*; **~s** Unterlagen, Akten; Prüfungsfragen; **~ bid** *Übernahmeangebot mit eigenen Aktien der übernehmenden Firma zu bezahlen*; **~ book** Aktenzusammenstellung für die höhere Instanz; **~ circulation** Papiergeldumlauf, Banknotenumlauf; **~ credit** offener Wechselkredit; **~ currency** Papiergeld, Papierwährung; **~ days** Sitzungstage; **~ duty** Papierzoll; **~ filed** Eingabe; **~ gold** goldwertes Papier (*Bezeichnung für Sonderziehungsrechte*); **~ hangings** Tapeten; **~ mill** Papierfabrik, Gerichtsarchiv; **~ logjam** Papierkrieg, Berg von Papieren; **~ money** → *money*; **~ of causes** Sitzungsliste; **~ of identity** Legitimationspapier; **~ office** *brit* Staatsarchiv; Gerichtsarchiv; **~s on appeal** Berufungsakten; **~ profit** → *profit*; **~ securities** Papierwerte, Papiereffekten; **~ shredder** Aktenwolf; **~ standard** → *standard*; **~ title** → *title*; **~ war** Zeitungskrieg, Pressekrieg; **~work** Schreibarbeit(en), „Papierkram", Durchsicht von Akten und Protokollen; **accommodation ~** Gefälligkeitswechsel; **ballot ~** →

ballot; **bank** ~ → *bank (1)*; **bond ~s** → *bond*; **bundle of ~s** → *bundle*; **commercial** ~ → *commercial paper*; **demand** ~ → *demand*; **eligible** ~ diskontfähiges Papier; beleihbare Effekten; **false ~s** gefälschte Papiere, schriftl Lüge, mittelbare Falschbeurkundung, falsche Schiffspapiere; **financial** ~ Handelsblatt, Börsenblatt; Finanzwechsel; **government** ~ → *government*; **green** ~ Ausschußbericht; **inconvertible** ~ reines Papiergeld; **long-dated** ~ langfristige Geldmarktpapiere; **mercantile** ~ Warenwechsel, Wertpapiere des Handelsrechts; **official ~s** amtliche Schriftstücke; **parliamentary ~s** Regierungsinformationsmaterial für Abgeordnete; **private ~s** Privatpapiere; **purchased** ~ im Wertpapierhandel erworbenes Papier; **registered** ~ Namenspapiere, vinkulierte Papiere; **revenue** ~ Liste von Steuersachen in der Rechtsmittelinstanz; **ship's ~s** → *ship*; **special** ~ Liste von Sonderterminen; **street** ~ über einen Makler gehandeltes Wertpapier (*nicht über die Bank*); **territorial ~s** → *territorial*; **testamentary** ~ Testament(surkunde); **three months'** ~ Dreimonatsakzept; **trade** ~ → *trade*; **moving ~s** Antragsschriftsatz mit Anlagen.

par Gleichheit *f*, Normalmaß *n*, Durchschnitt *m*; Pari *n*, Nennwert *m*, Parikurs *m*; ~ **clearance** Clearing zum Pariwert; ~ **collection** Inkasso zum Pariwert; ~ **emission** Pariemission; ~ **line** Aktienmittelwert; ~ **of exchange** Parikurs, Wechselparität; ~ **of stocks** Effektenparität; ~ **points** Pariplätze; ~ **rate of exchange** Parität, Währungsparität, Goldparität; ~ **redemption system** Parieinlösungssystem; ~ **remittance** Nettoüberweisung *ohne Abzüge*; ~ **value** → *value*; ~ **value share** → *share*; **no ~ value** → *no*; **no ~ value share** → *share*; **above** ~ über pari; **at** ~ zum Parikurs, Nennwert; **below** ~ unter pari; **exchange at** ~ Parikurs; **issue at** ~ Wert als pari; **nominal** ~ Nominalwert, Nennwert; **on a ~ with** gleichwertig mit; **to be on** ~ gleich sein; **to issue at** ~ zum Nennwert ausgeben; **to put on a ~ with** gleichstellen mit.

parachronism Parachronismus *m*, Zeitberechnungsfehler *m*.

parade | shed Vorführraum *m* zur Täteridentifizierung *f*; **identification** ~ → *identification*.

paradox of value Wertparadox *n*.

paragraph (*meist*) Absatz *m*, (*selten:*) Paragraph *m*; **consecutively numbered ~s** in numerischer Reihenfolge bezifferte Absätze.

paralegal Kanzleimitarbeiter *m*, rechtskundiger Vertreter *m*, Rechtsbeistand *m*.

parallelism Parallelismus *m*, Parallelität *f*, Übereinstimmung *f*; **conscious ~ of action** bewußte Parallelität *f* des Handelns, bewußtes gleichgerichtetes Verhalten *n*.

paramilitary militärähnlich.

paramount oberst(er, e, es), höchst(er, e, es), vorrangig, übergeordnet, überragend.

paramountcy Oberherrschaft *f*, Oberhoheit *f*, Vormachtstellung *f*, Vorrangstellung *f*.

paraph Paraphe *f*, Unterschrifts-Schnörkel *m*, Namenszug *m*, Unterschrift *f*.

paraphernalia Vorbehaltsgut *n* der Ehefrau.

paraphrase Paraphrase *f*, Interpretation *f*, freie Wiedergabe *f*.

parcel *s* Paket *n*, Bündel *n*, Ballen *m*, Partie *f*, Posten *m*, Stück *n*, Teil *n*; Grundstück *n*, Flurstück *n*, Parzelle *f*; ~ **goods** Stückgüter; ~ **makers** *hist* Steuereinzieher; ~ **of goods** Warenpartie; ~ **of land** Grundstück, Flurstück, Parzelle; ~ **of shares** Aktienpaket; ~ **office** Gepäckannahmestelle, Gepäckabfertigung; ~ **room** Handgepäckaufbewahrung; **by ~s** stückweise, in kleinen Posten; **by insured** ~ als Wertpaket; **bill of ~s** *bill (4)*.

parcel *v* abteilen, parzellieren, einpacken; ~ **an inheritance** e–e Erbteilung vornehmen.
parcelling Parzellierung *f*.
parcels Parzellen; *Grundstücksbeschrieb f in einer Auflassungsurkunde*; ~ **clause** *Abschnitt einer Auflassungsurkunde, der die Beschreibung des Grundstücks enthält.*
parcenary ungeteilter Nachlaßbesitz *m*, Eigentum *n* der Erbengemeinschaft am Nachlaßgrundstück.
parcener Miterbe *m*, Gesamthandelseigentümer *m* am Nachlaßgrundstück.
parchment Pergament *n*, Gerichtsurkunde *f*.
pardon *s* Begnadigung *f*, Gnadenerweis *m*, Straferlaß *m*, Gnadenrecht *n*, Pardon *n*; **absolute** ~ unbeschränkte Begnadigung; **act of** ~ Gnadenerweis; **board of** ~ Gnadenstelle, Gnadeninstanz; **conditional** ~ bedingter Straferlaß, Gnadenerweis mit Auflagen; **free** ~ unbeschränkte Begnadigung; **full** ~ volle Begnadigung; **general** ~ Amnestie; **partial** ~ Teilbegnadigung, teilweiser Straferlaß; **plea of** ~ Gnadengesuch.
pardon *v* begnadigen.
parent Elternteil *m*, Vater *m bzw* Mutter *f*; ~**s** Eltern; ~ **and child** Rechtsverhältnis zwischen Eltern und Kindern; ~ **branch** Hauptzweigstelle; ~ **company** → *company*; ~ **enterprise** Mutterunternehmen; ~ **firm** Stammhaus; ~ **store** Stammhaus; **custodial** ~ sorgeberechtigter Elternteil; **foster** ~**s** → *foster*; **intestate** ~ testamentslos verstorbener Elternteil; **natural** ~**s** natürliche Eltern, **non-custodial** ~ nicht-sorgeberechtigter Elternteil; **sole-custody** ~ (allein) sorgeberechtigter Elternteil; **surrogate** ~ Pflegevater bzw Pflegemutter, Ersatzelternteil.
parentage Abkunft *f*, Abstammung *f*, Familie *f*; **declaration of** ~ Vaterschaftsfeststellungsurteil; **of unknown** ~ unbekannter Abstammung.
parental elterlich, väterlich, mütterlich; ~ **rights and duties** elterliche Rechte und Pflichten, elterliche Sorge.
parentela Parentel *f*, Abkömmlinge *m*|*pl* e–s Stammvaters, Stamm *m*.
parenthesis Parenthese *f*, Klammer *f*, eingeklammerte Stelle *f*.
parenticide Elternmord *m*, Vatermord *bzw* Muttermord *m*.
pari mutuel Wettgemeinschaft *f*.
pari passu gleichrangig, gleichzeitig, gleichmäßig, in gleichen Quoten; ~ **agreement** Vereinbarung zur gleichrangigen Befriedigung; ~ **bonds** gleichrangig am Grundvermögen gesicherte Schuldverschreibungen; **to rank** ~ gleichen Rang haben, im Rang gleichstehen (*Forderungen*).
Paris | **Convention** Pariser (Verbands)Übereinkunft *f* (*über gewerblichen Rechtsschutz, erstmals 1883*); ~ **Declaration** Pariser Seerechtsdeklaration (1856); ~ **Treaties** Pariser Verträge (*1954 Aufhebung des Besatzungsstatuts der BRD*).
parish Gemeinde *f*, Gemeindebezirk *m*; Pfarrbezirk *m*, Kirchspiel *n*; Stadtbezirk *m*, Kommunalkörperschaft *f*, Landkreis *m*; Fürsorgebezirk *m*; ~ **church** Gemeindekirche, örtliche Kirchengemeinde; ~ **clerk** Küster, Kantor; ~ **constable** Gemeindepolizist; ~ **council** Gemeindevertretung, Gemeinderat; ~ **court** → *court*; ~ **law** Ortsrecht e–r Gemeinde; ~ **meeting** Gemeindeversammlung; ~ **officer** Küster, Gemeindevorstandsmitglied, Gemeindepolizist; ~ **property** gemeindeeigenes Grundstück; ~ **register** Kirchenbuch; ~ **relief** Fürsorge(unterstützung).
parishioner (*Grundsteuer zahlender*) Gemeindebewohner *m*.
paritor Gerichtsdiener *m*, Büttel *m*.
parity Parität *f*, Gleichheit *f*, Pariwert *m*, Währungsparität *f*, Umrechnungskurs *m*; ~ **clause** Paritätsklausel, Goldparitätsklausel; ~ **of notes** Nennwertparität von Banknoten; ~ **of stock** Effektenparität;

~ **payments** Zahlungen zum Parikurs; ~ **price** Parikurs; ~ **ratio** *Indexverhältnis von Agrarerzeugerpreisen zu den von den Landwirten bezahlten Preisen*; ~ **table** Paritätstabelle; **at the** ~ **of** zum Umrechnungskurs von; **commercial** ~ Handelsparität; **exchange** ~ → *exchange (2)*; **gold** ~ Goldparität; **nominal** ~ Nennwertparität; **purchasing power** ~ Kaufkraftparität.

parium judicium *Verfahren vor Richtern gleichen Ranges wie der Angeklagte.*

park *s* Park *m*, Parkgelände *n*, Naturschutzgebiet *n*, Jagdgehege *n*; **national** ~ Nationalpark, Naturschutzpark.

parking Parken *n*, Grünstreifen *m* (*am Bürgersteig und in Straßenmitte*), vorübergehendes Anlegen von Geldern; ~ **disk** (= *disc*) Parkscheibe; ~ **facilities** Parkmöglichkeiten; ~ **fee** Parkgebühr; ~ **place** Parkplatz; ~ **meter zone** Parkuhrbereich; ~ **regulations** Parkvorschriften; ~ **ticket** → *ticket*; ~ **under a street-light** „Laternengarage"; ~ **valet service** Parkabholdienst (*Flugplatz*); ~ **violation** Verstoß gegen Parkvorschriften; **covered** ~ überdachte Stellplätze; **dangerous** ~ verkehrsgefährdendes Parken; **double** ~ Parken in doppelter Reihe; **shoehorn** ~ Einparken auf engstem Raum; **street** ~ das Parken (*auf Straßen in Ortschaften*).

parkway Grünstreifen *m*; landschaftlich gestaltete Autostraße *f bzw* Autobahn *f*.

parlance Redeweise *f*, Sprache *f*; **common** ~ Umgangssprache; **in legal** ~ juristisch ausgedrückt; **legal** ~ Rechtssprache, juristische Ausdrucksweise.

parlementaire Parlamentär *m*, Unterhändler *m*.

parley *mil* Verhandlung *f*, Unterhandlung *f*.

parliament Parlament *n*, Abgeordnetenhaus *n*; Legislaturperiode *f*; **P~** das (*britische*) Parlament; **P~ Act** Parlamentsgesetz (*von 1911: Einschränkung der Macht des Oberhauses*); **P~ House** Justizpalast in Edinburgh (*die Justizgebäude des Court of Session qv*); ~ **rises** das Unterhaus vertagt sich; **P~ Rolls** = *Rolls of* ~ → *roll*; **duration of** ~ Legislaturperiode; **High Court of P~** → *high*; **letter of summons to** ~ Einberufungsdekret für Parlamentsabgeordnete; **prorogation of** ~ Beendigung der Sitzungsperiode des Parlaments; **session of** ~ Sitzungsperiode des Parlaments; **supremacy of** ~ Oberhoheit des Parlaments.

parliamentary parlamentarisch, den parlamentarischen Gepflogenheiten entsprechend; Parlaments . . .; **P~ Commissioner for Administration** *Parlamentsbeauftragter für Staatsverwaltungs-Überwachung*, „Ombudsman"; ~ **leader of a party** Fraktionsführer; **Parliamentary Undersecretary of State** parlamentarischer Staatssekretär.

parochial dörflich, Gemeinde . . ., Pfarr . . .; ~ **building** Kirchen- *bzw* Schulgebäude e–r Gemeinde; ~ **business** Gemeindeangelegenheiten; ~ **charity** gemeindegebundene Mildtätigkeit; ~ **church council** Gemeindekirchenrat; ~ **electors** Gemeindewahlberechtigte; ~ **officer** Gemeindebeamter; ~ **rates** Gemeindeabgaben; ~ **relief** Gemeindefürsorge.

parochialism Lokalpatriotismus *m*, Kirchturmpolitik *f*.

parol *adj* mündlich; formlos; ~ **evidence rule** Vermutung der Vollständigkeit und Richtigkeit e–r Urkunde, Unzulässigkeit des Zeugenbeweises bei Urkundenbeweismitteln.

parole *s* Ehrenwort *n*, *ehrenwörtliche Erklärung e–s Kriegsgefangenen, nicht wieder gegen den Gewahrsamsstaat zu kämpfen*; bedingter Straferlaß *f*; **P~ Board** Amt für bedingte Entlassung von Strafgefangenen, Gnadeninstanz; ~ **eligibility** Voraussetzung für bedingte Entlassung; ~ **officer** Bewährungshelfer; ~ **violation** Verstoß gegen die Auflagen der bedingten Entlassung; **discharge from** ~ endgültige Entlassung; **to be on** ~ bedingt entlassen sein.

parole *v* bedingt entlassen, auf Ehrenwort freilassen.

parolee *gegen Ehrenwort freigelassener Kriegsgefangener m*; bedingt Entlassener *m*.

parricide Vatermörder *m*, Vatermord *m*.

parsonage Pfarrhaus *n*, Ländereien *f/pl* und Pfründenrechte *f/pl* e–r Pfarrei.

part *s* Teil *m*, Stück *n*, Anteil *m*, Bestandteil *m*, Ausfertigung *f*, Glied *n*, Bezirk *m*, Gegend *f*; *adj* teilweise, Teil . . .; ~ **and parcel** wesentlicher Bestandteil; ~ **and pertinent** Grundstückszubehör; ~ **damage** Teilschaden; ~ **delivery** Teillieferung; ~ **loads** Stückgüter; ~**s of set** Einzelstück e–r Reihe; ~ **owner** → *owner*; ~ **ownership** → *ownership*; ~ **payment** Teilzahlung, teilweise Bezahlung; ~**s, pendicles and pertinents** Grundstückszubehör; ~ **performance** → *performance*; ~ **possession** Teilbesitz; ~**-time** Teilzeit; ~**-time employment** Teilzeitbeschäftigung; ~**-time job** nebenberufliche Beschäftigung; **accusatory** ~ → *accusatory*; **common** ~**s** zum Gemeinschaftseigentum gehörende Teile des Anwesens; gemeinsam genutzte Teile e–s Miethauses; **component** ~ Bestandteil, Bauteil, Komponente; **constituent** ~ Bestandteil; **copyrightable** ~ urheberrechtsfähiges Teilwerk; **in equal** ~**s** → *equal*; **in whole or in** ~ ganz oder teilweise; **integral** ~ Bestandteil (*e–r Sache*); **of the first** ~ erstgenannt „zu 1"; **of the one** ~ . . . **of the other** ~ einerseits . . . andererseits; **on the** ~ **of** seitens, von Seiten; **spare** ~ Ersatzteil; **substantial** ~ erheblicher Teil; **the privy** ~**s** die Scham- und Geschlechtsteile; **to do one's** ~ das Seine tun, seine Schuldigkeit tun; **wholly or in** ~ → *wholly*.

part *v/t* teilen, trennen, lösen, *v/i* sich trennen; verscheiden; ~ **with** sich (*e–r Sache*) entäußern, etwas aufgeben; ~ **with possession** den Besitz aufgeben.

partake of the profits am Gewinn teilnehmen.

partial voreingenommen, parteiisch; teilweise, Teil . . .; ~ **breach of contract** positive Vertragsverletzung, teilweise Schlechterfüllung.

partiality Voreingenommenheit *f*, Parteilichkeit *f*; **reasonable grounds for** ~ Besorgnis der Befangenheit.

partially teilweise, zum Teil; ~ **insured** teilversichert.

partibility Teilbarkeit *f*, Teilvererblichkeit *f*, Trennbarkeit *f*.

particeps criminis Tatbeteiligter *m*, Mittäter *m*, Komplize *m*.

participant Beteiligter *m*, Mitwirkender *m*, Teilhaber *m*.

participate beteiligt sein, zu gleichen Teilen beteiligt sein; teilnehmen, gemeinsam haben, teilhaben, sich beteiligen; am Gewinn beteiligt sein; ~ **equally in the profits** zu gleichen Teilen gewinnbeteiligt sein.

participating beteiligt, gewinnbeteiligt.

participation Teilhaberschaft *f*, Beteiligung *f*, Teilnahme *f*; ~ **account** → *account (2)*; ~ **agreement** Beteiligungsvertrag; ~ **certificate** → *certificate*; ~ **in an enterprise** Beteiligung an e–m Unternehmen; ~ **in earnings** Gewinnbeteiligung; ~ **in profits** Gewinnbeteiligung; **nominal** ~ formale Beteiligung.

participator Teilnehmer *m*, Teilhaber *m*, Gesellschafter *m*; ~ **in company** (*stiller*) Gesellschafter bzw Darlehensgläubiger *e–r close company qv*.

participatory decision making betriebliche Mitbestimmung *f*.

particular *s* Einzelangabe *f*, Einzelpunkt *m e–r Auskunft*; *pl* → *particulars*.

particular *adj* besonders, speziell, einzeln, individuell, örtlich, teilweise, ausführlich, umständlich, konkretisiert, privat.

particularism Partikularismus *m*, Kleinstaaterei *f*.

particularist Partikularist *m*, Lokalpatriot *m*.

particularity genügende Substantiierung; ~ **of pleading** ausreichend substantiierter schriftsätzl Vortrag.

particularize spezifizieren, substantiieren, auf Einzelheiten eingehen.

particulars besondere Umstände *m|pl*, nähere Umstände *m|pl*, Einzelheiten *f|pl*, Details *n|pl*; ~ **of an account** einzelne Posten e-r Abrechnung; ~ **of breaches and objections** genaue Angaben über die angebliche Schutzrechtsverletzung; ~ **of claim** Substantiierung der Klage(begründung); ~ **of criminal charges** Einzelheiten zur Anklage; ~ **of pleadings** Einzelheiten des schriftsätzlichen Vorbringens; ~ **of sale** Versteigerungsbeschreibung; ~ **of the risk** *ins* Gefahrenmerkmale; **application for** ~ Rüge der mangelnden Substantiierung; **application for further and better** ~ = *application for* ~ *qv*; **bill of** ~ → *bill (2)*; **full** ~ detaillierte Angaben, Spezifizierung; **material** ~ rechtserhebliche Tatsachenangaben; **personal** ~ Personalbeschreibung.

partisan Anhänger *m*, Partisan *m*; *adj:* parteilich, nicht neutral.

partitio legata Auseinandersetzung *f* aufgrund testamentarischer Teilungsanordnung.

partition *s* Teilung *f*, Grundstücksteilung *f*, Realteilung *f*, Aufteilung *f*, Auseinandersetzung *f*; Scheidewand *f*, Querwand *f*; ~ **action** → *action*; ~ **fences** Weidezäune; ~ **of a succession** Erbschaftsteilung, Nachlaßauseinandersetzung; ~ **of chattels** gerichtliche Teilungsanordnung bei beweglichen Sachen; ~ **of real estate** Grundvermögensaufteilung; Grundstücksauseinandersetzung; ~ **of the estate** Auseinandersetzung e-s Nachlasses; ~ **wall** → *wall*; **action for** ~ → *action*; **compulsory** ~ Zwangsteilung, Teilungsversteigerung; **deed of** ~ Teilungsurkunde, Teilungsauflassung; **distribution and** ~ Nachlaßauseinandersetzung; **owelty of** ~ → *owelty*; **procedure of** ~ Teilungsverfahren; **scheme of** ~ Teilungsplan; **voluntary** ~ vereinbarte Auseinandersetzung; **writ of** ~ → *writ*.

partition *v* teilen, verteilen, auseinandersetzen.

partner Partner *m*, Teilhaber *m*, Gesellschafter *m*; ~ **by estoppel** Gesellschafter kraft Rechtsscheins; ~**'s capital** Gesellschafterkapital; ~ **in interest** Beteiligter; ~ **in joint account** Teilhaber auf gemeinsame Rechnung; ~ **in name** Partner nur dem Namen nach; proforma Partner; ~**'s interest** Gesellschafteranteil; **acting** ~ tätiger Teilhaber; **active** ~ tätiger Gesellschafter, geschäftsführender Gesellschafter, persönlich haftender Gesellschafter; **actual** ~ firmierender, tätiger Gesellschafter; **admission of a** ~ Aufnahme e-s Gesellschafters; **associated** ~ unbeschränkt haftender Gesellschafter; **continuing** ~ verbleibender Gesellschafter; **dormant** ~ stiller Teilhaber; **expulsion of a** ~ Ausschließung e-s Gesellschafters; **fellow** ~ → *fellow*; **full** ~ persönlich haftender Gesellschafter, Komplementär; **general** ~ persönlich haftender Gesellschafter, Komplementär; **incoming** ~ neu eintretender Gesellschafter, **junior** ~ Juniorpartner; **limited** ~ Kommanditist; **liquidating** ~ Liquidator, Gesellschafter als Liquidator; **managing** ~ geschäftsführender Gesellschafter; **marital** ~ Ehegatte; **nominal** ~ Scheingesellschafter, Strohmann-Gesellschafter; **ordinary** ~ persönlich haftender Gesellschafter; **ostensible** ~ nomineller Gesellschafter, Scheingesellschafter; Gesellschafter kraft Rechtsscheins; **outgoing** ~ ausscheidender Gesellschafter; **personally liable** ~ persönlich haftender Gesellschafter, Komplementär; **quasi** ~ Mitbesitzer (*ohne Gesellschafter zu sein*), gesellschaftsähnlich Beteiligter; **responsible** ~ persönlich haftender Gesellschafter; **retiring** ~ ausscheidender Gesellschafter; **salaried** ~ Gesellschafter mit Anstellungsverhältnis; **secret** ~ *geheim gehaltener* stiller Teilhaber; **senior** ~ Seniorpartner, Hauptteilhaber; **silent** ~ stiller Teilhaber, (*auch:*) Kommanditist; **sleeping** ~ = *silent* ~ *qv*; **solvent** ~ vom Konkurs nicht betroffener Gesellschafter; **special** ~ Kommanditist; **surviving** ~ (*bei Tod des Mitgesellschafters*) die Gesellschaft fortsetzender Gesellschafter; **to buy out a** ~ e–n Teilhaber abfinden; **undisclosed** ~ stiller Teilhaber; **unlimited** ~ persönlich haftender Gesellschafter, Komplementär; **withdrawing** ~ ausscheidender Gesellschafter; **working** ~ tätiger Gesellschafter.

partnership Sozietät *f*, (Personal)Gesellschaft *f*, Teilhaberschaft *f*, Offene Handelsgesellschaft *f*; ~ **agreement** Gesellschaftsvertrag; ~ **articles** Gesellschaftsvertrag; ~ **assessment** gemeinsame Veranlagung der Gesellschafter; ~ **assets** Gesellschaftsvermögen; ~ **association** Gesellschaftsgründung (*e–r Personalgesellschaft*); ~ **at will** jederzeit kündbare Gesellschaft, Gesellschaft auf Widerruf; ~ **books** Bücher der Handelsgesellschaft; ~ **by estoppel** Gesellschaft kraft Rechtsscheins; ~ **capital** Gesellschaftskapital; ~ **certificate** Gründungsurkunde (*e–r Personalgesellschaft*); ~ **debts** Gesellschaftsschulden; ~ **firm** (Gesellschafts)Firma; ~ **funds** → *fund*; ~ **in commendam** Kommanditgesellschaft; ~ **in syndicate** Konsortialbeteiligung; ~ **insurance** Teilhaberversicherung; ~ **interest** Gesellschaftsanteil, Anteil am Gesellschaftskapital; ~ **property** Gesellschaftsvermögen; ~ **purpose** Gesellschaftszweck; **collaborative** ~ Arbeitsgemeinschaft (*ARGE*) *von Firmen*; **commercial** ~ (*meist: Offene*) Handelsgesellschaft; **dormant** ~ stille Gesellschaft; **general** ~ offene Handelsgesellschaft; **illegal** ~ rechtlich unzulässige Gesellschaft, Gesellschaft mit widerrechtlichen Zwecken; **implied** ~ faktische Gesellschaft; **industrial** ~ Gewinnbeteiligung der Arbeitnehmer; **leonine** ~ Societas leonia; **limited** ~ Kommanditgesellschaft; **memorandum of** ~ Gesellschaftsvertrag; **mercantile** ~ (*meist: Offene*) Handelsgesellschaft; **mining** ~ Bergbaugenossenschaft; Gewerkschaft; **mixed** ~ gemischte Sozietät (mit Nichtanwälten); **non-trading** ~ Sozietät, nicht gewerbliche Personalgesellschaft; **oral** ~ auf mündliche Vereinbarung beruhende Gesellschaft; **ordinary** ~ Offene Handelsgesellschaft; lang eingeführte Handelsgesellschaft; **particular** ~ Gelegenheitsgesellschaft; **presumption of** ~ Vermutung e–r Gesellschafterhaftung; **private** ~ *Personalgesellschaft mit nicht mehr als 50 Gesellschaftern*; **professional** ~ Sozietät; **secret** ~ stille Beteiligung; **shipping** ~ Reederei; **sleeping** ~ stille Gesellschaft; **special** ~ Gelegenheitsgesellschaft, Kommanditgesellschaft; **sub**~ Unterbeteiligung; **trading** ~ Handelsgesellschaft, *im Warenhandel tätige* offene Handelsgesellschaft; **universal** ~ *Personalgesellschaft mit Einbringen des Gesamtvermögens aller Gesellschafter*; **unlimited** ~ Offene Handelsgesellschaft.

parturition Entbindung *f*.

party *s* (pl: **parties** = ~**ies**) Partei *f* (= *P bzw* . . .*p*), Beteiligter *m*, Person *f*, streitender Teil *m*, Seite *f*; Abteilung *f*, Partie *f*, Interessent *m*; ~ **absolutely entitled** der Berechtigte; ~ **affiliation** Zugehörigkeit zu *e–r P*; ~ **aggrieved** die beschwerte *P*; ~ **and** ~ die streitenden *P–en* unmittelbar; ~ **and** ~ **costs** erstattungsfähige Kosten;

~ies' and privies die unmittelbaren Vertrags*p–en*; **~ appealing** Berufungsführer; **~ at fault** der schuldige Teil; **~ chargeable** die kostenpflichtige *P*; **~ concerned** Mitbeteiligter, Interessent; **~ entitled to claim** Anspruchsberechtigter; **~ entitled to receive** Empfangsberechtigter; **~ hardliners** getreue Parteianhänger; **~ in breach** vertragsbrüchige *P*; **~ in default** säumige *P*, in Verzug befindliche *P*; **~ insured** Versicherter; **~ in interest** beteiligte *P*; **~ interested** Mitbeteiligter, Mitinteressent; **~ies in actions** Prozeßparteien; **~ies in the cause** *P–en* des Schiedsverfahrens; Aussonderungsberechtigte; **~ jury** mehrsprachig *bzw mehrrassisch* zusammengesetztes Geschworenengericht; **~ labels** Dogmen e–r *P*; **~ leadership** Parteiführung; **~ liable** Schuldner, Verpflichteter, Haftender; **~ liable for costs** Kostenschuldner; **~ liable to recourse** Regreßpflichtiger, Regreßschuldner; **~ liable under a contract** vertraglich verpflichtete *P*; **~ line** *P*linie, *P*kurs; **~ machinery** *P*apparat; **~ man** *P*mann; **~ member** *P*mitglied; **~ of the first part** die erstgenannte (*Vertrags*) *P, P* zu 1); **~ official** Mitglied des *P*vorstandes; **~ opposed** Prozeßgegner; **~ or privy** Beteiligter (*an e–r Straftat*); **~ presenting** *den Wechsel* vorlegende *P*; **~ rally** *P*versammlung; **~ resolution** *P*versammlungsbeschluß, Fraktionsbeschluß; **~ ticket** Sammelfahrschein; **~ to a bill** Wechselverpflichteter; **~ to a contract** Vertrags*p*, Kontrahent, Vertragspartner; **~ to administrative proceedings** *P* e–s Verwaltungsstreitverfahrens; **~ to an action** Prozeß*p*; **~ to an agreement** Vertrags*p*, Vertragsgegner; **~ to an offence** Teilnehmer e–r strafbaren Handlung; **~ to be charged** die in Anspruch zu nehmende *P*, der Beklagte; **~ to the proceedings** Prozeß*p*; **~ to the suit** Prozeß*p*; **act of ~** → *act*; **additional ~** Streitverkündeter; zusätzlicher Kläger *bzw* Beklagter; **adverse ~** Gegenpartei; **charter ~** → *charter*; **contending ~ies** Prozeß*p–n*; **contracting ~ies** Vertrags*p–en*, vertragschließende *P–en*; **defaulting ~** säumige *P*, vertragsbrüchige *P*; **formal ~ies** unmittelbare *P–en (nur wirtschaftlich am Rechtsstreit interessiert)*; **indispensable ~ies** notwendige Streitgenossen; **injured ~** → *injure*; **innocent ~** der schuldlose Teil (*Ehescheidung*); **intervening ~** Nebenintervenient, Hauptintervenient; **litigant ~ies** *P–en* des Rechtsstreits, Prozeß*p–en*; **losing ~** (= *defeated* ~) unterliegende *P*; **moving ~** Antragsteller; **necessary ~ies** notwendige Streitgenossen; *P–en* deren Erscheinen absolut notwendig ist; **nominal ~** Streitgenosse ohne eigenes Prozeßinteresse; **non-defaulting ~** vertragstreue *P*; **non-observant ~** vertragsbrüchige *P*; **observant ~** vertragstreue *P*; **one ~'s act** einseitige Handlung; **opposing ~** Gegen*P*, Prozeßgegner; **opposite ~** Gegen*p*; **opposition ~** Oppositions*p*; **parliamentary ~** Fraktion; **prevailing ~** obsiegende *P*; **primary ~** Hauptschuldner; **private ~** private Gruppe, geschlossene Gesellschaft; **proper ~** die richtige *P*, der richtige Kläger *bzw* Beklagte; **real ~ (in interest)** die materiell berechtigte *P*, die aktiv legitimierte *P*; **restricted ~** Partei der Beschränkungen auferlegt sind; **secondary ~** Rückgriffsschuldner; Tatbeteiligter, Tatgehilfe; **the defaulting ~** die säumige, vertragsverletzende *P*; **the guilty ~** der schuldige Teil (*Scheidung*); **the High Contractings P~ies** die Hohen Vertrags*p–en*; **the immediate ~ies** die unmittelbar aufeinander folgenden *P–en* e–s Wechsels;**the innocent third ~** der gutgläubige Dritte; **the other ~** die Gegen*p*; **the ~ies concerned** die Beteiligten, die *P–en*; **the ~ies hereto** die *P–en (dieses Vertrages*); **the**

~ies, their successors and assigns die Parteien (und), ihre Gesamt- und Einzelrechtsnachfolger; **third ~** → *third*; **third ~ debtor** → *third*; **third ~ risk** → *third*; **unassisted ~** Partei ohne Prozeßkostenhilfe; **unsuccessful ~** unterlegene *P*, Verlierer; **wronged ~** Verletzter, Geschädigter.

party-wall Kommunmauer *f*, Gemeinschaftsmauer *f*; Brandmauer *f*.

pass *s* Passierschein *m*, Ausweis *m*; Durchgang *m*; Urlaubsschein *m*; Dauerkarte *f*, Freifahrkarte *f*; bestandenes Examen *n*; **~book** Kontogegenbuch, Bankbüchlein (*des Kunden*), Sparbuch; Einlagen-Kontobuch; *brit* Zollscheinheft; **~~** *savings account:* Spar(buch)konto; **~-check** Passierschein; **~ degree** Graduierung mit der Note „bestanden"; **~ office** Passierscheinstelle; **~ sheet** Grenzpassierschein; **~ word** Parole, Kennwort, Geheimwort; **free ~** Freikarte, Freifahrtschein.

pass *v* passieren, vorbeifahren, überholen; (Urteil) erlassen, abgeben; befinden (*über etw*), verhängen; verabschieden, unbeanstandet lassen; übergehen; übertragen; zukommen lassen; verbreiten, in Verkehr bringen; **~ a dividend** e–e Dividende nicht auszahlen; **~ a vote of thanks** e–e Danksagung beschließen; **~ an act** ein Gesetz verabschieden; **~ an entry** e–e Buchung vornehmen; **~ an item to an account** e–n Posten auf e–m Konto verbuchen; **~ and repass** auf Hin- und Rückweg passieren; **~ bad work** schlechte Arbeit durchgehen lassen (*Architekt*); **~ counterfeit money** Falschgeld in Verkehr bringen; **~ed by censor** von der Zensur freigegeben; **~ for** gelten als; **~ for military service** für diensttauglich erklären; **~ into law** Gesetz werden; **~ off as** ausgeben als; **~ sentence** über das Strafmaß entscheiden, e–e Strafe verhängen; **~ the chair** den Vorsitz übergeben; **~ title** Eigentum übertragen, übereignen; **~ to a person's account** jmdm in Rechnung stellen; **~ with the land** mit dem Grundstück übertragen werden, auf den jeweiligen Grundeigentümer übergehen; **the risk ~es** die Gefahr geht über; **title ~es** das Eigentum geht über; **to be ~ed** zur Genehmigung vorlegen, überprüfen, über etwas entscheiden.

passable begehbar, passierbar.

passage Durchgang *m*, Überfahrt *f*, Flug *m*; Verabschiedung *f* e–s Gesetzes; **~ broker** *brit* Auswanderungsagent; **~ contract** (Personen-)Beförderungsvertrag; **P~ Court** *Stadtgericht in Liverpool*; **~ home** Heimfahrt, Rückführungskosten in die Heimat; **~ money** Fahrgeld, Schiffspassagekosten, Personenbeförderungsentgelt; **by ~ of time** durch Zeitablauf; **final ~** dritte Lesung, Verabschiedung e–s Gesetzes; **innocent ~** friedliche Durchfahrt; **public ~** öffentl Durchfahrtsrecht; **right of ~** → *right*; **simple ~** bloße Durchfahrt.

passenger Fahrgast *m*, Fluggast *m*, Passagier *m*; **~ accommodation** Passagierräume; **~ agent** Fahrkartenschalterbeamter, Reiseagent; **~ and goods traffic** Personen- und Güterverkehr; **~ car** Personenwagen (*Eisenbahn*), Personenauto; **~ certificate** Zulassung für Personenbeförderung; **~ complaints table** Beschwerdetabelle von Passagieren; **~ concourses** Verkehrsflächen für Flugreisende; **~ contract** Personenbeförderungsvertrag; **~'s luggage** Reisegepäck; **~ mile** Passagiermeile; **~'s own risk** auf eigene Gefahr des Fahrgastes; **~ rates** Personentarif; **~ ship** Fahrgastschiff; **~ side of car** die Seite des Beifahrers; **~ traffic** Personenverkehr; **~ train** Personenzug, Eisenbahnzug für Personenbeförderung; **~ vehicle** Fahrzeug zur Personenbeförderung; **by ~ train** als Eilgut; **carriage of ~s** Personenbeförderung; **fare-paying ~** zahlender Passagier (*bzw Fluggast usw*).

passer-by Passant *m*.
passing Überholen *n*; **improper ~** falsches Überholen; **no ~** Überholverbot.
passing counterfeit money Inverkehrbringen von Falschgeld.
passing of title Eigentumsübergang *m*, Rechtsübergang *m*.
passing off Ursprungstäuschung *f*; Nachbau *m*, Nachahmung *f*, Warenzeichenmißbrauch *m*; **~ action** Klage wegen falscher Herkunftsangabe.
passion Leidenschaft *f*, Wut *f*, Ärger *m*, Zorn *m*; erotisches Verlangen *n*, Liebhaberei *f*; **in the heat of ~** in leidenschaftlicher Erregung, im Affekt.
passive passiv, untätig, duldend, mit Auflagen belastet; unverzinslich.
pass-over system Finanzausgleich *m* zwischen Händlern; **profit ~** Gewinnausgleichssystem (*an den geschützten Händler wird Teil des Verkaufsgewinns gezahlt*).
passport Paß *m*, Reisepaß *m*, Seepaß *m*, Passierschein *m*, Hafenpassierschein *m*, Schiffsmanifest *n*; Schiffspaß *m* (*für neutrales Schiff*); **~ control** Paßkontrolle; **~ forgery** Paßfälschung; **~ inspection** Paßkontrolle; **~ inspection point** (Paß-) Abfertigungsstelle; **alias ~** auf fremden Namen ausgestellter Reisepaß; **bearer of a ~** Inhaber e–s Passes; **collective ~** Sammelpaß; **diplomatic ~** Diplomatenpaß; **issuance of a ~** Ausstellung e–s Passes; **opened ~** aufgeschlagener Paß; **Nansen ~** → *Nansen*; **valid ~** gültiger Paß.
past due überfällig, in (Zahlungs-) verzug.
pasturage Weiderecht *n*.
pasture Weiderecht *n*, Weideland *n*; **~ lands** Weideland, Wiesengründe; **common of ~** → *common s*.
patent *adj* offen, offenkundig, unverborgen, ungesiegelt.
patent *s* Patent *n* (= *P bzw p*), Einzelkonzession *f*; Bestallungsurkunde *f*, Freibrief *m*, Privileg *n*; **P~ Act** *P*gesetz; **~ action** *P*klage, *P*prozeß; **~ advertising** *P*berühmung; **~ agency** Tätigkeit des *P*anwalts; **~ agent** (technischer) *P*anwalt; **~ amendment** *P*berichtigung; **~ applicant** *P*anmelder; **~ application** *P*anmeldung; *cf application (2)*; "**~ applied for**" „*P* angemeldet"; **~ article** gesetzlich geschützter Handelsartikel, Markenartikel; **~ attorney** (juristischer) *P*anwalt; **~ award** *P*gutachten; **P~ Bar** *P*anwaltschaft; **~ barred** Verweigerung der *P*erteilung; **P~ Bill Office** *Amt für königl Patente und Konzessionen (ohne Erfindungspatente)*; **~ branch** *P*fach; **~ case** *P*streitsache; **~ charges** *P*kosten; **~ claim** *P*anspruch; **~ class** *P*klasse; **~ classification** *P*klassifikation; **P~ Compensation Board** *P*entschädigungsamt (*US, zB Enteignung von nuklearen Patenten*); **~ consolidation** *P*zusammenfassung; **~ contest** *P*streit; **P~s Court** *P*gericht (*Abt des Chancery Ct*); **~ description** *P*beschreibung; **~ drawing** *P*zeichnung; **~ drawing and specification** *P*schrift; **~ examiner** *P*prüfer; **~ exchange agreement** *P*austauschvertrag; **~ exploitation** *P*ausübung, *P*verwertung; **~ fee** → *fee (1)*; **~ foods** Markennahrungsmittel; **~ for invention** *P*, Erfindungs*p*; **~ holder** *P*inhaber; **~ in force** gültiges *P*; **~ infringement** *P*verletzung; **~ infringement proceedings** *P*verletzungsverfahren; **~ law** → *law*; **~ law firm** *P*anwaltsbüro; **~ lawyer** *P*anwalt; **~ legislation** *P*gesetzgebung; **~ licence** *P*lizenz; **~ litigation** *P*prozeß, *P*streitsache; **~ medicine** warenzeichenrechtlich geschütztes (*nicht rezeptpflichtiges*) Arzneimittel; **~ monopoly** *P*monopol; **~ name** rechtlich geschützter Name; **~ of addition** Zusatz*p*; **~ of importation** Einfuhr*p*; **~ of improvement** Verbesserungs*p*; **~ of nobility** Adelsbrief; **~ of precedence** → *precedence*; **P~ Office** *P*amt; **P~ Office Journal** *P*blatt; **P~ Office procedure** patent-

amtlicher Geschäftsgang, Verfahren vor dem *P*amt; ~ **owner** *P*besitzer; ~ **pending** *P*anmeldung läuft; ~ **pool** Interessengemeinschaft an *P–en*, *P*kartell; ~ **power** Befähigung zur *P*erteilung; ~ **protection** *P*schutz; **P~ Register** *P*rolle; ~ **reports** *P*berichte; ~ **right** *P*anspruch, *P*recht; **~-right dealer** *P*makler; ~ **rolls** *GB amtliche Urkunden über königliche Konzessionen, Vergabe von Lehen und Privilegien*; **P~ Rules** patentamtliche Vorschriften; ~ **solicitor** → *solicitor*; ~ **specification** *P*beschreibung, *P*schrift; ~ **sued upon** Klage*p*, Streit*p*; ~ **suit** *P*streitsache, *P*klage; ~ **system** *P*wesen; ~ **writ** → *writ*; **abridgments of ~s** → *abridgment*; **active** ~ gültiges *P*, bestehender *P*schutz; **additional** ~ Zusatz*p*; **basic** ~ Grund*p*; **blocking-off** ~ Blockier*p*, Sperr*p*; **breach of** ~ Verletzung von *P*rechten; **chartered** ~ **agent** (eingetragener) *P*anwalt, zugelassener *P*anwalt; **Chartered Institute of P~ Agents** *P*anwaltskammer; **classification of ~s** → *classification*; **collateral** ~ Neben*p*; parallel laufendes *P*; **combination** ~ *P* für Kombinationserfindung; **Commissioner of P~s** *US* Präsident des *P*amts; **complete ~ specification** endgültige *P*beschreibung; **Comptroller-General of P~s** *brit* Präsident des *P*amts; **compulsory working of ~s** Ausübungszwang für *P–e*; **confirmation** ~ Bestätigungs*p*; Sicherungs*p*; **contents of** ~ *P*inhalt; **contributory infringement of a** ~ *P*verletzung; **dead wood** ~ Papier*p*; **defective** ~ mangelhaftes *P*; **design** ~ → *design*; **desire of** ~ *P*begehren; **device** ~ Vorrichtungs*p*; **divisional ~ application** → *application (2)*; **duration of** ~ Dauer e–s *P–s*, Laufzeit e–s *P–s*; **earlier** ~ älteres *P*, früher eingereichtes *P*; **expiration of a** ~ → *expiration*; **expired** ~ abgelaufenes *P*; **exploitation of a** ~ *P*verwertung; **extension of a** ~ → *extension*; **extent of a** ~ Geltungsbereich e–s *P–s*; **fencing-in** ~ Einkreisungs*p*; *Patent zur Entwertung e–s ähnlichen Patents*; **filing of an application for** ~ Einreichung e–r *P*anmeldung; **foreign** ~ Auslands*p*; **forfeiture of a** ~ Verfall e–s *P*; **free-lance** ~ Wegelagerer*p*; **freed** ~ zum Gebrauch freigegebenes *P*; **Government P~s Board** staatlicher *P*ausschuß, *P*amt; **grant of a** ~ → *grant*; **improvement** ~ Verbesserungs*p*, *P* auf e–e Verbesserungserfindung; **independent** ~ selbständiges *P*, Haupt*p*; **interfering** ~ Kollisions*p*; **International P~ Classification (IPC)** Internationale Klassifikation; **International P~ Office at The Hague** Internationales *P*amt, Den Haag; **issue of a** ~ Erteilung e–s *P–s*, *P*erteilung; **joint** ~ gemeinsames *P*; **joint applicants for a** ~ Mitanmelder e–s *P–s*; **lapsed** ~ verfallenes *P*; **later-dated** ~ Nach*p*; **lease of a** ~ Verpachtung e–s *P–s*; Überlassung e–s *P–s* zur Verwertung; **letters** ~ *P*, *P*urkunde, Konzession, **licence under a** ~ → *licence*; **life of a** ~ *P*dauer, Schutzdauer e–s *P–s*; **litigious** ~ Streit*p*, strittiges *P*, streitgegenständliches *P*; **main** ~ Haupt*p*; **master** ~ Grund*p*; **mate's** ~ → *mate*; **non-use of a** ~ Nichtverwertung e–s *P–s*, unterlassene *P*ausübung; **non-working of a** ~ Nichtausübung e–s *P–s*; **object matter of a** ~ Aufgabe e–s *P–s*; **opposition to the grant of a** ~ Einspruch gegen Erteilung e–s *P–s*; **original** ~ Haupt*p*, Stamm*p*; **ownership of the** ~ Eigentumsrecht am *P*; **paper** ~ nur auf dem Papier stehendes *P*, nutzloses *P*; **parent** ~ Haupt*p*, Stamm*p*; **pending** ~ laufendes *P*; **petty** Gebrauchsmuster; **pioneer** ~ bahnbrechendes *P*, Stamm*p*; **plant** ~ Pflanzen*p*; **President of the P~ Office** Präsident des *P*amts; **posthumous** ~ → *posthumous*; **printed ~ specification** *P*schrift; **prior** ~ älteres *P*, Vor*p*; **process** ~ Verfahrens*p*; **product** ~ Erzeugnis*p*, Stoff*p*; **provisional** ~ **specification** vorläufige *P*beschreibung; **refusal of** ~ Ablehnung des *P*antrags; **reissue** ~ Abänderungs*p*; **related** ~ Bezugs*p*, Haupt*p*; **restoration of lapsed** ~**s** Wiederherstellung verfallener *P–e*; **reversionary** ~ Anwartschafts*p*; **revocation of a** ~ → *revocation*; **sale of** ~ *P*verkauf; **scope of a** ~ (Schutz-) Umfang e–s *P–s*; **secret** ~ Geheim*p*; **shot-gun** ~ Wegelagerer*p*; **subject matter of a** ~ Gegenstand e–s *P–s*; *P*gegenstand; **subsequent** ~ jüngeres *P*, Nach*p*; **surrender of a** ~ Verzicht auf ein *P*; **term of a** ~ Laufzeit e–s *P–s*, *P*dauer; **to abandon a** ~ → *to abandon*; **universal** ~ Welt*p*, *P* von Weltbedeutung; **working of a** ~ Anwendung e–s *P–s*; Ausführung e–s *P–s*.

patent *v* patentieren, patentieren lassen; ~**ed article** patentrechtlich geschützter Gegenstand; Markenartikel; ~**ed process** patentiertes Verfahren.

patentability Patentfähigkeit *f*, Patentierbarkeit *f*.

patentable patentfähig, patentierbar; ~ **invention** → *invention*.

patentee Patentinhaber *m*, Erstinhaber *m* e–s Patents; **intended** ~ Patentanmelder; **joint** ~ Mitinhaber e–s Patents; **sole** ~ alleiniger Patentinhaber.

patentor Patentamt *n*.

paternal väterlich, Vater...; ~ **power** elterliche Gewalt; ~ **property** Vermögen väterlicherseits.

paternalism Paternalismus *m*, väterliche Fürsorge *f*.

paternity Vaterschaft *f*; ~ **suit** Abstammungsfeststellungsklage, Vaterschaftsklage; ~ **test** Untersuchung zum Abstammungsbeweis; **acknowledgment of** ~ Vaterschaftsanerkenntnis; **recognition of** ~ Vaterschaftsanerkenntnis.

patient Patient *m*; *bes Patient e–r Nervenheilanstalt*; Geisteskranker *m*; **mental** Patient in e–r Nervenheilanstalt; **voluntary** ~ freiwilliger Patient (*in Nervenheilanstalt*).

patrial Staatsbürger von Großbritannien: *brit Staatsangehöriger mit Wohnsitzrecht in GB und unbeschränkter Ein- und Ausreisemöglichkeit; seit 1981 ersetzt durch "British citizen"*.

patriation *v/t* einbürgern, in die eigene Stadt einbeziehen.

patricidal vatermörderisch; verräterisch.

patricide Vatermörder *m*, Vatermord *m*.

patrimonial ererbt, von väterlicher Seite ererbt.

patrimony Vermögen *n* väterlicherseits, väterliches Erbe *n*, Erbgut *n*.

patrol Streife *f*, Runde *f*, Patrouille *f*, Stoßtrupp *m*; ~ **car** Streifenwagen; ~ **wagon** Polizeiauto, Gefangenentransportwagen; **dog** ~ Streife mit Polizeihund, Hundestreife; **police** ~ → *police*.

patrolman Polizist *m*, Aufseher *m*; ~ **vessel** Küstenwachboot.

patron Patron *m*, Protektor *m*, Schirmherr *m*, Gönner *m*, Förderer *m*, Kunde *m*, Besucher *m*; Kirchenpatron *m*, Besitzer *m* e–s Patronats.

patronage Patronat *n*, Schirmherrschaft *f*, Schutz *m*, Protektion *f*; Pfründeverleihungsrecht *n*, Recht *n* auf Ämterbesetzung; Kundschaft *f*; ~ **dividend** Rabattmarke; ~ **letter** Patronatserklärung (*garantieähnliche Erklärung e–r Muttergesellschaft für Bonität der Tochter*); ~ **refund** Kundenrabatt; ~ **secretary** Parlamentssekretär des brit Premierministers, *zugleich chief government whip, vgl whip*; **Royal** ~ Vorzugsstellung als Hoflieferant.

patroness Förderin *f*, Beschützerin *f*, Schutzheilige *f*, Besitzerin *f* e–s Patronats, Kirchenpatronin *f*.

patronize unterstützen, protegieren, Stammkunde sein, Stammgast sein.

patter Rotwelsch *n*, Gaunersprache *f*, Jargon *m*.

pattern Muster *n*, Modell *n*, Warenprobe *f*, Probestück *n*; ~ **articles** Massenwaren; ~ **bombing** Flächenbombardierung; ~ **design** Probemodell, Schablone, Plan, Anlage, Struktur; ~ **maker** Modellmacher, Modelleur; ~ **parcel** Mustersendung; **behaviour** ~ Verhaltensweise; **reference** ~ Ausfallmuster, Warenprobe; **registered** ~ Gebrauchsmuster; registriertes Gebrauchsmustermodell; **standard** ~ Einheitsmuster.

pauper arme Partei *f*, *Kläger m oder Beklagter m, dem das Armenrecht bewilligt ist*; Unterstützungsempfänger *m*; ~ **grave** Armengrab; ~ **legislation** Armengesetzgebung; ~ **lunatic** Geisteskranker mit Gemeindefürsorgeunterstützung; ~ **petition** Armenrechtsantrag; ~ **relief** Armenunterstützung; **~'s oath** eidliche Versicherung der Mittellosigkeit; **~'s right** Armenrecht; **assignment to a** ~ Beiordnung im Armenrecht.

pauperism Massenarmut *f*.

pavage Beiträge *m|pl* für die Straßenpflasterung.

pavement till Straßenschalter e–r Bank.

paving Straßendecke *f*; ~ **rate** Straßenunkostenbeitrag.

pawn *s* Pfand *n*, Pfandstück *n*, Pfandobjekt *n*, Verpfändung *f*; ~ **bill of exchange** verpfändeter Wechsel; **~-receipt** Pfandschein; ~ **shop** Leihhaus, Pfandleihanstalt; ~ **ticket** Pfandschein; **in** ~ verpfändet; **public** ~ **house** Pfandleihanstalt; **taking out of** ~ Pfandeinlösung, Entlassung aus dem Pfandverband; **to deliver for** ~ verpfänden; **to give in** ~ verpfänden, versetzen; **to redeem a** ~ ein Pfand auslösen; **to take in** ~ sich etw verpfänden lassen, zum Pfand nehmen; **to take out a** ~ ein Pfand einlösen.

pawn *v* verpfänden, versetzen; lombardieren.

pawnable verpfändbar, lombardfähig.

pawnbroker Pfandleiher *m*.

pawnbroking Pfandleihgeschäft *n*, Pfandleihe *f*.

pawnee Pfandnehmer *m*, Pfandgläubiger *m*.

pawning Verpfändung *f*, Lombardierung *f*, Pfandbestellung *f*.

pawnor (= *pawner*) Verpfänder *m*, Pfandschuldner *m*.

pax regis Königsfriede *m*, öffentliche Ruhe *f* und Ordnung *f*.

pay *s* Entgelt *n*, Vergütung *f*, Bezahlung *f*, Auszahlung *f*, Lohn *m*, Gehalt *n*, Sold *m*; ~ **account** Lohnkonto; ~ **agreement** Lohnabkommen; ~ **bill** Zahlungsanweisung; **P~ Board** Lohnkontrollbehörde *GB*; ~ **book** Soldbuch, Wehrpaß; ~ **cheque** → *cheque*; ~ **day** → *day*; ~ **differential** Lohngefälle; ~ **envelope** Lohntüte; ~ **grade** Besoldungsgruppe; ~ **load** Nutzlast (*Schiff*); finanzielle Belastung durch Löhne und Gehälter; **~master** → *paymaster*; ~ **office** Zahlstelle, Lohnbüro; ~ **phone** Münztelefon; ~ **plan** Besoldungsordnung; ~ **sheet** → *sheet*; ~ **statement** Verdienstbescheinigung; *itemised* ~ ~: *spezifizierte Verdienstbescheinigung*; **~-TV** Abonnentenfernsehen; ~ **voucher** Kassenanweisung; **annual** ~ Jahresvergütung; **base** ~ Grundlohn; **basic** ~ Grundlohn, Grundgehalt; **dead heading** ~ Bezahlung für den Anmarschweg; **full** ~ volles Gehalt, ungekürzte Lohnzahlung; **make-up** ~ Lohnausgleich; **military** ~ → *military*; **overtime** ~ Überstundenzuschlag; **profit-related** ~ gewinnbezogene Bezahlung; gewinnabhängiger Arbeitslohn; **regular** ~ Normallohn (ohne Überstunden); **retroactive** ~ rückwirkende Lohnerhöhung; **take-home** ~ Nettolohn, Nettoverdienst.

pay *v* zahlen, bezahlen, begleichen, einlösen; ~ **a bill** e–n Wechsel einlösen; ~ **a dividend** Dividenden ausschütten; ~ **as may be paid thereon** e–e Zahlung als Rückversicherer decken; ~ **as you earn** (PAYE) Steuerabzug vom Arbeitslohn, Lohnsteuersystem; ~ **as you go** aus laufenden Erträgen bezahlen; ~ **as you go tax** → *tax*; ~ **as you see** (*television*) Münzfernsehen; ~ **back method** Kapitalrückflußberechnung, Investitionsabzahlungsberechnung; ~ **back period** Tilgungszeit; ~ **by instalments** in Raten zahlen; ~ **by way of damages** Schadenersatz leisten; ~ **cash** bar bezahlen; ~ **cash or order** an den Inhaber zahlen; ~ **down** e–e Anzahlung machen; ~ **duty on** versteuern, verzollen; ~ **in** einbezahlen; ~ **in kind** in Ware bezahlen; e–e Naturalvergütung leisten; ~ **into court** (Geld) bei Gericht hinterlegen; ~ **into the bank** bei der Bank einzahlen; ~ **off a debt** e–e Schuld zurückbezahlen, tilgen; ~ **off bonds** Obligationen einlösen; ~ **off period** Kapitalrückflußdauer; ~ **off shares** Aktien zurückkaufen; ~ **on presentation** bei Vorlage zahlen; ~ **out** auszahlen; ~ **over** abführen; **~-per-view TV** Münzfernsehen; ~ **self** (*Scheck*) zahlen Sie an mich; ~ **to order** an die Order *des Ausstellers* zahlen; ~ **under the table** „schwarz" zahlen; **ability to** ~ Zahlungsfähigkeit, Solvenz; **failure to** ~ Nichtzahlung; **inability to** ~ → *inability*; **notice to** ~ → *notice*; **promise to** ~ → *promise*.

payability Zahlbarkeit *f*, Fälligkeit *f*.

payable zahlbar, fällig, schuldig; ~ **abroad** im Ausland zahlbar; ~ **after sight** nach Sicht zahlbar; *zahlbar nach Akzept bzw nach Protest wegen Nichtannahme des Wechsels*; ~ **at sight** bei Sicht zahlbar, bei Vorlage zahlbar; ~ **in advance** im voraus zahlbar, pränumerando; ~ **in arrears** nachträglich zahlbar, postnumerando; ~ **in cash** in bar zahlbar; ~ **on delivery** zahlbar bei Lieferung; ~ **on demand** zahlbar bei Aufforderung, zahlbar bei Sicht; ~ **on sight** = ~ *at sight qv*; ~ **only through the clearing house** nur zur Verrechnung; ~ **to bearer** zahlbar an den Inhaber; ~ **to order** zahlbar an Order, an Order lautend; ~ **upon readiness for delivery** zahlbar bei Lieferbereitschaft; ~ **when due** bei Fälligkeit zahlbar; ~ **with exchange** zahlbar zuzüglich Einzugsspesen.

payables *bil* Kreditoren *m|pl*, Verbindlichkeiten *f|pl;* ~ **accrued** ~ antizipative Passiva.

payback|method Amortisationsrechnung; ~ **period** Amortisationsdauer, Tilgungsdauer.

payee Zahlungsempfänger *m*; Zahlungsberechtigter *m*; Remittent *m*; **alternative** ~**s** wahlweise Remittenten; **fictitious** ~ fingierter Remittent; **impersonal** ~ unbenannter Remittent; **joint** ~**s** gemeinsam empfangsberechtigte Remittenten.

payer Zahler *m*, Zahlungspflichtiger *m*, Bezogener *m*, Trassat *m*; ~ **bank** zahlende Bank; ~ **benefit** *US ins* Prämienbefreiung bei Tod oder Invalidität; ~ **for honour** Ehrenzahler, Honorant; **slow** ~ schlechter Zahler, säumiger Zahler; **tax** ~ Steuerzahler, Steuerschuldner.

paying|agent → *agent*; ~ **banker** die zahlende Bank; ~ **business** → *business*; ~ **concern** → *concern*; ~ **in** Einzahlung; **~-in slip** Einzahlungsbeleg; ~ **interest** → *interest (2)*; ~ **off** Abzahlung, Tilgung, Auszahlung; ~ **off creditors** Befriedigung von Gläubigern; ~ **office** Zahlstelle; ~ **out** Auszahlung, Wettzahlung leisten; ~ **quantities** gewinnbringende Mengen; **not** ~ unrentabel.

payload Nutzlast *f*, Lohnkosten *pl*.

paymaster Zahlmeister *m*, Kassenstelle *f*, Zahlstelle *f*; **P~ General** Generalzahlmeister, oberste staatliche Kassenstelle; ~ **robbery insurance** → *insurance*.

payment Zahlung *f* (= *Z bzw* . . .*z*), Bezahlung *f*, Einzahlung *f*, Auszahlung *f*, Vergütung *f*, Ausschüttung *f*, Bonifikation *f*, Erfüllung *f*, Begleichung *f*, Einlösung *f*; ~**s** *Z*–*s*verkehr; ~ **against documents** *Z* gegen Dokumente, *Bez* gegen Aushändigung der Verschiffungsdokumente; **~s agreement** *Z*–sabkommen, *Z*–svereinbarung; **~ appropriation** *Z*–sermächtigung; **~ at fixed or determinable future time** *Z* zu einem festen oder feststellbaren zukünftigen Zeitpunkt; **~ behaviour** *Z*–sverhalten, *Z*–smoral; **~ bill** Dokumentenwechsel; **~ by instalments** Raten*z*, Ab*z*; **~ by mistake** irrtümliche *Z*; **~ by post** *Z* auf dem Postwege (*durch Brief*); **~ by result** Leistungslohn; Bezahlung nach Erfolg; Erfolgshonorar; **~ cash against documents or delivery order** Bar*z* gegen Dokumente oder Auslieferungsanweisung; **~s deficit** Defizit in der *Z*–sbilanz; **~ on delivery** Nachnahme; **~s due** fällige *Z*–*en*; **~ for admission** Eintrittsgeld; **~ for breakage** Refaktie; **~ for hono(u)r** Ehren*z*; **~ for honour supra protest** Ehren*z* unter Protest; **~ in advance** Voraus*z*; **~ in anticipation** Voraus*z*; **~ in arrear** nachträgliche *Z*; **~ in cash** Bar*z*, Barausschüttung; **~ in due course** ordnungsgemäße *Z*; *Z* der Wechselsumme durch den Akzeptanten oder Wechselinhaber *bei oder nach Fälligkeit in gutem Glauben*; **~ in full** vollständige *Z*; **~ in kind** Naturallohn, Sachleistung; **~ in lieu of vacation** Urlaubsabgeltung; **~ in place of notice** Kündigungsabfindung; **~ into court** Hinterlegung von Geld bei Gericht; **~ of a bill** Einlösung e–s Wechsels; **~ of calls** Ein*z* auf Kapitalanteile gemäß Abruf; **~ of debts** Be*z* von Schulden, Tilgung von Verbindlichkeiten; **~ of dues** Beitrags*z*; **~ of duty** Verzollung, Versteuerung; **~ of money into court** gerichtl Hinterlegung (*unter Rücknahmeverzicht; im Kosteninteresse*); **~ of premiums** Prämien*z*; **~ of rent in advance** Mietvoraus*z*; **~ of tax credits** Anrechnung von Steuern; **~ on account** Anzahlung; Abschlags*z*; **~ on completion of purchase** *Z* bei Kaufabschluß; **~ on demand** *Z* bei Vorlage des Wechsels; **~ on the spot** sofortige Bar*z*; **~ out** Aus*z* *von Hinterlegungsgeld*; **~ out of court** Aus*z* der Gerichtskasse; **~ per account** Begleichung des Saldos, *Z* gem Rechnungssaldo; **~ received** eingegangene *Z*; **~ stopped** Schecksperre, Aus*z* gesperrt; **~ supra protest** *Z* unter Protest; **~s system** *Z*–ssystem; **~ under reserve** *Z* unter Vorbehalt; **additional ~** Nach*z*, Nachschuß; **against ~** gegen Be*z*, entgeltlich; **anticipated ~** Voraus*z*, Vorschuß; **application for ~** *Z*–santrag, Antrag auf Aus*z* von Hinterlegungsgeldern; **block ~s** zusammengefaßte *Z*–*n*, Gruppen*z*–*n*; **cash ~** → *cash*; **cashless ~** bargeldlose *Z*; **clean ~** Be*z* gegen offene Rechnung; **commutation ~** Abfindung, einmalige *Z*; Zahlung unter Vorbehalt; **confirmation of ~** *Z*–sbestätigung; **constructive ~** unterstellte *Z*, vermutete *Z*; **countermand of ~** *Z*–ssperre, Schecksperre; **current ~s** laufende *Z*–*n*; **date of ~** Fälligkeitstag; **day of ~** *Z*–stermin; **deferred ~** aufgeschobene Zahlung; **~s** Lieferantenkredit, Ratenzahlungen; **due ~** fällige *Z*, fristgerechte Be*z*; **ex gratia ~** Gratifikation, freiwillige Entschädigung (*ohne Rechtspflicht*), Liberalitätszahlung; **failing ~** mangels Zahlung; **final ~** Rest*z*, Abschluß*z*, Restquote; **for want of ~** mangels *Z*; **foreign ~s** *Z*–*en* in Devisen aus dem Ausland; **general ~s** allgemeiner *Z*–sverkehr; **in full and final ~** als endgültige Abfindung; **in lieu of ~** → *lieu*; **indefinite ~** allgemeine Schuldenbegleichung; *Z* ohne Bestimmung der Anrechnung; **initial ~** erste *Z*, An*z*; **interim ~** Abschlags*z*; **international ~s** internationaler *Z*–sverkehr; **late ~** verspätete *Z*; **lump ~** Pauschalbe*z*, Pauschalabfindung; **lump-sum ~** = *lump ~ qv*; **means of ~** → *means*; **mode of ~** → *mode*; **multilateral ~** multilaterale *Z*; **net ~** Netto-

Ausschüttung; **one-time** ~ Einmalz, einmalige *Z*; **order for** ~ → *order (1)*; **outstanding** ~ *Z*–*s*rückstand; **overdue** rückständige *Z*; **part** ~ → *part*; **partial** ~ teilweise *Z*; **periodical** ~**s** regelmäßige *Z*–*en*, laufende Unterhalts*z*–*en*; **preferential** ~**s** bevorzugte Befriedigung, Befriedigung bevorrechtigter Forderungen; **progress** ~**s** Abschlagszahlungen (*nach Baufortschritt etc.*); **pro rata** ~ quotenmäßige Befriedigung, anteilige *Z*; **receipts and** ~**s** Einnahmen und Ausgaben, Einzahlungen und Auszahlungen; **respite of** ~ *Z*–*s*aufschub; **restitution** ~**s** Wiedergutmachungs*z*–*en*; **rule of partial** ~**s** → *rule*; **subsequent** ~ Nach*z*, Nachschuß; **suspension of** ~**s** → *suspension*; **term of** ~ → *term*; **terms of** ~ → *term*; **time for** ~ → *time*; **to meet the** ~**s** die *Z*–*s*verpflichtungen einhalten; **to sue for** ~ auf *Z* klagen; **transitional** ~ Übergangs*z*; **voluntary** ~ freiwillige *Z*; **voucher for** ~ → *voucher*; **withdrawal of** ~ Entnahme, Antrag auf Rück*z* von Hinterlegungsgeldern; **without** ~ unentgeltlich, gratis.

payoff Schmiergeld(zahlung).

payor Zahlungspflichtiger *m*, *bes* Wechselschuldner *m*, Bezogener *m*.

payout Auszahlung *f*; Ausschüttung *f*; ~ **rate** Auszahlungssatz, Ausschüttungssatz; ~ **ratio** Auszahlungsquote, A.-kurs.

payroll Lohnliste *f*, Gehaltsliste *f*; ~**s** *US bil* Löhne und Gehälter; ~ **accounting** Lohnbuchhaltung; Lohn- bzw Gehaltsabrechnung; ~ **audit** Lohnbuchhaltungsrevision; ~ **book** Lohnliste; ~ **clerk** Lohnbuchhalter; ~ **credit** Sammellohnzahlungsanweisung; ~ **deduction** Einbehaltung vom Arbeitslohn; Lohn- bzw. Gehaltsabzug; ~ **manager** Leiter des Lohnbüros; ~ **overhead** Lohngemeinkosten; ~ **records** Lohnabrechnungen; ~ **sheet** Lohn- und Gehaltsliste; ~ **tax** → *tax*; **to pad a** ~ überhöhte Lohnkosten berechnen.

peace Friede *m*, öffentliche Sicherheit *f* und Ordnung *f*; *hist* Abschluß *m* des (*fiktiven*) Auflassungsstreitverfahrens; ~ **and quietude** öffentliche Ruhe und Ordnung; ~ **bond** → *bond (2)*; ~ **breaker** Störer der öffentlichen Ruhe und Ordnung; ~ **breaking** Störung der öffentlichen Ruhe und Sicherheit; ~ **campaigners** Demonstranten der Friedensbewegung; ~ **conference** Friedenskonferenz; ~ **maker** Friedensstifter; ~ **negotations** Friedensverhandlungen; ~ **of God** *Zustand außerhalb des Krieges*, (in) Friedenszeiten; ~ **of God and the Church** gerichtsfreie Zeiten; ~ **of the King (Queen)** öffentliche Ruhe und Sicherheit; ~ **of the State** öffentliche Ruhe und Sicherheit; ~ **offer** Friedensangebot; ~ **officer** Polizeibeamter, Polizist, Hilfsbeamter der Staatsanwaltschaft; ~ **settlement** friedensvertragliche Regelung; ~ **terms** Friedensbedingungen; ~ **treaty** Friedensvertrag; **appeal for** ~ Friedensappell; **articles of the** ~ → *articles*; **bill of** ~ → *bill (2)*; **enduring** ~ dauerhafter Friede; **public** ~ Landfrieden, öffentliche Ruhe und Sicherheit; **public** ~ **and quiet** öffentliche Ruhe und Sicherheit; **violation of the** ~ → *violation*.

peacable unangefochten, friedlich, ungestört, allseits geduldet.

peaceably and quietly ungestört, ohne Beeinträchtigung durch Dritte, gewaltlos.

peasent farmer Landwirt *m*, Bauer *m*.

pecking order Rangordnung *f*.

peculate öffentliche Gelder veruntreuen, unterschlagen.

peculation Veruntreuung *f*, Unterschlagung *f* öffentlicher Gelder.

peculator Veruntreuer *m*, Betrüger *m*.

peculiar *adj* besonders, eigentümlich, eigenartig.

peculiar *s* Vorrecht *n*, Privileg *n*, Privatinteresse *n*; autonome Zuständigkeit *f*, besondere Zuständigkeit *f*, autonome Kirchengemeinde *f*.

peculiarit|y Eigenheit *f*, Besonderheit *f*, Eigentümlichkeit *f*; **special ~ies** besondere Kennzeichen.

peculium Sondereigentum *n (der Frau bzw Kinder)*, persönliche Habe *f*.

pecuniary geldlich, Geld . . ., finanziell, pekuniär.

pecuniosity Wohlhabenheit *f*.

peddle hausieren.

peddler *US = pedlar qv*.

pederasty Päderastie *f*, Homosexualität *f (Mann mit Jugendlichen)*.

pedestrian Fußgänger *m*; **~ mall** Fußgängerzone; **~ crossing** Fußgängerüberweg; **oncoming ~** entgegenkommender Fußgänger.

pedigree Abstammung *f*, Stammbaum *m*, Ahnentafel *f*, Ahnenreihe *f*; **~ race** Zuchtstamm, Zuchtrasse.

pedlar Hausierer *m*, Wandergewerbetreibender *m*; **~'s licence** → *licence*.

pedlary Wandergewerbe *n*, Hausierhandel *m*.

peer Peer *m*, hoher Adliger *m*, Ebenbürtiger *m*, Mitglied *n* des Oberhauses; **~ review** *obergutachtliche bzw standesrechtliche* Überprüfung durch gleichrangige Kollegen; **cross-bench ~s** Oberhausmitglieder, die der Gegenpartei nahestehen; **life ~** Peer auf Lebenszeit, lebenslängliches Oberhausmitglied; **representative ~s** delegierte Oberhausmitglieder, *Vertreter Schottlands und Irlands im brit Oberhaus*.

peerage Peerswürde *f*, Hochadel *m*, Adelsstand *m*, *Anspruch m auf Strafverfahren vor Gleichrangigen bzw vor dem Oberhaus*; **life ~** Adelsprädikat auf Lebenszeit.

peeress Inhaberin *f* der Peerswürde, Gemahlin *f* eines Peers; **~ in her own right** Trägerin der Peerswürde aus eigenem Recht.

peers ranggleiche adlige Richter *m|pl*; **~ of fees** Vasallen des gleichen Lehnsherren als gleichberechtigte Richter; **judgment of his ~** → *judgment*; **trial by a jury of his ~** ranggleiches standesgemäßes Geschworenengericht.

peg *s* Pflock *m*, Markierungspflock *m*, Dübel *m*; **adjustable ~** = *crawling ~ qv*; **crawling ~** stufenweise Änderung des Interventionspunktes.

peg *v* stützen, festsetzen (*Preise, Kurse*); **~ged exchange** durch Zentralbanken gestützte Devisenkurse; **~ged market** gestützte Börsenkurse; **~ging operation** Intervention; **~ged prices** gestützte Preise.

pelfe (pelfre) Beute *f*, persönliche Habe *f* e–s Verurteilten, Verhaftungsprämie *f*.

pell Pergamentshaut *f*.

pells of issue and receipt Liste *f* (n) über Zahlungen und Zahlungseingänge der britischen Finanzbehörden.

penal strafbar, strafrechtlich, Straf-. . .

penalise mit e–r Strafe belegen, pönalisieren, benachteiligen.

penalty Strafe *f*; Konventionalstrafe *f*, Vertragsstrafe *f*; Reugeld *n*; **~ clause** → *clause*; **~ duty** Strafzoll; **~ envelope** frankierter Dienstumschlag; **~ for non-fulfilment** Konventionalstrafe; **~ freight** Vertragsstrafe auf die Fracht; **~ points** Strafpunkte (*Verkehrssünder*); **~ postage** Strafporto; **~ rate** höherer Lohnsatz (*für Überstunden*), Gefahrenzulage; **abatement of ~** Strafermäßigung; **administrative ~** Ordnungsstrafe; **assessment of ~** Strafzumessung; **civil ~** Bußgeld; **contractual ~** Vertragsstrafe; **conventional ~** Konventionalstrafe, Vertragsstrafe; **death ~** → *death*; **enhanced ~** verschärfte Strafe; **extramural ~** als Freigänger zu verbüßende Strafe; **fiscal ~** Steuerstrafe; **fixed ~ procedure** *etwa:* Strafbefehlsverfahren (*Verkehrsdelikte*); **fixed ~ system** Strafbefehlssystem, summarisches Strafverfahren ohne Verhandlung; **fixed ~ ticket** Strafmandat, Strafbefehl; **increased ~** verschärfte

Strafe; **maximum** ~ Höchststrafe; **on** ~ **of** bei Meidung e–r Strafe von; **on** ~ **of death** bei Todesstrafe; **pecuniary** ~ Geldstrafe; **substituted** ~ Ersatzstrafe, Ersatzfreiheitsstrafe; **summary** ~ Bußgeld; **to carry a** ~ mit Strafe bedroht sein; **to impose a** ~ zu e–r Strafe verurteilen, e–e Strafe verhängen; **to incur a** ~ sich strafbar machen; **under** ~ **of** bei Strafe von, unter Strafandrohung.

penance Kirchenbuße *f.*

pencil writing mit Bleistift Geschriebenes.

pendency Rechtshängigkeit *f*, Schweben *n*; Anhängigkeit *f*, Abhängigkeit *n*; ~ **of prosecution** Anhängigkeit e–s Strafverfahrens.

pendente lite während der Anhängigkeit des Rechtsstreits, in e–m schwebenden Verfahren.

pendentes ungeerntete Früchte *f/pl*, Früchte *f/pl* auf dem Halm.

pendicle Grundstücksteilfläche *f.*

pending *adj; prep* schwebend, unvollendet, unentschieden, bis zu, während, anhängig; ~ **action** anhängiger Rechtsstreit; für die Dauer des Prozesses; solange der Prozeß schwebt; ~ **appeal** noch nicht rechtskräftig; ~ **application** noch nicht verbeschiedene Anmeldung; ~ **arrangement** bis zur Erledigung; ~ **debts** Schulden; ~ **delivery** → *delivery*; ~ **final decision** während der Rechtshängigkeit; ~ **further investigation** während der weiteren Ermittlungen; ~ **further notice** bis auf weiteres; ~ **in court** rechtshängig; ~ **instructions** vorbehaltlich anderer Weisungen; ~ **litigation** anhängiger Rechtsstreit; ~ **proceedings** anhängige Strafsachen, Strafverfahren; ~ **risks** → *risk*; ~ **suit** für die Dauer des Prozesses; für den Fall der Rechtshängigkeit; ~ **the proceedings** für die Dauer des Verfahrens.

penetration Durchdringungsvermögen *n*, Penetration *f das (wenn auch geringe) Eindringen des Penis in die Vagina als Tatbestandsmerkmal bei Notzucht*; **foreign** ~ Überfremdung.

penitentiary Zuchthaus *n US*, Besserungsanstalt *f GB.*

pennant Stander *m.*

pennon Fähnlein *n*, Wimpel *m*, Standarte *f.*

pennyweight *Gaunersprache:* Schmuck *m*, Juwelen *m/pl.*

penology Strafvollzugswissenschaft *f.*

pension *s* Pension *f*, Ruhegehalt *n*, Rente *f*, Ehrensold *m*; ~ **account** Pensionskasse; ~ **age** Pensionsalter, Rentenalter; **P~s Appeal Tribunal** → *tribunal*; ~ **authority** Rentenbehörde; ~ **benefit** Rentenzahlung; ~ **commitment** Pensionszusage; *pl:* Pensionsverpflichtungen; ~ **fund** Pensionskasse; ~ ~ *portfeuille: Wertpapierbestand e–r Pensionskasse*; ~ **of churches** Kirchenabgaben (*an Stelle des Zehnten*); ~ **office** Versorgungsamt; ~ **plan** Altersversorgungsplan; ~ **pool** gemeinsame Pensionskasse *mehrerer Arbeitgeber*; ~ **reserve** Pensionsrückstellung; ~ **right** Pensionsberechtigung, Ruhegehaltsanspruch; ~ **scheme** Altersversorgungswerk, betriebliche Pensionskasse; **additional** ~ Zusatzrente; **basic** ~ Grundrente; **civil** ~ Ruhegeld (*für Zivilpersonen*), Beamtenpension; **contributory** ~ (*beiderseits*) beitragspflichtige Betriebsrente; **contributory** ~ **plan** beitragspflichtige Pensionskasse; **corporate** ~**s fund** betriebliche Altersversorgung; **director's** ~**s** Altersbezüge für Vorstandsmitglieder; **disablement** ~ Kriegsbeschädigtenrente; **early retirement** ~ vorgezogene Altersrente; **eligible for a** ~ → *eligible*; **graduated** ~ **scheme** *Rentensystem mit proportionalen Beiträgen und Leistungen*; **illhealth** ~ krankheitsbedingte Rente; **invalidity** ~ Erwerbsunfähigkeitsrente; **non-contributory retirement** ~ beitragsfreies Altersruhegeld; **life** ~ lebenslange Rente; **old age** ~

Altersrente, Alterspension; **retirement** ~ Altersruhegeld, Altersrente; **state retirement** ~ staatl. Altersruhegeld (*GB*); **survivor's** ~ Hinterbliebenenrente; **vested** ~ **right** unverfallbare Pensionsanwartschaft; **vested** ~ **plan** unentziehbare Ruhegeldanwartschaft; **war disability** ~ = *war* ~ *qv*; **war** ~ Kriegsbeschädigtenrente; **widow's** ~ Witwenrente, Witwengeld.

pension off *v* pensionieren, in den Ruhestand versetzen.

pensionable pensionsfähig, pensionsberechtigt.

pensionary *s* Pensionär *m*, Ruhegehaltsempfänger *m*.

pensioner Ehrensöldner *m*, Pensionär *m*, Rentner *m*, Ruhegehaltsempfänger *m*, Unterhaltsempfänger *m*, Beitragszahler *m*, Pensionsgast *m*, Kost und Wohnung zahlender Student *m*; *Präsident e–s Inn of Court qv*.

penultimate vorletzter (-e, -es).

penury Mangel *m*, Armut *f*.

peon Leibeigener *m*, arbeitsverpflichteter Schuldner *m*, Schuldknecht *m*.

peonage Leibeigenenrecht *n*; Verdingung *f* von Sträflingen an Unternehmen.

people Menschen *m|pl*, Bevölkerung *f*, Leute *pl*, Bürger *m|pl*, Wähler *m|pl*, Untertanen *m|pl*, Staatsangehörige *m|pl*, Wahlberechtigte *m|pl*, Nation *f*, Volk *n*, Staat *m*, Staatsgewalt *f*; ~**'s bank** Genossenschaftsbank; ~**'s front** Volksfront; **moneyed** ~ Geldleute, Kapitalisten.

peppercorn rent symbolischer Pachtzins.

per per, durch, über, i. V. (*in Vertretung von*); ~ **account rendered** → *account (2)*; ~ **agreement** gemäß Vereinbarung; ~ **and cui** auf Grund des Rechts eines Dritten; ~ **annum** pro Jahr, jährlich; ~ **autre vie** auf die Lebensdauer e–s Dritten; ~ **aversionem** Pauschalkauf (*ohne Prüfung*); ~ **balance** per Saldo; ~ **bearer** durch Überbringer; ~ **bouche** mündlich; ~ **capita** pro Kopf, nach Kopfteilen, (zu gleichen Teilen), nach Köpfen; ~ **cent** Prozent, vom Hundert; ~ **contra** Gegenbuchung; ~ **curiam** durch das Gericht, von Amtswegen, gerichtlich → ~ *totam curiam;* ~ **curiam opinion** → *opinion*; ~ **diem allowance** Tagegeld, tägl. Entschädigung, Tagesspesen; ~ **diem in lieu of subsistence** = ~ *diem allowance qv*; ~ **eundem** durch denselben (*Richter*); ~ **incuriam** durch Unachtsamkeit; durch das unzuständige Gericht; ~ **mensem** pro Monat; ~ **mille** Promille; ~ **mille interest** Tausendstel-Miteigentumsanteil; ~ **minas** durch Drohungen; ~ **misadventure** durch Unglücksfall; ~ **my et per tout** gesamthänderisch, intern zu gleichen Teilen; ~ **post** auf dem Postwege; ~ **pro** i. V. (*in Vertretung*), als Bevollmächtigter; ~ **procuration** (= *per proc., p.p.*), in Vollmacht, in Vertretung, (per) Prokura (*Wertpapierzeichnung*); ~ **quod** wodurch, aufgrund besonderer Tatumstände; ~ **sample** nach Probe; ~ **se** für sich allein, grundsätzlich, schlechthin, als solche(s); ~ **stirpes** nach Stämmen; ~ **subsequens matrimonium** durch nachfolgende Eheschließung; ~ **totam curiam** durch das Kollegialgericht, (als) Plenarentscheidung; ~ **unit price category** Stückpreiskategorie; ~ **universitatem** durch Gesamtrechtsnachfolge; ~ **vivam vocem** gesprochen; ~ **year** pro Jahr, jährlich; **trial** ~ **pais** Verfahren mit Geschworenen.

perambulation Grenzbegehung *f*; Gerichtssprengel *m*.

percentage Prozent *n*, Prozentsatz *m*, Provision *f*, Tantieme *f*; ~ **distribution** prozentuale Häufigkeit und Verteilung; ~ **lease** Umsatzpacht; ~ **of recovery** Konkursquote; ~ **of the profits** Gewinnanteil; **contract** ~ vertragliche Provision; **distribution on a** ~ **basis** prozentuale Aufteilung; **statutory** ~ gesetzlicher Zinssatz.

perception Wahrnehmung *f*, Besitzergreifung *f*, Auszählung *f* und Bezahlung *f*, geschuldete Verpflegung *f* (*Soldaten*).
perch Meßrute *f*, Meßlatte *f*; Rute *f* *Maßeinheit*.
percussion Schlag *m*, Stoß *m*, Erschütterung *f*.
perdurable langdauernd, unbegrenzt, immerwährend.
perempt *v* auf Rechtsmittel verzichten, e–s Rechtsmittels verlustig gehen; **an appeal is ~ed** jmd wird des Rechtsmittels verlustig erklärt.
peremption klageabweisendes Prozeßurteil *n*, Urteilsaufhebung *f*; Erledigung *f*.
peremptoriness Entschiedenheit *f*.
peremptory peremptorisch, bestimmt, entscheidend, endgültig, zwingend, willkürlich; ~ **order for time** gerichtliche Fristsetzung; ~ **paper** *vorrangige Sitzungsliste mit unerledigten oder auf Wunsch der Parteien anberaumter Sachen*.
perennial dauernd, beständig, immerwährend.
perfect *adj* vollkommen, vollendet, beendet, durchgeführt, durchsetzbar, mangelfrei, verkäuflich; ~ **attestation clause** *Bestätigung der formellen Voraussetzungen für eine gültige Testamentserrichtung*.
perfect *v/t* perfektionieren, rechtswirksam machen.
perfection Vollendung *f*; ~ **of gift** Vollziehung der Schenkung, Wirksamwerden der Schenkung; ~ **of security interest** Offenlegung e–r Darlehenssicherheit.
perfidious treulos, verräterisch, heimtückisch.
perfidy Heimtücke *f*, Treulosigkeit *f*.
perform erfüllen, leisten; ~ **an act** e–e Handlung vornehmen; **failure to** ~ Nichtleistung, Nichterfüllung; **failure to ~ a contract** Nichterfüllung e–s Vertrages.
performance Erfüllung *f*, Leistung *f*, *investm* Wertentwicklung e–s Investmentfonds; Ausführung *f*; Aufführung *f*, Vorführung *f*, Vorstellung *f*; ~ **appraisal** Leistungsbewertung; ~ **bond** → *bond (2)*; ~ **chart** Leistungsdiagramm; ~ **efficiency** Leistungsgrad; ~ **for profit** gewerbliche Vorführung; ~ **fund** auf überdurchschnittl Gewinn angelegter Investmentfonds; ~ **guarantee** → *guarantee*; ~ **in kind** Naturalerfüllung; ~ **in public** öffentliche Aufführung; ~ **of an obligation** Erfüllung e–r Verpflichtung; ~ **of contract** Vertragserfüllung; ~ **of duty** Diensterfüllung, Amtsführung; ~ **of services** Erbringung von Diensten; ~ **period** Leistungszeit(raum), Leistungsfrist; ~ **ratings** Leistungseinstufung; ~ **specifications** Leistungsverzeichnis, Leistungsbeschreibung; ~ **standard** Leistungsstandard; **contemporaneous** ~ gleichzeitige beiderseitige Erfüllung, Zug um Zug Leistung; **continuing** ~ Leistung e–r Dauerschuld; **defective** ~ mangelhafte Erfüllung; **first** ~ Uraufführung, Premiere; **impediment to** ~ Erfüllungshindernis; **impossibility of** ~ → *impossibility*; **indivisible** ~ unteilbare Leistung; **in lieu of** ~ an Erfüllungs statt; **part** ~ Teilleistung, Teilerfüllung; *cf principle of part* ~; **personal** ~ Leistung in Person; **positive** ~ Erfüllungsinteresse; **public** ~ öffentl Aufführung; **specific** ~ Naturalerfüllung, genaue Vertragserfüllung, Vornahme der geschuldeten Leistung; **substantial** ~ im wesentlichen richtige Vertragserfüllung; **timely** ~ fristgerechte Leistung; **to sue for** ~ auf Erfüllung klagen; **vicarious** ~ Erfüllungsübernahme der Leistung.
Performers Protection Act *GB, 1963* Urheberrechtsschutzgesetz für darstellende Künstler.
performing rights Aufführungsrechte *n/pl*; **P~ Right Society** *brit Gesellschaft zum Schutz musikalischer Aufführungsrechte*; ~ **right tribunal** → *tribunal*.
periculum in mora Gefahr *f* im Verzug; *cf: imminent peril*.

peril Gefahr *f*, Risiko *n*, Verantwortung *f*; ~**s clause** (Transport)Gefahrenklausel; ~**s insured against** versicherte Gefahren; ~ **of the lakes** Schiffahrtsgefahren auf den Großen Seen (*USA*) (*Bedeutung wie ~s of the sea qv*); ~ **of the road** Transportgefahren im Straßenverkehr; ~**s of the sea** Seerisiken, typische Seetransportgefahren; ~ **of transportation** Transportrisiko; ~**s of war** Kriegsgefahren, Kriegsrisiken; ~ **point** Gefahrenpunkt, Interventionspunkt; **at one's** ~ auf eigene Gefahr; **common** ~ gemeinschaftliche Gefahr (*Havarie*); **excepted** ~**s clause** → *to except*; **extraneous** ~**s** Sondergefahren; **imminent** ~ akute Gefahr, gegenwärtige Gefahr, Gefahr im Verzug.

perimeter wall Gefängnismauer *f*, Gefängnis-Außenmauer *f*.

period Zeitraum *m*, Frist *f*, Laufzeit *f*, Zeitabschnitt *m*; ~ **for appeal** Rechtsmittelfrist; ~ **for declaration** Anmeldefrist; ~ **for filing** *pat* Anmeldefrist; ~ **for objection** Einspruchsfrist; ~ **insured** Versicherungszeit; ~ **of a loan** Laufzeit e–r Anleihe; ~ **of appointment** Amtsdauer; ~ **of assessment** Veranlagungszeitraum; ~ **of childhood** Kindheit; ~ **of computation** Berechnungszeitraum; ~ **of copyright** Schutzfrist *e–s Urheberrechts*; ~ **of emergency** Notzeit; ~ **of entering an appearance** Einlassungsfrist; ~ **of extension** Verlängerungszeitraum, Stundungsfrist; ~ **of grace** Gnadenfrist, Nachfrist, Zahlungsfrist; ~ **of guarantee** Garantiefrist; ~ **of imprisonment** Dauer der Freiheitsstrafe; ~ **of insurance** Versicherungsdauer; ~ **of lease** Pachtzeit; ~ **of limitation** → *limitation*; ~ **of maintenance** Instandhaltungszeitfolge; ~ **of non-negotiability** Sperrfrist (*für Effekten*); ~ **of notice** Kündigungsfrist; ~ **of possible conception** Empfängniszeit; ~ **of prescription** Ersitzungsfrist; ~ **of probation** Bewährungsfrist, Probezeit; ~ **of qualification** Zulassungsfrist; ~ **of renunciation** Ausschlagungsfrist; ~ **of restriction** Karenzzeit; ~ **of shipment** Verladungsfrist; ~ **of summons** Ladungsfrist; ~ **of transition** Übergangszeit; ~ **of validity** Gültigkeitsdauer, Laufzeit; ~ **of vocational adjustment** Einarbeitungszeit; ~ **of warranty** Gewährleistungsfrist; ~ **to maturity** Laufzeit (*Obligationen*); ~ **to run** Laufzeit; **a** ~ **less than life** zeitliche Freiheitsstrafe; ~ **under review** Berichtszeitraum; **accounting** ~ → *accounting*; **basic** ~ Zuteilungsperiode (*Sonderziehungsrechte*); **blocked** ~ Sperrfrist; **comparable** ~ Vergleichszeitraum; **computation of** ~ Zeitberechnung, Fristberechnung; **contractual** ~ Vertragszeit; **cooling-off** ~ → *cooling*; **defects liability** ~ Mängelgewährleistungsfrist; **definite** ~ bestimmte Frist, fester Zeitraum; **fiscal** ~ Veranlagungszeitraum; **fixed** ~ Frist, fester Zeitraum; (*each*) **hourly** ~ **or fraction thereof** (jede) Stunde oder angefangene Stunde; **limitation** ~ → *limitation*; **limited** ~ beschränkte Zeit (*kann auch Lebenszeit bedeuten*); **ordering** ~ Bestellzeitraum, Bestellungsfrist; **peak** ~ Stoßzeit, Spitzenbelastungszeit; **rental** ~ Mietzahlungsperiode; **requisite** ~ gesetzliche Frist; **running of a** ~ Lauf e–r Frist; **specified** ~ bestimmte Frist; **statutory** ~ gesetzliche Frist; **statutory** ~ **of limitation** Verjährungsfrist; **statutory** ~ **of notice** gesetzliche Kündigungsfrist; **subscription** ~ Zeichnungsfrist; **taxable** ~ Besteuerungszeitraum, Veranlagungszeitraum; **testing** ~ Probezeit; **transitional** ~ Übergangszeit; **trial** ~ Probezeit, Versuchsstadium; **within a reasonable** ~ innerhalb angemessener Frist.

periodic periodisch, regelmäßig wiederkehrend.

periodical periodisch, regelmäßig

wiederkehrend; ~ **contribution** laufender Beitrag; ~ **meetings** regelmäßige Zusammenkünfte.

periphrasis Umschreibung *f*, Weitschweifigkeit *f*.

perish zugrunde gehen, verunglükken, verderben, umkommen, untergehen.

perishable leicht verderblich; **~s** leicht verderbliche Waren; ~ **commodity** leicht verderbliche Ware; ~ **goods** (= *perishables*) leicht verderbl Ware; **of ~ nature** leicht verderblich.

perjure (*to ~ oneself*) e–n Meineid leisten, falsch schwören.

perjurer Meineidige(r), e–n Falscheid Schwörende(r).

perjury Meineid *m*, Falscheid *m*, falsche Angaben *f/pl* unter Eid.

perks Nebenvergünstigungen für leitende Mitarbeiter.

permanent permanent, fest, dauernd, ständig, stabil, fortwährend; **P~ Boundary Commission** *brit ständige Kommission für Wahlkreisgrenzen*; ~ **building and loan association** *Bausparkasse mit ständiger Aktienausgabe (an jeden Antragsteller)*; ~ **building society** Bausparkasse; **P~ Court of Arbitration** → *court*; **P~ Court of International Justice** → *court*; **P~ Insurance Fund** *ständiger Fonds der US Bankeinlagenversicherung*; ~ **life insurance** jährlich kündbare Lebensversicherungspolice; ~ **working place** Dauerarbeitsplatz.

permeability Durchlässigkeit *f*, Überschreitbarkeit *f* (*e–r Zollgrenze*).

permissibility Zulässigkeit *f*.

permissible zulässig, erlaubt, statthaft; ~ **expenses** abzugsfähige Unkosten; ~ **load** → *load*.

permission Erlaubnis *f*, Genehmigung *f*, Gestattung *f*, Zulassung *f*, Konzession *f*; ~ **for building** Bauerlaubnis; **by special ~** mit besonderer Genehmigung; **government ~** staatliche Erlaubnis; **outline ~** (*to build a dwelling house*) grundsätzl. (Bau)Erlaubnis, Vorbescheid; **without ~** unbefugt.

permissive zulässig, erlaubt, zulassend, geduldet.

permit *s* Erlaubnis *f*, Konzession *f*, Lizenz *f*, Genehmigung *f*, Passierschein *m*; ~ **card** Erlaubnisschein; ~ **number** Zulassungsnummer; **building ~** → *building*; **discharging ~** Löscherlaubnis; **entry ~** → *entry*; **export ~** → *export*; **import ~** → *import*; **labo(u)r ~** → *labo(u)r*; **omnibus ~** allgemeine Erlaubnis; **residence ~** → *residence*; **special ~** Ausnahmegenehmigung; Sondererlaubnis; **transit ~** → *transit*; **visitor's ~** kurzfristige Aufenthaltserlaubnis, Besuchserlaubnis, Sprecherlaubnis (*Gefangenenbesuch*); **working ~** Arbeitserlaubnis.

permit *v* dulden, erlauben, gestatten, zulassen, einwilligen; ~ **an appeal** e–e Berufung zulassen; ~ **or suffer** gestatten oder dulden; **~ted by law** gesetzlich zulässig; **~ted hours** Schankstunden; **circumstances ~ting ~** → *circumstance*.

permittee Erlaubnisinhaber; Berechtigter *m*.

permutation Tauschgeschäft *n*.

pernancy Entgegennahme *f* von Erträgnissen.

pernor of profits Nutzungsberechtigter *m*.

perpars Erbteil *m*.

perpetrate begehen, verüben.

perpetration Begehung *f*, Verübung *f*.

perpetrator Täter *m*; ~ **in crime** Straftäter, Haupttäter.

perpetual fortwährend, immerwährend, ewig, lebenslänglich, unabsetzbar; ~ **bond** unkündbare Anleihe; ~ **charge** Reallast; **P~ Commissioners** ständige Urkundspersonen, Notare; ~ **floating rate capital notes** unkündbare, zinsvariable, kapitalersetzende Schuldscheine; ~ **interest** Dauerrecht (*mit ständiger Verlängerungs-*

klausel); ~ **inventory card** laufende Bestandskarte; ~**ly renewable lease** → *lease*; ~ **succession** Dauerbestand (*e–r juristischen Person*).

perpetuate verewigen.

perpetuating|evidence Beweissicherung; ~ **testimony** Beweissicherung von Zeugenaussagen.

perpetuity Fortdauer *f*, Dauerzustand *m*, Unaufhörlichkeit *f*, Unveräußerlichkeit *f*, ewige Generationenbindung *f* von Grundbesitz; ~ **of the king** *Fiktion des immerwährenden Bestandes der Krone*; **in** ~ für immer, auf unbegrenzte Zeit; **lease in** ~ → *lease*; **rule against** ~**ies** Fideikommißverbot.

perquisites Einkünfte *f/pl*; Nebeneinkünfte *f/pl*; Sachbezüge (*zB Kost und Logis*); Erwerb *m* unter Lebenden.

perquisitor Erwerber *m* (*unter Lebenden*), Ersterwerber *m*, Käufer *m*.

persecute verfolgen, drangsalieren.

persecutee (*politisch, rassisch oder aus religiösen Gründen*) Verfolgter *m*.

persecution Verfolgung *f* (*aus politischen, religiösen oder rassischen Gründen*).

persist beharren, bestehen auf; ~ **in a demand** auf e–r Forderung hartnäckig bestehen.

persistent beharrlich, anhaltend, hartnäckig; ~ **delay in paying rent** nachhaltiger Mietzahlungsverzug; ~ **shouter of abuse** ständiger Beschimpfungs-Schreihals.

person Person *f*, Individuum *n*, Mensch *m*; ~ **accounting** Kontoführer, der Rechnungslegende; ~ **acting in a fiduciary capacity** ein in treuhänderischer Eigenschaft Handelnder; ~ **acting in the administration** ein mit der Nachlaßverwaltung Befaßter, gesetzlicher Nachlaßpfleger; ~ **aggrieved** der Beschwerte, der in seinen Rechten Verletzte; ~ **appearing** der Erschienene; ~ **arrested** (*Untersuchungs*)Gefangener; ~ **carried over** Reportgeber; ~ **carrying over** Reportnehmer; ~ **charged** Beschuldigter; ~ **claiming through or under him** *jmd, der als Beauftragter oder Rechtsnachfolger Ansprüche erhebt*; ~ **convicted** Verurteilter, Vorbestrafter; ~ **detained for trial** Untersuchungsgefangener; ~ **disposing of property** Veräußerer; ~**s driving or riding in motor vehicles** PKW-Führer und Mitfahrende; ~ **distrained** Vollstreckungsschuldner *nach Beschlagnahme*; ~ **duly licensed** Konzessionsinhaber; ~ **employed** Arbeitnehmer; ~ **employed under the Post Office** Postbediensteter; ~ **entitled** Berechtigter, Rechtsinhaber, Anspruchsberechtigter; ~ **entitled to reversion** Heimfallsberechtigter; ~ **entitled to take** Erbberechtigter; ~ **for the time being entitled to possession** der jeweilige Besitzberechtigte; ~ **giving notice** Kündigender, Mitteilender, streitverkündende Partei; ~ **having agreed to buy goods** Kaufverpflichteter, Käufer; ~ **having management of road** Träger der Straßenbaulast; ~ **having superintendence entrusted to him** Aufsichtsführender, Verantwortlicher; ~ **holding office under Her Majesty** *brit* königl Beamter; Staatsbediensteter; ~ **in authority** Amtsperson; ~ **in charge** (*für das Fahrzeug*) unmittelbar Verantwortlicher, Fahrer; ~ **in his employ** sein Arbeitnehmer; ~ **in trust** Treuhänder; ~ **injured** Verletzter, Geschädigter; ~ **insured** der Versicherte; ~ **interested** Beteiligter, Betroffener; ~ **liable** Haftender; ~ **liable to make payment** Zahlungspflichtiger, Abgabenschuldner; ~ **liable to repair** Träger der Straßenunterhaltslast; ~ **making a complaint** Beschwerdeführer; ~ **needing care and attention** Pflegebedürftiger; ~ **non compos mentis** Unzurechnungsfähiger, Geisteskranker; ~ **notified** Streitverkündeter; ~ **of consequence** einflußreiche Person; ~ **of full age** Volljähriger; ~ **of incidence** Träger von Pflichten, Verpflichteter; ~

of independent means finanziell Unabhängiger; ~ **of inherence** Träger von Rechten, Berechtigter; ~ **of seniority** leitender Angestellter, Person in führender Stellung; ~ **of unsound mind** Geistesgestörter; ~ **on the run** Flüchtiger; ~**s using the road** Verkehrsteilnehmer *pl*; ~ **under disability** beschränkt Geschäftsfähiger *bzw* Geschäftsunfähiger; ~ **who served** der Zusteller; ~ **with criminal record** Vorbestrafter; ~ **wrongfully claiming** der unberechtigte Anspruchsteller; **accountable** ~ → *accountable*; **artificial** ~ juristische Person; **assessed** ~ der Steuerpflichtige, der Veranlagte; **body of** ~**s** → *body*; **British protected** ~ → *British*; **charitable** ~**s** Personen, die sich karitativen Zwecken widmen; **collective** ~ juristische Person; **deceased** ~ Verstorbener, Erblasser; **disorderly** ~**s** Ruhestörer, Erreger e–s öffentl Ärgernisses, Randalierer; **displaced** ~ →*displace*; **fictious** ~ fiktive (= *gedachte*) Person; juristische Person; **fit** ~ geeignete Person, taugliche Person; **incapacitated** ~ nicht geschäftsfähige erwachsene Person; **international** ~ Völkerrechtssubjekt; **irresponsible** ~ Unzurechnungsfähiger; **juristic** ~ juristische Person; **legal** ~ Rechtssubjekt; *to be a* [illegible]: *rechtsfähig sein*; **natural** ~ natürliche Person, physische Person, Mensch; **ordinary** ~**s** Durchschnittsmenschen; **protected** ~ Pflegling, Mündel; **single** ~ Alleinstehende(r), Single *m*; **taxable** ~ der (die) Steuerpflichtige; **to act in** ~ persönlich auftreten, e–n Prozeß persönlich (*ohne Anwalt*) führen; **unauthorized** ~ Unbefugter; **undesirable** ~ unerwünschter Ausländer; **wanted** ~ gesuchte Person, der (die) Gesuchte, jmd auf der Fahndungsliste; **young** ~ →*young person*.

persona non grata Persona *f* non grata, Persona *f* ingrata, unerwünschte Person *f* (*dipl Vertreter*).

personable rechtsfähig, prozeßfähig, empfangsfähig.

personal persönlich, Personen ..., Personal ..., schuldrechtlich, das bewegliche Vermögen betreffend; ~ **access to children** → *access*; ~ **accident insurance** Unfallversicherung; ~ **assets log** Privatvermögensverzeichnis; ~ **cheque service** vereinfachter Scheckdienst; ~ **consumption expenditures** Ausgaben des Privatverbrauchers, Privatverbrauch; ~ **credit agreement** Kreditvertrag, Personalkredit; ~ **data and testimonials** Bewerbungsunterlagen; **P**~ **Equity Plan** (*PEP*) steuerbegünstigter Kleinaktionärsbesitz; **P**~ **Identification Number** (*PIN*) persönl Kennziffer für elektronische Bankkarte; ~ **income tax** Einkommensteuer; ~ **liability insurance** → *insurance*; ~ **loan department** Personalkreditabteilung; ~ **saving rate** private Sparquote; ~ **service corporation** Dienstleistungs-Gesellschaft.

personalia Angaben *f*/*pl* zur Person; Privatangelegenheiten *f*/*pl*; private Habe *f*.

personaliter persönlich, in eigener Person.

personality Persönlichkeit *f*, Rechtsfähigkeit *f*; Personenbezogenheit *f*; **corporate** ~ Rechte und Pflichten e–r juristischen Person; **international** ~ Völkerrechtssubjekt, Völkerrechtspersönlichkeit; **juristic** ~ Rechtsfähigkeit; die Eigenschaft e–r juristischen Person; **legal** ~ Rechtspersönlichkeit, Rechtssubjekt; Eigenschaften e–r juristischen Person.

personalise personifizieren, verkörpern.

personalisation of cheques Namensaufdruck auf Scheckformularen.

personalty bewegliches Vermögen *n*, Fahrnis *f*, Mobiliarvermögen *n*; **mixed** ~ Liegenschaftsrechte, die zum beweglichen Vermögen gerechnet werden; **quasi** ~ →

quasi; **tangible** ~ bewegliche Sachen.

personat|e sich für jmdn anders ausgeben; **~ing an officer** sich als Polizist ausgeben.

personation Identitätstäuschung *f*; ~ **of juror** Unterschiebung *f* e–s Geschworenen; ~ **of voter** mittelbare Wahlscheinsfälschung; **false** ~ Identitätstäuschung, Personenstandsfälschung.

personnel Mitarbeiter *m|pl*, Betriebsangehörige *m|pl*, Belegschaft *f*; ~ **administration** Personalführung, Personalabteilung; ~ **department** Personalabteilung, Personalbüro; ~ **development** Mitarbeiterförderung; ~ **director** Personalchef; ~ **file** Personalkartei; ~ **management** Personalabteilung; Personalverwaltung; ~ **manager** Personalchef; ~ **records** Personalakten; ~ **relations** Arbeitgeber-Arbeitnehmer-Beziehungen; ~ **under his control and direction** ihm unterstelltes Personal; **administrative** ~ Verwaltungspersonal; **executive** ~ leitende Angestellte, Führungskräfte.

persuasion Überredung *f*, Überzeugung *f*, Meinungsrichtung *f*, Überzeugungskraft *f*; **political** ~ politische Richtung, p. Einstellung.

persuasive | authority einschlägige (*nicht bindende*) Vorentscheidung *f*; ~ **force** Überzeugungskraft.

pertinent anwendbar, relevant, zur Sache gehörig, sachdienlich, einschlägig, zugehörig; ~ **data** sachdienliche Angaben; ~ **information** sachdienliche Mitteilungen; ~ **literature** einschlägige Literatur.

pertinents Zubehör *n*, Dazugehöriges *n*.

perturbatrix friedensstörende Frau *f*.

perusal flüchtige Überprüfung *f*, Durchsicht *f*.

peruse durchsehen, Kenntnis nehmen, durchlesen.

perverse verkehrt, schlecht, unerträglich, pervers, verderbt, widernatürlich; ~ **delay** vorsätzliche Verzögerung; ~ **verdict** → *verdict*.

perversion Einstellung *f*, Verdrehung *f*, Travestie *f*, Perversion *f*; ~ **of justice** Rechtsbeugung, Justizskandal, Fehlurteil; ~ **of law** Rechtsbeugung.

perverting the course of justice Rechtsbeugung begehen.

pesage Wiegegebühr *f*.

petitio Klagebegehren *n*; ~ **principii** (=) Kreisschluß, Argument auf Grund e–r Wahrunterstellung.

petition *s* Petition *f*, Eingabe *f*, Ansuchen *n*, Bittschrift *f*, Klage *f*; Antrag *m*, Verfahrensantrag *m*, Konkursantrag *m*; Gesuch *n*; ~ **and complaint** Anklage wegen Amtsvergehen; ~ **at issue** anhängige (*Wahlanfechtungs*)klage; ~ **by creditor** Konkursantrag e–s Gläubigers; ~ **for arrangement** Vergleichsantrag; ~ **for clemency** Gnadengesuch; ~ **for discharge** Antrag auf Aufhebung des Konkursverfahrens *vgl discharge in bankruptcy*; ~ **for divorce** Scheidungsantrag, Scheidungsklage; ~ **for leave to appeal** Revisionszulassungsantrag; ~ **for mercy** Gnadengesuch; ~ **for more time** Fristverlängerungsgesuch; ~ **for naturalization** Einbürgerungsantrag; ~ **for nullification** Nichtigkeitsbeschwerde, Nichtigkeitsklage; ~ **for registration** Eintragungsantrag; ~ **for respite** Gesuch um Gewährung einer Frist; ~ **for restitution of conjugal community** Klage auf Wiederherstellung der ehelichen Gemeinschaft; ~ **for review** Rechtsmittel(schrift), Antrag auf Überprüfung (*e–s Militärgerichtsurteils*); ~ **for winding-up** Antrag auf Liquidation, Antrag auf Konkurseröffnung *gegen e–e Kapitalgesellschaft*; ~ **in bankruptcy** Konkursantrag; ~ **in error** Revisionsantrag; ~ **in liquidation** Liquidationsantrag, Vergleichsantrag, Konkursantrag (*Gesellschaftskonkurs*); ~ **in lunacy** Antrag auf Entmündigung (*wegen Geisteskrankheit*); ~ **of abandonment of property** Antrag (*des Konkursver-*

walters) auf Gestattung der Preisgabe wertloser Massegegenstände; ~ **of appeal** Berufungsantrag, Berufungsschrift; ~ **of course** Antrag auf e-n Beschluß im Bürowege, Antrag auf Erlaß eines Kostenfestsetzungsbeschlusses; ~ **of right** (*obs;* → *Crown Proceedings Act*) Schadensersatzklage gegen die Krone; **P~ of Rights** (=) *Bittschrift um Herstellung des Rechts (1629)*; **abatement of ~** Hauptsacheerledigung; **answer and cross ~** Klageerwiderung und Widerklage; **commitee on public ~s** Petitionsausschuß; **debtor's ~** Konkurseröffnungsantrag des Gemeinschuldners; **election ~** *GB* Wahlanfechtung(sklage); **hearing of ~** Verhandlung über den Konkursantrag; **right of ~** → *right*; **to file one's ~** den eigenen Konkurs anmelden; Konkurseröffnung beantragen; **to lodge a ~** Gesuch einbringen; **trial of ~** mündliche Verhandlung (*über die Klage*); **voluntary ~ (in bankruptcy)** Konkursanmeldung durch Schuldner; **winding up ~** = ~ *for winding up qv*.

petition *v* beantragen, Konkursantrag stellen; ein Gesuch einreichen; **~ing creditor** betreibender Konkursgläubiger.

petitioner Kläger(in) *im Equity-Verfahren*; Beschwerdeführer *m*; Bittsteller *m*, Antragsteller *m*; **Official P~** Staatsanwaltschaft als Konkursantragssteller.

petitum Petitum *n*, Ziel *n* e-s Anspruchs.

petrol Benzin (*GB*); ~ **bomb** Molotov-Cocktail, Benzinbombe; **unleaded ~** bleifreies Benzin; **four-star ~** Super(benzin); **two-star ~** Normal(benzin).

pettifog schikanieren; den Winkeladvokaten spielen.

pettifogger Winkeladvokat *m*, Rechtsverdreher *m*, Rabulist *m*.

pettifoggery Advokatenkniff *m*, Rechtsverdrehung *f*, Rabulismus *m*.

pettifogging shyster skrupelloser Winkeladvokat *m*.

pettines Geringfügigkeit *f*, Unbedeutendheit *f*, Kleinlichkeit *f*.

petty klein, geringfügig, unbedeutend; **P~ Bag Office** *Verwaltungsabteilung des Chancery Gerichts*; ~ **sessional court** Amtsgericht, Stadtgericht; ~ **sessional courthouse** Amtsgerichtsgebäude; ~ **sessional division** Amtsgerichtsbezirk; ~ **sessions** → *session*.

pew Kirchenbank *f*, Kirchenstuhl *m*; ~ **rents** Kirchstuhlgeld.

pharao (*faro*) Pharao *n* (*verbotenes Kartenglücksspiel*).

pharmacopoeia amtliches Arzneibuch *n*.

phasing out Auslaufen *m* (*e-s Programms*), Auslaufenlassen *n*, allmähliches Abschalten *n*.

Philadelphia plan *US Mietkaufvertrag mit Treuhandsicherung*.

philosophy of law Rechtsphilosophie *f*; **legal ~** Rechtsphilosophie.

phone tapping Abhören von Telefonleitungen, Fangschaltung.

photocopier Fotokopiergerät *n*.

photocopy Fotokopie *f*, Ablichtung *f*; **certified ~** beglaubigte Fotokopie, beglaubigte Ablichtung.

photograph Photographie *f*, Lichtbild *n*; Lichtbildwerk *n* (*Copyright Act*).

physical physisch, natürlich, wirklich, körperlich; ~ **capital maintenance** Substanzerhaltung; ~ **pain and suffering** (körperliche) Schmerzen.

physically disabled *s* Invalide, Versehrter; ~ **handicapped** körperbehindert.

physician Arzt *m*; **~'s prescription** (*ärztliches*) Rezept.

phytopathological pflanzenschutzrechtlich.

phytosanitary certificate Pflanzengesundheitszeugnis *n*.

picaroon Räuber *m*, Plünderer *m*.

pick of land schmale Grundstücksecke *f*.

pickage *Abgabe bei Errichtung von Messe- und Marktständen*.

picker Pflücker *m*; Dieb *m*, Dietrich *m*; **~-up** Schlepper, Zubringer e–s Spielsalons.

pickery Kleindiebstahl *m*.

picket Streikposten *m*, Streikwache *f*; **peaceful ~** friedlicher Streikposten; **secondary ~** Streikposten vor e–m nicht direkt beteiligten Betrieb.

picketer Streikposten *m*.

picketing Streikpostenstehen *n*; **mass ~** massenhafte Streikpostenaktion; **peaceable ~ (= peaceful ~)** gewaltloses Streikpostenstehen; **stranger ~** Streikposten von Betriebsfremden; **unlawful ~** widerrechtliche Behinderung durch Streikposten.

pickle kleines mit Hecken umgebenes Grundstück *n*.

picklock Nachschlüssel *m*, Dietrich *m*; Einbrecher *m*.

pickpocket Taschendieb *m*; **beware of ~s** Vorsicht Taschendiebe!

pickup Erholung *f*, Zufallsbekanntschaft *f*; Kleinlieferwagen *m*, Transporter *m*; **~ in orders** Auftragszunahme; **~-service** Abholdienst; **~** (= *pick-up*) **truck** Kleinlaster, Pritschenwagen.

pictorial advertising Bildwerbung *f*.

picture Bild *n*, Abbildung *f*, Gemälde *n*; **Identikit ~** Phantombild.

piece Stück *n*; Akkord *m*; Bühnenstück *n*; Komposition *f*; **~ broker** Restehändler; **~ goods** Stückgüter, Meterware; **~ number** Stückzahl; **~ of evidence** Beleg, Beweisstück; **~ of land** Grundstück, Parzelle; **~ of wine** ein Stück (= *Fass*) Wein; **~ rate** Akkordsatz; **~ rate plan** Akkordsystem; **~ wages** Akkordlohn, Stücklohn; **~ work** Arbeit nach Stücklohn, Akkordarbeit; **~ worker** Akkordarbeiter; **by the ~** stückweise, per Stück.

pier Pier *m*, Landungssteg *m*, Mole *f*, Kai *m*; **~s and harbours** Hafenanlagen.

pierage Hafengebühr *f*, Piergeld *n*, Ufergeld *n*, Hafeninstandhaltungsabgaben *f/pl*.

piercing (the) corporate veil Durchgriffshaftung bei jur. Personen.

pig of pork auf eigene Niederlassung gezogene Wechsel.

pigeonhole *s* Ablegefach *n*, Brieffach *n*; *v* in ein Fach legen, ablegen, nicht weiter behandeln.

piggyback „Huckepack"-Werbung (*für zwei verschiedene Produkte*).

piggy-back export scheme Huckepackausfuhrsystem *n* (*große Exportfirmen für kleinere Firmen*).

piggy bank Sparschwein *n*.

pignorative contract → *contract*.

pignus Pfand *n*, Faustpfand *n*.

piker kleiner Berufsspieler *m*, Nassauer *m*.

pile-up Kettenunfall *m*, Auffahrunfall *m*; Massenkarambolage *f*.

pilfer stehlen, klauen, mausen, filzen.

pilferage *m*, Kleindiebstahl *m*, Klauerei *f*, Diebstahl *m* aus Transportgut.

pilferer Dieb(in), Langfinger *m*.

pillage Plünderung *f*; *v* plündern.

pillion passenger Soziusfahrer(in) *m|f*.

pillory *s* Pranger *m*.

pillory *v* anprangern.

pilot *s* Lotse *m*, Pilot *m*, Flugzeugführer *m*; **~ boat** Lotsenboot; Vorversuch; **~'s fee** → *fee (1)*; **~-in-command** Kommandant (*Luftfahrzeug*); **~ instructor** Fluglehrer; **~ jack** Lotsenflagge; **~'s licence** Lotsenpatent; **~ trainee** Flugschüler; **branch ~** amtlicher Lotse; **compulsory ~** Zwangslotse.

pilot contractor federführender Unternehmer; **~ experiment** Vorversuch; **~ plant** Versuchsanlage, Versuchsanstalt, Musterbetrieb; **~ product** → *product*; **~ sample** Ausfallmuster; **~ scheme** Versuchsprojekt.

pilot *v* lotsen; **~ a bill** e–e Vorlage durchbringen.

pilotage Lotsentätigkeit *f*, Lotsen *n*; Lotsengeld *n*; **~ authorities** Lotsenämter; **~ certificate** Lotsenzulassungsurkunde; **~ inwards** Lotsengeld für Einlotsen; ~ **jurisdiction** Zuständigkeitsbereich e–s Lotsenamts; ~ **outwards** Lotsengeld für Auslotsen; **compulsory** ~ Lotsenzwang; *defense of ~ ~: Bestreiten der Haftung, da Unfallschiff von Zwangslotsen geführt wurde*; **free** ~ Lotsenfreiheit.

pimp Zuhälter *m*; ~**-tenure** *hist* Landpacht gegen Zuhälterdienste.

pimping Zuhälterei *f*.

pin-money Nadelgeld *n*, Taschengeld *n* der Ehefrau; Heimarbeiterinnenlohn *m*.

pinch *s* Klemme *f*, Notlage *f*, plötzliche Kurssteigerung *f*; Festnahme *f*; **money** ~ zeitweilige Geldknappheit.

pinch *v* klauen, Trickdiebstahl begehen, verhaften, einsperren; **to be** ~**ed** plötzlich zu Deckungskäufen gezwungen sein.

pincher Langfinger *m*, Geizhals *m*.

pink *adj* rosarot, *s* Kommunistenfreund *m*; **P**~ **Form Issue** Angebot zum Erwerb junger Aktien zum Vorzugskurs.

pint (=) *Hohlmaß von 1/8 Gallone*.

piracy Seeräuberei *f*; geistiger Diebstahl *m*, Plagiat *n*, Raubdruck *m*; ~ **copy** Raubdruck, unerlaubter Nachdruck; ~ **of an invention** Diebstahl e–r Erfindung; ~ **of dress designs** widerrechtliche Benutzung von Kleidermodellen; **design** ~ sklavische Nachahmung; **labo(u)r** ~ → *labo(u)r*; **literary** ~ Plagiat, Diebstahl geistigen Eigentums; **video** ~ Videokopierdiebstahl.

pirate *s* Seeräuber *m*; Nachdrucker *m*; ~ **radio station** Piratensender.

pirate *v* Seeräuberei treiben; unbefugt nachdrucken, Plagiat begehen, *Mitarbeiter* abwerben; ~**d edition** Raubdruck.

pirating Raubdruck *m*.

piscary Fischereirecht *n*, Dienstbarkeit *f* mit Fischereirecht.

pit (Kohlen)Zeche *f*, Grube *f*, Bergwerk *n*; Maklerstand *m* (*in der Produktenbörse von Chicago*); ~**s and veins** Gruben und Flöze; ~ **bottom** Füllort; ~ **head price** Preis ab Schacht; ~ **prop** (*Gruben*) Stempel; ~ **trader** → *trader*; ~ **umpire** Grubenschiedsobmann.

pitch Straßenverkaufsstand *m*, Börsenmaklerstand *m*; Verkaufsgespräch *n*.

pitch fee Standgeld, Dauercamping-Standgeld.

pitfall Falle *f*, Fallgrube *f*, Gefahr *f*; ~**s of the law** Fallstricke des Gesetzes.

pittance Hungerlohn *m*, spärliches Einkommen *n*, winzige Summe *f*; Almosen *n*, Lebensmittelspende *f*.

pivotal entscheidend, wichtig.

pix die Echtheit von Münzen prüfen.

placard *s* Plakat *n*, öffentlicher Anschlag *m*, Edikt *n*, Manifest *n*; *v* anschlagen, öffentlich anheften.

place *s* Ort *m*, Stelle *f*, Platz *m*, Dienst *m*, Amt *n*, Stellung *f*; ~ **and time designated** festgesetzter Termin; ~ **belonging to his (her) Majesty** im Eigentum der Krone stehendes Anwesen; ~ **for public refreshment** Gaststätte; ~ **of abode** Aufenthaltsort, Wohnort, Wohnung; ~ **of accident** Unfallort, Unfallstätte; ~ **of arrival** Ankunftsort; ~ **of birth** Geburtsort; ~ **of burial** Beerdigungsort; ~ **of business** Geschäftslokal, Betriebsstätte, Niederlassung; ~ **of business of a solicitor** Kanzleiort e–s Anwalts; ~ **of consignment** Versendungsort; ~ **of contract** Ort des Vertragsabschlusses; ~ **of crime** Tatort; ~ **of delivery** Lieferungsort, Leistungsort; ~ **of deposit** Hinterlegungsort; ~ **of destination** Bestimmungsort; ~ **of discharge** Löschplatz; ~ **of dramatic entertainment** Aufführungsort; ~ **of drawing** Ausstellungsort; ~ **of employment** Arbeitsplatz; ~ **of exchange** **Wechselplatz;** ~ **of execution** Errichtungsort, Ort der Ausfertigung; ~ **of exit** Austrittsort (Zoll); ~ **of fulfilment** Erfüllungsort; ~ **of issue** Ausgabeort, Ausstellungsort (*Wertpapier*); ~ **of payment** Zahlungsort; ~ **of per-**

formance Erfüllungsort, Leistungsort; ~ **of presentment** Vorlageort; ~ **of profit** mit Einkünften verbundenes Amt; ~ **of public entertainment** öffentliche Vergnügungsstätte; ~ **of public resort** Raum für öffentliche Veranstaltungen; ~ **of refuge** Zufluchtsort; ~ **of residence** Wohnort, Wohnungsanschrift, Aufenthaltsort, Wohnsitz; ~ **of safety** ungefährdeter Ort; ~ **of safety order** Unterbringungsbeschluß in e–m Fürsorgeheim; ~ **of sailing** Abgangsort, Versandort; ~ **of shelter** Unterschlupf, Zufluchtsort; ~ **of transshipment** Umschlagsort; ~ **of trial** Gerichtsort, Gerichtsstand; ~ ~ ~ *of the action: Terminsort*; ~ **of work** Arbeitsplatz, Arbeitsstätte; ~ **of worship** ein dem Gottesdienst gewidmeter Ort; ~ **to sue** Gerichtsstand; ~ **where** dort, wo; **dangerous** ~ eine Stelle besonderer Verkehrsgefährdung, Gefahrenstelle; **in** ~ **of** an Stelle von; **indication of** ~ Ortsangabe; **issuing** ~ Ausstellungsort; **loading** ~ Verladungsort; **open** ~ freier Platz, öffentliches Lokal; **permanent** ~ Dauerstellung; **petty sessional** ~ Sitz e–s Amtsgerichts (*magistrates' court*); **polling** ~ → *polling*; **populous** ~ größere Ortschaft; **principal** ~ **of business** Hauptgeschäftssitz, Hauptniederlassung; **privileged** ~**s** Orte mit Asylrecht; **public** ~ öffentlicher Ort, allgemein zugänglicher Ort; **secure** ~ geschlossene Anstalt; **shipping** ~ Verladungsort; **special** ~ Zahlstelle; **working** ~ Arbeitsplatz.

place *v* plazieren; anlegen, unterbringen; ~ **a contract** e–n Auftrag vergeben; ~ **a loan** e–e Anleihe plazieren, unterbringen; ~ **an insurance** e–e Versicherung abschließen; ~ **an order** e–n Auftrag erteilen; ~ **at interest** verzinslich anlegen; ~ **at one's disposal** zur Verfügung stellen; ~ **goods** Waren absetzen; ~ **money** Geld anlegen; ~ **on the same footing** gleichstellen; ~ **to account** in Rechnung stellen; ~ **to the credit** gutschreiben, kreditieren; ~ **under arrest** verhaften, beschlagnahmen.

placeman öffentlicher Bediensteter *m*, Postenjäger *m*, politischer Günstling *m*.

placement Stellung *f*, Unterbringung *f*, Anlage *f*; ~ **agency** Stellenvermittlung; ~ **of funds** Kapitalverwendung.

placer loses Mineralvorkommen *n*; ~ **claim** *Schürfanspruch auf öffentlichem Grund zur Gewinnung von losen mit dem Boden vermischten Mineralien*; ~ **location** *e–e Schürfstelle für lose Mineralien auf öffentlichem Grund.*

placing Plazierung *f*, Anlage *f*, Anlegen *n*, Unterbringung *f* von Wertpapieren *durch Maklerfirmen*; ~ **of an order** Auftragserteilung; ~ **price** Einführungspreis; **competitive** ~ Einstellung nach dem Wettbewerbsprinzip (*bes öffentlicher Dienst*); **private** ~ private Effektenplazierung.

placit Dekret *n*, Entscheidung *f*.

placitabile schlüssig, vorbringbar, vertretbar.

placitory Einrede(n) betreffend.

plagiarism Plagiat *n*, literarischer Diebstahl *m*.

plagiarist Plagiator *m*.

plagiarize plagiieren, ein Plagiat begehen, abschreiben.

plagiarizer Plagiator *m*.

plagiary Plagiat *n*.

plaideur Anwalt *m*.

plain clothes man Detektiv *m*, Geheimpolizist *m*.

plainant Kläger *m*.

plaint Klageschrift *f*, *beim County Court*; Beschwerde *f*; ~ **fee** gerichtl Prozeßgebühr.

plaintiff Kläger *m* (-in *f*), Klagepartei *f*; ~**'s description** nähere Bezeichnung des Klägers; ~ **in error** Revisionskläger; ~**-spouse** der klagende Ehegatte, Ehegatte(in) als Kläger, der Antragsteller/die Antragstellerin (*Scheidungsproz*); ~ **suing by a solicitor** Kläger bei Anwaltszwang, anwaltschaftlich vertretener Kläger; ~ **suing in person** nicht anwaltschaftlich vertretener Kläger; ~ **under disability** nicht prozeßfähiger Kläger; **infant** ~ minderjähriger Kläger; **joint** ~ Mitkläger; **nominal** ~ → *nominal*; **patient** ~ Geisteskranker als Kläger; **proper** ~ der richtige Kläger, aktivlegitimierter Kläger; **representative** ~ Kläger in Prozeßstandschaft *für e–e Gemeinschaft;* **suit-happy** ~**s** prozeßfreudige Kläger; **use** ~ der Drittbegünstigte *bei e–r Klage in Prozeßstandschaft.*

plan *s* Plan *m*, Entwurf *m*, Vorhaben *n*, Projekt *n*, Grundriß *m*, Bauplan *m*, Flächennutzungsplan *m*, Stadtplan *m*, Projekt *n*, technische Zeichnung *f*; ~ **of site** Lageplan *m*; **dead-on-arrival** ~ totgeborener Plan; **development** ~ → *development*; **eighty-twenty** ~ 80 zu 20 Schadensdeckungsplan (*Versicherung zahlt 80%, Versicherter 20%*); **fiscal** ~ Finanz-, Steuerplan; **general** ~ Übersichtsplan; **master** ~ Flächennutzungsplan.

plan *v* planen, entwerfen; ~**ned economy** Planwirtschaft; ~**ned parenthood** Familienplanung.

planning Planung *f*, Erschließung *f*; ~ **agency** Planungsstelle; ~ **authority** Planungsbehörde; ~ **permission** Bebauungs- und Nutzungsänderungs-Erlaubnis; ~ **scheme** Projekt; **city** ~ Stadtplanung; **economic** ~ Wirtschaftsplanung; **long-range** ~ langfristige Planung; **regional** ~ Landesplanung; **state** ~ staatliche Planung, *US* einzelstaatliche Planung.

plank Programmpunkt *m*, Artikel *m* im Parteiprogramm; ~ **bed** Pritsche (*Gefängnis*); ~ **way** Bohlenweg.

plant *s* Betriebsanlage *f*, Einrichtung *f*, Inventar *n*, Werk *n*, Fabrik *f*, Betrieb *m*, Maschinerie *f*, technische Anlage *f* und Einrichtung, Gerätschaften *f*|*pl*, Betriebsmaterial *n*; ausgemachter Schwindel *m*, (Polizei)Falle *f*, Polizeispitzel *m*; ~ **acceptance** → *acceptance*; ~ **and machinery** Betriebseinrichtung und Maschinen; ~ **capacity** Betriebskapazität; ~ **closing** Betriebsschließung(en); ~ **hire operator** gewerblicher Betriebsanlagenvermieter; ~ **ledger** Inventarverzeichnis, Betriebsanlagenbuch; ~ **regulations** Betriebsvorschriften; ~ **superintendent** Betriebsleiter; ~ **training** innerbetriebliche Ausbildung *am Arbeitsplatz*; **indivisible** ~ Betriebsanlagen, die nur für Großfertigung insgesamt geeignet sind; Großanlage.

plant *v* anbauen, pflanzen, errichten.

plastics Kunststoffe *m*|*pl*; ~ **industry** Kunststoffindustrie; ~ **processing industry** kunststoffverarbeitende Industrie.

plat Katasterplan *m*, Vermessungsplan *m*; Aufteilungsplan *m* für Bauland (= ~ *map*).

plate Schild *n*; Gold- und Silbergeschirr *n*, Gold- und Silberbestecke *n*|*pl*; ~**-glass insurance** → *insurance*; **display of** ~**s** gut sichtbare Anbringung von (Nummern)schildern; **rating** ~ Leistungsschild.

plateauing Einpendeln auf e–m Niveau.

platform Plattform *f*, Tribüne *f*, Podium *n*, Terrasse *f*, Parteiprogramm *n*, Wahlprogramm *n*.

plea *s* Einrede *f* (= *E*), Einwendung *f*, Vorbringen *n*, Antrag *m*, Gesuch *n*, Klageerwiderung *f*; ~ **bargaining** Absprachen über Schuldigerklärung *mit der Staatsanwaltschaft*; *Aushandeln, wie sich der Angeklagte einlassen soll*; ~ **for annulment** Nichtigkeitsklage; ~ **for clemency** Gnadengesuch; ~ **for infancy** Berufung auf Minderjährigkeit; ~ **in abatement** prozeßhindernde *E*; Antrag, die Eröffnung der Hauptverhandlung nicht zuzulassen; ~ **in bar** rechtsvernichtende *E*; prozeßhinderndes Verteidigungsvorbringen; ~ **in discharge** Einrede der Erfüllung (*oder sonstigen Erledigung*) des Klageanspruchs; ~ **in law** rechtshindernde *E*, ~ **in re-**

convention (*E* mit) Gegenvorbringen; ~**s in short by consent** einverständlich abgekürztes Beklagtenvorbringen; ~ **of confession and avoidance** Berufung auf anderweitige Erledigung des Klageanspruchs; ~ **of demurrer** Bestreiten der Zulässigkeit bzw Schlüssigkeit; ~ **of destitution** Notbedarfseinrede; ~ **of equitable lien** *E* des nicht erfüllten Vertrages; ~ **of estoppel per rem iudicatam** *E* der Rechtskraft; ~ **of guilty** Schuldigerklärung vor Gericht; ~ **of incompetency of plaintiff** *E* der mangelnden Aktivlegitimation; ~ **of insanity** Berufung auf Prozeßunfähigkeit des Klägers, *E* der mangelnden Geschäftsfähigkeit, *E* der Unzurechnungsfähigkeit; ~ **of justification** Rechtfertigungsvorbringen mit Angebot des Wahrheitsbeweises; ~ **of lapse of time** *E* der Verjährung, Berufung auf Ausschlußfrist; ~ **of necessity** Notbedarfseinrede; ~ **of negligent litigation** Hinweis auf grobfahrlässige Prozeßführung des Gegners; ~ **of never indebted** Bestreiten e–r Schuldverpflichtung; ~ **of nolo contendere** Erklärung des Angeklagten, die Anklage nicht bestreiten zu wollen; ~ **of not guilty** Nichtschuldigerklärung; ~ **of nullity** Nichtigkeitsbeschwerde, Einwand der Rechtsunwirksamkeit; ~ **of release** Berufung auf nachträgliche Entlassung aus der Verbindlichkeit; ~ **of set-off** Einrede der Aufrechnung; ~ **of sanctuary** Berufung auf Kirchenasylrecht; ~ **of superior orders** Berufung auf höheren Befehl; ~ **of suspension** Antrag auf Aussetzung des Verfahrens; ~ **of tender** sofortiges Anerkenntnis unter Hinweis auf Zahlungsangebot und Vorzeigen des geschuldeten Geldes im Termin; ~**s of the Crown** Strafklagen; ~ **of unexhausted remedies** Einrede der Vorausklage; ~**s roll** Liste der Schriftsätze e–s Prozesses; ~ **side** Streitgericht, Zivilprozeßabteilung e–s Gerichts; ~ **to indictment** formale Erklärung zur Anklage (*schuldig oder nicht schuldig*); ~ **to the action** materielle Einwendung; ~ **to the jurisdiction** *E* der Unzuständigkeit, Zuständigkeitsrüge; ~ **under intimidation** Schuldigerklärung bei Einschüchterung; **affirmative** ~ rechtsvernichtende Einwendung; **ambiguous** ~ mehrdeutige Einlassung, Schuldbekenntnis mit Vorbehalten; **anomalous** ~ rechtsvernichtende Einwendung mit bestreitendem Vorbringen; **bad** ~ unzulässige *bzw* unbegründete *E*; **common** ~**s** privatrechtlicher Prozeß; **counter-**~ Gegeneinwand; **declinatory** ~ *hist* Berufung auf Kirchenasylrecht; **defendant's** ~ Klageerwiderung; **dilatory** ~ verzögerliche (= dilatorische) *E*, prozeßhindernde *E*; **double** ~ Einwendung der unzulässigen Anspruchshäufung (*unzulässige Verbindung, zusammenhangloser Sachverhalte*); **duplicatious** ~ = *double ~ qv*; **equivocal** ~ widersprüchl Erklärung zur Anklage, eingeschränkte Schuldigerklärung; **false** ~ Scheineinrede; **foreign** ~ *E* der Unzuständigkeit; **frivolous** ~ unseriöses Vorbringen, schikanöser Einwand, frivoler Einwand; **general** ~ allgemeines Bestreiten der Klage; **issuable** ~ → *issuable*; **jurisdictional** ~ Rüge der Unzuständigkeit; **late** ~ nachträgliche Schuldigerklärung; **negative** ~ Bestreiten (nur) eines prozeßentscheidenden Punktes; **negotiated** ~ ausgehandelte Erklärung zur Anklage; **peremptory** ~ peremptorische *E*, rechtsvernichtende *E*; **permanent** ~ absolute Einrede; **pure** ~ auf Gegenansprüche gestützte *E*; **replication to** ~ Replik; **rolled-up** ~ kombinierte *E*, gestaffelte Hilfseinwendungen; *Berufung auf Wahrheit und Gutgläubigkeit gegen Beleidigungsanschuldigung*; **sham** ~ Scheineinrede, Verzögerungsmanöver, frivoles Gegenvorbringen; **special** ~ prozeßhindernde Einrede; substantiiertes Gegenvorbringen; **special ~ in bar** auf neues Vorbringen gestützte rechtsvernichtende *E*; **substituting ~** Hilfseinwendung; **to cop a ~** (*US sl*) sich aus taktischen Gründen für schuldig erklären (*um e–e Strafmilderung zu erreichen*).

plead vortragen, einwenden, plädieren, vor Gericht geltend machen, als Klageerwiderung vortragen, sich zur Anklage erklären; **~ a statute** e–e gesetzliche Vorschrift geltend machen, *e–n Tatbestand so vortragen, daß er subsumiert werden kann*; **~ as a defence** e–e Einrede vorbringen; **~ at the bar** vor Gericht plädieren; **~ bar of trial** e–e prozeßhindernde Einrede geltend machen; **~ guilty** sich schuldig (*im Sinne der Anklage*) bekennen; **~ guilty by post** sich auf postalischem Wege schuldig bekennen (*kleine Verkehrsdelikte*); **~ (one's) ignorance** sich auf Unwissenheit berufen; **~ ignorance of law** sich auf Gesetzesunkenntnis berufen; **~ in mitigation** strafmildernde Umstände vortragen, **~ in the alternative** hilfsweise (*schriftsätzlich*) vortragen; **~ issuably** Entscheidungserhebliches vortragen; **~ jus tertii** sich auf das Recht e–s Dritten berufen; **~ lapse of time** die Einrede des Fristablaufs geltend machen; **~ not guilty** sich für nichtschuldig erklären; **~ one's cause** seinen Fall vortragen, in eigener Sache plädieren; **~ over** rügelos hinnehmen (*über Fehler im gegnerischen Vorbringen rügelos hinweggehen*), allgemein bestreiten; **~ poverty** sich auf Armut berufen; **~ specifically** substantiiert vortragen; **~ the statute of limitations** Verjährung einwenden; **~ to the merits** materiell-rechtlich vortragen, zur Sache selbst ausführen.

pleadable vertretbar, triftig.

pleader Prozeßbevollmächtigter, *der bei Gericht mündl verhandelt*; der e–e Einrede (*plea*) Vorbringende; Hilfsanwalt *m* zur Vorbereitung von Schriftsätzen; schriftsätzliches Vorbringen; **faint ~** → *faint*; **special ~** Rechtsberater, Spezialist für Schriftsatzentwürfe, beratender Anwalt.

pleading anwaltliche Prozeßführung; schriftsätzliche Vorbereitung *f* der mündlichen Verhandlung, Schriftsatz *m*, Plädieren *n*; **~ guilty by post** Schuldigerklärung auf dem Postwege (*summarisches Verfahren*); **~ in the alternative** Hilfsvorbringen; **~ the "Baby Act"** sich auf die Minderjährigkeit des Vertragsschließenden (*oder auf Verjährung*) berufen (*abfällig*); **~ to the charge** Einlassung auf die Anklage; **adversarial ~** streitige schriftsätzl Vorbereitung; **colo(u)rable ~** Einwendungen durch Gegenvorbringen; **double ~** Anspruchshäufung (*Verbot der*) *mehrfachen Einwendung zur gleichen Behauptung*; **special ~** neues Gegenvorbringen; den persönlichen Vorteil bezweckendes Argument, geschickte anwaltschaftliche Vertretung; verdeckte Interessenvertretung; **special ~ legislation** *US* interessengebundene Gesetzgebung.

pleadings schriftlicher Vortrag *m*, beiderseitige schriftsätzliche Vorbereitung *f* der mündlichen Verhandlung; **~ out of time** verspäteter Schriftsatz; **close of ~** Ablauf der Frist zur schriftsätzlichen Vorbereitung; **default of ~** Versäumung der Zustellung vorbereitender Schriftsätze; **delivery of ~** Einreichung von Schriftsätzen; **oral ~** mündliche Ausführungen, Plädoyer; **subsequent ~** nachgereichte Schriftsätze; Schriftsätze nach Klageerwiderung; **to draw ~** Schriftsätze aufsetzen; **trial without ~** mündliche Verhandlung ohne (weitere) vorbereitende Schriftsätze; **written ~** Schriftsätze.

pleasure|grounds Erholungsflächen *f|pl*, Vergnügungspark *m*; **at (the) ~** kündbar, widerruflich, nach Belieben; **at the ~ of the owner** widerruflich; für den Eigentümer;

during Her Majesty's ~ solange es Ihrer Majestät beliebt, auf unbestimmte Zeit im Belieben Ihrer Majestät, bis auf königl Widerruf.

plebiscitary area Abstimmungsgebiet *n*.

plebiscite Volksabstimmung *f*, Volksentscheid *m*, Plebiszit *n*.

pledge *s* Bürge *m*; Mobiliarpfandrecht *n*, Verpfändung *f*, Faustpfand *m*, Gelübde *n*; ~ **of accounts** Verpfändung von Außenständen; ~ **of credit of firm** Inanspruchnahme von Kredit für die Firma; ~ **of secrecy** Geheimhaltungsverpflichtung; ~**s to restore** Bürgen als Sicherheitsleistung des pfändenden Arrestgläubigers; **by way of** ~ pfandweise; **dead** ~ Faustpfand; **documentary** ~ Dokumentenpfand; **forfeited** ~ verfallenes Pfand; **negative** ~ Verpfändungsunterlassungsverpflichtung; **to take in** ~ als Pfand nehmen; **to take s. th. out of** ~ etwas aus der Verpfändung auslösen; **unlawful** ~ widerrechtliche Verpfändung.

pledge *v* verpfänden, versetzen, geloben; ~ **as collateral security** verpfänden; ~ **one's credit** Kredit in Anspruch nehmen; ~ **one's honour** sich ehrenwörtlich verpflichten; ~ **one's own personal credit** sich persönlich feierlich verpflichten; ~ **one's word** sein Ehrenwort geben; ~**d article** Pfandobjekt; ~**d object** Pfandgegenstand; ~**d property** → *property*; ~**d securities** beliehene Wertpapiere.

pledgee Pfandnehmer *m*, Pfandgläubiger *m*.

pledgery Bürgschaft *f*.

pledging Verpfändung *f*; ~ **of accounts receivable** Sicherungsabtretung (von Außenständen).

pledgor Verpfänder *m*, Pfandschuldner *m*.

plene | **administravit** Einrede der abgeschlossenen Nachlaßabwicklung, E. des verteilten Nachlasses; ~ **comptavit** Einrede der erfolgten Rechnungslegung.

plenipotentiary *adj* bevollmächtigt; *s* Inhaber e–r Generalvollmacht; Bevollmächtigter *m*, Sonderbevollmächtigter *m*, Gesandter *m*; ~ **of governments** Regierungsbevollmächtigter.

plenum dominium Volleigentum *n* des Eigenbesitzers.

plevin gerichtlicher Befehl *m*, Zusicherung *f*.

plight hoffnungslose Lage *f*, Misere *f*; Landpachtbesitz *m*; Gelöbnis *n*, Eheversprechen *n*, Verlobung *f*.

Plimsoll Mark (line) gesetzliche Höchstlademarke *f* (*an Schiffsrümpfen*).

plot *(1)* Grundstück *n*, Parzelle *f*, Bauplan *m*; **building** ~ Baugrundstück; **landlocked** ~ zuwegsloses Grundstück, ohne Zufahrt.

plot *s (2)* Verschwörung *f*, Komplott *n*.

plot *v* anzetteln, sich verschwören; Verschwörung planen.

plottage Wertschätzung *f* von Grundstücken (*insbes zusammenliegender Parzellen*); ~ **increment** Mehrwert (*e–s Grundstücks*) durch Möglichkeit der Zusammenlegung.

plotter Verschwörer *m*, Ränkeschmied *m*, Anstifter *m*; Planzeichner *m*.

plotting Verschwörung *f*.

plough-bote Holzentnahmerecht (*für Pflüge und Gerätschaften*); ~**land** Ackerland.

plough-back *s* Reinvestierung *f* von Erträgen, Selbstfinanzierung *f* aus Gewinnen, Thesaurierung.

plow = *plough qv*.

plug für etwas Werbung treiben.

plum Sonderdividende *f*.

plump *parl* nur für e–n Kandidaten stimmen.

plunder *s* Plünderei *f*, Raub *m*; *v* plündern, rauben.

plunderage Unterschlagung *f* von Schiffsladung.

plunger Hazardeur *m*, waghalsiger Wetter *m*, Spekulant *m*.

plurality relative Mehrheit *f*, Vielheit *f*; ~ **of heirs** Mehrheit von Erben,

Erbengemeinschaft; ~ **of votes** relative Mehrheit.

pluries oft, häufig; **a ~ writ** dritte gerichtliche Aufforderung; **~ fi fa** neuer, wiederholter Vollstreckungsauftrag.

plutocracy Plutokratie *f*, Geldherrschaft *f*, Geldaristokratie *f*.

plying for hire auf Fahrgastsuche *f* herumfahren.

poach wildern.

poacher Wilddieb *m*.

poaching Wildern *n*, Jagdwilderei mit Fischwilderei *f*; ~ **(of) labour** Abwerben (von Arbeitskräften); **inter union** ~ Mitglieder-Abwerben zwischen Gewerkschaften; **night** ~ Wilderei bei Nacht.

poinding Zwangsvollstreckung *f*, Pfändung *f*; ~ **of the ground** = *real ~ qv*; **multiple** ~ → *multiple*; **personal** ~ Mobiliarpfändung; **real** ~ Zwangsverwaltung.

point *s* Punkt *m*, Gesichtspunkt *m*, Teil *m* e–s Vorbringens; (*Kursnotierung*) Einheit *f*; ~ **at issue** Kernpunkt, strittiger Punkt, entscheidungserhebliche Frage; ~ **duty** Verkehrsdienst; **~s of claim** Klagebegründung; ~ **of contact** Kontaktierungspunkt, Ansprechstelle; ~ **of controversy** Streitfrage; **~s of defence** → *defence*; ~ **of dispute** Streitpunkt; ~ **of entry** Grenzübergangsstelle; ~ **of fact** Tatfrage; ~ **of honour** Ehrensache; ~ **of law** Rechtsfrage, juristisches Argument; ~ ~ ~ *of general public importance: Rechtsfrage von grundsätzlicher öffentl Bedeutung*; ~ **of order** Geschäftsordnungspunkt; **~-of sale advertising** Verkaufspunktwerbung; ~ **of sale debit-card machine** Geldkarten-Kassenterminal; ~ **of sale terminal** Kassenterminal, bargeldlose Zahlung; elektronische Ladenkasse (*auch p. of sale*); ~ **of view** Gesichtspunkt, Standpunkt; ~ **plan** Punktsystem *für Arbeitsbewertung bzw für Prämien*; ~ **reserved** vorläufige Entscheidung e–r Frage unter Vorbehalt; ~ **system** Punktesystem (*Strafpunkte*); **at all ~s** vollinhaltlich; **at the ~ of death** bei Eintritt des Todes; **bullion** ~ Goldpunkt; **chief** ~ Hauptpunkt, Hauptsache; **in ~ of** in Hinsicht, hinsichtlich; **in ~ of fact** in tatsächlicher Hinsicht; **off the** ~ nicht zur Sache gehörig; **on a ~ of order** „zur Geschäftsordnung"; **to the** ~ zur Sache gehörig.

poison Gift *n*; **administering** ~ Giftbeibringung; **P~s Act** Giftgesetz *GB 1972*; ~ **pill** (*lit Giftpille*) *Abwehrmittel gegen Übernahmespekulanten* (*durch "stock dividends" ua*).

poisoning Vergiftung *f*; **murder by** ~ Giftmord.

police Polizei *f* (= *P bzw p*), Kriminalpolizei *f*, Amt *n* für öffentliche Ordnung; ~ **accountability** polizeiliche Rechenschaftspflicht; **P~ Act** Polizeigesetz *GB 1964*; ~ **authority** Polizei(*behörde*), *P*verwaltung; ~ **badge** *P*abzeichen; ~ **bash-in** *P*schelte; ~ **beat** *P*streife; ~ **blotter** Dienstbuch, *P*register; ~ **cadet** Polizeischüler; **~-community relations** Beziehungen der *P* zu den Bürgern; ~ **complaint** Beschwerde gegen die *P*; *P~ C~s Board: Beschwerdestelle gegen die Polizei*; ~ **court** → *court*; ~ **custody** *P*gewahrsam; ~ **detention** *P*gewahrsam; ~ **escort** *P*eskorte, *P*geleit; ~ **headquarters** *P*präsidium; ~ **informer** *P*spitzel; ~ **interrogation** polizeiliche Vernehmung; ~ **jury** Gemeinderat (*Louisiana*); ~ **justice** *P*richter, Schnellrichter; ~ **line-up** polizeiliche Gegenüberstellung zwecks Identifizierung; ~ **magistrate** Amtsrichter in *kleineren* Strafsachen, Schnellrichter, *P*richter; ~ **national computer** zentraler landesweiter Polizeicomputer *GB*; ~ **officer** *P*beamter, Polizist; ~ **order** *P*verfügung; ~ **ordinance** Polizeiverordnung; ~ **patrol** *P*streife; ~ **policy** Polizeiverwaltungsgrundsätze; polizeiliche Richtlinien; ~ **pound** polizeilicher Abstellplatz für abgeschleppte Fahrzeuge; ~ **power** *P*gewalt; ~ **power in court** Sitzungs*p*; ~ **pre-**

cautions polizeiliche Vorsichtsmaßnahmen; ~ **protection** *P*schutz, polizeilicher Schutz; ~ **purposes** polizeiliche Zwecke; ~ **record** Strafregister; ~ **reference** polizeiliches Führungszeugnis; ~ **registrations** polizeiliche Eintragungen, Vorstrafenregister; ~ **regulations** *P*vorschriften; ~ **spy** *P*spitzel; ~ **state** *P*staat; ~ **station** *P*revier, *P*station; ~ **supervision** *P*aufsicht; **P~ Support Group** *Spezialeinheit der Kriminalpolizei*; ~ **trap** Autofalle; ~ **witness** von der *P* gestellter Zeuge; **border** ~ Grenz*p*; **harbour** ~ Hafen*p*; **military** ~ Militär*p*, Feldgendarmerie; **political** ~ politische *P*, Geheim*p*; **railway** ~ Bahn*p*; **secret** ~ Geheim*p*; **wanted by the** ~ → *to want*.

policeman Polizeibeamter *m*, Polizist *m*; **undercover** ~ Geheimpolizist, Polizist in Zivil.

policy *(1)* Police *f* (= *P bzw p*), Versicherungsschein *m*; ~ **book** Policenregister; ~ **broker** Versicherungsmakler; ~ **drafting** *P–n*ausfertigung; **~-holder** *P–n*inhaber, Versicherungsnehmer; **~-holders' control** *Beherrschung des Versicherungsunternehmens durch Versicherungsnehmer*; **P~ holders' Protection Board** Entschädigungsstelle für Versicherungsnehmer (*bei Zahlungsunfähigkeit von Versicherungsgesellschaften*); ~ **loan** Beleihung e–r Versicherung; ~ **of insurance** Versicherungs*p*; ~ **owner** *P–n*besitzer, *P–n*inhaber; ~ **proof of interest** *P* genügt als Beweis des versicherbaren Interesses; ~ **terms** Versicherungsbedingungen; ~ **to bearer** Inhaber*p*; ~ **underwriter** Versicherungsgarant (*Seeversichg*); ~ **year** Ausstellungsjahr der *P*, Jahr des Versicherungsbeginns; **accident** ~ Unfallversicherungs*p*; **additional** ~ Zusatz*p*, Nachtrags*p*; **all risks** ~ Universalversicherung; **annual** ~ Jahres*p*; **antedated** ~ rückdatierte *P*; **assessable** ~ *Versicherungsvertrag mit Nachschußpflicht des Versicherten*; **automobile** ~ KFZ-Unfallversicherung; **bearer** ~ Inhaber*p*; **blank** ~ Blanko*p*, *P–n*formular; **blanket** ~ Pauschal*p*; **block** ~ General*p*; **builders' risk** ~ Bauunternehmerhaftpflichtversicherung; **burglary** ~ Einbruchsversicherung; **compound** ~ Pauschal*p*; **continuing** ~ automatisch fortlaufende *P*; **convertible term** ~ umwandelbare Lebensversicherungs*p*; **declaration** ~ *US Feuerversicherungspolice mit periodischer Wertangabepflicht*; **deferred annuity** ~ *P* über e–e aufgeschobene Rentenversicherung; **endowment (assurance)** ~ (Police e–r abgekürzten) Versicherung auf den Todes- und Erlebensfall, gemischte Lebensv.; **excess** ~ Versicherung für den nicht anderweitig gedeckten Schaden; **expired** ~ abgelaufene *P*; **extended** ~ beitragslos gestellte Lebensversicherung, prolongierte *P*; **family income** ~ Familien-Vorsorgeversicherung; **family protection** ~ Familien-Vorsorgeversicherung; **fidelity** ~ Veruntreuungsversicherung *f*; **fire** ~ → *fire*; **floater** ~ Pauschalversicherungs*p* für verschiedene Transportgefahren; **floating** ~ offene *P*, General*p*, laufende Versicherungs*p*, Ergänzungs*p*; **free** ~ prämienfreie *P*; **freight** ~ Fracht*p*; **freight and profits** ~ Seefracht- und Gewinnausfallversicherung; **general** ~ Sammel*p*; **general accident** ~ (*allgemeine*) Unfallversicherungs*p*; **general liability** ~ allgemeine Haftpflichtversicherung; **group** ~ Sammel*p*; **guaranteed dividend** ~ Versicherung mit Gewinnbeteiligungsgarantie; **health** ~ Krankenversicherung; **homeowners** ~ kombinierte Hausbesitzerhaftpflicht- und Hausratversicherung; **hull** ~ Schiffskaskoversicherung; **income** ~ Rentenversicherung zugunsten eines Dritten; **incontestable** ~ unwiderruflich gewordene *P*; **indisputable** ~ *P* ohne Zurückweisungsrecht; **industrial life** ~ Kleinlebens*p*; **inland transportation** ~ Binnenverkehrsschadensversicherung; **interest** ~ *P, der versicherungsfähiges Interesse zugrunde liegt*; **jeweller's block** ~ Pauschalschadensversicherung für Juweliere; **joint lives** ~ *P* über e–e Überlebensversicherung; **liability** ~ Haftpflicht*p*; **life** ~ Lebensversicherungs*p*; **life of a** ~ Laufzeit e–r *P*; **limited** ~ Versicherung mit beschränktem Risiko; **limited payment** ~ Versicherung mit begrenzter Prämienzahlung; **marine** ~ Seeversicherungs*p*, Schiffs*p*; **maritime** ~ = *marine* ~ *qv*; **master** ~ Hauptversicherung *bei Gruppenversicherung*, Haupt*p*, Rahmen*p*; **mixed** ~ (*Seeversicherung*) Zeit- und Reise*p*; **mutual** ~ *P* e–r Gesellsch auf Gegenseitigkeit; **named** ~ Seeversicherungs*p* mit Namensnennung *und Angaben über das Schiff*; **non-assessable** ~ *P* ohne Nachschußpflicht, nachschußfreie Versicherung; **non-concurrent** ~**ies** nicht gleichlautende Versicherungen (*von mehreren Versicherern*); **non-medical** ~ Lebensversicherung ohne ärztliche Untersuchung; **non-participating** ~ nicht gewinnberechtigte *P*; **office burglary** ~ → *office*; **open** ~ *P* ohne Wertangabe, offene *P*, General*p*; **ordinary life** ~ normale Lebensversicherung (*mit gleichen Prämien*); **original** ~ Original*p*, Haupt*p*; **package** ~ Sammel*p*; **paid-up** ~ vollbezahlte Versicherung, prämienfreie *P*; **participating (life)** ~ Lebensversicherung(spolice) mit Gewinnbeteiligung; **pluvius** ~ Regenversicherung(s*p*); **portion** ~ Aussteuerversicherung; **professional indemnity** ~ Berufshaftpflicht*p*; **reinstatement** ~ Neuwert*p*; **registered life** ~ amtlich registrierter Lebensversicherungsvertrag *beim US-einzelstaatlichen Versicherungsamt (state insurance commissioner), eingetragen und durch Hinterlegung von Wertpapieren in Höhe des Deckungskapitals gesichert*; **rental value** ~ Mietausfallversicherung; **reporting** ~ variable Globalversicherung *mit Wertmeldungspflicht des Versicherten*; **residence burglary** ~ Wohnungseinbruchsversicherungs*p*; **return premium** ~ Prämienrückgewährvertrag; **single** ~ Einzelpolice; **single premium life** ~ Einmalprämien-(Lebens)versicherung; **special computer** ~ Versicherung mit Sonderdeckung für Schäden durch Komputerbenutzung, Komputerhaftpflichtversicherung; **special risk** ~ kurzfristige *P* für bestimmtes Risiko; **standard** ~ Normal*p*, Einheits*p*; **stockbrokers' combined** ~ Börsenmaklerhaftpflicht*p*; **subsequent** ~ Nachtragspolice; **supplementary** ~ Nachtrgs*p*; **surrender value of a** ~ Rückkaufswert e–r *P*; **survivorship** ~ gemeinsame Lebensversicherung auf den Tod des Zuletztlebenden; **term** ~ Risikolebensversicherung(s*p*), zeitlich beschränkte Versicherung, Lebensversicherung ohne Rückkaufswert; **temporary assurance** ~ zeitl begrenzte Lebensversicherung; **three-D-**~ → *three*; **time** ~ Zeitversicherungs*p*, Zeit*p*, befristete *P (Seeversicherung)*; **time and distance** ~ *P mit zukünftiger Rückzahlung nebst Zinsen und laufenden Prämienzahlungen*; **tontine** ~ Tontineversicherung *mit befristeter Gruppenlebensversicherung, Anwachsungsrecht für die während der Versicherungsdauer überlebenden Versicherungsnehmer*; **tourist** ~ Reiseversicherung; **tourist floater** ~ Reisegepäckversicherung; **trader's** ~ Sammlung von *P–n* des gleichen Versicherten; **umbrella** ~ Zusatzhaftpflichtversicherung (*auf erhöhten Wert*); **unvalued** ~ *P* ohne Wertangabe, Pauschal*p*; **valued** ~ → *valued*; **voyage** ~ Reiseversicherungs*p*, *P* mit vereinbarter Wertangabe; **wager(ing)** ~ Versicherung mit Wettcharakter; *zB auf das Leben e–s Dritten*; **whole life** ~ Versicherung auf den Todesfall; **workmen's compensation** ~ gesetzliche Arbeitsunfallversicherung.

policy *(2)* Politik (= *P bzw p*), Richtlinie *f*, Grundsatz *m*, Richtlinien *f|pl* staatsmännischer Tätigkeit, politischer Grundsatz *m*, Gesetzeszweck *m*; ~ **bible** Grundsatzprogramm; ~ **document** Grundsatzdokument; ~ **guidelines** Richtlinien (*Politik, Verwaltung*); ~**-making** richtungweisend; ~**-**~ *bodies: Leitungsorgane*; ~ **of a statute** Gesetzeszweck; ~ **of alliances** Bündnis*p*; ~ **of appeasement** Beschwichtigungs*p*; ~ **of attrition** Zermürbungs*p*; ~ **of containment** Eindämmungs*p*; ~ **of economy** Spar*p*; ~ **of encirclement** Einkreisungs*p*; ~ **of force** Gewalt*p*; ~ **of legislation** gesetzgeberische Absicht; ~ **of the middle road** *P* der Mitte; ~ **of mutual understanding** Verständigungs*p*; ~ **of neutrality** Neutralitäts*p*; ~ **of non-interference** Nichteinmischungs*p*; ~ **of rapprochement** Annäherungs*p*; ~ **of the law** Rechtsgedanke, Rechtsgrundsatz; Absicht des Gesetzgebers; ~ **of wait and see** *P* des Abwartens; ~ **statement** Grundsatzerklärung; **business** ~ Betriebs*p*, Geschäfts*p*, Geschäftsgebaren; **business cycle** ~ Konjunktur*p*; **change in** ~ politischer Kurswechsel; **commercial** ~ Handels*p*; **co-ordinated** ~ abgestimmte *P*; **domestic** ~ Innen*p*; **economic** ~ Wirtschaftspolitik; **Fabian** ~ →*Fabian*; **financial** ~ Finanzpolitik, Finanzen; **fiscal** ~ Finanz*p*, steuerpolitische Maßnahmen; **foreign** ~ Außen*p*; **hands-off** ~ Nichteinmischungs*p*; **general** ~ allgemeine Richtlinien; **labo(u)r** ~ → *labo(u)r*; **long-range** ~ *P* auf weite Sicht; **monetary** ~ Währungspolitik; **open-door** ~ *P* der offenen Tür; **ostrich** ~ Vogel-Strauß-*P*; **price** ~ Preis*p*; **public** ~ Grundprinzipien von Recht und Ordnung; öffentl Interesse; ordre public, Staatsraison; **stop-go economic** ~ Wirtschaftspolitik des Bremsens und Wiedergasgebens; **tariff** ~ Zoll*p*; **wage** ~ Lohn*p*.

political politisch.

politician Politiker *m*, Staatsmann *m*, Berufspolitiker *m*, Parteipolitiker *m*.

politicize politisieren.

politico|-economical wirtschaftspolitisch; ~**-judicial** Justiz und Politik betreffend; ~**-social** sozialpolitisch.

politics Politik *f*, Staatswissenschaft *f*, Staatskunst *f*, Parteipolitik *f*, politische Machenschaften *f|pl*; **party** ~ Parteipolitik; **power** ~ Machtpolitik.

polity Staat *m*, Staatsform *f*, Verfassung *f*, politische Ordnung *f*.

poll *s* Kopf *m*, Einzelperson *f*, Personenregister *m*, Wählerverzeichnis *n*, Wahlteilnehmer *m*; Umfrage *f*, Befragung *f*; förmliche, namentliche Abstimmung *f*, (*bei Gesellschafterversammlungen meist durch Abstimmungsliste oder Stimmkarten*), Wahl *f*, Wählen *n*, Stimmabgabe *f*; Zahl *f* der Stimmen, Stimmenzählung *f*; ~**s** Wahllokal, Wahlurne; ~**-money** Kopfsteuer, Kopfgeld; ~ **permutations** Stimmenwanderungen; ~ **respondents** Umfrageteilnehmer; ~**-tax** → *tax*; **conduct of a** ~ Erhebung von Meinungsumfragen; **Gallup** ~ Gallupumfrage; **heavy** ~ große Wahlbeteiligung; **popularity** ~ Umfrage nach der Beliebtheit e-s Politikers; **small** ~ geringe Wahlbeteiligung; **to demand a** ~ e-e *namentliche, idR* schriftliche Abstimmung *mit Stimmzetteln und nach Kapitalanleihen* verlangen; **to go to the** ~**s** wählen, sich an der Wahl beteiligen.

poll *v* einzeln herausgreifen, einzeln befragen (*Geschworene*), wählen, abstimmen, in die Wählerliste eintragen; (*Stimmen*) erhalten, Stimmen auf sich vereinigen, Stimmen abgeben; zur Wahl auffordern; schriftlich abstimmen (*mit Stimmzetteln oder Stimmkarten, ggf nach Kapitalbeteiligung zB bei Widerspruch gegen Ab-*

stimmung durch Handzeichen oder Akklamation).

pollee Befragter *m*, Interviewter *m*.

poller Wahlhelfer *m*, Abstimmender *m*.

pollicitation noch nicht angenommenes Angebot *n*, einseitiges Versprechen *n*.

polling Wahlgang *m*, Stimmzählung *f*; Wahlbeteiligung *f*; ~ **agent** Wahlagent; ~ **booth** Wahlzelle; ~ **clerk** Wahlbeisitzer; ~ **district** → *district*; ~ **place** Wahllokal; ~ **station** Wahllokal; ~ **the jury** die Geschworenen einzeln über ihr Votum befragen.

pollster Meinungsforscher *m*, Interviewer *m*.

pollute beflecken, verunreinigen, schänden; verschmutzen, beschmutzen.

pollutant emissions Abgase *n|pl*.

pollution Verschmutzung *f*, Umweltverschmutzung *f*, Gewässerverschmutzung *f*; Befleckung *f*, Schändung *f*; ~ **abatement** Bekämpfung und Kontrolle der Umweltbelastung; ~ **control** Gewässerschutz; ~ **of sea** Meeresverschmutzung; ~ **of the air** Luftverschmutzung; ~ **of the atmosphere** Luftverschmutzung; **control of** ~ Umweltschutz; **cross-frontier** ~ grenzüberschreitende Umweltverschmutzung; **environmental** ~ Umweltverschmutzung; **land** ~ Bodenvergiftung; **marine** ~ Meeresverschmutzung.

polyandry Polyandrie *f (eheliche Gemeinschaft einer Frau gleichzeitig mit mehreren Männern)*.

Polyarchy Polyarchie *f*, Herrschaft *f* ~ von vielen oder mehreren, Kollegialherrschaft *f*.

polygamous polygam.

polygamy Polygamie *f*, Vielweiberei *f*; strafbare Bigamie *f*.

polygarchy → *polyarchy*.

polygraph *med|jur* Lügendetektor.

polypoly Polypol *n*.

ponce Zuhälter *m*.

pontage Brückenzoll *m*, Brückeninstandhaltungsabgabe *f*.

Pontifical State Kirchenstaat *m*.

pool *s* Pool *m*, Kartell *n*, Ring *m*, Trust *m*, gemeinsame Kasse *f*, gemeinsame Spielkasse *f*, Gewinnabrechnungsgemeinschaft *f*, Gewinnverteilungskartell *n*, Konsortium *n*, Verkehrsverband *m*, Syndikat *n*; ~ **car service** Sammelladungsspedition; ~ **support** Stützungskäufe der Pool-Beteiligten; **bear** ~ Baissespekulantengruppe; **blind** ~ unbeschränkte Vollmacht des Geschäftsführers; **buffer** ~ Ausgleichspool; **gross-money** ~ Gewinnbeteiligungskartell; **jury** ~ Geschworenenliste; **money** ~ Geldpool, Kapitalbereitstellungsgemeinschaft; **programming** ~ Programmierverbund; **purchasing** ~ Einkaufsgemeinschaft; **typing** ~ Schreibsaal.

pool *v* poolen, einen gemeinsamen Fonds schaffen, zu e–m Ring vereinigen; ~ **orders** Aufträge gemeinsam erteilen; ~**ed fund** gemeinsames Kapital.

pooling Poolung *f*, Poolbildung *f*; ~ **contracts** Verkehrsverbundsverträge, Arbeitsgemeinschaften; ~ **of accounts** Kontenzusammenlegung; ~ **of interests** Interessenzusammenführung *bil*; ~ **of risk** gemeinschaftliche Gefahrübernahme; ~ **of votes** Stimmenvereinigung.

poolroom Wettlokal *n*.

poor *adj* arm, ärmlich, dürftig, schwach; ~ **and needy** bedürftig; ~ **person** arme Partei, Partei im Armenrecht; ~ **prisoner** mittelloser *(zur Pflichtverteidigung berechtigter, in Haft befindlicher)* Beschuldigter.

poor *s* Bedürftiger *m*, arme Person *f*, mittellose Person *f*; ~ **laws** *obs* Fürsorgerecht, Armenpflegerecht; ~ **rate** Armensteuer, Gemeindeabgabe für Armenfürsorge; ~ **relief** Armenpflege.

populace Pöbel *m*, Plebs *f*, Menschenmasse *f*.

popular | **action** → *action*; ~ **initiative** Volksbegehren; ~**-priced** zu mäßigen Preisen; ~ **sense** allgemeine Bedeutung, laienhafte Bedeutung; ~ **will** Volkswille.

population Bevölkerung (= *B bzw b*), Population *f*; ~ **census** Volkszählung; ~ **data** Einwohnerdaten; ~ **density** *B–s*dichte; ~ **explosion** *B–s*explosion; ~ **increase** *B–s*zuwachs; ~ **migration** *B–s*wanderbewegung(en); ~ **mobility** *B–s*bewegung; ~ **policies** *b–s*politische Maßnahmen; ~ **pyramid** *B–s*pyramide; ~ **register** Einwohnerregister; ~ **statistics** *B–s*statistik; **civilian** ~ Zivil*b*; **congestion of** ~ → *congestion*; **dependent** ~ der unterhaltsabhängige Teil der *B*; **floating** ~ fluktuierende *B*; **prison** ~ → *prison*; **rural** ~ ländliche *B*; **urban** ~ Stadt*b*, städtische *B*; **voting** ~ wahlberechtigte *B*; **working** ~ die Beschäftigten; die berufstätige *B*; werktätige *B*.

pork barrel|amendment Zusatzantrag im Interesse der örtlichen Wähler; Änderungsantrag als Wahlgeschenk; ~ **project** populäres Vorhaben im lokalen Interesse, Wahlgeschenksvorhaben.

porrecting Vorlage *f* zur Prüfung *bzw* Kostenfestsetzung.

port Hafen *m* (= *H bzw h*); ~ **administration** *H*verwaltung; ~ **authority** *H*amt, *H*behörde; ~ **bill of lading** *H*konnossement; ~ **captain** *H*kapitän; ~ **charges** *H*gelder; ~ **court** *H*gericht; ~ **differential** Eisenbahnfrachtunterschied (*zu verschiedenen Häfen*); ~ **dues** *H*gelder; ~ **duties** → *duty (2)*; ~ **equipment** *H*anlagen; ~ **facilities** *H*einrichtungen; ~**-greve** *H*meister; ~ **health authority** *H*gesundheitsamt; ~ **of anchorage** Not*h*; ~ **of arrival** Ankunfts*h*; ~ **of call** anzulaufender *H*, Anlaufs*h*, Anlege*h*, Anflug*h*; ~ **of clearance** Abfertigungs*h*; ~ **of delivery** Lösch(ungs)*h*; ~ **of departure** Ladungs*h*, Abgangs*h*, Absende*h*; ~ **of destination** Bestimmungs*h*; ~ **of discharge** Löschungs*h*, Entlade*h*; ~ **of dispatch** Verlade*h*; ~ **of distress** Not*h*; ~ **of documentation** Heimat*h*; ~ **of embarcation** Einschiffungs*h*; ~ **of entry** Einlauf*h*, Lösch*h*, Zollabfertigungs*h*; ~ **of exit** Ausfuhr*h*; ~ **of lading** Einschiffungs*h*, Ladungs*h*; ~ **of loading** Ladungs*h*, Verlade*h*, Versand*h*; ~ **of refuge** Not*h*; ~ **of registry** Heimat*h*, Register*h*; ~ **of shipment** Verlade*h*; ~ **of transshipment** Umschlag*h*, Umlade*h*; ~ **of unloading** Entlade*h*; Auslade*h*; ~**-reeve** Bürgermeister (*bes e–r Hafenstadt*), *H*meister; ~ **regulation** *H*vorschrift, *H*ordnung; ~ **risk** *H*risiko (*e–s Schiffes*); ~ **sanitary authority** *H*gesundheitsbehörde; ~ **toll** *H*gebühr; ~**-warden** *H*meister, *H*aufseher; **approved** ~ zugelassener *H* (*für gefährliche Ladung bzw für Ausländer*); **courtesy of the** ~ Befreiung von der Zollrevision beim Gepäck; **custom(s) of the** ~ → *custom*; **domestic** ~ Inlands*h*; **final** ~ letzter Entladehafen; **foreign** ~ ausländischer *H*, fremder *H*; **free** ~ Frei*h*; **home** ~ Heimat*h*; **intermediate** ~ Zwischen*h*; **lading** ~ Verlade*h*; **nominated loading** ~ benannter Verlade*h*; **open roadstead** ~ Reede*h*; **registered** ~ Heimathafen; **shipping** ~ Versand*h*; **sub-**~ Nebenhafen.

portage Transport *m*, Transportkosten.

portal-to-portal pay *Lohn für die Zeit vom Betreten bis zum Verlassen des Betriebs,* Betriebsanwesenheitslohn *m* (*vom Werktor bis zum Arbeitsplatz und zurück, Bergwerk*).

porter Pförtner *m*, Portier *m*, Gepäckträger *m*, Dienstmann *m*, us Schlafwagenschaffner *m*, Steward *m*; *hist* Gerichtswachtmeister *m*.

porterage Trägergebühren *f|pl* (*Hafen*).

portfolio Geschäftsbereich *m*, Portefeuille *n*, Bestand *m*; ~ **analysis** Depotbewertung; ~ **bill** Portefeuillewechsel; ~ **company** Investmentgesellschaft; ~ **insurance** Portefeuille-Versicherung, Absicherung gegen größere Kursverluste (*durch Gegen-Termingeschäfte*); ~ **investment** (Kapital)anlage in Portefeuille-Wertpapieren; ~ **management** Effektenverwaltung; ~ **securities** Portefeuille-Effekten; **balanced ~ of assets** ausgewogenes Wertpapiervermögen; **diversified** ~ gestreutes Wertpapierportefeuille.

portio legitima Zwangserbteil *m*.

portion *s* Anteil *m*, Teil *m*, Erbteil *m*, Erbteil *m* für Abkömmlinge, Pflichtteil *m*, Ausstattung *an Kinder*; ~ **debt** Ausstattungsschuld; ~ **disponible** frei letztwillig veräußerlicher Vermögensteil; **~s for children** den Kindern bei Lebzeiten zugewendete Vermögensteile; ~ **of land** Parzelle; ~ **of proceeds** Ertragsanteil, Erlösanteil; ~ **of the cost** Kostenanteil; ~ **policy** → *policy (1)*; **aggressive** ~ risikoreicher Effektenbestand; **compulsory** ~ Pflichtteil; **defensive** ~ risikoarmer Effektenbestand; **equal ~s** zu gleichen Teilen; **disposable** ~ frei (letztwillig) verfügbarer Teil d. Vermögens; **double ~s** doppelte letztwillige Berücksichtigung von Kindern (*Zuwendung zugleich als Ausstattung und Schenkung*); **lawful** ~ gesetzlicher Erbteil; **legal** ~ gesetzlicher Erbteil; **to raise ~s** Abfindungszahlungen an weichende Erben aufbringen.

portion *v* teilen, einteilen, aussteuern.

portioner Kleinbauer *m*; Geistlicher *m* mit Pfründenbeteiligung.

portionist Anteilsempfänger *m*, Pfründenempfänger *m*.

position Position *f*, Stand *m*, Kontenstand *m*, Standpunkt *m*, Stellung *f*, Lage *f*, Situation *f*, Einstellung *f*; ~ **bond** Kaution (*für Angestellte*); ~ **in the Fund** (*International Monetary Fund*) Position gegenüber dem Fonds; ~ **of authority** verantwortungsvolle Stelle; ~ **of constraint** Zwangslage; ~ **of life** Stand, Lebensstellung; ~ **of trust** → *trust*; **bear** ~ Baisseposition; **bull** ~ Hausseposition; **cash** ~ Kassenlage; **change of** ~ → *change*; **competitive** ~ Wettbewerbslage, Konkurrenzfähigkeit; **creditor** ~ Gläubigerstellung; **current** ~ Liquiditätsanlage; **debtor** ~ Schuldnerstellung; **exchange** ~ Devisenlage; **executive** ~ leitende Stellung; **factual** ~ Sachlage; **fiduciary** ~ Vertrauensstellung, in treuhänderischer Eigenschaft; **financial** ~ finanzielle Lage, Vermögenslage; **honorary** ~ Ehrenamt; **legal** ~ Rechtslage, Rechtsstellung; **long** ~ Hausseposition; **net** ~ Nettoposition (*Unterschied zwischen Hausse- und Baisseposition*); **official** ~ Ausstellung, amtliche Eigenschaft; **permanent** ~ Dauerstellung; **short** ~ Baisseengagement; **uncovered** ~ Découvert, Stückemangel; **unpaid** ~ ehrenamtliche Tätigkeit; **vacant** ~ unbesetzte Stelle.

positive positiv, bejahend, zustimmend, ausdrücklich, vorgeschrieben, feststehend, einwandfrei, sicher, unumstößlich, überzeugt, wirklich, absolut.

positively no admission Zutritt streng verboten.

positivism Positivismus *m*; **legal** ~ Rechtspositivismus.

positivist theory of law Rechtspositivismus *m*.

possess (unmittelbar) besitzen, innehaben, im Gewahrsam haben, in Besitz nehmen; ~ **oneself of a thing** sich etwas aneignen; **intent to** ~ Besitzwille; **to be ~ed of** in Besitz haben, im Besitz sein, besitzen; **to become ~ed (of)** Besitz erlangen.

possessio Besitz *m* (*im römisch-rechtlichen Sinn*).

possession Besitz *m* (= *B bzw b*), Habe *f*, Besitztum *n*, Sachherrschaft *f*; **~s** Besitzungen *f/pl*, Liegenschaften *f/pl*; ~ **and enjoyment** *B* und Gebrauchvorteile, Nutzungen; ~ **in fact** (tatsächlicher) unmittelbarer *B*; ~ **in law** juristischer *B*; *B* ohne Gewahrsam; mittelbarer *B*; ~ **is nine points of the law** „sei im Besitz und du wohnst im Recht"; ~ **order** = *order for* ~ → *order (1)*; ~, **order or disposition** Verfügungsgewalt; ~ **proceedings** Räumungsverfahren; Räumungsklage; ~ **with intent to supply** Besitz mit der Absicht der Veräußerung (*Rauschgift*); **action for** ~ *B*schutzklage, *B*entziehungsklage; Räumungsklage; **actual** ~ unmittelbarer *B*; **adverse** ~ bestrittener *B* an e–m Grundstück, Ersitzungs*b*; **apparent** ~ (*anscheinend gegebener*) unmittelbarer *B*; **chose in** ~ → *chose*; **civil** ~ Rechts*b*, fiktiver *B*; **constructive** ~ vermuteter *B*, fiktiver *B*, mittelbarer *B*; **corporeal** ~ *B*, unmittelbarer *B*; **criminal** ~ strafbarer *B*, *B* als Straftatbestandsmerkmal; **de facto** ~ faktischer *B*; **defective** ~ fehlerhafter *B*; **delivery of** ~ → *delivery*; **derivative** ~ abgeleiteter *B*, *B* auf Grund e–s *B*mittlungsverhältnisses; **direct** ~ unmittelbarer *B*; **doubtful** ~ bestrittener *B*; **estate in** ~ → *estate*; **exclusive** ~ Allein*b*, ausschließlicher *B*; **faulty** ~ fehlerhafter *B*, widerrechtlicher *B*; **full** ~ unbeschränkter *B*; **hostile** ~ bestrittener Eigen*b*, Grundstückseigen*b* (*ohne Rücksicht auf Ansprüche anderer*); **immediate** ~ unmittelbarer *B*; **immemorial** ~ uralter *B*; **in (full)** ~ **of his faculties** in vollem Besitz seiner geistigen Kräfte; **indirect** ~ mittelbarer *B*; **interference with** ~ → *interference*; **joint** ~ Mit*b*; **lawful** ~ rechtmäßiger *B*; **legal** ~ rechtmäßiger *B*, rechtlicher *B*; Eigen*b*; *B* im Rechtssinn; **loss of** ~ *B*verlust; **naked** ~ Gewahrsam (*an e–m Grundstück*), bloße, tatsächliche Gewalt, *B ohne Rechtstitel*; **natural** ~ reiner *B*, unmittelbarer Eigen*b*; **notorius** ~ offenkundiger *B*, ortsbekannte *B*ausübung; **open** ~ offener (Grundstücks)*B*; **part** ~ → *part*; **peacable** ~ ungestörter *B*; **pedal** ~ Ersitzungs*b* am Grundstück; **physical** ~ unmittelbarer Besitz, Gewahrsam; **precarious** ~ jederzeit entziehbarer *B*; **proprietary** ~ Eigen*b*; **quasi** ~ → *quasi*; **quiet** ~ ungestörter *B*; **quiet enjoyment of** ~ ungestörter *B*, uneingeschränkte Sachherrschaft (*Rechtsmängelhaftung*); **recent** ~ kürzlicher (durch Diebstahl entzogener) *B*; **right of** ~ → *right*; **scrambling** ~ eigenmächtig erworbener *B*; **sole** ~ Allein*b*; **taking** ~ → *taking*; **to acquire by adverse** ~ ersitzen; **to award** ~ e–n Räumungs-(Herausgabe-)titel zusprechen; zur Räumung verurteilen; **to be in** ~ besitzen, im *B* sein; **to enjoy quiet** ~ ungestörten *B* haben; **to order** ~ e–e Räumungsverfügung erlassen; *auch:* zur Räumung verurteilen; **to take** ~ *B* ergreifen *cf take v|t*; **transfer of** ~ *B*übertragung; **unity of** ~ Mit*b*; **unlawful** ~ rechtswidriger *B*; **vacant** ~ aufgegebener *B*, Herrenlosigkeit; sofort beziehbar; mieter-/pächterloser Besitz, verlassenes Grundstück; **vested** ~ wohlerworbener *B*; **writ of** ~ → *writ*.

possessor Besitzer *m*, Inhaber *m*; ~**'s agent** Besitzdiener; ~ **bona fide** gutgläubiger Besitzer; ~ **mala fide** bösgläubiger Besitzer; **actual** ~ tatsächlicher (*unmittelbarer*) Besitzer; **adverse** ~ Ersitzer, gutgläubiger Eigenbesitzer *ohne Rücksicht auf Ansprüche anderer*; **lawful** ~ rechtmäßiger Besitzer; **naked** ~ Besitzer (*abstrakt, im Rechtssinne*).

possessory besitzrechtlich, possessorisch, Besitz . . ., auf Besitz begründet, zur Erlangung von Besitz.

possibility Möglichkeit *f*, Zulässigkeit *f*; ~ **coupled with an interest** Anwartschaft; ~ **of confusion** Verwechslungsgefahr; ~ **of contracting** (*inhaltliche*) Möglichkeit des Vertragsabschlusses; ~ **of reverter** theoretisches Heimfallsrecht; ~ **on a** ~ entfernte (*von einem ungewissen Ereignis abhängige*) Möglichkeit; **bare** ~ Chance, lediglich e–e Möglichkeit; **extraordinary** ~ = *remote* ~ *qv*; **near** ~

nähere Anwartschaft (*zB auf Nacherbschaft*); **naked** ~ = *bare* ~ *qv*; **ordinary** ~ = *near* ~ *qv*; **remote** ~ entfernte Möglichkeit.

possible möglich, durchführbar, zumutbar.

post nach, später; unten (*Zitierweise*); **~-act** Nachtat; ~ **and per** *auf Grund abgeleiteten und eigenen (höheren)* Rechts; ~ **audit** Rechnungsprüfung; ~ **commitment hearing** Verfahren nach Einweisung (*in e–e Heilanstalt*); ~ **conquestum** nach der (*normannischen*) Eroberung; **~-date** = *postdate v* vordatieren (*auf ein zukünftiges Datum*); **~-dated** vordatiert; ~ **design service** Änderungs- und Ergänzungsdienst (*Konstruktion u. Gestaltung*); ~ **diem** nach dem Fälligkeitstage; ~ **entry** nachträgliche Eintragung, Nachverzollung; ~ **facto** nachträglich; **~-factum** nachträgliche Handlung; ~ **liminium** → *postliminium*; ~ **litem motam** nach Rechtshängigkeit; ~ **meridiem** (= *p.m., P.M., PM*) nachmittags; **~-mortem** nach dem Tode; **~-mortem (examination)** Obduktion, Autopsie, Leichenöffnung, Leichenschau; **~-natal** nach der Geburt eintretend; ~ **natus** Nachkömmling, zweiter Sohn, Nachgeborener (*nach e–m bestimmten Ereignis*); **~-nuptial** nach der Eheschließung, während der Ehe; **~-obit (bond)** Schuldschein auf e–e erwartete Erbschaft; ~ **qualification experience** Berufserfahrung (*nach Anwaltszulassung*); **~-terminal sittings** Feriensitzungen; ~ **terminum** nach Fristablauf.

post *s (1)* Stand *m*, Posten *m*, Stellung *f*, Amt *n*, Anstellung *f*, Dienststellung *f*; Geländepunkt *m*; Garnison *f*, Ortsgruppe *f*, Standplatz *m*, Station *f*, Handelsniederlassung *f*, Börsenstand *m*; **P~ Exchange** *Kaufhaus für US-Streitkräfte*; **~-notes** Bankanleihe; **confidential** ~ Vertrauensstellung; **established** ~ Planstelle; **first aid** ~ Unfallstation; **judicial** ~ Richteramt.

post *s (2)* Post *f*, Postamt *n*, Postsendung *f*, Postsachen *f/pl*; ~ **address** Postanschrift; ~ **letter** mit der Post beförderter Brief; **~-mark** Poststempel; **date as ~-mark** Datum des Poststempels; ~ **office** Postamt, Postbehörde; ~ **office department** Postministerium; ~ **office box corporation** Briefkastenfirma; ~ **office receipt** → *receipt*; ~ **office savings bank** Postsparkasse; ~ **roads** Postwege; ~ **routes** *vorgeschriebene* Postrouten; ~ **savings bank** Postsparkasse; ~ **transfer account** Postgirokonto; **by return of** ~ postwendend, umgehend; **general** ~ (*mit der Morgenpost*); **letter** ~ Briefpost; **military** ~ Feldpost; **pneumatic** ~ Rohrpost; **registered** ~ Einschreiben (*versichert*).

post *v* absenden, zur Post geben, in den Briefkasten werfen; informieren, aushängen, öffentlich anschlagen; verbuchen, eintragen, übertragen; ~ **charges to customer's account** Belastungsanzeigen auf Kundenkonten verbuchen; **~ed by unrecorded mail** als gewöhnliche Postsendung aufgegeben; ~ **forward** vortragen, ~ **security** → *security*; ~ **up** ins reine schreiben, (*Buchungsposten*) übertragen; **to keep ~ed** auf dem laufenden halten.

postage Porto *n*; ~ **book** Portobuch; ~ **due** Nachgebühr, Strafporto; ~ **envelope** Freiumschlag; **~-free** freigemacht, frankiert; ~ **meter** Frankiermaschine; ~ **stamp** → *stamp*; ~ **underpaid** unterfrankiert; ~ **unpaid** unfrankiert; **exemption from** ~ Portofreiheit; **inland** ~ Inlandsporto; **liable to** ~ portopflichtig; **return** ~ Rückporto.

postal postalisch; Post . . .; ~ **address** Postanschrift; ~ **agreement** Postabkommen; ~ **authorities** → *authority*; ~ **charges** Postgebühren; ~ **cheque** Postscheck; ~ **clerk** Postbeamter, Bahnpostschaffner; ~ **collection order** Einziehungsauftrag; ~ **communication** → *com-*

munication; **P~ Convention** internationales Postabkommen; ~ **currency** Briefmarkenwährung; ~ **delivery** Postzustellung; ~ **district** → *district*; ~ **giro** → *giro*; ~ **item** Postsache; ~ **mark** Poststempel; ~ **order** → *order (2)*; ~ **power** Postkompetenz; ~ **privilege** → *privilege*; ~ **rates** Postgebühren; ~ **savings** Postsparguthaben; ~ **savings depository** Postsparkasse; ~ **savings system** Postsparkassensystem; ~ **service** → *service*; ~ **stamp** → *stamp*; **P~ Union** = *Universal P~ Union* Weltpostverein; ~ **voting** Briefwahl; ~ **wrapper** Streifband.

postcode Postleitzahl *f*.

postea *Angabe der Prozeßgeschichte (am Schluß der Gerichtsakte)*.

posted waters Privatgewässer *n* (*Fischen verboten!*).

poster Kontoführer *m*; Plakatanschlag *m*; ~ **advertising** Plakatwerbung.

poste restante postlagernd, Schalter für postlagernde Sendungen.

posteriority Nachrangigkeit *f*.

posterity Nachkommenschaft *f*, Nachwelt *f*.

posthumous | works nachgelassene Werke (*nach dem Tode des Verfassers veröffentlichte Schriften*); ~ **child** nach dem Tode des Vaters geborenes Kind; ~ **patent** nach dem Tode des Anmelders erteiltes Patent.

posting Postenbesetzung *f*, Stellenbesetzung *f*; **overseas** ~ Auslandseinsatz von Mitarbeitern.

posting | machine Buchungsmaschine *f*; ~ **period** Kontoübertragungszeitraum; ~ **run** Versandserie.

postliminium Postliminium *n Rückgabe von beschlagnahmtem Gut an Eigentümer, Wiederherstellung des früheren Rechtszustandes*.

postliminy = *postliminium qv*.

postmaster Postamtsvorsteher *m*, Postmeister *m*, Posthalter *m*; **P~ General** Postminister.

postpayment nachträgliche Bezahlung *f*.

postpone aufschieben, verschieben, vertagen, zurückstellen.

postponement Verschiebung *f*, Vertagung *f*; ~ **of payments** Moratorium *n*, Hinausschiebung *f* der Zahlungsfälligkeiten; ~ **of sentence** Strafaufschub; ~ **of trial** Verlegung der mündlichen Verhandlung (*bzw Hauptverhandlung*).

postscript Nachtrag *m*, Nachschrift *f*, Postskript *n*.

postulant Bewerber(in), Antragsteller(in).

postulate Postulat *n*, Bedingung *f*, Voraussetzung *f*.

postulation Gesuch *n*, Forderung *f*, Postulat *n*.

potentate Machthaber *m*, Herrscher *m*.

potential *adj* potentiell, latent, möglich; ~ **earnings** geschätzte Verdienstmöglichkeit.

potential *s* Potential *n*, Hilfsquellen *f|pl*, Möglichkeit *f*; **economic** ~ Wirtschaftspotential.

pothole Schlagloch *m*.

pound *(1) (lb)* Pfund *n* (*Gewichtseinheit*); Pfund Sterling *n*; ~ **sterling** Pfund Sterling; **avoirdupois** ~ = *16 Unzen = 453,59 g*; **troy** ~ Troygewichtspfund = *12 Unzen = 373,2418 g*.

pound *(2)* Pfandstall *m*, Gewahrsamsstelle *f*; Einzäunung *f* für streunende Tiere; ~**-breach** = *breach of ~ qv*; ~ **breacher** Täter e–s Verstrickungsbruchs.

poundage Gewicht *n* in Pfunden, Zentnerlast *f*, Provision pro Pfund; nach Gewicht erhobener Zoll *m*, Einsperrung *f*, Einschließung *f*, Einlösegebühr *f* für gepfändete (*bzw als Streuner eingefangene*) Tiere; Gerichtsvollziehergebühr (*Anteil am Erlös*).

pourparler vorbereitendes Gespräch *n*, Vorverhandlung *f*.

pourparty Auseinandersetzung *f* durch Naturalteilung von Grundstücken.

poursuivant königlicher Bote *m*, Staatsbote *m*.

poustie *scot* Machtbefugnis *f*.

poverty Armut *f*, Not *f*, Mangel *m*, Bedürftigkeit *f*, geringe Ergiebigkeit *f*; ~ **affidavit** eidliches Armenrechtszeugnis; ~ **gap** Abstand über dem Existenzminimum; ~ **line** Existenzminimum; ~ **of invention** mangelnde Erfindungshöhe; ~ **safety net** soziales Netz (*der Sozialhilfe*); **certificate of** ~ → *certificate*.

power *(1)* Macht *f*, Gewalt *f*, Staat *m*; Vollmacht *f*, Vollmachtsurkunde *f*, Ermächtigung *f*; Befugnis *f*, Recht *n*, Autorität *f*; Machtbefugnis *f*, Machtvollkommenheit *f*, Mandat *n*, Fähigkeit *f*, Talent *n*; ~ **coupled with an interest** *Vollmacht verbunden mit Vermögensinteresse des Bevollmächtigten am Gegenstand der Vollmacht*; ~ **in gross** *Verfügungsbefugnis e–s Grundbesitzers für die Zeit nach Ablauf seiner Rechte*; ~ **in trust** treuhänderische Befugnis; ~ **in the name of the trust** Vollmacht mit treuhänderischer Zweckbindung; ~ **of agency** (Handlungs)Vollmacht, Vertretungsmacht; ~ **of alienation** Veräußerungsbefugnis, Verfügungsbefugnis; ~ **of an authority** Befugnisse e–r Behörde; ~ **of appointment** Ernennungsbefugnis, Einsetzungsbefugnis; Ermächtigung, über Vermögensrechte zu verfügen; ~ **of attorney** schriftl Vollmacht, Vollmachtsurkunde; ~ ~ ~ *clause: Vollmacht des Pfandgläubigers zum Erwerb und damit Verkauf des Pfandobjekts*; ~ **of authority** Ermächtigung; Hoheitsbefugnis; ~ **of avoidance** → *avoidance*; ~ **of decision** Entscheidungsbefugnis, Entscheidungsgewalt; ~ **of discipline** Disziplinarbefugnis; ~ **of discretion** Ermessensfreiheit; ~ **of disposal** Verfügungsgewalt; ~ **of disposition** Verfügungsbefugnis, Veräußerungsbefugnis; Verfügungsgewalt; ~ **of expulsion** Ausschlußrecht; ~ **of incumbency** Amtsbonus; Machtstellung des Amtsinhabers; ~ **of intervention** Befugnis zur zeitweiligen Praxisübernahme durch Anwaltskammer; ~ **of procuration** Prokura; ~ **of removal** Abberufungsrecht; ~ **of revocation** Widerrufsrecht, Entziehungsrecht; ~ **of sale** Verwertungsrecht, Veräußerungsbefugnis, Recht des freihändigen Verkaufs (*des Pfandgegenstandes, bes des belasteten Grundstücks*); ~ **of search** Durchsuchungsbefugnis; ~ **of self-control** Selbstbeherrschung; ~ **of sentence** Strafgewalt; ~ **of substitution** Delegationsbefugnis; ~ **of testation** Testierfähigkeit; ~ **of the county** = *posse comitatus qv*; ~ **of the key** Hausgewalt, Hausrecht; ~ **of the purse** *brit* Zuständigkeit für Zuweisung von Mitteln; ~ **of visitation** *die e–m Kurator oder Treuhänder verliehene Aufsichts- und Amtseinsetzungsbefugnis*; ~ **politics** → *politics*; ~ **sharing** Beteiligung an der Macht; ~**s vested** (*jmdm*) eingeräumte Befugnisse, übertragene Befugnisse; ~ **to amend** Abänderungsbefugnis; ~ **to call for documents** Recht auf Urkundenvorlage; ~ **to collect** Inkassovollmacht; ~ **to compromise** Vollmacht zum Vergleichsabschluß; ~ **to convince** Überzeugungskraft; ~ **to hold land** *satzungsgemäße* Befugnis zum Liegenschaftsbesitz; ~ **to indorse** Indossamentsvollmacht; ~ **to negotiate** Begebungsrecht; ~ **to sell** Veräußerungsbefugnis, freihändiges Pfandverwertungsrecht; ~ **to sign** Unterschriftsbefugnis, Unterschriftsvollmacht; ~ **to transact business with bank** Bankvollmacht; ~ **to vary** Abänderungsbefugnis; ~ **vacuum** Machtvakuum; **abridgement of** ~**s** Machtbeschränkung; **absolute** ~ unbeschränkte Macht, Einfluß, Herrschaft, Ermächtigung; **abuse of** ~ Mißbrauch der Amtsgewalt; **administrative** ~ vollziehende Gewalt, Exekutive; **appendant** ~ mit Grundbesitz gekoppelte Befugnis; **appurtenant** ~ = *appendant* ~ *qv*; **arbitrary** ~ uneingeschränkte Ermessensbefugnis, willkürliche Macht; **assumption of** ~ Machtübernahme; **balance of** ~ → *balance*; **belligerent** ~ kriegführende Macht; **beneficial** ~ *Befugnis, die lediglich den Ermächtigten begünstigt*; **borrowing** ~**s** *satzungsgemäße* Befugnis zur Kreditaufnahme; **budgetary** ~**s** Budgetrecht; **buying** ~ Kaufkraft; **capricious** ~ willkürliche, sittenwidrige (Treuhänder)Ermächtigung; **collateral** ~ reine Vollmacht) ohne Eigeninteresse des Bevollmächtigten); **collecting** ~ Inkassovollmacht; **collective** ~ **of attorney** Gesamtvollmacht; **commercial** ~ Handlungsvollmacht; **compulsive** ~ physische Gewalt; **compulsory** ~ Erzwingungsrecht; **concurrent** ~ konkurrierende Gesetzgebung(szuständigkeit); **constituent** ~ verfassunggebende Gewalt; **constitutional** ~**s** verfassungsrechtliche Zuständigkeiten („*Gewalten*"); **corporate** ~**s** satzungsmäßige Befugnisse e–r juristischen Person, Rechtsfähigkeit juristischer Personen; **delaying** ~ Verzögerungsbefugnis (*Gesetzgebung*); **delegated** ~ delegierte Befugnis, Ermächtigung; **detaining** ~ Gewahrsamsmacht, Gewahrsamsstaat; **disciplinary** ~ Disziplinargewalt; **discretionary** ~**(s)** freie Verfügungsgewalt, Ermessensbefugnis; **dispensing** ~ Befugnis zu Ausnahmeregelungen, Dispensionsprivileg (*des Monarchen*); **disposing** ~ Verfügungsgewalt; **dispositive** ~ Veräußerungsbefugnis; **distributive** ~ Befugnis zu anteiligen Zuwendungen; **earning** ~ → *earning*; **economic** ~ Wirtschaftskraft; **emergency** ~**s** → *emergency*; **enduring** ~ → *enduring power*; **equitable** ~ Befugnis zur Einräumung von Billigkeitsrechten; **excess of** ~**s** Überschreiten der Befugnisse, Vollmachtsüberschreitung; **exclusive** ~ alleinige Befugnis; *Befugnis, bei Zuwendungen einzelne auszuschließen*; **executive** ~ vollziehende Gewalt, Exekutive; **foreign** ~ ausländische Macht; **full** ~ unbeschränkte Vollmacht, unbeschränkte Befugnisse; **full** ~**s** Sondervollmacht (*e–s diplomatisch Beauftragten*); **general** ~ Generalvollmacht, Vollmacht zur Veräußerung von Grundeigentum; **general** ~ **in trust** treuhänderische Veräußerungsbefugnis; **general** ~ **of appointment** unbeschränktes Bestimmungsrecht (*zur Einsetzung e–s Begünstigten bzw letztwillig Bedachten*); **implied** ~**s** abgeleitete Befugnisse, stillschweigend miteingeräumte Befugnisse; **in** ~ an der Macht; **incidental** ~**s** dazugehörige Befugnisse, Nebenbefugnisse; **inherent** ~**s** originäre Befugnisse, natürliche Rechte, naturrechtlich gegebene Befugnisse; **investigative** ~**s** kriminalpolizeiliche Befugnisse; **judicial** ~ → *judicial*; **legislative** ~ Legislative, gesetzgebende Gewalt; **licensing** ~ → *licensing*; **limited** ~ beschränkte Befugnis, Spezialvollmacht; **ministerial** ~ Befugnis des Grundstücksveräußerers zur Wahrung von Drittinteressen; *Befugnis zum Rechtserwerb an Grundstücken, die zugleich für Dritte ausgeübt werden muß*; **mixed** ~ *Befugnis zu anteiligen oder pauschalen Zuwendungen*; **monetary** ~ Währungskompetenz; **naked** ~ (*abstrakte*) Vollmacht, Befugnis ohne eigenes Interesse des Beauftragten; **naval** ~ Seemacht; **non-exclusive** ~ Befugnis zur anteiligen Zuwendung; **official** ~**s** Amtsgewalt, Behörde; **parental** ~ elterliche Gewalt; **particular** ~ Spezialvollmacht, *Befugnis zur Zuwendung an bestimmte Personen oder Personengruppen*; **plenary** ~ Generalvollmacht; *pol* ausschließliche Kompetenz; **primary** ~**s** Hauptvollmacht; **protecting** ~ Schutzmacht; **resulting** ~**s** Zuständigkeit aus der Natur der Sache; **revisory** ~ Überprüfungsbefugnis; **rule-making** ~ Rechtsetzungsbefugnis für das Verfahrensrecht; **sovereign** ~ Hoheitsgewalt, Hoheitsrecht, Staatshoheit, unumschränkte Gewalt; **special** ~ Spezialvollmacht,

Sondervollmacht, *Befugnis zur Grundstücksveräußerung an bestimmte Personen bzw Personengruppen*, beschränkte Veräußerungsbefugnis von Rechten an Grundstücken; **spending** ~ Ausgaberecht; **statutory** ~ gesetzliche Befugnis; **stop and search** ~**s** Anhalte- und Durchsuchungsbefugnisse; **summary provisional** ~ vorläufige generelle Amtsbefugnis; **taxing** ~ Besteuerungsrecht, Steuerhoheit; **testamentary** ~ letztwillige Einsetzungsbefugnis; **treaty-making** ~ Zuständigkeit zu völkerrechtlichen Vertragsabschlüssen; **unlimited** ~ unbegrenzte Vollmacht, Generalvollmacht, Blankovollmacht; **vesting** ~**s** Beschlagnahmerecht, Eigentumseinweisungsrecht; **visitorial** ~ Inspektionsbefugnis, Aufsichtsrecht.

power *(2)* elektrischer Strom *m*, Energie *f*; ~ **consumption** Stromverbrauch; ~ **economy** Energiewirtschaft; ~ **rating** Leistungsberechnung; ~ **supply** Stromversorgung; ~ **unit** Leistungseinheit.

practicability Durchführbarkeit *f*, Verwendbarkeit *f*, Brauchbarkeit *f*.

practicable durchführbar, anwendbar, brauchbar; begehbar, befahrbar; ~ **method** e-e brauchbare Methode.

practical praktisch angewandt; ~ **application** → *application (1)*; ~ **control** beherrschender Einfluß; ~ **knowledge** → *knowledge*; **a** ~ **joke** ein schlechter Scherz.

practice Praxis *f*, Prozeßpraxis *f*, Gerichtsverfahren *n*, Übung *f*, Berufsausübung *f*, Geschäftsgang *m*; **P~ Act** *US* Prozeßordnung; **P~ Court** *hist Abteilung des Court of King's Bench für Handelssachen ua*; **P~ Directions** richterliche Verfahrensrichtlinien; **P~ Master** *leitender Rechtspfleger der Hauptgeschäftsstelle*; ~ **note** Verfahrensanweisung; ~ **of law** anwaltschaftliche Tätigkeit, Ausübung des Anwaltsberufs; ~ **of the court** Gerichtspraxis, Rechtsgang; **administrative** ~ Verwaltungsverfahren; **banking** ~ Bankusance; **Civil P~ Act** *US* Zivilprozeßordnung; **commercial** ~ Geschäftspraxis, Handelsbrauch; **common** ~ allgemein übliches Verfahren; **constant** ~ (*of a court*) ständige Praxis, ständige Rechtsprechung; **corporate** ~ Tätigkeit als Syndikus *bzw* gesellschaftsrechtl spezialisierter Anwalt; **cross-frontier** ~ grenzüberschreitende Praxis, internationale P.; **established** ~ ständige (Gerichts)-Praxis, anerkannte Übung, feststehende Rechtsprechung; **general** ~ übliches Verfahren, allgemeine Praxis, **general and approved** ~ übliche, anerkannte Praxis; **in active** ~ tätig, praktizierend; **it is established** ~ es ist ständige Praxis; **legal** ~ Rechtsanwendung, Praxis; Rechtsprechung; **matter of** ~ **and procedure** → *matter*; **mercantile** ~ Handelsbrauch; **private** ~ (selbständige) Anwaltspraxis; **settled** ~ ständige Praxis, feststehende Rechtsprechung; **supreme court** ~ höchstrichterliche Rechtsprechung; **wholetime private** ~ hauptberufl Praxis.

practices Gepflogenheiten *f/pl*, gleichartige Handlungsfolge *f*; Praktiken *f/pl*; **anti-competitive** ~ wettbewerbsbeschränkendes Verhalten; **business** ~ Geschäftspraktiken, geschäftliche Gepflogenheiten; **corrupt** ~ Bestechung, Korruption; Wahlbestechung; **deceptive** ~ betrügerische Machenschaften; **electoral** ~ (unlautere) Wahlmachenschaften; **fair** ~ anständiges Geschäftsgebaren; **fraudulent** ~ betrügerische Machenschaften; **illegal** ~ verbotene Wahlkampfmethoden; Wahlkorruption; **improper** ~ unlautere Geschäftsmethoden; **legislative** ~ parlamentarische Machenschaften, Lobbyismus; **restrictive** ~ Wettbewerbsbeschränkungen; **sharp** ~ Manipulationen, unsaubere Geschäftsmethoden.

practis|e e–n Beruf ausüben, praktizieren; **licence to ~ medicine** ärztliche Approbation; **~ing barrister** (praktizierender) Rechtsanwalt; **~ing certificate** → *certificate*; **to ~ on one's own account alone in private practice** e–e Einzelpraxis betreiben.

practitioner freiberuflich Tätiger *m*, Anwalt *m*, Fachmann *m*; Arzt *m* für Allgemeinmedizin; **~ of law** praktizierender Anwalt (*bzw Rechtsbeistand*); **copyright ~** Spezialanwalt für Urheberrecht; **criminal ~** Strafrechts-Anwalt, Strafverteidiger; **general ~** praktischer Arzt; **legal ~** Rechtsberater; **matrimonial ~** Familienrechts-Anwalt; **medical ~** praktischer Arzt; **self-employed private ~** freiberuflicher Anwalt; **sole ~** allein praktizierender Anwalt.

pragmatic sanction pragmatische Sanktion *f*; hoheitlicher Rechtsspruch *m* e–s Monarchen, grundlegendes Staatsgesetz *n*.

pratique *Verkehrserlaubnis im Hafen bzw zwischen Schiff und Hafen nach Aufhebung der Quarantäne bzw nach Vorlegung des Gesundheitspasses.*

praxis Praxis *f*, Gepflogenheit *f*.

pray beantragen, bitten um; **~ in aid** um Hilfe ersuchen, zur Unterstützung e–s Rechts auffordern; sich berufen auf (*Präzedenzfall, Argument*).

prayer Klageantrag *m*, Sachantrag *m*; **~ for damages** Antrag der Schadensersatzklage; **~ for relief** Klagebegehren, Klageantrag; **~ of petitioner** Klageantrag, Klagebegehren; **~ of process** Antrag auf Zustellung der Klage und Ladung; **~ "that the said marriage be dissolved"** *Antrag: Die Ehe der Parteien wird geschieden*; **to amend the ~ of the petition** den Klageantrag abändern.

pre-accounting Vorkalkulation *f*.

pre-acquisition | losses frühere Verluste *m|pl der übernommenen Gesellschaft bzw Firma (vor Geschäftsübernahme)*; **~ profits** Gewinne vor der Übernahme (*durch die Muttergesellschaft*).

preamble Präambel *f*, Vorbemerkung *f|pl*.

pre-audience Vortritt *m* (*des Staatsanwalts bzw e–s Rechtsanwalts*).

pre-audit Vorprüfung *f*.

precarious widerruflich, kündbar, unsicher, vom Willen e–s anderen abhängig; **~ balance of forces** gefährdetes Mächtegleichgewicht; **~ circumstances** besorgniserregende Umstände; **~ loan** Leihe zu jederzeitiger Rückgabe; **possession** jederzeit entziehbarer Besitz; **~ right** → *right*; **~ trade** geduldeter Handel von neutralen Staaten mit Kriegführenden.

precarriage Vortransport *m*; (*auch pl*) Vorfracht *f*.

precatory e–e Bitte enthaltend, Bitt ..., bittend, ersuchend, empfehlend, e–n (*letztwilligen*) Wunsch enthaltend; **~ trust** → *trust*; **~ words** letztwillige Bitte.

precaution Vorkehrung *f*, Vorsichtsmaßregel *f*, Vorsicht *f*; vorausgegangenes Tun *n*.

precautionary vorbeugend, vorsorglich, Vorsichts ...; **~ measures** Vorbeugungsmaßnahmen; **~ motion** Hilfsantrag, vorsorglich gestellter Antrag.

precede vorausgehen, den Vortritt haben, den Vortritt lassen.

precedence Vortritt *m*, Vorrang *m*, Vorzug *m*, Vorrecht *n*, Rangordnung *f*, Priorität *f*, Präzedenz *f*; **list of ~** → *list*; **patent of ~** *ehrenhalber erteilter* Rangvortritt für Rechtsanwälte; **table of ~** protokollarische Rangordnung; **to have ~** im Rang vorgehen.

precedency = *precedence qv*.

precedent Präzedenzfall *m*, Vorentscheidung, *pl:* Rechtsprechung; Musterurkunde *f*; Standardformular; **~ letter** Musterschreiben; **authoritative ~** bindende höchstrichterliche Entscheidung; **binding ~** bindender Präzedenzfall; **declaratory ~** feststellende Präzedenzentscheidung (*Rechtsnorm*); **depar-**

ture from ~ Abweichung von der Rechtsprechung; **overruled** ~**s** aufgegebene Rechtsprechung; **original** ~ neues Richterrecht schaffender Präzedenzfall; **persuasive** ~ höchstrichterliche Entscheidung ohne Bindungswirkung; **propitious** ~ einschlägiger Präzedenzfall; **to cite a** ~ e–n Präzedenzfall anführen; **without** ~ noch nicht höchstrichterlich entschieden.

precedent vorhergehend, zuerst kommend, vorausgehend, vorangehend; ~ **condition** = *condition precedent* → *condition*.

precedented bereits durch Präzedenzfall entschieden.

preceding vorhergehend, früher.

pre-censorship Vorzensur *f*.

precept Anordnung *f*, Weisung *f*, Auftrag *m*, Vorschrift *f*, Verordnung *f*, Vorführungsbefehl *m*, Anordnung *f* der Parlamentswahl, Anordnung *f* zur Aufstellung von Geschworenen, Steueranforderung *f*; Umlageverfügung *f*; *hist* Anstiftung *f* zum Verbrechen; **to issue** ~**s** (*upon the rating authorities*) mit der Einziehung (*von Kommunalsteuern*) beauftragen.

precinct Bannmeile *f*, Umkreis *m*, Bezirk *m*, Polizeibezirk *m*, Wahlkreis *m*; **magisterial** ~ Amtsgerichtsbezirk; **pedestrians'** ~ Fußgängerzone; **police** ~ Polizeirevier.

precipe Weisung *f* an den Rechtspfleger.

precipitation beschleunigte Herbeiführung *f e–s Ereignisses*, Übereilung *f*, Überstürzung *f*.

precipitin test Präzipitin-Test *m*, Koagulin-Test *m* (*zur Feststellung von Menschenblut*).

preclosing trial balance Probebilanz *f*.

preclude ausschließen, ausschalten, vorbeugen, zuvorkommen; ~ **objections** Einwände vorwegnehmen.

preclusion Ausschließung *f*, Ausschluß *m*, Präklusion *f*; ~ **order** → *order (1)*.

preclusive period Ausschlußfrist *f*.

precognition Vorverhör *n*, Voruntersuchung *f*; Vorkenntnis *f*, frühere Erkenntnis *f*; schriftliche Festlegung *f* e–r Zeugenaussage *vor der Vernehmung*, vorprozessuale Vernehmung *f*.

pre-collection letter letzte Mahnung *f*.

preconceive sich im voraus ein Urteil bilden, vorher ausdenken; ~**d opinion** vorgefaßte Meinung, Vorurteil.

preconception vorgefaßte Meinung *f*.

preconcert *s* vorherige Vereinbarung *f*, Absprache *f*.

preconcert *v* vorher verabreden.

precondemn im voraus verurteilen.

precondition Voraussetzung *f*.

preconization Proklamation *f*, Präkonisation *f* (*Bekanntgabe e–r Botschafterernennung*).

pre-contract Vorvertrag *m*; zeitlich vorrangiger Vertrag.

precontractual vorvertraglich.

predate zurückdatieren, ein früheres Datum einsetzen.

predator Übernahmehai *m*, Übernahmepirat *m*.

predatory räuberisch; ~ **band** Räuberbande; ~ **exploitation** Raubbau; ~ **practices** Konkurrenzvernichtungsmethoden; ~ **price differentials** gezielte Kampfpreise; ~ **war** Raubkrieg.

predecease vorversterben, nicht überleben.

predeceased Vorverstorbene(r).

predecedent der (die) Vorversterbende.

predecessor Vorgänger *m*, Rechtsvorgänger *m*, Vorfahr *m*; ~ **company** Vorgesellschaft; ~ **in office** Amtsvorgänger; ~ **in title** Rechtsvorgänger, Voreigentümer.

predicate *s* Prädikat *n*, beigelegte Bezeichnung *f*, Titel *m*.

predicate *v* behaupten, e–e Aussage machen, begründen, basieren auf.

predication Aussage *f*, Behauptung *f*.

predisposed prädisponiert, anfällig,

empfänglich, e–e Neigung habend (*Krankheit, Handlungsweise*).

predominance Vorherrschaft *f*, Übergewicht *n*.

predominant vorherrschend, überwiegend.

predominate vorherrschen, überlegen sein, die Oberhand haben.

pre-election Vorwahl *f*; ~ **promise** Wahlversprechen.

pre-empt auf Grund e–s Vorkaufsrechts erwerben.

pre-emptible e–m Vorkaufsrecht unterliegend.

pre-emption Vorkauf *m*, Vorkaufsrecht *n*; ausschließliche Gesetzgebungskompetenz *f*; ~ **claimant** der das Vorkaufsrecht Ausübende (*Siedler*); Vorkaufsberechtigter; ~ **entry** → *entry*; ~ **right** Vorkaufsrecht (*bes von Siedlern, US*); **Federal** ~ *ausschließliche Gesetzgebungskompetenz des US Congress*.

pre-emptioner Vorkaufsberechtigter *m*, anwartschaftsberechtigter Siedler *m*.

preemptive Vorkaufs ..., Bezugs ... *cf right*.

pre-emptor Erwerber *m* auf Grund e–s Vorkaufsrechts.

pre-entry closed shops Betriebe *m|pl* mit absolutem Gewerkschaftsmonopol (*schon bei Einstellung*).

pre-estimate vorherige Schätzung *f*, Voranschlag *m*.

pre-exhaustion of rights Anspruchsverbrauch.

pre-exist vorher dasein, früher existieren.

pre-existent vorher vorhanden.

pre-existing bisherig, bisher vorhanden, bereits bestehend.

pre-fab Fertighaus *n*.

prefabricate vorfertigen.

prefabrication Vorfertigung *f*.

preface Vorwort *n*, Einleitung *f*, Vorrede *f*.

prefect Präfekt *m*, Statthalter *m*, Befehlshaber *m*, Ordner *m*.

prefecture Präfektur *f*.

prefer *(1)* vorziehen, bevorzugen, bevorzugt befriedigen, begünstigen.

prefer *(2)* vorbringen, einreichen, die Strafverfolgung durchführen, zur Verhandlung bringen; ~ **a bill of indictment** Anklage erheben; ~ **a charge** Anklage erheben; ~ **a claim** e–e Forderung geltend machen.

preferable bevorrechtigt, vorzugsweise.

preference Vorzug *m*, Vorrang *m*, Gläubigerbevorzugung *f*, Vorzugsrecht *n*, Präferenz *f*, Prioritätsrecht *n*, Vergünstigung *f*, Vorzugszoll *m*; ~ **dividend** Vorzugsdividende; ~ **freight** zu Vorzugsbedingungen beförderte Fracht; ~ **legacy** Vorausvermächtnis; ~ **loan** → *loan*; ~ **to creditors** (*over others*) Gläubigerbegünstigung; ~ **offer** Vorzugsangebot, Sonderangebot; ~ **shareholder** → *shareholder*; ~ **shares** → *share*; **Commonwealth** ~ Vorzugszollsystem im britischen Commonwealth; **cumulative** ~ **share** → *share*; **fraudulent** ~ (betrügerische) Gläubigerbegünstigung; **margin of** ~ → *margin*; **participating** ~ **shares** → *share*; **racial** ~ Bevorzugung aus rassischen Gründen (Antidiskriminierung); **recoverable** ~ Aussonderungsrecht; **voidable** ~ anfechtbare Gläubigerbevorzugung.

preferential bevorzugt, bevorrechtigt, Vorzugs ..., Sonder ...

preferment Vorzug *m*, Bevorzugung *f*; Beförderung *f*; Ehrenamt *n*; Vorlage der Anklageschrift, Anklageerhebung *f*.

preferred bevorrechtigt, bevorzugt.

pre-finance vorfinanzieren.

prefix voranstellen; im voraus bestimmen.

pregnancy Schwangerschaft *f*; ~ **leave** Mutterschaftsurlaub; Schwangerschaftsurlaub; ~ **per alium** Fremdschwangerschaft, außereheliche Schwangerschaft; **interruption of** ~ Schwangerschaftsabbruch; **plea of** ~ Gesuch um Exekutionsaufschub wegen Schwangerschaft; **to carry a** ~ **to**

full term e–e Schwangerschaft austragen.
pregnant schwanger.
pre-hearing assessment richterl Vorprüfung der Erfolgsaussichten.
pre-incorporation Vorgründungs . . .
preinstal vorinstallieren.
preinvoice *v* im voraus in Rechnung stellen, vorausberechnen.
prejudge im voraus urteilen, zu früh urteilen.
prejudication Präjudikat *n*, Präzedenzfall *m*.
prejudice *s* Schaden *m*, Vorurteil *n*, Präjudiz *f*, Rechtsnachteil *m*; **without** ~ unpräjudiziell, ohne Präjudiz, ohne Obligo, unbeschadet, unter Vorbehalt, ohne Anerkennung e–r Rechtspflicht.
prejudic|e *v* beeinträchtigen, verletzen, benachteiligen, schädigen, voreinnehmen; ~ **the due course of justice** das gerichtliche Verfahren behindern; ~**ing fair trial** Beeinträchtigung des schwebenden Verfahrens.
prejudiced befangen, voreingenommen.
prejudicial nachteilig; präjudiziell.
preliminaries Vorverhandlungen *f/pl*, Vorverfahren *n*, Präliminarien *n/pl*, vorbereitende Maßnahmen *f/pl*.
preliminary vorläufig, einleitend, vorbereitend, Vor . . .; ~ **application blank** Personalfragebogen; ~ **point of law** vorgreiflicher rechtlicher Gesichtspunkt.
pre-market dealings Vorbörse *f*.
premature voreilig, frühzeitig, vorzeitig.
premeditate (*vorher*) bedenken, überlegen, planen.
premeditated mit Vorbedacht; ~ **act** mit Vorbedacht begangene Handlung, vorsätzliche H; ~ **design** Vorbedacht, *vor der Tat gefaßter* Vorsatz; ~ **exculpation** vorbereiteter Rechtfertigungsgrund.
premeditation Vorbedacht *m*, Überlegung *f*.
premeeting Vorgesprächsrunde *f*.
premier Premierminister *m*, Ministerprasident *m*.
premise *s (1)* Voraussetzung *f*, Prämisse *f*, *pl*: Vorstehendes *n*; Rubrum *n* und Sachverhaltsschilderung *f* e–r Klage; Einleitungssätze *m/pl* e–r Urkunde.
premises *(2)* Beschreibung *f* des versicherten Gegenstandes; Anwesen *n*, (bebautes) Grundstück *n*, Lokal *n*, Örtlichkeit *f*, Betriebsgrundstück *n*; **dangerous** ~ nicht verkehrssicheres Grundstück; **decontrolled** ~ nicht mehr bewirtschafteter Wohnraum; **defective** ~ mängelbehaftetes Anwesen; **demised** ~ Mietgrundstück, Pachtgrundstück, Mieträume, Pachträume; **domestic** ~ Wohnraum, Wohnung; **dwelling** ~ Wohngrundstück, Wohngebäude, Mietobjekt; **industrial** ~ Gewerberaum, betrieblich genutzte Räume; **residential** ~ = *dwelling* ~ *qv*; **licensed** ~ Gaststätte mit Schankkonzession, Gastwirtschaft; **professional** ~ Kanzlei.
premium Prämie *f*, Belohnung *f*, Lehrgeld *n*; Aufgeld *n*, Agio *n*, Abstandsgeld *n (Wohnungen)*, Versicherungsprämie *f*, Beitrag *m*; ~ **annuity** Rente auf Grund von Prämienzahlungen; ~ **bonds** → *bond (1)*; ~ **bonus** Sonderleistungsprämie; ~ **drawing** Prämienziehung; ~ **due** Sollprämie, ausstehende Prämie; ~ **for export** Exportbonus; ~ **for the call** Vorprämie; ~ **for the put** Rückprämie; ~ **hunter** Kursspekulant; ~ **loan** Prämienanleihe; ~ **note** Schuldschein gegen Beleihung des Rückkaufwertes e–r Versicherung; ~ **pudicitiae** Kranzgeld; ~ **of insurance** Versicherungsprämie; ~ **offer** Zugabeangebot; ~ **on an issue** = *share* ~ → *share s*; ~ **on exchange** Agio, Aufgeld; ~ **on shares** = *share* ~ → *share s*; ~ **on stock** Aktienagio; ~ **pay** höherer Lohn (*für Überstunden*), Sondervergütung, Lohnzulage; ~ **rebate** Prämienrabatt, Beitragsermäßigung; ~ **reserve** Prä-

mienübertrag; ~ **reserve stock** Deckungsstock; ~ **savings bonds** Prämienanleihepapiere, Sparprämienobligationen; ~ **selling** Zugaben; ~ **statement** Prämienabrechnung; ~ **tax** → *tax*; **additional** ~ Zuschlagsprämie; **advance** ~ Voraus(zahlungs)prämie; **annual** ~ Jahresprämie; **at a** ~ **(issue)** über Pari (*Emission*); **compound** ~ Doppelprämie; **current** ~ Folgeprämie; **deferred** ~ → *deferred*; **earned** ~ verbrauchte Prämie (*von der Versicherung verdiente P.*); **fluctuating** ~ veränderliches Agio; **gold** ~ → *gold*; **grading of** ~ Beitragsstaffelung; **gross** ~ Bruttoprämie; **level** ~ gleichbleibende Prämie; **limited** ~ abgekürzte Prämienzahlung; **natural** ~ progressive Prämie, jährlich steigende Prämie (*Lebensversicherung*); durchschnittlicher Anfall von Sterbegeldauszahlungen; **net** ~ Nettoprämie, kostendeckende Prämie; **office** ~ Bruttoprämie; **outstanding** ~**s** Prämienaußenstände; **overdue** ~ rückständige Prämie; **pure** ~ Nettoprämie, reine Versicherungsprämie; **put** ~ → *put*; **rate of** ~ Prämiensatz; **return of** ~ Prämienrückgewähr; **self-liquidating** ~ aus dem Verkaufspreis gedeckter Bonus; laufende Versicherungsprämien, laufende Prämien; **share** ~ **account** → *share*; **single** ~ Einmalprämie; **step rate** ~ = *natural* ~ *qv*; **tabular** ~ Tarifprämie; **to be at a** ~ über pari stehen; **to sell at a** ~ mit Gewinn verkaufen; **unearned** ~**s** noch nicht verdiente Prämien; **unearned** ~ **reserve** → *reserve*; **uniform** ~ Einheitsprämie; **waiver of** ~ Prämienbefreiung.

premonition Warnung *f*, Mahnung *f*.

prender (= *prendre*) Entnahmerecht *n*.

preoccupation vorherige Besitzergreifung *f*; Vorurteil *n*, Befangenheit *f*.

prepack tray vorverpackter Fleischschalenbehälter.

prepaid vorausbezahlt, frankiert, freigemacht.

preparation Vorbereitung *f*, Vorbereitungshandlung *f*; Bereitschaft *f*, Aufstellung *f* (*Bilanz*); Bereitung *f*, Aufbereitung *f*, Vorbehandlung *f*, Präparat *n*; ~ **for trial** Prozeßvorbereitung, Vorbereitung d. mündl. Verhandlung bzw Hauptverhandlung.

preparatory vorbereitend.

prepare vorbereiten, anfertigen, bearbeiten, fertigmachen, herrichten, ausrüsten, bereitstellen, präparieren, zurichten, anfertigen, verfassen.

preparedness Bereitschaft *f*, Verteidigungsbereitschaft *f*.

prepay vorauszahlen, vor Fälligkeit zahlen.

prepayment Anzahlung *f*, Vorauszahlung *f*, vorzeitige Tilgung *f*, vorzeitige Rückzahlung *f*; ~**s** *bil* Anzahlungen an Lieferanten; ~ **penalty** Belastung wegen vorzeitiger Tilgung.

preponderance größeres Gewicht *n*, Schwergewicht *n*, Überwiegen *n*; Vorherrschaft *f*; ~ **of evidence** überwiegendes Ergebnis der Beweisaufnahme.

preponderant vorwiegend, überwiegend.

prepossessed eingenommen, voreingenommen.

prepossessor Vorbesitzer *m*, früherer Besitzer *m*.

prerequisite Vorbedingung *f*, Voraussetzung *f*.

prerogative Hoheitsrecht *n* der Krone, Vorrecht *n*, Vorrang *m*, Prärogative *f*, Privileg *n*; ~ **of mercy** Begnadigungsrecht (*des Souveräns*); ~ **of perfection** Indemnitätsvorrecht der Krone; **quintessentially important** ~ grundlegend wichtiges (Vor)Recht; **royal** ~**s** → *royal*.

prerogative bevorrechtigt, aufgrund e–s königl Vorrechts bestehend.

prescribable ersitzungsfähig.

prescribe vorschreiben, ersitzen, auf Grund e–s Ersitzungsrechtes geltend machen; ~**d industrial dis-**

ease *brit* Berufskrankheit; **~d limits of alcohol in blood** Blutalkoholgrenze; **as ~d** vorschriftsmäßig; **within the ~d period** fristgemäß, innerhalb der vorgesehenen Frist.

prescript Vorschrift *f*, Anordnung *f*.

prescription Vorschrift *f*; Ersitzung *f*, Versitzung *f*, Verjährung *f*; **~ in a que estate** Ersitzung *auf Grund ständiger Rechtsausübung aus unvordenklicher Zeit*; **~ in gross** = ~ *in the person qv*; **~ in the person** gewohnheitsrechtlich beschränktes persönliches Entnahmerecht am fremden Grundstück; **acquisitive ~** Ersitzung; **extinctive ~** Rechtsverlust durch Zeitablauf, Versitzung; **legal ~** gesetzl Vorschrift; **negative ~** Verjährung; Versitzung; **positive ~** Ersitzung; **the ~ runs** die Ersitzungs-(Verjährungs-)-frist läuft; **time of ~** Ersitzungsfrist, Versitzungsfrist, Verjährungsfrist; **to claim by ~** Ersitzung geltend machen.

prescriptive right ersessenes Recht, Recht kraft dauernder Ausübung; **~ title** dingliches Recht kraft Ersitzung, ersessenes Eigentum.

presence Anwesenheit *f*, Vorhandensein *n*, Präsenz *f*; **~ at commission of crime** Anwesenheit bei der Begehung der Tat; **~ chamber** Audienzzimmer; **~ of mind** Geistesgegenwart; **actual ~** physische Anwesenheit; **constructive ~** als Anwesenheit geltende Nähe, indirekte Präsenz; **hearing in ~** → *hearing*; **in ~ of an officer** in Gegenwart eines Beamten, in Sichtweite e–s Beamten; **in ~ of the court** in der Sitzung, im unmittelbaren Wahrnehmungsbereich des Gerichts; **in ~ of the testator** in Anwesenheit des Testierenden, in Hörweite des Testierenden; **your ~ is requested** Sie werden gebeten, zu erscheinen.

present *adj* gegenwärtig, zur Zeit bestehend, präsent, anwesend, vorliegend, laufend; **~ and future property** gegenwärtiges und künftiges Vermögen; **~ conveyance** sofort wirksame Übertragung; **~ enjoyment** gegenwärtiger Nutzungsbesitz; **~ interest** Recht auf sofortigen unmittelbaren Besitz; **~ price** → *price (1) bzw (2)*; **~ value** → *value*; **~ worth** der zur Kapitalbedienung erforderliche Investitionswert; **the ~ agreement** der vorliegende Vertrag, dieser Vertrag; **the ~ case** der vorliegende Fall; **those ~** die Anwesenden.

present *s* Geschenk *n*, Gratifikation *f*.

present *v* darbieten, vorlegen, präsentieren, für ein Amt vorschlagen; von Amts wegen beachten; einreichen, anbieten, darstellen; **~ a bill** e–e Vorlage einbringen; **~ a bill for acceptance** e–n Wechsel zur Annahme vorlegen; **~ for collection** zum Inkasso vorzeigen; **when ~ed** bei Vorlage.

presentation Präsentierung *f*, Aufmachung *f* (*der Ware*); Einreichung *f*; Vorzeigung *f*, Einführung *f*, Vorschlagsrecht *n*, Ernennung *f*; **~ copy** Freiexemplar; **~ for acceptance** Vorlage zum Akzept; **~ of goods** Gestellung der Waren (*Zoll*); **~ of petition** Klageerhebung, Einreichung e–s Scheidungsantrags; Stellung e–s Konkursantrags; **~ of the annual balance sheet** Vorlage des Jahresabschlusses; **~ office** Kirchenpfründenamt (*beim Lord Chancellor*); **on ~** bei Vorlage; **payable on ~** bei Sicht fällig.

presentative das Vorschlagsrecht besitzend, darstellend.

presentee vorgeschlagener Kandidat *m (für geistliches Amt)*, Beschenkter *m*, (*bei Hofe*) vorgestellte Person *f*; jmd, dem ein Wechsel vorgelegt wird.

presenter Geber *m*, Vorschlagender *m*, Präsentant *m*; Vorzeiger *m* (*e–s Wechsels oder Schecks*), Aufführender *m*, Darsteller *m*; Moderator *m*.

presentment Vorlage *f*, Vorlegung *f*, Darstellung *f*, Präsentation *f*; Feststellung *f* des dringenden Tatverdachts durch Geschworene (*Grand*

Jury qv); ~ **for acceptance** Vorlegung zur Annahme; ~ **for payment** Vorlage zur Einlösung, Scheckvorlage; ~ **of a bill of exchange** Wechselvorlage; ~ **to acceptor for honour** Vorlage zur Ehrenannahme; **special** ~ Anklageschrift.

presents die vorliegende Urkunde *f*; **these** ~ diese (*die vorliegende*) Urkunde, dieser Vertrag.

preservation Erhaltung *f*, Bewahrung *f*; Sicherstellung *f*; Instandhaltung *f*; ~ **from improper use** Bewahrung vor Mißbrauch; ~ **of amenity** Bestandserhaltung (*Gebäude, Umwelt, Bäume*); ~ **of testimony** Beweissicherung; ~ **of the public peace** Aufrechterhaltung der öffentlichen Ruhe und Ordnung; ~ **order** Veränderungssperre (*im Interesse des Denkmalschutzes*); **interim** ~ **of property** beweissichernde Erhaltungsanordnung; **tree** ~ Baumschutz.

preside (over) präsidieren, den Vorsitz haben, die Versammlung leiten, die Sitzung leiten.

presidency Präsidentschaft *f*.

president Präsident *m*, Staatspräsident *m*; Generaldirektor *m*, Direktor *m*, Vorstandsvorsitzender *m*, Vorsitzender *m*; ~ **elect** der gewählte Präsident; ~ **judge** Gerichtspräsident; **P~ of the Family Division** Präsident der Familiengerichtsabteilung (*des High Court*); **executive board** ~ *etwa:* Vorstandsvorsitzender; **the P~** der Präsident (der USA).

presidential | **campaign** Präsidentenwahlkampf; ~ **candidate** Präsidentschaftskandidat; ~ **election** Präsidentschaftswahl; ~ **electors** Wahlmänner (*für die US-Präsidentschaftswahlen*); ~ **democracy** Präsidialdemokratie; ~ **message** Botschaft des Präsidenten an den Kongreß; ~ **primary** *einzelstaatliche,* indirekte Wahl des US-Präsidenten; ~ **system** Präsidialsystem; ~ **tenure** Amtszeit des Präsidenten; ~ **year** Jahr der Präsidentenwahl.

press *s* Presse *f*, *hist* Gerichtspergamente *n|pl*; ~ **agency** Presseagentur, Nachrichtenbüro; ~ **amalgamation court** Untersuchungskommission für Pressekonzentration; ~ **campaign** Pressefeldzug; ~ **censorship** Pressezensur; ~ **conference** Pressekonferenz; ~ **controversy** Pressepolemik; ~ **council** Presserat; **P~ Gallery** Pressetribüne (*Parlament*); ~ **officer** Pressereferent, Leiter der Pressestelle; **freedom of the** ~ Pressefreiheit; **gutter** ~ Skandalpresse; **national** ~ überregionale Presse; **penny** ~ Boulevardpresse; Groschenblatt; **technical** ~ Fachpresse; **yellow** ~ Sensationspresse, Skandalpresse.

press *v* drängen, dringen; ~ **for payment** Zahlung anmahnen; ~ **in seamen** Seeleute zwangsweise anheuern; **~-gang** Zwangsrekrutierungsleute; **~ing social need** dringendes gesellschaftliches Bedürfnis.

pressure Druck *m*, Zwang *m*; ~ **for money** Geldknappheit; ~ **groups** Interessengruppen; **inflationary** ~ Inflationsdruck; **peaceful** ~ Ausübung von Druck (*ohne Kriegsmaßnahmen*); **undue** ~ Pression, Nötigung.

presumable vermutlich, mutmaßlich, wahrscheinlich, glaubwürdig.

presume vermuten, als wahr unterstellen, schließen aus, annehmen.

presumedly mutmaßlich, vermutet.

presumption Vermutung *f*, Folgerung *f*, Annahme *f*, Mutmaßung *f*, Präsumption *f*; ~ **against suicide** Vermutung, daß es sich nicht um einen Selbstmord handelt; ~ **of accuracy** Vermutung für die Genauigkeit von Meßinstrumenten; ~ **of advancement** → *advancement*; ~ **of agency** Vermutung der Aktiv- und Passivlegitimation des Beauftragten *e–s Ausländers*; ~ **of confiscation** Entziehungsvermutung (*Rückerstattungsrecht*); ~ **of consideration** Vermutung der Entgeltlichkeit; ~ **of continuance** Vermutung für die Fortdauer e–s Zustands; ~ **of correctness** Vermutung der Einhaltung von Formvorschriften; ~ **of death** Todesvermutung (*nach 7 Jahren*); ~ **of delivery** vermutete Übergabe, *unwiderlegbare Vermutung, daß die Übergabe e–s Wechsels an die gutgläubigen Wechselinhaber stattgefunden hat*; ~ **of fact** tatsächliche Vermutung, hoher Grad der Wahrscheinlichkeit; zur Überzeugung ausreichende Folgerung aus Tatsachen; ~ **of guilt** Schuldvermutung; ~ **of good faith and value** Vermutung für den gutgläubigen Besitz e–s Wechsels; ~ **of innocence** Nichtschuldvermutung; ~ **of intent** Folgerung, daß Vorsatz vorgelegen hat; ~ **of law** Rechtsvermutung; ~ **of lawful origin** Eigentumsvermutung; ~ **of legality** Vermutung für die förmliche Richtigkeit von Rechtsgeschäften; ~ **of legitimacy** Ehelichkeitsvermutung; ~ **of life** Lebensvermutung; ~ **of marriage validity** Vermutung für die Gültigkeit e–r Ehe; ~ **of negligence** Fahrlässigkeitsvermutung aufgrund der tatsächlichen Umstände; ~ **of non-dereliction** Vermutung gegen die territoriale Staatenlosigkeit; ~ **of ownership** Eigentumsvermutung; ~ **of paternity** Vaterschafsvermutung; ~ **of sanity** Vermutung für die Zurechnungsfähigkeit; ~ **of survivorship** Überlebensvermutung; ~ **of title** Eigentumsvermutung; ~ **of value** Vermutung der Entgeltlichkeit der Übertragung; **absolute** ~ unwiderlegbare Vermutung; **artificial** ~ gesetzliche Vermutung; **compelling** ~ zwingende Vermutung; **conclusive** ~ unwiderlegbare Vermutung; **decree of** ~ **of death and dissolution of marriage** gerichtliche Todeserklärung und Auflösung der Ehe; **disputable** ~ widerlegbare Vermutung; **inconclusive** ~ widerlegbare Vermutung; **irrebuttable** ~ unwiderlegbare Vermutung; **legitimate** ~ *völlig* gerechtfertigte Folgerung; **light** ~ Folgerung auf ungenügender Grundlage; **mixed** ~ gemischt tatsächliche und gesetzliche Vermutung; **natural** ~ natürliche Folgerung; **non-rebuttable** ~ unwiderlegbare Vermutung; **probable** ~ e–e Folgerung bei e–m hohen Wahrscheinlichkeitsgrad; **rash** ~ riskante Folgerung; **rebuttable** ~ widerlegbare Vermutung; **statutory** ~ gesetzliche Vermutung; **violent** ~ e–e sich aufdrängende Folgerung, zwingender Schluß.

presumptive vermutlich, wahrscheinlich, präsumptiv, mutmaßlich; ~ **deviser** (*of the invention*) mutmaßlicher Urheber (*der Erfindung*).

presuppose voraussetzen, zur Voraussetzung haben.

presupposition Voraussetzung *f*.

pre-tax | **income** Einkommen *f* vor (Abzug der) Steuern; ~ **profit** Gewinn vor Steuern, unversteuerter Gewinn.

pretence (*US: pretense*) zweifelhafter Anspruch *m*, Scheingrund *m*, Vorwand *m*, Verstellung *f*, Vorspiegelung *f*, Vorgeben *n*, Vortäuschung *f*; **false** ~**s** → *false pretences*; **fraudulent** ~**s** betrügerische Vorspiegelung e–r Tatsache, arglistige Täuschung.

pretend vorgeben, simulieren, sich ausgeben als, den Anschein erwecken, Anspruch erheben auf, sich anmaßen, bewerben.

pretended angeblich, vorgeblich; ~ **title to land** angebliches Grundstückseigentum.

pretender Anspruchsteller *m*, Bewerber *m*, Thronanwärter *m*, Prätendent *m*.

pretenses vorweggenommene Replik *f*.

pretension Anspruch *m*, Forderung *f*, Anmaßung *f*; **territorial** ~**s** angemaßte Gebietsansprüche.

pre-termination agreement Vereinbarung *f* für die Zeit der Vertragsbeendigung und danach.

pretermission Übergehung *f*, Auslassung *f*, Versäumnis *n*, Übergehung *f* e–s Abkömmlings bei der letztwilligen Verfügung; ~ **statute** *gesetzliche Erbersatzregelung bei versehentlichem Übergehen von Abkömmlingen im Testament.*

pretermit übergehen, auslassen, versäumen; ~**ted heir** übergangener Erbanwärter (*versehentlich im Testament nicht genannter erbberechtigter Abkömmling*).

pretext Vorwand *m*, Ausrede *f*, Ausflucht *f*.

pretium | affectionis Liebhaberwert *m*; ~ **periculi** Risikoprämie; Bodmereizins.

pre-trial diversion Resozialisierung vor Strafverfahren.

pre-trial review Vorverfahren *n (zivilrechtl, county court)*.

prevail wirksam sein, vorherrschen, maßgebend sein, gelten.

prevailing maßgebend, vorherrschend, üblich; ~ **case law** herrschende Rechtsprechung; ~ **wage** übliche Vergütung; ~ **wage law** (=) *Gesetz über die Pflicht zur angemessenen ortsüblichen Bezahlung von Arbeitskräften bei Staatsaufträgen.*

prevalence Vorherrschen *n*, Überhandnehmen *n*, Verbreitung *f*, Häufigkeit *f*.

prevalent vorherrschend, weit verbreitet; **to be** ~ verbreitet sein, grassieren.

prevaricate die Wahrheit verdrehen, Ausflüchte machen, *etw* verheimlichen, *etw* verdunkeln; Parteiverrat begehen, mit der Gegenpartei ins Einvernehmen treten.

prevarication Ausflucht *f*, Tatsachenverdrehung *f*, Winkelzug *m*; Parteiverrat *m*, Prävarikation *f*, Dienstwidrigkeit *f*, Amtsvergehen *n*.

prevaricator Wortverdreher *m*, Ausflüchtemacher *m*, Rechtsverdreher *m*; Anwalt *m*, der Parteiverrat begeht.

prevent verhindern, verhüten, hindern, zuvorkommen, dazwischentreten.

prevention Verhinderung *f*, Zuvorkommen *n*, Verhütung *f*, Vorbeugung *f*; Vorwegnahme *f* der Zuständigkeit; ~ **of crime** Generalprävention *f*, Verbrechensverhütung; **P~ of Cruelty to Children Act** Gesetz gegen Kindesmißhandlung *GB 1874*; ~ **of hardship** Vermeidung von Härten; ~ **of labour accidents** Arbeitsschutz; ~ **of loss** Schadensverhütung; **P~ of Terrorism Act** Terrorismus-Bekämpfungsgesetz.

preventive vorbeugend, verhütend.

previous vorhergehend, vorangehend, vorherig, früher, bevor; ~ **cessation of the patent protection** vorzeitige Aufgabe des Patentschutzes.

price *(1)* Preis *m* (= *P bzw* ...*p*), Kaufpreis *m*, Kosten *pl*, Belohnung *f*, Bestechungsgeld *n*, Kopfpreis *m*, Lohn *m*, Werklohn *m*, Entgelt *n*, Gegenleistung *f*, Verkehrswert *m*; ~ **adjustment levy** Abschöpfung, Abschöpfungsbetrag *EG*; ~ **administration** *US P*überwachung; ~ **advance** *P*steigerung; ~ **agreed upon** vereinbarter *P*; ~ **asked** geforderter *P*; ~ **boost** *P*erhöhung; ~ **catalogue** *P*liste; *P*verzeichnis; ~ **concession** *P*zugeständnis; ~ **control** *P*kontrolle, *P*überwachung; ~ **cutting** *P*herabsetzung im Wettbewerb; *P*unterbietung, *P*drückerei; ~ **decontrol** Aufhebung der *P*kontrolle; ~ **differential** *P*unterschied, Ausgleichsbetrag; ~ **discrimination** *P*differenzierung (*als unlauterer Wettbewerb*); ~**-discriminatory** *p*bewußt, *p*kritisch; ~ **distortion** *P*verzerrung; ~ **earnings ratio** Kurs-Gewinn-Verhältnis; ~ **elasticity** *P*elastizität; ~**-enhancing** *p*treibend; ~ **equalisation** *P*ausgleich, ~ **expectancy** *P*erwartung, erwarteter Einspielerlös; ~ **fixing** *P*festsetzung, *P*absprache; ~ **floor** Mindestpreis, *P*untergrenze; ~ **freeze** *P*stopp; ~ **gap** *P*gefälle; ~ **in contract of sale** Kauf*p*; ~ **increase** *P*steigerung; ~ **index** *P*index, *P*meßzahl; ~ **leader** attraktives Angebot zu Verlust*p–en* (*als un-*

lauterer Wettbewerb); ~ **leadership** *P*führung; ~ **level** *P*niveau; ~ **limit** *P*grenze, *P*limit; ~ **line** Einheits*p*; ~**-maintained goods** *p*gebundene Waren; ~ **maintenance agreement** Vereinbarung der *P*bindung; ~ **margin** *P*spanne; ~ **movements** Kursbewegungen; *tell-take* ~ ~: *aufschlußreiche K.*; ~ **number** *P*indexziffer; ~ **of adjudication** Höchstgebot, Zuschlagsgebot; ~ **of delivery** Liefer*p*, Bezugs*p*; ~ **of money** Kapitalmarktzins; ~ **paid** Kauf*p* bezahlt, Quittung; ~ **range** *P*lage, *P*skala; ~ **reduction** *P*senkung; ~ **regulations** *P*kontrolle, *P*vorschriften; ~ **ring** *P*kartell; ~ **rollback** *P*herabsetzung; ~**-sensitive** *adj p*reagibel, kursreagibel; ~ **shading** erzwungenes Nachgeben im *P (Konkurrenz)*; ~ **slashing** drastische *P*herabsetzung; ~ **structure** *P*gefüge; ~ **supervision** *P*überwachung; ~ **support** *P*stützung; ~ **tag** *P*etikett, *P*zettel; ~ **trend** *P*entwicklung; ~ **variance** *P*abweichung; ~ **variance clause** *P*gleitklausel; ~ **without engagement** *P* freibleibend; **acceptable** ~ annehmbarer *P*; **activating** ~ Auslösungs*p (Agrarmarktordnung)*; **actual** ~ Markt*p*, Tages*p*; **adjustable** ~ gestaffelter *P*; **administered** ~**s** bewirtschaftete *P–e*, Richt*p–e*; **allround** ~ Gesamt*p*, Pauschal*p*; **asking** ~ Verhandlungsbasis, Verkaufspreis(vorstellung), vom Verkäufer verlangter *P*; **at constant** ~ *p*bereinigt; **at the best** ~ **obtainable** bestens (*verkaufen*); **average** ~ Durchschnitts*p*; **base** ~ Grund*p*; **best** ~ der höchste (erzielbare) *P*; **bid** ~ Rücknahme*p* (Investm); **blanket** ~ Sammel*p*, Pauschal*p*; **blended** ~ Misch*p*; **bottom** ~ niedrigster *P*; **break in** ~**s** → *break*; **buying** ~ Einkaufs*p*, Anschaffungswert; **buying-in** ~ Ankaufs*p*; **cash** ~ → *cash*; **ceiling** ~ Höchst*p*, gesetzlicher Höchst*p*; **chattels** ~ *P* für mitverkaufte, bewegliche Sachen; **close** ~ scharf kalkulierter *P*; **closing** ~ Schluß*p*; **commercial contract** ~ vertragl vereinbarter Handels*p*; **competitive** ~ Konkurrenz*p*; **connoisseur's** ~ Liebhaber*p*; **consumer** ~ **index** → *consumer*; **call** ~ Rückprämien*p*; **contract** ~ Vertrags*p*, Liefer*p*, Binnenmarkt*p*; **controlled** ~ gebundener *P*, gesteuerter *P*; **cost** ~ Anschaffungs*p*, Inventurwert pro Einheit; **costplus** ~ *P auf Grundlage der Selbstkosten plus vereinbartem Zuschlag*; **current** ~ Tages*p*; **cushioning** ~ Stütz*p*; **cut-throat** ~ ruinöser *P*; **delivered** ~ *P* einschließlich Lieferkosten; **domestic** ~ Inlands*p*; **duty inclusive** ~ *P* verzollt; **equilibrium of** ~**s** *P*gleichgewicht; **exceptional** ~ Sonder*p*, Vorzugs*p*; **excessive** ~ Über*p*; **exorbitant** ~ überhöhter *P*, Wucher*p*; **factory** ~ *P* ab Werk, *pl* Fabrik*p–e*; **fair** ~ angemessener *P*; **fancy** ~ Affektionswert, Liebhaber*p*; **first** ~ Einkaufs*p*, Anschaffungs*p*; **fixed** ~ Fest*p*, gebundener *P*; **flat** ~ Einheits*p*, *einheitliche Preise für Kunden aller Art*, Fest*p*, Sammel*p*; **flexibility of** ~**s** *P*flexibilität; **fluctuations of** ~**s** *P*schwankungen; **forward** ~ *P* für künftige Lieferung; **free-at frontier** ~ *P* frei Grenze; **free domicile** ~ *P* frei Bestimmungsort; **graduated** ~ Staffel*p*; **gross** ~ Brutto*p*, *P* vor Abzug der (Grundstücks)Belastungen; **guide** ~ *P*vorstellung; **guiding** ~ Richt*p*; **inadequate** ~ in auffälligem Mißverhältnis zum Wert stehender *P*, zu niedriger *P*; **in bond** ~ *P* für unverzollte Ware im Zollager; **latest** ~ letzter *P*, aktueller *P*; **landed** ~ *P für Einfuhrgüter einschließlich Transport, Abladung und Zoll*; **leading** ~ Richt*p*; **limit** ~ → *limit*; **limited** ~ Limit*p*, Kurslimit; **liquidation** ~ → *liquidation*; **list** ~ Listen*p*, Katalog*p*; **loco** ~ *P* bei Übernahme am Lagerort; **long-run normal** ~ eingependelter stabiler *P*; **losing** ~ Verlust*p*; **lowest** ~ niedrigster *P*, äußerster *P*; **lump (sum)** ~ Pauschal*p*; **maintained ~s** gebundene *P–e*; **medium ~** mittlerer Durchschnitts*p*; **market ~** → *market*; **mill net ~** Netto*p* des Textilfabrikanten (*nach Abzug von Transportkosten*); **minimum resale ~** Mindestwiederverkaufs*p*; **net ~** Netto*p* (*Listenpreis minus Rabatt*); **nominal ~** theoretischer *P*; **non-sale ~** regulärer *P*; **offer ~** Angebots*p*, gebotener *P*; **offered ~** Angebots*p* des Verkäufers; **ordinary competitive ~** üblicher Wettbewerbs*p*; **original ~** Anschaffungs*p*; **overhead ~** *P einschließlich Generalunkosten und Nebenkosten*; **posted ~** (Erdöl)Listen*p*, fiktiver Verrechnungs*p* für Rohöl; **present ~** Tages*p*; **per-unit ~** Stück*p*; **prevailing ~** gegenwärtiger *P*, üblicher *P*, herrschender *P*; **private ~** Vorzugs*p*; **public ~** allgemeiner *P*, Laden*p*; **purchase ~** Kauf*p*, Einkaufs*p*; **quoted ~** → *quote*; **real ~** echter *P*, effektiver *P*; **recommended ~** empfohlener *P*; **reduced ~** ermäßigter *P*; **regulation of ~s** *P*kontrolle; **rendu ~** *P* frei Haus *des Käufers bzw Importeurs*; **resale ~** → *resale*; **resale ~ maintenance** → *resale*; **reserve ~** unteres Versteigerungslimit; **retail ~** → *retail*; **rock-bottom ~** absolut niedrigstes *P*angebot; **roll back ~** *auf den amtlichen Höchstpreis* zurückgeführter *P*; **ruling ~** Tages*p*, Markt*p*, geltender *P*; **sale ~** Sonderangebots*p*; **selling ~** Verkaufs*p*, Laden*p*; **single ~** Einheits*p*; **sluice-gate ~** Einschleusungs*p*; **spot ~** → *spot*; **stationary ~** stabiler *P*; **strike ~** Abschluß*p*, Einsteige*p*; **suggested ~** empfohlener *P*, (*Einzelhandel*)Richt*p*; **support ~** Stützungs*p*; **target ~** → *target*; **the payable ~** der zu zahlende *P*; **time ~** *P* bei Verkauf auf Lieferantenkredit; **to arrive ~** = *landed price qv*; **to build down to a ~** die Bauarbeiten e–m niedrigen Preis anpassen; **trade ~** Wiederverkäufer*p*, Großhandels*p*; **uniform ~** Einheits*p*; **uniform delivered ~** gleicher *P* an jedem Lieferort, Einheitsend*p*; **unit ~** Stück*p*, *P* je (*Gewichts- etc*) Einheit; **unreasonable ~** überhöhter *P*; **upset ~** unteres Versteigerungslimit, Mindestgebot; **wholesale ~** Großhandels*p*; **world ~s** Weltmarkt*p–e*.

price *(2)* Kurs *m* (= *K bzw* . . .*k*); **~ advance** *K*steigerung; **~ after hours** nachbörslicher *K*; **~ bid** Geld*k*; **~ current** Börsen*k*, *K*wert; **~ cushioning** Abfangen von *K*schwankungen; **~ decline** *K*rückgang; **~ drawn by lot** Los*k*, Börsen*k*, der durch Los bestimmt wird; **~ for cash** Kassa*k*; **~ for the account** Termin*k*; **~ for the settlement** Termin*k*; **~ improvement** *K*besserung; **~ index** *K*index; **~ limit** *K*begrenzung, Limit; **~ list** *K*zettel; **~ movement** *K*entwicklung; **~ nursing** *K*pflege; **~ of option** Prämien*k*; **~ of put** Rückprämien*k*; **~ of shares** Aktien*k*; **~s offered** Brief*k*; **~ quotation** *K*notierung; **~ quoted** notierter *K*; **asked ~** Brief*k*; **bid ~** Geld*k*; Rückkauf*k*, Rücknahme*k*; **buoyant ~s** hochschnellende *K–e*; **closing ~** Schluß*k*, Schlußnotierung; **crumbling of ~s** Abbröckeln der *K–e*; **decline of ~s** *K*rückgang, Baisse; **depression of ~s** *K*einbruch; **estimation ~** Tax*k*; **equalizing ~s** Ausgleich von *K–en*; **exhaust ~** untere *K*grenze *bei Erschöpfung der Sicherheit des Terminkäufers*; **firm ~s** feste *K–e*; **forward ~** *K* für Termingeschäfte; **issue ~** → *issue (1)*; **last ~** letzte Börsennotiz; **making up ~** Abrechnungs*k des Börsenmaklers*, Liquidations*k*; **middle ~** Mittel*k*; **offered ~** Brief*k*; **opening ~(s)** Eröffnungs*k*; **present ~** Tages*k*, *ausbezahlte Valuta für ein Wertpapier*; **put ~** → *put s*; **put and call ~** → *put s*; **rally in ~s** *K*erholung; **reported closing ~** festgestellter Schlußkurs; **settling**

~ Abrechnungs*k*; **slump in ~s** *K*sturz; **street ~s** → *street*.

priced mit Preisen versehen, ausgezeichnet.

pricing Preisfestsetzung *f*; ~ **of requisitions** Kostenbestimmung bei Materialanforderungen; ~ **system** Preiskalkulationssystem; **full cost** ~ Preiskalkulation einschließlich Gemeinkosten und Risikofaktor.

pricking Punktieren *n*, Lochen *n*; ~ **for sheriffs** Zufallsauswahl bei Ernennung der Sheriffs; ~ **note** Warenempfangsliste (*an Bord*).

primacy Vorrang *m*, Primat *n*.

prima facie (=) auf den ersten Anschein, nach dem Anscheinsbeweis; ~ **case** schlüssiges (*und bis zum Beweise des Gegenteils*) nachgewiesenes Vorbringen; *nach den Regeln des Anscheinsbeweises* glaubhaft gemachter Sachverhalt; *to make out a* ~ ~: *glaubhaft machen; schlüssig vortragen*; ~ **evidence** Glaubhaftmachung, Primafaciebeweis, Beweis des ersten Anscheins, Anscheinsbeweis, einstweilige Beweisführung; ~ **evidence of title** Glaubhaftmachung der Berechtigung; vorläufiger Eigentumsnachweis.

primage Frachtzuschlag *m*; *hist* Primage *f*; Primgeld *n*; ~ **duty** Einfuhrzoll.

primaries Vorwahlen *f/pl*.

primarily *adv* primär, in erster Linie.

primary *adj* primär, hauptsächlich.

primary purpose rule Haupteinreisezweck-Regel *f* (*Einwanderungsvorschriften*).

prime erst(er, -e, -es), vorzüglich, ursprünglich; ~ **banker's acceptances** Primadiskonten; ~ **bill** → *bill (3)*; ~ **collateral instruments** erstklassige Sicherheiten; ~ **contract** Vertrag mit den Generalunternehmen; ~ **contractor** Hauptunternehmer, Generalunternehmer; ~ **cost** Einstandspreis, Beschaffungskosten, Gestehungskosten, Gestehungspreis; Einkaufspreis; ~ **election** erste Wahl; ~ **entry** → *entry*; ~ **investment** erstklassige Kapitalanlage; ~ **minister** → *minister*; ~ **name** erste Adresse; ~ **paper** Primapapiere, erstklassige Wertpapiere; ~ **product** → *product*; ~ **rate** → *prime rate*; ~ **trade bill** erstklassiger Handelswechsel.

prime rate (=) Primarate *f*, Leitzins *m*, *UK: Diskontsatz für erstklassige Akzepte; US: Sollzinssatz amerikanischer Geschäftsbanken für erstklassige Kunden bei Dreimonatskredit.*

primo loco erstens, an erster Stelle.

primogeniture Erstgeburt *f*, Primogenitur *f*, Erstgeburtsrecht *n*, Nachfolge des ältesten Sohnes im Grundbesitz.

prince Fürst *m*, Prinz *m*; **~s and princesses of royal blood** nicht thronfolgeberechtigte königliche Prinzen und Prinzessinnen; ~ **consort** Prinzgemahl; ~ **regent** Prinzregent; **~s, rulers and peoples** Staatsgewalt.

principal *adj*, hauptsächlich, Haupt...; ~ **paying agent** Hauptzahlstelle; ~ **place of business** Hauptgeschäftssitz, Hauptniederlassung; ~ **subject-matter** Hauptsache.

principal *s (1)* Vorsteher *m*, Vorstand *m*, Vorgesetzter *m*, Chef *m*, Prinzipal *m*, Geschäftsherr *m*, Auftraggeber *m*, der (die) Vertretene, Vollmachtgeber *m*; Kommittent *m*, Bearbeiter *m*; aus eigenem Recht Handelnder *m*; Hauptschuldner *m*; Haupttäter *m*; Anführer *m*, Rädelsführer *m*; mittelbarer Täter *m*; ~ **and accessory** Teilnahme (*an Straftaten*); Teilnahmelehre; ~ **and agent** Stellvertretung; ~ **and surety** Bürgschaftsverhältnis; ~ **in the first degree** Mittäter; ~ **in the second degree** *am Tatort anwesender* Tatgehilfe; **~'s mandate** spezifizierte Bevollmächtigungsurkunde; ~ **of the house** Vorstand e–s Anwaltsvereins; **foreign** ~ ausländischer Auftraggeber (*e–s Propagandisten*); **undisclosed** ~ verdeckter Auftraggeber, mittelbar Vertretener, ungenannter Geschäftsherr.

principal *(2)* Hauptsumme *f*, Hauptsache *f*, Kapital *n*; ~ **and interest**

Hauptsache nebst Zinsen; **unpaid** ~ offene Hauptsacheforderung.

principle Regel *f*, Prinzip *n*, Grundsatz *m*, Grundlage *f*, Grundzug *m*, Grundbegriff *m*, Leitsatz *m*, Leitgedanke *m*, Rechtsgrundsatz *m*, Lehrsatz *m*; ~ **of conservatism** Vorsichtsprinzip (*Bewertung*); ~ **of derogation from grant** Grundsatz der eigenen Bindungswirkung e–r Bewilligung *bzw* Rechtsgewährung; ~ **of equality** Gleichheits(grund)satz; ~ **of equivalence** Gleichwertigkeitsgrundsatz *bei Enteignungsbeschluß*; **~s of good industrial relations practice** Grundsätze sozialer Arbeitnehmerbehandlung; ~ **of legality** „keine Strafe ohne Gesetz"; **~s of international law** völkerrechtl Grundsatz; ~ **of law** Rechtsgrundsatz; ~ **of majority** Majoritätsprinzip; ~ **of orality** Mündlichkeitsprinzip; ~ **of proportionality** Verhältnismäßigkeitsgrundsatz; ~ **of the most favoured nation** Meistbegünstigungsgrundsatz; **armchair** ~ Testamentsauslegung unter besonderer Berücksichtigung der Lebensverhältnisse des Testierenden; **as a matter of** ~ grundsätzlich; **"clean break"** ~ Grundsatz der sauberen Trennung (*beiderseitiger Unterhaltsverzicht*); **declaration of** ~ → *declaration*; **general ~s** allgemeine Grundsätze; **general ~s of law** allgemeine Rechtsgrundsätze; **guiding** ~ Leitsatz, Leitbild, Leitprinzip.

print *s* Druck *m*, Abdruck *m*, Stempel *m*; Gedrucktes *n*, Druckschrift *f*; **commercial** ~ gewerbliche gedruckte Darstellung; **non-commercial** ~ nicht gewerblich gedruckte Darstellung; **out of** ~ vergriffen; **the fine** ~ das Kleingedruckte.

print *v* drucken, in Druckbuchstaben schreiben; **~ed clause** vorgedruckte Klausel; **~ed document** Druckschrift; **~ed form** Vordruck; **~ed matter** → *matter*.

printing Druck *m*, Drucken *n* (*einschließlich Schreibmaschine und Vervielfältigung*); ~ **fee** Drucklegungsgebühr; ~ **industry** Druckereigewerbe; ~ **order** Druckauftrag; ~ **paper** Druckereipapier; **public** ~ Druck im Staatsauftrag.

print out (Computer)Ausdruck *m*.

prior früher, vor, älter, vorrangig, rangbesser, erststellig; ~ **applicant** *pat* früherer Anmelder, Voranmelder; ~ **application** frühere Anmeldung; ~ **claim** älterer Anspruch, bevorrechtigte Forderung; *pat*: Prioritätsanspruch; ~ **claim to satisfaction** Anspruch auf bevorrechtigte Befriedigung; ~ **conviction** Vorstrafe; ~ **estate** Volleigentum; ~ **grant** Prioritätsrecht; ~ **holder** Vorbesitzer; ~ **incumbrancer** vorrangiger Grundpfandgläubiger; ~ **indorser** Vormann; ~ **interest** vorrangiges Interesse; ~ **invention** ältere Erfindung; ~ **inventor** Ersterfinder; ~ **involvement** Vorbefassung (*e–s Richters*); ~ **judgment** früheres Urteil; ~ **mortgage** im Range vorgehende Hypothek; ~ **offence** Vortat; ~ **petens** der erste Antragsteller; ~ **preferred stock** Sondervorzugsaktie; ~ **redemption** vorzeitige Tilgung; ~ **taxable year** das vorangehende Steuerjahr; ~ **to maturity** vor Fälligkeit.

priority Vorrang *m*, Vorzug *m*, Vorzugsrecht *n*, Priorität *f*, Rangfolge *f*; Dringlichkeit *f*, Dringlichkeitsstufe *f*; Vorfahrtsrecht *n*; ~ **bonds** Prioritätsobligationen; ~ **caution** Vormerkung, Rangvorbehalt; ~ **date** → *date*; ~ **documents** → *document*; ~ **inhibition** Widerspruchseintragung *bei dinglichen Grundstücksrechten*; ~ **list** Dringlichkeitsliste; ~ **need for accommodation** Dringlichkeit der Wohnungsbeschaffung; ~ **notice** Vormerkung *für e–n Grundpfandrecht*; ~ **of creditors** → *creditor*; ~ **of debts of insolvent estate** Rangfolge der Nachlaßschulden bei Zahlungsunfähigkeit; ~ **of invention** Erfindungspriorität, Ersterfindung; ~

of lien Rangordnung von Pfandrechten; ~ **of time** zeitlicher Vorrang, zeitliches Rangverhältnis; ~ **rating** Festsetzung der Dringlichkeit; ~ **rehousing group** Wohnungssuchende mit Dringlichkeitsstufe I; ~ **sale** vorrangiger Verkauf (*an den prioritätsberechtigten Bieter, Wertpapierhandel*); ~ **share** → *share*; **application establishing** ~ prioritätsbegründende Anmeldung; **claim of earlier** ~ **date** prioritätsälterer Anspruch; **creditor by** ~ bevorrechtigter Gläubiger; **declaration of** ~ Prioritätserklärung; **degree of** ~ Dringlichkeitsstufe; **delay for filing** ~ Prioritätserklärungsfrist; **loss of** ~ → *loss*; **order of** ~ Rangordnung, Rangfolge; **to claim** ~ **for an application** Erstanmeldung beanspruchen; **to have** ~ **over s.o.** jmdm im Rang vorgehen; **with** ~ **over** mit Vorrang vor.

prisage Prisenanteil *m* der Krone.

prison Gefängnis *n*, Haftanstalt *f*, Strafanstalt *f*, Gefangenenanstalt *f*, Zuchthaus *n*; Gefängnisgelände *n*; ~ **bonds** den Gefangenen erlaubter Bereich bei der Gefangenenanstalt; ~ **breach** = ~ *breaking qv*; ~**-breaking** Ausbruch aus e–m Gefängnis, Selbstbefreiung; ~ **chaplain** Gefängnisgeistlicher; ~ **committal** ~ Einweisung in die Haftanstalt, Vollziehung des Haftbefehls; ~ **governor** Gefängnisdirektor; ~ **inmate** Gefängnisinsasse, Gefangener, Sträfling, Häftling; ~ **policy** Strafvollzugsgrundsätze; ~ **population** die (Gesamtheit der) Gefängnisinsassen; ~ **sentence** Freiheitsstrafe; ~ **system** Strafvollzugssystem; ~ **ward** Gefängnisabteilung; ~ **warden** Gefängnisdirektor.

prisoner Gefangener *m*; Angeklagter *m*; Häftling *m*, Sträfling *m*; ~ **at the bar** (*inhaftierter*) Angeklagter *in der Hauptverhandlung*; ~ **of war** Kriegsgefangener; ~ **on remand** Untersuchungsgefangener; ~ **on trial** (*inhaftierter*) Angeklagter; **arraignment of** ~ Befragung des Angeklagten zur Schuld bzw. Nichtschuld; **civil** ~ Inhaftierter im Zivilverfahren, in Beugehaft; **close** ~ streng bewachter Gefangener; **criminal** ~ Strafgefangener; **escape by** ~ Flucht e–s Strafgefangenen; **evidence of** ~ → *evidence*; **remand** ~ Untersuchungsgefangener.

privacy Ungestörtheit *f*, Heimlichkeit *f*, Nichtöffentlichkeit *f*, Geheimhaltung *f*; Individualsphäre *f*, Intimsphäre *f*, Privatsphäre *f*, Persönlichkeitssphäre *f*; ~ **of correspondence** Briefgeheimnis; **infringement of** ~ Verletzung der Intimsphäre; **invasion of** ~ Einbruch in die Privatsphäre; **right of** ~ Recht des Ausschlusses der Öffentlichkeit, Schutz der Privatsphäre; Anspruch auf ungestörte Intimsphäre; Schutz des Persönlichkeitsrechts.

private *adj* privat, eigen, persönlich, vertraulich, nicht öffentlich, intern, geheim, nicht amtlich, außergerichtlich; ~ **and confidential** vertraulich; ~ **chattels scheme** Entschädigung für Kriegsschäden an beweglichen Sachen; ~ **credit bank** Handelsbank, Geschäftsbank; ~ **enterprise** (privates) Unternehmen, freie Marktwirtschaft; ~ **evidentiary hearing** Beweisaufnahme unter Ausschluß der Öffentlichkeit; ~ **health care** privater Krankenversicherungsschutz, priv Krankheitsvorsorge; ~ **person's power of arrest** privates Festnahmerecht; ~ **rented sector** freier Wohnungsmarkt; ~ **sector economy** Privatwirtschaft; ~ **sector rents** freie Mieten; **going** ~ privatisiert werden; Umwandlung von Publikumsgesellschaften in *private company limited qv* durch Aktienerwerb.

privately *adv* privat, als Privatperson; freihändig; unter der Hand; ~ **owned** im Privatbesitz.

privation Wegnahme *f*, Entzug *m*.

privatisation (= *privatization*) Privatisierung *f*.

privies (pl von privy) Genossen *m*|*pl*, gemeinschaftlich Beteiligte *m*|*pl*, in gemeinsamer Beziehung Stehende *m/pl*; ~ **in estate** in Rechtsbeziehung zum gleichen Grundstück Stehende (*zB Verpächter u Pächter, Veräußerer u Erwerber*); ~ **in law** gesetzlich Beteiligte, gesetzlich in Gemeinschaft stehende Personen, notwendige Streitgenossen; ~ **in representation** gemeinschaftlich an Nachlaßverwaltung Beteiligte; ~ **in respect of contract** Vertragsbeteiligte; ~ **of blood** durch Blutsverwandtschaft verbundene Personen; ~ **to a judgment** Rechtsnachfolger e–r Prozeßpartei (*während des Prozesses*).

privilege *s* Recht *n*, Privileg *n*, Vorrecht *n*, Vorzug *m*, Vorrang *m*, Sonderrecht *n*; Rechtfertigungsgrund *m*; Wahrung *f* berechtigter Interessen; Aussageverweigerungsrecht *m*, Indemnität *f*; verbürgtes und unveräußerliches Recht *n*, Freiheit *f*, Spekulationsgeschäft *n*, Prämien- oder Stellagegeschäft *n*; ~**s and immunities** allgemeine Grundrechte (*nach US-Bundesrecht*); ~ **broker** Prämienmakler; ~ **of documents** Recht der Verweigerung der Urkundenvorlage; ~ **from arrest** (persönliche) Immunität; ~ **in land** Rechte an e–m Grundstück; ~ **of communication between client and solicitor** anwaltschaftliches Aussageverweigerungsrecht; ~ **of lawyers** anwaltliches Aussageverweigerungsrecht; ~ **of necessity** Notstand; ~ **of self-defence** Notwehr(recht); ~ **of the House** Vorrecht des Parlaments; Parlamentsimmunität; ~ **of transit** Anhalte- und Umladerechte e–s Versenders; ~ **of witness** Aussageverweigerungsrecht von Zeugen; Zeugenindemnität; Schutz des Zeugen vor ehrverletzenden Fragen; ~ **tax** *US* Konzessionssteuer; **absolute** ~ absolute Indemnität (*bei Beleidigung und Verleumdung*); **banker's** ~ (Recht der Berufung auf das) Bankgeheimnis; **breach of** ~ Zuständigkeitsüberschreitung, Eingriff in die Rechte anderer; **commercial** ~ Konzession; **conditional** ~ bedingte Immunität bzw Indemnität; **constitutional** ~ Vorrang von Anfragen wegen Gefährdung der Verfassung; **diplomatic** ~**s** diplomatische Vorrechte und Immunitäten; **exclusive** ~ ausschließliche Konzession; **executive** ~ Geheimhaltungsrecht der staatl Verwaltung; **informer's** ~ Anonymitätsprivileg für den Informanten; **instrument of** ~ Schutzrechtsurkunde (*gewerbl Rechtsschutz*); **justification and** ~ Wahrnehmung berechtigter Interessen; **legal** ~ Schutz der Vertraulichkeit anwaltschaftlicher Mitteilungen (*gegen Beschlagnahme, Verwertung im Strafverfahren*); **legal professional** ~ Anwaltsgeheimnis, berufl Aussageverweigerungsrecht des Rechtsanwalts; **marital** ~**s** Aussageverweigerungsrecht des Ehegatten (*bei Strafverfahren gegen den anderen*); **parliamentary** ~ Parlamentsprivilegien; Parlamentsimmunität, Abgeordnetenimmunität; Vorrang auf der Tagesordnung; **personal** ~ Abgeordneten-Immunität bzw Abgeordneten-Indemnität; **postal** ~ Postzwang, Postprivileg; **professional** ~ Berufsgeheimnis; **public** ~ Berufung auf Geheimhaltungsbedürftigkeit im öffentl Interesse; Berufung auf Wahrnehmung berechtigter Interessen; **qualified** ~ eingeschränkte Indemnität (*ohne Verleumdung*); **real** ~ an Grundstück gebundene Konzession; **royal** ~ Regal; **self-incrimination** ~ Aussageverweigerungsrecht wegen Gefahr der Selbstbezichtigung; **solicitors's** ~ Recht der Berufung auf Anwaltsgeheimnis; **special** ~ ausschließliches Privileg, Sonderrecht, Vorrecht; **tax** ~ → *tax*; **taxation** ~ → *taxation*; **writ of** ~ → *writ*.

privilege *v* bevorzugen, privilegieren, berechtigen, befreien.

privileged privilegiert, bevorrechtigt, berechtigt, in Wahrnehmung berechtigter Interessen handelnd, freigestellt (*von Lasten*); ~ **from discovery** nicht vorlegungspflichtig; ~ **from distress** unpfändbar.

privity gemeinsame Rechtsbeziehung *f*; Rechtsverhältnis *n* (*am gemeinsamen Vermögen bzw Recht*); gemeinsame Interessenbeziehung *f*, Interessengemeinschaft *f*; Gemeinschaft *f*, Treueverhältnis *n*; Mitwissen *n*, Mitwisserschaft *f*, Eingeweihtsein *n*; Rechtsnachfolge *f*; ~ **in deed** vertragliche Rechtsbeziehung; ~ **of blood** Abstammung, Verwandtschaftsverhältnis; ~ **of contract** unmittelbares Vertragsverhältnis, Vertragsbeziehung, Stellung als Vertragspartei; ~ **of estate** Lehensverhältnis, dingliches Gemeinschaftsverhältnis aus gleichem Rechtsgrund; dingliche Rechtsbeziehung, dingliches Rechtsverhältnis; ~ **of tenure** unmittelbares Lehensverhältnis; ~ **or knowledge** Kenntnis, Mitwisserschaft; **horizontal** ~ horizontale Verteilerbeziehung (*zum Verbraucher*); **legal** ~ unmittelbare Rechtsbeziehung; **vertical** ~ vertikale Verteilerbeziehung (*Produzentenhaftung*); **with his** ~ **and consent** mit seinem Wissen und Willen.

privy *adj* mitwissend, mitbeteiligt, mitschuldig, geheim.

Privy|Council *brit* Kronrat, geheimer Staatsrat; ~ **Councillor** Mitglied des Kronrates; **P~ Purse** königliche Privatschatulle (*der dem persönlichen Gebrauch des Monarchen vorbehaltene Teil der Zivilliste*).

privy *s* Beteiligter *m*, Mitwisser *m*; *pl* → *privies*.

prize *(1)* Prise *f*, Kriegsbeute *f*, Konfiskationsgut *n*; amtliche Belohnung *f*; aufgebrachtes (Feind)Schiff *n*; ~ **bounty** Prisensonderlöhnung, Prisengeld; ~ **case** Prisensache; ~ **commission** Prisenabteilung des Seegerichts; ~ **court** Prisengericht; ~ **crew** Prisenkommando; ~ **goods** Prisengüter; ~ **law** Prisenrecht; ~ **list** Gewinnliste, Liste der Offiziere und Mannschaften, die Prisengeld erhalten; ~ **money** Prisengeld, Geldpreis; ~ **of war** Prise, Kriegsprise; ~ **salvage** Prisengeldersatz bei Aufbringung e–s ursprünglich eigenen oder neutralen Schiffes; **naval** ~ Prise; **to make** ~ als Prise aufbringen.

prize *(2)* Preis *m*, Belohnung *f*, Auszeichnung *f*, Prämie *f*, Losgewinn *m*; ~ **competition** Preisausschreiben; ~ **drawing** Auslosung, Verlosung; ~ **fellow** Inhaber e–r Examensauszeichnung; ~ **fight** öffentlicher Boxkampf.

pro für, bezüglich, namens, an Stelle von, pro, Ja-Stimme *f*, zustimmende Äußerung *f*; ~ **and con** für und wider; ~ **bono et malo** im guten wie im bösen; ~ **bono publico work** unentgeltliche gemeinnützige Tätigkeit; ~ **confesso** als zugestanden gelten; ~ **forma** → *proforma*; ~ **querente** zugunsten des Klägers; ~ **rata** → *pro rata*; ~ **se** persönlich (erschienen), nicht (anwaltschaftlich) vertreten; ~ **tanto** insoweit, ebenso weitreichend wie, entsprechend; ~ **tem** provisorisch, derzeitig, (vorübergehend) amtierend, stellvertretend; ~ **tempore** = ~ *tem qv*.

probability Wahrscheinlichkeit *f*; ~ **calculus** Wahrscheinlichkeitsrechnung; ~ **of life** Lebenserwartung; **high** ~ **rule** *Recht der Schiffspreisgabe bei großer Wahrscheinlichkeit des Totalverlustes*; **with utmost** ~ mit an Sicherheit grenzender Wahrscheinlichkeit.

probable wahrscheinlich, vermutlich, mutmaßlich, einleuchtend, glaubhaft, glaubwürdig, nachweisbar; ~ **cause** dringender Tatverdacht; hinreichender Grund, glaubhaft gemachte Anspruchsgrundlage; ~ **cause certificate** Bescheinigung hinreichender Erfolgsaussicht (*Revision, habeas corpus*); ~ **future payments** voraussichtliche zukünftige Leistungen; kapitalisierte Rentenerwartung; ~ **ground** glaubhaft gemachter Anspruchsgrund; ~ **life** mutmaßliche Lebensdauer; ~ **reasoning** Wahrscheinlichkeitsbeweisführung; **date of ~ arrival** voraussichtlicher Ankunftstag.

probate gerichtliche Bestätigung der Gültigkeit e–es Testaments; Testamentsvollstreckungszeugnis *n*; **~ action** → *action*; **~ bond** Kaution des Testamentsvollstreckers bzw Nachlaßabwicklers; **~ case** Nachlaßsache; **~ code** Nachlaßrecht; **colonial ~s** in England zu bestätigende Erbschaftsurkunden aus den Kolonien; **~ copy** Ausfertigung des gerichtlich bestätigten Testaments; **~ court** → *court*; **~ decree** Feststellungsurteil über die Gültigkeit des Testaments; **~ denied** Bestätigung des Testaments verweigert; **P~, Divorce, and Admiralty Division** Abteilung des High Court of Justice für Nachlaß-, Ehescheidungs- und Seerechtsangelegenheiten *GB bis 1970, sodann: Family Division qv*; **~ duty** Erbschaftssteuer *auf beweglichen Nachlaß bei Testamentserbfolge*; **~ homestead** Pflichtteilseigenheim; **~ in common form** = *common form ~ qv*; **~ in solemn form** = *solemn form ~ qv*; **~ judge** Nachlaßrichter; **~ jurisdiction** → *jurisdiction*; **~ matter** Nachlaßsache; **~ of a will** gerichtliche Testamentsprüfung und Bestätigung; *etwa* Erbscheinsverfahren; **~ of estate** Nachlaßfeststellung; **~ of insolvent estate** *etwa:* Nachlaßkonkurs; **~ proceedings** Nachlaßverfahren; **~ registry** *brit* Nachlaßregister; Geschäftsstelle des Nachlaßgerichts; **~ rules** Verfahrensvorschriften für unstreitige Testamentsbestätigung; **~ valuation** (*vorläufige*) Nachlaßbewertung; **~ value** Gegenstandswert des Nachlaßverfahrens; **admissible to ~** bestätigungsfähig; **admitted to ~** gerichtlich bestätigt *als letztwillige Verfügung*; **ancillary ~** gegenständlich beschränktes Testamentsvollstreckerzeugnis (*für ausländ Testamentsvollstrecker*); **common form ~** *etwa:* Erbschein; = *non-contentious ~ qv*; **contentious ~** streitige Testamentsbestätigung (*durch Chancery Division*); **contested ~** streitige Testamentssache(n); **decree admitting a will to ~** Bestätigungsbeschluß; **District P~ Registry** *GB* örtliches Nachlaßregister; **evidence of ~** Nachweis der gerichtlichen Testamentsbestätigung; **facsimile ~** → *facsimile*; **grant of ~** → *grant*; **law of ~** formelles Nachlaßrecht, Nachlaßprozeßrecht; **non-contentious ~** einfache, nicht streitige Testamentsbestätigung (*durch die Family Division*); **non-contentious ~ rules** Nachlaßverfahrensbestimmungen; **Principal P~ Registry** *GB* Hauptnachlaßregister (*in London*); **Registrar of P~** Nachlaßrechtspfleger; **resealed ~** Ermächtigung zur Testamentsvollstreckung im Ausland; **solemn form (of) ~** rechtskräftige Feststellung der Testamentsgültigkeit *cf contentious ~ qv*; **to apply for ~** Bestätigungsantrag stellen; **to obtain ~** gerichtliche Testamentsbestätigung erwirken; **to renounce ~** das Nachlaßabwickleramt ablehnen, das testamentarische Erbe ausschlagen; **to take ~** das Nachlaßabwickleramt annehmen, ein Testament bestätigen lassen.

probate *v ein Testament* gerichtlich bestätigen; **~ a will** ein Testament gerichtlich bestätigen, die Gültigkeit des Testaments gerichtlich feststellen.

probation Bewährung *f*, Bewährungsfrist *f*, Probezeit *f*, Strafaussetzung *f* zur Bewährung; Beweismittel *n*, Beweis *m*, Prüfung *f*; **~ officer** Bewährungshelfer; **~ home** Wohnheim für auf Bewährung Entlassene; **~ hostel** = *~ home qv*; **~ order** Strafaussetzung(sbeschluß) zur Bewährung; **~ period** Bewährungsfrist, Probezeit; **~ service** Bewährungshilfe; **~ system** Bewährungssystem; **conditions of ~** Bewährungsauflagen; **on ~** auf Bewährung, auf Probe; **suspension of sentence on ~** →

suspension ; **to award** ~ Bewährung anordnen; Strafe zur Bewährung aussetzen; **to bind over on** ~ → *bind*; **to place on** ~ die Strafe zur Bewährung aussetzen.
probationary bedingt, auf Probe, auf Bewährung entlassen; ~ **appointment** Anstellung auf Probe; ~ **policeman** Polizeibeamter auf Probe.
probationer Proband *m*; Angestellter bzw Beamter auf Probe *m*.
probationship Probezeit *f*, Noviziat *n*.
probative beweiserheblich, beweiskräftig, als Beweis dienend, beweisrechtlich, Beweis . . .; ~ **fact** → *fact*; ~ **force** Beweiskraft; ~ **value** Beweiswert, Beweiskraft.
probatory = *probative qv*; ~ **drawings** Entwurfspläne *m*|*pl*; ~ **force** Beweiskraft; ~ **term** Frist zur Beweiserbringung.
probe *v* sondieren, gründlich prüfen; *s* Untersuchung *f*, Ermittlung *f*.
probing Sondierung *f*.
probity Rechtschaffenheit *f*, Redlichkeit *f*, Aufrichtigkeit *f*.
problem Problem *n*, Aufgabe *f*, Frage *f*, Schwierigkeit *f*; ~ **case** Problemfall.
procedural prozessual, verfahrensrechtlich, verfahrensmäßig, Verfahrens . . .; ~ **law** Verfahrensrecht, formelles Recht; ~ **niceties** Verfahrenstricks, Verfahrensraffinessen; ~ **provision** Verfahrensbestimmung; ~ **question** verfahrensrechtliche Frage, Verfahrensfrage; ~ **rule** prozessuale Vorschrift, Prozeßregel, Verfahrensregel.
procedure Verfahren *n* (= *V bzw . . .v*) Verfahrensart *f*, Verfahrensmethode *f*, Verfahrensrecht *n*, Prozeß *m*; Vorgehen *n*; ~ **in defended cases** Streit*v*, kontradiktorisches *V*; ~ **of appeal** Rechtsmittel*v*; **accusatorial** ~ Akkusationsmaxime, Beibringungsgrundsatz, Parteimaxime; **administrative** ~ Verwaltungs*v*, Verwaltungsmethode; **adversary** ~ kontradiktorisches *V*; **alternative** ~ wahlweise zulässiges *V*; **appellate** ~ Rechtsmittel*v*; **civil** ~ Zivilprozeß; **criminal** ~ Straf*v*, Strafprozeß; **dilatory** ~ schleppendes *V*; **election** ~ Wahl*v*; **electoral** ~ Wahl*v*; **flawed** ~ fehlerhaftes *V*; **inquisitorial** ~ *V* nach der Inquisitionsmaxime (= *Untersuchungsmaxime*); **legal** ~ rechtliches *V*, *V*–*s*recht; **legislative** ~ Gesetzgebungs*v*; **litigious** ~ Streit*v*, streitiges *V*; **mode of** ~ Art des Vorgehens; *pat:* Handlungsweise; **parliamentary** ~ parlamentarisches *V*, Geschäftsordnung; **rules of** ~ *V*–*s*vorschriften, *V*–*s*bestimmungen; **standard** ~ ordentliches *V*; **voting** ~ Abstimmungs*v*.
proceed ein Verfahren betreiben, mit etwas weitermachen, fortschreiten, fortfahren; promovieren; ~ **against** gegen jmdn gerichtlich vorgehen; ~ **from** ausgehen von; ~ **on the footing that it is true** als wahr unterstellen; ~ **to execution** die Zwangsvollstreckung betreiben; ~ **to next business** zum nächsten Tagesordnungspunkt übergehen; ~ **to the agenda** in die Tagesordnung eintreten; ~ **to the election** zur Wahl schreiten; ~ **to trial** in die mündliche Verhandlung eintreten.
proceeding Verfahren *n* (= *V bzw v*); ein *konkretes* Verfahren, Verfahrensschritt *m*; Verfahrensart (*vgl procedure*); ~**s** (*pl*; *dt meist sing*); Verfahren *n (als Sammelbegriff)*; Rechtsstreit *m*, Prozeß *m*; *protokollierter* Sitzungsverlauf *m*, Sitzung *f*; Prozeßgeschichte *f*; ~ **before trial** Ermittlungs*v*, gerichtliche Voruntersuchung; ~ **by public summons** Aufgebots*v*; ~**s for recovery** Leistungsklage; ~**s for taxation** Kostenfestsetzung; ~**s in bankruptcy** Konkurs*v*; ~**s in court** gerichtliches *V*; ~**s in error** Revisions*v*; ~**s instituted** anhängig gemachtes *V*; ~ **on one of several claims** prozessuale Weiterverfolgung einzelner Klageansprüche; ~ **on part of a claim** Teilverfolgung des Klage-

anspruchs, Geltendmachung e–r Teilklage; ~ **out of jurisdiction** Prozeßführung außerhalb des Gerichtsbezirks, *in dem die Sache anhängig ist*; ~**s pending** anhängiges *V*; **abatement of** ~**s** Unterbrechung e–s Prozesses; **abortive** ~**s** erfolglose Klage; **active** ~ rechtshängiges *V*; **administrative** ~ Verwaltungs*v*; **administrative** ~ **to exclude** *V* wegen Aufenthaltsverbots; **adversary** ~ kontradiktorisches *V*; **alien deportation** ~ Ausweisungs*v*; **appropriate** ~ zweckdienliches *V*; **arbitration** ~ Schiedsgerichts*v*; **assignment of** ~**s** geschäftsordnungsmäßige Zuweisung von Prozessen; **bankruptcy** ~ Konkurs; **cancellation** ~ Aufgebots*v*; **civil** ~ Zivilprozeß; **collateral** ~ Neben*v*, *Verfahren, bei dem eine Frage nur inzidenter zu entscheiden ist*; **consolidation of** ~**s** Verbindung von Prozessen; **contentious** ~ Streit*v*; **criminal** ~ Strafprozeß, Straf*v*; **declaratory** ~ Feststellungsklage; **domestic** ~**s** *V* in Unterhalts- und Vormundschaftssachen für Minderjährige; **driver's licence revocation** ~ *V* wegen Entzugs der Fahrerlaubnis; **earlier** ~**s** frühere Prozesse; **ex parte** ~ → *ex*; **executory** ~ Vollstreckbarkeits*v*; **false labelling** ~ *V* wegen irreführender Warenauszeichnung; **file of** ~**s** Prozeßverzeichnis; **form of** ~**s** äußere Form der Schriftsätze; **immigration** ~ Einbürgerungs*v*; **in rem** ~ *V* über dingliche Rechte; **interference** ~ Prioritätsstreit (*v*), Interferenz-*V*; **interlocutory** ~ Zwischen*v*, Neben*v*; **inter partes** ~**s** kontradiktorisches *V*; **irregular** ~ fehlerhaftes *V*, unübliches *V*; **judicial** ~**s** → *judicial*; **legal** ~**s** Prozeß, Gerichts*v*, *V* vor den Zivilgerichten; **litigation** ~**s** streitiges *V*, Rechtsstreit, Prozeß; **mandamus** ~ → *mandamus*; **misfeasance** ~ *V* wegen Untreue (*gegen ein Vorstandsmitglied*), *V* wegen Amtsmißbrauchs; **motion for staying** ~**s** Antrag auf Einstellung des *V–s*, Antrag auf einstweilige Einstellung der Zwangsvollstreckung; **non-contentious** ~ *V* der freiw Gerichtsbarkeit; **opposition** ~ → *opposition*; **oral** ~ mündliche Verhandlung; **ordinary** ~ ordentliches *V*, allgemeines Streit*v*; **penal** ~ Straf*v*; **preliminary** ~ Vor*v*; Voruntersuchung; **price-fixing** ~ Preisbindungs*v*; **prior** ~ Vor*v*, Vorprozeß; **probate** ~**s** → *probate*; **quo warranto** ~ → *quo w.*; **related** ~**s** ähnliche Prozesse; **remand** ~ Haftprüfungs*v*; **rent-fixing protest** ~ Widerspruchs*v* wegen Mietfestsetzung; **representative** ~ Musterprozeß, *V* e–s Mitglieds e–r notwendigen Streitgenossenschaft; **summary** ~**s** summarisches *V*, abgekürztes *V*; **supplementary** ~ Ergänzungs*v*, Vermögensoffenbarungs*v*; **suspension of** ~**s** → *suspension*; **tariff** ~ Zollstreit*v*; **tax** ~ Steuerrechtsstreit; **the** ~**s of a company** *die in der Niederschrift erfaßten Vorgänge auf den Hauptversammlungen e–r Gesellschaft*; **to commence** ~**s** Klage erheben; ein Verfahren anhängig machen; **to conduct the** ~**s** das *V* führen; **to institute a** ~ ein *V* einleiten; **to stay the** ~**s** das *V* aussetzen; **to take** ~**s** gerichtlich vorgehen; **transfer of** ~**s** → *transfer*; **wage and hour** ~**s** (Verwaltungs-) Rechtsstreit über Lohn- und Arbeitszeitvorschriften; **written** ~**s** schriftliches *V*; Akten.

proceeds Erlös *m*, Veräußerungserlös *m*, Verkaufserlös *m*, Versicherungsleistung *f*; Früchte *f/pl*, Einnahmen *f/pl*, Rohertrag *m*; ~ **from capital** Kapitalerträge; ~ **in cash** Barerlös; ~ **of (a) sale** Verkaufserlös; ~ **of an auction** Versteigerungserlös; ~ **of collection** Inkassoerträge; ~ **of the liquidation** Liquidationserlös; **annual** ~ Jahresertrag; **gross** ~ Bruttoertrag; **net** ~ Nettoerlös, Reinerlös.

proces-verbal Protokoll *n*, Bericht *m*.

process *s (1)* Verfahren *n*, Prozeß *m*,

Ladung *f* des Beklagten *bei Klageerhebung*, gerichtliche Anordnung *f*, prozeßleitende Verfügung *f*; Prozeßakte *f*; Erhebung *f* der öffentlichen Anklage; Vollstreckungsklausel *f*; ~ **agent** → *agent*; ~ **caption** Haftbefehl wegen Nichtrückgabe von Gerichtsakten; ~ **of distraint** Zwangsvollstreckung; ~ **of interpleader** Eigentumsfeststellungsklage; ~ **of law** gesetzliches Verfahren; ~ **of legislation** Gesetzgebungsverfahren; ~ **roll** Liste (*verjährungsunterbrechender*) prozeßleitender Verfügungen; ~ **server** Zusteller (e–r Ladung, Klage etc); **abuse of** ~ → *abuse*; **adjudicative** ~ Urteilsfindung; **compulsory** ~ gerichtliche Maßnahmen zur Erzwingung des Erscheinens (*Zeugen*); **criminal** ~ gerichtliche Ladung des Angeschuldigten; gerichtliche Verfügung zur Beweissicherung in Strafverfahren; **due** ~ **clause** Rechtsstaatsgarantie der US-Verfassung; **due** ~ **of law** rechtsstaatliches Verfahren, Rechtsstaatsprinzip, ordnungsgemäßes Verfahren; **executory** ~ Vollstreckungsverfahren; **final** ~ Zwangsvollstreckung, Vollstrekkungsklausel, Erteilung e–r vollstreckbaren Ausfertigung; **hortatory** ~ Mahnverfahren; **irregular** ~ mangelhaftes Verfahren, fehlerhafte Ladungsurkunde; **judicial** ~ gerichtliches Verfahren, Ladung und Klagemitteilung, Anklageerhebung; **legal** ~ gerichtliches Verfahren, rechtmäßiges Verfahren, gerichtliche Verfügung; **legislative** ~ Gesetzgebungsverfahren; **malicious** ~ mißbräuchliches schikanöses Verfahren; **mesne** ~ Zwischenverfahren; einstweilige Anordnung, Arrestverfahren *wegen Fluchtgefahr des Schuldners*; **original** ~ Klage, gerichtliche Mitteilung der Klage nebst Ladung; **originating** ~ verfahrenseinleitende Verfügung; **regular** ~ ordentliches Verfahren, regelmäßiges V; **service of** ~ → *service*; **simplified** ~ vereinfachte Ladung; **summary** ~ summarisches Verfahren, Schnellverfahren; **trustee** ~ Forderungspfändungsverfahren.

process *s (2)* Arbeitsgang *m*, Ablauf *m*, Verlauf *m*, (*Arbeits*)Verfahren *n*; ~ **account** Fabrikationskonto; ~ **chart** Arbeitsablaufdiagramm; ~ **costing** ~ spezielle fertigungsbedingte Kalkulation; ~ **of adjustment** Anpassungsprozeß; ~ **of distribution** Verteilungsprozeß; ~ **of manufacture** Herstellungsverfahren, Fertigungsverfahren; ~ **patent** → *patent*; **decision-making** ~ Entscheidungsfindung, Urteilsfindung; Entscheidungsverfahren; **finishing** ~ Veredelungsverfahren; **in** ~ **of construction** im Bau, während der Herstellung; **in** ~ **of time** im Laufe der Zeit; **industrial** ~ industrielles Herstellungsverfahren; **mechanical** ~ mechanisches Verfahren; **operating** ~ Arbeitsverfahren; **patentable** ~ patentfähiges Verfahren; **proprietary** ~ gesetzl. geschütztes Verfahren; **secret** ~ Geheimverfahren.

process *v* gerichtlich belangen, vorgehen, prozessieren; (*Ladung*) zustellen lassen; *econ:* bearbeiten; ~ **s.o. by writ** jmdn durch Gerichtsbefehl vorladen lassen.

processing Verarbeitung *f*, Bearbeitung *f*, Veredelung *f*; ~ **cost** Fertigungskosten; ~ **country** Veredelungsland; ~ **enterprise** Verarbeitungsbetrieb, Veredelungsbetrieb; ~ **fee** Bearbeitungsgebühr; ~ **industries** → *industry*; ~ **prohibition** Verarbeitungsverbot; ~ **security** Verarbeitungskaution; ~ **tax** Veredelungssteuer; **data** ~ Datenverarbeitung; **food** ~ **industry** Lebensmittelindustrie; **goods for further** ~ Vorerzeugnisse; **inward** ~ aktiver Veredelungsverkehr; **outward** ~ passiver Veredelungsverkehr; **stage of** ~ Verarbeitungsstufe.

procession Umzug *m*, Demonstrationsmarsch *m*; Grenzumgang *m*; **funeral** ~ Trauerzug.

processioning Grenzbegehung *f*, Abschreiten *n* der Grundstücksgrenzen.

processor Verarbeiter *m*.

prochronism irrtümliche Vordatierung *f*.

proclaim proklamieren, promulgieren, mitteilen, (*öffentlich*) bekanntgeben, verkünden; jmdn in ein Amt einsetzen.

proclamation Erklärung *f*, Proklamation *f*, Bekanntmachung *f*, Verordnung *f*, Aufruf *m* bei Sitzungseröffnung; ~ **by lord of manor** Aufforderung an die Erben des Hintersassen, das Erbe anzutreten; ~ **of a fine** *hist* wiederholte gerichtliche Verkündung e–r Auflassung *mit Ausschlußwirkung gegenüber Drittberechtigten*; ~ **of a state of emergency** Erklärung des Ausnahmezustands; ~ **of martial law** Verhängen des Standrechts; **royal** ~ königliche Proklamation (*königl Hoheitsrecht*); **statutory** ~ königl Proklamation auf Grund gesetzlicher Ermächtigung.

pro-consul Prokonsul *m*, Statthalter *m*, stellvertretender Konsul *m*.

procrastination Aufschub *m*, Verzögerung *f*.

procreation Zeugung *f*, Fortpflanzung *f*; **words of** ~ → *words*.

procreator Erzeuger *m*, Vater *m*.

proctor Prokurator *m*, Bevollmächtigter *m*, Vertreter *m*, Beauftragter *m*, Sachwalter *m*, Universitätsrektor *m*, Anwalt *m* (*Seegericht, Kirchengericht*); Disziplinarbeamter *m* (*in e–r Universität*); ~**s of the clergy** geistliche Abgeordnete; **King's (Queen's)** ~ → *king*.

proctorize maßregeln, Verweis erteilen.

procuracy Vollmachtsurkunde *f*.

procuration *(1)* Geschäftsbesorgung *f*, Verschaffung *f*, Vollmacht *f*, Bevollmächtigung *f*, Auftrag *m*; ~ **endorsement** Vollmachtsindossament; Prokuraind.; ~ **fee** Kreditvermittlungsprovision; ~ **money** = ~ *fee qv*; ~ **of a loan** Beschaffung e–s Darlehens; ~ **signature** Unterschrift als Bevollmächtigter, Prokuraunterschrift; **branch** ~ Filialhandlungsvollmacht; **joint** ~ Gesamtvollmacht; **per** ~ → *per*; **single** ~ Einzelhandlungsvollmacht; **tacit** ~ stillschweigend erteilte Vollmacht.

procuration *(2)* Kuppelei *f*; ~ **of women** Verkuppelung von Frauen.

procurator Bevollmächtigter *m*, Stellvertreter *m*, Beauftragter *m*, Anwalt *m*, Stellvertreter *m* e–s Oberhausabgeordneten; ~ **fiscal** *scot* Staatsanwalt(schaft); ~ **in rem suam** selbstkontrahierender Stellvertreter.

procuratory Vollmacht *f*; ~ **of resignation** Verfahren des Lehensverzichts; **letters of** ~ Vollmachts(urkunde).

procuratrix die Bevollmächtigte.

procure (1) einleiten, verschaffen, besorgen, vermitteln, verursachen, veranlassen; ~ **acceptance** Akzept einholen; ~ **capital** Kapital beschaffen; **to counsel and** ~ → *to counsel*.

procure (2) verkuppeln, e–e Frau der Unzucht zuführen.

procurement *s (1)* Beschaffung *f*, Erlangung *f*, Vermittlung *f*; ~ **agency** Beschaffungsstelle; ~**contract** Beschaffungsvertrag; ~ **division** Beschaffungsamt; ~ **fraud** Beschaffungsschwindel *US*; ~ **of absence** Besorgung des Nichterscheinens e–s Zeugen; ~ **of credit facilities** Kreditbeschaffung; ~ **of a judgment** Erwirkung e–s Urteils; ~ **of marriage** Heiratsvermittlung; ~ **officer** Leiter des Beschaffungsamtes.

procurement *(2)* Verkupplung *f*.

procurer Kuppler *m*, Zuhälter *m*.

procuring | **an offence** Verleitung zu e–r Straftat; ~ **breach of contract** Verleitung zum Vertragsbruch; ~ **instrumentalities to commit crime** Beschaffung von Verbrechenswerkzeugen.

prodigal *adj* verschwenderisch; *s* Verschwender *m*, wegen Verschwendungssucht Entmündigter *m*.

prodigality Verschwendungssucht *f*.

prodition Verrat *m*, Heimtücke *f*.

proditor Verräter *m*.

produce *s* Product *n*, Erzeugnis *n*, Bodenerzeugnis *n*, landwirtschaftliche Erzeugnisse, *n/pl*, Ertrag *m*, Gewinn *m*, Ausbeute *f*; ~ **advance** Produktionskredit; ~ **broker** → *broker*; ~ **business** Produktenhandel; ~ **exchange** Produktenbörse; ~ **market** Warenmarkt; ~ **of an invention** die Früchte e–r Erfindung; ~ **of the soil** Bodenfrüchte, Bodenerzeugnisse; **rude** ~ Rohprodukt(e).

produce *v* produzieren, erzeugen, herstellen, einbringen, vorbringen, vorlegen, Beweis antreten; verursachen; erzielen, sich rentieren; ~ **a prisoner** e–en Gefangenen vorführen (lassen); ~ **a witness** e–n Zeugen stellen; ~ **an alibi** ein Alibi beibringen; ~ **documents** Urkunden vorlegen; ~ **the accounts** die Rechnungen vorlegen; ~ **the authority** Vollmacht vorlegen.

producer Produzent *m*, Hersteller *m*, Erzeuger *m*; ~ **advertising** Herstellerwerbung; **~s' cooperative** landwirtschaftliche (Absatz)-Genossenschaft; **~s' liability insurance** Gewährleistungsversicherung des Warenherstellers; ~ **goods** Produktionsgüter; ~ **price** Erzeugerpreis; **primary** ~ Urerzeuger.

product Produkt *n*, Erzeugnis *n*, Ertrag *m*; ~ **advertising** Erzeugniswerbung; ~ **analysis** Warenkunde; ~ **cost card** Stückkalkulationskarte, Vorkalkulationskarte; ~ **costing** Erzeugniskalkulation; ~ **differentiation** Erzeugnis-Differenzierung; ~ **engineering** Fertigungs-Verfahren; ~ **family** Gruppe ähnlicher Erzeugnisse; **~s for commerce** Erzeugnisse für den (*zwischenstaatlichen*) Handel *US*; ~ **layout** Betriebsanlage; ~ **leadership** Führung und Qualität des Erzeugnisses; ~ **liability** Produzentenhaftung; ~ **licence** behördliche Zulassung e–s Erzeugnisses; ~ **mix** Sortiment, Fertigungssortiment; ~ **name** Produktname; **~s of the season** Früchte der Saison; **~s of the soil** Bodenprodukte; ~ **planning** Fertigungsplanung (*Planung und Gestaltung des zu fertigenden Erzeugnisses*); ~ **review** Produkt-Überprüfung; **basic ~s** Grunderzeugnisse; **compensating** ~ Veredelungserzeugnis (*Zoll*); **competitive ~s** Konkurrenzerzeugnisse; **defective ~s** mängelbehaftete Erzeugnisse, mangelhafte Waren; **farm ~s** landwirtschaftliche Erzeugnisse; **finished ~s** Fertigwaren; **homogeneous ~s** homogene Erzeugnisse (*vom Käufer als identisch angesehene Erzeugnisse verschiedener Hersteller*); **horticultural ~s** Gartenbauerzeugnisse; **joint** ~ Gesamterzeugnis; *pl*: gekoppelte Erzeugnisse, Verbundprodukte; **national** ~ *auch: N ~ Product,* Nationalprodukt, Sozialprodukt; **natural** ~ Naturerzeugnis, Naturstoff; **non-originating ~s** Nichtursprungsware (*Zoll*); **novel** ~ neuartiges Erzeugnis; **pilot** ~ Leitererzeugnis; ~ **placement** Schleichwerbung; **primary ~s** Urprodukte, Grundstoffe, Rohstoffe; **prime** ~ Rohprodukt; **raw** ~ Rohprodukt; **residual** ~ Abfallprodukt, Nebenprodukt; **tied** ~ gekoppeltes Erzeugnis; **waste** ~ Abfallprodukt.

production Produktion *f* (= *P bzw . . . p*), Erzeugung *f*, Herstellung *f*; Beibringung *f*, Vorlegung *f*; ~ **bonus** Leistungsprämie; ~ **certificate** Herstellertypenbescheinigung (*Flugzeug*); ~ **coefficient** *P*–skoeffizient; ~ **combination** *P*–skartell; ~ **control** Fertigungsüberwachung; ~ **costs** Herstellungskosten; ~ **credit associations** landwirtschaftliche Kreditgenossenschaften; ~ **cutback** *P*–skürzung; ~ **depreciation** Abschreibung nach proportionaler Gesamtleistung (*zB e–r Maschine*); ~ **engineer** Fertigungsingenieur, Betriebsingenieur; ~ **engineering** *P–s*technik, Ausarbeiten der Fertigungsunterlagen; ~ **equipment** Betriebseinrichtung; ~ **facilities** *P–s*anlagen; ~ **factors** *P–s*faktoren; ~ **flow** Fertigungsablauf; ~ **function** *P–s*funktion; ~ **goods** *P–s*mittel; ~ **grant** *P–s*beihilfe; ~ **in bulk** Massen*p*; ~ **index** Industrie-*P–s*index(ziffer); ~ **level** *P–s*höhe, *P–s*ausstoßmenge; ~ **line** Fließband, Arbeitsstrecke; ~ **load** Auslastung der Fertigung; ~ **manager** Betriebsleiter; ~ **method** Fertigungsverfahren; ~ **method (of depreciation)** Mengenabschreibung; ~ **of arguments** Beibringung von Beweisgründen; ~ **of business books** Vorlage von Geschäftsbüchern; ~ **of documents** Urkundenvorlage; ~ **of evidence** Beweisantritt, Vorlage von Beweismitteln; ~ **of suit** Klageformel; ~ **optimum** *P–s*optimum (*nach Standort von Rohstoffquellen*); ~ **prohibition** Herstellungsverbot; ~ **readiness** *P–s*bereitschaft; ~ **standard** Mengenvorgabe; ~ **target** *P–s*ziel, Leistungssoll; ~ **unit** *P–s*einheit, Arbeitsgruppe, Maschinengruppe; **industrial** ~ Industrie*p*; **line of** ~ *P–s*zweig; **loss of** ~ *P–s*ausfall; **primary** ~ Urerzeugung, Erzeugung von Lebensmitteln und Rohstoffen; **right of** ~ Herstellungsrecht; **under-warranty** ~ unter Garantie fallende Erzeugnisse.

productive produktiv, ertragreich, schöpferisch; ergiebig, ertragsfähig, fruchtbar, ideenreich; ~ **assets** werbende Aktiva; ~ **bed** abbauwürdige Lagerstätte; ~ **burden center** Fertigungskostenstelle; ~ **capacity** Produktionskapazität; ~ **department** Hauptkostenstelle; ~ **efficiency** Leistungsfähigkeit, Produktivität; ~ **labour** Fertigungslöhne; ~ **resources** Produktivkräfte; ~ **wages** produktiver Lohn, Fertigungslohn.

productivity measures Rationalisierungsmaßnahmen *f|pl*.

profanation Entweihung *f*, Entheiligung *f*.

profane profan, weltlich, gotteslästerlich; ~ **swearing** Fluchen.

profaneness = *profanity qv*.

profanity Gotteslästerung *f*, Ruchlosigkeit *f*; Weltlichkeit *f*.

profer Angebot *n*; Angebot *n*, ein Verfahren fortzusetzen; Rechnungslegung *f*.

profert Vorlage *f* e–r Urkunde bei Gericht.

profess erklären, angeben, bekennen, e–n Beruf ausüben; öffentlich erklären, öffentlich abschwören.

professed erklärt, offenkundig; ~**ly** erklärtermaßen, offenbar.

profession Beruf *m*, Stand *m*, akademischer Beruf *m*; öffentliche Erklärung *f*; Anwaltschaft *f*, Berufskollegen *m|pl*; Glaubensbekenntnis *n*; ~ **or business** Beruf; ~ **or vocation** Berufs(angabe); **independent** ~ freier Beruf; **learned** ~ akademischer Beruf; **legal** ~ Anwaltsberuf, Anwaltschaft (*solicitors und barristers*); Juristen(stand); **liberal** ~ freier Beruf; **fused** ~ einheitlicher Anwaltsstand; **paralegal** ~ juristische Hilfsberufe, Anwaltsgehilfenberuf; **the nonjudicial legal** ~ die Anwaltschaft.

professional *s* „Profi“ *m*, Fachkraft *f*, Spezialist *m*.

professional *adj* berufsmäßig, gewerbsmäßig, Berufs . . ., Standes . . .; ~ **indemnity cover** Berufshaftpflichtdeckung; ~ **(indemnity) insurance** Berufshaftpflichtversicherung; ~ **liability** Berufshaftung, anwaltschaftliche Haftung, Berufshaftpflicht; ~ **liability insurance** Berufshaftpflichtversicherung; ~ **man** Fachmann; Gelehrter, Akademiker; ~ **risks indemnity insurance** Berufshaftpflichtversicherung; **bad** ~ **work** mangelhafte anwaltschaftliche Leistung; **in a** ~ **capacity** beruflich; **in a** ~ **manner** fachmännisch; **the**

~ **classes** die freien Berufe, die akademischen Berufe.
professor Professor *m*, Dozent *m*, Hochschullehrer *m*.
professionalism Berufsqualifikation *f*, berufsständisches Verhalten *n*.
proficiency Tüchtigkeit *f*, Leistungsfähigkeit *f*, gute Leistungen *f/pl*, Sachverständigkeit *f*, Fertigkeit *f*; ~ **pay** *mil* Leistungszulage; **certificate of** ~ Befähigungsnachweis, Zeugnis.
profit Gewinn *m* (= *G bzw g*), Profit *m*, Nutzen *m*, Verdienst *m*; ~ **a prendre** Nutzungs- und Entnahmerecht am fremden Grundstück; ~ **a rendre** Nutzung(en); ~ **after taxes** *G* nach (Abzug der) Steuern; ~ **and loss** *G* und Verlust; ~ **and loss account** → *account (2)*; ~ **and loss format** Form (Gliederung) der *G*- und Verlustrechnung; ~ **and loss pooling agreement** Ergebnisübernahmevertrag; ~ **and loss sharing agreement** *G*- und Verlust-Gemeinschaftsvertrag; ~ **and loss statement** *G*- und Verlustrechnung; ~**s available for distribution** ausschüttungsfähiger *G*; ~ **balance** *G*saldo, *G*überschuß; ~ **basis** *G*basis; ~ **earning** *g*bringend, rentabel; ~ **figure** *G*ziffer; ~**s for the year** Jahres*g*; ~ **from operations** Unternehmer*g*; ~ **in gross** beschränktes persönliches Servitut; ~ **insurance** *G*ausfallversicherung (*bei Warenproduktion*); ~ **margin** *G*spanne; ~ **of each year** jährlicher *G*; ~**s of management** *G* aus der Geschäftsführung; ~ **of the business** Geschäfts*g*; ~ **of the company** Rein*g* der Gesellschaft; ~ **on a sale** Verkaufs*g*; ~ **on exchange** Kurs*g*; ~ **on real property** Einkünfte aus Grundbesitz; ~ **on sales** Umsatzrendite; ~ **rent** *G*beteiligungspacht; ~**s rise** *G*steigerung; ~ **share** *G*anteil; ~ **sharing** Beteiligung am *G*, *g*beteiligt; ~ **sharing bonds** → *bond (1)*; ~ **sharing plan** *G*beteiligungsplan; ~ **sharing scheme** *G*beteiligungsplan; ~ **sharing transactions** *G*beteiligungsgeschäfte; ~ **sharing trust** Investmentfond; ~ **taking** *G*realisierung, *G*mitnahme; ~**s tax** → *tax*; ~ **transfer** *G*abführung; **action of mesne** ~**s** Klage auf Nutzungsentschädigung wegen Räumungsverzug; **actual** ~ tatsächlich erzielter *G*; **anticipated** ~**s** erwarteter *G*; **apportionment of** ~ Aufteilung von *G–en auf mehrere Veranlagungszeiträume*; **appropriation of the** ~ → *appropriation*; **at a** ~ mit Gewinn; **balance of** ~ Rest*g*; **book** ~ Buch*g*; **business** ~ Unternehmens*g*; **capital** ~ Veräußerungs*g* von Investitionsgütern; **capitalization of** ~ → *capitalization*; **casual** ~ gelegentlicher *G*; **clear** ~ Netto*g*; **commercial** ~ gewerblicher *G*, Handelsbilanz*g*; **conjectural** ~ spekulative *G*erwartungen; **contingent** ~ eventueller *G*; **distributable** ~ verteilungsfähiger *G*; **distributed** ~ ausgeschütteter *G*; **distribution of** ~**s** → *distribution*; **easy** ~ müheloser *G*; **excess** ~ → *excess*; **excess** ~**s duty** → *excess*; **fair** ~ angemessener *G*; **for private** ~ gewerblich, gewinnorientiert; **for** ~ nutzbringend, gewinnträchtig; **gross** ~**s** Roh*g*, Brutto*g*; **gross** ~ **on sales** Bruttoerlös; **illicit** ~ unerlaubte *G*; **illusory** ~ Schein*g*; **imaginary** ~ imaginärer *G*; **industrial and commercial** ~**s** Einkünfte aus Gewerbebetrieb; **inflationary** ~ Inflations*g*, inflationsbedingter Schein*g*; **instant** ~**s** Augenblicks*g–e*; **loss of** ~**s** → *loss*; **marginal** ~ → *marginal*; **mesne** ~**s** zwischenzeitliche Nutzungen, *in der Zeit der Besitzentziehung erlangte Nutzungen des Nichtberechtigten*; **natural rate of** ~ natürliche Profitrate (= *normal profit qv*); **net** ~**s** Rein*g*, Reinertrag; **normal** ~ (=) *Durchschnittsprofitrate e–s Wirtschaftszweiges*; **operating** ~ Betriebs*g*, Geschäfts*g*; **paper** ~ noch nicht realisierter *G*, rechnerischer *G*, imaginärer *G*; **paper** ~**s** spekulative *G*erwartungen; **pretax** ~**s** *G–e* vor

Steuern, unversteuerter *G*; **prospective** ~ zu erwartender *G*; **remote** ~ entfernt möglicher *G*; **retained** ~**s** einbehaltene *G–e*, bil Gvortrag; **secret** ~**s** geheimgehaltene *G–e* (e–s Vertreters); **speculative** ~ Spekulations*g*; **surplus** ~ Rein*g*; **taxable** ~**s** steuerpflichtige *G–e*; **to allocate the** ~**s** den *G* verteilen; **to make a** ~ e–n *G* erzielen; **to make** ~**s from „the box"** *G–e* aus Eigengeschäften mit Investmentanteilen machen; **trading** ~ Roh*g*, Betriebs*g*; **unappropriated** ~**(s)** nicht ausgeschütteter *G*, unverteilter Rein*g*; **undistributed** ~ nicht ausgeschütteter *G*; **undivided** ~**s** nicht ausgeschütteter *G*; **utility** ~ Nutzungen; **winding-up** ~**s** Liquidationsgewinn.

profitability Rentabilität *f*; ~ **study** Wirtschaftlichkeitsberechnung; **limit of** ~ Rentabilitätsgrenze; **overall** ~ Gesamtrentabilität.

profitable gewinnbringend, einträglich, rentabel.

profiteer Profitmacher *m*.

profiteering gewinnsüchtiges Verhalten *n*; Preistreiberei *f*.

proforma (= *pro forma*) proforma als (reine) Formsache; ~ **account sales** Proforma-Abschluß (*als Kalkulationsvergleich*); ~ **invoice** → *invoice*; ~ **sale** Proformaverkauf, Scheinverkauf; ~ **transaction** Scheingeschäft; ~**trial** Proformaverfahren, Zwischenverfahren.

progenitor Vorfahre *m*, Ahn *m*.

progeny Nachkommenschaft *f*, Abkömmlinge *m*|*pl*.

program trading Programmhandel *m* (*elektronischer Aktienindex – Terminhandel*).

program(me) *s* Programm *n*, Plan *m*, Prospekt *m*; ~ **contractor** Programmveranstalter; ~ **updating service** Programmänderungsdienst; ~ (*Programm*) **trading** Programmhandel; **crash** ~ Sofortprogramm; **intercountry** ~ multinationales Programm, von mehreren Ländern durchgeführtes *P*.; **phased** ~ Programm mit zeitlichen Ausführungsstufen; **recreation** ~ Freizeitgestaltung; **relief** ~ Hilfsprogramm; **working** ~Arbeitsprogramm.

programme *v* programmieren.

progress *s* Fortschritt *m*, Fortgang *m*, Verbesserung *f*, Weiterentwicklung *f*; ~ **certificate** Arbeitsfortschrittsbescheinigung; ~ **control** Überwachung des Fortgangs der Arbeiten; ~ **of events** Gang der Ereignisse; ~ **of trial** Lauf der Hauptverhandlung; ~ **report** Tätigkeitsbericht, Zwischenbericht; Bericht über den Fortgang (*bzw Stand*) der Arbeiten; **engineering** ~ technischer Fortschritt; **negotiations in** ~ schwebende Verhandlungen; ~ **payment** Abschlagszahlung; Zahlung nach Leistungsabschnitten.

progression Progression *f*, Steigerung *f*, Staffelung *f*; **provision concerning** ~ Progressionsvorbehalt.

progressive progressiv, fortschreitend, stufenweise, fortschrittlich; ~ **abolition of customs duties** schrittweise Beseitigung der Zölle; ~ **approximation** schrittweise Annäherung; ~ **rate** progressiver (Steuer-, Zins-)Satz; ~ **rent** Miete (Pacht) mit automatischer Erhöhungsklausel; ~ **volume purchase agreement** Mengenstufen-Kaufvertrag.

prohibit (gesetzlich) verbieten, untersagen.

prohibited verboten; ~ **area** Sperrgebiet; ~ **class lists** nicht versicherbare Risikolisten; ~ **degress (of relationships)** verbotene Verwandtschaftsgrade (*als Ehehindernis*); ~ **goods** Schmuggelware, Konterbande; ~ **place** *mil* Sperrgebiet; ~ **transaction** verbotenes Rechtsgeschäft.

prohibition Verbot *n*, Untersagung *f*, obergerichtliche Zuständigkeitsentziehung *f* der unteren Instanz; *US* Prohibition *f* (*gesetzl Alkoholverbot*); ~ **notice** Untersagungsbescheid; ~ **of assembly** Versammlungsverbot; ~ **of delivery** Auslieferungsverbot (*Waren*); ~ **of importation** Einfuhrverbot; ~ **of issue** Emissionssperre; ~ **of trade** Handelsverbot; **statutory** ~ gesetzliches Verbot.

prohibitory untersagend, prohibitiv, Verbots . . .

project *s* Vorhaben *n*, Projekt *n*, Plan *m*; ~ **leader** Leitfirma, federführendes Unternehmen; ~ **management** Projekt-Management, Organisationsleitung bei e–m Vorhaben.

project *v* planen, vorhaben.

projection Vorbau *m*, vorstehender Gebäudeteil *m*.

prolicide Tötung *f* der Nachkommenschaft (*der Leibesfrucht bzw Kindestötung*).

proliferation Verbreitung *f* (*zB von Atomwaffen*); ~ **of illegal drugs** Verbreitung von verbotenen Betäubungsmitteln, Drogenhandel.

prolific ertragreich, fruchtbar.

prolix weitschweifig, umständlich.

prolixity Weitschweifigkeit *f*.

prolong verlängern, prolongieren (*Wechsel*).

prolongation Erneuerung *f*, Verlängerung *f*; Prolongation *f*, Aufschub *m*, Stundung *f*; ~ **business** *exch* Prolongationsgeschäfte; ~ **of a bill** Prolongation e–s Wechsels; ~ **of payment** Zahlungsaufschub, Stundung.

promise *s* Versprechen *n*, Zusage *f*, Verpflichtungserklärung *f*; ~ **of marriage** Eheversprechen, Verlöbnis; ~ **of reward** Auslobung; ~ **to make a gift** Schenkungsversprechen; ~ **to pay** Zahlungsversprechen; ~ **to pay the debt of another** Schuldübernahme; ~ **to perform** Leistungsversprechen; **breach of** ~ → *breach*; **collateral** ~ akzessorisches Versprechen; **dependent** ~ *von e–r Vorleistung* abhängiges Versprechen; **fictitious** ~ unterstellte Verpflichtung; gesetzlich fingiertes Vertragsversprechen; **gratuitous** ~ Gefälligkeitszusage; unentgeltliches Versprechen; **joint** ~ Gesamthandverpflichtung; **mercantile** ~ kaufmännischer Verpflichtungsschein; **mutual** ~ (*Übernahme e–r*) Gegenseitigkeitsverpflichtung; ~ *promises: reziprokbedingte Versprechen*; **naked** ~ Versprechen ohne Gegenleistung, abstraktes Schuldversprechen; **new** ~ Erneuerung e–s Vertragsversprechens; Schuldanerkenntnis; ~ **of credit** Kreditzusage; **to raise a** ~ ein rechtlich verbindliches Versprechen aus e–m Verhalten ableiten; **unconditional** ~ absolutes Versprechen.

promise *v* versprechen, sich verpflichten, zusichern.

promisee Versprechensempfänger *m*, Berechtigter *m*.

promisor Versprechender *m*, Versprechensgeber *m*, Verpflichteter *m*.

promissory versprechend, ein Versprechen enthaltend.

promissory note Solawechsel *m*, Eigenwechsel *m*; schriftliches Schuldversprechen *n*, Schuldschein *m*; ~ **made out to bearer** Inhabersolawechsel; ~ **made out to order** Solawechsel; **joint** ~ Gesamtschuldschein; **negotiable** ~ Solawechsel, Eigenwechsel; **to lift a** ~ → *to lift*.

promote fördern, gründen, unterstützen (*e–e Gesetzesvorlage*); ~ **a company** e–e Gesellschaft gründen.

promoter Initiator *m*, Förderer *m*, Gesellschaftsgründer *m*, Nebenkläger *m*, Antragsteller *m*; **professional** ~ gewerbsmäßiger Gesellschaftsgründer.

promoting Aufstellen *n* von Kandidaten; Vorgründungstätigkeit *f*; ~ **syndicate** Gründungskonsortium.

promotion Förderung *f*, Beförderung *f*, Gründung *f*; ~ **credit** Importförderungskredit; ~ **department** Werbeabteilung; ~ **expense** Gründungskosten; ~ **money** Gründervergütung; ~ **of fair trading** Förderung lauterer Geschäftsmethoden; ~ **of science** Förderung der Wissenschaft; ~ **of trade** Wirtschaftsförderung; ~ **shares** → *share*; ~ **to an office** Amtseinsetzung; **by** ~ beförderungshalber; **in-class** ~ Beförderung *in e–e höhere Gehaltsstufe*; **sales** ~ Verkaufs-, Absatzförderung.

promotional | chart Beförderungstabelle; ~ **literature** Werbeprospekte; ~ **money** Gründungskosten; ~ **roster** Beförderungsliste; ~ **selling** Werbeverkauf.

prompt sofort, prompt; ~ **payment discount** Skonto *n*.

promulgate promulgieren, bekanntmachen, verkünden, veröffentlichen.

promulgation öffentliche Bekanntmachung *f*, Verkündung *f*, Verbreitung *f*.

promulgator Verbreiter *m*, Verkünder *m*, Bekanntmacher *m*.

prone geneigt, anfällig.

proneness to crises Krisenanfälligkeit *f*.

pronotary erster Urkundsbeamter *m* des Gerichts.

pronounce verkünden (*Urteil*), aussprechen, behaupten, erklären; *v/i* (*on sth*) judizieren, gerichtl. befinden (*über*); ~ **dead** den Tod amtlich feststellen.

pronouncement Erklärung *f*, Verkündung *f*, Proklamation *f*; ~ **of judgment** Urteilsverkündung.

proof *s* Beweis *m* (= *B bzw b*), Nachweis *m*, Beweisergebnis *n*; ~ **beyond (any) reasonable doubt** vollständiger *B*, zur Verurteilung ausreichender *B*; Beweisergebnis, das keinen vernünftigen Zweifel übrig läßt; ~ **evident or presumption great** dringender Tatverdacht (*als Hindernis für Haftverschonung gegen Kaution*); ~ **in bankruptcy** Forderungsnachweis, Anmeldung e–r Konkursforderung; ~ **of a will** = *probate of a will* → *probate*; ~ **of conviction** Vorstrafennachweis; ~ **of will per testes** Testamentsbestätigung nach Zeugeneinvernahme (*im streitigen Verfahren über Gültigkeit e–s Testaments*); ~ **of a witness** Niederschrift der zu erwartenden Zeugenaussage; ~ **of ability** Befähigungsnachweis; ~ **of authenticity** Echtheits*b*; ~ **of authority** Nachweis der Vertretungsbefugnis; ~ **of claims** Forderungsnachweis; ~ **of death** Todes*b*, Nachweis des Todes; ~ **of debts** Forderungsnachweis; Anmeldung von Konkursforderungen; ~ **of default of appearance** gerichtliche Feststellung der Nichteinlassung; ~ **of fault** *B* des Verschuldens; ~ **of guilt** Schuld*b*; ~ **of identity** Identitätsnachweis, Personenausweis; ~ **of inability to pay** Nachweis der Zahlungsunfähigkeit; ~ **of indebtedness** Schuldtitel; ~ **of loss** Schadensnachweis; ~ **of nationality** Nachweis der Staatsangehörigkeit; ~ **of need** Bedürftigkeitsnachweis; ~ **of ownership** Eigentumsnachweis; ~ **of plaintiff's case** *B* des klägerischen Sachvortrags; ~ **of posting** Nachweis des richtigen Buchungsabschlusses; ~ **of previous convictions** Nachweis von Vorstrafen, Vorstrafenliste; ~ **of service** Zustellungsnachweis; ~ **of spirits** Feststellung des Alkoholgehalts; ~ **positive** voller *B*; ~ **to the contrary** Gegen*b*; **accessory** ~ Neben*b*, *B*indiz; **affirmative** ~ Nachweis e–r Tatsache; **burden of** ~ *B*last; **conclusive** ~ zwingender *B*, voller *B*; **convincing** ~ überzeugender *B*; **degree of** ~ Grad des Bewiesenseins; **documentary** ~ Urkunden*b*; **failing** ~ → *failing*; **from lack of** ~ aus Mangel an *B*–*n*, mangels *B*–*s*; **full** ~ voller *B*; **half** ~ unvollständiger *B*, Anscheins*b*, Glaubhaftmachung, *B* nur durch einen Zeugen; **in the absence of** ~ **to the contrary** → *absence*; **indubitable** ~ zweifelsfreier *B*; **judicial** ~ gerichtlicher *B*; **literal** ~ schriftliche *B*mittel; **negative** ~ negativer *B*; **offer of** ~ *B*angebot; **onus of** ~ → *onus*; **policy** ~ **of interest** → *policy (1)*; **positive** ~ positiver *B*, voller *B*; **preliminary** ~ vorläufiger *B*, Glaubhaftmachung, erster Schadensnachweis; **presumptive** ~ Wahrscheinlichkeits*b*; **reversal of the burden of** ~ Umkehr der *B*last; **shifting the burden of** ~ Übergang der *B*last (*auf die andere Partei*); **standard of** ~ → *standard*; **strict** ~ strenger *B*; **substantive** ~ schlüssiger *B*; **to lead** ~ *scot* Beweis antreten; **upon** ~ bei Nachweis; **written** ~ schriftlicher *B*.

proof *adj* sicher, undurchlässig, gefeit, bewährt, Probe ..., Prüf ...; **burglar** ~ einbruchsicher; **fire** ~ feuersicher, feuerhemmend.

propagate verbreiten, fortpflanzen, sich vermehren, propagieren.

propensity | **to commit crimes** kriminelle Neigungen; ~ **to consume** Konsumfreudigkeit *f*.

proper richtig, passend, angebracht, rechtmäßig, schicklich, eigen, eigentümlich, genau, wirklich, eigentlich, echt, tauglich; ~ **and convenient place** geeignete Stelle; ~ **and necessary powers** die sachlich erforderlichen Befugnisse; ~ **and workmanlike manner** fachgerecht; ~ **independent advice** unabhängiger, fachmännischer Rat, neutrale, anwaltschaftliche Beratung; ~ **law of contract** das auf den Vertrag anzuwendende Recht, Vertragsrecht, Vertragsstatut; ~ **state of repair** ordnungsgemäßer Erhaltungszustand.

property Eigentum *n*, eigentumsähnliches Recht *n*, absolutes Recht *n*; Vermögen *n*, Vermögensgegenstand *m*; Grundstück *n*; Sache *f*; ~ **account** → *account (2)*; ~ **adjustment order** Vermögensausgleichsanordnung, güterrechtlicher Ausgleich (*nach Scheidung*); ~ **and effects** Vermögen; ~ **assets** Vermögenswerte; ~ **at bank** die bei der Bank befindlichen Vermögensgegenstände; ~ **balance** Vermögensbilanz; ~ **company** Immobiliengesellschaft; ~ **control** Vermögensaufsicht; ~ **damage** Sachschaden; ~ **developers** Grundstückserschließungsgesellschaft, Bauträgerfirma; ~ **dividend** → *dividend*; ~ **held in trust** Treuhandvermögen; ~ **holdings** Vermögenswerte; ~ **in action** Forderungsrecht, Herausgabeanspruch; Immaterialgüterrecht; ~ **in expectancy** Anwartschaftsvermögen; ~ **in goods** Eigentum an bewegl Sachen, dingl Recht an bewegl Sachen; ~ **in land** Grundeigentum; Grundvermögen, Rechte an Grundstücken; ~ **in reversion** Grundvermögen des Heimfallberechtigten; ~ **law** Liegenschaftsrecht, Sachenrecht; ~ **ledger** Anlagenbuch; ~ **levy** Vermögensabgabe; ~ **loss** Vermögensschaden; ~ **management service** Hausverwaltungdienst; ~ **market** → *market*; ~ **of another** e–e fremde Sache, fremdes Hab und Gut; ~ **of debtor** Konkursmasse; ~ **passing on death of deceased** vererbliches Vermögen; ~ **qualification** *an Liegenschaftsbesitz gebundendes Wahlrecht*; ~ **record** → *record*; ~ **recovered or preserved** erstrittene oder gesicherte Vermögensgegenstände; **P~ Register** Bestandsverzeichnis (*Grundbuch*); ~ **rehabilitation** Sanierung, Altbausanierung; ~ **right** Vermögensrecht; ~**, rights and interests** Eigentums- und sonstige (dingliche) Rechte; ~ **risks** Vermögensschadensrisiko; ~ **room** Asservatenraum; ~ **settled** treuhänderisch überlassene Vermögensgegenstände; ~ **settlement** Vermögensregelung *im Scheidungsvertrag*; treuhänderische Vermögenszuwendung; ~ **transfer order** gerichtliche Ehewohnungszuweisung, Übertragung des Ehewohnungsgrundstücks *auf einen der Ehegatten durch Gerichtsbeschluß*; ~ **undisposed of by will** Nachlaß nach Abzug von Vermächtnissen; **abandoned** ~ herrenloses Gut, derelinquierte Sache; **abandonment of** ~ Dereliktion; **absolute** ~ (*unbeschränktes*) Eigentum; **accession of** ~ → *accession*; **after-acquired** ~ nachträglich (*nach der Eheschließung*) erworbenes Vermögen; **aggregate** ~ Gesamtvermögen; **aggregate**

taxable ~ steuerpflichtiges Gesamtvermögen; **alien** ~ → *alien*; **blocked** ~ eingefrorenes Kapital; **collective** ~ Gemeinschaftsvermögen; **commercial** ~ gewerbliche Immobilien, gewerblich genutzte Grundstücke, Renditehäuser; **common** ~ Miteigentum, gemeinschaftliches Vermögen, Gesamtgut; **community** ~ → *community*; **contributed** ~ eingebrachtes Gut *der Ehefrau*; Einlage *in eine Gesellschaft*; **copyhold** ~ → *copyhold*; **corporate** ~ Gesellschaftsvermögen; **corporeal** ~ Sachen, körperl Gegenstände; **corporeal personal** ~ bewegl Sachen, Fahrnis; **difficult-to-let** ~ schwer vermietbare Objekte; **discarded** ~ weggeworfener Gegenstand, herrenloses Gut; **disclaimed** ~ herrenlos gewordenes Gut, verlassenes Grundstück; **division of** ~ → *division*; **dotal** ~ → *dotal*; **encumbered** ~ belastetes Grundstück; **enemy** ~ Feindvermögen; Vermögen von Angehörigen feindlicher Staaten; **estate** ~ Gutsbesitz; **exempt** ~ unpfändbare Vermögensgegenstände; **free** ~ freies Vermögen (*Ehefrau, Mündel*); **freehold** ~ Grundeigentum; **funded** ~ Kapitalvermögen; **general** ~ Eigentumsanwartschaftsbesitz; **gifted** ~ Schenkung, geschenkter Vermögensgegenstand; **immovable** ~ unbewegliches Vermögen, Immobilien, Liegenschaften; **improved** ~ erschlossenes Grundstück; **income** ~ Rendite – Immobilien, gewerbliches Grundvermögen; **incorporeal** ~ immaterielle Vermögensgegenstände; **individual** ~ persönliches Vermögen; **industrial** ~ → *industrial*; **intangible** ~ nichtkörperliche Gegenstände, Immaterialgüterrecht; **intellectual** ~ geistiges Eigentum; **joint** ~ Gütergemeinschaft, Gesamthandseigentum; **jointly owned** ~ Grundstück in Miteigentumsgemeinschaft; **joint ownership of** ~ Gesamthandseigentum; **lakeside** ~ Seegrundstück; **landed** ~ Grundvermögen, Liegenschaften, Immobilien; **law of** ~ Sachenrecht; **leased** ~ Pachtgegenstand, Mietsache; **leasehold** ~ → *leasehold;* **literary** ~ literarisches Eigentum, geistiges E., Urheberrecht; **lost** ~ → *lost*; **marital** ~ eheliches Vermögen während der Ehe erworbenes *V*; **married women's** ~ Frauengut; **maternal** ~ mütterliches Vermögen, Muttergut; **mixed** ~ bewegliche Sachen mit Grundstückszubehöreigenschaft; **mortgaged** ~ hypothekarisch belastetes Grundstück; **movable** ~ bewegliches Vermögen, Fahrnis; **municipal** ~ öffentlicher Grundbesitz, gemeindeeigenes Grundstück, städtisches Grundstück, Gemeindeeigentum, Gemeindevermögen; **national** ~ Staatseigentum, Volksvermögen; **onerous** ~ rentables (*belastetes*) Grundstück; **own** ~ eigenes Vermögen, Sondergut; **paraphernal** ~ Vorbehaltsgut der Ehefrau; **pecuniary** ~ Geldvermögen; **personal** ~ bewegliches Vermögen, Mobiliarvermögen, bewegliche Sachen, Fahrnis, Mobiliarnachlaß; **pledged** ~ Pfandsache; **private** ~ Privateigentum, Privatvermögen; **privileged** ~ Vorbehaltsgut (*der Ehefrau*); **public** ~ Staatseigentum, Eigentum der öffentlichen Hand; **qualified** ~ Anrecht; beschränktes Eigentum; **real** ~ Liegenschaften, Grundvermögen, Grundstücke; *real* ~ **holdings** Grundstücksbesitz, Liegenschaften; **real** ~ **law** Liegenschaftsrecht, Immobilienrecht, Bodenrecht; **removal of** ~ **(by bankrupt)** Beiseiteschaffen von Vermögensgegenständen (*durch den zahlungsunfähigen Schuldner*); **requisitioned** ~ beschlagnahmtes Grundstück; **residential** ~ Wohngrundstück; **restricted** ~ Zweckvermögen; **separate** ~ Vorbehaltsgut; getrenntes eigenes Vermögen eines Ehegatten; **special** ~ Fremdbesitz; beschränktes dingliches Recht; **squatted** ~ hausbesetztes Anwesen; von Nichtseßhaften innegehabtes Grundstück; **tangible** ~ Sachen, körperl Gegenstände; **territorial** ~ Staatshoheitsgebiet; **true** ~ (echtes) Eigentum; **ultimate** ~ Obereigentum, eigentliches (Grundstücks)Eigentum; **unclaimed** ~ herrenlos gewordenes Gut; **unoccupied** ~ leerstehende Häuser.

propinquity Verwandtschaft *f*, Elternschaft *f*.

propone vorbringen, erklären.

proponent Antragsteller *m*; Darlegungspflichtiger *m*; präsumptiver Testamentserbe *m*; ~ **of a will** Antragsteller zwecks Testamentsbestätigung.

proportion *s* Anteil *m*, Vermächtnis *n*; *v* bemessen, in ein Verhältnis setzen.

proportional proportional, verhältnismäßig, pro rata; ~ **allotment** verhältnismäßiger Anteil; Quote.

proportionality Verhältnismäßigkeit *f*; ~ **principle** Verhältnismäßigkeitsgrundsatz.

proportionate im richtigen Verhältnis, angemessen, entsprechend, anteilig; ~ **share** verhältnismäßiger Anteil; anteilsmäßige Befriedigung; ~ **to the injury** im entsprechenden Verhältnis zur Verletzung.

proposal Vorschlag *m*, Angebot *n*, Vertragsantrag *m*, Antrag *m*, *bes Antrag in der freiwilligen Gerichtsbarkeit*, Entwurf *m*, Plan *m*, Heiratsantrag *m*; ~ **for amendment** Änderungsantrag; ~**s for paying the claim** Zahlungsvorschläge; ~ **for subscription** Subskriptionsangebot; ~ **of a motion** Antragstellung; ~ **of insurance** Versicherungsantrag; **indecent** ~ Angebot zur Unzucht; **to adopt a** ~ e–n Vorschlag annehmen; **to initiate a** ~ e–n Vorschlag machen.

propose vorschlagen, beabsichtigen, beantragen, einbringen; ~ **a resolution** e–n Entschließungsantrag einbringen; ~ **the names** benennen.

proposer Proponent *m*, Antragsteller *m*.

proposition (*logischer*) Satz *m*, Vorschlag *m*, Antrag *m*; ~ **of law** Rechtssatz.

propositus angeblicher Erzeuger *m*.

propound anbieten, vorlegen, unterbreiten, vorbringen, vorschlagen; ~ **a will** Antrag auf gerichtliche Bestätigung des Testaments stellen.

propounder Antragsteller *m beim Nachlaßgericht zwecks Testamentsbestätigung*.

proprietary *adj* eigentumsartig, eigentumsähnlich, eigen; besitzend; gesetzlich geschützt; ~ **company** Gründergesellschaft; Gesellschaft mit beschränkter Haftung (*Pty*); Holdinggesellschaft, Grundstücksgesellschaft; ~ **designation** unterscheidungsfähige Herstellerangabe; Wort-Warenzeichen, geschützte Bezeichnung; ~ **duties** Pflichten im eigenen Wirkungskreis (*e–r Gemeinde*); ~ **governments** autonome Verwaltungseinheiten; Regierung von Teilstaaten; ~ **industrial process** geschütztes Herstellungsverfahren; ~ **medicines** medizinische Markenartikel, gesetzlich geschützte Arzneimittel.

proprietary *s* Eigentümer *m*.

proprietor Eigentümer *m*, Inhaber *m*, Hausbesitzer *m*, Schutzrechtsinhaber *m*; ~ **in reversion** Eigentümer von verpfändetem Grundbesitz, Heimfallsberechtigter; ~ **of a trademark** Warenzeicheninhaber; **P~ Register** Eigentümer-Register (*vgl Grundbuch Abt. I*); ~**'s stake** Eigenkapitalsanteil; **individual** ~ Einzelunternehmer; **joint** ~**s** Teilhaber, Mitbesitzer; **landed** ~ Grundeigentümer, Grundbesitzer; **registered** ~ eingetragener Eigentümer; **riparian** ~ Eigentümer des Ufergrundstücks, Uferanlieger; **sole** ~ Alleineigentümer, Einzelunternehmer.

proprietorship Eigentumsrecht *n*, Eigentum *n*, Eigentumsverhältnisse; **individual** ~ Einzeleigentümer, Einzelunternehmen, Einzelfirma; **single** ~ Einzelfirma; **sole**

~ alleiniges Eigentumsrecht, Einzelfirma.

propriety Schicklichkeit *f*, Anstand *m*, Richtigkeit *f*, Angemessenheit *f*, *hist* Privatbesitz *m*, Eigentum *n*, Vermögensgegenstand *m*.

proprio motu auf eigenen Antrag, von Amts wegen; *eccl Anfangsworte e–r päpstlichen Entscheidung*.

propter affectum wegen Besorgnis der Befangenheit.

pro rata anteilig, quotenmäßig; ~ **apportionment** anteilsmäßige Aufteilung; ~ **distribution** quotenmäßige Verteilung; anteilige Deckung bei Sammelpolice; ~ **freight** Distanzfracht; ~ **itineris** (*Fracht*) anteilig zur Gesamtreisestrecke; ~ **temporis** anteilig zur Gesamtzeit *bzw zur vollen Frist*; **on a ~ basis** anteilsmäßig, anteilig.

prorate teilen, anteilig verteilen, umlegen.

proration anteilsmäßige Aufteilung *f*.

prorogation Beendigung der Sitzungsperiode; Vertagung *f* (*auf die nächste Legislaturperiode*).

prorogue (sich) vertagen, e–e Sitzungsperiode beenden; ~ **indefinitely** auf unbestimmte Zeit vertagen.

proscribe ächten, verbieten, verbannen, für vogelfrei erklären, unter Strafe stellen; ~**d blood alcohol level** unzulässiger Blutalkoholwert.

proscription Ächtung *f*, Verbot *n*, Ausschließung *f*.

prosecute verfolgen, weiterführen, gerichtlich verfolgen, belangen, strafrechtlich verfolgen, ein Verfahren betreiben, einklagen, jmdn verklagen; ~ **a claim** e–e Forderung gerichtl geltend machen; ~ **an action** e–n Prozeß betreiben; ~ **an application** e–e Anmeldung weiterverfolgen; ~ **the party accused** das Strafverfahren gegen den Angeklagten betreiben; ~ **with due diligence** ein Verfahren ohne Verzögerung betreiben; **neglect to** ~ → *neglect*.

prosecuting | attorney Anklagevertreter, Staatsanwalt; ~ **officer** Staatsanwalt; ~ **party** die (*das Verfahren*) betreibende Partei; ~ **witness** → *witness*.

prosecution Strafverfahren *n*, Strafverfolgung *f*; das Betreiben des Prozesses; Anklagebehörde *f*, Staatsanwaltschaft *f*, Ankläger *f*; ~ **by counsel** anwaltschaftliche Vertretung des Nebenklägers (*bzw sonstigen Geschädigten im Strafverfahren*); ~**'s case** das Anklagevorbringen, Beweisführung der Staatsanwaltschaft; ~ **minded** zugunsten der Staatsanwaltschaft eingestellt; ~ **of an action** Rechtsverfolgung; **criminal** ~ strafrechtliche Verfolgung; **malicious** ~ wissentlich falsche Anschuldigung, Verfolgung Unschuldiger; böswillige Rechtsverfolgung; Prozeßbetrug; **pending** ~ anhängiges Strafverfahren; **private** ~ private Strafverfolgung; Privatklage; **public** ~ Offizialverfolgung, Strafverfolgung durch den Staatsanwalt; **spurious** ~ vorgeschobene Strafverfolgung, unerwünschte Strafverfolgung; **to abort the** ~ die Strafverfolgung niederschlagen; **to mount** ~**s** Strafverfolgungen beginnen; **to stifle the** ~ die Strafverfolgung niederschlagen.

prosecutor Staatsanwalt *m*, Anklagevertreter *m*, Kläger *m*, Ankläger *m*, Privatkläger *m*, Geschädigter *m*, Anzeigeerstatter *m*; **private** ~ Anzeigeerstatter, Privatkläger; **public** ~ Staatsanwalt, öffentl Kläger; **senior** ~ Oberstaatsanwalt.

prosecutorial staatsanwaltschaftlich, die Strafverfolgung betreffend; ~ **discretion** Verfolgungsermessen, Opportunitätsprinzip.

prosecutrix Privatklägerin *f*, Anzeigeerstatterin *f*.

prospect *s* Anblick *m*, Aussicht *f*, Erwartung *f*, möglicher Kandidat *m*, Interessent *m*, voraussichtlicher Kunde *m*; Schürfstelle *f*, Minerallagerstätte *f*; ~**s for promotion** Beförderungsaussicht; ~ **of success**

Erfolgsaussicht(en); ~**s of the market** Konjunkturaussichten.
prospect *v* prospektieren, schürfen, auf Mineralvorkommen prüfen.
prospecting Prospektierung *f*, Schürfen *n*, Aufsuchen *n* von Bodenschätzen, *nebst Anwartschaft auf Ausbeutungskonzession*; ~ **contract** Prospektierungsvertrag; ~ **permit** Schürferlaubnis; ~ **shaft** Versuchsschaft, Probeschacht.
prospective in Aussicht stehend, voraussichtlich.
prospector Prospektor *m*, Schürfer *m*.
prospectus Prospekt *m*, Börsenprospekt *m*; ~ **company** → *company;* **pathfinder** ~ Einführungsprospekt.
prosperity Wohlstand *m*, Aufschwung *m*, Prosperität *f*, Wirtschaftsblüte *f*, Hochkonjunktur *f*; ~ **phase** Hochkonjunktur.
prosperous blühend, erfolgreich.
prostitute Prostituierte *f*; **common** ~ Dirne, Prostituierte.
prostitution Prostitution *f*, gewerbsmäßige Unzucht *f*.
protect schützen, bewahren; ~ **a bill at maturity** e–n Wechsel bei Verfall einlösen; ~ **a signature** den Aussteller durch Ehreneintritt stützen.
protected geschützt; ~ **articles** (*durch Einfuhrzölle*) geschützte Waren; ~ **by law** gesetzlich geschützt; ~ **by patent** patentrechtlich geschützt; ~ **furnished tenancy** möblierte Wohnung unter Mieterschutz; ~ **occupier** unter Mieterschutz stehender Bewohner; ~ ~ *by succession: Familienangehöriger e–s mietergeschützten verstorbenen Wohnungsinhabers;* ~ **shorthold tenancy** Kurzzeitpacht, (bzw -miete); mit Pächter-Mieterschutz.
protection Schutz *m*, Schutzzoll *m*, Schutzbrief *m*, Versicherungsschutz *m*, Zollschutz *m*; ~ **against accidents** Unfallschutz; ~ **by copyright** Urheber(rechts)schutz; ~ **gang** Erpresserbande; **P~ from Eviction Act** Räumungsschutzgesetz *GB 1977*; ~ **in bankruptcy** Haftverschonung e–s Gemeinschuldners; ~ **money** Erpressungszahlung *vgl* ~ *racket*; ~ **of animals** Tierschutz; ~ **of civil interests** Vollstreckungsschutz für Angehörige der Streitkräfte; ~ **of creditors** Gläubigerschutz; ~ **of debtor** Schuldnerschutz; ~ **of industrial property** gewerblicher Rechtsschutz; ~ **of inventors** Erfinderschutz; ~ **of labour** Arbeiterschutz; ~ **of literary and artistic works** Schutz von Werken der Literatur und Kunst; ~ **of minorities** Minderheitsschutz; ~ **of registered designs** Geschmacksmusterschutz; ~ **of the laws** (*gleicher*) Schutz durch die Gesetze; **P~ of Trading Interests Act** G. zum Schutz (britischer) Handelsinteressen *GB 1980*; ~ **order** einstweilige Anordnung zum Schutz des Frauenvermögens; vorläufiger Sicherstellungsbeschluß; vorläufige Verlängerung der Schankkonzession; ~ **racket** Schutzgelderpressung; **duration of** ~ Schutzdauer; **environmental** ~ Umweltschutz; **equal** ~ **(of the laws),** Gleichheits(grund)satz; *denial of equal* ~ *Verstoß gegen den Gleichheitssatz*; **legal** ~ Rechtsschutz.
protectionism Protektionismus *m*, Schutzzollsystem *n*.
protectionist Anhänger *m* des Protektionismus.
protective schützend, Schutz ...; ~ **clause** Schutzklausel; ~ **committee** Gläubigerschutzkommitee (*von Wertpapierbesitzern e–r notleidenden Gesellschaft*); ~ **device** Schutzvorrichtung; ~ **labour legislation** Arbeiterschutzgesetzgebung; ~ **power** Schutzmacht; ~ **trust** → *trust*.
protector Beschützer *m*, Pfleger *m*, Gebrechlichkeitspfleger *m*; Vormund *m*; Zuhälter *m*; ~ **of settlement** Vollstrecker *m* des Treugeberwillens; Beauftragter *m* zur Sicherstellung der Fideikommiß-

nachfolge; **criminal** ~ Begünstiger.

protectorate Protektorat *n*, Schutzgebiet *n*, Schutzherrschaft *f*.

protégé Schutzbefohlener *m*; Staat *m*, der unter Schutzherrschaft steht.

protest *s* Protest *m*, Einspruch *m*, Verwahrung *f*, Widerspruch *m*, Wechselprotest *m*, Wechselprotesturkunde *f*; Beteuerung *f*; ablehnendes Votum (*mit Gründen*) e–s Oberhausmitglieds; Seeprotest *m*, Verklarung *f*; ~ **by householder** Protest durch Haushaltsvorstand (*ohne Notar*); ~ **certificate** Protesturkunde; ~ **charges** Protestkosten; **protest fee** → *fee*; ~ **for better security** Protest bei Zahlungsunfähigkeit des Akzeptanten *vor Wechselfälligkeit*; ~ **for non-acceptance** Protest mangels Annahme; ~ **for non-delivery** Protest mangels Lieferung; ~ **for non-payment** Protest mangels Zahlung; ~ **in due course** rechtzeitig erhobener Protest; ~ **of the shipmaster** Seeprotest, Verklarung (*Beweissicherung bei Seeunfällen*); **entering of a** ~ Protesterhebung; **expenses of** ~ Protestkosten; **extended** ~ nachträglicher Wechselprotest *nach rechtzeitiger Notifizierung;* **extending the** ~ nachträgliche Protestaufnahme; *nach rechtzeitiger Notifizierung*; **formal** ~ förmlicher Protest; notariell festgestellter Wechselprotest; **householder's** ~ formloser privater (*nicht notarieller*) Wechselprotest; **note of** ~ → *note*; **notice of** ~ → *notice*; **past due** ~ zu spät erhobener Protest; **ship's** ~ Seeprotest, Verklarung; **supra** ~ unter Protest, nach Protest.

protest *v* protestieren, zu Protest gehen lassen; ~ **one's good faith** versichern, in gutem Glauben gehandelt zu haben; ~**ed bill** Protestwechsel (*Tratte*); ~**ed for nonpayment** mangels Zahlung protestiert; ~**ed note** Protest(sola)wechsel; **to have a bill** ~**ed** e–n Wechsel protestieren lassen.

protestable protestierbar.

protestation Beteuerung *f*, feierliche Versicherung *f*; Verwahrung *f*; Protesterhebung *f*, Einspruch *m*; ~ **of innocence** Unschuldbeteuerung.

protester Protestierender *m*, Demonstrant *m*; Protestgläubiger *m*.

prothonotary Leiter der Gerichtsgeschäftsstelle *in einigen Staaten der USA*.

protocol *s* Protokoll *n*, Verhandlungsprotokoll *n*, Niederschrift *f*, Ausfertigung *f*, Sitzungsprotokoll *n; scot* Urkundenrolle *f* (*des Notars*); Protokoll *n* (abteilung *f*); Staatsvertrag *m*, Zusatzübereinkunft *f*, Zusatzprotokoll *n*; diplomatische Etikette *f*; ~**s** Gerichtsakte *f* e–s Kirchenprozesses; ~ **of amendment** Berichtigungsprotokoll; ~ **of signature** Unterzeichnungsprotokoll; **final** ~ Schlußprotokoll; **supplementary** ~ Zusatzprotokoll; **textual** ~ Wortprotokoll.

protocol *v* protokollieren, in ein Protokoll aufnehmen.

protract in die Länge ziehen, verzögern; ~ **a litigation** e–n Prozeß verschleppen; ~**ed** langwierig.

protraction Verschleppung *f*, Verzögerung *f*.

protractor Prozeßverschlepper *m*, Verzögerer *m*.

provable nachweisbar.

prove beweisen, nachweisen, bestätigen, die Echtheit (e–s Testaments) bescheinigen; belegen, dokumentieren, beglaubigen, bekunden, unter Beweis stellen, prüfen, erproben, e–r Materialprüfung unterziehen; ~ **a debt** → *debt*; ~ **a will** → *will*; ~ **against the estate** e–e Nachlaßforderung anmelden; ~ **correct** sich als richtig erweisen; ~ **one's identity** sich ausweisen; ~ **the tenor** den Inhalt e–r (verlorengegangenen) Urkunde nachweisen; ~ **to the court** gerichtlich beweisen; ~ **to the satisfaction of the court** vor Gericht beweisen; **to** ~ **true** sich als wahr erweisen.

proved bewiesen, erwiesen, nachgewiesen; bewährt; ~ **damages** festgestellter Schadensersatzanspruch;

~ **debt** *vom Verwalter* anerkannte Forderung; ~ **up to the hilt** unwiderlegbar bewiesen; **as** ~ erwiesenermaßen; **until the contrary be** ~ bis zum Beweis des Gegenteils.

proven bewiesen, erwiesen, nachgewiesen; ~ **territory** ölträchtiges Gebiet; **not** ~ unbewiesen, beweisfällig; *scot* Freispruch mangels Beweises.

provenance Herkunft *f*, Provenienz *f*.

provide vorschreiben, vorsehen, bestimmen, verordnen, liefern, versehen, versorgen, anschaffen; ~ **as is** im Istzustand liefern; **~d by law** gesetzlich bestimmt, gesetzlich vorgeschrieben; **~d for** vorgesehen, vorgeschrieben; ~ **for payment** für Zahlung sorgen; ~ **for somebody** für den Lebensunterhalt jmds sorgen; ~ **payment** Deckung beschaffen, für Zahlung sorgen; **~d school** = *council school* → *school*; ~ **security** Sicherheit leisten; ~ **suitably** standesgemäßen Unterhalt leisten; **~d with funds** gedeckt; **as hereinafter ~d** gemäß nachstehenden Bestimmungen; **except as otherwise ~d** soweit nichts anderes bestimmt ist; **not otherwise ~d for** nicht anderweitig vorgesehen.

provided *conj* vorausgesetzt, vorgesehen, vorbehaltlich, unter der Bedingung, mit der Einschränkung, mit der Maßgabe, wenn, sofern (nur); ~ **always** vorbehaltlich; stets mit der Maßgabe, daß ... ~ **funds permit** soweit die Mittel verfügbar sind.

providence Voraussicht *f*, Vorsehung *f*, Vorsorge *f*; Sparsamkeit *f*; ~ **society** Unfallversicherungsgesellschaft.

provident voraussehend, vorsorglich, fürsorglich, haushälterisch.

provider Versorger *m*, Ernährer *m*, Lieferant *m*.

province Provinz *f*, Gebiet *n*; Fach *n*, Aufgabenbereich *m*, Wirkungskreis *m*, Zuständigkeit *f*; **the ~ of the jury** Sache der Geschworenen; **within my** ~ innerhalb meiner Zuständigkeit.

provincial | authorities Provinzbehörden; ~ **bank** Regionalbank; ~ **clearing** Regionalclearing; ~ **constitution** Dekrete von (*engl*) Kirchensynoden; ~ **exchange** Regionalbörse.

provision Klausel *f*, Bestimmung *f*, Vorschrift *f*, Rechtsnorm *f*, Verfügung *f*, Rückstellung *f*, Vorsorge *f*, Voraussicht *f*, zur Verfügung gestellte Valuta *f*; **~s** Lebensmittel *n*|*pl*; Bedarfsartikel *m*|*pl*; ~ **against engaging in competing business** Konkurrenzklausel; ~ **for automatic renewal** automatische Verlängerungsklausel; ~ **for contingencies** Rückstellung für unvorhergesehene Ausgaben; ~ **for diminution** Wertberichtigung (*Berücksichtigung der Wertminderungsabschreibung*); ~ **for doubtful accounts** Rückstellung für Dubiosen; ~ **for family and dependents** pflichtteilsähnliche Versorgungsansprüche der Angehörigen; ~ **for wife** Versorgung der Witwe aus dem Nachlaß durch gerichtl Anordnung; ~ **for taxation** Steuerrückstellung; ~ **governing inventions by employee** Arbeitnehmererfindungsklausel; **~s industry** Nahrungsmittelindustrie; ~ **merchant** Lebensmittelhändler; ~ **order** Gerichtsbeschluß über (vorläufige) Unterhaltsleistungen; ~ **out of the estate** (gesetzl) Unterhalt(sbeitrag) aus dem Nachlaß; **concluding** ~ Schlußbestimmung; **family** ~ → *family*; **deemed-to-satisfy ~s** Regelanforderungen (*Bauvorschriften*); **deeming** ~ Fiktionsbestimmung („gilt als"); **final** ~ Schlußbestimmung; **fiscal** ~ steuerrechtl Vorschrift; **grantback** ~ Rückübertragungsklausel für Patentverbesserungen des Lizenznehmers; **incidental ~s** Nebenbestimmungen; **legal** ~ gesetzliche Bestimmung; **legislative ~s** Rechtsvorschriften; **loan-loss** ~ Kreditausfallsrückstellung, Wertberichtigung für Anleihen; **operative** ~ Tenor, Entscheidungssatz; **optional** ~**s** → *optional*; **ousted** ~ abbedungene Vorschrift; **particular** ~**s** Spezialbestimmungen; **penal** ~**s** Strafbestimmungen; **peremptory** ~ zwingende Vorschrift; **permissive** ~ Kannbestimmung; **standard** ~**s** allgemeine (*Vertrags*)Bedingungen; **statutory** ~ gesetzliche Vorschrift; **supplementary** ~**s** ergänzende Bestimmungen; **sweeping-up** ~ Ermessensvorschrift für Sonderfälle; **transitional** ~**s** Übergangsbestimmungen; **voluntary** ~ freiwillige Unterhaltszahlung(en).

provisional vorläufig, einstweilig, provisorisch; ~ **licence to drive** vorläufige Fahrerlaubnis; ~ **lump sum** Vorsorgepauschale (*Werkvertrag*).

proviso *(pl oes)* Vorbehaltsklausel *f*, Einschränkung *f*, Vorbehalt *m*, Bedingung *f*, Abmachung *f*, Klausel *f*; ~ **clause** Vorbehaltsklausel; ~ **for redemption** Einlösungsvorbehalt (*Verpfändung, Sicherungsübereignung*); **to act under the** ~ unter Vorbehalt handeln; **trial by** ~ → *trial*; **with a** ~ mit Vorbehalt, vorbehaltlich; **with the usual** ~ unter dem üblichen Vorbehalt.

provisor Lieferant *m*, Hoflieferant *m*; Pfründenanwärter *m*.

provisory vorläufig, provisorisch.

provocation Herausforderung *f*, Provokation *f*, Erregung *f*, Aufreizung *f*; **at the slightest** ~ beim geringsten Anlaß.

provocative herausfordernd, aufreizend.

provoke aufreizen, herausfordern, provozieren, hervorrufen; ~ **a difficulty** e–e Auseinandersetzung provozieren; ~ **an attack** e–n Angriff provozieren.

provost Vorsteher *m*, Rektor *m*, Probst *m*; *scot* Bürgermeister *m*; Kriegsrichter *m*; ~ **court** Kriegsgericht; ~**-marshal** Kommandeur der Militärpolizei, Feldjägerkommandant, Leiter der Militärgefängnisbehörde, Marineprofos.

proximate unmittelbar, direkt, nächst, am nächsten in der Kausalreihe; ~ **cause** unmittelbare Ursache, Hauptursache; ~ **consequence** unmittelbare Folge; ~ **damages** → *damages*; ~ **in time** zeitlich am nächsten.

proximity Nähe *f*, nahe Lage *f*, Verwandtschaftsgrad *m*; ~ **of relationship** Verwandtschaftsgrad.

proximo (im) nächsten Monat.

proxy Stellvertreter *m*, Stimmrechtsbevollmächtigter *m*; Stellvertretung *f*, Vollmacht *f*, Vollmachtsurkunde *f*; ~ **battle** Kampf um Stimmvollmachten; ~ **holder** Stimmbevollmächtigter; ~ **paper** Stimmrechtsvollmacht(surkunde); ~ **statement** *vorgeschriebene Information an Aktionäre über die Voraussetzungen der Stimmrechtsvollmacht;* **by** ~ in Vertretung; **form of** ~ Stimmbevollmächtigungsformular; **general** ~ Generalvollmacht; **irrevocable** ~ unwiderrufliche Vollmacht; **to sign by** ~ in Vollmacht unterschreiben; **to stand** ~ **for** für jmdn die Stellvertretung ausüben; **to vote by** ~ sich im Stimmrecht vertreten lassen.

prudence Sorgfalt *f*, Vorsicht *f*.

prudent umsichtig, klug; ~ **investment** Kapitalanlage durch Beauftragten; ~ **man rule** (=) Sorgfaltspflicht bei Kapitalanlagen als Treuhänder.

prudential | **affairs** Maßnahmen *f*|*pl* des gemeindlichen Wohnungsbaus; ~ **insurance** Volksversicherung.

prudhommes *hist* Freisassen *m*|*pl*, Geschworene *m*|*pl*, Richter *m*|*pl*.

psephologist Wahl- und Meinungsumfrage-Analytiker *m*.

pseudograph gefälschte Schrift *f*.

pseudonym Pseudonym *n*, Deckname *m*.

public *adj* öffentlich, staatlich; offenkundig; ~ **accounts committee** Rechnungsprüfungsausschuß;

~ **auditors and valuers** öffentl bestellte Rechnungsprüfer und Schätzungssachverständige; ~ **benevolent institution** gemeinnützige Wohltätigkeitsorganisation; ~ **call box** öffentl Fernsprecher; ~ **capital expenditure** Investitionen der öffentl–n Hand; ~ **expenditure committee** Finanzausschuß; ~ **health** Volksgesundheit, *öffentl* Gesundheitswesen; ~ **health center** Gesundheitsamt; ~ **health service** staatlicher Gesundheitsdienst; ~ **housing agency** Wohnungsamt; ~ **index map** Katasterverzeichnis; ~ **interest immunity** Indemnität unter dem Gesichtspunkt des öffentlichen Interesses; ~ **land office** *US* staatl Bodenverwaltung; ~ **lending right** Autorenvergütungsanspruch für Benutzung der Werke in öffentl Bibliotheken (*cf Gema*); ~ **liability insurance** → *insurance*; ~ **local inquiries** öffentl Untersuchung von kommunalen Angelegenheiten; ~ **morals** allgemeine Moral, gute Sitten; ~ **navigable river** schiffbarer Fluß; ~ **power district** Stromversorgungsbezirk; **P~ Printer** Leiter der US Staatsdruckerei; ~ **prior use** offenkundige Vorbenutzung; ~ **records office** Staatsarchiv; ~ **relations** (=) Öffentlichkeitsbeziehungen, Öffentlichkeitsarbeit, Kontaktpflege, Vertrauenswerbung; **P~ Service Commission** Aufsichtsbehörde für öffentl Versorgungsbetriebe; ~ **service industries:** öffentl Versorgungsindustrie, staatl Unternehmen; ~ **service vehicle** Fahrzeug der öffentl Verkehrsbetriebe; ~ **use proceedings** Patenteinspruchsverfahren *wegen offenkundiger Vorbenutzung der Erfindung in USA*.

public utility Versorgungsbetrieb; **~ies** Versorgungswerke; **bonds** → *bond (1)*; ~ **commission** Aufsichtsbehörde für öffentl Versorgungsbetriebe; ~ **company** → *company*; ~ **services** öffentl Dienstleistungen; ~ **undertaking** Versorgungsunternehmen.

publican Schankwirt *m*, Gastwirt *m*.

publication Veröffentlichung *f*, Verkündung *f*, öffentliche Bekanntmachung *f*; *beleidigende* Äußerung gegenüber Dritten; Druckschrift *f*, Herausgabe *f* von Büchern; Erklärung *f* des letzten Willens; ~ **fee** Veröffentlichungsgebühr, Bekanntmachungsgebühr; ~ **of banns** Aufgebot; ~ **of libel** Verbreitung e–r verleumderischen (*schriftlichen oder gedruckten*) Äußerung; ~ **of seditious libel** Verbreitung einer hochverräterischen Schrift; **audible** ~ mündliche Mitteilung an die Öffentlichkeit; **indecent ~s** pornografische Veröffentlichung; **limited** ~ begrenzte und vertrauliche Mitteilung; **previous** ~ Vorveröffentlichung; **printed** ~ öffentliche Druckschrift; **right of** ~ → *right*; **treasonable** ~ publizistischer Landesverrat.

publicist Schriftsteller *m* des öffentl Rechts, Völkerrechtler *m*.

publicity Offenkundigkeit *f*, Öffentlichkeit *f*, Publizität *f*, Werbung *f*; ~ **agent** Werbeagent; ~ **campaign** Werbeaktion, Werbefeldzug; ~ **department** Werbeabteilung; ~ **expenses** Werbekosten; ~ **expert** Werbespezialist, Werbefachmann; ~ **man** Werbeberater, Werbefachmann; ~ **of proceedings** Öffentlichkeit des Verfahrens; ~ **purposes** Werbezwecke; **principle of** ~ Öffentlichkeitsprinzip.

publicize bekanntgeben, werben.

publish publizieren, veröffentlichen, verlegen, herausgeben, als echt in den Verkehr bringen; **~ing agreement** Verlagsvertrag; **~ing firm** Verlag.

publisher Verleger *m*, Herausgeber *m*; **~s' association** Verlegerverband.

pudicity Unberührtheit *f*, Enthaltsamkeit *f*, Unbescholtenheit *f*.

puffer Preistreiber *m*, Marktschreier *m*, Scheinbieter *m*.
puffering Preistreiberei *f*.
puffing Anpreisung *f*, Abgabe *f* von Scheingeboten, Preistreiberei *f*.
puffs übertriebene Werbung, überzogene Reklameanpreisung.
puisne jünger, nachrangig.
pull *v* ziehen, Zugkraft haben, sich vorwärtsarbeiten; ~ **back** zurückdatieren; ~ **down** abreißen (*Gebäude*); (*Kurse*) drücken; ~ **off** Erfolg haben; ~ **-tab can** Aufreißdose *US*; ~ **the job** das Ding drehen, schnappen, verhaften, e–e Razzia machen; **to be ~ed up by the police** von der Polizei festgenommen werden.
puller Schlager *m*, zugkräftiger Artikel *m*; **~-in** Anreißer; Kundenfänger.
pump ausholen, ausforschen; ~ **a witness** e–n Zeugen ausforschen.
pump priming Wirtschaftsankurbelung *f* durch Staatsaufträge.
puncheon Prägestempel *m*.
pundit Gelehrter *m*, Rechtsgelehrter *m*.
punish bestrafen, strafen, ahnden.
punishable strafbar, strafwürdig; ~ **act (offence)** strafbare Handlung; ~ **attempt** strafbarer Versuch; ~ **by death** mit Todesstrafe bedroht.
punishment Strafe *f*, Bestrafung *f*, Strafmaß *n*; **adequate** ~ angemessene Strafe; **alteration of** ~ Änderung der Strafzumessung; **arbitrary** ~ Strafe nach freiem Ermessen; **award of** ~ → *award*; **capital** ~ Todesstrafe; **combined** ~ Gesamtstrafe; **commencement of** ~ Strafantritt; **concurrent** ~ gleichzeitig zu verbüßende Strafen; **condign** ~ verdiente Strafe, gebührende Bestrafung, angemessene St.; **consecutive** ~ nacheinander zu verbüßende Strafen; **corporal** ~ körperliche Züchtigung; Prügelstrafe; **cruel and unusual** ~ grausame Bestrafung, Tortur; **cumulative** ~ erhöhte Strafe für Rückfallstäter; **disciplinary** ~ Disziplinarstrafe; **excessive** ~ übermäßig strenge Bestrafung; **exemplary** ~ als Abschreckung dienende Strafe; **exemption from** ~ → *exemption*; **infamous** ~ Zuchthausstrafe (*bes mit Zwangsarbeit*); **lawful** ~ gesetzliche Strafe; **lenient** ~ milde Strafe; **maximum** ~ Höchststrafe; **professional** ~ ehrengerichtliche Bestrafung; **repressive** ~ Ordnungsstrafe; **reprieve of** ~Straferlaß; **respite of** ~ Strafaufschub; **severe** ~ strenge Bestrafung; **substituted** ~ Ersatzstrafe; **termination of** ~ Ende der Strafe, Strafverkürzung; **to be liable to** ~ strafbar sein, straffällig geworden sein; **to incur a** ~ sich strafbar machen.
punitive strafend, Straf . . .; ~ **detention** Strafhaft (*für Jugendliche*); ~ **expedition** Strafexpedition; ~ **measures** Strafmaßnahmen; ~ **power** Strafgewalt.
punt Wette *f* Spekulation *f*.
punter Börsenspekulant *m*, kleiner (*berufsmäßiger*) Wetter *m*.
pupil Schüler *m*, Auszubildender *m*, etwa Anwaltsreferendar *m*; Minderjähriger *m*, Mündel *n*; ~ **master** Ausbildungsanwalt.
pupillage Unmündigkeit *f*, Minderjährigkeit *f*, Ausbildungsverhältnis, Anwaltsreferendarzeit; ~ **fee** Anwaltsausbildungsgebühr, Lehrgeld; **commercial** ~ Wirtschaftsausbildung für jüngere Anwälte.
pupillarity Kindheitsalter *n*.
pupillary minderjährig, unmündig.
puppet government → *government*.
pur autre vie auf Lebenszeit e–s Dritten.
purchasable käuflich, korrupt.
purchase *s* Kauf *m*, Ankauf *m*, Einkauf *m*; Grundstückserwerb *m*, Erwerb des dingl Rechts am Grundstück unter Lebenden; ~ **account** Wareneingangskonto, Einkaufskonto; ~ **annuity** Restkaufgeldrente, Leibrente; ~ **by description** Kauf nach Warenbeschreibung, Kauf nach Katalog; ~ **contingency** Verkaufsfall, Kaufmöglichkeit; ~ **contract** Kaufvertrag, Schlußnote; ~ **deed** Kaufurkunde;

(Grundstücks)Kaufvertrag; ~ **for cash** Kauf gegen bar, Barkauf; Kassakauf; ~ **for future delivery** Terminkauf, Lieferungskauf; ~ **for the settlement** Terminkauf; ~ **for value without notice** gutgläubiger käuflicher Erwerb; ~ **in bulk** Großeinkauf; ~ **ledger** Kreditorenbuch; ~ **money** Kaufgeld, Kaufpreis, Einkaufspreis, Anschaffungskosten; ~**-money bond** → *bond (1)*; ~**-money chattel mortgage** *US* Sicherungsübereignung zur Absicherung der Restkaufpreisschuld; ~**-money loan** Restkaufgelddarlehen, Warenbeschaffungskredit; ~**-money mortgage** Restkauf(geld)hypothek; ~**-money note** Restkaufgeldschuldschein; ~**-money obligation** Kaufpreisschuld; ~ **money resulting trust** Treuhand-Sicherungsrecht des Kaufpreisfinanzierers am Kaufobjekt; ~ **money security interest** Kaufpreis-Sicherungsrecht; ~ **notice** Bedarfsanmeldung; Aufforderung zum Grunderwerb (an e–e Behörde); Erklärung, das Ankaufsrecht ausüben zu wollen, Kauferklärung; ~ **of an estate** Erbschaftskauf; ~ **of an expectancy** Hoffnungskauf, Kauf e–s Anwartschaftsrechtes; ~ **of government supplies** Einkäufe für Bedarf der öffentlichen Hand; ~ **on approval** Kauf auf Probe; ~ **on commission** Kommissionseinkauf; ~ **on credit** Kreditkauf; ~ **on sample** Kauf nach Probe; ~ **order** → *order (2)*; ~ **order form** Bestellformular; ~ **period** Bestellzeitraum; ~ **price** → *price*; ~ **quota** Einkaufskontingent; ~ **returns book** Rückwarenbuch, Retourenjournal; ~ **right** Erwerbsrecht; ~ **tax** → *tax*; ~ **terms** Einkaufsbedingungen; ~ **trial** Abnahmeprüfung; **balance of ~ price** Restkaufgeld; **bona fide** ~ gutgläubiger käuflicher Erwerb; **chance** ~ Gelegenheitskauf; **compulsory** ~ Zwangsverkauf, Zwangsabtretung von Grund und Boden; **fictitious** ~ Scheinkauf; **forward** ~ Terminkauf, Kauf zur späteren Auslieferung; **hire ~ agreement** → *hire-purchase;* **multiple** ~ Sammeleinkauf; **outright** ~ fester Kaufabschluß; **quasi** ~ dem Kaufrecht unterstelltes Rechtsgeschäft; **unpaid ~ money** restliche Kaufpreisforderung, offene K.; **wholesale** ~ Engros-Einkauf, Großeinkauf; **words of** ~ rechtswirkende Ausdrücke beim Kauf, den Kauf bewirkende Formulierung.

purchase *v* kaufen, erwerben, käuflich erwerben; ~ **a leasehold** Pächter werden, e–en Mietvertrag schließen; ~ **for future delivery** auf Termin kaufen; ~ **forward** auf Termin kaufen; **authority to** ~ Ankaufsermächtigung.

purchaser Käufer *m*, Erwerber *m*, *Erwerber von Grundeigentum bzw e–s dingl Grundstücksrechts unter Lebenden*, Ersteigerer *m*; ~**s' association** Einkaufsgenossenschaft; ~ **for value without notice** gutgläubiger (entgeltlicher) Erwerber; ~ **in good faith** gutgläubiger Erwerber; ~ **of a note (bill)** Käufer e–s Wechsels (*ohne Indossament*); ~ **of land** Grundstückskäufer; ~ **of stolen goods** Hehler; **bona fide** ~ gutgläubiger Käufer, gutgläubiger Erwerber; **conditional** ~ Vorbehaltskäufer; **first** ~ Ersterwerber; **good faith** ~ gutgläubiger Käufer; **innocent** ~ gutgläubiger Käufer; **intending** ~ Kaufinteressent; ~ **without notice** gutgläubiger Erwerber (*vom Nichteigentümer*).

purchasing agent → *agent*; ~ **cooperative** Einkaufsgenossenschaft; ~ **power** Kaufkraft; Einkaufsvollmacht; ~ **power parity** → *parity*; ~ **value** Anschaffungswert; **at the ~ rate of exchange** zum Ankaufskurs.

purge *s* Reinigung *f*, Säuberung *f*, politische Säuberungsaktion *f*, Säuberungswelle *f*.

purge *v* säubern, reinigen, freisprechen, von e–m Verdacht reinigen, sühnen; ~**d of partial counsel**

Zeuge, bei dem Besorgnis der Befangenheit verneint wird.

purging Reinigung *f*, Säuberung *f*, Rechtfertigung *f*, Läuterung *f*; ~ **a tort** Rechtfertigung e–r unerlaubten Handlung durch Genehmigung; ~ **contempt** Lossprechen von Mißachtung des Gerichts; sich für Mißachtung des Gerichts entschuldigen.

purist Vertreter *m* der reinen Lehre; **legal** ~ Formaljurist; Positivist.

purlieu Land am Waldrand, Außenbezirk *m*, Nachbarbezirk *m*; ~**-men** Grundbesitzer mit eigenem Jagdrecht; ~**s** Nachbarschaft, Umgebung, Aufenthaltsgebiet.

purloin stehlen.

purloiner Dieb *m*.

purpart Anteil *m*, Teileigentum *n*.

purparty Anteil *m* aus e–r Auseinandersetzung; **to make** ~ aufteilen.

purport bedeuten, anscheinend bedeuten, anscheinend besagen, ausdrücken; **document** ~**ing to be a will** angebliche Testamentsurkunde.

purpose *s* Absicht *f*, Zweck *m*, Ziel *n*; ~**s of business** geschäftliche Zwekke; **commercial** ~ gewerblicher Zweck; **common** ~ gemeinsame Absicht; **criminal** ~ strafbarer Zweck; **domestic** ~**s** Wohnzwekke, häusliche Zwecke; **for the** ~**s of the Act** im Rahmen dieses Gesetzes; **for legal** ~**s** juristisch, im rechtlichen Sinn; **fraudulent** ~ Betrugszweck; **illegal** ~ widerrechtlicher Zweck; **lawful** ~ erlaubter Zweck; **legislative** ~ Absicht des Gesetzgebers; der gesetzgeberische Zweck; **on** ~ absichtlich, vorbedacht; **public** ~ öffentlicher Zweck, gemeinnütziger Zweck; **to answer the** ~ dem Zweck entsprechen; **trust** ~ → *trust*.

purpose *v* die Absicht haben, beabsichtigen.

purse Geldbörse *f*, Geld *n*, Fonds *m*, Preis *m*, Belohnung *f*, Auslobung *f*, Geldgeschenk *n*; ~ **bearer** Kassenwart; ~ **cutting** Geldtaschenraub (*durch Abschneiden*); ~ **snatching** Geldtaschenraub (*durch Wegreißen*); ~ **strings** Finanzkontrolle; ~ **trick** Münzwechseltrick; **common** ~ gemeinsame Kasse; **joint** ~ gemeinsame Kasse; **public** ~ Staatsschatz, Staatssäckel.

purser (Schiffs)Zahlmeister *m*, Proviantmeister *m*.

pursuant übereinstimmend mit, demgemäß, gemäß, zufolge, entsprechend.

purpose gerichtlich verfolgen, fahnden, nachsetzen; ausüben, betreiben.

pursuer Verfolger *m*; Kläger *m*.

pursuit Verfolgung *f*; Beschäftigung *f*, Beruf *m*, Ausübung *f*; ~ **of a trade** gewerbliche Tätigkeit; ~ **of happiness** Streben nach Glück, Persönlichkeitsentfaltung; ~ **of science** wissenschaftliche Betätigung; ~ **of the business of . . .** Betreiben des Gewerbes e–s . . .; **commercial** ~ Handelsbetrieb; **fresh** ~ Verfolgung auf frischer Tat; **hot** ~ Verfolgungsrecht, Nacheile *evt über die Staatsgrenze bzw über die Hoheitsgewässer hinaus*; **mercantile** ~**s** kaufmännische Tätigkeit.

purveyance Lieferung *f*, Anschaffung *f*, Belieferung *f* des Hofes.

purveyor Lieferant *m*, Beschaffer *m*; Beschaffungsbeamter *m*; ~ **to the Court** Hoflieferant; ~**s of cover** Deckungsbeschaffer; Versicherer.

purview Blickfeld *n*, Wirkungskreis *m*, Bereich *m*, Ressort *n*, Geltungsgebiet *n*, verfügender Teil *m* e–s Gesetzes.

push *s* Stoß *m*, Vorstoß *m*; Anstrengung *f*, Bemühung *f*; Diebesbande *f*; ~ **money** Verkaufsprämie für Ladenhüter; **to get a job by** ~ Stellung durch Protektion erhalten.

push *v* stoßen, energisch betreiben, propagieren; ~ **a claim** e–n Anspruch anmelden; ~ **a car** e–n Wagen schieben; ~ **s. o. for payment** jmd zur Zahlung drängen, mahnen; ~ **up prices** Preise hochtreiben.

pusher (*US slang*) Rauschgifthändler *m*.

pushing shares → *share pushing*.

put *s* Rückprämie *f*, Verkaufsoption *f*, Andienungsrecht *n*; Baisse *f*; ~ **and call** Stellage, Stellagegeschäft, Stell-Geschäft; ~ **and call option** Stellagegeschäft; ~ **and call price** Stellkurs; ~ **of more** Rückprämie mit Nachliefern, Nachgeschäft; ~ **option** (Termin)Verkaufsoption, Rückprämie; ~ **premium** Rückprämie; ~ **price** Rückprämienkurs.

put *v* setzen, stellen, legen, anbieten, liefern, ~ **ashore** an Land bringen; ~ **away** wegschaffen, beiseite schaffen, versetzen; ~ **down** niederschreiben, aufschreiben; ~ **down to a person's account** auf jmds Konto verbuchen; ~ **forward** zur Geltung bringen; zur Debatte stellen; ~ **in a caveat** e–e Vormerkung eintragen lassen; ~ **in a claim** e–n Anspruch erheben; ~ **in court** bei Gericht einreichen; ~ **in force** vollziehen, in Kraft setzen; ~ **in hotchpot** → *hotchpot*; ~ **in possession** in den Besitz setzen; ~ **in practice** praktisch anwenden; ~ **in repair** in einwandfreien Zustand versetzen; ~ **into circulation** in Umlauf setzen; ~ **into force** in Kraft setzen; ~ **into operation** in Betrieb nehmen; ~ **into port** e–n Hafen anlaufen; ~ **into writing** schriftlich niederlegen; ~ **off** aufschieben, vertagen, anderweitig verkaufen; ~ **off one's creditors** s–e Gläubiger hinhalten; ~ **on** aufschlagen; ~ **on at par with** gleichstellen mit; ~ **on the file** zu den Akten reichen; ~ **on trial** vor Gericht bringen; ~ **oneself before the country** sich dem Strafgericht im Strafmaß unterwerfen; ~ **out money at interest** Geld verzinslich ausleihen; ~ **s. o.'s income at** jmds Einkommen schätzen auf; ~ **s. o. upon oath** jmd den Eid zuschieben; ~ **up a candidate** e–n Kandidaten aufstellen; ~ **up for auction** versteigern, verauktionieren; ~ **up for parliament** für das Parlament kandidieren; ~ **up resistance** Widerstand leisten.

putage Mangel *m* an Enthaltsamkeit, Ausschweifung *f*.

putative vermeintlich, mutmaßlich, Putativ . . .

pyramiding of reserves Anhäufung *f* von Reserven.

pyramid sales scheme = **pyramid selling** (Vertrieb nach dem) Schneeballsystem.

pyromania Pyromanie *f*.

Q

QBD = *Queen's Bench Division qv.*
quadriennial vierjährig.
quadripartite vierseitig, vierteilig; in vierfacher Ausfertigung; ~ **agreement** Viermächteabkommen; ~ **status** Viermächtestatus.
quadruplicate vierfache Ausfertigung *f.*
quadruplication Quadruplik *f.*
qualification Eignung *f,* Tauglichkeit *f,* Bedingung *f,* Beschränkung *f,* Qualifikation *f,* Vorbehalt *m,* Bezeichnung *f,* Klassifizierung *f,* Kennzeichnung *f,* Anspruchsberechtigung *f,* notwendige Voraussetzung *f,* Modifikation *f;* ~ **for an office** Befähigung zu e–m Amt; ~ **for citizenship** Voraussetzung für den Erwerb der Staatsbürgerschaft; ~ **for public office** Befähigung für ein öffentliches Amt; ~ **of an offer** Einschränkung e–s Angebots; ~ **procedure** Zulassungsverfahren, Typenprüfung; ~ **requirements** Berechtigungserfordernisse; ~ **sample** Muster für die Typenprüfung; ~ **shares** → *share*; **certificate of** ~ Befähigungsnachweis; **personal** ~**s** persönliche Voraussetzungen; **professional** ~ Befähigung für e–n akademischen Beruf; **property** ~ → *property*; **with the** ~ mit der Einschränkung.
qualified qualifiziert, geeignet, einschränkend, bedingt, tauglich, berechtigt, befugt, autorisiert; ~ **medical practitioner** approbierter praktischer Arzt; ~ **oath** → *oath*; ~ **person** jmd, der die gesetzlichen Voraussetzungen erfüllt; ~ **pilot** zugelassener Pilot; ~ **plan** steuerabzugsfähiger Altersversorgungs- und Gewinnbeteiligungsplan (*e–r Firma*); ~ **to be elected** passiv wahlberechtigt.
qualify berechtigen, qualifizieren, befähigen, bezeichnen, beurteilen, einschränken, abschwächen; ~ **for a civil service position** für den öffentlichen Dienst qualifiziert sein; ~ **for the Bar** die Zulassungsvoraussetzungen zur Anwaltschaft erfüllen.
qualifying vgl. qualify; ~ **address** eine (*zu etwas*) berechtigende Postanschrift; ~ **capital interest** zur Abstimmung berechtigender Kapitalanteil, vollwertige Aktie, Beteiligung am Stammkapital; ~ **date** Stichtag für die Wahlberechtigung; ~ **diploma** Zulassungsdiplom; ~ **period** Anwartschaftszeit; ~ **service** anwartschaftsberechtigte Dienstzeit; ~ **shares** Pflichtaktien (*satzungsgemäß vorgeschriebener Aktienbesitz von Vorstandsmitgliedern*).
quality Qualität *f,* Eigenschaft *f,* Erstklassigkeit *f,* Talent *n,* Beschaffenheit *f,* Geeignetheit *f,* Güte *f,* Zustand *m;* ~ **categories** Güteklassen; ~ **certificate** Qualitätszeugnis; ~ **conformance** Qualitätsübereinstimmung; ~ **control** Qualitätskontrolle; ~ **gap** Qualitätslükke; ~ **label** Gütezeichen; ~ **of estate** Zeit und Art der Ausübung eines Herrschaftsrechtes (*an e–r Liegenschaft*); ~ **of life** Lebensqualität; ~ **subject to approval** Qualitätsprüfung vorbehalten; ~ **product** Qualitätserzeugnis; **acceptable** ~ einwandfreie Qualität; **accidental** ~ zufällige Eigenschaft; **agreed** ~ vereinbarte Qualität; **average** ~ Durchschnittsqualität; **bottom** ~ schlechteste Qualität; **choice** ~ erste Qualität; **commercial** ~ Handelswert; **defect of** ~ → *defect*; **essential** ~ notwendige Eigenschaft; **medium** ~ Mittelsorte, mittlere Qualität; **merchantable** ~ Tauglichkeit zum gewöhnlichen Gebrauch, mittlere Art und Güte; **of average kind and** ~ von durch-

schnittlicher Art und Güte; **promised** ~ zugesicherte Qualität; **sterling** ~ allererste Qualität; **warranted** ~ zugesicherte Eigenschaft.

qualm Skrupel *m*; **~s of conscience** Gewissensbisse.

quango halbstaatl Organisation *GB = quasi-autonomous non-governmental organization*.

quantity Quantität *f*, Menge *f*, Größe *f*, große Menge *f*, Anzahl *f*; ~ **buying** Mengenkauf; ~ **control** Mengenkontrolle; ~ **discount** → *discount*; ~ **of estate** Umfang eines Herrschaftsrechts an Liegenschaften; ~ **price group** Mengenpreisgruppe; ~ **receipt** Empfangsschein mit angenäherter Mengenangabe; ~ **sale** Mengenabsatz; ~ **scale** Mengenstaffelung.

quantum Quantum *n*, Menge *f*, Betrag *m*; ~ **meruit** angemessene Vergütung für Teilleistung; ~ **of damages** Höhe des Schadensersatzes.

quarantine *s* Quarantäne *f*, Isolierung *f*, Absonderung *f*; ~ **flag** Quarantäneflagge; ~ **harbour** Quarantänehafen; ~ **regulations** Quarantänebestimmungen; ~ **station** Quarantänestation, Infektionskrankenhaus.

quarantine *v* unter Quarantäne stellen.

quarrel Streit *m*, Streitigkeit *f*, Zank *m*, Hader *m*; **to pick a** ~ e–n Streit vom Zaun brechen.

quarreller Querulant *m*.

quarry Steinbruch *m*, offene Grube *f*.

quart Quartmaß *n (¼ Gallone)*.

quarter Viertel *n*; *US*: Länge *f* von 4 Zoll; *GB*: Viertelyard *n*; *US* 25-Cent-Münze; Stadtviertel *n*; Flächenquadratsviertel (*Katastereinteilung*); Vierteljahr *n*, Quartal *n*; Stelle *f*, Seite *f*, Quelle *f*; Quartier *n*, Unterkunft *f*, Kaserne *f*; Pardon *n*, Schonung *f*; **~annual(ly)** vierteljährlich, quartals...; ~ **chest of tea** Kiste Tee mit 25–30 lbs; ~ **cousins** → *cousin*; ~ **day** Quartalstag; Zahltag im Vierteljahr; (*gewohnheitsrechtlich in England: 25. 3., 24. 6., 29. 9. und 25. 12.; in Schottland: 2. 2., 15. 5., 1. 8., 11. 11.*); ~ **-eagle** Goldmünze von 2½ Dollar; **~'s instalment** Vierteljahreszahlung; ~ **notice** vierteljährliche Kündigung zum Quartalsende; ~ **of a year** Vierteljahr (*91 Tage*); **~'s of coverage** Beitragsdeckung nach Quartalen (*US-Sozialversicherung*); **~-rating** auf ein Viertel ermäßigte Grundsteuer und Kommunalabgaben; ~ **-sales** Erstattung eines Viertels des Kaufpreises bei Weiterverkauf; ~ **seal** → *seal*; ~ **section** ¼ Planquadrat (= *160 acres*); ~ **service** Werbung auf einem Viertel der Reklamefläche; **Q~ Sessions** *GB: bis 1971*, → *Crown Court*; vierteljährliche Gerichtssitzungen; Schöffengericht; **conventional ~s** der Erste jedes Kalenderquartals; **from official ~s** von amtlicher Seite; **residential** ~ Wohnviertel.

quarterage Vierteljahreszahlung *f*, Quartalszahlung *f*.

quartering Einquartierung *f*; *hist* Vierteilung *f* (*als Todesstrafe*); ~ **soldiers** Einquartierung von Militär.

quarterly vierteljährlich; ~ **payment** Quartalszahlung; ~ **statement** Vierteljahresbericht.

quartermaster Quartiermeister *m*; Steuermannsmaat *m*; **Q~ General** Generalquartiermeister *m*.

quarters Quartier *n*; **married** ~ Dienstwohnung für verheiratete Militärpersonen.

quash aufheben, verwerfen, niederschlagen, widerrufen, für nichtig erklären; ~ **a conviction** einen Schuldspruch aufheben; ~ **an indictment** e–e Anklage verwerfen, die Eröffnung der Hauptverhandlung ablehnen; ~ **the proceedings** das Verfahren einstellen; **~ing of a judgment** Aufhebung e–s Urteils; **~ing of a verdict** Aufhebung e–s Schuldspruchs (*der Geschworenen*).

quasi quasi, gleichsam, sozusagen, ähnlich; ~ **admission** widersprüchliche, belastende Einlassung; ~ **agreement** vertragsähnliche

Vereinbarung, aufeinander abgestimmtes Verhalten; ~**-arbitrator** Schiedsgutachter; ~ **contract** Quasikontrakt; ~ **contractual relationship** vertragsähnliches Verhältnis; ~ **connubial** eheähnlich; ~ **corporation** → *corporation*; ~ **crime** → *crime*; ~ **criminal act** Ordnungswidrigkeit; ~ **delict** Quasidelikt, fahrlässige unerlaubte Handlung; *Richterhaftung; Haftung für Verschulden Dritter*; ~ **derelict** → *derelict*; ~ **easement** → *easement*; ~ **fee** → *fee (2)*; ~ **group company** konzernnahe Gesellschaft; ~ **indorsement** Quasi-Indossament, nachträgliches Zwischenindossament; Indossament außerhalb der Ind.-kette; ~ **international law** → *international law*; ~ **judicial** → *judicial*; ~ **judicial functions** richterähnliche Funktionen; ~ **legislative international institutions** internationale Einrichtung mit Quasi-Gesetzgebungskompetenz; ~ **-loan** darlehensähnliches Geschäft; ~ **municipal bonds** (=) *nicht vollwertige Kommunalanleihen*; ~ **official** halbamtlich; ~ **partner** → *partner*; ~ **partnership association** faktische Gesellschaft; ~ **personality** (zum beweglichen Vermögen zählende) beschränkte Rechte am Grundstück; ~ **possession** besitzähnliches Verhältnis, Nutzungsherrschaft an e–m Recht; ~ **prosperity** Scheinkonjunktur; ~ **realty** → *realty*; ~ **rent** Quasirente, Produzentenrente; ~ **tenant at sufferance** → *tenant*; ~ **tort** → *tort*; ~ **trustee** → *trustee*; ~ **war** kriegsähnlicher Zustand, nicht erklärter Krieg.

quay Kai *m*, Schiffslandeplatz *m*; ~ **dues** Kaigebühren, Liegegeld; ~ **receipt** Kaiempfangsschein; **legal** ~ amtlicher Hafenkai.

quayage Kaigebühren *f|pl*, Liegegeld *n*.

queen Königin *f* (*vgl King*); ~**'s consent** königliche Zulassung von Parlamentsvorlagen (*die königliche Prärogativrechte betreffen*); ~ **consort** Gemahlin e–s regierenden Königs; ~ **dowager** → *dowager*; ~ **regnant** regierende Königin, Königin eigenen Rechts; **Q~ Anne's Bounty** = *Bounty of Q~ Anne* → *bounty*; **Q~'s Bench Division** *(=) Abteilung des High Court für allgemeine streitige Zivilsachen*; **Q~'s Counsel** (*Q.C.*) Senioranwalt, Justizrat (*Ehrentitel für barristers*); **Q~'s evidence** *Aussage e–s Mitangeklagten zugunsten der Staatsanwaltschaft*; *turning* ~ ~: *„Umfallen" e–s Zeugen der Verteidigung*; **Q~'s Remembrancer** → *remembrancer*; **Q~'s Prison** Schuldnergefängnis; **Q~'s Proctor** = Kronanwalt *zur Überwachung von Scheidungsprozessen*; **The Q~'s Speech** Parlamentseröffnungsrede der Königin.

quell unterdrücken; ~ **a riot** e–n Aufstand niederschlagen.

querist Anfragender *m*, ein Gutachten Anfordernder *m*.

querulous zänkisch, nörgelsüchtig, mürrisch, unzufrieden; ~ **person** Querulant.

query Frage *f*, Erkundigung *f*, Rückfrage *f*, Beanstandung *f*, Monitum *n*.

question *s* Frage *f*, Streitfrage *f*, Streitpunkt *m*; ~ **in dispute** Streitfrage, strittige Frage, entscheidungserhebliche Frage; ~ **in** (= at) **issue** Streitfrage, zur Entscheidung stehende Frage; ~ **of account** Rechnungslegungsfrage; ~ **of fact** Tatfrage; ~ **of guilt** Schuldfrage; ~ **of law** Rechtsfrage; ~ **of liability** Haftungsfrage; ~ **of merit** Sachfrage; ~ **of procedure** Verfahrensfrage; **Q~ Time** Fragestunde; **argumentative** ~ polemische Frage; **categorical** ~ kategorische Frage, (*eine nur mit ja oder nein zu beantwortende Frage*); **certified** ~ Rechtsfrage zur Revisionsvorlage; **controversial** ~ umstrittene Frage; **critical** ~ (die) entscheidende Frage; **federal** ~ bundesrechtliche Frage; **hypothetical** ~ hypothetische Frage; **in** ~ in Frage stehend, vorliegend; **incidental** ~ Zwischenfrage; **judicial** ~ richterliche Frage; **jurisdictional** ~ Zuständigkeitsfrage; **key** ~ entscheidende Frage; **leading** ~ Suggestivfrage; **legal** ~ Rechtsfrage; **mixed** ~**s** kollisionsrechtliche Fragen, rechtl und zugleich tatsächliche Fragen; **moot** ~ → *moot*; **political** ~ politische Frage; **preliminary** ~ Vorfrage; **previous** ~ vorangegangene Frage; der zuletzt behandelte Tagesordnungspunkt; *to move the* ~ ~: *Antrag auf Schluß der Debatte und Absetzung von der Tagesordnung stellen*; **putting the** ~ e–n Antrag auf Abstimmung stellen; **secondary** ~ Nebenfrage, Nebenproblem; **supplementary** ~ Zusatzfrage; **the** ~ **arises** die Frage erhebt sich; **the short** ~ die entscheidende Frage; **threshold** ~ Ausgangsfrage; **vexed** ~ schwierige Frage.

question *v* fragen, vernehmen, in Frage stellen; ~ **a witness** e–n Zeugen vernehmen; **to be** ~**ed by the police** von der Polizei vernommen (*verhört*) werden.

questionable bedenklich, fraglich, fragwürdig.

questionary Fragebogen *m*.

questioner Fragesteller *m*.

questioning *s* Befragung *f*, Infragestellen *n*; Verhör *n*, Vernehmung *f*; ~ **of suspects** polizeil Vernehmung von Tatverdächtigen.

quibble *s* Spitzfindigkeit *f*, Wortklauberei *f*.

quibble *v* Ausflüchte machen, Wortklauberei treiben.

quick asset ratio Liquiditätsverhältnis (*Verhältnis von liquiden Mitteln zu laufenden Verbindlichkeiten*).

quickening die ersten Kindesbewegungen *f|pl* im Mutterleib.

quid pro quo Gegenleistung *f* (*bei Vertragsschluß*).

quiet *adj* ruhig, lustlos, flau, ungestört, unbeeinträchtigt.

quiet *v* befrieden, e–e Beeinträchtigung beseitigen.

quinquennial fünfjährig; alle fünf Jahre; ~ **period** Fünfjahresfrist; ~ **valuation** *brit* alle 5 Jahre erfolgende Einheitswertfeststellung.

quinqueparite fünfseitig, fünfteilig.

quintal Quintal *n (100 lbs)*.

quire Bündel von 25 Zeitungen.

quit verzichten, aufgeben, ausziehen, räumen, verlassen, die Arbeit niederlegen, als Arbeitnehmer kündigen; ~ **and yield up a premise** ein Grundstück räumen und herausgeben; ~ **possession** den Besitz aufgeben, räumen; ~ **the ranks** desertieren, fahnenflüchtig werden.

quitclaim *s* Anspruchsverzicht *m*, Entlassung *f* aus Haftung; ~ **deed** Grundstücksüberlassungsurkunde (*mit Ausschluß der Rechtsmängelhaftung*); (Grundstücks-)Übergabevertrag.

quitclaim *v* auf e–n Anspruch verzichten, e–e Grundstücksveräußerungsurkunde errichten.

quittance Quittung *f*, Abfindung *f*, Erlaß *m*, Anspruchsverzicht *m*, Entlassung *f* aus der Haftung.

quo warranto proceeding Verfahren (*öffentliche Klage*) wegen Amtsanmaßung; Verfahren zur Entziehung der Rechtsfähigkeit bzw einer Konzession; Feststellungsklage.

quod computet Aufforderung *f* zur Rechnungslegung; **judgment** ~ Zwischenurteil auf Vorlage der Abrechnungsunterlagen.

quorum beschlußfähige Mindestzahl *f*, Beschlußfähigkeit *f*, Mehrzahl *f* der Mitglieder; die Friedensrichter *m|pl* (*kollektiv*); ~ **of directors** Beschlußfähigkeit im Verwaltungsrat; **absence of** ~ Beschlußunfähigkeit (*wegen zu geringer Beteiligung*); **justices of the** ~ → *justice*; **lack of** ~ Beschlußunfähigkeit; **maintenance of** ~ Aufrechterhaltung der Beschlußfähigkeit; **to constitute a** ~ ein beschlußfähiges Gremium bilden, beschlußfähig sein; **to muster a** ~ e–n Q. erreichen, beschlußfähig sein.

quota Quote *f*, Anteil *m*; Kontingent *n*; ~ **agent** Kontingentträger; ~

duty Kontigentszollsatz; ~ **goods** kontingentierte Waren; ~ **law** *US* Einwanderungsgesetz; ~ **of immigrants** Einwanderungskontingent; ~ **per capita** Kopfquote; ~ **restriction** Kontingentierung; ~ **sample** proportionaler Bevölkerungsausschnitt; ~ **share** Kontingentsanteil, Tranche e–s Kontingents; ~ **-share reinsurance** Schadensbeteiligungs-Rückversicherung; **special** ~ Sonderkontingent; ~ **treaty** → *treaty*; **global** ~ Globalkontingent; **quantitative** ~ mengenmäßiges Kontingent.

quotation Preisnotierung *f*, Notierung *f*, Kurs *m*, Börsenkurs *m*; Kostenanschlag *m*, Angabe der (Verbraucher)Kreditbedingungen; Zitat *n*, Anführung *f*; ~ **board** Kurstafel e–s Börsenmaklers; ~ **for futures** Terminnotierung; ~ **of exchange** Valutanotierung; ~**s of the day** Tageskurs, Tagesnotierung; ~ **service** Kursübermittlungsdienst; **bid** ~**s** Geldkurs; **closing** ~ Schlußnotierung; **current** ~ Tageskurs; **daily** ~ Tagenotierung; **demand** ~ → *demand*; **final** ~ Schlußkurs; **fluctuating** ~ schwankender Kurs; **list of** ~**s** → *list*; **market** ~ → *market*; **nominal** ~ Notiz ohne Umsätze; **offer** ~ → *offer*; **official** ~ amtlicher Kurs, amtliche Börsennotiz; **opening** ~ Eröffnungskurs, erste Notierung; **uniform** ~ Einheitskurs.

quote *s* Zitat *n*; Preisangebot *n*.

quote *v* zitieren, anführen, bemerken, notieren, im Kurs stehen; ~ **at par** pari notieren; ~ **one's authorities** seine Quellen angeben; ~**d investments at cost** *brit* börsengängige Wertpapiere zum Anschaffungspreis; ~**d list** amtlicher Kurszettel; ~**d price** angegebener Preis, Preisangebot; notierter Kurs; ~**d securities** notierte Wertpapiere; **to be** ~**d at the exchange** notiert werden; an der Börse gehandelt werden.

R

race Rennen *n*, Wettlauf *m*; ~ **course** Rennplatz, Rennbahn; *R~ C~ Betting Control Board: Aufsichtsbehörde für Pferderennen und Rennwetten*; ~ **track legislation** Gesetze über Pferde- und Hunderennen.

race Rasse *f*, Abstammung *f*, Rassenzugehörigkeit *f*; Geschlecht *n*, Stamm *m*, Familie *f*; ~ **equality** Rassengleichheit, rassische Gleichbehandlung; ~ **hatred** Rassenhaß; **R~ Relations Act** Rassendiskriminierungsverbotsgesetz *GB 1976*; ~ **riot** Rassenkrawall; ~ **segregation** Rassentrennung; **human** ~ Menschengeschlecht.

race recording statutes Gesetze über Prioritätsschutz bei Eintragung von Auflassungs- und Übereignungsurkunden.

rachat Rückkaufsrecht *n*.

racial rassisch, Rassen ... ~ **affinity** Rassenverwandtschaft; ~ **antagonism** Rassengegensätze; ~ **barriers** Rassenschranken; ~ **discrimination** → *discrimination*; ~ **group** rassisch bestimmte Bevölkerungsgruppe; ~ **hatred** Rassenhaß; ~ **persecution** Rassenverfolgung.

rack *s* Folter *f*, Streckfolter *f*.

rack rent volle erzielbare Jahresnettomiete (-pacht); *auch:* überhöhte Pacht (*bzw Miete*).

racket wilde Lärmszene *f*, Trubel *m*, Geschäftemacherei *f*, Gangstergeschäft *n*, Schiebung *f*, Gaunerei *f*, Dreh *m*, Masche *f*, Erpressung *f*.

racketeer Schieber *m*, Gangster *m*, Erpresser *m*, gewissenloser Geschäftemacher *m*.

racketeering organisierte Unterweltkriminalität *f*, organisierte Kriminalität *f*, Erpressung *f*, Schutzgelderpressung *f*, Schiebungsgeschäfte.

radiation | **hazard** Strahlungsgefahr; ~ **injury** Strahlungsschädigung.

raffle *s* Tombola *f*; *v* auf e–r Tombola verlosen; ~ **contract** Verlosungsvertrag.

raid *s* Überfall *m*, Einfall *m*, Razzia *f*; ~ **and detain policy** Razzia- und Verhaftungstaktik; **bank** ~ Bankraub.

raid *v* überfallen, einfallen.

raider Freibeuter *m*, plötzlicher Angreifer; **corporate** ~ Übernahmepirat, Firmenjäger, Firmenhai, aggressiver Aktienaufkäufer.

raiding Mitgliederabwerbung *f*.

rail charges Bahnfracht *f*.

railroad *s US* Eisenbahn *f*, Eisenbahnlinie *f*; Schienenweg *m*, Bahnkörper *m*.

railroad *v* mit der Eisenbahn befördern; durchpeitschen (*Gesetz*), summarisch aburteilen.

railway Eisenbahn *f*; Schienenweg *m*; ~ **agent** Bahnspediteur *m*; ~ **bonds** Eisenbahnobligationen; ~ **charges** Eisenbahnfrachttarif; ~ **commission** Eisenbahnaufsichtsamt; ~ **commissioners** Eisenbahnaufsichtsamt; ~ **company** Eisenbahngesellschaft; ~ **concession** Eisenbahnkonzession; ~ **crossing** Bahnübergang; ~ **delivery** Bahnzustellung; ~ **goods traffic** Eisenbahngüterverkehr; ~ **guide** Kursbuch; ~ **lands** Bahngelände, Eisenbahngrundstücke; ~ **luggage office** Handgepäckaufbewahrung; ~ **passenger duty** Beförderungssteuer; ~ **passenger insurance** Eisenbahnunfallversicherung; ~ **purposes** Bahnzwecke; **R~ Rates Tribunal** Bahntarifschiedsstelle; ~ **regulations** Eisenbahnverkehrsordnung; ~ **rolling stock** rollendes Material (der Bahn); ~ **securities** Eisenbahnwerte; ~ **station** Bahnhof; ~ **tracks** Gleise; **branch** ~ Nebenbahn, Nebenstrecke; **interurban** ~ Städteverbindungsbahn; Stadtbahn; **street** ~ Straßenbahn; **trunk** ~

Hauptstrecke, Bahnlinie über eine Hauptstrecke.

raise *s* Erhöhung *f*, Steigerung *f*; Gehaltserhöhung *f*, Lohnerhöhung *f*.

raise *v* erheben, heben, errichten, aufrichten, erhöhen; ~ **a claim** e–n Anspruch erheben; ~ **a credit** e–n Kredit aufnehmen; ~ **a loan** ein Darlehen aufnehmen; ~ **a presumption** e–e Vermutung entstehen lassen; ~ **a tax** e–e Steuer erheben; e–e Steuer erhöhen; ~ **an embargo** Beschlagnahme aufheben; ~**an objection** e–n Einwand erheben; ~ **capital** Kapital aufbringen; ~ **money** Geld aufbringen; ~ **revenue** Abgaben erheben.

raising of beasts Viehzucht *f*.

rake-off Provision *f*, Gewinnanteil *m* (*bei illegalen Geschäften*).

rallonge Aufstockung *f* des Plafonds, Rallonge *f*.

rally *s* Kurserholung *f*; *v/i* sich erholen (*Kurse*).

ramification Zweiggesellschaft *f*.

rampage Tumult *m*, Randalieren *n*, Randale *f*.

random Zufall *m*; ~ **breath tests** stichprobenweise Atemproben; ~ **check** Stichprobe; ~ **sample** → *sample*; ~ **testing** Stichprobenentnahme; **at** ~ zufällig; Zufalls ..., aufs Geratewohl.

range of action Tätigkeitsbereich; ~ **of goods** Sortiment; ~ **of punishment** Strafrahmen.

ranger Forstbeamter *m*, Förster *m*, Jagdaufseher *m*, Angehöriger *m* der berittenen Gendarmerie; Umherstreifender *m*.

rank *s* Stand *m*, Rang *m*, Rangordnung *f*; ~ **and file** Mannschaften, Reih und Glied, die große Masse, die schlichten (Partei)Mitglieder; ~ **of a debt** Rang e–r Forderung; ~ **of a mortgage** Rang e–r Hypothek; **of equal** ~ranggleich, im Range gleich; **of prior** ~ rangbesser; **senior in** ~ → *senior*; **to reduce to the** ~**s** degradieren.

rank *v* e–n Rang einnehmen, rangieren; ~ **after** im Rang nachgehen, nachrangig sein; ~ **alike** den gleichen Rang haben; ~ **before** vorgehen; ~ **first** an erster Stelle stehen, erststellig sein, erstrangig sein; ~ **for dividend** an der Konkursquote teilnehmen; ~ ~ ~ *pari passu inter se: zum gleichen Rang anteilig ... teilhaben*.

ranking Rang *m*, Rangfolge *f*, Rangordnung *f*; ~ **and sale** rangmäßige Befriedigung (*bei Zwangsversteigerung*); ~ **in priority** mit Vorrang vor; ~ **of claims** Rang(ordnung) der Forderungen; ~ **of creditors** Festlegung der Rangfolge der Gläubiger; ~ **pari passu with** gleichrangig mit.

ransom *s* Lösegeld *n*; ~ **bill** Lösegeldvertrag; ~ **money** Lösegeld; ~ **price** Wucherpreis.

ransom *v* loskaufen.

rape Vergewaltigung *f*, Notzucht *f*; ~ **and murder** Lustmord *m*; ~ **offence** Notzucht und Notzuchtbeihilfe; ~ **shield laws** Schutzgesetze gegen Vergewaltigung; ~ **victim** Opfer e–s Notzuchtverbrechens; **statutory** ~ Geschlechtsverkehr mit Minderjähriger unter dem zustimmungsfähigen Alter (*meist: 14 Jahre, nach US-Staaten verschieden*).

rapine Raub *m*, Plünderung *f*.

rapport à succession Ausgleichung *f* von Vorempfängen (*Erbauseinandersetzung*).

rapporteur Berichterstatter *m*.

rapprochement Annäherung *f*.

raptor Notzuchttäter *m*.

rascal Schurke *m*, Halunke *m*, Gauner *m*.

rashness Kopflosigkeit *f*, Leichtfertigkeit *f*; Unüberlegtheit *f*.

rasure Radieren *n*, ausradierte Stelle *f*, Rasur *f*.

rat *fig* Überläufer *m*, Abtrünniger *m*, Streikbrecher *m*.

ratability (= *rateability*) Abschätzbarkeit *f*; Kommunalabgabepflicht *f*, Umlagepflichtigkeit *f*; Verhältnismäßigkeit *f*.

ratable (= *rateable*) anteilig (*verhältnismäßig gleicher Anteil*), proportional; abschätzbar, zu bewerten; abgabepflichtig; ~ **estate of proper-**

ty steuerpflichtiges Vermögen; ~ **freight** Distanzfracht; ~ **hereditament** steuerpflichtiger Vermögenswert; ~ **occupation** steuerpflichtiger Besitz an Grundvermögen; ~ **value** → *value.*

ratal Veranlagungswert *m*, Steuermeßbetrag *m*.

rate *s*, Verhältnis *n*, Satz *m*, Taxe *f*, Tarif *m*, Rate *f*, Preis *m*, Betrag *m*, Gebühr *f*, Fracht *f*; Steuer *f*, Abgabe *f*, *bes* Kommunalabgabe *f*; für Grundbesitz; Grundsteuer *f*; ~**-aided** gemeindeabgabenbegünstigt; ~**-aided patient** Fürsorgepatient; ~ **asked** Briefkurs; ~ **authorized** zulässiger Tarif; ~ **band** Steuerprogressionsstufe; ~ **capping** Höchstbegrenzung der Kommunalabgaben; ~ **card** Inseratenpreisliste; ~ **cutting** Tarifherabsetzung; ~ **deficiency grant** staatlicher Zuschuß als Defizitausgleich (*an Gemeinde*); ~ **discrimination** diskriminierender Listenpreis; ~ **fixing** Kursfestsetzung; ~ **for advances on securities** Lombardsatz, Beleihungssatz; ~ **for day-to-day money** Tagesgeld; ~ **for loans on** (= *against*) **collateral** (*auch: on securities*) Lombardsatz; ~ **guarantee** Kurssicherung; ~ **holder** Dauerinserent (*zum ermäßigten Tarif*); ~ **making** Prämienfestsetzung; ~ **of assessment** → *assessment*; ~ **of charge** Gebührensatz; ~ **of commission** Provisionssatz; ~ **of consumption** Verbrauchssatz; ~ **of contango** Reportsatz; ~ **of contribution** Beitragssatz, Umlagesatz; ~ **of conversion** Umrechnungskurs; ~ **of depreciation** Abschreibungssatz; ~ **of discount** Diskontsatz; ~ **of duty** Zollsatz; *external* ~ ~ ~: *Außen-Zollsatz* (*EG*); ~ **of exchange** Wechselkurs, Umrechnungskurs; ~ **of freight** Frachtsatz; ~ **of growth** Wachstumsrate; ~ **of incarceration** Inhaftierungsquote; ~ **of increase** Zuwachsrate; ~ **of increment** Zuwachsrate; ~ **of interest** Zinssatz, Zinsfuß; ~ **of issue** Emissionskurs; ~ **of mortality** Sterblichkeitsrate; ~ **of option** Prämiensatz; ~ **of pay** Lohnsatz, Lohntarif, Besoldungssatz, Besoldungstarif; ~ **of profit** Gewinnrate; ~ **of return** Rendite, Kapitalverzinsungssatz; *required* ~ ~ ~: *Mindestrendite*; ~ **of subscription** Abonnementpreis; ~ **of the benefit** Unterstützungssatz; ~ **of turnover** Umschlagsgeschwindigkeit, Umsatzziffer; ~ **of waste** Schwundsatz; ~ **of wear and tear** Abnutzungssatz, Abschreibungsquote; ~**-payer** Gemeindesteuerzahler, umlagenpflichtiger Grundbesitzer; ~ **poundage** Kommunalabgabensatz *vom Steuerwert e–s Grundstückes gerechnet*; ~**s receipt** Kommunalsteuerquittung; ~ **scale** Tarif, Frachttarif; ~ **supervision** Versicherungstarif-Aufsicht; ~ **support grant** Staatszuschuß an Gemeinden; ~**-tariff** Frachttarifliste; **annual** ~ Jahresprämie; **agricultural** ~ Kommunalabgaben für landw. Grundstücke; **bank** ~→ *bank (1);* **base** ~ Grundzinssatz für Ausleihungen; Grundprämiensatz; **basic** ~ Grundlohn; **bill for** ~**s** Steueraufforderung; **birth** ~ Geburtenziffer; **blanket** ~Pauschalsatz; **buying** ~ Ankaufkurs, Geldkurs; **cable** ~ Kabelkurs, Kurs bei telegrafischer Auszahlung; **central** ~ Mittelkurs, Leitkurs; **class** ~ Sammeltarif; **closing** ~ Schlußkurs; **commodity** ~ → *commodity*; **cross** ~ → *cross*; **current** ~ Tageskurs, geltender Satz; **cut-off** ~ Mindestrendite; **death** ~ → *death*; **demand** ~ → *demand*; **deposit** ~ → *deposit*; **difference in** ~**s** → *difference*; **domestic** ~ Wassergeld für Wohnzwecke; **effective** ~ am Kapitalmarkt erzielbarer Zins (*bei Obligationen*), Effektivzinsen; **fine** ~ günstiger Zins bei erstklassigem Kreditnehmer; **flat** ~ Einheitsbetrag, Grundbetrag, Sockelbetrag; **floating** ~ frei fluktuierender Wechselkurs; **forward** ~ Terminkurs; **free** ~ freier Devisenkurs;

general ~s allgemeine Kommunalabgaben; **hourly** ~ Stundenhonorar, Stundenlohnsatz; **hurdle** ~ Mindestrendite; **indirect** ~s *brit* per Pfund notierte Devisenkurse; **interbank** ~ → *interbank*; **joint** ~s Verbundstarif, Tarifverbund; **judgment** ~ *US ins* nach eigenem Ermessen festgesetzte Prämie; **key** ~ nach Gefahrenkreisen eingeteilte Grundprämie; Ausgangstarif; **legal** ~ gesetzlicher Zinsfuß; **lifetime** ~Steuersatz bei Lebzeiten; **liner** ~s Linienfrachtraten; **local** ~s Gemeindesteuern; **lump sum** ~ Pauschalsatz, Einheitssatz; **market** ~ → *market*; **money market** ~ → *money*; **multiple** ~ *multiple;* **municipal** ~s → *municipal*; **net U.K.** ~ britischer Nettosteuersatz; **nil** ~ Nullsatz; **nominal** ~ **of interest** Nominalzinssatz; **official** ~ amtlicher Kurs; **open market** ~ → *open market*; **overall** ~ Pauschalsatz; **overtime** ~ Überstundentarif; **penal** ~ Kampfzoll; **piece** ~ Akkordlohn, Stücklohn; **preferential** ~ Vorzugstarif, Sondertarif; **prime** ~ → *prime*; **regular** ~ Normalsatz; Normallohn; **savings** ~ Sparquote; **selling** ~ Verkaufskurs; Briefkurs; **shift** ~s Tarif für Schichtarbeit; **spot** ~ → *spot*; **standard time** ~s Normalstundentarif; **tapering** ~s degressive Tarife (*Fracht*); **tariff** ~ Zollsatz; **tax** ~ Steuersatz; **telephone** ~ Telefontarif; **tel quel** ~ Telquel-Kurs; **term** ~ zeitlich begrenzter Prämiensatz; **to levy** ~s Kommunalsteuern erheben.

rate *v* einstufen, veranlagen, besteuern; ~ **up** höher versichern.

ratification Ratifizierung *f*, Bestätigung *f*, Vertragsbestätigung *f*, Genehmigung *f*; **subsequent** ~ Genehmigung, anschließende Ratifizierung

ratify ratifizieren, bestätigen, genehmigen.

rating Schätzung *f*, Veranlagung *f*, Bewertung *f*, Tarif *m*; Rationalisierungsstudie *f*; Leistungseinstufung *f*, Krediteinschätzung *f*, Bonitätsprüfung *f*; Einschaltquote *f*; ~ **agency** Rating Agentur (für Wertpapiereinstufung), ~ **agreement** Tarifvereinbarung; ~ **area** Steuerbezirk; ~ **authority** Kommunalsteueramt; ~ **bureau** gemeinschaftliche Tarif(bewertungs)stelle von Versicherungsgeschäften; ~ **for credit** Kreditauskunftsbeurteilung; ~ **plate** → *plate*; ~ **system** Tarifsystem; ~ **value** Steuereinheitswert.

ratio Verhältnis *n*, Proportion *f*, Rechtsfall *m*, Urteilsgründe *n|pl*; ~ **decidendi** tragender Entscheidungsgrund; ~ **legis** Sinn und Zweck des Gesetzes; ~ **of allotment** Zuteilungsquote; ~ **of working expenses** Betriebskostenkoeffizient; **cover** ~ → *cover*; **current** ~ Verhältnis von Umlaufvermögen zu kurzfristigen Verbindlichkeiten; **electoral** ~ Wahlquotient; **equity** ~ Eigenkapitalsquote (*im Verhältnis zu den Aktiva*); **expense** ~ Unkostensatz; Aufwendungsquote; **gross profit** ~ Rohgewinnquotient; **investment** ~ → *investment*; **operating** ~ Betriebswirtschaftlichkeitsquotient (*Verhältnis der veränderlichen Geschäftsunkosten zu den Roheinnahmen*); **quick asset** ~ Liquiditätsverhältnis; **reserve** ~ → *reserve*; **turnover** ~ Umschlagshäufigkeit; **working capital** ~ Betriebskapitalverhältnis.

ration *s* Ration *f*; ~ **card** Lebensmittelkarte; Bezugsschein; ~ **period** Zuteilungsperiode.

ration *v* bewirtschaften, kontingentieren.

rational vernunftgemäß, rational; ~ **basis test** „vernünftige Erwägungen des Gemeinwohls" (*als Maßstab der Einschränkung von Grundrechten*); ~ **doubt** begründeter Zweifel.

rationale logische Grundlage *f*; innerer Grund, Grundgedanke *m*, Sinn und Zweck.

rationalization Rationalisierung *f*, Wirtschaftlichkeitsgestaltung *f*.

rationing Bewirtschaftung *f*, Kontingentierung *f*, Rationierung *f*.
rattening Nötigung *f* zum Gewerkschaftsbeitritt (*durch Arbeitsbehinderung bes Wegnahme von Arbeitsgerät*); Sabotage *f durch Beschädigung von Arbeitsgeräten*.
ratter *pol* Überläufer *m*, Saboteur *m*.
ravish vergewaltigen, schänden, entführen.
ravisher Notzuchttäter *m*.
ravishment Vergewaltigung *f*, Schändung *f*, Entführung *f*; ~ **of ward** Heirat einer Minderjährigen ohne Zustimmung des gesetzlichen Vertreters, Entführung mit Willen der Minderjährigen.
raw roh, unbearbeitet; ~ **materials and supplies** Roh-, Hilfs- und Betriebsstoffe; ~ **or processed** unbearbeitet bzw bearbeitet.
raze vernichten, ausmerzen, (*Geschriebenes*) ausradieren, löschen.
re in Sachen, betreffs; bezüglich, wegen; **(in) R~ X (Deceased)** (in der) Nachlaßsache X; **(in) R~ X (a Bankrupt)** (in der) Konkurssache X; **(in) R~ X (a Minor, an Infant)** (in der) Kindschaftssache X.
reaccount Rückrechnung *f* (*e–s Wechsels*).
reaccuse erneut anklagen.
reacquire wiedererlangen, zurückerwerben.
reacquisition Wiedererlangung *f*, Wiedererwerb *m*.
reaction Reaktion *f*, Rückwirkung *f*.
reactivation Reaktivierung *f*, Wiederinvollzugsetzung *f*; ~ **of a suspended sentence** Anordnung des Strafvollzugs nach Widerruf der Strafaussetzung zur Bewährung.
read *v/t* ~ **in tandem (with)** parallel lesen mit; ~ **out** verlesen; ~ **law** Jura studieren.
read (*pp*) ~**, agreed and signed** vorgelesen, genehmigt und unterschrieben; ~ **and approved** gelesen und genehmigt.
reader in law außerordentlicher Professor der Rechtswissenschaften.
readiness Bereitschaft *f*, Promptheit *f*.
reading Vorlesung *f*, Auslegung *f*, Lesung *f*, Lesart *f*; ~ **of a bill** Lesung e–r Gesetzesvorlage; ~ **out** Verlesung; ~ ~ *judgments: Verlesen von Urteilen*; **ancient** ~**s** Rechtsquelle; rechtshistorische Vorlesung über alte engl Gesetze; **different** ~ Variante, verschiedene Lesart.
readjourn erneut vertagen.
readjournment Wiedervertagung *f*.
readjust wiederherstellen, wieder in Ordnung bringen.
readmission Wiederzulassung *f*.
ready bereit, verfügbar, prompt; ~ **and willing** bereit und in der Lage, verfügungsberechtigt und bereit; ~ **assets** verfügbare Vermögenswerte; ~ **business** Bargeschäft, Kassageschäft; ~ **capital** umlaufendes Vermögen; ~ **cash** Bargeld, Barzahlung; ~ **for delivery** lieferbereit, lieferbar, auf Abruf; ~ **for loading** ladebereit; ~ **for sea** zum Auslaufen bereit; reisefähig; ~ **for use** gebrauchsfertig, betriebsbereit; ~**-made** fertig, von der Stange; ~**-made clothing** Fertigkleidung; ~**-made furniture** Katalogmöbel; ~ **money** → *money*; ~ **quay berth** empfangsbereite Hafenanlegestelle; ~ **to be delivered** unterzeichnet und zur Verkündigung fertig (*Schiedsspruch*); ~ **to discharge** löschbereit; ~ **to sail** abreisefertig; **to be** ~ **to** bereit sein zu, sich verpflichten zu; **to find a** ~ **market** schnellen Absatz finden.
reafforested wiederaufgeforstet.
real dinglich, unbeweglich, Immobiliar . . .; real, tatsächlich, natürlich, unverfälscht, (geld)wertbereinigt; ~ **and personal estate** Gesamtvermögen, Gesamtnachlaß; ~ **resident, holder and occupier** Bewohner *e–s Schankkonzessions-Grundstücks*; **R~ Time Index** Echtzeit-Aktienindex (*an der Londonder Börse*).
real estate Immobilien *f/pl*, Grundvermögen *n*, unbewegliches Vermögen *n*, Liegenschaften *f/pl*, Grundstück *n*; ~ **agency** Grundstücksvermittlung, Immobilienbü-

ro; ~ **agent** Immobilienmakler; ~ **appreciation** Grundwertsteigerung; ~ **bonds** → *bond (1)*; ~ **broker** → *broker*; ~ **closing** Auflassung mit Eigentumsübertragung beim Grundstückskauf; ~ **company** (= ~ *corporation*), Terraingesellschaft, Immobiliengesellschaft; ~ **holdings** Grundstücksbeteiligungen; ~ **listing** → *listing*; ~ **loan** Immobiliendarlehen, Hypothekenkredit, Realkredit; ~ **market** Grundstücksmarkt, Immobilienmarkt; ~ **mortgage bond houses** Hypothekenbanken, Pfandbriefanstalten; ~ **operators** Grundstücksspekulanten; ~ **records** Grundstücksurkunden; ~ **register** Grundbuch; ~ **syndicate** Immobilienkonsortium; ~ **tax** → *tax*; ~ **trust** → *trust*; ~ **venture** Bodenspekulation, Grundstücksspekulation.

reality Realität *f*; Gegebenheit *f*; Dinglichkeit *f*.

realizable realisierbar, verwertbar, zu verwirklichen.

realization Realisierung *f*, Verwertung *f*, Verkauf *m*, Verwirklichung *f*, Liquidation *f*, *exch* Glattstellung *f*; ~ **account** → *account (2)*; ~ **of a pledge** Pfandverwertung, Pfandverkauf; ~ **of profits** Gewinnrealisierung, Gewinnmitnahme; ~ **order** Glattstellungsauftrag; ~ **sale** *exch* Verkauf zwecks Glattstellung; ~ **value** → *value*.

realize realisieren, verwirklichen, verwerten, erzielen, liquidieren, zu Geld machen; Erträge erzielen; ~ **a patent** ein Patent verwerten; ~ **a profit** e–n Gewinn realisieren; ~**d profits** realisierte Gewinne.

re-allocation Neuverteilung *f*, Neuzuteilung *f*, Umplazierung *f*.

re-allowance Rückvergütung *f*, Emissionsprovision *f*.

realm Reich *n*, Königreich *n*; **custom of the R~** → *custom*; **Estates of the R~** → *estate*; **maritime extent of the ~** in das Staatengebiet einbezogene Meeresfläche; **within the ~** im Inland.

realtor Immobilienmakler *m*.

realty Immobilie(n) *f*, Liegenschaften *f*|*pl*, unbewegliches Vermögen *n*, Eigentum und eigentumsähnliche Rechte an Grund und Boden; ~ **transfer tax** Grunderwerbssteuer; **quasi** ~ Grundstückszubehör.

ream Ries *n* (*Papierhandelsmaß*).

reapportionment Anpassung *f* der Wahlbezirke.

reappraisal Neueinschätzung *f*, Neubedeutung *f*.

reappraiser Zollbewertungsüberprüfer *m*.

reapsilver Ablösungsrente *f* für Erntedienste.

rear|-end collision Auffahrunfall; ~ **lights** Rücklichter.

reargue erneut *über e–n Fall* verhandeln.

rearmament Wiederaufrüstung *f*.

rearrange anders anordnen, umgruppieren.

rearrangement neue Anordnung *f*, Neuordnung *f*, Umgruppierung *f*.

rearrest *v* wieder verhaften, erneut festnehmen.

reason *s* Motiv *n*, Vernunft *f*, Verstand *m*, Grund *m*, Ursache *f*, Anlaß *m*; Beweggrund *m*, *pl*: Gründe, Begründung *f*; **Age of R~** die Aufklärung, das Zeitalter der Vernunft; **amplified ~s** ausführliche Begründung; **by ~ of** wegen; **by this ~** aus diesem Grund; **convincing ~** überzeugender Grund; **good ~** triftiger Grund; **it stands to ~ that** es versteht sich von selbst, daß; **ostensible ~s** anscheinend plausible Gründe; **overriding ~** ausschlaggebender Grund; **sound ~** triftiger Grund; **special ~** wichtiger Grund; **to give ~s** motivieren, begründen; **written ~s** schriftliche Begründung.

reason *v* erörtern, diskutieren, durchdenken; ~ **from s. th.** aus etwas schließen; ~**ed amendment** = *mit Begründung versehener Abänderungsantrag zur Blockierung e–r Verabschiedung*; ~**ed answer** wohlüberlegte Erwiderung, ~**ed decision** → *decision*.

reasonable vernünftig, plausibel, annehmbar, tragbar, zumutbar, gerecht, billig, üblich, ordnungsgemäß, angemessen, ausreichend, stichhaltig; ~ **act** zumutbare Handlung, zumutbare Tätigkeit; ~ **advance notice** angemessene Vorankündigung; ~ **and probable cause** dringender Tatverdacht; ~ **and proper** zulässig und angemessen; ~ **and proper speed** zulässige (und angemessene) Geschwindigkeit; ~ **and proportionate** angemessen; ~ **and sufficient** zumutbar und ausreichend; ~ **belief** vertretbare Überzeugung; ~ **care** angemessene Sorgfalt; die im Verkehr erforderliche Sorgfalt; ~ **care and diligence** die im Verkehr erforderliche Sorgfalt; ~ **cause** wichtiger Grund, erheblicher Anlaß; ~ **cause to believe** begründeter Anlaß zu der Annahme; **(with)** ~ **certainty** mit ausreichender Bestimmtheit; ~ **commuting reach** zumutbare Entfernung für Pendler; ~ **compensation** → *compensation*; ~ **contemplation test** Adäquanzprüfung bei der Schadenskausalität; ~ **creature** menschliches Lebewesen; ~ **deviation** gerechtfertigte Abweichung; ~ **diligence** → *diligence*; ~ **doubt** begründeter Zweifel, nicht unerheblicher Zweifel; ~ **doubt rule** in dubio pro reo (*bei begründetem Zweifel ist zugunsten des Angeklagten zu entscheiden*); ~ **excuse** ausreichende Entschuldigung; ~ **facilities** erforderliche Einrichtungen; ~ **financial provision** angemessene finanzielle Zuwendung; ~ **grounds** stichhaltiger Grund; ~ **hour** zumutbare Tageszeit; ~ **maintenance** → *maintenance*; ~ **man** ein (vernünftiger) Durchschnittsmensch; ~ **notice** → *notice*; ~ **opportunity** ausreichende Gelegenheit; ~ **part** Pflichterbteil der Witwe und der Kinder; ~ **price** angemessener Preis; ~ **satisfaction** vertretbare Überzeugung; ~ **security** ausreichende Sicherheitsleistung; ~ **skill** durchschnittliches Können; ~ **skill and knowledge** ausreichende Fachkenntnis; ~ **terms and conditions** angemessene Bedingungen; ~ **wear and tear** übliche Abnutzung.

reasonableness Zumutbarkeit *f*, Angemessenheit *f*, Billigkeit *f*; ~ **test** Zumutbarkeitsprüfung.

reasonably|accessible gut erreichbar, in zumutbarer Entfernung; ~ **fit for human habitation** für Wohnzwecke geeignet; ~ **incurred** berechtigterweise angefallen; ~ **necessary** erforderlich; ~ **practicable** zumutbar und praktisch möglich; ~ **required** in zumutbarem Umfang verlangt.

reasoning Beweisführung *f*, Schlußfolgerung *f*; ~ **leading to the decision** Entscheidungsbegründung.

reassessment Neubewertung *f* (*tax*).

reassign zurückabtreten, zurückübertragen; ~ **to active duty** aktivieren (*e–n Beamten im Wartestande*).

reassignment Wiederabtretung *f*, Retrozession *f*.

re-assurance Rückversicherung *f*.

reassure zusichern; rückversichern.

reassurer Rückversicherer *m*.

reattachment Wiederverhaftung *f*, wiederholte Pfändung *f*.

rebate *s* Rabatt *m*, Abzug *m*, Diskont *m*, Rückvergütung *f*, Erstattung *f*; ~ **certificate** Steuergutschein; **dealer's** ~ Händlerrabatt; **quantity** ~ Mengenrabatt; **rent** ~ → *rent*; **tax** ~ Steuernachlaß, Steuerrückvergütung.

rebate *v* e–n Rabatt gewähren.

rebel *s* Rebell *m*, Aufrührer *m*.

rebel *v* rebellieren, sich empören, sich auflehnen.

rebellion Aufruhr *f*, Auflehnung *f*, Rebellion *f*, offener Widerstand *m*; *hist* Ungehorsam *m* gegenüber dem Gericht; **commission of** ~ Anordnung der Beugestrafe.

rebellious|assembly aufrührerische Zusammenrottung; ~ **harangue** aufrührerische Hetzrede.

rebound Konjunkturerholung *f*, Wiederaufschwung *m*; *v|i* sich erholen.

rebuke e–n scharfen Verweis erteilen.

rebut den Gegenbeweis führen, entkräften, widerlegen, e–n Anspruch abwehren; ~ **the charges** Beschuldigungen (Vorwürfe) widerlegen; ~**ting evidence** = *evidence in rebuttal* → *evidence*.

rebuttable widerlegbar.

rebuttal Gegenbeweis *m*, Widerlegung *f*, Zurückweisung *f*; ~ **evidence** = *evidence in* ~ → *evidence*; ~ **testimony** gegenbeweisliche Zeugenaussage.

rebutter Quadruplik *f*, *schriftsätzliche Erwiderung auf eine Triplik*.

rebuy zurückkaufen.

recalcitrance Widerspenstigkeit *f*, Unbotmäßigkeit *f*.

recall *s* Aufkündigung *f*, Rückberufung *f*; Widerruf *n*; Abberufung *f*; ~ **election** Abberufungswahl; ~ **of a witness** erneute Vernehmung e–s Zeugen (*als Widerlegungszeuge*).

recall *v* sich ins Gedächtnis zurückrufen; aufkündigen, aufrufen, abberufen; ~ **a judgment** ein Urteil aufheben (*aus tatsächlichen Gründen*); ~ **a loan** ein Darlehen kündigen; ~ **the capital** Kapital kündigen; **until** ~**ed** bis auf Widerruf.

recant öffentlich widerrufen, abschwören, ein Geständnis widerrufen.

recantation öffentliche Widerrufung *f*.

recap = *recapitalization qv*.

recapitalization Kapitalumschichtung *f*; Kapitalumstrukturierung *f*; Kapitalberichtigung *f*; **leveraged** ~ K.umschichtung durch Aufnahme von Fremdmitteln.

recapitulate rekapitulieren, zusammenfassen, wiederholen.

recaption Wiederwegnahme *f*, Wiederinbesitznahme *f* (*nach widerrechtlicher Besitzentziehung*), Wegnahme *f* als Selbsthilfe; erneute Pfändung *f*; **writ of** ~ → *writ*.

recapture *s* Zurückeroberung *f*; Wiedererlangung *f*; Entziehung ungerechtfertigter Gewinne (*bei Staatsaufträgen*); ~ **clause** Rückforderungsklausel (*bei Staatsaufträgen, vgl renegotiation*).

recapture *v* wiedernehmen, wiedergefangennehmen, aufbringen.

recartelization Rückverflechtung *f*.

recede Abstand nehmen, zurückabtreten, nachgeben; ~ **from an opinion** die ablehnende Meinung aufgeben (*gegenüber der anderen Gesetzgebungskammer*).

recipient Empfänger *m*; **authorized** ~ Empfangsberechtigter.

receipt *s* Quittung *f*, Empfangsschein *m*, Empfangsbestätigung *f*, Empfang *m*, Zugang *m*, Eingang *m*, Einnahme *f*; Hehlerei *f*; Zulassung *f* als Nebenintervenient; ~ **book** Quittungsbuch; ~ **for shipment bill of lading** → *bill of lading;* ~ **for the balance** Quittung über Restzahlung, Schlußquittung; ~ **given** quittiert; ~ **in full** Quittung über den gesamten Betrag, Generalquittung; ~ **in part** Teilquittung; ~ **not signed** Quittung ohne Unterschrift; ~ **of debt** Überweisung der gepfändeten Forderung; ~ **of delivery** Rückschein, Empfangsquittung; ~ **of deposit** Depotschein; ~ **stamp** Eingangsstempel; ~ **voucher** Empfangsbescheinigung; **accountable** ~ → *accountable*; **acknowledgment of** ~ → *acknowledgment*; **advice of** ~ Empfangsanzeige; **against** ~ gegen Quittung; **bank** ~ → *bank (1)*; **blank** ~ Blankoquittung; **certificate of** ~ → *certificate*; **confirmation of** ~ Eingangsbestätigung, Empfangsbekenntnis; **date of** ~ → *date*; **dock** ~ Kaiempfangsbestätigung; **endorsed** ~ löschungsfähige Quittung; **full and effectual** ~ vollständige und gültige Quittung; **good** ~ gültige Quittung; **innocent** ~ gutgläubiger Empfang; **interim** ~ Zwischenquittung; **mate's** ~ → *mate*; **memorandum of** ~ Empfangsschein; **participating** ~ Anteilsschein, Partizipationsschein; **petty cash** ~ Eingangsbeleg der Handkasse; **postal** ~ Posteinlieferungsschein; **post**

office ~ Posteinlieferungsschein; **provisional** ~ vorläufige Quittung, Interimsquittung; Zwischenschein; **return** ~ Rückschein; **temporary** ~ = *provisional* ~ *qv*; **trust** ~ → *trust*; **warehouse** ~ Lagerschein.

receipt *v* quittieren; **~ed bill of exchange** quittierter Wechsel.

receiptor Quittierender *m*, Quittungsaussteller *m*, Verwahrer *m* von gepfändeten Sachen.

receipts Einnahmen *f/pl*; ~ **and expenditure** Einnahmen und Ausgaben; ~ **and payments** → *payment*; ~ **book** Einnahmebuch; **acutal** ~ Isteinnahmen; **current** ~ Umlaufsvermögen, Einnahmen aus laufender Rechnung; **daily** ~ Tageseinnahmen; **deficiency in** ~ Mindereinnahmen; **gross ~s** Bruttoeinnahmen; **net** ~ Nettoeinnahmen; **ordinary** ~ ordentliche (Staats)Einnahmen; **supposed** ~ Solleinnahmen.

receivable noch zu fordern, offen, unbezahlt; zulässig (*als Beweis*); **accounts** ~ → *account (2)*; **accruals** ~ → *accrual*; **deferred accounts** ~ →*deferred*; **notes** ~ → *note*; **to be** ~ **in evidence** als Beweismittel zugelassen sein.

receivables Forderungen *f/pl*, Außenstände *m/pl*, Debitoren *m/pl*; ~ **financing** Factoring, Inkassozession von Außenständen; ~ **from affiliated companies** Forderungen an verbundene Unternehmen; **accrued** ~ antizipative Aktiva; **current** ~ Umlaufvermögen; **doubtful** ~ Dubiosen, zweifelhafte Forderungen; **uncollectible** ~ Dubiosen, zweifelhafte Forderungen; **current** ~ Umlaufvermögen.

receive vereinnahmen, empfangen, erhalten, Geld einnehmen, etwas entgegennehmen; jmd aufnehmen; zulassen; ~ **a bribe** sich bestechen lassen; ~ **a legacy** ein Vermächtnis erhalten; ~ **a pardon** begnadigt werden; ~ **an oath** e–n Eid abnehmen; ~ **harbour and maintain** persönlich begünstigen durch Gewährung von Unterschlupf; ~ **stolen goods** Diebesgut an sich bringen, Hehlerei begehen; **~d for shipment** übernommen zur Beförderung; **~d for shipment bill of lading** → *bill of lading*; **~d on account** → *account (2)*; **~d or accrued** erhalten oder fällig; **duly ~d** → *duly*; **value ~d** → *value*; **when ~d** nach Erhalt, bei Empfang.

Received Eingang (*Stempel*).

receiver Empfänger *m*, Sequester *m*, vorläufiger Konkursverwalter *m*, Zwangsverwalter *m*, Liquidator *m*; Pfleger *m* (*e–s Geisteskranken*); Hehler *m*; ~ **and manager** Vermögensverwalter mit Geschäftsführungsbefugnis; **~s and triers of petitions** Petitionsausschuß; **~'s certificate** Verpfändungsurkunde über Zwangsverwaltungsgut; ~ **for debenture holders** Sequester für Schuldschein-Gläubiger; ~ **for partnership** Liquidator e–r OHG; ~ **in lunacy** Pfleger *m*, Vermögensverwalter e–s Geisteskranken; ~ **of customs** Zolleinnehmer; ~ **of goods** Konsignator, Warenempfänger; ~ **of rents** Zwangsverwalter; ~ **of stolen goods** Hehler; ~ **of wrecks** Strandvogt; **~'s office** Hebestelle, Steueramt; ~ **pendente lite** Sequester (*für die Dauer des Rechtsstreits*); **~'s register** *Verzeichnis des Zwangsverwalters über eingetragene Obligationen;* **ancillary** ~ Gehilfe e–s Konkursverwalters (*am Ort der Belegenheit der Massegegenstände*); inländischer Zwangsverwalter (*bei Insolvenz im Ausland*); **at ~'s account** zu Lasten des Empfängers; **bona fide** ~ gutgläubiger Empfänger; **interim** ~ vorläufiger Verwalter; **official** ~ vorläufiger Konkursverwalter, Zwangsverwalter, Sequester.

receivership Zwangsverwaltung *f*, Konkursverwaltung *f*, Verwaltung *f* durch Grundpfandgläubiger; Geschäftsaufsicht *f*; Amt *n* des Steuereinnehmers; **dry** ~ masselose Zwangsverwaltung; **official** ~ vorläufige Konkursverwaltung;

temporary ~ Sequestration, Geschäftsaufsicht; **to be under** ~ unter Zwangsverwaltung gestellt sein.

receiving *vgl to receive*; ~ **evidence out of court** außergerichtliche Beweiserhebung; ~ **order** → *order (1)*; ~ **place** Empfangsort; ~ **report** → *report*; ~ **state** → *state (2)*; ~ **stolen goods** Hehlerei → *handling (2)*; **teller** → *teller*.

recension Durchsicht *f*, Prüfung *f*, Rezension *f*, Revision *f* (*e–s Manuskripts*).

receptacle Behälter *m*, Gefäß *n*.

reception Empfang *m*, Annahme *f*; ~ **centre** Fürsorgeheim, Obdachlosenasyl; ~ **of verdict** Entgegennahme des Spruchs der Geschworenen (*durch den Richter in Anwesenheit des Angeklagten*); ~ **order** Einweisungsbeschluß in e–e Heil- und Pflegeanstalt; Verwahrungsbeschluß.

receptive aufnahmefähig, aufnahmebereit.

recess *s* (Parlaments-)Ferien *pl*, Unterbrechung *f*, (Sitzungs)Pause *f*; ~ **of the courts** Gerichtsferien.

recess *v* sich vertragen, Pause machen.

recession Rückgang *m*, Rezession *f*, Konjunkturflaute *f*; Rückabtretung *f*, Rückgabe *f*; ~ **period** Rezessionszeit.

recharter Unterfrachtvertrag *m*.

recidivism Rückfall *m*, Rückfälligkeit *f*.

recidivist Gewohnheitstäter *m*, Rückfälliger *m*.

recidivous rückfällig.

recipiendary akzeptierter Kandidat *m*.

recipient Empfänger *m*; **authorized** ~ Empfangsberechtigter, Zustellungsbevollmächtigter.

reciprocal wechselseitig, gegenseitig, umgekehrt.

reciprocity Gegenseitigkeit *f*, Wechselseitigkeit *f*; ~ **of treatment** Gegenseitigkeitsbehandlung.

recital Aufzählung *f*, Inventarverzeichnis *n*, einleitender Teil *m* e–r Urkunde, Präambel *f*, einleitende Sachdarstellung *f*; ~ **of debts** Schuldenverzeichnis; ~ **of facts** Darstellung des Sachverhalts; ~ **of parties** Rubrum.

recite einleitende Angaben machen, zitieren.

reckless rücksichtslos; grob fahrlässig, leichtfertig.

recklessness Leichtfertigkeit *f*, bewußte grobe Fahrlässigkeit *f*, *auch:* bedingter Vorsatz *m*.

reckon berechnen, errechnen, kalkulieren; halten für; achtgeben, ~ **on** auf etwas rechnen, sich auf jmd verlassen; ~**ed in the majority in value** die Mehrheit nach dem Werte (*der Forderungen*).

reckonable anrechenbar (*Rentenberechnung*).

reckoning time Fristberechnung *f*.

reclaim zurückverlangen, herausverlangen; *scot* Berufung einlegen; zähmen.

reclaimable besserungsfähig.

reclaimant Zurückforderer *m*, Beschwerdeführer *m*.

reclamation Zurückforderung *f*; Einspruch *m*, Mängelrüge *f*; Besserung *f*, Heilung *f*; Zurückgewinnung *f*, Urbarmachung *f*, Nutzbarmachung *f*; ~ **district** Verwaltungsbezirk zur Urbarmachung; ~ **proceedings** *US* Aussonderungsverfahren; **land** ~ Urbarmachung von Land.

recluse Einkerkerung *f*, Haft *f*.

reclusion Zuchthausstrafe *f*.

recognition Anerkennung *f*, Anerkenntnis *f*, Genehmigung *f*, Bestätigung *f*; Untersuchung *f* durch Geschworene; ~ **test** Wiedererkennungstest (*bei Werbung*).

recognizance (= *recognisance*) protokollierte Verpflichtung *f* vor Gericht, Übernahme e–r gerichtl Auflage, Kaution(s-Summe) *f*; ~ **of witness** Verpflichtungserklärung des Zeugen, zum Termin zu erscheinen; Sicherheitsleistung; **on one's own** ~ ohne Kaution (*von der Untersuchungshaft verschont werden*); **personal** ~ Verpflichtungser-

klärung (*im Hauptverhandlungstermin zu erscheinen*) ohne Kautionsstellung.
recognize anerkennen, gelten lassen, das Wort erteilen, zulassen (*zur Verhandlung*); ~ **a claim** e–n Anspruch anerkennen; ~**d agent** anerkannter Vertreter; ~**d gain or loss** zu versteuernder Gewinn *bzw* Verlust; ~**d holiday** gesetzlich geschützter Feiertag ~**d mortgage** (*für Agrarkredithilfe*) anerkannte Hypothek (*bzw Grundschuld*).
recognizee (= *recognisee*) der Begünstigte *m* e–r vor Gericht abgegebenen Verpflichtungserklärung.
recognizor (= *recognisor*) der sich vor Gericht Verpflichtende.
recoin umprägen, wiederprägen.
recoinage Umprägung *f*.
recollection Erinnerung *f*, Erinnerungsvermögen *n*, Gedächtnis *n*; **independent** ~ eigenes (unabhängiges) Erinnerungsvermögen; **refreshing** ~ **from notes** Aufzeichnungen zur Auffrischung des Gedächtnisses einsehen; **to the best of my** ~ soweit ich mich erinnern kann.
recommendation Empfehlung *f*, Befürwortung *f*, Vorschlag *m*; Lehensnahme *f* von Allodialland; ~ **is negatived** Vorschlag wird verworfen; ~ **of leniency** Gnadenempfehlung; ~ **to mercy** Gnadenempfehlung.
recommendatory empfehlend, bittend, beratend, anweisend.
recommit zurückverweisen; Haftfortdauer anordnen.
recommitment Zurückverweisung *f*; Anordnung *f* der Haftfortdauer.
recommittal Wiedereinlieferung *f* (*ins Gefängnis*); ~ **of bills** Zurückverweisung (*e–r Gesetzesvorlage an e–n Ausschuß*).
recompense *s* Belohnung *f*, Ersatz *m*, Schadenersatz *m*, Entschädigung *f*, Vergütung *f*.
recompense *v* belohnen, entschädigen, ersetzen.
reconcilability Abstimmbarkeit *f* (*Konten*).
reconcilable verträglich, vereinbar.
reconcile in Einklang bringen, versöhnen, aussöhnen; ~ **accounts** Konten abstimmen; ~**d** versöhnt, abgestimmt.
reconcilement Versöhnung *f*, Schlichtung *f*, Ausgleich *m*; Abstimmung *f*, Kollationierung *f*.
reconciliation Schlichtung *f*, Versöhnung *f*, Aussöhnung *f*, Verzeihung *f*, Abstimmung *f von Konten*; ~ **account** Berichtigungskonto; ~ **agreement** Schlichtungsvereinbarung; ~ **of accounts** Kontenabstimmung; ~ **of cash** Kassenabstimmung; ~ **procedure** Sühneverfahren; ~ **statement** Richtigbefundanzeige; Abklärung von Kontenabstimmungsdifferenzen.
recondite tiefgründig, schwer verständlich, abstrus.
reconditioning Instandsetzung *f*, Generalüberholung *f*.
reconduction Pachtverlängerung *f*.
reconsider erneut erwägen, nochmals behandeln, nochmals beraten, überprüfen.
reconsideration Überprüfung *f*, nochmalige Beratung *f*.
reconsign umadressieren, umdirigieren (*Ware unterwegs*).
reconsignment Umadressierung *f*, Umleitung *f*, Weitersendung *f*, Rücksendung *f*.
reconstitute wiederherstellen.
reconstruct neu aufbauen, neu errichten, sanieren, reorganisieren.
reconstruction Wiederaufbau *m*, Umstrukturierung *f*, Sanierung *f*, Reorganisation *f*; ~ **and reorganisation** Sanierungsumgründung; ~ **credit** Wiederaufbaukredit; ~ **of a company** Reorganisation e–r Gesellschaft, Sanierungsumgründung; ~ **of works** Wiedererrichtung von gewerblichen Anlagen.
recontinuance Fortsetzung *f* e–s (*unterbrochenen*) Nutzungsverhältnisses.
reconvention Widerklage *f*.
reconventional demand Widerklageforderung *f*.
re-conversion Rückumwandlung *f*,

Rückerstattung *f*; Wiederumstellung *f* auf Friedenswirtschaft.

re-convey zurückübertragen.

re-conveyance Rückübertragung *f* von Grundbesitz (*bes des verpfändeten Grundstücks*), Rückauflassung *f*.

reconvict *v/t, v/i* erneut verurteilen.

record *s* Gerichtsakte *f* (*der Tatsacheninstanz*), Beweisaufnahmeprotokoll *n*, Beweisurkunde *f*, Vorstrafenliste *f*, Prozeßmaterial *n*; Protokoll *n*, Niederschrift *f*, Sachverhalt *m*, Tonträger *m*; **~s** Aufzeichnungen *f/p*, Unterlagen; **~ commission** Staatsurkundenkommission; **~ date** Stichtag des Aktienerwerbs (*bei Namensaktien*); **~ day** Stichtag für die Feststellung d. Aktionäre; **~ inventory** Buchinventur; **~ of conveyance** Auflassungsurkunde; **~s of corporation** Gründungsurkunde und Satzung e–r Gesellschaft; **~ of evidence** Beweisaufnahmeprotokoll; **~ of interrogation** Vernehmungsprotokoll; **~ of nisi prius** Prozeßakte; **~s of original entry** Uraufzeichnungen; **~ of proceedings** Gerichtsakte; **R~Office** Staatsarchiv; Geschäftsstelle e–s Gerichts; **~ office copy** beglaubigte Abschrift aus e–m Staatsarchiv; **~s of the court** Gerichtsakten; **~ retention period** Aufbewahrungsfrist für Geschäftsunterlagen; **~ sheet** Tagebuchblatt, Aktenblatt; **~ title** eingetragene Berechtigung; **abstract of ~** Aktenauszug; **access to ~s** Akteneinsicht; **accounts receivable ~s** Aufzeichnungen der Kundenbuchhaltung; **bad ~** schlechte Vergangenheit; zweifelhafte Vorgeschichte; **books and ~s** Bücher und Geschäftspapiere; **case ~** Gerichtsakte, Prozeßakte; **criminal ~** Strafregister; Vorstrafenliste, Vorstrafe; *no ~ ~: nicht vorbestraft*; **diminuation of ~** Unvollständigkeit (*der erstinstanzlichen*) Gerichtsakte; **expense ~** Unkostenabrechnungen; **inventory ~s** Aufzeichnungen über Vorräte; **judicial ~** → *judicial*; **medical ~** Krankengeschichte, Krankenpapiere; **ministerial ~** eidliche Feststellung; **of ~** gerichtlich eingetragen, amtlich beurkundet, in amtlichen bzw gerichtlichen Urkunden enthalten; **off the ~** vertraulich, nicht zur Veröffentlichung bestimmt, außerhalb des Protokolls; **on ~** schriftlich niedergelegt; **operating ~s** Betriebsaufzeichnungen; **owner of ~** eingetragener Eigentümer; **personal ~** Lebenslauf; **property ~** Liegenschafts- und Inventarverzeichnis; **public ~** öffentliche Urkunde; **to ask for ~s** Akten anfordern; **to draw up a ~** ein Protokoll aufnehmen; **to have a long ~** erheblich vorbestraft sein; **to have a police ~** polizeilich bekannt sein; **to place on ~** schriftlich niederlegen, zu Protokoll geben; **to state for the ~** zu Protokoll erklären; **to take down on ~** protokollieren; **trial ~** Sitzungsprotokoll; **unilateral ~** einseitig unterzeichnete Niederschrift.

record *v* schriftlich festhalten, amtlich aufzeichnen, eintragen (*in ein Register usw*); beurkunden, protokollieren; **~ in the minutes** im Protokoll vermerken; **to have sth ~ed** etwas zu Protokoll geben.

recordable eintragungsfähig, registrierfähig.

recordare Vorlagebeschluß *m*, *ein Rechtsmittel gegen Urteile des Friedensrichters.*

recordation Eintragung *f*, Registrierung *f*.

recorded delivery form Rückschein (*bei Einschreiben mit R.*).

recorder Urkundsbeamter *m*, Protokollführer *m*, Archivar *m*, Registrator *m*; Polizeirichter *m*, Stadtjustitiar *m*, Stadtrichter *m*; (*nebenberufl*) Richter (*Crown Court, High Court, County Courts*), Einzelrichter, beauftragter Richter; **~ of deeds** (=) *etwa: Leiter des Grundbuchamts*; **~ of London** oberster Stadtrichter von London; **~ of**

mortgages and conveyances (=) *etwa: Leiter des Grundbuchamts.*

recording Aufzeichnung *f*, Eintragung *f*, Registrierung *f*; Protokollierung *f*, (Ton)Aufnahme *f*; ~ **act** Gesetz über amtliche Eintragungen *von Urkunden über Grundpfandrechte und sonstige Pfandurkunden*; ~ **clerk** Protokollführer; ~ **fee** Eintragungsgebühr; ~ **office** *etwa*: Grundbuchamt; ~ **system** Eintragungssystem, Grundbuchsystem.

recount *s* Nachzählung *f*, Überprüfung *f* der Stimmenauszählung.

recoup einbehalten, zurückbehalten, ein Zurückbehaltungsrecht ausüben; schadlos halten, e–n Verlust ersetzen, abrechnen; ~ **one's disbursements** s–e Auslagen erstattet erhalten.

recoupment Herabsetzung *f* (*e–r Klageforderung*), Aufrechnung *f*, Zurückbehaltungsrecht *n*, Leistungsverweigerungsrecht *m*.

recourse *s* Rückgriff *m*, Regreß *m*, Entschädigung *f*, Schadloshaltung *f*; ~ **basis** Rückgriffsmöglichkeit; ~ **factoring** Factoring mit Regreß bei Forderungsausfall, unechtes F.; ~ **of guarantee** Kautionsregreß; ~ **to a credit** Inanspruchnahme e–s Kredits; ~ **to a prior party** Sprungregreß; ~ **to the endorser** Rückgriff auf den Indossanten; **liable to** ~ regreßpflichtig; **person liable to** ~ → *person*; **right of** ~ Rückgriffrecht, Regreßanspruch; **without** ~ ohne Regreß.

recourse *v* Rückgriff nehmen, Regreß nehmen.

recover gerichtlich erlangen, erstreiten, erstattet erhalten, beitreiben, wiedererlangen, einklagen; ~ **additional expenses** zusätzliche Kosten erheben; ~ **damages** → *damages*; ~ **in one's suit** den Prozeß gewinnen; ~ **judgment** ein Urteil erlangen; ~ **one's expenses** die Auslagen erstattet bekommen; ~ **over** (*bei e–m Dritten*) Regreß nehmen; ~ **possession** den Besitz wiedererlangen, wieder an sich nehmen; ~ **tax** Steuer abwälzen; ~**ed as damages** als Schadenersatz zugesprochen erhalten; **sum** ~**ed** die Urteilssumme.

recoverable erstattungsfähig, gerichtlich durchsetzbar, klagbar, beitreibbar, zahlbar; ~ **by law** klagbar.

recoveree Regreßpflichtiger *m*.

recoverer Regreßnehmer *m*; *hist* Grundstückserwerber *m*.

recovery Erlangung durch Urteil; Obsiegen *n*; Prozeßergebnis *n*; Beitreibung *f*; Aufschwung *m*; Wiederbelebung *f*; ~ **charges** Einziehungsspesen; ~ **exclusion** teilweise Steuerbefreiung für die Beitreibung von Dubiosen; ~ **in business** Konjunkturbelebung; ~ **in kind** Naturalrestitution; ~ **of costs** Kostenerstattung; Kostenbeitreibung; ~ **of damages** Schadenersatzerlangung; ~ **of debts** gerichtliche Einziehung von Forderungen; ~ **of fines** Beitreibung von Geldstrafen; ~ **of freehold** (*rechtmäßige*) Entsetzung, Besitzkehrung; ~ **of land** Grundstückserlangung, *Verfahren auf* Räumung und Herausgabe *von Grundstücken*; Besitzentziehung durch den Grundstückseigentümer; ~ **of outstanding debts** Beitreibung von Außenständen; ~ **of possession** Wiedererlangung des Besitzes; ~ **of prices** Ansteigen der Preise, Kurserholung; ~ **of the market** Kurserholung, Festigung des Marktes; ~ **of title** Wiedererlangung des Eigentums; Herausgabeverlangen des Eigentümers; ~ **over** Regreß; ~ **value** Ersatzwert, voraussichtlicher Erlös bei Verkauf e–s Inventarstückes; **action for** ~ → *action*; **by way of** ~ auf dem Regreßwege; **double** ~ → *double*; **economic** ~ Wirtschaftsbelebung; **final** ~ obsiegendes Endurteil; rechtskräftiges Obsiegen; **unless** ~ **is had** außer im Erfolgsfall (*Honorar*).

recriminate Gegenbeschuldigung vorbringen.

recrimination Gegenbeschuldigung *f*.

recrudescence Wiederaufleben *n*.

recruit *v* rekrutieren, (*Arbeitskräfte*) anwerben, anheuern.

recruiter Personalbeschaffer *m*, Anwerber *m*.

recruitment Rekrutierung *f*; Anwerbung, Personalbeschaffung *f*, Einstellung *f* von Arbeitskräften; ~ **executive** Sachbearbeiter für Personal-Einstellungen; ~ **process** Einstellungsverfahren; ~ **by word of mouth** mündl Anwerbung; ~ **shortfall** Überschuß an unbesetzten Arbeitsplätzen; **professional** ~ Anwerbung von Freiberuflern.

rectifiable berichtigungsfähig.

rectification Berichtigung *f*, Verbesserung *f*, Richtigstellung *f*; ~ **of an entry** Berichtigung e–r Buchung; ~ **of boundaries** Grenzbereinigung; ~ **of contract** richterliche Vertragshilfe, richterl Ergänzung des Vertragsinhalts; ~ **of mistake** Berichtigung, Verbesserung; ~ **of the land register** Grundbuchberichtigung.

rectify berichtigen, verbessern, richtigstellen; ~**ing entry** Berichtigungsbuchung.

rectum esse vor Gericht im Recht sein.

rectus richtig; in gerader Linie abstammend.

recurring appropriation Bankkredit (zu üblichen Bedingungen).

recur sich wiederholen, immer wieder auftreten, periodisch auftreten; zurückgreifen, Regreß nehmen.

recurrent wiederkehrend; ~ **expenses** regelmäßig wiederkehrende Ausgaben.

recusable willkürlich, auf e–r Willenserklärung beruhend.

recusant Kirchenabtrünniger *m*, Rekusant *m*, Dissentierender *m*.

recusation Ablehnung *f* wegen Befangenheit; Erbausschlagung *f*.

recuse wegen Befangenheit ablehnen.

recycle regenerieren, Abfallstoffe zu Rohstoffen verarbeiten.

recycling (=) Wiederverwertung von Abfallstoffen.

red *adj* rot; *s* Roter *m*, Kommunist *m*; **R~ Book of the Exchequer** (=) *Landverzeichnis vor der normannischen Eroberung*; ~ **carpet** roter Teppich, feierlicher Staatsempfang; großer Bahnhof; ~ **clause** rotgedruckte Klausel, Akkreditivvorschußklausel; ~ **ensign** *brit* der rote Stander (*aller brit Privatschiffe*); ~**-handed** in flagranti, auf frischer Tat; ~**-herring** Ablenkungsmanöver; ~ **herring prospectus** vorläufiger Emissionsprospekt; ~ **ink entry** Verlusteintragung; ~ **interest** → *interest* (2); ~ **light** Rotlicht; Gefahr; ~ **light district** Bordellbezirk; **R~ Menace** Rote Gefahr; ~ **tape** Bürokratismus, Amtsschimmel, Paragraphenreiterei; ~**-tapist** Bürokrat; **to be in the** ~ Verluste haben, rote Zahlen schreiben.

reddendum Entgelt *n*; Zahlungsklausel *in e–m Pacht- bzw Mietvertrag*.

reddition Herausgabe *f*, Eigentumsanerkenntnis.

redecoration Renovierung *f*; **essential internal** ~ notwendige Schönheitsreparaturen.

redeem auslösen, retten, wiedererlangen, aufwiegen, wettmachen, erfüllen; zurückzahlen, amortisieren, (*von einer Belastung durch Zahlung*) befreien, tilgen, einziehen, einlösen; ~ **a bond** e–e Schuldverschreibung einlösen; ~ **a loan** ein Darlehen tilgen; ~ **a mortgage** e–e Hypothek tilgen, von e–m Grundpfandrecht durch Schuldtilgung befreien; ~ **a pledge** ein Pfand einlösen; ~ **an annuity** e–e Rente ablösen.

redeemability Rückkaufbarkeit *f*, Einlösbarkeit *f*, Ablösbarkeit *f*, Kündbarkeit *f*.

redeemable abzahlbar, einlösbar, tilgbar, zurückkaufbar, amortisierbar, erfüllbar, wiedergutzumachen; ~ **dead rent** feste Mindestpacht (*mit Anrechnungsklausel bei höherer Förderleistung*); ~ **equity shares**

rückkaufbare Kapitalanteile; ~ **in advance** vorzeitig tilgbar, ablösbar; ~ **on demand** auf Verlangen einlösbar; ~ **preference shares** → *share*; **not** ~ unkündbar.

re-defection Wiederabtrünnigwerden *n*.

redeliver zurückgeben, wieder abliefern, neu liefern; erneut einreichen.

redelivery Rückgabe *f*, Rücklieferung *f*, Neulieferung *f*; ~ **bond** → *bond* (2).

re-demise *s* Rückübertragung *f*, Rückauflassung *f*; *v* rückübertragen, die Rückauflassung vornehmen.

redemption Wiederkauf *m*, Rückkauf *m*, Amortisation *f*, Rückzahlung *f*, Tilgung *f*, Einlösung *f*, Ablösung *f*; ~ **account** Amortisationskonto; ~ **agreement** Tilgungsvereinbarung; ~ **bonds** neufundierte Obligationen, Umtauschobligationen; ~ **clause** Einlösungsklausel; ~ **date** Tilgungsdatum (*Obligationen zu pari*); ~ **fund** Tilgungsfonds, Amortisationsfonds; ~ **loan** Tilgungsanleihe; ~ **of a mortgage** Tilgung e–r Hypothek; ~ **of a pledge** Pfandeinlösung; ~ **of a promise** Einlösung e–s Versprechens; ~ **of land tax** Grundsteuerablösung; ~ **of legacies** Aufhebung von Vermächtnissen, Vermächtniswiderruf; ~ **of the national debt** Staatsschuldentilgung; ~ **period** (*meist gesetzl*) Nachfrist zur Pfandauslösung bzw Hypothekentilgung; ~ **plan** Tilgungsplan; ~ **premium** Rückzahlungsprämie; ~ **price** Rückkaufspreis, Rücknahmepreis (*Obligationen*); Tilgungskurs; ~ **rate** Tilgungskurs; ~ **reserve** Tilgungsrücklage; ~ **sum** Ablösungssumme; ~ **table** Tilgungsplan; ~ **value** Rückkaufswert; ~ **yield** Tilgungserlös, Rendite; **bill of** ~ Amortisationsschein, Rückkaufsvertrag; **mandatory** ~ Einlösung vor Verfall; **solicited** ~ beantragte Einlösung; **statutory right of** ~ gesetzliches Rückkaufsrecht; nachträgliches gesetzliches Pfandauslösungsrecht; **voluntary** ~ Pfandfreigabe.

redenomination Umbenennung, Währungsumbenennung (*durch Streichen von Nullen u. a.*).

redetermine *v*|*t* von neuem entscheiden, erneut festsetzen (*Kosten*).

re-development | **areas** städtische Sanierungsgebiete **n**|*pl*; ~ **plan** Sanierungsplan.

re-discount *v*|*t* rediskontieren.

redhibition Rückgängigmachung *f* (*e–s Kaufs*), Wandlung *f*.

redirect *adj* wiederum, unmittelbar *kurz für ~ examination qv*.

redirection Umadressierung *f*, Nachsendung *f*.

rediscount *s* Rediskont *m*; *v* rediskontieren; **eligible for** ~ rediskontfähig; **~ing by central banks** Zentralbankrediskontierung; **~ing bills of exchange** Wechselrediskontierung; ~ **rate** Diskontsatz der Zentralbank; Rediskontsatz.

rediscountable rediskontierbar.

redistribution Neuverteilung *f*, Umverteilung *f*.

redistributive umverteilend, Umverteilungs . . .

redraft *s* Ersatzwechsel *m* (*für e–n Protestwechsel*), revidierter Entwurf (*e–r Urkunde*); zweiter Wechsel *m*; ~ **charges** Kosten und Spesen des Ersatzwechsels *s. o.*

redraft *v* neu entwerfen, umformulieren.

redraw zurücktrassieren, e–n Wechsel auf den Vormann ziehen.

redress *s* Wiedergutmachung *f*, Entschädigung *f*; Abwehr e–s rechtswidrigen Zustandes; ~ **of a grievance** Abstellung e–s Übelstandes; **legal** ~ Rechtsbehelf, Rechtsschutz.

redress *v* abhelfen, Unrecht wiedergutmachen, schadlos halten, entschädigen.

redressing the balance of trade Ausgleich *m* der Handelsbilanz.

reduce reduzieren, herabsetzen; *scot* annullieren; ermäßigen, verringern, vermindern; ~ **in value** e–r

Wertminderung ausgesetzt sein; ~ **into money** versilbern, in Geld umsetzen; ~ **the capital stock** Grundkapital herabsetzen; ~ **to practice** praktisch anwenden; ~ **to writing** schriftlich niederlegen; **~d liquidity** → *liquidity*; **~d rate** ermäßigter Satz, ermäßigte Gebühr; **~d rate average clause** → *clause*; **~d rate contribution clause** geminderte Regulierung bei Unterversicherung; **„and ~d"** mit herabgesetztem Kapital.

reducible reduzierbar, herabsetzbar, umrechenbar, zurückführbar.

reducing balance (method of) depreciation → *depreciation*.

reducing working hours Arbeitszeitverkürzung *f*.

reduction Verminderung *f*, Reduzierung *f*, Entwertung *f*, Ermäßigung *f*, Verkleinerung *f*, Abbau *m*, Herabsetzung *f*, Kürzung *f*, Rabatt *m*; Anfechtungsklage *f* (*scot*); ~ **improbation** *scot* Anfechtungsklage wegen Fälschung e–r Urkunde; ~ **in the bank rate** Diskontsenkung; ~ **in value** Wertminderung; ~ **of capital** Kapitalherabsetzung; ~ **of consumption** Konsumverzicht; ~ **of damage** Schadensminderung; ~ **of dividend** Dividendenkürzung; ~ **of earning capacity** Minderung der Erwerbsfähigkeit; ~ **of prior provisions** Auflösung von Wertberichtigungen und Rückstellungen; ~ **of purchase price** Minderung; ~ **of taxes** Steuersenkung; ~ **to possession** Besitz- und Nutzungserlangung (*auf Grund e–s Anspruchs*); ~ **to practice** (*gewerblich*) Anwendbarkeit (*e–r Erfindung*); ~ **to present worth** Zurückführung (*zukünftigen Schadens*) auf den jetzigen Wert; **data** ~ Datenverarbeitung; **flat-rate** ~ pauschaler Abschlag; **no ~s** feste Preise.

redundancy Überflüssiges *n* (*in e–m Schriftsatz*), Weitschweifigkeit *f*, Überschuß *m*, Abbau von Arbeitskräften; Stellenlosigkeit *f*; ~ **letter** Kündigungsschreiben (des Arbeitgebers), Ausstellungsschr.; ~ **payment** soziale Abfindung für den Verlust des Arbeitsplatzes, Entlassungsabfindung; ~ **scheme** Sozialplan, Arbeitsausfallkasse; **compulsory ~ies** Massenentlassungen; **voluntary** ~ freiwilliger Verzicht auf den Arbeitsplatz.

redundant überzählig, überschüssig, überflüssig; **to be made** ~ voraussichtl als überflüssig entlassen werden; seinen Arbeitsplatz (*durch Rationalisierung etc*) verlieren.

re-education Umerziehung.

re-elect wiederwählen.

re-election Wiederwahl *f*; **to come up for** ~ für die Wiederwahl in Betracht kommen; **to stand for** ~ sich zur Wiederwahl stellen.

re-eligible wiederwählbar (*für ein Amt*).

re-employment Ersatzarbeitsplatz *m*, Wiederbeschäftigung *f*.

re-enact novellieren; erneut in Kraft setzen.

re-enactment erneute Inkraftsetzung *f*, Neufassung e–s Gesetzes, Gesetzesnovelle *f*; neue Darstellung *f*; ~ **of a crime** Rekonstruktion e–s Verbrechens.

re-engagement Wiedereinstellung *e–s entlassenen Arbeitnehmers*.

re-entry Wiederinbesitznahme *f*, Rücknahme des Besitzes; Neueintragung *f*, Wiedereintritt *m*.

re-establish wiederherstellen, wiedereinsetzen; **~ing credit** die Glaubwürdigkeit wiederherzustellen versuchen.

re-establishment Wiederherstellung *f*, Wiedereinsetzung *f*.

reeve Gemeindevorsteher *m*, Schulze *m*.

re-examination weitere Prüfung *f*, nochmalige Vernehmung *f* (*nach der Vernehmung von Zeugen durch die Gegenseite*).

re-examine nochmals überprüfen, erneut vernehmen.

re-execution Neuunterfertigung *f*, nochmalige Ausfertigung *f*.

re-exchange Wechselprotestunkosten *pl* im Ausland; Rückwechsel *m*, Rückrechnung *f*.

re-export *s* Wiederausfuhr *f*, Reexport *m*.
re-export *v* reexportieren.
re-extent erneute Zwangsverwaltung *f* (*vgl extent*).
refection Reparatur *f*, Wiederherstellung *f*; Erfrischung *f*, Imbiß *n*.
refer | a case to a court e–n Fall gerichtlich geltend machen; ~ **back** zurückverweisen; ~ **to arbitration** *Streitfall* e–m Schiedsgericht unterbreiten, ein Schiedsgericht anrufen; ~ **to drawer** (*R*/D) „nicht gedeckt", „zurück an den Aussteller" (*bei ungedecktem Scheck*).
referability Bezug *m*, innerer Zusammenhang *m*.
referee beauftragter Richter *m*, Einzelrichter *m*; Schiedsrichter *m*, Schlichter *m*; Referenz *f* (*Person*); Schiedsreferent *m*, Sachverständiger *m*, Sachbearbeiter *m*; ~ **in bankruptcy** Rechtspfleger im Konkursgericht; Konkursrichter; ~ **in case of need** Notadressat (*Wechsel*); **official r~ opinion** Schiedsgutachten; Berichterstatter, bestellter, beauftragter Richter; **special** ~ vereinbarter Schiedsrichter.
reference Bezugnahme *f*, Hinweis *m*, Aktenzeichen *n*, Verweisung *f*, Kreditwürdigkeitsprüfung *f*, Vorlage *f* an Schiedsgericht, Schiedsvereinbarung *f*, Referenz *f*, Zeugnis *m*; ~ **agency** Auskunftei; ~ **document** Bezugsurkunde; ~ **from the police** polizeiliches Führungszeugnis; ~ **in case of need** Notadresse; ~ **is made to** es wird Bezug genommen auf; ~ **library** Handbibliothek; Präsenzbibliothek; ~ **material** Quellen(material), Fundstellen, Literaturbeiträge; ~ **number** Geschäftszeichen, Aktenzeichen; ~ **of action** (*gerichtliche*) Verweisung eines *anhängigen Rechtsstreits* an Schiedsgutachten *bzw. Schiedsrichter;* ~ **patterns** zurückbehaltene Warenproben; ~ **statute** gesetzliche Vorschrift über Anwendung anderer Gesetze; ~ **to authorities** Quellenangabe; ~ **to record** Aktenzeichen; **banker's** ~ Bankauskunft, Bankreferenz; **compulsory** ~ Verweisung an den beauftragten Richter; **for ease of** ~ zur Erleichterung der Auffindung; **job** ~ Arbeitszeugnis; **our** ~ unser Aktenzeichen; **outside our** ~ außerhalb unserer Zuständigkeit; **police** ~ polizeiliches Führungszeugnis; **statutory** ~ gesetzlicher Hinweis.
referenced *adj* oben angegeben, gegenständlich, diesbezüglich.
referendum Volksentschied *m*, Volksbefragung *f*; Rückfrage *f* e–s Missionschefs bei seiner Heimatbehörde.
referral Verweisung *f*, Zwangsvorlage *f z. B. zur Überprüfung von Übernahmeangebot.*
re-finance Refinanzierung *f*; ~ **credit** Zwischenkredit *m*.
refine veredeln, raffinieren.
refinement überflüssiges Beiwerk *n* (*in Schriftsätzen*), Spitzfindigkeit *f*.
reflag *v/t* umflaggen, die Flagge wechseln.
reflagging Flaggenwechsel *m*, Umflaggen *n*.
reflation Reflation *f*; Konjunkturbelebung *f* durch Geldvermehrung.
reflection Erwägung *f*, Nachdenken *n*, tadelnde Bemerkung *f*, (*nachteilige*) Unterstellung *f*.
refloat sanieren, wieder flott machen; ~ **a loan** *e–e* Anleihe neu auflegen.
refloating of a company Reorganisation *f* e–r Gesellschaft.
reform *s* Reform *f*, Umbildung *f*, Neugestaltung *f*; Besserung *f* des Lebenswandels; ~ **act** Reformgesetz; ~ **of land tenure** Bodenreform; ~ **school** → *school*; **agrarian** ~ Bodenreform; **constitutional** ~ Verfassungreform; **financial** ~ Finanzrefrom, Steuerreform; **monetary** ~ Währungsreform; **penal** ~ Strafrechtsreform; **sweeping** ~ durchgreifende Reform.
reform *v* verbessern, reformieren, sich bessern, umgestalten; ~ **an instrument** e–e mit Formmängeln behaftete Urkunde als geheilt be-

handeln; ~**ed drunkard** geheilter Trinker.

reformation Besserung *f*, Neugestaltung *f*; Vertragsänderung *f*, Verurteilung *f* zur Vertragsberichtigung.

reformatory Jugendgefängis *n*; Besserungsanstalt *f*; **inebriate** ~ Trinkerheilanstalt.

refractoriness Widersetzlichkeit *f*.

refractory widersetzlich, störrisch, ungehorsam.

refrain from unterlassen, absehen von, Abstand nehmen von.

refresher außerordentliche Anwaltsgebühr *f* (*bei langdauerndem Prozeß bzw. mehrtätiger Verhandlung*); ~ **fee** = *refresher qv*.

refreshing (the) memory Auffrischung des Gedächtnisses (*durch Einsichtnahme in Schriftstücke*).

refuge Zufluchtsort *m*, Asyl *n*; ~ **for battered women** Frauenhaus.

refugee Flüchtling *m*; ~ **currency** Kapitalfluchtwährung; **admission of** ~**s** Aufnahme von Flüchtlingen.

refund *s* Erstattung *f*, Rückvergütung *f*, Kaufpreisrückzahlung; ~ **annuity contract** Rentenversicherung(svertrag); ~ **claim** Steuererstattungsanspruch; ~ **credit** Remboursgeschäft; ~ **of tax(es)** Steuerrückerstattung.

refund *v* zurückzahlen, vergüten, umfinanzieren; ~ **the costs** die Kosten erstatten.

refunding Refinanzierung *f* zur Ablösung e–r Schuld; Refundierung *f* (*Ablösung von Bankkrediten durch Emission von Aktien bzw. Obligationen)*; *Rückvergütung f*, Erstattung *f*; Ablösung *f*, ~ **bond** Umtauschobligation, Ablösungsschuldverschreibung; ~ **of a loan** Refundierung e–r Anleihe; ~ **of bonds** Refundierung von Obligationen (*durch Umtausch*); ~ **of postage** Portovergütung.

refurbish *v*|*t* renovieren.

refurbishment Renovierung *f*.

refurnish renovieren.

refusal Ablehnung *f*, Verweigerung *f*, abschlägiger Bescheid *m*; ~ **of acceptance** Annahmeverweigerung; ~ **of entry** Versagung der Einreiseerlaubnis; ~ **of goods** Abnahmeverweigerung; ~ **of justice** Rechtsverweigerung; ~ **to accept** Annahmeverweigerung, Ablehnung der Leistung; ~ **to answer questions** Aussageverweigerung; ~ **to give evidence** Zeugnisverweigerung, Aussageverweigerung; ~ **to undergo an examination** Weigerung sich (ärztlich) untersuchen zu lassen; **first** ~ → *first*; **in case of** ~ bei Ablehnung, im Weigerungsfall; **outright** ~ glatte Weigerung; **wilful** ~ willkürliche Ablehnung.

refuse *s* Abfall *m*, Müll *m*; Ausschußware *f*; **R**~ **Disposal (Amenity) Act** Abfallbeseitigungsgesetz; ~ **collector** Müll(abfuhr)mann; ~ **disposal** Müllabfuhr; **domestic** ~ Hausmüll; **house** ~ Wohnungsmüll.

refuse *v* ablehnen, zurückweisen, verweigern, abschlagen; ~ **a patent** ein Patent versagen; ~ **an appeal** ein Rechtsmittel nicht zulassen; ~ **delivery** Herausgabe verweigern; ~ **payment** Zahlung verweigern; ~ **to take delivery** die Annahme verweigern; **when** ~**d** bei Weigerung.

refutable widerlegbar.

refutation Widerlegung *f*, Zurückweisung *f*.

refute widerlegen.

regalia Regalien *n*|*pl*, Vorrechte *n*|*pl* der Krone; Krönungsinsignien *n*|*pl*.

regality Regal *n*, Souveränität *f*, Königswürde *f*, von der Krone verliehene Gerichtsbarkeit *f*; königliches Hoheitsrecht *n*, Gerichtsbezirk *m*, ein zum Richter eingesetzter Lord *m*.

regard *s* Beziehung *f*, Hinsicht *f*, Rücksicht *f*; *hist* Besichtigung *f*, Überwachung *f*; **having** ~ **to** im Hinblick auf, mit Rücksicht auf; **in** ~ **to** in bezug auf, bezüglich; **with** ~ **to** betreffs, bezüglich, in bezug auf; **with due** ~ unter gebührender Berücksichtigung.

regard *v* berücksichtigen, betrachten, betreffen.
regardless of ohne Rücksicht auf.
regency Herrschaft *f*, Regierungszeit *f*, Regentschaft *f*.
regent Regent *m*, Prinzregent *m*, Reichsverweser *m*; **board of ~s** Kuratorium (*Hochschule*).
regicide Königsmord *m*, Königsmörder *m*.
regime Regierungsform *f*, Regime *n*, Staatsform *f*, System *n*; Ordnung *f*, Regelung *f*; **~ of separation of goods** Gütertrennung; **contractual ~** vertragliches Güterrecht; **matrimonial ~** ehelicher Güterstand; **property ~** Güterstand; **statutory ~** gesetzlicher Güterstand.
regimental debts Nachlaßverwaltung von Militärpersonen; Vermögensverwaltung von geschäftsunfähigen Militärpersonen *bzw Deserteuren*.
Regina Reg. oder R brit. Königin *f* (*Rubrum bes in Strafsachen*); **R ~** vs. (= *versus*) **Smith** In der Strafsache gegen Smith.
region Gebiet *n*, Bereich *m*; Region *f*.
regional regional; **~ clearing house** regionale Scheckverrechnungsstelle; **~ differential** regionale Lohnunterschiede; **~ economic policy** Standortpolitik.
register *s* Register *n*, Liste *f*, Rolle *f*, Verzeichnis *n*; gerichtl Formularbuch *n*; Personenstandsbuch *n*, Schiffsregister *n*; Registerführer *m*; **~ book** Schiffshypothekenregister; **~ of accidents** Betriebsunfallverzeichnis; **~ of births** Geburtenbuch; **~ of births, deaths and marriages** Personenstandsbücher; **R ~ of Charges** amtl Verzeichnis der Belastungen von Kapitalgesellschaften; Pfandbuch, Hypothekenregister; **R ~ of Companies** Gesellschaftsregister, Handelsregister für Körperschaften; **~ of convictions** Strafregister; **~ of co-operative societies** Genossenschaftsregister; **~ of copyrights** Urheberrolle, Copyright-Register; **~ of debenture holders** Liste der Schuldverschreibungsinhaber; **~ of deeds** Grundbuchamt; Grundbuchbeamter, **R~ of Designs** Musterregister, Geschmacksmusterrolle; **~ of directors** Liste der Vorstandsmitglieder; **~ of directors' interests** Verzeichnis von persönl Beteiligungen von Vorstandsmitgl.; **~ of marriages** Heiratsbuch; **~ of members** *brit* Aktienbuch, Verzeichnis der Aktionäre; **R~ of Members' Interests** Verzeichnis von Beteiligungen der Abgeordneten des Unterhauses; **~ of mortgages** Hypothekenregister; **~ of (parliamentary) electors** Wählerliste; **R~ of European Patents** Europäisches Patentregister; **~ of patents** Patentrolle; **R~ of Sasines** → *sasine*; **~ of shareholders** Aktionärsregister, Aktienbuch; **~ of ships** Schiffsregister; **~ of trade marks** Warenzeichenrolle; **~ of transfers** Register für Aktienübertragungen; **~ of vital statistics** Personenstandsbücher; **~ of writs** Prozeßregister; **cash ~** Registrierkasse, Kassenbuch; **Charge R~** → *charge*; **commercial ~** Handelsregister; **debt ~** Schuldbuch; **electoral ~** Wählerverzeichnis; **estate ~** Grundbuch; **Federal R~** (=) Bundesanzeiger; **General R~ Office** Hauptstandesamt; **professional ~** Zulassungsregister (*Ärzte*), **property ~** (Grundstücks-)Bestandsverzeichnis; **public ~** amtl Verzeichnis, öffentl Register, Kunden-kredit-Register.
register *v* eintragen, (sich) einschreiben, registrieren, (sich anmelden).
registered eingetragen, registriert, eingeschrieben, gesetzlich geschützt; **~ agent for service of process** ständiger Zustellungsbevollmächtigter; **~ business name** eingetragene Firma; **~ holding company** registrierte Holdinggesellschaft (*US Securities and Exchange Comm.; Offenlegungspflichten*); **~ land** → *registered land*; **~ office** → *office*; **~ provident societies**

Versicherungsvereine auf Gegenseitigkeit.

registered land grundbuchmäßig erfaßte(s) Grundstück(e); ~ **areas** Gebiete mit Grundbuchzwang; ~ **certificate** amtlicher Grundbuchauszug.

registrability Eintragungsfähigkeit *f*, Zulässigkeit *f* der Eintragung.

registrable eintragungsfähig.

registrant Anmelder *m*; Zeicheninhaber *m*.

registrar Standesbeamter *m*, Registerführer *m*, Leiter des Registergerichts, Geschäftsstellenleiter *m*, Urkundsbeamter *m*, Rechtspfleger *m* mit richterlichen Aufgaben; *auch: beauftragter richterlicher Leiter e–r Außenstelle des Londoner Zentralgerichts; etwa:* Familienrichter; ~ **and merchants** beauftragter Rechtspfleger mit kaufmännischen Beisitzern (*zur Schadensfeststellung in Seesachen*); **R~ General** Leiter der Personenstandsbehörde; ~ *~'s license relating to marriage*: standesamtl. Sondererlaubnis zur Eheschließung an anderem Ort; ~ **in bankruptcy** Rechtspfleger im Konkursgericht; ~ **of births, deaths and marriages** Standesbeamter, Standesamt; **R~ of Companies** Leiter des Handelsregisters für Kapitalgesellschaften; ~ **of deeds** Registerführer im Grundbuchamt; **R~ of Friendly Societies** Leiter des Vereins- und Genossenschaftsregisters; **~'s office** Standesamt, Geschäftsstelle; **court** ~ Urkundsbeamter der Geschäftsstelle, Protokollführer; **deputy** ~ → *deputy*; **superintendent** ~ Bezirksstandesbeamter.

registration Registrierung *f*, Eintragung *f*, Anmeldung *f*; Immatrikulation *f*; ~ **authorities** Meldebehörden; ~ **dues** Eintragungsgebühr(en); ~ **fee** → *fee (1)*; ~ **for execution** Eintragung e–r Unterwerfungsklausel; ~ **for preservation** Eintragung zur Erhaltung e–r Urkunde; ~ **for publication** Eintragung zwecks Aufgebots; ~ **label** Einschreibezettel; ~ **law** Melderecht; ~ **of aliens** *obligatorische* Registrierung von Ausländern; ~ **of bills of sale** Eintragung von Sicherungsübereignungsverträgen; ~ **of births** standesamtliche Geburteneintragung, Geburtenregistrierung; ~ **of burials** registermäßige Erfassung von Beerdigungen; ~ **of business names** Firmeneintragung; *GB* gesetzlich vorgeschriebene Registrierung von Firmennamen, Unternehmensbezeichnungen und Sozietätsbezeichnungen (*außer bei Führung des Namens des Geschäftsinhabers*); ~ **of citizenship** Staatsangehörigkeitserfassung; ~ **of copyright** Urheberrechtseintragung; ~ **of design** Geschmacksmustereintragung; ~ **of estate contract** *etwa* Auflassungsvormerkung; ~ **of foreign nationals** Erfassung von Ausländern (*im Einwohnermeldeamt*); ~ **of land** Eintragung von Grundbesitz, Einführung des Grundbuchsystems, Grundbucheintragung; ~ **of patent** Eintragung in die Patentrolle; ~ **of road vehicles** Kraftfahrzeugzulassung; ~ **of stock** namentliche Erfassung der Aktionäre, Führung eines Aktienbuches; ~ **of title (to land)** Eintragung von Grundstückseigentumsurkunden (*bzw grundbuchmäßige Erfassung von Landbesitz, eigentumsähnlichen Herrschafts- und Besitzrechten*); ~ **of trade marks** Registrierung von Warenzeichen, Warenzeicheneintragung; ~ **period** Eintragungsdauer; ~ **statement** Angaben (*zB*) *im Börsenzulassungsantrag*; **application for** ~ → *application (1 bzw 2)*; **certificate of** ~ → *certificate*; **compulsory** ~ Eintragungszwang, Grundbuchzwang; Meldepflicht; **general** ~ allgemeine Eintragung, *bes Eintragung in die ständige Wählerliste*; **incapable of** ~ nicht eintragungsfähig, von Eintragung ausgeschlossen; **Land R~ Act** Grundbuchordnung; **new** ~ Neueintragung; **special** ~ Sondereintragung, *bes Wählereintragung für e–n einmaligen Zweck;* **subject to** ~ eintragungspflichtig; **to expunge a** ~ e–e Eintragung löschen.

registry Registrierung *f*, Registratur *f*, Register *n*, Registeramt *n*; Gerichtsgeschäftsstelle *f*; ~ **of deeds** (Grundstücks-)Urkundenregisteramt (*etwa: Grundbuchamt, US*), Urkundenrolle; ~ **of ships** Eintragung ins Schiffsregister; ~ **office** *US* Registerbehörde; *brit* Standesamt; **Company R**~ Handelsregister für Kapitalgesellschaften (*etwa: HRB*); **court** ~ Geschäftsstelle; **district**~ → *district*; **foreign** ~ ausländisches Schiffsregister, ausländ. Flagge; **land** ~ → *land*; **new** ~**ies** Neuzulassungen (*Kfz*); **port of** ~ → *port*; **probate** ~ → *probate*; **servants'** ~ Stellenvermittlung für Hausangestellte.

regnal | **day** Jahrestag des Regierungsantritts; ~ **years** Regierungsjahre, Regierungszeit (*e–s Monarchen*).

regnant herrschend, regierend.

regrade neu einstufen.

re-grant *s* Neugewährung *f*, Neubelehnung *f*, Wiederverpachung *f*.

regrating unzulässiger Lebensmitteleinkauf *m* auf Märkten (*zwecks Wiederverkauf*).

regress Wiederinbesitznahme *f*, Rückgang *m*, Rückgriff *m*; **letters of** ~ (=) *scot* Verpflichtungserklärung des Grundherrn, dem Grundpfandschuldner den Besitz des Pfandgrundstücks bei Schuldtilgung wieder zu überlassen.

regular regelmäßig, normal, ständig, ordnungsgemäß, ordentlich, formal; ~ **and established place of business** Betriebsstätte; ~ **course of business** normaler Geschäftsablauf; ~**-interval scheduling** Taktfahrplan(system); ~ **periodical payments** regelmäßig wiederkehrende Zahlungen, Rente; ~ **place of business** Betriebsstätte; ~ **way (delivery)** *exch Lieferung am 1. Werktag bei staatlichen Wertpapieren bzw am 2. Werktag bei sonstigen Obligationen, jeweils nach dem Tage des Abschlusses.*

regularity Regelmäßigkeit *f*, Richtigkeit *f*.

regularize regeln, regulieren, bereinigen.

regularly regelmäßig, ordnungsgemäß; ~ **employed** ständig beschäftigt.

regulars Ordensgeistliche *m|pl*, Berufssoldaten *m|pl*; treue Parteianhänger *m|pl*; Stammkunden *m|pl*.

regulate *v|t* regulieren, lenken, ordnen.

regulated *adj* reguliert, vorschriftsgebunden, formgebunden, kontrolliert; ~ **unofficial dealing** geregelter Freiverkehr.

regulation Vorschrift *f*, Verordnung *f*, Anordnung *f*, Ausführungsbestimmung *f*; ~**s** Satzung *f*; ~ **charge** Geschäftszulassungsabgabe; ~ **of an executive department** Verwaltungsverordnung; ~ **of banking** staatliche Ordnung des Kreditwesens; ~ **of business** Wirtschaftslenkung; ~ **of foreign trade** Außenhandelsregelung; ~ **of lending operations** staatl Kreditüberwachung; ~ **of private carriers** Vorschriften für Transportunternehmern; **according to** ~**s** vorschriftsmäßig; **administrative** ~**s** Ausführungsbestimmungen; Verwaltungsvorschriften; **agricultural** ~ Agrarordnung; **building** ~**s** → *building*; **censor** ~**s** Zensurvorschriften; **contrary to** ~**s** → *contrary*; **currency** ~**s** Devisenbestimmungen; **domestic** ~**s** innerstaatliche Vorschriften; **extraterritorial** ~ Versicherungsaufsicht über außerstaatliche Geschäftstätigkeit innerstaatlicher Gesellschaften; **factory** → *factory*; **internal** ~**s** Dienstvorschriften; **laws and** ~**s** Gesetze und Verordnungen; **obligatory** ~ Mußvorschrift; **postal** ~**s** Postvorschriften, Postordnung; **supplementary** ~**s** ergänzende Vorschriften.

regulator Überwachungsbeamter *m*, Kontrolleur *m*; Steuerbefugnis *f*.

regulatory regelnd, regulativ; ~ **body** Aufsichtsbehörde, Kontrollbehörde; ~ **function** Zuständigkeit für Erlaß von Verwaltungsvorschriften; ~ **order** Verwaltungsvorschrift; ~ **provisions** Verwaltungsvorschriften;

rehabilitate rehabilitieren, in frühere Rechte wiedereinsetzen.

rehabilitation Rehabilitierung *f*, Sanierung *f*, Wiedereinsetzung *f* in frühere Rechte; ~ **and settlement** Resozialisierung; ~ **order** Sanierungsanordnung ~ **period** Rehabilitierungszeit, Straftilgungszeit; **area** ~ → *area*; **vocational** ~ → *vocational*.

rehear (= *re-hear*) nochmals in die mündliche Verhandlung eintreten.

rehearing (*re-hearing*) erneute Verhandlung; erneuter Eintritt in die mündliche Verhandlung *bzw* Hauptverhandlung *f*, erneute Untersuchung *f*.

rehousing anderweitige Unterbringung *f*, Verschaffung e–r Ersatzwohnung; **permanent** ~ Ersatzwohnungsbeschaffung.

rehypothecation Weiterverpfändung *f* (*von Sicherheiten e–s Börsenkunden*); zweite Lombardierung *f*.

reign Herrschaft *f*, Regierung *f*, Regierungszeit *f*; ~ **of terror** Schreckensherrschaft.

reimbursable erstattungsfähig, rückzahlbar.

reimburse zurückzahlen, zurückerstatten, vergüten, entschädigen; **entitled to** ~ **himself** erstattungsberechtigt, entnahmeberechtigt (für Auslagen); **liable to** ~ erstattungspflichtig.

reimbursement Rückzahlung *f*, Rückvergütung *f*; ~ **credit** Rembourskredit, Trassierungskredit; ~ **of expenses** Erstattung von Auslagen; ~ **of taxes** Steuererstattung.

rein on costs (strenge) Kostenkontrolle, Maßhalten bei den Kosten.

reincorporation erneute Gründung e–r juristischen Person.

reinforcement Verstärkung *f*.

reinstall (*reinstal*) wiedereinsetzen (*in ein Amt*).

reinstal(l)ment Wiedereinsetzung *f*.

reinstate wiederinstandsetzen, wiedereinsetzen, wiederzulassen; Wiedereinsetzung in den vorigen Stand gewähren, wieder in Kraft setzen; ~ **a case** Wiedereinsetzung in den vorigen Stand gewähren, klageabweisendes Urteil aufheben; ~ **a policy holder** den Versicherungsvertrag wieder in Kraft setzen; ~ **workers** Arbeiter wiedereinstellen.

reinstatement Wiedereinstellung *f*; Wiederinstandsetzung *f*, Wiedereinsetzung *f* in den vorigen Stand, Wiederaufleben *n e–r Versicherung*; ~ **in civil employment** Wiedereinstellung (*vom Wehrdienst Entlassener*); ~ **order** Wiedereinstellungsverfügung.

reinsurance (*re-insurance*) Rückversicherung *f*; ~ **at original terms** = *back-to-back qv*; ~ **quota share** Rückversicherungsquote; **stop-loss** ~ Stopp-Loss Rückversicherung; (*pauschale Mehrbedarfsdekkung*); **surplus** ~ Exzendentenrückversicherung; ~ **company** Rückversicherungsgesellschaft; **back-to-back** ~ Rückversicherung zu Originalbedingungen (*dh. mit voller Schicksalsteilung in bezug auf das rückversicherte technische Risiko*); **excess** ~ Exzedentenrückversicherung; Rückversicherung für einen Spitzenbetrag; **excess loss** ~ Schadens-Exzedenten-Rückversicherung, unbegrenzte Rückversicherung; **flat** ~ unkündbare Rückversicherung; **treaty** ~ globale Rückversicherung durch Staatsverträge.

reinsure rückversichern.

reintegration Wiederherstellung *f*, Erneuerung *f*.

reinvest reinvestieren, wiederanlegen; jmdn wiedereinsetzen; ~ **profits** Gewinn wiederanlegen.

reinvestment Wiederanlage *f*, Reinvestierung *f*; ~ **discount** → *discount*.

reissue (= *re-issue*) erneute Herausgabe *f*; Neuauflage *f*; Neuausgabe *f*; ~ **of patents** Wiedererteilung von Patenten; ~ **patent** Abänderungspatent *n*.
reject versagen, verwerfen, zurückweisen, ablehnen, beanstanden.
rejection Zurückweisung *f*, Ablehnung *f* (*der Leistung, der Annahme*), Abnahmeverweigerung *f*; ~ **of a motion** Ablehnung e–s Antrags; ~ **of offer** Ablehnung e–s Angebots.
rejects Ausschußware *f*; fehlerhafte Stücke.
rejoin nochmals erwidern, duplizieren.
rejoinder Erwiderung *f*, Duplik *f*, erneute Einwendung *f*.
rejoining gratis nicht notwendige Duplik *f*.
rejudge neu untersuchen, nachprüfen, neu beurteilen, ein neues Urteil fällen.
relapse Rückfall *m*; Rückschlag *m*.
relapser Abtrünninger *m*, Renegat *m*.
related verbunden, verwandt; ~ **by blood** blutsverwandt; ~ **by marriage** verschwägert; ~ **company** Konzerngesellschaft.
relation Verhältnis *n*, Beziehung *f*, Tatbestandsangabe *f*; Rechtsbeziehung *f*, Vortrag *m* des Sachverhalts in der Klage; ~**s** Verwandte, Verwandte und Verschwägerte; ~ **back** Rückbeziehung, Rückwirkung; ~ **by blood** Verwandtschaft; ~**s by lineal descent** Verwandtschaft in gerader Linie; ~**s by marriage** Schwägerschaft, Verschwägerte; ~**s in direct line** Verwandte in gerader Linie; ~ **inter se** Innenverhältnis; ~ **to third parties** Außenverhältnis; **business** ~**s** Geschäftsverbindungen; **commercial** ~**s** wirtschaftl Beziehungen, Handelsbeziehungen; **confidential** ~ Vertrauensverhältnis; **conjugal** ~**s** eheliche Beziehungen; **consensual** ~**s** schuldrechtliche Beziehungen; **contractual** ~ Vertragsverhältnis, Vertragsbeziehung, Stellung als Vertragspartei; **diplomatic** ~**s** → *diplomatic*; **doctrine of** ~**s** *Fiktion der Zurückbeziehung auf den ersten Zeitpunkt bei mehrseitigen Rechtsgeschäften*; **domestic** ~ Familienbeziehungen; **fiduciary** ~ Vertrauensverhältnis, Treueverhältnis, Treuhandverhältnis; **filial** ~ Kindschaft(sbeziehung); **friendly** ~ freundschaftl. Beziehungen; **industrial** ~**s** → *industrial*; **obligatory** ~ schuldrechtliche Beziehung.
relationship Verhältnis *n*, Rechtsbeziehung *f*, Verwandtschaft *f* (Familien)Angehörigkeit *f*; Sippe *f*; **adoptive** ~ Adoptionsverhältnis, **confidential** ~ Vertrauensverhältnis; **degree of** ~ Verwandtschaftsgrad; **external** ~ Außenverhältnis; **illicit** ~ ehewidrige Beziehungen; Verhältnis; **internal** ~ Innenverhältnis; **legal** ~ Rechtsverhältnis; **special** ~ besondere Beziehungen.
relative *adj* relativ, bezüglich, verhältnismäßig.
relative *s* Verwandter bzw Verschwägerter, ~ **of the half blood** halbbürtiger Verwandter; ~ **of the whole blood** vollbürtiger Verwandter; **near** ~ Angehöriger; **remote** ~ entfernter Angehöriger.
relator Popularkläger *m*; Nebenkläger *m*; Popularklägerin *f*; Nebenklägerin *f*; Anzeigeerstatter *m*, Antragsteller *m*, Denunziant *m*; ~ **action** Popularklage (*Proforma-Kläger ist der Attorney General*).
relatrix Anzeigeerstatterin *f*, Antragstellerin *f*, Denunziantin *f*.
relax lockern, mildern, entspannen; ~ **requirements** Vorschriften mildern, Anforderungen herabsetzen.
relaxation Lockerung *f*, Milderung *f*, Entspannung *f*, Schuldentlassung *f*.
release *s* Freilassung *f*, Freigabe *f*, Freistellung *f*; Freigabe *f* zur Veröffentlichung, Entlassung *f*, Aufhebung *f*; Entlastung *f*, negatives Schuldanerkenntnis *f*; Veräußerung *f*; Treuhandaufhebungsurkunde; Eigentumsüberlassung *f* an den Grundbesitzer; ~ **by creditors on payment of composition** Erlaß der Restschulden bei Zahlung der

Vergleichsquote; ~ **from liability** Haftungsfreistellung, Entlastung; ~ **note** Freigabemitteilung; ~ **of a blocked account** Freigabe e–s gesperrten Kontos; ~ **of a debt** Erlaß e–r Schuld; ~ **of a reserve** Auflösung e–r Rückstellung; ~ **of a right** Verzicht auf ein Recht; ~ **of easement** Verzicht auf Dienstbarkeit, Löschung e–r Dienstbarkeit; ~ **of expectancy** Erbanwartschaftsverzicht; ~ **of funds** Freigabe von Mitteln; ~ **of liquidators** Entlastung und Amtsbeendigung von Liquidatoren; ~ **of mortgage** löschungsfähige Quittung mit Pfandfreigabe; ~ **of powers** Verzicht auf Veräußerungsbefugnis; ~ **on bail** Haftentlassung gegen Sicherheitsleistung; ~ **on licence** bedingte Entlassung; ~ **to uses** *hist* Grundstücksauflassung; **conditional** ~ bedingte Freilassung; **deed of** ~ → *deed*; **early** ~ vorzeitige Entlassung; **express** ~ formeller Erlaß e–r Schuld, beurkundeter Verzicht (*auf dingliches Recht*); **general** ~ allgemeine Abfindungserklärung, Verzicht auf alle gegenwärtigen und zukünftigen Ansprüche; **illegal** ~ widerrechtliche Freilassung; **implied** ~ stillschweigender Schulderlaß, konkludenter Verzicht.

release *v* freilassen, freigeben, befreien, entlassen; ~ **a debt** auf eine Forderung verzichten; ~ **from a guarantee** aus e–r Garantieverpflichtung entlassen; ~ **from custody** aus der Haft entlassen; ~ **from the oath** vom Eid entbinden; ~ **on probation** auf Bewährung entlassen.

re-lease neuverpachten, weiterverpachten.

releasee *durch e–n Verzicht* Begünstigter *m, von der Haftung* Freigestellter *m, bereits besitzender* Grundstückserwerber *m*.

releaser (= releasor) Verzichtender *m*, Freigebender *m*, Veräußerer *m e–s Grundstücksrechts*.

relegate *des Landes* verweisen.

relegation Landesverweisung *f*, Relegation *f*, Verbannung *f*.

re-let neuvermieten; weitervermieten (*an e–n Nachmieter*).

relevance Relevanz *f* (= *relevancy qv*).

relevancy Relevanz *f*, Erheblichkeit *f*, Wichtigkeit *f*; ~ **in law** Rechtserheblichkeit; ~ **of evidence** Beweiserheblichkeit; **legal** ~ formelle Zulässigkeit als Beweismittel.

relevant anwendbar, entscheidungserheblich, belangvoll, rechtserheblich, sachdienlich, einschlägig; ~ **to the issue** rechtserheblich, entscheidungserheblich; **legally** ~ **to** rechtserheblich für; ~ **document** rechtserhebliche Urkunde; ~ **evidence** sachdienlicher Beweis, zulässiges Beweismittel; ~ **in law** rechtlich relevant; ~ **information** zweckdienliche Angaben.

reliability Verlaß *m*, Verläßlichkeit *f*, Zuverlässigkeit *f*, Bonität *f*; ~ **run** Erprobungsfahrt.

reliable zuverlässig, vertrauenswürdig, kreditwürdig; ~ **authority** zuverlässige Quelle, Gewährsmann; ~ **firm** reelle Firma; ~ **person** Vertrauensperson; ~ **witness** glaubwürdiger Zeuge.

reliance Verlaß *m*, Vertrauen *n*, Stütze *f*, Hilfe *f*; **public** ~ öffentlicher Glaube.

relict Relikt *n*; überlebender Ehegatte *m*.

reliction Anwachsung *f* (*durch Zurückweichen von Gewässern*).

relief Entlastung *f*, Ablösung *f*, Abhilfe *f*, Rechtsbehelf *m*, Klagebegehren *n*, Klageantrag *m*, Rechtsschutz *m*, Steuerabzug *m*, Fürsorgeunterstützung *f*, Sozialhilfe *f*, Vertretung *f*, Aushilfe *f*; ~ **against forfeiture** Schuldnerschutz gegen Verfallsklauseln, Mieterschutz, Räumungsschutz, Behelf gegen Rechtsverlust; Wiedereinsetzung; ~ **association** Unterstützungsverein; ~ **committee** Hilfskomitee; ~ **fund** Unterstützungsfonds; ~ **population** Gesamtheit der Fürsorgeempfänger; ~ **sought** Klagebegehren; ~ **workers** Notstandsarbeiter *für Notstandsarbeiten vermittelte Arbeitslose*; **administrative** ~ Abhilfe im Verwaltungswege; **alternative** ~ Hilfsantrag; **ancillary** ~ (Antrag auf) Gewährung e–r einstweiligen Anordung bzw Scheidungsfolgenentscheidung; **consequential** ~ Rechtsschutzbegehren im nachfolgenden Prozeß (*nach Feststellungsurteil*); **declaratory** ~ Rechtsschutz durch Feststellungsverfahren; **dependant relatives** ~ Freibetrag für unterhaltsberechtigte Angehörige; **eligible to** ~ sozialhilfeberechtigt; **equitable** ~ billigkeitsrechtlicher Rechtsbehelf; **feudal** ~**s** Abgabe bei Lehensübergang auf den Erben; **general** ~ allgemeines Rechtsschutzbegehren; **indoor** ~ anstaltsinterne Unterstützung; **injunctive** ~ Abhilfe-Anordnung, Unterlassungsverfügung; **interim** ~ einstweilige Anordnung; **interlocutory** ~ vorläufiger Rechtsschutz; einstweilige Anordnung; **legal and equitable** ~ zivilrechtlicher Rechtsschutz; **outdoor** ~ Fürsorgeunterstützung; **personal** ~**s** persönliche Freibeträge; **poor** ~ → *poor*; **public** ~ öffentl. Fürsorge; **reduced rate** ~ gestaffelte Steuerermäßigung; **rollover** ~ Steuervergünstigung durch Überwälzung (*auf Neuinvestitionen*); **small income** ~ Freibetrag bei geringer Einkommensstufe; **substantive** ~ (materiell-rechtlicher) Rechtsschutz; **tapered** ~ allmählich geringer werdende Steuervergünstigungen; **temporary** ~ Überbrükkungshilfe; **the** ~ **prayed for** der Klageantrag; **to ask for** ~ e–n Sachantrag (*des Klägers*) stellen; den Antrag aus der Klage stellen; **to go on** ~ Sozialhilfe beziehen, Fürsorgeempfänger werden; **to pray for** = *to ask for qv*.

relieve abhelfen, unterstützen, befreien, freihalten, ablösen; ~ **hardship** Härten mildern.

relieving the enemy Feindunterstützung *f*, Kriegsverrat *m*.

religion Religion *f*, Kirche *f*, Konfession *f*, **established** ~ Konfession der englischen Staatskirche, Staatsreligion; **freedom of** ~ → *freedom*; **offenses against** ~ Straftaten gegen die Religion.

religious | **affiliation** Bekenntnis, Religionszugehörigkeit; ~ **belief** Glaube, Konfession; ~ **charity** → *charity*; ~ **corporation** → *corporation*; ~ **freedom** Religions- und Gewissensfreiheit; ~ **houses** kirchlichen Zwecken dienende Anwesen; ~ **impostor** religiöser Schwindler; ~ **instruction** Religionsunterricht; ~ **liberty** → *liberty*; ~ **men** Ordensangehörige, Mönche; ~ **orders** geistliche Orden; ~ **society** Religionsgesellschaft.

relinquish aufgeben, verlassen, verzichten, ausschlagen; ~ **an action** e–e Klage zurücknehmen; ~ **an inheritance** e–e Erbschaft ausschlagen; ~ **possession** Besitz (einseitig) aufgeben.

relinquishment Aufgabe *f*, Verzicht *m*, Dereliktion *f*; Ausschlagung *f*.

reliqua Restschuld *f*.

reliquary Schuldner *m* e–r Restschuld.

re-litigation erneutes Prozessieren.

relocate verlagern, versetzen; **to be** ~**d** versetzt werden.

relocation Verlagerung *f*, Umsiedlung *f*; Umzug *m*, Wiedervermietung *f*, Mietverlängerung *f*; ~ **allowance** Wohnungsverlegungsbeihilfe, Umzugsbeihilfe ~ **benefits** Umzugsbeihilfen; ~ **expenses** Umzugskosten *von Betriebsangehörigen bei Versetzung*; Verlagerungskosten; ~ **incentives** Betriebsverlagerungsanreize; ~ **of equipment** Verlegung der Einrichtung; ~ **of industry** Industrieverlagerung; ~ **package** (großzügige) Umzugsbeihilfen; **tacit** ~ stillschweigende Mietvertragsverlängerung.

remain bleiben, übrigbleiben; ~ **in existence** weiterbestehen; ~ **in force** in Kraft bleiben; ~**ing life** Restnutzungsdauer; ~**ing margin** Spitze.

remainder Restbestand *m*, Überrest *m*, Reinnachlaß *m*, Nacherbenrecht *n*; Recht zum Nachbesitz, Anwartschaft *f* (*auf Grundbesitz*); ~ **in fee** Nacherben-Volleigentum am Grundstück; ~ **of an account** Restbetrag, Passivsaldo; ~ **of any monies** das restliche Vermögen; ~ **of my property** mein restliches Vermögen; ~ **value** → *value*; **contingent** ~ aufschiebend bedingtes Herrschaftsrecht (*an Grundstück*), Nacherbenrecht, Recht zum Nachbesitz; **cross** ~**s** wechselseitige Anwartschaft auf Miteigentumserwerb (*an e–m Grundstück*); **estate in** ~ → *estate*; **executed** ~ *gegenwärtige Einräumung e–s Rechts am Grundstück, dessen Ausübung erst in Zukunft möglich ist*; **executory** ~ = *contingent* ~ *qv*; **vested** ~ unentziehbares Anwartschaftsrecht auf Nachbesitz.

remainderman Anwartschaftsberechtigter *m*, Anwärter auf den Nachbesitz, Nacherbe *m*, künftig Berechtigter *m*, Schlußerbe *m*.

remains (*the* ~), sterbliche Überreste, Leiche *f*.

remand *s* Überstellung e–s Angeklagten zur Hauptverhandlung; Haftprüfung *f*, Anordnung *f* der Haftfortdauer; Zurückverweisung *f*; ~ **cell** Haftzelle, U-Haft-Zelle; ~ **centres** Jugendhaftanstalten (*für 14- bis 21jährige in Untersuchungshaft*); ~ **court** Haftprüfungsgericht; ~ **facilities** Unterbringung(smöglichkeiten) von Untersuchungsgefangenen; ~ **food privilege** *Vorzugsrecht der Untersuchungshäftlinge, sich das Essen von außen bringen zu lassen;* ~ **hearing** Haftprüfungstermin; ~ **homes** Jugendarrestanstalten (*bis 17jährige*); ~ **in custody** Untersuchungshaft, Haftfortdauer ~ **on bail** Verschonung von der Untersuchungshaft gegen Sicherheitsleistung; ~ **prison** Untersuchungshaftanstalt; ~ **prisoner** Untersuchungsgefangener; ~ **section** Untersuchungshaft-Abteilung (*e–s Gefängnisses*); ~ **time** Untersuchungshaft; **on** ~ in Untersuchungshaft; **to appear on** ~ aus der Untersuchungshaft (*im Haftprüfungsverfahren*) vorgeführt werden; **weekly** ~ wöchentl Haftprüfung.

remand *v* zur Hauptverhandlung überstellen; e–n neuen Termin für die Hauptverhandlung ansetzen; die Haftfortdauer anordnen; zurückverweisen, zurücksenden; ~**ing a case** die Zurückverweisung e–r Sache anordnen; ~ **in custody** Haftfortdauer anordnen; ~ **into custody** in Untersuchungshaft nehmen, *gg jmd* U-Haft anordnen.

remanet Verbüßung *f* der ausgesetzten Reststrafe; noch nicht erledigter Gesetzesentwurf *m*; unerledigter Fall *m*; **to make a case a** ~ ein Verfahren ruhen lassen.

remargin nachschießen.

remargining Nachschußzahlung *f*.

remarking Nachauszeichnung *f* (*von Waren für den Verkauf*).

remarriage Wiederverheiratung *f*.

remarry sich wiederverheiraten, wieder heiraten.

remediable abhilfefähig, rechtsbehelfsfähig;

remedial Abhilfe gewährend, abhelfend, den Rechtsbehelf betreffend; ~ **action** Vorgehen gegen Mißstände, Abhilfemaßnahmen; ~ **loan society** gemeinnützige Pfandleihgesellschaft; ~ **measure** Abhilfemaßnahme; ~ **statute** Abhilfegesetz.

remed|y *s* Abhilfe *f*, Rechtsbehelf *m*, Rechtsschutz *m*, Rechtsverwirklichung *f*; Heilmittel *n*; Toleranz *f*; ~**ies for illegal arrest** Rechtsbehelfe gegen widerrechtliche Verhaftung; ~**ies have been exhausted** der Rechts(mittel)weg ist erschöpft; ~ **of fineness** zulässige Abweichung vom Feingehalt; ~ **over** Regress; **adequate** ~ → *adequate*; **administrative** ~ Rechtsbehelf in Verwaltungsangelegenheiten; **alternative** ~ wahlweise zulässiger Rechtsbehelf; **civil** ~ Rechtsbehelf in Zivilsachen; **concurrent** ~**ies** parallel bestehende

Rechtsbehelfe; **cumulative** ~ zusätzlicher Rechtsbehelf; **domestic ~ies** innerstaatliche Rechtsbehelfe; **equitable ~ies** billigkeitsrechtl Rechtsbehelfe (*zB specific performance*); **extrajudicial ~ies** außergerichtliche Rechtsbehelfe; **extraordinary ~-ies** außerordentliche Rechtsbehelfe (*habeas corpus, mandamus, quo warranto qv*); **judicial** ~ → *judicial*; **legal** ~ Rechtsbehelf, Klagemöglichkeit (*ursprünglich nur vor den common law Gerichten*); **local ~ies rule** Grundsatz der Notwendigkeit der Erschöpfung des innerstaatlichen Rechtswegs; **matter of** ~ prozeßrechtliche Frage; **post-conviction** ~ außerordentliches Rechtsmittel nach Verurteilung; **provisional** ~ vorläufiger Rechtsbehelf, einstweilige Anordnung; **speedy** ~ summarischer Rechtsbehelf; **to resort to a** ~ von e–m Rechtsbehelf Gebrauch machen.

remedy *v* abhelfen, abstellen, Abhilfe schaffen, wiedergutmachen ~ **a defect** e–n Mangel beheben, e–n Mangel heilen; ~ **a grievance** e–r Beschwerde abhelfen.

remember sich erinnern; ~ **someone in one's will** jmdn im Testament bedenken.

remembrance Erinnerung *f*, Gedächtnis *n*; Vorhaltung *f*.

remembrancer Sonderbeauftragter *m* zur Interessenwahrnehmung; Erinnerungshilfe *f*; *Justitiar der City of London*; **~s** *Finanzanwälte*; **R~ of the City of London** *hist* Zeremonienmeister der Stadt London; Sonderbeauftragter von London im Parlament und versch. Gremien; **Queen's R~** Sonderbeauftragter der Krone *am Londoner Zentralgericht* (*für Vermögensansprüche der Krone und Beitreibung von Außenständen*).

remind beanstanden, mahnen.

reminder Beanstandung *f*, Erinnerung *f*, Mahnung *f*; ~ **advertisement** Erinnerungsanzeige; ~ **of due date** Fälligkeitsavis; ~ **item** Merkposten.

remise aufgeben, überlassen, abtreten; ~ **a claim** sich e–s Anspruchs begeben.

remiss nachlässig, säumig, faul; **to be ~ed in one's duties** seine Pflichten vernachlässigen.

remissibility Begnadigungsmöglichkeit *f*.

remission Erlaß *m*, Verzicht *m*, Schulderlaß *n*, Straferlaß *m*, Ermäßigung *f*, Verweisung *f*, Vergebung *f*, Rückgängigmachen *n* e–r Verfallserklärung; Zurückverweisung *f an untere Instanz*; ~ **for good behavior** (Teil)Straferlaß wegen guter Führung; ~ **of arrears** Erlaß von Rückständen; ~ **of charges** Gebührenerlaß; ~ **of debt** Schulderlaß; ~ **of fines** Erlaß von Geldstrafen; ~ **of part of a sentence** teilweiser Straferlaß, Erlaß der Reststrafe; ~ **of sentence** Erlaß e–r Strafe; ~ **of taxes** Steuererlaß; **conventional** ~ Schulderlaß; **half** ~ bedingter Straferlaß nach Halbzeit.

remissness Nachlässigkeit *f*, Trägheit *f*, Verzug *m*; verspätete Erfüllung *f*, nachlässige Erfüllung *f*.

remit *s* Aufgabenbereich (*e–r Enquète*).

remit *v* überweisen, übersenden, zuweisen, erlassen, verweisen, aufgeben, annullieren, zurücksenden, zurückverweisen, zur Entscheidung unterbreiten, wiedereinsetzen; ~ **a claim** e–e Schuld erlassen; ~ **an offence** ein Strafverfahren einstellen, von Strafe absehen; **please** ~ um Überweisung (*des Rechnungsbetrages*) wird gebeten; **~ted actions** verwiesene Sachen.

remitment Abführen *n* in die Haft; Annullierung *f*.

remittal Erlaß *m*; ~ **of a debt** Schulderlaß; ~ **of a penalty** Straferlaß.

remittance Sendung *f*, Überweisung *f*, überwiesene Summe *f*, Rimesse *f*; ~ **account** Rimessenkonto; ~ **basis** beschränkte Besteuerung ins Inland überwiesener Einkünfte; ~ **by post** Zahlung auf dem Postwege;

~ **by wire** telegraphische (Geld-) Überweisung; ~ **in cash** = *cash* ~ → *cash*; ~ **of cover** Regulierung e–s überzogenen Kontos; ~ **slip** Überweisungsbegleitzettel, Überweisungsbegleitformular; **documentary** ~ dokumentäre Rimesse; **return** ~ Rücküberweisung.

remittee Empfänger *m*, Überweisungsempfänger *m*.

remitter Remittent *m*, Übersender *m*, Geldsender *m*, Einzahler *m*; Verweisungsbeschluß *m*.

remitting bank überweisende Bank *f*.

remittitur of record Zurücksendung *f* der Akte an die untere Instanz, Zurückverweisung *f*.

remittor Anweisender *m*, Übersender *m*.

remnant Rest *m*; **sale of ~s** Resteverkauf.

remodel neu gestalten, umgestalten, reorganisieren.

remonetization Wiederinkurssetzung *f* von Münzen, Wiedereinführung *f* des Metallwährungssystems.

remonetize wieder in Kurs setzen.

remonstrance Einwendung *f*, Einspruch *m*, Beschwerde *f*, Gegenvorstellung *f*, Protest *m*.

remonstrant Beschwerdeführer *m*.

remonstrate Einwände erheben, ernste Vorhaltungen machen, Vorwürfe erheben, jmdm etwas vorhalten; Gegenvorstellungen erheben.

remonstration Einwendung *f*, Vorhaltung *f*, Gegenvorstellung *f*.

remorse Reue *f*, Gewissensbisse *m*|*pl*.

remote entfernt, weitläufig, mittelbar.

remoteness Entlegenheit *f*, Ferne *f*; ~ **of damage** Inadäquanz des Schadens; Grad des Folgeschadens; ~ **of evidence** zu entfernte Beziehung zum Beweisthema, Beweisunerheblichkeit.

removable der Wegnahme zugänglich; transportabel, abnehmbar; absetzbar.

removal Entfernung *f*, Wegnahme *f*; Umzug *m*, Wechsel *m* des Aufenthaltsortes; Entlassung *f*, Beseitigung *f*, Abtransport *m*; Abschiebung *f*; Verlegung *f*; Verweisung *f auf Antrag des Beklagten wegen örtlicher bzw funktioneller Unzuständigkeit oder Besorgnis der Befangenheit*; ~ **bond** → *bond* (2); ~ **cost allowance** Umzugsbeihilfe; ~ **expenses** Umzugskosten; Abbruchkosten; ~ **from office** Absetzung, Amtsenthebung; ~ **from the stock exchange list** Absetzung von der amtlichen Notierung; ~ **from warehouse** Auslagerung; ~ **goods** Umzugsgut; ~ **jurisdiction** ausschließliche Zuständigkeit (*e–s US Bundesgerichts*); ~ **of actions** Verweisung; ~ **of business** Geschäftsverlegung; ~ **of causes** Verweisung (*bes an ein US-Bundesgericht*); ~ **of citizenship** Entzug der Staatsbürgerschaft (= *Staatsangehörigkeit*); ~ **of disqualification** (vorzeitige) Wiedererteilung der Fahrerlaubnis; ~ **of goods to prevent distress** Beiseiteschaffen zur Vereitelung des Vermieterpfandrechts; **R~ of Human Tissues Act** OrganverpflanzungsG *GB 1961*; ~ **of pauper** Abschieben von Fürsorgeempfängern; ~ **of property** → *property*; ~ **of surface soil** Entwendung von Humus; ~ **to avoid tax** Beiseiteschaffen zwecks Steuerhinterziehung; ~ **without notice** fristlose Entlassung; ~ **without proper cause** unbegründeter Wegzug; **fraudulent** ~ heimliches Entfernen (*von Sachen des Mieters*); **mandatory** ~ zwangsweise Entlassung; **order of** ~ Ortsverweisung; **wrongful** ~ **of child** widerrechtl Wegnahme e–s Kindes, Kindesentführung.

remove *s* Grad *m*, Schritt *m*, Stufe *f*, Verwandtschaftsgrad *m*; **~s to convertibility** schrittweiser Übergang zur Konvertierbarkeit.

remove *m* entfernen, entlassen, beiseite schaffen, verweisen, zwangsräumen, abschieben, versetzen; ~ **doubts** Zweifel ausräumen; ~ **from office** aus dem Amt entfernen, aus der Stellung entlassen, absetzen; ~ **from the agenda** von der Tagesordnung absetzen.

removing Beseitigung *f*, Umzug *m*, Räumung *f* (*vgl. removal*); ~ **cloud from title** Beseitigung von Rechtsmängeln; ~ **metals** Erzförderung.

removing expenses *brit* Umzugskosten.

remunerate belohnen, entlohnen.

remuneration Entschädigung *f*, Vergütung *f*, Belohnung *f*, Entlohnung *f*, Lohn *m*, Honorar *n*; ~ **from a profession** Einkünfte aus freiberuflicher Tätigkeit; ~ **of employment** Besoldung, Einkünfte aus nichtselbständiger Arbeit; ~ **package** Vergütungspaket; **fixed** ~ Fixum; **for** ~ gegen Entgelt; **non-cash** ~ Sachbezüge, Deputat; **variable** ~ veränderliche Vergütung; **without** ~ unentgeltlich.

remunerative vorteilhaft, entgeltlich, lohnend, gewinnbringend; ~ **business** lukratives Geschäft; ~ **employment** Erwerbstätigkeit; ~ **investment** einträgliche Anlage; ~ **undertaking** gewerbliches Unternehmen, rentables Unternehmen.

render übergeben, überreichen; beschreiben, wiedergeben; erlassen, (*Urteil*) fällen, verkünden; erteilen; ~ **a net statement** netto abrechnen; ~ **a person liable** jmdn haftbar machen; ~ **account** → *account* (*1*); ~ **an award** e–n Schiedsspruch fällen; ~ **an opinion** e–e Meinung abgeben, ein Gutachten erstatten; ~ **assistance** Beistand leisten; ~ **services** Dienste leisten; ~ **void** nichtig machen.

rendition Übergabe *f*, Überstellung *f*; Verkündung *f* e–r Entscheidung; ~ **of criminals** Überstellung von Straftätern (*ohne förmliche Auslieferung*); ~ **of judgment** Erlaß e–s Urteils; Urteilsfällung; Urteilsverkündung; **irregular** ~ formlose Überstellung (*e–s Tatverdächtigen*).

renegade Renegat *m*, Abtrünniger *m*, Apostat *m*, Überläufer *m*, Verräter *m*.

renegotiate erneut *über etwas* verhandeln, weiterbegeben.

renegotiation erneute Verhandlung *f*, Weiterbegebung *f*, vereinbarte nachträgliche Überprüfung *f* von Rechnungen (*wegen Möglichkeit überhöhten Gewinns bei Staatsaufträgen*), Umschuldung.

renew erneuern, verlängern; ~ **ed if required** mit Prolongationsrecht.

renewable erneuerbar, verlängerbar.

renewal Erneuerung *f*, Wiederaufnahme *f*, Prolongation *f*, Verlängerung *f*, Vertragsfortsetzung *f*; ~ **bill** Prolongationswechsel; ~ **certificate** Erneuerungsschein, Talon; ~ **clause** automatische Fortsetzungsklausel *um jeweils bestimmte Zeitabschnitte*; ~ **endorsement** (Paß)Verlängerungseintrag; ~ **fee** → *fee* (*1*); ~ **notice** *ins* Aufforderung zur Prämienzahlung; ~ **of a bill of exchange** Wechselprolongation; ~ **of a lease** Verlängerung des Miet- *(bzw Pacht)*verhältnisses; ~ **of a loan** Verlängerung der Kreditlaufzeit; ~ **of a licence** Lizenzverlängerung; ~ **of contract** Vertragsfortsetzung, Vertragsverlängerung; ~ **of a coupon sheets** Bogenerneuerung; ~ **of writs** Verlängerung der Gültigkeit der Prozeßeröffnungsverfügung (*zwecks Zustellung*); ~ **premium** Folgeprämie; ~ **order** Anschlußauftrag; ~ **rate** Prolongationssatz; ~ **reminder** Anmahnung der Verlängerungsgebühr, Abonnementsmahnung; **automatic** ~ automatische Verlängerung (*um bestimmte Zeitabschnitte*).

renounce verzichten auf, aufgeben, nicht anerkennen, von sich weisen, ausschlagen, sich lossagen von, kündigen; ~ **a claim** auf e–e Forderung verzichten; ~ **an allotment letter** ein (Bezugs-)Recht aufgeben; ~ **one's citizenship** seine Staatsangehörigkeit aufgeben; ~ **one's interest in an estate** e–e Erbschaft ausschlagen, auf sein Recht an e–m Grundstück verzichten; ~ **one's right** auf sein Recht verzichten.

renouncement Verzicht *m*, Entsagung *f*, Ausschlagung *f*; ~ **of succession** Erbschaftsausschlagung.

renovate erneuern, renovieren.

renovation Erneuerung *f*, Renovierung *f*.

rent s Mietzins *m*, Miete *f*, Pachtzins *m*, Pacht *f*; Leihgebühr *f*, Rente *f*; ~**s** (*unkündbare*) Staatsanleihen, Rente, Rentenpapiere, Staatspapiere; **R~ Acts** Miet(bewirtschaftungs)gesetze, Mietpreisgesetzgebung; ~ **agreed upon** vertraglich vereinbarte Miete|Pacht, Vertragsmiete|pacht; ~**s and profits of land** Einkünfte aus Grundbesitz; ~ **assessment board** Mietpreisbehörde; ~ **book** Mieterbüchlein; ~**-charge** Grundstücksbelastung, die zu regelmäßigen Leistungen verpflichtet; Rentenschuld, Reallast; ~ **control** Mietpreisbindung; ~ **due** geschuldete Miete | Pacht; ~**-fixing order** Mietbindungsanordnung; ~ **for life** dinglich gesicherte Leibrente, lebenslange Rentenschuld; ~**-free** mietfrei; ~ **gouging** *US* Mietwucher; ~ **in advance** Miet-|Pachtvorauszahlung; ~ **in arrear** Mietrückstand; ~ **insurance** → *insurance*; ~**s issues and profits** Erträge aus dem Grundstück; ~ **limit** Höchstmiete *bei regulated tenancy qv*; ~ **money** Mietzins *m*; ~ **of lands** Landüberlassung gegen Rentenschuld; ~ **officer** Beamter der Mietpreisschiedsstelle; ~ **rebate** Mietnachlaß, Mietermäßigung; ~ **receipts** Miet|Pachteinnahmen; ~ **recoverable under the Rent Acts** gesetzlich zulässige Miete (*Mietpreisbindungsgesetze*); ~**s resolute** Erbzins zugunsten der Krone; ~ **reserved** (vereinbarter) Mietzins, Pacht(zins), ausbedungene Miete; ~ **restriction** Wohnraummietenkontrolle; **R~ Restriction Acts** Mietpreisbindungsgesetze; ~ **review clause** Miet(pacht)zinsanpassungsklausel; ~ **review notice** Mietüberprüfungsaufforderung; ~**-roll** Miet|Pachtzinsverzeichnis; ~ **seck** = *dry* ~ *qv*; ~**-service** Bodenpachtzins als Ablösung für Lehensdienste; **cash and share** ~ *Vertrag auf Überlassung von Ackerland mit Erntebeteiligung und Barentlohnung des Pächters für Sonderdienste;* **chief** ~ Hauptpacht; Hauptmiete, Ewigrente (*dem Grundstücksveräußerer vorbehalten*); **contractual** ~ (vertragliche) Miete, Wohnungsmietzins; **dead** ~ Bergregalabgabe (*unabhängig vom Ertrag*); **distress for** ~ → *distress* (*1*); **double** ~ doppelte Nutzungsentschädigung bei Räumungsverzug; **dry** ~ vorbehaltener Bodenzins *(ohne Zwangsbeitreibungsklausel)*; **economic** ~ wirtschaftlich angemessene Miete; Kostenvergleichsmiete; Rente (*im volkswirtschaftlichen Sinn*); **fair** ~ angemessene Miete; **farm** ~ (*landwirtschaftlicher*) Pachtzins; **fee-farm** ~ ewige Leibrente, ewige Rentenschuld, Ewiggeld; **flat** ~ Pauschalmiete; **forehand** ~ im voraus zu zahlende Miete *bzw* Pacht; **ground** ~ Bodenrente, Bodenzins; **imputed** ~ Eigennutzungswert; **index-linked** ~ Miete mit Gleitklausel; **initial standard** ~ Grundmiete, anfängliche Grundmiete; **judicial** ~ angemessener Pachtzins; **net** ~ Nettopacht, Nettomiete; **nominal** ~ Anerkennungsbetrag für ein Pachtrecht; **occupation** ~ Nutzungsentschädigung (*Wohnraum*); **open-market** ~ Marktmiete, Miete auf d. freien Markt; **penal** ~ zusätzliche Pacht als Konventionalstrafe; **peppercorn** ~ symbolischer Pachtzins; **perpetual** ~ = *fee-farm* ~ *qv*; **progressive** ~ Miete | Pacht mit automatischer Erhöhungsklausel; **quit** ~ Ablösungsrente für Lehensdienste (*bes für Hand- und Spanndienste*); **rack** ~ → *rack rent*; **reserved** ~ Bodenzins, Pacht; **sleeping** ~ Bergregalabgabe, umsatzunabhängige Grundpacht; **standard** ~ gesetzlich zulässige Miete.

rent *v* vermietet werden, verpachtet werden; mieten, pachten; ~ **out** vermieten, verpachten;

rental *ajd* ~ **period** → *period*; ~ **purchase agreement** Wohnhaus-Abzahlungskauf.

rental *s* Jahresmiete *f*, Pachtzins *m*, Leasingzins *m*; Einkommen aus Vermietung und Verpachtung; Grundgebühr *f* (*Telefon*); Pächterverzeichnis *n*; ~ **fee** Leasingzins, Miete; **assessed** ~ steuerlicher Mietwert; **clear** ~ Nettomiete (*wobei der Mieter die Lasten zu tragen hat*); **net** ~ Nettopacht (*nach Abzug aller Unkosten*); ~ **rates** Mietsätze, Leihwagenpreise; **housing** ~**s** Wohnungsmieten; **standing** ~ fixe Dauerpacht.

renter Pächter *m*, Mieter *m*.

rentier Rentier *m*, Kapitalrentner *m*.

renunciation Verzicht *m*, Aufgabe *f*, Dereliktion *f*; Ausschlagung *f*, Ablehnung *f*; ~ **of a succession** Ausschlagung e–r Erbschaft; ~ **of a will** Ausschlagung der testamentarischen Erbeinsetzung bzw. Zuwendung *mit Anspruch auf Intestatserbe*; ~ **of agency** Widerruf des Vertretungsverhältnisses; ~ **of citizenship** Staatsangehörigkeitsverzicht; ~ **of contract** Erfüllungsverweigerung; ~ **of probate** Ablehnung des Testamentsvollstreckeramts.

renvoi Renvoi *m*, Rückverweisung *f*, Abschiebung *f* (*unerwünschter Ausländer*); **double** ~ = *total* ~ *qv*; **total** ~ Gesamtverweisung.

reo absente in Abwesenheit des Angeklagten.

reoffend *v/i* erneut straffällig werden; ~**ing rate** Rückfälligkeitsquote.

reopen wiedereröffnen, wiederbeginnen; ~ **a case** (= ~ *the proceedings* = ~ *judgment*) das Verfahren wiederaufnehmen; ~**ing clause** Neuverhandlungsklausel (*bei Weiterbestehen des Vertrages im übrigen*); ~**ing of appeal** Wiederaufnahme des Verfahrens; ~**ing the oral procedure** Wiedereröffnung der Verhandlung.

reorder *s* Nachbestellung *f*; *v* nachbestellen.

reorganization Liquidation *f* zu Sanierungszwecken, Umstrukturierung *f*; Sanierung *f*, Reorganisation *f*, Neugestaltung *f*, Neuregelung *f*; ~ **committee** Sanierungsausschuß der Gesellschaftsgläubiger; ~ **fund** Sanierungsfonds; **R**~ **of Corporations** *US gerichtliches Vergleichs- und Sanierungsverfahren bei Zahlungsunfähigkeit von Kapitalgesellschaften*; ~ **of finances** finanzielle Sanierung; ~ **of local government** Gebietsreform, Gemeinde- und Kreisreform; ~ **processing team** Umstrukturierungsgremium.

reorganize reorganisieren, neuregeln, sanieren.

repackaging Umpacken *n*; ~ **bag** Abpackbeutel; ~ **of a debt** Umschuldung.

repair *s* Reparatur *f*, Wiederherstellung *f*, Instandsetzung *f*; ~**s** Instandsetzungsarbeiten, Instandhaltung; ~ **order** Reparaturauftrag; **bad** ~ schlechter Erhaltungszustand; **beyond** ~ nicht mehr reparierbar; **decorative** ~**s** Schönheitsreparaturen; **emergency** ~**s** → *emergency*; **good** ~ guter Zustand; einwandfreier Erhaltungszustand; **necessary** ~**s** notwendige Instandhaltungsarbeiten; **non-warranty** ~**s** nicht unter Garantie fallende Reparaturen; **ordinary** ~**s** gewöhnliche Erhaltungsarbeiten und Schönheitsreparaturen; **out of** ~ in schlechtem Erhaltungszustand, in nicht verkehrssicherem Zustand; **state of** ~ → *state* (1); **tenantable** ~**s** einwandfreier (vermietungsfähiger) Erhaltungszustand *der Wohnung*; **warranty** ~**s** Garantiereparaturen; *no-charge* ~~: *kostenlose Garantiereparaturen*.

repair *v* wiedergutmachen, entschädigen, instand setzen; **covenant to** ~ = *repairing covenant qv*; **obligation to** ~ Unterhaltungspflicht, Instandsetzungspflicht.

repairing covenant → *covenant*.

reparation Instandsetzung *f*, Wiederherstellung *f*, Entschädigung *f*, Wiedergutmachung *f*; **~s** Reparationen, Wiedergutmachung; **to make ~s for** wiedergutmachen, Ersatz leisten für.

reparole erneute bedingte Entlassung *f*.

repartition Verteilung *f*, Auseinandersetzung *f*; **loss ~** *ins* Schadensverteilung.

repatriate *s* repatriierte Person *f*, Heimkehrer *m*.

repatriate *v* wieder einbürgern, repatriieren.

repatriation Wiedereinbürgerung *f*, Repatriierung *f*, Wiederverleihung *f* der Staatsangehörigkeit; **~ of capital** Rückführung von Kapital.

repay zurückzahlen, zurückvergüten, erstatten; **~ oneself** sich schadlos halten; **liable to ~** erstattungspflichtig.

repayable rückzahlbar.

repayment Rückzahlung *f*, Rückvergütung *f*; **~ of debts** Schuldenrückzahlung; **anticipated ~** vorzeitige Rückzahlung.

repeal *s* Aufhebung *f* (*von Gesetzen*); **~ of law** Gesetzesaufhebung, Außerkrafttretenlassen e–s Gesetzes.

repeal *v* aufheben, abschaffen; widerrufen.

repealer Widerruf *m*, Gesetzesbestimmung über die Aufhebung bestehender Vorschriften.

repeat option business Nochgeschäft *n* (*Optionsrecht, zum gleichen Kurs nachzufordern bzw zu liefern*).

repeater *US* Wähler *m*, der (*illegal*) mehrere Stimmen abgibt; rückfälliger Täter *m*, Wiederholungstäter *m*.

repent bereuen.

repentance Reue *f*.

repertory Informationssammlung *f*, Auswahl *f*, Vorrat *m*, Repertoire *n*; Urkundenrolle *f* des Notars.

repetition Wiederholung *f*, Verlesung *f* e–r Aussage vor Genehmigung; *scot* Rückzahlungsklage *f* wegen rechtsgrundloser Zahlung; **literal ~** wörtliche Wiedergabe;

replace ersetzen, an die Stelle setzen.

replacement Ersatz *m*, Ersatzleistung *f*, Ersatzlieferung *f*, Deckungskauf *f*; Ersatzperson *f*, Vertretung *f*; **~ cost** Wiederbeschaffungskosten; **~ fund** Wiederbeschaffungsrücklage; **~ goods** Ersatzware; **~ in kind** Naturalersatz; **~ investment** Ersatzinvestition; **~ method of depreciation** Abschreibung nach Wiederbeschaffungskosten; **~ price** Wiederbeschaffungspreis; **~ rate** Zu- und Abgangsrate; **~ reserve** Wiederbeschaffungsrücklage, Rückstellung für Ersatzbeschaffung; **~ value** Ersatzwert; **claim for ~** Wiederbeschaffungsanspruch; **provision for ~ of inventories** Rückstellung für die Ausführung des Lagerbestandes; **purchase of goods in ~** Deckungskauf.

replastering Neuverputzen *n*.

replead schriftsätzlich nochmals vortragen, neue Schriftsätze einreichen.

repledge weiter verpfänden.

replenish ergänzen, auffüllen; **~ the reserves** Reserven auffüllen.

replenishment Ergänzung *f*, Ersatz *n*, Auffüllung *f*; **~ ship** Versorgungsschiff.

repletion Fülle *f*, Übermaß *n*, ausreichende Pfründe *f*.

repleviable einlösbar, wiedererlangbar, der Herausgabeklage unterliegend.

replevin Herausgabeklage *f* wegen widerrechtlicher Besitzentziehung (*bes wegen Verpächterpfandrecht*); Klage auf Freigabe von Pfandgegenständen gegen Sicherheitsleistung; Feststellungsklage gegen Pfandverstrickung; **~ bond** Sicherheitsleistung zur Abwendung der Pfandverwertung; **personal ~** Haftprüfungsverfahren, Klage auf Entlassung aus dem Gewahrsam.

replevisable wiedererlangbar (*bes durch replevin qv*).

replevisor Interventionskläger *m*; Antragsteller in e–m *replevin (qv)* Verfahren.

replevy *s* Verfügung (Anordnung)

der Herausgabe gepfändeter Sachen an den Eigentümer *vgl replevin.*

replevy *v* e–e gepfändete Sache im replevin Verfahren zurückerlangen.

repliant = (*replivant*) replizierende Partei *f.*

replication Replik *f*, Reproduktion *f*, Kopie *f*; **general** ~ allgemeines Bestreiten der Einwendungen des Beklagten; **proof in** ~ *scot* Widerlegungsbeweismittel des Klägers; **special** ~ neues Gegenvorbringen zur Klageerwiderung; **to deliver a** ~ e–e Replik vorbringen.

reply Erwiderung *f*, Replik *f*; Gegenplädoyer *n* des Klägers *bzw* Staatsanwaltes; ~ **and defense to counterclaim** Replik (des Klägers) mit Erwiderung auf die Gegenklage; ~ **by return of mail** postwendende Antwort; ~ **of plaintiff** Replik; ~ **paid telegram** Telegramm mit bezahlter Rückantwort; **affirmative** ~ bejahende Antwort; **frivolous** ~ offensichtlich unhaltbare Erwiderung; **immediate** ~ postwendende Antwort; **negative** ~ abschlägige Antwort; **official** ~ amtlicher Bescheid; **right of** ~ → *right*; **sham** ~ zulässige aber völlig unbegründete Replik; **to make a** ~ erwidern.

report *s* Bericht *m*, (= *B bzw b*), Geschäftsbericht *m*, Rechenschaftsbericht *m*; Anzeige *f*, Meldung *f*; **R~s** Entscheidungssammlung(en); ~ **on title** anwaltsch. Prüfungsbericht über die Eigentumsurkunden (*als Beleihungsbedingung*); ~ **of committee** Ausschuß*b*; ~ **of proceedings** Verhandlungs*b*, Protokoll; **R~ Office** *Geschäftsstelle des Chancery Gerichts*; ~ **stage** Stadium der Beratung e–r Gesetzesvorlage; ~ **title** *B*–*s*überschrift; **action** ~ Tätigkeits*b*; **annual** ~ Jahres*b*; **annual financial** ~ jährlicher Haushalts*b* (*an die Legislative*); **annual popular** ~ abgekürzter Jahres*b* für die Öffentlichkeit; **audit** ~ Prüfer*b*, Prüfungs*b*; **auditors'** ~ Prüfer*b*, Prüfungs*b*; **budget** ~ Haushaltsvorbereitungs*b*; **by mere** ~ vom bloßen Hörensagen; **captain's** ~ → *captain*; **cash** ~ Kassen*b*; **classified** ~ Geheim*b*; **confidential** ~ vertraulicher *B*; **credit** ~ Kreditauskunft; **damage** ~ Schadensmeldung, Havarie*b*; **departmental** ~ Ministerial*b*, Abteilungs*b*; **directors'** ~ Geschäfts*b* des Vorstands; **exchange** ~ → *exchange* (*3*); **final** ~ Schluß*b*; **fiscal** ~ Finanzbericht; **interim** ~ Zwischen*b*; **law** ~**s** Entscheidungssammlung; **official** ~ dienstliche Meldung, amtlicher *B*, Parlamentsprotokoll; **over-the-counter** ~ Kursblatt; **period under** ~ *B*–*s*zeitraum; **receiving** ~ (Waren)Eingangsmeldung; **statutory** ~ gesetzlicher Gründungs*b*; **stock market** ~ Kursblatt; **The R~s** (=) *gesammelte Entscheidungen von Lord Coke 1552–1634.*

report *v* berichten, melden, anzeigen; ~ *v/i* (*to*) unterstellt sein, unterstellen; ~ **a bill** *brit* e–e Gesetzesvorlage dem Plenum (mit Ausschußbericht) wiedervorlegen; ~ **a person to the police** jmdn anzeigen; ~ **an offence to the police** Strafanzeige bei der Polizei erstatten; **to move to** ~ **progress** Antrag auf Unterbrechung der Debatte stellen; ~ **progress** über den Fortgang (*bzw Stand*) der Arbeiten berichten.

reportable anzeigepflichtig, meldepflichtig.

reporter Berichterstatter *m*, Protokollführer *m* bei Gericht; Reporter *m*; Referent *m*; **court** ~ Protokollführer (*bei Gericht*)).

reporting of fire Brandmeldung *f.*

reporting restrictions Beschränkung der (Gerichts)Berichterstattung.

repos = *executed repurchase agreement* ausgeführter Rückkaufvertrag.

repository Verwahrungsort *m.*

repossess wieder in Besitz nehmen; von Grundpfandgläubiger zur Verwertung beschlagnahmen;

repossession Wiederinbesitznahme *f*, Rücknahme *f.*

reprehensible verwerflich, tadelnswert.

reprehension Tadel *m*, Rüge *f.*

represent vertreten; schildern, darstellen; ~ **and warrant** zusichern; die Gewähr für etw übernehmen; ~**ed by counsel** anwaltschaftlich vertreten; ~ **oneself** ohne Anwalt auftreten, sich selbst vertreten; **to be legally ~ed** anwalt(schaft)lich vertreten sein.

representation Vertretung *f*, Stellvertretung *f*; Verkörperung *f*, Darstellung *f*, Vorstellung *f*, Schilderung *f*, tatsächliche Angabe(n) *f*, Zusicherung *f*; Erbfolge *f* nach Stämmen; Amt des Nachlaßabwicklers; **~s** Reklamationen *f|pl*, Einwendungen, Vorhaltungen *f|pl*, Gegenvorstellungen *f|pl*; ~ **abroad** Auslandsvertretung; ~ **by estoppel** Rechtsscheinvollmacht; ~ **expenses** Repräsentationskosten; ~ **of a design** Darstellung e–s Musters; ~ **of credit** Eigendarstellung über die Kreditfähigkeit, Selbstauskunft; ~ **of interest** Interessenvertretung; **R~ of the People Act** *GB* Wahlgesetz; ~ **of persons** Stellvertretung; **diplomatic** ~ diplomatische Vertretung; **estoppel by** ~ → *estoppel*; **exclusive** ~ Alleinvertretung; **false ~s** falsche Angaben, unrichtige Erklärungen bei Vertragsanbahnung; **fraudulent** ~ irreführende Angaben, Vorspiegelung falscher Tatsachen, arglistige Täuschung; **joint** ~ Gesamtvertretung; **legal** ~ Stellvertretung, anwaltschaftl. Vertretung; **legal and general** ~ gerichtliche und außergerichtliche Vertretung; **material ~s** wesentliche Angaben, *ins* versicherungswichtiger Umstand; **parliamentary** ~ Volksvertretung; parlamentarische Vertretung, Repräsentativsystem; **promissory ~s** Versprechungen, Zusagen bei Vertragsabschluß; **proportional** ~ Verhältniswahlrecht; **to make ~s** Vorhaltungen machen; **universal** ~ *scot* Gesamtnachfolge, Universalsukzession; **upon ~ of a claim** bei Geltendmachung e–s Anspruchs.

representative *adj* stellvertretend, repräsentativ, bezeichnend, typisch.

representative *s* Vertreter *m*, Stellvertreter *m*, Repräsentant *m*; ~ **to the U.N.** diplomatischer Vertreter bei der UNO; **authorized** ~ Bevollmächtigter; **consular** ~ → *consular*; **diplomatic** ~ diplomatischer Vertreter; **employees'** ~ → *employee*; **freely elected ~s** frei gewählte Vertreter; **House of R~s** → *house*; **lawful** ~ rechtmäßiger Vertreter; **legal ~s** Stellvertreter, Nachlaßtreuhänder; Erbanwärter; Testamentsvollstrecker *bzw* Nachlaßverwalter, Erben, Kinder, Nachkommen nach Stämmen; **natural** ~ blutsverwandter Rechtsnachfolger; **permanent** ~ ständiger Vertreter, Resident; **personal** ~ Rechtsnachfolger *des Erblassers*, Testamentsvollstrecker *bzw* Nachlaßverwalter; **real** ~ Liegenschaftsnachlaßverwalter, Immobiliarerbe; **sole** ~ Alleinvertreter; **special** ~ Sonderbeauftragter.

representee Erklärungsadressat, *derjenige demgegenüber e–e Erklärung oder Zusicherung abgegeben wird.*

repression Unterdrückung *f*.

repressive measures Ordnungsstrafen, Erzwingungsstrafen.

repricing staatliche Neufestsetzung *f* von Preisen (*bei Staatsaufträgen*).

reprieve *s* (Straf)Vollstreckungsaufschub *m*, Aussetzung der Vollstreckung; Nichtvollstreckung der Todesstrafe.

reprieve *v|t* Vollstreckungsaufschub *bzw* -aussetzung gewähren.

reprimand *s* (öffentlicher) Verweis *m*, Tadel *m*, Rüge *f*, Verwarnung *f*.

reprimand *v* rügen, e–n Verweis erteilen, tadeln, verwarnen.

reprint Neudruck *m*, Nachdruck *m*, **unauthorized** ~ unberechtigter Nachdruck.

reprisal Vergeltung *f*, Wegnahme *f* e–s Ersatzgegenstandes; **~s** Vergeltungsmaßnahmen, Repressalien; **general** ~ generelle Beschlagnahme als Repressalie; **negative** ~ Repressalie durch Erfüllungsverweigerung; **positive ~s** Repressalien durch Vornahme von Handlungen; **special ~s** einzelnen Staatsbürgern überlassenes Repressalienrecht.

reprises Nebenaufgaben *f/pl* des Pächters, Erbzins *m*; **beyond ~** die Abgaben abgerechnet.

reproach *v* vorwerfen, zum Vorwurf machen.

reprobate mißbilligen, verwerfen.

reprocessing Wiederaufbereitung *f*; ~ **plant** *for fuel from (light water) reactors* atomare Wiederaufbereitungsanlage.

reprobation Einwendungen *f/pl*.

reproduce reproduzieren, nachbilden, nachdrucken.

reproduction Nachbildung *f*, Reproduktion *f*; Abdruck *m*, Nachdruck *m*; **mechanical ~** Vervielfältigung auf mechanischem Wege.

reproof Verweis *m*, Tadel *m*.

reprove mißbilligen.

republication Wiederveröffentlichung *f*; Neudruck *m*, Neuauflage *f*; ~ **of a will** Neuerrichtung e–s widerrufenen Testaments.

republish *v/t* wiederveröffentlichen, neuerrichten (*Testament*).

repudiate nicht anerkennen, abweisen, ablehnen, verwerfen, zurückweisen, ausschlagen, bestreiten; *v/i* vom Vertrag zurücktreten; ~ **a claim** e–n Anspruch zurückweisen; ~ **a contract** e–n Vertrag als ungültig behandeln.

repudiation Nichtanerkennung *f*, Ablehnung *f*, Verwerfung *f*, Zurückweisung *f*; Verstoßung *f* e–r Ehefrau; ~ **of a debt** Nichtanerkennung e–r Schuld, Zahlungsverweigerung; ~ **of an inheritance** Erbausschlagung; ~ **of contract** Erfüllungsverweigerung, Bestreiten der Vertragsgültigkeit; Rücktritt vom Vertrag.

repudiator Befürworter *m* der Nichterfüllung (*von Auflagen e–r Siegermacht*).

repugnancy Widerwillen *m*, Unvereinbarkeit *f*, innerer Widerspruch *m*, Unstimmigkeit *f*; ~ **of allegations** Widersprüchlichkeit von Behauptungen.

repugnant im Widerspruch stehend zu, unvereinbar mit, zuwiderlaufend, widersprechend, im Gegensatz stehend zu; ~ **to English law** gegen das engl ordre public verstoßend, mit engl Recht unvereinbar.

repurchase *s* Rückkauf *m*, Wiederkauf *m*; ~ **agreement** Rückkaufsvertrag; Wertpapierpensionsgeschäft; ~ **cost** Wiederbeschaffungskosten; ~ **price** Rücknahmepreis (*Inventur*); **compulsory** ~ zwangsweise Rücknahme (*von Investmentanteilen*), Zwangsrückkauf.

repurchase *v* zurückkaufen; **right to ~** Rückkaufsrecht.

repurchaser Wiederkäufer *m*.

reputable angesehen; ~ **citizen** angesehener Mitbürger.

reputation Ruf *m*, Ansehen *n*; ~ **of prosecutrix** Leumund der Kindsmutter (*im Vaterschaftsprozeß bzw bei Unterhaltsklagen Nichtehelicher*); **business ~** geschäftliches Ansehen; **damage to ~** → *damage*; **stained ~** Bescholtenheit.

repute Ruf *m*, Leumund *m*, Wertschätzung *f*, Renommee *n*; **common ~** allgemein akzeptierte Ansicht, Ruf, Renommee; **good ~** einwandfreier Leumund; **ill ~** schlechter Ruf, übler Leumund.

reputed vermeintlich, angeblich, vermutlich, bekannt, berühmt, nach allgemeiner Anschauung.

requalify *v/i* erneut die Voraussetzungen für ein Amt, (e–e Zulassung) erwerben.

request *s* Bitte *f*, Verlangen *n*, Gesuch *n*, Ersuchen *n*, Nachfrage *f*; Zahlungsaufforderung *f*, Mahnung *f*; Klageantrag *m*; Klageschrift *f* zum County Court; **~s book** Beschwerdebuch; ~ **for an extension of time** Antrag auf Fristverlängerung, Stundungsgesuch; ~ **for an opinion** Einholung e–s Gutachtens; ~ **for cancellation**

Löschungsantrag; ~ **for cheques** Scheckanforderung; ~ **for delivery** Abruf *bestellter Ware*; ~ **for extradition** Auslieferungsantrag; ~ **for payment** Zahlungsaufforderung, Mahnung; ~ **for quotation** Aufforderung zur Preisaufgabe; ~ **for respite** Stundungsgesuch; ~ **in writing** schriftliche Aufforderung; ~ **note** Antrag auf Genehmigung zur Entnahme zollpflichtiger Waren; ~ **to arbitrate** Schiedsantrag; **at the** ~ **of** auf Antrag von, auf Verlangen von; **dying** ~ letztwillige Bitte; **special** ~ spezifische Bitte; **upon** ~ auf Anforderung, auf Wunsch.

request *v* (er)bitten, ersuchen, verlangen, beantragen, auffordern; ~ **permission** um Erlaubnis bitten; **the** ~**ed authority** die ersuchte Behörde; **the** ~**ing state** der ersuchende Staat (*Auslieferung*).

require etwas verlangen, fordern, ersuchen, begehren, anordnen, anweisen, auferlegen, zwingen.

required erforderlich; vorgeschrieben, zu kaufen gesucht; ~ **by law** gesetzl. vorgeschrieben; **as (and when)** ~ wie gewünscht, wunschgemäß, nach Bedarf; **if** ~ wenn nötig, falls erforderlich.

requirement Erfordernis *n*, erforderliche Eigenschaft *f*, Forderung *f*, Verlangen *n*, Anforderung *f*, Auflage *f* (*Bewährung*), Bedarf *m*, Voraussetzung *f*; ~ **contract** Pauschalbezugsvertrag zur Bedarfsdeckung; ~**s for admission** Zulassungsbedingungen; ~ **of form** Formerfordernis; **anticipated** ~ voraussichtlicher Bedarf; **educational** ~**s** Bildungsvorschriften; **evidentiary** ~ Beweiserfordernis, zu beweisende Behauptung; **formal** ~**s** Formvorschriften, Formerfordernis, Formzwang; **labour** ~**s** Bedarf an Arbeitskräften; **legal** ~**s** gesetzliche Voraussetzungen; gesetzlich vorgeschriebenes Deckungsverhältnis; **own** ~**s** Eigenbedarf; **preliminary** ~**s** Voraussetzungen; **to attach** ~**s** (*to an order*) Auflagen (*zu e–m Beschluß*) anordnen; **to impose** ~**s on s.o.** *jmdm* Auflagen machen; **total** ~**s** Gesamtbedarf.

requisite *adj* erforderlich.

requisite *s* Erfordernis *n*, Voraussetzung *f*.

requisition *s* gerichtliches Ersuchen *n*, Auslieferungsersuchen *n*, Aufforderung *f*, Anforderung *f*, Requisition *f*, Zwangsauflage *f*, Auflage *f*; Befähigung *f*, Eignung *f*, Bedürfnis *n*, Bedarf *m*, Zahlungsaufforderung *f*; ~ **note** Leistungsanforderung; ~**s on title** Verlangen auf Auskunftserteilung über Grundstückseigentumsnachweise; **material** ~ Materialanforderung; **personnel** ~ Personalanforderung.

requisition *v* beschlagnahmen, requirieren; ~**ed meeting** Hauptversammlung auf Antrag der Aktionäre.

requisitioning Inanspruchnahme von Dienst- und Sachleistungen; Requisition *f*.

requisitionists Antragsteller *m|pl*, *Aktionäre m|pl, die die Einberufung einer Hauptversammlung verlangen.*

requisitor Ermittler *m*, Untersuchungsführer *m*.

requital Belohnung *f*, Vergeltung *f*, Entschädigung *f*.

requite belohnen, vergelten, entschädigen.

re-rate *v|t den Kurs* neu bewerten.

re-registration Wiedereintragung *f*, Umschreibung *f*.

res Sache *f*, Gegenstand *n*; **gestae** (=), Sachverhalt, Tatumstände, Begleitumstände; ~ **ipsa loquitur** (=) *widerlegbare Vermutung von Fahrlässigkeit auf Grund der Tatumstände* (*Umkehr der Beweislast, Anscheinsbeweis*); ~ **judicata** rechtskräftig entschiedene Sache; ~ **judicata effect** Rechtskraftwirkung; ~ **judicata principle** Grundsatz der Rechtskraft gerichtl Entscheidungen; ~ **nova** noch nicht entschiedener Fall; ~ **nullius** herrenlose Sache.

resale Wiederverkauf *m*, Weiterverkauf *m*; Selbsthilfe-, Deckungs-,

Notverkauf; ~ **agreement** Wiederverkaufsvereinbarung; ~ **price** Wiederverkaufspreis; ~ **price fixing** Preisbindung der zweiten Hand; ~ **price maintenance** Preisbindung der zweiten Hand; ~ **service** Wiederverkaufsdienst (*Ferienwohnungen*).

rescheduling|charge Umdisponierungsgebühr *f*; ~ **of debts** Tilgungs- und Verzinsungsstreckung; ~ **package** Umschuldungspaket.

rescind anfechten, aufheben, für ungültig erklären, außer Kraft setzen; ~ **a judgment** ein Urteil aufheben; ~ **a law** ein Gesetz außer Kraft setzen.

rescission Annullierung *f*, Anfechtung *f*, Nichtigerklärung *f*, Aufhebungserklärung *f*; ~ **bonds** Ersatz-Schuldverschreibungen (*zur Ablösung von für ungültig erklärten Garantien*); ~ **of contract** rückwirkende Vertragsauflösung, Rücktritt vom Vertrag; **equitable** ~ Vertragsauflösung durch Gerichtsurteil (*nach Billigkeitsrecht*); **legal** ~ Vertragsaufhebung durch die Parteien; Rücktritt vom Vertrag.

rescissory action Anfechtungsklage *f*, Wandlungsklage *f*.

rescript Erlaß e–r Verordnung, Ausfertigung *f*; prozeßleitende Verfügung *f*, Beantwortung *f* e–r Anfrage; kirchenamtliche Stellungnahme *f*.

rescue *s* Rettung *f*, Hilfe *f*, Hilfeleistung *f*, gewaltsame Wiederinbesitznahme *f*, Gefangenenbefreiung *f*, Vollstreckungsvereitelung *f* (*durch Wegnahme gepfändeter Sachen*); Prisenrückeroberung *f*; ~ **cases** Schadensersatzprozesse wegen Nothilfehandlungen (*wegen Fahrlässigkeit von Nothelfern*); ~ **doctrine** Grundsatz des Aufwendungsersatzrechtes des Nothelfers; ~ **service** Rettungsdienst, Nothilfedienst.

rescue *v* retten, befreien, bergen, gewaltsam befreien, entsetzen.

rescussor *hist* Nothelfer *m*.

reseal a writ *einen Gerichtsbeschluß erneut mit dem Amtssiegel versehen (Fortsetzung der Gültigkeit bzw Behebung e–s Formfehlers)*.

resell wiederverkaufen, weiterverkaufen.

reseller Wiederverkäufer *m*.

resentencing erneute Aburteilung *f* (*e–r im Ausland abgeurteilten Tat im Inland*).

resentment Ressentiment *n*, Verärgerung *f*, Groll *m*, Hass *m*.

reservation Vorbehalt *m*, Zuständigkeitsbeschränkung *f*, Reservat *n*, Vorbehaltsklausel *f*; ~ **clause** Vorbehaltsklausel; ~ **of a right** Rechtsvorbehalt; ~ **of claim** Anspruchsvorbehalt; ~ **of the right of disposal** Veräußerungsvorbehalt, Eigentumsvorbehalt; ~ **of right to rescind** Rücktrittsvorbehalt; ~ **of title** Eigentumsvorbehalt; **central** ~ Mittelstreifen (*Autobahn*); **mental** ~ stiller Vorbehalt, geheimer Vorbehalt, Mentalreservation; **with** ~ unter Vorbehalt, vorbehaltlich; **without** ~ vorbehaltlos.

reserve *s* Reserve *f*, Rücklage *f*, Rückstellung *f*; Vorbehalt *m*; ~ **account** → *account* (*2*); ~ **assets** Reserveaktiva, zur Reservebildung geeignete Werte; ~ **balance** Rücklagenguthaben; ~ **bank** Federal Reserve Bank (US), Landeszentralbank; ~ **capital** → *capital*; ~ **city** Bankplatz zweiter Klasse; ~ **claim** Reserveforderung; ~ **currency** Reservewährung; ~ **depot** Ersatzteillager; ~ **earnings rate** *Zuschlag bei Berechnung von Versicherungsrücklagen*; ~ **for authorized expenditures** Rücklage für genehmigte Ausgaben; ~ **for bad debts** = *bad-debt* ~ *qv*; ~ **for contingencies** Rückstellung für Nichtvorgesehenes; ~ **for deferred dividends** Rückstellung für Dividendennachzahlungen; ~**s for depletion** Rücklage wegen Erschöpfung von Bodenschätzen, R. wegen Substanzverbrauchs; ~ **for encumbrances** Rückstellung für (Budget)-Belastungen; ~ **for inventories** Rücklage für Ersatzbeschaffung; ~

for loss on investments Rückstellung für Kursverluste; ~ **for outstanding claims** Schadensreserve; ~ **for sinking fund** Tilgungsrücklage; ~ **forces** Reserveeinheiten; ~ **fund** Gewinnrücklage; ~ **holding** Reserveguthaben (*Währung*); ~ **liability** Nachschußpflicht; nur bei Liquidation einforderbarer Teil des Aktienkapitals; ~ **maintained** Istreserve; ~ **of bills** Gesetzgebungsvorbehalt (*Vorbehalt der königlichen Zustimmung bei Gesetzesbeschlüssen*); ~ **of rights** Vorbehalt der Rechte; ~ **officer** Reserveoffizier; außerplanmäßiger Beamter; ~ **part** Ersatzteil; ~ **position in the Fund** IWF-Position (*Internationaler Währungsfonds*); ~ **price** → *price*; ~ **ratio** Deckungssatz, Liquidationskoeffizient; ~ **requirements** Vorschriften über die Bildung von Rücklagen; ~ **statement** Reserveausweis; ~ **strength** *Überschuß der Aktiva über die laufenden Verbindlichkeiten*; **actuarial** ~ Prämienreserve, Deckungskapital; **bad-debt** ~ Rückstellung für uneinbringliche Forderungen; **contingent** ~ Rückstellung (*für Nichtvorhergesehenes*); **creation of** ~**s** Rücklagenbildung; **debt reduction** ~ Rücklage für Schuldentilgung; **depletion** ~ Rückstellung wegen Erschöpfung von Bodenschätzen; **disclosed** ~**s** offene Rücklagen; **excess** ~**s** freie Reserven (*zB der Mitgliedsbanken bei Zentralbanken*); **exchange** ~ Devisenreserve; **extraordinary** ~ Sonderrücklage, Sonderrückstellung; **free** ~ freie Rücklage (*über Mindestreserve*); **funded** ~ in langfristigen Obligationen angelegte Rücklage; **gross** ~ *ins* Bruttoreserve; **hidden** ~**s** stille Rücklagen; **legal** ~ gesetzl Rücklage bzw gesetzl Rückstellung; **legal** ~ **ratio** gesetzlicher Rücklagensatz; **liquid** ~ Liquiditätsreserve; **loss** ~ → *loss*; **mathematical** ~ *ins* Deckungskapital, Deckungsrücklage; **minimum cash** ~ Pflichtreserve, Mindestreserve (*Bank*); **monetary** ~ Währungsreserven; **non-earning** ~ stillgelegte Gelder; **offsetting** ~**s** Rückstellungen; **operating** ~ Rückstellung für Betriebskostenmehrungen; **overall** ~ **needs** Gesamt(währungs)reservenbedarf; **required** ~**s** Pflichtreserven, Mindestreserven; **revenue** ~ → *revenue*; **secret** ~**s** stille Rücklagen; **special (contingency)** ~ Rückstellung; **special revaluation** ~ Neubewertungsrücklage; **specific** ~ Rückstellung; **statutory** ~ **fund** gesetzliche Rücklage; **tax** ~ → *tax*; **undistributable** ~ nicht ausschüttungsfähige Rücklage; **unearned premium** ~ Prämienreserve; Dekkungsrücklage, Deckungskapital, Deckungsstock; **valuation** ~ Wertberichtigung; Neubewertungsrückstellung; **without** ~ ohne Vorbehalt; ohne Mindestgebot.

reserve *v* vorbehalten, ausbedingen, reservieren; ~ **judgment** die Urteilsverkündung e–m besonderen Termin vorbehalten; ~ **points of law** die Entscheidung von Rechtsfragen (*dem Plenargericht*) vorbehalten; ~ **the defense** sich Einwendungen vorbehalten.

reserved|bidding → *bidding*; ~ **judgment** → *judgment*; ~ **land** unveräußerlicher Staatsgrund; ~ **powers** Vorbehaltsbefugnis; (*den Einzelstaaten der USA*) vorbehaltene Rechte; ~ **price** Mindestgebot; ~ **shares** genehmigte (*noch nicht begebene*) Aktien; ~ **speech** vorbehaltene Wortmeldung; ~ **surplus** zweckgebundene Rücklage; **all rights** ~ alle Rechte vorbehalten; Nachdruck verboten.

re-service erneute Zustellung.

reserving vorbehaltlich; ~ **points of law** Beratung und Entscheidung von Rechtsfragen vorbehalten.

reservoir of demand Nachfragevorrat *m*.

reship *v|t* weiterversenden.

resettlement Umsiedlung *f*, Neubegründung *f*, Wiedereingliederung ins Berufsleben, Resozialisierung; Neueinrichtung *f*; Neufestlegung *f* der Fideikommißbindung *bzw der Nacherbschaftstreuhand*; Urteilsergänzung *f*; ~ **administration** *US* Siedlungsbehörde; ~ **allowance** Umsiedlungsbeihilfe; ~ **fund** Wiedereingliederungsfonds; ~ **of offenders** Resozialisierung von Straffälligen; ~ **unit** Wohnheim für Nichtseßhafte; **occupational** ~ Umschulung.

reshuffle of the cabinet Kabinettsumbildung *f*.

reside wohnen, sich ständig aufhalten, seinen Wohnsitz haben.

residence Aufenthaltsort *m*, Wohnort *m*, ständiger Aufenthaltsort *m*, Wohnsitz *m* (*unjuristisch*); Geschäftsitz, Direktionssitz; Wohnhaus *n*, Herrenhaus *n*; ~ **abroad** Wohnort(sitz) im Ausland; ~ **ban** Aufenthaltsverbot; ~ **burglary insurance** → *insurance*; ~ **burglary policy** → *policy*; ~ **of a company** Sitz e–r Gesellschaft; ~ **permit** Aufenthaltserlaubnis; ~ **requirement** Wohnsitzerfordernis, Residenzpflicht; **actual** ~ tatsächlicher Wohnsitz; **change of** ~ Wohnsitzverlegung; **conjugal** ~ ehelicher Wohnsitz; **constructive** ~ fiktiver (*gemeinsamer*) Wohnsitz (*Unverheirateter*); **family** ~ Familienwohnsitz; Einfamilienhaus; **foreign** ~ Auslandswohnsitz; **free choice of** ~ Freizügigkeit; **habitual** ~ gewöhnlicher Aufenthalt; **legal** ~ Wohnort; **main** ~ Hauptwohnsitz; Eigenheim als Hauptwohnsitz; **official** ~ Amtssitz; **ordinary** ~ gewöhnlicher Aufenthalt(sort); **permanent** ~ ständiger Aufenthaltsort, Wohnsitz; **place of** ~ → *place*; **private** ~ Privatwohnung, Villa; **privately owned** ~ Eigenheim; **single** ~ Einfamilienhaus; **temporary** ~ vorübergehender Wohnort; **to be in** ~ am Amtsort wohnhaft sein.

resident *adj* ansässig, ortsansässig, wohnhaft, innewohnend, ausstehend; ~ **abroad** im Ausland wohnhaft; ~ **agent** Inlandsvertreter; Ortsvertreter; ~ **alien** im Inland ansässiger Ausländer; ~ **company** inländische (Handels)Gesellschaft; ~ **manager** örtlicher Geschäftsführer; ~ **minister** Ministerresident, Gesandter; *hist* Statthalter, Regierungsvertreter; ~ **sterling** *brit* Währungsbestände von Bewohnern des Sterling-Blocks; ~ **taxpayer** inländischer Steuerpflichtiger, unbeschränkt Steuerpflichtiger; **ordinarily** ~ wohnhaft.

resident *s* Einwohner *m*, Bewohner *m*; Deviseninländer *m*, Gebietsansässiger *m*; Ortsansässiger *m*, ansässige Person *f*; Resident *m*, Regierungsvertreter; ~ **in the UK** britischer Steuerinländer (*mind 183 Tage pro Jahr*); **national** ~ Inländer, Einwohner mit Staatsangehörigkeit des Wohnsitzlandes; ~ **status** → *status*; **to be a** ~ **of** in . . . wohnen.

residential care and custody Fürsorgeerziehung in e–r Anstalt; ~ **cluster** Wohn-Bebauungsgruppe; ~ **density** Bebauungsdichte; ~ **estate** Wohngrundstück; ~ ~ *agent*: *Wohnimmobilienmakler*; ~ **qualification for voters** Wohnsitzerfordernis für Wähler.

residual restlich, übrigbleibend, übrig.

residuary *adj* restlich, Rest . . .

residuary *s* Rest *m*, Reinnachlaß *m*, Restnachlaß *m*.

residue Rest *m*, Rückstand *m*, restlicher Nachlaß *m*, Reinnachlaß *m*; ~ **of action** Restprozeß (*nach Teilurteil*); ~ **of money** das restliche Geld, Rein(mobiliar)nachlaß; ~ **of my estate** mein Reinnachlaß; ~ **of my things** meine übrige Habe; **to carry to** ~ zum Restnachlaß rechnen.

residuum Rest *m*, Reinnachlaß *m*.

resign aufgeben, verzichten; ~ **a claim** auf e–e Forderung verzichten; ~ **in a body** geschlossen zurücktreten; ~ **the representation** die Vertretung niederlegen.

resignation Rücktritt *m*, Abdankung *f*; Kündigung *e–s Angestellten*, Amtsniederlegung *f*, Verzicht(sleistung), Aufgaben *f*, Lehensrückgabe *f*; ~ **of membership** Mandatsverzicht, Austritt (*aus e–m Verein*).

resignee der *e–n* Verzicht *bzw* e–e Amtsniederlegung Entgegenehmende.

resigner Verzichtleistender *m*.

resile (*from the contract*) Abstand nehmen, Zurücktreten.

resiliency rasche Erholungsfähigkeit (*Börse*).

resist Widerstand leisten, widerstehen, sich widersetzen; ~ **arrest** sich der Verhaftung widersetzen; ~ **claims** Ansprüche bestreiten.

resistance|movement Widerstandsbewegung; ~ **point** Widerstandpunkt; *Stand, auf dem sich der Kurs einpendelt*; ~ **to arrest** Widerstand gegen Festnahme; ~ **to officers of the law** Widerstand gegen Vollstreckungsbeamte; **armed** ~ bewaffneter Widerstand.

resisting|arrest Widerstandsleistung bei Verhaftung; ~ **an officer** Widerstand gegen Vollstreckungsbeamte; ~ **rape** Widerstand gegen Notzuchtversuch.

resit (*papers*) sich e–r Wiederholungsprüfung unterziehen.

resolution Lösung *f*, Auflösung *f*; Resolution *f*; Beschluß *m*, Entschließung *f*; ~ **of contract** Vertragsauflösung, Rücktritt; ~ **of the conflict** Konfliktlösung; ~ **to wind up** Liquidationsbeschluß; **borrowing** ~ Gesellschafterbeschluß über Kreditaufnahme; **circular** ~ Beschluß im Umlaufverfahren; **concurrent** ~**s** übereinstimmende Beschlüsse (*zweier gesetzgebender Körperschaften*); **extraordinary** ~ außerordentlicher Beschluß (*qualifizierte Mehrheit, besondere Ankündigung der Beschlußanträge*); **joint** ~ gemeinsame Entschließung (*zB Senat und Abgeordnetenhaus*); **notice of** ~ Ankündigung von qualifizierten Beschlußfassungen; **omnibus** ~ Beschluß mit genereller Ermächtigung zu Schuldaufnahmen; **ordinary** ~ (gewöhnlicher) Mehrheitsbeschluß; **special** ~ qualifizierter Beschluß *nach befristeter Vorankündigung*; **to adopt a** ~ → *to adopt*; **to pass a** ~ beschließen; **valid** ~ rechtsgültiger Beschluß.

resolve beschließen, lösen, auflösen; ~ **a contract** e–n Vertrag auflösen, von einem Vertrag zurücktreten.

resolved entschlossen, in dem Entschluß; beschlossen; **be it** ~ es ergeht folgender Beschluß.

resolving clause Einleitungsformel e–r Entschließung.

resort *s* (*1*) Hilfsmittel *n*, Zuflucht *f*, Hilfe *f*, Möglichkeit *f*; häufig besuchter Ort *m*; ~ **in case of need** Notadresse; **last** ~ letzte Instanz.

resort (*2*) Erholungsort *m*; Kurort *m*; **public** ~ Veranstaltungsstätte.

resort *v* sich wenden an, zurückgehen auf, sich begeben; ~ **to (a) court** ein Gericht anrufen, den Rechtsweg beschreiten; ~ **to litigation** ~ den Rechtsweg beschreiten, Klage erheben.

resource Ressource *f*; ständige Bezugsquelle; ~**s** Hilfsquellen *f|pl*, Hilfsmittel *n|pl*, Vermögenswerte *m|pl*, Geldmittel *n|pl*, Eigenmittel *n|pl*; ~ **recovery** Wiedernutzbarmachung von Ausgangsstoffen; **covering** ~**s** Deckungsmittel; **credit** ~**s** Kreditquellen; **financial** ~**s** finanzielle Mittel; **human** ~**s** Arbeitskräftepotential; **liquid** ~**s** flüssige Mittel; **national** ~**s** Bodenschätze e–s Landes; **natural** ~**s** Bodenschätze, Ressourcen; **non-monetary** ~**s** Sachmittel; **real** ~**s** Güter und Dienstleistungen; **pecuniary** ~**s** Geldmittel, Geldquellen; **without** ~**s** mittellos.

respect *s* Hinsicht *f*, Rücksicht *f*, Beziehung *f*, Bezug *m*; Hochachtung *f*, Wertschätzung *f*; Respekt *m*, Beachtung *f*, Rücksichtnahme *f*; ~ **for the law** Achtung vor dem Gesetz; **in** ~ **of** hinsichtlich, bezüglich.

respect *v* respektieren, beachten, achten, berücksichtigen, betreffen.

respite *s* Aufschub *m*, Nachfrist *f*; Stundung *f*, Zahlungsaufschub *m*; ~ **of a jury** Vertagung der Geschworenen (*wegen Mangel der Besetzung*); ~ **of appeal** Vertagung der Berufungsverhandlung; ~ **of a sentence** Vollstreckungsaufschub; ~ **of homage** Verzicht auf Lehenshuldigungsformalitäten; **additional** ~ Nachfrist; **days of** ~ Respekttage; **final** ~ letzte Zahlungsfrist; **forced** ~ vorläufige Einstellung der Vollstreckung.

respite *v* stunden, Frist gewähren, Aufschub bewilligen; ~ **a payment** stunden, Zahlungsfrist gewähren.

respond erwidern, e–e Klageerwiderung einreichen; haften, einstehen müssen; etwas wiedergutmachen; ~ **in damages** schadensersatzpflichtig sein.

respondeat ouster Zwischenurteil *n* auf Verwerfung e–r prozeßhindernden Einrede; ~ **superior** Haftung des Dienstherren für Erfüllungsgehilfen *bzw* Verrichtungsgehilfen.

respondent Beklagter *m*, Antragsgegner *m*, Beschwerdegegner *m*, Berufungsbeklagter *m*, Revisionsbeklagter *m*; ~**'s notice** Anschlußbeschwerde.

respondentia Bodmerei *f* auf die Schiffsladung; Notverpfändung *f* der Schiffsladung; ~ **loan** Bodmerei auf die Schiffsladung.

response Stellungsnahme *f*, Erwiderung *f*, Klagebeantwortung *f*.

responsibility Haftung *f*, Verantwortlichkeit *f*, Verantwortung *f*, Verpflichtung *f*, Obliegenheit *f*; **civil** ~ zivilrechtl Haftung; **collective** ~ Gesamtverantwortung (*des Kabinetts ggüb Parlament*); **criminal** ~ Schuldfähigkeit, strafrechtliche Haftung, **diminished** ~ verminderte Zurechnungsfähigkeit; **discharge on one's ~ies** Wahrnehmung von Aufgaben; **joint** ~ Gesamthaftung; **limited** ~ beschränkte Geschäftsfähigkeit; **ministerial** ~ Ministerverantwortung, Gesamtverantwortung der Minister *gegenüber dem Parlament*; **official** ~ Amtshaftung; **state** ~ Staatenverantwortlichkeit; **to shirk one's** ~ sich vor der Verantwortung drücken; **terminal** ~ Gesamtverantwortung bis zur Abnahme; **to claim** ~ sich (*zu e–r Tat*) bekennen (*Terrorismus*); **vicarious** ~ stellvertretende Haftung, Haftung für Erfüllungsgehilfen *bzw* Verrichtungsgehilfen.

responsible verantwortungsvoll, verantwortungsbewußt, verantwortlich haftbar ~ **age** Mündigkeit; ~ **bidder** geschäftlich angesehener Submittent; ~ **cause** Haftungsgrund, Rechtfertigungsgrund; ~ **contractor** geschäftlich angesehener Unternehmer (*bzw Submittent*); ~ **for recourse** regreßpflichtig; ~ **government** e–e dem Parlament verantwortliche Regierung; **jointly and severally** ~ solidarisch (= *samtverbindlich* = *gesamtschuldnerisch*) haftbar; **primarily** ~ unmittelbar haftbar, primär haftend.

responsive auf e–e Frage eingehend, reagibel.

responsiveness Direktheit *f* der Beantwortung der Frage; kein Ausweichen *n* vor der Frage.

rest *s* Rest *m*, Saldo m, Ruhe *f*, Arbeitsruhe *f*, Rechnungsabschluß *m*, *pl ~s*: regelmäßige Kontensaldierung *zwecks Hinzunahme zum Schuldbetrag* (*Zinseszins*); ~ **break** (= ~ *interval*) Ruhepause, Erholungspause; **for the** ~ im übrigen.

rest *v* beruhen, bleiben, ruhen; ~ **one's case** sein Vorbringen vorläufig abschließen; **the prosecution ~s** die Anklage hat ihre Beweisführung zunächst abgeschlossen.

restart programme Existenzneugründungsprogramm *m*.

restatement Neuaufstellung *f*, Neuformulierung *f*; **R~ (of American Law)** (=) *Darstellung des amerikanischen Privatrechts zur Rechtsvereinheitlichung*.

restitute (wieder) ersetzen, wiederherstellen, wiedergutmachen.

restitutee Rückerstattungsberechtigter *m*.

restitutio in integrum Wiederherstellung *f* des ursprünglichen Zustandes; Wiedereinsetzung *f* in den vorigen Stand.

restitution Rückerstattung *f*, Entschädigung *f*, Wiederherstellung *f*, Wiedereinsetzung *f* in den vorigen Stand, Herausgabe *f*, Rückgewähr, Rückgabe *f*; ~ **in quasi-contract** Herausgabe einer ungerechtfertigten Bereicherung; ~ **costs** Wiederherstellungskosten, Reparaturkosten; ~ **in kind** Naturalrestitution; ~ **in specie** Naturalrestitution; ~ **of action** Wiederaufnahme der mündlichen Verhandlung; ~ **of conjugal community** *obs* Wiederherstellung der ehelichen Lebensgemeinschaft; ~ **of conjugal rights** *obs* Wiederherstellung der ehel Rechte; ~ **of fine** Rückerstattung e–r Geldstrafe; ~ **of pledge** Herausgabe der Pfänder *durch Dritten*; ~ **of property** Rückerstattung von Vermögen; ~ **of rights** Wiederherstellung von Rechten; ~ **of stolen goods** Herausgabe gestohlener Gegenstände; ~ **order** Rückerstattungsbeschluß *m*, Anordnung der Rückgabe; gerichtliche Herausgabeverfügung; **action for** ~ → *action*; **claim for** ~ Rückerstattungsanspruch; **demand** ~ Herausgabe verlangen; **specific** ~ Herausgabe (*e–r bewegl Sache*).

restitutor Rückerstattungspflichtiger *m*.

restoration Wiederherstellung *f* (des bisherigen Zustandes); Rückerstattung in natura, Naturalrestitution; ~ **to an office** Wiedereinsetzung in ein Amt.

restore wiederherstellen, zurückerstatten, wiedereinsetzen; ~ **confiscated property** beschlagnahmtes Vermögen freigeben; ~ **order** die öffentliche Sicherheit und Ordnung wiederherstellen; ~ **peace** den Frieden wiederherstellen; ~ **to possession** wieder in den Besitz setzen.

restrain beschränken, einschränken, hemmen, hindern, verbieten, zwingen; in e–r geschlossenen Anstalt unterbringen; ~ **production** Produktion drosseln; ~ **trade** den Handel einschränken.

restraining|order → *order* (*1*); ~ **powers** Vollmachtsbeschränkung; ~ **statute** Veräußerungsverbot(sgesetz), *das Common Law* einschränkendes Gesetz; **agreements,** ~ **trade** wettbewerbsbeschränkende Vereinbarungen.

restraint Einschränkung *f*, Beschränkung *f*, Sicherungsverwahrung *f*; Freiheitsentzug *m*, Haft *f*, Verbot *n*, Wettbewerbsbeschränkung *f*; ~ **of marriage** (*vertragliche oder letztwillige*) Heiratsbeschränkung; ~ **of people** hoheitsrechtliche Eingriffe; ~ **of princes** hoheitsrechtliche Eingriffe; ~ **of ship** Schiffsarrest; ~ **of trade** Wettbewerbsbeschränkung, Konkurrenzverbot; ~ **of use** Gebrauchsbeschränkung; ~ **on** (= *of*) **alienation** Veräußerungsbeschränkung; ~ **on anticipation** Beschränkung der Vorausverfügung; ~ **on dealings with property** Vermögensverfügungsbeschränkung; ~ **on disposal** Verfügungsbeschränkung; **judicial** ~ → *judicial*.

restrict beschränken, einschränken.

restricted beschränkt, begrenzt, geheim; ~ **data** unter Geheimnisschutz stehende Angaben; ~ **district** Stadtbezirk mit Baubeschränkungen; ~ **government contracts** geheimhaltungsbedürftige Staatsaufträge; ~ **hours tariff** → *tariff*; ~ **matter** nur für den Dienstgebrauch, Verschlußsache; ~ **condition** Wiederherstellungsauflage (*bei Entnahmeerlaubnis*); ~ **use credit agreement** zweckgebundener Verbraucherkreditvertrag.

restriction Veräußerungsbeschränkung *f*, Verfügungsverbot *n*, Beschränkung *f*, Einschränkung *f*, Baubeschränkung *f*; Ausschluß der Ausübung von Rechten; ~ **of armaments** Rüstungsbegrenzung; ~ **of credit** Kreditverknappung, Krediteinschränkung; ~ **on culti-**

vation Anbaubeschränkung; ~ **on transfer of shares** Vinkulierung von Aktien; ~ **order** Verwahrungsbeschluß *in geschlossene Anstalt*; ~ **upon attendance** Beschränkung der Zulassung der Öffentlichkeit; **currency** ~ Devisenbewirtschaftung; **declaration of ~s** Gemeinschaftsordnung *von Wohnungseigentümern*; **field of use ~s** *pat* Benutzungsbeschränkungen; Einschränkungen auf eine Benutzungsart; **quantitative** ~ mengenmäßige Beschränkung; **territorial** ~ Gebietsbeschränkung; **tying ~s** Koppelungsbeschränkungen; über den Inhalt des Schutzrechtes hinausgehende Verpflichtungen.

restrictive beschränkend, einschränkend, wettbewerbsbehindernd; wettbewerbsbeschränkend.

restructuring Umstrukturierung *f*.

resubmission Wiedervorlage *f*, erneuter Antrag *m*; **for** ~ zur Wiedervorlage.

result Ergebnis *n*, Folge *f*; **incidental** ~ Nebenfolge, Nebenwirkung; **proximate** ~ unmittelbare Folge; **tangible ~s** greifbare Ergebnisse.

result *v* sich ergeben, folgen, enden, zurückfallen an; ~ **in a loss** mit Verlust abschließen, e–n Verlust mit sich bringen.

resume wiederaufnehmen, wiederannehmen.

resumé Lebenslauf *m*, berufl Werdegang *m*; ~ **faking** Falschangaben beim Lebenslauf.

resummon nochmals laden.

resummons nochmalige Ladung *f*.

resumption Wiederaufnahme *f*, Wiederbeginn *m*, Wiederannahme *f*; ~ **of business** Wiederaufnahme der Geschäftstätigkeit; ~ **of cohabitation** Wiederaufnahme der ehelichen Lebensgemeinschaft; ~ **of payments** Wiederaufnahme der Zahlungen.

resurrender Pfandfreigabe *f* von Pachtland, Grundschuldlöschung.

retail *s* Einzelhandel *m*, Kleinhandel *m*; ~ **banking** Privatkunden-Bankgeschäfte; ~ **ceiling price** Verbraucherhöchstpreis; ~ **consignment** Einzelsendungen; ~ **cost** Ladenpreis; Stückgut; ~ **firm** Einzelhandelsfirma; ~ **issue** Kleinverkauf; ~ **licence** Gewerbeschein für den Einzelhandel; ~ **markup** Einzelhandelsspanne; ~ **price** Einzelhandelspreis, Ladenpreis; ~ **prices index** Index der Einzelhandelspreise; ~ **sales** Einzelhandelsumsatz; ~ **shop** Einzelhandelsgeschäft; ~ **societies** *brit* Konsumgenossenschaften; **limited line ~ business** Spezialgeschäft.

retail *v* Einzelhandel betreiben; im Einzelhandel verkaufen.

retailer Einzelhändler *m*; **~'s excise** Einzelhandelsumsatzsteuer; ~ **of merchandise** Einzelhändler; **independent** ~ selbständiger Einzelhändler; **security** ~ Wertpapierhändler.

retain zurückbehalten, einbehalten, bestellen; einschalten, beauftragen; **a lawyer** → *lawyer*; ~ **income** Erträge einbehalten; thesaurieren; ~ **possession** den Besitz vorenthalten, nicht ausziehen; **to be ~ed** nicht zur Weitergabe bestimmt.

retainable einbehaltungsfähig.

retainer Gebührenvorschuß *m*; Anwaltsbestellung *f*, Mandat *n*, Mandatierung *f*; laufendes Festhonorar; ~ **of debts** Vorwegbefriedungsrecht des Testamentsvollstreckers *bzw* Nachlaßverwalters; **general** ~ allgemeine Anwaltsbestellung; **pure** ~ (ausschließliche) ständige anwaltschaftliche Vertretung; **special** ~ Anwaltsmandierung im Einzelfall.

retaining a cause Aufrechterhaltung *f* e–r (*zunächst nicht gegebenen*) Zuständigkeit.

retaking erneute Wegnahme *f*, Wiederinbesitznahme *f*.

retaliate Vergeltung üben.

retaliation Repressalie *f*, Gegenmaßnahme *f*, Vergeltung *f*.

retaliatory wiedervergeltend, Vergeltungs . . ., Retorsions . . .

retard verzögern.

retardation Verschleppung *f*, Verzögerung *f*.
retarded verzögert; (*geistig*) zurückgeblieben; ~ **protest** verspäteter Protest.
retention Selbstbehalt *m*, Eigenbehalt *m*, Zurückbehaltung *f*, Belassung *f* im Dienst; ~ **in office** Belassung im Dienst; ~ **manual** Handbuch über Aufbewahrungspflichten; ~ **money** Garantieeinbehalt; ~ **of deposit** Einbehaltung von hinterlegtem Geld; ~ **of documents** Zurückbehaltung von Urkunden, Aufbewahrung von Unterlagen; ~ **of earnings** Gewinnthesaurierung, Selbstfinanzierung, Finanzierung aus einbehaltenen Gewinnen; ~ **of name** Beibehaltung der Namensführung; ~ **of nationality** Beibehaltung der Staatsangehörigkeit; ~ **of title** Eigentumsvorbehalt; ~ **of wages** Einbehalten von Lohn; **net** ~ *ins* Selbstbehalt.
retentionist Befürworter der Beibehaltung der Todesstrafe.
reticence Zurückhaltung *f*, Verschwiegenheit *f*.
retire zurückziehen, zurücknehmen; einlösen, tilgen, zurücktreten, sich zurückziehen, sich zur Ruhe setzen, in Pension gehen, in den Ruhestand treten; ~ **a bill** e–n Wechsel einlösen; ~ **a debt** e–e Schuld tilgen; ~ **bonds** Obligationen aus dem Verkehr ziehen; ~ **coins from circulation** Münzen aus dem Verkehr ziehen; ~ **in rotation** turnusmäßig ausscheiden; ~**d list** Verzeichnis der Reserveoffiziere; ~**d pay** Pension, Ruhegehalt.
retiree im Ruhestand Lebender, Altersrentner(in), Pensionär(in).
retirement Rücktritt *m*, Austritt *m*, Pensionierung *f*, Ruhestand *m*; Abgang *m* (*Ausscheiden von Anlagegegenständen*); Verlassen des Sitzungssaals durch den (die) Richter am *Schluß der Sitzung*; ~ **age** Pensionsalter, Altersgrenze; buchmäßiger Abgang e–s Anlagegutes; ~ **annuity** Altersrente; ~ **benefits** Pensionsbezüge; ~ **credit** Anrechnung für die Pensionsanwartschaft; ~ **fund** Pensionsfonds, Pensionskasse; ~ **income** → *income*; ~ **of a loan** Rückzahlung e–r Anleihe; ~ **of (a) partner** (*freiwilliges*) Ausscheiden des Gesellschafters; ~ **of the jury** das Sichzurückziehen der Geschworenen (*zur Beratung*); ~ **on full pension** Pensionierung; ~ **pension** Altersversorgung; Altersrente; Pension; ~ **pensioner** Altersrentner; ~ **relief** Steuervergünstigung für Eintritt in den Ruhestand; **compulsory** ~ Zwangspensionierung; **debt** ~ Schuldtilgung, Schuldenablösung; **early** ~ vorzeitige Pensionierung, vorgezogener Ruhestand; Frühpensionierung; **optional** ~ freiwillige Pensionierung.
retool neu ausrüsten.
retooling Neuausrüstung *f* mit Werkzeugen *bzw* Maschinen.
retorsion Retorsion *f*, (Wieder)vergeltung *f*.
retort *s* scharfe Entgegnung *f*, Vergeltung *f*.
retort *v* erwidern, entgegnen, vergelten.
retortion Erwiderung *f* (*auf Beleidigung*); Vergeltung *f*, Retorsion *f*.
retrace zurückverfolgen, nachvollziehen.
retract zurückziehen, widerrufen; ~ **a confession** ein Geständnis widerrufen; ~ **a testimony** e–e Zeugenaussage widerrufen.
retractation Widerruf *m* e–s Verzichts, *bes e–r Erbausschlagung*.
retraction Zurücknahme *f* (*e–r Äußerung, e-er Ausschlagung*); Widerruf *m*.
retrain umschulen.
retraining Umschulung *f*; **occupatorial** ~ (berufliche) Umschulung.
retraite Rückwechsel *m*.
retransfer *s* Rückübertragung *f*.
retransfer *v* zurückübertragen.
retraxit Klagerücknahme *f* mit Anspruchsverzicht.
re-treat *v/t* nacharbeiten, nachbessern.
retreat *s* **to the wall** extreme Notwehrlage *f*.
retrench einschränken, kürzen.

retrenchement Einschränkung *f,* Kürzung *f.*
retrial Wiederaufnahme *f* des Verfahrens; erneute mündliche Verhandlung *f*; neuer Strafprozeß *m.*
retribution Vergeltung *f,* Gegenleistung *f,* Vergütung *f.*
retributive ausgleichend, vergeltend, strafend.
retrievable ersetzbar, wiederbringlich.
retrieve wiedergewinnen, wiedererlangen, wettmachen, wiedergutmachen; ~ **a loss** sich für e–n Verlust schadlos halten; e–n Verlust ausgleichen.
retroactive rückwirkend; ~**ly invoiced** nachberechnet.
retroactivity Rückwirkung *f,* rückwirkende Kraft *f;* ~ **of recognition** Rückwirkung der Anerkennung.
retrocede zurückabtreten.
retrocedent Retrozendent *m.*
retrocession Retrozession *f,* Risikoübertragung *f* des ersten auf den zweiten Rückversicherer; Rückabtretung *f.*
retrocessionary Retrozessionar *m,* Rückabtretungsempfänger *m.*
retrograde rückgängig, rückläufig; ~ **movement** rückläufige Bewegung.
retrospective zurückbezogen, rückbezüglich, rückwirkend.
retrospectivity Rückwirkung *f,* rückwirkende Kraft *f.*
retry *a case* e–n Prozeß neu aufrollen.
return *s* Rückgabe *f,* Erwiderung *f,* Entgegnung *f,* Herausgabe *f,* Erstattung *f,* Entgelt *n,* Gegenleistung *f;* Wiederwahl *f,* Ristorno *m,* Storno *m,* Ertrag *m,* Gewinn *m,* Umsatz *m,* Einkünfte *f/pl,* Rentabilität *f,* Rendite *f;* Rückvorlage *f,* Protokoll *n,* Zustellungsurkunde *f;* ~**s** Einnahmen, Umsatz, statistische Aufstellungen, laufende Berichte, Wahlergebnis, Wahlberichte; Vorlage e–s Antrags, Rücksendung, Rücklieferung, Remittenden; Rückschecks; ~ **account** Rückrechnung; ~**s-book** Retourenbuch, Buch für zurückgesandte Waren; Liste der gewählten Abgeordneten; ~ **cargo** Rückfracht, Rückladung; ~ **copies** Remittenden; ~ **-day** Terminstag, Zustellungstag, Wahlfeststellungstag; Gerichtstermin; ~ **freight** Rückfracht; ~ **goods** Rückwaren, ~**s inwards** erhaltene Waren; ~ **irreplevisable** Feststellung der Unzulässigkeit weiterer Herausgabeklagen (*vgl replevin*); ~ **of a charge** Gebührenrückerstattung; ~ **of duties** Gebührenrückvergütung; ~ **of empties** Rücksendung von Leergut; ~ **of expenses** Ausgabenaufstellung; ~ **of premium** → *premium;* ~ **of writs** Pfändungsbericht; ~ **office** Zustellungskanzlei; ~ **on equity** Eigenkapitalrendite; ~ **on investment** Gewinn im Verhältnis zu investiertem Kapital; ~ **on sales** Gewinnspanne; ~ **order** Rückgabeanordnung (*zugunsten des Vorbehaltsverkäufers*); ~**s and exchanges** Rücksendungen und Umtausch; ~ **stock** Aktienrendite; ~**s outwards** zurückgesandte Waren; ~ **shipment rate** verbilligter Frachtsatz für Leergut; ~ **shipping order** Rücklieferungsauftrag; ~ **unsatisfied** Pfandabstand(serklärung); **annual** ~ jährliche Meldung (*an Registergericht über Gesellschaftsverhältnisse und Verbindlichkeiten; Jahresbericht*); **average** ~**s** Durchschnittsertrag; **bank** ~ Bankausweis; **by** ~ **of post** → *post (2)*; **combined** ~ zusammengefaßte Bilanzerklärung (*von Konzernen*); **consolidated** ~ Konzernbilanz; **daily** ~**s** Tageseinnahmen, Tagesumsatz; **election** ~**s** → *election*; **fair** ~ angemessener Ertrag; **false** ~ Falschbeurkundung von Zustellungen; fehlerhafte Zustellungsbestätigung; **general** ~**-day** allgemeiner Gerichtstag, Schlußtermin für Zustellungserledigungen; **gross** ~**s** Bruttoeinnahmen, Bruttoertrag, Rohgewinn; **in** ~ **for** als Ersatz für, als Gegenleistung für; **interim** ~ Zwischenausweis; **joint**

~ gemeinsame Steuererklärung; **law of diminishing ~s** → *law*; **marginal ~s** Grenzertrag; **net ~s** Nettoumsatz; **official ~** amtliche Ziffern; **quick ~s** schneller Umsatz; **separate ~** getrennte Steuererklärung; **tax ~** → *tax*; **to falsify the ~s** Wahlergebnisse fälschen; **undue ~** fehlerhafte Feststellung des Wahlergebnisses; **unopposed ~** Wahl e-s Kandidaten ohne Gegenkandidat.

return *v* zurückkehren; zurückgeben, zurückgewähren; angeben, erklären, berichten; stornieren; **~ a profit** e-n Gewinn abwerfen; **~ guilty** für schuldig erkennen; **~ed for want of acceptance** mangels Annahme zurück.

returnable rückgabepflichtig, mit Bericht vorzulegen, zurückzugeben, zurückzusenden.

returning|board Wahlausschuß; **~ officer** Wahlleiter.

reus Beschuldigter *m*, Angeklagter *m*.

reuse Wiederverwendung *f*; **~ package** wiederverwendungsfähige Verpackung.

revalidate wieder gültig machen.

revalidation erneute Inkraftsetzung *f*.

revalorisation Aufwertung *f*, Revalorisierung *f*, Neubewertung *f*.

revaluation Neubewertung *f*, Aufwertung *f*; **~ of assets** Neubewertung von Vermögenswerten (*Zuschreibung, Erhöhung des Buchwerts*); **~ reserve** Neubewertungsrücklage; **~ surplus** Aufwertungsgewinn; **property ~** Grundstücksneubewertung.

revalue upward aufwerten.

revamp *v* reorganisieren, umstrukturieren; **~ debt** umschulden; **~ the cabinet** e-e Kabinettsumbildung vornehmen.

reveal enthüllen, offenbaren.

revendication Herausgabeanspruch *m* (*bes des unbefriedigten Verkäufers*); **~ action** Herausgabeklage.

revenue Einkommen *n*, Staatseinkommen *n*, Steueraufkommen *n*; Fiskus *m*, Kapitalrente *f*, Ertrag *m*, Nutzung *f*; **~ Acts** Steuergesetze; **~ agent** Steuerbeamter, Finanzbeamter; **~ authorities** Finanzbehörden, Fiskus; **R~ Bar** Steueranwaltschaft; **~ bill** Steuergesetzvorlage; **~ board** Finanzamt; **R~ Code** Abgabenordnung; **~ cutter** Zollschiff; **~ earning** gewinnbringend, einträglich; **~ estimates** Abgabenvorausschätzung; **~ expenditure** Investitionen zwecks kurzfristiger Kapitalerträge; **~ expense** Betriebsausgabe; **~ frauds** Steuer- *bzw* Zollhinterziehung; **~ freight** zahlende Ladung; **~ from taxation** Steueraufkommen; **R~ List** Gerichtsliste für Zahlungsklagen des Fiskus; **~ neutral** steueraufkommensneutral; **~ principle** Ertragswertberechnung; **~ protection** Schutz der Zollinteressen (*in Küstengewässern*); **~ receipts** Steuereinnahmen; **~ reserve** Gewinnrücklage; **~ ruling** Steuerrichtlinie(n), Finanzamtsbescheid; **~ side of the Exchequer** Gerichtsabteilung für Ansprüche des Kronfiskus; **~ sources** Steuerquellen; Abgabenquellen; **~ stamp** Steuermarken, Banderole; **~ statutes** Steuergesetze; **annual ~** Jahreseinkommen; **current ~s** laufende Erträge; **general fund ~** Steuern und sonstige allgemeine Staatseinkünfte; **gross ~** Bruttoertrag; **national ~** Nationaleinkommen; **net ~** Reinertrag; **non-operating ~** neutraler Erfolg; nicht aus dem Geschäftsbetrieb stammende Erträge; **operating ~** Betriebseinnahmen; **public ~** Staatseinkünfte, Einkünfte der öffentlichen Hand; **rental ~** Einkünfte aus Vermietung und Verpachtung; **unearned ~** transitorische Passiva.

reversal Aufhebung *f*, Umstoßung *f*, Kassation *f*, Abänderung *f*; Storno *m*, Rückbuchung *f*; *int Absichtserklärung, bestimmte Bedingungen trotz veränderter Umstände einzuhalten*; **~ of judgment** Urteilsaufhebung; **~ and remand** Aufhebung und Zurückverweisung.

reverse *v/t* abändern, aufheben, kassieren; umstoßen; stornieren; ~ **a policy** e–e Politik revidieren; *adj:* ~ **charge call** R-Gespräch; ~ **split** Aktienzusammenlegung; ~ **yield gap** negativer Renditeabstand (*zw Aktien u. Festverzinslichen bei inflationärer Konjunktur*).

reversible umkehrbar, revisibel, rechtsmittelfähig.

reversion (*Rest*)Eigentum *m* (*des langfristigen Verpächters*), Heimfallsrecht *n*; Eigentum *n* des mittelbaren Besitzers; Heimfall des dingl Rechts an den Oberberechtigten; ~ **agreement** *int* Rückgabevertrag; ~ **duty** Versicherungssumme *e–r Versicherung auf den Todesfall*); ~ **in fee** Recht auf Heimfall vollen Grundeigentums; **freehold** ~ Heimfall zu vollem (Grund)Eigentum; **immediate** ~ unmittelbares Heimfallrecht, unmittelbar anschließendes Recht der Wiederinbesitznahme; **legal** ~ Heimfallsrecht, *scot* Verfallsfrist zur Auflösung e–s verpfändeten Grundstücks; **right of** ~ Heimfallsrecht; **title to** ~ Eigentumsnachweis über das Pachtgrundstück; **to run with the** ~ dem jeweiligen Eigentümer zustehen; Bestandteil des (Grundstücks-)Eigentums bilden.

reversionary heimfallend; zukünftig in Kraft tretend

reversioner Heimfallsberechtigter *m*, Eigentümer *m* während der Pachtdauer, Anwartschaftsberechtigter *m*.

revert heimfallen, zurückkommen, letztwillig zugewendet werden.

reverter Heimfall *m* e–s Grundstücks; *vgl reversion*.

revertible heimfallend, zurückfallend.

revest zurückerwerben, ein Recht wiedererhalten.

review *s* Durchsicht *f*, Prüfung *f*, Untersuchung *f*, Revision *f*, Bericht *m*, Übersicht *f*; ~ **of remand cases** Haftprüfungsverfahren; ~ **of taxation** Erinnerungsverfahren bei der gerichtl Kostenfestsetzung; ~ **on appeal** Überprüfung e–s Urteils durch Rechtsmittelinstanz; **bill of** ~ → *bill* (*2*); **commission of** ~ → *commission*; **judicial** ~ → *judicial*; **market** ~ Markt-, Börsenbericht; **period under** ~ → *period*; **pre-trial** ~ Vor(untersuchungs)-Verfahren *im Crown Court qv*; **procedure on** ~ Verfahren in der Rechtsmittelinstanz.

review *v* prüfen, gerichtlich nachprüfen, revidieren; in der Rechtsmittelinstanz prüfen.

reviewability Rechtsmittelfähigkeit *f*.

reviewer Prüfer *m*, Rezensent *m*.

revile schmähen, öffentlich herabsetzen, verunglimpfen.

reviling the memory of the dead Verunglimpfung Verstorbener.

revindicate zurückfordern; erneut rechtfertigen.

revise durchsehen, revidieren, nachprüfen, ändern; ~ **a decision** e–e Entscheidung abändern.

revising|assessors Prüfer von Gemeindewählerlisten; ~ **authority** Überprüfungsbehörde, Wahlprüfungsbehörde; ~ **barrister** Anwalt zur Prüfung von Gemeindewählerlisten.

revision nochmalige Durchsicht *f*, Überprüfung *f*, Verbesserung *f*, Abänderung *f*, Revision *f*; ~ **of prices** Preisberichtigung; ~ **of statutes** Bereinigung und Neufassung von Gesetzen.

revisor Revisor *m*, Prüfer *m*.

revival Wiederbelebung *f*, Wiederinkrafttreten *n*, Aufschwung *m*, Erholung *f*, Erneuerung *f*; ~ **of action** Fortsetzung e–s ruhenden Verfahrens; Wiederaufnahme des Verfahrens; ~ **of business** Geschäftsbelebung; ~ **of treaties** Wiederanwendung von Verträgen; ~ **of will** Wiederinkraftsetzen e–s widerrufenen Testaments (*durch Testamentszusatz*).

revive erneuern, wiedereinführen, wiedereinsetzen, wieder aufleben lassen, wieder aufgreifen; eine verjährte Forderung anerkennen; ~ **an**

expired patent ein erloschenes Patent wiederherstellen.

revivor Wiederaufnahme *f* e–s Prozesses; **bill of ~** → *bill* (*2*); **writ of ~** neue Vollstreckungsklausel.

revocability Widerruflichkeit *f*.

revocable widerruflich.

revocation Aufhebung *f*, Widerruf *m*, Rücktritt *m*; **~ and new appointment** Entlassung und Neuberufung (*e–s Verwalters etc*); **~ clause** Testamentsbestimmung über den Widerruf früherer Verfügungen; **~ in law** = *constructive ~ qv*; **~ of (a) patent** Patententziehung, Patentlöschung; **~ of agency** Widerruf der Vertretungsmacht, Vollmachtsentzug; **~ of an authority** Widerruf e–r Vollmacht, V.entzug; **~ of banker's authority** Entziehung e–r Bankvollmacht; **~ of contract** Rücktritt vom Vertrag; **~ of donation** Schenkungswiderruf; **~ of gift** Schenkungswiderruf; **~ of licence** Lizenzentzug; **~ of offer** Zurücknahme e–s Angebots; **~ of patent** Widerruf e–s Patents; **~ of power** Erlöschen e–r Vollmacht, Widerruf e–r Befugnis (*kraft Gesetzes, Auslegung oder konkludenten Verhaltens*); **~ of probate** Widerruf der gerichtlichen Testamentsbestätigung, *etwa:* Aufhebung e–s Erbscheins; **~ of trust** Rücktritt von e–r Treuhanderrichtung; **~ of will** Widerruf des Testaments; **~ suit** Nichtigkeitsklage; **action for ~** Klage auf Widerruf; **constructive ~** gesetzliche Beendigung e–r Befugnis (*bzw e–r Vollmacht*); **general ~** allgemeiner Widerruf sämtlicher Willenserklärungen; **proceedings for ~** Nichtigkeitsverfahren; **special ~** Widerruf e–r einzelnen Erklärung *bzw* Vollmacht.

revoke widerrufen, anfechten, aufheben, für ungültig erklären; **~ a driving licence** e–n Führerschein entziehen; **~ a law** ein Gesetz aufheben; **~ a patent** ein Patent zurücknehmen; **~ a will** ein Testament widerrufen; **~ an offer** ein Angebot zurücknehmen; **~ an order** e–n Auftrag stornieren; **~ one's consent** seine Genehmigung zurückziehen.

revolv|e (sich) drehen, kreisen, rotieren; **~ing assets** Umlaufvermögen; **~ing credit** → *credit* (*2*); **~ing fund** → *fund*; **~ing letter of credit** → *letter of credit*; **~ing payments** wiederkehrende Zahlungen; **~ing underwriting facility** revolvierende Übernahmefazilität.

reward *s* Belohnung *f*, Entgelt *n*, Lohn *m*, Vergütung *f*; **~ claim** Mutungsanspruch; **~s for the return of goods** Versprechen e–r Belohnung (*„Auslobung"*) für Wiederbeschaffung verlorener Sachen; **~ system** Prämienlohnsystem; **due ~** gebührende Belohnung *bzw* Vergütung; **fair ~** angemessene Vergütung; **monetary ~** Belohnung in Geld; **pecuniary ~** finanzielle Entschädigung; **promise of ~** Auslobung, Aussetzung e–r Belohnung; **public offer of a ~** Auslobung.

reward *v* belohnen, vergelten, vergüten.

rewarehouse wieder einlagern.

rewarehousing Wiedereinlagerung *f*.

reweigh nachwiegen.

reweight nochmals ermitteltes Gewicht *n*.

rework nochmals bearbeiten, überarbeiten, umarbeiten, nachbearbeiten.

ribbon development Gestaltung *f* von Straßenanliegergrundstücken (*Stadtplanung*).

Richard Roe *fiktiver Name des Beklagten*.

ride fahren, lenken, vor Anker liegen; **~ on a side issue** auf e–r Nebenfrage herumreiten; **~ the goat** in e–n Geheimbund aufgenommen werden.

rider Allonge *f*, Zusatz *m*, Zusatzantrag *m*, Anhang *m* zu e–r Urkunde, Zusatzvereinbarung *f*; Zusatzklausel *f*, Nachtrag *m*, Zusatz zu e–m Geschworenenspruch (*bis 1972*); **~-roll** = *rider qv*.

ridership Fahrgastaufkommen *n*, Summe der Fahrgäste.

Riding (=) e–r der drei Teile der Grafschaft Yorkshire: East Riding, North Riding, West Riding (abgeleitet von trithings); Kreis *m*, Bezirk *m*.

rifle plündern, rauben.

rig durch unlautere Machenschaften beeinflussen, foppen; ~ **an election** Wahlschiebungen vornehmen; ~ **the market** (*künstlich*) Kurssteigerungen hervorrufen.

rigger Kurstreiber *m*.

right *adj* recht, richtig, angemessen; rechts; ~ **and wrong test** Prüfung der Unterscheidungsfähigkeit zwischen Recht und Unrecht; **(to be)** ~ **in court** postulationsfähig, parteifähig (sein); ~ **thinking** rechtschaffen, rechtlich gesonnen (~ ~ *members of society*); **to do s. b.** ~ *jmdm* Gerechtigkeit widerfahren lassen.

right *s* (subjektives) Recht *n (= R . . . bzw r)*, Anrecht *n*, Berechtigung *f*, Anspruch *m*; ~**s** *auch:* Grundrechte, Menschenrechte; Bezugsrecht(e) (→ *rights*); ~**s accrued** erworbene *R–e*; ~ **acquired** erworbenes *R*; ~**s and credits** *R–e* und Guthaben, bewegliche Habe; ~**s and liabilities** *R–e* und Verbindlichkeiten; ~ **and title** (das) Eigentums*r*; ~ **appendant** Neben*r*; ~ **apurtenant** zugehöriges *R*; ~**s dealings** Handel mit Bezugsrechten; ~ **ex lege** gesetzliches *R*, gesetzlicher Anspruch; ~**s issue** Bezugsrechtsausgabe; ~ **in action** = *chose in action* → *chose*; ~ **in gross** (*vom Grundstück*) unabhängiges *R*; ~ **in personam** obligatorisches *R*, Anspruch; ~ **in rem** dingliches *R*; ~**s inter se** *R–e* im Innenverhältnis; ~ **of abode** Aufenthaltsrecht; ~ **of access** *R* zur Einsichtnahme, Zutritts*r*; Umgangs*r*, Verkehrs*r* (*nach Scheidung*); ~ **of accrual** Anwachsungs*r*; ~ **of accused to counsel** *R* des Angeschuldigten auf Verteidiger seiner Wahl; ~ **of action** Klage*r*, Prozeßführungs*r*, klagbarer Anspruch, schlüssiger Klageanspruch; Besitzanspruch; Forderung; *auch:* = *chose in action qv*; ~ **of alienation** Veräußerungs*r*; ~ **of anchoring** Anker*r*; ~ **of angary** Angarien*r* *vgl angaria*; ~ **of anticipation** *R* auf Vorausverfügung; ~ **of appeal** *R*–smittel; ~ **of appropriation** Aneignungs*r*; ~ **of assembly** Versammlungs*r*, Versammlungsfreiheit; ~ **of assignment** Bewilligungs*r*; ~ **of association** Koalitions*r*; ~ **of aubaine** (= *droit d'aubaine*) Staatserb*r* an Ausländernachlaß, Heimfall*r*; ~ **of audience** Anspruch auf rechtliches Gehör, Anhörungsrecht, Postulationsfähigkeit (*R e–s Anwalts, bei Gericht aufzutreten und Anträge zu stellen*); ~ **of avoidance** Anfechtungs*r*; ~ **of calling** (*Prämiengeschäft*) das *R* zu nehmen; ~ **of cancellation** Rücktritts*r*, Aufhebungs*r*, Kündigungs*r*; ~ **of challenge** Geschworenenablehnungs*r*, *vgl challenge*; ~ **of coalition** Koalitions*r*; ~ **of coinage** Münzhoheit; ~ **of common** Entnahme*r* von fremdem Grund; ~ **of compensation** Entschädigungsanspruch; ~ **of complaint** Beschwerde*r*; ~ **of conscience** Gewissensfreiheit; ~ **of consolidation** *R* auf Mithaftung e–s zweiten Pfandes; ~ **of contiguity** Angrenzungs*r*, Anspruch auf angrenzendes Hoheitsgebiet; ~ **of continued use** Weiterbenutzungs*r*; ~ **of contribution** Ausgleichsanspruch *gegen Mithaftende*, Anspruch auf nachträgliche Einbezahlung *von gezeichneten Anteilen bei Gesellschaftsliquidation*; ~ **of courtesy** *gesetzliches* Witwererb*r* (*am Immobiliennachlaß der Frau*); ~ **of cure** Nachbesserungs*r*; ~ **of custody** Sorge*r*; ~ **of detention** Zurückbehaltungs*r*; ~ **of discovery** *R* auf Vorlage von Urkunden; ~ **of discussion** *scot* Einrede der Vorausklage; ~ **of disposal** Veräußerungs*r*, Verfügungs*r*; ~ **of division** anteilige Haftungsbeschränkung des Mitbürgen; ~ **of domicile** Niederlassungs*r*; ~ **of dower** Witwen*r*, Witwenanteil (*am Immobiliennachlaß des Mannes*), Witwenpflichtteilr; ~ **of easement** Anspruch aus e–r Grunddienstbarkeit; ~ **of eminent domain** Zwangsenteignungsr; ~ **of emption** Kaufr, Erwerbsr; ~ **of enclosure** Einhegungsr, Einfriedungsr; ~ **of enforcement** Vollstreckungsanspruch; ~ **of entry** *R* auf Inbesitznahme der (*durch Betreten des Grundstücks*); ~ **of escheat** Heimfallsr; ~ **of establishment** Niederlassungsr; ~ **of exploitation** Verwertungsr, Ausbeutungsr, Entnahmer; ~ **of first refusal** *R* der ersten Ablehnung; (*schuldrechtliches*) Vorkaufsr; ~ **of free entry** *R* auf ungehinderten Zugang; ~ **of habitation** (*kostenloses*) Wohnr; ~ **of his (her) Majesty** Kronr; ~ **of indemnity** Freistellungsanspruch, Aufwendungsersatzanspruch, Entschädigungsanspruch; ~ **of inheritance** Erbanspruch, *subjektives* Erbrecht; ~ **of issuing** Notenbankprivileg; ~ **of joint use** Mitbenutzungsr; ~ **of legation** das *R* auf diplomatische Vertretung; ~ **of local self-government** Selbstverwaltungsr; ~ **of maintenance** Unterhaltsanspruch; ~ **of meeting** Versammlungsr; ~**s of minorities** Minderheitenr; ~**s of (the) minority** Minderheitsr; ~ **of movement** Freizügigkeit; ~ **of navigation** Flußschiffahrtsr; ~ **of notice** Kündigungsr; ~ **of option** Optionsr; ~ **of passage** Weger, Fahrr; ~ **of pasturage** Weider; ~ **of patronage** Pfründenbesetzungsr; ~ **of performance** Aufführungsr; ~ **of persons** höchstpersönliches *R*; ~ **of petition** Petitionsr; ~ **of possession** *R* auf Besitz; ~ **of pre-emption** Vorkaufsr; ~ **of priority** Prioritätsr, Vorbenutzungsr; ~ **of priority on the road** Vorfahrtsr; ~ **of privacy** → *privacy*; ~ **of property** (*abstraktes*) Eigentumsr am Grundstück, Vermögensr; ~ **of prospect** Fensterr; ~ **of publication** Verlagsr, Veröffentlichungsr; ~ **of recovery** Entschädigungsanspruch, Regreßr, Rückgriffsr, Schadenersatzanspruch; ~ **of redemption** Pfandauslösungsr, Pfandrückübereignungsr (*nach Verfall*); ~ **of re-entry** *R* der Wiederinbesitznahme; ~ **of relief** Rückgriffsr (*bes des leistenden Bürgen gegen den Hauptschuldner*); ~ **of reply** Erwiderungsr (*bes des Antragstellers bei Debatte*); *R* auf Gegendarstellung; ~ **of representation and performance** Aufführungsr; ~ **of repurchase** Wiederkaufsr; ~ **of rescission** Anfechtungsr, Aufhebungsr; ~ **of restitution** Erstattungsanspruch; ~ **of restoration** Wiederherstellungsanspruch; ~ **of retainer** Zurückbehaltungsr; ~ **of retention** Zurückbehaltungsr; ~ **of reverter** Heimfallsr; ~ **of review** Überprüfungsr; ~ **of sale** Vertriebsr; ~ **of salvage** Strandr, Bergungsr; ~ **of sanctuary** Asylr; ~ **of search** Durchsuchungsr (*e–s neutralen Schiffes*); ~ **of seclusion** Absonderungsr, Aussonderungsr; ~ **of self-determination** Selbstbestimmungsr; ~ **of set-off** Aufrechnungsr; ~ **of severance** Abtrennungsr; ~ **of silence** (= ~ *to silence*) Schweigerecht (des Angeklagten); ~ **of succession** Erbfolger, Nachfolger; ~ **of support** *R* auf Grenzabstützung; ~ **of survivorship** Anwachsungsr des Überlebenden (*Partners*); ~ **of tanto** Vorkaufsr des Nießbrauchers; ~**s of things** *R–e* an Sachen; ~ **of translation** Übersetzungsr; ~ **of user** Gebrauchsr; ~ **of veto** Vetor; ~ **of visitation** → *visitation*; ~ **of way** Weger, Wegegerechtigkeit, Geh- und Fahrtr; Dienstbarkeit für Benutzung e–s Bahnkörpers, Vorfahrtsr; *public* ~ ~ ~: öffentl Weger; öffentl Begehungsr; ~**s over children** Personensorger an Kindern; ~ **patent** *hist* Eigentumsherausgabeklage auf Grundbesitz; ~ **to acquire** Bezugsr, Erwerbsberechtigung; ~ **to apply** Antragsberechtigung; ~ **to bail** *R* auf Haftverschonung gegen Sicherheitsleistung; ~ **to be consulted** Konsultationsr, *R* gefragt zu werden; ~ **to be elected** passives Wahl*r*; ~ **to begin** das *R* des ersten Plädoyers; *R* des ersten Sachvortrags; ~ **to benefit** Leistungsanspruch; ~ **to be heard** *R* auf Gehör; ~ **to bid reserved** Mitbietungs*r* des Verkäufers; ~ **to consult a solicitor** *R* auf Zuziehung e–s Rechtsanwalts; ~ **to convert** Umwandlungs*r*; ~ **to convey** das *R*, Grundstückseigentum zu übertragen, Grundstücksveräußerungs*r*; ~ **to counsel** → *counsel*; ~ **to demonstrate** Demonstrations*r*; ~ **to elect** Wahl*r*, Ersetzungsbefugnis; ~ **to exist** *R* auf Leben, Lebens*r*; ~ **to follow the asset** Folge*r*; ~ **to forbid** Untersagungs*r*; ~ **to future pension benefits** Pensionsanwartschaft; ~ **to information** Auskunfts*r*; ~ **to legal redress** Rechtsschutzanspruch; ~ **to legal representation** *R*, sich anwaltlich vertreten zu lassen; ~ **to light** Licht*r*; ~ **to merchandise exclusively** *R* zum ausschließlichen Vertrieb; ~ **to pass and repass** das *R* des Umhergehens auf öffentl Plätzen u Straßen; ~ **to protest** *R* zum Protestieren in der Öffentlichkeit; ~ **to quiet enjoyment** das *R* auf ungestörte Nutzung; ~ **to receive** Herausgabeanspruch; Empfangs*r*; ~ **to recovery** Herausgabeanspruch, Leistungsanspruch; ~ **to redeem** Auslösungs*r*, Tilgungs*r*; ~ **to refuse performance** Leistungsverweigerungs*r*; ~ **to relief** *R*–*s*schutzanspruch; ~ **to renew** Verlängerungs*r*; ~ **to repair** Instandsetzungsanspruch; ~ ~ ~ *default notice:* befristete Mahnung zwecks (Wohnungs)Instandsetzung, Selbsthilfeankündigung; ~ **to reproduce** Vervielfältigungs*r*; ~ **to silence** *R* keine Angaben zu machen, Schweige*r*; ~ **to strike** Streik*r*; ~ **to subscribe** Bezugs*r*; ~ **to succeed** (*subjektives*) Erbrecht, Anspruch auf Rechtsnachfolge; ~ **to sue in forma pauperis** Armen*r*; ~ **to sue in person** Prozeßfähigkeit im Parteiprozeß, persönl Klage*r*, ~ **to use a trade mark** Warenzeichenbenutzungs*r*; ~ **to vote** Wahl*r*, Stimm*r*; ~ **to work** *R* ohne Gewerkschaftszwang zu arbeiten; ~ **to work minerals** Bergwerks*r*, Schürf*r*; ~ **under a contract** Vertrags*r*; **absolute** ~ absolutes *R*, ausschließliches *R*; **abuse of ~s** → *abuse*; **accessory ~s** Neben*r*–*e*; **accrual of a** ~ → *accrual*; ~ **accruing** ~ anfallendes *R*, Anwachsungs*r*; **acquired ~s and ~s in course of acquisition** erworbene *R*–*e* und Anwartschafts*r*–*e*; **alienable** ~ veräußerliches *R*; **all ~s reserved** alle *R*–*e* vorbehalten; **antecedent ~s** originäre *R*–*e*, selbständige *R*–*e*; **appearance of a** ~ Anschein e–s *R*–*s*; **bare** ~ abstraktes *R*; **base** ~ Vasallen*r*, *R* des Unterlehensträgers; **bill of ~s** → *bill*; **by** ~ von *R*–*s* wegen; **by** ~ **of** kraft, auf Grund von; **call** ~ Kündigungs*r* (*Anleihe*); **chartered ~s** verbriefte *R*–*e*; **civic ~s** bürgerliche Ehren*r*–*e*, Grund*r*–*e*, Bürger*r*–*e*; **civil ~s** Grund*r*–*e*; **Civil R~s Acts** *US* Bürgerrechtsgesetze (*zur Rassengleichheit*); **common** ~ allgemein anerkanntes *R*; **composite** ~ Anspruch mit mehreren *R*–*s*grundlagen; **conditional** ~ bedingtes *R*; **conjugal ~s** eheliche *R*–*e*; **constitutional** ~ → *constitutional*; **contingent** ~ Aussicht, aufschiebend bedingtes *R*; **contract ~s** Vertragsansprüche; **contractual** ~ Vertrags*r*, obligatorisches *R*; **customary** ~ Gewohnheits*r*; gewohnheitsrechtl Anspruch; **dramatic ~s** Aufführungs*r*–*e*, Bühnen*r*–*e*; **duly acquired ~s** wohlerworbene *R*–*e*; **equality of ~s** → *equality*; **equitable** ~ billigkeitsrechtlicher Anspruch auf Equity beruhendes *R*; **ex ~s** → *ex*; **exclusive** ~ Alleinberechtigung, Ausschließlichkeits*r*; **exercise of a** ~ → *exercise*; **extrajudicial** ~ außergerichtlich durchsetzbares *R*; **film ~s** Verfilmungs*r*, Film*r*–*e*, Filmverwertungs*r*–*e*; **formal** ~ formaler Anspruch; *R*; **full** ~ volles *R* (*zB Eigentum und Besitz*); **fundamental** ~ grundlegendes *R*; Grund*r*; **future** ~ künftiges *R*; **grazing** ~**s** Weide*r–e*; **homestead** ~ Heimstättenvollstreckungsschutz (*für landwirtschaftliche Anwesen*); **human** ~**s** → *human*; **imperfect** ~ unvollkommenes *R*; nicht gerichtl erzwingbares *R*; **in** ~ **of sb** aus dem *R* von jmdm, auf Grund des *R–s* jmds; **inalienable** ~ nicht übertragbares *R*, unveräußerliches *R*; **inborn** ~ angeborenes *R*; **indefeasible** ~ unangreifbares *R*; **industrial** ~ gewerbliches Schutz*r*; **inchoate** ~ in der Entstehung begriffenes *R*, angemeldetes Patent*r*; **inherent** ~ angeborenes *R*, Natur*r*; originäres *R*; **intangible** ~ unkörperliches *R*, immaterielles *R*; **intellectual property** ~**s** gewerbliche Schutzrechte und Urheberrechte; **judicial** ~ gerichtlich durchsetzbares *R*; **junior** ~ jüngeres *R*, rangschlechteres *R*; **legal** ~ gesetzliches *R*, *R*–sanspruch *bes nach Common Law*, dingliches *R*; **licence of** ~ → *licence*; **magazine** ~**s** Nachdruck*r* für Zeitschriften; **mineral** ~**s** Schürf*r–e*; **mining** ~**s** Schürf*r–e*; **moral** ~ moralischer Anspruch; ~ ~*s of an author: Urheberpersönlichkeitsrecht*; **natural** ~ naturrechtlicher Anspruch; originäres *R*, Grund*r*; **note-issuing** ~ → *note*; **obligatory** ~ obligatorischer Anspruch; **ownership** ~ Eigentums*r*; **parental** ~**s** elterliche *R–e*; **participating** ~**s** Gewinnbeteiligungs*r–e*; Genuß*r–e*; **peremptory** ~ Ausschließlichkeits*r*, unabdingbares *R*; **perfect** ~ (vollkommenes) *R*; **performing** ~ Aufführungs*r*; **periferal** ~**s** Neben*r–e*; **personal** ~ obligatorischer Anspruch, Persönlichkeits*r*; absolutes e–r Person zustehendes Schutz*r*; **personal** ~**s** (verfassungsmäßige) Grund*r–e* der Person (*auf Leben, körperliche Unversehrtheit, Freiheit*); **Petition of R**~ → *petition*; **political** ~ staatsbürgerliches *R*, politisches *R*; **possessive** ~ Besitz*r*, *R* auf Besitz; **possessory** ~ possessorisches *R*; **precarious** ~ widerruflich gewährtes *R*; stets widerrufliche Gestattung; **preemptive** ~ Vorkaufs*r*, Vorzugs*r*, Bezugs*r auf junge Aktien*; **prescriptive** ~ → *prescriptive*; **present** ~ gegenwärtiges *R*; **preventive** ~ vorbeugendes *R*, Schutz*r*; **primary** ~ selbständiges *R*, Haupt*r*; **prior** ~ älteres *R*, Vorzugs*r*; **property** ~ Vermögens*r*; **proprietary** ~ Eigentums*r*, Befugnis des Eigentümers, Urheber*r*, Schutz*r*; **protective** ~ Schutz*r*; **public** ~**s** öffentl *R–e*, *R–e* der Allgemeinheit; **purchase** ~ → *purchase*; **qualified** ~ bedingtes *R*; **real** ~ dingliches *R*; **redeemable** ~ Heimfalls*r*, Ablösungs*r*, kündbares *R*; **relative** ~ relatives *R*, obligatorisches *R*; **remedial** ~ *R–s*-schutzanspruch; **rental** ~**s** → *rental s*; **reparative** ~ Wiederherstellungs*r*; **restitutory** ~ Rückerstattungs*r*; **reversionary** ~ (*vgl reversion*) durch Eintritt e–s zukünftigen Ereignisses bedingtes Anwartschafts*r*; **riparian** ~**s** Uferanlieger*r–e*; **secondary** ~ Neben*r*; **serial** ~**s** Abdrucks*r* in Fortsetzungen; **shop** ~ → *shop*; **sole** ~ alleiniges *R*; **sovereign** ~**s** Hoheits*r–e*; **sporting** ~**s** Jagd*r*; **stage** ~**s** Bühnen*r–e*, Aufführungs*r*; **status-based** ~ auf den Personenstand gegründes *R*, statusbedingter Anspruch; **substantial** ~ materielles *R*; erheblicher *R*–sanspruch; **substantive** ~ materielles *R*; **successor in** ~ *R*–snachfolger; **to abandon a** ~ → *abandon*; **to assert a** ~ → *to assert*; **to assign a** ~ ein *R* übertragen; e–n Anspruch abtreten; **to disclaim a** ~ auf ein *R* verzichten; **to infringe a** ~ ein *R* verletzen; **to relinquish a** ~ auf ein *R* verzichten; **to reserve** ~**s** sich *R–e* vorbehalten; **to stand on one's** ~**s** auf seinem *R* beharren; **treaty** ~**s** Vertrags*r–e*; **unalienable** ~ nicht übertragbares *R*, unveräußerliches *R*; **undivided** ~ ungeteiltes *R*, gemeinsames *R*;

use ~ Nutzungsr, Gebrauchsr; **valuable** ~ Vermögensr, vermögenswertes *R*; **vested** ~ → *vested*; **visiting** ~**s** Umgangsr (*zu e–m Kinde*), Besuchsr; **visitorial** ~ Durchsuchungsr; **without a semblance of** ~ ohne den Anschein e–s *R–s*; **writ of** ~ → *writ*.
rightful rechtmäßig, berechtigt.
rightist *pol* Rechter *m*, Konservativer *m*; Rechtsradikaler *m*; Frauenrechtlerin *f*.
rights Bezugsrechte *n*|*pl*; ~ **dealings** Handel mit Bezugsrechten; ~ **issue** Bezugsrechtsemission; ~ **letter** = *letters of* ~ *qv*; ~ **offering** Bezugsrechtsangebot; **letter of** ~ Bezugsrechtsmitteilung mit Angebot.
rights activist Menschenrechtskämpfer *m*.
right-thinking redlich, rechtlich denkend.
rigor mortis Totenstarre *f*.
ring Ring *m*, Verband *m*, Bande *f*, Clique *f*; kreisförmige Börsenschranke; Geländer; ~ **dropping** Trickdiebstahl; ~ **leader** Rädelsführer; **the** ~ *brit* die Buchmacher.
ringer betrügerisch vertauschtes Unfallwrack (*gegen Diebstahlswagen*).
ringing the changes Münzwechselschwindel *m*.
ringing up gegenseitige Abrechnung *f* der Kommissionäre und Makler.
riot *s* Aufruhr *m*, Auflauf *m*, Zusammenrottung *f*, Landfriedensbruch; = ~ **Act** *brit* Gesetz *von 1714* gegen Zusammenrottungen; *reading the R~ A~: Aufforderung an e–e Menschenmenge, friedlich auseinanderzugehen*; ~ **and civil commotions** Aufruhr und bürgerliche Unruhen; **R~ (Damages) Act** Tumultschädengesetz; ~ **gear** Ausrüstung für Tumulteinsatz; Tumultschutzkleidung; ~ **insurance** Aufruhrversicherung, Tumultschadensversicherung; ~ **police** Bereitschaftspolizei; ~ **shield** Schutzschild (*für Polizeibeamte*); ~ **squad** Überfallkommando; **prison** ~ Gefangenenmeuterei; **statutory** ~ Aufruhr im Sinne des Riot Act; **suppression of** ~ Bekämpfung von Landfriedensbruch.
riot *v* sich zusammenrotten.
rioter Aufrührer *m*.
riotous aufrührerisch.
rising of court Ende der Sitzung.
risk *s* Risiko *n*, Gefahr *f*, Risikosumme *f*; versicherte Person *f*, versicherter Gegenstand *m*; ~ **after discharge** Gefahr nach Löschung der Ladung; ~**s and perils** (gedeckte) Gefahren; ~ **arbitrage** Risikoarbitrage; ~**-asset ratio** Verhältnis des Risikos zum Eigenvermögen e–r Bank; ~**-bearer** Risikoträger; ~**-bearing capital** Spekulationskapital; ~ **begins to run** Versicherungsdeckung ab . . .; ~**s book** Liste der übernommenen Risiken; ~ **capital** Risikokapital; ~ **covered** gedecktes Risiko, versicherte Gefahr; ~ **excluded** ausgeschlossenes Risiko; ~**s incident to employment** Arbeitsgefahren; ~ **management** Risikobeherrschung; ~**-money** Fehlgeld, Mankogeld; ~ **note** schriftl Haftungsbeschränkung des Transportunternehmers; ~ **of carriage** Transportrisiko; ~ **of collision** Kollisionsgefahr; ~ **of contamination** Ansteckungsgefahr; ~ **of conveyance** Transportrisiko; ~ **of deterioration** Gefahr der zufälligen Verschlechterung; ~ **of escape** Fluchtgefahr; ~ **of insolvency** Insolvenzrisiko; ~ **of one's life** Lebensgefahr; ~ **of loss** Verlustrisiko, Gefahr des Untergangs; ~ **passes** *die* Gefahr (*des zufälligen Untergangs bzw der Beschädigung*) geht über (*auf*); ~**s of the sea** Seegefahren; ~ **premium** Risikoprämie; ~ **records** Übersichtspläne mit den wichtigsten Brandversicherungsobjekten; ~ **taking** Risikoübernahme; **accident** ~ Unfallrisiko; **accumulation of** ~ Risikohäufung; **against all** ~**s** gegen alle Gefahren; **aggravated** ~ erhöhtes Risiko; **all** ~**s policy** Universalversicherung; **allocation of** ~ Risikoverteilung; **amount at** ~ Risikosumme; **as-**

signed ~ (*vom Versicherungsverband einer Gesellschaft*) zugewiesenes Versicherungsrisiko; **assigned** ~ **pool** (=) *Pool von Versicherungsgesellschaften zur Versicherung „unerwünschter Fahrer"*; **assumption of** ~ Risikoübernahme, Gefahrenübernahme; **at consigner's** ~ auf Risiko des Absenders; **at one's own** ~ auf eigene Gefahr; **at receiver's** ~ auf Gefahr des Empfängers; **at the** ~ **and cost** auf Kosten und Gefahr; **attachment of** ~ → *attachment*; **automobile dealer's** ~ Autohändlerhaftpflicht; **automobile owner's** ~**s** Autohalterrisiken; **aviation** ~ Luftfahrtrisiko, Flugverkehrsrisiko; **bilateral** ~ zweiseitiges Risiko; **business** ~ Geschäftsrisiko; **change in the** ~ Risikoänderung; **classification of** ~**s** → *classification*; **commencement of** ~ Risikobeginn; **commercial** ~ wirtschaftliches Risiko, Unternehmerwagnis; **contractor's** ~ Unternehmerrisiko; **cooperative** ~ **carrying** gemeinschaftliche Risikotragung; **cover of** ~**s** Deckung von Risiken; **credit** ~ → *credit (2)*; **customary** ~**s** handelsübliche Risiken; **economic** ~ Konjunkturrisiko; **elimination of** ~ Risikobeseitigung; **entrepreneurial** ~ Unternehmerrisiko; **exchange** ~ → *exchange (2)*; **excluded** ~ ausgeschlossenes Risiko; **fair** ~**s** versicherbare Risiken; **fire** ~ → *fire*; **genuine** ~ echte Gefahr; **goods are at buyer's** ~ der Käufer trägt die Gefahr; **happening of the** ~ Eintritt des Versicherungsfalles; **increase of** ~ → *increase*; **individual** ~ Eigengefahr; **involving** ~ gefahrgeneigt; **insurable** ~ versicherbares Risiko; **lapse** ~ → *lapse*; **marginal** ~ Devisenkursschwankungsrisiko; **marine** ~ Seegefahr, Seerisiko; **marketing** ~ Absatzrisiko; **mean** ~ mittleres Risiko; **military** ~ Kriegsrisiko; **obvious** ~ offensichtliche Gefahr, leicht erkennbares Risiko; **ordinary** ~ gewöhnliches Berufsrisiko; **own** ~ auf eigene Gefahr, *ins* Selbstbehalt; **particular** ~ das Risiko im besonderen Fall; **passing of the** ~ Gefahrübergang; **pending** ~**s** laufende Versicherungsrisiken; **perceivable** ~ erkennbare Gefahr; unbestimmtes und ungewisses Risiko; **personal** ~ Personenrisiko (*Lebens- und Erwerbsunfähigkeitsrisiko*); **preferred** ~ Sondertarif für günstige Versicherungsrisiken; ~ ~*s plan: Schadensfreiheitssystem*; **price** ~ Kursrisiko; **primary** ~**s** Höchstrisikokategorie; **property** ~ Sachschadenrisiko; **pure** ~ Risiko im engeren Sinne, (*ohne Spekulationsrisiko*); **retained** ~ nicht rückversicherter Teil des Risikos; **secondary** ~**s** durchschnittliche Risikostufe; **selection** ~**s** → *selection*; **shifting** ~**s** Versicherungsdeckung e–s auswechselbaren Bestandes; **sole** ~ (auf) alleinige Gefahr; **special** ~ besonderes Risiko, tätigkeitsbedingtes R.; **speculative** ~ Spekulationsrisiko; **spreading of** ~**s** Risikostreuung, Risikoverteilung; **substantial** ~ erhebliches Risiko; **termination of** ~ Risikoende; **to run a** ~ ein Risiko auf sich nehmen; **transfer of** ~ → *transfer*; **uncovered** ~ nicht versichertes Risiko; **undesirable** ~**s** *(= the undesirables) wegen häufiger Unfälle* unerwünschte Fahrer; **unexpired** ~ Deckungszeit durch vorausbezahlte Prämie; **uninsurable** ~ nicht versicherbares Risiko; **uninsured** ~ ungedecktes Risiko; **voluntary assumption of** ~ freiwillige Gefahrenübernahme; **war** ~ → *war*.

ristorno Ristorno *m*.

rite *adv* ordnungsmäßig, formal richtig.

rite Ritus *m*.

rivage Flußzoll *m*.

rival *s* Mitbewerber *m*, Wettbewerber *m*; ~ **firm** Konkurrenzfirma.

rival *v* konkurrieren, wetteifern, rivalisieren.

rivalry Konkurrenz *f*, Wettbewerb *m*, Wetteifer *m*.

river Fluß *n*, Strom *m*; ~ **authorities**

Flußbauämter; ~ **bank** Flußufer (*vom Hochwasserstand aufwärts*); **R~ Board** Flußaufsichtsamt (*GB, bis 1963*); ~ **bill of lading** → *bill of lading*; ~ **power station** Flußkraftwerk; ~ **traffic** Flußverkehr; **international ~s** internationalisierte Flüsse; **internationalised ~s** internationalisierte Flüsse; **navigable** ~ schiffbarer Fluß; **pollution of ~s** Verschmutzung von Flüssen; **private** ~ Privatfluß; **public** ~ öffentlicher Fluß.

road Landstraße *f*, Wasserstraße *f*, Verkehrsweg *m*, Strecke *f*, Fahrbahn *f*, Bahnstrecke *f*, Geleise *n*, Gleisanlage *f*, Förderstrecke *f*; Gastspielgebiet *n*; ~ **accident** (Straßen)Verkehrsunfall; ~ **accident prevention campaigns** Unfallverhütungsaktionen; **~s advisory committee** Straßenverkehrsberatungsausschuß; ~ **authority** örtliche Straßenbehörde; **~bed** Bahnkörper; ~ **board** örtliches Straßenbauamt; ~ **carrying fast-moving traffic** *brit* Straße mit Schnellverkehr; ~ **districts** Straßenbauunterhaltsverbände; ~ **fund** Straßenbaufonds; ~ **haulage** Güterkraftverkehr; ~ **hog** rücksichtsloser, egoistischer Fahrer (*der anderen den Weg nicht freigibt*); ~ **patrols** Straßendienst; ~ **repair** (Straßen-) Ausbesserungsarbeiten; ~ **safety** Verkehrssicherheit; ~ **sense** Straßenverstand des Fahrers; ~ **sign** → *sign*; ~ **tax** Straßenunterhaltssteuer; ~ **toll** Maut; **R~ Traffic Act** Straßenverkehrsordnung; ~ **transport** Straßengüterverkehr; ~ **user** Verkehrsteilnehmer; ~ **warning** Straßenverkehrszeichen; ~ **works** Straßenarbeiten; **access** ~ Zufahrtstraße; **arterial** ~ Hauptverkehrsstraße; **at the** ~ auf der Reede, vor Anker; **by-** ~ → *byroad*; **hard-surface** ~ Straße mit staubfreiem Belag; **inner relief** ~ innerstädtische Entlastungsstraße; **law of the** ~ → *law*; **link** ~ Kreisstraße, Landstraße II. Ordnung; **main** ~ Hauptverkehrsstraße, Bundesstraße I. Ordnung; **major** ~ **ahead** Vorfahrt beachten!; **metalled** ~ geschotterte Straße, befestigte S.; **motor** ~ Schnellstraße; **occupation** ~ Anliegern vorbehaltene Straße; **on the** ~ auf Tournee; **orbital** ~ äußere Ringstraße, Ringautobahn; **private** ~ Privatweg; **public** ~ öffentliche Straße, Landstraße; **secondary** ~ Nebenstraße; **third class** ~ Gemeindeverbindungsweg; **trunk** ~ Fernverkehrsstraße; **unpaved** ~ Straße ohne staubfreien Belag, Schotterstraße.

roadholding Straßenlage *f* (*e–s Pkw*).

roadshow Lunch-Treffen der Hochfinanz.

roadstead Reede *f*.

roadworthiness Verkehrssicherheit *f* (*e–s Fahrzeugs*).

roadworthy verkehrssicher.

rob rauben, berauben, plündern, stehlen.

robber Räuber *m*.

robbery Raub *m*; Beraubung *f*, Raubüberfall *m*; ~ **by person armed** bewaffneter Raub; ~ **insurance** Raubüberfallversicherung; ~ **with aggravation** schwerer Raub; ~ **with violence** (gewalttätiger) Raub; **highway** ~ Straßenraub.

robe Robe *f*, Amtsrobe *f*, Amtstracht *f*; Talar *m*; **gentlemen of the (long)** ~ der Juristenstand, die Juristen; **master of the ~s** Oberkämmerer; **official** ~ Amtstracht; **the (long)** ~ Juristenberuf; Amtsrobe der Juristen, Juristenstand.

rodman Vermessungshelfer *m*.

rogation Fürbitte *f*, Rogation *f*; *hist* Gesetzesvorschlag *m*, Gesetz *n*.

rogatory commission Rechtshilfeersuchen um Zeugenvernehmung; ~ **letters** → *letter*.

rogue Landstreicher *m*, Bettler *m*; Vagabund *m*; **~'s gallery** Verbrecheralbum; ~ **virus** Hacker-Virus *m* (*in EDV-Anlagen*); **incorrigible** ~ unverbesserlicher Übeltäter.

roll Rolle *f*, Gerichtsakte *f*, Anwaltsliste *f*, Terminplan *m*; Verzeichnis *n*, Liste *f*, Protokoll *n*; **the R~s** *brit*

Staatsarchiv; ~ **call** namentlicher Aufruf; ~ **call vote** namentliche Abstimmung; **R~s Court** *hist Gerichtssaal des Masters of the Rolls qv*; ~ **of court** grundherrschaftliche Urkunden; ~ **of documents** Urkundenverzeichnis, Urkundenrolle; ~ **of honour** Ehrentafel der Gefallenen; **R~s of Parliament** Verzeichnis alter Parlamentsberichte und höchstrichterlicher Entscheidungen; ~ **of proceedings** Prozeßakte, Gerichtsakte; **~s of the exchequer** Abgabenverzeichnis; **~s of the temple** Beitragsliste der Mitglieder der Temple-Juristeninnung; **R~s Office of the Chancery** Urkundenzimmer des Chancery Gerichts; Sitzungssaal des Master of the Rolls; **admitted to the** ~ als Anwalt zugelassen; **assessment** ~ Verzeichnis der Steuerzahler *und der zu besteuernden Grundstücke*; **death** ~ Verlustliste; **electoral** ~ Wählerliste; **imparlance** ~ Vertagungsliste; **issue** ~ (*vorläufige*) Prozeßakte; **judgment** ~ → *judgment*; **Master of the R~s** → *master*; **nominal** ~ Namensliste; **patent** ~ Patentrolle; **plea(s)** ~ → *plea*; **process** ~ → *process*; **recognizance** ~ Liste der Kautionsverpflichtungen; **tax** ~ Verzeichnis der Steuerzahler; **to call the** ~ namentlich aufrufen; **warrant of attorney** ~ Verzeichnis der Prozeßbevollmächtigten.

roll fahren; rollen; rauben.

roll-back starke Preisherabsetzung; Zurückwerfen des Kommunismus; ~ **subsidies** Subventionen zur Preisherabsetzung.

rolling unterwegs, auf dem Transport; ~ **adjustment** branchenmäßiger Geschäftsvorgang; ~ **capital** Betriebskapital; ~ **freight** Rollgut; ~ **readjustment** allmähliche Anpassung; ~ **stock** rollendes Material; ~ **targets** flexible Zielvorgaben.

roll-over Kreditverlängerung; Abwälzung *f*; ~ **loan** längerfristiges Darlehen mit Zinsanpassungsklausel; ~ **relief** steuerliche Vergünstigung bei Wiederanlage.

roll over *v/t* umschulden, neu Kreditlinien festsetzen, refinanzieren; ~ **current lines of credit** neue Kreditlinien aushandeln.

Romalpa clause Vorbehaltsklausel bis zur vollständigen Zahlung.

romanist Romanist *m* (*Rechtsgelehrter auf dem Gebiet des römischen Rechts*).

Rome|Convention Konvention *f* von Rom 1928 (*internationales Verkehrsrecht*); **R~-Scot** *(Rome penny) hist* Peter-Pfennig; **Treaty of** ~ → *treaty*.

rood of land Viertelmorgen, *210 square yards*.

room Raum *m*, Zimmer *n*, Sitzungssaal *m*; **long** ~ Abfertigungshalle im Zollamt; **underground ~s** Souterrainsräume.

roomer Untermieter *m*.

rooming house Pension *f*.

Roosa-type bond Roosa-Bond *m*, einjähriger Schatzwechsel *m*.

root | of descent Abstammung *f*; ~ **of title** Eigentumsursprung; urkundlicher Eigentumsnachweis bei Grundstücken (*seit mindestens 30 Jahren*).

rope Strick *m*, Strang *m*; Tod *m* durch den Strang; **~s** Schliche, Kniffe.

roper-in Schlepper *m*, Zubringer *m e–s Spielsalons*.

ros noble Rosennobel *m*, Ryal *m (engl Münze 15. und 16. Jhd)*.

roster Dienstliste *f*, Liste *f*, Tabelle *f*, Geschworenenliste *f*.

rostrum Rednerpult *n*, Rednertribüne *f*.

rot Fäulnis *f*, Schwamm *m*; **dry** ~ Trockenfäule, Vermodern; **electoral** ~ Wählerschwund.

rota Turnus *m*, Namensliste *f*; kath. Kirchengerichte *n*.

rota clerk Geschäftsstelle *f* für turnusmäßige Bestellung von Vernehmungsanwälten (*vgl examiner*).

rotate turnusmäßig ausscheiden.

rotating|lines of credit Agrarkredit für Multikulturen; ~ **shift** Wechselschicht.

rotation turnusmäßiger Wechsel *m*,

turnusmäßiges Ausscheiden *n*; ~ **in office** turnusmäßiger Amtswechsel.

rotten faul, verfault, korrupt; ~ **clause** Haftungsausschluß bei Seeuntüchtigkeit (*wegen Fäulnis oder Korrosion*).

„roulette wheel" system of justice das Lotteriespiel der Justiz.

round *adj* rund, bogenförmig, abgerundet; ~ **lot** Schluß (= *Mindestmenge bzw. -betrag für den einzelnen Börsenabschluß; NY: 100 Aktien oder $ 1000 Nennwert bei Obligationen*); ~ **lot orders** → *order* (*2*); ~ **sum** runder Betrag; ~ **transaction** Börsengeschäft mit sofortiger Reinvestition; ~ **trip ticket** Rundreisebillet; *US* Hin- und Rückfahrkarte.

round *s* Rundung *f*; Runde *f*, Rundgang *m*, Streife *f*; Salve *f*, Schuß *m*.

round *v* runden, rund machen; denunzieren; ~ **off** arrondieren, abrunden.

round-about *brit* Kreisverkehr.

rounding Aufrundung *f bzw* Abrundung *f*.

roundup Razzia *f*, Zusammentreiben *n von Vieh*.

rout (Straßen)Auflauf *m*; Zusammenrottung *f*, Tumult *m*.

route *s* Route *f*, Weg *m*, Strecke *f*; ~ **card** Arbeitsablaufkarte; ~ **instructions** Leitvermerk; Anweisungen über die Reiseroute; ~ **man** für bestimmte Kundenroute eingesetzter Mitarbeiter; **intended** ~ vorgesehener Beförderungsweg; **forwarding** ~ Beförderungsweg.

route *v* Dokumente auf dem Amtsweg weiterleiten; ~**d** mit Leitvermerk versehen (*Postsendung*).

routing Festlegen *n* der Reiseroutine, Bestimmung *f* des Durchlaufs der Produktionsstufen.

routous aufrührerisch.

royal königlich; ~ **arms** das königliche Wappen; **R~ Assent** königliche Zustimmung (*Inkraftsetzung von Parlamentsgesetzen*); ~ **bounty** königliche Zuwendungen (*vgl bounty*); ~ **burgh** freie (Reichs-) Stadt; ~ **charter** königliche Verleihungsurkunde; **R~ College of Physicians** königliche Ärztekammer; ~ **commission** → *commission*; ~ **commissioner** → *commissioner*; **R~ Courts of Justice** (=) *Justizpalast in London*; ~ **draught** königliches Flußfischentnahmerecht; ~ **estate** → *estate*; **R~ Exchange** Londoner Börse; ~ **fish** → *fish*; ~ **forest** Kronforst; ~ **grant** → *grant*; ~ **honors** diplomatische Vorrechte des Monarchen; ~ **household** königlicher Hof; **R~ Humane Society** *brit* Lebensrettungsgesellschaft; **R~ Mail** der brit Postdienst; **R~ marine** kgl Seesoldat, Angehöriger des brit Marinekorps; **R~ Marriages Act** *brit Gesetz über Heiratserlaubnis für Angehörige der königlichen Familie (1972)*; **R~ Military Asylum** = Duke of York School (*Internat für Offizierssöhne, Kadettenschule*); ~ **mines** Silber- und Goldbergwerke als Prärogative der Krone; staatliches (*zum Münzregal gehörendes*) Ankaufsrecht von Edelmetallen; **R~ Mint** königl Münzamt; ~ **parks** königliche Wildgehege; **R~ personage** Mitglied der königlichen Familie; ~ **prerogatives** Regalien, königliche Vorrechte; ~ **privilege** → *privilege*; ~ **proclamation** königlicher Erlaß, königliche Proklamation; ~ **residence** königlicher Palast (*als Sitz des Königs*); **R~ Speech** Thronrede; ~ **standard** Königsstandarte; ~ **style and titles** der volle Titel des brit. Monarchen; **R~ warrant** *brit* Hoflieferantendiplom.

royalist Royalist *m*, Monarchist *m*, Königstreuer *m*.

royalty Königtum *n*, Königswürde *f*, königliches Vorrecht *n*, Regal *n*, Abgabe *f* an den König; Lizenzgebühr *f*, Patentabgabe *f*, Schürfrecht *n*, Bergregal *n*, Krongut *n*; Grundzehnt *m*; ~ **discrimination** unterschiedliche Lizenzgebühren; ~-**free licence** → *licence*; ~ **on patents** Patentlizenzabgabe; ~ **rent** Ertragspacht; **continuing** ~ **(on**

sales) laufende Lizenzgebühr (auf den Umsatz); **copyright** ~ → *copyright*; **director's** ~ Aufsichtsratstantieme; **overriding** ~ → *overriding*; **per unit** ~ Stücklizenzgebühr; **post-expiration** ~**ies** Lizenzgebühren nach Ablauf des Patentschutzes; **summed-up** ~**ies** kapitalisierte Gesamtlizenz.

rubber|cheque ungedeckter Scheck; ~ **stamp** Gummistempel; ~ **truncheon** Gummiknüppel.

rubbish claim Trivialforderung *f*.

rubric Rubrik *f*, Überschrift *f*, Titelkopf *m*; Weisung *f im Book of Common Prayers*; *scot* Leitsatz *m*; ~ **of a statute** Gesetzestitel.

rubricate mit Titelkopf versehen, rubrizieren, in Rubriken einteilen.

rudeness Grobheit *f*, Gewaltsamkeit *f*.

rule Regel *f*, Verfahrensregel *f*, Verfahrensnorm *f*, Verwaltungsvorschrift *f*, Ausführungsverordnung *f*, Anordnung *f*; Vorentscheid *m*, Offizialverfügung *f*; Herrschaft *f*, Regierung *f*; ~**s** Sondertermin; Termin für Beschlußsachen; ~ **absolute** rechtskräftige Verfügung; ~ **against accumulation** Verbot langfristiger Zinsthesaurierung; ~ **against perpetuities** Verbot von Zuwendungen auf „ewige" Zeit, *Verbot zukünftiger dingl Zuwendungen für die Zeit nach 21 Jahren seit dem Ableben e–r oder mehrerer bei der Verfügung lebender oder bereits gezeugter Personen;* ~**s and by-laws** Statuten, Satzung; ~**s and regulations** Durchführungsbestimmungen, Geschäftsordnung; **R**~**s Committee** höchstrichterlicher Prozeßordnungsausschuß; ~**s-day** Tag des Inkrafttretens (*e–r Verfügung bzw Auflage*); ~ **discharged** Verfügung aufgehoben; ~ **in Shelley's Case** → *Shelley's Case*; ~ **nisi** Vorbehaltsbeschluß (*bei dem der Gegenseite Einwendungen vorbehalten bleiben*); **R**~ **of 1756** (*int Verbot für neutrale Staaten, Handelsbereich mit Kriegsführenden zu erweitern*); ~**s of a prison** Außenbezirk e–s Gefängnisses; ~ **of apportionment** Ausgleichsregel bei Grundstücksaufteilung; ~**s of civil procedure** Zivilprozeßordnung; ~**s of conciliation and arbitration** Vergleichs- und Schiedsordnung; ~**s of conduct** Verhaltensmaßregeln; ~**s of construction** (richterliche) Auslegungsregeln; ~ **of course** antragsgemäß zu erlassende Verfügung; ~**s of court** gerichtliche Verfahrensvorschriften, Prozeßordnung; ~**s of criminal procedure** Strafprozeßordnung; ~**s of evidence** Beweisregeln, Beweisrecht; **R**~**s of Exchange** Börsenordnung; ~**s of good husbandry** Regeln der ordnungsgemäßen Landwirtschaft; ~ **of interpretation** Auslegungsregel; **r**~ **of law** Rechtsstaatlichkeit, Rechtsstaatsprinzip, Herrschaft des Rechts; Rechtsregel, Rechtsnorm, Rechtssatz; ~**s of law** Rechtssätze; ~ **of lenity** Grundsatz der milderen Auslegung; ~ **of last opportunities** Satz von der letzten Ausweichsmöglichkeit (*Mitverschulden*); ~**s of navigation** internationale Schiffahrtsregeln; ~ **of nondiscrimination** Diskriminierungsverbot (*aus rassischen oder ethnischen Gründen*); ~ **of partial payments** Anrechnungsvorschrift von Teilleistungen (*auf Zinsen, Hauptsache*); ~**s of practice** Verfahrensordnung, Prozeßordnung; ~ **of presumption** (*widerlegbare*) Vermutung; ~**s of procedure** → *procedure*; ~ **of property** eigentumsrechtlicher Grundsatz; ~ **of reason** Vernunftsregel; ~ **of substance** sachlichrechtliche (materielle) Norm; ~**s of the road** Straßenverkehrsregeln, Links- *bzw* Rechtsfahrgebot; ~**s of the road at sea** Schiffahrtsregeln, Seeverkehrsordnung; ~ **of the sea** = ~*s of the road at sea qv*; **R**~**s of the Supreme Court** Prozeßordnung (*des Londoner Zentralgerichts*); ~ **of the thumb** Faustregel; ~ **of uniformity** Gleichheitsgrundsatz; ~ **to plead** Ausschlußfrist zur Äußerung; ~ **to show cause** Ladung mit Aufforderung, etwaige Einwendungen vorzubringen; **administrative** ~ Verwaltungsvorschrift; **as a** ~ in der Regel; **common** ~**s** Richtlinien; **conflicting** ~**s** widersprechende Vorschriften; **cost-or-market** ~ Niederstwertprinzip; **disciplinary** ~**s** → *disciplinary*; **exclusionary** ~ Ausschlußregel; **foreign** ~ Fremdherrschaft; **formal** ~**s** Formvorschriften; **general** ~**s** allgemeine Regeln, Prozeßordnung, Norm; **golden** ~ Auslegungsregel, die absurde Ergebnisse vermeidet; **hard and fast** ~ strenge Regel, absolut bindende Vorschrift; **judges'** ~**s** → *judge*; **legal** ~ Rechtsnorm, Rechtssatz; **liberty of the** ~**s** → *liberty*; **literal** ~ wörtliche Auslegungsregel; **local trade** ~**s** Platzgebräuche, Platzusancen, Ortsgebrauch; **lower-of-cost-or-market** ~ Niederstwertprinzip; **majority** ~ Herrschaft der Mehrheit; Grundsatz der Mehrheitsentscheidung; **optional** ~ Kannvorschrift, dispositive Vorschrift; **peremptory** ~ zwingende Vorschrift; **practice** ~**s** Verfahrensordnung, Verfahrensregeln; **prison** ~**s** Gefängnisordnung; **procedural** ~ prozessuale Vorschrift; **special** ~ Beschluß nur auf Antrag, Sonderregel, Verweisung an den Einzelrichter; **standing** ~**s** Satzung, Geschäftsordnung; **„subjudice"** ~ Beschränkung der Berichterstattung bei rechtshängigen Verfahren; **technical** ~ technische Verfahrensregel, formaljuristische Norm; **ten minute** ~ Kurzdebatte von 10 Minuten (*bei Vorlage von Initiativanträgen*); **ten o'clock** ~ *Schlußzeit der regulären Parlamentssitzung um 22 Uhr*; **to discharge a** ~ e–n Beschluß aufheben.

rule *v* herrschen, regeln, entscheiden, lenken, leiten, anordnen, verfügen, festsetzen; ~ **off an account** ein Konto abschließen; ~ **out** ausschließen, ausstreichen.

ruler Herrscher *m*; **act of** ~**s** → *act*.

ruling *adj* vorherrschend, geltend, bestehend; ~ **cases** maßgebliche Entscheidungen; anerkannte Rechtsprechung; **R**~ **Case Law** = *Entscheidungssammlung in USA*.

ruling *s* Entscheidung *f*, Bescheid *m*; **administrative** ~ amtliche Verfügung, Bescheid, Verwaltungsverfügung; **declaratory** ~ Feststellungsbescheid.

rummage Ramsch *m*, Ausschußware *f*; Durchsuchung *f*; ~ **sale** Ramschverkauf.

run *s* Lauf *m*, Verlauf *m*, Ansturm *m*, Run *m*; ~ **of business** Geschäftsgang; ~ **of creditors** Ansturm der Gläubiger; ~**-of-mill** mittlere Durchschnittsqualität; ~**-of-mine** bergwergsüblicher Qualität; ~ **of office** Amtsdauer; ~**-of-paper** Plazierung der Anzeige bleibt der Redaktion vorbehalten; ~**-up** Vorgeschichte (*e–s Abschlusses*); ~ **upon a bank** Ansturm auf e–e Bank; **common** ~ übliche Art.

run *v* laufen (*Wechsel, Zinsen, Fristen*), in Kraft sein, betreiben; ~ **a business** → *business*; ~ **down prices** Preise drücken; ~ **for an office** kandidieren; ~ **for the presidency** für das Amt des Präsidenten kandidieren; ~ **into debts** in Schulden geraten; ~ **low** knapp werden; ~ **out** ablaufen, zu Ende gehen; ~ **up** anwachsen lassen, in die Höhe treiben, überbieten; ~ **with the land** dinglich wirken, dem Grundstückseigentum folgen; zugunsten des jeweiligen Eigentümers bestehen (wirken).

run-down costs Auslaufkosten *pl*.

running | **account credit** Dispositionskredit; Kontokorrentkredit; ~ **account mortgage** → *mortgage*; ~ **at large** streunend, umherziehend; ~ **down** Zusammenstoß; Anschwärzung; ~**-down case** Klage (*gegen den Fahrzeugführer*) bei Verkehrsunfall; Klage wegen Schiffskollision; ~**- down clause** (*Schiffs-*) Kollisionsklausel; ~ **of risks** das Aufsichnehmen von Gefahren; ~ **of the statute of limitations** der

Lauf der Verjährungsfrist; ~ **policy** laufende Police; ~ **powers** ständige Befugnisse; ~ **repairs** laufende Reparaturen; ~ **with the land** → *run with the land*; ~ **with the reversion** mit dem Eigentumsrecht (*des Heimfallberechtigten*) verbunden.

rupture Bruch *m*, Abbruch *m*; ~ **of diplomatic relations** Abbruch der diplomatischen Beziehungen.

rural ländlich, Land ...; ~ **authority** Landkreisbehörde; ~ **credit banks** Agrarbanken, landwirtschaftliche Genossenschaftsbanken; ~ **delivery service** Postzustellung auf dem Lande; ~ **rehabilitation** Resozialisierung ländlicher Gebiete, soziale Vorbeugung in ländlichen Gebieten; ~ **sanitary district** Kanalisierungszweckverband.

S

sabbath Sabbat *m*; ~ **breaking** Verletzung der Sonn- und Feiertagsruhe.

sabotage *s* Sabotage *f*; **economic** ~ Wirtschaftssabotage.

sabotage *v* sabotieren.

sack *s* Hinauswurf *m*; **to get the** ~ fristlos entlassen werden.

sack *v* jmdn fristlos entlassen.

sacrifice Opfer *n*; Verzicht *m* auf Gewinn, Einbuße *f*, Verlust *m*, Schaden; **at a** ~ mit Schaden; mit Verlust; **general average** ~**s** Aufopferung für große Havarie.

sacrilege Sakrileg *n*, Kirchenschändung *f*; Kirchenraub *m*.

safe *adj* sicher, zuverlässig; ~ **and sound** wohlbehalten; ~ **conduct** freies Geleit, Geleitbrief; ~**-keeping** Verwahrung, Aufbewahrung; ~ **limit of speed** gefahrlose Geschwindigkeit; ~ **loading place** sicherer Verladungsplatz; ~ **means of access** sicherer Zugang (*zur Arbeitsstelle*); ~ **place to work** (= ~ ~ *of work*) unfallsicherer Arbeitsplatz; ~**-pledge** Kautionsstellung *für das Erscheinen vor Gericht*; ~ **system of working** Arbeitsschutz.

safe *s* Safe *m*, Tresor *m* Bankfach *n*; ~**-room** Stahlkammer; ~ **vault** Stahlkammer, Banktresor.

safe custody Verwahrung *f*, *von Wertpapieren und Wertgegenständen im Banksafe*; ~ **receipt** Depotquittung; **to hold on** ~ im Depot verwahren.

safe deposit Verwahrung, Tresor-Verwahrung; ~ **box** Stahlfach, Stahlkammer, Schließfach, Tresor, Geldschrank; ~ **company** Gesellschaft zur Aufbewahrung von Wertgegenständen; ~ **vault** Stahlfachabteilung.

safeguard *s hist* Schutzbrief *m*, Freistellung *f* von Beschlagnahme; Sicherheit *f*, Bürgschaft *f*, Gewähr *f*, Schutz *m*; **contractual** ~**s** vertraglicher Schutz; vertragl Absicherungen; **procedural** ~**s** Verfahrenssicherungen.

safeguard *v* sichern, sicherstellen, Gewähr leisten, schützen; ~ **interests** Interessen wahren; ~**ing duty** Schutzzoll.

safekeeping Verwahrung *f*, Aufbewahrung *f*, Gewahrsam *m*.

safety Sicherheit *f*; ~ **appliances** Sicherheitsvorrichtungen; ~ **at sea** Sicherheitsvorschriften für die Seefahrt; ~ **clause** Nachschußklausel (*bei Versicherungsvereinen auf Gegenseitigkeit*); ~ **committee** Betriebsausschuß für gesicherten Arbeitsplatz; ~ **condition** Sicherheit; ~ **engineering department** technische Überwachungsabteilung; ~ **factor** Sicherheitsfaktor; ~ **first** Sicherheit hat Vorrang; ~ **fund** Reservefonds, Mindestreserven, Sicherungsfonds; ~ **fund system** Mindestreservensystem; ~ **inspection sticker** Prüfplakette (*TÜV*); ~ **island** Fußgängerinsel; ~ **load** zulässige Höchstbelastung; ~ **margin** Sicherheitsmarge, Sicherheitsfaktor; ~ **of goods** Konsumentenschutz; ~ **of principal** Sicherheit der Kapitalanlage (*gegen Wertminderung*); ~ **of work** Betriebssicherheit; ~ **officer** Sicherheitsbeamter, Sicherheitsbeauftragter; ~ **precautions** Sicherheitsvorkehrungen, Schutzmaßnahmen; ~ **regulation** Sicherheitsvorschriften, Arbeitsschutzbestimmungen; ~ **representative** Sicherheitsbeauftragter (*Arbeitsschutz*); ~ **zones** Verkehrsinseln, Fußgängerüberwege, Zebrastreifen; **industrial** ~ Betriebsschutz, Sicherheit am Arbeitsplatz; **national** ~ nationale Sicherheit; allgemeine Unfallverhütung; **public** ~ öffentl Sicherheit, Verkehrssicherheit.

sag vorübergehende Kursdepression *f*; *v* absacken.

said besagt, erwähnt, vorbenannt, (*oft mit dies (–er, –es) zu übersetzen*).

sailing Abfahrt *f*, Auslaufen *n*; ~ **date** Abfahrtsdatum; ~ **instructions** Fahrtanweisungen, Geleitzuganweisungen; **final** ~ Abreise vom letzten engl Hafen.

salability (= *saleability*) Gängigkeit *f*, Verkäuflichkeit *f*.

salable (= *saleable*) verkäuflich, gängig.

salary Besoldung *f*, Gehalt *n*; ~ **account** → *account* (2); ~ **advance** Gehaltsvorschuß; ~**ies and wages** Löhne und Gehälter; ~ **and wage ordinance** Tarifverordnung; ~ **bracket** Gehaltsklasse, Besoldungsgruppe; ~ **by arrangement** Gehalt nach Vereinbarung; ~ **class** Gehaltsgruppe, Besoldungsgruppe; ~ **differentials** Sonderzulagen (*für erschwerte Arbeitsbedingungen*); ~**-earner** Gehaltsempfänger, Angestellter; ~ **in lieu of leave** Gehalt anstelle von Urlaub, ausbezahlter Urlaub; ~ **review** Gehaltsüberprüfung; ~ **roll** Gehaltsabrechnung; ~ **tax** Lohnsteuer; **accrued** ~ Gehaltsrückstände; **annual** ~ Jahresgehalt; **appointive** ~ Eingangsgehalt, Gehalt bei Bestallung; **basic** ~ Grundgehalt; **commencing** ~ Anfangsgehalt; **desired** ~ Gehaltswünsche; **executive** ~**ies** Gehälter der leitenden Angestellten; **fixed** ~ festes Gehalt; **initial** ~ Anfangsgehalt; **staff** ~**ies** Mitarbeitergehälter; **starting** ~ Anfangsgehalt; **stating** ~ mit Angabe der Gehaltsansprüche; **straight** ~ reine Gehaltsbasis (*ohne Gewinnbeteiligung*); **top level** ~ Spitzengehalt.

sale Kauf *m*, Verkauf *m*, Kaufvertrag *m*, Veräußerung *f*, Absatz *m*, Vertrieb *m*, Ausverkauf *m*; ~**s** Umsatz, Absatz; ~**s account** → *account* (2); Warenverkaufskonto; ~**s agency** Verkaufsniederlassung, Verkaufsagentur; Handelsvertretung; ~**s agent** Vertreter, Reisender; ~**s agreement** Kaufvertrag; ~**s analysis** Verkaufsanalyse; ~ **and lease back** Rückvermietung durch die Leasinggesellschaft an den Verkäufer (*von Anlagegütern*); ~**s and marketing director** Leiter der Vertriebsabteilung; ~ **and return** Kauf mit Rückgaberecht; ~**s area** Absatzgebiet; ~ **at giveaway prices** Schleuderverkauf; ~**s bill** Rechnung; Warenwechsel; ~**s book** Warenausgangsbuch; ~**s branch** Verkaufsniederlassung; ~**s budget** Verkaufsumsatzplan; ~ **by auction** Versteigerung; ~ **by description** Kauf nach Beschreibung, Kauf nach Katalog; ~ **by lot** Partieverkauf; ~ **by private treaty** freihändiger Verkauf; ~ **by sample** Kauf nach Probe; ~ **by tender** Verkauf auf Grund e–r Ausschreibung; ~ **by the candle** Versteigerung (*Zuschlag bei Erlöschen e–r Kerze*); ~ **by the court** gerichtlicher Verkauf, gerichtl außerordentlicher Grundstückszwangsverkauf; ~**s cartel** Absatzkartell; ~ **catalogue** Auktionsliste; ~**s clerk** Ladenverkäufer; ~**s commission** Verkaufsprovision; ~**s company** Vertriebsgesellschaft; ~**s conditions** Verkaufsbedingungen, Lieferbedingungen; ~**s contract** Kaufvertrag, Liefervertrag; ~**s director** Leiter der Vertriebsabteilung; ~**s drive** Verkaufskampagne; ~**s executive** Leiter der Vertriebsabteilung; ~**s finance company** Kundenkreditbank; ~**s fluctuation** Absatzschwankung; ~ **for future delivery** Terminverkauf; ~ **for money** Verkauf gegen bar; ~ **for prompt delivery** Verkauf zur sofortigen Lieferung; ~ **for the account** Verkauf für zukünftige Lieferung; Verkauf auf Ziel; ~ **for the settlement** Terminverkauf; ~**s forecast** Absatzprognose; ~**s from the portfolio** Verkäufe aus dem Portefeuille, Verkäufe von Nostroeffekten; ~**s girl** Ladenmädchen; ~ **goods** Ausverkaufsware; ~**s increase** Umsatzsteigerung; ~ **in**

gross Partieverkauf; ~ in market overt Laden- und Marktverkauf; ~ in the open market Kaufgeschäft unter den Bedingungen des freien Wettbewerbs; ~s lady Verkäuferin; ~s ledger Debitorenbuch, Verzeichnis von Kunden mit Lieferkredit, Warenausgangsbuch; ~s load Vertriebskostenanteil, Verkaufsspesen; nicht investierter Teil des Verkaufserlöses von Investmentzertifikaten; ~ lot Auktionspartie; ~s management Vertriebsleitung; V.sorganisation; ~s manager → *manager*; ~s-note Schlußnote, Schlußschein (*des Maklers*); ~ of goods Kauf von beweglichen Sachen, Warenkauf; S~ of Goods Act Warenkaufgesetz, *GB Gesetz von 1893 über den Kauf beweglicher Sachen;* ~ of goodwill Verkauf des Goodwill (*des Firmenwerts*); ~ of land Grundstückskauf; ~ of land by auction Grundstücksversteigerung; ~ of offices Ämterkauf; ~ of reversion Verkauf des Stammeigentums, Verkauf des Heimfallsrechts, Verk. des Nachverpachtungsrechts; ~s of services Dienstleistungsgeschäfte; ~ of specific goods Spezieskauf, Stückkauf; ~ of unascertained goods Gattungskauf; ~ on approval Kauf auf Probe; ~ on consignment Kommissionsverkauf; ~ on credit Verkauf auf Ziel; ~ on inspection Kauf „wie besehen"; ~s on speculation Meinungskäufe; ~ on the spot Platzverkauf; ~ on trial Kauf auf Probe; ~s order Verkaufsauftrag; ~s organizations Absatzorganisationen; ~ out of court außergerichtlicher Verkauf; ~s pace Absatztempo; ~s people Verkaufspersonal; ~s person Verkäufer, Außendienstverkäufer, Vertreter; ~ per aversionem Pauschalverkauf; ~s potential erzielbarer Absatz, Absatzchancen; ~s premium Abschlußprämie; ~s pressure Abgabedruck *exch*; ~s price Verkaufspreis; ~s promotion Absatz-, Verkaufsförderung; ~ property Verkaufsobjekt; ~s prospects Absatzchancen; ~s quota Marktanteil; ~s resistance Kaufunlust; ~s return Retourwaren; ~s return journal → *journal*; ~s slump Absatzflaute; ~s talk Verkaufsgespräch, unverbindliche Anpreisungen; ~s tax → *tax*; ~s terms Lieferbedingungen; ~s turnover Warenumsatz; ~ under power Verkauf auf Grund e–r Ermächtigung; ~s value Verkaufswert; ~ with all faults Kauf ohne Gewähr, wie besichtigt, Kauf wie Ware steht und liegt; ~ with option to repurchase Verkauf mit Rückkaufsrecht; ~ with right of redemption Verkauf mit Rückkaufsrecht; absolute ~ Kaufvertrag ohne Eigentumsvorbehalt; accrued ~s getätigte Verkäufe; actual ~ Verkaufsabschluß; adjourned ~s (gerichtlich) ausgesetzter Kaufvertrag; advertisement of ~ Ankündigung des (gerichtlichen) Verkaufs durch Zeitungsinserat; after-~ service Kundendienst; all ~s final kein Umtausch; annual ~ Saisonverkauf; „as is" ~ Verkauf wie die Ware steht und liegt; bailment ~ Kommissionsverkauf mit Selbsteintrittsrecht; bargain ~ Gelegenheitskauf, Sonderangebot, Sonderausverkauf; bearish ~ Leerabgabe, Blankoverkauf; brisk ~s gute Umsätze; cash ~ Barverkauf, Kassageschäft; clearance ~ Ausverkauf; commission on ~ → *commission*; compulsory ~ Zwangsverkauf, Enteignung; conditional ~ Vorbehaltskauf, Verkauf unter Eigentumsvorbehalt; consignment ~ Konsignationsverkauf; consumer ~ Verkauf an den Endverbraucher; contract of ~ → *contract*; cross ~ → *cross*; daily ~s Tagesumsatz; deferred payment ~ Kreditkauf, Abzahlungskauf; direct ~ Direktverkauf, Engrosverkauf, Verkauf ohne Zwischenhändler; distressed ~ Ausverkauf wg Geschäftsaufgabe; duty paid ~ Verkauf nach Verzollung; effective ~ wirksamer

Verkauf; **exclusive** ~ Alleinverkauf; **executed** ~ Handkauf, erfüllter Kaufvertrag (*gleichzeitig mit Eigentumsübergang*); **execution** ~ Zwangsversteigerung; **executory** ~ noch zu erfüllender Kaufvertrag; **fair** ~ ordnungsgemäße Zwangsversteigerung mit angemessenem Erlös; **for** ~ zum Verkauf, zu verkaufen; **forced** ~ Zwangsversteigerung, Vollstreckungsverkauf, **foreclosure** ~ → *foreclosure*; **forward** ~ Terminverkauf; **fraudulent** ~ Verkauf zur Gläubigerschädigung; **gross** ~**s** Bruttowarenumsatz; **hedging** ~ Deckungsverkauf; **hire-purchase** ~ Abzahlungskauf, Kaufmiete; **instalment** ~ Ratenkauf; **intercompany** ~**s** → *intercompany*; **judicial** ~ → *judicial*; **jumble** ~ Ramschverkauf; **long** ~ Effektenverkauf aus eigenen Beständen; **lumping** ~ Gesamtzwangsverkauf; **matched** ~**s** gekoppelte Börsengeschäfte; **memorandum** ~ Kauf auf Probe, Kauf mit Rückgaberecht; **net** ~**s** Nettowarenumsatz; **no** ~**s** „ohne Umsatz"; **no longer on** ~ nicht mehr lieferbar; **not for** ~ unverkäuflich, „Muster ohne Wert"; **one-off** ~ einmaliger (Aus)Verkauf; **(open account) credit** ~ Verkauf auf Ziel; ~ **opening** ~ erster Abschluß *an e–m Börsentag*; **outright** ~ fester Verkaufsabschluß; Abschluß zu festem Verkaufspreis, Verkauf in Bausch und Bogen; **panic** ~ Angstverkauf; **partial** ~ Partieverkauf; Teilverkauf; **power of** ~ → *power (1)*; **present** ~ mit Vertragsschluß vollzogener (Ver)kauf; Handkauf; **priority** ~ → *priority*; **private** ~ Verkauf unter der Hand, freihändiger Verkauf; **pro forma** ~ → *pro forma*; **proceeds of** ~ → *proceeds*; **profit-taking** ~**s** Verkäufe zwecks Gewinnrealisierung; **public** ~ öffentliche Versteigerung, Zwangsversteigerung, Auktion; öffentlich angekündigter Verkauf; **quick** ~ leichter Verkauf, rascher V.; **rapid** ~**s** reißender Absatz; **ready** ~ schneller Absatz; **regular** ~ normaler Verkauf; Börsenverkauf für Lieferung am nächsten Tag; **remainder** ~ Verkauf von Restauflagen; **seasonal** ~ Saisonschlußverkauf; **sham** ~ → *sham*; **sheriff's** ~ Zwangsversteigerung; **short** ~**s** Leerverkäufe, Blankoverkäufe; **similar** ~**s** Vergleichsverkäufe (*Bewertung*); **slow** ~ langsamer Absatz; **slump in** ~**s** Absatzstockung; **special** ~**s** Sonderverkaufsveranstaltungen; **spot** ~ Barverkauf; **stimulative** ~**s** Sonderangebote zur Absatzförderung; **tax** ~ Zwangsvollstreckung wegen Steuerrückständen; **tie-in** ~ Kopplungsverkauf; **to take on** ~ zum Verkauf übernehmen; **voluntary** ~ Freiverkauf, freihändiger Verkauf; **wash** ~ Börsenscheingeschäft (*gleichzeitiger Kauf und Verkauf e–s Börsenpapiers*).

salesman Verkäufer *m*, Vertreter *m*, Handlungsreisender *m*; ~**'s base pay** Vertreterfixum; **missionary** ~ Werksvertreter; **outside** ~ Verkäufer im Außendienst.

sales company Vertriebsgesellschaft *f*.

salesmanship Verkaufstechnik *f*, Verkaufskunst *f*.

salesperson Verkäufer *m*, Werbevertreter *m*.

Salic Law salisches Recht *n*, Salisches Gesetz *n*, Lex salica *f* (*Erbfolge des Mannesstammes, Ausschluß der Frauen von der Thronfolge*).

salvage Bergelohn *m*, Bergegeld *n*; Hilfeleistung *f*, Bergung *f*, Wiedergewinnung *f*, Wiederverwertung *f*, soziale Rettungsarbeit *f*; geborgenes Gut *n*, Bergungsgut *n*; Restwert; ~ **bond** → *bond (2)*; ~ **charges** → *charge*; ~ **claims** Bergelohnforderung; ~ **company** Bergungsgesellschaft; ~ **goods** Strandgut; ~ **loss** → *loss*; ~ **money** → *money*; ~ **service** Beistandsleistung in Seenot, Bergungsdienst; ~ **value** Restwert, Bergewert.

salve bergen, aus Seenot retten.

salvor Berger *m* (e–s Schiffes), Hilfeleistender *m* in Seenot; **professional** ~ Bergeunternehmen.

same | case der gleiche Fall; ~ **cause** die gleiche Sache, die gleiche Tat, der gleiche Anlaß; ~ **cause of complaint** der gleiche Klagegrund; ~ **day funds** Gelder mit Wertstellung am gleichen Tage; ~ **invention** dieselbe Erfindung; ~ **offence** → *offence*; ~ **transaction** das gleiche Rechtsgeschäft, der gleiche Vorgang.

sample *s* Probe *f*, Stichprobe *f*, Repräsentativerhebung *f*, Warenmuster *n*; ~ **book** Musterbuch; ~ **card** Musterkarte; ~ **design** Auswahlplan, Stichprobenplan; ~ **exhibition** Musterausstellung, M.messe; ~ **make-up** Zusammensetzung der Repräsentativauswahl; ~**, no commercial value** Muster ohne Wert; ~ **not for sale** Muster ohne Wert; ~ **order** Probebestellung; ~ **post** Muster ohne Wert; ~ **rate** Tarif für Mustersendungen; ~ **taken off hand** Stichprobe; ~ **without value** Muster ohne Wert; **area** ~ Flächenstichprobe, gebietsweise statistische Auswahl; **commercial** ~ Warenmuster; **judgment** ~ ins Ermessen des Befragers gestellte Repräsentativauswahl; **picked** ~ entnommene Probe; **probability** ~ Repräsentativauswahl nach Wahrscheinlichkeitsregeln; **purposive** ~ gezieltes Auswahlverfahren; **quotal** ~ Quotaverfahren bei der Auswahl; **random** ~ Stichprobe; Auswahl aufs Geratewohl; **reference** ~ Vergleichsmuster; **representative** ~ Typenmuster, Serienmuster, repräsentative Stichprobe; **stratified** ~ Stichprobenauswahl nach Gruppen; **systematic** ~ systematische Auswahl; **to take** ~**s** Proben entnehmen; **to take** ~**s at random** Stichproben entnehmen; **traveler's** ~ Musterkollektion.

sample *v* Proben entnehmen, Muster ziehen; ~**d offer** bemustertes Angebot.

sampler Musterzieher *m*.

sampling Musterziehung *f*, Probeentnahme *f*, Bemusterung *f*, Repräsentativauswahl *f*, ~ **error** Auswahlfehler, Stichprobenfehler; **random** ~ Stichprobenentnahme; **representative** ~ Repräsentativ-Stichproben-Untersuchung.

sanction *s* Sanktion *f*, Strafandrohung *f*, Genehmigung *f*, Zwangsmittel *n*, Billigung *f*; Überziehungserlaubnis *f*; ~**s breakers** Sanktionen verletzende Staaten; ~**s evasion** Sanktionsumgehung; ~ **of court** gerichtliche Genehmigung, gerichtliche Billigung; ~ **of custom** Gewohnheitsrecht; **criminal** ~ Strafandrohung, strafrechtl. Sanktion; **economic** ~**s** Wirtschaftssanktionen; **legislative** ~ gesetzliche Strafandrohung; **penal** ~ = *punitive* ~ *qv*; **punitive** ~ Strafandrohung, Strafsanktion.

sanction *v* genehmigen, gutheißen, sanktionieren.

sanctity of contract Unantastbarkeit des Vertrages (= *der Verträge*).

sanctuary Asyl *n*, Schutzstätte *f*.

sandwich debenture Kreditsicherungsverteilung zw. Anlagevermögen und Umlaufvermögen des Schuldners (*zw Gläubigerbanken*).

sanitary | acts Hygienegesetze; ~ **affairs** allgemeine Hygiene, sanitäre Angelegenheiten; ~ **arrangements** sanitäre Einrichtungen; ~ **authorities** Gesundheitsämter, Gesundheitsbehörden; ~ **control** Gesundheitskontrolle; ~ **cordon** Quarantänesperre; ~ **inspectors** Inspektoren der Gesundheitsämter; ~ **police** Gesundheitspolizei.

sanitation Gesundheitswesen *n*.

sanity normaler Geisteszustand *m*, geistige Gesundheit *f*; **presumption of** ~ → *presumption*.

sans | frais ohne Kosten (*Wechsel*); ~ **recours** ohne Obligo (*Wechsel*), ohne eigene Rückgriffshaftung.

sap Totschläger *m* (*und ähnliche Verbrecherwaffen*).

satisfaction Befriedigung *f*, Bezahlung *f*, Begleichung *f*, Zufriedenstellung *f*, Tilgung *f*, Erfüllung *f*, Satisfaktion *f*, Genugtuung *f*, Ehrenerklärung *f*; ~ **for all damage** vollständige Entschädigung; ~ **of a creditor** Gläubigerbefriedigung; ~ **of bill of sale** Tilgung einer Sicherungsübereignungsschuld; ~ **of claim** Anspruchsbefriedigung; ~ **of condition** Erfüllung e–r Bedingung; ~ **of debts** Schuldbefriedigung; Schuldtilgung; ~ **of fine by serving time** Ersatzfreiheitsstrafe; ~ **of judgment** Quittierung des Titels; ~ **of lien** schriftl. Pfandfreigabe (wegen Erfüllung); ~ **of mortgage** Bescheinigung der Hypothekentilgung und Löschungsbewilligung; ~ **on the roll** gerichtl Vermerk der Befriedigung e–s vollstreckbaren Titels; **accord and** ~ → *accord*; **contracts of** ~ Verträge mit der Bedingung, daß zur Zufriedenheit des Auftraggebers geleistet wird; **discharge by** ~ Erlöschen der (Wechsel)Verbindlichkeit durch Einlösung des Wechsels; **in full** ~ zum vollständigen (Schadens)Ausgleich, zur Glattstellung; **in** ~ als Erfüllung, an Erfüllungs Statt; **pecuniary** ~ Geldentschädigung; **to the** ~ **of the court** zur Überzeugung des Gerichts.

satisfy befriedigen, zufriedenstellen, erfüllen, tilgen, bezahlen, sühnen, beheben, überzeugen; ~ **a claim** e–n Anspruch befriedigen; ~ **a debt** e–e Schuld bezahlen, tilgen; ~ **the court** das Gericht überzeugen.

save *prep u. conj* ausgenommen, abgesehen von; ~ **as otherwise agreed** wenn nichts anderes vereinbart wird; ~ **as provided** vorbehaltlich; ~ **as provided otherwise** soweit nichts anderes vereinbart ist; ~ **error and omission** Irrtum vorbehalten; ~ **for some error of law** außer bei e–m Rechtsfehler.

save *v* bergen, sparen, retten, bewahren, verhüten, vorbehalten; ~ **as you earn** Sparen im Lohnabzugsverfahren; ~ **harmless** schadlos halten, freistellen von.

saver Sparer *m*, Kleinsparer *m*.

saving *prep u. conj* außer, ausgenommen, unbeschadet.

saving *s* das Sparen, Ersparnis *f*, Einsparung *f*; **contractual** ~ laufendes Lohnabzugssparen.

savings Ersparnisse *n|pl*, Spargelder *n|pl*; ~ **account** → *account* (*2*); ~ **and loan associations** Bausparkassen; ~ **bank** Sparkasse; ~ **bank book** Sparbuch; ~ **bank deposit** Spareinlage, Sparguthaben; ~ **bank life insurance** Lebensversicherung(sgeschäft) von Sparkassen; ~ **bank trust** Sparkassentrust; ~ **bonds** Sparbonds, Sparanleihe; ~ **certificate** Sparbon; ~ **club** Sparverein; ~ **deposit** Spareinlage, Bankeinlage; ~ **depository** Sparkasse, Kapitalsammelstelle für Spargelder; ~ **investment** für Sparkassen zugelassene Anlage mündelsichere Kapitalanlage; ~ **passbook** Sparbüchlein; ~ **pool** Gesamtheit der Spargelder; ~ **rate** Sparrate; **business** ~ gewerblicher Gewinn, nicht entnommener Gewinn; **forced** ~ Zwangssparen, erzwungene Einsparungen; ~ **marginal** ~ geringfügige Einsparungen; **national** ~ Sparwesen, innerstaatliches Sparen; **negative** ~ Aufzehren des Vermögens, höherer Verbrauch als Einkommen; **personal** ~ Privatsparen, Privatersparnisse.

say sagen, berichten, erklären, behaupten; ~ **about** etwa; ~ **not less than** mindestens etwa.

scab unter Tarif Arbeitender *m*, Streikbrecher *m*.

scale Waagschale *f*; Stufenleiter *f*, Staffel *f*, Tarif *m*, Tabelle *f*; ~ **gradation** Tarifstaffelung; ~ **model** → *model*; ~ **of charges** Gebührentabelle; ~ **of discounts** Rabattstaffel; **S~s of Justice** Waage der Justiz, Gerechtigkeit; ~ **of preferences** Tabelle der Verbrauchsgewohnheiten; ~ **of premiums** Beitragsstaffelung; ~ **of salaries** Gehaltsstaffelung; ~ **order** → *order* (*2*); ~ **rate** Tarifpreis, Tabellensatz (Gebühren); ~**s tolerance** Toleranz zwischen Waagen; ~ **wages** Lohnskala; **on a** ~ zu verschiedenen Kurswerten; **pay** ~ Lohntabelle, Lohngruppe; **salary** ~ Besoldungsgruppe; **social** ~ Gesellschaftsstufe; **taxation** ~ → *taxation;* **to buy on a** ~ Teilkäufe machen (*zur Verringerung des Kursrisikos*); **to sell on a** ~ zum Durchschnittskurs weiterverkaufen.

scale *v* wiegen, auswiegen; einstufen, bemessen; maßstabgetreu zeichnen; ~ **down** (*Löhne*) heruntersetzen; (*Schuld*) nachlassen; *exch* repartieren, verkleinern.

scalp *v exch* mit kleinen Gewinnen spekulieren.

scalper kleiner Spekulant *m*.

scalping Mitnahme *f* kleinster Gewinne.

scandal Skandal *m*, öffentliches Ärgernis *n*; irrelevantes, beleidigendes Vorbringen *n* (*in Schriftsätzen*); ~ **monger** Verbreiter von Skandalgeschichten.

scandalising the court Beleidigung *f* des Gerichtes, Ärgerniserregung *f* bei Gericht.

scandalous skandalös, anstößig, ärgerniserregend; ~ **matter** irrelevante ehrenrührige Behauptungen, skandalöse Angelegenheiten; ~ **statement** ärgerniserregende Erklärung.

scare Panik *f*; ~ **buying** Panikkauf, Angstkäufe; ~ **mongering** Panikmache.

scene Tatort *m*, Schauplatz *m*; ~ **of the accident** Unfallstelle; ~ **of the crime** Tatort *m*.

schedule *s* Liste *f*, Tabelle *f*, Verzeichnis, Vertragsanhang *m*; Gesetzesanhang *m*; Prozeßgeschichte *f* (*für die Rechtsmittelinstanz*); Fahrplan *m*; ~ **bonds** Kautionslisten für Betriebsangehörige; ~ **of charges** Gebührenordnung; ~ **of creditors** Gläubigerverzeichnis, Konkurstabelle; ~ **of fees** Gebührenordnung; ~ **of investments** Verzeichnis der Anlagewerte; ~ **of plights** Mängelliste *bei Übernahme der Mietsache (bzw des Pachtgrundstückes);* ~ **of property** Vermögensverzeichnis; **equipment delivery** ~ Gerätelieferplan; **leave** ~ Urlaubsplan.

schedule *v* festlegen, bestimmen, klassifizieren, planen, verzeichnen; ~**d prices** Listenpreise; ~**d ship** fahrplanmäßiges Schiff; ~**d taxes** veranlagte Steuern; **S~d Territories** die Länder des Sterlingblocks; ~**d territory** das angegebene Gebiet; das Inland; ~**d work** Regiearbeit; **as** ~**d** planmäßig.

scheduling Planung *f*, Fertigungsplanung *f*; **master** ~ Gesamtplanung.

scheme *s* Diagramm *n*, schematische Darstellung *f*, Aufstellung *f*, Verzeichnis *n*, Projekt *n*, Aktionsprogramm *n*, Plan *m*, Entwurf *m*, System *n*; ~ **legally established** amtlich (*bzw gerichtlich*) errichtete (Treuhand)Verwaltung; ~ **of arrangement** Vergleichsplan *zur Abwendung des Konkurses*; ~ **of reconstruction or improvement** Sanierungsplan; **adoptive** ~ übernahmebedürftige Regelung, nicht zwingend vorgeschriebene Regelung; **allocation** ~ Zuteilungsplan; **irrigation** ~ Bewässerungsprojekt; **pension** ~ → *pension*.

scheme *v* heimlich planen, Ränke schmieden, intrigieren.

schemer Intrigant *m*, Ränkeschmied *m*.

schoolable schulpflichtig, im schulpflichtigen Alter stehend.

school|age schulpflichtiges Alter; ~ **attendance** Schulbesuch; ~ **attendance committee** Schulpflichtvollzugsausschuß; ~ **attendance order** Anweisung zum Schulbesuch; ~ **board** Schulamt; Schulaufsichtsbehörde, Schulbeirat; ~ **busing** Schulbusdienst für mehrrassige Gemeinschaftsschulen; ~ ~ *for desegregation (obligatorische) Schulbusdienste als Mittel gegen die Rassentrennung nach Schulen*; ~ **catchment**

area Schuleinzugsgebiet; ~ **certificate** Schulabgangszeugnis; ~ **crossing** Fußgängerüberweg bei e–r Schule; ~ **dame** Schulvorsteherin, Direktorin (*e–r Privatschule*); ~ **district** Schulzweckverband; ~ **fee** Schulgeld; ~ **for artisans** (Handwerker)Fachschule; ~ **lands** → *land*; ~ **leavers** Schulabgänger; ~ **of forestry** Forstakademie; ~ **regulations** Schulordnung; ~ **site** Schulgrundstück, Stiftungsland e–r Schule; ~ **training** Schulbildung; **aided** ~ Ersatzschule, öffentlich geförderte Privatschule; **approved** ~ Erziehungsanstalt (*GB, abgeschafft 1969*); **common** ~**s** öffentliche Schulen; **comprehensive** ~ (*höhere*) Gesamtschule; **compulsory** ~ **age** schulpflichtiges Alter; **consolidated** ~ **district** gemeinsamer Schulzweckverband; **continuation** ~ Fortbildungsschule; Fortbildungskursus; **controlled** ~ (*staatlich*) anerkannte Ersatzschule; **council** ~ Gemeindeschule, Kreisschule (*Schulträger: Landkreis oder kreisfreie Stadt*); **county** ~ Kreisschule, öffentliche Schule; **denominational** ~ Konfessionsschule; **desegregated** ~ Gemeinschaftsschule, Schule ohne Rassentrennung; **direct grant** ~**s** staatlich anerkannte Ersatzschulen (*traditionelle Privatgymnasien*); **district** ~ Volksschule (*e–s Schulbezirks*); **endowed** ~ Privatschule (*mit Stiftungskapital*); **evening** ~ Abendkurs(e), Volkshochschulkurs(e), Fortbildungskurs(e); **free** ~ gebührenfreie Schule; **grade** ~ (*mehrklassige*) Volksschule; **grammar** ~ Oberschule, Gymnasium; **high** ~ höhere Schule; **independent** ~ Privatschule, Ersatzschule; **industrial** ~ Berufsschulinternat; **infant** ~ Vorschule; **junior** ~ Vorschule; **language** ~ Sprachenschule; **law** ~ juristische Fakultät; **mixed** ~ gemischte (*Knaben- und Mädchen*) Schulen; **non-provided** ~ *private* Ersatzschule, Privatschule; **normal** ~ Einheitsschule; Lehrerseminar; **nursery** ~**s** Kindergarten; **preparatory** ~ (*private*) Vorschule *für höhere Schulen*; **primary** ~ Grundschule (*für 5- bis 11jähr.*); **provided** ~ = *council* ~ *qv*; **public** ~ *England:* private Internatsschule; *scot:* öffentliche Volksschule; *US:* öffentliche Schule; **public elementary** ~ Volksschule; **publicly maintained** ~ öffentliche Schule; **publicly provided** ~ öffentliche Schule, Schule in öffentl Trägerschaft; **reform** ~ *obs* (geschlossene) Erziehungsanstalt; **reformatory** ~ Erziehungsanstalt; **secondary** ~ Mittelschule, höhere Schule; **secondary modern** ~ Realgymnasium; **secondary technical** ~ Oberrealschule; **special** ~ Sonderschule; **technical** ~ Fachschule; Jugendstrafanstalt; **trade** ~ Gewerbeschule; **training** ~ Erziehungsanstalt; Lehrerseminar; **voluntary** ~ *etwa* staatlich anerkannte Ersatzschule.

scienter wissentlich, vorsätzlich; ~ **principle** Haftung bei Kenntnis von (Tat)Umständen; ~ **rule** erhöhte Tierhalterhaftung für Tiere, deren Bösartigkeit dem Eigentümer bekannt ist; **proof of** ~ Beweis der Kenntnis, Beweis der Bösgläubigkeit; **to prove** ~ den subjektiven Tatbestand nachweisen.

scilicet nämlich, das heißt.

scintilla | **juris** die Spur eines Rechts; ~ **of evidence** die Spur e–s Beweises, der geringste Beweis.

scion Abkömmling *m*, Sproß *m*.

scip tracing Anschriftenermittlung *f* von säumigen Schuldnern.

scire facias → *writ of* ~.

scission *Gesellschaftsteilung unter Übernahme von Aktiven und Passiven durch die Teilfirmen.*

scissors gap (*Preis-Lohn etc*) Schere; ~ **movement** Scherenbewegung.

scoff law Gesetzesverächter *m*.

scoop große Gewinnmitnahme *f*, großer Fang *m*, Exklusivmeldung *f*, „Knüller" *m*.

scope Bereich *m*, Gebiet *n*, Rahmen *m*, Umfang *m*, Wirkungskreis *m*,

Betätigungsfeld *n*, Ressort *n*, Feld *n*, Horizont *m*; ~ **of a law** Rahmen e–s Gesetzes, Anwendungsbereich e–s G–s; ~ **of a patent** → *patent*; ~ **of application** Anwendungsbereich, Geltungsbereich; ~ **of article** Anwendungsbereich des Artikels; ~ **of authority** (Amts)Zuständigkeit; ~ **of business** Umfang des Geschäftes; ~ **of employment** Rahmen der Beschäftigung; ~ **of power** Umfang der Vollmacht.

score erzielen, erringen, auf die Rechnung setzen, belasten; ~ **an advance** Kursgewinn verzeichnen; ~ **up debts** Schulden machen.

scot Abgabe *f*, Beitrag *m*; ~ **and lot** *hist* Gemeindeabgabe; ~ **and lot inhabitants** vermögenslose (*die Gemeindesteuer zum Armensatz zahlende*) Bewohner; ~ **and lot voters** vermögenlose, gemeindesteuerpflichtige Wähler; ~ **free** straffrei, steuerfrei, unbehelligt, ungeschoren; **to pay** ~ **and lot** auf Heller und Pfennig bezahlen.

Scotland Yard (=) Polizeipräsidium von London, Kriminalpolizei von London.

Scots law schottisches Recht *n*.

Scottish|bills nur Schottland betreffende Vorlagen; ~ **private legislation** *legislatives Sonderverfahren für Spezialvorlagen aus Schottland.*

scrap Schrott *m*, Abfall *m*, Ausschuß *m*; ~ **sales** Schrottverkäufe; ~ **value** Schrottwert.

screen|adaptation Filmbearbeitung; ~ **credit** (Vorspann)Benennung von Filmmitwirkenden; ~ **rights** Verfilmungsrechte; ~ **story** Filmstoff.

screening Abschirmung *f*, Überprüfung *f*, Aussonderung *f* ungeeigneter Bewerber; ~ **machine** Gepäckdurchleuchtungsgerät; ~ **panel** Prüfungsausschuß; ~ **test** Ausleseprüfung.

scrip Interimsschein *m*, Zwischenschein *m*, Gutschein *m*, Anteilschein *m*, unterwertiges Papiergeld; ~ **bonus** Gratisaktie; ~ **certificate** vorläufiges Aktienzertifikat; Notgeld; ~ **dividend** → *dividend*; ~ **holder** Inhaber e–s Zwischenscheins; ~ **issue** Ausgabe von Gratisaktien; ~ **money** Notgeld, Besatzungsgeld; ~ **or bonus issue of shares** Ausgabe von Gratisaktien; **land** ~ *US* staatlicher Landzuweisungsschein; **provisional** ~ Interimsschein; **registered** ~ auf den Namen lautender Interimsschein.

script Original *n*, Erstausfertigung *f*, Testamentsurkunde *f*, nicht formgerechtes Schriftstück *n* mit Testamentsinhalt; Urkunde *f* in Kursivschrift.

scrivener Schreiber *m*, Notar *m*; Geldmakler *m*; **money** ~ Finanzmakler.

scroll Handzeichen *n* als Siegel, Liste *f*, Rolle *f*.

scruple Skrupel *m*, Zweifel *m*, Gewissensnot *f*, Bedenken *n*; Skrupel *n* (*Apothekergewicht*).

scrupulous gewissenhaft.

scrutineer Wahlprüfer *m*.

scrutinize genau prüfen, untersuchen.

scrutiny Untersuchung *f*, Wahlprüfung *f*, Musterung *f*; ~ **of documents** Belegprüfung (*Zoll*); **public** ~ allgemeine Überprüfungsmöglichkeit; **to demand a** ~ die Wahl anfechten.

sculpture Skulptur *f*, Werk *n* der Bildhauerkunst.

scuttling Selbstversenkung *f*.

sea die See, das Meer; ~ **accident** Seeunfall; ~ **and land carriage** See- und Landtransport; ~ **bank** Seeuferanlage; ~**-battery** Mißhandlung von Matrosen (*durch den Kapitän*); ~**-bed** Meeresgrund; ~ **bill** Seewechsel, Bodmereibrief; ~**-borne** auf dem Seeweg befördert; ~**-borne trade** Überseehandel; ~**-brief** Schiffspaß; ~ **damage** Seeschaden, Havarie; ~ **fisheries** Hochseefischerei; ~ **fog** Küstennebel; ~ **freight** Seefracht; ~ **front** Seeseite; ~ **frontier** Meeresgrenze; ~**-going ship** Seeschiff; ~ **journal** Schiffstagebuch; ~**-laws** Regeln des Seerechts, Seehandelsrecht; ~ **lawyer** zänkischer Matrose; fauler, streitsüchtiger Hafenarbeiter; Amateuranwalt; ~ **letter** Schiffspaß (*e–s neutralen Schiffes*); ~ **mark** Seezeichen, Schiffahrtszeichen; ~ **mile** Seemeile; ~ **navigation** Seeschiffahrt; ~ **passage** Seereise, Überfahrt; ~ **peril** Seegefahr; ~ **port** Seehafen, Hafenstadt, ~ **protest** Verklarung, Seeprotest; ~**-risk** Seerisiko, Seegefahr; ~ **rovers** Piraten; ~**-shore** Seeküste, Ufer, Küstenstreifen (*zwischen dem gewöhnlichen Hoch- und Niedrigwasserstand*); ~ **trade** Seehandel; ~ **transit** Seeverkehr; ~ **transport** Ozeantransport; **beyond** ~ Übersee, außerhalb der britischen Inseln, außerhalb der USA; **by land and** ~ → *land*; **closed** ~ zum Hoheitsgebiet e–s Staates gehöriges Gewässer; **high ~s** die See, das (offene) Meer (*jenseits der Dreimeilenzone*); **main** ~ das (offene) Meer; **land-locked** ~ Binnenmeer; **narrow ~s** Meerengen (*um England*); **property on** ~ Seevermögen (*des Reeders*); **territorial** ~ Küstenmeer; **the four ~s** die vier Meere um Großbritannien; **the open** ~ das Meer.

seal *s* Siegel *n (= S bzw . . . s,)* Stempel *m*, Dienstsiegel *n*, Bestätigung *f*, Beglaubigungsstempel *m*, Prägesiegel *n*, Siegelabdruck *m*; ~ **book** Sbuch (*e–r Körperschaft, in das alle Siegelverwendungen eingetragen werden*); ~ **day** Antragsstellungseingangstag bei Gericht; ~ **of a company** Firmen*s*; ~ **of cause** *scot* Ermächtigung e–r Kommune, Tochterkörperschaften zu gründen; ~ **of confession** Beichtgeheimnis; ~ **of office** Diensts*s*; ~ **of secrecy** *S* der Verschwiegenheit; ~ **office** Gerichtseingangsstelle (*für Klagen*); ~**-paper** Geschäftsplan für Gerichte; **common** ~ Körperschafts*s*, Gesellschafts*s*; **company's** ~ Geschäfts*s*; **contract under** ~ gesiegelter Vertrag; verbriefter Vertrag; **corporate** ~ Gesellschafts*s*, Körperschafts*s*; **customs** ~ → *customs*; **forging ~s** *S*fälschung; **given under my hand and** ~ von mir unterzeichnet und gesiegelt; **Great S~** das große Staats*s* (*GB*); **impressed** ~ Präge*s*; **lead(en)** ~ (Blei)Plombe; **notarial** ~ (= *notary's* ~) Notariats*s*; **official** ~ Amts*s*, Diensts*s*; **private** ~ privatrechtliches *S*; **Privy S~** *brit* das kleine Staats*s*, Kabinetts*s*; **public** ~ Amts*s*; **quarter** ~ *scot* Neben*s*; **state** ~ Staats*s*, Bundesstaats*s*; **to affix a** ~ siegeln, ein *S* anbringen, ein *S* beidrücken; **to break a** ~ ein *S* erbrechen; **unbroken** ~ unverletztes *S*.

seal *v* siegeln, mit e–m Siegel versehen, plombieren, versiegeln, zukleben (*Brief*); ~ **a deed** e–e Urkunde siegeln; ~**ed and delivered** (*unterzeichnet,*) gesiegelt und begeben; ~**ed bid** verschlossenes und versiegeltes Submissionsangebot; ~**ed instrument** gesiegelte Urkunde; förmlicher Vertrag; ~**ed pattern** amtlich genehmigte Ausgabe (bzw . . . Form); ~**ed tender** → *tender*.

sealer Siegelbeamter *m* (*des Gerichts*), Eichmeister *m*.

sealing Siegeln *n*, Siegelung *f*, Versiegelung *f*, Plombierung *f*, Nachlaßverschluß *m* unter Gerichtssiegel; ~ **fee** → *fee* (*1*); ~ **of records** Strafregistersperre; ~ **up** Verdekken von Urkundenteilen durch Aufkleben (*die nicht offenbart werden müssen*); **official** ~ amtliche *bzw* gerichtliche Versiegelung.

seamen|'s agreement Heuervertrag; ~**'s custom** Seemannsbrauch; ~**'s employment agency** Heuerbüro; ~**'s wages** Matrosenheuer; ~**'s shore allowance** Landgangsgelder; **regulations for** ~ Seemannsordnung.

search *s* Suche *f*, Durchsuchung *f*, Haus(durch)suchung *f*, Fahndung *f*, Leibesvisitation *f*, Schiffsdurchsuchung *f*, Prüfung *f* von Grundstücksurkunden (*zur Feststellung von etwaigen Rechten Dritter*); Recherche *f*; ~ **and seizure** Durchsuchung und Beschlagnahme; ~**-for-drugs order** Rauschgift-Durchsuchungsbefehl; ~ **of private homes** Durchsuchung von Wohnungen; ~ **of title** Ermittlung der Eigentumsverhältnisse an Grundbesitz; ~ **party** Suchtrupp, Rettungsmannschaft; ~ **upon arrest** Durchsuchung bei Festnahme; ~ **warrant** Durchsuchungsbefehl; **bodily** ~ Leibesvisitation; körperliche Durchsuchung; **body** ~ = *bodily* ~ *qv*; **exploratory** ~ Ausforschungsdurchsuchung; **official** ~ grundbuchamtliche Nachforschung (*nach Belastungen*); **preliminary** ~ Vorprüfung; **to undergo a personal** ~ sich e–r Leibesvisitation unterziehen.

search *v* suchen, durchsuchen, untersuchen; ~ **s. b.** jmdn durchsuchen, e–r Leibesvisitation unterziehen.

searcher Untersucher *m*, Prüfer *m*, Zollfahnder *m*.

searching of documents Aktendurchsicht *f*.

season Jahreszeit *f*, Saison *f*, Jagdzeit *f*; ~ **business** Saisongeschäft *n*; ~ **ticket** Zeitkarte, Dauerkarte, Abonnementskarte; **closed** ~ Schonzeit, Hegezeit; **dead** ~ tote Saison, Sauregurkenzeit; **dull** ~ stille Jahreszeit, tote Saison; **early** ~ **business** Vorsaisongeschäft; **in the off** ~ außerhalb der Saison; **open** ~ Jagdzeit; **peak** ~ jahreszeitlich bedingte Hochkonjunktur.

seasonal saisonbedingt, Saison . . ., ~ **allowance** Frühbezugsrabatt; ~ **demand** saisonbedingte Nachfrage; ~ **employment** Saisonbeschäftigung; ~ **labourer** Saisonarbeiter; ~ **tolerance** Verzicht auf tarifvertragliche Sonderrechte außerhalb der Saison; ~ **variation** jahreszeitlich bedingte Veränderung, Saisonschwankungen; ~**ly adjusted** saisonberichtigt.

seat Sitz *m* (*e–r Behörde*); Sitz *m im Parlament bzw. e–m Gremium*, Mandat *n*, Börsensitz *m*; Mitgliedschaft *f*, Amtssitz *m*; ~ **in Parliament** (Abgeordneten)Mandat; ~ **in the cabinet** Kabinettssitz, Kabinettsrang, ~ **of government** Regierungssitz; ~ **of the court** Gerichtssitz; ~ **on a board** Sitz in e–m Verwaltungsrat; **allotment of** ~**s** Sitzverteilung; **country** ~ Landsitz; **county** ~ → *county*; **hot** ~ der elektrische Stuhl; eine riskante Situation (*bes auf dem Zeugenstuhl*); **open** ~ frei werdender Sitz; **reserved** ~ **ticket** Platzkarte; **senatorial** ~ Senatssitz, Senatsmandat; **to resign one's** ~ auf sein Mandat verzichten; **to secure a** ~ ein Mandat erringen; **to vacate one's** ~ sein Mandat niederlegen; **uncontested** ~ unbestrittener Wahlkreis.

seatless mandatslos, ohne Abgeordnetensitz.

seaworthiness Seetüchtigkeit *f*.

seaworthy seetüchtig.

secede sich lossagen, sich trennen.

secession Abspaltung *f*, Sezession *f*, Trennung *f*.

secessionist Sezessionist *m*, Abtrünniger *m*.

second class mail → *mail*; ~ **legal residence** Zweitwohnsitz; ~ **or subsequent conviction** Verurteilung wegen Rückfalls; ~ **sourcing** Vorsehen von zweiten Bezugsquellen.

second *s* Sekunden *m*, Zweiter *m*; Zweitschrift *f*; ~**s** zweite Wahl, Waren zweiter Qualität; Mittelsorte.

second *v* unterstützen, beistehen; ~ **a motion** e–n Antrag unterstützen, ~ **a petition** ein Gesuch befürworten.

secondary sekundär, hilfsweise, subsidiär, zweiten Ranges.

seconder Befürworter *m* (*e–s Antrags bei Abstimmungen*).

secondment Amtshilfe *f*, Unterstützung *f*.

secrecy Geheimhaltung *f*, Verschwiegenheit *f*, Diskretion *f*; ~ **of mails** Briefgeheimnis; **banking** ~ Bankgeheimnis; **official** ~ Amtsverschwiegenheit; **to be sworn to** ~ eidlich zur Geheimhaltung verpflichtet sein; **to exercise** ~ Verschwiegenheit bewahren.

secret *adj* geheim, heimlich.

secret *s* Geheimnis *n*; **business** ~ Betriebsgeheimnis, Geschäftsgeheimnis; **guilty** ~ gewissensbelastendes Geheimnis; **industrial** ~ Betriebsgeheimnis; **manufacturing** ~ Fabrikationsgeheimnis, Betriebsgeheimnis; **official** ~ Amtsgeheimnis; **Official S~s Act** → *act*; **professional** ~ Berufsgeheimnis; **top** ~ strenges Geheimnis, „streng geheim"; **trade** ~ Betriebsgeheimnis, Geschäftsgeheimnis, Zunftgeheimnis.

secretarial department Kanzleiabteilung.

secretary Sekretär *m*, Schriftführer *m*; Geschäftsführer *m* (*e–r Organisation*); Minister *m*; **S~ of Agriculture** (*US*) Landwirtschaftsminister; **S~ of Commerce** (*US*) Handelsminister; **~ of embassy** Botschaftsrat; **~'s office** Sekretariat, Geschäftsstelle; **S~ of Labor** (*US*) Arbeitsminister; **~ of legation** Gesandtschaftsrat; **S~ of Presentation** *hist* Pfründenverwalter (*Lord Chancellor*); **S~ of Senate** Leiter der Geschäftsstelle des (*US*) Senats; **~ of the briefs** *hist* Rechtspfleger der Ladungskanzlei; **S~ of the Interior** Innenminister; **S~ of the Treasury** Finanzminister; **S~ of State** → *Secretary of State*; **assistant** ~ *etwa* Ministerialdirektor; **Assistant Under S~ of State** Staatssekretär im US-Außenministerium; **Deputy Under S~ of State** Ministerialdirigent im US-Außenmin.; **executive** ~ Geschäftsführer; Chefsekretärin; **first** ~ Botschaftsrat 1. Klasse; **Foreign S~** Außenminister (*GB u. a.*); **parliamentary** ~ parlamentarischer Staatssekretär; **permanent under~ of state** (*beamteter*) Staatssekretär; **press** ~ Pressesekretär; **principal private** ~ Leiter des Ministerbüros; **private** ~ Privatsekretär; **second** ~ Legationsrat; **third** ~ *brit* Legationssekretär; **litigation** ~ Anwaltssekretär(in) für Prozeßsachen; **trade union** ~ Gewerkschaftssekretär.

Secretary of State *US:* Außenminister, *GB:* Minister; **~ for Defence** Verteidigungsminister; **~ for Education** Erziehungsminister; **~ for Employment** Arbeitsminister; **~ for Energy** Energieminister; **~ for Foreign and Commonwealth Affairs** Außenminister und Minister für Commonwealth-Angelegenheiten; **~ for North Ireland** Minister für Nord-Irland; **~ for Prices and Consumer Protection** Minister für Preise und Verbraucherschutz; **~ for Scotland** Minister für Schottland; **~ for Social Services** Sozialminister; **~ for the Environment** Umweltminister; **~ for the Home Department** Innenminister; **~ for Trade and Industry** Wirtschaftsminister; **~ for Transport** Verkehrsminister; **~ for Wales** Minister für Wales.

secrete verbergen, beiseiteschaffen.

section Abteilung *f*, Abschnitt *m*, Paragraph *m*, Schnitt *m*, Querschnitt *m*; Distrikt *m*, Effektengruppe *f*; Streckenabschnitt *m*, Abteil *n*; **~ of land** Landabschnitt (*von 1 Quadratmeile des US Katasters*); **~ of the law** Gesetzesparagraph; **cross** ~ Querschnitt; **longitudinal** ~ Längsschnitt; **vertical** ~ Aufriß.

sectional|interests Lokalinteressen; **~ ledger** Hauptbuch mit Unterkonten.

sector Sektor *m*, Bezirk *m*; **~ boundary** Sektorengrenze; **postal** ~ Postbezirk; **the private** ~ die (Privat)Wirtschaft; **the public** ~ die öffentl Hand, der staatl Bereich.

secure *v|t* sichern, Sicherheit gewähren, sicherstellen, garantieren; dinglich sichern, decken, schützen.

secured gesichert, dinglich gesichert; realisiert.

securitization Umwandlung von Darlehensschulden in verkehrsfähige Wertpapiere (*insbesondere Beteiligungspapiere*).

securitize umschulden in Beteiligungspapiere; umschulden zu börsenfähigen Anleihepapieren; refinanzieren durch Wertpapieremission.

security (*1*) Sicherheit *f* (= *S bzw ... s*), Sicherstellung *f*, Sicherung *f*, Sicherheitsleistung *f*, Kaution *f*, Pfand *n*, Bürge *m*, Schadloshaltung *f*; ~ **agreement** Besicherungsvereinbarung, Sicherheitsstellung; ~ **bond** → *bond* (*2*); ~ **by bond** *S*–*s*leistung durch Bürgschaft; ~ **by mortgage** hypothekarische *S*; ~ **by payment into court** *S* durch Hinterlegung; ~ **by undertaking to pay costs** eigene Kostenhaftungserklärung; ~ **clearance** Bescheid, daß keine sicherheitsmäßigen Bedenken bestehen, Unbedenklichkeitsbescheinigung; Erledigung der Sicherheitsüberprüfung; **S~ Council** Weltsicherheitsrat; ~ **credit** Bürgschaftskredit; ~ **deposit** *S*–*s*leistung, Mietkaution; ~ **for costs** Prozeßkosten*s*; ~ **for debt** *S* für e–e Forderung; ~ **for good behavior** Kautionsverpflichtung für künftiges Wohlverhalten; ~ **for keeping the peace** Kaution für die Auflage, keine öffentl Störung zu verursachen; ~ **for money** (*dingliche*) *S*; dinglich gesicherte Forderung; ~ **interest** dingliches *S*–*s*recht; ~ **lapse** Sicherheitsmanko; ~ **measures** *S*–*s*maßnahmen; ~ **note** lombardgesicherter Schuldschein; ~ **of tenure** sicheres (*längeres*) Mietverhältnis, Mietersicherheit; ~ **regulations** Verschlußsachenverordnung; ~ **risk** *S*–*s*risiko; ~ **sreening** Sicherheitsüberprüfung; ~ **surcharge** Sicherheitszuschlag (*Flugplatz*); ~ **transaction** Sicherungsgeschäft; **by way of** ~ gegen *S*; **collateral** ~ dingl *S*, besonders gestellte *S*, Sicherheitsleistung, Lombarddekkung; **collective** ~ kollektive *S*; **continuing** ~ fortlaufende *S*; **floating** ~ auswechselbare Kreditsicherung; aufschiebend bedingte *S*; **highgrade** ~ hochwertige *S*; **joint** ~ Solidarbürgschaft; **landed ~ies** → *landed*; **liquidator's** ~ vom Liquidator zu stellende Kaution; **loan without** ~ ungesichertes Darlehen; **national** ~ nationale *S*, Staatssicherh; **personal** ~ persönliche *S*; nicht dingl *S* (*Bürgschaft etc*); **property subject to a** ~ beliehene Sache; **public** ~ öffentl *S*; **real** ~ Immobiliar*s*, Grundpfandrecht; dingliche *S*; **special** ~ dingl *S*; **social** ~ → *social*; **to become** ~ **for a person** für jmdn e–e Bürgschaft übernehmen; **to give** ~ *S* geben, *S* stellen; **underlying** ~ dingliche *S*.

security (*2*) Wertpapier *n bes pl:* **~ies** (= *W, bzw w*); Effekten; ~ **account** Effektenkonto; **S~ies and Exchange Commission** *US*-Börsenaufsichtsamt; **~ies at cost** börsenfähige *W*–*e* zu Ankaufskursen; **~ies broker** Effektenmakler, Effektenhändler, *W*händler; **~ies company** Investmentgesellschaft; **~ies dealer** Effektenhändler; ~ **dealings** Effektenhandel; ~ **dividend** → *dividend*; **~ies exchange** *W*börse; **~ies firm** *W*handelsfirma, Effektenhaus; ~ **fraud** *W*schwindel; **~ies held in pledge** lombardierte Effekten; ~ **holder** *W*besitzer; ~ **holdings** *W*bestand; **~ies in hand** Effektenportefeuille; **~ies insurance** → *insurance*; **~ies ledger** Effektenbuch; **~ies lending** Ausleihen von *W*–*n* (*Eurobonds*); ~ **loans** Effektenlombard, *W*kredit; **~ies market** Effektenbörse, Effektenmarkt; **~ies payable to bearer** Inhaberpapiere; ~ **purchases** Effektenkäufe; **~ies quoted on the spot market** Kassawerte; **~ies research** Wertpapieranalyse; ~ **sales** Effektenverkäufe; ~ **stamp** Effektenstempel, E.-siegel; ~ **trading** Effektenhandel; ~ **trust** Holding-Syndikat; **active ~ies** Effekten mit täglichem Umsatz; **assessable** ~ beleihungsfähige *W*–*e*, nachschußpflichtige *W*–*e*; **authorized ~ies** mündelsichere *W*–*e*; **bearer** ~ Inhaberpapier; **exempted ~ies** von Börsenvorschriften befreite *W*–*e*; **fixed-interest-bearing ~ies** festverzinsliche *W–e*; **foreign ~ies** Auslandseffekten, ausl *W–e*; **gilt-edged ~ies** mündelsichere Papiere, erstklassige *W–e*; **government ~ies** Staatsanleihen; **inactive ~ies** selten gehandelte *W–e*; **industrial ~ies** Industriewerte; **interbourse ~ies** *brit* international gehandelte *W–e*; **investment ~ies** Anlagenwerte; **irredeemable ~ies** Obligationen ohne Tilgungsraten; **listed ~ies** börsenfähige *W–e*, zum Börsenhandel zugelassene *W–e*; **local ~** Kommunalpapiere; **marketable ~ies** börsengängige Effekten; **municipal ~ies** Kommunalanleihen; **non-marketable ~ies** nicht umlauffähige *W–e*, nicht handelbare *W–e*; **nonvoting ~ies** stimmrechtlose *W–e*; **outside ~ies** *US:* nicht notierte *W–e*; **outstanding ~ies** *W–e* im Privatbesitz, ungetilgte Obligationen; **over-the-counter ~ies** im Freiverkehr gehandelte Effekten; **personal ~ies** Namenspapiere; **public ~ies** Staatspapiere, Anleihen der öffentlichen Hand; **redeemable ~** kündbares Beteiligungspapier, kündbares Investmentzertifikat; **registered ~ies** Namenspapiere; **seasoned ~ies** gut eingeführte *W–e*; **senior ~ies** börsenfähige *W–e (Obligationen und Vorzugsaktien)*; **short-term ~ies** *W–e* mit kurzer Laufzeit; **speculative ~ies** Spekulationspapiere; **sundry ~s** Nebenwerte; **to borrow on ~ies** Effekten lombardieren, *W–e* beleihen; **treasury ~ies** →*treasury*; **trust ~**mündelsichere *W–e*; **undigested ~ies** nicht plazierte Effekten; **unlisted ~** nicht notiertes *W*, unkotierte *W*, Freiverkehrswerte; **voting ~ies** stimmberechtigte Wertpapiere.

secus anders, gegenteilig.

sedition Staatsgefährdung *f*, staatsgefährdende Propaganda *f*, aufrührerische Agitation *f*, Aufreizen *n* zum Aufruhr, Aufwiegelung *f*; **~-monger** revolutionärer Agent, staatsgefährdender Hetzer.

seditious aufrührerisch, hochverräterisch; **~ libel** → *libel*; **~ literature** staatsgefährdende Schriften; **~ utterance(s)** hochverräterische Äußerung(en).

seducing to leave service Abwerben *n* von Arbeitskräften.

seduction Verführung *f* (*zur Unzucht*); Verleitung zum Ungehorsam.

see sehen, einsehen, wahrnehmen; **~ back** vergleiche Rückseite, Bezugnahme auf rückseitige Bedingungen; **~ over** siehe nächste Seite; **~n** gesehen (*gilt als Annahme bei Wechseln*); **~n and approved** gesehen und genehmigt.

seek suchen, durchsuchen, verlangen, Zuflucht nehmen; **~ admission** Zulassung beantragen; **~ divorce** Scheidung begehren; **~ employment** Arbeit suchen; **~ information** Auskünfte einholen; **~ legal advice** sich anwaltschaftlich beraten lassen.

segregate absondern, abspalten, trennen, isolieren.

segregation Absonderung *f*, Trennung *f*, Isolierung *f*, Rassentrennung *f*.

seignior Grundherr *m*, Rittergutsbesitzer *m*; **~ in gross** Grundherr (*über Liegenschaften ohne Herrenhaus*).

seigniorage Prägeschutz *m*, Prägelohn *m*; königliche Münzgebühr *f*, Münzgewinn *m*; Verfasseranteil *m*; **~ profit** Münzgewinn.

seigniory Feudalherrschaft *f*, Privilegien e–s Feudalherrn; Grundherrschaft *f*; Domäne *f*.

seisin (= **seizin**) Belehnung *f*, freier Lehensbesitz *m*, rechtmäßiger Eigenbesitz *m* am Grundstück; **~ in deed** Eigenbesitz am freien Lehen; **~ in fact** = *actual ~ qv*; **~ in fee** = *actual ~ qv*; **~ in law** Rechtsbesitz am Lehensgrundstück (*zB nach Erbfall*), das Recht auf unmittelbaren Grundstücksbesitz; **~ ox** *scot hist* Naturalabgabe bei Lehensübergabe; **actual ~** freies Lehen in unmittelbarem Eigenbesitz; **constructive ~** freies Lehen in mittelbarem

Eigenbesitz; **covenant of** ~ → *covenant*; **equitable** ~ billigkeitsrechtlicher Anspruch auf Grundbesitz (*zB des Hypothekenschuldners*); **livery of** ~ → *livery*; **primer** ~ Abgabe des Lehenserben an den König; **quasi** ~ angenähert freier Lehensbesitz (*e–s Copyholder qv*).

seizable pfändbar.

seize festnehmen, ergreifen, verhaften, Besitz ergreifen, pfänden, *hist* Gewere erlangen, beschlagnahmen, sich bemächtigen; ~ **power** die Macht ergreifen; ~ **property on an execution** pfänden; ~ **the till** e–e Kassenpfändung vornehmen; **to be ~d with the matter** mit der Angelegenheit befaßt sein, zuständig sein.

seizing Beschlagnahme *f*.

seizor (der *bzw* die) Besitzergreifende *m*|*f*.

seizure Arrest *m*, Pfändung *f*, Beschlagnahme *f*, Besitznahme *f*, Konfiszierung *f*, Ergreifung *f*, Festnahme *f*; ~ **note** Quittung des Gerichtsvollziehers; ~ **of crops** Pfändung der Früchte auf dem Halm; ~ **of licence** Beschlagnahme des Führerscheins; ~ **of mortgaged goods** Pfändung von (*verpfändeten bzw*) sicherungsübereigneten Sachen; ~ **of prisoner** (Wieder)Ergreifung eines Gefangenen; **actual** ~ Beschlagnahme durch Wegnahme; **constructive** ~ Beschlagnahme durch Verfügungsverbot; **exemption from** ~ Unpfändbarkeit; **illegal** ~ rechtswidrige Beschlagnahme; **provisional** ~ Arrestbeschlagnahme; **to lift the** ~ die Pfändung aufheben.

selection Wahl *f*, Auswahl *f*; ~ **for dismissal** Auswahl der zu Entlassenden; ~ **in common** gemeinschaftliche Nominierung; ~ **of risks** Risikoauslese; ~ **procedure** Auswahlverfahren; **adverse** ~ negative Auslese (*Versicherungsrisiken*), Antiselektion (*Ausscheiden der besseren Risiken*).

selective auswählend, Auswahl ...; ~ **credit controls** Kreditlenkung; ~ **distribution** Vertrieb über ausgewählten Händlerkreis; ~ **driver plan** Schadenfreiheitsrabattsystem; ~ **employment tax** → *tax*; ~ **selling** Vertrieb über ausgewählten Händlerkreis; ~ **service** allgemeine Wehrpflichterfassung nach Musterung.

selectman Stadtverordneter *m*.

self selbst; ~**-accusation** Selbstbeschuldigung; ~**-acquired** selbsterworben; ~**-administration** → *administration*; ~**-assessable** selbstveranlagungspflichtig; ~**-assessment** Selbstveranlagung; ~**-benefit** Eigenvorteil; ~**-certificate** Selbstbescheinigung (*Krankheitsausfall*); ~**-confessed** geständig, eingestanden, nach eigenem Geständnis; ~**-constituted authority** angemaßte Autorität; ~**-contained** abgeschlossen, vollständig; ~**-contained flat** abgeschlossene Wohnung; ~**-contained house** Einfamilienhaus; ~**-contradiction** Widerspruch, innerer Widerspruch; ~**contradictory** in sich widerspruchsvoll; ~**-convicted** auf Grund eigener Aussagen überführt; ~**-dealing** Selbstkontrahieren, Rechtsgeschäft des Treuhänders im eigenen Interesse; ~**-defence** Notwehr, Selbstverteidigung; ~**-determination** Selbstbestimmung; ~**-discrimination** Selbstbenachteiligung; ~**-educated person** Autodidakt; ~**-employed** Freiberufler *m*; *adj*: freiberuflich, selbständig; ~ **employed retirement annuity** (*SERA*) Altersrente für Freiberufler; ~**-employer** Freiberufler, selbständiger Unternehmer; ~**-executing** unmittelbar geltend, direkt vollziehbar, sofort vollstreckbar; ~**-financing** Selbstfinanzierung, Eigenfinanzierung; ~**-firing explosives** Selbstschußanlagen; Selbstschüsse; ~**-government** Selbstverwaltung, Selbstregierung; ~**-help** Selbsthilfe; ~**-imposed** selbstauferlegt; ~**-incrimination** Selbstbezichtigung, Selbstbelastung; *compulsory* ~: *erzwungene*

Selbstbezichtigung; ~-**inflicted** selbstbeigebracht; ~-**inflicted wounds** Selbstverstümmelung; ~-**instruction** Selbstunterricht; ~-**insurance** eigene Betriebsversicherung, Eigenversicherung; ~-**interest** Eigennutz; ~-**justification** Rechtfertigung des eigenen Verhaltens; ~-**liquidating** sich selbst amortisierend; ~-**liquidating advances** Überbrückungskredit; ~-**liquidating credit** sich kurzfristig abdeckender Kredit, Warenkredit; ~-**liquidating paper** sich selbst amortisierende Obligation; ~-**liquidating premium** → *premium*; ~-**liquidating projects** sich selbst amortisierende Vorhaben; ~-**liquidity** Selbsttilgung; ~-**made man** Autodidakt, Selfmademan; ~-**misdirection** rechtsfehlerhafte Entscheidung (*e–s Richters*); ~-**murder** Selbstmord; ~ **neglect** Selbstgefährdung durch Verwahrlosung, selbst verursachte Verwahrlosung; ~-**policing** autonom, unter eigener Kontrolle stehend; ~-**preservation** Selbsterhaltung; ~-**protection** Notwehr; ~-**qualifying element** Element der immanenten Selbstbeschränkung, immanente Beschränkung; ~-**redress** Selbsthilfe; ~-**reducing clause** automatische Anpassungsklausel des Versicherungswertes (*bei beliehenen Versicherungen*); ~-**regulating** autonom; ~ **regulation** freiwillige Selbstkontrolle; ~-**renewing** sich automatisch verlängernd; ~-**retention** *ins* Selbstbehalt; ~-**rightous** selbstgerecht; ~-**rightousness** Selbstgerechtigkeit; ~-**same matter** genau die gleiche Angelegenheit, identischer Fall; ~-**service** Selbstbedienung; ~-**serving declaration** → *declaration*; ~-**slaughter** Selbstmord; ~-**sufficiency** wirtschaftliche Unabhängigkeit, Selbstversorgung; ~-**support** unterhaltsrechtl Selbständigkeit; *incapable of* ~ ~: *nicht imstande, für den eigenen Unterhalt aufzukommen*; ~-**supporting** selbstversorgend, autark; ~-**supporting idea** selbständiger Gedanke; ~ **tender** Verkaufsangebot von eigenen Aktien (*als Abwehr von Übernahmeversuch*).

sell verkaufen, veräußern, sich verkaufen lassen, Absatz finden; ~ **a bear** ohne Deckung verkaufen; auf Baisse spekulieren; ~ **ahead** für zukünftige Lieferung verk.; ~ **and dispose of** durch Verkauf veräußern; ~ **at a premium** mit Gewinn verkaufen; über Pari stehen; ~ **by private contract** freihändig verkaufen; ~ **by public sale** versteigern; ~ **by sample** nach Muster verkaufen; ~ **down the river** *hist, US*: verraten, in die Sklaverei verkaufen; unfair benachteiligen; ~ **for cash** gegen Barzahlung verkaufen; ~ **for future delivery** auf zukünftige Lieferung verkaufen; ~ **for the settlement** auf Termin verkaufen; ~ **hard** sich schwer verkaufen; ~ **in lots** etwas in Partien verkaufen; ~ **off** ausverkaufen; Glattstellungsverkauf vornehmen; ~ **off goods** Waren abstoßen; ~ **on time** auf Ziel verkaufen; ~ **on trust** auf Kredit verkaufen; ~ **one's bacon** auf den Strich gehen; ~ **or supply** verkaufen oder beliefern; ~ **out** ausverkaufen, ein Lager liquidieren, Wertpapierbestand restlos liquidieren; verraten, verkaufen, auspfänden, kahlpfänden; ~ **outright** → *outright*; ~ **privately** freihändig verkaufen; ~ **rapidly** reißend Absatz finden; ~ **readily** sich gut verkaufen lassen; ~ **short** ohne Deckung verkaufen, e–n Baisseverkauf tätigen; fixen; ~ **with vacant possession** geräumt verkaufen; **certain to** ~ mit sicherer Absatzmöglichkeit.

seller Verkäufer *m*, Veräußerer *m*; Auftragnehmer, Lieferfirma *f*; **„~s"** „Brief", offeriert; **~s ahead** *US exch* gehandelt und Brief; **~s and buyers** (*Kurszettel*) Brief und Geld; **~'s interest (policy)** Exportrisiko(versicherung); **~s' market** Verkäufermarkt; ~ **of a**

put and call Stellagegeber; ~ of a spread Stellagegeber; ~s' option →*option*; ~s over mehr Brief; bear ~ Baissespekulant; common ~ gewerbsmäßiger Verkäufer; forward ~ Terminverkäufer; intermediate ~ Zwischenverkäufer; unpaid ~ Kaufpreisgläubiger, nicht befriedigter Verkäufer.

selling | **at a loss** Verkauf zu Verlustpreisen; ~ **below cost price** Verkauf unter Selbstkosten; ~ **brokerage** Verkaufsprovision des Maklers; ~ **capacity** Verkaufskapazität; ~ **commission** Absatzprovision; ~ **conditions** Verkaufsbedingungen; ~ **contract** Schlußschein, Schlußnote; ~ **cost** Selbstkosten des Verkäufers; ~ **expense** Vertriebskosten, Verkaufsunkosten; ~ **forward** Terminverkäufe; ~ **group** Plazierungskonsortium; ~ **licence** Verkaufslizenz; ~ **machine** Warenautomat; ~ **methods** Vertriebsmethoden; ~ **off** Ausverkauf, Saisonausverkauf; ~ **office** Verkaufsbüro; ~ **order** Verkaufsauftrag; ~ **out** Selbsthilfeverkauf bei Abnahmeverzug (*von Effekten*); ~ **point** Verkaufsargument; ~ **price** → *price (1)*; ~ **public offices** Ämterkauf; ~ **rate** → *rate*; ~ **stocks short** Leerverkauf von Aktien; ~ **transactions** Verkaufsabschlüsse; ~ **value** Verkaufswert; ~ **with premium** Verkauf mit Zugaben; **common** ~ **agency** gemeinsames Verkaufsbüro; **indirect** ~ Verkauf durch Mittelsleute; **mail-order** ~ Versandgeschäft; **short** ~ Leerverkauf, Fixen; **stop-order** ~ limitierter Verkaufsauftrag.

sell-off Abstoßen *n*, Glattstellungsverkauf *m*, Privatisierungsverkauf *m*.

semblance of justice Anschein der Gerechtigkeit.

semble anscheinend, zweifelnd.

semi halb . . .; ~**-annual** halbjährlich; ~**-durable** beschränkt haltbar (*6 Monate bis 3 Jahre*); ~**-fixed fund** Investmentfonds mit begrenzt auswechselbarem Portefeuille; ~**-official** halbamtlich, offiziös; ~**-skilled labo(u)r** → *labo(u)r*; ~**-sovereign state** halbsouveräner Staat.

senate Senat *m*; **S~ Judiciary Committee** Justizausschuß des Senats *US*; ~ **inquiry** Untersuchung durch den Senat, Senatsenquete; **S~ of the Inns of Court and the Bar** Senat der Rechtsanwaltskammer *GB (seit 1974)*.

senator Senator *m*.

senatorial courtesy Kourtoisie der Senatoren (*Rücksichtnahme auf den gebietsmäßig zuständigen Senator*).

send senden, übersenden, absenden; ~ **cash on delivery** gegen Nachnahme (ver)senden; ~ **in** einreichen; ~ **in one's resignation** sein Rücktrittsgesuch einreichen; ~ **(in) money** Geld einsenden; ~ **on approval** zur Ansicht zuschicken.

sender Absender *m*, Versender *m*.

senior *adj* älter, dienstälter, rangälter; ~ **capital** *brit* Stammkapital; ~ **citizens' accommodation for single persons** Seniorenheim für Alleinstehende; ~ **civil servant** höherer Beamter; ~ **counsel** Hauptprozeßbevollmächtigter; ~ **district attorney** Oberstaatsanwalt; ~ **equity** das bessere (*ältere*) Billigkeitsrecht; ~ **executive** leitender Angestellter; ~ **high school** Oberstufe der höheren Schule; ~ **in rank** Vorgesetzter, Rangältester, Rangälterer; ~ **management shuffle** Umbesetzung der Führungskräfte; ~ **staff lawyer** Syndikus(anwalt).

senior *s* Senior, Chef, Vorgesetzter.

seniority höheres Dienstalter *n*, Anciennität *f*, höheres Alter, Vorrang *m*; Vorrang nach Dienstgrad; ~ **allowance** Dienstalterszulage; ~ **bonus** Alterszulage; ~ **in rank** Dienstrang, Dienstalter; ~ **list** Dienstrangliste; ~ **rule** Anciennitätsprinzip; **according to** ~ nach dem Dienstalter; **chairman by** ~ Vorsitzender wegen der längsten Zugehörigkeit (*zum Gremium*); **order of** ~ Anciennität(sprinzip).

sense Sinn *m*, Vernunft *f*, Verstand *m*,

Bedeutung *f*; ~ **of grievance** Gekränktheit, Groll; ~ **of justice** Rechtsgefühl, Gerechtigkeitssinn; **common** ~ gesunder Menschenverstand; **guilt-stricken** ~ Schuldbewußtsein; **in the legal** ~ im juristischen Sinn; **literal** ~ buchstäbliche Bedeutung; **metaphorical** ~ übertragene Bedeutung.

sensitive geheimhaltungsbedürftig, sicherheitsempfindlich, kritisch.

sensitivity analysis Sensitivitätsanalyse *f*, Empfindlichkeitsanalyse *f* (*Prüfung der Vorteilhaftigkeit von Investitionen bzw der Stabilität e–s Rechenergebnisses*).

sentence *s* Strafurteil *n*, Strafe *f*, Strafmaß *n*; Strafmaßfestsetzung, Strafzumessung (*durch Urteil*), Urteil *n* (*selten auch Zivilurteil*); ~ **in absentia** Abwesenheitsurteil; ~ **in contumacia** Abwesenheitsurteil; ~ **of death recorded** nicht zu vollstreckende Todesstrafe; **alteration of** ~ Änderung im Strafmaß; **alternative** ~ Ersatz(freiheits)strafe; **capital** ~ Todesstrafe; **concurrent** ~ *etwa:* Gesamtstrafe (*gleichzeitig zu verbüßende Einzelstrafen*); **conditional** ~ auf Bewährung ausgesetzte Freiheitsstrafe; **consecutive** ~**s** nacheinander zu verbüßende Strafen (*Einzelstrafen*); **cumulative** ~ *etwa:* Gesamtstrafe (*ohne Herabsetzung*); **cumulative** ~**s** Strafenhäufung; **convictional** ~ Verurteilung, Strafurteil; **custodial** ~ Freiheitsstrafe, Urteil zu Freiheitsentzug; **deferred** ~ aufgeschobene Urteilsverkündung zum Strafmaß; **definite** ~ Urteil mit bestimmter Freiheitsstrafe; **detention centre** ~ Jugendarrest; **determinate** ~ Freiheitsstrafe von bestimmter Dauer; **erroneous** ~ fehlerhaftes Strafurteil; **excessive** ~ übermäßig hohe Strafe; **execution of** ~ → *execution*; **extended** ~ **of imprisonment** Sicherungsverwahrung; **final** ~ abschließendes Strafurteil; **fixed** ~ bestimmte Einzelstrafe; **harsh** ~ übermäßig harte Strafe; **heavy** ~ schwere Strafe; **immediate** ~ nicht zur Bewährung ausgesetzte Strafe; **imposition of** ~ Verhängung e–r Strafe; **inadequate** ~ zu niedriges Strafmaß (*unter der Mindeststrafe*); **indeterminate** ~ Freiheitsstrafe mit unbestimmter Strafdauer; **irregular** ~ fehlerhaftes Strafurteil; **jail** ~ Gefängnisstrafe, Freiheitsstrafe; **judicial** ~ Gerichtsurteil; **just and lawful** ~ gerechte Strafe; **lenient** ~ mildes Urteil; **mandatory** ~ zwingend vorgeschriebene Strafe (*ohne Bewährung*); **maximum** ~ Höchststrafe; **measure of** ~ Strafmaß; **minimum** ~ Mindeststrafe; **mitigation of** ~ → *mitigation*; **non-custodial** ~ Strafe ohne Freiheitsentzug; **over-lenient** ~ viel zu mildes Urteil; **partly-served** ~ teilverbüßte Freiheitsstrafe; **partly-suspended** (= *partially-suspended*) ~ teilweise auf Bewährung ausgesetzte Freiheitsstrafe; **prison** ~ **in default** Ersatzfreiheitsstrafe; **pronouncement of** ~ Verkündung des Strafurteils (*des Strafmaßes*); **rehabilitative** ~ Verurteilung mit dem Ziel der Resozialisierung; **reasonable** ~ angemessene Strafe; **remainder of a** ~ Strafrest; **reprieve of** ~ → *reprieve*; **serving** ~ **in full** Strafe voll verbüßen; **single** ~ Einzelstrafe; **straight** ~ Urteil mit bestimmtem Strafmaß; **subsidiary** ~ Nebenstrafe; **suspended** ~ zur Bewährung ausgesetzte Strafe; **suspension of** ~ Strafaussetzung; **tariff** ~ Strafe mit gesetzl Strafrahmen; **termination of** ~ Ende der Strafzeit; Entlassung; **to award a** ~ auf Strafe erkennen; **to complete one's** ~ e–e Strafe voll verbüßen; **to execute a** ~ ein Urteil vollstrecken; **to reduce a** ~ e–e Strafe herabsetzen; **to serve one's** ~ seine Strafe verbüßen; **to uphold a** ~ ein Strafurteil bestätigen.

sentence *v* verurteilen, bestrafen, das Strafmaß aussprechen.

sentencer Strafrichter *m*.

sentencing Strafmaßverkündung *f*, Straf(maß)praxis *f*.

separability Trennbarkeit *f*; ~ **clause** salvatorische Klausel. *Vertragsbestimmung über die Gültigkeit des übrigen Vertrages bei Teilnichtigkeit.*

separable trennbar, teilbar; ~ **controversy** abtrennbarer Rechtsstreit.

separate *adj* getrennt, gesondert, selbständig; ~ **but equal doctrine** *Prinzip der Rassentrennung bei Gleichberechtigung der Farbigen.*

separate *v* trennen, sich trennen, teilen.

separation Trennung *f*; ~ **a mensa et thoro** Trennung von Tisch und Bett; ~ **agreement** Vereinbarung über das Getrenntleben, Trennungsvereinbarung; ~ **allowance** Trennungszulage; Trennungsgeld, Kündigungsabfindung; ~ **by consent** einverständliche Trennung; ~ **deed** Urkunde über das Getrenntleben; ~ **from bed and board** Trennung von Tisch und Bett; ~ **from service** Entlassung aus dem Amt; ~ **from the service** Entlassung aus dem Militärdienst; ~ **of claims** Absonderung; ~ **of partnership** Auflösung der Handelsgesellschaft; ~ **of patrimony** Absonderung des Nachlasses; ~ **of powers** Gewaltenteilung; ~ **of property** Gütertrennung; ~ **of spouses** eheliches Getrenntleben; ~ **order** gerichtliche Anordnung des Getrenntlebens; ~ **with consent** einverständliches Getrenntleben; **consensual** ~ einvernehmliches Getrenntleben; **decree for judicial** ~ → *decree*; **right to** ~ Recht zum Getrenntleben; **order for** ~ Anordnung des Getrenntlebens.

separatist Separatist *m*, Dissident *m*.

sequel Folge *f*, Nachspiel *n*, Fortsetzung *f*.

sequence Aufeinanderfolge *f*, Reihenfolge *f*, Nachfolge *f*; ~ **of courts** Instanzenzug; ~ **of priority** Rangfolge; **in** ~ aufeinanderfolgend.

sequent aufeinanderfolgend.

sequester *s* Sequester *m*.

sequester *v* absondern, beschlagnahmen, sequestrieren, requirieren.

sequestrable beschlagnahmefähig, sequestrierbar.

sequestrate sequestrieren, beschlagnahmen, der Zwangsverwaltung unterwerfen; ~ **a jury** die Klausur der Geschworenen vornehmen.

sequestration Sequestration *f*, Zwangsverwaltung *f*, gerichtl Beschlagnahme und Zwangsverwaltung (*als Erzwingungsmaßnahme*); **judicial** ~ gerichtl angeordnete Verwahrung, die Zwangsverwaltung; **writ of** ~→ *writ*.

sequestrator Sequester *m*, Zwangsverwalter *m*.

serf Leibeigener *m*, Sklave *m*.

serfdom Leibeigenschaft *f*.

sergeant Feldwebel *m*, Polizeiwachtmeister *m*.

serial reihenweise, periodisch, fortlaufend.

serialize in Fortsetzungen veröffentlichen; serienweise numerieren.

seriate serienweise anordnen; in Serien angeordnet.

seriately in Serien, in der Reihenfolge.

seriatim einzeln, eins nach dem anderen.

series Serie *f*, Reihe *f*, Kategorie *f*, Zusammenhang *m*; ~ **bonds** → *bond* (*1*).

serious | **and wilful misconduct** schwere vorsätzliche Verfehlung; ~ **bodily injury** → *injury*; ~ **buyer** ernsthafter Kaufinteressent; ~ **hardship** schwerer Härtefall; ~ **illness** schwere Krankheit; ~ **mistake** schwerer Fehler; ~ **offer** ernstgemeintes Angebot; ~ **promise** ernst gemeintes Versprechen; ~**ly disposed** mit ernsthaften Absichten.

serjeant königl Sicherheitsoffizier, Zeremonienbeamter, Gerichtswachtmeister *m*; ~ **at arms** Parlamentswachtmeister; ~ **at law** *hist* Angehöriger der höchsten Stufe der barristers *qv*, Ehrenrang für Anwälte; **S~ at the Mace** Stadtzeremonienmeister; ~ **of the peace** Gerichtswachtmeister, Gerichtsvollzieher; **Common S** → *Common Serjeant*.

serjeanty ritterliches Leben *n*.

serrated gezackt (*Rand von Pergamenten*).

servant Diener *m*, Bediensteter *m*, Arbeitnehmer *m*; ~ **in husbandry** Knecht *bzw* Magd; ~ **of the crown** Kronbeamter, Staatsbediensteter; **civil** ~ → *civil servant*; **domestic** ~ Hausangestellte(r), Hausgehilfin; **female** ~ weibl Bedienstete, Dienerin, Magd; **menial** ~ Diener, Hausdiener; **possessory** ~ Besitzdiener; **public** ~ (Staats)-Beamter, Staatsbediensteter, Angehöriger des öffentlichen Dienstes.

serve dienen, Dienst(e) leisten, angestellt sein, amtieren, fungieren; vollziehen; zustellen; abbüßen; ~ **a loan** e–e Anleihe bedienen; ~ **a sentence** e–e Strafe verbüßen; ~ **a sentence upon return** e–e Reststrafe nach Haftunterbrechung verbüßen; ~ **as a pretext** als Vorwand dienen; ~ **as collateral** → *collateral s*; ~ **copies** Abschriften zustellen; ~ **on a person** jmdm etwas persönlich zustellen; ~ **on juries** Geschworener sein; ~ **(on) the defendant** die Zustellung an den Beklagten vornehmen; **duly ~d** ordnungsgemäß zugestellt.

service (*1*) Dienstleistung *f*, Arbeitsleistung *f*; Service *m*, Tätigkeit *f*, Amt *n*; ~ **abroad** Auslandsdienst; ~ **agreement** → *agreement*; ~ **allowance** Aufwandsentschädigung; ~ **area** Versorgungsgebiet, Sendebereich; ~ **call** Dienstgespräch; ~ **center** Kundendienstzentrale; ~ **charges** Kommission, Verwaltungsgebühr; ~ **contract** Dienstleistungsvertrag, Werkvertrag; Wartungsvertrag; ~ **credit** → *credit*; ~ **declaration** Personalangaben für abwesende Wähler; ~ **department** Kundendienstabteilung; ~ **director** Vorstandsmitglied mit Dienstvertrag; ~ **establishment** Dienstleistungsbetrieb (*für allgemeine Kundschaft*); ~ **franchise** Wahlrecht als Bewohner einer Dienst- oder Werkswohnung; ~ **in aumone** *hist* Stiftung für Seelenmessen; ~ **industries** Dienstleistungsgewerbe; ~ **instructions** Betriebsvorschriften, Bedienungsanweisung; ~ **life** Verwendungsdauer; ~ **mark** Dienstleistungszeichen (*US: wie ein Warenzeichen geschützt*); ~ **occupancy** Werk(Dienst)wohnung; ~ **occupation** Wohnung im Hause des Dienstherrn; ~ **of an heir** *scot* Erbenfeststellung, Immobiliarnachlaßübertragung; ~ **of the loan** Anleihedienst, Zinsendienst; ~ **period for annuities** Dienstzeiten für die Pensionsberechnung; ~ **qualification** Einstellungsvoraussetzungen für den öffentlichen Dienst; **~s rendered** geleistete Dienste, Dienstleistung; ~ **trade** Dienstleistungsgewerbe; **~s transactions** Dienstleistungsverkehr; **banking ~s** → *banking*; ~ **business** → *business*; **cartage** ~ Rollfuhrdienst; **civil** ~ → *civil*; **collection** ~ Inkassodienst; **common** ~ gemeinsames Arbeitsverhältnis; **compulsory military** ~ allgemeine Wehrpflicht; **conditions of** ~ Arbeitsbedingungen; **contractual ~s** vertragliche Leistungen; **domestic** ~ Raumpflege, Hausbedienstetenarbeiten; **emergency** ~ Bereitschaftsdienst; **expediting** ~ Schnelldienst; **fiduciary ~s** Treuhandverwaltung (Bank); **field** ~ → *field*; **gratuitous ~s** unentgeltliche Dienste; **industrial ~s** Industrieberatungsdienste; **local ~s** Kommunalleistungen; **national** ~ Wehrdienst; **no-frills share dealing** ~ vereinfachter Aktienhandelsdienst; **ordinary** ~ übliche Leistungen; **pensionable** ~ pensions(anwartschafts)berechtigte Dienstleistungen; **post-design** ~ Änderungs- und Ergänzungsdienst; **postal** ~ Postdienst, Postverkehr; **preventive** ~ Zollfahndung; **professional ~s** freiberufliche Dienste, anwaltschaftliche Dienste; **public** ~ öffentlicher Dienst, Staatsdienst; **public utility** ~ öffentliches Versorgungsunternehmen (*Strom, Wasser, Gas usw*); **regular scheduled** ~ Linienverkehr; **representational ~s** Prozeßvertretung; **return** ~ Gegendienst; **same-day** ~ Erledigung am gleichen Tage; **technical** ~ Kundendienst; **to perform ~s** Dienstleistungen erbringen.

service (*2*) Zustellung *f* (= *Zst bzw zst*) ~ **abroad** Auslands*zst*; ~ **by plaintiff** (Partei)*Zst* durch den Kläger; ~ **by post** *Zst* durch Absendung auf dem Postwege; ~ **by publication** öffentliche *Zst*; ~ **by insertion through the letter box** *Zst* durch Einwurf in den Briefkasten des Empfängers; ~ **of notice** *Zst* e–r Kündigung, *Zst* e–r Erklärung; ~ **of process** Klage*zst*, *Zst* von Gerichtsurkunden, gerichtliche *Zst*; ~ **of summons** Ladungs*zst*; Klage*zst*; ~ **of the writ** Klage*zst*; ~ **out of the jurisdiction** Auslands*zst*, *Zst* außerhalb des Zuständigkeitsbereiches des Gerichts; ~ **through diplomatic channels** diplomatische *Zst*; **acceptance of** ~ → *acceptance*; **accepted** ~ angenommene Ersatz*zst*; **acknowledgment of** ~ → *acknowledgment*; **address for** ~ → *address* (*1*); **affidavit of** ~ → *affidavit*; **constructive ~ of process** Ersatz*zst*; **default of** ~ fehlende *Zst*; *Zst*mangel; **due** ~ ordnungsgemäße *Zst*; **evading** ~ Versuch, sich der *Zst* zu entziehen; **good** ~ ordnungsgemäße *Zst*; **personal** ~ persönliche *Zst*, *Zst* zu eigenen Händen; **postal** ~ Post*zst*; **substituted** ~ Ersatz*zst GB*, öffentliche *Zst US*; **substituted ~ by advertisement** öffentliche *Zst* durch Zeitungsinserat.

service *vt* warten, bedienen.

serviceable brauchbar, nützlich, zweckdienlich; **in a ~ condition** in gebrauchsfähigem Zustand.

servicetill Geldautomat *m*.

servicing Wartung *f*.

servitude Dienstbarkeit *f* (= *D bzw* . . . *d*), Dienstunterworfenheit *f*, Knechtschaft *f*, Leibeigenschaft *f*; Servitut *n*; **affirmative** ~ positive *D*; **international** ~ Staats*d*, völkerrechtliches Servitut; **involuntary** ~ Knechtschaft, Zwangsarbeit; **landed** ~ Grund*d*; **negative** ~ negative *D*; **penal** ~ Zuchthaus(strafe) *obs GB* + *D*; **personal** ~ beschränkt persönliche *D*; **positive** ~ positive *D*; **pr(a)edial** ~ *scot* Grund*d*; **real** ~ Grund*d*; **rural** ~ Grund*d* an landwirtschaftlichen Grundstücken; **urban** ~ Grund*d* an (*städtischen*) Hausgrundstücken.

session Tagung *f*, Sitzungsperiode *f*; Gerichtssitzung *f*; ~ **laws** Gesetze e–r Legislaturperiode; ~ **of Parliament** → *parliament*; ~ **of the peace** Gerichtstermin von Friedensrichtern; **closed** ~ nichtöffentliche Sitzung (*unter Ausschluß der Öffentlichkeit*); **closing** ~ Schlußsitzung; **contracting-parties** ~ Verhandlungsrunde; **emergency** ~ außerordentliche Sitzung, Krisensitzung; **executive** ~ nicht öffentl Sitzung (*e–r Behörde etc*); **full** ~ Plenarsitzung; **joint** ~ gemeinsame Sitzung; **legal** ~ gerichtl Sitzungsperiode; **opening** ~ Eröffnungssitzung; **ordinary** ~ ordentliche Sitzungsperiode; **parliamentary** ~ Legislaturperiode; **petty ~s** *etwa*: Amtsgericht in Strafsachen, *jetzt magistrates' court*; **plenary** ~ Plenarsitzung, Plenartagung; **quarter ~s** *obs* vierteljährliche Schöffengerichtstage; **regular** ~ ordentliche Sitzung, ordentl Tagung; **secret** ~ Geheimsitzung (*des Parlaments*); **special** ~ Sondertermin, Sondertagung; **special emergency** ~ Notstandsondertagung.

sessional eine Legislaturperiode betreffend; ~ **allowance** Diäten, Sitzungsgeld e–s Abgeordneten; ~ **committee** Ausschuß für e–e Legislaturperiode, ständiger Ausschuß (*der in jeder Legislaturperiode* *neu besetzt wird*); ~ **expense allowance** Diäten; ~ **orders** (*für e–e Legislaturperiode gültige*) Geschäftsordnung.

set *v* setzen, stellen; ~ **a price** e–n Preis festsetzen; ~ **apart** beiseite legen, reservieren, trennen, bereitstellen, getrennt verwahren; ~ **aside** abschaffen, aufheben, annullieren, außer Kraft setzen, reservieren, rückstellen; ~ **back** zurückstellen, hinausschieben (*Termin*); ~ **down** anberaumen, terminieren, niederschreiben, eintragen; ~ **down in writing** schriftlich niederlegen; ~ **down the action for trial** den Termin für die mündliche Verhandlung anberaumen; ~ **forth** darlegen, zeigen; ~ **forth grounds** Gründe vorbringen, begründen; ~ **free** auf freien Fuß setzen; ~ **off** aufrechnen, ausgleichen; ~ **off expenses** Auslagen in Anrechnung bringen; ~ **out** auseinandersetzen, darlegen, vortragen; ~ **up** aufstellen, vorbringen, einwenden, sich berufen auf, gründen, eröffnen, errichten; ~ **up a committee** e–n Ausschuß einsetzen; ~ **up a defence** e–e Einrede geltend machen, e–n Einwand vorbringen; ~ **up a good defence** sich geschickt verteidigen; ~ **up an account** ein Konto eröffnen; ~ **up and commence** neu eröffnen; ~ **up by way of counter-claim** aufrechnen; ~ **up in practice** e–e Praxis eröffnen; ~ **(oneself) up as a judge** sich zum Richter aufwerfen.

set-aside Rückstellung *f.*

setback Bauabstand *m.*

set-off *s* Aufrechnung *f.*

setting aside Aufhebung *f* (*e–r Entscheidung*).

setting down Terminanberaumung; ~ **for trial** Anberaumung des Termins für die Hauptverhandlung bzw d. mündl. Verhandlung; ~ **of action** Terminsanberaumung, Terminierung, Anberaumung des Haupttermins.

settle regeln, bezahlen, abfinden, bestimmen, errichten, festlegen, plazieren, billigen, abmachen, feststellen, liquidieren, e–n Streit beilegen; schlichten; sich niederlassen; ~ **a balance** e–n Saldo ausgleichen; ~ **a debt** e–e Schuld begleichen; ~ **a document** e–e Urkunde formgerecht errichten; ~ **amicably** sich gütlich einigen; ~ **an account** e–e Rechnung begleichen, abrechnen, e–n Saldo anerkennen; ~ **an annuity on a person** jmdm e–e Jahresrente aussetzen; ~ **an estate** e–n Nachlaß auseinandersetzen; ~ **by arbitration** durch Schiedsgericht regeln; ~ **by will** von Todes wegen treuhänderisch zuwenden, letztwillig e–n Fideikommiß gründen; ~ **out of court** sich außergerichtlich einigen; ~ **payments in dollars** Zahlungen in Dollar durchführen; ~ **property** treuhänderisch für nachfolgende Begünstigte festlegen; ~ **the average** die Dispache aufmachen; ~ **the terms** die Bedingungen vereinbaren; ~ **up** auseinandersetzen (*Nachlaß*).

settlement Regelung *f*, Vergleich *m*, Bezahlung *f*, Abfindung *f*, Abgeltung *f*, Glattstellung *f*, Tilgung *f*; Bildung e–s Sondervermögens mit Verfügungsbeschränkungen; treuhänderische Vermögensfestlegung *f*, treuhänderische Verfügung von Todes wegen; Fideikommiß *m*; Niederlassung *f*; Siedlung *f*; Absinken *n* (*e–s Gebäudes*); ~ **account** Liquidationskonto; ~ **agreement** Auseinandersetzungsvertrag, Abfindungsvereinbarung; ~ **bargain** Termingeschäft; ~ **by will** letztwillige Treuhandvermögensbildung; ~ **clerk** Abrechner; ~ **date** Ausgleichstermin; Liquidationstag, Liquidationstermin; ~ **day** Verrechnungstag, Liquidationstag; ~ **estate duty** Vorerbschaftssteuer; ~ **in a lump sum** Pauschalabfindung; ~ **negotiations** Schlichtungsverhandlungen; ~ **of a commitment** Begleichung e–r Verpflichtung; ~ **of accounts** Abrechnung; ~ **of action** Prozeßvergleich; ~ **of average** Havarieaufmachung, Dispache; ~ **of balances** Saldenausgleich; ~ **of claims** Schadensregulierung; ~ **of conflicts** Schlichtung von Streitigkeiten; ~ **of damage** Feststellung des Schadens; ~ **of debts** Schuldenregulierung; ~ **of estate** Liquidierung des Nachlasses; Nachlaßauseinandersetzung; ~ **of hardship cases** Härteregelung; ~ **of list of contributories** gerichtliche Feststellung der Nachschußverpflichteten; ~ **of paupers** Freizügigkeitsbeschränkung von Fürsorgeempfängern; ~ **of transactions** Ausgleich des Zahlungsverkehrs; ~ **option** Wahl(recht) der Auszahlungsart (*Lebensversicherung*); ~ **price** Terminkurs; ~ **statement** Abrechnung (*Grundstücksverkauf*); ~ **warrant** Auszahlungsanweisung; **Act of S~** → *act*; **ad hoc** ~ *Realisieren von Grundstücksbelastungen durch Bestellung des Eigentümers zum Treuhänder*; **amicable** ~ gütlicher Vergleich; **antenuptial** ~ → *antenuptial*; **buying** ~ Terminkauf; **claim** ~ Schadensregulierung; **commercial** ~ Handelsniederlassung; **compound** ~ Globaltreuhandbildung über Immobilien (*Gesamtheit der Treuhand- und Nießbrauchsurkunden bei e–r Familientreuhand*); **compulsory** ~ Zwangsvergleich; **concealment of** ~ (Untreue durch) Verheimlichung der Treuhandbindung; **daily** ~ tägliche Abrechnung; **door-of-the-court** ~ außergerichtl Vergleich (*zur Abwendung des Prozesses*); **end month** ~ Ultimoliquidation, Ultimoabrechnung; **equity of** ~ = *equity to a* ~ → *equity*; **family** ~ treuhänderische Vermögensfestlegung zugunsten der Familie bzw d. Ehegatten, Familientreuhand; **final** ~ Schlußabrechnung, Schlußverteilung; **fraudulent** ~ treuhänderische Vermögensverschiebung zur Gläubigerbenachteiligung; **freedom of** ~ → *freedom*; **full** ~ Gesamtvergleich, Vergleich zur Abgeltung aller beiderseitigen Ansprüche (*auch für die Vergangenheit*); **in** ~ **of** zur Abgeltung von; **judicial** ~ Liquidationsvergleich; **marriage** ~ → *marriage*; **midmonth** ~ Medioabrechnung; **mid-year** ~ Halbjahresabschluß; **monthly** ~ Monatsabschluß, Ultimoabschluß; **negotiated** ~ (ausgehandelter) Vergleich; **notional** ~ *treuhänderische, auflösend bedingte Grundbesitzübertragung*, gesetzliches Treuhandverhältnis (*Grundbesitz von Minderjährigen*); **out of court** ~ außergerichtlicher Vergleich; **overall** ~ Gesamtregelung, Gesamtvergleich; **peaceful** ~ **of international disputes** friedliche Beilegung internationaler Streitigkeiten; **periodical** ~ periodische Abrechnung; **postnuptial** ~ *Treuhandverfügung zugunsten e–r bereits Verheirateten;* **pretrial** ~ außergerichtlicher Vergleich (*zur Vermeidung e–s Prozesses*); **private** ~ gütliche Einigung, außergerichtlicher Vergleich; **property** ~ Vermögensauseinandersetzung *anläßlich Scheidung*; **pro rata** ~ anteilige Befriedigung; **referential** ~ erweiterte Treuhandbildung; **special** ~ Sonderabrechnung (*für neu eingeführte Börsenwerte*); **strict** ~ (Bildung e-r) Familientreuhandstiftung; Fideikommiß-Festlegung; **voluntary** ~ unentgeltliche treuhänderische Vermögensfestlegung; unentgeltl Nießbrauchbestellung (*für Ehefrau u. Kinder*).

settler Siedler *m*, Kolonist *m*; ~**'s claim** Siedleranspruch auf Landzuteilung.

settling | **bill of exceptions** tatbestandsmäßige Festlegung *f* von Verfahrensverstößen; ~ **interrogatories** Gerichtsbeschluß über (*Zulässigkeit von Fragen bei*) Rechtshilfevernehmung; ~ **issues** Festlegung der entscheidungserheblichen Fragen; ~ **of accounts** Abrechnung; ~ **period** Abrechnungsperiode.

settlor Treugeber *m*, Begründer e–s Treuhandvermögens *cf settlement*; Stifter *m* der Verfügende, der Zuwendende.

sever trennen, teilen; ~ **a joint ten-**

ancy Gesamthandseigentum auseinandersetzen; ~ **defences** sich unabhängig von Mitangeklagten verteidigen, das Verfahren abtrennen.

severable teilbar, abtrennbar; ~ **contract** → *contract.*

several einzeln, besonders, verschieden(e), getrennt.

severalty Einzelgrundbesitz(recht) *n*; Sondervermögen *n*, Bruchteilseigentum *n*; ~ **owner** Bruchteilseigentümer; **shifting ~s** Alleineigentum mit wechselndem Weiderecht; **to hold in** ~ allein berechtigt sein, Alleineigentümer sein.

severance Abtrennung *f*, Trennung *f*; Auseinandersetzung *f*, Teilung *f*; ~ **allowance** Trennungsentschädigung; ~ **in defence** gesondertes Verteidigungsvorbringen; ~ **of actions** Klagetrennung, Verfahrenstrennung; ~ **of contract** Aufrechterhaltung des Vertrages durch Umwandlung e–r nichtigen Bestimmung; ~ **of relations** Abbruch der (diplomatischen) Beziehungen; ~ **package** Gesamtabfindung (*bei Entlassung*); ~ **pay** Härteausgleich; Kündigungsabfindung; ~ **scheme** Personalabbauplan; ~ **tax** → *tax*; **words of** ~ → *word.*

severity Härte *f*, Strenge *f*; ~ **of a sentence** die Härte des Urteils; **the ~ of a test** die Genauigkeit e–r Prüfung.

sewage|system Abwässersystem *n*; ~ **disposal** Abwässerbeseitigung; ~ **disposal works** Kläranlage; ~ **farm** Rieselfeld.

sewer Abwässerkanal *m*, Abwässerungsanlage *f*; **Commissioners of S~s** *hist* Deichbehörde; Wasser- und Kanalbauamt; **main** ~ Hauptkanal; **public** ~ Hauptkanal; **trunk** ~ Hauptkanal.

sex Geschlecht *n*; ~ **discrimination** geschlechtsbezogene Benachteiligung , Benachteiligung von weiblichen Arbeitnehmern; ~ **disqualification** Diskriminierung der Frau; ~ **equality legislation** Gleichberechtigungsgesetze; ~ **establishment** Sexgeschäftsbetrieb; ~ **shop** Sexladen.

shack gemeinsames Weiderecht *n* der Grundnachbarn; **common of** ~ Weiderecht (*nach Ernte*).

shackles Fesseln *f|pl*, Handschellen *f|pl.*

shading geringfügiger Kursrückgang *m.*

shadow|cabinet Schattenkabinett; ~ **director** beherrschendes, indirektes Verwaltungsratsmitglied; Firmenchef hinter den Kulissen; ~ **portfolio** Ressort im Schattenkabinett.

shake schütteln, erschüttern; ~ **a witness's evidence** die Glaubwürdigkeit e–s Zeugen erschüttern; **by shaking hands** durch Handschlag.

shakeout Abschütteln *n*, Herausdrängen *n* der schwächeren Spekulanten; natürliche Auslese *f.*

shaking down Erpressen *n.*

shall müssen (*als zwingende Bestimmung in Verträgen auf Gesetzen, im Deutschen oft bloßer Indikativ!*); (*ausnahmsweise:*) sollen; ~ **and may be lawful** ist rechtlich zulässig; ~ **and may do s. th.** müssen, hat zu erfolgen (*meist zwingend; doch auch:*) hat nach pflichtgemäßen Ermessen zu handeln; ~ **be born** geboren werden; ~ **be construed** ist auszulegen; ~ **be final** rechtskräftig werden; ~ **be liable** haften; ~ **be recoverable** klagbar sein, eingeklagt werden können; ~ **be sufficient** reicht aus; ~ **deem it desirable** es für erwünscht halten; ~ **die** sterben (werden).

sham *adj* falsch, unecht, fiktiv, formgerecht doch inhaltlich falsch.

sham *s* Nachahmung *f*, Schein *m*, Schwindel *m.*

shanghai *v* durch Täuschung anheuern.

share *s* Aktie *f* (= *A bzw . . . a*), Kapitalanteil *m*, Stammeinlage *f*, Geschäftsanteil *m*; Teil *m*, Beitrag *m*, Quote *f*, Anteil *m*, Beteiligung *f*; **~s account** *A–n*konto; Stückekonto; **~s acquisition scheme** Projekt für Arbeitnehmer-Aktienbeteiligung; ~ **allotment** *A–n*zuteilung; ~**s bonus** *A–n*bonus; ~**broker** *A–n*makler, Börsenmakler, Effektenhändler, Fondsmakler; ~ **capital** → *capital*; ~ **certificate** *A–n*zertifikat, Kapitalanteilsurkunde; Gesamt*a*; ~**s deposited in escrow** treuhänderisch hinterlegte *A–n*; ~ **discount** Emissionsdisagio; ~ **fallout** Kurssturz; ~ **fraud** *A–n*betrug, *A–n*schwindel; ~ **hawking** Verkauf von *A–n* an der Haustüre; ~ **holding** *A–n*besitz; ~ **in a ship** Schiffspart; ~ **s in issue** begebene *A–n*; ~ **in the capital** Kapitalanteil; ~ **index** *A–n*index; ~ **ledger** *A–n*buch; ~ **list** Kurszettel; **low-voting** ~**s** *A–n* mit niedriger Stimmberechtigung; ~ **market** → *market*; ~ **of proceeds** Erlösanteil, Gewinnanteil, Tantieme; ~ **offering price** *A–n*-Emissionskurs; ~**s outstanding** ausgegebene *A–n*, Anteile im Umlauf; ~ **option** *A–n*terminoption; ~ **option scheme** Belegschafts*a–n*option; ~ **premium** Emissionsagio; ~ **premium account** Sonderkonto für Emissionsagio; ~ **pushing** aggressiver *A–n*verkauf, betrügerische Vermarktung dubioser *A–n*; ~ **quotation** *A–n*kurs, *A–n*notierung; ~**s ranking pari passu** Gleichrangigkeit der *A–n*; ~**s register** *A–n*buch; ~**s slump** Kurssturz; ~ **split** *A–n*split; ~ **splitting** Beteiligungsvereitelung; ~**s subscribed** gezeichnete *A–n*; ~ **transfer** Übertragungsurkunde von Kapitalanteilen; ~ **under an intestacy** gesetzlicher Erbteil; ~ **warrant** *A–n*zertifikat, *A–n*promesse (*auf den Inhaber lautender verkehrsfähiger Aktienberechtigungsschein, ähnl Inhaberaktie*); **allocation of** ~**s** → *allocation*; **allotment of** ~**s** Zuteilung von (neu emittierten) *A–n*; **baby** ~**s** Klein*a–n*; **bank** ~**s** Bank*a–n*, Bankwerte; **bearer** ~**s** Inhaber*a–n*; **block of** ~**s** *A–n*paket; **bonus** ~ → *bonus*; **cancellation of** ~**s** → *cancellation*; **charge on uncalled** ~ **capital** Verpfändung der Kapitaleinzahlungsforderungen; **charging order on** ~**s** Pfändung von *A–n*; **class of** ~**s** *A–n*gattung; **common** ~**s** Stamm*a–n*; **company's own** ~**s** eigene *A–n*, Vorrats*a–n*; **cumulative preference** ~ kumulative Vorzugs*a*, Vorzugs*a* mit Dividendennachzahlungsanspruch; **deferred** ~**s** Nachzugs*a–n*; **deferred** ~ **capital** Stammkapital; **deferred founders'** ~**s** Gründer*a–n* mit Anspruch auf Restdividende; **deferred ordinary** ~**s** Nachzugs*a–n*; Stamm*a–n* 2. Klasse (*Dividende nach der 1. Klasse*); **distributive** ~ gesetzl Erbteil am Mobiliarnachlaß; **division into** ~**s** Stückelung; **electricity** ~**s** Elektro*a–n*; **Eurotunnel** ~**s** Kanaltunnel*a–n*; **foreign** ~ Auslands*a*; **forfeiture of** ~**s** → *forfeiture*; **founders'** ~**s** Gründer*a–n*; **fractional** ~**s** Bruchteile von Aktien; **fully paid up** ~**s** voll eingezahlte *A–n*; **„golden"** ~ wertvolle Sperrminorität (*bei Privatisierungen*); **growth** ~ Wachstumsaktie; **half** ~ Hälfteanteil; **hereditary** ~ Erbteil; **holding of** ~**s** *A–n*besitz; **in equal** ~**s** zu gleichen Teilen; **industrial** ~**s** Industrie*a–n*; **initial** ~ Einlage, Gründungs*a*; **leading** ~**s** führende Werte; **lien on** ~**s** Pfandrecht (*der Gesellschaft*) an den *A–n*; **lion's** ~ Löwenanteil; **listed** ~**s** notierte *A–n*; **management** ~**s** *A–n im Besitz der Direktoren der Gesellschaft;* **mining** ~ Kux (*Anteil an e–r Bergbaugesellschaft*); **motor** ~**s** Automobil*a–n*; **multiple** ~**s** Mehrstimmen*a–n*; **new** ~**s** junge *A–n*; **no-par-value** ~**s** nennwertlose *A–n*, Quoten*a–n*; **non-voting** ~**s** stimmrechtslose *A–n*; **ordinary** ~**s** Stamm*a–n*; **ordinary preferred** ~**s** gewöhnliche Vorzugs*a–n*; **original** ~ Stamm*a–n* bei Gesellschaftsgründung; **paid-up** ~**s** voll einbezahlte *A–n*; **par value** ~**s** Nennwert*a–n*; **participating** ~ Anteilsschein; = *participating preference* ~ *qv*; **participating preference** ~**s** partizipierende

Vorzugs*a–n*, Vorzugs*a–n* mit zusätzlicher *nachrangiger* Dividendenberechtigung; **partly-paid ~s** nicht voll einbezahlte *A–n*; **personal ~s** Namens*a–n*; **preference ~s** Vorzugs*a–n*; **preferential ~s** Vorzugs*a–n*; **preferred ~s** Vorzugs*a–n*; **preferred ordinary ~s** Stamm*a–n* 1. Klasse; **presumptive ~** zu erwartender Anteil; **primary ~s** Vorzugs*a–n*; **promoters' ~s** Gründer*a–n*; **qualification ~s** Pflicht*a–n* der Vorstandsmitglieder; **railway ~s** Eisenbahn*a–n*; **redeemable preference ~s** rückkaufbare Vorzugs*a–n*; **registered ~s** Namens*a–n*; **rubber ~s** Gummi*a–n*, Gummiwerte; **shipping ~s** → *shipping*; **shop ~s** → *shop*; **surrender of ~s** Rückgabe von *A–n* an die Gesellschaft, Verzicht auf *A–n*; **title to ~s** *A–n*berechtigung; **to allot ~s** *A–n* zuteilen; **to hold ~s** → *to hold*; **to subscribe to ~s** → *to subscribe*; **transfer of ~s** *A–n*übertragung; **underwriting ~** Konsortialbeteiligung, Konsortialanteil; **unquoted ~** nicht amtl notierte *A*; Freiverkehrs*a*; **voting ~s** *A–n* mit Stimmrecht; **supervoting ~s** Mehrstimmrechts*a–n*.

share *v* teilen, teilhaben; **~ and ~ alike** Gewinne und Verluste zu gleichen Teilen teilen; **~ jointly** gemeinsam teilnehmen.

Shared National Credits *bankaufsichtl Kontrolle von gemeinsamen Großkrediten durch mehrere Banken, US.*

sharecropper Naturalpächter *m* (*Pächter auf Erntebeteiligungsbasis*).

shareholder Anteilseigner *m*; Aktionär *m*, (GmbH)Gesellschafter; Aktieninhaber *m*; **~s' bill** Aktionärsklage; **~s' derivative action** Prozeßstandschaftsklage von Aktionären; **~s' equity** Eigenkapital, Nettoanteil der Aktionäre; **~s' ledger** → *ledger*; **~s' meeting** → *meeting*; **~s' roll** Aktionärsliste, Aktienbuch; **"A" List and "B" List ~s** Aktionäre der Kategorien A bzw B; **controlling ~** Aktionär mit beherrschendem Einfluß; **corporate ~** → *corporate*; **dissentient (dissenting) ~s** (*gegen eine Fusion*) opponierende Aktionäre; **free ~s** Gesellschafter der Bausparkassen, die kein Darlehen in Anspruch nehmen; **institutional ~s** institutionelle Anteilseigner (*Banken, Versicherungsgesellschaften ua*); **joint ~s** Mitaktionäre, Aktionäre in Rechtsgemeinschaft; **minority ~** Minderheitsaktionär, Minderheits-GmbH-Gesellschafter; **nominee ~** Strohmann, als Aktionär vorgeschobener A; **ordinary ~** Stammaktionär; **preference ~** Vorzugsaktionär; **principal ~** Hauptaktionär, Großaktionär; **registered ~** Besitzer von Namensaktien.

shareholdings Aktienbesitz *m*; **~ index** Aktienindex; **nominee ~s** Strohmann-Aktienbeteiligung; **situs of ~** die Belegenheit des Aktienbesitzes; **valuation of ~** Bewertung des Aktienbesitzes.

shark repellent Abwehrmittel gegen aggressive Übernahmeversuche.

sharp *adj* skrupellos, unehrlich, gewinnsüchtig; sofort vollstreckbar; **~ clause** Unterwerfungsklausel.

sharper Gauner *m*, Betrüger *m*, Falschspieler *m*.

sharping Betrug *m*.

shave ausbeuten, erpressen, billig aufkaufen; **~ing the cost** Reduzierung der Kosten.

„shearing operation" nachträgliches Abkassieren (*durch den Fiskus*).

sheep|heaves Schafweide; **~-silver** *Ablösung für Dienstleistung des Schafewaschens*; **~ skin** gesiegelte Urkunde, Pergament; **~-walk** Schafweide, Recht auf Schafdüngung.

sheet Bogen *m*, Blatt *n*; **~ of letterpress** bedruckter Bogen; **agenda ~** Tagesordnung; **annual balance ~** → *balance sheet*; **attendance ~** Anwesenheitsliste; **charge ~** Anklageschrift; **cost ~** Kostenaufstellung; **coupon** → *coupon*; **pay ~** Gehaltsliste, Lohnliste, Soldliste; **time ~** Stundenzettel, Regiezettel, Präsenzliste.

shelf-warmer Ladenhüter *m.*

shell company Mantelfirma *f,* nur aus e–m Firmenmantel bestehende Gesellschaft; *bare shell: Aktienmantel.*

shelter Schutz *m,* Zuflucht *f,* Unterkunft *f;* ~**s for battered wives** Frauenhäuser.

shelterless obdachlos.

shelve zurückstellen, auf später verschieben; ~ **an issue** e–n Streitpunkt nicht weiter behandeln.

sheriff (Kreis)Polizeichef *m,* oberster Grafschaftsbeamter *m,* Obergerichtsvollzieher *m;* oberster Gerichtswachtmeister *m; scot* Richter; ~**-clerk** *scot* Urkundsbeamter *(e–s sheriff court);* ~**'s court** *scot → court;* ~**'s deed** Zuschlagsbeschluß in der Zwangsversteigerung; ~**'s jury** Untersuchungsgeschworene; ~**'s officer** Gerichtsvollzieher; ~**'s order** Pfändungsanordnung; ~**'s poundage** Gerichtsvollziehergebühr; ~**'s sale** → *sale;* ~**'s tourn** *hist, bis 1887 niederes Strafgericht;* **deputy** ~ → *deputy;* **high** ~ Polizeichef (= *sheriff qv zum Unterschied von stellvertretendem Sheriff);* **pocket** ~ unmittelbarer königlicher Sheriff.

sheriffalty Amtszeit *f* des Sheriff, Sheriffamt *m.*

sheriffwick Amtsbezirk *m* des Sheriff.

shewer ortskundige Führer *m* bei einem Lokaltermin.

shift *s* Veränderung *f,* Wechsel *m,* Schicht *f;* ~ **allowance** Schichtzuschlag; ~ **differential** Schichtzuschlag; ~ **marriage** *hist* Verheiratung e–r verschuldeten Witwe; ~ **of crops** Wechselwirtschaft; ~ **of resources** Ressourcentransfer; ~ **of the burden of proof** Beweislastverschiebung; ~ **of stowage** Verschiebung der Ladung; ~ **premium** Schichtzulage; ~ **work** Schichtarbeit; **extra** ~ Sonderschicht; **graveyard** ~ Nachtschicht; **lobster** ~ Nachtschicht *(durchgehend);* **night** ~ Nachtschicht; **rotating** ~ Wechselschicht; **to drop** ~**s** Feierschichten einlegen.

shift *v* verändern, verschieben; Ausflüchte gebrauchen; ~ **one's quarters** umziehen; ~ **the blame on s. o.** die Schuld auf jmdn schieben; ~ **the subject** das Thema wechseln.

shiftability Beweglichkeit *f (der Ausleihepolitik).*

shifting clause Bestimmung über den künftigen Anfall, B. über den bedingten Rechtsübergang, Ersatzklausel, Nachanfallklausel; ~ **income** Einkommensverlagerung; ~ **liens** Auswechselung von Sicherheiten; ~ **of influence** Schwerpunktverlagerung; ~ **of property** Vermögensverschiebung; ~ **of the burden of proof** Übergang der Beweislast *(auf).*

shingle Türschild *(e–s Anwalts ua);* **to hang out one's** ~ seine Praxis eröffnen.

ship *s* Schiff *n,* Wasserfahrzeug *n (einschließl Luftkissenboote und Wasserflugzeuge);* ~**'s agent** Schiffsagent, Schiffsmakler; ~ **anchored in a roadstead** auf Reede liegendes (See)Schiff; ~**s articles** Heuervertrag, Schiffsmusterrolle; ~ **bill of sale** Schiffsverkaufsbrief; ~**'s bill** Schiffskonnossement, Abschrift des Konnossements für den Kapitän; ~**'s books** Schiffstagebuch; ~ **breaking** Schiffseinbruch; ~**-broker** Schiffsmakler, Hafenagent der Reederei; ~ **brokerage** Schiffsmaklergeschäft, Frachtenmaklergeschäft; ~ **building** Schiffbau; ~ **canal** Seekanal, Binnenwasserstraße zur Seeküste; ~**'s certificate** Schiffsregisterbrief; ~ **chandler** Schiffslieferant, Schiffszubehörhändler; ~**-chandlery** Schiffsausrüstung, Schiffsbedarfshandlung, -magazin; ~**-channel** Schiffahrtskanal; ~ **clearance** Abladeerlaubnis für das Schiff, Abfahrterlaubnis für das Schiff; ~**'s company** Schiffsbesatzung; ~ **damage** Schiffsschaden, Havarie, Schaden durch Mangel am Schiff; ~ **deliv-**

ery order Lieferausweisung an das Schiff, Konnossement; **~'s equipment** Schiffsausrüstung; **~'s expense** in die Schiffsfracht eingeschlossen; **~'s husband** Generalagent des Schiffseigentümers; Korrespondentreeder, geschäftsführender Miteigentümer-Reeder, Schiffsinspektor; **~ in distress** Schiff in Seenot; **~'s inventory** Schiffsinventar; **~'s journal** Schiffstagebuch; **~ letter** zur Schiffsbeförderung mitgegebener Brief; **~ load** Schiffsladung; volle Schiffsladung als *Maßeinheit*; **~ log** Schiffsjournal, Logbuch; **~ man** Seemann, Schiffer, Matrose; **~ master** Schiffer, Kapitän, Schiffsführer; **~-money** *hist* Schiffsausrüstungssteuer; **~ mortgage** Schiffshypothek; **~ of state** Staatsschiff; **~'s office** Reederei; **~'s option** Wahlrecht des Schiffseigners (*betr Meßeinheit der Schiffsladung*); **~'s papers** Schiffspapiere; **~'s part** Schiffspart, Schiffsanteil; **~'s passport** Schiffspaß, Seebrief; **~ policy** Schiffsversicherungspolice; **~'s protest** → *protest*; **~'s rail** Reling des Schiffes; **~'s register** Schiffsregister, Schiffsregisterbrief; **~ store** Schiffsbedarfsmagazin; **~'s stores** Bordvorräte; **~'s supplies** Schiffsbedarf; **~ surveyor** Schiffsbesichtiger; **~ sweat** Schiffsschweiß; **~ under average** havariertes Schiff; **cargo ~** Frachtschiff; **ex ~** Eigentumsübergang bei Entladung im Ankunftshafen; **general ~s** Frachtschiffe für *den allgemeinen Verkehr*; **merchant ~** Handelsschiff, Kauffahrteischiff; **public ~** Staatsschiff; **the good ~** das Schiff, die „..." (*Schiffsname*) *bedeutet nicht, daß für Seetüchtigkeit Gewähr geleistet wird.*

ship *v* verladen, verschiffen, versenden, expedieren, sich einschiffen.

shipment Schiffsladung *f*, Verschiffung *f*, Verladung *f* auf Schiff, Absendung *f*, Versendung *f*, Transport *m*, Transportgut *n*; **~ as less than carload lot** Stückgutversand; **~ contract** Seefrachtvertrag; **~ on deck** Decksverladung; **advice of ~** Versandanzeige; **drop ~** Zulieferung; **foreign ~** Auslandssendung; **place of ~** Ladeplatz; **port of ~** Einschiffungshafen, Verladehafen; **ready for ~** versandbereit.

shipowner Schiffseigner *m*, Reeder *m*.

shipped versandt, verladen; **~ bill of lading** → *bill of lading*; **~ for exportation** Transportgut für Ausfuhrzwecke; **~ for sale** zwecks Verkauf verladen; **~ in good order and condition** Transportgut bei Verladung in einwandfreiem Zustand; **~ not billed** versandt, aber noch nicht in Rechnung gestellt; **when ~** nach Verladung.

shipper Verfrachter *m* (*Seefrachtvertrag*), *aber auch*: Befrachter *m*; Ablader *m*, Verlader *m*; *US*: Frachtführer; Stückgutspediteur; Schiffsführer *m*; Kapitän *m* (*vgl skipper*); **~'s manifest** Ausfuhrdeklaration; Zollausgangserklärung, Passagierliste; Schiffsmanifest, Ladungsmanifest, Ladungsverzeichnis, Frachtgüterliste; **~'s memorandum** Konnossement; **~'s order** die Order des Befrachters (*Eigentümers*); **~'s papers** Verladepapier; **~'s representative** Speditionsagent; **~'s risk** (auf) Gefahr des Befrachters.

shipping Schiffahrt *f*, Schiffe *n|pl*; Abladung *f*, Anbordnehmen *n* von Gütern; Verladung *f*, Verschiffung *f*; Schiffs ...; **~ advice** Versandanzeige, Verschiffungsanzeige; **~ agency** Schiffsagentur, Speditionsgeschäft, Speditionsbüro; **~ agent** Ablader, Schiffsmakler, Unternehmer e–r Schiffsagentur, Seehafenspediteur, Reedereivertreter im Ausland, Spediteur, Spedition, Verfrachter; **~ articles** Schiffsartikel, Heuervertrag; **~ bill** Verzeichnis verschiffter Waren, Manifest; **~ board** Seeamt; **~ book** Versandbuch, Expeditionsbuch; **~ business** Reederei, Schiffahrt, Seetransportgeschäft, Speditionsgeschäft; Spedition, Seehandel; **~ card** Liste der Abfahrtdaten; **~ certificate**

Verladungszeugnis, Konnossements-Teilschein; ~ **charges** Verladekosten; ~ **clerk** Expedient; ~ **commissioner** Seemannsamtsleiter; ~ **company** Reederei, Schifffahrtsgesellschaft; ~ **conference** Schiffahrtskonferenz; ~ **country** Ursprungsland, Herkunftsland; ~ **credit** Rembourskredit; ~ **date** Versandtermin, Verschiffungstag, Absendetag; ~ **department** Versandabteilung; ~ **documents** Verladepapiere, Versandpapiere, Begleitpapiere, Verschiffungsdokumente (*Rechnung, Versicherungspolice, Konnossement*); ~ **dues** Schifffahrtsabgaben, Schiffahrtsgebühren; ~ **exchange** Frachtenbörse; ~ **expenses** Versandkosten, Frachtkosten, Versandspesen; ~ **instructions** Versandanweisungen; ~ **law** Seerecht, Seehandelsrecht; ~ **line** Schiffahrtslinie; ~ **line bill-of-lading terms** Linienkonnossementsbedingungen; ~**-line service** Linienschiffahrt; ~ **list** Schiffsliste; ~ **master** Seemannsamtsleiter; ~ **note** Versandanzeige, Schiffszettel, Frachtannahmeschein, Ladeschein, Frachtbrief; ~ **office** Reederei, Speditionsbüro, Heuerbüro; ~ **order** Verschiffungsauftrag, Verladeorder, Versandauftrag, Speditionsauftrag; ~ **papers** Versandpapiere, Verschiffungsdokumente, Ladepapiere; ~ **permit** Ausfuhrerlaubnis; ~ **point** Versandort; Goldausfuhrpunkt; ~ **receipt** Frachtbrief; ~ **room** Verpackungsraum, Versandraum; ~ **shares** Schiffahrtswerte; ~ **space** Frachtraum; ~ **terms** Versandbedingungen; ~ **trade** Seehandel, Schiffahrt, Reederei, Seetransportgeschäft, Transportgeschäft, Spedition; ~ **value** Verschiffungswert (*Rechnungswert + 15%*); ~ **weight** Verschiffungsgewicht; **commercial** ~ Handelsschiffahrt; **idle** ~ aufgelegte Tonnage; **merchant** ~ Handelsschiffahrt.

shipyard Werft *f*; ~ **aid** Schiffbau-Hilfe.

shire Grafschaft *f*; ~ **clerk** Geschäftsstellenleiter des Grafschaftsgerichts; ~**-man** *hist* Grafschaftsrichter; ~**-mote** Grafschaftsthing; ~**-reeve** Grafschaftsschultheiß.

shirk sich drücken; ~ **important service** *mil* sich vor e–m wichtigen Dienst drücken (*gilt als Fahnenflucht*).

shock Schock *m*, Erschütterung *f*; ~ **loss** unerwartete ungünstige Schadenentwicklung; **mental** ~ Schock, Nervenschock; **nervous** ~ (Nerven)Schock; **physical** ~ Schlag, Aufprall.

shoot schießen, anschießen, treffen, feuern, erschießen; ~ **to kill** erschießen, scharf schießen (*zur Tötung, nicht nur Wehrlosmachung*).

shooting Schießen *n*, Schießerei *f*, Wettschießen *n*; Jagd *f*; Aufnahme *f* e–s Films; ~ **ground** Jagdrevier; ~ **licence** Jagdschein, Jagderlaubnisschein; ~ **rent** Jagdpacht; ~ **rights** Jagdrecht, Jagdberechtigung; ~ **season** Jagdzeit; ~ **tenant** Jagdpächter; ~ **with intent to murder** Schießen mit Mordabsicht.

shoot-out Schußwechsel *m*.

shop *s* Laden *m*, Ladengeschäft *n*, Werkstätte *f*, Werkhalle *f*, Fabrikgebäude *n*, Reparaturwerkstatt *f*; Gewerbebetrieb *n*, Geschäft *n*; ~ **agreement** Betriebsvereinbarung; ~ **assistant** Ladenangestellter, Handlungsgehilfe, Verkäufer; ~**-book** Geschäftsbuch, Journal; ~ **breaking** Ladeneinbruch; ~ **chairman** Betriebsratsvorsitzender; ~ **closing** Ladenschluß; ~ **club** Sparverein; ~ **committee** → *committee*; ~ **council** Betriebsrat; ~ **fitter** Ladenausstatter; ~ **fittings** Ladeneinrichtung; ~ **foreman** Werkmeister; ~ **front** Ladenfront; ~ **hours** Geschäftszeit, Arbeitsstunden; **S~ Hours Act** Ladenschlußgesetz; ~ **lifter** Ladendieb; ~**lifting** Ladendiebstahl; ~ **premises** Ladenräume, Geschäftsräume; ~ **regulation** Betriebsordnung, Betriebsvorschrift; ~ **right** Fabrikations- und Vertriebsrecht; ~ **selling** *exch* Berufsverkäufe; ~ **shares** Einführungsaktien; ~ **steward** Arbeitnehmervertreter, Gewerkschaftsvertreter, Betriebsratsmitglied; ~ **walker** aufsichtsführender Abteilungsleiter, Empfangschef; ~ **work** Werkstattarbeit; **anti-union** ~ gewerkschaftsfeindlicher Betrieb; **bucket** ~ Winkelbörse, Wettbüro, Büro e–s Freiverkehrsmaklers; Schwindelmaklerfirma; **closed** ~ voll gewerkschaftlich organisierter Betrieb, Betrieb nur für Gewerkschaftsmitglieder; **fittings** ~ Montagewerkstatt; **mobile** ~ fahrbarer Verkaufsstand; **open** ~ Betrieb ohne Gewerkschaftsmonopol, Tätigkeit auch für Nichtorganisierte; **preferential** ~ *Betrieb mit vorzugsweiser Beschäftigung von Gewerkschaftmitgliedern;* **taxfree** ~ Verkaufsstelle für abgabenfreie Waren; **union** ~ → *union.*

shopkeeper Ladenbesitzer *m*, Inhaber *m* e–s (kleinen) Einzelhandelsgeschäftes, Kleinhändler *m*.

shopman Ladenbesitzer *m*, Ladenangestellter *m*, Betriebsarbeiter *m*, Werkarbeiter *m*.

shopper Ladenbesucher *m*, Käufer *m*, anscheinend Kaufwilliger *m*.

shopping Einkaufen *n*, Einkäufe *m/pl*; ~ **center** Handelsplatz, Geschäftsviertel, Einkaufszentrum; ~ **goods** → *goods*; ~ **list credit** *Globalkredit mit Exportbürgschaft zur Aufteilung an Importeure des Bestimmungslandes*; ~ **mall** regionales Einkaufszentrum; **cashless** ~ bargeldloser Einkauf (*nur über Computer*).

shopworn angestaubt, als Ladenhüter angeboten.

shore Küste *f*, Ufer *n*, Strand *m*; ~ **duty** Dienst an Land; ~ **lands** Watt; ~ **leave** Landurlaub, Landgang; ~ **line boundary** Küstengrenze (*bei Flut*); ~ **patrol** Küstenstreife, Küstenpatrouille.

shore up *v/t* abstützen (*Währungskurs*).

short *adj* kurz, kurzfristig; ~ **cause list** Terminliste für kurze Prozesse (*ohne Geschworene*); ~ **lets** kurzfristige Vermietungen; ~ **notice of trial** abgekürzte Ladungsfrist; ~ **of war** bis an den Rand des Krieges, *noch keine Kriegshandlungen*; ~ **title clause** Zitiervorschrift; Hinweis auf Kurzbezeichnung des Gesetzes; **to go** ~ leer verkaufen.

short *s* Baissier *m*, Baissespekulant *m*; Fehlbetrag *m*, Defizit *n*; ~**s** Anleihepapiere mit kurzer Laufzeit, Kurzläufer (*bis 5 Jahre*); leerverkaufte Wertpapiere; ~ **interest** Baisse-Engagement; Eigenanteil des Baisse-Verkäufers an zurückgekauften Aktien; **cash** ~**s** Kassenfehlbeträge.

shortage Mangel *m*, Verknappung *f*; Fehlbetrag *m*, Defizit *n*, Manko *n*; ~ **goods** Mangelware; ~ **of capital** Kapitalmangel, Kapitalknappheit; ~ **of cash** Kassenfehlbetrag; ~ **of commodities** Warenknappheit.

short-change *v/t jmdm zu wenig Wechselgeld herausgeben,* beschwindeln.

short-dated kurzfristig.

shortcomings Unzulänglichkeiten *f/pl*, Fehler *m/pl*, Mängel *m/pl*.

short-covering Deckungskauf zum Ausgleich e–s Leerverkaufs.

shortening (Ver)Kürzung *f*, Abkürzung *f*, (Ver)Minderung *f*.

shortfall Fehlbetrag *m*, Defizit *n*; ~ **in receipts** Mindereinnahmen; ~ **of officers** Offiziersmangel.

shortford *hist* Grundpachtverfall *m*.

shorthand Kurzschrift *f*, Stenographie *f*; ~ **notes** Stenogramm; ~ **writer's notes** (*official* ~ *notes*) Kurzschriftaufzeichnungen des Protokollführers.

shorthold letting befristetes Wohnraummietverhältnis (*1 bis 5 Jahre*) *GB seit 1980 ohne gesetzl Mietverlängerungsmöglichkeit.*

shot Schuß *m*; **a** ~ **meant to kill** gezielter Todesschuß.

shoulder *s* Seitenstreifen *m*, Bankett *n*; **hard** ~ Bankett; **soft** ~ unbefestigtes Bankett.

short-termism Kurzfristigkeit *f*, rasche Gewinnerzielung *f*.

show *s* Schau *f*, Darbietung *f*, Auslage *f*, Ausstellung *f*; Augenscheinsobjekt *n*; ~ **of hands (vote)** (Abstimmung durch) Handzeichen; **~-trial** → *trial* (*1*); **on** ~ zur Besichtigung; **public** ~ öffentl Vorstellung, Aufführung.

show *v* zeigen, vorzeigen, nachweisen, ausweisen, dartun; ~ **a balance** ein Saldo aufweisen; ~ **a loss** e–n Verlust aufweisen; ~ **cause** Einwendungen vorbringen, Gegenvorstellungen vorbringen, Rechte im Nachverfahren geltend machen; ~ **cause order** = *order to ~ cause* → *order* (*1*); ~ **reasons** Gründe angeben; **as ~n by the books** buchmäßig, ausweislich der Geschäftsbücher.

shower (*ou*) s ortskundiger Führer *m* (*bei Lokaltermin*).

shredding Reißwolfvernichtung *f* (*von Akten*).

shrievalty Sheriffamt *n*, Sheriffwürde *f*, Amtszeit *f* e–s Sheriffs, Gerichtsbarkeit *f* e–s Sheriffs.

shrinkage Schwund *m*, Minderung *f*, Refaktie *f*; ~ **of exports** Exportschrumpfung.

shunting Auslandsarbitrage *f*, gemeinsamer Börsenhandel *m an verschiedenen Börsen*; Rangieren *n*, Verschieben *n*, ~ **station** Rangierbahnhof, Verschiebebahnhof; ~ **track** Rangiergleis.

shuttle Pendelverkehr *m*; ~ **diplomacy** Reisediplomatie; ~ **services** Pendelverkehr.

shyster Winkeladvokat *m*, unzuverlässiger Anwalt *m*.

sick|fund Krankenkasse; ~ **leave** Krankheitsurlaub; ~ **market** flaue Börse, uneinheitlicher Markt; ~ **pay** Krankheitsausgleichszahlung (*des Arbeitsgebers*); **to go** ~ krankgeschrieben sein; krank feiern; **to report** ~ sich krank melden.

sickness Krankheit *f*; ~ **allowance** Krankengeld; ~ **benefit** Krankengeld, Krankenversicherungsleistung; *contributory* ~ ~: *Krankengeld*; ~ **fund** Krankenkasse; ~ **insurance** → *insurance*; ~ **relief** Krankenbeihilfe; **last** ~ die Todeskrankheit.

sicut alias adj wie zuvor, *s* zweite Zustellung *f* (*e–r Klage bzw Verfügung*).

side|bar rules prozeßleitende Verfügungen; ~ **issue** Nebenfrage; ~ **kicker** Helfershelfer, Komplize, Spezi; ~ **letter** Begleitschreiben; ~ **line** Nebenbeschäftigung, Nebenartikel, Seitenbegrenzung; Industriegeleise; ~ **note** Randbemerkung, Randnotiz, Beisatz; ~ **partner** stiller Teilhaber; ~ **reports** nichtamtliche Fallsammlung; ~ **result** Nebeneffekt; ~ **scription** (Mit)Unterzeichnung zusammengeklebter Blätter durch eine Unterschrift, Abzeichnung; ~ **street** Nebenstraße, Querstraße; **instance** ~ als ordentliches Gericht; **on the father's** ~ väterlicherseits; **the civil** ~ zivilrechtliche Abteilung e–s Gerichts; **the equity** ~ Zuständigkeit für Billigkeitsrechtsfälle; **the law** ~ Zuständigkeit für Common-Law-Sachen; **the long** ~ die Haussepartei; **the near** ~ die eigene Fahrbahnhälfte; **the other** ~ die Gegenpartei; **the plea** ~ die Zivilgerichtsbarkeit; **this** ~ **of the house** meine Fraktion; **this** ~ **up!** nicht stürzen!; **to change ~s** zur anderen Partei übertreten.

side *v* Partei nehmen; ~ **against s. o.** gegen jmdn Partei nehmen.

sideways movement Börsenbewegung *f* ohne bestimmte Gesamttendenz.

siding Nebengleis *n*, Fabrikgleis *n*.

siege Belagerung *f*, **state of** ~ Belagerungszustand; **to proclaim the state of** ~ den Belagerungszustand verhängen.

sight *s* Sehvermögen *n*, Sicht *f*, Anblick *m*, Ansicht *f*, Vorzeigung *f*, Vorlage *f*, ~ **bill** →*bill* (*3*); ~ **credit** sofort auszahlbarer Kredit; ~ **deposit** Sichteinlage, täglich fälliges Guthaben; ~ **deposit accounts** Sichteinlagenkonten; ~ **draft**

Sichttratte, Sichtwechsel; ~ **rate** Sichtkurs; ~ **unseen** ohne Besicht, ohne Besichtigung; **at** ~ bei Sicht, bei Vorlage; **at first** ~ auf den ersten Blick, prima facie; **at long** ~ auf lange Sicht; **at short** ~ auf kurze Sicht; **due at** ~ fällig bei Sicht; **payable after (at, on)** ~ → *payable*; **(30) days'** ~ (30) Tage nach Sicht.

sight *v* **a bill** e–n Wechsel vorgelegt bekommen *und die Vorlage durch Abzeichnen bestätigen.*

sigil Siegel *n*, siegelähnliche Unterschrift *f*.

sign *s* Kennzeichen *n*, Zeichen *n*; Schild *n*, Tafel *f*, Anzeichen *n*, Spur *f*; **~-manual** die Unterschrift des Monarchen; ~ **of quality** Gütezeichen, Qualitätsmarke; ~ **of recognition** Zeichen der Anerkennung, Zeichen der Bestätigung; **~post** Wegweiser, Verkehrszeichen; ~ **posting** Straßenmarkierung, Beschilderung; **directional** ~ Richtzeichen, Wegweiser; **distinctive** ~ Unterscheidungszeichen, Unterscheidungsmerkmal; **informatory** ~ Hinweiszeichen; **mandatory** ~ Gebotszeichen; **prohibitive** ~ Verbotszeichen; **road** ~ Verkehrszeichen; **warning** ~ Warnzeichen; **„watch for ~"** „Verkehrszeichen beachten!"

sign *v* unterzeichnen, unterschreiben, zeichnen; ~ **by a mark** mit einem Kreuzchen unterzeichnen; ~ **for the goods** den Empfang der Ware(n) quittieren; ~ **in full** mit vollem Namen unterschreiben; ~ **off** kündigen, die Arbeit niederlegen, die Arbeitsbeendigung anzeigen, sich abmelden; ~ **on** Arbeitsvertrag abschließen, sich einstellen lassen, sich anmelden, sich anwerben lassen; ~ **on the dotted line** *e–n vorbereiteten Vertrag* unterschreiben; notgedrungen unterschreiben; ~ **personally** eigenhändig unterschreiben; ~ **the articles** sich anheuern lassen; **authorized to** ~ zeichnungsberechtigt; **power to** ~ → *power.*

signal Signal *n*, Signalisierung *f*, Zeichen *n*; ~ **book** Signalcode; ~ **of distress** Notsignal; **code of ~s** Flaggensignalsystem; **false ~s** Setzen von irreführenden Schiffssignalen; **left-turn** ~ Linksabbiegersignal; **off-~** Entwarnung; **on-~** Warnsignal.

signatory Unterzeichner *m*.

signatory|government Unterzeichnerregierung; ~ **power** Unterschriftsvollmacht; ~ **powers** (*to a treaty*) Signatarmächte; ~ **state** → *state (2)*.

signature Unterschrift *f* (= *U bzw ... u*), Unterzeichnung *f*, Signatur *f*, Namenszug *m*; ~ **book** *U–en*verzeichnis (*e–r Bank und dgl*); ~ **by agent** *U* in Vertretung (*i. V.*); ~ **by authorized representative** *U* durch bevollmächtigten Vertreter; ~ **card** Kärtchen mit hinterlegter Unterschriftsprobe; ~ **by mark** *U* durch Handzeichen; ~ **by procuration** *U* in Vollmacht; **„~differs"** „*U* ungenau". **"~ incomplete"** „unvollständige *U*"; **"~ incorrect"** „unrichtige *U*"; **„~ missing"** „*U* fehlt"; ~ **not authorized** *U* ohne Vertretungsbefugnis; ~ **on a bill** Wechsel *n*; ~ **page** Unterschriftsseite; ~ **per pro** Prokura-*U* (*gezeichnet in Vertretung*); ~ **per proc** = ~ *per pro qv*; ~ **per procuration** = ~ *per pro qv*; ~ **stamp** *U*–stempel, Faksimilestempel; **attestation of** ~ *U–s*beglaubigung, Bezeugung der *U*; **autograph** ~ eigenhändige *U*; **blank** ~ Blanko*u*; **corporate** ~ Firmenzeichnung *e–r Aktiengesellschaft*; **counter**~ Gegenzeichnung; **facsimile** ~ → *facsimile*; **forged** ~ gefälschte *U*; **genuine** ~ echte *U*; **joint** ~ gemeinschaftliche *U*, Gesamtzeichnung, Gesamtzeichnungsberechtigung, Gesamtprokura, Kollektivprokura; **manual** ~ eigenhändige *U*; **manuscript** ~ eigenhändige *U*; **single** ~ Alleinzeichnungsberechtigung, Alleinzeichnungsberechtigter; **specimen** ~ *U–s*probe; **to append ~s** unterzeichnen, unterfertigen; **to obtain a ~ by fraud** e–e *U* erschleichen; **to open for ~** zur (Unter)Zeichnung auflegen; **unauthorized ~** ohne Ermächtigung vorgenommene *U*.

signed, sealed and delivered unterschrieben, gesiegelt und begeben; unterfertigt (*Ausfertigung e–r deed qv*).

signer Unterzeichner *m*; Aussteller *m*.

signet Siegel *n*, Petschaft *n*; *bes* königliches Handsiegel *n*; **privy ~** königliches Handsiegel; **Queen's S~** (=) königl Handsiegel; *Gerichtssiegel des Court of Session qv*.

signification Bezeichnung *f*, Bedeutung *f*, Sinn *m*.

significavit bischöfliche Bestätigung *f* e–s Exkommunizierungsantrags.

signify bedeuten, andeuten, erklären, bekanntmachen, mitteilen, ankündigen.

signum Zeichen *n*, Siegel *n*.

silence Schweigen *n*, Stillschweigen *n*; **estoppel by ~** → *estoppel*.

silence *v* zum Schweigen bringen, beschwichtigen; **~ complaints** Beschwerden abhelfen; **~ criticism** Kritik zum Schweigen bringen.

silentiarius *hist* Mitglied *n* des Kronrats, Gerichtswachtmeister *m*.

silk Seide *f*; **~ gown** Robe des Senioranwalts (*Queen's Counsel – Q. C.*); **common law ~** Zivilprozeßanwalt; **specialist ~** Fachanwalt; **to take ~** zum Q. C. ernannt werden.

silver Silber *n*, Silbermünze *f*, Silbergeld *n*; **~ bullion** Barrensilber; **~ certificate** Silberdollarnote, Silberzertifikat; **~ coin** Silbermünze, Silbergeld; **~ coin and bullion** (Bank)Silberbestand; **~ coinage** Silbermünzprägung; **~ currency** Silbergeldwährung; **~ plate** Silbergeschirr, Tafelsilber; **~ point** Silberpunkt; **~ standard** Silberwährung.

similar ähnlich, gleichartig.

similarity Ähnlichkeit *f*, Gleichartigkeit *f*.

simony Simonie *f*, Kirchenämterkauf *m*, Handel *m* mit geistlichen Ämtern.

simple einfach, rein, nicht qualifiziert, nicht in gesiegelter Form.

simpliciter absolut, allgemeingültig, unbeschränkt; nur soweit ausdrücklich genannt.

simplification Vereinfachung *f*; **~ of design** Konstruktionsvereinfachung, Typenbereinigung.

simul cum gemeinsam mit (*anderen Tätern*).

simulate simulieren, nachahmen, vorgeben, heucheln, täuschen; **~d account** fingierte Rechnung, Proforma-Rechnung; **~d contract** Scheinvertrag; **~d fact** erfundene Tatsache; **~d judgment** erschlichenes Urteil; **~d sale** Scheinkauf.

simulation Simulierung *f*, Verstellung *f*, Vorspiegelung *f*.

simultaneous gleichzeitig; **~ death** gleichzeitiger Tod; **~ performance** Erfüllung Zug um Zug.

sine die ohne Zeitangabe, auf unbestimmte Zeit.

sinecure Sinekure *f*, Pfründe *f*.

single einzeln, einzig; hauptsächlich; unverheiratet, ledig; **~ entry bookkeeping** einfache Buchführung; **S~ European Act** *brit* Gesetz zum einheitlichen EWG-Markt; **~ exchange rate** Deviseneinheitskurs; **~ file traffic** einspuriges Fahren; **~ judge sitting** Einzelrichtersitzung; **~ line store** Spezialgeschäft; **~ member district** Einmann-Wahlbezirk (*mit nur einem Abgeordneten*); **~ name paper** nicht girierter Solawechsel; **~ part production** Einzelanfertigung; **~ payment annuity** → *annuity*; **~ personal allowance** Freibetrag für Alleinstehende; **~ venture partnership** Gelegenheitsgesellschaft.

sink abnehmen, sinken, versenken; **~ a controversy** e–e Streitigkeit beilegen; ~ **a loan** e–e Anleihe tilgen; ~ **money into an enterprise** Geld in ein Unternehmen stecken.

sinking Tilgung *f*, Amortisation *f*.

sinking fund Amortisationskasse *f*, Tilgungsfonds *m*; ~ **bond** Ablösungsanleihe, Tilgungsanleihe, Amortisationsobligation, Obligation mit Tilgungsplan; ~ **contributions** Zuweisungen zum Tilgungsfonds; ~ **debenture** Tilgungsfonds-Schuldverschreibung; ~ **income** Erträgnisse des Amortisationsfonds; ~ **instalment** Tilgungsrate; lineare Abschreibung; ~ **investments** Anlagen von Tilgungsfondsmitteln; ~ **loan** Tilgungsanleihe; ~ **reserve** Tilgungsrücklage; ~ **tax** → *tax*.

sister|company Schwestergesellschaft; ~ **ship** Schwesterschiff, Schiff der gleichen Bauweise; **half** ~ Halbschwester; **twin** ~ Zwillingsschwester.

sit sitzen, Sitzung abhalten, tagen, in die Tagesordnung eintreten; ~ **a hearing out** e–r mündlichen Verhandlung bis zum Schluß beiwohnen; ~ **for a constituency** e–n Wahlkreis vertreten; ~ **for an examination** sich e–r Prüfung unterziehen; ~ **in camera** unter Ausschluß der Öffentlichkeit verhandeln; ~ **in Congress** Kongreßmitglied sein; ~ **in judgment** zu Gericht sitzen; ~ **on a case** in e–r Sache verhandeln; ~ **on a jury** Geschworener sein; ~**ting magistrate** der amtierende Amtsrichter; ~**ting tenant** unmittelbarer Pachtbesitzer, derzeitiger Wohnungsmieter.

site Lage *f*, Örtlichkeit *f*, Bauplatz *m*; ~ **notice** Baustellenverfügung; ~ **owner** Grundstückseigentümer; ~ **plan** Lageplan; ~ **preparation costs** Montageort-Vorbereitungskosten; ~ **value** Bodenwert; *bare ~ ~: reiner Bodenwert*; ~ **value rating** Baulandbesteuerung; **building** ~ → *building*; **cleared** ~ abgeräumtes Grundstück; **fully serviced** ~ voll erschlossenes Grundstück, **in-town** ~ innerstädtische Lage.

sit-in *(=)* vorübergehende Protestbesetzung.

sitting Sitzung *f*, Gerichtssitzung *f*, Tagung *f*; ~**s** Sitzungsperiode, Gerichtszeiten *f|pl*; ~**s after term** Feriensitzungen; ~ **fee** Verhandlungsgebühr; ~**s in bank (banc)** → *banc*; ~**s in camera** nichtöffentl Sitzungen; ~ **of a court** Gerichtssitzung, Gerichtstermin; ~ **of Parliament** Parlamentssitzung; **final** ~ Schlußsitzung; **law** ~**s** reguläre Sitzungsperiode der Gerichte; **open** ~ öffentliche Sitzung.

situate *adj* belegen, gelegen (in), liegend; **property** ~ **in the U.K.** in Großbritannien belegenes Vermögen; ~ **within a town** innerstädtisch gelegen.

situate *v* plazieren, e–n Platz bestimmen; ~**d** gelegen, in e–r Lage befindlich, belegen.

situation Lage *f*, Stellung *f*, Situation *f*, Posten *m*; ~ **for life** Lebensstellung; ~ **map** Lagekarte; ~ **of danger** (*nicht mehr abwendbare*) Gefahrenlage; ~ **on the labour market** Arbeitsmarktlage; ~**s vacant** Stellenangebote; ~**s wanted** Stellengesuche; **legal** ~ Rechtslage, Rechtsposition; **market** ~ Marktlage, Börsenlage; **monetary** ~ Währungslage; **patent** ~ Patentlage; **permanent** ~ Dauerstellung; **the foreign** ~ außerpolitische Lage.

situs Situs *m*, Ort *m*, Lage *f*, Belegenheit *f*; **actual** ~ Ort der Niederlassung; **state of** ~ → *state (2)*.

sixes sechsprozentige Papiere *n|pl*.

„sixty-four dollar question" die Hauptfrage, der Knalleffekt (*zB beim Kreuzverhör*).

size *s* Größe *f*, Umfang *m*, Format *n*, Nummer *f*; **commercial** ~ marktgängige Größe; **odd** ~ nicht gangbare Größe; **out** ~ Übergröße; **standard** ~ Normalgröße.

size *v* nach Größe sortieren, in e–r bestimmten Größe anfertigen, zuschneiden; ~ **up** einschätzen, eintaxieren; **fair** ~**d** gangbare Größe; **full** ~**d** von genauen Abmaßen; **large** ~**d** große Nummern, Großformat; **standard ~d** normalgroß.

skeleton Skelett *n*, Rahmen *m*; ~ **agreement** Rahmenabkommen; ~ **bill** Wechselblankett; ~ **bill of exceptions** vorläufiger Einwendungsschriftsatz (*bei dem die Anlagen noch beizufügen sind*); ~ **case** gerüstartige Verpackung; ~ **construction** Stahlbauweise; ~ **contract** Rahmenvertrag; ~ **key** Generalschlüssel, Nachschlüssel, Dietrich; ~ **law** Rahmengesetz; ~ **letter** Blankoformular; ~ **map** Kartenskizze; ~ **organization** Rahmenorganisation; ~ **staff** Kader, Stammgruppe, Stammpersonal, reduzierte Belegschaft; ~ **tariff** Rahmentarif; ~ **wage agreement** Rahmentarifvertrag.

sketch Skizze *f*, Überschlag *m*, Berechnung *f*, Riß *m*, Zeichnung *f*, Ansichtszeichnung *f*; **rough** ~ Rohentwurf, Kurzgeschichte, Kurzdrama.

sketchy oberflächlich, lückenhaft, vage.

skid rutschen; ~ **mark** Rutschspur; ~**ding** Rutschen *n*, Schleudern *n*.

skill Fertigkeit *f*, Geschicklichkeit *f*, Können *n*; ~ **and knowledge** Fach- und Sachkenntnis; ~ **s shortage** Fachkräftemangel; **professional** ~ berufliche Qualifikation; **reasonable** ~ → *reasonable*.

skilled erfahren, geschickt, bewandert; ~ **in the art** fachlich ausgebildet, fachkundig.

skim abschöpfen, oberflächlich durchlesen, überfliegen; ~**ming of excess profit** Gewinnabschöpfung.

skinpop intramuskuläre Injektion *f*, Rauschgiftinjektion *f*.

skip unbekannt verzogener Schuldner *m*; ~**-tracer** Schuldnerermittlungsbeauftragter.

skipper Kapitän *m* (*Küstenschiffahrt*), Flugkapitän *m*.

skirt the law sich am Rande der Legalität bewegen; das Gesetz umgehen.

sky|sign Dachreklame *f*, Außenreklame *f*; ~ **marshal** Sicherheitsbeamter im Flugzeug; ~ **way(s)** Luftverkehrsweg, Flugverkehrslinie.

slacker Drückeberger *m*, Faulpelz *m*.

slackness Flaute *f*.

slade Grundstücksstreifen *m*.

slammer Arrestanstalt *f*, Polizeigefängnis *n*.

slander *s* mündliche Ehrverletzung, *Beleidigung durch gesprochenes Wort, Bild oder Geste, oder sonst in nicht dauerhafter Form*; üble Nachrede *f*, Verleumdung *f*, ~ **monger** Verbreiter von üblen Nachreden; ~ **of goods** Anschwärzung, Herabsetzung der Ware des Konkurrenten; ~ **of title** böswillige Eigentumsleugnung.

slander *v* verleumden, beleidigen.

slanderer Verleumder *m*.

slanderous beleidigend, ehrenkränkend, verleumderisch.

slant färben, frisieren (*Nachrichten*).

slap Schlag (*mit der flachen Hand bzw dem Handrücken*), Ohrfeige.

slap dash *adj* schlampig.

slate Schiefer(tafel) *f*, vorläufige Kandidatenliste *f*; ~ **club** Unterstützungsverein; **to clean the** ~ *auch*: *to wipe the ~ clean* reinen Tisch machen.

slaughter schlachten, *exch* mit Verlust verkaufen, verschleudern; **unlawful** ~**ing** Schwarzschlachtung.

slave Sklave *m*; ~ **driver** Menschenschinder; ~ **labour** Sklavenarbeit, Zwangsarbeit; ~**-trade** Sklavenhandel; **white** ~**-trade** Mädchenhandel.

slavery Sklaverei *f*, Sklavenhaltung *f*.

slavish sklavisch; ~ **imitation** → *imitation*.

slay erschlagen, töten, im Kampf töten, ermorden.

sleeper Schlafwagen *m*; schlechtgehender Artikel *m*; Artikel *m* mit unerkannten Absatzchancen.

sleeping dogs beware gegen die Gefahr der Verwirkung auf der Hut sein.

slice unbestimmter Anteil *m*, Tranche *f*.

slide *s exch* Absinken *n* (*der Kurse*).

sliding gleitend, veränderlich; ~ **budget** veränderlicher Etat; ~ **rate of interest** Staffelzins; ~ **scale of wages** gleitende Lohnskala; ~ **scale premium** gleitende Prämie; ~ **scale price** Staffelpreis, indexorientierter Preis; ~ **tariff** gleitender Tarif.

slimming down Gesundschrumpfen *n*.

slip Zettel *m*, Schein *m*, Beleg *m*, Bon *m*; vorläufige Deckungszusage *f*, Versicherungsabschlußbeleg *m*, Vorvertragsniederschrift *f*; Angeklagtenbank *f*, Kluft *f*; ~ **book** Belegbuch; ~ **law** *US* Einzelveröffentlichung von Gesetzen nach ihrem Erlaß während e–s Jahres; ~ **order** Urteilsberichtigung; ~ **rule** Berichtigungsmöglichkeit bei Schreibversehen (*in Gerichtsentscheidungen*); **binding** ~ *ins* vorläufige Deckungszusage; **packing** ~ Packzettel; **routing** ~ Laufzettel; **to give s.o. the** ~ jmdm entkommen; **wage** ~ → *wage*.

sloop Schaluppe *f*; Polizeiboot *n*, Geleitboot *n*.

slops Konfektionsware *f*.

slot machine Spielautomat *m*, Verkaufsautomat *m*.

slow langsam, säumig, flau; ~ **goods traffic** Frachtgutverkehr; ~ **mover** Ladenhüter; **to go** ~ e–n Bummelstreik machen.

sluggish flau, stagnierend.

slum Slum *m*; ~**s** Elendsviertel; ~ **clearance** Beseitigung von Elendsvierteln; Stadtsanierung; **irredeemable** ~ nicht sanierungsfähiges Elendsviertel.

slump Depression *f*, Wirtschaftskrise *f*; ~**-proof** krisenfest.

slush fund Bestechungsfonds *m*.

small estates procedure (*vereinfachtes*) Verfahren bei Kleinnachlassen.

smart-money Sonderbuße *f* (*als Schadensersatz bei grobem Fehlverhalten*); Abstandsgeld *n*; Versehrtengeld *n*.

smash Zusammenbruch *m*, Zusammenstoß *m*; Bankrott *m*, Pleite *f*, ~**-and-grab-raid** Schaufenstereinbruch; ~**-up** Zusammenstoß, Frontalzusammenstoß; **bank** ~ Bankkrach.

smear Herabsetzung *f*, Verunglimpfung *f*, ~ **device** Verleumdungstaktik.

smell Geruch *m*, Geruchssinn *m*, Geruchsbelästigung *f*.

smeller sachverständiger (Geruchs-) Zeuge *m* (*zur Alkoholfeststellung*).

smelting Verhüttung *f*.

smoke Rauch *m*, Rauchbelästigung *f*, ~ **control** Rauchbekämpfungsvorschriften; ~**-silver** Holzzehntenablösung.

smuggle schmuggeln.

smuggler Schmuggler *m*, Schleichhändler *m*; Schmuggelschiff *n*.

smuggling Schmuggler *m*.

smut Schund *m*, Zote *f*, Obszönität *f*.

„snake" die europ. Währungsschlange.

snare Falle *f*.

snaring Fallenstellerei *f* (*Wilderei*).

snitcher *sl* Spitzel *m*; Denunziant *m*.

so so, dermaßen, ebenso, in gleicher Weise, daher, diesbezüglich; ~ **far as conveniently could be** so bald wie möglich und zumutbar; ~ **help you God** so wahr dir Gott helfe; **or** ~ etwa.

soakage Schwund *m* durch Einsikkern (*im Behälter*).

sobriety test Alkoholprobe *f*.

socage Erblehen *n*, Dienstlehen *n* (*gegen niedere landwirtschaftliche Dienste*), Dienstgut *n*, Frongut *n*; **free** ~ Lehensbesitz e–s Freien.

social sozial, gesellschaftlich; ~ **accounting** Berechnung des Nationaleinkommens; ~ **adaption** (gesellschaftliche) Assimilation; ~ **adjustment** Resozialisierung; ~ **agency** Sozialbehörde; ~ **assistance** Sozialhilfe (*als Institution*); ~ **background** gesellschaftliche Herkunft; ~ **benefits** Sozialversicherungsleistungen; ~ **capital** Gemeinschaftsvermögen, Vermögen der öffentlichen Hand; ~ **class** Gesellschaftsklasse; ~ **clubs** Geselligkeitsvereine; ~ **compact** *selten für* ~ *contract qv*; ~ **conditions** soziale

Verhältnisse; ~ **contract** = *contract social* (*Aufklärung*) Gesellschaftsvertrag; Sozialkontrakt (*Konsens zwischen brit Regierung und Gewerkschaften 1974*); ~ **credit** Sozialkredit; ~ **democracy** Sozialdemokratie; ~, **domestic and pleasure purposes** Privatzwecke (*Kfz-haltung*); ~ **economy** → *economy*; ~ **expenditure** Sozialausgaben, Sozialleistungen; ~ **framework** soziales Gefüge, Gesellschaftssystem; ~ **functions** Repräsentationspflichten; ~ **habits** gesellschaftl Umgangsformen; ~ **income** Volkseinkommen; ~ **inquiry report** Sozialfürsorgebericht, Gutachten des Jugendamts; ~ **insurance** → *insurance*; ~ **justice** soziale Gerechtigkeit; ~ **legislation** → *legislation*; ~ **order** → *order* (*3*); ~ **organization** Geselligkeitsverein; ~ **product** Sozialprodukt; ~ **reform** Sozialreform; ~ **register** *US* Prominentenverzeichnis; ~ **saving** kollektives Sparen; ~ **science** Gesellschaftswissenschaft, Gesellschaftslehre; ~ **security** → *social security;* ~ **service** soziale Fürsorge; ~ **services** Sozialeinrichtungen; ~ **settlement** Fürsorgestiftung; ~ **standing** Status, gesellschaftlicher Rang; ~ **system** Gesellschaftsordnung, Sozialordnung; ~ **welfare** soziale Wohlfahrt, Wohl der Allgemeinheit; ~ **welfare activity** soziale Tätigkeit; ~ **work** soziale Arbeit, Sozialarbeit; ~ **worker** Fürsorger, Sozialarbeiter.

social security Sozialversicherung(swesen) *f*, soziales Netz *n*; **pension** (Sozialv) Rente; **S~ Board** Sozialversicherungsaufsichtsbehörde; **S~ S~ Commissioner** Sozialversicherungs-Aufsichtsbehörde; ~ **contributions** Sozialversicherungsbeiträge; ~ **payroll deductions** Sozialversicherungsabzüge; **services** Sozialversicherungsträger; ~**tax** → *tax*.

socialization Sozialisierung *f*, Vergesellschaftung *f*.

socialize *v/t* sozialisieren, vergesellschaften; *v/i*: gesellschaftlich betätigen, Kumpanei betreiben.

society Gesellschaft *f*, Vereinigung *f*, (nicht rechtsfähiger) Verein *m*, Verbindung *f*, Genossenschaft *f*; ~ **funds** Vereinskasse; **S~ of Friends** Quäker; **affiliated** ~ → *affiliated*; **affluent** ~ Wohlstandsgesellschaft; **agricultural** ~ Landwirtschaftsverband; **approved** ~ staatl anerkannter caritativer Verein; **benefit** ~ Unterstützungskasse; **benevolent** ~ Wohltätigkeitsverein; **building** ~ → *building*; **charitable** ~ Wohltätigkeitsverein; **co-operative** ~ Genossenschaft, Konsumverein; **deposit** ~ Sparkasse; **friendly** ~ Wohltätigkeitsverein; Unterstützungsverein auf Gegenseitigkeit, Unterstützungskasse, Versicherungsverein auf Gegenseitigkeit; **incorporated** ~ eingetragener Verein, rechtsfähiger Verein; **industrial** ~ Genossenschaft; **industrial and provident** ~ Erwerbs- und Wirtschaftsgenossenschaft; **law** ~ → *law*; **loan** ~ Darlehenskasse; **mutual** ~ Genossenschaft, Verein auf Gegenseitigkeit *vgl. mutual*; **non-in-corporated** (= *unicorporated*) ~ nichtrechtsfähiger Verein; **professional** ~ Berufsverband; **provident** ~ Versicherungsverein, Unterstützungsverein, Hilfsverein; **registered** ~ eingetragene Genossenschaft; **retail** ~ → *retail*; **secret** ~ Geheimbund; **trade protection** ~ → *trade;* **unlawful** ~ verbotene Vereinigung.

socio-political gesellschaftspolitisch.

sock *v/t* **away** in den Sparstrumpf stecken, sparen.

sodomite Sodomist *m*.

sodomy Sodomie *f*, widernatürliche Unzucht *f* mit Tieren.

soil Boden *m*, Oberfläche *f*, Land *n*; ~ **bank** Flächenstillegungsprogramm; ~ **erosion** Bodenerosion; ~ **improvement** Melioration; **to exhaust the** ~ Raubbau am Boden treiben.

sojourn *s* Aufenthalt *m*, Aufenthaltsort *m*; ~ **tax** Kurtaxe; **foreign** ~ Auslandsaufenthalt.

sojourn *v* sich vorübergehend aufhalten.

sola bill Wechsel in nur e-r Ausfertigung.

solace Entschädigung *f*, Schmerzensgeld *n*, *bes für seelisches Leid.*

solar|day Tageszeit (*Sonnenaufgang bis -untergang*); ~ **month** → *month.*

solatium Schmerzensgeld *n* für psychisches Leid.

sold verkauft; ~ **and delivered** geliefert; ~ **bill** → *bill* (*3*); ~ **by auction** versteigert; ~ **by weight** nach Gewicht verkauft; ~ **ledger** Verkaufsbuch, Verkaufsjournal; ~ **note** Verkaufsnote, Schlußschein (*Ausfertigung für den Verkäufer*); ~ **or offered for sale** verkauft oder feilgeboten; ~ **thing** Kaufsache, Kaufgegenstand; ~ **out** ausverkauft, vergriffen; ~ **up** bereits verkauft (*Produktion*); ~ **without resort to legal process** verkauft im Wege der Selbsthilfe, freihändig verkauft.

soldier Soldat m, Gefreiter *m*; ~ **acting under command** befehlsgemäßes militärisches Handeln (e-s Soldaten), Berufung auf höheren Befehl; **~'s will** (*mündl*) Soldatentestament; **common** ~ einfacher Soldat; **common ~s** Mannschaften und Unteroffiziere; **personation of ~s** Vortäuschung der Zugehörigkeit zu den Streitkräften.

soldiering Arbeitsverlangsamung *f*, Drückebergerei *f*, Krankfeiern *n*.

sole ledig, unverheiratet, allein, einzig, einzeln; ~ **actor doctrine** (=) *Kenntnis des Vertreters wird dem Vertretenen zugerechnet*; ~ **and unmarried** alleinstehend; ~ **bargaining agent** Alleinverhandlungspartner für Tarifverhandlungen; ~ **right of publication** Alleinveröffentlichungsrecht; ~ **right to sell** Alleinverkaufsrecht; ~ **selling agent** Alleinvertreter; ~ **selling right** Alleinverkaufsrecht, Alleinvertriebsrecht.

solemnization of marriage Trauung *f*, Eheschließung *f*.

solemnity Zeremonie *f*, Förmlichkeit *f*.

solemnize feierlich vornehmen (*bes. die Eheschließung*), die Ehe schließen; feierlich begehen, förmlich erledigen.

solicit bitten, nachsuchen, beantragen; verlocken, in Versuchung führen, anreizen; ~ **orders** sich um Aufträge bemühen, Werbung betreiben, seine Dienste anbieten; ~ **subscriptions** Abonnenten werben; ~ **votes** sich um Wahlstimmen bewerben.

solicitant Bittsteller *m*.

solicitation Anbieten *n*, Ersuchen *n*, Akquisition *f*; Antrag *m*, Bitte *f*, Verleitung *f*, Anstiftung *f*; ~ **for immoral purposes** Zuhälterwerbung; Aufforderung zur Unzucht; **for murder** Anstiftung zum Mord; ~ **of bribe** Anstiftung zur (aktiven) Bestechung; ~ **of business** Auftragswerbung, Akquisition; ~ **of chastity** Aufforderung zur Unzucht; ~ **of membership** Mitgliederwerbung; ~ **to commit crime** Anstiftung zum Verbrechen.

soliciting Straßenprostitution *f*, Strich *m*.

solicitor Rechtsanwalt *m* (*außergerichtlich und bei Gerichten unterer Instanzen*); **S~s at Law** (=) *Anwaltsverein in Edinburgh bei unteren Gerichten*; **~'s bank account** Anwalts-Bankkonto; **S~s before the Supreme Courts** (=) *Anwaltsverein in Edinburgh bei höheren Instanzen*; **~'s bill** (anwaltschaftliche) Kostenrechnung; **~'s costs** → *costs*; **~'s department** Rechtsabteilung; **S~s' Disciplinary Tribunal** Ehrengerichtshof *f* Rechtsanwälte; **~'s fees** Anwaltshonorar, Anwaltsgebühren; **S~ General** *brit* Kronanwalt, *US* Vertreter des Justizministers, (*einzelstaatlicher*) Justizminister; **~'s lien** anwaltschaftl Zurückbehaltungsrecht (*an Unterlagen etc*); ~ **of partner-**

ship calibre sozietätsfähiger Anwalt; ~ **of ten years' standing** Anwalt mit 10jähriger Berufszeit; ~ **of the Supreme Court** *GB*: zugelassener Rechtsanwalt; *scot* beim Court of Sessions zugelassener Anwalt; ~ **on secondment** beigeordneter Rechtsanwalt; **S~s' Practice Rules** Standesrichtlinien für Rechtsanwälte; **S~ to the Treasury** = *Treasury S~* → *treasury*; ~ **to the suitor's fund** Prozeßpfleger im Chancery Court; ~**'s undertaking** anwaltliche Verpflichtungserklärung (*gegenüber Bank u.a.*); **assigning ~ to poor prisoner** Beiordnung *e–s* Pflichtverteidigers; **assistant** ~ Anwaltsassessor; **city** ~ städtischer Justitiar; **duty** ~ präsenzpflichtiger abrufbereiter Pflichtverteidiger; ~ ~ *rota: Bereitschaftsplan der d.s.*; **employed** ~ Anwälte im Anstellungsverhältnis; **local panel** ~ ortsansässiger Anwalt; **non-contestation** ~ Anwalt für außergerichtliche Arbeit, für konsultatorische Praxis; **official** ~ Zivilstaatsanwalt; **patent** ~ Patentanwalt, beratender (*nicht auftretender*) Patentanwalt; **sole** ~ Anwalt mit Einzelpraxis; **voluntary duty** ~ zur Pflichtverteidigung bereiter Anwalt; **women ~s** Anwältinnen.

solicitorship anwaltschaftliche Tätigkeit *f*, anwaltschaftliche Stellung *f*.

solid waste management Abfallwirtschaft *f*.

solidarity Gesamtschuldverhältnis *n*, Solidarität *f*.

solidary gesamtschuldnerisch, samtverbindlich, solidarisch.

solidity Kreditfähigkeit *f*, Haltbarkeit *f*.

solo activity Einzeltätigkeit *f*, isolierte Handlung *f*.

solus agreement Alleinbezugsvertrag *m*.

solution Entlassung *f* aus e–r Verbindlichkeit, Lösung *f*, Auflösung *f*.

solvency Solvenz *f*, Zahlungsfähigkeit *f*, ~ **ratio** Liquiditätsquote; **crisis of** ~ Zahlungskrise; **financial** ~ Zahlungsfähigkeit, Liquidität.

solvent zahlungsfähig, solvent.

Somerset Hause Somerset Haus (*Gebäude der Zentralverwaltung, London; zentrales Handelsregister*).

somnambulism Traumwandeln *n*.

son Sohn *m*, ehelicher Sohn *m*; Abkömmling *m*; ~ **and heir** Stammhalter.

sooner determination vorzeitige Beendigung *f*, vorzeitige Kündigung *f*.

sophism Spitzfindigkeit *f*, Trugschluß *m*, Scheinargument *n*, Täuschung *f*.

soricide Schwesternmord *m*, Schwesternmörder *m*.

sorter Postsortierer *m*.

sorting Klassifizierung *f*, Aussuchen *n*; ~ **code number** Bankleitzahl auf Schecks.

sought after gesucht, gefragt; ~ **for** gesucht (*entwichener Häftling*); ~ **or obtained** herbeigeführt *bzw* erlangt.

sound *adj* unversehrt, unbeschädigt, in gutem Zustand, marktfähig, ohne Krankheit, ungefährlich, gesund, verständig; ~ **accounting practice** ordnungsmäßige Buchführung; ~ **of mind** geistig gesund, zurechnungsfähig.

sound *v* tönen, verkünden, lauten auf.

soundings Sondierungen *f/pl*.

soundness Bonität *f*, Fehlerfreiheit *f*, Kreditwürdigkeit *f*; gesunder Geisteszustand *m*.

source Quelle *f*, Ursprung *m*; ~ **code escrow** treuhänderische Hinterlegung der Quellcodes (*EDV*); ~ **documentation** Quellenbelegung; ~ **of error** Fehlerquelle; ~**s of evidence** Beweismittel; ~ **of income** Einkunftsquelle; ~ **of supply** Bezugsquelle; ~ **of law** Rechtsquelle; ~ **references** Fundstellen(verzeichnis); ~**s used** Quellenangabe; **from official ~s** aus amtlichen Quellen.

sovereign *adj* souverän, unumschränkt, höchst; **~-debt risk** Staatsschuldenrisiko; **~ emblem** Hoheitszeichen; **~ immunity** staatshoheitliche Immunität, die dem Souverän zustehende Immunität; **~ immunity of State from liability** hoheitlicher Ausschluß der Staatshaftung; **"~" lending** Euromarktanleihen an Regierungen; **~ people** Volkssouverän; **~ prerogative** (vorbehaltenes) Hoheitsrecht.

sovereign *s* Staatsoberhaupt *n*, Herrscher *m*, Souverän *m*; (=) *Goldmünze von e–m* £.

sovereignty Staatshoheit *f*, Herrschaft *f*, Souveränität *f*; **~ of Parliament** Parlamentshoheit; **~ of the air** Lufthoheit; **financial ~** Finanzhoheit; **monetary ~** Währungshoheit, Münzhoheit; **personal ~** Personalhoheit; **territorial ~** Gebietshoheit, Gebietsherrschaft, Hoheitsgewalt.

space Weltraum *m*; **~ law** Weltraumrecht; **~ protection program** Weltraumschutzprogramm *US*.

space|discount Mengenrabatt bei Anzeigen; **~ sharers** Bürogemeinschaft *f* (*Anwälte*).

spacing surface Abstandsfläche *f*.

spark off (*Streit*) auslösen.

speak sprechen, vortragen, plädieren, das Wort ergreifen, e–e Rede halten; **~ to the point** zur Sache sprechen; **~ing with prosecutor** (*gerichtlich gestattete*) Verhandlung des Angeklagten mit dem Staatsanwalt (*zur Strafminderung*).

speaker Sprecher *m*, Redner *m*; Vorsitzender *m*; **S~ of the House of Commons** Präsident des Unterhauses; **S~ of the House of Lords** Präsident des Oberhauses; **S~'s Counsel** Parlamentsjustitiar (*für Privateingaben und Vorlagen*); **S~'s ruling** Entscheidung des Parlamentspräsidenten; **S~'s Secretary** *der Sekretär des Parlamentspräsidenten*; **S~ takes the chair** der Präsident (des Unterhauses) eröffnet die Sitzung; **last ~** Vorredner.

special eigentümlich, besonders, außerordentlich, speziell, individuell; **S~ Drawing Rights** Sonderziehungsrechte (*auf den Internationalen Währungsfonds*); **~ errors** Erwiderung des Revisionsbeklagten (*mit verfahrensrechtlichen Rügen*); **~ hazard form** Versicherungsvertragsformular mit gegenständlich spezifizierten Deckungssummen; **~ licence for marriage** kirchliches Sondereheschließungsdispens (*zur Heirat an einem anderen Ort*); **~ matter** besonderes Beweismaterial (*seitens d Beklagten*); **~ offering** Sonderbörsenangebot e–s größeren Wertpapierpakets (*börsenaufsichtlich genehmigt*); **~ or particular manner** besondere oder eigentümliche Art; **~ paper days** Sondertermінstage; **~ parliamentary procedure** parlamentarisches Vorverfahren (*bei Enteignungen von Boden*); **~ personal representative** Erbschaftsverwalter e–s Treuhandimmobilienvermögens; **~ procedure order** delegierte Rechtsverordnung.

speciality Besonderheit *f*, Spezialgebiet *n*; Vertrag in gesiegelter Form; **~ies** *exch* Spezialwerte; **~ contract** → *contract*; **~ creditor** → *creditor*; **~ dealers** der Fachhandel; **~ debt** → *debt*; **~ gifts** Werbegeschenke.

specialize einzeln aufführen, substantieren; spezialisieren.

specie Hartgeld *n*, Metallgeld *n*, Münzsorte *f*, in natura, Speziessache *f*; **~ payment** Zahlung in Gold; **~ point** Goldpunkt; **a picture in ~** das bestimmte Bild; **bill in ~** Sortenzettel; **deposit in ~** Bardepot; **in ~** in natura, als Stückschuld, in bar; in Gold- bzw Silbermünzen; **performance in ~** Naturalerfüllung, vertragsgetreue Erfüllung; **statement of ~** Sortenzettel; **to pay in ~** in barer Münze zahlen.

species Gattung *f*, Art *f*, Sorte *f*; **endangered ~** gefährdete Arten; **protection of ~** Artenschutz.

specific spezifisch, genau formuliert, bestimmt; eigen, besonders; **~ res-**

titution of property Rückerstattung in natura.

specificatio Verarbeitung (*cf § 950 BGB*) Umbildung *von Material zu neuer Sache*.

specification (*esp* ~ *s*) Spezifizierung *f*; Spezifikation *f*; genaue Aufstellung *f*, Leistungsverzeichnis *n*; nähere Angaben *f/pl*, Patentbeschreibung *f*; *originärer* Eigentumserwerb *m* durch Verarbeitung *f*; ~ **of disbursements** Auslagenaufstellung, Spesenaufstellung; ~ **of errors** Aufführung der Revisionsrügen; ~ **of offence** genaue Angabe der Straftat; ~ **of witnesses** Zeugenbenennung; ~ **schedule** Leistungsverzeichnis; **complete** ~ vollständige Beschreibung, endgültige Beschreibung; **defective** ~**s** mangelhafte Patentbeschreibung; **patent** ~ → *patent*; **printed** ~ Patentschrift; **provisional** ~ vorläufige Beschreibung; **right by** ~ Rechtserwerb durch Verarbeitung.

specify spezifizieren, näher angeben, aufführen, substantiieren.

specimen Muster *n*, Probe *f*; ~ **copy** Musterexemplar; ~ **charge** formaler Anklagepunkt; ~ **evidence** Beweismittel von Blutproben (*bzw Meßwerten*); ~ **letter** Briefvorlage, Musterbrief; ~ **of breath** Atemprobe; ~ **signature** Unterschriftsprobe.

specious scheinbar, trügerisch, bestechend; ~ **argumentation** bestechende Begründung; ~ **reason** Scheingrund.

speculation Spekulation *f*; ~ **for a fall** Baissespekulation; ~ **for a rise** Haussespekulation; ~ **in futures** Terminspekulation; ~ **in landed property** Bodenspekulation; **bad** ~ Fehlspekulation; **rash and hazardous** ~**s** leichtsinnige Spekulationsgeschäfte.

speculative spekulativ, Spekulations ...

speculator Spekulant *m*, Börsenspekulant *m*; ~ **in property** Grundstücksspekulant; **professional** ~ berufsmäßiger Spekulant.

speech Rede *f*, Sprache *f*, Vortrag *m*; Ansprache *f*, ~**es** *brit* Entscheidungsbegründungen des Oberhauses; **attorney's** ~ Anwaltsplädoyer; **closing** ~ Schlußplädoyer; **defence** ~ Verteidigungsplädoyer; **election** ~ Wahlrede; **freedom of** ~ → *freedom*; **inaugural** ~ Antrittsrede; **inflammatory** ~ Hetzrede, aufrührerische Rede; **liberty of** ~ → *liberty*; **maiden** ~ *parl* Erstlingsrede, Jungfernrede; **order of** ~ Reihenfolge der Plädoyers; **prosecution** ~ Plädoyer des Staatsanwalts; **right of** ~ Sprecherlaubnis; Redefreiheit.

speechify große Worte machen.

speed Geschwindigkeit *f*, Schnelligkeit *f*, Eile *f*; ~ **indicator** Geschwindigkeitsmesser; ~ **limit** Geschwindigkeitsbeschränkung, Höchstgeschwindigkeit; ~ **regulations** Geschwindigkeitsvorschriften; ~ **restriction** Geschwindigkeitsbeschränkung; ~ **trap** Autofalle, Radarfalle; ~**way** Schnellstraße; **excessive** ~ überhöhte Geschwindigkeit; **maximum advisory** ~ Richtgeschwindigkeit; **posted advisory** ~ Richtgeschwindigkeit.

speeding Überschreiten *n* der Geschwindigkeitsgrenze, zu schnelles Fahren *n*.

spending Ausgabe(n) *f*, das Geldausgeben *n*; ~ **capacity** Verbraucherkaufkraft; ~ **estimate** Ausgabenschätzung; ~ **habit** Verbrauchergewohnheit; ~ **hold-down** Ausgabenbeschränkung; ~ **rate** Ausgabenquote; ~ **unit** Verbrauchereinheit; **consumer** ~ Verbraucherausgaben; **social** ~ Sozialausgaben.

spendthrift Verschwender *m*; ~ **trust** → *trust*.

sphere Bereich *m*, Gebiet *n*, Wirkungskreis *m*, Kompetenzbereich *m*; ~ **of activity** Tätigkeitsbereich, Wirkungkreis; ~ **of interest** Interessensphäre, Interessenbereich; ~ **of jurisdiction** Kompetenzbereich; Zuständigkeit; ~ **of**

responsibility Zuständigkeitsbereich.

spill control Geheimhaltungskontrolle *f*.

spin *v/i* sich drehend schleudern (~ *into a lamp-post*).

spin-off Ausgliederung *f*; Ausschüttung *f* von Aktien e–r Tochtergesellschaft an die Aktionäre der Muttergesellschaft; *v/t* abstoßen (*Tochtergesellschaften, Beteiligungen*).

spinster unverheiratete Frau *f*, *bei Namensangaben*: ledig.

spirits alkoholhaltige Getränke, Spirituosen; ~ **monopoly** Branntweinmonopol; **S~ Regulations** Branntweinverordnung.

spiritual geistlich, seelisch; ~ **advisor** geistlicher Berater, Seelsorger; ~ **corporation** → *corporation*; ~ **court** → *court*; ~ **tenure** → *tenure*.

spirituality Geistigkeit *f*, geistliches Wesen *n*; Kirchliches *n*; ~ **of benefices** Kirchenabgaben *f/pl*, der Zehnt; kirchliche Belange, geistliche Rechte.

spiv Gauner *m*; Schieber *m*, Nichtstuer *m*, Tag(e)dieb.

splinter party Splitterpartei *f*, Splittergruppe *f*.

split|commission geteilte Provision; ~ **currency system** System gespaltener Wechselkurse; ~ **income** → *income*; ~ **opening** Eröffnungsnotierung mit stark abweichenden Kursen; ~ **order** Kaufauftrag für Abschnitte zu verschiedenen Kursen; ~ **order for custody** aufgeteiltes Sorgerecht; ~ **quotation** Notierung in Bruchteilen; ~ **re-exportation** Teil-Wiederausfuhr; ~ **sentence** teilweise auf Bewährung ausgesetzte Strafe; ~ **session** aufgeteilte Sitzungsperiode (*zwischen Plenum und Ausschüssen*); ~ **shift** Arbeit in wechselnden Schichten; ~ **ticket** Wahlzettel mit verteilten Stimmen; ~ **transaction** Börsengeschäft zu verschiedenen Kursen; ~ **vote** geteilte Stimmabgabe.

split-off (=) Ausgliederung *f*; *Ausschüttung von Tochtergesellschaftsaktien gegen teilweise Überlassung von Aktien der Muttergesellschaft*.

split-up (=) Aufspaltung *f e–s Unternehmens, Gesamtübertragung des Gesellschaftsvermögens e–r Aktiengesellschaft an mehrere Neugründungen verbunden mit Eintausch der Aktien*; ~**s** geteilte Aktien.

splitting Splitting *n* (*Einkommenssteuer*); Spaltung *f*, Aktiensplit *n*, Aktienteilung *f*; ~ **a cause of action** Aufspaltung in Teilklagen; **fee** ~ Honorarteilung.

spoil *s* Beute *f*, Ausbeute *f*, Verderben *n*; ~**s system** Ämterpatronage *f bei Wahlsieg*; Futterkrippenwirtschaft *f*.

spoilage Verderb *m*, Ausschuß *m*.

spoilsmen Parteipolitiker *m*, Postenjäger *m*.

spoliation Pfründenentzug *m*, Plünderung *f*, Beraubung *f*, Sachbeschädigung *f*; Urkundenbeschädigung *f*, Unkenntlichmachen *n* von Urkunden, kriegsrechtliche Plünderung *f* neutraler Schiffe; Vernichtung *f* der Schiffspapiere (*zur Verschleierung der Identität oder Ladung*); unberechtigte Änderung *f* e–s Dokuments.

spoliator Schädiger *m*.

sponsion Verpflichtung *f*, Bürgschaft *f*; noch nicht ratifizierte internationale Verpflichtungserklärung *f*.

sponsor *s* Förderer *m*, Schirmherr *m*, Bürge *m*, Geldgeber *m*.

sponsor *v* fördern, empfehlen, vorschlagen, bürgen (für); **government** ~**ed** staatlich gefördert.

sponsorship Bürgschaft *f*, Patenschaft *f*; Schirmherrschaft *f*, finanzielle (Programm)Trägerschaft.

spontaneous spontan, freiwillig, von selbst, improvisiert; ~ **act** Willensakt; ~ **combustion** Selbstentzündung; ~ **deterioration** innerer Verderb; ~ **exclamation** spontaner Ausruf; ~ **statement** spontane Erklärung.

sporting Jagd *f*, Jagdrecht *n*.

Sporting Events Control of Alcohol Act Alkoholkontrollgesetz für Sportveranstaltungen *GB 1985*.

spot|audit sofortige Teilrevision; ~ **bargain** Lokogeschäft; ~ **broker** Platzmakler; ~ **check** Prüfung an Ort und Stelle, Stichprobe; ~ **conditions** Bedingungen bei sofortiger Barzahlung; ~ **contract** Platzgeschäft; ~ **deal** Kassageschäft; ~ **exchange rate** Devisenkassakurs; ~ **exchange transactions** → *transaction*; ~ **market** → *market*; ~ **payment** Barzahlung zur sofortigen Abrechnung; ~ **price** Preis bei sofortiger Lieferung, Kassakurs, Spotkurs, Lokopreis; ~ **purchase** Kauf von sofort lieferbaren Produkten *bzw Devisen*; Lokokauf; ~ **rate** Kassakurs, Tageskurs; ~ **rate** Kassakurs (*Devisenmarkt*); ~ **trading** Verkäufe gegen sofortige Kasse und Lieferung; ~ **transactions** → *transaction*; **over** ~ Report; **to sell for** ~ **delivery** loko verkaufen; **under** ~ Deport.

spots Lokoware *f*, Kassaware *f*.

spotter Polizeispitzel *m*, Hausdetektiv *m*, Privatdetektiv *m*.

spouse Ehegatte *m*; ~**s** Ehegatten, Eheleute; ~**-breach** *hist* Ehebruch; ~**s in occupation** *im Mitbesitz der ehelichen Wohnung befindlichen Ehegatten*; **complaining** ~ Kläger(in) (*Scheidungsprozeß*); **evidence of** ~ Ehegattenaussagen; **the non-entitled** ~ der nichtberechtigte Ehegatte.

spread *s* Spanne *f*, Kursdifferenz; Zinsdifferenz *f*, Marge *f*; Bandbreite *f*; Prämiengeschäft *n*, Stellagegeschäft *n*; ~ **between the intervention points** Wechselkursbandbreite.

spread *v* verbreiten, ausstreuen.

spreading|false news Verbreitung von Falschnachrichten (*über den Monarchen*); ~ **of risks** → *risk*.

spread sheet Arbeitsblatt *n*, Kalkulationstabelle *f*, tabellarische Bilanz *f*.

spring|guns Selbstschüsse; ~ **traps** Fußangeln.

spurious unecht, falsch; ~ **bank bill** gefälschte Banknote; ~ **note** Kellerwechsel; ~ **offspring** nichtehelicher Abkömmling.

spurt (Kurs)Sprung *m*, plötzliches Steigen *n*.

spy Spion *m*.

spying Spionage *f*.

squad Gruppe *f*, (Arbeits)Trupp *f*, Mannschaft *f*; **emergency** ~ Not(einsatz)kommando; **flying** ~ Überfallkommando; **homicide** ~ Mordkommission.

squander verschwenden, vergeuden; ~**-mania** Verschwendungssucht.

square *adj* ehrlich, anständig, deutlich; ~ **deal** faire Abmachung, gerechte Gesellschaftsordnung.

square *s* Platz *m*, unbebaute Fläche *f*; ~ **block** Straßenblock; **public** ~ öffentlicher Platz.

square *v* ausgleichen, abgleichen, saldieren; begleichen; ~ **accounts** Konten ausgleichen.

squash unterdrücken, aufheben; ~ **a riot** e–n Aufstand niederschlagen.

squat sich ohne Rechtstitel niederlassen, wild siedeln.

squatter unberechtigter Siedler *m*; Hausbesetzer *m*; ~**'s title** Ersitzungsrecht (*e–s ursprünglich illegalen Siedlers*).

squeal „singen" (*beim Verhör*), auspacken, ein Geständnis ablegen (*zum Nachteil von Tatbeteiligten*); verpfeifen.

squealer Informant *m* der Polizei; Verräter *m von Gangstern*.

squeeze Druck *m*, Klemme *f*, Knappheit *f*, Engpaß *m*; **bear** ~ *exch* Zwang zu Deckungskäufen mit Verlust; **credit** ~ → *credit (2)*.

squeezing out (*employees*) Hinausekeln *n* (*von Arbeitnehmern*).

squeezing the bears Zwang zu Verlustdeckungskäufen, Druckausübung auf Baissiers.

squire Patronatsherr *m*, Friedensrichter *m*.

squirearchy Herrschaft des Landadels.

stab stechen, auf jmdn einstechen, erdolchen.

stabber Meuchelmörder *m*.

stability Stabilität *f*, Beständigkeit *f*; ~ **of prices** Preisstabilität; **currency** ~ Währungsstabilität.

stabilization Stabilisierung *f*; ~ **fund** Stabilisierungsfonds.

stabilize stabilisieren; ~ **prices** Preise stabil halten; ~**d loan** Stabilisierungsanleihe; ~**d standard** stabilisierte Währung.

staff Stab *m*, Personal *n*, Gefolgschaft *f*; ~ **bonus** Gratifikation, Extrazahlung für Mitarbeiter; ~**-controlled** mitarbeiterbestimmt, arbeitnehmerbestimmt; ~ **department** Personalabteilung; ~**-herding** Weidenlassen von Rindern im Wald; ~ **manager** Personalchef; ~ **officer** planmäßiger Beamter; Stabsoffizier; ~ **pension fund** Angestellten-Pensionskasse; ~ **provident fund** Angestelltenunterstützungskasse; ~ **reduction** Personalabbau; ~ **regulations** Dienstordnung, Personalstatut; ~ **room** Lehrerzimmer, Aufenthaltsraum für Mitarbeiter; ~ **shares** Belegschaftsaktien; ~ **shortage** Personalmangel; **casual** ~ Gelegenheitsarbeitskräfte; **clerical** ~ Büropersonal; Schreibkräfte; **expatriate** ~ *im Ausland wohnender Mitarbeiter, ins Ausland gezogene bzw versetzte Mitarbeiter*; **high calibre** ~ Spitzenkräfte, hochqualifizierte Mitarbeiter; **indoor** ~ Mitarbeiter im Innendienst; **junior** ~ die dienstjüngere Belegschaft; **managerial** ~ leitende Angestellte; **technical** ~ Fachpersonal; **temporary** ~ Angestellte auf Zeit, Aushilfspersonal; **upgraded** ~ spezialisiertes Personal, höher eingestufter Mitarbeiter; **voluntary** ~ unbezahlter Mitarbeiter.

staffer Mitarbeiter *m*, Angestellter *m*.

staffing Personalplanung *f*, Personalaufbau *m*; ~ **schedule** Stellenbesetzungsplan.

stag Konzertzeichner *m*, spekulativer Aufkäufer *m* von Aktienmissionen; zum Kronzeugen gewordener Beschuldigter.

stage (*1*) Stufe *f*, Stadium *n*; ~ **carriage** Postkutsche, Linienbus; ~**s of appeal** Instanzenweg; ~ **of proceedings** Stand des Verfahrens, Prozeßlage; ~**s of production** Produktionsstufen; ~ **of trial** Prozeßphase; **experimental** ~ Versuchsstadium; **in the initial** ~ im Anfangsstadium; **manufactured** ~ abgeschlossenes Produktionsstadium; **operational** ~ Betriebsstadium; **raw material** ~ Rohstoffstadium.

stage (*2*) Bühne *f*; ~ **director** Regisseur.

stagflation *f* (=) (*stagnierende Konjunktur mit Inflation*).

staggering Staffelung *f*; ~ **of credit** Kreditstaffelung; ~ **the timing of cases** gestaffelte Terminanberaumung, Anberaumung von Einzelterminen.

stagging *brit* Konzertzeichnung *f*; ~ **the market** Beeinflussung des Marktes durch Konzertzeichnungen, *vgl stag*.

stagnancy Stockung *f*, Stille *f*, Lustlosigkeit *f*.

stagnant stagnierend, flau, still.

stagnation Stille *f*, Flaute *f*, Stagnation *f*, Stillstand *m*.

stake *s* Einsatz *m*, Einlage *f*, Anteil *m*, Beteiligung *f*; ~ **money** Einsatz.

stakeholder Verwahrer *m*, Verwahrer der Kaufpreisanzahlung (*bzw e–s Geldbetrages zwischen mehreren Parteien*), Treuhandverwahrer, Anwartschaftsberechtigter *m bei Landzuteilungen bzw Schürfrechtsvergabe*; ~**'s interpleader** → *interpleader*.

stake out observieren (*Polizei, Detektive*), beschatten.

stake-out squad Sonderkommando für die Unschädlichmachung e–s Schwerverbrechers.

stale verjährt, verwirkt, unwirksam; schal, abgestanden, alt(backen), veraltet, abgedroschen.

stallholder (Markt)Standbesitzer *m*, Marktbudenverkäufer *m*.

stall-money Standgeld *m*.

stallage Recht *n*, e–n Marktstand zu errichten; Standgeld *n*, Marktgeld *n*.

stalling tactics Verzögerungstaktik *f*.

stamp Stempel *m*, Briefmarke *f*,

Steuerprägestempel *m*, Stempelsteuermarke *f*; ~ **acts** Stempelsteuergesetze; ~ **collection** Briefmarkensammlung; ~ **duty** Stempelsteuer, Urkundensteuer; ~ **duty on bills of exchange** Wechselsteuer; ~ **duty on securities** Effektensteuer, Wertpapierstempelsteuer; ~ **machine** Wertzeichenautomat; ~ **paper** Stempelpapier; ~ **trading** Briefmarkenhandel; **bill** ~ Wechselsteuermarke; **date** ~ Tagesstempel, Eingangsstempel; **deed** ~ Urkundensteuer; **exempt from** ~ **duty** stempel(steuer)frei; **firm** ~ Firmenstempel; **forgery of** ~**s** Wertzeichenfälschung; **green** ~**s** Rabattmarken; **impressed** ~ eingedruckter Stempel, Prägestempel; **liable to** ~ **duty** stempelsteuerpflichtig; **postage** ~ **(= postal** ~**)** Briefmarke, Postwertzeichen; **revenue** ~ → *revenue*; **rubber** ~ Gummistempel; **signature** ~ → *signature*.

stamping office Direktionsbüro *n* für Genehmigung von Versicherungsverträgen.

stand *s* Zeugenstand *m*; **to take the** ~ aussagen.

stand *v* stehen, in Kraft bleiben, vor Gericht erscheinen, kandidieren; ~ **adjourned** (sich) vertagen; ~ **aside** (*jurors*) vorläufig zurückstellen (*Geschworene*); ~ **bail** → *bail*; ~ **by** beistehen, unterstützen; in (Alarm-) Bereitschaft stehen; ~ **by the terms of a contract** sich an die Vertragsbestimmungen halten; ~ **convicted** überführt sein; verurteilt werden; ~ **corrected** e–n Fehler zugeben; ~ **delcredere** das Delkredere übernehmen; ~ **for parliament** (für e–n Sitz im Parlament) kandidieren; ~ **for re-election** → *re-election*; ~ **in for s. o.** jmdn vertreten; ~ **on one's right** auf seinem Recht bestehen; ~ **over** aufgeschoben werden, zurückstellen; ~ **the loss** den Schaden tragen; ~ **trial** → *trial*; ~ **unsatisfied** noch nicht befriedigt sein; ~ **up for** eintreten für.

standage Ernteabzug *m*, *Abzug von der Pacht für Früchte auf dem Halm bei vorzeitiger Pachtbeendigung*.

standard|average clause → *clause*; ~ **bullion** Münzgold; ~ **capacity** Durchschnittsleistung; ~ **coin** Münze mit gesetzl vorgesehenem Feingehalt; ~ **commercial article** eingeführter Artikel des (freien) Warenmarktes; ~ **cost** Standardkosten, Richtkosten; ~ **costing** Plankostenrechnung; ~ **deviation** Standardabweichung; ~ **fire insurance policy** Einheitsfeuerversicherungspolice; ~ **form** Standardformular, Einheitsformular; ~ **form contract** Formularvertrag, Einheitsvertrag, Typenvertrag; ~**s in industry** Industrienormen; ~ **interest** üblicher Zinsfuß; **S**~ **International Trade Classification** Internationales Warenverzeichnis für den Außenhandel; ~ **mark** Feingehaltsstempel; ~ **market** Einheitsmarkt; ~ **measure** Normalmaß, Eichmaß; ~ **money** vollwichtige Münze, Währungsgeld; ~**s of dimensions, designs or quality** Abmessungs-, Konstruktions- oder Qualitätsnormen; ~ **of care** Sorgfaltsmaßstab; ~ **of excellence** hervorragendes Qualitätsniveau; ~ **of fineness** Feingehalt; ~ **of life** Lebensstandard, Lebenshaltungsindex; ~ **of need** Bedürftigkeitsschwelle; ~ **of performance** Leistungsstandard, Leistungsniveau; Solleistung, Leistungsvorgabe; ~ **of proof** Grad der Beweisführung; Anforderung auf Grund der Beweislast, Grad der Beweislast; *strict* ~ ~ ~: *strenge Anforderungen an die Beweisführung*; ~ **of value** Wertmesser, Wertmaßstab; ~ **piece wage** Einheitsstücklohn; ~ **practice** übliches Verfahren; ~ **price** Einheitspreis; ~ **provision** Standardbestimmung; ~ **quality** Einheitsqualität durchschnittlicher Güte; ~ **quotation** Einheitskurs; ~ **rate** Einheitssatz, Normalsatz; ~ ~ *of taxation: normaler Steuersatz*; ~ **rent** → *rent*; ~ **sil-**

ver Münzsilber; ~ **size** → *size*; ~ **stocks** Standardwerte, Spitzenwerte; ~ **terms** → *terms*; ~ **time** → *time*; ~ **value** Normalwert; Einheitswert; ~ **wage** → *wage*; ~ **weight** Normalgewicht, Eichgewicht; **accepted engineering ~s** anerkannte Regeln der Technik; **American S~s Association** Amerikanischer Normenverband; **ascertainable ~ of guilt** feststellbare Schuldnorm; **bimetallic** ~ bimetallisches Währungssystem; **British S~s Institution** Britischer Normenverband; **Bureau of S~s** (Bundes)Eichamt (*USA*); **commercial** ~ handelsübliche Qualität; **compensated** ~ kaufkraftberichtigtes Metallwährungssystem; **credit ~s** Kreditrichtlinien; **descriptive** ~ äußerliche Warenmerkmale; **double currency** ~ → *double*; **engineering ~s** Regeln der Technik; *generally accepted ~ ~s: allgemein gültige Regeln der Technik*; **established ~s** anerkannte Normen; **executive** ~ staatlich kontrollierte Währung; **fiat** ~ Papier(geld)währung, Staatsgeld; **fiat exchange** ~ devisengesichertes Staatsgeld; **fiduciary money** ~ Staatsgeld, Papierwährung; **gold** ~ → *gold*; **gold bullion** ~ → *gold*; **gold coin** ~ → *gold*; **gold exchange** ~ → *gold*; **gold specie** ~ Goldumlaufswährung; **high ~ of ethics** hohes sittliches Niveau; **ideal** ~ optimale Standardkosten *e–s Erzeugnisses*; **inconvertible silver** ~ nicht konvertierbare Silbergeldwährung; **industrial ~s** Industrie-Normen; **international ~s** internationale Richtlinien, völkerrechtliche Verhaltensnormen; **metallic** ~ Metallwährung; **monetary** ~ Währungsstandard, Münzfuß, Währungseinheit; **multiple** ~ Indexwährung; **paper (money)** ~ Papiergeldwährung; **performance** ~ → *performance*; **professional ~s** standesrechtliche Richtlinien; **safety** ~ Sicherheitsnormen; **tabular** ~ Währungsstandard nach Kauftkrafttabellen; **universal ~s** *(=) Qualitätsbezeichnung für Baumwolle.*

standardization Standardisierung *f*, Vereinheitlichung *f*, Normung *f*; Warennormung *f*; ~ **of tariffs** Tarifvereinheitlichung.

standardize normieren, in Normwerten ausdrücken.

standby *s* ständiger Vertreter (*e–s Anwalts*).

stand-by|agreement Abkommen über e–n Bereitschaftskredit, Stand-by-Vereinbarung; ~ **arrangement** Beistandsabkommen; Bereitschaftskreditzusage; ~ **charges** Bereithaltungsgebühr (Anwalt); ~ **credit** → *credit*; ~ **facility** Bereitschaftskredit; ~ **judge** Richter mit Bereitschaftsdienst; ~ **letter of credit** Bankgarantie, Garantieakkreditiv, Bereitschaftsakkreditiv; ~ **supply** Spitzenversorgung (*Strom*); ~ **tax increase** Steuererhöhung bei Bedarf; ~ **time** Wartezeit; **office** ~ Bereitschaftsdienst (*Kanzlei*).

standing *adj* stehend, dauernd, laufend, üblich.

standing *s* Status *m*, Stand *m*, Rang *m*; **credit** ~ Kreditwürdigkeit, Bonität, **financial** ~ Finanzlage, Kreditwürdigkeit; **legal** ~ gesetzlicher Status; **of long** ~ langjährig, seit langem bestehend.

standing order Geschäftsordnungsregel, Dauerauftrag; feste Vorschrift; *pl* Geschäftsordnung *GB parl*; ~ **~s committee** Geschäftsordnungsausschuß.

standing to sue Prozeßführungsrecht *m*, Klagebefugnis *f*.

standstill|agreement Stillhalteabkommen; ~ **credit** Stillhaltekredit.

stannaries Zinngruben *f/pl*, *Zinnbergwerksbezirk in Devon und Cornwall.*

staple Markt *m*, Stapelplatz *m*, Handelserlaubnis *f* für Ausländer; ~ **commodities** Stapelware, Hauptprodukte; ~ **industries** Hauptindustriezweige; **S~ Inn** (=) *Anwaltsinnung beim Chancery-Gericht*; ~ **law** Marktrecht; ~ **privilege** Marktgerechtigkeit; ~ **towns** *hist königlich bestimmte Hafenstädte für*

Export von Landeserzeugnissen; **statute** ~ *hist* Schuldverschreibung (*unter dem Gültigkeitssiegel e–r Marktstadt*); **Statute of the S~** (=) *G. v. 1353 betr. staple towns qv*; **statutory** ~ *hist* dingliche und persönliche Vollstreckung bei Verfall e–s *statute ~ qv*.

Star-Chamber *hist* Sternkammer von 1641 (*geheimes Strafgericht*); **s~-c~-justice** Geheimjustiz, Willkürjustiz.

Star War Contract SDI-Vertrag *m*.

stare decisis Grundsatz *m* der Bindung an Vorentscheidungen.

start-up Ingangsetzung *f*.

state *s* (*1*) Zustand *m*, Stand *m*; ~ **of affairs** Sachlage; ~ **of business** Geschäftslage, Konjunktur; ~ **of emergency** Ausnahmezustand, Notlage; ~ **of facts** Tatbestand, Sachverhalt; ~ **of facts and proposals** Bericht über den zu Entmündigenden; ~ **of intoxication** Betrunkenheit; ~ **of mind** Geistesverfassung, innere Verfassung, subjektiver Tatumstand; ~ **of necessity** *öffentlicher* Notstand, Staatsnotstand; ~ **of repair** baulicher Zustand, Erhaltungszustand; ~ **of siege** → *siege*; ~ **of the art** Stand der Technik; ~ **of the books** bilanzmäßiger Status; ~ **of the case** Sachverhaltsdarstellung, Klagebegründung; **S~ of the Union Message** Botschaft zur Lage der Nation; ~ **of war** Kriegszustand; **current** ~ derzeitiger Zustand; jeweiliger Z.; **deliverable** ~ übergabefähiger Zustand, lieferfähiger Zustand; **married** ~ Ehestand; **mental** ~ = ~ *of mind qv*.

state *s* (*2*) Staat *m*, Einzelstaat *m*, Bundesland *m*; *adj* staatlich, einzelstaatlich; ~ **act** staatlicher Hoheitsakt; ~ **action** Staatshaftungsklage; ~ **administrator** Verwaltungschef für ein Staatsgebiet; ~ **affairs** Staatsgeschäfte; ~ **agent** Regierungsbeauftragter; ~ **aid** staatliche Unterstützung; ~ **aided** staatlich subventioniert; **S~ attorney** *US* Staatsanwalt (*e–s US Einzelstaates*); ~ **auditor** → *auditor*; **S~ bank** Staatsbank, Staatsbank e–s US Einzelstaates, Länderbank; nur in e–m US-Staat zugelassene Bank; ~ **banking department** staatliche Bankenaufsicht; ~ **borrowing** Staatsschuldenaufnahme; ~ **ceremony** feierlicher Staatsakt; ~ **citizenship** Staatszugehörigkeit *in US Einzelstaat*; ~ **comptroller** → *comptroller*; ~ **control** Staatskontrolle, Beherrschung durch die öffentliche Hand; ~ **controlled** unter staatlicher Aufsicht; bewirtschaftet; ~ **courts** Gerichte in *US* Einzelstaaten; ~**craft** Staatskunst, das politische Handwerk; ~ **criminal** *US* Straftäter nach einzelstaatlichem Recht; ~ **earnings related pension scheme** staatl Zusatz-Versorgungskasse; ~ **enterprise** Staatsbereich; **S~'s evidence** → *evidence*; ~ **finance** Staatsfinanzen; ~ **government** Staatsregierung (*US Einzelstaat*); ~ **grant** staatlicher Zuschuß; **S~ House** Parlamentsgebäude (*e–s US Einzelstaates*); ~ **immunity** Staatenimmunität, Befreiung von der inländischen Gerichtsbarkeit, Exterritorialität; ~ **insurance** staatliche Versicherung; ~ **jurisdiction** (einzel)staatliche Zuständigkeit; ~ **lands** staatlicher Grundbesitz; ~ **machinery** Staatsapparat; ~ **monopoly** Staatsmonopol, Regie; ~ **of domicile** Wohnsitzstaat; ~ **of origin** Ursprungsland, Heimatland; ~ **of situs** Belegenheitsstaat; ~**owned** staatseigen, in Staatseigentum befindlich; ~ **owned enterprise** staatseigener Betrieb; ~ **owned property** Staatseigentum, Staatsvermögen; **S~ Paper Office** Staatsurkundenamt, *GB*; ~ **papers** Staatsurkunden, Staatsanzeiger; ~ **policy** Staatspolitik; Richtlinien der Staatspolitik; ~ **property** Staatseigentum; ~ **relief administration** (einzel)staatliche Fürsorgeverwaltung; ~ **responsibility** Staatshaftung; ~ **revenue** Staatseinnahmen, Staatseinkünfte; ~

rights den Einzelstaaten vorbehaltene Rechte; ~ **secret** Staatsgeheimnis; **S~ securities** Staatsanleihen; einzelstaatliche Anleihepapiere; ~ **succession** = *succession of ~s* → *succession*; ~ **supervision** staatliche Aufsicht; ~ **tax** → *tax*; ~ **territory** staatliches Hoheitsgebiet; ~ **trading corporation** staatliche Handelsgesellschaft; ~ **transfer tax** Börsenumsatzsteuer; ~ **trial** politischer Prozeß, Hochverratsprozeß; ~ **visit** Staatsbesuch; **act of** ~ → *act*; **confederated** ~ Staat e–s Staatenbundes; **contracting** ~ Vertragsstaat; **creditor** ~ Gläubigerstaat; **Department of S~** → *department*; **dependent** ~ Vasallenstaat; **enemy** ~ Feindstaat; **federal** ~ Bundesstaat; **for reason of** ~ aus Gründen der Staatsräson; **friendly** ~ befreundeter Staat; **frontline S~s** Frontstaaten; **head of** ~ Staatsoberhaupt; **landlocked** ~ Binnenstaat (*ohne Zugang zum Meer*); **littoral** ~ Uferstaat, Küstenstaat, Anliegerstaat; **member** ~ Mitgliedsstaat; **multi-national** ~ Nationalitätenstaat; **sovereign** ~ Staat, souveräner Staat; (Staat als) Völkerrechtssubjekt; **peripheral** ~ Randstaat; **protected** ~ unter brit Schutzherrschaft stehender Commonwealth-Staat; **puppet** ~ Marionettenstaat; **receiving** ~ Empfangsstaat; **requesting** ~ ersuchender Staat (*Auslieferung*); **riparian** ~ Uferstaat, Stromanliegerstaat; **satellite** ~ Satellitenstaat; **sending** ~ Entsendestaat; **signatory** ~ Signatarstaat, Unterzeichnerstaat; **unitary** ~ Zentralstaat, Einheitsstaat; **welfare** ~ Wohlfahrtsstaat.

state *v* angeben, erklären, feststellen; ~ **a case** e–e Begründung vortragen, e–n Fall schlüssig vortragen; ~ **an account** e–e Rechnung vorlegen; ~ **facts** Tatsachen vorbringen; ~ **full particulars** genaue Einzelheiten angeben; substantiieren, detaillieren; ~ **one's grievance** sich beschweren; ~ **the average** die Dispache aufmachen; ~ **the issue** zur entscheidungserheblichen Frage vortragen; **(as) ~d above** oben angegeben, oben erwähnt; **~d account** = *account stated* → *account* (*2*); **~d amount** der angegebene Betrag; **~d capital** ausgewiesenes Kapital; **~d date** angegebenes Datum; **~d liabilities** Buchschulden; **~d meeting** → *meeting*; **~d period** angegebene Frist; **~d term** reguläre Sitzungszeit *e–s Gerichts*; **at ~d periods** regelmäßig, periodisch; **at ~d times** in regelmäßigen Zeitabständen; **by ~d instalments** in festgesetzten Raten.

statehood (Eigen)Staatlichkeit *f*; **recognition of** ~ Anerkennung *f* als souveräner Staat.

stateless staatenlos; ~ **person** Staatenloser *m*.

statelessness Staatenlosigkeit *f*.

statement Angabe *f*, Darlegung *f*, Erklärung *f*, Aussage *f*, Ausführung *f*, Sachvortrag *m*, Prozeßbehauptung *f*; Aufstellung *f*; ~ **analysis** Statusprüfung, Bilanzanalyse; ~ **by prisoner** Aussage e–s (Untersuchungs)Gefangenen; ~ **by witness** Zeugenaussage; ~ **in lieu of prospectus** Vorgründungsbericht (*an das Handelsregister*), Prospektersatzerklärung (*vereinfachte Gründung*); ~ **of account** → *account* (*1*), (*2*); ~ **of accused** → *accused*; ~ **of affairs** Vermögensaufstellung, Geschäftslage; Bericht über die Vermögenslage, Status e–s Gemeinschuldners; ~ **of all property** Vermögensverzeichnis; ~ **of assets and liabilities** Status; ~ **of average** Havarie, Dispache; ~ **of case** Vorlagebericht; ~ **of charges** Kostenrechnung; ~ **of claim** Klagebegründung; ~ **of condition** Status; ~ **of confession** Unterwerfungserklärung; ~ **of consideration** Angabe über die vereinbarte Gegenleistung; ~ **of contents** Inhaltsangabe; ~ **of damage** Schadensaufstellung; ~ **of defence** Klageerwiderung, Verteidigungsschrift; ~ **of deposit** Depotauszug; ~ **of expenses** Spesenaufstellung; ~ **of fact** tatsächliche Behauptung; ~ **of facts** Tatbestand, Sachverhalt, Sachdarstellung; ~ **of incidental powers** Aufzählung der satzungsgemäßen Befugnisse *e–r Körperschaft*; ~ **of income** Gewinn- und Verlustrechnung; ~ **of income and surplus** Jahresbericht nebst Bilanz und Gewinn- und Verlustrechnung, ~ **of information and belief** indirekte Zeugenerklärung; ~ **of intent** Absichtserklärung; ~ **of operating results** Ergebnisrechnung; ~ **of opinion** Meinungsäußerung; ~ **of origin** Ursprungsbescheinigung; ~ **of particulars** Substantiierung der Klage (*nachträgliche Substantiierung der Klage bei Säumnis des Beklagten*); ~ **of policy** Grundsatzerklärung; ~ **of proof** anwaltschaftlich aufgenommene Zeugenerklärung; ~ **of reasons** schriftl. Begründung *e–r Entscheidung*; ~ **of the insured** Angaben des Versicherungsnehmers; ~ **on oath** eidliche Erklärung; **admitted** ~ Geständnis; **annual** ~ Jahresbericht; **annual financial** ~ Finanzbericht, Bilanz; **average** ~ Dispache; **bank** ~ → *bank* (*1*); **cash** ~ → *cash*; **consonant** ~ indirekte Aussage zur Bestätigung der Glaubwürdigkeit; **corporate** ~ Bilanz e–r AG; **defamatory** ~ beleidigende Behauptung, Verleumdung; **discretion** ~ → *discretion*; **false** ~ falsche Angabe an Eides Statt; **false** ~**s as to candidates** Wahltäuschung; **financial** ~ Finanzbericht, Haushaltserklärung, Status, Ausweis, Abschluß, Bilanz; **fraudulent** ~ betrügerische Angaben über Aktiengesellschaften, betrügerische Bilanzverschleierung, Vorspiegelung falscher Tatsachen; **full** ~ umfassende Erklärung, vollständige Darstellung; **government** ~ **of policy** Regierungserklärung; **interest** ~ → *interest* (*2*); **jurisdictional** ~ Angaben zum Streitwert; **mixed** ~ Einlassung der Beschuldigten mit e–r Mischung von Teilgeständnissen und exkulpatorischen Angaben; **official** ~ amtliche Erklärung, Kommuniqué; **operating** ~ Betriebsergebnisrechnung; **partial** ~**s** einseitige Behauptungen; **profit and loss** ~ Gewinn- und Verlustrechnung; **self-serving** ~ Angaben zur eigenen Entlastung; exkulpatorische Angaben; **sworn** ~ eidliche schriftliche Zeugenerklärung; **royalty** ~ Lizenzabrechnung; **true** ~ wahrheitsgemäße Angaben; **to retract a** ~ e–e Aussage widerrufen; **unsworn** ~ uneidliche schriftliche Einlassung des Beschuldigten; **untrue** ~ unwahre Zeugenerklärung; **written** ~ schriftliche Erklärung.

statesman Staatsmann *m*; Grundbesitzer *m*; **elder** ~ erfahrener älterer Staatsmann, Politiker im Ruhestand.

statesmanship Staatskunst *f*, Regierungskunst *f*.

static ratio statische Verhältniszahl *f* (*Bilanzanalyse*).

stating-part of the bill Klagebegründung *f*.

station Bahnhof *m*, Reede *f*, Standort *m*, Stützpunkt *m*; Amt *n*, Beruf *m*, Geschäft *n*; Rang *m*, Stand *m*; ~ **in life** Lebensstellung; ~ **of arrival** Ankunftsbahnhof; ~ **of departure** Abgangsbahnhof; ~ **of destination** Bestimmungsbahnhof; **forwarding** ~ → *forwarding*; **goods** ~ Güterbahnhof; **jamming** ~ Störsender; **life boat** ~ Rettungsstation; **police** ~ → *police*; **polling** ~ → *polling*; **power** ~ Kraftwerk; **social** ~ Stand, soziale Stellung; **trading** ~ Handelsniederlassung.

stationer Schreibwarenhändler *m*; **S~s' Company** (=) *Schreibwarenhändler-Innung London, Zensurbehörden*; **S~s' Hall** (=) *Sitz der Stationers' Company*; ~**s' register** Verzeichnis von Neuerscheinungen *GB*.

stationery Büromaterial *n*, Bürobedarf *m*; ~ **department** Büromaterialverwaltung; **H.M.S.~ Office** (=) *brit Staatsverlag und Verkaufsstelle für amtl Veröffentlichungen*.

statism Staatssystem *n*, Staatswirtschaftsprinzip *n*, Dirigismus *m*; Staatskunst.

statistical|data statistische Angaben; ~ **inquiry** statistische Umfrage, Rundfrage.

statistics Statistik *f* (-en) *pl*; ~ **of employment** Beschäftigungsstatistik; **cradle-to-grave** ~ Statistik von der Wiege bis zur Bahre; **criminal** ~ Kriminalstatistik; **foreign trade** ~ Außenhandelsstatistik; **official** ~ amtliche Statistik; **sales** ~ Umsatzstatistik; **vital** ~ → *vital*.

status Status *m*, Personenstand *m*, rechtliche Stellung *f* (*e–r Person*); Zustand *m*, Stellung *f*; ~ **enquiries and reports** (*auch:* ~ *enquiry*) Kreditauskunft; ~ **of forces agreement** Truppenstatut; ~ **of aliens** Ausländereigenschaft; ~ **of irremovability** Recht auf Seßhaftigkeit (*e–s Armen*); ~ **of legitimacy** ehelicher Status, Ehelichkeit; ~ **of members** Status der Aktionäre, Zugehörigkeit zu e–r Aktiengattung; ~ **quo** derzeitiger Zustand; ~ **quo ante** vorheriger Zustand; **civil** ~ Personenstand, Familienstand; **dominion** ~ Dominionstatus; **equality of** ~ staatsrechtliche und diplomatische Ebenbürtigkeit; **financial** ~ Vermögenslage; **law of** ~ → *law*; **legal** ~ Personenstand, statusrechtliche Stellung, Rechtslage, Rechtsposition, Rechtspersönlichkeit, Rechtsfähigkeit, Rechtsstellung; **marital** ~ Familienstand; **national** ~ Staatsangehörigkeit; **neutral** ~ Neutralität; **occupational** ~ Berufsverhältnis, Berufsangabe; **official** ~ Amtsstellung; **personal** ~ Familienstand, Personenstand; Personalstatut; **resident** ~ Daueraufenthaltsberechtigung; **social** ~ gesellschaftliche Stellung; **trustee** ~ Mündelsicherheit.

statutable = *statutory qv*.

statute Gesetz *n* (= *G bzw* . . . *g*), geschriebenes Recht *n*, Statut *n*, Satzung *f*; **~s at large** sämtliche Gesetze (*in ihrer ursprünglichen Fassung*); **S~s at Large** (=) *amtliche Sammlung von US Bundesgesetzen*; **~-barred** verjährt; ~ **book** *G*buch; *G–es*sammlung; die geltenden Gesetze; ~ **fair** Markt für Gelegenheitsarbeiter; ~ **in blank** Blankett*g*; ~ **labour** *hist* Hand- und Spanndienste zum Straßenbau; ~ **law** → *law*; ~ **law revision** *G–es*bereinigung; **~-merchant** *hist* exekutorische Schuldverschreibung (*an engl Marktplätzen*); ~ **of amendments and jeofailes** gesetzliche Berichtigungsmöglichkeit des eigenen Sachvortrags; ~ **of descent** gesetzliche Erbfolge bei unbeweglichem Vermögen; ~ **of distributions** → *distribution*; **S~ of Frauds** → *frauds*; ~ **of limitations** gesetzliche Verjährungsvorschriften, Verjährung (*evt Ersitzung*); ~ **of minorities** Minderheitenstatut; ~ **of monopolies** Kartell*g*; **S~s of the Realm** *Sammlung brit Reichsgesetze Anfang 19. Jhd*; **S~ of Uncertain Date** *Gesetze unbestimmten Datums von Eduard III*; **S~ of Uses** → *use*; **S~ of Vagabonds** → *vagabond*; **S~ of Westminster** Westminster-Statut (*1931 betr staatsrechtliche Stellung der Dominions*); **S~s of Westminster** *hist Gesetzessammlung von 1275, 1285 u 1290*; **S~ of Wills** (=) *Gesetz unter Heinrich VIII. betr letztwillige Verfügungen über Grundbesitz*; **S~s Revised** Amtliche (Gesetzes)Sammlung; ~ **roll** *G–es*rolle, *G–es*pergament; ~ **staple** → *staple*; **affirmative** ~ → *affirmative*; **alteration of** ~ *G–es*änderung; **codifying** ~ Kodifizierungs, Kodifikation; **consolidated ~s** Gesetzessammlung, Bereinigte Sammlung; **consolidating** ~ zusammenfassendes *G*, Bereinigungsgesetz; **criminal** ~ Straf*g*; **declaratory** ~ Ausführungs*g*, Erläuterungs*g*; **directory** ~ Sollvorschrift, Gesetz mit Sollbestimmungen; **disabling** ~ *G* über Entziehung der Rechtsfähigkeit, *G* über Entzug von Privilegien; **enabling** ~ → *enabling*; **expositry** ~ Erläuterungs*g*; **gener-**

al ~ allgemeines *G*; **immunity** ~ Immunitäts*g*; **local** ~ örtlich beschränkte *G–e*, Orts*g–e*; Ortsstatuten; **mandatory** ~ zwingendes *G*; **negative** ~ Verbots*g*; **penal** ~ Straf*g*, Strafbestimmung; **No Fault S~s** Regreßgesetze gegen Versicherungen; **perpetual** ~ zeitlich unbeschränktes *G*; **personal** ~ Personalstatut, auf bestimmte Personen bezogenes *G*; **private** ~ Spezial*g*, auf bestimmte Personen bezogenes *G*, personenrechtliche Norm; **public** ~ allgemeines *G*; **punitive** ~ Straf*g*, pönalisierendes *G*; **real** ~ Realstatut, sachenrechtliche Norm; **reference** ~ → *reference*; **regulatory** ~ Ausführungsbestimmungen; **remedial** ~ → *remedial*; **repeal of** ~ Aufhebung e–s Gesetzes (*bzw e–r Gesetzesvorschrift*); **Revised S~s** → *revised*; **special** ~ Sonder*g* (*auf bestimmte Personen bezogenes Gesetz*); **temporary** ~ befristetes Übergangs*g*; **validating** ~ Ratifizierungs*g*, Bereinigungs*g*; *G* zur Heilung von fehlerhaften Verwaltungsakten.

statutory gesetzlich (= *g*) *im Sinne des durch Gesetzgebungsorgane geschaffenen Rechts*, auf geschriebenem Recht beruhend, gesetzlich vorgeschrieben; ~ **alien** Ausländer britischer Geburt; ~ **authority** *g–e* Befugnis; ~ **bar** *g–er* Hinderungsgrund; ~ **body** öffentlich-rechtliche Anstalt, ö.-r. Körperschaft; ~ **bond** Schuldurkunde in *g–er* Form; ~ **books** → *book*; ~ **company** → *company*; ~ **construction** Vertragsauslegung durch innerstaatliches Gesetz; ~ **corporation** → *corporation*; ~ **crime** → *crime*; ~ **damages** Schadenersatz; ~ **declaration** → *declaration*; ~ **dedication** → *dedication*; ~ **defence** zulässige Einwendung; ~ **duty** *g–e* Verpflichtung; ~ **exposition** *g–e* Auslegung; ~ **factor's lien** → *lien*; ~ **forced share** *US* Pflichterbteil; ~ **foreclosure** → *foreclosure*; ~ **form** *g–e* Form; ~ **guardian** *g–er* Vormund; ~ **heir** *g–er* Erbe; ~ **holiday** *g–er* Feiertag; ~ **instrument** Rechtsverordnung, Ausführungsverordnung; ~ **interest** → *interest* (*2*); ~ **interpretation** *g–e* Auslegung (*von Gesetzen*); ~ **law** gesetztes Recht, Gesetzesrecht; ~ **language** Gesetzessprache, Gesetzeswortlaut; ~ **liability** *g–e* Haftung; ~ **lien** → *lien*; ~ **meeting** → *meeting*; ~ **obligation** *g–e* Verpflichtung; ~ **offences** *g–e* Straftatbestände; ~ **office** Amt, *g* vorgesehenes Amt; ~ **order** → *order* (*1*); ~ **owner** *g–er* Eigentümer; Treuhandseigentümer *bei Liegenschaftstreuhand für minderjährigen Nießbraucher bzw bei Wegfall des Nießbrauchers*; ~ **period** → *period*; ~ **portion** *g–er* Erbteil; ~ **power** → *power* (*1*); ~ **power of removal** gesetzl Abschiebungsbefugnis; ~ **provision** → *provision*; ~ **receipt** löschungsfähige Quittung; ~ **redundancy scheme** Arbeitslosenunterbringungsprojekt; ~ **regime (in ordinary)** *g–er* Güterstand; ~ **regulations** *g–e* Vorschriften; ~ **release** Auflassung in *g–er* Form; ~ **report** → *report*; ~ **requirements** *g–e* Voraussetzungen, *g–e* Vorschriften; ~ **reserves** *g–e* Rücklage; ~ **restriction** *g–e* Beschränkung; ~ **rules** Vorschriften durch Rechtsverordnung, *g–e* Vorschriften; ~ **rules and orders** Rechtsverordnungen; ~ **sales price** vorgeschriebener Preis, amtlicher Einzelhandelspreis; ~ **sick pay** Lohnausgleichszahlung im Krankheitsfall; ~ **staple** → *staple*; ~ **tenancy** → *tenancy*; ~ **tenant** → *tenant*; ~ **trust** → *trust*; ~ **undertaker** → *undertaker*; ~ **value** gesetzlich festgesetzter Wert.

stay *s* Aufenthalt *m*, Stütze *f*, Stillstand *m*, Aussetzung *f*, Vollstreckungsaufschub *m*; ~ **abroad** Auslandsaufenthalt; ~ **laws** Vollstreckungsschutzgesetze; ~ **of action** → *action*; ~ **of execution** → *execution*; ~ **of proceedings** Aussetzung des Verfahrens.

stay *v* sich aufhalten; die Zwangsvollstreckung vorläufig einstellen, Vollstreckungsaufschub gewähren; ~ **and trade** zu Handelszwecken verbleiben (*Seeschiffahrtspolice*).

staying access Dauerumgangsrecht *n* (*zu Kindern*).

steadiness Festigkeit *f*, Stabilität *f*.

steady fest, beständig, stabil, behauptet.

steal stehlen; ~ **into** sich einschleichen.

stealing Stehlen *n*, Diebstahl *m*; ~ **by finding** Fundunterschlagung; ~ **children** Kindesraub.

steaming Massenplündern *n*.

steel|cartell Stahlkartell; ~ **industry** Eisen- und Stahlindustrie; ~ **stock(s)** Montanaktien, Stahlaktien; ~ **using industry** stahlverarbeitende Industrie; ~ **vault** Stahlkammer.

steering Lenkung *f*; ~ **column** Lenksäule; ~ **committee** → *committee*; ~ **mechanism** Lenkvorrichtung; ~ **wheel** Lenkrad; **power-assisted** ~ Servolenkung.

steersman Lenker (*Kfz*), Steuermann.

stellionate betrügerische Handlung *f*, betrügerische Mehrfachveräußerung *f*.

stenographer Stenograf *m*; **court** ~ Protokollführer(in).

step Schritt *m*, Stufe *f*; ~ **in the proceedings** Verfahrensschritt, Prozeßhandlung; ~**-rate premium** = *natural premium* → *premium*; **appropriate** ~**s** geeignete Maßnahmen; **introductory** ~**s** einleitende Schritte; **inventive** ~ Erfindungsleistung, zusätzliche Erfindungshöhe.

step|child Stiefkind *n*; ~**-daughter** Stieftochter; ~**-father** Stiefvater; ~**-mother** Stiefmutter; ~**-parents** Stiefeltern; ~**-son** Stiefsohn.

sterilize unfruchtbar machen, sterilisieren.

sterling *adj* echt, zuverlässig.

sterling *s* Sterling *m*, Sterlingsilber *n* (0,925 Feingehalt); *obs*: gesetzliche Münze *f*, gesetzliches Silbergeld *n*; ~ **account** Konto in brit Währung; ~ **area** Sterlinggebiet; ~ **bloc** Sterlingblock; ~ **bonds** auf engl Pfund lautende Schuldverschreibungen; ~ **invoices** in engl Pfund zahlbare Rechnungen; **external** ~ brit Auslandsguthaben; **resident** ~ Währungsbestände von Bewohnern des Sterlingblocks.

stevedore *s* Schauermann *m* (*pl* Schauerleute), Güterpacker *m*, Stauer *m*, Schiffsbelader *m*, Schiffsentlader *m* (*als Unternehmer*).

stevedore *v* stauen, verladen, entladen.

steward Verwalter *m*; Versammlungsleiter *m*; ~ **of a manor** Gerichtsbeamter e-s Patronatsgerichtes; **S~ of all England** *hist* (=) *Vorsitzender bei Gerichten über Adlige*; **chief** ~ (Speisewagen)Oberkellner; **land** ~ → *land*; **shop** ~ → *shop*.

stewartry *scot* Grafschaft *f*.

stick befestigen, ankleben; ~ **to the text** sich genau an den Wortlaut halten.

sticker Aufklebezettel *m*; Ladenhüter *m*.

stick fast foil lid festklebender Foliendeckel *m*.

stickler beharrlicher Befürworter *m*, Verfechter *m*; *hist* Schiedsrichter *m*.

stick-up Überfall *m* mit Schußwaffe.

stiffen sich versteifen, fester werden (*Kurs*).

stifling | a prosecution entgeltliche Abrede, von der Strafverfolgung Abstand zu nehmen; ~ **of competition** Wettbewerbsbeschränkung.

still Brennerei *f*; **illicit** ~ Schwarzbrennerei.

still-not-in-force *adj* noch nicht in Kraft befindlich.

sting Polizeifalle *f*.

stint Begrenzung *f*, beschränkte Anzahl *f*; Aushilfstätigkeit *f*, zugewiesene Arbeit *f*; Schicht *f*; Tagewerk *n*; ~ **tickets** Weideberechtigungsscheine.

stipe = *stipendiary magistrate qv*.

stipend Besoldung *f*, Gehalt *f*, Pfarrergehalt *n*.

stipital nach Stämmen (Erbfolge); ~

distribution Nachlaßverteilung nach Stämmen.

stipulate ausbedingen, vereinbaren, festsetzen, verabreden, unstreitig stellen; ~ **by contract** vertraglich festlegen; ~ **for a reward** Belohnung vereinbaren; ~ **in writing** schriftlich vereinbaren.

stipulated vereinbart, ausbedungen; ~ **and conditioned** vereinbart (und als Bedingung festgelegt); ~ **by contract** vertraglich vereinbart; ~ **damages** → *damages*; ~ **premium** Vertragsprämie; ~ **quality** ausbedungene Qualität; **as** ~ wie vereinbart.

stipulation Vereinbarung *f*, Abmachung *f*, Vertragsbestimmung *f*, Bestimmung *f*, Klausel *f*, Kautionsstellung *f*, gegenseitige Parteiabrede *f*; ~ **as to time** Zeitbestimmung; ~ **of contract** Vertragsbedingung; V-sbestimmung; ~ **proceedings** Einigungsverfahren; ~ **to the contrary** gegenteilige Bestimmung; **by** ~ einverständlich; **contrary** ~ gegenteilige Vertragsbestimmung; **express** ~ ausdrückliche Bestimmung.

stipulator Vertragspartei *f*, Kontrahent *m*.

stock (*1*) Aktie (= *A bzw . . . a pl A–n bzw . . . a–n*) Grundkapital *n*, Gesellschaftskapital *n*, Stammkapital *n*, Anleihekapital *n*; Kapital *n*, Fonds *m*, Anleihepapier *n*, öffentliche Schuldverschreibung *f*; ~ **account** → *account* (*2*); ~ **appreciation right** Wertsteigerungsanspruch bei Aktien-Bezugsrechtsabfindung; ~ **arbitrage** Effektenarbitrage; ~ **assessment** *A–n*nachschußverpflichtung; ~ **association** *A–n*gesellschaft; ~ **book** *A–n*buch; ~**-broker** Broker *m*, Börsenhändler für fremde Rechnung; ~**-broker's bargain book** Schlußnotenbuch; ~**-broking** Maklergeschäft, Effektengeschäft; ~**-broking transaction** Börsenkommissionsgeschäft; ~ **buyback** *A–n*-Rückkauf; ~ **call** Aufruf der notierten Effekten, Terminkauf; ~ **capital** → *capital*; ~ **certificate** *A–n*urkunde, *A–n*zertifikat; ~ **carrying rights** mit Bezugsrechten ausgestattete *A–n*; ~ **clearing corporation** Abrechnungsstelle (*New Yorker Börsenhändler*); ~ **company** *A–n*gesellschaft; ~ **corporation** *A–n*gesellschaft; ~ **deals** *A–n*abschlüsse; ~ **department** Wertpapierabteilung, Effektenabteilung; ~ **dividend** → *dividend*; ~ **insurance companies** Versicherungsgesellschaften auf *A–n*; ~ **issue** *A–n*ausgabe; ~**-index futures** *A–n*index-Termingeschäfte; ~ **index number** Wertpapier-Kenn-Nummer; ~**-jobber** Börsenspekulant, Börsenhändler; ~ **jobbing** Wertpapierhandel, Spekulation; ~**-jobbing Act** (=) *brit Börsenspekulationsverbotsgesetz von 1733*; ~ **list** Kurszettel; ~ **market** → *stock market*; ~**-note** *A–n*empfangsbestätigung; ~ **option** *A–n*erwerbsoption (*bes für leitende Mitarbeiter*); *A–n*bezugsrecht; ~ **order** Effektenorder; ~ **pooling agreement** *A–n*pool-Vereinbarung; ~ **power** Vollmacht zum Verkauf von *A–n*; ~ **price** *A–n*kurs; ~ **purchase plan** Belegschafts*a–n*-Programm; ~ **purchase warrant** Berechtigungsschein, Optionsschein; ~ **receipt** (=) Quittung über *A–n*zertifikate *für die Bezahlung von Aktien als Berechtigungsnachweis*; ~ **register** *A–n*buch, Obligationsverzeichnis; ~ **registrar** (=) *Kontrollbeauftragter für Übertragungen von Namensaktien*; ~ **right** *A–n*bezugsrecht; ~ **split** *A–n*split, *A–n*zusammenlegung; ~ **ticker** Börsentelegraf, Börsenfernschreiber; ~ **transfer** *A–n*übertragung; ~ **transfer agent** Transferagent für *A–n*; ~ **transfer journal** *A–n*buch; ~ **transfer tax** Börsenumsatzsteuer; ~ **warrant** *brit A–n*bezugsrechtsschein, *A–n*zertifikat (*entspricht praktisch der Inhaberaktie*); **accumulative** ~ kumulative Vorzugs*a–n*; **active** ~ lebhaft gehandelte Effekten; **assented** ~ im Sammeldepot hinterlegte Effekten;

assessable ~ nachschußpflichtige *A–n*; **assigned** ~ Namens*a–n* mit Übertragungsvermerk; **authorized** ~ Grundkapital, Stammkapital, *pl* zum Börsenverkehr zugelassene Aktien; **bearer** ~ Inhaber*a–n*; **block of ~s** *A–n*paket; **blue-chip** ~ hochwertige *A–n*, absolut erstklassige *A–n*; **bonus** ~ → *bonus*; **callable** ~ kündbare Vorzugs*a–n*; **capital** ~ → *capital*; **certificate of** ~ →*stock certificate*; **classified** ~ *A–n* mehrerer Gattungen; **clearing-house** ~ börsenfähige *A–n*; **common** ~ Stamm*a–n*; **consent** ~ dividendenberechtigte Stamm*a–n*; **consolidated ~s** konsolidierte Schuldverschreibungen; **control** ~ beherrschendes *A–n*paket; **convertible** ~ Vorzugs*a* mit Umtauschberechtigung; **corporate ~s** Kapitalanteile, Effekten, *A–n*; **corporation ~s** *brit* kommunale Schuldverschreibungen; **cumulative** ~ kumulative Vorzugs*a–n*; **cumulative preferred** ~ kumulative Vorzugs*a–n*; **curb** ~ Freiverkehrswert; **dated** ~ Anleihen mit fester Laufzeit; **dead** ~ Verwaltungs*a–n*; **deferred** ~ Nachzugs*a–n*; **delinquent** ~ *A–n* in Einzahlungsverzug; **double liability** ~ in voller Höhe nachschußpflichtige *A–n*; **fancy ~(s)** unsichere Spekulationspapiere; **fictitious** ~ verwässerte *A–n*; **floating** ~ Spekulations*a–n*; **foreign** ~ Auslandswerte; **founders' ~s** Gründer*a–n*; **full** ~ *A–n* mit vollem Nennwert ($ *100*); **fully paid** ~ voll eingezahlte *A–n*; **fund** ~ *A–n*kapital, Stammkapital; **general** ~ Stamm*a–n*; Grundkapital; **gilt-edged** ~ mündelsichere Obligationen, Staatsanleihepapiere; **government ~s** → *government*; **growth** ~ Wachstums*a–n*; **guarantee(d)** ~ *A–n* mit Dividendengarantie; **half-~** *US* Fünfzig-Dollar-*A–n*; **industrial** ~ Industrie*a–n*; **inscribed** ~ Anleihestücke ohne Zertifikate; börsenmäßig gehandelte Buchwerte; **international** ~ an Auslandsbörsen zugelassene *A–n*; **joint** ~ → *joint*; **junior** ~ junge Emissionen; **letter** ~ *brieflich vinkulierte, nicht freiveräußerliche, nicht registrierte Kapitalanteile (Aktien)*; **listed** ~ notierte *A–n*, börsenfähige *A–n*; **management** ~ Verwaltungs*a–n*; **motor ~s** Automobil*a–n*; **no-par value** ~ Quoten*a–n*; nennwertlose *A–n*; **non-assented** ~ *A–n*, bei denen keine Zustimmung erteilt wurde (*die nicht im Sammeldepot verwahrt werden; bzw die nicht am Sanierungsumtausch teilnehmen*); **non assessable** ~ nicht nachschußpflichtige *A–n*; **non par** ~ Quoten*a–n*; **non-cumulative preferred** ~ Vorzugs*a–n* ohne Nachbezugrecht; **non-voting** ~ stimmrechtslose *A–n*; **option** ~ Prämienwerte; **ordinary** ~ Stamm*a–n*; **original** ~ Stammkapital, Stamm*a–n*; **outstanding** ~ ausgegebene (*und nicht zurückerworbene*) *A–n*; *A–n* im Publikumsbesitz; **over-the-counter** ~ nicht im Börsenhandel zugelassene *A–n*; **paid-up** ~ voll einbezahlte *A–n*; **par-value** ~ Nennwert*a–n*; **participating** ~ dividendeberechtigte *A–n*; **participating preferred** ~ partizipierende Vorzugs*a-n* (*Gewinnteilnahme nach Vorzugsdividende*); **partly paid** ~ nicht voll einbezahlte *A–n*; **penny** ~ Klein*a–n*, billige Spekulations*a–n*; **potential** ~ genehmigte (*noch nicht ausgegebene*) *A–n*; **preferred** ~ Vorzugs*a–n*; **premium** ~ zu e–m Agio ausgegebene *A–n*; **prior preference** ~ Vorzugs*a–n* mit primärer Dividendenberechtigung; **profit sharing** ~ *A–n* mit Gewinnbeteiligung; **promotional** ~ Gründer*a-n*; **public ~s** Staatsanleihen, Staatspapiere; Obligationen der öffentlichen Hand; **re-acquired** ~ zurückerworbene *A–n*, Verwaltungs*a–n*; **redeemable** ~ rückkaufbare Vorzugs*a–n*; **registered** ~ Namensanleihepapiere, *GB*; an der Börse zugelassene *A–n*, *US*; **restricted ~s** noch nicht zum Börsenhandel zugelassene *A–n*; **rubber**

~ Gummi*a-n*, Gummiwerte; **second preferred** ~ Vorzugs*a–n* zweiter Klasse; **special** ~ rückkaufbare Sonder*a–n* (*USA, Massachusetts*); **steel** ~ → *steel*; **treasury** ~ Verwaltungs*a–n*, zurückerworbene eigene *A–n*; **unified** ~ → *unified*; **unissued** ~ genehmigtes (*noch nicht begebenes*) Kapital; **unissued capital** ~ nicht ausgegebenes *A–n*kapital; **unlisted** ~ nicht an der Börse notierte Effekten; **unsubscribed** ~ nicht gezeichnete *A–n*; **unvalued** ~ nennwertlose *A–n*, Quoten*a–n*; **vetoing** ~ zur Sperrminorität (*Beschlußverhinderung*) ausreichender *A–n*besitz; **voting** ~ stimmberechtigte *A–n*; **voting capital** ~ stimmberechtigtes *A–n*kapital; **watered** ~ verwässertes *A–n*kapital; unseriöse *A–n*; **widely held** ~ Streubesitz (*von A–n*); **without par value** ~ nennwertlose *A–n*, Quoten*a–n*.

stock (*2*) Vorrat *m*, Lagerbestand *m*; Bestand *m*, Warenbestand *m*; Inventar *n*, Vieh *n*; ~ **account** → *account* (*2*); ~ **book** Lagerbuch; Bestandsbuch; ~ **check** Bestandsaufnahme; ~ **control** Lagerwirtschaft, Inventursystem; ~ **in bank** Bankguthaben; ~ **in trade** Betriebsausstattung, Handwerkszeug, Warenbestand; ~ **of codified law** Bestand an kodifiziertem Recht; ~ **of goods** Warenlager; ~ **of merchandise** Warenbestand, Lager(bestand); ~ **on commission** Kommissionslager; ~ **on hand** Lagerbestand; ~ **out** nicht am Lager; ~ **pile** Vorräte, Vorratslager; ~ **purse** Gemeinschaftskasse; ~ **raising homesteads** Eigenhöfe mit Viehzucht; ~ **record card** Lagerbestandskarte; ~ **reduction** Lagerabbau; ~ **relief** Steuervergünstigung durch einstweilige Unterbewertung von Vorratsvermögen; ~ **sheet** Lagerliste, Bestandsliste; ~ **taking** Bestandsaufnahme, Inventur; **~-taking sale** Inventurausverkauf; ~ **turnover** Lagerumschlag, Warenumsatz; **base** ~ eiserner Bestand; **closing** ~ Schlußbestand; **consignment** ~ Konsignationslager; **dead** ~ totes Inventar, unverkäufliche Ware; **distributing** ~ Auslieferungslager; **farm** ~ → *farm*; **in** ~ auf Lager, vorrätig; **live** ~ lebendes Inventar, Vieh; **open** ~ Ware, die ständig auf Lager ist; **small** ~ Kleinvieh.

stock exchange Börse *f*, Wertpapierbörse *f*; ~ **account** Börsenbericht; ~ **broker** Börsenmakler; ~ **clearing house** Effektenberechnungsstelle; ~ **collateral** verpfändete (*börsenfähige*) Aktien; ~ **commitment** Börsenengagement; ~ **committee** Börsenausschuß, B.vorstand; ~ **hours** Börsenstunden; ~ **introduction** Börsenzulassung von Aktien; ~ **list** Kurszettel; ~ **loans** Lombardvorschüsse, kurzfristige Darlehen an Börsenmakler; ~ **operations** Börsengeschäfte; ~ **operator** Börsenspekulant; ~ **order** Börsenauftrag; ~ **parlance** Börsensprache; ~ **practices** Börsengepflogenheiten; ~ **price** Börsenkurs; ~ **procedure** Börsenverfahren; ~ **regulations** Börsenordnung; ~ **rules** Börsenvorschriften; ~ **securities** börsengängige Papiere, an der Börse gehandelte Effekten; ~ **settlement** Börsenabrechnung, Liquidation; ~ **tax** Börsenumsatzsteuer; ~ **transactions** Börsengeschäfte; **closing of the** ~ Börsenschluß; **listed on the** ~ börsengängig; **recognised** ~ amtliche Wertpapierbörse.

stockholder Aktionär *m*; **~'s derivative suit** Prozeßstandschaftsklage e–s Aktionärs; **~s' equity** Eigenkapital e–r Gesellschaft; **~s' ledger** Aktienbuch; **~s' liability** Nachschußhaftung von Aktionären; **~s' meeting** Hauptversammlung; ~ **of record** eingetragener Aktionär; **~s' representative action** Prozeßstandschaftsklage e–s Aktionärs (*zugleich für die übrigen Aktionäre*); **~s' suit** Prozeßstandschaftsklage e–s Aktionärs im Interesse der Gesellschaft.

stockholding Aktienbesitz *m*.

stockist Händler *m* mit eigenem Lager.

stock market (= *stockmarket*) Börse, Aktienmarkt; ~ **launch** Börsenpremiere, Emission; ~ **watchdog agency** Börsenaufsichtsamt.

stockmaster Börsenkursregistriergerät.

stockpiling Bevorratung *f*, Lagerbildung *f*; ~ **policy** Vorratspolitik.

stocks *hist* Stock *m*, Fußblock *m*.

stolidity Teilnahmslosigkeit *f* (*eines Tatverdächtigen*).

stonewall *v* nicht reagieren; Obstruktionspolitik betreiben; ~**ing performance** Sichausschweigen *n*.

stooge Handlanger *m*, Helfershelfer *m*, willenloses Werkzeug *n*, Vertrauensmann *m* der Polizei.

stool Lockspitzel *m*.

stool pigeon Lockspitzel *m*.

stop *s* Stopp *m*, Halt *m*, Hemmung *f*, Stillstand *m*; ~ **and search powers** Anhalte- und Durchsuchungsbefugnis; ~**day** Schlußtermin; Stichtag; ~**-gap** Lückenbüßer, Notmaßnahme; ~**-gap loan** Überbrückungskredit; Schecksperrung; ~ **loss order** → *order (2)*; ~ **notice** Veräußerungsverbot (*bei Insolvenz*), Einstellungsverfügung, Unterlassungsverfügung; ~ **order** → *order (1) und (2)*; ~ **payment** Zahlungssperre; ~ **press** letzte Nachrichten; ~ **price** Stopppreis.

stop *v* stoppen, sperren, anhalten; ~ **a quotation** e–e Kursnotierung aussetzen; ~ **an account** ein Konto sperren; ~ **business** den Betrieb einstellen; ~ **payments** die Zahlungen einstellen; ~ **the proceedings** das Verfahren einstellen.

stoppage Hemmung *f*, Stockung *f*, Sperre *f*, Aufrechnung *f*; ~ **in payment** Sperrung e–s Schecks, Zahlungseinstellung e–r Bank; ~ **in transitu** Anhaltsrecht, Rückrufsrecht, Verfolgungsrecht (*unbezahlter Unterwegsware*); ~ **of business** Betriebseinstellung, Geschäftsstillstand; ~ **of credit** Kreditsperre; ~ **of leave** Urlaubssperre; ~ **of work** Arbeitseinstellung.

storage Lagergeld *n*, Lagerung *f*; ~ **audit** → *audit*; ~ **business** Lagergeschäft; ~ **charge** Lagergebühr, Aufbewahrungsgebühr; ~ **credit** → *credit* (*2*); ~ **door delivery** Ablieferung beim Empfänger; ~ **expenses** Lagerkosten; ~ **loss** Lagerschwund; **dead** ~ zwischenzeitlich nicht zugängliche Einlagerung; **live** ~ jederzeit zugängliche Einlagerung, PKW-Einstellung zur tägl Benutzung.

store Vorrat *m*, Magazin *n*, Speicher *m*, Laden *m*, Geschäft *n*; *pl*; Proviantmagazin *n*, Schiffsvorräte *m*|*pl*; ~ **account** Lagerkonto, Lagerrechnung; ~**s accounting** Lagerbuchhaltung; ~ **book** Lagerbuch, Bestandsbuch; ~ **business** Lagerhaltung; ~ **charges** Lagergebühren, Lagergeld, Lagerkosten; ~ **ledger** Lagerbuch; ~ **of value** Wertaufbewahrungsmittel; ~ **order act** Lohnbarzahlungsgesetz; ~ **rental** Ladenmiete; ~**s requisitions** Materialanforderungen; ~**s shares** Warenhausaktien; **chain** ~ Filialgeschäft, Einzelhandelsgeschäft e–r Kette; **department** ~ Warenhaus, Kaufhaus; **marine** ~**s** → *marine*; **multiple** ~ Supermarkt; **public** ~ staatliches Magazin.

storehouse Lagerhaus *n*, Speicher *m*.

storekeeper Ladenbesitzer *m*, Lagerhalter, Lagerverwalter *m*, Magazinverwalter *m*; ~**'s burglary policy** Geschäftsraum-Einbruchsversicherung.

storeroom Vorratskammer *f*; Lagerraum *m*.

storing conditions Lagerbedingungen *f*|*pl*.

Stormont *das Parlament von Nordirland*.

stowage Verstauung *f*, Stauerlohn *m*, Lagergebühr *f*; Laderaum *m*, Ladung *f*; ~ **certificate** Stauattest; **improper** ~ fehlerhafte Verladung.

stowaway blinder Passagier *m*.

straddle Stellagegeschäft *n*, Stellgeschäft *n*; kombiniertes Vor- und Rückprämiengeschäft *n*.

straddling the market gleichzeitiger Haussekauf *m* und Baisseverkauf *m* von Effekten auf Termin.
straggler Bummler *m*, Versprengter *m*, vorschriftswidrig abwesender Matrose *m*.
straight gerade, unmittelbar, reell, ehrlich, ohne Rabatt, zum Nettopreis; ~ **bill of lading** → *bill of lading*; ~ **commission** vorbehaltlose Provision; ~ **dealings** korrektes Geschäftsgebaren; ~ **life insurance** → *life insurance*; ~ **line depreciation** lineare Abschreibung; ~ **line method** → *method*; ~ **loan** → *loan*; ~ **shipment** Versand an bestimmten Empfänger (*nicht an Order*); ~ **ticket** → *ticket*.
strain Spannung *f*, Anspannung *f*, Beanspruchung *f*; ~ **on credit** Kreditanspannung, Kreditbeanspruchung; ~**s on liquidity** Liquiditätsanspannung; **monetary** ~ Anspannung des Geldmarktes.
straitjacket Zwangsjacke *f*.
Straits Convention Meerengenabkommen (*1841*).
stranger Dritter *m*, Außenstehender *m*, Fremder *m*, Ausländer *m*; ~**s' gallery** → *gallery*; ~ **in blood** nicht blutsverwandte Person; **I spy** ~**s** *parl* ich beantrage den Ausschluß der Öffentlichkeit.
strangle strangulieren, erdrosseln, erwürgen; ~ **a bill** e–e Gesetzesvorlage abwürgen.
stranglehold Würgegriff *m*.
strangulation Strangulation *f*, Erdrosselung *f*, Erwürgung *f*.
strapped in höchsten Nöten, ohne e–n Pfenning.
strata | **estate** Wohnungseigentum; ~ **plan** Aufteilungsplan; ~ **title** Stockwerkseigentum.
stratocracy Militärregierung *f*, Militärstaat *m*.
stratum (*pl strata*) Schicht *f*; Stockwerkseigentum *n*; Wohnungseigentum *n*; Eigentumswohnung *f*.
straw | **bail** → *bail*; ~ **bid** Scheingebot; ~ **bond** → *bond* (*2*); ~ **boss** Kapo, Vorarbeiter; ~ **man** Strohmann; ~ **name** Proforma-Indossament; ~ **party** Strohmann; ~ **vote** Probeabstimmung.
stray verirrtes bzw streunendes Tier; herrenloses Gut *n*.
stream Fluß *m*, Wasserlauf *m*; **private** ~ Privatfluß.
street Straße *f*, Ortsstraße *f*; öffentl Verkehrsfläche *f*; ~ **accident** Verkehrsunfall; ~ **betting** Wetten auf offener Straße; ~ **brawl** Straßenauflauf; ~ **broker** freier Makler; ~ **certificate** blankoindossiertes Aktienzertifikat; ~ **collection** Straßensammlung; ~ **crime** Verbrechen auf offener Straße; ~ **hawker** ambulanter Händler; ~ **improvement bonds** kommunale Schuldverschreibungen zur Straßenbaufinanzierung; ~ **loan** → *loan*; ~ **market** Nachbörse, Freiverkehrsmarkt; ~ **market price** Freiverkehrskurs; ~ **name** Wertpapierkauf im Namen des Effektenhändlers; ~ **offences** Straftaten und Ordnungswidrigkeiten auf öffentlichen Straßen; ~ **paper** → *paper*; ~ **parking** → *parking*; ~ **performances** Straßendarbietungen, ~ **playgrounds** Spielstraßen; ~ **prices** nachbörsliche Kurse, Freiverkehrskurs; ~ **trader** Straßenhändler; ~ **trading** Straßenhandel; ~ **walker** Prostituierte, Straßenmädchen; ~ **walking** Prostitution; ~ **works** Straßenarbeiten, Straßenbau; **arterial** ~ städtische Hauptstraße; **favoured** ~ Vorfahrtsstraße; **in the** ~ nach Börsenschluß; **one-way** ~ Einbahnstraße; **potholed** ~ mit Schlaglöchern übersäte Straße; **two-way** ~ Straße mit Gegenverkehr.
strength *s* Kraft *f*, Stärke *f*; Festigkeit *f*, stetiges Anwachsen *n*; ~ **of an argument** Überzeugungskraft e–s Arguments; ~ **of judgment** Urteilsfähigkeit; ~ **of memory** Gedächtniskraft; **actual** ~ Iststärke; **competitive** ~ Wettbewerbsfähigkeit; **economic** ~ Wirtschaftskraft; **required** ~ Sollstärke; **the** ~ **of testimony** die Beweiskraft e–r Aussage.

strengthen *v* verstärken, festigen, sich festigen; ~**ing** Verstärkung, Festigung.

stress *s* Betonung *f*, Nachdruck *m*; Druck *m*; ~ **of competition** Wettbewerbsdruck.

stretch *s* Strecke *f*, Zeitraum *m*; Strafe *f*, Strafzeit *f*; ~**-out** vermehrte Arbeit ohne entsprechende Bezahlung.

stretch *v* überspannen, überschreiten, ausdehnen, hängen; aufgehängt werden; ~ **a rule** e–e Vorschrift zu weit auslegen; ~ **one's credit** seinen Kredit übermäßig in Anspruch nehmen; ~ **the law (in s.o.'s favour)** es mit dem Recht (zu jmds Gunsten) nicht genau nehmen.

strict streng, genau; ~ **inquiry and search** umfassende und nachhaltige Nachforschung; ~ **line of duty** unmittelbarer Pflichtenkreis; ~ **ministerial duty** strenge Amtspflicht (*ohne Ermessensspielraum*).

strike *s* Streik *m* (= *Str bzw ... str*), Ausstand *m*; ~**-benefits** *Str*gelder; ~ **bound** bestreikt, vom *Str* betroffen; ~ **breaker** *Str*brecher; ~ **committee** *Str*ausschuß; ~ **fund** → *fund*; ~ **notice** *Str*ankündigung; ~ **order** *Str*befehl; ~ **pay** *Str*gelder; ~ **picket** *Str*posten; ~ **prone** *str*anfällig; ~ **target** *Str*ziel; ~ **threat** *Str*drohung; ~ **vote** Urabstimmung; **coal** ~ Kohlenbergarbeiter*str*; **defensive** ~ Abwehr*str*; **flash** ~ wilder *Str*; **freedom of** ~ *Str*recht; **general** ~ General*str*; **go slow** ~ Dienst nach Vorschrift; **guerrilla** ~ Überraschungs*str*, wilder *Str*; **hunger** ~ Hunger*str*; **illegal** ~ widerrechtlicher *Str*, wilder *Str*; **jurisdictional** ~ Zuständigkeits*str*, *Str* wegen Abgrenzungskämpfen zwischen Gewerkschaften; **negative** ~ Defensiv*str*; **official** ~ offizieller *Str*, gewerkschaftlich organisierter *Str*; **outlaw** ~ wilder *Str*; **pin-point** ~ Schwerpunkt*str*; **positive** ~ Angriffs*str*; **quickie** ~ unangekündigter *Str*, wilder *Str*; **rail** ~ Eisenbahner*str*; **rolling** ~ *Str* mit wechselnden Schwerpunkten; **secondary** ~ mittelbarer Boykott*str*; **sitdown** ~ Sitz*str*; **slowdown** ~ Bummel*str*; **stay-in** ~ mehrtägiger Sitz*str*; **sympathy** ~ Sympathie*str*; **token** ~ symbolischer *Str*; **wildcat** ~ wilder *Str*; **warning** ~ Warn*str*.

strike *v* schlagen, treffen; streichen; ~ **a balance** Saldo ziehen, Konto abschließen, Bilanz ziehen; ~ **a bargain** Vertrag abschließen, handelseinig werden; ~ **an average** den Durchschnitt nehmen; ~ **broadside** auf die Fahrzeugmitte aufprallen; ~ **off** zuschlagen, den Zuschlag erteilen; e–n Fall absetzen; die Zulassung entziehen; ~ **off the register** im Register löschen; ~ **off 3%** 3% abziehen, e–n Abzug von 3% machen; ~ **oil** auf Öl stoßen; ~ **one's colours** seine Flagge streichen; ~ **words not applicable** nicht Zutreffendes streichen.

striking|a docket Konkursanmeldung; ~ **off the roll(s)** Löschung in e–r Berufsliste (*Ärzteschaft usw*); Entziehung der Zulassung; ~ **out a defendant** Verweisung e–s Beklagten aus dem Prozeß (*Zwischenurteil*); ~ **out a defense** Zurückweisung eines Verteidigungsvorbringens *als unzulässig*; ~ **out a plaintiff** Verweisung e–s Klägers aus dem Prozeß (*mangels Prozeßführungsbefugnis*); ~ **out a pleading** *Unzulässigerklärung (e–s Teils) des schriftsätzlichen Vortrags*; ~ **out indorsement** Streichung des Indossaments (*durch den honorierenden Indossatar, erneutes Wechselgiro mögl*); ~ **price** Optionskurs; ~ **the action out** die Ungültigkeit des Verfahrens feststellen; die Klage für unzulässig erklären.

strike off Zulassungsentzug *m*.

strike suit *Prozeßstandschaftsklage e–s Aktionärs zum eigenen Vorteil*.

stringency Knappheit *f*, Strenge *f*, zwingende Kraft *f*; **credit** ~ → *credit (2)*.

stringent knapp, hart, streng, bindend, zwingend; ~ **form** strenge

Form; ~ **necessity** absolute Notwendigkeit.
strip abräumen, widerrechtlich entnehmen.
structural strukturell, baulich, Bau . . .; ~ **additions** Anbauten, Hinzugebautes; ~ **alteration or change** bauliche Änderung(en); ~ **crisis** Strukturkrise; ~ **damage** Gebäudesubstanzschaden; ~ **engineering** Bautechnik.
structure Beschaffenheit *f*, Aufbau *m*, Gefüge *n*, Anordnung *f*, Bau *m*, Konstruktion *f*, Gebäude *n*; ~ **or work** Bauwerk; ~ **plan** Flächennutzungsplan; **economic** ~ Wirtschaftsstruktur; **financial** ~ Kapitalstruktur; **price** ~ → *price* (*1*).
stub Kontrollabschnitt *m*, Talon *m*; Kapitalbeteiligungsoption; vorläufiges Aktienzertifikat.
student letting Vermietung an Studenten.
study studieren, prüfen; ~ **law** Jura studieren.
stuff gown *brit* (*gewöhnliche*) Anwaltsrobe *f*, Prozeßanwalt *m* (*der noch kein Queen's Counsel ist*).
stultification Darstellung als lächerlich *bzw* absurd, Hinderung *f*, Blockierung *f*; ~ **of the very purpose of the company** Ad-absurdum-Führen des Sinns und Zwecks der Gesellschaft.
stultify *jmdn* als unzurechnungsfähig hinstellen; ad absurdum führen, lächerlich machen.
stumer (= *stumour*) gefälschter Scheck *m*, ungedeckter Scheck, gefälschte Münze *f* oder Banknote *f*.
stump *v* als Wahlredner bereisen.
stumpage Vergütung *f* für Holzfällerei.
stumper Wahlredner *m*.
stun gun elektrische Keule *f*.
stupration Notzucht *f*.
stuprum unerlaubter Geschlechtsverkehr *m*.
style *s* Stil *m*, Typ *m*; Art *f* und Weise *f*, Manier *f*, Titel *m*, Anrede *f*; Firmenbezeichnung *f*; Firmenname *m*, Fabrikzeichen *n*, Fabrikationsname *m*; ~ **of a company** Firmenname; ~ **of life** Lebenshaltungsniveau; **business** ~ Geschäftsstil; **judicial** ~ Kanzleistil; **new** ~ neue Zeitrechnung (*in GB ab 1752*); **under the** ~ **of** unter der Firma von.
style *v* nennen, betiteln; **to be ~d** firmieren, die Firma tragen.
styling (industrielle) Formgebung *f*.
stymie *v/t* blockieren, behindern.
suability Klagbarkeit *f*, Einklagbarkeit *f*.
suable klagbar, einklagbar.
suasion Überredung *f*.
subagency Untervollmacht *f*, Untervertretung *f*, Unteragentur *f*.
subagent Unterbevollmächtigter *m*, Unteragent *m*; Zwischenspediteur *m*.
subagreement Nebenabrede *f*.
subaltern untergeordnet, subaltern, untergeben.
subassembly Teilmontage *f*; Untergruppe *f*.
sub-bailee Unterverwahrer *m*, Erfüllungsgehilfe des Verwahrers.
sub-branch Zweigstelle *f*, Fachgruppe *f*.
sub-charge Unterverpfändung *f* e–s Grundpfandrechts.
subcharter *v* unterchartern, unterverfrachten.
sub-clause Absatz, Unterabschnitt.
subcontract *s* Nebenvertrag *m*, Untervertrag *m*, Subunternehmervertrag *m*, Nachunternehmervertrag *m*.
subcontract *v* an e–n Sub(Nach)unternehmer vergeben, untervergeben.
subcontractor Subunternehmer *m*, Nachunternehmer *m*, Unterlieferant *m*; **higher tier** ~ Hauptsubunternehmer.
subdivide unterteilen, aufteilen, stückeln.
subdivision Unterteilung *f*, Untergliederung *f*; parzelliertes Areal, Parzellierung; ~ **of shares** Aktienstückelung; ~ **plan** Aufteilungsplan; **governmental** ~ Behörde; **political** ~ Gebietskörperschaft, Verwaltungsgebiet.
subduct zurücknehmen.

subfolder Beiakte *f*.

subhastation *hist* Zwangsversteigerung *f*.

subheading Untertitel *m*, Tarifstelle *f* (*Zoll*).

subinfeudation Unterlehensgewährung *f*, Afterbelehnung *f*.

subitem Unterposten *m*; Buchstabe *m*; Ziffer *f* (*e–r Aufstellung bzw von Vertragsabschnitten*).

subjacent unterliegend.

subject *adj* untertan, unterworfen, abhängig von, vorbehaltlich, gemäß; ~ **as hereafter provided** gemäß nachstehenden Bedingungen; ~ **to a fee** gebührenpflichtig; ~ **to alterations** Änderungen vorbehalten; ~ **to appeal** rechtsmittelfähig; revisibel; ~ **to approval** genehmigungspflichtig; ~ **to authorization** genehmigungspflichtig; ~ **to average** unter der Bedingung der eigenen proportionalen Schadenstragung bei Unterversicherung; ~ **to call** täglich kündbar; ~ **to change without notice** freibleibend, Änderungen vorbehalten; ~ **to collection** Eingang vorbehalten (*E.v.*); ~ **to commission** provisionspflichtig; ~ **to confirmation** gültig nur bei Bestätigung; ~ **to contract** gültig nur bei förmlichem Vertragsabschluß; ~ **to control** im Beherrschungsbereich, weisungsunterworfen; ~ **to death duties** erbschaftssteuerpflichtig, Erbschaftssteuer vom Bedachten zu tragen; ~ **to duty thereon** insoweit anfallende Erbschaftssteuer vom Bedachten zu tragen; ~ **to equities** unter Aufrechterhaltung der persönlichen Einreden; ~ **to execution** pfändbar, vollstreckbar; ~ **to fluctuations** Schwankungen unterworfen; ~ **to (a) formal contract** gültig erst bei förmlichem Vertragsabschluß; ~ **to licence** lizenzpflichtig, genehmigungspflichtig; ~ **to modifications** → *modification*; ~ **to notice** kündbar; ~ **to planning permission** vorbehaltl e–r Bauerlaubnis; vorausgesetzt, daß ein Bebauungsplan erlassen wird; ~ **to prior sale** Zwischenverkauf vorbehalten; ~ **to redemption** tilgbar, kündbar; ~ **to shipment** falls diese Ware versandt wird; ~ **to survey** vorbehaltlich der Vermessung; ~ **to taxation** steuerpflichtig; ~ **to the terms of a lease** nur gültig, falls ein Pachtvertrag zustande kommt; ~ **to this** unter diesem Vorbehalt; ~ **to war clause** der Kriegsrisikoklausel unterworfen; **to be ~ to limitation** der Verjährung unterliegen; **to be ~ to the consent of** von der Zustimmung des ... abhängen; **to be ~ to the jurisdiction** der Gerichtsbarkeit unterworfen sein; **to be ~ to ratification** der Ratifikation bedürfen, erst bei Ratifizierung (Genehmigung) gültig sein.

subject *s* Subjekt *n*; Untertan *m*, Staatsangehöriger *m*; Gegenstand *m*, der Betreffende, Betroffener *m*; Anlaß *m*, Ursache *f*; *scot* Vertragsgegenstand *m*, Vermögen *n*, Grundbesitz *m*; ~ **catalogue** Sachkatalog; ~ **index** Sachverzeichnis, Sachregister; ~ **of international law** Völkerrechtssubjekt; ~ **of litigation** Streitgegenstand; ~ **of rights and duties** Träger von Rechten und Pflichten; ~ **of records** Aktenvorgang; **British** ~ → *British*; **denizen** ~ Staatsangehöriger kraft Einbürgerung; **foreign** ~ Ausländer, ausländische Staatsangehörige; **legal** ~ Rechtssubjekt; **natural-born** ~ Staatsangehöriger kraft Geburt (*im britischen Hoheitsgebiet geboren*); **to be a ~ of law** Rechtspersönlichkeit haben.

subject-matter Gegenstand, Streitgegenstand, Hauptinhalt; ~ **insured** versicherter Gegenstand, Versicherungsgegenstand; ~ **of an agreement** Inhalt e–r Vereinbarung; ~ **of complaint** Beschwerdepunkt; ~ **of gift** zugewendeter Gegenstand; ~ **of invention** Erfindungsgegenstand; ~ **of the action** Streitgegenstand, Prozeßergebnis; ~ **of the contract** Vertragsgegenstand; ~ **of the disposition** Gegenstand der Verfügung.

subject specialist Sachbearbeiter *m*, Referent *m*.

subjection Unterworfensein *n*, Unterordnung *f*.

subjective subjektiv, persönlich, individuell, unsachlich.

subjoin beifügen, hinzusetzen.

subjoinder Beifügung *f*, Zusatz *m*.

subjudice rechtshängig; ~ **rule** Verbot der Vorverurteilung durch die Medien, Rechtshängigkeit.

sublease Unterpacht *f*, Untermiete *f* (*von Grundstücken*).

sublessee Untermieter *m*, Unterpächter *m*.

sublessor Untervermieter *m*, Unterverpächter *m*.

sub-let untervermieten, abvermieten; weitervergeben (*Auftrag*).

sub-letting Untervermietung *f*.

sub-licence (*–se, US*) Unterlizenz *f*.

sub-licensee Unterlizenznehmer *m*.

sub-licensor Unterlizenzgeber *m*.

submarginal nicht mehr rentabel.

submission Unterwerfung *f*, Duldung *f*, Kompromiß *m*; Vortrag *m*, Vorlage *f*, Antrag *m*; ~ **bond** → *bond* (*2*); ~ **of account** Rechnungsvorlage; ~ **of evidence** Beweisantritt, Vorlage von Beweismaterial; ~ **that there is no case to answer** Einwendung, daß die Klage (*bzw. Anklage*) nicht schlüssig sei; ~ **to arbitration** → *arbitration* (*1*); **alternative** ~ Hilfsvorbringen; **final** ~**(s)** Schlußplädoyer; **spurious** ~**s** unseriöser Vortrag.

submit (*bei Gericht*) vortragen, unterwerfen, überlassen, zur Entscheidung stellen, vorlegen, beantragen; ~ **a proposition** e–n Gesichtspunkt vortragen; ~ **for approval** zur Genehmigung vorlegen; ~ **for signature** zur Unterschrift vorlegen.

submittal Sach- und Rechtsvortrag *m*.

submitter Antragsteller(in).

sub modo unter der Bedingung, mit der Einschränkung, mit der Maßgabe, daß ...

sub-mortgage Unterverpfändung *f* e–r Grundschuld, nachrangige Grundschuld.

sub-mortgage *v* unterverpfänden, eine nachrangige Hypothek (*bzw* Grundschuld) bestellen.

subnormality geistige Behinderung *f*, Schwachsinn *m*.

subnotations königliche Rechtsbemerkungen *f/pl*.

suboffice Nebenstelle *f*, Zweigstelle *f*.

subordinate *adj* untergeordnet, Unter ..., Neben ...

subordinate *s* Untergebener *m*.

subordination Unterordnung *f*.

suborn verleiten, zur falschen Aussage verleiten, anstiften; ~ **witnesses** Zeugen zum Meineid verleiten.

subornation Verleitung zu e–r Straftat; ~ **of perjury** Verleitung zum Meineid.

suborner Anstifter *m*, Verleiter *m* zum Meineid.

subparagraph Absatz *m*, Unterabschnitt *m*.

subparticipation Unterbeteiligung *f*.

subpoena Zwangsvorladung *f*, förmliche Ladung (*vor Gericht, unter Strafandrohung*); ~ **ad testificandum** förmliche Zeugenladung *f*; ~ **duces tecum** Ladung mit Auflage, Urkunden mitzubringen; ~ **of witness** förmliche Zeugenladung (*mit Zwangsandrohung*); ~ **office** Ladungskanzlei; **administrative** ~ behördliche Vorladung; **witness under** ~ förmlich geladener Zeuge; **writ of** ~ → *writ*.

sub-post-office Posthilfestelle *f*, Postagentur *f*.

subpurchaser nachfolgender Käufer *m*, Abnehmer *m* des Käufers.

subreption Erschleichung *f* e–r Kirchenpfründe.

subrogate übergehen auf, in die Rechte einsetzen, Rechte übergehen lassen auf; **s.o. is** ~**d to a claim** ein Anspruch ist auf jemanden übergegangen.

subrogation Rechtsübergang *m*, Forderungsübergang *m*, Eintritt in die Gläubigerstellung; Sonderrechtsnachfolge *f*; ~ **by operation of law** = *legal* ~ *qv*; ~ **clause** → clause; ~ **of rights** Rechtseintritt; **conventional** ~ gewillkürte Sonderrechtsnachfolge, Abtretung, vertraglicher Forderungsübergang; ~~ *receipt: Bestätigung des Forderungsübergangs (seitens des Empfängers)*; **legal** ~ gesetzlicher Forderungsübergang, Regreß, Rückgriff, Durchgriff.

subrogee Sonderrechtsnachfolger *m*.

sub rosa geheim, streng vertraulich.

subscribe zeichnen, unterschreiben, abonnieren, beitragen, beisteuern; ~ **for a loan** e–e Anleihe zeichnen; ~ **in excess** überzeichnen; ~ **to shares** Aktien zeichnen; ~**d capital** → *capital*; ~**d demand tariff** → *tariff*; ~**d risk** übernommene Gefahr; **amount** ~**d** Zeichungsbetrag.

subscriber Unterzeichner *m*, Zeichner *m*, Abonnent *m*, Fernsprechteilnehmer *m*; ~**'s contract** Teilnehmerverhältnis (Telefon); ~**s' insurance** Abonnentenversicherung; ~**s' number** Fernsprechnummer; ~ **ticket** Abonnementkarte, Dauerkarte; **list of** ~**s** Zeichnungsliste; **original** ~ Zeichner, Ersterwerber, Gründer (*e–r Kapitalgesellschaft*).

subscription Unterzeichnung *f*, Unterschrift *f*, Zeichnung *f*, Subskription *f*, Mitgliedsbeitrag *m*; ~ **agent** Abonnentenwerber; ~ **contract** Abonnementsvertrag; ~ **fee** Abonnementspreis, Bezugsgebühr; ~ **form** Bestellschein; ~ **in kind** Sachgründung; ~ **library** Mietbücherei, Leihbibliothek; ~ **list** Zeichnungsliste; ~ **list price** Subskriptionspreis, Vorbestellpreis; **offer** Zeichnungsangebot; ~ **period** Zeichnungsfrist; ~ **privilege** Bezugsrecht; ~ **rental** Grundgebühr; ~ **right** Bezugsrecht; ~ **shares** Anteilszeichnung auf Raten, die nach Ratenplan gezeichneten Anteile (*Baugenossenschaft*); ~ **warrant** Optionsschein; **annual** ~ Jahresabonnement; **capital stock** ~ Aktienzeichnung, Zeichnung von Kapitalanteilen; **initial** ~ Erstzeichnung; **minimum** ~ Mindestzeichnung, Mindestbarertrag e–r Wertpapieremission; **terms of** ~ → term; **to invite** ~**s** zur Zeichnung auflegen.

subsection Absatz *m*, Unterabschnitt *m*.

subsequent nachträglich, nachfolgend, später, rangjünger, Nach . . .

subservience Dienstbarkeit *f*; untergeordnete Stellung *f*, Unterwürfigkeit *f*.

subshare Unterbeteiligung *f*.

subsidiary Tochtergesellschaft *f*; **majority-owned** ~ im (Aktien) Mehrheitsbesitz stehende Tochtergesellschaft; **participating** ~**ies** (*am Vertrag*) teilnehmende Tochtergesellschaften; **wholly-owned** ~ 100%ige Tochtergesellschaft.

subsidiary subsidiär, dienend; ~ **account** Nebenkonto, Hilfskonto; ~ **activity** Nebentätigkeit; ~ **agreement** Nebenabrede; ~ **contract** Nebenvertrag, Untervertrag; ~ **establishment** Nebenbetrieb, Niederlassung; ~ **law** subsidiär geltendes Recht; ~ **organs** nachgeordnete Organe.

subsidizable bezuschußbar, subventionsfähig.

subsidize subventionieren; ~**d lunch** verbilligtes Mittagessen.

subsidy Beihilfe *f*, Zuschuß *m*, Subvention *f*; ~ **on exports** Exportsubvention; **agricultural** ~ Agrarsubvention; **basic residual** ~ Wohnungsbaubeihilfe; **governmental** ~ Staatszuschuß; **operating** Betriebszuschuß.

subsist unterhalten, sich ernähren, weiterbestehen, noch bestehen; ~ **in the person** an die Person gebunden sein; ~**ing bill** gültiger (*noch nicht eingelöster*) Wechsel.

subsistence Unterhalt *m*, Auskommen *n*; Aufenthaltskosten (*geschäftlich*); ~ **allowance** Unterhaltszuschuß; ~ **costs** Übernachtungs- und Verpflegungskosten (*Tage-*

geld); ~ **economy** Wirtschaft am Rande des Existenzminimums; ~ **expenses** Lebenshaltungskosten; ~ **farm** Kleinbauernhof, bäuerlicher Familienbetrieb; ~ **level** Existenzminimum; ~ **theory** ehernes Lohngesetz; ~ **wage** (*zur bescheidenen Lebenshaltung erforderlicher*) Mindestlohn; **means of** ~ → *means*; **minimum of** ~ Existenzminimum; **reasonable** ~ angemessener Unterhalt; **support and** ~ öffentliche Unterstützung.

substance Substanz *f*, Stoff *m*, (wesentlicher) Inhalt *m*; ~ **of the action** wesentlicher Inhalt der Klage, Gegenstand der Klage; **defect in** ~ → *defect*; **foreign** ~ körperfremder Stoff; **man of** ~ vermögender Mann; **matter of** ~ materiellrechtliche Frage; **subsisting** ~**s** Rückstände.

substandard unter der Norm liegend; normunterschreitend, unter der gesetzlichen Mindestqualität liegend; nicht vollwertig.

substantial erheblich, wesentlich, wertvoll, von Wert; ~ **compliance** Einhaltung in allen wesentlichen Punkten; ~ **compliance rule** (=) *Grundsatz, daß es genügt, wenn der Versicherungsnehmer alles zur Änderung der Begünstigung Erforderliche unternommen hat*; ~ **damages** → *damages;* ~ **equivalence of patented device** praktisch gleiche Wirkung und gleicher Wert mehrerer patentierter Erfindungen.

substantiate begründen, nachweisen, substantiieren, festigen; ~ **a claim** e–n Anspruch substantiieren; ~ **an action** e–e Klage substantiieren.

substantiation nähere Begründung *f*, Substantiierung *f*.

substantive wesentlich, materiellrechtlich, vollendet; abgeschlossen; ~ **and permanent employment** Dauerstellung.

substitute *s* Substitut *m*, Stellvertreter *m*, Vertreter *m*, Bevollmächtigter *m*, *scot* Ersatzerbe *m*; Unterprozeßbevollmächtigter *m*; ~ **to a legatee** Ersatzvermächtnisnehmer; **beware of** ~**s** vor Nachahmungen wird gewarnt; **money** ~ → *money*.

substitute *v* ersetzen, an die Stelle setzen; ~ **an heir** e–n Ersatzerben bestellen; ~**d contract** neuer Vertrag, Novationsvertrag; ~**d executor** Ersatztestamentsvollstrekker; ~**d expenses** *ins* stellvertretende Kosten (*bei Havarie grosse*); ~**d heir** Ersatzerbe; ~**d penalty** → *penalty*; ~**d security** Ersatzsicherheit; ~**d service** → *service*.

substitute performance Ersatzvornahme *f*.

substitution Substituierung *f*, Stellvertretung *f*, Vertretung *f*, Ersetzung *f*, Einsetzung *f* e–s Nacherben, Eintritt des Ersatzfalls; Bestimmung *f* e–s Ersatzvermächtnisnehmers; ~ **of an heir** Einsetzung e–s Ersatzerben; ~ **of child** Kindesunterschiebung; ~ **of debt** Novation, Schuldauswechslung; ~ **of invoices** Rechnungsaustausch; ~ **of parties** Parteiwechsel.

substitutional *adj* ersetzend, stellvertretend, ersatzweise; Ersatz . . .

substitutionary *adj* = *substitutional qv*.

substitutionary *s* Ersatzerbe *m*, Ersatzvermächtnisnehmer *m*.

substitutive limitation Ersatznacherbfolge.

substraction Abzug *m*.

substratum Grundlage *f*, Basis *f*, Geschäftsgrundlage *f*.

subsumption Subsumption *f*; *scot* Tatbestandsangabe *f* in der Anklageschrift.

subtenant (= *sub-tenant*) Untermieter *m*, Unterpächter *m*.

subtippee *jmd, der indirekt e–n Börsentip erhält*.

subtotal Teilsumme *f*; ~ **carried forward** Übertrag.

subtraction Unterschlagung *f*, Nachlaßveruntreuung *f*; ~ **of conjugal rights** unberechtigte Verweigerung der ehelichen Pflichten.

sub-trust Untertreuhand *f*.

sub-underwriter Unterversicherer Subemittent, Unterkonsorte *m*.

sub-underwriting Übernahme *f* e–r Versicherung als Unterversicherer; ~ **agreement** Subemissionsvertrag.

subvention Subvention *f*, staatlicher Zuschuß *m*.

subversion Unterwühlung *f*, Unterwanderung *f*, Umsturz *m*.

subversive movement staatsgefährdende Bewegung *f*.

subvert untergraben, unterwühlen, stürzen.

succeed Erfolg haben, obsiegen, nachfolgen; ~ **to an estate** e–e Erbschaft machen, beerben; **entitled to** ~ zur Erbfolge berufen.

successful erfolgreich; ~ **party** obsiegende Partei.

succession Rechtsnachfolge *f*, Erbfolge *f*, Intestatserbfolge *f*; Sukzession *f*, Erblinie *f*; Nachlaß; Reihenfolge *f*; ~ **ab intestato** Intestatserbfolge, gesetzl. Erbfolge; ~ **by inheritance** Erbfolge; ~ **by testament** testamentarische Erbfolge; ~ **duty** Erbschaftssteuer; ~ **in title** Rechtsnachfolge; ~ **in office** Nachfolge im Amt; ~ **of crops** Fruchtwechsel; ~ **of states** Staatensukzession, Staatennachfolge; ~ **on intestacy** Intestatserbfolge, gesetzliche Erbfolge; ~ **per stirpes** Erbfolge nach Stämmen; ~ **tax** → *tax*; **artificial** ~ theoretische Dauerexistenz *e–r juristischen Person*, Konstanz der Rechtspersönlichkeit; **escheated** ~ Heimfallrechtsnachfolge, Erbfolge an den Staat; **general** ~ Gesamtrechtsnachfolge; **hereditary** ~ Erbfolge, Beerbung; **in** ~ **to** als Nachfolger von; **intestate** ~ Intestatserbfolge, gesetzliche Erbfolge; **irregular** ~ gesetzliche Ersatzerbfolge; **legal** ~ gesetzliche Erbfolge, Rechtsnachfolge; **lineal** ~ Erbfolge in gerader Linie; **natural** ~ Erbfolge (*zwischen natürlichen Personen*); gesetzliche Erbfolge; **negative** ~ Staatennachfolge ohne Übernahme der Verbindlichkeiten des Vorgängers; **new** ~ neue unabhängige Kette von Rechtsnachfolgern; **perpetual** ~ ununterbrochene Rechtsfähigkeit (*e–r jur Person*); **reversionary** ~ Nacherbfolge; **right of** ~ → *right*; **singular** ~ Einzelrechtsnachfolge; **testamentary** ~ testamentarische Erbfolge; **testate** ~ testamentarische Erbfolge; **universal** ~ Gesamtrechtsnachfolge, Universalsukzession; **vacant** ~ erbenloser Nachlaß.

successive nachfolgend, sukzessiv; ~**ly** nach und nach, nacheinander.

successor Rechtsnachfolger *m*, Amtsnachfolger *m*, Erbe *m*; ~ **in business** Nachfolgefirma, Firmennachfolger; ~ **in interest** Rechtsnachfolger, wirtschaftlicher Nachfolger, Unternehmensfortführer bei Identität der Gesellschaft; ~ **in title** Rechtsnachfolger; ~ **in trade** Geschäftsnachfolger; ~ **on the premises** Raumnachfolger; ~ **states** Nachfolgestaaten; ~ **trustee** Nachfolgetreuhänder, Ersatztreuhänder; **intestate** ~ gesetzlicher Erbe; **legal** ~ Rechtsnachfolger, rechtmäßiger Erbe; **legitimate** ~ rechtmäßiger Nachfolger; **singular** ~ Einzelrechtsnachfolger (*Rechtsnachfolger bezüglich e–s bestimmten Gegenstandes*); **universal** ~ Gesamt(rechts)nachfolger.

such dieser Art, der genannten Art; wie benannt, dies (*dieser, diese, dieses*); ~ **as shall survive** diejenigen die (*den Erblasser*) überleben; ~ **issue** die betreffenden Nachkommen; ~ **other person** der (betreffende) Dritte.

suchlike dergleichen *adj, pron*.

sudden plötzlich, überraschend, unvorhergesehen, unvermutet; ~ **affray** plötzliche Rauferei, Krawall; ~ **heat or passion** Affekt, hochgradige Erregung; ~ **or violent injury** plötzlich zugefügte oder gewaltsame Verletzung.

sue klagen, verklagen, prozessieren; ~ **and labour clause** (= *brit für suing and laboring clause*) → *suing*; ~

for a debt e–e Geldforderung einklagen; ~ **in a representative capacity** in Prozeßstandschaft klagen; ~ **forma pauperis** im Armenrecht klagen; ~ **on a contract** aus (e–m) Vertrag klagen; ~ **out** einklagen, beantragen, bei Gericht erlangen; ~ **s.o. for damages** jmdn auf Schadensersatz verklagen; **capacity to** ~ Aktivlegitimation; Prozeßfähigkeit; **capacity to be ~d** Passivlegitimation, passive Prozeßfähigkeit; ~ ~ ~ ~ *in tort: Deliktsfähigkeit*; **title to** ~ → *title*.

suffer dulden, gestatten, erleiden; ~ **a default** ein Versäumnisurteil gegen sich ergehen lassen; ~ **a loss** Verlust erleiden; ~ **damages** Schaden haben, geschädigt sein; ~ **judicial proceedings** e–n Prozeß (ohne Einwendungen) hinnehmen; ~ **pecuniary loss** e–n Vermögensschaden erleiden; ~ **punishment** bestraft werden; **s.o. ~s an injustice** jmdm geschieht Unrecht.

sufferance Duldung *f*; **light on** ~ Fensterrecht, Lichtrecht.

sufferer der Geschädigte (*Feuerversicherung*).

suffering Leid *n*; **mental** ~ seelisches Leid.

suffering a recovery *hist* Veräußerung e–s Grundstücks durch Auflassung.

sufficiency Angemessenheit *f*, Genüge *f*; Erfindungseigenschaft *f*; ~ **of motion** Zulässigkeit *f* der Antragstellung.

sufficient genügend, ausreichend, hinlänglich; ~ **cause** wichtiger Grund, triftiger Grund; ~ **evidence** → *evidence;* ~ **in law** rechtsgültig, rechtlich zulässig; ~ **security** ausreichende Sicherheit; ~ **witness** ausreichender Zeuge(nbeweis).

suffragan Weihbischof *m*.

suffrage Wahlrecht *n*; **direct universal** ~ unmittelbares gleiches allgemeines Wahlrecht; **universal** ~ allgemeines Wahlrecht; **universal adult** ~ allgemeines Erwachsenenwahlrecht; **women's** ~ Frauenwahlrecht.

suffragette Frauenrechtlerin *f*.

suggest dartun, meinen, anregen, vorschlagen, nahelegen, empfehlen; **~ed price** → *price* (*1*).

suggestion Vorschlag *m*, Anregung *f*, Empfehlung *f*; Vortrag *m* vor Gericht; ~ **selling** *US* Kundenbeeinflussung; ~ **system** Prämienplan für betriebliche Verbesserungsvorschläge; **auto-~** Autosuggestion, Selbsttäuschung.

suggestive | **interrogation** Vernehmung *f* mit Suggestivfragen; ~ **question** Suggestivfrage; ~ **selling** Verkaufswerbung.

sui | **generis** eigener Art, einzigartig; ~ **juris** aus eigenem Recht; geschäftsfähig.

suicidal intent *ins* Selbstmordabsicht *f*.

suicide Selbstmord *m*, Selbsttötung *f*; ~ **clause** Selbstmordklausel (*Lebensversicherung*); ~ **pact** Verabredung zum Selbstmord; **~, sane or insane** *ins* Selbstmordklausel; **agreement to commit** ~ Verabredung zum (gemeinsamen) Selbstmord; **assisting** ~ Beihilfe zum Selbstmord; **attempt to commit** ~ Selbstmordversuch; **inciting to commit** ~ Anstiftung zum Selbstmord; **procuring** ~ Herbeiführung des Selbstmordes; Überredung zum Selbstmord.

suing and laboring clause *Klausel über Schadensminderungspflicht durch Prozeß oder eigene Leistung des Versicherungsnehmers*; Beteiligungszusage *f* der Versicherung bei Klageerhebung.

suit (*1*) Klage *f*, *bes* Klage *f* im Equity-Verfahren; Prozeß *m*, Rechtsfall *m*, Verfahren *n*; Liste *f* der Zeugen des Klägers; ~ **at law** (Zivil)Prozeß; ~ **for contribution** Klage auf Ausgleichszahlung (unter Gesamtschuldnern); ~ **for discontinuance** Unterlassungsklage; ~ **for jactitation of marriage** Klage auf Unterlassung der Behauptung, mit jmdm verheiratet zu sein; ~ **for restitution of conjugal community** *GB: vor 1969* Klage auf die Wiederherstellung der ehelichen Lebensgemeinschaft; ~ **money** Prozeßkostenvorschuß (*für die Ehefrau*); ~ **of a civil nature** Zivilklage; ~ **of the kings's peace** Strafklage; ~ **of the peace** Anklage wegen Hochverrats; ~ **pending** anhängiger Prozeß; ~ **to establish priorities** Klage auf Feststellung der Gläubigerrangfolge; **administration** ~ Nachlaßverfahren; **civil** ~ Zivilklage, Zivilprozeß; **class** ~**s** → *class*; **common** ~ allgem zivilrechtl Klage; **counter** ~ Gegenklage; **criminal** ~ Strafverfahren; **defended** ~ streitiger (Scheidungs) Prozeß; **derivative** ~ Prozeßstandschaftsklage (*zB e–s Aktionärs*), Modellprozeß; **divorce** ~ Scheidungsklage; **equity** ~ Klage nach dem Billigkeitsrecht; **federal** ~ Klage vor e–m Bundesgericht *(US)*; **foreclosure** ~ Pfandverfallsklage, *Klage e–s Grundpfandgläubigers auf Feststellung des Eigentumsüberganges durch Pfandverfall*; **fresh** ~ neue Klage; **friendly** ~ Klage ohne feindl Absicht, Kl. zur Regulierung oder Feststellung e–s Rechtsverhältnisses; **infringement** ~ → *infringement;* **institution of** ~ Klageerhebung; **nullity** ~ → *nullity;* **party to a** ~ Prozeßpartei; **paternity** ~ → *paternity;* **penal** ~ Strafverfahren; **plenary** ~ ordentl Verfahren, Hauptprozeß; **redemption** ~ Klage auf Grundstücksrückauflassung nach Tilgung; **to bring (a)** ~ **against a person** jmdn verklagen; **to file** ~ → *to file*.

suit (*2*) Vasallendienst *m*, Gefolgepflicht *f*; ~ **covenant** Hofgefolgeverpflichtung; ~ **custom** Hofdienste seit unvordenklicher Zeit; ~ **of court** Hofgefolgepflicht des Lehensmannes; ~ **silver** *hist* Schilling als Ersatz für Hofgefolgepflicht.

suit (*3*) Werbung *f*, Anliegen *n*, Antrag *m*, Heiratsantrag *m*; **at the plaintiffs's** ~ auf Antrag des Klägers.

suitability Eignung *f*, Tauglichkeit *f*, Zweckmäßigkeit *f*.

suitable geeignet, sachdienlich, angemessen, passend; ~ **alternative accommodation** geeignete Ersatzwohnung; ~ **employment** geeignete Beschäftigung, zumutbare Ersatzarbeit.

suitor Kläger *m*, Partei *f*, Antragsteller *m*, Bewerber (*Fusion*); Übernahmespekulant *m*, Freier *m*, Bittsteller *m*; ~**'s deposit account** Gerichtskonto für (*verzinsliche Anlage von*) Sicherheitsleistungen des Klägers; ~**'s fee fund** Gerichtskasse, *gerichtliches Sammelvermögen aus den Gerichtsgebühren für gerichtliche Personalkosten*.

sum Summe *f*, Betrag *m*, Geldbetrag *m*; *hist* juristische Abhandlung *f*; ~ **adjudged (to be paid)** Urteilssumme; ~ **assured** Versicherungssumme; ~ **certain** ein bestimmter Geldbetrag; ~ **charged on** gesicherter Betrag; ~ **claimed** Klagebetrag, Streitgegenstand; ~ **due** geschuldeter Betrag, fälliger Betrag; ~ **employed** verwendeter Betrag; ~ **in dispute** eingeklagter Betrag, Streitwert; ~ **in excess of** Mehrbetrag; ~ **in full settlement of all claims** Betrag zur Abgeltung aller Ansprüche; Abfindungssumme; ~ **insured** Versicherungssumme; ~ **of-digits depreciation** digitale Abschreibung, arithmetisch degressive Abschreibung; ~**s of money due and owing** Außenstände; ~ **owing** geschuldeter Betrag, Rechnungssumme; ~ **paid in** Einlage; ~ **payable** Wechselbetrag, Rechnungssumme; ~ **recoverable summarily** im summarischen Verfahren klagbarer Betrag; ~ **total** Gesamtbetrag; ~ **usually expended** gewöhnlich aufgewendeter Geldbetrag; **aggregate** ~ Gesamtbetrag; **deposited** ~ hinterlegter Betrag; **equivalent** ~ Gegenwert; **even** ~ runde Summe; **flat** ~ Pauschalbetrag; **gross** ~ Gesamtsumme, Bruttobetrag; **lump** ~ → *lump*; **net** ~ Nettobetrag; **nominal** ~ pro forma angesetzter

Betrag, nomineller Betrag; **penal** ~ Konventionalstrafe, Strafgeld, Reugeld; **principal** Hauptbetrag.

sum up zusammenfassen, addieren, plädieren; ~ **evidence** zum Beweisergebnis plädieren; ~ **the items** die Rechnungsposten aufaddieren.

summarily summarisch, ohne Formalitäten; **to be dismissed** ~ fristlos entlassen werden.

summariness summarische Kürze *f*, Bündigkeit *f*, sofortige Maßnahmen *f/pl* (*ohne Ankündigung*).

summary *adj* summarisch, abgekürzt, beschleunigt; ~ **award of punishment** Bestrafung im Strafbefehlsverfahren (*oder ähnlichen summarischen Verfahren*); ~ **court martial** Standgericht; **S~ Jurisdiction Acts** (=) *Gerichtsverfassungsgesetze für Amtsgerichte*; ~ **procedure on bills of exchange** Wechselprozeß; ~ **reception order** (vorläufiger) Verwahrungsbeschluß (*Nervenheilanstalt*).

summary *s* Auszug *m*, Übersicht *f*, Zusammenstellung *f*; Zusammenfassung *f*; Schlußplädoyer *n*; ~ **of evidence** Ergebnis der Beweisaufnahme; ~ **of the facts** Zusammenfassung des Sachverhalts, Tatbestand; **executive** ~ Zusammenfassung für Führungskräfte.

summation Schlußplädoyer *n*; **accusatory** ~ Schlußplädoyer der Anklage (des Staatsanwalts).

summing-up Schlußplädoyer *n*, abschließende Belehrung *f* der Geschworenen (*Zusammenfassung des Beweisergebnisses durch den Richter für die Geschworenen*); ~ **of evidence** abschließende Beweiswürdigung (*Richter bzw Anwalt*).

summiteers Gipfelkonferenz-Politiker *m/pl*.

summitry Gipfelkonferenz-Diplomatie *f*.

summon *v* laden, auffordern zu erscheinen; ~ **a witness** e–n Zeugen laden; ~ **for trial** zur Hauptverhandlung laden; ~**ed personally** durch eigenhändige Zustellung geladen; **duly** ~ **to appear** ordnungsgemäß laden (lassen).

summoner Ladungsbeamter *m*.

summons Ladung (*des Beklagten mit Klagezustellung*), Klageerhebung *f*, Vorladung *f*, Antrag an den Richter im Bürowege; Strafbefehl *m*; Bußgeldbescheid *m*; ~ **and order** Beschluß im Bürowege auf Antrag; ~ **and severance** Zwischenurteil auf abgetrenntes Verfahren; ~ **by publication** Ladung durch öffentliche Zustellung; ~ **for an injunction** Ladung zum Verhandlungstermin zum Erlaß e–r einstweiligen Verfügung; ~ **for directions** Ladung zum frühen ersten Termin vor dem Einzelrichter; prozeßleitende Verfügung, gerichtliche Anordnung; ~ **for entry of satisfaction** Ladung zum Anhörungstermin über die gerichtliche Eintragung e–r Pfandfreigabe; ~ **for time** Ladung zur Verhandlung über e–e Fristverlängerung; ~ **to admit to bail** Ladung zum Bürotermin über Kautionsstellung; ~ **to deliver bill of costs** Ladung zum Anhörungstermin im Kostenfestsetzungsverfahren; ~ **to pay** Mahnbescheid; ~ **to review the taxation** Erinnerungen gegen den Kostenfestsetzungsbeschluß; **application by (way of)** ~ → *application*; **concurrent** ~ weitere Ausfertigung e–r Terminsladung mit Klageankündigung; **dismissal of** ~ Zurückweisung des Antrags auf Entscheidung im summarischen Verfahren; **ex parte originating** ~ Terminsanberaumung im einseitigen Verfahren; **fixed date** ~ Terminsladung; **directions on** ~ gerichtliche Anordnungen; **infant settlement** ~ Terminladung zur Vergleichsprotokollierung über den Anspruch e–s Minderjährigen; **interpleader** ~ Terminladung bei Zwangsvollstreckungsintervention; **misfeasance** ~ Klage im abgekürzten Verfahren wegen unerlaubter Handlung; **originating** ~ (*Form der*) Klageerhebung, *verfah-*

renseinleitende Verfügung mit Ladung; Klage mit Ladung (*bei Feststellungsklagen und diversen Anträgen*); **personal** ~ unmittelbare Ladung; **public** ~ Ladung durch öffentliche Zustellung des Aufgebots; **short** ~ Ladung mit abgekürzter Frist; **time for** ~ gerichtliche Ladungsfrist; **to apply to court on** ~ vorläufige Entscheidung beantragen; **to take out a** ~ **against s.o.** jmdn laden lassen, jmdn verklagen; **writ of** ~ → *writ*.

sumptuary | laws Gesetze gegen Luxus; ~ **principle** *tax* Aufwandsprinzip.

Sunday|observance Acts Gesetze *n|pl* zur Erhaltung der Sonntagsruhe; ~ **trading** Ladenverkaufszeiten an Sonntagen.

sundries Verschiedenes *n*, Diverses *n*; ~ **account** Konto „Verschiedenes".

sunset law *Gesetz für Nullstellung laufender Bewilligungen zum Ende des Haushaltsjahrs (keine Fortschreibung) US; Gesetz, wonach Behörden ihre Existenzberechtigung periodisch der Legislative nachweisen müssen.*

sunshine law *Gesetz, das Öffentlichkeit von Behördensitzungen vorschreibt.*

superannuate *v|i* überaltern, aus Altersgründen ausscheiden, in Rente gehen; verjähren; *v|t* wegen Erreichen des Rentenalters entlassen.

superannuated *adj* überaltert, veraltet; zu alt bzw verbraucht für Dienstleistungen, erwerbsunfähig.

superannuation Überalterung *f*, Ausscheiden aus Altersgründen, Entlassung wegen Erreichen der Altersgrenze, Verrentung; **S~ Act** Altersversorgungsgesetz; ~ **fund** Pensionskasse, Versorgungswerk; **S~ Regulations** Rechtsverordnung zur (*kommunalen*) Altersversorgung; ~**scheme** Altersversorgungswerk.

supercargo Frachtaufseher *m*, Ladungsaufseher *m*, Superkargo *f*, Kargadeur *m* (*Bevollmächtigter m des Eigentümers der Ladung*).

superdividend Superdividende *f*, Zusatzdividende *f*.

superficiarius Erbbauberechtigter *m*.

superficies Einräumung *f* von Erbbaurecht; Bauwerk *n* im Erbbaurecht; ~ **solo cedit** keine Sonderrechtsfähigkeit von Gebäuden.

superfluous lands überflüssiger (*nicht zum Bahnbau benötigter zwangsabgetretener*) Grund *m*.

supergrass Polizeizeuge *m*, Zeuge aus der Terroristenszene.

superimpose hinzufügen; ~ **a punishment** e–e zusätzliche Strafe verhängen.

superintendence Aufsichtsführung *f*, Überordnung *f*, Oberaufsicht *f*, Betriebsleitung *f*.

superintendent Aufsichtsführender *m*, Betriebsleiter *m*, Werkmeister *m*; ~ **of banking** Leiter der Bankaufsichtsbehörde; ~ **of schools** Schulrat; **S~ Registrar** Oberstandesbeamter; ~ ~ *'s certificate relating to marriage; standesamtliche Aufgebotsbescheinigung*; **erection** ~ Bauleiter, Montageleiter.

supernumerary überzählig, außerplanmäßig.

superscription (= *act of* ~) notarieller Beurkundungsvermerk *m*.

supersed|e außer Kraft setzen, aufheben, ungültig machen, vorgehen, ersetzen; ~**ing cause** Ergebnis mit überholender Kausalität.

supersedeas obergerichtliche Anordnung *f* der Einstellung des Verfahrens; vorläufige Aufhebung *f* der Vollstreckbarkeit; Aussetzung der Amtsbefugnis von Friedensrichtern; ~ **bond** → *bond* (*2*).

supersession Ablösung *f*; ~ **of treaties** Außerkraftsetzung früherer durch spätere Verträge.

superstitious use abergläubische Auflage *f* bei e–r letztwilligen Zuwendung.

superstructure Aufbau(ten), Bebauung *f*.

super-tax Übersteuer *f*, Zusatzsteuer *f*.

supervening überholend, kausal, zusätzlich kausal.

supervis|e beaufsichtigen, überwachen; **~ing authority** Aufsichtsbehörde; **~ing duty** Aufsichtspflicht; **~ing judge** aufsichtsführender Richter.

supervision Beaufsichtigung *f*, Oberaufsicht *f*, Überwachung *f*; ~ **of aliens** Ausländerüberwachung; ~ **of manufacture** Fertigungskontrolle; ~ **order** → *order* (*1*); **bank** ~ Bankaufsicht; **governmental** ~ Staatsaufsicht; **judicial** ~ gerichtliche Geschäftsüberwachung; **power of** ~ Aufsichtsbefugnis; **price** ~ → *price* (*1*).

supervisor Inspektor *m*, Aufseher *m*, Dienstvorgesetzter *m*, Kontrolleur *m*; Straßenbaubeamter *m*; Gemeindevorsteher *m*; **~s of elections** Wahlprüfer; **board of ~s** → *board* (*1*).

supervisory | authority → *authority*; ~ **board** Überwachungsstelle, Aufsichtsbehörde; Aufsichtsrat; ~ **control** Rechtsaufsicht; Zuständigkeit als Rechtsmittelinstanz; ~ **council** Kuratorium; **in a** ~ **capacity** als Aufsichtsbehörde, in aufsichtsführender Eigenschaft.

supplement *s* Nachtrag *m*, Ergänzung *f*, Zuschlag *m*, Zulage *f*; **letters of** ~ Prozeßerstreckung *auf Personen außerhalb der Gerichtsbarkeit*; **special** ~ Sonderbeilage.

supplement *v* ergänzen, nachtragen.

supplemental ergänzend, Nachtrags . . .

supplementary zusätzlich, ergänzend.

supplementary benefits *GB* Sozialhilfe(leistung); **S~ B~ Act** Sozialhilfegesetz (*GB, 1976*); **S~ B~ Appeal Tribunal** Sozialhilfe-Rechtsmittelinstanz; **S~ B~ Commission** Sozialhilfeverwaltung, Fürsorgebehörde.

supplementation Ergänzung *f*, Vervollständigung *f*.

suppliant Bittsteller *m*, Petent *m*; Kläger *im Petition-of-Rights-Verfahren*.

supplier Lieferant *m (außer Einzelhandel)*; Zulieferer *m*, Leistungserbringer *m*; ~ **country** → *country*; ~ **credit** → *credit*; ~ **of goods** Warenlieferant; ~ **of services** Auftragnehmer, Erbringer von Dienstleistungen; **~'s account** Lieferantenkonto; **~'s credit** Lieferkredit, Lieferantenkredit; **~s' ledger** Wareneingangsbuch; **mail-order** ~ Versandhauslieferant.

supplies Vorräte *m|pl*, Betriebsstoffe *m|pl*; *parl* gesondert zu bewilligende Gelder *n|pl*; Versorgung *f*, Belieferung *f*, Bedarf *m*; ~ **area** Versorgungsgebiet; ~ **of labour** Angebot an Arbeitskräften; **commercial** ~ handelsübliche Betriebsmittel; **essential** ~ lebenswichtiger Bedarf; **excess** ~ Überangebot; **floating** ~ laufendes Angebot; **operating** ~ Betriebsmittel; **to vote** ~ Haushaltsmittel bewilligen.

supply *s* Lieferung *f*, Zuschuß *m*, Beitrag *m*; ~ **and demand** Angebot und Nachfrage; ~ **bottleneck** Versorgungsengpaß; ~ **of goods** Warenlieferung, Versorgung mit Gütern; ~ **of money** Geldversorgung, Geldangebot; ~ **services** aus allgemeinen Haushaltsmitteln finanzierte Staatsausgaben; **commissioner of** ~ *scot* Grundsteuerbehörde; **Committee of S~** → *committee*; **floating** ~ tägliches Angebot.

supply *v* liefern, beschaffen, beibringen, versorgen, ausstatten, ergänzen, ausgleichen, befriedigen, abhelfen, nachzahlen, zuschießen; ~ **collateral** Sicherheiten anschaffen; ~ **evidence** Beweismaterial beibringen; ~ **the market** den Markt beliefern.

support *s* Unterstützung *f*, Beistand *m*, Lebensunterhalt *m*, Stützung *f*; ~ **operation** Stützungsmaßnahme; ~ **price** Stützungspreis; ~ **services** unterstützende Dienstleistungen; **action for** ~ Unterhaltsklage; **banking** ~ Stützungsaktion der Banken; **domestic** ~ haushaltsmäßige Betreuung; **easement of** ~ → *easement*; **farm-price ~s** Agrarpreissubventionen; **lateral** ~ das

Recht auf seitliche Grundstücksabstützung; **liability for ~** Unterhaltspflicht; **memorandum in ~ of opposition** Einspruchsschriftsatz; **price ~** → *price*; **public ~** Unterhaltsbeihilfe aus öffentl Mitteln; **right of ~** → *right*; **sold ~** gebührenpflichtige Dienstleistungen; **subjacent ~** Recht auf Grundstücksabstützung durch den talwärtigen Anlieger; **vouchers in ~ of an account** Rechnungsbelege.

support *v* tragen, unterstützen, unterhalten, aufkommen für, finanzieren, befürworten; begründen, beweisen; decken; **~ a charge** e–e Anklage erhärten; **~ a claim** e–n Anspruch begründen *bzw* unterbauen; **~ by the relevant documentary evidence** durch einschlägige Unterlagen belegen; **~ed by voluntary subscriptions** finanziert durch freiwillige Beiträge; **~ed price** Stützungspreis, gestützter Preis; **~ing authorities** Belegstellen; **~ing purchases** *exch* Stützungskäufe, Interventionskäufe.

supporter Anhänger *m*, Verfechter *m*; Ernährer *m*, Beistand *m*.

suppose vermuten, annehmen, voraussetzen, vorschlagen; **~d deceased** Verschollener.

supposition Voraussetzung *f*, Annahme *f*; Unterstellung *f*.

suppress unterdrücken, verbieten, verheimlichen; **~ a will** ein Testament unterschlagen; **~ the truth** die Wahrheit unterdrücken; **~ing evidence of crime** Verdunkelung e–r Straftat.

suppression Unterdrückung *f*, Verheimlichung *f*, Verhehlen *n*; **~ of crime** Verbrechensbekämpfung; **~ of documents** Unterdrücken von Urkunden; **~ of evidence** Unterdrückung von Beweismaterial; **~ of facts** Verschweigen von Tatsachen; **~ of terrorism** Terrorismusbekämpfung; **S~ of Terrorism Act** Terrorismusbekämpfungsgesetz *GB 1978*.

supra siehe oben (*Zitierhinweis*); **pro-test** → *protest*; **~-riparian** als Oblieger *e–s Flusses*.

supranational supranational, übernational.

supremacy höchste Gewalt *f*, Souveränität *f*, Oberhoheit *f*, Vorrang *m*; **~ clause** Verfassungsbestimmung über den Vorrang des Bundesrechts (*US*); **~ of law** → *law*; **Act of S~** (=) *Gesetz von 1558; Vereinigung weltlicher und geistlicher Oberhoheit*; **judicial ~** → *judicial*; **national ~** *US* Bundeshoheit, Vorrang des Bundesrechts; **oath of ~** *hist* weltlicher Treueid der Geistlichkeit *in England*.

supreme | authority oberste Gewalt; **S~ Court of Judicature** → *court*; **S~ Court Taxing Office** Kostenfestsetzungsstelle des Supreme Court *qv*; **~ law of the land** höchstes staatliches Recht; **~ penalty** Todesstrafe; **~ power** oberste Staatsgewalt.

supreption Erschleichung *f* e–r Pfründe *durch Verheimlichung*.

surcharge *s* Gebührenzuschlag *m*, Steuerzuschlag *m*, Ergänzungsabgabe *f*; Aufschlag *m*, Gebührenerhebung *f*, Sonderzoll *m*; nachrangiges Grundpfandrecht *n*.

surcharge *v* aufschlagen, mit Zuschlag belegen; zuviel berechnen; Ergänzung der Rechnungslegung verlangen; Regreß nehmen (*gg Rechnungsleger*); Weiderecht überbeanspruchen; **~ and falsify** Beschluß auf Nachprüfung und Berichtigung e–r Rechnungslegung *durch den Antragsteller*; **~ liability notice** Säumniszuschlagsbescheid; **~ the account** die fälschliche Unterlassung e–r Gutschrift bei e–r Rechnungslegung nachweisen.

surety Bürge *m* (*bes selbstschuldnerischer B.*); Garant *m*; **~ bond** → *bond (2)*; **~ company** Kautionsversicherungsgesellschaft; **~ credit** Avalkredit; **~ for a debt** Bürge (*für e–e Forderung*); **~ for a surety** Rückbürge, Afterbürge; **~ for payment** Bürge, Wechselbürge; **~ insurance** → *insurance*; **~ of the**

peace Bürge für das Wohlverhalten e–r *Person, vorbeugende Kautionsstellung bei Wiederholungstätern*; ~ **of the peace and good behaviour** = → *of the peace qv*; ~ **warrant** Bürgschaftserklärung; **bill** ~ Wechselbürge; **co-**~ Mitbürge, Mitgarant, Rückbürge; **collateral** ~ Nebenbürge; **compensated** ~ bezahlter Bürge; **counter** ~ Rückbürge; **joint** ~ Mitbürge; **paying** ~ der leistende Bürge; **proper** ~ tauglicher Bürge; **to stand** ~ e–e Bürgschaft übernehmen, bürgen.

suretyship Bürgschaft *f*; **contract of** ~ Bürgschaftsvertrag *m*.

surface|damage Oberflächenschaden (*des Bodens über dem Bergwerk*); ~ **of land** Boden über e–m Bergwerk; ~ **rights** Oberflächenrechte, *Rechte am Boden über e–m Bergwerk;* ~ **waters** → *water*; ~ **working** Tagebau.

surmise vermuten, mutmaßen, vortragen.

surname Familienname *m*, Zuname *m*, Nachname *m*; ~ **at marriage** Familienname bei der Heirat, Ehename.

surplice fees Kirchengebühren *f/pl*.

surplus Überschuß *m*, Mehrbetrag *m*, Mehrertrag *m*, Zugewinn *m*; Mehrwert *m*; ~ **account** Gewinnkonto; ~ **assets** Liquidationswert e–r Gesellschaft; **brought forward** Gewinnvortrag; ~ **dividend** Superdividende, außerordentliche Dividende; ~ **earnings** unverteilter Reingewinn; ~ **in taxes** Steuerüberschuß; ~ **interest** Zinseszinsen; ~ **line** zur Rückversicherung bestimmter Teil der Versicherungssumme; ~ **moneys** Überschuß(beträge); ~ **of a corporation** Nettovermögen e–r Gesellschaft (*ohne Abzug des Nennkapitals*); ~ **of births over deaths** Geburtenüberschuß; ~ **of imports** Importüberschuß; ~ **population** Bevölkerungsüberschuß; ~ **reinsurance** Exzedenten-Rückversicherung; ~ **requirements** Emissionsmindestagio (*Bankgründung*); ~ **reserve** außerordentliche Reserve; ~ **value** → *value*; ~ **war property** überschüssiges Kriegsmaterial; **accumulated** ~ Gewinnvortrag, thesaurierter Gewinn, Kapitalrücklagefonds; **appraisal** ~ Überschuß durch Bewertungserhöhung; **appreciated** ~ Überschuß nach Auflösung der stillen Reserven, Mehrwert; **appreciation** ~ Kapitalzuwachs aus Werterhöhungen; **appropriated** ~ Rückstellung, zweckgebundene Rückstellung; **capital** ~ → *capital*; **contributed** ~ = *paid-in* ~ *qv*; **corporate** ~ Gesellschaftsreingewinn; **earned** ~ Geschäftsgewinn, thesaurierter Gewinn; **external** ~ Zahlungsbilanzüberschuß; **gross** ~ Rohüberschuß; **initial** ~ Überschußvortrag; **net** ~ Reinüberschuß; **operating** ~ Reingewinn (*e–s Geschäftsjahres nach Dividendenausschüttung*); **paid-in** ~ Emissionsgewinn (*über pari*); **revaluation** ~ Überschuß als Wertsteigerung des Anlagekapitals; **total** ~ Gesamtüberschuß; **unappropriated** ~ allgemeine Rücklagen, allgemeiner Überschuß; **unappropriated budget** ~ Haushaltsüberschuß; **unappropriated earned** ~ unverteilter Reingewinn; **unearned** ~ nicht gewerblich erwirtschafteter Gewinn.

surplusage Überschuß *m*; überflüssiges Vorbringen *n*.

surprise Überraschung *f*, Überraschungsmanöver *n*, überraschende Situation *f*; **elimination of** ~ Ausschaltung des Überraschungsmoments (*Strafrechtsreform*).

surrebut *v* e–e Quintuplik einreichen.

surrebutter Quintuplik *f*, Erwiderung *f* des Klägers auf e–e Quadruplik (*obs*).

surrejoin triplizieren.

surrejoinder Triplik *f*, Erwiderung *f* des Klägers auf e–e Duplik.

surrender *s* Übergabe *f*, Herausgabe *f*, Aufgabe *f*, Überlassung *f*, Auslieferung *f*, Hingabe *f*, Preisgabe *f*,

Kapitulation *f*; ~ **by bail** Übergabe des Beschuldigten zur Entlastung des Kautionsverpflichteten; ~ **by operation of law** gesetzlich vermuteter (Pachtrecht)Verzicht; ~ **charge** Gebühr bei Aufgabe e–r Lebensversicherung; Einbehalt, Deckungsrücklage bei Rückkauf von Versicherung; ~ **in deed** Aufgabe des Nießbrauchs am Grundstück; ~ **of a patent** → *patent*; ~ **of a preference** *Konkurs*: Verzicht auf e–e Vorzugsstellung; ~ **of charter** Verzicht auf Konzession, Selbstauflösung e–r Aktiengesellschaft; ~ **of copyhold** Auflösung und Übertragung von Copyhold-Pachtbesitz; ~ **of criminals** Auslieferung von Straftätern; ~ **of fugitives** Auslieferung von flüchtigen Straftätern; ~ **of lease** Verzicht auf ein Mietrecht (*bzw Pachtrecht*); Räumung, Rückgabe der Mietsache; ~ **of possession** (*vertragliche*) Rückgabe des Besitzes; ~ **of profits** Gewinnabführung; ~ **of rights** Aufgabe von Rechten, Rechtsverzicht; ~ **of shares** → *shares*; ~ **of tenancy** einvernehmliche Beendigung des Miet/Pachtverhältnisses; ~ **to uses of will** letztwillige Übertragung e–s Pachtrechts; ~ **value** → *value;* **against** ~ gegen Einreichung; **compulsory** ~ *scot* Enteignung; **terms of** ~ Übergabebedingungen; **unconditional** ~ bedingungslose Kapitulation.

surrender *v* aufgeben, herausgeben, überlassen, ausliefern, kapitulieren; *v/i* die Strafe antreten; ~ **a patent** auf ein Patent verzichten; ~ **an estate** ein Besitzrecht aufgeben; ~ **foreign currency** Devisen abführen; ~ **to the police** sich der Polizei stellen.

surrenderee Erwerber *m*, Übernehmer *m*, Entgegennehmender *m*.

surrenderor Veräußerer *m*, Abtretender *m*, Zedent *m*.

surrogacy Leihmutterschaftsverhältnis *n*; ~ **agency** Leihmutter(schafts)vermittlungsbüro; **S~ Arrangements Act** LeihmutterschaftsG (*GB 1985*); ~ **brokerage** Leihmuttervermittlung; ~ **mother** Leihmutter.

surrogate Stellvertreter *m* im Amt; *GB*: Beauftragter des Bischofs für Heiratserlaubnisse; *US*: Vormundschafts- und Nachlaßrichter *m*; ~**s' court** → *court*; ~ **guardian** gerichtlich ernannter Gegenvormund.

surtax Zusatzsteuer *f*, Ergänzungssteuer *f*, Ergänzungsabgabe *f*.

surveillance Beaufsichtigung *f*, Überwachung *f*, Kontrolle *f*; ~ **monitoring** elektronische Überwachung; **electronic** ~ elektronische Überwachung, Abhöranlagen; **surreptitious** ~ heimliches Abhören, Lauschangriff.

survey *s* Vermessung *f*, Besichtigung *f*, Befragung *f*, Erhebung *f*, Begutachtung *f*; ~ **certificate** Besichtigungsschein; ~ **fees** Gebühren für Gutachter; ~ **of a vessel** Schiffszeugnis; ~ **of schools** Schulinspektion; ~ **report** Befundbericht, Besichtigungsbericht; **governmental** ~ allgemeine staatliche Landvermessung (*US*); **judicial** ~ Ortsbesichtigung, Augenscheinseinnahme; **Ordnance S~** *brit* amtliche Landvermessung; **structural** ~ Gebäudewertschätzung.

survey *v* vermessen, besichtigen, schätzen.

surveyor Geometer *m*, Vermessungsbeamter *m*; Schadensexperte *m*, Begutachter *m*, Zollinspektor *m*, Aufsichtsbeamter *m*; ~ **and valuer** Katasterbeamter; ~ **general** Generalinspektor, Aufsichtsbeamter für Staatsländereien; ~ **of customs** Zollbeamter; ~ **of highways** Straßenmeister; ~ **of the port** Leiter des Hafenamtes; **S~'s Office** Baubehörde; **land** ~ Vermessungsbeamter; **mine** ~ Bergwerksinspektor; **quantity** ~ Bausachverständiger für Massenberechnungen.

survival Überleben *n*; ~ **action** → *action*; ~**of causes of action** Fortbestehen von Ansprüchen nach dem Tode des Schuldners; ~ **rate**

Geburtenüberschuß; ~ **statutes** *gesetzliche Vorschriften über die Aufrechterhaltung von Ansprüchen des verstorbenen Verletzten*; **in case of** ~ im Überlebensfall; **presumption of** ~ Überlebensvermutung; **with** ~ **of cause of action** ohne Verzicht auf den Klageanspruch.

surviv|e überleben, überdauern, fortdauern (*nach Ablauf usw*); ~**ing debts** Restschulden; ~**ing spouse** der überlebende Ehegatte; ~ ~ *statutory legacy on an intestacy: etwa Ehegattenpflichtteil, (gesetzl Ehegatten-Pflichtvermächtnis bei Intestatserbfolge)*.

survivor Überlebener *m*, Letztlebender *m*; Anwachsungsberechtigung *beim Tode e–s Mitberechtigten*; Hinterbliebener *m*; ~ **benefits** → *benefit*; **the** ~ **of my children** das Letztlebende meiner Kinder.

survivorship Überlebensfall *m*; Rechte des überlebenden Gesamthandseigentümers (*unter Ausschluß der Nachlaßabwickler*); Anwachsung im Überlebensfall; ~ **account** → *account (2)*; **right of** ~ → *right*.

susceptible fähig; ~ **of proof** beweisfähig.

suspect *s* Verdächtiger *m*, Verdächtige *f*; **criminal** ~ Strafverdächtiger.

suspect *v* verdächtigen, annehmen, vermuten, den Verdacht haben; ~**ed bill (of health)** Gesundheitspaß mit Vermerk „ansteckungsverdächtig"; ~**ed carcase** krankheitsverdächtiger Tierkörper; ~**ed person** ein Tatverdächtiger.

suspend suspendieren, einstellen, aussetzen, vorläufig entlassen; ~ **a sentence** Strafaussetzung gewähren, e–e Strafe zur Bewährung aussetzen; ~ **from office** des Amtes vorläufig entheben; ~ **payments** die Zahlungen einstellen; ~ **proceedings** das Verfahren aussetzen; ~ **the judgment** die (Urteils)Vollstreckung vorläufig einstellen; ~ **the running of time** die Verjährung hemmen.

suspense Ungewißheit *f*, Aufschub *m*, Unterbrechung *f*; ~ **account** → *account (2)*; ~ **entry** → *entry*; ~ **items** vorläufige Posten; ~ **of mind** Nervenanspannung; **to hold in** ~ hinhalten (*Gläubiger*), notleiden lassen (*Wechsel*).

suspension Suspendierung *f*, Einstellung *f* (*der Zwangsvollstreckung*), Aussetzung *f*, Ausschließung *f*, vorläufige Amtsenthebung *f*; ~ **credit** Überbrückungskredit; ~ **from exercise of profession or trade** befristete Untersagung der Berufsausübung; ~ **of a law** zeitweises Außerkrafttreten e–s Gesetzes; ~ **of a statute** zeitweises Außerkraftsetzen e–s Gesetzes; ~ **of arms** *zeitlich und örtlich begrenzte* Waffenruhe; ~ **of banks** Liquidation von Banken; ~ **of business** Einstellung des Geschäftsbetriebs; ~ **of civic rights** (*zeitlich begrenzte*) Aberkennung der bürgerlichen Ehrenrechte; ~ **of diplomatic relations** Unterbrechung der diplomatischen Beziehungen; ~ **of driver's license** *befristeter* Führerscheinentzug; ~ **of earnings** Verdienstausfall; ~ **of execution** vorläufige Einstellung der Zwangsvollstreckung, Vollstreckungsaufschub, Aufschub *bzw* Unterbrechung des Strafvollzugs; ~ **of execution of sentence** Strafaussetzung, Aussetzung der Strafvollstreckung; ~ **of gold standard** zeitweiliges Abgehen vom Goldstandard; ~ **of hostilities** Einstellung der Kampfhandlungen, Waffenstillstand; ~ **of imposition of sentence** Aussetzung der Urteilsverkündung zum Strafmaß (*während der Berufung gegen Schuldspruch*); ~ **of legislation** Suspendierung von Gesetzen; ~ **of members** vorübergender Mitgliederausschluß; ~ **of payments** Zahlungseinstellung; ~ **of prescription** Hemmung der Verjährung; ~ **of privileges** Aufhebung von Immunitätsvorrechten; ~ **of (the) proceedings** Aussetzung des Verfahrens, Ruhen des Verfahrens; ~ **of sentence on probation** Strafaussetzung zur Bewährung; ~ **of sitting** Unterbrechung der Sitzung; ~ **of work** Arbeitseinstellung; ~ **on suggestion of insanity** Strafaussetzung wegen nachträglicher Geisteskrankheit; **notice of** ~ → *notice*; **permanent** ~ unbefristete Strafaussetzung; **plea in** ~ dilatorische Einrede; **temporary** ~ einstweilige Strafaussetzung.

suspicion Verdacht *m*, Argwohn *m*, Verdächtigung *f*, Mißtrauen *m*; **above** ~ = *beyond* ~ *qv*; **beyond** ~ über jeden Verdacht erhaben, absolut unverdächtig; **gratuitous** ~ grundloser Verdacht; **on strong** ~ wegen dringenden Tatverdachts; **reasonable** ~ **of an offence** hinreichender Tatverdacht; **to dispel** ~ e–n Verdacht zerstreuen; **to incur** ~ in Verdacht geraten.

suspicious verdächtig; ~ **character** (*als Gewohnheitstäter*) Verdächtiger; ~ **fact** Verdachtsmoment.

sustain ertragen, stützen, aufrechterhalten, bestätigen, tragen, erleiden, sich unterziehen; ~ **a claim** e–n Anspruch aufrechterhalten; ~ **a loss** e–n Schaden haben; ~ **a will** (*gerichtl*) ein Testament (*als gültig*) aufrechterhalten; ~ **a motion** e–m Antrag stattgeben; ~ **competition** sich gegen die Konkurrenz behaupten; ~ **damages** Schaden haben; ~ **injury** verletzt werden; ~ **loss** Schaden erleiden; ~ **the burden of proof** den obliegenden Beweis erbringen.

sustenance Unterhalt *m*, Versorgung *f*, Nährwert *m*.

sustentation fund Unterstützungsfonds *m für Geistliche*; Streikunterstützungsfonds *m*.

suzerain Suzerän *m*, Kronvasall.

suzerainty Suzeränität *f*, Oberherrschaft *f*, Schutzhoheit *f*, Protektorat *n*.

swap Tausch *m*, Swap *m*, Swapgeschäft *n*; Devisenreportgeschäft *n*; ~ **facility** Swap-Fazilität; ~ **rate** Swapsatz; ~ **issue** Swap-Emission (*mit Zins- und Währungsswapgeschäften verbundene Emission*).

swatch Stoffprobe *f*.

swear schwören, beeidigen, den Eid leisten; fluchen; ~ **a witness (in)** e–n Zeugen beeiden (*vor der Aussage*); ~ **an affidavit** e–e schriftliche Aussage beschwören; ~ **an oath** e–n Eid leisten; ~ **an official in** e–m Beamten den Diensteid abnehmen; ~ **falsely** falsch schwören, e–n Meineid leisten; ~ **in** vereidigen, den Eid abnehmen; ~ **out a warrant of arrest** e–n Haftbefehl durch beschworene Strafanzeige erwirken; ~ **to a fact** e–e Tatsache beschwören; ~ **to a statement** e–e schriftliche Aussage beschwören.

swearing Schwören *n*, Eidesleistung *f*; Fluchen *n*; ~ **in** Beeidigung; ~ **of witness** Zeugenbeeidigung; ~ **the peace** Bitte um gerichtlichen Schutz bei Bedrohung; **false** ~ außergerichtlicher Falscheid.

sweat *v* für e–n Hungerlohn arbeiten, ausgebeutet werden.

sweat damage Schiffsdunstschaden *m*.

sweat-shop Betrieb *m* mit Hungerlohn-Akkordsätzen.

sweating Ausbeutung *f*, Aussageerpressung *f*, scharfes Verhör *n*; ~ **system** Ausbeutung durch Heimarbeit.

sweep Großrazzia *f*.

sweepstake Rennwette *f*.

sweetener Anreiz *m*.

sweetheart|contract spezielle freundschaftliche Betriebsvereinbarung mit Gewerkschaft (*mit Sondervergünstigungen zwecks Ausschaltung konkurrierender Gewerkschaft*); ~ **deals** Gefälligkeitsvereinbarungen.

swindle Schwindel *m*; **insurance** ~ Versicherungsbetrug.

swindler Hochstapler *m*, Schwindler *m*, Betrüger *m*.

swindling Betrug *m*, Betrügerei *f*.

swing Schwung *m*, Kreditmarge *f*, Swing *m*; Wahlrundreise *f*; ~ **back** *pol* Umschwung; ~ **in the balance of payments** Zahlungsbilanzschwankung; ~ **shift** Sonderschicht.

switch limits Rangierbahnhofsbereich *m*.
switch selling *Verkaufstrick durch Übergang auf ein teureres Modell.*
switching operation Rangierbetrieb; ~ **service** Rangierdienst; **anomaly** ~ Ausnutzung besonderer Kursverhältnisse zu Gewinnmitnahmen; **coupon** ~ kurzfristige Ertragsumdisposition; **policy** ~ langfristige Anlageumdisposition.
swordstick Stockdegen *m*.
sworn beeidigt, vereidigt; ~ **appraiser** beeidigter Schätzer; ~ **brothers** verbrüderte Genossen; ~ **expert** beeidigter Sachverständiger; ~ **statement** → *statement*; ~ **testimony** → *testimony*; ~ **translator** → *translator*; ~ **witness** beeidigter Zeuge.
syllabus Lehrplan *m*, Zusammenfassung *f*, kurze Urteilsabgabe *f*, Leitsatz *m*; Inhaltsangabe *f*.
syllogism Syllogismus *m*, Vernunftsschluß *m*, Spitzfindigkeit *f*; **false** ~ Trugschluß.
symbol Symbol *n*, Kennzeichen *n*.
symbolaeography Urkundenformulierungskunst *f*.
syndic Syndikus *m*, Anwalt *m*, Konkursverwalter *m*.
syndicalism Syndikalismus *m* (*revolutionär-gewerkschaftliche Bewegung*); **criminal** ~ strafbarer Syndikalismus, Anarchieverbot.
syndicate Syndikat *n*, Konsortium *n*, Konzern *m*, Gelegenheitsgesellschaft *f*, Universitätsausschuß *m*; ~ **account** Konsortialkonto; ~ **credit** Konsortialkredit; ~ **transactions** Konsortialgeschäfte; **banking** ~ → *banking*; **issuing** ~ Emissionskonsortium, Begebungsk.; **original** ~ Übernahmekonsortium; **share in a** ~ Konsortialbeteiligung; **underlying** ~ Gründungskonsortium.
syndication Syndizierung *f*, Konsortial-Plazierung *f*.
syndicus Syndikus *m*, Rechtsvertreter *m*, rechtskundiger Verwaltungsbeamter *m*.
synergy Gemeinschaftsaktion *f*.
syngraph gesiegelte mehrseitige Urkunde *f*.
synmetallism Doppelwährung *f*, *alternative Gold- und Silberwährung.*
synopsis Synopsis *f*, Zusammenfassung *f*.
system System *n*, Plan *m*, Ordnung *f*; ~ **of accounts** Buchführungssystem; ~ **of checks and balances** System der wechselseitigen Kontrolle der Verfassungsorgane; ~ **of government** Regierungssystem; ~ **of judicature** Gerichtsordnung, Gerichtsverfassung; ~ **of law** Rechtsordnung; ~ **of measurement** Maßsystem; ~ **of railroads** Eisenbahnnetz; ~ **of working** Arbeitsmethode; **air mail** ~ Luftpostdienst; **competitive** ~ Wettbewerbssystem; **elective** ~ Wahlsystem; **fiscal** ~ Steuersystem; **hire purchase** ~ Abzahlungsplan; **inquisitorial** ~ Untersuchungsgrundsatz, Inquisitionsmaxime; **interlinked** ~ Verbund; **judicial** ~ → *judicial*; **lay-by** ~ Abzahlungskauf (*bei Lebensmitteln*); **legal** ~ Rechtssystem, Rechtsordnung; **levy** ~ Abgabensystem; **monetary** ~ Münzsystem, Währungssystem; **parliamentary** ~ parlamentarisches Regierungssystem; **penal** ~ Strafrechtssystem; **ticket-of-leave** ~ bedingte Strafentlassung.

T

table *s* Tabelle *f*, Register *n*, Verzeichnis *n*, Anhang *m*; **T~ A** (=) gesetzliche Mustersatzung für brit Kapitalgesellschaften; ~ **of birth** Geburtenregister; ~ **of cases** Verzeichnis von Präzedenzfällen (*in juristischen Werken*); ~ **of costs** (Gerichts)kostentabelle; ~ **of depreciation** Abschreibungstabelle; ~ **of descent** Stammbaum; ~ **of exchange** Umrechnungstabelle, Kurstabelle; ~ **of fees** Gebührentabelle; ~ **of interest** Zinstabelle; ~ **of the House** Präsidiumstisch (*Unterhaus*); ~ **of wages** Lohntabelle; ~ **office** Geschäftsstelle für Eingaben (*Unterhaus*); **adoption of T~ A** Aufnahme der „Table A" in die Gesellschaftssatzung; **American Experience T~** (=) *amtliche Sterblichkeitstafel;* **genealogical** ~ (Darstellung e–s) Familienstammbaum(es); **interest** ~ Zinstabelle.

table *v* einreichen, vorlegen, einbringen, eintragen; *US parl* verschieben, die Behandlung zurückstellen; ~ **a bill** e–n Gesetzesentwurf einbringen; *US*: die Beratung e–s Gesetzentwurfs auf unbestimmte Zeit vertagen.

table bumping Mit-der-Faust-auf-den-Tisch-Schlagen *n*.

tachigraph Fahrtenschreiber *m*.

tacit stillschweigend, konkludent.

taciturnity Verwirkung *f* (durch Stillschweigen).

tack *v* anheften, hinzufügen; im Rang aufrücken; e–en Rangvorbehalt ausüben, *Rangvortritt erlangen durch Einbeziehung in erststelliges Grundpfandrecht.*

tagging elektronische Aufenthaltsüberwachung *von Freigängern etc.*

tail Nachkommenschaft *f*; ~ **female** auf die weiblichen Nachkommen beschränkte Immobiliarerbfolge; ~ **general** auf e–n Mann und dessen leiblichen Nachkommen beschränkte Erbfolge; ~ **male** auf männliche Nachkommen im Mannesstamm beschränkte Immobiliarerbfolge; ~ **special** auf bestimmte Abkömmlinge beschränkte Erbfolge; **estate (in)** ~ → *estate*; **heir in** → *heir;* **issue in** ~ → *issue* (*3*); **several** ~ *Fideikommißbindung an zwei Erbenstämme*, getrennte Miterbenbegünstigung; **tenant in** ~ Nacherbe.

tailback (Rück)Stau *m*.

tailers Mitläufer *m*|*pl* von Großspekulanten.

tailor to the trade Lohnschneider *m*.

taint Makel *m*; **hereditary** ~ ungünstige Erbanlage, erbliche Belastung.

take ergreifen, nehmen wegnehmen; erben; Gericht halten, den Geschworenenspruch entgegennehmen; beschlagnahmen; verhaften, entziehen; erwerben; **"~"** (= *accept offer*) „annehme Angebot"; ~ **a benefit under a will** in e–m Testament bedacht werden; e–e letztwillige Zuwendung erhalten; ~ **a flier** Spekulation riskieren; ~ **a loss** e–n Verlust in Kauf nehmen; ~ **a mortgage on a property** e–e Hypothek (Grundschuld) auf ein Grundstück aufnehmen; ~ **action** → *action*; ~ **an oath** Eid leisten; ~ **and appropriate** in Zueignungsabsicht wegnehmen; ~ **and carry away** wegnehmen und wegschaffen; ~ **away** wegnehmen, entführen; ~ **back** zurücknehmen, widerrufen, zurückziehen; ~ **by descent** auf Grund gesetzlicher Erbfolge erben; ~ **by stealth** stehlen; ~ **care of** sorgen, versorgen, (e–e Schuld) bezahlen, sich um etw kümmern; ~ **charge of s. th.** die Verantwortung für etw übernehmen; ~ **delivery** abnehmen, in Empfang nehmen; ~ **down** abreißen; ~ **effect** in Kraft treten, wirksam werden; ~ **evidence** → *evidence*; ~ **home pay** Nettolohn; ~ **in** übernehmen, aufnehmen, *exch* hereinnehmen, in Report nehmen; fremdes Vieh in Pension nehmen; ~ **in execution** pfänden; ~ **in pawn** → *pawn*; ~ **in payment** in Zahlung nehmen; erfüllungshalber annehmen; ~ **in satisfaction** an Erfüllungs Statt hereinnehmen; ~ **into account** berücksichtigen, in Betracht ziehen, einrechnen; ~ **into consideration** in Betracht ziehen; ~ **into custody** in Gewahrsam nehmen, verhaften; ~ **legal measures** gerichtliche Maßnahmen treffen; ~ **liberties with s. o.** sich jmdm gegenüber Freiheiten herausnehmen; ~ **notice** beachten, (*von etwas*) Kenntnis nehmen; ~ **off the price** vom Preis nachlassen; ~ **on credit** auf Kredit kaufen; anschreiben lassen; ~ **on intestacy** gesetzlich erben; **~-or-pay agreement** Festvertrag mit unbedingter Abnahmepflicht; ~ **out a patent** ein Patent erhalten, patentieren lassen; ~ **out a pawn** → *pawn*; ~ **out an insurance policy** e–e Versicherung abschließen; ~ **possession** etwas in Besitz nehmen, Besitz ergreifen; ~ ~ *of the goods: die Ware abnehmen*, ~ **priority** e–n Vorrang haben; ~ **profits** Gewinne mitnehmen, Gewinne realisieren; ~ **red-handed** auf frischer Tat ertappen; ~ **the chair** den Vorsitz übernehmen, den Vorsitz haben; ~ **the execution of the work** den Auftrag übernehmen; als Auftragnehmer tätig werden; ~ **the floor** das Wort ergreifen; ~ **under a will** testamentarisch erben; ~ **undue advantage** in sittenwidriger Weise ausnutzen; ~ **up a loan** e–n Kredit aufnehmen; ~ **up an option** ein Bezugsrecht ausüben; ~ **up money** Geld aufnehmen; ~ **up shares** Aktien beziehen.

takeaway food shop Schnellimbiß mit Straßenverkauf.

take-off ticket Effektenumsatzjournal e–s Börsenhändlers.

take-over *auch: takeover s* Übernahme *f*, Geschäftsübernahme *f*, Kontrollübernahme *f*; Abnahme *f*; ~ **bid** Übernahmeangebot; **T~ Code** Regeln für Kapitalübernahmen und Fusionen (*London*); ~ **offer** Übernahmeangebot (*von Kapitalanteilen*); **T~ Panel** Fusionskontrollorgan; ~ **sharks** Übernahmehaie, unredliche Fusionsarrangeure; ~ **target** angestrebtes Übernahmeobjekt; **reverse** ~ umgekehrte Übernahme (*die große Gesellschaft durch die kleine*).

taker Hereinnehmer *m*, Abnehmer *m*, Käufer *m*, Erbe *m*, Vermächtnisnehmer *m*; ~ **(of an option)** Stillhalter; ~ **for a call** Verkäufer e–r Vorprämie; ~ **for a call of more** Verkäufer e–s Rechts zur Nachforderung.

taker-over Übernehmender *m*, Firmenakquisiteur *m*.

taking Wegnahme *f* (bei Diebstahl), Nehmen *n*, Abnahme *f*; **~s** Einnahmen, Kasseneinnahmen; ~ **and asportation** Wegnahme und Wegschaffen; ~ **at sea** Entwendung auf See; ~ **delivery** Abnahme (*Kauf*); ~ **kickbacks** passive Bestechung; Annahme von Schmiergeldern; ~ **of motor vehicle** Gebrauchsdiebstahl e–s Kfz (= ~ *cars*); **of stock** Abnahme der Aktien; ~ **possession** Besitzergreifung, Inbesitznahme; ~ **samples** Musterziehung; ~ **the view** Lokaltermin, Augenscheinnahme; ~ **up of capital** Kapitalaufnahme; **constructive** ~ *die als Wegnahme geltende Aneignung (e–r nicht im Gewahrsam des Täters befindlichen Sache)*; **delayed** ~ Abnahmeverzug; **profit** ~ →*profit*; **surreptitious** ~ geheime Wegnahme; **unlawful** ~ widerrechtliche Wegnahme.

tale Geldzählung *f*; Geschichtserzählung *f* in der Klagebegründung; ~ **quale** = tel quel = wie die Sache steht und liegt; **by** ~ dem nominellen Wert entsprechend.

tales Ersatzmänner *m|pl* (der Geschworenen); ~ **de circumstantibus** Benennung von Geschworenen aus den zufällig Anwesenden; **to pray a** ~ Ladung von Ersatzgeschworenen beantragen.

talesman Hilfsgeschworener *m*, Ersatzgeschworener *m*.

talion Vergeltungsprinzip *n*.

Talisman *Zentrales Wertpapierhandels- und Börsenabrechnungssystem (EDV, GB)*.

talk *s* Gespräch *n*, Unterredung *f*, Besprechung *f*; **exploratory** ~**s** Sondierungen; **preliminary** ~**s** Vorverhandlungen.

talkathon Marathondebatte *f*.

talking out (=) *den Beginn der Lesung e–r Vorlage verhindern durch überlanges Debattieren des vorangehenden Tagesordnungspunktes (e–e Art Filibuster)*.

talking-shop Schwatzbude *f*.

tallager *hist* Steuereinzieher *m*.

tally Kerbholz *n*, Kerbstock *m*, Kerbzettel *m*; Kontogegenbuch *n*, Gegenbuch *n*, Duplikat *n*n, Etikett *n*, Marke *f*, Kennzeichen *n*; Warenliste *f*, Stückmaß *n*, Kupon *m*; ~ **clerk** Kontrolleur, Stimmenzähler; ~ **man** Tallymann (*der mit dem Kerbholz rechnet*); Inhaber e–s Abzahlungsgeschäftes, Musterreisender, Kontrolleur; ~ **sheet** Zahlbogen, Rechnungsbogen; ~ **system** Teilscheinsystem; ~ **trade** fortlaufender Lieferantenkredit.

talon Talon *m*, Erneuerungsschein *m*; ~ **tax** → *tax*.

Talweg (= Thalweg) Schiffahrtsrinne (*bei Grenzflüssen, Mündungsbuchten usw*).

tamquam *Rechtsmittel gegen Urteilstenor und die Vollstreckungsklausel*; **venire** ~ Einberufung von Geschworenen zur Entscheidung über Grund und Höhe des Anspruchs.

tamper sich mit etwas heimlich zu schaffen machen, fälschen, beeinflussen, bestechen; ~**ing with customs seals** Manipulation der Zollverschlüsse; ~ **with mail** das Briefgeheimnis verletzen; Post heimlich öffnen; ~**ing with witnesses** Beeinflussung von Zeugen; ~**ing with jurors** Geschworenenbeeinflussung; ~**ing with nomination papers** Kandidaturlistenfälschung.

tangible körperlich, physisch existent, wirklich, erheblich; ~ **fixed assets** Sachanlagen; ~ **movable assets** realisierbare Gegenstände des Betriebsvermögens.

tap *unbegrenzt emittierte festverzinsliche Staatspapiere, die den Banken von der Zentralbank angeboten werden*; ~ **bills** direkt emittierte Schatzwechsel; ~ **issue** Daueremission; **longer** ~ *langfristige Staatsobligationen*; **short** ~ *kurz- und mittelfristige (bis zu 5 Jahren) Staatsobligationen bzw Schatzbriefe*.

tap anzapfen, erschließen; **telephone** ~**ping** Abhören von Telefongesprächen.

tape Tonband *n*, Papierstreifen *m* (Tape), auf dem Kurse verzeichnet werden, Börsenticker; ~ **abbreviations** Börsentickerabkürzungen; ~ **quotation** Börsentickernotierung; ~ **-recording** Bandaufnahme.

tara Tara *f s* (= *T bzw . . .t*); ~ **and tret** *T* und Gutgewicht; ~ **weight** *T*gewicht, Bruttogewicht einschließlich Verpackung, Leergewicht e–s Flugzeugs; **actual** ~ reine *T*, wirkliche *T*; **average** ~ Durchschnitts*t*; **customary** ~ handelsübliche *T*, Usotara; **customs** ~ Zoll*t*; **super** ~ zusätzliche *T*vergütung.

tare *v* Tara vergüten, die Tara bestimmen.

target Ziel *n*, Planziel *n*, Vorgabe *f*, Soll *n*; Ansprechpartner (*Telephonwerbung*); ~ **company** Zielgesellschaft e–s Übernahmemanövers; Objekt e–s Ü; ~ **date** planmäßiger Termin; ~ **population** werbemäßig zu erreichender Bevölkerungsteil, Zielgruppe; ~ **price** Richtpreis, angestrebter Preis, Garantiepreis *für Ausgleichszahlung*;

on ~ unter Einhaltung des Planungssolls.

tarif de combat Konkurrenztarif *m*, Kampftarif *m*.

tariff Tarif *m*, Zolltarif *m*, Zoll *m*, Taxe *f*, Preisliste *f*; Strafenverzeichnis *n*; ~ **adjustment** Zolltarifanpassung; ~ **agreement** Zollabkommen; ~ **barriers** Zollschranken; ~ **bills** Zollvorlagen; ~ **business** Versicherungsgeschäfte nach Einheitstarifen; ~ **classification** Tarifierung; **T~ Commission** US-Bundeszollbehörde; ~ **companies** Versicherungsgesellschaften mit einheitlichen Tarifen; ~ **concessions** Zugeständnisse auf dem Gebiet des Zollwesens; ~ **cut** Zollsenkung; ~ **description** zolltarifl Benennung; ~ **differential** Zollunterschied; ~ **discrimination** benachteiligende Zollbehandlung; ~ **fed** (= ~ *protected*) durch Zölle geschützt; ~ **in force** gültiger Tarif; ~ **increase** Zollerhöhung; ~ **item** Tarifnummer; ~ **law** Zollgesetz; ~ **legislation** Zollgesetzgebung; ~ **making** Tariffestsetzung; ~ **negotiations** Zollverhandlungen; ~ **policy** → *policy* (*2*); ~ **protection** Schutzzoll, Schutz durch Zölle; ~ **quota** Zollkontingent; ~ **rate** Tarifsatz, Zollsatz; ~ **reduction** Zollsenkung; ~ **regulations** Zollbestimmungen; ~ **ridden** mit hohen Zöllen belastet; ~ **union** Zollverein, Zollverband; **ad valorem** ~ Wertzoll; **agricultural** ~ Agrarzoll; **anti-dumping** ~ Dumpingbekämpfungszoll; **bulk supply** ~ Mengentarif; **block** ~ degressiv gestaffelter Tarif; **compensating** ~ Ausgleichszoll, Zoll gemäß zollpflichtigem Rohstoffanteil am Fertigprodukt; **compensatory** = *compensating* ~ *qv*; **compound** ~ gemischter Zolltarif (aus Wertzoll und Stückzoll); **countervailing** ~ Ausgleichszoll; **customs** ~ Zolltarif; **differential** ~ Differentialtarif, Staffeltarif; **electricity** ~ Stromtarif; **export** ~ Ausfuhrzoll(tarif); **flat-rate** ~ Pauschaltarif, Kleinabnehmertarif; **flexible** ~ flexibler Zolltarif; **flexible use of** ~ **protection** elastische Handhabung des Zollschutzes; **freight** ~ → *freight*; **graduated** ~ Staffeltarif; **import** ~ → *import*; **installed load** ~ Grundgebühr (*nach Umfang der elektrischen Installation*); **insurance** ~ → *insurance*; **internal** ~ Binnenzoll; **load-rate** ~ Tarif nach normalem Verbrauch; **local** ~ Binnentarif; **maximum demand** ~ Höchstverbrauchertarif; **most-favoured-nation** ~ Meistbegünstigungszolltarif; **multiple** ~ Mehrfachzoll; **preferential** ~ Präferenztarif, Vorzugszoll; **protective** ~ Schutzzoll; **restricted hour** ~ Nachtstromtarif; **retaliatory** ~ Vergeltungszoll; **revenue** ~ Finanzzoll; **seasonal** ~ jahreszeitlich verschiedener Tarif; **sliding ~-scale** Gleitzoll; **special** ~ Sondertarif, Ausnahmetarif; **specific** ~ Gewichtszoll; Stückzoll; **subscribed demand** ~ gemischter Stromtarif (*Grundgebühr und Verbrauch*); **time-of-day** ~ Tag- und Nachtstromtarif; **two-part** ~ Grundgebühr plus Verbrauchertarif; **uniform** ~ Einheitstarif.

tariffication Tariffestsetzung *f*, Tarifierung *f*.

task Aufgabe *f*, Arbeitspensum *n*; Auftrag *m* (*e–s Beschaffungsamts*); ~ **force** *mil* Sonderkommando, Einsatzgruppe; *zivil*: Arbeitsgruppe, Arbeitsstab, Sonderarbeitsgruppe; ~ **behaviour** aufgabenorientiertes Verhalten; ~ **master** Aufseher, Vorarbeiter; ~ **wage** Akkordlohn; ~ **work** Akkordarbeit, Stückarbeit, zugeteilte Arbeit; **onerous** ~ Bürde.

tasking document Auftragsschein *m* (*e–s Beschaffungsamts*).

tautology Wiederholsamkeit *f*, Tautologie *f*.

tax Steuer *f* (= *St bzw . . . st*), Abgabe *f*, Besteuerung *f*; Gebühr *f*; ~ **abatement** *St*nachlaß; ~ **accounting** → *accounting*; ~ **advantages** *St*vorteile; ~ **adviser** *St*berater; ~ **allocation right** *St*bewilligungsrecht; ~ **allowance** *St*freibetrag; ~ **anticipation note** *St*gutschein; ~ **appeal** → *appeal*; ~ **arrears** *St*rückstände; ~**es assessed** veranlagte *St–n*; ~ **assessment** *St*veranlagung, *St*bescheid; ~ **at the source** Quellen*st*; ~ **attorney** Anwalt für *St*sachen; ~ **audit** *St*prüfung; ~ **auditor** *St*prüfer; ~ **authorities** *St*behörden; ~ **avoidance** Vermeidung von *St–n*; ~ **base** Besteuerungsgrundlage; *St*bemessungsgrundlage; ~**-bought** aus steuerlichen Gründen erworben; ~ **burden** *St*last; ~ **certificate** *St*abzugsbescheinigung (*Quellenst, Dividende*); ~ **class** *St*klasse; ~ **collection** *St*erhebung, *St*einziehung; ~ **compliance** Einhaltung der *St*gesetze; ~ **concession** *St*vergünstigung; ~ **convention** *St*abkommen; ~ **court** → *court*; ~ **credit** *St*anrechnung, *St*gutschrift; *foreign ~ ~: Anrechnung im Ausland gezahlter Stn*; **cut** *St*senkung; ~ **declaration** *St*erklärung; ~ **deduction** *St*abzug; ~ **deduction at source** *St*abzugsverfahren; Quellenbesteuerung; ~**-deed** Grunderwerbsurkunde bei Veräußerung wegen *St*rückständen; ~ **deferral** *St*stundung; ~ **delinquency** *St*säumnis; ~ **demand** *St*bescheid; ~ **disc** *St*plakette; ~ **discount** *St*skonto; ~ **dodger** *St*drückeberger, *St*hinterzieher; ~**es due** *St*schuld; ~ **efficient** *st*wirksam; *st*günstig; ~ **evader** *jmd, der Stverkürzung begeht, evt:* *St*hinterzieher; ~ **evasion** = *evasion of tax(es)* → *evasion*; ~ **exempt** *st*frei, gebührenfrei; ~ **exempt bonds** *st*freie Obligationen; ~ **exemption** *St*befreiung; ~ **exile** *St*exil; im *St*exil lebende Person; ~ **expert** *St*berater; *St*sachverständiger; ~ **ferret** (*privater*) *St*ermittler; ~ **foreclosure** Zwangsversteigerung für das Finanzamt; ~ **fraud** → *fraud*; ~ **free** *st*frei; ~ **haven** *St*oase; ~ **home** steuerlich relevanter beruflicher Wohnsitz; ~ **incidence** *St*anfall; ~ **law** *St*recht; ~ **lease** Pachtrechtsübertragung bei Zwangsveräußerung wegen *St*rückständen; ~ **legislation** *St*gesetze; ~**es levied by assessment** veranlagte *St–n*; ~ **levy** *St*erhebung, Gesamtertrag e–r *St*, *St*aufkommen; ~ **liability** *St*pflicht, *St*schuld; ~**-lien** *St*grundpfandrecht; ~**-lien property** für *St*schulden haftendes Vermögen; ~ **litigator** Prozeßanwalt in *St*sachen; ~ **on capital** Kapital*st*; ~ **on corporations** Körperschafts*st*; ~ **on donations** Schenkungs*st*; ~ **on income** Einkommens*st*; ~ **on scale charge** Tarifbesteuerung; ~ **on stock exchange dealings** Börsenumsatz*st*; ~ **on the total amount of wages or salaries** Lohnsummen*st*; ~ **on tobacco** Tabak*st*; ~ **overhaul** *St*reform; ~ ~ *package*: *St*reformpaket; ~**-paid** versteuert; ~ **penalty** *St*säumnizuschlag, *St*strafe; ~ **privilege** *St*vergünstigung; ~ **progression** *St*progression; ~ **purchaser** Erwerber bei *St*zwangsverkauf (*e–s Grundstücks*); ~ **rate** *St*satz; ~ **rebate** *St*rückvergütung; ~ **receipts** *St*einnahmen; ~ **reform** *St*reform; ~ **relief** *St*entlastung; *St*vorteil; *St*freibetrag; ~ **remission** *St*erlaß; ~ **reserve** *St*rückstellung; ~ **reserve certificate** verzinslicher *St*gutschein; ~ **return** *St*erklärung; ~ **revenue** *St*aufkommen, *St*ertrag; ~ **ridden** mit *St–n* überlastet; ~ **roll** → *roll*; ~ **sale** → *sale*; ~ **secrecy** *St*geheimnis; ~ **shelter** *St*oase; Niedrig*st*; ~ **sheltered accounts** Konten mit *st*freien Zinsen; ~ **shifting** *St*überwälzung; ~ **sovereignty** *St*hoheit; ~ **sparing** Quellensteuerbefreiung (*Doppelbesteuerungsabkommen*); ~ **statement** *St*aufstellung; ~ **statutes** *St*gesetze; ~ **table** *St*tabelle; ~**-title** Grunderwerbsnachweis bei *St*zwangsversteigerung; ~**es withheld at (the) source** Quellen*st–n*, im Abzugsverfahren erhobene *St–n*; ~ **year** *St*jahr, *GB ab 6. April e–s Jahres*; ~ **yield** *St*aufkommen,

*St*anfall; *St*erträgnisse; ~ **warrant** *St*-Vollstreckungsanordnung; **accrued ~es** *St*schulden; **accumulated earnings** ~ Körperschafts*st auf thesaurierte Gewinne*; **ad valorum** ~ Wert*st*; **added value** ~ Mehrwert*st*; **additional** ~ Zusatz*st*, Ergänzungsabgabe, *St*zuschlag; **after ~es** nach Abzug der *St-n;* **alternative** ~ Alternativ*st*; **amusement** ~ Vergnügungs*st*; **apportioned** ~ Repartitions*st*; **assessed** ~ direkte *St*, veranlagte *St*; **automobile** ~ Kraftfahrzeug*st*; **bank deposit** ~ Depot*st*; **basic rate** ~ Einkommen*st* zum Eingangstarif; **beverage** ~ Getränke*st*; **border** ~ Grenzausgleich; **building** ~ Bauabgabe; **business** ~ Gewerbe*st*; **capital gains** ~ (= *CGT*) Veräußerungsgewinn*st*; Spekulationsgewinn*st*; Spekulations*st*; **capital income** ~ Kapitalertrag*st*; **capital investment** ~ Investitions*st*; **capital stock** ~ Aktien*st*; **capital transfer** ~ Vermögensübertragungs*st*; gemeinsame Erbschafts- und Schenkungs*st*; **capitation** ~ Kopf*st*; **chain store** ~ Filialladen*st*; **car** ~ Zusatzumsatz*st* auf Kraftfahrzeuge; **circulation** ~ *US* Geldverkehrs*st*; **collateral inheritance** ~ *St* auf Nachlaß für Verwandte der Seitenlinie; **computation of** ~ *St*berechnung, *St*satz; **consumption** ~ Verbrauchs*st*; **corporate franchise** ~ Körperschaftsgründungs*st*; **corporate income** ~ Körperschafts*st*; **corporation profits** ~ Körperschafts*st*, Gewinnsonder*st* für Kapitalgesellschaften; **corporation sur~ on net income** Sonder*st* auf Körperschaftsgewinne; **corporation** ~ Körperschafts*st GB (auch für nichtrechtsfähige Vereine)* **cotton futures** ~ Umsatz*st* bei Baumwolltermingeschäften; **death** ~ Erbschafts*st*; **deduction of** ~ *St*abzug; **deferred ~es** latente *St–n*; **defrauded** ~ hinterzogene *St*; **degressive** ~ degressive *St*; **delinquent ~es** *St*rückstände; **direct** ~ direkte *St*; **dues** ~ *St* auf Mitgliedsbeiträge; **employment** ~ *US*: Sozialversicherungsbeiträge in Form e-r Lohnsummen*st*; **entertainment** ~ Vergnügungs*st*; **estate** ~ Nachlaß*st*, Erbschafts*st*; **estimated** ~ geschätzte *St*schuld, *St*schätzung; **excess profits** ~ Übergewinn*st*, Zusatzkörperschafts*st*; **excise** ~ Verbrauchs*st*, Gewerbe*st*; **excise lien property** ~ Versicherungsprämien*st*; **exemption from income** ~ Einkommens*st*freiheit; **export** ~ Ausfuhr*st*, Exportabgabe; **development land** ~ Bodenerschließungszuwachs*st* *(bei Veräußerung)*; **farmer's** ~ Landwirtschafts*st*, Grundertrags*st*; **federal income** ~ Bundeseinkommen*st*; **federal social security** ~ Sozialversicherungsbeiträge (*US*); **floor stocks** ~ Lagervorrats*st* (*Alkohol, Tabak*); **franchise** ~ Konzessions*st*; **general property** ~ Vermögens*st*; **gift** ~ Schenkungs*st*; **graded** ~ stufenweise *St*vergünstigung (*z. B. für Neubauten*); **graduated** ~ progressive *St*; **grand total of** ~ **revenue** Gesamt*st*aufkommen; **hidden** ~ verschleierte *St*; **illegal** ~ (völker)rechtswidrige Besteuerung; **immunity from ~es** *St*freiheit; **imperial ~es** brit Staats*st–n*; **impersonal ~es** Sach*st–n*; **import equalization** ~ Einfuhr-Ausgleichsabgabe; **import excise** ~ Einfuhrumsatz*st*; **imposition of** ~ Besteuerung; **income** → *income tax*; **income** ~ **return** Einkommen*st*erklärung; *joint* ~ ~ ~: *gemeinsame Einkst. erklärung*; **increment value** ~ Wertzuwachs*st*; **indirect** ~ indirekte *St*; **inheritance** ~ Erbschafts*st*; **input** ~ *Vorst* (*bei der Mehrwertst*); **interest equalization** ~ Zinsausgleichs*st*; **internal revenue** ~ *St–n*; **"knowledge"** ~ „Wissens*st*" (= *Mehrwertst auf Bücher, Zeitschriften u Zeitungen*); **land** ~ → *land*; **landed property** ~ Grund*st*; **license** ~ Konzessions*st*, Gewerbe*st*; **lien for** ~ gesetzliches Pfandrecht wegen *St*schulden; **lim-**

ited ~ **liability** beschränkte *St*pflicht; **liquor** ~ Alkohol*st* (*alkoholische Getränke und denaturierter Alkohol*); **local** ~ Kommunal*st*, Gemeinde*st*; **luxury** ~ Luxus*st*; **manufacturer's excise** ~ Produzentenumsatz*st* (*auf Industrieerzeugnisse*); **matured** ~**es** fällige *St–n*; **mileage** ~ Güterverkehrs*st* (*im zwischenstaatlichen Verkehr in USA*); **motor vehicle** ~ Kraftfahrzeug*st*; **municipal** ~ Kommunal*st*; **narcotic** ~ Rauschmittel*st*; **National T~ Association** Bund der *St*zahler; **net worth** ~ Vermögen*st*; **non-resident** ~ Fremden*st*, Kurtaxe; **normal** ~ Basis*st* (*US income tax*); **occupation** ~ Gewerbe*st*; **old age security** ~ **on income** Sozialabgaben vom Einkommen für die Altersversicherung; **oleomargarine** ~ Margarine*st*; **oppressive** ~**es** drückende Steuerlast; **organization** ~ Gründungs*st* (*Körperschaften*); **parafiscal** ~ steuerähnliche Abgabe; **parliamentary** ~**es** staatliche *St–n* (*durch das Zentralparlament eingeführt*); **pay as you go** ~ Quellen*st*; **payroll** ~ Lohnsummen*st*; Arbeitgeberbeiträge zur Sozialversicherung *US*; **perpetual** ~**es** stehende Abgaben; **personal** ~ Personal*st*, Kopf*st*, *St-n* auf das bewegliche Vermögen; **personal property** ~ *St–n* auf das bewegliche Vermögen; **poll** ~ Kopf*st*, Bürger*st esp Community charge qv*; **premium** ~ Versicherungs*st*, Prämien*st*; **profits** ~ Körperschafts*st*, Gewinn*st*; **progressive** ~ progressive *St*; **property** ~ *brit* Grund*st*, *US* Vermögens*st*; **proportional** ~ proportionale Vermögens*st*; **public** ~**es** staatliche *St-n;* **purchase** ~ Kauf*st*, Umsatz*st auf Güter des gehobenen Bedarfs; GB: abgeschafft seit 1972*; **racing** ~ Rennwett*st*; **rate of** ~**(es)** *St*satz; **rates and** ~**es** Kommunal*st–n* und Staats*st–n*; **real** ~ Real*st*; **real estate** ~ (= *real property* ~) Grund*st*; **refund of** ~**es** → *refund;* **regressive** ~ regressive *St* (*gemäß Stwert*); **remittance** ~ Besteuerungssatz für Erträge aus dem Ausland (*GB*); **retail sales** ~ Umsatz*st* im Einzelhandel, Warenverkaufs*st*; **road-using** ~ Straßenbenutzungsgebühr; **safe deposit** ~ Tresor*st*; **sales** ~ Warenumsatz*st*, Umsatz*st*; **selective employment** ~ Arbeitgeberzusatzabgabe (*GB 1966–1972*); **self-employment** ~ Einkommen*st* für Freiberufler; **severance** ~ Schürf*st*; **single** ~ Global*st*, Einheits(grund)*st*; **sinking fund** ~ Anleihe*st*, *St* zur Amortisation von Staatsanleihen; **snuff** ~ Schnupftabak*st*; **social security** ~ Sozialversicherungsbeitrag; **specific** ~ Stück*st*; **stamp** ~ Stempel*st*; **state** ~ staatliche *St*, *US* einzelstaatliche *St*; **state income** ~ einzelstaatliche Einkommen*st*; **stock transfer** ~ *US* Börsenumsatz*st*; **succession** ~ Erbschafts*st*; **sugar** ~ Zucker*st*; **talon** ~ Zinsbogen*st*, Kapitalertrag*st*; **tobacco** ~ Tabak*st*; **tobacco peddler's** ~ Umsatz*st* auf Tabakwaren im Wandergewerbe; **to bring into** ~ der *St* unterwerfen, besteuern; **trade** ~ Gewerbe*st*; **transportation** ~ (Personen)Beförderungs*st*; **turnover** ~ Umsatz*st*; **undistributed profits** ~ *St* auf unausgeschüttete Körperschaftsgewinne; **uniform** ~ Einheits*st*; **use** ~ *US* Gebrauchs*st*; **value added** ~ Mehrwert*st*; **vehicle** ~ Kraftfahrzeug*st*; **wage** ~ Lohn*st*; **war** ~**es** Krieg*st–n*; **water** ~ Wassergebühr; **wealth** ~ Vermögens*st*; **withholding** ~ Abzugs*st*, abzugsfähige *St*; Quellen*st*; *US*: Lohn*st*; **withholding** ~ **on dividends** Dividenden*st*, Kapitalertrag*st* im *St*abzugsverfahren; **windfall** ~ Sondergewinn*st*.

tax *v* besteuern; Kosten festsetzen (*Gerichts- und Anwaltskosten*); ~**ed off** bei der Kostenfestsetzung gekürzt.

taxable steuerpflichtig, abgabenpflichtig; festsetzbar, erstattungsfähig (*Kostenerstattung*).

taxation Besteuerung *f*, Taxierung *f*, Schätzung *f*, Kostenfestsetzung *f*; ~

as between solicitor and client Kostenfestsetzung bezügl des eigenen Mandanten; ~ **at the source** Quellenbesteuerung; ~ **between party and party** Kostenfestsetzung gegen den Prozeßgegner; ~ **discrimination** steuerliche Diskriminierung; ~ **equalization reserve** Steuerausgleichsrücklage; ~ **of costs** Kostenfestsetzung; ~ **privilege** Steuervergünstigung; ~ **scale** Steuersatz; **basis of** ~ Steuergrundlage; **certificate of** ~ → *certificate*; **deferred** ~ Steuerabgrenzung; **double** ~ Doppelbesteuerung; **double** ~ **arrangements** Vereinbarung zur Vermeidung der Doppelbesteuerung; **double** ~ **relief** Doppelbesteuerungsvergünstigung; **economic double** ~ wirtschaftliche Doppelbesteuerung; **future** ~ Steuerrückstellung; **juridical double** ~ juristische Doppelbesteuerung; **law of** ~ → *law;* **light** ~ geringe Besteuerung; **multiple** ~ mehrfache Besteuerung; **progressive** ~ progressive Besteuerung; **proportional** ~ proportionale Besteuerung (*nach dem gleichen Satz*); **recurrent** ~ Mehrfachbesteuerung; **redistributive** ~ Umverteilungsbesteuerung; **retroactive** ~ rückbezügliche Besteuerung; **to lodge a bill for** ~ e–e Kostenrechnung zur Festsetzung vorlegen; **to review** ~ die Kostenfestsetzung überprüfen; über Erinnerungen gegen e–n Kostenfestsetzungsbeschluß entscheiden; **unitary** ~ unbeschränkte Einheitsbesteuerung *des Konzerns* (*incl. Auslandstöchter*).

taximeter Taxameter *n*.

taxing master (Rechtspfleger als) Kostenbeamter *m*.

taxpayer Steuerzahler *m*; Steuerpflichtiger *m*; ~ **company** steuerpflichtige Gesellschaft; ~**s at large** die Steuerzahler; ~ **in arrears** säumiger Steuerpflichtiger; ~**s' list** Vermögensaufstellung (*der Steuerbehörde*); ~**'s suit** Popularklage; **nonresident** ~ beschränkt Steuerpflichtiger; **resident** ~ inländischer Steuerpflichtiger, unbeschränkt Steuerpflichtiger; **standard rate** ~ Einkommensteuerpflichtiger zum Normalsatz, mittelständischer Steuerzahler.

tea chest Teekiste *f* (*75 bis 80 lbs*).

teamster Fuhrmann *m*, Lastwagenfahrer *m*.

technical technisch, fachlich, formal, regelrecht.

technicality formale Eigentümlichkeit *f*, technische Feinheit *f*; Förmlichkeit *f* des Verfahrens, Raffinesse *f*, Formalismus *m*.

technobandit Technologie-Räuber *m*.

technobanditry Technologieraub *m*, Technologie-Banditentum, T.-Kriminalität.

technological | **change** technische Veränderung; ~ **improvement** Verbesserungen nach dem Stand der Technik; ~ **transfer** Technologietransfer; ~ **unemployment** durch die technische Entwicklung bedingte Arbeitslosigkeit.

technology Technologie *f*, Technik *f*; ~ **smuggler** Technologie-Schmuggler; ~ **transfer agreement** Technologie-Überlassungsvertrag; **copy-protect** ~ Kopierschutztechnik.

telecommunications Fernmeldeverkehr *m*.

telegram Telegramm *n* (= *T bzw ... t*), telegrafische Mitteilung *f*; ~ **address** *T*anschrift, Drahtanschrift; ~ **by telephone** vom Amt zugesprochenes *T*; ~**s' counter** *T*annahmeschalter; ~ **delivered by mail** Brief*t*; ~ **in cipher** Chiffre*t*; ~ **in plain language** unchiffriertes *T*, offenes *T*; ~ **with answer paid** Anwort*t*; ~ **with notice of delivery** *T* mit Empfangsbenachrichtigung; ~ **with repetition** *T* mit Wiederholung; **deferred** ~ gewöhnliches *T*; **exchange** ~ Kursdepesche; **forgery of** ~ *T*fälschung; **money order** ~ telegrafische Geldüberweisung; **prepaid** ~ *T* mit bezahlter

Rückantwort; **service** ~ Dienst*t*; **wireless** ~ Funk*t*.

telegraphic | **address** Telegrammadresse; ~ **communication** telegrafische Mitteilung; ~ **reply** Drahtantwort; ~ **transfer** telegrafische Überweisung.

telephone Fernsprecher *m*, Telefon *n*; ~ **answering machine** Anrufbeantworter; ~ **bill** Telefonrechnung; ~ **booth** Fernsprechzelle; ~ **box** Fernsprechzelle; ~ **charges** Fernsprechgebühren; ~ **conversation** fernmündliche Unterredung; ~ **dialling code** Vorwahlnummer; ~ **directory** Fernsprechbuch; ~ **exchange** Fernsprechamt; ~ **sales representative** telephonischer Werbeagent; ~ **subscriber** Fernsprechteilnehmer; ~ **tapping** „Anzapfen" des Telephons; ~ **trade** → *trade*.

telephoto Bildfunk *m*.

teleprinter Fernschreiber *m*.

telesales Vertrieb über das Telefon.

tell berichten, sagen; zählen; ~ **the plain truth** die reine Wahrheit sagen; ~ **the votes** Stimmen zählen.

teller Zähler *m*, Kassierer *m*, Kassenführer *m* im Schatzamt, Schalterbeamter *m*; Stimmenzähler *m*; **~'s cash book** Bank-Kassenjournal; **~s in parliament** mit der Stimmenzählung beauftragte Abgeordnete; ~ **terminal** eletronischer Bankschalter, Schalterautomat; **paying** ~ Auszahlungskassierer; **receiving** ~ Kassierer, Beamter am Einzahlungsschalter.

temp *s* vorübergehend Beschäftigter *m*.

temp *v*|*i* Gelegenheitsarbeit leisten, vorübergehend arbeiten.

temperance Mäßigkeit *f* in der Lebensführung; ~ **hotel** alkoholfreies Hotel; ~ **movement** Antialkoholbewegung; ~ **union** (=) Blaues Kreuz.

temperate in habits mäßig im Alkoholgenuß.

Templar Angehöriger *m* des Templer-Ordens; Angehöriger *m* der Temple Juristeninnung.

Temple (=) *e–e der Londoner Juristeninnungen bzw deren Gebäude.*

temporal weltlich.

temporalities *eccl* Temporalien *n*|*pl*, Kircheneinnahmen *f*|*pl*, weltliche Lehensgüter *n*|*pl* der Kirche.

temporarily | **lent or let on hire** als Leiharbeiter verwendet, ausgeliehen; ~ **used** vorübergehend verwendet.

temporary *s* Zeitarbeiter *m*, Leiharbeitskraft *f*.

temporary vorübergehend, zeitweilig, kurzfristig, zeitlich begrenzt, vorläufig, einstweilig; ~ **assurance policy** → *policy*; ~ **cessation of work** Betriebsunterbrechung; ~ **crisis accommodation** Notunterkunft; ~ **housing accommodation** vorläufige Ersatzwohnung; ~ **restraining order** einstweilige Unterlassungsanordnung.

temporization beabsichtigte Verzögerung *f*, Verschleppung *f*, Abwarten *n* (*um Zeit zu gewinnen*), *vgl temporize*.

temporize Zeit zu gewinnen suchen; verhandeln, um Zeit zu gewinnen; sich nicht festlegen; sich opportunistisch verhalten; e–n Kompromiß schließen.

tenable haltbar, vertretbar.

tenancy Mietverhältnis *n*, Pachtverh *n*, *hist* Lehensbesitz am Grundstück; dingliche Berechtigung (*meist an Grundstücken*), Grundstücksmiete, Grundstückspacht; ~ **agreement** Miet(Pacht)vertrag; ~ **at sufferance** Nutzungsverhältnis (*nach Ablauf der Miet/Pachtzeit*); ~ **at will** jederzeit fristlos kündbares Pachtverhältnis; ~ **by estoppel** Mietverhältnis kraft Rechtsscheins oder konkludenten Verhaltens; ~ **by the entirety** → *entirety;* ~ **for life** lebenslängliches Pachtrecht, Nießbrauch an Grundstück, lebenslängliches Besitzrecht; ~ **for years** Mietverhältnis auf bestimmte Zeit; ~ **from year to year** jahrweise festgesetztes Miet(Pacht)verhältnis; ~ **in common** Miteigentum nach Bruchteilen, Bruchteilsgemeinschaft (*GB 1925 ohne Anwachsungsrecht im Todesfall*); ~ **year** Miet(Pacht)jahr; ~ **of business premises** Geschäftsraummiete; ~ **pur autre vie** Miete (Pacht) auf Lebenszeit eines Dritten; **assured** ~ *frei vereinbartes Mietverh mit Kündigungsschutz*; **business** ~ Geschäftsraummiete; **contractual** ~ vertragliches Mietverh; **controlled** ~ *dem Mieterschutz und der Mietpreisbindung unterliegendes Mietverhältnis,* geschütztes, preisgebundenes Mietverhältnis; *GB bis 1980*; *dann protected* ~ *qv*; **entire** ~ Einzelmietvertrag, Alleinpacht, Miete (Pacht) mit alleinigem Mieter (Pächter); **expiration of** ~ Ablauf des Miet(Pacht)verhältnisses; **extension of** ~ Pacht(Miet)verlängerung; **farm** ~ Landpacht, landwirtschaftliches Pachtverhältnis; **furnished** ~ Vermietung von möblierter Wohnung; **general** ~ unbefristetes Pachtverhältnis; Mietverhältnis auf unbestimmte Zeit; **housing association** ~ Mietverh auf Grund e–s Kapitalanteils des Vermieters an einer Wohnungsbaugesellschaft; **joint** ~ gemeinsames Mietverhältnis, Gesamthandsgemeinschaft, Gesamthandseigentum; Miteigentum *am Grundstück* zur gesamten Hand; **long** ~ langfristiges Mietverh (über 21 Jahre); **month-to-month** ~ monatlich sich verlängerndes Miet(Pacht)verhältnis; **periodic** ~ sich stets verlängerndes Mietverhältnis; **presently-subsisting** ~ derzeit bestehendes Mietverhältnis; **protected** ~ geschütztes Mietverh; **regulated** ~ geschütztes Mietverh; **secure** ~ geschütztes Mietverh; **several** ~ Einzelpachtverhältnis, Einzelbesitzrecht am Grundstück; **shorthold** ~ kurzfristiges Mietverhältnis; **statutorily protected** ~ geschütztes Mietverh, Wohnung unter Mieterschutzrecht; **statutory** ~ gesetzliches Nutzungsverhältnis *nach Ablauf der Mietzeit*; **sub**~ Unterpacht (-miete); **yearly** ~ jährlich sich verlängerndes Mietverhältnis.

tenant zum Besitz am Grundstück Berechtigter; Grundstücksbesitzer *m* auf Zeit, Pächter *m*, Mieter *m*; ~ **at sufferance** widerrufl geduldeter Nutzungsausübender; faktischer Mieter (*nach Ablauf der Mietzeit*); ~ **at will** jederzeit kündbarer Pächter; **business** ~ Mieter von Geschäftsraum; ~ **by copy of court roll** = *copyholder qv*; ~ **by elegit** zwangsverwaltender Gläubiger; ~ **by the curtesy** (= *courtesy*) Witwer mit Nießbrauch am Immobiliennachlaß der Ehefrau; ~ **by the manner** Pachtbesitzer; ~ **farmer** landwirtschaftl Pächter; ~**s' fixtures** Einbauten des Mieters/Pächters; ~ **for life** (Grundstücks)Nießbraucher auf (*eigene oder fremde*) Lebenszeit; ~ **for life by will** Vorerbe auf Lebenszeit; ~ **for a term of years** Pächter auf bestimmte Zeit; ~ **from year to year** Jahrespächter auf unbestimmte Zeit, zum Jahresende kündbarer bzw kündigungsberechtigter P. (*mit halbjähriger, bei landwirtschaftl Pacht ganzjähriger Kündigungsfrist*); ~ **in capite** Kronvasall; ~**-inchief** Kronvasall, unmittelbarer Lehensträger; ~**s in common** Miteigentümer nach Bruchteilen, Mitbesitzer (*auf Grund verschiedener Rechtstitel*); ~ **in dower** Witwe als Pflichtteilsnießbraucherin (*zu ⅓ am Ehegattengrundbesitz*); ~ **in fee** (= ~ *in fee-simple*) Grundeigentümer (*ohne Erbfolgebindungen*); ~ **in occupation under a lease** unmittelbarer Pachtbesitzer; ~ **in paravail** = ~ *paravail qv*; ~ **in possession** Mieter (Pächter) im unmittelbaren Besitz; Wohnungsinhaber; Vorerbe; ~ **in severalty** alleinberechtigter Pachtbesitzer; ~ **in tail** Grundbesitzer mit Fideikommißbeschränkung; ~ **in tail in remainder** Nacherbe; ~ **of a trust fund** Begünstigter e–s Treuhandvermögens; ~ **of the demesne** Unterpächter, Unterlehensträger; ~ **paravail(e)** Unterpächter, Unterlehensträger; ~ **pur autre vie** Grundbesitzer auf Lebenszeit e–s

Dritten; ~ **purchase loan** Hoferwerbsdarlehen (*aus US Bundesmitteln für landwirtsch. Siedlung*); ~**s' repairs** vom Mieter (*bzw Pächter*) auszuführende Instandhaltungsarbeiten; ~ **right** Mieterrecht; Aufwendungsersatzanspruch des weichenden Pächters; ~**-right of renewal** Anwartschaftsbesitz; ~**s' risk** Pächter(Mieter)haftung; ~**-stockholder** Mitglied einer Wohnungs-Genossenschaft (*mit einbezahltem Kapital*); **agricultural** ~ landwirtschaftlicher Pächter; **base** ~ Grundhöriger; **cash** ~ Pächter bei Geldzahlungspacht; **cash-share** ~ Pächter bei gemischter Geldzahlungs- und Naturalpacht; **conventionary** ~**s** *Hörige auf Grund vertraglicher Unterwerfung;* **council** ~ Mieter e–r gemeindeeigenen Sozialwohnung; **customary** ~ = *copyhold* ~ *qv*; **flat** ~ Wohnungsmieter, Etagenwohnungsm.; **game** ~ Jagdpächter; **holdover** ~ vertragslos weiterwohnende ehem Mieter; **incoming** ~ neuer (Pächter) Mieter; **joint** ~**s** Gesamthandsberechtigter, Gesamthandseigentümer; **new** ~ Nachmieter, Nachpächter; **occupying** ~ Wohnungsinhaber als Mieter bzw Nutzungsberechtigter; **outgoing** ~ weichender Pächter, ausziehender Mieter; **particular** ~ Teilpächter; **protected** ~ geschützter Mieter (*Räumungsschutz nach Vertragsablauf bei eigengenutzter Wohnung*); **public sector** ~**s** Mieter von Wohnungen der öffentl Hand; **quasi** ~ **at sufferance** rechtsgrundloser, stillschweigend geduldeter Gewahrsamsinhaber, geduldeter Unterpächter (*nach Ende der Hauptpacht*); **residential** ~ Wohnungsmieter; **secure** ~ Sozialmieter mit Erwerbsrecht an der Wohnung; **share** ~ Naturalpächter (*zu e–m Ernteanteil*); **shooting** ~ Jagdpächter; **sitting** ~ bereits vorhandener Mieter; **sole** ~ Einzelpächter, Einzelmieter, Einzelbesitzer auf Zeit (*an e–m Grundstück*); **statutory** ~ unter Räumungsschutz stehender Wohnungsinhaber (*nach Mietbeendigung*); **statutory** ~ **by succession** Nachfolger (Erbe) des unter Räumungsschutz stehenden Mieters.

tenantable verpachtbar, vermietbar, in bewohnbarem Zustand; **repair** → *repair*.

tenantless unverpachtet, unvermietet.

tendency Tendenz *f*, Richtung *f*, Neigung *f*, Stimmung *f*; **bearish** ~ Baissetendenz; **bullish** ~ → *bullish*.

tender Zahlungsangebot *n*, Leistungsangebot *n*, Lieferungsangebot *n*, befristetes Börsenangebot; Angebot *n*, Offerte *f*, Submission *f*, Kostenvoranschlag *m*, Realangebot *n*, Anbieten *n* (*der geschuldeten Leistung*), Andienung *f*; vorprozessuale Zahlungsbereitschaft *f*; Angebot, Schatzwechsel (*von der Bank of Engl*) zu kaufen (*im Tenderverfahren*); ~ **bills** im Ausschreibungsverfahren (*tender*) gehandelte (*brit*) Schatzwechsel; ~ **bond** Bietungsgarantie; ~ **closing date** Submissionstermin; ~ **guarantee** Bietungsgarantie; ~ **of amends** → *amends*; ~ **offer** → *tender offer*; ~ **of issue** Antrag auf Sachentscheidung; ~ **of payment** Zahlungsangebot; ~ **of performance** Leistungsangebot, Erfüllungsangebot; ~ **of resignation** Rücktrittsgesuch, Abschied; ~ **of services** Anerbieten von Diensten; ~ **of the price** Kaufpreisbereithaltung; ~ **system** Tenderverfahren, Zeichnungsangebot mit bestimmtem Kurs; **acceptance of** ~ → *acceptance*; **allocation by** ~**s** Ausschreibung, Vergabe im Submissionswege; **allocation to the lowest** ~ Vergebung an das niedrigste Submissionsangebot; **by** ~ auf dem Submissionswege, durch Ausschreibung; **common** ~ gesetzliches Zahlungsmittel; **form of** ~ Vordruck für Submissionsofferten, Leistungsverzeichnis; **government** ~ staatliche Ausschreibung; **invitation for** ~**s** → *invitation*;

joint ~ agreement Vertrag über die Abgabe e-s Konsortialangebots, volles Zahlungsangebot; **legal** ~ gesetzliche(s) Zahlungsmittel; **plea of** ~ → *plea*; **public** ~ (öffentl) Ausschreibung; **sealed** ~ Submissionsangebot in versiegeltem Umschlag; **terms of the** ~ Ausschreibungsbedingungen; **to make a** ~ ein Submissionsangebot machen; **to participate in a** ~ an e–r Ausschreibung teilnehmen.

tender *v* anbieten, offerieren, einreichen, ein Angebot machen, sich um etwas bewerben; ~ **an oath to s.o.** jmdm den Eid zuschieben; ~ **bail** Kaution zur Haftverschonung anbieten; ~ **delivery** Lieferung anbieten; ~ **documents** Urkunden vorlegen; ~ **evidence** Beweis antreten; ~ **one's resignation** seinen Rücktritt anbieten; ~ **one's services** seine Dienste anbieten.

tender offer befristetes Aktienkauf-Angebot (*zur Erlangung von Mehrheit bzw Sperrminorität*); Übernahmeangebot zum festen Kurs.

tenderee Auftraggeber *m* (*bei Ausschreibungen*), die vergebene Stelle.

tenderer Submittent *m*, (An)Bieter *m*; **the lowest** ~ der billigste Submittent.

tenement *hist* Lehensbesitz am Grundstück, Grundstück *n*, Wohnhaus *n*, Mietskaserne *f*, (Miet)Wohnung; ~ **house** Mietskaserne, Slumwohnung; ~ **resident** Mietshausbewohner; **dominant** ~ herrschendes Grundstück (*Dienstbarkeit*); **idle** ~ leerstehendes Wohnhaus; **servient** ~ dienendes Grundstück (*Dienstbarkeit*).

tenendum *formelle Besitztitelbeschreibung in Grundstücksübertragungsurkunden.*

tenens Pächter *m*, Beklagter *m* (*bei dinglichen Klagen*).

tenet Grundsatz *m*, Dogma *n*, Meinung *f*, Ansicht *f*.

tenner zehnjährige Zuchthausstrafe *f*; Zehndollarnote *f*.

tenor Tenor *m*, Wortlaut *m*, wesentlicher Inhalt *m*, Sinn *m*, Fassung *f*, Text *m*; Laufzeit *f*; Abschrift *f*, Kopie *f*; ~ **of a bill** Laufzeit e–s Wechsels; ~ **of a deed** Inhalt e–r gesiegelten Urkunde; **according to the** ~ nach dem Inhalt der Urkunde; **original** ~ ursprüngl Wortlaut.

tentative versuchsweise, probeweise.

tenure Landbesitzrecht *n*, Pachtverhältnis *n*, Grundbesitz *m*, Lehen *n*; Amtsdauer *f*, Amtszeit *f*, Amtsinhaberschaft *f*; ~ **at will** = *tenancy at will* → *tenancy*; ~ **by divine service** Kirchenlandbesitz gegen Verpflichtung zur Seelenmesse und Armenpflege; ~ **by lease** Pachtbesitz, Zeitpacht; Lehensbesitz; ~ **of land** (Recht zum) Besitz am Grundstück; ~ **in capite** Kronlehen, Oberlehen, unmittelbares Lehen; ~ **of land** Landpacht; ~ **of office** Amt, Amtsdauer, Amtsführung; **base** ~ nachgeordneter Lehensbesitz; **customary** ~ Lehensform nach Ortsgebrauch; **feudal** ~ Lehen, Lehensbesitz, Lehenswesen; **free** ~ freies Lehen; **lay** ~ weltliches Lehen; **life** ~ → *life*; **multiple** ~ gemeinsamer Landbesitz; **nonfree** ~ unfreies Lehen; = *copyhold qv*; **quam diu** ~ Amt auf Lebenszeit; **security of** ~ → *security*; **spiritual** ~ geistliches Lehen; **statutory** ~ gesetzliche Amtszeit.

tenured fest angestellt, verbeamtet.

term *s* Zeitdauer *f*, Frist *f*, Sitzungsperiode *f*, Mietzeit *f*, Pachtzeit *f*, Besitz *m* auf unbestimmte Zeit, Dauer *f*, Laufzeit *f*, Gefängnisstrafe *f*, Strafzeit *f*; Begriff *m*, Kunstwort *n*, Terminus *m*, Fachausdruck *m*, Bedingung *f*; Termin *m*; Zahlungsfrist *f*, Ziel *n*; Quartalstermin *m*; **~s** Bedingungen, Bestimmungen; **~s and conditions** Geschäftsbedingungen; **~s and conditions of an issue** Emissionsbedingungen; **~s and conditions of sale** Lieferbedingungen; ~ **bill** Terminwechsel, Tagwechsel; **~s, cash** Barzahlung bei Kaufabschluß; **~s control** AGB-überwachung beim Ratenkauf; ~ **credit** Akzeptkredit; ~

date Ablaufstag e–r Frist bzw festen Mietzeit; ~ **days** Mietfälligkeitstage, Zahltage; ~ **deposit** Festgeldeinlage; langfristig kündbare Einlage; ~ **draft** Zieltratte; ~ **fee** Prozeßgebühr (*des Anwalts pro Gerichtsperiode*); ~ **for deliberating** Ausschlagungsfrist; ~ **for filing** Einreichungsfrist, Anmeldefrist; ~ **for years** Pacht(verhältnis); ~ **in gross** (*nicht erbrechtlich bzw treuhänderisch gebundenes*) Grundbesitzrecht; ~**s inclusive** alles inbegriffen, Pauschalpreis; ~ **insurance** → *insurance*; ~ **loan** mittelfristiger Kredit, befristetes Darlehen (*1–10 Jahre*); ~ **note** mittelfristiger Eigenwechsel; ~ **of a bill** Wechselfrist, Laufzeit; ~ **of a guarantee** Dauer e–r Garantie, Garantiefrist; ~ **of a licence** Lizenzdauer; ~ **of a patent** → *patent*; ~ **of acceptance** Akzeptfrist, Annahmefrist; ~**s of admission** Zulassungsbedingungen; ~**s of amortization** Amortisationsbedingungen, Amortisationsplan, Tilgungsbedingungen; ~**s of an award** Inhalt e–s Schiedsspruchs; ~**s of business** Geschäftsbedingungen; ~**s of composition** Vergleichsbedingungen; ~ **of contract** bestimmte Vertragsdauer; ~**s of contract** Vertragsbedingungen; ~ **of copyright** Urheberrechtsschutzfrist; ~ **of court** Sitzungsperiode e–s Gerichts; ~**s of delivery** Lieferbedingungen, Bezugsbedingungen; Bedingungen der Lieferkostentragung; ~**s of freight** Frachtbedingungen, Transportbedingungen; ~ **of gestation** → *gestation;* ~**s of interest** Zinsbedingungen; ~**s of issue** Ausstattung (*Schuldverschreibung*); ~ **of years absolute** Erbpacht; ~ **of lease** Pachtzeit, Mietzeit; ~ **of life** Lebensdauer, Lebenszeit; ~ **of limitation** Verjährungsfrist; ~ **of military service** Militärdienstzeit; ~ **of notice** Kündigungsfrist; ~ **of office** Dienstzeit, Amtsdauer, Amtszeit; ~ **of Parliament** Legislaturperiode; ~ **of payment** Zahlungsfrist, Zahlungstermin; ~**s of payment** Zahlungsbedingungen, Zahlungsgewohnheiten im Außenhandel; ~ **of preclusion** Ausschlußfrist; ~ **of prescription** Verjährungsfrist; ~ **of presentation** Vorlagefrist; ~ **of protection** Schutzdauer; ~ **of redemption** Tilgungsfrist; ~**s of redemption** Tilgungsplan, Amortisationsplan; ~**s of reference** Auftrag (*e–s Ausschusses*), Mandat, Zuständigkeitsbereich; ~ **of subscription** Bezugsfrist; ~**s of subscription** Zeichnungsbedingungen; ~ **of the insurance** Versicherungsdauer; ~**s of the policy** Versicherungsbedingungen; ~**s of trade** (=) Handelsbedingungen, Außenhandelsmeßzahl, Verhältnis von Ausfuhr- zu Einfuhrpreisen; ~**s of trust** Treuhandbestimmung; ~ **of validity** Gültigkeitsdauer; ~ **of years** fester mehrjähriger Zeitraum, feste Pacht/Mietzeit; ~ **of years absolute** Zeitpacht, Erbpacht (*auf bestimmte Zeit*), dingliches Pachtrecht (*zeitlich begrenztes, ausschließliches Besitzrecht an e–m Grundstück*); ~ **policy** → *policy* (*1*); ~ **refresher** erneuter Anwaltskostenvorschuß; ~**s rent** Quartalsmiete(pacht); ~ **shares** befristet gesperrte Einlagen bei Baugenossenschaft; ~**s strictly cash** nur gegen Barzahlung; ~ **to conclude** Schlußfrist für beiderseitiges Parteivorbringen; ~ **transfer** Laufzeitumstrukturierung; **at reasonable** ~**s** zu vernünftigen Bedingungen; **concurrent** ~**s** gleichzeitige Verbüßung von Freiheitsstrafen; **consecutive** ~**s** aufeinanderfolgende Verbüßung von Freiheitsstrafen; **contract** ~**s** Vertragsbedingungen; **conventional** ~**s** übliche Zahlungsfristen; **default of** ~ Fristversäumnis; **deferred** ~**s** auf Abzahlung; **descriptive** ~ beschreibende Angabe; **easy** ~**s** günstige Kreditbedingungen, Zahlungserleichterungen; **exact** ~**s** genauer Wortlaut; **expired** ~ abgelaufene Frist; **express** ~ ausdrückliche Bedingung, ausdrückl übernommene Verpflichtung; **fair ~s** angemessen Bedingungen; **fixed ~** Frist, fester Zeitraum; feste Vertragsdauer, Befristung; **general ~** allgemeine Sitzungsperiode; **implied ~** stillschweigende Bedingung; **in ~s of** in Form von, ausgedrückt in; **in set ~s** festgelegt; **inclusive ~s** Inklusivpreis; **initial ~** Erstdauer, Dauer von zunächst . . .: **landed ~s** → *landed*; **legal ~** juristischer Begriff, juristischer Fachausdruck; **local ~s** Platzbedingungen, Lokalbedingungen; **maximum ~** längste befristete Freiheitsstrafe; **on mutual ~s** auf Gegenseitigkeit; **peace ~s** Friedensbedingungen; **penal ~** Strafzeit; **peremptory ~** Notfrist; **preclusive ~** Ausschlußfrist; **preference ~s** Vorzugsbedingungen; **presidential ~** Amtszeit des *US* Präsidenten; **prison ~** Strafzeit; **real ~s** geldwertbereinigt; **regular ~** richterliche Frist; **running of a ~** Lauf e–r Frist; **satisfied ~** durch Erfüllung erledigte Pachtzeit; **special ~** Verhandlung vor dem Einzelrichter; **special ~s** Sonderbedingungen; **standard ~s** Einheitsbedingungen, allgemeine Geschäftsbedingungen; **surrender ~s** Kapitulationsbedingungen; **technical ~** Fachausdruck; **the ~s of section 12 have been satisfied** die Bestimmungen von § 12 sind erfüllt; **to be under ~s** an gerichtl Auflagen (*bei Nachsichtsgewährung oder Fristverlängerung*) gebunden sein; **to come to ~s** → *to come;* **to keep ~s** → *to keep;* **under ~s** mit gerichtlichen Auflagen beschwert; **unexpired ~** unverbrauchte Miet(Pacht)zeit; **unread ~s** nicht gelesene Vertragsbestimmungen (*verbindlich*); **usual ~s** → *usual.*

termer zu zeitiger Freiheitsstrafe Verurteilter.

terminable begrenzbar, kündbar, rückzahlbar; **~ at pleasure** jederzeit kündbar; **~ by notice** ordentlich kündbar, befristet kündbar; **~ annuity** zeitlich begrenzte Rente; **~ association** kündbare Produzentenvereinigung, Kartell; **~ contract** kündbarer Vertrag.

terminal *adj* abschließend, End . . .; **~ benefit** (Entlassungs-)Abfindung; **~ market** Terminmarkt, Produktenbörse; **~ payment** Zahlung der letzten Rate, Schlußzahlung; **~ point of transportation** Endpunkt der Beförderung; **~ price** Preis für künftige Lieferung; ; **~ property** Besitz auf Zeit; **~ wage** Entlassungsabfindung.

terminal Endstation *f*, Hauptbahnhof *m*; **~ charges** (Fracht)Zustellgebühren.

terminate beenden, kündigen, enden, erlöschen; **~ a contract** e–n Vertrag kündigen, e–n V. einseitig beenden; **~ by notice** ordentlich (*unter Einhaltung e–r Kündigungsfrist*) kündigen.

terminating building society Baugenossenschaft *f* auf Zeit.

termination Ablauf *m*, Abschluß *m*, Ende *n*; Kündigung *f*, Beendigung *f*; **~ clause** Bestimmung über Vertragsbedingung; **~ date** Tag des Außerkrafttretens; **~ for convenience** Kündigung nach Belieben; **~ of contract** Vertragsbeendigung; **~ of authority** Erlöschen der Vollmacht; **~ of power of attorney** Erlöschen der Vollmacht

terminer *gerichtliche* (End)Entscheidung.

terminology Terminologie *f*, Fachsprache *f*; **legal ~** Rechtsterminologie, Rechtssprache.

terminus Ende *n*, Endstation *f*, Grenze *f*, Begrenzung *f*; **~ a quo** Ausgangspunkt; **~ ad quem** Endpunkt; **~ juris** richterliche Frist; **final ~** Endpunkt, Ankunftsort; **initial ~** Ausgangspunkt (*e–r Reise*).

termor Landpächter *m*, langfristiger bzw lebenslänglich berechtigter Grundbesitzer *m* auf Zeit.

terrace Reihenhausgruppe *f*.

terre-tenant unmittelbarer Grundbesitzer *m*.

terrier Flurbuch *n*.

territorial | **air space** Lufthoheitsgebiet; ~ **application** örtlicher Geltungsbereich; ~ **army** Territorialarmee (*Wehrpflichtigen-Einheiten*); ~ **bay** Bucht im Staatshoheitsgebiet; ~ **changes** Gebietsveränderungen; ~ **claim** territorialer Anspruch, Gebietsanspruch; ~ **corporation** Gebietskörperschaft; ~ **courts** Gerichte in den Territorien der USA; ~ **frontier** Dreimeilengrenze, Hoheitsgrenze; ~ **papers** Staatsurkunden betr US-Territorien (*bzw Gliedstaaten vor Gründung*); ~ **practice acts** Prozeßordnungen von US-Territorien; ~ **zone** Dreimeilenzone, Hoheitsgewässer.

territoriality Territorialität *f*, Zugehörigkeit *f* zu e–m Staatsgebiet; **principle of** ~ Territorialitätsprinzip.

territory Staatsgebiet *n*, Hoheitsgebiet *n*; Territorium *n* (*Schutzgebiet*) der USA; ~ **allocation** Marktaufteilung; ~ **covered** Geltungsbereich; ~ **of a judge** örtliche Zuständigkeit e–s Richters (Gerichts); **acquisition of** ~ → *acquisition*; **administrative** ~ Verwaltungsgebiet; **ceded** ~ abgetretenes Gebiet; **customs** ~ → *customs*; **dependent** ~ abhängiges Gebiet, Schutzgebiet; **enemy** ~ Feindesland; **exchange of** ~ Gebietsaustausch; **duty-paid** ~ Zollinland; **federal** ~ Bundesgebiet; **hostile** ~ Feindgebiet; **national** ~ Staatsgebiet; **neutral** ~ neutrales Hoheitsgebiet; **occupied** ~ besetzes Gebiet; **protected** ~ Protektoratsgebiet; **sales** ~ Absatzgebiet; **scheduled** ~ → *to schedule*; **sovereign** ~ Hoheitsgebiet; **state** ~ → *state* (*2*); **violation of** ~ Gebietsverletzung.

terror Terror *m*, Schreckensherrschaft *f*; plötzliches Erschrecken *n*, Panik *f*; ~ **raid** Terrorangriff.

terrorism Terrorismus *m*; **professional criminal** ~ berufsmäßiger (*verbrecherischer*) Terrorismus.

test Probe *f*, Versuch *m*, Untersuchung *f*, Prüfung *f*; Prüfungsmaßstab *m*, Maßstab *m*; ~ **action** Musterprozeß; ~ **audit** stichprobenweise Rechnungsprüfung; ~ **ballot** Probeabstimmung; **T~ Ban Treaty** Atomsperrvertrag; ~ **case** Musterprozeß; ~ **oath** Treueid, Amtseid; ~ **of relation** Feststellungskriterien für die Tatbeteiligung; ~-**paper** Beweisurkunde; ~ **period** Probezeit; ~ **period return** Probezeitergebnis; ~ **series** Versuchsserie; ~ **site** Versuchsgelände; **blood** ~ Blutprobe, Blutgruppenuntersuchung; **breath** ~ Alkohol-Atemtest; *roadside* ~ ~: *Alkoholtest an Ort und Stelle*; **capacity** ~ Eignungsprüfung; **check** ~ Gegenprobe; **endurance** ~ → *endurance*; **material** ~ Materialprüfung; **means** ~ → *means;* **mundane** ~**s** *med jur* Routineunterschungen; **punishment** ~ Zerreißprobe.

test-tube baby Retortenbaby *n*.

testable prüfbar, testierfähig.

testacy Testierfähigkeit *f*; Ableben unter Hinterlassung e–s Testaments; gewillkürte Erbfolge *f*.

testament Testament *n* (= *T bzw* . . . *t*), letzter Wille *m*, letztwillige Verfügung *f* über das bewegliche Vermögen; ~-**dative** *scot* vom Gericht ernannter *T*–*s*vollstrecker; ~-**testamentar** *scot* Bestätigung als vom Erblasser ernannter *T*–*s*vollstrekker; **holograph** ~ eigenhändiges (*handgeschriebenes*) *T*; **inofficious** ~ *Testament mit sittenwidriger Enterbung naher Angehöriger*; **last will and** ~ *T*, letztwillige Verfügung; **military** ~ Soldaten*t*; **mutual** ~**s** gegenseitiges *T*, wechselbezügliches *T*; **mystic** ~ geheimes Notariats*t*.

testamentary testamentarisch, letztwillig, Testaments- . . .

testate *adj adv* testamentarisch, ein Testament errichtet habend, Testaments . . .; **to die** ~ unter Hinterlassung e–s Testaments sterben.

testate *s* Testator *m*, Testierender *m*.

testate *v* testieren; ein Testament errichten, ein Testament hinterlassen.

testation Zeuge *m*, Beweismaterial *n*; testamentarische Verfügung *f*.

testator Testator *m*, Testierender *m*; testamentarischer Erblasser *m* (*bei testamentarischer Erbfolge*); von Todes wegen Verfügender.

testatrix Erblasserin *f* (*bei testamentarischer Erbfolge*).

testatum Hauptteil *m* e–r Urkunde (*nach den Worten "this indenture witnesseth"*); ~ **writ** Rechtshilfeersuchen zur auswärtigen Zustellung.

teste (*of a writ*) Beglaubigungsvermerk *m*.

tested geprüft; beglaubigt.

tester Prüfer *m*, Prüfungsbeamter *m*.

testificate bezeugen, beweisen, unter Eid aussagen.

testify aussagen, bezeugen; ~ **by affirmation** durch eidesstattliche Versicherung bekunden; ~ **in court** vor Gericht aussagen; **refusal to** ~ Aussageverweigerung.

testimonial Zeugnis *n*, Attest *n*, Arbeitszeugnis *n*; Dienstzeugnis *n*, *hist* Einreisebescheinigung *f*.

testimonium (clause) Schlußklausel *f* (*in e–r Urkunde*), Unterschriftsformel (*in witness whereof . . .*).

testimony Zeugenaussage *f*, Bekundung *f* von Zeugen *bzw* Sachverständigen; **action to perpetuate** ~ Beweissicherungsverfahren, Beweissicherungsantrag; **compulsory** ~ Aussagepflicht; **conflicting** ~ sich widersprechende Zeugenaussagen; **experimental** ~ Sachverständigenaussage über wissenschaftliche Versuche (*zur Überführung des Täters*); **expert** ~ Aussage e–s sachverständigen Zeugen; mündl Gutachten e–s Sachverständigen; **false** ~ Falschaussage(n); **in** ~ **whereof** zu Urkund dessen; **negative** ~ negative Aussage (*als Indiz, daß etw nicht geschehen ist*); **oral** ~ mündlicher Beweis, Zeugenaussage; **perpetuating** ~ → *perpetuating*; **postive** ~ Aussage e–s unmittelbaren Zeugen; **sponsal** ~ Ehegattenaussagen; **sworn** ~ eidliche Aussage; **to bear** ~ bezeugen; **to refuse** ~ die Aussage verweigern; **to withdraw the** ~ die Zeugenaussage widerrufen.

testing agency Prüfstelle *f*.

text Text *m*, Worlaut *m*; ~**book** (*juristisches*) Lehrbuch, Gesetzeskommentar, Erläuterungswerk; ~ **of the law** Gesetzestext; ~ **with notes** Text mit Anmerkungen; ~ **writer** Kommentator; **abridged** ~ gekürzter Text, verbindlicher Text; **draft** ~ Textentwurf; **legal** ~ Gesetzestext; **official** ~ amtlicher Wortlaut; **original** ~ Original(text), Urschrift; **the English** ~ **prevails** der englische Wortlaut ist maßgebend; **unabridged** ~ ungekürzte Ausgabe.

textually (wort)wörtlich; auf den Text bezogen.

theater (theatre) Theater *n*, Theatergebäude *n*, Schauplatz *m*; ~ **of operation** Operationsgebiet; ~ **of war** Kriegsschauplatz; **picture** ~ Kino, Filmtheater.

theatrical performance Bühnenaufführung *f*.

theft Diebstahl *m* (= *D bzw. . . d*), *GB seit 1968: auch Unterschlagung*; ~**-bote** Begünstigung e–s Räubers durch Nichtanzeige; ~ **by breaking and entering** Einbruchs*d*; ~ **by jostling the victim** Anrempelungs*d*; ~ **by using false keys** Nachschlüssel*d*; ~ **insurance** Diebstahlsversicherung; ~, **pilferage and non-delivery** Diebstahl und Abhandenkommen; ~ **prevention device** Sicherheitsvorrichtung; ~ **risk** Diebstahlsrisiko; **aggravated** ~ schwerer Diebstahl; **car** ~ → *car*; **mail** ~ Postdiebstahl; **open** ~ Diebstahl in flagranti (*bei dem der Dieb auf frischer Tat ertappt wird*); **petty** ~ Klein*d*; Gelegenheits*d*.

then damals, dann, damalig, künftig, in dem Falle, hierauf, ferner, außerdem, also; ~ **and there** sofort, auf der Stelle; ~ **dead** dann (*zu dem betr Zeitpunkt*) bereits verstorben; ~ **entitled** zu dem betr Zeitpunkt (*zB Todesfall*) berechtigt; ~ **in being** dann (*zu dem betr Zeitpunkt*) bereits geboren oder gezeugt; ~ **living** dann (*zB beim Tode des Bedachten*) lebend.

thence von da an.
thenceforth von dann ab, von da an.
theocracy Theokratie *f*.
theorem Theorem *n*, Lehrsatz *m*.
theoretical|competition vollständige Konkurrenz, automatische Konkurrenz; ~ **strength** Sollstärke.
theory Theorie *f*, Lehre *f*; ~ **of interests** Theorie der Interessenjurisprudenz; ~ **of prices** Preistheorie; ~ **of probabilities** Wahrscheinlichkeitstheorie; ~ **of taxation** Steuertheorie, allgemeine Steuerlehre; **equilibrium** ~ → *equilibrium*; **in** ~ theoretisch; **production** ~ **of value** Produktionskostentheorie.
thereabouts mehr oder weniger, etwa.
thereafter danach, daraufhin, nachstehend; ~ **to be born** später (*nach e–m bestimmten Zeitpunkt*) geboren (werdend).
therein dahin, dort.
thereinafter nachstehend, im folgenden.
thereinbefore vorstehend, im vorstehenden.
thereof dessen, deren; **for the duration** ~ während dessen (deren) Gültigkeitsdauer.
thereto dazu, daran; ~ **adjoining** daran angrenzend.
theretofore bisher, zuvor, bis dahin, früher; ~ **demised** bisher vermietet.
thereunto = *thereto qv*.
thereupon daraufhin, danach, unverzüglich danach, infolgedessen.
therewith damit; ~ **occupied** als . . . benutzt; **lands held** ~ dazu gehöriger Landbesitz.
thesaurer Schatzmeister *m*.
thesaurus Thesaurus *m*, Wörterbuch *n*, Wissensschatz *m*; *hist* Schatzkammer *f*, Vorratshaus *n*; ~ **inventus** *hist* Schatzfund.
thesmothete Gesetzgeber *m*.
thief Dieb *m*, Diebin *f*; ~**-proof** diebessicher; **common** ~ gewerbsmäßiger Dieb; **shop** ~ Ladendieb, Warenhausdieb.
thievery Dieberei *f*; **petty** ~ Bagatelldiebstahl, Klauerei.
thievishness Stehlsucht *f*, Kleptomanie *f*.
thing Gegenstand *m*; Vermögensgegenstand *m*, körperlicher Gegenstand *m*; Sache *f* (*im Sinne von körperlichen Gegenständen*); Angelegenheit *f*, Tat *f*; ~**s in action** Forderungsrechte, Ansprüche auf Erlangung von Geld oder beweglichen Sachen; ~**s in possession** Sachen, körperliche Gegenstände (*Gegensatz zu ~s in action*); ~ **of value** Wertgegenstand; ~**s personal** persönliche Habe, bewegliches Vermögen, Mobilien; ~**s real** unbewegliche Sachen, Immobilien; **aggregate of** ~**s** Sachinbegriff; **consumable** ~**s** verbrauchbare Sachen; **entirety of** ~**s** Sachinbegriff; **fungible** ~**s** vertretbare Sachen, Gattungssachen; **nonfungible** ~**s** nicht vertretbare Sachen; **tangible** ~ körperlicher Gegenstand.
think denken, glauben, sich erinnern, meinen, folgern aus; ~ **fit** für tunlich halten, nach pflichtgemäßem Ermessen für richtig halten.
third|arbitrator Obmann e–s Schiedsgericht; ~**-class** drittklassig; ~**-class mail** → *mail*; ~ **conviction** die dritte Verurteilung (*nach zwei Strafen wegen Verbrechen*); ~ **country** Drittland; ~**-degree practices** verschärftes Verhör, Folterungsverhör; ~ **opposition** Drittwiderspruchsklage, Interventionsklage; ~ **party claim proceeding** Drittwiderspruchsklage; ~ **party complaint** Streitverkündung durch den Beklagten; ~ **penny** Einbehalt von einem Drittel (*der Gerichtsgebühr von Strafen für die Gerichtskasse*); ~ **possessor** lastenfreier Grundstückserwerber; ~ **-rate** drittklassig; ~ **term** dritte Amtsperiode (*des US Präsidenten; durch Verfassungsänderung untersagt*).
third party der Dritte, ein Dritter, ein Unbeteiligter; Nebeninterve-

nient; ~ **acting in good faith** gutgläubiger Dritter.

third-party | **accident insurance** Unfallhaftpflichtversicherung; ~ **beneficiary** Drittbegünstigter, Drittberechtigter, begünstigter Dritter; ~ **damage** Drittschaden; ~ **debtor** Drittschuldner; ~ **directions** Beweisbeschluß im Nebeninterventionsverfahren; ~ **funds** Fremdgelder; ~ **indemnity** Haftpflicht; ~ **indemnity insurance** → *insurance*; ~ **insurance** → *insurance*; ~ **notice** Streitverkündung; ~ **order** Leistungsverbot an Drittschuldner; Pfändungsüberweisungsbeschluß; ~ **procedure** Nebeninterventionsverfahren, Streitverkündungsverfahren; ~ **proceedings** Regressprozeß; ~ **rights** Rechte Dritter; ~ **risk** Haftpflicht.

thirds Waren dritter (*bzw minderwertiger*) Qualität; Witwendrittel *n*|*pl* am beweglichen Nachlaß.

this dies, *das vorstehend* (*zuletzt*) *Erwähnte* ...; ~ **day six months** auf 6 Monate zurückgestellt (*Vorlage kann in der betreffenden Legislaturperiode nicht mehr behandelt werden*); ~ **my will** mein (*hiermit errichtetes*) Testament.

thoroughfare Durchfahrt *f*, öffentliche Straße *f* (*die keine Sackstraße ist*), durchfahrbare Straße *f*; **no** ~ kein Durchgang, Straße gesperrt, Einfahrt verboten; **public** ~ öffentlicher Durchgang, öffentlicher Weg.

those present die Anwesenden *m*|*pl*.

thread Mittellinie *f*, Schiffahrtslinie *f*.

threat Drohung *f*, Bedrohung *f*; ~**s action** *brit* Klage wegen grundlos behaupteter Patentverletzung; ~ **of dismissal** Androhung der Entlassung; ~ **of legal procceedings** Klageandrohung, Androhung e–s Prozesses, Androhung der Patentverletzungsklage; ~**s to jobs** Gefährdung von Arbeitsplätzen; **illegitimate** ~ widerrechtl. D.; **wrongful** unrechtmäßige D.

threaten androhen, bedrohen.

threatener Mahnbrief mit Androhung gerichtlicher Schritte.

Threatening Communications Act *US*: *Gesetz gegen Versendung von Drohbriefen*.

three drei; ~**-D-policy** Kautionsversicherung (*gegen Unehrlichkeit, Verschwinden und Zerstörung: dishonesty, disappearance, destruction*); ~**-fourths value clause** Einsatz bis zu ¾ des versicherten Wertes (*Feuerversicherung*); ~**-judge panel** Spruchkörper mit 3 Richtern (*Kammer bzw Senat*); ~**-mile zone** Dreimeilenzone; ~ **month's bill** Dreimonatswechsel; ~**-name paper** Tratte, Orderpapier *mit drei Unterschriften*.

threshold Schwelle *f*; Freibetragsgrenze *f*; ~ **price** Schwellenpreis, Einschleusungspreis; ~ **payment** Lohnerhöhung bei Erreichen e–r Indexstufe; ~ **worker** unerfahrener Arbeiter *m*, Anlernling *m*; **12 months'** ~ Mindeststrafzeit von 12 Monaten.

thrift Sparsamkeit *f*, Sparen *n*; ~**account** → *account* (*2*); ~ **deposit** → *deposit*; ~ **institutions** Sparkassen und ähnl Kreditinstitute sowie Bausparkassen.

throne Thron *m*; **abdication of the** ~ Abdankung, Thronverzicht; **accession to the** ~ Thronbesteigung; **disclaimer to the** ~ Thronverzicht; **speech from the** ~ Thronrede (*bei Parlamentseröffnung*); **successor to the** ~ Thronfolger.

through durch, bis einschließlich; innerhalb, namens, in Vertretung; ~ **an agent** durch (*bzw über*) e–n Vertreter; ~ **bill of lading** → *bill of lading*; ~ **bookings** Pauschalreisen; ~ **document of transport** Durchfrachttransportpapier; ~ **freight** Durchgangs-, Transitfracht; ~ **lot** durchgehendes Baugrundstück; ~ **rate** Durchgangstarif; ~ **route** Durchgangsverbindung; ~ **traffic** Durchgangsverkehr.

throughput agreement Öl-/Erdgasleitungs-Finanzierungsvertrag (*nach Durchsatz der Leitung*).

throw in draufgeben, umsonst dazugeben.

throw out verwerfen, als unzulässig zurückweisen; ~ **a bill** *parl* e–n Gesetzesentwurf verwerfen.

throwaway Reklamezettel *m*, Wurfsendung *f*.

thrust stechen, (*auf jmdn mit spitzem Gegenstand*) zustoßen, auf jmdn einstechen.

thug Schurke *m*; Rohling *m*; Meuchelmörder *m*; Gewaltverbrecher *m*.

thumb mark Daumenabdruck; ~ **print** Daumenabdruck.

tick *s* Anschreibenlassen *n*, Häkchen *n*, *sl* Kredit m; Nachkontrolle zur Buchungsfehlersuche.

tick *v* anstreichen, ankreuzen, abhaken; ~ **off** abhaken; ~ **the box** das Kästchen ankreuzen.

ticker Börsenfernschreiber *m*; ~ **abbreviations** Börsenabkürzungen; ~ **firm** Börsenmakler; ~ **service** Tickerdienst.

ticket Fahrkarte *f*, Zettel *m*, Karte *f*, Billet *n*, Strafzettel *m*, Berechtigungsschein *m*; gebührenpflichtige Verwarnung *f*; Wahlliste *f*; ~ **agent** Verkaufsstelle; ~ **book** Fahrscheinheft; ~ **day** = *name day qv*; ~ **of leave** Urlaubsschein, vorläufiger Entlassungsschein *aus der Haftanstalt*; **~-of-leave man** bedingt Entlassener; Freigänger; **balance** ~ Depotschein für hinterlegte Aktien; **banker's** ~ → *banker*; **complimentary** ~ Freifahrschein, Freikarte, Ehrenkarte; **delivery** ~ Lieferschein; **deposit** ~ → *deposit*; **job** ~ → *job*; **fixed penalty** ~ *etwa* Strafbefehl; **mixed** ~ Koalitionswahlliste; **multiple** ~ Mehrfahrtenausweis; **parking** ~ gebührenpflichtige Verwarnung (*bzw. Vorladung*) wegen Parkübertretung; **pawn** ~ → *pawn*; **reserved seat** ~ Platzkarte; **scratch** ~ ungültiger Wahlschein; **single** ~ einfache Fahrt (Fahrkarte); **straight** ~ Einheitsliste (*bei Wahlen*).

ticketing Auszeichnung *f*, Etikettierung *f*.

tickler Terminkalender *m*, Mahnkartei *f*; ~ **file** Wiedervorlagemappe.

tide | **land** Watt; ~ **surveyor** Seezollinspektor; ~ **waiter** = *tidesman qv*.

tide-me-over plan Überbrükkungsplan *m*, vorläufiger Firmenrettungsplan.

tidesman Seezollbeamter *m* (*der an Bord e–s einlaufenden Schiffes kommt*).

tie *s* Stimmengleichheit *f*; ~ **break** Entscheidung bei Stimmengleichheit, Stichwahl; ~ **division** → *division*; ~ **vote** unentschiedene Abstimmung.

tie *v* binden; ~ **money** Geld fest anlegen; **~d house** brauereigebundene Gaststätte; **~d loan** zweckgebundene Anleihe.

tie-in Verbindung *f*; ~ **arrangement** Koppelungsverkauf; ~ **clause** → *clause*; ~ **sale** → *sale*.

tie-on label Anhängeadresse *f*.

tie-up Vereinigung *f*, Verbindung *f*; Stockung *f*, Stillstand *m*; ~ **shop** an e–e Lieferfirma gebundenes Geschäft.

tier Rang *m*, Stufe (*e–r Verwaltungshierarchie bzw Gerichtsordnung*); **in ~s** abgestuft, hierarchisch, in verschiedenen Ebenen.

tight *econ* knapp, angespannt, *jur* sofort vollstreckbar; ~ **bargain** Geschäft mit kleiner Marge; ~ **money** knappes Geld; ~ **money market** angespannter Geldmarkt, künstlich verknappte Geldversorgung; ~ **times** äußerst knappe (Produktions)Fristen.

tightness Verknappung *f*, Knappheit *f*; ~ **in money** Geldknappheit.

till Ladenkasse *f*, Geldkassette *f*, Kassenbestand *m*; ~ **book** Kassenbuch; ~ **money** Kassenbestand; **~-tapping** (Registrier)Kassendiebstahl.

till-forbid laufende Inserierung *f* bis auf Widerruf (*Werbung*).

timber Bauholz *n*, Nutzholz *n* (*ursprünglich nur Eichen-, Eschen-, Ulmenholz*); ~ **culture entry** → *entry*; ~ **estate** forstwirtschaftlich genutztes Grundstück; ~ **merchant** Holzhändler; ~**-trees** (*Eichen, Eschen und Ulmen*); Bauholzbestände.

time Zeit *f*, Zeitpunkt *m*, Zeitdauer *f*; Frist *f*; ~ **allowed** Frist; ~ **allowed for appearance** Einlassungsfrist; ~ **and materials contract** Werklieferungsvertrag; ~ **and motion study** REFA-Studie, Zeit- und Bewegungsstudie; ~**-bargain** Börsentermingeschäft, Zeitgeschäft; ~**-bar** zeitl Schranke; Ausschlußfrist; ~ **barred** verjährt; ~ **begins to run** die Frist beginnt, die Verjährung beginnt; ~ **bill** Zeitwechsel, Wechsel mit bestimmter Laufzeit; ~ **book** Arbeits(stunden)buch; ~ **certain** ein bestimmter Zeitpunkt; ~ **charge** Zeitgebühr, Stundenhonorar; ~ **charter** Zeitfrachtvertrag, Zeitcharter; ~ **charter party** = *charter qv*; ~ **check** Lohnstundennachweis; ~ **constraints** Zeitnot; ~**costing** Zeitkostenkalkulation; ~ **deposit** Termineinlage, kündbare Einlage, Festgeld; ~ **draft** → *draft*; ~ **effeciency** Zeitausnutzungsgrad; ~ **elapsing** Fristablauf, verstreichende Zeit; ~ **expired** abgelaufen; ~ **fixed for payment** Zahlungstermin; ~ **for acceptance** Annahmefrist; Angebotsbindefrist; ~ **for answer** Erwiderungsfrist; ~ **for ante-natal care** Freistellung für Schwangerschaftsvorsorge; ~ **for appeal** Rechtsmittelfrist; ~ **for application** Anmeldefrist; ~ **for carrying out directions** Auflagenfrist; ~ **for consideration** Bedenkzeit; ~ **for delivery** Lieferfrist; ~ **for (entering an) appearance** Einlassungsfrist; ~ **for filing claims** (Schadens)Anmeldefrist; ~ **for loading** Ladezeit; ~ **for payment** Zahlungsfrist, Ziel; ~ **for performance** Erfüllungsfrist, Ausführungsfrist, Leistungsfrist; ~ **for presenting bills** Vorlegungsfrist (*Wechsel*); ~ **for reply** Erwiderungsfrist; ~ **for summons** Ladungsfrist; ~ **granted** eingeräumte Frist; Ziel; ~ **immemorial** unvordenkliche Zeit; *GB: vor 1189*; ~ **insurance** Versicherung auf Zeit; ~ **interest charges** Festgeldzinsen; ~ **is of the essence** Fristeinhaltung ist Vertragsgrundlage (*Fixgeschäft*); ~ **lag** Verzögerung, zeitlicher Abstand; ~ **limit** → *time limit*; ~ **loan(s)** → *loan*; ~ **money** → *money*; ~ **note** Sichtwechsel; ~ **of accident** Unfallszeit; ~ **of arrival** Ankunftszeit; ~**-of-day tariff** tageszeitlich gestaffelter (Strom-)Tarif; ~ **of delivery** Lieferzeit, Zeit der Zustellung; ~ *of proposed delivery: in Aussicht gestellte Lieferzeit*; ~ **of departure** Abfahrtszeit; ~ **off (work)** Freistellung von der Arbeit; ~ **of memory** zurückverfolgbare Zeit bis 1189, *Thronbesteigung von Richard I*; ~ **of payment** Zahlungstermin; ~ **of preclusion** Ausschlußfrist; ~ **of protection** Schutzdauer, Schutzfrist; ~ **of summons** Ladefrist; ~ **of validity** Gültigkeitsdauer; ~ **on remand** Dauer der Untersuchungshaft; ~ **order** → *order* (*1*) *u order* (*2*); ~**s over** mehrfach; ~ **out of memory** = ~ *immemorial qv*; ~ **out of mind** = ~ *immemorial qv*; ~ **paid for but not worked** vergütete arbeitsfreie Lohnstunden; ~ **payment** Ratenzahlung; ~ **policy** → *policy* (*1*); ~ **purchase** Terminkauf; ~ **rates** Zeitlohnsätze; ~ **recording devoice** Arbeitszeitmeßgerät, Stechuhr; ~ **records** Arbeitszeitnachweis; ~ **scales** Zeitstufen (*e–s Projekts*); ~ **selling** Abzahlungsgeschäfte, Abzahlungssystem; ~**-server** Opportunist; ~**-serving** Opportunismus; ~ **sheets** Stundenlisten, Anwesenheitslisten; ~ **summons** Verlängerung der Zustellungsfrist; ~ **table** Zeitplan; ~ **to prepare for trial** Frist zur Vorbereitung der mündlichen Verhandlung (*bzw Hauptverhandlung*); **abridging** ~ e–e Frist verkürzen; **abridgment of** ~ Verkürzung e–r Frist; **allotted** ~ Frist, Zahlungsfrist; **appointed** ~ Termin; **apt** ~ geeigneter Zeitpunkt; **at the fixed** ~ zur festgesetzten Zeit; **by passage of** ~ → *passage*; **calculation of** ~ Zeitberechnung, Fristberechnung; **case processing** ~ Bearbeitungszeit (*pro Fall*); **check-in** ~ Meldezeit, spätestes Eintreffen; **closing** ~ Geschäftsschluß, Polizeistunde; **computation of** ~ → *computation*; **contract** ~ Vertragszeit, Vertragstermin(e); **cooling** ~ Aussetzung des Arbeitskampfes; Beruhigungsfrist; **customary** ~ die übliche Frist (*Wechselannahme*); **dead** ~ tote Zeit, nicht ausgenutzte Zeit, Lohnausfall; **equal** ~ Ausgewogenheitsgrundsatz bei der Sendezeit; **expiration of** ~ Fristablauf; **extension of** ~ → *extension*; **failure to observe the** ~ **limit** Fristversäumnis, Fristüberschreitung; **for a certain** ~ auf e–e im voraus bestimmte Zeit; **for the** ~ **being** jeweils, zum jeweiligen Zeitpunkt, derzeitig; **for want of** ~ aus Zeitmangel; **from time to** ~ → *from*; **free** ~ Freizeit, freie Liegezeit, Abladefrist; **full** ~ ganztätig; **in due** ~ rechtzeitig; **in point of** ~ in zeitl Hinsicht; **in the specified** ~ fristgemäß; **lapse of** ~ → *lapse*; **lead** ~ Lieferzeit (*von Auftragsvergabe bis Lieferung*), Vorgabezeit, Vorlaufzeit; Zeit bis zur Terminierung; **legal** ~ gesetzliche Frist; **limitation of** ~ → *limitation*; **limited in** ~ befristet, zeitlich begrenzt; **local** ~ Ortszeit; **loss of** ~ → *loss*; **material** ~ Tatzeit, entscheidungserheblicher Zeitpunkt; **new** ~ Börsengeschäft am 2. Tag vor dem Reporttag; **on** ~ termingerecht; **out of** ~ verspätet, nach Fristablauf, nicht fristgerecht, verjährt; **processing** ~ Bearbeitungszeit; **productive** ~ Stückheit; **reasonable** ~ angemessene Frist; **regular** ~ Normalarbeitszeit; **shipping** ~ Versandtermin; **short** ~ Kurzarbeit; **standard** ~ Normalzeit; **traveling** ~ Reisezeit, Wegezeit; **unexpired** ~ offene Frist.

time limit Frist *f*; ~ **for claims** Rügefrist; ~ **for payments** Zahlungsfrist, Aufschubsfrist (*Zoll*); **strict** ~ strenge Frist, Notfrist.

timely rechtzeitig, zeitgemäß, zeitlich passend.

timeous pünktlich, zeitgerecht.

timeshare zeitanteilige Nutzung, Kauf auf Zeitanteilsbasis (*von Ferienhäusern, Ferieneigentumswohnungen etc*); ~ **interests** timeshare-Vermögensrechte; ~ **sale contract** zeitanteiliger (Ferienwohnungs-) Kaufvertrag; ~ **title** Eigentum bzw Dauernutzungsrecht auf Timeshare-Basis.

timesharer Teilzeitmieter *m*, Teilzeitnutzungsberechtigter *m*, Ferienwohnungbesitzer auf Zeit.

timing Wahl *f* des richtigen Zeitpunkts (*zB für Investitionen*).

timocracy Timokratie *f* (*vermögensorientierte Staatsform*), Geldaristokratie *f*.

tinbounding Zinnschürfrechte *n*|*pl*.

Tinewald (=) *Parlament der Insel Man.*

tin parachute *großzügige Mitarbeiterabfindung bei Entlassung (wegen Firmenübernahme).*

tippee *jmd* der e–n Börsentip erhält.

tipper Tippgeber *m* (*Insidergeschäfte*).

tippling Zecherei *f*, gewohnheitsmäßiges Trinken *n* (*in mäßigem Umfang*); **T~ Act** Zechschuldengesetz; ~ **house** → *house*.

tipstaff Gerichtswachtmeister *m* (*für Inhaftnahme im Gericht*).

tipster Tipster *m*, Börsentipgeber *m*.

tissue (Organ)Gewebe *n*; **Human T~ Act** 1961 *GB:* Transplantationsgesetz.

tit-for-tat Zug um Zug, Gegenzug *m*, Retorsion *f*, sofortige Vergeltung *f*.

tithe Zehnt *m*.

tithing Zehntschaft *f*, kleiner Verwaltungsbezirk *m*; **~-man** Vorsteher der Zehntschaft, *Gemeindebeamter für Einhaltung der Sonntagsruhe*; ~**-penny** örtliche Steuer.

title Titel *m*, Bezeichnung *f*, Überschrift *f*, Klagerubrum *n*; Betreffsangabe *f*; Eigentumsrecht *n*, urkundlicher Rechtsnachweis *m* (*bes e–s dinglichen Rechts*); dingliche Berechtigung *f*; Rechtstitel *m* (*bes zum Besitz*); Grundeigentum *n*; Anspruch *m*; ~ **by abandonment** Eigentumserwerb auf Grund von Dereliktion; ~ **by accretion** Eigentumserwerb durch Anwachsung *bzw* Anlandung; ~ **by adverse possession** Eigentums(erwerb) durch Ersitzung; ~ **by bequest** Eigentum(serwerb) durch Vermächtnis; ~ **by descent** auf Erbfolge beruhende dingliche Berechtigung; ~ **by devise** Eigentum(serwerb) durch letztwillige Verfügung *über Immobilien*; ~ **by discovery** Eigentum(serwerb) durch Fund; ~ **by estoppel** Recht(sstellung) kraft Rechtsscheins *bzw* durch Verwirkung; ~ **by inheritance** Eigentum(serwerb) durch Erbschaft; ~ **by operation of law** Eigentum(serwerb) kraft Gesetzes; ~ **by prescription** Ersitzungseigentum; ~ **by will** Eigentum(serwerb) durch letztwillige Verfügung; ~ **certificate** Eigentumsnachweis, Bescheinigung über das Grundstückseigentum; ~ **company** Versicherungsgesellschaft für Rechtsmängelhaftpflicht bei Grundstücken; ~ **deeds** Grundeigentumsurkunden; *urkundl Nachweis der Herrschaftsrechte am Grundstück;* ~ **defective in form** formal fehlerhafter Eigentumsnachweis; ~ **documents** Eigentums- bzw Eigentumsübertragungsurkunden; ~ **guarantee** Gewährleistung gegen Rechtsmängel bei Grunderwerb; ~ **guaranty company** Immobilienbesitz-Prüfungs- und Garantie-Gesellschaft; ~**-hunters** *hist* Spitzel zur Aufdekkung von formalen Rechtsmängeln an Grundbesitz; ~ **insurance** Versicherung gegen Rechtsmängel bei Grundstückserwerb; ~ **of a cause** Klagerubrum; ~ **of an act** Gesetzestitel; ~ **of an action** Klagerubrum; ~ **of costs** Kostenurteil, Kostentitel; ~ **of declaration** Klagerubrum; ~ **of entry** Betretungsrecht; ~ **of invention** Kurztitel e–r Erfindung; ~ **of nobility** Adelstitel, -prädikat; ~ **of office** Amtsbezeichnung; ~ **of ownership** Eigentumstitel; ~ **of patent** kurze Bezeichnung der Erfindung; ~ **of presentation** das Recht, für e–e Pfründe vorgeschlagen zu werden; ~ **of record** verbrieftes Eigentum (*durch öffentliche Urkunden nachgewiesen*); ~ **of the action** Klagerubrum; ~ **paramount** oberstes Lehensrecht; Obereigentum; ~ **plant** Grundstücksurkundenverzeichnis; ~ **record** Grundbuchauszug, Eigentumsnachweis; ~ **retaining note** Eigentumsvorbehaltsurkunde; ~ **retention** Sicherungsübereignung; ~**-search** Ermittlung und Prüfung der Eigentums- und Belastungsverhältnisse am Grundstück (*vor dem Verkauf*); ~ **theory** *US*: Lehre vom treuhänderischen Eigentumsübergang auf den Hypothekengläubiger; ~ **to exclude** Ausschließlichkeitsrecht, besseres Recht am Grundstück; ~ **to goods** Eigentumsrecht an Waren; ~ **to land** Grundstückseigentum, eigentumsähnliches Recht am Grundstück; ~ **to orders** Ordensaufnahmeberechtigung; ~ **to sue** Aktivlegitimation; **absolute** ~ Grundeigentum, unbeschränktes (dingliches) Herrschaftsrecht; rechtsgültiges dingl Pachtrecht; Volleigentum; **abstract of** ~ → *abstract*; **acquisition of** ~ Eigentumserwerb; **adverse** ~ ersessene Berechtigung; **assignment of** ~ Rechtsübertragung; **bad** ~ fehlendes Eigentumsrecht, Mangel im Recht, mit Rechtsmängeln behaftetes Eigentum; **best** ~ das stärkste Recht (*an einer Sache, bes Grundstück*); **bond for** ~ → *bond*; **by onerous** ~ gegen Entgelt; **certifi-**

cate of ~ → *certificate*; **chain of** ~ → *chain*; **chartered** ~ verbrieftes Recht; **clear** ~ unbestrittenes Recht; lastenfreies (Grundstücks-) Eigentum; **clear** ~ **of record** einwandfreier Rechtsanspruch, rechtsmängelfreier Eigentumstitel; **clear record** ~ = *clear* ~ *of record qv*; **closing of** ~ Auflassung mit Eigentumsübertragung; **collective** ~ Sammelbezeichnung (*von Einzelgesetzen*); **colo(u)rable** ~ Rechtsscheinsanspruch; anscheinend begründeter Rechtstitel; **defective** ~ mit Rechtsmängeln behafteter Rechtstitel; **derivative** ~ derivativ (*mit Eigentumsübertragung*) erworbenes Eigentum; **dispute of** ~ Eigentumsstreit; **document of** ~ → *document*; **dormant** ~ ruhender, ungebrauchter Rechtstitel; **doubtful** ~ zweifelhafter Rechtstitel; zweifelhafter Nachweis des Grundstückseigentums; **equitable** ~ (*nur*) billigkeitsrechtlich anerkannter Besitztitel; Übertragungsanspruch, Eigentumsanwartschaft, vorläufiges Eigentum, wirtschaftl Eigentum; **good** ~ rechtmäßiges Eigentum, gültiger Rechtstitel; **having the first** ~ erstberechtigt (nächstberechtigt) sein; **historical** ~ Eigentum kraft Ersitzung; **immarketable** ~ nicht verkehrsfähiges Recht, Eigentumstitel bei bestrittener Rechtslage; **imperfect** ~ vorläufiges Eigentum, aufschiebend bedingtes Eigentum; **inchoate** ~ Anwartschaft; **indefeasible** ~ unentziehbares Eigentum, absolutes E.; **investigation of** ~ → *investigation*; **joint** ~ Mitberechtigung, Miteigentum; **legal** ~ (volles) Eigentum; **legitimate** ~ gültiger Rechtstitel; **long** ~ vollständiger Titel e–s Gesetzes; **lucrative** ~ unentgeltlich erworbenes Recht od. Eigentum; **marketable** ~ → *marketable*; **merchantable** ~ → *merchantable*; **non-merchantable** ~ → *non-merchantable*; **official** ~ Amtsbezeichnung; **onerous** ~ entgeltlich erworbenes Eigentum; **outstanding** ~ besseres Recht; **paper** ~ Grundstücksurkunde(n); nur auf dem Papier stehendes Eigentum an Liegenschaften; **paramount** ~ → *paramount*; **passive** ~ *scot* Eigentum e–s unbeschränkt haftenden Erben, Passivlegitimation; **perfect** ~ einwandfreier Rechtstitel, volles Eigentumsrecht; **plaintiff's** ~ klägerischer Rechtsanspruch; **possessory** ~ Besitztitel, Recht zum Besitz; **predecessor in** ~ → *predecessor*; **preliminary** ~ vorläufiger Rechtstitel; **prescriptive** ~ → *prescriptive*; **presumptive** ~ vermutetes Eigentum, vermutete Berechtigung; Ersitzungsrecht; **proof of** ~ Eigentumsnachweis; **qualified** ~ beschränktes eigentumsähnliches Recht; Besitztitel unter Vorbehalt älterer Rechte; **record** ~ Grundeigentum gemäß verbrieftem und eingetragenem Recht; **short** ~ Kurztitel (e–s Gesetzes); **singular** ~ Einzeltitel, Eigentum als Einzelrechtsnachfolge; **sound** ~ einwandfreier Rechtstitel; **superior** ~ rangbesseres Recht; **to claim** ~ **to** Anspruch auf . . . erheben; **to clear the** ~ das Eigentum von Belastungen freistellen, lastenfrei übergeben; **to have good** ~ vollberechtigt sein; Eigentümer sein; **vested** ~ verbrieftes Recht, übertragenes Recht; **unendorsable** ~ Rektapapier; **unmarketable** ~ nicht verkehrsfähiger Besitztitel; **waiver of** ~ Rechtsverzicht; **want of** ~ Fehlen e–s Rechtsanspruchs, Rechtsmangel, rechtsfehlerhaftes Besitzrecht; **worthier** ~ rangbesseres Recht.

titular *adj* Titel . . ., e–n Titel führend; Titular . . ., nominell, nur dem Titel nach; ~ *s* Titular *m*, nomineller Amtsinhaber.

to zu, bis zu (*den letzten Tag nicht mitgerechnet*); nach, an; ~ **all intents and purposes** in jeder Hinsicht; ~ **and amongst** an (*mehrere Beteiligte*); ~ **and from** hin und zurück; ~ **arrive** termingerechte Lieferung (*als Fixgeschäft*); ~ **arrive price** =

landed price → *price*; ~ **be left till called for** auf Abruf; ~ **continue** kaufen mit Wiederkaufsverpflichtung zum Termin; ~ **have and to hold** (*darüber einig*) daß das Eigentum übergehen soll (Auflassungsklausel); ~ **his knowledge** seines Wissens; ~ **order** an Order; ~ **the best of my knowledge and belief** nach meinem besten Wissen und Gewissen; ~ **the extent** bis zu, höchstens; ~ **whom it may concern** (*an wen es angeht*) Erklärung, Bestätigung; ~ **wit** → *wit*.

toe *v* **the line** sich streng an die Parteilinie halten, Parteidisziplin wahren.

toft Hofstätte *f*, Anwesen *n*, Hof *m*, Grundfläche *f* (*e–s nicht mehr vorhandenen Hauses*); ~ **and croft** Haus und Hof, das *gesamte* Anwesen.

toftman Besitzer *m* e–r Hofstelle.

token Zeichen *n*, Symbol *n*, Automatenmünze *f*, Metallmarke *f*, Wertmarke *f*; ~ **coin** Scheidemünze(n); ~ **money** Zeichengeld, Notgeld, Papiergeld, Münzen *ohne entsprechenden Edelmetallgehalt*; ~ **payment** symbolische Zahlung, Draufgeld; Draufgabe; ~ **strike** Warnstreik; **false** ~ gefälschte Wertmarke; **obtaining money by false** ~ betrügerische Beschaffung von Geld, Kreditbetrug.

tolerance Toleranz *f*, Gewichtsabweichung *f*.

toleration Duldung *f*, Duldsamkeit *f*, Toleranz *f*, Nachsicht *f*; **T~ Act** Toleranzgesetz *GB 1689*.

toll *s* Wegegeld *n*, Maut *f*, Brückenzoll *m*, Straßenbenutzungsgebühr *f*, Marktgebühr *f*, Standgeld *n*, Fuhrlohn *m*, Transportgebühr *f*, Fernsprechgebühr *f*; Zollregal *n*; ~ **and team** Markt- und Hofherrschaft; ~ **bar** Schranke, Schlagbaum; ~ **bridge** mautpflichtige Brücke; ~ **call** Ferngespräch (*im Vorortsverkehr*); ~ **dish** Naturzollmeßbehälter; ~ **gatherer** Maut-Kassierer, Stadtzolleinnehmer; ~ **of death** Todesopfer *n*|*pl*, tödliche Unfallsquote *f*; ~ **road** mautpflichtige Straße; ~**-thorough** Straßen- und Brückenzoll, Durchfahrzoll; ~**-traverse** Entschädigung für Benutzung e–s Privatweges bzw. Durchfahrt; Recht auf gebührenpflichtige Durchfahrt; ~ **turn** Wegezoll für Tiere (*die von e–m Markt zurückgebracht werden*); **lighthouse** ~ Leuchtfeuergebühr.

toll *v* versperren, abschneiden, wegnehmen; ~ **an entry** das Betretungsrecht blockieren; ~ **the statute of limitations** den Nichteintritt der Verjährung nachweisen.

tollage Bezahlung *f* e–r Maut (*vgl toll*), Mautrecht *n*.

tolsey Kaufmannshalle *f*; **T~ Court** Ortsgericht in Bristol.

tombstone Grabstein *m*; Emittentenliste *f*.

Tomlin Order Protokollierung e–s Prozeßvergleichs mit Ruhen des Verfahrens.

tommy Naturallohn *m*; ~ **shop** werkseigenes Lebensmittelgeschäft.

ton Tonne *f* (= *T bzw. . . t*); ~ **cost** Durchschnittstransportkosten per *T* und Meile; ~**s deadweight** Tragfähigkeit (*in Gewichtst–n*); ~ **mile** *T–n*meile (*Transport e–r britischen T e–e Meile lang*); **American** ~ amerikanische *T* (= *net* ~ = *short* ~ *qv*); **displacement** ~ Verdrängungs*st*; **English** ~ (*imperial* ~, = *long* ~ = *gross* ~ = *shipping* ~) brit Tonne; **freight** ~ Fracht; **gross** ~ = *long* ~ *qv*; **gross register** ~ Bruttoregister (*Rauminhalt e–s Schiffs*); **imperial** ~ = *English* ~ *qv*; **long** ~ englisches Gewicht*st*; **measurement** ~ Tonne als Raummaß, Raum*t*, Fracht*t*; **metric** ~ metrische *T*; **net** ~ = *short* ~ *qv*; **register** ~ Register*t*; **revenue** ~ vergütete Transportleistung pro *T* und Meile; **shipping** ~ = *freight* ~; **short** ~ Gewichtstonne von 2000 lbs.

tonnage Tonnage *f*, Ladegewicht *n*, Tragfähigkeit *f*, Schiffsraum *m*; ~ **duty** Tonnengeld, Schiffssteuer, Einfuhr- *bzw* Ausfuhrzoll nach Gewicht; ~ **length** Vermessungslänge; ~ **opening** Ladeluke; ~ **rate** Lohnsatz pro Tonne; ~**-rent** Pacht nach Produktionsmenge (*Bergwerk*); **cargo** ~ Ladefähigkeit (*Schiff*); **certificate of** ~ → *certificate*; **deadweight** ~ → *deadweight*; **displacement** ~ Verdrängungstonnage; **gross** ~ Bruttotonnage, Schiffsraum; **idle** ~ aufgelegte Tonnage; **net** ~ Nettotonnage, nutzbarer Schiffsraum.

tontine Tontine, Tontineversicherung *f*; ~ **annuity** thesaurierende Überlebensrente; ~ **policy** → *policy (1)*.

tool Werkzeug *n*, Gerät *n*; ~**s and implements of trade** Werkzeuge und Geräte zur Berufsausübung; ~**s of trade** Werkzeuge für die Berufsausübung, Handwerkszeug; **measuring** ~ Meßgerät; **perishable** ~ Verschleißwerkzeug; **simple** ~**(s)** gewöhnliche Werkzeuge; **simple** ~**s doctrine** Haftungsfreiheit des Unternehmers für Zustand einfacher Werkzeuge; **to lay down** ~**s** die Arbeit niederlegen, streiken.

tooling Werkzeug- und Maschinenausstattung *f*.

top-level | **executives** Führungsspitze; ~ **tax rate** Spitzensteuersatz.

topics of conversation Besprechungsthemen *n|pl* (*keine vorvertragliche Bindung*).

topping-out ceremony Richtfest *n*.

topping-up clause → *clause*.

tort unerlaubte Handlung *f* (*im zivilrechtlichen Sinn*), Delikt *n*, Schädigung *f*; ~ **of negligence** fahrlässig begangene unerlaubte Handlung; ~ **per se** selbständige unerlaubte Handlung; **action in** ~ Klage aus unerlaubter Handlung; **actionable** ~ → *actionable*; **constitutional** ~ Staatsdienerhaftung für Verletzung von Grundrechten; **derivative** ~ Haftung für Delikte Dritter; **innominate** ~ allgemeiner Tatbestand der unerlaubten Handlung; **joint** ~ gemeinsam begangene unerlaubte Handlung; **personal** ~ unerlaubte Handlung gegen Personen; **property** ~ vermögensrechtliche unerlaubte Handlung, unerlaubte Handlung gegen Sachen; **quasi** ~ deliktsähnliche Haftung; **wilful** ~ vorsätzliche unerlaubte Handlung.

tortfeasor deliktisch Handelnder, Täter *m*, Schädiger *m* (*zivilrechtlich*); **concurrent** ~ selbständiger Mittäter (*zivilrechtlich*); **joint** ~**s** Mittäter, gemeinschaftliche Schädiger, deliktische Gesamtschuldner.

tortious deliktisch, unerlaubte Handlungen betreffend; ~ **act** unerlaubte Handlung *im Sinne des Zivilrechts*; ~ **duty** Pflicht, unerlaubte Handlungen zu unterlassen; ~ **liability** → *liability*; ~ **professional liability** Berufshaftung für unerlaubte Handlungen, deliktische Berufshaftung (*von Rechtsanwälten*).

torture Tortur *f*, Folterung *f*.

tot addieren; Schuldsummen bestätigen.

total | **charge for credit** effektive Kreditkosten; ~ **current assets** Gesamtumlaufvermögen; ~ **gross income before depreciation** Bruttoeinkünfte vor Abschreibung; ~ **votes cast** Gesamtstimmenzahl.

totalisator (= totalizator) Totalisator *m*, Wettapparat *m*.

toties quoties so oft, wie sich die Gelegenheit bietet.

totting up Zusammenzählen *n*: ~ **law** gesetzl Vorschriften über das Zusammenrechnen von Strafpunkten (*wegen Entzugs der Fahrerlaubnis*).

touch *v* berühren, in Kontakt kommen, (*Hafen*) anlaufen; ~**-and-go** auf Grund laufen und gleich wieder flott werden (*Seeversicherung*); ~ **and stay** e–n Hafen anlaufen und dort verweilen; ~**ing a dead body** das Berühren der Leiche (*zur Überführung des Mörders*); ~**ing the land** mit dinglicher Wirkung (*am Grundstück*).

touch signature Fingerabdruck zur Identitätskontrolle (*bei Abhebung*).

tour Reise *f*, Rundgang *m*; ~ **of duty** Einsatz (*e–s Beamten*); ~ **operator** Reiseunternehmer; ~ **organizer**

Reiseveranstalter; **all expense** ~ Pauschalreise; **guided** ~ Gesellschaftsreise; **official** ~ Dienstreise; **package** ~ → *package*.

touring Touristenverkehr *m* (*Zoll*).

tout *s* Kundensucher *m*, Schlepper *m*; Akquisiteur *m*.

tout *v* Kunden werben; Wähler schleppen.

touter = *tout, s, qv*.

touting Kundenwerbung *f*; Stimmenwerbung *f*.

towage Schlepplohn *m*, Bugsierlohn *m*; Schleppschiffahrt *f*; ~ **contractor** Schleppschiffahrtsunternehmer; ~ **service** Schleppdienst.

towing-away Abschleppen *n*; ~ **team** Abschleppleute.

town Stadt *f*; ~ **agent** Alkoholmonopolbeauftragter e–r Stadtgemeinde (*New England*); ~ **and country planning** Regionalplanung; ~ **cause** vor e–m Stadtrichter zu verhandelnde Sache; ~ **cheque** → *cheque*; ~ **clearing** sofortiges Scheck-clearing in London; ~**-clerk** Leiter der Stadtkanzlei; ~ **collector** Leiter des Stadtsteueramtes; ~ **commissioner** Stadtdirektor (*kommissarischer Leiter der Stadtverwaltung*); ~ **council** Stadtrat; ~**-crier** Gemeinde-Ausrufer; ~ **development** Stadtentwicklung; ~ **hall** Rathaus; ~ **management** Stadtverwaltung; ~ **mayor** Ortsbürgermeister, Bürgermeister e–r Kleinstadt; ~ **meeting** Bürgerversammlung (*aller wahlberechtigter Bürger e–r Stadt*); ~ **order** städtische Zahlungsanweisung; ~ **planning** Ortsplanung; ~ **pound** Stadtgefängnis; ~ **property** städtischer Grundbesitz; ~ **purpose** für Zwecke des städtischen Gemeinwohls; ~ **reeve** Bürgermeister; ~ **tax** kommunale Steuer; ~ **treasurer** Stadtkämmerer; ~**-twinning** Bildung von Städtepartnerschaften; ~ **warrant** städtische Zahlungsanweisung; **company** ~ Firmensiedlung.

township Stadtgemeinde *f*; Katastermaßeinheit *f* von 6 Quadratmeilen; ~ **trustee** kommissarischer Leiter der Stadtverwaltung; **rural** ~ Marktgemeinde; Flur; ländliche Fläche von 36 Quadratmeilen.

trace *s* Spur *f*; Fährte *f*; **no** ~ unbekannt verzogen, unzustellbar; **to remove the ~s** die Spuren verwischen.

trace *v* nachforschen, Spuren verfolgen.

traceless spurlos, ohne Spuren zu hinterlassen.

tracer Laufzettel *m*.

tracing Suchen *n*, Nachforschung; ~ **enquiries** Anschriftenermittlung, Wohnsitzermittlung(en); ~ **of stolen property** Sachfahndung; ~ **of stolen vehicles** Kraftfahrzeugfahndung; ~ **order** Nachforschungsanordnung; ~ **trust** Nachforschung über den Verbleib von Treuhandsvermögenswerten.

tracker Verfolger *m*.

track record Leistungsnachweis *m*.

tracks Eisenbahngeleise *n*; ~ **delivery shipments** Massengutabfertigung per Bahn; **industrial** ~ Betriebsgleis.

tract (*of land*) Landstrich *m*, Gelände *n*, Grundstück *n*, Parzelle *f*; *min* Oberflächenfündigkeit *f*; *US*: Wohnsiedlung; ~ **house** *US*: Reihenhaus.

trade Handel *m* (= *H bzw. . . h*), Gewerbe *n*, erlernter Beruf *m*, Handwerk *n*; Wirtschaftsverkehr *m*, Branche *f*, Geschäft *n*, Verkehr *m*; ~ **acceptance** *H*–sakzept, *H*–swechsel, Warenwechsel; ~ **accounts payable** *bil* Warenschulden; ~ **accounts receivable** *bil* Forderungen aus Lieferungen und Leistungen; ~ **agreement** → *agreement*; ~ **allowance** Großhandelsrabatt; ~ **and commerce** *H* und Verkehr, Wirtschaft, gewerbliche Tätigkeit; ~ **and industry** Industrie und *H*, Wirtschaft; ~ **association** Unternehmerverband, Wirtschaftsverband; ~ **balance** *H*–sbilanz; ~ **barriers** → *barrier*; ~ **bill** → *bill* (*1*) *bzw* (*3*); ~ **board** *brit* Arbeitgeber-Arbeitnehmer-Ausschuß; Mindestlohnfestsetzungsamt (*seit 1945: Wages Council*); ~ **branch** Gewerbezweig; ~ **channels** *H*–*s*wege, Absatzwege; ~ **commissioner** britischer Wirtschaftsbeauftragter in den Dominions; *US* Mitarbeiter des *H*–*s*attachés; ~ **competition** Wirtschaftskampf; ~ **connections** *H*–*s*beziehungen; ~ **consul** Wahlkonsul; ~ **control** Gewerbeaufsicht; ~ **credit** → *credit*; ~ **creditors** → *creditor*; ~ **cycle** Konjunkturzyklus; ~ **debts** → *debt*; ~ **debtors** → *debtor*; ~ **description** Warenbeschreibung; (*Warenangaben über Menge, Qualität, Zusammensetzung, Funktion u dgl*); **T** ~ **Descriptions Act 1968** GB) *G. über wahrheitsgemäße Angaben auf Waren und Verpackungen*; ~ **directory** → *directory*; ~**discount** → *discount*; ~ **disease** Berufskrankheit; ~ **dispute** Arbeitskampf, arbeitsrechtliche Auseinandersetzung; ~ **dollar** Silberdollar; ~ **dress** *H*–*s*form, Ausstattung; ~ **effluent** Industrieabwässer; ~ **embargo** *H*–*s*embargo; ~ **establishment** kaufmännisches Unternehmen; ~ **expense** Betriebsausgaben; ~ **facilities** Kreditförderung *zur Arbeitsbeschaffung*; ~ **fair** Messe; ~ **fixtures** → *fixture*; ~ **gap** Außenhandelsdefizit; ~ **group** Wirtschaftszweig; ~ **imbalance** Außenhandelsungleichgewicht; ~**-in** in Zahlung gegebene Ware; **trade-in allowance** Rabatt bei Inzahlungnahme; ~**-in car** Eintauschwagen; ~**-in value** Eintauschwert, Verrechnungswert; ~ **interest** Geschäftswert; ~ **investments** geschäftliche Investitionen; Beteiligungen an Konzernunternehmen; ~ **label** Warenetikett; ~ **letter** *brit* Nachnahmebrief; ~ **libel** Anschwärzung; ~ **licence** Betriebskonzession; ~ **losses** gewöhnlicher Gewichtsabgang und Schwund unterwegs; ~ **machinery** Maschinen als Zubehör, betriebliche Maschinen; ~ **margin** *H*–*s*spanne; ~ **money order** Nachnahmepostanweisung; ~ **monopoly** *H*–*s*monopol; ~ **name** → *trade name*; ~**-off** (*gegenseitige*) Abstimmung, Koordinierungsmaßnahme; ~ **study** Koordinierungsstudie, Abstimmungsstudie; ~ **or business** gewerblicher Betrieb; ~ **or calling** Gewerbe oder Beruf; ~ **paper** Warenwechsel, *H*–*s*wechsel, Kundenwechsel: Fachzeitschrift; ~ **policy** *H*–*s*politik; ~ **practice** *H*–*s*gepflogenheiten; ~ **practice rules** *US* Wettbewerbsregeln; ~ **premises** gewerbliche Räume; ~ **price** → *price* (*1*); ~ **protection society** Kreditschutzverein; ~ **publication** Fachzeitschrift; ~**receivables** *bil* Forderungen aus Lieferungen und Leistungen; ~ **reference** Kreditauskunft; ~ **refuse** Industriemüll; ~ **regulations** *H*–*s*vorschriften, Gewerbeordnung; ~ **relations** Wirtschaftsbeziehungen; ~ **report** *H*–*s*bericht; ~ **representative** *H*–*s*vertreter; ~ **returns** *H*–*s*statistik; ~ **risk** Geschäftsrisiko; ~ **school** → *school*; ~ **secret** → *secret*; ~ **settlement** *H*–*s*niederlassung; ~ **shown** Einspielergebnis; ~ **sign** Firmenschild; ~ **stoplist** schwarze Liste e–s Wirtschaftsverbandes; ~ **surplus** Außenhandelsüberschuß; ~ **tax** Gewerbesteuer; ~ **terms** *h*–*s*übliche Vertragsformeln, Lieferbedingungen; ~ **union** → *trade-union*; ~ **usage** *H*–*s*brauch, *H*–*s*usance; ~ **value** *H*–*s*wert, Marktwert, Verkaufswert; **active** ~ Aktiv*h*, Export; **adverse balance of** ~ passive *H*–*s*bilanz; **balanced** ~ ausgeglichener *H*; **barter terms of** ~ → *term*; **basic** ~ Schlüsselindustrie; **Board of T**~ → *board* (*1*); **branch of** ~ Wirtschaftszweig; **by** ~ gelernt, von Beruf; **carrying** ~ Transportgewerbe; **chain** ~ Ketten*h*; **commodity** ~ Rohstoff*h*; **contraband** ~ Schmuggel, Schleich*h*; **crude** ~ **gap** Außenhandelsdefizit (*zwischen cif-Importen und fob-Exporten*); **distributive** ~ Handel, Verteilergewerbe; **domestic** ~ Binnen*h*; **export** ~ Ausfuhr*h*; **external** ~ Außen*h*; Transit*h* *bei dem die Ware nicht über das Land des Transithändlers geleitet wird*; **fair** → *fair*; **flow of** ~ Wirtschaftsfluß; **foreign** ~ → *foreign*; **free** ~ freier Handel, Freihandel; **freedom of** ~ → *freedom*; **illegal** ~ Schmuggel, Schleich*h*, rechtswidriger (*bzw völkerrechtswidriger*) *H*; **illicit** ~ Schwarz*h*, Schleich*h*; **import** ~ Einfuhr*h*; **intercoastal** ~ Küsten*h*; **intermediate** ~ Zwischen*h*; **internal** ~ Binnen*h*; **international** ~ Welt*h*; **invisible** ~ unsichtbare Auslandsumsätze (*Dienstleistungsverkehr*); **itinerant** ~ Wandergewerbe; **jobber** ~ Maklerberuf; **lawful** ~ erlaubter *H*; **licenced** ~ konzessioniertes Gewerbe; **local** ~ **rules** → *rule*; **manufacturing** ~ Industrie; **maritime** ~ See*h*; **monopoly of** ~ *H*–*s*monopol; **offensive** ~ Gewerbe von dem e–e Geruchs- oder Geräuschbelästigung ausgeht; **overseas** ~ → *overses*; **over-the-counter** ~ Freiverkehr; **passive** ~ Einfuhr*h*; **precarious** ~ geduldeter *H* von neutralen Staaten mit Kriegführenden; **preferential** ~ begünstigter Warenverkehr; **prime** ~ **(bill)** → *prime*; **private** ~ Eigen*h*; **public** ~ Gewerbe; **restraint of** ~ → *restraint*; **retail** ~ Einzel*h*, Detailgeschäft; **seaborne** ~ See*h*; **stock in** ~ Lagerbestand, Warenlager, Betriebskapital; **telephone** ~ *exch* Telefon*h*; **to sell to the** ~ an Wiederverkäufer verkaufen; **unfair** ~ **practices** unlautere Geschäftsmethoden, unlauterer Wettbewerb; **wholesale** ~ Großhandel.

trade *v* handeln, Handel treiben; ~ **in** in Zahlung geben (nehmen); ~ **in bills** Wechselreiterei treiben; ~ **up** zu besseren Bedingungen abschließen.

trade mark *s* (*GB adj: trade-mark; US: trademark*) Warenzeichen *n*, Schutzmarke *f*; ~ **at common law** gewohnheitsrechtl anerkanntes Warenzeichen; ~ **commodity** Markenware; ~ **law** Warenzeichengesetz; ~ **licence** Warenzeichenlizenz; ~ **protection** Markenschutz; ~ **register** Warenzeichenrolle; ~ **registration Act** Warenzeichengesetz; **arbitrary** ~ willkürlich gewähltes Zeichen; **associated** ~**s** verbundene Warenzeichen; **cancellation of a** ~ Löschung e–s Warenzeichens; **certification of** ~ Warenzeichenbescheinigung; **collective** ~ Kollektivzeichen, Verbandszeichen; **common law** ~ nicht eingetragenes Warenzeichen mit Verkehrsgeltung; **community** ~ Gemeinschaftsmarke; **defensive** ~ Defensivzeichen; **distinctive** ~ Unterscheidungsmarke, unterscheidungskräftiges Warenzeichen; **lapse of a** ~ Erlöschen e–s Warenzeichens; **pictorial** ~ Bildzeichen; **register of** ~**s** → *register*; **registered** ~ eingetragenes Warenzeichen; **service** ~ Dienstleistungsmarke, geschützte Bezeichnung für e–e Dienstleistung; **slogan** ~ Wortzeichen; **word** ~ → *word*.

trade name Handelsmarke, geschützte Warenbezeichnung; Firmenname, Etablissementsbezeichnung.

trade union Gewerkschaft *f*; **T~ U~ Act** (*brit Gesetz von 1871 über gewerkschaftliche Koalitionsfreiheit*); ~ **affiliation** Gewerkschaftszugehörigkeit; ~ **ballot** gewerkschaftsinterne Abstimmung; **T~ U~ Congress** (TUC) (=) brit Gewerkschaftsverband; ~ **delegate** Gewerkschaftsvertreter; ~ **freedom** Koalitionsfreiheit für Gewerkschaften; ~ **movement** Gewerkschaftsbewegung; ~ **official** Gewerkschaftsfunktionär; **independent** ~ unabhängige Gewerkschaft.

trade unionism Gewerkschaftsbewegung *f*.

trade-weighted depreciation gewichtete Außenwertminderung *des engl Pfundes, Index*.

trader (*1*) Händler *m*, Kaufmann *m*, Gewerbetreibender *m*; Eigenhändler *m*; Wertpapierhändler *m*; Trader *m*; **floor** ~ zugelassener Börsenhändler, selbständiges Börsenmitglied; **petty** ~ kleiner Geschäftsmann; **pit** ~ Terminhändler an der Produktenbörse; **private** ~ selbständiger Unternehmer; **retail** ~ Einzelhändler; **sole** ~ Einzelkaufmann; **stock** ~ Effektenhändler; **whole-sale** ~ Großhändler.

trader (*2*) Handelsschiff *n*; **constant** ~ ständig auf e–r Route eingesetztes Schiff.

tradesman *brit* Ladeninhaber *m*, *US* Handwerker *m*; **tradesmen's bank** ~ Gewerbebank.

tradespeople kleine Gewerbetreibende *m*|*pl*.

tradeswoman Kauffrau *f*, Händlerin *f*, Ladenbesitzerin *f*.

trading | **account** → *account* (*2*); ~ **activity** gewerbl Tätigkeit, Gewerbe; ~ **agreement** Kartellvereinbarung; ~ **area** Vertriebsgebiet, Absatzgebiet, Verkaufsgebiet; ~ **as** firmierend als; ~ **bank** Handelsbank; ~ **business** Handelsgeschäft (*auf Warenumsatz gerichtetes Handelsgeschäft*); ~ **capital** → *capital*; ~ **certificate** → *certificate*; ~ **cheques** Wareneinkaufs-Schecks; ~ **company** Handelsgesellschaft; ~ **concern** Handelsunternehmen; ~ **conditions** Geschäftsbedingungen; ~ **corporation** → *corporation*; ~ **days** Börsentage; ~ **difference** Aufschlag für kleinere Aktienposten (*unter 100 Stück*); ~ **estates** Industriegebiet; ~ **failure** Geschäftszusammenbruch; ~ **firm** Handelshaus; ~ **floor** der Börsensaal; ~ **fund** Betriebskapital; ~ **in calls** *brit exch* Vorprämiengeschäft; ~ **in futures** Termingeschäft; ~ **in . . . or selling** vertreiben; ~ **in prostitution** Zuhälterei; ~ **income** → *income*; **(vessels)** ~ **inwards** frachtführende einlaufende Schiffe; ~ **licence** → *licence*; ~ **loss** → *loss*; ~ **on margin** Reportgeschäft; ~ **on the equity** Fremdfinanzierung; **(vessels)** ~ **outwards** frachtführende auslaufende Schiffe; ~ **pace** Umsatzgeschwindigkeit; ~ **partnership** → *partnership*; ~ **post** Handelsniederlassung; ~ **profit** → *profit*; ~ **receipts** Einkünfte aus Erwerbstätigkeit; ~ **results** Betriebsergebnisse; ~ **session** Börsentag; ~ **stamps** Rabattmarken; ~ **standards** Normen des kaufmännischen Geschäftsverkehrs; ~ **stock in hand** Lagerbestand; ~ **stocks** Lagerbestände; ~ **stopped** Kurs gestrichen; ~ **unit** *exch* Handelseinheit; ~ **value** Handelswert; ~ **volume** Handelsvolumen; ~ **voyage** Trampschiffahrtsroute; ~ **with the enemy** geschäftlicher Verkehr mit feindlichen Ausländern; ~ **year** Geschäftsjahr; **fraudulent** ~ betrügerische Geschäftstätigkeit *zur Gläubigerbenachteiligung*; **illicit** ~ unlauterer Wettbewerb; **insider** → *insider*; **light** ~ schwache Umsätze (*Börse*); **listless** ~ lustlose Börse; **mutual** ~ gegenseitige Geschäftsbeziehungen; **official** ~ amtlicher Handel (*Börse*); **over the counter** ~ Freiverkehr; Handel mit nicht notierten Wertpapieren; **professional** ~ Berufshandel; **unfair** ~ unlauterer Wettbewerb; **wrongful** ~ rechtswidrige Geschäftstätigkeit bei Insolvenz.

tradition Tradition *f*; Übergabe *f* (*beweglicher Sachen*); **legal** ~ Rechtsüberlieferung.

traditional herkömmlich.

traducer Verleumder *m*.

traffic *s* Verkehr *m*, Handelsverkehr *m*; ~ **accident** → *accident*; ~ **beacon** Fußgängerampel; ~ **cases** Verkehrsstrafsachen; ~ **census** Verkehrszählung; ~ **commissioner** (=) *brit* Straßenverkehrszulassungsbehörde (*für Güter- und Personenverkehr*); ~ **congestion** Verkehrsstauung; ~ **density** Verkehrsdichte; ~ **diversion** Umleitung; ~ **hold up** Verkehrsstockung; ~ **in arms** Waffenhandel; ~ **in children and women** Kinder- und Frauenhandel; ~ **in votes** Stimmenkauf, Wahlschiebung; ~ **junction** Verkehrsknotenpunkt; ~ **lights** = ~ *signals qv*; ~ **management** Versandwesen; ~ **orders** Verkehrsvorschriften; ~ **planning** Verkehrsplanung; ~ **queue** Schlange, Verkehrsstau; ~ **regulations** Verkehrsvorschriften; ~ **requirements** Verkehrsbedürfnisse; ~ **signals** Verkehrsampeln; ~ **signs** Verkehrszeichen; **T~ Signs Regulations** Verkehrszeichenverordnung *f*; ~ **violation** Verstoß gegen Verkehrsvorschriften; ~ **warden** Polizeihelfer im Straßenverkehr, Politesse; **commercial** ~ Handelsverkehr; **competitive** ~ Verkehrsbedienung zu Wettbewerbsbedingungen; **freight** ~ → *freight*; **goods** ~ Güterverkehr; **joint** ~ → *joint*; **left-hand** ~ Linksverkehr; **liner** ~ Linienfahrt; **local** ~ Ortsverkehr; **long distance** ~ Fernverkehr; **oncoming** ~ Gegenverkehr; **public** ~ öffentl Verkehr; **rush hour** ~ Berufsverkehr; **tourist** ~ Reiseverkehr; **Uniform T~ Code** Straßenverkehrsordnung (*einheitliches Gesetz der US-Einzelstaaten*); **vehicular** ~ Fahrzeugverkehr.

traffic *v* feilschen, handeln; ~ **s. th. away** etwas verschachern.

trafficker Händler *m*, Hausierer *m*, Schwarzhändler *m*.

trafficking Einzelhandel *m*, Hausieren *n*; Schleichhandel *m*.

train driver Lokomotivführer *m*.

trainee Auszubildender *m*, Praktikant *m*.

training Ausbildung *f*; Schulung *f*; ~ **allowance** Berufsausbildungsunterstützung; ~ **centre** Ausbildungsstätte; ~ **on the job** Fortbildung am Arbeitsplatz; ~ **school** Jugendstrafanstalt; **T~ Opportunities Scheme** Berufsausbildungswerk; ~ **workshop** Lehrwerkstätte; **additional** ~ **requirements** erforderliche Zusatzausbildung; **compulsory** ~ Pflichtausbildung; **executive** ~ Weiterbildung von Führungskräften; **in-plant** ~ Ausbildung am Arbeitsplatz, betriebl Ausbildung; **legal** ~ juristische Ausbildung; **mercantile** ~ kaufmännische Ausbildung; **methods** ~ Ausbildung in den Arbeitsmethoden; **military** ~ militärische Ausbildung; **occupational** ~ Berufsausbildung; **pre-employment** ~ Berufsausbildung; Ausbildung vor Arbeitsaufnahme; **re-**~ Umschulung; **technical** ~ Fachausbildung; **industrial** ~ gewerbl Berufsausbildung; **vocational** ~ Berufsausbildung, berufliche Bildung.

traitor Verräter *m*; jmd, der Treubruch begeht.

traitorously in (*landes- bzw hoch-*) verräterischer Absicht.

tramp Vagabund *m*, Landstreicher *m*; Trampschiff *n*; ~ **navigation** Trampschiffahrt; ~ **ship owner** Trampreeder.

tranche Tranche *f*, Teilbetrag *m* e–r Wertpapieremission *bzw* e–r Darlehensauszahlung.

transact abschließen, verhandeln, unterhandeln, tätigen; ~ **business** e–e geschäftliche Tätigkeit ausüben.

transaction Geschäft *n*, Rechtsgeschäft *n*, Rechtshandlung *f*; Verfügung *f*; Abschluß *m*, Vergleich *m*, Durchführung *f*, Verhandlung *f*, Verrichtung *f*; ~ **by will** Verfügung von Todes wegen; ~ **for cash** Bargeschäft; ~ **for future delivery** Termingeschäft (*Produktenbörse*); ~ **for the settlement** Termingeschäft; ~ **for value** entgeltliches Rechtsgeschäft; ~ **in foreign exchange** Devisengeschäft; ~ **inter vivos** Rechtsgeschäft unter Lebenden; ~ **loan** kurzfristiger zweckbestimmter Kredit; ~ **on credit** Kreditgeschäft; ~ **on the exchange** Börsengeschäft; **barter** ~ Kompensationsgeschäft, Tauschgeschäft; **bilateral** ~ zweiseitiges Rechtsgeschäft; **capital ~s** → *capital*; **closed** ~ abgeschlossenes Geschäft; **colo(u)rable** ~ vorgetäuschtes Geschäft; verdeckendes G; **current ~s** laufende Geschäfte; **day-to-day ~s** laufende Geschäfte; **evening up** ~ Glattstellungsgeschäft; **fiduciary** ~ treuhänderisches Rechtsgeschäft, fiduziarisches R.; **foreign ~s** Geschäfte mit dem Ausland; **forward ~** Termingeschäft; **invisible ~s** unsichtbare Umsätze; **legal ~** Rechtsgeschäft, juristisch vollzogenes Geschäft; **linked ~** Koppelungsgeschäft; **local ~** Platzgeschäft, Lokogeschäft; **mercantile ~** Handelsgeschäft (*oft: beiderseitiges*); **monetary ~** Geldgeschäft; **non-cash ~s** bargeldloser Zahlungsverkehr; **property ~s** Immobiliengeschäfte; **protected ~s** unter Konkursanfechtung fallende Geschäfte; **secured ~s** Sicherungsgeschäfte; **sham ~** Scheingeschäft, fingiertes Geschäft; **spot ~** Spotgeschäft, Kassageschäft, Lokogeschäft; **spot exchange ~s** Devisenkassageschäfte; **transnational ~s** grenzüberschreitende Geschäfte; **unconscionable ~** sittenwidriges Ausbeutungsgeschäft; **underlying ~s** Grundgeschäfte; **unilateral ~** einseitiges Rechtsgeschäft; **unofficial stock ~s** Freiverkehr; **void ~** nichtiges Rechtsgeschäft.

transactionable verfügbar, abdingbar.

transcribe abschreiben, umschreiben, übertragen.

transcript Abschrift *f*, Ausfertigung *f*, Kopie *f*, Übertragung *f* aus der Urschrift *bzw. aus der Kurzschrift;* **~ of a bill** Wechselabschrift, **~ of the oral evidence** Zeugenvernehmungsprotokoll; **~ of witnesses' evidence** Zeugenvernehmungsprotokoll, Beweisaufnahmeprotokoll; **~ of record** Aktenabschrift.

transcription Umschreibung *f*.

transfer *s* Übertragung *f* (= *Ü bzw ...ü*), Überweisung *f*, Übertrag *m*, Umbuchung *f*, Transfer *m*; Veräußerung *f*, Übergang *m*, Übereignung *f*; Umschreibung *f*, Verlegung *f*; **~ account** Girokonto; **~ agent** Transferagent (*treuhänderischer Aktienbuchverwahrer und Aktienübertragungsbeauftragter*); Umschreibestelle; **~ agreement** Abtretungsvertrag; **~ allowance** Umzugskostenbeihilfe; **~ and counter warrant** Stornoverfügung, Berichtigungsbuchung; **~ book** Aktienbuch; **~ by cheque** Überweisung per Scheck; **~ by death** Übertragung von Todes wegen; **~ by operation of law** gesetzlicher Forderungsübergang; **~ by way of gift** schenkungsweise Veräußerung; **~ by way of security** Sicherungsübereignung; **~ certificate** (Aktien) *Ü–s*bescheinigung; **~ company** Bahnhofsspeditionsgesellschaft; **~ cost** Transferkosten, Kostenschwelle (*bei Anreiz für e–e Standortveränderung*); **~ credit** Überweisungskredit; **~ deed** Auflassungsurkunde, Abtretungsurkunde, *Ü–s*urkunde; **~ duty** Umschreibungsgebühr, Börsenumsatzsteuer; **~ earnings** Höchstertragsalternative (*bei Standortveränderung von Produktionsfaktoren*); **~ fee** *Ü–s*gebühr; **~ for disciplinary reasons** Strafversetzung; **~ for use** Gebrauchsüberlassung; **~ form** Aktienübertragungsformular; **~ in blank** Blankoübertragungsformular; **~ in contemplation of death** Verfügung angesichts des Todes; **~ into an account** Überweisung auf ein Konto; **~ of a cause** Abgabe e–s Falles (*an ein anderes Gericht*); Verweisung; **~ of a debt** Abtretung e–r Forderung; **~ of action** Verweisung e–s Rechtsstreits; **~ of an entry** Umbuchung; **~ of balance** Saldoübertrag; **~ of bill** Wechsel*ü*; **~ of business** Geschäftsverlegung; **~ of capital abroad** Kapitalexport, Kapitalausfuhr; **~ of claim** Forderungs*ü*; **~ of convicts** Verschubung, Verlegung von Strafgefangenen; **~ of domicile** Wohnsitzverlegung; **~ of expectancy** *Ü* e–r (Erb)Anwartschaft; **~ of fee simple** Grundeigentums*ü*, Auflassung; **~ of land** Grundstücks*ü*; **~ of mortgage** Hypotheken*ü*, Grundpfand*ü*; **~ of ownership** Eigentums*ü*, Eigentumsübergang; **~ of prisoner** Verschubung e–s Gefangenen; **~ of**

proceedings Verweisung des Rechtsstreits; ~ **of property** Eigentums*ü*, Übereignung; ~ **of risk** Gefahrübergang; ~ **of shares** → *share*; ~ **of title** Eigentums*ü*, Übereignung; *Ü* e–s absoluten Rechts; ~ **on sale** Veräußerung im Wege des Verkaufs; ~ **or delivery** Veräußerung, Sicherungsübereigung (*bei Gläubigerbenachteiligung*); ~ **order** Überweisungsauftrag, Lagergut-*Ü*–*s*anweisung; ~ **out an out** absolute *Ü*; ~ **payments** Unterstützungszahlungen staatlicher Stellen; Transferzahlungen; ~ **receipt** *Ü*–*s*quittung (*Aktien*); ~ **risk** Devisentransferrisiko; ~ **tax** Erbschaftssteuer; Wertpapierumsatzsteuer; ~ **ticket** Umsteigekarte; ~ **to the Commercial List** *etwa*: Verweisung an die Kammer für Handelssachen; **absolute** ~ unbedingte *Ü*; **bank** ~ → *bank (1)*; **blank** ~ Blanko*ü*, (*Aktien*)Blankoindossament; **cashless money** ~ bargeldloser Zahlungsverkehr; **currency** ~ Devisentransfer; **fraudulent** ~ (Gesamt-)Übertragung des Schuldnervermögens zur Gläubigerbenachteiligung; **inter-bank money** ~ Überweisungsverkehr; **manual** ~ Übergabe; **money** ~ Geldüberweisung; **unilateral** ~ Zession.

transfer *v* übertragen, übereignen, transferieren, abtreten, zedieren, überweisen; ~ **a right** ein Recht abtreten; ~ **foreign currency** Devisen transferieren.

transferability Übertragbarkeit *f*, Veräußerbarkeit *f*, Abtretbarkeit *f*; ~ **of a debt** Abtretbarkeit e–r Forderung.

transferable übertragbar, transferierbar.

transferee Erwerber *m*, Zessionar *m*, Empfänger *m*, Abnehmer *m*; Übernehmer *m*; ~ **company** übernehmende Gesellschaft; **bona fide** ~ gutgläubiger Erwerber.

transference Fortsetzung *f* des Rechtsstreits mit Erben; ~ **of ownership** Eigentumsübertragung, ~ **of property** Besitzübergang, Übereignung.

transferor Zedent *m*, Veräußerer *m*, Übertragender *m*, Indossant *m*; ~ **company** übertragende Gesellschaft.

transformation Verarbeitung *f*, Umbildung *f*; **doctrine of** ~ → *doctrine*.

transgress überschreiten; verletzen.

transgression Rechtsverletzung *f*, Überschreitung *f*, Übertretung *f*.

transient | **arrangement** Zwischenabkommen; ~ **business** Zwischenhandel; ~ **foreigner** ausländischer Tourist; ~ **merchant** Wandergewerbetreibender; ~ **person** Person ohne festen Wohnsitz, sich vorübergehend Aufhaltender; ~ **visitor** Durchreisender.

transire Zollpassierschein *m*.

transit Transit *m*, Durchfuhr *f*; Durchgang *m*, Durchreise *f*, Durchgangsverkehr *m*, Transport *m*; Durchfuhrverkehr *m*; ~ **agent** Zwischenspediteur, Durchfuhrspediteur; ~ **bond** Transitschein; ~ **cargo** Transitladung; ~ **counterfoil** Transitblatt (*Stammabschnitt, Zoll*); ~ **document** Beförderungspapier; Durchfuhrpapier; ~ **country** Durchfuhrland; ~ **duty** Durchfuhrzoll; ~ **entry** Durchfuhrerklärung; ~ **goods** Transitgüter, Transitware; ~ **in rem judicatam** (*etwa*) hat Rechtskraft erlangt; ~ **insurance** Gütertransportversicherung; ~ **number** Bankleitzahl US; ~ **passenger** Durchreisender; ~ **permit** Durchfuhrbewilligung; ~ **trade** Transitverkehr, Transithandel; ~ **traffic** Transitverkehr; ~ **voucher** Transitblatt (*Trennabschnitt*; *Zoll*); **damaged in** ~ auf dem Transport beschädigt; **freedom of** ~ Freiheit des Durchgangsverkehrs; **in** ~ auf dem Transport, unterwegs; **metropolitan** ~ (großstädtisches) Verkehrswesen, Verkehrsverbund; **ordinary course of** ~ gewöhnliche Route.

transition Übergang *m*, Überleitung *f*; ~ **period** Übergangszeit.

transitional | **arrangements** Übergangslösungen; ~ **period** → *period*; ~ **provisions** Übergangsbestimmungen, Überleitungsvorschriften.

transitory vorübergehend, transitorisch, nicht ortsgebunden; ~ **action** → *action*; ~ **item** Durchlaufposten.

translation Übersetzung *f*; *eccl* Versetzung *f* e–s Bischofs; ~ **of evidence** Dolmetschen von Aussagen; **close** ~ wortgetreue Übersetzung; **near** ~ sinngetreue Übersetzung; **rough** ~ Rohübersetzung; **word for word** ~ wörtliche Übersetzung.

translative fact Übertragstatbestand *m*.

translator Übersetzer *m*, (*evt auch*) Dolmetscher *m*; **free-lance** ~ freiberuflicher Übersetzer; **officially certified** ~ öffentlich bestellter Übersetzer; **sworn** ~ (öffentlich bestellter und) beeidigter Übersetzer.

translocate verlagern; verlegen; versetzen.

translocation Verlagerung *f*, Verlegung *f*, Versetzung *f*.

transmigrant Durchwanderer *m*.

transmissibility Vererblichkeit *f*, Übersendbarkeit *f*.

transmissible übertragbar, vererblich.

transmission Übertragung *f*, Übermittlung *f*, Überstellung (*e–s Verhafteten*), Überlassung *f*, Übergang *m*; ~ **by post** Postversendung; ~ **of action** Übertragung e–s streitbefangenen Gegenstandes; ~ **of goods** Versendung von Gütern; ~ **of intelligence** Weitergabe von Geheimnachrichten; ~ **of rights** Rechtsübergang; ~ **of shares** gesetzl Übergang von Aktien (etc); ~ **on death** Übergang von Todes wegen.

transmit übertragen, übersenden, versenden, überlassen; ~ **onward** weiterleiten.

transnational übernational.

transport *s* Beförderung *f*, Transport *m*, Versendung *f*, Übertragung *f*; Auflassung *f* von Grundstücken; ~ **agency** Speditionsfirma; ~ **authorities** Verkehrsbehörden; ~ **charges** Transportkosten, Beförderungskosten; **T~ Commission** (=) (*GB*) Eisenbahn- und Binnenschiffahrtsbehörde; ~ **company** Speditionsgesellschaft; ~ **contractor** Transportunternehmer; ~ **executives** Verkehrsbehörden; ~ **in transit** Durchgangstransport; ~ **insurance** → *insurance*; ~ **policy** Verkehrspolitik; ~ **risk** Transportgefahr, Transportrisiko; **T~ Tribunal** → *tribunal;* ~ **users** Fahrgäste, Beförderungskunden; **air** ~ Luftverkehr, Beförderung auf dem Luftwege; **by public** ~ mit öffentlichen Verkehrsmitteln; **collective** ~ Sammeltransport; **conditions of** ~ Beförderungsbedingungen; **international** ~ grenzüberschreitende Beförderung; **interstate** ~ *US* zwischenstaatlicher Binnenverkehr; **intrastate** ~ innerstaatlicher (Güter)Verkehr (*US Gliedstaaten*); **Ministry of T~ and Civil Aviation** Verkehrsministerium (*GB*); **on-ward** ~ Weitertransport.

transport *v* befördern, transportieren.

transportable transportierbar, versandfähig.

transportation Transport *m*, Verkehrsmittel *n|pl*; Beförderung *f*, Verschickung *f*, Versendung *f*, Transportwesen *n*; Deportation *f*, *hist. in e–e Strafkolonie*; ~ **bond** Versandkaution; ~ **facilities** Verkehrsanlagen; ~ **of the body** (Leichen)Überführung; ~ **rate** Transporttarif; ~ **tax** → *tax*; **interference with** ~ Transportgefährdung; **public** ~ öffentliche Verkehrsmittel.

transpose umstellen, versetzen.

transposition Umstellung *f*, Versetzung *f*; Zahlenverdrehung *f*.

transship umladen, umschlagen, expedieren, umsteigen.

transshipment Umladung *f*, Umschlag *m*, Umexpedierung *f*; ~ **bill of lading** → *bill of lading;* ~ **charge** Umladegebühr.
trap Falle *f*; Hinterhalt *m*, Polizeispitzel *m*; **doctrine of** ~ *Gefährdungshaftung für Fallen, Fußeisen u dgl.*
trash wertlose Waren *f|pl*, Ausschußwaren *f|pl*.
trassans Wechselaussteller *m*.
trassatus Bezogener *m*.
traveaux préparatoires Gesetzgebungsmaterialien *f|pl*.
travel Reise *f*; ~ **advance** Reisekostenvorschuß; ~ **agent** Reisevermittler, Reisebüro; ~ **allowance** Reisespesenpauschale, Devisenzuteilung für Reisezwecke; ~ **allowances in foreign currencies** Reisedevisen; ~ **and subsistence expenses** Reisekosten; ~ **expenses** Reisekosten, Reisespesen; ~ **packing services** Pauschalreise-Dienstleistungen; ~ **souvenirs and gifts** Reisemitbringsel; ~ **report** Reisespesenabrechnung; **business** ~ Geschäftsreise; **international** ~ grenzüberschreitender Reiseverkehr; **official** ~ Dienstreise; **ordinary** ~ allgemein übliche Straßenbenutzung.
travel(l)er Reisender *m*; ~ **at her Majesty's expense** transportierter Strafgefangener (*jocular*); ~**'s cheque** → *cheque*; ~**'s health insurance** Reise-Krankenversicherung; ~**'s letter of credit** Reisekreditbrief; ~ **on commission** Provisionsreisender; **commercial** ~ Handlungsreisender, Vertreter im Außendienst; **fellow** ~ → *fellow*; **town** ~ Platzvertreter.
travel(l)ing | **agent** Handlungsreisender; ~ **allowance** Reisekostenpauschale; ~ **auditor** Außenrevisor; ~ **benefit** Reisekostenvergütung (*an ein arbeitssuchendes Gewerkschaftsmitglied*); ~ **exhibition** Wanderausstellung; ~ **expenses** Reisekosten; ~ **salesman** Handlungsreisender, Geschäftsreisender; ~ **salesman on straight salary** Außendienstmitarbeiter im Angestelltenverhältnis; ~ **time** Reisezeit, Wegezeit; ~ **ways** Verkehrsstollen (*Bergwerk*); ~ **without prepayment** Fahren ohne Fahrschein, Schwarzfahren.
traversable bestreitbar.
traverse *s* Bestreiten *n*, Einwendung *f*; ~ **by denial** das (*allgemeine*) Bestreiten; ~ **jury** Geschworene in der Hauptverhandlung; ~ **of indictment** Nichtschuldigerklärung zur Anklage; ~ **upon a** ~ das Gegenbestreiten; **common** ~ allgemeines Bestreiten; **general** ~ allgemeines Bestreiten; **special** ~ substantiiertes Bestreiten; **technical** ~ Formaleinwand.
traverse *v* bestreiten; die Einlassung verzögern.
traverser der Bestreitende, der bestreitende Beklagte; der Angeklagte.
traversing | **answer** vorweggenommenes Bestreiten *n* in der Klageschrift; ~ **note** = ~ *answer qv*.
travesty | **of facts** Tatsachenverdrehung *f*; ~ **of justice** Justizskandal *m*, schreiendes Unrecht *n*.
trawling Schleppfischerei *f*.
treacherous heimtückisch.
treachery Verrat *m*, Heimtücke *f*, Kriegsverrat *m*.
tread Profil *n* (*Sohlen, Reifen*).
treason Verrat *m*, Landesverrat *m*, Hochverrat *m*; (*US: nur Landesverrat*), ~**-felony** Vorbereitung zum Hochverrat, hochverräterische Drohung *bzw* Anstiftung; Verbrechen gegen die Staatssicherheit; **constructive** ~ gesetzlich vermuteter Verrat, als Hochverrat geltende Verschwörung; **high** ~ Hochverrat (*bes gegen das Staatsoberhaupt*); **misprision of** ~ → *misprision;* **petit** ~ Lehensherrentotschlag; Tötung des Ehemannes; **petty** ~ = *petit* ~ *qv*.
treasonable verräterisch, Landesverrats-, Hochverrats-; ~ **misdemeanour** leichteres Hochverratsdelikt; ~ **publication** → *publication*.
treasure (*verborgener, zufällig entdeck-*

ter) Schatz *m*, Schatzfund *m*; **~-trove** Schatzfund (*gold- bzw silberhaltig, GB: der Krone gehörend*).

treasurer Kämmerer *m*, Schatzmeister *m*, Kassenwart *m*, Leiter *m* der Finanzabteilung; **T~ of the United States** *US* Schatzminister; **~'s remembrancer** Schatzamtsbeauftragter der Krone.

treasury Schatzamt *n*, Finanzministerium *n*, Staatskasse *f*, Fiskus *m*, oberste Finanzbehörde *f*; **~ authorities** Finanzbehörden; **~ bench** *brit* Regierungsbank, Ministerbank; **~ bill** → *bill* (*4*); **T~** *GB* Finanzministerium; **T~ Board** *brit* Finanzministerium; **~ bond** Schatzanweisung *brit; US:* firmeneigene Schuldverschreibung; **~ cash** Staatskassenbestand; **~ certificate** Schatzwechsel, kurzfristige Schuldverschreibung (*verzinslich, Laufzeit bis 1 Jahr*); **~ chest fund** Dispositionsfonds *der brit Staatskasse;* **T~ Counsel** Rechtsanwälte (*barristers*), die als Staatsanwälte auftreten; **~ currency outstanding** von der Staatskasse ausgegebenes Geld; **~ department** Finanzministerium; **~ deposit receipt** verzinsliche Schatzamtsquittungen *für Banken* (*Vorläufer der ~ bills* →*bill* (*3*); **~ directive** Weisung des brit Finanzministeriums *an Banken über Kreditplafond;* **~ savings certificates** Bundessparbonds; **~ securities** Eigenbestand an Wertpapieren; Wertpapierportefeuille e–r Kapitalgesellschaft; **T~ Solicitor** (=) *leitender Justitiar des britischen Finanzministeriums*; **~ statements** Wochenausweis des Schatzamtes; **~ stock** → *stock* (*1*); **~ warrant** Schatzanweisung; **First Lord of the T ~** *brit* erster Lord des Schatzamtes (*von Amts wegen der Ministerpräsident*); **market ~ bill** wöchentliche Schatzwechsel für den Kapitalmarkt; **public ~** Staatskasse, Fiskus; **tap ~ bills** unmittelbar *an Staatsbehörden* ausgegebene Schatzwechsel.

treating Bewirtung *f* zwecks Wählerbeeinflussung.

treatment Bearbeitung *f*, Behandlung *f*; **~ of aliens** Ausländerbehandlung; **~ of offender** Strafvollzug; **competent ~** fachgerechte (ärztliche) Behandlung; **customs ~** zollrechtliche Behandlung, Zollabfertigung; **discriminative ~** diskriminierende Behandlung; unterschiedliche Behandlung; **equal ~** Gleichbehandlung; **medical ~** ärztliche Behandlung, Heilverfahren; **national ~** Inländerbehandlung; **non-custodial ~** Strafen und Maßregeln ohne Freiheitsentzug; **preferential ~** Präferenzbehandlung, Vorzugsbehandlung, Bevorzugung; **unskillful ~** fehlerhafte (ärztliche) Behandlung, ärztlicher Kunstfehler.

treaty Staatsvertrag *m*, (*völkerrechtlicher*) Vertrag *m* (= *V bzw. . . . v*), Übereinkunft *f*, Übereinkommen *n*; **~ credibility** Glaubwürdigkeit als Vertragspartner, Vertragstreue, **~ duties** *V–s*zölle; **~-making power** → *power*; **~ of accession** Beitritts*v;* **~ of alliance** Bündnisv; **~ of arbitration and conciliation** Schieds- und Schlichtungs*v;* **~ of cession** Abtretungs*v;* **~ of commerce** Handels*v*, Wirtschaftsabkommen; **~ of guarantee** Garantie*v*; **~ of navigation** Schiffahrtsabkommen; **~ of peace** Friedens*v*; **T~ of Rome** die Römischen Verträge, EWG-*V*; **~ powers** *V–s*mächte; **~ tariff** *V–s*zoll, vertraglicher Zollsatz; **arbitration ~** → *arbitration* (*1*); **bilateral ~** zweiseitiges Abkommen, zweiseitiger Vertrag; **binding ~** fester *V*; **commercial ~** Handels*v*; **declaratory ~** *V* mit Feststellungscharakter; **dispositive ~** dinglicher völkerrechtlicher *V*; **draft ~** *V–s*-entwurf; **lawmaking ~** Staats*v* mit gesetzgeberischer Wirkung; normativer *V*; **legislative ~** = *lawmaking ~ qv;* **multilateral ~**

mehrseitiger *V*; **naval** ~ Flotten*v*; **non-proliferation** ~ Atomsperr*v*; **preliminary** ~ Vor*v*; **quota** ~ Schadensteilungsabkommen (*zwischen Versicherern*); **reciprocity** ~ Gegenseitigkeits*v*; **reinsurance** ~ Rückversicherungs*v*; **retroactive** ~ *V* mit rückwirkender Kraft; **self-executing** ~ Staats*v* mit unmittelbarer innerstaatlicher Wirkung; **space** ~ Weltraum*v*; **tariff** ~ Zoll*v*; **Test Ban T**~ →*test*.

trebellanic portion Eigenanteil des gesetzlichen Erben bei Vermächtnisbeschwerung.

trend Richtung *f*, Tendenz *f*; ~ **in prices** Preis-, Kurstendenz; ~ **of thoughts** Gedankenrichtung; **cyclical** ~ zyklischer (Konjunktur) Trend; **economic** ~ Konjunktur, Wirtschaftstrend.

trespass Besitzstörung *f*, widerrechtliches Betreten *n*; rechtswidrige Einwirkung, Verletzung des Eigentums, Verletzung absoluter Rechte; ~ **de bonis asportatis** Schadenersatzklage wegen widerrechtlichen Wegnehmens von Sachen; ~ **for mesne profits** Schadenersatzklage wegen widerrechtlichen Nutzungsentzugs; ~ **in law only** gewaltloses unerlaubtes Eindringen; ~ **on the case** Schadenersatzklage wegen widerrechtlicher Verletzung von Rechtsgütern (*bei mittelbarem Schaden*); ~ **quare clausum fregit** Schadenersatzklage wegen Hausfriedensbruchs; ~ **to chattels** Verletzung des Besitzes an fremden bewegl Sachen; ~ **to goods** = ~ *to chattels qv;* ~ **to land** Störung des Besitzes an Grundstücken, unbefugtes Betreten fremden Grundbesitzes; ~ **to property** Verletzung des Eigentums; ~ **to the person** Verletzung der personalen Integrität, V. der körperlichen Unversehrtheit (*Körperverletzung bzw Freiheitsberaubung*); ~ **to try title** Grundstücksherausgabeklage zur Eigentumsfeststellung; ~ **vi et armis** Schadenersatzklage wegen gewaltsamer und bewaffneter Verletzung e–s Rechtsgutes; **action of** ~ → *action*; **continuing** ~ fortgesetzte Besitzstörung *bzw*. Besitzentziehung; **forcible** ~ Besitzstörung, unberechtigte Eigenmacht; **criminal** ~ Hausfriedensbruch; **innocent** ~ versehentliches widerrechtliches Betreten e–s Grundstücks; **joint** ~ gemeinsam begangene unerlaubte Handlung; **malicious** ~ mutwillige Sachbeschädigung; **permanent** ~ unerlaubte Handlung als Dauertat.

trespasser Besitzstörer *m*, Rechtsverletzer *m*; ~ **ab initio** rückwirkend als Besitzstörer behandelter Täter; **assault on** ~ Gewaltanwendung gegen einen Eindringling; **defiant** ~ mutwilliger Rechtsbrecher; **homicide of** ~ Tötung e–s Eindringlings; **innocent** ~ *jmd, der Besitzverletzung in gutem Glauben und aus entschuldbarem Rechtsirrtum begeht*; **joint** ~ Mittäter e–r unerlaubten Handlung.

tret Refaktie *f*, Gutgewicht *n*, Gewichtsvergütung *f* (*Gewichtsnachlaß wegen Wertminderung bei Transport durch Eindringen von Wasser oder Staub*).

triable verhandelbar, verfolgbar.

trial (*1*) Gerichtsverhandlung *f*, mündliche Verhandlung *f*, Haupttermin *m*, Hauptverhandlung *f*; ~ **advocacy** Prozeßanwaltschaft, forensische Anwaltstätigkeit; ~ **amendment** Änderung des Sachvortrags; ~ **at bar** Plenarsitzung des Gerichts, Plenarverhandlung; ~ **at nisi prius** ordentlicher Prozeß vor dem Einzelrichter; ~ **before a judge sitting with assessors** Kammersitzung; ~ **by ambush** Überraschungstaktik im Prozeß; ~ **by battle** Zweikampf (*Ordal*); ~ **by certificate** Verfahren nur auf Grund schriftlicher Glaubhaftmachung; ~ **by commissioners** Verhandlung und Beweisaufnahme durch beauftragte *bzw* ersuchte Richter, Verfahren im Rechtshilfewege; ~ **by compurgation** Prozeß durch Eideshelfer; ~ **by ex-**

amination = ~ *by inspection qv;* ~ **by fire** Feuerordal; ~ **by inspection** Verhandlung *nur* nach Augenscheinsbeweis (*ohne Geschworene*); ~ **by jury** Geschworenenprozeß; ~ **by master** dem Rechtspfleger übertragenes Verfahren; ~ **by ordeal** Prozeß gemäß Gottesurteil; ~ **by pair** Geschworenenverfahren; ~ **by peers** Aburteilung durch Gleichrangige (*Adelige bzw Offiziere*); ~ **by proviso** Geschworenenverhandlung auf (*zunächst zurückgestellte*) Klage und (*spätere*) Widerklage; ~ **by record** *obs* Urkundenprozeß, Feststellungsprozeß über das Vorhandensein e–r Urkunde; ~ **by wager of battle** Prozeß durch Zweikampf; ~ **by wager of law** Zivilprozeß mit Bestreiten unter Eid und durch Eideshelfer; ~ **by witnesses** Prozeß ohne Geschworene; ~ **conduct** Prozeßführung, Prozeßverhalten; ~ **court** Prozeßgericht, erkennendes Gericht, Gericht erster Instanz; ~ **date** (Gerichts-)Termin; ~ **de novo** erneute Verhandlung (*über den gesamten Prozeßstoff*); ~ **docket** gerichtlicher Terminkalender; ~ **examiner** mit Rechtshilfevernehmung beauftragter Verwaltungsbeamter; ~ **for costs** Verfahren zur Herbeiführung e–r Kostenentscheidung; ~ **in camera** nichtöffentliche Verhandlung; ~ **in long vacation** Verhandlung als Feriensache; ~ **in short cause list** Verhandlung im summarischen Verfahren (*vor dem Master qv*); ~ **judge** → *judge;* ~ **judge advocate** Militärstaatsanwalt *in der Hauptverhandlung*; ~ **jury** → *jury*; ~ **lawyer** → *lawyer*; ~ **list** Terminkalender (*des Gerichts*), Sitzungsliste; ~ **of an action** mündliche Verhandlung; ~ **of issues** mündliche Verhandlung *in der Tatsacheninstanz*; ~ **of peers** *Strafverfahren gegen Adelige bzw Offiziere vor gleichrangigen Richtern;* ~ **of the action** die mündl Verhandlung; ~ **on circuit** Gerichtstagung außerhalb des Gerichtssitzes; ~ **on merits** Verhandlung über materiellrechtliche Streitpunkte; Verhandlung zur Sache; ~ **per testes** Einzelrichterverhandlung (*ohne Geschworene*); ~ **procedure** Gang der Hauptverhandlung; ~ **record** → *record;* ~ **date** → *date;* ~ **with assessors** mündliche Verhandlung mit (*sachverständigen*) Beisitzern, Verhandlung vor der Kammer, Hauptverhandlung e–s Kollegialgerichts; **adjournment of** ~ Terminverlegung; **application for** ~ Antrag auf Anberaumung e–s Termins; **bar of** ~ → *bar*; **bifurcated** ~ zweigeteiltes Verfahren (*zB Grund- u. Betragsverf*); **civil** ~ Zivilprozeß; **committal for** ~ → *committal;* **conclusion of** ~ Prozeßbeendigung; **criminal** ~ Strafverfahren; **defended** ~ streitige (= kontradiktorische) Verhandlung; **entry for** ~ → *entry*; **examining** ~ Voruntersuchungsverhandlung; **fair** ~ gerechtes Verfahren; **fair and impartial** ~ gerechtes und objektives Verfahren; **final** ~ (letzte) mündliche Verhandlung erster Instanz, Hauptverhandlung; **joint** ~ gemeinsame Hauptverhandlung; ~ **judge** → *judge*; **jury** ~ → *jury*; **mock** ~ Scheinprozeß; **multi-defendant** ~ Hauptverhandlung mit mehreren Angeklagten; **murder** ~ Mordprozeß; **new** ~ Wiederaufnahmeverfahren, Verfahren nach Rückverweisung; **new** ~ **paper** Sitzungsliste für Sachen im Nachverfahren (*bzw nach Einspruch*); **non-jury** ~ Prozeß ohne Geschworene, Hauptverhandlung ohne Geschw.; **notice of** ~ → *notice*; **preliminary** ~ Vorverhandlung, früher erster Termin; **public** ~ öffentliche Verhandlung; **publicity of** ~ Öffentlichkeit bei der Gerichtsverhandlung; **record of** ~ Sitzungsprotokoll, Gerichtsakte; **separate** ~ abgetrennte Verhandlung (*gesonderte Hauptverhandlung gegen einzelne Mitangeklagte*); **sham** ~ Scheinprozeß; **show-**~ Schauprozeß; **speedy** ~ Verfahren ohne

Verzögerung, unverzüglich anberaumte Hauptverhandlung; **state** ~ → *state* (*2*); **summary** ~ Schnellverfahren (vor dem *magistrate*); **writ of** ~ → *writ*; **to adjourn the** ~ das Verfahren unterbrechen, das Verfahren aussetzen; **to attend at the** ~ vor Gericht erscheinen; **to be on** ~ vor Gericht stehen, angeklagt sein; **to bring to** ~ vor Gericht bringen, zur Aburteilung bringen; **to charge for** ~ anklagen; **to close the** ~ die mündliche Verhandlung schließen; **to commit for** ~ → *to commit*; **to order a new** ~ die Sache an die erste Instanz zurückverweisen; **to set down for** ~ **on** terminieren auf; **to stand** ~ vor Gericht stehen, sich vor Gericht verantworten.

trial (*2*) Versuch *m*, Untersuchung *f*; Probe *f*; ~ **balance** Probebilanz, Rohbilanz, Verprobung; ~ **balance book** Zwischenbilanzbuch; ~ **balloon** Versuchsballon; ~ **engagement** Anstellung auf Probe; ~ **lot** Probesendung; ~ **of the pyx** Münzprüfung, Prüfung neugeprägter Münzen (*durch vereidigte Goldschmiede*); ~ **order** Probebestellung, Probeauftrag; ~ **period** Probezeit, Billigungsfrist; ~ **purchase** Probekauf; ~ **run** Probelauf; ~ **without pleadings** mündliche Verhandlung ohne (weitere) vorbereitende Schriftsätze; **undergoing** ~**s** im Versuchsstadium.

triangular exchange Dreiecksarbitrage *f*.

tribal lands Indianerreservatsgebiete *n|pl*; ~ **law** Stammesrecht.

tribe Volksstamm *m*, Stamm *m*, Sippe *f*.

tribunal Gericht *n*, Gerichtshof *m*, Tribunal *n*; Sondergericht *n*, Standesgericht *n*, Schiedsstelle *f*; ~ **of inquiry** parlamentarische Untersuchungskommission; **T**~ **of the Hague** = *Hague Tribunal* → *Hague*; **administrative** ~ Verwaltungsgericht (*meist auf besonderen Gebieten*), *Verw–s*behörde als Spruchstelle; Widerspruchsinstanz; **arbitral** ~ Schiedsgericht; **civil service arbitration** ~ Schiedsgericht für Tarifkonflikte im öffentlichen Dienst; **DHSS** ~ Sozialgericht; **disciplinary** ~ Standesgericht, Disziplinargericht, Ehrengerichtshof; **domestic** ~ → *domestic;* **International Military T**~ Internationaler Militärgerichtshof (*in Nürnberg*); **Lands T**~ → *land*; **mental health review** ~ Beschwerdeinstanz gegen Einweisungen in Nervenheilanstalten; **military** ~ Militärgerichtshof; **mixed arbitral** ~ gemischter Schiedsgerichtshof; **Pensions Appeal T**~ Sozialgericht, Beschwerdegericht für Veteranenrenten; **performing rights** ~ Bühnenschiedsgericht, Urheberrechtsschiedsstelle; **rent** ~ Schiedsstelle für Wohnungsmietstreitigkeiten *GB*; **Transport T**~ Schiedsstelle für Eisenbahn- und Straßenbeförderungstarife.

tribute Tribut *m*, Staatsabgabe *f*, Zins *m*; **the** ~ **system** Bergwerksnaturallohn (*durch Überlassung e–s Anteils an der Förderung*).

trickery List *f*, Betrügerei *f*, Betrug *m*.

trichotomy of governmental powers Gewaltenteilungslehre *f*.

tried and discharged freigesprochen.

triens Witwendrittel *n* am Grundbesitz.

trier of fact Tatrichter *m*.

trigger Abzug(shahn) *m*; ~ **clause** auslösende Klausel; ~ **mechanism** Auslösevorrichtung, auslösendes Moment; ~ **notice** Mieterhöhungsverlangen.

trim *s* Gleichgewichtslage *f*, Trimm *m*; Innenausstattung (*Auto*).

trimm *v* trimmen, stauen; ~ **the hold** seemäßig stauen.

Trinity | House (=) *Brit* Seeamt *n*; *Piloten- u. Leuchtturmbehörde f*; ~ **House outport districts** Pilotenbezirke (*an der brit Küste*); ~ **Masters** Vorstandsmitglieder des Trinity House (*sachverständige Beisitzer beim Seegericht*); ~ **sittings** Sommersitzungszeit (*Dienstag nach der Pfingstwoche bis 8. August*); ~ **term** *Sitzungsperiode vom 22. 5. bis 12. 6.*

trior(s) Prüfer *m* bei Geschworenenablehnung; Richter *m* von Adligen im Oberhaus.

tripartite dreifach (ausgefertigt), dreiteilig, dreiseitig, zwischen drei Mächten abgeschlossen, in dreifacher Ausfertigung; **T~ Alliance** *pol* Dreierbündnis (*hist der Mittelmächte Deutsches Kaiserreich, Österreich-Ungarn und Italien*); **T~ Entente** *hist* die Drei-Mächte Entente (*Rußland, Frankreich, Großbritannien*); ~ **indenture** Vertragsurkunde in dreifacher Ausfertigung.

triple-A *(AAA)* erstklassig (*Anleihebewertung*).

triplicate dreifach, dritte Ausfertigung; ~ **bill of exchange** → *bill* (*3*).

triplicatio Triplik *f*.

triptique Tryptik *n* *Grenzübergangsschein für Kraft- und Wasserfahrzeuge.*

trithing Drittelgrafschaft *f*, Dreihundertschaft *f*.

triumvir Mitglied *n* e–s Triumvirats, Schulze *m* e–s *trithing qv*.

trivial geringfügig.

triviality Geringfügigkeit *f*, Trivialität *f*.

trouble *pol* öffentliche Unruhe *f*, Wirren *f|pl*, Krawall *m*, Unfrieden *m*; ~ **notice** Anzeige e–s Versicherungsfalles bei Kautionsversicherung; ~ **spot** Krisenherd.

trough Talsohle *f* (*im Konjunkturzyklus*); ~ **of recession** Talsohle (der Rezession).

trousseau Brautausstattung *f*, Mitgift *f*.

trove Schatzfund *m*.

trover *hist* Fund *m*, Fundunterschlagung *f*; Schadenersatzklage wegen rechtswidriger Aneignung beweglicher Sachen (= *action of* ~ → *action*).

troy weight Troygewicht *n* (*für Edelmetalle, Edelsteine und Arzneien*).

truancy Schulschwänzerei *f*, Bummelantentum *n*.

truant Schulschwänzer *m*, Bummelant *m*, Drückeberger *m*; ~ **officer** Vollzugsbeamter der Schulbehörde (*für Schulschwänzerei*).

truce Waffenruhe *f*, Waffenstillstand *m*.

Trucial States *GB hist* Protektoratsstaaten *m|pl* am Persischen Golf.

truck (*1*) Umtausch *m*, Naturallohn *m* in betriebseigenen Unternehmen; Tauschhandel *m*; **T~ Acts** (=) *brit Lohnzahlungsgesetzes (1887 und 1896) mit Verbot der Naturalvergütung bzw. Einkaufsverpflichtung in Geschäften des Arbeitgebers.*

truck (*2*) Lastkraftwagen *m*; offener Güterwagen (*brit*); ~ **load** Waggonladung; **motor** ~ LKW.

truckage *brit* Transport *m* auf Güterwagen, *US* Transport *m* auf Lastkraftwagen; Güterkraftverkehr *m*; Rollgeld *n*.

trucking company LKW-Transportunternehmen *n*.

true|and first inventor → *inventor*; ~ **in substance and in fact** wahrheitsgemäß; ~ **value rule** Grundsatz der Bareinzahlungspflicht zum Nennwert (*Aktienemission*).

truly set forth richtig angegeben.

trumped-up erdichtet, aus den Fingern gesogen; ~ **charge** *jmdm* angedichtete Verfehlung; vorsätzlich falsche Anschuldigung.

truncated verkürzt, summarisch.

truncation *Nichtvorlage e–s Schecks mangels Deckung im Bankverkehr; US: Nichtrückgabe entwerteter eingelöster Schecks; belegloses Scheckeinzugsverfahren.*

truncheon Gummiknüppel *m*, Schlagstock *m*.

trunk Hauptstrecke *f*, Hauptfahrrinne *f*; Fernleitung *f*; ~ **call** Ferngespräch; ~ **exchange** Fernamt; ~ **line** Hauptverkehrsstraße, Hauptstecke; ~ **network** Telefonnetz; ~ **offence** Verkehrsdelikt; ~ **road** → *road*.

trust Vertrauen *n*, Treuhand *f*, (= *T bzw . . . t*); Treuhandverhältnis *n*; *ein auf Marktbeherrschung gerichteter* Unternehmenszusammenschluß;

Trust *m*; Syndikat *n*, Kartell *n*, Konzern *m*, Fideikommiß *n*; ~ **account** *T*konto, Anderkonto; ~ **administration** *T*verwaltung; ~ **agreement** *T*vertrag; ~ **allotment** treuhänderische Landzuweisung (*an Indiander in USA*); ~ **and agency funds** Gelder e–r öffentlichen *T* und Auftragsverwaltung; ~ **assets** *T*vermögen; ~ **certificates** Anteilscheine e–s Massachusetts Trust; *T*zertifikate (*mit dinglicher Sicherung am Treugut*); ~ **company** *T*-Aktiengesellschaft; ~ **corporation** öffentlich-rechtliche *T*anstalt; ~ **declaration** Stiftungsurkunde; *T*errichtungsurkunde; ~ **deed** *T*vertrag, treuhänderische Grundstücksübertragung *als Grundpfandrecht*; ~ **department** *T*abteilung (*e–r Bank*); ~ **deposit** *T*deposit, Einzeldepot; ~ **estate** → *estate*; ~ **ex delicto** = ~ *ex maleficio qv;* ~ **ex maleficio** gesetzliche *T*haftung wegen unredlichen Verhaltens; ~ **for sale** Veräußerungs*t* (*Treuhand an Liegenschaftsbesitz mit zwingender Verkaufsauflage*), Verwertungs*t*, Verkaufs*t*; ~ **fund** *T*gelder, Treugut, *T*vermögen; ~ **fund doctrine** Lehre von der Haftung des Vermögensübernehmers; ~ **in invitum** gesetzliche *T*haftung; ~ **indenture** (*gesiegelte*) *T*urkunde; ~ **instrument** *T*urkunde; ~ **investment** mündelsichere Kapitalanlage; ~ **letter** = *receipt qv*; ~ **money** *T*gelder; Mündelgelder; ~ **mortgage** Sicherungsübereignung; ~ **officer** Leiter der *T*abteilung (*Bank*); ~ **patent** *T*urkunde; ~ **powers** Befugnisse des Treuhänders; *T*geschäftserlaubnis (*Banken*); ~ **property** *T*vermögen; ~ **receipt** (=) *T*quittung (*Urkunde über besitzloses Pfandrecht mit Sicherungsabtretung des Veräußerungserlösanspruchs; Dokument bei Sicherungsübereignung an zwischenfinanzierende Bank*); ~ **relationship** *T*verhältnis; ~ **res** *T*vermögen; ~ **settlement** treuhänderische Vermögensübertragung; ~ **share** *T*zertifikat; ~ **stock** mündelsichere Wertpapiere; ~ **territory** *T*gebiet; **accumulation** ~ Thesaurierungs*t*; **active** ~ aktive *T*, *T* mit Tätigkeitspflichten, Auftrags*t*, weisungsgebundene *T*; **alimentary** *T*vermögen zur Sicherung von Unterhaltsansprüchen; Unterhaltsfonds, Rentenfonds; **annuity** ~ *T* mit festen jährl Zuwendungen; **bare** ~ schlichtes *T*verhältnis; **beneficial** ~ entgeltliches *T*verhältnis; **breach of** ~ → *breach*; **blind** ~ Schein*t*; **business** ~ (=) Kapitalgesellschaft in *T*form; **car** ~ → *car*; **cestui que** ~ → *cestui*; **charitable** ~ mildtätige (= gemeinnützige) *T*, Wohltätigkeitsstiftung; **Civic T**~ (=) *brit öffentliche Stiftung für städtebauliche Gestaltung*; **common** ~ **fund** Sammelvermögen mehrerer Treuhänder; **community** ~ gemeinnützige Stiftung; **complete** ~ *T* mit abschließender Zweckbindung; **complete voluntary** ~ spezifiziertes *T*verhältnis; **completely constituted** ~ vollendete *T*errichtung; **constructive** ~ als *T*verhältnis geltender Sachverhalt, gesetzliches *T*verhältnis; **contingent** ~ bedingtes *T*verhältnis; **controlled** ~ anwaltschaftl verwaltetes *T*vermögen; **corporate** ~ Aktienkonzern, *T*verwaltung durch Kreditanstalt; **creditor in** ~ Treugeber; **court** ~ gerichtlich angeordnete *T*verwaltung; **derivative** ~ (*von Treuhänder*) abgeleitete *T*, sekundäre *T*, Unter*t*; **direct** ~ ausdrücklich erklärtes *T*verhältnis; **directory** ~ *nur in den Grundzügen festgelegtes Treuhandverhältnis*; **discretionary** ~ *T* mit uneingeschränkter Ermessensbefugnis (*bei der Verfügung über T-Kapital und -Erträge*); **dry** ~ abstraktes *T*verhältnis; **educational** ~ Stiftung für e–e Bildungsanstalt; **estate** ~ eheliche Zugewinn-Nachlaß *T*; **executed** ~ abgeschlossene *T*, vollständig festgelegtes *T*verhältnis; **executory** ~ ergänzungsbedürftige *T*errichtung (*durch gerichtl Verfügung zu ergänzen*); unvollständige *T*errichtung, Vereinbarung zur Errichtung e–r *T*-Urkunde; **express** ~ ausdrücklich erklärtes *T*verhältnis, gewillkürtes *T*verhältnis; **fixed** ~ Investmentfonds mit feststehendem Investitionsprogramm; **flexible** ~ Investmentfonds mit veränderlichem Portefeuille; **general management** ~ → *management*; **grantor** ~ vom Errichter der *T* beherrschtes *T*vermögen (*wird diesem steuerl zugerechnet*); **illusory** ~ unechte *T*, widerrufl Grundstücks*t*; **imperfect** ~ unvollständige *T*errichtung *cf executory* ~; **implied** ~ durch Auslegung angenommenes *T*verhältnis; kraft Gesetzes entstandenes *T*verhältnis, vermutetes *T*verhältnis; stillschweigend begründetes *T*verhältnis; **in** ~ zu treuen Händen, treuhänderisch; **incompletely constituted** ~ unvollständige *T*bildung; **industrial** ~ Finanzierungsgesellschaft für den Industriebedarf; **investment** ~ → *investment*; **involuntary** ~ gesetzliches *T*verhältnis; **irrevocable** ~ unwiderrufliche *T*bestellung; **limited** ~ für kurze Zeit errichteter Konzern; **living** ~ lebenslängl *T*verwaltung; *T*verhältnis unter Lebenden; **managed list** ~ Anlagegesellschaft mit Austauschrechten der Investitionseffekten; **management** ~ → *management*; **Massachusetts T**~ (=) *amerikanische Kapitalgesellschaft in Tform;* **ministerial** ~ Verwaltungs*t*; weisungsgebundenes *T*verhältnis; **money in** ~ → *money*; **naked** ~ schlichte *T*, *T* ohne Weisungen und ohne Pflicht zu aktivem Tun, *T*verhältnis ohne Verwaltungsfunktion; **National T**~ → *national*; **nominee** ~ *T* für unbenannten Begünstigten; **non-discretionary** ~ *T*verwaltung mit strengen Anlagevorschriften; **non-expendable fund** → *non-expendable*; **on** ~ **for sale** *T*besitz mit Verkaufsauftrag; **oral** ~ mündliche *T*; **overriding** ~ → *overriding*; **particular** ~ Einzel*t*, *T* an einzelnen Vermögensgegenständen; **passive** ~ passive *T* (*ohne Verwaltungsfunktion*); **perfect** ~ = *executed* ~ *qv*; *T*verhältnis; **perpetual** ~ Dauer*t*; **personal** ~ *T* zugunsten e–r Privatperson; **position of** ~ Vertrauensstellung; **precatory** ~ auf letztwilliger Bitte beruhende *T*; **presumptive** ~ vermuteter *T*verhältnis; **private** ~ *T* zugunsten bestimmter Privatpersonen; *T* mit bestimmten begünstigten Personen; **proprietary** ~ *scot* schlichte *T* (*ohne Verwaltungsfunktion*); **protective** ~ Schutz, *T* für Schutzbedürftige; Schutzklausel zum Wegfall des Treuhänders (*bei dessen Konkurs ua*); **public** ~ Stiftung, gemeinnützige *T*; **purpose** ~ *T* mit objektiver Zweckbestimmung; **real estate** ~ Immobilienanlagegesellschaft, Terraingesellschaft; **resulting** ~ gesetzlich vermutetes *T*verhältnis *zugunsten des Tgebers*; auf hypothetischem Willen des Erblassers basierende *T*; an den *T*geber zurückfallende Zuwendung; **revocable** ~ widerrufliche *T*bestellung; **secret** ~ verdecktes *T*verhältnis (*mündliche treuhänderische Auflage an Vermächtnisnehmer*); **sheltering** ~ *T*verhältnis zum Schutz gegen Verschwendung; **shifting** ~ *T* mit festgelegtem Ersatzbegünstigten; **simple** ~ schlichte *T* (*ohne Vorschriften des Treugebers u. ohne Verwaltungspflichten des Treuhänders*); **special** ~ *T* mit besonderem Zweck; auftragsgebundene *T*; **spendthrift** ~ (=) *T*verwaltung zur Verhinderung von Verschwendung (*seitens des Begünstigten*); **sprinkling** ~ „Gießkannen"*T*; **statutory** ~ *T*schaft kraft Gesetzes; gesetzliches *T*verhältnis, normiertes *T*verhältnis (*zur Grundstücksveräußerung*); **statutory ~s** Intestatsnachlaß*t*; ~~ *for issue: T des Intestatsnachlasses zugunsten der Abkömmlinge* (*zu gleichen Teilen, nach Stämmen*); **testamentary** ~ testamentarische *T*, *T* kraft letztwilliger Verfügung, letztwillige *T*bestellung; **to be under** ~ treuhänderisch verwaltet werden; e–r treuhänderischen Bindung unterliegen; **to hold in** (*upon*) ~ als Treuhänder verwalten; **terms of** ~ → *term*; **totten** ~ (=) *widerrufliche Treuhandbindung eigenen Vermögens zugunsten eines Dritten*; **transgressive** ~ unzulässige Dauer*t*; **unit** ~ → *unit*; **unlawful** ~ rechtswidrige *T*bindung; **variation of** ~ Vertragshilfe zur Änderung des *T*verhältnisses; **vertical** ~ vertikaler Konzern; **voluntary** ~ rechtsgeschäftl *T*; unentgeltliche *T*; uneigennützige *T*, *T*schenkung, unselbständige Stiftung; Konzernbildung durch treuhänderische Aktienkonzentrierung; Kapitalgesellschaft in Form e–r treuhänderischen Vereinigung; **voting** ~ Aktienkonzentration zur Stimmrechtsausübung, Syndikatsvertrag; **wasting** ~ *T mit zulässiger Inangriffnahme der Substanz*.

trustee Treuhänder *m*, Verwalter *m*, Pfleger *m*, Kurator *m*, Fiduziar *m*, Sicherungsnehmer *m*; **T~ Acts** (=) *brit Gesetze von 1852 über gerichtliche Ersatztreuhänderbestellung*; **~'s certificate** Verwahrungsschein, Hinterlegungsschein; ~ **clause** *dingliche Unterwerfungsklausel des Hypothekenschuldners*; **~'s cost basis** Kostenentnahmeregeln für Treuhänder; ~ **de son tort** Scheintreuhänder, ein widerrechtlich Verfügender mit gesetzlicher Treuhandhaftung; ~ **ex maleficio** unredlicher Verwalter unter gesetzlicher Treuhandhaftung; ~ **in bankruptcy** Konkursverwalter; ~ **investment** →*investment*; ~ **of a bankrupt's estate** Nachlaßkonkursverwalter; ~ **process** → *process (1)*; **T~ Relief Act** *brit Gesetz von 1849 mit Hinderlegungsbefugnis für Treuhänder*; ~ **savings banks** = (*staatlich überwachte*) Sparkassen; ~ **security** mündelsicheres Wertpapier; ~ **under a will** letztwillig bestellter Nachlaßtreuhänder; **bare** ~ (*schlichter*) Treuhänder (*ohne Nebenpflichten*); **constructive** ~ der als Treuhänder Geltende, unwiderlegbar vermuteter *T*; **custodian** ~ Treuhänder von Mündelvermögen; **joint** ~ gemeinschaftlicher Treuhänder; **judicial** ~ → *judicial*; **naked** ~ = *bare* ~ *qv*; **official** ~ amtlicher Treuhänder; **private** ~ gewillkürter Treuhänder; **public** ~ staatlicher Treuhänder, staatliche Treuhandstelle, öffentliches Treuhänderamt, öffentl bestellter *T*; **qualified** ~ an Kaufgrundstück dinglich gesicherter Verkäufer; **quasi** ~ *Treuhandhaftung bei unredlicher Verwaltung*; **refusing** ~ seine Berufung ausschlagender Treuhänder; **sole** ~ Einzeltreuhänder, Alleintreuhänder; **solicitor** ~ Anwalt als Treuhänder; **successor** ~ → *successor*; **testamentary** ~ letztwillig bestellter Treuhänder.

trusteeship Treuhandschaft *f*, Treuhänderschaft *f*, Stellung *f* als Treuhänder; Treuhandverwaltung *f*, Kuratel *n*, Kuratorium *n*; ~ **agreement** Treuhandabkommen; **T~ Council** UNO-Treuhandschaftsrat; ~ **territories** Treuhandgebiete.

trustor Treugeber *m*, Errichter *m* e–er Treuhand.

trustworthiness Vertrauenswürdigkeit *f*, Glaubwürdigkeit *f*.

trustworthy vertrauenswürdig, glaubwürdig.

trusty Vertrauenshäftling *m*.

truth Wahrheit *f*, Wirklichkeit *f*; ~ **and veracity of accused** die Glaubwürdigkeit des Angeklagten ~ **in lending** wahrheitsgemäße Kreditkostenangaben (Effektivzins u. a.) ~ **of libel** Wahrheitsbeweis bei Ehrverletzungen; ~ **serum** Wahrheitsserum; **contrary to the** ~ wahrheitswidrig; **evidence of** ~ Wahrheitsbeweis; **nothing but the** ~ die reine Wahrheit; **plain** ~ reine Wahrheit; **to admonish to tell the** ~ zur Wahrheit ermahnen; **to suppress the** ~ → *to suppress*; **to swear the** ~ die Wahrheit e–r Aussage beschwören; **to tell the**

~ **and nothing but the** ~ die reine Wahrheit sagen (*und nichts verschweigen*).

truthfulness Wahrheitsliebe *f*; ~ **of reproduction** Genauigkeit *f* der Wiedergabe.

try gerichtlich prüfen, gerichtlich entscheiden, über den Fall verhandeln; untersuchen, verhören; versuchen; ~ **a case** über e–n Fall gerichtlich verhandeln; ~ **an offence** über e–e Straftat verhandeln; ~ **charges** in Strafsachen verhandeln; ~ **jointly** Prozesse verbinden, gleichzeitig verhandeln.

tub (=) Tub *n*, Faß *n*, Fäßchen *n*, kleine Tonne *f f* (*etwa 4 Gallonen, Gin*); *min* Förderwagen, Hund.

tub-man Anwalt *m* mit Vortrittsrecht.

tug Schlepper *m*, Schleppdampfer *m*; ~ **and tow** Schleppdienst.

tuition Erziehung *f*, Unterricht *m*, Vormundschaft *f*; Studiengebühren *f|pl*; Schulgeld *n*; **postal** ~ Fernunterricht; **private** ~ Privatstunden, Privatunterricht.

tumbrel Schandstuhl *m*, Pranger *m*.

tumult Tumult *m*, Aufruhr *m*, Auflauf *m*.

tumultuous petitioning Petitionseinreichung *f* mit Demonstration.

tungreve Schulze *m*, Gerichtsdiener *m*.

tunnage Weinzoll *m*, Tonnengeld *n*.

turbary Torfgerechtigkeit *f*; **common of** ~ → *common s*.

turf and twig Torf *m* und Zweig *m* (*Auflassungssymbole*); ~ **cutting** Torfstechen.

turmoil Tumult *m*, Unruhe *f*, Aufruhr *m*; **civil** ~ innere Unruhen.

turn *s* Wendung *f*, Wende *f*, Abbiegen *n*, Abbiegung *f*; Veränderung *f*, Umschwung *m*; Turnus *m*, Richterwechsel *m*; Differenz zw Brief- und Geldkurs; ~ **of mind** Denkweise, Gedankenrichtung; ~ **of the market** Kursgewinn; **by** ~**s** der Reihe nach, abwechselnd; **in** ~ turnusmäßig, abwechselnd.

turn *v* verwandeln, drehen; ~ **down** abweisen, verwerfen; ~ **into money** zu Geld machen; ~ **out** sich erweisen, sich herausstellen; zur Räumung zwingen; ~ **to a right** auf den Rechtsweg verweisen (*Herausgabe von Lehensbesitz*); ~ **to account** verwerten, sich zunutze machen.

turnaround Wendefläche *f*.

turncoat Abtrünniger *m*, Überläufer *m*.

turnkey *s* Gefängniswärter *m*.

turnkey *adj, s* schlüsselfertig; gebrauchsfertige Ablieferung *f*; ~- **contract** (*auch turn-key contract*) pauschaler Werkvertrag bis zur Abnahme, Bauvertrag bis zur schlüsselfertigen Übergabe.

turn-off Autobahnausfahrt *f*.

turnout Versammlung *f*, Wahlbeteiligung *f*; Gesamtproduktion *f*; Nebengleis *n*.

turnover Absatz *m*, Umsatz *m*; Umschlaghäufigkeit *f*; ~ **in stock** Lagerumschlag; ~ **rate** Umschlagsgeschwindigkeit, Umsatzziffer; ~ **ratio** Umsatzquote; ~ **tax** Umsatzsteuer; **active** ~ reger Umsatz; **annual** ~ Jahresumsatz; **average** ~ durchschnittlicher Umsatz; **capital** ~ → *capital*; **employment** ~ Fluktuation (von Arbeitskräften); **goods** ~ Güterumschlag; **gross** ~ Bruttoumsatz.

turnpike Schlagbaum *m*, Mautschranke *f*, mautpflichtige Straße *f*; ~ **charges** Maut(gebühr); Straßenbenutzungsgebühr, Straßenzoll; ~ **road** mautpflichtige Straße.

turnround Wende *f* (zum Besseren).

turntable doctrine Haftungsgrundsatz *m* für Kinderspielattraktionen (*vgl attractive nuisance doctrine*).

turpitude Verworfenheit *f*, Niedertracht *f*, niedere Beweggründe *m|pl*; **moral** ~ = *turpitude qv*.

tutelage Bevormundung *f*, Vormundschaft *f*, Pflegschaft *f*.

tutor Vormund *m*, Pfleger *m*, Tutor *m*, Privatlehrer *m*, *GB*: Studienleiter *m*; *US*: Assistent *m*; Lektor *m*; ~ **dative** *scot* gerichtlich bestellter Vormund; ~ **nominate** *scot* von den Eltern eingesetzter Vormund.

tutorial vormundschaftlich.
tutorship Pflegschaft *f*; (*US Louisiana:*) Vormundschaft *f*; Stelle *f* als Hauslehrer; ~ **by nature** elterliche Gewalt; ~ **by will** letztwillige Einsetzung e–s Vormunds.
tutrix weiblicher Vormund *m*, Pflegerin *f*.
twelve-day writ Wechselklage *f*.
twelvemonth *hist* Jahresfrist.
twelve months 12 Monate zu 28 Tagen (*nach Common Law*).
twenty-four calendar months 24 Kalendermonte *m|pl* = 2 Jahre = 730 Tage (*amerik. Rechtsprechung*).
twice in jeopardy Risiko *n* e–r erneuten Strafgerichtsverhandlung (*ne bis in idem*).
twist verdrehen, entstellen; ~ **the law** das Recht verdrehen; ~ **the truth** die Wahrheit entstellen.
twisting Verdrehung *f*, Verleitung *f* zum Übergang auf eine andere Versicherung; **a criminal** ~ e–e kriminelle Veranlagung.
two|-dollar broker Auftragsmakler; ~ **independent brakes** zwei voneinander unabhängige Bremssysteme; ~**-job man** Doppelverdiener; ~**-name account** → *account*; ~**-name paper** Solawechsel, Orderpapier mit mindestens zwei Haftenden; ~**-thirds majority** Zweidrittelmehrheit; ~**-thousand hour clause** Überstundenvergütung ab 2000 Arbeitsstunden pro Jahr; ~**-tier gold price** gespaltener Goldpreis; ~ **way street** Straße mit Gegenverkehr; ~ **years** zwei Jahre (*730 Tage für Fristberechnung nach amerik. Rechtsprechung*).
tycoon Industriemagnat *m*, Großkapitalist *m*.
Tynwald Court Parlament *n* der Insel Man.
type Typ *m*, Muster *n*, Bauart *f*, Modell *n*; ~ **acceptance test** Typenprüfung, Zulassungsprüfung; ~ **sample** Ausfallmuster; ~ **script** maschinegeschriebener Text, Schreibmaschinenmanuskript.

U

U-turn Wenden *n* (*auf der Straße*); **no ~** Wenden verboten.

uberrima fides höchste Gutgläubigkeit *f* und Redlichkeit *f*, *ohne irgend etwas zu verschweigen*; (*z. B. bei Versicherungsanträgen*).

ubiquity Allgegenwart *f*; **legal ~** juristisch fingierte Allgegenwart (*des Königs in den engl Gerichten*).

ukase Ukas *m*, Erlaß *m*.

ullage Flüssigkeitsverlust *m*, Schwund *m*, Fehlquantum *n*.

ultimatum Ultimatum *n*, äußere Grenze *f*.

ultimo Letzter *m* des Monats, Ultimo *m*.

ultimogeniture Erbfolge *f* auf den jüngsten Sohn.

ultra ultra, jenseits, radikal; **~ reprises** nach Abzug von Rabatten, nach Abzug von Auslagen; **~ vires** (=) in Überschreitung der satzungsgemäßen Befugnisse; **~ vires action** Vollmachtsüberschreitung; **~ vires borrowing** durch die Satzung nicht autorisierte Kreditaufnahme.

umpirage oberschiedsrichterliche Entscheidung *f*, Schiedsentscheid *m*.

umpire Schiedsobmann *m*, Schiedsrichter *m*.

umbrella|company Dachgesellschaft; **~ coverage** *ins* Globaldeckung *f*; **~ grouping** gemeinschaftliche Dachorganisation, Dachkonzern.

unabated unvermindert.

unabbreviated unverkürzt.

unabetted ohne Helfershelfer.

unable unfähig, nicht in der Lage; **~ or unwilling** nicht in der Lage bzw (*ohne Angabe von Gründen*) nicht bereit; **~ to pay** zahlungsunfähig.

unabridged ungekürzt.

unacceptable unannehmbar.

unaccommodating ungefällig, unkulant.

unaccountability Nichtverantwortlichkeit *f*, fehlende Rechenschaftspflicht.

unaccountable nicht rechenschaftspflichtig.

unaccounted for nicht ausgewiesen.

unaccrued noch nicht angefallen, noch nicht fällig.

unacknowledged unbestätigt, nicht anerkannt, nicht zugestanden.

unaddressed ohne Adressenangabe; **~ mailing** Postwurfsendung *f*.

unadjudged noch streitbefangen.

unadjusted ungewiß, noch nicht vereinbart, noch nicht reguliert.

unadmitted nicht zugelassen; **~ assets** nicht bewertbare Aktiva.

unadulterated ohne Beimischung.

unadvanced noch nicht befördert; noch nicht zuteilungsberechtigt.

unaffiliated selbständig, nicht angeschlossen.

unalienable unveräußerlich, unverkäuflich.

unallotted noch nicht zugeteilt, noch nicht begeben.

unalterable unabänderlich, unumstößlich.

unambiguous präzis, eindeutig.

unanimity Einstimmigkeit *f*, Einhelligkeit *f*.

unanimous einstimmig.

unappealable nicht rechtsmittelfähig, rechtskräftig.

unapplied nicht zugewiesen, nicht angewendet; frei verfügbar.

unapportionable nicht aufteilbar.

unapprehended flüchtig.

unappropriated nicht angeeignet, nicht zugewiesen.

unargued unbesprochen; unbestritten.

unascertained unbestimmt, noch nicht festgelegt, noch nicht konkretisiert.

unassessed untaxiert, nicht veranlagt.
unassignable nicht übertragbar, nicht abtretbar.
unattached nicht zugehörig, parteilos; nicht beschlagnahmt.
unattended ohne Begleitung (*e–s zugelassenen Anwalts*).
unattested unbeglaubigt, unbestätigt.
unauthenticated unbeglaubigt, unverbürgt.
unauthorized nicht ermächtigt, unbefugt; ~ **practice of law** unzulässige Rechtsausübung.
unavailability Nichtverfügbarkeit *f*.
unavailable nicht verfügbar.
unavailed nicht in Anspruch genommen.
unavailing nutzlos, vergeblich, unnütz.
unavoidable unvermeidlich, unabwendbar.
unaware unbewußt, nichtsahnend.
unbalanced unausgeglichen, nicht saldiert, ohne Gegenbuchung.
unbankable nicht bankfähig, nicht diskontfähig.
unbanked ohne Bankkonto.
unbar *v* offenlegen, sich öffnen, aufschließen.
unbiassed unvoreingenommen, unparteiisch, unbefangen.
unblemished unbescholten; **a person of ~ character** e–e unbescholtene Person.
unblock *v* freigeben; ~**ing** Freigabe, Entsperrung.
unborn person Ungeborene(r), Nasciturus *m*, künftig entstehende Person *f* (*natürliche evtl auch juristische Person*).
unbought unverkauft.
unbound ungebunden, broschiert.
unbribable unbestechlich.
unbroken ungebrochen, unverletzt; ununterbrochen.
unbuilt unbebaut.
unbusinesslike unkaufmännisch, nicht geschäftsmäßig, unsachlich.
uncalled unaufgefordert, noch nicht eingefordert, nicht aufgerufen, nicht abgerufen.
uncensored nicht zensiert, unzensiert, ungerügt.
uncertain ungewiß, unbestimmt.
uncertainty Ungewißheit *f*, Unbestimmtheit *f*; ~ **as to what the law is** Rechtsunsicherheit; ~ **of pleading** mangelnde Bestimmtheit des Schriftsatzvortrags; (*conditions*) **void for** ~ wegen Unbestimmtheit nichtig.
uncertificated ohne amtliche Zulassung, nicht diplomiert.
unchallengable unangreifbar, unwiderlegbar.
unchallenged unangefochten, unbeanstandet.
unchanged unverändert.
uncharged nicht in Rechnung gestellt; franko; nicht angeklagt.
unchaste unkeusch.
unchastity Unkeuschheit *f*.
unclaimed nicht beansprucht, nicht eingelöst (*Scheck*); unverlangt.
unclean hands principle *Grundsatz der Unzulässigkeit der Rechtsausübung wegen eigenen unredlichen Verhaltens.*
uncleared nicht abgefertigt; nicht verrechnet (*Schecks*).
uncollected noch nicht erhoben, noch nicht eingefordert, nicht abgeholt.
uncollectible uneinbringlich, nicht beitreibbar.
uncollectibles uneinbringliche Forderungen *f/pl*.
uncommitted nicht gebunden, blockfrei.
uncommunicative wenig mitteilsam.
uncompromising kompromißlos, unnachgiebig.
unconcerned uninteressiert, unbeteiligt.
unconditional unbedingt, bedingungslos, vorbehaltlos.
unconfirmed unbestätigt.
unconformity Nichtübereinstimmung *f*, Unvereinbarkeit *f*.
unconfutable unwiderlegbar.
unconscionable skrupellos, sittenwidrig, gewissenlos.
unconscionability Übervorteilung *f*, Sittenwidrigkeit *f*.

unconscious unbewußt, bewußtlos.
unconstitutional verfassungswidrig.
unconstitutionality Verfassungswidrigkeit *f.*
unconsummated unvollzogen (*Ehe*).
uncontended unbestritten.
uncontestable unbestreitbar.
uncontested unbestritten, unstreitig.
uncontrollable unbeherrschbar; ~ **impulse** unwiderstehliche Reaktion, Affekt.
uncontrollables nicht disponible Haushaltsposten *m|pl.*
uncontrolled unkontrolliert, nicht bewirtschaftet, unbeaufsichtigt.
uncopyrighted nicht urheberrechtlich geschützt.
uncovenanted nicht vertraglich, nicht vereinbart.
uncovered ungedeckt.
uncustomed unverzollt.
undamaged unbeschädigt, unversehrt.
undated nicht datiert, ohne Datumsangabe.
undecided unbestimmt, unentschieden.
undeclared nicht deklariert.
undefended unbestritten, unstreitig, auf der Beklagtenseite nicht vertreten, ohne Anzeige der Verteidigungsbereitschaft.
undeliverable unzustellbar.
undelivered nicht zugestellt.
undeniable unbestreitbar, unleugbar.
under unter, auf Grund von, gemäß, jmdm untergeordnet, nach, laut; ~ **a contract** nach dem Vertrag, gemäß Vertrag, vertraglich gebunden; ~ **an act** auf Grund e–s Gesetzes; ~ **an execution** auf Grund e–r Vollstreckung; ~ **and subject** belastet mit; ~ **any circumstances** unter allen Umständen; ~ **bond** unter Zollverschluß; ~ **command** manövrierfähig; ~ **control** unter Aufsicht, beherrscht von, geführt (Fahrzeug), unter Kontrolle; ~ **hand** unterzeichnet; ~ **hand and seal** unterzeichnet und gesiegelt; ~ **my hand** von mir unterschrieben; ~ **or by virtue of** auf Grund von; ~ **protest** unter Vorbehalt; ~ **repair** in Reparatur; ~ **the counter** schwarz (*verkaufen, zahlen*); ~ **the hammer** versteigert (*werden*), unter den Hammer (*kommen*); ~ **the influence of (intoxicating) liquor** unter Alkoholeinfluß; ~ **the rules** börsenamtlich (*Vollziehung e–s Effektenengagements*); ~ **the rules of the House** nach der Geschäftsordnung des Parlaments.
underabsorbed indirect costs Gemeinkostenunterdeckung *f.*
underbid unterbieten.
underbill zu niedrig deklarieren, zu niedrig berechnen.
underborrowed unterverschuldet.
undercapitalized unterkapitalisiert.
under-chamberlains of the Exchequer (=) *hist* Finanzbeamte *m|pl.*
under-cover man Detektiv *m*, Vertrauensmann *m.*
undercut unterbieten, unterschreiten.
underdeveloped areas unterentwickelte Gebiete *n|pl*, Entwicklungsgebiete *n|pl.*
underemployment Unterbeschäftigung *f.*
underestimate Unterbewertung *f*, Unterschätzung *f*, zu geringer Kostenanschlag *m.*
underfunding ungenügende finanzielle Ausstattung *f.*
undergo durchmachen, erfahren, sich unterziehen; ~ **an examination** vernommen werden, e–e Prüfung ablegen; ~ **the prescription** verjähren.
under-insurance Unterversicherung *f.*
underinsure unterversichern.
underlease *s* (= *under-lease*) Unterpacht *f*, Unterverpachtung *f*; Untermiete *f.*
underlessee Unterpächter *m*, Untermieter *m.*
underlet untervermieten.
underling Untergebener *m*, Mitarbeiter *m.*

underlying zugrunde liegend.

underpay schlecht bezahlen, unterfrankieren.

underpayment Minderzahlung *f*, Unterbezahlung *f*.

underpin abfangen (*Fundamente*); sichern (*Kapital*).

underprice Schleuderpreis *m*.

underprivileged sozial oder wirtschaftlich benachteiligt, unterprivilegiert.

underrate unterbewerten, unterschätzen.

underrating Unterbewertung *f*.

under-recovery zu geringe Wiedergewinnung; defizitäres Wirtschaften.

underreporting *s* zu niedrige Einkunftsangaben.

undersecretary Staatssekretär *m*.

undersell unter dem Wert verkaufen, verschleudern; jmdn unterbieten.

under-sheriff Sheriff-Stellvertreter; Gerichtswachtmeister *m*.

undersign unterschreiben, unterzeichnen; **the ~ed** der Unterzeichnete bzw die Unterzeichneten.

understand verstehen, erfahren, als sicher annehmen, voraussetzen.

understanding Absprache *f*, Einigung *f*, Vereinbarung *f*, Verständigung *f*, Nebenabrede *f*, formlose Vereinbarung *f*; **on the ~ (with the ~; upon the ~)** mit der Maßgabe (, *daß* . . .); unter der (stillschweigenden) Voraussetzung, daß . . .; **tacit ~** stillschweigendes Einverständnis; **written ~** schriftliche provisorische Vereinbarung.

understood es besteht Einigkeit darüber, daß; einverstanden.

undersubscribed nicht in voller Höhe gezeichnet.

undertake sich verpflichten, unternehmen, übernehmen; **~ a guarantee** e–e Bürgschaft (*bzw Garantie*) übernehmen; **~ a risk** ein Risiko eingehen; **~ an engagement** e–e Verpflichtung eingehen.

undertaker Unternehmer *m* (*Werkvertrag*); Leichenbestatter *m*.

undertaking (*1*) Unternehmen *n*, Betrieb *m*; Vorhaben *n*; **agricultural ~** landwirtschaftlicher Betrieb; **commercial ~** Handelsunternehmen, kaufmännischer Geschäftsbetrieb, Handelsfirma; **industrial ~** Industrieunternehmen; **private ~** Privatunternehmen; **statutory ~s** Versorgungsbetriebe (*im öffentlichen Auftrag*).

undertaking (*2*) Verpflichtung *f*, Verpflichtungserklärung *f* (*bes gegenüber dem Gericht*); Versprechen *n*; **~ of title** Zusicherung der Rechtsmängelfreiheit; **~ to pay** Zahlungsversprechen, Zahlungszusage; **~ to tell the truth** Wahrheitsbekräftigung; **collateral ~** formlose zusätzliche Verpflichtung, Nebenverpflichtung; **cross-~** Gegenverpflichtung; **peremptory ~** zwingende Verpflichtung; *ua Verpflichtung des Klägers, zur Verhandlung in der nächsten Gerichtssitzung zu erscheinen*; **voluntary ~** Versprechen *n*, Verpflichtung zur Einhaltung e–r Auflage.

undertenancy Untermietverhältnis *n*; Untermiete *f*, Unterpacht(verhältnis).

undertenant Untermieter *m*, Unterpächter *m*.

undertutor Gegenvormund *m*.

undervaluation Unterbewertung *f*.

under-value *s* Unterbewertung *f*; zu niedriger Wert *m*.

undervalue *v* unterbewerten; **~d currency** unterbewertete Währung.

underweight Untergewicht *n*, Mindergewicht *n*.

underwrite unterschreiben; e–e Wertpapieremission garantieren bzw übernehmen; versichern; (*als Versicherer*) übernehmen, Versicherungsschutz gewähren.

underwriter Emissionsbank *f*, Unterschreiber *m*, Versicherer *m* (*Feuer bzw Leben*), Lebensversicherungsagent; **leading ~** Erstversicherer; **marine ~** Seeversicherer; *pl* **~s** Emissionskonsortium; **private ~** Privatversicherer.

underwriting *s* Garantie *f* für neue

Effektenemission; Versicherungsgeschäft *n.*

underwriting|agent Versicherungsvertreter, Abschlußagent; ~ **agreement** Emissionskonsortialvertrag; ~ **business** Effektenemissionsgeschäft; ~ **commission** → *commission*; ~ **commitment** Übernahme *f* e–r Emission; ~ **contract** → *contract*; ~ **deficit** Versicherungsverlust; ~ **expenses** Konsortialaufwendungen; ~ **guarantee** Abnahmegarantie (*Wertpapieremission*); ~ **group** Emissionskonsortium; ~ **house** Mitglied e–s Emissionskonsortiums; ~ **limit** Zeichnungsgrenze; ~ **member** Einzelversicherer; ~ **price** Übernahmekurs; ~ **syndicate** Emissionskonsortium.

undesignated nicht angegeben.

undesigned ohne Absicht, nicht vorsätzlich.

undeveloped unerschlossen, noch nicht baureif.

undisbursed noch nicht ausgezahlt, erstattungsfähig.

undischarged unerledigt, unbezahlt, ungelöscht; nicht rehabilitiert.

undisclosed nicht offengelegt, verdeckt.

undisposed nicht verfügt, nicht vermacht.

undisputed unbestritten, unstreitig.

undistributed unverteilt, unausgeschüttet.

undivided ungeteilt, noch nicht auseinandergesetzt.

undo ungeschehen machen, lösen, glattstellen, liquidieren; ~ **a bargain** ein Geschäft rückgängig machen; ~ **the damage** den Schaden wiedergutmachen.

undocumented nicht dokumentiert; nicht durch Beweisurkunden belegt; keine Papiere habend.

undoubtful zweifellos, unzweifelhaft.

undrawn | portion of a loan noch nicht in Anspruch genommener Teil e–s Kredits; ~ **profit** nicht entnommener Gewinn.

undue noch nicht fällig, ungebührlich, ungehörig, unangemessen, unzulässig.

unearned unverdient, noch nicht verdient, nicht erarbeitet, nicht aus Erwerbstätigkeit stammend, aus Kapitalanlage stammend.

unelectable nicht wählbar.

unemancipated minderjährig, noch vom Elternhause abhängig.

unemployability Erwerbsunfähigkeit *f*; Nichtvermittelbarkeit *f*; ~ **supplement** Zusatzrente bei Erwerbsunfähigkeit.

unemployable *adj* nicht vermittelbar, nicht verwendungsfähig.

uneducated ungebildet.

unemployed arbeitslos, erwerbslos, nicht genutzt.

unemployment Arbeitslosigkeit *f*; ~ **beneficiary** Bezieher von Arbeitslosenunterstützung; ~ **benefits** Arbeitslosengeld; ~**-Benefit-Office** Arbeitsamt; ~ **blackspot** Gebiet mit hoher Arbeitslosigkeit; ~ **contributions** Arbeitslosenversicherungsbeiträge; ~ **insurance** Arbeitslosenversicherung; ~ **insurance tax** *US* Arbeitslosenversicherungsbeitrag; ~ **pay** Arbeitslosengeld; ~ **rate** Arbeitslosigkeitsquote; ~ **relief** Arbeitslosenhilfe; Maßnahmen gegen Arbeitslosigkeit; ~ **relief projects** Notstandsvorhaben; **U~ Trust Fund** Vermögen der Arbeitslosenversicherung *US*; **cyclical** ~ konjunkturbedingte Arbeitslosigkeit; **disguised** ~ verdeckte Arbeitslosigkeit; **frictional** ~ fluktuierende Arbeitslosigkeit; **mass** ~ Massenarbeitslosigkeit; **seasonal** ~ jahreszeitlich bedingte Arbeitslosigkeit; **structural** ~ strukturbedingte Arbeitslosigkeit; **technological** ~ entwicklungstechnische Freisetzung von Arbeitskräften; **voluntary** ~ selbstgewollte Arbeitslosigkeit.

unenclosed nicht umfriedet, nicht eingezäunt.

unencumbered unbelastet, lastenfrei, unverpfändet.

unendorsable nicht indossabel, nicht girierbar.

unendowed nicht dotiert.

unenforceability Nichteinklagbarkeit *f*, Nichtdurchsetzbarkeit *f*.

unenforceable nicht erzwingbar, nicht klagbar, nicht vollstreckbar.

unentered nicht deklariert.

unequal ungleich, unverhältnismäßig, unfair, voreingenommen, unzulässig.

unequivocal klar, zweifelsfrei, eindeutig, widerspruchslos.

unerring unfehlbar.

unethical sittenwidrig; standeswidrig.

unexceptionable makellos.

unexcised verbrauchssteuerfrei.

unexcused unentschuldigt.

unexecuted nicht vollzogen; nicht schriftlich ausgefertigt, nicht unterfertigt.

unexhausted nicht verbraucht, unerschöpft.

unexpired noch nicht abgelaufen; noch nicht fällig.

unfair unfair, unbillig, unredlich, unlauter; ~ **business practices** unlautere Geschäftsmethoden; ~ **competition** → *competition*; ~ **consumer practices** Verbraucher-Benachteiligung; ~ **contract terms** unfaire Vertragsbedingungen; **U~ Contract Terms Act** Gesetz gegen unfaire Vertragsbedingungen (*das brit AGB-Gesetz*); ~ **dimissal** → *dismissal*; ~ **industrial action** sozialwidriger Arbeitskampf; ~ **labo(u)r practices** unlautere Arbeitskampfmethoden, gewerkschaftsdiskriminierendes Verhalten; ~ **to union labo(u)r** gewerkschaftsfeindlich; ~ **trade doctrine** *Verbot der Warenursprungsfälschung (ua)*; ~ **trade practices** → *trade*.

unfairness Unfairneß *f*, Ungerechtigkeit *f*, Unredlichkeit *f*, Unbilligkeit *f*.

unfaithful untreu, treulos, bösgläubig.

unfavo(u)rable ungünstig.

unfeasible undurchführbar.

unfilled unausgefüllt; unbesetzt; unerledigt.

unfinished unfertig, unerledigt.

unfit untüchtig, untauglich, ungeeignet; ~ **for human consumption** für menschlichen Verzehr ungeeignet; ~ **for human habitation** für Wohnzwecke ungeeignet; ~ **for publication** nicht zur Veröffentlichung geeignet; ~ **for service** dienstunfähig; ~ **for use as a beverage** als Getränk ungeeignet; ~ **to act** handlungsunfähig, inkompetent; ~ **to plead** (*strafrechtlich*) prozeßunfähig.

unfitness Untauglichkeit *f*, Unfähigkeit *f*; ~ **for work** Arbeitsunfähigkeit.

unforeseen unvorhergesehen, nicht vorausgesehen; ~ **contingencies excepted** Ausschluß bei unvorhergesehenen Ereignissen.

unfounded unbegründet, grundlos.

unfreeze aufheben, deblockieren; ~ **funds** Guthaben freigeben.

unfulfilled unerfüllt.

unfunded unfundiert, schwebend, von kurzer Laufzeit.

unhung nicht blockiert (*Gremium, Geschworene*).

unicameral legislation Einkammerngesetzgebung *f*; ~ **system** *parl* Einkammernsystem.

unifactoral einseitig verpflichtend.

unification Einigung *f*, Vereinheitlichung *f*; ~ **of law** → *law*.

unified vereinigt, vereinheitlicht; ~ **bonds** Ablösungsschuldverschreibungen; ~ **debt** unifizierte (konsolidierte) Schuld; ~ **stock** konsolidierte Anleihe.

uniform einheitlich, gleichförmig, gleichmäßig; ~ **accounting system** einheitliches Buchführungssystem; ~ **acknowledgment form** Einheitsbeglaubigungsformel; **U~ Acts** vereinheitlichte Gesetze (*der US-Gliedstaaten*); Modellkodifikation; **U~ Commercial Code** (= *UCC*) Einheitliches Handelsgesetzbuch (*der US-Bundesländer*); ~ **conveyance** Einheitsauflassung; ~ **delivered price** → *price* (*1*); ~ **law** gemeinsames allgemeines Recht; *US:* Vereinheitlichungsgesetz; ~

system of accounts Kontenrahmen.
uniformity Einheitlichkeit *f*, Gleichmäßigkeit *f*; ~ **in taxation** gleichmäßige Besteuerung; ~ **of arguments** Übereinstimmung der Beweisgründe; **U~ of Process Act** *brit Gesetz von 1832 über einheitliche Klageförmlichkeiten*; ~ **requirement** Gleichheitsgrundsatz; **legal** ~ Rechtseinheit(lichkeit).
unify vereinigen, vereinheitlichen.
unigeniture alleinige Nachkommenschaft *f*.
unilateral einseitig.
unimpaired unbehindert, unbeschädigt (*Person*), unbeeinträchtigt.
unimpeachable zuverlässig, nicht widerlegbar, unangreifbar.
unimproved unerschlossen, unentwickelt.
uninclosed = *unenclosed qv*.
unincorporated nicht rechtsfähig, nicht eingetragen (*Gemeinschaft, Verein*); nicht als juristische Person bestehend, keine Körperschaft bildend.
unincumbered → *unencumbered*.
uninhabitable unbewohnbar.
uninsurable nicht versicherbar.
uninsured nicht versichert, unversichert.
unintelligible unverständlich, nicht entzifferbar.
unintended unbeabsichtigt, ungewollt.
unintentional unbeabsichtigt, ungewollt.
uninterrupted ununterbrochen, fortlaufend.
union Zusammenschluß *m*, Verband *m*, nicht rechtsfähiger Verein *m*, Verein *m*, Vereinigung *f*, Bund *m*, Union *f*, Gewerkschaft *f*; ~ **agreement** Tarifvertrag; **~-bashing** Eindreschen auf die Gewerkschaften; ~ **card** Mitgliedsausweis e-r Gewerkschaft; ~ **certification** gewerkschaftlicher Unbedenklichkeitsvermerk; ~ **committee-man** gewerkschaftl Betriebsratsmitglied; ~ **contract** Betriebsvereinbarung; **U~ Convention** Pariser Verbandsübereinkunft; **U~ country** Mitgliedsstaat des Weltpostvereins, Verbandsland; ~ **dues** Gewerkschaftsbeiträge; **U~ Jack** britische Flagge; ~ **jurisdiction** gewerkschaftliche Zuständigkeit; ~ **label** Etikett für Erzeugnisse gewerkschaftlich organisierter Herstellerfirmen; ~ **labo(u)r** gewerkschaftlich organisierte Arbeitnehmer; ~ **leader** Gewerkschaftsführer; ~ **mortgage clause** *Feuerversicherungsklausel zugunsten des Grundpfandgläubigers;* ~ **negotiations** Tarifverhandlungen; ~ **of parishes** Gemeindezweckverband; ~ **rate** Mindesttariflohn; ~ **representative** Gewerkschaftsvertreter; ~ **security clauses** Schutzklauseln für Gewerkschaften; ~ **shop** geschlossen gewerkschaftlich organisierter Betrieb; ~ **shop system** Gewerkschaftsmonopol; Ausschluß nicht organisierter Arbeitnehmer; ~ **steward** gewerkschaftl Betriebsratsmitglied; ~ **termination** Tarifkündigung; **affiliated** ~ angeschlossene Gewerkschaft, Einzelgewerkschaft; **amalgamated** ~ Gewerkschaftsverband; **closed** ~ Gewerkschaft mit Mitgliederbeschränkung; **company** ~ → *company*; **craft** ~ → *craft*; **customs** ~ Zollunion; **dual** ~ Gegengewerkschaft; **economic** ~ einheitliches Wirtschaftsgebiet; **horizontal** ~ fachliche Einheitsgewerkschaft; **independent** ~ unabhängige (*örtliche*) Gewerkschaft; unabhängige Fachgewerkschaft; **industrial** ~ Industriegewerkschaft; **international** ~ internationaler Gewerkschaftsverband; internationaler Verband, Weltverband; **labo(u)r** ~ → *labo(u)r*; **local** ~ Einzelgewerkschaft (*auf örtlicher Ebene*); **monetary** ~ Währungsunion; **multicraft** ~ Einheitsgewerkschaft; **national** ~ Zentralverband; *gesamtstaatlicher* Gewerkschaftsverband; **open** ~ Gewerkschaft mit freier Mitgliederaufnahme; **personal** ~ Personalunion; **real** ~

Realunion; **the U~** *Vereinigung Englands und Schottlands 1707;* Kurzbezeichnung für USA; **vertical ~** Industriegewerkschaft.

unionism Unionismus *m;* Bewegung *f* für Zugehörigkeit Irlands zu Großbritannien; Sezession *f* der Südstaaten; Gewerkschaftsbewegung *f.*

unionist Gewerkschaftler *m.*

unionize gewerkschaftlich organisieren.

unissued noch nicht ausgegeben, unbegeben; noch nicht ausgestellt, (noch) nicht emittiert.

unit Einheit *f,* Sondereigentumseinheit (*Wohnungseigentum*); Investmentzertifikat *n;* **~s** Anlageeinheiten; **~ amount** Betrag pro Einheit; **~ assurance** mit Investmentfond gekoppelte Lebensversicherung; **~ banking** Einzelbankwesen; **~ bank** unabhängige Einzelbank; **~ control** Inventur, buchmäßige Mengenkontrolle; **~ cost** Einheitskosten, Stückkosten; **~ cost standard** Mindesteinheitskosten; **~ entitlement** Sondereigentum; **~-holder** Zertifikatsinhaber (*Investment Trust*), Fondsanteilseigner; **~ investment trust** Investmentfonds; **~-linked assurance** = **~** *assurance qv;* **~ load** Verladeeinheit; **~ of account** Rechnungseinheit; Verrechnungseinheit; **~ of assessment** Veranlagungsobjekt; **~ of currency** Währungseinheit; **~ of performance** Leistungseinheit; **~ pricing** Preisangabe per Stück; **~ of production** Produktionseinheit; **~ of production method** Abschreibung nach Lebensdauer der Produktionseinheit; **~ of trade** *exch* Handelseinheit; **~ replacement** Ersatz- und Austauschverfahren; **~ rule** *Kursbildungsmethode ausgehend von e–m einzelnen Börsenumsatz;* **~ trust** offener Investmentfonds (*mit Anteilsscheinen = units, Treuhänder-portefeuille*); **~ valuation** Einzelbewertung; **~ value** Wert pro Einheit; **~ voting** gleiches Mitgliederstimmrecht; **~ wage** Stücklohn, Akkordlohn; **average ~ cost** Durchschnittskosten pro Einheit; **bargaining ~** Tarifvertragspartei; **cost ~** Kosteneinheit; **denominational ~** Stükkelung; **monetary ~** Währungseinheit; **standard ~ cost** Normalkosten pro Einheit; **taxable ~** Steuergegenstand.

unitary einheitlich, zentralistisch, Einheits . . .

unite sich vereinigen, sich zusammenschließen, sich einigen.

United Association for the Protection of Trade *(=) GB: Kreditauskunftsorganisation ähnl Schufa;* **~ Kingdom (of Great Britain and Northern Ireland)** Vereinigtes Königreich (von Großbritannien und Nordirland); **~ Nations Charter** Satzung der Vereinten Nationen; **~ Nations Organisation** die UNO.

United States die Vereinigten Staaten *m*|*pl* von Nordamerika, USA; **~ bonds** US-Bundesanleihen; **~ citizenship** Staatsangehörigkeit der USA; **~ Commissioner** (=) richterlicher Beauftragter in Bundesstrafsachen; **~ Code** (=) → *code;* **~ Courts** Bundesgerichte der USA; **~ currency** US-Währung (*jedes zulässige Zahlungsmittel in USA*); **~ notes** amerikanische Bundesschatzwechsel, Geldscheine der USA; **~ officer** Bundesbeamter, Inhaber eines Amtes der USA-Bundesregierung; **~ rule** *amerikanische Anrechnungsregel bei Teilzahlung (zunächst auf Zinsen, dann Kapital);* **~ Supreme Court** Oberster Bundesgerichtshof der USA; **~ value** USA-Binnenwert (*Zoll*).

unity Einheit *f,* Einheitlichkeit *f,* Einigkeit *f,* Gleichförmigkeit *f;* **~ of crime** Tateinheit; **~ of interest** Beteiligung aus gleichem Rechtsgrund, Rechtsgemeinschaft; **~ of invention** Einheitlichkeit der Erfindung; **~ of possession** Gesamtbesitz; Besitz in e–r Hand; gemeinsamer Besitz, Mitbesitz; **~ of seisin** *Vereinigung des dienenden Grund-*

stücks mit dem des Dienstbarkeitsberechtigten; Miteigentum (*am Grundstück*); ~ **of time** Einheit der Zeitdauer (*des Mitbesitzrechtes*); ~ **of title** einheitlicher Rechtsgrund (*Grundstücksmitbesitz*).

universal universal, universell, allgemein, Gesamt . . .; **U~ Copyright Convention** Welturheberrechtsabkommen; **U~ Declaration of Human Rights** Allgemeine Erklärung der Menschenrechte; ~ **military training** allgemeine Wehrpflicht; **U~ Numerical System** *US* Bankleitzahlensystem; **U~ Postal Union** Weltpostverein.

universality Allgemeingültigkeit *f*, universelle Bedeutung *f*, Vielseitigkeit *f*.

university Universität *f*; **U~ courts** *ordentliche Gerichte und Disziplinargerichte der Universitäten Cambridge und Oxford*; ~ **admissions policy** Immatrikulationsgrundsätze; ~ **education** akademische Bildung; ~ **statutes** Universitätssatzung.

unjust ungerecht, unbillig, ungerechtfertigt.

unjustifiable extravagance in living unvertretbar aufwendiger Lebensaufwand *m*.

unjustified ungerechtfertigt.

unkept nicht beachtet, nicht eingehalten.

unlading Abladen *n*, Löschen *n*.

unlawful rechtswidrig, unerlaubt, ungesetzlich, widerrechtlich; ~ **harrassment of a debtor** unzulässige Pression gegen e–n Schuldner, Schuldner-Nötigung; ~ **touching of person's body** widerrechtliches Berühren e–s anderen.

unlawfully widerrechtlich; ~ **fail to . . .** es widerrechtlich unterlassen; ~ **obtained evidence** widerrechtlich erlangtes Beweismittel.

unlawfulness Widerrechtlichkeit *f*.

unless wenn nicht; vorausgesetzt, daß nicht; falls nicht, außer, es sei denn; ~ **and until** solange nicht; ~ **countermanded** Abbestellung vorbehalten; ~ **general** *keine Haftung außer bei Havarie grosse, vgl average*; "~" **lease** auflösend bedingter (Erdöl)Bohrvertrag; "~ **order**" befristeter Auflagenbeschluß mit Ausschlußanordnung; ~ **otherwise (mutually) agreed** soweit nichts anderes vereinbart; unbeschadet anderweitiger Vereinbarung.

unlevied unerhoben, nicht besteuert.

unlicensed unkonzessioniert; ohne Schankkonzession, unerlaubt.

unlimited unbegrenzt, unbeschränkt.

unliquidated offen, unbezahlt, unbeziffert, nicht bezifferbar, der Höhe nach unbestimmt.

unlisted unnotiert, nicht notiert.

Unlisted Securities Market Freiverkehrsbörse, Markt für nicht notierte Werte (*GB*).

unlivery Löschung *f* (*Fracht*).

unload entladen, abladen, ausladen, löschen; auf den Markt werfen.

unloading Abladen *n*, Löschen *n*; Massenverkauf von Effekten; ~ **berth** Ausladeplatz, Löschplatz; ~ **charges** Kosten für Löschung; **days for** ~ Ausladezeit, Löschzeit.

unlocking oil Öl-Erschließung *f*.

unmanifested nicht im Ladungsmanifest aufgeführt.

unmarketable unverkäuflich, nicht gangbar, nicht marktfähig.

unmatured noch nicht fällig.

unmistakeable unmißverständlich, unverkennbar.

unmortgaged nicht verpfändet, nicht hypothekarisch belastet.

unnecessary nicht erforderlich, unnötig, unnütz, überflüssig; ~ **danger or peril** unnötige Gefährdung; ~ **hardship** unnötige Härte.

unnegotiable nicht begebbar, nicht negoziierbar, Rekta . . .

unneutral services neutralitätswidrige Dienste *m*|*pl*.

unobjectionable nicht zu beanstanden.

unoccupancy Unbewohntsein *n*; Leerstehen *n*.

unoccupied unbewohnt, leerstehend.

unofficial nicht amtlich, inoffiziell.

unopposed unwidersprochen, ohne Gegenkandidaten; ohne verteidigungsbereiten Gegner.
unorganized nicht (gewerkschaftlich) organisiert, gewerkschaftsfrei.
unowned herrenlos, ohne Eigentümer; nicht anerkannt.
unpaid unbezahlt, offen, rückständig; ehrenamtlich; unfrankiert.
unparticularised nicht spezifiziert, unsubstantiiert.
unpatented unpatentiert, nicht geschützt.
unpegged ohne Kursbindung.
unpledged unverpfändet.
unpolled nicht von e–r Meinungsumfrage erfaßt; nicht abgegeben (*Wahlstimme*).
unpossessed besitzerlos, ohne Besitzer; leerstehend; herrenlos.
unprecedented ohne Präzedenzfall, beispiellos, neuartig.
unprejudiced unvoreingenommen, vorurteilslos.
unpremeditated ohne Vorbedacht, nicht vorsätzlich, unüberlegt.
unprintable nicht druckfähig, nicht zur Veröffentlichung geeignet.
unproductive unproduktiv; ~ **capital** → *capital*; ~ **wages** → *wage*.
unprofessional nicht berufsmäßig; nicht freiberuflich; unfachmännisch; laienhaft; standeswidrig.
unprofitable unvorteilhaft, uneinträglich, unrentabel.
unproved unbewiesen.
unprovided for unversorgt, nicht vorgesehen.
unpunished ungestraft, unbestraft, ungeahndet.
unqualified unbeschränkt; ungeeignet.
unquoted nicht (amtlich) notiert, nicht angeführt.
unrealized nicht realisiert; nicht verwertet, nicht verwirklicht; unerkannt.
unreasonable unvernünftig, unzumutbar, unangemessen, unverhältnismäßig; ~ **refusal to submit to operation** unbegründete Operationsverweigerung; ~ **restraint of trade** Wettbewerbsbehinderung; ~ **restraint of alienation** unzumutbare Veräußerungsbehinderung.
unreasonably refused grundlos verweigert; ~ **withheld** ohne wichtigen Grund vorenthalten (bzw verweigert).
unrebuttable unwiderlegbar.
unrecallable unwiderruflich.
unreceipted nicht quittiert.
unrecoverable nicht beitreibbar, nicht realisierbar.
unrecovered nicht realisiert, nicht beigetrieben; ~ **cost** Restwert, nicht versicherter Schaden.
unredeemable untilgbar, unkündbar.
unredeemed uneingelöst, nicht zurückbezahlt.
unregistered nicht registriert, nicht (*im Grundbuch bzw sonstigen öffentl Büchern*) eingetragen.
unrelated business income steuerpflichtiger Einkommensteil *m*.
unreported unveröffentlicht (*Entscheidung*).
unreprievable unaufschiebbar, ohne Gnadenfrist.
unrequited unerwidert, unbelohnt, unvergolten.
unrescinded unwiderrufen, nicht angefochten.
unreserved vorbehaltslos, ohne Mindestgebot.
unrestricted unbeschränkt, uneingeschränkt.
unreturned *pol* nicht wiedergewählt.
unroadworthy nicht verkehrssicher.
unruly and dangerous wild und gefährlich (*Tiere*).
unsafe gefährlich, nicht verkehrssicher.
unsalable unverkäuflich.
unsalaried unbesoldet, unbezahlt, ehrenamtlich.
unsatisfied unbezahlt, unbeglichen, nicht befriedigt, nicht erfüllt.
unseal *v* ein Siegel brechen; e–n Brief öffnen.
unsealed unversiegelt, unverschlossen (*Brief*).

unseat (*a Member of Parliament*) *e–m Abgeordneten* das Mandat entziehen; ausschließen; e–n Abgeordneten (*bei der Wahl*) schlagen.
unseated *parl* nicht wiedergewählt.
unseaworthiness Seeuntauglichkeit *f*.
unseaworthy nicht seetüchtig, seeuntauglich.
unsecured ungesichert, nicht dingl gesichert.
unseemly ungebührlich, unpassend.
unseizable unpfändbar.
unsettled unbezahlt, unerledigt; unbesiedelt; schwankend; noch nicht auseinandergesetzt.
unsheltered schutzlos; zollpolitisch nicht geschützt.
unship ausladen.
unshipment Löschung *f*, Ausladung.
unsigned nicht unterzeichnet, ohne Unterschrift.
unsinkable unamortisierbar, untilgbar.
unskilled ungelernt, unfachmännisch.
unsolemn ohne Rechtsförmlichkeit, schlicht, formlos.
unsolicited unaufgefordert, freiwillig, aus freien Stücken.
unsound ungesund, nicht stichhaltig, nicht schlüssig.
unsoundness Unrichtigkeit *f*, Unzuverlässigkeit *f*, Unwahrheit *f*; ~ **of mind** Geistesschwäche.
unspent credit balance offene Kreditlinie, nicht abgerufene Kreditbeträge.
unstatesmanlike nicht staatsmännisch, e–m Staatsmann nicht entsprechend; politisch unklug.
unsubstantiated nicht substantiiert, nicht detailliert.
unsuitable unzulässig, unangemessen, ungeeignet, unpassend.
unsuited ungeeignet (*für ein Amt*).
unsworn unbeeidigt, nicht beschworen, uneidlich.
untaxable nicht besteuerungsfähig, nicht zu versteuern, steuerfrei.
untaxed unbesteuert, unversteuert, steuerfrei.
untenable unhaltbar; ~ **argument** unhaltbares Argument; ~ **statement** unhaltbare Behauptung.
untenantable unvermietbar; ~ **condition** unvermietbarer Zustand.
untenanted unbewohnt, unvermietet.
unthrift Verschwendung *f*, Unwirtschaftlichkeit *f*.
until bis; ~ **and included February 1st** bis einschließlich 1. Februar; ~ **countermanded** → *to countermand*; ~ **further order** → *order* (*1*); ~ **lately** bis vor kurzem; ~ **she shall marry again** bis zu ihrer Wiederverheiratung; ~ **she shall take the veil** bis zu ihrer Verheiratung.
untimely zur Unzeit, ungelegen, vor der Zeit.
untitled ohne Rechtstitel, unberechtigt.
unto and the use of an *jmdn* zu dessen Eigentum (*Auflassungsformel*).
untraceable unauffindbar, nicht feststellbar, nicht zu ermitteln.
untried nicht entschieden; *noch* nicht abgeurteilt, unerprobt.
untrue unrichtig, unwahr; ~ **statement** → *statement*.
untrustworthy unzuverlässig, unglaubwürdig.
unvalued nicht bewertet, nicht taxiert.
unwarranted unverbürgt, ohne Gewähr, unberechtigt.
unwholesome nicht bekömmlich, ungesund, nicht zum Verzehr geeignet.
unwillingness to pay Zahlungsunwilligkeit *f*.
unwitting unbewußt, unbeabsichtigt.
unwitnessed ohne Zeugenunterschrift(en); nicht von Zeugen wahrgenommen, unbeobachtet.
unworkable nicht betriebsfähig, nicht ausführbar.
unworthy unwürdig, ohne ausreichenden Wert.
unwritten ungeschrieben.
unyielding unnachgiebig, unbeugsam.
up | **to** bis (einschließlich); ~ **to date**

bis heute, bisher; ~ **to standard** vollwertig.

update *s* Aktualisierung *f*, Nachlieferung *f* (*auf dem neuesten Stand*); Neufassung *f*; **legal** ~ Rechtsprechungsübersicht.

update *v/t* aktualisieren, auf den neuesten Stand bringen, fortschreiben.

updating Anpassung an den neuesten Stand, Aktualisierung *f*, Fortschreibung *f*; ~ **of the body of laws** Fortschreibung der Gesetzesbestände.

upgrade Nachfolgegeschäft *n* (zur Leistungsverbesserung).

upgrade *v* höher einstufen, befördern; ~**d area** saniertes Baugebiet.

uphold aufrechterhalten, verteidigen; ~ **a conviction** e–n Strafurteil bestätigen; ~ **a decision** e–e Entscheidung bestätigen.

upkeep Instandhaltung *f*.

uplands Ufergrundstücke *n/pl*.

uplifted hand Schwurhand *f*.

upon bei, unter der Bedingung, daß; vor, während oder danach; ~ **appeal** bei Rechtsmitteleinlegung; ~ **either side** auf jeder Seite; ~ **the death** im Todesfall; ~ **the merits** in der Sache; ~ **the trial** bei (oder kurz nach) der Verhandlung; ~ **trust** treuhänderisch; ~ **your introducing a purchaser** bei Vermittlung e–s Käufers durch Sie.

uprating Erhöhung *f*, Heraufsetzung *f* (*Rente etc*).

uprising Volkserhebung *f*, Aufruhr *m*, Volksaufstand *m*.

uproar Radau *m*, Krawall *m*, Tumult *m*.

upset price → *price* (*1*).

upstream stromaufwärts; näher zum Produzenten; näher zur Muttergesellschaft; ~ **loan** Darlehen der Tochtergesellschaft an die Muttergesellschaft.

upsurge Aufschwung *m*, rascher Anstieg *m*.

upswing Aufschwung *m*, Aufstieg *m*.

uptrend steigende Tendenz *f*, Aufschwung *m*.

upturn Aufschwung *m*, Wiederanstieg *m*; Steigerung *f*; ~ **in growth** Wachstumssteigerung *f*.

upwards-only rent review Mietüberprüfungsklausel nur für Mieterhöhung.

urban städtisch, Stadt . . .; ~ **development areas** Sanierungsgebiete, ~ **district council** Gemeinderat; ~ **renewal** Stadtsanierung.

urbanization Verstädterung *f*, städtische Wohnsiedlung *f*.

urgency Dringlichkeit *f*, dringende Bitte *f*, Gesuch *n*; ~ **motion** Dringlichkeitsantrag; ~ **order** Verwahrungsbeschluß (*Einweisung e–s Geisteskranken*).

urgent dringend, dringlich; ~ **case** Dringlichkeitsfall; ~ **need** → *need*.

urn Urne *f*, Wahlurne *f*.

usability (= *useability*) Anwendbarkeit *f*, Brauchbarkeit *f*.

usage Brauch *m*, Usance *f*, Übung *f*, Handelsbrauch *m*, Gewohnheit *f*; ~ **contract** → *contract*; ~ **of the port** Hafenusance; ~ **of the trade** Handelsbrauch, Usance; **ancient** ~**s** alte Sitten und Gebräuche; **commercial** ~ Handelsbrauch; **compulsory** ~ Benutzungszwang; **established** ~ ständiger Brauch; **fair** ~ → *fair*; **general** ~ allgemeiner Brauch; **immemorial** ~ unvordenkliche Gewohnheit, althergebrachter Gebrauch (bzw Brauch); **local** ~ örtlicher Brauch, Platzusance; **mercantile** ~ Handelsbrauch.

usance Uso *m*, Wechselfrist *f*; Gebrauch *m*; ~ **draft** Usowechsel; **at** ~ nach Uso; **bill at** ~ Usowechsel.

use Gebrauch *m*, Anwendung *f*, Benutzung *f*, Nutzen *m*, Inanspruchnahme *f*; Nutzungsrecht *n*, Nutznießung *f*; *hist* Treuhand *f*, Verwendungszweck *m*; **(for the)** ~ **and benefit** zugunsten von; ~ **and occupancy insurance** Betriebsunterbrechungsversicherung; ~ **and occupation** vertragsloser Nutzungsbesitz; ~ **classes** Gebrauchskategorien (*Gebäude, Stadtplanung*); ~ **immunity** Verwendungsverbot selbstbelastender Zeugenaussagen (*gegen den Zeugen*); ~ **of a right** Ausübung e–s Rechts; ~ **plaintiff** → *plaintiff*; ~ **value** Gebrauchswert; ~ **variance** Gebrauchsabweichung; **accessory** ~ Nebengebrauch(szweck); **active** ~ gegenwärtiges Besitzerrecht; **adverse** ~ unbefugter Gebrauch; **agricultural** ~ landwirtschaftliche Nutzung; **beneficial** ~ unbeschränktes Nutzungsrecht, Nießbrauch; **charitable ~s** mildtätige (gemeinnützige) Zwecke; **common** ~ Gemeingebrauch, ~ **compensation for** ~ → *compensation*; **contingent** ~ aufschiebend, bedingtes Nutzungsrecht, *hist* bedingtes Treuhandverhältnis; **continued** ~ Weiterbenutzung; **dead** ~ zukünftiges Nießbrauchrecht; **double** ~ Patientierung e–r neuen Benutzungsmöglichkeit; **duration of** ~ Nutzungsdauer; **economic** ~ wirtschaftl Gebrauch, Nutzung; **end** ~ → *end*; **exclusive** ~ ausschließliche Benutzung, alleiniges Nutzungsrecht; **executed** ~ Besitz und Nutzungsüberlassung; **executory** ~ aufschiebend bedingtes Nutzungsrecht, Vorerbschaft, Vorvermächtnis; **fair** ~ (*copyright*) redlicher Gebrauch, allgemein zulässige Benutzung (*geschützter Werke*); **for home** ~ zum Verbrauch im Inland; **grant to ~s** *hist* rechtsgeschäftliches Treuhandverhältnis; **improper** ~ mißbräuchliche Verwendung, vorschriftswidriger Gebrauch; **industrial** ~ gewerblicher Zweck, gewerbliche Verwendung; **intermediate** ~ Zwischenbenutzung; **intervening** ~ Zwischennutzung; **joint** ~ Mitbenutzung; **loss of** ~ → *loss*; **mixed** ~ gemischte Nutzung (*Grundstück*); **natural** ~ gewöhnliche Benutzung; **official** ~ Dienstgebrauch; **ordinary** ~ gewöhnlicher Gebrauch; **passive** ~ = *permissive* ~ *qv*; **permissive** ~ *hist* Scheinnutzungsrecht; **permitted** ~ zulässige Benutzung; **personal** ~ Eigenbedarf; **pious ~s** seelsorgerische Zwecke; **prior** ~ Vorbenutzung; **prior notorious** ~ offenkundige Vorbenutzung; **private** ~ Privatgebrauch; **public** ~ öffentlicher Nutzen; öffentliche Benutzung; **restricted** ~ zweckgebundene Verwendung; **resulting** ~ vermutetes (billigkeitsrechtliches) Nutzungsrecht des Veräußerers (*von Lehensland*); **right of** ~ Nutzungsrecht; **secondary** ~ nachrangiges Nutzungsrecht, aufschiebend bedingtes Nutzungsrecht; **shifting** ~ Treuhand mit bedingtem Anfall an Ersatz- oder Nachberechtigten; **sole** ~ Alleinbenutzung(srecht); **springing** ~ aufschiebend bedingtes Nutzungsrecht; **Statute of U~s** (=) *engl Gesetz von 1536 über Abschaffung des Scheinnießbrauchs, Verdinglichung der Treuhandnutzung*; **to hold to the** ~ *hist* treuhänderisch besitzen, treuhänderisch verwalten; **unauthorized** ~ unbefugte Benutzung, widerrechtlicher Gebrauch; ~ ~ *of premises: Wohnungszweckentfremdung*; **unrestricted** ~ freie Verwendung.

use gebrauchen, verwenden; ~ **and enjoy** den Besitzgenuß haben; die Nutzungen haben; ~ **their best endeavo(u)rs** sich nach besten Kräften bemühen; **~d area** Nutzfläche.

usee Partei *f*, für die in Prozeßstandschaft geklagt wird.

useful brauchbar, nützlich; ~ **life** → *life*; ~ **load** Nutzlast.

usefulness Nützlichkeit *f*, Verwendbarkeit *f*, Brauchbarkeit *f*.

useless unbrauchbar, nutzlos.

user Benutzer *m*, Nutznießer *m*; Benutzung *f*, Benutzungsrecht *n*, Gebrauch *m*, Nutzung *f*, Nießbrauch *m*; ~ **cost** Benutzungskosten; ~ **as of right** Gebrauchsrecht; ~ **in good faith** gutgläubiger Benutzer; **adverse** ~ eigenmächtige Nutzung; **concurrent ~s** Mitbenutzer, Mitbenutzungsrecht; **industrial** ~ gewerblicher Verwender; **intervening** ~ Zwischenbenutzung; **joint ~s** Mitbenutzer; **prior**

~ Vorbenutzung, Vorbenutzer; **public** ~ Vorbenutzung; **registered** ~ eingetragener Warenzeichenbenutzer; **right of** ~ → *right*; **road** ~ → *road*; **ultimate** ~ Endabnehmer.

usher Gerichswachtmeister *m*; **U~ of the Black Rod** (=) königlicher Parlamentswachtmeister.

using|mail to defraud Postmißbrauch zu Betrugszwecken; ~ **the service of another for pay** jmdn entgeltlich beschäftigen.

usual gebräuchlich, gewöhnlich, üblich; ~ **agency terms** übliche Honorarregelung für unterbevollmächtigte Anwälte; ~ **banker's charges** die übliche Bankprovision; ~ **channels** → *channels*; ~ **clauses** (zu den) üblichen Vertragsbedingungen; ~ **common form** (unter Einhaltung der) übliche(n) Formalitäten; ~ **course** im gewöhnlichen Geschäftsbetrieb; ~ **Lloyd's conditions** die allgemeinen Versicherungsbedingungen von Lloyds; ~ **medical attendant** Hausarzt; ~ **place of abode** gewöhnlicher Aufenthaltsort; ~ **terms** übliche Bedingungen (*auch: e–n Prozeß des Beklagten wie üblich streitig vorbereiten*); ~ **trade name** die übliche Geschäftsbezeichnung.

usucaption Ersitzung *f*.

usufruct Nießbrauch *m*; ~ **for life** lebenslänglicher Nießbrauch; **imperfect** = *quasi* ~ *qv*; **legal** ~ gesetzliches Nießbrauchsrecht; **perfect** ~ Naturalnießbrauch; **quasi** ~ uneigentlicher Nießbrauch, Nießbrauch an verbrauchbaren Sachen.

usufructuary Nießbraucher *m*, Nießbrauchsberechtigter *m*, Nutznießer *m*.

usurer Wucherer *m*.

usurious wucherisch.

usurp usurpieren, sich anmaßen.

usurpation Usurpation *f*, widerrechtliche Besitzstörung *f*, widerrechtlicher Nutzungsentzug *m*; ~ **of advowson** widerrechtlicher Pfründenentzug; ~ **of franchise** Rechtsanmaßung, Amtsanmaßung; ~ **of office** Amtsanmaßung.

usurper Usurpator *m*.

usury Wucher *m*, Kreditwucher *m*, Wucherzinsen *m|pl*; *hist* Kreditzinsen *m|pl*; ~ **in matters of credit** Kreditwucher; ~ **law** Gesetz gegen den Wucher; **to practice** ~ Wucher treiben.

utensils Arbeitsgerät *n*.

uterine von der gleichen Mutter abstammend; ~ **brother** Halbbruder (*mit gleicher Mutter, aber verschiedenem Vater*).

utero-gestation Schwangerschaft *f*.

utilization Ausnutzung *f*, Nutzbarmachung *f*; ~ **of the soil** Bodenbewirtschaftung.

utilize ausnutzen, nutzbar machen, verwerten.

utilitarian | considerations Nützlichkeitserwägungen; ~ **purposes** nützliche Zwecke.

utility Nützlichkeit *f*, gewerbliche Verwertbarkeit *f*, Nutzen *m*; ~ **bonds** Versorgungsanleihen (*öffentliche Anleihen mit Verpfändung von Versorgungsbetrieben*); ~ **deposits** Hinterlegungsgelder bei öffentlichen Versorgungsbetrieben; ~ **fund** Sondervermögen von öffentlichen Versorgungsbetrieben, ~ **goods** Gebrauchsgüter; ~ **model** Gebrauchsmuster; **~-operated stores** betriebseigene Läden von Versorgungsunternehmen; ~ **optimum** Nutzungsoptimum, Nutzenmaximum; ~ **patent** Gebrauchsmuster; ~ **sinking fund** Amortisationsfonds für Versorgungsanleihen; **marginal** ~ → *marginal*; **total** ~ Nutzenmaximum; totale Konsumentenbefriedigung.

utmost äußerst; ~ **care** → *care*; ~ **good faith** = *uberimae fides qv*; ~ **resistance** größtmöglicher Widerstand (*Notzucht*).

utter *v* äußern, aussprechen, in Verkehr bringen; ~ **calumnies** verleumden.

utter | **bar** = *outer bar qv*; ~ **barrister** jüngerer Prozeßanwalt.
utterance Äußerung *f*, Aussprache *f*.
uttering | **counterfeit coin** Inverkehrbringen *n* von Falschgeld; ~ **forged documents** Weitergabe von Falschurkunden; ~ **threatening letters** Erpressungsbriefe übermitteln.
uxoricide Tötung *f* der Ehefrau.

V

vacancy Vakanz *f*, unbesetzte Stelle *f*, freiwerdender Sitz *m*, Leerstehen *n*; unvermessenes Staatsland *n*; ~ **arises** ein Sitz wird frei (*in e–m Gremium*); ~ **ratio** (= *vacancy rate*) Prozentsatz der leerstehenden Wohnungen; **casual** ~ zufälliges Freiwerden (*e–s Vorstandssitzes*); **to fill a** ~ e–e offene Stelle besetzen.

vacant leer, unbesetzt, sofort beziehbar, unbebaut, unbewohnt, herrenlos.

vacate räumen, den Besitz aufgeben; aufheben, annullieren, löschen (*im Register*); ~ **a judgment** ein Urteil aufheben; ~ **one's office** → *office*; ~ **one's residence** ausziehen; **notice to** ~ → *notice*.

vacation (*1*) Räumung *f*; Aufhebung *f*, Kassation *f*; ~ **of judgment** Urteilsaufhebung *wegen schwerer Mängel*; ~ **of sentence** Aufhebung des Urteils im Strafmaß.

vacation (*2*) Gerichtsferien *pl*, Universitätsferien *pl*; *US* Schulferien *pl*, Urlaub *m*; sitzungsfreie Zeit *f*; ~ **barrister** → *barrister*; ~ **court** Ferienkammer; ~ **judge** → *judge*; ~ **of the court** Gerichtsferien; ~ **sittings** Ferientermine; ~ **with pay** bezahlter Urlaub; **Long V~** Gerichtsferien (*GB: 1. Aug.–30. Sept.*); **payless** ~ unbezahlter Urlaub.

vaccination (Schutz)Impfung *f*; **compulsory** ~ Impfzwang.

vaccine damage Impfschaden *m*.

vadium mortuum *hist* Todsatzung, Verfallspfand; ~ **vivum** *hist* Lebendsatzung, Nutzpfand.

vagabond Vagabund *m*, Landstreicher *m*; **Statute of V~s** (=) *brit Gesetz von 1547 gegen Landstreicherei*.

vagrancy Landstreicherei *f*.

vagrant Vagabund *m*, Landstreicher *m*, Nichtstuer *m*, Herumtreiber *m*.

vague unbestimmt, zweideutig.

vagueness mangelnde Bestimmtheit (*zB des Straftatbestandes*).

valid gültig, rechtsgültig, rechtswirksam, stichhaltig, schlüssig, triftig; ~ **and sufficient reason** rechtlich ausreichender Grund; ~ **for one day** *exch* börsengültig, nur am Börsentag gültig; ~ **until recalled** bis auf Widerruf gültig; **legally** ~ rechtsgültig.

validat|e legalisieren, die Gültigkeit prüfen, rechtsgültig machen, bestätigen; ~**ing statute** → *statute*.

validation Gültigkeitserklärung *f*, Bestätigung *f*, Ratifizierung *f*.

validity Rechtswirksamkeit *f*, Rechtsgültigkeit *f*, Gültigkeit *f*, Gültigkeitsdauer *f*, Stichhaltigkeit *f*; ~ **check** Plausibilitätskontrolle; ~ **in law** Rechtsgültigkeit; **extent of** ~ Geltungsbereich; **formal** ~ Formgültigkeit; **legal** ~ Rechtsgültigkeit, Rechtsbestand; **of general** ~ allgemeingültig; **period of** ~ → *period*; **universal** ~ Allgemeingültigkeit.

valorization Aufwertung *f*, Valorisation *f*; staatliche Maßnahmen *f|pl* zur Erzeugerpreisstützung; ~ **scheme** Preisstützungsmaßnahmen.

valorize aufwerten.

valuable wertvoll, entgeltlich, von finanziellem Wert, e–n Vermögenswert darstellend.

valuables Wertsachen *f|pl*, Wertgegenstände *m|pl*.

valuation Bewertung *f*, Wertansatz *m*, Bestimmung *f* des Rückkaufwertes (*Lebensversicherung*); ~ **account** → *account* (*28*; ~ **allowance** Wertberichtigung; ~ **charge** Wertzuschlag für Luftfrachtbrief (*bei Wertdeklaration*); ~ **clause** Wertklausel; ~ **fee** Wertschätzungsgebühr; ~ **for duty purposes** Zollwertermittlung; ~ **for rating** Grundstücksbewertung (*zwecks Kommunalabgaben*); ~ **list** Grundbesitzwertverzeichnis; ~ **of assets** Bewertung der Aktiva; ~ **of claim** Bewertung e–r Forderung; ~ **of probate** Nachlaßbewertung; ~ **of property** Vermögensbewertung; ~ **price** Taxkurs; ~ **reserve** Wertberichtigung; **actuarial** ~ versicherungstechnische Bewertung; **assessed** ~ steuerliche Bewertung; **conservative** ~ vorsichtige Bewertung; **fair** ~ Bewertung zum Verkehrsw; **inventory** ~ → *inventory*; **judicial** ~ gerichtliche Schätzung; **mortgage** ~ Beleihungswertgutachten; **official** ~ amtliche Bewertung, zollamtl B.; **stock** ~ Aktienbewertung.

value Wert *m (= W bzw ...w)*, Nutzwert *m*, Valuta *f*; Entgeltlichkeit *f*; Gegenwert *m*, erhaltener *W*, Verkehrswert *m*; ~ **added** Mehr*w*, *W*schöpfung; ~ **added tax** → *tax*; ~ **adjustment** *W*berichtigung; ~ **analysis** Leistungsanalyse (*Rationalisierung*); ~ **as a going concern** Betriebs*w*; ~ **as per invoice** Rechnungs*w*, *W* auf Faktura; ~ **at cost** = *cost* ~ *qv*; ~ **compensated** Valuta kompensiert; ~ **date** Wert, Valuta, Tag der *W*stellung; ~ **engineering** technische Rationalisierung; ~ **for use** Gebrauchs*w (zu besonderem Zweck*); ~ **given clause** Valutaklausel; ~ **guarantee** *W*sicherung; ~ **in cash** Bar*w*; ~ **in dispute** Streit*w*; ~ **insured** Versicherungs*w*; ~ **judgment** *W*urteil; ~ **of cargo** Ladungs*w*; ~ **of marriage** *hist* Heiratsabgabe der Hintersassen; *Klage wegen Heiratsverweigerung von Lehensabhängigen*; ~ **of matter in controversy** Streit*w*; ~ **of money** Geld*w*; ~ **of plant in successful operation** Betriebs*w*; ~ **of service principle** *Monopoltarifprinzip nach Dienstleistungswert*; ~ **of the business as a whole** Unternehmens*w*; ~ **of the property** Grundstücks*w*; ~ **payment** *W*ausgleichszahlung (*bei Ersatz für Kriegsschäden*); ~ **received** *W* erhalten (*Valutaklausel auf Wechseln*); **acquisition** ~ Anschaffungs*w*; **actual** ~ gewöhnlicher Verkaufs*w*, Verkehrs*w*, wirklicher *W*, Real*w*; **actual cash** ~ *ins* Ist*w* (*Wiederbeschaffungswertminimum, Abzug: neu für alt*); **added** ~ Mehr*w*, (*zusätzliche*) *W*schöpfung; **adventitious** ~ zufälliger *W*, außergewöhnl *W*; **aggregate** ~ Gesamt*w*; **annual** ~ Jahresertrags*w*; **appraised** ~ Schätz*w*, Tax*w*; **appreciation in** ~ → *appreciation*; **arbitrary or fictitious** ~ willkürlich angenommener *W*, fiktiver *W*; **assessable** ~ → *assessable*; **assessed** ~ → *assessed*; **asset** ~ → *asset*; **assumed** ~ → *to assume*; **book** ~ → *book value*; **breakup** ~ (Zwangs)Liquidations*w* (e–s Unternehmens); Einzel*w* bei Konzernentflechtung; **capital** ~ Vermögens*w*, Substanz*w*, Kapital*w*; **carrying** ~ Buch*w*; *W*ansatz; Beleihungs*w*; **cash** ~ → *cash*; **cash surrender** ~ → *cash*; **commercial** ~ Handels*w*, Markt*w*; **comparative** ~ Vergleichs*w*; **commuted** ~ zurückgerechneter *W*; Zeit*w* e–s künftigen Vermögensrechts; **condemnation** ~ Beschlagnahme*w*; **contributive** ~ → *contributive*; **cost** ~ Einstands*w*, Anschaffungs*w*, Erwerbs*w*; **current** ~ Tages*w*, Zeit*w*; Verkehrs*w*; **customs** ~ Zoll*w*; **customs assessment** ~ Zoll*w*; **declaration of** ~ → *declaration*; **double** ~ doppelte Nutzungsentschädigung (*bei Räumungsverzug*); **dutiable** ~ Zoll*w*; Außen*w*; **equal** ~ gleicher *W*, Gleichwertigkeit; **estimated** ~ Schätz*w*, Tax*w*; **exchange** ~ → *exchange* (*1*); **external** ~ Außen*w*; **face** Nenn*w*, Nominal*w*; **fair** ~ angemessener *W*, Verkehrs*w*, Zeit*w*, innerer *W*, Wiederbeschaffungs*w*; **fanciful** ~ Liebhaber*w*; **foreign** ~**s** → *foreign*; **going** ~ Teil*w*; **going-concern** ~ Teil*w*, Unternehmenswert bei Fortführung des Betriebs; **gross** ~ Bruttojahrespachtwert; **holder for** ~ → *holder*; **imaginary** ~ Affektions*w*; **increment** ~ *W*zuwachs; **insurable** ~ versicherbarer *W*; **insurance** ~ Versicherungs*w*, Versicherungstaxe; **insured** ~ Versicherungs*w*, V.-ssumme; **intangible** ~ immaterieller *W*, Firmen*w*, Goodwill; **intrinsic** ~ innerer *W*; **invoice** ~ Rechnungs*w*, Rechnungsposten; **junk** ~ Schrott*w*; **labour theory of** ~ Arbeitswerttheorie; **land** ~ Grundstücks*w*, Boden*w*; **lettable** ~ Miet*w*, Pacht*w*; **letting** ~ Miet*w*, Pacht*w*; **liquidation** ~ Liquidations*w*; **marginal** ~ → *marginal*; **market** ~ → *market*; **marketable** ~ Markt*w*, gewöhnlicher Verkaufs*w*; **mean** ~ Durchschnitts*w*; **monetary** ~ *W* in Geld, Geld*w*; finanzieller *W*; **net** ~ Netto*w*, Prämienreserve, Deckungskapital (*Lebensversicherung*); ~ ~ *of tangible assets: Substanzw*; **net annual** ~ → *net*; **net asset** ~ → *net*; **no par** ~ → *no*; **nominal** ~ Nenn*w*, Nominal*w*; **nuisance** ~ *W* der Beeinträchtigung; **ordinary** ~ gewöhnlicher *W*; **original** ~ Anschaffungs*w*, Nenn*w*, Stamm*w*; **paid-up** ~ Rückkaufs*w*; **par** ~ Pari*w*, Nenn*w*, Nominal*w*; **policy** ~ Policen*w*, Rückkauf*w*; **present** ~ jetziger *W*, Gegenwarts*w*, Kapital*w* e–r Rente; **present cash** ~ gegenwärtiger Bar*w*; **principal** ~ gemeiner *W*; **productive** ~ Ertrags*w*; **prospective** ~ voraussichtlicher *W*; **ratable** ~ Steuer*w*, Einheits*w*; **real** ~ effektiver *W*, echter *W*, Sach*w*; **realization** ~ Veräußerungs*w*, Liquidations*w*; **realised development** ~ erschließungsbedingter Mehr*w*; **redemption** ~ Rückkaufs*w*; **relevant base** ~ der einschlägige Grund*w*; **rental** ~ Miet*w*; **remainder** ~ Rest*w*; **reminder** ~ Erinnerungs*w*; **repaired** ~ Wert in repariertem Zustand; **replacement** ~ Wiederbeschaffungs*w*; **reproduction** ~ Wiederbeschaffungs*w*; **reserve** ~ **fund** Deckungsstock, Prämienreservefonds; **residual** ~ Rest(buch)*w*; **salable** ~ gewöhnl Verkaufs*w*; **sale** ~ Veräußerungs*w*; **salvage** ~ Berge*w*, Rest*w*; **scarcity** ~ Seltenheits*w*; **service** ~ Eignungs*w*, Gebrauchs*w*; **specific** ~ innerer *W*; **scrap** ~ Schrott*w*; **sentimental** ~ Liebhaber*w*, Affektions*w*; **sound** ~ Herstellungs*w*; **standard** ~ Richt*w*; **statement of** ~ Wertangabe; **surplus** ~ Mehr*w*, Überschuß; **surrender** ~ Rückkaufs*w* (*e–r Versicherung*); **tangible** ~ materieller *W*, Substanz*w*, Sachvermögens*w*; **taxable** ~ Steuer*w*, Versteuerungs*w*, Einheits*w*; **trade** ~ → *trade*; **true** ~ echter *W*, innerer *W*; Verkehrs*w*; **unimproved** ~ → *unimproved*; **usable** ~ Zeit*w*; **use** ~ Gebrauchs*w*; **utility** ~ Nutzungs*w*; **written-down** ~ abgeschriebener Wert.

valued | **policy** taxierte Police, *Police mit vereinbarter Wertangabe*; ~ **policy law** Gesetz mit zwingender Bestimmung über Auszahlung zum vollen Versicherungswert (*Schadens- und Feuerversicherung*).

valueless wertlos.

valuer Taxator *m*, Schätzer *m*.

vandalism Rowdytum *n*, vorsätzliche Sachbeschädigung *f*.

vandalize tumultartig zerstören; rowdyhaft belästigen.

vandals Vandalen *m*|*pl*, schadensstiftende Rowdies.

variability Veränderlichkeit *f*.

variable veränderlich, schwankend; ~**-yield securities** Wertpapiere mit schwankendem Ertrag; ~ **rate contract** Abzahlungsvertrag mit variablem Zins; ~ **rate mortgage** variabel verzinsliche Hypothek.

variance Abweichung *f*, Uneinigkeit *f*, Nichtübereinstimmung *f* von Klagebehauptung und Beweisergebnis; Widerspruch *m*; **adverse** ~ Defizit, negative Differenz; **gross** ~ Gesamtabweichung der Istkosten von den Standardkosten; **immaterial** ~ geringfügige Abweichung; **price** ~ → *price*; **quantity** ~ Mengenabweichung.

variation Veränderung *f*, Abänderung *f*, Abweichung *f*, Schwankung *f*; Vertragsänderung *f*; ~ **ap-**

plication Abänderungsantrag (*Unterhalt*); ~ **of contract** (*gerichtliche*) Vertragsabänderung; ~ **of the circumstances** Änderung der Verhältnisse; ~ **of trust** gerichtliche Änderung von Treuhandbedingungen (*für Geschäftsunfähige*); ~ **order** → *order* (*1*); **allowed** ~ zulässige Abweichung, Toleranz; **colo(u)rable** ~ → *colo(u)rable*.

varied verschiedenartig, mannigfaltig; geändert, verändert.

variety Sorte *f*, Qualität *f*, Auswahl *f*; ~ **limiting** Typenbeschränkung; ~ **store** Billigwarengeschäft; Gemischtwarenhandlung.

vary sich ändern, verändern, auswechseln, abweichen.

vasectomy Vasektomie *f* (*Sterilisierung von Männern*).

vassal Vasall *m*, Lehensmann *m*, Untertan *m*; ~ **state** Vasallenstaat, Satellitenstaat; **rear** ~ Hintersasse.

vassalage Vasallenland *n*.

vault Tresor *m*, Stahlkammer *f*.

veer *v/i* schleudern; ~ **off the road** von der Fahrbahn abkommen.

vehicle Fahrzeug *n*; ~ **and traffic laws** Verkehrsvorschriften *f/pl*; ~ **(own damage) insurance** Fahrzeug(kasko)versicherung; ~ **interference** Straßenverkehrsbehinderung; Fahrzeuggebrauchsdiebstahl; ~ **lifting truck** Abschleppfahrzeug; ~ **turning left** (= *left-turning* ~) Linksabbieger; **adverse** ~ Fahrzeug der Gegenpartei; **commercial** ~ Nutzfahrzeug, gewerbliches Fahrzeug; **disabled drivers' ~s** maschinell angetriebene Krankenfahrstühle.

vein Erzader *f*, Flöz *n*; **discovery** ~ ursprünglich entdeckte Erzader; **original** ~ *min* Hauptader.

velocity of circulation Umlaufgeschwindigkeit *f*.

velvet *US* leicht erzielter Börsengewinn *m*.

venal käuflich, bestechlich; ~ **justice** käufliche Justiz; ~ **politician** käuflicher Politiker.

venality Käuflichkeit *f*, Bestechlichkeit *f*.

venary jagdbares Wild *n*.

vend verkaufen, hausieren.

vendee Käufer *m*, Erwerber *m* (*bes. von Grundstücken*).

vendetta Blutfehde *f*; Blutrache *f*.

vendible verkäuflich, handelsfähig.

vending machine Verkaufsautomat *m*.

vendition Verkauf *m*, Verkaufsgeschäft *n*.

vendor Verkäufer *m* (*bes von Grundstücken*), Veräußerer *m*, Lieferant *m*; ~ **and purchaser** Grundstückskaufrecht; ~ **company** Lieferfirma; einbringende Gesellschaft; **~'s covenants for title** Rechtsmängelgewährleistung des (Grundstücks-) Verkäufers; **~'s lien** → *lien*; **~s' list** Lieferantenliste; ~ **placing** Unterbringung von Emissionen bei Außenstehenden; ~ **rating scheme** Zulieferer-Bewertungstabelle; **~'s rights** Vorbehaltsrechte des Grundstücksverkäufers vor Verbriefung und Bezahlung; **~'s shares** eingebrachte Aktien, Gründeraktien; **~-supplied items of equipment** von Zulieferanten gelieferte Geräte; **conditional** ~ Vorbehaltsverkäufer.

vendue Auktion *f*, Zwangsversteigerung *f*; ~ **master** Auktionator.

venial verzeihlich, (er)läßlich.

venire Geschworenenvorladung *f*; ~ **de novo** Wiederaufnahme des Verfahrens (*bei schweren Verfahrensfehlern*); Restitutionsklage; ~ **facias** Ladung des Beschuldigten (*bei kleineren Vergehen*).

venireman geladener Geschworener *m*.

venter Mutterleib *m*; **by the first** ~ von der ersten Frau (*geboren*).

venture Wagnis *m*, Spekulation *f*, Unternehmen *n*; schwimmendes Gut *n*; ~ **capital** Risikokapital; **business** ~ geschäftliches Unternehmen; **collaborative** ~ Arbeitsgemeinschaft, Gemeinschaftsprojekt; **joint** ~ → *joint venture*; **joint equity** ~ Joint Venture mit Kapitalbeteiligung; **real estate** ~ → *real estate*.

venue (= *venue of proceeding*) Gerichtsbezirk *m*, Gerichtsstand *m*, zuständiger Gerichtsort *m*, örtliche Zuständigkeit *f*; ~ **facts** Tatbestand e–s besonderen Gerichtsstandes; ~ **jurisdiction** Gerichtshoheit, Gerichtsbarkeit e–s einzelnen Gerichtes; **change of** ~ → *change*; **jurisdictional** ~ Gerichtsstand; **local** ~ ausschließlicher örtlicher Gerichtsstand; **to lay the** ~ die örtliche Zuständigkeit begründen.

veracity Wahrheitsliebe *f*, Glaubwürdigkeit *f*.

verbal *adj* wörtlich, in Worten ausgedrückt, wortgetreu, mündlich formlos, schriftlich doch ohne Unterschrift; ~ **acts** mündliche Äußerungen (*anläßlich der Tat*); ~ **act doctrine** Beweiszulässigkeit von mündlichen Äußerungen bei Rechtsgeschäften; ~ **agreement** → *agreement*; ~ **contract** → *contract*; **offer** → *offer*; ~ **process** = *procès-verbal qv*; ~ **remonstrance** mündliche Vorhaltungen; ~ **statement** mündliche Erklärung, mündliche Äußerung; ~ **translation** wortgetreue Übersetzung.

verbals Worte e–s Tatverdächtigen ggüber Polizeibeamten; zu Protokoll abgegebene Erklärung.

verbalism Spiel *n* mit Worten, Wortklauberei *f*.

verbatim wörtlich, Wort für Wort; ~ **et literatim** buchstäblich, wortgetreu.

verderer Forstaufseher *m*.

verdict Spruch *m (der Geschworenen)*; Urteil *n (zur Schuldfrage bzw tatsächlichen Fragen)*; ~ **by lot** Geschworenenspruch durch das Los; ~ **contrary to law** rechtswidrige Geschworenenentscheidung; ~ **for the defendant** klageabweisender Urteilsspruch; ~ **of guilty** Schuldspruch; ~ **of guilty but insane** Freispruch wegen Unzurechnungsfähigkeit (*trotz Erfüllung des objektiven Tatbestands*); ~ **of no cause of action** Klageabweisung durch Geschworene (*wegen Unschlüssigkeit der Klage*); ~ **of not guilty** Freispruch; ~ **of not proven** *scot* Freispruch mangels Beweises; **alternative** ~ Verurteilung auf Grund geänderten rechtl Gesichtspunkts; **chance** ~ → *chance*; **compromise** ~ (*unzulässige*) Kompromißentscheidung der Geschworenen; **directed** ~ Geschworenenentscheidung auf (Grund bindender) Weisung des Richters; **false** ~ rechtsbeugender Spruch der Geschworenen; **general** ~ Geschworenenspruch zur Schuldfrage; Geschworenenurteil (*in Zivilsachen: absoluter Spruch für Kläger bzw Beklagten*); **impeachment of** ~ Anfechtung e–s Geschworenenurteils; **inconsistent** ~ Geschworenenspruch mit innerem Widerspruch; **majority** ~ Mehrheitsvotum der Geschworenen; **open** ~ richterliche Feststellung, daß Todesursache unbekannt ist; **partial** ~ Teilverurteilung *bei Freispruch im übrigen*; **perverse** ~ rechtsfehlerhaftes Geschworenenurteil (*Nichtbefolgung der Rechtsbelehrung des Richters*); **privy** ~ geheime Mitteilung des Spruchs der Geschworenen; **public** ~ Geschworenenspruch in öffentlicher Sitzung; **quotient** ~ Geschworenenentscheidung zur Höhe des Anspruchs (*nach dem arithmetischen Mittel der Einzelbewertungen der Geschworenen*); **sealed** ~ → *sealed*; **special** ~ Tatsachenfeststellung durch Geschworene; qualifizierter Geschworenenspruch (*schuldig, jedoch unzurechnungsfähig*); **split** ~ Geschworenenspruch durch Stimmenmehrheit; **to return a** ~ ein Geschworenenurteil fällen; **to upset a** ~ ein Geschworenenurteil aufheben; **true** ~ rechtsgültiger Geschworenenspruch; **unanimous** ~ einstimmiger Geschworenenspruch; **unreasonable** ~ unhaltbares Geschworenenurteil.

verge Bereich *m*, Bannkreis *m*, Zuständigkeitsbereich *m*, Gerichtsbezirk *m (um den Königshof)*; Straßenschulter, nicht befestigter Nebenweg an der Landstraße; ~ **of a**

court Zuständigkeitsbereich e–s Gerichts.
verifiable belegbar, nachweislich, beweisbar; ~ **allegations** nachprüfbare Angaben.
verification (*eidliche*) Beglaubigung *f*, Überprüfung *f*, Nachprüfung *f*, Bestätigung *f*; Ankündigung *f* von Beweisangeboten; ~ **of an assertion** Glaubhaftmachung e–r Behauptung; ~ **of execution** Unterschriftsbeglaubigung; ~ **of prices** Preisprüfung; ~ **of quality** Qualitätsprüfung; ~ **of quantity** Mengenprüfung; ~ **of signature** Unterschriftsbestätigung; ~ **of the cash** Kassenrevision; **after** ~ nach Richtigbefund; **delivery** ~ Wareneingangsbescheinigung; **in** ~ **whereof** zu Urkund dessen (*Beglaubigungsvermerk*).
verify eidlich bestätigen, beglaubigen, überprüfen, bestätigen, beweisen; ~**ied copy** beglaubigte Abschrift.
verily wahrlich.
verity Wahrheit *f*, Richtigkeit *f*; **oath of** ~ eidliche Bestätigung.
versed bewandert, erfahren.
versedness in trade Geschäftserfahrung *f*.
version Darstellung *f*, Fassung *f*, Lesart *f*; **amended** ~ geänderte Fassung; **unamended** ~ alte Fassung.
versus (= *v* = *vs*) gegen, kontra.
vertical | **combination** vertikale Verflechtung *f*, Vertikalkonzern; ~ **integration** vertikale Verflechtung, vertikaler Unternehmensverbund, Unterordnungskonzern; ~ **price fixing** vertikale Preisbindung der zweiten Hand.
vessel Schiff *n*, Wasserfahrzeug *n*; Gefäß *n*; **cargo** ~ Frachtschiff; **factory** ~ Fischverarbeitungsschiff; **foreign** ~ Schiff unter fremder Flagge; **idle** ~ stilliegendes Schiff; **light** ~ unbeladenes Schiff; **merchant** ~ Handelsschiff; **privileged** ~ vorfahrtberechtigtes Schiff; **public** ~ Staatsschiff; **sea-going** ~ Seeschiff.
vest *v*|*t*: verleihen, übertragen, einräumen; *v*|*i*: übergehen, zufallen, übertragen werden; ~ **s.o. with authority** jmdn ermächtigen.
vested fest erworben, wohlerworben, zugefallen, absolut besitzend, nicht entziehbar, unverfallbar.
vestibule | **school** Lehrwerkstatt *f*; ~ **training** Anlernen von Arbeitskräften.
vesting *s* Rechtsübergang *m*, Eigentumsübergang *m*; Eintritt der Unverfallbarkeit (*e–r Anwartschaft*).
vesting|**assent** → *assent*; ~ **date** Übertragungsdatum; ~ **day** Tag des Eigentumswechsels, Tag der Besitzübertragung; ~ **declaration** Übertragserklärung (*Treugut*); ~ **deed** *dingl* Übertragungsurkunde e–s Grundstücks auf den Treuhänder; Bestallungsurkunde; ~ **instrument** Übertragungsurkunde, Übereignungsurkunde; ~ **order** gerichtliche Auflassungsverfügung, Zwangsübereignungsbeschluß, Enteignungsbeschluß.
vet *v*|*t* überprüfen (*Personen, Kandidaten, Geschworene*).
veteran Veteran, Kriegsteilnehmer; **disabled** ~ Kriegsversehrter; Kriegsbeschädigter.
veto *s* Veto *n*, Einspruch *m*; ~**is sustained** Veto wird aufrechterhalten; ~ **power** Vetorecht; **item** ~ Veto bei Einzelpunkten e–r Vorlage, punktuelles V.; **line-item** ~ punktuelles Veto; **pocket** ~ indirektes Veto (*durch Schweigen des Präsidenten bis nach Schluß der Legislaturperiode, US*); **qualified** ~ überstimmbares Veto; **right of** ~ → *right*; **suspensive** ~ aufschiebendes Veto; **to exercise a** ~ Vetorecht ausüben; **to override a** ~ ein Veto überstimmen, trotz des Vetos beschließen; **voting** ~ Sperrminorität, Abstimmungsveto.
veto *v* ein Veto einlegen.
veto-bearing vetoberechtigt.
vex belästigen, schikanieren.
vexation Schikane *f*.
vexatious schikanös; querulatorisch.
viability Lebensfähigkeit *f*, Existenzfähigkeit *f*.

viable lebensfähig, praktikabel, wirtschaftlich, existenzfähig; ~ **construction** brauchbare Auslegung; **economically** ~ wirtschaftlich lebensfähig.

vicarious stellvertretend; für (durch) e–n Dritten; ~ **act** stellvertretende Handlung; Handlung e–s Erfüllungsgehilfen bzw Verrichtungsgehilfen; ~ **agent** → *agent*; ~ **liability** → *liability*; ~ **performance** Leistung durch einen Dritten; ~ **responsibility** → *responsibility*.

vice Mangel *m*, Fehler *m*; Laster *n*, unmoralischer Lebenswandel *m*; ~ **crimes** Sittlichkeitsdelikte; ~ **squad** Sittenpolizei; **constitutional** ~ Körperfehler; **inherent** ~ → *inherent*; **redhibitory** ~ Sachmangel, Gewährleistungsmangel.

vice|-chancellor Vizekanzler, Präsident der *Chancery Division qv*, geschäftsführender Rektor; ~**-chancellorship** Amt des Vizekanzlers; ~**-commercial agent** Vizehandelsreferent e–s Konsulats; ~**-consul** Vizekonsul, Wahlkonsul; ~**-dean** Unterdekanat, Unterdekan; ~**-gerence** Statthaltung; ~**-gerent** Stellvertreter, Statthalter, Verweser; ~**-president** Vizepräsident, zweiter Vorsitzender, stellvertretender Verwaltungsratsvorsitzender; ~**-principal** leitender Angestellter, Geschäftsführer, Werkmeister.

vice versa umgekehrt, in umgekehrter Reihenfolge.

vicennial 20jährig.

viceroy Vizekönig *m*.

vicinage Nachbarschaft *f*, nähere Umgebung *f*; die Geschworenen *m|pl* der Grafschaft des Gerichtsortes.

vicinity Nähe *f*, nähere Umgebung *f*.

vicious fehlerhaft, unvollkommen, mangelhaft, bösartig; ~ **intent** rechtswidrige, böswillige Absicht; ~ **intromission** unbefugte Machenschaften mit fremden Nachlaß; ~ **propensity** bösartige Veranlagung, Bösartigkeit (*e–s Tieres*).

vico(u)ntiel gräflich; Sheriffs . . .; ~ **jurisdiction** Zuständigkeit der Grafschaftsbeamten (*des Sheriff, Coroner ua*).

victim Opfer *n*, Geschädigter *m*, Verletzter *m*, Leidtragender *m*; ~ **advocacy group** Verbrechensopferhilfe (-organisation); ~**'s bill of rights** Katalog der Verbrechensopferrechte; **unintended** ~ zufälliges Opfer.

victimization Opferung *f*; Schikanierung *f*.

victimize verfolgen, schikanieren.

victualler Gastwirt *m*, (Proviant) Lieferant *m*, Marketender *m*; Versorgungsschiff *n*; **common** ~ Gastwirt; **licensed** ~ → *to license*.

victualling|bill *brit* Zollschein für Schiffsproviant; ~ **house** Speiselokal, Gaststätte.

victuals Speisen *f|pl*, Lebensmittel *n|pl*, Proviant *m*.

vide licet nämlich; das heißt; wie folgt; (*viz*).

vidnews Bildschirmzeitung *f*.

videotaping (*private*) Video(recorder)aufzeichnung *f*.

vidimus beglaubigte Abschrift *f* (*e–r Urkunde*).

viduity Witwenschaft *f*.

view *s* Ansicht *f*, Recht *n* auf Aussicht; Dienstbarkeit *f* gegen die Verbauung der Aussicht, Fensterrecht; Sicht *f* (*Verkehr*), Besichtigung *f*, Augenscheinnahme *f*; ~ **and delivery** besondere Zuweisung e–r Allmende; ~ **by jury** Lokaltermin, Augenscheinseinnahme durch Geschworene; ~ **of an inquest** Ortsbesichtigung durch Geschworene; ~ **of frankpledge** Überprüfung der Treueidsleistung; **demand of** ~ Antrag auf Augenscheinseinnahme; **exchange of** ~**s** Meinungsaustausch; **in** ~ **of . . .** im Hinblick auf, in Anbetracht, angesichts; **legal** ~**point** Rechtsstandpunkt; **private** ~ geschlossene Besichtigung; **retrospective** ~ Rückblick.

view *v* besichtigen, prüfen, in Augenschein nehmen.

viewer Augenscheinsbeauftragter *m*;

Geschworener beim Augenscheinstermin.
viewing | **of land** amtliche Grundstücksbesichtigung; ~ **the scene** Tatortbesichtigung, Lokaltermin.
vif-gage *hist* Lebendsatzung *f* (Nutzpfand).
vigilance Wachsamkeit *f*, Vorschrift *f*, rechtzeitiges Geltendmachen *n* von Ansprüchen; ~ **committee** Bürgerwehr- und Polizeiausschuß.
vigilante Hilfspolizist *m*, Mitglied e–r freiwilligen Sicherheitspatrouille, Bürgerwehrmitglied *m*, Selbsthilfe-Täter *m*.
vilification Schmähung *f*, Verleumdung *f*.
vill *hist* Unterteilung *f* e–r Hundertschaft; Weiler *m*, Herrenhaus *n*; **demi-**~ *hist* Ortsteil.
village Dorf *n*, Ortschaft *f*, ländliche Gemeinde *f*, selbständige Kleinstadt *f*; ~ **community** Dorfgemeinde; ~ **council** Gemeinderat; ~ **green** Erholungsfläche e–r Dorfgemeinde.
villain Schurke *m*.
villein Leibeigener *m*, Unfreier *m*, Zinsbauer *m*, Hintersasse *m*; ~ **in gross** persönlicher Leibeigener des Grundherrn; ~ **regardant** zum Landgut gehörender Hintersasse; ~ **services** niedrige Gutsdienste; ~ **socage** Landpacht gegen bestimmte Gutsdienste; ~ **tenure** Fronbesitz, *unfreier Landbesitz gegen unbestimmte Gutsdienste*.
vindicate verteidigen, rechtfertigen, schützen; ~ **one's rights** seine Rechte geltend machen.
vindicatio Herausgabeklage *f* des Eigentümers.
vindication Rechtfertigung *f*.
vindictive rachsüchtig, pönalisierend; ~ **damages** → *damages*.
vintner Weinkaufmann *m*; ~**s company** Weinhändler-Innung.
violate verletzen, übertreten; schänden; ~ **a law** gegen ein Gesetz verstoßen; ~ **a treaty** e–n Vertrag verletzen.
violation Verletzung *f*, Übertretung *f*, Rechtsbruch *m*, Rechtsverletzung *f*; Schändung *f*, Verführung *f*; ~ **of contract** Vertragsverletzung; ~ **of covenants** Verletzung von Vereinbarungen; ~ **of international law** Völkerrechtsverletzung; ~ **of neutrality** Neutralitätsverletzung; ~ **of official duties** Amtspflichtverletzung; ~ **of one's oath** Eidesverletzung; ~ **of professional secrecy** Verletzung des Berufsgeheimnisses; ~ **of professional standards** standeswidriges Verhalten; ~ **of safe conduct** Verletzung des freien Geleits; ~ **of the border** Grenzverletzung; ~ **of the peace** Störung der öffentlichen Ordnung, Landfriedensbruch; ~ **of the professional honour** Verstoß gegen die Standesehre; ~ **of the rules** Regelwidrigkeit; ~ **of trust** Vertrauensbruch; ~ **of women** Notzucht; **flagrant** ~ krasse Verletzung; **good faith** ~ **of law** rechtsirrtümliche Gesetzesverletzung; **frontier** ~ Grenzverletzung; **reciprocal** ~ **of law** beiderseitige Rechtsverletzung; **traffic** ~ Verkehrsübertretung.
violator Verletzer *m*, Übertreter *m*.
violence Gewalt *f*, Gewalttätigkeit *f*, Tätlichkeit *f*, Gewalttat; ~ **for securing entry** gewalttätiger Hausfriedensbruch; **actual** ~ Gewaltanwendung; **criminal** ~ Gewaltverbrechen; **domestic** ~ → *domestic*; ~ **family** ~ → *family*; **insidious** ~ heimtückische Gewaltanwendung; **physical** ~ physische Gewalt, Gewalttätigkeit.
violent gewalttätig; **by** ~ **means** gewaltsam.
virement Übertragung von Etatposten, Ermächtigung zum interministeriellen Ausgleich nicht verbrauchter Etatposten.
vires of legality Legalitätskompetenz *f*.
virtuous jungfräulich, tugendhaft.
vis Gewalt *f*; ~ **major** höhere Gewalt.
visa Sichtvermerk *m*, Visum *n*; **immigration** ~ Einwanderungsvi-

sum; **transit** ~ Durchreisevisum; **visitor's** ~ Besuchervisum.

vis-à-vis gegenüber; ~ **third parties** im Verhältnis zu Dritten.

viscera innere Organe *n*|*pl*, Eingeweide *n*|*pl* (*Autopsie*).

viscount Vicomte *m*, Stellvertreter *m* e–s Grafen; Sheriff *m* (*e–r Grafschaft*).

visé gesehen.

visible sichtbar, bemerkbar, unterscheidbar, deutlich, offen; ~ **envelope** Fensterumschlag; ~ **exports** sichtbare Ausfuhr; ~ **imports** sichtbare Einfuhr; ~ **injury** äußerlich sichtbare Verletzung; ~ **reserves** offene Reserven; ~ **supply** die dem Markt zur Verfügung stehende Warenmenge; ~ **trade** sichtbarer Handel; Außenhandel mit Gütern (*zum Unterschied von Dienstleistungen*); **without** ~ **means** ersichtlich mittellos.

vision Sehen *n*, Sehvermögen *n*, Blick *m*, Sicht *f*; **impaired** ~ behinderte Sicht; **obscured** ~ behinderte Sicht.

visit Besuch *m*, Besichtigung *f*, Visitation *f*, Durchsuchung *f*; ~ **and search** Durchsuchung (*von Schiffen*); ~ **to the scene** Ortsbesichtigung; **domiciliary** ~ Haussuchung; **first** ~ Antrittsbesuch; **right of** ~ Recht der Flaggenkontrolle.

visitation Visitation *f*, Besuch *m*, Inspektion *f*, Kirchenvisitation *f*; ~ **books** *hist* standesamtliche Bücher; **right of** ~ Besuchsrecht des getrennt lebenden Elternteils; Durchsuchungsrecht (*auf See*).

visiting rights → *right*.

visitor Inspekteur *m*; Besucher *m*, Gast *m*; ~ **of manners** *hist* Forstaufseher; ~**'s permit** → *permit*; **board of** ~**s** → *board*; **district** ~ Fürsorger(in); **lawful** ~ berechtigt Betretender.

visual sichtbar; ~ **evidence** → *evidence*; ~ **merchandising** optisch wirksame Verkaufsförderung.

vital lebenswichtig; ~ **interests** lebenswichtige Interessen; ~ **statistics** Bevölkerungsstatistik, Standesamtsregister; **V~ Statistics Office** Standesamt (*USA*).

vitality Lebenskraft *f*, Keimfähigkeit *f*.

vitiate aufheben, ungültig machen; (*Luft*) verpesten, verderben.

vitiation Ungültigmachen *n*, Aufhebung *f*; ~ **of patent** Nichtigkeitserklärung e–s Patents.

vitiligate aus Streitsucht prozessieren.

viva voce mündlich; durch Zuruf, per Akklamation (*Abstimmung*); ~ **evidence** mündl Beweiserhebung; **a** ~ **examination** → *examination*.

vivary Wildgehege *n*; Fischteich *m*.

viz nämlich (*kurz für vide licet qv*).

vocation Beruf *m*, Beschäftigung *f*; **in pursuance of his** ~ in Ausübung seines Berufes; **inability to follow** ~ Berufsunfähigkeit.

vocational beruflich, Berufs . . .; ~ **rehabilitation** berufliche Rehabilitierung, Wiedereingliederung ins Berufsleben (*nach Strafhaft*); **period of** ~ **adjustment** Einarbeitungszeit, Umschulungszeit.

voice and data recorder Flugschreiber *m*.

voice in the management Mitbestimmungsrecht *n* (bei der Geschäftsführung); Mitspracherecht *n*.

void *adj* nichtig, ungültig, unwirksam; ~ **ab initio** von Anfang an nichtig, ex tunc nichtig; ~ **at law** nach strengem Recht (*Common Law*) unwirksam; ~ **by law** rechtsunwirksam, nichtig; ~ **for vagueness rule** Grundsatz der Unwirksamkeit wegen Unbestimmtheit (*von Gesetzen*); ~ **pro tanto** teilweise nichtig; ~ **pro toto** insgesamt nichtig, in vollem Umfang nichtig; **absolutely** ~ (null und) nichtig; **null and** ~ (null und) nichtig.

void *v* anfechten, ungültig machen, aufheben.

voidability Vernichtbarkeit *f*, Anfechtbarkeit *f*.

voidable anfechtbar, annullierbar.

voir dire vorläufige Befragung *f* von Laienrichtern bzw Zeugen (*bei Einwendung bzw Ablehnungsantrag*).

voisinage *int* nachbarstaatliche Gepflogenheiten.

volatility Umschlagshäufigkeit *f*; Unsicherheit an der Börse, heftige Kursschwankungen, Sprunghaftigkeit, Volatilität *f*.

volition Wille *m*, Willensäußerung *f*; **act of ~** Willensäußerung, Willensakt.

volitional willensmäßig, gewollt, auf dem Willen beruhend, mit Wissen und Wollen.

volte face völlige Abkehr *f*, radikale Meinungsänderung *f*, plötzlicher Gesinnungswandel.

volume Band *n*, Volumen *n*, Masse *f*; **~ cost** Volumenkosten, fixe Kosten; **~ discount** Mengenrabatt, Mengenbonus; **~ of business** Geschäftsumfang; **~ of credit** Kreditvolumen, Umfang der Ausleihungen; **~ of freight handled** beförderte Gütermenge.

voluntariness Freiwilligkeit *f*.

voluntary freiwillig, aus eigenem Willen, spontan, absichtlich, gewillkürt, rechtsgeschäftlich, unentgeltlich.

volunteer *s* Volontär *m*, unentgeltlich Beschäftigter *m*; unentgeltlicher Erwerber *m*, uneigennütziger Treuhänder *m*; Freiwilliger *m*; Geschäftsführer *m* ohne Auftrag.

volunteer *v* sich freiwillig melden, freiwillig übernehmen; **illegal ~ing** Freischärlerei.

votable zur Beschlußfassung geeignet.

votary Verfechter *m*, Vorkämpfer *m*.

vote *s* Stimme *f*, Stimmrecht *n*, Abstimmung *f*, Abstimmungsergebnis *n*, Beschluß *m*; Wahlrecht *n*; Budgetposten *m*, Bewilligung *f*, bewilligter Betrag *m*; **~s and proceedings** (*tägliches*) Kurzprotokoll des Parlaments; **~ by acclamation** Abstimmung durch Zuruf; **~ by ballot** geheime Abstimmung (mit Stimmzetteln), geheime Wahl; **~ by correspondence** schriftliche Stimmabgabe, Briefwahl; **~ by division** Hammelsprung, Abstimmung durch getrennte Zählung; **~ by open ballot** offene Abstimmung; **~ by proxy** → *proxy*; **~ by rising and sitting** Stimmabgabe durch Sichерheben bzw Sitzenbleiben; **~ by secret ballot** geheime Abstimmung; **~ by show of hands** Abstimmung durch Handaufheben, Abstimmung durch Handzeichen; **~s cast** abgegebene Stimmen; **~ catcher** Stimmenfänger, Wahllokomotive; **~-catching** Stimmenfang; **~ of censure** Mißbilligungsvotum; **~ of confidence** Abstimmung über die Vertrauensfrage; Vertrauensvotum; **~ of no(n)confidence** Mißtrauensvotum; **~ of thanks** Danksagungsbeschluß; **~ office** Amt für Parlamentsdrucksachen; **~ on account** Haushaltsbeschluß; **~s polled** abgegebene Stimmen; **~s to be struck off** abzuziehende Stimmen; **~ to remove s.o.** (*from the board*) Abberufungsabstimmung; **~ viva voce** Abstimmung durch Zuruf; **affirmative ~** Jastimme; Mehrheit von Jastimmen; positives Abstimmungsergebnis; **aggregate of ~s** → *aggregate*; **block ~** geschlossene Stimmabgabe; **branch ~** auf eine Ortsgruppe beschränkte Personalwahl; **casting ~** ausschlaggebende Stimme (*bei Stimmengleichheit*); **close ~** knappes Abstimmungsergebnis; **cumulative ~** → *cumulative*; **derivative ~** (*vom Mann*) abgeleitetes (Frauen)Stimmrecht; **direct ~** unmittelbare Wahl; Abstimmung zur Sache; **equality of ~s** → *equality*; **final ~** Schlußabstimmung; **floating ~** Wechselwähler; **free ~** Abstimmung ohne Fraktionszwang; **majority ~** → *majority*; **minority ~** → *minority*; **negative ~** Nein-Stimme; ablehnende Abstimmung; **open ~** öffentliche Abstimmung; **original ~; plural ~** Mehrstimmenwahlrecht; **plurality of ~s** → *plurality*; **pooling of ~s** → *pooling*; **postal ~** Briefwahl;

private ~ interne (Vor)Abstimmung; **proportional** ~ Verhältniswahl; **right to** ~ → *right*; **roll-call** ~ → *roll*; **supplementary** ~ *parl* Nachbewilligung; **to ask for a** ~ **of confidence** die Vertrauensfrage stellen; **to cast one's** ~ → *cast*; **to poll** ~**s** Stimmen erhalten; **to put to the** ~ zur Abstimmung bringen, abstimmen lassen; **to split** ~**s** Stimmen auf mehrere Kandidaten verteilen, panaschieren; **unanimous** ~ einstimmiger Beschluß; **voice** ~ Abstimmung durch Zuruf.

vote *v* wählen, abstimmen, beschließen, stimmen; ~ **down** (*durch Beschluß*) ablehnen; ~ **funds** Gelder bewilligen; ~ **solidly for** geschlossen für etwas stimmen; ~ **the budget** den Haushalt genehmigen.

voteless stimmrechtslos.

voter Wähler *m*, Wählerin *f*; **qualified** ~ Wahlberechtigter *m*; **service** ~ wehrdienstangehöriger Wähler.

voting | **age** Wahlalter; ~ **box** Wahlurne; ~ **by ballot** geheime Abstimmung; ~ **by correspondence** schriftl Abstimmung; ~ **by proxies** Abstimmung durch Stellvertreter; ~ **by show of hands** Abstimmung durch Handzeichen; ~ **capital stock** → *stock* (*1*); ~ **certificate** Wahlschein; ~ **figures** Abstimmungsergebnisse; ~ **hours** Wahlstunden; ~ **machine** Abstimmungsmaschine; ~ **offences** Wahldelikte; ~ **on a poll** schriftliche Abstimmung (*nach Kapitalanteilen usw, vgl poll*); ~ **on division** Abstimmung im Hammelsprung; ~ **paper** Stimmzettel; ~ **pool** Stimmrechtsbindung; ~ **power** Stimmrecht; ~ **procedure** Abstimmungsverfahren; ~ **right** Stimmrecht, Wahlrecht; ~ **securities** stimmberechtigte Aktien (*bzw sonstige verbriefte Kapitalanteile*); ~ **share** → *share*; ~ **station** Wahlort, Wahllokal; ~ **stock** → *stock* (*1*); ~ **trust** → *trust*; ~ **trust agreement** Stimmbindungsvertrag; ~ **procedure** → *procedure*; ~ **trust certificate** Stimmbindungs-Treuhandzertifikat; ~ **trustee's certificate** → *certificate*; **absentee** ~ Briefwahl; **abstention from** ~ Stimmenthaltung; **compulsory** ~ Wahlpflicht; **cumulative** ~ → *cumulative*; **direct** ~ direkte Wahl; **disqualification from** ~ Verlust des Wahlrechts; **first** ~ erster Wahlgang; **method of** ~ → *method*; **plural** ~ Mehrstimmenwahlrecht; **service** ~ Wahlteilnahme der Streitkräfte; **to abstain from** ~ → *to abstain*.

vouch einstehen für, bürgen, versichern, sich berufen auf; bekräftigen; laden; bezeugen; ~ **for repairs** für Reparaturen die Verantwortung übernehmen.

vouchee Bürge *m*, Gewährsmann *m*; Geladener *m*; *fiktiver* Beklagter *m*; **common** ~ *hist* öffentlicher Gewährsmann, fiktiver Beklagter.

voucher Zeuge *m*, Bürge *m*, Gewährsmann *m*, Zeugnis *n*, Urkunde *f*; Auszahlungsbestätigung *f*, (Buchungs)Beleg *m*; Quittung *f*, Schein *m*, Gutschein *m*; ~ **attached** Beleg anliegend; ~ **audit** Belegprüfung; ~ **bookkeeping** Belegbuchhaltung; ~ **check** *US* Scheck mit Rechnungsabschnitt; Marke (*zB Garderobenmarke*); ~ **clerk** Kreditorenbuchhalter; ~ **copy** Belegdoppel; ~ **for payment** Zahlungsbeleg, Ausgabenbeleg; Kassenanweisung; ~ **number** Belegnummer; ~**s payable** zur Zahlung freigegebene Beträge, Kreditoren; ~ **register** Einkaufsbuch, Zahlungsnachweis, Belegregister, einfache Ausgabenbuchführung; ~ **system** Belegbuchhaltung; **approved** ~ anerkannter Beleg; **audited** ~ geprüfter Beleg; **cash** ~ Kassenanweisung; **cheque** ~ Belegabschnitt an e–m Scheck; **disbursement** ~ → *disbursement*; **expense** ~ Ausgabenbeleg; **external** ~ Fremdbeleg; **internal** ~ Eigenbeleg; **journal** ~ Buchungsbeleg,

Journalbeleg, Belegbuchhaltung; **payroll** ~ Lohnauszahlungsbeleg; **purchase** ~ Einkaufsbeleg.
vouching vorbereitende Belegsichtung *f*, stichprobenartige Prüfung *f*.
vouching-in Streitverkündung *f*.
voyage Reise *f*, *bes* Seereise *f*; Fahrt *f*, Flugreise *f*; ~ **charter(-party)** Reisecharter (*für eine Reise bzw die gleiche Reise wiederholt*); ~ **freight** Fracht für die ganze Reise; ~ **insurance** Reiseversicherung; ~ **insured** versicherte Reise; ~ **policy** → *policy* (*1*); **foreign** ~ Auslandsreise, Überseereise.

W

wafer Oblate *f*; Siegelmarke *f* (*aufgeklebtes rotes Papierstück an Stelle von Siegelwachs*); ~ **seal** Prägesiegel; **the** ~ **great seal** (*vereinfachtes*) Staatssiegel.

wage Lohn *m*, Arbeitsvergütung *f*, Heuer *f*, *hist* Sicherheitsleistung *f*; ~ **advance** Vorschuß; ~**(s) agreement** Lohnvereinbarung, Tarifvertrag; ~ **and price controls** Lohn- und Preisüberwachung; ~**s and salaries** Löhne und Gehälter; ~ ~ ~ *account* → *account* (*2*); ~ ~ ~ *owing: Lohn- und Gehaltsschulden*; ~ **and salary ordinance** kommunale Lohn- und Gehaltstarifordnung; ~ **and salary receipts** Arbeitseinkommen; ~ **arbitration** Lohnschlichtung; ~ **bargaining** Tarifverhandlungen; ~ **base** Grundfreibetrag; ~ **bracket** Lohngruppe; ~ **ceiling** Höchstlohngrenze; ~ **cheque** Lohnscheck; ~ **class** Lohnstufe, Tarifklasse; ~ **continuation** Lohnfortzahlung; ~ **control** staatliche Reglementierung von Löhnen und Gehältern; ~**s council** Tarifkommission; ~**s declaration** Jahresmeldung über bezahlte Löhne und Gehälter (*der Versicherten*); ~ **differential** Lohnniveauunterschied (*standortbedingt, bzw betriebsbedingt*); ~ **dispute** Lohnstreitigkeit, Lohnkampf; ~ **drift** Differenz der übertariflichen Bezahlung; ~ **earner** Lohnempfänger, Arbeitnehmer; ~ **earner's plan** gerichtlich überwachter Abzahlungsvergleich *mit Teilschulderlaß, bei berufstätigem Schuldner*; ~**-earning employment** lohnsteuerpflichtige Beschäftigung, abhängige Beschäftigung; ~ **freeze** Lohnstopp; ~ **fund theory** Lohnfondstheorie; ~ **garnishment** Lohnpfändung; ~ **hour law** Arbeitszeitgesetz; ~**s in kind** Naturallohn; ~ **incentive(s)** Lohnanreiz, Leistungsanreiz; ~ **increase** Lohnerhöhung; ~ **inequality** Lohnungleichheit, Lohnungerechtigkeit; ~ **level** Lohnniveau; ~ **on piece-work basis** Stücklohn; ~ **packet** Lohn- und Gehaltspaket *m mit Sondervergütungen*; Lohn(erhöhungs)paket; ~**-price spiral** Lohn-Preis-Spirale; ~ **rate** Lohnsatz, Tarifsatz; ~ **regulation** Lohnregelung; ~**-related** lohnbezogen; ~ **reopening clause** Klausel über Wiederaufnahme von Lohnverhandlungen (*ohne Tarifvertragskündigung*); ~ **schedule** Lohntabelle; ~ **slip** Lohnzettel; ~ **structure** Lohngefüge; ~ **tax** → *tax*; **actual** ~**s** Reallohn; **assignment of** ~**s** → *assignment*; **basic** ~ Grundlohn; **bootleg** ~**s** überhöhte Löhne; **current** ~ → *current*; **garnishment of** ~**s** Lohnpfändung; **guaranteed minimum** ~ garantierter Mindestlohn; **industrial** ~**s** Industriearbeiterlöhne; **job** ~ → *job*; **living** ~ zum Lebensunterhalt (gerade) ausreichender Lohn; **peak** ~ Spitzenlohn; **piece** ~**s** Akkordlohn, Stücklohn; **minimum** ~**s** Mindestlohn; **nominal** ~ symbolische Entlohnung; **productive** ~**s** → *productive*; **real** ~ Reallohn; **saving** ~ Sparkapital bildender Lohnanteil; vermögenswirksame Leistung; **sliding** ~ **scale** gleitende Lohnskala; **standard** ~ ortsüblicher Lohn, Tariflohn; **standard** ~ **rate** normaler Lohnsatz, Tariflohn; **unproductive** ~ Gemeinkostenlöhne; **weekly** ~ Wochenlohn.

wager *s* Wette *f*, Einsatz *m*, Wettvertrag *m*, *hist* Pfand *m*, Bürgschaft *f*; ~ **of battle** *hist* Gottesurteil durch Zweikampf; ~ **of law** *hist* Verpflichtung zum Erscheinen und zur Stellung von Eideshelfern; ~ **policy** → *policy* (*1*).

wager *v hist* sich zum Zweikampf anbieten; wetten.

wagering das Wetten *n*, die Wetten *n|pl*; ~ **and gaming** Glücksspiel und Wette; ~ **contract** → *contract*.

wag(g)on Wagen *m*, Güterwagen *m*, Waggon *m*, Gepäckwagen *m*; **by** ~ per Achse.

wagonage Fuhrgeld *n*, Transport *m* mit Wagen, Transportkosten *pl*, Wagenpark *m*.

waif(s) herrenloses Gut *n*, weggeworfene Sachen *f|pl*, weggeworfenes Diebesgut *n*; Aneignungsrecht an herrenlosen Sachen; verwahrloster Hund *m*, Ausgestoßener *m*, streunendes Tier *n*; ~ **and strays** heimatlose, verwahrloste Kinder.

wainwright Wagner *m*, Stellmacher *m*.

wait-and-see policy Politik *f* des Abwartens, abwartende Haltung *f*.

waiter Börsendiener *m*; Bereitschaftsverteidiger *m (Anwalt, der im Gericht auf die Zuteilung e–s Angeklagten wartet)*.

waiting | **list** Warteliste; ~ **period** Wartezeit, *ins* Karenzzeit, Sperrfrist; ~ **time** Wartezeit, anrechenbare Zeit, Anwartschaftszeit, Verlustzeit (*wegen Produktionsausfall*).

waive *v* verzichten, ausschlagen, den Besitz aufgeben; ~ **a claim** auf e–n Anspruch verzichten; ~ **a remedy** auf einen Rechtsbehelf verzichten; ~ **a right** auf ein Recht verzichten; ~ **a tort** auf den Rechtsbehelf gegen e–e unerlaubte Handlung verzichten; ~ **informality** die Nichteinhaltung von Förmlichkeiten hinnehmen; ~ **one's privilege** auf sein Zeugnisverweigerungsrecht verzichten; ~ **the age-limit** Altersdispens erteilen.

waiver Aufgabe *f*, Verzicht *m*, Verzichtleistung *f*, Wechselrückgriffsverzicht *m*; Verzichtsurkunde *f*; ~ **clause** (Haftungs)Verzichtklausel; ~ **of a fee** Gebührenerlaß; ~ **of allocution** Verzicht auf das letzte Wort; ~ **of an action** → *action*; ~ **of exemption** Verzicht auf Pfändungsschutz; ~ **of immunity** Verzicht auf Selbstbezichtigungsschutz; ~ **of indictment** Verzicht auf förmliche Anklage (*vor einem Geschworenengericht*); ~ **of jury trial** Verzicht auf Geschworenenverfahren; ~ **of pleas** Verzicht auf Erklärung zur Schuldfrage; ~ **of privilege** Verzicht auf Zeugnisverweigerungsrecht; ~ **of prosecution** Einstellung des Strafverfahrens; ~ **of protest** Protestverzicht; ~ **of tort** Verzicht auf Anspruch aus unerlaubter Handlung; *zB bei Übergang von deliktischer zu schuldrechtlicher Anspruchsgrundlage*; ~ **of venue** Verzicht auf Strafverhandlung vor dem Gericht des Heimatortes; **doctrine of** ~ stillschweigendes Hinnehmen von Stornierungstatbeständen, Verwirkung; **express** ~ (ausdrücklicher) Verzicht; **implied** ~ konkludenter Verzicht; **oral** ~ mündlicher Verzicht.

wakening Wiederaufnahme *f* e–s Verfahrens.

walk *s* Route *f*, Runde *f*; ~**s** Schecks auf Nichtmitglieder des Londoner Clearing House; ~**s clerk** Bankbote, Inkassobote; ~**s department** Botenabteilung (*zur Scheckvorlage bei Banken, die nicht dem Clearing angeschlossen sind*); ~ **of life** Lebensstellung, soziale Stellung.

walk *v* gehen, e–e Strecke zu Fuß zurücklegen; ~ **a person off** jmdn abführen; ~ **out** die Arbeit niederlegen; ~ **the streets** auf den Strich gehen.

walking | **charges** Beitreibungskosten; ~ **inspector** Reiseinspektor; ~ **time** Wegezeit.

walkout spontane Arbeitsniederlegung *f*; plötzliches Verlassen des Konferenzsaals; **orchestrated** ~ geplante gemeinsame Arbeitsniederlegung.

wall Mauer *f*; **common** ~ Kommunmauer; **ancient** ~ alte Kommunmauer (*über 20 Jahre geduldet*); **customs** ~**s** Zollschranken; **division** ~ Grenzmauer; **enclosing** ~ Umfassungsmauer; **load-bearing**

~s tragende Wände; **partition-~** Trennmauer, Brandmauer; **party-~** Kommunmauer; **perimeter ~** Umfassungsmauer, äußere Gefängnismauer.

wand Amtsstab *m*; ~ **of peace** *scot* Amtsstab des Gerichtsvollziehers.

wangle schieben; ~ **accounts** Kontenschiebung begehen.

want *s* Mangel *m*, Bedürfnis *n*, Bedarf *m*, Erfordernis *n*; ~ **ad** Suchanzeige, Stellenangebot; **(for)** ~ **of acceptance** mangels Annahme; ~ **of capital** Kapitalmangel; ~ **of care** mangelnde Sorgfalt; ~ **of defence** Säumnis, Einwendungen (*fristgemäß*) geltend zu machen; ~ **of form** Formfehler, Formmangel; ~ **of jurisdiction** Unzuständigkeit, mangelnde Zuständigkeit; ~ **of mutuality** fehlende Gegenleistung; ~ **of novelty** mangelnde Neuheit; ~ **of ordinary care** Nichtbeachtung der verkehrsüblichen Sorgfalt; ~ **of title** → *title*; **for** ~ **of** mangels . . . (*cf "for", "consideration", "time"*); **in** ~ **of repair** reparaturbedürftig.

want *v* verlangen, benötigen; ~**ed** verlangt, gesucht; ~**ed by the police** steckbrieflich gesucht; auf der Fahndungslise eingetragen; ~**ed immediately** für sofort gesucht.

wantage Mangel *m*, Knappheit *f*, Fehlbetrag *m*, Defizit *n*, Manko *n*; Fehlmenge *f* durch Leck.

wanted persons list Fahndungsbuch *n*.

wanton *adj* rücksichtslos, böswillig, mutwillig; ~ **act** mutwillige Handlung; ~ **and furious driving** grob verkehrswidrige und rücksichtslose Fahrweise; ~ **driving** rücksichtsloses Fahren; ~ **misconduct** mutwilliges Fehlverhalten, grobe Rücksichtslosigkeit.

wantonness Mutwilligkeit *f*.

war Krieg *m* (= *K bzw . . .k*); ~ **baby** *K*-skind; *k*-sbegünstigte Industrie; ~ **bonus** *K*-szulage; ~ **charities** mildtätige Stiftung (*bzw Vermächtnis*) für *K*-sopfer; ~ **chest** *K*-skasse; Streikkasse; ~ **clause** Vorbehalt für den *K*-sfall; ~ **crime** *K*-sverbrechen, *K*-sstraftat; *conventional* ~ ~*s*: herkömmliche K-sverbrechen; gewohnheitsrechtl anerkannte K-sverbr.; ~ **criminal** *K*-sverbrecher, *K*-sstraftäter; ~ **damage** *K*-sschaden; ~ **debts** *K*-sschulden; ~ **economy** *K*-swirtschaft; ~ **factory** Rüstungsfabrik; ~ **guilt** *K*-sschuld; ~ **indemnity** *K*-sentschädigung; ~ **injury** *K*-sverletzung, Verwundung; ~ **legislation** *K*-sgesetzgebung; ~ **loan** → *loan*; ~ **monger** *K*-streiber, *K*-shetzer; **W~ Mothers** (=) *amerik. Frauenvereinigung von Müttern von Soldaten oder Veteranen bzw Gefallenen*; ~ **of attrition** Zermürbungs*k*; ~ **of fixed positions** Stellungs*k*; ~ **order** Rüstungsauftrag; ~ **pension** → *pension*; ~ **pensioners** *K*-sinvaliden; ~ **plant** Rüstungsbetrieb; ~ **power** *K*führungsbefugnis; ~ **proscription pact** *K*-sächtungspakt; ~ **region** *K*-sgebiet; ~ **reserve** *ins K*-srücklage; ~ **risk** *K*-srisiko; ~ **risk clause** *K*-sklausel; ~ **risk for buyer's account** *K*-srisiko ist Sache des Käufers; ~ **risk hazard** *ins K*-srisiko; ~ **risk hazard compensation** Entschädigung wegen *k*-sbedingter Gefahren (*Zivilarbeiter für US-Regierung*); ~ **risk injury** *K*-sfolgen, Verletzung von Handelsmarineangehörigen auf See; ~ **risk insurance** *K*-srisikoversicherung; ~ **savings certificates** *K*-ssparanleihen *f*|*pl*; ~ **service injury** *K*-sverletzung, zivile *K*-sverletzung; ~**-time economy** *K*-swirtschaft; **aggressive** ~ Angriffs*k*, Aggressions*k*; **articles of** ~ Militärstrafgesetzbuch; **civil** ~ Bürger*k*; **cold** ~ kalter *K*; **contraband of** ~ *K*-skonterbande; **customs of** ~ *K*-sbräuche, *K*-sgewohnheitsrecht; **defensive** ~ Verteidigungs*k*; **imperfect** ~ begrenzter *K*; **laws of** ~ → *law*; **levying** ~ **against the king** Hochverrat; **measures short of** ~ *k*-sähnliche Maßnahmen (*ohne Kampfhandlungen*); **perfect** ~ allgemeiner *K*;

preventive ~ Präventiv*k*; **private** ~ Privat*k*, Privatfehde; **public** ~ Völker*k*, *K im völkerrechtlichen Sinn*; **rights of** ~ (*angemaßtes*) *K*–srecht; **solemn** ~ erklärter *K*; **to resort to** ~ es auf e–n *K* ankommen lassen; e–n *K* führen; **undeclared** ~ *K* ohne *K*–serklärung; **to be at** ~ **with** sich im *K*–szustand befinden mit.

ward Mündel *n*; Stadtbezirk *m*, Abteilung *f*, Revier *n* (*Polizei*), Anstaltsrevier *n*, Saal *m*, Station *f*, Anstaltsabteilung *f*; ~**-holding** ritterliches Lehen; ~ **in chancery** Schutzbefohlener des (Vormundschafts)-Gerichts, unter vormundschaftsgerichtlicher Aufsicht stehender Minderjähriger; ~ **of court** Mündel unter gerichtlicher Vormundschaft; Pflegling unter gerichtl Schutz; ~**'s money** Mündelgeld; ~**-mote** Stadtbezirksgericht, Bezirksversammlung; ~**s of admiralty** Schutzbefohlene der Admiralität (*zivilrechtlicher Schutz von Matrosen gegen Ausbeutung*); ~**-penny** Burgwachenlohn, Wachtgeld; ~**-staff** Polizeistock; ~**-wit** Befreiung vom Wachtdienst; **electoral** ~ Wahlbezirk; **prison** ~ → *prison*.

wardage Wachtgeld *n*.

warden Vorsteher *m*, Leiter *m*, Wächter *m*, Aufseher *m*; Präsident *m*, *hist* Gouverneur *m*, Gefängnisdirektor *m*, Zunftmeister *m*, Bürgermeister *m*, Vormund *m*, Kustor *m*; **W~ of the Cinque Ports** Gouverneur der Cinque Ports *qv*; ~ **of the forest** Forstaufseher; **W~ of the Marches** Landeshauptmann an der schottischen Grenze; **W~ of the Mint** Münzdirektor.

warder Wachtmann *m*, Posten *m*, Gefängnisaufseher *m*, Gefangenenwärter *m*.

wardship Vormundschaft *f*, Pflegschaft *f*; ~ **of infants** Vormundschaft über Minderjährige; ~ **proceeding** Sorgerechtsverfahren.

warehouse Lager *n*, Magazin *n*, Lagerhaus *n*; ~ **account** Lagerkonto; ~ **bond** Lagerschein; Zollverschlußschein; ~ **book** Lagerbuch, Inventurbuch; ~ **charges** Lagergeld; ~ **goods** Lagergut, Waren auf Lager; ~ **money** → *money*; ~ **receipt** → *receipt*; ~ **system** Zollverschluß(system); ~ **to** ~ **clause** Von-Haus-zu-Haus-Klausel (*Seeversicherung*); ~ **warrant** Lagerpfandschein; **bonded** ~ Lager gegen Zoll- bzw Steuersicherung, Zollager; **ex** ~ ab Lager; **exise** ~ Steuerdepot, Steuerlager; **field** ~ **receipt** Lagerschein für sicherungsübereignete Waren; **inward processing** ~ Lager für den aktiven Veredelungsverkehr; **public** ~ öffentliches Lagerhaus.

warehousekeeper Lagerhalter *m*; ~**'s certificate** Lagerempfangsschein; ~**'s lien** Lagerhalterpfandrecht; ~**'s receipt** Lagerempfangsschein; ~**'s warrant** Orderlagerschein.

warehouseman Lagerhalter *m*; ~**'s lien** Lagerhalterpfandrecht.

warehousing Lagereigewerbe *n*; Lagerhaltung *f*; Wertpapierkauf und -verwahrung zur Kurssicherung; Ansammlung von Kapitalanteilen für verdeckte Übernahmespekulation; ~ **company** Lagerhausgesellschaft; ~ **credit system** Warenumschlagskredit; ~ **system** Zollagersystem; **field** ~ → *field*.

warming-up time Anlaufzeit *f* (*Produktion, Arbeitskräfte*).

warn warnen, verwarnen, androhen, *scot* kündigen.

warning Mahnung *f*, Warnung *f*, Verwarnung *f*; Drohung *f*, Abmahnung *f*, Androhung *f* (e–r Ausschlußfrist), Vorladung *f*, Ankündigung *f*, Kündigung *f*, Warnsignal *n*, Voraussage *f*, Bescheid *m*; ~ **and watching** (*lehensrechtliche*) Wachdienste; ~ **notice** Verwarnung, Abmahnung; ~ **of a caveat** Aufforderung zu Begründung e–r Vormerkung (*caveat qv*) vor Gericht; ~ **strike** →*strike*; ~ **to strike** Streikdrohung; **a month's** ~ monatliche Kündigung, Kündigungsfrist von 1 Monat; **at a minute's** ~ auf jeder-

zeitige Kündigung, fristlos; auf Abruf, sofort; **early** ~ rechtzeitiger Voralarm (*Atomangriff*); **fair** ~ rechtzeitige Verwarnung; **road ~s** → *road*; **to give s.o. a fair** ~ jmdn rechtzeitig (auf etwas) aufmerksam machen; **without a moment's** ~ ohne Ankündigung, unerwartet; **without further** ~ ohne weitere Androhung; **written** ~ schriftl Verwarnung.

warrant *s* Ermächtigung *f*, Bescheinigung *f*, Beleg *m*, Garantie *f*, Lagerschein *m*, Pfandschein *m*; Bezugsrecht *n*, Schuldschein *m*; Zahlungsanweisung *f*, Haftbefehl *m*, Haussuchungsbefehl *m*, Ladung *f*; ~ **backed for bail** Haftbefehl mit Kautionserlaubnis; ~ **card** Legitimationspapier (*des Detektivs*); ~ **creditor** → *creditor*; ~ **for goods** Lagerschein; ~ **for payment of money** Zahlungsanweisung; ~ **in bankruptcy** Konkursbeschlagnahme; ~ **issue** Optionsanleihe (*mit Option auf Aktienerwerb*); ~ **of apprehension** Steckbrief, Haftbefehl; ~ **of arrest** Haftbefehl; ~ **of attachment** Beschlagnahmeverfügung, Pfändungsbeschluß; ~ **of attorney** unwiderrufliche Prozeßvollmacht zur .Erklärung e–s Anerkenntnisses vor Gericht, Unterwerfungserklärung; ~ **of attorney roll** → *roll*; ~ **of commitment** Einlieferungsbefehl, Haftbefehl; ~ **of deposit** Depotschein, Hinterlegungsschein; ~ **of distraint** Wegnahmeermächtigung, Bewilligung der Pfandverwertung; ~ **of distress** = *distress* ~ *qv*; ~ **of execution** Pfändungsauftrag; ~ **officer** → *officer*; **~s payable** fällige Zahlungsanweisungen; ~ **to appear** Vorführungsbefehl; ~ **to bearer** Inhaberzertifikat; Inhaberaktie; ~ **to sue and defend** Prozeßvollmacht; **alias** ~ → *alias*; **bench** ~ richterlicher Haftbefehl; **bond** ~ *brit* Zollbegleitschein, Inhaberlagerschein; **county** ~ kommunales Schuldscheindarlehen, Zahlungsanweisung auf die Kreisverwaltung; **death** ~ Befehl zur Vollstreckung der Todesstrafe; **deposit** ~ → *deposit*; **distress** ~ Pfändungsauftrag; *vgl distress*; **dividend** ~ → *dividend*; **fractional** ~ Berechtigungsschein auf gestückelte neue Aktien; **general** ~ unbenannter Haftbefehl oder Durchsuchungsbefehl; **interest** ~ Zinsschein; **land** ~ → *land*; **landlord's** ~ → *landlord's*; **municipal** ~ kommunaler Schatzwechsel, kommunale Zahlungsanweisung; **outstanding** ~ noch nicht vollzogener Haftbefehl; **royal** ~ → *royal*; **search** ~ → *search*; **share** ~ → *share*; **stock** ~ → *stock* (*1*); **to execute a** ~ e–n Haftbefehl ausfertigen; **withdrawal** ~ Auszahlungsermächtigung.

warrant *v* einstehen für, zusichern, gewährleisten, die Freiheit von Rechtsmängeln zusichern; rechtfertigen; **~ed free** Versicherungshaftung ausgeschlossen; **~ed free from capture** Haftungsausschuß bei Beschlagnahme; **~ed free of all average** haftet nur bei Totalschaden; **~ed pure** garantiert rein; **~ed sound** Mängelfreiheit zugesichert; garantierte Gesundheit (*Pferdekauf*); **~ed uninsured** Zusicherung des unversicherten Eigenrisikos (*in Höhe des Selbstbehalts*).

warrantable berechtigt, zu rechtfertigen; ~ **title** garantierbarer Rechtstitel.

warrantee Empfänger *m* e–r Zusicherung *bzw* Garantie *vgl warranty*.

warrantor der Zusichernde, der Gewährleistende.

warranty Gewähr *f*, Gewährleistung *f*, Gewährleistungserklärung *f*, Zusicherung (*e–r Eigenschaft bzw Tatsache*); Garantie *f*; Versicherung *f* der Richtigkeit der Angaben (*in e–m Versicherungsantrag*); ~ **deed** Urkunde mit Gewährleistungsversprechen; Grundstückskaufvertrag mit Auflassung *und Rechtsmängelgewährleistungsversprechen*; Auflassungsurkunde; ~ **defence** Gewährleistungseinrede; ~ **of au-**

thority Einstehen für die Gültigkeit der Vertretungsmacht; ~ **of fitness** Gewährleistung der Eignung für den vertragl Zweck; ~ **of habitability** Gewährleistung des Wohnungsvermieters (*für den Zustand der Wohnung*); ~ **of merchantability** Gewährleistung der marktgängigen Qualität; ~ **of quality** Sachmängelhaftung für mittlere Art und Güte; ~ **of quiet enjoyment** Zusicherung des ungestörten Besitzes; ~ **of title** Gewährleistung für Rechtsmängel, Rechtsmängelhaftung; ~**ies on bills and cheques** *bil* Wechsel- und Scheckbürgschaften; ~ **period** Gewährleistungsfrist; **affirmative** ~ Zusicherung der Richtigkeit von tatsächlichen Angaben (*Versicherung*); **breach of** ~ Verletzung e–r Gewährleistungspflicht, Nichteinhaltung e–r Zusicherung, Garantieverletzung; ~~~ *of authority: Fehlen behaupteter Vertretungsmacht*; **collateral** ~ Gewährleistung des ungestörten Zwischenbesitzes (*Erbrecht*); **construction** ~ Baugewährleistung; **continuing** ~ Dauergarantie (*für die gesamte Vertragszeit*); **contract of** ~ → *contract*; **covenant of** ~ → *covenant*; **exclusion of** ~ Gewährleistungsausschluß; **express** ~ ausdrückliche Zusicherung; **full** ~ Garantie, **general** ~ absolute Freistellung von Rechten Dritter; **implied** ~ gesetzliche Gewährleistung; konkludente Gewährleistung; **joint** ~ Solidargewährleistung; **limited** ~ (*meist auf Arbeits- und Materialkosten*) beschränkte Garantie; **lineal** ~ Rechtsmängelgewähr durch den Aszendenten (*Erblasser*); **on-site** ~ Gewährleistung am Einsatzort; **period of** ~ → *period*; **personal** ~ Bürgschaft; **promissory** ~ Verpflichtungserklärung auf Dauer e–r Versicherung; **return-to-factory** ~ Gewährleistung bei Rücksendung an das Lieferwerk; **special** ~ Freistellung von Ansprüchen des Veräußerers oder dessen Erben; **statutory** ~ gesetzl Mängelgewährleistung; **to hono(u)r a** ~ e–e Gewährleistungsverpflichtung einhalten.

warren Wildgehege *n*, Privileg *n* für Wildgehegehaltung; **fowl of** ~ jagdbares Geflügel (*in Wildgehegen*); **free** ~ Wildgehegeprivileg.

washing of dirty linen Schmutzige-Wäsche-Waschen *n*.

washout Fiasko *n*, Reinfall *m*.

wash sale → *sale*.

wastage Abgang *m*, Verlust *m*, Materialschwund *m*, Wertverlust *m* durch Abnützung und Substanzminderung e–r Sache; **natural** ~ natürlicher Personalabgang.

waste *s* übermäßiger Verbrauch *m*, Verschleiß *m*, Verschwendung *f*, Vergeudung *f*, Verfall *m*, Abnützung *f*, Verschlechterung *f* (*bes während der Pachtzeit*), Wertminderung *f*, Substanzminderung *f*, Vernachlässigung *f*, Verschwendungssucht *f*; Schutt *m*, Müll *m*, Überschüsse *m|pl*, Ausschuß *m*, Spillage *f*; Verschleiß *m*, Abnahme *f*, Schwund *m*, Abgang *m*, Beschädigung *f*; ~ **accounting** Abfallverrechnung; ~**-book** Kladde (*e–s Kaufmanns*); ~ **land** Ödland; ~ **of a manor** Brachland e–s Landguts; ~ **product** → *product*; ~**-treatment plant** Kläranlage; ~ **utilization** Abfallverwertung; ~**-water disposal** Abwässerbeseitigung; ~ **water treatment** Abwasserbehandlung; **active** = *positive* ~ *qv*; **ameliorating** ~ werterhöhende Veränderungen an der Grundstückssubstanz; (*zB Urbarmachung von Ödland*); **atomic** ~ Atommüll; **commissive** ~ Beschädigung (*am Pachtgrundstück*); Substanzschädigung *cf positive* ~; **double** ~ mehrfache Substanzverringerung (*zB Gebäude u Wald*); **equitable** ~ *billigkeitsrechtlich* unzulässige Substanzschädigung (*willkürliche Substanzschädigung durch den unbeschränkt Nutzungsberechtigten als unzulässige Rechtsausübung*); **impeachment of** ~ → *impeachment*; **low-level** ~ ge-

ring verstrahler Atommüll; **meliorating** ~ = *ameliorating* ~ *qv*; **natural** ~ innerer Verderb, natürlicher Schwund, gewöhnliche Verschlechterung, Abnutzung; **nul** ~ Bestreiten des Substanzschadens (*an der Pachtsache*); **permissive** ~ Unterlassen notwendiger Instandsetzung, Verletzung der Instandhaltungspflicht; **positive** ~ vorsätzliche Substanzschädigung *cf voluntary*; **rate of** ~ Schwundsatz; **roadside** ~**s** Straßenböschungen; **voluntary** ~ vorsätzliche Substanzschädigung, vorsätzliche Zerstörung oder Beschädigung der Pachtsache; übermäßige, mißbräuchliche Fruchtziehung; **unlicensed disposal of** ~ unbefugte Mülldeponie, wilde Müllablagerung; **wanton** ~ mutwillige Substanzschädigung.

waste *v* vernachlässigen, verschwenden, in Verfall geraten lassen, e–e Substanzverschlechterung verursachen (*bzw zulassen*).

wasting kurzlebig, schwindend, zehrend, abbaufähig; ausbeutungsfähig.

watch *s* Wache *f*, Wachkommando *n*; ~ **and ward** Wachpflicht bei Tag und Nacht; ~ **and warning service** Kreditinformationsdienst auf Gegenseitigkeit; ~ **brief** Beobachtungsauftrag (*im Prozeß*); ~ **committee** *obs* Gemeindeausschuß zur Polizeiüberwachung; ~ **rate** Gemeindepolizeisteuer.

watching and besetting Beschatten *n*, Auflauern *n*; ~ **out** Achtgeben.

watchman Wachmann *m*; **night** ~ Nachtwächter.

water Wasser *n* (= *W bzw* . . .*w*), Gewässer *n*; **W~ Act** *W*gesetz (*GB 1973*); **W~ Authority** Wasserwirtschaftsamt; ~**-bailiff** Hafenzollbeamter, Fischereiaufseher, Strompolizist; ~ **board** = ~ *authority qv*; ~ **bonds** → *bond* (*2*); ~ **canon** *W*werfer; ~ **damage** *W*schaden, ~ **damage insurance** → *insurance*; ~**-gavel** *hist* Fischereipacht; ~**-guard** Flußpolizei, Hafenpolizei, Hafenzollwache; ~ **in an underground stratum** unterirdisches Gewässer, Grund*w*; ~ **line** *W*linie, Ladelinie; ~**-logged** manövrierunfähig wegen eingedrungenen *W–s*; ~**-mark** *W*zeichen; ~**s of the United States** Binnenschiffahrtsgewässer in USA; ~ **ordeal** → *ordeal*; ~**-packed** → *to pack*; ~ **pollution** *W*verschmutzung; ~ **power** *Wkraft;* ~ **privilege** *W*benutzungsrecht; ~ **rate** *W*geld; **W~ Resources Act** *W*haushaltsg. *GB 1963*; ~ **right** *W*nutzungsrecht, *W*entnahmerecht; ~ **right claim** *W*entnahmeanspruch; ~ **supply** *W*versorgung; ~ **table** Grundwasserspiegel; ~**-way** *W*weg, Schifffahrtsweg; ~ **works** *W*versorgungsanlage(n); **coast** ~**s** → *coast*; **developed** ~ an die Oberfläche gebrachtes Nutz*w*; **flood** ~**s** → *flood*; **foreign** ~**s** ausländische Hoheitsgewässer; **high** ~ **mark** Hochwasserstandszeichen; Flutlinie; oberer normaler *W*stand; **inland** ~**s** → *inland*; **international** ~**s** internationale Gewässer; **jurisdictional** ~ Hoheitsgewässer; **low** ~ Niedrigwasser, niedrigster Gezeitenstand, niedrigste Ebbe; **low** ~ **mark** Tiefwasserzeichen, niedrigster *W*stand *bei Ebbe*; Tiefstand; **national** ~**s** Hoheitsgewässer; **navigable** ~**s** schiffbare Gewässer; **percolating** ~ Sicker*w*; **private** ~**s** Privatgewässer; **public** ~**s** öffentliche Gewässer; **subsoil** ~ Grund*w*; **subterranean** ~**s** unterirdische Gewässer; **surface** ~**s** Oberflächen*w*; **surplus** ~ Überschuß*w*; **territorial** ~**s** Hoheitsgewässer; **tidal** ~**s** Gezeiten*w*, den Gezeiten unterworfenes Gewässer, Flutgebiet; **underground** ~ Grund*w*.

waterage Transport *m* auf dem Wasserweg *m*; Wasserfracht *f*.

watercourse fließendes Gewässer *n*.

watering of stock Kapitalverwässerung *f*.

way Weg *m*, Straße *f*, Wegerecht *n*, Art *f* und Weise *f*; ~**s and means**

Mittelbeschaffung; **~s and means advances** Staatsbankenvorschüsse auf Steuereinkommen; **~s and means committee** → *committee*; **~-bill** Frachtbrief, Beförderungsschein, **~-going crop** nach Pachtablauf reifendes Erntegut; ~ **of necessity** Notweg; ~ **station** Zwischenstation; **common** ~ öffentliche Straße, Landstraße; **private** ~ Wegerecht (*Dienstbarkeit*), Privatweg; **public** ~ öffentl Weg, Landstraße; **right of** ~ → *right*; **under** ~ unterwegs.

waybill Passagierliste *f*, Frachtliste *f*, Warenbegleitschein *n*.

wayleave Wegerecht *n*, Durchfahrtsrecht *n (bes. für Bergbau*); Überführungsrecht (*für Stromleitungen*).

waywarden Straßenbauamtsleiter *m*, Gemeindebeauftragter *m* für Straßenunterhalt.

weakness Hinfälligkeit *f*, Schwäche *f*; ~ **of mind** Geistesschwäche.

weal Wohl *n*; **common** (= *public* ~) Gemeinwohl.

wealth Vermögen *n*, Reichtum *m*; ~ **tax** → *tax*; **creation of** ~ (= *wealth-creation*) Vermögensbildung; **monetary** ~ Geldvermögensbildung; **national** ~ Volksvermögen.

weapon Waffe *f*; ~ **of offence** = *offensive W. qv*; **atomic ~s** Atomwaffen, **conventional** ~ konventionelle Waffe; **dangerous ~s** gefährliche Waffen; **deadly** ~ tödliche Waffe; **letal** ~ = *dealthy* ~ *qv*; **offensive** ~ gefährliche Waffe, zum Angriff geeignete Waffe.

wear and tear Abnutzung *f*, Verschleiß *m*, übliche Abnutzung *f*; **admissibility of** ~ Zulässigkeit der Beweiserhebung über Abnützung; **depreciation of** ~ Abschreibung für Abnutzung; **fair** ~ normale Abnutzung; **reasonable** ~ angemessene Abnutzung.

wearing apparel Kleidungsstücke *n|pl* (*einschließlich Unterwäsche*).

weather | **permitting** (*wp*) falls es das Wetter zuläßt, bei günstigen Wetterbedingungen; ~ **working days** (*wwd*) wetterabhängige Arbeitstage (*falls wettermäßig gearbeitet werden kann*).

wed trauen, heiraten, die Ehe eingehen.

wedlock Ehe *f*, Ehestand *m*; **born in lawful** ~ ehelich geboren; **born out of** ~ nichtehelich geboren; **lawful** ~ Ehe(stand); **the bonds of** ~ Eheband, Ehe.

week Woche *f*; ~ **days** Wochentage; **~'s notice** wöchentliche Kündigung; ~ **order** → *order* (*2*); ~ **under review** Berichtswoche; **~-work** wöchentliche Dienstleistung für den Grundherrn; **working** ~ Arbeitswoche, Wochenarbeitszeit.

weekly wöchentlich; ~ **account of work done** wöchentliche Arbeitsfortschrittsabrechnung; ~ **payment** wöchentliche Zahlung; ~ **return** Wochenbericht.

weighage Wiegegeld *n*.

weighing | **bureau** Eichamt; ~ **fee** Wiegegeld; ~ **regulations** Wiegeordnung; ~ **stamp** Wiegestempel; **check** ~ Nachwiegen.

weight Gewicht *n*, Bedeutung *f*, Wichtigkeit *f*, Last *f*; ~ **allowed free** Freigewicht; **~s and measures** Maße und Gewichte; **W~s and Measures Acts** G. über Maße und Gewichte *GB 1963–74*; ~ **certificate** Gewichtsbescheinigung; ~ **limit** Gewichtsgrenze, Höchstgewicht; ~ **note** Wiegeschein; ~ **of evidence** → *evidence*; ~ **of fine gold** Feingoldgewicht; ~ **of testimony** Wert e–r Zeugenaussage; ~ **variation allowance** Gewichtstoleranz, Franchise; **allowance of** ~ Gutgewicht; **boxed** ~ Gewicht nach Verpackung; **by** ~ nach Gewicht; **commercial** ~ Handelsgewicht; **dead** ~ → *dead*; **deficiency in** ~ → *deficiency*; **dry** ~ Trockengewicht; **dutiable** ~ zollpflichtiges Gewicht; **gross** ~ Bruttogewicht (*einschließlich Verpackung*); **live** ~ Lebendgewicht; **loss in** ~ Gewichtsverlust; **miner's** ~ (=) *vereinbarte Fördermenge zur Gewinnung 1 Tonne Kohle*; **net** ~ Nettogewicht; **short** ~ Untergewicht,

Fehlgewicht; **surplus** ~ Mehrgewicht; **true** ~ genaues Gewicht.

weighting Gewichtung *f*; Einräumen von Sonderkonditionen e–r Bank.

welfare Wohlfahrt *f*, Wohlergehen *n*, Fürsorge *f*, Sozialhilfe *f*; ~ **agency** Sozialamt, Fürsorgebehörde; ~ **benefits** Sozialhilfeleistungen; ~ **centre** Sozialhilfestelle; ~ **dead beat** Wohlfahrtsschmarotzer, heruntergekommener Wohlfahrtsempfänger; ~ **expenditure** Fürsorgelasten, Sozialausgaben; ~ **fund** Unterstützungsfonds; ~ **institution** Sozialeinrichtung, soziales Hilfswerk; ~ **law** Sozialrecht, Recht der sozialen Sicherheit; Wohlfahrtsrecht; ~ **officer** Versöhnungshelfer (*Ehescheidung*); Sozialhelfer(in); ~ *~'s report: Gutachten des Jugendamts, Bericht des Sozialamts*; ~ **services** Sozialleistungen; ~ **state** → *state* (*2*); ~ **visitor** Hausfürsorgerin; ~ **work** Fürsorge, Sozialarbeit; ~ **worker** Wohlfahrtspfleger, Fürsorger; Sozialhelfer(in); **child** ~ Kinderfürsorge; *~'s ~: Kindeswohl*; **economic** ~ materielles Wohlergehen; **industrial** ~ betriebliche Sozialfürsorge; **infant** ~ Säuglingsfürsorge, Kleinkinderfürsorge; **maternity** ~ **service** Mütter(beratungs)dienst; **maternity and child** ~ Fürsorge für Mutter und Kind; **national** ~ Volkswohl, Volksfürsorge; **public** ~ öffentliche Fürsorge; Wohlergehen der Allgemeinheit, Gemeinwohl.

well|-acquired wohlerworben; ~ **and truly** ordnungsgemäß (*ausführen*); **~-born men** *hist* Bürgerschöffen; **~-established** wohlbegründet, wohlerworben; **~-founded** (wohl)begründet; **~-grounded** wohlbegründet; **~-informed** gut unterrichtet; ~ **knowing** bewußt; ~ **known** wohlbekannt, im Vertrauen auf; ~ **timed** rechtzeitig, zur richtigen Zeit; **warranted** ~ einwandfreier Zustand zugesichert.

well *s* Quelle *f*; Bohrloch *n*, Bohrung *f* (*Öl, Erdgas, Wasser*).

welsher betrügerischer Buchmacher *m*.

welshing Wettuntreue *f*, Wettbetrug *m*; **larceny by** ~ Unterschlagung von Wettgeldern.

whack aufteilen, parzellieren, auseinandersetzen.

wharf *s* Kai *m*, Dock *n*, Pier *m*, Landeplatz *m*, Löschplatz *m*, *pl* (*wharves*) Lagerhäuser *n|pl* (*für nichtzollpflichtige Waren*); ~ **dues** Kaigeld, Kaigebühr; ~ **labo(u)rer** Schiffsladearbeiter; **~'s receipt** Kaiablieferungsschein; **approved ~ves** amtlich zugelassene Lade- und Löschplätze für zollpflichtige Waren; **private** ~ Privatpier; **public** ~ öffentlicher Kai, öffentlicher Anlegeplatz; **sufferance ~ves** Kaianlagen für Zollzwecke, Freihafen.

wharf *v* am Kai anlegen, ausladen, löschen.

wharfage Kaigebühr *f*; ~ **charges** Löschungskosten, Kaigebühren.

wharfing out ausschließliches Recht *n* am Unterwasserboden zur Errichtung von Kaianlagen.

wharfinger Kaibesitzer *m*, Kaimeister *m*.

what remains was übrig bleibt, meine restliche Habe.

wheelage Wegegeld *n*, Rollgeld *n*.

wheelers Ladespeditionsarbeiter *m*; ~ **and dealers** skrupellose Geschäftemacher.

when wann, zu welcher Zeit, zu der betreffenden Zeit, bei, während, nach, unmittelbar nach; falls; unter der Bedingung, daß; ~ **and as** bei (*Erreichen e–s bestimmten Alters*); ~ **and where** wann und wo auch immer; **~, as, and if issued** (*bei Emissionen*) mit dem Vorbehalt, daß die Effektenausgabe tatsächlich erfolgt; ~ **issued** bei Erscheinen, bei Ausgabe (*Wertpapier*); ~ **the matter of complaint arose** bei (seit) Entstehen des Klageanspruchs.

whence woher, von wannen, woraus, wodurch, von wo, weshalb, dahin.

whenever wenn auch immer, zu je-

der Zeit, solange wie, so bald als, bei, falls.

where who, falls; ~ **appropriate** gegebenenfalls; ~ **it is shown** sofern nachgewiesen wird, daß ...; ~ **occasion requires** soweit erforderlich.

whereabouts *s* Aufenthaltsort *m*, Verbleib *m*, Adresse *f*; **to establish** ~ den jeweiligen Aufenthaltsort feststellen.

whereas davon ausgehend, daß; in Anbetracht (*der Tatsache, daß*); angesichts; in der Erwägung, daß; im Hinblick darauf, daß (*Präambelformel*).

whereby wodurch.

wherefore weshalb.

wheresoever wo auch immer, gleich wo; ~ **arising** wo auch immer entstehend (*bzw entstanden*).

whereupon worauf, wonach.

whether ob, falls; ~ **or not ...** gleichgültig ob.

whichever is the later der spätere dieser Zeitpunkte (ist maßgeblich).

whig Whig *m*, Liberaler *m*, *US*: Nationalrepublikaner *m* (*im Gegensatz zu Loyalist m*); *Oppositionspartei gegen die Democrats* (*19. Jhd.*).

while während, währenddessen, solange wie, wenn auch, obwohl, obgleich, wohingegen.

whilst bei, wobei, währenddem, solange wie; ~ **under the influence** unter Alkoholeinfluß.

whip *s parl* Fraktionsgeschäftsführer *m*; Fraktionszwang *m*, Fraktionsrundschreiben *n* mit Aufforderung, zur Abstimmung zu erscheinen; **chief government** ~ Fraktionsgeschäftsführer der Regierungspartei; **one-line** ~ Fraktionsanwesenheitsaufforderung; **three-line** ~ äußerst dringende Fraktionsanwesenheitsaufforderung; **to break the** ~ den Fraktionszwang nicht einhalten; **to heel to the party** ~ Fraktionsdisziplin wahren; **to take off the** ~**s** den Fraktionszwang aufheben; **to vote by** ~ unter Fraktionszwang abstimmen; **two-line** ~ dringende Fraktionsanwesenheitsaufforderung.

whip in *v* zur Abstimmung zusammentrommeln.

whipping Prügelstrafe *f*, Auspeitschen *n*; ~**-post** Pfahl (*zum Anbinden des Auszupeitschenden*).

whipsaw *pol* sich von beiden Seiten bestechen lassen; ~**ed** in allen Punkten besiegt; **to be** ~**ed** *exch US* doppelten Verlust erleiden.

whipsawing Schaukelbewegung (*der Kurse*).

whisk *v/t* **through** durchwinken (*Grenzposten*).

white | **acre** das Grundstück A (*fiktive Grundstücksbezeichnung*) *vgl black acre*; **W**~ **Book** Prozeßordnung des Supreme Court (*GB*); ~ **book of London** *Sammlung mittelalterlichen Londoner Stadtrechts*; ~ **collar crime** *US* Wirtschaftsverbrechen; ~ **collar worker** Büroangestellte(r); ~ **elephant** unrentables Geschäft; ~ **flag** weiße Fahne, Parlamentärflagge; ~ **goods** weiße Ware (*Küchengeräte etc*); ~ **knight** Retter in der Not (*gegen Übernahmespekulation durch Überbieten des Angreifers*); ~ **meats** Molkereiprodukte; ~ **paper** Weißbuch; erstklassiger Handelswechsel; ~ **persons** Weiße, Angehörige der weißen Rasse, Personen europäischer Abstammung; ~ **rents** Bodenzins in Geld (*Silber*); ~ **slave** Opfer des Mädchenhandels; ~ **slave traffic** Mädchenhandel; ~ **tithes** der kleine Zehnt (*verschiedene Ortsbedeutungen*).

whitewash *s* Schönfärberei *f*, Schuldentlastung *f*.

whitewash *v* beschönigen, reinwaschen, rehabilitieren; e–n „Persilschein" ausstellen.

whoever wer, derjenige welcher.

whole ganz, gesund, stark; ~ **blood** → *blood*; ~ **chest** e–e Kiste Tee (*über 100 lbs*); ~ **debt** die gesamte Forderung (*bzw Schuld*); ~ **life assurance** → *assurance*; ~ **life insurance** → *life insurance*; ~ **life**

policy → *policy* (*1*); ~ **time job** hauptberufliche Tätigkeit; **on the** ~ im ganzen gesehen; **the** ~ **of one's property** sein gesamtes Vermögen.

wholesale Großhandel *m;* ~ **banking** Firmenkundengeschäft, Großbankengeschäft, Interbankengeschäft; ~ **business** Großhandel, Engrosgeschäft; ~ **cost** Gestehungskosten des Einzelhändlers (*vom Großhandel oder Produzenten*); ~ **society** Großeinkaufsgenossenschaft.

wholesaler Großhändler *m*; Großhandelskaufmann *m*, Grossist *m*; **full-service** ~ Großhandelsvollkaufmann (*mit eigener Lagerhaltung*); **limited-service** ~ Zwischenverkäufer; **merchant** ~ Großhändler; **(security)** ~ Emissionsbank (*Übernahme von Gesamtemissionen*).

wholesome gesund, gesundheitsfördernd.

wholly ganz, gänzlich, vollständig, ausschließlich, gleichermaßen; ~ **and permanently disabled** (dauernd) erwerbsunfähig; ~ **dependant** vollständig unterhaltsabhängig; ~ **liable** unbeschränkt persönlich haftend; ~ **or in part** ganz oder teilweise; ~ **owned by its employees** ganz im Eigentum seiner Belegschaft; ~**-owned corporation** Gesellschaft in ausschließlichem Schachtelbesitz, 100%ige Tochtergesellschaft; ~**-owned government corporation** staatseigene Kapitalgesellschaft; ~**-owned subsidiary** 100%ige Tochtergesellschaft.

whosoever wer, wer auch immer.

wide | opening *exch* weite Spanne *f* zwischen Angebots- und Nachfragekurs; ~ **prices** *exch* Kurse mit großer Spanne zwischen Geld- und Briefkurs.

widow Witwe *f*; ~**'s allowance** (allgemeines) staatliches Witwengeld (*für 26 Wochen*) *GB*; ~ **and orphan stock** mündelsichere Wertpapiere; ~**'s annuity** Witwenrente; ~**-bench** Witwenteil; ~**'s benefits** Witwengeld, Hinterbliebenenbezüge für Witwen; ~**s bereavement allowance** Steuerfreibetrag für Witwen (*im Todesjahr des Mannes*); ~**'s chamber** → *chamber*; ~**'s election** Wahlrecht der Witwe (*Testament oder Pflichtteil in Höhe des Intestatserbteils*); ~ **insurance** Witwenversicherung; ~**'s pension** → *pension*; ~**'s quarantine** 40tägiges Wohnrecht der Witwe im Herrenhaus; **grass** ~ Strohwitwe, getrennt lebende Ehefrau, verlassene Ehefrau, geschiedene Frau.

widowed verwitwet; ~ **mother** Witwe mit Kindern; ~ *~'s allowance* Rente für Witwe mit Kind(ern).

widower Witwer *m*.

wife Ehefrau *f*, Gattin *f*; ~ **and children** Frau und Kinder; (*for the benefit of* ~ *and children:*) Zuwendung an die Kinder mit lebenslänglichem Nießbrauch für die Ehefrau (*bzw Witwe*); ~**'s equity** → *equity*; ~**'s non-privileged property** eingebrachtes Gut der Ehefrau; ~**'s part** Pflichterbteil der Witwe; ~ **swapping agreement** Vereinbarung, die beiderseitigen Ehefrauen auszutauschen; ~ **to hold property to her separate use** es wird Vorbehaltsgut vereinbart; **coercion of** ~ *crim* Berufung auf Nötigung durch Ehemann; **common-law** ~ Lebensgefährtin; **lawful wedded** ~ rechtmäßige Ehefrau.

wild | animals wilde Tiere; ~ **bank** *US* Schwindelbank; **W**~ **Creatures and Forest Laws Act** Wild- und Forstrechtsgesetz (*GB 1971; Kodifizierung, Aufhebung alter Forstrechte*).

wildcat *adj* unseriös, riskant, spontan, ungeregelt; spekulativ; ~ **banking** unseriöses Bankunternehmen; ~ **finance** unseriöse Finanzierung; ~ **strike** → *strike*.

wildcat *s* spekulative Versuchsbohrung *f*, unsolides Geschäftsunternehmen *n*.

wildlife | resources Wildbestände; ~ **sanctuary** Wildreservat.

wilful *US: willful* vorsätzlich (= *v*), absichtlich, störrisch, widersetzlich; ~ **act, default or neglect** Vorsatz oder Fahrlässigkeit, Verschulden; ~ **and malicious** böswillig; ~ **and malicious injury** *v–e* Schädigung, *v–e* Verletzung; ~ **and wanton injuring** *v–e* Schädigung, *v–e* Verletzung; ~ **infringement for profit** strafbare Handlung mit Bereicherungsabsicht; ~ **interference to the safety of others** *v–e* Gefährdung anderer Personen; ~ **neglect to maintain** *v–e* Verletzung der Unterhaltspflicht; ~ **omission of duty** *v–e* Nichterfüllung e–r Pflicht; ~ **refusal to consummate** *v–e Weigerung der Vollziehung der Ehe;* ~**ly holding over** bewußt widerrechtliches Verbleiben (*nach Pachtablauf*).

wilfullness (*US willfullness*) böse Absicht; **legal** ~ absichtliches Außerachtlassen der Sorgfaltspflicht, Rücksichtslosigkeit.

will (*1*) Wille *m*, Willenskraft *f*, Wunsch *m*; **ill** ~ böser Wille; **of one's free** ~ freiwillig.

will (*2*) Testament *n* (= *T bzw . . .t*), letzter Wille *m*; letztwillige Verfügung (*jeder Art*); *im engeren Sinn:* letztw. Verfüg. über Immobilien; ~ **contest** *T–s*anfechtungsprozeß, *T–s*prüfungsverfahren; ~ **in contemplation of marriage** *T* in Erwartung e–r Eheschließung; ~ **in local form** *T* in Ortsform (*nach den Formerfordernissen des Wohnsitzlandes*); **W~s Act** *T–s*gesetz (*GB, 1837, 1968*); ~ **suit** *T–s*feststellungsklage; **alternative** ~ *T* mit Alternativklausel (*der letztwilligen Gültigkeit e–s anderen T–s bei Eintritt e–s Ereignisses*); **ambulatory** ~ widerrufliches *T*; **alteration of** ~ *T–sänderung*; **attestation of** ~ → *attestation*; **attested** ~ von Zeugen unterschriebenes *T*; **avoidance of** ~ *T–s*anfechtung; **beneficiary under a** ~ testamentarisch Bedachter; **by** ~ letztwillig, testamentarisch; **capacity to make a** ~ Testierfähigkeit; **common** ~ gemeinsames *T*; **concurrent** ~ gleichzeitig in verschiedenen Staaten errichtetes (*gegenständlich beschränktes*) *T*; **conditional** ~ bedingtes *T*; **conjoint** ~ gemeinsames *T*; **counter** ~ gegenseitiges *T*; **disposition by** ~ → *disposition*; **double** ~ gegenseitige Erbeinsetzung; **drafted** ~ vorbereitetes *T*, (*vom Anwalt*) aufgesetztes *T*; **execution of a** ~ Errichtung e–s *T–s*; *T–s*errichtung, *T–s*unterfertigung; **gift by** ~ → *gift*; **holographic** ~ eigenhändiges *T*; selbst geschriebenes (*und unterschriebenes*) *T*; **informal** ~ formloses *T*; **international** ~ international gültiges *T*; **joint** ~ gemeinschaftliches (*wechselbezügliches*) *T*; **joint and mutual** ~ wechselbezügliches (*gleichzeitig errichtetes*) *T*; **last** ~ *T*, letztwillige Verfügung; **last** ~ **and testament** *T*, letzter Wille; **living** ~ *schriftliche Untersagung aussichtsloser lebensverlängernder Maßnahmen als letzter Wunsch*; **lost** ~ nicht auffindbares *T*; **mariner's** ~ → *mariner*; **mutual** ~ gemeinschaftliches wechselbezügliches *T*, Ehegatten*t*; **mutual** ~**s** *getrennte* wechselbezügliche *T–e*; **mystic** ~ geheimes Notariats*t*; **non-intervention** ~ *T mit Testamentsvollstreckereinsetzung bei Ausschluß der Überwachung durch das Nachlaßgericht*; **notarial** ~ notariell beurkundetes *T*, Notariats*t* (*nicht. GB/US*); **nuncupative** ~ mündliches, vor Zeugen errichtetes (*später niedergeschriebenes*) *T*; **officious** ~ → *officious*; **oral** ~ mündliches Zeugen*t*; **original** ~ Original*t*; **private** ~ Privat*t*; **privileged** ~ formfreies (*schriftl oder mündl*) Not*t*; **probate of** ~ → *probate*; **proof of** ~ *T–s*nachweis; **proved** ~ als gültig bestätigtes *T*; **reciprocal** ~ wechselbezügliches *T*, gegenseitiges *T*; **renunciation of a** ~ → *renunciation*; **revival of** ~ → *revival*; **revocation of** ~ → *revocation*; **sealed** ~ *T* in verschlossenem, versiegeltem Umschlag; **self-proved** ~ *T* ohne Unterschriftszeugen; **settlement**

by ~ letztwillige Treuhandsbildung; Vorerbschaftsanordnung; **soldier's** ~ → *soldier*; **statutory** ~ amtliches *T* (*für Testierunfähige*); **succession by** ~ testamentarische Erbfolge; *tenancy*; **title by** ~ → *title*; **to administer a** ~ ein *T* vollziehen; **to benefit by a** ~ in e–m *T* bedacht werden; **to dispose by** ~ → *to dispose*; **to draw** ~ ein *T* aufsetzen; **to execute a** ~ ein *T* errichten; ein *T* unterfertigen; **to leave by** ~ testamentarisch vermachen; **to probate a** ~ → *probate*; **to propound a** ~ → *to propound*; **to prove a** ~ = *to probate a* ~ *qv*; **unnatural** ~ ungewöhnliche letztwillige Verfügung (*an Außenstehende*); **unofficious** ~ willkürliches *T* (*ohne Beachtung der Familienbande*); **unsolemn** ~ *T* ohne Testamentsvollstrecker; **valid** ~ gültiges *T*.

will *v/t* letztwillig verfügen, vermachen.

willful → *wilful*.

willing bereit, willens, willig; ~ **seller** verkaufsbereiter (*freihändiger*) Veräußerer.

willingly aus freien Stücken, freiwillig.

willingness to pay Zahlungswille *m*.

win gewinnen, siegen, obsiegen; schürfen; ~ **one's case** s–n Prozeß gewinnen.

wind up abwickeln, liquidieren; ~ **an estate** e–n Nachlaß auseinandersetzen.

windbill Gefälligkeitswechsel *m*; Reitwechsel *m*, Kellerwechsel *m*.

windbreak Windschutzhecke *f*.

windfall Windschlag *m*, Windbruch *m*, unerwarteter Gewinn *m*; ~ **receipts** Zufallseinnahmen; ~ **profits** unerwartete Gewinne, große Zufallsgewinne; ~ **tax** → *tax*.

winding-up Abwicklung *f*, Liquidation *f*; ~ **by the court** Liquidation, Zwangsliquidation, Gesellschaftskonkurs; ~ **in stanneries court** Bergwerkskonkursverfahren; ~ **order** gerichtlicher Liquidationsbeschluß; ~ **petition** Antrag auf Genehmigung der Liquidation; ~ **resolution** (Selbst)Liquidationsbeschluß; ~ **rules** Vorschriften für (Gesellschaft)Liquidation; ~ **sale** Ausverkauf wegen Aufgabe des Geschäfts; ~ **subject to supervision** freiwillige Liquidation unter Aufsicht des Gerichts; **compulsory** ~ Zwangsliquidation, Gesellschaftskonkurs; **compulsory ~ order** Zwangsliquidationsbeschluß, Gesellschaftskonkurseröffnungsbeschluß; **creditor's voluntary** ~ → *creditor*; **debt provable in** ~ Konkursforderung; **members' voluntary** ~ Eigenliquidation durch Beschluß der Hauptversammlung; **resolution for voluntary** ~ Liquidationsbeschluß der Hauptversammlung; **voluntary** ~ (freiwillige) Liquidation.

window Fenster *n*, Fensterrecht *n*; Sonderliquiditätsbereitstellung der Zentralbank; ~ **box** Fensterstock (*Vertiefung für Schiebefenstergewichte*); ~ **display** Schaufensterauslage; ~ **dressing** Schaufensterarrangement; Bilanzkosmetik; ~ **envelope** Fensterumschlag; ~ **tax** *hist* Fenstersteuer.

windshielding seitlicher Windschutz *m* auf Brücken.

wine Wein *m*; (*selten*) Most *m*; ~ **doctoring** Weinpanscherei; ~ **duty** Weinsteuer; ~ **licence** Weinausschankkonzession; ~ **merchant** Weinhändler; **adulteration of** ~ Weinfälschung.

winter Winter *m* (*kalendermäßig, bzw die Monate Dez., Jan., Febr.*); ~ **heyning** Winterschonzeit (*11. Nov. bis 23. April*) *GB*.

wintner Winzer *m*.

wire Draht *m*, Telegramm *n*; ~ **answer** telegrafische Antwort; ~ **collect** *US* Telegramm mit bezahlter Rückantwort; ~ **communication** telegrafische Übermittlung; **~-drawn reply** spitzfindige Erwiderung; **~-tapping** Anzapfen von Telefonleitungen; ~ **transfer of funds** telegrafische Geldüberweisung; **by** ~ telegrafisch; **hot** ~ heißer Draht.

wish *s* Wunsch *m*, Wille *m*.

wish *v* wünschen, letztwillig anordnen.

wit wissen, erfahren; **to** ~ das heißt; nämlich; wie folgt.

with mit, bei; ~ **a view of** *bzw* **to** in der Absicht; ~ **all convenient speed** so schnell wie möglich; ~ **all despatch** unverzüglich; ~ **all faults** → *fault*; ~ **all liberties** mit allen Rechten; ~ **consent** mit Zustimmung, einvernehmlich, im Benehmen mit; ~ **costs** → *costs*; ~ **creditable records** im Dienst bewährt; ~ **effect** (*as of*) rechtswirksam (*seit*); ~ **exchange** Einzugskosten zahlt Remittent; ~ **intent** vorsätzlich; ~ **intent to deceive** in Täuschungsabsicht; ~ **interest** plus Zinsen, verzinslich (*zum gesetzlichen Zinssatz*); ~ **no strings attached** ohne Nebenbedingungen, ohne Auflagen; ~ **particular average** mit Deckung für besondere Havarie-Schäden *vgl average*; ~ **prejudice** mit materieller Rechtskraft; ~ **profits (policy)** mit Gewinnbeteiligung, Police mit Gewinnbeteiligung; ~ **recourse** als Indossament, mit Rückgriffshaftung, mit Gewähr; ~ **reference to** unter Bezugnahme auf; ~ **respect** bezüglich; ~ **strong hand** gewaltsam; ~ **the option of renewal** mit Verlängerungsoption.

withdraw entziehen, zurücknehmen, entfernen, ausscheiden; ~ **a charge** ein Verfahren einstellen, Anklage fallen lassen; ~ **a claim** e–n Anspruch fallen lassen; ~ **a power of attorney** e–e Vollmacht entziehen; ~ **a statement** e–e Aussage zurücknehmen; ~ **an action** e–e Klage zurücknehmen; ~ **an attachment** e–n Arrest (*bzw e–e Beschlagnahme*) aufheben; ~ **an order** e–n Auftrag stornieren; ~ **from circulation** aus dem Verkehr ziehen; ~ **money from an account** Geld von e–m Konto abheben; ~ **opposition** Einspruch zurücknehmen; ~ **restrictions** Beschränkungen aufheben.

withdrawable entziehbar, kündbar; ~ **at one year's notice** mit einjähriger Kündigungsfrist abhebbar.

withdrawal Rückzug *m*, Entziehung *f*, Zurücknahme *f*, Abhebung *f*, Entnahme *f*, Mandatsniederlegung *f*; Austritt *m*; ~ **from candidature** Aufgabe der Kandidatur; ~ **from prosecution** (*unzulässige*) Einstellung der Strafverfolgung; ~ **notice** Kreditkündigung; ~ **of acknowledgement** Widerruf der Zustellungsbestätigung; ~ **of a juror** Abberufung e–s Geschworenen; ~ **of a partner** Ausscheiden e–s Gesellschafters; ~ **of a patent** Zurücknahme e–s Patents; ~ **of a power of attorney** Vollmachtswiderruf, Vollmachtsentzug, Mandatsentzug; ~ **of an action** → *action*; ~ **of an order** Stornierung e–s Auftrags; ~ **of capital** Kapitalentnahme; ~ **of charges** Rücknahme des Strafantrags; ~ **of counsel** Mandatsniederlegung; ~ **of credit** Zurückziehung des Kredits, Kreditkündigung; ~ **of driving-licence** Führerscheinentzug; ~ **of issue from jury** Klageabweisung durch den Richter (*wegen Beweisfälligkeit*); ~ **of members** Ausscheiden von Mitgliedern; ~ **of money** Abhebung von Geld; ~ **of motion** Antragsrücknahme; ~ **of plea** Zurücknahme der Schuldigerklärung; ~ **of prosecution** Einstellung e–s Verfahrens (*durch den Staatsanwalt*); **corrupt** ~ eigennützige Rücknahme e–s Wahlprüfungsantrags; **day-to-day** ~**s** tägliche Abhebungen; **mandatory** ~ notwendige Mandatsniederlegung; **permissive** ~ freigestellte Mandatsniederlegung.

withdrawing | **a juror** Abberufung e–s Geschworenen, Einstellung des Verfahrens; ~ **a licence** Konzessionsentzug; ~ **the record** Nichtweiterbetreiben e–s Prozesses; Ruhen des Verfahrens.

withhold | **a document** e–e Urkunde nicht herausgeben; ~ **a patent** ein Patent versagen; ~ **one's assent** seine Zustimmung versagen; ~

payment die Zahlung vorenthalten.

withholding | **agent** Lohnsteuerabzugspflichtiger; ~ **certificate** Lohnsteuerbescheinigung; ~ **exemption** Lohnsteuerfreibetrag; ~ **of the truth** Verschweigen der Wahrheit; ~ **regulations** Lohnsteuerrichtlinien; ~ **statement** Bescheinigung über vom Arbeitgeber bezahlte Lohnsteuer; ~ **tax** → *tax*.

within binnen, innerhalb; ~ **a reasonable scientific certainty** mit an Sicherheit grenzender Wahrscheinlichkeit; ~ **a reasonable time** in angemessener Frist; ~ **due time** fristgemäß, rechtzeitig; ~-**grade salary advancements** laufbahnmäßige Gehaltserhöhungen; ~ **or under** in und unter (*dem Boden*); ~ **the ambit** im Rahmen, im Bereich; ~ **the jurisdiction** im Gerichtsbezirk, im Staatsgebiet; ~ **the meaning of the Act** im Sinne des Gesetzes; ~ **the prescribed time** fristgemäß; ~ **the realm** im Vereinigten Königreich; ~ **the set period** fristgemäß; ~ **time** fristgemäß.

without ohne, außerhalb, jenseits; ~ **advice** ohne Bericht; ~ **affecting** unbeschadet; ~ **anticipation** Vorausverfügung nicht zulässig; ~ **any deduction** ohne Abzug, rein netto; ~ **benefit of clergy** Kirchenasylrecht ausgeschlossen (*Bestimmung in älteren Strafgesetzen*); ~ **cause** ohne zureichenden Grund; ~ **charge of any kind** lastenfrei, ~ **day** ohne neuen Termin; ~ **debt** schuldenfrei; ~ **delay** unverzüglich; ~ **dispute** unstreitig, ohne Einwendungen; ~ **dividend** ex Dividende; ~ **engagement** → *engagement*; ~ **expenses** ohne Kosten; ~ **giving compensation therefor** ohne Vergütung; ~ **good cause** ohne berechtigten Grund; ~ **her consent** gegen ihren Willen; ~ **impeachment of waste** → *impeachment*; ~ **interest** ex-Zinsen, zinslos; ~ **interruption** ununterbrochen; ~ **issue** ohne Nachkommen; ~ **just cause** ohne rechtl Grund, ohne Rechtsgrund; ~ **justification** ohne rechtfertigenden Grund, ohne Berechtigung; ~ **lawful excuse** ohne Rechtfertigungsgrund; ~ **leave** unerlaubt; ~ **leave of absence** unerlaubte Entfernung *von der Truppe*; ~ **leave of the court** ohne gerichtliche Erlaubnis; ~ **leaving issue** kinderlos; ~ **let or hindrance** ohne Behinderung; ~ **negligence** ohne Verschulden; ~ **notice** → *notice*; ~ **par value stock** → *stock* (*1*); ~ **prejudice** → *prejudice*; ~ **P/L (profit/loss) effect** erfolgsneutral; ~ **reasonable and proper cause** unberechtigterweise; ~ **reasonable cause** ohne triftigen Grund; ~ **reasonable excuse** ohne ausreichende Entschuldigung; ~ **recourse (to me)** ohne Obligo, ohne Regreß, ohne Gewähr, nur als Zessionar; ~ **remedy** nicht rechtsmittelfähig; ~ **reserve** → *reserve*; ~ **respect of person** ohne Ansehen der Person; ~ **risk** unter Ausschluß der Gefahr, ohne Risiko; ~ **sales** umsatzlos; ~ **stint** ohne Begrenzung, ohne Ziffernangabe; ~ **sufficient cause** ohne ausreichenden Grund; ~ **the state** außerhalb des Staatsgebietes (*e–s Gliedstaates der USA*); ~ **valid excuse** ohne ausreichende Entschuldigung.

witness *s* Zeuge *m* (= *Z bzw . . .z*); ~ **box** *Z–n*stand, *Z–n*stuhl; ~ **fee** → *fee* (*1*); ~ **for the character** Leumunds*z*; ~ **for the Crown** Belastungs*z*; ~ **for the defence** Entlastungs*z*, von der Verteidigung benannter *Z*; ~ **for the prosecution** *Z* der Anklage, Belastungs*z*; ~ **stand** *Z–n*stand; ~**'s oath** Zeugeneid; ~ **order** gerichtl. Anordnung des Erscheinens e–s *Z–n*; ~ **sequestration** *Z–n*ausschluß (als betroffenes Opfer); ~ **to a marriage** Trau*z*; ~ **to a will** Testaments*z*; ~ **urged to give false testimony** Verleitung zur Falschaussage; ~ **warrant** *Z–n*ladung; **accomplice** ~ Beteiligter als Zeuge; **adverse** ~ feindlicher *Z* (*gegenüber der benen-*

nenden Partei); **apprehension of** ~ → *apprehension*; **attendance of** ~**es** Erscheinen von *Z–n*; **attesting** ~ *Z* bei der Unterschriftsleistung; **auricular** ~ Ohren*z*; **bribing of** ~**es** *Z–n*bestechung; **called as a** ~ als *Z* geladen; **(compelling accused to be)** ~ **against himself** (Zwang zur) Selbstbezichtigung; **character** ~ Leumunds*z*; **compellable** ~ aussagepflichtiger *Z*; **competency of** ~ → *competency*; **competent** ~ geeigneter *Z*, zulässiger *Z*; **contumacious** ~ unentschuldigt ausgebliebener *Z*, widersetzlicher *Z*; **corroboration of** ~ Bestätigung der *Z–n*aussage; **corruption of** ~**es** → *corruption*; **credibility of** ~ Glaubwürdigkeit des *Z–n*; **credible** ~ glaubwürdiger *Z*; **disinterested** ~ neutraler *Z*, unbeteiligter *Z*; **ear-**~ Ohren*z*; **evidence of** ~**es** *Z–n*beweis; **examination of** ~ *Z–n*vernehmung; **expenses of** ~ Auslagen des *Z–n*; **expert** ~ sachverständiger *Z*, Sachverständiger (*vor Gericht*); **eye-**~ Augen*z*; **forsworn** ~ meineidiger *Z*; **friendly** ~ eigener *Z*; **hostile** ~ *Z*, der gegen die benennende Partei aussagt, *Z* mit (*unerwarteter*) feindlicher Einstellung; **interested** ~ *Z* mit eigenem Interesse am Ausgang des Rechtsstreits; parteiischer *Z*; **key** ~ Haupt*z*, Kron*z*; **ocular** ~ Augen*z*; **non-compellable** ~ *Z*, dessen Erscheinen nicht erzwungen werden kann; *Z* mit Aussageverweigerungsrecht; **non-expert** ~ (*gewöhnlicher*) *Z*; **plain-spoken** ~ klare Aussagen machender *Z*; **principal** ~ Haupt*z*; **privileged** ~ *Z* mit Aussageverweigerungsrecht; **production of** ~**es** Mitbringen von *Z–n*; **prosecuting** ~ Nebenkläger als *Z*; *Z* der Anklage, Belastungs*z*; **scientific** ~ sachverständiger *Z* auf wissenschaftlichem Gebiet; **skilled** ~ sachverständiger *Z*, sachkundiger *Z*; **soliciting** ~ **to remain away from court** strafbare Aussageverhinderung; **subscribing** ~ (*mitunterzeichnender*) Unterschrifts*z*; **swift** ~ eilfertiger *Z*, voreingenommener *Z*; **to appear as a** ~ als *Z* erscheinen; **to bear** ~ → *to bear*; **to call a** ~ → *to call*; **to examine a** ~ e–n *Z–n* vernehmen; **unfavo(u)rable** ~ feindlicher *Z*; **unimpeachable** ~ verläßlicher *Z*; **unsworn** ~ nicht beeidigter *Z*; **unwilling** ~ *Z*, der sich nur widerwillig vernehmen läßt, widerspenstiger *Z*; **veracity of** ~ Wahrhaftigkeit e–s *Z–n*; **zealous** ~ übereifriger *Z*.

witness *v* als Zeuge wahrnehmen; bei der Unterschrift zugegen sein; ~ **my hand** (von mir) unterzeichnet; ~**ed by official means** amtlich bescheinigt, amtlich beglaubigt; **as** ~ **our hands** unterschriftlich von uns bestätigt; von uns unterzeichnet.

witnesseth es wird bezeugt; **this agreement** ~ hiermit wird (urkundlich folgendes) vereinbart; **this deed** ~ es soll hiermit folgendes urkundlich festgehalten werden.

witnessing|clause Beglaubigungsklausel; ~ **part** *Formel in Urkunden beginnend mit dem Wort "witnesseth", Teil e–r Urkunde mit Hauptverpflichtungen und Gegenleistung der Parteien.*

witword Rechtsanspruch *m*, Herausgabeanspruch *m* mit eidlicher Bekräftigung.

wolf *exch* gerissener Börsianer *m*.

woman Frau *f*; (*pl: alle weiblichen Personen außer Kindern*); ~ **driver** Fahrerin; ~ **executive** Unternehmerin; ~ **magistrate** Amtsrichterin; ~ **solicitor** Anwältin; ~ **suffrage** → *suffrage*; **innocent** ~ unbescholtene Frau.

womanizing Weibergeschichten *f/pl*; Affairen *f/pl*.

womb-leasing Geburt in fremdem Auftrag; Leihmutterschaft.

"won't pays" zahlungsunwillige Schuldner.

woolsack *brit* Wollsack *m*; Sitz *m* des Präsidenten des Oberhauses; **to take the seat on the** ~ die Sitzung (*im Oberhaus*) eröffnen.

word *s* Wort *n*; **~s** Wörter, Worte, Fachausdrücke *m|pl*; **~ of art** Fachausdruck, Terminus technicus; **~s of contract** vertragsbegründende Worte; **~s of description** beschreibende Ausdrücke; **~s of expectation** Worte vorvertraglicher Erwartung; **~ of hono(u)r** Ehrenwort; **~s of limitation** Fideikomißklausel, erbrechtl Nachfolgebeschränkung; **~s of procreation** Nachkommensklausel; **~s of purchase** den Kaufabschluß bewirkende Worte; **~s of severance** Teilungsanordnung (*zB je zur Hälfte, nicht Gesamthand, sondern Eigentum nach Bruchteilen*); **~ trade mark** Wortmarke; **apt ~s** zutreffende Formulierung; **blasphemous ~s** gotteslästerliche Worte; **by ~ of mouth** mündlich; **defamatory ~s** beleidigende Worte; **distinctive ~** kennzeichnendes Wort; unterscheidungsfähige Wortbildung; **generic ~** Gattungsbezeichnung; **obscene ~s** unzüchtige Worte; **operative ~s** rechtsgestaltende Worte, e–e Rechtsänderung begründende Worte; **overt ~s** eindeutige, klare Worte; **precatory ~s** letztwillige Bitte; **seditious ~s** hochverräterische Worte; **special and distinctive ~** Kennwort, Spezialausdruck; **treasonable ~s** hochverräterische Worte; **vestigial ~s** gegenstandslos gewordene (Gesetzes)Worte.

word *v* in Worte fassen, formulieren.

wording Formulierung *f*, Ausdrucksweise *f*, Wortlaut *m*, Fassung *f*; **~ of the law** Gesetzestext; **~ of the oath** Eidesformel; **original ~** ursprünglicher Wortlaut.

work *s* Arbeit (= *A bzw* ...*a*), Arbeitsleistung, Werk *n*; **~ ahead schedule** Maschineneinsatzplan; *A*–sverteilungsprogramm; **~ and labo(u)r** werkvertragliche Leistungen (*Arbeit und Material*); **~-beast** *A*–stier; **~ by order** Werkauftrag; **~ by the contract** werkvertragliche Leistung; **~ creation** *A*–sbeschaffung; **~ experience** *A*–serfahrung, Praktikum für Schüler; **~-horse** *A*–spferd; **~ hours** *A*–szeit; **~-house** *A*–shaus; **~ in process** = *in progress qv*; **~ in progress** in Bearbeitung befindliche Aufträge; Halbfabrikate, Halberzeugnisse; **~ layout** *A*–splatzgestaltung; **~ of art** Kunstwerk, Kunstgegenstand; **~ of national importance** staatswichtige *A–n*; **~ of necessity** (*für die Öffentlichkeit*) notwendige *A–n* (*die an Sonntagen verrichtet werden dürfen*); **~ of reference** Nachschlagewerk; **~ on hand** in Bearbeitung befindlicher Auftrag; **~ order** *A*–sauftrag; **~ permit ~** *A*–serlaubnis (*staatlich bzw gewerkschaftlich*); **~~~** *laws: gesetzliche Arbeitserlaubnisvorschriften*; **~ place** *A*–splatz; **~ programme** *A*–sprogramm; **~ relief** *A*–sfürsorge, *A*–slosenunterstützung; **~ satisfaction** *A*–szufriedenheit; **~ sharing** Streckung und Verteilung von *A*–smöglichkeiten, *A*–splatzteilung; **~ sheet** *A*–sbogen, Auftragsblatt; **~ terms** *A*–sbedingungen; **~ stoppage** *A*–seinstellung; **~ study** Zeitstudie(n); **~ to rule** → *working to rule qv*; **~ undertaken** übernommene *A*; **~ unit** Leistungseinheit; **~ week** *A*–swoche; **accident at ~** Betriebsunfall; **artistic ~** Kunstwerk; **brain ~** geistige *A*; **casual ~** Gelegenheits*a*; **contract ~** werkvertragliche Leistung; im Stücklohn geleistete *A*; **contract processing ~** Lohnveredelung; **derivative ~** abgeleitetes Werk; **dramatic ~** Werk der Theaterkunst; **flow of ~** → *flow*; **home ~** → *home*; **illicit ~** Schwarz*a*; **job ~** → *job*; **manual ~** → *manual*; **off ~** nicht in *A*, krankgeschrieben; von der *A* freigestellt; **out of ~** erwerbslos; *a*–slos; **piece ~** → *piece*; **plastic ~** plastisches Kunstwerk; **routine ~** alltägliche *A*, tägliche Klein*a*; **rush ~** Eilauftrag; **shop ~** Werkstatt*a*; **short-time ~** Kurz*a*; **spare-time ~** Nebenbeschäftigung; **the ~ outstanding** die noch nicht geleisteten *A–en*; **time ~** Teilzeit*a*; **volume of ~** *A*–sanfall.

work *v* arbeiten, bearbeiten, betreiben, bewirken; ~ **a patent** ein Patent nutzen.

workable praktisch durchführbar, brauchbar.

workaway zusätzliche freiwillige Arbeitskraft *f.*

workday Werktag *m*, Arbeitstag *m*, tägl Arbeitszeit *f.*

worker Arbeiter *m* (= *A bzw . . .a*), Arbeitnehmer *m*; ~**-director** Arbeitsdirektor; ~**s' participation in management** betriebl Mitbestimmung (*der Arbeiter*); ~**'s housing estate** *A*siedlung; ~ **retraining scheme** Umschulungsprogramm für Arbeiter; **casual** ~ Gelegenheits*a*; **clerical** ~ Bürokraft, Büroangestellter; **foreign** ~ Fremd*a*, Gast*a*; **job** ~ Akkord*a*; **key** ~ Schlüsselkraft; **loan** ~ Leih*a*; **managerial** ~ leitender Angestellter; **manual** ~ Hand*a*; **part-time** ~ Teilzeitbeschäftigter; **professional** ~ geistiger *A*, Akademiker; Fachmann; **qualified** ~ Spezial*a*; **salaried** ~ Gehaltsempfänger; **seasonal** ~ Saison*a*; **semiskilled** ~ angelernter *A*; **shop floor** ~ Industrie*a*, Hand*a*; **skilled** ~ gelernter *A*, Fach*a*; **unskilled** ~ ungelernter *A*, Hilfs*a*.

workforce Belegschaft *f*, Arbeiterschaft *f*, Betriebsangehörige *pl*.

workhand Arbeitskraft *f*, Arbeiter *m*.

work-in Arbeitsplatzbesetzung mit Fortsetzung der Produktion.

working agreement Absprache, sich bewährende Abmachung; ~ **assets** → *assets*; ~ **balance** Betriebsmittel, Betriebsmittelguthaben; ~ **capacity** Arbeitskraft, Arbeitsfähigkeit; ~ **capital** Betriebskapital; Nettoumlaufvermögen; ~ **capital loan** Betriebsmittelkredit; ~ **capital ratio** → *ratio*; ~ **card** *US* Gewerkschaftsmitgliedskarte; ~ **classes** Arbeiterklasse, Arbeiterstand; ~ **climate** Betriebsklima; ~ **conditions** Arbeitsbedingungen; ~ **director** geschäftsführendes Vorstandsmitglied; ~ **environment reserve** Rücklage für Betriebsverschönerung; ~ **expenses** Betriebsausgaben; ~ **face** Ort (*im Stollen*); ~ **facilities** Arbeitsplatzeinrichtung; ~ **foreman** Vorarbeiter; ~ **funds** Betriebsmittel; ~ **group** Arbeitsgruppe, Team; *joint ~ ~: Arbeitsgemeinschaft*; ~ **hatch** benutzte Ladeluke; ~ **holiday** Feiertag, der als gewöhnlicher Arbeitstag gerechnet wird; ungeschützter Feiertag; ~ **hours** Arbeitsstunden, Arbeitszeit; ~ **instructions** Arbeitsanweisungen; ~ **interest** Nutzungsvergütung; Ausbeutebeteiligung, Beteiligungsprozentsatz, Lizenzabgaben; ~ **language** Verhandlungssprache, Arbeitssprache (*bei Konferenzen*); ~ **life** Lebenszeit bei Erwerbsfähigkeit (ab 16); ~ **load** Höchstbelastung e–s Maschinenteils; ~ **luncheon** Arbeitsessen; ~ **order** betriebsfähiger Zustand; ~ **owner** wirtschaftlicher Eigentümer; mitarbeitender Betriebsinhaber; ~ **paper** vorläufige Aufstellung, Verhandlungspapier; ~ **papers** Arbeitspapiere, Arbeitsunterlagen; ~ **partner** → *partner*; ~ **party** Arbeitsgruppe; ~ **performance** Arbeitsleistung, Leistung (*e–er Maschine*); ~ **platform** Arbeitspodest, Staffelei; ~ **population** → *population*; **proprietors** wirtschaftliche Eigentümer; ~ **regulations** Betriebsvorschriften, Betriebsordnung; ~ **shaft** in Betrieb befindlicher Aufzugsschacht (*Bergwerk*); ~ **to rule** Dienst streng nach Vorschrift; Bummelstreik; ~ **trial balance** Bilanzentwurf.

working *s* Verarbeitung *f*, Bearbeitung *f*, Bewirtschaftung *f*; ~ **of goods** Bearbeitung (*Veredelung*).

workingwoman Arbeiterin *f*.

workload Arbeitsbelastung; ~ **pressure(s)** Arbeitsüberlastung.

workman (*pl workmen*) Arbeiter *m*.

workmanlike fachgerecht.

workmanship Ausführung *f*, technische Ausführung *f*; Arbeit *f*; **good** ~ fachgerechte Ausführung, gute

Arbeit; **scamped** ~ schlampige Arbeit.
workmate Arbeitskollege *m*.
workmen's compensation *US: gesetzlicher* Arbeitsunfallschutz; ~ **insurance** *etwa:* Berufsgenossenschaft.
workplace Arbeitsplatz *m;* ~ **democracy** Demokratie am Arbeitsplatz; Mitbestimmung; ~ **safety** Arbeitsschutz, Sicherheit am Arbeitsplatz.
works Werk *n*, Fabrik *f*, Anlagen *f/pl*, Bauten *pl;* ~ **accountant** leitender Betriebsbuchhalter; ~ **area** Fabrikgelände; ~ **council** *etwa:* Betriebsrat (*gemeinsam mit Arbeitgeberseite*); ~ **manager** Betriebsleiter; ~ **oncost** Produktionsgemeinkosten; ~ **outing** Betriebsausflug; ~ **superintendent** Betriebsleiter; ~ **supervisor** Betriebsleiter; **capital** ~ Großbauten, öffentliche Bauten; **clerk of the** ~ Bauaufseher; **ex** ~ ab Werk; **gas** ~ Gaswerk; **Ministry of W**~ Ministerium für öffentliche Bauten; **new** ~ Neubau; **public** ~ öffentliche Bauten, öffentliche Arbeiten; **steel** ~ Stahlwerk.
workshop Werkstatt *f*, Fabrikraum *m*; ~ **regulation** Arbeitsordnung.
world|court Internationaler Gerichtshof (*Den Haag*); ~ **depression** Weltwirtschaftskrise; **W**~ **Intellectual Property Organisation** (*Wipo*) Weltorganisation für geistiges Eigentum; ~ **trade** Welthandel; ~**-wide letter of credit** Reisekreditbrief; ~**-wide reputation** Weltruf; **all the** ~ (*gegenüber*) jedermann.
worldly weltlich, irdisch; ~ **employment or business** weltliche Arbeits- oder Geschäftstätigkeit; **my** ~ **estate** mein (*gesamtes*) irdisches Vermögen; **my** ~ **goods** meine irdische Habe.
worth *adj* wert (*in Geld*); **to be** ~ wert sein, *Vermögen* besitzen.
worth *s* Wert *m*, Gegenwert *m*, Preis *m*; **net** ~ → *net*.
worthiest of blood männliche Nachkommen *m/pl*.
worthiness guter Zustand *m*.
worthless wertlos; ~ **cheque** ungedeckter Scheck; ~ **security** Nonvaleur.
wound Wunde *f*, Verletzung *f*; **incised** ~ Schnittwunde; **punctured** ~ Stichwunde.
wounding Zufügung e–r Wunde, schwere Körperverletzung *f*; ~ **with intent** vorsätzliche schwere Körperverletzung; ~ **with intent to murder** Körperverletzung mit Mordvorsatz; **malicious** ~ heimtückische schwere Körperverletzung.
wreck *s* Schiffbruch *m*, Wrack *n*, Strandgut *n*; ~ **cargo** durch Schiffbruch verlorengegangene Fracht; ~ **commissioner** Strandvogt; ~ **master** Strandvogt; ~ **site** Lageplatz e–s gesunkenen Schiffes; **total** ~ *ins* Totalverlust.
wreck *v* zerstören, abwracken, verschrotten.
wreckfree frei von Beschlagnahme als Wrack *bzw* Strandgut.
writ gerichtlicher Befehl *m*, gerichtliche Verfügung *f*; gerichtl Anordnung; Beschluß, *bes hist:* Klage; Rechtsbehelf; *Kurzform für* ~ *of summons qv*; Schriftstück *n*, Urkunde *f*; ~ **de estoveriis habendis** Unterhaltsklage e–r geschiedenen Frau; ~ **de perambulatione facienda** Grenzfeststellungsklage; ~ **for by-elections** Anordnung der Ausschreibung von Nachwahlen; ~ **ne exeat regno** gerichtl Ausreiseverbot; ~ **of allocate** *hist Zuweisung von Freibeträgen an Exchequerbeamte*; ~ **of assistance** *obs* Besitzeinweisungsbeschluß; Zolldurchsuchungsbefehl; ~ **of assize** *hist* Grundstücksherausgabeklage; ~ **of attachment** Arrestbefehl, Vorführungsbefehl; Beschlagnahmebeschluß; ~ **of capias** → *capias*; ~ **of certiorari** → *certiorari*; ~ **of commission** Rechtshilfeersuchen; ~ **of computate** = *writ of allocate qv*; ~ **of consimili casu** *hist* Räumungsklage des Heimfallsberechtigten; ~ **of conspiracy** Klage wegen wider-

rechtlicher Verbindung (*zur Schädigung des Klägers*); ~ **of covenant** Klage wegen Vertragsverletzung (*aus e–m gesiegelten Vertrag*); ~ **of debt** Klage auf Zahlung e–r Geldschuld; ~ **of deceit** Schadenersatzklage wegen arglistiger Täuschung *gegen betrügerischen Vertreter ohne Vertretungsmacht*; ~ **of delivery** Herausgabeanordnung; richterliche Vollstreckungsanordnung *auf Herausgabe e–r beweglichen Sache*; ~ **of detainer** Anordnung der Haftfortdauer; ~ **of detinue** Herausgabeklage; ~ **of distringas** Vollstreckungsbeschluß (*vgl distringas*); ~ **of dower** Klage auf Witwenteil am Grundstück *vgl dower*; ~ **of elegit** Mobiliarvollstreckung mit Zwangsverwaltung des Grundbesitzes; ~ **of ejectment** Herausgabeklage des Grundstückseigentümers, Räumungsklage; ~ **of entry** (*GB bis 1833*) Räumungsklage (*des Grundeigentümers*); ~ **of error** Revisionszulassungsbeschluß (*des Revisionsgerichts mit Anordnung der Aktenvorlage*); ~ **of error coram nobis** Antrag auf Urteilsberichtigung, Urteilsberichtigungsbeschluß (*des erkennenden Gerichts*); ~ **of error coram vobis** Aktenvorlagebeschluß an das Rechtsmittelgericht; Revisionsbeschluß; ~ **of execution** Zwangsvollstreckungsklausel; Vollstreckungsauftrag; ~ **of extradition** (*gerichtlicher*) Auslieferungsbeschluß; ~ **of false judgment** Berufung (*zum High Court*); ~ **of fieri facias** Pfändungsanordnung; ~ **of formedon** Besitzeinräumungsklage (*des Heimfallsberechtigten, vgl formedon*); ~ **of habeas corpus** Anordnung der Anwesenheit des Inhaftierten vor Gericht zwecks Haftprüfung; ~ **of habere facias possessionem** Beschluß über die Einweisung in den Besitz des Schuldners; ~ **of injunction** einstweilige Verfügung (*mit gerichtlichem Verbot bzw Gebot*); ~ **of inquiry** Betragsverfahren (*Verfahren zur Feststellung der Schadenshöhe*); ~ **of levari facias** Pfändungsanordnung mit Wegnahmeermächtigung; ~ **of liberate** Freigabebeschluß, Zahlungsanweisung e–r Rente; ~ **of mainprize** Haftentlassungsanordnung gegen Kaution; ~ **of mandamus** → *mandamus*; ~ **of mandate** = *writ of mandamus* → *mandamus*; ~ **of partition** Teilungsklage; ~ **of possession** Vollstreckungsklausel bei Räumungsurteil, Zwangsräumungsanordnung; ~ **of praecipe** Klage auf Vollziehung der Auflassung; ~ **of prevention** vorbeugende Unterlassungsverfügung; ~ **of privilege** Antrag auf Haftentlassung wegen parlamentarischer Immunität; ~ **of possession** Zwangsräumungsanweisung an den Gerichtsvollz.; ~ **of probable cause** einstweilige Einstellung (*nach Berufungseinlegung*); ~ **of procedendo** obergerichtl Verfahrensanweisung; Zurückverweisungsbeschluß, Vorlagebeschluß; ~ **of process** gerichtliche Ladung des Beklagten (*bei Klageerhebung*); ~ **of proclamation** Androhung der Acht; ~ **of prohibition** Zuständigkeitsentziehung durch ein oberes Gericht *vgl prohibition*; ~ **of protection** *befristeter* königlicher Immunitätsbefehl *in zivilen Arrestverfahren für abwesende Staatsbedienstete*; ~ **of quo warranto** Antrag im quo-warranto-Verfahren → *quo warranto proceeding*; ~ **of recaption** Herausgabeanordnung an den interventionsberechtigten Eigentümer; ~ **of replevin** Interventionsklage, Herausgabeklage; *vgl replevin*; ~ **of restitution** Anordnung der Rückgabe der gepfändeten Sache; ~ **of review** Zulassung des Rechtsmittels (*durch das obere Gericht*); ~ **of revivor** erneuter Vollstreckbarkeitsbeschluß (*Parteiänderung ua*); ~ **of right** Herausgabeklage des Eigentümers, Klage auf Grund e–s Rechtsanspruchs; ~ **of right close** Herausgabeklage des (*verdrängten*) Grundpächters; ~ **of scire facias** *gerichtliche Aufforde-*

rung, Einwendungegen gegen e–e Urkunde vorzubringen oder diese anzuerkennen; Einleitung e–s Urkundenprozesses; Urkundenannullierungsverfahren; Titelumschreibungsverfahren; ~ **of scire facias to repeal letters patent** Patentnichtigkeitsklage; ~ **of seisin** Klage des Eigentümers auf Herausgabe des Grundstücks; ~ **of sequestration** gerichtliche Einsetzung e–s Zwangsverwalters; ~ **of subpoena** Ladung unter Strafandrohung; ~ **of summons** Prozeßeröffnungsverfügung mit Ladung und Klage; *etwa:* Klageerhebung; *the ~~~ was issued ...: die Klage wurde erhoben ... (Schadensersatz- u. andere Leistungsklagen*); ~ **of supersedeas** Einstellungsbeschluß (*vgl supersedeas*); ~ **of supervisory control** Eingriff des Revisionsgerichts in ein schwebendes Verfahren; ~ **of transgressione** Klage wegen Besitzstörung; ~ **of trial** Verweisungsbeschluß an untere Instanz; ~ **of venditioni exponas** Anordnung der Pfandverwertung; ~ **of warrant** Vollstreckungsbefehl; ~ **of waste** Klage wegen Substanzschädigung seitens des Pächters; **alias** ~ zweite Ausfertigung e–s Vollstreckungstitels; zweiter Vollstreckungsauftrag; zweite Aufforderung des Gerichts; **alternative** ~ Auflagenbeschluß mit Hinweis evtl Einwendungen vorzubringen; **close** ~ königliche Geheimverfügung; **concurrent** ~ zweite Ausfertigung e–r Klage; **concurrent ~s** Ladungsurkunde in mehreren Ausfertigungen; **interlocutory** ~ Zwischenurteil; **issue of** ~ gerichtliche Anordnung der Klagezustellung und Ladung; **judicial** ~ richterliche Verfügung; prozeßleitende Verfügung; **junior** ~ später zugestellte Klage; **optional** ~ Alternativklage (*facultas alternativa des Bekl*); **original** ~ *hist* Klagezustellung und Klage (*Chancery Gericht*); **patent** ~ offenes Sendschreiben; **peremptory** ~ Klagezustellung und Ladung mit Einlassungszwang; **prerogative ~s** außerordentliche Rechtsmittel (*i.e. ~s of habeas corpus, mandamus, procedendo, prohibition, quo warranto qv*); **to issue a** ~ Klage erheben; e–n verfahrenseinleitenden Antrag stellen; **to meet the** ~ die Urteilssumme tilgen; den Vollstreckungstitel befriedigen; **to serve a** ~ e–e Klage zustellen; e–e Klage erheben; **to take out a** ~ **against s.o.** jmdn verklagen.

writ server Zusteller *m*, Zustellungsbeamter *m*.

write-down *s* Abschreibung *f*; Wertberichtigung *f*; ~ **to the going (concern) value** Teilwertabschreibung.

write down *v* Abschreibungen vornehmen; teilweise abschreiben, niedriger bewerten.

write-off *s* Ausbuchung, vollständige Abschreibung *f*; Totalschaden *m*; **anticipatory** ~ vorzeitige Abschreibung; **tax ~s** Steuerabschreibungen.

write off *s* ausbuchen, (*als uneinbringlich*) abschreiben.

write-up Höherbewertung *f*, Aktivierung *f*, Zuschreibung *f*.

write up *v* höher bewerten; den Buchwert hinaufsetzen.

writer Verfasser *m*; Optionsverkäufer; ~ **to the signet** *scot* Rechtsanwalt *m*; ~ **of the statement** der Erklärende, Verfasser der Erklärung; ~ **of the tallies** Zählbeamter (*Excheque*); **the** ~ der Autor, der Verfasser (*dieser Zeilen*).

writing Schriftstück *n*, Schreiben *n*, Urkunde *f*, Schriftform *f*; Schriftlichkeit einschließlich Druck, Fotographie, Lithographie u. a. Reproduktionsarten; ~ **back** Rückbuchung, Storno; ~ **limit** Zeichnungsgrenze; ~ **obligatory** gesiegelte Schuldurkunde; ~ **under his hand** eigenhändiges Schriftstück; **in** ~ schriftlich; **legal** ~ juristische Abhandlung; **must be in** ~ bedarf der Schriftform; **proof of** ~ Echtheitsbeweis e–r Handschrift; **to re-**

duce to ~ schriftlich fixieren, niederlegen.

written geschrieben, schriftlich; ~ **particulars of employment** Bescheinigung über die Bedingungen des Arbeitsverhältnisses, schriftl Arbeitsvertrag.

wrong *s* Unrecht *n*, Ungerechtigkeit *f*, Rechtsverletzung *f*, unerlaubte Handlung *f*, Delikt *n*; **actionable** ~ klagbare unerlaubte Handlung; **civil** ~ unerlaubte Handlung, Delikt; **continuing** ~ andauernde unerlaubte Handlung; Dauerdelikt; **international** ~ völkerrechtswidriges Delikt; **positive** ~ vorsätzl unerlaubte Handlung; **private** ~ unerlaubte Handlung (*des Privatrechts*), Delikt; **public** ~ strafbare Handlung; Verletzung des öffentlichen Rechts; **real** ~ widerrechtliche Entziehung des Grundeigentums.

wrong *v* ungerecht behandeln, Unrecht tun; ~ **a person** jmdm Unrecht antun; ~**ed party** → *party*.

wrong-doer Schädiger *m*, Täter *m* (*derjenige, der e–e unerlaubte Handlung begeht*); Übeltäter *m*.

wrongful unrechtmäßig, rechtswidrig, schädlich, zu Unrecht; ~ **act, neglect or default** unerlaubte Handlung bzw Unterlassung; ~ **death** widerrechtliche Tötung; ~ **interference with goods** Entwendung von bewegl Sachen bzw Sachbeschädigung.

wrongfully | affected geschädigt; ~ **and without legal authority** rechtswidrig; ~ **intending** in böswilliger Absicht.

X

xenodochy Aufnahme *f* von Fremden, Gastfreundschaft *f*.

xenophilia Fremdenfreundlichkeit *f*.

xenophobia Fremdenhaß *m*.

Y

yard Yard *n (= 0,9144 m)*; **square** ~ Quadratyard.

yard Hof *m*, Hofraum *m*, Werkplatz *m*; **marshalling ~s** Rangierbahnhof; **prison** ~ Gefängnishof; **repair** ~ Ausbesserungswerft; **shipbuilding** ~ Schiffswerft; **stock** ~ Viehhof; **wood** ~ Holzlager.

yard(d)age Recht *n* auf Werkplatznutzung *bzw Lagerplatznutzung*, Lagergebühr *f*.

yardsman Werftarbeiter *m*.

year Jahr *n* (= *J . . . j*) (= *12 Kalendermonate = 365 Tage*); ~ **and day** *J*–*s*frist; ~ **book** *J*buch; **Y~ Books** *hist juristische Fallsammlung 1292–1534*; **~'s contract** *J*–*s*vertrag; **~, day, and waste** *obs königlicher Bußanspruch auf die Jahresnutzung und Substanzentnahme bei Verurteilung wegen Schwerverbrechen, bes Hochverrat*; **~'s earnings** *J*–*es*gewinn; **~-end adjustment** Ultimoausgleich; **~-end closing** *J*-*es*abschluß; **~-end dividend** *J*–*es*-schlußdividende; **~-end entry** *J*–*es*schlußbuchung; ~ **of assessment** Veranlagungs*j*; Steuer*j*; ~ **of issue** *J* des Versicherungsbeginns, Ausstellungs*j*; ~ **of manufacture** Herstellungs*j*; ~ **of maturity** Fälligkeits*j*; ~ **of mourning** Trauer*j*; **~s of office** Dienst*j*–*e*; **~'s purchase** Jahresertragswert; ~ **of our Lord** (im) *J* des Herrn; ~ **under review** Berichts*j*; **~'s wages** *J*–*es*-lohn; **account** ~ → *account* (*2*); **budgetary** ~ Haushaltsjahr; **business** ~ Geschäfts*j*; **civil** ~ bürgerliches *J*, Kalender*j*; **common** ~ bürgerliches *J*; **company's** ~ Geschäfts*j*; **financial** ~ Geschäfts*j*; Haushalts*j*; Finanz*j* *(GB 1. April bis 31. März)* = *fiscal* ~ *qv*; **fiscal** ~ Etat*j*, Wirtschafts*j*, Geschäfts*j*, Haushalts*j*, Rechnungs*j*, Finanz*j*; **leap** ~ Schalt*j*; **legal** ~ Gerichts*j*, bürgerliches *J*; Kalender*j*; **policy** ~ → *policy* (*1*); **preparatory** ~ Vorbereitungs*j*; **present** ~ laufendes *J*; **taxable** ~ Steuer*j*, Veranlagungs*j*; **two ~s** → *two*; **vintage** ~ Wein*j*, Erfolgs*j*.

yearling bond Kommunalanleihe *f*.

yearly | **account** Jahresrechnung; ~ **income** Jahreseinkommen; ~ **interest** Jahreszins; ~ **output** Jahresertrag, Jahresleistung; ~ **settlement** Jahresabrechnung, Jahresabschluß; ~ **tenancy** Pacht au[illegible] resbasis, Jahrespacht.

yeas and nays Ja- und Neinstim[illegible] *f/pl*.

yellow dog contract Arbeitsvert[illegible] mit Gewerkschaftsbeitrittsverbo[illegible]

yeoman der Freie *m*, freier Bauer [illegible] Pächter *m*, kleiner Grundbesitzer [illegible] Gehilfe *m* e–s Beamten, Diener [illegible] im königlichen Haushalt, Verwal[illegible] tungsunteroffizier *m*; ~ **usher** (=[illegible] *Stellvertreter des Black Rod qv*.

yes lobby Vorraum für die mit „Ja“ [illegible] stimmenden Abgeordneten.

yield *s* Ertrag *m*, Ausbeute *f*, Ernte *f*, Rendite *f*; ~ **gap** Abstand der Rendite von Dividendepapieren zu Staatsanleihen; ~ **mix** Ertragsmischung, Durchschnittsrendite; ~ **of depreciation** Abschreibungsertrag; ~ **on (upon) investment** Rendite; ~ **to maturity** langfristige Rendite (*für die restliche Laufzeit e–s festverzinslichen Papiers*); **current** ~ kurzfristige Rendite; **estimated** ~ Sollaufkommen; **flat** ~ laufende Rendite; Pauschalertrag; **gross** ~ Bruttorendite; **lowest** ~ Mindestertrag; **marginal** ~ → *marginal*; **net** ~ Nettorendite (*nach Steuern*), Reinertrag, Effektivverzinsung; **peak** ~ Ertragsspitze; **running** ~ Umlaufrendite.

yield *v* erbringen, abwerfen; nachgeben, sich fügen, überlassen; jmdm

das Wort überlassen; ~ **one's rights** seine Rechte aufgeben; ~ **the right of way** die Vorfahrt gewähren; ~ **to conditions** auf Bedingungen eingehen; ~ **up** (premises) (ein Grundstück bzw e–e Wohnung) räumen, herausgeben.

yielding | and paying *Einleitungsklausel in Pachtverträgen mit Vorbehalt des vom Verpächter zu zahlenden Grundzinses*; ~ **law** nachgiebiges Recht; **profit** ~ ertragreich.

York-Antwerp rules York-Antwerpener Regeln (*Seeversichg, Havarie, zuletzt 1974*).

young adult offender Heranwachsender *m* (*17–20*) (*als Straftäter*).

young offender jugendlicher bzw heranwachsender Straftäter.

young person Jugendliche(r) *m bzw f*, Minderjährige(r) *m bzw f* (*zwischen 14 und 18*); **Y~ P~s Employment Act** Jugendarbeitsschutzgesetz; **abandonment of ~s** Aussetzung von Minderjährigen; **abduction of ~s** Entführung Minderjähriger; **custody of ~s** Personensorge über Minderjährige.

youth Jugend *f*; Jugendlicher *m*; ~ **custody** Jugendstrafe; ~~ *sentence* Jugendstrafe; ~ **custody centre** Jugendstrafanstalt; ~ **employment** Beschäftigung von Jugendlichen; ~ **service** Jugendorganisation, Jugendbetreuung; ~ **welfare office** Jugendamt.

youthful jugendlich.

Z

zebra crossing Zebrastreifen; **uncontrolled** ~ nicht überwachter Zebrastreifen.

zero Null *f*; ~ **balance** Nullsaldo; ~ **coupon bonds** Zero-Bonds, Nullkupon-Anleihe, Anleihe ohne Zinskupon; ~ **budgeting** von Null ausgehender Jahreshaushalt (*ohne fortgeschriebene Posten*); ~ **growth** Nullwachstum; ~**-rated** von der MWSt befreit; ~**-rating** Mehrwertsteuerbefreiung; ~ **tariffs** Nulltarif-Zölle, Zollfreiheit.

zeroing Nullstellung *f*, Zurückstellen des Kilometerstandes auf Null.

zip | **area** *US* Postleitzone *f*; ~ **code** Postleitzahl.

zombie drogenabhängiger „lebender Leichnam".

zonal border Zonengrenze *f*.

zone Zone *f*, Bezirk *m*, Bereich *m*; ~ **of employment** Bereich der Arbeitsstätte; ~ **of influence** Einflußzone, Einflußbereich; ~ **of occupation** Besatzungszone; ~ **of operations** Einflußzone; ~ **price** Einheitspreis für e–e Zone; ~ **time** Landeszeit, Ortszeit; **danger** ~ Gefahrenzone; **floating** ~ noch nicht festgelegtes gewerblich nutzbares Gebiet; **free** ~ Freihafenzone; **littoral** ~ Gezeitenzone, Küstenland; **operational** ~ Kriegsgebiet; **pedestrian** ~ Fußgängerzone; **plebiscite** ~ Abstimmungsgebiet; **postal** ~ Post(zustell)bezirk; **prohibited** ~ Sperrgebiet; **residential** ~ Wohnbezirk; **spot** ~ Gebiet mit Bauausnahmegenehmigungen (*für Geschäftshäuser*); **unrestricted** ~ freies Baugebiet.

zoning Einteilung *f* in Zonen, Bauleitplanung *f*; ~ **classification** Bebauungsvorschriften; Ortsklasseneinteilung; ~ **laws** Bebauungsvorschriften; ~ **map** Bebauungsplan; ~ **ordinance** Flächennutzungssatzung, Baunutzungsverordnung; ~ **variance** Abweichung von Bebauungsvorschriften; **cluster** ~ Wohndichte-Planungsvorschriften; **density** ~ Wohndichteplanung; **Euclidean** ~ Flächennutzungsplan; **spot** ~ Änderung des Bebauungsplans im Einzelfall.